# ACCOUNTING PRINCIPLES

## FOURTH EDITION

# ACCOUNTING PRINCIPLES

►**JERRY J. WEYGANDT** *Ph.D., C.P.A.*

Arthur Andersen Alumni Professor of Accounting
University of Wisconsin
Madison, Wisconsin

►**DONALD E. KIESO** *Ph.D., C.P.A.*

KPMG Peat Marwick Emeritus Professor of Accountancy
Northern Illinois University
DeKalb, Illinois

►**WALTER G. KELL** *Ph.D., C.P.A.*

Professor Emeritus of Accounting
University of Michigan
Ann Arbor, Michigan

 **JOHN WILEY & SONS, INC.**

New York • Chichester • Brisbane • Toronto • Singapore

ACQUISITIONS EDITOR   Susan Elbe
SENIOR DEVELOPMENTAL EDITOR   Nancy Perry
SENIOR MARKETING MANAGER   Karen D. Allman
PRODUCTION COORDINATOR   Elm Street Publishing Services, Inc.
DESIGNER   Kevin Murphy
MANUFACTURING MANAGER   Mark Cirillo
PHOTO EDITOR   Mary Ann Price
PHOTO RESEARCHER   Jennifer Atkins
ILLUSTRATION COORDINATOR   Anna Melhorn
COVER PHOTO   John Kelly/The Image Bank

This book was set in 10.5/12 Palatino by CRWaldman Graphic Communications, Inc. and printed and bound by Von Hoffmann Press. The cover was printed by Phoenix Color Corp.


Recognizing the importance of preserving what has been written, it is a
policy of John Wiley & Sons, Inc. to have books of enduring value published
in the United States printed on acid-free paper, and we exert our best
efforts to that end.

The paper in this book was manufactured by a mill whose forest management programs include
sustained yield harvesting of its timberlands. Sustained yield harvesting principles ensure that
the number of trees cut each year does not exceed the amount of new growth. The specimen
financial statements, Appendix A, are printed with permission of PepsiCo, Inc.

*Library of Congress Cataloging-in-Publication Data*
Weygandt, Jerry J.
    Accounting principles / Jerry J. Weygandt, Donald E. Kieso, Walter
G. Kell.—4th ed.
        p.   cm.
    Includes index.
    ISBN 0-471-03661-7 (cloth : alk. paper)
    1. Accounting.     I. Kieso, Donald E.     II. Kell, Walter Gerry,
1921–     .
    HF5635.W524     1995                                         95-38872
    657—dc20                                                          CIP

Printed in the United States of America

10  9  8  7  6  5  4

Dedicated to our wives

Enid
Donna
Linda

for their love and support

# STUDENT OWNER'S MANUAL

## STUDENT TO STUDENT

Hi—

You are about to begin your first accounting class. You may not plan on becoming an accountant, so you may feel that this course will be difficult for you. But it doesn't have to be. Feeling comfortable with the course from the start is the key to success in this beginning accounting course. I'd like to share some tips that I picked up while I took this class and used this text:

- Each chapter contains a lot of information. To retain that information better, try answering the **Before You Go On** questions throughout the chapter. You can really benefit from this if you write your answers on a sheet of paper as you go through the chapter and then at the end of the chapter review your answers. You will have a better understanding about the material you just read.

- Read the **Accounting in Action** boxes located throughout the chapter. These sections can be very helpful because they allow you to see a particular idea from a real-world perspective. They also answer the question, "When am I ever going to use this stuff?" by providing you with examples of real-world accounting applications in many different industries.

- The biggest tip that I can give you really isn't a secret. Do the homework! I know that I sound like your professor right now, but I'm telling you that doing the homework is the difference between passing and failing this course. A good way to approach the exercises and problems at the end of the chapters is to read what is required of you before you begin to read the exercise or problem itself. You will pick up on key parts of the exercises and problems this way.

I took this course because I needed it for my undergraduate business degree. I have taken several upper-level business courses since then, but I occasionally find myself referring to this accounting book for information because this course teaches the fundamentals of accounting. The knowledge you learn here will serve as the foundation for all your other business classes. That is the main reason to take this course seriously and be successful with it.

Good luck!

*Gary T. Hedden*

Gary T. Hedden
Central Michigan University

# HOW TO USE THE STUDY AIDS
# IN THIS BOOK

**Concepts for Review,** listed at the beginning of each chapter from Chapter 2 on, are the accounting concepts you learned in previous chapters that you will need to know in order to understand the topics you are about to cover. Page references are provided if you need to review before reading the chapter.

## Concepts for Review

**Before studying this chapter, you should know or, if necessary, review:**

**a.** *How cash transactions are journalized in special journals.*
   *(Ch. 6, pp. 244–47, 250–52)*
**b.** *How postings are made to the cash account from special journals.*
   *(Ch. 6, pp. 244–47, 250–52)*
**c.** *The phases in developing an accounting system. (Ch. 6, pp. 237–38)*

## No Free Lunch

NEW YORK, NY — At Columbia University, thousands of dollars in cash changes hands between students and dining facility cashiers. Making sure that all of the money received by cashiers gets to where it's supposed to go requires various control measures. In accounting, these measures are called internal control.

One control measure used in the cafeteria at Columbia is that the register tape that records the sale and the amount of cash received must reconcile with the amount of cash in the cash drawer at the end of the day. "We see if there are significant overages or shortages at the end of each day for each register," says Susan McLaughlin, director of Columbia's dining facilities. Do cash differences happen very often? "No, because the cashier knows that if there are repeated or significant shortages, disciplinary action will be

taken," she says. "Ther_ be a variance of more _ either over or under, a time—or else it indica_ handling."

If a student buying _ register sees that a sale

The **Chapter-Opening Vignette** is a brief story that helps you picture how the topics of the chapter relate to the real worlds of accounting and business. Throughout the chapter, references to the opening vignette will help you put new ideas in context, organize them, and remember them.

**Study Objectives** appear at the beginning of each chapter to provide you with a learning framework. Each study objective then reappears at the point within the chapter where the concept is discussed and each is also summarized at the end of the chapter.

CHAPTER · **7**

# *I*NTERNAL CONTROL AND CASH

### ▶ STUDY OBJECTIVES ◀

**After studying this chapter, you should be able to:**

1. *Define internal control.*
2. *Identify the principles of internal control.*
3. *Explain the applications of internal control principles to cash receipts.*
4. *Describe the applications of internal control principles to cash disbursements.*
5. *Explain the operation of a petty cash fund.*
6. *Indicate the control features of a bank account.*
7. *Prepare a bank reconciliation.*
8. *Explain the reporting of cash.*

283

The **Preview** starts with an introductory paragraph linking the vignette with the major topics of the chapter. It is followed by a graphic outline of major topics and subtopics that will be discussed. This narrative and visual preview gives you a mental framework upon which to arrange the new information you are learning.

**Technology in Action** sections, identified by a CD icon, show how computers are one of the most important tools to the accountant and users of accounting information.

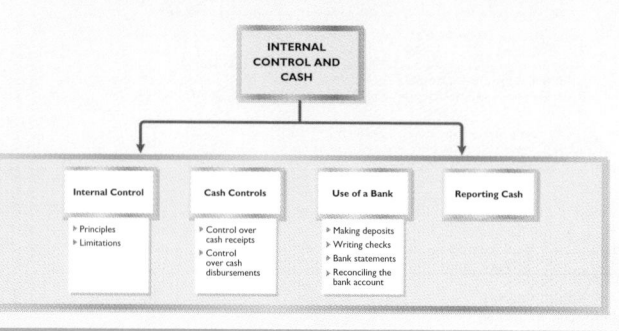

► **PREVIEW OF CHAPTER 7**

As the story about the dining facilities at Columbia University indicates, control of cash is important. Similarly, controls are needed to safeguard other types of assets. For example, Columbia University undoubtedly has controls to prevent the theft of food served in the cafeteria and controls to prevent the theft of computer equipment and supplies from its computer laboratories.

In this chapter, we explain the essential features of an internal control system and then describe how those controls apply to cash. The applications include some controls with which you may be already familiar. Toward the end of the chapter, we describe the use of a bank and explain how cash is reported on the balance sheet. The organization and content of Chapter 7 are as follows:

**INTERNAL CONTROL AND CASH**

**Internal Control**
- ► Principles
- ► Limitations

**Cash Controls**
- ► Control over cash receipts
- ► Control over cash disbursements

**Use of a Bank**
- ► Making deposits
- ► Writing checks
- ► Bank statements
- ► Reconciling the bank account

**Reporting Cash**

*Use of a Bank* • 303

► **Technology in Action**

A malfunctioning computer software program doubled all withdrawals and transfers made at Chemical Bank automatic teller machines (ATMs) in New York state for about 12 hours. The printed record of transactions spit out by the ATM was accurate, but the computerized posting of the transactions was automatically doubled. The bank corrected all errors, which in the aggregate may have been $15 million.

*Source: Denver Post, February 19, 1994.*

The incidence of errors depends on the effectiveness of the internal controls maintained by the depositor and the bank. Bank errors are infrequent. However, either party could inadvertently record a $450 check as $45 or $540. In addition, the bank might mistakenly charge a check drawn by C. D. Berg to the account of C. D. Burg.

### Reconciliation Procedure

**To obtain maximum benefit from a bank reconciliation, the reconciliation should be prepared by an employee who has no other responsibilities pertaining to cash.** When the internal control principle of independent internal verification is not followed in preparing the reconciliation, cash embezzlements may escape unnoticed. For example, a cashier who prepares the reconciliation can embezzle cash and conceal the embezzlement by misstating the reconciliation. Thus, the bank accounts would reconcile and the embezzlement would not be detected.

In reconciling the bank account, it is customary to reconcile the balance per books and balance per bank to their adjusted (correct or true) cash balances. The reconciliation schedule is divided into two sections, as shown in Illustration 7-12. The starting point in preparing the reconciliation is to enter the balance per bank statement and balance per books on the schedule. The following steps should reveal all the reconciling items that cause the difference between the two balances.

1. Compare the individual deposits on the bank statement with deposits in transit from the preceding bank reconciliation and with the deposits per company records or copies of duplicate deposit slips. Deposits recorded by the depositor that have not been recorded by the bank represent deposits in transit and are added to the balance per bank.

2. Compare the paid checks shown on the bank statement or the paid checks returned with the bank statement with (a) checks outstanding from the preceding bank reconciliation and (b) checks issued by the company as recorded in the cash payments journal. Issued checks recorded by the company that have not been paid by the bank represent outstanding checks that are deducted from the balance per bank.

3. Note any **errors** discovered in the foregoing steps and list them in the appropriate section of the reconciliation schedule. For example, if a paid check correctly written by the company for $195 was mistakenly recorded by the company for $159, the error of $36 is deducted from the balance per books. All errors made by the depositor are reconciling items in determining the adjusted cash balance per books. In contrast, all errors made by the bank are reconciling items in determining the adjusted cash balance per bank.

**Helpful hint** Deposits in transit and outstanding checks are reconciling items because of time lags.

st employees in the business that you own or manage? ver sometimes is Yes. For example, the financial press lowing:

small company diverted $750,000 of bill payments to a nt over a 3-year period.

th 28 years of service shipped $125,000 of merchandise

r embezzled $21 million from Wells Fargo Bank over a

borrowed" $150,000 of church funds to finance a friend's

size the need for a good system of internal control.

**Helpful Hints** in the margins help clarify concepts being discussed.

**Key Terms** and concepts are printed in blue where they are first explained in the text and are defined again in the end-of-chapter glossary.

**Accounting in Action** boxes give you more glimpses into the real world of accounting by discussing actual challenges faced by accountants. Each type of issue—business, ethics, and international—is identified by its own icon. Don't skip over the photos, figures, and tables.

---

302    CHAPTER 7 ► Internal Control and Cash

### ▲Accounting in Action ► Business Insight

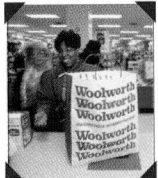

As copying machines have become ever more sophisticated, check counterfeiting has flourished. For example, in the second quarter of a recent fiscal year, the Woolworth Corporation had a $5 million loss from bad checks. Most of the total occurred in the Foot Locker division of the company, a spokesperson said. In the U.S. business community as a whole, some $10 billion worth of bad checks are written every year.

Checkmate Electronic Inc. thinks it has at least a partial answer to this problem. It makes electronic devices that read the magnetic ink used to print account and routing numbers on checks. By identifying the magnetic frequencies as well as the precise shape and size of the numbers, the machine can determine if a check is a fake. Checkmate has a machine small enough to be installed beside cash registers, and it is now in use by such retailers as J.C. Penney, Neiman-Marcus, and Pier 1 Imports.

*Source: Wall Street Journal, March 31, 1994, p. C2; and Business Week, May 23, 1994, p. 9.*

### Credit Memorandum

A depositor may ask the bank to collect its notes receivable. In such a case, the bank will credit the depositor's account for the cash proceeds of the note, as illustrated on the bank statement by the symbol CM. It will issue a credit memorandum which is sent with the statement to explain the entry. Many banks also offer interest on checking accounts. The interest earned may be indicated on the

with the depositor's name and address. Each check and with both a bank and a depositor identification number computer processing of the transaction.

Many companies have more than one bank accoun ations and better control, national retailers like Wal-Ma have regional bank accounts. Similarly, a company such as Exxon with more than 150,000 employees may have a payroll bank account, as well as one or more general bank accounts. In addition, a company may maintain several bank accounts in order to have more than one source for obtaining short-term loans when needed.

### Making Bank Deposits

Bank deposits should be made by an authorized employee, such as the head cashier. Each deposit must be documented by a deposit slip (ticket), as shown in Illustration 7-9.

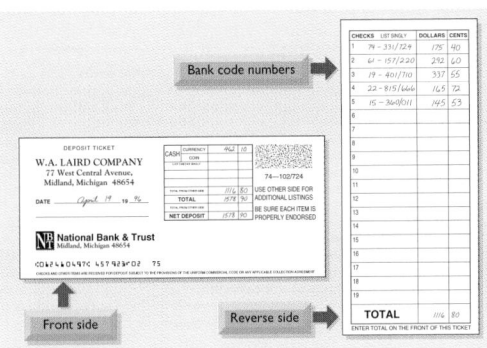

**Illustration 7-9**
*Deposit slip*

**Color Illustrations** visually reinforce important concepts and therefore often contain material that may appear on exams.

Deposit slips are prepared in duplicate. The original is retained by the bank; the duplicate, machine stamped by the bank to establish its authenticity, is retained by the depositor.

---

Internal Control ◄ 289

Independent internal verification is especially useful in comparing recorded accountability with existing assets. The reconciliation of the cash register tape with the cash in the register in the Columbia University dining facility is an example of this internal control principle. Another common example is the reconciliation by an independent person of the cash balance per books with the cash balance per bank. The relationship between this principle and the segregation of duties principle is shown graphically in Illustration 7-3.

**Infographics,** a special type of illustration, pictorially link concepts to the real world.

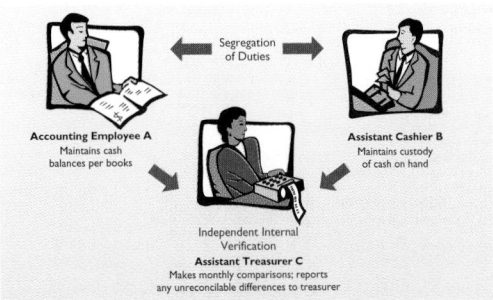

**Illustration 7-3**
*Comparison of segregation of duties principle with independent internal verification principle*

**Before You Go On** *Review It* questions serve as a learning check. If you cannot answer these questions, you should go back and read the section again. Brief *Do It* exercises help you apply what you are learning; their solutions help you see how the problem should be solved. (Keyed to homework exercises.)

A petty cash fund should be replenished at the end of the accounting period regardless of the cash in the fund. Replenishment at this time is necessary in order to recognize the effects of the petty cash payments on the financial statements.

Internal control over a petty cash fund is strengthened by (1) having a supervisor make surprise counts of the fund to ascertain whether the paid vouchers and fund cash equal the imprest amount and (2) canceling or mutilating the paid vouchers so they cannot be resubmitted for reimbursement.

### *Before You Go On . . .*

#### ► *Review It*

1. How do the principles of internal control apply to cash receipts?
2. How do the principles of internal control apply to cash disbursements?
3. When are entries required in a petty cash system?

#### ► *Do It*

L. R. Cortez is concerned about the control over cash receipts in his fast-food restaurant, Big Cheese. The restaurant has two cash registers. At no time do more than two employees take customer orders and ring up sales. Work shifts for employees range from 4 to 8 hours. Cortez asks your help in installing a good system of internal control over cash receipts.

**Reasoning:** Cortez needs to understand the principles of internal control, especially the principles of establishing responsibility, the use of electronic controls, and independent internal verification. Using this knowledge, an effective system of control over cash receipts can be designed and implemented.

**Solution:** Cortez should assign a cash register to each employee at the start of each work shift, with register totals set at zero. Each employee should be instructed to use only the assigned register and to ring up all sales. At the end of each work shift, Cortez or a supervisor/manager should total the register and make a cash count to see whether all cash is accounted for.

*Related exercise material:* BE7–3 and E7–2.

## Use of a Bank

**STUDY OBJECTIVE**
••••••••••••• 6
*Indicate the control features of a bank account.*

**The use of a bank contributes significantly to good internal control over cash.** A company can safeguard its cash by using a bank as a depository and clearing house for checks received and checks written. Use of a bank minimizes the amount of currency that must be kept on hand. In addition, the use of a bank facilitates the control of cash because a double record is maintained of all bank transactions—one by the business and the other by the bank. The asset account, Cash, maintained by the depositor is the reciprocal of the bank's liability account for each depositor. It should be possible to **reconcile these accounts** (make them agree) at any time.

Opening a bank checking account is a relatively simple procedure. Typically, the bank makes a credit check on the new customer and the depositor is required to sign a **signature card**. The card should contain the signatures of each person authorized to sign checks on the account. The signature card is used by bank employees to validate signatures on the checks.

As soon as possible after an account is opened, the bank will provide the depositor with a book of serially numbered checks and deposit slips imprinted

---

**EASTMAN KODAK COMPANY**

Current assets (in millions)
Cash and cash equivalents

Cash equivalents are highly liquid investments, with m[...]
less when purchased, that can be converted into a specif[...]
include money market funds, money market savings certi[...]
of deposit, and U.S. Treasury bills and notes.

A company may have cash that is restricted for a spe[...]
include a payroll bank account for paying salaries and w[...]
sion fund cash for financing new construction. If the res[...]
to be used within the next year, the amount should be rep[...]
However, when this is not the case, the restricted funds [...]
noncurrent asset. Since a payroll bank account will be u[...]
payday for employees, it is reported as a current asset. [...]
new construction will begin within the next year, plant [...]
classified as a noncurrent asset.

In making loans to depositors, it is common for banks to require the borrowers to maintain minimum cash balances. These minimum balances, called compensating balances, provide the bank with support for the loans. Compensating balances are a restriction on the use of cash that may affect a company's liquidity. Accordingly, compensating balances should be disclosed in the financial statements.

### *Before You Go On . . .*

#### ► *Review It*

1. What is generally reported as cash on a company's balance sheet?
2. What is meant by cash equivalents and compensating balances?

#### ► *A Look Back at Columbia University*

Refer to the opening story about Columbia University, and answer the following questions:

1. Does Susan McLaughlin have a valid basis for establishing responsibility for overages or shortages? Why or why not?
2. What internal control principles are applicable to reconciling cash register tapes and the amount of cash in the cash drawer at the end of the day?
3. What internal control principle is involved in seeing that a student gets a receipt when buying a meal at a register? How does this requirement contribute to good internal control?
4. Do you think the cashiers are, or should be, bonded?

**Solution**

1. Establishing responsibility for overages or shortages is made only at the end of the day. This will provide a valid basis for evaluation only if one person worked the register for the entire day. If more than one person works the register during the day, the single count will not provide a valid basis for establishing who is responsible for the overage or shortage.
2. Applicable internal control principles are: (a) Segregation of duties—the cashier(s) should not be involved in performing the reconciliation. (b) Documentation proce-

The last **Before You Go On** exercise takes you back for a critical look at the chapter-opening vignette.

Under the Foreign Corrupt Practices Act of 1977, all major U.S. corporations are required to maintain an adequate system of internal control. Companies that fail to comply are subject to fines, and company officers may be imprisoned. Also, the National Commission on Fraudulent Financial Reporting concluded that all companies whose stock is publicly traded should maintain internal controls that can provide reasonable assurance that fraudulent financial reporting will be prevented or subject to early detection.[1]

### Principles of Internal Control

To safeguard its assets and enhance the accuracy and reliability of its accounting records, a company follows specific control principles. Of course, internal control measures vary with the size and nature of the business and with management's control philosophy. However, the six principles listed in Illustration 7-1 apply to most enterprises:

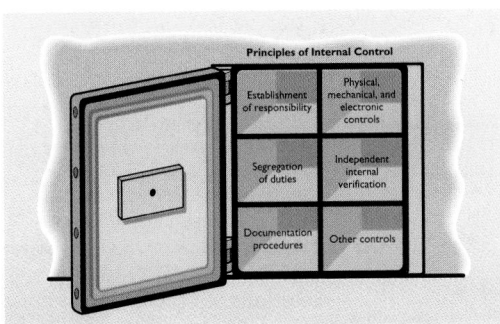

▸ *International note*
U.S. companies also adopt model business codes that guide their international operations to provide for a safe and healthy workplace, avoid child and forced labor, abstain from bribes, and follow sound environmental practices.

**International Notes** provide a helpful way of introducing international issues and problems in accounting.

**STUDY OBJECTIVE**
**2**
*Identify the principles of internal control.*

**Study Objectives** reappear in the margins at each point that the topic is discussed. End-of-chapter exercises and problems are keyed to study objectives.

**Illustration 7-1**
*Principles of internal control*

▸ *Ethics note*
Fundamental to internal control systems is the assumption that employees are honest and ethical and will not commit wrongdoing. As a result, most control measures are more effective in preventing and detecting errors than irregularities.

**Ethics Notes** help sensitize you to the real-world ethical dilemmas of accounting.

[1]Report of the National Commission on Fraudulent Financial Reporting, October 1987, p. 11.

---

dures—the cash register tape provides the documentation for total receipts for the day. (c) Independent internal verification—a supervisor should perform the reconciliation.
3. The internal control principle of documentation procedures is involved. The control does not reside in the receipt itself. For example, there will not be any subsequent reconciliation of cash register receipts with cash at the end of the day. The control is forcing the cashier to ring up each sale so that a receipt is produced. Each receipt is recorded on the cash register tape. At the end of the day, the tape is used in determining overages or shortages.
4. If the dining facility has nonstudent employees who work as cashiers, they may be bonded. However, if students work part-time as cashiers, it is doubtful that they are bonded. From the employer's standpoint, bonding is protection against major embezzlements. The risk of this occurring with student help is relatively low.

The **Summary of Study Objectives** relates the chapter summary to the study objectives located throughout the chapter. It gives you another opportunity to review as well as to see how all the key topics within the chapter are related.

## ▾ Summary of Study Objectives

**1.** *Define internal control.* Internal control is the plan of organization and related methods and procedures adopted within a business to safeguard its assets and to enhance the accuracy and reliability of its accounting records.

**2.** *Identify the principles of internal control.* The principles of internal control are: establishment of responsibility; segregation of duties; documentation procedures; physical, mechanical, and electronic controls; independent internal verification; and other controls.

**3.** *Explain the applications of internal control principles to cash receipts.* Internal controls over cash receipts include: (a) designating only personnel such as cashiers to handle cash; (b) assigning the duties of receiving cash, recording cash, and custody of cash to different individuals; (c) obtaining remittance advices for mail receipts, cash register tapes for over-the-counter receipts, and deposit slips for bank deposits; (d) using company safes and bank vaults to store cash with access limited to authorized personnel, and using cash registers in executing over-the-counter receipts; (e) making independent daily counts of register receipts and daily comparisons of total receipts with total deposits; and (f) bonding personnel that handle cash and requiring them to take vacations.

**4.** *Describe the applications of internal control principles to cash disbursements.* Internal controls over cash disbursements include: (a) having only specified individuals such as the treasurer authorized to sign checks; (b) assigning the duties of approving items for payment, paying the items, and recording the payment to different individuals; (c) using

prenumbered checks and accounting for all checks, with each check supported by an approved invoice; (d) storing blank checks in a safe or vault with access restricted to authorized personnel, and using a checkwriter to imprint amounts on checks; (e) comparing each check with the approved invoice before issuing the check, and making monthly reconciliations of bank and book balances; and (f) after payment, stamping each approved invoice "paid."

**5.** *Explain the operation of a petty cash fund.* In operating a petty cash fund, it is necessary to establish the fund, make payments from the fund, and replenish the fund.

**6.** *Indicate the control features of a bank account.* A bank account contributes to good internal control by providing physical controls for the storage of cash, minimizing the amount of currency that must be kept on hand, and creating a double record of a depositor's bank transactions.

**7.** *Prepare a bank reconciliation.* In reconciling the bank account, it is customary to reconcile the balance per books and balance per bank to their adjusted balances. The steps in determining the reconciling items are to ascertain deposits in transit, outstanding checks, errors by the depositor or the bank, and unrecorded bank memoranda.

**8.** *Explain the reporting of cash.* Cash is listed first in the current assets section of the balance sheet. In some cases, cash is reported together with cash equivalents. Cash restricted for a special purpose is reported separately as a current asset or as a noncurrent asset depending on when the cash is expected to be used.

The **Glossary** defines all the terms and concepts introduced in the chapter.

## ▾ Glossary

**Bank service charge** A fee charged by a bank for the use of its services. (p. 301).
**Bank statement** A statement received monthly from the bank that shows the depositor's bank transactions and balances. (p. 300).

**Cash** Resources that consist of coins, currency, checks, money orders, and money on hand or on deposit in a bank or similar depository. (p. 291).

**Cash equivalents** Highly liquid investments, with matur-

**End-of-Chapter Appendices** address topics considered optional by some instructors.

# APPENDIX ▸ *Alternative Treatment of Prepaid Expenses and Unearned Revenues*

In our discussion of adjusting entries for prepaid expenses and unearned revenues, we illustrated transactions for which the initial entries were made to balance sheet accounts. That is, in the case of prepaid expenses, the prepayment was debited to an asset account, and in the case of unearned revenue, the cash received was credited to a liability account. Some businesses use an alternative treatment: (1) At the time an expense is prepaid, it is debited to an expense account; (2) at the time of a receipt for future services, it is credited to a revenue account. The circumstances that justify such entries and the different adjusting entries that may be required are described below. The alternative treatment of prepaid expenses and unearned revenues has the same effect on the financial statements as the procedures described in the chapter.

**STUDY OBJECTIVE**
▼
*After studying this appendix, you should be able to:*

9. *Prepare adjusting entries for the alternative treatment of prepayments.*

## DEMONSTRATION PROBLEM

Trillo Company's bank statement for May 1996 shows the following data:

| | | | |
|---|---|---|---|
| Balance 5/1 | $12,650 | Balance 5/31 | $14,280 |
| Debit memorandum: | | Credit memorandum: | |
| NSF check | $ 175 | Collection of note receivable | $ 505 |

The cash balance per books at May 31 is $13,319. Your review of the data reveals the following:

1. The NSF check was from Hup Co., a customer.
2. The note collected by the bank was a $500, three-month, 12% note. The bank charged a $10 collection fee. No interest has been accrued.
3. Outstanding checks at May 31 total $2,410.
4. Deposits in transit at May 31 total $1,752.
5. A Trillo Company check for $352 dated May 10 cleared the bank on May 25. This check, which was a payment on account, was journalized for $325.

*Instructions*

(a) Prepare a bank reconciliation at May 31.
(b) Journalize the entries required by the reconciliation.

**Demonstration Problems** are the final step before you begin homework. These sample problems provide you with **Problem-Solving Strategies** and **Solutions**.

### *Solution to Demonstration Problem*

(a)

**TRILLO COMPANY**
**Bank Reconciliation**
**May 31, 1996**

| | | |
|---|---|---|
| Cash balance per bank statement | | $14,280 |
| Add: Deposits in transit | | 1,752 |
| | | 16,032 |
| Less: Outstanding checks | | 2,410 |
| Adjusted cash balance per bank | | $13,622 |
| Cash balance per books | | $13,319 |
| Add: Collection of note receivable $500, plus $15 interest less collection fee $10 | | 505 |
| | | 13,824 |

**Problem-Solving Strategies**
1. Follow the four steps used in reconciling items (pp. 303–4).
2. Work carefully to minimize mathematical errors in the reconciliation.
3. All entries are based on reconciling items per books.
4. Make sure the cash ledger balance after posting the reconciling entries agrees with the adjusted cash balance per books.

| | | | |
|---|---|---|---|
| ...heck | $175 | | |
| ...r books | 27 | | 202 |
| | | | $13,622 |
| | | | |
| ...Expense | | 505 | |
| ...able | | 10 | |
| | | | 500 |
| ...nue | | | 15 |
| ...collection of note by bank) | | | |
| ...vable—Hup Co. | | 175 | |
| | | | 175 |
| ...NSF check from Hup Co.) | | | |
| ...le | | 27 | |
| | | | 27 |
| ...error in recording check) | | | |

## SELF-STUDY QUESTIONS

**Self-Study Questions** are a practice test, keyed to Study Objectives, that gives you an opportunity to check your knowledge of important topics. Answers appear on the last page of the chapter.

Answers are at the end of the chapter.

(SO 1) 1. Internal control is used in a business to enhance the accuracy and reliability of its accounting records and to:
   a. safeguard its assets.
   b. prevent fraud.
   c. produce correct financial statements.
   d. deter employee dishonesty.

(SO 2) 2. The principles of internal control do not include:
   a. establishment of responsibility.
   b. documentation procedures.
   c. management responsibility.
   d. independent internal verification.

(SO 2) 3. Physical controls do not include:
   a. safes and vaults to store cash.
   b. independent bank reconciliations.
   c. locked warehouses for inventories.
   d. bank safety deposit boxes for important papers.

(SO 3) 4. Which of the following items in a cash drawer at November 30 is not cash?
   a. Money orders.
   b. Coins and currency.
   c. A customer check dated December 1.
   d. A customer check dated November 28.

(SO 3) 5. Permitting only designated personnel such as cashiers to handle cash receipts is an application of the principle of:
   a. segregation of duties.
   b. establishment of responsibility.
   c. independent check.
   d. other controls.

(SO 4) 6. The use of prenumbered checks in disbursing cash is an application of the principle of:
   a. establishment of responsibility.
   b. segregation of duties.
   c. physical, mechanical, and electronic controls.
   d. documentation procedures.

(SO 5) 7. A check is written to replenish a $100 petty cash fund when the fund contains receipts of $94 and $3 in cash. In recording the check,
   a. Cash Over and Short should be debited for $3.
   b. Petty Cash should be debited for $94.
   c. Cash should be credited for $94.
   d. Petty Cash should be credited for $3.

(SO 6) 8. The control features of a bank account do not include:
   a. having bank auditors verify the correctness of the bank balance per books.
   b. minimizing the amount of cash that must be kept on hand.
   c. providing a double record of all bank transactions.
   d. safeguarding cash by using a bank as a depository.

(SO 7) 9. In a bank reconciliation, deposits in transit are:
   a. deducted from the book balance.
   b. added to the book balance.
   c. added to the bank balance.
   d. deducted from the bank balance.

(SO 7) 10. The reconciling item in a bank reconciliation that will result in an adjusting entry by the depositor is:
   a. outstanding checks.
   b. deposit in transit.
   c. a bank error.
   d. bank service charges.

(SO 8) 11. The statement that correctly describes the reporting of cash is:
   a. Cash cannot be combined with cash equivalents.
   b. Restricted cash funds may be combined with Cash.
   c. Cash is listed first in the current asset section.
   d. Restricted cash funds cannot be reported as a current asset.

**Questions** allow you to explain your understanding of concepts and relationships covered in the chapter.

# QUESTIONS

1. "Internal control is concerned only with enhancing the accuracy of the accounting records." Do you agree? Explain.

2. What principles of internal control apply to most business enterprises?

3. In the corner grocery store, all sales clerks make change out of one cash register drawer. Is this a violation of internal control? Why?

4. J. Duma is reviewing the principle of segregation of duties. What are the two common applications of this principle?

5. How do documentation procedures contribute to good internal control?

6. What internal control objectives are met by physical, mechanical, and electronic controls?

7. (a) Explain the control principle of independent internal verification. (b) What practices are important in applying this principle?

8. The management of Cobo Company asks you, as the company accountant, to explain (a) the concept of reasonable assurance in internal control and (b) the importance of the human factor in internal control.

9. Midwest Inc. owns the following assets at the balance sheet date:

| | |
|---|---:|
| Cash in bank-savings account | $ 5,000 |
| Cash on hand | 850 |
| Cash refund due from the IRS | 1,000 |
| Checking account balance | 12,000 |
| Postdated checks | 500 |

What amount should be reported as cash in the balance sheet?

10. What principle(s) of internal control is (are) involved in making daily cash counts of over-the-counter receipts?

11. Dent Department Stores has just installed new electronic cash registers in its stores. How do cash registers improve internal control over cash receipts?

12. In Allen Wholesale Company, two mail clerks open all mail receipts. How does this strengthen internal control?

13. "To have maximum effective internal control over cash disbursements, all payments should be made by check." Is this true? Explain.

14. Handy Company's internal controls over cash disbursements provide for the treasurer to sign checks imprinted by a checkwriter after comparing the check with the approved invoice. Identify the internal control principles that are present in these controls.

15. How do the principles of (a) physical, mechanical, and electronic controls and (b) other controls apply to cash disbursements?

16. (a) What is a voucher system? (b) What principles of internal control apply to a voucher system?

17. What is the essential feature of an electronic funds transfer (EFT) procedure?

18. (a) Identify the three activities that pertain to a petty cash fund, and indicate an internal control principle that is applicable to each activity. (b) When are journal entries required in the operation of a petty cash fund?

19. "The use of a bank contributes significantly to good internal control over cash." Is this true? Why?

20. Paul Pascal is confused about the lack of agreement between the cash balance per books and the balance per the bank. Explain the causes for the lack of agreement to Paul, and give an example of each cause.

21. What are the four steps involved in finding differences between the balance per books and balance per banks?

22. Mary Mora asks your help concerning an NSF check. Explain to Mary (a) what an NSF check is, (b) how it is treated in a bank reconciliation, and (c) whether it will require an adjusting entry per bank.

23. (a) "Cash equivalents are the same as cash." Do you agree? Explain. (b) How should restricted cash funds be reported on the balance sheet?

**Brief Exercises** help you focus on one Study Objective at a time and thus help you build confidence in your basic skills and knowledge. (Keyed to Study Objectives.)

# BRIEF EXERCISES

BE7–1  Gina Milan is the new owner of Liberty Parking. She has heard about internal control but is not clear about its importance for her business. Explain to Gina the two purposes of internal control and give her one application of each purpose for Liberty Parking.

*Explain the importance of internal control.*
*(SO 1).*

BE7–2  The internal control procedures in Marion Company provide that:

(a) Employees who have physical custody of assets do not have access to the accounting records.

*Identify internal control principles.*
*(SO 2).*

# EXERCISES

*Identify the principles of internal control.*
*(SO 2).*

E7–1  Joe Marino is the owner of Marino's Pizza. Marino's is operated strictly on a carryout basis. Customers pick up their orders at a counter where a clerk exchanges the pizza for cash. While at the counter, the customer can see other employees making the pizzas and the large ovens in which the pizzas are baked.

**Instructions**
Identify the six principles of internal control and give an example of each principle that you might observe when picking up your pizza. (Note: It may not be possible to observe all the principles.)

**Exercises,** which gradually increase in skills, understanding, and time necessary to complete them, help you continue to build your confidence. (Keyed to Study Objectives.)

Certain exercises or problems marked with an icon ▦══▶ help you practice business **writing skills**.

**Instructions**
(a) List the weaknesses in internal control over cash disbursements.
(b) ▦══▶ Write a memo to your boss indicating your recommendations for improvement.

E7–5  Ramona Company uses an imprest petty cash system. The fund was established on March 1 with a balance of $100. During March the following petty cash receipts were found in the petty cash box:

*Prepare journal entries for a petty cash fund.*
*(SO 5).*

| Date | Receipt No. | For | Amount |
|---|---|---|---|
| 3/5 | 1 | Stamp Inventory | $38 |
| 7 | 2 | Freight-in | 19 |
| 9 | 3 | Miscellaneous Expense | 12 |
| 11 | 4 | Travel Expense | 24 |
| 14 | 5 | Miscellaneous Expense | 5 |

There was no cash over or short. The fund was replenished on March 15. On March 20, the amount in the fund was increased to $150.

*Problems* ◂ 315

*Instructions*

(a) Prepare the bank reconciliation at September 30.
(b) Prepare the adjusting entries at September 30, assuming (1) the NSF check was from a customer on account, and (2) no interest had been accrued on the note.

**E7–10** The cash records of Kuwait Company show the following:

1. The June 30 bank reconciliation indicated that deposits in transit total $850. During July the general ledger account Cash shows deposits of $15,750, but the bank statement indicates that only $15,600 in deposits were received during the month.
2. The June 30 bank reconciliation also reported outstanding checks of $920. During the month of July, Kuwait Company books show that $17,200 of checks were issued, yet the bank statement showed that $16,400 of checks cleared the bank in July.
3. In September, deposits per the bank statement totaled $26,700, deposits per books were $25,400, and deposits in transit at September 30 were $2,400.
4. In September, cash disbursements per books were $23,700, checks clearing the bank were $25,000, and outstanding checks at September 30 were $2,100.

There were no bank debit or credit memoranda, and no errors were made by either the bank or Kuwait Company.

*Instructions*

Answer the following questions:

(a) In situation (1), what were the deposits in transit at July 31?
(b) In situation (2), what were the outstanding checks at July 31?
(c) In situation (3), what were the deposits in transit at August 31?
(d) In situation (4), what were the outstanding checks at August 31?

*Compute deposits in transit and outstanding checks for two bank reconciliations. (SO 7).*

## PROBLEMS

**P7–1** Red River Theater is located in the Red River Mall. A cashier's booth is located near the entrance to the theater. Two cashiers are employed. One works from 1–5 P.M., the other from 5–9 P.M. Each cashier is bonded. The cashiers receive cash from customers and operate a machine that ejects serially numbered tickets. The rolls of tickets are inserted and locked into the machine by the theater manager at the beginning of each cashier's shift.

After purchasing a ticket, the customer takes the ticket to a doorperson stationed at the entrance of the theater lobby some 60 feet from the cashier's booth. The doorperson tears the ticket in half, admits the customer, and returns the ticket stub to the customer. The other half of the ticket is dropped into a locked box by the doorperson.

At the end of each cashier's shift, the theater manager removes the ticket rolls from the machine and makes a cash count. The cash count sheet is initialed by the cashier. At the end of the day, the manager deposits the receipts in total in a bank night deposit vault located in the mall. In addition, the manager sends copies of the deposit slip and the initialed cash count sheets to the theater company treasurer for verification and to the company's accounting department. Receipts from the first shift are stored in a safe located in the manager's office.

*Instructions*

(a) Identify the internal control principles and their application to the cash receipts transactions of the Red River Theater.
(b) If the doorperson and cashier decide to collaborate to misappropriate cash, what actions might they take?

*Identify internal control weaknesses over cash receipts. (SO 2, 3).*

**P7–2** MTR Company maintains a petty cash fund for small expenditures. The following transactions occurred over a 2-month period:

July 1 Established petty cash fund by writing a check on Metro Bank for $200.
15 Replenished the petty cash fund by writing a check for $194.30. On this date the fund consisted of $5.70 in cash and the following petty cash receipts: Freight-in $94.00, postage expense $42.40, entertainment expense $46.60, and miscellaneous expense $10.70.
31 Replenished the petty cash fund by writing a check for $192.00. At this date, the fund consisted of $8.00 in cash and the following petty cash receipts: Freight-in

*Journalize and post petty cash fund transactions. (SO 5).*

---

Each **Problem** helps you pull together and apply several concepts of the chapter. Included in these are problems that help you develop the writing skills that are so important in business. (Keyed to multiple Study Objectives.)

**General Ledger Problems,** identified by an icon are selected problems that can be solved using the General Ledger Software package.

---

Paired with the Problems, **Alternate Problems** provide additional opportunities to apply concepts learned in the chapter. (Each Alternate Problem is keyed to the same Study Objectives as its counterpart in the Problems set.)

**Spreadsheet Problems** identified by an icon are selected exercises and problems that can be solved using *Solving Principles of Accounting Problems Using Lotus 1-2-3 or Excel.*

---

230　CHAPTER 5 ▸ *Accounting for Merchandising Operations*

*Prepare correct multiple-step and single-step income statements. (SO 5, 7).*

**P5–5A** A part-time bookkeeper prepared the following income statement for the Tao Company for the year ending December 31, 1996.

**TAO COMPANY**
**Income Statement**
**December 31, 1996**

| | | |
|---|---:|---:|
| Revenues | | |
| Sales | | $702,000 |
| Less: Freight-in | $ 17,200 | |
| Discounts | 4,100 | 21,300 |
| Net sales | | 680,700 |
| Other revenues (net) | | 1,300 |
| Total revenues | | 682,000 |
| Expenses | | |
| Purchases | 470,000 | |
| Selling expenses | 100,000 | |
| Administrative expenses | 50,000 | |
| L. Tao, Drawings | 12,000 | |
| Total expenses | | 632,000 |
| Net income | | $ 50,000 |

As an experienced, knowledgeable accountant you review the statement and determine the following facts:

1. Sales includes $10,000 of deposits from customers for future sales orders.
2. Discounts consist of purchase discounts earned $7,200 and sales discounts granted $11,300.
3. Other revenues contains two items: interest expense $4,000 and interest revenue $5,300.
4. Purchases includes freight-out $14,000 less purchase returns and allowances $9,000.
5. Ending merchandise inventory increased $20,000 from a beginning inventory of $35,000.
6. Selling expenses consist of sales salaries $76,000, advertising $10,000, depreciation on store equipment $7,500, and sales commissions expense $6,500.
7. Administrative expenses consist of office salaries $19,000, utilities expense $8,000, rent expense $16,000, and insurance expense $7,000. Insurance expense includes $1,200 of insurance applicable to 1994.

# ▼*B*roadening Your Perspective

The **Broadening Your Perspective** section helps you pull together various concepts covered in the chapter and apply them to real-life business decisions.

C

## *F*INANCIAL REPORTING PROBLEM

The financial statements of PepsiCo, Inc. are presented in Appendix A of this textbook together with two reports: (1) a management report, Management's Responsibility for Financial Statements, and (2) an auditor's report, Report of Independent Auditors.

*Instructions*
Using the financial statements and reports, answer the following questions about PepsiCo's internal controls and cash.
1. What comments, if any, concerning the company's system of internal control are included in each report?
2. What reference, if any, is made to internal auditors in each report?
3. What comments, if any, are made about cash in the report of the independent auditors?
4. What data about cash and cash equivalents are shown in the consolidated balance sheet (statement of financial condition)?
5. What activities are identified in the consolidated statement of cash flows as being responsible for the changes in cash during 1994?
6. How are cash equivalents defined under the Notes to Consolidated Financial Statements?

A **Financial Reporting Case** familiarizes you with the format, content, and uses of financial statements prepared by major U.S. companies.

E

## *D*ECISION CASE

The board of trustees of a local church is concerned about the internal accounting controls pertaining to the offering collections made at weekly services. They ask you to serve on a three-person audit team with the internal auditor of the university and a CPA who has just joined the church.
    At a meeting of the audit team and the board of trustees you learn the following:
1. The church's board of trustees has delegated responsibility for the financial management and audit of the financial records to the finance committee. This group prepares the annual budget and approves major disbursements but is not involved in collections or record keeping. No audit has been made in recent years because the same trusted employee has kept church records and served as financial secretary for 15 years. The church does not carry any fidelity insurance.
2. The collection at the weekly service is taken by a team of ushers who volunteer to serve one month. The ushers take the collection plates to a basement office at the rear of the church. They hand their plates to the head usher and return to the church service. After all plates have been turned in, the head usher counts the cash received. The head usher then places the cash in the church safe along with a notation of the amount counted. The head usher volunteers to serve for 3 months.
3. The next morning the financial secretary opens the safe and recounts the collection. The secretary withholds $150–$200 in cash, depending on the cash expenditures expected for the week, and deposits the remainder of the collections in the bank. To facilitate the deposit, church members who contribute by check are asked to make their checks payable to "cash."
4. Each month, the financial secretary reconciles the bank statement and submits a copy of the reconciliation to the board of trustees. The reconciliations have rarely contained any bank errors and have never shown any errors per books.

*Instructions*
(a) Indicate the weaknesses in internal accounting control over the handling of collections.

A **Decision Case** helps you build your decision-making skills by analyzing accounting information in a less structured situation. At the same time it provides practice in your writing skills.

(b) List the improvements in internal control procedures that you plan to make at the next meeting of the audit team for (1) the ushers, (2) the head usher, (3) the financial secretary, and (4) the finance committee.
(c) What church policies should be changed to improve internal control?

**Communication Activities** ask you to engage in real-life business situations using your writing, speaking, or presentation skills.

## *C*OMMUNICATION ACTIVITY

E

As a new auditor for the CPA firm of Rawls, Keoto, and Landry you have been assigned to review the internal controls over mail cash receipts of Adirondack Company. Your review reveals the following: Checks are promptly endorsed "For Deposit Only," but no list of the checks is prepared by the person opening the mail. The mail is opened either by the cashier or by the employee who maintains the accounts receivable records. Mail receipts are deposited in the bank weekly by the cashier.

*Instructions*
Write a letter to L. S. Osman, owner of the Adirondack Company, explaining the weaknesses in internal control and your recommendations for improving the system.

**Group Activities** prepare you for the business world, where you will be working with many people, by giving you practice in solving problems with colleagues.

## *G*ROUP ACTIVITY

AN

From your employment or personal experiences, identify situations in which cash was received or disbursed.

*Instructions*
In groups of five or six students:
(a) Identify the internal control principles used for cash receipts.
(b) Identify the internal control principles used for cash disbursements.
(c) Identify any weaknesses in internal control related to cash receipts and disbursements.

Through the **Ethics Cases** you will reflect on ethical situations an accountant typically confronts.

## ETHICS CASE

E

You are the assistant controller in charge of general ledger accounting at Lemon Twist Bottling Company. Your company has a large loan from an insurance company. The loan agreement requires that the company's cash account balance be maintained at $200,000 or more as reported monthly. At June 30 the cash balance is $80,000, which you report to Sam Williams, the financial vice-president. Sam excitedly instructs you to keep the cash receipts book open for one additional day for purposes of the June 30 report to the insurance company. Sam says, "If we don't get that cash balance over $200,000, we'll default on our loan agreement. They could close us down, put us all out of our jobs!" Sam continues, "I talked to Grochum Distributors (one of Lemon Twist's largest customers) this morning and they said they sent us a check for $150,000 yesterday. We should receive it tomorrow. If we include just that one check in our cash balance, we'll be in the clear. It's in the mail!"

**Instructions**

(a) Who will suffer negative effects if you do not comply with Sam Williams' instructions? Who will suffer if you do comply?
(b) What are the ethical considerations in this case?
(c) What alternatives do you have?

---

AN ## CRITICAL THINKING CASE
▶ *A Real-World Focus: Alternative Distributor Corp.*
..................................................................

*Alternative Distributor Corp., a distributor of groceries and related products, is headquartered in Medford, Massachusetts. It was founded in 1980 and today has seven employees, with a total sales of $7 million.*

During its audit, the Alternative Distributor Corp. was advised that previously existing internal controls necessary for the company to develop reliable financial statements were inadequate. The audit report stated that the current system of accounting for sales, receivables, and cash receipts constituted a material weakness.

Among other items, the report focused on non-timely deposit of cash receipts, exposing Alternative Distributor to potential loss or misappropriation; excessive past due accounts receivable due to lack of collection efforts; disregard of advantages offered by vendors for prompt payment of invoices; absence of appropriate segregation of duties by personnel consistent with appropriate control objectives; inadequate procedures for applying accounting principles; lack of qualified management personnel; lack of supervision by an outside board of directors; and overall poor recordkeeping.

**Instructions**
Identify the principles of internal control violated by Alternative Distributor Corporation.

---

*Answers to Self-Study Questions*
1. a    2. c    3. b    4. c    5. b    6. d    7. a    8. a    9. c    10. d    11. c

**Critical Thinking: A Real-World Focus** asks you to decide how to apply the concepts you have learned to specific situations faced by actual companies.

**Answers to Self-Study Questions** provide feedback on your understanding of concepts.

# HOW DO YOU LEARN BEST?

Now that you have looked at your Owner's Manual, take time to find out how you learn best. This quiz was designed to help you find out something about your preferred learning method. Research on left brain/right brain differences and also on learning and personality differences suggests that each person has preferred ways to receive and communicate information. After taking the quiz, we will help you pinpoint the study aids in this text that will help you learn the material based on your learning style.

Circle the letter of the answer that best explains your preference. If a single answer does not match your perception, please circle two or more choices. Leave blank any question that does not apply.

1. You are about to give directions to a person. She is staying in a hotel in town and wants to visit your house. She has a rental car. Would you
   V) draw a map on paper?
   R) write down the directions (without a map)?
   A) tell her the directions?
   K) pick her up at the hotel in your car?

2. You are staying in a hotel and have a rental car. You would like to visit friends whose address/location you do not know. Would you like them to
   V) draw you a map on paper?
   R) write down the directions (without a map)?
   A) tell you the directions by phone?
   K) pick you up at the hotel in their car?

3. You have just received a copy of your itinerary for a world trip. This is of interest to a friend. Would you
   A) call her immediately and tell her about it?
   R) send her a copy of the printed itinerary?
   V) show her on a map of the world?

4. You are going to cook a dessert as a special treat for your family. Do you
   K) cook something familiar without need for instructions?
   V) thumb through the cookbook looking for ideas from the pictures?
   R) refer to a specific cookbook where there is a good recipe?
   A) ask for advice from others?

5. A group of tourists has been assigned to you to find out about national parks. Would you
   K) drive them to a national park?
   R) give them a book on national parks?
   V) show them slides and photographs?
   A) give them a talk on national parks?

6. You are about to purchase a new stereo. Other than price, what would most influence your decision?
   A) A friend talking about it.
   K) Listening to it.
   R) Reading the details about it.
   V) Its distinctive, upscale appearance.

7. Recall a time in your life when you learned how to do something like playing a new board game. (Try to avoid choosing a very physical skill, e.g., riding a bike.) How did you learn best? By

V) visual clues—pictures, diagrams, charts?
A) listening to somebody explaining it?
R) written instructions?
K) doing it?

8. Which of these games do you prefer?
   V) *Pictionary*
   R) *Scrabble*
   K) Charades

9. You are about to learn to use a new program on a computer. Would you
   K) ask a friend to show you?
   R) read the manual that comes with the program?
   A) telephone a friend and ask questions about it?

10. You are not sure whether a word should be spelled "dependent" or "dependant." Do you
    R) look it up in the dictionary?
    V) see the word in your mind and choose the best way it looks?
    A) sound it out in your mind?
    K) write both versions down?

11. Apart from price, what would most influence your decision to buy a particular textbook?
    K) Using a friend's copy.
    R) Skimming parts of it.
    A) A friend talking about it.
    V) It looks OK.

12. A new movie has arrived in town. What would most influence your decision to go or not to go?
    A) Friends talked about it.
    R) You read a review of it.
    V) You saw a preview of it.

13. Do you prefer a lecturer/teacher who likes to use
    R) handouts and/or a textbook?
    V) flow diagrams, charts, slides?
    K) field trips, labs, practical sessions?
    A) discussion, guest speakers?

**Results:** To determine your learning preference, add up the number of individual Vs, As, Rs, and Ks you have circled. Take the letter you have the greatest number of and match it to the same letter in the Learning Styles Chart. Next to each letter in the Chart are suggestions that will refer you to different learning aids throughout this text.

# LEARNING STYLES CHART

| TYPE | WHAT TO DO IN CLASS | WHAT TO DO WHEN STUDYING | TEXT FEATURES THAT MAY HELP YOU THE MOST | WHAT TO DO PRIOR TO AND DURING EXAMS |
|---|---|---|---|---|
| **V** VISUAL | Underline. Use different colors. Use symbols, charts, arrangements on the page. | Use the "In Class" strategies. Reconstruct images in different ways. Redraw pages from memory. Replace words with symbols and initials. | **Preview** **Infographics/ Illustrations** **Photos** **Accounting in Action** **Technology in Action** **Key Terms in blue** **Words in bold** **Questions/Exercises/ Problems** **Financial Reporting Problem** | Recall the "pictures of the pages." Draw, use diagrams where appropriate. Practice turning visuals back into words. |

| TYPE | WHAT TO DO IN CLASS | WHAT TO DO WHEN STUDYING | TEXT FEATURES THAT MAY HELP YOU THE MOST | WHAT TO DO PRIOR TO AND DURING EXAMS |
|---|---|---|---|---|
| **A** AURAL | Attend lectures and tutorials. Discuss topics with students. Explain new ideas to other people. Use a tape recorder. Describe overheads, pictures, and visuals to somebody not there. Leave space in your notes for later recall. | You may take poor notes because you prefer to listen. Therefore: Expand your notes. Put summarized notes on tape and listen. Read summarized notes out loud. Explain notes to another "aural" person. | **Infographics/Illustrations** **Accounting in Action** **Technology in Action** **Review It/Do It** **Summary of Study Objectives** **Glossary** **Demonstration Problem** **Self-Study Questions** **Questions/Exercises/ Problems** **Financial Reporting Problem** **Decision Case** **Communication Activity** **Group Activity** **Ethics Case** **Critical Thinking** **Videos** | Listen to your "voices" and write them down. Speak your answers. Practice writing answers to old exam questions. |

*Source*: Adapted from Neil D. Fleming and Colleen Mills, "Not Another Inventory, Rather a Catalyst for Reflections," *To Improve the Academy*, Volume II (1992), pp. 137-155. Used by permission.

| TYPE | WHAT TO DO IN CLASS | WHAT TO DO WHEN STUDYING | TEXT FEATURES THAT MAY HELP YOU THE MOST | WHAT TO DO PRIOR TO AND DURING EXAMS |
|---|---|---|---|---|
|  **R** READING/WRITING | Use lists, headings.<br>Use dictionaries and definitions.<br>Use handouts and textbooks.<br>Read.<br>Use lecture notes. | Write out words again and again.<br>Reread notes silently.<br>Rewrite ideas into other words.<br>Organize diagrams into statements. | **Study Objectives**<br>**Preview**<br>**Review It/Do It**<br>**Summary of Study Objectives**<br>**Glossary**<br>**Self-Study Questions**<br>**Questions/Exercises/Problems**<br>**Writing Problems**<br>**Financial Reporting Problem**<br>**Decision Case**<br>**Communication Activity**<br>**Group Activity**<br>**Ethics Case**<br>**Critical Thinking** | Practice with multiple-choice questions.<br>Write out lists.<br>Write paragraphs, beginnings and endings. |

| TYPE | WHAT TO DO IN CLASS | WHAT TO DO WHEN STUDYING | TEXT FEATURES THAT MAY HELP YOU THE MOST | WHAT TO DO PRIOR TO AND DURING EXAMS |
|---|---|---|---|---|
| **K** KINESTHETIC  | Use all your senses.<br>Go to labs, take field trips.<br>Use trial-and-error methods.<br>Listen to real-life examples.<br>Use hands-on approach. | You may take notes poorly because topics do not seem relevant. Therefore:<br>Put examples in note summaries.<br>Use pictures and photos to illustrate.<br>Talk about notes with another "kinesthetic" person. | **Concepts for Review**<br>**Vignettes**<br>**Preview**<br>**Infographics/Illustrations**<br>**Review It/Do It**<br>**A Look Back at . . .**<br>**Summary of Study Objectives**<br>**Demonstration Problem**<br>**Self-Study Questions**<br>**Questions/Exercises/Problems**<br>**Financial Reporting Problem**<br>**Decision Case**<br>**Communication Activity**<br>**Group Activity** | Write practice answers.<br>Role-play the exam situation. |

# SPECIAL STUDENT SUPPLEMENTS THAT HELP YOU GET THE BEST GRADE YOU CAN

## Working Papers, Volume I: Chapters 1-13 and Volume II: Chapters 13-27

These partially completed accounting forms can be used for all end-of-chapter exercises, problems, and cases. They demonstrate how to set up solution formats correctly and are directly tied to textbook assignments.

## Student Study Guide, Volume I: Chapters 1-13 and Volume II: Chapters 13-27

The Student Study Guide is a comprehensive review of accounting and a powerful tool. In addition to guiding you through chapter content, it provides resources for use during lectures, including a chapter outline with room for lecture notes and blank working papers for problems worked in class. With additional opportunities to practice your knowledge and skills, this is an excellent resource when preparing for exams.

## Self-Study Problems/Solutions Book, Volume I: Chapters 1-13 and Volume II: Chapters 13-27

This tutorial is designed to improve your ability in solving accounting principles homework assignments and exam questions through a wide selection of multiple-choice questions, exercises, and cases. The Self-Study Book also provides additional insights on how to study accounting and tips to alert you to common pitfalls.

## Career Supplement

This valuable resource gives a broad perspective of accounting and its applications in business, presents an overview of various career paths that you may pursue, and provides a listing of each of the companies discussed in the textbook with contact information, allowing you to explore these companies for more information.

## Practice Sets

Practice sets expose you to a real-world simulation of maintaining a complete set of accounting records for a business. You'll find that practice sets reinforce the concepts and procedures learned in each chapter of the textbook and show you how they are brought together to generate the accounting information that is essential in assessing the financial position and operating results of a company. The practice sets available are:

**Campus Cycle Shop: A Business Papers Practice Set**
**Heritage Home Furniture: A Narrative Practice Set**
**University Bookstore, Inc.: A Corporate Practice Set**
**Olympic Mowers Co.: A Manufacturing Practice Set**
**Flint Hills Salon: A Case Analysis**

## General Ledger Software

Available for either DOS or Windows, the General Ledger Software program allows you to solve selected end-of-chapter text problems using a computerized accounting system. The software also allows you to complete the Campus Cycle Shop, Heritage Home Furniture, and University Bookstore, Inc., practice sets on a computer.

## Solving Accounting Principles Problems Using Lotus 1-2-3 and Solving Accounting Principles Problems Using Excel for Windows

These electronic spreadsheet templates (available in either Lotus or Excel) allow you to complete selected end-of-chapter exercises and problems. The manuals, which include the disks, guide you step-by-step from an introduction to computers and Lotus or Excel, to completing preprogrammed spreadsheets, to designing your own spreadsheets.

## Microstudy, a Computerized Study Guide

A computerized version of the Student Study Guides I and II, Microstudy is designed to provide more flexible movement through the content to meet your particular needs. You can select from a number of self-study options including: chapter summaries, chapter Study Objectives, and self-test questions. Multiple-choice questions offer you explanations of why the wrong choices are not correct.

## Overture: An Interactive Guide to Mastering Principles of Accounting

This CD introduces you to the content and pedagogy of the text, while emphasizing the importance of accounting in the business world. Includes an electronic version of the Learning Styles Survey and the first chapter of the Study Guide and the Self-Study Problems/Solutions Book for free.

## Profiles: A Multimedia Look at Uses of Accounting Information

This interactive CD uses a variety of sound, graphics, animation and spreadsheet material to help you make the connection between the accounting systems and the effective business decisions that are made by using that information. The 12 modules use interactive simulations to bring the key concepts of accounting to life and reinforce your knowledge. Each module requires you to assume the identity of the person featured in the case and make decisions based on the information provided.

# ACKNOWLEDGMENTS

During the course of the development of *Accounting Principles*, Fourth Edition, the authors benefited greatly from feedback from numerous instructors of accounting principles courses throughout the country, including many users of the Third Edition of the text. The criticism, constructive suggestions, and innovative ideas helped to focus the revision on the needs of the students. We are indebted to the contributions of the following accounting professionals.

## Reviewers and Focus Group Participants for Prior Editions of *Accounting Principles*

Hector Agostini, Middlesex Community College; Linda Alderson, Cabrillo College; Walter Allen, North Virginia Community College; Peter Barton, University of Wisconsin–Whitewater; Abdul Baten, North Virginia Community College; Steven Becker, University of Wisconsin–Platteville; Harold Bland, Roosevelt University; Dennis Bolen, Augustana College; Lana Bone, West Valley College; Eugene Braun, North Virginia Community College; Russell Breslaur, Chabot College; Virginia Brunell, Diablo Valley College; Jim Bryant, Catonsville Community College; Terry Bullock, College of Dupage; Ashley Burrowes, California State University–Bakersfield; Madeline Carlin, University of Pittsburgh; Barbara Chiapetta, Nassau Community College; John Corradetti, Joliet Junior College; Randy Castello, West Valley College; Carolyn Craig, Shepherd College; Mark Dawson, Indiana University of Pennsylvania; Michael Deda, Fairleigh Dickinson University; Irene Douma, Montclair State College; Charles Downing, Massasoit Community College; Roger DuFresne, Northern Essex Community College; David Erlich, Queens College; Carl Fisher, Foothills College; Michael Foland, Belleville Area College; Angelo Gazzola, University of Wisconsin–Fox Valley; Robert Giacoletti, Eastern Kentucky University; Debra Goorbin, Westchester Community College; Ed Gordon, Triton College; Michael Gough, DeAnza College; Gloria Halpern, Montgomery College; Margie Hamilton, Lewis & Clark Community College; Clo Hampton, West Valley College; Ken Hardy, Catonsville Community College; Patricia Harrison, University of New Orleans; Nabil Hassan, Wright State University; Alene Helling, Stark Technical College; Keith Hendrick, Wallace State College; Sid Hyder, Indiana University of Pennsylvania; Lou Jacoby, Saginaw Valley State University; Garry K. Lym, Golden Gate University; Joe Kaderabek, Baldwin–Wallace College; Janice Kelley, St. Louis Community College; Robert Kirsch, Bowling Green State University; Carol Klinger, Queens College; Jeanette Klosterman, Hutchinson Community College; John Lannen, Salem State College; Doug Larson, Salem State College; Kathy Larson, Middlesex Community College; Larry Larson, Triton College; Henri LeClerc, Suffolk Community College; Mary Maury, St. John's University; Lynn Mazzola Paluska, Nassau Community College; Jean McKenzie, Fergus Falls Community College; Greg Mostyn, Mission College; Rhonda Mulkonen, University of South Dakota; Deborah Niemer, Oakland Community College–Royal Oak; Betty Nolen, Floyd Junior College; Cletus O'Drobinak, South Suburban College; Sandra Penn, Wayne State University; Wayne Pfingsten, Belleville Area College; Rose Marie Pilcher, Abilene Christian University; Beverly Piper, Ashland University; Paul Polachek, Loyola University of Chicago; Kay Poston, Arizona State University–West Campus; Charles Reilly, Suffolk Community College; Bill Reynolds, St. Charles Community College; James Rosa, Queensborough Community College; Victoria Rymer, University of Maryland; Stephen Schaefer, Contra Costa College; Barry Smith, DeAnza College; Jerome Spallino, Westmoreland Community College; Carolyn Strickler, Ohlone College; John Sullivan, North Shore Community College; Du Wayne Wacker, University of North Dakota; Janis Waivio, Delta College; Daniel Ward, Southwest Louisiana State University; John Wells, Triton College; Robert Wernagel, College of the Mainland; Kathleen Wessman, Montgomery College.

## Survey Respondents

James Abbott, Broome Community College; Jill Estes Bailey, Abilene Christian University; Peter Barton, University of Wisconsin, Whitewater; Chris Bennett, Taylor University; Mary Bochnak, Hamline University; Michael Brown, Abilene Christian University; M. Patrick Joseph Cahill, R.S.H.M., Marymount University; Joseph D'Adamo, Providence College; S. T. Desai, Cedar Village College; Pamela Druger, Augustana College; Jim Dunigan, University of Wisconsin, Stevens Point; Larry Edwards, Tarrant County South Junior College; Harold Goldde, Marshall University; Mary Greenawalt, The Citadel; Vicki Greshik, Jamestown College; Sue Gunkel, Albuquerque T–VI; John Hartwick, Bucks County Community College; Candie Humphrey, University of Dubuque; Thomas Kam, Hawaii Pacific University; Kenneth Koerber, Bucks County Community College; Teresa Mack, Loras College; Don McDaniel, Clatsop Community College; Jean McKenzie, Fergus Falls Community College; Noel McKeon, Florida Community College; Ben Milchman, Queensborough Community College; Charles Mitchell, Central Carolina Community College; Sally Nelson, Northeast Iowa Community College and University of Dubuque; Jon Nitschke, Montana State University; Daniel Oliveras, Inter American University; William Radig, Marshall University; Reed Reynolds, Sheldon Jackson College; S. C. Schaefer, Contra Costa College; Richard Seek, University of South Alabama; James Segar, Southern College of Seventh-Day Adventists; Robbie Sheffy, Tarrant County South Junior College; Frank Urbancic, University of South Alabama; Du Wayne Wacker, University of North Dakota; Bea Wallace, St. Phillips College; Jack Wiehler, San Joaquin Delta College; Carolyn Woodbury, University of Montana–Missoula.

## Reviewers and Focus Group Participants for *Accounting Principles,* Fourth Edition

Marilyn Allan, Central Michigan University; Melody Ashenfelter, Southwestern Oklahoma State University; Don Baynham, Eastfield College; William Brooks, Southwestern Oklahoma State University; Janet Cassagio, Nassau Community College; Sharon Cotton, Schoolcraft College; Dean Eiteman, Indiana University of Pennsylvania; Mary Kathryn Gardner, Johnson & Wales University; W. Michael Gough, De Anza College; Don Green, State University of New York–Farmingdale; John Hartwick, Bucks County Community College; Roann Kopel, Eastern Illinois University; Marcella Lecky, University of Southwestern Louisiana; Johnnie Mapp, Norfolk State University; Greg Mostyn, Mission College; Noel McKeon, Florida Community College, Jacksonville; Lynn Mazzola Paluska, Nassau Community College; Victoria Rymer, University of Maryland; Paul Shinal, Cayuga Community College; Karen Ulbrich, Parkland College; Michael Watters, New Mexico State University; Steven Wong, San Jose City College.

## Student Reviewers—Schools

Appalachian State University; Hofstra University; Nassau Community College; North Carolina A & M University; Ohlone State College; Phoenix College; Providence College; Queensborough Community College; University of Maine–Bangor; University of Texas–San Antonio; Wake Forest Technical College.

Special thanks also to our proofers, checkers, and others who provided help with the text: John C. Borke, University of Wisconsin–Platteville; Wayne M. Higley, Buena Vista College; James M. Emig, Villanova University; Larry Falcetto, Emporia State University; and Anne Lee Bain, St. Cloud State University.

We would like to provide special recognition to Paul Kimmel, University of Wisconsin–Milwaukee, who provided much insight and help in this edition. His contribution was exceptional and much appreciated. In addition, Ann Torbert gave us much help and direction in making sure the text was well-written and accurate. Cathy Manu Ka'iama of the University of Hawaii–Manoa and Martha J. King of Emporia State University provided wonderful material on accounting education changes. Larry A. Ponemon of Binghamton University contributed ethics material, Rachel Bunin lent research support, Marjorie Singer Anderson analyzed reviews, and Shirley Glass of Macomb Community College brought the learning styles survey and its use in the classroom to our attention.

We also sincerely appreciate the work of our supplements authors: Margaret Dwyer of the University of Wisconsin–Eau Claire, Larry Falcetto of Emporia State University, Jessica Frazier of Eastern Kentucky University, Marilyn F. Hunt of the University of Central Florida, Douglas W. Kieso of Aurora University, David Koeppen and Diane English of Boise State University, Kathlynn Lockhard of Northern Illinois University, Garry Lubin of Leon Levin, and Eugene R. Rozanski of Illinois State University. In addition, special recognition goes to Ivan Pagan of the University of Wisconsin–Madison and Jo Koehn of Central Missouri State University for their work in applying Bloom's Taxonomy.

We also thank the editorial, marketing, design, and production staff of John Wiley & Sons. The following individuals were particularly helpful: Susan Elbe, Karen Allman, Nancy Perry, Charlotte Hyland, Joe Heider, David Kear, Laura Eckley, Barbette Lherisson, Bill Fleischer, Francine Banner, Robert Meador, Theresa Fiorenza, Kevin Murphy, Madelyn Lesure, Anna Melhorn, Mary Ann Price, Jennifer Atkins, Mark Cirillo, Susan Stetzer, Rita Kerrigan, Jeanie Berke, Romayne Ponleithner, and Marsheela Evans. In addition, a note of gratitude to Martha Beyerlein and Barb Lange of Elm Street Publishing Services and Mike Klinman of CRWaldman for their help on this project.

Finally, our thanks for the support provided by Will Pesce, Senior Vice-President of the College Division, and Bonnie Lieberman, Editorial Director.

Suggestions and comments from users—instructors and students alike—will be appreciated.

Jerry J. Weygandt
*Madison, Wisconsin*

Donald E. Kieso
*DeKalb, Illinois*

Walter G. Kell
*Ann Arbor, Michigan*

# BRIEF CONTENTS

# CONTENTS

# Strike Three?

MILWAUKEE, Wis. — "It might be . . . it could be . . . it IS . . . a home run!" That phrase was not heard in major league baseball stadiums from August 11, 1994, until April 25, 1995. During that time major league baseball was benched by a players' strike. Who was at fault? Some argue that the reason for the strike was the greed of *both* the players and the owners. Each side—players and owners—thinks the other makes too much money, and each believes its side should be receiving more.

It would seem easy to prove how much the owners make—or lose—each year. Interim baseball commissioner Bud Selig stated that "losses for many teams are not only real, they are staggering." Selig points out that teams like the Kansas City Royals and the Detroit Tigers would have lost over $20 million if play had continued in 1994. Thus, owners argue they need

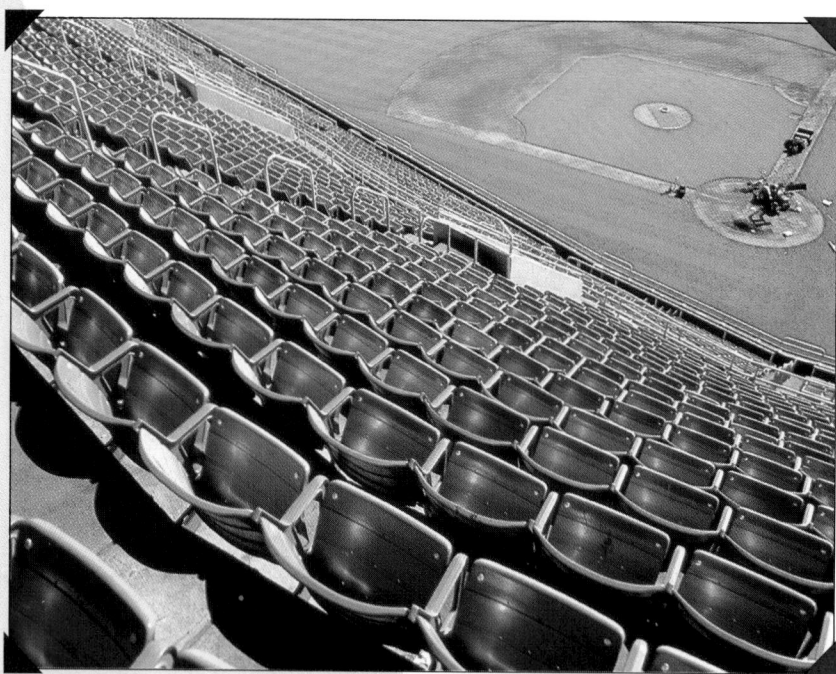

to limit salaries and other expenses in order to bring financial stability to the nation's pastime. Players' association union chief Donald Fehr, on the other hand, has said repeatedly that you can do anything with numbers. He contends that better management and more honest book-keeping would show that most baseball teams are making money. And, he notes, the value of a baseball franchise is increasing yearly.

Which argument makes more sense to you—that of the owners or the players? ◄

# CHAPTER 1

# ACCOUNTING IN ACTION

> ► STUDY OBJECTIVES ◄

**After studying this chapter, you should be able to:**

1. *Explain the meaning of accounting.*
2. *Identify the users and uses of accounting.*
3. *Understand why ethics is a fundamental business concept.*
4. *Explain the meaning of generally accepted accounting principles and the cost principle.*
5. *Explain the meaning of the monetary unit assumption and the economic entity assumption.*
6. *State the basic accounting equation and explain the meaning of assets, liabilities, and owner's equity.*
7. *Analyze the effect of business transactions on the basic accounting equation.*
8. *Prepare an income statement, owner's equity statement, balance sheet, and statement of cash flows.*

The opening story about the major league baseball strike highlights the need for accurate and sound reporting of financial information. It follows that regardless of one's pursuits or occupation, the need for financial information is inescapable. You cannot earn a living, spend money, buy on credit, make an investment, or pay taxes without receiving, using, or dispensing financial information. Good decision making depends on good information.

The purpose of this chapter is to show you that accounting is the system used to provide useful financial information. The content and organization of the chapter are as follows:

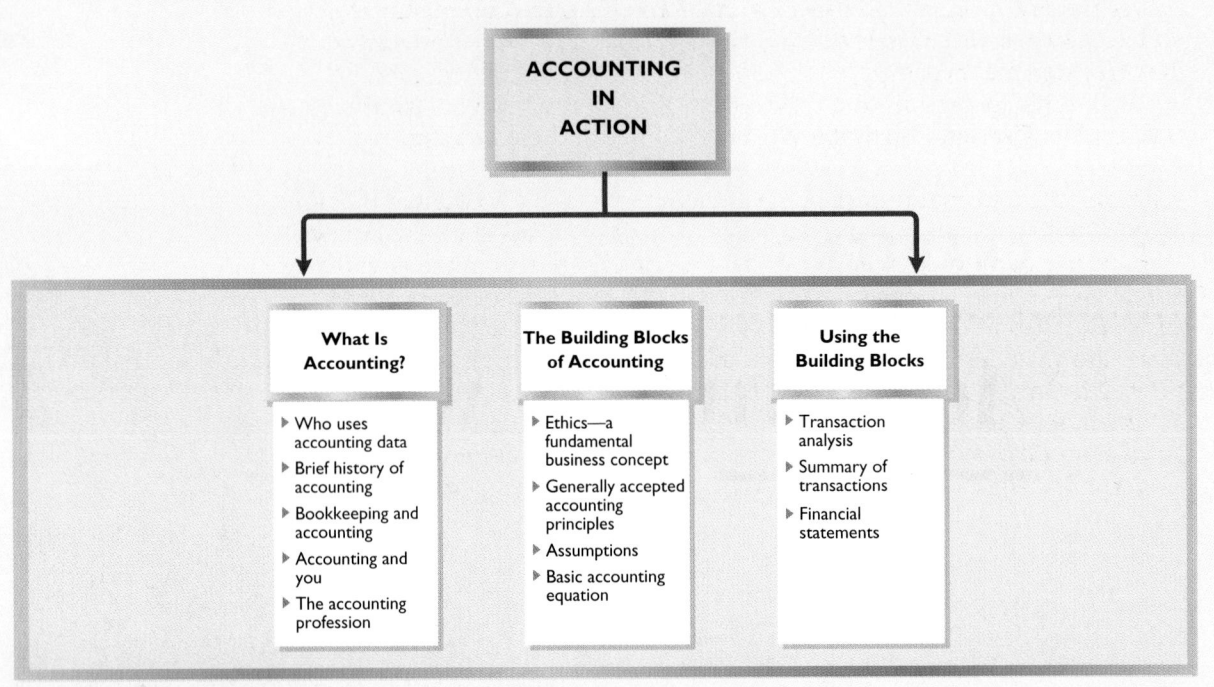

The Preview describes and outlines the major topics and subtopics you will see in the chapter. It will also help you when it is time to review the chapter before exams.

## What Is Accounting?

**STUDY OBJECTIVE**
••••••••••1••••••••••
*Explain the meaning of accounting.*

As a financial information system, accounting is a process of three activities: **identifying**, **recording**, and **communicating** the economic events of an organization (business or nonbusiness) to interested users of the information. Let's take a closer look at these three activities:

1. The first part of the process—**identifying**—involves selecting those events that are considered **evidence of economic activity relevant to a particular organization**. The sale of goods by J.C. Penney Company, the rendering of services by American Telephone & Telegraph, the payment of wages by Ford Motor Company, and the collection of ticket and broadcast money and the payment of expenses by major league baseball teams are examples of economic events.

2. Once identified and measured in dollars and cents, economic events are **recorded** to provide a permanent history of the financial activities of the or-

ganization. Recording consists of keeping a **chronological diary of measured events in an orderly and systematic manner**. In recording, economic events are also classified and summarized.

3. This identifying and recording activity is of little use unless the information is **communicated** to interested users. The information is communicated through the **preparation and distribution of accounting reports**, the most common of which are called **financial statements**. To make the reported financial information meaningful, accountants describe and report the recorded data in a standardized way. Information resulting from similar transactions is accumulated and totaled. Such data are said to be reported **in the aggregate**. For example, all sales transactions of Apple Computer are accumulated over a certain period of time and reported as one amount in the financial statements of Apple Computer. By presenting the recorded data in the aggregate, the accounting process simplifies a multitude of transactions and renders a series of activities understandable and meaningful.

A vital element in communicating economic events is the accountant's ability and responsibility to **analyze** and **interpret** the reported information. Analysis involves the use of ratios, percentages, graphs, and charts to highlight significant financial trends and relationships. Interpretation involves **explaining the uses, meaning, and limitations of reported data**. Included in Appendix A of this textbook are specimen financial statements and accompanying notes and graphs from PepsiCo, Inc. We will refer to them at various places throughout the text. At this point, they probably strike you as complex and confusing. By the end of this course, you'll be surprised at how much about them you understand.

In summary, the accounting process may be diagrammed as follows:

Illustrations such as the one below convey information in pictorial form to help you visualize and apply the information as you study.

**Illustration 1-1**

*Accounting process*

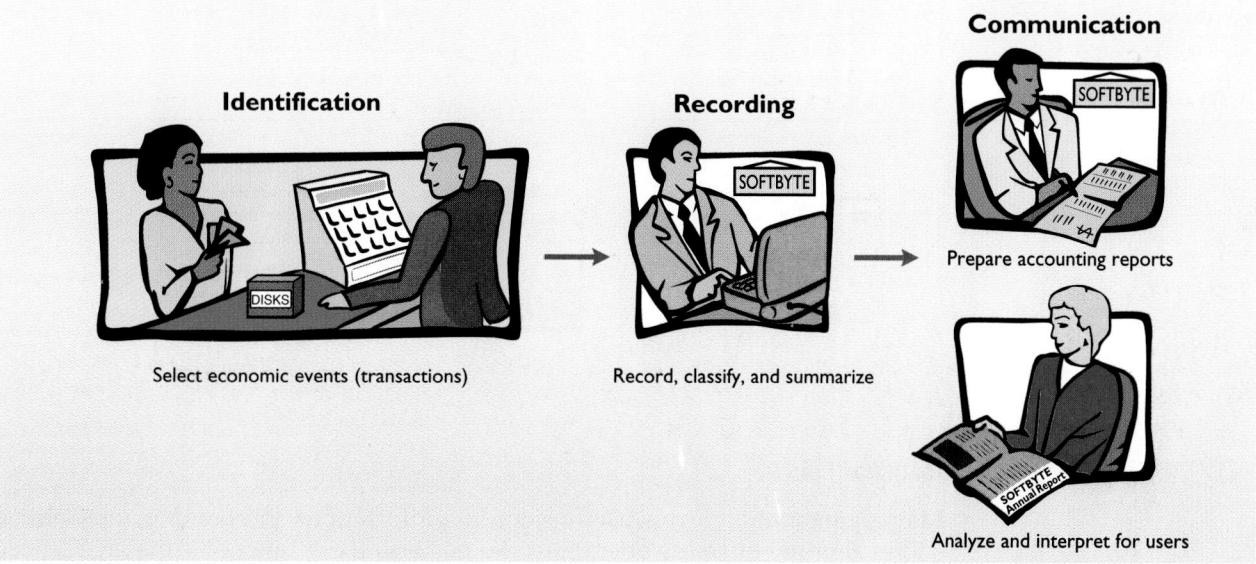

**Communication**

**Identification**

Select economic events (transactions)

**Recording**

SOFTBYTE

Record, classify, and summarize

SOFTBYTE

Prepare accounting reports

Analyze and interpret for users

Accounting should consider the needs of the users of financial information. As a consequence, you should know who these users are and something about their needs for information.

## Who Uses Accounting Data

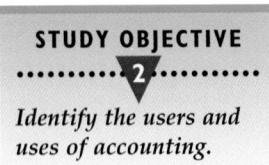

**STUDY OBJECTIVE**
••••••••••**2**••••••••••
*Identify the users and uses of accounting.*

Because it communicates financial information about a business enterprise, accounting is often called "the language of business." The information that a specific user of financial information needs depends upon the kinds of decisions that user makes. The differences in the decisions divide the users of financial information into two broad groups: internal users and external users. **Internal users** are those who manage the business (officers and other decision makers). **External users** are those outside the business who have either a **present or potential direct financial interest** (investors and creditors) or an **indirect financial interest** (taxing authorities, regulatory agencies, labor unions, customers, and economic planners). The relationship of these users to the accounting process and to one another is diagrammed in Illustration 1-2.

**Illustration 1-2**

*Users of accounting information*

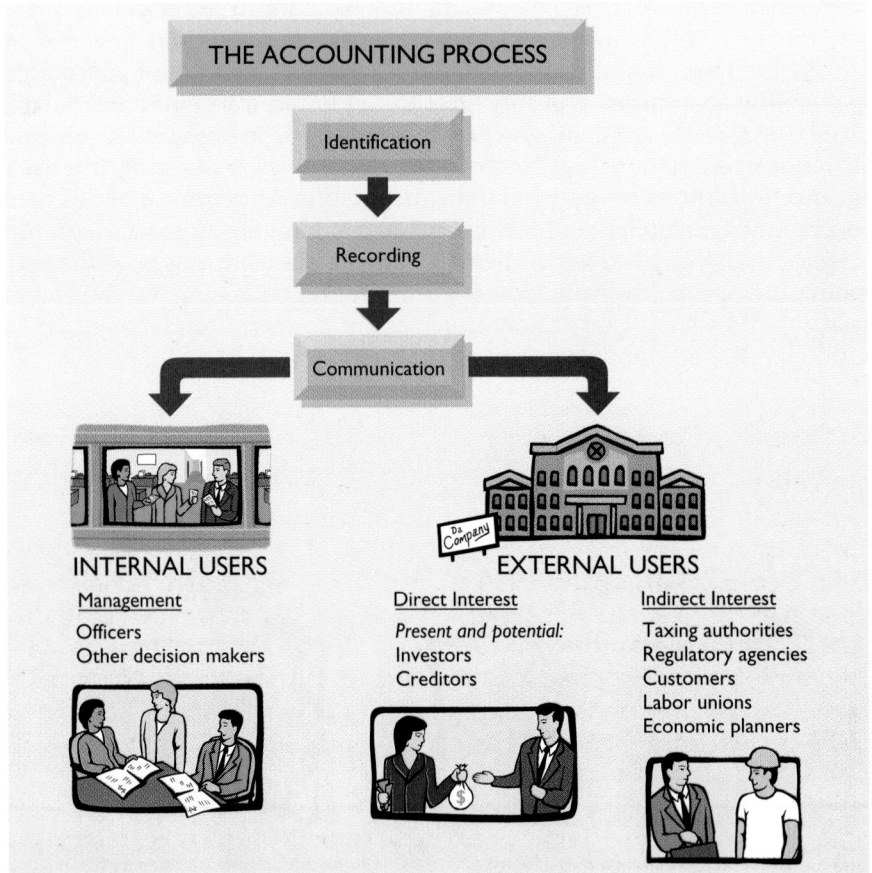

### Internal Users

**Management** at all levels uses accounting information in planning, controlling, and evaluating business operations. To perform these functions, managers need detailed information on a timely basis. For example, the managers of a company might ask:

Is cash sufficient to pay our debts?
Are customers paying their bills promptly?

What is the cost of manufacturing each unit of product?
What costs exceed budget?
Can we afford to give employee pay raises this year?
Which product line is the most profitable?
How much money must be borrowed to expand the factory?

To assist management in answering these questions, accounting provides **internal reports**. Examples include financial comparisons of operating alternatives, projections of income from new sales campaigns, and forecasts of cash needs for the next year. In addition, statements on the financial position and results of operations of the entire business are prepared.

### External Users—Direct Interest

External users with a direct interest are the company's investors and creditors. **Investors** (owners) make their decisions to buy, hold, or sell their financial interests on the basis of accounting information. **Creditors** (suppliers and bankers) evaluate the risks of granting credit or lending money on the basis of available accounting information. Some of the questions asked by investors and creditors about a company might be:

Is the company earning satisfactory income?
How does the company compare in size and profitability with competitors?
Will the company be able to pay its debts as they come due?
Are interest payments and dividends protected by an adequate inflow of cash from operations?

### External Users—Indirect Interest

The information needs and questions of those with indirect financial interests vary considerably. **Taxing authorities** (such as the Internal Revenue Service) want to know if the company complies with the tax laws. **Regulatory agencies** (such as the Securities and Exchange Commission or the Federal Trade Commission) want to know if the company is operating within prescribed rules. **Customers** are interested in whether a company will continue to honor product warranties and otherwise support its product lines. **Labor unions** (such as the major league players' association in the opening story) want to know if the owners have the ability to pay increased wages and benefits. **Economic planners** use accounting information to analyze and forecast economic activity.

The many and varied uses of accounting information clearly attest to its importance. **Without accounting, our existing systems of production, investment, credit, and taxation would be seriously impaired.**

## Brief History of Accounting

The **origins of accounting** are generally attributed to the work of Luca Pacioli, a famous Italian Renaissance mathematician. Pacioli was a close friend and tutor to Leonardo da Vinci and a contemporary of Christopher Columbus. In his text *Summa de Arithmetica, Geometria, Proportione et Proportionalite*, Pacioli described a system to ensure that financial information was recorded efficiently and accurately.

With the advent of the **industrial age** in the nineteenth century and, later, the emergence of large corporations, a separation of the owners from the man-

## ▲Accounting in Action ▸ *International Insight*

When the chief engineer of Irkutsk Energo, a public utility in Moscow, addressed a gathering of international investors recently, he provided them with all kinds of financial information about the company. The reason: Russians are learning that corporate openness lures much-needed foreign investment. Foreign investors, however, have been reluctant to invest because Russian firms have been secretive (and sometimes deceptive) about their financial affairs. Now, however, things will probably change because firms such as Irkutsk Energo have enjoyed stock price surges after providing candid accounting information. In short, good accounting information may help Russia solve some of its economic problems.

*Source: Wall Street Journal,* June 9, 1995, p. A-6.

Throughout this textbook, you will find Accounting in Action examples highlighted like this. These examples illustrate important and interesting information as it relates to actual accounting situations in business. Different icons highlight each type of issue—a globe, as here, for international insights, scales for ethics insights, and a city skyline for business insights.

agers of businesses took place. As a result, the need to report the status of the business enterprise took on increasing importance, to ensure that managers acted in accord with owners' wishes. In addition, transactions between businesses became more complex, making necessary improved approaches for reporting financial information.

Our economy has now evolved into a post-industrial age—**the information age**—in which the "products" are information services. The computer, as the information processor, has been the driver of the information age.

The pace of business change has also increased, partly in response to international competition. Companies must remake themselves rapidly, and they are doing it by a whole assortment of actions: downsizing, worker empowerment, process reengineering, mergers, alliances, and novel financial instruments. Accounting is constantly adapting to this changing environment, by examining carefully the types of financial information needed in this fast-paced environment.

### Distinguishing between Bookkeeping and Accounting

Many individuals mistakenly consider bookkeeping and accounting to be one and the same. This confusion is understandable because the accounting process **includes the bookkeeping function**. However, accounting also includes much more. Bookkeeping usually involves only the **recording of economic events** and is therefore just one part of the accounting process. In total, accounting involves the **entire process** of identification, recording, and communication.

The bookkeeping function is often performed by individuals with limited skills in accounting. As a result, it is not surprising that the increased use of computers by business enterprises has resulted in much of the detailed work that is part of the bookkeeping process being performed by machines.

### Accounting and You

One question frequently asked by students of accounting is, "How will the study of accounting help me?" It should help you a great deal, because a working knowledge of accounting is desirable for virtually every field of endeavor. Some illustrations of how accounting is used in other careers include:

> **General management:** Imagine running General Motors, a major hospital, a school, a McDonald's franchise, a bike shop; all general managers need to understand and have access to accounting data in order to make wise business decisions.

## ►*Technology* in *Action*

With the phenomenal growth in computers, more and more record keeping is being performed electronically. Businesses, small as well as large, are finding that through the use of the computer the entire recording process has become more efficient. However it is important to know the procedures used in a manual system to understand the operations a computer performs.

Throughout this textbook you will find computer notes highlighted like this. These notes are designed to show how computer technology is used in accounting and business.

**Marketing/Advertising:** A marketing specialist is someone who develops strategies to help the sales force be successful. But making a sale is meaningless unless it is a profitable sale. Marketing people must be sensitive to costs and benefits, which accounting helps them quantify and understand.

Marketing people are also involved in advertising. What would a flashy field such as advertising have to do with accounting? Just ask anybody who works in the media department of a company or an ad agency: If you buy a commercial on a radio station, you'll want to know the cost per thousand listeners. You'll deal in ratings numbers and budgets all day. And ad agencies are always under pressure to cut costs, because their clients can be very fickle—particularly if the ad campaign doesn't work.

**Finance:** Do you want to be a banker, an investment analyst, a stock broker? These fields rely heavily on accounting. Suppose you decide to go into banking. You could become a lending officer, a money manager, a deal-maker, a foreign currency trader, or a retail branch supervisor. You could work with huge companies or with a mom-and-pop business down the street. You might specialize in one industry, such as health care, or be a generalist. Whatever the situation, you will regularly examine financial statements to understand the financial standing of your customer. In fact, it is difficult to get a good job in a finance function without two or three courses in accounting.

**Real estate:** Perhaps the most prevalent career in real estate is that of a broker, a person who sells residential or commercial real estate. Because a third party—the bank—is almost always involved in financing a real estate transaction, brokers must understand the numbers involved: Can the buyer of the house afford to make the payments to the bank on a given salary? Does the cash flow from the industrial property justify the purchase price in this market? What are the tax benefits of making the purchase?

Accounting is useful even for occupations you might think completely unrelated. If you become a doctor, a lawyer, a social worker, a teacher, an engineer, an architect, or an entrepreneur—you name it—a working knowledge of accounting is relevant.

## The Accounting Profession

What would you do if you joined the accounting profession? You probably would apply your expertise in one of three major fields—public accounting, private accounting, or not-for-profit accounting.

### *Public Accounting*

In public accounting, you would offer expert service to the general public in much the same way that a doctor serves patients and a lawyer serves clients. A major portion of public accounting practice is involved with auditing. In this area, a certified public accountant (CPA) examines the financial statements of companies and expresses an opinion as to the fairness of presentation. When the presentation is fair, users consider the statements to be **reliable**. In the opening story, audited financial statements should be required by the major league baseball players' association in assessing the financial soundness of baseball franchises.

Taxation is another major area of public accounting. The work performed by tax specialists includes tax advice and planning, preparing tax returns, and representing clients before governmental agencies such as the Internal Revenue Service.

A third area in public accounting is management consulting. Management consulting ranges from the installing of basic computerized accounting systems to helping companies determine whether they should use the space shuttle for high-tech research and development projects.

### Private Accounting

Instead of working in public accounting, an accountant may be an employee of a business enterprise. In private (or managerial) accounting, you would be involved in one of the following activities:

1. **Cost accounting**—determining the cost of producing specific products.
2. **Budgeting**—assisting management in quantifying goals concerning revenues, costs of goods sold, and operating expenses.
3. **General accounting**—recording daily transactions and preparing financial statements and related information.
4. **Accounting information systems**—designing both manual and computerized data processing systems.
5. **Tax accounting**—preparing tax returns and engaging in tax planning for the company.
6. **Internal auditing**—reviewing the company's operations to determine compliance with management policies and evaluating the efficiency of operations.

From the above, you can see that within a specific company, private accountants perform as wide a variety of duties as the public accountant.

Illustration 1-3 presents the general career paths in public and private accounting.

### Not-for-Profit Accounting

Like businesses that exist to make a profit, not-for-profit organizations also need sound financial reporting and control. Donors to such organizations as the United Way, the Ford Foundation, and the Red Cross want information about how well the organization has met its objectives and whether continued support is justified. Hospitals, colleges, and universities must make decisions about the allocation of funds. Local, state, and federal governmental units are continually providing financial information to legislators, citizens, employees, and creditors. In each of these cases, accounting expertise is highly valued. At the federal level, for example, the largest employers of accountants are the Internal Revenue Service, the General Accounting Office, the Federal Bureau of Investigation, and the Securities and Exchange Commission.

**Illustration 1-3**

*Career paths in public and private accounting*

## ACCOUNTING CAREER LADDER

**Business and Industry
(Private Accounting)**

Public Accounting

**VP Finance
and CFO**

10+ years

Partner

**Corporate
Controller**

6 to 8 years

Audit Manager

**Senior Accountant**

2 to 4+ years

Senior Auditor

**Junior Accountant**

Entry level

Junior Auditor

## ▶ **A**ccounting in **A**ction ► *Business Insight*

### *Help Wanted: Forensic CPAs*

Tom Taylor's job at the FBI has changed. He used to pack a .357 magnum; now he wields a No. 2 pencil. Taylor, age 37, for two years an FBI agent, is a forensic accountant, somebody who sniffs through company books to ferret out white-collar crime.

Demand for this service has surged in the past few years. In one recent year, a recruiter for San Diego's Robert Half International, a headhunting firm, had requests for more than 1,000 such snoops.

Qualification: a CPA with FBI, IRS, or similar government experience. Interestingly, despite its macho image, the FBI has long hired mostly accountants and lawyers as agents.

## Before You Go On . . .

### ▶ Review It

1. What is accounting?
2. Who uses accounting information?
3. What is the difference between bookkeeping and accounting?
4. How can you use your accounting knowledge?

# The Building Blocks of Accounting

Every profession develops a body of theory consisting of principles, assumptions, and standards. Accounting is no exception. Just as a doctor follows certain standards in treating a patient's illness, an accountant follows certain standards in reporting financial information. For these standards to work, however, a fundamental business concept is followed—ethical behavior.

### Ethics—A Fundamental Business Concept

**STUDY OBJECTIVE**

**3**

*Understand why ethics is a fundamental business concept.*

Wherever you make your career—whether in accounting, marketing, management, finance, government, or elsewhere—your behavior and actions will affect other people and organizations. The standards of conduct by which one's actions are judged as right or wrong, honest or dishonest, fair or not fair, are ethics. Imagine trying to carry on a business, perform an audit, or invest money if you could not depend on the individuals you deal with to be honest. If managers, customers, investors, co-workers, and creditors all consistently lied, effective communication and economic activity would be impossible. Information would have no credibility.

Fortunately most individuals in business are ethical. Their actions are both legal and responsible, and they consider the organization's interests in their decision making. However, in some situations public officials, business executives, and respected leaders act unethically. For example, a former chief of the finance committee of the House of Representatives was indicted for possible illegal behavior; Sears was accused of widespread customer overcharging on car repairs; Woolworth Corp. executives were dismissed because they reported false income numbers. As one business leader noted: "We are all embarrassed by the events that make *The Wall Street Journal* read like the *Police Gazette*."

To sensitize you to ethical situations and to give you practice at solving ethical dilemmas, we have included in the book three types of ethics materials: (1) marginal notes that provide helpful hints for developing ethical sensitivity, (2) ethics in accounting boxes that highlight ethics situations and issues, and (3) an ethics case simulating a business situation at the end of the chapter. In the process of analyzing these ethics cases, you should apply the steps outlined in Illustration 1-4.

### Generally Accepted Accounting Principles

**STUDY OBJECTIVE**

**4**

*Explain the meaning of generally accepted accounting principles and the cost principle.*

The accounting profession has attempted to develop a set of standards that is generally accepted and universally practiced. Its efforts have resulted in a common set of standards called generally accepted accounting principles (GAAP). These standards indicate how to report economic events.

Two organizations are primarily responsible for establishing generally accepted accounting principles. The first is the Financial Accounting Standards

**Illustration 1-4**

*Steps in analyzing ethics cases*

### Solving an Ethical Dilemma

**1. Recognize an ethical situation and the ethical issues involved.**

Use your personal ethics to identify ethical situations and issues. Some businesses and professional organizations provide written codes of ethics for guidance in some business situations.

**2. Identify and analyze the principal elements in the situation.**

Identify the *stakeholders*— persons or groups who may be harmed or benefited. Ask the question: What are the responsibilities and obligations of the parties involved?

**3. Identify the alternatives, and weigh the impact of each alternative on various stakeholders.**

Select the most ethical alternative, considering all the consequences. Sometimes there will be one right answer. Other situations involve more than one right solution; these situations require an evaluation of each and a selection of the best alternative.

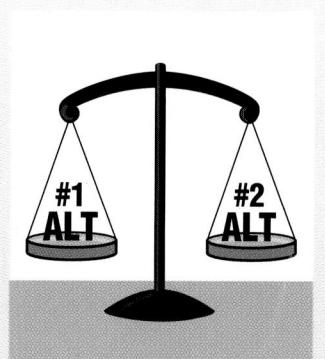

Board (FASB), a private organization that establishes broad reporting standards of general applicability as well as specific accounting rules. The second, the Securities and Exchange Commission (SEC), is a governmental agency that requires companies filing financial reports with it to follow generally accepted accounting principles. In situations where no principles exist, the SEC often mandates that certain guidelines be used. In general, the FASB and the SEC work hand in hand to assure that timely and useful accounting principles are developed.

One important principle is the cost principle, which states that assets should be recorded at their cost. **Cost is the value exchanged at the time something is acquired.** If you buy a house today, the cost is the amount you pay for it, say $100,000. If you sell the house in two years for $120,000, the sales price is its **market value**—the value determined by the market for homes at that time. At the time of acquisition, cost and fair market value are the same. In subsequent periods, cost and fair market value may vary, **but the cost amount continues to be used**.

For example, at one time, Greyhound Corporation had 128 bus stations nationwide that cost approximately $200 million. The current market value of the stations is approximately $1 billion. Under the cost principle, the bus stations are recorded and reported at $200 million, not $1 billion. Until the bus stations are actually sold, estimates of market values are considered too subjective.

As the Greyhound example indicates, cost has an important advantage over other valuations: it is reliable. Cost is definite and verifiable. The values exchanged at the time something is acquired generally can be objectively measured. To rely on the information supplied, users must know that the information is based on fact. However, critics argue that cost is often not relevant and that market values provide more useful information. Despite its shortcomings, cost continues to be used in the financial statements because of its reliability.

## Assumptions

In developing generally accepted accounting principles, certain basic assumptions are made. These assumptions provide a foundation for the accounting process. Two main assumptions are the **monetary unit assumption** and the **economic entity assumption**.

► **International note**

The standard-setting processes in Canada, Mexico, and the United States are quite similar in most respects. All three have relatively open deliberations on new rules, and they support efforts to follow international standards. The use of similar accounting principles within North America has implications for the success of the North American Free Trade Agreement (NAFTA).

## Monetary Unit Assumption

**STUDY OBJECTIVE**
••••••••• ▼5▼ •••••••••

*Explain the meaning of the monetary unit assumption and the economic entity assumption.*

The monetary unit assumption requires that only transaction data that can be expressed in terms of money be included in the accounting records of the economic entity. Because money is the commonly used medium of exchange, this assumption enables accounting to quantify (measure) the economic event. The monetary unit assumption is vital to applying the cost principle discussed earlier. This assumption prevents such relevant information as the health of the owner, the quality of service, and the morale of employees from being included in the accounting records because they cannot be quantified in terms of money.

**An important corollary to the monetary unit assumption is the added assumption that the unit of measure remains sufficiently constant over time.** However, the assumption of a stable monetary unit has been challenged because of the significant decline in the purchasing power of the dollar. For example, what used to cost $1.00 in 1960, costs over $4.00 in 1996, an increase of fourfold. In such situations, adding, subtracting, or comparing 1960 dollars with 1996 dollars is highly questionable. The profession has recognized this problem and encourages companies to disclose the effects of changing prices.

## Economic Entity Assumption

**▶ Ethics note**

An IRS investigation uncovered the following violation of the economic entity assumption: Gucci Shops, the international retail chain, issued checks payable to "Gucci," supposedly to pay for expenses of acquiring merchandise through a buying office in Italy. However, the checks actually went into founder Aldo Gucci's personal bank accounts, and the cash diverted from the business was divided among Gucci family members. (*Source: Wall Street Journal,* 1/20/86.)

**An economic entity can be any organization or unit in society.** It may be a business enterprise (such as General Electric Company), a governmental unit (such as the state of Ohio), a municipality (such as Seattle), a school district (such as St. Louis District 48), or a social organization such as a church (Southern Baptist), a fraternity (Theta Chi), or a sorority (Chi Omega). The economic entity assumption states that economic events can be identified with a particular unit of accountability. This assumption requires that the activities of the entity be kept separate and distinct from (1) the activities of its owner and (2) all other economic entities. To illustrate, if Sally Rider, owner of Sally's Boutique, charges any of her personal living costs as expenses of the Boutique, the economic entity assumption is violated. Similarly, the economic entity assumption assumes that the activities of McDonald's, Wendy's, and Burger King can each be segregated into separate economic entities for accounting purposes.

Although the economic entity assumption can be applied to any unit of accountability, we will generally discuss it in relation to a business enterprise, which may be organized as a proprietorship, partnership, or corporation.

## ▶ Accounting in Action ▸ *Ethics Insight*

⚖ A violation of the entity assumption contributed to the recent resignation by the chief executive of W.R. Grace and Company. Investors were angered to learn that company funds were used for personal medical care, a Manhattan apartment, and a personal chef for the company's chief. Funds were also used to support a hotel interest owned by the chief executive's son.

*Source: New York Times,* March 10, 1995.

**Proprietorship.**   A business owned by one person is generally a proprietorship. The owner is often the manager/operator of the business. Small service-type businesses (barber shops, law offices, plumbing companies, and auto repair shops), farms, and small retail stores (antique shops, clothing stores, and book stores) are often sole proprietorships. **Usually only a limited amount of money (capital) is necessary to start in business as a proprietorship, and the owner receives any profits, suffers any losses, and is personally liable for all debts**

**of the business.** Although there is no legal distinction between the business as an economic unit and the owner, the records of the business activities are kept separate from the personal records and activities of the owner. Although sole proprietorships represent the largest number of businesses in the United States, they are typically the smallest in size and volume of business.

**Partnership.** A business owned by two or more persons associated as partners is a partnership. In most respects a partnership is similar to a sole proprietorship except that more than one owner is involved. When a partnership is created, an agreement (written or oral) should set forth such terms as initial investment of each partner, duties of each partner, division of net income (or net loss), and settlement to be made upon death or withdrawal of a partner. Each partner generally has unlimited personal liability for the debts of the partnership. **Like a proprietorship, for accounting purposes the partnership affairs must be kept separate from the personal activities of the partners.** Partnerships are often used to organize retail and service-type businesses, including professional practices (lawyers, doctors, architects, and certified public accountants).

**Corporation.** A business organized as a separate legal entity under state corporation law and having ownership divided into transferable shares of stock is called a corporation. The holders of the shares (stockholders) **enjoy limited liability**; they are not personally liable for the debts of the corporate entity. Stockholders **may transfer all or part of their shares to other investors at any time** (i.e., sell their shares in the securities market). The ease with which ownership can change adds to the attractiveness of investing in a corporation. Because ownership can be transferred without dissolving the corporation, the corporation **enjoys an unlimited life**.

Although the combined number of proprietorships and partnerships in the United States is more than five times the number of corporations, the revenue produced by corporations is eight times greater. Most of the largest enterprises in the United States—for example, Exxon, General Motors, Sears Roebuck, Citicorp, and Pacific Gas and Electric—are corporations.

## Basic Accounting Equation

Other essential building blocks of accounting are the categories into which economic events are classified. The two basic elements of a business are what it owns and what it owes. **Assets** are the resources owned by a business. For example, Eastman Kodak has total assets of approximately $15 billion. **Equities** are the rights or claims against these resources. Thus, a company such as Eastman Kodak that has $15 billion of assets also has $15 billion of claims against those assets. This relationship can be shown in equation form as follows:

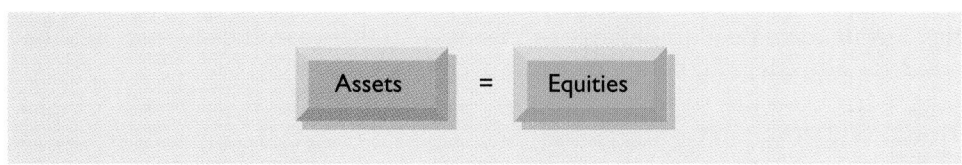

Equities may be further subdivided into two categories: claims of creditors and claims of owners. Claims of creditors are called **liabilities**. Claims of owners are called **owner's equity**. For example, Eastman Kodak has liabilities of $11 billion and owners' equity of $4 billion. The equation above can, then, be expanded as follows:

**Helpful hint** Principles and assumptions will be discussed throughout the text. Here is a full list; those discussed so far are shown in bold:

Principles
─────────────
**Cost**
Revenue recognition
Matching
Full disclosure

Assumptions
─────────────
**Monetary unit**
**Economic entity**
Time period
Going concern

**STUDY OBJECTIVE**
·········▼**6**·········
*State the basic accounting equation and explain the meaning of assets, liabilities, and owner's equity.*

**Illustration 1-5**
*Relationship between assets and equities*

**Illustration 1-6**

*The basic accounting equation*

This equation is referred to as the basic accounting equation. Assets must equal the sum of liabilities and owner's equity. Because creditors' claims are paid before ownership claims if a business is liquidated, liabilities are shown before owner's equity in the basic accounting equation.

The accounting equation applies to all **economic entities** regardless of size, nature of business, or form of business organization. Thus, it applies to a small proprietorship such as a corner grocery store as well as to a giant corporation such as AT&T. The equation provides the underlying framework for recording and summarizing the economic events of a business enterprise.

Let's look in more detail at the categories in the basic accounting equation.

### Assets

As indicated above, assets are resources owned by a business. Thus, they are the things of value used in carrying out such activities as production, consumption, and exchange. The common characteristic possessed by all assets is the capacity to provide future services or benefits to the entities that use them. In a business enterprise, that service potential or future economic benefit eventually results in cash inflows (receipts) to the enterprise.

For example, the enterprise Campus Pizza owns a delivery truck that provides economic benefits because it is used in delivering pizzas. Other assets of Campus Pizza are tables, chairs, jukebox, cash register, oven, mugs and silverware, and, of course, cash.

### Liabilities

Liabilities are claims against assets. Put more simply, **liabilities are existing debts and obligations**. For example, businesses of all sizes and degrees of success usually find it necessary to borrow money and to purchase merchandise on credit. Campus Pizza, for instance, purchases cheese, sausage, flour, and beverages on credit from suppliers; these obligations are called **accounts payable**. Additionally, Campus Pizza has a **note payable** to First National Bank for the money borrowed to purchase its delivery truck. Campus Pizza may also have **wages payable** to employees, and **sales and real estate taxes payable** to the local government. Persons or entities to whom Campus Pizza owes money are called **creditors**.

Most claims of creditors attach to **total** enterprise assets rather than to the specific assets provided by the creditor. In the event of nonpayment, creditors may legally force the liquidation of a business. In that case, the law requires that creditor claims be paid before ownership claims.

### Owner's Equity

The ownership claim on total assets is known as owner's equity. It is equal to total assets minus total liabilities. Here is why: The assets of a business are supplied or claimed by either creditors or owners. To determine what belongs to owners, we therefore subtract creditors' claims—the liabilities—from assets. The remainder—owner's equity—is the owner's claim on the assets of the business. Since the claims of creditors take precedence over ownership claims, the latter are often referred to as **residual equity**.

In a proprietorship, owner's equity is increased by owner's investments and revenues. It is decreased by owner's drawings and expenses.

**Investments by Owner.** Investments by owner are the assets put into the business by the owner. These investments in the business increase owner's equity.

**Drawings.** An owner may withdraw cash or other assets during the accounting period for personal use. These withdrawals could be recorded as a direct decrease of owner's equity. However, it is generally considered preferable to use a separate classification referred to as drawings to determine the total withdrawals for the accounting period. **Drawings decrease total owner's equity.**

**Revenues.** Revenues are the gross increase in owner's equity resulting from business activities entered into for the purpose of earning income. Generally, revenues result from the sale of merchandise, the performance of services, the rental of property, and the lending of money.

> **Helpful hint** The effect of revenues is positive—an increase in owner's equity coupled with an increase in assets or a decrease in liabilities.

Revenues usually result in an increase in an asset. They may arise from different sources and are identified by various names depending on the nature of the business. Campus Pizza, for instance, has two categories of sales revenues—pizza sales and beverage sales. Other titles for and sources of revenue common to many businesses are: sales, fees, services, commissions, interest, dividends, royalties, and rent.

**Expenses.** Expenses are **the decreases in owner's equity that result from operating the business.** They are the cost of assets consumed or services used in the process of earning revenue. Expenses represent actual or expected cash outflows (payments). Like revenues, expenses take many forms and are identified by various names depending on the type of asset consumed or service used. For example, Campus Pizza recognizes the following types of expenses: cost of ingredients (meat, flour, cheese, tomato paste, mushrooms, etc.); cost of beverages; wages expense; utility expense (electric, gas, and water expense); telephone expense; delivery expense (gasoline, repairs, licenses, etc.); supplies expense (napkins, detergents, aprons, etc.); rent expense; interest expense; and property tax expense.

> **Helpful hint** The effect of expenses is negative—a decrease in owner's equity coupled with a decrease in assets, or an increase in liabilities.

In summary, the principal sources (increases) of owner's equity are (1) investments by owners and (2) revenues from business operations. In contrast, reductions in owner's equity are a result of (1) withdrawals of assets by owners and (2) expenses. Net income results when revenues exceed expenses; conversely, a net loss occurs when expenses exceed revenues.

These relationships are shown in Illustration 1-7.

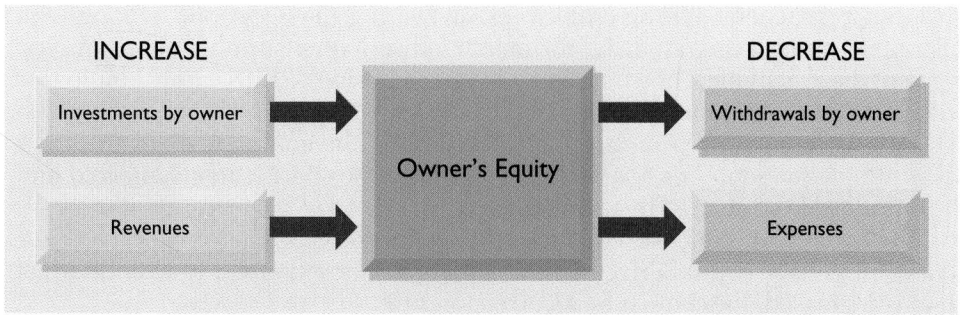

**Illustration 1-7**

*Increases and decreases in owner's equity*

## Before You Go On . . .

### ▶ Review It

1. Why is ethics considered a fundamental business concept?
2. What are generally accepted accounting principles? Give an example of an accounting principle.
3. Explain the monetary unit and the economic entity assumption.
4. What is the basic accounting equation?
5. What are assets, liabilities, and owner's equity?

*Do It* exercises give you immediate practice of the material just covered. These exercises outline the reasoning necessary to complete the exercise and a solution.

### ▶ Do It

Classify the following items as investment by owner (I), owner's drawings (D), revenues (R), or expenses (E), and indicate whether these items increase or decrease owner's equity: (1) Rent Expense, (2) Service Revenue, (3) Drawings, and (4) Salaries Expense.

**Reasoning:** Both investments and service revenue increase owner's equity; however, service revenue arises from the sale of merchandise, the performance of services, the rental of property, or the lending of money. Investments are resources contributed to the business by the owner. Similarly, expenses and drawings decrease owner's equity; however, expenses arise from consuming assets or services. Drawings are withdrawals of cash or other assets from the business for personal use.

**Solution:**
(1) Rent Expense is classified as an expense (E); it decreases owner's equity.
(2) Service Revenue is classified as revenue (R); it increases owner's equity.
(3) Drawings is classified as owner's drawings (D); it decreases owner's equity.
(4) Salaries Expense is classified as an expense (E); it decreases owner's equity.

*Related exercise material: BE1–1, BE1–2, BE1–3, BE1–4, BE1–5, BE1–6, BE1–7, BE1–9, E1–1, E1–2, E1–3, E1–4, E1–6, and E1–7.*

# Using the Building Blocks

**STUDY OBJECTIVE**
**7**

*Analyze the effect of business transactions on the basic accounting equation.*

**Helpful hint** Transactions are events that cause a change in individual assets, liabilities, or one of the subdivisions of owner's equity.

Transactions (often referred to as business transactions) are the economic events of the enterprise that are recorded. Transactions may be identified as external or internal. **External transactions involve economic events between the company and some outside enterprise or party.** For example, for Campus Pizza the purchase of cooking equipment from a supplier, the payment of monthly rent to the landlord, and the sale of pizzas to customers are external transactions. **Internal transactions are economic events that occur entirely within one company.** The use of office supplies illustrates this type of transaction for Campus Pizza.

A company may carry on many activities that do not in themselves represent business transactions. Hiring employees, answering the telephone, talking with customers, and placing an order for merchandise with a supplier are examples. Some of these activities, however, may lead to a business transaction: employees will earn wages, and merchandise will be delivered by the supplier. Each transaction must be analyzed in terms of its effect on the components of the basic accounting equation. This analysis must identify the specific items affected and the amount of the change in each item.

The equality of the basic equation must be preserved. Therefore, each transaction must have a dual effect on the equation. For example, if an individual asset is increased, there must be a corresponding:

1. Decrease in another asset, or
2. Increase in a specific liability, or
3. Increase in owner's equity.

It follows that two or more items could be affected when an asset is increased. For example, as one asset is increased $10,000, another asset could decrease $6,000, and a specific liability could increase $4,000. Note also that any change in an individual liability or ownership claim is subject to similar analysis.

## Transaction Analysis

The following examples are business transactions for a new computer programming business during its first month of operations. You will want to study these transactions until you are sure you understand them. They are not difficult but they are important to your success in this course. The ability to analyze transactions in terms of the basic accounting equation is essential for an understanding of accounting.

**Transaction (1). Investment by Owner.** Ray Neal decides to open a computer programming service. On September 1, 1996, he invests $15,000 cash in the business, which he names Softbyte. This transaction results in an equal increase in assets and owner's equity. In this case, there is an increase in the asset Cash, $15,000, and an equal increase in the owner's equity, R. Neal, Capital, $15,000. The effect of this transaction on the basic equation is:

|   | Assets | = | Liabilities | + | Owner's Equity | |
|---|---|---|---|---|---|---|
|   | Cash | = |   |   | R. Neal, Capital | |
| (1) | +$15,000 | = |   |   | +$15,000 | Investment |

Observe that the equality of the basic equation has been maintained. Note also that the source of the increase in owner's equity is indicated, to make clear that the increase is an investment rather than revenue from operations. Why does this matter? Because investments by the owner do not represent revenues, and they are excluded in determining net income.

**Transaction (2). Purchase of Equipment for Cash.** Softbyte purchases computer equipment for $7,000 cash. This transaction results in an equal increase and decrease in total assets, though the composition of assets is changed: Cash is decreased $7,000, and the asset Equipment is increased $7,000. Both the specific effect of this transaction and the cumulative effect of the first two transactions are:

|   |   | Assets | | | = | Liabilities | + | Owner's Equity |
|---|---|---|---|---|---|---|---|---|
|   |   | Cash | + | Equipment | = |   |   | R. Neal, Capital |
|   | Old Bal. | $15,000 |   |   | = |   |   | $15,000 |
| (2) |   | −7,000 |   | +$7,000 |   |   |   |   |
|   | New Bal. | $ 8,000 | + | $7,000 | = |   |   | $15,000 |
|   |   | | $15,000 | | | | | |

Observe that total assets are still $15,000 and Neal's equity also remains at $15,000, the amount of his original investment.

**Transaction (3).   Purchase of Supplies on Credit.**   Softbyte purchases computer paper and other supplies expected to last several months from Acme Supply Company for $1,600. Acme Company agrees to allow Softbyte to pay this bill in October, a month later. This transaction is often referred to as a purchase on account or a credit purchase. Assets are increased by this transaction because of the expected future benefits of using the paper and supplies, and liabilities are increased by the amount due Acme Company. The asset Supplies is increased $1,600, and the liability Accounts Payable is increased by the same amount. The effect on the equation is:

|  |  | Assets | | | = | Liabilities | + | Owner's Equity |
|---|---|---|---|---|---|---|---|---|
|  |  |  |  |  |  | Accounts |  | R. Neal, |
|  |  | Cash | + Supplies | + Equipment = | | Payable | + | Capital |
|  | Old. Bal. | $8,000 |  | $7,000 |  |  |  | $15,000 |
| (3) |  |  | +$1,600 |  |  | +$1,600 |  |  |
|  | New Bal. | $8,000 + | $1,600 + | $7,000 | = | $1,600 | + | $15,000 |
|  |  |  | $16,600 | | | | $16,600 | |

Total assets are now $16,600. This total is matched by a $1,600 creditor's claim and a $15,000 ownership claim.

**Transaction (4).   Services Rendered for Cash.**   Softbyte receives $1,200 cash from customers for programming services it has provided. This transaction represents the principal revenue-producing activity of Softbyte. Recall that **revenue increases owner's equity**. Both assets and owner's equity are, then, increased by this transaction: In this case, Cash is increased $1,200, and R. Neal, Capital, is increased $1,200. The new balances in the equation are:

|  |  | Assets | | | = | Liabilities | + | Owner's Equity | |
|---|---|---|---|---|---|---|---|---|---|
|  |  |  |  |  |  | Accounts |  | R. Neal, |  |
|  |  | Cash | + Supplies | + Equipment = | | Payable | + | Capital | |
|  | Old Bal. | $8,000 | $1,600 | $7,000 |  | $1,600 |  | $15,000 | |
| (4) |  | +1,200 |  |  |  |  |  | +1,200 | Service Revenue |
|  | New Bal. | $9,200 + | $1,600 + | $7,000 | = | $1,600 | + | $16,200 | |
|  |  |  | $17,800 | | | | $17,800 | | |

The two sides of the equation balance at $17,800. Note that owner's equity is increased when revenues are earned. The source of the increase in owner's equity is indicated as service revenue. Service revenue is included in determining Softbyte's net income.

**Transaction (5).   Purchase of Advertising on Credit.**   Softbyte receives a bill for $250 from the *Daily News* for advertising the opening of its business but postpones payment of the bill until a later date. This transaction results in an increase in liabilities and a decrease in owner's equity. The specific items involved are Accounts Payable and R. Neal, Capital. The effect on the equation is:

| | | Assets | | | | = | Liabilities | + | Owner's Equity | |
|---|---|---|---|---|---|---|---|---|---|---|
| | | Cash | + Supplies | + Equipment | = | | Accounts Payable | + | R. Neal, Capital | |
| (5) | Old Bal. | $9,200 | $1,600 | $7,000 | | | $1,600 +250 | | $16,200 −250 | Advertising Expense |
| | New Bal. | $9,200 + | $1,600 + | $7,000 | = | | $1,850 | + | $15,950 | |
| | | | $17,800 | | | | | $17,800 | | |

The two sides of the equation still balance at $17,800. Observe that owner's equity is decreased when the expense is incurred, and the specific cause of the decrease (advertising expense) is noted. Expenses do not have to be paid in cash at the time they are incurred. When payment is made at a later date, the liability Accounts Payable will be decreased and the asset Cash will be decreased [see Transaction (8)]. The cost of advertising is considered an expense, as opposed to an asset, because the benefits have been used. This expense is included in determining net income.

**Transaction (6). Services Rendered for Cash and Credit.** Softbyte provides programming services of $3,500 for customers. Cash amounting to $1,500 is received from customers, and the balance of $2,000 is billed to customers on account. This transaction results in an equal increase in assets and owner's equity. Three specific items are affected: Cash is increased $1,500; Accounts Receivable is increased $2,000; and R. Neal, Capital is increased $3,500. The new balances are as follows:

| | | | Assets | | | | = | Liabilities | + | Owner's Equity | |
|---|---|---|---|---|---|---|---|---|---|---|---|
| | | Cash | + Accounts Receivable | + Supplies | + Equipment | = | | Accounts Payable | + | R. Neal, Capital | |
| (6) | Old Bal. | $9,200 +1,500 | +2,000 | $1,600 | $7,000 | | | $1,850 | | $15,950 +3,500 | Service Revenue |
| | New Bal. | $10,700 + | $2,000 + | $1,600 + | $7,000 | = | | $1,850 | + | $19,450 | |
| | | | | $21,300 | | | | | $21,300 | | |

Why increase owner's equity by $3,500 when only $1,500 has been collected? Because the inflow of assets resulting from the earning of revenues does not have to be in the form of cash. Remember that owner's equity is increased when revenues are earned, and in Softbyte's case that is when the service is provided. When collections on account are received at a later date, Cash will be increased and Accounts Receivable will be decreased [see Transaction (9)].

**Transaction (7). Payment of Expenses.** Expenses paid in cash for September are store rent, $600, salaries of employees, $900, and utilities, $200. These payments result in an equal decrease in assets and owner's equity. Cash is decreased $1,700 and R. Neal, Capital is decreased by the same amount. The effect of these payments on the equation is:

|  |  | **Assets** |  |  |  | **= Liabilities +** | **Owner's Equity** |  |
|---|---|---|---|---|---|---|---|---|
|  |  |  | Accounts |  |  | Accounts | R. Neal, |  |
|  | Cash | + Receivable | + Supplies | + Equipment = | Payable | + Capital |  |
| Old Bal. | $10,700 | $2,000 | $1,600 | $7,000 | $1,850 | $19,450 |  |
| (7) | −1,700 |  |  |  |  | −600 | Rent Expense |
|  |  |  |  |  |  | −900 | Salaries Expense |
|  |  |  |  |  |  | −200 | Utilities Expense |
| New Bal. | $ 9,000 + | $2,000 + | $1,600 + | $7,000 = | $1,850 + | $17,750 |  |
|  |  |  | $19,600 |  |  | $19,600 |  |

The two sides of the equation now balance at $19,600. Three lines are required in the analysis to indicate the different types of expenses that have been incurred.

**Transaction (8).   Payment of Accounts Payable.**  Softbyte pays its *Daily News* advertising bill of $250 in cash. In analyzing the effect of this transaction, we must recall that the bill has previously been recorded in Transaction (5) as an increase in Accounts Payable and a decrease in owner's equity. Thus, this payment "on account" decreases both assets and liabilities. In this case, the asset Cash and the liability Accounts Payable are decreased by $250. The effect of this transaction on the equation is:

|  |  |  | **Assets** |  |  | **= Liabilities +** | **Owner's Equity** |
|---|---|---|---|---|---|---|---|
|  |  |  | Accounts |  |  | Accounts | R. Neal, |
|  | Cash | + | Receivable | + Supplies | + Equipment = | Payable | + Capital |
| Old Bal. | $9,000 |  | $2,000 | $1,600 | $7,000 | $1,850 | $17,750 |
| (8) | −250 |  |  |  |  | −250 |  |
| New Bal. | $8,750 + |  | $2,000 + | $1,600 + | $7,000 = | $1,600 + | $17,750 |
|  |  |  |  | $19,350 |  | $19,350 |  |

Observe that the payment of a liability related to an expense that has previously been recorded does not affect owner's equity.

**Transaction (9).   Receipt of Cash on Account.**  The sum of $600 in cash is received from customers who have previously been billed for services in Transaction (6). This transaction does not change total assets, but it changes the composition of Softbyte's assets. Cash is increased $600 and Accounts Receivable is decreased $600. The new balances are:

|  |  |  | **Assets** |  |  | **= Liabilities +** | **Owner's Equity** |
|---|---|---|---|---|---|---|---|
|  |  |  | Accounts |  |  | Accounts | R. Neal, |
|  | Cash | + | Receivable | + Supplies | + Equipment = | Payable | + Capital |
| Old Bal. | $8,750 |  | $2,000 | $1,600 | $7,000 | $1,600 | $17,750 |
| (9) | +600 |  | −600 |  |  |  |  |
| New Bal. | $9,350 + |  | $1,400 + | $1,600 + | $7,000 = | $1,600 + | $17,750 |
|  |  |  |  | $19,350 |  | $19,350 |  |

Note that a collection on account for services previously billed and recorded does not affect owner's equity. Revenue was already recorded in Transaction (6) and should not be recorded again.

**Transaction (10). Withdrawal of Cash by Owner.** Ray Neal withdraws $1,300 in cash from the business for his personal use. This transaction results in an equal decrease in assets and owner's equity. Thus, both Cash and R. Neal, Capital are decreased $1,300, as shown below:

| | | Assets | | | | | | | = | Liabilities + | Owner's Equity | |
|---|---|---|---|---|---|---|---|---|---|---|---|---|
| | | Cash | + | Accounts Receivable | + | Supplies | + | Equipment | = | Accounts Payable | + | R. Neal, Capital | |
| | Old Bal. | $9,350 | | $1,400 | | $1,600 | | $7,000 | | $1,600 | | $17,750 | |
| (10) | | −1,300 | | | | | | | | | | −1,300 | Drawings |
| | New Bal. | $8,050 + | | $1,400 + | | $1,600 + | | $7,000 | = | $1,600 | + | $16,450 | |
| | | | | | | $18,050 | | | | | | $18,050 | |

Observe that the effect of a cash withdrawal by the owner is the opposite of the effect of an investment by the owner. **Owner's drawings do not represent expenses.** Like owner's investment, they are not included in determining net income.

## Summary of Transactions

The transactions of Softbyte are summarized in Illustration 1-8 to show their cumulative effect on the basic accounting equation. The transaction number, the

**Illustration 1-8**

*Tabular summary of Softbyte transactions*

| | | Assets | | | | | | | = | Liabilities + | | Owner's Equity | |
|---|---|---|---|---|---|---|---|---|---|---|---|---|---|
| Transaction | | Cash | + | Accounts Receivable | + | Supplies | + | Equipment | = | Accounts Payable | + | R. Neal, Capital | |
| (1) | | +$15,000 | | | | | | | | | | +$15,000 | Investment |
| (2) | | −7,000 | | | | | | +$7,000 | | | | | |
| | | 8,000 | | | + | | | 7,000 | = | | | 15,000 | |
| (3) | | | | | | +$1,600 | | | | +$1,600 | | | |
| | | 8,000 | | | + | 1,600 + | | 7,000 | = | 1,600 | + | 15,000 | |
| (4) | | +1,200 | | | | | | | | | | +1,200 | Service Revenue |
| | | 9,200 | | | + | 1,600 + | | 7,000 | = | 1,600 | + | 16,200 | |
| (5) | | | | | | | | | | +250 | | −250 | Advertising Expense |
| | | 9,200 | | | + | 1,600 + | | 7,000 | = | 1,850 | + | 15,950 | |
| (6) | | +1,500 | | +$2,000 | | | | | | | | +3,500 | Service Revenue |
| | | 10,700 + | | 2,000 + | | 1,600 + | | 7,000 | = | 1,850 | + | 19,450 | |
| (7) | | −1,700 | | | | | | | | | | −600 | Rent Expense |
| | | | | | | | | | | | | −900 | Salaries Expense |
| | | | | | | | | | | | | −200 | Utilities Expense |
| | | 9,000 + | | 2,000 + | | 1,600 + | | 7,000 | = | 1,850 | + | 17,750 | |
| (8) | | −250 | | | | | | | | −250 | | | |
| | | 8,750 + | | 2,000 + | | 1,600 + | | 7,000 | = | 1,600 | + | 17,750 | |
| (9) | | +600 | | −600 | | | | | | | | | |
| | | 9,350 + | | 1,400 + | | 1,600 + | | 7,000 | = | 1,600 | + | 17,750 | |
| (10) | | −1,300 | | | | | | | | | | −1,300 | Drawings |
| | | $ 8,050 + | | $1,400 + | | $1,600 + | | $7,000 | = | $1,600 | + | $16,450 | |
| | | | | | | $18,050 | | | | | | $18,050 | |

specific effects of the transaction, and the balances after each transaction are indicated. The illustration demonstrates a number of significant facts:

1. Each transaction must be analyzed in terms of its effect on:
   a. the three components of the basic accounting equation.
   b. specific types (kinds) of items within each component.
2. The two sides of the equation must always be equal.
3. The causes of each change in the owner's claim on assets must be indicated in the owner's equity column.

There! You made it through transaction analysis. If you feel a bit shaky on any of the transactions, it would probably be a good idea at this point to get up, take a short break, and come back again for a 10- to 15-minute review of the transactions, to make sure you understand them before you go on to the next section.

## Financial Statements

**STUDY OBJECTIVE**

*Prepare an income statement, owner's equity statement, balance sheet, and statement of cash flows.*

After transactions are identified, recorded, and summarized, four financial statements are prepared from the summarized accounting data:

1. An income statement presents the revenues and expenses and resulting net income or net loss of a company for a specific period of time.
2. An owner's equity statement summarizes the changes in owner's equity for a specific period of time.
3. A balance sheet reports the assets, liabilities, and owner's equity of a business enterprise at a specific date.
4. A statement of cash flows summarizes information concerning the cash inflows (receipts) and outflows (payments) for a specific period of time.

**Helpful hint** The income statement, owner's equity statement, and statement of cash flows are all for a *period* of time, whereas the balance sheet is for a *point* in time.

Each statement provides management, owners, and other interested parties with relevant financial data. The financial statements of Softbyte and their interrelationships are shown in Illustration 1-9. The statements are interrelated: **(1) Net income of $2,750 shown on the income statement is added to the beginning balance of owner's capital in the owner's equity statement. (2) Owner's capital of $16,450 at the end of the reporting period shown in the owner's equity statement is reported on the balance sheet. (3) Cash of $8,050 on the balance sheet is reported on the statement of cash flows.**

Additionally, every set of financial statements is accompanied by explanatory notes and supporting schedules that are an integral part of the statements. Examples of these notes and schedules are illustrated in later chapters of this textbook.

Be sure to carefully examine the format and content of each statement. The essential features of each are briefly described in the following sections.

### Income Statement

The income statement for Softbyte is prepared from the data appearing in the owner's equity column of Illustration 1-8. The heading of the statement identifies the company, the type of statement, and the time period covered by the statement. Note that the primary focus of the income statement is on reporting the success or profitability of the company's operations over a specified period of time. To indicate that it applies for a period of time, the income statement is dated "For the Month Ended September 30, 1996."

**Illustration 1-9**

*Financial statements and their interrelationships*

## SOFTBYTE
## Income Statement
## For the Month Ended September 30, 1996

| | | |
|---|---:|---:|
| Revenues | | |
| Service revenue | | $4,700 |
| Expenses | | |
| Salaries expense | $900 | |
| Rent expense | 600 | |
| Advertising expense | 250 | |
| Utilities expense | 200 | |
| Total expenses | | 1,950 |
| Net income | | $2,750 |

## SOFTBYTE
## Owner's Equity Statement
## For the Month Ended September 30, 1996

| | | |
|---|---:|---:|
| R. Neal, Capital, September 1 | | $ –0– |
| Add: Investments | $15,000 | |
| Net income | 2,750 | 17,750 |
| | | 17,750 |
| Less: Drawings | | 1,300 |
| R. Neal, Capital, September 30 | | $16,450 |

## SOFTBYTE
## Balance Sheet
## September 30, 1996

### Assets

| | |
|---|---:|
| Cash | $ 8,050 |
| Accounts receivable | 1,400 |
| Supplies | 1,600 |
| Equipment | 7,000 |
| Total assets | $18,050 |

### Liabilities and Owner's Equity

| | |
|---|---:|
| Liabilities | |
| Accounts payable | $ 1,600 |
| Owner's Equity | |
| R. Neal, Capital | 16,450 |
| Total liabilities and owner's equity | $18,050 |

## SOFTBYTE
## Statement of Cash Flows
## For the Month Ended September 30, 1996

| | | |
|---|---:|---:|
| Cash flows from operating activities | | |
| Cash receipts from revenues | $ 3,300 | |
| Cash payments for expenses | (1,950) | |
| Net cash provided by operating activities | | 1,350 |
| Cash flows from investing activities | | |
| Purchase of equipment | | (7,000) |
| Cash flows from financing activities | | |
| Investments by owner | $15,000 | |
| Drawings by owner | (1,300) | 13,700 |
| Net increase in cash | | 8,050 |
| Cash at the beginning of the period | | 0 |
| Cash at the end of the period | | $ 8,050 |

① ② ③

On the income statement, revenues are listed first, followed by expenses. Finally net income (or net loss) is determined. Although practice varies, we have chosen in our illustrations and homework solutions to list expenses in order of magnitude. Alternative formats for the income statement will be considered in later chapters.

Note that investment and withdrawal transactions between the owner and the business are not included in the measurement of net income. For example, the withdrawal by Ray Neal of cash from Softbyte was not regarded as a business expense, as explained earlier.

### Owner's Equity Statement

Data for the preparation of the owner's equity statement are obtained from the owner's equity column of the tabular summary (Illustration 1-8) and from the income statement. The heading of this statement identifies the company, the type of statement, and the time period covered by the statement. The time period is the same as that covered by the income statement and therefore is dated "For the Month Ended September 30, 1996." The beginning owner's equity amount is shown on the first line of the statement. Then, the owner's investments, net income, and the owner's drawings are identified in the statement. The information provided by this statement indicates the reasons why owner's equity has increased or decreased during the period.

What if Softbyte reported a net loss in its first month? Let's assume that during the month of September, 1996, Softbyte lost $10,000. The presentation in the owner's equity statement of a net loss appears in Illustration 1-10.

**Illustration 1-10**

*Presentation of additional investment*

| SOFTBYTE<br>Owner's Equity Statement<br>For the Month Ended September 30, 1996 | | |
| --- | --: | --: |
| R. Neal, Capital, September 1 | | $   –0– |
| Add: Investments | | 15,000 |
| | | 15,000 |
| Less: Drawings | $ 1,300 | |
|      Net loss | 10,000 | 11,300 |
| R. Neal, Capital, September 30 | | $3,700 |

If there are additional investments, they are reported as investments in the owner's equity statement.

### Balance Sheet

The balance sheet for Softbyte is prepared from the column headings and the month-end data shown in the last line of the tabular summary (Illustration 1-8). The heading of a balance sheet must identify the company, the statement, and the date. To indicate that the balance sheet is at a specific date, it is dated "September 30, 1996." Observe that the assets are listed at the top, followed by liabilities and owner's equity. Total assets must equal total liabilities and owner's equity. In the Softbyte illustration, only one liability, accounts payable, is reported on the balance sheet. In most cases, there will be more than one liability. When two or more liabilities are involved, a customary way of listing is as follows:

Illustration 1-11

*Presentation of liabilities*

| Liabilities | |
|---|---|
| Notes payable | $10,000 |
| Accounts payable | 63,000 |
| Salaries payable | 18,000 |
| Total liabilities | $91,000 |

The balance sheet is like a snapshot of the company's financial condition at a specific moment in time (usually the month-end or year-end).

### Statement of Cash Flows

The primary purpose of a statement of cash flows is to provide financial information about the cash receipts and cash payments of an enterprise for a specific period of time. To achieve this purpose and to aid investors, creditors, and others in their analysis of cash, the statement of cash flows reports (1) the cash effects of a company's operations during a period, (2) its investing transactions, (3) its financing transactions, (4) the net increase or decrease in cash during the period, and (5) the cash amount at the end of the period.

**Helpful hint** Investing activities pertain to investments made by the company, not investments made by the owner.

Reporting the sources, uses, and net increase or decrease in cash is useful because investors, creditors, and others want to know what is happening to a company's most liquid resource. The statement of cash flows, therefore, provides answers to the following simple but important questions:

1. Where did the cash come from during the period?
2. What was the cash used for during the period?
3. What was the change in the cash balance during the period?

A statement of cash flows for Softbyte, Inc., is provided in Illustration 1-9.

As shown in the statement, cash increased $8,050 during the year. This increase resulted because net cash flow provided from operating activities increased cash $1,350, cash flow from investing transactions decreased cash $7,000 and cash flow from financing transactions increased cash $13,700. At this time, you need not be concerned with how these amounts are determined. Chapter 18 will examine in detail how the statement is prepared.

## Before You Go On . . .

### ▶ Review It

1. If an asset increases, what are the three possible effects on the basic accounting equation?
2. What are the income statement, statement of owner's equity, balance sheet, and statement of cash flows?
3. Indicate how the financial statements are interrelated.

### ▶ A Look Back at the Baseball Strike

The final set of exercises refers back to the chapter opening story. These exercises help you analyze that real-world situation in terms of the accounting topic of the chapter.

Refer to the opening story about the baseball strike, and answer the following questions:

1. If you represented the baseball players' union, what two financial statements would you request from the owners?
2. What would these financial statements tell you?
3. Would you request audited financial statements? Explain.
4. Will the financial statements show the market value of the baseball team? Explain.

**Solution:**

1. The two statements that you would probably want to request are the balance sheet and the income statement.

2. The balance sheet reports the assets, liabilities, and owner's equity of the team. The income statement presents the revenues and expenses and resulting net income (or net loss) for a specific period of time. The balance sheet is like a snapshot of the team's financial condition at a point in time. The income statement should give you a good indication of the profitability of the team. Also, the sources of the team's revenues and a picture of its expenses are provided in the income statement.

3. The players should request **audited** financial statements—statements that a CPA has examined and expressed an opinion as to the fairness of presentation. Players should not make decisions without having audited financial statements.

4. The financial statements will not show the market value of the team. As indicated, one important principle of accounting is the cost principle, which states that assets should be recorded at cost. Cost has an important advantage over other valuations: it is reliable.

# ▼*Summary of Study Objectives*

**1.** *Explain the meaning of accounting.* Accounting is the process of identifying, recording, and communicating the economic events of an organization (business or nonbusiness) to interested users of the information.

**2.** *Identify the users and uses of accounting.* The major users and uses of accounting are: (a) Management uses accounting information in planning, controlling, and evaluating business operations. (b) Investors (owners) judge the wisdom of buying, holding, or selling their financial interests on the basis of accounting data. (c) Creditors (suppliers and bankers) evaluate the risks of granting credit or lending money to particular businesses on the basis of the accounting information obtained about those businesses. Other groups with an indirect interest are taxing authorities, regulatory agencies, customers, labor unions, and economic planners.

**3.** *Understand why ethics is a fundamental business concept.* Ethics are the standards of conduct by which one's actions—both personal and business—are judged as right or wrong. If you cannot depend on the honesty of the individuals you deal with, effective communication and economic activity would be impossible and information would have no credibility.

**4.** *Explain the meaning of generally accepted accounting principles and the cost principle.* Generally accepted accounting principles are a common set of standards used by accountants. One important principle is the cost principle, which states that assets should be recorded at their cost.

**5.** *Explain the meaning of the monetary unit assumption and the economic entity assumption.* The monetary unit as-sumption requires that only transaction data capable of being expressed in terms of money be included in the accounting records of the economic entity. The economic entity assumption states that economic events can be identified with a particular unit of accountability.

**6.** *State the basic accounting equation and explain the meaning of assets, liabilities, and owner's equity.* The basic accounting equation is:

$$\text{Assets} = \text{Liabilities} + \text{Owner's Equity}$$

Assets are resources owned by a business. Liabilities are creditorship claims on total assets. Owner's equity is the ownership claim on total assets. It is often referred to as residual equity.

**7.** *Analyze the effect of business transactions on the basic accounting equation.* Each business transaction must have a dual effect on the accounting equation. For example, if an individual asset is increased, there must be a corresponding (1) decrease in another asset, or (2) increase in a specific liability, or (3) increase in owner's equity.

**8.** *Prepare an income statement, owner's equity statement, balance sheet, and statement of cash flows.* An income statement presents the revenues and expenses of a company for a specified period of time. An owner's equity statement summarizes the changes in owner's equity that have occurred for a specific period of time. A balance sheet reports the assets, liabilities, and owner's equity of a business at a specific date. A statement of cash flows summarizes information concerning the cash inflows (receipts) and outflows (payments) for a specific period of time.

# GLOSSARY

**Accounting**   The process of identifying, recording, and communicating the economic events of an organization to interested users of the information. (p. 2).

**Assets**   Resources owned by a business. (p. 14).

**Auditing**   The examination of financial statements by a certified public accountant in order to express an opinion as to the fairness of presentation. (p. 7).

**Balance sheet**   A financial statement that reports the assets, liabilities, and owner's equity at a specific date. (p. 22).

**Basic accounting equation**   Assets = Liabilities + Owner's equity. (p. 14).

**Bookkeeping**   A part of accounting that involves only the recording of economic events. (p. 6).

**Corporation**   A business organized as a separate legal entity under state corporation law having ownership divided into transferable shares of stock. (p. 13).

**Cost principle**   An accounting principle that states that assets should be recorded at their cost. (p. 11).

**Drawings**   Withdrawal of cash or other assets from an unincorporated business for the personal use of the owner(s). (p. 15).

**Economic entity assumption**   An assumption that economic events can be identified with a particular unit of accountability. (p. 12).

**Ethics**   The standards of conduct by which one's actions are judged as right or wrong, honest or dishonest, fair or not fair. (p. 10).

**Expenses**   The cost of assets consumed or services used in the process of earning revenue. (p. 15).

**Financial Accounting Standards Board (FASB)**   A private organization that establishes generally accepted accounting principles. (p. 10).

**Generally accepted accounting principles (GAAP)**   A common set of standards that indicate how to report economic events. (p. 10).

**Income statement**   A financial statement that presents the revenues and expenses and resulting net income or net loss of a company for a specific period of time. (p. 22).

**Investments by owner**   The assets put into the business by the owner. (p. 15).

**Liabilities**   Creditorship claims on total assets. (p. 14).

**Management consulting**   An area of public accounting involving financial planning and control and the development of accounting and computer systems. (p. 8).

**Monetary unit assumption**   An assumption stating that only transaction data that can be expressed in terms of money be included in the accounting records of the economic entity. (p. 12).

**Net income**   The amount by which revenues exceed expenses. (p. 15).

**Net loss**   The amount by which expenses exceed revenues. (p. 15).

**Owner's equity**   The ownership claim on total assets. (p. 14).

**Owner's equity statement**   A financial statement that summarizes the changes in owner's equity for a specific period of time. (p. 22).

**Partnership**   An association of two or more persons to carry on as co-owners of a business for profit. (p. 13).

**Private (or managerial) accounting**   An area of accounting within a company that involves such activities as cost accounting, budgeting, and accounting information systems. (p. 8).

**Proprietorship**   A business owned by one person. (p. 12).

**Public accounting**   An area of accounting in which the accountant offers expert service to the general public. (p. 7).

**Revenues**   The gross increase in owner's equity resulting from business activities entered into for the purpose of earning income. (p. 15).

**Securities and Exchange Commission (SEC)**   A governmental agency that requires companies to file financial reports in accordance with generally accepted accounting principles. (p. 11).

**Statement of cash flows**   A financial statement that provides information about the cash inflows (receipts) and cash outflows (payments) of an entity for a specific period of time. (p. 22).

**Taxation**   An area of public accounting involving tax advice, tax planning, and preparing tax returns. (p. 8).

**Transactions**   The economic events of the enterprise recorded by accountants. (p. 16).

# DEMONSTRATION PROBLEM

Mary Malone opens her own law office on July 1, 1996. During the first month of operations, the following transactions occurred:

1. Invested $10,000 in cash in the law practice.
2. Paid $800 for July rent on office space.
3. Purchased office equipment on account, $3,000.

The Demonstration Problems are a final review before you begin homework. The problem-solving strategies in the margins give you tips about how to approach the problem, and the solutions provided demonstrate both the form and content of complete answers.

4. Rendered legal services to clients for cash, $1,500. (use Fees Earned)
5. Borrowed $700 cash from a bank on a note payable.
6. Rendered legal services to client on account, $2,000.
7. Paid monthly expenses: salaries, $500; utilities, $300; and telephone, $100.

**Instructions**

(a) Prepare a tabular summary of the transactions.
(b) Prepare the income statement, owner's equity statement, and balance sheet at July 31 for Mary Malone, Attorney at Law.

## Solution to Demonstration Problem

**Problem-Solving Strategies**

1. Remember that assets must equal liabilities and owner's equity after each transaction.
2. Investments and revenues increase owner's equity.
3. Withdrawals and expenses decrease owner's equity.
4. The income statement shows revenues and expenses for a period of time.
5. The owner's equity statement shows the changes in owner's equity for a period of time.
6. The balance sheet reports assets, liabilities, and owner's equity at a specific date.

(a)

| | | Assets | | = | Liabilities | + | Owner's Equity | |
|---|---|---|---|---|---|---|---|---|
| Trans-action | Cash | + Accounts Receivable + | Equipment = | Notes Payable + | Accounts Payable + | | Mary Malone, Capital | |
| (1) | +$10,000 | | | | | | +$10,000 | Investment |
| (2) | −800 | | | | | | −800 | Rent Expense |
| | 9,200 | | | = | | | 9,200 | |
| (3) | | | +$3,000 | | +$3,000 | | | |
| | 9,200 | + | 3,000 = | | 3,000 + | | 9,200 | |
| (4) | +1,500 | | | | | | +1,500 | Fees Earned |
| | 10,700 | + | 3,000 = | | 3,000 + | | 10,700 | |
| (5) | +700 | | | +$700 | | | | |
| | 11,400 | + | 3,000 = | 700 + | 3,000 + | | 10,700 | |
| (6) | | +$2,000 | | | | | +2,000 | Fees Earned |
| | 11,400 + | 2,000 + | 3,000 = | 700 + | 3,000 + | | 12,700 | |
| (7) | −900 | | | | | | −500 | Salaries Expense |
| | | | | | | | −300 | Utilities Expense |
| | | | | | | | −100 | Telephone Expense |
| | $10,500 + | $2,000 + | $3,000 = | $700 + | $3,000 + | | $11,800 | |

(b)

**MARY MALONE**
**Attorney at Law**
**Income Statement**
**For the Month Ended July 31, 1996**

| | | |
|---|---|---|
| Revenues | | |
| Fees earned | | $3,500 |
| Expenses | | |
| Rent expense | $800 | |
| Salaries expense | 500 | |
| Utilities expense | 300 | |
| Telephone expense | 100 | |
| Total expenses | | 1,700 |
| Net income | | $1,800 |

**MARY MALONE**
**Attorney at Law**
**Owner's Equity Statement**
**For the Month Ended July 31, 1996**

| | | |
|---|---|---|
| Mary Malone, Capital, July 1 | | $   −0− |
| Add: Investments | $10,000 | |
| Net income | 1,800 | 11,800 |
| Mary Malone, Capital, July 31 | | $11,800 |

**MARY MALONE**
**Attorney at Law**
**Balance Sheet**
**July 31, 1996**

Assets

| | |
|---|---:|
| Cash | $10,500 |
| Accounts receivable | 2,000 |
| Equipment | 3,000 |
| Total assets | $15,500 |

Liabilities and Owner's Equity

| | |
|---|---:|
| Liabilities | |
| Notes payable | $ 700 |
| Accounts payable | 3,000 |
| Total liabilities | 3,700 |
| Owner's Equity | |
| Mary Malone, Capital | 11,800 |
| Total liabilities and owner's equity | $15,500 |

# SELF-STUDY QUESTIONS

Answers are at the end of the chapter.

(SO 1)   1. The accounting process does *not* include:
   a. identification
   b. verification
   c. recording
   d. communication

(SO 2)   2. One of the following statements about users of accounting information is *incorrect*. The incorrect statement is:
   a. Management is considered an internal user.
   b. Taxing authorities are considered external users.
   c. Present creditors are considered external users.
   d. Regulatory authorities are considered internal users.

(SO 2)   3. The public accountant generally provides the following services:
   a. auditing, taxation, and management consulting.
   b. auditing, budgeting, and management consulting.
   c. auditing, budgeting, and cost accounting.
   d. internal auditing, budgeting, and management consulting.

(SO 4)   4. The cost principle states that:
   a. assets should be recorded at cost and adjusted when the market value changes.
   b. activities of an entity be kept separate and distinct from its owner.
   c. assets should be recorded at their cost.
   d. only transaction data capable of being expressed in terms of money be included in the accounting records.

(SO 5)   5. Which of the following statements about basic assumptions is *incorrect*?
   a. Basic assumptions are the same as accounting principles.
   b. The economic entity assumption states that there should be a particular unit of accountability.
   c. The monetary unit assumption enables accounting to measure economic events.
   d. An important corollary to the monetary unit assumption is the stable monetary unit assumption.

(SO 6)   6. Net income will result during a time period when:
   a. assets exceed liabilities.
   b. assets exceed revenues.
   c. expenses exceed revenues.
   d. revenues exceed expenses.

(SO 7)   7. The effects on the basic accounting equation of performing services on account are:
   a. increase assets and decrease owner's equity.
   b. increase assets and increase owner's equity.
   c. increase assets and increase liabilities.
   d. increase liabilities and increase owner's equity.

(SO 7)   8. As of December 31, 1996, Stoneland Company has assets of $3,500 and owner's equity of $2,000. What are the liabilities for Stoneland Company as of December 31, 1996?
   a. $1,500.
   b. $1,000.
   c. $2,500.
   d. $2,000.

9. Genesis Company buys a $900 machine on credit. This transaction will affect the:
a. income statement only.
b. balance sheet only.
c. income statement and owner's equity statement only.
d. income statement, owner's equity statement, and balance sheet.

10. The financial statement that reports assets, liabilities, and owner's equity is the:
a. income statement.
b. owner's equity statement.
c. balance sheet.
d. statement of cash flow.

# QUESTIONS

1. "Accounting is ingrained in our society and it is vital to our economic system." Do you agree? Explain.

2. Identify and describe the steps in the accounting process.

3. (a) Who are internal users of accounting data?
   (b) How does accounting provide relevant data to these users?

4. Distinguish between the two types of external users of accounting data and give examples of each.

5. "Bookkeeping and accounting are the same." Do you agree? Explain.

6. Vince Gill Travel Agency purchased land for $75,000 cash on December 10, 1996. At December 31, 1996, the land's value has increased to $93,000. What amount should be reported for land on Vince Gill's balance sheet at December 31, 1996? Explain.

7. What is the monetary unit assumption? What impact does inflation have on the monetary unit assumption?

8. What is the economic entity assumption?

9. What are the three basic forms of business organizations for profit-oriented enterprises?

10. Martha Ross is the owner of a successful printing shop. Recently her business has been increasing, and Martha has been thinking about changing the organization of her business from a proprietorship to a corporation. Discuss some of the advantages Martha would enjoy if she were to incorporate her business.

11. What is the basic accounting equation?

12. (a) Define the terms assets, liabilities, and owner's equity. (b) What items affect owner's equity?

13. Which of the following items are liabilities of Kool-Jewelry Stores?
    (a) Cash.            (f) Equipment.
    (b) Accounts payable. (g) Salaries payable.
    (c) Drawings.        (h) Service revenue.
    (d) Accounts receivable. (i) Rent expense.
    (e) Supplies.

14. Can a business enter into a transaction in which only the left side of the basic accounting equation is affected? If so, give an example.

15. Are the following events recorded in the accounting records? Explain your answer in each case.
    (a) The owner of the company dies.
    (b) Supplies are purchased on account.
    (c) An employee is fired.
    (d) The owner of the business withdraws cash from the business for personal use.

16. Indicate how the following business transactions affect the basic accounting equation.
    (a) Paid cash for janitorial services.
    (b) Purchased equipment for cash.
    (c) Invested cash in the business.
    (d) Paid an accounts payable in full.

17. Listed below are some items found in the financial statements of Ruth Weber, M.D. Indicate in which financial statement(s) the following items would appear.
    (a) Service revenue.
    (b) Equipment.
    (c) Advertising expense.
    (d) Accounts receivable.
    (e) Ruth Weber, Capital.
    (f) Wages payable.

18. In February 1996, Paul Jonas invested an additional $10,000 in his business, Jonas's Pharmacy, which is organized as a proprietorship. Jonas's accountant, Donna Wortham, recorded this receipt as an increase in cash and revenues. Is this treatment appropriate? Why or why not?

19. A company's net income appears directly on the income statement and the owner's equity statement, and it is included indirectly in the company's balance sheet. Do you agree? Explain.

20. Hernandez Enterprises had a capital balance of $158,000 at the beginning of the period. At the end of the accounting period, the capital balance was $198,000.
    (a) Assuming no additional investment or withdrawals during the period, what is the net income for the period?

(b) Assuming an additional investment of $13,000 but no withdrawals during the period, what is the net income for the period?

21. Summarized operations for the Cora L. King Co. for the month of July are as follows:

Revenues earned: for cash $45,000; on account $70,000.

Expenses incurred: for cash $26,000; on account $40,000.

Indicate for Cora L. King Co. (a) the total revenues, (b) the total expenses, and (c) net income for the month of July.

# BRIEF EXERCISES

**BE1-1** Presented below is the basic accounting equation. Determine the missing amounts:

*Basic accounting equation.*
*(SO 6)*

|     | Assets | = | Liabilities | + | Owner's Equity |
|-----|--------|---|-------------|---|----------------|
| (a) | $90,000 |  | $50,000 |  | ? |
| (b) | ? |  | $48,000 |  | $70,000 |
| (c) | $94,000 |  | ? |  | $72,000 |

**BE1-2** Given the accounting equation, answer each of the following questions:

*Basic accounting equation.*
*(SO 6)*

1. The liabilities of Hogan Company are $90,000 and the owner's equity is $240,000. What is the amount of Hogan Company's total assets?
2. The total assets of Potter Company are $170,000 and its owner's equity is $90,000. What is the amount of its total liabilities?
3. The total assets of Barren Co. are $700,000 and its liabilities are equal to one half of its total assets. What is the amount of Barren Co.'s owner's equity?

**BE1-3** At the beginning of the year, Lamson Company had total assets of $700,000 and total liabilities of $500,000. Answer the following questions:

*Basic accounting equation.*
*(SO 6)*

1. If total assets increased $150,000 during the year and total liabilities decreased $80,000, what is the amount of owner's equity at the end of the year?
2. During the year, total liabilities increased $100,000 and owner's equity decreased $70,000. What is the amount of total assets at the end of the year?
3. If total assets decreased $90,000 and owner's equity increased $110,000 during the year, what is the amount of total liabilities at the end of the year?

**BE1-4** Presented below are three business transactions. On a sheet of paper, list the letters a, b, c with columns for assets, liabilities, and owner's equity. For each column, indicate whether the transactions increased (+), decreased (−) or had no effect (NE) on assets, liabilities, and owner's equity:

*Determine effect of transactions on basic accounting equation.*
*(SO 7)*

(a) Purchased supplies on account.
(b) Received cash for providing a service.
(c) Expenses paid in cash.

**BE1-5** Follow the same format as BE1-4 above. Determine the effect on assets, liabilities, and owner's equity of the following three transactions:

*Determine effect of transactions on basic accounting equation.*
*(SO 7)*

(a) Invested cash in the business.
(b) Withdrawal of cash by owner.
(c) Received cash from a customer who had previously been billed for services provided.

**BE1-6** Classify each of the following items as owner's drawing (D), revenue (R), or expense (E).

*Determine effect of transactions on owner's equity.*
*(SO 7)*

_____ Advertising expense          _____ T. Quick, Drawing
_____ Commission revenue           _____ Rent revenue
_____ Insurance expense            _____ Utilities expense
_____ Salaries expense

*Determine effect of*
*transactions on owner's*
*equity.*
*(SO 7)*

**BE1–7**  Presented below are three transactions. Mark each transaction as affecting owner's investment (I), owner's drawings (D), revenue (R), expense (E), or not affecting owner's equity (NOE):

_____ Received cash for services performed
_____ Paid cash to purchase equipment
_____ Paid employee salaries

**BE1–8**  In alphabetical order below are balance sheet items for Gidget Company at December 31, 1996. Sally Fried is the owner of Gidget Company. Prepare a balance sheet, following the format of Illustration 1-9.

| | |
|---|---|
| Accounts payable | $90,000 |
| Accounts receivable | $81,000 |
| Cash | $40,500 |
| Sally Fried, Capital | $31,500 |

*Identify assets, liabilities, and*
*owner's equity.*
*(SO 6)*

**BE1–9**  Indicate whether each of the following items is an asset (A), liability (L), or part of owner's equity (OE).

_____ Accounts receivable       _____ Office supplies
_____ Salaries payable          _____ Owner's investment
_____ Equipment                 _____ Notes payable

*Determine where items appear*
*on financial statements.*
*(SO 8)*

**BE1–10**  Indicate whether the following items would appear on the income statement (IS), balance sheet (BS), or owner's equity statement (OE).

_____ Notes payable           _____ Cash
_____ Advertising expense     _____ Fees earned
_____ R. Harrison, Capital

# EXERCISES

••••••••••••••••••••••••••••••••••••••••••••••••••••••••••••••••••••••••••••••••••••••

**E1–1**  The Ace Cleaners has the following balance sheet items:

| | |
|---|---|
| Accounts payable | Accounts receivable |
| Cash | Notes payable |
| Cleaning equipment | Salaries payable |
| Cleaning supplies | H. Ace, Capital |

*Classify accounts as assets,*
*liabilities, and owner's equity.*
*(SO 6)*

*Instructions*
Classify each item as an asset, liability, or owner's equity.

**E1–2**  Selected transactions for Green Lawn Care Company are listed below:

1. Made cash investment to start business.
2. Paid monthly rent.
3. Purchased equipment on account.
4. Billed customers for services performed.
5. Withdrew cash for owner's personal use.
6. Received cash from customers billed in (4).
7. Incurred advertising expense on account.
8. Purchased additional equipment for cash.
9. Received cash from customers when service was rendered.

*Instructions*
List the numbers of the above transactions and describe the effect of each transaction on assets, liabilities, and owner's equity. For example, the first answer is: (1) Increase in assets and increase in owner's equity.

**E1–3**  Li Wang Computer Timeshare Company entered into the following transactions during May 1996.

1. Purchased computer terminals for $19,000 from Digital Equipment on account.
2. Paid $4,000 cash for May rent on storage space.

*Analyze the effect of*
*transactions on assets,*
*liabilities, and owner's equity.*
*(SO 6, 7)*

3. Received $15,000 cash from customers for contracts billed in April.
4. Provided computer services to Brieske Construction Company for $3,000 cash.
5. Paid Southern States Power Co. $11,000 cash for energy usage in May.
6. Li Wang invested an additional $32,000 in the business.
7. Paid Digital Equipment for the terminals purchased in (1) above.
8. Incurred advertising expense for May of $1,000 on account.

**Instructions**
Indicate with the appropriate letter whether each of the transactions above results in:

   (a) an increase in assets and a decrease in assets.
   (b) an increase in assets and an increase in owner's equity.
   (c) an increase in assets and an increase in liabilities.
   (d) a decrease in assets and a decrease in owner's equity.
   (e) a decrease in assets and a decrease in liabilities.
   (f) an increase in liabilities and a decrease in owner's equity.
   (g) an increase in owner's equity and a decrease in liabilities.

**E1–4**  A tabular analysis of the transactions made by Roberta Mendez & Co., a certified public accounting firm, for the month of August is shown below. Each increase and decrease in owner's equity is explained.

*Analyze transactions and compute net income.*
*(SO 7)*

| | Cash | + | Accounts Receivable | + | Supplies | + | Office Equipment | = | Accounts Payable | + | Owner's Equity R. Mendez, Capital |
|---|---|---|---|---|---|---|---|---|---|---|---|
| 1. | +$15,000 | | | | | | | | | | +$15,000  Investment |
| 2. | −2,000 | | | | | | +$5,000 | | +$3,000 | | |
| 3. | − 750 | | | | +$750 | | | | | | |
| 4. | +4,600 | | +3,400 | | | | | | | | +8,000  Fees Earned |
| 5. | −1,500 | | | | | | | | −1,500 | | |
| 6. | −2,000 | | | | | | | | | | −2,000  Drawings |
| 7. | − 650 | | | | | | | | | | − 650  Rent Expense |
| 8. | + 450 | | −450 | | | | | | | | |
| 9. | −2,900 | | | | | | | | | | −2,900  Salaries Expense |
| 10. | | | | | | | | | + 500 | | − 500  Utilities Expense |

**Instructions**
   (a) ▭▭▭▷ Describe each transaction that occurred for the month.
   (b) Determine how much owner's equity increased for the month.
   (c) Compute the amount of net income for the month.

**E1–5**  The tabular analysis of transactions for Roberta Mendez & Co. is presented in E1–4.

*Prepare an income statement and owner's equity statement.*
*(SO 8)*

**Instructions**
Prepare an income statement and an owner's equity statement for August and a balance sheet at August 31, 1996.

**E1–6**  The Debra Company had the following assets and liabilities on the dates indicated:

*Determine net income (or loss).*
*(SO 7)*

| December 31 | Total Assets | Total Liabilities |
|---|---|---|
| 1996 | $380,000 | $250,000 |
| 1997 | $460,000 | $310,000 |
| 1998 | $590,000 | $400,000 |

Debra began business on January 1, 1996, with an investment of $100,000.

**Instructions**
From an analysis of the change in owner's equity during the year, compute the net income (or loss) for:

   (a) 1996, assuming Debra's drawings were $15,000 for the year.
   (b) 1997, assuming Debra made an additional investment of $50,000 and had no drawings in 1997.
   (c) 1998, assuming Debra made an additional investment of $10,000 and had drawings of $20,000 in 1998.

*Analyze financial statements items.*
*(SO 6, 7)*

**E1–7**   Two items are omitted from each of the following summaries of balance sheet and income statement data for two proprietorships for the year 1996, Kate Cordova, D.D.S., and Maxim Enterprises.

|  | Kate Cordova, D.D.S. | Maxim Enterprises |
|---|---|---|
| **Beginning of year:** | | |
| Total assets | $ 90,000 | $130,000 |
| Total liabilities | 80,000 | (c) |
| Total owner's equity | (a) | 95,000 |
| **End of year:** | | |
| Total assets | 160,000 | 180,000 |
| Total liabilities | 120,000 | 50,000 |
| Total owner's equity | 40,000 | 130,000 |
| **Changes during year in owner's equity:** | | |
| Additional investment | (b) | 25,000 |
| Drawings | 24,000 | (d) |
| Total revenues | 215,000 | 100,000 |
| Total expenses | 165,000 | 80,000 |

**Instructions**
Determine the missing amounts.

*Prepare income statement and owner's equity statement.*
*(SO 8)*

**E1–8**   The following information relates to Tone Kon Co. for the year 1996.

| | | | |
|---|---|---|---|
| Tone Kon, Capital, January 1, 1996 | $45,000 | Advertising expense | 1,800 |
| Tone Kon, Drawing, during 1996 | 5,000 | Rent expense | 10,400 |
| Fees earned | 50,000 | Utilities expense | 3,100 |
| Salaries expense | 28,000 | | |

**Instructions**
After analyzing the data, prepare an income statement and an owner's equity statement for the year ending December 31, 1996.

*Correct an incorrectly prepared balance sheet.*
*(SO 8)*

**E1–9**   Kit Lucas is the bookkeeper for Aurora Company. Kit has been trying to get the balance sheet of Aurora Company to balance. Aurora's balance sheet is as follows:

**AURORA COMPANY**
**Balance Sheet**
**December 31, 1996**

| Assets | | Liabilities | |
|---|---|---|---|
| Cash | $16,500 | Accounts payable | $20,000 |
| Supplies | 8,000 | Accounts receivable | (10,000) |
| Equipment | 46,000 | Aurora, Capital | 67,500 |
| Aurora, Drawing | 7,000 | Total liabilities and | |
| Total assets | $77,500 | owner's equity | $77,500 |

**Instructions**
Prepare a correct balance sheet.

*Compute net income and prepare a balance sheet.*
*(SO 8)*

**E1–10**   Rick Stead is the sole owner of Deer Park, a public camping ground near the Lake Mead National Recreation Area. Rick has compiled the following financial information as of December 31, 1996.

| | | | |
|---|---|---|---|
| Revenues during 1996—camping fees | $147,000 | Market value of equipment | 140,000 |
| Revenues during 1996—general store | 40,000 | Notes payable | 60,000 |
| Accounts payable | 11,000 | Expenses during 1996 | 150,000 |
| Cash on hand | 7,000 | Supplies on hand | 2,500 |
| Original cost of equipment | 115,500 | | |

**Instructions**
(a) Determine Rick Stead's net income from Deer Park for 1996.
(b) Prepare a balance sheet for Deer Park as of December 31, 1996.

**E1–11**  Presented below is financial information related to the 1996 operations of the Duchess Cruise Company.

*Prepare an income statement.*
*(SO 8)*

| | |
|---|---:|
| Maintenance expense | $ 90,000 |
| Property tax expense (on dock facilities) | 10,000 |
| Salaries expense | 142,000 |
| Advertising expense | 3,500 |
| Ticket revenue | 325,000 |

*Instructions*
Prepare the 1996 income statement for the Duchess Cruise Company.

**E1–12**  Presented below is information related to the single proprietorship of Grace Olsen, attorney.

*Prepare an owner's equity statement.*
*(SO 8)*

| | |
|---|---:|
| Legal fees earned—1996 | $380,000 |
| Total expenses—1996 | 205,000 |
| Assets, January 1, 1996 | 85,000 |
| Liabilities, January 1, 1996 | 62,000 |
| Assets, December 31, 1996 | 168,000 |
| Liabilities, December 31, 1996 | 70,000 |
| Drawings—1996 | ? |

*Instructions*
Prepare the 1996 owner's equity statement for Grace Olsen's legal practice.

# PROBLEMS

**P1–1**  On April 1, Laura Seall established the Seall Travel Agency. The following transactions were completed during the month:

*Analyze transactions and compute net income.*
*(SO 6, 7)*

1. Invested $20,000 cash in Corner State Bank in the name of the agency.
2. Paid $400 cash for April office rent.
3. Purchased office equipment for $2,500 cash.
4. Incurred $300 of advertising costs in the Chicago Tribune, on account.
5. Paid $600 cash for office supplies.
6. Earned $9,000 for services rendered: Cash of $1,000 is received from customers, and the balance of $8,000 is billed to customers on account.
7. Withdrew $200 cash for personal use.
8. Paid Chicago Tribune amount due in transaction (4).
9. Paid employees' salaries, $1,200.
10. Received $8,000 in cash from customers who have previously been billed in transaction (6).

*Instructions*
(a) Prepare a tabular analysis of the transactions using the following column headings: Cash, Accounts Receivable, Supplies, Office Equipment, Accounts Payable, and Laura Seall, Capital.
(b) From an analysis of the column, Laura Seall, Capital, compute the net income or net loss for April.

**P1–2**  Ivan Izo opened a law office, Ivan Izo, Attorney at Law, on July 1, 1996. On July 31, the balance sheet showed Cash $4,000, Accounts Receivable $1,500, Supplies $500, Office Equipment $5,000, Accounts Payable $4,200, and Ivan Izo, Capital, $6,800. During August the following transactions occurred:

*Analyze transactions and prepare income statement and owner's equity statement.*
*(SO 6, 7, 8)*

1. Collected $1,400 of accounts receivable.
2. Paid $2,700 cash on accounts payable.
3. Earned fees of $6,400, of which $3,000 is collected in cash and the balance is due in September.
4. Purchased additional office equipment for $1,000, paying $400 in cash and the balance on account.
5. Paid salaries $1,500, rent for August $900, and advertising expenses $350.

6. Withdrew $550 in cash for personal use.
7. Received $2,000 from Standard Federal Bank—money borrowed on a note payable.
8. Incurred utility expenses for month on account, $250.

**Instructions**

(a) Prepare a tabular analysis of the August transactions beginning with July 31 balances. The column heading should be as follows: Cash + Accounts Receivable + Supplies + Office Equipment = Notes Payable + Accounts Payable + Ivan Izo, Capital.

(b) Prepare an income statement for August, an owner's equity statement for August, and a balance sheet at August 31.

*Prepare income statement, owner's equity statement, and balance sheet.*
*(SO 8)*

**P1–3** On June 1, Clarice Thies started Glamor Cosmetics Co., a company that provides individual skin care treatment to clients at their residence, by investing $26,200 cash in the business. Following are the assets and liabilities of the company at June 30 and the revenues and expenses for the month of June.

| | | | |
|---|---|---|---|
| Cash | $11,000 | Notes Payable | $13,000 |
| Accounts Receivable | 4,000 | Accounts Payable | 1,200 |
| Fees Earned | 6,500 | Supplies Expense | 1,200 |
| Cosmetic Supplies | 2,400 | Gas and Oil Expense | 800 |
| Advertising Expense | 500 | Utilities Expense | 300 |
| Equipment | 25,000 | | |

Clarice made no additional investment in June, but withdrew $1,700 in cash for personal use during the month.

**Instructions**

(a) Prepare an income statement and owner's equity statement for the month of June and a balance sheet at June 30, 1996.

(b) Prepare an income statement and owner's equity statement for June assuming the following data are not included above: (1) $800 of fees were earned and billed but not collected at June 30, and (2) $100 of gas and oil expense was incurred but not paid.

*Prepare income statement and owner's equity statement.*
*(SO 8)*

**P1–4** Michael Upton organized the Upton Consulting Co. on March 1, 1996. The owner's equity column of the tabular summary for the month of March contained the following recorded data:

| Transaction | Amount | Description |
|:-----------:|-------:|-------------|
| (1) | $15,000 | Investment |
| (4) | 750 | Rent expense |
| (6) | 3,250 | Fees earned |
| (8) | 400 | Advertising expense |
| (11) | 1,000 | Salaries expense |
| (12) | 2,100 | Fees earned |
| (15) | 250 | Utilities expense |
| (18) | 500 | Drawings |
| (20) | 3,200 | Fees earned |
| (22) | 200 | Repair expense |
| (24) | 1,000 | Advertising expense |
| (27) | 300 | Drawings |
| (29) | 1,100 | Fees earned |
| (32) | 900 | Salaries expense |
| (34) | 200 | Property tax expense |
| (36) | 150 | Utilities expense |

All data were properly recorded except the following:

In transaction (22), $150 of the repair expense was applicable to Michael Upton's personal residence.

In transaction (36), $80 was applicable to repairs on business property.

**Instructions**
(a) Prepare an income statement for the month of March.
(b) Prepare an owner's equity statement for March.

**P1–5** Financial statement information about four different companies is as follows:

*Determine financial statement amounts and prepare owner's equity statements.*
(SO 7, 8)

| | Santa Fe Company | San Jose Company | Tucson Company | Tempe Company |
|---|---|---|---|---|
| **January 1, 1996:** | | | | |
| Assets | $ 80,000 | $100,000 | (g) | $150,000 |
| Liabilities | 50,000 | (d) | 75,000 | (j) |
| Owner's equity | (a) | 60,000 | 45,000 | 90,000 |
| **December 31, 1996:** | | | | |
| Assets | (b) | 130,000 | 180,000 | (k) |
| Liabilities | 55,000 | 62,000 | (h) | 80,000 |
| Owner's equity | 45,000 | (e) | 110,000 | 145,000 |
| **Owner's equity changes in year:** | | | | |
| Additional investment | (c) | 8,000 | 10,000 | 15,000 |
| Drawings | 10,000 | (f) | 12,000 | 10,000 |
| Total revenues | 350,000 | 400,000 | (i) | 500,000 |
| Total expenses | 330,000 | 385,000 | 360,000 | (l) |

**Instructions**
(a) Determine the missing amounts.
(b) Prepare the owner's equity statement for Santa Fe Company.
(c) �▸ Write a memorandum explaining the sequence for preparing financial statements and the interrelationship of the owner's equity statement to the income statement and balance sheet.

# ALTERNATE PROBLEMS

**P1–1A** Tony's Repair Shop was started on May 1 by R. Antonio. A summary of May transactions is presented below.

*Analyze transactions and compute net income.*
(SO 6, 7)

1. Invested $15,000 cash in the Fox Valley Bank in the name of the business.
2. Purchased equipment for $5,000 cash.
3. Paid $400 cash for May office rent.
4. Paid $500 cash for supplies.
5. Incurred $250 of advertising costs in the Beacon News on account.
6. Received $4,100 in cash from customers for repair service.
7. Withdrew $500 cash for personal use.
8. Paid part-time employee salaries $1,000.
9. Paid utility bills $140.
10. Provided repair service on account to customers, $200.
11. Collected cash of $120 for services billed in transaction (10).

**Instructions**
(a) Prepare a tabular analysis of the transactions, using the following column headings: Cash, Accounts Receivable, Supplies, Equipment, Accounts Payable, and R. Antonio, Capital. Revenue is called service revenue.
(b) From an analysis of the column, R. Antonio, Capital, compute the net income or net loss for May.

**P1–2A** Donna Corso opened a veterinary business in Hills, Iowa, on August 1. On August 31, the balance sheet showed Cash $9,000, Accounts Receivable $1,700, Supplies $600, Office Equipment $6,000, Accounts Payable $3,600, and D. Corso, Capital, $13,700. During September the following transactions occurred:

*Analyze transactions and prepare income statement and owner's equity statement.*
(SO 6, 7, 8)

1. Paid $3,100 cash on accounts payable.
2. Collected $1,300 of accounts receivable.

3. Purchased additional office equipment for $2,100, paying $800 in cash and the balance on account.
4. Earned fees of $5,900, of which $2,500 is paid in cash and the balance is due in October.
5. Withdrew $600 cash for personal use.
6. Paid salaries $700, rent for September $900, and advertising expense $100.
7. Incurred utility expenses for month on account, $170.
8. Received $7,000 from Hilldale Bank—money borrowed on a note payable.

**Instructions**
(a) Prepare a tabular analysis of the September transactions beginning with August 31 balances. The column headings should be as follows: Cash + Accounts Receivable + Supplies + Office Equipment = Notes Payable + Accounts Payable + Donna Corso, Capital.
(b) Prepare an income statement for September, an owner's equity statement for September, and a balance sheet at September 30.

*Prepare income statement, owner's equity statement, and balance sheet.*
*(SO 8)*

**P1–3A**   On May 1, Steve O'Hare started Aero Flying School, a company that provides flying lessons to would-be pilots, by investing $45,000 cash in the business. Following are the assets and liabilities of the company on May 31, 1996, and the revenues and expenses for the month of May.

| | | | |
|---|---|---|---|
| Cash | $ 7,800 | Notes Payable | $30,000 |
| Accounts Receivable | 7,200 | Rent Expense | 1,200 |
| Equipment | 64,000 | Repair Expense | 400 |
| Fees Earned | 9,600 | Fuel Expense | 2,200 |
| Advertising Expense | 500 | Insurance Expense | 400 |
| | | Accounts Payable | 800 |

Steve O'Hare made no additional investment in May, but he withdrew $1,700 in cash for personal use.

**Instructions**
(a) Prepare an income statement and owner's equity statement for the month of May and a balance sheet at May 31.
(b) Prepare an income statement and owner's equity statement for May assuming the following data are not included above: (1) $900 of fees were earned and billed but not collected at May 31, and (2) $3,300 of fuel expense was incurred but not paid.

*Prepare income statement and owner's equity statement.*
*(SO 8)*

**P1–4A**   Presented below are the November 1996 transactions that affected the owner's equity account of the Lars Larsson Co.

| Transaction | Amount | Description |
|---|---|---|
| (7) | $ 700 | Property tax expense |
| (9) | 6,000 | Service revenue |
| (10) | 350 | Utilities expense |
| (13) | 4,000 | Wage expense |
| (16) | 300 | Utilities expense |
| (18) | 1,250 | Rent expense |
| (19) | 450 | Advertising expense |
| (22) | 2,000 | Service revenue |
| (23) | 800 | Drawings |
| (25) | 600 | Repair expense |
| (27) | 400 | Auto expense |
| (31) | 9,000 | Service revenue |
| (32) | 1,600 | Drawings |
| (33) | 4,000 | Wage expense |
| (34) | 500 | Utilities expense |

In reviewing the account, Lars realized that the new bookkeeper had made the following errors:

Transaction (23) was actually a drawing of $1,000 by L. Larsson.

Transaction (27) was a disbursement for work on L. Larsson's family car.

## Instructions

(a) Prepare an income statement for the month of November.

(b) Prepare a statement of owner's equity for November, assuming that Lars Larsson's beginning equity balance was $9,500 on November 1.

**P1–5A**  Financial statement information about four different companies is as follows:

*Determine financial statement amounts and prepare owner's equity statements.*
*(SO 7, 8)*

|  | Amin Company | Petino Company | Keino Company | Korbut Company |
|---|---|---|---|---|
| January 1, 1996: |  |  |  |  |
| Assets | $ 90,000 | $110,000 | (g) | $170,000 |
| Liabilities | 50,000 | (d) | 75,000 | (j) |
| Owner's equity | (a) | 60,000 | 55,000 | 90,000 |
| December 31, 1996: |  |  |  |  |
| Assets | (b) | 150,000 | 200,000 | (k) |
| Liabilities | 55,000 | 65,000 | (h) | 80,000 |
| Owner's equity | 58,000 | (e) | 130,000 | 170,000 |
| Owner's equity changes in year: |  |  |  |  |
| Additional investment | (c) | 15,000 | 10,000 | 15,000 |
| Drawings | 25,000 | (f) | 14,000 | 20,000 |
| Total revenues | 350,000 | 420,000 | (i) | 520,000 |
| Total expenses | 320,000 | 385,000 | 350,000 | (l) |

## Instructions

(a) Determine the missing amounts.

(b) Prepare the owner's equity statement for Petino Company.

(c) ▱▱▱▭⟹  Write a memorandum explaining the sequence for preparing financial statements and the interrelationship of the owner's equity statement to the income statement and balance sheet.

# ▶*B*roadening Your Perspective

## *F*INANCIAL REPORTING PROBLEM
• • • • • • • • • • • • • • • • • • • • • • • • • • • • • • • • • • • • • • • • • • • • • • • • • • •

The actual financial statements of PepsiCo, Inc., as presented in the company's 1994 Annual Report, are contained in Appendix A (at the back of the textbook). Refer to PepsiCo's financial statements and answer the following questions:

1. What were PepsiCo's total assets at December 31, 1994? At December 25, 1993?
2. How much cash (and cash equivalents) did PepsiCo have on December 31, 1994?
3. What amount of accounts payable did PepsiCo report on December 31, 1994? On December 25, 1993?
4. What were PepsiCo's net sales in 1992? In 1993? In 1994?
5. What is the amount of the change in PepsiCo's net income from 1993 to 1994?
6. The accounting equation is: Assets = Liabilities + Owner's Equity. Replacing the words in that equation with dollar amounts, what is PepsiCo's accounting equation at December 31, 1994? (Hint: Owner's equity is equivalent to shareholders' equity.)

## *D*ECISION CASE
• • • • • • • • • • • • • • • • • • • • • • • • • • • • • • • • • • • • • • • • • • • • • • • • • • •

Betsy and Bill Kite, local golf stars, opened the Parmor Driving Range on March 1, 1996, by investing $10,000 of their cash savings in the business. A caddy shack was constructed for cash at a cost of $4,000 and $800 was spent on golf balls and golf clubs. The Kites leased five acres of land at a cost of $1,000 per month and paid the first month's rent. During the first month, advertising costs totaled $750 of which $150 was unpaid at March 31, and $400 was paid to members of the high school golf team for retrieving golf balls. All fees from customers were deposited in the company's bank account. On March 15, Betsy and Bill withdrew a total of $800 in cash for personal living expenses. A $100 utility bill was received on March 31 but it was not paid. On March 31, the balance in the company's bank account was $8,550.

Betsy and Bill thought they had a pretty good first month of operations. However, their estimates of profitability ranged from a loss of $1,450 to net income of $3,100.

**Instructions**
(a) How could the Kites have concluded that the business operated at a loss of $1,450? Was this a valid basis on which to determine net income?
(b) How could the Kites have concluded that the business operated at a net income of $3,100? (Hint: Prepare a balance sheet at March 31.) Was this a valid basis on which to determine net income?
(c) Without preparing an income statement, determine the actual net income for March.
(d) What were the fees earned in March?

# COMMUNICATION ACTIVITY

Amy Joan is the bookkeeper for Vermont Company. Amy has been trying to get the balance sheet of Vermont Company to balance. Vermont's balance sheet is as follows:

**VERMONT COMPANY**
**Balance Sheet**
**For the Month Ended December 31, 1996**

| Assets | | Liabilities | |
|---|---|---|---|
| Equipment | $20,500 | Vermont, Capital | $21,000 |
| Cash | 9,000 | Accounts receivable | (3,000) |
| Supplies | 2,000 | Vermont, Drawing | (2,000) |
| Accounts payable | (5,000) | Notes payable | 10,500 |
| | $26,500 | | $26,500 |

**Instructions**
Explain to Amy Joan in a memo why the original balance sheet is incorrect and what should be done to correct it.

# GROUP ACTIVITY

Mary Company had the following account balances:

| | | | |
|---|---|---|---|
| Rent expense | $   800 | Utilities expense | $  300 |
| Notes payable | 700 | Accounts receivable | 2,000 |
| Cash | 10,500 | Telephone expense | 100 |
| Capital, July 1 | 10,000 | Accounts payable | 3,000 |
| Salaries expense | 500 | Equipment | 3,000 |
| Revenue | 3,500 | | |

**Instructions**
Your instructor will divide the class into groups of five or six students. When you are told to begin, prepare Mary Company's income statement, owner's equity statement, and balance sheet for July 31. The first group to finish with the correct answer wins!

# ETHICS CASE

After numerous campus interviews, Joe Catmus, a senior at Great Eastern College, received two office interview invitations from the Baltimore offices of two large firms. Both firms offered to cover his out-of-pocket expenses (travel, hotel, and meal). He scheduled the interviews for both firms on the same day, one in the morning and one in the afternoon. At the conclusion of each interview, he submitted to both firms his total out-of-pocket expenses for the trip to Baltimore, $244: mileage $70 (280 miles at $.25), hotel $120, meals $36, parking and tolls $18, for a total of $244. He believes this approach is appropriate. If he had made two trips, his cost would have been two times $244. He is also certain that neither firm knew he had visited the other on that same trip. Within ten days Joe received two checks in the mail, each in the amount of $244.

*Instructions*
    (a) Who are the stakeholders (affected parties) in this situation?
    (b) What are the ethical issues in this case?
    (c) What would you do in this situation?

# CRITICAL THINKING
## ► *A Real-World Focus: Air Transportation Holding Company Inc.*

*Founded in 1980, **Air Transportation Holding Company** operates contract cargo shipping, specializing in small, overnight deliveries throughout the eastern United States. The company flies approximately 80 routes, as specified in its contracts with Federal Express. It has hangars and maintenance facilities in North Carolina, Michigan, and South Carolina.*

The specific assets, liabilities, and subdivisions of owner's equity of any business depend on the type of business being operated. Management of Air Transportation Holding Company explained the year's results of operations as follows:

    Operating expenses increased $5,498,000 (29.9%) to $23,904,000 for 1993 compared to 1992. The increase in operating expenses consisted of the following changes: cost of flight operations increased $2,313,000 (25.7%) as a result of increases in pilot and flight personnel and costs associated with travel and landing fees which were partially offset by decreased aircraft lease and fuel costs; maintenance expense increased $2,850,000 (42.9%) primarily as a result of increases in aircraft parts purchases and mechanic and maintenance personnel costs (due to start-up of satellite maintenance facility and the operation of additional aircraft); the general and administrative expense increase of $470,000 (17.3%) resulted from increases in operational and clerical staffing related to expansion of the aircraft fleet operated.

*Instructions*
    (a) Recall the definition of an asset. Can you identify three specific types of assets owned by Air Transportation Holding Company?
    (b) The discussion above is largely about the operating expenses of the company. Identify five expenses of operations that Air Transportation incurs.
    (c) When this company renders service by providing air transportation, what account affecting owner's equity is increased?

---

*Answers to Self-Study Questions*
1. b    2. d    3. a    4. c    5. a    6. d    7. b    8. a    9. b    10. c

# Her Classroom Is the Real World

SAN DIEGO, Calif. — Gabriella Torres of San Diego learned how to record transactions on a computer before she took her first accounting course. The reason: by day, she manages the office of Diabetes & Endocrine Associates, a medical practice with an office located near San Diego State University. The doctors' office uses a computer package that makes recording transactions quite easy for Gabriella. She attends night school and hopes to graduate within six years. "The doctors have really been accommodating to my school schedule."

Working during the day allows Gabriella to bring a real-world perspective to the classroom. In turn, studying business subjects at night makes her job easier. She is in charge of paying the bills for the medical practice, making sure the bank statement reconciles with the checkbook, hiring office staff, preparing patient bills, and maintaining accounts receivable. "I really love my job," she says, which is one reason she prefers to work days and go to school at night.

Taking her first accounting course helped Gabriella understand how the journal entries, the accounts, and financial statements fit together. Unlike doing homework assignments, though, the computer package at work catches some of her errors. "It won't let you proceed from one accounting entry to the next unless the entry balances," she says. In fact, there are no "books" at all, just diskettes and printouts. ◀

CHAPTER · **2**

# $T$HE RECORDING PROCESS

▶ **STUDY OBJECTIVES** ◀

**After studying this chapter, you should be able to:**

1. *Explain what an account is and how it helps in the recording process.*
2. *Define debits and credits and explain how they are used to record business transactions.*
3. *Identify the basic steps in the recording process.*
4. *Explain what a journal is and how it helps in the recording process.*
5. *Explain what a ledger is and how it helps in the recording process.*
6. *Explain what posting is and how it helps in the recording process.*
7. *Prepare a trial balance and explain its purposes.*

In Chapter 1, we analyzed business transactions in terms of the accounting equation and presented the cumulative effects of these transactions in tabular form. Imagine a medical practice such as Diabetes & Endocrine Associates using the same tabular format as Softbyte to keep track of every one of its transactions. In a single day, this medical practice engages in hundreds of business transactions. To record each transaction this way would be impractical, expensive, and unnecessary.

As a result, a set of procedures and records are used to make it possible to keep track of and accumulate transaction data more easily. In this chapter we will introduce and illustrate the basic procedures and records that are used. The organization and content of the chapter are as follows:

## The Account

**STUDY OBJECTIVE**

•••••••• 1 ••••••••

*Explain what an account is and how it helps in the recording process.*

An account is an individual accounting record of increases and decreases in a specific asset, liability, or owner's equity item. For example, Softbyte (discussed in Chapter 1) would have separate accounts for Cash, Accounts Receivable, Accounts Payable, Service Revenue, Salaries Expense, and so on. In its simplest form, an account consists of three parts: (1) the title of the account, (2) a left or debit side, and (3) a right or credit side. Because the alignment of these parts of an account resembles the letter T, it is referred to as a T account. The basic form of an account is shown in Illustration 2-1.

**Illustration 2-1**

*Basic form of account*

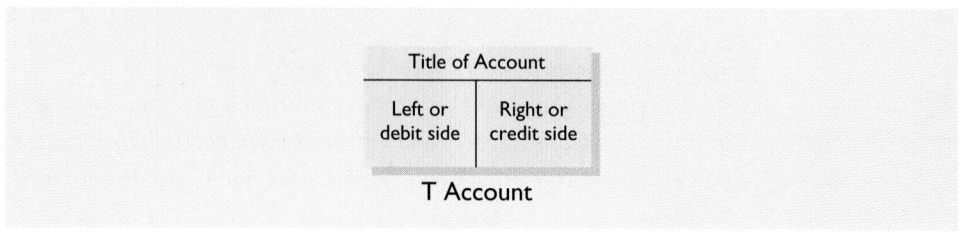

**Helpful hint** The T account is a standard shorthand in accounting that helps make clear the effects of transactions on individual accounts.

This form of account will be used often throughout this book to explain basic accounting relationships.

# ▶Technology in Action

 Computerized and manual accounting systems basically parallel one another. Most of the procedures are handled by electronic circuitry in computerized systems. They seem to occur invisibly. Therefore, to fully comprehend how computerized systems operate, it is necessary to illustrate and understand manual approaches for processing accounting data.

## Debits and Credits

The terms debit and credit mean left and right, respectively. They are commonly abbreviated as Dr. for debit and Cr. for credit.[1] These terms do not mean increase or decrease. The terms debit and credit are used repeatedly in the recording process. For example, the act of entering an amount on the left side of an account is called **debiting** the account, and making an entry on the right side is **crediting** the account. When the totals of the two sides are compared, an account will have a **debit balance** if the total of the debit amounts exceeds the credits. Conversely, an account will have a **credit balance** if the credit amounts exceed the debits.

The procedure of having debits on the left and credits on the right is an accounting custom, or rule. We could function just as well if debits and credits were reversed. However, the custom of having debits on the left side of an account and credits on the right side (like the custom of driving on the right-hand side of the road) has been adopted in the United States. **This rule applies to all accounts.**

The procedure of recording debits and credits in an account is shown in Illustration 2-2 for the cash transactions of Softbyte. The data are taken from the cash column of the tabular summary in Illustration 1-8.

**STUDY OBJECTIVE**
••••••••••▼2••••••••••
*Define debits and credits and explain how they are used to record business transactions.*

**Helpful hint** The word credit has a different meaning in accounting than it has in everyday life. For accounting purposes, think of the terms debit and credit solely as directional signals. Debit—use the left side of the account; credit—use the right side.

**Illustration 2-2**

*Tabular summary compared to account form*

| Tabular Summary | Account Form | | | |
|---|---|---|---|---|
| Cash | Cash | | | |
| $15,000 | (Debits) | 15,000 | (Credits) | 7,000 |
| −7,000 | | 1,200 | | 1,700 |
| 1,200 | | 1,500 | | 250 |
| 1,500 | | 600 | | 1,300 |
| −1,700 | Balance | 8,050 | | |
| −250 | (Debit) | | | |
| 600 | | | | |
| −1,300 | | | | |
| $ 8,050 | | | | |

Every positive item in the tabular summary represents a receipt of cash; every negative amount constitutes a payment of cash. Notice that in the account form the increases in cash are recorded as debits, and the decreases in cash are recorded as credits. Having increases on one side and decreases on the other helps in determining the totals of each side of the account as well as the balance in the account. The account balance, a debit of $8,050, indicates that Softbyte has had $8,050 more increases than decreases in cash. That is, it has $8,050 in its Cash account.

[1]These abbreviations come from the Latin words *debere* (Dr.) and *credere* (Cr.).

## *Debit and Credit Procedure*

In Chapter 1 you learned the effect of a transaction on the basic accounting equation. Remember that each transaction must affect two or more accounts to keep the basic accounting equation in balance. In other words, for each transaction debits must equal credits in the accounts. The equality of debits and credits provides the basis for the double-entry system of recording transactions (sometimes referred to as double-entry bookkeeping).

Under the universally used double-entry system, the dual (two-sided) effect of each transaction is recorded in appropriate accounts. This system provides a logical method for recording transactions. It also offers a means of proving the accuracy of the recorded amounts. If every transaction is recorded with equal debits and credits, then the sum of all the debits to the accounts must equal the sum of all the credits.

The double-entry system for determining the equality of the accounting equation is much more efficient than the plus/minus procedure used in Chapter 1. There, it was necessary after each transaction to compare total assets with total liabilities and owner's equity to determine the equality of the two sides of the accounting equation.

**Assets and Liabilities.**   In the Softbyte illustration above, increases in cash—an asset—were entered on the left side, and decreases in cash were entered on the right side. We know that both sides of the basic equation (assets = liabilities + owner's equity) must be equal; it then follows that increases and decreases in liabilities will have to be recorded opposite from increases and decreases in assets. Thus, increases in liabilities must be entered on the right or credit side, and decreases in liabilities must be entered on the left or debit side. The effects that debits and credits have on assets and liabilities are summarized as follows:

**Illustration 2-3**

*Debit and credit effects— assets and liabilities*

| Debits | Credits |
|---|---|
| Increase assets | Decrease assets |
| Decrease liabilities | Increase liabilities |

Debits to a specific asset account should exceed the credits to that account, and credits to a liability account should exceed debits to that account. Thus, asset accounts normally show debit balances, and liability accounts normally show credit balances. The normal balances may be diagrammed as follows:

**Illustration 2-4**

*Normal balances—assets and liabilities*

| Assets | | Liabilities | |
|---|---|---|---|
| Increase Debit ↓ Normal Balance | Decrease Credit | Decrease Debit | Increase Credit ↓ Normal Balance |

An awareness of the normal balance in an account may help you when you are trying to trace errors. For example, a credit balance in an asset account such as Land or a debit balance in a liability account such as Wages Payable would indicate errors in recording. Occasionally, however, an abnormal balance may

## ►*T*echnology in *A*ction

In automated systems, the computer is programmed to flag these normal balance exceptions and to print out error or exception reports. In manual systems, careful visual inspection of the accounts is required to detect normal balance problems.

be correct. The Cash account, for example, will have a credit balance when a company has overdrawn its bank balance (i.e., written a "bad" check).

**Owner's Equity.** As indicated in Chapter 1, owner's equity is increased by owner's investments and revenues. It is decreased by owner's drawings and expenses. In a double-entry system, accounts are kept for each of these types of transactions, as explained below.

*Owner's Capital.* Investments by owners are credited to the owner's capital account. The owner's capital account is increased by credits and decreased by debits. For example, when cash is invested in the business, cash is debited and owner's capital is credited. Conversely, owner's capital is debited when the owner's investment in the business is reduced.

The rules of debit and credit for the owner's capital account are stated as follows:

| Debits | Credits |
| --- | --- |
| Decrease owner's capital | Increase owner's capital |

**Illustration 2-5**

*Debit and credit effects—owner's capital*

The normal balance in this account may be diagrammed as follows:

| Owner's Capital | |
| --- | --- |
| Decrease | Increase |
| Debit | Credit |
| | ↓ |
| | Normal |
| | Balance |

**Illustration 2-6**

*Normal balance—owner's capital*

**Helpful hint** The rules for debit and credit and the normal balance of owner's capital are the same as for liabilities.

*Owner's Drawing.* An owner may withdraw cash or other assets for personal use. Withdrawals could be debited directly to owner's capital to indicate a decrease in owner's equity. However, it is preferable to establish a separate account, referred to as the owner's drawing account, in order to determine the total withdrawals for the accounting period. **The drawing account decreases owner's equity. It is not an income statement account like revenues and expenses.** Owner's drawing is increased by debits and decreased by credits. Normally, the drawing account will have a debit balance. The rules of debit and credit for the drawing account are stated as follows:

| Debits | Credits |
| --- | --- |
| Increase owner's drawing | Decrease owner's drawing |

**Illustration 2-7**

*Debit and credit effects—owner's drawing*

The normal balance may be diagrammed as follows:

**Illustration 2-8**

*Normal balance—owner's drawing*

| Owner's Drawing | |
|---|---|
| Increase<br>Debit<br>↓<br>Normal<br>Balance | Decrease<br>Credit |

***Revenues and Expenses.***   When revenues are earned, owner's equity is increased. Accordingly, **the effect of debits and credits on revenue accounts is identical to their effect on owner's capital**. Revenue accounts are increased by credits and decreased by debits.

On the other hand, expenses decrease owner's equity. As a result, expenses are recorded by debits. Since expenses are the negative factor in the computation of net income, and revenues are the positive factor, it is logical that the increase and decrease sides of expense accounts should be the reverse of revenue accounts. Thus, expense accounts are increased by debits and decreased by credits. The effect of debits and credits on revenues and expenses may be stated as follows:

**Helpful hint**  Because revenues increase owner's equity, a revenue account has the same debit and credit rules as does the owner's capital account. Conversely, expenses have the opposite effect.

**Illustration 2-9**

*Debit and credit effects—revenues and expenses*

| Debits | Credits |
|---|---|
| Decrease revenues | Increase revenues |
| Increase expenses | Decrease expenses |

Credits to revenue accounts should exceed the debits, and debits to expense accounts should exceed credits. Thus, revenue accounts normally show credit balances and expense accounts normally show debit balances. The normal balances may be diagrammed as follows:

**Illustration 2-10**

*Normal balances—revenues and expenses*

| Revenues | | Expenses | |
|---|---|---|---|
| Decrease<br>Debit | Increase<br>Credit<br>↓<br>Normal<br>Balance | Increase<br>Debit<br>↓<br>Normal<br>Balance | Decrease<br>Credit |

## ▸Accounting in Action ▸ *Business Insight*

The Chicago Cubs baseball team has the following major revenue and expense accounts:

| *Revenues* | *Expenses* |
|---|---|
| Admissions (ticket sales) | Players' salaries |
| Concessions | Administrative salaries |
| Television and radio | Travel |
| Advertising | Ballpark maintenance |

## Expansion of Basic Equation

You have already learned the basic accounting equation. Illustration 2-11 expands this equation to show the accounts that comprise owner's equity. In addition, the debit/credit rules and effects on each type of account are illustrated. Study this diagram carefully. It will help you understand the fundamentals of the double-entry system. Like the basic equation, the expanded basic equation must be in balance (total debits equal total credits).

**Illustration 2-11**

*Expanded basic equation and debit/credit rules and effects*

# Before You Go On . . .

### ► Review It

1. What do the terms debit and credit mean?
2. What are the debit and credit effects on assets, liabilities, and owner's equity?
3. What are the debit and credit effects on revenues, expenses, and owner's drawing?
4. What are the normal balances for individual asset, liability, and owner's equity accounts?

### ► Do It

Kate Browne has just rented space in a shopping mall for the purpose of opening and operating a beauty salon, to be called "Hair It Is." Long before opening day and before purchasing equipment, hiring assistants, and remodeling the space, Kate is strongly advised to set up a double-entry set of accounting records in which to record all of her business transactions.

Identify the balance sheet accounts that Kate will likely need to record the transactions necessary to establish and open her business. Also, indicate whether the normal balance of each account is a debit or a credit.

*Reasoning:* To start her business, Kate will need to have asset accounts for each different type of asset invested in the business. In addition, Kate will need liability accounts for debts incurred by the business. Kate will only need one owner's equity account, owner's capital, when she begins the business. The other owner's equity accounts will only be needed after business has commenced.

*Solution:* Kate would likely need the following accounts in which to record the transactions necessary to establish and ready her beauty salon for opening day: Cash (debit balance); Equipment (debit balance); Supplies (debit balance); Accounts Payable (credit balance); Notes Payable (credit balance), if she borrows money; K. Browne, Capital (credit balance).

*Related exercise material:* BE2–1, BE2–2, E2–1, E2–3, and E2–10.

# Steps in the Recording Process

Although it is possible to enter transaction information directly into the accounts, few businesses do so. In practically every business, the basic steps in the recording process are:

1. Analyze each transaction in terms of its effect on the accounts.
2. Enter the transaction information in a journal (book of original entry).
3. Transfer the journal information to the appropriate accounts in the ledger (book of accounts).

The actual sequence of events begins with the transaction. Evidence of the transaction comes in the form of a **business document**, such as a sales slip, a check, a bill, or a cash register tape. This evidence is analyzed to determine the effect of the transaction on specific accounts. The transaction is then entered in the journal. Finally, the journal entry is transferred to the designated accounts in the ledger. The sequence of events in the recording process can be diagrammed as follows:

**Illustration 2-12**

*The recording process*

**The Recording Process**

Analyze each transaction

Enter transaction in a journal

Transfer journal information to ledger accounts

The basic steps in the recording process occur repeatedly in every business enterprise. The analysis of transactions has already been illustrated, and further examples of this step will be given in this and later chapters. The other steps in the recording process are explained in the next sections.

## The Journal

Transactions are initially recorded in chronological order in a journal before being transferred to the accounts. Thus, the journal is referred to as the book of original entry. For each transaction the journal shows the debit and credit effects on specific accounts. Companies may use various kinds of journals, but every company has the most basic form of journal, a general journal. Typically, a general journal has spaces for dates, account titles and explanations, references, and two money columns. Whenever the term journal is used in this textbook without a modifying adjective, it will mean the general journal.

The journal makes several significant contributions to the recording process:

1. It discloses in one place the complete effect of a transaction.
2. It provides a chronological record of transactions.
3. It helps to prevent or locate errors because the debit and credit amounts for each entry can be readily compared.

### Journalizing

Entering transaction data in the journal is known as journalizing. Separate journal entries are made for each transaction. A complete entry consists of: (1) the date of the transaction, (2) the accounts and amounts to be debited and credited, and (3) a brief explanation of the transaction.

To illustrate the technique of journalizing, the first two transactions of Softbyte are journalized in Illustration 2-13 using the first page (J1) of the general journal. These transactions were: September 1, Ray Neal invested $15,000 cash in the business, and computer equipment was purchased for $7,000 cash.

**Illustration 2-13**

*Technique of journalizing*

| GENERAL JOURNAL | | | | J1 |
|---|---|---|---|---|
| Date | Account Titles and Explanation | Ref. | Debit | Credit |
| 1996 Sept. 1 | Cash | | 15,000 | |
| | R. Neal, Capital | | | 15,000 |
| | (Invested cash in business) | | | |
| 1 | Computer Equipment | | 7,000 | |
| | Cash | | | 7,000 |
| | (Purchased equipment for cash) | | | |

The standard form and content of journal entries are as follows:

1. The date of the transaction is entered in the Date column. The date recorded should include the year, month, and day of the transaction.
2. The debit account title (that is, the account to be debited) is entered first at the extreme left margin of the column headed Account Titles and Explanation. The credit account title (that is, the account to be credited) is then entered on the next line, indented under the line above. The indentation decreases the possibility of switching the debit and credit amounts.
3. The amounts for the debits are recorded in the Debit (left) column and the amounts for the credits are recorded in the Credit (right) column.
4. A brief explanation of the transaction is given.
5. A space is left between journal entries. The blank space separates individual journal entries and makes the entire journal easier to read.
6. The column entitled Ref. (which stands for reference) is left blank at the time the journal entry is made. The Reference column is used later when the journal entries are transferred to the ledger accounts. At that time, the ledger account number is placed in the Reference column to indicate where the amount in the journal entry was transferred.

**It is important to use correct and specific account titles in journalizing.** Since most accounts appear later in the financial statements, erroneous account titles lead to incorrect financial statements. Some flexibility exists initially in selecting account titles. The main criterion is that each title must appropriately describe the content of the account. For example, the account title used for the cost of delivery trucks may be Delivery Equipment, Delivery Trucks, or Trucks. Once a company chooses the specific title to use, all subsequent transactions involving the account should be recorded under that account title.[2]

If an entry involves only two accounts, one debit and one credit, it is considered a simple entry. For some transactions, however, it may be necessary to use more than two accounts in journalizing. Imagine, for example, the numerous accounts needed by General Electric to record the acquisition of all the assets and liabilities of RCA in what was one of the largest mergers ever completed. When three or more accounts are required in one journal entry, the entry is referred to as a compound entry. To illustrate, assume that on July 1, Butler Company purchases a delivery truck costing $14,000 by paying $8,000 cash and the balance on account (to be paid at a later date). The entry is as follows:

**Illustration 2-14**

*Compound journal entry*

| GENERAL JOURNAL | | | | J1 |
|---|---|---|---|---|
| Date | Account Titles and Explanation | Ref. | Debit | Credit |
| 1996<br>July  1 | Delivery Equipment<br>   Cash<br>   Accounts Payable<br>   (Purchased truck for cash with balance on<br>   account) | | 14,000 | <br>8,000<br>6,000 |

In a compound entry, it is important to determine that the total debit and credit amounts are equal. Also, the standard format requires that all debits be listed before the credits are listed.

## Before You Go On . . .

### ▶ Review It

1. What is the correct sequence of the steps in the recording process?
2. What contribution does the journal make to the recording process?
3. What is the standard form and content of a journal entry made in the general journal?

### ▶ Do It

In establishing her beauty salon, Hair It Is, Kate Browne engaged in the following activities:

1. Opened a bank account in the name of Hair It Is and deposited $20,000 of her own money in this account as her initial investment.
2. Purchased on account (to be paid in 30 days) equipment, for a total cost of $4,800.
3. Interviewed three persons for the position of beautician.

In what form (type of record) should Kate record these three activities? Prepare the entries to record the transactions.

---

[2]In homework problems, when specific account titles are given, they should be used. When account titles are not given, you may select account titles that identify the nature and content of each account. The account titles used in journalizing should not contain explanations such as Cash Paid or Cash Received.

**Reasoning:** Kate should record the transactions in a journal, which is a chronological record of the transactions. The record should be a complete and accurate representation of the transactions' effects on her business's assets, liabilities, and owner's equity.

**Solution:** Each transaction that is recorded is entered in the general journal. The three activities would be recorded as follows:

1. Cash                                             20,000
      K. Browne, Capital                                           20,000
        (Invested cash in the business)

2. Equipment                                      4,800
      Accounts Payable                                             4,800
        (Purchased equipment on account)

3. No entry because no transaction has occurred.

*Related exercise material: BE2–3, BE2–5, BE2–6, E2–2, E2–4, E2–6, E2–7, and E2–8.*

## The Ledger

The entire group of accounts maintained by a company is referred to collectively as the ledger. The ledger keeps in one place all the information about changes in specific account balances.

Companies may use various kinds of ledgers, but every company has a general ledger. A general ledger contains all the assets, liabilities, and owner's equity accounts, as shown in Illustration 2-15. A business can use a looseleaf binder or card file for the ledger with each account kept on a separate sheet or card. Whenever the term ledger is used in this textbook without a modifying adjective, it will mean the general ledger.

**STUDY OBJECTIVE**
5
*Explain what a ledger is and how it helps in the recording process.*

**Illustration 2-15**

*The general ledger*

The ledger should be arranged in statement order beginning with the balance sheet accounts. First in order are the asset accounts, followed by liability accounts, owner's capital, owner's drawing, revenues, and expenses. Each account is numbered for easier identification.

The information in the ledger provides management with the balances in various accounts. For example, the Cash account enables management to determine the amount of cash that is available to meet current obligations. Amounts due from customers and the amounts owed to creditors can be determined by examining the Accounts Receivable and Accounts Payable accounts, respectively.

## ▸Accounting in Action ▸ *Business Insight*

In his autobiography Sam Walton described the double-entry accounting system he began the Wal-Mart empire with: "We kept a little pigeonhole on the wall for the cash receipts and paperwork of each [Wal-Mart] store. I had a blue binder ledger book for each store. When we added a store, we added a pigeonhole. We did this at least up to twenty stores. Then once a month, the bookkeeper and I would enter the merchandise, enter the sales, enter the cash, and balance it."

*Source:* Sam Walton, *Made in America* (New York: Doubleday, 1992), p. 53.

### Standard Form of Account

The simple T-account form of an account used in an accounting textbook is often very useful for illustration and analysis purposes. However, in practice, the account forms used in ledgers are much more structured. A form widely used in a manual system is shown in Illustration 2-16, using assumed data from a cash account.

**Illustration 2-16**

*Three-column form of account*

| CASH | | | | | No. 10 |
|---|---|---|---|---|---|
| Date | Explanation | Ref. | Debit | Credit | Balance |
| 1996 | | | | | |
| June 1 | | | 25,000 | | 25,000 |
| 2 | | | | 8,000 | 17,000 |
| 3 | | | 4,200 | | 21,200 |
| 9 | | | 7,500 | | 28,700 |
| 17 | | | | 11,700 | 17,000 |
| 20 | | | | 250 | 16,750 |
| 30 | | | | 7,300 | 9,450 |

This form has three money columns—debit, credit, and balance. The balance in the account is determined after each transaction. Thus, this form is often called the three-column form of account. Note that the explanation space and reference columns are used to provide special information about the transaction.

**STUDY OBJECTIVE**
•••••••••6•••••••••

*Explain what posting is and how it helps in the recording process.*

### Posting

The procedure of transferring journal entries to the ledger accounts is called posting. **This phase of the recording process accumulates the effects of journalized transactions in the individual accounts.**

## ▸Technology in Action

Determining what to record is the most critical (and for most businesses the most expensive) point in the accounting process. In computerized systems, after this phase is completed, your input and all further processing just boil down to file merging and report generation. Programmers and management information system types with good accounting backgrounds (such as they should gain from a good principles textbook) are better able to develop effective computerized systems.

Posting involves the following steps:

1. In the ledger, enter in the appropriate columns of the account(s) debited the date, journal page, and debit amount shown in the journal.
2. In the reference column of the journal, write the account number to which the debit amount was posted.
3. In the ledger, enter in the appropriate columns of the account(s) credited the date, journal page, and credit amount shown in the journal.
4. In the reference column of the journal, write the account number to which the credit amount was posted.

**Helpful hint** Posting is essentially a copying procedure that should be done carefully if correct account balances are to be obtained.

These four steps are diagrammed in Illustration 2-17 using the first journal entry of Softbyte. The boxed numbers indicate the sequence of the steps.

**Illustration 2-17**

*Posting a journal entry*

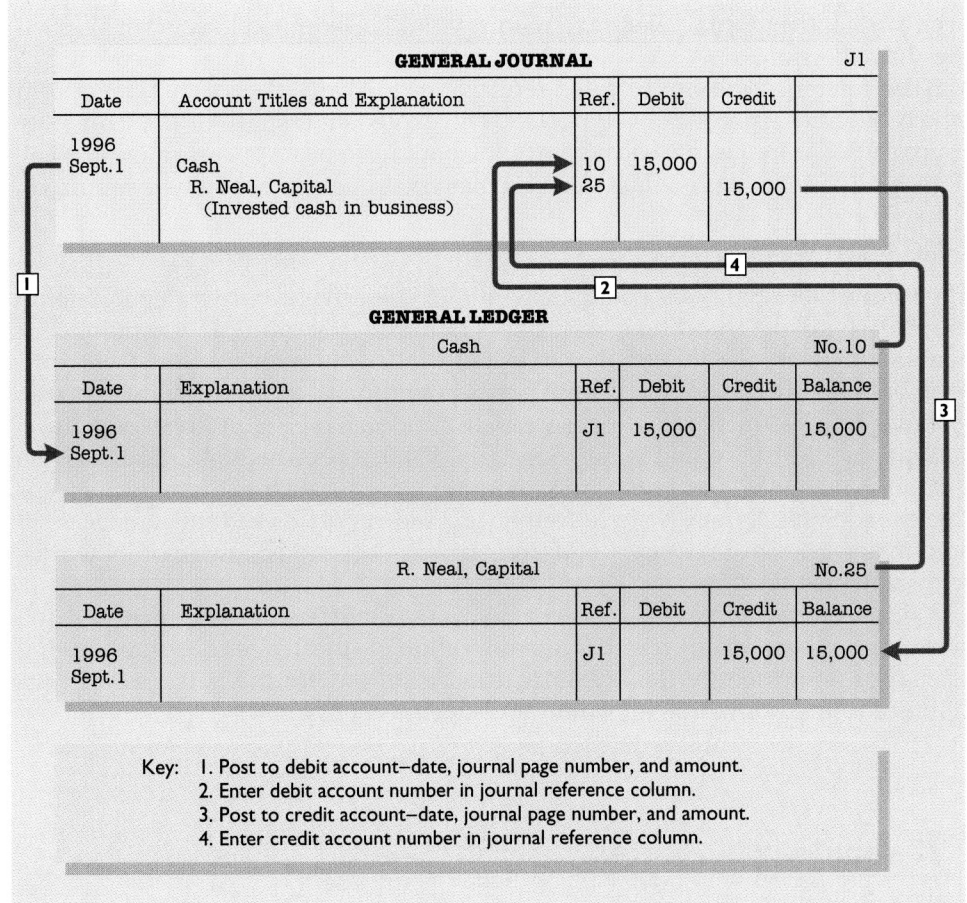

Key: 1. Post to debit account—date, journal page number, and amount.
2. Enter debit account number in journal reference column.
3. Post to credit account—date, journal page number, and amount.
4. Enter credit account number in journal reference column.

Posting should be performed in chronological order. That is, all the debits and credits of one journal entry should be posted before proceeding to the next journal entry. Under the journalizing procedures described in this chapter, postings should be made on a timely basis to ensure that the ledger is up to date.[3]

The reference column **in the journal** serves several purposes. The numbers in this column indicate the entries that have been posted. After the last entry has

---

[3]In homework problems, it will be permissible to journalize all transactions before posting any of the journal entries.

## ▶Accounting in Action ▸ *Business Insight*

The numbering system used to identify accounts can be quite sophisticated or relatively simple. For example, at Goodyear Tire & Rubber Company an 18-digit system is used. The first three digits identify the division or plant. The second set of three-digit numbers contains the following account classifications:

| | |
|---|---|
| 100–199 Assets | 300–399 Revenues |
| 200–299 Liabilities and Owner's Equity | 400–599 Expenses |

Other digits describe the location of a specific plant, product line, region of the country, and so on.

been posted, the journal reference column should be scanned to see that all postings have been made.

The reference column **of a ledger** account indicates the journal page from which the transaction has been posted. The explanation space of the ledger account is used infrequently because an explanation already appears in the journal. It generally is used only when detailed analysis of account activity is required.

### Chart of Accounts

The number and type of accounts used differ for each enterprise, depending on the size, complexity, and type of business involved. For example, the number of accounts depends on the amount of detail desired by management. The management of one company may want one account for all types of utility expense. Another may keep separate expense accounts for each type of utility expenditure, such as gas, electricity, and water. Similarly, a single proprietorship like Softbyte will not have many accounts compared with a corporate giant like Ford Motor Company. Softbyte may be able to manage and report its activities in 20 to 30 accounts, while Ford requires thousands of accounts to keep track of its worldwide activities.

Most companies have a chart of accounts that lists the accounts and the account numbers which identify their location in the ledger. The numbering system used to identify the accounts usually starts with the balance sheet accounts and follows with the income statement accounts.

## ▶Technology in Action

The first step in designing a computerized accounting system is to create a chart of accounts. The chart of accounts establishes the framework for the entire data base of accounting information.

From the chart of accounts, the general ledger can be created. Journal entries are simultaneously posted to the ledger accounts when the journal entry is made in most computerized systems. The balances are available at any point in time in such systems.

Obvious errors in the recording process (e.g., unbalanced entries or use of nonexistent accounts) are "flagged" by the system and are not processed until corrected. This correction usually takes place immediately after the error is discovered by the system. Because the initial entry is so important, many systems search for more subtle errors, such as unreasonable dollar amounts for specific accounts.

In this and the next two chapters, we will be explaining the accounting for the proprietorship, Pioneer Advertising Agency (a service enterprise). Accounts 1–19 indicate asset accounts; 20–39 indicate liabilities; 40–49 indicate owner's equity accounts; 50–59, revenues; and 60–69, expenses. The chart of accounts for Pioneer Advertising Agency (C. R. Byrd, owner) is shown in Illustration 2-18. Accounts shown in red are used in this chapter; accounts shown in black are explained in later chapters.

**Illustration 2-18**

*Chart of accounts*

**Pioneer Advertising Agency**

| Assets | Owner's Equity |
| --- | --- |
| **1. Cash** | **40. C. R. Byrd, Capital** |
| 6. Accounts Receivable | **41. C. R. Byrd, Drawing** |
| **8. Advertising Supplies** | 49. Income Summary |
| **10. Prepaid Insurance** | **Revenues** |
| **15. Office Equipment** | |
| 16. Accumulated Depreciation—Office Equipment | **50. Fees Earned** |
| **Liabilities** | **Expenses** |
| **25. Notes Payable** | **60. Salaries Expense** |
| **26. Accounts Payable** | 61. Advertising Supplies Expense |
| 27. Interest Payable | **62. Rent Expense** |
| **28. Unearned Fees** | 63. Insurance Expense |
| 29. Salaries Payable | 64. Interest Expense |
| | 65. Depreciation Expense |

You will notice that there are gaps in the numbering system of the chart of accounts for Pioneer Advertising. Gaps are left to permit the insertion of new accounts as needed during the life of the business.

# The Recording Process Illustrated

Illustration 2-19 through Illustration 2-28 show the basic steps in the recording process, using the October transactions of the Pioneer Advertising Agency. Its accounting period is a month. A basic analysis and a debit-credit analysis precede the journalizing and posting of each transaction. Study these transaction analyses carefully. **The purpose of transaction analysis is first to identify the type of account involved, and then to determine whether a debit or a credit to the account is required.** You should always perform this type of analysis before preparing a journal entry. Doing so will help you understand the journal entries discussed in this chapter as well as more complex journal entries to be described in later chapters.

Keep in mind that every journal entry affects one or more of the following items: assets, liabilities, owner's capital, owner's drawing, revenues, or expenses. By becoming skilled at transaction analysis, you will be able to recognize quickly the impact of any transaction on these six items. For simplicity, the T-account form is used in the illustrations instead of the standard account form.

**Helpful hint** To correctly record a transaction, you must carefully analyze the event and translate that analysis into debit and credit language.
First: Determine what type of account is involved.
Second: Determine what items increased or decreased and by how much.
Third: Translate the increases and decreases into debits and credits.

**Illustration 2-19**

*Investment of cash by owner*

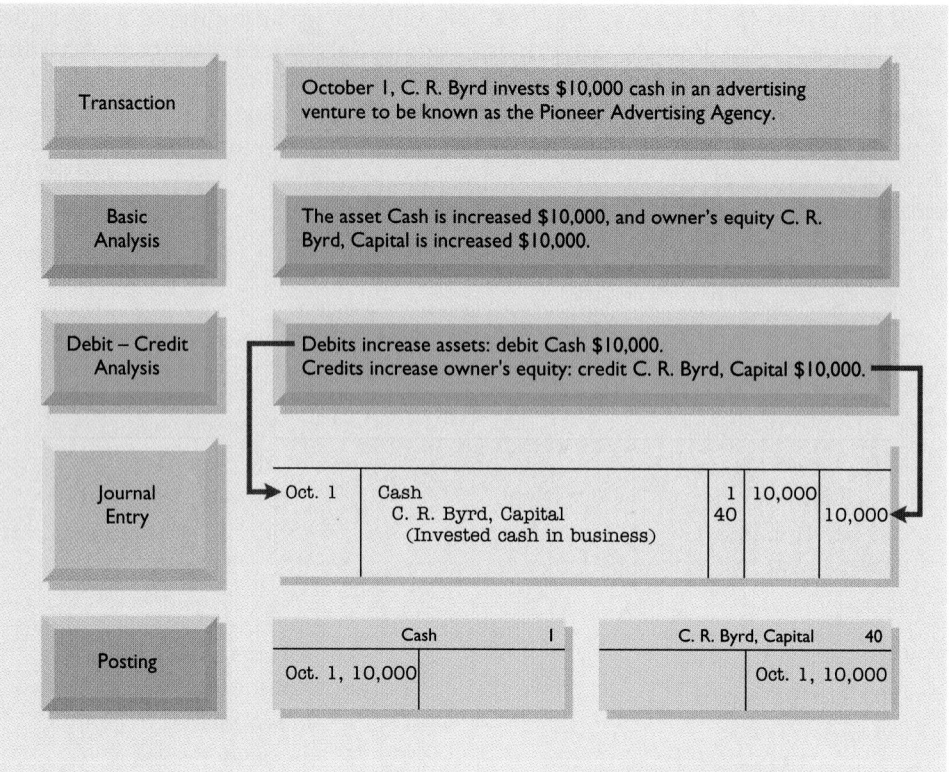

**Illustration 2-20**

*Purchase of office equipment*

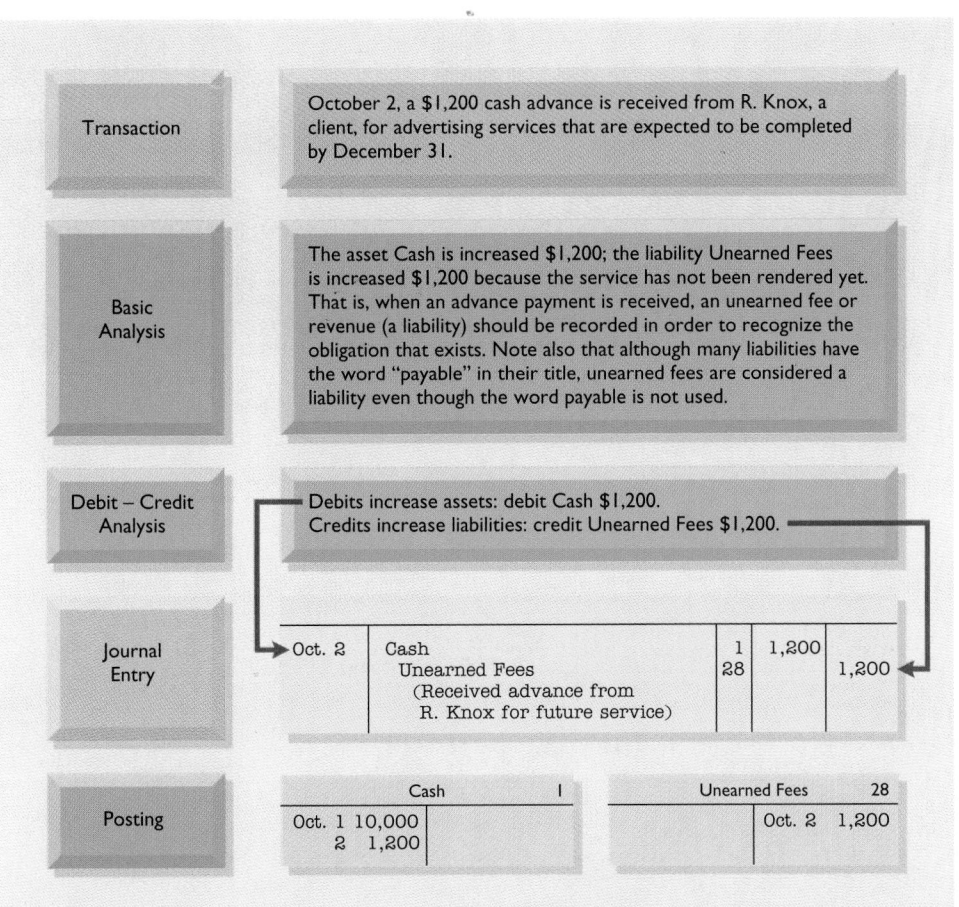

**Illustration 2-21**

*Receipt of cash for future service*

**Transaction**

October 2, a $1,200 cash advance is received from R. Knox, a client, for advertising services that are expected to be completed by December 31.

**Basic Analysis**

The asset Cash is increased $1,200; the liability Unearned Fees is increased $1,200 because the service has not been rendered yet. That is, when an advance payment is received, an unearned fee or revenue (a liability) should be recorded in order to recognize the obligation that exists. Note also that although many liabilities have the word "payable" in their title, unearned fees are considered a liability even though the word payable is not used.

**Debit – Credit Analysis**

Debits increase assets: debit Cash $1,200.
Credits increase liabilities: credit Unearned Fees $1,200.

**Journal Entry**

| Oct. 2 | Cash | 1 | 1,200 | |
| | Unearned Fees | 28 | | 1,200 |
| | (Received advance from R. Knox for future service) | | | |

**Posting**

| Cash | 1 |
|---|---|
| Oct. 1 10,000 | |
| 2 1,200 | |

| Unearned Fees | 28 |
|---|---|
| | Oct. 2 1,200 |

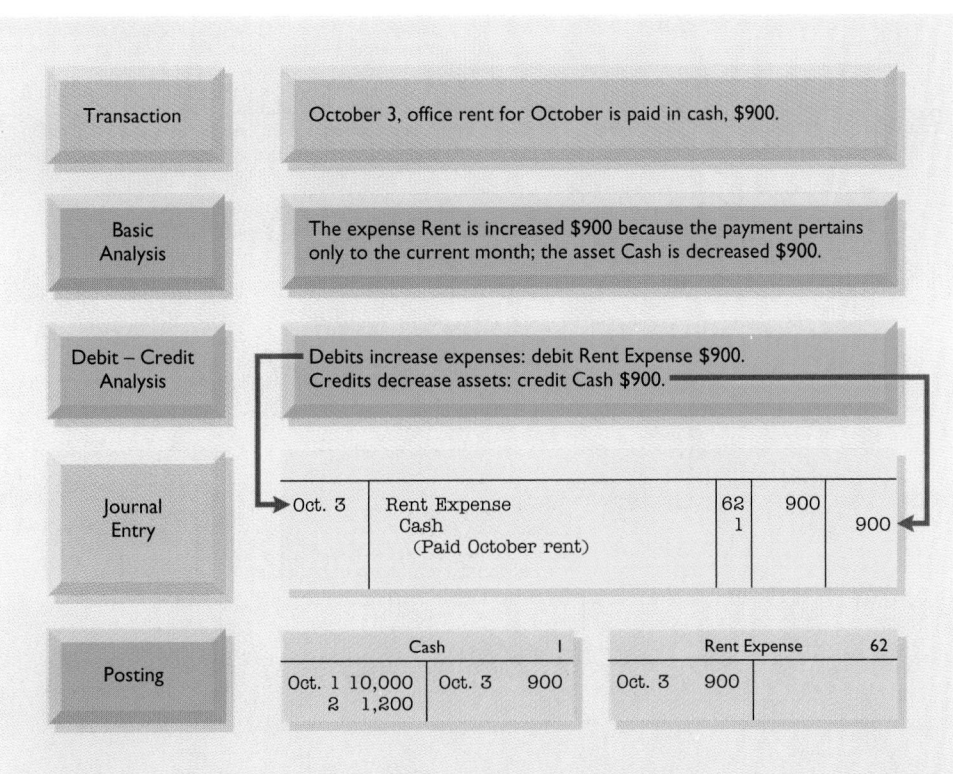

**Illustration 2-22**

*Payment of monthly rent*

**Transaction**

October 3, office rent for October is paid in cash, $900.

**Basic Analysis**

The expense Rent is increased $900 because the payment pertains only to the current month; the asset Cash is decreased $900.

**Debit – Credit Analysis**

Debits increase expenses: debit Rent Expense $900.
Credits decrease assets: credit Cash $900.

**Journal Entry**

| Oct. 3 | Rent Expense | 62 | 900 | |
| | Cash | 1 | | 900 |
| | (Paid October rent) | | | |

**Posting**

| Cash | 1 |
|---|---|
| Oct. 1 10,000 | Oct. 3 900 |
| 2 1,200 | |

| Rent Expense | 62 |
|---|---|
| Oct. 3 900 | |

**Illustration 2-23**

*Payment for insurance*

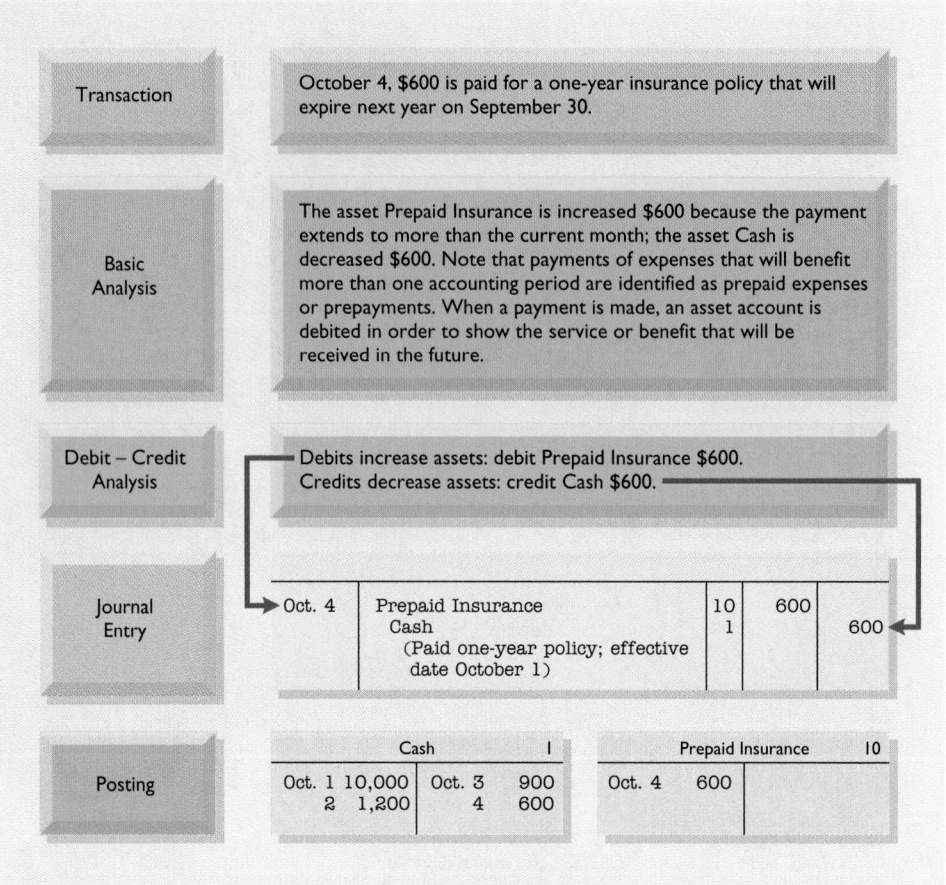

**Illustration 2-24**

*Purchase of supplies on credit*

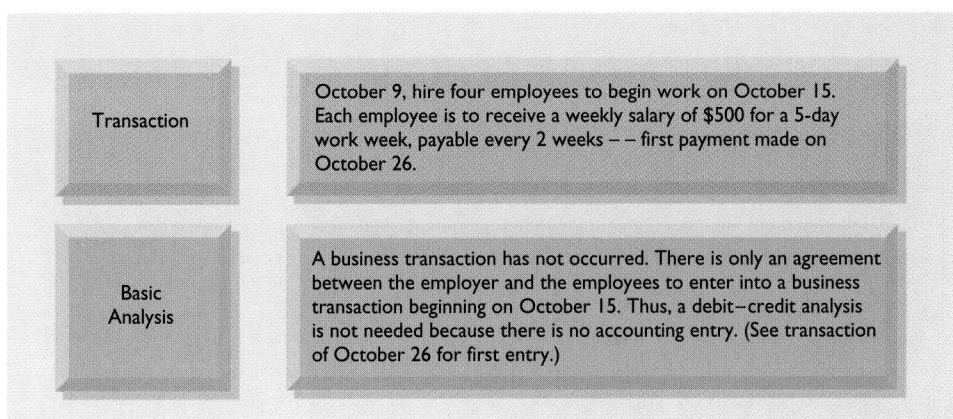

**Illustration 2-25**

*Hiring of employees*

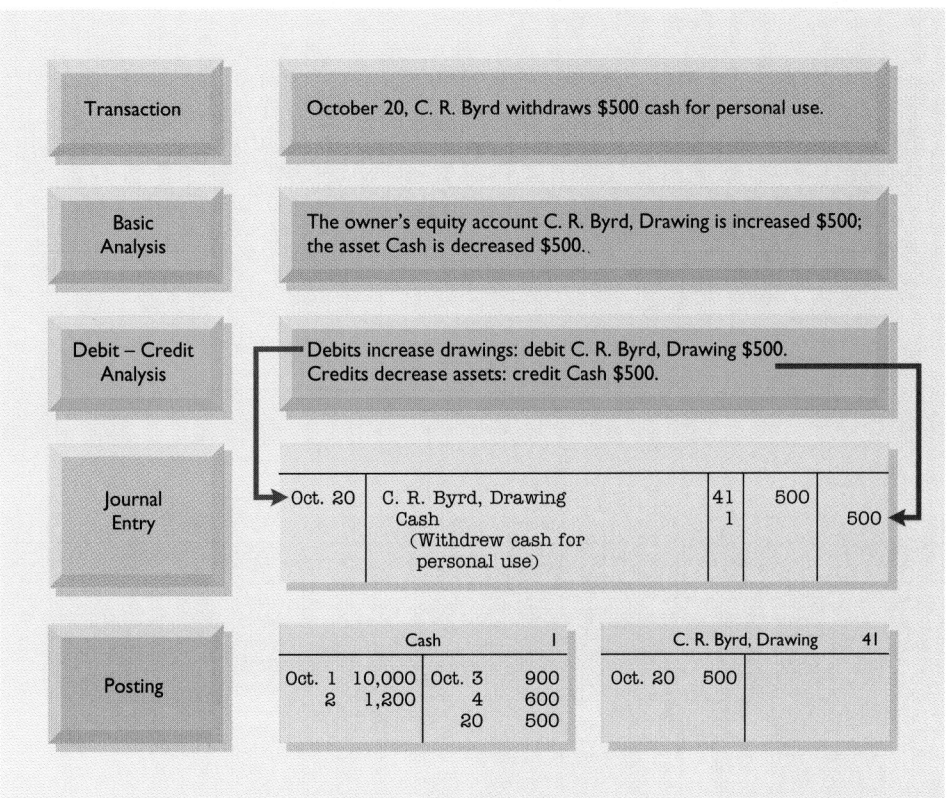

**Illustration 2-26**

*Withdrawal of cash by owner*

**Illustration 2-27**

*Payment of salaries*

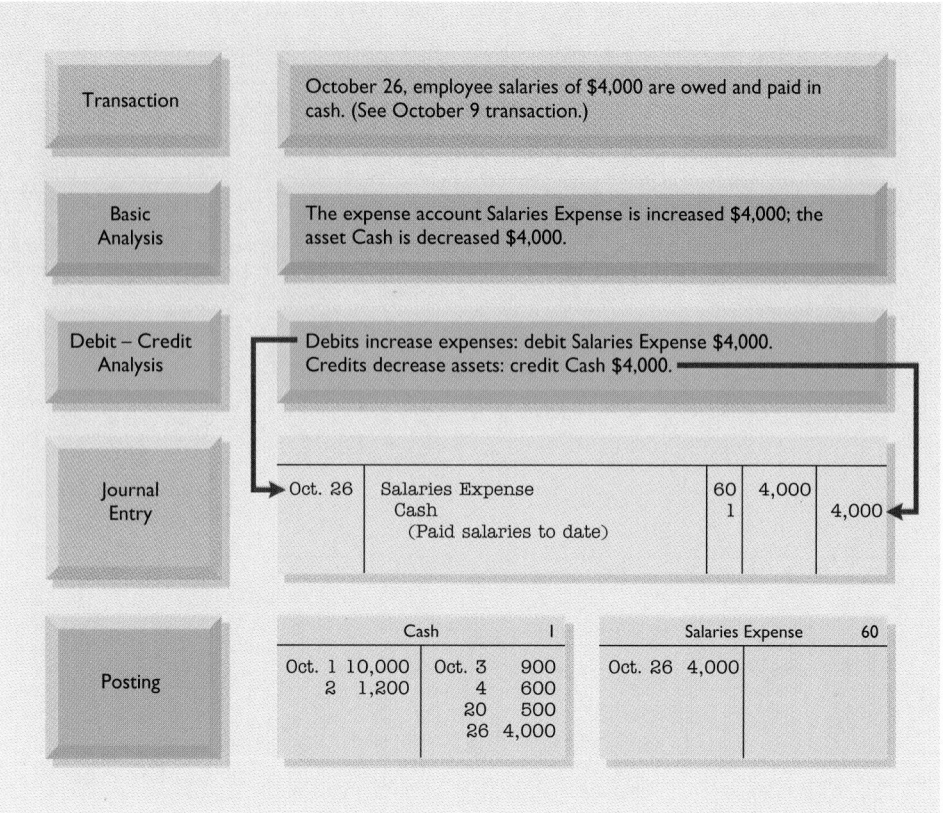

**Illustration 2-28**

*Receipt of cash for fees earned*

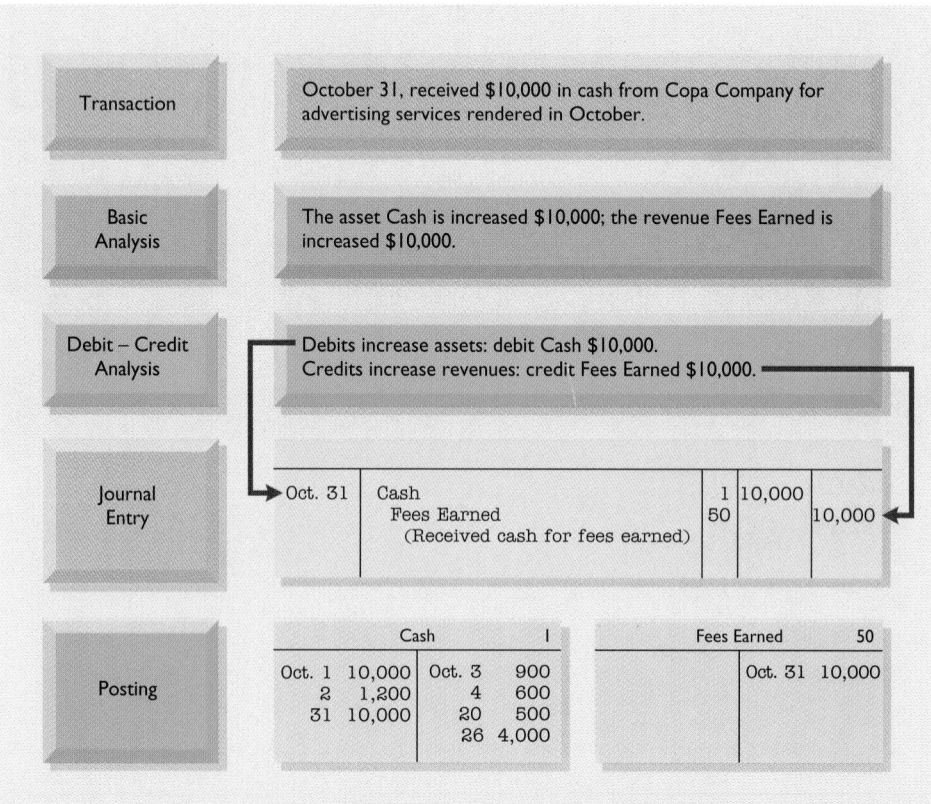

## Summary Illustration of Journalizing and Posting

The journal for Pioneer Advertising Agency for the month of October is summarized in Illustration 2-29. The ledger is shown in Illustration 2-30 with all balances in color.

| GENERAL JOURNAL | | | | Page J1 |
|---|---|---|---|---|
| Date | Account Titles and Explanation | Ref. | Debit | Credit |
| 1996 | | | | |
| Oct. 1 | Cash | 1 | 10,000 | |
| |    C. R. Byrd, Capital | 40 | | 10,000 |
| |    (Invested cash in business) | | | |
| 1 | Office Equipment | 15 | 5,000 | |
| |    Notes Payable | 25 | | 5,000 |
| |    (Issued three-month, 12% note for office equipment) | | | |
| 2 | Cash | 1 | 1,200 | |
| |    Unearned Fees | 28 | | 1,200 |
| |    (Received advance from R. Knox for future services) | | | |
| 3 | Rent Expense | 62 | 900 | |
| |    Cash | 1 | | 900 |
| |    (Paid October rent) | | | |
| 4 | Prepaid Insurance | 10 | 600 | |
| |    Cash | 1 | | 600 |
| |    (Paid one-year policy; effective date, October 1) | | | |
| 5 | Advertising Supplies | 8 | 2,500 | |
| |    Accounts Payable | 26 | | 2,500 |
| |    (Purchased supplies on account from Aero Supply) | | | |
| 20 | C. R. Byrd, Drawing | 41 | 500 | |
| |    Cash | 1 | | 500 |
| |    (Withdrew cash for personal use) | | | |
| 26 | Salaries Expense | 60 | 4,000 | |
| |    Cash | 1 | | 4,000 |
| |    (Paid salaries to date) | | | |
| 31 | Cash | 1 | 10,000 | |
| |    Fees Earned | 50 | | 10,000 |
| |    (Received cash for fees earned) | | | |

**Illustration 2-29**

*General journal entries*

## Before You Go On . . .

### ► Review It

1. How does journalizing differ from posting?
2. What is the purpose of (a) the ledger and (b) a chart of accounts?

### ► Do It

In the week following her successful grand opening of Hair It Is, Kate Browne collected $2,280 in cash for hair styling services, and she paid $400 in wages and $92 for utilities. Kate recorded these transactions in a general journal and posted the entries to the general ledger. Explain the purpose and process of journalizing and posting these transactions.

***Reasoning:*** Every business must keep track of its financial activities (receipts, payments, receivables, payables, etc.); journalizing does this. However, just recording every transaction in chronological order does not make the entries useful. To be useful, the entries need to be classified and summarized; posting the entries to specific ledger accounts does this.

***Solution:*** The purpose of journalizing is to record in chronological order every transaction. Journalizing involves dating every transaction, measuring the dollar amount of each transaction, identifying or labeling each amount with account titles, and recording in a standard format equal debits and credits. Posting involves transferring the journalized debits and credits to specific accounts in the ledger.

*Related exercise material:* BE2–7, BE2–8, E2–2, E2–5, and E2–8.

**Illustration 2-30**

*General ledger*

## GENERAL LEDGER

### Cash　　No. 1

| Date | Explanation | Ref. | Debit | Credit | Balance |
|---|---|---|---|---|---|
| 1996 | | | | | |
| Oct.　1 | | J1 | 10,000 | | 10,000 |
| 　　2 | | J1 | 1,200 | | 11,200 |
| 　　3 | | J1 | | 900 | 10,300 |
| 　　4 | | J1 | | 600 | 9,700 |
| 　20 | | J1 | | 500 | 9,200 |
| 　26 | | J1 | | 4,000 | 5,200 |
| 　31 | | J1 | 10,000 | | **15,200** |

### Advertising Supplies　　No. 8

| Date | Explanation | Ref. | Debit | Credit | Balance |
|---|---|---|---|---|---|
| 1996 | | | | | |
| Oct.　5 | | J1 | 2,500 | | **2,500** |

### Prepaid Insurance　　No. 10

| Date | Explanation | Ref. | Debit | Credit | Balance |
|---|---|---|---|---|---|
| 1996 | | | | | |
| Oct.　4 | | J1 | 600 | | **600** |

### Office Equipment　　No. 15

| Date | Explanation | Ref. | Debit | Credit | Balance |
|---|---|---|---|---|---|
| 1996 | | | | | |
| Oct.　1 | | J1 | 5,000 | | **5,000** |

### Notes Payable　　No. 25

| Date | Explanation | Ref. | Debit | Credit | Balance |
|---|---|---|---|---|---|
| 1996 | | | | | |
| Oct.　1 | | J1 | | 5,000 | **5,000** |

### Accounts Payable　　No. 26

| Date | Explanation | Ref. | Debit | Credit | Balance |
|---|---|---|---|---|---|
| 1996 | | | | | |
| Oct.　5 | | J1 | | 2,500 | **2,500** |

### Unearned Fees　　No. 28

| Date | Explanation | Ref. | Debit | Credit | Balance |
|---|---|---|---|---|---|
| 1996 | | | | | |
| Oct.　2 | | J1 | | 1,200 | **1,200** |

### C. R. Byrd, Capital　　No. 40

| Date | Explanation | Ref. | Debit | Credit | Balance |
|---|---|---|---|---|---|
| 1996 | | | | | |
| Oct.　1 | | J1 | | 10,000 | **10,000** |

### C. R. Byrd, Drawing　　No. 41

| Date | Explanation | Ref. | Debit | Credit | Balance |
|---|---|---|---|---|---|
| 1996 | | | | | |
| Oct.　20 | | J1 | 500 | | **500** |

### Fees Earned　　No. 50

| Date | Explanation | Ref. | Debit | Credit | Balance |
|---|---|---|---|---|---|
| 1996 | | | | | |
| Oct.　31 | | J1 | | 10,000 | **10,000** |

### Salaries Expense　　No. 60

| Date | Explanation | Ref. | Debit | Credit | Balance |
|---|---|---|---|---|---|
| 1996 | | | | | |
| Oct.　26 | | J1 | 4,000 | | **4,000** |

### Rent Expense　　No. 62

| Date | Explanation | Ref. | Debit | Credit | Balance |
|---|---|---|---|---|---|
| 1996 | | | | | |
| Oct.　3 | | J1 | 900 | | **900** |

# *T*he Trial Balance

A trial balance is a list of accounts and their balances at a given time. Customarily, a trial balance is prepared at the end of an accounting period. The accounts are listed in the order in which they appear in the ledger, with debit balances listed in the left column and credit balances in the right column. The totals of the two columns must be in agreement.

**The primary purpose of a trial balance is to prove the mathematical equality of debits and credits after posting.** Under the double-entry system this equality will occur when the sum of the debit account balances equals the sum of the credit account balances. **A trial balance also uncovers errors in journalizing and posting. In addition, it is useful in the preparation of financial statements**, as will be explained in the next two chapters. The procedures for preparing a trial balance consist of:

1. Listing the account titles and their balances.
2. Totaling the debit and credit columns.
3. Proving the equality of the two columns.

The trial balance prepared from the ledger of Pioneer Advertising Agency is presented below:

**STUDY OBJECTIVE**

**7**

*Prepare a trial balance and explain its purposes.*

**Helpful hint** A trial balance is so named because it is a test to determine if the sum of the debit balances equals the sum of the credit balances.

| PIONEER ADVERTISING AGENCY<br>Trial Balance<br>October 31, 1996 | | |
|---|---|---|
| | Debit | Credit |
| Cash | $15,200 | |
| Advertising Supplies | 2,500 | |
| Prepaid Insurance | 600 | |
| Office Equipment | 5,000 | |
| Notes Payable | | $ 5,000 |
| Accounts Payable | | 2,500 |
| Unearned Fees | | 1,200 |
| C. R. Byrd, Capital | | 10,000 |
| C. R. Byrd, Drawing | 500 | |
| Fees Earned | | 10,000 |
| Salaries Expense | 4,000 | |
| Rent Expense | 900 | |
| | $28,700 | $28,700 |

**Illustration 2-31**

*A trial balance*

**Helpful hint** If only the debit portion of a journal entry is posted, what procedure should bring this error to light? Answer: Taking a trial balance.

Note that the total debits $28,700 equal the total credits $28,700. Account numbers are sometimes shown to the left of the account titles in the trial balance.

## Limitations of a Trial Balance

**A trial balance does not prove that all transactions have been recorded or that the ledger is correct.** Numerous errors may exist even though the trial balance columns agree. For example, the trial balance may balance even when (1) a transaction is not journalized, (2) a correct journal entry is not posted, (3) a journal entry is posted twice, (4) incorrect accounts are used in journalizing or posting, or (5) offsetting errors are made in recording the amount of a transaction. In

**Helpful hint** A trial balance is a necessary check point before proceeding to other steps in the accounting process.

## ▸Technology in Action

In a computerized system, the trial balance is often only one column (no debit or credit columns), and the accounts have plus and minus signs associated with them. The final balance therefore is zero. Any errors that develop in a computerized system will undoubtedly involve the initial recording rather than some error in the posting or preparation of a trial balance.

other words, as long as equal debits and credits are posted, even to the wrong account or in the wrong amount, the total debits will equal the total credits.

### Locating Errors

The procedure for preparing a trial balance is relatively simple. However, in manual systems if the trial balance does not balance, locating an error can be time-consuming, tedious, and frustrating. The error(s) generally results from mathematical mistakes, incorrect postings, or simply transcribing the data incorrectly.

What happens if you are faced with a trial balance that does not balance? First determine the amount of the difference between the two columns of the trial balance. After this amount is known, the following steps are often helpful:

▸*Ethics note*

Auditors are required to differentiate errors from irregularities when evaluating the accounting system. An error is the result of an unintentional mistake; as such, it is neither ethical nor unethical. An irregularity, on the other hand, is an intentional misstatement, which is generally viewed as highly unethical.

1. If the error is $1, $100, or $1,000, re-add the trial balance columns and recompute the account balances.
2. If the error is divisible by two, scan the trial balance to see whether a balance equal to half the error has been entered in the wrong column.
3. If the error is divisible by nine, retrace the account balances on the trial balance to see whether they are incorrectly copied from the ledger. For example, if a balance was $12 and it was listed as $21, a $9 error has been made. Reversing the order of numbers is called a transposition error.
4. If the error is not divisible by two or nine (for example, $365), scan the ledger to see whether an account balance of $365 has been omitted from the trial balance, and scan the journal to see whether a $365 posting has been omitted.

## ▸Accounting in Action ▸ *Business Insight*

If you've ever made an arithmetic error in your checkbook register, you may take some comfort from an accountant's mistake at Fidelity Investments, the world's largest mutual-fund investment company. The accountant failed to include a minus sign while doing a tax calculation, making what was actually a $1.3 billion loss look like a $1.3 billion gain. No one expects that kind of mistake at a firm like Fidelity, which manages over $300 billion in investment funds, with sophisticated computer systems and top investment managers. In explaining the mistake to shareholders, Fidelity's manager director, J. Gary Burkhead, wrote: "Some people have asked how, in this age of technology, such a mistake could be made. While many of our processes are computerized, the requirements of the tax code are complex and dictate that some steps must be handled manually by our tax managers and accountants, and people can make mistakes." Evidently so. That's why it pays to do a "reasonableness check"—presumably someone at Fidelity had a sense that the year's results weren't as rosy as the the accounting numbers first indicated.

## Use of Dollar Signs

Note that dollar signs do not appear in the journals or ledgers. Dollar signs are usually used only in the trial balance and the financial statements. Generally, a dollar sign is shown only for the first item in the column and for the total of that column. A single line is placed under the column of figures to be added or subtracted; the total amount is double underlined to indicate the final sum.

## *Before You Go On . . .*

### ► *Review It*

1. What is a trial balance and how is it prepared?
2. What is the primary purpose of a trial balance?
3. What are the limitations of a trial balance?

### ► *A Look Back at Gabriella Torres, Diabetes & Endocrine Associates*

Now that you have learned the details of the recording process, think back to the beginning of the chapter to Gabriella Torres and her position as office manager at Diabetes & Endocrine Associates, and answer the following questions:

1. What accounting entries would Gabriella be likely to make to record (a) the rent payment, (b) billing a patient for services rendered, and (c) collecting cash from a patient on account.
2. In what way might Gabriella's day-time job as office manager help in her studies as a night student in accounting and business?
3. Prepare a likely list of asset accounts Gabriella has in her general ledger at Diabetes & Endocrine Associates.

**Solution:**

1. Gabriella would likely make the following entries:
   (a) Rent Expense
   　　Cash
   　　　(Paid rent)
   (b) Accounts Receivable
   　　Fees Earned
   　　　(Billed a patient for services performed)
   (c) Cash
   　　Accounts Receivable
   　　　(Collected cash for amount due)
2. As a result of her office manager's position, Gabriella is able to relate the subject matter as well as much of the assignment material in her business courses to a real-world context. From her job she knows how bills are paid; how to reconcile a bank statement; how employees are hired, managed, evaluated, and paid; how the individual accounts receivable accounts are maintained; how accounting functions are performed on a computer; and much more.
3. A likely list of asset accounts is: Cash, Accounts Receivable, Medical Supplies, Land and Building (if owned), Medical Equipment, Office Furniture and Fixtures, and Pre-paid Insurance.

# Summary of Study Objectives

**1. *Explain what an account is and how it helps in the re-cording process.*** An account is an individual accounting record of increases and decreases in specific asset, liability, and owner's equity items.

**2. *Define debits and credits and explain how they are used to record business transactions.*** The terms debit and credit are synonymous with left and right. Assets, drawings, and expenses are increased by debits and decreased by credits. Liabilities, owner's capital, and revenues are increased by credits and decreased by debits.

**3. *Identify the basic steps in the recording process.*** The basic steps in the recording process are: (a) analyze each transaction in terms of its effect on the accounts, (b) enter the transaction information in a journal, (c) transfer the journal information to the appropriate accounts in the ledger.

**4. *Explain what a journal is and how it helps in the re-cording process.*** The initial accounting record of a transaction is entered in a journal before the data are entered in the accounts. A journal (a) discloses in one place the complete effect of a transaction, (b) provides a chronological record of transactions, and (c) prevents or locates errors because the debit and credit amounts for each entry can be readily compared.

**5. *Explain what a ledger is and how it helps in the recording process.*** The entire group of accounts maintained by a company is referred to collectively as a ledger. The ledger keeps in one place all the information about changes in specific account balances.

**6. *Explain what posting is and how it helps in the recording process.*** Posting is the procedure of transferring journal entries to the ledger accounts. This phase of the recording process accumulates the effects of journalized transactions in the individual accounts.

**7. *Prepare a trial balance and explain its purposes.*** A trial balance is a list of accounts and their balances at a given time. The primary purpose of the trial balance is to prove the mathematical equality of debits and credits after posting. A trial balance also uncovers errors in journalizing and posting and is useful in preparing financial statements.

# Glossary

**Account** An individual accounting record of increases and decreases in a specific asset, liability, or owner's equity items. (p. 44).

**Chart of accounts** A list of accounts and the account numbers which identify their location in the ledger. (p. 56).

**Compound entry** An entry that involves three or more accounts. (p. 52).

**Credit** The right side of an account. (p. 45).

**Debit** The left side of an account. (p. 45).

**Double-entry system** A system that records the dual effect of each transaction in appropriate accounts. (p. 46).

**General journal** The most basic form of journal. (p. 50).

**General ledger** A ledger that contains all asset, liability, and owner's equity accounts. (p. 53).

**Journal** An accounting record in which transactions are initially recorded in chronological order. (p. 50).

**Journalizing** The procedure of entering transaction data in the journal. (p. 51).

**Ledger** The entire group of accounts maintained by a company. (p. 53).

**Posting** The procedure of transferring journal entries to the ledger accounts. (p. 54).

**Simple entry** An entry that involves only two accounts. (p. 52).

**T account** The basic form of an account. (p. 44).

**Three-column form of account** A form containing money columns for debit, credit, and balance amounts in an account. (p. 54).

**Trial balance** A list of accounts and their balances at a given time. (p. 65).

# DEMONSTRATION PROBLEM

Bob Sample opened the Campus Laundromat on September 1, 1996. During the first month of operations the following transactions occurred:

Sept. 1 Invested $20,000 cash in the business.

2 Paid $1,000 cash for store rent for the month of September.

3 Purchased washers and dryers for $25,000 paying $10,000 in cash and signing a $15,000 6-month 12% note payable.

4 Paid $1,200 for one-year accident insurance policy.

10 Received bill from the Daily News for advertising the opening of the laundromat, $200.

20 Withdrew $700 cash for personal use.

30 Determined that cash receipts for laundry fees for the month were $6,200.

The chart of accounts for the company is the same as in Pioneer Advertising Agency except for the following: No. 15 Laundry Equipment and No. 61 Advertising Expense.

## Instructions

(a) Journalize the September transactions. (Use J1 for the journal page number.)

(b) Open ledger accounts and post the September transactions.

(c) Prepare a trial balance at September 30, 1996.

## Solution to Demonstration Problem

(a)                          **GENERAL JOURNAL**                          **J1**

| Date | Account Titles and Explanation | Ref. | Debit | Credit |
|---|---|---|---|---|
| 1996 | | | | |
| Sept. 1 | Cash | 1 | 20,000 | |
| | Bob Sample, Capital | 40 | | 20,000 |
| | (Invested cash in business) | | | |
| 2 | Rent Expense | 62 | 1,000 | |
| | Cash | 1 | | 1,000 |
| | (Paid September rent) | | | |
| 3 | Laundry Equipment | 15 | 25,000 | |
| | Cash | 1 | | 10,000 |
| | Notes Payable | 25 | | 15,000 |
| | (Purchased laundry equipment for cash and 6-month 12% note payable) | | | |
| 4 | Prepaid Insurance | 10 | 1,200 | |
| | Cash | 1 | | 1,200 |
| | (Paid one-year insurance policy) | | | |
| 10 | Advertising Expense | 61 | 200 | |
| | Accounts Payable | 26 | | 200 |
| | (Received bill from Daily News for advertising) | | | |
| 20 | Bob Sample, Drawing | 41 | 700 | |
| | Cash | 1 | | 700 |
| | (Withdrew cash for personal use) | | | |
| 30 | Cash | 1 | 6,200 | |
| | Fees Earned | 50 | | 6,200 |
| | (Received cash for laundry fees earned) | | | |

**Problem-Solving Strategies**

1. Separate journal entries are made for each transaction.

2. In journalizing, make sure debits equal credits.

3. In journalizing, use specific account titles taken from the chart of accounts.

4. Provide appropriate description of journal entry.

5. Arrange ledger in statement order, beginning with the balance sheet accounts.

6. Post in chronological order.

7. Numbers in the reference column indicate the amount has been posted.

8. The trial balance lists accounts in the order in which they appear in the ledger.

9. Debit balances are listed in the left column, and credit balances in the right column.

**(b)**

## GENERAL LEDGER

### Cash                                                                 No. 1

| Date | Explanation | Ref. | Debit | Credit | Balance |
|------|-------------|------|-------|--------|---------|
| 1996 |             |      |        |        |         |
| Sept. 1 |          | J1   | 20,000 |        | 20,000  |
| 2    |             | J1   |        | 1,000  | 19,000  |
| 3    |             | J1   |        | 10,000 | 9,000   |
| 4    |             | J1   |        | 1,200  | 7,800   |
| 20   |             | J1   |        | 700    | 7,100   |
| 30   |             | J1   | 6,200  |        | 13,300  |

### Prepaid Insurance                                               No. 10

| Date | Explanation | Ref. | Debit | Credit | Balance |
|------|-------------|------|-------|--------|---------|
| 1996 |             |      |       |        |         |
| Sept. 4 |          | J1   | 1,200 |        | 1,200   |

### Laundry Equipment                                              No. 15

| Date | Explanation | Ref. | Debit | Credit | Balance |
|------|-------------|------|-------|--------|---------|
| 1996 |             |      |        |        |         |
| Sept. 3 |          | J1   | 25,000 |        | 25,000  |

### Notes Payable                                                    No. 25

| Date | Explanation | Ref. | Debit | Credit | Balance |
|------|-------------|------|-------|--------|---------|
| 1996 |             |      |       |        |         |
| Sept. 3 |          | J1   |       | 15,000 | 15,000  |

### Accounts Payable                                               No. 26

| Date | Explanation | Ref. | Debit | Credit | Balance |
|------|-------------|------|-------|--------|---------|
| 1996 |             |      |       |        |         |
| Sept. 10 |         | J1   |       | 200    | 200     |

### Bob Sample, Capital                                            No. 40

| Date | Explanation | Ref. | Debit | Credit | Balance |
|------|-------------|------|-------|--------|---------|
| 1996 |             |      |       |        |         |
| Sept. 1 |          | J1   |       | 20,000 | 20,000  |

### Bob Sample, Drawing                                           No. 41

| Date | Explanation | Ref. | Debit | Credit | Balance |
|------|-------------|------|-------|--------|---------|
| 1996 |             |      |      |        |         |
| Sept. 20 |         | J1   | 700  |        | 700     |

### Fees Earned                                                        No. 50

| Date | Explanation | Ref. | Debit | Credit | Balance |
|------|-------------|------|-------|--------|---------|
| 1996 |             |      |       |        |         |
| Sept. 30 |         | J1   |       | 6,200  | 6,200   |

### Advertising Expense                                            No. 61

| Date | Explanation | Ref. | Debit | Credit | Balance |
|------|-------------|------|-------|--------|---------|
| 1996 |             |      |      |        |         |
| Sept. 10 |         | J1   | 200  |        | 200     |

### Rent Expense                                                      No. 62

| Date | Explanation | Ref. | Debit | Credit | Balance |
|------|-------------|------|-------|--------|---------|
| 1996 |             |      |       |        |         |
| Sept. 2 |          | J1   | 1,000 |        | 1,000   |

**(c)**

### CAMPUS LAUNDROMAT
### Trial Balance
### September 30, 1996

|                     | Debit    | Credit   |
|---------------------|----------|----------|
| Cash                | $13,300  |          |
| Prepaid Insurance   | 1,200    |          |
| Laundry Equipment   | 25,000   |          |
| Notes Payable       |          | $15,000  |
| Accounts Payable    |          | 200      |
| Bob Sample, Capital |          | 20,000   |
| Bob Sample, Drawing | 700      |          |
| Fees Earned         |          | 6,200    |
| Advertising Expense | 200      |          |
| Rent Expense        | 1,000    |          |
|                     | $41,400  | $41,400  |

# SELF-STUDY QUESTIONS

Answers are at the end of the chapter.

(SO 1) 1. Which of the following statements about an account is true?
  a. In its simplest form, an account consists of two parts.
  b. An account is an individual accounting record of increases and decreases in specific asset, liability, and owner's equity items.
  c. There are separate accounts for specific assets and liabilities but only one account for owner's equity items.
  d. The left side of an account is the credit or decrease side.

(SO 2) 2. Debits:
  a. increase both assets and liabilities.
  b. decrease both assets and liabilities.
  c. increase assets and decrease liabilities.
  d. decrease assets and increase liabilities.

(SO 2) 3. A revenue account:
  a. is increased by debits.
  b. is decreased by credits.
  c. has a normal balance of a debit.
  d. is increased by credits.

(SO 2) 4. Accounts that normally have debit balances are:
  a. assets, expenses, and revenues.
  b. assets, expenses, and owner's capital.
  c. assets, liabilities, and owner's drawings.
  d. assets, owner's drawings, and expenses.

(SO 3) 5. Which of the following is not part of the recording process?
  a. Analyzing transactions.
  b. Preparing a trial balance.
  c. Entering transactions in a journal.
  d. Posting transactions.

(SO 4) 6. Which of the following statements about a journal is false?
  a. It is not a book of original entry.
  b. It provides a chronological record of transactions.
  c. It helps to locate errors because the debit and credit amounts for each entry can be readily compared.
  d. It discloses in one place the complete effect of a transaction.

(SO 5) 7. A ledger:
  a. contains only asset and liability accounts.
  b. should show accounts in alphabetical order.
  c. is a collection of the entire group of accounts maintained by a company.
  d. is a book of original entry.

(SO 6) 8. Posting:
  a. normally occurs before journalizing.
  b. transfers ledger transaction data to the journal.
  c. is an optional step in the recording process.
  d. transfers journal entries to ledger accounts.

(SO 7) 9. A trial balance:
  a. is a list of accounts with their balances at a given time.
  b. proves the mathematical accuracy of journalized transactions.
  c. will not balance if a correct journal entry is posted twice.
  d. proves that all transactions have been recorded.

(SO 7) 10. A trial balance will not balance if:
  a. a correct journal entry is posted twice.
  b. the purchase of supplies on account is debited to Supplies and credited to Cash.
  c. a $100 cash drawing by the owner is debited to Owner's Drawing for $1,000 and credited to Cash for $100.
  d. a $450 payment on account is debited to Accounts Payable for $45 and credited to Cash for $45.

# QUESTIONS

1. Why is an account referred to as a T account?

2. The terms *debit* and *credit* mean increase and decrease, respectively. Do you agree? Explain.

3. José Amaro, a fellow student, contends that the double-entry system means each transaction must be recorded twice. Is José correct? Explain.

4. Teresa Alvarez, a beginning accounting student, believes debit balances are favorable and credit balances are unfavorable. Is Teresa correct? Discuss.

5. State the rules of debit and credit as applied to (a) asset accounts, (b) liability accounts, and (c) owner's equity account.

6. What is the normal balance for each of the following accounts? (a) Accounts Receivable. (b) Cash. (c) Owner's Drawing. (d) Accounts Payable. (e) Fees Earned. (f) Salaries Expense. (g) Owner's Capital.

7. Indicate whether each of the following accounts is an asset, a liability, or an owner's equity account and whether it would have a debit or credit balance: (a) Accounts Receivable, (b) Accounts Payable, (c) Equipment, (d) Owner's Drawing, (e) Supplies.

8. For the following transactions, indicate the account debited and the account credited:
   (a) Supplies are purchased on account.

(b) Cash is received on signing a note payable.

(c) Employees are paid salaries in cash.

9. Presented below is a series of accounts. Indicate whether these accounts generally will have (a) debit entries only, (b) credit entries only, (c) both debit and credit entries.

(1) Cash.

(2) Accounts Receivable.

(3) Owner's Drawing.

(4) Accounts Payable.

(5) Salaries Expense.

(6) Fees Earned.

10. What are the basic steps in the recording process?

11. What are the advantages of using the journal in the recording process?

12. (a) When entering a transaction in the journal, should the debit or credit be written first?

(b) Which should be indented, the debit or credit?

13. Give an example of a compound entry.

14. (a) Can business transaction debits and credits be recorded directly in the ledger accounts?

(b) What are the advantages of first recording transactions in the journal and then posting to the ledger?

15. The account number is entered as the last step in posting the amounts from the journal to the ledger. What is the advantage of this step?

16. Journalize the following business transactions.

(a) Doris Wang invests $9,000 in the business.

(b) Insurance of $800 is paid for the year.

(c) Supplies of $1,500 are purchased on account.

(d) Cash of $7,500 is received for services rendered.

17. (a) What is a ledger?   (b) Why is a chart of accounts important?

18. What is a trial balance and what are its purposes?

19. Kap Shin is confused about how accounting information flows through the accounting system. He believes the flow of information is as follows:

(a) Debits and credits posted to the ledger.

(b) Business transaction occurs.

(c) Information entered in the journal.

(d) Financial statements are prepared.

(e) Trial balance is prepared.

Indicate to Kap the proper flow of the information.

20. Two students are discussing the use of a trial balance. They wonder whether the following errors, each considered separately, would prevent the trial balance from balancing.

(a) The bookkeeper debited Cash for $600 and credited Wages Expense for $600 for payment of wages.

(b) Cash collected on account was debited to Cash for $900 and Fees Earned was credited for $90. What would you tell them?

## BRIEF EXERCISES

*Indicate debit and credit effects and normal balance.*

(SO 2)

**BE2–1**   For each of the following accounts indicate (a) the effect of a debit or a credit on the account and (b) the normal balance.

1. Accounts Payable.

2. Advertising Expense.

3. Fees Earned.

4. Accounts Receivable.

5. A. J. Takamoto, Capital.

6. A. J. Takamoto, Drawing.

*Identify accounts to be debited and credited.*

(SO 2)

**BE2–2**   Transactions for the H. J. Oslo Company for the month of June are presented below. Identify the accounts to be debited and credited for each transaction.

June  1   H. J. Oslo invests $2,500 cash in a small welding business of which he is the sole proprietor.

     2   Buys equipment on account for $900.

     3   Pays $500 to landlord for June rent.

    12   Bills J. Kronsnoble $300 for welding work done.

*Journalize transactions.*

(SO 4)

**BE2–3**   Using the data in BE2–2, journalize the transactions. (You may omit explanations.)

*Identify and explain steps in recording process.*

(SO 3)

**BE2–4**   ▭▬▶   Tage Shumway, a fellow student, is unclear about the basic steps in the recording process. Identify and briefly explain the steps in the order in which they occur.

*Indicate basic and debit-credit analysis.*

(SO 4)

**BE2–5**   J. A. Norris has the following transactions during August of the current year. Indicate (a) the basic analysis and (b) the debit-credit analysis illustrated on pages 58–62 of the text.

Aug.  1   Opens an office as a financial advisor, investing $5,000 in cash.

     4   Pays insurance in advance for 6 months, $1,800.

    16   Receives $900 from clients for services rendered.

    27   Pays secretary $500 salary.

**BE2–6** Using the data in BE2–5, journalize the transactions. (You may omit explanations.)

**BE2–7** Selected transactions for the Gonzales Company are presented in journal form below. Post the transactions to T accounts.

J1

| Date | | Account Titles and Explanation | Ref. | Debit | Credit |
|---|---|---|---|---|---|
| May | 5 | Accounts Receivable | | 3,200 | |
| | | Fees Earned | | | 3,200 |
| | 12 | Cash | | 2,400 | |
| | | Accounts Receivable | | | 2,400 |
| | 15 | Cash | | 2,000 | |
| | | Fees Earned | | | 2,000 |

**BE2–8** Selected journal entries for the Gonzales Company are presented in BE2–7. Post the transactions using the standard form of account.

*Post journal entries to*
*standard form of account.*
*(SO 6)*

**BE2–9** From the ledger balances given below, prepare a trial balance for the P. J. Carland Company at June 30, 1996. List the accounts in the order shown on page 65 of the text. All account balances are normal.

Accounts Payable $4,000, Cash $3,800, P. J. Carland, Capital $20,000, P. J. Carland, Drawing $1,200, Equipment $17,000, Fees Earned $6,000, Accounts Receivable $3,000, Salaries Expense $4,000, and Rent Expense $1,000.

**BE2–10** An inexperienced bookkeeper prepared the following trial balance that does not balance. Prepare a correct trial balance, assuming all account balances are normal.

**GOMEZ COMPANY**
**Trial Balance**
**December 31, 1996**

| | Debit | Credit |
|---|---|---|
| Cash | $18,800 | |
| Prepaid Insurance | | $ 3,500 |
| Accounts Payable | | 3,000 |
| Unearned Fees | 2,200 | |
| Lea Gomez, Capital | | 17,000 |
| Lea Gomez, Drawing | | 4,500 |
| Fees Earned | | 25,600 |
| Salaries Expense | 18,600 | |
| Rent Expense | | 2,400 |
| | $39,600 | $56,000 |

# EXERCISES

**E2–1** Selected transactions for A. Mane, an interior decorator, in her first month of business, are as follows:

1. Invested $10,000 cash in business.
2. Purchased used car for $4,000 cash for use in business.
3. Purchased supplies on account for $500.
4. Billed customers $1,800 for services performed.
5. Paid $200 cash for advertising start of business.
6. Received $700 cash from customers billed in (4) above.
7. Paid creditor $300 cash on account.
8. Withdrew $500 cash for personal use of owner.

*Instructions*

For each transaction indicate (a) the basic type of account debited and credited (asset, liability, owner's equity); (b) the specific account debited and credited (cash, rent expense, fees earned, etc.); (c) whether the specific account is increased or decreased; and (d) the normal balance of the specific account. Use the following format, in which transaction (1) is given as an example:

| | Account Debited | | | | Account Credited | | | |
|---|---|---|---|---|---|---|---|---|
| Trans-action | (a) Basic Type | (b) Specific Account | (c) Effect | (d) Normal Balance | (a) Basic Type | (b) Specific Account | (c) Effect | (d) Normal Balance |
| (1) | Asset | Cash | Increase | Debit | Owner's Equity | A. Mane, Capital | Increase | Credit |

*Journalize transactions and post using standard account form.*
(SO 4, 6)

**E2–2**  Data for A. Mane, interior decorator, are presented in E2–1.

**Instructions**
Journalize the transactions using journal page J1.

*Analyze transactions and determine their effect on accounts.*
(SO 2)

**E2–3**  Presented below is information related to Marx Real Estate Agency:

Oct.  1  Lynn Marx begins business as a real estate agent with a cash investment of $13,000.
  2  Hires an administrative assistant.
  3  Buys office furniture for $1,900, on account.
  6  Sells a house and lot for B. Rollins; fees due from Rollins, $3,200 (not paid by Rollins at this time).
 10  Receives cash of $140 as fees for renting an apartment for the owner.
 27  Pays $700 on the balance indicated in the transaction of October 3.
 30  Pays the administrative assistant $960 in salary for October.

**Instructions**
Prepare the debit-credit analysis for each transaction as illustrated on pages 58–62.

*Journalize transactions.*
(SO 4)

**E2–4**  Transaction data for Marx Real Estate Agency are presented in E2–3.

**Instructions**
Journalize the transactions.

*Post journal entries and prepare a trial balance.*
(SO 6, 7)

**E2–5**  Selected transactions from the journal of J. L. Kang, investment broker, are presented below.

| Date | | Account Titles and Explanation | Ref. | Debit | Credit |
|---|---|---|---|---|---|
| Aug. | 1 | Cash | | 1,600 | |
| | | J. L. Kang, Capital | | | 1,600 |
| | 10 | Cash | | 2,400 | |
| | | Fees Earned | | | 2,400 |
| | 12 | Office Equipment | | 4,000 | |
| | | Cash | | | 1,000 |
| | | Notes Payable | | | 3,000 |
| | 25 | Accounts Receivable | | 1,400 | |
| | | Fees Earned | | | 1,400 |
| | 31 | Cash | | 900 | |
| | | Accounts Receivable | | | 900 |

**Instructions**
(a) Post the transactions to T accounts.
(b) Prepare a trial balance at August 31, 1996.

*Journalize transactions from account data and prepare a trial balance.*
(SO 4, 7)

**E2–6**  The T accounts below summarize the ledger of Lush Landscaping Company at the end of the first month of operations:

| Cash | | | No. 101 |
|---|---|---|---|
| 4/1 | 8,000 | 4/15 | 600 |
| 4/12 | 900 | 4/25 | 1,500 |
| 4/29 | 400 | | |
| 4/30 | 800 | | |

| Accounts Receivable | | | No. 112 |
|---|---|---|---|
| 4/7 | 3,200 | 4/29 | 400 |

| Supplies | | | No. 126 |
|---|---|---|---|
| 4/4 | 1,800 | | |

| Accounts Payable | | | No. 201 |
|---|---|---|---|
| 4/25 | 1,500 | 4/4 | 1,800 |

| Unearned Fees | | | No. 205 |
|---|---|---|---|
| | | 4/30 | 800 |

| R. A. Lush, Capital | | | No. 301 |
|---|---|---|---|
| | | 4/1 | 8,000 |

| Fees Earned | | | No. 400 |
|---|---|---|---|
| | | 4/7 | 3,200 |
| | | 4/12 | 900 |

| Salaries Expense | | | No. 726 |
|---|---|---|---|
| 4/15 | 600 | | |

**Instructions**

(a) Prepare the complete general journal (including explanations) from which the postings to Cash were made.

(b) Prepare a trial balance at April 30, 1996.

**E2–7** Presented below is the ledger for Holly Co.

*Journalize transactions from account data and prepare a trial balance.*
*(SO 4, 7)*

| Cash | | | No. 101 |
|---|---|---|---|
| 10/1 | 4,000 | 10/4 | 400 |
| 10/10 | 650 | 10/12 | 1,500 |
| 10/10 | 5,000 | 10/15 | 250 |
| 10/20 | 500 | 10/30 | 300 |
| 10/25 | 2,000 | 10/31 | 500 |

| Accounts Receivable | | | No. 112 |
|---|---|---|---|
| 10/6 | 800 | 10/20 | 500 |
| 10/20 | 940 | | |

| Supplies | | | No. 126 |
|---|---|---|---|
| 10/4 | 400 | | |

| Furniture | | | No. 149 |
|---|---|---|---|
| 10/3 | 2,000 | | |

| Notes Payable | | | No. 200 |
|---|---|---|---|
| | | 10/10 | 5,000 |

| Accounts Payable | | | No. 201 |
|---|---|---|---|
| 10/12 | 1,500 | 10/3 | 2,000 |

| L. Holly, Capital | | | No. 301 |
|---|---|---|---|
| | | 10/1 | 4,000 |
| | | 10/25 | 2,000 |

| L. Holly, Drawing | | | No. 306 |
|---|---|---|---|
| 10/30 | 300 | | |

| Service Revenue | | | No. 407 |
|---|---|---|---|
| | | 10/6 | 800 |
| | | 10/10 | 650 |
| | | 10/20 | 940 |

| Store Wages Expense | | | No. 628 |
|---|---|---|---|
| 10/31 | 500 | | |

| Rent Expense | | | No. 729 |
|---|---|---|---|
| 10/15 | 250 | | |

**Instructions**

(a) Reproduce the journal entries for the transactions that occurred on October 1, 10, and 20 and provide explanations for each.

(b) Prepare a trial balance at October 31, 1996.

**E2–8** Selected transactions for the Basler Company during its first month in business are presented below.

*Prepare journal entries and post using standard account form.*
*(SO 4, 6)*

Sept. 1 Invested $15,000 cash in the business.

5   Purchased equipment for $10,000 paying $5,000 in cash and the balance on account.

25   Paid $3,000 cash on balance owed for equipment.

30   Withdrew $500 cash for personal use.

Basler's chart of accounts shows: Cash, No. 101; Equipment, No. 157; and Accounts Payable, No. 201; Shirley Basler, Capital, No. 301; and Shirley Basler, Drawing, No. 306.

**Instructions**
(a) Journalize the transactions on page J1 of the journal.
(b) Post the transactions using the standard account form.

*Analyze errors and their effects on trial balance.*
*(SO 7)*

**E2–9**   The bookkeeper for John Castle's Equipment Repair made a number of errors in journalizing and posting, as described below:

1. A credit posting of $400 to Accounts Receivable was omitted.
2. A debit posting of $750 for Prepaid Insurance was debited to Insurance Expense.
3. A collection on account of $100 was journalized and posted as a debit to Cash $100 and a credit to Fees Earned $100.
4. A credit posting of $300 to Property Taxes Payable was made twice.
5. A cash purchase of supplies for $250 was journalized and posted as a debit to Supplies $25 and a credit to Cash $25.
6. A debit of $465 to Advertising Expense was posted as $456.

**Instructions**
For each error, indicate (a) whether the trial balance will balance; if the trial balance will not balance, indicate (b) the amount of the difference, and (c) the trial balance column that will have the larger total. Consider each error separately. Use the following form, in which error (1) is given as an example.

| Error | (a)<br>In Balance | (b)<br>Difference | (c)<br>Larger Column |
|:-----:|:-----------------:|:-----------------:|:--------------------:|
| (1)   | No                | $400              | debit                |

*Prepare a trial balance.*
*(SO 2, 7)*

**E2–10**   The accounts in the ledger of Speedy Delivery Service contain the following balances on July 31, 1996:

| | | | |
|---|---:|---|---:|
| Accounts Receivable | $ 8,642 | Prepaid Insurance | $ 1,968 |
| Accounts Payable | 7,396 | Repair Expense | 961 |
| Cash | ? | Service Revenue | 10,610 |
| Delivery Equipment | 49,360 | T. Weld, Drawing | 700 |
| Gas and Oil Expense | 758 | T. Weld, Capital | 44,636 |
| Insurance Expense | 523 | Salaries Expense | 4,428 |
| Notes Payable | 18,450 | Salaries Payable | 815 |

**Instructions**
Prepare a trial balance with the accounts arranged as illustrated in the chapter and fill in the missing amount for Cash.

# PROBLEMS

*Journalize a series of transactions.*
*(SO 2, 4)*

**P2–1**   The Surepar Miniature Golf and Driving Range was opened on March 1 by Jim McInnes. The following selected events and transactions occurred during March:

Mar. 1   Invested $50,000 cash in the business.

3   Purchased Lee's Golf Land for $38,000 cash. The price consists of land, $23,000, building, $9,000, and equipment, $6,000. (Make one compound entry.)

5   Advertised the opening of the driving range and miniature golf course, paying advertising expenses of $1,600.

6   Paid cash $1,480 for a one-year insurance policy.

10   Purchased golf clubs and other equipment for $1,600 from Palmer Company payable in 30 days.

18  Received golf fees of $800 in cash.

19  Sold 100 coupon books for $15.00 each. Each book contains 10 coupons that enable the holder to one round of miniature golf or to hit one bucket of golf balls.

25  Withdrew $500 cash for personal use.

30  Paid salaries of $600.

30  Paid Palmer Company in full.

31  Received $500 of fees in cash.

Jim McInnes uses the following accounts: Cash; Prepaid Insurance; Land; Buildings; Equipment; Accounts Payable; Unearned Golf Fees; Jim McInnes, Capital; Jim McInnes, Drawing; Golf Fees Earned; Advertising Expense; and Salaries Expense.

**Instructions**
Journalize the March transactions.

**P2-2**  Patricia Perez is a licensed architect. During the first month of the operation of her business, the following events and transactions occurred.

*Journalize transactions, post, and prepare trial balance.*
*(SO 2, 4, 6, 7)*

April 1  Invested $13,000 cash.

1  Hired a secretary-receptionist at a salary of $300 per week payable monthly.

2  Paid office rent for the month, $800.

3  Purchased architectural supplies on account from Halo Company, $1,500.

10  Completed blueprints on a carport and billed client $900 for services.

11  Received $500 cash advance from R. Welk for the design of a new home.

20  Received $1,500 cash for services completed and delivered to P. Donahue.

30  Paid secretary-receptionist for the month, $1,200.

30  Paid $600 to Halo Company on account.

Patricia uses the following chart of accounts: No. 101 Cash, No. 112 Accounts Receivable, No. 126 Supplies, No. 201 Accounts Payable, No. 205 Unearned Fees, No. 301 Patricia Perez, Capital, No. 400 Fees Earned, No. 726 Salaries Expense, and No. 729 Rent Expense.

**Instructions**
(a) Journalize the transactions.
(b) Post to the ledger accounts.
(c) Prepare a trial balance on April 30, 1996.

**P2-3**  The trial balance of Jane's Laundry on September 30 is shown below:

*Journalize transactions, post, and prepare a trial balance.*
*(SO 2, 4, 6, 7)*

**JANE'S LAUNDRY**
**Trial Balance**
**September 30, 1996**

| Account No. | | Debit | Credit |
|---|---|---|---|
| 101 | Cash | $ 8,500 | |
| 112 | Accounts Receivable | 2,200 | |
| 126 | Supplies | 1,700 | |
| 157 | Equipment | 8,000 | |
| 201 | Accounts Payable | | $ 5,000 |
| 206 | Unearned Revenue | | 700 |
| 301 | Jane Kent, Capital | | 14,700 |
| | | $20,400 | $20,400 |

The October transactions were as follows:

Oct. 5  Received $900 cash from customers on account.

10  Billed customers for services performed $5,500.

15  Paid employee salaries $1,200.

17  Performed $400 of services for customers who paid in advance in August.

20  Paid $1,600 to creditors on account.

29  Withdrew $500 for personal use.

31  Paid utilities $600.

## Instructions

(a) Enter the opening balances in the ledger accounts as of October 1. Write "Balance" in the explanation space and insert a check mark (√) in the reference column. Provision should be made for the following additional accounts: No. 306 Jane Kent, Drawing; No. 426 Laundry Revenue; No. 726 Salaries Expense; and No. 732 Utilities Expense.

(b) Journalize the transactions.

(c) Post to the ledger accounts.

(d) Prepare a trial balance on October 31, 1996.

*Prepare a correct trial balance.*
*(SO 7)*

**P2–4**  The trial balance of Thom Wargo Co. shown below does not balance.

### THOM WARGO CO.
### Trial Balance
### June 30, 1996

|  | Debit | Credit |
|---|---|---|
| Cash |  | $ 2,840 |
| Accounts Receivable | $ 3,231 |  |
| Supplies | 800 |  |
| Equipment | 3,000 |  |
| Accounts Payable |  | 2,666 |
| Unearned Fees | 1,200 |  |
| T. Wargo, Capital |  | 9,000 |
| T. Wargo, Drawing | 800 |  |
| Fees Earned |  | 2,380 |
| Salaries Expense | 3,400 |  |
| Office Expense | 910 |  |
|  | $13,341 | $16,886 |

Each of the listed accounts has a normal balance per the general ledger. An examination of the ledger and journal reveals the following errors.

1. Cash received from a customer on account was debited for $570 and Accounts Receivable was credited for the same amount. The actual collection was for $750.

2. The purchase of a typewriter on account for $340 was recorded as a debit to Supplies for $340 and a credit to Accounts Payable for $340.

3. Services were performed on account for a client for $890. Accounts Receivable was debited for $890 and Fees Earned was credited for $89.

4. A debit posting to Salaries Expense of $600 was omitted.

5. A payment on account for $206 was credited to Cash for $206 and credited to Accounts Payable for $260.

6. The withdrawal of $400 cash for Wargo's personal use was debited to Salaries Expense for $400 and credited to Cash for $400.

## Instructions

Prepare a correct trial balance.

*Journalize transactions, post,*
*and prepare a trial balance.*
*(SO 2, 4, 6, 7)*

**P2–5**  The Star Theater, owned by Leo Baerga, will begin operations in March. The Star will be unique in that it will show only triple features of sequential theme movies. As of February 28, the ledger of Star showed: No. 101 Cash $16,000; No. 140 Land $42,000; No. 145 Buildings (concession stand, projection room, ticket booth, and screen) $18,000; No. 157 Equipment $16,000; No. 201 Accounts Payable $12,000; and No. 301 L. Baerga, Capital $80,000. During the month of March the following events and transactions occurred:

Mar. 2  Acquired the three *Star Wars* movies (*Star Wars, The Empire Strikes Back*, and *The Return of the Jedi*) to be shown for the first 3 weeks of March. The film rental was $12,000; $4,000 was paid in cash and $8,000 will be paid on March 10.

3  Ordered the first three *Star Trek* movies to be shown the last 10 days of March. It will cost $400 per night.

9  Received $6,500 cash from admissions.

10  Paid balance due on *Star Wars* movies rental and $3,000 on February 28 accounts payable.

11  Hired M. Brewer to operate concession stand. Brewer to pay Star Theater 15% of gross receipts payable monthly.

12  Paid advertising expenses $800.
20  Received $7,200 cash from admissions.
20  Received the *Star Trek* movies and paid the rental fee of $4,000.
31  Paid salaries of $3,800.
31  Received statement from M. Brewer showing gross receipts from concessions of $8,000 and the balance due to Star Theater of $1,200 for March. Brewer paid one-half the balance due and will remit the remainder on April 5.
31  Received $12,500 cash from admissions.

In addition to the accounts identified above, the chart of accounts includes: No. 112 Accounts Receivable, No. 405 Admission Revenue, No. 406 Concession Revenue, No. 610 Advertising Expense, No. 632 Film Rental Expense, and No. 726 Salaries Expense.

*Instructions*
(a)  Enter the beginning balances to the ledger. Insert a check mark (√) in the reference column of the ledger for the beginning balance.
(b)  Journalize the March transactions.
(c)  Post the March journal entries to the ledger. Assume that all entries are posted from page 1 of the journal.
(d)  Prepare a trial balance on March 31, 1996.

# ALTERNATE PROBLEMS

● ● ● ● ● ● ● ● ● ● ● ● ● ● ● ● ● ● ● ● ● ● ● ● ● ● ● ● ● ● ● ● ● ● ● ● ● ● ● ● ● ● ● ● ● ● ● ● ● ● ● ● ● ● ● ● ● ● ● ● ● ● ● ● ● ● ● ● ●

**P2–1A**  The Frontier Park was started on April 1 by Ed Quinn. The following selected events and transactions occurred during April.

*Journalize a series of transactions.*
(SO 2, 4)

Apr.  1  Invested $60,000 cash in the business.
4  Purchased land costing $30,000 for cash.
8  Incurred advertising expense of $1,800 on account.
11  Paid salaries to employees $1,500.
12  Hired park manager at a salary of $4,000 per month, effective May 1.
13  Paid $1,500 for a one-year insurance policy.
17  Withdrew $600 cash for personal use.
20  Received $5,700 in cash for admission fees.
25  Sold 100 coupon books for $25 each. Each book contains 10 coupons that entitle the holder to one admission to the park.
30  Received $5,900 in cash admission fees.
30  Paid $700 on account for advertising incurred on April 8.

Ed Quinn uses the following accounts: Cash; Prepaid Insurance; Land; Accounts Payable; Unearned Admissions; Ed Quinn, Capital; Ed Quinn, Drawing; Admission Revenue; Advertising Expense; and Salaries Expense.

*Instructions*
Journalize the April transactions.

**P2–2A**  Iva Holz is a licensed CPA. During the first month of operations of her business, the following events and transactions occurred:

*Journalize transactions, post, and prepare a trial balance.*
(SO 2, 4, 6, 7)

May  1  Invested $42,000 cash.
2  Hired a secretary-receptionist at a salary of $1,000 per month.
3  Purchased $1,200 of supplies on account from Read Supply Company.
7  Paid office rent of $900 for the month.
11  Completed a tax assignment and billed client $1,100 for services rendered.
12  Received $3,500 advance on a management consulting engagement.
17  Received cash of $1,200 for services completed for H. Arnold Co.
31  Paid secretary-receptionist $1,000 salary for the month.
31  Paid 40% of balance due Read Supply Company.

Iva uses the following chart of accounts: No. 101 Cash, No. 112 Accounts Receivable, No. 126 Supplies, No. 201 Accounts Payable, No. 205 Unearned Fees, No. 301 Iva Holz, Capital, No. 400 Fees Earned, No. 726 Salaries Expense, and No. 729 Rent Expense.

*Instructions*
(a) Journalize the transactions.
(b) Post to the ledger accounts.
(c) Prepare a trial balance on May 31, 1996.

*Journalize transactions, post,
and prepare a trial balance.*
(SO 2, 4, 6, 7)

**P2–3A**  The trial balance of Sterling Dry Cleaners on June 30 is shown below.

**STERLING DRY CLEANERS**
**Trial Balance**
**June 30, 1996**

| Account No. | | Debit | Credit |
|---|---|---|---|
| 101 | Cash | $12,532 | |
| 112 | Accounts Receivable | 10,536 | |
| 126 | Supplies | 4,844 | |
| 157 | Equipment | 25,950 | |
| 201 | Accounts Payable | | $15,878 |
| 206 | Unearned Revenue | | 1,730 |
| 301 | R. Sterling, Capital | | 36,254 |
| | | $53,862 | $53,862 |

The July transactions were as follows:

July  8  Collected $4,936 in cash on June 30 accounts receivable.
9  Paid employee salaries $2,100.
11  Received $4,325 in cash for services rendered.
14  Paid June 30 creditors $10,750 on account.
17  Purchased supplies on account $554.
22  Billed customers for services rendered, $4,700.
30  Paid employee salaries $3,114, utilities $1,384, and repairs $692.
31  Withdrew $700 cash for personal use of owner.

*Instructions*
(a) Enter the opening balances in the ledger accounts as of July 1. Write "Balance" in the
explanation space and insert a check mark (√) in the reference column. Provision
should be made for the following additional accounts: No. 306 R. Sterling, Drawing;
No. 428 Dry Cleaning Revenue; No. 622 Repair Expense; No. 726 Salaries Expense;
and No. 732 Utilities Expense.
(b) Journalize the transactions.
(c) Post to the ledger accounts.
(d) Prepare a trial balance on July 31, 1996.

*Prepare a correct trial balance.*
(SO 7)

**P2–4A**  The trial balance of the Saginaw Company shown below does not balance.

**SAGINAW COMPANY**
**Trial Balance**
**May 31, 1996**

| | Debit | Credit |
|---|---|---|
| Cash | $ 5,850 | |
| Accounts Receivable | | $ 2,750 |
| Prepaid Insurance | 700 | |
| Equipment | 8,000 | |
| Accounts Payable | | 4,500 |
| Property Taxes Payable | 560 | |
| M. A. Fox, Capital | | 11,700 |
| Fees Earned | 6,690 | |
| Salaries Expense | 4,200 | |
| Advertising Expense | | 1,100 |
| Property Tax Expense | 800 | |
| | $26,800 | $20,050 |

Your review of the ledger reveals that each account has a normal balance. You also discover the following errors.

1. The totals of the debit sides of Prepaid Insurance, Accounts Payable, and Property Tax Expense were each understated $100.
2. Transposition errors were made in Accounts Receivable and Fees Earned. Based on postings made, the correct balances were $2,570 and $6,960, respectively.
3. A debit posting to Salaries Expense of $200 was omitted.
4. A $700 cash drawing by the owner was debited to M. A. Fox, Capital for $700 and credited to Cash for $700.
5. A $420 purchase of supplies on account was debited to Equipment for $420 and credited to Cash for $420.
6. A cash payment of $250 for advertising was debited to Advertising Expense for $25 and credited to Cash for $25.
7. A collection from a customer for $210 was debited to Cash for $210 and credited to Accounts Payable for $210.

**Instructions**
Prepare a correct trial balance. (Note: The chart of accounts includes the following: M. A. Fox, Drawing; Supplies; and Supplies Expense.

**P2–5A** The Lake Theater is owned by Frances Hill. All facilities were completed on March 31. At this time, the ledger showed: No. 101 Cash $6,000; No. 140 Land $10,000; No. 145 Buildings (concession stand, projection room, ticket booth, and screen) $8,000; No. 157 Equipment $6,000; No. 201 Accounts Payable $2,000; No. 275 Mortgage Payable $8,000; and No. 301 Frances Hill, Capital $20,000. During April, the following events and transactions occurred.

*Journalize transactions, post, and prepare a trial balance.* (SO 2, 4, 6, 7)

Apr. 2 Paid film rental of $800 on first movie.
    3 Ordered two additional films at $500 each.
    9 Received $1,800 cash from admissions.
   10 Made $2,000 payment on mortgage and $1,000 on accounts payable.
   11 Hired R. Thoms to operate concession stand. Thoms to pay The Lake Theater 17% of gross receipts payable monthly.
   12 Paid advertising expenses $300.
   20 Received one of the films ordered on April 3 and was billed $500. The film will be shown in April.
   25 Received $4,200 cash from admissions.
   29 Paid salaries $1,600.
   30 Received statement from R. Thoms showing gross receipts of $1,000 and the balance due to The Lake Theater of $170 for April. Thoms paid one-half of the balance due and will remit the remainder on May 5.
   30 Prepaid $700 rental on special film to be run in May.

In addition to the accounts identified above, the chart of accounts shows: No. 112 Accounts Receivable, No. 136 Prepaid Rentals, No. 405 Admission Revenue, No. 406 Concession Revenue, No. 610 Advertising Expense, No. 632 Film Rental Expense, and No. 726 Salaries Expense.

**Instructions**
(a) Enter the beginning balances in the ledger as of April 1. Insert a check mark (√) in the reference column of the ledger for the beginning balance.
(b) Journalize the April transactions.
(c) Post the April journal entries to the ledger. Assume that all entries are posted from page 1 of the journal.
(d) Prepare a trial balance on April 30, 1996.

# ▶*Broadening Your Perspective*

## *F*INANCIAL REPORTING PROBLEM
••••••••••••••••••••••••••••••••••••••••••••••••••••••••••••••••••••••••••••••••

The financial statements of PepsiCo in Appendix A at the back of this textbook and the notes accompanying the statements contain the following selected accounts, and stated in millions of dollars:

| | | | |
|---|---|---|---|
| Accounts Payable | $1,451.6 | Income Taxes Payable | 671.7 |
| Accounts Receivable | 2,050.9 | Interest Income | 90.4 |
| Interest Expense | 645.0 | Prepaid Expenses | 563.2 |
| Land | 1,321.6 | | |

### *Instructions*
(a) Answer the following questions:
  1. What is the increase and decrease side for each account?
  2. What is the normal balance for each account?
(b) Identify the probable other account in the transaction and the effect on that account when
  1. Accounts Receivable is decreased.
  2. Income Taxes Payable is decreased.
  3. Prepaid Expenses are increased.
(c) Identify the other account(s) that ordinarily would be involved when
  1. Interest Expense is increased.
  2. Land is increased.

## *D*ECISION CASE
••••••••••••••••••••••••••••••••••••••••••••••••••••••••••••••••••••••••••••••••

Lucy Lars operates the Lucy Riding Academy. The academy's primary sources of revenue are riding fees and lesson fees, which are provided on a cash basis. Lucy also boards horses for owners, who are billed monthly for boarding fees. In a few cases, boarders pay in advance of expected use. For its revenue transactions, the academy maintains the following accounts: No. 1 Cash, No. 5 Boarding Accounts Receivable, No. 27 Unearned Boarding Fees, No. 51 Riding Fees Earned, No. 52 Lesson Fees Earned, and No. 53 Boarding Fees Earned.

The academy owns 10 horses, a stable, a riding corral, riding equipment, and office equipment. These assets are accounted for in accounts No. 11 Horses, No. 12 Building, No. 13 Riding Corral, No. 14 Riding Equipment, and No. 15 Office Equipment.

The academy employs stable helpers and an office employee, who receive weekly salaries. At the end of each month, the mail usually brings bills for advertising, utilities, and veterinary service. Other expenses include feed for the horses and insurance. For its expenses, the academy maintains the following accounts: No. 6 Hay and Feed Supplies, No. 7 Prepaid Insurance, No. 21 Accounts Payable, No. 60 Salaries Expense, No. 61 Advertising Expense, No. 62 Utilities Expense, No. 63 Veterinary Expense, No. 64 Hay and Feed Expense, and No. 65 Insurance Expense.

Lucy Lars' sole source of income is the academy. Thus, she makes periodic withdrawals of cash for personal living expenses. To record Lucy's equity in the business and her drawings, two accounts are maintained: No. 50 Lucy Lars, Capital, and No. 51 Lucy Lars, Drawing.

During the first month of operations an inexperienced bookkeeper was employed. Lucy Lars asks you to review the following nine entries of the 50 entries made during the month. In each case, the explanation for the entry is correct.

| | | | |
|---|---|---|---|
| May  1 | Cash | 15,000 | |
| | Lucy Lars, Capital | | 15,000 |
| | (Invested $15,000 cash in business) | | |

| | | | |
|---|---|---|---|
| 5 | Cash | 250 | |
| | Riding Fees Earned | | 250 |
| | (Received $250 cash for lesson fees) | | |
| 7 | Cash | 500 | |
| | Boarding Fees Earned | | 500 |
| | (Received $500 for boarding of horses beginning June 1) | | |
| 9 | Hay and Feed Expense | 1,700 | |
| | Cash | | 1,700 |
| | (Purchased estimated two months' supply of feed and hay for $1,700 on account) | | |
| 14 | Riding Equipment | 80 | |
| | Cash | | 800 |
| | (Purchased desk and other office equipment for $800 cash) | | |
| 15 | Salaries Expense | 400 | |
| | Cash | | 400 |
| | (Issued check to Lucy Lars for personal use) | | |
| 20 | Cash | 145 | |
| | Riding Fees Earned | | 154 |
| | (Received $154 cash for riding fees) | | |
| 31 | Veterinary Expense | 75 | |
| | Accounts Payable | | 75 |
| | (Received bill of $75 from veterinarian for services rendered) | | |

**Instructions**

(a) For each journal entry that is correct, so state. For each journal entry that is incorrect, prepare the entry that should have been made by the bookkeeper.
(b) Which of the incorrect entries would prevent the trial balance from balancing?
(c) What was the correct net income for May, assuming the bookkeeper reported net income of $4,500 after posting all 50 entries?
(d) What was the correct cash balance at May 31, assuming the bookkeeper reported a balance of $12,475 after posting all 50 entries?

# COMMUNICATION ACTIVITY

Milly Maid Company offers home cleaning service. Two recurring transactions for the company are billing customers for services rendered and paying employee salaries. For example, on March 15 bills totaling $6,000 were sent to customers and $2,000 was paid in salaries to employees.

**Instructions**

Write a memorandum to your instructor that explains and illustrates the steps in the recording process for each of the March 15 transactions. Use the format illustrated in the text under the heading, "The Recording Process Illustrated" (p. 58).

# GROUP ACTIVITY

The expanded basic accounting equation contains six account categories: assets, liabilities, owner's capital, owner's drawing, revenues, and expenses.

*Instructions*

With the class divided into six groups, each group should choose one of the six account categories and should:

    (a) Explain for its category: (1) the increase/decrease side of the account, and (2) the normal balance of the account.

    (b) Give an example of a transaction that will result in an increase in the assigned category.

# *E*THICS CASE

Mary Vonesh is the assistant chief accountant at Staples Company, a manufacturer of computer chips and cellular phones. The company presently has total sales of $20 million. It is the end of the first quarter and Mary is hurriedly trying to prepare a general ledger trial balance so that quarterly financial statements can be prepared and released to management and the regulatory agencies. The total credits on the trial balance exceed the debits by $1,000. In order to meet the 4 p.m. deadline, Mary decides to force the debits and credits into balance by adding the amount of the difference to the Equipment account. She chose Equipment because it is one of the larger account balances: percentage-wise it will be the least misstated. Mary plugs the difference! She believes that the difference is quite small and will not affect anyone's decisions. She wishes that she had another few days to find the error but realizes that the financial statements are already late.

*Instructions*

    (a) Who are the stakeholders in this situation?

    (b) What are the ethical issues involved in this case?

    (c) What are Mary's alternatives?

# *C*RITICAL THINKING
## ▸ *A Real-World Focus: Automated Security Holdings*

*Automated Security Holdings operates multinationally, with principal markets in the United States and the United Kingdom. The company designs, produces, installs, and maintains security systems to safeguard life and property from a wide range of hazards. The markets for these security products include commercial, industrial, and residential customers.*

The following notes to the financial statements identify a few of the accounts found in the general ledger of Automated Security Holdings.

FINANCIAL NOTES:

|  | November 30, | |
|---|---|---|
|  | 1993 | 1994 |
|  | (thousands of dollars) | |
| Income Tax Payable | 3,929 | 3,919 |
| Accounts Payable | 6,499 | 9,620 |
| Salaries Expense | 16,353 | 9,213 |
| Cash | 4,749 | 2,869 |
| Unearned Fees | 1,211 | 1,434 |
| Notes Payable | 52,000 | 40,000 |
| Prepaid Insurance | 1,333 | 2,000 |

*Instructions*

    (a) Identify the accounts of Automated Security Holdings that have debit balances in the trial balance.

(b) What date has Automated Security Holdings adopted for its accounting year-end?

(c) Are the accounts listed above in the order in which they would appear in Automated Security Holdings' general ledger? Explain.

---

***Answers to Self-Study Questions***

1. b   2. c   3. d   4. d   5. b   6. a   7. c   8. d   9. a   10. c

# When Students Leave Campus, This College Adjusts Its Books

TEMPE, Ariz. — Like many colleges, Arizona State University (ASU) uses a June 30 date as the end of its annual accounting period. Rather than using December 31, most colleges use the school year as their primary period of activity. Having an ending date like that seems neat and tidy—and it is in many respects. (If it were not, schools would choose an end-date that made more sense.) But colleges, just like any business organization, have some loose ends that need tying up at the end of the accounting period. For example, at ASU, the second summer session begins around July 5, but registration for the session takes place the prior February. The school collects tuition for the session in one accounting period but will provide the services in the next accounting period. "We have lots of students who are paying tuition in February for a session that begins in July," says Carol Balk, ASU's manager of student tuition payments. In the new accounting year, following completion of the summer session, "we have to account for the revenue collection of five months earlier."

Similarly, ASU has to account for supplies purchased in one accounting year but used the next. Supplies purchased on April 1 for use in the summer session will need to be reported as an expense in the new accounting year. ◀

# CHAPTER · 3

# ADJUSTING THE ACCOUNTS

## ▶ STUDY OBJECTIVES ◀

**After studying this chapter, you should be able to:**

1. Explain the time period assumption.
2. Distinguish between the revenue recognition principle and the matching principle.
3. Explain why adjusting entries are needed.
4. Identify the major types of adjusting entries.
5. Prepare adjusting entries for prepayments.
6. Prepare adjusting entries for accruals.
7. Describe the nature and purpose of an adjusted trial balance.
8. Explain the accrual basis of accounting.

In Chapter 2 we examined the basic steps in the recording process through the preparation of the trial balance. Before we will be ready to prepare financial statements from the trial balance, additional steps need to be taken. The timing mismatch between revenues and expenses of Arizona State University illustrates the types of situations that make these additional steps necessary. For example, computer equipment purchased in the prior accounting year is being used to keep student records and accounts in the current year. What portion of the computer cost, if any, should be recognized as an expense of the current period? Before financial statements can be prepared, these and other questions relating to the recognition of revenues and expenses must be answered. With the answers in hand, the relevant account balances can then be adjusted.

The organization and content of the chapter are as follows:

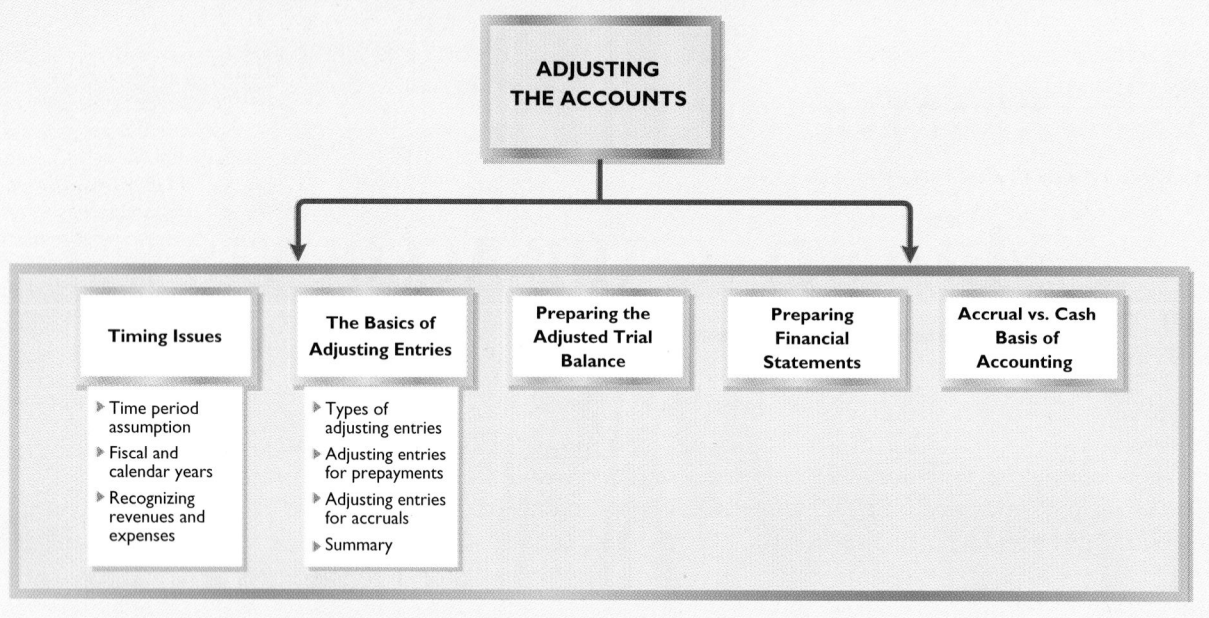

## Timing Issues

**STUDY OBJECTIVE**

▼

*Explain the time period assumption.*

No adjustments would be necessary if we waited to prepare financial statements until a company ended its operations. At that point, we could readily determine its final balance sheet and the amount of lifetime income it earned. The following anecdote illustrates one way to compute lifetime income:

A grocery store owner from the old country kept his accounts payable on a spindle, accounts receivable on a note pad, and cash in a cigar box. His daughter, having just passed the CPA exam, chided the father: "I don't understand how you can run your business this way. How do you know what your profits are?"

"Well," the father replied, "when I got off the boat 40 years ago, I had nothing but the pants I was wearing. Today your brother is a doctor, your sister is a college professor, and you are a CPA. Your mother and I have a nice car, a well-furnished house, and a lake home. We have a good business and everything is paid for. So, you add all that together, subtract the pants, and there's your profit."

## Selecting an Accounting Time Period

Although the old grocer may be correct in his evaluation, it is impractical to wait so long for the results of operations. All entities, from the corner grocery, to a global company like PepsiCo, to your college or university, find it desirable and necessary to report the results of their activities more frequently. For example, management usually wants monthly financial statements, and the Internal Revenue Service requires all businesses to file annual tax returns. As a consequence, **accountants make the assumption that the economic life of a business can be divided into artificial time periods.** This assumption is referred to as the time period assumption.

Many business transactions affect more than one of these arbitrary time periods. For example, the milking machine bought by Farmer Brown in 1995 and the airplanes purchased by Delta Airlines 5 years ago are still in use today. Therefore it is necessary to determine the relevance of each business transaction to specific accounting periods. Doing so may involve subjective judgments and estimates. Generally, the shorter the time period (e.g., a month or a quarter of a year), the more difficult it becomes to determine the proper adjustments to be made.

## Fiscal and Calendar Years

Both small and large companies prepare financial statements on a periodic basis in order to assess their financial condition and results of operations. **Accounting time periods are generally a month, a quarter, or a year.** Monthly and quarterly time periods are often referred to as interim periods. Most large companies are required to prepare both interim (quarterly) and annual financial statements.

An accounting time period that is one year in length is referred to as a fiscal year. A fiscal year usually begins with the first day of a month and ends 12 months later on the last day of a month. The accounting period used by most businesses coincides with the calendar year (January 1 to December 31). Companies whose fiscal year differs from the calendar year include Delta Air Lines, June 30; Walt Disney Productions, September 30; Kmart Corp., January 31; and Dunkin' Donuts, Inc., October 31. Arizona State University's fiscal year is July 1 through June 30, which is typical of universities and governmental agencies.

## Recognizing Revenues and Expenses

Determining the amount of revenues and expenses to be reported in a given accounting period can be difficult. Therefore, accountants have developed two principles as part of generally accepted accounting principles (GAAP) that help in this determination: the revenue recognition principle and the matching principle.

The revenue recognition principle dictates that revenue be recognized in the accounting period in which it is earned. In a service enterprise, revenue is considered to be earned at the time the service is performed. To illustrate, assume that a dry cleaning business cleans clothing on June 30 but customers do not claim and pay for their clothes until the first week of July. Under the revenue recognition principle, revenue is earned in June when the service is performed and not in July when the cash is received. At June 30, the dry cleaner would report a receivable on its balance sheet and revenue in its income statement for the service performed.

In recognizing expenses, accountants follow the approach of "let the expenses follow the revenues." Thus, expense recognition is tied to revenue recognition. In the preceding example, this principle means that the salary expense incurred in performing the cleaning service on June 30 should be reported in the income statement for the same period in which the service revenue is recognized.

▶ **Ethics note**

In addition to annual numbers, many investors rely on interim reports. The Securities and Exchange Commission recently charged two former executives of the Union Corporation with intentionally reporting in one quarter revenues that were earned in a different quarter, in order to meet quarterly income targets. The misstatement had no effect on year-end totals.

**STUDY OBJECTIVE 2**

*Distinguish between the revenue recognition principle and the matching principle.*

**Helpful hint** Another example is ASU's need to account for supplies purchased in one year but used in the next.

## ▲*Accounting in Action* ▸ *Business Insight*

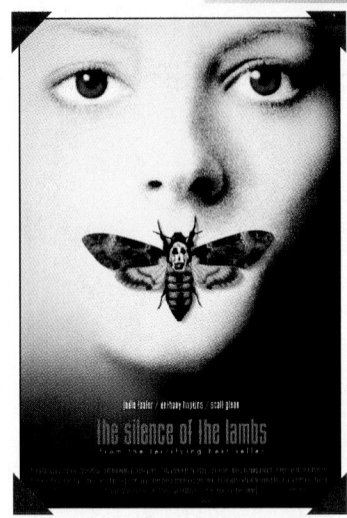

Suppose you are a filmmaker and spend $15 million to produce a film. Over what period should the $15 million be expensed? Yes, it should be expensed over the economic life of the film. But what is its economic life? The filmmaker must estimate how much revenue will be earned from box office sales, video sales, and television—a period that easily can stretch five years or more. If a filmmaker allocates the cost over five years, and the film produces revenue in the sixth year, proper matching has not occurred. Furthermore, in some cases, films flop, and yet the costs are spread out over five years in the hopes that the films will eventually succeed. For example, in the mid-1980s Orion Pictures (now bankrupt) earned $7.3 million in one year, but lost $32 million the next year because it expensed 40 films that were not producing revenue. It was alleged that the company had overstated its income in earlier years because it did not expense these costs earlier. This case demonstrates the difficulty of properly matching expenses to revenues.

The critical issue in expense recognition is when the expense makes its contribution to revenue. This may or may not be the same period in which the expense is paid. If the salary incurred on June 30 is not paid until July, the dry cleaner would report salaries payable on its June 30 balance sheet. The practice of expense recognition is referred to as the matching principle because it dictates that efforts (expenses) be matched with accomplishments (revenues).

Once the assumption is made that the economic life of a business can be divided into artificial time periods, it follows that the revenue recognition and matching principles can be applied. This one assumption and two principles thus provide guidelines as to when revenues and expenses should be reported. These relationships are shown in Illustration 3-1.

**Illustration 3-1**

*GAAP relationships in revenue and expense recognition*

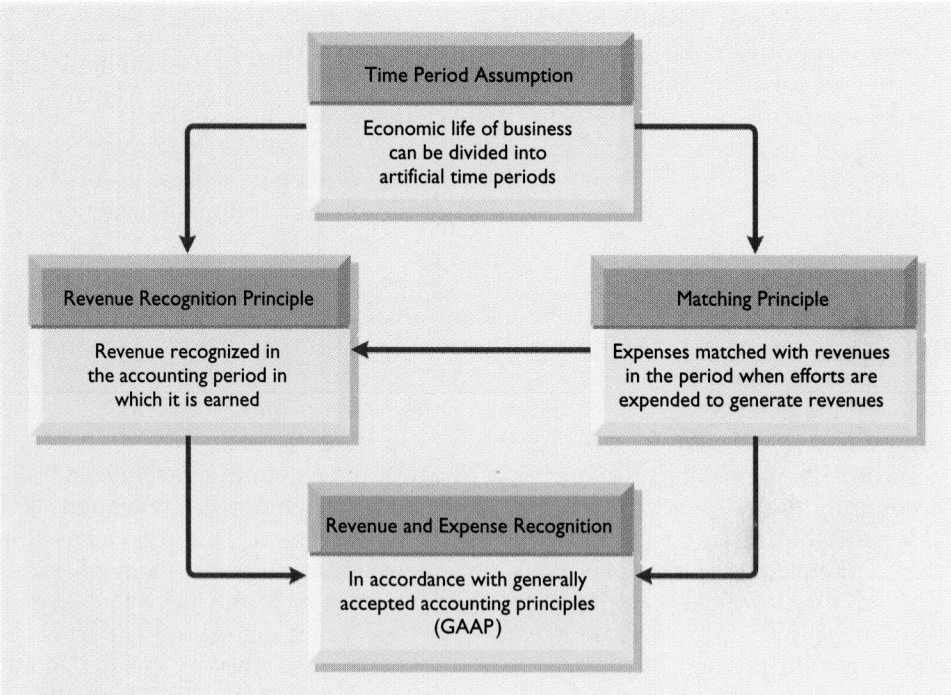

## *Before You Go On . . .*

### ▸ *Review It*

1. What is the relevance of the time period assumption to accounting?
2. What are the revenue recognition and matching principles?

# The Basics of Adjusting Entries

In order for revenues to be recorded in the period in which they are earned, and for expenses to be recognized in the period in which they are incurred, adjusting entries are made at the end of the accounting period. In short, adjusting entries **are needed to ensure that the revenue recognition and matching principles are followed.**

**STUDY OBJECTIVE**
▼ 3

*Explain why adjusting entries are needed.*

The use of adjusting entries makes it possible to report on the balance sheet the appropriate assets, liabilities, and owner's equity at the statement date and to report on the income statement the proper net income (or loss) for the period. However, the trial balance—the first pulling together of the transaction data—may not contain up-to-date and complete data. This is true for the following reasons:

1. Some events are not journalized daily because it is inexpedient to do so. Examples are the consumption of supplies and the earning of wages by employees.
2. Some costs are not journalized during the accounting period because these costs expire with the passage of time rather than as a result of recurring daily transactions. Examples of such costs are building and equipment deterioration and rent and insurance.
3. Some items may be unrecorded. An example is a utility service bill that will not be received until the next accounting period.

**Helpful hint** Adjusting entries are needed to enable financial statements to be in conformity with GAAP.

**Adjusting entries are required every time financial statements are prepared.** An essential starting point is an analysis of each account in the trial balance to determine whether it is complete and up-to-date for financial statement purposes. The analysis requires a thorough understanding of the company's operations and the interrelationship of accounts. The preparation of adjusting entries is often an involved process. In accumulating the adjustment data, the company may need to make inventory counts of supplies and repair parts. Also it may be desirable to prepare supporting schedules of insurance policies, rental agreements, and other contractual commitments. Adjustments are often prepared after the balance sheet date. However, the adjusting entries are dated as of the balance sheet date.

## Types of Adjusting Entries

Adjusting entries can be classified as either prepayments or accruals. Each of these classes has two subcategories as shown below:

**STUDY OBJECTIVE**
▼ 4

*Identify the major types of adjusting entries.*

**Prepayments**
1. **Prepaid Expenses.** Expenses paid in cash and recorded as assets before they are used or consumed.
2. **Unearned Revenues.** Revenues received in cash and recorded as liabilities before they are earned.

**Accruals**
3. **Accrued Revenues.** Revenues earned but not yet received in cash or recorded.
4. **Accrued Expenses.** Expenses incurred but not yet paid in cash or recorded.

Specific examples and explanations of each type of adjustment are given in subsequent sections. Each example is based on the October 31 trial balance of Pioneer Advertising Agency, reproduced in Illustration 3-2 from Chapter 2.

**Illustration 3-2**

*Trial balance*

| PIONEER ADVERTISING AGENCY Trial Balance October 31, 1996 | Debit | Credit |
|---|---|---|
| Cash | $15,200 | |
| Advertising Supplies | 2,500 | |
| Prepaid Insurance | 600 | |
| Office Equipment | 5,000 | |
| Notes Payable | | $ 5,000 |
| Accounts Payable | | 2,500 |
| Unearned Fees | | 1,200 |
| C. R. Byrd, Capital | | 10,000 |
| C. R. Byrd, Drawing | 500 | |
| Fees Earned | | 10,000 |
| Salaries Expense | 4,000 | |
| Rent Expense | 900 | |
| | $28,700 | $28,700 |

We assume that Pioneer Advertising uses an accounting period of one month. Thus, monthly adjusting entries will be made. The entries will be dated October 31.

## Adjusting Entries for Prepayments

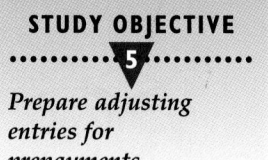

**STUDY OBJECTIVE**

5

*Prepare adjusting entries for prepayments.*

**Helpful hint** Remember that credits decrease assets and increase revenues. Debits increase expenses and decrease liabilities.

As indicated earlier, prepayments are either prepaid expenses or unearned revenues. Adjusting entries for prepayments are required at the statement date to record the portion of the prepayment that represents the **expense incurred or the revenue earned** in the current accounting period. Assuming an adjustment is needed for both types of prepayments, the asset and liability are overstated and the related expense and revenue are understated. For example, in the trial balance, the balance in the asset, Supplies, shows only supplies purchased. This balance is overstated; the related expense account, Supplies Expense, is understated because the cost of supplies used has not been recognized. Thus the adjusting entry for prepayments will decrease a balance sheet account and increase an income statement account. The effects of adjusting entries for prepayments are graphically depicted in Illustration 3-3.

### Prepaid Expenses

As stated on page 91, expenses paid in cash and recorded as assets before they are used or consumed are identified as prepaid expenses. When a cost is prepaid, an asset account is debited to show the service or benefit that will be received in the future. Prepayments often occur in regard to insurance, supplies, advertising, and rent. In addition, prepayments are made when buildings and equipment are purchased.

**Prepaid expenses expire either with the passage of time (e.g., rent and insurance) or through use and consumption (e.g., supplies).** The expiration of these costs does not require daily recurring entries, which would be unnecessary and impractical. Accordingly, it is customary to postpone the recognition of such cost expirations until financial statements are prepared. At each statement date, adjusting entries are made to record the expenses that apply to the current accounting period and to show the unexpired costs in the asset accounts.

**An asset-expense relationship exists with prepaid expenses.** Prior to adjustment, assets are overstated and expenses are understated. **Thus, the prepaid**

**Illustration 3-3**

*Adjusting entries for
prepayments*

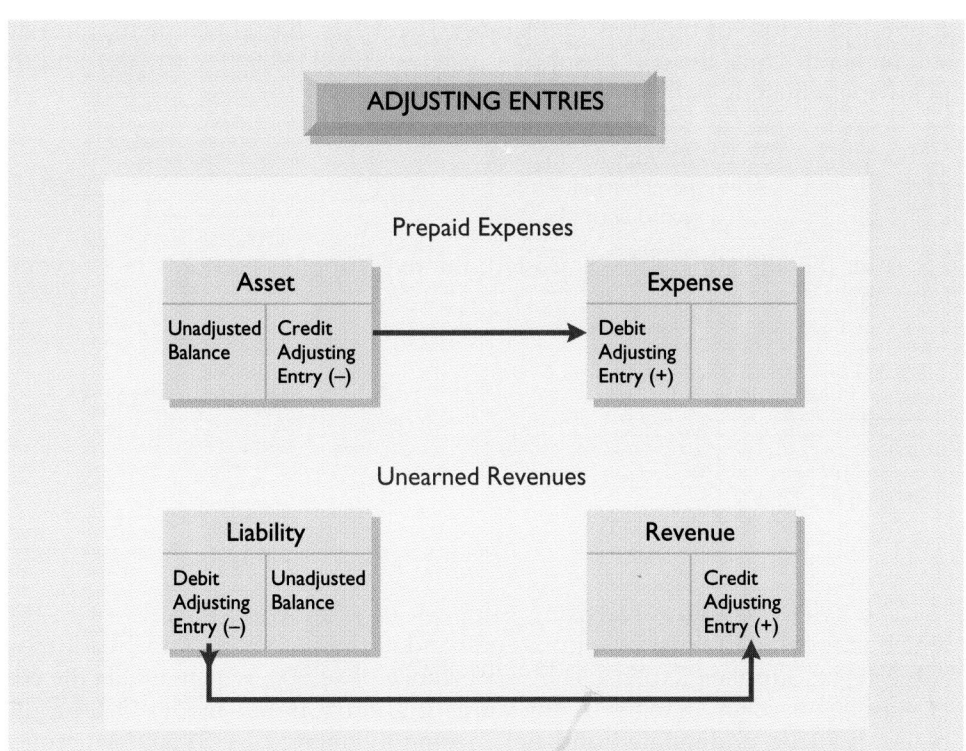

**ADJUSTING ENTRIES**

Prepaid Expenses

| Asset | |
|---|---|
| Unadjusted Balance | Credit Adjusting Entry (−) |

→

| Expense | |
|---|---|
| Debit Adjusting Entry (+) | |

Unearned Revenues

| Liability | |
|---|---|
| Debit Adjusting Entry (−) | Unadjusted Balance |

| Revenue | |
|---|---|
| | Credit Adjusting Entry (+) |

expense adjusting entry results in a debit to an expense account and a credit to an asset account.

**Supplies.** Several different types of supplies are used in a business enterprise. For example, a CPA firm will have **office supplies** such as stationery, envelopes, and accounting paper. In contrast, an advertising firm will have **advertising supplies** such as graph paper, video film, and poster paper. Supplies are generally debited to an asset account when they are acquired. During the course of operations, supplies are depleted or entirely consumed. However, recognition of supplies used is deferred until the adjustment process when a physical inventory (count) of supplies is taken. The difference between the balance in the Supplies (asset) account and the cost of supplies on hand represents the supplies used (expense) for the period.

Pioneer Advertising Agency purchased advertising supplies costing $2,500 on October 5. The debit was made to the asset Advertising Supplies, and this account shows a balance of $2,500 in the October 31 trial balance. An inventory

**Supplies**

Oct.5

Supplies purchased;
record asset

Oct.31
Supplies used;
record supplies expense

▶**Accounting in Action** ▶ *Business Insight*

The costs of advertising on radio, television, and magazines for such products as burgers, bleaches, athletic shoes, and so on are sometimes considered prepayments. As a manager for Procter & Gamble noted, "If we run a long ad campaign for soap and bleach, we sometimes report the costs as prepayments if we think we'll receive sales benefits from the campaign down the road." Presently it is a judgment call whether these costs should be prepayments or expenses in the current period. Developing guidelines consistent with the matching principle is difficult because situations vary widely from company to company. The issue is important since the outlays for advertising can be substantial. Recent big spenders: Procter & Gamble, the biggest U.S. advertiser, spent $2.3 billion, Sears Roebuck spent $1.5 billion, and McDonald's $760 million.

count at the close of business on October 31 reveals that $1,000 of supplies are still on hand. Thus, the cost of supplies used is $1,500 ($2,500 − $1,000), and the following adjusting entry is made:

| Oct. 31 | Advertising Supplies Expense | 1,500 | |
| |    Advertising Supplies | | 1,500 |
| |      (To record supplies used) | | |

After the adjusting entry is posted, the two supplies accounts in T-account form show:

**Illustration 3-4**

*Supplies accounts after adjustment*

| Advertising Supplies | | | | Advertising Supplies Expense | | |
|---|---|---|---|---|---|---|
| 10/5 | 2,500 | 10/31 Adj. | 1,500 | 10/31 Adj. | 1,500 | |
| 10/31 Bal. | 1,000 | | | | | |

The asset account Advertising Supplies now shows a balance of $1,000, which is equal to the cost of supplies on hand at the statement date. In addition, Advertising Supplies Expense shows a balance of $1,500, which equals the cost of supplies used in October. **If the adjusting entry is not made, October expenses will be understated and net income overstated by $1,500. Moreover, both assets and owner's equity will be overstated by $1,500 on the October 31 balance sheet.**

**Insurance.**    Most companies have fire and theft insurance on merchandise and equipment, personal liability insurance for accidents suffered by customers, and automobile insurance on company cars and trucks. The cost of insurance protection is determined by the payment of insurance premiums. The term and coverage are specified in the insurance policy. The minimum term is usually one year, but three- to five-year terms are available and offer lower annual premiums. Insurance premiums normally are charged to the asset account Prepaid Insurance when paid. At the financial statement date it is necessary to debit Insurance Expense and credit Prepaid Insurance for the cost that has expired during the period.

On October 4, Pioneer Advertising Agency paid $600 for a one-year fire insurance policy. The effective date of coverage was October 1. The premium was charged to Prepaid Insurance when it was paid, and this account shows a balance of $600 in the October 31 trial balance. An analysis of the policy reveals that $50 ($600 ÷ 12) of insurance expires each month. Thus, the following adjusting entry is made:

| Oct. 31 | Insurance Expense | 50 | |
| |    Prepaid Insurance | | 50 |
| |      (To record insurance expired) | | |

After the adjusting entry is posted, the accounts show:

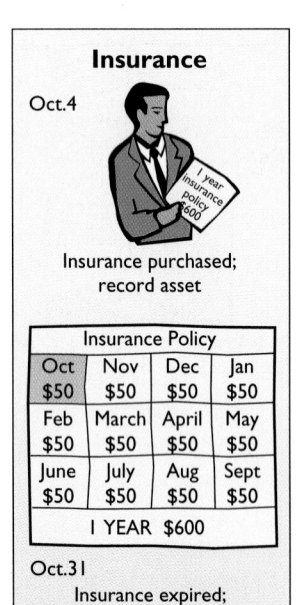

Insurance

Oct.4

Insurance purchased; record asset

| Insurance Policy | | | |
|---|---|---|---|
| Oct $50 | Nov $50 | Dec $50 | Jan $50 |
| Feb $50 | March $50 | April $50 | May $50 |
| June $50 | July $50 | Aug $50 | Sept $50 |
| I YEAR $600 | | | |

Oct.31

Insurance expired; record insurance expense

**Illustration 3-5**

*Insurance accounts after adjustment*

| Prepaid Insurance | | | | Insurance Expense | | |
|---|---|---|---|---|---|---|
| 10/4 | 600 | 10/31 Adj. | 50 | 10/31 Adj. | 50 | |
| 10/31 Bal. | 550 | | | | | |

The asset Prepaid Insurance shows a balance of $550, which represents the unexpired cost applicable to the remaining 11 months of coverage. At the same time, the balance in Insurance Expense is equal to the insurance cost that has expired in October. **If this adjustment is not made, October expenses will be understated by $50 and net income overstated by $50. Moreover, both assets and owner's equity also will be overstated by $50 on the October 31 balance sheet.**

**Depreciation.**   A business enterprise typically owns a variety of productive facilities such as buildings, equipment, and motor vehicles. These assets provide a service for a number of years. The term of service is commonly referred to as the useful life of the asset. Because an asset such as a building is expected to provide service for many years, it is recorded as an asset, rather than an expense, in the year it is acquired. As explained in Chapter 1, such assets are recorded at cost, as required by the cost principle.

According to the matching principle, a portion of the cost of a long-lived asset should be reported as an expense during each period of the asset's useful life. Depreciation is the process of allocating the cost of an asset to expense over its useful life in a rational and systematic manner.

***Need for Depreciation Adjustment.***   From an accounting standpoint, the acquisition of productive facilities is viewed essentially as a long-term prepayment for services. The need for making periodic adjusting entries for depreciation is, therefore, the same as described before for other prepaid expenses; that is, to recognize the cost that has expired (expense) during the period and to report the unexpired cost (asset) at the end of the period.

In determining the useful life of a productive facility, the primary causes of depreciation are actual use, deterioration due to the elements, and obsolescence. At the time an asset is acquired, the effects of these factors cannot be known with certainty, so they must be estimated. Thus, you should recognize that depreciation is an estimate rather than a factual measurement of the cost that has expired. A common procedure in computing depreciation expense is to divide the cost of the asset by its useful life. For example, if cost is $10,000 and useful life is expected to be 10 years, annual depreciation is $1,000.[1]

For Pioneer Advertising, depreciation on the office equipment is estimated to be $480 a year, or $40 per month. Accordingly, depreciation for October is recognized by the following adjusting entry:

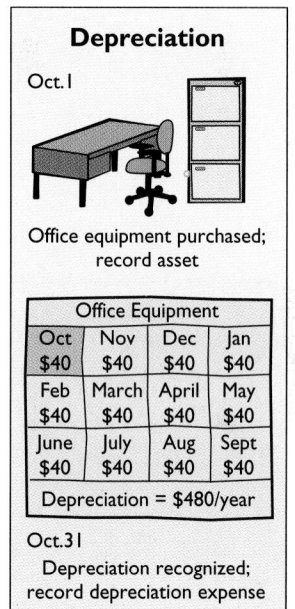

| Oct. 31 | Depreciation Expense | 40 | |
| | Accumulated Depreciation—Office Equipment | | 40 |
| | (To record monthly depreciation) | | |

After the adjusting entry is posted, the accounts show:

---

[1]Additional consideration is given to computing depreciation expense in Chapter 10.

The balance in the accumulated depreciation account will increase $40 each month. Therefore, after journalizing and posting the adjusting entry at November 30, the balance will be $80.

**Helpful hint**  All contra accounts have increases, decreases, and normal balances opposite to the account to which they relate.

**Statement Presentation.**    Accumulated Depreciation—Office Equipment is a contra asset account. A contra asset account is an account that is offset against an asset account on the balance sheet. This means that the accumulated depreciation account is offset against Office Equipment on the balance sheet and that its normal balance is a credit. This account is used instead of crediting Office Equipment in order to permit disclosure of **both the original cost** of the equipment **and the total cost that has expired to date**. In the balance sheet, Accumulated Depreciation—Office Equipment is deducted from the related asset account as follows:

**Illustration 3-7**

*Balance sheet presentation of accumulated depreciation*

| | | |
|---|---:|---:|
| Office equipment | $5,000 | |
| Less: Accumulated depreciation—office equipment | 40 | $4,960 |

The difference between the cost of any depreciable asset and its related accumulated depreciation is referred to as the book value of that asset. In Illustration 3-7, the book value of the equipment at the balance sheet date is $4,960. It is important to realize that the book value and the market value of the asset are generally two different values. The reason the two are different is that depreciation is not a matter of valuation but rather, a means of cost allocation.

Note also that depreciation expense identifies that portion of the asset's cost that has expired in October. As in the case of other prepaid adjustments, the omission of this adjusting entry would cause total assets, total owner's equity, and net income to be overstated and depreciation expense to be understated.

If additional equipment is involved, such as delivery or store equipment, or if the company has buildings, depreciation expense is recorded on each of these items. Related accumulated depreciation accounts also are established. These accumulated depreciation accounts would be described in the ledger as follows: Accumulated Depreciation—Delivery Equipment; Accumulated Depreciation—Store Equipment; and Accumulated Depreciation—Buildings.

### Unearned Revenues

As stated on page 91, revenues received in cash and recorded as liabilities before they are earned are called unearned revenues. Such items as rent, magazine subscriptions, and customer deposits for future service may result in unearned revenues. Airlines such as United, American, and Delta treat receipts from the sale of tickets as unearned revenue until the flight service is provided. Similarly, tuition received prior to the start of a semester, as in the opening story about Arizona State University, is considered to be unearned revenue. Unearned revenues are the opposite of prepaid expenses. Indeed, unearned revenue on the books of one company is likely to be a prepayment on the books of the company that has made the advance payment. For example, if identical accounting periods are assumed, a landlord will have unearned rent revenue when a tenant has prepaid rent.

When the payment is received for services to be provided in a future accounting period, an unearned revenue (a liability) account should be credited to recognize the obligation that exists. Unearned revenues are subsequently earned through rendering service to a customer. During the accounting period it may not be practical to make daily recurring entries as the revenue is earned. In such cases, the recognition of earned revenue is delayed until the adjustment process. Then an adjusting entry is made to record the revenue that has been earned and to show the liability that remains. **A liability–revenue account relationship therefore exists with unearned revenues.** In the typical case, liabilities are over-stated and revenues are understated prior to adjustment. Thus, **the adjusting entry for unearned revenues results in a debit (decrease) to a liability account and a credit (increase) to a revenue account.**

Pioneer Advertising Agency received $1,200 on October 2 from R. Knox for advertising services expected to be completed by December 31. The payment was credited to Unearned Fees, and this account shows a balance of $1,200 in the October 31 trial balance. When analysis reveals that $400 of those fees has been earned in October, the following adjusting entry is made:

**Unearned Revenues**

| Oct. 31 | Unearned Fees | 400 | |
| |    Fees Earned | | 400 |
| |      (To record fees earned) | | |

After the adjusting entry is posted, the accounts show:

| Unearned Fees | | | | | Fees Earned | | |
|---|---|---|---|---|---|---|---|
| 10/31 **Adj.** | 400 | 10/2 | 1,200 | | | 10/31 **Bal.** | 10,000 |
| | | 10/31 **Bal.** | 800 | | | 31 **Adj.** | 400 |

**Illustration 3-8**

*Fees accounts after prepayments adjustment*

The liability Unearned Fees now shows a balance of $800, which represents the remaining advertising services expected to be performed in the future. At the same time, Fees Earned shows total revenue earned in October of $10,400. **If this adjustment is not made, revenues and net income will be understated by $400 in the income statement. Moreover, liabilities will be overstated and owner's equity will be understated by $400 on the October 31 balance sheet.**

## Before You Go On . . .

### ▶ Review It

1. What are the four types of adjusting entries?
2. What is the effect on assets, owner's equity, expenses, and net income if a prepaid expense adjusting entry is not made?
3. What is the effect on liabilities, owner's equity, revenues, and net income if an unearned revenue adjusting entry is not made?

### ▶ Do It

The ledger of Hammond, Inc., on March 31, 1996, includes the following selected accounts before adjusting entries are prepared:

| | Debit | Credit |
|---|---|---|
| Prepaid Insurance | 3,600 | |
| Office Supplies | 2,800 | |
| Office Equipment | 25,000 | |
| Accumulated Depreciation—Office Equipment | | 5,000 |
| Unearned Fees | | 9,200 |

An analysis of the accounts shows the following:

1. Insurance expires at the rate of $100 per month.
2. Supplies on hand total $800.
3. The office equipment depreciates $200 a month.
4. One-half of the unearned fees were earned in March.

Prepare the adjusting entries for the month of March.

***Reasoning:*** In order for revenues to be recorded in the period in which they are earned, and for expenses to be recognized in the period in which they are incurred, adjusting entries are made at the end of the accounting period. Adjusting entries for prepayments are required at the statement date to record the portion of the prepayment that represents the expense incurred or the revenue earned in the current accounting period. The failure to adjust for the prepayment leads to overstatement of the asset or liability and a related understatement of the expense or revenue.

**Solution:**

| | | |
|---|---|---|
| 1. Insurance Expense | 100 | |
|    Prepaid Insurance | | 100 |
|       (To record insurance expired) | | |
| 2. Office Supplies Expense | 2,000 | |
|    Office Supplies | | 2,000 |
|       (To record supplies used) | | |
| 3. Depreciation Expense | 200 | |
|    Accumulated Depreciation | | 200 |
|       (To record monthly depreciation) | | |
| 4. Unearned Fees | 4,600 | |
|    Fees Earned | | 4,600 |
|       (To record fees earned) | | |

*Related exercise material:* BE3–3, BE3–4, BE3–5, BE3–6, E3–1, E3–2, E3–3, E3–4, E3–5, E3–6, E3–7, E3–8 and E3–9.

## Adjusting Entries for Accruals

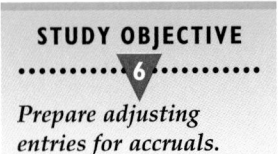

**STUDY OBJECTIVE**
••••••••• 6 •••••••••
*Prepare adjusting entries for accruals.*

The second category of adjusting entries is **accruals**. Adjusting entries for accruals are required to record revenues earned and expenses incurred in the current accounting period that have not been recognized through daily entries. If an accrual adjustment is needed, the revenue account (and the related asset account) and/or the expense account (and the related liability account) is understated. Thus, the adjusting entry for accruals will **increase both a balance sheet and an income statement account**. Adjusting entries for accruals are graphically depicted in Illustration 3-9.

### Accrued Revenues

As explained on page 91, revenues earned but not yet received in cash or recorded at the statement date are accrued revenues. Accrued revenues may accumulate (accrue) with the passing of time, as in the case of interest revenue and rent revenue. Or they may result from services that have been performed but neither billed nor collected, as in the case of commissions and fees. The former are unrecorded because the earning of interest and rent does not involve daily transactions; the latter may be unrecorded because only a portion of the total service has been provided.

An adjusting entry is required to show the receivable that exists at the balance sheet date and to record the revenue that has been earned during the period. **An asset-revenue account relationship exists with accrued revenues.** Prior to adjustment both assets and revenues are understated. Accordingly, **an adjusting**

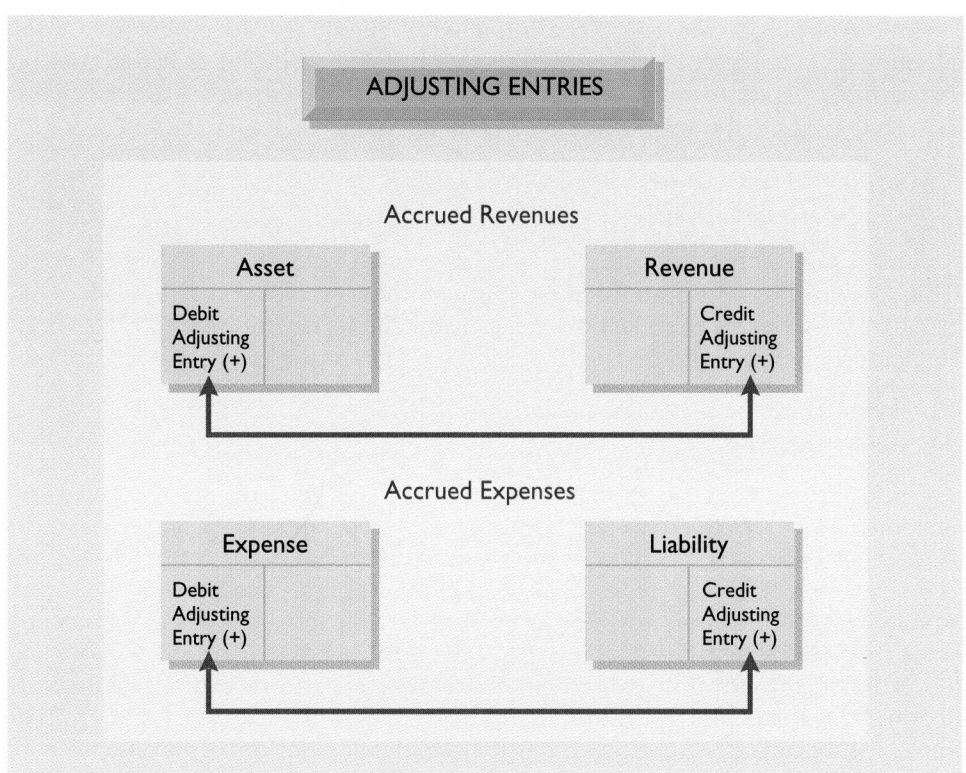

**Illustration 3-9**

*Adjusting entries for accruals*

**Helpful hint** For accruals, there may be no prior entry and the accounts requiring adjustment may both have zero balances prior to adjustment.

**entry for accrued revenues results in a debit (increase) to an asset account and a credit (increase) to a revenue account.**

In October Pioneer Advertising Agency earned $200 in fees for advertising services that were not billed to clients before October 31. Because these services have not been billed, they have not been recorded. Thus, the following adjusting entry is made:

| Oct. 31 | Accounts Receivable | 200 | |
| | Fees Earned | | 200 |
| | (To accrue fees earned but not billed or collected) | | |

After the adjusting entry is posted, the accounts show:

| Accounts Receivable | | | Fees Earned | | |
|---|---|---|---|---|---|
| 10/31 **Adj.** 200 | | | | 10/31 | 10,000 |
| | | | | 31 | 400 |
| | | | | 31 **Adj.** | 200 |
| | | | | 10/31 **Bal.** | 10,600 |

**Accrued Revenues**

Oct. 31

Revenue and receivable are recorded for unbilled services

Nov.

Cash is received; receivable is reduced

**Illustration 3-10**

*Receivable and revenue accounts after accrual adjustment*

The asset Accounts Receivable shows that $200 is owed by clients at the balance sheet date. The balance of $10,600 in Fees Earned represents the total fees earned during the month ($10,000 + $400 + $200). **If the adjusting entry is not made, assets and owner's equity on the balance sheet, and revenues and net income on the income statement, will all be understated.**

In the next accounting period, the clients will be billed. When this occurs, the entry to record the billing should recognize that $200 of fees earned in October have already been recorded in the October 31 adjusting entry. To illustrate, assume that bills totaling $3,000 are mailed to clients on November 10. Of this amount, $200 represents fees earned in October and recorded as Fees Earned in the October 31 adjusting entry. The remaining $2,800 represents fees earned in November. Thus, the following entry is made:

| Nov. 10 | Accounts Receivable | 2,800 | |
| | Fees Earned | | 2,800 |
| | (To record fees billed) | | |

This entry records the amount of fees earned between November 1 and November 10. The subsequent collection of fees from clients (including the $200 earned in October) will be recorded with a debit to Cash and a credit to Accounts Receivable.

### Accrued Expenses

As indicated on page 91, expenses incurred but not yet paid or recorded at the statement date are called accrued expenses. Interest, rent, taxes, and salaries can be accrued expenses. Accrued expenses result from the same causes as accrued revenues. In fact, an accrued expense on the books of one company is an accrued revenue to another company. For example, the $200 accrual of fees by Pioneer is an accrued expense to the client that received the service.

Adjustments for accrued expenses are necessary to record the obligations that exist at the balance sheet date and to recognize the expenses that apply to the current accounting period. **A liability–expense relationship exists with accrued expenses.** Prior to adjustment both liabilities and expenses are understated. Therefore, **the adjusting entry for accrued expenses results in a debit (increase) to an expense account and a credit (increase) to a liability account.**

**Accrued Interest.**   Pioneer Advertising Agency signed a 3-month note payable in the amount of $5,000 on October 1. The note requires interest at an annual rate of 12%. The amount of the interest accumulation is determined by three factors: (1) the face value of the note, (2) the interest rate, which is always expressed as an annual rate, and (3) the length of time the note is outstanding. In this instance, the total interest due on the $5,000 note at its due date 3 months hence is $150 ($5,000 $\times$ 12% $\times$ 3/12), or $50 for one month. The formula for computing interest and its application to Pioneer Advertising Agency for the month of October[2] are shown in Illustration 3-11.

**Helpful hint**  Interest is a cost of borrowing money that accumulates with the passage of time.

**Illustration 3-11**

*Formula for computing interest*

Note that the time period is expressed as a fraction of a year. The accrued expense adjusting entry at October 31 is as follows:

| Oct. 31 | Interest Expense | 50 | |
| | Interest Payable | | 50 |
| | (To accrue interest on notes payable) | | |

[2]The computation of interest will be considered in more depth in later chapters.

After this adjusting entry is posted, the accounts show:

| Interest Expense | | | Interest Payable | | |
|---|---|---|---|---|---|
| 10/31 | 50 | | | 10/31 | 50 |

**Illustration 3-12**

*Interest accounts after adjustment*

Interest Expense shows the interest charges applicable to the month of October. The amount of interest owed at the statement date is shown in Interest Payable. It will not be paid until the note comes due at the end of three months. The Interest Payable account is used instead of crediting Notes Payable to disclose the two types of obligations (interest and principal) in the accounts and statements. **If this adjusting entry is not made, liabilities and interest expense will be understated, and net income and owner's equity will be overstated.**

**Accrued Salaries.** Some types of expenses, such as employee salaries and commissions, are paid for after the services have been performed. At Pioneer Advertising, salaries were last paid on October 26; the next payment of salaries will not occur until November 9. As shown in the calendar below, three working days remain in October (October 29–31).

At October 31, the salaries for these days represent an accrued expense and a related liability to Pioneer Advertising. As explained on page 61, the employees receive total salaries of $2,000 for a five-day work week, or $400 per day. Thus, accrued salaries at October 31 are $1,200 ($400 × 3), and the adjusting entry is:

| Oct. 31 | Salaries Expense | | 1,200 | |
|---|---|---|---|---|
| | Salaries Payable | | | 1,200 |
| | (To record accrued salaries) | | | |

After this adjusting entry is posted, the accounts show:

| Salaries Expense | | | | Salaries Payable | | | |
|---|---|---|---|---|---|---|---|
| 10/26 | | 4,000 | | | 10/31 | Adj. | 1,200 |
| 31 | Adj. | 1,200 | | | | | |
| 10/31 | Bal. | 5,200 | | | | | |

**Illustration 3-13**

*Salary accounts after adjustment*

After this adjustment, the balance in Salaries Expense of $5,200 (13 days $\times$ $400) is the actual salary expense for October. The balance in Salaries Payable of $1,200 is the amount of the liability for salaries owed as of October 31. **If the $1,200 adjustment for salaries is not recorded, Pioneer's expenses will be understated $1,200, and its liabilities will be understated $1,200.**

At Pioneer Advertising, salaries are payable every two weeks. Consequently, the next payday is November 9, when total salaries of $4,000 will again be paid. The payment consists of $1,200 of salaries payable at October 31 plus $2,800 of salaries expense for November (7 working days as shown in the November calendar $\times$ $400). Therefore, the following entry is made on November 9:

| Nov. 9 | Salaries Payable | 1,200 | |
|---|---|---|---|
| | Salaries Expense | 2,800 | |
| |     Cash | | 4,000 |
| |       (To record November 9 payroll) | | |

This entry eliminates the liability for Salaries Payable that was recorded in the October 31 adjusting entry and records the proper amount of Salaries Expense for the period between November 1 and November 9.

## Before You Go On . . .

### ► Review It

1. What is the effect on assets, owner's equity, revenues, and net income if an accrued revenue adjusting entry is not made?
2. What is the effect on liabilities, owner's equity, and interest expense if an accrued expense adjusting entry is not made?

### ► Do It

Calvin and Hobbs are the new owners of Micro Computer Services. At the end of August 1996, their first month of ownership, Calvin and Hobbs are trying to prepare a monthly financial statement. The following information relates to August:

1. At August 31, Calvin and Hobbs owed their employees $800 in salaries that will be paid on September 1.
2. On August 1, Calvin and Hobbs borrowed $30,000 from a local bank on a 15-year mortgage. The annual interest rate is 10%.
3. Fees earned but unrecorded for August totaled $1,100.

Prepare the adjusting entries needed at August 31, 1996.

**Reasoning:** Adjusting entries for accruals are required to record revenues earned and expenses incurred in the current accounting period that have not been recognized through daily entries. An adjusting entry for accruals will increase both a balance sheet and an income statement account.

**Solution:**

| 1. Salaries Expense | 800 | |
|---|---|---|
|     Salaries Payable | | 800 |
|       (To record accrued salaries) | | |
| 2. Interest Expense | 250 | |
|     Interest Payable | | 250 |
|       (To record accrued interest) | | |
|       ($30,000 $\times$ 10% $\times$ 1/12 = $250) | | |
| 3. Accounts Receivable | 1,100 | |
|     Fees Earned | | 1,100 |
|       (To accrue fees earned but not billed or collected) | | |

*Related exercise material:* BE3–7, E3–1, E3–2, E3–3, E3–4, E3–5, E3–6, E3–7, E3–8, and E3–9.

## Summary of Basic Relationships

Pertinent data on each of the four basic types of adjusting entries are summarized in Illustration 3-14. Take some time to study and analyze the adjusting entries shown in the summary. Be sure to note that **each adjusting entry affects one balance sheet account and one income statement account**.

**Illustration 3-14**

*Summary of adjusting entries*

| Type of Adjustment | Account Relationship | Accounts before Adjustment | Adjusting Entry |
|---|---|---|---|
| 1. Prepaid expenses | Assets and expenses | Assets overstated Expenses understated | Dr. Expenses Cr. Assets |
| 2. Unearned revenues | Liabilities and revenues | Liabilities overstated Revenues understated | Dr. Liabilities Cr. Revenues |
| 3. Accrued revenues | Assets and revenues | Assets understated Revenues understated | Dr. Assets Cr. Revenues |
| 4. Accrued expenses | Expenses and liabilities | Expenses understated Liabilities understated | Dr. Expenses Cr. Liabilities |

**Helpful hint** (1) Remember that adjusting entries should not involve debits and credits to cash. (2) Evaluate whether the adjustment makes sense. For example, an adjustment to recognize supplies used should increase supplies expense. (3) Double-check all computations.

The journalizing and posting of adjusting entries for Pioneer Advertising Agency on October 31 are shown in Illustrations 3-15 and 3-16. All adjustments are identified in the ledger by the reference J2 because they are journalized on page 2 of the general journal. A center caption entitled Adjusting Entries may be inserted between the last transaction entry and the first adjusting entry to identify these entries. When reviewing the general ledger in Illustration 3-16, note that the adjustments are highlighted in color.

**Illustration 3-15**

*General journal showing adjusting entries*

| | GENERAL JOURNAL | | | J2 |
|---|---|---|---|---|
| Date | Account Titles and Explanation | Ref. | Debit | Credit |
| 1996 | Adjusting Entries | | | |
| Oct. 31 | Advertising Supplies Expense | 61 | 1,500 | |
| |    Advertising Supplies | 8 | | 1,500 |
| |    (To record supplies used) | | | |
| 31 | Insurance Expense | 63 | 50 | |
| |    Prepaid Insurance | 10 | | 50 |
| |    (To record insurance expired) | | | |
| 31 | Depreciation Expense | 65 | 40 | |
| |    Accumulated Depreciation—Office Equipment | 16 | | 40 |
| |    (To record monthly depreciation) | | | |
| 31 | Unearned Fees | 28 | 400 | |
| |    Fees Earned | 50 | | 400 |
| |    (To record fees earned) | | | |
| 31 | Accounts Receivable | 6 | 200 | |
| |    Fees Earned | 50 | | 200 |
| |    (To accrue fees earned but not billed or collected) | | | |
| 31 | Interest Expense | 64 | 50 | |
| |    Interest Payable | 27 | | 50 |
| |    (To accrue interest on notes payable) | | | |
| 31 | Salaries Expense | 60 | 1,200 | |
| |    Salaries Payable | 29 | | 1,200 |
| |    (To record accrued salaries) | | | |

**Illustration 3-16**

*General ledger after adjustment*

## GENERAL LEDGER

### Cash — No. 1

| Date | Explanation | Ref. | Debit | Credit | Balance |
|---|---|---|---|---|---|
| 1996 Oct. 1 | | J1 | 10,000 | | 10,000 |
| 2 | | J1 | 1,200 | | 11,200 |
| 3 | | J1 | | 900 | 10,300 |
| 4 | | J1 | | 600 | 9,700 |
| 20 | | J1 | | 500 | 9,200 |
| 26 | | J1 | | 4,000 | 5,200 |
| 31 | | J1 | 10,000 | | 15,200 |

### Accounts Receivable — No. 6

| Date | Explanation | Ref. | Debit | Credit | Balance |
|---|---|---|---|---|---|
| 1996 Oct. 31 | Adj. entry | J2 | 200 | | 200 |

### Advertising Supplies — No. 8

| Date | Explanation | Ref. | Debit | Credit | Balance |
|---|---|---|---|---|---|
| 1996 Oct. 5 | | J1 | 2,500 | | 2,500 |
| 31 | Adj. entry | J2 | | 1,500 | 1,000 |

### Prepaid Insurance — No. 10

| Date | Explanation | Ref. | Debit | Credit | Balance |
|---|---|---|---|---|---|
| 1996 Oct. 4 | | J1 | 600 | | 600 |
| 31 | Adj. entry | J2 | | 50 | 550 |

### Office Equipment — No. 15

| Date | Explanation | Ref. | Debit | Credit | Balance |
|---|---|---|---|---|---|
| 1996 Oct. 1 | | J1 | 5,000 | | 5,000 |

### Accumulated Depreciation—Office Equipment — No. 16

| Date | Explanation | Ref. | Debit | Credit | Balance |
|---|---|---|---|---|---|
| 1996 Oct. 31 | Adj. entry | J2 | | 40 | 40 |

### Notes Payable — No. 25

| Date | Explanation | Ref. | Debit | Credit | Balance |
|---|---|---|---|---|---|
| 1996 Oct. 1 | | J1 | | 5,000 | 5,000 |

### Accounts Payable — No. 26

| Date | Explanation | Ref. | Debit | Credit | Balance |
|---|---|---|---|---|---|
| 1996 Oct. 5 | | J1 | | 2,500 | 2,500 |

### Interest Payable — No. 27

| Date | Explanation | Ref. | Debit | Credit | Balance |
|---|---|---|---|---|---|
| 1996 Oct. 31 | Adj. entry | J2 | | 50 | 50 |

### Unearned Fees — No. 28

| Date | Explanation | Ref. | Debit | Credit | Balance |
|---|---|---|---|---|---|
| 1996 Oct. 2 | | J1 | | 1,200 | |
| 31 | Adj. entry | J2 | 400 | | 800 |

### Salaries Payable — No. 29

| Date | Explanation | Ref. | Debit | Credit | Balance |
|---|---|---|---|---|---|
| 1996 Oct. 31 | Adj. entry | J2 | | 1,200 | 1,200 |

### C. R. Byrd, Capital — No. 40

| Date | Explanation | Ref. | Debit | Credit | Balance |
|---|---|---|---|---|---|
| 1996 Oct. 1 | | J1 | | 10,000 | 10,000 |

### C. R. Byrd, Drawing — No. 41

| Date | Explanation | Ref. | Debit | Credit | Balance |
|---|---|---|---|---|---|
| 1996 Oct. 20 | | J1 | 500 | | 500 |

### Fees Earned — No. 50

| Date | Explanation | Ref. | Debit | Credit | Balance |
|---|---|---|---|---|---|
| 1996 Oct. 31 | | J1 | | 10,000 | 10,000 |
| 31 | Adj. entry | J2 | | 400 | 10,400 |
| 31 | Adj. entry | J2 | | 200 | 10,600 |

### Salaries Expense — No. 60

| Date | Explanation | Ref. | Debit | Credit | Balance |
|---|---|---|---|---|---|
| 1996 Oct. 26 | | J1 | 4,000 | | 4,000 |
| 31 | Adj. entry | J2 | 1,200 | | 5,200 |

### Advertising Supplies Expense — No. 61

| Date | Explanation | Ref. | Debit | Credit | Balance |
|---|---|---|---|---|---|
| 1996 Oct. 31 | Adj. entry | J2 | 1,500 | | 1,500 |

### Rent Expense — No. 62

| Date | Explanation | Ref. | Debit | Credit | Balance |
|---|---|---|---|---|---|
| 1996 Oct. 3 | | J1 | 900 | | 900 |

### Insurance Expense — No. 63

| Date | Explanation | Ref. | Debit | Credit | Balance |
|---|---|---|---|---|---|
| 1996 Oct. 31 | Adj. entry | J2 | 50 | | 50 |

### Interest Expense — No. 64

| Date | Explanation | Ref. | Debit | Credit | Balance |
|---|---|---|---|---|---|
| 1996 Oct. 31 | Adj. entry | J2 | 50 | | 50 |

### Depreciation Expense — No. 65

| Date | Explanation | Ref. | Debit | Credit | Balance |
|---|---|---|---|---|---|
| 1996 Oct. 31 | Adj. entry | J2 | 40 | | 40 |

# Preparing the Adjusted Trial Balance

After all adjusting entries have been journalized and posted, another trial balance is prepared from the ledger accounts. This trial balance is called an adjusted trial balance. It shows the balances of all accounts, including those that have been adjusted, at the end of the accounting period. The purpose of an adjusted trial balance is to **show the effects of all financial events that have occurred during the accounting period.** The procedures for preparing an adjusted trial balance are identical to those described in Chapter 2 for preparing a trial balance.

An adjusted trial balance proves the equality of the total debit balances and the total credit balances in the ledger after all adjustments have been made. The proof provided by an adjusted trial balance, like the proof contained in a trial balance, extends only to the mathematical accuracy of the ledger. Because the accounts contain all data that are needed for financial statements, the adjusted trial balance provides the primary basis for the preparation of financial statements.

The adjusted trial balance for Pioneer Advertising Agency presented in Illustration 3-17 has been prepared from the ledger accounts shown in Illustration 3-16. To facilitate the comparison of account balances before and after adjustment, the adjusted data are presented with the trial balance data shown in Illustration 3-2, on page 92. In addition, the amounts affected by the adjusting entries are highlighted in color in the After Adjustment columns.

**STUDY OBJECTIVE**

▼ 7

*Describe the nature and purpose of an adjusted trial balance.*

**Illustration 3-17**

*Trial balance and adjusted trial balance compared*

| PIONEER ADVERTISING AGENCY Trial Balances October 31, 1996 | | | | |
|---|---|---|---|---|
| | Before Adjustment | | After Adjustment | |
| | Dr. | Cr. | Dr. | Cr. |
| Cash | $15,200 | | $15,200 | |
| Accounts Receivable | | | 200 | |
| Advertising Supplies | 2,500 | | 1,000 | |
| Prepaid Insurance | 600 | | 550 | |
| Office Equipment | 5,000 | | 5,000 | |
| Accumulated Depreciation— Office Equipment | | | | $ 40 |
| Notes Payable | | $ 5,000 | | 5,000 |
| Accounts Payable | | 2,500 | | 2,500 |
| Interest Payable | | | | 50 |
| Unearned Fees | | 1,200 | | 800 |
| Salaries Payable | | | | 1,200 |
| C. R. Byrd, Capital | | 10,000 | | 10,000 |
| C. R. Byrd, Drawing | 500 | | 500 | |
| Fees Earned | | 10,000 | | 10,600 |
| Salaries Expense | 4,000 | | 5,200 | |
| Advertising Supplies Expense | | | 1,500 | |
| Rent Expense | | | 900 | |
| | 900 | | | |
| Insurance Expense | | | 50 | |
| Interest Expense | | | 50 | |
| Depreciation Expense | | | 40 | |
| | $28,700 | $28,700 | $30,190 | $30,190 |

## ▶Technology in Action

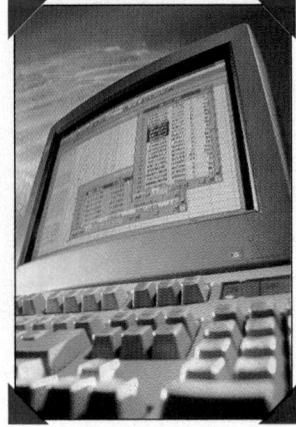

In many computer systems, the adjusting process is handled like any other transaction, with the accountant inputting the adjustment at the time required. The main difference between adjusting entries and regular transactions is that with adjusting entries, one part of the computer system may perform the required calculation for such items as depreciation or interest and then "feed" these figures to the journalizing process.

Such systems are also able to display information before and after changes were made. Management may be interested in such information to highlight the impact that adjustments have on the various accounts and financial statements.

## *P*reparing Financial Statements

**Financial statements can be prepared directly from an adjusted trial balance.**
The preparation of financial statements from the adjusted trial balance of Pioneer Advertising Agency and the interrelationship of data are presented in Illustrations 3-18 and 3-19. As shown in Illustration 3-18 the income statement is prepared from the revenue and expense accounts; the owner's equity statement is derived from the owner's capital and drawing accounts and the net income (or net loss) shown in the income statement. As shown in Illustration 3-19 the balance sheet is then prepared from the asset and liability accounts and the ending owner's capital balance as reported in the owner's equity statement.

**Illustration 3-18**

*Preparation of the income statement and owner's equity statement from the adjusted trial balance*

### PIONEER ADVERTISING AGENCY
### Adjusted Trial Balance
### October 31, 1996

| Account | Debit | Credit |
|---|---|---|
| Cash | $15,200 | |
| Accounts Receivable | 200 | |
| Advertising Supplies | 1,000 | |
| Prepaid Insurance | 550 | |
| Office Equipment | 5,000 | |
| Accumulated Depreciation— Office Equipment | | $ 40 |
| Notes Payable | | 5,000 |
| Accounts Payable | | 2,500 |
| Interest Payable | | 50 |
| Unearned Fees | | 800 |
| Salaries Payable | | 1,200 |
| C. R. Byrd, Capital | | 10,000 |
| C. R. Byrd, Drawing | 500 | |
| Fees Earned | | 10,600 |
| Salaries Expense | 5,200 | |
| Advertising Supplies Expense | 1,500 | |
| Rent Expense | 900 | |
| Insurance Expense | 50 | |
| Interest Expense | 50 | |
| Depreciation Expense | 40 | |
| | $30,190 | $30,190 |

### PIONEER ADVERTISING AGENCY
### Income Statement
### For the Month Ended October 31, 1996

| | | |
|---|---|---|
| Revenues | | |
| Fees earned | | $10,600 |
| Expenses | | |
| Salaries expense | $5,200 | |
| Advertising supplies expense | 1,500 | |
| Rent expense | 900 | |
| Insurance expense | 50 | |
| Interest expense | 50 | |
| Depreciation expense | 40 | |
| Total expenses | | 7,740 |
| Net Income | | $ 2,860 |

### PIONEER ADVERTISING AGENCY
### Owner's Equity Statement
### For the Month Ended October 31, 1996

| | | |
|---|---|---|
| C. R. Byrd; Capital, October 1 | | $  –0– |
| Add: Investments | | 10,000 |
| Net income | | 2,860 |
| | | 12,860 |
| Less: Drawings | | 500 |
| C. R. Byrd, Capital, October 31 | | $12,360 |

**Illustration 3-19**

*Preparation of the balance sheet from the adjusted trial balance*

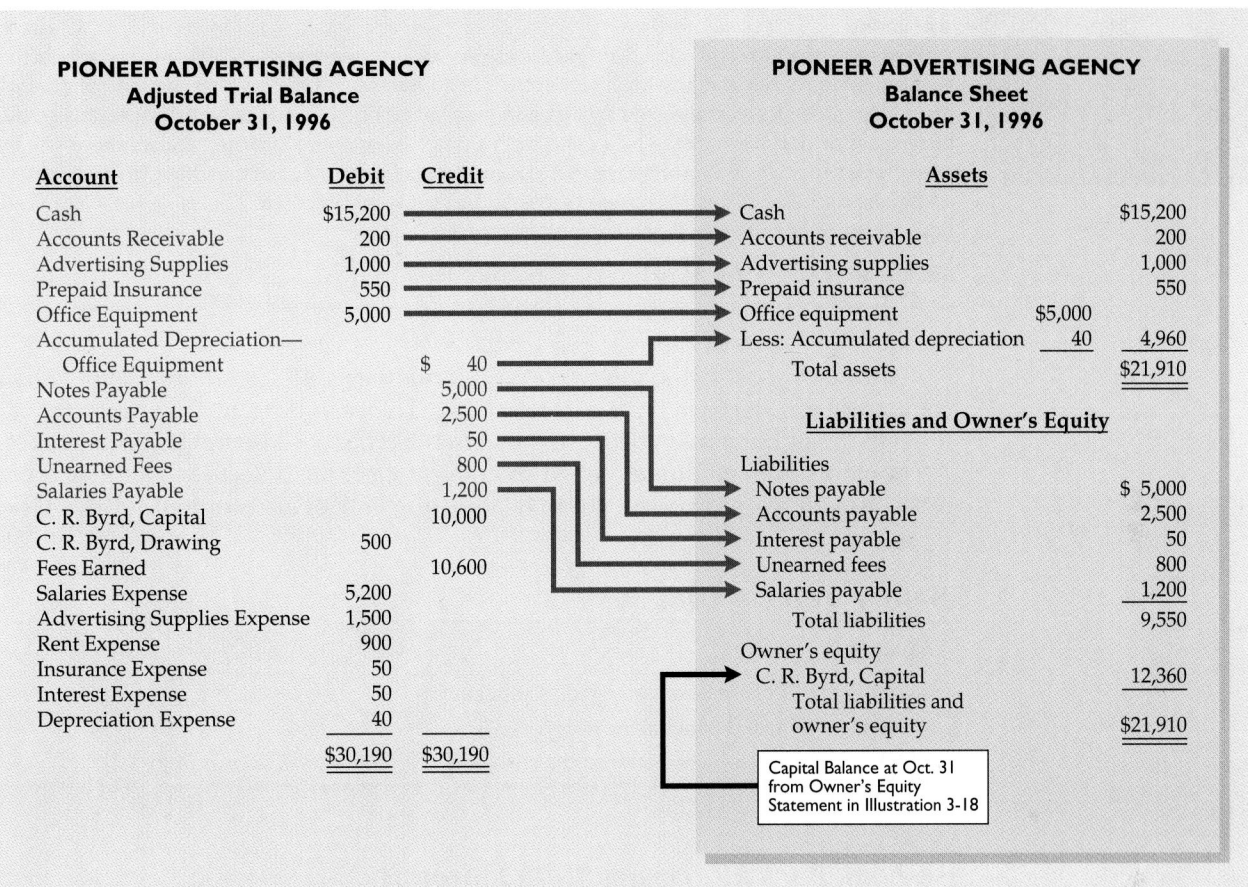

## Accrual vs. Cash Basis of Accounting

What you have learned in this chapter is the accrual basis of accounting. Accrual basis accounting means that transactions that change a company's financial statements are recorded **in the periods in which the events occur**, rather than in the periods in which the company receives or pays cash. For example, using the accrual basis to determine net income means recognizing revenues when earned rather than when the cash is received, and recognizing expenses when incurred rather than when paid. Information presented on an accrual basis reveals relationships that are likely to be important in predicting future results. To illustrate, under accrual accounting, revenues are generally recognized when services are performed so they can be related to the economic environment in which they occur. Trends in revenues are thus more meaningful for decision-making purposes.

Under cash basis accounting, revenue is recorded only when the cash is received, and an expense is recorded only when cash is paid. As a result, the cash basis of accounting often leads to misleading financial statements. For example, it fails to record revenue which has been earned but for which the cash has not been received, violating the revenue recognition principle. In addition, expenses are also not matched with earned revenues and therefore the matching principle is not followed. Therefore, **the cash basis of accounting is not in accordance with generally accepted accounting principles.**

**STUDY OBJECTIVE**

▼
**8**

*Explain the accrual basis of accounting.*

▶ *International note*

Although different accounting standards are often used in other major industrialized countries, the accrual basis of accounting is followed by all these countries.

## ▶Accounting in Action ▸ *Business Insight*

If you are upset about the billions of dollars of taxpayers' money that will be needed to make good on Uncle Sam's guarantees related to the savings and loan bailout, here's one thing you might do: Suggest that your congressional representatives learn accrual accounting.

Presently, the U.S. federal budget measures only cash transactions—how many dollar bills the government pays out and how many it receives in a given year. Let's say that the federal government guarantees loans made by a savings and loan. Since no cash outlay takes place initially, the budget deficit doesn't increase by a cent, even though everyone concerned knows there will be credit losses that Uncle Sam will have to make good. As a former head of the Office of Management and Budget noted, "loan guarantees are the budget's invisible Pacmen. You can't see them now, but sooner or later they will gobble up your money."

*Source:* Adapted from "Phony Bookkeeping," *Forbes*, May 1990.

Although most companies use the accrual basis of accounting, some small companies use the cash basis of accounting. The cash basis of accounting is justified by these businesses because they often have few receivables and payables. Accountants are sometimes asked to convert cash basis records to the accrual basis. As you might expect, extensive adjusting entries are required for this task.

## *Before You Go On . . .*

### ▶ *Review It*

1. What is the purpose of an adjusted trial balance?
2. How is an adjusted trial balance prepared?
3. What are the differences between the cash and accrual bases of accounting?

### ▸ *A Look Back at Arizona State University*

Refer to the opening story about Arizona State University, and answer the following questions.

1. What are the purposes of adjusting entries?
2. Why should Arizona State be concerned about the period in which revenue is recognized?
3. What adjusting entries should be made for tuition revenue and supplies expense at the end of the summer session?
4. What other types of adjusting entries do you believe Arizona State University might make?

*Solution:*

1. Adjusting entries are necessary to make the financial statements complete and accurate. Adjusting entries are made to record revenues in the period in which they are earned and to recognize expenses in the period in which they are incurred. Therefore, adjustments ensure that the revenue recognition and matching principles are followed.
2. As a not-for-profit institution Arizona State University must operate within its state appropriations and its own budget. It must know what revenues are attributable to each operating/accounting period. Assignment of revenues to the proper operating periods (namely, in the period earned) is necessary in order to make operating/accounting periods (years) comparable.
3. ASU probably used Unearned Tuition Revenue because tuition is generally received before the semester begins. The adjusting entry is debit Unearned Tuition Revenue

and credit Tuition Revenue. When supplies were purchased, ASU probably debited Supplies. The adjusting entry is a credit to Supplies and a debit to Supplies Expense.

4. (a) Accrued expenses: rent, salaries, utilities, interest.
   (b) Accrued revenues: unpaid tuition, lab fees, interest earned.
   (c) Prepaid expenses: insurance, depreciation.
   (d) Unearned revenues: tuition, lab fees, theatre tickets, athletic tickets.

# ▼ *Summary of Study Objectives*

**1.** *Explain the time period assumption.* The time period assumption assumes that the economic life of a business can be divided into artificial time periods.

**2.** *Distinguish between the revenue recognition principle and the matching principle.* The revenue recognition principle dictates that revenue be recognized in the accounting period in which it is earned. The matching principle dictates that expenses be recognized when they make their contribution to revenues.

**3.** *Explain why adjusting entries are needed.* Adjusting entries are made at the end of an accounting period. They ensure that revenues are recorded in the period in which they are earned and that expenses are recognized in the period in which they are incurred.

**4.** *Identify the major types of adjusting entries.* The major types of adjusting entries are prepaid expenses, unearned revenues, accrued revenues, and accrued expenses.

**5.** *Prepare adjusting entries for prepayments.* Prepayments are either prepaid expenses or unearned revenues. Adjusting entries for prepayments are required at the statement date to record the portion of the prepayment that represents the expense incurred or the revenue earned in the current accounting period.

**6.** *Prepare adjusting entries for accruals.* Accruals are either accrued revenues or accrued expenses. Adjusting entries for accruals are required to record revenues earned and expenses incurred in the current accounting period that have not been recognized through daily entries.

**7.** *Describe the nature and purpose of an adjusted trial balance.* An adjusted trial balance is a trial balance that shows the balances of all accounts, including those that have been adjusted, at the end of an accounting period. The purpose of an adjusted trial balance is to show the effects of all financial events that have occurred during the accounting period.

**8.** *Explain the accrual basis of accounting.* Accrual basis accounting means that events that change a company's financial statements are recorded in the periods in which the events occur, rather than in the periods in which the company receives or pays cash.

# ▼ *A*PPENDIX ▸ *Alternative Treatment of Prepaid Expenses and Unearned Revenues*

In our discussion of adjusting entries for prepaid expenses and unearned revenues, we illustrated transactions for which the initial entries were made to balance sheet accounts. That is, in the case of prepaid expenses, the prepayment was debited to an asset account, and in the case of unearned revenue, the cash received was credited to a liability account. Some businesses use an alternative treatment: (1) At the time an expense is prepaid, it is debited to an expense account; (2) at the time of a receipt for future services, it is credited to a revenue account. The circumstances that justify such entries and the different adjusting entries that may be required are described below. The alternative treatment of prepaid expenses and unearned revenues has the same effect on the financial statements as the procedures described in the chapter.

**STUDY OBJECTIVE**

▼

*After studying this appendix, you should be able to:*

9. *Prepare adjusting entries for the alternative treatment of prepayments.*

# Prepaid Expenses

Prepaid expenses become expired costs either through the passage of time, as in the case of insurance, or through consumption, as in the case of advertising supplies. If, at the time of purchase, the company expects to consume the supplies before the next financial statement date, **it may be more convenient initially to debit (increase) an expense account rather than an asset account**. Assume, for example, that Pioneer Advertising expects that all of the supplies purchased on October 5 will be used before October 31. A debit of $2,500 to Advertising Supplies Expense rather than to the asset account, Advertising Supplies, on October 5 will eliminate the need for an adjusting entry on October 31, if all the supplies are used. At October 31, the Advertising Supplies Expense account will show a balance of $2,500, which is equal to the cost of supplies used between October 5 and October 31.

Assume, however, that the company does not use all the supplies, and an inventory of $1,000 of advertising supplies remains on October 31. What then? Obviously, in such a case an adjusting entry is needed. Prior to adjustment, the expense account, Advertising Supplies Expense, is overstated $1,000, and the asset account, Advertising Supplies, is understated $1,000. Thus the following adjusting entry is made:

| Oct. 31 | Advertising Supplies | 1,000 | |
| |     Advertising Supplies Expense | | 1,000 |
| |       (To record supplies inventory) | | |

After posting the adjusting entry, the accounts show:

**Illustration 3A-1**

*Prepaid expenses accounts after adjustment*

| Advertising Supplies | | | |
|---|---|---|---|
| 10/31 Adj. | 1,000 | | |

| Advertising Supplies Expense | | | |
|---|---|---|---|
| 10/5 | 2,500 | 10/31 Adj. | 1,000 |
| 10/31 Bal. | 1,500 | | |

After adjustment, the asset account, Advertising Supplies, shows a balance of $1,000, which is equal to the cost of supplies on hand at October 31. In addition, Advertising Supplies Expense shows a balance of $1,500, which is equal to the cost of supplies used between October 5 and October 31. If the adjusting entry is not made, expenses will be overstated and net income will be understated by $1,000 in the October income statement. Moreover, both assets and owner's equity will be understated by $1,000 on the October 31 balance sheet.

A comparative summary of the entries and accounts for advertising supplies is shown in Illustration 3A-2.

**Illustration 3A-2**

*Adjustment approaches— a comparison*

| | Prepayment Initially Debited to Asset Account (per chapter) | | | | Prepayment Initially Debited to Expense Account (per appendix) | | |
|---|---|---|---|---|---|---|---|
| Oct. 5 | Advertising Supplies | 2,500 | | Oct. 5 | Advertising Supplies | | |
| |   Accounts Payable | | 2,500 | |     Expense | 2,500 | |
| | | | | |       Accounts Payable | | 2,500 |
| Oct. 31 | Advertising Supplies | | | Oct. 31 | Advertising Supplies | 1,000 | |
| |   Expense | 1,500 | | |     Advertising Supplies | | |
| |     Advertising Supplies | | 1,500 | |       Expense | | 1,000 |

After posting the entries, the accounts appear as follows:

|  | (per chapter) Advertising Supplies |  |  |  |  | (per appendix) Advertising Supplies |  |  |  |
|---|---|---|---|---|---|---|---|---|---|
| 10/5 | 2,500 | 10/31 | Adj. | 1,500 | 10/31 | Adj. | 1,000 |  |  |
| 10/31 Bal. | 1,000 |  |  |  |  |  |  |  |  |

| Advertising Supplies Expense |  |  |  | Advertising Supplies Expense |  |  |  |
|---|---|---|---|---|---|---|---|
| 10/31 Adj. | 1,500 |  |  | 10/5 | 2,500 | 10/31 Adj. | 1,000 |
|  |  |  |  | 10/31 Bal. | 1,500 |  |  |

Note that the account balances under each alternative are the same at October 31; that is, Advertising Supplies $1,000, and Advertising Supplies Expense $1,500.

# Unearned Revenues

Unearned revenues become earned either through the passage of time, as in the case of unearned rent, or through rendering the service, as in the case of unearned fees. Like prepaid expenses, a revenue account may be credited when cash is received for future services and a different adjusting entry may be necessary.

To illustrate, assume that when Pioneer Advertising received $1,200 in fees for future services on October 2 the services were expected to be performed before October 31.[3] In such a case, Fees Earned would be credited. If these fees are in fact earned before October 31, no adjustment is needed. However, if, at the statement date, $800 of the services have not been provided, an adjusting entry is required. Prior to adjustment, the revenue account, Fees Earned, is overstated $800, and the liability account, Unearned Fees, is understated $800. Thus, the following adjusting entry is made:

| Oct. 31 | Fees Earned |  | 800 |  |
|---|---|---|---|---|
|  | Unearned Fees |  |  | 800 |
|  | (To record unearned fees) |  |  |  |

After posting the adjusting entry, the accounts show:

| Unearned Fees |  |  |  | Fees Earned |  |  |  |
|---|---|---|---|---|---|---|---|
|  | 10/31 Adj. | 800 | 10/31 Adj. | 800 | 10/2 | 1,200 |  |
|  |  |  |  |  | 10/31 Bal. | 400 |  |

[3]This example focuses only on the alternative treatment of unearned revenues. In the interest of simplicity, the entries to Fees Earned pertaining to the immediate earning of fees ($10,000) and the adjusting entry for accrued fees ($200) have been ignored.

The liability account, Unearned Fees, shows a balance of $800, which is equal to the services that will be rendered in the future. In addition, the balance in Fees Earned equals the services rendered in October. If the adjusting entry is not made, both revenues and net income will be overstated by $800 in the October income statement. Moreover, liabilities will be understated by $800, and owner's equity will be overstated by $800 on the October 31 balance sheet.

A comparative summary of the entries and accounts for fees earned and unearned is presented in Illustration 3A-5:

**Illustration 3A-5**

*Adjustment approaches— a comparison*

| | Unearned Revenue Initially Credited to Liability Account (per chapter) | | | Unearned Revenue Initially Credited to Revenue Account (per appendix) | |
|---|---|---|---|---|---|
| Oct. 2 | Cash | 1,200 | Oct. 2 | Cash | 1,200 |
| | Unearned Fees | 1,200 | | Fees Earned | 1,200 |
| Oct. 31 | Unearned Fees | 400 | Oct. 31 | Fees Earned | 800 |
| | Fees Earned | 400 | | Unearned Fees | 800 |

After posting the entries, the accounts will show:

**Illustration 3A-6**

*Comparison of accounts*

| (per chapter) Unearned Fees | | | | | (per appendix) Unearned Fees | | |
|---|---|---|---|---|---|---|---|
| 10/31 Adj. | 400 | 10/2 | 1,200 | | | 10/31 Adj. | 800 |
| | | 10/31 Bal. | 800 | | | | |

| Fees Earned | | | | | Fees Earned | | |
|---|---|---|---|---|---|---|---|
| | | 10/31 Adj. | 400 | 10/31 Adj. | 800 | 10/2 | 1,200 |
| | | | | | | 10/31 Bal. | 400 |

Note that the balances in the accounts are the same under the two alternatives: Unearned Fees $800, and Fees Earned $400.

# **S**ummary of Additional Adjustment Relationships

The use of alternative adjusting entries requires additions to the summary of basic relationships presented earlier in Illustration 3-14. The additions are shown in color in Illustration 3A-7.

Alternative adjusting entries do not apply to accrued revenues and accrued expenses because **no entries occur before these types of adjusting entries are made**. Hence, the summary data shown in Illustration 3-14 for these two types of adjustments remains unchanged.

**Illustration 3A-7**

*Summary of basic relation-
ships for prepayments*

| Type of Adjustment | Account Relationship | Reason for Adjustment | Account Balances before Adjustment | Adjusting Entry |
|---|---|---|---|---|
| 1. Prepaid Expenses | Assets and Expenses | (a) Prepaid expenses initially recorded in asset accounts have been used. | Assets overstated Expenses understated | Dr. Expenses Cr. Assets |
| | | (b) Prepaid expenses initially recorded in expense accounts have not been used. | Assets understated Expenses overstated | Dr. Assets Cr. Expenses |
| 2. Unearned Revenues | Liabilities and Revenues | (a) Unearned revenues initially recorded in liability accounts have been earned. | Liabilities overstated Revenues understated | Dr. Liabilities Cr. Revenues |
| | | (b) Unearned revenues initially recorded in revenue accounts have not been earned. | Liabilities understated Revenues overstated | Dr. Revenues Cr. Liabilities |

# Summary of Study Objectives for Chapter 3 Appendix

**9. Prepare adjusting entries for the alternative treatment of prepayments.** When prepayments are initially recorded in expense and revenue accounts, these accounts are overstated prior to adjustment. The adjusting entries for prepaid expenses are a debit to an asset account and a credit to an expense account. Adjusting entries for unearned revenues are a debit to a revenue account and a credit to a liability account.

# GLOSSARY

**Accrual basis of accounting** Accounting basis in which transactions that change a company's financial statements are recorded in the periods in which the events occur, rather than in the periods in which the company receives or pays cash. (p. 107).

**Accrued expenses** Expenses incurred but not yet paid in cash or recorded. (p. 100).

**Accrued revenues** Revenues earned but not yet received in cash or recorded. (p. 98).

**Adjusted trial balance** A list of accounts and their balances after all adjustments have been made. (p. 105).

**Adjusting entries** Entries made at the end of an accounting period to ensure that the revenue recognition and matching principles are followed. (p. 91).

**Book value** The difference between the cost of a depreciable asset and its related accumulated depreciation. (p. 96).

**Calendar year** An accounting period that extends from January 1 to December 31. (p. 89).

**Cash basis accounting** Revenue is recorded only when

cash is received and an expense is recorded only when cash is paid. (p. 107).

**Contra asset account** An account that is offset against an asset account on the balance sheet. (p. 96).

**Depreciation** The process of allocating the cost of an asset to expense over its useful life in a rational and systematic manner. (p. 95).

**Fiscal year** An accounting period that is one year in length. (p. 89).

**Interim periods** Monthly or quarterly accounting time periods. (p. 89).

**Matching principle** The principle that efforts (expenses) be matched with accomplishments (revenues). (p. 90).

**Prepaid expenses** Expenses paid in cash and recorded as assets before they are used or consumed. (p. 92).

**Revenue recognition principle** The principle that revenue be recognized in the accounting period in which it is earned. (p. 89).

**Time period assumption**   An assumption that the economic life of a business can be divided into artificial time periods. (p. 89).

**Unearned revenues**   Revenues received in cash and recorded as liabilities before they are earned. (p. 96).

**Useful life**   The length of service of a productive facility. (p. 95).

---

# DEMONSTRATION PROBLEM

Terry Thomas opens the Green Thumb Lawn Care Company on April 1. At April 30, the trial balance shows the following balances for selected accounts:

| | |
|---|---:|
| Prepaid Insurance | $ 3,600 |
| Equipment | 28,000 |
| Notes Payable | 20,000 |
| Unearned Fees | 4,200 |
| Fees Earned | 1,800 |

Analysis reveals the following additional data pertaining to these accounts:

1. Prepaid insurance is the cost of a two-year insurance policy, effective April 1.
2. Depreciation on the equipment is $500 per month.
3. The note payable is dated April 1. It is a six-month, 12% note.
4. Seven customers paid for the company's six months' lawn service package of $600 beginning in April. These customers were serviced in April.
5. Lawn services rendered other customers but not billed at April 30 totaled $1,500.

*Instructions*
Prepare the adjusting entries for the month of April. Show computations.

## Solution to Demonstration Problem

**Problem-Solving Strategies**
1. Note that adjustments are being made for one month.
2. Make computations carefully.
3. Select account titles carefully.
4. Make sure debits are made first and credits are indented.
5. Check that debits equal credits for each entry.

**GENERAL JOURNAL**                                                J2

| Date | | Account Titles and Explanation | Ref. | Debit | Credit |
|---|---|---|---|---:|---:|
| | | *Adjusting Entries* | | | |
| Apr. | 30 | Insurance Expense | | 150 | |
| | |    Prepaid Insurance | | | 150 |
| | |    (To record insurance expired: | | | |
| | |    $3,600 ÷ 24 = $150 per month) | | | |
| | 30 | Depreciation Expense | | 500 | |
| | |    Accumulated Depreciation—Equipment | | | 500 |
| | |    (To record monthly depreciation) | | | |
| | 30 | Interest Expense | | 200 | |
| | |    Interest Payable | | | 200 |
| | |    (To accrue interest on notes payable: | | | |
| | |    $20,000 × 12% × 1/12 = $200) | | | |
| | 30 | Unearned Fees | | 700 | |
| | |    Fees Earned | | | 700 |
| | |    (To record fees earned: $600 ÷ 6 = $100; | | | |
| | |    $100 per month × 7 = $700) | | | |
| | 30 | Accounts Receivable | | 1,500 | |
| | |    Fees Earned | | | 1,500 |
| | |    (To accrue fees earned but not billed or | | | |
| | |    collected) | | | |

*Note:* All **asterisked** Questions, Exercises, and Problems relate to material contained in the Appendix to the chapter.

# SELF-STUDY QUESTIONS

Answers are at the end of the chapter.

(SO 1)  1. The time period assumption states that:
   a. revenue should be recognized in the accounting period in which it is earned.
   b. expenses should be matched with revenues.
   c. the economic life of a business can be divided into artificial time periods.
   d. the fiscal year should correspond with the calendar year.

(SO 2)  2. The principle which dictates that efforts (expenses) be matched with accomplishments (revenues) is the:
   a. matching principle.
   b. cost principle.
   c. periodicity principle.
   d. revenue recognition principle.

(SO 3)  3. Adjusting entries are made to ensure that:
   a. expenses are recognized in the period in which they are incurred.
   b. revenues are recorded in the period in which they are earned.
   c. balance sheet and income statement accounts have correct balances at the end of an accounting period.
   d. All of the above.

(SO 4)  4. Each of the following is a major type (or category) of adjusting entries *except*:
   a. prepaid expenses.
   b. accrued revenues.
   c. accrued expenses.
   d. earned revenues.

(SO 5)  5. The trial balance shows Supplies $1,350 and Supplies Expense $0. If $600 of supplies are on hand at the end of the period, the adjusting entry is:
   a. Supplies                600
          Supplies Expense          600
   b. Supplies            750
          Supplies Expense          750
   c. Supplies Expense    750
          Supplies                   750
   d. Supplies Expense    600
          Supplies                   600

(SO 5)  6. Adjustments for unearned revenues:
   a. decrease liabilities and increase revenues.
   b. have an assets and revenues account relationship.
   c. increase assets and increase revenues.
   d. decrease revenues and decrease assets.

(SO 6)  7. Adjustments for accrued revenues:
   a. have a liabilities and revenues account relationship.

   b. have an assets and revenues account relationship.
   c. decrease assets and revenues.
   d. decrease liabilities and increase revenues.

(SO 6)  8. Kathy Kiska earned a salary of $400 for the last week of September. She will be paid on October 1. The adjusting entry for Kathy's employer at September 30 is:
   a. No entry is required
   b. Salaries Expense          400
          Salaries Payable                 400
   c. Salaries Expense          400
          Cash                             400
   d. Salaries Payable          400
          Cash                             400

(SO 7)  9. Which of the following statements is *incorrect* concerning the adjusted trial balance?
   a. An adjusted trial balance proves the equality of the total debit balances and the total credit balances in the ledger after all adjustments are made.
   b. The adjusted trial balance provides the primary basis for the preparation of financial statements.
   c. The adjusted trial balance lists the account balances segregated by assets and liabilities.
   d. The adjusted trial balance is prepared after the adjusting entries have been journalized and posted.

(SO 8)  10. One of the following statements about the accrual basis of accounting is *false*. That statement is:
   a. Events that change a company's financial statements are recorded in the periods in which the events occur.
   b. Revenue is recognized in the period in which it is earned.
   c. This basis is in accord with generally accepted accounting principles.
   d. Revenue is recorded only when cash is received, and expense is recorded only when cash is paid.

(SO 9)  *11. The trial balance shows Supplies $0 and Supplies Expense $1,500. If $800 of supplies are on hand at the end of the period, the adjusting entry is:
   a. debit Supplies $800 and credit Supplies Expense $800.
   b. debit Supplies Expense $800 and credit Supplies $800.
   c. debit Supplies $700 and credit Supplies Expense $700.
   d. debit Supplies Expense $700 and credit Supplies $700.

# QUESTIONS

1. (a) How does the time period assumption affect an accountant's analysis of business transactions?
   (b) Explain the terms *fiscal year*, *calendar year*, and *interim periods*.

2. Identify and state two generally accepted accounting principles that relate to adjusting the accounts.

3. Tony Galego, a lawyer, accepts a legal engagement in March, performs the work in April, and is paid in May. If Connel's law firm prepares monthly financial statements, when should it recognize revenue from this engagement? Why?

4. In completing the engagement in (3) above, Galego incurs $2,000 of expenses in March, $2,500 in April, and none in May. How much expense should be deducted from revenues in the month the revenue is recognized? Why?

5. "Adjusting entries are required by the cost principle of accounting." Do you agree? Explain.

6. Why may a trial balance not contain up-to-date and complete financial information?

7. Distinguish between the two categories of adjusting entries and identify the types of adjustments applicable to each category.

8. What account relationship exists with prepaid expenses? What is the debit/credit effect of a prepaid expense adjusting entry?

9. "Depreciation is a process of valuation that results in the reporting of the fair market value of the asset." Do you agree? Explain.

10. Explain the differences between depreciation expense and accumulated depreciation.

11. Cher Company purchased equipment for $12,000. By the current balance sheet date, $7,000 had been depreciated. Indicate the balance sheet presentation of the data.

12. What account relationships exist with unearned revenues? What is the debit/credit effect of an unearned revenue adjusting entry?

13. A company fails to recognize revenue earned but not yet received. Which of the following accounts are involved in the adjusting entry: (a) asset, (b) liability, (c) revenue, or (d) expense? For the accounts selected, indicate whether they would be debited or credited in the entry.

14. A company fails to recognize an expense incurred but not paid. Indicate which of the following accounts is debited and which is credited in the adjusting entry: (a) asset, (b) liability, (c) revenue, or (d) expense.

15. A company makes an accrued revenue adjusting entry for $900 and an accrued expense adjusting entry for $600. How much was net income understated prior to these entries? Explain.

16. On January 9, a company pays $5,000 for salaries of which $1,700 was reported as Salaries Payable on December 31. Give the entry to record the payment.

17. For each of the following items before adjustment, indicate the type of adjusting entry (prepaid expense, unearned revenue, accrued revenue, and accrued expense) that is needed to correct the misstatement. If an item could result in more than one type of adjusting entry, indicate each of the types.
   (a) Assets are understated.
   (b) Liabilities are overstated.
   (c) Liabilities are understated.
   (d) Expenses are understated.
   (e) Assets are overstated.
   (f) Revenue is understated.

18. One half of the adjusting entry is given below. Indicate the account title for the other half of the entry.
   (a) Salaries Expense is debited.
   (b) Depreciation Expense is debited.
   (c) Interest Payable is credited.
   (d) Supplies is credited.
   (e) Accounts Receivable is debited.
   (f) Unearned Fees is debited.

19. "An adjusting entry may affect more than one balance sheet or income statement account." Do you agree? Why or why not?

20. Why is it possible to prepare financial statements directly from an adjusted trial balance?

21. Why do accrual basis financial statements provide more useful information than cash basis statements?

*22. The Alpha Company debits Supplies Expense for all purchases of supplies and credits Rent Revenue for all advanced rentals. For each type of adjustment, give the adjusting entry.

# BRIEF EXERCISES

*Indicate why adjusting entries are needed.*

(SO 3)

**BE3–1**  The ledger of the Lena Company includes the following accounts. Explain why each account may require adjustment.
   a. Prepaid Insurance          c. Unearned Fees
   b. Depreciation Expense      d. Interest Payable

**BE3–2** The Riko Company accumulates the following adjustment data at December 31. Indicate (a) the type of adjustment (prepaid expense, accrued revenues and so on), (b) the account relationships (asset/revenue, liability/expense, and so on), and (c) the accounts before adjustment (overstated or understated).

1. Supplies of $600 are on hand.
2. Fees earned but unbilled total $900.
3. Interest of $200 has accumulated on a note payable.
4. Rent collected in advance totaling $800 has been earned.

*Identify the major types of adjusting entries.*
*(SO 4)*

**BE3–3** The Sain Advertising Company's trial balance at December 31 shows Advertising Supplies $9,700 and Advertising Supplies Expense $0. On December 31, there are $1,500 of supplies on hand. Prepare the adjusting entry at December 31 and, using T accounts, enter the balances in the accounts, post the adjusting entry, and indicate the adjusted balance in each account.

*Prepare adjusting entry for supplies.*
*(SO 5)*

**BE3–4** At the end of its first year, the trial balance of the Shah Company shows Equipment $25,000 and zero balances in Accumulated Depreciation—Equipment and Depreciation Expense. Depreciation for the year is estimated to be $3,000. Prepare the the adjusting entry for depreciation at December 31, post the adjustments to T accounts, and indicate the balance sheet presentation of the equipment at December 31.

*Prepare adjusting entries for depreciation.*
*(SO 5)*

**BE3–5** On July 1, 1996, Bere Co. pays $15,000 to Marla Insurance Co. for a three-year insurance contract. Both companies have fiscal years ending December 31. For Bere Co. journalize and post the entry on July 1 and the adjusting entry on December 31.

*Prepare adjusting entries for prepaid expense.*
*(SO 5)*

**BE3–6** Using the data in BE3–5, journalize and post the entry on July 1 and the adjusting entry on December 31 for Marla Insurance Co. Marla uses the accounts Unearned Insurance Revenue and Insurance Revenue.

*Prepare adjusting entry for unearned revenue.*
*(SO 5)*

**BE3–7** The bookkeeper for the DeVoe Company asks you to prepare the following accrued adjusting entries at December 31.

1. Interest on notes payable of $400 is accrued.
2. Fees earned but unbilled total $1,400.
3. Salaries earned by employees of $700 have not been recorded.

Use the following account titles: Fees Earned, Accounts Receivable, Interest Expense, Interest Payable, Salaries Expense, and Salaries Payable.

*Prepare adjusting entries for accruals.*
*(SO 6)*

**BE3–8** The trial balance of the Hoi Company includes the following balance sheet accounts. Identify the accounts that require adjustment. For each account that requires adjustment, indicate (a) the type of adjusting entry (prepaid expenses, unearned revenues, accrued revenues, and accrued expenses) and (b) the related account in the adjusting entry.

*Analyze accounts in an adjusted trial balance.*
*(SO 7)*

| | |
|---|---|
| Accounts Receivable | Notes Payable |
| Prepaid Insurance | Interest Payable |
| Equipment | Unearned Fees |
| Accumulated Depreciation—Equipment | |

**BE3–9** The adjusted trial balance of the Lumas Company at December 31, 1996, includes the following accounts: T. Lumas, Capital $15,600; T. Lumas, Drawing $6,000; Fees Earned $35,400; Salaries Expense $13,000; Insurance Expense $2,000; Rent Expense $4,000; Supplies Expense $1,500; and Depreciation Expense $1,000. Prepare an income statement for the year.

*Prepare an income statement from an adjusted trial balance.*
*(SO 7)*

**BE3–10** Partial adjusted trial balance data for the Lumas Company is presented in BE3–9. The balance in T. Lumas, Capital is the balance as of January 1. Prepare an owner's equity statement for the year assuming net income is $14,000 for the year.

*Prepare an owner's equity statement from an adjusted trial balance.*
*(SO 7)*

**\*BE3–11** The Tower Company records all prepayments in income statement accounts. At April 30, the trial balance shows Supplies Expense $2,800, Fees Earned $9,200, and zero balances in related balance sheet accounts. Prepare the adjusting entries at April 30 assuming (a) $1,300 of supplies on hand and (b) $900 of the fees are unearned.

*Prepare adjusting entries under alternative treatment of prepayments.*
*(SO 9)*

# EXERCISES

························································································································

*Identify types of adjustments and account relationships.*
(SO 4, 5, 6, 7)

**E3–1**   The Rafael Company accumulates the following adjustment data at December 31.

1. Fees earned but unbilled total $600.
2. Store supplies of $300 have been used.
3. Utility expenses of $225 are unpaid.
4. Fees of $260 collected in advance have been earned.
5. Salaries of $800 are unpaid.
6. Prepaid insurance totaling $350 has expired.

**Instructions**
For each of the above items indicate:

(a) The type of adjustment (prepaid expense, unearned revenue, accrued revenue, or accrued expense).
(b) The account relationship (asset/revenue, liability/revenue, and so on).
(c) The accounts before adjustment (overstatement or understatement).

*Prepare adjusting entries from selected account data.*
(SO 5, 6, 7)

**E3–2**   The ledger of Easy Rental Agency on March 31 of the current year includes the following selected accounts before adjusting entries have been prepared.

|  | Debit | Credit |
|---|---|---|
| Prepaid Insurance | $ 3,600 | |
| Supplies | 2,800 | |
| Equipment | 25,000 | |
| Accumulated | | |
|    Depreciation—Equipment | | $ 8,400 |
| Notes Payable | | 20,000 |
| Unearned Rent Revenue | | 9,300 |
| Rent Revenue | | 60,000 |
| Interest Expense | –0– | |
| Wage Expense | 14,000 | |

An analysis of the accounts shows the following:

1. The equipment depreciates $500 per month.
2. One-third of the unearned rent was earned during the quarter.
3. Interest of $600 is accrued on the notes payable.
4. Supplies on hand total $850.
5. Insurance expires at the rate of $200 per month.

**Instructions**
Prepare the adjusting entries at March 31, assuming that adjusting entries are made quarterly. Additional accounts are: Depreciation Expense, Insurance Expense, Interest Payable, and Supplies Expense.

*Prepare adjusting entries.*
(SO 5, 6, 7)

**E3–3**   Kay Ong, D.D.S., opened a dental practice on January 1, 1996. During the first month of operations the following transactions occurred.

1. Performed services for patients who had dental plan insurance. At January 31, $750 of such services was earned but not yet billed to the insurance companies.
2. Utility expenses incurred but not paid prior to January 31 totaled $650.
3. Purchased dental equipment on January 1 for $80,000, paying $20,000 in cash and signing a $60,000, three-year-note payable. The equipment depreciates $400 per month. Interest is $600 per month.
4. Purchased a one-year malpractice insurance policy on January 1 for $12,000.
5. Purchased $1,800 of dental supplies. On January 31, determined that $500 of supplies were on hand.

**Instructions**
Prepare the adjusting entries on January 31. Account titles are: Accumulated Depreciation—Dental Equipment, Depreciation Expense, Fees Earned, Accounts Receivable, Insurance Expense, Interest Expense, Interest Payable, Prepaid Insurance, Supplies, Supplies Expense, Utilities Expense, and Utilities Payable.

**E3–4** The trial balance for the Pioneer Advertising Agency is shown in Illustration 3-2, p. 92. In lieu of the adjusting entries shown in the text at October 31, assume the following adjustment data:

1. Advertising supplies on hand at October 31 total $1,300.
2. Expired insurance for the month is $100.
3. Depreciation for the month is $50.
4. Unearned fees earned in October total $500.
5. Fees earned but unbilled at October 31 are $300.
6. Interest accrued at October 31 is $70.
7. Accrued salaries at October 31 are $1,600.

*Prepare adjusting entries.*
(SO 5, 6, 7)

**Instructions**
Prepare the adjusting entries for the items above.

**E3–5** The income statement of Weller Co. for the month of July shows net income of $1,400 based on Fees Earned $5,500, Wages Expense $2,300, Supplies Expense $1,200, and Utilities Expense $600. In reviewing the statement, you discover the following:

*Prepare correct income statement.*
(SO 2, 5, 6, 7)

1. Insurance expired during July of $300 was omitted.

   ...upplies that are still on hand at July 31.

   ...was omitted.

   ...l of $300 were not included.

   ...750.

...y.

...he Cordero Company at January 31, 1996, shows

*Analyze adjusted data*
(SO 2, 4, 5, 6, 7)

**...d Trial Balance**

| | Debit | Credit |
|---|---|---|
| | $ 800 | |
| | 2,400 | |
| | | 700 |
| | | 750 |
| | 950 | |
| | 400 | |
| | 1,800 | |
| | | 2,500 |

...the year begins January 1:

...s the January 31 adjusting entry, and $850 of sup-
...t was the balance in Supplies on January 1?
...is the January 31 adjusting entry, and the origi-
...year, what was the total premium and when was

...ary, what was the balance in Salaries Payable at

...ary for services performed in January, what was
...ember 31, 1995?

...pany are shown below:

*Journalize basic transactions and adjusting entries.*
(SO 5, 6, 7)

| Supplies | | | | Salaries Payable | |
|---|---|---|---|---|---|
| 7/1 Bal. | 1,100 | 7/31 | 400 | 7/31 | 1,200 |
| 7/10 | 300 | | | | |

| Accounts Receivable | | | | Unearned Fees | | | | |
|---|---|---|---|---|---|---|---|---|
| 7/31 | 500 | | | 7/31 | 800 | 7/1 | Bal. | 1,500 |
| | | | | | | 7/20 | | 700 |

| Salaries Expense | | | | Fees Earned | | |
|---|---|---|---|---|---|---|
| 7/15 | 1,200 | | | | 7/14 | 3,000 |
| 7/31 | 1,200 | | | | 7/31 | 800 |
| | | | | | 7/31 | 500 |

**Instructions**

After analyzing the accounts, journalize (a) the July transactions and (b) the adjusting entries that were made on July 31. (Hint: July transactions were for cash.)

*Prepare adjusting entries from analysis of trial balances.*
*(SO 5, 6, 7)*

**E3–8**  The trial balances before and after adjustment for the Apachi Company at the end of its fiscal year are presented below.

**APACHI COMPANY**
**Trial Balance**
**August 31, 1996**

| | Before Adjustment | | After Adjustment | |
|---|---|---|---|---|
| | Dr. | Cr. | Dr. | Cr. |
| Cash | $10,400 | | $10,400 | |
| Accounts Receivable | 8,800 | | 9,500 | |
| Office Supplies | 2,300 | | 700 | |
| Prepaid Insurance | 4,000 | | 2,500 | |
| Office Equipment | 14,000 | | 14,000 | |
| Accumulated Depreciation—Office Equipment | | $ 3,600 | | $ 4,800 |
| Accounts Payable | | 5,800 | | 5,800 |
| Salaries Payable | | –0– | | 1,000 |
| Unearned Rent Revenue | | 1,500 | | 700 |
| R. Roni, Capital | | 15,600 | | 15,600 |
| Fees Earned | | 34,000 | | 34,700 |
| Rent Revenue | | 11,000 | | 11,800 |
| Salaries Expense | 17,000 | | 18,000 | |
| Office Supplies Expense | –0– | | 1,600 | |
| Rent Expense | 15,000 | | 15,000 | |
| Insurance Expense | –0– | | 1,500 | |
| Depreciation Expense | –0– | | 1,200 | |
| | $71,500 | $71,500 | $74,400 | $74,400 |

**Instructions**

Prepare the adjusting entries that were made.

*Prepare financial statements from adjusted trial balance.*
*(SO 5, 6, 7)*

**E3–9**  The adjusted trial balance for the Apachi Company is given in E3–8.

**Instructions**

Prepare the income and owner's equity statements for the year and the balance sheet at August 31.

*Distinguish between cash and accrual basis of accounting.*
*(SO 8)*

**E3–10**  On numerous occasions proposals have surfaced to put the federal government on the accrual basis of accounting. This is no small issue because if this basis were used, it would mean that billions in unrecorded liabilities would have to be booked and the federal deficit would increase substantially.

**Instructions** ▯▭▭▶

(a) What is the difference between accrual basis accounting and cash basis accounting?
(b) Comment on why politicians prefer a cash basis accounting system over an accrual basis system.
(c) Write a letter to your senator explaining why you think the federal government should adopt the accrual basis of accounting.

**\*E3–11**  At the Devereaux Company, prepayments are debited to expense when paid and unearned revenues are credited to revenue when received. During January of the current year, the following transactions occurred:

*Journalize transactions and adjusting entries using appendix.*
*(SO 9)*

Jan.  2  Paid $3,600 for fire insurance protection for the year.
  10  Paid $1,700 for supplies.
  15  Received $5,100 in fees for services to be performed in the future.

On January 31, it is determined that $1,200 of the services fees have been earned and that there are $800 of supplies on hand.

**Instructions**
  (a) Journalize and post the January transactions. (Use T accounts.)
  (b) Journalize and post the adjusting entries at January 31.
  (c) Determine the ending balance in each of the accounts.

# PROBLEMS

**P3–1**  The trial balance before adjustment of Scenic Tours at the end of its first month of operations is presented below:

*Prepare adjusting entries, post, and prepare an adjusted trial balance.*
*(SO 5, 6, 7)*

**SCENIC TOURS**
**Trial Balance**
**June 30, 1996**

|  | Debit | Credit |
|---|---|---|
| Cash | $    3,000 | |
| Prepaid Insurance | 7,200 | |
| Office Equipment | 1,800 | |
| Buses | 140,000 | |
| Notes Payable | | $ 62,000 |
| Unearned Fees | | 15,000 |
| Eldon Kaplan, Capital | | 70,000 |
| Fees Earned | | 15,900 |
| Salaries Expense | 9,000 | |
| Advertising Expense | 800 | |
| Gas and Oil Expense | 1,100 | |
| | $162,900 | $162,900 |

Other data:

  1. The insurance policy has a one-year term beginning June 1, 1996.
  2. The monthly depreciation is $50 on office equipment and $2,000 on buses.
  3. Interest of $700 accrues on the notes payable each month.
  4. Deposits of $1,500 each were received for advanced tour reservations from 10 school groups. At June 30, three of these deposits have been earned.
  5. Bus drivers are paid a combined total of $400 per day. At June 30, 3 days' salaries are unpaid.
  6. A senior citizen's organization that had not made an advance deposit took a Canyon tour on June 30 for $1,200. This group was not billed for the services rendered until July 3.

**Instructions**
  (a) Journalize the adjusting entries at June 30, 1996.
  (b) Prepare a ledger using the three-column form of account. Enter the trial balance amounts and post the adjusting entries. (Use J2 as the posting reference.)
  (c) Prepare an adjusted trial balance at June 30, 1996.

*Prepare adjusting entries,*
*adjusted trial balance, and*
*financial statements.*
(SO 5, 6, 7)

**P3–2**  The River Run Motel opened for business on May 1, 1996. Its trial balance before adjustment on May 31 is as follows:

**RIVER RUN MOTEL**
**Trial Balance**
**May 31, 1996**

|  | Debit | Credit |
|---|---|---|
| Cash | $ 2,500 | |
| Prepaid Insurance | 1,800 | |
| Supplies | 1,900 | |
| Land | 15,000 | |
| Lodge | 70,000 | |
| Furniture | 16,800 | |
| Accounts Payable | | $ 4,700 |
| Unearned Rent Revenue | | 3,600 |
| Mortgage Payable | | 35,000 |
| Carla Damon, Capital | | 60,000 |
| Rent Revenue | | 9,200 |
| Salaries Expense | 3,000 | |
| Utilities Expense | 1,000 | |
| Advertising Expense | 500 | |
| | $112,500 | $112,500 |

Other data:

1. Insurance expires at the rate of $200 per month.
2. An inventory of supplies shows $1,350 of unused supplies on May 31.
3. Annual depreciation is $3,600 on the lodge and $3,000 on furniture.
4. The mortgage interest rate is 12%. (The mortgage was taken out on May 1.)
5. Unearned rent of $1,500 has been earned.
6. Salaries of $300 are accrued and unpaid at May 31.

*Instructions*
(a) Journalize the adjusting entries on May 31.
(b) Prepare a ledger using the three-column form of account. Enter the trial balance amounts and post the adjusting entries. (Use J1 as the posting reference.)
(c) Prepare an adjusted trial balance on May 31.
(d) Prepare an income statement and an owner's equity statement for the month of May and a balance sheet at May 31.

*Prepare adjusting entries and*
*financial statements.*
(SO 5, 6, 7)

**P3–3**  The Ozaki Co. was organized on July 1, 1996. Quarterly financial statements are prepared. The trial balance and adjusted trial balance on September 30 are shown below.

| | Trial Balance | | Adjusted Trial Balance | |
|---|---|---|---|---|
| | **Dr.** | **Cr.** | **Dr.** | **Cr.** |
| Cash | $ 6,700 | | $ 6,700 | |
| Accounts Receivable | 400 | | 800 | |
| Prepaid Rent | 1,500 | | 900 | |
| Supplies | 1,200 | | 1,000 | |
| Equipment | 15,000 | | 15,000 | |
| Accumulated Depreciation—Equipment | | | | $ 350 |
| Notes Payable | | $ 5,000 | | 5,000 |
| Accounts Payable | | 1,510 | | 1,510 |
| Salaries Payable | | | | 600 |
| Interest Payable | | | | 50 |
| Unearned Rent Revenue | | 900 | | 600 |
| Aoko Ozaki, Capital | | 14,000 | | 14,000 |
| Aoko Ozaki, Drawing | 600 | | 600 | |
| Commission Revenue | | 14,000 | | 14,400 |

| | | 400 | | 700 |
|---|---|---|---|---|
| Rent Revenue | | | | |
| Salaries Expense | 9,000 | | 9,600 | |
| Rent Expense | 900 | | 1,500 | |
| Depreciation Expense | | | 350 | |
| Supplies Expense | | | 200 | |
| Utilities Expense | 510 | | 510 | |
| Interest Expense | | | 50 | |
| | $35,810 | $35,810 | $37,210 | $37,210 |

**Instructions**
(a) Journalize the adjusting entries that were made.
(b) Prepare an income statement and an owner's equity statement for the 3 months ending September 30 and a balance sheet at September 30.
(c) If the note bears interest at 12%, how many months has it been outstanding?

**P3–4** A review of the ledger of the Montana Company at December 31, 1996, produces the following data pertaining to the preparation of annual adjusting entries:

*Prepare adjusting entries.*
*(SO 5, 6)*

1. Prepaid Insurance $12,800. The company has separate insurance policies on its buildings and its motor vehicles. Policy B4564 on the building was purchased on July 1, 1995, for $9,600. The policy has a term of 3 years. Policy A2958 on the vehicles was purchased on January 1, 1996, for $4,800. This policy has a term of 2 years.
2. Unearned Subscription Revenue $49,000. The company began selling magazine subscriptions in 1996 on an annual basis. The selling price of a subscription is $50. A review of subscription contracts reveals the following:

| Subscription Date | Number of Subscriptions |
|---|---|
| October 1 | 200 |
| November 1 | 300 |
| December 1 | 480 |
| | 980 |

3. Notes Payable, $50,000. This balance consists of a note for 6 months at an annual interest rate of 9%, dated September 1.
4. Salaries Payable $0. There are eight salaried employees. Salaries are paid every Friday for the current week. Five employees receive a salary of $600 each per week, and three employees earn $700 each per week. December 31 is a Wednesday. Employees do not work weekends. All employees worked the last 3 days of December.

**Instructions**
Prepare the adjusting entries at December 31, 1996.

**P3–5** On November 1, 1996, the account balances of Alou Equipment Repair were as follows:

*Journalize transactions and follow through accounting cycle to preparation of financial statements.*
*(SO 5, 6, 7)*

| No. | Debits | | No. | Credits | |
|---|---|---|---|---|---|
| 101 | Cash | $ 2,790 | 154 | Accumulated Depreciation | $ 500 |
| 112 | Accounts Receivable | 2,510 | 201 | Accounts Payable | 2,100 |
| 126 | Supplies | 1,000 | 209 | Unearned Service Revenue | 400 |
| 153 | Store Equipment | 10,000 | 212 | Salaries Payable | 500 |
| | | | 301 | R. Alou, Capital | 12,800 |
| | | $16,300 | | | $16,300 |

During November the following summary transactions were completed.

Nov. 8 Paid $1,100 for salaries due employees, of which $600 is for November.
10 Received $1,200 cash from customers on account.
12 Received $1,400 cash for services performed in November.
15 Purchased store equipment on account $3,000.
17 Purchased supplies on account $1,500.
20 Paid creditors on account $2,500.
22 Paid November rent $300.

25  Paid salaries $1,000.

27  Performed services on account and billed customers for services rendered $700.

29  Received $550 from customers for future service.

Adjustment data consist of:

1.  Supplies on hand $1,600.
2.  Accrued salaries payable $500.
3.  Depreciation for the month is $120.
4.  Unearned service revenue of $300 is earned.

**Instructions**

(a)  Enter the November 1 balances in the ledger accounts.

(b)  Journalize the November transactions.

(c)  Post to the ledger accounts. Use J1 for posting reference and No. 407 Service Revenue, No. 615 Depreciation Expense, No. 631 Supplies Expense, No. 726 Salaries Expense, and No. 729 Rent Expense.

(d)  Prepare a trial balance at November 30.

(e)  Journalize and post adjusting entries.

(f)  Prepare an adjusted trial balance.

(g)  Prepare an income statement and an owner's equity statement for November and a balance sheet at November 30.

*Prepare adjusting entries, adjusted trial balance, and financial statements using appendix.*
*(SO 5, 6, 7, 9)*

*P3-6  The Global Graphics Company was organized on January 1, 1996, by Nancy Glover. At the end of the first 6 months of operations, the trial balance contained the following accounts:

| **Debits** | | **Credits** | |
|---|---|---|---|
| Cash | $  9,500 | Notes Payable | $ 17,000 |
| Accounts Receivable | 14,000 | Accounts Payable | 9,000 |
| Equipment | 45,000 | Nancy Glover, Capital | 25,000 |
| Insurance Expense | 1,800 | Graphic Fees Earned | 52,100 |
| Salaries Expense | 30,000 | Consulting Fees Earned | 5,000 |
| Supplies Expense | 2,700 | | |
| Advertising Expense | 1,900 | | |
| Rent Expense | 1,500 | | |
| Utilities Expense | 1,700 | | |
| | $108,100 | | $108,100 |

Analysis reveals the following additional data:

1.  The $2,700 balance in Supplies Expense represents supplies purchased in January. At June 30, there was $1,500 of supplies on hand.
2.  The note payable was issued on February 1. It is a 12%, 6-month note.
3.  The balance in Insurance Expense is the premium on a one-year policy, dated March 1, 1996.
4.  Consulting fees are credited to revenue when received. At June 30, consulting fees of $1,000 are unearned.
5.  Graphic fees earned but unbilled at June 30 total $2,000.
6.  Depreciation is $2,000 per year.

**Instructions**

(a)  Journalize the adjusting entries at June 30 (assume adjustments are recorded every 6 months).

(b)  Prepare an adjusted trial balance.

(c)  Prepare an income statement and owner's equity statement for the 6 months ended June 30 and a balance sheet at June 30.

# ALTERNATE PROBLEMS

*Prepare adjusting entries, post, and prepare an adjusted trial balance.*
*(SO 5, 6, 7)*

P3-1A  The Ortega Security Service began operations on January 1, 1996. At the end of the first year of operations, the trial balance before adjustment shows the following:

**ORTEGA SECURITY SERVICE**
**Trial Balance**
**December 31, 1996**

|  | Debit | Credit |
|---|---|---|
| Cash | $ 12,400 |  |
| Accounts Receivable | 3,200 |  |
| Prepaid Insurance | 3,600 |  |
| Automobiles | 58,000 |  |
| Notes Payable |  | $ 45,000 |
| Unearned Fees |  | 2,500 |
| C. Ortega, Capital |  | 18,000 |
| Fees Earned |  | 84,000 |
| Salaries Expense | 57,000 |  |
| Repairs Expense | 6,000 |  |
| Gas and Oil Expense | 9,300 |  |
|  | $149,500 | $149,500 |

Other data:

1. Fees earned but unbilled $1,500 at December 31.
2. Insurance coverage began on January 1 under a 2-year policy.
3. Automobile depreciation is $15,000 for the year.
4. Interest of $5,400 accrued on notes payable for the year.
5. $1,000 of the unearned fees has been earned.
6. Drivers' salaries total $500 per day. At December 31, 4 days' salaries are unpaid.
7. Repairs to automobiles of $650 have been incurred, but bills have not been received prior to December 31. (Use Accounts Payable.)

*Instructions*
(a) Journalize the annual adjusting entries at December 31, 1996.
(b) Prepare a ledger using the three-column account form. Enter the trial balance amounts and post the adjusting entries. (Use J15 as the posting reference.)
(c) Prepare an adjusted trial balance at December 31, 1996.

**P3–2A** The Highland Cove Resort opened for business on June 1 with eight air-conditioned units. Its trial balance before adjustment on August 31 is as follows:

*Prepare adjusting entries, adjusted trial balance, and financial statements.*
*(SO 5, 6, 7)*

**HIGHLAND COVE RESORT**
**Trial Balance**
**August 31, 1996**

|  | Debit | Credit |
|---|---|---|
| Cash | $ 19,600 |  |
| Prepaid Insurance | 5,400 |  |
| Supplies | 3,300 |  |
| Land | 25,000 |  |
| Cottages | 125,000 |  |
| Furniture | 26,000 |  |
| Accounts Payable |  | $ 6,500 |
| Unearned Rent Revenue |  | 6,800 |
| Mortgage Payable |  | 80,000 |
| Tina Leone, Capital |  | 100,000 |
| Tina Leone, Drawing | 5,000 |  |
| Rent Revenue |  | 80,000 |
| Salaries Expense | 51,000 |  |
| Utilities Expense | 9,400 |  |
| Repair Expense | 3,600 |  |
|  | $273,300 | $273,300 |

Other data:

1. Insurance expires at the rate of $300 per month.

2. An inventory count on August 31 shows $700 of supplies on hand.
3. Annual depreciation is $4,800 on cottages and $2,400 on furniture.
4. Unearned rent of $5,000 was earned prior to August 31.
5. Salaries of $400 were unpaid at August 31.
6. Rentals of $800 were due from tenants at August 31. (Use Accounts Receivable.)
7. The mortgage interest rate is 12% per year. (The mortgage was taken out on August 1.)

**Instructions**
(a) Journalize the adjusting entries on August 31 for the 3-month period June 1–August 31.
(b) Prepare a ledger using the three-column form of account. Enter the trial balance amounts and post the adjusting entries. (Use J1 as the posting reference.)
(c) Prepare an adjusted trial balance on August 31.
(d) Prepare an income statement and an owner's equity statement for the 3 months ending August 31 and a balance sheet as of August 31.

*Prepare adjusting entries and financial statements.*
*(SO 5, 6, 7)*

**P3–3A**   The Grant Advertising Agency was founded by Thomas Grant in January of 1992. Presented below are both the adjusted and unadjusted trial balances as of December 31, 1996.

### GRANT ADVERTISING AGENCY
### Trial Balance
### December 31, 1996

|  | Unadjusted | | Adjusted | |
| --- | --- | --- | --- | --- |
|  | Dr. | Cr. | Dr. | Cr. |
| Cash | $ 11,000 |  | $ 11,000 |  |
| Accounts Receivable | 20,000 |  | 21,000 |  |
| Art Supplies | 8,400 |  | 5,000 |  |
| Prepaid Insurance | 3,350 |  | 2,500 |  |
| Printing Equipment | 60,000 |  | 60,000 |  |
| Accumulated Depreciation |  | $ 28,000 |  | $ 35,000 |
| Accounts Payable |  | 5,000 |  | 5,000 |
| Interest Payable |  | 0 |  | 150 |
| Notes Payable |  | 5,000 |  | 5,000 |
| Unearned Advertising Revenue |  | 7,000 |  | 5,600 |
| Salaries Payable |  | 0 |  | 1,800 |
| T. Grant, Capital |  | 25,500 |  | 25,500 |
| T. Grant, Drawing | 12,000 |  | 12,000 |  |
| Advertising Revenue |  | 58,600 |  | 61,000 |
| Salaries Expense | 10,000 |  | 11,800 |  |
| Insurance Expense |  |  | 850 |  |
| Interest Expense | 350 |  | 500 |  |
| Depreciation Expense |  |  | 7,000 |  |
| Art Supplies Expense |  |  | 3,400 |  |
| Rent Expense | 4,000 |  | 4,000 |  |
|  | $129,100 | $129,100 | $139,050 | $139,050 |

**Instructions**
(a) Journalize the annual adjusting entries that were made.
(b) Prepare an income statement and a statement of owner's equity for the year ending December 31, 1996, and a balance sheet at December 31.
(c) Answer the following questions:
  (1) If the note has been outstanding 3 months, what is the annual interest rate on that note?
  (2) If the company paid $13,500 in salaries in 1996, what was the balance in Salaries Payable on December 31, 1995?

*Prepare adjusting entries.*
*(SO 5, 6)*

**P3–4A**   A review of the ledger of Greenberg Company at December 31, 1996, produces the following data pertaining to the preparation of annual adjusting entries.

1. Salaries Payable $0. There are eight salaried employees. Salaries are paid every Friday for the current week. Five employees receive a salary of $600 each per week, and three

employees earn $500 each per week. December 31 is a Tuesday. Employees do not work weekends. All employees worked the last 2 days of December.

2. Unearned Rent Revenue $369,000. The company began subleasing office space in its new building on November 1. Each tenant is required to make a $5,000 security deposit that is not refundable until occupancy is terminated. At December 31, the company had the following rental contracts that are paid in full for the entire term of the lease.

| Date | Term (in months) | Monthly Rent | Number of Leases |
|------|------------------|--------------|------------------|
| Nov. 1 | 6 | $4,000 | 5 |
| Dec. 1 | 6 | $8,500 | 4 |

3. Prepaid Advertising $13,200. This balance consists of payments on two advertising contracts. The contracts provide for monthly advertising in two trade magazines. The terms of the contracts are as follows:

| Contract | Date | Amount | Number of Magazine Issues |
|----------|------|--------|---------------------------|
| A650 | May 1 | $6,000 | 12 |
| B974 | Sept. 1 | 7,200 | 24 |

The first advertisement runs in the month in which the contract is signed.

4. Notes Payable $80,000. This balance consists of a note for one year at an annual interest rate of 12%, dated June 1.

**Instructions**

Prepare the adjusting entries at December 31, 1996. (Show all computations.)

**P3–5A** On September 1, 1996, the account balances of Rijo Equipment Repair were as follows:

*Journalize transactions and follow through accounting cycle to preparation of financial statements.*
(SO 5, 6, 7)

| No. | Debits | | No. | Credits | |
|-----|--------|--|-----|---------|--|
| 101 | Cash | $ 4,880 | 154 | Accumulated Depreciation | $ 1,500 |
| 112 | Accounts Receivable | 3,520 | 201 | Accounts Payable | 3,400 |
| 126 | Supplies | 1,000 | 209 | Unearned Service Revenue | 400 |
| 153 | Store Equipment | 15,000 | 212 | Salaries Payable | 500 |
| | | | 301 | R. Rijo, Capital | 18,600 |
| | | $24,400 | | | $24,400 |

During September the following summary transactions were completed.

Sept. 8 Paid $1,100 for salaries due employees, of which $600 is for September.
   10 Received $1,200 cash from customers on account.
   12 Received $3,400 cash for services performed in September.
   15 Purchased store equipment on account $3,000.
   17 Purchased supplies on account $1,500.
   20 Paid creditors $4,500 on account.
   22 Paid September rent $500.
   25 Paid salaries $1,050.
   27 Performed services on account and billed customers for services rendered $900.
   29 Received $650 from customers for future service.

Adjustment data consist of:

1. Supplies on hand $1,800.
2. Accrued salaries payable $400.
3. Depreciation is $200 per month.
4. Unearned service revenue of $350 is earned.

**Instructions**

(a) Enter the September 1 balances in the ledger accounts.
(b) Journalize the September transactions.

(c) Post to the ledger accounts. Use J1 for posting reference and No. 407 Service Revenue, No. 615 Depreciation Expense, No. 631 Supplies Expense, No. 726 Salaries Expense, and No. 729 Rent Expense.
(d) Prepare a trial balance at September 30.
(e) Journalize and post adjusting entries.
(f) Prepare an adjusted trial balance.
(g) Prepare an income statement and an owner's equity statement for September and a balance sheet at September 30.

# ▶**B**roadening *Your Perspective*

## **F**INANCIAL REPORTING PROBLEM
••••••••••••••••••••••••••••••••••••••••••••••••••••••••••••••••••••••••

The financial statements of PepsiCo are presented in Appendix A at the end of this textbook.

*Instructions*
(a) Using the consolidated income statement and balance sheet, identify items that may result in adjusting entries for prepayments.
(b) Using the consolidated income statement, identify two items that may result in adjusting entries for accruals.
(c) Using the Notes to Consolidated Financial Statements section, what was the amount of depreciation expense for 1994 and 1993? How was depreciation expense reported in the income statement? Do you have any suggestions for improving PepsiCo's presentation of accumulated depreciation?
(d) Using the Selected Financial Data section, what has been the trend since 1990 for (a) interest expense and (b) interest income?
(e) Using the Consolidated Income Statement and the Consolidated Statement of Cash Flows, how much interest was paid in 1994? Where is the remainder presumably reported in the balance sheet?

## **D**ECISION CASE
••••••••••••••••••••••••••••••••••••••••••••••••••••••••••••••••••••••••

(SO 1, 2, 5, 6, 7)  ∼    The Holiday Travel Court was organized on April 1, 1995, by Alice Adare. Alice is a good manager but a poor accountant. From the trial balance prepared by a part-time bookkeeper, Alice prepared the following income statement for the quarter that ended March 31, 1996.

**HOLIDAY TRAVEL COURT**
**Income Statement**
**For the Quarter Ended March 31, 1996**

| | | |
|---|---:|---:|
| Revenues | | |
|   Travel court rental fees | | $95,000 |
| Operating expenses | | |
|   Advertising | $ 5,200 | |
|   Wages | 29,800 | |
|   Utilities | 900 | |
|   Depreciation | 800 | |
|   Repairs | 4,000 | |
|     Total operating expenses | | 40,700 |
| Net income | | $54,300 |

Alice knew that something was wrong with the statement because net income had never exceeded $20,000 in any one quarter. Knowing that you are an experienced accountant, she asks you to review the income statement and other data.

You first look at the trial balance. In addition to the account balances reported above in the income statement, the ledger contains the following additional selected balances at March 31, 1996.

| | |
|---|---|
| Supplies | $ 5,200 |
| Prepaid Insurance | 7,200 |
| Notes Payable | 12,000 |

You then make inquiries and discover the following:

1. Travel court rental fees include advanced rentals for summer month occupancy $28,000.
2. There were $1,300 of supplies on hand at March 31.
3. Prepaid insurance resulted from the payment of a one-year policy on January 1, 1996.
4. The mail on April 1, 1996, brought the following bills: advertising for week of March 24, $110; repairs made March 10, $260; and utilities, $180.
5. There are four employees who receive wages totaling $350 per day. At March 31, 2 days' wages have been incurred but not paid.
6. The note payable is a 3-month, 10% note dated January 1, 1996.

*Instructions*
(a) Prepare a correct income statement for the quarter ended March 31, 1996.
(b) Explain to Alice the generally accepted accounting principles that she did not recognize in preparing her income statement and their effect on her results.

# COMMUNICATION ACTIVITY

In reviewing the accounts of the Marylee Co. at the end of the year, you discover that adjusting entries have not been made.

*Instructions*
Write a memorandum to Mary Lee Virgil, the owner of Marylee Co., that explains the following: the nature and purpose of adjusting entries, why adjusting entries are needed, and the types of adjusting entries that may be made.

# GROUP ACTIVITY

The following types of adjusting entries were introduced in this chapter: (1) prepaid expenses, (2) unearned revenues, (3) accrued revenues, and (4) accrued expenses.

*Instructions*
With the class divided into four groups, each group will choose one type of adjusting entry. Each group is to report to the class on the following: (a) the account relationship that is involved, (b) the status of the accounts before adjustment, (c) the debit/credit effect of the adjusting entry, and (d) the effects on the balance sheet and income statement if the adjusting entry is not made.

# ETHICS CASE

Diamond Company is a pesticide manufacturer. Its sales declined greatly this year due to the passage of legislation outlawing the sale of several of Diamond's chemical pesticides. During the coming year, Diamond will have environmentally safe and competitive replacement chemicals to replace these discontinued products. Sales in the next year are expected to greatly exceed any prior year's. The development in sales and profits appears to be a one-year aberration. But even so, the company president believes that a large dip in current year's profits could cause a significant drop in the market price of Diamond's stock and make it a takeover target. To avoid this possibility, the company president urges Carol Denton, controller, in making this period's year-end adjusting entries to accrue every possible revenue and to defer as many expenses as possible. The president says to Carol, "We need the revenues this year, and next year can easily absorb expenses deferred from this year. We can't let our stock price be hammered down!" Carol didn't get around to recording the adjusting entries until January 17, but she dated the entries December 31 as if they were recorded then. Carol also made every effort to comply with the president's request.

*Instructions*
(a) Who are the stakeholders in this situation?
(b) What are the ethical considerations of (1) the president's request and (2) Carol's dating the adjusting entries December 31?
(c) Can Carol accrue revenues and defer expenses and still be ethical?

# CRITICAL THINKING
## ▶ *A Real-World Focus: Laser Recording Systems Incorporated*
..................................................................................................

*Laser Recording Systems, founded in 1981, produces laser disks for use in the home market. Sales since 1985 have increased approximately 15 percent per year.*

The following is an excerpt from Laser Recording Systems' 1994 financial statements (all dollars in thousands):

**Management Discussion**
Accrued liabilities increased to $1,642 at January 31, 1994, from $138 at the end of fiscal year 1993. Compensation and related accruals increased $195 due primarily to increases in accruals for severance, vacation, commissions, and relocation expenses. Accrued professional services increased by $137 primarily as a result of legal expenses related to several outstanding contractual disputes. Other expense increased $35, of which $18 was for interest payable.

*Instructions*
(a) Can you tell from the discussion whether Laser Recording has prepaid their legal expenses and is now making an adjustment to the asset account Prepaid Legal Expenses, or whether they are handling the legal expense via an accrued expense adjustment?
(b) Identify each of the adjustments Laser Recording is discussing as one of the four types of possible adjustments discussed in the chapter. How is net income ultimately affected by each of the adjustments?
(c) What journal entry did Laser Recording make to record their accrued interest?

---

*Answers to Self-Study Questions*
1. c     2. a     3. d     4. d     5. c     6. a     7. b     8. b     9. c     10. d     11. a

# Concepts for Review

**Before studying this chapter you should know or, if necessary, review:**

**a.** *How to apply the revenue recognition and matching principles. (Ch. 3, pp. 89–90)*

**b.** *How to make adjusting entries. (Ch. 3, pp. 92–102)*

**c.** *How to prepare an adjusted trial balance. (Ch. 3, p. 105)*

**d.** *How to prepare a balance sheet, income statement, and owner's equity statement. (Ch. 3, pp. 106–107)*

# A Little Knowledge Brings a Lot of Profits

WOODRIDGE, Ill. — Employee training in financial accounting has paid off for Jack Stack at SRC Corporation which rebuilds engines. President and owner of SRC, he was really concerned when his company lost $61,000 on sales of $16 million. He decided that the "only way to turn things around was to get employees to think like owners." But how to do it? He decided to "teach anyone who moved a broom or operated a grinder everything a bank lender would know. That way they would really understand how each nickel saved could make a difference."

Therefore, in 1994 alone SRC spent $300,000 on financial accounting training for its employees. Each week the company stopped its operations for half an hour while its 800 employees broke into small groups to study the latest financial statements. "At first it wasn't easy for everyone to understand the numbers," concedes Craig Highbarger (an employee), "but we've been over the different figures enough times now, if you hand any one of us a financial statement and leave out a few numbers, we can fill them in." Employees now understand how much it costs to copy a document or turn on a light.

Has it made a difference? In 1994 SRC earned $6 million on sales of $100 million. As a result of this turnaround, SRC has handed out $1.4 million in bonuses to its employees, who are now wealthier in both cash and knowledge. ◄

## CHAPTER · 4

# COMPLETION OF THE ACCOUNTING CYCLE

▶ STUDY OBJECTIVES ◀

After studying this chapter, you should be able to:

1. Prepare a work sheet.
2. Explain the process of closing the books.
3. Describe the content and purpose of a post-closing trial balance.
4. State the required steps in the accounting cycle.
5. Explain the approaches to preparing correcting entries.
6. Identify the sections of a classified balance sheet.

As was true at SRC Corporation, financial statements can help employees understand what is happening in the business. In Chapter 3, we prepared financial statements directly from the adjusted trial balance. However, with so many details involved in the end-of-period accounting procedures, it is easy to make errors. Locating and correcting errors can cost much time and effort. One way to minimize errors in the records and to simplify the end-of-period procedures is to use a work sheet.

In this chapter we will explain the role of the work sheet in accounting as well as the remaining steps in the accounting cycle, most especially, the closing process, again using Pioneer Advertising Agency as an example. Then we will consider (1) correcting entries and (2) classified balance sheets. The organization and content of the chapter are as follows:

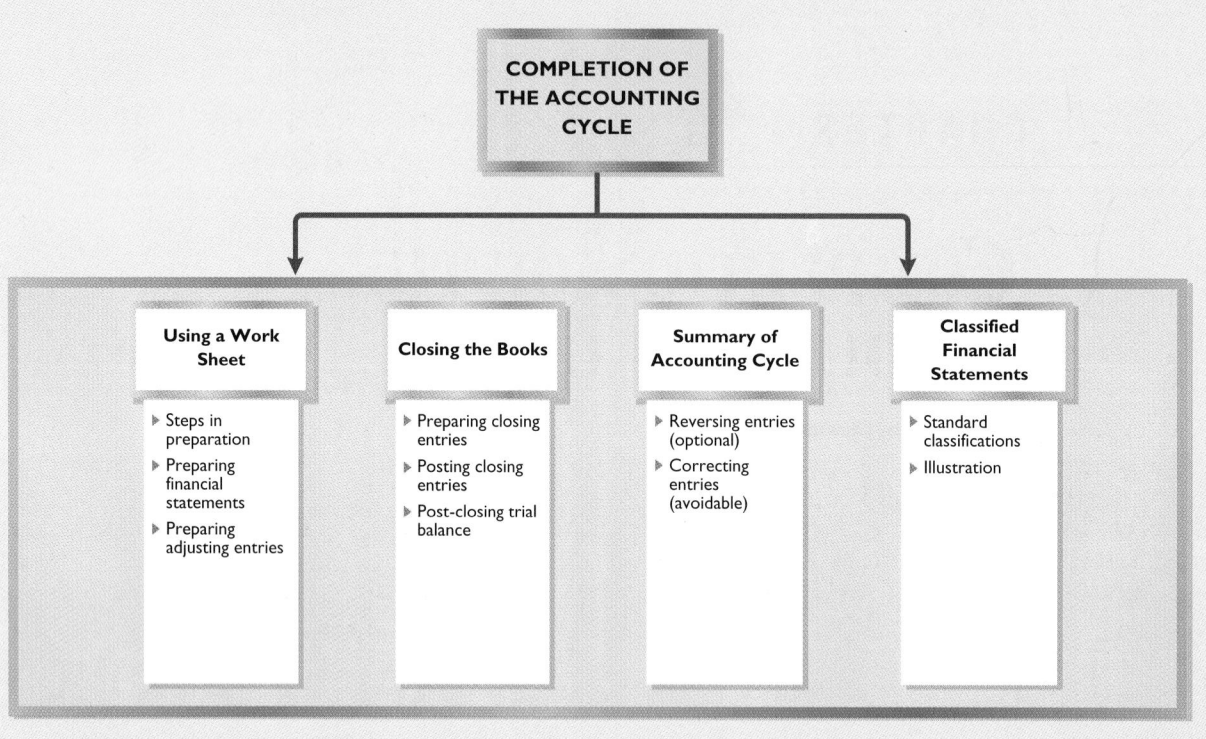

## Using a Work Sheet

**STUDY OBJECTIVE**

▼

*Prepare a work sheet.*

A work sheet is a multiple-column form that may be used in the adjustment process and in preparing financial statements. As its name suggests, the work sheet is a working tool or a supplementary device for the accountant. **A work sheet is not a permanent accounting record;** it is neither a journal nor a part of the general ledger. The work sheet is merely a device used to make it easier to prepare adjusting entries and the financial statements. In small companies with relatively few accounts and adjustments, a work sheet may not be needed. In large companies with numerous accounts and many adjustments, it is almost indispensable.

The basic form of a work sheet and the procedure (5 steps) for preparing a work sheet are shown in Illustration 4-1.

**Illustration 4-1**

*Form and procedure for a work sheet*

**Work Sheet**

| Account Titles | Trial Balance | | Adjustments | | Adjusted Trial Balance | | Income Statement | | Balance Sheet | |
|---|---|---|---|---|---|---|---|---|---|---|
| | Dr. | Cr. | Dr. | Cr. | Dr. | Cr. | Dr. | Cr. | Dr. | Cr. |
| (Ledger account titles) | | | | | | | | | | |
| (Additional account titles for adjustments) | | | | | | | | | | |

| 1. Prepare a trial balance on the work sheet | 2. Enter adjustment data | 3. Enter adjusted balances | 4. Extend adjusted balances to appropriate statement columns |
|---|---|---|---|
| | | | 5. Total the statement columns, compute net income, (or net loss), and complete work sheet |

Each of the steps in preparing the work sheet must be performed in the prescribed sequence.

**The use of a work sheet is optional.** When a work sheet is used, financial statements are prepared from the work sheet. The adjustments are entered in the work sheet columns and are then journalized and posted after the financial statements have been prepared. Thus, management and other interested parties can receive the financial statements at an earlier date than without a work sheet.

## Steps in Preparing a Work Sheet

We will use the October 31 trial balance and adjustment data of Pioneer Advertising in Chapter 3 to illustrate the preparation of a work sheet. Each step of the process is described below and demonstrated in Illustrations 4-2 and 4-3A, B, C, and D following page 137.

**Step 1. Prepare a Trial Balance on the Work Sheet.** The account title space and trial balance columns are used to prepare a trial balance. The data for the trial balance come directly from the ledger accounts. The trial balance for Pioneer Advertising Agency is entered in the trial balance columns of the work sheet as shown in Illustration 4-2.

**Step 2. Enter the Adjustments in the Adjustment Columns. Turn over the first transparency, Illustration 4-3A.** When a work sheet is used, all adjustments are entered in the adjustment columns. In entering the adjustments, applicable trial balance accounts should be used. If additional accounts are needed, they should be inserted on the lines immediately below the trial balance totals. Each adjustment is indexed and keyed to facilitate the journalizing of the adjusting entry in the general journal. **It is important to recognize that the adjustments are not journalized until after the work sheet is completed and the financial statements have been prepared.**

The adjustments for Pioneer Advertising Agency are the same as the adjustments illustrated on page 103. They are keyed in the adjustment columns of the work sheet as follows:

**(a)** An additional account, Advertising Supplies Expense, is debited $1,500 for the cost of supplies used, and Advertising Supplies is credited $1,500.

**(b)** An additional account, Insurance Expense, is debited $50 for the insurance that has expired, and Prepaid Insurance is credited $50.

**(c)** Two additional accounts are needed. Depreciation Expense is debited $40 for the month's depreciation, and Accumulated Depreciation—Office Equipment is credited $40.

**(d)** Unearned Fees is debited $400 for fees earned, and Fees Earned is credited $400.

**(e)** An additional account, Accounts Receivable, is debited $200 for fees earned but not billed, and Fees Earned is credited $200.

**(f)** Two additional accounts are needed. Interest Expense is debited $50 for accrued interest, and Interest Payable is credited $50.

**(g)** Salaries Expense is debited $1,200 for accrued salaries, and an additional account, Salaries Payable, is credited $1,200.

Note in the Illustration that after all the adjustments have been entered, the adjustment columns are totaled and the equality of the column totals is proved.

**Step 3.   Enter Adjusted Balances in the Adjusted Trial Balance Columns.** **Turn over the second transparency, Illustration 4-3B.** The adjusted balance of an account is obtained by combining the amounts entered in the first four columns of the work sheet for each account. For example, the Prepaid Insurance account in the trial balance columns has a $600 debit balance. When this is combined with the $50 credit in the adjustment columns, the result is a $550 debit balance recorded in the adjusted trial balance columns. **For each account on the work sheet, the amount in the adjusted trial balance columns is equal to the account balance that will appear in the ledger after the adjusting entries have been journalized and posted.** The balances in these columns are the same as those in the adjusted trial balance in Illustration 3-17 on page 105.

## ▸*Technology in Action*

The work sheet can be computerized using an electronic spreadsheet program. The LOTUS 1–2–3 supplement for this textbook is one of the most popular versions of such spreadsheet packages. With a program like LOTUS 1–2–3, you can produce any type of work sheet (accounting or otherwise) that you could produce with paper and pencil on a columnar pad. The tremendous advantage of an electronic work sheet over the paper and pencil version is the ability to change selected data. When data are changed, the computer updates the balance of your computations instantly. More specific applications of electronic spreadsheets will be noted as we proceed.

**Helpful hint**   Every adjusted trial balance amount must be extended to one of the four statement columns. Debit amounts go to debit columns and credit amounts go to credit columns.

After the balances of all accounts have been entered in the adjusted trial balance columns, the columns are totaled and their equality is proved. The agreement of the column totals facilitates the completion of the work sheet. If these columns are not in agreement, the statement columns will not balance and the financial statements will be incorrect.

**Step 4.   Extend Adjusted Trial Balance Amounts to Appropriate Financial Statement Columns.**   Turn over the third transparency, Illustration 4-3C. This step involves the extension of adjusted trial balance amounts to the last four columns of the work sheet. Balance sheet accounts such as Cash and Notes Payable are entered in the balance sheet debit and credit columns, respectively. The balance in accumulated depreciation is extended to the balance sheet credit column. This results because accumulated depreciation is a contra-asset account with a credit balance.

Because the work sheet does not have columns for the owner's equity statement, the balance in owner's capital is extended to the balance sheet credit column. In addition, the balance in owner's drawing is extended to the balance sheet debit column because it is an owner's equity account with a debit balance. The expense and revenue accounts such as Salaries Expense and Fees Earned are entered in the appropriate income statement columns. These extensions are shown in Illustration 4-3C.

**Step 5. Total the Statement Columns, Compute the Net Income (or Net Loss), and Complete the Work Sheet. Turn over the fourth transparency, Illustration 4-3D.** Each of the statement columns must be totaled. The net income or loss for the period is then found by computing the difference between the totals of the two income statement columns. If total credits exceed total debits, net income has resulted. In such a case, as shown in Illustration 4-3D, the words "net income" are inserted in the account title space. The amount then is entered in the income statement debit column and the balance sheet credit column. **The debit amount balances the income statement columns and the credit amount balances the balance sheet columns.** In addition, the credit in the balance sheet column indicates the increase in owner's equity resulting from net income. Conversely, if total debits in the income statement columns exceed total credits, a net loss has occurred. The amount of the net loss is entered in the income statement credit column and the balance sheet debit column.

After the net income or net loss has been entered, new column totals are determined. The totals shown in the debit and credit income statement columns will be identical. The totals shown in the debit and credit balance sheet columns will also be identical. If either the income statement columns or the balance sheet columns are not equal after the net income or net loss has been entered, an error has been made in completing the work sheet. The completed work sheet for Pioneer Advertising Agency is shown in Illustration 4-3D.

**Helpful hint** All pairs of columns must balance for a work sheet to be complete.

## Preparing Financial Statements from a Work Sheet

After a work sheet has been completed, the statement columns contain all the data that are required for the preparation of financial statements. The income statement is prepared from the income statement columns, and the balance sheet and owner's equity statement are prepared from the balance sheet columns. The financial statements prepared from the work sheet for Pioneer Advertising Agency are shown in Illustration 4-4. At this point, adjusting entries have not been journalized and posted. Therefore, the ledger does not support all financial statement amounts.

The amount shown for owner's capital on the work sheet is the account balance **before considering drawings and net income (or loss).** When there have been no additional investments of capital by the owner during the period, this amount is the balance at the beginning of the period.

Using a work sheet, accountants can prepare financial statements before adjusting entries are journalized and posted. **However, the completed work sheet is not a substitute for formal financial statements.** Data in the financial statement columns are not properly arranged for statement purposes. Moreover, as noted above, the financial statement presentation for some accounts differs from their statement columns on the work sheet. **A work sheet is essentially a working tool of the accountant and is not distributed to management and other parties.**

(**Note**: Text continues on page 140, following acetate overlays.)

ILLUSTRATION 4-2

*Preparing a trial balance*

### PIONEER ADVERTISING AGENCY
### Work Sheet
### For the Month Ended October 31, 1996

| Account Titles | Trial Balance Dr. | Trial Balance Cr. | Adjustments Dr. | Adjustments Cr. | Adjusted Trial Balance Dr. | Adjusted Trial Balance Cr. | Income Statement Dr. | Income Statement Cr. | Balance Sheet Dr. | Balance Sheet Cr. |
|---|---|---|---|---|---|---|---|---|---|---|
| Cash | 15,200 | | | | | | | | | |
| Advertising Supplies | 2,500 | | | | | | | | | |
| Prepaid Insurance | 600 | | | | | | | | | |
| Office Equipment | 5,000 | | | | | | | | | |
| Notes Payable | | 5,000 | | | | | | | | |
| Accounts Payable | | 2,500 | | | | | | | | |
| Unearned Fees | | 1,200 | | | | | | | | |
| C. R. Byrd, Capital | | 10,000 | | | | | | | | |
| C. R. Byrd, Drawing | 500 | | | | | | | | | |
| Fees Earned | | 10,000 | | | | | | | | |
| Salaries Expense | 4,000 | | | | | | | | | |
| Rent Expense | 900 | | | | | | | | | |
| Totals | 28,700 | 28,700 | | | | | | | | |

Include all accounts from ledger with balances.

Trial balance amounts are taken directly from ledger accounts.

ILLUSTRATION 4-4

*Financial statements from a
work sheet*

**PIONEER ADVERTISING AGENCY**
**Income Statement**
**For the Month Ended October 31, 1996**

Revenues
  Fees earned               $10,600

Expenses
  Salaries expense      $5,200
  Advertising supplies expense  1,500
  Rent expense         900
  Insurance expense      50
  Interest expense       50
  Depreciation expense    40

    Total expenses        7,740
Net Income               $ 2,860

**PIONEER ADVERTISING AGENCY**
**Owner's Equity Statement**
**For the Month Ended October 31, 1996**

C. R. Byrd, Capital, October 1     $ –0–
Add: Investments    $10,000
    Net income     2,860  12,860
                    12,860
Less: Drawings          500
C. R. Byrd, Capital, October 31  $12,360

**PIONEER ADVERTISING AGENCY**
**Balance Sheet**
**October 31, 1996**

**Assets**

Cash                $15,200
Accounts receivable       200
Advertising supplies     1,000
Prepaid insurance       550
Office equipment     $5,000
Less: Accumulated depreciation  40  4,960
    Total assets        $21,910

**Liabilities and Owner's Equity**

Liabilities
  Notes payable        $ 5,000
  Accounts payable     2,500
  Interest payable       50
  Unearned fees       800
  Salaries payable     1,200
    Total liabilities    9,550
Owner's equity
  C. R. Byrd, Capital    12,360
    Total liabilities and
    owner's equity    $21,910

## Preparing Adjusting Entries from a Work Sheet

**A work sheet is not a journal, and it cannot be used as a basis for posting to ledger accounts.** To adjust the accounts, it is necessary to journalize and post the adjustments to the ledger. **The adjusting entries are prepared from the adjustment columns of the work sheet.** The reference letters in the adjustment columns and the explanation of the adjustments that appear at the bottom of the work sheet help identify entries. However, writing the explanation to the adjustments at the bottom of the work sheet is not required. As indicated previously, the journalizing and posting of adjusting entries **follows** the preparation of financial statements when a work sheet is used. The adjusting entries on October 31 for Pioneer Advertising Agency are the same as those shown in Illustration 3-15 (page 103).

## *Before You Go On . . .*

### ▸ *Review It*

1. What are the five steps in preparing a work sheet?
2. How is net income or net loss shown in a work sheet?
3. How does a work sheet relate to preparing financial statements and adjusting entries?

### ▸ *Do It*

Merlynn Kimmel is preparing a work sheet. Explain to Merlynn how the following adjusted trial balance accounts should be extended to the financial statement columns of the work sheet: Cash; Accumulated Depreciation; Accounts Payable; R. Kerr, Drawing; Fees Earned; and Salaries Expense.

**Reasoning:** Asset and liability balances and drawing are extended to the balance sheet debit and credit columns respectively except for accumulated depreciation which is extended to the balance sheet credit column. The expenses are extended to the income statement debit column. Revenue accounts are extended to the income statement credit column.

**Solution:**
Income statement debit column—Salaries Expense
Income statement credit column—Fees Earned
Balance sheet debit column—Cash; and R. Kerr, Drawing.
Balance sheet credit column—Accumulated Depreciation; Accounts Payable
As indicated in the Technology in Action box on page 136, the work sheet is an ideal application for electronic spreadsheet software like Microsoft Excel and LOTUS 1–2–3.

*Related exercise material: BE4–1, BE4–2, BE4–3, E4–1, E4–2, E4–4, and E4–5.*

# *C*losing the Books

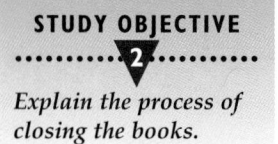

**STUDY OBJECTIVE**

**2**

*Explain the process of closing the books.*

In closing the books, it is necessary to distinguish between temporary and permanent accounts. Temporary or nominal accounts relate only to a given accounting period. They include all income statement accounts and owner's drawing. All temporary accounts are closed. In contrast, permanent or real accounts relate to one or more future accounting periods. They consist of all balance sheet accounts including owner's capital. Permanent accounts are not closed. Instead, their balances are carried forward into the next accounting period. Illustration 4-5 identifies the accounts in each category.

**Illustration 4-5**

*Temporary versus permanent accounts*

| TEMPORARY (NOMINAL) These accounts are closed | PERMANENT (REAL) These accounts are not closed |
|---|---|
| All revenue accounts | All asset accounts |
| All expense accounts | All liability accounts |
| Owner's drawing | Owner's capital account |

## Preparing Closing Entries

At the end of the accounting period, the temporary account balances are transferred to the permanent owner's equity account, owner's capital, through the preparation of closing entries.[1] Closing entries formally recognize in the ledger the transfer of net income or net loss and owner's drawing to owner's capital as shown in the owner's equity statement. **These entries also produce a zero balance in each temporary account so it can be used to accumulate data in the next accounting period separate from the data of prior periods.** Permanent accounts are not closed.

**Journalizing and posting closing entries is a required step in the accounting cycle.** This step is performed after financial statements have been prepared. In contrast to the steps in the cycle that you have already studied, closing entries are generally journalized and posted **only at the end of a company's annual accounting period.** This practice facilitates the preparation of annual financial statements because all temporary accounts will contain data for the entire year.

In preparing closing entries, each income statement account could be closed directly to owner's capital. However, to do so would result in excessive detail in the permanent owner's capital account. Accordingly, the revenue and expense accounts are closed to another temporary account, Income Summary, and only the net income or net loss is transferred from this account to owner's capital.

**Closing entries are journalized in the general journal.** A center caption entitled Closing Entries may be inserted in the journal between the last adjusting entry and the first closing entry to identify these entries. Then the closing entries are posted to the ledger accounts. Closing entries may be prepared directly from the adjusted balances in the ledger, from the income statement and balance sheet columns of the work sheet, or from the income and owner's equity statements. Separate closing entries could be prepared for each nominal account, but the following four entries accomplish the desired result more efficiently:

**Helpful hint** When the work sheet is used, revenue and expense account data are found in the income statement columns, and owner's drawing is in the balance sheet debit column.

1. Debit each revenue account for its balance and credit Income Summary for total revenues.
2. Debit Income Summary for total expenses and credit each expense account for its balance.
3. Debit Income Summary and credit owner's capital for the amount of net income.

**Helpful hint** Owner's Drawing is closed directly to capital and *not* to Income Summary because Owner's Drawing is not an expense.

---

[1]Closing entries for a partnership and for a corporation are explained in Chapters 13 and 14, respectively.

**4.** Debit owner's capital for the balance in the owner's drawing account and credit owner's drawing for the same amount.

**Illustration 4-6**

*Diagram of closing process—proprietorship*

The four entries are referenced in the diagram of the closing process shown in Illustration 4-6 and in the journal entries in Illustration 4-7. The posting of closing entries is shown in Illustration 4-8.

| (Individual) Expenses | | | (Individual) Revenues |
|---|---|---|---|

[2]  [1]

**Income Summary**

[3]

**Owner's Capital**

Owner's Capital is a permanent account; all other accounts are temporary accounts.

[4]

**Owner's Drawing**

If there were a net loss because expenses exceeded revenues, entry 3 in Illustration 4-6 would be reversed: Credit Income Summary and debit Owner's Capital.

## ▶ *Accounting in Action* ▸ *Business Insight*

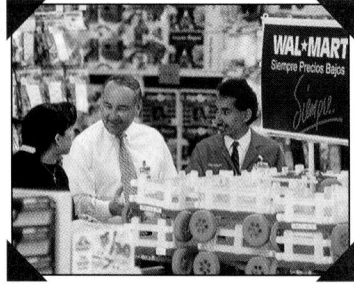

Until Sam Walton had opened twenty Wal-Mart stores, he used what he called the "ESP method" of closing the books. ESP was a pretty basic method: If the books didn't balance, Walton calculated the amount by which they were off and entered that amount under the heading ESP—which stood for "Error Some Place." As Walton noted, "It really sped things along when it came time to close those books."

*Source:* Sam Walton, *Made in America* (New York: Doubleday Publishing Company, 1992), p. 53.

### Closing Entries Illustrated

As explained above, closing entries are generally prepared only at the end of a company's annual accounting period. However, to illustrate the journalizing and posting of closing entries, we will assume that Pioneer Advertising Agency closes its books monthly. The closing entries at October 31 are shown in Illustration 4-7.

**Illustration 4-7**

*Closing entries journalized*

| GENERAL JOURNAL | | | | J3 |
|---|---|---|---|---|
| Date | Account Titles and Explanation | Ref. | Debit | Credit |
| | Closing Entries | | | |
| | (1) | | | |
| 1996 | | | | |
| Oct. 31 | Fees Earned | 50 | 10,600 | |
| | Income Summary | 49 | | 10,600 |
| | (To close revenue account) | | | |
| | (2) | | | |
| 31 | Income Summary | 49 | 7,740 | |
| | Salaries Expense | 60 | | 5,200 |
| | Advertising Supplies Expense | 61 | | 1,500 |
| | Rent Expense | 62 | | 900 |
| | Insurance Expense | 63 | | 50 |
| | Interest Expense | 64 | | 50 |
| | Depreciation Expense | 65 | | 40 |
| | (To close expense accounts) | | | |
| | (3) | | | |
| 31 | Income Summary | 49 | 2,860 | |
| | C. R. Byrd, Capital | 40 | | 2,860 |
| | (To close net income to capital) | | | |
| | (4) | | | |
| 31 | C. R. Byrd, Capital | 40 | 500 | |
| | C. R. Byrd, Drawing | 41 | | 500 |
| | (To close drawings to capital) | | | |

**Helpful hint** Income Summary is a very descriptive title: total revenues are closed to Income Summary, total expenses are closed to Income Summary, and the balance in the Income Summary is a net income or net loss.

Note that the amounts for Income Summary in entries (1) and (2) are the totals of the income statement credit and debit columns, respectively, in the work sheet.

A couple of cautions in preparing closing entries: (1) Avoid unintentionally doubling the revenue and expense balances rather than zeroing them. (2) Do not close owner's drawing through the Income Summary account. **Owner's drawing is not an expense, and it is not a factor in determining net income.**

## Posting Closing Entries

The posting of the closing entries and the ruling of the accounts are shown in Illustration 4-8. Note that all temporary accounts have zero balances after posting the closing entries. In addition, you should realize that the balance in Owner's Capital represents the total equity of the owner at the end of the accounting period. This balance is shown on the balance sheet and is the ending capital reported on the owner's equity statement, as shown in Illustration 4-4 on page 139. **The Income Summary account is used only in closing.** No entries are journalized and posted to this account during the year.

As part of the closing process, the **temporary accounts** (revenues and expenses) in T-account form are totaled, balanced, and double ruled as shown in Illustration 4-8. The **permanent accounts** (assets, liabilities, and owner's capital)

**Helpful hint** The balance in Income Summary before it is closed must equal the net income or net loss for the period.

are not closed: A single rule is drawn beneath the current period entries, and the account balance carried forward to the next period is entered below the single rule. (For example, see C. R. Byrd, Capital.)

## Preparing a Post-Closing Trial Balance

STUDY OBJECTIVE

•••••••••▾3▾•••••••••

*Describe the content and purpose of a post-closing trial balance.*

After all closing entries have been journalized and posted, another trial balance, called a post-closing trial balance, is prepared from the ledger. A post-closing trial balance is a list of permanent accounts and their balances after closing entries have been journalized and posted. **The purpose of this trial balance is to prove the equality of the permanent account balances that are carried forward into the next accounting period.** Since all temporary accounts will have zero balances, **the post-closing trial balance will contain only permanent—balance sheet—accounts.**

**Illustration 4-8**

*Posting of closing entries*

The procedure for preparing a post-closing trial balance again consists entirely of listing the accounts and their balances. These balances are the same as those reported in the company's balance sheet in Illustration 4-4. The post-closing trial balance for Pioneer Advertising is shown in Illustration 4-9.

**Illustration 4-9**

*Post-closing trial balance*

| PIONEER ADVERTISING AGENCY<br>Post-Closing Trial Balance<br>October 31, 1996 | | |
| --- | --- | --- |
| | Debit | Credit |
| Cash | $15,200 | |
| Accounts Receivable | 200 | |
| Advertising Supplies | 1,000 | |
| Prepaid Insurance | 550 | |
| Office Equipment | 5,000 | |
| Accumulated Depreciation—Office Equipment | | $ 40 |
| Notes Payable | | 5,000 |
| Accounts Payable | | 2,500 |
| Interest Payable | | 50 |
| Unearned Fees | | 800 |
| Salaries Payable | | 1,200 |
| C. R. Byrd, Capital | | 12,360 |
| | $21,950 | $21,950 |

The post-closing trial balance is prepared from the permanent accounts in the ledger. The permanent accounts of Pioneer Advertising are shown in the general ledger in Illustration 4-10. Remember that the balance of each permanent account is computed after every posting. Therefore, no additional work on these accounts is needed as part of the closing process. The remaining accounts in the general ledger are temporary accounts (shown in Illustration 4-11 on page 147). After the closing entries are posted, each temporary account has a zero balance. These accounts are double-ruled to finalize the closing process.

A post-closing trial balance provides evidence that the journalizing and posting of closing entries has been properly completed. In addition, it shows that the accounting equation is in balance at the end of the accounting period. However, as in the case of the trial balance, it does not prove that all transactions have been recorded or that the ledger is correct. For example, the post-closing trial balance will balance if a transaction is not journalized and posted or if a transaction is journalized and posted twice.

# Summary of the Accounting Cycle

The required steps in the accounting cycle are shown graphically in Illustration 4-12. From the graphic you can see that the cycle begins with the analysis of business transactions and ends with the preparation of a post-closing trial balance. The steps in the cycle are performed in sequence and are repeated in each accounting period.

Steps 1–3 may occur daily during the accounting period, as explained in Chapter 2. Steps 4–7 are performed on a periodic basis, such as monthly, quarterly, or annually. Steps 8 and 9, closing entries, and a post-closing trial balance, are usually prepared only at the end of a company's **annual** accounting period.

**STUDY OBJECTIVE**

••••••••••**4**••••••••••

*State the required steps in the accounting cycle.*

**Illustration 4-10**

*General ledger, permanent accounts*

## (Permanent Accounts Only)

| GENERAL LEDGER |
|---|

| | Cash | | | | No. 1 | | | Accounts Payable | | | | No. 26 |
|---|---|---|---|---|---|---|---|---|---|---|---|---|
| Date | Explanation | Ref. | Debit | Credit | Balance | | Date | Explanation | Ref. | Debit | Credit | Balance |
| 1996 | | | | | | | 1996 | | | | | |
| Oct. 1 | | J1 | 10,000 | | 10,000 | | Oct. 5 | | J1 | | 2,500 | 2,500 |
| 2 | | J1 | 1,200 | | 11,200 | | | Interest Payable | | | | No. 27 |
| 3 | | J1 | | 900 | 10,300 | | Date | Explanation | Ref. | Debit | Credit | Balance |
| 4 | | J1 | | 600 | 9,700 | | | | | | | |
| 20 | | J1 | | 500 | 9,200 | | 1996 | | | | | |
| 26 | | J1 | | 4,000 | 5,200 | | Oct. 31 | Adj. entry | J2 | | 50 | 50 |
| 31 | | J1 | 10,000 | | 15,200 | | | | | | | |

| | Accounts Receivable | | | | No. 6 | | | Unearned Fees | | | | No. 28 |
|---|---|---|---|---|---|---|---|---|---|---|---|---|
| Date | Explanation | Ref. | Debit | Credit | Balance | | Date | Explanation | Ref. | Debit | Credit | Balance |
| 1996 | | | | | | | 1996 | | | | | |
| Oct. 31 | Adj. entry | J2 | 200 | | 200 | | Oct. 2 | | J1 | | 1,200 | 1,200 |
| | Advertising Supplies | | | | No. 8 | | 31 | Adj. entry | J2 | 400 | | 800 |
| Date | Explanation | Ref. | Debit | Credit | Balance | | | Salaries Payable | | | | No. 29 |
| 1996 | | | | | | | Date | Explanation | Ref. | Debit | Credit | Balance |
| Oct. 5 | | J1 | 2,500 | | 2,500 | | 1996 | | | | | |
| 31 | Adj. entry | J2 | | 1,500 | 1,000 | | Oct. 31 | Adj. entry | J2 | | 1,200 | 1,200 |

| | Prepaid Insurance | | | | No. 10 | | | C. R. Byrd, Capital | | | | No. 40 |
|---|---|---|---|---|---|---|---|---|---|---|---|---|
| Date | Explanation | Ref. | Debit | Credit | Balance | | Date | Explanation | Ref. | Debit | Credit | Balance |
| 1996 | | | | | | | 1996 | | | | | |
| Oct. 4 | | J1 | 600 | | 600 | | Oct. 1 | | J1 | | 10,000 | 10,000 |
| 31 | Adj. entry | J2 | | 50 | 550 | | 31 | Closing entry | J3 | | 2,860 | 12,860 |
| | Office Equipment | | | | No. 15 | | 31 | Closing entry | J3 | 500 | | 12,360 |

*Note:* The permanent accounts for Pioneer Advertising Agency are shown here; the temporary accounts are shown in Illustration 4-11. Both permanent and temporary accounts are part of the general ledger; they are segregated here to aid in learning.

| | Office Equipment | | | | No. 15 |
|---|---|---|---|---|---|
| Date | Explanation | Ref. | Debit | Credit | Balance |
| 1996 | | | | | |
| Oct. 1 | | J1 | 5,000 | | 5,000 |

| | Accumulated Depreciation—Office Equipment | | | | No. 16 |
|---|---|---|---|---|---|
| Date | Explanation | Ref. | Debit | Credit | Balance |
| 1996 | | | | | |
| Oct. 31 | Adj. entry | J2 | | 40 | 40 |

| | Notes Payable | | | | No. 25 |
|---|---|---|---|---|---|
| Date | Explanation | Ref. | Debit | Credit | Balance |
| 1996 | | | | | |
| Oct. 1 | | J1 | | 5,000 | 5,000 |

**Illustration 4-11**

*General ledger, temporary accounts*

## (Temporary Accounts Only)

### GENERAL LEDGER

| C. R. Byrd, Drawing | | | | | No. 41 |
|---|---|---|---|---|---|
| Date | Explanation | Ref. | Debit | Credit | Balance |
| 1996 | | | | | |
| Oct. 20 | | J1 | 500 | | 500 |
| 31 | Closing entry | J3 | | 500 | –0– |

| Income Summary | | | | | No. 49 |
|---|---|---|---|---|---|
| Date | Explanation | Ref. | Debit | Credit | Balance |
| 1996 | | | | | |
| Oct. 31 | Closing entry | J3 | | 10,600 | 10,600 |
| 31 | Closing entry | J3 | 7,740 | | 2,860 |
| 31 | Closing entry | J3 | 2,860 | | –0– |

| Fees Earned | | | | | No. 50 |
|---|---|---|---|---|---|
| Date | Explanation | Ref. | Debit | Credit | Balance |
| 1996 | | | | | |
| Oct. 31 | | J1 | | 10,000 | 10,000 |
| 31 | Adj. entry | J2 | | 400 | 10,400 |
| 31 | Adj. entry | J2 | | 200 | 10,600 |
| 31 | Closing entry | J3 | 10,600 | | –0– |

| Salaries Expense | | | | | No. 60 |
|---|---|---|---|---|---|
| Date | Explanation | Ref. | Debit | Credit | Balance |
| 1996 | | | | | |
| Oct. 26 | | J1 | 4,000 | | 4,000 |
| 31 | Adj. entry | J2 | 1,200 | | 5,200 |
| 31 | Closing entry | J3 | | 5,200 | –0– |

| Advertising Supplies Expense | | | | | No. 61 |
|---|---|---|---|---|---|
| Date | Explanation | Ref. | Debit | Credit | Balance |
| 1996 | | | | | |
| Oct. 31 | Adj. entry | J2 | 1,500 | | 1,500 |
| 31 | Closing entry | J3 | | 1,500 | –0– |

| Rent Expense | | | | | No. 62 |
|---|---|---|---|---|---|
| Date | Explanation | Ref. | Debit | Credit | Balance |
| 1996 | | | | | |
| Oct. 3 | | J1 | 900 | | 900 |
| 31 | Closing entry | J3 | | 900 | –0– |

| Insurance Expense | | | | | No. 63 |
|---|---|---|---|---|---|
| Date | Explanation | Ref. | Debit | Credit | Balance |
| 1996 | | | | | |
| Oct. 31 | Adj. entry | J2 | 50 | | 50 |
| 31 | Closing entry | J3 | | 50 | –0– |

| Interest Expense | | | | | No. 64 |
|---|---|---|---|---|---|
| Date | Explanation | Ref. | Debit | Credit | Balance |
| 1996 | | | | | |
| Oct. 31 | Adj. entry | J2 | 50 | | 50 |
| 31 | Closing entry | J3 | | 50 | –0– |

| Depreciation Expense | | | | | No. 65 |
|---|---|---|---|---|---|
| Date | Explanation | Ref. | Debit | Credit | Balance |
| 1996 | | | | | |
| Oct. 31 | Adj. entry | J2 | 40 | | 40 |
| 31 | Closing entry | J3 | | 40 | –0– |

*Note:* The temporary accounts for Pioneer Advertising Agency are shown here; the permanent accounts are shown in Illustration 4-10. Both permanent and temporary accounts are part of the general ledger; they are segregated here to aid in learning.

**Illustration 4-12**

*Required steps in the accounting cycle*

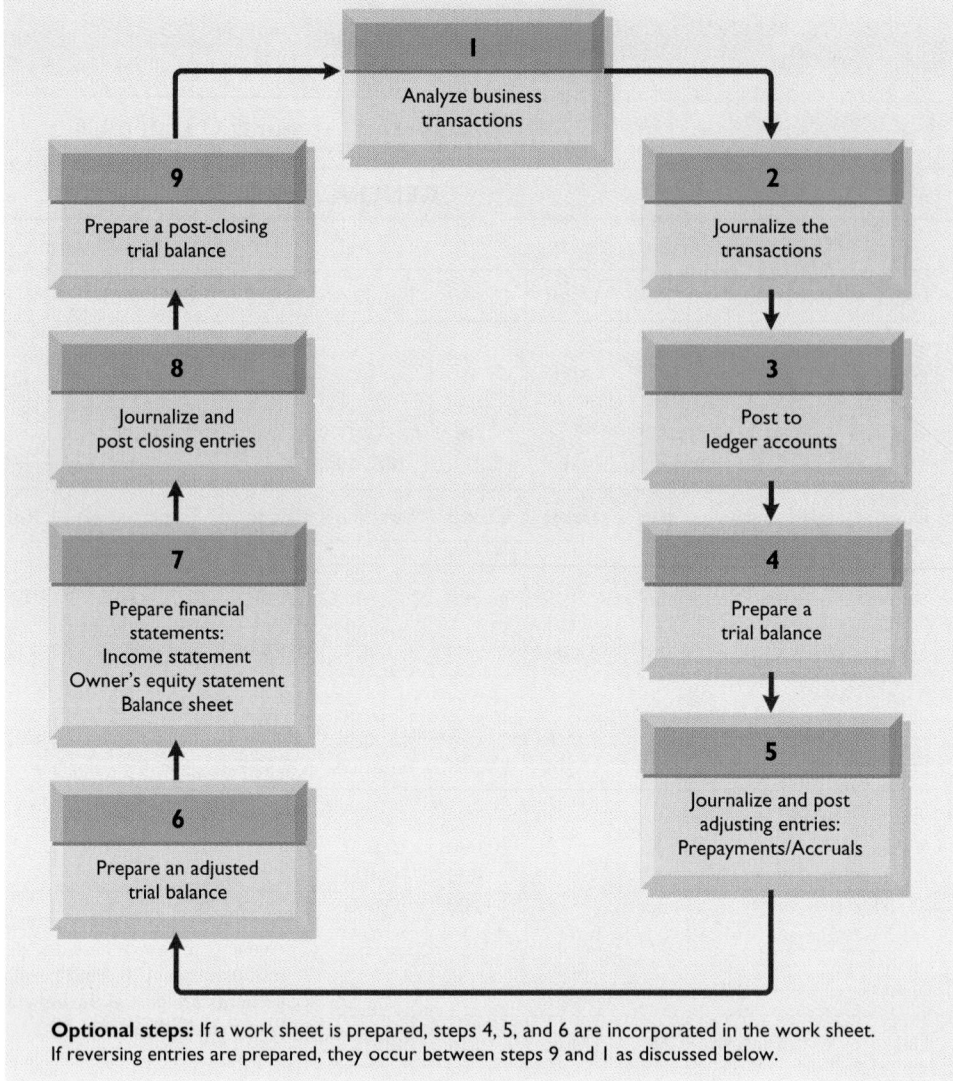

**Optional steps:** If a work sheet is prepared, steps 4, 5, and 6 are incorporated in the work sheet. If reversing entries are prepared, they occur between steps 9 and 1 as discussed below.

There are also two optional steps in the accounting cycle. As you have seen, a work sheet may be used in preparing adjusting entries and financial statements. In addition, reversing entries may be used as explained in the following section.

### Reversing Entries—An Optional Step

Some accountants prefer to reverse certain adjusting entries at the beginning of a new accounting period. A reversing entry is made at the beginning of the next accounting period and is the exact opposite of the adjusting entry made in the previous period. **The preparation of reversing entries is an optional bookkeeping procedure that is not a required step in the accounting cycle.** Accordingly, we have chosen to cover this topic in an appendix at the end of the chapter.

### Correcting Entries—An Avoidable Step

**STUDY OBJECTIVE**

**5**

*Explain the approaches to preparing correcting entries.*

If the accounting records are free of errors, no correcting entries are necessary. Unfortunately, errors may occur in the recording process. Errors should be corrected **as soon as they are discovered** by journalizing and posting correcting entries. You should recognize several significant differences between correcting entries and adjusting entries. First, adjusting entries are an integral part of the accounting cycle, whereas correcting entries are unnecessary if the records are free of errors. Second, **adjustments are journalized and posted only at the end of an accounting period; in contrast, correcting entries are made whenever an error is discovered**. Finally, adjusting entries always affect at least one balance sheet account and one income statement account. In contrast, correcting entries may involve any combination of accounts in need of correction. Correcting entries must be posted before closing entries.

To determine the correcting entry, it is useful to compare the incorrect entry with the correct entry. Doing so helps identify the accounts and amounts that should—and should not—be corrected. After comparison, a correcting entry is made to correct the accounts. This approach is illustrated in the following two cases.

**Case I.** On May 10, a $50 cash collection on account from a customer is journalized and posted as a debit to Cash $50 and a credit to Fees Earned $50. The error is discovered on May 20, when the customer pays the remaining balance in full.

▶ *Ethics note*

In 1991 Citicorp reported a correcting entry reducing reported revenue by $23 million, while firing 11 employees. Citicorp officials did not specify why the employees had apparently intentionally inflated the revenue figures, although it was noted that their bonuses were tied to their unit's performance.

**Illustration 4-13**

*Comparison of entries*

| Incorrect Entry (May 10) | | | Correct Entry (May 10) | | |
|---|---|---|---|---|---|
| Cash | 50 | | Cash | 50 | |
|    Fees Earned | | 50 |    Accounts Receivable | | 50 |

A comparison of the incorrect entry with the correct entry reveals that the debit to Cash $50 is correct. However, the $50 credit to Fees Earned should have been credited to Accounts Receivable. As a result, both Fees Earned and Accounts Receivable are overstated in the ledger. The following correcting entry is required:

**Illustration 4-14**

*Correcting entry*

| | Correcting Entry | | |
|---|---|---|---|
| May 20 | Fees Earned | 50 | |
| |    Accounts Receivable | | 50 |
| |    (To correct entry of May 10) | | |

**Case 2.** On May 18, office equipment costing $450 is purchased on account. The transaction is journalized and posted as a debit to Delivery Equipment $45, and a credit to Accounts Payable $45. The error is discovered on June 3, when the monthly statement for May is received from the creditor.

**Illustration 4-15**

*Comparison of entries*

| Incorrect Entry (May 18) | | | Correct Entry (May 18) | | |
|---|---|---|---|---|---|
| Delivery Equipment | 45 | | Office Equipment | 450 | |
|    Accounts Payable | | 45 |    Accounts Payable | | 450 |

A comparison of the two entries shows that three accounts are incorrect. Delivery Equipment is overstated $45; Office Equipment is understated $450; and Accounts Payable is understated $405. The correcting entry is:

**Illustration 4-16**

*Correcting entry*

| | Correcting Entry | | |
|---|---|---|---|
| June 3 | Office Equipment | 450 | |
| |    Delivery Equipment | | 45 |
| |    Accounts Payable | | 405 |
| |    (To correct May 18 entry) | | |

Instead of preparing a correcting entry, **it is possible to reverse the incorrect entry and then prepare the correct entry**. This approach will result in more entries and postings than a correcting entry, but it will accomplish the desired result.

## ▸Accounting in Action ▸ *Business Insight*

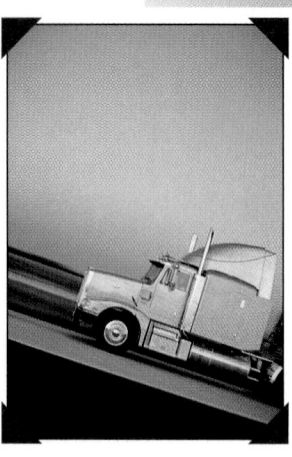

Yale Express, a short-haul trucking firm, turned over much of its cargo to local truckers for delivery completion. Yale collected the entire delivery charge and, when billed by the local trucker, remitted payment for the final phase to the local trucker. Yale used a cutoff period of 20 days into the next accounting period in making its adjusting entries for accrued liabilities. That is, it waited 20 days to receive the local truckers' bills to determine the amount of the unpaid but incurred delivery charges as of the balance sheet date.

On the other hand, Republic Carloading, a nationwide, long-distance freight forwarder, frequently did not receive transportation bills from truckers to whom it passed on cargo until months after the year end. In making its year-end adjusting entries, Republic waited for months in order to include all of these outstanding transportation bills.

When Yale Express merged with Republic Carloading, Yale's vice-president employed the 20-day cutoff procedure for both firms. As a result, millions of dollars of Republic's accrued transportation bills went unrecorded. When the erroneous procedure was detected and correcting entries were made, these and other errors changed a reported profit of $1.14 million into a loss of $1.88 million!

## *Before You Go On . . .*

### ▸ *Review It*

1. How do permanent accounts differ from temporary accounts?
2. What four different types of entries are required in closing the books?
3. What is the content and purpose of a post-closing trial balance?
4. What are the required and optional steps in the accounting cycle?

### ▸ *Do It*

The work sheet for Hancock Company shows the following in the financial statement columns: R. Hancock, Drawing $15,000, R. Hancock, Capital $42,000, and net income $18,000. Prepare the closing entries at December 31 that affect owner's capital.

***Reasoning:*** Closing entries are made in sequence. The first two entries close revenues and expenses. The remaining two entries close net income and owner's drawing to owner's capital.

***Solution:***

| | | | |
|---|---|---|---|
| Dec 31 | Income Summary | 18,000 | |
| |     R. Hancock, Capital | | 18,000 |
| |     (To close net income to capital) | | |
| 31 | R. Hancock, Capital | 15,000 | |
| |     R. Hancock, Drawing | | 15,000 |
| |     (To close drawings to capital) | | |

*Related exercise material:* BE4–4, BE4–5, BE4–6, E4–3, E4–6, and E4–8.

# Classified Financial Statements

The financial statements illustrated up to this point were purposely kept simple. We classified items as assets, liabilities, and owner's equity in the balance sheet, and as revenues and expenses in the income statement. **Financial statements, however, become more useful to management, creditors, and potential investors when the elements are classified into significant subgroups.** In the remainder of this chapter we will introduce you to the primary balance sheet classifications. The classified income statement is presented in Chapter 5. The classified financial statements are what Jack Stack, the president of SRC Corporation, gave to his employees to understand what was happening in the business.

**STUDY OBJECTIVE**

**6**

*Identify the sections of a classified balance sheet.*

## Standard Classifications

A classified balance sheet generally contains the following standard classifications:

| Assets | Liabilities and Owner's Equity |
|---|---|
| Current Assets | Current Liabilities |
| Long-Term Investments | Long-Term Liabilities |
| Property, Plant, and Equipment | Owner's (Stockholders') Equity |
| Intangible Assets | |

**Illustration 4-17**

*Standard balance sheet classifications*

These sections help the financial statement user to determine such matters as (1) the availability of assets to meet debts as they come due and (2) the claims of short- and long-term creditors on total assets. A classified balance sheet also makes it easier to compare companies in the same industry, such as GM, Ford, and Chrysler in the automobile industry. Each of the sections is explained below, except for owner's equity, which has already been discussed.

A complete set of specimen financial statements for PepsiCo, Inc. is shown in Appendix A at the back of the book.

### Current Assets

Current assets are cash and other resources that are reasonably expected to be realized in cash or sold or consumed in the business within one year of the balance sheet date or the company's operating cycle, whichever is longer. For example, accounts receivable are included in current assets because they will be realized in cash through collection within one year. In contrast, a prepayment such as supplies is a current asset because of its expected use or consumption in the business within one year.

The operating cycle of a company is the average time that is required to go from cash to cash in producing revenues. The term "cycle" suggests a circular flow, which in this case, starts and ends with cash. For example, in municipal transit companies, the operating cycle would tend to be very short since services are rendered entirely on a cash basis. On the other hand, the operating cycle in public utility companies is longer: they bill customers for services rendered and the collection period may extend for several months. Most companies have operating cycles of less than one year. More will be said about operating cycles in later chapters.

In a service enterprise, it is customary to recognize four types of current assets: (1) cash, (2) marketable securities such as U.S. government bonds held as

▶ *International note*

Other countries use a different format for the balance sheet. In Great Britain, for example, property, plant, and equipment are reported first on the balance sheet; assets and liabilities are netted and grouped into net current and net total assets.

a temporary (short-term) investment, (3) receivables (notes receivable, accounts receivable, and interest receivable), and (4) prepaid expenses (insurance and supplies). **These items are listed in the order of liquidity**, that is, in the order in which they are expected to be converted into cash. This arrangement is illustrated below in the presentation of UAL, Inc. (United Airlines).

**Illustration 4-18**

*Current asset section*

| UAL, INC. (United Airlines) | |
|---|---:|
| **Current assets (in thousands)** | |
| Cash | $    52,368 |
| Marketable securities | 389,862 |
| Receivables | 721,479 |
| Aircraft fuel, spare parts, and supplies | 178,840 |
| Prepaid expenses | 83,662 |
| Total current assets | $1,426,211 |

A company's current assets are important in assessing the company's short-term debt-paying ability, as explained later in the chapter.

### Long-Term Investments

Like current assets, long-term investments are resources that can be realized in cash. However, the conversion into cash is not expected within one year or the operating cycle, whichever is longer. In addition, long-term investments are not intended for use or consumption within the business. This category, often just called "investments," normally includes stocks and bonds of other corporations. Deluxe Check Printers Incorporated reported the following in its balance sheet:

**Illustration 4-19**

*Long-term investment section*

| DELUXE CHECK PRINTERS INCORPORATED | | |
|---|---:|---:|
| **Long-term investments** | | |
| Investment in stock of Data Card Corporation | $20,468,000 | |
| Other long-term investments | 16,961,000 | $37,429,000 |

### Property, Plant, and Equipment

Property, plant, and equipment are tangible resources of a relatively permanent nature that are used in the business and not intended for sale. This category includes land, buildings, machinery and equipment, delivery equipment, and furniture and fixtures. Assets subject to depreciation should be reported at cost less accumulated depreciation. This practice is illustrated in the following presentation of Delta Airlines:

**Illustration 4-20**

*Property, plant, and equipment section*

| DELTA AIRLINES, INC. | | | |
|---|---:|---:|---:|
| **Property, plant, and equipment** **(in thousands)** | | | |
| Flight equipment | $3,985,796 | | |
| Less: Accumulated depreciation | 1,713,059 | $2,272,737 | |
| Ground equipment | 865,628 | | |
| Less: Accumulated depreciation | 325,618 | 540,010 | $2,812,747 |

## Intangible Assets

Intangible assets are noncurrent resources that do not have physical substance. Intangible assets include patents, copyrights, and trademarks or trade names that give the holder **exclusive right** of use for a specified period of time. Their value to a company is generally derived from the rights or privileges granted by governmental authority.

In its balance sheet, Brunswick Corporation reported:

| **BRUNSWICK CORPORATION** | |
| --- | --- |
| Intangible assets | |
| Patents, trademarks, and other intangibles | $10,460,000 |

**Illustration 4-21**

*Intangible assets section*

## Current Liabilities

Listed first in the liabilities and owner's equity section of the balance sheet are current liabilities. Current liabilities are obligations that are reasonably expected to be paid from existing current assets or through the creation of other current liabilities. As in the case of current assets, the time period for payment is one year or the operating cycle, whichever is longer. Current liabilities include (1) debts related to the operating cycle, such as accounts payable and wages and salaries payable, and (2) other short-term debts, such as bank loans payable, interest payable, taxes payable, and current maturities of long-term obligations (payments to be made within the next year on long-term obligations).

The arrangement of items within the current liabilities section has evolved through custom rather than from a prescribed rule. Notes payable is usually listed first, followed by accounts payable. Other items are then listed in any order. The current liability section adapted from the balance sheet of UAL, Inc. (United Airlines) is as follows:

| **UAL, INC. (United Airlines)** | |
| --- | --- |
| Current liabilities (in thousands) | |
| Notes payable | $  297,518 |
| Accounts payable | 382,967 |
| Current maturities of long-term obligations | 81,525 |
| Unearned ticket revenue | 432,979 |
| Salaries and wages payable | 435,622 |
| Taxes payable | 80,390 |
| Other current liabilities | 240,652 |
| Total current liabilities | $1,951,653 |

**Illustration 4-22**

*Current liabilities section*

Users of financial statements look closely at the relationship between current assets and current liabilities. This relationship is important in evaluating a company's liquidity—its ability to pay obligations that are expected to become due within the next year or operating cycle. When current assets exceed current liabilities at the balance sheet date, the likelihood for paying the liabilities is favorable. When the reverse is true, short-term creditors may not be paid, and the company may ultimately be forced into bankruptcy.

### Long-Term Liabilities

Obligations expected to be paid after one year are classified as long-term liabilities (or long-term debt). Liabilities in this category include bonds payable, mortgages payable, long-term notes payable, lease liabilities, and obligations under employee pension plans. Many companies report long-term debt maturing after one year as a single amount in the balance sheet and show the details of the debt in the notes that accompany the financial statements. Others list the various sources of long-term liabilities. In its balance sheet, Consolidated Freightways, Inc. reported:

**Illustration 4-23**

*Long-term liabilities section*

| CONSOLIDATED FREIGHTWAYS, INC. | |
|---|---:|
| **Long-term liabilities (in thousands)** | |
| Bank notes payable | $10,000 |
| Mortgage payable | 2,900 |
| Bonds payable | 53,422 |
| Other long-term debt | 9,597 |
| Total long-term liabilities | $75,919 |

### Owner's Equity

The content of the owner's equity section varies with the form of business organization. In a proprietorship, there is one capital account. In a partnership, there is a capital account for each partner. For a corporation, owners' equity is divided into two accounts—Capital Stock and Retained Earnings. Investments of assets in the business by the stockholders is recorded in the Capital Stock account. Income retained for use in the business is recorded in the Retained Earnings account. These two accounts are combined and reported as stockholders' equity on the balance sheet. (We'll learn more about these corporation accounts in later chapters.)

In its balance sheet, the Americana Corporation reported its owners' (stockholders') equity section as follows:

**Illustration 4-24**

*Stockholders' equity section*

| AMERICANA CORPORATION | | |
|---|---:|---:|
| **Stockholders' equity** | | |
| Capital stock | $1,000,000 | |
| Retained earnings | 200,000 | |
| Total stockholders' equity | | $1,200,000 |

### Classified Balance Sheet Illustrated

An unclassified balance sheet of Pioneer Advertising Agency was presented in Illustration 3-19 on page 107. Using the same adjusted trial balance accounts for Pioneer at October 31, 1996, we can prepare the classified balance sheet shown in Illustration 4-25. For illustrative purposes, we have assumed that $1,000 of the notes payable is due currently and $4,000 is long-term.

The balance sheet is most often presented in **report form**, as in Illustration 4-25, with the assets shown above the liabilities and owner's equity. The balance sheet may also be presented in **account form** with the assets section placed on the left and the liabilities and owner's equity sections on the right.

**Illustration 4-25**

*Classified balance sheet in report form*

| PIONEER ADVERTISING AGENCY | | |
|---|---|---|
| Balance Sheet | | |
| October 31, 1996 | | |

### Assets

| | | |
|---|---|---|
| Current assets | | |
| Cash | | $15,200 |
| Accounts receivable | | 200 |
| Advertising supplies | | 1,000 |
| Prepaid insurance | | 550 |
| Total current assets | | 16,950 |
| Property, plant, and equipment | | |
| Office equipment | $5,000 | |
| Less: Accumulated depreciation | 40 | 4,960 |
| Total assets | | $21,910 |

### Liabilities and Owner's Equity

| | |
|---|---|
| Current liabilities | |
| Notes payable | $ 1,000 |
| Accounts payable | 2,500 |
| Interest payable | 50 |
| Unearned fees | 800 |
| Salaries payable | 1,200 |
| Total current liabilities | 5,550 |
| Long-term liabilities | |
| Notes payable | 4,000 |
| Total liabilities | 9,550 |
| Owner's equity | |
| C. R. Byrd, Capital | 12,360 |
| Total liabilities and owner's equity | $21,910 |

# Before You Go On . . .

## ► Review It

1. What are the major sections in a classified balance sheet?
2. What is the difference between the report form and the account form of the classified balance sheet?

## ► A Look Back at SRC Corporation

Refer to the opening story about SRC Corporation, and answer the following questions:

1. What is the lesson of the SRC story and Jack Stack's innovations?
2. How did Craig Highbarger's knowledge of financial statements, especially the income statement, contribute to his effectiveness as an employee?

*Solution:*

1. If you give employees equity in the company and provide them with the training and the information to understand the financial consequences of their decisions and actions, they will act more responsibly and make a greater contribution to the sales and income of the company. In other words, they begin to think like owners.
2. By understanding the income statement, he now recognizes the impact of revenues and expenses in arriving at net income—as well as how they affect his bonus.

# Summary of Study Objectives

**1.** *Prepare a work sheet.* The steps in preparing a work sheet are: (a) prepare a trial balance on the work sheet, (b) enter the adjustments in the adjustment columns, (c) enter adjusted balances in the adjusted trial balance columns, (d) extend adjusted trial balance amounts to appropriate financial statement columns, and (e) total the statement columns, compute net income (or net loss), and complete the work sheet.

**2.** *Explain the process of closing the books.* Closing the books occurs at the end of an accounting period. The process is to journalize and post closing entries and then rule and balance all accounts. In closing the books, separate entries are made to close revenues and expenses to Income Summary, Income Summary to owner's capital, and owner's drawings to owner's capital. Only temporary accounts are closed.

**3.** *Describe the content and purpose of a post-closing trial balance.* A post-closing trial balance contains the balances in permanent accounts that are carried forward to the next accounting period. The purpose of this trial balance is to prove the equality of these balances.

**4.** *State the required steps in the accounting cycle.* The required steps in the accounting cycle are: (a) analyze business transactions, (b) journalize the transactions, (c) post to ledger accounts, (d) prepare a trial balance, (e) journalize and post adjusting entries, (f) prepare an adjusted trial balance, (g) prepare financial statements, (h) journalize and post closing entries, and (i) prepare a post-closing trial balance.

**5.** *Explain the approaches to preparing correcting entries.* One approach for determining the correcting entry is to compare the incorrect entry with the correct entry. After comparison, a correcting entry is made to correct the accounts. An alternative to a correcting entry is to reverse the incorrect entry and then prepare the correct entry.

**6.** *Identify the sections of a classified balance sheet.* In a classified balance sheet, assets are classified as current assets; long-term investments; property, plant, and equipment; or intangibles. Liabilities are classified as either current or long-term. There is also an owner's equity section, which varies with the form of business organization.

# APPENDIX ▸ *Reversing Entries*

**STUDY OBJECTIVE**

*After studying this appendix, you should be able to:*

7. Prepare reversing entries.

After the financial statements are prepared and the books are closed, it is often helpful to reverse some of the adjusting entries before recording the regular transactions of the next period. Such entries are called reversing entries. **A reversing entry is made at the beginning of the next accounting period and is the exact opposite of the adjusting entry made in the previous period.** The recording of reversing entries is an **optional** step in the accounting cycle.

The purpose of reversing entries is to simplify the recording of a subsequent transaction related to an adjusting entry. In Chapter 3, you may recall, the payment of salaries after an adjusting entry resulted in two debits: one to Salaries Payable and the other to Salaries Expense. With reversing entries, the entire subsequent payment can be debited to Salaries Expense. **The use of reversing entries does not change the amounts reported in the financial statements. It does, however, simplify the recording of subsequent transactions.**

## Illustration of Reversing Entries

Reversing entries are most often used to reverse two types of adjusting entries: accrued revenues and accrued expenses. They are seldom made for prepaid expenses and unearned revenues. To illustrate the optional use of reversing entries for accrued expenses, we will use the salaries expense transactions for Pioneer Advertising Agency. The transaction and adjustment data are as follows:

1. October 26 (initial salary entry): $4,000 of salaries earned between October 15 and October 26 are paid.
2. October 31 (adjusting entry): Salaries earned between October 29 and October 31 are $1,200. These will be paid in the November 9 payroll.
3. November 9 (subsequent salary entry): Salaries paid are $4,000. Of this amount, $1,200 applied to accrued wages payable and $2,800 was earned between November 1 and November 9.

The comparative entries with and without reversing entries are shown in Illustration 4A-1.

**Illustration 4A-1**

*Comparative entries— not reversing vs. reversing*

| When Reversing Entries Are Not Used (per chapter) | | | | When Reversing Entries Are Used (per appendix) | | | |
|---|---|---|---|---|---|---|---|
| **Initial Salary Entry** | | | | **Initial Salary Entry** | | | |
| Oct. 26 | Salaries Expense | 4,000 | | Oct. 26 | Salaries Expense | 4,000 | |
| | Cash | | 4,000 | | Cash | | 4,000 |
| **Adjusting Entry** | | | | **Adjusting Entry** | | | |
| Oct. 31 | Salaries Expense | 1,200 | | Oct. 31 | Salaries Expense | 1,200 | |
| | Salaries Payable | | 1,200 | | Salaries Payable | | 1,200 |
| **Closing Entry** | | | | **Closing Entry** | | | |
| Oct. 31 | Income Summary | 5,200 | | Oct. 31 | Income Summary | 5,200 | |
| | Salaries Expense | | 5,200 | | Salaries Expense | | 5,200 |
| **Reversing Entry** | | | | **Reversing Entry** | | | |
| Nov. 1 | No reversing entry is made. | | | Nov. 1 | Salaries Payable | 1,200 | |
| | | | | | Salaries Expense | | 1,200 |
| **Subsequent Salary Entry** | | | | **Subsequent Salary Entry** | | | |
| Nov. 9 | Salaries Payable | 1,200 | | Nov. 9 | Salaries Expense | 4,000 | |
| | Salaries Expense | 2,800 | | | Cash | | 4,000 |
| | Cash | | 4,000 | | | | |

The comparative entries show that the first three entries are the same whether or not reversing entries are used. The last two entries, however, are different. The November 1 **reversing entry** eliminates the $1,200 balance in Salaries Payable that was created by the October 31 adjusting entry. The reversing entry also creates a $1,200 credit balance in the Salaries Expense account. As you know, it is unusual for an expense account to have a credit balance. The balance is correct in this instance, though, because it anticipates that the entire amount of the first salary payment in the new accounting period will be debited to Salaries Expense. This debit will eliminate the credit balance, and the resulting debit balance in the expense account will equal the salaries expense incurred in the new accounting period ($2,800 in this example).

▶**Technology in Action**

Using reversing entries in a computerized accounting system is more efficient than in a manual system. The reversing entry saves writing a program to locate the amount accrued from the preceding period and making the more complicated entry in the current period. That is, the computer does not have to be programmed to determine whether any accrued items exist.

When reversing entries are made, all cash payments of expenses can be debited to the expense account. This means that on November 9 (and every payday) Salaries Expense can be debited for the amount paid without regard to the existence of any accrued salaries payable. Being able to make the same entry each time simplifies the recording process. Note that when reversing entries are used, the recording of subsequent transactions is simplified because they can be recorded as if the related adjusting entry had never been made.

The posting of the entries with reversing entries is shown in Illustration 4A-2.

| Salaries Expense | | | | | | Salaries Payable | | | | | |
|---|---|---|---|---|---|---|---|---|---|---|---|
| 10/26 | Paid | 4,000 | 10/31 | Closing | 5,200 | 11/1 | Reversing | 1,200 | 10/31 | Adjusting | 1,200 |
| 31 | Adjusting | 1,200 | | | | | | | | | |
| | | 5,200 | | | 5,200 | | | | | | |
| 11/9 | Paid | 4,000 | 11/1 | Reversing | 1,200 | | | | | | |

**Illustration 4A-2**

*Postings with reversing entries*

Reversing entries may also be made for accrued revenue adjusting entries. For Pioneer Advertising, the adjusting entry was: Accounts Receivable (Dr.) $200 and Fees Earned (Cr.) $200. Thus, the reversing entry on November 1 is:

| Nov. 1 | Fees Earned | 200 | |
|---|---|---|---|
| | Accounts Receivable | | 200 |
| | (To reverse October 31 adjusting entry) | | |

When the accrued fees are collected, Cash is debited and Fees Earned is credited.

# Summary of Study Objective for Chapter 4 Appendix

**7.** *Prepare reversing entries.* Reversing entries are the direct opposite of the adjusting entry made in the preceding period. They are made at the beginning of a new accounting period to simplify the recording of later transactions related to the adjusting entry. In most cases, only accrued adjusting entries are reversed.

# Glossary

**Classified balance sheet**   A balance sheet that contains a number of standard classifications or sections. (p. 151).

**Closing entries**   Entries at the end of an accounting period to transfer the balances of temporary accounts to a permanent owner's equity account, owner's capital. (p. 141).

**Correcting entries**   Entries to correct errors made in recording transactions. (p. 148).

**Current assets**   Cash and other resources that are reasonably expected to be realized in cash or sold or consumed in the business within one year or the operating cycle, whichever is longer. (p. 151).

**Current liabilities**   Obligations reasonably expected to be paid from existing current assets or through the creation of other current liabilities within the next year or operating cycle, whichever is longer. (p. 153).

**Income Summary**   A temporary account used in closing revenue and expense accounts. (p. 141).

**Intangible assets**   Noncurrent resources that do not have physical substance. (p. 153).

**Liquidity**   The ability of a company to pay obligations that are expected to become due within the next year or operating cycle. (p. 153).

**Long-term investments** Resources not expected to be realized in cash within the next year or operating cycle. (p. 152).

**Long-term liabilities (Long-term debt)** Obligations expected to be paid after one year. (p. 154).

**Operating cycle** The average time required to go from cash to cash in producing revenues. (p. 151).

**Permanent (real) accounts** Balance sheet accounts whose balances are carried forward to the next accounting period. (p. 140).

**Post-closing trial balance** A list of permanent accounts and their balances after closing entries have been journalized and posted. (p. 144).

**Property, plant, and equipment** Assets of a relatively permanent nature that are being used in the business and not intended for resale. (p. 152).

**Reversing entry** An entry at the beginning of the next accounting period that is the exact opposite of the adjusting entry made in the previous period. (p. 145).

**Stockholders' equity** The ownership claim of shareholders on total assets. It is to a corporation what owner's equity is to a proprietorship. (p. 154).

**Temporary (nominal) accounts** Revenue, expense, and drawing accounts whose balances are transferred to owner's capital at the end of an accounting period. (p. 140).

**Work sheet** A multiple-column form that may be used in the adjustment process and in preparing financial statements. (p. 134).

# DEMONSTRATION PROBLEM

At the end of its first month of operations, the Watson Answering Service has the following unadjusted trial balance:

### WATSON ANSWERING SERVICE
### August 31, 1996
### Trial Balance

| | Debit | Credit |
|---|---|---|
| Cash | $ 5,400 | |
| Accounts Receivable | 2,800 | |
| Prepaid Insurance | 2,400 | |
| Supplies | 1,300 | |
| Equipment | 60,000 | |
| Notes Payable | | $40,000 |
| Accounts Payable | | 2,400 |
| Ray Watson, Capital | | 30,000 |
| Ray Watson, Drawing | 1,000 | |
| Fees Earned | | 4,900 |
| Salaries Expense | 3,200 | |
| Utilities Expense | 800 | |
| Advertising Expense | 400 | |
| | $77,300 | $77,300 |

**Problem-Solving Strategies**

1. In completing the work sheet, be sure to (a) key the adjustments, (b) extend adjusted balances to the correct statement columns, and (c) enter net income (or net loss) in the proper columns.

2. In preparing a classified balance sheet, know the contents of each of the sections.

3. In journalizing closing entries, remember that there are only four entries and that owner's drawing is closed to owner's capital.

Other data consist of the following:

1. Insurance expires at the rate of $200 per month.
2. There are $1,000 of supplies on hand at August 31.
3. Monthly depreciation is $900 on the equipment.
4. Interest of $500 has accrued during August on the notes payable.

*Instructions*

(a) Prepare a work sheet.
(b) Prepare a classified balance sheet assuming $35,000 of the notes payable are long-term.
(c) Journalize the closing entries.

## Solution to Demonstration Problem

(a)

**WATSON ANSWERING SERVICE**
**Work Sheet**
**For the Month Ended August 31, 1996**

| Account Titles | Trial Balance Dr. | Cr. | Adjustments Dr. | Cr. | Adjusted Trial Balance Dr. | Cr. | Income Statement Dr. | Cr. | Balance Sheet Dr. | Cr. |
|---|---|---|---|---|---|---|---|---|---|---|
| Cash | 5,400 | | | | 5,400 | | | | 5,400 | |
| Accounts Receivable | 2,800 | | | | 2,800 | | | | 2,800 | |
| Prepaid Insurance | 2,400 | | | (a) 200 | 2,200 | | | | 2,200 | |
| Supplies | 1,300 | | | (b) 300 | 1,000 | | | | 1,000 | |
| Equipment | 60,000 | | | | 60,000 | | | | 60,000 | |
| Notes Payable | | 40,000 | | | | 40,000 | | | | 40,000 |
| Accounts Payable | | 2,400 | | | | 2,400 | | | | 2,400 |
| Ray Watson, Capital | | 30,000 | | | | 30,000 | | | | 30,000 |
| Ray Watson, Drawing | 1,000 | | | | 1,000 | | | | 1,000 | |
| Fees Earned | | 4,900 | | | | 4,900 | | 4,900 | | |
| Salaries Expense | 3,200 | | | | 3,200 | | 3,200 | | | |
| Utilities Expense | 800 | | | | 800 | | 800 | | | |
| Advertising Expense | 400 | | | | 400 | | 400 | | | |
| Totals | 77,300 | 77,300 | | | | | | | | |
| Insurance Expense | | | (a) 200 | | 200 | | 200 | | | |
| Supplies Expense | | | (b) 300 | | 300 | | 300 | | | |
| Depreciation Expense | | | (c) 900 | | 900 | | 900 | | | |
| Accumulated Depreciation— Equipment | | | | (c) 900 | | 900 | | | | 900 |
| Interest Expense | | | (d) 500 | | 500 | | 500 | | | |
| Interest Payable | | | | (d) 500 | | 500 | | | | 500 |
| Totals | | | 1,900 | 1,900 | 78,700 | 78,700 | 6,300 | 4,900 | 72,400 | 73,800 |
| Net Loss | | | | | | | | 1,400 | 1,400 | |
| Totals | | | | | | | 6,300 | 6,300 | 73,800 | 73,800 |

Explanation: (a) Insurance expired, (b) Supplies used, (c) Depreciation expensed, (d) Interest accrued.

(b)

**WATSON ANSWERING SERVICE**
**Balance Sheet**
**August 31, 1996**

Assets

| | | |
|---|---|---|
| Current assets | | |
| Cash | | $ 5,400 |
| Accounts receivable | | 2,800 |
| Prepaid insurance | | 2,200 |
| Supplies | | 1,000 |
| Total current assets | | 11,400 |
| Property, plant, and equipment | | |
| Equipment | $60,000 | |
| Less: Accumulated depreciation—equipment | 900 | 59,100 |
| Total assets | | $70,500 |

Liabilities and Owner's Equity

| | | |
|---|---|---|
| Current liabilities | | |
| Notes payable | | $ 5,000 |
| Accounts payable | | 2,400 |
| Interest payable | | 500 |
| Total current liabilities | | 7,900 |

Long-term liabilities
  Notes payable                                                                35,000
    Total liabilities                                                          42,900
Owner's equity
  Ray Watson, Capital                                                          27,600*
    Total liabilities and owner's equity                                       $70,500

*Ray Watson, Capital, $30,000 less drawings $1,000 and net loss $1,400.

(c)

| | | | |
|---|---|---|---|
| Aug. 31 | Fees Earned | 4,900 | |
| | Income Summary | | 4,900 |
| | (To close revenue account) | | |
| 31 | Income Summary | 6,300 | |
| | Salaries Expense | | 3,200 |
| | Depreciation Expense | | 900 |
| | Utilities Expense | | 800 |
| | Interest Expense | | 500 |
| | Advertising Expense | | 400 |
| | Supplies Expense | | 300 |
| | Insurance Expense | | 200 |
| | (To close expense accounts) | | |
| 31 | Ray Watson, Capital | 1,400 | |
| | Income Summary | | 1,400 |
| | (To close net loss to capital) | | |
| 31 | Ray Watson, Capital | 1,000 | |
| | Ray Watson, Drawing | | 1,000 |
| | (To close drawings to capital) | | |

**\*Note:** All **asterisked** Questions, Exercises, and Problems relate to material contained in the appendix to the chapter.

# SELF-STUDY QUESTIONS

Answers are at the end of the chapter.

(SO 1)  1. Which of the following statements is *incorrect* concerning the work sheet?
  a. The work sheet is essentially a working tool of the accountant.
  b. The work sheet is distributed to management and other interested parties.
  c. The work sheet cannot be used as a basis for posting to ledger accounts.
  d. Financial statements can be prepared directly from the work sheet before journalizing and posting the adjusting entries.

(SO 1)  2. In a work sheet, net income is entered in the following columns:
  a. income statement (Dr) and balance sheet (Dr).
  b. income statement (Cr) and balance sheet (Dr).
  c. income statement (Dr) and balance sheet (Cr).
  d. income statement (Cr) and balance sheet (Cr).

(SO 2)  3. An account that will have a zero balance after closing entries have been journalized and posted is:
  a. Fees Earned.
  b. Advertising Supplies.
  c. Prepaid Insurance.
  d. Accumulated Depreciation.

(SO 2)  4. When a net loss has occurred, Income Summary is:
  a. debited and owner's capital is credited.
  b. credited and owner's capital is debited.
  c. debited and owner's drawing is credited.
  d. credited and owner's drawing is debited.

(SO 2)  5. The closing process involves separate entries to close (1) expenses, (2) drawings, (3) revenues and (4) net income (or loss). The correct sequencing of the entries is:
  a. (4), (3), (2), (1)
  b. (1), (2), (3), (4)
  c. (3), (1), (4), (2)
  d. (3), (2), (1), (4)

(SO 3)  6. Which types of accounts will appear in the post-closing trial balance?
  a. Permanent (real) accounts.
  b. Temporary (nominal) accounts.

c. Accounts shown in the income statement columns of a work sheet.
d. None of the above.

(SO 4)    7. All of the following are required steps in the accounting cycle *except*:
a. journalizing and posting closing entries.
b. preparing an adjusted trial balance.
c. preparing a post-closing trial balance.
d. preparing a work sheet.

(SO 5)    8. Cash of $100 received at the time the service was rendered was journalized and posted as a debit to Cash $100 and a credit to Accounts Receivable $100. Assuming the incorrect entry is not reversed, the correcting entry is:
a. debit Fees Earned $100 and credit Accounts Receivable $100.
b. debit Accounts Receivable $100 and credit Fees Earned $100.
c. debit Cash $100 and credit Fees Earned $100.
d. debit Accounts Receivable $100 and credit Cash $100.

(SO 6)    9. In a classified balance sheet, assets are usually classified as:
a. current assets; long-term assets; property, plant, and equipment; and intangible assets.

b. current assets; long-term investments; property, plant, and equipment; and other assets.
c. current assets; long-term investments; tangible assets; and intangible assets.
d. current assets; long-term investments; property, plant, and equipment; and intangible assets.

10. Current assets are listed:                                    (SO 6)
a. by liquidity.
b. by importance.
c. by longevity.
d. alphabetically.

*11. On December 31, the Mott Company correctly    (SO 7)
made an adjusting entry to recognize $2,000 of accrued salaries payable. On January 8 of the next year, total salaries of $3,400 were paid. Assuming the correct reversing entry was made on January 1, the entry on January 8 will result in a credit to Cash $3,400, and the following debit(s):
a. Salaries Payable $1,400 and Salaries Expense $2,000.
b. Salaries Payable $2,000 and Salaries Expense $1,400.
c. Salaries Expense $3,400.
d. Salaries Payable $3,400.

# Questions

1. "A work sheet is a permanent accounting record and its use is required in the accounting cycle." Do you agree? Explain.

2. The use of a work sheet affects two steps of the accounting cycle after preparing the trial balance. What steps are they, and how are they affected by the work sheet?

3. What is the relationship, if any, between the amount shown in the adjusted trial balance column for an account and that account's ledger balance?

4. If a company's revenues are $122,000 and its expenses are $113,000, in which financial statement columns of the work sheet will the net income of $9,000 appear? When expenses exceed revenues, in which columns will the difference appear?

5. Why is it necessary to prepare formal financial statements when all of the data are in the statement columns of the work sheet?

6. Identify the account(s) debited and credited in each of the four closing entries, assuming the company has net income for the year.

7. Describe the nature of the Income Summary account and identify the types of summary data that may be posted to this account.

8. What are the content and purpose of a post-closing trial balance?

9. Which of the following accounts would not appear in the post-closing trial balance? Interest Payable; Equipment; Depreciation Expense; Ben Alschuler, Drawing; Unearned Fees; Accumulated Depreciation—Equipment; and Fees Earned.

10. Distinguish between a reversing entry and an adjusting entry. Are reversing entries required?

11. Indicate, in the sequence in which they are made, the three required steps in the accounting cycle that involve journalizing.

12. Identify, in the sequence in which they are prepared, the three trial balances that are required in the accounting cycle.

13. How do correcting entries differ from adjusting entries?

14. What standard classifications are used in preparing a classified balance sheet?

15. What is meant by the term "operating cycle"?

16. Define current assets. What basis is used for arranging individual items within the current asset section?

17. Distinguish between long-term investments and property, plant, and equipment.

18. How do current liabilities differ from long-term liabilities?

19. (a) What is the term used to describe the owner's equity section of a corporation? (b) Identify the two owner's equity accounts in a corporation and indicate the purpose of each.

20. How does a report form balance sheet differ from an account form balance sheet?

*21. Kimbria Shumway Company prepares reversing entries. If the adjusting entry for interest payable is reversed, what type of an account balance, if any, will there be in Interest Payable and Interest Expense after the reversing entry is posted?

*22. At December 31, accrued salaries payable totaled $4,500. On January 10, total salaries of $7,000 are paid. (a) Assume that reversing entries are made at January 1. Give the January 10 entry and indicate the Salaries Expense account balance after the entry is posted. (b) Repeat part (a) assuming reversing entries are not made.

# BRIEF EXERCISES

**BE4–1** The steps in using a work sheet are presented in random order below. List the steps in the proper order.

_____ Total the statement columns, compute net income (loss), and complete the work sheet.
_____ Enter adjustment data.
_____ Prepare a trial balance on the work sheet.
_____ Enter adjusted balances.
_____ Extend adjusted balances to appropriate statement columns.

*List the steps in preparing a work sheet.*
*(SO 1)*

**BE4–2** The ledger of Ingram Company includes the following unadjusted balances: Prepaid Insurance $4,200, Fees Earned $58,000, and Salaries Expense $24,000. Adjusting entries are required for (a) expired insurance $1,600, (b) accrued fees earned $900, and (c) accrued salaries payable $800. Enter the unadjusted balances and adjustments into a work sheet and complete the work sheet for all accounts. Note: You will need to add the following accounts: Accounts Receivable, Salaries Payable, and Insurance Expense.

*Prepare partial work sheet.*
*(SO 1)*

**BE4–3** The following selected accounts appear in the adjusted trial balance columns of the work sheet for the Khanna Company: Accumulated Depreciation; Depreciation Expense; H. Khanna, Capital; H. Khanna, Drawing; Fees Earned; Supplies; and Accounts Payable. Indicate the financial statement column (income statement Dr., balance sheet Cr., etc.) to which each balance should be extended.

*Identify work sheet columns for selected accounts.*
*(SO 1)*

**BE4–4** The ledger of the Batan Company contains the following balances: T. Batan, Capital $30,000; T. Batan, Drawing $2,000; Fees Earned $41,000; Salaries Expense $26,000; and Supplies Expense $4,000. Prepare the closing entries at December 31.

*Prepare closing entries from ledger balances.*
*(SO 2)*

**BE4–5** Using the data in BE4–4, enter the balances in T accounts, post the closing entries, and rule and balance the accounts.

*Post closing entries and rule and balance T accounts.*
*(SO 2)*

**BE4–6** The income statement for the Edgebrook Golf Club for the month ending July 31 shows Green Fees Earned $16,000, Salaries Expense $6,200, Maintenance Expense $2,500, and Net Income $7,300. Prepare the entries to close the revenue and expense accounts. Post the entries to the revenue and expense accounts and complete the closing process for these accounts using the three-column form of account.

*Journalize and post closing entries using the three-column form of account.*
*(SO 2)*

**BE4–7** Using the data in BE4–3, identify the accounts that would be included in a post-closing trial balance.

*Identify post-closing trial balance accounts.*
*(SO 3)*

**BE4–8** The required steps in the accounting cycle are listed in random order below. List the steps in proper sequence.

_____ Prepare a post-closing trial balance.
_____ Prepare an adjusted trial balance.
_____ Analyze business transactions.
_____ Prepare a trial balance.
_____ Journalize the transactions.
_____ Journalize and post closing entries.
_____ Prepare financial statements.
_____ Journalize and post adjusting entries.
_____ Post to ledger accounts.

*List the required steps in the accounting cycle in sequence.*
*(SO 4)*

*Prepare correcting entries.*
(SO 5)

**BE4–9**   At Key Company, the following errors were discovered after the transactions had been journalized and posted. Prepare the correcting entries.

1. A collection on account from a customer for $780 was recorded as a debit to Cash $780 and a credit to Fees Earned $780.
2. The purchase of store supplies on account for $1,530 was recorded as a debit to Store Supplies $1,350 and a credit to Accounts Payable $1,350.

*Prepare the current asset section of a balance sheet.*
(SO 6)

**BE4–10**   The balance sheet debit column of the work sheet for Swann Company includes the following accounts: Accounts Receivable $16,500; Prepaid Insurance $3,600; Cash $18,400; Supplies $5,200, and Marketable Securities $8,200. Prepare the current asset section of the balance sheet listing the accounts in proper sequence.

*Prepare reversing entries.*
(SO 7)

**\*BE4–11**   At October 31, Diana Company made an accrued expense adjusting entry of $500 for salaries. Prepare the reversing entry on November 1 and indicate the balances in Salaries Payable and Salaries Expense after posting the reversing entry.

# EXERCISES

*Complete work sheet.*
(SO 1)

**E4–1**   The adjusted trial balance columns of the work sheet for Rey Sanchez Company are as follows:

## REY SANCHEZ COMPANY
### (Partial) Work Sheet
### For the Month Ended April 30, 1996

| Account Titles | Adjusted Trial Balance Dr. | Adjusted Trial Balance Cr. | Income Statement Dr. | Income Statement Cr. | Balance Sheet Dr. | Balance Sheet Cr. |
|---|---|---|---|---|---|---|
| Cash | 18,052 | | | | | |
| Accounts Receivable | 7,840 | | | | | |
| Prepaid Rent | 2,280 | | | | | |
| Equipment | 23,050 | | | | | |
| Accumulated Depreciation | | 4,921 | | | | |
| Notes Payable | | 5,700 | | | | |
| Accounts Payable | | 5,972 | | | | |
| R. Sanchez, Capital | | 33,960 | | | | |
| R. Sanchez, Drawing | 3,650 | | | | | |
| Fees Earned | | 12,590 | | | | |
| Salaries Expense | 6,840 | | | | | |
| Rent Expense | 760 | | | | | |
| Depreciation Expense | 671 | | | | | |
| Interest Expense | 57 | | | | | |
| Interest Payable | | 57 | | | | |
| Totals | 63,200 | 63,200 | | | | |

**Instructions**
Complete the work sheet.

*Prepare financial statements from work sheet.*
(SO 1, 6)

**E4–2**   Work sheet data for the Rey Sanchez Company are presented in E4–1.

**Instructions**
Prepare an income statement, an owner's equity statement, and a classified balance sheet.

*Journalize and post closing entries and prepare a post-closing trial balance.*
(SO 2, 3)

**E4–3**   Work sheet data for the Rey Sanchez Company are presented in E4–1.

**Instructions**
(a) Journalize the closing entries at April 30.
(b) Post the closing entries to Income Summary and R. Sanchez, Capital. Use T accounts.
(c) Prepare a post-closing trial balance at April 30.

**E4–4** The adjustments columns of the work sheet for Betsy Company are shown below.

*Prepare adjusting entries from a work sheet and extend balances to work sheet columns.*
*(SO 1)*

| | Adjustments | |
| --- | --- | --- |
| Account Titles | Debit | Credit |
| Accounts Receivable | 700 | |
| Prepaid Insurance | | 400 |
| Accumulated Depreciation | | 1,000 |
| Salaries Payable | | 600 |
| Fees Earned | | 700 |
| Salaries Expense | 600 | |
| Insurance Expense | 400 | |
| Depreciation Expense | 1,000 | |
| | 2,700 | 2,700 |

**Instructions**
(a) Prepare the adjusting entries.
(b) Assuming the adjusted trial balance amount for each account is normal, indicate the financial statement column to which each balance should be extended.

**E4–5** Selected work sheet data for Nikon Company are presented below.

*Derive adjusting entries from work sheet data.*
*(SO 1)*

| Account Titles | Trial Balance | | Adjusted Trial Balance | |
| --- | --- | --- | --- | --- |
| | Dr. | Cr. | Dr. | Cr. |
| Accounts Receivable | ? | | 34,000 | |
| Prepaid Insurance | 24,000 | | 18,000 | |
| Supplies | 9,000 | | ? | |
| Accumulated Depreciation | | 12,000 | | ? |
| Salaries Payable | | ? | | 7,000 |
| Fees Earned | | 90,000 | | 94,000 |
| Insurance Expense | | | ? | |
| Depreciation Expense | | | 10,000 | |
| Supplies Expense | | | 4,000 | |
| Salaries Expense | ? | | 49,000 | |

**Instructions**
(a) Fill in the missing amounts.
(b) Prepare the adjusting entries that were made.

**E4–6** The adjusted trial balance of Batra Company at the end of its fiscal year on July 31, 1996, is as follows:

*Journalize and post closing entries and prepare a post-closing trial balance.*
*(SO 2, 3)*

**BATRA COMPANY**
**Adjusted Trial Balance**
**July 31, 1996**

| No. | Account Titles | Debits | Credits |
| --- | --- | --- | --- |
| 101 | Cash | $ 11,940 | |
| 112 | Accounts Receivable | 8,780 | |
| 157 | Equipment | 15,900 | |
| 167 | Accumulated Depreciation | | $ 5,400 |
| 201 | Accounts Payable | | 6,220 |
| 208 | Unearned Rent Revenue | | 1,800 |
| 301 | R. Batra, Capital | | 45,200 |
| 306 | R. Batra, Drawing | 14,000 | |
| 404 | Commission Revenue | | 63,100 |
| 429 | Rent Revenue | | 6,500 |
| 711 | Depreciation Expense | 4,000 | |
| 720 | Salaries Expense | 58,700 | |
| 732 | Utilities Expense | 14,900 | |
| | | $128,220 | $128,220 |

*Instructions*

(a) Prepare the closing entries using page J15.

(b) Post to C. Batra, Capital and No. 350 Income Summary accounts. (Use the three-column form.)

(c) Prepare a post-closing trial balance at July 31.

*Prepare financial statements.*
*(SO 6)*

**E4–7**    The adjusted trial balance for Batra Company is presented in E4–6.

*Instructions*

(a) Prepare an income statement and an owner's equity statement for the year. Batra did not make any capital investments during the year.

(b) Prepare a classified balance sheet at July 31.

*Prepare closing entries and an owner's equity statement.*
*(SO 2)*

**E4–8**    Selected accounts for Barb's Beauty Salon are presented below. All June 30 postings are from closing entries.

| Salaries Expense | | | | Fees Earned | | | | Barb Ost, Capital | | | |
|---|---|---|---|---|---|---|---|---|---|---|---|
| 6/10 | 3,200 | 6/30 | 7,800 | 6/30 | 15,600 | 6/15 | 7,200 | 6/30 | 2,500 | 6/1 | 12,000 |
| 6/28 | 4,600 | | | | | 6/24 | 8,400 | | | 6/30 | 2,800 |
| | | | | | | | | | | Bal. | 12,300 |

| Supplies Expense | | | | Rent Expense | | | | Barb Ost, Drawing | | | |
|---|---|---|---|---|---|---|---|---|---|---|---|
| 6/12 | 800 | 6/30 | 1,500 | 6/1 | 3,500 | 6/30 | 3,500 | 6/13 | 1,000 | 6/30 | 2,500 |
| 6/24 | 700 | | | | | | | 6/25 | 1,500 | | |

*Instructions*

(a) Prepare the closing entries that were made.

(b) Post the closing entries to Income Summary.

*Prepare correcting entries.*
*(SO 5)*

**E4–9**    The Choi Company has an inexperienced accountant. During the first 2 weeks on the job, the following errors were made in journalizing transactions. All entries were posted as made.

1. A payment on account to a creditor of $530 was debited to Accounts Payable $350 and credited to Cash $350.

2. The purchase of supplies on account for $500 was debited to Equipment $50 and credited to Accounts Payable $50.

3. A $400 withdrawal of cash for L. Choi's personal use was debited to Salaries Expense $400 and credited to Cash $400.

*Instructions*

Prepare the correcting entries.

*Prepare a classified balance sheet.*
*(SO 6)*

**E4–10**    The adjusted trial balance for Summit's Bowling Alley at December 31, 1996, contains the following accounts.

| Debits | | Credits | |
|---|---|---|---|
| Building | $125,800 | T. Bolgos, Capital | $110,000 |
| Accounts Receivable | 14,520 | Accumulated Depreciation—Building | 45,600 |
| Prepaid Insurance | 4,680 | Accounts Payable | 13,480 |
| Cash | 20,840 | Mortgage Payable | 93,600 |
| Equipment | 62,400 | Accumulated Depreciation—Equipment | 18,720 |
| Land | 61,200 | Interest Payable | 2,600 |
| Insurance Expense | 780 | Bowling Revenues | 14,180 |
| Depreciation Expense | 5,360 | | $298,180 |
| Interest Expense | 2,600 | | |
| | $298,180 | | |

*Instructions*

(a) Prepare a classified balance sheet; assume that $13,600 of the mortgage payable will be paid in 1997.

(b) ▨▨▨▶ Comment on the liquidity of the company.

*E4–11 On December 31, the adjusted trial balance of Goode Employment Agency shows the following selected data:

*Prepare closing and reversing entries.*
(SO 2, 4, 7)

| | | | |
|---|---|---|---|
| Accounts Receivable | $5,000 | Commission Revenue | $97,000 |
| Interest Expense | 7,800 | Interest Payable | 2,000 |

Analysis shows that adjusting entries were made to (a) accrue $5,000 of commission revenue and (b) accrue $2,000 interest expense.

**Instructions**
(a) Prepare the closing entries for the temporary accounts at December 31.
(b) Prepare the reversing entries on January 1.
(c) Post the entries in (a) and (b). Rule and balance the accounts. (Use T accounts.)
(d) Prepare the entries to record (1) the collection of the accrued commissions on January 10 and (2) the payment of all interest due ($2,700) on January 15.
(e) Post the entries in (d) to the temporary accounts.

# PROBLEMS

P4–1 The trial balance columns of the work sheet for Everlast Roofing at March 31, 1996, are as follows:

*Prepare a work sheet, financial statements, and adjusting and closing entries.*
(SO 1, 2, 3, 6)

**EVERLAST ROOFING**
**Work Sheet**
**For the Month Ended March 31, 1996**

| Account Titles | Trial Balance | |
|---|---|---|
| | Dr. | Cr. |
| Cash | $ 2,700 | |
| Accounts Receivable | 1,600 | |
| Roofing Supplies | 1,100 | |
| Equipment | 6,000 | |
| Accumulated Depreciation—Equipment | | $ 1,200 |
| Accounts Payable | | 1,100 |
| Unearned Fees | | 300 |
| J. Cambo, Capital | | 7,000 |
| J. Cambo, Drawing | 600 | |
| Fees Earned | | 3,000 |
| Salaries Expense | 500 | |
| Miscellaneous Expense | 100 | |
| | $12,600 | $12,600 |

Other data:

1. A physical count reveals only $420 of roofing supplies on hand.
2. Depreciation for March is $200.
3. Unearned fees amounted to $100 after adjustment on March 31.
4. Accrued salaries are $400.

**Instructions**
(a) Enter the trial balance on a work sheet and complete the work sheet.
(b) Prepare an income statement and owner's equity statement for the month of March and classified balance sheet at March 31.
(c) Journalize the adjusting entries from the adjustments columns of the work sheet.
(d) Journalize the closing entries from the financial statement columns of the work sheet.

*Complete work sheet and*
*prepare financial statements,*
*closing entries, and post-*
*closing trial balance.*
(SO 1, 2, 3, 6)

**P4–2**  The adjusted trial balance columns of the work sheet for Diaz Company, owned by Carl Diaz, is as follows:

### DIAZ COMPANY
### Work Sheet
### For the Year Ended December 31, 1996

| Account No. | Account Titles | Adjusted Trial Balance Dr. | Adjusted Trial Balance Cr. |
|---|---|---|---|
| 101 | Cash | 14,600 | |
| 112 | Accounts Receivable | 15,400 | |
| 126 | Supplies | 1,500 | |
| 130 | Prepaid Insurance | 2,800 | |
| 151 | Office Equipment | 34,000 | |
| 152 | Accumulated Depreciation—Office Equipment | | 8,000 |
| 200 | Notes Payable | | 16,000 |
| 201 | Accounts Payable | | 6,000 |
| 212 | Salaries Payable | | 3,000 |
| 230 | Interest Payable | | 500 |
| 301 | C. Diaz, Capital | | 25,000 |
| 306 | C. Diaz, Drawing | 10,000 | |
| 400 | Fees Earned | | 88,000 |
| 610 | Advertising Expense | 14,000 | |
| 631 | Supplies Expense | 5,700 | |
| 711 | Depreciation Expense | 4,000 | |
| 722 | Insurance Expense | 5,000 | |
| 726 | Salaries Expense | 39,000 | |
| 905 | Interest Expense | 500 | |
| | | 146,500 | 146,500 |

### Instructions

(a) Complete the work sheet by extending the balances to the financial statement columns.

(b) Prepare an income statement, owner's equity statement, and a classified balance sheet. (Note: $10,000 of the notes payable become due in 1997.)

(c) Prepare the closing entries. Use J14 for the journal page.

(d) Post the closing entries and rule and balance the accounts. Use the three-column form of account. Income Summary is No. 350.

(e) Prepare a post-closing trial balance.

*Prepare financial statements,*
*closing entries, and post-*
*closing trial balance.*
(SO 1, 2, 3, 6)

**P4–3**  The completed financial statement columns of the work sheet for Melinda Company are shown below.

### MELINDA COMPANY
### Work Sheet
### For the Year Ended December 31, 1996

| Account No. | Account Titles | Income Statement Dr. | Income Statement Cr. | Balance Sheet Dr. | Balance Sheet Cr. |
|---|---|---|---|---|---|
| 101 | Cash | | | 13,600 | |
| 112 | Accounts Receivable | | | 13,500 | |
| 130 | Prepaid Insurance | | | 3,500 | |
| 157 | Equipment | | | 26,000 | |
| 167 | Accumulated Depreciation | | | | 5,600 |
| 201 | Accounts Payable | | | | 13,300 |
| 212 | Salaries Payable | | | | 3,000 |
| 301 | Ann Melinda, Capital | | | | 36,000 |
| 306 | Ann Melinda, Drawing | | | 12,000 | |
| 400 | Fees Earned | | 54,000 | | |
| 622 | Repair Expense | 1,800 | | | |

| | | | | | |
|---|---|---|---|---|---|
| 711 | Depreciation Expense | 2,600 | | | |
| 722 | Insurance Expense | 2,200 | | | |
| 726 | Salaries Expense | 35,000 | | | |
| 732 | Utilities Expense | 1,700 | | | |
| | Totals | 43,300 | 54,000 | 68,600 | 57,900 |
| | Net Income | 10,700 | | | 10,700 |
| | | 54,000 | 54,000 | 68,600 | 68,600 |

**Instructions**

(a) Prepare an income statement, owner's equity statement, and a classified balance sheet.

(b) Prepare the closing entries.

(c) Post the closing entries and rule and balance the accounts. Use T-accounts. Income Summary is No. 350.

(d) Prepare a post-closing trial balance.

**P4–4** Porter Management Services began business on January 1, 1996, with a capital investment of $120,000. The company manages condominiums for owners (Fees Earned) and rents space in its own office building (Rent Revenue). The trial and adjusted trial balance columns of the work sheet at the end of the first year are as follows:

*Complete work sheet and prepare classified balance sheet, entries, and post-closing trial balance.*
*(SO 1, 2, 3, 6)*

## PORTER MANAGEMENT SERVICES
### Work Sheet
### For the Year Ended December 31, 1996

| Account Titles | Trial Balance | | Adjusted Trial Balance | |
|---|---|---|---|---|
| | Dr. | Cr. | Dr. | Cr. |
| Cash | 12,500 | | 12,500 | |
| Accounts Receivable | 23,600 | | 23,600 | |
| Prepaid Insurance | 3,100 | | 1,600 | |
| Land | 56,000 | | 56,000 | |
| Building | 106,000 | | 106,000 | |
| Equipment | 48,000 | | 48,000 | |
| Accounts Payable | | 10,400 | | 10,400 |
| Unearned Rent Revenue | | 4,000 | | 1,800 |
| Mortgage Payable | | 100,000 | | 100,000 |
| B. Porter, Capital | | 120,000 | | 120,000 |
| B. Porter, Drawing | 20,000 | | 20,000 | |
| Fees Earned | | 75,600 | | 75,600 |
| Rent Revenue | | 24,000 | | 26,200 |
| Salaries Expense | 32,000 | | 32,000 | |
| Advertising Expense | 17,000 | | 17,000 | |
| Utilities Expense | 15,800 | | 15,800 | |
| Totals | 334,000 | 334,000 | | |
| Insurance Expense | | | 1,500 | |
| Depreciation Expense—Building | | | 2,500 | |
| Accumulated Depreciation—Building | | | | 2,500 |
| Depreciation Expense—Equipment | | | 3,900 | |
| Accumulated Depreciation—Equipment | | | | 3,900 |
| Interest Expense | | | 12,000 | |
| Interest Payable | | | | 12,000 |
| Totals | | | 352,400 | 352,400 |

**Instructions**

(a) Prepare a complete work sheet.

(b) Prepare a classified balance sheet. (Note: $10,000 of the mortgage payable is due for payment next year.)

(c) Journalize the adjusting entries.
(d) Journalize the closing entries.
(e) Prepare a post-closing trial balance.

*Complete all steps in accounting cycle.*
(SO 1, 2, 3, 4, 6)

**P4–5** Jan Jansen opened Jan's Window Washing on July 1, 1996. During July the following transactions were completed.

July  1  Invested $8,000 cash in the business.
      1  Purchased used truck for $6,000, paying $3,000 cash and the balance on account.
      3  Purchased cleaning supplies for $900 on account.
      5  Paid $1,200 cash on one-year insurance policy effective July 1.
     12  Billed customers $2,500 for cleaning services.
     18  Paid $1,000 cash on amount owed on truck and $500 on amount owed on cleaning supplies.
     20  Paid $1,200 cash for employee salaries.
     21  Collected $1,400 cash from customers billed on July 12.
     25  Billed customers $3,000 for cleaning services.
     31  Paid gas and oil for month on truck $200.
     31  Withdrew $600 cash for personal use.

The chart of accounts for Jan's Window Washing contains the following accounts: No. 101 Cash, No. 112 Accounts Receivable, No. 128 Cleaning Supplies, No. 130 Prepaid Insurance, No. 157 Equipment, No. 158 Accumulated Depreciation—Equipment, No. 201 Accounts Payable, No. 212 Salaries Payable, No. 301 Jan Jansen, Capital, No. 306 Jan Jansen, Drawing, No. 350 Income Summary, No. 400 Fees Earned, No. 633 Gas & Oil Expense, No. 634 Cleaning Supplies Expense, No. 711 Depreciation Expense, No. 722 Insurance Expense, No. 726 Salaries Expense.

*Instructions*
(a) Journalize and post the July transactions. Use page J1 for the journal and the three-column form of account.
(b) Prepare a trial balance at July 31 on a work sheet.
(c) Enter the following adjustments on the work sheet and complete the work sheet.
    (1) Earned but unbilled fees at July 31 were $1,100.
    (2) Depreciation on equipment for the month was $200.
    (3) One-twelfth of the insurance expired.
    (4) An inventory count shows $600 of cleaning supplies on hand at July 31.
    (5) Accrued but unpaid employee salaries were $400.
(d) Prepare the income statement and owner's equity statement for July and a classified balance sheet at July 31.
(e) Journalize and post adjusting entries. Use page J2 for the journal.
(f) Journalize and post closing entries and complete the closing process. Use page J3 for the journal.
(g) Prepare a post-closing trial balance at July 31.

*Analyze errors and prepare correcting entries.*
(SO 5)

**P4–6** Michael Mears, CPA, was retained by Campus TV Repair to prepare financial statements for April 1996. Mears accumulated all the ledger balances per Morris's records and found the following:

**CAMPUS TV REPAIR**
**Trial Balance**
**April 30, 1996**

|  | Debit | Credit |
|---|---|---|
| Cash | $ 5,100 | |
| Accounts Receivable | 3,200 | |
| Supplies | 800 | |
| Equipment | 10,600 | |
| Accumulated Depreciation | | $ 1,350 |
| Accounts Payable | | 2,100 |
| Salaries Payable | | 500 |
| Unearned Fees | | 890 |

| | | |
|---|---:|---:|
| S. Morris, Capital | | 13,900 |
| Fees Earned | | 5,450 |
| Salaries Expense | 3,300 | |
| Advertising Expense | 400 | |
| Miscellaneous Expense | 290 | |
| Depreciation Expense | 500 | |
| | $24,190 | $24,190 |

Michael Mears reviewed the records and found the following errors:

1. Cash received from a customer on account was recorded as $650 instead of $560.
2. The purchase, on account, of a typewriter costing $340 was recorded as a debit to supplies and a credit to accounts payable for $340.
3. A payment of $30 for advertising expense was entered as a debit to Miscellaneous Expense $30 and a credit to Cash $30.
4. The first salary payment this month was for $1,900, which included $500 of salaries payable on March 31. The payment was recorded as a debit to Salaries Expense $1,900 and a credit to Cash $1,900. (No reversing entries were made on April 1.)
5. A cash payment of repair expense on equipment for $86 was recorded as a debit to Equipment $68 and a credit to Cash $68.

*Instructions*
(a) Prepare an analysis of each error showing (1) the incorrect entry, (2) the correct entry, and (3) the correcting entry.
(b) Prepare a correct trial balance.

# ALTERNATE PROBLEMS

**P4–1A** Pierre Mason began operations as a private investigator on January 1, 1996. The trial balance columns of the work sheet for Mason P.I. at March 31 are as follows:

*Prepare work sheet, financial statements, and adjusting and closing entries.*
*(SO 1, 2, 3, 6)*

### MASON P.I.
### Work Sheet
### For the Quarter Ended March 31, 1996

| | Trial Balance | |
|---|---:|---:|
| Account Titles | Dr. | Cr. |
| Cash | $12,400 | |
| Accounts Receivable | 5,620 | |
| Supplies | 1,050 | |
| Prepaid Insurance | 2,400 | |
| Equipment | 30,000 | |
| Notes Payable | | $10,000 |
| Accounts Payable | | 12,350 |
| P. Mason, Capital | | 20,000 |
| P. Mason, Drawing | 600 | |
| Fees Earned | | 13,620 |
| Salaries Expense | 1,200 | |
| Travel Expense | 1,300 | |
| Rent Expense | 1,200 | |
| Miscellaneous Expense | 200 | |
| | $55,970 | $55,970 |

Other data:

1. Supplies on hand total $750.
2. Depreciation is $400 per quarter.
3. Interest accrued on six months note payable, issued January 1, $300.
4. Insurance expires at the rate of $150 per month.
5. Fees earned but unbilled at March 31 total $750.

### Instructions
(a) Enter the trial balance on a work sheet and complete the work sheet.
(b) Prepare an income statement and owner's equity statement for the quarter and a classified balance sheet at March 31.
(c) Journalize the adjusting entries from the adjustments columns of the work sheet.
(d) Journalize the closing entries from the financial statement columns of the work sheet.

*Complete work sheet and prepare financial statements, closing entries, and post-closing trial balance.*
*(SO 1, 2, 3, 6)*

**P4–2A**   The adjusted trial balance columns of the work sheet for Ohno Company is as follows:

### OHNO COMPANY
### Work Sheet
### For the Year Ended December 31, 1996

| Account No. | Account Titles | Adjusted Trial Balance Dr. | Cr. |
|---|---|---|---|
| 101 | Cash | 24,800 | |
| 112 | Accounts Receivable | 15,400 | |
| 126 | Supplies | 2,300 | |
| 130 | Prepaid Insurance | 4,800 | |
| 151 | Office Equipment | 44,000 | |
| 152 | Accumulated Depreciation—Office Equipment | | 18,000 |
| 200 | Notes Payable | | 20,000 |
| 201 | Accounts Payable | | 8,000 |
| 212 | Salaries Payable | | 3,000 |
| 230 | Interest Payable | | 1,000 |
| 301 | Y. Ohno, Capital | | 36,000 |
| 306 | Y. Ohno, Drawing | 12,000 | |
| 400 | Fees Earned | | 79,000 |
| 610 | Advertising Expense | 12,000 | |
| 631 | Supplies Expense | 3,700 | |
| 711 | Depreciation Expense | 6,000 | |
| 722 | Insurance Expense | 4,000 | |
| 726 | Salaries Expense | 35,000 | |
| 905 | Interest Expense | 1,000 | |
| | | 165,000 | 165,000 |

### Instructions
(a) Complete the work sheet by extending the balances to the financial statement columns.
(b) Prepare an income statement, owner's equity statement, and a classified balance sheet. $10,000 of the notes payable become due in 1997.
(c) Prepare the closing entries. Use J14 for the journal page.
(d) Post the closing entries and rule and balance the accounts. Use the three-column form of account. Income Summary is No. 350.
(e) Prepare a post-closing trial balance.

*Prepare financial statements, closing entries, and post-closing trial balance.*
*(SO 1, 2, 3, 6)*

**P4–3A**   The completed financial statement columns of the work sheet for Batavia Company are shown below.

### BATAVIA COMPANY
### Work Sheet
### For the Year Ended December 31, 1996

| Account No. | Account Titles | Income Statement Dr. | Cr. | Balance Sheet Dr. | Cr. |
|---|---|---|---|---|---|
| 101 | Cash | | | 8,200 | |
| 112 | Accounts Receivable | | | 7,500 | |
| 130 | Prepaid Insurance | | | 1,800 | |
| 157 | Equipment | | | 28,000 | |
| 167 | Accumulated Depreciation | | | | 8,600 |

| | | | | | |
|---|---|---|---|---|---|
| 201 | Accounts Payable | | | | 12,000 |
| 212 | Salaries Payable | | | | 3,000 |
| 301 | Millie Batavia, Capital | | | | 34,000 |
| 306 | Millie Batavia, Drawing | | | 7,200 | |
| 400 | Fees Earned | | 42,000 | | |
| 622 | Repair Expense | 3,200 | | | |
| 711 | Depreciation Expense | 2,800 | | | |
| 722 | Insurance Expense | 1,200 | | | |
| 726 | Salaries Expense | 36,000 | | | |
| 732 | Utilities Expense | 3,700 | | | |
| | Totals | 46,900 | 42,000 | 52,700 | 57,600 |
| | Net Loss | | 4,900 | 4,900 | |
| | | 46,900 | 46,900 | 57,600 | 57,600 |

### Instructions

(a) Prepare an income statement, owner's equity statement, and a classified balance sheet.

(b) Prepare the closing entries.

(c) Post the closing entries and rule and balance the accounts. Use T-accounts. Income Summary is No. 350.

(d) Prepare a post-closing trial balance.

**P4–4A** Space Amusement Park has a fiscal year ending on September 30. Selected data from the September 30 work sheet are presented below:

*Complete work sheet and prepare classified balance sheet, entries, and post-closing trial balance.*

*(SO 1, 2, 3, 6)*

### SPACE AMUSEMENT PARK
### Work Sheet
### For the Year Ended September 30, 1996

| | Trial Balance | | Adjusted Trial Balance | |
|---|---|---|---|---|
| | Dr. | Cr. | Dr. | Cr. |
| Cash | 37,400 | | 37,400 | |
| Supplies | 18,600 | | 1,200 | |
| Prepaid Insurance | 31,900 | | 3,900 | |
| Land | 80,000 | | 80,000 | |
| Equipment | 120,000 | | 120,000 | |
| Accumulated Depreciation | | 36,200 | | 43,000 |
| Accounts Payable | | 14,600 | | 14,600 |
| Unearned Admissions | | 2,700 | | 1,700 |
| Mortgage Payable | | 50,000 | | 50,000 |
| L. A. Sparks, Capital | | 109,700 | | 109,700 |
| L. A. Sparks, Drawing | 14,000 | | 14,000 | |
| Admission Revenue | | 278,500 | | 279,500 |
| Salaries Expense | 109,000 | | 109,000 | |
| Repair Expense | 30,500 | | 30,500 | |
| Advertising Expense | 9,400 | | 9,400 | |
| Utilities Expense | 16,900 | | 16,900 | |
| Property Taxes Expense | 18,000 | | 21,000 | |
| Interest Expense | 6,000 | | 12,000 | |
| Totals | 491,700 | 491,700 | | |
| Insurance Expense | | | 28,000 | |
| Supplies Expense | | | 17,400 | |
| Interest Payable | | | | 6,000 |
| Depreciation Expense | | | 6,800 | |
| Property Taxes Payable | | | | 3,000 |
| Totals | | | 507,500 | 507,500 |

**Instructions**

(a) Prepare a complete work sheet.

(b) Prepare a classified balance sheet. (Note: $10,000 of the mortgage payable is due for payment in the next fiscal year.)

(c) Journalize the adjusting entries using the work sheet as a basis.

(d) Journalize the closing entries using the work sheet as a basis.

(e) Prepare a post-closing trial balance.

*Complete all steps in accounting cycle.*
*(SO 1, 2, 3, 4, 6)*

**P4–5A**   Helga Kohl opened Helga's Carpet Cleaners on March 1. During March, the following transactions were completed.

| | | |
|---|---|---|
| July | 1 | Invested $10,000 cash in the business. |
| | 1 | Purchased used truck for $6,000, paying $4,000 cash and the balance on account. |
| | 3 | Purchased cleaning supplies for $1,200 on account. |
| | 5 | Paid $1,800 cash on one-year insurance policy effective March 1. |
| | 14 | Billed customers $2,800 for cleaning services. |
| | 18 | Paid $1,500 cash on amount owed on truck and $500 on amount owed on cleaning supplies. |
| | 20 | Paid $1,500 cash for employee salaries. |
| | 21 | Collected $1,600 cash from customers billed on July 14. |
| | 28 | Billed customers $3,200 for cleaning services. |
| | 31 | Paid gas and oil for month on truck $200. |
| | 31 | Withdrew $900 cash for personal use. |

The chart of accounts for Helga's Carpet Cleaners contains the following accounts: No. 101 Cash, No. 112 Accounts Receivable, No. 128 Cleaning Supplies, No. 130 Prepaid Insurance, No. 157 Equipment, No. 158 Accumulated Depreciation—Equipment, No. 201 Accounts Payable, No. 212 Salaries Payable, No. 301 H. Kohl, Capital, No. 306 H. Kohl, Drawing, No. 350 Income Summary, No. 400 Fees Earned, No. 633 Gas & Oil Expense, No. 634 Cleaning Supplies Expense, No. 711 Depreciation Expense, No. 722 Insurance Expense, No. 726 Salaries Expense.

**Instructions**

(a) Journalize and post the March transactions. Use page J1 for the journal and the three-column form of account.

(b) Prepare a trial balance at March 31 on a work sheet.

(c) Enter the following adjustments on the work sheet and complete the work sheet.

(1) Earned but unbilled fees at March 31 were $600.

(2) Depreciation on equipment for the month was $250.

(3) One-twelfth of the insurance expired.

(4) An inventory count shows $400 of cleaning supplies on hand at March 31.

(5) Accrued but unpaid employee salaries were $500.

(d) Prepare the income statement and owner's equity statement for March and a classified balance sheet at March 31.

(e) Journalize and post adjusting entries. Use page J2 for the journal.

(f) Journalize and post closing entries and complete the closing process. Use page J3 for the journal.

(g) Prepare a post-closing trial balance at March 31.

# ▼*B*roadening Your Perspective

## *F*INANCIAL REPORTING PROBLEM

The financial statements of PepsiCo, Inc. are presented in Appendix A at the end of this textbook.

*Instructions*
Answer the following questions using the Consolidated Balance Sheet and the Notes to Consolidated Financial Statements section.

1. What were PepsiCo's total current assets at December 31, 1994, and December 25, 1993?
2. Are assets included in current assets listed in proper order? Explain.
3. How are PepsiCo's assets classified?
4. What are "cash equivalents"?
5. What were PepsiCo's total current liabilities at December 31, 1994, and December 25, 1993?
6. What was the composition of the company's short-term borrowing balance at December 31, 1994?

## *D*ECISION CASE

Moody Janitorial Service was started 2 years ago by Pat Moody. Because business has been exceptionally good, Pat decided on July 1, 1996, to expand operations by acquiring an additional truck and hiring two more assistants. To finance the expansion, Pat obtained on July 1, 1996, a $25,000, 10% bank loan, payable $10,000 on July 1, 1997, and the balance on July 1, 1998. The terms of the loan require the borrower to have $10,000 more current assets than current liabilities at December 31, 1996. If these terms are not met, the bank loan will be refinanced at 15% interest.

At December 31, 1996, the accountant for Moody Janitorial Service prepared the following balance sheet:

### MOODY JANITORIAL SERVICE
### Balance Sheet
### December 31, 1996

#### Assets

| | | |
|---|---:|---:|
| Current assets | | |
| Cash | | $ 6,500 |
| Accounts receivable | | 9,000 |
| Janitorial supplies | | 5,200 |
| Prepaid insurance | | 4,800 |
| Total current assets | | 25,500 |
| Property, plant, and equipment | | |
| Cleaning equipment (net) | $22,000 | |
| Delivery trucks (net) | 34,000 | 56,000 |
| Total assets | | $81,500 |

#### Liabilities and Owner's Equity

| | | |
|---|---:|---:|
| Current liabilities | | |
| Notes payable | | $10,000 |
| Accounts payable | | 2,500 |
| Total current liabilities | | 12,500 |
| Long-term liability | | |
| Notes payable | | 15,000 |
| Total liabilities | | 27,500 |

Owner's equity
    Pat Moody, Capital          54,000
    Total liabilities and owner's equity    $81,500

Pat presented the balance sheet to the bank's loan office on January 2, 1997, confident that the company had met the terms of the loan. The loan officer was not impressed. She said, "We need financial statements audited by a CPA."

A CPA was hired and immediately realized that the balance sheet had been prepared from a trial balance and not from an adjusted trial balance. The adjustment data at the balance sheet date consisted of the following:

1. Earned but unbilled janitorial services were $2,400.
2. Janitorial supplies on hand were $3,500.
3. Prepaid insurance was a three-year policy dated January 1, 1996.
4. December expenses incurred but unpaid at December 31, $250.
5. Interest on the bank loan was not recorded.
6. The amounts for plant assets were net of accumulated depreciation of $4,000 for cleaning equipment and $5,000 for delivery trucks as of January 1, 1996. Depreciation for 1996 was $2,000 for cleaning equipment and $5,000 for delivery trucks.

*Instructions*
(a) Prepare a correct balance sheet.
(b) Were the terms of the bank loan met? Explain.


# COMMUNICATION ACTIVITY

The accounting cycle is important in understanding the accounting process.

*Instructions*
Write a memorandum to your instructor which lists the required steps in the order in which they should be completed. Complete your memorandum with a paragraph that explains the optional steps in the accounting cycle.


# GROUP ACTIVITY

A classified balance sheet has the following sections: current assets; property, plant, and equipment; long-term investments; intangible assets; current liabilities; long-term liabilities; and stockholders' equity.

*Instructions*
With the class divided into seven groups, each group should choose one section of the classified balance sheet. Each group is to explain its section and illustrate the section using an example from a published annual report.


# ETHICS CASE

As the controller of Breathless Perfume Company, you discover a significant misstatement that overstated net income in the prior year's financial statements. The misleading financial statements are contained in the company's annual report which was issued to banks and other creditors less than a month ago. After much thought about the consequences of telling the president, Eddy Kadu, about this misstatement, you gather your courage to inform him. Eddy says, "Hey! What they don't know won't hurt them. But, just so we set the record straight, we'll adjust this year's financial statements for last year's misstatement. We can absorb that misstatement better in this year than in last year anyway! Just don't make that kind of mistake again."

*Instructions*

    (a)  Who are the stakeholders in this situation?

    (b)  What are the ethical issues in this situation?

    (c)  What would you do as a controller in this situation?

# CRITICAL THINKING
## ▸ *A Real-World Focus: Bethlehem Corporation*

......................................................................................

*Located in Easton, Pennsylvania, **Bethlehem Corp.** was established in 1856. Today it offers contract services for industrial products, rebuilding and remanufacturing industrial and military equipment per customer specifications and designs. The company also manufactures and sells a line of equipment used in the chemical, environmental, and food industries.*

Bethlehem Corporation has a net loss for 1994 of $239,251. One reason for the loss is that Bethlehem established an accrual to provide for expenses and costs associated with certain legal proceedings against Bethlehem.

*Instructions*

    (a)  Indicate how the net loss would be shown in Bethlehem's 1994 work sheet.

    (b)  Where in the general ledger would you expect to find the two accounts related to the accrual for expenses and costs associated with legal proceedings?

    (c)  Identify the financial statement columns to which the balances of the two accounts in part (b) would be extended on the work sheet.

---

*Answers to Self-Study Questions*

1. b    2. c    3. a    4. b    5. c    6. a    7. d    8. b    9. d    10. a    11. c

**Before studying this chapter, you should know or, if necessary, review:**

**a.** *How to prepare a work sheet. (Ch. 4, pp. 135–39)*
**b.** *How to close revenue, expense, and drawing accounts. (Ch. 4, pp. 140–44)*
**c.** *The steps in the accounting cycle. (Ch. 4, p. 148)*

# Dropped Courses Produce Bookstore Headaches

PULLMAN, Wash. — Larry Martin is in charge of ordering textbooks for the Washington State University bookstore in Pullman, Washington. The bookstore sells about $4 million in textbooks each year. The average inventory at any point in time is 2,500 titles.

Mr. Martin's big challenge is to order enough books to satisfy demand—but not to order too many. For example, say a course historically has sold 75 books; he'll order 85 to be on the safe side. The reason: if he orders short, he'll have to order additional books by second-day air express—which is expensive and cuts into profits. However, if Martin orders too many, the publisher won't accept for return more than 20% of his original order.

Of course, returns occur all the time, especially when students drop courses during the first week of class. If the returned books are in "new and resalable" condition, the publisher will accept the return of such books and issue Martin a credit memo.

Washington State University starts its fall term before Labor Day. The busy book selling and return period lasts three to four weeks. Therefore, Martin waits until the end of September to take the inventory and determine his returns. That count also tells him his beginning inventory for the next term. At that point, he is ready to order more books. ◀

CHAPTER · **5**

# *A*CCOUNTING FOR MERCHANDISING OPERATIONS

---

▶ **STUDY OBJECTIVES** ◀

**After studying this chapter, you should be able to:**

**1.** *Identify the components in measuring net income in a merchandising company.*

**2.** *Explain the entries for sales revenues.*

**3.** *State the steps in determining cost of goods sold.*

**4.** *Explain the computation and importance of gross profit.*

**5.** *Identify the unique features of the income statement for a merchandising company.*

**6.** *Explain the steps in the accounting cycle for a merchandising company.*

**7.** *Distinguish between a multiple-step and a single-step income statement.*

As indicated in the opening story, Washington State University Bookstore buys and sells goods rather than performs services to earn a profit. Merchandising companies that purchase and sell directly to consumers—such as Kmart, Washington State Bookstore, Safeway, and Toys "R" Us—are called **retailers**. In contrast, merchandising companies that sell to retailers are known as **wholesalers**. For example, retailer Walgreens might buy goods from wholesaler McKesson & Robbins; Office Depot might buy office supplies from wholesaler United Stationers.

The steps in the accounting cycle for a merchandising company are the same as the steps for a service enterprise. However, merchandising companies use additional accounts and entries which are required in recording merchandising transactions. The content and organization of this chapter are as follows:

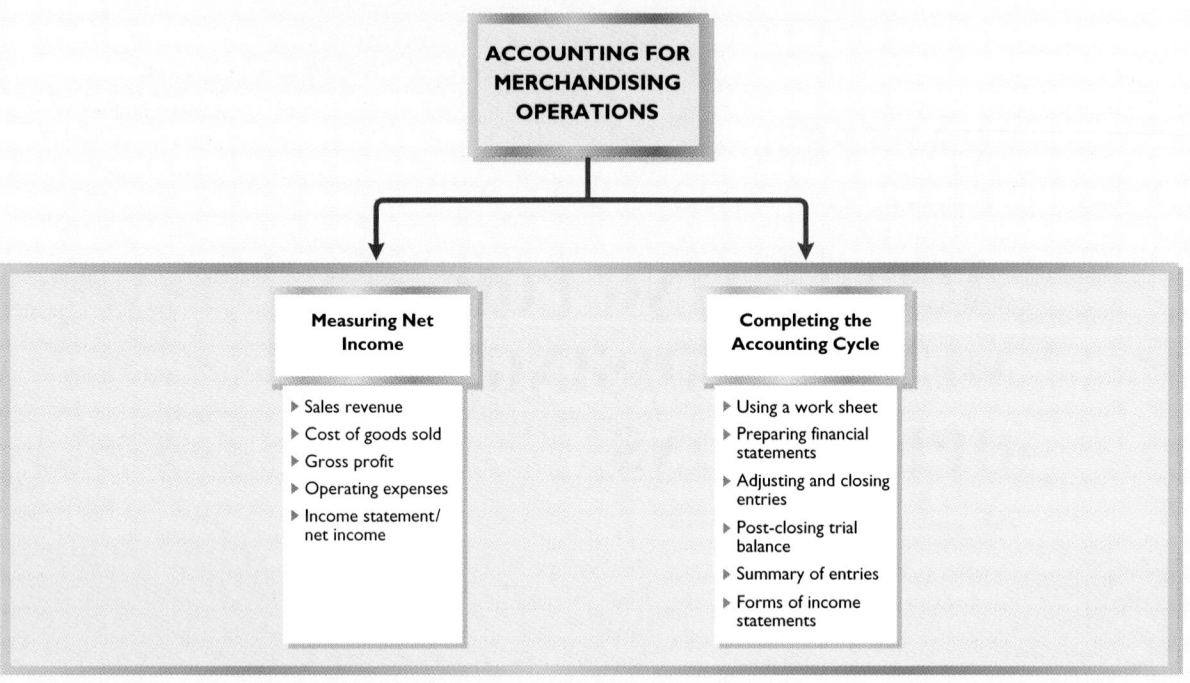

## SECTION 1 ► *Measuring Net Income*

**STUDY OBJECTIVE**
•••••••••• 1 ••••••••••
*Identify the components in measuring net income in a merchandising company.*

Measuring net income for a merchandising company is conceptually the same as for a service enterprise. That is, net income (or loss) results from the matching of expenses with revenues. In a merchandising company, the primary source of revenues is the sale of merchandise, often referred to simply as sales revenue or sales. Unlike expenses for a service company, expenses for a merchandising company are divided into two categories: (1) the cost of goods sold and (2) operating expenses.

The cost of goods sold is the total cost of merchandise sold during the period. This expense is directly related to the revenue recognized from the sale of the goods. You will see later in this chapter exactly how cost of goods sold is calculated.

Sales revenue less cost of goods sold is called gross profit (or gross margin) on sales. For example, when a pocket calculator costing $15 is sold for $25, the gross profit is $10. Merchandising companies customarily report gross profit on sales in the income statement.

After gross profit is calculated, operating expenses are deducted to determine net income (or loss). Operating expenses are expenses incurred in the process of earning sales revenue. Examples of operating expenses are sales salaries, advertising expense, and insurance expense. The operating expenses of a merchandising company include many of the expenses found in a service enterprise.

The income measurement process for a merchandising company may be diagrammed as shown in Illustration 5-1. The items in the two blue boxes are peculiar to a merchandising company; they are not used by a service company.

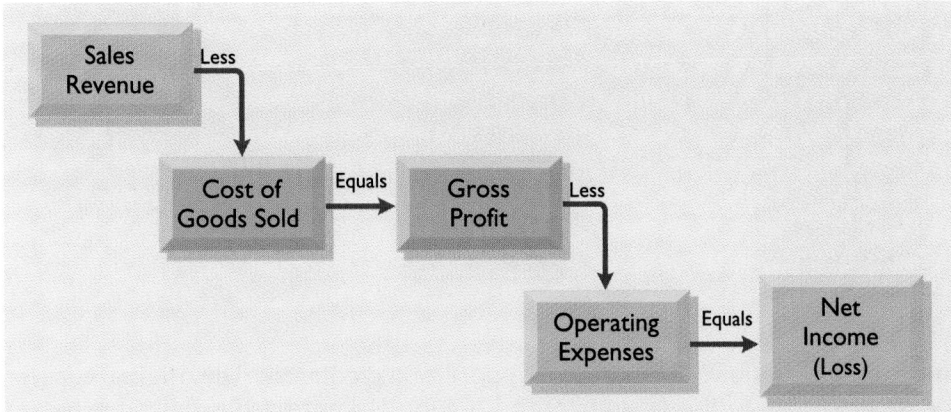

**Illustration 5-1**

*Income measurement process for a merchandising company*

While measuring income for a merchandising company is conceptually the same as for a service company, their operating cycles differ. The normal operating cycle of a merchandising company ordinarily is longer than that of a service company. The purchase of merchandise inventory and its eventual sale lengthens the cycle. Graphically, the operating cycles of service and merchandising companies can be contrasted as shown in Illustration 5-2. Note that the added asset account for a merchandising company is an **inventory** account (usually entitled Merchandise Inventory).

# Sales Revenue

Sales revenues, like service revenues, are recorded when earned. This is in accordance with the revenue recognition principle. Typically, sales revenues are earned when the goods are transferred from the seller to the buyer. At this point, the sales transaction is completed and the sales price is established.

Sales may be made on credit or for cash. Every sales transaction should be supported by a **business document** that provides written evidence of the sale. **Cash register tapes** provide evidence of cash sales. A sales invoice, like the one

**STUDY OBJECTIVE**
▼ 2

*Explain the entries for sales revenues.*

**Illustration 5-2**

*Operating cycles for a service company and a merchandising company*

**Service Company**

**Merchandising Company**

shown in Illustration 5-3, provides support for a credit sale. The original copy of the invoice goes to the customer, and a copy is kept by the seller for use in recording the sale. The invoice shows the date of sale, customer name, total sales price, and other relevant information.

To record a sale, an asset account is debited, and the revenue account, Sales, is credited. For cash sales, the Cash account is debited. For credit sales, Accounts Receivable is debited. The following entry is made by Highpoint Electronic to record the credit sale for the sales invoice shown in Illustration 5-3.

| May 4 | Accounts Receivable | 3,800 | |
| |    Sales | | 3,800 |
| |      (To record credit sale per invoice #731) | | |

As indicated by this entry, sales revenues can be recorded before cash is actually collected. For credit sales, the amount due may not be collected until the next period. Therefore, the sales revenues earned during a particular period may be significantly different from the cash collected from sales during that same period.

To illustrate a sale for cash, assume that Highpoint's cash register total for cash sales on May 4 is $6,210. The entry, therefore, is:

| May 4 | Cash | 6,210 | |
| |    Sales | | 6,210 |
| |      (To record daily cash sales) | | |

**Helpful hint** The Sales account is credited only for sales of goods held for resale. Sales of assets not held for resale, such as equipment or land, are credited directly to the asset account.

Merchandising companies may use more than one sales account. For example, Highpoint Electronic may decide to keep separate sales accounts for its sales of television sets, videocassette recorders, and microwave ovens. Because sales are the principal source of revenue for a merchandising company, the amount and trend of sales are of critical importance. For example, an increase in sales

Illustration 5-3

*Sales invoice*

```
                                          INVOICE NO. 731

                              ▲
                             ▲▲▲
                    HIGHPOINT ELECTRONIC
                          27 CIRCLE DRIVE
                      HARDING, MICHIGAN 48281
                              ▼
```

| | | |
|---|---|---|
| **S** Firm Name | Chelsea Video | |
| **O** | | |
| **L** Attention of | James Hoover, Purchasing Agent | |
| **D** | | |
| **T** Address | 125 Main Street | |
| **O** | | |
| Chelsea | Illinois | 60915 |
| City | State | Zip |

| Date 5/4/96 | Salesperson Malone | Terms 2/10, n/30 | Freight FOB Sh.Pt. – Collect | | |
|---|---|---|---|---|---|
| Catalogue No. | Description | | Quantity | Price | Amount |
| X572Y9820 | Printed Circuit Board-prototype | | 1 | 2,300 | $2,300 |
| A2547Z45 | Production Model Circuits | | 5 | 300 | 1,500 |
| **IMPORTANT:** ALL RETURNS MUST BE MADE WITHIN 10 DAYS | | | | **TOTAL** | $3,800 |

**Helpful hint** To better understand the contents of this invoice, identify the:
(1) Seller.
(2) Invoice date.
(3) Purchaser.
(4) Salesperson.
(5) Credit terms.
(6) Freight terms.
(7) Goods sold:
    Catalogue no.
    Description.
    Quality.
    Price per unit.
(8) Total invoice amount.

from the preceding year signifies a growing business and often leads to higher net income. An unfavorable trend may suggest lower future earnings.

## Sales Returns and Allowances

A customer may be dissatisfied with the merchandise received because the goods are damaged or defective, of inferior quality, or not in accord with the customer's specifications. In such cases, the customer may return the goods to the seller for credit if the sale was made on credit, or for a cash refund if the sale was originally for cash. This transaction is known as a **sales return**. Alternatively, the customer may choose to keep the merchandise if the seller is willing to grant an allowance (deduction) from the selling price. This transaction is known as a **sales allowance**. For accounting purposes, sales returns and sales allowances are combined into one account, Sales Returns and Allowances.

To give the customer a sales return or allowance, the seller normally prepares a credit memorandum. This document informs a customer that a credit has been made to the customer's account receivable for a sales return or allowance. The credit memorandum shown in Illustration 5-4 relates to the sales invoice shown in Illustration 5-3.

The original copy of the credit memorandum is sent to the customer, and a copy is kept by the seller as evidence of the transaction. The seller's entry to

► *Ethics note*

Large retailers of electronics often have generous return policies, allowing returns for any reason within the first 30 days. Unfortunately, unscrupulous customers will "buy" video cameras or large stereos for special events such as weddings, use them, and then return them after the event. The retailer suffers a loss because they must then sell the item as returned merchandise.

**Illustration 5-4**

*Credit memorandum*

```
                                                          CREDIT-CM126

                              ▲
                        HIGHPOINT ELECTRONIC
                            27 CIRCLE DRIVE
                        HARDING, MICHIGAN  48281
                                 ▼

  S    Firm Name ____ Chelsea Video _____
  O
  L    Attention of __ James Hoover, Purchasing Agent _____
  D
  T    Address _____ 125 Main Street _____
  O
       Chelsea                 Illinois              60915
         City                    State                Zip


  Date  5/8/96 │ Salesperson  Malone │ Invoice No.  731 │ Invoice Date 5/4/96 │ Approved  Reid

  Catalogue No. │        Description          │ Quantity │ Price │ Amount

   A2547Z45     │ Production Model            │          │       │
                │ Circuits                    │    1     │  300  │  $300
                │ (Inoperative)               │          │       │




  Cash Refund ☐     Credit Account ☒     Other ☐
```

record a credit memorandum involves a debit to the Sales Returns and Allowances account and a credit to Accounts Receivable, as shown below:

| | | | |
|---|---|---|---|
| May 8 | Sales Returns and Allowances | 300 | |
| | Accounts Receivable | | 300 |
| | (To record allowance for damaged goods per credit memorandum CM126) | | |

For a sales return or allowance on a cash sale, a cash refund is normally made. In such case, Sales Returns and Allowances is debited and Cash is credited.

Sales Returns and Allowances is a contra revenue account to Sales. The normal balance of Sales Returns and Allowances is a debit. A contra account is used, instead of debiting Sales, to disclose the amount of sales returns and allowances in the accounts and in the income statement. Disclosure of this information is important to management: Excessive returns and allowances suggest inferior merchandise, inefficiencies in filling orders, errors in billing customers, and mistakes in delivery or shipment of the goods. Moreover, a debit directly to Sales would obscure the relative importance of sales returns and allowances as a percentage of sales. It also could distort comparisons between total sales in different accounting periods.

## ►Accounting in Action ► *Business Insight*

How high is too high? Returns can become so high that it is questionable whether sales revenue should have been recognized in the first place. An example of high returns is Florafax International Inc., a floral supply company, which was alleged to ship its product without customer authorization on 10 holiday occasions, including 8,562 shipments of its product to customers for Mother's Day and 6,575 for Secretary's Day. The return rate on these shipments went as high as 69% of sales. As one employee noted: "products went out the front door and came in the back door."

An offshoot of high returns is "channel stuffing." In channel stuffing, the seller "sells" its product by providing substantial inducement to buy. Although this helps the sellers' revenue in the short run, the long term can be devastating when the merchandise bought remains on the purchasers' shelves for a long period of time.

## Sales Discounts

The terms of a credit sale may include an offer of a cash discount, called a sales discount, to the customer for prompt payment of the balance due. This incentive offers advantages to both parties: The purchaser saves money, and the seller is able to convert the accounts receivable into cash earlier.

The **credit terms** specify the amount and time period for the cash discount. They also indicate the length of time in which the purchaser is expected to pay the full invoice price. In the sales invoice in Illustration 5-3, credit terms are 2/10, n/30, which is read "two-ten, net thirty." This means that a 2% cash discount may be taken on the invoice price (less any returns or allowances) if payment is made within 10 days of the invoice date (the **discount period**); otherwise, the invoice price less any returns or allowances is due 30 days from the invoice date. Alternatively, the discount period may extend to a specified number of days following the month in which the sale occurs. For example, 1/10 EOM (end-of-month) means that a 1% discount is available if the invoice is paid within the first 10 days of the next month.

When the seller elects not to offer a cash discount for prompt payment, credit terms will specify only the maximum time period for paying the balance due. For example, the time period may be stated as n/30, n/60, or n/10 EOM.

When cash discounts are taken by customers, the seller debits Sales Discounts. To illustrate, assume Chelsea Video pays the balance due of $3,500 (Sales $3,800 less Sales Returns and Allowances $300) on May 14, the last day of the discount period. The cash discount is $70 ($3,500 × 2%), and the amount of cash paid by Chelsea Video is $3,430 ($3,500 − $70). Assuming the payment is received by Highpoint Electronic on May 15, the entry is:

**Helpful hint** The term "net" in "net 30" means the remaining amount due after subtracting any sales returns and allowances and partial payments.

| May 15 | Cash | 3,430 | |
| | Sales Discounts | 70 | |
| |    Accounts Receivable | | 3,500 |
| |     (To record collection within 2/10, n/30 | | |
| |     discount period) | | |

Sales Discounts is a **contra revenue account** to Sales. Its normal balance is a debit. This account is used, instead of debiting Sales, to disclose the amount of cash discounts taken by customers. If the discount is not taken, Highpoint Electronic debits Cash for $3,500 and credits Accounts Receivable for the same amount at the date of collection.

## Statement Presentation

As contra revenue accounts, sales returns and allowances and sales discounts are deducted from sales in the income statement to arrive at net sales. The sales revenues section of the income statement based on assumed data for Highpoint Electronic is as follows:

**Illustration 5-5**

*Statement presentation of sales revenues section*

| HIGHPOINT ELECTRONIC Partial Income Statement | | |
|---|---:|---:|
| Sales revenues | | |
| Sales | | $480,000 |
| Less: Sales returns and allowances | $12,000 | |
| Sales discounts | 8,000 | 20,000 |
| Net sales | | $460,000 |

This presentation discloses the significant aspects of the company's principal revenue producing activities.

## *Before You Go On . . .*

### ▶ *Review It*

1. How do the components in measuring net income in a merchandising company differ from those in a service enterprise?
2. What entries are made to record sales, sales returns and allowances, and sales discounts?
3. How are sales and contra revenue accounts reported in the income statement?

## ◢ Cost of Goods Sold

**STUDY OBJECTIVE**

**3**

*State the steps in determining cost of goods sold.*

As you learned earlier in this chapter, the second factor in measuring net income in a merchandising company is the cost of goods sold. The cost of goods sold may be determined each time a sale occurs or at the end of an accounting period. To make the determination when the sale occurs, a company uses a perpetual inventory system. Under this system, detailed records of the cost of each inventory item are maintained and continuously show the inventory that should be on hand. For example, a Ford dealership will have separate inventory records for each Escort, Tempo, Taurus, and Thunderbird. When a car is sold, its cost is obtained from the inventory records. Perpetual inventory systems have traditionally been used by companies that sell high unit-value items such as automobiles, furniture, television sets, and large home appliances.

When cost of goods sold is determined only at the end of an accounting period, a company is said to be using a periodic inventory system. This system is widely used by companies that sell thousands of low unit-value items, such as Wal-Mart, True Value hardware stores, and Rexall drugstores. Most businesses employ the periodic inventory system because they can control merchandise and manage day-to-day operations without detailed inventory records. In addition, perpetual systems are expensive, and often the benefits they offer do not justify their cost.

Illustration 5-6 compares the sequence of activities and the timing of the cost of goods sold computation under the two inventory methods.

**Illustration 5-6**

*Comparing periodic to perpetual inventory*

To determine the cost of goods sold under a periodic inventory system, it is necessary to (1) record purchases of merchandise, (2) determine the cost of goods purchased, and (3) determine the cost of goods on hand at the beginning and end of the accounting period. These procedures are illustrated in the following sections. The perpetual inventory system is discussed more fully in an appendix to this chapter.

## Recording Purchases of Merchandise

When merchandise is purchased for resale to customers, the temporary account, Merchandise Purchases, or simply Purchases, is debited for the cost of the goods. Thus, Larry Martin, as manager of the Washington State University Bookstore, would debit Purchases for books purchased for resale to students. However, not all purchases are debited to Purchases. Purchases of assets acquired for use and not for resale, such as supplies, equipment, and similar items, should be debited to specific asset accounts rather than to Purchases. For example, Larry would debit Supplies for the supplies he buys and uses to make shelf signs and labels that identify which books are for which courses.

**Helpful hint** Be careful not to fall into the trap of debiting purchases of equipment or supplies to Purchases.

Like sales, purchases may be made for cash or on account (credit). The purchase is normally recorded by the purchaser when the goods are received from the seller. Every purchase should be supported by business documents that provide written evidence of the transaction. Each cash purchase should be supported by a canceled check or cash register receipt indicating the items purchased. Cash purchases are recorded by a debit to Purchases and a credit to Cash. Each credit purchase should be supported by a purchase invoice indicating the total purchase price and other relevant information. The purchaser does not prepare a separate purchase invoice. Instead, the copy of the sales invoice sent by the seller becomes a purchase invoice to the buyer. The entry by Chelsea Video for the invoice (Illustration 5-3) shown on page 183 is:

| | | | |
|---|---|---|---|
| May 4 | Purchases | 3,800 | |
| | Accounts Payable | | 3,800 |
| | (To record goods purchased on account, terms 2/10, n/30) | | |

### Purchase Returns and Allowances

A sales return and allowance on the seller's books is recorded as a **purchase return and allowance** on the books of the purchaser. The purchaser initiates the request for a reduction of the balance due through the issuance of a debit memorandum. A debit memorandum is a document issued by a buyer to inform a seller that a debit has been made to the seller's account. The original copy of the memorandum is sent to the seller and one copy is retained by the purchaser. The information contained in a debit memorandum is similar to the information found in the credit memorandum in Illustration 5-4 (p. 184). The entry by Chelsea Video for the merchandise returned on May 8 is:

| | | | |
|---|---|---|---|
| May 8 | Accounts Payable | 300 | |
| | Purchase Returns and Allowances | | 300 |
| | (To record allowance for damaged goods) | | |

**Helpful hint**   Only returns of goods held for resale are credited to Purchase Returns and Allowances. Returns of supplies, for example, should be credited to the Supplies account.

Purchase Returns and Allowances represents a reduction in the cost of goods purchased for resale. It is a **contra account** to Purchases and its normal balance is a credit. The contra account is used instead of crediting Purchases in order to disclose both the dollar amount of returns and allowances and the percentage of gross purchases that have proven to be unsatisfactory. Excessive purchase returns and allowances may indicate inefficiencies in a company's purchasing procedures or the need to find more reliable suppliers.

Credit memorandums and debit memorandums derive their names from the action that the issuer takes on the accounts receivable or payable carried on its books. The purchaser sends a debit memorandum to indicate a **debit** to Accounts Payable and a credit to Purchase Returns and Allowances. Similarly, a seller issues a credit memorandum to indicate a **credit** to Accounts Receivable and a debit to Sales Returns and Allowances.

### Purchase Discounts

Credit terms may permit the buyer to claim a cash discount for the prompt payment of a balance due. The buyer calls this discount a purchase discount. Like a sales discount, a purchase discount is based on the invoice cost less returns and allowances, if any. Purchase Discounts is credited for discounts that are taken. The entry to record the May 14 payment by Chelsea Video to Highpoint Electronic is as follows:

**Helpful hint**   See the same transaction recorded by the seller on page 185.

| | | | |
|---|---|---|---|
| May 14 | Accounts Payable | 3,500 | |
| | Purchase Discounts | | 70 |
| | Cash | | 3,430 |
| | (To record payment within discount period) | | |

Like Purchase Returns and Allowances, Purchase Discounts represents a reduction in the cost of goods purchased for resale. Purchase Discounts is a **contra account** to Purchases. Its normal balance is a credit. If Chelsea Video fails to take the discount and full payment is made on June 3, Chelsea makes the following entry:

| | | | |
|---|---|---|---|
| June 3 | Accounts Payable | 3,500 | |
| | Cash | | 3,500 |
| | (To record payment with no discount taken) | | |

## ▸Accounting in Action ▸ *Business Insight*

In the early 1990s, Sears wielded its retail clout by telling its suppliers that, rather than pay its obligations in the standard 30-day period, it would now pay in 60 days. This practice is often adopted by firms that are experiencing financial distress from a shortage of cash. A Sears spokesperson insisted, however, that Sears did not have cash problems, but, rather, was simply utilizing "vendor-financed inventory methods to improve its return on investment." Supplier trade groups have been outspoken critics of Sears' new policy, and have suggested that consumers will be the ultimate victims, because the financing costs will eventually be passed on to them.

*Source: The Wall Street Journal,* August 15, 1991.

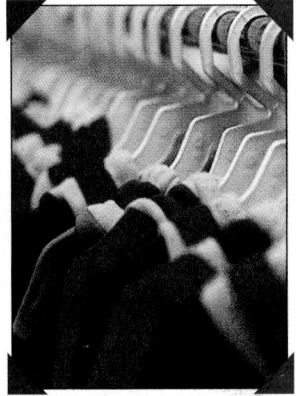

A buyer usually should take all available discounts. For example, if Chelsea Video takes the discount, it pays $70 less in cash. Conversely, if it forgoes the discount and invests the $3,500 in a bank savings account for 20 days at 10% interest, it will earn only $19.44 in interest. The savings obtained by taking the discount is computed as follows:

| | |
|---|---|
| Discount of 2% on $3,500 | $70.00 |
| Interest received on $3,500 | |
| (for 20 days at 10%) | 19.44 |
| Savings by taking the discount | $50.56 |

**Illustration 5-7**

*Savings obtained by taking purchase discount*

Alternatively, passing up the discount may be viewed as **paying an interest rate of 2%** for the use of $3,500 for 20 days. This is the equivalent of an annual interest rate of 36% (2% × 360/20).[1] Obviously, it would be better for Chelsea Video to borrow at prevailing bank interest rates of 8–12% than to lose the discount.

### *Freight Costs*

The sales agreement should indicate whether the seller or the buyer is to pay the cost of transporting the goods to the buyer's place of business. When a common carrier such as a railroad, trucking company, or airline is used, the transportation company prepares a freight bill (often called a bill of lading) in accordance with the sales agreement. Freight terms are expressed as either **FOB shipping point** or **FOB destination**. The letters FOB mean **free on board**. Thus, FOB shipping point means that goods are placed free on board the carrier by the seller, and the buyer pays the freight costs. Conversely, FOB destination means that the goods are placed free on board at the buyer's place of business, and the seller pays the freight. For example, the sales invoice in Illustration 5-3 on page 183 indicates that freight is FOB shipping point. Thus, the buyer (Chelsea Video) pays the freight charges.

When the purchaser directly incurs the freight costs, the account Freight-in (or Transportation-in) is debited. For example, if upon delivery of the goods on May 6, Chelsea Video pays Acme Freight Company $150 for freight charges, the entry on Chelsea's books is:

| | | | |
|---|---|---|---|
| May 6 | Freight-in | 150 | |
| | Cash | | 150 |
| | (To record payment of freight, terms FOB shipping point) | | |

**Helpful hint** So as not to miss purchase discounts, unpaid invoices should be filed by due dates. For example, Chelsea Video should have a file dated May 14 in which all bills to be paid on this date are filed. This procedure helps the purchaser remember the discount date, prevents early payment of bills, and maximizes the time that cash can be used for other purposes.

[1]For simplicity, we use 360 days rather than 365.

Like Purchases, Freight-in is a **temporary account** whose normal balance is a debit.

**Freight-in is part of cost of goods purchased.** The reason is that cost of goods purchased should include any freight charges necessary to bring the goods to the purchaser. The use of a Freight-in account enables management to determine the materiality of these costs. If freight costs are significant, management may want to compare the cost of truck, rail, or air freight to find the least expensive alternative. Freight costs are not subject to a purchase discount. Purchase discounts apply on the invoice cost of the merchandise.

In contrast, **freight costs incurred by the seller on outgoing merchandise are an operating expense to the seller.** These costs are debited to Freight-out or Delivery Expense. For example, if the freight terms on invoice no. 731 in Illustration 5-3 had specified FOB destination and Highpoint Electronic paid the $150 freight charges, the entry by Highpoint would be:

| May 4 | Freight-out | 150 | |
|-------|-------------|-----|-----|
| |    Cash | | 150 |
| |    (To record payment of freight on goods | | |
| |    sold FOB destination) | | |

When the freight charges are paid by the seller, the seller will usually establish a higher invoice price for the goods, to cover the expense of shipping.

### Determining Cost of Goods Purchased

In explaining the accounting for goods purchased for resale, we discussed the following temporary accounts:

**Illustration 5-8**

*Normal balances: cost of goods purchased accounts*

| Account | Normal Balance |
|---------|----------------|
| Purchases | Debit |
| Purchase Returns and Allowances | Credit |
| Purchase Discounts | Credit |
| Freight-in | Debit |

The procedure for determining the cost of goods purchased is as follows:

1. The accounts with credit balances (Purchase Returns and Allowances and Purchase Discounts) are subtracted from Purchases to produce net purchases.
2. Freight-in is then added to net purchases to produce cost of goods purchased.

To illustrate, assume that Highpoint Electronic shows the following balances for the accounts above: Purchases $325,000; Purchase Returns and Allowances $10,400; Purchase Discounts $6,800; and Freight-in $12,200. Net purchases and cost of goods purchased are $307,800 and $320,000, respectively, as computed in Illustration 5-9:

| | | |
|---|---:|---:|
| Purchases | | $325,000 |
| (1) Less: Purchase returns and allowances | $10,400 | |
| Purchase discounts | 6,800 | 17,200 |
| Net purchases | | 307,800 |
| (2) Add: Freight-in | | 12,200 |
| Cost of goods purchased | | $320,000 |

**Illustration 5-9**

*Computation of net purchases and cost of goods purchased*

## ▶Accounting in Action ▸ *Ethics Insight*

Inventory losses can be substantial. Shoplifting is a big crime in the United States, with a cost of more than $18 billion annually, or 5% of retail sales, not including thefts by store employees. Shoplifting losses have led to the demise of many companies. For example, Dayton-Hudson closed its landmark store in downtown Detroit, in part, because of excessive shoplifting losses. Many department stores are trying to reduce shoplifting losses by use of electronic tags on merchandise and by continuous surveillance of customers on closed circuit television.

## Determining Cost of Goods on Hand

To **determine the cost of inventory on hand, it is necessary to take a physical inventory**. Taking a physical inventory involves:

1. Counting the units on hand for each item of inventory.
2. Applying unit costs to the total units on hand for each item of inventory.
3. Aggregating the costs for each item of inventory to determine the total cost of goods on hand.

A physical inventory should be taken at or near the balance sheet date. To improve the accuracy of the count, many businesses suspend operations while inventory is being taken.

The account Merchandise Inventory is used to record the cost of inventory on hand at the balance sheet date. This amount becomes the beginning inventory for the next accounting period. For Highpoint Electronic, the balance in Merchandise Inventory at December 31, 1995, is $36,000. This amount is also the January 1, 1996, balance in Merchandise Inventory. During 1996, **no entries are made to Merchandise Inventory**. At December 31, 1996, entries will be made to eliminate the beginning inventory and to record the ending inventory, which we will assume is $40,000. These entries are illustrated later in the chapter.

## Computing Cost of Goods Sold

We have now reached the point where we can compute cost of goods sold. Doing so involves two steps:

1. Add the cost of goods purchased to the cost of goods on hand at the beginning of the period (beginning inventory) to obtain the cost of goods available for sale
2. Subtract the cost of goods on hand at the end of the period (ending inventory) from the cost of goods available for sale to arrive at the **cost of goods sold**.

For Highpoint Electronic the cost of goods available for sale and the cost of goods sold are $356,000 and $316,000, respectively, as shown below.

**Illustration 5-10**

*Computation of cost of goods available for sale and cost of goods sold*

|  |  |  |
|---|---|---|
| | Beginning inventory | $ 36,000 |
| (1) | Add: Cost of goods purchased | 320,000 |
| | Cost of goods available for sale | 356,000 |
| (2) | Less: Ending inventory | 40,000 |
| | Cost of goods sold | $316,000 |

# Gross Profit

**STUDY OBJECTIVE**

**4**

*Explain the computation and importance of gross profit.*

From Illustration 5-1, you learned that cost of goods sold is deducted from sales revenue to determine **gross profit**. Sales revenue used for this computation is **net sales** (which takes into account sales returns and allowances and sales discounts). On the basis of the sales data presented in Illustration 5-5 and the cost of goods sold data in Illustration 5-10, the gross profit for Highpoint Electronic is $144,000, computed as follows:

**Illustration 5-11**

*Computation of gross profit*

|  |  |
|---|---|
| Net sales | $460,000 |
| Cost of goods sold | 316,000 |
| Gross profit | $144,000 |

A company's gross profit may also be expressed as a percentage by dividing the amount of gross profit by net sales. For Highpoint Electronic the gross profit rate is 31.3% ($144,000 ÷ $460,000). The gross profit rate is generally considered to be more useful than the gross profit amount because it expresses a more meaningful (qualitative) relationship between net sales and gross profit. For example, a gross profit of $1,000,000 may be impressive. But, if it is the result of a gross profit rate of only 7%, it is not so impressive.

Gross profit represents the **merchandising profit** of a company. It is not a measure of the overall profitability of a company, because operating expenses have not been deducted. Nevertheless, the amount and trend of gross profit is closely watched by management and other interested parties. Comparisons of current gross profit with past amounts and rates and with those in the industry

▶**Accounting in Action** ▸ *Business Insight*

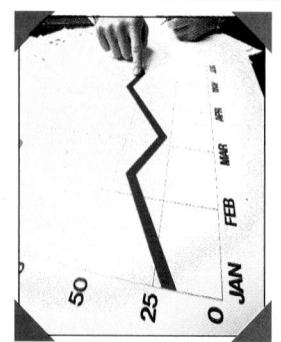

In a recent year, Woolworth Corporation reported a gross profit rate of 32%; J.C. Penney, 31%; Kmart, 24%; and Wal-Mart, 20%. Gross profit is critical. "If you don't have someone monitoring it," says one business consultant, "you are asking for instant death." A decline should trigger a search for the cause. The drop could be due to an increase in cost of goods sold or a decrease in sales revenue, either of which needs prompt attention. The change may be temporary and easily reversed, or it may signal the beginning of a bad trend.

indicate the effectiveness of its purchasing function and the soundness of its pricing policies.

# *O*perating Expenses

Operating expenses are the third component in measuring net income for a merchandising company. As indicated earlier, these expenses are similar in merchandising and service enterprises. At Highpoint Electronic, operating expenses were $114,000. The firm's net income is determined by subtracting operating expenses from gross profit. Thus, net income is $30,000 as shown below:

**Illustration 5-12**

*Operating expenses in computing net income*

| | |
|---|---:|
| Gross profit | $144,000 |
| Operating expenses | 114,000 |
| Net income | $ 30,000 |

The net income amount is the "bottom line" of a company's income statement.

## *Before You Go On . . .*

### ► *Review It*

1. Identify the three steps in determining cost of goods sold.
2. What accounts are used in determining the cost of goods purchased?
3. In what ways is a perpetual inventory system different from a periodic inventory system?

### ► *Do It*

Aerosmith Company's accounting records show the following at year-end: Purchase Discounts $3,400; Freight-in $6,100; Sales $240,000; Purchases $162,500; Beginning Inventory $18,000; Ending Inventory $20,000; Sales Discounts $10,000; Purchase Returns $5,200; and Operating Expenses $57,000. Compute the following amounts for Aerosmith Company: net sales, cost of goods purchased, cost of goods sold, gross profit, and net income.

**Reasoning:** To compute the required amounts, it is important to know the relationships in measuring net income for a merchandising company. For example, it is necessary to know the difference between the following: sales and net sales, goods available for sale and cost of goods sold, and gross profit and net income.

**Solution:**
Net sales: $240,000 − $10,000 = $230,000.
Cost of goods purchased: $162,500 − $5,200 − $3,400 + $6,100 = $160,000.
Cost of goods sold: $18,000 + $160,000 − $20,000 = $158,000.
Gross profit: $230,000 − $158,000 = $72,000.
Net income: $72,000 − $57,000 = $15,000.

*Related exercise material:* BE5–3, BE5–5, B5–6, E5–2, E5–4, E5–5, E5–7 and E5–10

**STUDY OBJECTIVE**
**5**

*Identify the unique features of the income statement for a merchandising company.*

# *I*ncome Statement

The income statement for retailers and wholesalers contains three features not found in the income statement of a service enterprise. These features are: (1) a sales revenue section, (2) a cost of goods sold section, and (3) gross profit. Using assumed data for specific operating expenses, the income statement for Highpoint Electronic is shown in Illustration 5-13.

**Illustration 5-13**

*Income statement for a merchandising company*

| HIGHPOINT ELECTRONIC<br>Income Statement<br>For the Year Ended December 31, 1996 | | | |
|---|---|---|---|
| Sales revenues | | | |
|   Sales | | | $480,000 |
|   Less: Sales returns and allowances | | $ 12,000 | |
|       Sales discounts | | 8,000 | 20,000 |
|   Net sales | | | 460,000 |
| Cost of goods sold | | | |
|   Inventory, January 1 | | 36,000 | |
|   Purchases | $325,000 | | |
|   Less: Purchases returns and allowances | $10,400 | | |
|       Purchase discounts | 6,800 | 17,200 | |
|   Net purchases | | 307,800 | |
|   Add: Freight-in | | 12,200 | |
|   Cost of goods purchased | | 320,000 | |
|   Cost of goods available for sale | | 356,000 | |
|   Inventory, December 31 | | 40,000 | |
|     Cost of goods sold | | | 316,000 |
| Gross profit | | | 144,000 |
| Operating expenses | | | |
|   Store salaries expense | | 45,000 | |
|   Rent expense | | 19,000 | |
|   Utilities expense | | 17,000 | |
|   Advertising expense | | 16,000 | |
|   Depreciation expense—store equipment | | 8,000 | |
|   Freight-out | | 7,000 | |
|   Insurance expense | | 2,000 | |
|     Total operating expenses | | | 114,000 |
| Net income | | | $ 30,000 |

**Helpful hint**  The far right column identifies the major subdivisions of the income statement. The next column identifies the primary items comprising cost of goods sold of $316,000 and operating expenses of $114,000; in addition, contra revenue items of $20,000 are reported. The third column explains cost of goods purchased of $320,000. The fourth column reports contra purchase items of $17,200.

▼**SECTION** *2* ▸ *Completing the Accounting Cycle*

**STUDY OBJECTIVE**
••••••••• **6** •••••••••

*Explain the steps in the accounting cycle for a merchandising company.*

Up to this point, we have been primarily concerned with measuring net income in a merchandising company. We have also illustrated the basic entries in recording transactions relating to sales and purchases. Now it is time to consider the remaining steps in the accounting cycle that were identified in Chapter 4.

Each of the required steps in the cycle applies to a merchandising company. Again, a work sheet is an optional step. To illustrate the steps in the cycle, we will assume that Highpoint Electronic uses a work sheet.

# Using a Work Sheet

As indicated in Chapter 4, a work sheet enables financial statements to be prepared before the adjusting entries are journalized and posted. The steps in preparing a work sheet for a merchandising company are the same as they are for a service enterprise (see pp. 134–35). The work sheet for Highpoint Electronic, shown in Illustration 5-14, contains all the income statement data explained above plus other data. The unique accounts for a merchandising company are shown in capital letters in red.

**Illustration 5-14**

*Work sheet for merchandising company*

**HIGHPOINT ELECTRONIC**
**Work Sheet**
**For the Year Ended December 31, 1996**

| | Trial Balance Dr. | Trial Balance Cr. | Adjustments Dr. | Adjustments Cr. | Adjusted Trial Balance Dr. | Adjusted Trial Balance Cr. | Income Statement Dr. | Income Statement Cr. | Balance Sheet Dr. | Balance Sheet Cr. |
|---|---|---|---|---|---|---|---|---|---|---|
| Cash | 9,500 | | | | 9,500 | | | | 9,500 | |
| Accounts Receivable | 16,100 | | | | 16,100 | | | | 16,100 | |
| MERCHANDISE INVENTORY | 36,000 | | | | 36,000 | | 36,000 | 40,000 | 40,000 | |
| Prepaid Insurance | 3,800 | | | (a) 2,000 | 1,800 | | | | 1,800 | |
| Store Equipment | 80,000 | | | | 80,000 | | | | 80,000 | |
| Accumulated Depreciation | | 16,000 | | (b) 8,000 | | 24,000 | | | | 24,000 |
| Accounts Payable | | 20,400 | | | | 20,400 | | | | 20,400 |
| R. A. Lamb, Capital | | 83,000 | | | | 83,000 | | | | 83,000 |
| R. A. Lamb, Drawing | 15,000 | | | | 15,000 | | | | 15,000 | |
| SALES | | 480,000 | | | | 480,000 | | 480,000 | | |
| SALES RETURNS AND ALLOWANCES | 12,000 | | | | 12,000 | | 12,000 | | | |
| SALES DISCOUNTS | 8,000 | | | | 8,000 | | 8,000 | | | |
| PURCHASES | 325,000 | | | | 325,000 | | 325,000 | | | |
| PURCHASE RETURNS AND ALLOWANCES | | 10,400 | | | | 10,400 | | 10,400 | | |
| PURCHASE DISCOUNTS | | 6,800 | | | | 6,800 | | 6,800 | | |
| FREIGHT-IN | 12,200 | | | | 12,200 | | 12,200 | | | |
| Freight-out | 7,000 | | | | 7,000 | | 7,000 | | | |
| Advertising Expense | 16,000 | | | | 16,000 | | 16,000 | | | |
| Rent Expense | 19,000 | | | | 19,000 | | 19,000 | | | |
| Store Salaries Expense | 40,000 | | (c) 5,000 | | 45,000 | | 45,000 | | | |
| Utilities Expense | 17,000 | | | | 17,000 | | 17,000 | | | |
| Totals | 616,600 | 616,600 | | | | | | | | |
| Insurance Expense | | | (a) 2,000 | | 2,000 | | 2,000 | | | |
| Depreciation Expense | | | (b) 8,000 | | 8,000 | | 8,000 | | | |
| Salaries Payable | | | | (c) 5,000 | | 5,000 | | | | 5,000 |
| Totals | | | 15,000 | 15,000 | 629,600 | 629,600 | 507,200 | 537,200 | 162,400 | 132,400 |
| Net Income | | | | | | | 30,000 | | | 30,000 |
| Totals | | | | | | | 537,200 | 537,200 | 162,400 | 162,400 |

Key: (a) Insurance expired, (b) Depreciation expensed, (c) Salaries accrued.

## Trial Balance Columns

Data for the trial balance are obtained from the ledger balances of Highpoint Electronic at December 31. The amount shown for Merchandise Inventory, $36,000, is the beginning inventory.

## Adjustments Columns

A merchandising company generally has the same types of adjustments as a service company. As you see in the work sheet, adjustments (a), (b), and (c) are for insurance, depreciation, and salaries. These adjustments were also required for Pioneer Advertising Agency, as illustrated in Chapters 3 and 4.

After all adjustment data are entered on the work sheet, the equality of the adjustment column totals is established. The balances in all accounts are then extended to the adjusted trial balance columns.[2]

## Adjusted Trial Balance

The adjusted trial balance shows the balance of all accounts after adjustment at the end of the accounting period. Note that beginning inventory was not adjusted. Therefore it is extended to the adjusted trial balance in the amount of $36,000.

## Income Statement Columns

The accounts and balances that affect the income statement are transferred from the adjusted trial balance columns to the income statement columns. For Highpoint Electronic, Sales of $480,000 is shown in the credit column whereas the contra revenue accounts, Sales Returns and Allowances of $12,000 and Sales Discounts of $8,000, are shown in the debit column. Thus, the difference of $460,000 is the net sales shown on the income statement. Similarly, Purchases of $325,000 and Freight-in of $12,200 are extended to the debit column. The contra purchase accounts, Purchase Returns and Allowances of $10,400 and Purchase Discounts of $6,800, are extended to the credit columns.

The work sheet procedures for the account Merchandise Inventory merit specific comment. The procedures are:

1. The beginning balance, $36,000, is extended from the adjusted trial balance column to the **income statement debit column**. From there it can be used (added) in reporting cost of goods available for sale in the income statement.
2. The ending inventory, $40,000, is added to the work sheet by an **income statement credit and a balance sheet debit**. The credit makes it possible to deduct ending inventory from the cost of goods available for sale in the income statement to determine cost of goods sold. The debit means the ending inventory can be reported as an asset on the balance sheet.

These two procedures are specifically illustrated below:

**Illustration 5-15**

*Work sheet procedures for inventories*

| | Income Statement | | Balance Sheet | |
|---|---|---|---|---|
| | Dr. | Cr. | Dr. | Cr. |
| **Merchandise Inventory** | (1) 36,000 | 40,000 ◂——(2)——▸ 40,000 | | |

[2]Conceptually, it can be argued that the change between the beginning and ending inventory balances should be shown on the work sheet as an adjustment. We have elected to consider the change in inventory to be part of the closing process. Both approaches are acceptable and accomplish the same objective. The adjusting entry approach is explained and illustrated in Appendix 5B at the end of the chapter.

The computation for cost of goods sold, taken from the income statement columns in Illustration 5-14, is as follows:

**Illustration 5-16**

*Computation of cost of goods sold from work sheet columns*

| Debit Column | | Credit Column | |
| --- | --- | --- | --- |
| Beginning inventory | $ 36,000 | Ending inventory | $40,000 |
| Purchases | 325,000 | Purchase returns and allowances | 10,400 |
| Freight-in | 12,200 | Purchase discounts | 6,800 |
| Total debits | 373,200 | Total credits | $57,200 |
| Less: Total credits | 57,200 | | |
| Cost of goods sold | $316,000 | | |

Finally, all the credits in the income statement column should be totaled and compared to the total of all the debits in the income statement column. If the credits exceed the debits, then the company has net income. In Highpoint Electronic's case there was net income of $30,000. Conversely if the debits exceed the credits, the company would report a net loss.

**Helpful hint** In a periodic system, cost of goods sold is a computation—it is not a separate account with a balance.

### Balance Sheet Columns

The major difference between the balance sheets of a service company and a merchandising company is inventory. For Highpoint Electronic, the ending inventory amount of $40,000 is shown in the balance sheet debit column. Note also that the information to prepare the owner's equity statement is also found in these columns. That is, the capital account of R. A. Lamb is $83,000. The drawings for R. A. Lamb are $15,000. Net income results when the total of the debit column exceeds the total of the credit column in the balance sheet columns of the work sheet. Conversely, a net loss results when the total of the credits exceeds the total of the debit balances.

## Preparing Financial Statements

As is true in a service enterprise, financial statements for a merchandising company are prepared from the financial statement columns of the work sheet. The income statement for Highpoint Electronic has already been illustrated (see Illustration 5-13).

The owner's equity statement is as follows:

**Illustration 5-17**

*Owner's equity statement*

| HIGHPOINT ELECTRONIC<br>Owner's Equity Statement<br>For the Year Ended December 31, 1996 | |
| --- | --- |
| R. A. Lamb, Capital, January 1 | $ 83,000 |
| Add: Net income | 30,000 |
| | 113,000 |
| Less: Drawings | 15,000 |
| R. A. Lamb, Capital, December 31 | $ 98,000 |

The classified balance sheet, then, is as follows:

**Illustration 5-18**

*Classified balance sheet*

**HIGHPOINT ELECTRONIC**
**Balance Sheet**
**December 31, 1996**

Assets

Current assets

| | | |
|---|---|---|
| Cash | | $ 9,500 |
| Accounts receivable | | 16,100 |
| **Merchandise inventory** | | **40,000** |
| Prepaid insurance | | 1,800 |
| Total current assets | | 67,400 |

Property, plant, and equipment

| | | |
|---|---|---|
| Store equipment | $80,000 | |
| Less: Accumulated depreciation—store equipment | 24,000 | 56,000 |
| Total assets | | $123,400 |

Liabilities and Owner's Equity

Current liabilities

| | | |
|---|---|---|
| Accounts payable | | $ 20,400 |
| Salaries payable | | 5,000 |
| Total current liabilities | | 25,400 |

Owner's equity

| | | |
|---|---|---|
| R. A. Lamb, Capital | | 98,000 |
| Total liabilities and owner's equity | | $123,400 |

In the balance sheet, merchandise inventory is reported as a current asset immediately below accounts receivable. Recall that items are listed under current assets in the order of liquidity. Merchandise inventory is less liquid than accounts receivable because the goods must first be sold and then collection must be made from the customer.

## ▶*A*ccounting in *A*ction ▸ *Ethics Insight*

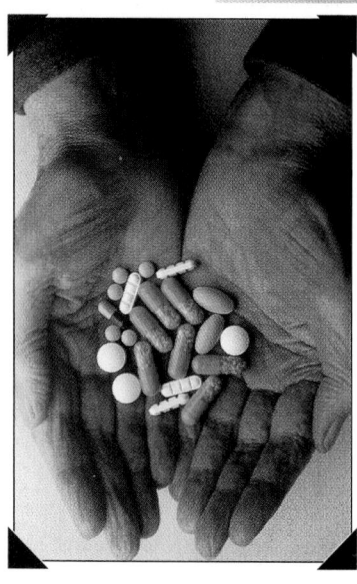

Phar Mor was one of the largest and fastest growing retail pharmacy chains in the United States until a massive fraud was discovered in 1992 by the company's auditors, Coopers and Lybrand. Based on reports in *The Wall Street Journal*, the assets of the company were overstated by more than $400 million, or about one-third of Phar Mor's gross revenue. Most of this overstatement pertained to fake or overvalued merchandise inventories at various store locations which was perpetrated by the company's top financial managers.

## *A*djusting Entries and Closing Entries

Adjusting entries are journalized from the adjustment columns of the work sheet. Because the journalizing and posting of the entries are the same as they are for a service enterprise, they are not illustrated here.

For a merchandising company, like a service enterprise, all accounts that affect the determination of net income are closed to Income Summary. Data for the preparation of closing entries may be obtained from the income statement columns of the work sheet. In journalizing, all debit column amounts are credited, and all credit column amounts are debited. To close the merchandise inventory:

1. The beginning inventory balance is debited to Income Summary and credited to Merchandise Inventory.
2. The ending inventory balance is debited to Merchandise Inventory and credited to Income Summary.

The two entries for Highpoint Electronic are:

|  |  | (1) |  |  |
|---|---|---|---|---|
| Dec. 31 | Income Summary |  | 36,000 |  |
|  |    Merchandise Inventory |  |  | 36,000 |
|  |      (To close beginning inventory) |  |  |  |
|  |  | (2) |  |  |
| 31 | Merchandise Inventory |  | 40,000 |  |
|  |    Income Summary |  |  | 40,000 |
|  |      (To record ending inventory) |  |  |  |

After posting, the Merchandise Inventory and Income Summary accounts will show the following:

| Merchandise Inventory | | Income Summary | |
|---|---|---|---|
| 1/1   Bal.   36,000 | 12/31  **Close 36,000** | 12/31  **Close 36,000** | 12/31  **Close 40,000** |
| 12/31  **Close 40,000** | | | |
| 12/31  Bal.   40,000 | | | |

**Illustration 5-19**

*Posting closing entries for merchandise inventory*

Often, the closing of merchandise inventory is included with other closing entries, as shown below for Highpoint Electronic.

| Dec. 31 | Merchandise Inventory (Dec. 31) | 40,000 |  |
|---|---|---|---|
|  | Sales | 480,000 |  |
|  | Purchase Returns and Allowances | 10,400 |  |
|  | Purchase Discounts | 6,800 |  |
|  |    Income Summary |  | 537,200 |
|  |      (To record ending inventory and close |  |  |
|  |      accounts with credit balances) |  |  |
| 31 | Income Summary | 507,200 |  |
|  |    Merchandise Inventory (Jan. 1) |  | 36,000 |
|  |    Sales Returns and Allowances |  | 12,000 |
|  |    Sales Discounts |  | 8,000 |
|  |    Purchases |  | 325,000 |
|  |    Freight-in |  | 12,200 |
|  |    Store Salaries Expense |  | 45,000 |
|  |    Rent Expense |  | 19,000 |
|  |    Freight-out |  | 7,000 |
|  |    Advertising Expense |  | 16,000 |
|  |    Utilities Expense |  | 17,000 |
|  |    Depreciation Expense |  | 8,000 |
|  |    Insurance Expense |  | 2,000 |
|  |      (To close beginning inventory and other |  |  |
|  |      income statement accounts with debit |  |  |
|  |      balances) |  |  |

**Helpful hint** Except for merchandise inventory, the easiest way to prepare the first two closing entries is to identify the temporary accounts by their balances and then prepare one entry for the credits and one for the debits.

**Helpful hint** Close inventory with other accounts in homework problems unless stated otherwise.

| | | | |
|---|---|---|---|
| 31 | Income Summary | 30,000 | |
| | R. A. Lamb, Capital | | 30,000 |
| | (To transfer net income to capital) | | |
| | | | |
| 31 | R. A. Lamb, Capital | 15,000 | |
| | R. A. Lamb, Drawing | | 15,000 |
| | (To close drawings to capital) | | |

After the closing entries are posted, all temporary accounts have zero balances. In addition, R. A. Lamb, Capital has a credit balance of $98,000: beginning balance + net income − drawings ($83,000 + $30,000 − $15,000).

## ▶reparing the Post-Closing Trial Balance

After the closing entries are posted, the post-closing trial balance is prepared. The only new account in the post-closing trial balance is Merchandise Inventory. The post-closing trial balance for Highpoint Electronic at December 31, 1996, is shown in Illustration 5-20.

**Illustration 5-20**

*Post-closing trial balance*

| | | Debit | Credit |
|---|---|---|---|
| **HIGHPOINT ELECTRONIC** | | | |
| **Post-Closing Trial Balance** | | | |
| **December 31, 1996** | | | |
| Cash | | $ 9,500 | |
| Accounts receivable | | 16,100 | |
| **Merchandise inventory** | | **40,000** | |
| Prepaid insurance | | 1,800 | |
| Store equipment | | 80,000 | |
| Accumulated depreciation | | | $ 24,000 |
| Accounts payable | | | 20,400 |
| Salaries payable | | | 5,000 |
| R. A. Lamb, Capital | | | 98,000 |
| | | $147,400 | $147,400 |

## ▶ummary of Merchandising Entries

The entries for the merchandising accounts are summarized in Illustration 5-21.

**Illustration 5-21**

*Daily recurring and closing entries*

| Transactions | Daily Recurring Entries | Dr. | Cr. |
|---|---|---|---|
| Selling merchandise to customers | Cash or Accounts Receivable | XX | |
| | Sales | | XX |
| Granting sales returns or allowances to customers | Sales Returns and Allowances | XX | |
| | Cash or Accounts Receivable | | XX |
| Receiving payment from customers within discount period | Cash | XX | |
| | Sales Discounts | XX | |
| | Accounts Receivable | | XX |

| Transactions | Daily Recurring Entries | Dr. | Cr. |
|---|---|---|---|
| Purchasing merchandise for resale | Purchases | XX | |
| | Cash or Accounts Payable | | XX |
| Paying freight costs on merchandise purchased; FOB shipping point | Freight-in | XX | |
| | Cash | | XX |
| Paying freight costs on sales; FOB destination | Freight-out | XX | |
| | Cash | | XX |
| Receiving purchase returns or allowances from suppliers | Cash or Accounts Payable | XX | |
| | Purchase Returns and Allowances | | XX |
| Paying suppliers within discount period | Accounts Payable | XX | |
| | Purchase Discounts | | XX |
| | Cash | | XX |

| Events | Closing Entries | | |
|---|---|---|---|
| Recording ending inventory and closing accounts with credit balances | Merchandise Inventory | XX | |
| | Sales | XX | |
| | Purchase Returns and Allowances | XX | |
| | Purchase Discounts | XX | |
| | Income Summary | | XX |
| Closing beginning inventory and accounts with debit balances | Income Summary | XX | |
| | Merchandise Inventory | | XX |
| | Sales Returns and Allowances | | XX |
| | Sales Discounts | | XX |
| | Purchases | | XX |
| | Freight-in | | XX |
| | Freight-out | | XX |

# Before You Go On . . .

## ► Review It

1. How does a work sheet for a merchandising company differ from a work sheet for a service company? In what ways is the work sheet similar for a merchandising company and a service company?
2. In what columns of the work sheet will (a) the beginning inventory and (b) the ending inventory be shown?
3. What merchandising account(s) will appear in the post-closing trial balance?

## ► Do It

The trial balance of Revere Clothing Company at December 31 shows Merchandise Inventory $25,000, Sales $162,400, Sales Returns and Allowances $4,800, Purchases $151,000, Purchase Discounts $3,600, and Freight-in $2,700. Prepare the closing entries for the above accounts, assuming the ending merchandise inventory is $28,000.

*Reasoning:* The first closing entry for a merchandising company recognizes the ending inventory and closes temporary accounts with credit balances. The second closing entry closes beginning inventory and temporary accounts with debit balances.

*Solution:* The two closing entries are:

| Dec. 31 | Merchandise inventory (Dec. 31) | 28,000 | |
|---|---|---|---|
| | Sales | 162,400 | |
| | Purchase Discounts | 3,600 | |
| | Income Summary | | 194,000 |
| | (To recognize ending inventory and close accounts with credit balances) | | |

| Dec. 31 | Income Summary | 183,500 | |
|---|---|---|---|
| | Merchandise Inventory (Jan. 1) | | 25,000 |
| | Sales Returns and Allowances | | 4,800 |
| | Purchases | | 151,000 |
| | Freight-in | | 2,700 |
| | (To close beginning inventory and accounts with debit balances) | | |

*Related exercise material:* BE5–8, E5–4, and E5–5.

# Forms of Income Statements

Two forms of the income statement are widely used by merchandising companies. These income statements are explained below.

## Multiple-Step Income Statement

The multiple-step income statement is so named because it shows the numerous steps in determining net income (or net loss). The Highpoint Electronic income statement in Illustration 5-13 is an example. It shows two steps: (1) cost of goods sold was subtracted from net sales, and (2) operating expenses were deducted from gross profit. These steps pertain to the company's principal operating activities. A multiple-step statement provides users with more information about a company's income performance by distinguishing between **operating** and **nonoperating activities**. The statement also highlights intermediate components of income and shows subgroupings of expenses.

### Nonoperating Activities

**Nonoperating activities** consist of (1) revenues and expenses that result from secondary or auxiliary operations and (2) gains and losses that are unrelated to the company's operations. The results of nonoperating activities are shown in two sections: Other revenues and gains and Other expenses and losses. For a merchandising company, these sections will typically include the following items:

▶ *International note*

When the owner of a Russian business was recently asked, "What is net income?" he responded, "We don't have that concept here." Then, after consulting his colleagues, he explained that although he thinks he understands the concept, he isn't comfortable with it. The conversation highlights the difficulties that countries like Russia face in attempting to develop a market-based economy.

**Illustration 5-22**

*Items reported in nonoperating sections*

| Other Revenues and Gains | Other Expenses and Losses |
|---|---|
| Interest revenue from notes receivable and marketable securities | Interest expense on notes and loans payable |
| Dividend revenue from investments in capital stock | Casualty losses from recurring causes such as vandalism and accidents |
| Rent revenue from subleasing a portion of the store | Loss from the sale or abandonment of property, plant, and equipment |
| Gain from the sale of property, plant, and equipment | Loss from strikes by employees and suppliers |

The nonoperating sections are reported in the income statement immediately after the sections that pertain to the company's primary operating activities. These sections are illustrated in Illustration 5-23 using assumed data for Highpoint Electronic.

## ▶Accounting in Action ▸ *Business Insight*

The distinction between operating and nonoperating activities is crucial to many external users of financial data. The reason is that operating income is viewed as sustainable and therefore long-term, and nonoperating is viewed as nonrecurring and therefore short-term. For example, it was reported that a large cinema chain in North America was selling some of its assets and counting the gains as part of operating income. As a result, operating losses were being offset by these gains. Because of unfavorable press reaction to this practice, the company revised its financial statements. By not counting its nonrecurring items as part of operating income, its first quarter results changed from $24.9 million operating income to a $22.6 million loss. Although the net income figure didn't change, investors were able to see that income was derived from selling assets rather than from selling movie tickets. Thus, with this new information, investors were able to make a more informed decision about the company's earnings.

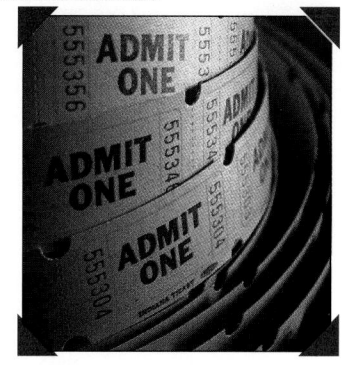

**Illustration 5-23**

*Multiple-step income statement—nonoperating sections and subgrouping of operating expenses*

| HIGHPOINT ELECTRONIC<br>Income Statement<br>For the Year Ended December 31, 1996 | | | |
|---|---|---|---|
| Sales revenues | | | |
|   Sales | | | $480,000 |
|   Less: Sales returns and allowances | | $ 12,000 | |
|       Sales discounts | | 8,000 | 20,000 |
|   Net sales | | | 460,000 |
| Cost of goods sold | | | |
|   Inventory, January 1 | | 36,000 | |
|   Purchases | $325,000 | | |
|   Less: Purchase returns and allowances | $10,400 | | |
|       Purchase discounts | 6,800 | 17,200 | |
|   Net purchases | | 307,800 | |
|   Add: Freight-in | | 12,200 | |
|   Cost of goods purchased | | 320,000 | |
|   Cost of goods available for sale | | 356,000 | |
|   Inventory, December 31 | | 40,000 | |
|     Cost of goods sold | | | 316,000 |
| Gross profit | | | 144,000 |
| Operating expenses | | | |
|   **Selling expenses** | | | |
|     Store salaries expense | 45,000 | | |
|     Advertising expense | 16,000 | | |
|     Depreciation expense—store equipment | 8,000 | | |
|     Freight-out | 7,000 | | |
|       Total selling expenses | | 76,000 | |
|   **Administrative expenses** | | | |
|     Rent expense | 19,000 | | |
|     Utilities expense | 17,000 | | |
|     Insurance expense | 2,000 | | |
|       Total administrative expenses | | 38,000 | |
|       Total operating expenses | | | 114,000 |
| Income from operations | | | 30,000 |
| Other revenues and gains | | | |
|   Interest revenue | 3,000 | | |
|   Gain on sale of equipment | 600 | 3,600 | |
| Other expenses and losses | | | |
|   Interest expense | 1,800 | | |
|   Casualty loss from vandalism | 200 | 2,000 | 1,600 |
| Net income | | | $ 31,600 |

**Helpful hint**   Operating income relates to the sale of primary goods in the ordinary course of business.

When the two nonoperating sections are included, the label Income from operations (or Operating income) precedes them. It clearly identifies the results of the company's normal operations. Income from operations is determined by subtracting cost of goods sold and operating expenses from net sales.

Observe that the results of the two nonoperating sections are netted. The difference is added to or subtracted from income from operations to determine net income. Finally, within the nonoperating sections, items are generally reported at the net amount. Thus, if a company received a $2,500 insurance settlement on vandalism losses of $2,700, the loss is reported at $200.

▶ *Ethics note*

How would *you* account for this expense? At the end of a celebratory lunch the employees of a sales department each gave the manager $10, and the manager paid the bill with his charge card. During the next week you notice that the manager reported the full amount of the lunch bill on his expense report (and requested reimbursement). When this question was posed to the CEO of Intel, he suggested that an appropriate action would be to report the problem anonymously to the internal audit staff for investigation.

### *Subgrouping of Operating Expenses*

In larger companies, operating expenses are often subdivided into selling expenses and administrative expenses, as illustrated in the income statement in Illustration 5-23. Selling expenses are those associated with making sales. They include sales promotional expenses as well as expenses of completing the sale, such as delivery and shipping expenses. Administrative expenses (sometimes called general expenses) relate to general operating activities such as personnel management, accounting, and store security.

When subgroupings are made, some expenses may have to be pro-rated, e.g., 70% to selling and 30% to administrative expenses. For example, if a store building is used for both selling and general functions, building expenses such as depreciation, utilities, and property taxes will need to be allocated.

Any reasonable classification of expenses that serves to inform those who use the statement is satisfactory. For example, the present tendency in statements prepared for management is to present in considerable detail expense data grouped along lines of responsibility.

## Single-Step Income Statement

Another format for income statement presentation is the single-step income statement. The statement is so named because only one step, subtracting total expenses from total revenues, is required in determining net income (or net loss).

In a single-step statement, all data are classified under two categories: (1) **Revenues**, which includes both operating revenues and other revenues and gains, or (2) **Expenses**, which includes cost of goods sold, operating expenses, and other expenses and losses. A condensed single-step statement for Highpoint Electronic is illustrated in Illustration 5-24.

**Illustration 5-24**

*Single-step income statement*

| HIGHPOINT ELECTRONIC<br>Income Statement<br>For the Year Ended December 31, 1996 | | |
|---|---:|---:|
| **Revenues** | | |
| Net sales | | $460,000 |
| Interest revenue | | 3,000 |
| Gain on sale of equipment | | 600 |
| Total revenues | | 463,600 |
| **Expenses** | | |
| Cost of goods sold | $316,000 | |
| Selling expenses | 76,000 | |
| Administrative expenses | 38,000 | |
| Interest expense | 1,800 | |
| Casualty loss from vandalism | 200 | |
| Total expenses | | 432,000 |
| Net income | | $ 31,600 |

There are two primary reasons for using the single-step form: (1) A company does not realize any type of profit or income until total revenues exceed total expenses, so it makes sense to divide the statement into these two categories. (2) The form is simpler and easier to read than the multiple-step form. For homework problems, the single-step form of income statement should be used only when it is specifically requested.

## Before You Go On . . .

### ▶ Review It

1. What are nonoperating activities and how are they reported in the income statement?
2. How does a single-step income statement differ from a multiple-step income statement?

## ▶ A Look Back at Washington State University Bookstore

Refer to the opening story about the Washington State University bookstore, and answer the following questions:

1. What entry, if any, would the WSU bookstore make when ordering books? When books are received? When returning books? When allowing the students to return books? When purchasing used books from students?
2. How often is it necessary for Larry Martin to take a physical inventory? Why is it necessary to take an inventory? For the inventory taken in September, does Larry need both quantities and costs? Explain.

### Solution

1. No entry is made at the time books are ordered. Probably an open purchase order file or memo record is maintained for keeping track of open (unfilled) purchase orders. When books are received, the bookstore would record the purchases at invoice cost as follows:

Purchases
   Accounts Payable
      (To record goods purchased on account)

When books are returned to the publisher, the WSU bookstore would prepare a debit memo from which the following entry is made:

Accounts Payable
   Purchase Returns and Allowances
      (To record purchase returns and allowances)

When the bookstore gives a refund for a returned book (not a used book purchase), the following entry would be made at the book's selling price:

Sales Returns and Allowances
   Cash
      (To record payment for returned goods)

When used books are bought from students, the bookstore would record the following entry:

Purchases—Used Books
   Cash
      (To record purchase of used goods)

2. Larry Martin waits about 4 weeks after the school term, when the busy book selling and return period ends, to take a physical inventory of books. He does that each school term. In addition Larry takes a physical inventory when the financial statements are prepared at least once a year.

It is necessary for Larry to take accurate inventory counts in order to make good ordering and return decisions. Accurate ordering coupled with efficient return practices is a must for profitable bookstore operations. In addition, inventory counts are necessary for financial statement preparation, most especially income determination.

Larry uses the September inventory for ordering books. Thus, only quantities—not costs—are needed by Larry.

# Summary of Study Objectives

**1.** *Identify the components in measuring net income in a merchandising company.* The major components in measuring net income in a merchandising company are sales revenue, cost of goods sold, gross profit, and operating expenses.

**2.** *Explain the entries for sales revenues.* In recording sales revenues, entries are required for (a) cash and credit sales, (b) sales returns and allowances, and (c) sales discounts.

**3.** *State the steps in determining cost of goods sold.* The steps in determining cost of goods sold are (a) recording the purchase of merchandise, (b) determining the cost of goods purchased, and (c) determining the cost of goods on hand at the beginning and end of the accounting period.

**4.** *Explain the computation and importance of gross profit.* Gross profit is computed by subtracting cost of goods sold from net sales. Gross profit represents the merchandising profit of a company, and the amount and trend of gross profit is closely watched by management and other interested parties.

**5.** *Identify the unique features of the income statement for a merchandising company.* The income statement for a merchandising company contains three sections: sales revenues, cost of goods sold, and operating expenses.

**6.** *Explain the steps in the accounting cycle for a merchandising company.* Each of the required steps in the accounting cycle for a service enterprise applies to a merchandising company. A work sheet is again an optional step.

**7.** *Distinguish between a multiple-step and a single-step income statement.* A multiple-step income statement shows numerous steps in determining net income including nonoperating sections. In a single-step income statement all data are classified under two categories, revenues or expenses, and net income is determined by one step.

# ▶APPENDIX 5A ▸ *Perpetual Inventory Systems*

As indicated earlier in this chapter, under a perpetual inventory system, records are kept of the quantity and cost of each item as it is bought, held in inventory, and sold. Because of the detailed information available under a perpetual inventory system, management is able to respond to inquiries of salespersons and customers about merchandise availability, to maintain optimum inventory levels, and to avoid running out of stock.

Under a perpetual system, the cost of each item is debited to the Merchandise Inventory account when purchased. **At the time of sale**, the cost of each item is transferred from the Merchandise Inventory account to the Cost of Goods Sold account. Thus, the Cost of Goods Sold account **at all times** equals the cost of merchandise sold during the period, and the Merchandise Inventory account **at all times** equals the cost of merchandise on hand.

# Merchandise Transactions under a Perpetual Inventory System

Because all increases and decreases related to merchandise are recorded directly in the Merchandise Inventory account under a perpetual system, accounts for purchases, purchase returns and allowances, purchase discounts, and freight-in are not used. To illustrate the recording of merchandise transactions under a perpetual system, we will use selected transactions of Country Clothiers Co. The beginning inventory on July 1 is $68,000 and the ending inventory on July 31 is $93,940.

**Purchase of Merchandise on Credit.**   Only July 5, Country Clothiers purchased $40,000 of merchandise on account from Wear Apparel Co., terms 2/10, n/30. The entry to record the purchase is:

| July 5 | Merchandise Inventory | 40,000 | |
| |     Accounts Payable | | 40,000 |
| |     (To record goods purchased on account, | | |
| |     terms 2/10, n/30) | | |

**Purchase Returns and Allowances.**   On July 6, Country Clothiers returned merchandise received from Wear Apparel Co. on July 5 for a credit of $2,000. The entry is:

| July 6 | Accounts Payable | 2,000 | |
| |     Merchandise Inventory | | 2,000 |
| |     (To record returned merchandise) | | |

**Freight Costs on Purchases.**   Country Clothiers received a bill on July 8 from Overhand Trucking Co. for freight charges on the July 5 purchase, terms n/30, $200. The entry to record payment is:

| July 8 | Merchandise Inventory | 200 | |
| |     Accounts Payable | | 200 |
| |     (To record freight costs, on account) | | |

**Payment on Account with a Discount.**   On July 14, Country Clothiers paid Wear Apparel Co. in full for the July 5 purchase, less $2,000 that was returned on July 6 and less the discount of $760 [($40,000 − $2,000) × 2%]. The entry is:

| July 14 | Accounts Payable | 38,000 | |
| |     Cash | | 37,240 |
| |     Merchandise Inventory | | 760 |
| |     (To record payment within discount | | |
| |     period) | | |

**Sale of Merchandise on Credit.**   On July 16, Country Clothiers sold merchandise on credit to Squire Men's Wear, terms 1/10, n/30, FOB destination, $24,000. The merchandise cost $12,000. Entries to record the transaction are:

| July 16 | Accounts Receivable | 24,000 | |
| |    Sales | | 24,000 |
| |      (To record credit sale, terms 1/10, n/30) | | |
| | | | |
| | Cost of Goods Sold | 12,000 | |
| |    Merchandise Inventory | | 12,000 |
| |      (To record cost of goods sold) | | |

**Return of Merchandise Sold.**   Country Clothiers on July 18 accepted for full credit the return of $1,000 of merchandise sold to Squire Men's Wear on July 16, the cost of which was $500. Entries to record the return are:

| July 18 | Sales Returns and Allowances | 1,000 | |
| |    Accounts Receivable | | 1,000 |
| |      (To record allowance for returned goods) | | |
| | | | |
| | Merchandise Inventory | 500 | |
| |    Cost of Goods Sold | | 500 |
| |      (To record cost of returned goods) | | |

**Cash Received on Account with a Discount.**   On July 25, Country Clothiers received payment in full of the account from Squire Men's Wear, less the return of July 18 and less the discount of $230 [($24,000 − $1,000) × 1%].

| July 25 | Cash | 22,770 | |
| | Sales Discounts | 230 | |
| |    Accounts Receivable | | 23,000 |
| |      (To record collection within 1/10, n/30 | | |
| |      discount period) | | |

# Comparison of Entries

The perpetual inventory entries above are shown in Illustration 5A-1 next to those that would be made if Country Clothiers used a periodic inventory system. The differing effects of the two inventory methods on the general ledger Merchandise Inventory account are more clearly depicted in Illustration 5A-2, which shows the transactions of Country Clothiers Co. entered in the Merchandise Inventory accounts.

Note the differences in these accounts: Under the perpetual system, the Merchandise Inventory account balance changes with every change in amount or cost of the inventory. Under the periodic system, the Merchandise Inventory account balance does not change until the closing entries are made. To summarize, the differences between the periodic and the perpetual systems are:

1. The **perpetual inventory system** records all purchases in the Merchandise Inventory account; it uses no Purchases account. The **periodic inventory system** uses a Purchases account.

2. The **perpetual inventory system** records returns of purchased merchandise by directly reducing the Merchandise Inventory account. The **periodic inventory system** uses a Purchase Returns and Allowances account.

3. The **perpetual inventory system** increases the Merchandise Inventory account for additional costs of purchases like freight-in and decreases Mer-

**Helpful hint**  An advantage of the perpetual inventory system is that a comparison can be made between the physical counts and the recorded inventory. Thus inventory losses due to theft or waste can be computed. Under the periodic inventory system, the cost of theft or waste cannot be determined and is included in cost of goods sold.

| Transaction | | Perpetual Inventory System | | | Periodic Inventory System | | |
|---|---|---|---|---|---|---|---|
| July 5 | Purchase of merchandise on credit. | Merchandise Inventory | 40,000 | | Purchases | 40,000 | |
| | | Accounts Payable | | 40,000 | Accounts Payable | | 40,000 |
| July 6 | Purchase returns and allowances. | Accounts Payable | 2,000 | | Accounts Payable | 2,000 | |
| | | Merchandise Inventory | | 2,000 | Purchase Returns and Allowances | | 2,000 |
| July 8 | Freight costs on purchases. | Merchandise Inventory | 200 | | Freight-in | 200 | |
| | | Accounts Payable | | 200 | Accounts Payable | | 200 |
| July 14 | Payment on account with a discount. | Accounts Payable | 38,000 | | Accounts Payable | 38,000 | |
| | | Cash | | 37,240 | Cash | | 37,240 |
| | | Merchandise Inventory | | 760 | Purchase Discounts | | 760 |
| July 16 | Sale of merchandise on credit. | Accounts Receivable | 24,000 | | Accounts Receivable | 24,000 | |
| | | Sales Revenue | | 24,000 | Sales Revenue | | 24,000 |
| | | Cost of Goods Sold | 12,000 | | No entry | | |
| | | Merchandise Inventory | | 12,000 | | | |
| July 18 | Return of merchandise sold. | Sales Returns and Allowances | 1,000 | | Sales Returns and Allowances | 1,000 | |
| | | Accounts Receivable | | 1,000 | Accounts Receivable | | 1,000 |
| | | Merchandise Inventory | 500 | | No entry | | |
| | | Cost of Goods Sold | | 500 | | | |
| July 25 | Cash received on account with a discount. | Cash | 22,770 | | Cash | 22,770 | |
| | | Sales Discounts | 230 | | Sales Discounts | 230 | |
| | | Accounts Receivable | | 23,000 | Accounts Receivable | | 23,000 |

chandise Inventory directly for reductions in purchases like purchase discounts. The **periodic inventory system** uses Freight-in and Purchase Discounts accounts.

4. The **perpetual inventory system** increases Cost of Goods Sold and decreases Merchandise Inventory when merchandise is sold. The **periodic inventory system** computes cost of goods sold based on the inventory count at the end of the period.

5. The **perpetual inventory system** records customer returns and allowances by decreasing Cost of Goods Sold and increasing the Merchandise Inventory account. The periodic inventory system makes no entry for the cost of a sales return.

**Illustration 5A-1**

*Comparison of journal entries under perpetual and periodic inventory systems*

Under the perpetual inventory system, the cost of goods sold and the amount of inventory are continuously updated, and the balances are readily available at any time. Under the periodic inventory system, cost of goods sold and inventory amounts are not available until they are computed and are accompanied by a physical inventory count.

**Illustration 5A-2**

*Effects of inventory methods on merchandise inventory accounts*

### PERIODIC INVENTORY SYSTEM

**Merchandise Inventory**

| | | | | | |
|---|---|---|---|---|---|
| Bal. 7/1 | | 68,000 | 7/31 | Closing | 68,000 |
| 7/31 | Closing | 93,940 | | | |
| Bal. 8/1 | | 93,940 | | | |

### PERPETUAL INVENTORY SYSTEM

**Merchandise Inventory**

| | | | | | |
|---|---|---|---|---|---|
| Bal. 7/1 | | 68,000 | 7/6 | Purchase Return | 2,000 |
| 7/5 | Purchases | 40,000 | 7/14 | Discount | 760 |
| 7/8 | Freight-in | 200 | 7/16 | Cost of Goods Sold | 12,000 |
| 7/18 | Sales Return | 500 | | | |
| Bal. 8/1 | | 93,940 | | | |

# Summary of Study Objective for Appendix 5A

**8.** *Record merchandising transactions using the perpetual inventory system.* Under a perpetual system, the cost of each item is debited to the Merchandise Inventory account when purchased. **At the time of sale**, the cost of each item is transferred from the Merchandise Inventory account to the Cost of Goods Sold account. Thus, the Cost of Goods Sold account **at all times** equals the cost of merchandise sold during the period, and the Merchandise Inventory account **at all times** equals the cost of merchandise on hand.

# Appendix 5B ► Adjusting Entry Method for Merchandise Inventory

**STUDY OBJECTIVE**

*After studying this appendix, you should be able to:*

9. *Explain how the adjusting entry method is used in the work sheet.*

As stated in this chapter, the change between the beginning and ending inventory balances may be made through adjusting entries rather than through closing entries. Some favor this method because they believe that changes in merchandise inventory should receive the same accounting treatment as changes in the cost of supplies on hand between two points in time. The adjusting entry method is just as acceptable as the closing entry method, and it accomplishes the same objective.

The adjusting entry method affects several steps in the accounting cycle, beginning with the use of a work sheet. Again, these effects are explained and illustrated using Highpoint Electronic as an example.

## Using a Work Sheet

In Illustration 5B-1, you will see a work sheet similar to the work sheet presented in the chapter (Illustration 5-14). The major difference in these two work sheets relates to merchandise inventory. In Illustration 5B-1, the accounting for merchandise inventory uses the adjusting entry method. In Illustration 5-14, the closing entry method was used. The unique accounts for the adjusting entry method are shown in capital letters in red.

### Trial Balance Columns

The trial balance columns are self-explanatory. The inventory before adjustment is the beginning inventory.

### Adjustments Columns

In the adjustments columns of Illustration 5B-1, you will see two adjusting entries related to inventory. The objective of preparing adjusting entries for mer-

## ►Technology in Action

The adjusting entry method is used in most computerized systems since the programming logic involved is more straightforward. That is, in a computerized system, the command to close the books will close all the temporary accounts to Income Summary. However, if the inventory has not been adjusted, it will not be up-to-date and therefore a misstatement can occur. Some accountants favor the adjusting entry method in manual systems as well.

**HIGHPOINT ELECTRONIC**
**Work Sheet**
**For the Year Ended December 31, 1996**

| | Trial Balance Dr. | Trial Balance Cr. | Adjustments Dr. | Adjustments Cr. | Adjusted Trial Balance Dr. | Adjusted Trial Balance Cr. | Income Statement Dr. | Income Statement Cr. | Balance Sheet Dr. | Balance Sheet Cr. |
|---|---|---|---|---|---|---|---|---|---|---|
| Cash | 9,500 | | | | 9,500 | | | | 9,500 | |
| Accounts Receivable | 16,100 | | | | 16,100 | | | | 16,100 | |
| MERCHANDISE INVENTORY | 36,000 | | (e) 40,000 | (d) 36,000 | 40,000 | | | | 40,000 | |
| Prepaid Insurance | 3,800 | | | (a) 2,000 | 1,800 | | | | 1,800 | |
| Store Equipment | 80,000 | | | | 80,000 | | | | 80,000 | |
| Accumulated Depreciation | | 16,000 | | (b) 8,000 | | 24,000 | | | | 24,000 |
| Accounts Payable | | 20,400 | | | | 20,400 | | | | 20,400 |
| R. A. Lamb, Capital | | 83,000 | | | | 83,000 | | | | 83,000 |
| R. A. Lamb, Drawing | 15,000 | | | | 15,000 | | | | 15,000 | |
| SALES | | 480,000 | | | | 480,000 | | 480,000 | | |
| SALES RETURNS AND ALLOWANCES | 12,000 | | | | 12,000 | | 12,000 | | | |
| SALES DISCOUNTS | 8,000 | | | | 8,000 | | 8,000 | | | |
| PURCHASES | 325,000 | | | | 325,000 | | 325,000 | | | |
| PURCHASE RETURNS AND ALLOWANCES | | 10,400 | | | | 10,400 | | 10,400 | | |
| PURCHASE DISCOUNTS | | 6,800 | | | | 6,800 | | 6,800 | | |
| FREIGHT-IN | 12,200 | | | | 12,200 | | 12,200 | | | |
| Freight-out | 7,000 | | | | 7,000 | | 7,000 | | | |
| Advertising Expense | 16,000 | | | | 16,000 | | 16,000 | | | |
| Rent Expense | 19,000 | | | | 19,000 | | 19,000 | | | |
| Store Salaries Expense | 40,000 | | (c) 5,000 | | 45,000 | | 45,000 | | | |
| Utilities Expense | 17,000 | | | | 17,000 | | 17,000 | | | |
| Totals | 616,600 | 616,600 | | | | | | | | |
| Insurance Expense | | | (a) 2,000 | | 2,000 | | 2,000 | | | |
| Depreciation Expense | | | (b) 8,000 | | 8,000 | | 8,000 | | | |
| Salaries Payable | | | | (c) 5,000 | | 5,000 | | | | 5,000 |
| INCOME SUMMARY | | | (d) 36,000 | (e) 40,000 | 36,000 | 40,000 | 36,000 | 40,000 | | |
| Totals | | | 91,000 | 91,000 | 669,600 | 669,600 | 507,200 | 537,200 | 162,400 | 132,400 |
| Net Income | | | | | | | 30,000 | | | 30,000 |
| Totals | | | | | | | 537,200 | 537,200 | 162,400 | 162,400 |

Key: (a) Insurance expired, (b) Depreciation expensed, (c) Salaries accrued, (d) Beginning merchandise inventory, (e) Ending merchandise inventory.

**Illustration 5B-1**

*Work sheet—adjusting inventory method*

chandise inventory is to adjust the asset balance to the cost of goods on hand at the balance sheet date. To accomplish this objective for merchandise inventory, two adjusting entries are made: (1) the beginning inventory amount is removed from merchandise inventory, and (2) the ending inventory amount is recorded in merchandise inventory. The entries, using the inventory data for Highpoint Electronic, are as follows:

| Dec. 31 | Income Summary | 36,000 | |
| | Merchandise Inventory | | 36,000 |
| | (To remove beginning inventory) | | |

| 31 | Merchandise Inventory | 40,000 | |
| | Income Summary | | 40,000 |
| | (To record ending inventory) | | |

These entries are identified as adjustments (d) and (e), respectively, in the work sheet.

These entries should be familiar to you. They are exactly the same as the closing entries illustrated on page 199. The only difference is that changes in inventory are reported in the adjustments columns when the adjusting entry approach is used.

After posting, the accounts will show:

**Illustration 5B-2**

*Posting of adjustments for merchandise inventory*

| Merchandise Inventory | | Income Summary | |
|---|---|---|---|
| Jan.  1 Bal.  36,000 | Dec.31 Adj.  36,000 | Dec.31  Adj.  36,000 | Dec.31  Adj.  40,000 |
| Dec.31 Adj.  40,000 | | | |
| Dec.31 Bal.  40,000 | | | |

## Adjusted Trial Balance Columns

In Illustration 5B-1, the merchandise inventory amount is extended to the adjusted trial balance debit column. **This amount is the ending inventory for the period.** Both amounts reported in Income Summary are transferred to the adjusted trial balance columns to ensure that these two amounts are reported in the income statement columns. Therefore the net amount, in this case, $4,000 ($40,000 − $36,000), is not reported.

## Financial Statement Columns

Complete financial statements are prepared directly from the income statement and balance sheet columns of the work sheet. The use of the financial statement columns should be familiar to you. One difficult subject is the treatment of merchandise inventory and income summary adjustments. A partial work sheet showing just these two items is presented below:

**Illustration 5B-3**

*Partial work sheet*

| | Trial Balance | | Adjustments | | Adjusted Trial Balance | | Income Statement | | Balance Sheet | |
|---|---|---|---|---|---|---|---|---|---|---|
| | Dr. | Cr. | Dr. | Cr. | Dr. | Cr. | Dr. | Cr. | Dr. | Cr. |
| Merchandise Inventory | 36,000 | | (e) 40,000 | (d) 36,000 | 40,000 | | | | 40,000 | |
| Income Summary | | | (d) 36,000 | (e) 40,000 | 36,000 | 40,000 | 36,000 | 40,000 | | |

In the merchandise inventory line, the $40,000 in the balance sheet debit column is the ending inventory. In the income summary line, the debit in the income statement column indicates the cost of the beginning inventory, and the credit in the income statement column shows the cost of the ending inventory. Complete financial statements are then prepared directly from the income statement and balance sheet columns of the work sheet.

# *J*ournalizing and Posting Closing Entries

When the adjusting entry method is followed, merchandise inventory is not part of the closing process. As a result, entries to close the books are as follows:

| Dec. 31 | Sales | 480,000 | |
| | Purchase Returns and Allowances | 10,400 | |
| | Purchase Discounts | 6,800 | |
| |    Income Summary | | 497,200 |
| |      (To close income statement accounts with | | |
| |      credit balances) | | |
| | | | |
| 31 | Income Summary | 471,200 | |
| |    Sales Returns and Allowances | | 12,000 |
| |    Sales Discounts | | 8,000 |
| |    Purchases | | 325,000 |
| |    Freight-in | | 12,200 |
| |    Store Salaries Expense | | 45,000 |
| |    Rent Expense | | 19,000 |
| |    Freight-out | | 7,000 |
| |    Advertising Expense | | 16,000 |
| |    Utilities Expense | | 17,000 |
| |    Depreciation Expense | | 8,000 |
| |    Insurance Expense | | 2,000 |
| |      (To close income statement accounts with | | |
| |      debit balances) | | |

These entries produce a credit balance in the Income Summary account of $30,000. This amount equals the net income reported for Highpoint Electronic using the closing method. The postings to Income Summary are as follows:

**Income Summary**

| | | | | | | |
|---|---|---|---|---|---|---|
| Dec. 31 | Adj. | 36,000 | Dec. 31 | Adj. | 40,000 |
| 31 | Close | 471,200 | 31 | Close | 497,200 |
| 31 | to Cap. | 30,000 | | | |
| | | 537,200 | | | 537,200 |

**Illustration 5B-4**

*Postings to Income Summary*

Both the closing entry method and the adjusting entry method result in the same accounts and amounts reported in the financial statements. It is a matter of personal preference which method is used.

# Summary of Study Objective for Appendix 5B

**9.** *Explain how the adjusting entry method is used in the work sheet.* Under the adjusting entry method, the two adjustments for inventories are entered in the adjustments columns of the work sheet. The balance in Merchandise Inventory is extended to the adjusted trial balance and balance sheet debit columns. The adjustments to Income Summary are extended to the adjusted trial balance and income statement columns. The adjusting entry method is just as acceptable as the closing entry method, and it accomplishes the same objective.

# GLOSSARY

**Administrative expenses** Expenses relating to general operating activities such as personnel management, accounting, and store security. (p. 204).

**Contra revenue account** An account that is offset against a revenue account on the income statement. (p. 184).

**Cost of goods available for sale**   The sum of the beginning merchandise inventory plus the cost of goods purchased. (p. 191).

**Cost of goods purchased**   The sum of net purchases plus freight-in. (p. 190).

**Cost of goods sold**   The total cost of merchandise sold during the period, determined by subtracting ending inventory from the cost of goods available for sale. (p. 180).

**Credit memorandum**   A document issued by a seller to inform a customer that a credit has been made to the customer's account receivable for a sales return or allowance. (p. 183).

**Debit memorandum**   A document issued by a buyer to inform a seller that a debit has been made to the seller's account because of unsatisfactory merchandise. (p. 188).

**FOB destination**   Freight terms indicating that the goods will be placed free on board at the buyer's place of business, and the seller pays the freight costs. (p. 189).

**FOB shipping point**   Freight terms indicating that goods are placed free on board the carrier by the seller, and the buyer pays the freight costs. (p. 189).

**Gross profit**   The excess of net sales over the cost of goods sold. (p. 181).

**Income from operations**   Income from a company's principal operating activity determined by subtracting cost of goods sold and operating expenses from net sales. (p. 204).

**Multiple-step income statement**   An income statement that shows numerous steps in determining net income (or net loss). (p. 202).

**Net purchases**   Purchases less purchase returns and allowances and purchase discounts. (p. 190).

**Net sales**   Sales less sales returns and allowances and sales discounts. (p. 186).

**Operating expenses**   Expenses incurred in the process of earning sales revenues that are deducted from gross profit in the income statement. (p. 181).

**Other expenses and losses**   A nonoperating section of the income statement that shows expenses from auxiliary operations and losses unrelated to the company's operations. (p. 202).

**Other revenues and gains**   A nonoperating section of the income statement that shows revenues from auxiliary operations and gains unrelated to the company's operations. (p. 202).

**Periodic inventory system**   An inventory system in which detailed records are not maintained and the cost of goods sold is determined only at the end of an accounting period. (p. 186).

**Perpetual inventory system**   A detailed inventory system in which the cost of each inventory item is maintained and the records continuously show the inventory that should be on hand. (p. 186).

**Purchase discount**   A cash discount claimed by a buyer for prompt payment of a balance due. (p. 188).

**Purchase invoice**   A document that supports each credit purchase. (p. 187).

**Sales discount**   A reduction given by a seller for prompt payment of a credit sale. (p. 185).

**Sales invoice**   A document that provides support for credit sales. (p. 181).

**Sales revenue**   Primary source of revenue in a merchandising company. (p. 180).

**Selling expenses**   Expenses associated with the making of sales. (p. 204).

**Single-step income statement**   An income statement that shows only one step in determining net income (or net loss). (p. 204).

# DEMONSTRATION PROBLEM

The adjusted trial balance columns of the work sheet for the year ended December 31, 1996, for Dykstra Company are as follows:

| **Debit** | | **Credit** | |
|---|---|---|---|
| Cash | $ 14,500 | Accumulated Depreciation | $ 18,000 |
| Accounts Receivable | 11,100 | Notes Payable | 25,000 |
| Merchandise Inventory | 32,000 | Accounts Payable | 10,600 |
| Prepaid Insurance | 2,500 | Gene Dykstra, Capital | 81,000 |
| Store Equipment | 95,000 | Sales | 520,000 |
| Gene Dykstra, Drawing | 12,000 | Purchase Returns and Allowances | 9,600 |
| Sales Returns and Allowances | 6,700 | Purchase Discounts | 7,200 |
| Sales Discounts | 5,000 | Interest Revenue | 2,500 |
| Purchases | 352,000 | | $673,900 |
| Freight-in | 8,400 | | |
| Freight-out | 7,600 | | |
| Advertising Expense | 12,000 | | |
| Store Salaries Expense | 56,000 | | |

| | Debit | Credit |
|---|---|---|
| Utilities Expense | 18,000 | |
| Rent Expense | 24,000 | |
| Depreciation Expense | 9,000 | |
| Insurance Expense | 4,500 | |
| Interest Expense | 3,600 | |
| | $673,900 | |

**Instructions**

(a)  Enter the adjusted trial balance data on a work sheet. Complete the work sheet assuming that ending merchandise inventory is $29,000.

(b)  Prepare an income statement assuming Dykstra Company does not use subgroupings for operating expenses.

## Solution to Demonstration Problem

(a)

**DYKSTRA COMPANY**
**Work Sheet**
**For the Year Ended December 31, 1996**

| Account Titles | Adjusted Trial Balance | | Income Statement | | Balance Sheet | |
|---|---|---|---|---|---|---|
| | Dr. | Cr. | Dr. | Cr. | Dr. | Cr. |
| Cash | 14,500 | | | | 14,500 | |
| Accounts Receivable | 11,100 | | | | 11,100 | |
| Merchandise Inventory | 32,000 | | 32,000 | 29,000 | 29,000 | |
| Prepaid Insurance | 2,500 | | | | 2,500 | |
| Store Equipment | 95,000 | | | | 95,000 | |
| Accumulated Depreciation | | 18,000 | | | | 18,000 |
| Notes Payable | | 25,000 | | | | 25,000 |
| Accounts Payable | | 10,600 | | | | 10,600 |
| Gene Dykstra, Capital | | 81,000 | | | | 81,000 |
| Gene Dykstra, Drawing | 12,000 | | | | 12,000 | |
| Sales | | 520,000 | | 520,000 | | |
| Sales Returns and Allowances | 6,700 | | 6,700 | | | |
| Sales Discounts | 5,000 | | 5,000 | | | |
| Purchases | 352,000 | | 352,000 | | | |
| Purchase Returns and Allowances | | 9,600 | | 9,600 | | |
| Purchase Discounts | | 7,200 | | 7,200 | | |
| Freight-in | 8,400 | | 8,400 | | | |
| Freight-out | 7,600 | | 7,600 | | | |
| Advertising Expense | 12,000 | | 12,000 | | | |
| Store Salaries Expense | 56,000 | | 56,000 | | | |
| Utilities Expense | 18,000 | | 18,000 | | | |
| Rent Expense | 24,000 | | 24,000 | | | |
| Depreciation Expense | 9,000 | | 9,000 | | | |
| Insurance Expense | 4,500 | | 4,500 | | | |
| Interest Expense | 3,600 | | 3,600 | | | |
| Interest Revenue | | 2,500 | | 2,500 | | |
| Totals | 673,900 | 673,900 | 538,800 | 568,300 | 164,100 | 134,600 |
| Net Income | | | 29,500 | | | 29,500 |
| Totals | | | 568,300 | 568,300 | 164,100 | 164,100 |

**Problem-Solving Strategies**

1. Make sure in the adjusted trial balance that debits and credits are equal before transferring amounts to the income statement and balance sheet columns.

2. Transfer all amounts in the adjusted trial balance to either the income statement or balance sheet columns.

3. The merchandise inventory reported in the adjusted trial balance is the beginning inventory.

4. Record the ending inventory by debiting the balance sheet column and crediting the income statement column.

5. The net income or net loss is the reconciling item in both the income statement and the balance sheet columns.

(b)

## DYKSTRA COMPANY
### Income Statement
### For the Year Ended December 31, 1996

| | | | |
|---|---|---:|---:|
| Sales revenues | | | |
| Sales | | | $520,000 |
| Less: Sales returns and allowances | | $ 6,700 | |
| Sales discounts | | 5,000 | 11,700 |
| Net sales | | | 508,300 |
| Cost of goods sold | | | |
| Inventory, January 1 | | 32,000 | |
| Purchases | $352,000 | | |
| Less: Purchase returns and allowances | $9,600 | | |
| Purchase discounts | 7,200 | 16,800 | |
| Net purchases | | 335,200 | |
| Add: Freight-in | | 8,400 | |
| Cost of goods purchased | | 343,600 | |
| Cost of goods available for sale | | 375,600 | |
| Inventory, December 31 | | 29,000 | |
| Cost of goods sold | | | 346,600 |
| Gross profit | | | 161,700 |
| Operating expenses | | | |
| Store salaries expense | | 56,000 | |
| Rent expense | | 24,000 | |
| Utilities expense | | 18,000 | |
| Advertising expense | | 12,000 | |
| Depreciation expense | | 9,000 | |
| Freight-out | | 7,600 | |
| Insurance expense | | 4,500 | |
| Total operating expenses | | | 131,100 |
| Income from operations | | | 30,600 |
| Other revenues and gains | | | |
| Interest revenue | | 2,500 | |
| Other expenses and losses | | | |
| Interest expense | | 3,600 | 1,100 |
| Net income | | | $ 29,500 |

**\*Note:** All **asterisked** Questions, Exercises, and Problems relate to material contained in the appendixes to this chapter.

# SELF-STUDY QUESTIONS

Answers are at the end of the chapter.

(SO 1)   1. Gross profit will result if:
  a. operating expenses are less than net income.
  b. sales revenues are greater than operating expenses.
  c. sales revenues are greater than cost of goods sold.
  d. operating expenses are greater than cost of goods sold.

(SO 2)   2. The sales accounts that normally have a debit balance are:
  a. sales discounts.
  b. sales returns and allowances.
  c. Both (a) and (b).
  d. Neither (a) nor (b).

(SO 2)   3. A credit sale of $750 is made on June 13, terms 2/10, net/30, on which a return of $50 is granted on June 16. The amount received as payment in full on June 23 is:
  a. $700.
  b. $686.
  c. $685.
  d. $650.

(SO 3) 4. When goods are purchased for resale by a company:
   a. purchases on account are debited to Merchandise Inventory.
   b. purchases on account are debited to Purchases.
   c. purchase returns are debited to Purchase Returns and Allowances.
   d. freight costs are debited to Purchases.

(SO 3) 5. In determining cost of goods sold:
   a. purchase discounts are deducted from net purchases.
   b. freight-out is added to net purchases.
   c. purchase returns and allowances are deducted from net purchases.
   d. freight-in is added to net purchases.

(SO 3) 6. If beginning inventory is $60,000, cost of goods purchased is $380,000, and ending inventory is $50,000, cost of goods sold is:
   a. $390,000.
   b. $370,000.
   c. $330,000.
   d. $420,000.

(SO 4) 7. If sales revenues are $400,000, cost of goods sold is $310,000, and operating expenses are $60,000, the gross profit is:
   a. $30,000.
   b. $90,000.
   c. $340,000.
   d. $400,000.

(SO 5) 8. The income statement for a merchandising company shows each of the following features *except*:
   a. gross profit.
   b. cost of goods sold.
   c. a sales revenue section.
   d. operating income section.

(SO 6) 9. In a work sheet, ending merchandise inventory is shown in the following columns (assuming the closing entry method is used):
   a. Adjusted trial balance credit and balance sheet debit.
   b. Income statement debit and balance sheet debit.
   c. Income statement credit and balance sheet debit.
   d. Income statement credit and adjusted trial balance debit.

(SO 7) 10. In a single-step income statement:
   a. gross profit is reported.
   b. cost of goods sold is not reported.
   c. sales revenues and other revenues and gains are reported in the revenues section of the income statement.
   d. operating income is separately reported.

(SO 8) *11. Which of the following accounts will normally appear in the ledger of a merchandising company that uses a perpetual inventory system?
   a. Purchases.
   b. Freight-in.
   c. Cost of Goods Sold.
   d. Purchase Discounts.

(SO 9) *12. In using the adjusting entry method to prepare a work sheet:
   a. changes in merchandise inventory are made in the adjustments columns of the work sheet.
   b. financial statements can be prepared only after closing entries are made.
   c. ending inventory appears only in the balance sheet debit column.
   d. beginning inventory is not reported on the trial balance before adjustment.

# QUESTIONS

1. (a) "The steps in the accounting cycle for a merchandising company are different from the accounting cycle for a service enterprise." Do you agree or disagree? (b) Is the measurement of net income in a merchandising company conceptually the same as in a service enterprise? Explain.

2. (a) How do the components of revenues and expenses differ between a merchandising company and a service enterprise? (b) Explain the income measurement process in a merchandising company.

3. How does income measurement differ between a merchandising company and a service company?

4. Chuck Rudy Co. has sales revenue of $100,000, cost of goods sold of $70,000, and operating expenses of $20,000. What is its gross profit?

5. Joan Hollins believes revenues from credit sales may be earned before they are collected in cash. Do you agree? Explain.

6. (a) What is the primary source document for recording (1) cash sales, (2) credit sales, and (3) sales returns and allowances? (b) Using XXs for amounts, give the journal entry for each of the transactions in part (a).

7. A credit sale is made on July 10 for $900, terms 2/10, n/30. On July 12, $100 of goods are returned for credit. Give the journal entry on July 19 to record the receipt of the balance due within the discount period.

8. Identify the accounts that are added to or deducted from purchases to determine the cost of goods purchased. For each account, indicate (a) whether it is added or deducted and (b) its normal balance.

9. Goods costing $1,600 are purchased on account on July 15 with credit terms of 2/10, n/30. On July 18 a $100 credit memo is received from the supplier for damaged goods. Give the journal entry on July 24 to record payment of the balance due within the discount period.

10. Distinguish between FOB shipping point and FOB destination. Identify the freight terms that will result in a debit to Freight-in by the purchaser and a debit to Freight-out by the seller.

11. Why is it inappropriate for a company to include freight-out expense within the Cost of Goods Sold account?

12. In the following separate mini cases, using a periodic inventory system, identify the item(s) designated by letter.
    (a) Purchases − X − Y = Net purchases.
    (b) Cost of goods purchased − Net purchases = X.
    (c) Beginning inventory + X = Cost of goods available for sale.
    (d) Cost of goods available for sale − Cost of goods sold = X.
    (e) Cost of goods sold + Gross profit = X.

13. Anna Ford Company reports net sales $800,000, gross profit of $580,000, and net income of $300,000. What are its operating expenses?

14. Identify the distinguishing features of an income statement for a merchandising company.

15. Indicate the columns of the work sheet in which (a) the beginning merchandise inventory, and (b) the ending merchandise inventory will be shown.

16. Why is the normal operating cycle for a merchandising company likely to be longer than for a service company?

17. Prepare the closing entries for the merchandise inventory account, assuming a beginning inventory of $48,000 and an ending inventory of $58,000.

18. What merchandising account(s) will appear in the post-closing trial balance?

19. Identify the sections of a multiple-step income statement that relate to (a) operating activities, and (b) nonoperating activities.

20. Distinguish between the types of functional groupings of operating expenses. What problem is created by these groupings?

21. How does the single-step form of income statement differ from the multiple-step form?

*22. What types of businesses are most likely to use a perpetual inventory system?

*23. Beginning inventory is $79,000 and ending inventory is $72,000. Assuming a work sheet is used with adjusting entries for merchandise inventory:
    (a) What amount will appear in the balance sheet debit column for merchandise inventory?
    (b) What amounts will appear in the adjustments debit and credit columns for Income Summary?

# BRIEF EXERCISES

*Compute missing amounts in determining net income.*
*(SO 1)*

**BE5-1**  Presented below are the components in Sang Nam Company's income statement. Determine the missing amounts.

|     | Sales | Cost of Goods Sold | Gross Profit | Operating Expenses | Net Income |
|-----|-------|--------------------|--------------|--------------------|------------|
| (a) | $75,000 | ? | $43,500 | ? | $10,800 |
| (b) | $108,000 | $65,000 | ? | ? | 29,500 |
| (c) | ? | $71,900 | $109,600 | $39,500 | ? |

*Journalize sales transactions.*
*(SO 2)*

**BE5-2**  Prepare the journal entries to record the following transactions on H. Hunt Company's books using a periodic inventory system.
    (a) On March 2, H. Hunt Company sold $900,000 of merchandise to B. Streisand Company, terms 2/10, n/30.
    (b) On March 6, B. Streisand Company returned $130,000 of the merchandise purchased on March 2 because it was defective.
    (c) On March 12, H. Hunt Company received the balance due from B. Streisand Company.

*Journalize purchases transactions.*
*(SO 3)*

**BE5-3**  From the information in BE5-2, prepare the journal entries to record these transactions on B. Streisand Company's books under a periodic inventory system.

*Prepare sales revenue section of income statement.*
*(SO 2)*

**BE5-4**  A. Cosby Company provides the following information for the month ended October 31, 1996: Sales on credit $300,000, Cash sales $100,000, Sales discounts $5,000, Sales returns and allowances $20,000. Prepare the sales revenues section of the income statement based on this information.

**BE5–5**  Assume that K. Bassing Company uses a periodic inventory system and has the following account balances: Purchases $400,000, Purchase Returns and Allowances $11,000, Purchase Discounts $8,000, and Freight-in $16,000. Determine (a) net purchases and (b) cost of goods purchased.

*Compute net purchases and cost of goods purchased.*
(SO 3)

**BE5–6**  Assume the same information as in BE5–5, and also that K. Bassing Company has beginning inventory of $60,000, ending inventory of $90,000, and net sales of $630,000. Determine the amounts to be reported for cost of goods sold and gross profit.

*Compute cost of goods sold and gross profit.*
(SO 3, 4)

**BE5–7**  Presented below is the format of the work sheet presented in the chapter.

*Identify work sheet columns for selecting accounts.*
(SO 6)

| Trial Balance | | Adjustments | | Adjusted Trial Balance | | Income Statement | | Balance Sheet | |
|---|---|---|---|---|---|---|---|---|---|
| Dr. | Cr. | Dr. | Cr. | Dr. | Cr. | Dr. | Cr. | Dr. | Cr. |

Indicate where the following items will appear on the work sheet: (a) cash, (b) beginning inventory, (c) purchases, (d) ending inventory.
*Example:*
     Cash: Trial balance debit column; Adjusted trial balance debit column; and Balance sheet debit column.

**BE5–8**  Pema Company has the following merchandise account balances: Sales $180,000, Sales Discounts $2,000, Purchases $120,000, Purchase Returns and Allowances $30,000. In addition, it has a beginning inventory of $50,000 and an ending inventory of $30,000. Prepare the entries to record the closing of these items to Income Summary.

*Prepare closing entries for merchandise accounts.*
(SO 6)

**BE5–9**  ▭▭▭▷ Explain where each of the following items would appear on (1) a multiple-step income statement and on (2) a single-step income statement: (a) gain on sale of equipment, (b) casualty loss from vandalism, and (c) cost of goods sold.

*Contrast presentation in multiple-step and single-step income statements.*
(SO 7)

*\*BE5–10*  Keo Company buys merchandise on account from Mayo Company. The selling price of the goods is $900, and the cost of the goods is $600. Both companies use perpetual inventory systems. Journalize the transaction on the books of both companies.

*Journalize perpetual inventory entries.*
(SO 8)

*\*BE5–11*  Using the information from BE5–7, indicate how these items are presented on the work sheet if the adjusting entry method illustrated in the chapter appendix is used.

*Adjusting entry method.*
(SO 9)

# *E*XERCISES

• • • • • • • • • • • • • • • • • • • • • • • • • • • • • • • • • • • • • • • • • • • • • • • • • • •

**E5–1**  Presented below are the following transactions related to C. Pippen Company.

*Journalize sales transactions.*
(SO 2)

   1. On December 3, C. Pippen Company sold $400,000 of merchandise to I. Thomas Co., terms 2/10, n/30, FOB shipping point.
   2. On December 8, I. Thomas Co. was granted an allowance of $20,000 for merchandise purchased on December 3.
   3. On December 13, C. Pippen Company received the balance due from I. Thomas Co.

**Instructions**
   (a) Prepare the journal entries to record these transactions on the books of C. Pippen Company.
   (b) Assume that C. Pippen Company received the balance due from I. Thomas Co. on January 2 of the following year instead of December 13. Prepare the journal entry to record the receipt of payment on January 2.

**E5–2**  Presented below is the following information related to Hans Olaf Co.

*Journalize purchases transactions.*
(SO 3)

   1. On April 5, purchased merchandise from D. DeVito Company for $18,000 terms 2/10, net/30, FOB shipping point.
   2. On April 6 paid freight costs of $900 on merchandise purchased from D. DeVito.
   3. On April 7, purchased equipment on account for $26,000.
   4. On April 8, returned damaged merchandise to D. DeVito Company and was granted a $3,000 allowance.
   5. On April 15 paid the amount due to D. DeVito Company in full.

**Instructions**

(a) Prepare the journal entries to record these transactions on the books of Hans Olaf Co.

(b) Assume that Hans Olaf Co. paid the balance due to D. DeVito Company on May 4 instead of April 15. Prepare the journal entry to record this payment.

*Prepare sales revenues section and closing entries.*
(SO 2, 5, 6)

**E5–3**    The adjusted trial balance of Cecilie Company shows the following data pertaining to sales at the end of its fiscal year October 31, 1996: Sales $900,000, Freight-out $12,000, Sales Returns and Allowances $24,000, and Sales Discounts $15,000.

**Instructions**

(a) Prepare the sales revenues section of the income statement.

(b) Prepare separate closing entries for (1) sales, and (2) the contra accounts to sales.

*Prepare purchase entries and closing entries.*
(SO 3, 6)

**E5–4**    On June 10, L. Pele Company purchased $5,000 of merchandise from R. Duvall Company FOB shipping point, terms 2/10, n/30. L. Pele pays the freight costs of $300 on June 11. Damaged goods totaling $300 are returned to R. Duvall for credit on June 12. On June 19, L. Pele pays R. Duvall Company in full, less the purchase discount.

**Instructions**

(a) Prepare separate entries for each transaction on the books of L. Pele Company.

(b) Prepare separate closing entries on June 30 for the temporary accounts with (1) debit balances, and (2) credit balances.

*Prepare cost of goods sold section and closing entries.*
(SO 3, 6)

**E5–5**    The trial balance of G. Garbo Company at the end of its fiscal year, August 31, 1996, includes the following accounts: Merchandise Inventory $17,200, Purchases $142,400, Sales $190,000, Freight-in $4,000, Sales Returns and Allowances $3,000, Freight-out $1,000, and Purchase Returns and Allowances $2,000. The ending merchandise inventory is $26,000.

**Instructions**

(a) Prepare a cost of goods sold section for the year ending August 31.

(b) Prepare the closing entries for all accounts.

(c) Post the closing entries to Merchandise Inventory.

*Prepare an income statement.*
(SO 6)

**E5–6**    Presented is information related to Baja Co. for the month of January 1996.

| | | | |
|---|---|---|---|
| Freight-in | $10,000 | Rent expense | 20,000 |
| Freight-out | 7,000 | Salary expense | 61,000 |
| Insurance expense | 12,000 | Sales discounts | 8,000 |
| Purchases | 200,000 | Sales returns and allowances | 13,000 |
| Purchase discounts | 3,000 | Sales | 312,000 |
| Purchase returns and allowances | 6,000 | | |

Beginning merchandise inventory was $42,000 and ending inventory was $63,000.

**Instructions**

Prepare an income statement using the format presented on page 194. Operating expenses should not be segregated into selling and administrative expenses.

*Compute missing amounts in determining gross profit.*
(SO 3, 4)

**E5–7**    Financial information is presented below for three different companies:

| | Liz's Cosmetics | Monroe Grocery | Allied Wholesalers |
|---|---|---|---|
| Sales | $90,000 | (c) | $144,000 |
| Sales returns | (a) | $  6,000 | 12,000 |
| Net sales | 74,000 | 94,000 | 132,000 |
| Beginning inventory | 14,000 | (d) | 44,000 |
| Purchases | 88,000 | 100,000 | (e) |
| Purchase returns | 6,000 | 10,000 | 8,000 |
| Ending inventory | (b) | 50,000 | 30,000 |
| Cost of goods sold | 64,000 | 72,000 | (f) |
| Gross profit | 10,000 | 22,000 | 24,000 |

**Instructions**

Determine the missing amounts. Show all computations.

**E5–8** Presented below are selected accounts for B. Milia Company as reported in the work sheet at the end of May 1996. Ending merchandise inventory is $72,000.

*Complete work sheet and identify accounts for post-closing trial balance.*
*(SO 6)*

| Accounts | Adjusted Trial Balance | | Income Statement | | Balance Sheet | |
|---|---|---|---|---|---|---|
| | Dr. | Cr. | Dr. | Cr. | Dr. | Cr. |
| Cash | 9,000 | | | | | |
| Merchandise Inventory | 80,000 | | | | | |
| Purchases | 240,000 | | | | | |
| Purchase Returns and Allowances | | 30,000 | | | | |
| Sales | | 450,000 | | | | |
| Sales Returns and Allowances | 10,000 | | | | | |
| Sales Discounts | 5,000 | | | | | |
| Rent Expense | 42,000 | | | | | |

**Instructions**
(a) Complete the work sheet by extending amounts reported in the adjusted trial balance to the appropriate columns in the work sheet. The closing entry method is used to account for merchandise inventory. Do not total individual columns.
(b) Identify the merchandising account(s) that are in the post-closing trial balance.

**E5–9** In its income statement for the year ended December 31, 1996, Chevalier Company reported the following condensed data:

*Prepare multiple-step and single-step income statements.*
*(SO 7)*

| | | | |
|---|---|---|---|
| Administrative expenses | $435,000 | Selling expenses | $ 690,000 |
| Cost of goods sold | 989,000 | Loss on sale of equipment | 10,000 |
| Interest expense | 70,000 | Net sales | 2,359,000 |
| Interest revenue | 45,000 | | |

**Instructions**
(a) Prepare a multiple-step income statement.
(b) Prepare a single-step income statement.

**E5–10** An inexperienced accountant for Churchill Company made the following errors in recording merchandising transactions:

*Prepare correcting entries for sales and purchases.*
*(SO 2, 3)*

1. A $150 refund to a customer for faulty merchandise was debited to Sales $150 and credited to Cash $150.
2. A $250 credit purchase of supplies was debited to Purchases $250 and credited to Cash $250.
3. An $80 sales discount was debited to Purchase Discounts.
4. A $50 purchase return was recorded as a debit to Accounts Payable $50 and a credit to Purchases $50.
5. A cash payment of $30 for freight on merchandise purchases was debited to Purchases $300 and credited to Cash $300.

**Instructions**
Prepare separate correcting entries for each error, assuming that the incorrect entry is not reversed. (Omit explanations.)

**\*E5–11** On September 1, Campus Office Supply had an inventory of 30 deluxe pocket calculators at a cost of $20 each. The company uses a perpetual inventory system. During September, the following transactions occurred.

*Journalize perpetual inventory entries.*
*(SO 8)*

Sept.  6  Purchased 60 calculators at $20 each from Digital Co. for cash.
     9  Paid freight of $60 on calculators purchased from Digital Co.
    10  Returned 2 calculators to Digital Co. for $40 credit because they did not meet specifications.
    12  Sold 26 calculators costing $20 (including freight-in) for $30 each to Campus Book Store, terms, n/30.

14    Granted credit of $30 to Campus Book Store for the return of one calculator that was not ordered.

20    Sold 30 calculators costing $20 for $30 each to Varsity Card Shop, terms, n/30.

### Instructions
Journalize the September transactions.

*Identify work sheet columns using adjusting entry method.*
(SO 8)

**\*E5–12**    Tastie Candy Company prepares adjusting entries for merchandise inventory at the end of the accounting period. On January 1, the balance in Merchandise Inventory was $29,500 and the inventory on hand at December 31 is $34,700.

### Instructions
(a) Determine the amounts and the work sheet columns in which merchandise inventory will appear.
(b) Journalize the adjusting entries for merchandise inventory at December 31.

# PROBLEMS
• • • • • • • • • • • • • • • • • • • • • • • • • • • • • • • • • • • • • • • • • • • • • • • • • • • • • • • • • • • • • • • • • • • •

*Journalize, post, and prepare partial income statement.*
(SO 2, 3, 4, 5)

**P5–1**    Eagle Hardware Store completed the following merchandising transactions in the month of May. At the beginning of May, the ledger of Eagle showed Cash of $5,000 and S. Dorn, Capital, of $5,000.

May  1    Purchased merchandise on account from Depot Wholesale Supply $5,000, terms 2/10, n/30.

2    Sold merchandise on account $4,000, terms 2/10, n/30.

5    Received credit from Depot Wholesale Supply for merchandise returned $200.

9    Received collections in full, less discounts, from customers billed on sales of $4,000 on May 2.

10    Paid Depot Wholesale Supply in full, less discount.

11    Purchased supplies for cash $900.

12    Purchased merchandise for cash $2,400.

15    Received refund for poor quality merchandise from supplier on cash purchase $230.

17    Purchased merchandise from Harlow Distributors $1,900, FOB shipping point, terms 2/10, n/30.

19    Paid freight on May 17 purchase $250.

24    Sold merchandise for cash $6,200.

25    Purchased merchandise from Horicon Inc. $1,000, FOB destination, terms 2/10, n/30.

27    Paid Harlow Distributors in full, less discount.

29    Made refunds to cash customers for defective merchandise $100.

31    Sold merchandise on account $1,600, terms n/30.

Eagle Hardware's chart of accounts includes the following: No. 101 Cash, No. 112 Accounts Receivable, No. 120 Merchandise Inventory, No. 126 Supplies, No. 201 Accounts Payable, No. 301 S. Dorn, Capital, No. 401 Sales, No. 412 Sales Returns and Allowances, No. 414 Sales Discounts, No. 510 Purchases, No. 512 Purchase Returns and Allowances, No. 514 Purchase Discounts, No. 516 Freight-in.

### Instructions
(a) Journalize the transactions.
(b) Enter the beginning cash and capital balances and post the transactions. (Use J1 for the journal reference.)
(c) Prepare an income statement through gross profit for the month of May 1996, assuming ending inventory is $2,400, and no beginning inventory.

*Journalize, post, and prepare trial balance and partial income statement.*
(SO 2, 3, 4, 5)

**P5–2**    Chi Chi Ramos, a former professional golf star, operates Chi Chi's Pro Shop at Bay Golf Course. At the beginning of the current season on April 1, the ledger of Chi Chi's Pro Shop showed Cash $2,500, Merchandise Inventory $3,500, and Chi Chi Ramos, Capital $6,000. The following transactions were completed during April.

Apr. 5 Purchased golf bags, clubs, and balls on account from Balata Co. $1,600, FOB shipping point, terms 2/10, n/60.

7 Paid freight on Balata purchase $80.

9 Received credit from Balata Co. for merchandise returned $100.

10 Sold merchandise on account to members $900, terms n/30.

12 Purchased golf shoes, sweaters, and other accessories on account from Arrow Sportswear $660, terms 1/10, n/30.

14 Paid Balata Co. in full.

17 Received credit from Arrow Sportswear for merchandise returned $60.

20 Made sales on account to members $700, terms n/30.

21 Paid Arrow Sportswear in full.

27 Granted credit to members for clothing that did not fit $30.

30 Made cash sales $600.

30 Received payments on account from members $1,100.

The chart of accounts for the pro shop includes the following: No. 101 Cash, No. 112 Accounts Receivable, No. 120 Merchandise Inventory, No. 201 Accounts Payable, No. 301 C. Ramos, Capital, No. 401 Sales, No. 412 Sales Returns and Allowances, No. 510 Purchases, No. 512 Purchase Returns and Allowances, No. 514 Purchase Discounts, No. 516 Freight-in.

**Instructions**

(a) Journalize the April transactions.

(b) Enter the beginning balances in the ledger accounts and post the April transactions. (Use J1 for the journal reference.)

(c) Prepare a trial balance on April 30, 1996.

(d) Prepare an income statement through gross profit, assuming merchandise inventory on hand at April 30 is $4,200.

**P5–3** The trial balance of Mesa Wholesale Company contained the following accounts at December 31, the end of the company's fiscal year:

*Complete accounting cycle beginning with a work sheet. (SO 5, 6, 7)*

## MESA WHOLESALE COMPANY
### Trial Balance
### December 31, 1996

|  | Debit | Credit |
|---|---|---|
| Cash | $ 33,400 |  |
| Accounts Receivable | 37,600 |  |
| Merchandise Inventory | 62,400 |  |
| Land | 92,000 |  |
| Buildings | 197,000 |  |
| Accumulated Depreciation—Buildings |  | $ 54,000 |
| Equipment | 83,500 |  |
| Accumulated Depreciation—Equipment |  | 42,400 |
| Notes Payable |  | 50,000 |
| Accounts Payable |  | 37,500 |
| G. Mesa, Capital |  | 267,800 |
| G. Mesa, Drawing | 10,000 |  |
| Sales |  | 886,100 |
| Sales Discounts | 4,600 |  |
| Purchases | 725,100 |  |
| Purchase Discounts |  | 16,000 |
| Freight-in | 12,400 |  |
| Salaries Expense | 69,800 |  |
| Utilities Expense | 9,400 |  |
| Repair Expense | 5,900 |  |
| Gas and Oil Expense | 7,200 |  |
| Insurance Expense | 3,500 |  |
|  | $1,353,800 | $1,353,800 |

Adjustment data:

1. Depreciation is $10,000 on buildings and $9,000 on equipment. (Both are administrative expenses.)
2. Interest of $7,000 is due and unpaid on notes payable at December 31.

Other data:

1. Merchandise inventory on hand at December 31, 1996, is $90,000.
2. Salaries are 80% selling and 20% administrative.
3. Utilities expense, repair expense, and insurance expense are 100% administrative.
4. $15,000 of the notes payable are payable next year.
5. Gas and oil expense is a selling expense.

*Instructions*
(a) Enter the trial balance on a work sheet and complete the work sheet.
(b) Prepare a multiple-step income statement and owner's equity statement for the year, and a classified balance sheet at December 31, 1996.
(c) Journalize the adjusting entries.
(d) Journalize the closing entries.
(e) Prepare a post-closing trial balance.

*Prepare financial statements and adjusting and closing entries.*
*(SO 5, 6, 7)*

**P5–4**   Metro Department Store is located in midtown Metropolis. During the past several years, net income has been declining because of suburban shopping centers. At the end of the company's fiscal year on November 30, 1996, the following accounts appeared in two of its trial balances:

| | Trial Balances | |
| --- | --- | --- |
| | Unadjusted | Adjusted |
| Accounts Payable | $ 37,310 | $ 37,310 |
| Accounts Receivable | 11,770 | 11,770 |
| Accumulated Depreciation—Delivery Equipment | 15,680 | 19,680 |
| Accumulated Depreciation—Store Equipment | 32,300 | 41,800 |
| Cash | 8,000 | 8,000 |
| Delivery Expense | 8,200 | 8,200 |
| Delivery Equipment | 57,000 | 57,000 |
| Depreciation Expense—Delivery Equipment | | 4,000 |
| Depreciation Expense—Store Equipment | | 9,500 |
| Freight-in | 5,060 | 5,060 |
| B. Howit, Capital | 84,200 | 84,200 |
| B. Howit, Drawing | 12,000 | 12,000 |
| Insurance Expense | | 9,000 |
| Interest Expense | 8,000 | 8,000 |
| Interest Revenue | 5,000 | 5,000 |
| Merchandise Inventory | 34,360 | 34,360 |
| Notes Payable | 46,000 | 46,000 |
| Prepaid Insurance | 13,500 | 4,500 |
| Property Tax Expense | | 3,500 |
| Purchases | 640,000 | 640,000 |
| Purchase Discounts | 7,000 | 7,000 |
| Purchase Returns and Allowances | 3,000 | 3,000 |
| Rent Expense | 19,000 | 19,000 |
| Salaries Expense | 120,000 | 120,000 |
| Sales | 860,000 | 860,000 |
| Sales Commissions Expense | 8,000 | 14,000 |
| Sales Commissions Payable | | 6,000 |
| Sales Returns and Allowances | 10,000 | 10,000 |
| Store Equipment | 125,000 | 125,000 |
| Property Taxes Payable | | 3,500 |
| Utilities Expense | 10,600 | 10,600 |

Analysis reveals the following additional data:

1. Salaries expense is 70% selling and 30% administrative.
2. Insurance expense is 50% selling and 50% administrative.
3. Merchandise inventory at November 30, 1996, is $36,200.
4. Rent expense, utilities expense, and property tax expense are administrative expenses.
5. Notes payable are due in 2002.

**Instructions**

(a) Prepare a multiple-step income statement, an owner's equity statement, and a classi-fied balance sheet.
(b) Journalize the adjusting entries that were made.
(c) Journalize the closing entries that are necessary.

**P5–5** An inexperienced accountant prepared the following condensed income statement for Zambrana Company, a retail firm that has been in business for a number of years.

*Prepare correct multiple-step and single-step income statements.*
*(SO 5, 7)*

### ZAMBRANA COMPANY
### Income Statement
### For Year Ended December 31, 1996

| | | |
|---|---|---|
| Revenues | | |
| Net sales | $740,000 | |
| Other revenues | 24,000 | $764,000 |
| Cost of goods sold | | |
| Purchases (net) | 540,000 | |
| Inventory increase | 15,000 | |
| Cost of goods sold | | 555,000 |
| Gross profit | | 209,000 |
| Operating expenses | | |
| Selling expenses | 104,000 | |
| Administrative expenses | 69,000 | 173,000 |
| Net earnings | | $ 36,000 |

As an experienced, knowledgeable accountant you review the statement and determine the following facts:

1. Net sales consist of sales $800,000, less delivery expense on merchandise sold $30,000, and sales returns and allowances $30,000.
2. Other revenues consist of purchase discounts $16,000 and rent revenue $8,000.
3. Net purchases include purchases $520,000 and delivery costs on incoming merchan-dise $20,000.
4. The inventory did increase $15,000, which amounted to 25% of the beginning in-ventory.
5. Selling expenses consist of salespersons' salaries $80,000, depreciation on accounting equipment $8,000, advertising $10,000, and sales commissions $6,000. The commis-sions represent commissions paid. At December 31, $4,000 of commissions have been earned by salespersons, but have not been paid.
6. Administrative expenses consist of office salaries $27,000, owner's drawing $4,000, utilities $12,000, interest expense $2,000, and rent $24,000, which includes prepay-ments totaling $6,000 for the first quarter of 1997.

**Instructions**

(a) Prepare a correct detailed multiple-step income statement.
(b) Prepare a correct condensed single-step income statement.

**\*P5–6** Presented below are selected transactions for the Norlan Company during September of the current year. Norlan Company uses the perpetual inventory system.

*Journalize entries under a perpetual inventory system.*
*(SO 8)*

Sept. 2 Purchased delivery equipment on account for $28,000.
   4 Purchased merchandise on account from Hillary Company at a cost of $60,000, terms FOB shipping point, 2/10, n30.
   5 Paid freight charges of $2,000 on merchandise purchased from Hillary Company on September 4.

5  Returned damaged goods costing $7,000 received from Hillary Company on September 4.

6  Sold merchandise to Kimmel Company costing $15,000 on account for $21,000, terms 1/10, n30.

14  Paid Hillary balance due related to September 4 transaction.

15  Purchased supplies costing $4,000 for cash.

16  Received balance due from Kimmel Company.

18  Purchased merchandise for cash $6,000.

22  Sold to Waldo Company on account for $28,000 inventory costing $20,000, terms 1/10, n30.

**Instructions**

Journalize the September transactions.

*Complete a work sheet using the adjusting entry method, prepare adjusting and closing entries and post to some accounts.*
*(SO 9)*

**\*P5–7**  The trial balance of World Enterprises for the year ending December 31, 1996, is shown below.

### WORLD ENTERPRISES
### Trial Balance
### December 31, 1996

|  | Debit | Credit |
|---|---|---|
| Cash | $ 14,000 | |
| Accounts Receivable | 27,600 | |
| Merchandise Inventory | 27,500 | |
| Prepaid Insurance | 1,800 | |
| Store Equipment | 42,000 | |
| Accumulated Depreciation—Store Equipment | | $ 9,000 |
| Accounts Payable | | 31,200 |
| R. Roger, Capital | | 50,300 |
| Sales | | 238,500 |
| Sales Returns and Allowances | 4,600 | |
| Sales Discounts | 3,900 | |
| Purchases | 172,000 | |
| Freight-in | 5,000 | |
| Purchase Returns and Allowances | | 1,200 |
| Purchase Discounts | | 2,000 |
| Salaries Expense | 27,700 | |
| Utilities Expense | 6,100 | |
| | $332,200 | $332,200 |

Other data:

1. Merchandise inventory on hand at December 31, $38,600.
2. Insurance expired $800.
3. Depreciation expense, $3,000.
4. The company uses the adjusting entry method for merchandise inventory.

**Instructions**

(a) Enter the trial balance on a work sheet and complete the work sheet using the adjusting entry method.
(b) Journalize the adjusting entries.
(c) Prepare the closing entries.
(d) Post the entries in (b) and (c) to Merchandise Inventory and Income Summary.

# ALTERNATE PROBLEMS

*Journalize, post, and prepare a partial income statement.*
*(SO 2, 3, 4, 5)*

**P5–1A**  The Nisson Distributing Company completed the following merchandising transactions in the month of April. At the beginning of April, the ledger of Nisson showed cash of $9,000 and S. Nisson capital of $9,000.

Apr. 2 Purchased merchandise on account from Kentucky Supply Co. $4,900, terms 2/10, n/30.

4 Sold merchandise on account $5,000, FOB destination, terms 2/10, n/30.

5 Paid $200 freight on April 4 sale.

6 Received credit from Kentucky Supply Co. for merchandise returned $300.

11 Paid Kentucky Supply Co. in full, less discount.

13 Received collections in full, less discounts, from customers billed on April 4.

14 Purchased merchandise for cash $4,400.

16 Received refund from supplier on cash purchase of April 14, $500.

18 Purchased merchandise from Pigeon Distributors $4,200, FOB shipping point, terms 2/10, n/30.

20 Paid freight on April 18 purchase $100.

23 Sold merchandise for cash $6,400.

26 Purchased merchandise for cash $2,300.

27 Paid Pigeon Distributors in full, less discount.

29 Made refunds to cash customers for defective merchandise $90.

30 Sold merchandise on account $3,700, terms n/30.

Nisson Company's chart of accounts includes the following: No. 101 Cash, No. 112 Accounts Receivable, No. 120 Merchandise Inventory, No. 201 Accounts Payable, No. 301 S. Nisson, Capital, No. 401 Sales, No. 412 Sales Returns and Allowances, No. 414 Sales Discounts, No. 510 Purchases, No. 512 Purchase Returns and Allowances, No. 514 Purchase Discounts, No. 516 Freight-in, and No. 644 Freight-out.

*Instructions*
(a) Journalize the transactions.
(b) Enter the beginning cash balances, and post the transactions (Use J1 for the journal reference.)
(c) Prepare the income statement through gross profit for the month of April, 1996, assuming ending inventory is $9,700 and no beginning inventory.

**P5–2A** Billy Jean Evert, a former professional tennis star, operates B.J.'s Tennis Shop at the Jackson Lake Resort. At the beginning of the current season, the ledger of B.J.'s Tennis Shop showed Cash $2,500, Merchandise Inventory $1,700, and B.J. Evert, Capital $4,200. The following transactions were completed during April:

*Journalize, post, and prepare a trial balance and partial income statement.*
(SO 2, 3, 4, 5)

Apr. 4 Purchased racquets and balls from Robert Co. $640 FOB shipping point, terms 3/10, n/30.

6 Paid freight on Robert purchase $40.

8 Sold merchandise to members $900, terms n/30.

10 Received credit of $40 from Robert Co. for a damaged racquet that was returned.

11 Purchased tennis shoes from Niki Sports for cash, $300.

13 Paid Robert Co. in full.

14 Purchased tennis shirts and shorts from Martina's Sportswear $700, FOB shipping point, terms 2/10, n/60.

15 Received cash refund of $50 from Niki Sports for damaged merchandise that was returned.

17 Paid freight on Martina's Sportswear purchase $30.

18 Sold merchandise to members, $800, terms n/30.

20 Received $500 in cash from members in settlement of their accounts.

21 Paid Martina's Sportswear in full.

27 Granted credit of $30 to members for tennis clothing that did not fit.

30 Sold merchandise to members $900, terms n/30.

30 Received cash payments on account from members, $500.

The chart of accounts for the tennis shop includes the following: No. 101 Cash, No. 112 Accounts Receivable, No. 120 Merchandise Inventory, No. 201 Accounts Payable, No. 301 B.J. Evert, Capital, No. 401 Sales, No. 412 Sales Returns and Allowances, No. 510 Purchases, No. 512 Purchase Returns and Allowances, No. 514 Purchase Discounts, No. 516 Freight-in.

*Instructions*

  (a) Journalize the April transactions.

  (b) Enter the beginning balances in the ledger accounts and post the April transactions. (Use J1 for the journal reference.)

  (c) Prepare a trial balance on April 30.

  (d) Prepare an income statement through gross profit, assuming merchandise inventory on hand at April 30 is $1,800.

*Complete accounting cycle beginning with a work sheet.*
*(SO 5, 6, 7)*

**P5–3A**  The trial balance of Ivanna Fashion Center contained the following accounts at November 30, the end of the company's fiscal year.

**IVANNA FASHION CENTER**
**Trial Balance**
**November 30, 1996**

| | Debit | Credit |
|---|---|---|
| Cash | $ 16,700 | |
| Accounts Receivable | 33,700 | |
| Merchandise Inventory | 38,000 | |
| Store Supplies | 5,500 | |
| Store Equipment | 85,000 | |
| Accumulated Depreciation—Store Equipment | | $ 18,000 |
| Delivery Equipment | 48,000 | |
| Accumulated Depreciation—Delivery Equipment | | 6,000 |
| Notes Payable | | 51,000 |
| Accounts Payable | | 48,500 |
| L. Ivanna, Capital | | 110,000 |
| L. Ivanna, Drawing | 12,000 | |
| Sales | | 746,600 |
| Sales Returns and Allowances | 4,200 | |
| Purchases | 503,600 | |
| Purchase Returns and Allowances | | 6,900 |
| Purchase Discounts | | 3,700 |
| Freight-in | 10,800 | |
| Salaries Expense | 140,000 | |
| Advertising Expense | 26,400 | |
| Utilities Expense | 14,000 | |
| Repair Expense | 12,100 | |
| Delivery Expense | 16,700 | |
| Rent Expense | 24,000 | |
| | $990,700 | $990,700 |

Adjustment data:

  1. Store supplies on hand totaled $3,500.

  2. Depreciation is $9,000 on the store equipment and $7,000 on the delivery equipment.

  3. Interest of $11,000 is accrued on notes payable at November 30.

Other data:

  1. Merchandise inventory on hand at November 30, 1996 is $45,000.

  2. Salaries expense is 70% selling and 30% administrative.

  3. Rent expense and utilities expense are 80% selling and 20% administrative.

  4. $30,000 of notes payable are due for payment next year.

  5. Repair expense is 100% administrative.

*Instructions*

  (a) Enter the trial balance on a work sheet and complete the work sheet.

  (b) Prepare a multiple-step income statement and owner's equity statement for the year and a classified balance sheet as of November 30, 1996.

(c) Journalize the adjusting entries.
(d) Journalize the closing entries.
(e) Prepare a post-closing trial balance.

**P5–4A** The N-Mart Department Store is located near the Village shopping mall. At the end of the company's fiscal year on December 31, 1996, the following accounts appeared in two of its trial balances.

*Prepare financial statements and adjusting and closing entries.*
*(SO 5, 6, 7)*

| | Trial Balances | |
| --- | --- | --- |
| | Unadjusted | Adjusted |
| Accounts Payable | $ 89,300 | $ 89,300 |
| Accounts Receivable | 50,300 | 50,300 |
| Accumulated Depreciation—Building | 42,100 | 52,500 |
| Accumulated Depreciation—Equipment | 29,600 | 42,900 |
| Building | 190,000 | 190,000 |
| Cash | 23,000 | 23,000 |
| Depreciation Expense—Building | | 10,400 |
| Depreciation Expense—Equipment | | 13,300 |
| Equipment | 110,000 | 110,000 |
| Freight-in | 3,600 | 3,600 |
| Insurance Expense | | 7,200 |
| Interest Expense | 3,000 | 11,000 |
| Interest Payable | | 8,000 |
| Interest Revenue | 4,000 | 4,000 |
| Merchandise Inventory | 40,500 | 40,500 |
| Mortgage Payable | 80,000 | 80,000 |
| Office Salaries Expense | 32,000 | 32,000 |
| Prepaid Insurance | 9,600 | 2,400 |
| Property Taxes Payable | | 4,800 |
| Purchases | 462,000 | 462,000 |
| Purchase Discounts | 12,000 | 12,000 |
| Purchase Returns and Allowances | 6,400 | 6,400 |
| Sales Salaries Expense | 76,000 | 76,000 |
| Sales | 618,000 | 618,000 |
| Sales Commissions Expense | 11,000 | 14,500 |
| Sales Commissions Payable | | 3,500 |
| Sales Returns and Allowances | 8,000 | 8,000 |
| S. Newsom, Capital | 176,600 | 176,600 |
| S. Newsom, Drawing | 28,000 | 28,000 |
| Property Taxes Expense | | 4,800 |
| Utilities Expense | 11,000 | 11,000 |

Analysis reveals the following additional data:

1. Merchandise inventory on December 31, 1996, is $75,000.
2. Insurance expense and utilities expense are 60% selling and 40% administrative.
3. $20,000 of the mortgage payable is due for payment next year.
4. Depreciation on the building and property tax expense are administrative expenses; depreciation on the equipment is a selling expense.

*Instructions*
(a) Prepare a multiple-step income statement, an owner's equity statement, and a classi-fied balance sheet.
(b) Journalize the adjusting entries that were made.
(c) Journalize the closing entries that are necessary.

*Prepare correct multiple-step and single-step income statements.*
*(SO 5, 7)*

**P5–5A**   A part-time bookkeeper prepared the following income statement for the Tao Company for the year ending December 31, 1996.

**TAO COMPANY**
**Income Statement**
**December 31, 1996**

| | | |
|---|---|---|
| Revenues | | |
| Sales | | $702,000 |
| Less: Freight-in | $ 17,200 | |
| Discounts | 4,100 | 21,300 |
| Net sales | | 680,700 |
| Other revenues (net) | | 1,300 |
| Total revenues | | 682,000 |
| Expenses | | |
| Purchases | 470,000 | |
| Selling expenses | 100,000 | |
| Administrative expenses | 50,000 | |
| L. Tao, Drawings | 12,000 | |
| Total expenses | | 632,000 |
| Net income | | $ 50,000 |

As an experienced, knowledgeable accountant you review the statement and determine the following facts:

1. Sales includes $10,000 of deposits from customers for future sales orders.
2. Discounts consist of purchase discounts earned $7,200 and sales discounts granted $11,300.
3. Other revenues contains two items: interest expense $4,000 and interest revenue $5,300.
4. Purchases includes freight-out $14,000 and purchase returns and allowances $9,000.
5. Ending merchandise inventory increased $20,000 from a beginning inventory of $35,000.
6. Selling expenses consist of sales salaries $76,000, advertising $10,000, depreciation on store equipment $7,500, and sales commissions expense $6,500.
7. Administrative expenses consist of office salaries $19,000, utilities expense $8,000, rent expense $16,000, and insurance expense $7,000. Insurance expense includes $1,200 of insurance applicable to 1994.

*Instructions*
(a)  Prepare a correct detailed multiple-step income statement.
(b)  Prepare a correct condensed single-step income statement.

# ▼*B*roadening Your Perspective

## *F*INANCIAL REPORTING PROBLEM

Bob Evans Farms, Inc., operates 315 restaurants in 19 states and produces fresh and fully cooked sausage products, fresh salads, and related products distributed to grocery stores in the Midwest, Southwest, and Southeast. For a recent 3-year period, Bob Evans Farms reported the following selected income statement data (in millions of dollars):

| | 1994 | 1993 | 1992 |
|---|---|---|---|
| Sales | $699.0 | $653.2 | $556.3 |
| Cost of goods sold | 514.4 | 480.3 | 424.3 |
| Selling and administrative expenses | 85.0 | 83.6 | 72.0 |
| Net income | 48.2 | 43.1 | 39.3 |

In his letter to the stockholders, the chairman of the board and CEO made the following comments:

"I am looking forward to a record-setting year at Bob Evans Farms. We have excellent leadership in place, great traditions on which to build, and the teamwork and knowledge to move ahead."

*Instructions*

(a) Compute the percentage change in sales and in net income from year to year for the years 1993 and 1994.
(b) What contribution, if any, did the company's gross profit rate make to the improved earnings?
(c) What was Bob Evans' percentage of net income to net sales in each of the 3 years? Comment on any trend in this percentage.

# DECISION CASE
............................................................................

Three years ago, Kathy Webb and her brother-in-law John Utley opened FedCo. Department Store. For the first 2 years, business was good, but the following condensed income results for 1996 were disappointing.

**FEDCO. DEPARTMENT STORE**
**Income Statement**
**For the Year Ended December 31, 1996**

| | | |
|---|---|---|
| Net sales | | $700,000 |
| Cost of goods sold | | 546,000 |
| Gross profit | | 154,000 |
| Operating expenses | | |
| Selling expenses | $100,000 | |
| Administrative expenses | 25,000 | 125,000 |
| Net income | | $ 29,000 |

Kathy believes the problem lies in the relatively low gross profit rate (gross profit divided by net sales) of 22%. John believes the problem is that operating expenses are too high.

Kathy thinks the gross profit rate can be improved by making both of the following changes: (1) Increase average selling prices by 17%; this increase is expected to lower sales volume so that total sales will increase only 6%. (2) Buy merchandise in larger quantities and take all purchase discounts; these changes are expected to increase the gross profit rate by 3%. Kathy does not anticipate that these changes will have any effect on operating expenses.

John thinks expenses can be cut by making both of the following changes: (1) Cut 1996 sales salaries of $60,000 in half and give sales personnel a commission of 2% of net sales. (2) Reduce store deliveries to one day per week rather than twice a week; this change will reduce 1996 delivery expenses of $30,000 by 40%. John feels that these changes will not have any effect on net sales.

Kathy and John come to you for help in deciding the best way to improve net income.

*Instructions*

(a) Prepare a condensed income statement for 1997 assuming (1) Kathy's changes are implemented and (2) John's ideas are adopted.
(b) What is your recommendation to Kathy and John?
(c) Prepare a condensed income statement for 1997 assuming both sets of proposed changes are made.

# COMMUNICATION ACTIVITY
............................................................................

The following situation is in chronological order:

1. Dexter decides to buy a surfboard.
2. He calls Surfing USA Co. to inquire about their surfboards.

3. Two days later he requests Surfing USA Co. to make him a surfboard.
4. Three days later, Surfing USA Co. sends him a purchase order to fill out.
5. He sends back the purchase order.
6. Surfing USA Co. receives the completed purchase order.
7. Surfing USA Co. completes the surfboard.
8. Dexter picks up the surfboard.
9. Surfing USA Co. bills Dexter.
10. Surfing USA Co. receives payment from Dexter.

**Instructions**

In a memo to the President of Surfing USA Co., explain the following:

(a) When should Surfing USA Co. record the sale?
(b) Suppose that with his purchase order, Dexter is required to make a down payment. Would that change your answer?

# GROUP ACTIVITY

The following information is taken from the accounting records of Grant Company:

| | |
|---|---|
| Sales | $150,000 |
| Purchase Returns and Allowances | 20,000 |
| Beginning Merchandise Inventory | 20,000 |
| Sales Discounts | 8,000 |
| Purchases | 100,000 |
| Operating Expenses | 30,000 |
| Freight-in | 12,000 |
| Purchase Discounts | 9,000 |
| Sales Returns and Allowances | 10,000 |
| Ending Merchandise Inventory | 8,000 |

**Instructions**

Working in groups of four or five students, determine the following:

(a) Net sales.
(b) Cost of goods purchased.
(c) Cost of goods sold.
(d) Gross profit.
(e) Net income.

# ETHICS CASE

Rita Pelzer was just hired as the assistant treasurer of Yorkshire Stores, a specialty chain store company consisting of nine retail stores concentrated in one metropolitan area. Among other things, the payment of all invoices is centralized in one of the departments Rita will manage. Her primary responsibility is to maintain the company's high credit rating by paying all bills when due and to take advantage of all cash discounts. Jamie Caterino, the former assistant treasurer, who has been promoted to treasurer, is training Rita in her new duties. He instructs Rita that she is to continue the practice of preparing all checks "net of discount" and dating the checks the last day of the discount period. "But," Jamie continues, "we always hold the checks at least four days beyond the discount period before mailing them. That way we get another four days of interest on our money. Most of our creditors need our business and don't complain. And, if they scream about our missing the discount period, we blame it on the mail room or the post office. We've only lost one discount out of every hundred we take that way. I think everybody does it. By the way, welcome to our team!"

**Instructions**

(a) What are the ethical considerations in this case?
(b) Who are the stakeholders that are harmed or benefitted in this situation?
(c) Should Rita continue the practice started by Jamie? Does she have any choice?

# CRITICAL THINKING
## ► *A Real-World Focus: A.L. Laboratories*

........................................................

**A.L. Laboratories** *is headquartered in Ft. Lee, N.J., and also has operations in Scandinavia and Indonesia. The company develops and produces generic pharmaceuticals, specializing in both over-the-counter and prescription creams and ointments, aerosol inhalants, and liquids such as cough syrups. A significant share of its income is also derived from the development and distribution of animal health products such as food additives for poultry. The company was founded in 1975 and today has over 2,700 employees.*

Gross profit at A.L. Laboratories declined in both dollars and as a percentage of revenues. The decline was attributed to lower sales volume, customer credits associated with product recalls, inventory disposals, and the impact of higher inventory costs. In addition to the above, the gross profit percentage declined as a result of lower production volumes.

### Instructions
   (a) What account is affected when A.L. Laboratories has a product recall?
   (b) What factors caused gross profit to decline?
   (c) What factors could cause this company to have to dispose of inventory?

---

*Answers to Self-Study Questions*
1. c   2. c   3. b   4. b   5. d   6. a   7. b   8. d   9. c   10. c   11. c
12. a

Before studying this chapter, you should know, or, if necessary, review:

**a.** *How to perform each of the steps in the accounting cycle.*
(Ch. 4, pp. 147–48)
**b.** *How to record transactions for a merchandising company.*
(Ch. 5, pp. 181–190)
**c.** *How to prepare financial statements for a merchandising company.*
(Ch. 5, pp. 197–98)

# "It Just Kind of Ate Things"

FORT WASHINGTON, Pa. — After years of fighting a computerized bookkeeping system, Debbie Goodeve was glad to toss out the machine that had made her bookkeeping job at an orthodontics office a nightmare. "The computer has totally messed up everybody's accounts," groused Debbie. "It just kind of ate things."

The office didn't have the money to upgrade the computer or buy a new one, so they dusted off the carbon-backed check ledger, made by Safeguard Business Systems—the old-fashioned kind that leaves a paper record each time a check is written.

For 36 years, Safeguard Business Systems Inc. has churned out low-tech, low-cost ledgers. In effect, the company has written a survival manual for manual products in a computer age. Its strategy for prolonging the life expectancy of its ledgers is simple: It figures that most entrepreneurs can't afford a computerized bookkeeping system or don't write enough checks to warrant one.

The company's sales force tries to persuade prospective customers,

even those that already own computers, that Safeguard's system is faster and less costly to use than a computer. When a check is written, records are simultaneously created: there are no stubs or invoices to fill out separately. Sales reps emphasize that entrepreneurs didn't go into business to keep books—that if they get bogged down with that task, they aren't doing what they do best.

Although Safeguard has found a profitable niche market, it also recognizes that the world is changing.

The number of small businesses switching to computer systems is growing rapidly. Recognizing that all the sales expertise in the world won't stop progress, the company has begun to sell computer forms and accounting software that can be used with its manual ledgers. Although this new line currently represents a small fraction of total business, it is the company's fastest growing product. Says Safeguard's chairperson, Vinton Bacon, "You can't fight the technology. You've got to try to work with it." ◄

# CHAPTER · 6

# ACCOUNTING INFORMATION SYSTEMS

---

### ▶ STUDY OBJECTIVES ◀

**After studying this chapter, you should be able to:**

1. *Identify the basic principles of accounting information systems.*
2. *Explain the major phases involved in the development of an accounting system.*
3. *Describe the nature and purpose of a subsidiary ledger.*
4. *Explain how special journals are used in journalizing.*
5. *Indicate how a columnar journal is posted.*
6. *Distinguish between computer hardware and accounting software and the principal methods of data processing.*
7. *Identify the key points in comparing manual and electronic accounting systems.*

As you see from the opening story, although many businesses continue to use manual systems, an increasing number are becoming computerized. Whether you use pen, pencil, or computers in maintaining accounting records, certain principles and procedures apply. The purpose of this chapter is to explain and illustrate these features. The content and organization of this chapter are as follows:

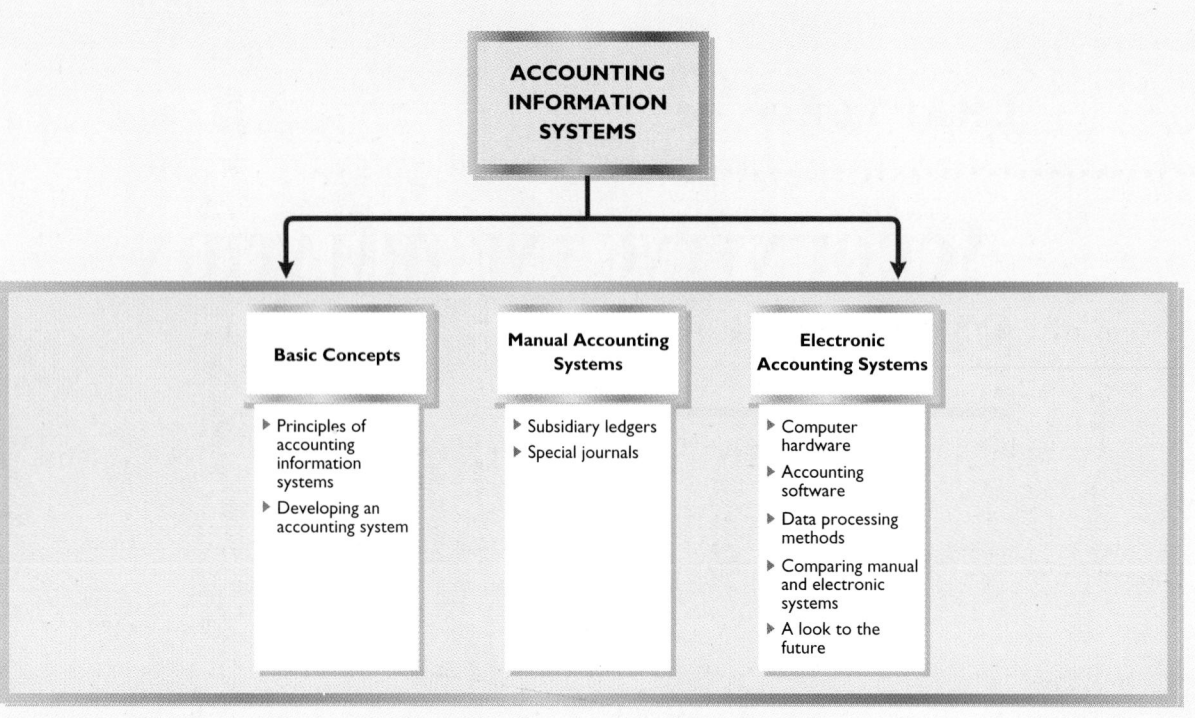

---

## ▼SECTION 1 ▶ Basic Concepts

The system of collecting and processing transaction data and disseminating financial information to interested parties is known as the accounting information system. It includes each of the steps in the accounting cycle that you have studied in earlier chapters, the documents that provide evidence of the transactions and events, and the records, trial balances, work sheets, and financial statements that result. An accounting information system may be either manual or electronic.

### ▼Principles of Accounting Information Systems

**STUDY OBJECTIVE**
••••••••••▼••••••••••

*Identify the basic principles of accounting information systems.*

To have an efficient and effective accounting information system (hereafter referred to simply as the accounting system), certain basic principles must be followed. These principles are:

1. **Cost awareness.** The system must be cost effective: the benefits obtained from the information disseminated must outweigh the cost of providing it. For example, the value of each accounting report should be at least equal to the cost of producing it.

2. **Useful output.** To be useful, information must be understandable, relevant, reliable, timely, and accurate. Designers of accounting systems must consider the needs and knowledge of various users so that the system's output (reports and statements) will be useful to them. For example, sales managers may need weekly reports of sales, and factory supervisors may need daily reports of production. Others with differing responsibilities (such as vice-presidents) may need such reports only monthly or quarterly.

3. **Flexibility.** The accounting system should be able to accommodate a variety of users and changing information needs. The business environment changes as a result of technological advances, organizational growth, increased competition, government regulation, or changes in accounting principles. When it does, the accounting system should be sufficiently flexible to meet the resulting changes in the demands made upon it.

If the accounting system is cost effective, provides useful output, and has the flexibility to meet future needs, it can provide a valuable service and make a major contribution to both individual and organizational goals.

# Developing an Accounting System

Good accounting systems do not just happen. They are carefully planned, designed, installed, managed, and refined. Generally, developing an accounting system involves the following four phases:

1. **Analysis.** The starting point of analysis is to determine the information needs of internal and external users. Once this is established, the system analyst proceeds to identify the sources of the information and the records and procedures for collecting and reporting the data. If an existing system is being analyzed, its strengths and weaknesses must be identified.

2. **Design.** For a new system, forms and documents must be designed; methods and procedures selected from alternatives; job descriptions prepared; controls integrated; reports formatted; and equipment selected. Redesigning an existing system may involve only minor changes, a complete overhaul, or replacement of a manual system by a computerized system.

3. **Implementation.** Implementation of either new or revised systems requires that documents, procedures, reports, and processing equipment must be installed and made operational. Personnel must be hired, trained, and closely supervised through a start-up or transition period.

4. **Follow-up.** After the system is up and running, it must be evaluated and monitored for weaknesses and breakdowns. Also, its effectiveness and efficiency must be compared to design and organizational objectives. Corrections in design or changes in implementation may be necessary.

**STUDY OBJECTIVE**

**2**

*Explain the major phases involved in the development of an accounting system.*

Illustration 6-1 highlights the relationship of these four phases in the life cycle of the accounting system.

These phases, which represent the life cycle of an accounting system, suggest that few systems remain the same forever. As experience and knowledge are obtained, and as technological and organizational changes occur, the accounting system may also have to grow and change.

The accounting system in the first five chapters is satisfactory in a company where the volume of transactions is extremely low. However, in most companies, it is necessary to add additional ledgers and journals to the accounting system to record transaction data efficiently.

**Illustration 6-1**

*Phases in the development of an accounting system*

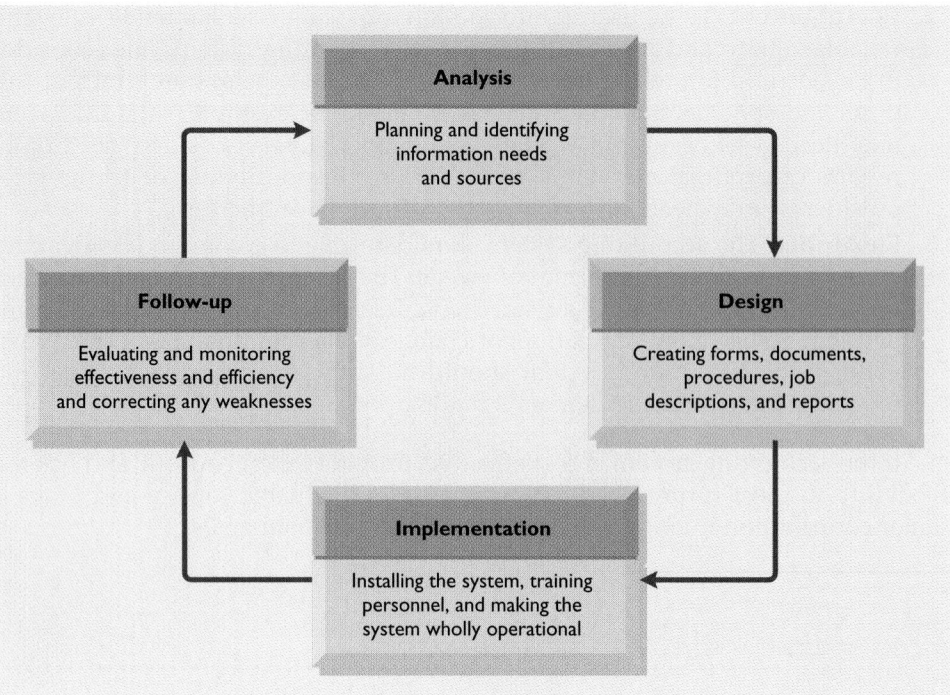

# ▼SECTION 2 ▸ *Manual Accounting Systems*

In a manual accounting system, each of the steps in the accounting cycle is performed by hand. For example, each accounting transaction is entered manually in the journal and posted manually to the ledger. To obtain ledger account balances and to prepare a trial balance and financial statements, additional manual computations must be made. In this section, therefore, we discuss how the manual processing system can be more efficiently used to process accounting data.

At this point you might be wondering, "Why cover manual accounting systems if the real world uses computerized systems?" First, small businesses still abound. Most of them begin operations with manual (or even "shoe box") accounting systems and convert to computerized systems as the business grows. Second, to understand what computerized accounting systems do, you need to understand how manual accounting systems work.

## Subsidiary Ledgers

**STUDY OBJECTIVE**

**3**

*Describe the nature and purpose of a subsidiary ledger.*

Imagine a business that has several thousand charge (credit) customers and shows the transactions with these customers in only one account—Accounts Receivable—in the general ledger. It would be virtually impossible to determine the balance owed by an individual customer at any specific time. Similarly, the amount payable to one creditor would be difficult to locate quickly from a single Accounts Payable account in the general ledger.

To provide such information, companies use subsidiary ledgers to keep track of individual balances. A subsidiary ledger is a group of accounts with a common characteristic (for example, all customer accounts—that is, accounts receivable). The subsidiary ledger frees the general ledger from the details of individual balances. A subsidiary ledger is an addition to, and an expansion of, the general ledger.

Two common subsidiary ledgers are:

1. The accounts receivable (or customers') ledger which accumulates transaction data with individual customers.
2. The accounts payable (or creditors') ledger which maintains transaction data with individual creditors.

In each of these subsidiary ledgers, individual accounts are usually arranged in alphabetical order.

The detailed data shown in a subsidiary ledger are summarized in a general ledger account. The accounts for the two ledgers above are Accounts Receivable and Accounts Payable, respectively. The general ledger account that summarizes subsidiary ledger data is called a control account. **Each general ledger control account balance must equal the composite balance of the individual accounts in the related subsidiary ledger at the end of an accounting period.** An overview of the relationship of subsidiary ledgers to the general ledger is shown in Illustration 6-2, with the general ledger control accounts in color.

**Illustration 6-2**

*Relationship of general ledgers and subsidiary accounts*

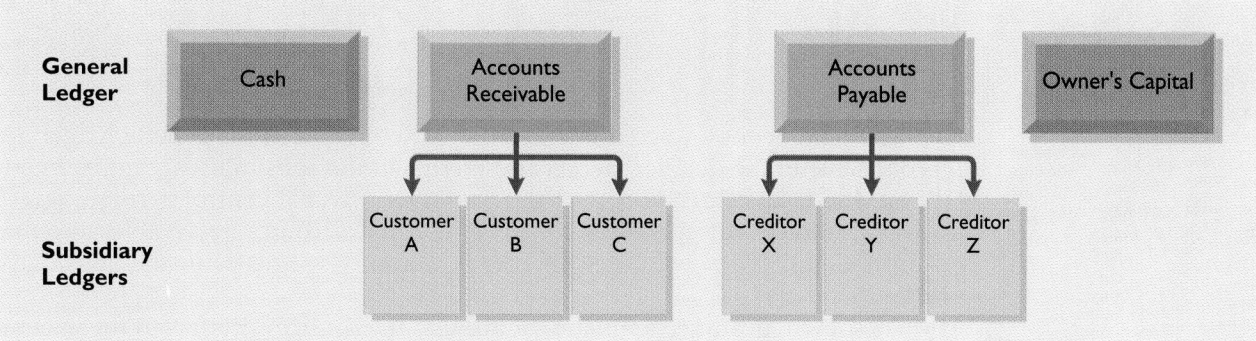

Note that cash and owner's capital are not control accounts.

## Illustration

An example of a control account and subsidiary ledger for Larson Enterprises is provided in Illustration 6-3. The explanation column in these accounts is not shown in this and subsequent illustrations due to space considerations.

**Illustration 6-3**

*Relationship between ledgers*

## ▲*Technology in Action*

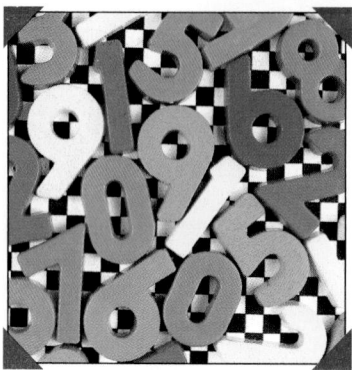

Rather than relying on customer or creditor names in a subsidiary ledger, a computer system expands the account number of the control account in a pre-specified manner. For example, if accounts receivable was numbered 10010, the first account in the accounts receivable subsidiary ledger might be numbered 10010-0001. Most systems allow inquiries about specific accounts in the subsidiary ledger (by account number) or about the control account. With the latter, the system would automatically total all the subsidiary accounts whenever an inquiry to the control account was made.

**Illustration 6-4**

*Sales and collection transactions*

The example is based on the following transactions:

| | Credit Sales | | | Collections on Account | |
|---|---|---|---|---|---|
| Jan. 10 | Aaron Co. | $ 6,000 | Jan. 19 | Aaron Co. | $ 4,000 |
| 12 | Branden Inc. | 3,000 | 21 | Branden Inc. | 3,000 |
| 20 | Caron Co. | 3,000 | 29 | Caron Co. | 1,000 |
| | | $12,000 | | | $ 8,000 |

The total debits and credits in Accounts Receivable in the general ledger are reconcilable to the detailed debits and credits in the subsidiary accounts. In addition, the balance of $4,000 in the accounts receivable control account agrees with the total of the balances in the individual accounts receivable accounts (Aaron Co. $2,000 + Branden Inc. $0 + Caron Co. $2,000) in the subsidiary ledger.

As shown, postings are made monthly to the control accounts in the general ledger so that monthly financial statements may be prepared. Postings to the individual accounts in the subsidiary ledger are made daily. The rationale for posting daily is to ensure that current account information can be used as a basis for monitoring credit limits, billing customers, and answering inquiries from customers about their account balances.

### Advantages of Subsidiary Ledgers

The advantages of using subsidiary ledgers are that they:

1. **Show transactions affecting one customer or one creditor in a single account**, thus providing necessary up-to-date information on specific account balances.
2. **Free the general ledger of excessive details**. As a result, a trial balance of the general ledger does not contain vast numbers of individual account balances.
3. **Help locate errors in individual accounts** by reducing the number of accounts combined in one ledger and by using controlling accounts.
4. **Make possible a division of labor** in posting by having one employee post to the general ledger and a different employee(s) post to the subsidiary ledgers.

## *Before You Go On . . .*

### ▶ *Review It*

1. What are the basic principles to be followed in designing and developing an efficient and effective accounting information system?

**2.** What are the major phases in the development of an accounting information system?

**3.** What is a subsidiary ledger, and what purpose does it serve?

### ► *Do It*

Presented below is information related to Sims Company for its first month of operations. Identify the balances that appear in the accounts payable subsidiary ledger and the accounts payable balance that appears in the general ledger at the end of January.

| | Credit Purchases | | | Cash Paid | |
|---|---|---|---|---|---|
| Jan 5 | Devon Co. | $11,000 | Jan 9 | Devon Co. | $7,000 |
| Jan 11 | Shelby Co. | 7,000 | Jan 14 | Shelby Co. | 2,000 |
| Jan 22 | Taylor Co. | 14,000 | Jan 27 | Taylor Co. | 9,000 |

*Reasoning:* Note that only one account appears in the general ledger, but the detail related to this account is shown in the subsidiary ledger.

*Solution:* Subsidiary ledger balances: Devon Co. $4,000 ($11,000 − $7,000); Shelby Co. $5,000 ($7,000 − $2,000); Taylor Co. $5,000 ($14,000 − $9,000). General ledger Accounts Payable balance $14,000 ($32,000 − $18,000).

*Related exercise material:* BE6–3, BE6–4, E6–1, E6–2, E6–3, E6–4, E6–5, and E6–9.

# ◣ Special Journals

So far you have learned to journalize transactions in a two-column general journal and post these entries individually to the general ledger. This procedure is satisfactory in only the very smallest companies. To expedite journalizing and posting transactions, most companies use special journals **in addition to the general journal**.

A special journal is used to record similar types of transactions, such as all sales of merchandise on account, or all cash receipts. The types of special journals used depend largely on the types of transactions that occur frequently in a business enterprise. Most merchandising enterprises use the journals shown in Illustration 6-5 to record transactions daily:

**STUDY OBJECTIVE**

**4**

*Explain how special journals are used in journalizing.*

**Illustration 6-5**

*Use of special journals and the general journal*

| Sales Journal | Cash Receipts Journal | Purchases Journal | Cash Payments Journal | General Journal |
|---|---|---|---|---|
| Used for: | Used for: | Used for: | Used for: | Used for: |
| All sales of merchandise on account | All cash received (including cash sales) | All purchases of merchandise on account | All cash paid (including cash purchases) | Transactions that cannot be entered in a special journal, including correcting, adjusting, and closing entries |

**If a transaction cannot be recorded in a special journal, it is recorded in the general journal.** For example, if you had special journals only for the four types of transactions listed above, purchase returns and allowances or sales returns and allowances would be recorded in the general journal. Similarly, **cor-**

**recting, adjusting, and closing entries are recorded in the general journal**. Other types of special journals may be used in some situations. For example, when purchase returns and allowances or sales returns and allowances are frequent, special journals may be used to record these transactions.

Special journals **permit greater division of labor** because several individuals can record entries in different journals at the same time. For example, one employee may be responsible for journalizing all cash receipts, and another for journalizing credit sales. In addition, the use of special journals **reduces the time necessary to complete the posting process**. When special journals are used, monthly postings to some accounts may be substituted for daily postings, as will be illustrated later in the chapter.

## Sales Journal

**Helpful hint**  Will a special journal or the general journal have fewer daily entries? Answer: The general journal, because in a properly designed system all recurring daily entries should be recorded in a special journal.

The sales journal is used to record sales of merchandise on account. Cash sales of merchandise are entered in the cash receipts journal. Credit sales of assets other than merchandise are entered in the general journal.

### Journalizing Credit Sales

All entries in a sales journal are made from sales invoices. Each invoice is prenumbered to ensure that all invoices are journalized. To illustrate, assume that Karns Wholesale Supply has the following credit sales transactions:

**Illustration 6-6**

*Credit sales transactions*

| Date | Customer | Invoice No. | Amount | Date | Customer | Invoice No. | Amount |
|------|----------|-------------|--------|------|----------|-------------|--------|
| 5/3 | Abbot Sisters | 101 | $10,600 | 5/21 | Abbot Sisters | 105 | $15,400 |
| 5/7 | Babson Co. | 102 | 11,350 | 5/24 | Deli Co. | 106 | 21,210 |
| 5/14 | Carson Bros. | 103 | 7,800 | 5/27 | Babson Co. | 107 | 14,570 |
| 5/19 | Deli Co. | 104 | 9,300 | | | | |

Each entry in the sales journal used here results in a debit to Accounts Receivable and a credit to Sales. Since each sale on account involves a debit to Accounts Receivable and a credit of equal amount to Sales, only one line is needed in this sales journal to record each transaction. The sales journal is presented in Illustration 6-7.

**Illustration 6-7**

*Journalizing the sales journal*

| | KARNS WHOLESALE SUPPLY | | | |
|---|---|---|---|---|
| | **Sales Journal** | | | **S1** |
| Date | Account Debited | Invoice No. | Ref. | Accts. Receivable Dr. Sales Cr. |
|------|-----------------|-------------|------|----------------------------------|
| 1996 | | | | |
| May  3 | Abbot Sisters | 101 | | 10,600 |
| 7 | Babson Co. | 102 | | 11,350 |
| 14 | Carson Bros. | 103 | | 7,800 |
| 19 | Deli Co. | 104 | | 9,300 |
| 21 | Abbot Sisters | 105 | | 15,400 |
| 24 | Deli Co. | 106 | | 21,210 |
| 27 | Babson Co. | 107 | | 14,570 |
| | | | | 90,230 |

The reference (Ref.) column is not used in journalizing. It is used in posting the sales journal, as explained in the next section. Also, note that, unlike the general journal, an explanation is not required for each entry in a special journal.

If management wishes to record its sales by department, additional columns may be provided in the sales journal. For example, a department store may have columns for home furnishings, sporting goods, shoes, etc. In addition, practically all states and cities require a sales tax be charged on items sold, which the company must remit to the state or city. In this case, it is desirable to add an additional credit column to the sales journal for sales tax payable. Sales tax payable is posted in total at the end of the month, similar to sales.

### *Posting the Sales Journal*

Postings from the sales journal are made **daily to the individual accounts receivable** in the subsidiary ledger and **monthly to the general ledger**, as shown in Illustration 6-8.

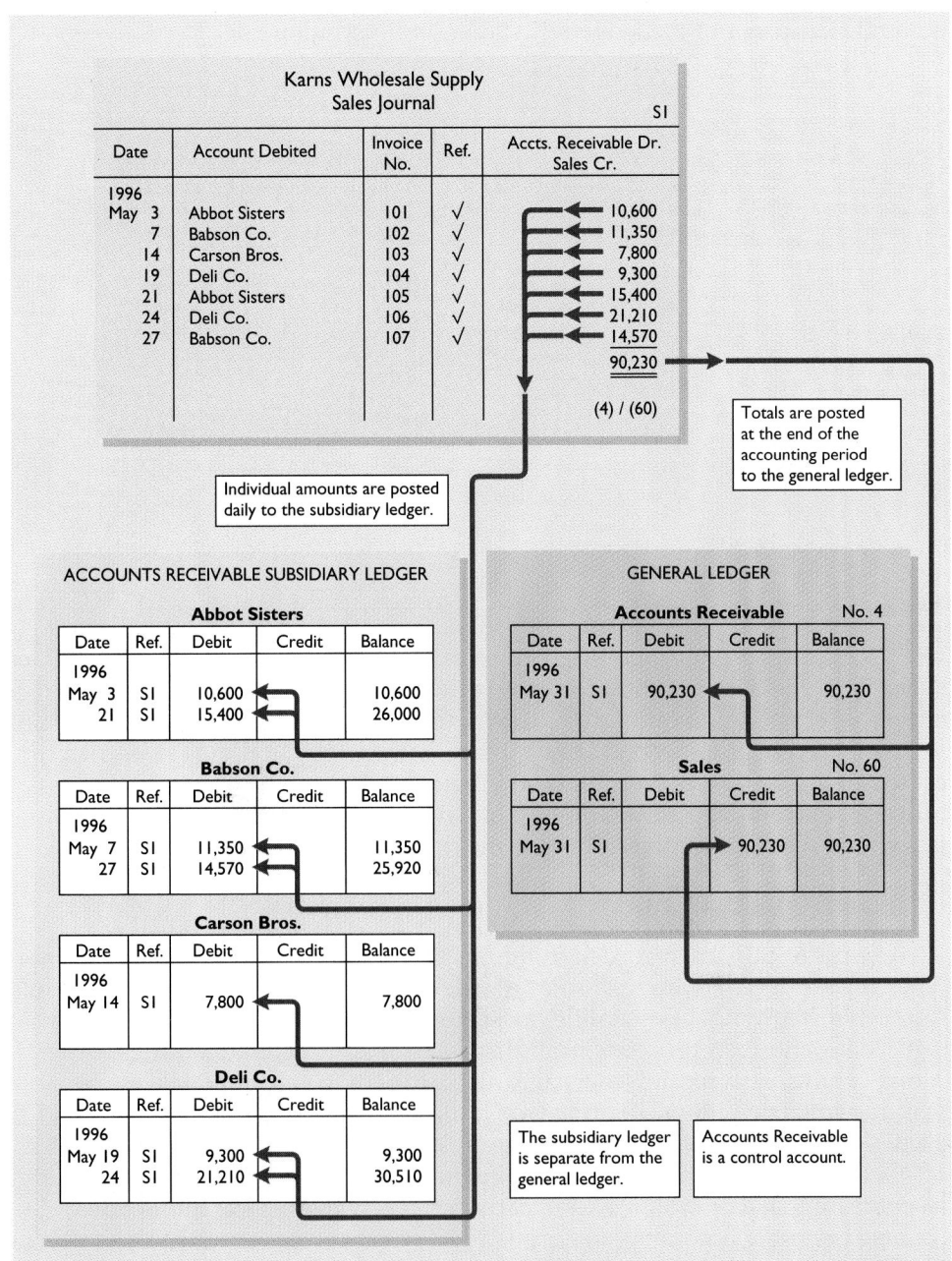

**Illustration 6-8**

*Posting the sales journal*

A check mark (√) is inserted in the reference posting column to indicate that the daily posting to the customer's account has been made. A check mark (√) is used in this illustration because the subsidiary ledger accounts are not numbered. At the end of the month, the column total of the sales journal ($90,230) is posted to the general ledger—as a debit to Accounts Receivable (account No. 4) and a credit to Sales (account No. 60). The insertion of the respective account numbers below the column total indicates that the postings have been made. In both the general ledger and subsidiary ledger accounts, the reference **S1** indicates that the posting came from page 1 of the sales journal.

### Proving the Ledgers

To prove the ledgers it is necessary to determine that (1) the total of the general ledger debit balances equals the total of the general ledger credit balances and (2) the sum of the subsidiary ledger balances equals the balance in the control account. The proof of the ledgers is shown in Illustration 6-9.

**Illustration 6-9**

*Proving the ledgers*

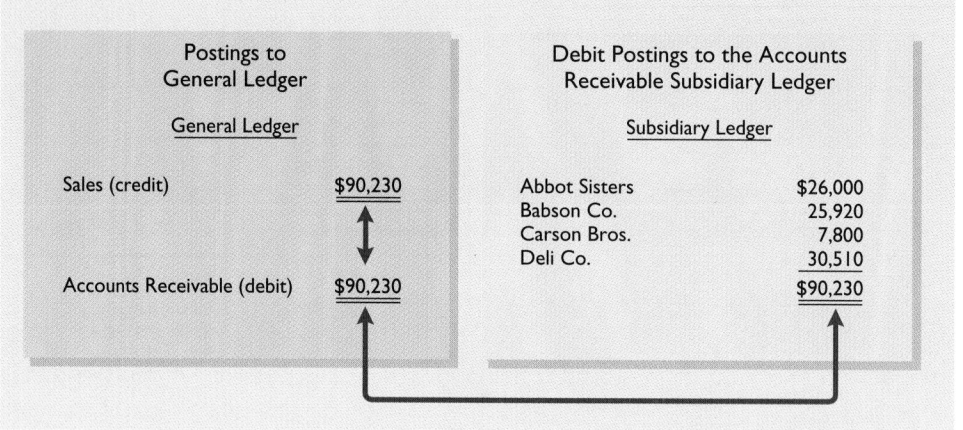

### Advantages of the Sales Journal

The use of a special journal to record sales on account has a number of advantages. First, the one-line entry for each sales transaction **saves time**, because it is not necessary to write out a debit to Accounts Receivable and a credit to Sales for each transaction. Second, only totals, rather than individual entries, are posted to the general ledger, thus **saving posting time and reducing the possibilities of errors in posting**. Finally, **a division of labor results**, because one individual can take responsibility for the sales journal.

## Cash Receipts Journal

All receipts of cash are recorded in the cash receipts journal. The most common types of cash receipts are cash sales of merchandise and collections of accounts receivable. Many other possibilities exist, however, such as receipt of money from bank loans and cash proceeds from disposals of equipment, buildings, or land. A one-column cash receipts journal is not sufficient to accommodate all possible cash receipt transactions. Therefore, a multiple-column cash receipts journal is used.

Generally, a cash receipts journal includes debit columns for cash and sales discounts and credit columns for accounts receivable, sales, and "other" accounts. The other accounts category is used when the cash receipt does not involve a cash sale or a collection of accounts receivable. A five-column cash receipts journal is shown in Illustration 6-10. When a special journal has more than one account column it is referred to as a columnar journal.

**Illustration 6-10**

*Journalizing and posting the cash receipts journal*

**Karns Wholesale Supply
Cash Receipts Journal**

CRI

| Date | Accounts Credited | Ref. | Cash Dr. | Sales Discounts Dr. | Accounts Receivable Cr. | Sales Cr. | Other Accounts Cr. |
|---|---|---|---|---|---|---|---|
| 1996 | | | | | | | |
| May 1 | D.A Karns, Capital | 50 | 5,000 | | | | 5,000 |
| 7 | | | 1,900 | | | 1,900 | |
| 10 | Abbot Sisters | √ | 10,388 | 212 | 10,600 | | |
| 12 | | | 2,600 | | | 2,600 | |
| 17 | Babson Co. | √ | 11,123 | 227 | 11,350 | | |
| 22 | Notes Payable | 20 | 6,000 | | | | 6,000 |
| 23 | Carson Bros. | √ | 7,644 | 156 | 7,800 | | |
| 28 | Deli Co. | √ | 9,114 | 186 | 9,300 | | |
| | | | 53,769 | 781 | 39,050 | 4,500 | 11,000 |
| | | | (1) | (61) | (4) | (60) | (x) |

| Individual amounts are posted daily to the subsidiary ledger. | Totals are posted at the end of the accounting period to the general ledger. |
|---|---|

**ACCOUNTS RECEIVABLE SUBSIDIARY LEDGER**

**Abbot Sisters**

| Date | Ref. | Debit | Credit | Balance |
|---|---|---|---|---|
| 1996 | | | | |
| May 3 | SI | 10,600 | | 10,600 |
| 10 | CRI | | 10,600 | -------- |
| 21 | SI | 15,400 | | 15,400 |

**Babson Co.**

| Date | Ref. | Debit | Credit | Balance |
|---|---|---|---|---|
| 1996 | | | | |
| May 7 | SI | 11,350 | | 11,350 |
| 17 | CRI | | 11,350 | -------- |
| 27 | SI | 14,570 | | 14,570 |

**Carson Bros.**

| Date | Ref. | Debit | Credit | Balance |
|---|---|---|---|---|
| 1996 | | | | |
| May 14 | SI | 7,800 | | 7,800 |
| 23 | CRI | | 7,800 | ------- |

**Deli Co.**

| Date | Ref. | Debit | Credit | Balance |
|---|---|---|---|---|
| 1996 | | | | |
| May 19 | SI | 9,300 | | 9,300 |
| 24 | SI | 21,210 | | 30,510 |
| 28 | CRI | | 9,300 | 21,210 |

| Accounts Receivable is a control account. | The subsidiary ledger is separate from the general ledger. |
|---|---|

**GENERAL LEDGER**

**Cash** — No. 1

| Date | Ref. | Debit | Credit | Balance |
|---|---|---|---|---|
| 1996 | | | | |
| May 31 | CRI | 53,769 | | 53,769 |

**Accounts Receivable** — No. 4

| Date | Ref. | Debit | Credit | Balance |
|---|---|---|---|---|
| 1996 | | | | |
| May 31 | SI | 90,230 | | 90,230 |
| 31 | CRI | | 39,050 | 51,180 |

**Notes Payable** — No. 20

| Date | Ref. | Debit | Credit | Balance |
|---|---|---|---|---|
| 1996 | | | | |
| May 22 | CRI | | 6,000 | 6,000 |

**D.A. Karns, Capital** — No. 50

| Date | Ref. | Debit | Credit | Balance |
|---|---|---|---|---|
| 1996 | | | | |
| May 1 | CRI | | 5,000 | 5,000 |

**Sales** — No. 60

| Date | Ref. | Debit | Credit | Balance |
|---|---|---|---|---|
| 1996 | | | | |
| May 31 | SI | | 90,230 | 90,230 |
| 31 | CRI | | 4,500 | 94,730 |

**Sales Discounts** — No. 61

| Date | Ref. | Debit | Credit | Balance |
|---|---|---|---|---|
| 1996 | | | | |
| May 31 | CRI | 781 | | 781 |

Additional credit columns may be used if they significantly reduce postings to a specific account. For example, the cash receipts of a loan company, such as Household International, include thousands of collections from customers. These collections are credited to Loans Receivable and Interest Revenue. A significant saving in posting would result from using separate credit columns for Loans Receivable and Interest Revenue, rather than using the other accounts credit column for these amounts. In contrast, a retailer that has only one interest collection a month would not find it useful to have a separate column for interest revenue.

### Journalizing Cash Receipts Transactions

To illustrate the journalizing of cash receipts transactions, we will continue with the transactions of Karns Wholesale Supply during the month of May. Collections from customers relate to the entries recorded in the sales journal in Illustration 6-7. The entries in the cash receipts journal are based on the following cash receipts transactions:

May 1  D. A. Karns makes an investment of $5,000 in the business.
   7  Cash sales of merchandise total $1,900.
   10  A check for $10,388 is received from Abbot Sisters in payment of invoice No. 101 for $10,600 less a 2% discount.
   12  Cash sales of merchandise total $2,600.
   17  A check for $11,123 is received from Babson Co. in payment of invoice No. 102 for $11,350 less a 2% discount.
   22  Cash is received by signing a note for $6,000.
   23  A check for $7,644 is received from Carson Bros. in full for invoice No. 103 for $7,800 less a 2% discount.
   28  A check for $9,114 is received from Deli Co. in full for invoice No. 104 for $9,300 less a 2% discount.

Further information about the columns in the cash receipts journal (see Illustration 6-10) is as follows:

### Debits:

1. **Cash.** The amount of cash actually received in each transaction is entered in this column; the column total indicates the total cash receipts for the month.
2. **Sales Discounts.** The Sales Discounts column is included so that it is not necessary to enter sales discount items in the general journal. As a result, the collection of an account receivable within the discount period is expressed on one line in the appropriate columns of the cash receipts journal.

### Credits:

3. **Accounts Receivable.** The Accounts Receivable column is used to record cash collections on account. The amount entered in this column is the amount to be credited to the individual customer's account.
4. **Sales.** The Sales column records all cash sales of merchandise. Cash sales of plant assets, for example, are not reported in this column.
5. **Other Accounts.** The Other Accounts column, often referred to as the **sundry accounts column**, is used whenever the credit is other than to Accounts Receivable or Sales. For example, in the first entry, $5,000 is entered as a credit to D. A. Karns, Capital.

**Helpful hint** When is an account title entered in the "Accounts Credited" column of the cash receipts journal? Answer: A *subsidiary ledger* title is entered there whenever the entry involves a collection of accounts receivable. A *general ledger* account title is entered there whenever the entry involves an account that is not the subject of a special column (and an amount must be entered in the "Other Accounts" column). No account title is entered there if neither of the foregoing apply.

In a columnar journal, as in a single-column journal, only one line is needed for each entry. There must be equal debit and credit amounts for each line. When the collection from Abbot Sisters on May 10 is journalized, for example, three amounts are indicated. Note also that the Accounts Credited column is used to identify both general ledger and subsidiary ledger account titles. The former is illustrated in the May 1 entry for Karns' investment; the latter is illustrated in the May 10 entry for the collection in full from Abbot Sisters.

When the journalizing of a columnar journal has been completed, the amount columns are totaled, and the totals are balanced to prove the equality of debits and credits. The proof for Karns Wholesale Supply is as follows:

Illustration 6-11

*Proving the accuracy of the cash receipts journal*

| Debits | | Credits | |
| --- | --- | --- | --- |
| Cash | $53,769 | Accounts Receivable | $39,050 |
| Sales Discounts | 781 | Sales | 4,500 |
| | $54,550 | Other Accounts | 11,000 |
| | | | $54,550 |

Totaling the columns of a journal and proving the equality of the totals is called **footing** and **cross-footing** a journal.

### Posting the Cash Receipts Journal

Posting a columnar journal involves the following procedures.

1. All column totals except the total for the Other Accounts column are posted **once at the end of the month** to the account title specified in the column heading, such as Cash or Accounts Receivable. Account numbers are entered below the column totals to show that they have been posted.
2. The total of the Other Accounts column is not posted. Instead, the **individual amounts comprising the total are posted separately** to the general ledger accounts specified in the Accounts Credited column. See, for example, the credit posting to D. A. Karns, Capital. The symbol (X) is inserted below the total to this column to indicate that the amount has not been posted.
3. The individual amounts in a column, posted in total to a control account (Accounts Receivable, in this case), are posted **daily to the subsidiary ledger** account specified in the Accounts Credited column. See, for example, the credit posting of $10,600 to Abbot Sisters.

Therefore, cash is posted to account No. 1, accounts receivable to account No. 4, sales to account No. 60, and sales discounts to account No. 61. The symbol **CR** is used in the ledgers to identify postings from the cash receipts journal.

### Proving the Ledgers

After the posting of the cash receipts journal is completed, it is necessary to prove the ledgers. As shown in Illustration 6-12, the general ledger totals are in agreement and the sum of the subsidiary ledger balances equals the control account balance.

## Purchases Journal

All purchases of merchandise on account are recorded in the purchases journal. Each entry in this journal results in a debit to Purchases and a credit to Accounts Payable. When a one-column purchases journal is used, other types of purchases on account and cash purchases cannot be journalized in it. For example, credit purchases of equipment or supplies must be recorded in the general journal, and all cash purchases are entered in the cash payments journal. As illustrated later,

**Helpful hint** A single-column purchases journal only needs to be footed to prove the equality of debits and credits.

**Illustration 6-12**

*Proving the ledgers*

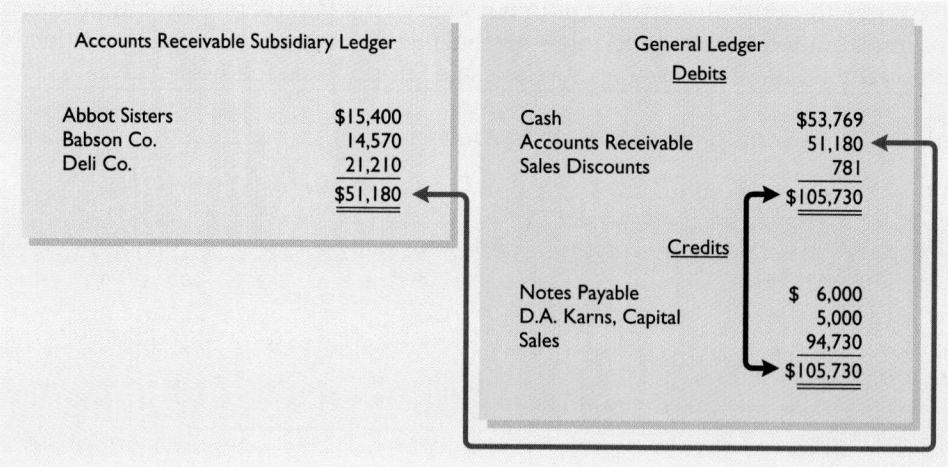

**Illustration 6-13**

*Journalizing and posting purchases journal*

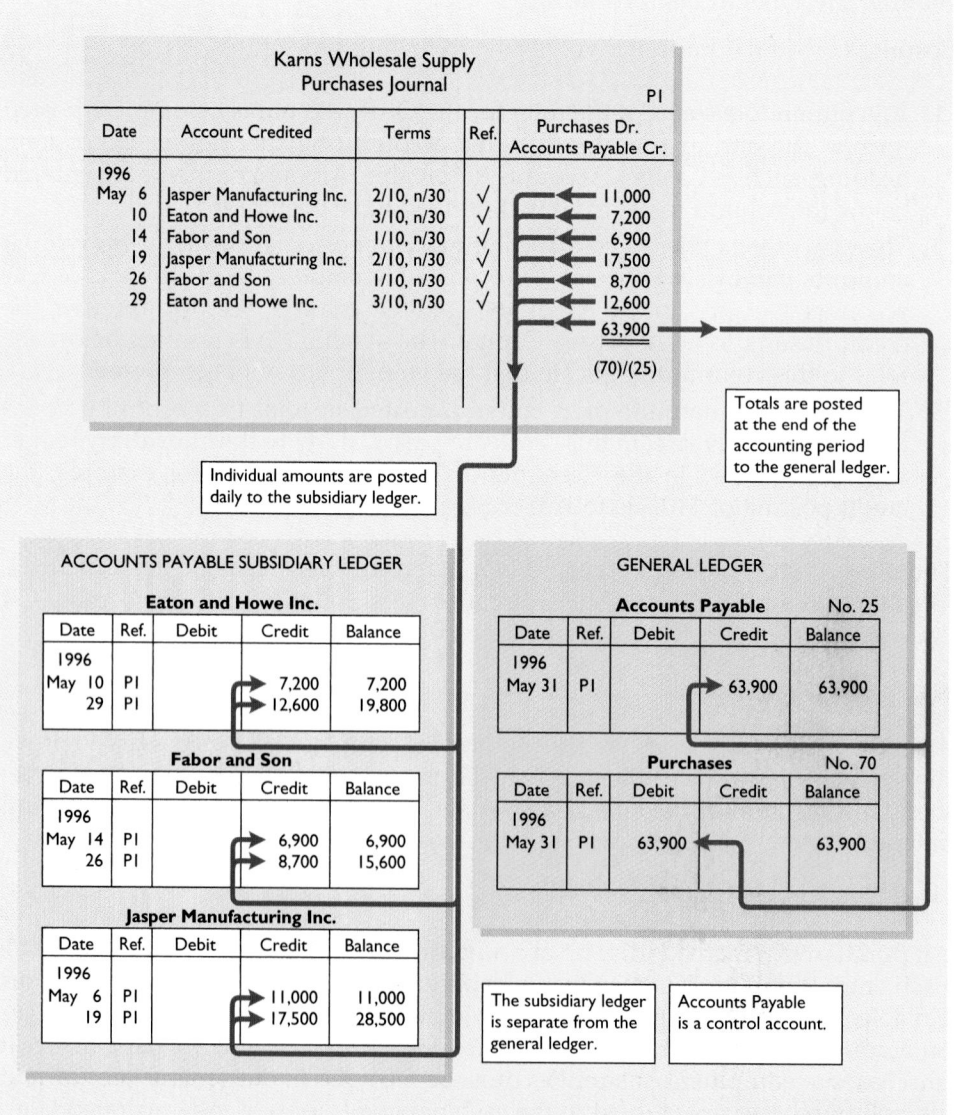

where credit purchases for items other than merchandise are numerous, the purchases journal is often expanded to a multi-column format. The single-column purchases journal for Karns Wholesale Supply is shown in Illustration 6-13.

## Journalizing Credit Purchases of Merchandise

Entries in the purchases journal are made from purchase invoices. The journalizing procedure is similar to the procedures for a single-column sales journal. In contrast to the sales journal, the purchases journal may not have an invoice number column, because invoices received from different suppliers will not be in numerical sequence. To assure that all purchase invoices are recorded, however, some companies consecutively number each invoice upon receipt and then provide for an internal document number column in the purchases journal.

The entries for Karns Wholesale Supply are based on the following assumed transactions:

| Date | Supplier | Amount | Date | Supplier | Amount |
|------|----------|--------|------|----------|--------|
| 5/6 | Jasper Manufacturing Inc. | $11,000 | 5/19 | Jasper Manufacturing Inc. | $17,500 |
| 5/10 | Eaton and Howe, Inc. | 7,200 | 5/26 | Fabor and Son | 8,700 |
| 5/14 | Fabor and Son | 6,900 | 5/29 | Eaton and Howe, Inc. | 12,600 |

**Illustration 6-14**

*Credit purchases transactions*

## Posting the Purchases Journal

The procedures for posting the purchases journal are similar to those for the sales journal. In this case, postings are made **daily** to the **accounts payable ledger** and **monthly** to Purchases and Accounts Payable in the general ledger. In both ledgers, the letter P1 is used in the reference column to show that the postings are from page 1 of the purchases journal.

Proof of the accuracy of the postings to both ledgers in this example is shown by the following tabulation:

**Helpful hint** Postings to subsidiary ledger accounts are done daily because it is often necessary to know a current balance for the subsidiary accounts.

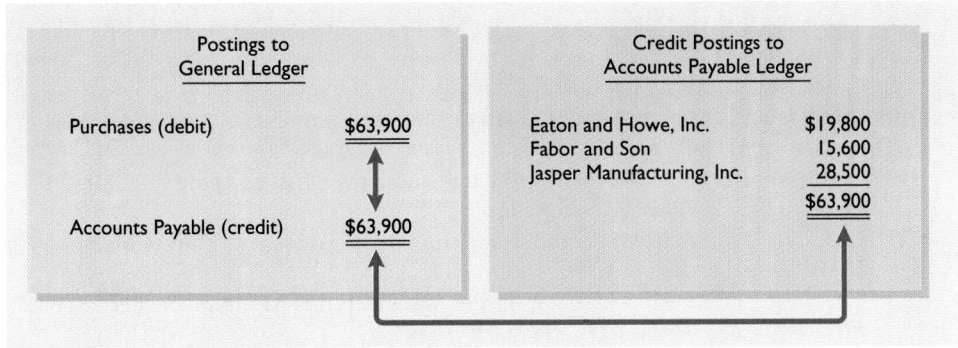

**Illustration 6-15**

*Proving the ledgers*

## Expanding the Purchases Journal

Some companies expand the purchases journal to include all types of purchases on account. Instead of one column for purchases and accounts payable, a multiple-column format is used. The multiple-column format usually includes a credit column for accounts payable and debit columns for purchases of merchandise, purchases of office supplies, purchases of store supplies, and other accounts. Illustration 6-16 is an example of a multiple-column purchases journal for Hanover Co. The posting procedures are similar to those used for posting the cash receipts journal illustrated earlier.

**Helpful hint** A multiple-column purchases journal must be footed and cross-footed to prove the equality of debits and credits.

| | | | Accounts Payable Cr. | Purchases Dr. | Office Supplies Dr. | Store Supplies Dr. | Other Accounts Dr. | | |
|---|---|---|---|---|---|---|---|---|---|
| Date | Accounts Credited | Ref. | | | | | Account | Ref. | Amount |
| 1996 June 1 | Signe Audio | √ | 2,000 | | 2,000 | | | | |
| 3 | Wright Co. | √ | 1,500 | 1,500 | | | | | |
| 5 | Orange Tree Co. | √ | 2,600 | | | | Equipment | 18 | 2,600 |
| 30 | Sue's Business Forms | √ | 800 | | | 800 | | | |
| | | | 56,600 | 43,000 | 7,500 | 1,200 | | | 4,900 |

HANOVER CO.
Purchases Journal                                                                  P 1

**Illustration 6-16**

*Columnar purchases journal*

## Cash Payments Journal

All disbursements of cash are entered in a cash payments journal. Entries in this journal are made from prenumbered checks. Because cash payments may be made for a variety of purposes, the cash payments journal has multiple columns. A four-column journal is shown in Illustration 6-17.

### Journalizing Cash Payments Transactions

The procedures for journalizing transactions in this journal are similar to those described earlier for journalizing transactions in the cash receipts journal. For example, each transaction is entered on one line, and for each line there must be equal debit and credit amounts. The entries in the cash payments journal shown in Illustration 6-17 are based on the following transactions for Karns Wholesale Supply:

May  1   Check No. 101 for $1,200 issued for the annual premium on a fire insurance policy.
    3   Check No. 102 for $100 issued in payment of freight when terms were FOB shipping point.
    8   Check No. 103 for $400 issued for the purchase of merchandise.
   10   Check No. 104 for $10,780 sent to Jasper Manufacturing Inc. in payment of May 6 invoice for $11,000 less a 2% discount.
   19   Check No. 105 for $6,984 mailed to Eaton and Howe, Inc. in payment of May 10 invoice for $7,200 less a 3% discount.
   23   Check No. 106 for $6,831 sent to Fabor and Son in payment of May 14 invoice for $6,900 less a 1% discount.
   28   Check No. 107 for $17,150 sent to Jasper Manufacturing Inc. in payment of May 19 invoice for $17,500 less a 2% discount.
   30   Check No. 108 for $500 issued to D. A. Karns as a cash withdrawal for personal use.

Note that whenever an amount is entered in the Other Accounts column, a specific general ledger account must be identified in the Accounts Debited column. The entries for check Nos. 101, 102, and 103 illustrate this situation. Similarly, a subsidiary account must be identified in the Accounts Debited column whenever an amount is entered in the Accounts Payable column, as, for example, the entry for check No. 104.

When the journalizing of the cash payments journal has been completed, the amount columns are totaled. The totals are then balanced to prove the equality of debits and credits.

**Illustration 6-17**

*Journalizing and posting the cash payments journal*

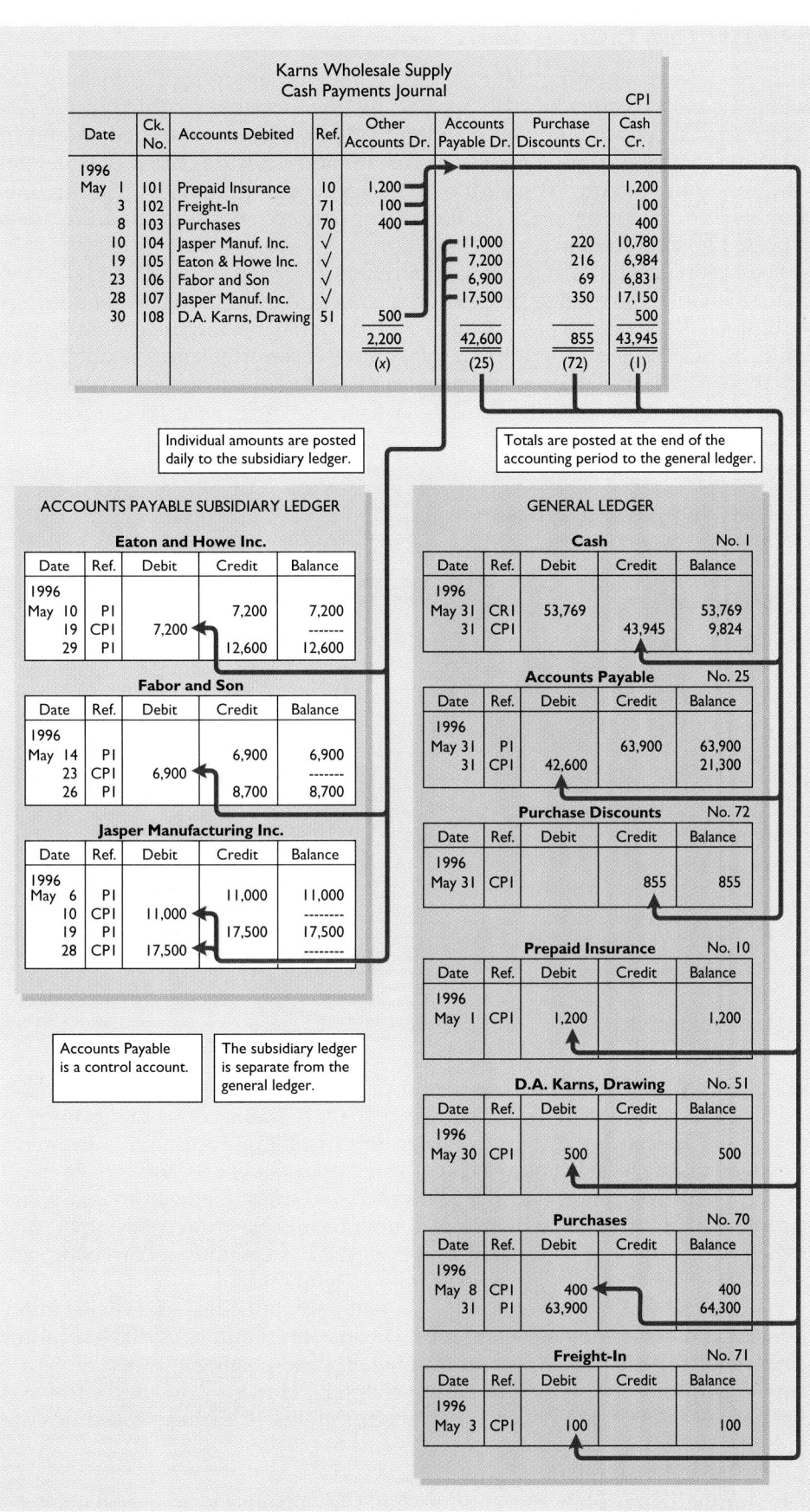

### *Posting the Cash Payments Journal*

The procedures for posting the cash payments journal are similar to those for posting the cash receipts journal. Specifically, the amounts recorded in the Accounts Payable column are posted individually to the subsidiary ledger and in total to the control account. Purchase Discounts and Cash are posted only in total at the end of the month. When a transaction is recorded in the Other Accounts column, it is posted individually to the appropriate account(s) affected. No totals are posted for this column.

The posting of the cash payments journal is shown in Illustration 6-17. Note that the symbol **CP** is used as the posting reference for this journal. After postings are completed, the equality of the debit and credit balances in the general ledger should be determined. In addition, the control account balances should agree with the subsidiary ledger total balance. The agreement of these balances is shown in Illustration 6-18.

**Illustration 6-18**

*Proving the ledgers*

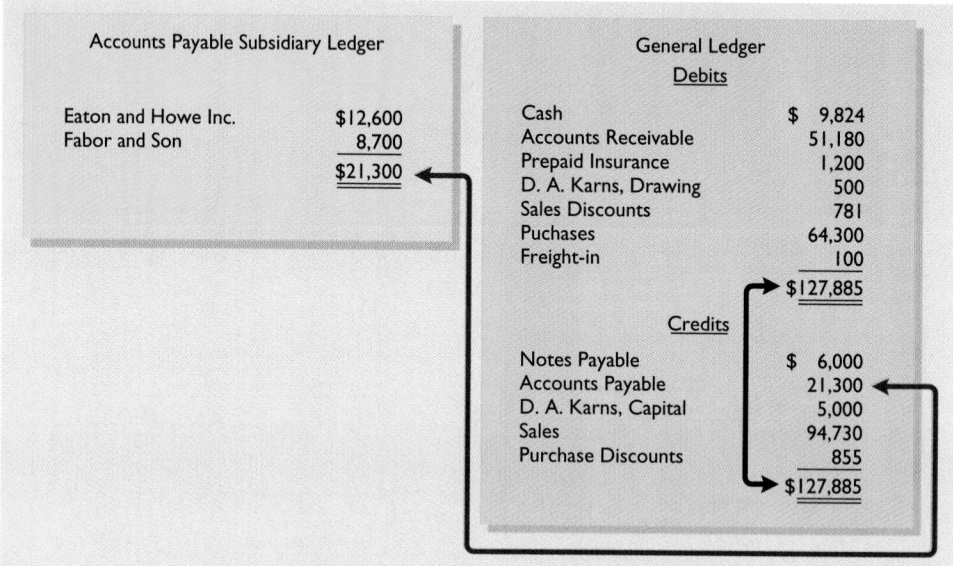

### Effects on General Journal

Special journals for sales, purchases, and cash substantially reduce the number of entries that are made in the general journal. **Only transactions that cannot be entered in a special journal are recorded in the general journal.** For example, the general journal may be used to record such transactions as granting of credit to a customer for a sales return or allowance, receipt of credit from a supplier for purchases returned, acceptance of a note receivable from a customer, and purchase of equipment by issuing a note payable. In addition, correcting, adjusting, and closing entries are made in the general journal.

The general journal has columns for date, account titles and explanation, reference, and debit and credit amounts. When control and subsidiary accounts are not involved, the procedures for journalizing and posting of transactions are identical with those described in earlier chapters. However, when control and subsidiary accounts are involved, two modifications of earlier procedures are required:

1. In **journalizing**, both the control and the subsidiary accounts must be identified.

**2.** In **posting**, there must be a **dual posting**: once to the control account and once to the subsidiary account.

To illustrate, assume that on May 31, Karns Wholesale Supply returns $500 of merchandise for credit to Fabor and Son because of an error in filling its May 26 order. The entry in the general journal and the posting of the entry are shown in Illustration 6-19. Note that if cash is received instead of credit granted on this return, then the transaction is recorded in the cash receipts journal.

**Illustration 6-19**

*Journalizing and posting the general journal*

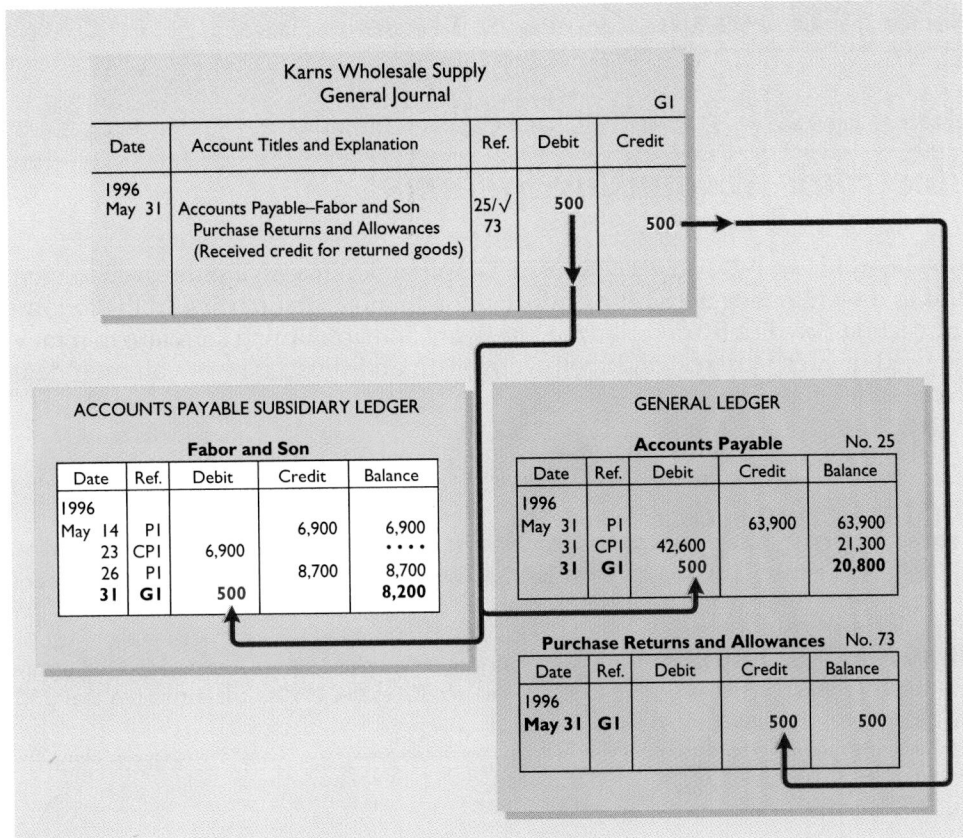

Observe in the journal that two accounts are indicated for the debit and two postings are indicated in the reference column. One amount is posted to the control account and the other to the creditor's account in the subsidiary ledger.

## Before You Go On . . .

### ▶ Review It

1. What type of special journals are usually used to record transactions? Why are special journals used?
2. Explain how transactions recorded in the sales journal and the cash receipts journal are posted.
3. Indicate the types of transactions that are recorded in the general journal when special journals are used.

### ▶ Do It

The Vilas Company has the following selected transactions: (1) purchase of equipment for cash, (2) cash sale, (3) sales returns and allowances, (4) withdrawal of cash for proprietor's personal use, and (5) sale of merchandise on account. Identify the journals in which each transaction should be entered.

**Reasoning:** It is necessary to know the content of each special journal and the effect of special journals on the general journal. For example, the sales journal contains only sales on account, and the cash payments journal is used for all cash payments.

**Solution:** (1) Purchase of equipment for cash—cash payments journal. (2) Cash sale—cash receipts journal. (3) Sales return and allowance—general journal. (4) Withdrawal of cash for proprietor's personal use—cash payments journal. (5) Sale of merchandise on account—sales journal.

*Related exercise material:* BE6–5, BE6–6, E6–1, E6–4, E6–5, E6–6, E6–7, and E6–8.

# ▸SECTION *3* ▸ *Electronic Accounting Systems*

An electronic accounting system uses computers in processing transaction data and in disseminating accounting information to interested parties. In the following sections, we briefly describe the hardware and accounting software that may be used in such systems, and then we explain and illustrate two common data processing methods.

## ▸Accounting in Action ▸ *Business Insight*

The growth of computers has been phenomenal. The first experimental computers were developed in the 1940s, and primitive computers were used in business in the early 1950s. The first serious business applications for computers were put into use in the mid-1960s. From the time of their invention in the 1940s up to 1980, there were approximately one million computer systems of all kinds. In the middle of the 1990s, it is estimated that *250 million* personal computers (PCs) alone are in use.

## Computer Hardware

**STUDY OBJECTIVE**

·········**6**·········

*Distinguish between computer hardware and accounting software and the principal methods of data processing.*

Computers can be divided into three classes, by size: mainframes, minicomputers, and microcomputers. **Mainframes** are large, powerful, very expensive computers that are used by major corporations to process huge volumes of transactions. Mainframes are able to serve many users and perform different processing functions at one time. **Minicomputers** are less powerful and not as expensive as mainframes. They can perform different tasks for several users at a time. The **microcomputer** is commonly referred to as a personal computer (PC). It has speed and power (though generally less than minicomputers), and it is very affordable. In many companies, each employee has his or her own PC.

Computer hardware is the physical equipment associated with a computerized accounting system. The basic hardware configuration consists of the central processing unit (CPU) and peripheral devices. The **central processing unit (CPU)** is composed of three parts:

1. The control unit, which directs and coordinates the entire system, including the entry and removal of information from storage.

## ►Accounting in Action ► *Ethics Insight*

The Internet is our new frontier—a digital Wild West, with its own forms of lawlessness. By some estimates, roughly $2 billion worth of software was stolen from "the Net" in a recent year. In October 1994, an international software piracy ring stole 140,000 telephone credit card numbers and sold them to computer hackers who used them to make $140 million worth of long-distance phone calls. Such thievery is not likely to stop, because the current prevailing ethic of the Internet is "shareware": Digital socialism rules the Net, not copyright capitalism.

*Source: Newsweek,* November 14, 1994, pp. 46–47.

2. The **internal storage unit**, or computer memory, which stores the program instructions and the data to be processed.
3. The **arithmetic-logic unit**, which performs mathematical computations (addition, subtraction, multiplication, division) and certain logical operations (such as comparisons).

Common types of computer hardware are shown in Illustration 6-20.

**Illustration 6-20**

*Computer hardware*

**Central Processing
Unit (CPU)**
Control unit
Computer memory
Arithmetic-logic unit

**Peripheral Equipment**
Keyboard
Magnetic disk / tape drive
CD-ROM
Display screen
Printer

A computer linked with one or more other computers and running with a common software package is called a **network**. A computer network may be as small as two computers in the same dormitory room. In contrast, the Internet is a worldwide network, with a hookup of some 40 million computers.

## ►Accounting Software

Accounting software consists of programs that relate to specific parts of the accounting process. For example, there are programs for the general ledger and each subsidiary ledger, and there are programs for performing the steps in the accounting cycle such as journalizing, posting, and preparing a trial balance. In addition, there is software for business functions such as billing customers, preparing the payroll, and budgeting.

Accounting software can be purchased "off the shelf," or it can be custom-made by individual companies and users. For maximum efficiency, related programs are generally used together. For example, a program for paying creditors

► *International note*

It has recently been noted that, in an unusual turning of the tables, some companies in countries such as Brazil that were slow to adopt computer systems early on are often now more advanced than U.S. corporations. The reason: The systems they are buying today are far more sophisticated than many systems that U.S. corporations bought years ago and continue to use.

## ▸*T*echnology in *A*ction

 For PCs, leading off-the-shelf accounting software packages are Peachtree's **Accounting**®, Intuit's **Quick Books**®, M-USA's **Pacioli 2000**®, and DAC Easy's **Accounting**®. Quick Books® offers, among other products, complete accounts receivable; painless accounts payable; powerful, flexible management information; and easy inventory.

would be used with programs for journalizing the payments and maintaining both the general ledger and the accounts payable subsidiary ledger. When programs are used together, the company is said to be using **integrated accounting software**.

## ▸*D*ata Processing Methods

The term **data processing methods** refers to how data are entered into and processed by a computer. That is, it includes *both* data entry *and* the processing of the data once entered into the system. Two widely used data processing methods are batch processing and on-line processing.

### Batch Processing

In batch processing, data are accumulated by classes of transactions and are periodically entered into the computer and processed in batches. A batch may include such transaction classes as credit sales, collections on account, or cash payments to creditors.

As shown in Illustration 6-21, transaction data are entered into the computer and coded by batch as they occur. At specified intervals—such as daily or weekly—the coded transactions are sorted (transferred) to a batch transaction file that is the equivalent of a special journal in a manual system.

**Illustration 6-21**

*Batch processing*

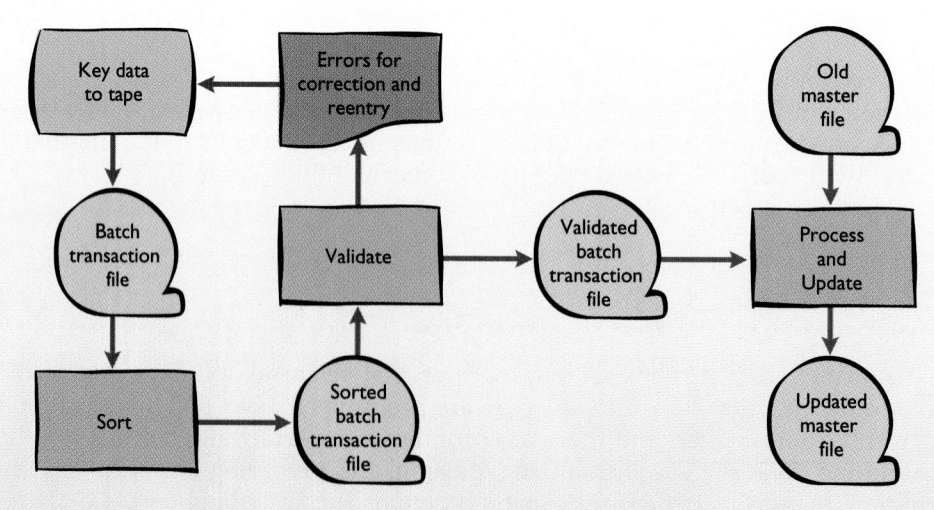

Next, as illustrated, the transaction file is **validated**. Validations confirm the accuracy of such items as code numbers and account numbers. Subsequently, as

## ►Accounting in Action ► Business Insight

Under a system called *electronic data interchange (EDI)*, a company's computer can use dial-up communication lines to communicate electronically with other businesses. Recently, EDI was being used in the accounting systems of about 75% of the Fortune 100 companies and 39% of the Fortune 500. For example, computers at over 3,000 suppliers to Chrysler accept purchase orders transmitted by computers from assembly plants, and in turn electronically invoice Chrysler's computers for parts shipped. Wal-Mart, which operates the largest EDI program in the retail industry, processes about 75% of its payments to suppliers using EDI.

shown, the validated transaction file is used to update the master files. This step is similar to posting in a manual system.

Batch processing is an efficient method because similar transactions are processed together. The principal disadvantage of batch processing is that files may not always contain up-to-date information. For such files as subsidiary ledgers for accounts receivable and accounts payable, lack of current information could be, at the least, an annoyance.

## On-line Processing

In on-line processing, files are updated as data entry takes place. In addition, a transaction log (or tape) is produced that shows a chronological record of all transactions. This processing method is used in airline and hotel reservation systems, among others.

A common accounting application of on-line processing is found in many retail stores, where electronic cash registers are connected directly with the central processing unit of the store's computer. An example of on-line processing in a grocery store is shown in Illustration 6-22.

**Illustration 6-22**

*On-line processing*

Data about the sale are scanned into the cash register/computer.

General and subsidiary ledgers are updated for sales and inventory.

Reports and other documents are generated.

A critical feature of on-line processing is a **bar code identification** for each product. In our grocery store example, the computerized accounting system is activated by the cashier, who moves the product over a scanner. The scanner reads the product being sold and the selling price and enters the information

## ▲*T*echnology in *A*ction

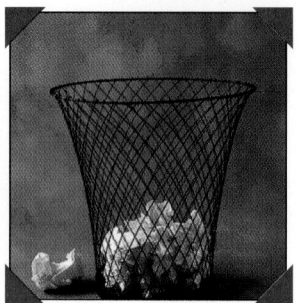

Data processing professionals use the acronym GIGO—garbage-in, garbage-out—to indicate that a computer system is only as good as the data it receives. Data entry is the garbage-in stage of the acronym. Garbage-in is not automated, garbage-out is. The real trick—and the expensive part—of both manual and automated systems (either micros, minis, or mainframes) is to get what we might call DIIO, that is, data-in, information-out.

directly into the CPU. At the same time, the cash register shows the same information on a screen for the customer.[1]

As the data about the sale are entered into the computer, the total sale is recorded in the sales journal. In this case, the sales journal includes both cash and credit card sales. The sale is also posted to the general ledger and filed for sales analysis. In addition, the system immediately updates the inventory records. As illustrated, the system can also print out a purchase order when an inventory item reaches a programmed reorder point, and it can generate inventory reports.

## ▲*C*omparing Manual and Electronic Systems

Despite the tremendous capabilities of computers, one should not conclude that electronic systems are always better. As with any choice, the costs and benefits of each alternative should be weighed before the choice is made. The following key points should be considered when evaluating and comparing manual and electronic systems.

### Dollar Costs

The costs of bookkeepers' salaries and manual accounting records must be compared to the costs of computer hardware and software. Electronic systems also have some hidden costs that must be considered, such as computer training of personnel and salary differences between bookkeepers and competent computer operators. Another consideration is the possibility that fewer individuals are needed to run an electronic system. As noted in the opening story about Safeguard Business Systems, with microcomputers widely available, as well as an abundance of user-friendly software packages, the manual system is losing its comparative advantage in even the smallest businesses.

### Processing Speed

When the number of transactions is large, electronic systems offer real advantages. Thousands of transactions can be processed quickly by a computer, and high-speed printers can generate reports. However, delays in computer processing can occur because of power shortages and computer breakdowns.

### Processing Errors

Unless a hardware failure occurs, the computer will not make a processing error. Both hardware and software controls generally ensure accurate processing. Be-

▶ *Ethics note*

Most auditors and fraud investigators would emphasize that a poorly controlled computer-based accounting system gives "clever" criminals opportunities to steal from a company because it provides an environment in which detection is easily evaded. Thus, one should not conclude that, simply because an accounting system employs a computer, it is less likely to be victimized by theft.

---

[1]When a product does not have an attached bar code, the cashier must "punch in" the code number and price using the keyboard on the register.

cause humans perform the processing in a manual system, the potential for processing errors is greater in the manual system. However, humans may be involved with data entry in an electronic system, so some errors may creep into the system.

## Report Generation

A definite advantage of electronic systems is the ease with which reports can be prepared. Once the system contains the information, reports can be printed in a matter of minutes. The computer can also bring together information from different parts of the system, such as sales transactions and the accounts receivable subsidiary ledger.

## ▶Accounting in Action ► *Business Insight*

 Although the software industry has long touted its sophisticated accounting programs, four out of five financial executives responding to a recent survey said their companies' accounting technology falls short—producing useful data too slowly and inefficiently, providing useless data, requiring too many manual steps, and costing too much to maintain. Almost 70 percent said they plan to replace their system in the next two years, but of those that had recently replaced systems, three-quarters said they were "very unsatisfied." Although none of these big firms would want to go back to a manual system, there is clearly room for improvement in their computerized systems. As one disgruntled executive put it, software developers "should get their act together."

*Source: Wall Street Journal, February 2, 1995.*

## ◢ Look to the Future

Accountants are now beginning to use electronic systems to capture all the organizational information and then provide this information to analysts and decision makers in the forms they desire. As one writer noted: Accountants are becoming organization historians by (a) recording complete histories of organizational events and (b) interpreting these histories for decision makers. Thus, an organizational database of events is developed. This database is then used to provide information for decision making for both internal and external purposes. These new developments will make accounting even more enjoyable and useful in the future.[2]

## *Before You Go On . . .*

### ▶ *Review It*

1. Identify the components of computer hardware.
2. Distinguish between batch and on-line processing.
3. What are the advantages of using a computerized system to record business transactions?

---

[2]Adapted from an article by Eric L. Denna, "Real Time Accounting," *New Accounting* (December 1990).

### ▸ *A Look Back at Safeguard Business Systems Inc.*

Refer to the opening story about Safeguard, and answer the following questions:

1. Why did bookkeeper Debbie Goodeve want to go back to a manual system?
2. What is causing many small businesses to switch to computer bookkeeping systems?
3. Is it likely that in the future some businesses will continue to use manual systems?

*Solution:*

1. Debbie Goodeve found that the computerized system they were using was complicated and inaccurate, and she thought switching to a new computerized system would be too costly.
2. As discussed in the chapter, more and more small businesses are switching to computerized systems because computers are becoming cheaper, faster, and more reliable, and software is becoming increasingly user-friendly. Furthermore, since a business may have already purchased computers for other parts of its business, it makes sense to employ them for record keeping as well.
3. While the percentage of businesses using manual systems will likely decline, it will probably always make sense for certain businesses to use manual systems. For many start-up businesses, or businesses with few transactions, the advantages of installing a computerized system do not appear to outweigh the costs.

## *S*ummary of Study Objectives

**1.** *Identify the basic principles of accounting information systems.* The basic principles in developing an accounting information system are cost awareness, useful output, and flexibility.

**2.** *Explain the major phases involved in the development of an accounting system.* The major phases in the development of an accounting system are analysis, design, implementation, and follow-up.

**3.** *Describe the nature and purpose of a subsidiary ledger.* A subsidiary ledger is a group of accounts with a common characteristic. It facilitates the recording process by freeing the general ledger from details of individual balances.

**4.** *Explain how special journals are used in journalizing.* A special journal is used to group similar types of transactions. In a special journal, only one line is used to record a complete transaction.

**5.** *Indicate how a columnar journal is posted.* In posting a columnar journal:
(a) all column totals except for the Other Accounts column

are posted once at the end of the month to the account title specified in the column heading.
(b) the total of the Other Accounts column is not posted. Instead, the individual amounts comprising the total are posted separately to the general ledger accounts specified in the Accounts column.
(c) the individual amounts in a column posted in total to a control account are posted daily to the subsidiary ledger accounts specified in the Accounts column.

**6.** *Distinguish between computer hardware and accounting software and the principal methods of data processing.* Computer hardware is the physical equipment associated with a computerized accounting system. Accounting software consists of programs that relate to specific parts of the accounting process. The principal methods of data processing are batch processing and on-line processing.

**7.** *Identify the key points in comparing manual and electronic accounting systems.* The key points in comparing manual and electronic accounting systems are (a) dollar costs, (b) processing speed, (c) processing errors, and (d) report generation.

## *G*LOSSARY

**Accounting information system**   A system that involves collecting and processing transaction data, and disseminating financial information to interested parties. (p. 236).

**Accounting software**   Programs that relate to specific parts of the accounting process. (p. 255).

**Accounts payable (creditors') ledger**   A subsidiary ledger that contains accounts with individual creditors. (p. 239).

**Accounts receivable (customers') ledger**   A subsidiary ledger that contains individual customer accounts. (p. 239).

**Batch processing**   A method in which data are accumulated by classes of transactions and are entered into the computer and processed in batches. (p. 256).

**Cash payments journal** A special journal used to record all cash paid. (p. 250).

**Cash receipts journal** A special journal used to record all cash received. (p. 244).

**Columnar journal** A special journal with more than one column. (p. 245).

**Computer hardware** The physical equipment associated with an electronic accounting system. (p. 254).

**Control account** An account in the general ledger that controls a subsidiary ledger. (p. 239).

**Electronic accounting system** A system that uses comput-

ers in processing transaction data and in disseminating accounting information to interested parties. (p. 254).

**Manual accounting system** A system in which each of the steps in the accounting cycle is performed by hand. (p. 238).

**On-line processing** A method in which files are updated concurrently with data entry. (p. 257).

**Purchases journal** A special journal used to record all purchases of merchandise on account. (p. 247).

**Sales journal** A special journal used to record all sales of merchandise on account. (p. 242).

**Special journal** A journal that is used to record similar types of transactions such as all credit sales. (p. 241).

**Subsidiary ledger** A group of accounts with a common characteristic. (p. 238).

# *D*EMONSTRATION PROBLEM

Emelia Company uses a five-column cash receipts journal with columns for Cash (Dr.), Sales Discounts (Dr.), Accounts Receivable (Cr.), Sales (Cr.), and Other Accounts (Cr.). Cash receipts transactions for the month of July 1996 are as follows:

July 3  Cash sales total $5,800.

   5  A check for $6,370 is received from the Jeltz Company in payment of invoice dated June 26 for $6,500 terms 2/10, n/30.

   9  An additional investment of $5,000 in cash is made in the business by Betty Emelia, the proprietor.

   10  Cash sales total $12,519.

   12  A check for $7,275 is received from R. Eliot & Co. in payment of a $7,500 invoice dated July 3, terms 3/10, n/30.

   15  A customer advance of $700 cash is received for future sales.

   20  Cash sales total $15,472.

   22  A check for $5,880 is received from Beck Company in payment of $6,000 invoice dated July 13, terms 2/10, n/30.

   29  Cash sales total $17,660.

   31  Cash of $200 is received on interest earned for July.

*Instructions*

(a)  Journalize the transactions in the cash receipts journal.

(b)  Contrast the posting of the Accounts Receivable and Other Accounts columns.

## *Solution to Demonstration Problem*

(a)

**EMELIA COMPANY**
**Cash Receipts Journal**

CR1

| Date | Accounts Credited | Ref. | Cash Dr. | Sales Discounts Dr. | Accounts Receivable Cr. | Sales Cr. | Other Accounts Cr. |
|------|-------------------|------|----------|---------------------|-------------------------|-----------|--------------------|
| 1996 | | | | | | | |
| 7/3 | | | 5,800 | | | 5,800 | |
| 5 | Jeltz Company | | 6,370 | 130 | 6,500 | | |
| 9 | Betty Emelia, Capital | | 5,000 | | | | 5,000 |
| 10 | | | 12,519 | | | 12,519 | |

**Problem-Solving Strategies**

1. All cash receipts are recorded in the cash receipts journal.

2. The "accounts credited" indicate items posted individually to the subsidiary ledger or general ledger.

3. Cash sales are recorded in the cash receipts journal—not in the sales journal.

4. The total debits must equal the total credits.

| Date | Accounts Credited | Ref. | Cash Dr. | Sales Discounts Dr. | Accounts Receivable Cr. | Sales Cr. | Other Accounts Cr. |
|------|-------------------|------|----------|---------------------|-------------------------|-----------|--------------------|
| 12 | R. Eliot & Co. | | 7,275 | 225 | 7,500 | | |
| 15 | Unearned Revenues | | 700 | | | | 700 |
| 20 | | | 15,472 | | | 15,472 | |
| 22 | Beck Company | | 5,880 | 120 | 6,000 | | |
| 29 | | | 17,660 | | | 17,660 | |
| 31 | Interest Revenue | | 200 | | | | 200 |
| | | | 76,876 | 475 | 20,000 | 51,451 | 5,900 |

(b) The Accounts Receivable column is posted as a credit to Accounts Receivable. The individual amounts are credited to the customers' accounts identified in the Accounts Credited column, which are maintained in the accounts receivable subsidiary ledger.

The amounts in the Other Accounts Column are only posted individually. They are credited to the account titles identified in the Accounts Credited column.

# SELF-STUDY QUESTIONS

Answers are at the end of the chapter.

(SO 1)   1. The basic principles of an accounting information system include all of the following except:
a. cost awareness.
b. flexibility.
c. useful output.
d. periodicity.

(SO 2)   2. Which of the following is *not* a major phase in the development of an accounting information system?
a. Design.
b. Responsiveness.
c. Implementation.
d. Follow-up.

(SO 3)   3. Which of the following is *incorrect* concerning subsidiary ledgers?
a. The purchases ledger is a common subsidiary ledger for creditor accounts.
b. The accounts receivable ledger is a subsidiary ledger.
c. A subsidiary ledger is a group of accounts with a common characteristic.
d. An advantage of the subsidiary ledger is that it permits a division of labor in posting.

(SO 4)   4. A sales journal will be used for:

| | Credit sales | Cash sales | Sales discounts |
|----|------|------|------|
| a. | no | yes | yes |
| b. | yes | no | yes |
| c. | yes | no | no |
| d. | yes | yes | no |

(SO 5)   5. Which of the following statements is correct?
a. The sales discount column is included in the cash receipts journal.

b. The purchases journal records all purchases of merchandise whether for cash or on account.
c. The cash receipts journal records sales on account.
d. Merchandise returned by the buyer is recorded by the seller in the purchases journal.

(SO 5)   6. Which of the following is *incorrect* concerning the posting of the cash receipts journal?
a. The total of the Other Accounts column is not posted.
b. All column totals except the total for the Other Accounts column are posted once at the end of the month to the account title specified in the column heading.
c. The total of all columns are posted daily to the accounts specified in the column heading.
d. The individual amounts in a column posted in total to a control account are posted daily to the subsidiary ledger account specified in the Accounts Credited column.

(SO 5)   7. Postings from the purchases journal to the subsidiary ledger are generally made:
a. yearly.
b. monthly.
c. weekly.
d. daily.

(SO 4)   8. Which statement is *incorrect* regarding the general journal?
a. Only transactions that cannot be entered in a special journal are recorded in the general journal.
b. Dual postings are always required in the general journal.
c. The general journal may be used to record acceptance of a note receivable for an accounts receivable.

d. Correcting, adjusting, and closing entries are made in the general journal.

(SO 6)  9. Computer hardware consists of the:
a. central processing unit.
b. accounting software.
c. peripheral equipment.
d. Both (a) and (c).

10. Which of the following is *not* a key point in eval-   (SO 7)
uating and comparing manual and electronic systems?
a. Cost considerations and processing speed.
b. Processing errors and responsiveness.
c. Posting general journals and special journals.
d. Report generation.

# QUESTIONS

1. (a) What is an accounting information system? (b) "An accounting information system applies only to a manual system." Do you agree? Explain.

2. Certain principles should be followed in the development of an accounting information system. Identify and explain each of the principles.

3. Sandi Scott Company is considering changing its accounting system for its accounts receivable billing procedure. At present, the procedure is performed manually by three clerks. A consultant has recommended that a new computer and related software be purchased for $1,000,000. What basic principle of designing and developing an effective accounting system might be violated by this proposal?

4. There are four phases in the life cycle of an accounting system. Identify and briefly explain each phase.

5. What are the advantages of using subsidiary ledgers?

6. (a) When are postings normally made to (1) the subsidiary accounts and (2) the general ledger control accounts? (b) Describe the relationship between a control account and a subsidiary ledger.

7. Identify and explain the four specific journals discussed in the chapter. List an advantage of using each of these journals rather than using only a general journal.

8. A. Mega Company uses special journals. A sale made on account to K. Hansen for $435 was recorded in a single-column sales journal. A few days later, Hansen returns $70 worth of merchandise for credit. Where should A. Mega Company record the sales return? Why?

9. A $400 purchase of merchandise on account from Julia Company was properly recorded in the purchases journal. When posted, however, the amount recorded in the subsidiary ledger was $40. How might this error be discovered?

10. Why would special journals used in different businesses not be identical in format? Can you think of a business that would maintain a cash receipts journal but not include a column for accounts receivable?

11. The cash and the accounts receivable columns in the cash receipts journal were mistakenly over-added by $4,000 at the end of the month. (a) Will the customers' ledger agree with the Accounts Receivable control account? (b) Assuming no other errors, will the trial balance totals be equal?

12. The column total of a special journal is posted at month end to only two general ledger accounts. One of these two accounts is Accounts Receivable. What is the name of this special journal? What is the other general ledger account to which the month-end total is posted?

13. In what journal would the following transactions be recorded? (Assume that a single-column sales journal and a single-column purchases journal are used.)
(a) Recording of depreciation expense for the year.
(b) Gave credit to a customer for merchandise purchased on credit and returned.
(c) Sales of merchandise for cash.
(d) Sales of merchandise on account.
(e) Collection of cash on account from a customer.
(f) Purchase of office supplies on account.

14. In what journal would the following transactions be recorded? (Assume that a single-column sales journal and a single-column purchases journal are used.)
(a) Cash received from signing a note payable.
(b) Investment of cash by the owner of the business.
(c) Closing of the expense accounts at the end of the year.
(d) Purchase of merchandise on account.
(e) Received credit for merchandise purchased and returned to supplier.
(f) Payment of cash on account due a supplier.

15. What transactions might be included in a multiple-column purchases journal that would not be included in a single-column purchases journal?

16. Give an example of a transaction in the general journal that causes an entry to be posted twice (i.e., to two accounts), one in the general ledger, the other in the subsidiary ledger. Does this affect the debit/credit equality of the general ledger?

17. Give some examples of appropriate general journal transactions for an organization using special journals.

18. (a) Identify and explain the units that comprise the central processing unit (CPU). (b) What types of equipment are considered to be peripheral?

19. (a) What is accounting software? (b) What is integrated computer software?

20. Identify and distinguish between the two widely used methods of data processing in an electronic system.

21. What are the key points to be considered in evaluating and comparing manual and electronic systems?

# BRIEF EXERCISES

*Identify basic principles of accounting information system development.*

*(SO 1)*

**BE6–1**   Indicate whether each of the following statements is true or false.

1. When designing an accounting system, we need to think about the needs and knowledge of both the top management and other various users.
2. When the environment changes as a result of technological advances, increased competition, or government regulation, an accounting system does not have to be sufficiently flexible to meet the changes in order to save money.
3. In developing an accounting system, cost is relevant. The system must be cost effective; that is, the benefits obtained from the information disseminated must outweigh the cost of providing it.

*Identify major phases in accounting system development.*

*(SO 2)*

**BE6–2**   The development of an accounting system involves four phases: analysis, design, implementation, and follow-up. Identify the statement that best describes each of these four phases.

1. Determining internal and external information needs, identifying information sources and the needs for controls, and studying alternatives.
2. Evaluation and monitoring of effectiveness and efficiency, and correction of weaknesses, implementation, and design.
3. Creation of forms and documents, selection of procedures, and preparation of job descriptions.
4. Implementing new or revised documents, procedures, reports, and processing equipment; hiring and training personnel through a start-up or transition period.

*Identify subsidiary ledger balances.*

*(SO 3)*

**BE6–3**   Presented below is information related to Bradley Company for its first month of operations. Identify the balances that appear in the accounts receivable subsidiary ledger and the accounts receivable balance that appears in the general ledger at the end of January.

| | **Credit Sales** | | | **Cash Collections** | |
|---|---|---|---|---|---|
| Jan. 7 | Avon Co. | $9,000 | Jan. 17 | Avon Co. | $7,000 |
| 15 | Barto Inc. | $6,000 | 24 | Barto Inc. | $5,000 |
| 23 | Cecil Co. | $9,000 | 29 | Cecil Co. | $9,000 |

*Identify subsidiary ledger accounts.*

*(SO 3)*

**BE6–4**   Identify in what ledger (general or subsidiary) each of the following accounts is shown.

1. Rent Expense
2. Accounts Receivable—Oliva
3. Notes Payable
4. Accounts Payable—Kerns

*Identify special journals.*

*(SO 4)*

**BE6–5**   Identify the journal in which each of the following transactions is recorded.

1. Cash sales
2. Owner withdrawal of cash
3. Cash purchase of land
4. Credit sales
5. Purchase of merchandise on account
6. Receipt of cash for services performed

*Identify entries to cash receipts journal.*

*(SO 4)*

**BE6–6**   Indicate whether each of the following debits and credits is included in the Cash Receipts journal. (Use "Yes" or "No" to answer this question.)

1. Debit to Sales
2. Credit to Purchase Discounts
3. Credit to Accounts Receivable
4. Debit to Accounts Payable

*Indicate postings to cash receipts journal.*

*(SO 5)*

**BE6–7**   Sterling Computer Components Inc. uses a columnar Cash Receipts journal. Indicate which column(s) is/are posted only in total, only daily, or both in total and daily.

1. Accounts Receivable
2. Sales Discounts
3. Cash
4. Other Accounts

**BE6–8**  Cohen Co. uses special journals and a general journal. Identify the journal in which each of the following transactions is recorded.

1. Purchased equipment on account.
2. Purchased merchandise on account.
3. Paid utility expense in cash.
4. Sold merchandise on account.

*Identify transactions for special journals.*
*(SO 4),* **C**

**BE6–9**  Identify the special journal(s) in which the following column headings appear.

1. Sales Discounts Dr.
2. Accounts Receivable Cr.
3. Cash Dr.
4. Purchase Discount Cr.
5. Purchase Dr.
6. Sales Cr.

*Identify transactions for special journals.*
*(SO 4),* **C**

**BE6–10**  (a) Prepare a flowchart of the on-line processing method in an electronic accounting system. (b) Explain the manual system equivalent of this method of data processing.

*Prepare a flowchart of the on-line processing method.*
*(SO 6),* **C**

# EXERCISES

**E6–1**  Toyama Company uses both special journals and a general journal as described in this chapter. On June 30, after all monthly postings had been completed, the Accounts Receivable controlling account in the general ledger had a debit balance of $320,000 and the Accounts Payable controlling account had a credit balance of $97,000.

The July transactions recorded in the special journals are summarized below. No entries affecting accounts receivable and accounts payable were recorded in the general journal for July.

*Determine control account balances and explain posting of special journals.*
*(SO 3, 5)*

| | |
|---|---|
| Sales journal | Total sales, $161,400 |
| Purchases journal | Total purchases, $54,360 |
| Cash receipts journal | Accounts receivable column total, $135,000 |
| Cash payments journal | Accounts payable column total, $47,500 |

**Instructions**
(a) What is the balance of the Accounts Receivable control account after the monthly postings on July 31?
(b) What is the balance of the Accounts Payable control account after the monthly postings on July 31?
(c) To what account(s) is the column total of $161,400 in the sales journal posted?
(d) To what account(s) is the accounts receivable column total of $135,000 in the cash receipts journal posted?

**E6–2**  Presented below is the subsidiary accounts receivable account of Rene Lopaz.

*Explain postings to subsidiary ledger.*
*(SO 3),* **C**

| Date | | Ref | Debit | Credit | Balance |
|---|---|---|---|---|---|
| 1996 | | | | | |
| Sept. | 2 | S31 | 61,000 | | 61,000 |
| | 9 | G4 | | 12,000 | 49,000 |
| | 27 | CR8 | | 49,000 | — |

**Instructions**
▭▭▭▷  Write a memo that explains each transaction.

**E6–3**  On September 1 the balance of the Accounts Receivable controlling account in the general ledger of Crampton Company was $10,960. The customers' subsidiary ledger contained account balances as follows: Bannister, $1,440; Crowley, $2,640; Dotson, $2,060; Seaver, $4,820. At the end of September the various journals contained the following information:

*Post various journals to control and subsidiary accounts.*
*(SO 3, 5)*

**Sales Journal:** Sales to Seaver, $800; to Bannister, $1,350; to DeLeon, $1,030; to Dotson, $1,100.

**Cash receipts journal:** Cash received from Dotson, $1,310; from Seaver, $2,300; from DeLeon, $410; from Crowley, $1,800; from Bannister, $1,240.

**General journal:** An allowance is granted to Seaver, $120.

### Instructions

(a) Set up control and subsidiary accounts and enter the beginning balances. Do not construct the journals.

(b) Post the various journals. Post the items as individual items or as totals, whichever would be the appropriate procedure. (No sales discounts given)

(c) Prepare a list of customers and prove the agreement of the controlling account with the subsidiary ledger at September 30, 1996.

*Record transactions in sales and purchases journal.*

*(SO 3, 4)*

**E6–4**   Hariett Company uses special journals and a general journal. The following transaction occurred during September 1996.

Sept.  2   Sold merchandise on account to B. Vell, invoice no. 101, $600, terms n/30.
    10   Purchased merchandise on account from C. Cosgrove $700, terms 2/10, n/30.
    12   Purchased office equipment on account from J. Wells, $6,500.
    21   Sold merchandise on account to L. Scott, invoice no. 102 for $800, terms 2/10, n/30.
    25   Purchased merchandise on account from P. Lewis $900, terms n/30.
    27   Sold merchandise to R. Cowan for $700 cash.

### Instructions

(a) Draw a single-column sales journal (see Illustration 6-8) and a single-column purchase journal (see Illustration 6-13). (Use page 1 for each journal.)

(b) Record the transaction(s) for September that should be journalized in the sales journal and the purchases journal.

*Record transactions in cash receipts and cash payments journal.*

*(SO 3, 4)*

**E6–5**   Reese Inc. uses special journals and a general journal. The following transactions occurred during May 1996.

May  1   L. Reese invested $72,000 cash in the business.
     2   Sold merchandise to L. Bean for $6,000 cash.
     3   Purchased merchandise for $8,000 from R. L. Sanchez using check no. 101.
    14   Paid salary to F. Sparks $700 by issuing check no. 102.
    16   Sold merchandise on account to B. Ready for $900, terms n/30.
    22   A check of $9,000 is received from C. Moody in full for invoice 101; no discount given.

### Instructions

(a) Draw a multiple-column cash receipts journal (see Illustration 6-10) and a multiple-column cash payments journal (see Illustration 6-17). (Use page 1 for each journal.)

(b) Record the transaction(s) for May that should be journalized in the cash receipts journal and cash payments journal.

*Explain journalizing in cash journals.*

*(SO 4)*

**E6–6**   Alda Company uses the columnar cash journals illustrated in the textbook. In April, the following selected cash transactions occurred:

1. Made a refund to a customer for the return of damaged goods.
2. Received collection from customer within the 3% discount period.
3. Purchased merchandise for cash.
4. Paid a creditor within the 3% discount period.
5. Received collection from customer after the 3% discount period had expired.
6. Paid freight on merchandise purchased.
7. Paid cash for office equipment.
8. Received cash refund from supplier for merchandise returned.
9. Withdrew cash for personal use of owner.
10. Made cash sales.

### Instructions

Indicate (a) the journal, and (b) the columns in the journal that should be used in recording each transaction.

**E6–7** Vernor Company has the following selected transactions during March:

*Journalize transactions in general journal and post.*
*(SO 3, 4)*

Mar. 2 Purchased equipment costing $6,000 from Lifetime Company.

  5 Received credit memorandum for $300 from Lynch Company for merchandise damaged in shipment to Vernor.

  7 Issued a credit memorandum for $400 to Frey Company for merchandise the customer returned.

Vernor Company uses a one-column purchases journal, a sales journal, the columnar cash journals used in the text, and a general journal.

**Instructions**

(a) Journalize the transactions in the general journal.
(b) ▭▭▭➤ In a brief memo to the president of Vernor Company, explain the postings to the control and subsidiary accounts.

**E6–8** Below are some typical transactions incurred by Duluth Company.

*Indicate journalizing in special journals.*
*(SO 4)*

1. Payment of creditors on account.
2. Return of merchandise sold for credit.
3. Collection on account from customers.
4. Sold land for cash.
5. Sale of merchandise on account.
6. Sale of merchandise for cash.
7. Received credit for merchandise purchased on credit.
8. Sales discount taken on goods sold.
9. Payment of employee wages.
10. Close income summary to owner's capital.
11. Depreciation on building.
12. Purchase of office supplies for cash.
13. Purchase of merchandise on account.

**Instructions**

For each transaction, indicate whether it would normally be recorded in a cash receipts journal, cash payments journal, single-column sales journal, single-column purchases journal, or general journal.

**E6–9** The general ledger of the Gonya Company contained the following Accounts Payable control account (in T-account form). Also shown is the related subsidiary ledger.

*Explain posting to control account and subsidiary ledger.*
*(SO 3, 5)*

**General Ledger**

**Accounts Payable**

| | | | | |
|---|---|---|---|---|
| Feb. 15 General Journal | 1,200 | Feb. 1 | Balance | 26,025 |
| 28 ? | ? | 5 | General Journal | 265 |
| | | 11 | General Journal | 550 |
| | | 28 | Purchases | 13,700 |
| | | Feb. 28 | Balance | 9,640 |

**Accounts Payable Ledger**

**Patee**

| | | |
|---|---|---|
| Feb. 28 | Bal. | 4,600 |

**Wagner**

| | | |
|---|---|---|
| Feb. 28 | Bal. | ? |

**Gruber**

| | | |
|---|---|---|
| Feb. 28 | Bal. | 3,000 |

**Instructions**

(a) Indicate the missing posting reference and amount in the control account and the missing ending balance in the subsidiary ledger.
(b) Indicate the amounts in the control account that were dual-posted (i.e., posted to the control account and the subsidiary accounts).

*Prepare purchases and general journals.*
(SO 3, 4)

**E6–10**   Selected accounts from the ledgers of Alps Company at July 31 showed the following:

## GENERAL LEDGER

**Store Equipment**                              **No. 153**

| Date | Explanation | Ref. | Debit | Credit | Balance |
|------|-------------|------|-------|--------|---------|
| July  1 |  | G1 | 3,600 |  | 3,600 |

**Accounts Payable**                             **No. 201**

| Date | Explanation | Ref. | Debit | Credit | Balance |
|------|-------------|------|-------|--------|---------|
| July  1 |  | G1 |  | 3,600 | 3,600 |
| 15 |  | G1 |  | 400 | 4,000 |
| 18 |  | G1 | 100 |  | 3,900 |
| 25 |  | G1 | 200 |  | 3,700 |
| 31 |  | P1 |  | 8,600 | 12,300 |

**Purchases**                                    **No. 510**

| Date | Explanation | Ref. | Debit | Credit | Balance |
|------|-------------|------|-------|--------|---------|
| July 31 |  | P1 | 8,600 |  | 8,600 |

**Freight-in**                                   **No. 516**

| Date | Explanation | Ref. | Debit | Credit | Balance |
|------|-------------|------|-------|--------|---------|
| July 15 |  | G1 | 400 |  | 400 |

**Purchase Returns and Allowances**             **No. 512**

| Date | Explanation | Ref. | Debit | Credit | Balance |
|------|-------------|------|-------|--------|---------|
| July 18 |  | G1 |  | 100 | 100 |
| 25 |  | G1 |  | 200 | 300 |

## ACCOUNTS PAYABLE LEDGER

**Andrew Equipment Co.**

| Date | Explanation | Ref. | Debit | Credit | Balance |
|------|-------------|------|-------|--------|---------|
| July  1 |  | G1 |  | 3,600 | 3,600 |

**Bradley Co.**

| Date | Explanation | Ref. | Debit | Credit | Balance |
|------|-------------|------|-------|--------|---------|
| July  3 |  | P1 |  | 2,000 | 2,000 |
| 20 |  | P1 |  | 700 | 2,700 |

**Craig Materials**

| Date | Explanation | Ref. | Debit | Credit | Balance |
|------|-------------|------|-------|--------|---------|
| July 17 |  | P1 |  | 1,400 | 1,400 |
| 18 |  | G1 | 100 |  | 1,300 |
| 29 |  | P1 |  | 2,300 | 3,600 |

**David Co.**

| Date | Explanation | Ref. | Debit | Credit | Balance |
|------|-------------|------|-------|--------|---------|
| July 14 |  | P1 |  | 1,100 | 1,100 |
| 25 |  | G1 | 200 |  | 900 |

**Erick Co.**

| Date | Explanation | Ref. | Debit | Credit | Balance |
|------|-------------|------|-------|--------|---------|
| July 12 |  | P1 |  | 500 | 500 |
| 21 |  | P1 |  | 600 | 1,100 |

**Gary Transit**

| Date | Explanation | Ref. | Debit | Credit | Balance |
|------|-------------|------|-------|--------|---------|
| July 15 |  | G1 |  | 400 | 400 |

### Instructions
From the data prepare:

(a)  the single-column purchases journal for July.

(b)  the general journal entries for July.

*Determine correct posting amount to control account.*
(SO 5)

**E6–11**   Olsen Products uses both special journals and a general journal as described in this chapter. Olsen also posts customers' accounts in the accounts receivable subsidiary ledger. The postings for the most recent month are included in the subsidiary T accounts below.

**Edmonds**

| | |
|---|---|
| Bal.  340 | 250 |
| 180 | |

**Roemer**

| | |
|---|---|
| Bal.  150 | 150 |
| 190 | |

**Schulz**

| | |
|---|---|
| Bal.  –0– | 145 |
| 145 | |

**Park**

| | |
|---|---|
| Bal.  120 | 120 |
| 190 | |
| 170 | |

## Instructions

Determine the correct amount of the end-of-month posting from the sales journal to the Accounts Receivable controlling account.

# PROBLEMS

**P6–1** Kimbell Company's chart of accounts includes the following selected accounts:

| 101 Cash | 401 Sales |
|---|---|
| 112 Accounts Receivable | 414 Sales Discounts |
| 301 A. J. Kimbell, Capital | 512 Purchase Returns and Allowances |

Journalize transactions in cash receipts journal and post to control account and subsidiary ledger.
(SO 3, 4, 5)

On June 1 the accounts receivable ledger of the Kimbell Company showed the following balances: Block & Son, $2,500; Field Co., $1,900; Green Bros., $1,600; and Mastin Co., $900. The June transactions involving the receipt of cash were as follows:

June 1 The owner, A. J. Kimbell, invested additional cash in the business, $9,000.
  3 Received check in full from Mastin Co. less 2% cash discount.
  6 Received check in full from Field Co. less 2% cash discount.
  7 Made cash sales of merchandise totaling $6,135.
  9 Received check in full from Block & Son less 2% cash discount.
  11 Received cash refund from a supplier for damaged merchandise, $200.
  15 Made cash sales of merchandise totaling $5,250.
  20 Received check in full from Green Bros., $1,600.

## Instructions

(a) Journalize the transactions above in a five-column cash receipts journal with columns for Cash, Dr.; Sales Discounts, Dr.; Accounts Receivable, Cr.; Sales, Cr.; and Other Accounts, Cr. Foot and crossfoot the journal.
(b) Insert the beginning balances in the Accounts Receivable control and subsidiary accounts and post the June transactions to these accounts.
(c) Prove the agreement of the control account and subsidiary account balances.

**P6–2** Creek Company's chart of accounts includes the following selected accounts:

| 101 Cash | 306 V. Creek, Drawing |
|---|---|
| 130 Prepaid Insurance | 510 Purchases |
| 157 Equipment | 514 Purchase Discounts |
| 201 Accounts Payable | |

Journalize transactions in cash payments journal and post to the general and subsidiary ledger.
(SO 3, 4, 5)

On November 1 the accounts payable ledger of the Creek Company showed the following balances: R. Huff & Co., $3,750; G. Paul, $2,350; R. Snyder, $1,000; and Wicks Bros., $1,900. The November transactions involving the payment of cash were as follows:

Nov. 1 Purchased merchandise, check no. 11, $900.
  3 Purchased store equipment, check no. 12, $1,650.
  5 Paid Wicks Bros. balance due of $1,900, less 1% discount, check no. 13, $1,881.
  11 Purchased merchandise, check no. 14, $2,000.
  15 Paid R. Snyder balance due of $1,000, less 3% discount, check no. 15, $970.
  16 V. Creek, the owner, withdraws $500 cash for own use, check no. 16.
  19 Paid G. Paul in full for invoice no. 1245, $1,500 less 2% discount, check no. 17, $1,470.
  25 Paid premium due on one year insurance policy, check no. 18, $3,000.
  30 Paid R. Huff & Co. in full for invoice no. 832, $2,250, check no. 19.

## Instructions

(a) Journalize the transctions above in a five-column cash payments journal with columns for Other Accounts, Dr.; Accounts Payable, Dr.; Purchases, Dr.; Purchase Discounts, Cr.; and Cash, Cr. Foot and crossfoot the journal.
(b) Insert the beginning balances in the Accounts Payable control and subsidiary accounts and post the November transactions to these accounts.
(c) Prove the agreement of the control account and the subsidiary account balances.

*Journalize transactions in multicolumn purchases journal and post to the general and subsidiary ledgers.*
(SO 3, 4, 5)

**P6–3**    The chart of accounts of Ventura Company includes the following selected accounts:

| | |
|---|---|
| 112 Accounts Receivable | 412 Sales Returns and Allowances |
| 126 Supplies | 510 Purchases |
| 157 Equipment | 512 Purchase Returns and Allowances |
| 201 Accounts Payable | 516 Freight-in |
| 401 Sales | 610 Advertising Expense |

In May the following selected transactions were completed. All purchases and sales were on account except as indicated.

May  2  Purchased merchandise from Vons Company, $8,000.
      3  Received freight bill from Acme Freight on Vons purchase, $400.
      5  Sales were made to Penner Company, $2,600; Hendrix Bros., $2,700; and Nelles Company, $1,500.
      8  Purchased merchandise from Golden Company, $8,000 and Dorn Company, $8,700.
     10  Received credit on merchandise returned to Dorn Company, $500.
     15  Purchased supplies from Engle Supply, $900.
     16  Purchased merchandise from Vons Company, $4,500; and Golden Company, $6,000.
     17  Returned supplies to Engle Supply, receiving credit, $100. (Hint: Credit Supplies.)
     18  Received freight bills on May 16 purchases from Acme Freight, $500.
     20  Returned merchandise to Vons Company receiving credit, $300.
     23  Made sales to Hendrix Bros., $2,400; and Nelles Company, $2,200.
     25  Received bill for advertising from Ball Advertising, $900.
     26  Granted allowance to Nelles Company for merchandise damaged in shipment, $200.
     28  Purchased equipment from Engle Supply, $250.

**Instructions**
(a) Journalize the transactions above in a purchases journal, a one-column sales journal, and a general journal. The purchases journal should have the following column headings: Date, Accounts Credited (Debited), Ref., Other Accounts Dr., Purchases Dr., Freight-in Dr., and Accounts Payable Cr.
(b) Post to both the general and subsidiary ledger accounts. (Assume that all accounts have zero beginning balances.)
(c) Prove the agreement of the control and subsidiary accounts.

*Journalize transactions in special journals.*
(SO 3, 4, 5)

**P6–4**    Selected accounts from the chart of accounts of Susan Company are shown below.

| | |
|---|---|
| 101 Cash | 401 Sales |
| 112 Accounts Receivable | 414 Sales Discounts |
| 126 Supplies | 510 Purchases |
| 140 Land | 512 Purchase Returns and Allowances |
| 145 Buildings | 514 Purchase Discounts |
| 201 Accounts Payable | 610 Advertising Expense |

During October, Susan Company completed the following transactions:

Oct.  2  Purchased merchandise on account from Mason Company, $16,500.
      4  Sold merchandise on account to Parker Co., $8,100. Invoice no. 204; terms 2/10, n/30.
      5  Purchased supplies for cash, $80.
      7  Made cash sales for the week totaling $9,160.
      9  Paid in full the Mason Company on account less a 2% discount.
     10  Purchased merchandise on account from Quinn Corp., $4,200.
     12  Received payment from Parker Co. for invoice no. 204.
     13  Issued a debit memorandum to Quinn Corp. and returned $250 worth of damaged goods.
     14  Made cash sales for the week totaling $8,180.
     16  Sold a parcel of land for $27,000 cash, the land's book value.

17 Sold merchandise on account to L. Boyton & Co., $5,350, invoice no. 205, terms 2/10, n/30.

18 Purchased merchandise for cash, $2,125.

21 Made cash sales for the week totaling $8,465.

23 Paid in full the Quinn Corp. on account for the goods kept (no discount).

25 Purchased supplies on account from Frey Co., $260.

25 Sold merchandise on account to Green Corp., $5,220, invoice no. 206, terms 2/10, n/30.

25 Received payment from L. Boyton & Co. for invoice no. 205.

26 Purchased for cash a small parcel of land and a building on the land to use as a storage facility. The total cost of $35,000 was allocated $21,000 to the land and $14,000 to the building.

27 Purchased merchandise on account from Schmid Co., $8,500.

28 Made cash sales for the week totaling $8,540.

30 Purchased merchandise on account from Mason Company, $14,000.

30 Paid advertising bill for the month from the Gazette, $400.

30 Sold merchandise on account to L. Boyton & Co., $4,600. Invoice no. 207; terms 2/10, n/30.

Susan Company uses the following journals:

1. Single-column sales journal.
2. Single-column purchases journal.
3. Cash receipts journal with columns for Cash, Dr.; Sales Discounts, Dr.; Accounts Receivable, Cr.; Sales, Cr.; and Other Accounts, Cr.
4. Cash payments journal with columns for Other Accounts, Dr.; Accounts Payable, Dr.; Supplies, Dr.; Purchase Discounts, Cr.; and Cash, Cr.
5. General journal.

*Instructions*

Using the selected accounts provided:

(a) Record, in the appropriate journals, the October transactions.

(b) Foot and crossfoot all special journals.

(c) Show how postings would be made by placing ledger account numbers and check marks as needed in the journals. (Actual posting to ledger accounts is not required.)

**P6–5** Presented below are the sales and cash receipts journals for Taco Co. for its first month of operations.

*Journalize in purchase and cash payments journals, post, prepare a trial balance, prove control to subsidiary, prepare adjusting entries, and prepare an adjusted trial balance.*
*(SO 3, 4, 5)*

### SALES JOURNAL                                                    S1

| Date | Account Debited | Ref. | Accounts Receivable Debit Sales Credit |
|---|---|---|---|
| Feb. 3 | H. Adams | | 5,000 |
| 9 | R. Babcock | | 6,500 |
| 12 | B. Chambers | | 7,000 |
| 26 | L. Dawson | | 6,000 |
| | | | 24,500 |

### CASH RECEIPTS JOURNAL                                            CR1

| Date | Accounts Credited | Ref. | Cash Debit | Sales Discounts Debit | Accounts Receivable Credit | Sales Credit | Other Accounts Credit |
|---|---|---|---|---|---|---|---|
| Feb. 1 | B. Taco, Capital | | 30,000 | | | | 30,000 |
| 2 | | | 6,500 | | | 6,500 | |
| 13 | H. Adams | | 4,950 | 50 | 5,000 | | |
| 18 | Purchase Returns and Allowances | | 150 | | | | 150 |
| 26 | R. Babcock | | 6,500 | — | 6,500 | — | — |
| | | | 48,100 | 50 | 11,500 | 6,500 | 30,150 |

In addition, the following transactions have not been journalized for February 1996.

Feb.  2  Purchased merchandise on account from S. Healy for $2,000, terms 1/10, n/30.
     7  Purchased merchandise on account from L. Held for $30,000, terms 1/10, n/30.
     9  Paid cash of $1,000 for purchase of supplies.
    12  Paid $1,980 to S. Healy in payment for $2,000 invoice, less 1% discount.
    15  Purchased equipment for $8,000 cash.
    16  Purchased merchandise on account from R. Landly, $2,400, terms 2/10, n/30.
    17  Paid $29,700 to L. Held in payment of $30,000 invoice, less 1% discount.
    20  Withdrew cash of $1,100 from business for personal use.
    21  Purchased merchandise on account from J. Able for $6,500, terms 1/10, n/30.
    28  Paid $2,400 to R. Landly in payment of $2,400 invoice.

*Instructions*

(a)  Open the following accounts in the general ledger.

| | | | |
|---|---|---|---|
| 101 | Cash | 306 | B. Taco, Drawing |
| 112 | Accounts Receivable | 401 | Sales |
| 126 | Supplies | 414 | Sales Discounts |
| 157 | Equipment | 510 | Purchases |
| 158 | Accumulated Depreciation—Equipment | 512 | Purchase Returns and Allowances |
| 201 | Accounts Payable | 514 | Purchase Discounts |
| 301 | B. Taco, Capital | 631 | Supplies Expense |
| | | 711 | Depreciation Expense |

(b)  Journalize the transactions that have not been journalized in a one-column purchases journal, and the cash payments journal (see Illustration 6-17).

(c)  Post to the accounts receivable and accounts payable subsidiary ledgers. Follow the sequence of transactions as shown in the problem.

(d)  Post the individual entries and totals to the general ledger.

(e)  Prepare a trial balance at February 28, 1996.

(f)  Determine that the subsidiary ledgers agree with the control accounts in the general ledger.

(g)  The following adjustments at the end of February are necessary.
    1.  A count of supplies indicates that $300 is still on hand.
    2.  Depreciation on equipment for February is $200.
    Prepare the adjusting entries and then post the adjusting entries to the general ledger.

(h)  Prepare an adjusted trial balance.

*Journalize in special journals, post, and prepare a trial balance.*
(SO 3, 4, 5)

**P6–6**  The post-closing trial balance for Garcia Co. is as follows:

**GARCIA CO.**
**Post-Closing Trial Balance**
**December 31, 1996**

| | Debit | Credit |
|---|---|---|
| Cash | $ 39,500 | |
| Accounts Receivable | 15,000 | |
| Notes Receivable | 45,000 | |
| Merchandise Inventory | 23,000 | |
| Equipment | 6,450 | |
| Accumulated Depreciation—Equipment | | $  1,500 |
| Accounts Payable | | 43,000 |
| S. Garcia, Capital | | 84,450 |
| | $128,950 | $128,950 |

The subsidiary ledgers contain the following information: (1) accounts receivable—R. Barton $2,500; B. Cole $7,500; S. Devine $5,000; (2) accounts payable—S. Field $10,000; R. Gilson $18,000; and D. Harms $15,000.

The transactions for January 1997 are as follows:

Jan.  3  Sell merchandise to B. Senton, $2,000, terms 2/10, n/30.

5   Purchase merchandise from S. Warren, $2,200, terms 2/10, n/30.

7   Receive a check from S. Devine, $3,500.

11  Pay freight on merchandise purchased, $300.

12  Pay rent of $1,000 for January.

13  Receive payment in full from B. Senton.

14  Post all entries to the subsidiary ledgers. Issue a credit memo to acknowledge receipt of damaged merchandise of $700 returned by R. Barton.

15  Send D. Harms a check for $14,850 in full payment of account, discount, $150.

17  Purchase merchandise from D. Lapeska, $1,600, terms 2/10, n/30.

18  Pay sales salaries of $2,800 and office salaries, $1,500.

20  Give R. Gilson a 60-day note for $18,000 in full payment of accounts payable.

23  Total cash sales amount to $8,600.

24  Post all entries to the subsidiary ledgers. Sells merchandise on account to B. Cole, $7,700, terms 1/10, n/30.

27  Send S. Warren a check for $950.

29  Receive payment on a note of $40,000 from S. Lava.

30  Return merchandise of $500 to D. Lapeska for credit. Post all journals to the subsidiary ledger.

### Instructions

(a)  Open general and subsidiary ledger accounts for the following:

| | |
|---|---|
| 101  Cash | 412  Sales Returns and Allowances |
| 112  Accounts Receivable | 414  Sales Discounts |
| 115  Notes Receivable | 510  Purchases |
| 120  Merchandise Inventory | 512  Purchase Returns and Allowances |
| 157  Equipment | 514  Purchase Discounts |
| 158  Accumulated Depreciation—Equipment | 516  Freight-in |
| 200  Notes Payable | 726  Sales Salaries Expense |
| 201  Accounts Payable | 727  Office Salaries Expense |
| 301  S. Garcia, Capital | 729  Rent Expense |
| 401  Sales | |

(b)  Record the January transactions in a single-column sales journal, a single-column purchases journal, a cash receipts journal (see Illustration 6-10), a cash payments journal (see Illustration 6-17), and a general journal.

(c)  Post the appropriate amounts to the general ledger.

(d)  Prepare a trial balance at January 31, 1997.

(e)  Determine whether the subsidiary ledgers agree with controlling accounts in the general ledger.

# ALTERNATE PROBLEMS

**P6–1A**  Lemont Company's chart of accounts includes the following selected accounts:

| | |
|---|---|
| 101  Cash | 401  Sales |
| 112  Accounts Receivable | 414  Sales Discounts |
| 301  F. Lemont, Capital | 512  Purchase Returns and Allowances |

*Journalize transactions in cash receipts journal and post to control account and subsidiary ledger.*

(SO 3, 4, 5)

On April 1 the accounts receivable ledger of Lemont Company showed the following balances: Harris, $1,550; Kerl, $1,200; Northeast Co., $2,900; and Smith, $1,600. The April transactions involving the receipt of cash were as follows:

Apr.  1   The owner, F. Lemont, invested additional cash in the business, $6,000.

4   Received check for payment of account from Smith less 2% cash discount.

5   Received check for $620 in payment of invoice no. 307 from Northeast Co.

8   Made cash sales of merchandise totaling $7,245.

10  Received check for $900 in payment of invoice no. 309 from Harris.

11  Received cash refund from a supplier for damaged merchandise, $550.

23    Received check for $1,600 in payment of invoice no. 310 from Northeast Co.

29    Received check for payment of account from Kerl.

### Instructions

(a) Journalize the transactions above in a five-column cash receipts journal with columns for Cash, Dr.; Sales Discounts, Dr.; Accounts Receivable, Cr.; Sales, Cr.; and Other Accounts, Cr. Foot and crossfoot the journal.

(b) Insert the beginning balances in the Accounts Receivable control and subsidiary accounts and post the April transactions to these accounts.

(c) Prove the agreement of the control account and subsidiary account balances.

*Journalize transactions in cash payments journal and post to control account and subsidiary ledger.*
*(SO 3, 4, 5)*

**P6–2A**    McCarty Company's chart of accounts includes the following selected accounts:

| | |
|---|---|
| 101  Cash | 306  L. McCarty, Drawing |
| 130  Prepaid Insurance | 510  Purchases |
| 157  Equipment | 514  Purchase Discounts |
| 201  Accounts Payable | |

On October 1 the accounts payable ledger of the McCarty Company showed the following balances: Newton Company, $1,600; Martin & Sons, $2,500; Lien Co., $1,400; and Watson Company, $3,700. The October transactions involving the payment of cash were as follows:

Oct.  1    Purchased merchandise, check no. 63, $700.

3    Purchased equipment, check no. 64, $800.

5    Paid Newton Company balance due of $1,600, less 2% discount, check no. 65, $1,568.

10    Purchased merchandise, check no. 66, $2,250.

15    Paid Lien Co. balance due of $1,400, check no. 67.

16    L. McCarty, the owner, pays his personal insurance premium of $400, check no. 68.

19    Paid Martin & Sons in full for invoice no. 610, $1,400 less 2% cash discount, check no. 69, $1,372.

29    Paid Watson Company in full for invoice no. 264, $2,300, check no. 70.

### Instructions

(a) Journalize the transactions above in a five-column cash payments journal with columns for Other Accounts, Dr.; Accounts Payable, Dr.; Purchases, Dr.; Purchase Discounts, Cr.; and Cash, Cr. Foot and crossfoot the journal.

(b) Insert the beginning balances in the Accounts Payable control and subsidiary accounts and post the October transactions to these accounts.

(c) Prove the agreement of the control account and the subsidiary account balances.

*Journalize transactions in multi-column purchases journal and post to the general and subsidiary ledgers.*
*(SO 3, 4, 5)*

**P6–3A**    The chart of accounts of Dong Lai Company includes the following selected accounts:

| | |
|---|---|
| 112  Accounts Receivable | 412  Sales Returns and Allowances |
| 126  Supplies | 510  Purchases |
| 157  Equipment | 512  Purchase Returns and Allowances |
| 201  Accounts Payable | 516  Freight-in |
| 401  Sales | 610  Advertising Expense |

In July the following selected transactions were completed. All purchases and sales were on account.

July  1    Purchased merchandise from Jansen Company, $8,000.

2    Received freight bill from Johnson Shipping on Jansen purchase, $400.

3    Made sales to Lyons Company, $1,300; and Franklin Bros., $1,900.

5    Purchased merchandise from Maxwell Company, $3,200.

8    Received credit on merchandise returned to Maxwell Company, $300.

13    Purchased store supplies from Apollo Supply, $720.

15    Purchased merchandise from Jansen Company, $3,600; and Sparky Company, $2,800.

16    Made sales to Jackson Company, $3,450; and Franklin Bros., $1,570.

18    Received bill for advertising from Nancy's Advertisements, $600.

21    Sales were made to Lyons Company, $310; and Jeff Company, $2,200.

22    Granted allowance to Lyons Company for merchandise damaged in shipment, $40.

24  Purchased merchandise from Maxwell Company, $3,000.
26  Purchased equipment from Apollo Supply, $600.
28  Received freight bill from Johnson Shipping on Maxwell purchase of July 24, $380.
30  Sales were made to Jackson Company, $3,900.

**Instructions**
(a) Journalize the transactions above in a purchases journal, a one-column sales journal, and a general journal. The purchases journal should have the following column headings: Date, Accounts Credited (Debited), Ref., Other Accounts Dr., Purchases Dr., Freight-in Dr., and Accounts Payable Cr.
(b) Post to both the general and subsidiary ledger accounts. (Assume that all accounts have zero beginning balances.)
(c) Prove the agreement of the control and subsidiary accounts.

**P6–4A**  Selected accounts from the chart of accounts of Ripple Company are shown below.

*Journalize transactions in special journals.*
(SO 3, 4, 5)

| | |
|---|---|
| 101 Cash | 412 Sales Returns and Allowances |
| 112 Accounts Receivable | 414 Sales Discounts |
| 126 Supplies | 510 Purchases |
| 157 Equipment | 512 Purchase Returns and Allowances |
| 201 Accounts Payable | 514 Purchase Discounts |
| 401 Sales | 726 Salaries Expense |

During January, Ripple completed the following transactions:

Jan. 3  Purchased merchandise on account from Bell Co., $8,900.
4  Purchased supplies for cash, $80.
4  Sold merchandise on account to Gilbert, $7,550, invoice no. 371, terms 1/10, n/30.
5  Issued a debit memorandum to Bell Co. and returned $300 worth of damaged goods.
6  Made cash sales for the week totaling $3,150.
8  Purchased merchandise on account from Law Co., $4,500.
9  Sold merchandise on account to Mays Corp., $5,600, invoice no. 372, terms 1/10, n/30.
11  Purchased merchandise on account from Hatch Co., $3,700.
13  Paid in full the Bell Co. on account less a 2% discount.
13  Made cash sales for the week totaling $5,340.
15  Received payment from Mays Corp. for invoice no. 372.
15  Paid semi-monthly salaries of $14,300 to employees.
17  Received payment from Gilbert for invoice no. 371.
17  Sold merchandise on account to Amber Co., $1,200, invoice no. 373, terms 1/10, n/30.
19  Purchased equipment on account from Johnson Corp., $5,500.
20  Cash sales for the week totaled $3,200.
20  Paid in full the Law Co. on account less a 2% discount.
23  Purchased merchandise on account from Bell Co., $7,800.
24  Purchased merchandise on account from Levine Corp., $4,690.
27  Made cash sales for the week totaling $3,730.
30  Received payment from Amber Co. for invoice no. 373.
31  Paid semi-monthly salaries of $13,200 to employees.
31  Sold merchandise on account to Gilbert, $9,330, invoice no. 374, terms 1/10, n/30.

Ripple Company uses the following journals:

1. Single-column sales journal.
2. Single-column purchases journal.
3. Cash receipts journal with columns for Cash, Dr.; Sales Discounts, Dr.; Accounts Receivable, Cr.; Sales, Cr.; and Other Accounts, Cr.
4. Cash payments journal with columns for Other Accounts, Dr.; Accounts Payable, Dr.; Purchase Discounts, Cr.; and Cash, Cr.
5. General journal.

**Instructions**

Using the selected accounts provided:

(a) Record, in the appropriate journal noted, the January transactions.

(b) Foot and crossfoot all special journals.

(c) Show how postings would be made by placing ledger account numbers and check-marks as needed in the journals. (Actual posting to ledger accounts is not required.)

*Journalize in sales and cash receipts journals, post, prepare a trial balance, prove control to subsidiary, prepare adjusting entries, and prepare an adjusted trial balance.*

*(SO 3, 4, 5)*

**P6–5A**   Presented below are the purchases and cash payments journal for Pinckney Co. for its first month of operations.

**PURCHASES JOURNAL**                                                         **P1**

| Date | | Account Credited | Ref. | Purchases Debit Accounts Payable Credit |
|---|---|---|---|---|
| July | 4 | J. Dixon | | 6,800 |
| | 5 | W. Engel | | 7,500 |
| | 11 | R. Gamble | | 3,720 |
| | 13 | M. Hill | | 15,300 |
| | 20 | D. Jacob | | 7,800 |
| | | | | 41,120 |

**CASH PAYMENTS JOURNAL**                                                     **CP1**

| Date | | Accounts Debited | Ref. | Other Accounts Debit | Accounts Payable Debit | Purchase Discounts Credit | Cash Credit |
|---|---|---|---|---|---|---|---|
| July | 4 | Store Supplies | | 600 | | | 600 |
| | 10 | W. Engel | | | 7,500 | 75 | 7,425 |
| | 11 | Prepaid Rent | | 6,000 | | | 6,000 |
| | 15 | J. Dixon | | | 6,800 | | 6,800 |
| | 19 | Pinckney, Drawing | | 2,500 | | | 2,500 |
| | 21 | M. Hill | | | 15,300 | 153 | 15,147 |
| | | | | 9,100 | 29,600 | 228 | 38,472 |

In addition, the following transactions have not been journalized for July.

July  1   The founder, A. Pinckney, invests $80,000 in cash.

6   Sell merchandise on account to Hardy Co., $6,400 terms 1/10, n/30.

7   Make cash sales totaling $4,000.

8   Sell merchandise on account to D. Washburn, $3,600, terms, 1/10, n/30.

10   Sell merchandise on account to L. Lemansky, $4,900, terms 1/10, n/30.

13   Receive payment in full from D. Washburn.

16   Receive payment in full from L. Lemansky.

20   Receive payment in full from Hardy Co.

21   Sell merchandise on account to S. Kane, $3,000, terms, 1/10, n/30.

29   Return damaged goods to J. Dixon and received cash refund of $450.

**Instructions**

(a) Open the following accounts in the general ledger.

| | |
|---|---|
| 101 Cash | 401 Sales |
| 112 Accounts Receivable | 412 Sales Returns and Allowances |
| 127 Store Supplies | 414 Sales Discounts |
| 131 Prepaid Rent | 510 Purchases |
| 201 Accounts Payable | 512 Purchase Returns and Allowances |
| 301 Pinckney, Capital | 514 Purchase Discounts |
| 306 Pinckney, Drawing | 631 Supplies Expense |
| | 729 Rent Expense |

(b) Journalize the transactions that have not been journalized in the single-column sales journal, the cash receipts journal (see Illustration 6-10), and the general journal.

(c) Post to the accounts receivable and accounts payable subsidiary ledgers. Follow the sequence of transactions as shown in the problem.

(d) Post the individual entries and totals to the general ledger.

(e) Prepare a trial balance at July 31, 1996.

(f) Determine whether the subsidiary ledgers agree with the controlling accounts in the general ledger.

(g) The following adjustments at the end of July are necessary.
1. A count of supplies indicates that $140 is still on hand.
2. Recognize rent expense for July, $500.
Prepare the necessary entries in the general journal. Post the entries to the general ledger.

(h) Prepare an adjusted trial balance at July 31, 1996.

# ►*B*roadening *Your Perspective*

## *F*INANCIAL REPORTING PROBLEM—A MINI PRACTICE SET

(The working papers that accompany this textbook are needed in order to work this mini practice set.)

Hunt Co. uses both an accounts receivable and an accounts payable subsidiary ledger. Balances related to both the general ledger and the subsidiary ledger for Hunt are indicated in the working papers. Presented below are a series of transactions for Hunt Co. for the month of January. Credit sales terms are 2/10, n/30.

Jan. 3 Sell merchandise on credit to B. Sargent $3,100, invoice No. 510, and to J. Eaton $1,800, invoice No. 511.

5 Purchase merchandise from S. Walden $3,000 and D. Landell $2,200, terms n/30.

7 Receive checks from S. Lowell, $4,000 and B. Jaggar $2,000 after discount period has lapsed.

8 Pay freight on merchandise purchased $180.

9 Send checks to S. Lee for $9,000 less 2% cash discount and D. Nordin for $11,000 less 1% cash discount.

9 Issue credit memo for $300 to J. Eaton for merchandise returned.

10 Summary daily cash sales total $15,500.

11 Sell merchandise on credit to R. Dansig $1,300, invoice No. 512, and to S. Lowell $900, invoice No. 513.

12 Pay rent of $1,000 for January.

13 Receive payment in full from B. Sargent and J. Eaton less cash discounts.

15 Withdraw $800 cash by S. Hunt for personal use.

15 Post all entries to the subsidiary ledgers.

16 Purchase merchandise from D. Nordin $15,000, terms 1/10, n/30; S. Lee $14,200, terms 2/10, n/30; and S. Walden $1,500, terms n/30.

17 Pay $400 cash for office supplies.

18 Return $200 of merchandise to S. Lee and receive credit.

20 Summary daily cash sales total $17,500.

21 Issue $15,000 note to R. Mannon in payment of balance due.

21 Receive payment in full from S. Lowell less cash discount.

22 Sell merchandise on credit to B. Sargent $1,700, invoice No. 514 and to R. Dansig $800, invoice No. 515.

22 Post all entries to the subsidiary ledger.

23 Send checks to D. Nordin and S. Lee in full payment less cash discounts.

25 Sell merchandise on credit to B. Jaggar $3,500, invoice No. 516 and to J. Eaton $6,100, invoice No. 517.

27   Purchase merchandise from D. Nordin $14,500, terms 1/10, n/30; D. Landell $1,200, terms n/30; and S. Walden $2,800, terms n/30.

27   Post all entries to the subsidiary ledger.

28   Pay $200 cash for office supplies.

31   Summary daily cash sales total $21,300.

31   Pay sales salaries $4,300 and office salaries $2,600.

*Instructions*

(a) Record the January transactions in a single-column sales journal, a single-column purchases journal, a cash receipts journal as shown on page 245, a cash payments journal as shown on page 251, and a two-column general journal.

(b) Post the journals to the general ledger.

(c) Prepare a trial balance at January 31, 1997, in the trial balance columns of the work sheet. Complete the work sheet using the following additional information.

(1) Office supplies at January 31 total $500.

(2) Insurance coverage expires on October 31, 1997.

(3) Annual depreciation on the equipment is $1,500.

(4) Interest of $60 has accrued on the note payable.

(5) Merchandise inventory at January 31 is $16,000.

(d) Prepare a multiple-step income statement and an owner's equity statement for January and a classified balance sheet at the end of January.

(e) Prepare and post adjusting and closing entries.

(f) Prepare a post-closing trial balance and determine whether the subsidiary ledgers agree with the controlling accounts in the general ledger.

# DECISION CASE

Smith & Young is a wholesaler of small appliances and parts. Smith & Young is operated by two owners, Paul Smith and Ann Young. In addition, the company has one employee, a repair specialist, who is on a fixed salary. Revenues are earned through the sale of appliances to retailers (approximately 75% of total revenues), appliance parts to do-it-yourselfers (10%), and the repair of appliances brought to the store (15%). Appliance sales are made on both a credit and cash basis. Customers are billed on prenumbered sales invoices. Credit terms are always net/30 days. All parts sales and repair work are cash only.

Merchandise is purchased on account from the manufacturers of both the appliances and the parts. Practically all suppliers offer cash discounts for prompt payments, and it is company policy to take all discounts. Most cash payments are made by check. Checks are most frequently issued to suppliers, to trucking companies for freight on merchandise purchases, and to newspapers, radio, and TV stations for advertising. All advertising bills are paid as received. Paul and Ann each make a monthly drawing in cash for personal living expenses. The salaried repairman is paid twice monthly.

Smith & Young currently has a manual accounting system. However, the business is growing and some consideration is being given to an electronic accounting system.

*Instructions*

(a) Identify the special journals that Smith & Young should have in its manual system. List the column headings appropriate for each of the special journals.

(b) What control and subsidiary accounts should be included in Smith & Young's manual system? Why?

(c) Identify for Paul and Ann the key points they should consider in deciding whether to install an electronic system.

# COMMUNICATION ACTIVITY

Demi Morris, a classmate, has a part-time bookkeeping job. She is concerned about the inefficiencies in journalizing and posting transactions. Rami Ali is the owner of the company where Demi works. In response to numerous complaints from Demi and others, Rami hired two additional bookkeepers a month ago. However, the inefficiencies have continued at an even higher rate. The accounting information system for the company has only a general journal and a general ledger. Rami refuses to install an electronic accounting system.

*Instructions*
Now that Demi is an expert in manual accounting information systems, she decides to send a letter to Rami Ali explaining (1) why the additional personnel did not help and (2) what changes should be made to improve the efficiency of the accounting department. Write the letter that you think Demi should send.

# GROUP ACTIVITY

Hard Hat Construction uses a general journal and the following special journals: single-column sales journal, cash receipts journal, single-column purchases journal, and a cash payments journal. Hard Hat also uses control accounts and subsidiary ledgers for accounts receivable and accounts payable.

*Instructions*
With the class divided into six groups, five groups will choose one journal each and should report to the class on the journalizing and posting of the journal and proving the postings. The sixth group will consider control accounts and subsidiary ledgers. This group should report to the class on the relationship of the accounts, postings to the accounts, and proving the agreement of the accounts.

# ETHICS CASE

Triport Products Company operates three divisions, each with its own manufacturing plant and marketing/sales force. The corporate headquarters and central accounting office are in Triport with the plants in Freeport, Rockport, and Bayport, all within 50 miles of Triport. Corporate management treats each division as an independent profit center and encourages competition among them. They each have similar but different product lines. As a competitive incentive, bonuses are awarded each year to the employees of the fastest growing and most profitable division.

Ron Hermann is the manager of Triport's centralized computer accounting operation that keyboards the sales transactions and maintains the accounts receivable for all three divisions. Ron came up in the accounting ranks from the Bayport division where his wife, several relatives, and many friends still work.

As sales documents are keyboarded into the computer, the originating division is identified by code. Most sales documents (95%) are coded, but some (5%) are not coded or are coded incorrectly. As the manager, Ron has instructed the keyboard operators to assign the Bayport code to all uncoded and incorrectly coded sales documents. This is done he says, "in order to expedite processing and to keep the computer files current since they are updated daily." All receivables and cash collections for all three divisions are handled by Triport as one subsidiary accounts receivable ledger.

*Instructions*
(a) Who are the stakeholders in this situation?
(b) What are the ethical issues in this case?
(c) How might the system be improved to prevent this situation?

# CRITICAL THINKING
▶ *A Real-World Focus: Alco Standard Corporation*

*Alco Standard Corporation's operations are divided into two business groups: Alco Office Products and Unisource. Alco Office Products sells, leases, and rents various electronic office machines; Unisource markets and distributes papers primarily for office use. The company owns or leases facilities in 49 states and 9 foreign countries.*

**ALCO** Standard Corporation

The President of Alco wrote the following in his letter in a recent annual report:

The creation of Unisource allows us to pursue strategies that are practical only on a unified basis. Our efforts to upgrade information technology, for example, will now be directed to building a common system throughout North America. This unified approach will give us online electronic link suppliers, cutting order entry costs and improving inventory management. As a result, we will be able to improve service to customers with more timely and more accurate order fulfillment, faster inquiry response and enhanced technical support.

### Instructions
  (a) When a company computerizes customer order entry, what equivalent special journal type must be programmed into such an electronic system?
  (b) When a company computerizes inventory management (which involves more timely ordering of new merchandise), what special journal type must be programmed into such an electronic system?

---

### Answers to Self-Study Questions
1. d    2. b    3. a    4. c    5. a    6. c    7. d    8. b    9. d    10. c

•••••• ▶ **Concepts for Review**

**Before studying this chapter, you should know or, if necessary, review:**

**a.** *How cash transactions are journalized in special journals.*
   *(Ch. 6, pp. 244–47. 250–52)*
**b.** *How postings are made to the cash account from special journals.*
   *(Ch. 6, pp. 244–47, 250–52)*
**c.** *The phases in developing an accounting system. (Ch. 6, pp. 237–38)*

# No Free Lunch

NEW YORK, NY — At Columbia University, thousands of dollars in cash changes hands between students and dining facility cashiers. Making sure that all of the money received by cashiers gets to where it's supposed to go requires various control measures. In accounting, these measures are called internal control.

One control measure used in the cafeteria at Columbia is that the register tape that records the sale and the amount of cash received must reconcile with the amount of cash in the cash drawer at the end of the day. "We see if there are significant overages or shortages at the end of each day for each register," says Susan McLaughlin, director of Columbia's dining facilities. Do cash differences happen very often? "No, because the cashier knows that if there are repeated or significant shortages, disciplinary action will be taken," she says. "There should not be a variance of more than $5, either over or under, at any given time—or else it indicates poor cash handling."

If a student buying a meal at a register sees that a sale isn't rung up or if the student doesn't get a receipt, there is a possibility that the cashier is stealing. "We know that taking the receipt is an annoyance," says Ms. McLaughlin, "but issuing receipts is an absolutely mandatory control for us." ◀

# INTERNAL CONTROL AND CASH

As the story about the dining facilities at Columbia University indicates, control of cash is important. Similarly, controls are needed to safeguard other types of assets. For example, Columbia University undoubtedly has controls to prevent the theft of food served in the cafeteria and controls to prevent the theft of computer equipment and supplies from its computer laboratories.

In this chapter, we explain the essential features of an internal control system and then describe how those controls apply to cash. The applications include some controls with which you may be already familiar. Toward the end of the chapter, we describe the use of a bank and explain how cash is reported on the balance sheet. The organization and content of Chapter 7 are as follows:

## Internal Control

Could there be dishonest employees in the business that you own or manage? Unfortunately, the answer sometimes is Yes. For example, the financial press recently reported the following:

A bookkeeper in a small company diverted $750,000 of bill payments to a personal bank account over a 3-year period.

A shipping clerk with 28 years of service shipped $125,000 of merchandise to himself.

A computer operator embezzled $21 million from Wells Fargo Bank over a 2-year period.

A church treasurer "borrowed" $150,000 of church funds to finance a friend's business dealings.

These situations emphasize the need for a good system of internal control.

# ►*T*echnology in *A*ction

Good internal control must be designed into computerized systems. The starting point is usually flow charts that graphically depict each component of a firm's operations. The assembled flow charts serve as the basis for writing detailed programs. An example of flow charting is given in this chapter. When attempts to automate or improve accounting systems fail, it is often due to the absence of such well-documented procedures.

Internal control consists of the plan of organization and all the related methods and measures adopted within a business to:

1. **Safeguard its assets** from employee theft, robbery, and unauthorized use.
2. **Enhance the accuracy and reliability of its accounting records** by reducing the risk of errors (unintentional mistakes) and irregularities (intentional mistakes and misrepresentations) in the accounting process.

Under the Foreign Corrupt Practices Act of 1977, all major U.S. corporations are required to maintain an adequate system of internal control. Companies that fail to comply are subject to fines, and company officers may be imprisoned. Also, the National Commission on Fraudulent Financial Reporting concluded that all companies whose stock is publicly traded should maintain internal controls that can provide reasonable assurance that fraudulent financial reporting will be prevented or subject to early detection.[1]

## Principles of Internal Control

To safeguard its assets and enhance the accuracy and reliability of its accounting records, a company follows specific control principles. Of course, internal control measures vary with the size and nature of the business and with management's control philosophy. However, the six principles listed in Illustration 7-1 apply to most enterprises:

▶ **International note**

U.S. companies also adopt model business codes that guide their international operations to provide for a safe and healthy workplace, avoid child and forced labor, abstain from bribes, and follow sound environmental practices.

**STUDY OBJECTIVE**
············**2**············

*Identify the principles of internal control.*

**Illustration 7-1**

*Principles of internal control*

▶ **Ethics note**

Fundamental to internal control systems is the assumption that employees are honest and ethical and will not commit wrongdoing. As a result, most control measures are more effective in preventing and detecting errors than irregularities.

**Principles of Internal Control**

| | |
|---|---|
| Establishment of responsibility | Physical, mechanical, and electronic controls |
| Segregation of duties | Independent internal verification |
| Documentation procedures | Other controls |

---

[1]Report of the National Commission on Fraudulent Financial Reporting, October 1987, p. 11.

Each principle is explained in the following sections.

### Establishment of Responsibility

An essential characteristic of internal control is the assignment of responsibility to specific individuals. **Control is most effective when only one person is responsible for a given task.** To illustrate, assume that the cash on hand at the end of the day in a Safeway supermarket is $10 short of the cash rung up on the cash register. If only one person has operated the register, responsibility for the shortage can be assessed quickly. However, if two or more individuals have worked the register, it may be impossible to determine who is responsible for the error unless each person is assigned a separate cash drawer and register key. The principle of establishing responsibility was followed by Columbia University's dining services (in the opening story) by assigning a cashier to a cash register and keeping each cashier's cash drawer separate from others.

Establishing responsibility includes the authorization and approval of transactions. For example, the vice-president of sales should have the authority to establish policies for making credit sales. The policies ordinarily will require written credit department approval of credit sales.

### Segregation of Duties

This principle (also identified as separation of functions or division of work) is indispensable in a system of internal control. There are two common applications of this principle:

1. The responsibility for related activities should be assigned to different individuals.
2. The responsibility for establishing the accountability (keeping the records) for an asset should be separate from the physical custody of that asset.

**The rationale for segregation of duties is that the work of one employee should, without a duplication of effort, provide a reliable basis for evaluating the work of another employee.**

**Related Activities.**   Related activities that should be assigned to different individuals arise in both the purchasing and selling areas. **When one individual is responsible for all of the related activities, the potential for errors and irregularities is increased.** Related purchasing activities include ordering the merchandise, receiving the goods, and paying (or authorizing payment) for the merchandise. In purchasing, for example, orders could be placed with friends or with suppliers who give kickbacks. Similarly, only a cursory count and inspection could be made upon receiving the goods, which could lead to errors and poor quality merchandise. In addition, payment might be authorized without a careful review of the invoice, or even worse, fictitious invoices might be approved for payment. When the responsibility for ordering, receiving, and paying are assigned to different individuals or departments, the risk of such abuses is minimized.

Similarly, related sales activities should be assigned to different individuals. Related selling activities include making a sale, shipping (or delivering) the goods to the customer, and billing the customer. When one person is responsible for related sales transactions, a salesperson could make sales at unauthorized prices to increase sales commissions; a shipping clerk could ship goods to himself, as indicated at the beginning of the chapter; a billing clerk could understate

## ►*Accounting in Action* ► *Ethics Insight*

A former electronic data processing employee of Texaco, Inc., and his wife were indicted for stealing thousands of dollars from the company in an accounts payable-type fraud. The employee instructed Texaco's computer to pay his wife rent for land she allegedly leased to Texaco by assigning her an alphanumeric code as a lessor and then ordering that payments be made. The lesson here is simple: "*never* allow the same person to both authorize and pay for goods and services." Doing otherwise violates the segregation-of-duties principle of internal control.

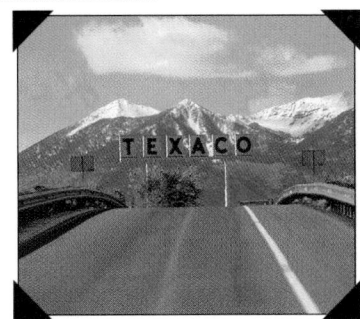

the amount billed for sales made to friends and relatives. These abuses are reduced when salespersons make the sale, shipping department employees ship the goods on the basis of the sales order, and billing department employees prepare the sales invoice after comparing the sales order with the report of goods shipped.

**Accountability for Assets.** If accounting is to provide a valid basis of accountability for an asset, the accountant should have neither physical custody of the asset nor access to it. Moreover, the custodian of the asset should not maintain or have access to the accounting records. **When one employee maintains the record of the asset that should be on hand, and a different employee has physical custody of the asset, the custodian of the asset is not likely to convert the asset to personal use.** The separation of accounting responsibility from the custody of assets is especially important for cash and inventories because these assets are very vulnerable to unauthorized use or misappropriation.

### *Documentation Procedures*

Documents provide evidence that transactions and events have occurred. In the Columbia University cafeteria, the cash register tape was the university's documentation for the sale and the amount of cash received. Similarly, the shipping document indicates that the goods have been shipped, and the sales invoice indicates that the customer has been billed for the goods. By adding signatures (or initials) to the documents, the individual(s) responsible for the transaction or event can be identified. Documentation of transactions should be made when the transaction occurs. Documentation of events, such as those leading to adjusting entries, is generally developed when the adjustments are made.

Several procedures should be established for documents. First, whenever possible, **documents should be prenumbered and all documents should be accounted for.** Prenumbering helps to prevent a transaction from being recorded more than once, or conversely, to prevent the transactions from not being recorded. Second, documents that are **source documents for accounting entries should be promptly forwarded to the accounting department to help ensure timely recording of the transaction and event.** Thus, this control measure contributes directly to the accuracy and reliability of the accounting records.

**Helpful hint** An important corollary to prenumbering is that voided documents be kept until all documents are accounted for.

### *Physical, Mechanical, and Electronic Controls*

Use of physical, mechanical, and electronic controls is essential. Physical controls relate primarily to the safeguarding of assets. Mechanical and electronic controls safeguard assets and enhance the accuracy and reliability of the accounting records. Examples of these controls are shown in Illustration 7-2.

**Illustration 7-2**

*Physical, mechanical, and electronic controls*

### Physical Controls

Safes, vaults, and safety deposit boxes for cash and business papers

Locked warehouses and storage cabinets for inventories and records

Computer facilities with pass key access

### Mechanical and Electronic Controls

Alarms to prevent break-ins

Television monitors and garment sensors to deter theft

Time clocks for recording time worked

### Independent Internal Verification

Most systems of internal control provide for independent internal verification. This principle involves the review, comparison, and reconciliation of data prepared by one or several employees. To obtain maximum benefit from independent internal verification:

1. The verification should be made periodically or on a surprise basis.
2. The verification should be done by an employee who is independent of the personnel responsible for the information.
3. Discrepancies and exceptions should be reported to a management level that can take appropriate corrective action.

## ▶Accounting in Action ▸ *Business Insight*

John Patterson, a young Ohio merchant, couldn't understand why his retail business didn't show a profit. There were lots of customers, but the money just seemed to disappear.

Patterson suspected pilferage and sloppy bookkeeping by store clerks. Frustrated, he placed an order with a Dayton, Ohio, company for two rudimentary cash registers. A year later, Patterson's store was in the black.

"What is a good thing for this little store is a good thing for every retail store in the world," he observed. A few months later, in 1884, John Patterson and his brother, Frank, bought the tiny cash register maker for $6,500. The word around Dayton was that the Patterson boys got stung.

In the following 37 years, John Patterson built National Cash Register Co. into a corporate giant. Patterson died in 1922, the year in which NCR sold its two millionth cash register.

*Source: Wall Street Journal.* January 28, 1989.

Independent internal verification is especially useful in comparing recorded accountability with existing assets. The reconciliation of the cash register tape with the cash in the register in the Columbia University dining facility is an example of this internal control principle. Another common example is the reconciliation by an independent person of the cash balance per books with the cash balance per bank. The relationship between this principle and the segregation of duties principle is shown graphically in Illustration 7-3.

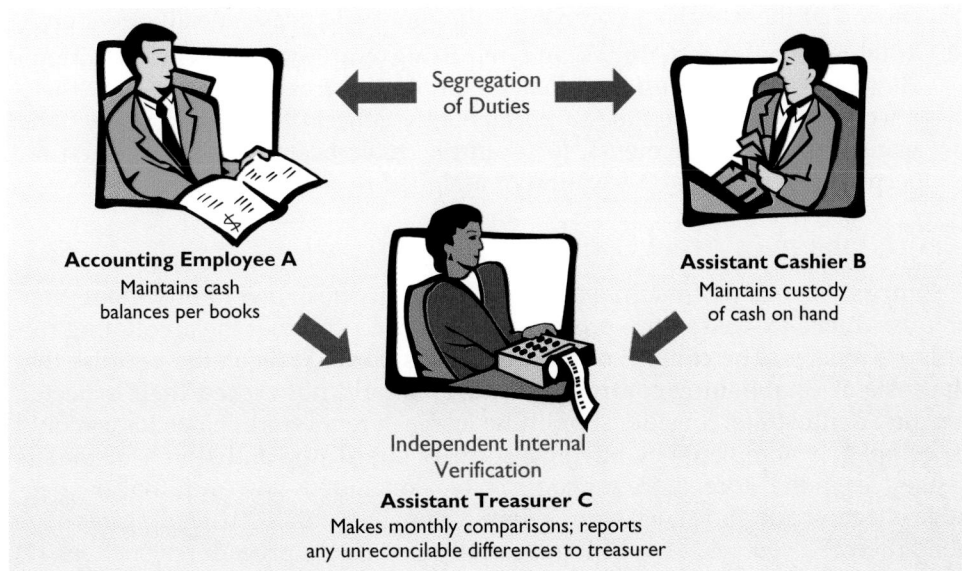

**Accounting Employee A**
Maintains cash
balances per books

Segregation
of Duties

**Assistant Cashier B**
Maintains custody
of cash on hand

Independent Internal
Verification
**Assistant Treasurer C**
Makes monthly comparisons; reports
any unreconcilable differences to treasurer

**Illustration 7-3**

*Comparison of segregation of duties principle with independent internal verification principle*

In large companies, independent internal verification is often assigned to internal auditors. **Internal auditors** are employees of the company who evaluate on a continuous basis the effectiveness of the company's system of internal control. They periodically review the activities of departments and individuals to determine whether prescribed internal controls are being followed and to make recommendations for improvement. The importance of this function is illustrated by the number of internal auditors employed by companies. In a recent year, AT&T had 350 internal auditors, Exxon had 395, and IBM had 142.

## ►*T*echnology in *A*ction

Program controls are controls built into the computer to prevent intentional or unintentional errors or unauthorized access. To prevent unauthorized access, the computer system may require that passwords be entered and random personal questions be correctly answered before system access is allowed. Once access has been allowed, other program controls identify data having a value higher or lower than a predetermined amount (limit checks), validate computations (math checks), and detect improper processing order (sequence checks).

A crucial consideration in programming computerized systems is building in controls that limit unauthorized or unintentional tampering. Entire books and movies have been produced with computer system tampering as a major theme. Most programmers would agree that tamper proofing and debugging programs are the most difficult and time-consuming phases of their jobs.

### Other Controls

Other control measures include the following:

1. **Bonding of employees who handle cash.** Bonding involves obtaining insurance protection against misappropriation of assets by dishonest employees. This measure contributes to the safeguarding of cash in two ways: First, the insurance company carefully screens all individuals before adding them to the policy and may reject risky applicants. Second, bonded employees know that the insurance company will vigorously prosecute all offenders.

2. **Rotating employees' duties and requiring employees to take vacations.** These measures are designed to deter employees from attempting any thefts since they will not be able to permanently conceal their improper actions. Many bank embezzlements, for example, have been discovered when the perpetrator has been on vacation or assigned to a new position.

## Limitations of Internal Control

A company's system of internal control is generally designed to provide reasonable assurance that assets are properly safeguarded and that the accounting records are reliable. **The concept of reasonable assurance rests on the premise that the costs of establishing control procedures should not exceed their expected benefit.** To illustrate, consider shoplifting losses in retail stores. Such losses could be completely eliminated by having a security guard stop and search customers as they leave the store. Store managers have concluded, however, that the negative effects of adopting such a procedure cannot be justified. Instead, stores have attempted to "control" shoplifting losses by less costly procedures such as: (1) posting signs saying, "We reserve the right to inspect all packages," and "All shoplifters will be prosecuted," (2) using hidden TV cameras and store detectives to monitor customer activity, and (3) using sensoring equipment at exits.

The **human element** is also an important factor in every system of internal control. A good system can become ineffective as a result of employee fatigue, carelessness, or indifference. For example, a receiving clerk may not bother to count goods received or may just "fudge" the counts. Occasionally, two or more individuals may work together to get around prescribed controls. Such **collusion** can significantly impair the effectiveness of a system, because it eliminates the protection anticipated from segregation of duties. If a supervisor and a cashier collaborate to understate cash receipts, the system of internal control may be negated (at least in the short run). No system of internal control is perfect.

The size of the business may impose limitations on internal control. In a small company, for example, it may be difficult to apply the principles of segregation of duties and independent internal verification.

▶ *Ethics note*

Managements who tolerate weak internal controls invite unethical practices and biased information in financial reports. Examples: cost of sales manipulation due to poor inventory records; ambiguity of expense classifications and arbitrary usage of them.

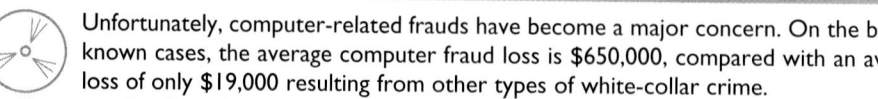

## ▶ Technology in Action

Unfortunately, computer-related frauds have become a major concern. On the basis of known cases, the average computer fraud loss is $650,000, compared with an average loss of only $19,000 resulting from other types of white-collar crime.

Computer fraud can be perpetrated almost invisibly and done with electronic speed. Psychologically, stealing with impersonal computer tools can seem far less criminal. Therefore, the moral threshold to commit computer fraud is far lower than in fraud involving person-to-person contact.

Preventing and detecting computer fraud represents a major challenge. One of the best ways for a company to minimize the likelihood of computer fraud is to have a good system of internal control that allows the benefits of computerization to be gained without opening the possibility for rampant fraud.

## *Before You Go On . . .*

### ► *Review It*

1. What are the two primary objectives of internal control?
2. Identify and describe the principles of internal control.
3. What are the limitations of internal control?

### ► *Do It*

Li Song owns a small retail store. Li wants to establish good internal control procedures but is confused about the difference between segregation of duties and independent internal verification. Explain the differences to Li.

**Reasoning:** In order to help Li, you need to thoroughly understand each principle. From this knowledge, and a study of Illustration 7-1, it should be possible to explain the differences between the two principles.

**Solution:** Segregation of duties pertains to the assignment of responsibility so that the work of one employee will permit the evaluation of the work of another employee. Segregation of duties occurs daily in executing and recording transactions. In contrast, independent internal verification involves reviewing, comparing, and reconciling data prepared by one or several employees. Independent internal verification occurs after the fact, as in the case of reconciling cash register totals at the end of the day with cash on hand.

*Related exercise material:* BE7–1, BE7–2, E7–1, E7–2, and E7–3.

# Cash Controls

Just as cash is the beginning of a company's operating cycle, it is usually the starting point for a company's system of internal control. Cash is the one asset that is readily convertible into any other type of asset; it is easily concealed and transported; and it is highly desired. Because of these characteristics, cash is the asset most susceptible to improper diversion and use. Moreover, because of the large volume of cash transactions, numerous errors may occur in executing and recording cash transactions. To safeguard cash and to assure the accuracy of the accounting records for cash, effective internal control over cash is imperative.

Cash consists of coins, currency (paper money), checks, money orders, and money on hand or on deposit in a bank or similar depository. The general rule is that if the bank will accept it for deposit, it is cash. Items such as postage stamps and postdated checks (checks payable in the future) are not cash. Stamps are a prepaid expense; the postdated checks are accounts receivable. The application of internal control principles to cash receipts and cash disbursements is explained in the following sections.

► **International note**

Other countries also have control problems. For example, a judge in France has issued a 36-page "book" detailing many of the scams that are widespread, such as kickbacks in public-works contracts, the skimming of development aid money to Africa, and bribes on arms sales.

## ►*Accounting in Action* ► *Business Insight*

In 1891 James C. Fargo, president of American Express Co., gave one of his managers a challenge: Devise a piece of paper that will be accepted as money around the world.

Mr. Fargo, just back from a long trip in Europe, was frustrated by cumbersome bank letters of credit and confusing exchange rates. He asked Marcellus Fleming Berry, a manager, to come up with a negotiable instrument secure against loss, theft, counterfeit, fraud, and forgery. Mr. Berry created the "Travelers Cheque," using the British spelling.

The checks were a small sideline for American Express, whose principal business then was forwarding freight. But American Express kept its early lead. In 1891 the company sold checks with a face amount of $9,120, or about $122,000 in today's dollars. Not too long ago, American Express sold a record $22 billion in checks, giving it more than half of what has become a $40-billion-a-year market.

*Source: Wall Street Journal, January 13, 1989.*

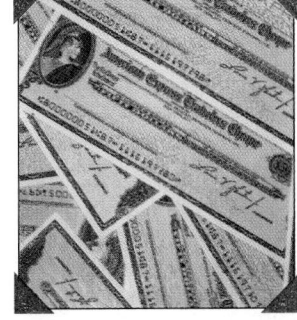

**STUDY OBJECTIVE**
•••••••• **3** ••••••••

*Explain the applications of internal control principles to cash receipts.*

# Internal Control over Cash Receipts

Cash receipts may result from a variety of sources: cash sales; collections on account from customers; the receipt of interest, rents, and dividends; investments by owners; bank loans; and proceeds from the sale of noncurrent assets. The internal control principles explained earlier apply to cash receipts transactions as shown in Illustration 7-4:

**Internal Control over Cash Receipts**

| Establishment of Responsibility | Segregation of Duties | Documentation Procedures | Physical, Mechanical, and Electronic Controls | Independent Internal Verification | Other Controls |
|---|---|---|---|---|---|
| Only designated personnel authorized to handle cash receipts (cashiers) | Different individuals receive cash, record cash receipts, and hold the cash | Use remittance advice (mail receipts), cash register tapes, and deposit slips | Store cash in safes and bank vaults; limit access to storage areas; use cash registers | Supervisors count cash receipts daily; treasurer compares total receipts to bank deposits daily | Bond personnel who handle cash; required vacations; all cash deposited in bank daily |

**Illustration 7-4**

*Application of internal control principles to cash receipts*

As might be expected, companies vary considerably in how they apply these principles. To illustrate internal control over cash receipts, we will examine control measures for a retail store with both over-the-counter and mail receipts.

## Over-the-Counter Receipts

Control of over-the-counter receipts in retail businesses is centered on cash registers that are visible to customers. In supermarkets and variety stores such as Kmart, cash registers are placed in check-out lines near the exit(s). In Sears, Roebuck & Co. and J. C. Penney stores each department has its own cash register. When a cash sale occurs, the sale is "rung up" on a cash register **with the amount clearly visible to the customer**. This measure prevents the cashier from ringing up a lower amount and pocketing the difference. The customer receives an itemized cash register receipt slip and is expected to count the change received. A cash register tape, which is locked into the register until removed by a supervisor or manager, accumulates the daily transactions and totals. When the tape is removed, the supervisor compares the total with the amount of cash in the register. It should show all registered receipts accounted for. The supervisor's findings are reported on a cash count sheet that is signed by both the cashier and supervisor. The cash count sheet used by Alrite Food Mart is shown in Illustration 7-5.

The count sheets, register tapes, and cash are then given to the head cashier. This individual prepares a daily cash summary showing the total cash received and the amount from each source, such as cash sales and collections on account. The head cashier sends one copy of the summary to the accounting department for entry into the cash receipts journal. The other copy goes to the treasurer's office for subsequent comparison with the daily bank deposit. Next, the head cashier prepares a deposit slip (see Illustration 7-9 on page 299) and makes the

**Helpful hint** The cashier registers a cash sale manually by punching the appropriate keys on the register or electronically by using electronic scanning equipment.

▶ *Ethics note*

In terms of cash receipts, most American car dealerships do not have adequate internal controls in parts sales. According to a recent study, this lack of controls can cost the average dealership between $40,000 and $65,000 per year in theft and lost profits.

**Illustration 7-5**

*Cash count sheet*

| Store No. 8 | Date March 8, 1996 |
|---|---|
| 1. Opening cash balance | $ 50.00 |
| 2. Cash sales per tape (attached) | 6,956.20 |
| 3. Total cash to be accounted for | 7,006.20 |
| 4. Cash on hand (see list) | 6,996.10 |
| 5. Cash (short) or over | $ (10.10) |
| 6. Ending cash balance | $ 50.00 |
| 7. Cash for deposit (Line 4 – Line 6) | $6,946.10 |

Cashier *J. Cruse*          Supervisor *M. Braun*

bank deposit. The total amount deposited should be equal to the total receipts on the daily cash summary. This will assure that all receipts have been placed in the custody of the bank. In accepting the bank deposit, the bank stamps (authenticates) the duplicate deposit slip and sends it to the company treasurer, who makes the comparison with the daily cash summary. The foregoing measures for cash sales are graphically presented in Illustration 7-6. The activities of

**Illustration 7-6**

*Executing over-the-counter cash sales*

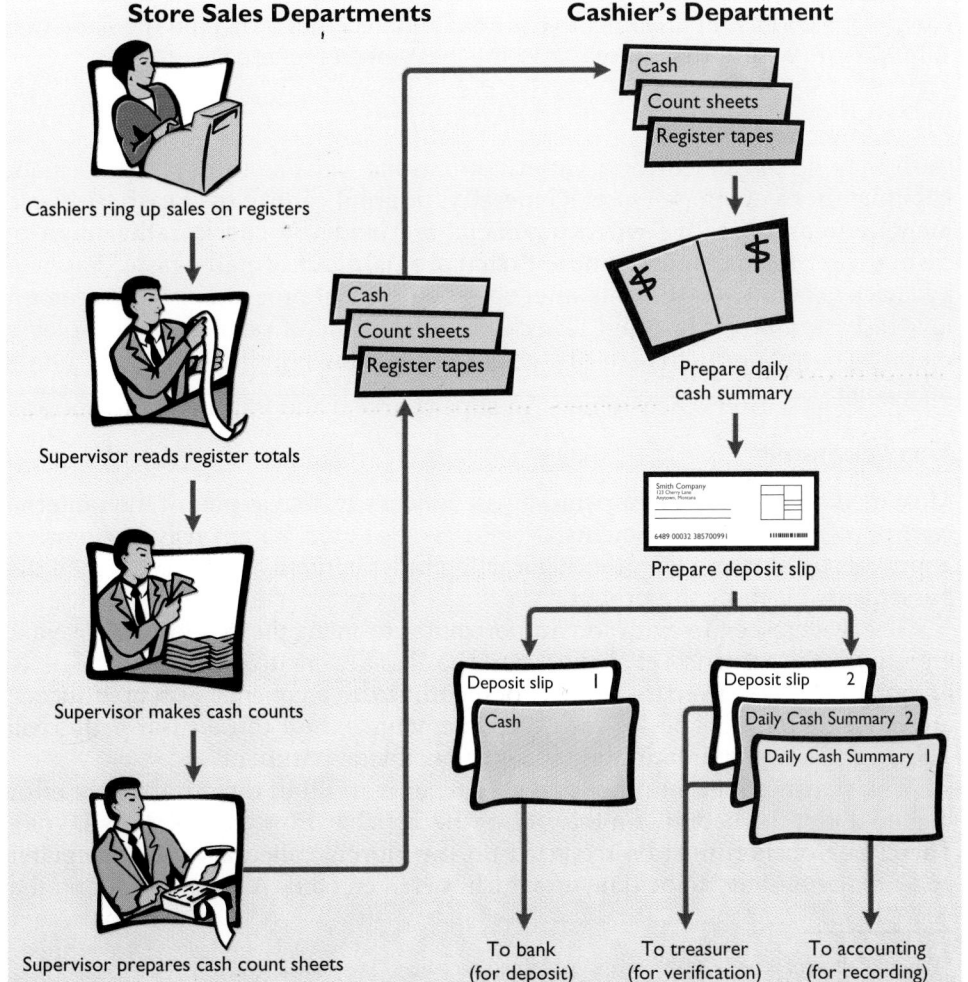

**Store Sales Departments**

Cashiers ring up sales on registers

Supervisor reads register totals

Supervisor makes cash counts

Supervisor prepares cash count sheets

**Cashier's Department**

Cash / Count sheets / Register tapes

Prepare daily cash summary

Prepare deposit slip

Deposit slip 1 / Cash

Deposit slip 2 / Daily Cash Summary 2 / Daily Cash Summary 1

To bank (for deposit)    To treasurer (for verification)    To accounting (for recording)

**Helpful hint** Flowcharts enhance the understanding of the flow of documents, the processing steps, and the internal control procedures.

the sales department are shown separate from those of the cashier's department to indicate the segregation of duties in handling cash.

### Mail Receipts

Because of your experience as an individual customer, you may be more familiar with over-the-counter receipts than with mail receipts. However, mail receipts resulting from billings and credit sales are by far the most common way cash is received by the greatest variety of businesses. Think, for example, of the number of checks received through the mail daily by a national retailer such as Land's End or L.L. Bean.

All mail receipts should be received in the presence of two mail clerks. These receipts are generally in the form of checks or money orders and frequently are accompanied by a remittance advice stating the purpose of the check. Each check should be promptly endorsed "For Deposit Only" by use of a company stamp. This **restrictive endorsement** reduces the likelihood that the check will be diverted to personal use because banks will not give an individual any cash under this type of endorsement.

A list of the checks received each day should be prepared in duplicate showing the name of the issuer of the check, the purpose of the payment, and the amount of the check. Each mail clerk should sign the list to establish responsibility for the data. The original copy of the list, along with the checks and remittance advices, are then sent to the cashier's department, where they are added to over-the-counter receipts (if any) in preparing the daily cash summary and in making the daily bank deposit. In addition, a copy of the list is sent to the treasurer's office for comparison with the total mail receipts shown on the daily cash summary, to assure that all mail receipts have been included.

## Internal Control over Cash Disbursements

**STUDY OBJECTIVE**
•••••••••◀ 4 ▶•••••••••
*Describe the applications of internal control principles to cash disbursements.*

Cash may be disbursed for a variety of reasons, such as to pay expenses and liabilities, or to purchase assets. **Generally, internal control over cash disbursements is more effective when payments are made by check, rather than by cash, except for incidental amounts that are paid out of petty cash.**[2] Payment by check generally occurs only after specified control procedures have been followed. In addition, the "paid" check provides proof of payment. Principles of internal control apply to cash disbursements as shown in Illustration 7-7 on the next page.

### Voucher System

Most medium and large companies use a voucher system as part of their internal control over cash disbursements. A voucher system is an extensive network of approvals by authorized individuals acting independently to ensure that all disbursements by check are proper.

The system begins with the authorization to incur the cost or expense and ends with the issuance of a check for the liability incurred. A voucher is an authorization form prepared for each expenditure in a voucher system. Vouchers are required for all types of cash disbursements except those from petty cash. The voucher is prepared in the accounts payable department.

The starting point in preparing a voucher is to fill in the appropriate information about the liability on the face of the voucher from the vendor's invoice. Then, the voucher must be recorded (in the journal called a **voucher register**) and filed according to the date on which it is to be paid. A check is sent on that

---

[2]The operation of a petty cash fund is explained on pages 296–98.

**Internal Control over Cash Disbursements**

| Establishment of Responsibility | Segregation of Duties | Documentation Procedures | Physical, Mechanical, and Electronic Controls | Independent Internal Verification | Other Controls |
|---|---|---|---|---|---|
| Only designated personnel authorized to sign checks (treasurer) | Different individuals approve and make payments; check signers do not record disbursements | Use prenumbered checks and account for them in sequence; each check must have approved invoice | Store blank checks in safes, with limited access; print check amounts by machine in indelible ink | Compare checks to invoices; reconcile bank statement monthly | Stamp invoices PAID |

date, the voucher is stamped "paid," and the paid voucher is sent to the accounting department for recording (in a journal called the **check register**).

### Electronic Funds Transfer (EFT) System

To account for and control cash is an expensive and time-consuming process. For example, it was estimated recently that the cost to process a check through a bank system ranges from $0.55 to $1.00 and is increasing. It is not surprising, therefore, that new approaches are being developed to transfer funds among parties without the use of paper (deposit tickets, checks, etc.). Such a procedure is called an electronic funds transfer (EFT). EFT is a disbursement system that uses wire, telephone, telegraph, or computer to transfer cash from one location to another. Use of EFT is quite common. For example, the authors receive no formal payroll checks from their universities, which simply send magnetic tapes to the appropriate banks for deposit. Regular payments such as those for house, car, or utilities are frequently made by EFT.

## ►Technology in Action

The development of EFT will continue. Already it is estimated that 80% of the total volume of bank transactions in the United States is performed using EFT. The computer technology is available to create a "checkless" society. The only major barriers appear to be the individual's concern for privacy and protection and certain legislative constraints. It should be noted that numerous safeguards have been built into EFT systems. However, the possibility of errors and fraud still exists because only a limited number of individuals are involved in the transfers, which may prevent appropriate segregation of duties.

### Petty Cash Fund

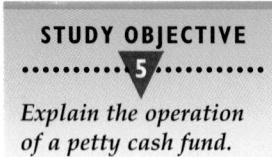

**STUDY OBJECTIVE**

⋯⋯⋯⋯ **5** ⋯⋯⋯⋯

*Explain the operation of a petty cash fund.*

As you learned earlier in the chapter, better internal control over cash disbursements is possible when payments are made by check. However, using checks to pay such small amounts as those for postage due, employee lunches, and taxi fares is both impractical and a nuisance. A common way of handling such payments, while maintaining satisfactory control, is to use a petty cash fund. A **petty cash fund** is a cash fund used to pay relatively small amounts. The operation of a petty cash fund, often called an **imprest system**, involves (1) establishing the fund, (2) making payments from the fund, and (3) replenishing the fund.[3]

**Establishing the Fund.**    Two essential steps in establishing a petty cash fund are (1) appointing a petty cash custodian who will be responsible for the fund and (2) determining the size of the fund. Ordinarily, the amount is expected to cover anticipated disbursements for a 3- to 4-week period. When the fund is established, a check payable to the petty cash custodian is issued for the stipulated amount. If the Laird Company decides to establish a $100 fund on March 1, the entry in general journal form is:

| Mar. 1 | Petty Cash | 100.00 | |
|---|---|---|---|
| |     Cash | | 100.00 |
| |      (To establish a petty cash fund) | | |

The check is then cashed and the proceeds are placed in a locked petty cash box or drawer. Most petty cash funds are established on a fixed amount basis. Moreover, no additional entries will be made to the Petty Cash account unless the stipulated amount of the fund is changed. For example, if Laird Company decides on July 1 to increase the size of the fund to $250, it would debit Petty Cash $150 and credit Cash $150.

**Making Payments from the Fund.**    The custodian of the petty cash fund has the authority to make payments from the fund that conform to prescribed management policies. Usually, management limits the size of expenditures that may be made and does not permit use of the fund for certain types of transactions (such as making short-term loans to employees). Each payment from the fund must be documented on a prenumbered petty cash receipt (or petty cash voucher), as shown in Illustration 7-8. Note that the signatures of both the cus-

**Illustration 7-8**

*Petty cash receipt*

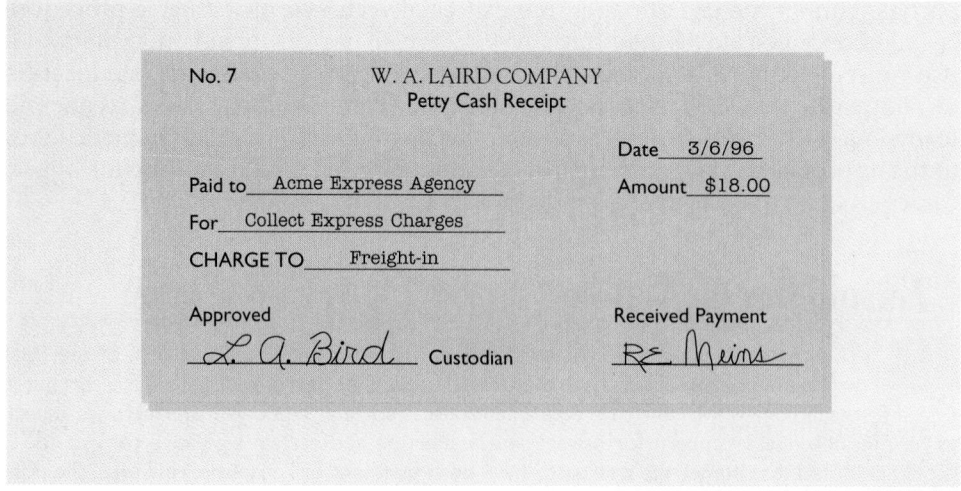

---

[3]The term "imprest" means an advance of money for a designated purpose.

todian and the individual receiving payment are required on the receipt. If other supporting documents such as a freight bill or invoice are available, they should be attached to the petty cash receipt.

The receipts are kept in the petty cash box until the fund is replenished. As a result, the sum of the petty cash receipts and money in the fund should equal the established total at all times. This means that surprise counts can be made at any time by an independent person, such as an internal auditor, to determine whether the fund is being maintained intact.

No accounting entry is made to record a payment at the time it is made from petty cash. It is considered to be both inexpedient and unnecessary to do so. Instead, the accounting effects of each payment are recognized when the fund is replenished.

**Replenishing the Fund.**   When the money in the petty cash fund reaches a minimum level, the fund is replenished. The request for reimbursement is initiated by the petty cash custodian. This individual prepares a schedule (or summary) of the payments that have been made and sends the schedule, supported by petty cash receipts and other documentation, to the treasurer's office. The receipts and supporting documents are examined in the treasurer's office to verify that they were proper payments from the fund. The treasurer then approves the request and a check is prepared to restore the fund to its established amount. At the same time, all supporting documentation is stamped "paid" so that it cannot be submitted again for payment.

To illustrate, assume that on March 15 the petty cash custodian requests a check for $87. The fund contains $13 cash and petty cash receipts for postage $44, freight-in $38, and miscellaneous expenses $5. The entry, in general journal form, to record the check is:

| Mar. 15 | Postage Expense | 44 | |
| | Freight-in | 38 | |
| | Miscellaneous Expense | 5 | |
| | Cash | | 87 |
| | (To replenish petty cash fund) | | |

Note that the Petty Cash account is not affected by the reimbursement entry. Replenishment changes the composition of the fund by replacing the petty cash receipts with cash, but it does not change the balance in the fund.

It may be necessary in replenishing a petty cash fund to recognize a cash shortage or overage. To illustrate, assume in the example above that the custodian had only $12 in cash in the fund plus the receipts as listed. The request for reimbursement would, therefore, have been for $88, and the following entry would be made:

| Mar. 15 | Postage Expense | 44 | |
| | Freight-in | 38 | |
| | Miscellaneous Expense | 5 | |
| | Cash Over and Short | 1 | |
| | Cash | | 88 |
| | (To replenish petty cash fund) | | |

Conversely, if the custodian had $14 in cash, the reimbursement request would have been for $86 and Cash Over and Short would have been credited for $1. A debit balance in Cash Over and Short is reported in the income statement as miscellaneous expense; a credit balance is reported as miscellaneous revenue. Cash Over and Short is closed to Income Summary at the end of the year.

A petty cash fund should be replenished at the end of the accounting period regardless of the cash in the fund. Replenishment at this time is necessary in order to recognize the effects of the petty cash payments on the financial statements.

Internal control over a petty cash fund is strengthened by (1) having a supervisor make surprise counts of the fund to ascertain whether the paid vouchers and fund cash equal the imprest amount and (2) canceling or mutilating the paid vouchers so they cannot be resubmitted for reimbursement.

## *Before You Go On . . .*

### ▶ *Review It*

1. How do the principles of internal control apply to cash receipts?
2. How do the principles of internal control apply to cash disbursements?
3. When are entries required in a petty cash system?

### ▶ *Do It*

L. R. Cortez is concerned about the control over cash receipts in his fast-food restaurant, Big Cheese. The restaurant has two cash registers. At no time do more than two employees take customer orders and ring up sales. Work shifts for employees range from 4 to 8 hours. Cortez asks your help in installing a good system of internal control over cash receipts.

*Reasoning:* Cortez needs to understand the principles of internal control, especially the principles of establishing responsibility, the use of electronic controls, and independent internal verification. Using this knowledge, an effective system of control over cash receipts can be designed and implemented.

*Solution:* Cortez should assign a cash register to each employee at the start of each work shift, with register totals set at zero. Each employee should be instructed to use only the assigned register and to ring up all sales. At the end of each work shift, Cortez or a supervisor/manager should total the register and make a cash count to see whether all cash is accounted for.

*Related exercise material:* BE7–3 and E7–2.

## Use of a Bank

**STUDY OBJECTIVE**

········▼**6**·········

*Indicate the control features of a bank account.*

**The use of a bank contributes significantly to good internal control over cash.** A company can safeguard its cash by using a bank as a depository and clearing house for checks received and checks written. Use of a bank minimizes the amount of currency that must be kept on hand. In addition, the use of a bank facilitates the control of cash because a double record is maintained of all bank transactions—one by the business and the other by the bank. The asset account, Cash, maintained by the depositor is the reciprocal of the bank's liability account for each depositor. It should be possible to **reconcile these accounts** (make them agree) at any time.

Opening a bank checking account is a relatively simple procedure. Typically, the bank makes a credit check on the new customer and the depositor is required to sign a **signature card**. The card should contain the signatures of each person authorized to sign checks on the account. The signature card is used by bank employees to validate signatures on the checks.

As soon as possible after an account is opened, the bank will provide the depositor with a book of serially numbered checks and deposit slips imprinted

## ▲Technology in Action

The first big consumer business on the information highway is shaping up as a set of financial household chores: balancing the checkbook, paying bills, and saving for retirement. Several major U.S. banks now offer electronic home banking. For customers, the new capabilities mean more convenient service, more up-to-date information about their finances, and more control over their money. Several hundred thousand households now do a substantial amount of their money management electronically from home, and this number is expected to increase significantly.

with the depositor's name and address. Each check and deposit slip is imprinted with both a bank and a depositor identification number in magnetic ink to permit computer processing of the transaction.

Many companies have more than one bank account. For efficiency of operations and better control, national retailers like Wal-Mart Stores and Kmart may have regional bank accounts. Similarly, a company such as Exxon with more than 150,000 employees may have a payroll bank account, as well as one or more general bank accounts. In addition, a company may maintain several bank accounts in order to have more than one source for obtaining short-term loans when needed.

### Making Bank Deposits

Bank deposits should be made by an authorized employee, such as the head cashier. Each deposit must be documented by a deposit slip (ticket), as shown in Illustration 7-9.

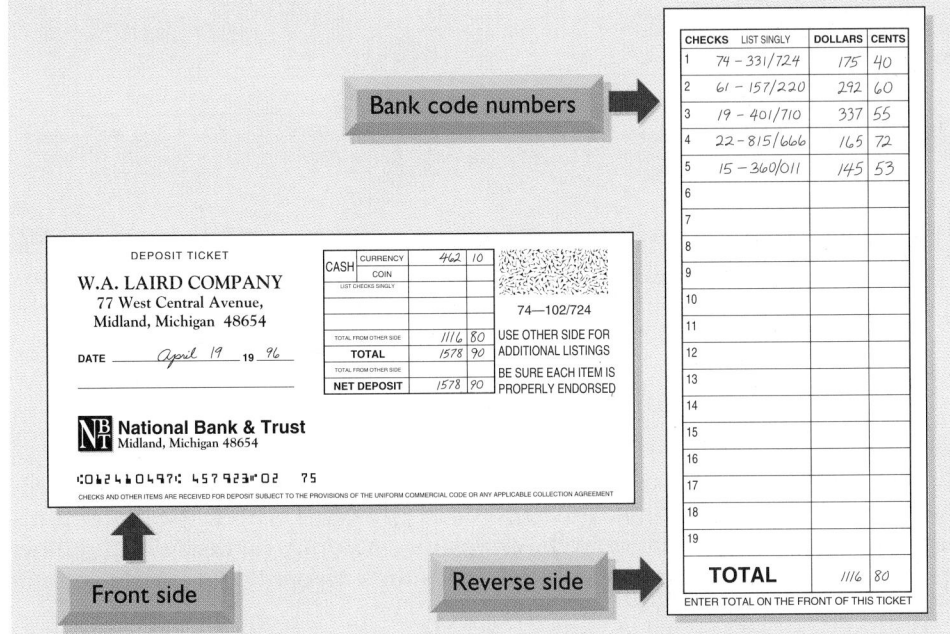

**Illustration 7-9**

*Deposit slip*

Deposit slips are prepared in duplicate. The original is retained by the bank; the duplicate, machine stamped by the bank to establish its authenticity, is retained by the depositor.

## Writing Checks

A check is a written order signed by the depositor directing the bank to pay a specified sum of money to a designated recipient. Thus, there are three parties to a check: the **maker** (or drawer) who issues the check, the **bank** (or payer) on which the check is drawn, and the **payee** to whom the check is payable. A check is a negotiable instrument that can be transferred to another party by endorsement. Each check should be accompanied by an explanation of its purposes. In many businesses, this is done by attaching a remittance advice to the check, as shown in Illustration 7-10.

**Illustration 7-10**

*Check with remittance advice*

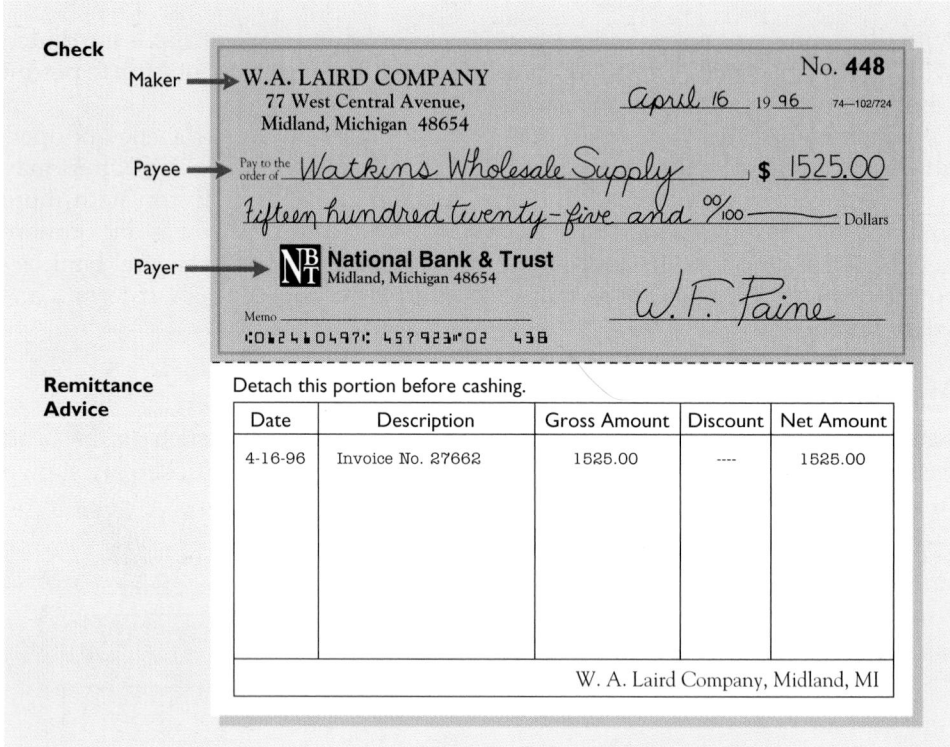

For both individuals and businesses, it is important to know the balance in the checking account at all times. To keep the balance current, each deposit and check should be entered on running balance memorandum forms provided by the bank or on the check stubs contained in the checkbook.

## Bank Statements

**Helpful hint**  Essentially, the bank statement is a copy of the bank's records sent to the customer for periodic review.

Each month, the depositor receives a bank statement from the bank. A bank statement shows the depositor's bank transactions and balances. For example, the statement, like the one in Illustration 7-11, shows (1) checks paid and other debits that reduce the balance in the depositor's account, (2) deposits and other credits that increase the balance in the depositor's account, and (3) the account balance after each day's transactions.

Most banks offer depositors the option of receiving "paid" checks with their bank statements. For those who decline, the bank keeps a record of each check on microfilm. Irrespective of the depositor's choice, all "paid" checks are listed in numerical sequence on the bank statement along with the date the check was paid and its amount. Upon paying a check, the bank stamps the check "paid"; a paid check is sometimes referred to as a **canceled** check. In addition, the bank

Illustration 7-11

*Bank statement*

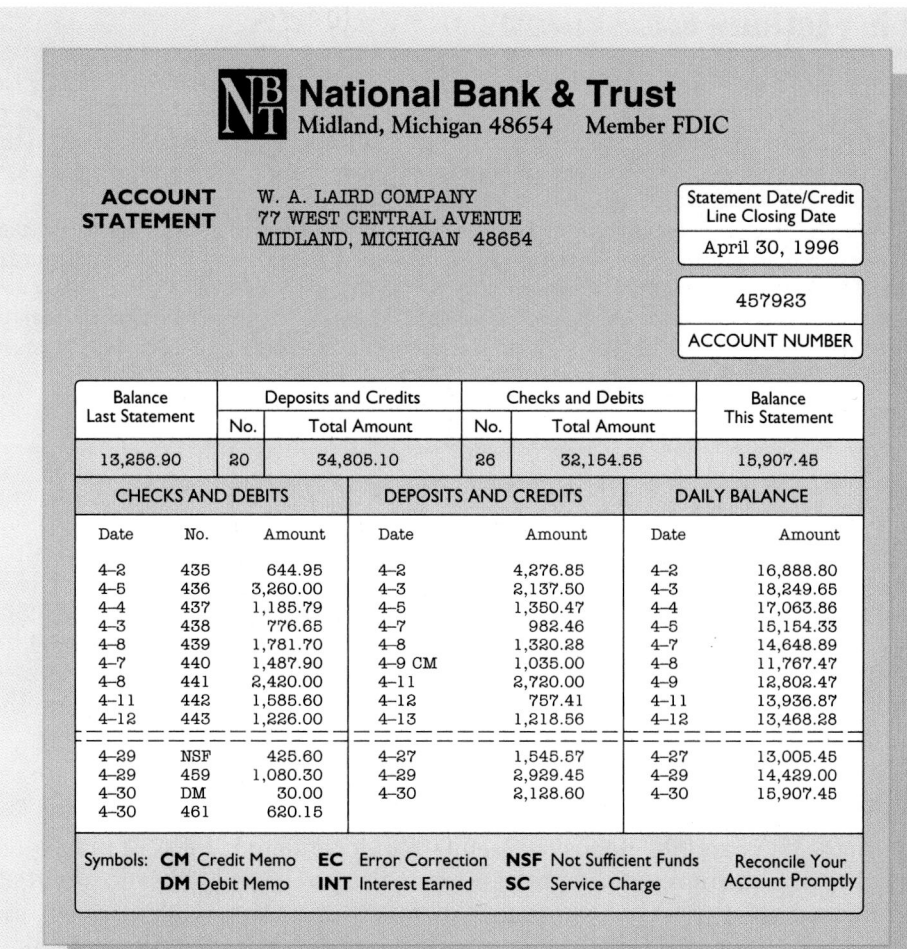

**National Bank & Trust**
Midland, Michigan 48654    Member FDIC

ACCOUNT
STATEMENT

W. A. LAIRD COMPANY
77 WEST CENTRAL AVENUE
MIDLAND, MICHIGAN  48654

Statement Date/Credit
Line Closing Date

April 30, 1996

457923

ACCOUNT NUMBER

| Balance Last Statement | Deposits and Credits | | Checks and Debits | | Balance This Statement |
|---|---|---|---|---|---|
| | No. | Total Amount | No. | Total Amount | |
| 13,256.90 | 20 | 34,805.10 | 26 | 32,154.55 | 15,907.45 |

| CHECKS AND DEBITS | | | DEPOSITS AND CREDITS | | DAILY BALANCE | |
|---|---|---|---|---|---|---|
| Date | No. | Amount | Date | Amount | Date | Amount |
| 4-2 | 435 | 644.95 | 4-2 | 4,276.85 | 4-2 | 16,888.80 |
| 4-5 | 436 | 3,260.00 | 4-3 | 2,137.50 | 4-3 | 18,249.65 |
| 4-4 | 437 | 1,185.79 | 4-5 | 1,350.47 | 4-4 | 17,063.86 |
| 4-3 | 438 | 776.65 | 4-7 | 982.46 | 4-5 | 15,154.33 |
| 4-8 | 439 | 1,781.70 | 4-8 | 1,320.28 | 4-7 | 14,648.89 |
| 4-7 | 440 | 1,487.90 | 4-9 CM | 1,035.00 | 4-8 | 11,767.47 |
| 4-8 | 441 | 2,420.00 | 4-11 | 2,720.00 | 4-9 | 12,802.47 |
| 4-11 | 442 | 1,585.60 | 4-12 | 757.41 | 4-11 | 13,936.87 |
| 4-12 | 443 | 1,226.00 | 4-13 | 1,218.56 | 4-12 | 13,468.28 |
| 4-29 | NSF | 425.60 | 4-27 | 1,545.57 | 4-27 | 13,005.45 |
| 4-29 | 459 | 1,080.30 | 4-29 | 2,929.45 | 4-29 | 14,429.00 |
| 4-30 | DM | 30.00 | 4-30 | 2,128.60 | 4-30 | 15,907.45 |
| 4-30 | 461 | 620.15 | | | | |

Symbols: **CM** Credit Memo    **EC** Error Correction    **NSF** Not Sufficient Funds    Reconcile Your Account Promptly
**DM** Debit Memo    **INT** Interest Earned    **SC** Service Charge

includes with the bank statement memoranda explaining other debits and credits made by the bank to the depositor's account.

### Debit Memorandum

Banks charge a monthly fee for the use of their services. Often the fee is charged only when the average monthly balance in a checking account falls below a specified amount. The fee, called a bank service charge, is often identified on the bank statement by a code symbol such as SC. A debit memorandum explaining the charge is included with the bank statement. Separate debit memoranda may also be issued for other bank services such as the cost of printing checks, issuing traveler's checks, and wiring funds to other locations. The symbol DM is often used for such charges.

A debit memorandum is used by the bank when a previously deposited customer's check "bounces" because of insufficient funds. In such a case, the check is marked NSF (not sufficient funds) by the customer's bank and is returned to the depositor's bank. The bank then debits the depositor's account, as shown by the symbol NSF on the bank statement in Illustration 7-11, and sends the NSF check and debit memorandum to the depositor as notification of the charge. The NSF check creates an accounts receivable for the depositor and reduces cash in the bank account.

## ▶Accounting in Action ▸ *Business Insight*

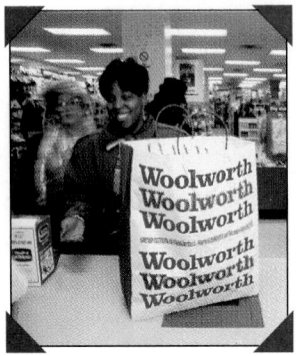

As copying machines have become ever more sophisticated, check counterfeiting has flourished. For example, in the second quarter of a recent fiscal year, the Woolworth Corporation had a $5 million loss from bad checks. Most of the total occurred in the Foot Locker division of the company, a spokesperson said. In the U.S. business community as a whole, some $10 billion worth of bad checks are written every year.

Checkmate Electronic Inc. thinks it has at least a partial answer to this problem. It makes electronic devices that read the magnetic ink used to print account and routing numbers on checks. By identifying the magnetic frequencies as well as the precise shape and size of the numbers, the machine can determine if a check is a fake. Checkmate has a machine small enough to be installed beside cash registers, and it is now in use by such retailers as J.C. Penney, Neiman-Marcus, and Pier 1 Imports.

*Source: Wall Street Journal*, March 31, 1994, p. C2; and *Business Week*, May 23, 1994, p. 9.

### *Credit Memorandum*

A depositor may ask the bank to collect its notes receivable. In such a case, the bank will credit the depositor's account for the cash proceeds of the note, as illustrated on the bank statement by the symbol CM. It will issue a credit memorandum which is sent with the statement to explain the entry. Many banks also offer interest on checking accounts. The interest earned may be indicated on the bank statement by the symbol CM or INT.

## Reconciling the Bank Account

**STUDY OBJECTIVE**

•••••••••**7**••••••••••

*Prepare a bank reconciliation.*

Because the bank and the depositor maintain independent records of the depositor's checking account, you might assume that the respective balances will always agree. In fact, the two balances are seldom the same at any given time, and it is necessary to make the balance per books agree with the balance per bank—a process called **reconciling the bank account**. The lack of agreement between the two balances is due to:

1. **Time lags** that prevent one of the parties from recording the transaction in the same period.
2. **Errors** by either party in recording transactions.

Time lags occur frequently. For example, several days may elapse between the time a check is mailed to a payee and the date the check is paid by the bank.

## ▶Accounting in Action ▸ *Ethics Insight*

Some firms have used time lags to their advantage. For example, E. F. Hutton managers at one time overdrew their accounts by astronomical amounts—on some days the overdrafts totaled $1 billion—creating interest-free loans they could invest. The loans lasted as long as it took for the covering checks to be collected. Although not technically illegal at the time, Hutton's actions were wrong because it did not have bank permission to do so.

Similarly, when the depositor uses the bank's night depository to make its deposits, there will be a difference of one day between the time the receipts are recorded by the depositor and the time they are recorded by the bank. A time lag also occurs whenever the bank mails a debit or credit memorandum to the depositor.

# ►Technology in Action

A malfunctioning computer software program doubled all withdrawals and transfers made at Chemical Bank automatic teller machines (ATMs) in New York state for about 12 hours. The printed record of transactions spit out by the ATM was accurate, but the computerized posting of the transactions was automatically doubled. The bank corrected all errors, which in the aggregate may have been $15 million.

*Source: Denver Post,* February 19, 1994.

The incidence of errors depends on the effectiveness of the internal controls maintained by the depositor and the bank. Bank errors are infrequent. However, either party could inadvertently record a $450 check as $45 or $540. In addition, the bank might mistakenly charge a check drawn by C. D. Berg to the account of C. D. Burg.

## *Reconciliation Procedure*

**To obtain maximum benefit from a bank reconciliation, the reconciliation should be prepared by an employee who has no other responsibilities pertaining to cash.** When the internal control principle of independent internal verification is not followed in preparing the reconciliation, cash embezzlements may escape unnoticed. For example, a cashier who prepares the reconciliation can embezzle cash and conceal the embezzlement by misstating the reconciliation. Thus, the bank accounts would reconcile and the embezzlement would not be detected.

In reconciling the bank account, it is customary to reconcile the balance per books and balance per bank to their adjusted (correct or true) cash balances. The reconciliation schedule is divided into two sections, as shown in Illustration 7-12. The starting point in preparing the reconciliation is to enter the balance per bank statement and balance per books on the schedule. The following steps should reveal all the reconciling items that cause the difference between the two balances.

1. Compare the individual deposits on the bank statement with deposits in transit from the preceding bank reconciliation and with the deposits per company records or copies of duplicate deposit slips. Deposits recorded by the depositor that have not been recorded by the bank represent deposits in transit and are added to the balance per bank.

   **Helpful hint** Deposits in transit and outstanding checks are reconciling items because of time lags.

2. Compare the paid checks shown on the bank statement or the paid checks returned with the bank statement with (a) checks outstanding from the preceding bank reconciliation and (b) checks issued by the company as recorded in the cash payments journal. Issued checks recorded by the company that have not been paid by the bank represent outstanding checks that are deducted from the balance per the bank.

3. Note any **errors** discovered in the foregoing steps and list them in the appropriate section of the reconciliation schedule. For example, if a paid check correctly written by the company for $195 was mistakenly recorded by the company for $159, the error of $36 is deducted from the balance per books. All errors made by the depositor are reconciling items in determining the adjusted cash balance per books. In contrast, all errors made by the bank are reconciling items in determining the adjusted cash balance per the bank.

4. Trace **bank memoranda** to the depositor's records. Any unrecorded memoranda should be listed in the appropriate section of the reconciliation schedule. For example, a $5 debit memorandum for bank service charges is deducted from the balance per books, and $32 of interest earned is added to the balance per books.

### Bank Reconciliation Illustrated

The bank statement for the Laird Company is shown in Illustration 7-11. It shows a balance per bank of $15,907.45 on April 30, 1996. On this date the balance of cash per books is $11,589.45. From the foregoing steps, the following reconciling items are determined.

|   |   |
|---|---:|
| 1. **Deposits in transit:** April 30 deposit (received by bank on May 1). | $2,201.40 |
| 2. **Outstanding checks:** No. 453 $3,000.00; No. 457 $1,401.30; No. 460 $1,502.70. | 5,904.00 |
| 3. **Errors:** Check No. 443 was correctly written by Laird for $1,226.00 and was correctly paid by the bank. However, it was recorded for $1,262.00 by Laird Company. | 36.00 |
| 4. **Bank memoranda:** | |
|     **a.** Debit—NSF check from J. R. Baron for $425.60 | 425.60 |
|     **b.** Debit—Printing company checks charge, $30.00 | 30.00 |
|     **c.** Credit—Collection of note receivable for $1,000 plus interest earned $50, less bank collection fee $15.00 | 1,035.00 |

*Helpful hint* Note in the bank statement that checks No. 459 and 461 have been paid but check No. 460 is not listed. Thus, this check is outstanding. If a complete bank statement were provided, checks No. 453 and 457 would also not be listed. The amounts for these three checks are obtained from the company's cash payments records.

The bank reconciliation is as follows:

**Illustration 7-12**

*Bank reconciliation*

*Helpful hint* The terms *adjusted balance*, *true cash balance*, and *correct cash balance* may be used interchangeably.

| LAIRD COMPANY<br>Bank Reconciliation<br>April 30, 1996 | | |
|---|---:|---:|
| Cash balance per bank statement | | $15,907.45 |
| Add: Deposits in transit | | 2,201.40 |
| | | 18,108.85 |
| Less: Outstanding checks | | |
|     No. 453 | $3,000.00 | |
|     No. 457 | 1,401.30 | |
|     No. 460 | 1,502.70 | 5,904.00 |
| Adjusted cash balance per bank | | $12,204.85 |
| Cash balance per books | | $11,589.45 |
| Add: Collection of note receivable, $1,000 plus interest | | |
|       earned $50, less collection fee $15 | $1,035.00 | |
|     Error in recording check No. 443 | 36.00 | 1,071.00 |
| | | 12,660.45 |
| Less: NSF check | 425.60 | |
|     Bank service charge | 30.00 | 455.60 |
| Adjusted cash balance per books | | $12,204.85 |

## ▸Accounting in Action ▸ *Business Insight*

Imagine reconciling a bank statement when you have an employee like Billie Hurst. She worked as a librarian at Southwest Missouri State University for 30 years, yet she never got around to cashing paychecks totaling more than $100,000 because she didn't need the money.

The 72-year-old woman got the money anyway when State Treasurer Wendell Bailey presented an $88,100.85 check to Hurst's cousin and guardian, Frances Jane Gleghorn, after a special act of the Legislature made it possible to pay checks more than 5 years old.

Bailey's office said it already had re-issued checks amounting to $20,024.53 for uncashed checks not more than 5 years old, bringing the total reimbursement to $108,125.38.

Hurst occasionally cashed a paycheck, Gleghorn said, but co-workers tried for years to get her to cash the rest of the checks.

*Source: Bay City Times, March 24, 1989.*

### Entries from Bank Reconciliation

Each reconciling item in determining the **adjusted cash balance per books** should be recorded by the depositor. If these items are not journalized and posted, the Cash account will not show the correct balance. The entries for the Laird Company on April 30 are as follows:

**Collection of Note Receivable.** This entry involves four accounts. Assuming that the interest of $50 has not been accrued and the collection fee is charged to Miscellaneous Expense, the entry is:

| | | | |
|---|---|---|---|
| Apr. 30 | Cash | 1,035.00 | |
| | Miscellaneous Expense | 15.00 | |
| | Notes Receivable | | 1,000.00 |
| | Interest Revenue | | 50.00 |
| | (To record collection of notes receivable by bank) | | |

**Helpful hint** These entries are adjusting entries. In prior chapters, Cash was an account that did not require adjustment because a bank reconciliation had not been explained.

**Book Error.** An examination of the cash disbursements journal shows that check No. 443 was a payment on account to Andrea Company, a supplier. The correcting entry is:

| | | | |
|---|---|---|---|
| Apr. 30 | Cash | 36.00 | |
| | Accounts Payable—Andrea Company | | 36.00 |
| | (To correct error in recording check No. 443) | | |

**NSF Check.** As indicated earlier, an NSF check becomes an accounts receivable to the depositor. The entry is:

| | | | |
|---|---|---|---|
| Apr. 30 | Accounts Receivable—J. R. Baron | 425.60 | |
| | Cash | | 425.60 |
| | (To record NSF check) | | |

**Bank Service Charges.** Check printing charges (DM) and other bank service charges (SC) are debited to Miscellaneous Expense because they are usually nominal in amount. The entry is:

| | | | |
|---|---|---|---|
| Apr. 30 | Miscellaneous Expense | 30.00 | |
| | Cash | | 30.00 |
| | (To record charge for printing company checks) | | |

The foregoing entries could also be combined into one compound entry. After the entries are posted, the cash account will show the following:

**Illustration 7-13**

*Adjusted balance in cash account*

| Cash | | | | |
|---|---|---|---|---|
| Apr. 30  Bal. | 11,589.45 | Apr. 30 | | 425.60 |
| 30 | 1,035.00 | | | 30.00 |
| 30 | 36.00 | | | |
| Apr. 30  Bal. | 12,204.85 | | | |

The adjusted cash balance in the ledger should agree with the adjusted cash balance per books in the bank reconciliation in Illustration 7-12.

What entries does the bank make? If any bank errors are discovered in preparing the reconciliation, the bank should be notified so it can make the necessary corrections on its records. The bank does not make any entries for deposits in transit or outstanding checks. Only when these items reach the bank will the bank record these items.

## Before You Go On . . .

### ▶ Review It

1. Why is it necessary to reconcile a bank account?
2. What steps are involved in the reconciliation procedure?
3. What information is included in a bank reconciliation?

### ▶ Do It

Sally Kist owns Linen Kist Fabrics. Sally asks you to explain how the following reconciling items should be treated in reconciling the bank account at December 31: (1) a debit memorandum for an NSF check, (2) a credit memorandum for a note collected by the bank, (3) outstanding checks, and (4) a deposit in transit.

**Reasoning:** Sally needs to understand that one cause of a reconciling item is time lags. Items (1) and (2) are reconciling items because Linen Kist Fabrics has not yet recorded the memoranda. Items (3) and (4) are reconciling items because the bank has not recorded the transactions.

**Solution:** In reconciling the bank account, the reconciling items are treated as follows:

NSF check: Deducted from balance per books.
Collection of note: Added to balance per books.
Outstanding checks: Deducted from balance per bank.
Deposit in transit: Added to balance per bank.

*Related exercise material: BE7–6, BE7–7, BE7–8, BE7–9, E7–7, E7–8, E7–9, and E7–10.*

# Reporting Cash

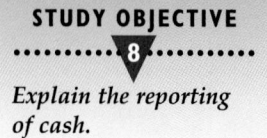

**STUDY OBJECTIVE**

•••••••••**8**•••••••••

*Explain the reporting of cash.*

Cash on hand, cash in banks, and petty cash are often combined and reported simply as **Cash**. Because it is the most liquid asset owned by a company, cash is listed first in the current asset section of the balance sheet. Some companies use the designation "cash and cash equivalents" in reporting cash as illustrated by the following:

**Illustration 7-14**

*Presentation of cash and cash equivalents*

| **EASTMAN KODAK COMPANY** | | |
|---|---|---|
| | 1994 | 1993 |
| Current assets (in millions) | | |
| Cash and cash equivalents | $2,020 | $1,635 |

Cash equivalents are highly liquid investments, with maturities of 3 months or less when purchased, that can be converted into a specific amount of cash. They include money market funds, money market savings certificates, bank certificates of deposit, and U.S. Treasury bills and notes.

A company may have cash that is restricted for a special purpose. Examples include a payroll bank account for paying salaries and wages, and plant expansion fund cash for financing new construction. If the restricted cash is expected to be used within the next year, the amount should be reported as a current asset. However, when this is not the case, the restricted funds should be reported as a noncurrent asset. Since a payroll bank account will be used as early as the next payday for employees, it is reported as a current asset. In contrast, unless the new construction will begin within the next year, plant expansion fund cash is classified as a noncurrent asset.

In making loans to depositors, it is common for banks to require the borrowers to maintain minimum cash balances. These minimum balances, called compensating balances, provide the bank with support for the loans. Compensating balances are a restriction on the use of cash that may affect a company's liquidity. Accordingly, compensating balances should be disclosed in the financial statements.

## *Before You Go On . . .*

### ▶ *Review It*

1. What is generally reported as cash on a company's balance sheet?
2. What is meant by cash equivalents and compensating balances?

### ▶ *A Look Back at Columbia University*
• • • • • • • • • • • • • • • • • • • • • • • • • • • • • • • • • • • • • • • • • • • • • •

Refer to the opening story about Columbia University, and answer the following questions:

1. Does Susan McLaughlin have a valid basis for establishing responsibility for overages or shortages? Why or why not?
2. What internal control principles are applicable to reconciling cash register tapes and the amount of cash in the cash drawer at the end of the day?
3. What internal control principle is involved in seeing that a student gets a receipt when buying a meal at a register? How does this requirement contribute to good internal control?
4. Do you think the cashiers are, or should be, bonded?

*Solution*

1. Establishing responsibility for overages or shortages is made only at the end of the day. This will provide a valid basis for evaluation only if one person worked the register for the entire day. If more than one person works the register during the day, the single count will not provide a valid basis for establishing who is responsible for the overage or shortage.
2. Applicable internal control principles are: (a) Segregation of duties—the cashier(s) should not be involved in performing the reconciliation. (b) Documentation proce-

dures—the cash register tape provides the documentation for total receipts for the day. (c) Independent internal verification—a supervisor should perform the reconciliation.

3. The internal control principle of documentation procedures is involved. The control does not reside in the receipt itself. For example, there will not be any subsequent reconciliation of cash register receipts with cash at the end of the day. The control is forcing the cashier to ring up each sale so that a receipt is produced. Each receipt is recorded on the cash register tape. At the end of the day, the tape is used in determining overages or shortages.

4. If the dining facility has nonstudent employees who work as cashiers, they may be bonded. However, if students work part-time as cashiers, it is doubtful that they are bonded. From the employer's standpoint, bonding is protection against major embezzlements. The risk of this occurring with student help is relatively low.

# ▼ Summary of Study Objectives

•••••••••••••••••••••••••••••••••••••••••••••••••••••••••••••••••••••••••••••••••••••

**1.** *Define internal control.* Internal control is the plan of organization and related methods and procedures adopted within a business to safeguard its assets and to enhance the accuracy and reliability of its accounting records.

**2.** *Identify the principles of internal control.* The principles of internal control are: establishment of responsibility; segregation of duties; documentation procedures; physical, mechanical, and electronic controls; independent internal verification; and other controls.

**3.** *Explain the applications of internal control principles to cash receipts.* Internal controls over cash receipts include: (a) designating only personnel such as cashiers to handle cash; (b) assigning the duties of receiving cash, recording cash, and custody of cash to different individuals; (c) obtaining remittance advices for mail receipts, cash register tapes for over-the-counter receipts, and deposit slips for bank deposits; (d) using company safes and bank vaults to store cash with access limited to authorized personnel, and using cash registers in executing over-the-counter receipts; (e) making independent daily counts of register receipts and daily comparisons of total receipts with total deposits; and (f) bonding personnel that handle cash and requiring them to take vacations.

**4.** *Describe the applications of internal control principles to cash disbursements.* Internal controls over cash disbursements include: (a) having only specified individuals such as the treasurer authorized to sign checks; (b) assigning the duties of approving items for payment, paying the items, and recording the payment to different individuals; (c) using

prenumbered checks and accounting for all checks, with each check supported by an approved invoice; (d) storing blank checks in a safe or vault with access restricted to authorized personnel, and using a checkwriter to imprint amounts on checks; (e) comparing each check with the approved invoice before issuing the check, and making monthly reconciliations of bank and book balances; and (f) after payment, stamping each approved invoice "paid."

**5.** *Explain the operation of a petty cash fund.* In operating a petty cash fund, it is necessary to establish the fund, make payments from the fund, and replenish the fund.

**6.** *Indicate the control features of a bank account.* A bank account contributes to good internal control by providing physical controls for the storage of cash, minimizing the amount of currency that must be kept on hand, and creating a double record of a depositor's bank transactions.

**7.** *Prepare a bank reconciliation.* In reconciling the bank account, it is customary to reconcile the balance per books and balance per bank to their adjusted balances. The steps in determining the reconciling items are to ascertain deposits in transit, outstanding checks, errors by the depositor or the bank, and unrecorded bank memoranda.

**8.** *Explain the reporting of cash.* Cash is listed first in the current assets section of the balance sheet. In some cases, cash is reported together with cash equivalents. Cash restricted for a special purpose is reported separately as a current asset or as a noncurrent asset depending on when the cash is expected to be used.

# GLOSSARY

•••••••••••••••••••••••••••••••••••••••••••••••••••••••••••••••••••••••••••••••••••••

**Bank service charge** A fee charged by a bank for the use of its services. (p. 301).

**Bank statement** A statement received monthly from the bank that shows the depositor's bank transactions and balances. (p. 300).

**Cash** Resources that consist of coins, currency, checks, money orders, and money on hand or on deposit in a bank or similar depository. (p. 291).

**Cash equivalents** Highly liquid investments, with maturities of three months or less when purchased, that can be converted to a specific amount of cash. (p. 307).

**Check** A written order signed by the depositor directing the bank to pay a specified sum of money to a designated recipient. (p. 300).

**Compensating balances** Minimum cash balances required by a bank in support of bank loans. (p. 307).

**Deposits in transit** Deposits recorded by the depositor that have not been recorded by the bank. (p. 303).

**Electronic funds transfer (EFT)** A disbursement system that uses wire, telephone, telegraph, or computer to transfer cash from one location to another. (p. 295).

**Internal auditors** Company employees who evaluate on a continuous basis the effectiveness of the company's system of internal control. (p. 289).

**Internal control** The plan of organization and all the related methods and measures adopted within a business to safeguard its assets and enhance the accuracy and reliability of its accounting records. (p. 285).

**NSF check** A check that is not paid by a bank because of insufficient funds in a customer's bank account. (p. 301).

**Outstanding checks** Checks issued and recorded by a company that have not been paid by the bank. (p. 303).

**Petty cash fund** A cash fund used to pay relatively small amounts. (p. 296).

**Voucher** An authorization form prepared for each payment by check in a voucher system. (p. 294).

**Voucher system** An extensive network of approvals by authorized individuals acting independently to ensure that all disbursements by check are proper. (p. 294).

# *D*EMONSTRATION PROBLEM

Trillo Company's bank statement for May 1996 shows the following data:

| | | | |
|---|---|---|---|
| Balance 5/1 | $12,650 | Balance 5/31 | $14,280 |
| Debit memorandum: | | Credit memorandum: | |
| NSF check | $ 175 | Collection of note receivable | $ 505 |

The cash balance per books at May 31 is $13,319. Your review of the data reveals the following:

1. The NSF check was from Hup Co., a customer.
2. The note collected by the bank was a $500, three-month, 12% note. The bank charged a $10 collection fee. No interest has been accrued.
3. Outstanding checks at May 31 total $2,410.
4. Deposits in transit at May 31 total $1,752.
5. A Trillo Company check for $352 dated May 10 cleared the bank on May 25. This check, which was a payment on account, was journalized for $325.

*Instructions*

(a) Prepare a bank reconciliation at May 31.
(b) Journalize the entries required by the reconciliation.

## *Solution to Demonstration Problem*

(a)

**TRILLO COMPANY**
**Bank Reconciliation**
**May 31, 1996**

| | |
|---|---:|
| Cash balance per bank statement | $14,280 |
| Add: Deposits in transit | 1,752 |
| | 16,032 |
| Less: Outstanding checks | 2,410 |
| Adjusted cash balance per bank | $13,622 |
| | |
| Cash balance per books | $13,319 |
| Add: Collection of note receivable $500, plus $15 interest less collection fee $10 | 505 |
| | 13,824 |

**Problem-Solving Strategies**

1. Follow the four steps used in reconciling items (pp. 303–4).
2. Work carefully to minimize mathematical errors in the reconciliation.
3. All entries are based on reconciling items per books.
4. Make sure the cash ledger balance after posting the reconciling entries agrees with the adjusted cash balance per books.

| | | | |
|---|---|--:|--:|
| Less: NSF check | | $175 | |
| Error in recording check | | 27 | 202 |
| Adjusted cash balance per books | | | $13,622 |

(b)

| | | | | |
|---|---|---|--:|--:|
| May 31 | Cash | | 505 | |
| | Miscellaneous Expense | | 10 | |
| | Notes Receivable | | | 500 |
| | Interest Revenue | | | 15 |
| | (To record collection of note by bank) | | | |
| 31 | Accounts Receivable—Hup Co. | | 175 | |
| | Cash | | | 175 |
| | (To record NSF check from Hup Co.) | | | |
| 31 | Accounts Payable | | 27 | |
| | Cash | | | 27 |
| | (To correct error in recording check) | | | |

# SELF-STUDY QUESTIONS

Answers are at the end of the chapter.

(SO 1)   1. Internal control is used in a business to enhance the accuracy and reliability of its accounting records and to:
   a. safeguard its assets.
   b. prevent fraud.
   c. produce correct financial statements.
   d. deter employee dishonesty.

(SO 2)   2. The principles of internal control do not include:
   a. establishment of responsibility.
   b. documentation procedures.
   c. management responsibility.
   d. independent internal verification.

(SO 2)   3. Physical controls do not include:
   a. safes and vaults to store cash.
   b. independent bank reconciliations.
   c. locked warehouses for inventories.
   d. bank safety deposit boxes for important papers.

(SO 3)   4. Which of the following items in a cash drawer at November 30 is not cash?
   a. Money orders.
   b. Coins and currency.
   c. A customer check dated December 1.
   d. A customer check dated November 28.

(SO 3)   5. Permitting only designated personnel such as cashiers to handle cash receipts is an application of the principle of:
   a. segregation of duties.
   b. establishment of responsibility.
   c. independent check.
   d. other controls.

(SO 4)   6. The use of prenumbered checks in disbursing cash is an application of the principle of:
   a. establishment of responsibility.
   b. segregation of duties.
   c. physical, mechanical, and electronic controls.
   d. documentation procedures.

7. A check is written to replenish a $100 petty cash   (SO 5)
fund when the fund contains receipts of $94 and $3 in cash. In recording the check,
   a. Cash Over and Short should be debited for $3.
   b. Petty Cash should be debited for $94.
   c. Cash should be credited for $94.
   d. Petty Cash should be credited for $3.

8. The control features of a bank account do not   (SO 6)
include:
   a. having bank auditors verify the correctness of the bank balance per books.
   b. minimizing the amount of cash that must be kept on hand.
   c. providing a double record of all bank transactions.
   d. safeguarding cash by using a bank as a depository.

9. In a bank reconciliation, deposits in transit are:   (SO 7)
   a. deducted from the book balance.
   b. added to the book balance
   c. added to the bank balance.
   d. deducted from the bank balance.

10. The reconciling item in a bank reconciliation that   (SO 7)
will result in an adjusting entry by the depositor is:
   a. outstanding checks.
   b. deposit in transit.
   c. a bank error.
   d. bank service charges.

11. The statement that correctly describes the report-   (SO 8)
ing of cash is:
   a. Cash cannot be combined with cash equivalents.
   b. Restricted cash funds may be combined with Cash.
   c. Cash is listed first in the current asset section.
   d. Restricted cash funds cannot be reported as a current asset.

# QUESTIONS

1. "Internal control is concerned only with enhancing the accuracy of the accounting records." Do you agree? Explain.

2. What principles of internal control apply to most business enterprises?

3. In the corner grocery store, all sales clerks make change out of one cash register drawer. Is this a violation of internal control? Why?

4. J. Duma is reviewing the principle of segregation of duties. What are the two common applications of this principle?

5. How do documentation procedures contribute to good internal control?

6. What internal control objectives are met by physical, mechanical, and electronic controls?

7. (a) Explain the control principle of independent internal verification. (b) What practices are important in applying this principle?

8. The management of Cobo Company asks you, as the company accountant, to explain (a) the concept of reasonable assurance in internal control and (b) the importance of the human factor in internal control.

9. Midwest Inc. owns the following assets at the balance sheet date:

| | |
|---|---|
| Cash in bank-savings account | $ 5,000 |
| Cash on hand | 850 |
| Cash refund due from the IRS | 1,000 |
| Checking account balance | 12,000 |
| Postdated checks | 500 |

What amount should be reported as cash in the balance sheet?

10. What principle(s) of internal control is (are) involved in making daily cash counts of over-the-counter receipts?

11. Dent Department Stores has just installed new electronic cash registers in its stores. How do cash registers improve internal control over cash receipts?

12. In Allen Wholesale Company, two mail clerks open all mail receipts. How does this strengthen internal control?

13. "To have maximum effective internal control over cash disbursements, all payments should be made by check." Is this true? Explain.

14. Handy Company's internal controls over cash disbursements provide for the treasurer to sign checks imprinted by a checkwriter after comparing the check with the approved invoice. Identify the internal control principles that are present in these controls.

15. How do the principles of (a) physical, mechanical, and electronic controls and (b) other controls apply to cash disbursements?

16. (a) What is a voucher system? (b) What principles of internal control apply to a voucher system?

17. What is the essential feature of an electronic funds transfer (EFT) procedure?

18. (a) Identify the three activities that pertain to a petty cash fund, and indicate an internal control principle that is applicable to each activity. (b) When are journal entries required in the operation of a petty cash fund?

19. "The use of a bank contributes significantly to good internal control over cash." Is this true? Why?

20. Paul Pascal is confused about the lack of agreement between the cash balance per books and the balance per the bank. Explain the causes for the lack of agreement to Paul, and give an example of each cause.

21. What are the four steps involved in finding differences between the balance per books and balance per banks?

22. Mary Mora asks your help concerning an NSF check. Explain to Mary (a) what an NSF check is, (b) how it is treated in a bank reconciliation, and (c) whether it will require an adjusting entry per bank.

23. (a) "Cash equivalents are the same as cash." Do you agree? Explain. (b) How should restricted cash funds be reported on the balance sheet?

# BRIEF EXERCISES

**BE7–1**   Gina Milan is the new owner of Liberty Parking. She has heard about internal control but is not clear about its importance for her business. Explain to Gina the two purposes of internal control and give her one application of each purpose for Liberty Parking.

*Explain the importance of internal control.*
*(SO 1)*

**BE7–2**   The internal control procedures in Marion Company provide that:

(a) Employees who have physical custody of assets do not have access to the accounting records.

*Identify internal control principles.*
*(SO 2)*

(b) Each month the assets on hand are compared to the accounting records by an internal auditor.

(c) A prenumbered shipping document is prepared for each shipment of goods to customers.

Identify the principles of internal control that are being followed.

*Identify the internal control principles applicable to cash receipts.*
*(SO 3)*

**BE7–3**   The Tene Company has the following internal control procedures over cash receipts. Identify the internal control principle that is applicable to each procedure.

1. All over-the-counter receipts are registered on cash registers.
2. All cashiers are bonded.
3. Daily cash counts are made by cashier department supervisors.
4. The duties of receiving cash, recording cash, and custody of cash are assigned to different individuals.
5. Only cashiers may operate cash registers.

*Identify the internal control principle applicable to cash disbursements.*
*(SO 4)*

**BE7–4**   Hills Company has the following internal control procedures over cash disbursements. Identify the internal control principle that is applicable to each procedure.

1. Company checks are prenumbered.
2. The bank statement is reconciled monthly by an internal auditor.
3. Blank checks are stored in a safe in the treasurer's office.
4. Only the treasurer or assistant treasurer may sign checks.
5. Check signers are not allowed to record cash disbursement transactions.

*Prepare entry to replenish a petty cash fund.*
*(SO 5)*

**BE7–5**   On March 20, Gimbal's petty cash fund of $100 is replenished when the fund contains $12 in cash and receipts for postage $52, freight-in $26, and travel expense $10. Prepare the journal entry to record the replenishment of the petty cash fund.

*Identify the control features of a bank account.*
*(SO 6)*

**BE7–6**   T. J. Boad is uncertain about the control features of a bank account. Explain the control benefits of (a) a signature card, (b) a check, and (c) a bank statement.

*Indicate location of reconciling items in a bank reconciliation.*
*(SO 7)*

**BE7–7**   The following reconciling items are applicable to the bank reconciliation for Ashley Company: (1) outstanding checks, (2) bank debit memorandum for service charge, (3) bank credit memorandum for collecting a note for the depositor, (4) deposit in transit. Indicate how each item should be shown on a bank reconciliation.

*Identify reconciling items that require adjusting entries.*
*(SO 7)*

**BE7–8**   Using the data in BE7–7, indicate (a) the items that will result in an adjustment to the depositor's records and (b) why the other items do not require adjustment.

*Prepare partial bank reconciliation.*
*(SO 7)*

**BE7–9**   At July 31, Dana Company has the following bank information: cash balance per bank, $7,420, outstanding checks $762, deposits in transit $1,700, and a bank service charge $20. Determine the adjusted cash balance per bank at July 31.

*Prepare partial bank reconciliation.*
*(SO 7)*

**BE7–10**   At August 31, Kahn Company has a cash balance per books of $9,200 and the following additional data from the bank statement: charge for printing Kahn Company checks $35, interest earned on checking account balance $40, and outstanding checks $800. Determine the adjusted cash balance per books at August 31.

*Explain the statement presentation of cash balances.*
*(SO 8)*

**BE7–11**   Tijuana Company has the following cash balances: Cash in Bank $12,742, Payroll Bank Account $6,000, and Plant Expansion Fund Cash $25,000. Explain how each balance should be reported on the balance sheet.

# EXERCISES

• • • • • • • • • • • • • • • • • • • • • • • • • • • • • • • • • • • • • • • • • • • • • • • • • • • • • • • • • •

*Identify the principles of internal control.*
*(SO 2)*

**E7–1**   Joe Marino is the owner of Marino's Pizza. Marino's is operated strictly on a carryout basis. Customers pick up their orders at a counter where a clerk exchanges the pizza for cash. While at the counter, the customer can see other employees making the pizzas and the large ovens in which the pizzas are baked.

**Instructions**
Identify the six principles of internal control and give an example of each principle that you might observe when picking up your pizza. (Note: It may not be possible to observe all the principles.)

**E7–2** The following control procedures are used in the Tolan Company for over-the-counter cash receipts.

1. Cashiers are experienced; thus they are not bonded.
2. All over-the-counter receipts are registered by three clerks who use a cash register with a single cash drawer.
3. To minimize the risk of robbery, cash in excess of $100 is stored in an unlocked attaché case in the stock room until it is deposited in the bank.
4. At the end of each day, the total receipts are counted by the cashier on duty and reconciled to the cash register total.
5. The company accountant makes the bank deposit and then records the day's receipts.

*List internal control weaknesses over cash receipts and suggest improvements. (SO 2, 3)*

**Instructions**
(a) For each procedure, explain the weakness in internal control and identify the control principle that is violated.
(b) For each weakness, suggest a change in procedure that will result in good internal control.

**E7–3** The following control procedures are used in Ann's Botique Shoppe for cash disbursements.

1. Each week, Ann leaves 100 company checks in an unmarked envelope on a shelf behind the cash register.
2. The store manager personally approves all payments before signing and issuing checks.
3. The company checks are unnumbered.
4. After payment, bills are "filed" in a paid invoice folder.
5. The company accountant prepares the bank reconciliation and reports any discrepancies to the owner.

*List internal control weaknesses over cash disbursements and suggest improvements. (SO 2, 4)*

**Instructions**
(a) For each procedure, explain the weakness in internal control and identify the internal control principle that is violated.
(b) For each weakness, suggest a change in the procedure that will result in good internal control.

**E7–4** In the O'Malley Company, checks are not prenumbered because both the purchasing agent and the treasurer are authorized to issue checks. Each signer has access to unissued checks kept in an unlocked file cabinet. The purchasing agent pays all bills pertaining to goods purchased for resale. Prior to payment, the purchasing agent determines that the goods have been received and verifies the mathematical accuracy of the vendor's invoice. After payment, the invoice is filed by vendor, and the purchasing agent records the payment in the cash disbursements journal. The treasurer pays all other bills following approval by authorized employees. After payment, the treasurer stamps all bills PAID, files them by payment date, and records the checks in the cash disbursements journal. Webber Company maintains one checking account that is reconciled by the treasurer.

*Identify internal control weaknesses for cash disbursements and make recommendations for improvement. (SO 4)*

**Instructions**
(a) List the weaknesses in internal control over cash disbursements.
(b) ▮▮▮▮▬▶ Write a memo to your boss indicating your recommendations for improvement.

**E7–5** Ramona Company uses an imprest petty cash system. The fund was established on March 1 with a balance of $100. During March the following petty cash receipts were found in the petty cash box:

*Prepare journal entries for a petty cash fund. (SO 5)*

| Date | Receipt No. | For | Amount |
|------|------------|-----|--------|
| 3/5 | 1 | Stamp Inventory | $38 |
| 7 | 2 | Freight-in | 19 |
| 9 | 3 | Miscellaneous Expense | 12 |
| 11 | 4 | Travel Expense | 24 |
| 14 | 5 | Miscellaneous Expense | 5 |

There was no cash over or short. The fund was replenished on March 15. On March 20, the amount in the fund was increased to $150.

**Instructions**

Journalize the entries in March that pertain to the operation of the petty cash fund.

*Prepare bank reconciliation and adjusting entries.*
*(SO 7)*

**E7–6**   Ono LoKo is unable to reconcile the bank balance at January 31. Ono's reconciliation is as follows:

| | |
|---|---|
| Cash balance per bank | $3,560.20 |
| Add: NSF check | 530.00 |
| Less: Bank service charge | 25.00 |
| Adjusted balance per bank | $4,065.20 |
| Cash balance per books | $3,875.20 |
| Less: Deposits in transit | 490.00 |
| Add: Outstanding checks | 730.00 |
| Adjusted balance per books | $4,115.20 |

**Instructions**

(a)  Prepare a correct bank reconciliation.

(b)  Journalize the entries required by the reconciliation.

*Determine outstanding checks.*
*(SO 7)*

**E7–7**   On April 30, the bank reconciliation of Drofo Company shows three outstanding checks: No. 254 $650, No. 255 $820, and No. 257 $410. The May bank statement and the May cash payments journal show the following:

| Bank Statement | | | Cash Payments Journal | | |
|---|---|---|---|---|---|
| Checks Paid | | | Checks Issued | | |
| Date | Check No. | Amount | Date | Check No. | Amount |
| 5/4 | 254 | 650 | 5/2 | 258 | 159 |
| 5/2 | 257 | 410 | 5/5 | 259 | 275 |
| 5/17 | 258 | 159 | 5/10 | 260 | 925 |
| 5/12 | 259 | 275 | 5/15 | 261 | 500 |
| 5/20 | 261 | 500 | 5/22 | 262 | 750 |
| 5/29 | 263 | 480 | 5/24 | 263 | 480 |
| 5/30 | 262 | 750 | 5/29 | 264 | 360 |

**Instructions**

Using step 2 in the reconciliation procedure, list the outstanding checks at May 31.

*Prepare bank reconciliation and adjusting entries.*
*(SO 7)*

**E7–8**   The following information pertains to Mohammed Company.

1.  Cash balance per bank, July 31, $7,463.
2.  July bank service charge not recorded by the depositor $15.
3.  Cash balance per books, July 31, $7,190.
4.  Deposits in transit, July 31, $1,700.
5.  Note for $1,200 collected for Mohammed in July by the bank, plus interest $36 less fee $20. The collection has not been recorded by Mohammed, and no interest has been accrued.
6.  Outstanding checks, July 31, $772.

**Instructions**

(a)  Prepare a bank reconciliation at July 31.

(b)  Journalize the adjusting entries at July 31 on the books of Mohammed Company.

*Prepare bank reconciliation and adjusting entries.*
*(SO 7)*

**E7–9**   The information below relates to the Cash account in the ledger of Reston Company.

Balance September 1—$17,150; Cash deposited—$64,000.

Balance September 30—$17,404; Checks written—$63,746.

The September bank statement shows a balance of $16,422 on September 30 and the following memorandum:

| Credits | | Debits | |
|---|---|---|---|
| Collection of $1,500 note plus interest $30 | $1,530 | NSF check: J. Hower | $410 |
| Interest earned on checking account | $45 | Safety deposit box rent | $30 |

At September 30, deposits in transit were $4,500 and outstanding checks totaled $2,383.

*Instructions*
(a) Prepare the bank reconciliation at September 30.
(b) Prepare the adjusting entries at September 30, assuming (1) the NSF check was from a customer on account, and (2) no interest had been accrued on the note.

**E7–10**   The cash records of Kuwait Company show the following:

*Compute deposits in transit and outstanding checks for two bank reconciliations.*
(SO 7)

1. The June 30 bank reconciliation indicated that deposits in transit total $850. During July the general ledger account Cash shows deposits of $15,750, but the bank statement indicates that only $15,600 in deposits were received during the month.
2. The June 30 bank reconciliation also reported outstanding checks of $920. During the month of July, Kuwait Company books show that $17,200 of checks were issued, yet the bank statement showed that $16,400 of checks cleared the bank in July.
3. In September, deposits per the bank statement totaled $26,700, deposits per books were $25,400, and deposits in transit at September 30 were $2,400.
4. In September, cash disbursements per books were $23,700, checks clearing the bank were $25,000, and outstanding checks at September 30 were $2,100.

There were no bank debit or credit memoranda, and no errors were made by either the bank or Kuwait Company.

*Instructions*
Answer the following questions:

(a) In situation (1), what were the deposits in transit at July 31?
(b) In situation (2), what were the outstanding checks at July 31?
(c) In situation (3), what were the deposits in transit at August 31?
(d) In situation (4), what were the outstanding checks at August 31?

# PROBLEMS

**P7–1**   Red River Theater is located in the Red River Mall. A cashier's booth is located near the entrance to the theater. Two cashiers are employed. One works from 1–5 P.M., the other from 5–9 P.M. Each cashier is bonded. The cashiers receive cash from customers and operate a machine that ejects serially numbered tickets. The rolls of tickets are inserted and locked into the machine by the theater manager at the beginning of each cashier's shift.

*Identify internal control weaknesses over cash receipts.*
(SO 2, 3)

After purchasing a ticket, the customer takes the ticket to a doorperson stationed at the entrance of the theater lobby some 60 feet from the cashier's booth. The doorperson tears the ticket in half, admits the customer, and returns the ticket stub to the customer. The other half of the ticket is dropped into a locked box by the doorperson.

At the end of each cashier's shift, the theater manager removes the ticket rolls from the machine and makes a cash count. The cash count sheet is initialed by the cashier. At the end of the day, the manager deposits the receipts in total in a bank night deposit vault located in the mall. In addition, the manager sends copies of the deposit slip and the initialed cash count sheets to the theater company treasurer for verification and to the company's accounting department. Receipts from the first shift are stored in a safe located in the manager's office.

*Instructions*
(a) Identify the internal control principles and their application to the cash receipts transactions of the Red River Theater.
(b) If the doorperson and cashier decide to collaborate to misappropriate cash, what actions might they take?

**P7–2**   MTR Company maintains a petty cash fund for small expenditures. The following transactions occurred over a 2-month period:

*Journalize and post petty cash fund transactions.*
(SO 5)

July  1   Established petty cash fund by writing a check on Metro Bank for $200.
     15   Replenished the petty cash fund by writing a check for $194.30. On this date the fund consisted of $5.70 in cash and the following petty cash receipts: Freight-in $94.00, postage expense $42.40, entertainment expense $46.60, and miscellaneous expense $10.70.
     31   Replenished the petty cash fund by writing a check for $192.00. At this date, the fund consisted of $8.00 in cash and the following petty cash receipts: Freight-in

$82.10, charitable contributions expense $30.00, postage expense $47.80, and miscellaneous expense $32.10.

Aug. 15  Replenished the petty cash fund by writing a check for $188.00. On this date, the fund consisted of $12.00 in cash and the following petty cash receipts: Freight-in $74.40, entertainment expense $43.00, postage expense $33.00, and miscellaneous expense $38.00.

16  Increased the amount of the petty cash fund to $300 by writing a check for $100.

31  Replenished petty cash fund by writing a check for $283.00. On this date, the fund consisted of $17 in cash and the following petty cash receipts: Postage expense $145.00, entertainment expense $90.60, and freight-in $45.40.

**Instructions**
(a) Journalize the petty cash transactions.
(b) Post to the Petty Cash account.
(c) What internal control features exist in a petty cash fund?

*Prepare a bank reconciliation and adjusting entries.*
*(SO 7)*

**P7–3**   On July 31, 1996, Lori Company had a cash balance per books of $6,815.30. The statement from Tri-County Bank on that date showed a balance of $7,075.80. A comparison of the bank statement with the cash account revealed the following facts:

1. The bank service charge for July was $25.
2. The bank collected a note receivable of $1,200 for Lori Company on July 15, plus $48 of interest. The bank made a $10 charge for the collection. Lori has not accrued any interest on the note.
3. The July 31 receipts of $1,819.60 were not included in the bank deposits for July. These receipts were deposited by the company in a night deposit vault on July 31.
4. Company check No. 2480 issued to J. Brokaw, a creditor, for $492 that cleared the bank in July was incorrectly entered in the cash payments journal on July 10 for $429.
5. Checks outstanding on July 31 totaled $1,480.10.
6. On July 31, the bank statement showed an NSF charge of $550 for a check received by the company from R. Close, a customer, on account.

**Instructions**
(a) Prepare the bank reconciliation as of July 31.
(b) Prepare the necessary adjusting entries at July 31.

*Prepare a bank reconciliation and adjusting entries from detailed data.*
*(SO 7)*

**P7–4**   The bank portion of the bank reconciliation for London Company at October 31, 1996, was as follows:

**LONDON COMPANY**
**Bank Reconciliation**
**October 31, 1996**

| | | | |
|---|---|---|---:|
| Cash balance per bank | | | $12,367.90 |
| Add: Deposits in transit | | | 1,530.20 |
| | | | 13,898.10 |
| | | | |
| Less: Outstanding checks | | | |
| | Check Number | Check Amount | |
| | 2451 | $1,260.40 | |
| | 2470 | 720.10 | |
| | 2471 | 844.50 | |
| | 2472 | 426.80 | |
| | 2474 | 1,050.00 | 4,301.80 |
| Adjusted cash balance per bank | | | $ 9,596.30 |

The adjusted cash balance per bank agreed with the cash balance per books at October 31.

The November bank statement showed the following checks and deposits:

| Bank Statement | | | | |
|---|---|---|---|---|
| Checks | | | Deposits | |
| Date | Number | Amount | Date | Amount |
| 11-1 | 2470 | $ 720.10 | 11-1 | $ 1,530.20 |
| 11-2 | 2471 | 844.50 | 11-4 | 1,211.60 |
| 11-5 | 2474 | 1,050.00 | 11-8 | 990.10 |
| 11-4 | 2475 | 1,640.70 | 11-13 | 2,575.00 |
| 11-8 | 2476 | 2,830.00 | 11-18 | 1,472.70 |
| 11-10 | 2477 | 600.00 | 11-21 | 2,945.00 |
| 11-15 | 2479 | 1,750.00 | 11-25 | 2,567.30 |
| 11-18 | 2480 | 1,330.00 | 11-28 | 1,650.00 |
| 11-27 | 2481 | 695.40 | 11-30 | 1,186.00 |
| 11-30 | 2483 | 575.50 | Total | $16,127.90 |
| 11-29 | 2486 | 900.00 | | |
| | Total | $12,936.20 | | |

The cash records per books for November showed the following:

| Cash Payments Journal | | | | | | Cash Receipts Journal | |
|---|---|---|---|---|---|---|---|
| Date | Number | Amount | Date | Number | Amount | Date | Amount |
| 11-1 | 2475 | $1,640.70 | 11-20 | 2483 | $ 575.50 | 11-3 | $ 1,211.60 |
| 11-2 | 2476 | 2,830.00 | 11-22 | 2484 | 829.50 | 11-7 | 990.10 |
| 11-2 | 2477 | 600.00 | 11-23 | 2485 | 974.80 | 11-12 | 2,575.00 |
| 11-4 | 2478 | 538.20 | 11-24 | 2486 | 900.00 | 11-17 | 1,472.70 |
| 11-8 | 2479 | 1,570.00 | 11-29 | 2487 | 398.00 | 11-20 | 2,954.00 |
| 11-10 | 2480 | 1,330.00 | 11-30 | 2488 | 800.00 | 11-24 | 2,567.30 |
| 11-15 | 2481 | 695.40 | Total | | $14,294.10 | 11-27 | 1,650.00 |
| 11-18 | 2482 | 612.00 | | | | 11-29 | 1,186.00 |
| | | | | | | 11-30 | 1,225.00 |
| | | | | | | Total | $15,831.70 |

The bank statement contained two bank memoranda:

1. A credit of $2,105.00 for the collection of a $2,000 note for London Company plus interest of $120 and less a collection fee of $15. London Company has not accrued any interest on the note.
2. A debit for the printing of additional company checks, $50.00.

At November 30 the cash balance per books was $11,123.90, and the cash balance per the bank statement was $17,604.60. The bank did not make any errors, but two errors were made by London Company.

### Instructions
(a) Using the four steps in the reconciliation procedure described on pages 303–4, prepare a bank reconciliation at November 30.
(b) Prepare the adjusting entries based on the reconciliation. (*Note:* The correction of any errors pertaining to recording checks should be made to Accounts Payable. The correction of any errors relating to recording cash receipts should be made to Accounts Receivable.)

*Prepare a bank reconciliation and adjusting entries.*
(SO 7)

**P7–5**  Mayo Company's bank statement from Lane National Bank at August 31, 1996, shows the following information:

| | | | |
|---|---|---|---|
| Balance, August 1 | $17,400 | Bank credit memorandum: | |
| August deposits | 73,000 | Collection of note | |
| Checks cleared in August | 68,660 | receivable plus $90 | |
| Balance, August 31 | 24,850 | interest | $3,090 |
| | | Interest earned | 45 |
| | | Bank debit memorandum | |
| | | Safety deposit box rent | 25 |

A summary of the Cash account in the ledger for August shows: Balance, August 1, $16,900; receipts $77,000; disbursements $73,570; and balance, August 31, $20,330. Analysis reveals that the only reconciling items on the July 31 bank reconciliation were a deposit in transit for $4,000 and outstanding checks of $4,500. The deposit in transit was the first deposit recorded by the bank in August. In addition, you determine that there were two errors involving company checks drawn in August: (1) a check for $400 to a creditor on account that cleared the bank in August was journalized and posted for $420, and (2) a salary check to an employee for $275 was recorded by the bank for $285.

**Instructions**
(a)  Prepare a bank reconciliation at August 31.
(b)  Journalize the adjusting entries to be made by Mayo Company at August 31. Assume the interest on the note has been accrued by the company.

# ALTERNATE PROBLEMS

**P7–1A**  Segal Office Supply Company recently changed its system of internal control over cash disbursements. The system includes the following features.

*Identify internal control principles over cash disbursements.*
(SO 2, 4)

Instead of being unnumbered and manually prepared, all checks must now be pre-numbered and written by using the new checkwriter purchased by the company. Before a check can be issued, each invoice must have the approval of Cindy Morris, the purchasing agent, and Ray Mills, the receiving department supervisor. Checks must be signed by either Frank Malone, the treasurer, or Mary Arno, the assistant treasurer. Before signing a check, the signer is expected to compare the amounts of the check with the amounts on the invoice.

After signing a check, the signer stamps the invoice PAID and inserts within the stamp, the date, check number, and amount of the check. The "paid" invoice is then sent to the accounting department for recording.

Blank checks are stored in a safe in the treasurer's office. The combination to the safe is known only by the treasurer and assistant treasurer. Each month, the bank statement is reconciled with the bank balance per books by the assistant chief accountant.

**Instructions**
Identify the internal control principles and their application to cash disbursements of Segal Office Supply Company.

**P7–2A**  Dockers Company maintains a petty cash fund for small expenditures. The following transactions occurred over a 2-month period:

*Journalize and post petty cash fund transactions.*
(SO 5)

July  1  Established petty cash fund by writing a check on Metro Bank for $200.
    15  Replenished the petty cash fund by writing a check for $195.00. On this date the fund consisted of $5.00 in cash and the following petty cash receipts: Freight-in $94.00, postage expense $42.40, entertainment expense $46.60, and miscellaneous expense $11.90.
    31  Replenished the petty cash fund by writing a check for $192.00. At this date, the fund consisted of $8.00 in cash and the following petty cash receipts: Freight-in $82.10, charitable contributions expense $40.00, postage expense $27.80, and miscellaneous expense $42.10.

Aug. 15   Replenished the petty cash fund by writing a check for $187.00. On this date, the fund consisted of $13.00 in cash and the following petty cash receipts: Freight-in $74.60, entertainment expense $43.00, postage expense $33.00, and miscellaneous expense $37.00.

16   Increased the amount of the petty cash fund to $300 by writing a check for $100.

31   Replenished petty cash fund by writing a check for $283.00. On this date, the fund consisted of $17 in cash and the following petty cash receipts: Postage expense $140.00, travel expense $95.60, and freight-in $46.40.

**Instructions**
(a) Journalize the petty cash transactions.
(b) Post to the Petty Cash account.
(c) What internal control features exist in a petty cash fund?

**P7–3A**   On May 31, 1996, Maloney Company had a cash balance per books of $5,781.50. The bank statement from Community Bank on that date showed a balance of $6,804.60. A comparison of the statement with the cash account revealed the following facts:

*Prepare a bank reconciliation and adjusting entries.*
*(SO 7)*

1.  The statement included a debit memo of $40 for the printing of additional company checks.
2.  Cash sales of $836.15 on May 12 were deposited in the bank. The cash receipts journal entry and the deposit slip were incorrectly made for $846.15. The bank credited Maloney Company for the correct amount.
3.  Outstanding checks at May 31 totaled $1,276.25, and deposits in transit were $936.15.
4.  On May 18, the company issued check No. 1181 for $685 to M. Helms, on account. The check, which cleared the bank in May, was incorrectly journalized and posted by Maloney Company for $658.
5.  A $2,000 note receivable was collected by the bank for Maloney Company on May 31 plus $80 interest. The bank charged a collection fee of $20. No interest has been accrued on the note.
6.  Included with the cancelled checks was a check issued by Teller Company to P. Jonet for $600 that was incorrectly charged to Maloney Company by the bank.
7.  On May 31, the bank statement showed an NSF charge of $700 for a check issued by W. Hoad, a customer, to Maloney Company on account.

**Instructions**
(a) Prepare the bank reconciliation at May 31, 1996.
(b) Prepare the necessary adjusting entries for Maloney Company at May 31, 1996.

**P7–4A**   The bank portion of the bank reconciliation for Sandra Company at November 30, 1996, was as follows:

*Prepare a bank reconciliation and adjusting entries from detailed data.*
*(SO 7)*

**SANDRA COMPANY**
**Bank Reconciliation**
**November 30, 1996**

| | | |
|---|---|---:|
| Cash balance per bank | | $14,367.90 |
| Add: Deposits in transit | | 2,530.20 |
| | | 16,898.10 |
| | | |
| Less: Outstanding checks | | |

| Check Number | Check Amount | |
|---|---|---:|
| 3451 | $2,260.40 | |
| 3470 | 720.10 | |
| 3471 | 844.50 | |
| 3472 | 1,426.80 | |
| 3474 | 1,050.00 | 6,301.80 |
| Adjusted cash balance per bank | | $10,596.30 |

The adjusted cash balance per bank agreed with the cash balance per books at November 30.

The December bank statement showed the following checks and deposits:

| Bank Statement | | | | |
| --- | --- | --- | --- | --- |
| **Checks** | | | **Deposits** | |
| Date | Number | Amount | Date | Amount |
| 12-1 | 3451 | $ 2,260.40 | 12-1 | $ 2,530.20 |
| 12-2 | 3471 | 844.50 | 12-4 | 1,211.60 |
| 12-7 | 3472 | 1,426.80 | 12-8 | 2,365.10 |
| 12-4 | 3475 | 1,640.70 | 12-16 | 2,672.70 |
| 12-8 | 3476 | 1,300.00 | 12-21 | 2,945.00 |
| 12-10 | 3477 | 2,130.00 | 12-26 | 2,567.30 |
| 12-15 | 3479 | 3,080.00 | 12-29 | 2,836.00 |
| 12-27 | 3480 | 600.00 | 12-30 | 1,025.00 |
| 12-30 | 3482 | 475.50 | Total | $18,152.90 |
| 12-29 | 3483 | 1,140.00 | | |
| 12-31 | 3485 | 540.80 | | |
| | Total | $15,438.70 | | |

The cash records per books for December showed the following:

| Cash Payments Journal | | | | | | Cash Receipts Journal | |
| --- | --- | --- | --- | --- | --- | --- | --- |
| Date | Number | Amount | Date | Number | Amount | Date | Amount |
| 12-1 | 3475 | $1,640.70 | 12-20 | 3482 | $  475.50 | 12-3 | $ 1,211.60 |
| 12-2 | 3476 | 1,300.00 | 12-22 | 3483 | 1,140.00 | 12-7 | 2,365.10 |
| 12-2 | 3477 | 2,130.00 | 12-23 | 3484 | 832.00 | 12-15 | 2,672.70 |
| 12-4 | 3478 | 538.20 | 12-24 | 3485 | 450.80 | 12-20 | 2,954.00 |
| 12-8 | 3479 | 3,080.00 | 12-30 | 3486 | 1,389.50 | 12-25 | 2,567.30 |
| 12-10 | 3480 | 600.00 | Total | | $14,384.10 | 12-28 | 2,836.00 |
| 12-17 | 3481 | 807.40 | | | | 12-30 | 1,025.00 |
| | | | | | | 12-31 | 1,190.40 |
| | | | | | | Total | $16,822.10 |

The bank statement contained two memoranda:

1. A credit of $2,145 for the collection of a $2,000 note for Sandra Company plus interest of $160 and less a collection fee of $15.00. Sandra Company has not accrued any interest on the note.
2. A debit of $547.10 for an NSF check written by A. Jordan, a customer. At December 31, the check had not been redeposited in the bank.

At December 31 the cash balance per books was $13,034.30, and the cash balance per the bank statement was $18,680.00. The bank did not make any errors, but two errors were made by Sandra Company.

**Instructions**

(a) Using the four steps in the reconciliation procedure, prepare a bank reconciliation at December 31.
(b) Prepare the adjusting entries based on the reconciliation. (*Note:* The correction of any errors pertaining to recording checks should be made to Accounts Payable. The correction of any errors relating to recording cash receipts should be made to Accounts Receivable.)

*Prepare a bank reconciliation and adjusting entries.*
(SO 7)

**P7–5A**  Palmeiro Company maintains a checking account at the Marine City Bank. At July 31, selected data from the ledger balance and the bank statement are as follows:

**Cash in Bank**

| | Per Books | Per Bank |
|---|---|---|
| Balance, July 1 | $17,600 | $19,200 |
| July receipts | 82,000 | |
| July credits | | 80,070 |
| July disbursements | 76,900 | |
| July debits | | 74,740 |
| Balance, July 31 | $22,700 | $24,530 |

Analysis of the bank data reveals that the credits consist of $78,000 of July deposits and a credit memorandum of $2,070 for the collection of a $2,000 note plus interest revenue of $70. The July debits per bank consist of checks cleared, $74,700 and a debit memorandum of $40 for printing additional company checks.

You also discover the following errors involving July checks: (1) a check for $230 to a creditor on account that cleared the bank in July was journalized and posted as $320, and (2) a salary check to an employee for $255 was recorded by the bank for $155.

The June 30 bank reconciliation contained only two reconciling items: deposits in transit $5,000 and outstanding checks of $6,600.

**Instructions**
(a) Prepare a bank reconciliation at July 31.
(b) Journalize the adjusting entries to be made by Palmeiro Company at July 31, 1996. Assume that the interest on the note has been accrued.

**P7–6A** Acura Company is a very profitable small business. It has not, however, given much consideration to internal control. For example, in an attempt to keep clerical and office expenses to a minimum, the company has combined the jobs of cashier and bookkeeper. As a result, Rob Rowe handles all cash receipts, keeps the accounting records, and prepares the monthly bank reconciliations.

*Prepare comprehensive bank reconciliation with defalcation and internal control deficiencies.*
*(SO 2, 3, 4, 7)*

The balance per the bank statement on October 31, 1996, was $18,380. Outstanding checks were: No. 62 for $126.75, No. 183 for $150, No. 284 for $253.25, No. 862 for $190.71, No. 863 for $226.80, and No. 864 for $165.28. Included with the statement was a credit memorandum of $200 indicating the collection of a note receivable for the Acura Company by the bank on October 25. This memorandum has not been recorded by Acura Company.

The company's ledger showed one cash account with a balance of $21,892.72. The balance included undeposited cash on hand. Because of the lack of internal controls, Rowe took for personal use all of the undeposited receipts in excess of $3,795.51. He then prepared the following bank reconciliation in an effort to conceal his theft of cash.

| | | |
|---|---|---|
| Cash balance per books, October 31 | | $21,892.72 |
| Add: Outstanding checks | | |
| No. 862 | $190.71 | |
| No. 863 | 226.80 | |
| No. 864 | 165.28 | 482.79 |
| | | 22,375.51 |
| Less: Undeposited receipts | | 3,795.51 |
| Unadjusted balance per bank, October 31 | | 18,580.00 |
| Less: Bank credit memorandum | | 200.00 |
| Cash balance per bank statement, October 31 | | $18,380.00 |

**Instructions**
(a) Prepare a correct bank reconciliation. (*Hint:* Deduct the amount of the theft from the adjusted balance per books.)
(b) Indicate the three ways that Rowe attempted to conceal the theft and the dollar amount pertaining to each method.
(c) What principles of internal control were violated in this case?

# ▼*Broadening Your Perspective*

## *F*INANCIAL REPORTING PROBLEM

The financial statements of PepsiCo, Inc. are presented in Appendix A of this textbook together with two reports: (1) a management report, Management's Responsibility for Financial Statements, and (2) an auditor's report, Report of Independent Auditors.

*Instructions*
Using the financial statements and reports, answer the following questions about PepsiCo's internal controls and cash.

1. What comments, if any, concerning the company's system of internal control are included in each report?
2. What reference, if any, is made to internal auditors in each report?
3. What comments, if any, are made about cash in the report of the independent auditors?
4. What data about cash and cash equivalents are shown in the consolidated balance sheet (statement of financial condition)?
5. What activities are identified in the consolidated statement of cash flows as being responsible for the changes in cash during 1994?
6. How are cash equivalents defined under the Notes to Consolidated Financial Statements?

## *D*ECISION CASE

The board of trustees of a local church is concerned about the internal accounting controls pertaining to the offering collections made at weekly services. They ask you to serve on a three-person audit team with the internal auditor of the university and a CPA who has just joined the church.

At a meeting of the audit team and the board of trustees you learn the following:

1. The church's board of trustees has delegated responsibility for the financial management and audit of the financial records to the finance committee. This group prepares the annual budget and approves major disbursements but is not involved in collections or record keeping. No audit has been made in recent years because the same trusted employee has kept church records and served as financial secretary for 15 years. The church does not carry any fidelity insurance.
2. The collection at the weekly service is taken by a team of ushers who volunteer to serve one month. The ushers take the collection plates to a basement office at the rear of the church. They hand their plates to the head usher and return to the church service. After all plates have been turned in, the head usher counts the cash received. The head usher then places the cash in the church safe along with a notation of the amount counted. The head usher volunteers to serve for 3 months.
3. The next morning the financial secretary opens the safe and recounts the collection. The secretary withholds $150–$200 in cash, depending on the cash expenditures expected for the week, and deposits the remainder of the collections in the bank. To facilitate the deposit, church members who contribute by check are asked to make their checks payable to "cash."
4. Each month, the financial secretary reconciles the bank statement and submits a copy of the reconciliation to the board of trustees. The reconciliations have rarely contained any bank errors and have never shown any errors per books.

*Instructions*
(a) Indicate the weaknesses in internal accounting control over the handling of collections.

(b) List the improvements in internal control procedures that you plan to make at the next meeting of the audit team for (1) the ushers, (2) the head usher, (3) the financial secretary, and (4) the finance committee.

(c) What church policies should be changed to improve internal control?

# COMMUNICATION ACTIVITY

As a new auditor for the CPA firm of Rawls, Keoto, and Landry you have been assigned to review the internal controls over mail cash receipts of Adirondack Company. Your review reveals the following: Checks are promptly endorsed "For Deposit Only," but no list of the checks is prepared by the person opening the mail. The mail is opened either by the cashier or by the employee who maintains the accounts receivable records. Mail receipts are deposited in the bank weekly by the cashier.

*Instructions*
Write a letter to L. S. Osman, owner of the Adirondack Company, explaining the weaknesses in internal control and your recommendations for improving the system.

# GROUP ACTIVITY

From your employment or personal experiences, identify situations in which cash was received or disbursed.

*Instructions*
In groups of five or six students:

(a) Identify the internal control principles used for cash receipts.

(b) Identify the internal control principles used for cash disbursements.

(c) Identify any weaknesses in internal control related to cash receipts and disbursements.

# ETHICS CASE

You are the assistant controller in charge of general ledger accounting at Lemon Twist Bottling Company. Your company has a large loan from an insurance company. The loan agreement requires that the company's cash account balance be maintained at $200,000 or more as reported monthly. At June 30 the cash balance is $80,000, which you report to Sam Williams, the financial vice-president. Sam excitedly instructs you to keep the cash receipts book open for one additional day for purposes of the June 30 report to the insurance company. Sam says, "If we don't get that cash balance over $200,000, we'll default on our loan agreement. They could close us down, put us all out of our jobs!" Sam continues, "I talked to Grochum Distributors (one of Lemon Twist's largest customers) this morning and they said they sent us a check for $150,000 yesterday. We should receive it tomorrow. If we include just that one check in our cash balance, we'll be in the clear. It's in the mail!"

*Instructions*
(a) Who will suffer negative effects if you do not comply with Sam Williams' instructions? Who will suffer if you do comply?

(b) What are the ethical considerations in this case?

(c) What alternatives do you have?

# CRITICAL THINKING CASE
## ▸ *A Real-World Focus: Alternative Distributor Corp.*

........................................................................................................

***Alternative Distributor Corp.,*** *a distributor of groceries and related products, is headquartered in Medford, Massachusetts. It was founded in 1980 and today has seven employees, with a total sales of $7 million.*

During its audit, the Alternative Distributor Corp. was advised that previously existing internal controls necessary for the company to develop reliable financial statements were inadequate. The audit report stated that the current system of accounting for sales, receivables, and cash receipts constituted a material weakness.

Among other items, the report focused on non-timely deposit of cash receipts, exposing Alternative Distributor to potential loss or misappropriation; excessive past due accounts receivable due to lack of collection efforts; disregard of advantages offered by vendors for prompt payment of invoices; absence of appropriate segregation of duties by personnel consistent with appropriate control objectives; inadequate procedures for applying accounting principles; lack of qualified management personnel; lack of supervision by an outside board of directors; and overall poor recordkeeping.

### Instructions
Identify the principles of internal control violated by Alternative Distributor Corporation.

------------

### Answers to Self-Study Questions
1. a    2. c    3. b    4. c    5. b    6. d    7. a    8. a    9. c    10. d    11. c

## Concepts for Review

**Before studying this chapter, you should know or, if necessary, review:**

**a.** *How to record sales transactions (Ch. 5, pp. 181–85)*
**b.** *Why adjusting entries are made (Ch. 3, p. 91)*
**c.** *How to compute interest (Ch. 3, p. 100)*

# How Long Should the Check Be in the Mail?

RALEIGH, N.C. — Take a look at your campus newspaper. Read the advertisements—the nearby pizza parlor, a local clothing merchant, maybe a review course for the Law School Admission Test. In many cases these advertisers set up accounts with the campus paper and pay their bills 30 days after the ad runs. The paper keeps track of these accounts and bills them on a timely basis.

For more than 70 years, the North Carolina State University newspaper, the *Technician*, has published stories by student writers and run ads by local merchants. "Eighty-five percent of our $400,000 annual operating budget comes from advertising," says Tim Ellington, General Manager—a graduate of NC State. "The rest comes from student fees."

Ellington says that the paper requires prepayment from new advertising accounts. After a trial period, the advertiser will be granted a 30-day payment period. From time to time, however, advertisers don't pay on time. "When it comes to bill paying time, our bill often gets put on the bottom of the pile," says Ellington. "If they are going to anger somebody, they'll anger us before they do a supplier."

The newspaper follows a series of steps in trying to collect late accounts: Once a bill is 30 days past due, the advertiser is sent a letter that says, nicely, "If you haven't sent your payment, please do." At 45 days, the letter isn't as nice: "If we don't receive payment in 30 days, then we could pursue it through small claims court." At 75 days, the newspaper files a small claims suit. ◀

CHAPTER · **8**

# ACCOUNTING FOR RECEIVABLES

## ▶ STUDY OBJECTIVES ◀

**After studying this chapter, you should be able to:**

1. Identify the different types of receivables.
2. Explain how accounts receivable are recognized in the accounts.
3. Distinguish between the methods and bases used to value accounts receivable.
4. Describe the entries to record the disposition of accounts receivable.
5. Compute the maturity date of, and interest on, notes receivable.
6. Explain how notes receivable are recognized in the accounts.
7. Describe how notes receivable are valued.
8. Describe the entries to record the disposition of notes receivable.
9. Explain the statement presentation of receivables.

As you read this chapter, you will learn what journal entries the *Technician* makes when it sells its ad space, when it collects the cash for those sales, and when it writes off an uncollectible account. The types of entries the *Technician* makes are typical of most businesses, because our economy depends heavily on the use of credit, which takes the form of accounts and notes receivable.

The content and organization of this chapter are as follows:

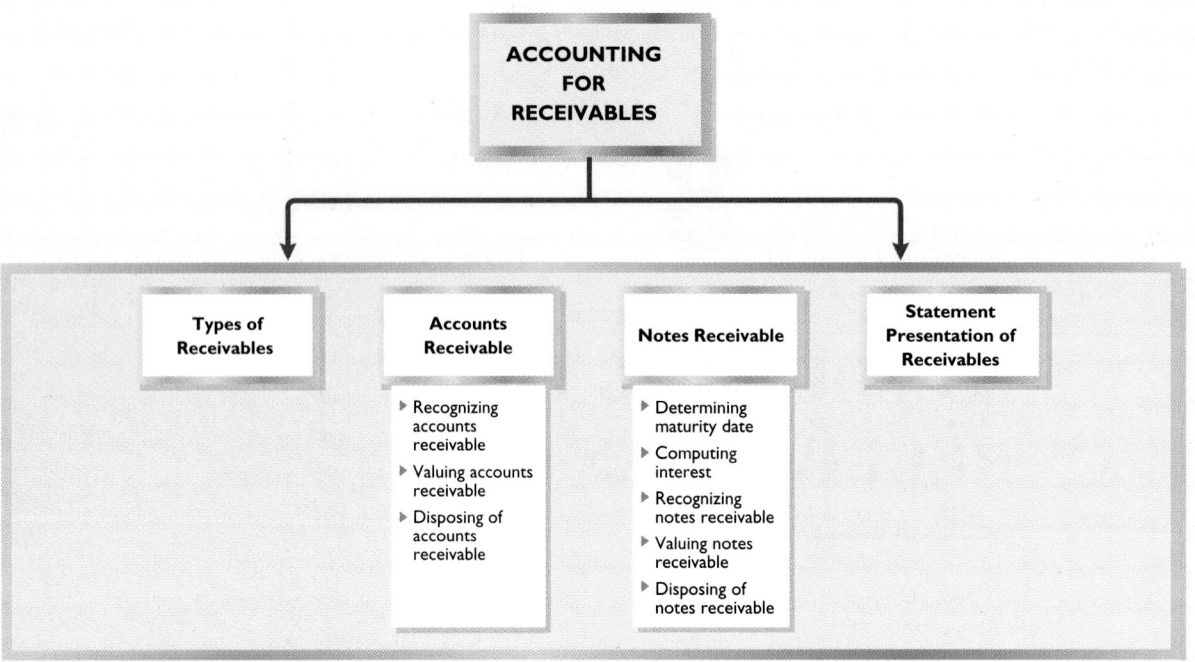

# Types of Receivables

The term "receivables" refers to amounts due from individuals and other companies. Receivables are claims that are expected to be collected in cash. Receivables are frequently classified as (1) accounts, (2) notes, and (3) other.

**Accounts receivable** are amounts owed by customers on account. They result from the sale of goods and services. These receivables generally are expected to be collected within 30 to 60 days. They are the most significant type of claim held by a company.

**Notes receivable** represent claims for which formal instruments of credit are issued as evidence of the debt. The credit instrument normally requires the debtor to pay interest and extends for time periods of 60–90 days or longer. Notes and accounts receivable that result from sales transactions are often called trade receivables.

**Other receivables** include nontrade receivables such as interest receivable, loans to company officers, advances to employees, and income taxes refundable. These are unusual; therefore, they are generally classified and reported as separate items in the balance sheet.

# Accounts Receivable

The three primary accounting problems associated with accounts receivable are:

1. **Recognizing** accounts receivable.
2. **Valuing** accounts receivable.
3. **Disposing of** accounts receivable.

## Recognizing Accounts Receivable

Recognizing accounts receivable is relatively straightforward. In Chapter 5 we saw how accounts receivable are affected by the sale of merchandise. To illustrate, assume that Jordache Co. on July 1, 1996, sells merchandise on account to Polo Company for $1,000 terms 2/10, n/30. On July 5, merchandise worth $100 is returned to Jordache Co. On July 11, payment is received from Polo Company for the balance due. The journal entries to record these transactions on the books of Jordache Co. are as follows:

> **STUDY OBJECTIVE**
> **2**
>
> *Explain how accounts receivable are recognized in the accounts.*

| | | | |
|---|---|---|---|
| July 1 | Accounts Receivable | 1,000 | |
| | Sales | | 1,000 |
| | (To record sales on account) | | |
| July 5 | Sales Returns and Allowances | 100 | |
| | Accounts Receivable | | 100 |
| | (To record merchandise returned) | | |
| July 11 | Cash ($900 − $18) | 882 | |
| | Sales Discounts ($900 × .02) | 18 | |
| | Accounts Receivable | | 900 |
| | (To record collection of accounts receivable) | | |

The opportunity to receive a cash discount usually occurs when a manufacturer sells to a wholesaler or a wholesaler sells to a retailer. A discount is given in these situations either to encourage prompt payment or for competitive reasons.

On the other hand, retailers rarely grant cash discounts to customers. For example, we would be surprised if you ever received a cash discount in purchasing goods from any well-known retailer, such as Kmart, Sears, Wal-Mart, and so on. In these situations, most sales are either cash or credit card sales. In fact, when you use a retailer's credit card (J. C. Penney or Sears, for example), instead of giving a discount, the retailer charges interest on the balance due if not paid within a specified period (usually 25–30 days).

To illustrate, assume that you charge on your J. C. Penney credit card a new outfit that costs $300. J. C. Penney will make the following entry at the date of sale:

| | | |
|---|---|---|
| Accounts Receivable | 300 | |
| Sales | | 300 |
| (To record sale of merchandise) | | |

J. C. Penney will then send you a monthly statement of this transaction and any others that have occurred during the month. If you fail to pay in full within 30 days, J. C. Penney adds an interest (financing) charge to the balance due. Although interest rates vary from state to state and from time to time (depending in part on federal monetary policy), a common rate for retailers is 18% per year or 1.5% per month.

When financing charges are added, the seller recognizes interest revenue. Assuming that you owe $300 at the end of the month, and J. C. Penney charges 1.5% per month on the balance due, the entry to record interest revenue of $4.50 ($300 × 1.5%) is as follows:

| | | |
|---|---|---|
| Accounts Receivable | 4.50 | |
|     Interest Revenue | | 4.50 |
|         (To record interest on amount due) | | |

Interest revenue is often substantial for many retailers.

## ▸Accounting in Action ▸ *Business Insight*

Interest rates on most credit cards are quite high, averaging approximately 18.8%. As a result, consumers are often looking for companies that charge lower rates. But be careful—some companies offer lower interest rates but have eliminated the standard 25-day grace period before finance charges are incurred. Other companies encourage consumers to get more in debt by advertising that only a $1 minimum payment is due on a $1,000 account balance! They, of course, earn more interest! Chase Manhattan Corp. markets a credit card that allows cardholders to skip a payment twice a year. However, the outstanding balance continues to incur interest. Other credit card companies calculate finance charges initially on two-month, rather than one-month averages, a practice which often translates into higher interest charges. In short, read the fine print. Because of rising competition among banks to issue MasterCard and VISA credit cards, interest rates in 1994 ranged between 9.5% with annual fees (of $18 to $35) to 21% with no annual fees.

*Source: Wall Street Journal, February 21, 1992, and Fortune, November 28, 1994.*

## Valuing Accounts Receivable

STUDY OBJECTIVE
▼ 3
*Distinguish between the methods and bases used to value accounts receivable.*

Once receivables are recorded in the accounts, the next question is: How should these receivables be reported on the balance sheet? Determining the amount to report as an asset is important because some receivables will become uncollectible. To ensure that receivables are not overstated on the balance sheet, they are stated at their cash (net) realizable value. Cash (net) realizable value is the net amount expected to be received in cash. The cash realizable value excludes amounts that the company estimates it will not be able to collect. Receivables are therefore reduced by estimated uncollectible receivables on the balance sheet.

The income statement also is affected by the amount of uncollectibles. An expense for estimated uncollectibles is recorded to make certain that expenses are not understated and are matched with related sales revenue. This expense is reported as **bad debts expense** on the income statement.

### *Uncollectible Accounts Receivable*

Although each customer must satisfy the credit requirements of the seller before the credit sale is approved, inevitably some accounts receivable become uncollectible. For example, a company may experience a decline in sales because of a downturn in the economy. Similarly, individuals may be laid off from their jobs or be faced with unexpected hospital bills.

In accounting, credit losses are debited to Bad Debts Expense (or Uncollectible Accounts Expense). Such losses are considered a normal and necessary risk of doing business on a credit basis. In fact, from a management point of view, a reasonable amount of uncollectible accounts is evidence of a sound credit policy. When bad debts are abnormally low, the company may be losing profitable business by following a credit policy that is too strict. Of course, abnormally high bad debts indicate a credit policy that is too lenient.

Two methods are used in accounting for uncollectible accounts: (1) the allowance method and (2) the direct write-off method. Each of these methods is explained in the following sections.

**Allowance Method.** The allowance method is required for financial reporting purposes when bad debts are material in amount. Its essential features are:

**Helpful hint** In this context, *material* means significant or important.

1. Uncollectible accounts receivable are estimated and matched against sales in the same accounting period in which the sales occurred.
2. Estimated uncollectibles are debited to Bad Debts Expense and credited to Allowance for Doubtful Accounts through an adjusting entry at the end of each period.
3. Actual uncollectibles are debited to Allowance for Doubtful Accounts and credited to Accounts Receivable at the time the specific account is written off.

*Recording Estimated Uncollectibles.* To illustrate the allowance method, assume that Hampson Furniture has credit sales of $1,200,000 in 1996, of which $200,000 remain uncollected at December 31. The credit manager estimates that $12,000 of these sales will prove uncollectible. The adjusting entry to record the estimated uncollectibles is:

| Dec. 31 | Bad Debts Expense | 12,000 | |
| |     Allowance for Doubtful Accounts | | 12,000 |
| |     (To record estimate of uncollectible | | |
| |     accounts) | | |

Bad Debts Expense is reported in the income statement as an operating expense (usually as a selling expense). Thus, the estimated uncollectibles are **matched** with sales in 1996 because the expense is recorded in the same year the sales are made.

Allowance for Doubtful Accounts is a contra asset account that shows the claims on customers that are expected to become uncollectible in the future. A contra account is used instead of a direct credit to Accounts Receivable because we do not know which customers will not pay. The credit balance in this account will absorb the specific write-offs when they occur. **Allowance for Doubtful Accounts is not closed at the end of the fiscal year.** It is deducted from Accounts Receivable in the current asset section of the balance sheet as follows:

| | | |
|---|---|---|
| Current assets | | |
|   Cash | | $ 14,800 |
|   Accounts receivable | $200,000 | |
|   Less: Allowance for doubtful accounts | 12,000 | 188,000 |
|   Merchandise inventory | | 310,000 |
|   Prepaid expense | | 25,000 |
|   Total current assets | | $537,800 |

**Illustration 8-1**

*Presentation of allowance for doubtful accounts*

▶ **International note**

The Finance Ministry in Japan recently noted that financial institutions should make better disclosure of bad loans. This disclosure would help depositors pick healthy banks.

The amount of $188,000 represents the expected **cash realizable value** of the accounts receivable at the statement date.

***Recording the Write-off of an Uncollectible Account.*** Companies use various methods of collecting past-due accounts, such as the sequence of letters, calls, and legal action described by Tim Ellington of the NCSU *Technician* in the opening story. When all means of collecting a past-due account have been exhausted and collection appears impossible, the account should be written off. To prevent premature write-offs, each write-off should be formally approved in writing by authorized management personnel.

Assume, for example, that the vice-president of finance of Hampson Furniture authorizes the write-off of the $500 balance owed by R. A. Ware on March 1, 1997. The entry to record the write-off is:

| Mar. 1 | Allowance for Doubtful Accounts | 500 | |
| | Accounts Receivable—R. A. Ware | | 500 |
| | (Write-off of R. A. Ware account) | | |

Bad Debts Expense is not debited when the write-off occurs. **Under the allowance method, every bad debt write-off is debited to the allowance account and not to Bad Debts Expense.** A debit to Bad Debts Expense would be incorrect, because the expense is recognized when the adjusting entry is made for estimated bad debts. After posting, the general ledger accounts will show:

**Illustration 8-2**

*General ledger balances after write-off*

| Accounts Receivable | | | | Allowance for Doubtful Accounts | | | |
|---|---|---|---|---|---|---|---|
| 1/1/97 Bal. | 200,000 | 3/1/97 | 500 | 3/1/97 | 500 | 1/1/97 Bal. | 12,000 |
| 3/1/97 Bal. | 199,500 | | | | | 3/1/97 | 11,500 |

A write-off affects only balance sheet accounts. The write-off of the account reduces both Accounts Receivable and the Allowance for Doubtful Accounts. Cash realizable value in the balance sheet, therefore, remains the same as illustrated below.

**Illustration 8-3**

*Cash realizable value comparison*

| | Before Write-off | After Write-off |
|---|---|---|
| Accounts receivable | $200,000 | $199,500 |
| Allowance for doubtful accounts | 12,000 | 11,500 |
| Cash realizable value | $188,000 | $188,000 |

***Recovery of an Uncollectible Account.*** Occasionally, a company collects from a customer after the account has been written off as uncollectible. Two entries are required to record the recovery of a bad debt: (1) The entry made in writing off the account is reversed to reinstate the customer's account. (2) The collection is journalized in the usual manner. To illustrate, assume that on July 1, R. A. Ware pays the $500 amount that had been written off on March 1. The entries are:

(1)

| July 1 | Accounts Receivable—R. A. Ware | 500 | |
| | Allowance for Doubtful Accounts | | 500 |
| | (To reverse write-off of R. A. Ware account) | | |

(2)

| 1 | Cash | 500 | |
| | Accounts Receivable—R. A. Ware | | 500 |
| | (To record collection from R. A. Ware) | | |

Note that the recovery of a bad debt, like the write-off of a bad debt, affects only balance sheet accounts. The net effect of the two entries above is a debit to Cash and a credit to Allowance for Doubtful Accounts for $500. Accounts Receivable is debited and the Allowance for Doubtful Accounts is credited for two reasons: First, the company made an error in judgment when it wrote off the account receivable. Second, R. A. Ware did pay, and therefore the Accounts Receivable account should show this collection for possible future credit purposes.

**Helpful hint** Like the write-off, a recovery does not involve the income statement.

**Bases Used for Allowance Method.** To simplify the preceding explanation, the amount of the expected uncollectibles was given. However, in "real life" companies must estimate that amount if they use the allowance method. Two bases are used to determine this amount: **(1) percentage of sales**, and **(2) percentage of receivables**. Both bases are generally accepted in accounting. The choice is a management decision. It depends on the relative emphasis that management wishes to give to expenses and revenues on the one hand or to cash realizable value of the accounts receivable on the other. The choice is whether to emphasize income statement or balance sheet relationships. Illustration 8-4 compares the two bases.

**Illustration 8-4**

*Comparison of bases of estimating uncollectibles*

The percentage of sales basis results in a better matching of expenses with revenues—an income statement viewpoint. In contrast, the percentage of receivables basis produces the better estimate of cash realizable value—a balance sheet viewpoint. Under both bases, it is necessary to determine the company's past experience with bad debt losses.

**Percentage of Sales.** In the percentage of sales basis, management establishes a percentage relationship between the amount of credit sales and expected losses from uncollectible accounts. The percentage is based on past experience and anticipated credit policy.

The percentage is usually applied to either total credit sales or net credit sales of the current year. To illustrate, assume that Gonzalez Company elects to use the percentage of sales basis and concludes that 1% of net credit sales will become uncollectible. If net credit sales for 1996 are $800,000, the estimated bad debts expense is $8,000 (1% × $800,000). The adjusting entry is:

| Dec. 31 | Bad Debts Expense | 8,000 | |
| |    Allowance for Doubtful Accounts | | 8,000 |
| |      (To record estimated bad debts for year) | | |

**This basis of estimating uncollectibles emphasizes the matching of expenses with revenues.** As a result, Bad Debts Expense will show a direct percentage relationship to the sales base on which it is computed. **When the adjusting entry is made, the existing balance in the Allowance for Doubtful Accounts is disregarded**. The adjusted balance in this account should result in a reasonable approximation of the realizable value of the receivables. If actual write-offs differ significantly from the amount estimated, the percentage for future years should be modified.

## ▸Technology in Action

 In computerized accounts receivable systems, percentage of sales relationships can be readily obtained from the database of information on customer accounts. Such analysis is often referred to as a history search.

*Percentage of Receivables.*    Under the percentage of receivables basis, management establishes a percentage relationship between the amount of receivables and expected losses from uncollectible accounts. A schedule (often called an **aging schedule**) is prepared, in which customer balances are classified by the length of time they have been unpaid. Because of its emphasis on time, the analysis is often called aging the accounts receivable.

After the accounts are aged, the expected bad debt losses are determined by applying percentages based on past experience to the totals of each category. The longer a receivable is past due, the less likely it is to be collected. As a result, the estimated percentage of uncollectible debts increases as the number of days past due increases. An aging schedule for Dart Company is shown in Illustration 8-5. Note the increasing percentages from 2% to 40%.

**Illustration 8-5**

*Aging schedule*

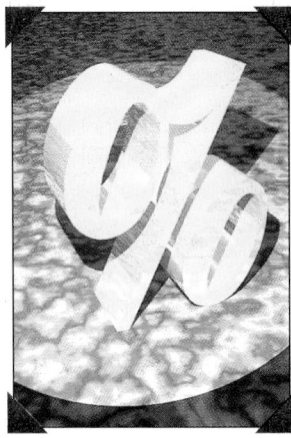

**Helpful hint**   The higher percentages are used for the older categories because the longer an account is past due, the more susceptible it is to being uncollectible.

| Customer | Total | Not Yet Due | Number of Days Past Due | | | |
|---|---|---|---|---|---|---|
| | | | 1–30 | 31–60 | 61–90 | Over 90 |
| T. E. Adert | $    600 | | $  300 | | $  200 | $  100 |
| R. C. Bortz | 300 | $    300 | | | | |
| B. A. Carl | 450 | | 200 | $  250 | | |
| O. L. Diker | 700 | 500 | | | 200 | |
| T. O. Ebbet | 600 | | | 300 | | 300 |
| Others | 36,950 | 26,200 | 5,200 | 2,450 | 1,600 | 1,500 |
| | $39,600 | $27,000 | $5,700 | $3,000 | $2,000 | $1,900 |
| Estimated Percentage Uncollectible | | 2% | 4% | 10% | 20% | 40% |
| Total Estimated Bad Debts | $ 2,228 | $   540 | $   228 | $   300 | $   400 | $   760 |

Total uncollectibles for Dart Company ($2,228) represent the amount of existing customer claims expected to become uncollectible in the future. Thus, this amount represents the **required balance** in Allowance for Doubtful Accounts at the balance sheet date. Accordingly, **the amount of the bad debt adjusting entry is the difference between the required balance and the existing balance in the**

## ►Technology in Action

The aging schedule is another example of output that can be obtained from a computerized accounts receivable system. Manually, preparation of this schedule is an onerous and time-consuming task. However, the schedule can be done in minutes on computer systems.

**allowance account.** If the trial balance shows Allowance for Doubtful Accounts with a credit balance of $528, an adjusting entry for $1,700 ($2,228 − $528) is necessary, as shown below:

| | | | |
|---|---|---|---|
| Dec. 31 | Bad Debts Expense | 1,700 | |
| |     Allowance for Doubtful Accounts | | 1,700 |
| |       (To adjust allowance account to total | | |
| |       estimated uncollectibles) | | |

After the adjusting entry is posted, the accounts of the Dart Company will show:

| Bad Debts Expense | | Allowance for Doubtful Accounts | |
|---|---|---|---|
| 12/31 Adj. 1,700 | | Bal. 528 | |
| | | 12/31 Adj. 1,700 | |
| | | Bal. 2,228 | |

**Illustration 8-6**

*Bad debt accounts after posting*

Occasionally the allowance account will have a **debit balance** prior to adjustment, because write-offs during the year have exceeded previous provisions for bad debts. In such a case **the debit balance is added to the required balance** when the adjusting entry is made. Thus, if there had been a $500 debit balance in the allowance account before adjustment, the adjusting entry would have been for $2,728 ($2,228 + $500) to arrive at a credit balance of $2,228.

The percentage of receivables method will normally result in the better approximation of cash realizable value. This method, however, will not result in the better matching of expenses with revenues if some customers' accounts are more than one year past due. Under such circumstances, bad debts expense for the current period would include amounts applicable to the sales of a prior period.

**Direct Write-off Method.** Under the direct write-off method, bad debt losses are not estimated and no allowance account is used. When an account is determined to be uncollectible, the loss is charged to Bad Debts Expense. Assume, for example, that Warden Co. writes off M. E. Doran's $200 balance as uncollectible on December 12. The entry is:

| | | | |
|---|---|---|---|
| Dec. 12 | Bad Debts Expense | 200 | |
| |     Accounts Receivable—M. E. Doran | | 200 |
| |       (To record write-off of M. E. Doran | | |
| |       account) | | |

When this method is used, bad debts expense will show only actual losses from uncollectibles. Accounts receivable will be reported at its gross amount.

Under the direct write-off method, bad debts expense is often recorded in a period different from the period in which the revenue was recorded. Thus, no attempt is made to match bad debts expense to sales revenues in the income statement or to show the cash realizable value of the accounts receivable in the balance sheet. **Consequently, unless bad debt losses are insignificant, the direct write-off method is not acceptable for financial reporting purposes.** The direct write-off method is, however, used for tax purposes. The Internal Revenue Service allows a tax deduction for uncollectible accounts only when specific accounts receivable are deemed uncollectible.

## Disposing of Accounts Receivable

**STUDY OBJECTIVE**

·········▼·········
**4**

*Describe the entries to record the disposition of accounts receivable.*

In the normal course of events, accounts receivable are collected in cash and removed from the books. However, as credit sales and receivables have grown in size and significance, the "normal course of events" has changed. In order to accelerate the receipt of cash from receivables, companies frequently sell the receivables to another company for cash, thereby shortening the cash-to-cash operating cycle.

There are several reasons for the sale of receivables. **First, for competitive reasons, sellers** (retailers, wholesalers, and manufacturers) **often must provide financing to purchasers of their goods.** For example, in the sale of durable goods, such as automobiles, trucks, industrial and farm equipment, computers, and appliances, a majority of the sales are on a credit basis. Many major companies in these industries have therefore created companies that accept responsibility for accounts receivable financing. General Motors has General Motors Acceptance Corp. (GMAC), Sears has Sears Roebuck Acceptance Corp. (SRAC), Ford has Ford Motor Credit Corp. (FMCC), and Chrysler has Chrysler Finance Corporation (CFC). These companies are referred to as captive finance companies because they are wholly owned by the company making the product. The purpose of captive financing companies is to encourage the sale of their product by assuring financing to buyers.

## ▶ Accounting in Action ▸ *Business Insight*

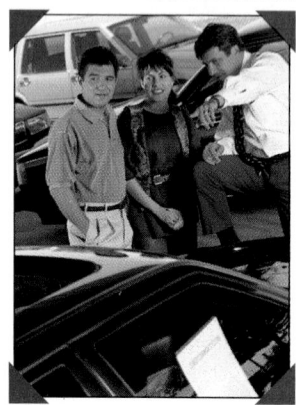

For example, consider the local car dealer. Most local dealers simply do not have the financial resources to finance the sale of cars because most loans today are quite large in relationship to the cost of the car. Recently, the percentage of the price financed by the Big Three automobile manufacturers in the United States was 93% of the selling price of the automobile. In addition, the average length of the loan was 53.5 months, compared to 35 months a decade ago. It is no wonder, therefore, that a captive finance subsidiary like General Motors Acceptance Corporation, if it were a bank, would rank third in total assets behind Citicorp and Chase Manhattan.

**Second, receivables may be sold because they may be the only reasonable source of cash.** When money is tight, companies may not be able to borrow money in the usual credit markets. If money is available, the cost of borrowing may be prohibitive. A final reason for selling receivables is that **billing and collection are often time consuming and costly.** As a result, it is often easier for a retailer to sell the receivable to another party with expertise in billing and collection matters. Credit card companies such as MasterCard, VISA, American Express, and Diners Club specialize in billing and collecting accounts receivable.

### *Sale of Receivables*

A common sale of receivables is a sale to a factor. A factor is a finance company or bank that buys receivables from businesses for a fee and then collects the payments directly from the customers. Factoring was traditionally associated

## ►Accounting in Action ► *Business Insight*

"They're the devil in disguise," is how CEO Barry Weinstein describes factors. Unable to raise capital from bankers or outside investors, Weinstein turned to factoring receivables. The arrangement was pricey: the factor charged interest of 5% a month, to a maximum of 13% of the total invoice, on any uncollected invoices that were factored. The deal became an endless cycle. Soon Weinstein was factoring all new invoices to get the cash to pay the interest on the older factored invoices.

*Source: Inc., July 1994, p. 97.*

with the textiles, apparel, footwear, furniture, and home furnishing industries. It has now spread to many other types of businesses and is a multibillion dollar business. For example, Sears, Roebuck and Co. recently sold $14.8 billion of customer accounts receivable.

Factoring arrangements vary widely, but typically the factor (purchaser of the receivables) charges a commission. It ranges from 1% to 3% of the amount of receivables purchased. To illustrate, assume that Hendredon Furniture factors $600,000 of receivables to Federal Factors, Inc. Federal Factors assesses a service charge of 2% of the amount of receivables sold. The journal entry to record the sale by Hendredon Furniture is as follows:

| | | |
|---|---|---|
| Cash | 588,000 | |
| Service Charge Expense (2% × $600,000) | 12,000 | |
| Accounts Receivable | | 600,000 |
| (To record the sale of accounts receivable) | | |

If the company usually sells its receivables, the service charge expense incurred by Hendredon Furniture is recorded as selling expense. If receivables are sold infrequently, this amount may be reported in the Other Expenses and Losses section of the income statement.

### Credit Card Sales

Approximately 1 billion credit cards were estimated to be in use recently—more than three credit cards for every man, woman, and child in this country. A common type of credit card is a national credit card such as VISA, MasterCard, and American Express. Three parties are involved when national credit cards are used in making retail sales: (1) the credit card issuer, who is independent of the retailer, (2) the retailer, and (3) the customer. A retailer's acceptance of a national credit card is another form of selling (factoring) the receivable.

The major advantages of these national credit cards to the retailer are shown in Illustration 8-7.

In exchange for these advantages, the retailer pays the credit card issuer a fee of 2–6% of the invoice price for its services.

**VISA and MasterCard Sales.** Sales resulting from the use of VISA and MasterCard are considered cash sales by the retailer. These cards are issued by banks. Upon receipt of credit card sales slips from a retailer, the bank immediately adds the amount to the seller's bank balance. These credit card sales slips are therefore recorded in the same manner as checks deposited from a cash sale. Banks generally charge a fee of 2–4% of the credit card sales slips for this service. To illustrate, Anita Ferreri purchases a number of compact discs for her restaurant from Karen Kerr Music Co. for $1,000 using her VISA First Bank Card. The

**Illustration 8-7**

*Advantages of credit cards to the retailer*

service fee that First Bank charges is 3%. The entry to record this transaction by Karen Kerr Music is as follows:

| | | |
|---|---|---|
| Cash | 970 | |
| Service Charge Expense | 30 | |
|     Sales | | 1,000 |
|       (To record Visa credit card sales) | | |

**American Express Sales.**   Sales using American Express cards are reported as credit sales, not cash sales. Conversion into cash does not occur until American Express remits the net amount to the seller. To illustrate, assume that Four Seasons restaurant accepts an American Express card for a $300 bill. The entry for the sale by Four Seasons (assuming a 5% fee) is:

| | | |
|---|---|---|
| Accounts Receivable—American Express | 285 | |
| Service Charge Expense | 15 | |
|     Sales | | 300 |
|       (To record American Express credit card sales) | | |

Thus American Express will subsequently pay the restaurant $285 which the restaurant will record as follows:

| | | |
|---|---|---|
| Cash | 285 | |
|     Accounts Receivable—American Express | | 285 |
|       (To record redemption of credit card billings) | | |

Service Charge Expense is reported as a selling expense in the income statement by the restaurant.

## ►Accounting in Action ► *Business Insight*

Many *are* leaving home without it! Despite long-standing advertisements that urge customers not to leave home without it, two million users cut up their AmEx (American Express) cards between 1991 and 1993 and went in search of better bargains in credit cards. Now AmEx is staking its future on a new set of twelve different types of credit cards. All will offer revolving credit at rates comparable to AmEx's principal rivals, Visa and MasterCard. The U.S. market is saturated with 1 *billion* cards issued by 6,500 companies. Competition is fierce because the pool of potential new customers is shrinking at the same time America's plastic habit is growing. The industry average for bad debt losses on credit cards is 5%.

*Source: Time*, September 12, 1994, p. 60.

## *Before You Go On . . .*

### ► *Review It*

1. How are accounts receivable recognized in the accounts?
2. What are the essential features of the allowance method?
3. Explain the difference between the percentage of sales and the percentage of receivables methods.
4. Why do companies sell their receivables?
5. What is the journal entry when a company sells its receivables to a factor?

### ► *Do It*

Peter M. Dell Wholesalers Co. has been expanding faster than it can raise capital and, according to its local banker, the company has reached its debt ceiling. Dell's customers are slow in paying (60–90 days), but its suppliers (creditors) are demanding 30-day payment. Dell has a cash flow problem.

Dell needs to raise $120,000 in cash to safely cover next Friday's employee payroll. Dell's present balance of outstanding receivables totals $750,000. What might Dell do to alleviate this cash crunch? Record the entry that Dell would make when it raises the needed cash.

**Reasoning:** One source of immediate cash at a competitive cost is the sale of receivables to a factor. Rather than waiting until it can collect receivables, Dell may raise immediate cash by selling its receivables. The last thing Dell (or any employer) wants to do is miss a payroll.

**Solution:** Assuming that Dell Co. factors $125,000 of its accounts receivable at a 1% service charge, the following entry would be made:

| | | |
|---|---|---|
| Cash | 123,750 | |
| Service Charge Expense | 1,250 | |
| Accounts Receivable | | 125,000 |
| (To record sale of receivables to factor) | | |

*Related exercise material: BE8–9 and E8–5.*

## **N**otes Receivable

Credit may also be granted in exchange for a formal credit instrument known as a **promissory note**. A **promissory note** is a written promise to pay a specified amount of money on demand or at a definite time. Promissory notes may be used (1) when individuals and companies lend or borrow money, (2) when the amount of the transaction and the credit period exceed normal limits, and (3) in settlement of accounts receivable.

**Helpful hint** Note the similarities and differences between a note and a check. *Similarities:* Both are instruments (documents that are readily transferable by endorsement). Both have a maker and a payee. *Differences:* A check is a cash instrument that does not bear interest. A note is a credit instrument that may bear interest.

In a promissory note, the party making the promise to pay is called the maker; the party to whom payment is to be made is called the payee. The payee may be specifically identified by name or may be designated simply as the bearer of the note. In the note shown in Illustration 8-8, Brent Company is the maker and Wilma Company is the payee. To the Wilma Company, the promissory note is a note receivable; to the Brent Company, the note is a note payable.

**Illustration 8-8**

*Promissory note*

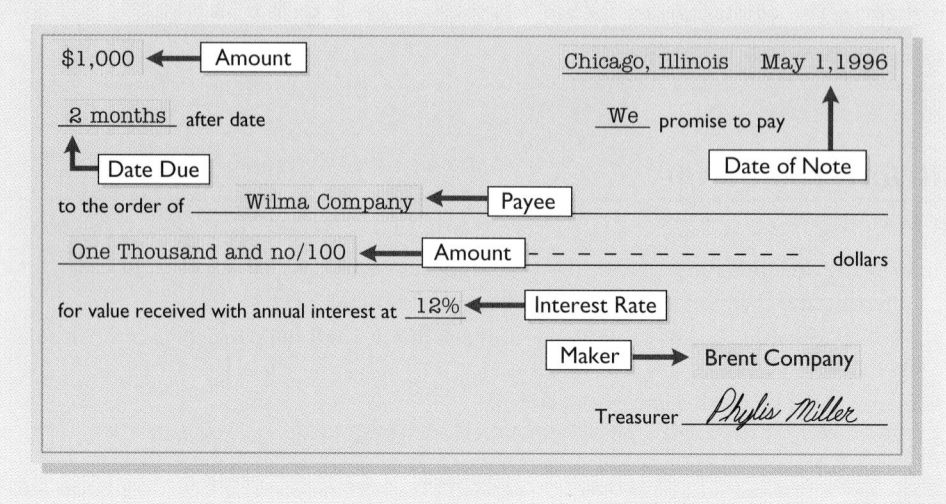

Notes receivable gives the holder a stronger legal claim to assets than accounts receivable. Like accounts receivable, notes receivable can be readily sold to another party. Promissory notes are negotiable instruments (as are checks), which means that, when sold they can be transferred to another party by endorsement.

Notes receivable are frequently accepted from customers who need to extend the payment of an outstanding account receivable and are often required from high-risk customers. In some industries (e.g., the pleasure and sport boat industry) all credit sales are supported by notes. The majority of notes, however, originate from lending transactions. The basic issues in accounting for notes receivable are the same as those for accounts receivable.

1. **Recognizing** notes receivable.
2. **Valuing** notes receivable.
3. **Disposing of** notes receivable.

On the following pages, we will look at each of these issues. Before we do, though, we need to consider two issues that did not apply to accounts receivable: the maturity date and the computation of interest.

### Determining the Maturity Date

**STUDY OBJECTIVE**

▼
**5**

*Compute the maturity date of, and interest on, notes receivable.*

When the life of a note is expressed in terms of months, the due date is found by counting the months from the date of issue. For example, the maturity date of a 3-month note dated May 1 is August 1. A note drawn on the last day of a month matures on the last day of a subsequent month; that is, a July 31 note due in 2 months matures on September 30. When the due date is stated in terms of days, it is necessary to count the exact number of days to determine the maturity date. In counting, **the date the note is issued is omitted but the due date is**

**included**. For example, the maturity date of a 60-day note dated July 17 is September 15, computed as follows:

| | | |
|---|---|---|
| Term of note | | 60 |
| July (31 – 17) | 14 | |
| August | 31 | 45 |
| **Maturity date, September** | | **15** |

**Illustration 8-9**

*Computation of maturity date*

The due date (maturity date) of a promissory note may be stated in one of three ways, as shown in Illustration 8-10.

**Illustration 8-10**

*Maturity date of different notes*

## Computing Interest

As indicated in Chapter 3, the basic formula for computing interest on an interest-bearing note is:

**Illustration 8-11**

*Formula for computing interest*

The interest rate specified on the note is an **annual** rate of interest. The time factor in the computation above expresses the fraction of a year that the note is outstanding. When the maturity date is stated in days, the time factor is frequently the number of days divided by 360. When the due date is stated in months, the time factor is the number of months divided by 12. The computation of interest is shown in Illustration 8-12.

**Helpful hint** The interest rate specified is the *annual* rate.

| Terms of Note | Interest Computation | | | | |
|---|---|---|---|---|---|
| | Face | × Rate × | Time | = | Interest |
| $ 730, 18%, 120 days | $ 730 × | 18% × | 120/360 | = | $ 43.80 |
| $1,000, 15%, 6 months | $1,000 × | 15% × | 6/12 | = | $ 75.00 |
| $2,000, 12%, 1 year | $2,000 × | 12% × | 1/1 | = | $240.00 |

**Illustration 8-12**

*Computation of interest*

There are many different ways to calculate interest. For example, the computation above assumed the total days to be used for the year are 360. Many financial institutions use 365 days to compute interest. It is more profitable, though, to use 360 days because the holder of the note receives more interest than if 365 days are used. For homework problems, assume 360 days.

## Recognizing Notes Receivable

*Explain how notes receivable are recognized in the accounts.*

To illustrate the basic entry for notes receivable, we will use the $1,000, 2-month, 12% promissory note on page 340. Assuming that the note was written to settle an open account, the entry for the receipt of the note by Wilma Company is:

| May 1 | Notes Receivable | 1,000 | |
|---|---|---|---|
| | Accounts Receivable—Brent Company | | 1,000 |
| | (To record acceptance of Brent Company note) | | |

Observe that the note receivable is recorded at its **face value**, the value shown on the face of the note. No interest revenue is reported when the note is accepted because the revenue recognition principle does not recognize revenue until earned. Interest is earned (accrued) as time passes.

If a note is exchanged for cash, the entry is a debit to Notes Receivable and a credit to Cash in the amount of the loan.

## Valuing Notes Receivable

*Describe how notes receivable are valued.*

Like accounts receivable, short-term notes receivable are reported at their **cash (net) realizable value**. The notes receivable allowance account is Allowance for Doubtful Accounts. Valuing short-term notes receivable is the same as valuing accounts receivable. The computations and estimations involved in determining cash realizable value and in recording the proper amount of bad debt expense and related allowance are similar.

Long-term notes receivable, however, pose additional estimation problems. As an example, we need only look at the problems a number of large U.S. banks are having in collecting their receivables. Loans to less-developed countries are particularly worrisome. Developing countries need loans for development but often find repayment difficult. U.S. loans (notes) to less-developed countries at one time totaled approximately $135 billion. In Brazil alone, Citibank at one time had loans equivalent to 80% of its stockholders' equity; Chemical Bank had 77% of its equity lent out in Mexico. Determining the proper allowance is understandably difficult for these types of long-term receivables.

## Disposing of Notes Receivable

*Describe the entries to record the disposition of notes receivable.*

Notes may be held to their maturity date, at which time the face value plus accrued interest is due. In some situations, the maker of the note defaults and appropriate adjustment must be made. In other situations, similar to accounts receivable, the holder of the note speeds up the conversion to cash by selling the receivables. The entries for honoring and dishonoring notes are illustrated below.

### *Honor of Notes Receivable*

A note is **honored** when it is paid in full at its maturity date. For each interest-bearing note, the amount due at maturity is the face value of the note plus interest for the length of time specified on the note.

To illustrate, assume that Wolder Co. lends Higly Inc. $10,000 on June 1, accepting a 4-month, 9% interest note. In this situation, interest is $300 ($10,000 ×

9% × 4/12); the amount due, the maturity value, is $10,300. To obtain payment, Wolder (the payee) must present the note either to Higly Inc. (the maker) or to the maker's duly appointed agent, such as a bank. Assuming that Wolder presents the note to Higly Inc. on October 1, the maturity date, the entry by Wolder to record the collection is:

| | | | |
|---|---|---|---|
| Oct. 1 | Cash | 10,300 | |
| |     Notes Receivable | | 10,000 |
| |     Interest Revenue | | 300 |
| |       (To record collection of Higly Inc. note) | | |

If Wolder Co. prepares financial statements as of September 30, it would be necessary to accrue interest. In this case, the adjusting entry by Wolder would be for 4 months, or $300, as shown below:

| | | | |
|---|---|---|---|
| Sept. 30 | Interest Receivable | 300 | |
| |     Interest Revenue | | 300 |
| |       (To accrue four months' interest) | | |

When interest has been accrued, it is necessary to credit Interest Receivable at maturity. The entry by Wolder to record the honoring of the Higly note on October 1 is:

| | | | |
|---|---|---|---|
| Oct. 1 | Cash | 10,300 | |
| |     Notes Receivable | | 10,000 |
| |     Interest Receivable | | 300 |
| |       (To record collection of note at maturity) | | |

In this case, Interest Receivable is credited because the receivable was established in the adjusting entry.

# ▶Accounting in Action ▸ *International Insight*

Varied plans have been proposed to solve the international debt problem. These plans range from encouraging more lending to reducing or forgiving the debt. At one time, this debt burden to banks worldwide exceeded $1.3 trillion. (As an aside, a trillion is a lot of money—enough money to give every man, woman, and child in the world approximately $250 each. Why were these loans made in the first place? The reasons are numerous, but the three major ones are: (1) to provide stability to these governments and thereby increase trade, (2) the belief that governments would never default on payment, and (3) the desire by banks to increase their income by lending to these countries.

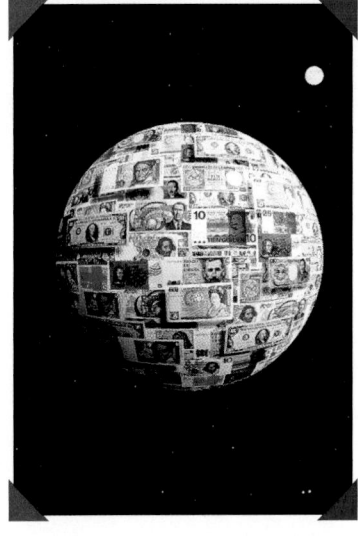

## Dishonor of Notes Receivable

A dishonored note is a note that is not paid in full at maturity. A dishonored note receivable is no longer negotiable. However, the payee still has a claim against the maker of the note. Therefore the Notes Receivable account is usually transferred to an Account Receivable.

To illustrate, assume that Higly Inc. on October 1 indicates that it cannot pay at the present time. The entry to record the dishonor of the note depends on whether eventual collection is expected. If Wolder Co. expects eventual collection, the amount due (face value and interest) on the note is debited to Accounts Receivable. Wolder Co. would make the following entry at the time the note is dishonored (assuming no previous accrual of interest):

| Oct. 1 | Accounts Receivable | 10,300 | |
| | Notes Receivable | | 10,000 |
| | Interest Revenue | | 300 |
| | (To record the dishonor of the note) | | |

If there is no hope of collection, the face value of the note should be written off by debiting the Allowance for Doubtful Accounts. No interest revenue would be recorded because collection will not occur.

### Sale of Notes Receivable

The accounting for the sales of notes receivable is recorded in a manner similar to the sale of accounts receivable. The Accounting in Action discussion that follows demonstrates how notes receivable are sold and resold. The accounting entries for the sale of notes receivable are left for a more advanced course.

## Before You Go On . . .

### ▸ Review It

1. What is the basic formula for computing interest?
2. At what value are notes receivable reported on the balance sheet?
3. Explain the difference between honoring and dishonoring a note receivable.

### ▸ Do It

Gambit Stores accepts from Leonard Co. a $3,400, 90-day, 12% note dated May 10 in settlement of Leonard's overdue open account. What is the maturity date of the note? What is the entry made by Gambit at the maturity date, assuming Leonard pays the note and interest in full at that time?

**Reasoning:** When the due date is stated in terms of days, it is necessary to count the exact number of days to determine the maturity date. In counting, the date the note is issued is omitted, but the due date is included. The entry to record interest at maturity in this solution assumes that no interest is accrued on this note.

**Solution:** The maturity date is August 8, computed as follows:

| Term of note: | | 90 days |
|---|---|---|
| May (31 − 10) | 21 | |
| June | 30 | |
| July | 31 | 82 |
| Maturity date, August | | 8 |

The interest payable at maturity date is $102, computed as follows:

$$\text{Face} \times \text{Rate} \times \text{Time} = \text{Interest}$$
$$\$3,400 \times 12\% \times 90/360 = \$102$$

The entry recorded by Gambit Stores at the maturity date is:

| Cash | 3,502 | |
| | Notes Receivable | | 3,400 |
| | Interest Revenue | | 102 |
| | (To record collection of Leonard note) | | |

*Related exercise material:* BE8–8, BE8–10, E8–8, and E8–9.

## ►Accounting in Action ► *Business Insight*

### How One Receivable Crisscrossed the U.S.

Consider how the following note receivable of $120,000 was sold and resold in different markets in the United States and abroad.

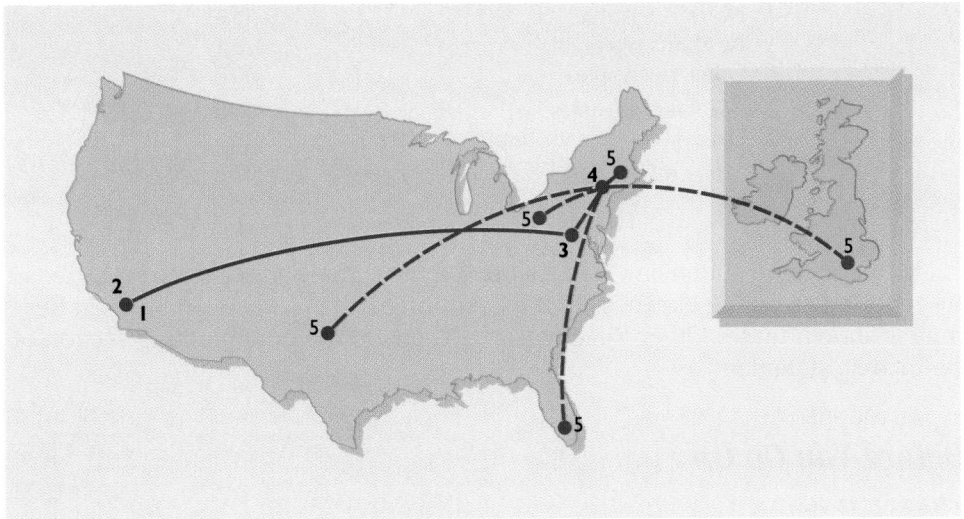

Step 1 *September 1987.* Jim and Erica Vogel bought a four-bedroom house in San Dimas, Calif. They got a $120,000 loan from First Federal S&L of San Gabriel.

Step 2 *December 1987.* First Federal sold the Vogels' receivable to the Federal Home Loan Mortgage Corp., known as Freddie Mac.

Step 3 *December 1987.* In Reston, Va., Freddie Mac put the Vogels' receivable into a giant pool with more than 6,000 other receivables.

Step 4 *May 1988.* Part of that pool was bought by First Boston Corp. in New York. The pool went into a $550 million pool.

Step 5 *May/June 1988.* In Hartford, Conn., Cigna Investments Inc. bought $10 million of this pool for its pension accounts.

*May/June 1988.* In El Reno, Okla., Globe Savings Bank bought $66 million of the pool to expand its receivable portfolio.

*May/June 1988.* In Florida an S&L bought $40 million of the pool as an interest rate hedge.

*May/June 1988.* Other buyers of the pool ranged from a Pittsburgh S&L, to a London commercial bank.

*Source: Wall Street Journal, August 17, 1988.*

## ▼Statement Presentation of Receivables

Each of the major types of receivables should be identified in the balance sheet or in the notes to the financial statements. Short-term receivables are reported within the current asset section of the balance sheet below temporary investments. Temporary investments appear before short-term receivables, because these investments are more liquid, or nearer to cash. Both the gross amount of receivables and the allowance for doubtful accounts should be reported. Illus-

**STUDY OBJECTIVE**
••••••••••▼9••••••••••

*Explain the statement presentation of receivables.*

tration 8-13 shows the current asset presentation of receivables for CPC International Inc.

**Illustration 8-13**

*Balance sheet presentation of receivables*

| CPC INTERNATIONAL INC. | |
| --- | --- |
| Receivables (in millions) | |
| Notes receivable | $ 16.6 |
| Accounts receivable | 375.1 |
| Other receivables | 60.7 |
| Total receivables | 452.4 |
| Less: Allowance for doubtful accounts | 10.5 |
| Net receivables | $441.9 |

In the income statement, Bad Debts Expense and Service Charge Expense are reported as selling expenses in the Operating Expenses section. Interest Revenue is shown under Other Revenues and Gains in the nonoperating section of the income statement.

## *Before You Go On . . .*

### ► *Review It*

1. Explain where accounts and notes receivable are reported on the balance sheet.
2. Where are bad debts expense, service charge expense, and interest revenue reported on the income statement?

### ► *A Look Back at North Carolina State University*

Refer back to the story about the North Carolina State University newspaper at the beginning of the chapter, and answer the following questions:

1. If you had sold advertising space to a tardy paying client, how would you persuade them to pay?
2. At what point would you recommend that the newspaper write-off uncollectible receivables?
3. Indicate the accounts to be debited and credited for each of the following transactions of the newspaper: (a) ad space is sold on account; (b) ad space is sold and prepaid; (c) cash is collected on account; (d) the ad is run for the advertiser who prepaid; (e) an uncollectible account is written off.

**Solution:**

1. The collection process used by the newspaper: a friendly letter at the end of 30 days, a less-than-friendly letter at the end of 45 days, and the filing of a suit in small claims court at the end of 75 days. In addition, a tactful, persuasive telephone call might be added to the attempts to collect.
2. An unpaid receivable should be written off when it is determined that it is uncollectible. Past experience with small unpaid ad bills will usually dictate the appropriate point at which bills are deemed uncollectible. With the limited information given in this case, the write-off would seem proper at the conclusion of an unsuccessful court claim.
3. (a) Debit Accounts Receivable, credit Advertising Revenue.
   (b) Debit Cash, credit Unearned Advertising Revenue.
   (c) Debit Cash, credit Accounts Receivable.
   (d) Debit Unearned Advertising Revenue, credit Advertising Revenue.
   (e) Debit Allowance for Doubtful Accounts, credit Accounts Receivable.

# Summary of Study Objectives

**1.** *Identify the different types of receivables.* Receivables are frequently classified as (1) accounts, (2) notes, and (3) other. Accounts receivable are amounts owed by customers on account. Notes receivable represent claims that are evidenced by formal instruments of credit. Other receivables include nontrade receivables such as interest receivable, loans to company officers, advances to employees, and income taxes refundable.

**2.** *Explain how accounts receivable are recognized in the accounts.* Accounts receivable are recorded at invoice price. They are reduced by Sales Returns and Allowances. Cash discounts reduce the amount received on accounts receivable. When interest is charged on a past due receivable, this interest is added to the accounts receivable balance and is recognized as interest revenue.

**3.** *Distinguish between the methods and bases used to value accounts receivable.* There are two methods of accounting for uncollectible accounts: (1) the allowance method and (2) the direct write-off method. Either the percentage of sales or the percentage of receivables basis may be used to estimate uncollectible accounts using the allowance method. The percentage of sales basis emphasizes the matching principle. The percentage of receivables basis emphasizes the cash realizable value of the accounts receivable. An aging schedule is frequently used with this basis.

**4.** *Describe the entries to record the disposition of accounts receivable.* When an account receivable is collected, Accounts Receivable is credited. When an account receivable is sold, a service charge expense is charged which reduces the amount collected.

**5.** *Compute the maturity date of, and interest on, notes receivable.* The maturity date of a note must be computed unless the due date is specified or the note is payable on demand. For a note stated in months, the maturity date is found by counting the months from the date of issue. For a note stated in days, the number of days is counted, omitting the issue date and counting the due date. The formula for computing interest is face value × interest rate × time.

**6.** *Explain how notes receivable are recognized in the accounts.* Notes receivable are recorded at face value. In some cases, it is necessary to accrue interest prior to maturity. In this case, Interest Receivable is debited and Interest Revenue is credited.

**7.** *Describe how notes receivable are valued.* Like accounts receivable, notes receivable are reported at their cash (net) realizable value. The notes receivable allowance account is the Allowance for Doubtful Accounts. The computation and estimations involved in valuing notes receivables at cash realizable value, and in recording the proper amount of bad debt expense and related allowance are similar to accounts receivable.

**8.** *Describe the entries to record the disposition of notes receivable.* Notes can be held to maturity, at which time the face value plus accrued interest is due and the note is removed from the accounts. However, in many cases, similar to accounts receivable, the holder of the note speeds up the conversion by selling the receivable to another party. In some situations, the maker of the note dishonors the note (defaults), and the note is written off.

**9.** *Explain the statement presentation of receivables.* Each major type of receivable should be identified in the balance sheet or in the notes to the financial statements. Short-term receivables are considered current assets. The gross amount of receivables and allowance for doubtful accounts should be reported. Bad debts and service charge expenses are reported in the income statement as operating (selling) expenses, and interest revenue is shown as other revenues and gains in the nonoperating section of the statement.

# GLOSSARY

**Aging of accounts receivable** The analysis of customer balances by the length of time they have been unpaid. (p. 334).

**Cash (net) realizable value** The net amount expected to be received in cash. (p. 330).

**Dishonored note** A note that is not paid in full at maturity. (p. 343).

**Factor** A finance company or bank that buys receivables from businesses for a fee and then collects the payments directly from the customers. (p. 336).

**Maker** The party in a promissory note who is making the promise to pay. (p. 339).

**Payee** The party to whom payment of a promissory note is to be made. (p. 339).

**Percentage of receivables basis** Management establishes a percentage relationship between the amount of receivables and the expected losses from uncollectible accounts. (p. 334).

**Percentage of sales basis** Management establishes a percentage relationship between the amount of credit sales and expected losses from uncollectible accounts. (p. 333).

**Promissory note** A written promise to pay a specified amount of money on demand or at a definite time. (p. 339).

**Trade receivables** Notes and accounts receivable that result from sales transactions. (p. 328).

# DEMONSTRATION PROBLEM

Presented below are selected transactions related to B. Dylan Corp.

Mar.  1  Sold $20,000 of merchandise to Potter Company, terms 2/10, n/30.

11  Received payment in full from Potter Company for balance due.

12  Accepted Juno Company's $20,000 6-month, 12% note for balance due.

13  Made Dylan Corp. credit card sales for $13,200.

15  Made American Express credit sales totaling $6,700. A 5% service fee is charged by American Express.

30  Received payment in full from American Express Company less 5% service charge.

Apr. 11  Sold accounts receivable of $8,000 to Harcot Factor. Harcot Factor assesses a service charge of 2% of the amount of receivables sold.

13  Received collections of $8,200 on Dylan Corp. credit card sales and added finance charges of 1.5% to the remaining balances.

May 10  Wrote off as uncollectible $16,000 of accounts receivable. Dylan uses the percentage of sales basis to estimate bad debts.

June 30  Credit sales for the first six months total $2,000,000 and the bad debt percentage is 1%. At June 30, the balance in the allowance account is $3,500.

July 16  One of the accounts receivable written off in May pays the amount due, $4,000, in full.

## Instructions

Prepare the journal entries for the transactions.

## Solution to Demonstration Problem

### Problem-Solving Strategies

1. Accounts receivable are generally recorded at invoice price.

2. Sales returns and allowances and cash discounts reduce the amount received on accounts receivable.

3. When accounts receivable are sold, a service charge expense is incurred by the seller.

4. Bad debts expense is an adjusting entry.

5. Percentage of sales basis ignores any balance in the allowance account. Percentage of receivables basis does not ignore this balance.

6. Write-offs of accounts receivable affect only balance sheet accounts.

| | | | |
|---|---|---:|---:|
| Mar. 1 | Accounts Receivable—Potter | 20,000 | |
| | Sales | | 20,000 |
| | (To record sales on account) | | |
| Mar. 11 | Cash | 19,600 | |
| | Sales Discounts (2% × $20,000) | 400 | |
| | Accounts Receivable—Potter | | 20,000 |
| | (To record collection of accounts receivable) | | |
| Mar. 12 | Notes Receivable | 20,000 | |
| | Accounts Receivable—Juno | | 20,000 |
| | (To record acceptance of Juno Company note) | | |
| Mar. 13 | Accounts Receivable | 13,200 | |
| | Sales | | 13,200 |
| | (To record company credit card sales) | | |
| Mar. 15 | Accounts Receivable—American Express | 6,365 | |
| | Service Charge Expense (5% × $6,700) | 335 | |
| | Sales | | 6,700 |
| | (To record credit card sales) | | |
| Mar. 30 | Cash | 6,365 | |
| | Accounts Receivable—American Express | | 6,365 |
| | (To record redemption of credit card billings) | | |
| Apr. 11 | Cash | 7,840 | |
| | Service Charge Expense (2% × $8,000) | 160 | |
| | Accounts Receivable | | 8,000 |
| | (To record sale of receivables to factor) | | |

| | | | |
|---|---|---|---|
| Apr. 13 | Cash | 8,200 | |
| |     Accounts Receivable | | 8,200 |
| |       (To record collection of accounts receivable) | | |
| | Accounts Receivable [($13,200 − $8,200) × 1.5%] | 75 | |
| |     Interest Revenue | | 75 |
| |       (To record interest on amount due) | | |
| May 10 | Allowance for Doubtful Accounts | 16,000 | |
| |     Accounts Receivable | | 16,000 |
| |       (To record write-off of accounts receivable) | | |
| June 30 | Bad Debts Expense ($2,000,000 × 1%) | 20,000 | |
| |     Allowance for Doubtful Accounts | | 20,000 |
| |       (To record estimate of uncollectible accounts) | | |
| July 16 | Accounts Receivable | 4,000 | |
| |     Allowance for Doubtful Accounts | | 4,000 |
| |       (To reverse write-off of accounts receivable) | | |
| | Cash | 4,000 | |
| |     Accounts Receivable | | 4,000 |
| |       (To record collection of accounts receivable) | | |

# SELF-STUDY QUESTIONS

Answers are at the end of the chapter.

(SO 2)

1. Jones Company on June 15 sells merchandise on account to Bullock Co. for $1,000 terms 2/10, n/30. On June 20, Bullock Co. returns merchandise worth $300 to Jones Company. On June 24, payment is received from Bullock Co. for the balance due. What is the amount of cash received?
   a. $700.
   b. $680.
   c. $686.
   d. None of the above.

(SO 3)

2. Which of the following approaches for bad debts is best described as a balance sheet method?
   a. Percentage of receivables basis.
   b. Direct write-off method.
   c. Percentage of sales basis.
   d. Both a and b.

(SO 3)

3. Net sales for the month are $800,000 and bad debts are expected to be 1.5% of net sales. The company uses the percentage of sales basis. If the Allowance for Doubtful Accounts has a credit balance of $15,000 before adjustment, what is the balance after adjustment?
   a. $15,000.
   b. $27,000.
   c. $23,000.
   d. $31,000.

(SO 3)

4. In 1996, D. H. Lawrence Company had net credit sales of $750,000. On January 1, 1996, Allowance for Doubtful Accounts had a credit balance of $18,000. During 1996, $30,000 of uncollectible ac-

counts receivable were written off. Past experience indicates that 3% of net credit sales become uncollectible. What should be the adjusted balance of Allowance for Doubtful Accounts at December 31, 1996?
   a. $10,050.
   b. $10,500.
   c. $22,500.
   d. $40,500.

(SO 3)

5. An analysis and aging of the accounts receivable of Machiavelli Company at December 31 reveals the following data:

| | |
|---|---|
| Accounts Receivable | $800,000 |
| Allowance for Doubtful Accounts per books before adjustment | 50,000 |
| Amounts expected to become uncollectible | 65,000 |

The cash realizable value of the accounts receivable at December 31, after adjustment, is:
   a. $685,000.
   b. $750,000.
   c. $800,000.
   d. $735,000.

(SO 6)

6. One of the following statements about promissory notes is incorrect. The incorrect statement is:
   a. The party making the promise to pay is called the maker.
   b. The party to whom payment is to be made is called the payee.

c. A promissory note is not a negotiable instrument.

d. A promissory note is more liquid than an accounts receivable.

(SO 4) 7. Which of the following statements about VISA credit card sales is incorrect?

a. The credit card issuer makes the credit investigation of the customer.

b. The retailer is not involved in the collection process.

c. Two parties are involved.

d. The retailer receives cash more quickly than it would from individual customers.

(SO 4) 8. Morgan Retailers accepted $50,000 of Citibank VISA credit card charges for merchandise sold on July 1. Citibank charges 4% for its credit card use. The entry to record this transaction by Morgan Retailers will include a credit to sales of $50,000 and a debit(s) to:

| | |
|---|---|
| a. Cash | $48,000 |
| and Service Charge Expense | $2,000 |
| b. Accounts Receivable | $48,000 |
| and Service Charge Expense | $2,000 |
| c. Cash | $50,000 |
| d. Accounts Receivable | $50,000 |

9. Sorenson Co. accepts a $1,000, 3-month, 12% promissory note in settlement of an account with Parton Co. The entry to record this transaction is as follows: (SO 6)

| | | |
|---|---|---|
| a. Notes Receivable | 1,030 | |
| Accounts Receivable | | 1,030 |
| b. Notes Receivable | 1,000 | |
| Accounts Receivable | | 1,000 |
| c. Notes Receivable | 1,000 | |
| Sales | | 1,000 |
| d. Notes Receivable | 1,020 | |
| Accounts Receivable | | 1,020 |

10. Schlicht Co. holds Osgrove Inc.'s $10,000, 120-day, 9% note. The entry made by Schlicht Co. when the note is collected, assuming no interest has been accrued, is (SO 8)

| | | |
|---|---|---|
| a. Cash | 10,300 | |
| Notes Receivable | | 10,300 |
| b. Cash | 10,000 | |
| Notes Receivable | | 10,000 |
| c. Accounts Receivable | 10,300 | |
| Notes Receivable | | 10,000 |
| Interest Revenue | | 300 |
| d. Cash | 10,300 | |
| Notes Receivable | | 10,000 |
| Interest Revenue | | 300 |

# QUESTIONS

1. What is the difference between an account receivable and a note receivable?

2. What are some common types of receivables other than accounts receivable or notes receivable?

3. Texaco Oil Company issues its own credit cards. Assume that Texaco charges you $50 on an unpaid balance. Prepare the journal entry that Texaco makes to record this revenue.

4. What are the essential features of the allowance method of accounting for bad debts?

5. Soo Eng cannot understand why cash realizable value does not decrease when an uncollectible account is written off under the allowance method. Clarify this point for Soo Eng.

6. Distinguish between the two bases that may be used in estimating uncollectible accounts.

7. Kersee Company has a credit balance of $3,200 in Allowance for Doubtful Accounts. The estimated bad debts expense under the percentage of sales basis is $4,100, and the total estimated uncollectibles under the percentage of receivables basis is $5,800. Prepare the adjusting entry under each basis.

8. How are bad debts accounted for under the direct write-off method? What are the disadvantages of this method?

9. Allmar Company accepts both its own credit cards and national credit cards. What are the advantages of accepting both types of cards?

10. An article recently appeared in *The Wall Street Journal* indicating that companies are selling their receivables at a record rate. Why are companies selling their receivables?

11. Southern Textiles decides to sell $700,000 of its accounts receivable to First Central Factors Inc. First Central Factors assesses a service charge of 2% of the amount of receivables sold. Prepare the journal entry that Southern Textiles makes to record this sale.

12. Your roommate is uncertain about the advantages of a promissory note. Compare the advantages of a note receivable with those of an accounts receivable.

13. How may the maturity date of a promissory note be stated?

14. Indicate the maturity date of each of the following promissory notes:

| Date of Note | Terms |
|---|---|
| (a) March 13 | one year after date of note |
| (b) May 4 | 3 months after date |
| (c) June 10 | 30 days after date |
| (d) July 2 | 60 days after date |

15. Compute the missing amounts for each of the following notes:

| | Principal | Annual Interest Rate | Time | Total Interest |
|---|---|---|---|---|
| (a) | ? | 9% | 120 days | $ 360 |
| (b) | $30,000 | 10% | 3 years | ? |
| (c) | $60,000 | ? | 5 months | $2,500 |
| (d) | $50,000 | 11% | ? | $1,375 |

16. In determining interest revenue, some financial institutions use 365 days per year whereas others use 360 days. Why might a financial institution use 360 days?

17. May Company dishonors a note at maturity. What actions by May may occur with the dishonoring of the note?

18. Paula Company has accounts receivable and notes receivable. How should the receivables be reported on the balance sheet?

# BRIEF EXERCISES

**BE8–1** Presented below are three receivable transactions. Indicate whether these receivables are reported as accounts receivable, notes receivable, or other receivables on a balance sheet.

*Different types of receivables*
*(SO 1)*

1. Advanced $10,000 to an employee.
2. Received a promissory note of $57,000 for services performed.
3. Sold merchandise on account for $60,000 to a customer.

**BE8–2** Record the following transactions on the books of Essex Co.

*Basic accounts receivable transactions*
*(SO 2)*

1. On July 1, Essex Co. sold merchandise on account to Cambridge Inc. for $14,000, terms 2/10, n/30.
2. On July 8, Cambridge Inc. returned merchandise worth $3,800 to Essex Co.
3. On July 11, Cambridge Inc. paid for the merchandise.

**BE8–3** During its first year of operations, Wendy Company had credit sales of $3,000,000, of which $600,000 remained uncollected at year-end. The credit manager estimates that $40,000 of these receivables will become uncollectible. (a) Prepare the journal entry to record the estimated uncollectibles. (b) Prepare the current asset section of the balance sheet for Wendy Company, assuming that in addition to the receivables it has cash of $90,000, merchandise inventory of $130,000, and prepaid expenses of $13,000.

*Entries for allowance method and classifications*
*(SO 3, 9)*

**BE8–4** At the end of 1996, Searcy Co. has accounts receivable of $700,000 and an allowance for doubtful accounts of $54,000. On January 24, 1997, it is learned that the company's receivable from Hutley Inc. is not collectible and therefore management authorizes a write-off of $8,000. (a) Prepare the journal entry to record the write-off. (b) What is the cash realizable value of the accounts receivable (1) before the write-off and (2) after the write-off?

*Entries for write-off and determining cash realizable value*
*(SO 3)*

**BE8–5** Assume the same information as BE8–4 and that on March 4, 1997, Searcy Co. receives payment of $8,000 in full from Hutley Co. Prepare the journal entries to record this transaction.

*Entries for collection of bad debt write-off*
*(SO 3)*

**BE8–6** Alex Co. elects to use the percentage of sales basis in 1996 to record bad debts expense and concludes that 2% of net credit sales will become uncollectible. Sales are $700,000 for 1996, sales returns and allowances are $50,000, and the allowance for doubtful accounts has a credit balance of $12,000. Prepare the adjusting entry to record bad debts expense in 1996.

*Entry using percentage of sales method*
*(SO 3)*

**BE8–7** Massey Co. uses the percentage of accounts receivable basis to record bad debt expense, and concludes that 1% of accounts receivable will become uncollectible. Accounts receivable are $500,000 at the end of the year, and the allowance for doubtful accounts has a credit balance of $3,000. (a) Prepare the adjusting journal entry to record bad debt expense for the year. (b) If the allowance for doubtful accounts had a debit balance of $800 instead of credit balance of $3,000, determine the amount to be reported for bad debt expense.

*Entry using percentage of receivables method*
*(SO 3)*

**BE8–8** Presented below are three promissory notes. Determine the missing amounts.

*Compute maturity date and interest on note.*
*(SO 5)*

| Date of Note | Terms | Maturity Date | Principal | Annual Interest Rate | Total Interest |
|---|---|---|---|---|---|
| (a) April 1 | 60 days | ? | $900,000 | 10% | ? |
| (b) July 2 | 30 days | ? | 79,000 | ? | $592.50 |
| (c) March 7 | 6 months | ? | 56,000 | 12% | ? |

*Disposition of accounts receivable*
*(SO 4)*

**BE8–9**   Presented below are the following transactions.

1. St. Pierre Restaurant accepted a Visa card in payment of a $100 lunch bill. The bank charges a 3% fee. What entry should St. Pierre make?
2. Mayfield Company sold its accounts receivable of $70,000. What entry should Mayfield make, given a service charge of 3% on the amount of receivables sold?

*Notes receivable exchanged for accounts receivable*
*(SO 6)*

**BE8–10**   On January 10, 1995, Raja Co. sold merchandise on account to R. Opal for $12,000, n/30. On February 9, R. Opal gave Raja Co. a 10% promissory note in settlement of this account. Prepare the journal entry to record the sale and the settlement of the accounts receivable.

# EXERCISES

*Journalize entries for recognizing accounts receivable.*
*(SO 2)*

**E8–1**   Presented below are two independent situations that occurred during the year.

1. On January 6, Nicklaus Co. sells merchandise on account to Watson Inc. for $4,000, terms 2/10, n/30. On January 16, Watson pays the amount due. Prepare the entries on Nicklaus' books to record the sale and related collection.
2. On January 10, Margaret Giger uses her Salizar Co. credit card to purchase merchandise from Salizar Co. for $11,000. On February 10, Giger is billed for the amount due of $11,000. On February 12, Giger pays $5,000 on the balance due. On March 10, Giger is billed for the amount due, including interest at 2% per month on the unpaid balance as of February 12. Prepare the entries on Salizar Co.'s books related to the transactions that occurred on January 10, February 12, and March 10.

*Journalize entries to record allowance for doubtful accounts using two different bases.*
*(SO 3)*

**E8–2**   The ledger of the Patillo Company at the end of the current year shows Accounts Receivable $80,000, Sales $940,000, and Sales Returns and Allowances $40,000.

**Instructions**

(a) If Allowance for Doubtful Accounts has a credit balance of $800 in the trial balance, journalize the adjusting entry at December 31, assuming bad debts are expected to be (1) 1% of net sales, and (2) 10% of accounts receivable.
(b) If Allowance for Doubtful Accounts has a debit balance of $500 in the trial balance, journalize the adjusting entry at December 31, assuming bad debts are expected to be (1) .75% of net sales and (2) 8% of accounts receivable.

*Determine bad debts expense and prepare the adjusting entry for bad debts expense.*
*(SO 3)*

**E8–3**   Grevina Company has accounts receivable of $92,500 at March 31. An analysis of the accounts shows the following:

| Month of Sale | Balance, March 31 |
|---|---|
| March | $65,000 |
| February | 12,600 |
| December and January | 8,500 |
| November and October | 6,400 |
| | $92,500 |

Credit terms are 2/10, n/30. At March 31, there is a $1,600 credit balance in Allowance for Doubtful Accounts prior to adjustment. The company uses the percentage of receivables basis for estimating uncollectible accounts. The company's estimate of bad debts are as follows:

| Age of Accounts | Estimated Percentage Uncollectible |
|---|---|
| Current | 2.0% |
| 1–30 days past due | 10.0% |
| 31–90 days past due | 30.0% |
| Over 90 days | 50.0% |

**Instructions**

(a) Determine the total estimated uncollectibles.
(b) Prepare the adjusting entry at March 31 to record bad debts expense.

**E8–4** On December 31, 1996, Lisa Ceja Co. estimates that 2% of its net sales of $300,000 will become uncollectible and records this amount as an addition to Allowance for Doubtful Accounts. On May 11, 1997, Lisa Ceja Co. determined that Robert Worthy's account was uncollectible and wrote off $900. On June 12, 1997, Worthy paid the amount previously written off.

*Percentage of sales basis, write-off, recovery.*
*(SO 3)*

**Instructions**
Prepare the journal entries on December 31, 1996, May 11, 1997, and June 12, 1997.

**E8–5** Presented below are two independent situations:

*Journalize entries for the sale of accounts receivable.*
*(SO 4)*

1. On March 3, Soyka Appliances sells $900,000 of its receivables to Potter Factors Inc. Potter Factors Inc. assesses a finance charge of 3% of the amount of receivables sold. Prepare the entry on Soyka Appliances' books to record the sale of the receivables.
2. On May 10, Monee Company sold merchandise for $3,000 and accepted the customer's First Business Bank MasterCard. At the end of the day, the First Business Bank MasterCard receipts were deposited in the company's bank account. First Business Bank charges a 4% service charge for credit card sales. Prepare the entry on Monee Company's books to record the sale of merchandise.

**E8–6** Presented below are two independent situations that occurred during the year.

*Journalize entries for credit card sales.*
*(SO 4)*

1. On April 2, P. Zachos uses her J. C. Penney credit card to purchase merchandise from a J. C. Penney store for $1,300. On May 1, Zachos is billed for the $1,300 amount due. Zachos pays $900 on the balance due on May 3. On June 1, Zachos receives a bill for the amount due, including interest at 1.0% per month on the unpaid balance as of May 3. Prepare the entries on J. C. Penney Co.'s books related to the transactions that occurred on April 2, May 3, and June 1.
2. On July 4, Robyn's Restaurant accepts an American Express card for a $300 dinner bill. American Express charges a 5% service fee. On July 10, American Express pays Robyn $285. Prepare the entries on Robyn's books related to the transactions.

**E8–7** Kasko Stores accepts both its own and national credit cards. During the year the following selected summary transactions occurred.

*Journalize credit card sales and indicate the statement presentation of financing charges and service charge expense.*
*(SO 4)*

Jan. 15   Made Kasko credit card sales totaling $16,000.
    20   Made American Express credit card sales (service charge fee, 5%) totaling $2,800.
    30   Received payment in full from American Express less a 5% service charge.
Feb. 10   Collected $12,000 on Kasko credit card sales.
    15   Added finance charges of 1.5% to Kasko credit card balance.

**Instructions**
(a) Journalize the transactions for Kasko Stores.
(b) Indicate the statement presentation of the financing charges and the credit card service expense for Kasko Stores.

**E8–8** Indiana Supply Co. has the following transactions related to notes receivable during the last 2 months of the year.

*Journalize entries for notes receivable transactions.*
*(SO 5, 6)*

Nov. 1   Loaned $24,000 cash to A. Gomez on a 1-year, 10% note.
Dec. 11   Sold goods to R. Wright, Inc., receiving a $3,600, 90-day, 12% note.
    16   Received a $4,000, 6-month, 12% note on account from B. Barnes.
    31   Accrued interest revenue on all notes receivable.

**Instructions**
Journalize the transactions for Indiana Supply Co.

**E8–9** Record the following transactions for the Rather Co. in the general journal:

*Journalize entries for notes receivable.*
*(SO 5, 6)*

1996
May 1   Received a $6,000, 1-year, 10% note on account from T. Jones.
Dec. 31   Accrued interest on the Jones' note.
Dec. 31   Closed the interest revenue account.
1997
May 1   Received principal plus interest on the Jones note. (No interest has been accrued in 1997)

*Journalize entries for dishonor of notes receivable.*
(SO 5, 8)

**E8–10**   On May 2, P. Brey Company lends $4,000 to Feingold Inc., issuing a 6-month, 10% note. At the maturity date, November 2, Feingold indicates that it cannot pay.

**Instructions**
(a) Prepare the entry to record the dishonor of the note, assuming that Brey Company expects collection will occur.
(b) Prepare the entry to record the dishonor of the note, assuming that Brey Company does not expect collection in the future.

# PROBLEMS

*Prepare journal entries related to bad debt expense.*
(SO 2, 3)

**P8–1**   At December 31, 1996, Trisha Underwood Imports reported the following information on its balance sheet:

| | |
|---|---|
| Accounts receivable | $1,000,000 |
| Less: Allowance for doubtful accounts | 60,000 |

During the first quarter of 1997, the company had the following transactions related to receivables.

| | |
|---|---|
| 1. Sales on account | $2,600,000 |
| 2. Sales returns and allowances | 40,000 |
| 3. Collections of accounts receivable | 2,300,000 |
| 4. Write-offs of accounts receivable deemed uncollectible | 80,000 |
| 5. Recovery of bad debts previously written off as uncollectible | 25,000 |

**Instructions**
(a) Prepare the journal entries to record each of these five transactions. Assume that no cash discounts were taken on the collections of accounts receivable.
(b) Enter the January 1, 1996, balances in Accounts Receivable and Allowance for Doubtful Accounts, post the entries to the two accounts (use T accounts), and determine the balances.
(c) Prepare the journal entry to record bad debts expense for the first quarter of 1997, assuming that an aging of accounts receivable indicates that estimated bad debts are $70,000.

*Computation of bad debts amounts*
(SO 3)

**P8–2**   Information related to Aris Company for 1996 is summarized below:

| | |
|---|---|
| Total credit sales | $1,800,000 |
| Accounts receivable at December 31 | $600,000 |
| Bad debts written off | $26,000 |

**Instructions**
(a) What amount of bad debts expense will Aris Company report if it uses the direct write-off method of accounting for bad debts?
(b) Assume that Aris Company decides to estimate its bad debts expense to be 3% of credit sales. What amount of bad debts expense will Aris Company record if Allowance for Doubtful Accounts has a credit balance of $3,000?
(c) Assume that Aris Company decides to estimate its bad debts expense based on 4% of accounts receivable. What amount of bad debts expense will Aris Company record if Allowance for Doubtful Accounts balance has a credit balance of $4,000?
(d) Assume the same facts as in (c), except that there is a $2,000 debit balance in Allowance for Doubtful Accounts. What amount of bad debts expense will Aris record?
(e) ▥▭▭▷   What is the weakness of the direct write-off method of reporting bad debts expense?

**P8–3**  Presented below is an aging schedule for Boitano Company.

*Journalize entries to record transactions related to bad debts.*
*(SO 2, 3)*

| Customer | Total | Not Yet Due | Number of Days Past Due | | | |
| --- | --- | --- | --- | --- | --- | --- |
| | | | 1–30 | 31–60 | 61–90 | Over 90 |
| Aber | $ 20,000 | | $ 9,000 | $11,000 | | |
| Bohr | 30,000 | $ 30,000 | | | | |
| Case | 50,000 | 15,000 | 5,000 | | $30,000 | |
| Datz | 38,000 | | | | | $38,000 |
| Others | 120,000 | 92,000 | 15,000 | $13,000 | | |
| | $258,000 | $137,000 | $29,000 | $24,000 | $30,000 | $38,000 |
| Estimated Percentage Uncollectible | | 3% | 6% | 12% | 24% | 50% |
| Total Estimated Bad Debts | $ 34,930 | $ 4,110 | $ 1,740 | $ 2,880 | $ 7,200 | $19,000 |

At December 31, 1996, the unadjusted balance in Allowance for Doubtful Accounts is a credit of $9,000.

**Instructions**
(a) Journalize and post the adjusting entry for bad debts at December 31, 1996.
(b) Journalize and post to the allowance account the following 1997 events and transactions.
   (1) March 1, an $800 customer balance originating in 1996 is judged uncollectible.
   (2) May 1, a check for $800 is received from the customer whose account was written off as uncollectible on March 1.
(c) Journalize the adjusting entry for bad debts on December 31, 1997, assuming that the unadjusted balance in Allowance for Doubtful Accounts is a debit of $1,100 and the aging schedule indicates that total estimated bad debts will be $27,100.

**P8–4**  Carlo Fassi Co. uses 2% of net sales to determine its bad debts expense for the period. At the beginning of the current period, Fassi had Allowance for Doubtful Accounts of $10,000 (credit). During the period, it had net sales of $900,000 and wrote off as uncollectible accounts receivable of $6,000. However, one of the accounts written off as uncollectible in the amount of $3,000 was recovered before the end of the current period.

*Journalize entries to record transactions related to bad debts.*
*(SO 3)*

**Instructions**
(a) Prepare the entry to record bad debts expense for the current period.
(b) Prepare the entry to record the write-off of uncollectible accounts during the current period.
(c) Prepare the entries to record the recovery of the uncollectible accounts during the current period.
(d) Determine the ending balance in Allowance for Doubtful Accounts.

**P8–5**  The Bon Ton Company closes its books monthly. On June 30, selected ledger account balances are

*Prepare entries for various note receivable transactions.*
*(SO 2, 4, 5, 8, 9)*

| | |
| --- | --- |
| Notes Receivable | $19,800 |
| Interest Receivable | $132.80 |

Notes Receivable include the following:

| Date | Maker | Face | Term | Interest |
| --- | --- | --- | --- | --- |
| May 21 | Alder Inc. | $6,000 | 60 days | 12% |
| May 25 | Dorn Co. | 4,800 | 60 days | 11% |
| June 30 | MJH Corp. | 9,000 | 6 months | 9% |

During July, the following transactions were completed.

July  5   Made sales of $6,200 on Bon Ton credit cards.

14   Made sales of $700 on VISA credit cards. The credit card service charge is 3%.

16   Added $415 to Bon Ton charge customer balances for finance charges on unpaid balances.

20   Received payment in full from Alder Inc. on the amount due.

25   Received notice that Dorn note has been dishonored. (Assume that Dorn is expected to pay in the future.)

**Instructions**

(a) Journalize the July transactions and the July 31 adjusting entry for accrued interest receivable. (Interest is computed using 360 days.)

(b) Enter the balances at July 1 in the receivable accounts and post the entries to all of the receivable accounts.

(c) Show the balance sheet presentation of the receivable accounts at July 31.

*Prepare entries for various receivables transactions.*
*(SO 2, 4, 5, 6, 7, 8)*

**P8–6**   On January 1, 1996, Comaneci Company had Accounts Receivable $54,200 and Allowance for Doubtful Accounts $4,700. Comaneci Company prepares financial statements annually. During the year the following selected transactions occurred.

Jan.  5   Sold $6,000 of merchandise to Garth Brooks Company, terms n/30.

Feb.  2   Accepted a $6,000, 4-month, 12% promissory note from Garth Brooks Company for balance due.

12   Sold $7,200 of merchandise to Gage Company and accepted Gage's $7,200 two-month, 10% note for the balance due.

26   Sold $5,000 of merchandise to Mathias Co., terms n/10.

Apr.  5   Accepted a $5,000, 3-month, 8% note from Mathias Co. for balance due.

12   Collected Gage Company note in full.

June  2   Collected Garth Brooks Company note in full.

July  5   Mathias Co. dishonors its note of April 5. It is expected that Mathias will eventually pay the amount owed.

15   Sold $3,000 of merchandise to Tritt Inc. and accepted Tritt's $3,000, 3-month, 12% note for the amount due.

Oct. 15   The Tritt Inc. note was dishonored. Tritt Inc. is bankrupt, and there is no hope of future settlement.

**Instructions**

Journalize the transactions.

# ALTERNATE PROBLEMS
• • • • • • • • • • • • • • • • • • • • • • • • • • • • • • • • • • • • • • • • • • • • • • • • • • • • • • • • • • • • • • • • • • • •

*Prepare journal entries related to bad debts expense.*
*(SO 2, 3, 4)*

**P8–1A**   At December 31, 1996, Bordeaux Inc. reported the following information on its balance sheet.

| | |
|---|---:|
| Accounts Receivable | $960,000 |
| Less: Allowance for doubtful accounts | 70,000 |

During the first quarter of 1997, the company had the following transactions related to receivables.

| | |
|---|---:|
| 1. Sales on account | $3,200,000 |
| 2. Sales returns and allowances | 50,000 |
| 3. Collections of accounts receivable | 2,800,000 |
| 4. Write-offs of accounts receivable deemed uncollectible | 90,000 |
| 5. Recovery of bad debts previously written off as uncollectible | 35,000 |

**Instructions**

(a) Prepare the journal entries to record each of these five transactions. Assume that no cash discounts were taken on the collections of accounts receivable.

(b) Enter the January 1, 1997, balances in Accounts Receivable and Allowance for Doubtful Accounts, post the entries to the two accounts (use T accounts), and determine the balances.

(c) Prepare the journal entry to record bad debts expense for the first quarter of 1997, assuming that an aging of accounts receivable indicates that expected bad debts are $100,000.

**P8–2A** Information related to Volkov Company for 1996 is summarized below:

*Computation of bad debts amounts.* (SO 3)

| | |
|---|---|
| Total credit sales | $2,000,000 |
| Accounts receivable at December 31 | $800,000 |
| Bad debts written off | $36,000 |

**Instructions**
(a) What amount of bad debts expense will Volkov Company report if it uses the direct write-off method of accounting for bad debts?
(b) Assume that Volkov Company decides to estimate its bad debts expense to be 3% of credit sales. What amount of bad debts expense will Volkov Company record if it has an Allowance for Doubtful Accounts credit balance of $4,000?
(c) Assume that Volkov Company decides to estimate its bad debts expense based on 5% of accounts receivable. What amount of bad debts expense will Volkov Company record if it has an Allowance for Doubtful Accounts credit balance of $3,000?
(d) Assume the same facts as in (c), except that there is a $3,000 debit balance in Allowance for Doubtful Accounts. What amount of bad debts expense will Volkov record?
(e) What is the weakness of the direct write-off method of reporting bad debts expense?

**P8–3A** Presented below is an aging schedule for Deep Canyon Company.

*Journalize entries to record transactions related to bad debts.* (SO 2, 3)

| Customer | Total | Not Yet Due | 1–30 | 31–60 | 61–90 | Over 90 |
|---|---|---|---|---|---|---|
| | | | Number of Days Past Due | | | |
| Anita | $ 22,000 | | $10,000 | $12,000 | | |
| Barry | 40,000 | $ 40,000 | | | | |
| Chagnon | 57,000 | 16,000 | 6,000 | | $35,000 | |
| David | 34,000 | | | | | $34,000 |
| Others | 126,000 | 96,000 | 16,000 | 14,000 | | |
| | $279,000 | $152,000 | $32,000 | $26,000 | 35,000 | $34,000 |
| Estimated Percentage Uncollectible | | 4% | 7% | 13% | 25% | 50% |
| Total Estimated Bad Debts | $ 37,450 | $ 6,080 | $ 2,240 | $ 3,380 | $ 8,750 | $17,000 |

At December 31, 1996, the unadjusted balance in Allowance for Doubtful Accounts is a credit of $10,000.

**Instructions**
(a) Journalize and post the adjusting entry for bad debts at December 31, 1996.
(b) Journalize and post to the allowance account the following 1997 events and transactions.
  (1) March 31, an $800 customer balance originating in 1996 is judged uncollectible.
  (2) May 31, a check for $800 is received from the customer whose account was written off as uncollectible on March 31.
(c) Journalize the adjusting entry for bad debts on December 31, 1997, assuming that the unadjusted balance in Allowance for Doubtful Accounts is a debit of $800 and the aging schedule indicates that total estimated bad debts will be $28,300.

**P8–4A** Huang Co. uses 3% of net sales to determine its bad debts expense for the period. At the beginning of the current period, Huang had Allowance for Doubtful Accounts of $9,000 (credit). During the period, it had net sales of $800,000 and wrote off as uncollectible accounts

*Journalize entries to record transactions related to bad debts.* (SO 3)

receivable of $7,000. However, one of the accounts written off as uncollectible in the amount of $4,000 was recovered before the end of the current period.

**Instructions**

(a) Prepare the entry to record bad debts expense for the current period.

(b) Prepare the entry to record the write-off of uncollectible accounts during the current period.

(c) Prepare the entries to record the recovery of the uncollectible account during the current period.

(d) Determine the ending balance in Allowance for Doubtful Accounts.

*Prepare entries for various note receivable transactions.*
(SO 2, 4, 5, 8, 9)

**P8–5A**    Selica Company closes its books monthly. On September 30, selected ledger account balances are:

| | |
|---|---|
| Notes Receivable | $23,400 |
| Interest Receivable | $182.40 |

Notes Receivable include the following:

| Date | Maker | Face | Term | Interest |
|------|-------|------|------|----------|
| Aug. 16 | Foran Inc. | $ 8,000 | 60 days | 12% |
| Aug. 25 | Drexler Co. | 5,200 | 2 months | 12% |
| Sept. 30 | MGH Corp. | 10,200 | 6 months | 9% |

Interest is computed using a 360-day year. During October, the following transactions were completed.

Oct.  7  Made sales of $6,900 on Selica credit cards.

12  Made sales of $750 on VISA credit cards. The credit card service charge is 4%.

15  Added $485 to Selica charge customer balance for finance charges on unpaid balances.

15  Received payment in full from Foran Inc. on the amount due.

25  Received notice that Drexler note has been dishonored. (Assume that Drexler is expected to pay in future.)

**Instructions**

(a) Journalize the October transactions and the October 31 adjusting entry for accrued interest receivable.

(b) Enter the balances at October 1 in the receivable accounts and post the entries to all of the receivable accounts.

(c) Show the balance sheet presentation of the receivable accounts at October 31.

*Prepare entries for various receivable transactions.*
(SO 2, 4, 5, 6, 7, 8)

**P8–6A**    On January 1, 1996, Ricardo Company had Accounts Receivable $146,000, Notes Receivable $15,000, and Allowance for Doubtful Accounts $13,200. The note receivable is from the Annabelle Company. It is a 4-month, 12% note dated December 31, 1995. Uptown Company prepares financial statements annually. During the year the following selected transactions occurred.

Jan.  5  Sold $12,000 of merchandise to George Company, terms n/15.

20  Accepted George Company's $12,000, 3-month, 9% note for balance due.

Feb. 18  Sold $8,000 of merchandise to Swaim Company and accepted Swaim's $8,000, 6-month, 10% note for the amount due.

Apr. 20  Collected George Company note in full.

30  Received payment in full from Annabelle Company on the amount due.

May 25  Accepted Avery Inc.'s $7,000, 3-month, 8% note in settlement of a past-due balance on account.

Aug. 18  Received payment in full from Swaim Company on note due.

25  The Avery Inc. note was dishonored. Avery Inc. is not bankrupt and future payment is anticipated.

Sept.  1  Sold $10,000 of merchandise to Young Company and accepted a $10,000, 6-month, 10% note for the amount due.

**Instructions**

Journalize the transactions.

# ▼*B*roadening *Your Perspective*

## *F*INANCIAL REPORTING PROBLEM

Arvada Company sells office equipment and supplies to many organizations in the city and surrounding area on contract terms of 2/10, n/30. In the past, over 75% of the credit customers have taken advantage of the discount by paying within 10 days of the invoice date.

The number of customers taking the full 30 days to pay has increased within the last year. Current indications are that less than 60% of the customers are now taking the discount. Bad debts as a percentage of gross credit sales have risen from the 1.5% provided in past years to about 4% in the current year.

The controller has responded to a request from the Finance Committee for more information on the collections of accounts receivable with the report reproduced below.

### ARVADA COMPANY
### Accounts Receivable Collections
### May 31, 1997

The fact that some credit accounts will prove uncollectible is normal. Annual bad debt write-offs have been 1.5% of gross credit sales over the past five years. During the last fiscal year, this percentage increased to slightly less than 4%. The current Accounts Receivable balance is $1,400,000. The condition of this balance in terms of age and probability of collection is as follows:

| Proportion of Total | Age Categories | Probability of Collection |
|---|---|---|
| 66% | not yet due | 99% |
| 16% | less than 30 days past due | 96½% |
| 9% | 30 to 60 days past due | 95% |
| 5% | 61 to 120 days past due | 91% |
| 2½% | 121 to 180 days past due | 75% |
| 1½% | over 180 days past due | 20% |

The Allowance for Doubtful Accounts had a credit balance of $29,500 on June 1, 1996. Arvada has provided for a monthly bad debts expense accrual during the current fiscal year based on the assumption that 4% of gross credit sales will be uncollectible. Total gross credit sales for the 1996–97 fiscal year amounted to $2,800,000. Write-offs of bad accounts during the year totaled $96,000.

*Instructions*
    (a) Prepare an accounts receivable aging schedule for Arvada Company using the age categories identified in the controller's report to the Finance Committee showing:
        1. The amount of accounts receivable outstanding for each age category and in total.
        2. The estimated amount that is uncollectible for each category and in total.
    (b) Compute the amount of the year-end adjustment necessary to bring Allowance for Doubtful Accounts to the balance indicated by the age analysis. Then prepare the necessary journal entry to adjust the accounting records.
    (c) In a recessionary environment with tight credit and high interest rates:
        1. Identify steps Arvada Company might consider to improve the accounts receivable situation.
        2. Then evaluate each step identified in terms of the risks and costs involved.

## *D*ECISION CASE

Johanna and Jake Berkvom own Campus Fashions. From its inception Campus Fashions has sold merchandise on either a cash or credit basis, but no credit cards have been accepted. During the past several months, the Berkvoms have begun to question their sales policies.

First, they have lost some sales because of refusing to accept credit cards. Second, representatives of two metropolitan banks have been persuasive in convincing them to accept their national credit cards. One bank, City National Bank, has stated that (1) its credit card fee is 4%, and (2) it pays the retailer 96 cents on each $1 of sales within 3 days of receiving the credit card billings.

The Berkvoms decide that they should determine the cost of carrying their own credit sales. From the accounting records of the past three years they accumulate the following data:

|  | 1996 | 1995 | 1994 |
|---|---|---|---|
| Net credit sales | $500,000 | $600,000 | $400,000 |
| Collection agency fees for slow paying customers | 2,450 | 2,500 | 1,600 |
| Salary of part-time accounts receivable clerk | 3,800 | 3,800 | 3,800 |

Credit and collection expenses as a percentage of net credit sales: uncollectible accounts 1.6%, billing and mailing costs 0.5%, and credit investigation fee on new customers 0.15%.

Johanna and Jake also determine that the average accounts receivable balance outstanding during the year is 5% of net credit sales. The Berkvoms estimate that they could earn an average of 10% annually on cash invested in other business opportunities.

*Instructions*
(a) Prepare a tabulation showing for each year total credit and collection expenses in dollars and as a percentage of net credit sales.
(b) Determine the net credit and collection expense in dollars and as a percentage of sales after considering the revenue not earned from other investment opportunities. (*Note:* The income lost on the cash held by the bank for 3 days is considered to be immaterial.)
(c) Discuss both the financial and nonfinancial factors that are relevant to the decision.

# COMMUNICATION ACTIVITY
. . . . . . . . . . . . . . . . . . . . . . . . . . . . . . . . . . . . . . . . . . . . . . . . . . . . . . . . . . . . . . . . .

Lois, a friend of yours who knows little about accounting, asks you to help make sense of a discussion she overheard at work about changes her employer wants to make in accounting for uncollectible accounts. Specifically, she asks you to explain the differences between the percentage of sales, percentage of receivables, and the direct write-off methods for uncollectible accounts.

*Instructions*
In a letter of one page (or less), explain to Lois the three methods of accounting for uncollectibles. Be sure to discuss differences among these methods.

# GROUP ACTIVITY
. . . . . . . . . . . . . . . . . . . . . . . . . . . . . . . . . . . . . . . . . . . . . . . . . . . . . . . . . . . . . . . . .

Sherie Mitchell, controller for S & J Mitchell Co., provides you with the following list of accounts receivable that were written off during the current year.

| Date | Customer | Amount |
|---|---|---|
| February 26 | Kadlec Corp. | $ 8,700 |
| April 17 | Lois Hamilton Shops | 13,219 |
| June 30 | Ilsa Kosinsky Co. | 5,500 |
| October 4 | Eleanor Scheave | 3,187 |

S & J Mitchell Co. follows the policy of debiting Bad Debts Expense as accounts are written off. Sherie Mitchell maintains that this practice is appropriate for financial statement purposes because the Internal Revenue Service will not accept other methods for recognizing bad debts.

All of S & J Mitchell's sales are on a 30-day credit basis. Sales for the current year total $2,470,000. Experience has determined that bad debt losses approximate 2% of sales.

*Instructions*
In groups of four or five students, answer the following questions.

   (a) Do you agree or disagree with S & J Mitchell's policy concerning recognition of bad debts? Why or why not?
   (b) By what amount would net income differ if bad debts expense were computed using the percentage of sales approach?

# *E*THICS CASE

Shirt Co. is a subsidiary of Clothes Corp. The controller believes that the yearly allowance for doubtful accounts for Shirt Co. should be 2% of net credit sales. The president of Shirt Co., nervous that the parent company might expect the subsidiary to sustain its 10% growth rate, suggests that the controller increase the allowance for doubtful accounts to 4%. The president thinks that the lower net income, which reflects a 6% growth rate, will be a more sustainable rate for Shirt Co.

*Instructions*
   (a) Who are the stakeholders in this case?
   (b) Does the president's request pose an ethical dilemma for the controller?
   (c) Should the controller be concerned with Shirt Co.'s growth rate in estimating the allowance? Explain your answer.

# *C*RITICAL THINKING
### ► *A Real-World Focus: Art World Industries, Inc.*

*Art World Industries, Inc. was incorporated in 1986 in Delaware, though it is located in Los Angeles. The company employs 25 people to print, publish, and sell limited edition graphics and reproductive prints in the wholesale market.*

The operating expenses for the year ended August 1994 for Art World Industries, Inc., include bad debts expense of $6,715.50. The balance sheet shows an allowance for doubtful accounts of $175,477. The allowance was set up against certain Japanese accounts receivable which average over one year in age. The Japanese acknowledge the amount due, but with the slow economy in Japan lack the resources to pay at this time.

*Instructions*
   (a) Which basis for estimating uncollectible accounts does Art World Industries use?
   (b) When Art World makes its adjusting entry to record bad debts expense must it consider a previous existing balance in the Allowance for Doubtful Accounts?
   (c) Explain the difference between the percentage of sales and percentage of receivables methods. In applying either of these methods, based on Art World's disclosure above, what important factor would you have to consider in arriving at appropriate percentages to apply?

*Answers to Self-Study Questions*
1. c    2. a    3. b    4. b    5. d    6. c    7. c    8. a    9. b    10. d

# Keeping the Books on the Books

BUFFALO, N.Y. — If you go to a large college or university, chances are that your bookstore or student union has state-of-the-art computer technology for tracking inventories. In an instant, the clerk at the checkout stand "wooshes" your purchases over a scanning machine that automatically rings up the price and deducts the item from inventory.

Not all schools have such state-of-the-art technology. Some bookstores are even small enough that the person managing it can take a "mom-and-pop corner grocery" approach. One such bookstore is at Erie Community College in Buffalo, New York, which produces annual sales of $500,000 per year. Instead of using "point-of-sale" computer technology, the bookstore uses an old-fashioned cash register. The inventory of textbooks, notebooks, art supplies, and so on is counted every month by Joel Damiani, manager. Because the quantity of inventory is relatively small, Damiani, or his two assistants, can specifically

identify each item when sold. A larger bookstore would have too much inventory to use that approach; instead, they would use inventory costing methods that do not specifically match the cost of inventory to the actual sale of goods.

Damiani is candid, too, about some problems at his store. For one thing, the accounting records were in disarray when he took the

job. "They told me it was going to be a challenge," he says. "And I like challenges." His challenges have included working with the school's accountant to produce a monthly balance sheet and income statement for the bookstore and making sure he has enough inventory of books and supplies on hand for the start of classes. "Sometimes, students say we're not quick enough." ◄

# CHAPTER · 9

# *I*NVENTORIES

---

## ► STUDY OBJECTIVES ◄

### After studying this chapter, you should be able to:

1. Describe the steps in determining inventory quantities.
2. Explain the basis of accounting for inventories and describe the inventory cost flow methods.
3. Explain the financial statement and tax effects of each of the inventory cost flow methods.
4. List the essential accounting features of a perpetual inventory system.
5. Explain the lower of cost or market basis of accounting for inventories.
6. Describe the two methods of estimating inventories.
7. Indicate the effects of inventory errors on the financial statements.

As indicated in the opening story about the bookstore at Erie Community College, how to account for inventory can be time-consuming and complex. In this chapter we will explain the procedures for determining inventory quantities and the methods used in determining the cost of inventory on hand at the balance sheet date. In addition, we will discuss how inventory valuation differs in periodic and perpetual inventory systems, the use of estimates in determining inventory amounts, and the effects of inventory errors on a company's financial statements. The content and organization of this chapter are as follows:

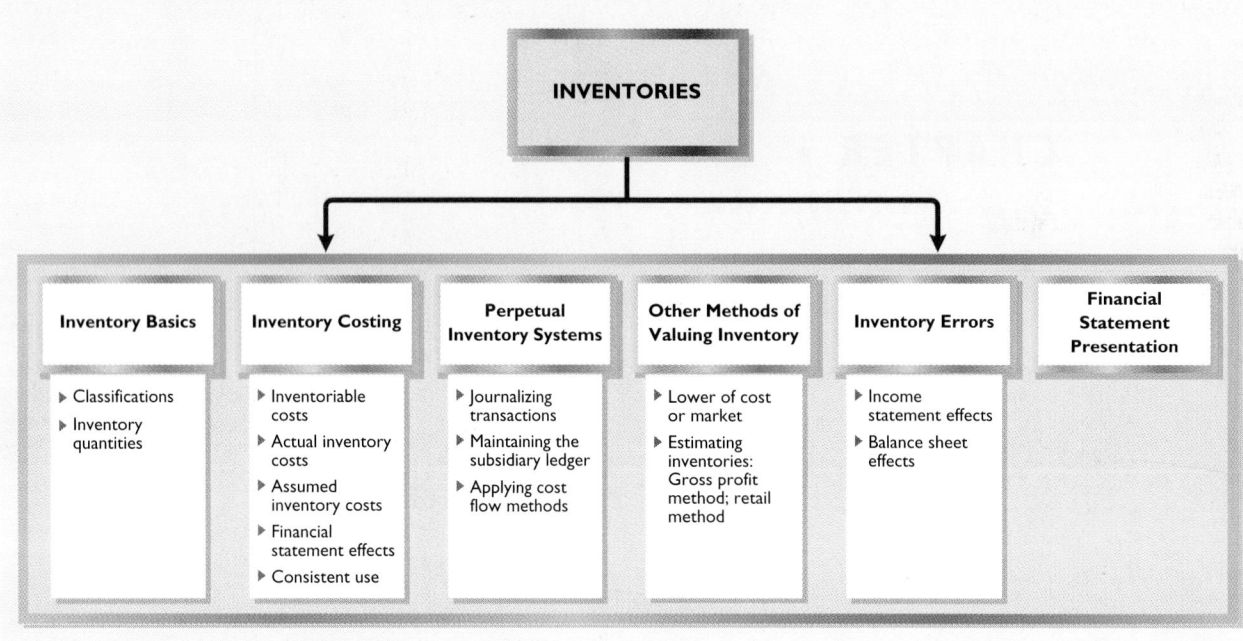

# *I*nventory Basics

In our economy, inventories are an important barometer of business activity. The U.S. Commerce Department, for example, publishes monthly combined inventory data for retailers, wholesalers, and manufacturers. The amount of inventories and the time required to sell the goods on hand are two indicators that are closely watched. During downturns in the economy, there is an initial build-up of inventories, as the length of time needed to sell existing quantities increases. The reverse effects are generally associated with an upturn in business activity. A delicate balance must be maintained between too little inventory and too much. A merchandiser or manufacturer with too little inventory to meet demand will have dissatisfied customers and sales personnel. One with too much inventory will be burdened with unnecessary costs.

Inventories affect both the balance sheet and the income statement. In the **balance sheet** of merchandising companies, inventory is frequently the most significant current asset. Of course, its amount and relative importance can vary, even for enterprises in the same industry. For example, Wal-Mart reported inventory of $14 billion, representing 90% of total current assets, whereas for the same period, J.C. Penney Company reported $3.9 billion of inventory, representing 41% of total current assets. In the **income statement**, inventory is vital

**Helpful hint** An important inventory management concept is inventory turnover. Inventory that turns means sales and profit; inventory that doesn't turn means costs and losses.

in determining the results of operations for a particular period. Moreover, gross profit (net sales less cost of goods sold) is closely watched by management, owners, and other interested parties (as explained in Chapter 5).

## Classifying Inventory

How a company classifies its inventory depends on whether the firm is a merchandiser or a manufacturer. In a **merchandising enterprise**, inventory consists of many different items. For example, in a grocery store, canned goods, dairy products, meats, and produce are just a few of the inventory items on hand. These items have two common characteristics: (1) they are owned by the company, and (2) they are in a form ready for sale to customers in the ordinary course of business. Thus, only one inventory classification, **merchandise inventory**, is needed to describe the many different items that make up the total inventory.

In a **manufacturing enterprise**, inventories are also owned by the company, but some goods may not yet be ready for sale. As a result, inventory is usually classified into three categories: finished goods, work in process, and raw materials. For example, General Motors classifies automobiles completed and ready for sale as **finished goods**. The automobiles on the assembly line in various stages of production are classified as **work in process**. The steel, glass, upholstery, and other components that are on hand waiting to be used in the production of automobiles are identified as **raw materials**.

The accounting principles and concepts discussed in this chapter apply to inventory classifications of both merchandising and manufacturing companies. In this chapter we will focus on merchandise inventory. In later chapters we will discuss the accounting for the three inventory classifications used by manufacturers.

**Helpful hint** Regardless of the classification, all inventories are reported under Current Assets on the balance sheet.

## Determining Inventory Quantities

In order to prepare financial statements, it is necessary to determine the number of units of inventory owned by the company at the statement date. For many companies, determining inventory quantities consists of two steps: (1) taking a physical inventory of goods on hand, and (2) determining the ownership of goods.

**STUDY OBJECTIVE**

*Describe the steps in determining inventory quantities.*

### Taking a Physical Inventory

Taking a physical inventory involves actually counting, weighing, or measuring each kind of inventory on hand. In many companies, taking an inventory is a formidable task. Retailers, such as Kmart, True Value Hardware, or your favorite music store have thousands of different inventory items. An inventory count is generally more accurate when goods are not being sold or received during the counting. Consequently, companies often "take inventory" when the business is closed or when business is slow. Many retailers, for example, close early on a chosen day in January—after the holiday sales and returns—to count their inventory.

To minimize errors in taking the inventory, a company should adhere to the following **internal control** principles by adopting certain procedures:

1. The counting should be done by employees who do not have custodial responsibility for the inventory. (Segregation of duties)
2. Each counter should establish the authenticity of each inventory item, e.g., each box does contain a 25-inch television set, and each storage tank does contain gasoline. (Establishment of responsibility)
3. There should be a second count by another employee. (Independent internal verification)

4. Prenumbered inventory tags should be used, and all inventory tags should be accounted for. (Documentation procedures)
5. A designated supervisor should ascertain at the conclusion of the count that all inventory items are tagged and that no items have more than one tag. (Independent internal verification)

After the physical inventory is taken, the quantity of each kind of inventory is listed on **inventory summary sheets**. To assure the accuracy of the summary sheets, the listing should be verified by a second employee or supervisor. Subsequently, unit costs will be applied to the quantities in order to determine a total cost of the inventory—which is the topic of later sections.

## ▸Accounting in Action ▸ *Business Insight*

Failure to observe the foregoing internal control procedures contributed to the Great Salad Oil Swindle. In this case, management intentionally overstated its salad oil inventory, which was stored in large holding tanks. Three procedures contributed to overstating the oil inventory: (1) Water added to the bottom of the holding tanks caused the oil to float to the top. Inventory-taking crews who viewed the holding tanks from the top observed only salad oil, when, in fact, as much as 37 out of 40 feet of many of the holding tanks contained water. (2) The company's inventory records listed more holding tanks than it actually had. The company repainted numbers on the tanks after inventory crews examined them, so the crews counted the same tanks twice. (3) Underground pipes pumped oil from one holding tank to another during the inventory taking; therefore, the same salad oil was counted more than once. Although the salad oil swindle was unusual, it demonstrates the complexities involved in assuring that inventory is properly counted.

### Determining Ownership of Goods

Before we can begin to calculate the cost of inventory, we need to consider the ownership of goods: specifically, we need to be sure that we have not included in the inventory any goods that do not belong to the company.

**Goods in Transit.** Goods are considered to be **in transit** when they are in the hands of a public carrier, such as a railroad, trucking, or airline company at the statement date. Goods in transit should be included in the inventory of the party that has legal title to the goods. Legal title is determined by the terms of sale, as shown in Illustration 9-1 and described below:

1. When the terms are **FOB (free on board) shipping point**, ownership of the goods passes to the buyer when the public carrier accepts the goods from the seller.

**Illustration 9-1**

*Terms of sale*

2. When the terms are **FOB destination**, legal title to the goods remains with the seller until the goods reach the buyer.

Significant errors may occur in determining inventory quantities if goods in transit at the statement date are ignored. Assume, for example, that Hargrove Company has 20,000 units of inventory on hand on December 31 and the following goods in transit: (1) **sales** of 1,500 units shipped December 31 FOB destination, and (2) **purchases** of 2,500 units shipped FOB shipping point by the seller on December 31. Hargrove has legal title to both the units sold and the units purchased. Consequently, inventory quantities would be understated by 4,000 units (1,500 + 2,500) if units in transit are ignored.

# ►Technology in Action

 Many companies have invested large amounts of time and money in automated inventory systems. One of the most sophisticated is Federal Express' Digitally Assisted Dispatch System (DADS). This system uses hand-held "SuperTrackers" to transmit data about the packages and documents to the firm's computer system. Based on bar codes, the system allows the firm to know where any package is at any time to prevent losses and to fulfill the firm's delivery commitments. More recently, FedEx's newly developed software enables customers to track shipments on their own PCs.

**Consigned Goods.** In some lines of business, it is customary to acquire merchandise on consignment. Under a consignment arrangement, the holder of the goods (called the *consignee*) does not own the goods. Ownership remains with the shipper of the goods (called the *consignor*) until the goods are actually sold to a customer. Because consigned goods are not owned by the consignee, they should not be included in the consignee's physical inventory count. Conversely, the consignor should include merchandise held by the consignee as part of its inventory.

## *Before You Go On . . .*

### ► *Review It*

1. What steps are involved in determining inventory quantities?
2. How is ownership determined for goods in transit at the balance sheet date?
3. Who has title to consigned goods?

### ► *Do It*

Hasbeen Corporation completed its inventory count, arriving at a total value for inventory of $200,000. You have been informed of the information listed below. Discuss how this information affects the reported cost of inventory.

1. Goods held on consignment for Falls Corp., costing $15,000, were included in the inventory.
2. Purchased goods of $10,000 which were in transit (terms: FOB shipping point) were not included in the count.
3. Sold inventory with a cost of $12,000 which was in transit (terms: FOB shipping point) was not included in the count.

*Reasoning:* For goods in transit, ownership is determined by the freight terms. For consigned goods, ownership rests with the consignor until the goods are sold by the consignee.

*Solution:* The goods held on consignment of $15,000 should be deducted from the inventory count. The goods of $10,000 purchased FOB shipping point should be added to the inventory count. Sold goods of $12,000 which were in transit FOB shipping point should not be included in the ending inventory.

*Related exercise material:* BE9–1 and E9–1.

# *I*nventory Costing

**STUDY OBJECTIVE**
•••••••••• 2 ••••••••••
*Explain the basis of accounting for inventories and describe the inventory cost flow methods.*

With a reliable physical count of the inventory (considering both goods in transit and consigned goods), we are now ready to assign costs to the inventory. Remember that the purpose of inventory costing is to determine the amount to be reported for inventory in the financial statements.

## Inventoriable Costs

The cost and matching principles of accounting are essential to an explanation of inventoriable costs.

1. In accordance with the **cost principle**, the primary basis of accounting for inventories is cost.
2. Under the **matching principle**, the major objective in accounting for inventories is the matching of appropriate costs with sales revenues.

These two principles guide the decisions about determining and allocating inventoriable costs.

### *Determining Inventoriable Costs*

All expenditures necessary to acquire the goods and to make them ready for sale are included as inventoriable costs. Inventoriable costs may be regarded as a pool of costs that consists of two elements: (1) the cost of the beginning inventory and (2) the cost of goods purchased during the year. As explained in Chapter 5, the sum of these two elements equals the cost of goods available for sale. The individual items included in cost of goods purchased are shown in Illustration 9-2.

**Illustration 9-2**

*Items included in cost of goods purchased*

| Item | Account Title | Effect on Inventoriable Costs |
|---|---|---|
| Invoice price | Purchases | Increase |
| Freight charges paid by purchaser | Freight-in | Increase |
| Purchase discounts taken by purchaser | Purchase Discounts | Decrease |
| Purchase returns and allowances granted by the seller | Purchase Returns and Allowances | Decrease |

What about the costs of the purchasing, receiving, and warehousing departments whose efforts make the goods available for sale? Conceptually those costs should also be included in inventoriable costs. However, because of the practical difficulties in allocating these costs to inventory, they are generally accounted for as **operating expenses** in the period in which they are incurred.

### *Allocating Inventoriable Costs*

**Helpful hint** Under a perpetual inventory system, described in Chapter 5 and later in this chapter, the allocation is continuously recognized as purchases and sales are made.

Inventoriable costs are allocated to ending inventory and to cost of goods sold. Under a periodic inventory system (illustrated in Chapter 5), the allocation is made at the end of the accounting period. First, the costs assignable to the ending inventory are determined. Second, the cost of the ending inventory is subtracted from the cost of goods available for sale to determine the cost of goods sold. Cost of goods sold is then deducted from sales revenues in accordance with the matching principle.

To illustrate, assume that General Suppliers Inc. has a cost of goods available for sale of $120,000, based on a beginning inventory of $20,000 and cost of goods purchased of $100,000. The physical inventory indicates that 5,000 units are on hand. The costs applicable to the units are $3.00 per unit. The allocation of the pool of costs is shown in Illustration 9-3. As shown, the $120,000 of goods available for sale are allocated $15,000 to ending inventory and $105,000 to cost of goods sold.

**Illustration 9-3**

*Allocation (matching) of pool of costs*

| Pool of Costs | |
| --- | --- |
| **Cost of Goods Available for Sale** | |
| Beginning inventory | $ 20,000 |
| Cost of goods purchased | 100,000 |
| Cost of goods available for sale | $120,000 |

| Step 1 | | | Step 2 | |
| --- | --- | --- | --- | --- |
| **Ending Inventory** | | | **Cost of Goods Sold** | |
| Units | Unit Cost | Total Cost | Cost of goods available for sale | $120,000 |
| | | | Less: Ending inventory | 15,000 |
| 5,000 | $3.00 | $15,000 | Cost of goods sold | $105,000 |

## Using Actual Physical Flow Costing—Specific Identification

Costing of the inventory is complicated because the units on hand for a specific item of inventory may have been purchased at different prices. For example, in a period of rising prices, a company may experience several increases in the cost of identical goods within a given year. Alternatively, unit costs may decline. Under such circumstances, how should the different unit costs in the cost of goods available for sale be allocated between the ending inventory and cost of goods sold?

One answer is to use specific identification of the units purchased. This method tracks the **actual physical flow** of the goods. **Each item of inventory is marked, tagged, or coded with its "specific" unit cost.** Items still in inventory at the end of the year are specifically costed to arrive at the total cost of the ending inventory. Assume, for example, that Southland Music Company purchases three 46-inch television sets at costs of $700, $750, and $800, respectively. During the year, two sets are sold at $1,200 each. At December 31, the company determines that the $750 set is still on hand. Accordingly, the ending inventory is $750 and the cost of goods sold is $1,500 ($700 + $800).

Specific identification is possible when a company sells a limited variety of high-unit cost items that can be clearly identified from the time of purchase through the time of sale. Examples of such companies are automobile dealerships (cars, trucks, and vans), music stores (pianos and organs), and antique shops (tables and cabinets). Although the bookstore at Erie Community College uses specific identification, it is somewhat unusual to do so for that type of business.

Ordinarily, however, the identity of goods purchased at a specific cost is lost between the date of purchase and the date of sale. For example, drug, grocery, and hardware stores sell thousands of relatively low unit-cost items of inventory. These items are often indistinguishable from one another, making it impossible or impractical to track each item's cost.

When feasible, specific identification seems to be the ideal method of allocating cost of goods available for sale. Under this method, the ending inventory is reported at actual cost and the actual cost of goods sold is matched against sales revenue. This method, however, may enable management to manipulate net income. For example, assume that a music store has three identical Steinway grand pianos that were purchased at different costs. When selling one piano, management could maximize its net income by selecting the piano with the lowest cost to match with revenues. Alternatively, it could minimize net income by selecting the highest-cost piano.

## Using Assumed Cost Flow Methods—FIFO, LIFO, and Average Cost

Because specific identification is often impractical, other cost flow methods are allowed. These differ from specific identification in that they assume flows of costs that may be unrelated to the physical flow of goods. For this reason we call them **assumed cost flow methods** or **cost flow assumptions**. They are:

1. First-in, first-out (FIFO).
2. Last-in, first-out (LIFO).
3. Average cost.

▸ *International note*

A survey of accounting standards in 21 major industrial countries found that all three methods were permissible. In Ireland and the U.K., LIFO is permitted only in extreme circumstances.

**There is no accounting requirement that the cost flow assumption be consistent with the physical movement of the goods.** The selection of the appropriate cost flow assumption (method) is made by management. The management of companies in the same industry may reach different conclusions as to the most appropriate method.

To illustrate these three inventory cost flow methods, we will assume that Bow Valley Electronics uses a periodic inventory system and has the information shown below for its Z202 Astro condenser.

**Illustration 9-4**

*Inventoriable costs*

### BOW VALLEY ELECTRONICS
### Z202 Astro Condensers

| Date | Explanation | Units | Unit Cost | Total Cost |
|------|-------------|-------|-----------|------------|
| 1/1 | Beginning inventory | 100 | $10 | $ 1,000 |
| 4/15 | Purchase | 200 | 11 | 2,200 |
| 8/24 | Purchase | 300 | 12 | 3,600 |
| 11/27 | Purchase | 400 | 13 | 5,200 |
| | Total | 1,000 | | $12,000 |

During the year, 550 units were sold and 450 units are on hand at December 31.

### First-in, First-out (FIFO)

The FIFO method assumes that the **earliest goods** purchased are the first to be sold. FIFO often parallels the actual physical flow of merchandise because it generally is good business practice to sell the oldest units first. Under the FIFO method, therefore, the **costs** of the earliest goods purchased are the first to be recognized as cost of goods sold. The allocation of the cost of goods available for sale at Bow Valley Electronics under FIFO is shown in Illustration 9-5.

**Pool of Costs**

**Cost of Goods Available for Sale**

| Date | Explanation | Units | Unit Cost | Total Cost |
|------|-------------|-------|-----------|------------|
| 1/1 | Beginning inventory | 100 | $10 | $ 1,000 |
| 4/15 | Purchase | 200 | 11 | 2,200 |
| 8/24 | Purchase | 300 | 12 | 3,600 |
| 11/27 | Purchase | 400 | 13 | 5,200 |
| | Total | 1,000 | | $12,000 |

**Illustration 9-5**

*Allocation of costs—FIFO method*

**Helpful hint** Note the sequencing of the allocation: (1) compute ending inventory and (2) determine cost of goods sold.

| Step I | | | | Step 2 | |
|--------|---|---|---|--------|---|
| **Ending Inventory** | | | | **Cost of Goods Sold** | |
| Date | Units | Unit Cost | Total Cost | | |
| 11/27 | 400 | $13 | $5,200 | Cost of goods available for sale | $12,000 |
| 8/24 | 50 | 12 | 600 | Less: Ending inventory | 5,800 |
| Total | 450 | | $5,800 | Cost of goods sold | $ 6,200 |

Note that the ending inventory is based on the latest units purchased. That is, **the cost of the ending inventory is obtained by taking the unit cost of the most recent purchase and working backward until all units of inventory have been costed**.

We can verify the accuracy of the cost of goods sold by recognizing that the **first units acquired are the first units sold**. The computations for the 550 units sold are shown in Illustration 9-6.

**Helpful hint** Note that ending inventory of $5,800 and the cost of goods sold of $6,200 equals cost of goods available for sale.

| Date | Units | | Unit Cost | | Total Cost |
|------|-------|---|-----------|---|------------|
| 1/1 | 100 | × | $10 | = | $1,000 |
| 4/15 | 200 | × | 11 | = | 2,200 |
| 8/24 | 250 | × | 12 | = | 3,000 |
| Total | 550 | | | | $6,200 |

**Illustration 9-6**

*Proof of cost of goods sold*

### Last-in, First-out (LIFO)

The LIFO method assumes that the **latest goods** purchased are the first to be sold. LIFO seldom coincides with the actual physical flow of inventory. Under the LIFO method, the **costs** of the latest goods purchased are the first to be recognized as cost of goods sold. The allocation of the cost of goods available for sale at Bow Valley Electronics under LIFO is shown in Illustration 9-7.

**Illustration 9-7**

*Allocation of costs—LIFO method*

### Pool of Costs
### Cost of Goods Available for Sale

| Date | Explanation | Units | Unit Cost | Total Cost |
|---|---|---|---|---|
| 1/1 | Beginning inventory | 100 | $10 | $ 1,000 |
| 4/15 | Purchase | 200 | 11 | 2,200 |
| 8/24 | Purchase | 300 | 12 | 3,600 |
| 11/27 | Purchase | 400 | 13 | 5,200 |
| | Total | 1,000 | | $12,000 |

| Step 1 | | | | Step 2 | |
|---|---|---|---|---|---|
| **Ending Inventory** | | | | **Cost of Goods Sold** | |

| Date | Units | Unit Cost | Total Cost | | |
|---|---|---|---|---|---|
| 1/1 | 100 | $10 | $1,000 | Cost of goods available for sale | $12,000 |
| 4/15 | 200 | 11 | 2,200 | Less: Ending inventory | 5,000 |
| 8/24 | 150 | 12 | 1,800 | Cost of goods sold | $ 7,000 |
| Total | 450 | | $5,000 | | |

Under the LIFO method, **the cost of the ending inventory is obtained by taking the unit cost of the earliest goods available for sale and working forward until all units of inventory are costed**. As a result, the first costs assigned to ending inventory are the costs of the beginning inventory. Proof of the costs allocated to cost of goods sold is shown in Illustration 9-8.

**Illustration 9-8**

*Proof of cost of goods sold*

| Date | Units | | Unit Cost | | Total Cost |
|---|---|---|---|---|---|
| 11/27 | 400 | × | $13 | = | $5,200 |
| 8/24 | 150 | × | 12 | = | 1,800 |
| Total | 550 | | | | $7,000 |

Note that the cost of the **last** goods in are the **first** to be assigned to cost of goods sold. Under a periodic inventory system, which we are using here, **all goods purchased during the period are assumed to be available for the first sale, regardless of the date of purchase**.

### Average Cost

The average cost method assumes that the goods available for sale are homogeneous. Under this method, the allocation of the cost of goods available for sale is made on the basis of the **weighted average unit cost** incurred. The formula and a sample computation of the weighted average unit cost are:

**Illustration 9-9**

*Formula for weighted average unit cost*

The weighted average unit cost is then applied to the units on hand to determine the cost of the ending inventory. The allocation of the cost of goods available for sale at Bow Valley Electronics using average cost is shown in Illustration 9-10.

| Pool of Costs | | | | |
| --- | --- | --- | --- | --- |
| Cost of Goods Available for Sale | | | | |
| Date | Explanation | Units | Unit Cost | Total Cost |
| 1/1 | Beginning inventory | 100 | $10 | $ 1,000 |
| 4/15 | Purchase | 200 | 11 | 2,200 |
| 8/24 | Purchase | 300 | 12 | 3,600 |
| 11/27 | Purchase | 400 | 13 | 5,200 |
| | Total | 1,000 | | $12,000 |

**Illustration 9-10**

*Allocation of costs—average cost method*

| Step 1 | | | Step 2 | |
| --- | --- | --- | --- | --- |
| Ending Inventory | | | Cost of Goods Sold | |
| $12,000 ÷ 1,000 = $12.00 | | | Cost of goods available for sale | $12,000 |
| | Unit | Total | Less: Ending inventory | 5,400 |
| Units | Cost | Cost | Cost of goods sold | $ 6,600 |
| 450 × $12.00 = $5,400 | | | | |

We can verify the cost of goods sold under this method by multiplying the units sold by the weighted average unit cost (550 × $12 = $6,600). Note that this method does not use the average of the unit costs. That average is $11.50 ($10 + $11 + $12 + $13 = $46; $46 ÷ 4). The average cost method instead uses the average **weighted** by the quantities purchased at each unit cost.

## Financial Statement Effects of Cost Flow Methods

Each of the three cost flow methods is acceptable. For example, Black and Decker Manufacturing Company and Northwest Industries, Inc., currently use the FIFO method of inventory costing. Campbell Soup Company, Krogers, and Walgreen Drugs use LIFO for part or all of their inventory. Bristol-Myers and Motorola use the average cost method. A company may also use more than one cost flow method at the same time. Del Monte Corporation, for example, uses LIFO for domestic inventories and FIFO for foreign inventories. Illustration 9-11 shows the use of the three cost flow methods in the 600 largest companies in the U.S. The reasons why companies adopt different inventory cost flow methods are varied, but they usually involve one of the following factors:

1. Income statement effects
2. Balance sheet effects
3. Tax effects

### *Income Statement Effects*

To understand why companies might choose a particular cost flow method, let's examine the effects of the different flow assumptions on the financial statements of Bow Valley Electronics. The condensed income statements in Illustration 9-12

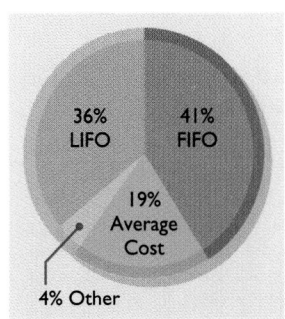

assume that Bow Valley sold its 550 units for $11,500, its operating expenses were $2,000, and its income tax rate is 30%.

**Illustration 9-12**

*Comparative effects of cost flow methods*

**BOW VALLEY ELECTRONICS**
**Condensed Income Statements**

| | FIFO | LIFO | Average Cost |
|---|---|---|---|
| Sales | $11,500 | $11,500 | $11,500 |
| Beginning inventory | 1,000 | 1,000 | 1,000 |
| Purchases | 11,000 | 11,000 | 11,000 |
| Cost of goods available for sale | 12,000 | 12,000 | 12,000 |
| Ending inventory | **5,800** | **5,000** | **5,400** |
| Cost of goods sold | 6,200 | 7,000 | 6,600 |
| Gross profit | 5,300 | 4,500 | 4,900 |
| Operating expenses | 2,000 | 2,000 | 2,000 |
| Income before income taxes[1] | 3,300 | 2,500 | 2,900 |
| Income tax expense (30%) | 990 | 750 | 870 |
| Net income | $ 2,310 | $ 1,750 | $ 2,030 |

Although the cost of goods available for sale ($12,000) is the same under each of the three inventory cost flow methods, both the ending inventories and cost of goods sold are different. This difference is due to the unit costs that are allocated to cost of goods sold and to ending inventory. Each dollar of difference in ending inventory results in a corresponding dollar difference in income before income taxes. For Bow Valley, there is an $800 difference between FIFO and LIFO. In a period of inflation, FIFO produced a higher net income because the lower unit costs of the first units purchased are matched against revenues. In a period of rising prices (as is the case here), FIFO reports the highest net income ($2,310) and LIFO the lowest ($1,750); average cost falls in the middle ($2,030). If prices are falling, the results from the use of FIFO and LIFO are reversed. FIFO will report the lowest net income and LIFO the highest. To management, higher net income is an advantage: it causes external users to view the company more favorably. In addition, if management bonuses are based on net income, FIFO will provide the basis for higher bonuses.

Some argue that the use of LIFO in a period of inflation enables the company to avoid reporting **paper or phantom profit** as economic gain. To illustrate, assume that Kralik Company buys 200 XR492s at $20 per unit on January 10 and 200 more on December 31 at $24 each. During the year, 200 units are sold at $30 each. The results under FIFO and LIFO are shown in Illustration 9-13.

**Illustration 9-13**

*Income statement effects compared*

| | FIFO | | LIFO | |
|---|---|---|---|---|
| Sales (200 × $30) | $6,000 | | $6,000 | |
| **Cost of goods sold** | 4,000 | (200 × $20) | 4,800 | (200 × $24) |
| Gross profit | $2,000 | | $1,200 | |

Under LIFO, the company has recovered the current replacement cost ($4,800) of the units sold. Thus, the gross profit in economic terms is real. However, under

---

[1]It is assumed that Bow Valley is a corporation, and corporations are required to pay income taxes.

FIFO, the company has recovered only the January 10 cost ($4,000). To replace the units sold, it must reinvest $800 (200 × $4) of the gross profit. Thus, $800 of the gross profit is said to be phantom or illusory. As a result, reported net income is also overstated in real terms.

### Balance Sheet Effects

A major advantage of the FIFO method is that in a period of inflation, the costs allocated to ending inventory will approximate their current cost. For example, for Bow Valley, 400 of the 450 units in the ending inventory are costed at the November 27 unit cost of $13.

Conversely, a major shortcoming of the LIFO method is that in a period of inflation, the costs allocated to ending inventory may be significantly understated in terms of current cost. This is true for Bow Valley, where the cost of the ending inventory includes the $10 unit cost of the beginning inventory. The understatement becomes greater over prolonged periods of inflation if the inventory includes goods purchased in one or more prior accounting periods.

### Tax Effects

We have seen that both inventory on the balance sheet and net income on the income statement are higher when FIFO is used in a period of inflation. Yet, many companies have switched to LIFO. The reason is that LIFO results in the lowest income taxes (because of lower net income). For example, at Bow Valley Electronics, income taxes are $750 under LIFO, compared to $990 under FIFO. The tax saving of $240 makes more cash available for use in the business.

## ►Accounting in Action ► *Business Insight*

Most small firms use the FIFO method. But fears of rising inflation often cause many firms to switch to LIFO. For example, Chicago Heights Steel Co. in Illinois boosted cash "by 5% to 10% by lowering income taxes" when it switched to LIFO. Electronic games distributor Atlas Distributing Inc., Chicago, considered a switch "because the costs of our games, made in Japan, are rising 15% a year," says Joseph Serpico, treasurer. When inflation heats up, "the number of companies electing LIFO will rise dramatically," says William Spiro of BDO Seidman, New York.

## Using Inventory Cost Flow Methods Consistently

Whatever cost flow method a company chooses, it should be used consistently from one accounting period to another. Consistent application enhances the comparability of financial statements over successive time periods. In contrast, using the FIFO method in one year and the LIFO method in the next year would make it difficult to compare the net incomes of the two years.

Although consistent application is preferred, it does not mean that a company may *never* change its method of inventory costing. When a company adopts a different method, the change and its effects on net income should be disclosed in the financial statements. A typical disclosure is shown in Illustration 9-14, using information from recent financial statements of the Quaker Oats Company.

**Helpful hint** As you will learn in Chapter 12, consistency is one of the important characteristics of accounting information.

**Illustration 9-14**

*Disclosure of change in cost flow method*

**Notes to the Financial Statements:**

**Note 1** Effective July 1, the Company adopted the LIFO cost flow assumption for valuing the majority of U.S. Grocery Products inventories. The Company believes that the use of the LIFO method better matches current costs with current revenues. The effect of this change on the current year was to decrease net income by $16.0 million.

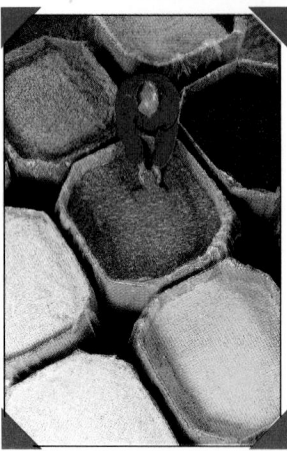

## ▶Accounting in Action ▸ *International Insight*

U.S. companies typically choose between LIFO and FIFO. Many choose LIFO because it reduces inventory profits and taxes. However, the international community recently considered rules that would ban LIFO entirely and force companies to use FIFO. This proposed rule was defeated, but the issue will not go away.

The issue is sensitive. As John Wulff, controller for Union Carbide noted, "We were in support of the international effort up until the proposal to eliminate LIFO." Wulff says that if Union Carbide had been suddenly forced to switch from LIFO to FIFO recently, its reported $632 million pretax income would have jumped by $300 million. That would have increased Carbide's income tax bill by as much as $120 million.

Do you believe that accounting principles and rules should be the same around the world?

## *Before You Go On . . .*

### ▶*Review It*

1. How do the cost and matching principles apply to inventoriable costs?
2. How are the three assumed cost flow methods applied in allocating inventoriable costs?
3. What factors should be considered by management in selecting an inventory cost flow method?
4. Which inventory cost flow method produces (a) the highest net income in a period of rising prices, and (b) the lowest income taxes?

### ▶*Do It*

The accounting records of Shumway Ag Implement show the following data:

| | |
|---|---|
| Beginning inventory | 4,000 units at $3 |
| Purchases | 6,000 units at $4 |
| Sales | 5,000 units at $12 |

Determine the cost of goods sold during the period under (a) the FIFO method, (b) the LIFO method, and (c) the average cost method.

***Reasoning:*** Because the units of inventory on hand and available for sale may have been purchased at different prices, a systematic method must be adopted to allocate the costs between the goods sold and the goods on hand (ending inventory).

***Solution:***

(a) FIFO:   (4,000 @ $3) + (1,000 @ $4) = $12,000 + $4,000 = $16,000.

(b) LIFO:   5,000 @ $4 = $20,000

(c) Average cost: [(4,000 @ $3) + (6,000 @ $4)] ÷ 10,000 = ($12,000 + $24,000) ÷ 10,000 = $3.60 per unit; 5,000 @ $3.60 = $18,000.

*Related exercise material:* BE9–2, BE9–3, BE9–4, BE9–5, E9–1, E9–2, E9–3, and E9–4.

## ▼*P*erpetual Inventory Systems

**STUDY OBJECTIVE**
••••••••••4••••••••••

*List the essential accounting features of a perpetual inventory system.*

To this point in the chapter we have assumed a periodic inventory system. We now turn our attention to a perpetual inventory system. Perpetual systems have traditionally been used by companies that sell merchandise with high unit values, such as automobiles, furniture, and major home appliances. The recent widespread use of computers and electronic scanners has enabled more companies to install perpetual inventory systems. The perpetual inventory system is so named because the accounting records continuously—perpetually—show the quantity and cost of the inventory that should be on hand at any time. The accounting features of a perpetual inventory system are:

1. Purchases of merchandise for resale are debited to Inventory rather than to Purchases.
2. Freight-in, purchase returns and allowances, and purchase discounts are recorded in Inventory rather than in separate accounts.
3. Cost of goods sold is recognized for **each sale** by debiting the account, Cost of Goods Sold, and crediting Inventory.
4. Inventory is a control account that is supported by a subsidiary ledger of individual inventory records. The subsidiary records show the quantity and cost of each type of inventory on hand.

## Journalizing Transactions

To illustrate the journalizing of transactions under a perpetual inventory system, we will compare how entries are recorded in perpetual and periodic inventory systems. Transaction and other data pertaining to solar panels, Model A2776 sold by Astro Energy Inc. are as follows:

| Periodic System | | Perpetual System | |
|---|---|---|---|
| **1. There are 4 units in beginning inventory at a cost of $3,000 each.** | | | |
| The inventory account shows the inventory on hand at $12,000 | | The inventory account shows the inventory on hand at $12,000 | |
| **2. Purchase 12 panels on account at $3,000 each.** | | | |
| Purchases | 36,000 | Merchandise Inventory | 36,000 |
| Accounts Payable | 36,000 | Accounts Payable | 36,000 |
| **3. Return one defective panel for $3,000 credit.** | | | |
| Accounts Payable | 3,000 | Accounts Payable | 3,000 |
| Purchase Returns and Allowances | 3,000 | Merchandise Inventory | 3,000 |
| **4. Sell 7 panels on account for $5,000 each.** | | | |
| Accounts Receivable | 35,000 | Accounts Receivable | 35,000 |
| Sales | 35,000 | Sales | 35,000 |
| | | Cost of Goods Sold | 21,000 |
| | | Merchandise Inventory | 21,000 |
| **5. End of period entries for inventory accounts (8 units on hand at $3,000 each)** | | | |
| **Closing entries are necessary:** | | **No entries are necessary:** | |
| Income Summary | 12,000 | The account, Merchandise Inventory, shows the ending balance, $24,000 ($12,000 + $36,000 − $3,000 − $21,000) | |
| Merchandise Inventory (Beginning) | 12,000 | | |
| Merchandise Inventory (Ending) | 24,000 | | |
| Income Summary | 24,000 | | |

**Illustration 9-15**

*Comparative entries— periodic vs perpetual*

**Helpful hint** Additional entries are explained and illustrated in the Appendix to Chapter 5.

Note that in a perpetual system, two entries are required when a sale occurs. Also no closing entries are required for the inventory account at the end of an accounting period. The reason is that the account balance shows the amount of goods that should be on hand. If the physical inventory count confirms this amount, no entries are needed. However, if the physical inventory count does not agree with the balance shown in the control account, an entry will be necessary to make the inventory balance agree with the goods actually on hand. A difference is usually a shortage caused by spoilage or theft. In such a case, an adjusting entry is made in which Inventory Losses is debited and Inventory is credited.

## Maintaining the Subsidiary Ledger

As indicated above, the subsidiary ledger consists of individual inventory records for each type of inventory. A typical record is shown in Illustration 9-16, using assumed data. The record shows transaction data for purchases and sales, and the balance on hand. In addition, the record gives the type and model number of the inventory, the location of the goods in the storeroom or warehouse, and suggested minimum and maximum quantities. As in the case of individual customer accounts in the accounts receivable subsidiary ledger, **the individual inventory records in the subsidiary ledger are updated after each transaction**.

**Illustration 9-16**

*Subsidiary ledger inventory record*

| Item | | 12″ Television Sets | | | | | Location: Warehouse 2 | | Aisle 4 | |
| Model No. TR65 | | | | | | | Maximum Units 30 | | Minimum Units 5 | |

| | Purchases | | | | Sales | | | Balance | | |
| Date | Units | Cost | Total | Units | Cost | Total | Units | Cost | Total |
|------|-------|------|-------|-------|------|-------|-------|------|-------|
| 1/1 | | | | | | | 10 | $120 | $1,200 |
| 5 | | | | 4 | $120 | $480 | 6 | 120 | 720 |
| 8 | 15 | $120 | $1,800 | | | | 21 | 120 | 2,520 |
| 14 | | | | 5 | 120 | 600 | 16 | 120 | 1,920 |
| 20 | | | | 7 | 120 | 840 | 9 | 120 | 1,080 |
| 24 | 10 | 120 | 1,200 | | | | 19 | 120 | 2,280 |
| 30 | | | | 8 | 120 | 960 | 11 | 120 | 1,320 |

A perpetual inventory system contributes to better control over inventories than a periodic system. Since the inventory records show the quantities that should be on hand, the goods can be counted at any time to see whether they actually exist. Any shortages uncovered can be investigated immediately. Fur-

## ▶*Technology in Action*

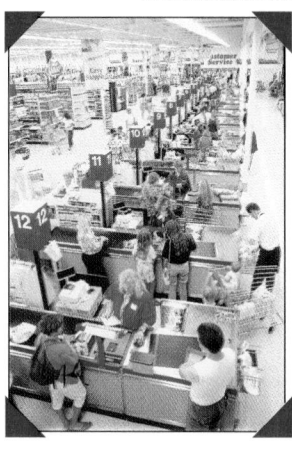

A major benefit of automated accounting systems is that transactions are processed soon after actual occurrence. Large department stores and supermarkets use electronic point-of-sales systems. In these systems, the cash registers are, in effect, computer terminals. Information that can be gathered and processed at the time of an ordinary sale of merchandise includes:

1. Update the perpetual inventory records, indicating if more items need to be ordered from suppliers.
2. Identify the time, date, and place of sale and who sold the item.
3. Verify the selling price of the item, taking any markdowns into account.
4. Check the credit standing of the customer, alerting the checker if the customer is over the credit limit, delinquent in payment, or is using a stolen card.

The use of scanners permits faster, more accurate, and less costly data entry.

ther, the maximum quantity shown on the inventory record helps prevent over-investment in inventory, and the minimum quantity protects the company from losing sales on "out-of-stock" items.

A perpetual inventory system involves additional clerical work and cost involved in maintaining the subsidiary ledger. This cost is minimized when a computerized system is used.

## Applying Cost Flow Methods

The inventory cost flow methods described earlier for periodic inventory systems also apply to perpetual systems. The specific identification method is the same for either system. However, there are several significant differences in using the cost flow assumption methods. These differences are explained and illustrated in the appendix to this chapter.

# Other Methods of Valuing Inventory

Special circumstances sometimes call for inventory valuation methods other than those presented in the chapter. For example, consider the following situations:

- Suppose you are the owner of a retail store that sells Compaq Desk Pro computers. During a recent 12-month period, the cost of the computers dropped $1,800 (almost 50%). At the end of your fiscal year, you have some of these computers in inventory. Do you think your inventory should be stated at cost, in accordance with the cost principle, or at its lower replacement cost?
- Or, suppose that your inventory of lumber was destroyed by fire. Without having the inventory available for a physical count, how can you value it in order to determine the loss?

The first situation requires a departure from the cost basis of accounting. The second situation requires that inventory be estimated, rather than counted, to determine its ending balance. Each of these approaches is discussed below.

## Valuing Inventory at the Lower of Cost or Market (LCM)

When the value of inventory is lower than its cost, the inventory is written down to its market value. This is accomplished by valuing the inventory at the lower of cost or market (LCM) in the period in which the price decline occurs. LCM is an example of the accounting concept of conservatism. **Conservatism** means that when choosing among accounting alternatives, the best choice is to select the method that is least likely to overstate assets and net income.

Under the LCM basis, market is defined as current replacement cost, not selling price. For a merchandising company, market is the cost of purchasing the same goods at the present time from the usual suppliers in the usual quantities. Current replacement cost is used because a decline in the replacement cost of an item usually leads to a decline in the selling price of the item.

The lower of cost or market basis may be applied to individual items of inventory, major categories of inventory, or total inventory. For example, assume that Len's TV has the following lines of merchandise with costs and market values as indicated. LCM produces the following three results:

**STUDY OBJECTIVE**

**5**

*Explain the lower of cost or market basis of accounting for inventories.*

**Illustration 9-17**

*Alternative lower of cost or market results*

| | Cost | Market | Lower of Cost or Market by: Individual Items | Lower of Cost or Market by: Major Categories | Lower of Cost or Market by: Total Inventory |
|---|---|---|---|---|---|
| Television sets | | | | | |
|   Consoles | $ 60,000 | $ 55,000 | $ 55,000 | | |
|   Portables | 45,000 | 52,000 | 45,000 | | |
| Total | 105,000 | 107,000 | | $105,000 | |
| Video equipment | | | | | |
|   Recorders | 48,000 | 45,000 | 45,000 | | |
|   Movies | 15,000 | 14,000 | 14,000 | | |
| Total | 63,000 | 59,000 | | 59,000 | |
| Total inventory | $168,000 | $166,000 | $159,000 | $164,000 | $166,000 |

The amount entered in the individual items column is the lower of the cost or market amount for **each item**. For the major categories column, the amount is the lower of the total cost or total market for **each category**. Finally, the amount for the total inventory column is the lower of the cost or market for the **entire inventory**. The common practice is to use individual items in determining the LCM valuation. This approach gives the most conservative valuation for balance sheet purposes and also the lowest net income. LCM should be applied consistently from period to period.

## Estimating Inventories

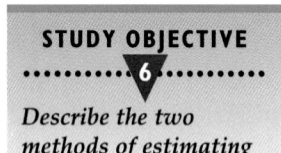

**STUDY OBJECTIVE**
••••••••••6••••••••••

*Describe the two methods of estimating inventories.*

We have assumed throughout the chapter that a company would be able to do a physical count of its inventory. But what if it cannot, as in the example of the lumber inventory destroyed by fire? In that case, we would use an estimate.

Two circumstances explain the reasons for estimating rather than counting inventories. First, management may want monthly or quarterly financial statements but a physical inventory is taken only annually. Second, a casualty such as fire, flood, or earthquake may make it impossible to take a physical inventory. The need for estimating inventories is associated primarily with a periodic inventory system because of the absence of detailed inventory records.

There are two widely used methods of estimating inventories: (1) the gross profit method and (2) the retail inventory method.

### *Gross Profit Method*

The gross profit method estimates the cost of ending inventory by applying a gross profit rate to net sales. It is used in preparing monthly financial statements when physical inventories are not taken. This method is a relatively simple but effective estimation technique. To use this method, a company needs to know its net sales, cost of goods available for sale, and gross profit rate. The company then uses the gross profit rate to estimate its gross profit for the accounting period. The formulas for using the gross profit method are given in Illustration 9-18.

To illustrate, assume that Williams Company wishes to prepare an income statement for the month of January, when its records show net sales $200,000; beginning inventory $40,000; and cost of goods purchased $120,000. In the preceding year, the company realized a 30% gross profit rate, and it expects to earn the same rate this year. Given these facts and assumptions, the estimated cost of

**Illustration 9-18**

*Gross profit method formulas*

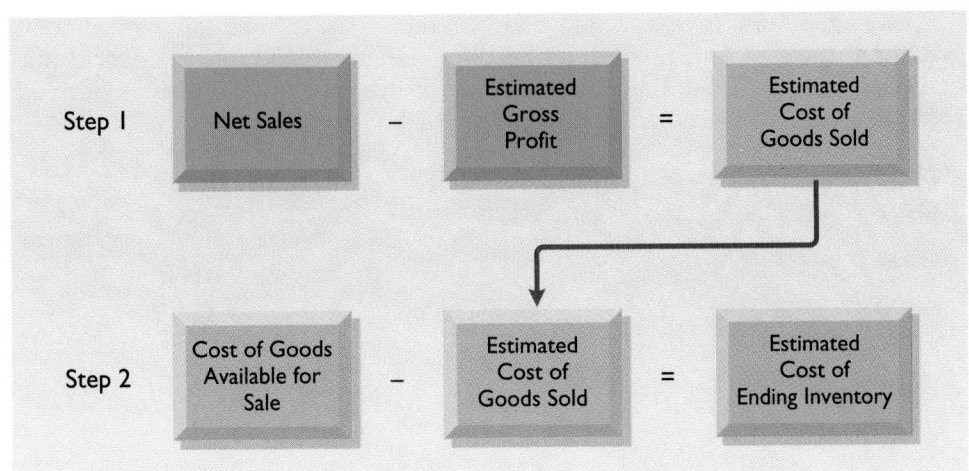

the ending inventory at January 31 under the gross profit method is $20,000, computed as follows:

**Illustration 9-19**

*Example of gross profit method*

| | |
|---|---:|
| Step 1: | |
| Net sales | $200,000 |
| Less: Estimated gross profit (30% × $200,000) | 60,000 |
| **Estimated cost of goods sold** | **$140,000** |
| | |
| Step 2: | |
| Beginning inventory | $ 40,000 |
| Cost of goods purchased | 120,000 |
| Cost of goods available for sale | 160,000 |
| Less: Estimated cost of goods sold | 140,000 |
| **Estimated cost of ending inventory** | **$ 20,000** |

The gross profit method is based on the assumption that the rate of gross profit will remain constant from one year to the next. It may not remain constant, though, because of a change either in merchandising policies or in market conditions. In such cases, the rate of the prior period should be adjusted to reflect current operating conditions. In some cases, a more accurate estimate may be obtained by applying this method on a department or product-line basis.

The gross profit method should not be used in preparing a company's financial statements at the end of the year. These statements should be based on a physical inventory count.

### Retail Inventory Method

A retail store such as Kmart, Ace Hardware, or Wal-Mart has thousands of different types of merchandise at low unit costs. In such cases the application of unit costs to inventory quantities is difficult and time-consuming. An alternative is to use the retail inventory method to estimate the cost of inventory. In most retail concerns, a relationship between cost and sales price can be established. Under the retail inventory method, the cost to retail percentage is then applied to the ending inventory at retail prices to determine inventory at cost.

To use the retail inventory method, a company must maintain records that show both the cost and retail value of the goods available for sale. Under the retail inventory method, the estimated cost of the ending inventory is derived from the formulas presented in Illustration 9-20.

**Illustration 9-20**

*Retail inventory method formulas*

The logic of the retail method can be demonstrated by using unit cost data. Assume that 10 units purchased at $7.00 each are marked to sell for $10 per unit. Thus, the cost to retail ratio is 70% ($70 ÷ $100). If 4 units remain unsold, their retail value is $40 and their cost is $28 ($40 × 70%), which agrees with the total cost of goods on hand on a per unit basis (4 × $7).

The application of the retail method based on the accounting records and supplementary data for Lacy Co. is shown in Illustration 9-21. Note that it is not necessary to take a physical inventory to determine the estimated cost of goods on hand at any given time.

**Illustration 9-21**

*Example of retail inventory method*

|  | At Cost | At Retail |
|---|---|---|
| Beginning inventory | $14,000 | $ 21,500 |
| Goods purchased | 61,000 | 78,500 |
| Goods available for sale | $75,000 | 100,000 |
| Net sales |  | 70,000 |
| (1) Ending inventory at retail |  | $ 30,000 |

(2) Cost to retail ratio = ($75,000 ÷ $100,000) = 75%
(3) Estimated cost of ending inventory = ($30,000 × 75%)    $22,500

The retail inventory method also facilitates taking a physical inventory at the end of year. With this method, the goods on hand can be valued at the prices marked on the merchandise. The cost to retail ratio is then applied to the goods actually on hand at retail to determine the ending inventory at cost.

The major disadvantage of the retail method is that it is an averaging technique. It may produce an incorrect inventory valuation if the mix of the ending inventory is not representative of the mix in the goods available for sale. Assume, for example, that the cost to retail ratio of 75% in the Lacy Co. consists of equal proportions of inventory items that have cost to retail ratios of 70%, 75%, and 80%, respectively. If the ending inventory contains only items with a 70% ratio, an incorrect inventory cost will result. This problem can be minimized by applying the retail method on a departmental or product-line basis.

# *I*nventory Errors

Unfortunately, errors occasionally occur in taking or costing inventory. In some cases, errors are caused by failure to count or price the inventory correctly. In other cases, errors occur because proper recognition is not given to the transfer of legal title to goods that are in transit. When errors occur, they affect both the income statement and the balance sheet.

**STUDY OBJECTIVE**
**7**

*Indicate the effects of inventory errors on the financial statements.*

## Income Statement Effects

As you know, both the beginning and ending inventories appear in the income statement. The ending inventory of one period automatically becomes the beginning inventory of the next period. Inventory errors affect the determination of cost of goods sold and net income.

The effects on cost of goods sold can be determined by entering the incorrect data in the following formula and then substituting the correct data.

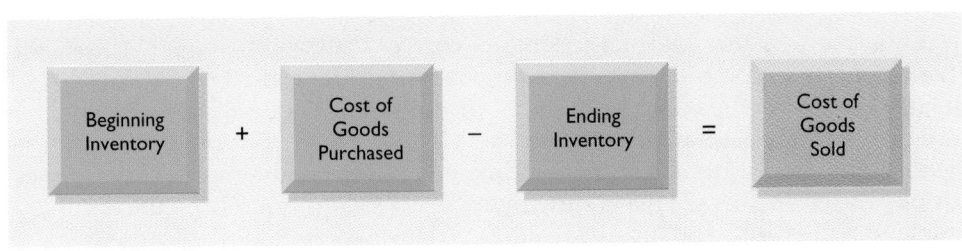

**Illustration 9-22**

*Formula for cost of goods sold*

► *Ethics note*

Inventory fraud increases during recessions. Such fraud includes pricing inventory at amounts in excess of their actual value, or claiming to have inventory when no inventory exists. Inventory fraud is usually done to overstate ending inventory, thereby understating cost of goods sold and creating higher income.

If beginning inventory is understated, cost of goods sold will be understated. On the other hand, an understatement of ending inventory will overstate cost of goods sold. The effects of inventory errors on the current year's income statement are shown in Illustration 9-23.

**Illustration 9-23**

*Effects of inventory errors on current year's income statement*

| Inventory Error | Cost of Goods Sold | Net Income |
|---|---|---|
| Understate beginning inventory | Understated | Overstated |
| Overstate beginning inventory | Overstated | Understated |
| Understate ending inventory | Overstated | Understated |
| Overstate ending inventory | Understated | Overstated |

An error in ending inventory of the current period will have a **reverse effect on net income of the next accounting period**. This is shown in Illustration 9-24. Note that the understatement of ending inventory in 1996 results in an under-

**Illustration 9-24**

*Effects of inventory errors on 2 years' income statements*

statement of beginning inventory in 1997 and an overstatement of net income in 1997.

| | Condensed Income Statement | | | | | | | |
|---|---|---|---|---|---|---|---|---|
| | **1996** | | | | **1997** | | | |
| | Incorrect | | Correct | | Incorrect | | Correct | |
| Sales | | $80,000 | | $80,000 | | $90,000 | | $90,000 |
| Beginning inventory | $20,000 | | $20,000 | | $12,000 | | $15,000 | |
| Cost of goods purchased | 40,000 | | 40,000 | | 68,000 | | 68,000 | |
| Cost of goods available for sale | 60,000 | | 60,000 | | 80,000 | | 83,000 | |
| Ending inventory | 12,000 | | 15,000 | | 23,000 | | 23,000 | |
| Cost of goods sold | | 48,000 | | 45,000 | 57,000 | | 60,000 | |
| Gross profit | | 32,000 | | 35,000 | 33,000 | | 30,000 | |
| Operating expenses | | 10,000 | | 10,000 | 20,000 | | 20,000 | |
| Net income | | $22,000 | | $25,000 | $13,000 | | $10,000 | |

($3,000)
Net income
understated

$3,000
Net income
overstated

Total income for
2 years correct

Over the 2 years, total net income is correct because the errors offset one another. Notice that total income using incorrect data is $35,000 ($22,000 + $13,000), which is the same as the total income of $35,000 ($25,000 + $10,000) using correct data. Also note in this example that an error in the beginning inventory does not result in a corresponding error in the ending inventory for that period. The correctness of the ending inventory depends entirely on the accuracy of taking and costing the inventory at the balance sheet date.

## Balance Sheet Effects

The effect of ending inventory errors on the balance sheet can be determined by using the basic accounting equation: assets equal liabilities plus owner's equity. Errors in the ending inventory have the following effects on these components:

**Illustration 9-25**

*Ending inventory error—balance sheet effects*

| Ending Inventory Error | Assets | Liabilities | Owner's Equity |
|---|---|---|---|
| Overstated | Overstated | None | Overstated |
| Understated | Understated | None | Understated |

The effect of an error in ending inventory on the subsequent period was shown in Illustration 9-24. Recall that if the error is not corrected, total net income for the two periods would be correct. Thus, total owner's equity reported on the balance sheet at the end of 1997 in Illustration 9-24 will also be correct.

# Financial Statement Presentation

As indicated in an earlier chapter, inventory is classified as a current asset after receivables in the balance sheet, and cost of goods sold is subtracted from sales in the income statement. In addition, there should be disclosure of (1) the major inventory classifications, (2) the basis of accounting (cost or lower of cost or market), and (3) the costing method (FIFO, LIFO, or average).

Colgate-Palmolive Company, for example, reported inventory of $616,067,000 under current assets in a recent balance sheet. The accompanying notes to the financial statements, as shown in Illustration 9-26, disclosed the following information:

---

### Colgate-Palmolive Company

**Note 1. Inventories**

Inventories are valued at the lower of cost or market. The last-in, first-out (LIFO) method is used to value substantially all inventories in the U.S. as well as in certain overseas locations. The remaining inventories are valued using the first-in, first-out (FIFO) method.

---

**Illustration 9-26**

*Inventory disclosures*

## Before You Go On . . .

### ►Review It

1. Why is it appropriate to report inventories at the lower of cost or market?
2. How is ending inventory estimated under the gross profit method?
3. How is ending inventory estimated under the retail inventory method?
4. How do inventory errors affect financial statements?

### ► A Look Back at Erie Community College

Refer back to the opening story concerning the bookstore at Erie Community College, and answer the following questions.

1. Why might a small bookstore use specific identification to determine inventory?
2. If the inventory is overstated at the end of the month, what effect does this error have on the balance sheet and the income statement?

*Solution:*

1. A small bookstore, as opposed to a large bookstore, might use specific identification because of:
   a. A smaller number of any one book in inventory.
   b. Fewer different books in inventory.
   c. The familiarity of the owner/manager (who handles sales) with the books being sold.
2. An end-of-month, inventory overstatement will result in overstated inventory in the balance sheet along with overstated owner's equity, due to overstated net income on the income statement. Cost of goods sold will be understated on the income statement. The next month's income statement will have overstated beginning inventory and understated net income.

# ▼Summary of Study Objectives

**1.** *Describe the steps in determining inventory quantities.* The steps in determining inventory quantities are (1) taking a physical inventory of goods on hand and (2) determining the ownership of goods in transit.

**2.** *Explain the basis of accounting for inventories and describe the inventory cost flow methods.* The primary basis of accounting for inventories is cost. Cost includes all expenditures necessary to acquire goods and place them in condition ready for sale. Inventoriable costs include (1) cost of beginning inventory and (2) the cost of goods purchased. The inventory cost flow methods are: specific identification, FIFO, LIFO, and average cost.

**3.** *Explain the financial statement and tax effects of each of the inventory cost flow methods.* The cost of goods available for sale may be allocated to cost of goods sold and ending inventory by specific identification or by a method based on an assumed cost flow. These methods have different effects on financial statements during periods of changing prices. When prices are rising, the first-in, first-out method (FIFO) results in lower cost of goods sold and higher net income than the average and the last-in, first-out (LIFO) methods. The reverse is true when prices are falling. In the balance sheet, FIFO results in an ending inventory that is closest to current value, whereas the inventory under LIFO is the farthest from current value. LIFO results in the lowest income taxes (because of lower net income).

**4.** *List the essential accounting features of a perpetual inventory system.* Under a perpetual inventory system, (a) purchases of merchandise for resale are debited to Inventory, (b) all transactions that affect cost of goods purchased are recorded in Inventory, (c) the cost of goods sold is recognized each time a sale occurs by a debit to Cost of Goods Sold and a credit to Inventory, and (d) Inventory is a control account that is supported by a subsidiary ledger of individual inventory records.

**5.** *Explain the lower of cost or market basis of accounting for inventories.* The lower of cost or market basis (LCM) may be used when the current replacement cost (market) is less than cost. Under LCM, the loss is recognized in the period in which the price decline occurs. LCM may be applied to individual inventory items, major categories of inventory, or to total inventory.

**6.** *Describe the two methods of estimating inventories.* The two methods of estimating inventories are the gross profit method and the retail inventory method. Under the gross profit method, a gross profit rate is applied to net sales to determine estimated cost of goods sold. Estimated cost of goods sold is then subtracted from cost of goods available for sale to determine the estimated cost of the ending inventory. Under the retail inventory method, a cost to retail ratio is computed by dividing the cost of goods available for sale by the retail value of the goods available for sale. This ratio is then applied to the ending inventory at retail to determine the estimated cost of the ending inventory.

**7.** *Indicate the effects of inventory errors on the financial statements.* In the income statement of the current year: (a) an error in beginning inventory will have a reverse effect on net income (overstatement of inventory results in understatement of net income) and (b) an error in ending inventory will have a similar effect on net income (overstatement of inventory results in overstatement of net income). If ending inventory errors are not corrected in the following period, their effect on net income for that period is reversed, and total net income for the two years will be correct. In the balance sheet, ending inventory errors will have the same effect on total assets and total owner's equity and no effect on liabilities.

# ▼APPENDIX ▸ *Inventory Cost Flow Methods in Perpetual Inventory Systems*

**STUDY OBJECTIVE**

·········**8**·········

*After studying this appendix, you should be able to:*

**8.** *Apply the inventory cost flow methods to perpetual inventory records.*

Each of the inventory cost flow methods described in the chapter for a periodic inventory system may be used in a perpetual inventory system. To illustrate the application of the three assumed cost flow methods (FIFO, average cost, and LIFO), we will use the data shown below for model X268L4 Econo radios in the Home Appliance Mart.

| Date | Purchases | Sale | Balance in Units |
|------|-----------|------|------------------|
| April　3 | 4,000 @ $8.00 | | 4,000 |
| April 10 | 12,000 @ $8.80 | | 16,000 |
| April 26 | | 8,000 units | 8,000 |
| April 29 | 4,000 @ $8.30 | | 12,000 |

# First-In, First-Out (FIFO)

Under FIFO, the cost of the earliest goods on hand prior to each sale is charged to cost of goods sold. Therefore, the cost of goods sold on April 26 consists of the items purchased on April 3 and April 10. The inventory on a FIFO method perpetual system is shown in Illustration 9A-1.

| Date | Purchases | Sales | Balance | |
|---|---|---|---|---|
| April 3 | (4,000 @ $8.00)  $ 32,000 | | (4,000 @ $8.00)  $ 32,000 | |
| April 10 | (12,000 @ $8.80)  $105,600 | | (4,000 @ $8.00) ⎫<br>(12,000 @ $8.80) ⎬  $137,600 | |
| April 26 | | (4,000 @ $8.00)<br>(4,000 @ $8.80) | (8,000 @ $8.80)  $ 70,400 | |
| | | ($67,200) | | |
| April 29 | (4,000 @ $8.30)  $ 33,200 | | (8,000 @ $8.80) ⎫<br>(4,000 @ $8.30) ⎬  $103,600 | |

**Illustration 9A-1**

*Perpetual system—FIFO*

The ending inventory in this situation is $103,600 and the cost of goods sold is $67,200 [(4,000 @ $8.00) + (4,000 @ $8.80)].

The results under FIFO in a perpetual system are the **same as in a periodic system**. Regardless of the system, the first costs in are the first costs assigned to cost of goods sold.

# Average Cost

The average cost method in a perpetual inventory system is called the **moving average method**. Under this method a new average is computed **after each purchase**. The average cost is computed by dividing the cost of goods available for sale by the units on hand. The average cost is then applied to: (1) the units sold, to determine the cost of goods sold, and (2) the remaining units on hand, to determine the ending inventory amount. The application of the average cost method for Home Appliance Mart is shown in Illustration 9A-2.

| Date | Purchases | Sales | Balance |
|---|---|---|---|
| April 3 | (4,000 @ $8.00)  $ 32,000 | | (4,000 @ $8.00)  $ 32,000 |
| April 10 | (12,000 @ $8.80)  $105,600 | | (16,000 @ $8.60)  $137,600 |
| April 26 | | 8,000 @ $8.60<br>($68,800) | (8,000 @ $8.60)  $ 68,800 |
| April 29 | (4,000 @ $8.30)  $ 33,200 | | (12,000 @ $8.50)  $102,000 |

**Illustration 9A-2**

*Perpetual system—average cost*

As indicated above, a new average is computed each time a purchase is made. On April 10, after 12,000 units are purchased for $105,600, a total of 16,000 units costing $137,600 ($32,000 + $105,600) are on hand. The average unit cost is $137,600 divided by 16,000, or $8.60. This unit cost is used in costing withdrawals until another purchase is made, when a new unit cost is computed. Accordingly, the unit cost of the 8,000 units sold on April 26 is shown at $8.60, and the total cost of goods sold is $68,800. On April 29, following the purchase of 4,000 units for $33,200, there are 12,000 units on hand costing $102,000 ($68,800 + $33,200). The new average cost is $8.50 ($102,000 ÷ 12,000).

# Last-In, First-Out (LIFO)

Under the LIFO method using a perpetual system, the cost of the most recent purchase prior to sale is allocated to the units sold. Therefore, the cost of the goods sold on April 26 consists entirely of goods from the April 10 purchase. The ending inventory on a LIFO method is computed in Illustration 9A-3.

**Illustration 9A-3**

*Perpetual system—LIFO*

| Date | Purchases | | Sales | Balance | |
|------|-----------|---|-------|---------|---|
| April 3 | (4,000 @ $8.00) | $ 32,000 | | (4,000 @ $8.00) | $ 32,000 |
| April 10 | (12,000 @ $8.80) | $105,600 | | (4,000 @ $8.00)⎱ (12,000 @ $8.80)⎰ | $137,600 |
| April 26 | | | 8,000 @ $8.80 ($70,400) | (4,000 @ $8.00)⎱ (4,000 @ $8.80)⎰ | $ 67,200 |
| April 29 | (4,000 @ $8.30) | $ 33,200 | | (4,000 @ $8.00)⎱ (4,000 @ $8.80)⎬ (4,000 @ $8.30)⎰ | $100,400 |

The use of LIFO in a perpetual system will usually produce cost allocations that differ from using LIFO in a periodic system. In a perpetual system, the latest units incurred **prior to each sale** are allocated to cost of goods sold. In contrast, in a periodic system, the latest units incurred during the period are allocated to cost of goods sold.[2] The ending inventory in this example is $100,400 and the cost of goods sold is $70,400.

# Summary of Study Objective for Chapter 9 Appendix

**8. Apply the inventory cost flow methods to perpetual inventory records.** Under FIFO, the cost of the earliest goods on hand prior to each sale is charged to cost of goods sold. Under the average cost method, a new average cost is computed after each purchase. Under LIFO, the cost of the most recent purchase prior to sale is charged to cost of goods sold.

# Glossary

**Average cost method** An inventory costing method that assumes that the goods available for sale are homogeneous. (p. 372).

**Consigned goods** Goods shipped by a consignor, who retains ownership, to another party called the consignee. (p. 367).

**Current replacement cost** The current cost to replace an inventory item. (p. 379).

**First-in, first-out method (FIFO)** An inventory costing method that assumes that the costs of the earliest goods acquired are the first to be recognized as cost of goods sold. (p. 370).

---

[2]Thus, when a purchase is made after the last sale for the period, the periodic method will apply this purchase to the previous sale. In the example, 4,000 at $8.30 and 4,000 at $8.80, or $68,400 would be allocated to cost of goods sold in April under the LIFO periodic method—leaving an ending inventory of $102,400.

**Gross profit method** A method for estimating the cost of the ending inventory by applying a gross profit rate to net sales. (p. 380).

**Inventoriable costs** The pool of costs that consists of two elements: (1) the cost of the beginning inventory and (2) the cost of goods purchased during the period. (p. 368).

**Last-in, first-out method (LIFO)** An inventory costing method that assumes that the costs of the latest units purchased are the first to be allocated to cost of goods sold. (p. 371).

**Lower of cost or market basis (LCM) (inventories)** A basis whereby inventory is stated at the lower of cost or market (current replacement cost). (p. 379).

**Perpetual inventory system** An inventory system in which the quantity and cost of each inventory item is maintained and the records continuously show the inventory that should be on hand at any time. (p. 376).

**Retail inventory method** A method used to estimate the cost of the ending inventory by applying a cost to retail ratio to the ending inventory at retail. (p. 381).

**Specific identification method** An actual physical flow costing method in which items still in inventory are specifically costed to arrive at the total cost of the ending inventory. (p. 369).

# DEMONSTRATION PROBLEM

Gerald D. Englehart Company has the following inventory, purchases, and sales data for the month of March:

|            |          |                     |          |
|------------|----------|---------------------|----------|
| Inventory, March 1 | | 200 units @ $4.00 | $ 800 |
| Purchases: | | | |
| | March 10 | 500 units @ $4.50 | 2,250 |
| | March 20 | 400 units @ $4.75 | 1,900 |
| | March 30 | 300 units @ $5.00 | 1,500 |
| Sales: | | | |
| | March 15 | 500 units | |
| | March 25 | 400 units | |

Gerald D. Englehart Company uses a periodic inventory system. The physical inventory count on March 31 shows 500 units on hand.

### Instructions

Determine the cost of inventory on hand at March 31 and the cost of goods sold for March under the (a) first-in, first-out (FIFO) method, (b) last-in, first-out (LIFO) method, and (c) average cost method.

## Solution to Demonstration Problem

The cost of goods available for sale is $6,450:

|            |          |                     |          |
|------------|----------|---------------------|----------|
| Inventory | | 200 units @ $4.00 | $ 800 |
| Purchases: | | | |
| | March 10 | 500 units @ $4.50 | 2,250 |
| | March 20 | 400 units @ $4.75 | 1,900 |
| | March 30 | 300 units @ $5.00 | 1,500 |
| Total cost of goods available for sale | | | $6,450 |

The allocation of the pool of costs is as follows:

### FIFO Method

Ending Inventory:

| Date | Units | Unit Cost | Total Cost | |
|------|-------|-----------|-----------|---|
| March 30 | 300 | $5.00 | $1,500 | |
| March 20 | 200 | 4.75 | 950 | $2,450 |

Cost of goods sold: $6,450 − $2,450 =    $4,000

**Problem-Solving Strategies**

1. For FIFO, the latest costs are allocated to inventory.
2. For LIFO, the earliest costs are allocated to inventory.
3. For average costs, use a weighted average.
4. Remember, the costs allocated to cost of goods sold can be proved.
5. Total purchases are the same under all three cost flow methods.

### LIFO Method

Ending Inventory:

| Date | Units | Unit Cost | Total Cost | |
|------|-------|-----------|-----------|------|
| March 1 | 200 | $4.00 | $ 800 | |
| March 10 | 300 | 4.50 | 1,350 | $2,150 |

Cost of goods sold: $6,450 − $2,150 =                                    $4,300

### Average Cost Method

Weighted average unit cost: $6,450 ÷ 1,400 = $4.607
Ending inventory: 500 × $4.607 =                                    $2,303.50

Cost of goods sold: $6,450 − $2,303.50 =                            $4,146.50

*Note:** All **asterisked** Questions, Exercises, and Problems relate to material contained in the appendix to the chapter.

## SELF-STUDY QUESTIONS

Answers are at the end of the chapter.

(SO 1)   1. Which of the following should *not* be included in the physical inventory of a company?
  a. Goods held on consignment from another company.
  b. Goods shipped on consignment to another company.
  c. Goods in transit from another company shipped FOB shipping point.
  d. None of the above.

(SO 2)   2. Inventoriable costs consist of two elements: beginning inventory and
  a. ending inventory.
  b. cost of goods purchased.
  c. cost of goods sold.
  d. cost of goods available for sale.

(SO 2)   3. Kam Company has the following:

| | Units | Unit Cost |
|---|-------|-----------|
| Inventory, Jan. 1 | 8,000 | $11 |
| Purchase, June 19 | 13,000 | 12 |
| Purchase, Nov. 8 | 5,000 | 13 |

If 9,000 units are on hand at December 31, the cost of the ending inventory under FIFO is:
  a. $99,000.
  b. $108,000.
  c. $113,000.
  d. $117,000.

(SO 2)   4. Using the data in (3) above, the cost of the ending inventory under LIFO is:
  a. $113,000.
  b. $108,000.
  c. $99,000.
  d. $100,000.

(SO 3)   5. In periods of rising prices, LIFO will produce:
  a. higher net income than FIFO.
  b. the same net income as FIFO.
  c. lower net income than FIFO.
  d. higher net income than average costing.

(SO 3)   6. Factors that affect the selection of an inventory costing method do *not* include:
  a. tax effects.
  b. balance sheet effects.
  c. income statement effects.
  d. perpetual vs. periodic inventory system.

(SO 4)   7. Which of the following statements is *incorrect* concerning a perpetual inventory system?
  a. A perpetual inventory system contributes to better control over inventories.
  b. Accounting records continuously show the inventory that should be on hand at any point in time.
  c. The cost of goods sold is recognized when each sale occurs by debiting Cost of Goods Sold and crediting Purchases.
  d. Purchases are debited to Inventory.

(SO 5)   8. The lower of cost or market basis may be applied to:
  a. categories of inventories.
  b. individual items of inventories.
  c. total inventory.
  d. all of the above.

(SO 6)   9. Somers Company has sales of $150,000 and cost of goods available for sale of $135,000. If the gross profit rate is 30%, the estimated cost of the ending inventory under the gross profit method is:
  a. $15,000.
  b. $30,000.

c. $45,000.
d. $75,000.

(SO 7) 10. In Fran Company, ending inventory is understated $4,000. The effects of this error on the current year's cost of goods sold and net income, respectively, are:
   a. understated, overstated.
   b. overstated, understated.
   c. overstated, overstated.
   d. understated, understated.

*11. In a perpetual inventory system,  (SO 8)
   a. LIFO cost of goods sold will be the same as in a periodic inventory system.
   b. average costs are based entirely on unit cost averages.
   c. a new average is computed under the average cost method after each sale.
   d. FIFO cost of goods sold will be the same as in a periodic inventory system.

# QUESTIONS

1. "The key to successful business operations is effective inventory management." Do you agree? Explain.

2. An item must possess two characteristics to be classified as inventory. What are these two characteristics?

3. Your friend Tom Wetzel has been hired to help take the physical inventory in Casey's Hardware Store. Explain to Tom Wetzel what this job will entail.

4. (a) Janine Company ships merchandise to Laura Corporation on December 30. The merchandise reaches the buyer on January 5. Indicate the terms of sale that will result in the goods being included in (1) Janine's December 31 inventory, and (2) Laura's December 31 inventory.
   (b) Under what circumstances should Janine Company include consigned goods in its inventory?

5. Mary Ann's Hat Shop received a shipment of hats for which it paid the wholesaler $2,940. The price of the hats was $3,000, but Mary Ann's was given a $60 cash discount and required to pay freight charges of $70. In addition, Mary Ann's paid $100 to cover the travel expenses of an employee who negotiated the purchase of the hats. What amount should Mary Ann's include in inventory? Why?

6. What is the primary basis of accounting for inventories? What is the major objective in accounting for inventories? What accounting principles are involved here?

7. Dave Wier believes that the allocation of inventoriable costs should be based on the actual physical flow of the goods. Explain to Dave why this may be both impractical and inappropriate.

8. What is a major advantage and a major disadvantage of the specific identification method of inventory costing?

9. "The selection of an inventory cost flow method is a decision made by accountants." Do you agree? Explain.

Once a method has been selected, what accounting requirement applies?

10. Which assumed inventory cost flow method:
   (a) usually parallels the actual physical flow of merchandise?
   (b) assumes that goods available for sale during an accounting period are homogeneous?
   (c) assumes that the latest units purchased are the first to be sold?

11. In a period of rising prices, the inventory reported in Plato Company's balance sheet is close to the current cost of the inventory, whereas York Company's inventory is considerably below its current cost. Identify the inventory cost flow method being used by each company. Which company has probably been reporting the higher gross profit?

12. Shaunna Corporation has been using the FIFO cost flow method during a prolonged period of inflation. During the same time period, Shaunna has been paying out all of its net income as dividends. What adverse effects may result from this policy?

13. Pedro Lord is uncertain about the accounting features of a perpetual inventory system. Explain these features to Pedro.

14. Mia Mullen believes a perpetual inventory system requires a great deal of work for only marginal benefit. Explain to Mia the advantages of a perpetual inventory system.

15. Lucy Ritter is studying for the next accounting midterm examination. What should Lucy know about (a) departing from the cost basis of accounting for inventories and (b) the meaning of "market" in the lower of cost or market method?

16. Rock Music Center has 5 CD players on hand at the balance sheet date that cost $400 each. The current replacement cost is $320 per unit. Under the lower of cost or market basis of accounting for inventories, what value should be reported for the CD players on the balance sheet? Why?

17. What methods may be used under the lower of cost or market basis of accounting for inventories? Which method will produce the lowest inventory value?

18. When is it necessary to estimate inventories?

19. Both the gross profit method and the retail inventory method are based on averages. For each method, indicate the average used, how it is determined, and how it is applied.

20. Pat Voga Company has net sales of $400,000 and cost of goods available for sale of $300,000. If the gross profit rate is 30%, what is the estimated cost of the ending inventory? Show computations.

21. Miller Shoe Shop had goods available for sale in 1996 with a retail price of $120,000. The cost of these goods was $84,000. If sales during the period were $90,000, what is the ending inventory at cost using the retail inventory method?

22. Mila Company discovers in 1996 that its ending inventory at December 31, 1995, was $5,000 understated. What effect will this error have on (a) 1995 net income, (b) 1996 net income, and (c) the combined net income for the 2 years?

23. Maureen & Nathan Company's balance sheet shows Inventories $162,800. What additional disclosures should be made?

*24. "When perpetual inventory records are kept, the results under the FIFO and LIFO methods are the same as they would be in a periodic inventory system." Do you agree? Explain.

*25. How does the average method of inventory costing differ between a perpetual inventory system and a periodic inventory system?

# BRIEF EXERCISES

*Identify items to be included in taking a physical inventory.*
*(SO 1)*

**BE9–1**   Ginger Helgeson Company identifies the following items for possible inclusion in the taking of a physical inventory. Indicate whether each item should be included or excluded from the inventory taking.

1. Goods shipped on consignment by Helgeson to another company.
2. Goods in transit from a supplier shipped FOB destination.
3. Goods sold but being held for customer pickup.
4. Goods held on consignment from another company.

*Identify the components of inventoriable costs.*
*(SO 2)*

**BE9–2**   The ledger of Wharton Company includes the following items: (1) Freight-in, (2) Purchase Returns and Allowances, (3) Purchases, (4) Sales Discounts, (5) Purchase Discounts. Identify which items are included in inventoriable costs.

*Compute ending inventory using FIFO.*
*(SO 2)*

**BE9–3**   In its first month of operations, Quilt Company made three purchases of merchandise in the following sequence: (1) 300 units at $6, (2) 400 units at $7, and (3) 300 units at $8. Compute the cost to be allocated to ending inventory under the FIFO method, assuming there are 400 units on hand.

*Compute ending inventory using LIFO.*
*(SO 2)*

**BE9–4**   Data for Quilt Company are presented in BE9–3. Compute the cost to be allocated to the ending inventory under the LIFO method, assuming there are 400 units on hand.

*Compute the ending inventory using average costs.*
*(SO 2)*

**BE9–5**   Data for Quilt Company are presented in BE9–3. Compute the cost to be allocated to the ending inventory under the average cost method, assuming there are 400 units on hand.

*Journalize transactions in a perpetual inventory system.*
*(SO 4)*

**BE9–6**   Zina Company uses a perpetual inventory system. In March, its first month of operations, it has the following transactions: March 3 purchased on account 20 units of Product X at $25 per unit, March 6 returned 3 units for credit, and March 21 sold on account 10 units at $45 per unit. Journalize the three transactions.

*Determine the LCM valuation using inventory categories.*
*(SO 5)*

**BE9–7**   Hawkeye Appliance Center accumulates the following cost and market data at December 31:

| Inventory Categories | Cost Data | Market Data |
|---|---|---|
| Cameras | $12,000 | $10,200 |
| Camcorders | 9,000 | 9,500 |
| VCRs | 14,000 | 12,800 |

Compute the lower of cost or market valuation using categories.

*Apply the gross profit method.*
*(SO 6)*

**BE9–8**   At May 31, Jansen Company has net sales of $300,000 and cost of goods available for sale of $210,000. Compute the estimated cost of the ending inventory assuming the gross profit rate is 40%.

**BE9–9** On June 30, Faber's Fabrics has the following data pertaining to the retail inventory method: Goods available for sale: at cost $35,000, at retail $50,000; net sales $30,000, and ending inventory at retail $20,000. Compute the estimated cost of the ending inventory using the retail inventory method.

*Apply the retail inventory method.*
*(SO 6)*

**BE9–10** Creole Company reports net income of $90,000 in 1996. However, ending inventory was understated $7,000. What is the correct net income for 1996? What effect, if any, will this error have on total assets as reported in the balance sheet at December 31, 1996?

*Determine correct income statement amounts.*
*(SO 7)*

**\*BE9–11** Graf Department Store uses a perpetual inventory system. Data for product XX include the following purchases:

*Apply FIFO to perpetual records.*
*(SO 8)*

| Date | Number of Units | Unit Price |
|------|-----------------|------------|
| May 5 | 50 | $10 |
| July 29 | 25 | 12 |

On June 1 Graf sold 30 units, and on August 27, 28 more units. Prepare the perpetual inventory card for the above transactions using the FIFO method of inventory costing.

# EXERCISES

**E9–1** First Bank and Trust is considering giving Novotna Company a loan. Before doing so, they decide that further discussions with Novotna's accountant may be desirable. One area of particular concern is the inventory account, which has a year-end balance of $295,000. Discussions with the accountant reveal the following:

*Determine the correct inventory amount.*
*(SO 1)*

1. Novotna sold goods costing $35,000 to Moghul Company FOB shipping point on December 28. The goods are not expected to arrive in India until January 12. The goods were not included in the physical inventory because they were not in the warehouse.
2. The physical count of the inventory did not include goods costing $95,000 that were shipped to Novotna FOB destination on December 27, and were still in transit at year-end.
3. Novotna received goods costing $25,000 on January 2. The goods were shipped FOB shipping point on December 26 by Cellar Co. The goods were not included in the physical count.
4. Novotna sold goods costing $40,000 to Sterling of Canada FOB destination on December 30. The goods were received in Canada on January 8. They were not included in Novotna's physical inventory.
5. Novotna received goods costing $44,000 on January 2 that were shipped FOB destination on December 29. The shipment was a rush order that was supposed to arrive December 31. This purchase was included in the ending inventory of $295,000.

*Instructions*
Determine the correct inventory amount on December 31.

**E9–2** Mawmey Inc. uses a periodic inventory system. Its records show the following for the month of May, in which 78 units were sold.

*Compute inventory and cost of goods sold using FIFO and LIFO.*
*(SO 2)*

| | | Units | Unit Cost | Total Cost |
|--------|-----------|-------|-----------|------------|
| May 1 | Inventory | 30 | $ 8 | $240 |
| 15 | Purchases | 25 | 10 | 250 |
| 24 | Purchases | 35 | 12 | 420 |
| | Totals | 90 | | $910 |

*Instructions*
Compute the ending inventory at May 31 using the FIFO and LIFO methods. Prove the amount allocated to cost of goods sold under each method.

*Compute inventory and cost of goods sold using FIFO and LIFO.*
*(SO 2, 3)*

**E9–3**   In June, Dakota Company reports the following for the month of June.

|  | | Units | Unit Cost | Total Cost |
|---|---|---|---|---|
| June | 1  Inventory | 200 | $5 | $1,000 |
|  | 12  Purchases | 300 | 6 | 1,800 |
|  | 23  Purchases | 500 | 7 | 3,500 |
|  | 30  Inventory | 180 | | |

**Instructions**

(a) Compute the cost of the ending inventory and the cost of goods sold under (1) FIFO and (2) LIFO.

(b) Which costing method gives the higher ending inventory? Why?

(c) Which method results in the higher cost of goods sold? Why?

*Compute inventory and cost of goods sold using average costs.*
*(SO 2, 3)*

**E9–4**   Inventory data for Dakota Company are presented in E9–3.

**Instructions**

(a) Compute the cost of the ending inventory and the cost of goods sold using the average cost method.

(b) Will the results in (a) be higher or lower than the results under (1) FIFO and (2) LIFO?

(c) Why is the average unit cost not $6?

*Journalize and post using a perpetual inventory system.*
*(SO 4)*

**E9–5**   On September 1, Collegiate Office Supply had an inventory of 10 high-speed deluxe pocket calculators at a cost of $15 each. The company uses a perpetual inventory system. During September, the following transactions and events occurred.

Sept.  2   Purchased 90 calculators at $15 each from Digital Inc., terms n/30.

   5   Received credit of $60 for the return of four calculators purchased on September 2 that were defective.

   8   Sold 50 calculators for $25 each to University Bookstore, terms 2/10, n/30.

   12   Sold 30 calculators for $25 each to Hilltop Card Shop, terms n/30.

   20   Purchased 15 calculators at $16 each from Sterling Electronics, terms n/30.

   30   Determined that there were 31 calculators on hand.

**Instructions**

Journalize the September transactions and events.

*Determine ending inventory under lower of cost or market inventory method.*
*(SO 5)*

**E9–6**   Cody Camera Shop uses the lower of cost or market basis for its inventory. The following data are available at December 31:

| Item | Units | Unit Cost | Market |
|---|---|---|---|
| Cameras | | | |
| Minolta | 5 | $175 | $160 |
| Canon | 7 | 150 | 152 |
| Light Meters | | | |
| Vivitar | 12 | 125 | 110 |
| Kodak | 10 | 115 | 135 |

**Instructions**

Determine the amount of the ending inventory by applying the lower of cost or market basis to (a) individual items, (b) inventory categories, and (c) the total inventory.

*Determine merchandise lost using the gross profit method of estimating inventory.*
*(SO 6)*

**E9–7**   The inventory of Susan Company was destroyed by fire on March 1. From an examination of the accounting records, the following data for the first 2 months of the year are obtained: Sales $51,000, Sales Returns and Allowances $1,000, Purchases $28,200, Freight-in $1,200, and Purchase Returns and Allowances $1,400.

**Instructions**

Determine the merchandise lost by fire, assuming:

(a) A beginning inventory of $20,000 and a gross profit rate of 30% on net sales.

(b) A beginning inventory of $25,000 and a gross profit rate of 25% on net sales.

**E9–8** Sharp Shoe Store uses the retail inventory method for its two departments: Women's Shoes and Men's Shoes. The following information for each department is obtained:

*Determine ending inventory at cost using retail method.*
(SO 6)

| Item | Women's Department | Men's Department |
|---|---|---|
| Beginning inventory at cost | $ 32,000 | $ 46,450 |
| Cost of goods purchased at cost | 148,000 | 137,300 |
| Net sales | 185,000 | 195,000 |
| Beginning inventory at retail | 45,000 | 60,000 |
| Cost of goods purchased at retail | 180,000 | 185,000 |

**Instructions**
Compute the estimated cost of the ending inventory for each department under the retail inventory method.

**E9–9** Seles Hardware reported cost of goods sold as follows:

*Determine effects of inventory errors.*
(SO 7)

| | 1996 | 1997 |
|---|---|---|
| Beginning inventory | $ 20,000 | $ 30,000 |
| Cost of goods purchased | 150,000 | 175,000 |
| Cost of goods available for sale | 170,000 | 205,000 |
| Ending inventory | 30,000 | 35,000 |
| Cost of goods sold | $140,000 | $170,000 |

Seles made two errors: (1) 1996 ending inventory was overstated $4,000 and (2) 1997 ending inventory was understated $3,000.

**Instructions**
Compute the correct cost of goods sold for each year.

**E9–10** Aruba Company reported the following income statement data for a 2-year period.

*Prepare correct income statements.*
(SO 7)

| | 1996 | 1997 |
|---|---|---|
| Sales | $210,000 | $250,000 |
| Cost of goods sold | | |
|   Beginning inventory | 32,000 | 40,000 |
|   Cost of goods purchased | 173,000 | 202,000 |
|   Cost of goods available for sale | 205,000 | 242,000 |
|   Ending inventory | 40,000 | 52,000 |
|     Cost of goods sold | 165,000 | 190,000 |
| Gross profit | $ 45,000 | $ 60,000 |

Aruba uses a periodic inventory system. The inventories at January 1, 1996, and December 31, 1997, are correct. However, the ending inventory at December 31, 1996, was overstated $6,000.

**Instructions**
(a) Prepare correct income statement data for the 2 years.
(b) What is the cumulative effect of the inventory error on total gross profit for the 2 years?
(c) ▯▯▯▯▶ Explain in a letter to the president of Aruba Company what has happened—i.e., the nature of the error and its effect on the financial statements.

**\*E9–11** Stracka Appliance uses a perpetual inventory system. For its model B47 television sets, the January 1 inventory was four sets at $600 each. During January, the following purchase was made: Jan. 10, 6 units at $640 each. That month, the company had the following sales: Jan. 8, 2 units and Jan. 15, 4 units.

*Apply cost flow methods to perpetual records.*
(SO 8)

**Instructions**
Compute the ending inventory under (1) FIFO, (2) LIFO, and (3) average cost.

# PROBLEMS

●●●●●●●●●●●●●●●●●●●●●●●●●●●●●●●●●●●●●●●●●●●●●●●●●●●●●●●●●●●●●●●●●●●●●●●●●●●●●●●●

*Determine cost of goods sold and ending inventory, using FIFO, LIFO, and average cost with analysis.*
*(SO 2, 3)*

**P9–1**   Kane Company had a beginning inventory on January 1 of 100 units of Product SXL at a cost of $20 per unit. During the year, the following purchases were made.

| Mar. 15 | 300 units at $24 | Sept. 4 | 300 units at $28 |
|---------|------------------|---------|------------------|
| July 20 | 200 units at  25 | Dec.  2 | 100 units at  30 |

850 units were sold. Kane Company uses a periodic inventory system.

### Instructions

(a) Determine the cost of goods available for sale.
(b) Determine (1) the ending inventory, and (2) the cost of goods sold under each of the assumed cost flow methods (FIFO, LIFO, and average). Prove the accuracy of the cost of goods sold under the FIFO and LIFO methods.
(c) Which cost flow method results in (1) the highest inventory amount for the balance sheet and (2) the highest cost of goods sold for the income statement?

*Compute ending inventory, prepare income statements, and answer questions using FIFO and LIFO.*
*(SO 2, 3)*

**P9–2**   The management of Tumatoe Inc. asks your help in determining the comparative effects of the FIFO and LIFO inventory cost flow methods. For 1996, the accounting records show the following data:

| | |
|---|---|
| Inventory, January 1 (10,000 units) | $ 35,000 |
| Cost of 110,000 units purchased | 460,000 |
| Selling price of 95,000 units sold | 665,000 |
| Operating expenses | 120,000 |

Units purchased consisted of 40,000 units at $4.00 on May 10; 50,000 units at $4.20 on August 15; and 20,000 units at $4.50 on November 20. Income taxes are 30%.

### Instructions

(a) Prepare comparative condensed income statements for 1996 under FIFO and LIFO. (Show computations of ending inventory.)
(b) ▭▬▬▶  Answer the following questions for management in the form of a business letter:
   (1) Which inventory cost flow method produces the most meaningful inventory amount for the balance sheet? Why?
   (2) Which inventory cost flow method produces the most meaningful net income? Why?
   (3) Which inventory cost flow method is most likely to approximate actual physical flow of the goods? Why?
   (4) How much additional cash will be available for management under LIFO than under FIFO? Why?
   (5) How much of the gross profit under FIFO is illusionary in comparison with the gross profit under LIFO?

*Compute gross profit rate and inventory loss using gross profit method.*
*(SO 6)*

**P9–3**   M. Chang Company lost all of its inventory in a fire on December 28, 1996. The accounting records showed the following gross profit data for November and December.

| | November | December (to 12/28) |
|---|---|---|
| Net sales | $400,000 | $300,000 |
| Beginning inventory | 22,100 | 29,100 |
| Purchases | 314,975 | 236,000 |
| Purchase returns and allowances | 11,800 | 4,000 |
| Purchase discounts | 8,577 | 6,000 |
| Freight-in | 4,402 | 3,700 |
| Ending inventory | 29,100 | ? |

M. Chang is fully insured for fire losses but must prepare a report for the insurance company.

### Instructions

(a) Compute the gross profit rate for November.
(b) Using the gross profit rate for November, determine the estimated cost of the inventory lost in the fire.

**P9–4** Barker's Book Store uses the retail inventory method to estimate its monthly ending inventories. The following information is available for two of its departments at October 31, 1996.

*Compute ending inventory using retail method.*
*(SO 6)*

|  | Hardcovers | | Paperbacks | |
|---|---|---|---|---|
|  | Cost | Retail | Cost | Retail |
| Beginning inventory | $ 260,000 | $ 400,000 | $ 63,000 | $ 90,000 |
| Purchases | 1,180,000 | 1,800,000 | 268,000 | 380,000 |
| Freight-in | 5,000 |  | 2,000 |  |
| Purchase discounts | 15,000 |  | 4,000 |  |
| Net sales |  | 1,810,000 |  | 363,000 |

At December 31, Barker's Book Store takes a physical inventory at retail. The actual retail values of the inventories in each department are: Hardcovers $400,000 and Paperbacks $100,000.

**Instructions**
(a) Determine the estimated cost of the ending inventory for each department at **October 31**, 1996, using the retail inventory method.
(b) Compute the ending inventory at cost for each department at **December 31**, assuming the cost to retail ratios for the year are 65% for hardcovers and 70% for paperbacks.

**P9–5** Varsity Auto Sales uses a perpetual inventory system. On April 1, the new car inventory records show total inventory of $140,000 consisting of the following:

*Journalize transactions under a perpetual inventory system.*
*(SO 4)*

| Model | Units | Unit Cost |
|---|---|---|
| Custom Sedans | 4 | $14,000 |
| Convertibles | 3 | 16,000 |
| Recreational Vans | 2 | 18,000 |

During April, the following purchases and sales were made on account.

April 5 Purchased three custom sedans for $14,000 each.
　　 7 Sold two custom sedans for $18,200 each.
　 13 Purchased two recreational vans for $18,000 each.
　 17 Sold one custom sedan for $18,500.
　 20 Purchased two convertibles for $16,000 each.
　 22 Returned one convertible purchased on April 20 for $16,000 credit.
　 24 Sold three recreational vans for $24,000 each.
　 28. Sold one convertible for $21,000.

**Instructions**
(a) Journalize the transactions using (1) a periodic inventory system and (2) a perpetual inventory system.
(b) Explain the end-of-year entries, if any, for the inventory account under each inventory system.

# ALTERNATE PROBLEMS

**P9–1A** Steward Company had a beginning inventory of 400 units of Product MLN at a cost of $8.00 per unit. During the year, purchases were:

*Determine cost of goods sold and ending inventory, using FIFO, LIFO, and average cost.*
*(SO 2, 3)*

| Feb. 20 | 700 units at $9.00 | Aug. 12 | 300 units at $11.00 |
|---|---|---|---|
| May 5 | 500 units at $10.00 | Dec. 8 | 100 units at $12.00 |

Steward Company uses a periodic inventory system. Sales totaled 1,550 units.

**Instructions**
(a) Determine the cost of goods available for sale.

(b) Determine (1) the ending inventory, and (2) the cost of goods sold under each of the assumed cost flow methods (FIFO, LIFO, and average). Prove the accuracy of the cost of goods sold under the FIFO and LIFO methods.

(c) Which cost flow method results in (1) the lowest inventory amount for the balance sheet, and (2) the lowest cost of goods sold for the income statement?

*Compute ending inventory, prepare income statements, and answer questions using FIFO and LIFO.*
*(SO 2, 3)*

**P9–2A**  The management of Real Novelty Inc. is reevaluating the appropriateness of using its present inventory cost flow method, which is average cost. They request your help in determining the results of operations for 1996 if either the FIFO method or the LIFO method had been used. For 1996, the accounting records show the following data:

| **Inventories** | | **Purchases and Sales** | |
|---|---|---|---|
| Beginning (15,000 units) | $34,000 | Total net sales (225,000 units) | $865,000 |
| Ending (20,000 units) | | Total cost of goods purchased | |
| | | (230,000 units) | 578,500 |

Purchases were made quarterly as follows:

| Quarter | Units | Unit Cost | Total Cost |
|---|---|---|---|
| 1 | 60,000 | $2.30 | $138,000 |
| 2 | 50,000 | 2.50 | 125,000 |
| 3 | 50,000 | 2.60 | 130,000 |
| 4 | 70,000 | 2.65 | 185,500 |
| | 230,000 | | $578,500 |

Operating expenses were $147,000, and the company's income tax rate is 30%.

**Instructions**

(a) Prepare comparative condensed income statements for 1996 under FIFO and LIFO. (Show computations of ending inventory.)

(b) ▭▭▭▭▷  Answer the following questions for management:

(1) Which cost flow method (FIFO or LIFO) produces the more meaningful inventory amount for the balance sheet? Why?

(2) Which cost flow method (FIFO or LIFO) produces the more meaningful net income? Why?

(3) Which cost flow method (FIFO or LIFO) is more likely to approximate actual physical flow of the goods? Why?

(4) How much additional cash will be available for management under LIFO than under FIFO? Why?

(5) Will gross profit under the average cost method be higher or lower than (a) FIFO and (b) LIFO? (*Note:* It is not necessary to quantify your answer.)

*Estimate inventory loss using gross profit method.*
*(SO 6)*

**P9–3A**  Vanessa Company lost 80% of its inventory in a fire on March 23, 1996. The accounting records showed the following gross profit data for February and March.

| | February | March (to 3/23) |
|---|---|---|
| Net sales | $270,000 | $260,000 |
| Net purchases | 200,800 | 191,000 |
| Freight-in | 2,900 | 3,500 |
| Beginning inventory | 16,500 | 20,400 |
| Ending inventory | 20,400 | ? |

Vanessa Company is fully insured for fire losses but must prepare a report for the insurance company.

**Instructions**

(a) Compute the gross profit rate for the month of February.

(b) Using the gross profit rate for February, determine both the estimated total inventory and inventory lost in the fire in March.

**P9–4A** Martinez Department Store uses the retail inventory method to estimate its monthly ending inventories. The following information is available for two of its departments at August 31, 1996.

*Compute ending inventory and cost of inventory lost using retail method.*
*(SO 6)*

|  | Sporting Goods | | Jewelry and Cosmetics | |
|---|---|---|---|---|
|  | **Cost** | **Retail** | **Cost** | **Retail** |
| Net sales |  | $1,020,000 |  | $1,160,000 |
| Purchases | $670,000 | 1,066,000 | $731,000 | 1,158,000 |
| Purchase returns | (26,000) | (40,000) | (12,000) | (20,000) |
| Purchase discounts | (15,360) | — | (9,440) | — |
| Freight-in | 6,000 | — | 8,000 | — |
| Beginning inventory | 47,360 | 74,000 | 38,440 | 62,000 |

At December 31, Martinez Department Store takes a physical inventory at retail. The actual retail values of the inventories in each department are: Sporting Goods $75,000, and Jewelry and Cosmetics $44,000.

**Instructions**

(a) Determine the estimated cost of the ending inventory for each department on August 31, 1996, using the retail inventory method.

(b) Compute the ending inventory at cost for each department at December 31, assuming the cost-to-retail ratios are 60% for Sporting Goods and 65% for Jewelry and Cosmetics.

**\*P9–5A** The Family Home Appliance Mart begins operations on May 1. It uses a perpetual inventory system. During May the company had the following purchases and sales for its Model 25 Sureshot camera.

*Prepare subsidiary ledger records under a perpetual inventory system.*
*(SO 8)*

|  | Purchases | |  |
|---|---|---|---|
| **Date** | **Units** | **Unit Cost** | **Sales Units** |
| May 1 | 7 | $150 |  |
| 4 |  |  | 5 |
| 8 | 8 | $170 |  |
| 12 |  |  | 5 |
| 15 | 5 | $180 |  |
| 20 |  |  | 4 |
| 25 |  |  | 3 |

**Instructions**

(a) Determine the inventory under a perpetual inventory system using (1) FIFO, (2) average cost, and (3) LIFO. Follow the format shown in the appendix.

(b) Which costing method produces (1) the highest ending inventory valuation and (2) the lowest ending inventory valuation?

# ►**B**roadening Your Perspective

## **F**INANCIAL REPORTING PROBLEM
••••••••••••••••••••••••••••••••••••••••••••••••••••••••••••••

The notes that accompany a company's financial statements provide informative details that would clutter the amounts and descriptions presented in the statements. Refer to the financial statements of PepsiCo and the Notes to Consolidated Financial Statements in Appendix A.

**Instructions**
Answer the following questions. Complete the requirements in millions of dollars, as shown in PepsiCo's annual report.

(a) What did PepsiCo report for the amount of inventories in its Consolidated Balance Sheet at December 31, 1994? December 25, 1993?
(b) Compute the dollar amount of change and the percentage change in inventories between 1993 and 1994. Compute inventory as a percentage of current assets for 1994.
(c) How does PepsiCo value its inventories? Which inventory cost flow method does PepsiCo use?
(d) What two categories of inventories are classified in the note on "Inventories"? Briefly explain what you think is contained in each category.
(e) What is the cost of sales (cost of goods sold) reported by PepsiCo for 1994, 1993, and 1992? Compute the percentage of cost of sales to net sales in 1994.

# DECISION CASE

On April 10, 1996, fire damaged the office and warehouse of Gibson Company. Most of the accounting records were destroyed but the following account balances were determined as of March 31, 1996: Merchandise Inventory, January 1, 1996, $80,000; Sales (January 1–March 31, 1996), $150,000; Purchases (January 1–March 31, 1996), $84,000.

The company's fiscal year ends on December 31, and it uses a periodic inventory system.

From an analysis of the April bank statement you discover cancelled checks of $4,200 during the period April 1–10 for cash purchases. Deposits during the same period totaled $18,500 of which 60% were collections on accounts receivable and the balance was cash sales.

Correspondence with the company's principal suppliers revealed $12,400 of purchases on account from April 1 to April 10 of which $1,800 was for merchandise in transit on April 10 that was shipped FOB destination.

Correspondence with the company's principal customers produced acknowledgments of credit sales totaling $28,000 from April 1 to April 10. It was estimated that $4,600 of credit sales will never be acknowledged or recovered from customers.

Gibson Company reached an agreement with the insurance company that its fire-loss claim should be based on the average of the gross profit rates for the preceding 2 years. The financial statements for 1994 and 1995 showed the following data:

|  | 1995 | 1994 |
|---|---|---|
| Net sales | $600,000 | $480,000 |
| Cost of goods purchased | 416,000 | 356,000 |
| Beginning inventory | 60,000 | 40,000 |
| Ending inventory | 80,000 | 60,000 |

Inventory with a cost of $19,000 was salvaged from the fire.

*Instructions*
(a) Determine the balances in (1) Sales and (2) Purchases at April 10.
(b) Determine the average profit rate for the years 1994 and 1995. (*Hint:* Find the gross profit rate for each year and divide the sum by 2.)
(c) Determine the inventory loss as a result of the fire, using the gross profit method.

# COMMUNICATION ACTIVITY

You are the controller of Small Toys Inc. Joe Paisley, the president, recently mentioned to you that he found an error in the 1994 financial statements which he believes has corrected itself. He determined, in discussions with the Purchasing Department, that 1994 ending inventory was overstated by $1 million. Joe says that the 1995 ending inventory is correct, thus he assumes that 1995 income is correct. Joe says to you, "What happened has happened—there's no point in worrying about it anymore."

*Instructions*
You conclude that Joe is incorrect. Write a brief, tactful memo to Joe, clarifying the situation.

# GROUP ACTIVITY

In groups of four or five students, choose one of the following inventory cost flow methods: FIFO periodic, FIFO perpetual, LIFO periodic, LIFO perpetual, average cost, specific identification.

*Instructions*
- (a) Discuss the inventory methodology and its effects on the financial statements if adopted.
- (b) Explain to the class how to implement the method you chose and its effects on the financial statements that you discussed earlier.

# ETHICS CASE

Lonergan Wholesale Corp. uses the LIFO method of inventory costing. In the current year, profit at Lonergan is running unusually high. The corporate tax rate is also high this year, but it is scheduled to decline significantly next year. In an effort to lower current year's net income and to take advantage of the changing income tax rate, the president of Lonergan Wholesale instructs the plant accountant to recommend to the purchasing department a large purchase of inventory for delivery 3 days before the end of the year. The price of the inventory to be purchased has doubled during the year and the purchase will represent a major portion of the ending inventory value.

*Instructions*
- (a) What is the effect of this transaction on this year's and next year's income statement and income tax expense? Why?
- (b) If Lonergan Wholesale had been using the FIFO method of inventory costing, would the president give the same directive?
- (c) Should the plant accountant order the inventory purchase to lower income? What are the ethical implications of this order?

# CRITICAL THINKING
## ► *A Real-World Focus: General Motors Corporation*

*General Motors is the largest producer of automobiles in the world, as well as the world's biggest industrial enterprise. After stumbling in the early 1990s, GM has enacted numerous cost-cutting measures, including downsizing and renegotiating contracts with suppliers. In addition, it has shifted more of its resources to the hot-selling truck market.*

The annual report of General Motors Corporation disclosed the following information about its accounting for inventories:

**Note 12. Inventories**
Major Classes of Inventories

| (Dollars in millions) | 1994 | 1993 |
|---|---|---|
| Productive material, work in process, and supplies | $ 5,478.3 | $4,671.9 |
| Finished product, service parts, etc. | 4,649.5 | 3,943.2 |
| Total | $10,127.8 | $8,615.1 |
| Memo: Increase in LIFO inventories if valued at first-in, first-out (FIFO) | $ 2,535.9 | $2,519.0 |

Inventories are stated generally at cost, which is not in excess of market. The cost of substantially all U.S. inventories other than the inventories of Saturn Corporation (Saturn) and GMHE is determined by the last-in, first-out (LIFO) method. The cost of non-U.S., Saturn, and GMHE inventories is determined generally by FIFO or average cost methods.

*Instructions*

(a) What is meant by ''inventories are stated generally at cost, which is not in excess of market''?

(b) The company uses LIFO for most of its inventory. What impact does this have on reported ending inventory if prices are increasing?

(c) General Motors uses different inventory methods for different types of inventory. Why might it do this?

---

*Answers to Self-Study Questions*

1. a     2. b     3. c     4. d     5. c     6. d     7. c     8. d     9. b     10. b     *11. d

▶ **Concepts for Review**

**Before studying this chapter, you should know or, if necessary, review:**

**a.** *The time period assumption. (Ch. 3, p. 89)*
**b.** *The cost principle. (Ch. 1, p. 11) and the matching principle (Ch. 3, p. 90)*
**c.** *What is depreciation? (Ch. 3, p. 95)*
**d.** *How to make adjustments for depreciation. (Ch. 3, pp. 95–6)*

# On the Books, Your Classroom May Be Worthless

PORTLAND, Maine — Take a stroll around your campus. Some of those buildings were built before you were born. How much do you think they cost to build? Are they depreciating? Are they appreciating?

These questions are not merely academic. It costs millions of dollars to construct, maintain, and sometimes demolish these campus buildings. Where does the money come from? Partly your tuition, perhaps tax dollars, perhaps from contributions of wealthy alumni, or from long-term borrowing. How these dollars are allocated can depend upon a reasonable estimate of a building's condition, its remaining life—and of course, how much it would cost to replace (its replacement cost).

At Westbrook College in Portland, Maine, Ms. Betty-Ann Doucette, the school's controller, recently researched the age of cer-

tain buildings on campus. The reason: a recent Financial Accounting Standards Board rule mandates that private colleges report fixed assets and depreciate them. Ms. Doucette found that some of the college's buildings go back to the nineteenth century. In order to value each building, she tried to find original construction costs and periodic renovations costs, as well as current replacement costs.

"For example, the building I'm

in, Goddard Hall, was built in the early part of this century," says Ms. Doucette. "It's now being depreciated over 40 years, and because it's over eighty years old, I show it as fully depreciated." If it is fully depreciated, does that mean it has a zero value? "On the books it says it does," she says. Of course, that doesn't mean it's worthless. An asset can have a zero value on the books yet have a substantial market value. ◀

# CHAPTER 10

# *P*LANT ASSETS, NATURAL RESOURCES, AND INTANGIBLE ASSETS

## ▶ STUDY OBJECTIVES ◀

### After studying this chapter, you should be able to:

1. *Describe the application of the cost principle to plant assets.*
2. *Explain the concept of depreciation.*
3. *Compute periodic depreciation using different methods.*
4. *Describe the procedure for revising periodic depreciation.*
5. *Distinguish between revenue and capital expenditures and explain the entries for these expenditures.*
6. *Explain how to account for the disposal of a plant asset through retirement, sale, or exchange.*
7. *Identify the basic accounting issues related to natural resources.*
8. *Contrast the accounting for intangible assets with the accounting for plant assets.*
9. *Indicate how plant assets, natural resources, and intangible assets are reported on the balance sheet.*

As you can see, the accounting for campus buildings at Westbrook College is complex. In this chapter, we explain the application of the cost principle of accounting to buildings like those at Westbrook, as well as to natural resources and intangible assets such as Westbrook's school logo. We also describe the methods that may be used to allocate an asset's cost over its useful life. In addition, the accounting for expenditures incurred during the useful life of assets is discussed. The organization and content of this chapter are as follows:

# ► SECTION *1* ► Plant Assets

Plant assets are tangible resources that are used in the operations of the business and are not intended for sale to customers. They are also called **property, plant, and equipment; plant and equipment;** or **fixed assets**. These assets are generally long-lived and are expected to provide services to the company for a number of years. Except for land, plant assets decline in service potential over their useful lives.

Many companies have substantial investments in plant assets. In public utility companies, for example, net plant assets (plant assets less accumulated depreciation) often represent more than 75% of total assets. Recently net plant assets were 79% of Consolidated Edison's total assets and 92% of Pennsylvania Power & Light Company's. In other types of companies the percentages of plant assets to total assets were:

| McDonald's | 86% | Delta Airlines | 82% |
| Marriott Corporation | 63% | General Motors Corporation | 37% |
| Caterpillar | 26% | Wal-Mart | 44% |

**Illustration 10-1**

*Percentages of plant assets to total assets*

In the income statement, the relationship of depreciation expense and maintenance expense to total operating expenses was 10.4% for Consolidated Edison, 9.6% for Delta Airlines, and 6.2% for General Motors.

Plant assets are often subdivided into four classes:

1. **Land**, such as a building site.
2. **Land improvements**, such as driveways, parking lots, fences, and underground sprinkler systems.
3. **Buildings**, such as stores, offices, factories, and warehouses.
4. **Equipment**, such as store check-out counters, cash registers, coolers, office furniture, factory machinery, and delivery equipment.

Like the purchase of a home by an individual, the acquisition of plant assets is an important decision for a business enterprise. It is also important for a business enterprise to (1) keep the asset in good operating condition, (2) replace wornout or outdated facilities, and (3) expand its productive resources as needed. The decline of rail travel in the United States can be traced in part to the failure of railroad companies to meet the first two conditions. Conversely, the growth of air travel in this country can be attributed in part to the general willingness of airline companies to observe these essential conditions.

# Determining the Cost of Plant Assets

Plant assets are recorded at cost in accordance with the **cost principle** of accounting. Thus the buildings at Westbrook College are recorded at cost. Cost consists of all expenditures necessary to acquire the asset and make it ready for its intended use. For example, the purchase price, freight costs paid by the purchaser, and installation costs are all considered part of the cost of factory machinery.

Cost is measured by the cash paid in a cash transaction or by the cash equivalent price paid when noncash assets are used in payment. **The cash equivalent price is equal to the fair market value of the asset given up or the fair market value of the asset received, whichever is more clearly determinable.** Once cost is established, it becomes the basis of accounting for the plant asset over its useful life. Current market or replacement values are not used after acquisition. The application of the cost principle to each of the major classes of plant assets is explained in the following sections.

**STUDY OBJECTIVE**
▼
1

*Describe the application of the cost principle to plant assets.*

## Land

The cost of land includes (1) the cash purchase price, (2) closing costs such as title and attorney's fees, (3) real estate brokers' commissions, and (4) accrued property taxes and other liens on the land assumed by the purchaser. For example, if the cash price is $50,000 and the purchaser agrees to pay accrued taxes of $5,000, the cost of the land is $55,000.

All necessary costs incurred in making land **ready for its intended use** are debited to the Land account. When vacant land is acquired, these costs include

**Helpful hint** Management's intended use is important in applying the cost principle.

▸ **International note**

The United Kingdom (UK) is more flexible regarding asset valuation. Most companies in the UK make occasional revaluations to fair value when they believe this information is more relevant. Other examples of countries that permit revaluations are Switzerland and the Netherlands.

expenditures for clearing, draining, filling, and grading. Sometimes the land has a building on it that must be removed to make the site suitable for construction of a new building. In this case, all demolition and removal costs less any proceeds from salvaged materials are chargeable to the Land account. To illustrate, assume that Hayes Manufacturing Company acquires real estate at a cash cost of $100,000. The property contains an old warehouse that is razed at a net cost of $6,000 ($7,500 in costs less $1,500 proceeds from salvaged materials). Additional expenditures consist of the attorney's fee, $1,000, and the real estate broker's commission, $8,000. Given these factors, the cost of the land is $115,000, computed as follows:

**Illustration 10-2**

*Computation of cost of land*

| Land | |
| --- | --- |
| Cash price of property | $100,000 |
| Net removal cost of warehouse | 6,000 |
| Attorney's fee | 1,000 |
| Real estate broker's commission | 8,000 |
| Cost of land | $115,000 |

In recording the acquisition, Land is debited for $115,000 and Cash is credited for $115,000.

## Land Improvements

The cost of land improvements includes all expenditures necessary to make the improvements ready for their intended use. For example, the cost of a new company parking lot will include the amount paid for paving, fencing, and lighting. These improvements have limited useful lives and their maintenance and replacement are the responsibility of the company. Thus, these costs are debited to Land Improvements and are depreciated over the useful lives of the improvements.

## Buildings

All necessary expenditures relating to the purchase or construction of a building are charged to the Buildings account. When a building is purchased, such costs include the purchase price, closing costs (attorney's fees, title insurance, etc.), and real estate broker's commission. Costs to make the building ready for its intended use consist of expenditures for remodeling rooms and offices and replacing or repairing the roof, floors, electrical wiring, and plumbing.

When a new building is constructed, such as a new science building by Westbrook College, cost consists of the contract price plus payments made by the owner for architects' fees, building permits, and excavation costs. In addition, interest costs incurred to finance the project are included in the cost of the asset when a significant period of time is required to get the asset ready for use. In these circumstances, interest costs are considered as necessary as materials and labor. The inclusion of interest costs in the cost of a constructed building is **limited to the construction period**. When construction has been completed, subsequent interest payments on funds borrowed to finance the construction are debited to Interest Expense.

## Equipment

The cost of equipment consists of the cash purchase price, sales taxes, freight charges, and insurance during transit paid by the purchaser. It also includes expenditures required in assembling, installing, and testing the unit. However, motor vehicle licenses and accident insurance on company trucks and cars are expensed as incurred, because they represent annual recurring expenditures and do not benefit future periods.

To illustrate, assume that the Lenard Company purchases a delivery truck at a cash price of $22,000. Related expenditures consist of sales taxes $1,320, painting and lettering $500, motor vehicle license $80, and a 3-year accident insurance policy $1,600. The cost of the delivery truck is $23,820, computed as follows:

**Illustration 10-3**

*Computation of cost of delivery truck*

| Delivery Truck | |
|---|---|
| Cash price | $22,000 |
| Sales taxes | 1,320 |
| Painting and lettering | 500 |
| Cost of delivery truck | $23,820 |

The motor vehicle license is expensed when incurred and the insurance policy is a prepaid asset. Thus, the summary entry to record the purchase of the truck and related expenditures is:

| | | |
|---|---|---|
| Delivery Truck | 23,820 | |
| License Expense | 80 | |
| Prepaid Insurance | 1,600 | |
|     Cash | | 25,500 |
|     (To record purchase of delivery truck and related expenditures) | | |

For another example, assume the Merten Company purchases factory machinery at a cash price of $50,000. Related expenditures consist of sales taxes $3,000, insurance during shipping $500, and installation and testing $1,000. The cost of the factory machinery is $54,500 computed as follows:

**Illustration 10-4**

*Computation of cost of factory machinery*

| Factory Machinery | |
|---|---|
| Cash price | $50,000 |
| Sales taxes | 3,000 |
| Insurance during shipping | 500 |
| Installation and testing | 1,000 |
| Cost of factory machinery | $54,500 |

The summary entry to record the purchase and related expenditures is:

| | | |
|---|---|---|
| Factory Machinery | 54,500 | |
|     Cash | | 54,500 |
|     (To record purchase of factory machine) | | |

# ▼Depreciation

**STUDY OBJECTIVE**

**▼2**

*Explain the concept of depreciation.*

As explained in Chapter 3, **depreciation is the process of allocating to expense the cost of a plant asset over its useful (service) life in a rational and systematic manner.** Cost allocation is designed to provide for the proper matching of expenses with revenues in accordance with the matching principle.

**Helpful hint**  Once cost is established, then the matching principle applies under GAAP.

**Depreciation is a process of cost allocation, not a process of asset valuation.** Accountants make no attempt to measure the change in an asset's market value during ownership, because plant assets are not held for resale. Thus, the **book value** (cost less accumulated depreciation) of a plant asset may differ significantly from its market value. This is why Goddard Hall, in the opening story, can have zero book value and still have substantial market value.

Depreciation applies to three classes of plant assets: land improvements, buildings, and equipment. Each of these classes is considered to be a **depreciable asset**, because the usefulness to the company and revenue-producing ability of each class will decline over the asset's useful life. Depreciation does not apply to land because its usefulness and revenue-producing ability generally remain intact as long as the asset is owned. In fact, in many cases, the usefulness of land is greater over time because of the scarcity of good land sites. Thus, **land is not a depreciable asset**.

**Helpful hint**  Land does not depreciate because it does not wear out.

During a depreciable asset's useful life its revenue-producing ability will decline because of **wear and tear**. A delivery truck that has been driven 100,000 miles will be less useful to a company than one driven only 800 miles. Similarly, trucks and planes exposed to snow and salt will deteriorate faster than equipment that is not exposed to these elements.

A decline in revenue-producing ability may also occur because of **obsolescence**. Obsolescence is the process of becoming out of date before the asset physically wears out. The rerouting of major airlines from Chicago's Midway Airport to Chicago-O'Hare International Airport because Midway's runways were too short for jumbo jets is an example. Likewise, diesel train engines made coal-burning locomotives obsolete, and municipal buses sent streetcars to the scrap heap.

**Helpful hint**  Remember that depreciation is the process of allocating cost over the useful life of an asset. It is not a measure of value.

**Recognition of depreciation does not result in the accumulation of cash for the replacement of the asset.** The balance in Accumulated Depreciation represents the total cost that has been charged to expense; it is not a cash fund.

### Factors in Computing Depreciation

Three factors affect the computation of depreciation, as shown in Illustration 10-5.

**Illustration 10-5**

*Three factors in computing depreciation*

**Helpful hint**  Recall that depreciation expense is reported on the income statement and accumulated depreciation is reported as a deduction from plant assets.

**Cost:** all expenditures necessary to acquire the asset and make it ready for intended use

**Useful life:** estimate of the expected life based on need for repair, service life, and vulnerability to obsolescence

**Salvage value:** estimate of the asset's value at the end of its useful life

1. **Cost.** Considerations affecting the cost of a depreciable asset have been explained earlier in this chapter. You will recall that plant assets are recorded at cost, in accordance with the cost principle of accounting.

2. **Useful life.** Useful life is an estimate of the expected productive life, also called service life, of the asset. Useful life may be expressed in terms of time, units of activity such as machine hours, or in units of output. Like salvage value, useful life is an estimate. In making the estimate, management should

consider such factors as the intended use of the asset, its expected repair and maintenance policies, and its vulnerability to obsolescence. The company's past experience with similar assets is often helpful in deciding on expected useful life.

3. **Salvage value.** Salvage value is an estimate of the asset's value at the end of its useful life. The value may be based on the asset's worth as scrap or salvage or on its expected trade-in value. Salvage value is an estimate. In making the estimate, management should consider how it plans to dispose of the asset and its experience with similar assets.

## ►Accounting in Action ► *Business Insight*

Not all companies use the same useful life for assets. Compare the useful lives used by the Big Three automakers, for example: At one time General Motors depreciated its machinery over 10 years, compared to Ford's 12 years and Chrysler's 11 years. GM also depreciated its buildings over 28 years while Ford used 30 years and Chrysler used 26 years. General Motors also depreciated its dies and equipment used to manufacture car bodies about twice as fast as Ford and three times as fast as Chrysler. Now GM has changed and aligned itself with its principal competitors by applying more liberal depreciation policies that have increased annual income. Should companies in the same industry be required to use the same useful life for the same type of assets?

## Before You Go On . . .

### ► Review It

1. What are plant assets? What are the major classes of plant assets? How is the cost principle applied to accounting for plant assets?
2. What is the relationship, if any, of depreciation to (a) cost allocation, (b) asset valuation, and (c) cash accumulation?
3. Explain the factors that affect the computation of depreciation.

### ► Do It

Assume that a delivery truck is purchased for $15,000 cash, plus sales taxes of $900 and delivery costs to the dealer of $500. The buyer also pays $200 for painting and lettering, $600 for an annual insurance policy, and $80 for a motor vehicle license. Explain how each of these costs would be accounted for.

*Reasoning:* The cost principle applies to all expenditures made in order to get delivery equipment ready for its intended use. The principle does not apply to operating costs incurred during the useful life of the equipment, such as gas and oil, motor tune-ups, and insurance.

*Solution:* The first four payments ($15,000, $900, $500, and $200) are considered to be expenditures necessary to make the truck ready for its intended use. Thus, the cost of the truck is $16,600. The payments for insurance and the license are considered to be operating expenses incurred during the useful life of the asset.

*Related exercise material:* BE10–1, BE10–2, E10–1, E10–2, and E10–3.

## Depreciation Methods

Depreciation is generally computed using one of the following methods:

1. Straight-line
2. Units-of-activity
3. Declining-balance

**STUDY OBJECTIVE**

··········▼**3**··········

*Compute periodic depreciation using different methods.*

**Illustration 10-6**

*Use of depreciation methods in major U.S. companies*

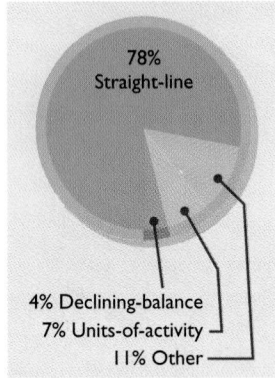

78% Straight-line

4% Declining-balance
7% Units-of-activity
11% Other

Like the inventory methods discussed in Chapter 9, each method is acceptable under generally accepted accounting principles. Management selects the method or methods it believes to be appropriate in the circumstances. The objective is to select the method that best measures the asset's contribution to revenue over its useful life. Once a method is chosen, it should be applied consistently over the useful life of the asset. Consistency enhances the comparability of financial statements.

Depreciation affects the balance sheet through accumulated depreciation and the income statement through depreciation expense. Illustration 10-6 shows the use of the different depreciation methods in 600 of the largest companies in the United States.

To facilitate the comparison of the three depreciation methods, we will base all computations on the following data applicable to a small delivery truck purchased by Barb's Florists on January 1, 1996:

**Illustration 10-7**

*Delivery truck data*

**Helpful hint**  The adjusting entry for depreciation is a debit to Depreciation Expense and a credit to Accumulated Depreciation.

| | |
|---|---|
| Cost | $13,000 |
| Expected salvage value | $ 1,000 |
| Estimated useful life in years | 5 |
| Estimated useful life in miles | 100,000 |

### Straight-Line

Under the straight-line method, depreciation is the same for each year of the asset's useful life. It is measured solely by the passage of time. In order to compute depreciation expense, it is necessary to determine depreciable cost. Depreciable cost is the cost of the asset less its salvage value. It is the total amount subject to depreciation. Depreciable cost is then divided by the asset's useful life to determine depreciation expense. The formula and computation of depreciation expense in the first year for Barb's Florists are shown in Illustration 10-8.

**Illustration 10-8**

*Formula for straight-line method*

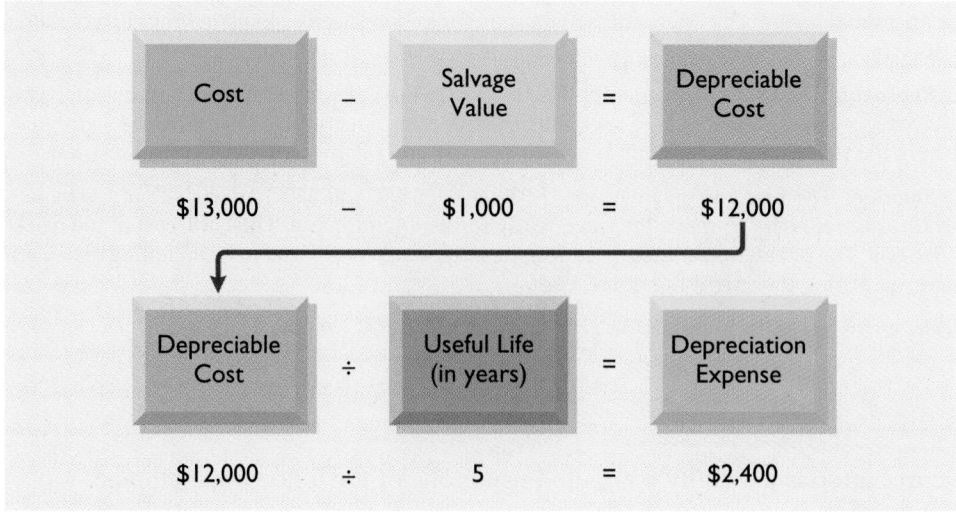

| Cost | − | Salvage Value | = | Depreciable Cost |
|---|---|---|---|---|
| $13,000 | − | $1,000 | = | $12,000 |

| Depreciable Cost | ÷ | Useful Life (in years) | = | Depreciation Expense |
|---|---|---|---|---|
| $12,000 | ÷ | 5 | = | $2,400 |

Alternatively, we also can compute an annual rate at which the delivery truck is being depreciated. In this case, the rate is 20% (100% ÷ 5 years). When an annual rate is used under the straight-line method, the percentage rate is applied to the depreciable cost of the asset, as shown in the following **depreciation schedule**:

**Illustration 10-9**

*Straight-line depreciation schedule*

| | Computation | | | | End of Year | |
|---|---|---|---|---|---|---|
| **BARB'S FLORISTS** | | | | | | |
| Year | Depreciable Cost | × Depreciation Rate | = | Annual Depreciation Expense | Accumulated Depreciation | Book Value |
| 1996 | $12,000 | 20% | | $2,400 | $ 2,400 | $10,600* |
| 1997 | 12,000 | 20 | | 2,400 | 4,800 | 8,200 |
| 1998 | 12,000 | 20 | | 2,400 | 7,200 | 5,800 |
| 1999 | 12,000 | 20 | | 2,400 | 9,600 | 3,400 |
| 2000 | 12,000 | 20 | | 2,400 | 12,000 | 1,000 |

*($13,000 − $2,400).

Note that the depreciation expense of $2,400 is the same each year, and that the book value at the end of the useful life is equal to the estimated $1,000 salvage value.

What happens when an asset is purchased **during** the year, rather than on January 1, as in our example? In that case, it is necessary to **prorate the annual depreciation** for the proportion of time used. If Barb's Florists had purchased the delivery truck on April 1, 1996, the depreciation for 1996 would be $1,800 ($12,000 × 20% × 9/12 of a year).

The straight-line method predominates in practice, as shown in Illustration 10-6. For example, such large companies as Campbell Soup, Marriott Corporation, and General Mills use the straight-line method. It is simple to apply, and it matches expenses with revenues appropriately when the use of the asset is reasonably uniform throughout the service life. In the opening story, Westbrook College is probably using the straight-line method of depreciation for its buildings.

### Units-of-Activity

Under the units-of-activity method, instead of expressing the life as a time period, useful life is expressed in terms of the total units of production or use expected from the asset. The units-of-activity method is ideally suited to factory machinery: production can be measured in terms of units of output or in terms of machine hours used in operating the machinery. It is also possible to use this method for such items as delivery equipment (miles driven) and airplanes (hours in use). The units-of-activity method is generally not suitable for such assets as buildings or furniture, because depreciation for these assets is more a function of time than of use.

To use this method, the total units of activity for the entire useful life are estimated, the amount is divided into depreciable cost to determine the depreciation cost per unit. The depreciation cost per unit is then applied to the units of activity during the year to determine the annual depreciation. To illustrate, assume that the delivery truck of Barb's Florists is driven 15,000 miles in the first year. The formula and computation of depreciation expense in the first year are:

**Helpful hint** Depreciation stops when the asset's book value equals expected salvage value.

**Illustration 10-10**

*Formula for units-of-activity method*

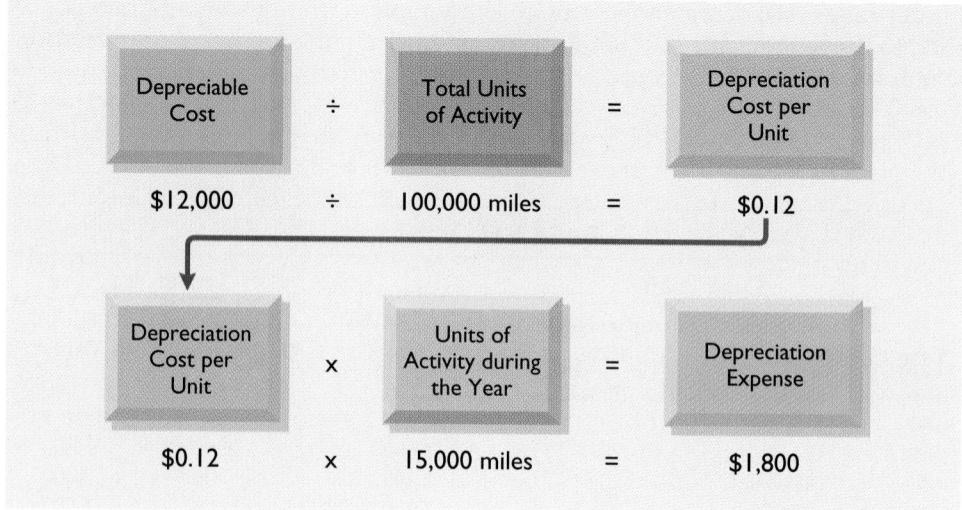

The depreciation schedule, using assumed mileage data, is as follows:

**Illustration 10-11**

*Units-of-activity depreciation schedule*

| | Computation | | | Annual | End of Year | |
|---|---|---|---|---|---|---|
| Year | Units of Activity | × | Depreciation Cost/Unit = | Depreciation Expense | Accumulated Depreciation | Book Value |
| 1996 | 15,000 | | $.12 | **$1,800** | $ 1,800 | $11,200* |
| 1997 | 30,000 | | .12 | **3,600** | 5,400 | 7,600 |
| 1998 | 20,000 | | .12 | **2,400** | 7,800 | 5,200 |
| 1999 | 25,000 | | .12 | **3,000** | 10,800 | 2,200 |
| 2000 | 10,000 | | .12 | **1,200** | 12,000 | **1,000** |

**BARB'S FLORISTS**

*($13,000 − $1,800).

The units-of-activity method is not nearly as popular as the straight-line method (see, for example, Illustration 10-6), primarily because it is often difficult to make a reasonable estimate of total activity. However, this method is used by some very large companies, such as Standard Oil Company of California and Boise Cascade Corporation. When the productivity of the asset varies significantly from one period to another, the units-of-activity method results in the best matching of expenses with revenues. This method is easy to apply when assets are purchased during the year. In such a case, the productivity of the asset for the partial year is used in computing the depreciation.

### Declining-Balance

The declining-balance method produces a decreasing annual depreciation expense over the useful life of the asset. The method is so named because the computation of periodic depreciation is based on a **declining book value** (cost less accumulated depreciation) of the asset. Annual depreciation expense is computed by multiplying the book value at the beginning of the year by the declining-balance depreciation rate. **The depreciation rate remains constant from year to year, but the book value to which the rate is applied declines each year.**

Book value for the first year is the cost of the asset, because the balance in accumulated depreciation at the beginning of the asset's useful life is zero. In subsequent years, book value is the difference between cost and accumulated depreciation at the beginning of the year. **Unlike the other depreciation methods, salvage value is ignored in determining the amount to which the declining balance rate is applied.** Salvage value, however, does limit the total depreciation that can be taken. Depreciation stops when the asset's book value equals expected salvage value.

A common declining-balance rate is double the straight-line rate. As a result, the method is often referred to as the **double-declining-balance method**. If Barb's Florists uses the double-declining-balance method, the depreciation rate is 40% (2 × the straight-line rate of 20%). The formula and computation of depreciation for the first year on the delivery truck are:

**Illustration 10-12**

*Formula for declining-balance method*

The depreciation schedule under this method is as follows:

**BARB'S FLORISTS**

| Year | Computation Book Value Beginning of Year | × | Depreciation Rate | = | Annual Depreciation Expense | End of Year Accumulated Depreciation | Book Value |
|------|------|---|------|---|------|------|------|
| 1996 | $13,000 | | 40% | | **$5,200** | $ 5,200 | $7,800 |
| 1997 | 7,800 | | 40 | | **3,120** | 8,320 | 4,680 |
| 1998 | 4,680 | | 40 | | **1,872** | 10,192 | 2,808 |
| 1999 | 2,808 | | 40 | | **1,123** | 11,315 | 1,685 |
| 2000 | 1,685 | | 40 | | 685* | 12,000 | **1,000** |

*Computation of $674 ($1,685 × 40%) is adjusted to $685 in order for book value to equal salvage value.

**Illustration 10-13**

*Double-declining-balance depreciation schedule*

**Helpful hint**  Book value is variable and the depreciation rate is constant for this method.

You can see that the delivery equipment is 69% depreciated ($8,320 ÷ $12,000) at the end of the second year. Under the straight-line method it would be depreciated 40% ($4,800 ÷ $12,000) at that time. Because the declining-balance method produces higher depreciation expense in the early years than in the later years, it is considered an accelerated-depreciation method. The declining-balance method is compatible with the matching principle. The higher depreciation expense in early years is matched with the higher benefits received in these years. Conversely, lower depreciation expense is recognized in later years when the asset's contribution to revenue is less. Also, some assets lose usefulness rapidly because of obsolescence. In these cases, the declining-balance method provides a more appropriate depreciation amount.

When an asset is purchased during the year, it is necessary to prorate the declining-balance depreciation in the first year on a time basis. For example, if Barb's Florists had purchased the delivery equipment on April 1, 1996, depre-

**Helpful hint**  The method to be used for an asset that is expected to be more productive in the first half of its useful life is the declining-balance method.

ciation for 1996 would become $3,900 ($13,000 × 40% × 9/12). The book value for computing depreciation in 1997 then becomes $9,100 ($13,000 − $3,900), and the 1997 depreciation is $3,640 ($9,100 × 40%).

## ▸Accounting in Action ▸ *Business Insight*

Why does Gingiss Formal Wear have 70 depreciation accounts and use the units-of-activity method for its tuxedos? The reason is that Gingiss wants to track wear and tear on each of its 16,000 dinner jackets individually. So each tuxedo has a bar code, like a box of cereal at the supermarket. When a tux is rented, a clerk runs its code across an electronic scanner. At year-end, the computer adds up the total rentals for each of 15 styles, then divides by expected total use to compute the rate. For instance, on one dolphin-gray tux, Gingiss expects a life of 30 rentals. In a recent year the tux was rented 13 times. So depreciation that period was 43% (13 ÷ 30) of the total cost.

### Comparison of Methods

A comparison of annual and total depreciation expense under each of the three methods is shown for Barb's Florists in Illustration 10-14.

**Illustration 10-14**

*Comparison of depreciation methods*

| Year | Straight-Line | Units-of-Activity | Declining-Balance |
|------|--------------|-------------------|-------------------|
| 1996 | $ 2,400 | $ 1,800 | $ 5,200 |
| 1997 | 2,400 | 3,600 | 3,120 |
| 1998 | 2,400 | 2,400 | 1,872 |
| 1999 | 2,400 | 3,000 | 1,123 |
| 2000 | 2,400 | 1,200 | 685 |
| | **$12,000** | **$12,000** | **$12,000** |

Observe that periodic depreciation varies considerably among the methods, but total depreciation is the same for the 5-year period. Each method is acceptable in accounting, because each recognizes the decline in service potential of the asset in a rational and systematic manner. The depreciation expense pattern under each method is presented graphically in Illustration 10-15.

## Depreciation and Income Taxes

**Helpful hint** Depreciation per GAAP usually will be different from depreciation per IRS rules.

The Internal Revenue Service (IRS) allows corporate taxpayers to deduct depreciation expense when computing taxable income. However, the tax regulations of the IRS do not require the taxpayer to use the same depreciation method on the tax return that is used in preparing financial statements. Consequently, many large corporations use straight-line depreciation in their financial statements to

## ▸*Technology in Action*

Software packages to account for plant assets exist for both large and small computer systems. Though varying in complexity, even the least sophisticated packages can maintain a control and subsidiary ledger for plant assets and make the necessary depreciation computations and adjusting entries. Many packages also maintain separate depreciation schedules for both financial statement and income tax purposes, with reconciliations made for any differences. Even spreadsheet packages contain embedded formulas or functions for calculating depreciation using a variety of methods.

**Illustration 10-15**

*Patterns of depreciation*

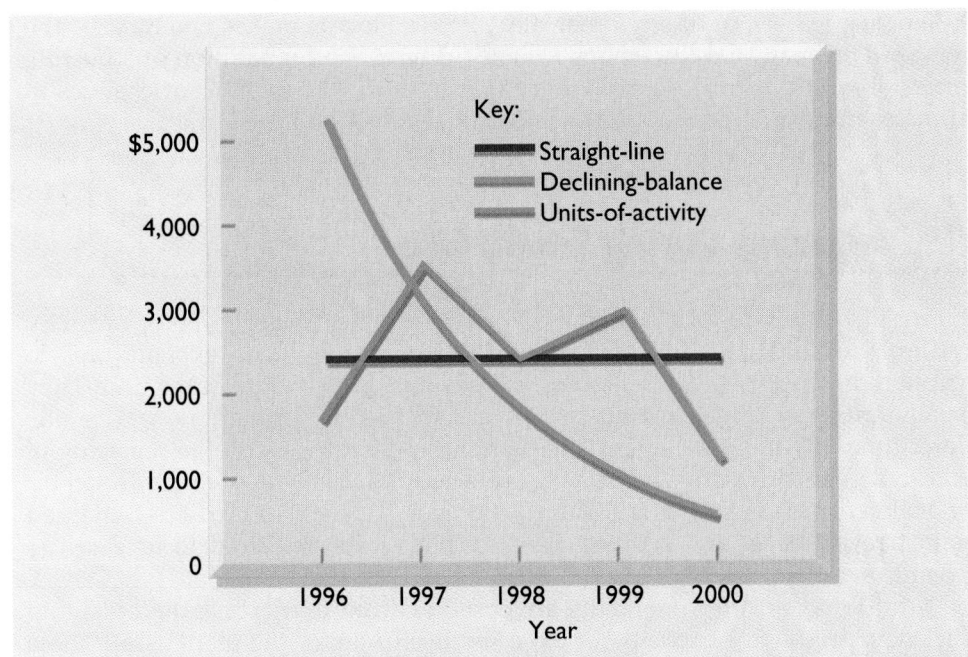

maximize net income, and at the same time, a special accelerated-depreciation method is generally used on their tax returns to minimize their income taxes. For tax purposes, taxpayers must use on their tax returns either the straight-line method or a special accelerated-depreciation method called **Modified Accelerated Cost Recovery System** (MACRS).

► **International note**

In Germany, tax laws have a strong influence on financial accounting. Depreciation expense determined by the tax code must also be used for preparing financial statements.

## Revising Periodic Depreciation

Depreciation is one example of the estimation procedures that are part of the accounting process. Annual depreciation expense should be reviewed periodically by management. If wear and tear or obsolescence indicate that annual depreciation is inadequate or excessive, a change in the amount should be made.

When a change in an estimate is required, the change is made in **current and future years but not to prior periods**. Thus, when a change is made, (1) there is no correction of previously recorded depreciation expense, and (2) depreciation expense for current and future years is revised. The rationale for this treatment is that continual restatement of prior periods would adversely affect the reader's confidence in financial statements.

To determine the new annual depreciation expense, we compute the asset's depreciable cost at the time of the revision and divide it by remaining useful life. To illustrate, assume that Barb's Florists decides on January 1, 1999, to extend the useful life of the truck one year because of its excellent condition. The company has used the straight-line method to depreciate the asset to date, and book value is $5,800 ($13,000 − $7,200). The new annual depreciation is $1,600, computed as follows:

**STUDY OBJECTIVE**
▼ **4**

*Describe the procedure for revising periodic depreciation.*

**Helpful hint** Use a step-by-step approach: (1) determine new depreciable cost; (2) divide by remaining useful life.

**Illustration 10-16**

*Revised depreciation computation*

| | | |
|---|---|---|
| Book value, 1/1/99 | $5,800 | |
| Less: Salvage value | 1,000 | |
| Depreciable cost | $4,800 | |
| Remaining useful life | 3 years | (1999–2001) |
| **Revised annual depreciation ($4,800 ÷ 3)** | **$1,600** | |

On January 1, 1999, or at any other time, Barb's Florists makes no entry for the change in estimate. On December 31, 1999, during the preparation of adjusting entries, it would record depreciation expense of $1,600. Significant changes in estimates must be described in the financial statements.

## Expenditures during Useful Life

**STUDY OBJECTIVE**

**5**

*Distinguish between revenue and capital expenditures and explain the entries for these expenditures.*

**Helpful hint** These expenditures occur after all costs have been incurred to make the asset ready for its intended use when it was acquired.

During the useful life of a plant asset a company may incur costs for ordinary repairs, additions, and improvements. Ordinary repairs are expenditures to maintain the operating efficiency and expected productive life of the unit. They usually are fairly small amounts that occur frequently throughout service life. Motor tune-ups and oil changes, the painting of buildings, and the replacing of worn-out gears on factory machinery are examples. They are debited to Repair (or Maintenance) Expense as incurred. Because they are immediately charged against revenues as an expense, these costs are often referred to as revenue expenditures.

Additions and improvements are costs incurred to increase the operating efficiency, productive capacity, or expected useful life of the plant asset. These expenditures are usually material in amount and occur infrequently during the period of ownership. Expenditures for additions and improvements increase the company's investment in productive facilities and are generally debited to the plant asset affected. Accordingly, they are often referred to as capital expenditures. Most major U.S. corporations disclose the amount of their annual capital expenditures. In a recent year, both IBM and General Motors reported capital expenditures slightly in excess of $6 billion. The accounting for capital expenditures varies depending on the nature of the expenditure.

## ▶ Accounting in Action ▸ *Business Insight*

Northwest Airlines is spending $120 million to spruce up forty DC9–30 jets. The improvements are designed to extend the lives of the planes, meet stricter government noise limits, and save money. The capital expenditure will extend the life of the jets by 10 to 15 years and save about $560 million over the cost of buying new planes. The DC9 jets now have an average age of 24 years.

*Source: Ann Arbor News, August 9, 1994.*

## Plant Asset Disposals

**STUDY OBJECTIVE**

**6**

*Explain how to account for the disposal of a plant asset through retirement, sale, or exchange.*

Plant assets of various types may be disposed of in three ways, as shown in Illustration 10-17. Whatever the method of disposal, at the time of disposal it is necessary to determine the book value of the plant asset. The book value is the difference between the cost of the plant asset and the accumulated depreciation to date. If the disposal occurs at any time during the year, depreciation for the fraction of the year to the date of disposal must be recorded. The book value is then eliminated by debiting Accumulated Depreciation for the total depreciation to the date of disposal and crediting the asset account for the cost of the asset.

In this section we will examine the accounting for each of the three methods of plant asset disposal.

**Retirement**
Equipment is scrapped or discarded.

**Sale**
Equipment is sold to another party.

**Exchange**
Existing equipment is traded for new equipment.

**Illustration 10-17**

*Methods of plant asset disposal*

## Retirement of Plant Assets

To illustrate the accounting for a retirement of plant assets, assume that Hobart Enterprises retires its computer printers, which cost $32,000. The accumulated depreciation on these printers is also $32,000; the equipment, therefore, is fully depreciated (zero book value). The entry to record this retirement is as follows:

| | | |
|---|---|---|
| Accumulated Depreciation—Printing Equipment | 32,000 | |
|     Printing Equipment | | 32,000 |
|       (To record retirement of fully depreciated equipment) | | |

What happens if a fully depreciated plant asset is still useful to the company? In this case, the plant asset and the related accumulated depreciation continue to be reported on the balance sheet without further depreciation or adjustment until the asset is retired. Reporting the asset and related accumulated depreciation on the balance sheet informs the reader of the financial statements that the asset is still being used by the company. However, once an asset is fully depreciated, even if it is still being used, no additional depreciation should be taken. In no situation can the accumulated depreciation on the plant asset exceed its cost.

If a plant asset is retired before it is fully depreciated, and no scrap or salvage value is received, a loss on disposal occurs. For example, assume that Sunset Company discards delivery equipment that cost $18,000 and has accumulated depreciation of $14,000 at the date of retirement. The entry is as follows:

**Helpful hint** When a plant asset is disposed of, all amounts related to the asset must be removed from the accounts. This includes the original cost in the asset account and the total depreciation to date in the accumulated depreciation account.

| | | |
|---|---|---|
| Accumulated Depreciation—Delivery Equipment | 14,000 | |
| Loss on Disposal | 4,000 | |
|     Delivery Equipment | | 18,000 |
|       (To record retirement of delivery equipment at a loss) | | |

The loss on disposal is reported in the Other Expenses and Losses section of the income statement.

## Sale of Plant Assets

In a disposal by sale, the book value of the asset is compared with the proceeds received from the sale. If the proceeds of the sale exceed the book value of the plant asset, a **gain on disposal** occurs. If the proceeds of the sale are less than the book value of the plant asset sold, a **loss on disposal** occurs.

Only by coincidence will the book value and the fair market value of the asset be the same at the time the asset is sold. Gains and losses on sales of plant assets are, therefore, quite common. As an example, Delta Airlines, Inc. reported a $94,343,000 gain on the sale of five Boeing B-727-200 aircraft and five Lockheed L-1011-1 aircraft.

### Gain on Disposal

To illustrate a gain, assume that on July 1, 1996, Wright Company sells office furniture for $16,000 cash. The office furniture originally cost $60,000 and as of January 1, 1996, had accumulated depreciation of $41,000. Depreciation for the first 6 months of 1996 is $8,000. The entry to record depreciation expense and update accumulated depreciation to July 1 is as follows:

| July 1 | Depreciation Expense | 8,000 | |
| | Accumulated Depreciation—Office Furniture | | 8,000 |
| | (To record depreciation expense for the first six months of 1996) | | |

After the accumulated depreciation balance is updated, a gain on disposal of $5,000 is computed:

**Illustration 10-18**

*Computation of gain on disposal*

| Cost of office furniture | $60,000 |
| Less: Accumulated depreciation ($41,000 + $8,000) | 49,000 |
| Book value at date of disposal | 11,000 |
| Proceeds from sale | 16,000 |
| **Gain on disposal** | **$ 5,000** |

The entry to record the sale and the gain on disposal is as follows:

| July 1 | Cash | 16,000 | |
| | Accumulated Depreciation—Office Furniture | 49,000 | |
| | Office Furniture | | 60,000 |
| | Gain on Disposal | | 5,000 |
| | (To record sale of office furniture at a gain) | | |

The gain on disposal is reported in the Other Revenues and Gains section of the income statement.

### Loss on Disposal

Assume that instead of selling the office furniture for $16,000, Wright sells it for $9,000. In this case, a loss of $2,000 is computed:

**Illustration 10-19**

*Computation of loss on disposal*

| Cost of office furniture | $60,000 |
| Less: Accumulated depreciation | 49,000 |
| Book value at date of disposal | 11,000 |
| Proceeds from sale | 9,000 |
| **Loss on disposal** | **$ 2,000** |

The entry to record the sale and the loss on disposal is as follows:

| July 1 | Cash | 9,000 | |
| | Accumulated Depreciation—Office Furniture | 49,000 | |
| | Loss on Disposal | 2,000 | |
| | Office Furniture | | 60,000 |
| | (To record sale of office furniture at a loss) | | |

The loss on disposal is reported in the Other Expenses and Losses section of the income statement.

## Exchanges of Plant Assets

Plant assets may also be disposed of through exchange. Exchanges can be for either similar or dissimilar assets. Because exchanges of similar assets are more common, they are discussed here.

An exchange of similar assets involves assets of the same type. This occurs, for example, when old delivery equipment is exchanged for new delivery equipment or when old office furniture is exchanged for new office furniture. In an exchange of similar assets, the new asset performs the **same function** as the old asset.

In exchanges of similar plant assets, it is necessary to determine (1) the cost of the asset acquired and (2) the gain or loss on the asset given up. Because a noncash asset is given up in the exchange, cost is equal to the **cash equivalent price** paid. Cost, therefore, is the fair market value of the asset given up plus the cash paid. The gain or loss on disposal is the **difference between the fair market value and the book value of the asset given up**. These determinations and the resulting accounting entries are explained and illustrated below.

### *Loss Treatment*

When a loss occurs on the exchange of similar assets, it is recognized immediately. To illustrate the accounting for a loss, assume that Roland Company exchanged old office equipment for similar new office equipment. The book value of the old office equipment is $26,000 (cost $70,000 less accumulated depreciation $44,000), its fair market value is $10,000, and cash of $81,000 is paid. The cost of the new office equipment, $91,000, is computed as follows:

**Helpful hint** As indicated earlier, immediate recognition of the loss also occurs in disposals by retirement and sale.

| | |
|---|---:|
| Fair market value of old office equipment | $10,000 |
| Cash | 81,000 |
| **Cost of new office equipment** | **$91,000** |

**Illustration 10-20**

*Computation of cost of new office equipment*

Through this exchange, a loss on disposal of $16,000 is incurred. A loss results when the book value is greater than the fair market value of the asset given up. The computation is as follows:

| | |
|---|---:|
| Book value of old office equipment ($70,000 − $44,000) | $26,000 |
| Fair market value of old office equipment | 10,000 |
| **Loss on disposal** | **$16,000** |

**Illustration 10-21**

*Computation of loss on disposal*

In recording an exchange at a loss it is necessary to (1) eliminate the book value of the asset given up, (2) record the cost of the asset acquired, and (3) recognize the loss on disposal. The entry for the Roland Company is as follows:

| | | |
|---|---:|---:|
| Office Equipment (new) | 91,000 | |
| Accumulated Depreciation—Office Equipment (old) | 44,000 | |
| Loss on Disposal | 16,000 | |
|    Office Equipment (old) | | 70,000 |
|    Cash | | 81,000 |
|     (To record exchange of old office equipment for similar new equipment) | | |

### *Gain Treatment*

When a gain occurs on the exchange of similar assets, it is not recognized immediately. Instead, the gain is deferred by reducing the cost basis of the new asset. Thus, in determining the cost of the asset acquired, it is necessary to compute the **cost before deferral of the gain** and then the **cost after deferral of the gain**.

To illustrate the accounting for similar assets, assume that Mark's Express Delivery decides to exchange its old delivery equipment plus cash of $3,000 for new delivery equipment. At this time, the book value of the old delivery equipment is $12,000 (cost $40,000 less accumulated depreciation $28,000). In addition, it is determined that the fair market value of the old delivery equipment is $19,000.

The cost of the new asset received (before deferral of the gain) is equal to the **fair market value of the old asset exchanged plus any cash or other consideration given up**. The cost of the new delivery equipment (before deferral of the gain) is $22,000, computed as follows:

**Illustration 10-22**

*Cost of new equipment (before deferral of gain)*

| | |
|---|---:|
| Fair market value of old delivery equipment | $19,000 |
| Cash | 3,000 |
| Cost of new delivery equipment (before deferral of gain) | $22,000 |

A gain results when the fair market value is greater than the book value of the asset given up. For Mark's Express, there is a gain of $7,000, computed as follows, on the disposal:

**Illustration 10-23**

*Computation of gain on disposal*

| | |
|---|---:|
| Fair market value of old delivery equipment | $19,000 |
| Book value of old delivery equipment ($40,000 − $28,000) | 12,000 |
| Gain on disposal | $ 7,000 |

The $7,000 gain on disposal is then offset against the $22,000 cost of the new delivery equipment. The result is a $15,000 cost of the new delivery equipment, after deferral of the gain, as shown in Illustration 10-24.

**Illustration 10-24**

*Cost of new delivery equipment (after deferral of gain)*

| | |
|---|---:|
| Cost of new delivery equipment (before deferral of gain) | $22,000 |
| Less: Gain on disposal | 7,000 |
| Cost of new delivery equipment (after deferral of gain) | $15,000 |

The entry to record the exchange is as follows:

| | | |
|---|---:|---:|
| Delivery Equipment (new) | 15,000 | |
| Accumulated Depreciation—Delivery Equipment (old) | 28,000 | |
|     Delivery Equipment (old) | | 40,000 |
|     Cash | | 3,000 |
|       (To record exchange of old delivery equipment for | | |
|       similar new delivery equipment) | | |

This entry does not eliminate the gain; it just postpones or defers it to future periods. The deferred gain of $7,000 reduces the $22,000 cost to $15,000. As a result, net income in future periods increases because depreciation expense on the newly acquired delivery equipment is less by $7,000.

Summarizing, the rules for accounting for exchanges of similar assets are as follows:

| Type of Event | Recognition |
|---|---|
| Loss | Recognize immediately by debiting Loss on Disposal |
| Gain | Defer and reduce cost of new asset |

**Illustration 10-25**

*Accounting rules for plant exchanges*

# Before You Go On . . .

## ► Review It

1. What are the formulas for computing annual depreciation under each of the depreciation methods?
2. How do the methods differ in terms of their effects on annual depreciation over the useful life of the asset?
3. Are revisions of periodic depreciation made to prior periods? Explain.
4. How does a capital expenditure differ from a revenue expenditure?
5. What is the proper accounting for the retirement and sale of plant assets?
6. What is the proper accounting for the exchange of similar plant assets?

## ► Do It

Overland Trucking has an old truck that cost $30,000, has accumulated depreciation of $16,000, and a fair value of $17,000. It has a choice of either selling the truck for cash of $17,000 or exchanging the old truck and $3,000 cash for a new truck. What is the entry that Overland Trucking would record under each option?

**Reasoning:** Gains and losses on the sale or exchange of plant assets are determined by the difference between the book value and the fair value of the company's asset. Gains on the exchange of similar assets are deferred.

**Solution:**
Sale of truck for cash:

| | | |
|---|---|---|
| Cash | 17,000 | |
| Accumulated Depreciation—Truck (old) | 16,000 | |
|   Truck (old) | | 30,000 |
|   Gain on Disposal [$17,000 − ($30,000 − $16,000)] | | 3,000 |
|     (To record sale of truck at a gain) | | |

Exchange of old truck and cash for new truck:

| | | |
|---|---|---|
| Truck (new)* | 17,000 | |
| Accumulated Depreciation—Truck (old) | 16,000 | |
|   Truck (old) | | 30,000 |
|   Cash | | 3,000 |
|     (To record exchange of old truck for similar new truck) | | |

*($20,000 − $3,000)

If the old truck is exchanged for the new truck, the $3,000 gain is deferred, and the recorded cost of the new truck is reduced by $3,000.

*Related exercise material:* BE10–8, BE10–9, BE10–10, BE10–11, E10–10, E10–11, E10–12, E10–13, and E10–14.

# ▼Section 2 ▸ *Natural Resources*

**Helpful hint**  On a balance sheet, natural resources may be described as Timberlands, Mineral Deposits, Oil Reserves, and so on.

Natural resources consist of standing timber and underground deposits of oil, gas, and minerals. Such resources include the much-publicized offshore oil deposits of major petroleum companies and the oil deposits for which the Alaskan pipeline was built. These long-lived productive assets have two distinguishing characteristics: (1) they are physically extracted in operations (such as mining, cutting, or pumping), and (2) they are replaceable only by an act of nature. Because of these characteristics, natural resources are frequently called **wasting assets.**

## ▲Acquisition Cost

**STUDY OBJECTIVE**
••••••••••7••••••••••

*Identify the basic accounting issues related to natural resources.*

The acquisition cost of a natural resource is the cash or cash equivalent price necessary to acquire the resource and prepare it for its intended use. For an already discovered resource, such as an existing coal mine, cost is the price paid for the property.

Determining acquisition cost becomes a problem when exploration is involved. For example, some argue that the costs of unsuccessful exploration as well as successful exploration should be capitalized. They believe that, using an oil well as an example, the cost of drilling the dry holes is a cost that is needed to find the commercially profitable wells. As a result, both successful and unsuccessful explorations are capitalized, and the costs are written off to expense over the useful life of the successful wells. This method is often referred to as the full cost approach.

Others disagree, arguing that the costs of only successful projects should be capitalized and unsuccessful projects should be expensed. They maintain that if only one of ten exploratory wells becomes commercially viable, it is inappropriate to assign the costs of the nine unsuccessful wells to the cost of the successful well. This method is referred to as the successful efforts approach. At present, both approaches are used in accounting for natural resources. For example, such companies as American Petrofina, DuPont, Callahan Mining, and Copperweld use full costing, whereas Texaco, Mobil, and Gulf use successful efforts.

## ▲Accounting in Action ▸ *Business Insight*

Should both full cost and successful efforts be permitted in accounting? Views are particularly strong on this subject. As one financial expert, commenting on the full-cost method, noted: "It lets them call a dry hole an asset, and as far as I am concerned, any company that uses full-cost accounting is guilty until proven innocent." On the other hand, companies using the full-cost method argue that "it enables us to undertake risky exploration projects without having sharp swings in reported earnings." Or as one writer noted: "Forcing companies to use successful efforts accounting would retard domestic oil and gas exploration and imperil national security." The debate raises an interesting question—should accounting be concerned with national security, or should it "tell it like it is"?

# Depletion

The process of allocating the cost of natural resources to expense in a rational and systematic manner over the resource's useful life is called depletion. **The units-of-activity method is generally used to compute depletion, because periodic depletion generally is a function of the units extracted during the year.** Under this method, the total cost of the natural resource minus salvage value, if any, is divided by the number of units estimated to be in the resource. The result is a depletion cost per unit of product. The depletion cost per unit is then multiplied by the number of units extracted and sold, to compute the depletion expense. The formula is as follows:

**Illustration 10-26**

*Formula to compute depletion expense*

**Helpful hint** The computation for depletion is similar to the computation for depreciation using the units-of-activity method of depreciation.

To illustrate, assume that the Lane Coal Company invests $5 million in a mine estimated to have 10 million tons of coal and no salvage value. In the first year, 800,000 tons of coal are extracted and sold. Using the formulas above, the computations are as follows:

$$\$5,000,000 \div 10,000,000 = \$.50 \text{ depletion cost per ton}$$

$$\$.50 \times 800,000 = \$400,000 \text{ depletion expense}$$

The entry to record depletion expense for the first year of operation is as follows:

| | | | |
|---|---|---|---|
| Dec. 31 | Depletion Expense | 400,000 | |
| |     Accumulated Depletion | | 400,000 |
| |     (To record depletion expense on coal | | |
| |     deposits) | | |

The account Depletion Expense is reported as a part of the cost of producing the product. Accumulated Depletion, a contra asset account similar to accumulated depreciation, is deducted from the cost of the natural resource in the balance sheet as follows:

**Helpful hint** Natural resources are generally reported as part of Property, Plant, and Equipment on the balance sheet.

**Illustration 10-27**

*Statement presentation of accumulated depletion*

| | | |
|---|---|---|
| Coal mine | $5,000,000 | |
| **Less: Accumulated depletion** | **400,000** | $4,600,000 |

However, in many companies an Accumulated Depletion account is not used, and the amount of depletion is credited directly to the natural resource account.

Sometimes, natural resources extracted in one accounting period will not be sold until a later period. In this case, depletion is not expensed until the resource is sold. The amount not sold is reported in the Current Asset section as inventory.

## ▶*Technology in Action*

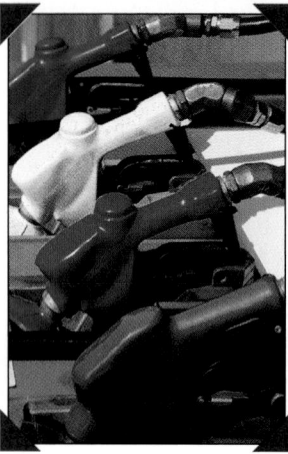

Firms in the oil and gas industry maintain extensive computerized data bases on their natural resources. Depletion amounts (in both monetary and physical units) are constantly monitored by these systems. Revisions in cost projections are automatically updated as new deposits are located or as estimates on existing deposits are changed. We all see the end result of this accounting at the gas pump.

## *Before You Go On . . .*

### ▶ *Review It*

1. What is the difference between the full-cost and successful efforts methods in accounting for natural resources?
2. How is depletion expense computed?

### ▶ *Do It*

Explain the method used in computing depletion and show the computation, assuming Hard Rock Mining Corporation invests $12 million in a mine estimated to have 10 million tons of ore and a $2 million salvage value. In the first year 40,000 tons of ore are mined and sold.

**Reasoning:** There are many similarities between depreciation and depletion. In computing depletion expense, the units-of-activity method is generally used.

**Solution:** Under the units-of-activity method, a depletion cost per unit is determined by dividing total cost minus salvage value by the total estimated units. The computation is as follows:

$$(\$12,000,000 - \$2,000,000) \div 10,000,000 = \$1 \text{ depletion cost per ton}$$

The cost per unit is then multiplied by the number of units extracted and sold to determine depletion expense. Depletion expense for Hard Rock is $40,000 ($1 × 40,000).

*Related exercise material:* BE10–12 and E10–15.

## ▶*SECTION 3 ▸ Intangible Assets*

Intangible assets are rights, privileges, and competitive advantages that result from the ownership of long-lived assets that do not possess physical substance. Evidence of intangibles may exist in the form of contracts, licenses, and other documents. Intangibles may arise from:

1. Government grants such as patents, copyrights, franchises, trademarks, and trade names.
2. Acquisition of another business in which the purchase price includes a payment for goodwill.

**3.** Private monopolistic arrangements arising from contractual agreements, such as franchises and leases.

Some widely known intangibles are the patents of Polaroid, the franchises of McDonald's, the trade name of Col. Sander's Kentucky Fried Chicken, and the trademark 3M of Minnesota Mining and Manufacturing Company.

# Accounting for Intangible Assets
........................................................

In general, accounting for intangible assets parallels the accounting for plant assets. That is, **intangible assets are recorded at cost**, and this cost is expensed **over the useful life of the intangible asset in a rational and systematic manner**. At disposal, the book value of the intangible asset is eliminated, and a gain or loss, if any, is recorded.

There are, however, differences between accounting for intangible assets and accounting for plant assets. First, the term used to describe the allocation of the cost of an intangible asset to expense is amortization, rather than depreciation. To record amortization of an intangible, an amortization expense is debited and the specific intangible asset is credited. An alternative is to credit an accumulated amortization account, similar to accumulated depreciation. Most companies, however, choose simply to reduce the cost of the intangible asset.

There is also a difference in determining cost. For plant assets, cost includes both the purchase price of an asset and the costs incurred by a company in designing and constructing the plant asset. In contrast, cost for an intangible asset includes only the purchase price. Costs incurred in developing an intangible asset are expensed as incurred.

A third difference is that **the amortization period of an intangible asset cannot be longer than 40 years**. For example, even if the useful life of an intangible asset is 60 years, it must be written off over 40 years. Conversely, if the useful life is less than 40 years, the useful life is used. This rule ensures that all intangibles, especially those with indeterminable lives, will be written off in a reasonable period of time.

Unlike plant assets, intangible assets are typically amortized on a straight-line basis. The widespread use of this method adds comparability in accounting for intangible assets.

**STUDY OBJECTIVE**
············ ▼ 8 ············
*Contrast the accounting for intangible assets with the accounting for plant assets.*

## Patents

A patent is an exclusive right issued by the United States Patent Office that enables the recipient to manufacture, sell, or otherwise control an invention for a period of 17 years from the date of the grant. A patent is nonrenewable, but the legal life of a patent may be extended beyond its original term by obtaining new patents for improvements and other changes in the basic design.

**The initial cost of a patent is the cash or cash equivalent price paid to acquire the patent.** It should be noted that the saying, "A patent is only as good as the money you're prepared to spend defending it," is very true. Most patents are subject to some type of litigation by competitors. A well-known example is the patent infringement suit won by Polaroid against Eastman Kodak in protecting its patent on instant cameras. If the owner incurs legal costs in successfully defending the patent in an infringement suit, such costs are considered necessary to establish the validity of the patent. Thus, **they are added to the Patent account and amortized over the remaining life of the patent**.

**The cost of a patent should be amortized over its 17-year legal life or its useful life, whichever is shorter.** In determining useful life, obsolescence, inadequacy, and other factors should be considered; these may cause a patent to become economically ineffective before the end of its legal life. To illustrate the computation of patent expense, assume that National Labs purchases a patent at a cost of $60,000. If the useful life of the patent is 8 years, the annual amortization expense is $7,500 ($60,000 ÷ 8). The entry to record the annual amortization is:

| Dec. 31 | Patent Expense | 7,500 | |
| | Patents | | 7,500 |
| | (To record patent amortization) | | |

Patent Expense is classified as an **operating expense** in the income statement.

## Copyrights

Copyrights are granted by the federal government, giving the owner the exclusive right to reproduce and sell an artistic or published work. Copyrights extend for the life of the creator plus 50 years. The cost of the copyright consists of the **cost of acquiring and defending it**. The cost may be only the $10 fee paid to the U.S. Copyright office, or it may amount to a great deal more if a copyright infringement suit is involved.

The useful life of a copyright generally is significantly shorter than its legal life. Similar to other intangible assets, the maximum write-off is 40 years. However, because of the difficulties of determining the period over which benefits are to be received, copyrights usually are amortized over a relatively short period of time.

## ▶**A**ccounting in **A**ction ▸ *International Insight*

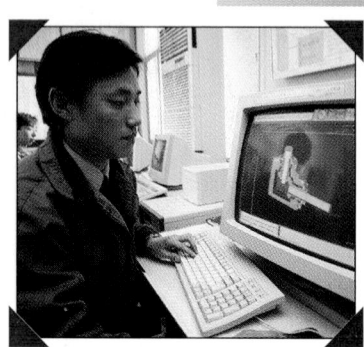

One of the significant new items copyrighted today is computer software. Lotus Development Corporation (Lotus 1-2-3), Microsoft (Windows), and WordPerfect Corporation (WordPerfect) are some examples. These intangible assets—copyrights, in this case—are one of the most valuable assets of these corporations. To illustrate how important copyrights are, consider that in China only $1 million in computer software was sold in two recent years because China had no copyright law to discourage software piracy. Now an agreement has been reached with the Chinese that will provide protection against unlicensed copying of software. As one software maker observed, "If copyrights are protected, the value of the computer-software market in China will skyrocket."

## Trademarks and Trade Names

A trademark or trade name is a word, phrase, jingle, or symbol that distinguishes or identifies a particular enterprise or product. Trade names like Wheaties, Trivial Pursuit, Sunkist, Kleenex, Coca-Cola, Big Mac, and Cadillac create immediate product identification and generally enhance the sale of the product. The creator or original user may obtain exclusive legal right to the trademark or trade name by registering it with the U.S. Patent Office. Such registration provides 20 years' protection and may be renewed indefinitely as long as the trademark or trade name is in use.

If the trademark or trade name is purchased, the cost is the purchase price. If it is developed by the enterprise itself, the cost includes attorney's fees, registration fees, design costs, successful legal defense costs, and other expenditures directly related to securing it.

As with other intangibles, the cost of trademarks and trade names must be amortized over the shorter of its useful life or 40 years. Because of the uncertainty involved in estimating the useful life, the cost is frequently amortized over a much shorter period.

## ▶ **A**ccounting in **A**ction ▸ *Business Insight*

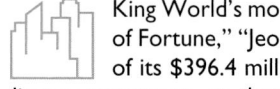

Consider the trademarks that Kohlberg, Kravis, Roberts and Company (KKR) received when it purchased RJR Nabisco. First RJR Nabisco owned 30% of the cigarette market, with such trade names as Camel, Salem, Doral, and Vantage. In the food area, RJR Nabisco owned Oreo, Ritz, Chips Ahoy, Premium Saltines (crackers), Fleischmann's and Blue Bonnet (margarine), Grey Poupon (mustard), Milk Bone, Ortega (Mexican foods), Shredded Wheat, Peek Freans (cookies), Hawaiian Punch, Del Monte, Planters, Life Savers, Baby Ruth, and Butterfinger. It is no wonder that KKR paid approximately $25 billion for the company!

## Franchises and Licenses

When you drive down the street in your Trans-Am purchased from a General Motors dealer, fill up your tank at the corner Standard Oil station, eat lunch at Wendy's, and vacation at a Club Med resort, you are dealing with franchises. A franchise is a contractual arrangement under which the franchisor grants the franchisee the right to sell certain products, to render specific services, or to use certain trademarks or trade names, usually within a designated geographical area.

Another type of franchise is that entered into between a governmental body (commonly municipalities) and a business enterprise. This type of franchise permits the enterprise to use public property in performing its services. Examples are the use of city streets for a bus line or taxi service, use of public land for telephone and electric lines, and the use of airwaves for radio or TV broadcasting. Such operating rights are referred to as licenses.

Franchises and licenses may be granted for a definite period of time, an indefinite period, or perpetual. **When costs can be identified with the acquisition of the franchise or license, an intangible asset should be recognized.** In the case of a limited life, the cost of a franchise (or license) should be amortized as operating expense over the useful life. If the life is indefinite or perpetual, the cost may be amortized over a reasonable period not to exceed 40 years. Annual payments made under a franchise agreement should be recorded as **operating expenses** in the period in which they are incurred.

▶ *Ethics note*

A pharmaceutical company was growing rapidly by buying unwanted drug licensing rights held by larger companies. These licensing rights, reported as intangible assets, represented over 70% of the company's total assets. At first considered a "hot stock" because of its quick growth in profits, it sustained a 50% drop in value when the market realized the rights were being amortized over 40 years. If a more reasonable life had been used to amortize the rights, the company's reported profits would, instead, have been huge losses.

## ▶ **A**ccounting in **A**ction ▸ *Business Insight*

King World's most valuable asset is the right to license television shows such as "Wheel of Fortune," "Jeopardy," "The Oprah Winfrey Show," and "Inside Edition." Almost 90% of its $396.4 million in a recent year came from the fees associated with the rights to license agreements on these intangible assets.

## Goodwill

Usually, the largest intangible asset that appears on a company's balance sheet is goodwill. Goodwill is the value of all favorable attributes that relate to a business enterprise. These include exceptional management, desirable location, good customer relations, skilled employees, high-quality products, fair pricing policies, and harmonious relations with labor unions. Some view goodwill as expected earnings in excess of normal earnings. Goodwill is, therefore, unusual: unlike other assets such as investments, plant assets, and other intangibles that can be sold individually in the marketplace, goodwill can be identified only with the business as a whole.

If goodwill can be identified only with the business as a whole, how can it be determined? Certainly, many of the factors above (exceptional management, desirable location, and so on) are present in many business enterprises. However, to determine the amount of goodwill in these types of situations would be too difficult and very subjective. In other words, to recognize goodwill without an exchange transaction would lead to subjective valuations that do not contribute to the reliability of financial statements. **Therefore, goodwill is recorded only when there is an exchange transaction that involves the purchase of an entire business. When an entire business is purchased, goodwill is the excess of cost over the fair market value of the net assets (assets less liabilities) acquired.**

In recording the purchase of a business, the net assets are shown at their fair market values, goodwill is recorded at its cost, and cash is credited for the purchase price. Subsequently, goodwill is written off over its useful life, not to exceed 40 years. The amortization entry generally results in a debit to Goodwill Expense and a credit to Goodwill. Goodwill is reported in the balance sheet under Intangible Assets.

## ▶ **A**ccounting in **A**ction ▸ *International Insight*

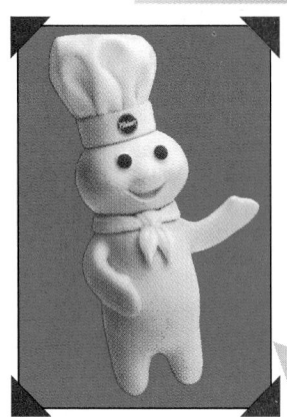

Does the amortization requirement for goodwill create a disadvantage for U.S. companies? British companies, for example, do not have to amortize goodwill against earnings. Rather, they bypass the income statement completely and charge goodwill directly to stockholders' equity. For example, Pillsbury was purchased by Grand Met, a British firm. Many complained that U.S. companies were reluctant to bid for Pillsbury because it would mean that they would have to record a large amount of goodwill, which would substantially depress income in the future. What should be done when accounting practices are different among countries and perhaps give one country a competitive edge?

## ▶ **R**esearch and Development Costs

Research and development costs are not intangible costs, but because these expenditures may lead to patents and copyrights, they are discussed in this section. Many companies spend considerable sums of money on research and development in an ongoing effort to develop new products or processes. For example, in a recent year IBM spent over $2.5 billion on research and development, an amount greater than the total expenditure budget of many state governments.

Research and development costs present accounting problems: (1) it is sometimes difficult to assign the costs to specific projects, and (2) there are uncertainties in identifying the extent and timing of future benefits. As a result, research and development costs are **usually recorded as an expense when incurred**, whether the research and development is successful or not.

To illustrate, assume that Laser Scanner Company spent $3 million on research and development. These research and development costs resulted in the development of two highly successful patents. The R&D costs, however, cannot be included in the cost of the patent. Rather, they are recorded as an expense when incurred.

Many disagree with this accounting approach. They argue that to expense these costs leads to understated assets and net income. Others, however, argue that capitalizing these costs will lead only to highly speculative assets on the balance sheet. Who is right is difficult to determine. The controversy, however, illustrates how difficult it is to establish proper guidelines for financial reporting.

▶ *International note*

Many factors, including differences in accounting treatment of R&D, contribute to differences in R&D expenditures across nations. R&D as a percentage of gross domestic product in 1994 was 2.6% in the United States, 2.4% in France, 2.5% in Germany, 3% in Japan, and 1.8% in Korea.

# *F*inancial Statement Presentation
•••••••••••••••••••••••••••••••••••••••••••••••••••••••••••••••

Usually plant assets and natural resources are combined under Property, Plant, and Equipment, and intangibles are shown separately under Intangible Assets. Either within the balance sheet or in the notes, there should be disclosure of the balances of the major classes of assets, such as land, buildings, and equipment, and accumulated depreciation by major classes or in total. In addition, the depreciation and amortization methods used should be described and the amount of depreciation and amortization expense for the period disclosed.

Illustration 10-28 is an excerpt from Owens-Illinois' balance sheet. The notes to the financial statements of Owens-Illinois identify the major classes of property, plant, and equipment. They also indicate that depreciation is by the straight-line method, depletion is by the units-of-activity method, and amortization is by the straight-line method.

**STUDY OBJECTIVE**
•••••••••▼9▼•••••••••

*Indicate how plant assets, natural resources, and intangible assets are reported on the balance sheet.*

| OWENS-ILLINOIS, INC.<br>Partial Balance Sheet<br>(In millions of dollars) | | | |
|---|---|---|---|
| Property, plant, and equipment | | | |
| Timberlands, at cost, less accumulated depletion | | $ 95.4 | |
| Buildings and equipment, at cost | $2,207.1 | | |
| Less: Accumulated depreciation | 1,229.0 | 978.1 | |
| Total property, plant, and equipment | | | $1,073.5 |
| Intangibles | | | |
| Patents | | | 410.0 |
| Total | | | $1,483.5 |

**Illustration 10-28**

*Presentation of property, plant, and equipment and intangible assets*

# *Before You Go On . . .*

▶ *Review It*

1. What are the main differences between accounting for intangible assets and plant assets?
2. Identify the major types of intangibles and the proper accounting for them.
3. Explain the accounting for research and development costs.

# ▸ *A Look Back at Westbrook College*
••••••••••••••••••••••••••••••••••••••••••••••••••••••••••••••••

Refer back to the opening story about Westbrook College, and answer the following questions:

1. Why should Westbrook College depreciate its buildings?
2. How can Westbrook College have a building with a zero book value yet a substantial market value?
3. Give some examples of intangibles other than a trademark that you might find on your college campus.

4. Give some examples of company or product trademarks or trade names. Are trade names and trademarks reported on a company's balance sheet? Explain.

**Solution:**

1. Westbrook College should depreciate its buildings because depreciation is necessary in order to allocate the cost of the buildings to the periods in which they are used.
2. A building can have a zero book value if it has no salvage value and it is fully depreciated—that is, if it has been used for a period longer than its expected life. Because depreciation is used to allocate cost rather than to reflect actual value, it is not at all unlikely that a building could have a low or zero book value, but a positive market value.
3. Examples of other intangibles that might be found on a college campus are franchise of a bookstore chain, license to operate a radio station, patents developed by professors, and a permit to operate a bus service.
4. Typical company or product trade names are:
   Clothes—Gap, Gitano, Dockers, Calvin Klein, Chaus, Guess.
   Perfume—Passion, Ruffles, Chanel No. 5, Diamonds.
   Cars—TransAm, Nova, Prelude, Coupe DeVille, Eclipse.
   Shoes—Nike, Florsheim, L.A. Gear, Adidas.
   Breakfast cereals—Cheerios, Wheaties, Frosted Mini-Wheats, Rice Krispies.

Trade names and trademarks are reported on a balance sheet if there is a cost attached to them. If the trade name or trademark is purchased, the cost is the purchase price. If it is developed by the enterprise, the cost includes attorney's fees, registration fees, design costs, successful legal defense costs, and other expenditures directly related to securing the trade name or trademark.

# ◣ Summary of Study Objectives

**1. Describe the application of the cost principle to plant assets.** The cost of plant assets includes all expenditures necessary to acquire the asset and make it ready for its intended use. Cost is measured by the cash or cash equivalent price paid.

**2. Explain the concept of depreciation.** Depreciation is the process of allocating to expense the cost of a plant asset over its useful (service) life in a rational and systematic manner. Depreciation is not a process of valuation, and it is not a process that results in an accumulation of cash. Depreciation is caused by wear and tear and by obsolescence.

**3. Compute periodic depreciation using different methods.** There are three depreciation methods:

| Method | Effect on Annual Depreciation | Formula |
|---|---|---|
| Straight-line | Constant amount | Depreciable cost ÷ useful life (in years) |
| Units-of-activity | Varying amount | Depreciation cost per unit × units of activity during the year |
| Declining-balance | Decreasing amount | Book value at beginning of year × declining-balance rate |

**4. Describe the procedure for revising periodic depreciation.** Revisions of periodic depreciation are made in present and future periods, not retroactively. The new annual depreciation is determined by dividing the depreciable cost at the time of the revision by the remaining useful life.

**5. Distinguish between revenue and capital expenditures and explain the entries for these expenditures.** Revenue expenditures are incurred to maintain the operating efficiency and expected productive life of the asset. These expenditures are debited to Repair Expense as incurred. Capital expenditures increase the operating efficiency, productive capacity, or expected useful life of the asset. These expenditures are generally debited to the plant asset affected.

**6. Explain how to account for the disposal of a plant asset through retirement, sale, or exchange.** The accounting for disposal of a plant asset through retirement or sale is as follows:
(a) Eliminate the book value of the plant asset at the date of disposal.
(b) Record cash proceeds, if any.
(c) Account for the difference between the book value and the cash proceeds as a gain or loss on disposal.

In accounting for exchanges of similar assets:
(a) Eliminate the book value of the old asset at the date of the exchange.
(b) Record the acquisition cost of the new asset.
(c) Account for the loss or gain, if any, on the old asset.
   1. If a loss, recognize it immediately.
   2. If a gain, defer and reduce the cost of the new asset.

**7.** *Identify the basic accounting issues related to natural resources.* The basic accounting issues related to natural resources are whether exploration costs on unsuccessful explorations should be capitalized or expensed. Under the full-cost approach, both successful and unsuccessful explorations are capitalized and the costs amortized to expense over the useful life of the successful wells. The other approach is to capitalize only the costs of successful explorations. This is referred to as the successful efforts approach.

**8.** *Contrast the accounting for intangible assets with the accounting for plant assets.* The accounting for intangible assets and plant assets is much the same. One difference is that the term used to describe the write-off of an intangible asset is amortization, rather than depreciation. In addition,

the amortization of the intangible asset cannot be longer than 40 years. The straight-line method is normally used for amortizing intangible assets.

**9.** *Indicate how plant assets, natural resources, and intangible assets are reported on the balance sheet.* Usually plant assets and natural resources are combined under Property, Plant, and Equipment; intangibles are shown separately under Intangible Assets. Either within the balance sheet or in the notes, the balances of the major classes of assets, such as land, buildings, and equipment, and accumulated depreciation by major classes or in total should be disclosed. Also, the depreciation and amortization methods used should be described, and the amount of depreciation and amortization expense for the period should be disclosed.

# GLOSSARY

**Accelerated-depreciation method** A depreciation method that produces higher depreciation expense in the early years than in the later years. (p. 415).

**Additions and improvements** Costs incurred to increase the operating efficiency, productive capacity, or expected useful life of a plant asset. (p. 418).

**Amortization** The allocation of the cost of an intangible asset to expense. (p. 427).

**Capital expenditures** Expenditures that increase the company's investment in productive facilities. (p. 418).

**Cash equivalent price** An amount equal to the fair market value of the asset given up or the fair market value of the asset received, whichever is more clearly determinable. (p. 407).

**Copyright** An exclusive right granted by the federal government allowing the owner to reproduce and sell an artistic or published work. (p. 428).

**Declining-balance method** A depreciation method that applies a constant rate to the declining book value of the asset and produces a decreasing annual depreciation expense over the useful life of the asset. (p. 414).

**Depletion** The process of allocating the cost of a natural resource to expense in a rational and systematic manner over the resources's useful life. (p. 425).

**Depreciable cost** The cost of a plant asset less its salvage value. (p. 412).

**Franchise (license)** A contractual arrangement under which the franchisor grants the franchisee the right to sell certain products, to render specific services, or to use certain trademarks or trade names, usually within a designated geographical area. (p. 429).

**Full-cost approach** Method in which both successful and unsuccessful exploration costs are included in the cost of a natural resource and the costs are written off to expense over the useful life of the successful wells. (p. 424).

**Goodwill** The value of all favorable attributes that relate to a business enterprise. (p. 429).

**Intangible assets** Rights, privileges, and competitive advantages that result from the ownership of long-lived assets that do not possess physical substance. (p. 426).

**Licenses** Operating rights to use public property, granted by a governmental agency to a business enterprise. (p. 429).

**Natural resources** Assets that consist of standing timber and underground deposits of oil, gas, and minerals. Also called *wasting assets*. (p. 424).

**Ordinary repairs** Expenditures to maintain the operating efficiency and expected productive life of the unit. (p. 418).

**Patent** An exclusive right issued by the U.S. Patent Office that enables the recipient to manufacture, sell, or otherwise control an invention for a period of 17 years from the date of the grant. (p. 427).

**Plant assets** Tangible resources that are used in the operations of the business and are not intended for sale to customers. (p. 406).

**Research and development costs** Expenditures that may lead to patents, copyrights, new processes, and products. (p. 430).

**Revenue expenditures** Expenditures that are immediately charged against revenues as an expense. (p. 418).

**Straight-line method** A method in which periodic depreciation is the same for each year of the asset's useful life. (p. 412).

**Successful efforts approach** Method in which only the costs of successful exploration are included in the cost of a natural resource. (p. 424).

**Trademark (trade name)** A word, phrase, jingle, or symbol that distinguishes or identifies a particular enterprise or product. (p. 428).

**Units-of-activity method** A depreciation method in which useful life is expressed in terms of the total units of production or use expected from the asset. (p. 413).

## DEMONSTRATION PROBLEM 1

DuPage Company purchases a factory machine at a cost of $18,000 on January 1, 1996. The machine is expected to have a salvage value of $2,000 at the end of its 4-year useful life.

During its useful life, the machine is expected to be used 160,000 hours. Actual annual hourly use was: Year 1, 40,000; Year 2, 60,000; Year 3, 35,000; and Year 4, 25,000.

### Instructions
Prepare depreciation schedules for the following methods: (a) the straight-line, (b) units-of-activity, and (c) declining-balance using double the straight-line rate.

## Solution to Demonstration Problem

(a)

**Problem-Solving Strategies**

1. Under the straight-line method, the depreciation rate is applied to depreciable cost.

2. Under the units-of-activity method, depreciation cost per unit is computed by dividing depreciable cost by total units of activity.

3. Under the declining-balance method, the depreciation rate is applied to **book value** at the beginning of the year.

### Straight-Line Method

| Year | Depreciable Cost | × | Depreciation Rate | = | Annual Depreciation Expense | Accumulated Depreciation | Book Value |
|------|------|---|------|---|------|------|------|
| 1996 | $16,000 | | 25% | | $4,000 | $ 4,000 | $14,000* |
| 1997 | 16,000 | | 25% | | 4,000 | 8,000 | 10,000 |
| 1998 | 16,000 | | 25% | | 4,000 | 12,000 | 6,000 |
| 1999 | 16,000 | | 25% | | 4,000 | 16,000 | 2,000 |

*End of Year*

*$18,000 − $4,000.

(b)

### Units-of-Activity Method

| Year | Units of Activity | × | Depreciation Cost/Unit | = | Annual Depreciation Expense | Accumulated Depreciation | Book Value |
|------|------|---|------|---|------|------|------|
| 1996 | 40,000 | | $.10 | | $4,000 | $ 4,000 | $14,000 |
| 1997 | 60,000 | | .10 | | 6,000 | 10,000 | 8,000 |
| 1998 | 35,000 | | .10 | | 3,500 | 13,500 | 4,500 |
| 1999 | 25,000 | | .10 | | 2,500 | 16,000 | 2,000 |

*Computation* | *End of Year*

(c)

### Declining-Balance Method

| Year | Book Value Beginning of Year | × | Depreciation Rate | = | Annual Depreciation Expense | Accumulated Depreciation | Book Value |
|------|------|---|------|---|------|------|------|
| 1996 | $18,000 | | 50% | | $9,000 | $ 9,000 | $9,000 |
| 1997 | 9,000 | | 50% | | 4,500 | 13,500 | 4,500 |
| 1998 | 4,500 | | 50% | | 2,250 | 15,750 | 2,250 |
| 1999 | 2,250 | | 50% | | 250* | 16,000 | 2,000 |

*End of Year*

*Adjusted to $250 because ending book value should not be less than expected salvage value.

## DEMONSTRATION PROBLEM 2

On January 1, 1994, the Skyline Limousine Co. purchased a limousine at an acquisition cost of $28,000. The vehicle has been depreciated by the straight-line method using a 4-year service life and a $4,000 salvage value. The company's fiscal year ends on December 31.

**Instructions**

Prepare the journal entry or entries to record the disposal of the limousine assuming that it was:

(1) Retired and scrapped with no salvage value on January 1, 1998.

(2) Sold for $5,000 on July 1, 1997.

(3) Traded in on a new limousine on January 1, 1997. The fair market value of the old vehicle was $9,000 and $22,000 was paid in cash.

(4) Traded in on a new limousine on January 1, 1997. The fair market value of the old vehicle was $11,000 and $2,000 was paid in cash.

## Solution to Demonstration Problem

| | | | | |
|---|---|---|---|---|
| (1) | 1/1/98 | Accumulated Depreciation—Limousine | 24,000 | |
| | | Loss on Disposal | 4,000 | |
| | |    Limousine | | 28,000 |
| | |    (To record retirement of limousine) | | |
| (2) | 7/1/97 | Depreciation Expense | 3,000 | |
| | |    Accumulated Depreciation—Limousine | | 3,000 |
| | |    (To record depreciation to date of disposal) | | |
| | | Cash | 5,000 | |
| | | Accumulated Depreciation—Limousine | 21,000 | |
| | | Loss on Disposal | 2,000 | |
| | |    Limousine | | 28,000 |
| | |    (To record sale of limousine) | | |
| (3) | 1/1/97 | Limousine (new) | 31,000 | |
| | | Accumulated Depreciation—Limousine | 18,000 | |
| | | Loss on Disposal | 1,000 | |
| | |    Limousine | | 28,000 |
| | |    Cash | | 22,000 |
| | |    (To record exchange of limousines) | | |
| (4) | 1/1/97 | Limousine (new)* | 12,000 | |
| | | Accumulated Depreciation—Limousine (old) | 18,000 | |
| | |    Limousine (old) | | 28,000 |
| | |    Cash | | 2,000 |
| | |    (To record exchange of limousines) | | |

*($11,000 + $2,000 − $1,000)

### Problem-Solving Strategies

1. At the time of disposal, determine the book value of the asset.

2. Recognize any gain or loss from disposal of the asset.

3. Remove the book value of the asset from the records by debiting accumulated depreciation for the total depreciation to date of disposal and crediting the asset account for the cost of the asset.

# SELF-STUDY QUESTIONS

Answers are at the end of the chapter.

(SO 1)

1. Corrieten Company purchased equipment and the following costs were incurred:

| | |
|---|---|
| Cash price | $24,000 |
| Sales taxes | 1,200 |
| Insurance during transit | 200 |
| Installation and testing | 400 |
|   Total costs | $25,800 |

What amount should be recorded as the cost of the equipment?
a. $24,000.
b. $25,200.
c. $25,400.
d. $25,800.

2. Depreciation is a process of:   (SO 2)
a. valuation.
b. cost allocation.
c. cash accumulation.
d. appraisal.

3. Cuso Company purchased equipment on January  (SO 3) 1, 1995, at a total invoice cost of $400,000. The equipment has an estimated salvage value of $10,000 and an estimated useful life of 5 years. The amount of accumulated depreciation at December 31, 1996, if the straight-line method of depreciation is used is:
a. $80,000.
b. $160,000.
c. $78,000.
d. $156,000.

(SO 3)    4. Kant Enterprises purchased a truck for $11,000 on January 1, 1995. The truck will have an estimated salvage value of $1,000 at the end of 5 years. Using the units-of-activity method, the balance in accumulated depreciation at December 31, 1996, can be computed by the following formula:
a. ($11,000 ÷ Total estimated activity) × Units of activity for 1996.
b. ($10,000 ÷ Total estimated activity) × Units of activity for 1996.
c. ($11,000 ÷ Total estimated activity) × Units of activity for 1995 and 1996.
d. ($10,000 ÷ Total estimated activity) × Units of activity for 1995 and 1996.

(SO 4)    5. When there is a change in estimated depreciation:
a. previous depreciation should be corrected.
b. current and future years' depreciation should be revised.
c. only future years' depreciation should be revised.
d. None of the above.

(SO 5)    6. Additions are:
a. revenue expenditures.
b. debited to a Repair Expense account.
c. debited to a Purchases account.
d. capital expenditures.

(SO 6)    7. Schopenhauer Company exchanged an old machine, with a book value of $39,000 and a fair market value of $35,000, and paid $10,000 cash for a similar new machine. At what amount should the machine acquired in the exchange be recorded on the books of Schopenhauer?
a. $45,000.
b. $46,000.
c. $49,000.
d. $50,000.

(SO 6)    8. In exchanges of similar assets:
a. neither gains nor losses are recognized immediately.

b. gains, but not losses, are recognized immediately.
c. losses, but not gains, are recognized immediately.
d. both gains and losses are recognized immediately.

(SO 7)    9. Averroes Company expects to extract 20 million tons of coal from a mine that cost $12 million. If no salvage value is expected, and 2 million tons are mined and sold in the first year, the entry to record depletion will include a:
a. debit to Accumulated Depletion of $2,000,000.
b. credit to Depletion Expense of $1,200,000.
c. debit to Depletion Expense of $1,200,000.
d. credit to Accumulated Depletion of $2,000,000.

(SO 8, 9)    10. Pierce Company incurred $150,000 of research and development costs in its laboratory to develop a patent granted on January 2, 1995. On July 31, 1995, Pierce paid $35,000 for legal fees in a successful defense of the patent. The total amount debited to Patents through July 31, 1995, should be:
a. $150,000.
b. $35,000.
c. $185,000.
d. some other amount.

(SO 9)    11. Indicate which of the following statements is *true*.
a. Since intangible assets lack physical substance they need be disclosed only in the notes to the financial statements.
b. Goodwill should be reported as a contra-account in the Stockholder's Equity section.
c. Totals of major classes of assets can be shown in the balance sheet, with asset details disclosed in the notes to the financial statements.
d. Intangible assets are typically combined with plant assets and natural resources and then shown in the Property, Plant, and Equipment section.

# QUESTIONS

1. Susan Dey is uncertain about the applicability of the cost principle to plant assets. Explain the principle to Susan.

2. How is cost for a plant asset measured in (a) a cash transaction, and (b) a noncash transaction?

3. Jamie Company acquires the land and building owned by Smitt Company. What types of costs may be incurred to make the asset ready for its intended use if Jamie Company wants to use (a) only the land, and (b) both the land and the building?

4. In a recent newspaper release, the president of Lawsuit Company asserted that something has to be done about depreciation. The president said,

"Depreciation does not come close to accumulating the cash needed to replace the asset at the end of its useful life." What is your response to the president?

5. Cecile is studying for the next accounting examination. She asks your help on two questions: (a) What is salvage value? (b) Is salvage value used in determining depreciable cost under each depreciation method? Answer Cecile's questions.

6. Contrast the straight-line method and the units-of-activity method as to (a) useful life, and (b) the pattern of periodic depreciation over useful life.

7. Contrast the effects of the three depreciation methods on annual depreciation expense.

8. In the fourth year of an asset's 5-year useful life, the company decides that the asset will have a 6-year service life. How should the revision of depreciation be recorded? Why?

9. Distinguish between revenue expenditures and capital expenditures during useful life.

10. How is a gain or loss on the sale of a plant asset computed?

11. Ewing Corporation owns a machine that is fully depreciated but is still being used. How should Ewing account for this asset and report it in the financial statements?

12. When similar assets are exchanged, how is the gain or loss on disposal computed?

13. Ice-Master Refrigeration Company trades in an old machine on a new model when the fair market value of the old machine is greater than its book value. Should Ice-Master recognize a gain on disposal? If the fair market value of the old machine is less than its book value, should Ice-Master recognize a loss on disposal?

14. Hakeem Company experienced a gain on disposal when exchanging similar machines. In accordance with generally accepted accounting principles, the gain was not recognized. How will Hakeem's future financial statements be affected by not recognizing the gain?

15. What are natural resources, and what are their distinguishing characteristics?

16. Sandy Shaw and Jo Koehn are arguing about the full-cost approach and the successful efforts approach. Shaw says that the full-cost approach will provide a greater reported asset value, while Koehn says that the successful efforts approach would. Who is correct?

17. What are the similarities and differences between the terms depreciation, depletion, and amortization?

18. Heflin Company hires an accounting intern who says that intangible assets should always be amortized over their legal lives. Is the intern correct? Explain.

19. Goodwill has been defined as the value of all favorable attributes that relate to a business enterprise. What types of attributes could result in goodwill?

20. Bob Leno, a business major, is working on a case problem for one of his classes. In this case problem, the company needs to raise cash to market a new product it developed. Saul Cain, an engineering major, takes one look at the company's balance sheet and says, "This company has an awful lot of goodwill. Why don't you recommend that they sell some of it to raise cash?" How should Bob respond to Saul?

21. Under what conditions is goodwill recorded?

22. Often research and development costs provide companies with benefits that last a number of years. (For example, these costs can lead to the development of a patent that will increase the company's income for many years.) However, generally accepted accounting principles require that such costs be recorded as an expense when incurred. Why?

# BRIEF EXERCISES

**BE10–1**  The following expenditures were incurred by Gene Shumway Company in purchasing land. Cash price $50,000, accrued taxes $3,000, attorneys' fees $2,500, real estate broker's commission, $2,000, and clearing and grading $3,500. What is the cost of the land?

*Determine the cost of land.*
*(SO 1)*

**BE10–2**  Shirley Basler Company incurs the following expenditures in purchasing a truck: cash price $18,000, accident insurance $2,000, sales taxes $900, motor vehicle license $100, and painting and lettering $400. What is the cost of the truck?

*Determine the cost of a truck.*
*(SO 1)*

**BE10–3**  Joy Cunningham Company acquires a delivery truck at a cost of $22,000. The truck is expected to have a salvage value of $2,000 at the end of its 4-year useful life. Compute annual depreciation for the first and second years using the straight-line method.

*Compute straight-line depreciation.*
*(SO 3)*

**BE10–4**  Depreciation information for Joy Cunningham Company is given in BE10–3. Assuming the declining-balance depreciation rate is double the straight-line rate, compute annual depreciation for the first and second years under the declining-balance method.

*Compute declining-balance depreciation.*
*(SO 3)*

**BE10–5**  Jerry Englehart Taxi Service uses the units-of-activity method in computing depreciation on its taxicabs. Each cab is expected to be driven 120,000 miles. Taxi No. 10 cost $24,500 and is expected to have a salvage value of $500. Taxi No. 10 is driven 30,000 miles in Year 1 and 20,000 miles in Year 2. Compute the depreciation for each year.

*Compute depreciation using the units-of-activity method.*
*(SO 3)*

*Compute revised depreciation.*
*(SO 4)*

**BE10–6**   On January 1, 1997, the Asler Company ledger shows Equipment $32,000 and Accumulated Depreciation $12,000. The depreciation resulted from using the straight-line method with a useful life of 10 years and salvage value of $2,000. On this date, the company concludes that the equipment has only a remaining useful life of 4 years with the same salvage value. Compute the revised annual depreciation.

*Disposal by retirement*
*(SO 6)*

**BE10–7**   Prepare journal entries to record the following:

  (a) Ruiz Company retires its delivery equipment, which cost $41,000. Accumulated depreciation is also $41,000 on this delivery equipment. No salvage value is received.

  (b) Assume the same information as (a), except that accumulated depreciation for Ruiz Company is $35,000, instead of $41,000.

*Disposal by sale*
*(SO 6)*

**BE10–8**   Wiley Company sells office equipment on September 30, 1996, for $21,000 cash. The office equipment originally cost $72,000 and as of January 1, 1996, had accumulated depreciation of $42,000. Depreciation for the first 9 months of 1996 is $6,250. Prepare the journal entries to (a) update depreciation to September 30, 1996, and (b) record the sale of the equipment.

*Disposal by exchange*
*(SO 6)*

**BE10–9**   Concord Company exchanges old delivery equipment for similar new delivery equipment. The book value of the old delivery equipment is $31,000 (cost $61,000 less accumulated depreciation $30,000), its fair market value is $19,000, and cash of $3,000 is paid. Prepare the entry to record the exchange.

*Disposal by exchange*
*(SO 6)*

**BE10–10**   Assume the same information as BE10–9, except that the fair market value of the old delivery equipment is $42,000. Prepare the entry to record the exchange.

*Accounting for natural resources*
*(SO 7)*

**BE10–11**   Sunshine Mining Co. purchased for $7 million a mine which is estimated to have 28 million tons of ore and no salvage value. In the first year, 4 million tons of ore are extracted and sold. (a) Prepare the journal entry to record depletion expense for the first year. (b) Show how this mine is reported on the balance sheet at the end of the first year.

*Accounting for intangibles—patents*
*(SO 8)*

**BE10–12**   Popper Company purchases a patent for $180,000 on January 2, 1996. Its estimated useful life is 10 years. (a) Prepare the journal entry to record patent expense for the first year. (b) Show how this patent is reported on the balance sheet at the end of the first year.

*Classification of long-lived assets on balance sheet*
*(SO 9)*

**BE10–13**   Presented below is information related to plant assets, natural resources and intangibles at the end of 1996 for Joker Company: buildings $800,000; accumulated depreciation—buildings $650,000; goodwill $410,000; coal mine $200,000; accumulated depletion—coal mine $108,000. Prepare a partial balance sheet of Joker Company for these items.

# EXERCISES

• • • • • • • • • • • • • • • • • • • • • • • • • • • • • • • • • • • • • • • • • • • • • • • • • • • • • • • • • • •

*Determine cost of plant acquisitions.*
*(SO 1)*

**E10–1**   The following expenditures relating to plant assets were made by John Kosinski Company during the first 2 months of 1996.

  1. Paid $250 to have company name and advertising slogan painted on new delivery truck.

  2. Paid $75 motor vehicle license fee on the new truck.

  3. Paid $850 sales taxes on new delivery truck.

  4. Paid $17,500 for parking lots and driveways on new plant site.

  5. Paid $5,000 of accrued taxes at time plant site was acquired.

  6. Paid $8,000 for installation of new factory machinery.

  7. Paid $900 for one-year accident insurance policy on new delivery truck.

  8. Paid $200 insurance to cover possible accident loss on new factory machinery while the machinery was in transit.

**Instructions**

  (a) ▭▭▭▭▷ Explain the application of the cost principle in determining the acquisition cost of plant assets.

  (b) List the numbers of the foregoing transactions, and opposite each indicate the account title to which each expenditure should be debited.

*Determine acquisition costs on land.*
*(SO 1)*

**E10–2**   On March 1, 1996, Roy Orbis Company acquired real estate, on which they planned to construct a small office building, by paying $100,000 in cash. An old warehouse on the property was razed at a cost of $6,600; the salvaged materials were sold for $1,700. Additional expenditures before construction began included $1,100 attorney's fee for work concerning the land purchase, $4,000 real estate broker's fee, $7,800 architect's fee, and $14,000 to put in driveways and a parking lot.

**Instructions**
    (a) Determine the amount to be reported as the cost of the land.
    (b) For each cost not used in part (a), indicate the account to be debited.

**E10–3**   Interstate Bus Lines uses the units-of-activity method in depreciating its buses. One bus was purchased on January 1, 1996, at a cost of $108,000. Over its 4-year useful life, the bus is expected to be driven 100,000 miles. Salvage value is expected to be $8,000.

*Compute depreciation under units-of-activity method.*
*(SO 3)*

**Instructions**
    (a) Compute the depreciation cost per unit.
    (b) Prepare a depreciation schedule assuming actual mileage was: 1996, 28,000; 1997, 30,000; 1998, 25,000; and 1999, 17,000.

**E10–4**   Elvis Costello Company purchased a new machine on October 1, 1996, at a cost of $96,000. The company estimated that the machine will have a salvage value of $12,000. The machine is expected to be used for 84,000 working hours during its 6-year life.

*Determine depreciation for partial periods.*
*(SO 3)*

**Instructions**
Compute the depreciation expense under the following methods for the year indicated: (1) straight-line for 1996, (2) units-of-activity for 1996, assuming machine usage was 1,700 hours, and (3) declining-balance using double the straight-line rate for 1996 and 1997.

**E10–5**   Lindy Weink, the new controller of the Waterloo Company, has reviewed the expected useful lives and salvage values of selected depreciable assets at the beginning of 1996. Her findings are as follows:

*Compute revised annual depreciation.*
*(SO 3, 4)*

| Type of Asset | Date Acquired | Cost | Accumulated Depreciation 1/1/96 | Useful Life in Years | | Salvage Value | |
|---|---|---|---|---|---|---|---|
| | | | | Old | Proposed | Old | Proposed |
| Building | 1/1/90 | $800,000 | $114,000 | 40 | 45 | $40,000 | $62,000 |
| Warehouse | 1/1/93 | 100,000 | 11,400 | 25 | 20 | 5,000 | 3,600 |

All assets are depreciated by the straight-line method. Waterloo Company uses a calendar year in preparing annual financial statements. After discussion, management has agreed to accept Lindy's proposed changes.

**Instructions**
    (a) Compute the revised annual depreciation on each asset in 1996. (Show computations.)
    (b) Prepare the entry (or entries) to record depreciation on the building in 1996.

**E10–6**   Presented below are selected transactions at Beck Company for 1996.

*Journalize entries for disposal of plant assets.*
*(SO 6)*

Jan.  1  Retired a piece of machinery that was purchased on January 1, 1986. The machine cost $62,000 on that date, and had a useful life of 10 years with no salvage value.

June 30  Sold a computer that was purchased on January 1, 1993. The computer cost $35,000, and had a useful life of 7 years with no salvage value. The computer was sold for $28,000.

Dec. 31  Discarded a delivery truck that was purchased on January 1, 1990. The truck cost $27,000 and was depreciated based on an 8-year useful life with a $3,000 salvage value.

**Instructions**
Journalize all entries required on the above dates, including entries to update depreciation, where applicable, on assets disposed of. Beck Company uses straight-line depreciation. (Assume depreciation is up to date as of December 31, 1995.)

**E10–7**   Presented below are two independent transactions:

*Journalize entries for exchange of similar assets.*
*(SO 6)*

    1. Noyes Co. exchanged trucks (cost $64,000 less $22,000 accumulated depreciation) plus cash of $17,000 for new trucks. The old trucks had a fair market value of $36,000. Prepare the entry to record the exchange of similar assets by Noyes Co.

2. Greg Inc. trades its used accounting machine (cost $12,000 less $4,000 accumulated depreciation) for a new accounting machine. In addition to exchanging the old accounting machine (which had a fair market value of $9,000), Greg also paid cash of $2,000. Prepare the entry to record the exchange of similar assets by Greg Inc.

*Journalize entries for the exchange of similar plant assets.*
*(SO 6)*

**E10–8**  Mueller Company exchanges similar equipment with the Logan Company. Also Evert Company exchanges similar equipment with Flader Company. The following information pertains to these two exchanges:

|  | Mueller Co. | Evert Co. |
|---|---|---|
| Equipment (cost) | $28,000 | $22,000 |
| Accumulated depreciation | 20,000 | 5,000 |
| Fair market value of equipment | 12,000 | 15,000 |
| Cash paid | 3,000 | –0– |

**Instructions**
Prepare the journal entries to record the exchange on the books of Mueller Company and Evert Company.

*Journalize entries for the exchange of similar plant assets.*
*(SO 6)*

**E10–9**  Abner's Delivery Company and Wainwright's Express Delivery exchanged similar delivery trucks on January 1, 1996. Abner's truck cost $18,000, had accumulated depreciation of $13,000, and has a fair market value of $3,000. Wainwright's truck cost $10,000, had accumulated depreciation of $8,000, and has a fair market value of $3,000.

**Instructions**
(a) Journalize the exchange for Abner's Delivery Company.
(b) Journalize the exchange for Wainwright's Express Delivery.

*Journalize entries for natural resources depletion.*
*(SO 7)*

**E10–10**  On July 1, 1996, Phillips Inc. invested $360,000 in a mine estimated to have 600,000 tons of ore of uniform grade. During the last 6 months of 1996, 100,000 tons of ore were mined and sold.

**Instructions**
(a) Prepare the journal entry to record depletion expense.
(b) Assume that the 100,000 tons of ore were mined, but only 80,000 units were sold. How are the costs applicable to the 20,000 unsold units reported?

*Prepare adjusting entries for amortization.*
*(SO 8)*

**E10–11**  The following are selected 1996 transactions of Graf Corporation.

Jan. 1  Purchased a small company and recorded goodwill of $120,000. The goodwill has a useful life of 55 years.

May 1  Purchased a patent with an estimated useful life of 5 years and a legal life of 17 years for $15,000.

**Instructions**
Prepare all adjusting entries at December 31 to record amortization required by the events above.

*Prepare entries to set up appropriate accounts for different intangibles; amortize intangible assets.*
*(SO 8)*

**E10–12**  Collins Company, organized in 1996, has the following transactions related to intangible assets.

| | | |
|---|---|---|
| 1/2/96 | Purchased patent (7-year life) | $350,000 |
| 4/1/96 | Goodwill purchased (indefinite life) | 360,000 |
| 7/1/96 | 10-year franchise; expiration date 7/1/2006 | 450,000 |
| 9/1/96 | Research and development costs | 185,000 |

**Instructions**
Prepare the necessary entries to record these intangibles. All costs incurred were for cash. Make the entries as of December 31, 1996, recording any necessary amortization and reflecting all balances accurately as of that date.

# PROBLEMS

**P10–1**  Jay Weiseman Company was organized on January 1. During the first year of operations, the following plant asset expenditures and receipts were recorded in random order.

*Determine acquisition costs of land and building.*
*(SO 1)*

### Debits

| | |
|---|---:|
| 1. Cost of real estate purchased as a plant site (land $100,000 and building $25,000) | $125,000 |
| 2. Installation cost of fences around property | 4,000 |
| 3. Cost of demolishing building to make land suitable for construction of new building | 13,000 |
| 4. Excavation costs for new building | 20,000 |
| 5. Accrued real estate taxes paid at time of purchase of real estate | 2,000 |
| 6. Cost of parking lots and driveways | 12,000 |
| 7. Architect's fees on building plans | 10,000 |
| 8. Real estate taxes paid for the current year on land | 3,000 |
| 9. Full payment to building contractor | 600,000 |
| | $789,000 |

### Credits

| | |
|---|---:|
| 10. Proceeds from salvage of demolished building | $  2,500 |

**Instructions**
Analyze the foregoing transactions using the following tabular arrangement. Insert the number of each transaction in the Item space and insert the amounts in the appropriate columns. For amounts entered in the Other Accounts column also indicate the account title.

| Item | Land | Building | Other Accounts |
|---|---|---|---|

**P10–2**  In recent years, Wind Company has purchased three machines. Because of heavy turnover in the accounting department, a different accountant was in charge of selecting the depreciation method for each machine, and various methods have been selected. Information concerning the machines is summarized below:

*Compute depreciation under different methods.*
*(SO 3)*

| Machine | Acquired | Cost | Salvage Value | Useful Life in Years | Depreciation Method |
|---|---|---|---|---|---|
| 1 | 1/1/93 | $ 86,000 | $ 6,000 | 10 | Straight-line |
| 2 | 1/1/94 | 100,000 | 10,000 | 8 | Declining-balance |
| 3 | 11/1/96 | 78,000 | 6,000 | 6 | Units-of-activity |

For the declining-balance method, Wind Company uses the double-declining rate. For the units-of-activity method, total machine hours are expected to be 24,000. Actual hours of use in the first 3 years were: 1996, 4,000; 1997, 4,500; and 1998, 5,000.

**Instructions**
  (a) Compute the amount of accumulated depreciation on each machine at December 31, 1996.
  (b) If machine 2 was purchased on April 1 instead of January 1, what is the depreciation expense for this machine in (1) 1994 and (2) 1995?

**P10–3**  Keith Whitley Corporation purchased machinery on January 1, 1996, at a cost of $100,000. The estimated useful life of the machinery is 4 years, with an estimated residual value at the end of that period of $10,000. The company is considering different depreciation methods that could be used for financial reporting purposes.

*Compute depreciation under different methods.*
*(SO 3, 4)*

**Instructions**
  (a) Prepare separate depreciation schedules for the machinery using the straight-line method, and the declining-balance method using double the straight-line rate. Round to the nearest dollar.

(b) Which method would result in the higher reported 1996 income? In the highest total reported income over the 4-year period?

(c) Which method would result in the lower reported 1996 income? In the lowest total reported income over the 4-year period?

*Journalize a series of equipment transactions related to purchase, sale, retirement, and depreciation.*
*(SO 6, 9)*

**P10–4**   At December 31, 1996, Jerry Hamsmith Corporation reported the following as plant assets:

| | | |
|---|---:|---:|
| Land | | $ 3,000,000 |
| Buildings | $26,500,000 | |
| Less: Accumulated depreciation—buildings | 12,100,000 | 14,400,000 |
| Equipment | 40,000,000 | |
| Less: Accumulated depreciation—equipment | 5,000,000 | 35,000,000 |
| Total plant assets | | $52,400,000 |

During 1997, the following selected cash transactions occurred:

April  1  Purchased land for $2,200,000.

May  1  Sold equipment that cost $600,000 when purchased on January 1, 1993. The equipment was sold for $350,000.

June  1  Sold land purchased on June 1, 1987 for $1,800,000. The land cost $500,000.

July  1  Purchased equipment for $1,200,000.

Dec. 31  Retired equipment that cost $500,000 when purchased on December 31, 1987. No salvage value was received.

**Instructions**

(a) Journalize the above transactions. Hamsmith uses straight-line depreciation for buildings and equipment. The buildings are estimated to have a 40-year useful life and no salvage value; the equipment is estimated to have a 10-year useful life and no salvage value. Update depreciation on assets disposed of at the time of sale or retirement.

(b) Record adjusting entries for depreciation for 1997.

(c) Prepare the plant asset section of Hamsmith's balance sheet at December 31, 1997.

*Journalize a series of transactions related to disposals of plant assets.*
*(SO 6)*

**P10–5**   Express Co. has delivery equipment that cost $48,000 and that has been depreciated $20,000. Record the disposal under the following assumptions:

(a) It was scrapped as having no value.

(b) It was sold for $31,000.

(c) It was sold for $18,000.

(d) It was exchanged for similar delivery equipment. The old delivery equipment has a fair market value of $12,000 and $32,000 was paid.

(e) It was exchanged for similar delivery equipment. The old delivery equipment has a fair market value of $35,000 and $9,000 was paid.

*Prepare entries to record transactions related to acquisition and amortization of intangibles; prepare the intangible asset section.*
*(SO 8, 9)*

**P10–6**   The intangible asset section of Roberts Corporation at December 31, 1996, is presented below:

| | |
|---|---:|
| Patent ($60,000 cost less $6,000 amortization) | $54,000 |
| Copyright ($36,000 cost less $14,400 amortization) | 21,600 |
| Total | $75,600 |

The patent was acquired in January of 1996 and has a useful life of 10 years. The copyright was acquired in January of 1993 and also has a useful life of 10 years. The following cash transactions may have affected intangible assets during 1997:

Jan. 2  Paid $9,000 legal costs to successfully defend the patent against infringement by another company.

Jan.–June  Developed a new product incurring $140,000 in research and development costs. A patent was granted for the product on July 1, and its useful life is equal to its legal life.

Sept. 1  Paid $60,000 to a quarterback to appear in commercials advertising the company's products. The commercials will air in September and October.

Oct. 1  Acquired a copyright for $100,000. The copyright has a useful life of 50 years.

## Instructions

(a) Prepare journal entries to record the transactions above.
(b) Prepare journal entries to record the 1997 amortization expense for intangible assets.
(c) Prepare the intangible asset section of the balance sheet at December 31, 1997.
(d) ▮▮▮▮▮▬► Prepare the note to the financials on Roberts' intangibles as of December 31, 1997.

**P10–7**  Due to rapid turnover in the accounting department, a number of transactions involving intangible assets were improperly recorded by Riley Corporation in 1997.

*Prepare entries to correct errors made in recording and amortizing intangible assets.*
*(SO 8)*

1. Riley developed a new manufacturing process, incurring research and development costs of $102,000. The company also purchased a patent for $37,400. In early January, Riley capitalized $139,400 as the cost of the patents. Patent amortization expense of $8,200 was recorded based on a 17-year useful life.
2. On July 1, 1997, Riley purchased a small company and as a result acquired goodwill of $60,000. Riley recorded a half-year's amortization in 1997, based on a 50-year life ($600 amortization).

## Instructions

Prepare all journal entries necessary to correct any errors made during 1997. Assume the books have not yet been closed for 1997.

# ALTERNATE PROBLEMS

**P10–1A**  Jule Kadlec Company was organized on January 1. During the first year of operations, the following plant asset expenditures and receipts were recorded in random order.

*Determine acquisition costs of land and building.*
*(SO 1)*

### Debits

| | |
|---|---:|
| 1. Cost of real estate purchased as a plant site (land $100,000 and building $45,000) | $145,000 |
| 2. Accrued real estate taxes paid at time of purchase of real estate | 2,000 |
| 3. Cost of demolishing building to make land suitable for construction of new building | 12,000 |
| 4. Cost of filling and grading the land | 4,000 |
| 5. Excavation costs for new building | 20,000 |
| 6. Architect's fees on building plans | 10,000 |
| 7. Full payment to building contractor | 700,000 |
| 8. Cost of parking lots and driveways | 14,000 |
| 9. Real estate taxes paid for the current year on land | 5,000 |
| | $912,000 |

### Credits

| | |
|---|---:|
| 10. Proceeds for salvage of demolished building | $ 3,500 |

## Instructions

Analyze the foregoing transactions using the following tabular arrangement. Insert the number of each transaction in the Item space and insert the amounts in the appropriate columns. For amounts entered in the Other Accounts column, also indicate the account titles.

| Item | Land | Building | Other Accounts |
|---|---|---|---|

**P10–2A**  In recent years, Rapid Transportation purchased three used buses. Because of frequent turnover in the accounting department, a different accountant selected the depreciation method for each bus, and various methods have been selected. Information concerning the buses is summarized below:

*Compute depreciation under different methods.*
*(SO 3)*

| Bus | Acquired | Cost | Salvage Value | Useful Life in Years | Depreciation Method |
|-----|----------|------|---------------|----------------------|---------------------|
| 1 | 1/1/94 | $ 96,000 | $ 6,000 | 5 | Straight-line |
| 2 | 1/1/94 | 120,000 | 10,000 | 4 | Declining-balance |
| 3 | 1/1/95 | 80,000 | 8,000 | 5 | Units-of-activity |

For the declining balance method, Rapid Transportation uses the double-declining rate. For the units-of-activity method, total miles are expected to be 120,000. Actual miles of use in the first 3 years were: 1995, 24,000; 1996, 34,000; and 1997, 30,000.

**Instructions**
(a) Compute the amount of accumulated depreciation on each bus at December 31, 1996.
(b) If Bus No. 2 was purchased on April 1 instead of January 1, what is the depreciation expense for this bus in (1) 1994 and (2) 1995?

*Compute depreciation under different methods.*
*(SO 3, 4)*

**P10–3A**  Scott Piper Corporation purchased machinery on January 1, 1996, at a cost of $243,000. The estimated useful life of the machinery is 5 years, with an estimated residual value at the end of that period of $12,000. The company is considering different depreciation methods that could be used for financial reporting purposes.

**Instructions**
(a) Prepare separate depreciation schedules for the machinery using the straight-line method, and the declining-balance method using double the straight-line rate.
(b) Which method would result in the higher reported 1996 income? In the highest total reported income over the 5-year period?
(c) Which method would result in the lower reported 1996 income? In the lowest total reported income over the 5-year period?

*Journalize a series of equipment transactions related to purchase, sale, retirement, and depreciation.*
*(SO 6, 9)*

**P10–4A**  At December 31, 1996, Yount Corporation reported the following as plant assets:

| | | |
|---|---:|---:|
| Land | | $ 4,000,000 |
| Buildings | $28,500,000 | |
| Less: Accumulated depreciation—buildings | 12,100,000 | 16,400,000 |
| Equipment | 48,000,000 | |
| Less: Accumulated depreciation—equipment | 5,000,000 | 43,000,000 |
| Total plant assets | | $63,400,000 |

During 1997, the following selected cash transactions occurred:

April 1   Purchased land for $2,630,000.
May 1    Sold equipment that cost $600,000 when purchased on January 1, 1993. The equipment was sold for $370,000.
June 1   Sold land purchased on June 1, 1987, for $1,800,000. The land cost $200,000.
July 1    Purchased equipment for $1,200,000.
Dec. 31  Retired equipment that cost $500,000 when purchased on December 31, 1987. No salvage value was received.

**Instructions**
(a) Journalize the above transactions. Yount uses straight-line depreciation for buildings and equipment. The buildings are estimated to have a 40-year life and no salvage value; the equipment is estimated to have a 10-year useful life and no salvage value. Update depreciation on assets disposed of at the time of sale or retirement.
(b) Record adjusting entries for depreciation for 1997.
(c) Prepare the plant asset section of Yount's balance sheet at December 31, 1997.

*Journalize a series of transactions related to disposals of plant assets.*
*(SO 6)*

**P10–5A**  Walker Co. has office furniture that cost $80,000 and that has been depreciated $47,000. Record the disposal under the following assumptions:
(a) It was scrapped as having no value.
(b) It was sold for $21,000.
(c) It was sold for $61,000.
(d) It was exchanged for similar office furniture. The old office furniture has a fair market value of $46,000 and $8,000 was paid.
(e) It was exchanged for similar office furniture. The old office furniture has a fair market value of $25,000 and $29,000 was paid.

**P10–6A**  The intangible asset section of Eikel Company at December 31, 1996, is presented below:

*Prepare entries to record transactions related to acquisition and amortization of intangibles; prepare the intangible asset section.*
(SO 8, 9)

| | |
|---|---|
| Patent ($70,000 cost less $7,000 amortization) | $63,000 |
| Copyright ($48,000 cost less $19,200 amortization) | 28,800 |
| Total | $91,800 |

The patent was acquired in January of 1996 and has a useful life of 10 years. The copyright was acquired in January of 1993 and also has a useful life of 10 years. The following cash transactions may have affected intangible assets during 1997:

Jan. 2   Paid $9,000 legal costs to successfully defend the patent against infringement by another company.

Jan.–June   Developed a new product incurring $140,000 in research and development costs. A patent was granted for the product on July 1, and its useful life is equal to its legal life.

Sept. 1   Paid $80,000 to an extremely large defensive lineman to appear in commercials advertising the company's products. The commercials will air in September and October.

Oct. 1   Acquired a copyright for $80,000. The copyright has a useful life of 50 years.

**Instructions**
(a)  Prepare journal entries to record the transactions above.
(b)  Prepare journal entries to record the 1997 amortization expense.
(c)  Prepare the intangible asset section of the balance sheet at December 31, 1997.

**P10–7A**  Due to rapid turnover in the accounting department, a number of transactions involving intangible assets were improperly recorded by the Glover Company in 1997.

*Prepare entries to correct for errors made in recording and amortizing intangible assets.*
(SO 8)

1. Glover developed a new manufacturing process, incurring research and development costs of $136,000. The company also purchased a patent for $39,100. In early January, Glover capitalized $175,100 as the cost of the patents. Patent amortization expense of $10,300 was recorded based on a 17-year useful life.
2. On July 1, 1997, Glover purchased a small company and as a result acquired goodwill of $76,000. Glover recorded a half-year's amortization in 1997, based on a 50-year life ($760 amortization).

**Instructions**
Prepare all journal entries necessary to correct any errors made during 1997. Assume the books have not yet been closed for 1997.

# ▶**B**roadening Your Perspective

## **F**INANCIAL REPORTING PROBLEM
••••••••••••••••••••••••••••••••••••••••••••••••••••••••••••••

Refer to the financial statements and the Notes to Consolidated Financial Statements of PepsiCo, Inc. in Appendix A, and answer the following questions:

(a)  What was the total cost and book value of property, plant, and equipment at December 31, 1994?
(b)  What method or methods of depreciation are used by PepsiCo for financial reporting purposes?
(c)  What was the amount of depreciation expense for each of the three years 1992–1994?
(d)  Using the Statement of Cash Flows, what is the amount of property, plant, and equipment purchased (capital spending) in 1994 and 1993?
(e)  Identify the primary reason why PepsiCo has goodwill and other intangibles.
(f)  What was the amortization for goodwill and other intangibles in 1994, and where

was it reported in the income statement? Was it more or less than 1993? What useful life was used to amortize goodwill and other intangibles?
(g) What was the amount of research and development expenses PepsiCo incurred in 1994?

# DECISION CASE

Tammy Company and Hamline Company are two proprietorships that are similar in many respects except that Tammy Company uses the straight-line method and Hamline Company uses the declining-balance method at double the straight-line rate. On January 2, 1994, both companies acquired the following depreciable assets.

| Asset | Cost | Salvage Value | Useful Life |
|---|---|---|---|
| Building | $320,000 | $20,000 | 40 years |
| Equipment | 110,000 | 10,000 | 10 years |

Including the appropriate depreciation charges, annual net income for the companies in the years 1994, 1995, and 1996 and total income for the 3 years were as follows:

| | 1994 | 1995 | 1996 | Total |
|---|---|---|---|---|
| Tammy Company | $84,000 | $88,400 | $90,000 | $262,400 |
| Hamline Company | 68,000 | 76,000 | 85,000 | 229,000 |

At December 31, 1996, the balance sheets of the two companies are similar except that Hamline Company has more cash than Tammy Company.

Dawna Tucci is interested in buying one of the companies, and she comes to you for advice.

*Instructions*
(a) Determine the annual and total depreciation recorded by each company during the 3 years.
(b) Assuming that Hamline Company also uses the straight-line method of depreciation instead of the declining-balance method as in (a), prepare comparative income data for the 3 years.
(c) Which company should Mrs. Tucci buy? Why?

# COMMUNICATION ACTIVITY

The following was published with the financial statements to American Exploration Company:

**Property, Plant and Equipment**—The Company accounts for its oil and gas exploration and production activities using the successful efforts method of accounting. Under this method, acquisition costs for proved and unproved properties are capitalized when incurred.... The costs of drilling exploratory wells are capitalized pending determination of whether each well has discovered proved reserves. If proved reserves are not discovered, such drilling costs are charged to expense.... Depletion of the cost of producing oil and gas properties is computed on the units-of-activity method.

*Instructions*
Write a brief memo to your instructor discussing American Exploration Company's footnote regarding property, plant and equipment. Your memo should address what is meant by the "successful efforts method" and "units-of-activity method."

# GROUP ACTIVITY

With the class divided into three groups, each group should be assigned one of the following depreciation methods: straight-line, units-of-activity, declining-balance.

*Instructions*
    (a) Think of an example using the methodology assigned. Calculate depreciation for the first 2 years of useful life.
    (b) Present your example to the class. Include necessary journal entries.

# ETHICS CASE

Imporia Container Company is suffering declining sales of its principal product, nonbiodegradeable plastic cartons. The president, Benny Benson, instructs his controller, John Straight, to lengthen asset lives to reduce depreciation expense. A processing line of automated plastic extruding equipment, purchased for $2.7 million in January 1996 was originally estimated to have a useful life of 8 years and a salvage value of $300,000. Depreciation has been recorded for 2 years on that basis. Benny wants the estimated life changed to 12 years total, and the straight-line method continued. John is hesitant to make the change, believing it is unethical to increase net income in this manner. Benny says, "Hey, the life is only an estimate, and I've heard that our competition uses a 12-year life on their production equipment."

*Instructions*
    (a) Who are the stakeholders in this situation?
    (b) Is the change in asset life unethical or simply a good business practice by an astute president?
    (c) What is the effect of Benny Benson's proposed change on income before taxes in the year of change?

# CRITICAL THINKING
## ▸ *A Real-World Focus: Clark Equipment Company*

*Clark Equipment Company was originally formed in 1902 as a general manufacturing company. During its history it has specialized in the manufacture of drills, gears, towing tractors, and truck transmissions. Today the company operates throughout the U.S. and Europe in the design, manufacture, and sale of skid steer loaders, construction machinery, and transmissions for on-highway trucks and for off-highway equipment. It also is involved in a 50–50 joint venture with Volvo in the manufacture of construction equipment.*

The following information relates to the plant assets of Clark Equipment:

| | (All amounts in millions) | |
| | 1993 | 1994 |
|---|---|---|
| Land | $ 7.4 | $ 13.2 |
| Land improvements | 5.9 | 8.8 |
| Buildings | 77.3 | 126.0 |
| Machinery and equipment | 398.4 | 451.7 |
| Totals | 489.0 | 599.7 |
| Accumulated depreciation | 272.8 | 315.9 |
| Total plant assets | $216.2 | $283.8 |

**Instructions**

(a) What type of costs would Clark Equipment capitalize in the land category of plant assets?

(b) Cite several possible types of land improvements that Clark Equipment might have made.

(c) What is the book value of Clark Equipment's plant assets?

---

**Answers to Self-Study Questions**

1. d    2. b    3. d    4. d    5. b    6. d    7. a    8. c    9. c    10. b    11. c

**Before studying this chapter, you should know or, if necessary, review:**

**a.** *The importance of liquidity in evaluating the financial position of a company. (Ch. 4, p. 153)*

**b.** *How to make adjusting entries related to unearned revenue (Ch. 3, pp. 96–7) and accrued expenses. (Ch. 3, pp. 100–102)*

**c.** *The principles of internal control. (Ch. 7, p. 285)*

# No Computer? Your Paycheck May Be Late

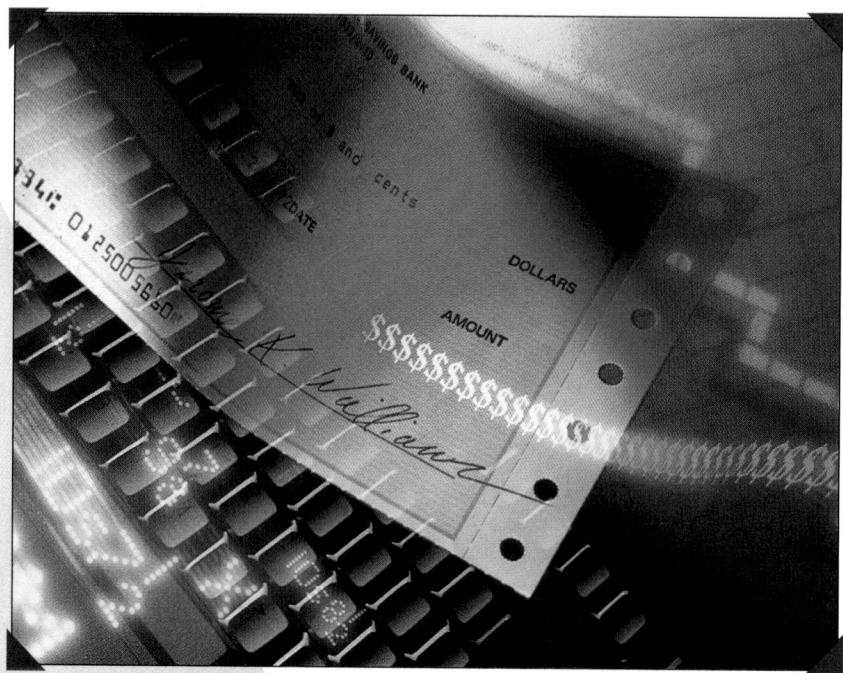

CASPER, Wyo. — When it comes to payroll, colleges are very much like the "real world." There's a payroll supervisor, a few clerks, a giant computer, reams of computer printouts—and, of course, paychecks.

Mrs. Dianna Webb is the payroll supervisor at Casper College in Casper, Wyoming, a school with 6,000 students and 550 people on the payroll. "I take out tax deductions, credit union contributions, contributions to tax-sheltered annuities, United Way donations, and even garnishments when an employee has been ordered by a court to pay a debt. Wyoming has no state income tax, so that's one deduction I don't have to worry about."

The payroll staff consists of just Mrs. Webb and the computer. Their job: To process monthly checks for the faculty, administrators, and students and semi-monthly checks for staff. What if she didn't have a computer? "I doubt I'd be able to pay as many people," she laughs.

Just as in any other business, Dianna Webb keeps timecards for all hourly employees. The faculty and administrators—salaried employees—are on the honor system to work the required number of hours, but even their pay has to be authorized.

The computer provides Dianna Webb with many useful reports: The main report shows the payroll in alphabetical order, listing gross pay, tax deductions, other payroll deductions, and net pay. She also gets a report that lists year-to-date totals. "In May, faculty members get paid the balance on their contracts, so I need to know those year-to-date totals."

Student employees provide one extra wrinkle: They don't have Social Security (FICA) taxes withheld during the school year. The reason: Federal regulations consider students who work for the college and are enrolled and attend classes to be exempt from Social Security and Medicare taxes. For work done during the summer months, though, Social Security taxes are withheld. ◄

# CHAPTER · 11

# CURRENT LIABILITIES AND PAYROLL ACCOUNTING

## ▶ STUDY OBJECTIVES ◀

### After studying this chapter, you should be able to:

1. *Explain a current liability and identify the major types of current liabilities.*
2. *Describe the accounting for notes payable.*
3. *Explain the accounting for other current liabilities.*
4. *Describe the accounting and disclosure requirements for contingent liabilities.*
5. *Discuss the objectives of internal control for payroll.*
6. *Compute and record the payroll for a pay period.*
7. *Describe and record employer payroll taxes.*
8. *Identify additional fringe benefits associated with employee compensation.*

Whether it be a college like Casper College, a pizza parlor like Pizza Hut, a public accounting firm like Arthur Andersen & Co., or a large multinational company like IBM, all enterprises have liabilities for payroll. In addition, they also have many other types of liabilities. Examples are the purchase of supplies on account, the borrowing of money on a bank loan, and the obligation to pay interest. Liabilities are classified as current or long-term on the balance sheet. We will explain current liabilities in this chapter and long-term liabilities in Chapter 16. The content and organization of this chapter are as follows:

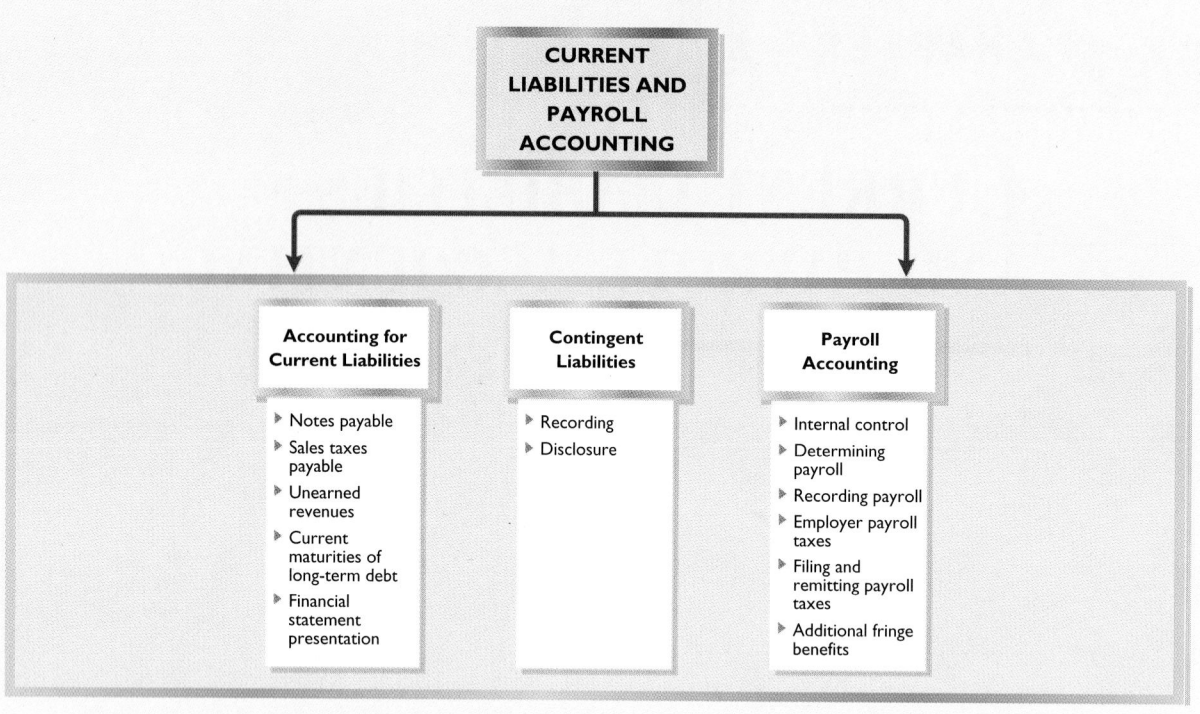

## Accounting for Current Liabilities

As explained in Chapter 4, a **current liability** is a debt that can reasonably be expected to be paid (1) from existing current assets or through the creation of other current liabilities, and (2) within one year or the operating cycle, whichever is longer. Debts that do not meet both criteria are classified as long-term liabilities. In most companies, current liabilities are paid within one year out of current assets, rather than through the creation of other liabilities.

Companies must carefully monitor the relationship of current liabilities to current assets. This relationship is critical in evaluating a company's liquidity, or short-term debt paying ability. A company that has more current liabilities than current assets is usually the subject of some concern because the company may not be able to meet its current obligations when they become due.

Current liabilities include notes payable, accounts payable, unearned revenues, and accrued liabilities such as taxes, salaries and wages, and interest payable. The entries for accounts payable and adjusting entries for some current liabilities have been explained in previous chapters. Other types of current liabilities that are frequently encountered in practice are discussed in the following sections.

## Notes Payable

Obligations in the form of written promissory notes are recorded as notes payable. Notes payable are often used instead of accounts payable. Doing so gives the lender written documentation of the obligation in case legal remedies are needed to collect the debt. Notes payable usually require the borrower to pay interest and frequently are issued to meet short-term financing needs.

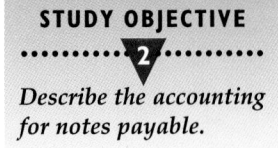

**STUDY OBJECTIVE**
············**2**············

*Describe the accounting for notes payable.*

Notes are issued for varying periods. **Those due for payment within one year of the balance sheet date are usually classified as current liabilities.** Most notes are interest bearing. To illustrate the accounting for notes payable, assume that First National Bank agrees to lend $100,000 on March 1, 1996, if Cole Williams Co. signs a $100,000, 12%, 4-month note. With an interest-bearing promissory note, the amount of assets received upon issuance of the note generally equals the note's face value. Cole Williams Co. therefore will receive $100,000 cash and will make the following journal entry:

| | | | |
|---|---|---|---|
| Mar. 1 | Cash | 100,000 | |
| |     Notes Payable | | 100,000 |
| |     (To record issuance of 12%, 4-month note to | | |
| |     First National Bank) | | |

Interest accrues over the life of the note and must be recorded periodically. If Cole Williams Co. prepares financial statements semiannually, an adjusting entry is required to recognize interest expense and interest payable of $4,000 ($100,000 × 12% × 4/12) at June 30. The adjusting entry is:

| | | | |
|---|---|---|---|
| June 30 | Interest Expense | 4,000 | |
| |     Interest Payable | | 4,000 |
| |     (To accrue interest for 4 months on First | | |
| |     National Bank note) | | |

In the June 30 financial statements, the current liability section of the balance sheet will show notes payable $100,000 and interest payable $4,000. In addition, interest expense of $4,000 will be reported under Other Expenses and Losses in the income statement. If Cole Williams Co. prepared financial statements monthly, the adjusting entry at the end of each month would have been $1,000 ($100,000 × 12% × 1/12).

At maturity (July 1), Cole Williams Co. must pay the face value of the note ($100,000) plus $4,000 interest ($100,000 × 12% × 4/12). The entry to record payment of the note and accrued interest is as follows:

| | | | |
|---|---|---|---|
| July 1 | Notes Payable | 100,000 | |
| | Interest Payable | 4,000 | |
| |     Cash | | 104,000 |
| |     (To record payment of First National Bank | | |
| |     interest-bearing note and accrued interest at | | |
| |     maturity) | | |

## Sales Taxes Payable

As consumers, we are well aware that many of the products we purchase at retail stores are subject to sales taxes. The tax is expressed as a stated percentage of the sales price. The retailer (or selling company) collects the tax from the customer when the sale occurs, and periodically (usually monthly) remits the collections to the state's department of revenue.

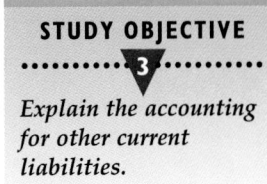

**STUDY OBJECTIVE**
············**3**············

*Explain the accounting for other current liabilities.*

Under most state sales tax laws, the amount of the sale and the amount of the sales tax collected must be rung up separately on the cash register. (Gasoline

**Helpful hint**  Watch how sales are rung up at local retailers, to see whether the sales tax is computed separately.

sales are a major exception.) The cash register readings are then used to credit Sales and Sales Taxes Payable. For example, assuming that the March 25 cash register readings for Cooley Grocery show sales of $10,000 and sales taxes of $600 (sales tax rate of 6%), the entry is:

| | | | |
|---|---|---|---|
| Mar. 25 | Cash | 10,600 | |
| | Sales | | 10,000 |
| | Sales Taxes Payable | | 600 |
| | (To record daily sales and sales taxes) | | |

When the taxes are remitted to the taxing agency, Sales Taxes Payable is debited and Cash is credited. The company does not report sales taxes as an expense; it simply forwards the amount paid by the customer to the government. Thus, Cooley Grocery serves only as a **collection agent** for the taxing authority.

When sales taxes are not rung up separately on the cash register, total receipts are divided by 100% plus the sales tax percentage to determine sales. To illustrate, assume in the above example that Cooley Grocery "rings up" total receipts, which are $10,600. Because the amount received from the sale is equal to the sales price 100% plus 6% of sales, or 1.06 times the sales total, we can compute sales as follows:

$$\$10,600 \div 1.06 = \$10,000.$$

Thus, the sales tax amount of $600 is found either by (1) subtracting sales from total receipts ($10,600 − $10,000) or (2) multiplying sales by the sales tax rate ($10,000 × 6%).

## ▶ Accounting in Action ▸ *Business Insight*

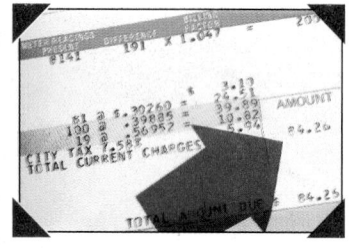

Sales taxes do not apply exclusively to retail companies. They also apply to manufacturing companies, service companies, and public utilities, and the extent of the taxes is increasing. There are now over 9,000 state and local sales taxes. "Compliance is becoming much more complex as states expand their sales taxes," says an American Telephone and Telegraph (AT&T) tax attorney. They are also becoming more costly. AT&T employs 76 people to file the company's sales tax returns each year. They also handle the 200 sales tax audits AT&T is presently undergoing.

*Source: Forbes, September 30, 1991.*

### Unearned Revenues

A magazine publisher such as Sports Illustrated may receive a customer's check when magazines are ordered, and an airline company, such as American Airlines, often receives cash when it sells tickets for future flights. How do these companies account for unearned revenues that are received before goods are delivered or services are rendered?

1. When the advance is received, Cash is debited, and a current liability account identifying the source of the unearned revenue is credited.
2. When the revenue is earned, the unearned revenue account is debited, and an earned revenue account is credited.

To illustrate, assume that Superior University sells 10,000 season football tickets at $50 each for its five-game home schedule. The entry for the sales of season tickets is:

| Aug. 6 | Cash | 500,000 | |
|---|---|---|---|
| |     Unearned Football Ticket Revenue | | 500,000 |
| |     (To record sale of 10,000 season tickets) | | |

As each game is completed, the following entry is made:

| Sept. 7 | Unearned Football Ticket Revenue | 100,000 | |
|---|---|---|---|
| |     Football Ticket Revenue | | 100,000 |
| |     (To record football ticket revenues earned) | | |

Unearned Football Ticket Revenue is, therefore, unearned revenue and is reported as a current liability in the balance sheet. As revenue is earned, a transfer from unearned revenue to earned revenue occurs. Unearned revenue is material for some companies: In the airline industry, tickets sold for future flights represent almost 50% of total current liabilities. At United Air Lines, unearned ticket revenue is the largest current liability, recently amounting to over $1 billion.

Illustration 11-1 shows specific unearned and earned revenue accounts used in selected types of businesses.

| Type of Business | Account Title | |
|---|---|---|
| | **Unearned Revenue** | **Earned Revenue** |
| Airline | Unearned Passenger Ticket Revenue | Passenger Revenue |
| Magazine publisher | Unearned Subscription Revenue | Subscription Revenue |
| Hotel | Unearned Rental Revenue | Rental Revenue |

**Illustration 11-1**

*Unearned and earned revenue accounts*

## Current Maturities of Long-Term Debt

Companies often have a portion of long-term debt that comes due in the current year. For example, assume that Wendy Construction issues a 5-year interest-bearing $25,000 note on January 1, 1996. This note specifies that each January 1, starting January 1, 1997, $5,000 of the note should be paid. When financial statements are prepared on December 31, 1996, $5,000 should be reported as a current liability and $20,000 as a long-term liability. Current maturities of long-term debt are often identified on the balance sheet as **long-term debt due within one year**.

It is not necessary to prepare an adjusting entry to recognize the current maturity of long-term debt. The proper statement classification of each balance sheet account is recognized when the balance sheet is prepared.

## Financial Statement Presentation

As indicated in Chapter 4, current liabilities are the first category under liabilities on the balance sheet. Each of the principal types of current liabilities is listed separately within the category. In addition, the terms of notes payable and other pertinent information concerning the individual items are disclosed in the notes to the financial statements.

Current liabilities are seldom listed in the order of maturity because of the varying maturity dates that may exist for specific obligations such as notes payable. A more common, and entirely satisfactory, method of presenting current liabilities is to list them by **order of magnitude**, with the largest obligations first. Many companies, as a matter of custom, show notes payable and accounts payable first, regardless of amount. The following adapted excerpt from a recent balance sheet of USX Corp. illustrates this practice.

**Helpful hint** For another example of a current liability section refer to the PepsiCo balance sheet in Appendix A.

**Illustration 11-2**

*Balance sheet presentation of current liabilities*

| USX CORP. | |
|---|---|
| **Current Liabilities (in millions)** | |
| Notes payable | $ 138 |
| Accounts payable | 2,196 |
| Payroll and benefits payable | 243 |
| Taxes payable | 415 |
| Interest payable | 113 |
| Long-term debt due within one year | 197 |
| Total current liabilities | 3,302 |

# Contingent Liabilities

**STUDY OBJECTIVE**

**4**

*Describe the accounting and disclosure requirements for contingent liabilities.*

**Helpful hint** Another example of a contingency is toxic waste. Corporations have increasingly been held liable for toxic waste cleanup. Some expect that insurance will cover these costs, but insurance companies are arguing that (1) intentional discharges are not covered and (2) general liability policies were never meant to cover this type of situation.

With notes payable, interest payable, accounts payable, and sales taxes payable, we know that an obligation exists to make payment. But suppose that your company is currently involved in a dispute with the Internal Revenue Service (IRS) over the amount of its income tax liability. Do you have to report the disputed amount on the balance sheet as a liability? Or suppose your company is the defendant in a lawsuit in which an adverse decision might result in bankruptcy. How should this major contingency be reported? The answers to these questions are difficult, because these liabilities are dependent—contingent—upon some future event. In other words, a contingent liability is a potential liability that may become an actual liability in the future.

How, then, should contingent liabilities be reported? Guidelines have been adopted that are helpful in resolving these problems. The guidelines require that:

1. If the contingency is **probable**—if it is likely to occur—**and** the amount can be **reasonably estimated**, the liability should be recorded in the accounts.
2. If the contingency is only **reasonably possible**—if it could happen—then it need be disclosed only in the notes accompanying the financial statements.
3. If the contingency is **remote**—if it is unlikely to occur—it need not be recorded or disclosed.

## Recording a Contingent Liability

Product warranties are a good example of a contingent liability that should be recorded in the accounts. Warranty contracts result in future costs that may be incurred in replacing defective units or repairing malfunctioning units without

## ▸Accounting in Action ▸ *Business Insight*

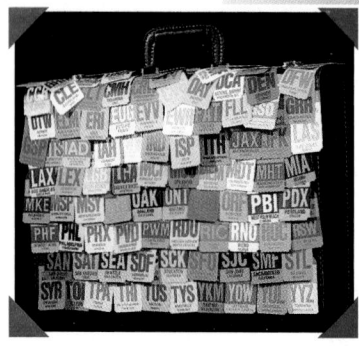

Contingent liabilities abound in the real world. Consider the following: Manville Corp. filed bankruptcy when it was hit by billions of dollars in asbestos product liability claims. Companies having multiple toxic waste sites are faced with cleanup costs that average $10 to $30 million and can reach as high as $500 million depending on the type of waste. For life and health insurance companies and their stockholders, the cost of AIDS is like an iceberg—everybody wonders how big it really is and what damage it might do in the future; according to the U.S. Centers for Disease Control treatment costs could be $8 billion to $16 billion. And frequent-flyer programs are so popular that airlines at one time owed participants more than 3 million round-trip domestic tickets. That's enough to fly at least 5.4 billion miles—free for the passengers but at what future cost to the airlines?

charge to the customer for a specified period after the product is sold. Generally, a manufacturer, such as Black & Decker, knows that some warranty costs will be incurred. Moreover, on the basis of prior experience with the product (or similar products), the company usually can make a reasonable estimate of the anticipated cost of servicing (honoring) the contract.

The accounting for warranty costs is based on the matching principle. To comply with this principle, **the estimated cost of honoring product warranty contracts should be recognized as an expense in the period in which the sale occurs**. To illustrate, assume that in 1996 Denson Manufacturing Company sells 10,000 washers and dryers at an average price of $600 each. The selling price includes a one-year warranty on parts. It is expected that 500 units (5%) will be defective and that warranty repair costs will average $80 per unit. In the year of sale, warranty contracts are honored on 300 units at a total cost of $24,000.

At December 31, it is necessary to accrue the estimated warranty costs on the 1996 sales. The computation is as follows:

**Illustration 11-3**

*Computation of estimated product warranty liability*

| | |
|---|---:|
| Number of units sold | 10,000 |
| Estimated rate of defective units | × 5% |
| Total estimated defective units | 500 |
| Average warranty repair cost | × $80 |
| **Estimated product warranty liability** | **$40,000** |

The adjusting entry, therefore, is:

**Helpful hint** The effects of the warranty adjusting entry are an increase in expenses and an increase in liabilities; the effects of the entry to record the honoring of the warranty are a decrease in one liability and either a decrease in assets or an increase in another liability.

| Dec. 31 | Warranty Expense | 40,000 | |
|---|---|---|---|
| | Estimated Warranty Liability | | 40,000 |
| | (To accrue estimated warranty costs) | | |

The entry to record repair costs incurred in 1996 to honor warranty contracts on 1996 sales is shown in summary form below:

| Jan. 1– | Estimated Warranty Liability | 24,000 | |
|---|---|---|---|
| Dec. 31 | Repair Parts/Wages Payable | | 24,000 |
| | (To record honoring of 300 warranty contracts on 1996 sales) | | |

Warranty expense of $40,000 is reported under selling expenses in the income statement, and estimated warranty liability of $16,000 ($40,000 − $24,000) is classified as a current liability on the balance sheet.

In the following year, all expenses incurred in honoring warranty contracts on 1996 sales should be debited to Estimated Warranty Liability. To illustrate, assume that 20 defective units are replaced in January 1997, at an average cost of $80 in parts and labor. The summary entry for the month of January is:

| Jan. 31 | Estimated Warranty Liability | 1,600 | |
|---|---|---|---|
| | Repair Parts/Wages Payable | | 1,600 |
| | (To record honoring of 20 warranty contracts on 1996 sales) | | |

## Disclosure of Contingent Liabilities

When a contingent liability meets one but not both conditions for recording the contingency described above, or when the contingent liability is only reasonably possible, only disclosure of the contingency is required. Examples of contingen-

► ***International note***

International accounting standards basically use the same criteria in determining how to account for contingencies.

cies that may require disclosure are pending or threatened lawsuits and assessment of additional income taxes pending an IRS audit of the tax return.

The disclosure should identify the nature of the item, and if known, the amount of the contingency and the expected outcome of the future event. Disclosure is usually accomplished through a note to the financial statements, as illustrated by the following:

**Illustration 11-4**

*Disclosure of contingent liability*

| **USAir** |
| --- |
| **Legal Proceedings** |
| The Company and various subsidiaries have been named as defendants in various suits and proceedings which involve, among other things, environmental concerns about noise and air pollution and employment matters. These suits and proceedings are in various stages of litigation, and the status of the law with respect to several of the issues involved is unsettled. For these reasons the outcome of these suits and proceedings is difficult to predict. In the Company's opinion, however, the disposition of these matters is not likely to have a material adverse effect on its financial condition. |

## Before You Go On . . .

### ▸ Review It

1. What are the two criteria for classifying a debt as a current liability?
2. What entries are made for an interest-bearing note payable?
3. How are sales taxes recorded by a retailer? Identify three unearned revenues.
4. What are the accounting guidelines for contingent liabilities?

### ▸ Do It

You and several classmates are studying for the next accounting examination. They ask you to answer the following questions: (1) How is the sales tax amount determined when the cash register total includes sales taxes? (2) When should a contingency be recorded in the accounts?

**Reasoning:** To answer the first question, you must remove the sales taxes from the total sales. To answer the second question, you need to know the criteria for recording and disclosing contingent liabilities.

**Solution:**

(1) First, divide the total proceeds by 100% plus the sales tax percentage to find the sales amount; second, subtract the sales amount from the total proceeds to determine the sales taxes.

(2) A contingency should be recorded when it is *probable* that it will happen and the amount can be *reasonably* estimated.

*Related exercise material:* BE11–3, BE11–4, BE11–5, E11–2, E11–3, E11–4, and E11–5.

## �*P*ayroll Accounting

Payroll and related fringe benefits often constitute a substantial percentage of current liabilities. In addition, employee compensation is often the most significant expense that a company incurs. For example, General Motors recently reported total employees of 516,000 and labor costs of $31.3 billion. Add to labor costs such fringe benefits as health insurance, life insurance, disability insurance, and so on, and you can see why proper accounting and control of payroll are so important.

It should be emphasized that payroll accounting involves more than paying employees' wages. Companies are required by law to maintain payroll records for each employee, file and pay payroll taxes, and comply with numerous state and federal tax laws applicable to employee compensation. Accounting for payroll has become much more complex as a result of these regulations.

The term "payroll" pertains to all salaries and wages paid to employees. Managerial, administrative, and sales personnel are generally paid salaries, which are often expressed in terms of a specified amount per month or per year. For example, in the opening story the faculty and administrative personnel at Casper College are paid salaries. In contrast, store clerks, factory employees, and manual laborers are normally paid wages, which are based on a rate per hour or on a piecework basis (such as per unit of product). Frequently, the terms "salaries" and "wages" are used interchangeably.

The term "payroll" does not extend to payments made for personal service by professionals such as certified public accountants, attorneys, and architects. Such professionals are independent contractors, and payments to them are called **fees**, rather than salaries or wages. This distinction is important because government regulations relating to the payment and reporting of payroll taxes apply only to employees.

## Internal Control

Internal control was introduced in Chapter 7. As applied to payrolls, the objectives of internal control are (1) to safeguard company assets against unauthorized payments of payrolls and (2) to assure the accuracy and reliability of the accounting records pertaining to payrolls.

Unfortunately, irregularities often result if internal control is lax. Overstating hours, using unauthorized pay rates, adding fictitious employees to the payroll, continuing terminated employees on the payroll, and distributing duplicate payroll checks are all methods of stealing from a company. Moreover, inaccurate records will result in incorrect paychecks, financial statements, and payroll tax returns.

Payroll activities involve four functions: hiring employees, timekeeping, preparing the payroll, and paying the payroll. For an internal control system to work effectively, these four functions should be assigned to different departments or individuals. To illustrate these functions in more detail, we will examine the case of Academy Company and one of its employees, Michael Jordan.

### STUDY OBJECTIVE
••••••••••▼**5**••••••••••
*Discuss the objectives of internal control for payroll.*

## ▲*Technology in Action*

  A Senate hearing revealed that the U.S. Army spent $8 million on unauthorized pay, including payments to 76 deserters and six "ghost" soldiers. The underlying cause was a computer system so lax that it was possible to create new pay records and destroy old ones without leaving an audit trail.

*Source: Ann Arbor News, April 13, 1994, p. A4.*

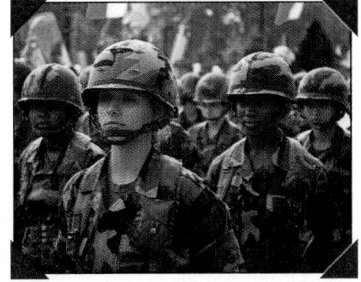

### *Hiring Employees*

Posting job openings, screening and interviewing applicants, and hiring employees are responsibilities of the personnel department. From a control standpoint, the personnel department provides significant documentation and authorization. When an employee is hired, the personnel department prepares an authorization form like the one used by Academy Company for Michael Jordan shown in Illustration 11-5.

**Illustration 11-5**

*Personnel authorization form*

**Hiring Employees**

Personnel department documents and authorizes employment.

### ACADEMY COMPANY

| | |
|---|---|
| Employee Name __Jordan,__ __Michael__ ___ | Starting Date __9/01/92__ |
| LAST · FIRST · MI | |
| Classification __Skilled-Level 10__ | Social Security No. __329-36-9547__ |
| Department __Shipping__ | Division __Entertainment__ |

| | |
|---|---|
| **NEW HIRE** | Classification __Clerk__     Salary Grade __Level 10__   Trans. from Temp. ☐ <br> Rate $__10.00__ per __hour__    Bonus __N/A__   Non-exempt ☒ Exempt ☐ |
| **RATE CHANGE** | New Rate $ __12.00__    Effective Date __9/1/94__ <br> Present Rate $ __10.00__ <br> Merit ☒ Promotion ☐ Decrease ☐   Other _____ <br> Previous Increase Date __None__   Amount $____ per____ Type____ |
| **SEPARATION** | Resignation ☐ Discharge ☐ Retirement ☐   Reason _____ <br> <br> Leave of absence ☐ From____ to____ Type_____ <br> Last Day Worked _____ |
| **APPROVALS** | *BEW*    9/1/92      *EMW*    9-1-94 <br> BRANCH OR DEPT. MANAGER   DATE     DIVISION V.P.    DATE <br>                                       *James E. Speer* <br>                                    PERSONNEL DEPARTMENT |

The authorization form is sent to the payroll department, where it is used to place the new employee on the payroll. A chief concern of the personnel department is ensuring the accuracy of this form. The reason is quite simple: one of the most common types of payroll frauds is adding fictitious employees to the payroll.

The personnel department is also responsible for authorizing (1) changes in pay rates during employment and (2) terminations of employment. In each instance, the authorization should be in writing, and a copy of the change in status should be sent to the payroll department. Note in Illustration 11-5 that Jordan received a pay increase of $2 per hour.

### Timekeeping

**Timekeeping**

Supervisors monitor hours worked through time cards and time reports.

Another area in which internal control is important is timekeeping. Hourly employees are usually required to record time worked by "punching" a time clock. The time of arrival and departure are automatically recorded by the employee when he or she inserts a time card into the clock. The time card for Michael Jordan is shown in Illustration 11-6.

In large companies, time clock procedures are often monitored by a supervisor or security guard to make sure an employee punches only one card. At the end of the pay period, the employee's supervisor is required to approve the hours shown by signing the time card. When overtime hours are involved, approval by a supervisor is usually mandatory to guard against unauthorized overtime.

**Illustration 11-6**

*Time card*

| | | | PAY PERIOD ENDING | |
|---|---|---|---|---|
| No. 17 | | | | 1/14/96 |

NAME  Michael Jordan

| EXTRA TIME | | | REGULAR TIME |
|---|---|---|---|
| | | 1st Day | A.M. IN | 8:58 |
| | | | NOON OUT | 12:00 |
| | | | IN | 1:00 |
| | | | P.M. OUT | 5:01 |
| | | 2nd Day | A.M. IN | 9:00 |
| | | | NOON OUT | 11:59 |
| | | | IN | 12:59 |
| | | | P.M. OUT | 5:00 |
| | THIS SIDE OUT | 3rd Day | A.M. IN | 8:59 |
| | | | NOON OUT | 12:01 |
| | | | IN | 1:01 |
| | | | P.M. OUT | 5:00 |
| 5:00 | | 4th Day | A.M. IN | 9:00 |
| 9:00 | | | NOON OUT | 12:00 |
| | | | IN | 1:00 |
| | | | P.M. OUT | 5:00 |
| | | 5th Day | A.M. IN | 8:57 |
| | | | NOON OUT | 11:58 |
| | | | IN | 1:00 |
| | | | P.M. OUT | 5:01 |
| | | 6th Day | A.M. IN | 8:00 |
| | | | NOON OUT | 1:00 |
| | | | IN | |
| | | | P.M. OUT | |
| | | 7th Day | A.M. IN | |
| | | | NOON OUT | |
| | | | IN | |
| | | | P.M. OUT | |
| TOTAL 4 | | | TOTAL | 40 |

## ▶*A*ccounting in *A*ction ▶ *Business Insight*

The annual pay raise may soon be passé. Large companies such as American Express and Eastman Kodak and some small companies are linking pay more directly to the performance of both the worker and the company. The performance measures include product quality, on-time delivery, and customer satisfaction. If the company and the worker have a good year, a fatter paycheck is the reward. If the reverse is true, down goes the paycheck. Under the plan, a worker's base annual salary remains the same from year to year.

The approved time card is then sent to the payroll department. For salaried employees, a manually prepared weekly or monthly time report kept by a supervisor may be used to record time worked.

### Preparing the Payroll

The payroll is prepared in the payroll department on the basis of two sources of input: (1) personnel department authorizations and (2) approved time cards. Because of the numerous calculations involved in determining gross wages and payroll deductions, it is customary for a second payroll department employee, working independently, to verify all amounts, and a payroll department supervisor then approves the payroll. The payroll department is also responsible for preparing (but not signing) payroll checks, maintaining payroll records, and preparing payroll tax returns.

**Preparing the Payroll**

Two (or more) employees verify payroll amounts; supervisor approves.

## ▸Accounting in Action ▸ *Business Insight*

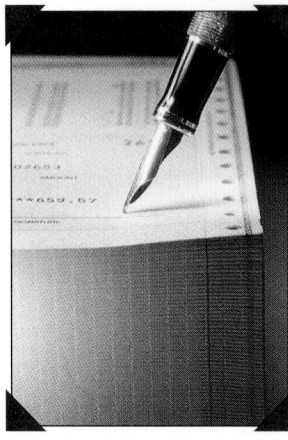

Payroll processing is considered by many small business owners to be a tedious and painful chore fraught with legal and tax headaches. As a result, service bureaus that process payrolls for small businesses are becoming increasingly popular. Small businesses appreciate the advantages service bureaus offer: relatively low cost, simplicity, confidentiality, accuracy, and keeping up to date on changes in tax rates and laws.

### Paying the Payroll

The payroll is paid by the treasurer's department. **Payment by check minimizes the risk of loss from theft, and the endorsed check provides proof of payment.** For good internal control, payroll checks should be prenumbered, and all checks should be accounted for. All checks must be signed by the treasurer (or a designated agent), and their distribution to employees should be controlled by the treasurer's department. Checks may be distributed by the treasurer or paymaster.

If the payroll is paid in currency, it is customary to have a second person count the cash in each pay envelope and for the paymaster to obtain a signed receipt from the employee upon payment. Thus, if alleged discrepancies arise, adequate safeguards have been established to protect each party involved.

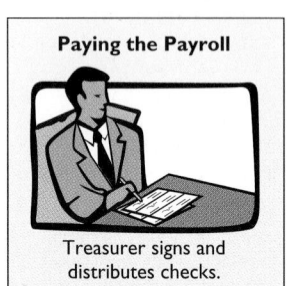

**Paying the Payroll**

Treasurer signs and distributes checks.

## Determining the Payroll

Determining the payroll involves computing (1) gross earnings, (2) payroll deductions, and (3) net pay.

### Gross Earnings

Gross earnings are the total compensation earned by an employee. There are three major types of gross earnings: wages, salaries, and bonuses.

Total **wages** for an employee are determined by multiplying the hours worked by the hourly rate of pay. In addition to the hourly pay rate, most companies are required by law to pay hourly workers a minimum of one and one-half times the regular hourly rate for overtime work in excess of 8 hours per day or 40 hours per week. For example, companies involved in interstate commerce are required by the Federal Fair Labor Standards Act to pay one and one-half times the regular wage rate. In addition, many employers pay overtime rates for work done at night, on weekends, and on holidays. The computation of Michael Jordan's gross earnings (total wages) for the 44 hours shown on his time card for the weekly pay period ending January 14 is as follows:

**Illustration 11-7**

*Computation of total wages*

| Type of Pay | Hours | × | Rate | = | Gross Earnings |
|---|---|---|---|---|---|
| Regular | 40 | × | $12.00 | = | $480.00 |
| Overtime | 4 | × | 18.00 | = | 72.00 |
| **Total wages** | | | | | **$552.00** |

This computation assumes that Jordan receives one and one-half times his regular hourly rate ($12.00 × 1.5) for his overtime hours. Union contracts often require that overtime rates be as much as twice the regular rates.

The **salary** for an employee is generally based on a monthly or yearly rate rather than on an hourly basis. These rates are then applied ratably to the payroll periods used by the company. Most executive and administrative positions are salaried. The Federal Fair Labor Standards Act does not require overtime pay

## ▶*Accounting in Action* ▸ *Business Insight*

In 1995 Amoco Corporation employees received shares of the company's stock equal to 3.5% of their salaries as a result of the company's strong total return to shareholders. Amoco's performance plan awards shares to employees when the return to shareholders meets or exceeds the average of seven major oil companies. Amoco's return of 18.8% was the second highest of the group of competitors.

*Source: Denver Post,* January 6, 1995.

for such positions. In the Casper College example at the beginning of the chapter, overtime is not given to either faculty or administrative personnel.

Many companies have bonus agreements for management personnel and other employees. For example, a recent survey indicated that over 94% of the largest manufacturing companies in the United States provide annual bonuses to their key executives. Bonus arrangements may be based on such factors as increased sales or net income. Bonuses may be paid in cash and/or by granting executives and employees the opportunity to acquire shares of stock in the company at favorable prices (called stock option plans). Bonuses have become very lucrative, as companies attempt to retain the services of key executives—so lucrative, in fact, that they have come under intense public scrutiny.

### *Payroll Deductions*

As anyone who has received a paycheck knows, gross earnings are usually very different from the amount actually received. The difference is attributable to payroll deductions. Payroll deductions do not result in payroll tax expense to the employer. The employer serves only as a collection agency, and it subsequently transfers the deductions to the government and designated recipients. Payroll deductions may be mandatory or voluntary. The former are required by law and consist of FICA taxes and income taxes. The latter are at the option of the employee. Illustration 11-8 summarizes the types of payroll deductions.

▶*Ethics note*

Bonuses often reward outstanding individual performance; however, a successful corporation also needs considerable teamwork. A challenge is to motivate individuals while preventing an unethical team member from taking another's idea for his or her own advantage.

**Illustration 11-8**

*Payroll deductions*

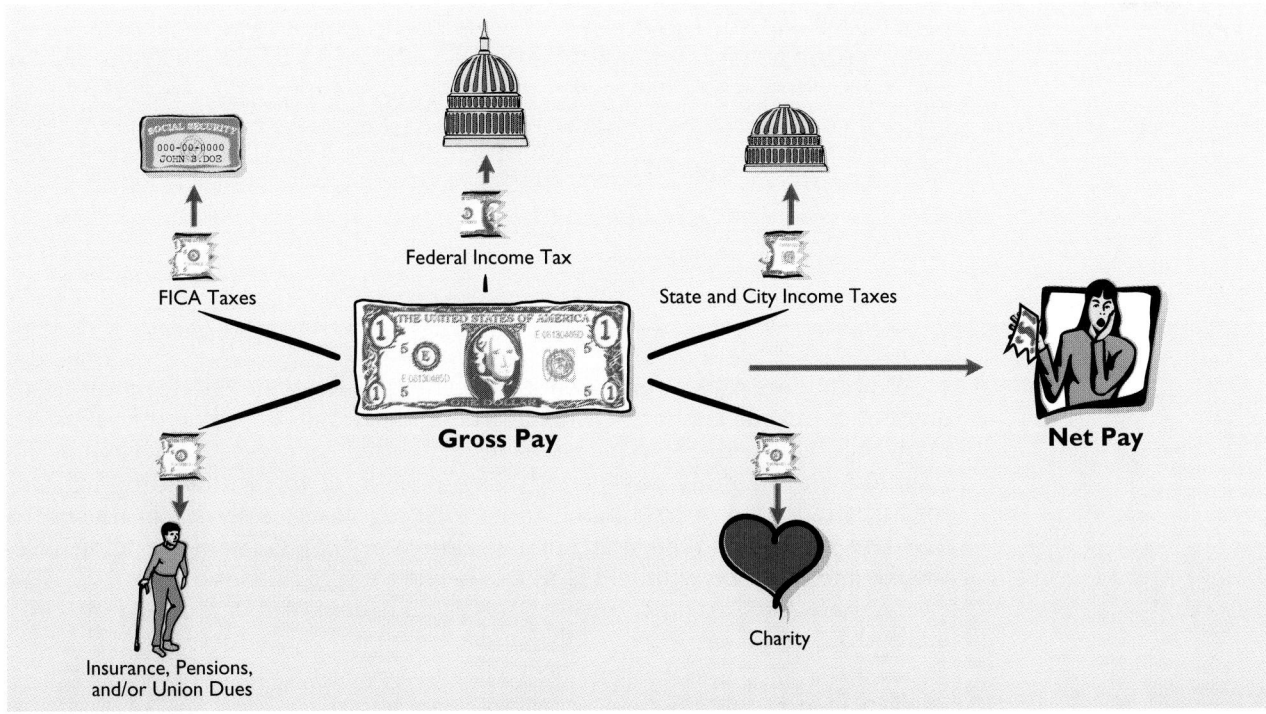

**FICA Taxes.** In 1937 Congress enacted the Federal Insurance Contribution Act (FICA). FICA taxes **are designed to provide workers with supplemental retirement, employment disability, and medical benefits.** In 1965, benefits were expanded to include Medicare for individuals over 65 years of age. The benefits are financed by a tax levied on employees' earnings. FICA taxes are commonly referred to as **social security taxes**.

The tax rate and the tax base for FICA taxes are set by Congress, and they are changed intermittently. When FICA taxes were first imposed, the rate was 1% on the first $3,000 of gross earnings, or a maximum of $30 per year. The rate and base have changed dramatically since that time! In 1995, that rate was 7.65% (6.2% Social Security and 1.45% Medicare) on the first $61,200 of gross earnings for each employee, or a maximum of $4,681.80.[1] For purpose of illustration in this chapter, we will assume a rate of 8% on the first $60,000 of gross earnings, or a maximum of $4,800. Using the 8% rate, the FICA withholding for Jordan for the weekly pay period ending January 14 is $44.16 ($552 × 8%).

**Income Taxes.** Under the United States pay-as-you-go system of federal income taxes, employers are required to withhold income taxes from employees each pay period. The amount to be withheld is determined by three variables: (1) the employee's gross earnings; (2) the number of allowances claimed by the employee for herself or himself, his or her spouse, and other dependents; and (3) the length of the pay period. **To indicate to the Internal Revenue Service the number of allowances claimed, the employee must complete an** Employee's Withholding Allowance Certificate (Form W-4). As shown in Illustration 11-9, Michael Jordan claims two allowances on his W-4.

**Illustration 11-9**

*W-4 form*

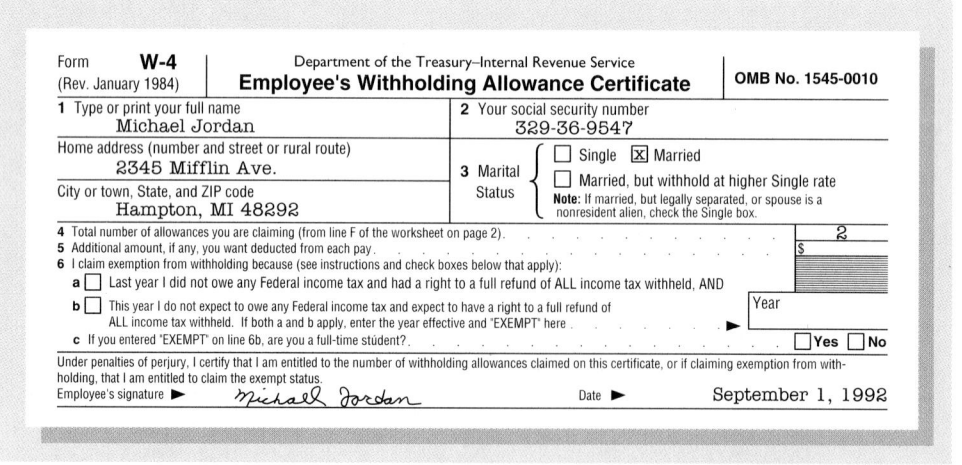

Withholding tables furnished by the Internal Revenue Service indicate the amount of income tax to be withheld from gross wages based on the number of allowances claimed. Separate tables are provided for weekly, biweekly, semi-monthly, and monthly pay periods. The portion of the withholding tax table for Michael Jordan (assuming he earns $552 per week) is shown in Illustration 11-10. As indicated in the table, for a weekly salary of $552 with two allowances, the income tax to be withheld is $50.

---

[1] The Medicare provision also includes a tax of 1.45% on gross earnings in excess of $61,200. In our end-of-chapter materials, gross earnings will not exceed $61,200.

**Illustration 11-10**

*Withholding tax table*

| **MARRIED** Persons — **WEEKLY** Payroll Period | | | | | | | | | | | | |
|---|---|---|---|---|---|---|---|---|---|---|---|---|
| (For Wages Paid in 1995) | | | | | | | | | | | | |
| If the wages are – | | And the number of withholding allowances claimed is – | | | | | | | | | | |
| At least | But less than | 0 | 1 | 2 | 3 | 4 | 5 | 6 | 7 | 8 | 9 | 10 |
| | | The amount of income tax to be withheld is – | | | | | | | | | | |
| 490 | 500 | 56 | 49 | 41 | 34 | 27 | 20 | 13 | 5 | 0 | 0 | 0 |
| 500 | 510 | 57 | 50 | 43 | 36 | 28 | 21 | 14 | 7 | 0 | 0 | 0 |
| 510 | 520 | 59 | 52 | 44 | 37 | 30 | 23 | 16 | 8 | 1 | 0 | 0 |
| 520 | 530 | 60 | 53 | 46 | 39 | 31 | 24 | 17 | 10 | 3 | 0 | 0 |
| 530 | 540 | 62 | 55 | 47 | 40 | 33 | 26 | 19 | 11 | 4 | 0 | 0 |
| 540 | 550 | 63 | 56 | 49 | 42 | 34 | 27 | 20 | 13 | 6 | 0 | 0 |
| 550 | 560 | 65 | 58 | **50** | 43 | 36 | 29 | 22 | 14 | 7 | 0 | 0 |
| 560 | 570 | 66 | 59 | 52 | 45 | 37 | 30 | 23 | 16 | 9 | 1 | 0 |
| 570 | 580 | 68 | 61 | 53 | 46 | 39 | 32 | 25 | 17 | 10 | 3 | 0 |
| 580 | 590 | 69 | 62 | 55 | 48 | 40 | 33 | 26 | 19 | 12 | 4 | 0 |
| 590 | 600 | 71 | 64 | 56 | 49 | 42 | 35 | 28 | 20 | 13 | 6 | 0 |
| 600 | 610 | 72 | 65 | 58 | 51 | 43 | 36 | 29 | 22 | 15 | 7 | 0 |
| 610 | 620 | 74 | 67 | 59 | 52 | 45 | 38 | 31 | 23 | 16 | 9 | 2 |
| 620 | 630 | 75 | 68 | 61 | 54 | 46 | 39 | 32 | 25 | 18 | 10 | 3 |
| 630 | 640 | 77 | 70 | 62 | 55 | 48 | 41 | 34 | 26 | 19 | 12 | 5 |
| 640 | 650 | 78 | 71 | 64 | 57 | 49 | 42 | 35 | 28 | 21 | 13 | 6 |
| 650 | 660 | 80 | 73 | 65 | 58 | 51 | 44 | 37 | 29 | 22 | 15 | 8 |
| 660 | 670 | 81 | 74 | 67 | 60 | 52 | 45 | 38 | 31 | 24 | 16 | 9 |
| 670 | 680 | 83 | 76 | 68 | 61 | 54 | 47 | 40 | 32 | 25 | 18 | 11 |
| 680 | 690 | 84 | 77 | 70 | 63 | 55 | 48 | 41 | 34 | 27 | 19 | 12 |

Most states and some cities also require employers to withhold income taxes from the earnings of employees. As a general rule, the amounts to be withheld are determined by applying a percentage specified in the state revenue code to the amount withheld for the federal income tax or to the employee's earnings. For the sake of simplicity, we have assumed that Jordan's wages are subject to state income taxes of 2%, or $11.04 (2% × $552).

There is no limit on the amount of gross earnings subject to income tax withholdings. In fact, the higher the earnings, the higher the amount of taxes withheld.

**Voluntary Deductions.** Employees may voluntarily authorize withholdings for charitable, retirement, and other purposes. All voluntary deductions from gross earnings should be authorized in writing by the employee. The authorization(s) may be made individually or as part of a group plan. Deductions for charitable organizations, such as the United Fund, or for financial arrangements, such as U.S. savings bonds and repayment of loans from company credit unions are made individually. In contrast, deductions for union dues, health and life insurance, and pension plans are often made on a group basis. For purpose of illustration, we will assume that Jordan has voluntary deductions of $10 for the United Fund and $5 for union dues.

## ►Technology in Action

With the widespread use of microcomputers, the error-prone task of manually searching tax tables for the proper payroll deductions is becoming extinct even in small businesses. Now computers with entire tax tables stored internally perform this table lookup function without error and accurately calculate all payroll information.

### Net Pay

Net pay is determined by subtracting payroll deductions from gross earnings. For Michael Jordan, net pay for the pay period is $431.80, computed as follows:

**Illustration 11-11**

*Computation of net pay*

| | | |
|---|---|---|
| Gross earnings | | $552.00 |
| Payroll deductions: | | |
| FICA taxes | $44.16 | |
| Federal income taxes | 50.00 | |
| State income taxes | 11.04 | |
| United Fund | 10.00 | |
| Union dues | 5.00 | 120.20 |
| Net pay | | $431.80 |

Assuming that Michael Jordan's wages for each week during the year are $552, total wages for the year are $28,704 (52 × $552). Thus, all of Jordan's wages are subject to FICA tax during the year. However, if an employee's wages are $1,200 per week, or $62,400 for the year, only the first $60,000 is subject to FICA taxes. In such case, the maximum FICA withholdings would be $4,800 ($60,000 × 8%).

## Recording the Payroll

Recording the payroll involves maintaining payroll department records, recognizing payroll expenses and liabilities, and recording payment of the payroll.

### Maintaining Payroll Department Records

To comply with state and federal laws, an employer must keep a cumulative record of each employee's gross earnings, deductions, and net pay during the year. The record that provides this information and other essential data is the employee earnings record. Michael Jordan's employee earnings record is shown in Illustration 11-12.

**Illustration 11-12**

*Employee earnings record*

**ACADEMY COMPANY**
**Employee Earnings Record**
**For the Year 1996**

| Name | Michael Jordan | Address | 2345 Mifflin Ave. |
|---|---|---|---|
| Social Security Number | 329-36-9547 | | Hampton, Michigan 48292 |
| Date of Birth | December 24, 1962 | Telephone | 238-9051 |
| Date Employed | September 1, 1992 | Date Employment Ended | |
| Sex | Male | Exemptions | 2 |
| Single _____ | Married ___X___ | | |

| 1996 Period Ending | Total Hours | Gross Earnings | | | | Deductions | | | | | | Payment | |
|---|---|---|---|---|---|---|---|---|---|---|---|---|---|
| | | Regular | Overtime | Total | Cumulative | FICA | Fed. Inc. Tax | State Inc. Tax | United Fund | Union Dues | Total | Net Amount | Check No. |
| 1/7 | 42 | 480.00 | 36.00 | 516.00 | 516.00 | 41.28 | 44.00 | 10.32 | 10.00 | 5.00 | 110.60 | 405.40 | 974 |
| 1/14 | 44 | 480.00 | 72.00 | 552.00 | 1,068.00 | 44.16 | 50.00 | 11.04 | 10.00 | 5.00 | 120.20 | 431.80 | 1028 |
| 1/21 | 43 | 480.00 | 54.00 | 534.00 | 1,602.00 | 42.72 | 47.00 | 10.68 | 10.00 | 5.00 | 115.40 | 418.60 | 1077 |
| 1/28 | 42 | 480.00 | 36.00 | 516.00 | 2,118.00 | 41.28 | 44.00 | 10.32 | 10.00 | 5.00 | 110.60 | 405.40 | 1133 |
| Jan. Total | | 1,920.00 | 198.00 | 2,118.00 | | 169.44 | 185.00 | 42.36 | 40.00 | 20.00 | 456.80 | 1,661.20 | |

A separate earnings record is kept for each employee, and it is updated after each pay period. The cumulative payroll data on the earnings record are used by the employer in (1) determining when an employee has earned the maximum earnings subject to FICA taxes, (2) filing state and federal payroll tax returns (as explained later in the chapter), and (3) providing each employee with a statement of gross earnings and tax withholdings for the year, as shown in Illustration 11-15 on page 472. In the opening story about Casper College, Dianna Webb's report that lists the year-to-date totals is the employee earnings record.

In addition to employee earnings records, many companies find it useful to prepare a payroll register to accumulate the gross earnings, deductions, and net pay by employee for each pay period. It provides the documentation for preparing a paycheck for each employee. The payroll register is presented in Illustration 11-13, with the data for Michael Jordan shown in the wages section. In this example, Academy Company's total payroll is $17,210, as shown in the gross pay column.

**Illustration 11-13**

*Payroll register*

## ACADEMY COMPANY
### Payroll Register
### For the Week Ending January 14, 1996

| Employee | Total Hours | Earnings | | | Deductions | | | | | | Paid | | Accounts Debited | |
| | | Regular | Over-time | Gross | FICA | Federal Income Tax | State Income Tax | United Fund | Union Dues | Total | Net Pay | Check No. | Office Salaries Expense | Wages Expense |
|---|---|---|---|---|---|---|---|---|---|---|---|---|---|---|
| Office Salaries | | | | | | | | | | | | | | |
| Arnold, Patricia | 40 | 580.00 | | 580.00 | 46.40 | 62.00 | 11.60 | 15.00 | | 135.00 | 445.00 | 998 | 580.00 | |
| Canton, Matthew | 40 | 590.00 | | 590.00 | 47.20 | 64.00 | 11.80 | 20.00 | | 143.00 | 447.00 | 999 | 590.00 | |
| | | | | | | | | | | | | | | |
| Mueller, William | 40 | 530.00 | | 530.00 | 42.40 | 55.00 | 10.60 | 11.00 | | 119.00 | 411.00 | 1000 | 530.00 | |
| Subtotal | | 5,200.00 | | 5,200.00 | 416.00 | 1,090.00 | 104.00 | 120.00 | | 1,730.00 | 3,470.00 | | 5,200.00 | |
| Wages | | | | | | | | | | | | | | |
| Bennett, Robin | 42 | 480.00 | 36.00 | 516.00 | 41.28 | 44.00 | 10.32 | 18.00 | 5.00 | 118.60 | 397.40 | 1025 | | 516.00 |
| **Jordan, Michael** | **44** | **480.00** | **72.00** | **552.00** | **44.16** | **50.00** | **11.04** | **10.00** | **5.00** | **120.20** | **431.80** | **1028** | | **552.00** |
| | | | | | | | | | | | | | | |
| Milroy, Lee | 43 | 480.00 | 54.00 | 534.00 | 42.72 | 47.00 | 10.68 | 10.00 | 5.00 | 115.40 | 418.60 | 1029 | | 534.00 |
| Subtotal | | 11,000.00 | 1,010.00 | 12,010.00 | 960.80 | 2,400.00 | 240.20 | 301.50 | 115.00 | 4,017.50 | 7,992.50 | | | 12,010.00 |
| Total | | 16,200.00 | 1,010.00 | 17,210.00 | 1,376.80 | 3,490.00 | 344.20 | 421.50 | 115.00 | 5,747.50 | 11,462.50 | | 5,200.00 | 12,010.00 |

Note that this record is a listing of each employee's payroll data for the pay period. In some companies, a payroll register is a journal or book of original entry, and postings are made directly to ledger accounts from the register. In other companies, the payroll register is a memorandum record that provides the data for a general journal entry and subsequent posting to the ledger accounts. In the Academy Company situation, the latter procedure is followed. The main payroll report provided by the computer at Casper College is the payroll register.

## ►*T*echnology in *A*ction

In addition to supplying the entry to record the payroll, the output for a computerized payroll system would include (1) payroll checks, (2) a payroll check register sorted by check and department, and (3) updated employee earnings records which become the source for monthly, quarterly, and annual reporting of wages to taxing agencies.

### *Recognizing Payroll Expenses and Liabilities*

From the payroll register in Illustration 11-13, a journal entry is made to record the payroll. For the week ending January 14 the entry is:

| | | | |
|---|---|---|---|
| Jan. 14 | Office Salaries Expense | 5,200.00 | |
| | Wages Expense | 12,010.00 | |
| |     FICA Taxes Payable | | 1,376.80 |
| |     Federal Income Taxes Payable | | 3,490.00 |
| |     State Income Taxes Payable | | 344.20 |
| |     United Fund Payable | | 421.50 |
| |     Union Dues Payable | | 115.00 |
| |     Salaries and Wages Payable | | 11,462.50 |
| |     (To record payroll for the week ending January 14) | | |

Specific liability accounts are credited for the mandatory and voluntary deductions made during the pay period. In the example, debits to Office Salaries and Wages Expense are used for gross earnings because office workers are on a salary and other employees are paid on an hourly rate. In other cases, there may be additional debits such as Store Salaries and Sales Salaries. The amount credited to Salaries and Wages Payable is the sum of the individual checks the employees will receive.

### *Recording Payment of the Payroll*

Payment by check is made either from the employer's regular bank account or a payroll bank account. Each check is usually accompanied by a detachable statement of earnings document that shows the employee's gross earnings, payroll deductions, and net pay. The Academy Company uses its regular bank account for payroll checks. The check and statement of earnings for Michael Jordan are shown in Illustration 11-14.

**Illustration 11-14**

*Check and statement of earnings*

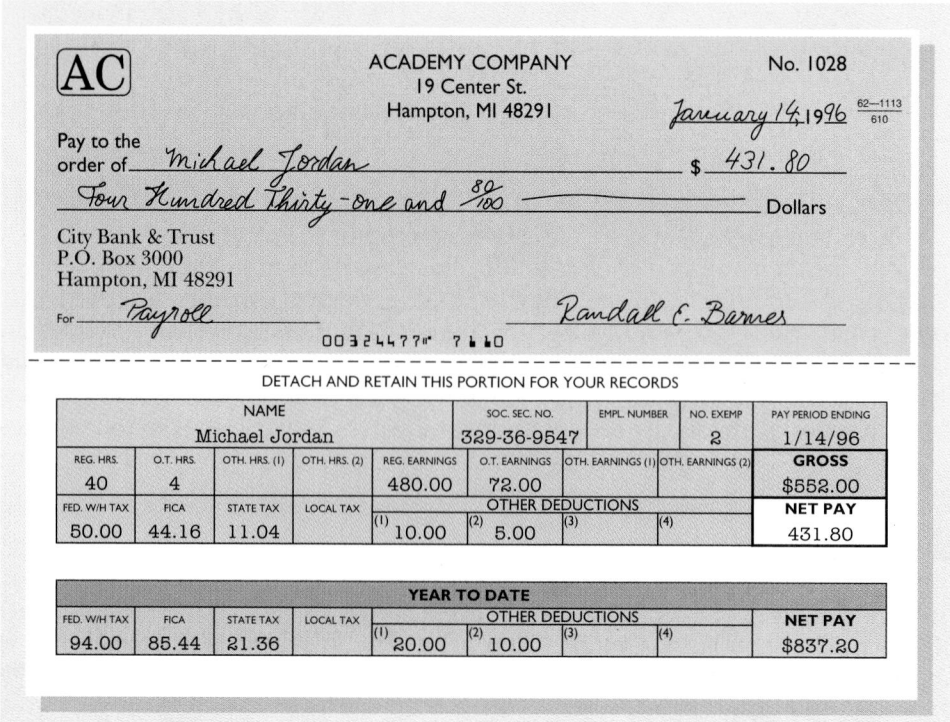

Following payment of the payroll, the check numbers are entered in the payroll register. The entry to record payment of the payroll for Academy Company is as follows:

| | | | |
|---|---|---|---|
| Jan. 14 | Salaries and Wages Payable | 11,462.50 | |
| | Cash | | 11,462.50 |
| | (To record payment of payroll) | | |

When currency is used in payment, one check is prepared for the net pay. The check is then cashed, and the coins and currency are inserted in individual pay envelopes for disbursement to individual employees.

## Before You Go On . . .

### ▶ Review It

1. Identify two internal control procedures that are applicable to each payroll function.
2. What are the primary sources of gross earnings?
3. What payroll deductions are (a) mandatory and (b) voluntary?
4. What account titles are used in recording a payroll, assuming only mandatory payroll deductions are involved?

### ▶ Do It

Your cousin Stan is establishing a house-cleaning business and will have a number of employees working for him. From his prior work experience, he is aware that documentation procedures are an important part of internal control. However, he is confused about the difference between an employee earnings record and a payroll register. He asks you to explain the principal differences, because he wants to be sure that he sets up the proper payroll procedures.

**Reasoning:** You may need to review the material on payroll department records and study Illustrations 11-12 and 11-13 in order to identify and explain the differences for Stan.

**Solution:** An employee earnings record is kept for *each* employee. It shows gross earnings, payroll deductions, and net pay for each pay period. It provides cumulative payroll data for that employee. In contrast, a payroll register is a listing of *all* employees' gross earnings, payroll deductions, and net pay for each pay period. It is the documentation for preparing paychecks and for recording the payroll. Of course, Stan will need to keep both documents.

*Related exercise material:* BE11–6, BE11–7, BE11–8, E11–6, E11–7, E11–8, and E11–9.

## Employer Payroll Taxes

Payroll tax expense for businesses and educational institutions, like Casper College, results from three taxes **levied on employers** by governmental agencies. These taxes are: FICA, federal unemployment tax, and state unemployment tax. Each of these taxes plus such items as paid vacations and pensions are collectively referred to as "fringe benefits." As indicated earlier, the cost of fringe benefits in many companies is substantial.

> **STUDY OBJECTIVE**
> ·········▼7·········
> *Describe and record employer payroll taxes.*

### FICA Taxes

We have seen that each employee must pay FICA taxes. The employer must match each employee's FICA contribution. The matching contribution results in **payroll tax expense** to the employer. The employer's tax is subject to the same rate and maximum earnings applicable to the employee. The account, FICA Taxes Payable, is used for both the employee's and the employer's FICA contri-

## ▸Accounting in Action ▸ *Business Insight*

Facing a rising tide of disability applications and a backlog of more than 1 million cases, the Social Security Administration plans to shorten the time for processing a claim by two-thirds. One part of the plan is to streamline routing systems in order to reduce by two-thirds the number of people that handle a claim. With 65,000 employees, the Administration collects payroll taxes from 135 million Americans and sends 45 million checks monthly. Only 20% of the checks go to recipients of disability benefits, but the handling of such claims takes slightly more than half of the agency's $4.9 billion budget. Clearly, more efficient systems will be beneficial.

butions. For the January 14 payroll, Academy Company's FICA tax is $1,376.80 ($17,210.00 × 8%).

### Federal Unemployment Taxes

**Helpful hint** FICA taxes are paid both by the employer and employee. Federal unemployment taxes and (in most states) the state unemployment taxes are borne entirely by the employer.

The Federal Unemployment Tax Act (FUTA) is another feature of the federal social security program. Federal unemployment taxes provide benefits for a limited period of time to employees who lose their jobs through no fault of their own. Under provisions of the Act, the employer is required to pay a tax of 6.2% on the first $7,000 of gross wages paid to each employee during a calendar year. The law, however, allows the employer a maximum credit of 5.4% on the federal rate for contributions to state unemployment taxes. Because of this provision, state unemployment tax laws generally provide for a 5.4% rate, and the effective federal unemployment tax rate becomes 0.8% (6.2% − 5.4%). This tax is borne **entirely by the employer**; there is no deduction or withholding from employees. The account Federal Unemployment Taxes Payable is used to recognize this liability. The federal unemployment tax for Academy Company for the January 14 payroll is $137.68 ($17,210.00 × 0.8%).

### State Unemployment Taxes

All states have unemployment compensation programs under state unemployment tax acts (SUTA). Like federal unemployment taxes, state unemployment taxes provide benefits to employees who lose their jobs. These taxes are levied on employers.[2] The basic rate is usually 5.4% on the first $7,000 of wages paid to an employee during the year. The basic rate is adjusted according to the employer's experience rating: Companies with a history of unstable employment may pay more than the basic rate. Companies with a history of stable employment may pay less than 5.4%. Regardless of the rate paid, the credit on the federal unemployment tax is still 5.4%. The account State Unemployment Taxes Payable is used for this liability. The state unemployment tax for Academy Company for the January 14 payroll is $929.34 ($17,210.00 × 5.4%).

### Recording Employer Payroll Taxes

Employer payroll taxes are usually recorded at the same time the payroll is journalized. The entire amount of gross pay ($17,210.00) shown in the payroll register in Illustration 11-13 is subject to each of the three taxes mentioned above. Accordingly, the entry to record the payroll tax expense associated with the January 14 payroll is:

---

[2]In a few states, the employee is also required to make a contribution. In this textbook, including the homework, we will assume that the tax is only on the employer.

| Jan. 14 | Payroll Tax Expense | 2,443.82 | |
|---|---|---|---|
| | FICA Taxes Payable | | 1,376.80 |
| | Federal Unemployment Taxes Payable | | 137.68 |
| | State Unemployment Taxes Payable | | 929.34 |
| | (To record employer's payroll taxes on January 14 payroll) | | |

Separate liability accounts are used instead of a single credit to Payroll Taxes Payable, because these liabilities are payable to different taxing authorities at different dates. The liability accounts are classified as current liabilities since they will be paid within the next year. Payroll Tax Expense is classified on the income statement as an operating expense.

## Filing and Remitting Payroll Taxes

Preparation of payroll tax returns is the responsibility of the payroll department; payment of the taxes is made by the treasurer's department. Much of the information for the returns is obtained from employee earnings records.

For purposes of reporting and remitting, FICA taxes and federal income taxes withheld are combined. **The taxes must be reported quarterly**, no later than one month following the close of each quarter. The remitting requirements depend on the amount of taxes withheld and the length of the pay period. Remittances are made through deposits in either a Federal Reserve Bank or an authorized commercial bank.

Federal unemployment taxes are generally filed and remitted **annually** on or before January 31 of the subsequent year. Earlier payments are required, however, when the tax exceeds a specified amount. State unemployment taxes usually must be filed and paid by the **end of the month following each quarter**. When payroll taxes are paid, payroll liability accounts are debited and cash is credited.

The employer is also required to provide each employee with a Wage and Tax Statement (Form W-2) by January 31 following the end of a calendar year. This statement shows gross earnings, FICA taxes withheld, and income taxes withheld for the year. The required W-2 form for Michael Jordan, using assumed annual data, is shown in Illustration 11-15.

The employer must send a copy of each employee's Wage and Tax Statement to the Social Security Administration. This agency subsequently furnishes the Internal Revenue Service with the income data required.

## ►*A*ccounting in *A*ction ► *Business Insight*

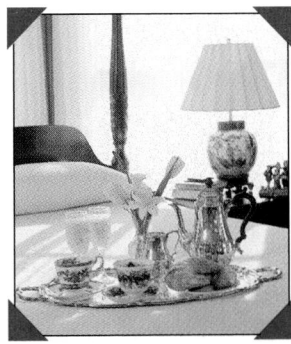

The owner of a newly restored Victorian hotel, nestled in a small Massachusetts town, skipped payment of withholding taxes for three quarters because of cash flow problems. Before long, he received a call from the IRS. After months of haggling, the hotel owner was told that unless he paid the $70,000 owed, the IRS would be forced to liquidate the hotel, the land, and dozens of antiques in the inn, which had taken him and his wife years to acquire.

As this story indicates, cash-hungry small businesses are often tempted to skip or delay paying withholding taxes. Increasingly, federal and state agencies are cracking down on such cheaters. Penalties for late or nonpayment can be devastating: Fines are levied at the rate of 5% of taxes owed for each month a payroll tax isn't filed. And in cases where nothing is paid, penalties of 100% can be applied, with interest added, to the unpaid balance. Under the 100% penalty, the government can padlock the doors, seize assets, and hold the officers or certain other employees personally responsible for the penalties.

What happened to the Massachusetts hotel owner? He's now working on a repayment plan, rather than lose his years of hard work.

**Illustration 11-15**

*W-2 form*

| Form **W-2 Wage and Tax Statement** | | |
|---|---|---|

**1** Control number

OMB No. 1545-0008

**2** Employer's name, address and ZIP code

Academy Company
19 Center St.
Hampton, MI 48291

**3** Employer's identification number
36-2167852

**4** Employer's State number

**5** Stat. employee    Deceased    Legal rep.    942 emp.    Subtotal    Void
□    □    □    □    □

**6** Allocated tips

**7** Advance EIC payment

**8** Employee's social security number
329-36-9547

**9** Federal income tax withheld
$3240.00

**10** Wages, tips, other compensation
$26,300.00

**11** Social security tax withheld
$2,104.00

**12** Employee's name, address, and ZIP code

Michael Jordan
2345 Mifflin Ave.
Hampton, MI 48292

**13** Social security wages
$26,300.00

**14** Social security tips

**16**

**17** State income tax
$526.00

**18** State wages, tips, etc.

**19** Name of State
Michigan

**20** Local income tax

**21** Local wages, tips, etc.

**22** Name of locality

# Before You Go On . . .

## ▶ Review It

1. What payroll taxes are levied on employers?
2. What accounts are involved in accruing employer payroll taxes?

## ▶ Do It

In January, the payroll supervisor determines that gross earnings in Halo Company are $70,000. All earnings are subject to 8% FICA taxes, 5.4% state unemployment taxes, and 0.8% federal unemployment taxes. You are asked to record the employer's payroll taxes.

**Reasoning:** In recording the taxes, you should remember that (1) the total expense can be debited to one account and (2) separate accounts are required for each of the three liabilities.

**Solution:** The entry to record the employer's payroll taxes is:

| | | |
|---|---|---|
| Payroll Tax Expense | 9,940 | |
|     FICA Taxes Payable ($70,000 × 8%) | | 5,600 |
|     Federal Unemployment Taxes Payable ($70,000 × 0.8%) | | 560 |
|     State Unemployment Taxes Payable ($70,000 × 5.4%) | | 3,780 |
|     (To record employer's payroll taxes on January | | |
|     payroll) | | |

*Related exercise material:* BE11–9, E11–8, and E11–10.

**STUDY OBJECTIVE**

● ● ● ● ● ● ● ● ● ● **8** ● ● ● ● ● ● ● ● ● ●

*Identify additional fringe benefits associated with employee compensation.*

## Additional Fringe Benefits

In addition to the three payroll tax fringe benefits, employers incur other substantial fringe benefit costs. Two of the most important are paid absences and postretirement benefits.

## Paid Absences

Employees often have rights to receive compensation for future absences when certain conditions of employment are met. The compensation may pertain to paid vacations, sick pay benefits, and paid holidays. When the payment of such compensation is **probable** and the amount can be **reasonably estimated**, a liability should be accrued for paid future absences. When the amount cannot be reasonably estimated, the potential liability should be disclosed. Ordinarily, vacation pay is the only paid absence that is accrued; the other types of paid absences are only disclosed.[3]

To illustrate, assume that Academy Company employees are entitled to one day's vacation for each month worked. If thirty employees earn an average of $110 per day in a given month, the accrual for vacation benefits in one month is $3,300. The liability is recognized at the end of the month by the following adjusting entry:

| Jan. 31 | Vacation Benefits Expense | 3,300 | |
| |     Vacation Benefits Payable | | 3,300 |
| |     (To accrue vacation benefits expense) | | |

This accrual is required by the matching principle. Vacation Benefits Expense is reported as an operating expense in the income statement, and Vacation Benefits Payable is reported as a current liability in the balance sheet. When vacation benefits are paid, Vacation Benefits Payable is debited and Cash is credited. For example if the above benefits for ten employees are paid in July, the entry is:

| July 31 | Vacation Benefits Payable | 1,100 | |
| |     Cash | | 1,100 |
| |     (To record payment of vacation benefits) | | |

The magnitude of unpaid absences has gained employers' attention. Consider the case of an assistant superintendent of schools who worked for around 20 years and rarely took a vacation or sick day. A month or so before she retired, the school district discovered that she was due nearly $30,000 in accrued benefits. Yet the liability was never accrued.

## Postretirement Benefits

Postretirement benefits consist of payments by employers to retired employees for (1) health care and life insurance and (2) pensions. For many years the accounting for postretirement benefits was on a cash basis. However, both types of postretirement benefits are now accounted for on the accrual basis.

**Postretirement Health Care and Life Insurance Benefits.** Providing medical and related health care benefits for retirees—at one time an inexpensive and highly effective way of generating employee goodwill—has turned into one of corporate America's most worrisome financial problems. Runaway medical costs, early retirement, and increased longevity are sending the liability for retiree health plans through the roof for many companies.

Many companies began offering retiree health care coverage in the form of Medicare supplements in the 1960s. Almost all plans operated on a pay-as-you-go basis—the companies simply paid for the bills as they came in, rather than setting aside funds to meet the cost of future benefits. These plans were ac-

---

[3]The typical U.S. company provides an average of 12 days of paid vacations for its employees at an average cost of 5% of gross earnings.

## ▸Accounting in Action ▸ *Business Insight*

The battle over fringe benefits has grabbed a starring role in the corporate drama of the 1990s, as benefits continue to outpace wages and salaries. Growing far faster than pay, benefits equaled 38% of wages and salaries in a recent year. While vacations and other forms of paid leave still take the biggest bite of the benefits pie, medical costs are the fastest-growing item.

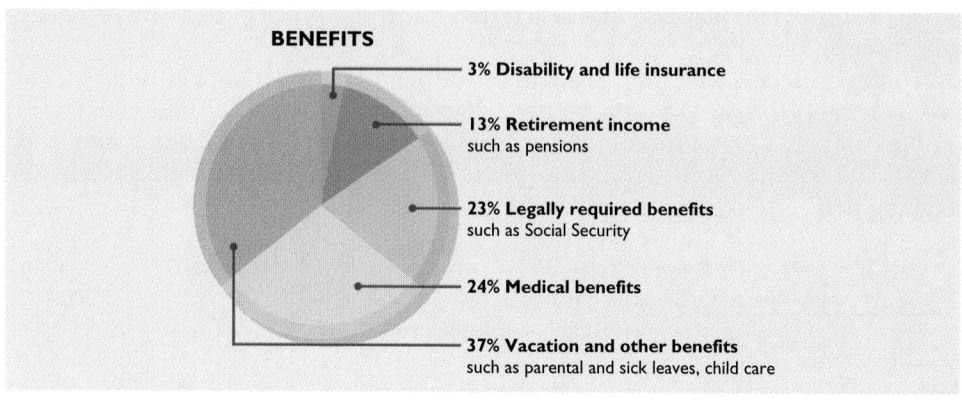

**BENEFITS**

- 3% Disability and life insurance
- 13% Retirement income such as pensions
- 23% Legally required benefits such as Social Security
- 24% Medical benefits
- 37% Vacation and other benefits such as parental and sick leaves, child care

counted for on the cash basis rather than the accrual basis. However, the FASB concluded that shareholders and creditors should know the amount of the employer's obligations. As a result, employers must now use the **accrual basis** in accounting for postretirement health care and life insurance benefits.

**Pension Plans.**    A pension plan is an agreement whereby an employer provides benefits (payments) to employees after they retire. Over 50 million workers currently participate in pension plans in the United States. The need for proper administration of and good accounting for pension plans becomes apparent when one appreciates the size of existing pension funds. Most pension plans are subject to the provisions of ERISA (Employee Retirement Income Security Act), a law enacted to curb abuses in the administration and funding of such plans.

Three parties are generally involved in a pension plan. The **employer** (company) sponsors the pension plan. The **plan administrator** receives the contributions from the employer, invests the pension assets, and makes the benefit payments to the **pension recipients** (retired employees). Illustration 11-16 shows the three distinct parties involved in a pension plan and indicates the flow of cash among them.

**Illustration 11-16**

*Parties in a pension plan*

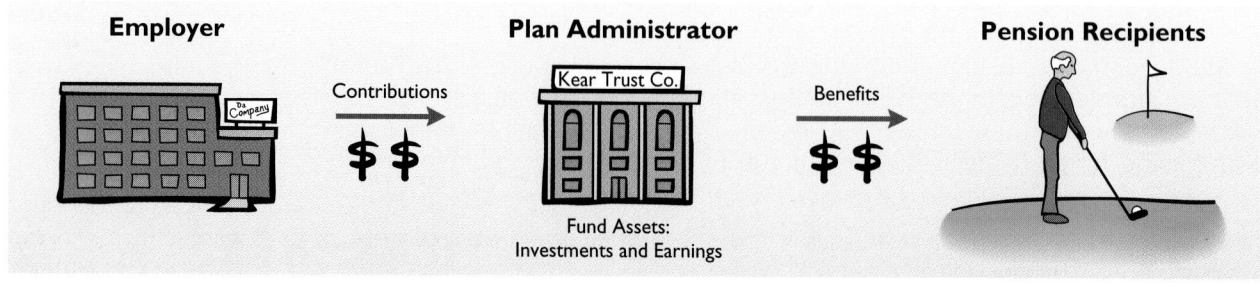

**Employer**                    **Plan Administrator**                    **Pension Recipients**

Contributions                    Kear Trust Co.                    Benefits

Fund Assets:
Investments and Earnings

The provisions of ERISA establish the minimum contribution that a company must make each year. The company uses the accrual basis of accounting in recognizing pension expense for the year. When a company makes only the minimum contribution, the difference between the accrued liability and the amount contributed is reported as a **current liability** in the balance sheet. Pension expense is reported as an **operating expense** in the income statement. Further consideration of the accounting for pension plans is left for more advanced courses.

## Before You Go On . . .

► *Review It*

1. What accounts are involved in accruing and paying vacation benefits?
2. What basis should be used in accounting for postretirement benefits?

## ► *A Look Back at Casper College*

Refer back to the story about Casper College at the beginning of the chapter, and answer the following questions:

1. In addition to taxes withheld from employees, what employer payroll taxes are remitted by Casper College to governmental agencies?
2. For each of the four payroll functions, give examples of internal control procedures used by Casper College.

*Solution:*

1. In addition to the amounts withheld for FICA and federal income taxes, Casper College must match the FICA taxes withheld from employees and must pay federal and state unemployment taxes.
2. *Hiring:* Contracts are issued to faculty and administrative personnel, and their pay must be approved.

   *Timekeeping:* Timecards are used for hourly employees.

   *Preparing the payroll:* Deductions from gross earnings for each employee are documented. For example, there must be a W-4 form for withholding federal income taxes. The computer prepares useful reports that include maintaining a payroll record for each employee.

   *Paying the payroll:* Although these procedures are not explicitly stated, the payroll checks generated by the computer would be signed by the chief financial officer of Casper College, and paychecks would be distributed directly to employees through this officer.

# ◢ *Summary of Study Objectives*

**1.** *Explain a current liability and identify the major types of current liabilities.* A current liability is a debt that can reasonably be expected to be paid (1) from existing current assets or through the creation of other current liabilities, and (2) within one year or the operating cycle, whichever is longer. The major types of current liabilities are notes payable, accounts payable, sales taxes payable, unearned revenues, and accrued liabilities such as taxes, salaries and wages, and interest payable.

**2.** *Describe the accounting for notes payable.* When a promissory note is interest-bearing, the amount of assets received upon the issuance of the note is generally equal to the face value of the note, and interest expense is accrued over the life of the note. At maturity, the amount paid is equal to the face value of the note plus accrued interest.

**3.** *Explain the accounting for other current liabilities.* Sales taxes payable are recorded at the time the related sales occur. The company serves as a collection agent for the taxing authority. Sales taxes are not an expense to the company. Unearned revenues are initially recorded in an unearned revenue account. As the revenue is earned, a transfer from unearned revenue to earned revenue occurs. The current maturities of long-term debt should be reported as a current liability in the balance sheet.

**4. Describe the accounting and disclosure requirements for contingent liabilities.** If it is probable that (likely to occur) the contingency will happen and the amount is reasonably estimable, the liability should be recorded in the accounts. However, if it is only reasonably possible (it could happen), then it need be disclosed only in the notes to the financial statements. If the possibility that the contingency will happen is remote (unlikely to occur), it need not be recorded or disclosed.

**5. Discuss the objectives of internal control for payroll.** The objectives of internal control for payroll are (1) to safeguard company assets against unauthorized payments of payrolls, and (2) to assure the accuracy and reliability of the accounting records pertaining to payrolls.

**6. Compute and record the payroll for a pay period.** The computation of the payroll involves gross earnings, payroll deductions, and net pay. In recording the payroll, salaries (or wages) expense is debited for gross earnings, individual tax and other liability accounts are credited for payroll deductions, and salaries (wages) payable is credited for net pay. When the payroll is paid, Salaries and Wages Payable is debited, and Cash is credited.

**7. Describe and record employer payroll taxes.** Employer payroll taxes consist of FICA, federal unemployment taxes, and state unemployment taxes. The taxes are usually accrued at the time the payroll is recorded by debiting Payroll Tax Expense and crediting separate liability accounts for each type of tax.

**8. Identify additional fringe benefits associated with employee compensation.** Additional fringe benefits associated with wages are paid absences (paid vacations, sick pay benefits, and paid holidays), and postretirement benefits (health care and life insurance and pensions). Both types of benefits should be accounted for on the accrual basis.

# Glossary

**Bonus** Compensation to management personnel and other employees, based on factors such as increased sales or the amount of net income. (p. 463)

**Contingent liability** A potential liability that may become an actual liability in the future. (p. 456)

**Employee earnings record** A cumulative record of each employee's gross earnings, deductions, and net pay during the year. (p. 466)

**Employee's Withholding Allowance Certificate (Form W-4)** An Internal Revenue Service form on which the employee indicates the number of allowances claimed for withholding federal income taxes. (p. 464)

**Federal unemployment taxes** Taxes imposed on the employer that provides benefits for a limited time period to employees who lose their jobs through no fault of their own. (p. 470)

**FICA taxes** Taxes designed to provide workers with supplemental retirement, employment disability, and medical benefits. (p. 464)

**Gross earnings** Total compensation earned by an employee. (p. 462)

**Net pay** Gross earnings less payroll deductions. (p. 466)

**Payroll deductions** Deductions from gross earnings to determine the amount of a paycheck. (p. 463)

**Payroll register** A payroll record that accumulates the gross earnings, deductions, and net pay by employee for each pay period. (p. 467)

**Pension plan** An agreement whereby an employer provides benefits to employees after they retire. (p. 474)

**Postretirement benefits** Payments by employers to retired employees for health care, life insurance, and pensions. (p. 473)

**Salaries** Specified amount per month or per year paid to executive and administrative personnel. (p. 459)

**Statement of earnings** A document attached to a paycheck that indicates the employee's gross earnings, payroll deductions, and net pay. (p. 468)

**State unemployment taxes** Taxes imposed on the employer that provide benefits to employees who lose their jobs. (p. 470)

**Wage and Tax Statement (Form W-2)** A form showing gross earnings, FICA taxes withheld, and income taxes withheld which is prepared annually by an employer for each employee. (p. 471)

**Wages** Amounts paid to employees based on a rate per hour or on a piece-work basis. (p. 459)

# DEMONSTRATION PROBLEM

Indiana Jones Company had the following selected transactions:

Feb. 1 Signs a $50,000 6-month 9%-interest-bearing note payable to CitiBank receiving $50,000 in cash.

10 Cash register sales total $43,200 which includes an 8% sales tax.

28 The payroll for the month consists of Sales Salaries $32,000 and Office Salaries $18,000. All wages are subject to 8% FICA taxes. A total of $8,900 federal income taxes are withheld. The salaries are paid on March 1.

28 The following adjustment data are developed:
1. Interest expense of $375 has been incurred on the note.
2. Employer payroll taxes include 8% FICA taxes, a 5.4% state unemployment tax, and a 0.8% federal unemployment tax.
3. Some sales were made under warranty. Of the units sold under warranty, 350 are expected to become defective. Repair costs are estimated to be $40 per unit.

## Instructions

(a) Journalize the February transactions.

(b) Journalize the adjusting entries at February 28.

## Solution to Demonstration Problem

| | | | |
|---|---|---:|---:|
| (a) Feb. 1 | Cash | 50,000 | |
| |   Notes Payable | | 50,000 |
| |     (Issued 6-month 9%-interest-bearing note to CitiBank) | | |
| 10 | Cash | 43,200 | |
| |   Sales ($43,200 ÷ 1.08) | | 40,000 |
| |   Sales Taxes Payable ($40,000 × 8%) | | 3,200 |
| |     (To record sales and sales taxes payable) | | |
| 28 | Sales Salaries Expense | 32,000 | |
| | Office Salaries Expense | 18,000 | |
| |   FICA Taxes Payable (8% × $50,000) | | 4,000 |
| |   Federal Income Taxes Payable | | 8,900 |
| |   Salaries Payable | | 37,100 |
| |     (To record February salaries) | | |
| (b) Feb. 28 | Interest Expense | 375 | |
| |   Interest Payable | | 375 |
| |     (To record accrued interest for February) | | |
| 28 | Payroll Tax Expense | 7,100 | |
| |   FICA Taxes Payable | | 4,000 |
| |   Federal Unemployment Taxes Payable | | 400 |
| |   (0.8% × $50,000) | | |
| |   State Unemployment Taxes Payable | | 2,700 |
| |   (5.4% × $50,000) | | |
| |     (To record employer's payroll taxes on February payroll) | | |
| 28 | Warranty Expense (350 × $40) | 14,000 | |
| |   Estimated Warranty Liability | | 14,000 |
| |     (To record estimated product warranty liability) | | |

**Problem-Solving Strategies**

1. The formula for determining sales is cash register total divided by 100% plus the sales tax percentage.

2. All payroll taxes are based on gross earnings.

3. Warranty costs are expensed in the period in which the sale occurs.

# SELF-STUDY QUESTIONS

Answers are at the end of the chapter.

(SO 1) 1. The time period for classifying a liability as current is one year or the operating cycle, whichever is:
a. longer.
b. shorter.
c. probable.
d. possible.

(SO 1) 2. To be classified as a current liability, a debt must be expected to be paid:
a. out of existing current assets.
b. by creating other current liabilities.
c. within two years.
d. both (a) and (b).

(SO 2) 3. Julie Gilbert Company borrows $88,500 on September 1, 1997 from the Sandwich State Bank by signing an $88,500 12%, one-year note. What is the accrued interest at December 31, 1997?
a. $2,655.
b. $3,540.
c. $4,425.
d. $10,620.

(SO 3) 4. Reeves Company has total proceeds from sales of $4,515. If the proceeds include sales taxes of 5%, the amount to be credited to Sales is:
a. $4,000.
b. $4,300.
c. $4,289.25.
d. No correct answer given.

(SO 4) 5. A contingency should be recorded in the accounts when:
a. It is probable the contingency will happen but the amount cannot be reasonably estimated.
b. It is reasonably possible the contingency will happen and the amount can be reasonably estimated.

c. It is probable the contingency will happen and the amount can be reasonably estimated.
d. It is reasonably possible the contingency will happen but the amount cannot be reasonably estimated.

(SO 4) 6. At December 31, Hanes Company prepares an adjusting entry for a product warranty contract. Which of the following accounts is/are included in the entry?
a. Miscellaneous Expense.
b. Estimated Warranty Liability.
c. Repair Parts/Wages Payable.
d. Both (a) and (b).

(SO 5) 7. The department that should pay the payroll is the:
a. timekeeping department.
b. personnel department.
c. payroll department.
d. treasurer's department.

(SO 6) 8. J. Barr earns $14 per hour for a 40-hour week and $21 per hour for any overtime work. If Barr works 45 hours in a week, gross earnings are:
a. $560.
b. $630.
c. $650.
d. $665.

(SO 7) 9. Employer payroll taxes do not include:
a. federal unemployment taxes.
b. state unemployment taxes.
c. federal income taxes.
d. FICA taxes.

(SO 8) 10. Which of the following is *not* an additional fringe benefit?
a. Postretirement pensions.
b. Paid absences.
c. Paid vacations.
d. Salaries.

# QUESTIONS

1. Li Feng believes a current liability is a debt that can be expected to be paid in one year. Is Li correct? Explain.

2. Rio Grande Company obtains $25,000 in cash by signing a 9%, 6-month $25,000 note payable to First Bank on July 1. Rio Grande's fiscal year ends on September 30. What information should be reported for the note payable in the annual financial statements?

3. (a) Your roommate says, "Sales taxes are reported as an expense in the income statement." Do you agree? Explain.
(b) Hard Walk Cafe has cash proceeds from sales of $10,400. This amount includes $400 of sales taxes. Give the entry to record the proceeds.

4. Aurora University sold 10,000 season football tickets at $90 each for its five-game home schedule. What entries should be made (a) when the tickets were sold and (b) after each game?

5. What is a contingent liability? Give an example of a contingent liability that is usually recorded in the accounts.

6. Under what circumstances is a contingent liability disclosed only in the notes to the financial statements? Under what circumstances is a contingent liability not recorded in the accounts nor disclosed in the notes to the financial statements?

7. You are a newly hired accountant with Steeples Company. On your first day, the controller asks you to identify the main internal control objectives

related to payroll accounting. How would you respond?

8. What are the four functions associated with payroll activities?

9. What is the difference between gross pay and net pay? Which amount should a company record as wages or salaries expense?

10. Which payroll tax is levied on both employers and employees?

11. Are the federal and state income taxes withheld from employee paychecks a payroll tax expense for the employer? Explain your answer.

12. What do the following acronyms stand for: FICA, FUTA, and SUTA?

13. What information is shown on a W-4 statement? A W-2 statement?

14. Distinguish between the two types of payroll deductions and give examples of each.

15. What are the primary uses of the employee earnings record?

16. (a) Identify the three types of employer payroll taxes. (b) How are tax liability accounts and payroll tax expense classified in the financial statements?

17. Identify three additional types of fringe benefits associated with employees' compensation.

18. Often during job interviews, the candidate asks the potential employer about the firm's paid absences policy. What are paid absences? How are they accounted for?

19. What are the two types of postretirement benefits? During what years does the FASB advocate expensing the employer's costs of these postretirement benefits?

20. What basis of accounting for the employer's cost of postretirement health care and life insurance benefits has been used by most companies, and what basis does the FASB now require? Explain the basic difference between these methods in accounting for postretirement benefit costs.

21. Identify the three parties in a pension plan. What role does each party have in the plan?

## BRIEF EXERCISES

**BE11–1** Fresno Company has the following obligations at December 31: (a) a note payable for $100,000 due in 2 years, (b) a 10-year mortgage payable of $200,000 payable in 10 $20,000 annual payments, (c) interest payable of $15,000 on the mortgage, and (d) accounts payable of $60,000. For each obligation, indicate whether it should be classified as a current liability.

*Identify whether obligations are current liabilities.*
*(SO 1)*

**BE11–2** Romez Company borrows $60,000 on July 1 from the bank by signing a $60,000 10%, one-year note payable. Prepare the journal entries to record (a) the proceeds of the note and (b) accrued interest at December 31, assuming adjusting entries are made only at the end of the year.

*Prepare entries for an interest-bearing note payable.*
*(SO 2)*

**BE11–3** Grandy Auto Supply does not segregate sales and sales taxes at the time of sale. The register total for March 16 is $9,975. All sales are subject to a 5% sales tax. Compute sales taxes payable and make the entry to record sales taxes payable and sales.

*Compute and record sales taxes payable.*
*(SO 3)*

**BE11–4** Outstanding University sells 3,000 season basketball tickets at $60 each for its 12-game home schedule. Give the entry to record (a) the sale of the season tickets and (b) the revenue earned by playing the first home game.

*Prepare entries for unearned revenues.*
*(SO 3)*

**BE11–5** On December 1, Irma Company introduces a new product that includes a one-year warranty on parts. In December 1,000 units are sold. Management believes that 4% of the units will be defective and that the average warranty costs will be $60 per unit. Prepare the adjusting entry at December 31 to accrue the estimated warranty cost.

*Prepare adjusting entry for warranty costs.*
*(SO 4)*

**BE11–6** Lukas Company has the following payroll procedures:

1. Supervisor approves overtime work.
2. The personnel department prepares hiring authorization forms for new hires.
3. A second payroll department employee verifies payroll calculations.
4. The treasurer's department pays employees.

Identify the payroll function to which each procedure pertains.

*Identify payroll functions.*
*(SO 5)*

**BE11–7** Pat Broka's regular hourly wage rate is $14, and she receives an hourly rate of $21 for work in excess of 40 hours. During a January pay period, Pat works 43 hours. Pat's federal income tax withholding is $70, and she has no voluntary deductions. Compute Pat Broka's gross earnings and net pay for the pay period.

*Compute gross earnings and net pay.*
*(SO 6)*

*Record a payroll and the payment of wages.*
(SO 6)

**BE11–8**  Data for Pat Broka are presented in BE11–7. Prepare the journal entries to record (a) Pat's pay for the period and (b) the payment of Pat's wages. Use January 15 for the end of the pay period and the payment date.

*Record employer payroll taxes.*
(SO 7)

**BE11–9**  In January, gross earnings in the Nigel Company totaled $50,000. All earnings are subject to 8% FICA taxes, 5.4% state unemployment taxes, and 0.8% federal unemployment taxes. Prepare the entry to record January payroll tax expense.

*Record estimated vacation benefits.*
(SO 8)

**BE11–10**  At Welch Company employees are entitled to one day's vacation for each month worked. In January, 50 employees worked the full month. Record the vacation pay liability for January assuming the average daily pay for each employee is $120.

# EXERCISES

••••••••••••••••••••••••••••••••••••••••••••••••••••••••••••••••••••••••••••••••

*Prepare entries for interest-bearing notes.*
(SO 2)

**E11–1**  Cairo Company borrows $50,000 from First Bank on a 6-month, $50,000, 12% note.

*Instructions*
(a) Prepare the entry on June 1.
(b) Prepare the adjusting entry on June 30.
(c) Prepare the entry at maturity (December 1), assuming monthly adjusting entries have been made through November 30.
(d) What was the total financing cost (interest expense)?

*Journalize sales and related taxes.*
(SO 3)

**E11–2**  In providing accounting services to small businesses, you encounter the following situations pertaining to cash sales:

1. Nash Company rings up sales and sales taxes separately on its cash register. On April 10, the register totals are sales $25,000 and sales taxes $1,500.
2. Pontiac Company does not segregate sales and sales taxes. Its register total for April 15 is $13,780, which includes a 6% sales tax.

*Instructions*
Prepare the entry to record the sales transactions and related taxes for each client.

*Journalize unearned subscription revenue.*
(SO 3)

**E11–3**  Westland Company publishes a monthly sports magazine, *Fishing Preview*. Subscriptions to the magazine cost $24 per year. During November 1996, Westwood sells 6,000 subscriptions beginning with the December issue. Westwood prepares financial statements quarterly and recognizes subscription revenue earned at the end of the quarter. The company uses the accounts Unearned Subscription Revenue and Subscription Revenue.

*Instructions*
(a) Prepare the entry in November for the receipt of the subscriptions.
(b) Prepare the adjusting entry at December 31, 1996, to record subscription revenue earned in December of 1996.
(c) Prepare the adjusting entry at March 31, 1997, to record subscription revenue earned in the first quarter of 1997.

*Record estimated liability and expense for warranties.*
(SO 4)

**E11–4**  Redland Company sells automatic can openers under a 75-day warranty for defective merchandise. Based on past experience, Redland estimates that 3% of the units sold will become defective during the warranty period. Management estimates that the average cost of replacing or repairing a defective unit is $10. The units sold and units defective that occurred during the last 2 months of 1996 are as follows:

| Month | Units Sold | Units Defective Prior to December 31 |
|---|---|---|
| November | 30,000 | 600 |
| December | 32,000 | 400 |

*Instructions*
(a) Determine the estimated warranty liability at December 31 for the units sold in November and December.
(b) Prepare the journal entries to record the estimated liability for warranties and the costs (assume actual costs of $10,000) incurred in honoring 1,000 warranty claims.

(c) Give the entry to record the honoring of 400 warranty contracts in January at an average cost of $10.

**E11–5** Paddy O'Day Company has the following liability accounts after posting adjusting entries: Accounts Payable $62,000, Unearned Ticket Revenue $24,000, Estimated Warranty Liability $18,000, Interest Payable $12,000, Mortgage Payable $120,000, Notes Payable $80,000, and Sales Taxes Payable $10,000.

*Prepare the current liability section of the balance sheet.*
*(SO 1, 2, 3, 4)*

**Instructions**
(a) Prepare the current liability section of the balance sheet, assuming $30,000 of the mortgage is payable next year.
(b) Comment on Paddy O'Day Company's liquidity, assuming total current assets are $300,000.

**E11–6** Rose Reed's regular hourly wage rate is $15.00, and she receives a wage of 1½ times the regular hourly rate for work in excess of 40 hours. During a March weekly pay period Rose worked 42 hours. Her gross earnings prior to the current week were $19,000. Rose is married and claims three withholding allowances. Her only voluntary deduction is for group hospitalization insurance at $10.00 per week.

*Compute net pay and record pay for one employee.*
*(SO 6)*

**Instructions**
(a) Compute the following amounts for Rose's wages for the current week.
   1. Gross earnings.
   2. FICA taxes (assume 8% rate on maximum of $60,000).
   3. Federal income taxes withheld (use wage-bracket table in text).
   4. State income taxes withheld (assume 2.0% rate).
   5. Net pay.
(b) Record Rose's pay, assuming she is an office computer operator.

**E11–7** Employee earnings records for Kokomo Company reveal the following gross earnings for four employees through the pay period of December 15.

*Compute maximum FICA deductions.*
*(SO 6)*

| R. Sunberg | $58,500 | D. Myers | $59,200 |
| C. Carlsen | $59,700 | P. Otto | $60,000 |

For the pay period ending December 31, each employee's gross earnings is $1,000. The FICA tax rate is 8% on gross earnings of $60,000.

**Instructions**
Compute the FICA withholdings that should be made for each employee for the December 31 pay period. (Show computations.)

**E11–8** Ahmad Company has the following data for the weekly payroll ending January 31.

*Prepare payroll register and record payroll and payroll tax expense.*
*(SO 6, 7)*

| | | | Hours | | | | Hourly | Federal Income Tax | Health |
| Employee | M | T | W | T | F | S | Rate | Withholding | Insurance |
| --- | --- | --- | --- | --- | --- | --- | --- | --- | --- |
| A. Hope | 8 | 8 | 9 | 8 | 10 | 0 | $10 | $34 | $10 |
| B. Innes | 8 | 8 | 8 | 8 | 8 | 2 | 12 | 37 | 15 |
| C. Stone | 9 | 10 | 8 | 8 | 9 | 0 | 12 | 58 | 15 |

Employees are paid 1½ times the regular hourly rate for all hours worked in excess of 40 hours per week. FICA taxes are 8% on the first $60,000 of gross earnings. Ahmad Company is subject to 5.4% state unemployment taxes and 0.8% federal unemployment taxes on the first $7,000 of gross earnings.

**Instructions**
(a) Prepare the payroll register for the weekly payroll.
(b) Prepare the journal entry to record the payroll and Ahmad's payroll tax expense.

*Compute missing payroll amounts and record payroll.*
*(SO 6)*

**E11–9**   Selected data from a February payroll register for Tia Yue Company are presented below with some amounts intentionally omitted.

| Gross earnings: | | State income taxes | $ (3) |
|---|---|---|---|
| Regular | $8,900 | Union dues | 100 |
| Overtime | (1) | | |
| Total | (2) | Total deductions | (4) |
| Deductions: | | Net pay | 7,310 |
| FICA taxes | $ 760 | Accounts debited: | |
| Federal income taxes | 1,140 | Warehouse wages | (5) |
| | | Store wages | $4,000 |

FICA taxes are 8% and state income taxes are 2% of gross earnings.

**Instructions**
(a) Fill in the missing amounts.
(b) Journalize the February payroll and the payment of the payroll.

*Determine employer's payroll taxes and record payroll tax expense.*
*(SO 7)*

**E11–10**   According to a payroll register summary of Modesco Company, the amount of employee's gross pay in December was $700,000, of which $60,000 was not subject to FICA tax and $680,000 was not subject to state and federal unemployment taxes.

**Instructions**
(a) Determine the employer's payroll tax expense for the month, using the following rates: FICA, 8%; state unemployment, 5.4%; federal unemployment, 0.8%.
(b) Prepare the journal entry to record December payroll tax expense.

*Prepare adjusting entries for fringe benefits.*
*(SO 8)*

**E11–11**   Roanoke Company has two fringe benefit plans for its employees:

1. It grants employees 2 days' vacation for each month worked. Ten employees worked the entire month of March at an average daily wage of $120 per employee.
2. In its pension plan the company recognizes 10% of gross earnings as an expense. Gross earnings in March were $35,000. No contribution has been made to the pension fund.

**Instructions**
Prepare the adjusting entries at March 31.

# PROBLEMS

*Prepare current liability entries, adjusting entries, and current liability section.*
*(SO 1, 2, 3, 4)*

**P11–1**   On January 1, 1996, the ledger of Calcutta Company contains the following liability accounts.

| Accounts Payable | $42,500 |
|---|---|
| Sales Taxes Payable | 5,600 |
| Unearned Service Revenue | 15,000 |

During January the following selected transactions occurred:

Jan.  1   Borrowed $15,000 in cash from Midland Bank on a 4-month, 10%, $15,000 note.
   5   Sold merchandise for cash totaling $7,800 which includes 4% sales taxes.
   12   Provided services for customers who had made advance payments of $8,000. (Credit Service Revenue.)
   14   Paid state treasurer's department for sales taxes collected in December 1995 $5,600.
   20   Sold 500 units of a new product on credit at $52 per unit, plus 4% sales tax. This new product is subject to a 1-year warranty.
   25   Sold merchandise for cash totaling $11,440, which includes 4% sales taxes.

**Instructions**
(a) Journalize the January transactions.
(b) Journalize the adjusting entries at January 31 for (1) the outstanding note payable, and (2) estimated warranty liability, assuming warranty costs are expected to equal 8% of sales of the new product.
(c) Prepare the current liability section of the balance sheet at January 31, 1996. Assume no change in Accounts Payable.

**P11–2** Banner Drug Store has four employees who are paid on an hourly basis plus time-and-one-half for all hours worked in excess of 40 a week. Payroll data for the week ended February 15, 1996, are presented below:

*Prepare payroll register and payroll entries.*
(SO 6, 7)

| Employees | Hours Worked | Hourly Rate | Federal Income Tax Withholdings | United Fund |
|---|---|---|---|---|
| B. Creek | 39 | $13.00 | $ ? | $ –0– |
| C. Crowley | 42 | 12.00 | ? | 5.00 |
| E. Irvine | 44 | 13.00 | 56 | 7.50 |
| G. Klamath | 46 | 12.00 | 33 | 5.00 |

Creek and Crowley are married. They claim 2 and 4 withholding allowances, respectively. The following tax rates are applicable: FICA 8%, state income taxes 3%, state unemployment taxes 5.4%, and federal unemployment 0.8%. The first three employees are sales clerks (store wages expense), and the other employee performs administrative duties (office wages expense).

**Instructions**
(a) Prepare a payroll register for the weekly payroll. (Use the wage-bracket withholding table in the text for federal income tax withholdings.)
(b) Journalize the payroll on February 15, 1996, and the accrual of employer payroll taxes.
(c) Journalize the payment of the payroll on February 16, 1996.
(d) Journalize the deposit in a federal reserve bank on February 28, 1996, of the FICA and federal income taxes payable to the government.

**P11–3** The payroll procedures used by three different companies are described below:

*Identify internal control weaknesses and make recommendations for improvement.*
(SO 5)

1. In Lindy Company each employee is required to mark the hours worked on a clock card. At the end of each pay period, the employee must have this clock card approved by the department manager. The approved card is then given to the payroll department by the employee. Subsequently, the treasurer's department pays the employee by check.
2. In Selina Company clock cards and time clocks are used. At the end of each pay period, the department manager initials the cards, indicates the rates of pay, and sends them to payroll. A payroll register is prepared from the cards by the payroll department. Cash equal to the total net pay in each department is given to the department manager, who pays the employees in cash.
3. In Winker Company employees are required to record hours worked on clock cards by "punching" a time clock. At the end of each pay period, the clock cards are collected by the department manager. The manager prepares a payroll register in duplicate and forwards the original to payroll. In payroll, the summaries are checked for mathematical accuracy and a payroll supervisor pays each employee by check.

**Instructions**
(a) �\[□▤▤➤ Indicate the weakness(es) in internal control in each company.
(b) ▢▤▤➤ For each weakness, describe the control procedure(s) that will provide effective internal control. Use the following format for your answer:

| **(a) Weaknesses** | **(b) Recommended Procedures** |
|---|---|
| | |

**P11–4** The following payroll liability accounts are included in the ledger of Carlos Costa Company on January 1, 1996:

*Journalize payroll transactions and adjusting entries.*
(SO 6, 7, 8)

| | |
|---|---|
| FICA Taxes Payable | $ 662.20 |
| Federal Income Taxes Payable | 954.60 |
| State Income Taxes Payable | 102.15 |
| Federal Unemployment Taxes Payable | 2,400.00 |
| State Unemployment Taxes Payable | 1,954.40 |
| Union Dues Payable | 250.00 |
| U.S. Savings Bonds Payable | 350.00 |

In January, the following transactions occurred:

Jan. 10  Sent check for $250.00 to union treasurer for union dues.
     12  Deposited check for $1,616.80 in Federal Reserve Bank for FICA taxes and federal income taxes withheld.
     15  Purchased U.S. Savings Bonds for employees by writing check for $350.00.
     17  Paid state income taxes withheld from employees.
     20  Paid federal and state unemployment taxes.
     31  Completed monthly payroll register, which shows office salaries $14,600, store wages $27,400, FICA taxes withheld $3,360, federal income taxes payable $1,654, state income taxes payable $360, union dues payable $400, United Fund contributions payable $1,688 , and net pay $34,538.
     31  Prepared payroll checks for the net pay and distributed checks to employees.

At January 31, the company also makes the following accruals pertaining to employee compensation:

1. Employer payroll taxes: FICA taxes (8%), state unemployment taxes (5.4%), and federal unemployment taxes (0.8%).
2. Vacation pay: 4% of gross earnings.

**Instructions**
(a) Journalize the January transactions.
(b) Journalize the adjustments pertaining to employee compensation at January 31.

*Prepare entries for payroll and payroll taxes, and prepare W-2 data.*
*(SO 6, 7, 8)*

**P11-5**  For the year ended December 31, 1996, Valley Electric Company reports the following summary payroll data:

| Gross earnings: | |
|---|---|
| Administrative salaries | $180,000 |
| Electricians' wages | 370,000 |
| Total | $550,000 |

| Deductions: | |
|---|---|
| FICA taxes | $ 38,000 |
| Federal income taxes withheld | 168,000 |
| State income taxes withheld (2.6%) | 14,300 |
| United Fund contributions payable | 27,500 |
| Hospital insurance premiums | 17,200 |
| Total | $265,000 |

Valley Company's payroll taxes are: FICA 8%, state unemployment 2.5% (due to a stable employment record), and 0.8% federal unemployment. Gross earnings subject to (1) FICA taxes total $475,000, and (2) unemployment taxes total $400,000.

**Instructions**
(a) Prepare a summary journal entry at December 31 for the full year's payroll.
(b) Journalize the adjusting entry at December 31 to record the employer's payroll taxes.
(c) The W-2 Wage and Tax Statement requires the following dollar data:

| Wages, Tips, Other Compensation | Federal Income Tax Withheld | State Income Tax Withheld | FICA Wages | FICA Tax Withheld |
|---|---|---|---|---|
| | | | | |

Complete the required data for the following employees:

| Employee | Gross Earnings | Federal Income Tax Withheld |
|---|---|---|
| A. Osa | $60,000 | $27,500 |
| B. Bama | 26,000 | 10,200 |

*Journalize and post note transactions and show balance sheet presentation.*
*(SO 2)*

**P11-6**  The following are selected transactions of Eldorado Company. Eldorado prepares financial statements *quarterly*.

Jan.  2  Purchased merchandise on account from McCoy Company, $15,000, terms 2/10, n/30.
Feb.  1  Issued a 10%, 2-month, $15,000 note to McCoy in payment of account.

Mar. 31  Accrued interest for 2 months on McCoy note.

Apr.  1  Paid face value and interest on McCoy note.

July  1  Purchased equipment from Scottie Equipment paying $11,000 in cash and signing a 10%, 3-month, $24,000 note.

Sept. 30  Accrued interest for 3 months on Scottie note.

Oct.  1  Paid face value and interest on Scottie note.

Dec.  1  Borrowed $10,000 from the Federation Bank by issuing a 3-month, 9%-interest-bearing note with a face value of $10,000.

Dec. 31  Recognized interest expense for 1 month on Federation Bank note.

**Instructions**

(a) Prepare journal entries for the above transactions and events.

(b) Post to the accounts, Notes Payable, Interest Payable, and Interest Expense.

(c) Show the balance sheet presentation of notes payable at December 31.

(d) What is total interest expense for the year?

# ALTERNATE PROBLEMS

**P11–1A**  On January 1, 1996, the ledger of El Paso Company contains the following liability accounts:

| | |
|---|---|
| Accounts Payable | $52,000 |
| Sales Taxes Payable | 7,500 |
| Unearned Service Revenue | 16,000 |

*Prepare current liability entries, adjusting entries, and current liability section.*
(SO 1, 2, 3, 4)

During January the following selected transactions occurred:

Jan.  5  Sold merchandise for cash totaling $16,632, which includes 8% sales taxes.

12  Provided services for customers who had made advance payments of $9,000. (Credit Service Revenue)

14  Paid state revenue department for sales taxes collected in December 1995 ($7,500).

20  Sold 500 units of a new product on credit at $50 per unit, plus 8% sales tax. This new product is subject to a 1-year warranty.

21  Borrowed $18,000 from Midland Bank on a 3-month, 10%, $18,000 note.

25  Sold merchandise for cash totaling $11,340, which includes 8% sales taxes.

**Instructions**

(a) Journalize the January transactions.

(b) Journalize the adjusting entries at January 31 for (1) the outstanding notes payable, and (2) estimated warranty liability, assuming warranty costs are expected to equal 8% of sales of the new product. (Hint: Use one-third of a month for the Midland Bank note.)

(c) Prepare the current liability section of the balance sheet at January 31, 1996. Assume no change in accounts payable.

**P11–2A**  Sure-Value Hardware has four employees who are paid on an hourly basis plus time-and-one-half for all hours worked in excess of 40 a week. Payroll data for the week ended March 15, 1996, are presented below:

*Prepare payroll register and payroll entries.*
(SO 6, 7)

| Employee | Hours Worked | Hourly Rate | Federal Income Tax Withholdings | United Fund |
|---|---|---|---|---|
| A. Pima | 40 | $13.00 | $? | $5.00 |
| C. Zuni | 42 | 13.00 | ? | 5.00 |
| E. Hopi | 44 | 13.00 | 42 | 8.00 |
| G. Mohav | 46 | 13.00 | 48 | 5.00 |

Pima and Zuni are married. They claim 0 and 4 withholding allowances, respectively. The following tax rates are applicable: FICA 8%, state income taxes 3%, state unemployment taxes 5.4%, and federal unemployment 0.8%. The first three employees are sales clerks (store wages expense) and the other employee performs administrative duties (office wages expense).

**Instructions**

(a) Prepare a payroll register for the weekly payroll. (Use the wage-bracket withholding table in the text for federal income tax withholdings.)

(b) Journalize the payroll on March 15, 1996, and the accrual of employer payroll taxes.

(c) Journalize the payment of the payroll on March 16, 1996.

(d) Journalize the deposit in a federal reserve bank on March 31, 1996, of the FICA and federal income taxes payable to the government.

*Identify internal control weaknesses and make recommendations for improvement.*
*(SO 5)*

**P11–3A**    Selected payroll procedures of Chen Wee Company are described below:

1. Department managers interview applicants and on the basis of the interview either hire or reject the applicants. When an applicant is hired, the applicant fills out a W-4 form (Employer's Withholding Exemption Certificate). One copy of the form is sent to the personnel department and one copy is sent to the payroll department as notice that the individual has been hired. On the copy of the W-4 sent to payroll, the managers manually indicate the hourly pay rate for the new hire.

2. The payroll checks are manually signed by the chief accountant and given to the department managers for distribution to employees in their department. The managers are responsible for seeing that any absent employees receive their checks.

3. There are two clerks in the payroll department. The payroll is divided alphabetically with one clerk having employees A to L and the other employees M to Z. Each clerk computes the gross earnings, deductions, and net pay for employees in the section and posts the data to the employee earning records.

**Instructions**

(a) ▯▯▭▭▭▷  Indicate the weaknesses in internal control.

(b) ▯▯▭▭▭▷  For each weakness, describe the control procedures that will provide effective internal control. Use the following format for your answer:

| **(a) Weaknesses** | **(b) Recommended Procedures** |
| --- | --- |

*Journalize payroll transactions and adjusting entries.*
*(SO 6, 7, 8)*

**P11–4A**    The following payroll liability accounts are included in the ledger of Amora Company on January 1, 1996:

| | |
| --- | --- |
| FICA Taxes Payable | $  760.00 |
| Federal Income Taxes Payable | 954.60 |
| State Income Taxes Payable | 108.95 |
| Federal Unemployment Taxes Payable | 288.95 |
| State Unemployment Taxes Payable | 1,954.40 |
| Union Dues Payable | 870.00 |
| U.S. Savings Bonds Payable | 360.00 |

In January, the following transactions occurred:

Jan. 10   Sent check for $870.00 to union treasurer for union dues.

12   Deposited check for $1,714.60 in Federal Reserve Bank for FICA taxes and federal income taxes withheld.

15   Purchased U.S. Savings Bonds for employees by writing check for $360.00.

17   Paid state income taxes withheld from employees.

20   Paid federal and state unemployment taxes.

31   Completed monthly payroll register, which shows office salaries $14,600, store wages $28,400, FICA taxes withheld $3,440, federal income taxes payable $1,684, state income taxes payable $360, union dues payable $400, United Fund contributions payable $1,888, and net pay $35,228.

31   Prepared payroll checks for the net pay and distributed checks to employees.

At January 31, the company also makes the following accrued adjustments pertaining to employee compensation:

1. Employer payroll taxes: FICA taxes (8%), federal unemployment taxes (0.8%), and state unemployment taxes (5.4%).

2. Vacation pay: 4% of gross earnings.

**Instructions**

(a) Journalize the January transactions.

(b) Journalize the adjustments pertaining to employee compensation at January 31.

**P11–5A** For the year ended December 31, 1996, Wynn Electrical Repair Company reports the following summary payroll data:

*Prepare entries for payroll and payroll taxes and prepare W-2 data.*
*(SO 6, 7, 8)*

| Gross earnings: | |
|---|---|
| Administrative salaries | $180,000 |
| Electricians' wages | 470,000 |
| Total | $650,000 |

| Deductions: | |
|---|---|
| FICA taxes | $ 48,000 |
| Federal income taxes withheld | 188,000 |
| State income taxes withheld (2.6%) | 16,900 |
| United Fund contributions payable | 32,500 |
| Hospital insurance premiums | 20,300 |
| Total | $305,700 |

Wynn Company's payroll taxes are: FICA 8%, state unemployment 2.5% (due to a stable employment record), and 0.8% federal unemployment. Gross earnings subject to (1) FICA taxes total $600,000; and (2) unemployment taxes total $450,000.

**Instructions**
(a) Prepare a summary journal entry at December 31 for the full year's payroll.
(b) Journalize the adjusting entry at December 31 to record the employer's payroll taxes.
(c) The W-2 Wage and Tax Statement requires the following dollar data:

| Wages, Tips, Other Compensation | Federal Income Tax Withheld | State Income Tax Withheld | FICA Wages | FICA Tax Withheld |
|---|---|---|---|---|
| | | | | |

Complete the required data for the following employees:

| Employee | Gross Earnings | Federal Income Tax Withheld |
|---|---|---|
| A. Ute | $62,000 | $28,500 |
| B. Yuma | 28,000 | 10,800 |

# ▶*B*roadening Your Perspective

## *F*INANCIAL REPORTING PROBLEM
••••••••••••••••••••••••••••••••••••••••••••••••••••••••••••

Refer to the financial statements of PepsiCo, Inc. and the Notes to Consolidated Financial Statements in Appendix A.

**Instructions**
Answer the following questions about current and contingent liabilities and payroll costs:
(a) What were PepsiCo's total current liabilities at December 31, 1994? What was the increase/decrease in PepsiCo's total current liabilities from the prior year?
(b) How much were the "short-term borrowings" at December 31, 1994?
(c) What were the components of total current liabilities on December 31, 1994 (other than "short-term borrowings" already discussed in b above)?
(d) Where does PepsiCo report its contingent liabilities?
(e) What is management's opinion as to the ultimate effect of the "various claims, lawsuits, and other matters" pending against the company?
(f) What is the amount for which PepsiCo is contingently liable under guarantees at December 31, 1994, and December 25, 1993?

# DECISION CASE

Quicko Processing Company provides word-processing services for clients and students in a university community. The work for clients is fairly steady throughout the year, but the work for students peaks significantly in December and May as a result of term papers, research project reports, and dissertations.

Two years ago, the company attempted to meet the peak demand by hiring part-time help. However, this led to numerous errors and considerable customer dissatisfaction. A year ago, the company hired four experienced employees on a permanent basis instead of using part-time help. This proved to be much better in terms of productivity and customer satisfaction. However, it has caused an increase in annual payroll costs and a significant decline in annual net income.

Recently, Sue Stone, a sales representative of Hiawatha Services Inc. has made a proposal to the company. Under the plan, Hiawatha Services will provide up to four experienced workers at a daily rate of $100 per person for an 8-hour workday. Hiawatha workers are not available on an hourly basis. Quicko Processing would have to pay only the daily rate for the workers used.

The owner of Quicko Processing, Denise Denby, asks you, as the company's accountant, to prepare a report on the expenses that are pertinent to the decision. If the Hiawatha plan is adopted, Denise will terminate the employment of two permanent employees who are each earning an average annual salary of $28,000. The remaining permanent employees each earn an annual income of $28,000. Quicko Processing pays 8% FICA taxes, 0.8% Federal Unemployment Taxes, and 5.4% State Unemployment Taxes. The unemployment taxes apply to only the first $7,000 of gross earnings. In addition, Quicko Processing pays $40 per month for each employee for medical and dental insurance.

Denise indicates that if the Hiawatha Services plan is accepted, her needs for workers will be as follows:

| Months | Number | Working Days per Month |
|---|---|---|
| January–March | 2 | 20 |
| April–May | 3 | 25 |
| June–October | 2 | 18 |
| November–December | 3 | 23 |

*Instructions*
  (a) Prepare a report showing the comparative payroll expense of continuing to employ permanent workers compared to adopting the Hiawatha Services Inc. plan.
  (b) What other factors should Denise consider before finalizing her decision?

# COMMUNICATION ACTIVITY

Prentice Berg, president of the Flying Eagle Company, has recently hired a number of additional employees. He recognizes that additional payroll taxes will be due as a result of this hiring, and that the company will serve as the collection agent for other taxes.

*Instructions*
In a memorandum to Prentice Berg explain each of the taxes, and identify the taxes that result in payroll tax expense to the employer.

# GROUP ACTIVITY

There are five topics in the section on Accounting for Current Liabilities: notes payable, sales taxes payable, unearned revenues, current maturities of long-term debt, and financial statement presentation.

*Instructions*

With the class divided into five groups, each group should choose one topic and prepare a presentation to explain to the class the key points about the assigned topic.

# ETHICS CASE

. . . . . . . . . . . . . . . . . . . . . . . . . . . . . . . . . . . . . . . . . . . . . . . . . . . . . . . . .

Jack Sprat owns and manages the Spicy-Saucer Restaurant, a 24-hour restaurant near the city's medical complex. Jack employs nine full-time employees and sixteen part-time employees. He pays all of the full-time employees by check, the amounts of which are determined by Jack's public accountant, Clara Hankes. Jack pays all of his part-time employees in currency that he computes and withdraws directly from his cash register. Clara has repeatedly urged Jack to pay all employees by check. But as Jack has told his competitor and friend, Bud Juice, who owns the Tasty Diner, "First of all, my part-time employees prefer the currency over a check, and secondly I don't withhold or pay any taxes or workmen's compensation insurance on those wages because they go totally unrecorded and unnoticed."

*Instructions*
  (a) Who are the stakeholders in this situation?
  (b) What are the legal and ethical considerations regarding Jack's handling of his payroll?
  (c) Clara Hankes is aware of Jack's payment of the part-time payroll in currency. What are her ethical responsibilities in this case?
  (d) What internal control principle is violated in this payroll process?

# CRITICAL THINKING
► *A Real-World Focus: Capitol American Financial Corporation*
. . . . . . . . . . . . . . . . . . . . . . . . . . . . . . . . . . . . . . . . . . . . . . . . . . . . . . . . .

*Formed in 1970, today* **Capitol American Financial Corporation** *is licensed throughout most of the United States, Puerto Rico, and the U.S. Virgin Islands. The company's 285 employees develop, underwrite, market, and distribute individual supplemental health and accidental insurance. A primary product line is cancer insurance.*

CAPITOL**A**MERICAN
Capitol American Financial Corporation

Presented below is a note to the financial statement of Capitol American Financial Corporation:

The Company is the subject of an employment tax examination by the Internal Revenue Service ("IRS") with respect to the treatment of its agents as independent contractors rather than employees for financial reporting and tax purposes for 1987 and 1988. The IRS has proposed for 1987 and 1988 an increase in the tax liability of the Company in the aggregate amount of approximately $6.1 million, including approximately $1.5 million in penalties, for assessment of Federal Insurance Contributions Act ("FICA") taxes, federal unemployment compensation taxes and federal income taxes on wages not withheld by the Company. Management believes, based in part on the opinion of legal counsel, that the Company's treatment of its agents as independent contractors rather than employees is correct for federal tax purposes and that the Company should prevail. Accordingly, no liability or loss that could result upon adverse resolution of this matter has been recognized in the Company's consolidated financial statements. If the Company does not prevail, it can be expected that the Company would be assessed similar, but generally increasing, amounts for the years 1989 through 1992 (representing a total potential liability to the Company, including penalties, of approximately $28.1 million, for 1987 through 1992), and also for 1993 and future years unless the Company changes certain of its practices regarding the treatment of its agents. In addition, an adverse resolution of this matter could also be expected to have an adverse effect on the Company with respect to certain state and local taxes.

*Instructions*
  (a) How is the company's net income affected by hiring work to be done by independent contractors rather than employees?

      (b) If Capitol American Financial Corporation loses the lawsuit which accounts will
           have been understated by using the independent contractor arrangement?

      (c) What assessment has the Corporation made with respect to the likelihood and esti-
           matability of this contingent liability?

---

*Answers to Self-Study Questions*

1. a    2. d    3. b    4. b    5. c    6. b    7. d    8. d    9. c    10. d

**Before studying this chapter, you should know or, if necessary, review:**

**a.** *The two organizations primarily responsible for setting accounting standards. (Ch. 1, pp. 10–11)*

**b.** *The monetary unit assumption, the economic entity assumption, and the time period assumption. (Chs. 1 and 3, pp. 12, 89, 89–90)*

**c.** *The cost principle, the revenue recognition principle, and the matching principle. (Chs. 1 and 3, pp. 11, 89–90)*

# Is Online "Off-Track"?

VIENNA, Va. — In the world of interactive media, subscribers pay a monthly fee ($9.95 or so) for limited access to electronic data systems. America Online (AOL) is one of the success stories in this industry. Its stock has increased from $11.50 in 1992, when the company went public, to $71.50 in late 1994. However, an accounting controversy over some of its costs has raised questions about the amount of its earnings.

AOL's biggest expenditure is the cost of attracting subscribers. The company sends out millions of mail solicitations, and works deals to give away a trial subscription with each new computer. Such promotion is expensive; in 1994, subscription-acquisition costs totaled $37 million. Are those an expense against revenue? Or are they an investment undertaken to create an asset?

AOL believes they are the latter. The company capitalizes the costs and amortizes them over 18 months. The other treatment would reduce earnings more: If it had expensed the $37 million as incurred, AOL would have reported a net loss of about $6 million—rather than net income of $6 million. AOL's practice has the FASB's blessing: it considers the cost of obtaining the subscriptions from direct-mail campaigns to be assets. Magazine publishers, similarly, often capitalize such costs.

However, AOL's biggest competitor, CompuServe, takes a more conservative approach by expensing subscriber-acquisition costs as they occur. As CompuServe's controller noted, "We didn't want to taint [our earnings] or dilute them by following [AOL's] accounting."

AOL defends its accounting as a policy of matching expenses with revenues. As its CFO notes, "We're writing these costs off much more rapidly than the ongoing revenue stream." One test of the wisdom of AOL's accounting practice may be the long-term loyalty of subscribers: If they stay with AOL in the face of increasing competition, the subscription-acquisition costs will have created long-term assets. ◀

CHAPTER · **12**

# ACCOUNTING PRINCIPLES

► **STUDY OBJECTIVES** ◄

**After studying this chapter, you should be able to:**

1. *Explain the meaning of generally accepted accounting principles and identify the key items of the conceptual framework.*
2. *Describe the basic objectives of financial reporting.*
3. *Discuss the qualitative characteristics of accounting information and elements of financial statements.*
4. *Identify the basic assumptions used by accountants.*
5. *Identify the basic principles of accounting.*
6. *Identify the two constraints in accounting.*
7. *Explain the accounting principles used in international operations.*

As indicated in the opening story, it is important that general guidelines be available to resolve accounting issues such as that faced by America Online. Without these basic guidelines, each enterprise would have to develop its own set of accounting practices. If this happened, we would have to become familiar with every company's peculiar accounting and reporting rules in order to understand their financial statements. Thus, it would be difficult, if not impossible, to compare the financial statements of different companies.

This chapter explores the basic accounting principles followed in developing specific accounting guidelines. The content and organization of the chapter are as follows:

# *T*he Conceptual Framework of Accounting

The accounting profession has established a set of standards and rules that are recognized as a general guide for financial reporting purposes. This recognized set of standards is called generally accepted accounting principles (GAAP). "Generally accepted" means that these principles must have "substantial authoritative support." Such support usually comes from two standard-setting bodies: the Financial Accounting Standards Board (FASB) and the Securities and Exchange Commission (SEC).[1]

Since the early 1970s the business and governmental communities have given the FASB the responsibility for developing accounting principles in this country.

---

[1]The SEC is an agency of the U.S. government that was established in 1933 to administer laws and regulations relating to the exchange of securities and the publication of financial information by U.S. businesses. The agency has the authority to mandate generally accepted accounting principles for companies under its jurisdiction. However, throughout its history, the SEC has been willing to accept the principles set forth by the FASB and similar bodies.

## ▶A̲ccounting in A̲ction ▸ *International Insight*

You should recognize that different political and cultural influences affect the accounting that occurs in foreign countries. For example, in the Near East, Islamic accounting is presently being considered. If adopted, the changes would introduce religious tenets into accounting practice. In Sweden, accounting is considered an instrument to be used to shape fiscal policy. In Europe, more emphasis is given to social reporting (more information on employment statistics, health of workers, and so on) because employees and their labor organizations are strong and demand that type of information from management.

This job is an ongoing process in which accounting principles change to reflect changes in the business environment and in the needs of users of accounting information.

Prior to the establishment of the FASB, accounting principles were developed on a problem-by-problem basis. Thus, rule-making bodies developed and issued accounting rules and methods to solve specific problems. Critics charged that the problem-by-problem approach led to inconsistent rules and practices over time. Unfortunately, no clearly developed conceptual framework of accounting existed for the accounting rule makers to refer to in solving problems.

In response to these criticisms, the FASB developed a conceptual framework to serve as the basis for resolving accounting and reporting problems. The FASB spent considerable time and effort on this project. The Board views its conceptual framework as "... a constitution, a coherent system of interrelated objectives and fundamentals."[2]

The FASB's conceptual framework consists of the following four items:

1. Objectives of financial reporting.
2. Qualitative characteristics of accounting information.
3. Elements of financial statements.
4. Operating guidelines (assumptions, principles, and constraints).

We will discuss each of these items on the following pages.

### Objectives of Financial Reporting

In developing the conceptual framework, the FASB concluded that the first level of study was to determine the objectives of financial reporting. Determining these objectives required answers to such basic questions as: Who uses financial statements? Why? What information do they need? How knowledgeable about business and accounting are the users of financial statements? How should financial information be reported so that it is best understood?

In answering these questions, the FASB concluded that the objectives of financial reporting are to provide information that:

1. Is useful to those making investment and credit decisions.
2. Is helpful in assessing future cash flows.
3. Identifies the economic resources (assets), the claims to those resources (liabilities), and the changes in those resources and claims.

**STUDY OBJECTIVE**
·········▼**2**·········
*Describe the basic objectives of financial reporting.*

---

[2]"Conceptual Framework for Financial Accounting and Reporting: Elements of Financial Statements and Their Measurement," *FASB Discussion Memorandum* (Stamford, Conn.: 1976), p. 1.

The FASB then undertook to describe the characteristics that make accounting information useful.

## Qualitative Characteristics of Accounting Information

**STUDY OBJECTIVE**

**▸ 3 ◂**

*Discuss the qualitative characteristics of accounting information and elements of financial statements.*

How does a company like Microsoft decide on the amount of financial information to disclose? In what format should its financial information be presented? How should assets, liabilities, revenues, and expenses be measured? **The FASB concluded that the overriding criterion by which such accounting choices should be judged is decision usefulness.** The accounting practice selected or the policy adopted should be the one that generates the most useful financial information for making a decision. To be useful, information should possess the following qualitative characteristics: relevance, reliability, comparability, and consistency.

### Relevance

**Helpful hint** What makes accounting information relevant? Answer: Relevant accounting information provides feedback, serves as a basis for predictions, and is timely (current).

Accounting information is relevant if it makes a difference in a decision. Relevant information has either predictive or feedback value or both. **Predictive value** helps users forecast future events. For example, when Exxon issues financial statements, the information in the statements is considered relevant because it provides a basis for forecasting (predicting) future earnings. **Feedback value** confirms or corrects prior expectations. When Exxon issues financial statements, in addition to helping predict future events, it confirms or corrects prior expectations about the financial health of the company.

In addition, for accounting information to be relevant it must be **timely**. That is, it must be available to decision makers before it loses its capacity to influence decisions. If Exxon reported its financial information only every 5 years, the information would have limited usefulness for decision making purposes.

### Reliability

**Helpful hint** What makes accounting information reliable? Answer: Reliable accounting information is free of error and bias, is factual, verifiable, and neutral.

Reliability of information means that the information is free of error and bias; it can be depended on. To be reliable, accounting information must be **verifiable**—we must be able to prove that it is free of error and bias. The information must be a **faithful representation** of what it purports to be—it must be factual. If Sears, Roebuck's income statement reports sales of $100 billion when it had sales of $51 billion, then the statement is not a faithful representation. Finally, accounting information must be **neutral**—it cannot be selected, prepared, or presented to favor one set of interested users over another. To ensure reliability, certified public accountants audit financial statements, just as the Internal Revenue Service audits tax returns for the same purpose.

### Comparability and Consistency

Accounting information about an enterprise is most useful when it can be compared with accounting information about other enterprises. Comparability results when different companies use the same accounting principles. For example, Sears, Roebuck, Montgomery Ward, and J.C. Penney all use the cost principle in reporting plant assets on the balance sheet. Moreover, each company uses the revenue recognition and matching principles in determining its net income.

Conceptually, comparability should also extend to the methods used by companies in complying with an accounting principle. Accounting methods include the FIFO and LIFO methods of inventory costing, and various depreciation methods. At this point, comparability of methods is not required, even for companies in the same industry, as the opening story about America Online demonstrates. Thus, Ford, General Motors, and Chrysler may use different inventory costing and depreciation methods in their financial statements. The only accounting requirement is that each company **must disclose** the accounting methods used. From the disclosures, the external user can determine whether the financial information is comparable.

Consistency means that a company uses the same accounting principles and methods from year to year. Thus, if a company selects FIFO as the inventory costing method in the first year of operations, it is expected to continue to use FIFO in succeeding years. When financial information has been reported on a consistent basis, the financial statements permit meaningful analysis of trends within a company.

A company can change to a new method of accounting if management can justify that the new method results in more meaningful financial information. In the year in which the change occurs, the change must be disclosed in the notes to the financial statements so that users of the financial statements are aware of the lack of consistency.

The qualitative characteristics of accounting information are summarized in Illustration 12-1.

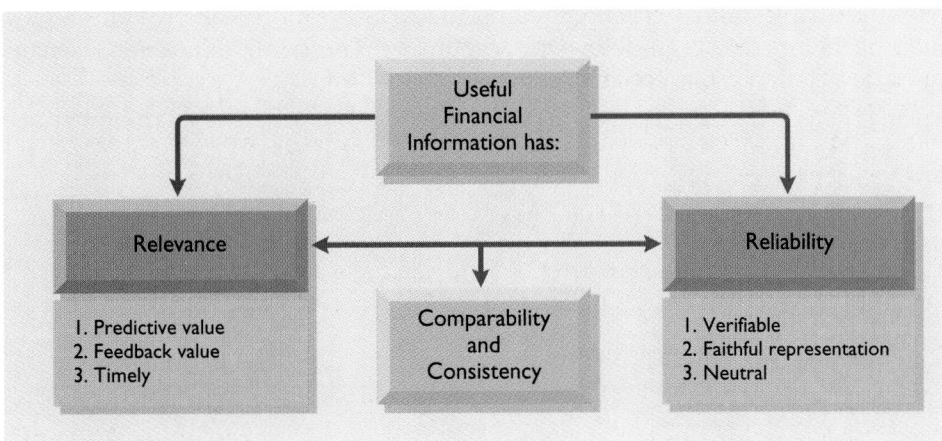

**Illustration 12-1**

*Qualitative characteristics of accounting information*

## Elements of Financial Statements

An important part of an accounting conceptual framework is a set of definitions that describe the basic terms used in accounting. The FASB refers to this set of definitions as the elements of financial statements. They include such terms as assets, liabilities, equity, revenues, and expenses.

Because these elements are so important, it is imperative that they be precisely defined and universally understood and applied. Finding the appropriate definition for many of these elements is not easy. For example, how should an

►**A**ccounting in **A**ction ► *Business Insight*

There is an old story that professors often tell students about a company looking for an accountant. The company approached the first accountant and asked: "What do you believe our net income will be this year?" The accountant said $4 million dollars. The company asked the second accountant the same question, and the answer was "What would you like it to be?" Guess who got the job? The reason we tell the story here is that, because accounting principles offer flexibility, it is important that a consistent treatment be provided from period to period. Otherwise it would be very difficult to interpret financial statements. Perhaps *no* alternative methods should be permitted in accounting. What do you think?

asset be defined? Should the value of a company's employees be reported as an asset on a balance sheet? Should the death of the company's president be reported as a loss? A good set of definitions should provide answers to these types of questions. Because you have already encountered most of these definitions in earlier chapters, they are not repeated here.

## Operating Guidelines

The objectives of financial statements, the qualitative characteristics of accounting information, and the elements of financial statements are very broad. However, because practicing accountants and standard-setting bodies must solve practical problems, more detailed guidelines are needed. In its conceptual framework, the FASB recognized the need for operating guidelines. We have chosen to classify these guidelines as assumptions, principles, and constraints. These guidelines are well-established and accepted in accounting.

**Assumptions** provide a foundation for the accounting process. **Principles** are specific rules that indicate how economic events should be reported in the accounting process. **Constraints** on the accounting process allow for a relaxation of the principles under certain circumstances. Illustration 12-2 provides a roadmap of the operating guidelines of accounting. These guidelines are discussed in more detail in the following sections.

**Illustration 12-2**

*The operating guidelines of accounting*

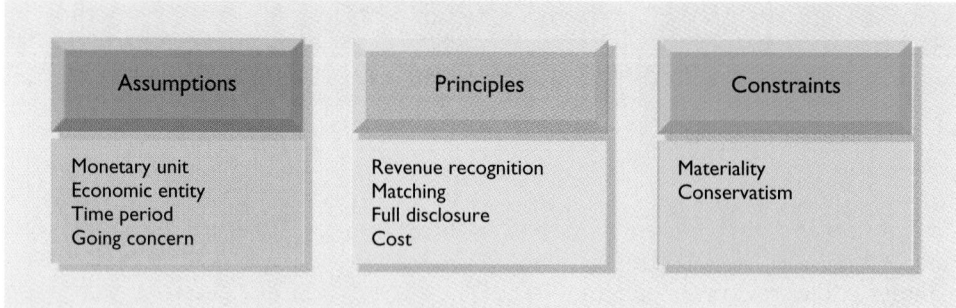

| Assumptions | Principles | Constraints |
|---|---|---|
| Monetary unit | Revenue recognition | Materiality |
| Economic entity | Matching | Conservatism |
| Time period | Full disclosure | |
| Going concern | Cost | |

## Before You Go On . . .

▶ **Review It**

1. What are generally accepted accounting principles?
2. What are the basic objectives of financial information?
3. What are the qualitative characteristics that make accounting information useful? Identify two elements of the financial statements.

# Assumptions

**STUDY OBJECTIVE**

**4**

*Identify the basic assumptions used by accountants.*

As noted above, assumptions provide a foundation for the accounting process. You have already studied three of the major assumptions in preceding chapters—the monetary unit, economic entity, and time period assumptions. The fourth is called the going concern assumption.

## Monetary Unit Assumption

The monetary unit assumption states that only transaction data capable of being expressed in terms of money should be included in the accounting records of the economic entity. For example, the death of a company president would not be reported in a company's financial records as a loss because the event cannot be expressed easily in dollars.

An important corollary to the monetary unit assumption is the added assumption that the unit of measure remains sufficiently constant over time. This point will be discussed in more detail later in this chapter.

## Economic Entity Assumption

The economic entity assumption states that economic events can be identified with a particular unit of accountability. For example, it is assumed that the activities of IBM can be distinguished from those of other computer companies such as Apple, Compaq, and Hewlett-Packard.

## Time Period Assumption

The time period assumption states that the economic life of a business can be divided into artificial time periods. Thus, it is assumed that the activities of business enterprises such as General Electric, America Online, Exxon, or any enterprise can be subdivided into months, quarters, or a year for meaningful financial reporting purposes.

## Going Concern Assumption

The going concern assumption assumes that the enterprise will continue in operation long enough to carry out its existing objectives. Experience indicates that, in spite of numerous business failures, companies have a fairly high continuance rate, and it has proved useful to adopt a going concern assumption for accounting purposes.

The accounting implications of adopting this assumption are critical. If a going concern assumption is not used, then plant assets should be stated at their liquidation value (selling price less cost of disposal)—not at their cost. As a result, depreciation and amortization of these assets would not be needed. Each period these assets would simply be reported at their liquidation value. Also, without this assumption, the current–noncurrent classification of assets and liabilities would have little significance. Labeling anything as fixed or long-term would be difficult to justify.

Acceptance of the going concern assumption gives credibility to the cost principle. If, instead, liquidation were assumed, assets would be better stated at liquidation value than at cost. Only when liquidation appears imminent is the going concern assumption inapplicable.

These basic accounting assumptions are illustrated graphically in Illustration 12-3.

▶ *International note*

In a recent action that sent shock-waves through the French business community, the CEO of Alcatel-Alsthom was taken into custody for an apparent violation of the economic entity assumption. Allegedly, the executive improperly used company funds to install an expensive security system in his home.

# *P*rinciples

On the basis of these fundamental assumptions of accounting, the accounting profession has developed principles that dictate how transactions and other economic events should be recorded and reported. In earlier chapters we discussed the cost principle (Chapter 1) and the revenue recognition and matching principles (Chapter 3). We now examine a number of reporting issues related to these principles. In addition, another principle, the full disclosure principle, is discussed.

**STUDY OBJECTIVE**
**5**
*Identify the basic principles of accounting.*

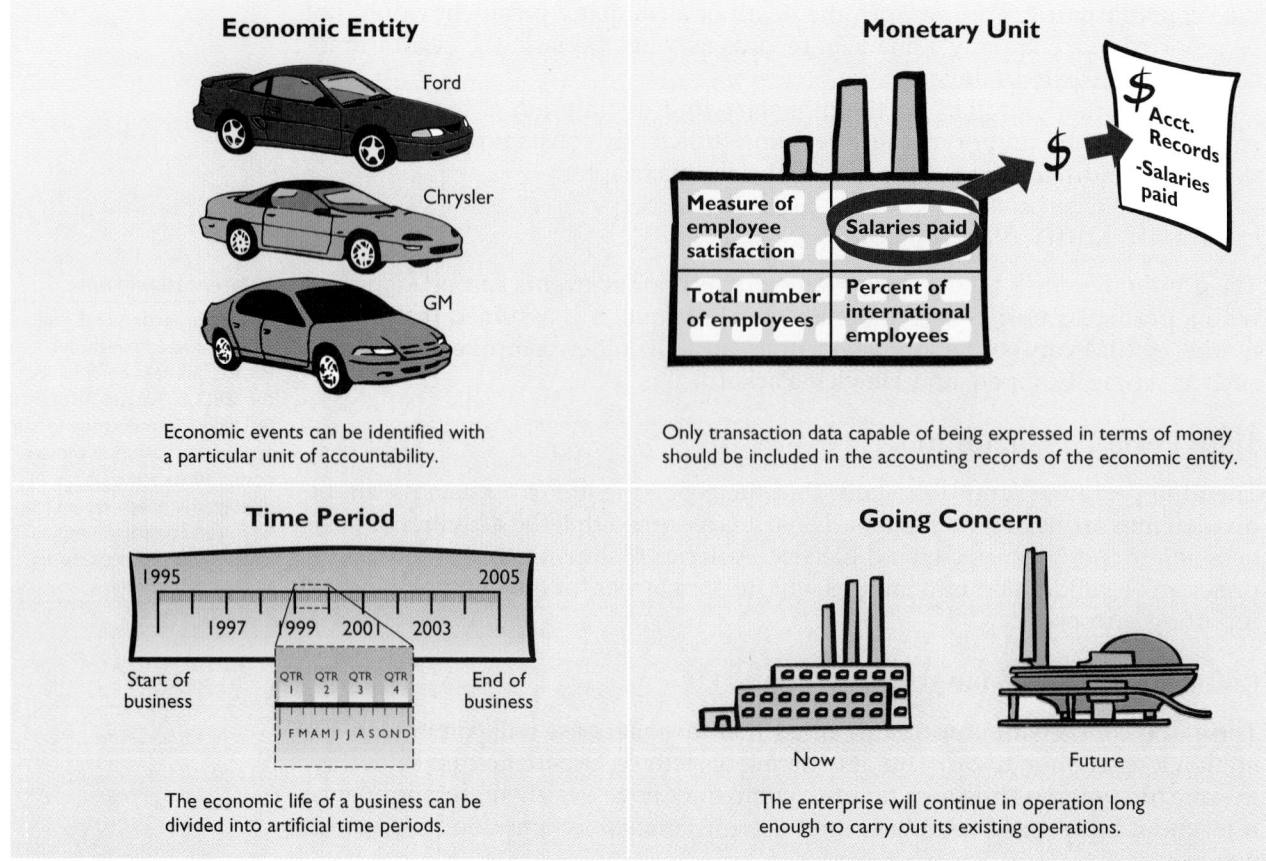

**Economic Entity**

Ford

Chrysler

GM

Economic events can be identified with
a particular unit of accountability.

**Monetary Unit**

$ Acct.
Records
-Salaries
paid

Measure of employee satisfaction

Salaries paid

Total number of employees

Percent of international employees

Only transaction data capable of being expressed in terms of money
should be included in the accounting records of the economic entity.

**Time Period**

1995                    2005

1997   1999   2001   2003

Start of
business

QTR QTR QTR QTR
 1   2   3   4

J F M A M J J A S O N D

End of
business

The economic life of a business can be
divided into artificial time periods.

**Going Concern**

Now

Future

The enterprise will continue in operation long
enough to carry out its existing operations.

**Illustration 12-3**

*Assumptions used in
accounting*

**Helpful hint** Revenue
should be recognized in the
accounting period in which it is
earned, which may not be the
period in which the related
cash is received. In a retail establishment the point of sale is
often the critical point in the
process of earning revenue.

## Revenue Recognition Principle

The revenue recognition principle dictates that revenue should be recognized
in the accounting period in which it is earned. Applying this general principle
in practice, however, can be difficult. For example, it was reported that Automatic Inc. was improperly recognizing revenue on goods that had not been
shipped to customers. Similarly, many questioned the revenue recognition practices of the savings and loan industry, which until recently recorded a large
portion of its fees for granting a loan as revenue immediately rather than spread-
ing those fees over the life of the loan.

When a sale is involved, revenue is recognized at the point of sale. The **sales
basis** involves an exchange transaction between the seller and buyer, and the
sales price provides an objective measure of the amount of revenue realized.
There are, however, two exceptions to the sales basis for revenue recognition that
have become generally accepted.

### *Percentage-of-Completion Method*

**Helpful hint** In accounting
for long-term construction
contracts, it is appropriate
to use the percentage-of-
completion method of revenue
recognition because the critical
event in the earning process is
making progress toward completion. The ultimate sale and
selling price are assured by the
contract.

In long-term construction contracts, recognition of revenue is usually required
before the contract is completed. For example, assume that Warrior Construction
Co. had a contract to build a dam for the U.S. Bureau of the Interior for $400
million. Construction is estimated to take 3 years (starting in 1994) at a construction cost of $360 million. If Warrior applies the point-of-sale basis, it will report
no revenues and no profit in the first two years. But, in 1996 when completion
and sale take place, Warrior will report $400 million in revenues, costs of $360
million, and the entire profit of $40 million. Was Warrior really producing no
revenues and earning no profit in 1994 and 1995? Obviously not. The dam will

be as good as sold when Warrior completes the project according to specifications. Although technically an exchange transaction (transfer of ownership) has not occurred until completion of the dam, the earning process is considered substantially completed at various stages as construction progresses.

In recognizing revenue, Warrior can apply the percentage-of-completion method. This method recognizes revenue and income over the life of a long-term project on the basis of reasonable estimates of the project's progress toward completion. Progress toward completion is measured by comparing the costs incurred in a year to the total estimated costs for the entire project. That percentage is multiplied by the total revenue for the project; the result is then recognized as revenue for the period. The formulas for this method are as follows:

**Illustration 12-4**

*Formula to recognize revenue in the percentage-of-completion method*

The costs incurred in the current period are then subtracted from the revenue recognized during the current period to arrive at the gross profit.

Let's look at an illustration of the percentage-of-completion method. Assume that Warrior Construction Co. incurs costs of $54 million in 1994, $180 million in 1995, and $126 million in 1996 on the dam project. The portion of the $400 million of revenue recognized in each of the 3 years is shown in Illustration 12-5.

**Illustration 12-5**

*Revenue recognized—percentage-of-completion method*

| Year | Costs Incurred (Current Period) | ÷ | Total Estimated Cost | = | Percent Complete (Current Period) | × | Total Revenue | = | Revenue Recognized (Current Period) |
|------|------|---|------|---|------|---|------|---|------|
| 1994 | $ 54,000,000 | | $360,000,000 | | 15% | | $400,000,000 | | $ 60,000,000 |
| 1995 | 180,000,000 | | 360,000,000 | | 50% | | 400,000,000 | | 200,000,000 |
| 1996 | 126,000,000 | | | | Balance required to complete the contract | | | | 140,000,000 |
| Totals | $360,000,000 | | | | | | | | $400,000,000 |

Note that no estimate is made of the percentage of work completed during the final period. In the final period, all remaining revenue is recognized. In this example, the company's cost estimates have been very accurate; the costs incurred in the third year were 35% of the total estimated cost ($126,000 ÷ $360,000). The gross profit recognized each period is as follows:

**Illustration 12-6**

*Gross profit recognized—percentage-of-completion method*

| Year | Revenue Recognized (Current Period) | − | Actual Cost Incurred (Current Period) | = | Gross Profit Recognized (Current Period) |
|------|------|---|------|---|------|
| 1994 | $ 60,000,000 | | $ 54,000,000 | | $ 6,000,000 |
| 1995 | 200,000,000 | | 180,000,000 | | 20,000,000 |
| 1996 | 140,000,000 | | 126,000,000 | | 14,000,000 |
| Totals | $400,000,000 | | $360,000,000 | | $40,000,000 |

Application of the percentage-of-completion method involves some subjectivity. As a result, there is the possibility of error in determining the amount of revenue recognized and net income reported. Yet to wait until completion would seriously distort each period's financial statements. Naturally, **if it is not possible to obtain dependable estimates of costs and progress, then the revenue should be recognized at the completion date** and not by the percentage-of-completion method.

### Installment Method

Another basis for revenue recognition is the receipt of cash. The cash basis is generally used only when it is difficult to determine the revenue amount at the time of a credit sale because collection is so uncertain. One popular approach to the recognition of revenue using the cash basis is the installment method.

Under the installment method, each cash collection from a customer consists of (1) a partial recovery of the cost of the goods sold, and (2) partial gross profit from the sale. For example, if the gross profit rate at date of sale is 40%, each subsequent receipt consists of 60% recovery of cost of goods sold and 40% gross profit. The formula to recognize gross profit is as follows:

**Illustration 12-7**

*Gross profit formula—installment method*

To illustrate, assume that an Iowa farm machinery dealer in the first year of operations had installment sales of $600,000 and a cost of goods sold on installment of $420,000. Total gross profit is, therefore, $180,000 ($600,000 − $420,000), and the gross profit percentage is 30% ($180,000 ÷ $600,000). The collections on the installment sales were as follows: First year, $280,000 (down payment plus monthly payments); second year, $200,000; and, third year, $120,000. The collections of cash and recognition of the gross profit are summarized in Illustration 12-8 (interest charges are ignored in this illustration):

**Illustration 12-8**

*Gross profit recognized—installment method*

| Year | Cash Collected | × | Gross Profit Percentage | = | Gross Profit Recognized |
|------|------|---|------|---|------|
| 1994 | $280,000 | | 30% | | $ 84,000 |
| 1995 | 200,000 | | 30% | | 60,000 |
| 1996 | 120,000 | | 30% | | 36,000 |
| Total | $600,000 | | | | $180,000 |

## ►*Accounting in Action* ► *Business Insight*

Datapoint Corp. encouraged its customers to load up with large shipments at the end of the year, allowing Datapoint to report these shipments as revenues, even though payment hadn't been collected. Unfortunately, some of the customers either went broke or quit before paying for the equipment received. As a result, the company had to record substantial bad debts or in some cases reverse previously recorded sales. If Datapoint had used the installment method, this revenue would not have been reported. As a result, revenue recognition practices that are cash-basis oriented, such as the installment method, are becoming more acceptable as it becomes difficult to tell when a sale is a sale.

Under the installment method of accounting, gross profit is therefore recognized **in the period in which the cash is collected**.

As indicated earlier, use of the installment method is justified when the risk of not collecting an account receivable may be such that the sale is not sufficient evidence for revenue to be recognized.

## Matching Principle (Expense Recognition)

Expense recognition is traditionally tied to revenue recognition: "Let the expense follow the revenue." This practice is referred to as the matching principle: it dictates that expenses be matched with revenues in the period in which efforts are expended to generate revenues. Expenses are not recognized when cash is paid, or when the work is performed, or when the product is produced; they are recognized when the labor (service) or the product actually makes its contribution to revenue.

The problem is that it is sometimes difficult to determine the accounting period in which the expense contributed to the generation of revenues. Several approaches have therefore been devised for matching expenses and revenues on the income statement.

To understand these approaches, it is necessary to examine the nature of expenses. Costs that will generate revenues only in the current accounting period are expensed immediately. They are reported as operating expenses in the income statement. Examples include such costs as advertising, sales salaries, and repairs. These expenses are often called **expired costs**.

> **Helpful hint** Costs are the source of expenses. Costs become expenses when they are charged against revenue.

Costs that will generate revenues in future accounting periods are recognized as assets. For example, this is the basis on which America Online accounts for its subscription-acquisition costs. Other examples include merchandise inventory, prepaid expenses, and plant assets. These costs represent **unexpired costs**. Unexpired costs become expenses in two ways:

1. **Cost of goods sold.** Costs carried as merchandise inventory are expensed as cost of goods sold in the period when the sale occurs. Thus, there is a direct matching of expenses with revenues.
2. **Operating expenses.** Unexpired costs become operating expenses through use or consumption (as in the case of store supplies) or through the passage of time (as in the case of prepaid insurance and prepaid rent). The cost of plant assets and other long-lived productive resources is expensed through rational and systematic allocation methods which result in periodic depreciation and amortization. Operating expenses contribute to the revenues of the period but their association with revenues is less direct than for cost of goods sold.

> ►*Ethics note*
>
> Many appear to do it, but few like to discuss it: it's earnings management, and it's a clear violation of the revenue recognition and matching principles. Banks sometimes time the sale of investments or the expensing of bad debts to accomplish earnings objectives. Prominent companies, such as GE, have been accused of matching one-time gains with one-time charge-offs so that current period earnings are not so high that they can't be surpassed next period.

These points about expense recognition are illustrated in Illustration 12-9.

**Illustration 12-9**

*Expense recognition pattern*

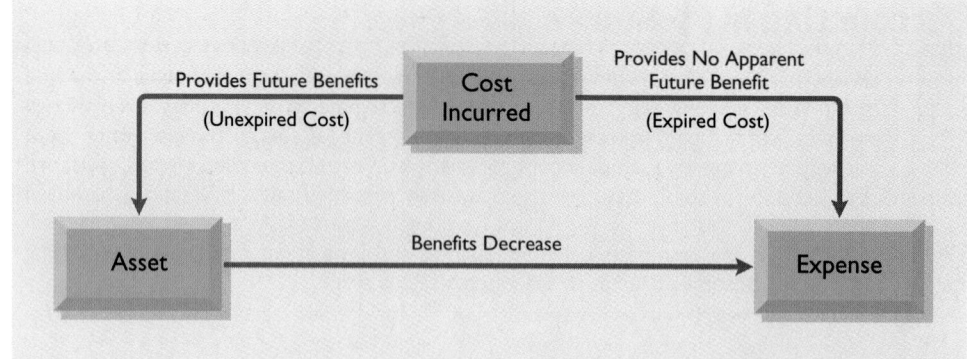

## ▶ Accounting in Action ▸ *Business Insight*

Implementing expense recognition guidelines can be difficult. Consider, for example, Harold's Club (a gambling casino) in Reno, Nevada. How should it report expenses related to the payoff of its progressive slot machines? Progressive slot machines, which generally have no ceiling on their jackpots, are capable of providing a lucky winner with all the money that many losers had previously put in. Payoffs tend to be huge, but infrequent; at Harold's, the progressive slots pay off on average every 4½ months. The basic accounting question is: Can Harold's deduct the millions of dollars sitting in its progressive slot machines from the revenue recognized at the end of the accounting period? One might argue that no, you cannot deduct the money until the "winning handle pull." However, a winning handle pull might not occur for many months or even years. Although admittedly an estimate would have to be used, the better answer is to match these costs with the revenue recognized, assuming that an average 4½ months' payout is well documented. This example demonstrates that the matching principle can be difficult to apply in practice.

*Source:* Adapted from *Fortune*, July 7, 1986, p. 100.

## Full Disclosure Principle

The **full disclosure principle** requires that circumstances and events that make a difference to financial statement users be disclosed. For example, most accountants would agree that Manville Corporation should have disclosed the 52,000 asbestos liability suits (totaling $2 billion) pending against it so that interested parties were made aware of this contingent loss. Similarly, it is generally agreed that companies should disclose the major provisions of employee pension plans and long-term lease contracts.

Compliance with the full disclosure principle occurs through the data contained in the financial statements and the information in the notes that accompany the statements. The first note in most cases is a **summary of significant accounting policies**. The summary includes, among others, the methods used by the company for inventory costing, depreciation of plant assets, and amortization of intangible assets.

**Helpful hint** See the specimen financial statements of PepsiCo illustrated in Appendix A for an example of information disclosed in a summary of significant accounting policies.

Deciding how much disclosure is enough can be difficult. Accountants could disclose every financial event that occurs and every contingency that exists. However, accounting information must be condensed and combined to make it understandable. Providing additional information entails a cost, and the benefits of providing this information in some cases may be less than the costs. Many companies complain of an accounting standards overload. In addition, they object to requirements that force them to disclose confidential information. Determining where to draw the line on disclosure is not easy.

One thing is certain: financial statements were much simpler years ago, when many companies provided little additional information regarding the financial statements. In 1930, General Electric had no notes to the financial statements; today it has over 10 pages of notes! Why this change? A major reason is that the objectives of financial statements have changed. In the past, information was generally presented on what the business had done. Today the objectives of financial reporting are more future-oriented; accounting is trying to provide information that makes it possible to predict the amount, timing, and uncertainty of future cash flows.

## ►*T*echnology in *A*ction

Some accountants are reconsidering the current means of financial reporting. These accountants propose a data base concept of financial reporting. In such a system, all the information from transactions would be stored in a computerized data base to be accessed by various user groups. The main benefit of such a system is the ability to tailor the information requested to the needs of each user.

What makes it controversial? Discussion currently revolves around access and aggregation issues. Questions such as "Who should be allowed to make inquiries of the system?" "What is the lowest/smallest level of information to be provided?" and "Will such a system necessarily improve on the current means of disclosure?" must be answered before such a system can be implemented on a large scale.

## Cost Principle

As you know, the cost principle dictates that assets are recorded at their cost. Cost is used because it is both relevant and reliable. Cost is **relevant** because it represents the price paid, the assets sacrificed, or the commitment made at date of acquisition. Cost is **reliable** because it is objectively measurable, factual, and verifiable. It is the result of an exchange transaction. Cost is the basis used in preparing financial statements.

The cost principle, however, has come under much criticism. It is criticized by some as irrelevant. Subsequent to acquisition, the argument goes, cost is not equivalent to market value or current value. For that matter, as the purchasing power of the dollar changes, so also does the meaning associated with the dollar that is used as the basis of measurement. Consider the classic story about the individual who went to sleep and woke up 10 years later. Hurrying to a telephone, he got through to his broker and asked what his formerly modest stock portfolio was worth. He was told that he was a multi-millionaire—his General Motors stock was worth $5 million and his AT&T stock was up to $10 million. Elated, he was about to inquire about his other holdings, when the telephone operator cut in with "Your time is up. Please deposit $100,000 for the next 3 minutes."[3]

This story demonstrates that prices can and do change over a period of time, and that one is not necessarily better off when they do. Although the numbers in the story are extreme, consider some more realistic data that compare prices in 1980 with what is expected in 1996, assuming average price increases of 6% and 12% per year.

---

[3]Adapted from *Barron's*, January 28, 1980, p. 27.

**Illustration 12-10**

*Example of changing prices*

**Helpful hint**  Are you a winner or loser when you hold cash in a period of inflation? Answer: A loser, because the value of the cash declines as inflation climbs.

| | 1980 | 1996 | |
|---|---|---|---|
| **Assumed average price increase** | | 6% | 12% |
| Public college, yearly average cost | $ 3,350.00 | $ 8,510.00 | $ 20,537.00 |
| Average taxi ride, New York City (before tip) | 2.95 | 7.49 | 18.08 |
| Slice of pizza | .65 | 1.65 | 3.98 |
| First-class postage stamp | .15 | .38 | .92 |
| Run-of-the-mill suburban house, New York City | 150,000.00 | 381,052.00 | 919,559.00 |
| McDonald's milk shake | .75 | 1.91 | 4.60 |

Despite the inevitability of changing prices during a period of inflation, the accounting profession still follows the stable monetary unit assumption in preparing a company's primary financial statements. While admitting that some changes in prices do occur, the profession believes the unit of measure—the dollar—has remained sufficiently constant over time to provide meaningful financial information.

If presented, the **disclosure of price-level adjusted data is in the form of supplemental information** presented with financial statements. The two most widely used approaches to show the effects of changing prices on a company's financial statements are (1) constant dollar accounting and (2) current cost accounting.

### Constant Dollar Accounting

The real value of the dollar is determined by the goods or services for which it can be exchanged. This real value is commonly called purchasing power. As the economy experiences **inflation** (rising price levels) or **deflation** (falling price levels), the amount of goods or services for which a dollar can be exchanged changes; that is, the purchasing power of the dollar changes from one period to the next. These changes are referred to as **general price level changes**.

**Helpful hint**  With constant dollar accounting, the unit of measure is the purchasing power of a dollar. All items are expressed in terms of units of purchasing power rather than units of money.

Constant dollar accounting restates financial statement items into dollars that have equal purchasing power. As one executive from Shell Oil Company explained, "Constant dollar accounting is a restatement of the traditional financial information into a common unit of measurement." In other words, constant dollar accounting changes the **unit** of measurement; it does not, however, change the underlying accounting principles used to report cost amounts. **Constant dollar accounting is cost based.**

### Current Cost Accounting

The price of a specific item may be affected not only by a change in the general price level, but also by individual market forces. For example, during a recent 6-year period, certain items changed more or less than the general price level. To illustrate, during this period of time, the cost of a local telephone call increased 150%, guaranteed overnight mail delivery increased 4,575%, a gallon of gasoline decreased over 30%, and a flawless one-carat diamond decreased over 70%. Thus, changes in the specific price of items may be very different from the change in the general price level. These changes are referred to as **specific price level changes**.

A popular means to measure the change in a specific price is current cost. Current cost is the cost of replacing the identical asset owned. Current cost may be approximated by reference to current catalog prices or by applying a specific index to the book value of the asset. Unlike the constant dollar approach, which is simply a restatement of historical dollars into constant purchasing power, the current cost approach **changes the basis of measurement from cost to current value.**

The basic principles of accounting are summarized in Illustration 12-11.

**Illustration 12-11**

*Basic principles used in accounting*

### Revenue Recognition

At end of production

At time of order

At time of sale

During production

At time cash received

Revenue should be recognized in the accounting period in which it is earned (generally point of sale).

### Matching

Costs

Match

Sales Revenue

Materials

Labor

Delivery

AD

Advertising          Utilities

Operating Expenses

Expenses should be matched with revenues

### Cost

Assets should be recorded at cost.

### Full Disclosure

✓ Financial Statements
✓ Balance Sheet
✓ Income Statement
✓ Retained Earnings Statement
✓ Cash Flow Statement

Circumstances and events that make a difference to financial statement users should be disclosed.

# Constraints in Accounting

**Constraints** permit a company to modify generally accepted accounting principles without reducing the usefulness of the reported information. The constraints are materiality and conservatism.

## Materiality

**Materiality** relates to an item's impact on a firm's overall financial condition and operations. An item is material when it is likely to influence the decision of a reasonably prudent investor or creditor. It is immaterial if its inclusion or omission has no mpact on a decision maker. In short, if the item does not make a

**STUDY OBJECTIVE**

•••••••• ▼ 6 ••••••••

*Identify the two constraints in accounting.*

difference, GAAP does not have to be followed. To determine the materiality of an amount, that is, to determine its financial significance, the accountant usually compares it with such items as total assets, total liabilities, and net income.

To illustrate how the constraint of materiality is applied, assume that Rodriguez Co. purchases a number of low-cost plant assets, such as wastepaper baskets. Although the proper accounting would appear to be to depreciate these wastepaper baskets over their useful life, they are usually expensed immediately. This practice is justified because these costs are considered immaterial. Establishing depreciation schedules for these assets is costly and time-consuming and will not make a material difference on total assets and net income. Other applications of the materiality constraint are the expensing of small tools or the expensing of any plant assets under a certain dollar amount.

## Conservatism

Conservatism in accounting means that when in doubt the accountant should choose the method that will be least likely to overstate assets and income. It does **not** mean **understating** assets or income. Conservatism gives the accountant a guide in difficult situations, and the guide is a reasonable one: do not overstate assets and income.

A common application of the conservatism constraint is the use of the lower of cost or market method for inventories. As indicated in Chapter 9, inventories are reported at market value if market value is below cost. This practice results in a higher cost of goods sold and lower net income. In addition, inventory on the balance sheet is stated at a lower amount when market value is below cost. Other examples of conservatism in accounting are the use of the LIFO method for inventory valuation when prices are rising and the use of accelerated depreciation methods for plant assets. Both these methods result in lower asset carrying values and lower net income than alternative methods.

The two constraints are graphically depicted in Illustration 12-12.

**Illustration 12-12**

*Constraints in accounting*

**Materiality**

Account for under GAAP

If dollar amounts of costs are small, GAAP does not have to be followed.

**Conservatism**

When in doubt, choose the solution that will be least likely to overstate assets and income.

## Summary of Conceptual Framework

As we have seen, the conceptual framework for developing sound reporting practices starts with a set of objectives for financial reporting and follows with the development of qualities that make information useful. In addition, elements of financial statements are defined. Operating guidelines in the form of assumptions and principles are then provided. The conceptual framework also recognizes that important constraints exist on the reporting environment. These points are illustrated graphically in Illustration 12-13:

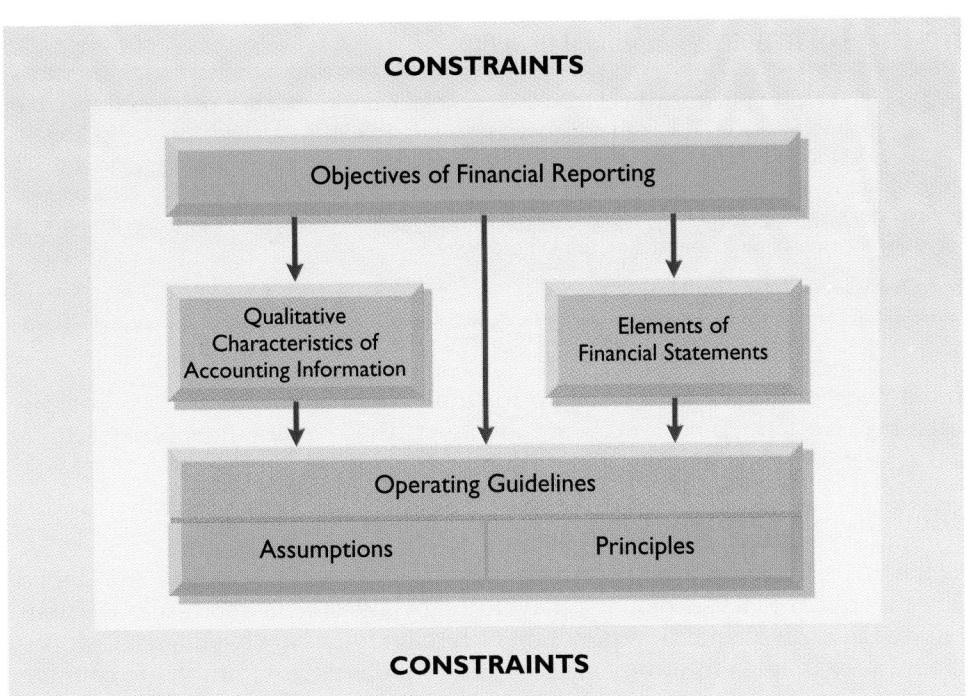

**Illustration 12-13**

*Conceptual framework*

# *I*nternational Accounting Standards

World markets are becoming increasingly intertwined. Foreigners use American computers, eat American breakfast cereals, read American magazines, listen to American rock music, watch American movies and TV shows, and drink American soda. And, Americans drive Japanese cars, wear Italian shoes and Scottish woolens, drink Brazilian coffee and Indian tea, eat Swiss chocolate bars, sit on Danish furniture, and use Arabian oil. The tremendous variety and volume of both exported and imported goods indicates the extensive involvement of U.S. business in international trade. For many U.S. companies, the world is their market.

**STUDY OBJECTIVE**

**7**

*Explain the accounting principles used in international operations.*

The following table illustrates the magnitude of foreign sales and type of product sold by U.S. companies.

**Illustration 12-14**

*Foreign sales and type of product*

| Company | Foreign Sales as a % of Total | Product |
|---|---|---|
| Caterpillar | 22.6 | Heavy machinery, engines, turbines |
| Coca-Cola | 68.3 | Beverages |
| Eastman Kodak | 52.5 | Photographic equipment and supplies |
| E.I. duPont de Nemours | 42.1 | Specialty chemicals |
| Exxon | 77.4 | Petroleum, chemicals |
| Ford Motor | 29.6 | Motor vehicles and parts |
| General Motors | 28.4 | Motor vehicles and parts |
| Hewlett-Packard | 54.1 | Computers, electronics |
| IBM | 62.3 | Computers and related equipment |
| Philip Morris Cos. | 30.4 | Tobacco, beverages, food products |

Firms that conduct their operations in more than one country through subsidiaries, divisions, or branches in foreign countries are referred to as **multina-**

## ▶ Accounting in Action ▸ *International Insight*

In 1991, for the first time, McDonald's opened more restaurants overseas than in the United States: 427 abroad compared with just 188 in the United States. The top 10 McDonald's restaurants in sales and profits are on foreign soil. The busiest McDonald's are in Moscow, on the Champs-Elysees in Paris, and in central Rome. In 1992 McDonald's opened its first store in Beijing, China. Recently, 37% of McDonald's sales and 40% of the company's operating income came from outside the United States.

*Source: The New York Times, April 17, 1992.*

tional corporations. The accounting for multinational corporations is complicated because foreign currencies are involved. These international transactions and operations must be translated into U.S. dollars.

### Differences in Standards

As the "world economy" is becoming globalized to the point where the United States is only one in a set of major players, many investment and credit decisions require the analysis and interpretation of foreign financial statements. Unfortunately, there is little uniformity in accounting standards from country to country, and there are few recognized worldwide accounting standards. This lack of uniformity is the result of different legal systems, different processes for developing accounting standards, different governmental requirements, and different economic environments.

## ▶ Accounting in Action ▸ *International Insight*

Research and development costs are an example of different international accounting standards. Compare how four countries account for research and development:

| Country | Accounting treatment |
|---|---|
| United States | Expenditures are expensed. |
| United Kingdom | Certain expenditures may be capitalized. |
| Germany | Expenditures are expensed. |
| Japan | Expenditures may be capitalized and amortized over 5 years. |

Thus, a research and development expenditure of $100 million is charged totally to expense in the current period in the United States and Germany. This expense could range from zero to $100 million in the United Kingdom and from $20 million to $100 million in Japan!

Do you believe that accounting principles should be comparable across countries?

### Uniformity in Standards

Some efforts have been made to obtain uniformity in international accounting practices. In 1973 the International Accounting Standards Committee (IASC) was formed by agreement of accounting organizations in the United States, the United Kingdom, Canada, Australia, France, Germany, Japan, Mexico, and the Netherlands. More than 80 accounting organizations representing more than 60 countries now participate in the development of international accounting standards.

To date, over 30 International Accounting Standards have been issued for IASC members to introduce to their respective countries. But, because the IASC has no enforcement powers, these standards are by no means universally applied. They are, however, generally followed by the large multinational companies that are audited by international public accounting firms. Thus, the foundation has been laid for considerable progress toward greater uniformity in international accounting.

## Before You Go On . . .

### ▶ Review It

1. What are the monetary unit assumption, the economic entity assumption, the time period assumption, and the going concern assumption?
2. What are the revenue recognition principle, the matching principle, the full disclosure principle, and the cost principle?
3. What are the materiality constraint and the conservatism constraint?
4. What is the purpose of the International Accounting Standards Committee?

### ▶ A Look Back at America Online

Refer back to the opening story and answer the following questions.

1. CompuServe expenses its subscriber acquisition costs as incurred; America Online capitalizes these costs and amortizes them over 18 months. Are the concepts of comparability or consistency violated in this situation? Explain.
2. The controller for CompuServe stated, "We consider our earnings strong. We didn't want to taint them or dilute them by following [America Online's] accounting." Explain this statement.

#### Solution:

1. Comparability results when different companies use the same accounting principles. In this case, comparability does not occur because CompuServe and America Online use different practices to account for subscriber acquisition costs. Consistency means that a company uses the same accounting principles and methods from year to year. Both companies are consistent in that they continue to use the same accounting method from year to year.
2. CompuServe expenses its subscriber acquisition costs as incurred. Its earnings are therefore conservatively reported (often referred to as "high-quality earnings"). That is, earnings may be understated because of the expensing of subscriber acquisition costs.

## ◣ Summary of Study Objectives

**1.** *Explain the meaning of generally accepted accounting principles and identify the key items of the conceptual framework.* Generally accepted accounting principles are a set of rules and practices that are recognized as a general guide for financial reporting purposes. Generally accepted means that these principles must have "substantial authoritative support." The key items of the conceptual framework are: (1) objectives of financial reporting; (2) qualitative characteristics of accounting information; (3) elements of financial statements; and (4) operating guidelines (assumptions, principles, and constraints).

**2.** *Describe the basic objectives of financial reporting.* The basic objectives of financial reporting are to provide information that is (1) useful to those making investment and

credit decisions; (2) helpful in assessing future cash flows; and (3) helpful in identifying economic resources (assets), the claims to those resources (liabilities), and the changes in those resources and claims.

**3.** *Discuss the qualitative characteristics of accounting information and elements of financial statements.* To be judged useful, information should possess the following qualitative characteristics: relevance, reliability, comparability, and consistency. The elements of financial statements are a set of definitions that can be used to describe the basic terms used in accounting.

**4.** *Identify the basic assumptions used by accountants.* The major assumptions are: monetary unit, economic entity, time period, and going concern.

**5.** *Identify the basic principles of accounting.* The major principles are revenue recognition, matching, full disclosure, and cost.

**6.** *Identify the two constraints in accounting.* The major constraints are materiality and conservatism.

**7.** *Explain the accounting principles used in international operations.* There are few recognized worldwide accounting standards. The International Accounting Standards Committee (IASC), of which the United States is a member, is making efforts to obtain conformity in international accounting practices.

# Glossary

**Comparability**   Ability to compare accounting information of different companies because they use the same accounting principles. (p. 496).

**Conceptual framework**   A coherent system of interrelated objectives and fundamentals that can lead to consistent standards. (p. 495).

**Conservatism**   The approach of choosing an accounting method when in doubt that will least likely overstate assets and net income. (p. 508).

**Consistency**   Use of the same accounting principles and methods from year to year within a company. (p. 497).

**Constant dollar accounting**   A type of accounting that restates financial statement items into dollars that have equal purchasing power. (p. 506).

**Cost principle**   Accounting principle that assets should be recorded at their historical cost. (p. 505).

**Current cost**   The cost of replacing the identical asset owned; a measure of the change in a specific price. (p. 506).

**Economic entity assumption**   Accounting assumption that economic events can be identified with a particular unit of accountability. (p. 499).

**Elements of financial statements**   Definitions of basic terms used in accounting. (p. 497).

**Full disclosure principle**   Accounting principle that circumstances and events that make a difference to financial statement users should be disclosed. (p. 504).

**Generally accepted accounting principles (GAAP)**   A set of rules and practices, having substantial authoritative support, that are recognized as a general guide for financial reporting purposes. (p. 494).

**Going concern assumption**   The assumption that the enterprise will continue in operation long enough to carry out its existing objectives and commitments. (p. 499).

**Installment method**   A method of recognizing revenue using the cash basis; each cash collection consists of a partial recovery of cost of goods sold and partial gross profit from the sale. (p. 502).

**Matching principle**   Accounting principle that expenses should be matched with revenues in the period when efforts are expended to generate revenues. (p. 503).

**Materiality**   The constraint of determining if an item is important enough to likely influence the decision of a reasonably prudent investor or creditor. (p. 507).

**Monetary unit assumption**   Accounting assumption that only transaction data capable of being expressed in monetary terms should be included in accounting records. (p. 498).

**Percentage-of-completion method**   Recognizes revenue and income on a construction project on the basis of costs incurred during the period to the total estimated costs for the entire project. (p. 501).

**Purchasing power**   The amount of goods and services for which a dollar can be exchanged. (p. 506).

**Relevance**   The quality of information that indicates the information makes a difference in a decision. (p. 496).

**Reliability**   The quality of information that gives assurance that it is free of error and bias. (p. 496).

**Revenue recognition principle**   Accounting principle that revenue should be recognized in the accounting period in which it is earned (generally at the point of sale). (p. 500).

**Time period assumption**   Accounting assumption that the economic life of a business can be divided into artificial time periods. (p. 499).

## Demonstration Problem 1

Carver Construction Company is under contract to build a condominium at a contract price of $2,000,000. The building will take 18 months to complete at an estimated cost of $1,400,000. Construction began in November, 1995, and was finished in April, 1997. Actual construction costs incurred in each year were: 1995, $140,000; 1996; $910,000; and 1997, $350,000.

*Instructions*
Compute the gross profit to be recognized in each year.

## Solution to Demonstration Problem

| Year | Costs Incurred (Current Period) | ÷ Total Estimated Cost = | Percent Complete (Current Period) | × Total Revenue = | Revenue Recognized (Current Period) |
|---|---|---|---|---|---|
| 1995 | $ 140,000 | $1,400,000 | 10% | $2,000,000 | $ 200,000 |
| 1996 | 910,000 | 1,400,000 | 65% | 2,000,000 | 1,300,000 |
| 1997 | 350,000 | Balance to complete contract | | | 500,000 |
| | $1,400,000 | | | | $2,000,000 |

| Year | Revenue Recognized (Current Period) | − Actual Costs Incurred (Current Period) | = Gross Profit Recognized (Current Period) |
|---|---|---|---|
| 1995 | $ 200,000 | $ 140,000 | $ 60,000 |
| 1996 | 1,300,000 | 910,000 | 390,000 |
| 1997 | 500,000 | 350,000 | 150,000 |
| | $2,000,000 | $1,400,000 | $600,000 |

**Problem-Solving Strategies**

(1) Percent complete is determined by dividing costs incurred by total estimated costs.

(2) Percent complete is multiplied by contract price to find revenue recognized.

(3) Gross profit equals revenue recognized less actual costs incurred.

(4) Percentage-of-completion method recognizes revenue as the construction occurs—it is viewed as a series of sales.

## DEMONSTRATION PROBLEM 2

Valdes Inc. uses the installment method in accounting for its sales. During its first year of operations, it had installment sales of $900,000 and a cost of goods sold on installments of $600,000. The collections on installment sales were as follows: Year 1, $330,000; Year 2, $420,000; and Year 3, $150,000.

### Instructions
Compute the amount of gross profit to be recognized each year.

## Solution to Demonstration Problem

| Year | Cash Collected | × | Gross Profit Percentage* | = | Gross Profit Recognized |
|---|---|---|---|---|---|
| 1 | $330,000 | | 33⅓% | | $110,000 |
| 2 | 420,000 | | 33⅓% | | 140,000 |
| 3 | 150,000 | | 33⅓% | | 50,000 |
| | $900,000 | | | | $300,000 |

*$900,000 − $600,000 = $300,000; $300,000 ÷ $900,000 = 33⅓%

**Problem-Solving Strategies**

(1) Installment method used when cash collection is uncertain.

(2) Must always find gross profit percentage.

(3) Gross profit recognized each period results from cash collected times gross profit percentage.

## SELF-STUDY QUESTIONS

Answers are at the end of the chapter.

(SO 1) 1. Generally accepted accounting principles are:
   a. a set of standards and rules that are recognized as a general guide for financial reporting.
   b. usually established by the Internal Revenue Service.
   c. the guidelines used to resolve ethical dilemmas.
   d. fundamental truths that can be derived from the laws of nature.

(SO 2) 2. Which of the following is *not* an objective of financial reporting?

   a. Provide information that is useful in investment and credit decisions.
   b. Provide information about economic resources, claims to those resources, and changes in them.
   c. Provide information that is useful in assessing future cash flows.
   d. Provide information on the liquidation value of a business.

3. The primary criterion by which accounting information can be judged is: (SO 3)
   a. consistency.

b. predictive value.
c. decision-usefulness.
d. comparability.

(SO 3)    4. Verifiable is an ingredient of:

|     | Reliability | Relevance |
| --- | --- | --- |
| a. | Yes | Yes |
| b. | No | No |
| c. | Yes | No |
| d. | No | Yes |

(SO 4, 5, 6)    5. Valuing assets at their liquidation value rather than their cost is *inconsistent* with the:
a. time period assumption.
b. matching principle.
c. going concern assumption.
d. materiality constraint.

(SO 5)    6. Gonzalez's Construction Company began a long-term construction contract on January 1, 1996. The contract is expected to be completed in 1997 at a total cost of $20,000,000. Gonzalez's revenue for the project is $24,000,000. Gonzalez incurred contract costs of $4,000,000 in 1996. What gross profit should be recognized in 1996?
a. $800,000.
b. $1,000,000.
c. $2,000,000.
d. $4,000,000.

(SO 5)    7. Glackin Company had installment sales of $1,000,000 in their first year of operations. The cost of goods sold on installment was $650,000, and Glackin collected a total of $500,000 on the install-

ment sales. Using the installment method, how much gross profit should be recognized in the first year?
a. $140,000.
b. $175,000.
c. $350,000.
d. $500,000.

8. Which of the following statements is correct?    (SO 5)
a. Constant dollar accounting reports the cost of replacing the identical asset owned at current prices.
b. Current cost accounting restates financial statement items into dollars of equal purchasing power.
c. Current cost accounting is cost based.
d. Constant dollar accounting is cost based.

9. The accounting constraint that refers to the tendency of accountants to resolve uncertainty in favor of understating assets and revenues is known as (the):    (SO 4, 5,
a. matching principle.
b. materiality.
c. conservatism.
d. monetary unit assumption.

10. The organization that issues international accounting standards is the:    (SO 7)
a. Financial Accounting Standards Board.
b. International Accounting Standards Committee.
c. International Auditing Standards Committee.
d. None of the above.

# QUESTIONS

1. (a) What are generally accepted accounting principles (GAAP)? (b) What bodies provide authoritative support for GAAP?

2. What elements comprise the FASB's conceptual framework?

3. (a) What are the objectives of financial reporting? (b) Identify the qualitative characteristics of accounting information.

4. Ray Aldag, the president of Raynard Company, is pleased. Raynard substantially increased its net income in 1995 while keeping its unit inventory relatively the same. Tom Erhardt, chief accountant, cautions Aldag, however. Erhardt says that since Raynard changed from the LIFO to the FIFO method of inventory valuation, there is a consistency problem and it would be difficult to determine if Raynard is better off. Is Erhardt correct? Why?

5. What is the distinction between comparability and consistency?

6. Why is it necessary for accountants to assume that an economic entity will remain a going concern?

7. When should revenue be recognized? Why has the date of sale been chosen as the point at which to recognize the revenue resulting from the entire producing and selling process?

8. Ryder Construction Company has a $200 million contract to build a bridge. Its total estimated cost for the project is $170 million. Costs incurred in the first year of the project were $34 million. Ryder appropriately uses the percentage-of-completion method. How much revenue and gross profit should Ryder recognize in the first year of the project?

9. Merchandise with a cost of $80,000 was sold during the year for $100,000. Cash collected for the year amounted to $40,000. How much gross profit should be recognized during the year if the company uses the installment method?

10. Distinguish between expired costs and unexpired costs.

11. (a) Where does the accountant disclose information about an entity's financial position, operations, and cash flows? (b) The full disclosure principle recognizes that the nature and amount of

information included in financial reports reflects a series of judgmental trade-offs. What are the objectives of these trade-offs?

12. Sue Leonard is the president of Better Books. She has no accounting background. Leonard cannot understand why current cost is not used as the basis for accounting measurement and reporting. Explain what basis is used and why.

13. (a) What is meant by constant dollar accounting? (b) What is purchasing power?

14. What is current cost accounting? How does it differ from constant dollar accounting?

15. What is the accounting profession's position on reporting changing price information?

16. Describe the two constraints inherent in the presentation of accounting information.

17. Your roommate believes that international accounting standards are uniform throughout the world. Is your roommate correct? Explain.

18. What organization establishes international accounting standards?

# *B*RIEF EXERCISES

**BE12–1**   Indicate whether each of the following statements is true or false.

1. ____ GAAP is a set of rules and practices established by the accounting profession to serve as a general guide for financial reporting purposes.
2. ____ Substantial authoritative support for GAAP usually comes from two standard-setting bodies: the FASB and the IRS.
3. ____ "*Generally accepted*" means that these principles must have "substantial authoritative support."

*Generally accepted accounting principles.*
*(SO 1)*

**BE12–2**   Indicate which of the following items is(are) included in the FASB's conceptual framework. (Use "Yes" or "No" to answer this question.)

1. ____ Analysis of financial statement ratios.
2. ____ Objectives of financial reporting.
3. ____ Qualitative characteristics of accounting information.

*Items included in conceptual framework.*
*(SO 1)*

**BE12–3**   According to the FASB's conceptual framework, which of the following are objectives of financial reporting? (Use "Yes" or "No" to answer this question.)

1. ____ Provide information that is helpful in assessing past cash flows and stock prices.
2. ____ Provide information that is useful to those making investment and credit decisions.
3. ____ Provide information that identifies the economic resources (assets), the claims to those resources (liabilities), and the changes in those resources and claims.

*Objectives of financial reporting.*
*(SO 2)*

**BE12–4**   Presented below is a chart of the qualitative characteristics of accounting information. Fill in the blanks from (a) to (e).

*Qualitative characteristics.*
*(SO 3)*

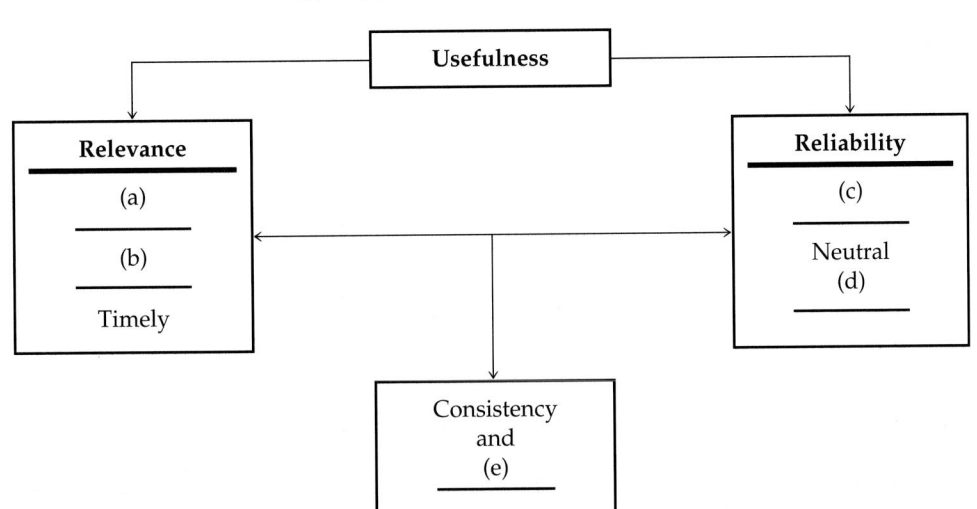

*Qualitative characteristics.*
(SO 3)

**BE12–5**    Given the *qualitative characteristics* of accounting established by the FASB's conceptual framework, complete each of the following statements:

1. ____ For information to be ____, it should have predictive or feedback value, and it must be presented on a timely basis.
2. ____ is the quality of information that gives assurance that it is free of error and bias; it can be depended on.
3. ____ means using the same accounting principles and methods from year to year within a company.

*Qualitative characteristics.*
(SO 3)

**BE12–6**    Presented below is a set of qualitative characteristics of accounting information.

   (a) Predictive value     (c) Verifiable
   (b) Neutral          (d) Timely

   Match these qualitative characteristics to the following statements, using letters a through d.

1. ____ Accounting information should help users make predictions about the outcome of past, present, and future events.
2. ____ Accounting information cannot be selected, prepared, or presented to favor one set of interested users over another.
3. ____ Accounting information must be proved to be free of error and bias.
4. ____ Accounting information must be available to decision makers before it loses its capacity to influence their decisions.

*Operating guidelines.*
(SO 4, 5, 6)

**BE12–7**    Presented below are four concepts discussed in this chapter.

   (a) Time period assumption     (c) Full disclosure principle
   (b) Cost principle           (d) Conservatism

   Match these concepts to the following accounting practices. Each letter can be used only once.

1. ____ Recording inventory at its purchase price.
2. ____ Using notes and supplementary schedules in the financial statements.
3. ____ Preparing financial statements on an annual basis.
4. ____ Using the lower of cost or market method for inventory valuation.

*Revenue recognition principle—percentage of completion.*
(SO 5)

**BE12–8**    Hard Hat Construction Company is under contract to build a commercial building at a price of $4,000,000. Construction began in January 1996 and was finished in December 1998. Total estimated construction costs are $2,800,000. Actual construction costs incurred in each year were: 1996, $560,000; 1997, $1,820,000; 1998, $420,000. Compute the revenue to be recognized in each year using the *percentage-of-completion* method.

*Revenue recognition method—installment method.*
(SO 5)

**BE12–9**    Waldo Co. uses the installment method to determine its net income. During its first year of operations, it had installment sales of $800,000 and a cost of goods sold of $600,000. The collections on installment sales were as follows: Year 1, $360,000; Year 2, $440,000. Determine the gross profit recognized for Year 1 and 2.

*Identify the constraints that have been violated.*
(SO 6)

**BE12–10**    The Emelda Company uses the following accounting practices:

1. Inventory is reported at cost when market value is lower.
2. Revenue on installment sales is recognized at the time of sale.
3. Small tools are recorded as plant assets and depreciated.
4. The income statement shows paper clips expense of $10.

Indicate the accounting constraint, if any, that has been violated by each practice.

*Identify the assumption, principle, or constraint that has been violated.*
(SO 4, 5, 6)

# EXERCISES

**E12–1**    A number of accounting reporting situations are described below.

1. Tercek Company recognizes revenue at the end of the production cycle, but before sale. The price of the product, as well as the amount that can be sold, is not certain.
2. In preparing its financial statements, Seco Company omitted information concerning its method of accounting for inventories.

3. Shea Company uses the direct write-off method of accounting for uncollectible accounts.

4. Ravine Hospital Supply Corporation reports only current assets and current liabilities on its balance sheet. Property, plant, and equipment and bonds payable are reported as current assets and current liabilities, respectively. Liquidation of the company is unlikely.

5. Barton Inc. is carrying inventory at its current market value of $100,000. Inventory had an original cost of $110,000.

6. Bonilla Company is in its fifth year of operation and has yet to issue financial statements. (Do not use full disclosure principle.)

7. Watts Company has inventory on hand that cost $400,000. Watts reports inventory on its balance sheet at its current market value of $425,000.

8. Steph Wolfson, president of the Classic Music Company, bought a computer for her personal use. She paid for the computer by using company funds and debited the "computers" account.

**Instructions**

For each of the above, list the assumption, principle, or constraint that has been violated, if any. List only one term for each case.

**E12–2** Presented below are some business transactions that occurred during 1996 for Marietta Co.

*Identify the assumption, principle, or constraint that has been violated and prepare correct entries.*

*(SO 4, 5, 6)*

(a) Merchandise inventory with a cost of $208,000 is reported at its market value of $260,000. The following entry was made:

| | | |
|---|---|---|
| Merchandise Inventory | 52,000 | |
| Gain | | 52,000 |

(b) Equipment worth $90,000 was acquired at a cost of $72,000 from a company that had water damage in a flood. The following entry was made:

| | | |
|---|---|---|
| Equipment | 90,000 | |
| Cash | | 72,000 |
| Gain | | 18,000 |

(c) An account receivable has been deemed to be a bad debt. The following entry was made:

| | | |
|---|---|---|
| Allowance for Doubtful Accounts | 7,000 | |
| Accounts Receivable | | 7,000 |

(d) The president of Marietta Co., George Winston, purchased a truck for personal use and charged it to his expense account. The following entry was made:

| | | |
|---|---|---|
| Travel Expense | 18,000 | |
| Cash | | 18,000 |

(e) An electric pencil sharpener costing $50 is being depreciated over 5 years. The following entry was made:

| | | |
|---|---|---|
| Depreciation Expense—Pencil Sharpener | 10 | |
| Accumulated Depreciation—Pencil Sharpener | | 10 |

**Instructions**

In each of the situations above, identify the assumption, principle, or constraint that has been violated, if any, and discuss the appropriateness of the journal entries. Give the correct journal entry, if necessary.

**E12–3** Presented below are the assumptions, principles, and constraints discussed in this chapter:

*Identify accounting assumptions, principles, and constraints to different situations.*

*(SO 4, 5, 6)*

(a) Economic entity assumption
(b) Going concern assumption
(c) Monetary unit assumption
(d) Time period assumption
(e) Cost principle

(f) Matching principle
(g) Full disclosure principle
(h) Revenue recognition principle
(i) Materiality
(j) Conservatism

**Instructions**

Identify by letter the accounting assumption, principle, or constraint that describes each situation below. Do not use a letter more than once.

1. Is the rationale for why plant assets are not reported at liquidation value. (Do not use historical cost principle.)
2. Indicates that personal and business record-keeping should be separately maintained.
3. Ensures that all relevant financial information is reported.
4. Assumes that the dollar is the "measuring stick" used to report on financial performance.
5. Requires that the operational guidelines be followed for all significant items.
6. Separates financial information into time periods for reporting purpose.
7. Requires recognition of expenses in the same period as related revenues.
8. Indicates that market value changes subsequent to purchase are not recorded in the accounts.

*Determine the amount of revenue to be recognized.*
*(SO 5)*

**E12–4**    Consider the following transactions of Kokomo Company for 1996.

1. Sold a 6-month insurance policy to Taylor Corporation for $9,000 on March 1.
2. Leased office space to Excel Supplies for a 1-year period beginning September 1. The rent of $36,000 was paid in advance.
3. A sales order for merchandise costing $9,000 that had a sales price of $12,000 was received on December 28 from Warfield Company. The goods were shipped FOB shipping point on December 31 and Warfield received them on January 3, 1997.
4. Signed a long-term contract to construct a building at a total price of $1,800,000. Total estimated cost of construction is $1,200,000. During 1996, the company incurred $300,000 of costs and collected $330,000 in cash. The percentage of completion method is used to recognize revenue.
5. Merchandise inventory on hand at year-end amounted to $160,000. Kokomo expects to sell the inventory in 1997 for $180,000.

**Instructions**

For each item above, indicate the amount of revenue Kokomo should recognize in calendar year 1996. Explain.

*Determine gross profit for construction projects.*
*(SO 5)*

**E12–5**    Qi Shen Construction Company currently has one long-term construction project. The project has a contract price of $150,000,000 with total estimated costs of $100,000,000. Qi Shen appropriately uses the percentage-of-completion method. After 2 years of construction, the following costs have been accumulated:

| | |
|---|---|
| Actual cost incurred, Year 1 | $30,000,000 |
| Total estimated cost remaining after Year 1 | 70,000,000 |
| Actual cost incurred, Year 2 | 50,000,000 |
| Total estimated cost remaining after Year 2 | 20,000,000 |

**Instructions**

Determine the gross profit for each of the first 2 years of the construction contract.

*Determine gross profit using installment sales and point-of-sale bases.*
*(SO 5)*

**E12–6**    Waco Company sold equipment for $300,000 in 1995. Collections on the sale were as follows: 1995, $70,000; 1996, $190,000; 1997, $40,000. Waco's cost of goods sold is typically 75% of sales.

**Instructions**

(a) Determine Waco's gross profit for 1995, 1996, and 1997, assuming that Waco recognizes revenue under the installment method.
(b) Determine Waco's gross profit for 1995, 1996, and 1997, assuming that Waco recognizes revenue under the point-of-sale basis.

*Analyze transactions to identify accounting principle or assumption violated and preparation of correct entries.*
*(SO 4, 5)*

# PROBLEMS

**P12–1**    Garner and Simon are accountants for Desktop Computers. They are having disagreements concerning the following transactions that occurred during the calendar year 1996.

1. A 1-year insurance policy was purchased by Desktop on September 1, 1996 for $12,000. Garner believes that the following entry should be made on September 1:

| Insurance Expense | 12,000 | |
| Cash | | 12,000 |

2. Desktop purchased equipment for $35,000 at a going-out-of-business sale. The equipment was worth $45,000. Garner believes that the following entry should be made:

| Equipment | 45,000 | |
| Cash | | 35,000 |
| Gain | | 10,000 |

3. Land costing $60,000 was appraised at $90,000. Garner suggests the following journal entry:

| Land | 30,000 | |
| Gain on Appreciation of Land | | 30,000 |

4. Depreciation for the year was $18,000. Since net income is expected to be lower this year, Garner suggests deferring depreciation to a year when there is more net income.
5. Desktop bought a custom-made piece of equipment for $18,000. This equipment has a useful life of 6 years. Desktop depreciates equipment using the straight-line method. "Since the equipment is custom-made, it will have no resale value and, therefore, shouldn't be depreciated but instead expensed immediately," argues Garner. "Besides, it provides for lower net income."
6. Garner suggests that equipment should be reported on the balance sheet at its liquidation value, which is $15,000 less than its cost.

Simon disagrees with Garner on each of the above situations.

### Instructions

For each transaction, indicate why Simon disagrees. Identify the accounting principle or assumption that Garner would be violating if his suggestions were used. Prepare the correct journal entry for each transaction, if any.

**P12–2** Presented below are a number of business transactions that occurred during the current year for Hialeah, Inc.

*Determine the appropriateness of journal entries in terms of generally accepted accounting principles or assumptions. (SO 4, 5)*

1. Because the general level of prices increased during the current year, Hialeah, Inc. determined that there was a $20,000 understatement of depreciation expense on its equipment and decided to record it in its accounts. The following entry was made:

| Depreciation Expense | 20,000 | |
| Accumulated Depreciation | | 20,000 |

2. Materials were purchased on March 31 for $65,000 and this amount was entered in the Materials account. On December 31, the materials would have cost $85,000, so the following entry was made:

| Inventory | 20,000 | |
| Gain on Inventories | | 20,000 |

3. An order for $30,000 has been received from a customer for products on hand. This order is to be shipped on January 9 next year. The following entry was made:

| Accounts Receivable | 30,000 | |
| Sales | | 30,000 |

4. The president of Hialeah, Inc. used his expense account to purchase a new Saab 9000 solely for personal use. The following entry was made:

| Miscellaneous Expense | 34,000 | |
| Cash | | 34,000 |

5. Because of a "flood sale," equipment obviously worth $230,000 was acquired at a cost of $150,000. The following entry was made:

| Equipment | 230,000 | |
| Cash | | 150,000 |
| Gain on Purchase of Equipment | | 80,000 |

*Recognize gross profit using the percentage-of-completion method.*
(SO 5)

**Instructions**

▸ In each of the situations above, discuss the appropriateness of the journal entries in terms of generally accepted accounting principles.

**P12–3**  Beaver Construction Company is involved in a long-term construction contract to build an office building at a total estimated cost of $30 million and contract price of $40 million. Additional information follows:

| | Office Building | |
|---|---|---|
| | **Cash Collections** | **Actual Costs Incurred** |
| 1995 | $ 9,000,000 | $ 4,500,000 |
| 1996 | 9,000,000 | 6,000,000 |
| 1997 | 12,500,000 | 12,000,000 |
| 1998 | 9,500,000 | 7,500,000 |

The project is completed in 1998 and all cash to be received from the contract has been received.

*Recognize gross profit using the installment method.*
(SO 5)

**Instructions**

Prepare a schedule to determine the gross profit in each year for the long-term construction contract using the percentage-of-completion method.

**P12–4**  Beaver Construction sold apartments it had constructed to Mattson Management Company for $2.5 million. Beaver's cost to construct the apartments was $2 million. Beaver appropriately uses the installment method. Additional information follows:

| | **Cash Collected** |
|---|---|
| 1995 | $ 800,000 |
| 1996 | 1,200,000 |
| 1997 | 500,000 |

(a) Determine the gross profit for each year using the installment method.
(b) Repeat (a) assuming the constructions costs were $1.9 million.

*Identify accounting assumptions, principles, and constraints.*
(SO 4, 5, 6)

**P12–5**  Presented below are the assumptions, principles, and constraints used in this chapter.

(a) Economic entity assumption
(b) Going concern assumption
(c) Monetary unit assumption
(d) Time period assumption
(e) Full disclosure principle

(f) Revenue recognition principle
(g) Matching principle
(h) Cost principle
(i) Materiality
(j) Conservatism

Identify by letter the accounting assumption, principle, or constraint that describes each situation below. Do not use a letter more than once.

1. Repair tools are expensed when purchased. (Do not use conservatism)
2. Allocates expenses to revenues in proper period.
3. Assumes that the dollar is the measuring stick used to report financial information.
4. Separates financial information into time periods for reporting purposes.
5. Market value changes subsequent to purchase are not recorded in the accounts. (Do not use revenue recognition principle.)
6. Indicates that personal and business record keeping should be separately maintained.
7. Ensures that all relevant financial information is reported.
8. Lower of cost or market is used to value inventories.

# ALTERNATE PROBLEMS

*Analyze transactions to identify accounting principle or assumption violated and preparation of correct entries.*
(SO 4, 5)

**P12–1A**  Ava and Brad are accountants for Qwik Printers. They are having disagreements concerning the following transactions that occurred during the year.

1. Qwik bought equipment for $30,000, including installation costs. The equipment has a useful life of 5 years. Qwik depreciates equipment using the straight-line method. "Since the equipment as installed into our system cannot be removed without consid-

erable damage, it will have no resale value, and therefore should not be depreciated but instead expensed immediately," argues Ava. "Besides, it lowers net income."

2. Depreciation for the year was $26,000. Since net income is expected to be lower this year, Ava suggests deferring depreciation to a year when there is more net income.

3. Qwik purchased equipment at a fire sale for $21,000. The equipment was worth $26,000. Ava believes that the following entry should be made:

| | | |
|---|---|---|
| Equipment | 26,000 | |
| Cash | | 21,000 |
| Gain | | 5,000 |

4. Ava suggests that Qwik should carry equipment on the balance sheet at its liquidation value, which is $20,000 less than its cost.

5. Qwik rented office space for 1 year starting October 1, 1995. The total amount of $24,000 was paid in advance. Ava believes that the following entry should be made on October 1:

| | | |
|---|---|---|
| Rent Expense | 24,000 | |
| Cash | | 24,000 |

6. Land costing $41,000 was appraised at $49,000. Ava suggests the following journal entry:

| | | |
|---|---|---|
| Land | 8,000 | |
| Gain on Appreciation of Land | | 8,000 |

Brad disagrees with Ava on each of the situations above.

**Instructions**
For each transaction, indicate why Brad disagrees. Identify the accounting principle or assumption that Ava would be violating if her suggestions were used. Prepare the correct journal entry for each transaction, if any.

**P12–2A** Presented below are a number of business transactions that occurred during the current year for Chita, Inc.

*Determine the appropriateness of journal entries in terms of generally accepted accounting principles or assumptions. (SO 4, 5)*

1. An order for $70,000 has been received from a customer for products on hand. This order is to be shipped on January 9 next year. The following entry was made:

| | | |
|---|---|---|
| Accounts Receivable | 70,000 | |
| Sales | | 70,000 |

2. Because of a "flood sale," equipment obviously worth $300,000 was acquired at a cost of $250,000. The following entry was made:

| | | |
|---|---|---|
| Equipment | 300,000 | |
| Cash | | 250,000 |
| Gain on Purchase of Equipment | | 50,000 |

3. Because the general level of prices increased during the current year, Chita, Inc. determined that there was a $40,000 understatement of depreciation expense on its equipment and decided to record it in its accounts. The following entry was made:

| | | |
|---|---|---|
| Depreciation Expense | 40,000 | |
| Accumulated Depreciation | | 40,000 |

4. The president of Chita, Inc. used his expense account to purchase a pre-owned Mercedes-Benz 190 solely for personal use. The following entry was made:

| | | |
|---|---|---|
| Miscellaneous Expense | 28,000 | |
| Cash | | 28,000 |

5. Land was purchased on April 30 for $200,000 and this amount was entered in the Land account. On December 31, the land would have cost $230,000, so the following entry was made:

| | | |
|---|---|---|
| Land | 30,000 | |
| Gain on Land | | 30,000 |

*Instructions*

▦▦▦▦▷  In each of the situations above, discuss the appropriateness of the journal entries in terms of generally accepted accounting principles.

*Recognize gross profit using the percentage-of-completion.*
*(SO 5)*

**P12–3A**  Builders Construction Company is involved in a long-term construction contract. Builders contracted to build a health club with a total estimated cost of $20 million and contract price of $25 million. Additional information follows:

**Health Club**

|  | Cash Collections | Actual Costs Incurred |
|---|---|---|
| 1995 | $ 4,500,000 | $3,000,000 |
| 1996 | 10,000,000 | 9,000,000 |
| 1997 | 7,000,000 | 5,000,000 |
| 1998 | 3,500,000 | 3,000,000 |

The project was completed in 1998 and all cash collections related to the contract have been received.

*Instructions*

Prepare a schedule to determine the gross profit for each year for the long-term construction contract, using the percentage-of-completion method.

*Recognize gross profit using the installment method.*
*(SO 5)*

**P12–4A**  Tunis Inc. sold condominiums it had constructed to Parker Management Company for $6 million. Tunis's cost to construct the condominiums was $4.5 million. Tunis appropriately uses the installment method. Additional information follows:

**Cash Collected**

| 1995 | $  900,000 |
|---|---|
| 1996 | 3,800,000 |
| 1997 | 1,300,000 |

*Instructions*

(a) Prepare a schedule to determine the gross profit for each year using the installment method.
(b) Repeat (a) assuming construction costs were $4.8 million.

*Identify accounting assumptions, principles, and constraints.*
*(SO 4, 5, 6)*

**P12–5A**  Presented below are the assumptions, principles, and constraints used in this chapter.

(a) Economic entity assumption
(b) Going concern assumption
(c) Monetary unit assumption
(d) Time period assumption
(e) Full disclosure principle

(f) Revenue recognition principle
(g) Matching principle
(h) Cost principle
(i) Materiality
(j) Conservatism

Identify by letter the accounting assumption, principle, or constraint that describes each situation below. Do not use a letter more than once.

1. Assets are not stated at their liquidation value. (Do not use cost principle.)
2. The death of the president is not recorded in the accounts.
3. Pencil sharpeners are expensed when purchased.
4. An allowance for doubtful accounts is established. (Do not use conservatism.)
5. Each entity is kept as a unit distinct from its owner or owners.
6. Reporting must be done at defined intervals.
7. Revenue is recorded at the point of sale.
8. When in doubt, it is better to understate rather than overstate net income.
9. All important information related to inventories is presented in the footnotes or in the financial statements.

# ▼*B*roadening Your Perspective

## *F*INANCIAL REPORTING PROBLEM
·······················································································

Sue Federco has successfully completed her first accounting course during the spring semester and is now working as a management trainee for First Arizona Bank during the summer. One of her fellow management trainees, Bill Harlow, is taking the same accounting course this summer and has been having a "lot of trouble." On the second examination, for example, Bill became confused about inventory valuation methods and completely missed all the points on a problem involving LIFO and FIFO.

Bill's instructor recently indicated that the third examination will probably have a number of essay questions dealing with accounting principle issues. Bill is quite concerned about the third examination for two reasons. First, he has never taken an accounting examination where essay answers were required. Second, Bill feels he has to do well on this examination to get an acceptable grade in the course.

Bill has therefore asked Sue to help him prepare for the next examination. Sue agrees, and suggests that Bill develop a set of possible questions on the accounting principles material that they might discuss.

### Instructions
Answer the following questions that were developed by Bill.

  (a) What is a conceptual framework?
  (b) Why is there a need for a conceptual framework?
  (c) What are the objectives of financial reporting?
  (d) If you had to explain generally accepted accounting principles to a nonaccountant, what essential characteristics would you include in your explanation?
  (e) What are the qualitative characteristics of accounting? Explain each one.
  (f) Identify the basic assumptions used in accounting.
  (g) What are two major constraints involved in financial reporting? Explain both of them.

## *D*ECISION CASE
·······················································································

Hague Industries has two operating divisions—Devany Construction Division and German Securities Division. Both divisions maintain their own accounting system and method of revenue recognition.

### Devany Construction Division
During the fiscal year ended November 30, 1996, Devany Construction Division had one construction project in process. A $30,000,000 contract for construction of a civic center was granted on June 19, 1996, and construction began on August 1, 1996. Estimated costs of completion at the contract date were $26,000,000 over a 2-year time period from the date of the contract. On November 30, 1996, construction costs of $8,000,000 had been incurred. The construction costs to complete the remainder of the project were reviewed on November 30, 1996, and were estimated to amount to only $16,000,000 because of an expected decline in raw materials costs. Revenue recognition is based upon a percentage-of-completion method.

### German Securities Division
German Securities Division works through manufacturers' agents in various cities. Orders for alarm systems and down payments are forwarded from agents, and the division ships the goods f.o.b. factory directly to customers (usually police departments and security guard companies). Customers are billed directly for the balance due plus actual shipping costs. The firm received orders for $6,000,000 of goods during the fiscal year ended November 30, 1996. Down payments of $600,000 were received and goods with a selling price of $5,000,000 were billed and shipped. Actual freight costs of $100,000 were also billed. Commissions of 10% on product price are paid manufacturing agents after goods are shipped to customers. Such

goods are warranted for 90 days after shipment, and warranty returns have been about 1% of sales. Revenue is recognized at the point of sale by this division.

*Instructions*

(a) There are a variety of methods of revenue recognition. Define and describe each of the following methods of revenue recognition and indicate whether each is in accordance with generally accepted accounting principles.
   1. Point of sale.
   2. Percentage-of-completion.
   3. Installment contract.

(b) Compute the revenue to be recognized in fiscal year 1996 for both operating divisions of Hague Industries in accordance with generally accepted accounting principles.

# COMMUNICATION ACTIVITY

If you go on to advanced accounting courses, you'll study the differences between accounting in the business world and university accounting. You'll find that there's one major similarity: both depend heavily on the matching principle.

At Long Beach City College, a two-year community college with 30,000 students, most of the revenues come from the state of California and the federal government. As a condition of receiving these grants, "we must match expenses against revenues in the right fiscal year," says Catalina Cruz, accounting manager.

For example, the college receives federal funding under the Job Training Partnership Act. "We receive funding from the federal government, which allows us to offer classes to students for job preparation. The government specifies the grant periods, for instance, from July 1 to June 30. We therefore have to ensure that all transactions for that project are completed within that fiscal year." Another project is the amnesty program, the federal government's legalization of foreign nationals. Expenses to offset the grant money are mostly teaching salaries and instructional materials.

By year-end, the goal is to break even. Excess funds, if any, have to be returned. But program managers do not want a deficit, either, because these projects are accountable to the college administration and any overspending will come from the college's general fund.

*Instructions*

Write a letter to your instructor covering the following points:

1. Why is the matching principle important in accounting for government grants?
2. Give some examples of grant or special programs to which the matching principle might be applied at your college or university.
3. What are some examples of costs that Long Beach Community College might properly charge to its grant or special programs?

# GROUP ACTIVITY

Assume that the FASB has decided to address the problem of information overload. It has agreed to eliminate one of the principles, assumptions, constraints, or qualitative characteristics listed below. This concept will be deleted from all textbooks and will no longer be considered important in accounting literature.

*Instructions*

With the class divided into groups, each group will be assigned one or more of the following:

| | |
|---|---|
| Relevance | Revenue recognition |
| Reliability | Matching |
| Comparability and consistency | Full disclosure |
| Economic entity | Cost |
| Monetary unit | Materiality |
| Time period | Conservatism |

(a) Discuss within your group why your specific concept(s) should *not* be eliminated.
(b) Pick a group leader who will present to the class the group's reasons why the FASB should not delete the group's concept(s).
(c) At the end of all presentations, the class should vote on which concept to delete.

# ETHICS CASE

•••••••••••••••••••••••••••••••••••••••••••••••••••••••••••••••••••••••••••••

When the Financial Accounting Standards Board issues new standards, the required implementation date is usually 12 months or more from the date of issuance, with early implementation encouraged. Kathy Johnston, accountant at Redondo Corporation, discusses with her financial vice-president the need for early implementation of a recently issued standard that would result in a much fairer presentation of the company's financial condition and earnings. When the financial vice-president determines that early implementation of the standard will adversely affect reported net income for the year, he strongly discourages Kathy from implementing the standard until it is required.

*Instructions*
(a) Who are the stakeholders in this situation?
(b) What, if any, are the ethical considerations in this situation?
(c) What does Kathy have to gain by advocating early implementation? Who might be affected by the decision against early implementation?

# CRITICAL THINKING
## ▸ *A Real-World Focus: Newcor Incorporated*

•••••••••••••••••••••••••••••••••••••••••••••••••••••••••••••••••••••••••••••

*Newcor Inc. designs, manufactures, and sells specialty-purpose equipment and also manufactures and sells precision-machined parts and molded rubber and plastic products. The company previously had operating facilities in Belgium and Canada, both of which were sold. The company employs 747 employees and has roughly 2,000 shareholders.*

The annual report of Newcor Inc. reports the following information in the President's letter to stockholders:

> As indicated in last year's report, we were considering adoption of the percentage-of-completion method of accounting for long-term contracts. During the first quarter of 1994, we did adopt this method which has the effect of better matching revenues with work performed when compared to the completed-contract method of accounting that had previously been used to report financial results.

*Instructions*
(a) Which two accounting principles are discussed in Newcor's President's letter?
(b) Explain how the change in method will provide better matching of revenues with work performed.

---

*Answers to Self-Study Questions*
1. a   2. d   3. c   4. c   5. c   6. a   7. b   8. d   9. c   10. b

**Before studying this chapter, you should know or, if necessary, review:**

**a.** *The cost principle of accounting. (Ch. 1, p. 11)*
**b.** *The owner's equity statement. (Ch. 1, p. 24)*
**c.** *How to make closing entries and prepare the post-closing trial balance. (Ch. 4, pp. 141–43)*
**d.** *The steps in the accounting cycle. (Ch. 4, p. 148)*
**e.** *The format of classified financial statements. (Ch. 4, pp. 151–55)*

# From Trials to Top Ten

NEW YORK, N.Y. — Razor & Tie Music opened its doors in 1990 when Cliff Chenfield and Craig Balsam gave up the razors, ties, and six-figure salaries they had become accustomed to as New York lawyers to set up a partnership in Cliff's living room. In 1995 the label is at the forefront of marketing contemporary music—the only record company in the country that has achieved success by selling music both on television and in the stores. Razor & Tie's entertaining and effective TV commercials have yielded unprecedented sales for multi-artist music compilations, while its hot young retail label has been behind some of the most recent original, progressive releases.

Razor & Tie's first TV release, *Those Fabulous '70s* (100,000 copies sold), was followed by *Disco Fever* (over 300,000). These albums generated so much publicity that partners Cliff and Craig were guests on dozens of TV interview shows. Their charm and humor contributed to a genuine '70s revival.

After restoring respectability to the musically oft-maligned 1970s, the partners forged into the '80s.

Razor & Tie released *Totally '80s*, a collection of top singles from the 1980s that has sold over 400,000 copies, making it one of the best-selling direct response albums in the country.

More recently the partners have achieved impressive success on the retail level with the release of brand-new studio albums from legendary rocker Graham Parker and the meteorically rising young folk singer, Dar Williams. These, coupled with the critically lauded career compilations the label has been releasing since its inception (Arthur Alexan-

der, James Carr, Merle Haggard), have raised Razor & Tie's profile considerably. Without question it is a force to be reckoned with in a competitive music industry.

How has Razor & Tie carved out such a sizable piece of the market? Through the complementary talents of the two committed partners. Their imagination and savvy, along with exciting new releases planned for the coming years, ensure Razor & Tie of such continued growth that the partnership form of organization may be challenged to its limits. ◀

# CHAPTER · 13

# ACCOUNTING FOR PARTNERSHIPS

▶ STUDY OBJECTIVES ◀

**After studying this chapter, you should be able to:**

1. *Identify the characteristics of the partnership form of business organization.*
2. *Explain the accounting entries for the formation of a partnership.*
3. *Identify the bases for dividing net income or net loss.*
4. *Describe the form and content of partnership financial statements.*
5. *Explain the effects of the entries when a new partner is admitted.*
6. *Describe the effects of the entries when a partner withdraws from the firm.*
7. *Prepare the entries to record the liquidation of a partnership.*

It is not surprising that when Cliff Chenfield and Craig Balsam began Razor & Tie, they decided to use the partnership form of organization. Both saw the need for hands-on control of their product and its promotion. In this chapter, we will discuss reasons why the partnership form of organization is often selected and explain the major issues in accounting for partnerships. The content and organization of this chapter are as follows:

# ▼*P*artnership Form of Organization

The Uniform Partnership Act provides the basic rules for the formation and operation of partnerships in more than 90% of the states. This act defines a partnership as "an association of two or more persons to carry on as co-owners of a business for profit." Partnerships are common in retail establishments and in small manufacturing companies. Similarly, if you enter a profession such as accounting, law, or medicine, you may find it desirable to form a partnership with other professionals in your field. Professional partnerships vary in size from a medical partnership of 3 to 5 doctors to 150 to 200 partners in a large law firm and more than 2,000 partners in a Big Six international accounting firm.

## Characteristics of Partnerships

**STUDY OBJECTIVE**

·········▼·········

*Identify the characteristics of the partnership form of business organization.*

Partnerships are fairly easy to form. They can be formed by a verbal agreement, although partners who have not taken the next step—to put in writing the rights and obligations of the partners—have found that the characteristics of partnerships can sometimes lead to later difficulties.

The principal characteristics of the partnership form of business organization are shown in Illustration 13-1 and explained in the following sections.

**Illustration 13-1**

*Partnership characteristics*

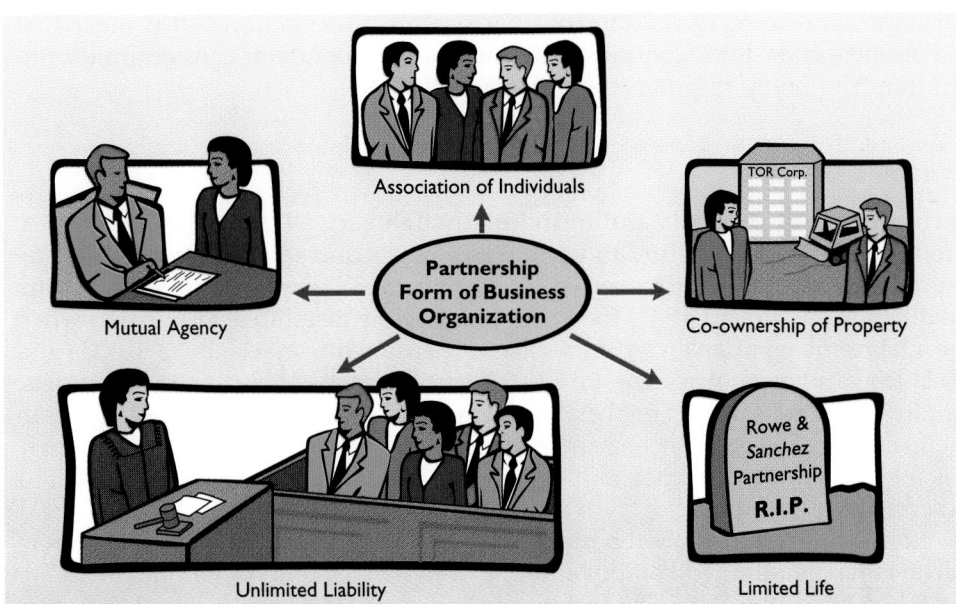

### Association of Individuals

The voluntary association of two or more individuals in a partnership may be based on as simple an act as a handshake. However, it is preferable to state the agreement in writing. Under the Uniform Partnership Act, a partnership is considered a legal entity for certain purposes. For instance, property (land, buildings, equipment) can be owned in the name of the partnership, and the firm can sue or be sued. **A partnership also represents an accounting entity for financial reporting purposes.** Thus, the purely personal assets, liabilities, and transactions of the partners are excluded from the accounting records of the partnership, just as they are in a proprietorship.

The net income of a partnership is not taxed as a separate entity. However, a partnership is required to file an information tax return showing partnership net income and each partner's share of net income. Each partner's share is taxable at personal tax rates, regardless of the amount of net income withdrawn from the business during the year.

### Mutual Agency

Mutual agency means that each partner acts on behalf of the partnership when engaging in partnership business. The act of any partner is binding on all other partners, even when partners act beyond the scope of their authority, so long as the act appears to be appropriate for the partnership. For example, a partner of a grocery store who purchases a delivery truck creates a binding contract in the name of the partnership, even if the partnership agreement denies this authority. On the other hand, if a partner in a law firm purchased a snowmobile for the partnership, such an act would not be binding on the partnership, because it is clearly outside the scope of partnership business.

**Helpful hint** Because of mutual agency, an individual should be extremely cautious in selecting partners.

### Limited Life

A partnership does not have unlimited life. A partnership may be ended voluntarily at any time through the acceptance of a new partner into the firm or the withdrawal of a partner. A partnership may be ended involuntarily by the death or incapacity of a partner. Thus the life of a partnership is indefinite. Partnership dissolution occurs whenever there is a change in the number of partners, regardless of the cause. Dissolution of a partnership does not necessarily mean that the business ends. If the continuing partners agree, operations can continue without interruption by forming a new partnership.

### Unlimited Liability

Each partner is **personally and individually liable** for all partnership liabilities. Creditors' claims attach first to partnership assets and then to the personal resources of any partner, irrespective of that partner's equity in the partnership. To illustrate, assume that: (1) the Rowe-Sanchez partnership is terminated when the claims of company creditors exceed partnership assets by $30,000, and (2) L. Rowe's personal assets total $40,000 but B. Sanchez has no personal assets. Creditors can collect their total claims from Rowe regardless of Rowe's equity in the firm, even though Sanchez and Rowe may be equal partners. Rowe, in turn, has a legal claim on Sanchez, but this would be worthless under the conditions described.

Some states allow limited partnerships. In a limited partnership, one or more partners have unlimited liability and one or more partners have limited liability for the debts of the firm. The former are called general partners and the latter are called limited partners. The responsibility of limited partners for the debts of the partnership is limited to their investment in the firm. For the privilege of limited liability, the limited partner usually accepts less compensation than a general partner and exercises less influence in the affairs of the firm. This form of organization works well in large partnerships where the partners do not work together closely. In such cases, partners want some protection from liability caused by the acts of partners they may hardly know.

## ►Accounting in Action ► *Business Insight*

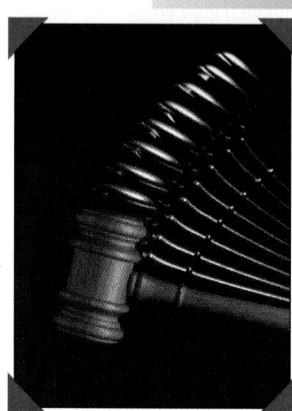

The prestigious New York law firm of Kaye, Scholer, Fierman, Hays, & Handler, accused of withholding damaging information during a federal investigation of its client, Lincoln Savings & Loan, settled out of court for $41 million. The firm's liability insurance covered only $25 million of the total. Thus, its 109 partners had to pay the remaining $16 million out of their own pockets.

In a recent year, court damage awards in malpractice suits against U.S. accountants and attorneys was close to $1 billion.

*Source: The Wall Street Journal, June 10, 1992, p. A1.*

### Co-Ownership of Property

Partnership assets are owned jointly by all the partners. If the partnership is terminated, the assets do not legally revert to the original contributor. Each partner has a claim on total assets equal to the balance in his or her respective capital account. This claim does not attach to specific assets that an individual partner contributed to the firm.

Similarly, if a partner invests a building in the partnership valued at $100,000 and the building is later sold at a gain of $20,000, that partner does not personally receive the entire gain. Partnership net income (or net loss) is also co-owned. **If the partnership contract does not specify to the contrary, all net income or net loss is shared equally by the partners.** As you will see later, however, partners may agree to unequal sharing of net income or net loss.

## ▶ Accounting in Action ▶ *Business Insight*

With surprising speed, states are creating a new form of business organization that tax experts predict will be adopted by many small companies. Known as a **limited liability company (LLC)**, it combines the advantages of partnerships and corporations by shielding owners from personal liability while taxing income at the individual level. The new structure may soon be an option for many sole proprietorships as well.

*Source: Nation's Business, August 1994, p. 36.*

## Advantages and Disadvantages of Partnerships

Why do people choose to form partnerships? One major advantage of doing so is that the **skills and resources of two or more individuals can be combined**. For example, a large public accounting firm such as Price Waterhouse must have combined expertise in auditing, taxation, and management consulting, not to mention specialists within each of these areas. In addition, a partnership does not have to contend with the "red tape" that a corporation must face. That is, a partnership is **easily formed and is relatively free from governmental regulations and restrictions**. Decisions can be made quickly on substantive matters affecting the firm, whereas in a corporation, formal meetings with the board of directors are often needed.

On the other hand, partnerships also have some major disadvantages: **mutual agency**, **limited life**, and **unlimited liability**. Unlimited liability is particularly troublesome to many individuals, because they may lose not only their initial investment but also their personal assets, if those assets are needed to pay partnership creditors. As a result, partnerships often find it difficult to obtain large amounts of investment capital. That is one reason why the largest business enterprises in the United States are corporations, not partnerships.

The advantages and disadvantages of the partnership form of business organization are summarized in Illustration 13-2.

▶ *International note*

The largest CPA firms (referred to as the "Big Six") are international partnerships. Arthur Andersen, one of the Big Six, reported that revenues in a recent year were up 14% in the Americas, up 50% in Asia/Pacific, and were flat in Europe, the Middle East, India, and Africa.

**Illustration 13-2**

*Advantages and disadvantages of a partnership*

| Advantages | Disadvantages |
|---|---|
| Combining skills and resources of two or more individuals | Mutual agency |
| Ease of formation | Limited life |
| Freedom from governmental regulations and restrictions | Unlimited liability |
| Ease of decision making | |

## The Partnership Agreement

Ideally, the voluntary agreement of two or more individuals to form a partnership should be expressed in writing. This written contract is often referred to as the partnership agreement or **articles of co-partnership**. The partnership agreement contains such basic information as the name and principal location of the firm, the purpose of the business, and date of inception. In addition, different relationships that will exist among the partners should be specified, such as the following:

1. Names and capital contributions of partners.
2. Rights and duties of partners.
3. Basis for sharing net income or net loss.
4. Provision for withdrawals of assets.

5. Procedures for submitting disputes to arbitration.
6. Procedures for the withdrawal or addition of a partner.
7. Rights and duties of surviving partners in the event of a partner's death.

The importance of a written contract cannot be overemphasized. The agreement should be drawn with care and should attempt to anticipate all possible situations, contingencies, and disagreements. The help of a lawyer is highly desirable in preparing the agreement. A poorly drawn contract may create friction among the partners and eventually cause the termination of the partnership.

## Before You Go On . . .

### ▶ *Review It*

1. What are the distinguishing characteristics of a partnership?
2. What are the principal advantages and disadvantages of a partnership?
3. What are the major items in a partnership agreement?

# ◢ *B*asic Partnership Accounting

We now turn our attention to the basic accounting for partnerships. The major accounting issues relate to forming the partnership, dividing net income or net loss, and preparing financial statements.

## Forming a Partnership

**STUDY OBJECTIVE**
••••••••**2**••••••••
*Explain the accounting entries for the formation of a partnership.*

Each partner's initial investment in a partnership should be recorded at the **fair market value of the assets at the date of their transfer to the partnership.** The values assigned must be agreed to by all of the partners.

To illustrate, assume that A. Rolfe and T. Shea combine their proprietorships to start a partnership named U.S. Software. The firm will specialize in developing financial modeling software packages. Rolfe and Shea have the following assets prior to the formation of the partnership:

**Illustration 13-3**

*Book and market value of assets invested*

|  | Book Value | | Market Value | |
|---|---|---|---|---|
|  | **A. Rolfe** | **T. Shea** | **A. Rolfe** | **T. Shea** |
| Cash | $ 8,000 | $ 9,000 | $ 8,000 | $ 9,000 |
| Office equipment | 5,000 | | 4,000 | |
| Accumulated depreciation | (2,000) | | | |
| Accounts receivable | | 4,000 | | 4,000 |
| Allowance for doubtful accounts | | (700) | | (1,000) |
|  | $11,000 | $12,300 | $12,000 | $12,000 |

**Helpful hint** The cost principle applies—cash and the fair-market value of non-cash assets are recorded at date of acquisition.

The entries to record the investments are:

**Investment of A. Rolfe**

| | | |
|---|---|---|
| Cash | 8,000 | |
| Office Equipment | 4,000 | |
|   A. Rolfe, Capital | | 12,000 |
|     (To record investment of Rolfe) | | |

### Investment of T. Shea

| | | |
|---|---|---|
| Cash | 9,000 | |
| Accounts Receivable | 4,000 | |
|    Allowance for Doubtful Accounts | | 1,000 |
|    T. Shea, Capital | | 12,000 |
|     (To record investment of Shea) | | |

Note that neither the original cost of the equipment ($5,000) nor its book value ($5,000 − $2,000) is recorded by the partnership. The equipment is recorded at its fair market value, $4,000. Since the equipment has not been used by the partnership, there can be no accumulated depreciation. In contrast, the gross claims on customers ($4,000) are carried forward to the partnership, and the allowance for doubtful accounts is adjusted to $1,000 to arrive at a cash (net) realizable value of $3,000. A partnership may start with an Allowance for Doubtful Accounts account, because this balance pertains to existing accounts receivable that are expected to be uncollectible in the future. In addition, this procedure maintains the control and subsidiary relationship between accounts receivable and the accounts receivable subsidiary ledger.

After the partnership has been formed, the accounting for transactions is similar to any other type of business organization. For example, all transactions with outside parties, such as the purchase or sale of merchandise inventory and the payment or receipt of cash, should be recorded in the same manner for a partnership as for a proprietorship.

The steps in the accounting cycle described in Chapter 4 for a proprietorship also apply to a partnership. For example, it is necessary to prepare a trial balance and to journalize and post adjusting entries. In addition, a work sheet may be used. There are minor differences in journalizing and posting closing entries and in preparing financial statements, as explained in the following sections. The differences occur because there is more than one owner in a partnership.

## Dividing Net Income or Net Loss

**Partnership net income or net loss is shared equally unless the partnership contract specifically indicates otherwise.** The same basis of division usually applies to both net income and net loss. As a result, it is customary to refer to the basis as the **income ratio**, the **income and loss ratio**, or the **profit and loss ratio**. Because of its wide acceptance, we will use the term income ratio to identify the basis for dividing both net income and net loss. A partner's share of net income or net loss is recognized in the accounts through closing entries.

### Closing Entries

As in the case of a proprietorship, four entries are required in preparing closing entries for a partnership. The entries are:

1. Debit each revenue account for its balance and credit Income Summary for total revenues.
2. Debit Income Summary for total expenses and credit each expense account for its balance.
3. Debit Income Summary for its balance and credit each partner's capital account for his or her share of net income. Conversely, credit Income Summary and debit each partner's capital account for his or her share of net loss.
4. Debit each partner's capital account for the balance in that partner's drawing account, and credit each partner's drawing account for the same amount.

The first two entries are the same as in a proprietorship. The last two entries are different because (1) there are two or more owners' capital and drawing accounts and (2) it is necessary to divide net income (or net loss) among the partners.

To illustrate the last two closing entries, we will assume that the AB Company has net income of $32,000 for 1996. The partners, L. Arbor and D. Barnett, share net income and net loss equally, and drawings for the year were Arbor $8,000 and Barnett $6,000. The last two closing entries are:

**Illustration 13-4**

*Closing net income and drawing accounts*

| | | | | |
|---|---|---|---|---|
| Dec. 31 | Income Summary | | 32,000 | |
| | L. Arbor, Capital ($32,000 × 50%) | | | 16,000 |
| | D. Barnett, Capital ($32,000 × 50%) | | | 16,000 |
| | (To transfer net income to owners' capital accounts) | | | |
| 31 | L. Arbor, Capital | | 8,000 | |
| | D. Barnett, Capital | | 6,000 | |
| | L. Arbor, Drawing | | | 8,000 |
| | D. Barnett, Drawing | | | 6,000 |
| | (To close drawing accounts to capital accounts) | | | |

Assuming the beginning capital balance is $47,000 for Arbor and $36,000 for Barnett, the capital and drawing accounts will show the following after posting the closing entries:

**Illustration 13-5**

*Partners' capital and drawing accounts after closing*

**L. Arbor, Capital**

| | | | |
|---|---|---|---|
| 12/31 **Clos.** 8,000 | 1/1 Bal. 47,000 | | |
| | 12/31 **Clos.** 16,000 | | |
| | 12/31 Bal. 55,000 | | |

**D. Barnett, Capital**

| | | | |
|---|---|---|---|
| 12/31 **Clos.** 6,000 | 1/1 Bal. 36,000 | | |
| | 12/31 **Clos.** 16,000 | | |
| | 12/31 Bal. 46,000 | | |

**L. Arbor, Drawing**

| | |
|---|---|
| 12/31 Bal. 8,000 | 12/31 **Clos.** 8,000 |

**D. Barnett, Drawing**

| | |
|---|---|
| 12/31 Bal. 6,000 | 12/31 **Clos.** 6,000 |

As in a proprietorship, the partners' capital accounts are permanent accounts; the partners' drawing accounts are temporary accounts. Normally, the capital accounts will have credit balances and the drawing accounts will have debit balances. Drawing accounts are debited when partners withdraw cash or other assets from the partnership for personal use. For example, the partnership agreement may permit each partner to withdraw cash monthly for personal living expenses.

### Income Ratios

**STUDY OBJECTIVE**

**3**

*Identify the bases for dividing net income or net loss.*

As indicated earlier, the partnership agreement should specify the basis for sharing net income or net loss. The following are typical of the ratios that may be used:

1. A fixed ratio, expressed as a proportion (6:4), a percentage (70% and 30%), or a fraction (2/3 and 1/3).
2. A ratio based either on capital balances at the beginning of the year or on average capital balances during the year.

3. Salaries to partners and the remainder on a fixed ratio.
4. Interest on partners' capitals and the remainder on a fixed ratio.
5. Salaries to partners, interest on partners' capitals, and the remainder on a fixed ratio.

The objective is to reach agreement on a basis that will equitably reflect the differences among partners in terms of their capital investment and service to the partnership.

A fixed ratio is easy to apply, and it may be an equitable basis in some circumstances. Assume, for example, that Hughes and Lane are partners. Each contributes the same amount of capital, but Hughes expects to work full-time in the partnership and Lane expects to work only half-time. Accordingly, the partners agree to a fixed ratio of 2/3 to Hughes and 1/3 to Lane.

A ratio based on capital balances may be appropriate when the funds invested in the partnership are considered the critical factor. Capital balances may also be equitable when a manager is hired to run the business and the partners do not plan to take an active role in daily operations.

The three remaining ratios (3, 4, and 5) give specific recognition to differences that may exist among partners. These ratios provide salary allowances for time worked and interest allowances for capital invested. Then, any remaining net income or net loss is allocated on a fixed ratio. Some caution needs to be exercised in working with these types of income ratios. These ratios pertain exclusively to **the computations that are required in dividing net income or net loss.**

**Salaries to partners and interest on partners' capitals are not expenses of the partnership. Therefore, these items do not enter into the matching of expenses with revenues and the determination of net income or net loss.** For a partnership, as well as for other entities, salaries expense pertains to the cost of services performed by employees, and interest expense relates to the cost of borrowing money from creditors. Partners in their ownership capacity are not considered either **employees** or **creditors**. Thus, when the income ratio includes a salary allowance for partners, some partnership agreements permit the partner to make monthly withdrawals of cash based on their "salary." In such cases, the withdrawals are debited to the partner's drawing account.

## ►Accounting in Action ► *Business Insight*

Partners in professional firms can and do make substantial incomes. For example, in one large international public accounting firm, the average earnings of all partners in a recent year was $200,000, and the individual earnings of the five most highly compensated partners ranged from $500,000 to $900,000. Note, however, that the compensation of partners in most large partnerships differs in both form and substance from the compensation of a corporate executive. Partners are not guaranteed an annual salary. Compensation depends entirely on each year's operating results. Substantial investment is required of each partner. This capital is at risk for the partner's entire career—often 25–30 years—without an established return. Upon leaving, it is repayable without adjustment for inflation or appreciation in value.

### *Salaries, Interest, and Remainder on a Fixed Ratio*

Under this income ratio (item 5 in the list above), the provisions for salaries and interest must be applied **before** the remainder is allocated on the specified fixed ratio. **This is true even if the provisions exceed net income or the partnership has suffered a net loss for the year.** Detailed information concerning the division of net income or net loss should be shown at the bottom of the income statement.

To illustrate this income ratio, assume that Sara King and Ray Lee are co-partners in the Kingslee Company. The partnership agreement provides for (1) salary allowances of $8,400 to King and $6,000 to Lee, (2) interest allowances of 10% on capital balances at the beginning of the year, and (3) the remainder equally. Capital balances on January 1 were King, $28,000, and Lee, $24,000. In 1996, partnership net income is $22,000. The division of net income is as follows:

**Illustration 13-6**

*Income statement with division of net income*

### KINGSLEE COMPANY
### Income Statement
### For the Year Ended December 31, 1996

| | Sales | | | $200,000 |
|---|---|---|---|---|
| | Net Income | | | $ 22,000 |

**Division of Net Income**

| | Sara King | Ray Lee | Total |
|---|---|---|---|
| Salary allowance | $ 8,400 | $6,000 | $14,400 |
| Interest allowance | | | |
|   Sara King ($28,000 × 10%) | 2,800 | | |
|   Ray Lee ($24,000 × 10%) | | 2,400 | |
|     Total interest | | | 5,200 |
| Total salaries and interest | 11,200 | 8,400 | 19,600 |
| **Remaining income, $2,400** | | | |
|   ($22,000 − $19,600) | | | |
|   Sara King ($2,400 × 50%) | 1,200 | | |
|   Ray Lee ($2,400 × 50%) | | 1,200 | |
|     Total remainder | | | 2,400 |
| **Total division** | $12,400 | $9,600 | $22,000 |

The entry to record the division of net income is:

| Dec. 31 | Income Summary | 22,000 | |
|---|---|---|---|
| | Sara King, Capital | | 12,400 |
| | Ray Lee, Capital | | 9,600 |
| | (To close net income to partners' capitals) | | |

To illustrate a situation in which the salary and interest allowances exceed net income, assume that net income in the Kingslee Company is only $18,000. In this case, the salary and interest allowances will create a deficiency of $1,600 ($19,600 − $18,000). Since the computations of the allowances are the same as those in the preceding example, we will begin the division of net income with total salaries and interest as follows:

**Illustration 13-7**

*Division of net income—income deficiency*

| | Sara King | Ray Lee | Total |
|---|---|---|---|
| Total salaries and interest | $11,200 | $8,400 | $19,600 |
| Remaining deficiency ($1,600) | | | |
|   ($18,000 − $19,600) | | | |
|   Sara King ($1,600 × 50%) | (800) | | |
|   Ray Lee ($1,600 × 50%) | | (800) | |
|     Total remainder | | | (1,600) |
| **Total division** | $10,400 | $7,600 | $18,000 |

## Partnership Financial Statements

The financial statements of a partnership are similar to those of a proprietorship. The differences are related to the fact that a number of owners are involved in a partnership. The income statement for a partnership is identical to the income statement for a proprietorship except for the division of net income, as shown earlier.

> **STUDY OBJECTIVE**
> ·········▼·········
> 4
> *Describe the form and content of partnership financial statements.*

The owners' equity statement for a partnership is called the partners' capital statement. Its function is to explain the changes in each partner's capital account and in total partnership capital during the year. As in a proprietorship, changes in capital may result from three causes: additional capital investment, drawings, and net income or net loss.

The partners' capital statement for the Kingslee Company shown below is based on the division of $22,000 of net income in Illustration 13-6. The statement includes assumed data for the additional investment and drawings.

**Illustration 13-8**

*Partners' capital statement*

| KINGSLEE COMPANY Partners' Capital Statement For the Year Ended December 31, 1996 | | | |
|---|---|---|---|
| | Sara King | Ray Lee | Total |
| Capital, January 1 | $28,000 | $24,000 | $52,000 |
| Add: Additional investment | 2,000 | | 2,000 |
| Net income | 12,400 | 9,600 | 22,000 |
| | 42,400 | 33,600 | 76,000 |
| Less: Drawings | 7,000 | 5,000 | 12,000 |
| Capital, December 31 | $35,400 | $28,600 | $64,000 |

**Helpful hint** As in a proprietorship, owner's capital may change due to (1) additional investment, (2) drawings, and (3) net income or loss.

The partners' capital statement is prepared from the income statement and the partners' capital and drawing accounts.

The balance sheet for a partnership is the same as for a proprietorship except in the owner's equity section. In a partnership, the capital balances of each partner are shown in the balance sheet. The owners' equity section for Kingslee Company would show the following:

**Illustration 13-9**

*Owners' equity section of a partnership balance sheet*

| KINGSLEE COMPANY Partial Balance Sheet December 31, 1996 | | |
|---|---|---|
| Total liabilities (assumed amount) | | $115,000 |
| Owners' equity | | |
| Sara King, Capital | $35,400 | |
| Ray Lee, Capital | 28,600 | |
| Total owners' equity | | 64,000 |
| Total liabilities and owners' equity | | $179,000 |

## *Before You Go On . . .*

► *Review It*

1. How should a partner's initial investment of assets be valued?

**2.** What are the closing entries for a partnership?

**3.** What income ratios may be used in a partnership?

**4.** How do partnership financial statements differ from proprietorship financial statements?

### ▶ *Do It*

LeMay Company reports net income of $57,000. The partnership agreement provides for salaries of $15,000 to L. Lee and $12,000 to R. May, with the remainder to be shared on a 60:40 basis, respectively. L. Lee asks your help to divide the net income between the partners and to prepare the closing entry.

***Reasoning:*** Salaries to partners and interest on partners' capital are not expenses of the partnership. These items do not enter into the matching of expenses with revenues and the determination of net income or net loss. Therefore, after net income for LeMay is computed, salaries are deducted and then the income ratios are applied to the remainder. The closing entry for net income in a partnership is the same as in a proprietorship except that more than one capital account is credited.

***Solution:*** The division of net income is as follows:

|  | L. Lee | R. May | Total |
|---|---|---|---|
| Salary allowance | $15,000 | $12,000 | $27,000 |
| Remaining income ($57,000 − $27,000) | | | |
| L. Lee (60% × $30,000) | 18,000 | | |
| R. May (40% × $30,000) | | 12,000 | |
| Total remaining income | | | 30,000 |
| Total division of income | $33,000 | $24,000 | $57,000 |

The closing entry for net income therefore is:

| | | |
|---|---|---|
| Income Summary | 57,000 | |
| L. Lee, Capital | | 33,000 |
| R. May, Capital | | 24,000 |
| (To close net income to partners' capitals) | | |

*Related exercise material:* BE13–3, BE13–4, BE13–5, and E13–2.

# Admission and Withdrawal of Partners

We have seen how the basic accounting for a partnership works. We now look at how to account for a common occurrence in partnerships—the addition or withdrawal of a partner.

## Admission of a Partner

**STUDY OBJECTIVE**
••••••••• **5** •••••••••

*Explain the effects of the entries when a new partner is admitted.*

The admission of a new partner results in the **legal dissolution of the existing partnership** and **the beginning of a new partnership**. From an economic standpoint, however, the admission of a new partner (or partners) may be of minor significance in the continuity of the business. For example, in large public accounting or law firms, partners are admitted annually without any change in operating policies established by the continuing partners. **To recognize the economic effects, it is necessary only to open a capital account for each new partner.** The entries described and illustrated below are based on the assumption that the accounting records of the predecessor firm will continue to be used by the new partnership.

A new partner may be admitted either by (1) purchasing the interest of one or more existing partners or (2) investing assets in the partnership, as shown in Illustration 13-10. The former affects only the capital accounts of the partners

**Illustration 13-10**

*Procedures in adding partners*

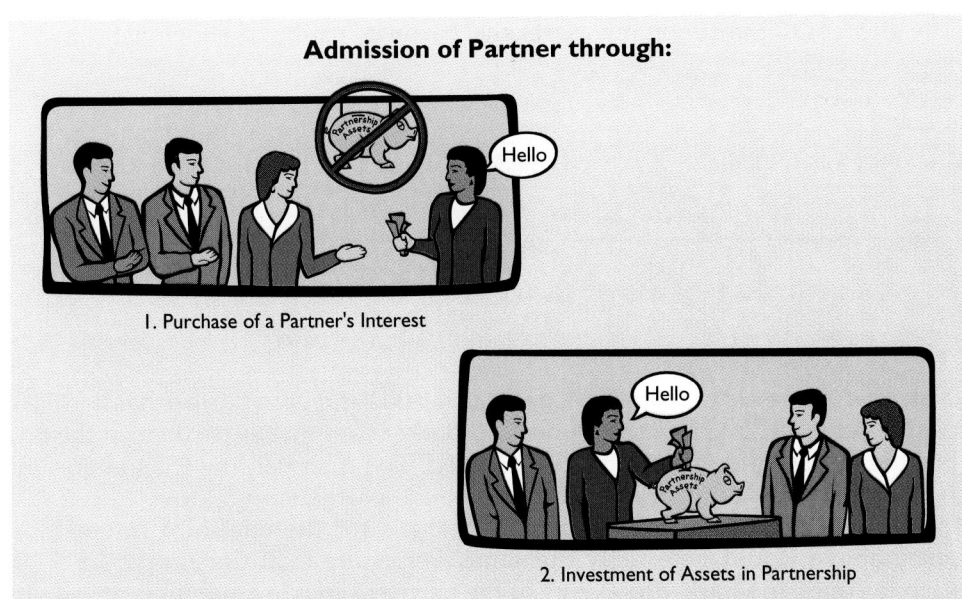

**Admission of Partner through:**

1. Purchase of a Partner's Interest

2. Investment of Assets in Partnership

who are parties to the transaction. The latter increases both net assets (total assets less total liabilities) and total capital of the partnership.

### Purchase of a Partner's Interest

The admission of a partner by purchase of an interest in the firm is a personal transaction between one or more existing partners and the new partner. Each party acts as an individual separate from the partnership entity. The price paid is negotiated and determined by the individuals involved. It may be equal to or different from the capital equity acquired. The amount of the purchase price passes directly from the new partner to the partners who are giving up part or all of their ownership claims. Any money or other consideration exchanged is the personal property of the participants and **not** the property of the partnership. Upon purchase of an interest, the new partner acquires each selling partner's capital interest and income ratio. A partner does not have to obtain the approval of the other partners to sell his or her interest. However, the Uniform Partnership Act provides that the purchaser does not become a partner until he or she is accepted into the firm by the continuing partners.

**Helpful hint** In a purchase of an interest, the partnership is **not** a participant in the transaction. For example, no cash is contributed to the partnership.

Accounting for the purchase of an interest is straightforward. As far as the partnership is concerned, only the realignment of partners' capital is recorded. **Each partner's capital account is debited for the ownership claims that have been relinquished, and the new partner's capital account is credited with the capital equity purchased.** Total assets, total liabilities, and total capital remain unchanged, as do all individual asset and liability accounts.

To illustrate, assume that L. Carson agrees to pay $10,000 each to C. Ames and D. Barker for 33⅓% (one third) of their interest in the Ames–Barker partnership. At the time of the admission of Carson, each partner has a $30,000 capital balance. Both partners, therefore, give up $10,000 of their capital equity. The entry to record the admission of Carson is:

| | | |
|---|---:|---:|
| C. Ames, Capital | 10,000 | |
| D. Barker, Capital | 10,000 | |
|    L. Carson, Capital | | 20,000 |
|     (To record admission of Carson by purchase) | | |

**Illustration 13-11**

*Ledger balances after purchase of a partner's interest*

The effect of this entry on net assets and partners' capital is shown below:

| Net Assets | | C. Ames, Capital | | D. Barker, Capital | | L. Carson, Capital |
|---|---|---|---|---|---|---|
| 60,000 | | 10,000 | 30,000 | 10,000 | 30,000 | 20,000 |
| | | | Bal.  20,000 | | Bal.  20,000 | |

Note that net assets remain unchanged at $60,000 and each partner has a $20,000 capital balance. Note also that Ames and Barker continue as partners in the firm but the capital interest of each has changed. The cash paid by Carson goes directly to the individual partners and not to the partnership.

**Regardless of the amount paid by Carson for the one-third interest, the entry above would be exactly the same.** For example, if Carson pays $12,000 each to Ames and Barker for 33⅓% of the partnership, the foregoing entry is still made.

### Investment of Assets in a Partnership

The admission of a partner by an investment of assets is a transaction between the new partner and the partnership. Often referred to simply as admission by investment, the transaction **increases both the net assets and total capital of the partnership**. To illustrate, assume that instead of purchasing an interest, Carson invests $30,000 in cash in the Ames–Barker partnership for a 33⅓% capital interest. In such a case, the entry is:

| | | |
|---|---|---|
| Cash | 30,000 | |
|   L. Carson, Capital | | 30,000 |
|   (To record admission of Carson by investment) | | |

**Illustration 13-12**

*Ledger balances after investment of assets*

The effects of this transaction on the partnership accounts may be shown as follows:

| Net Assets | | C. Ames, Capital | | D. Barker, Capital | | L. Carson, Capital |
|---|---|---|---|---|---|---|
| 60,000 | | | 30,000 | | 30,000 | 30,000 |
| 30,000 | | | | | | |
| Bal.  90,000 | | | | | | |

Note that both net assets and total capital have increased by $30,000.

Remember that Carson's one-third capital interest might not result in a one-third income ratio. Carson's income ratio should be specified in the new partnership agreement, and it may or may not be equal to the one-third capital interest.

The different effects of the purchase of an interest and admission by investment are shown in the comparison of the net assets and capital balances in Illustration 13-13.

| Purchase of an Interest | | Admission by Investment | |
|---|---|---|---|
| Net Assets | $60,000 | Net Assets | $90,000 |
| Capital | | Capital | |
| C. Ames | $20,000 | C. Ames | $30,000 |
| D. Barker | 20,000 | D. Barker | 30,000 |
| L. Carson | 20,000 | L. Carson | 30,000 |
| Total capital | $60,000 | Total capital | $90,000 |

**Illustration 13-13**

*Comparison of purchase of an interest and admission by investment*

When an interest is purchased, the total net assets and total capital of the partnership do not change. However, when a partner is admitted by investment, both the total net assets and the total capital change.

In the case of admission by investment, further complications occur when the new partner's investment differs from the capital equity acquired. When those amounts are not the same, the difference is considered a bonus either to (1) the existing (old) partners or (2) the new partner.

**Bonus to Old Partners.** The existing partners may be unwilling to admit a new partner without receiving a bonus for both personal and business reasons. In an established firm, existing partners may insist on a bonus as compensation for the work they have put into the company over the years. Two accounting-related factors underlie the business reason: First, total partners' capital equals the **book value** of the recorded net assets of the partnership. At the time the new partner is admitted, the fair market values of assets such as land and buildings may be higher than their book values. Second, when the partnership has been profitable, goodwill may exist. However, the goodwill will not be recorded or included in total partners' capital. In such cases the new partner is usually willing to pay the bonus to become a partner.

A bonus to old partners results when the new partner's capital credit on the date of admittance is less than his or her investment in the firm. The bonus results in **an increase in the capital balances of the old partners that is allocated to them on the basis of their income ratios before the admission of the new partner**.

To illustrate, assume that the Bart–Cohen partnership owned by Sam Bart and Tom Cohen has total capital of $120,000 when Lea Eden is admitted to the partnership. Lea acquires a 25% ownership (capital) interest by making a cash investment of $80,000 in the partnership. The procedure for determining Eden's capital credit and the bonus to the old partners is as follows:

> **Helpful hint** (1) The debit to Cash is greater than the new partner's capital credit. (2) Credits to old partners' capitals are needed for equal debits and credits.

1. **Determine the total capital of the new partnership** by adding the new partner's investment to the total capital of the old partnership. In this case the total capital of the new firm is $200,000, computed as follows:

   | | |
   |---|---|
   | Total capital of existing partnership | $120,000 |
   | Investment by new partner, Eden | 80,000 |
   | Total capital of new partnership | $200,000 |

2. **Determine the new partner's capital credit** by multiplying the total capital of the new partnership by the new partner's ownership interest. Eden's capital credit is $50,000 ($200,000 × 25%).

3. **Determine the amount of bonus** by subtracting the new partner's capital credit from the new partner's investment. The bonus in this case is $30,000 ($80,000 − $50,000).

**4. Allocate the bonus to the old partners on the basis of their income ratios.** Assuming the ratios are Bart, 60%, and Cohen, 40%, the allocation is: Bart, $18,000 ($30,000 × 60%) and Cohen, $12,000 ($30,000 × 40%).

The entry to record the admission of Eden is:

| | | |
|---|---|---|
| Cash | 80,000 | |
|     Sam Bart, Capital | | 18,000 |
|     Tom Cohen, Capital | | 12,000 |
|     Lea Eden, Capital | | 50,000 |
|       (To record admission of Eden and bonus to old partners) | | |

**Bonus to New Partner.**   A bonus to a new partner results when the new partner's capital credit is greater than his or her investment of assets in the firm. This may occur when the new partner possesses resources or special attributes that are desired by the partnership. For example, when bank interest rates are high, the new partner may be able to supply cash that is urgently needed for expansion or to meet maturing debts. Alternatively, the new partner may be a recognized expert or authority in a relevant field. Thus, an engineering firm may be willing to give a world-renowned engineer a bonus to join the firm. Similarly, the partners of a restaurant may offer a bonus to a sports celebrity in order to add the athlete's name to the partnership name. A bonus to a new partner may also result when recorded book values on the partnership books are higher than their market values.

A bonus to a new partner results in a **decrease in the capital balances of the old partners based on their income ratios before the admission of the new partner**. To illustrate, assume that Lea Eden invests $20,000 in cash for a 25% ownership interest in the Bart–Cohen partnership. Using the procedures described in the preceding section, the computations for Eden's capital credit and the bonus are as follows:

**Illustration 13-14**

*Computation of capital credit and bonus to new partner*

| | | |
|---|---|---|
| 1. | Total capital of Bart–Cohen partnership | $120,000 |
| | Investment by new partner, Eden | 20,000 |
| | Total capital of new partnership | $140,000 |
| 2. | Eden's capital credit (25% × $140,000) | $ 35,000 |
| 3. | **Bonus to Eden** ($35,000 − $20,000) | $ 15,000 |
| 4. | Allocation of bonus: | |
| |     Bart ($15,000 × 60%)     $9,000 | |
| |     Cohen ($15,000 × 40%)   6,000 | $ 15,000 |

The entry to record the admission of Eden is as follows:

| | | |
|---|---|---|
| Cash | 20,000 | |
| Sam Bart, Capital | 9,000 | |
| Tom Cohen, Capital | 6,000 | |
|     Lea Eden, Capital | | 35,000 |
|     (To record Eden's admission and bonus) | | |

**STUDY OBJECTIVE**

••••••••• **6** •••••••••

*Describe the effects of the entries when a partner withdraws from the firm.*

## Withdrawal of a Partner

Now let's look at the opposite situation—the withdrawal of a partner. A partner may withdraw from a partnership **voluntarily** by selling his or her equity in the firm or **involuntarily** by reaching mandatory retirement age or by dying. The withdrawal of a partner, like the admission of a partner, legally dissolves the partnership. The legal effects may be recognized in accounting for a withdrawal by dissolving the firm. However, it is customary to record only the economic effects. As indicated earlier, the partnership agreement should specify the terms of withdrawal. The withdrawal of a partner may be accomplished by (1) payment from partners' personal assets or (2) payment from partnership assets, as shown in Illustration 13-15. The former affects only the partners' capital accounts. The latter decreases total net assets and total capital of the partnership.

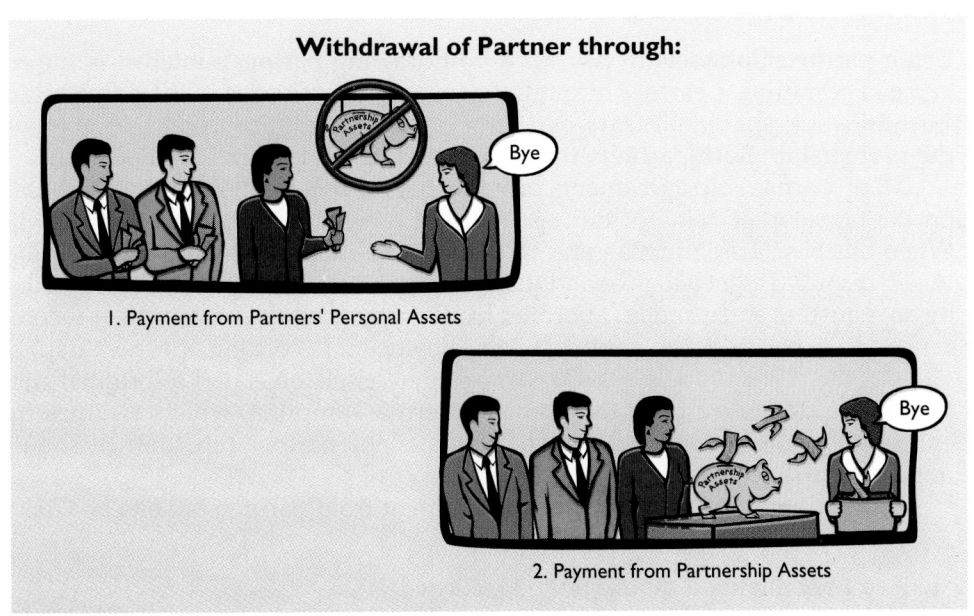

**Withdrawal of Partner through:**

1. Payment from Partners' Personal Assets

2. Payment from Partnership Assets

**Illustration 13-15**

*Procedures in partnership withdrawal*

### Payment from Partners' Personal Assets

**The withdrawal of a partner when payment is made from partners' personal assets is the direct opposite of admitting a new partner who purchases a partner's interest.** Withdrawal by payment from partners' personal assets is a personal transaction between the partners. Payment to the retiring partner is made directly from the remaining partners' personal assets. **Partnership assets are not involved in any way, and total capital does not change.** Thus, the effect on the partnership is limited to a realignment of the partners' capital balances.

To illustrate, assume that Anne Morz, Mary Nead, and Jill Odom have capital balances of $25,000, $15,000, and $10,000, respectively, when Morz and Nead agree to buy out Odom's interest. Each of them agrees to pay Odom $8,000 in exchange for one-half of Odom's total interest of $10,000. The entry to record the withdrawal is:

| | | |
|---|---|---|
| Jill Odom, Capital | 10,000 | |
|     Anne Morz, Capital | | 5,000 |
|     Mary Nead, Capital | | 5,000 |
|       (To record purchase of Odom's interest) | | |

The effect of this entry on the partnership accounts is shown below:

**Helpful hint** If each purchaser acquires one-fourth of Odom's total interest for $8,000 each, the debit becomes $5,000 and the credits $2,500.

**Illustration 13-16**

*Ledger balances after payment from partners' personal assets*

| Net Assets | | Anne Morz, Capital | | Mary Nead, Capital | | Jill Odom, Capital | |
|---|---|---|---|---|---|---|---|
| 50,000 | | | 25,000 | | 15,000 | 10,000 | 10,000 |
| | | | 5,000 | | 5,000 | | |
| | | Bal. | 30,000 | Bal. | 20,000 | | Bal.  –0– |

Note that net assets and total capital remain the same at $50,000. Note also that the $16,000 paid to Odom is not recorded. Odom's capital is debited only for $10,000, not for the $16,000 that she received. Similarly, both Morz and Nead credit their capital accounts for only $5,000, not the $8,000 they each paid. Morz and Nead will share net income or net loss equally unless they specifically indicate another income ratio in the partnership agreement.

### *Payment from Partnership Assets*

Using partnership assets to pay for a withdrawing partner's interest is the **reverse** of admitting a partner through the investment of assets in the partnership. Withdrawal by payment from partnership assets is a transaction that involves the partnership. **Both partnership net assets and total capital are decreased.**

Many partnership agreements provide that the amount paid should be based on the fair market value of the assets at the time of the partner's withdrawal. When this basis is required, some accountants maintain that any differences between recorded asset balances and their fair market values should be (1) recorded by an adjusting entry and (2) allocated to all partners on the basis of their income ratios. This position has serious flaws, however. Recording the revaluations violates the cost principle, which requires that assets be stated at original cost. It also is a departure from the going-concern assumption, which assumes the entity will continue indefinitely. The terms of the partnership contract should not dictate the accounting for the event.

In accounting for a withdrawal by payment from partnership assets:

1. Asset revaluations should not be recorded.
2. Any difference between the amount paid and the withdrawing partner's capital balance should be considered a bonus to the retiring partner or a bonus to the remaining partners.

**Bonus to Retiring Partner.**   A bonus may be paid to a retiring partner when:

1. The fair market value of partnership assets is more than their book value,
2. There is unrecorded goodwill resulting from the partnership's superior earnings record, or
3. The remaining partners are anxious to remove the partner from the firm.

**The bonus is deducted from the remaining partners' capital balances on the basis of their income ratios at the time of the withdrawal.**

To illustrate, assume that the following capital balances exist in the RST partnership: Fred Roman $50,000, Dee Sand $30,000, and Betty Terk $20,000. The partners share income in the ratio of 3:2:1, respectively. Terk retires from the partnership and receives a cash payment of $25,000 from the firm. The procedure for determining the bonus to the retiring partner and the allocation of the bonus to the remaining partners is as follows:

1. **Determine the amount of the bonus** by subtracting the retiring partner's capital balance from the cash paid by the partnership. The bonus in this case is $5,000 ($25,000 − $20,000).
2. **Allocate the bonus to the remaining partners on the basis of their income ratios.** The ratios of Roman and Sand are 3:2. Thus, the allocation of the $5,000 bonus is: Roman $3,000 ($5,000 × 3/5) and Sand $2,000 ($5,000 × 2/5).

The entry to record the withdrawal of Terk is:

| | | |
|---|---|---|
| Betty Terk, Capital | 20,000 | |
| Fred Roman, Capital | 3,000 | |
| Dee Sand, Capital | 2,000 | |
|     Cash | | 25,000 |
|       (To record withdrawal of and bonus to Terk) | | |

The remaining partners, Roman and Sand, will recover the bonus given to Terk as the undervalued assets are sold or used in the partnership.

**Bonus to Remaining Partners.**   The retiring partner may give a bonus to the remaining partners when:

1.  Recorded assets are overvalued,
2.  The partnership has a poor earnings record, or
3.  The partner is anxious to leave the partnership.

In such cases, the cash paid to the retiring partner will be less than the retiring partner's capital balance. **The bonus is allocated (credited) to the capital accounts of the remaining partners on the basis of their income ratios.**

To illustrate, assume that, instead of the example above, Terk is paid only $16,000 for her $20,000 equity upon withdrawing from the RST partnership. In such case:

1.  The bonus to remaining partners is $4,000 ($20,000 − $16,000).
2.  The allocation of the $4,000 bonus is: Roman $2,400 ($4,000 × 3/5) and Sand $1,600 ($4,000 × 2/5).

The entry to record the withdrawal is:

| | | |
|---|---|---|
| Betty Terk, Capital | 20,000 | |
|     Fred Roman, Capital | | 2,400 |
|     Dee Sand, Capital | | 1,600 |
|     Cash | | 16,000 |
|       (To record withdrawal of Terk and bonus to remaining partners) | | |

It is important to note that if Sand had withdrawn from the partnership, any bonus would be divided between Roman and Terk on the basis of their income ratio which is 3:1 or 75% and 25%.

### Death of a Partner

The death of a partner dissolves the partnership, but provision generally is made for the surviving partners to continue operations. When a partner dies, it usually is necessary to determine the partner's equity at the date of death. This is done by (1) determining the net income or loss for the year to date, (2) closing the books, and (3) preparing financial statements. The partnership agreement may also require an audit of the financial statements by independent auditors and a revaluation of assets by an independent appraisal firm.

The surviving partners may agree either to (1) purchase the deceased partner's equity from their personal assets or (2) use partnership assets to settle with the deceased partner's estate. In both instances, the entries to record the withdrawal of the partner are similar to those presented in previous illustrations.

To facilitate payment from partnership assets, some partnerships obtain life insurance policies on each partner with the partnership as the beneficiary. The proceeds from the insurance policy on the deceased partner are then used to settle with the estate.

## *Before You Go On . . .*

### ▶ *Review It*

1. How does the accounting for admission by purchase of an interest differ from admission by investing assets in the partnership?
2. Contrast the accounting effects of the withdrawal of a partner by payment from (a) personal assets and (b) partnership assets.

### ▶ *Do It*

Curly, Moe, and Larry have a partnership. Each partner has a $40,000 balance in his capital account. Record journal entries for each of the independent events listed below.

1. Curly, Moe, and Larry agree to admit Stan as a new one-quarter-interest partner. Stan pays $10,000 in cash directly to each partner.
2. Curly, Moe, and Larry agree to admit Stan as a new one-quarter-interest partner. Stan contributes $40,000 into the partnership.
3. Curly and Moe agree to let Larry withdraw from the partnership, and $30,000 of partnership cash is distributed to Larry. Curly and Moe share income and losses equally.
4. Curly and Moe agree to let Larry withdraw from the partnership. Each pays Larry $25,000 out of his personal assets. Curly and Moe share income and losses equally.

***Reasoning:*** You need to understand that admission (withdrawal) by purchase (sale) of an interest is a personal transaction between one or more existing partners and the new (withdrawing) partner. In contrast, admission (withdrawal) by investment (distribution) of partnership assets is a transaction between the new (withdrawing) partner and the partnership.

***Solution:***

1.

| | | |
|---|---:|---:|
| Curly, Capital | 10,000 | |
| Moe, Capital | 10,000 | |
| Larry, Capital | 10,000 | |
|    Stan, Capital | | 30,000 |
|      (To record admission of Stan by purchase) | | |

2.

| | | |
|---|---:|---:|
| Cash | 40,000 | |
|    Stan, Capital | | 40,000 |
|      (To record admission of Stan by investment) | | |

3.

| | | |
|---|---:|---:|
| Larry, Capital | 40,000 | |
|    Cash | | 30,000 |
|    Curly, Capital | | 5,000 |
|    Moe, Capital | | 5,000 |
|      (To record withdrawal of Larry and bonus to remaining partners) | | |

4.

| | | |
|---|---:|---:|
| Larry, Capital | 40,000 | |
|    Curly, Capital | | 20,000 |
|    Moe, Capital | | 20,000 |
|      (To record purchase of Larry's interest) | | |

*Related exercise material:* BE13–6, BE13–7, BE13–8, BE13–9, E13–4, E13–5, E13–6, and E13–7.

# Liquidation of a Partnership

The liquidation of a partnership terminates the business. It entails selling the assets of the firm, paying liabilities, and distributing any remaining assets to the partners. Liquidation may result from the sale of the business by mutual agreement of the partners, from the death of a partner, or from bankruptcy. In contrast to the dissolution of a partnership, partnership liquidation ends both the legal and economic life of the entity.

From an accounting standpoint, liquidation should be preceded by completing the accounting cycle for the partnership for the final operating period. This includes preparing adjusting entries and financial statements. It also involves preparing closing entries and a post-closing trial balance. Thus, only balance sheet accounts should be open as the liquidation process begins.

The liquidation process may occur at a specific point in time or it may occur over a period of time. In liquidation, the sale of noncash assets for cash is called **realization**, and the difference between book value and the cash proceeds is called the **gain or loss on realization**. To liquidate a partnership, it is necessary to:

**STUDY OBJECTIVE**

**▼**
**7**

*Prepare the entries to record the liquidation of a partnership.*

1. Sell noncash assets for cash and recognize a gain or loss on realization.
2. Allocate gain/loss on realization to the partners based on their income ratios.
3. Pay partnership liabilities in cash.
4. Distribute remaining cash to partners on the basis of their capital balances.

**Helpful hint** These steps are indispensable to correct homework and examination results.

**Each of the steps must be performed in sequence** because creditors must be paid **before** partners receive any cash distributions. Each step also must be recorded by an accounting entry.

When a partnership is liquidated, all partners may have credit balances in their capital accounts—a situation termed no capital deficiency; or at least one partner's capital account may have a debit balance—a situation termed a capital deficiency. To illustrate each of these conditions, assume that the Ace Company is liquidated when its ledger shows the following assets, liabilities, and owners' equity accounts:

| Assets | | Liabilities and Owners' Equity | |
|---|---|---|---|
| Cash | $ 5,000 | Notes payable | $15,000 |
| Accounts receivable | 15,000 | Accounts payable | 16,000 |
| Inventory | 18,000 | R. Arnet, Capital | 15,000 |
| Equipment | 35,000 | P. Carey, Capital | 17,800 |
| Accum. depr.—equipment | (8,000) | W. Eaton, Capital | 1,200 |
| | $65,000 | | $65,000 |

**Illustration 13-17**

*Account balances prior to liquidation*

## No Capital Deficiency

The partners of Ace Company agree to liquidate the partnership on the following terms: (1) a cash sale of the noncash assets of the partnership to Jackson Enterprises for $75,000, and (2) payment of partnership liabilities by the partnership. The income ratios of the partners are 3:2:1, respectively. The steps in the liquidation process are as follows:

1. The noncash assets (accounts receivable, inventory, and equipment) are sold for $75,000. Since the book value of these assets is $60,000 ($15,000 +

$18,000 + $35,000 − $8,000), a gain of $15,000 is realized on the sale. The entry is:

**(1)**

| | | |
|---|---:|---:|
| Cash | 75,000 | |
| Accumulated Depreciation—Equipment | 8,000 | |
|    Accounts Receivable | | 15,000 |
|    Inventory | | 18,000 |
|    Equipment | | 35,000 |
|    Gain on Realization | | 15,000 |
|      (To record realization of noncash assets) | | |

2. The gain on realization of $15,000 is allocated to the partners on their income ratios, which are 3:2:1. The entry is:

**(2)**

| | | |
|---|---:|---:|
| Gain on Realization | 15,000 | |
|    R. Arnet, Capital ($15,000 × 3/6) | | 7,500 |
|    P. Carey, Capital ($15,000 × 2/6) | | 5,000 |
|    W. Eaton, Capital ($15,000 × 1/6) | | 2,500 |
|      (To allocate gain to partners' capitals) | | |

**Helpful hint** Unless the partnership agreement states to the contrary, the income ratio also applies to realization gains and losses.

3. Partnership liabilities consist of Notes Payable $15,000 and Accounts Payable $16,000. Creditors are paid in full by a cash payment of $31,000. The entry is:

**(3)**

| | | |
|---|---:|---:|
| Notes Payable | 15,000 | |
| Accounts Payable | 16,000 | |
|    Cash | | 31,000 |
|      (To record payment of partnership liabilities) | | |

4. The remaining cash is distributed to the partners on the basis of **their capital balances**. After the entries in the first three steps are posted, all partnership accounts, including Gain on Realization, will have zero balances except for four accounts: Cash $49,000; R. Arnet, Capital $22,500; P. Carey, Capital $22,800; and W. Eaton, Capital $3,700, as shown below:

**Illustration 13-18**

*Ledger balances before distribution of cash*

| Cash | | | | R. Arnet, Capital | | | P. Carey, Capital | | | W. Eaton, Capital | |
|---|---|---|---|---|---|---|---|---|---|---|---|
| Bal. | 5,000 | (3) | 31,000 | | Bal. | 15,000 | | Bal. | 17,800 | | Bal. | 1,200 |
| (1) | 75,000 | | | | (2) | 7,500 | | (2) | 5,000 | | (2) | 2,500 |
| Bal. | 49,000 | | | | Bal. | 22,500 | | Bal. | 22,800 | | Bal. | 3,700 |

The entry to record the distribution of cash is as follows:

**(4)**

| | | |
|---|---:|---:|
| R. Arnet, Capital | 22,500 | |
| P. Carey, Capital | 22,800 | |
| W. Eaton, Capital | 3,700 | |
|    Cash | | 49,000 |
|      (To record distribution of cash to partners) | | |

After this entry is posted, all partnership accounts will have zero balances, as shown in Illustration 13-19.

Illustration 13-19

*Ledger balances after distribution of cash*

| Cash | | | | R. Arnet, Capital | | | P. Carey, Capital | | | W. Eaton, Capital | | |
|---|---|---|---|---|---|---|---|---|---|---|---|---|
| Bal. | 5,000 | (3) | 31,000 | (4) 22,500 | Bal. | 15,000 | (4) 22,800 | Bal. | 17,800 | (4) 3,700 | Bal. | 1,200 |
| (1) | 75,000 | (4) | 49,000 | | (2) | 7,500 | | (2) | 5,000 | | (2) | 2,500 |
| Bal. | –0– | | | | Bal. | –0– | | Bal. | –0– | | Bal. | –0– |

A word of caution: **Cash should not be distributed to partners on the basis of their income-sharing ratios.** On this basis, for example, Arnet would receive three-sixths, or $24,500, which would produce an erroneous debit balance of $2,000. The income ratio is a proper basis for allocating net income or loss, **but it is not a proper basis for making the final distribution of cash to the partners.**

**Helpful hint** Zero balances after posting is a quick proof of the accuracy of the cash distribution entry.

### Schedule of Cash Payments

Some accountants prepare a cash payments schedule to determine the distribution of cash to the partners in the liquidation of a partnership. The schedule of cash payments, sometimes called a **safe cash payments schedule**, is organized around the basic accounting equation. The schedule for the Ace Company is shown in Illustration 13-20. The numbers in parentheses refer to the four required steps in the liquidation of a partnership. They also identify the accounting entries that must be made. The cash payments schedule is especially useful when the liquidation process extends over a period of time.

Illustration 13-20

*Schedule of cash payments, no capital deficiency*

| | | | ACE COMPANY | | | | | | | | |
|---|---|---|---|---|---|---|---|---|---|---|---|
| | | **Schedule of Cash Payments** | | | | | | | | | |
| Item | | Cash | + | Noncash Assets | = | Liabilities | + | R. Arnet Capital | + | P. Carey Capital | + W. Eaton Capital |
| Balances before liquidation | | 5,000 | + | 60,000 | = | 31,000 | + | 15,000 | + | 17,800 | + 1,200 |
| Sales of noncash assets and allocation of gain | (1)&(2) | 75,000 | + | (60,000) | = | | | 7,500 | + | 5,000 | + 2,500 |
| New balances | | 80,000 | + | –0– | = | 31,000 | + | 22,500 | + | 22,800 | + 3,700 |
| Pay liabilities | (3) | (31,000) | | | = | (31,000) | | | | | |
| New balances | | 49,000 | + | –0– | = | –0– | + | 22,500 | + | 22,800 | + 3,700 |
| Cash distribution to partners | (4) | (49,000) | | | = | | | (22,500) | + | (22,800) | + (3,700) |
| Final balances | | –0– | | –0– | | –0– | | –0– | | –0– | –0– |

## Capital Deficiency

A capital deficiency may be caused by recurring net losses, excessive drawings before liquidation, or by losses from realization suffered during liquidation. To illustrate, assume that Ace Company is on the brink of bankruptcy. The partners decide to liquidate by having a "going-out-of-business" sale in which merchandise is sold at substantial discounts, and the equipment is sold at auction. Cash proceeds from these sales and collections from customers total only $42,000. Accordingly, the loss from liquidation is $18,000 ($60,000 − $42,000). The steps in the liquidation process are as follows:

**1.** The entry for the realization of noncash assets is:

**(1)**

| | | |
|---|---:|---:|
| Cash | 42,000 | |
| Accumulated Depreciation—Equipment | 8,000 | |
| Loss on Realization | 18,000 | |
|     Accounts Receivable | | 15,000 |
|     Inventory | | 18,000 |
|     Equipment | | 35,000 |
|       (To record realization of noncash assets) | | |

**2.** The loss on realization is allocated to the partners on the basis of their income ratios. The entry is:

**(2)**

| | | |
|---|---:|---:|
| R. Arnet, Capital ($18,000 × 3/6) | 9,000 | |
| P. Carey, Capital ($18,000 × 2/6) | 6,000 | |
| W. Eaton, Capital ($18,000 × 1/6) | 3,000 | |
|     Loss on Realization | | 18,000 |
|       (To allocate loss on realization to partners) | | |

**3.** Partnership liabilities are paid. This entry is the same as in the previous example.

**(3)**

| | | |
|---|---:|---:|
| Notes Payable | 15,000 | |
| Accounts Payable | 16,000 | |
|     Cash | | 31,000 |
|       (To record payment of partnership liabilities) | | |

**4.** After posting the three entries, two accounts will have debit balances—Cash, $16,000, and W. Eaton, Capital, $1,800—and two accounts will have credit balances—R. Arnet, Capital, $6,000, and P. Carey, Capital, $11,800, as shown below:

**Illustration 13-21**

*Ledger balances before distribution of cash*

| Cash | | | | R. Arnet, Capital | | | | P. Carey, Capital | | | | W. Eaton, Capital | | | |
|---|---|---|---|---|---|---|---|---|---|---|---|---|---|---|---|
| Bal. | 5,000 | (3) | 31,000 | (2) | 9,000 | Bal. | 15,000 | (2) | 6,000 | Bal. | 17,800 | (2) | 3,000 | Bal. | 1,200 |
| (1) | 42,000 | | | | | Bal. | 6,000 | | | Bal. | 11,800 | Bal. | 1,800 | | |
| Bal. | 16,000 | | | | | | | | | | | | | | |

Eaton has a capital deficiency of $1,800. Eaton, therefore, owes the partnership $1,800, and Arnet and Carey have a legally enforceable claim against Eaton's personal assets. The distribution of cash is still made on the basis of capital balances. However, the amount will vary depending on how the deficiency is settled.

### Payment of Deficiency

If the partner with the capital deficiency pays the amount owed the partnership, the deficiency is eliminated. To illustrate, assume that Eaton pays $1,800 to the partnership. The entry is:

**(a)**

| | | |
|---|---:|---:|
| Cash | 1,800 | |
|     W. Eaton, Capital | | 1,800 |
|       (To record payment of capital deficiency by Eaton) | | |

After posting this entry, account balances are as follows:

| Cash | | | | R. Arnet, Capital | | | | P. Carey, Capital | | | | W. Eaton, Capital | | | |
|---|---|---|---|---|---|---|---|---|---|---|---|---|---|---|---|
| Bal. | 5,000 | (3) | 31,000 | (2) | 9,000 | Bal. | 15,000 | (2) | 6,000 | Bal. | 17,800 | (2) | 3,000 | Bal. | 1,200 |
| (1) | 42,000 | | | | | | | | | | | | | (a) | 1,800 |
| (a) | 1,800 | | | | | Bal. | 6,000 | | | Bal. | 11,800 | | | | |
| | | | | | | | | | | | | | | Bal. | –0– |
| Bal. | 17,800 | | | | | | | | | | | | | | |

*Illustration 13-22*

*Ledger balances after paying capital deficiency*

The cash balance of $17,800 is now equal to the credit balances in the capital accounts (Arnet $6,000 + Carey $11,800), and cash is distributed on the basis of these balances. The entry is:

| | | |
|---|---|---|
| R. Arnet, Capital | 6,000 | |
| P. Carey, Capital | 11,800 | |
| Cash | | 17,800 |
| (To record distribution of cash to the partners) | | |

After this entry is posted, all accounts will have zero balances.

### Nonpayment of Deficiency

If a partner with a capital deficiency is unable to pay the amount owed to the partnership, the partners with credit balances must absorb the loss. The loss is allocated on the basis of the income ratios that exist between the partners with credit balances. The income ratios of Arnet and Carey are 3:2 or 3/5 and 2/5, respectively. Thus, the following entry is made to remove Eaton's capital deficiency:

| (a) | | |
|---|---|---|
| R. Arnet, Capital ($1,800 × 3/5) | 1,080 | |
| P. Carey, Capital ($1,800 × 2/5) | 720 | |
| W. Eaton, Capital | | 1,800 |
| (To record write-off of capital deficiency) | | |

*Illustration 13-23*

*Ledger balances after non-payment of capital deficiency*

After posting this entry, the cash and capital accounts will have the following balances:

| Cash | | | | R. Arnet, Capital | | | | P. Carey, Capital | | | | W. Eaton, Capital | | | |
|---|---|---|---|---|---|---|---|---|---|---|---|---|---|---|---|
| Bal. | 5,000 | (3) | 31,000 | (2) | 9,000 | Bal. | 15,000 | (2) | 6,000 | Bal. | 17,800 | (2) | 3,000 | Bal. | 1,200 |
| (1) | 42,000 | | | (a) | 1,080 | | | (a) | 720 | | | | | (a) | 1,800 |
| Bal. | 16,000 | | | | | Bal. | 4,920 | | | Bal. | 11,080 | | | Bal. | –0– |

The cash balance of $16,000 now equals the sum of the credit balances in the capital accounts (Arnet $4,920 + Carey $11,080). The entry to record the distribution of cash is:

| | | |
|---|---|---|
| R. Arnet, Capital | 4,920 | |
| P. Carey, Capital | 11,080 | |
| Cash | | 16,000 |
| (To record distribution of cash to partners) | | |

After this entry is posted, all accounts will have zero balances.

## Before You Go On . . .

### ▶ Review It

1. Identify the steps in liquidating a partnership.
2. What basis is used in making the final distribution of cash to the partners?

### ▸ A Look Back at Razor & Tie Music

Refer back to the opening story about Razor & Tie Music, and answer the following questions:

1. Speculate as to why Razor & Tie selected the partnership form of organization for its business.
2. What do you believe are the major items written into the partnership agreement for Razor & Tie?
3. How is net income or loss divided if the partnership is silent regarding the percentage allocation?

#### Solution:

1. Cliff Chenfield and Craig Balsam may have chosen to form a partnership, rather than a corporation, for a number of reasons. First, the partnership is much quicker and easier to form, with little of the red tape associated with a corporation. Second, the partnership form has distinct tax advantages relative to a corporation. Third, since the two partners knew each other well prior to beginning Razor & Tie, their concerns about the risk of unlimited liabilities that might be incurred due to inappropriate actions by the other partner are reduced.
2. A partnership agreement of Razor & Tie should specify the capital contributed by both partners, and the basis for sharing income and losses and for withdrawing funds from the partnership. In addition, it is good to specify a mechanism for resolving disputes, adding or removing a partner, or what to do in the event of the death of one of the partners. A well-written partnership agreement can significantly reduce conflicts as the firm grows.
3. In this case, income and losses are shared equally.

## Summary of Study Objectives

**1. Identify the characteristics of the partnership form of business organization.** The principal characteristics of a partnership are: (a) association of individuals, (b) mutual agency, (c) limited life, (d) unlimited liability, and (e) co-ownership of property.

**2. Explain the accounting entries for the formation of a partnership.** When a partnership is formed, each partner's initial investment should be recorded at the fair market value of the assets at the date of their transfer to the partnership.

**3. Identify the bases for dividing net income or net loss.** Net income or net loss is divided on the basis of the income ratio, which may be (a) a fixed ratio, (b) a ratio based on beginning or average capital balances, (c) salaries to partners and the remainder on a fixed ratio, (d) interest on partners' capitals and the remainder on a fixed ratio, and (e) salaries to partners, interest on partners' capitals, and the remainder on a fixed ratio.

**4. Describe the form and content of partnership financial statements.** The financial statements of a partnership are similar to those of a proprietorship. The principal differences are: (a) the division of net income is shown on the income statement, (b) the owners' equity statement is called a partners' capital statement, and (c) each partner's capital is reported on the balance sheet.

**5. Explain the effects of the entries when a new partner is admitted.** The entry to record the admittance of a new partner by purchase of a partner's interest affects only partners' capital accounts. The entries to record the admittance by investment of assets in the partnership (a) increases both net assets and total capital and (b) may result in recognition of a bonus to either the old partners or the new partner.

**6. Describe the effects of the entries when a partner withdraws from the firm.** The entry to record a withdrawal from the firm when payment is made from partners' personal assets only affects partners' capital accounts. The entry to record a withdrawal when payment is made from partnership assets (a) decreases net assets and total capital and (b) may result in recognizing a bonus either to the retiring partner or the remaining partners.

**7. Prepare the entries to record the liquidation of a partnership.** When a partnership is liquidated, it is necessary to record the (a) sale of noncash assets, (b) allocation of the gain or loss on realization, (c) payment of partnership liabilities, and (d) distribution of cash to the partners.

# GLOSSARY

**Admission by investment** Admission of a partner by investing assets in the partnership, in which both partnership net assets and total capital increase. (p. 540).

**Admission by purchase of an interest** Admission of a partner in a personal transaction between one or more existing partners and the new partner, which does not change total partnership assets or total capital. (p. 539).

**Capital deficiency** A debit balance in a partner's capital account after allocation of gain or loss. (p. 547).

**General partner** A partner who has unlimited liability for the debts of the firm. (p. 530).

**Income ratio** The basis for dividing both net income and net loss in a partnership. (p. 533).

**Limited partner** A partner who has limited liability for the debts of the firm. (p. 530).

**Limited partnership** A partnership in which one or more general partners have unlimited liability and one or more partners have limited liability for the obligations of the firm. (p. 530).

**No capital deficiency** All partners have credit balances after allocation of gain or loss. (p. 547).

**Partners' capital statement** The owners' equity statement for a partnership which shows the changes in each partner's

capital balance and in total partnership capital during the year. (p. 537).

**Partnership** An association of two or more persons to carry on as co-owners of a business for profit. (p. 528).

**Partnership agreement** A contract expressing the voluntary agreement of two or more individuals in a partnership. (p. 531).

**Partnership dissolution** A change in the number of partners which does not necessarily terminate the business. (p. 529).

**Partnership liquidation** An event that ends both the legal and economic life of a partnership. (p. 547).

**Schedule of cash payments** A schedule showing the distribution of cash to the partners in the liquidation of a partnership. (p. 549).

**Withdrawal by payment from partners' personal assets** Withdrawal of a partner in a personal transaction between partners, which does not change total partnership assets or total capital. (p. 543).

**Withdrawal by payment from partnership assets** Withdrawal of a partner in a transaction involving the partnership which decreases both partnership net assets and total capital. (p. 544).

# DEMONSTRATION PROBLEM

On January 1, 1996, the capital balances in Hollingsworth Company are Lois Holly $26,000, and Jim Worth $24,000. In 1996, the company reports net income of $30,000. The income ratio provides for salary allowances of $12,000 for Holly and $10,000 to Worth and the remainder equally. Neither partner had any drawings in 1996.

In 1997, assume that the following independent transactions occur on January 1:

1. Donna Reichenbacher purchases one-half of Holly's capital interest for $25,000.
2. Marsha Mears is admitted with a 25% capital interest by a cash investment of $40,000.
3. Stan Wells is admitted with a 35% capital interest by a cash investment of $40,000.

*Instructions*

(a) Prepare a schedule showing the distribution of net income in 1996.

(b) Journalize the division of 1996 net income to the partners.

(c) Journalize each of the independent transactions that occurred on January 1, 1997.

**Problem-Solving Strategies**

1. Journalizing the division of net income is a closing entry.
2. The entry for purchase of an interest involves only capital accounts.
3. The entry for admission by investment must have a debit to cash.
4. Allocation of a bonus occurs only in admission by investment.

## Solution to Demonstration Problem

(a) Net income　　　　　　　　　　　　　　　　　　　　　　$30,000

### Division of Net Income

|  | Lois Holly | Jim Worth | Total |
|---|---|---|---|
| Salary allowance | $12,000 | $10,000 | $22,000 |
| Remaining income $8,000 ($30,000 − $22,000) |  |  |  |
| Lois Holly ($8,000 × 50%) | 4,000 |  |  |
| Jim Worth ($8,000 × 50%) |  | 4,000 |  |
| Total remainder |  |  | 8,000 |
| Total division | $16,000 | $14,000 | $30,000 |

(b) 12/31/96　Income Summary　　　　　　　　　　　　30,000
　　　　　　　　　Lois Holly, Capital ($12,000 + $4,000)　　　　　16,000
　　　　　　　　　Jim Worth, Capital ($10,000 + $4,000)　　　　　14,000
　　　　　　　　　　(To close net income to partners' capitals)

(1)

(c) 1/1/97　Lois Holly, Capital ($26,000 + $16,000) × ½)　21,000
　　　　　　　　Donna Reichenbacher, Capital　　　　　　　　　21,000
　　　　　　　　　(To record purchase of one-half of Holly's
　　　　　　　　　interest)

(2)

1/1/97　Cash　　　　　　　　　　　　　　　40,000
　　　　　　Lois Holly, Capital　　　　　　　　　　　　5,000
　　　　　　Jim Worth, Capital　　　　　　　　　　　　5,000
　　　　　　Marsha Mears, Capital　　　　　　　　　　30,000
　　　　　　　(To record admission of Mears and bonus to
　　　　　　　old partners)

Total capital after investment: $120,000
　(Holly, $42,000, Worth $38,000, Mears
　investment $40,000)

Mears' capital credit (25% × $120,000)　　　　　　$30,000

Bonus to old partners ($40,000 − $30,000)　　　　$10,000

Allocation of bonus:
　Holly ($10,000 × 50%)　　　　　$ 5,000
　Worth ($10,000 × 50%)　　　　　　5,000　$10,000

(3)

1/1/97　Cash　　　　　　　　　　　　　　　40,000
　　　　　　Lois Holly, Capital　　　　　　　　　　　　1,000
　　　　　　Jim Worth, Capital　　　　　　　　　　　　1,000
　　　　　　Stan Wells, Capital　　　　　　　　　　　42,000
　　　　　　　(To record Wells' admission and bonus)

Wells' capital credit (35% × $120,000)　　　　　　$42,000

Bonus to Wells ($42,000 − $40,000)　　　　　　　$ 2,000

Allocation of bonus:
　Holly ($2,000 × 50%)　　　　　　$1,000
　Worth ($2,000 × 50%)　　　　　　1,000　$ 2,000

# SELF-STUDY QUESTIONS

Answers are at the end of the chapter.

(SO 1)

1. Which of the following is *not* a characteristic of a partnership?
   a. Taxable entity
   b. Co-ownership of property
   c. Mutual agency
   d. Limited life

(SO 1)

2. The advantages of a partnership do *not* include:
   a. ease of formation.
   b. unlimited liability.
   c. freedom from government regulation.
   d. ease of decision making.

(SO 2)

3. Upon formation of a partnership, each partner's initial investment of assets should be recorded at their:
   a. book values.
   b. cost.
   c. market values.
   d. appraised values.

(SO 3)

4. The ABC Company reports net income of $60,000. If partners A, B, and C have an income ratio of 50%, 30%, and 20%, respectively, C's share of the net income is:
   a. $30,000.
   b. $12,000.
   c. $18,000.
   d. No correct answer is given.

(SO 3)

5. Using the data in (4) above, what is B's share of net income if the percentages are applicable after each partner receives a $10,000 salary allowance?
   a. $12,000
   b. $20,000
   c. $19,000
   d. $21,000

(SO 4)

6. Which of the following statements about partnership financial statements is true?
   a. Details of the distribution of net income are shown in the owners' equity statement.
   b. The distribution of net income is shown on the balance sheet.
   c. Only the total of all partner capital balances is shown in the balance sheet.

d. The owners' equity statement is called the partners' capital statement.

(SO 5)

7. R. Ranken purchases 50% of L. Lar's capital interest in the K & L partnership for $22,000. If the capital balances of Kim and L. Lars are $40,000 and $30,000, respectively, Ranken's capital balance following the purchase is:
   a. $22,000.
   b. $35,000.
   c. $20,000.
   d. $15,000.

(SO 5)

8. Capital balances in the DEA partnership are D Capital $60,000, E Capital $50,000, and A Capital $40,000, and income ratios are 5:3:2, respectively. The DEAR partnership is formed by admitting R to the firm with a cash investment of $60,000 for a 25% capital interest. The bonus to be credited to A Capital in admitting R is:
   a. $10,000.
   b. $7,500.
   c. $3,750.
   d. $1,500.

(SO 6)

9. Capital balances in the TERM partnership are T Capital $50,000, E Capital $40,000, R Capital $30,000, and M Capital $20,000, and income ratios are 4:3:2:1, respectively. M withdraws from the firm following payment of $29,000 in cash from the partnership. E's capital balance after recording the withdrawal of M is:
   a. $36,000.
   b. $37,000.
   c. $38,000.
   d. $40,000.

(SO 7)

10. In the liquidation of a partnership it is necessary to (1) distribute cash to the partners, (2) sell non-cash assets, (3) allocate any gain or loss on realization to the partners, and (4) pay liabilities. These steps should be performed in the following order:
    a. (2), (3), (4), (1)
    b. (2), (3), (1), (4)
    c. (3), (2), (1), (4)
    d. (3), (2), (4), (1)

# QUESTIONS

1. The characteristics of a partnership include the following: (a) association of individuals, (b) limited life, and (c) co-ownership of property. Explain each of these terms.

2. Carla Cardosa is confused about the partnership characteristics of (a) mutual agency and (b) unlimited liability. Explain these two characteristics for Carla.

3. V.K. Nasser and T. Yoko are considering a business venture. They ask you to explain the advantages and disadvantages of the partnership form of organization.

4. S. Brown and D. Barclay form a partnership. Brown contributes land with a book value of $50,000 and a fair market value of $65,000. Brown also contributes equipment with a book value of

$52,000 and a fair market value of $57,000. The partnership assumes a $20,000 mortgage on the land. What should be the balance in Brown's capital account upon formation of the partnership?

5. R. Hay, S. Innis, and L. Joyce have a partnership called Express Wings. A dispute has arisen among the partners because Hay has invested twice as much in assets as the other two partners and believes net income and net losses should be shared in accordance with the capital ratios. The partnership agreement does not specify the division of profits and losses. How will net income and net loss be divided?

6. S. Hark and R. Green are discussing how income and losses should be divided in a partnership they plan to form. What factors should be considered in determining the division of net income or net loss?

7. R. Leno and A. Hall have capital balances of $40,000 and $80,000, respectively, in a partnership. The partnership agreement indicates that net income or net loss should be shared equally. If the net income for the partnership is $24,000, how should the net income be divided?

8. H. Astro and S. Sund share net income and net loss equally. (a) Which account(s) is (are) debited and credited to record the division of net income between the partners? (b) If H. Astro withdraws $30,000 in cash for personal use in lieu of salary, which account is debited and which is credited?

9. Partners R. Rowe and B. Zander are provided salary allowances of $30,000 and $25,000, respectively. They divide the remainder of the partnership income in a ratio of 60:40. If partnership net income is $50,000, how much is allocated to Rowe and Zander?

10. Are the financial statements of a partnership similar to those of a proprietorship? Discuss.

11. Holly Canter decides to pay Mark Waller $30,000 for a one-third interest in the partnership of Waller and Rose. What effect does this transaction have on partnership net assets?

12. R. Minoa decides to invest $15,000 in a partnership for a one-sixth capital interest. How much do the partnership's net assets increase? Does Minoa also acquire a one-sixth income ratio through this investment?

13. Santos purchases Ramos' interest in the Morgan–Ramos partnership for $72,000. Assuming that Ramos has a $65,000 capital balance in the partnership, what journal entry is made by the partnership to record this transaction?

14. Won Jang has a $37,000 capital balance in a partnership. She sells her interest to Karen Crest for $42,000 cash. What entry is made by the partnership for this transaction?

15. Rorey Rolf retires from the partnership of Suarez, Tanks, and Rolf. She receives $87,000 of partnership assets in settlement of her capital balance of $75,000. Assuming that the income-sharing ratios are 5:3:2, respectively, how much of Rolf's bonus is debited to Tanks' capital account?

16. Your roommate argues that partnership assets should be revalued in situations like those in question 15. Why is this generally not done?

17. How is a deceased partner's equity determined?

18. How does the liquidation of a partnership differ from the dissolution of a partnership?

19. Joe and Jean are discussing the liquidation of a partnership. Joe maintains that all cash should be distributed to partners on the basis of their income ratios. Is he correct? Explain.

20. In continuing their discussion, Jean says that even in the case of a capital deficiency, all cash should still be distributed on the basis of capital balances. Is Jean correct? Explain.

21. Mike, Larry, and Joan have income ratios of 5:3:2 and capital balances of $34,000, $31,000, and $28,000, respectively. Noncash assets are sold at a gain. After creditors are paid, $109,000 of cash is available for distribution to the partners. How much cash should be paid to Larry?

22. Before the final distribution of cash, account balances are: Cash $24,000; R. Katz, Capital $18,000 (cr); M. Moss, Capital $12,000 (cr); and T. Zaret, Capital $6,000 (dr). Zaret is unable to pay any of the capital deficiency. If the income-sharing ratios are 5:3:2, respectively, how much cash should be paid to M. Moss?

# BRIEF EXERCISES

• • • • • • • • • • • • • • • • • • • • • • • • • • • • • • • • • • • • • • • • • • • • • • • • •

*Journalize entries in forming a partnership.*
(SO 2)

**BE13–1**   R. Alfredo and B. Starr decide to organize the ALL-Star partnership. Alfredo invests $15,000 cash, and Starr contributes $10,000 cash and equipment having a book value of $3,500. Prepare the entry to record Starr's investment in the partnership, assuming the equipment has a fair market value of $4,000.

*Prepare portion of opening balance sheet for partnership.*
(SO 2)

**BE13–2**   C. Held and G. Kamp decide to merge their proprietorships into a partnership called HeldKamp Company. The balance sheet of Kamp Co. shows:

| Accounts Receivable | $15,000 | |
| Less: Allowance for Doubtful Accounts | 1,200 | $13,800 |
| Equipment | 20,000 | |
| Less: Accumulated Depreciation | 8,000 | 12,000 |

The partners agree that the net realizable value of the receivables is $12,500 and that the fair market value of the equipment is $11,000. Indicate how the four accounts should appear in the opening balance sheet of the partnership.

**BE13-3**  B&R Co. reports net income of $60,000. The income ratios are: B 60% and R 40%. Indicate the division of net income to each partner and prepare the entry to distribute the net income.

*Journalize the division of net income using fixed income ratios.*
*(SO 3)*

**BE13-4**  Met Co. reports net income of $50,000. Partner salary allowances are M $10,000, E $5,000, and T $5,000. Indicate the division of net income to each partner, assuming the income ratio is 50:30:20, respectively.

*Compute division of net income with a salary allowance and fixed ratios.*
*(SO 3)*

**BE13-5**  S&T Co. reports net income of $20,000. Interest allowances are S $6,000 and T $5,000; salary allowances are S $15,000 and T $10,000; the remainder is shared equally. Show the distribution of income on the income statement.

*Show division of net income when allowances exceed net income.*
*(SO 3)*

**BE13-6**  In ABC Co. capital balances are: Ali $30,000, Babson $25,000, and Carter $20,000. The partners share income equally. Daniel is admitted to the firm by purchasing one-half of Carter's interest for $12,000. Journalize the admission of Daniel to the partnership.

*Journalize admission by purchase of an interest.*
*(SO 5)*

**BE13-7**  In the EZ Co., capital balances are Edie $40,000 and Zane $30,000. The partners share income equally. Kerns is admitted to the firm with a 40% interest by an investment of cash of $42,000. Journalize the admission of Kerns.

*Journalize admission by investment.*
*(SO 5)*

**BE13-8**  Capital balances in DEB Co. are Ditka $40,000, Embs $30,000, and Boyd $28,000. Ditka and Embs each agree to pay Boyd $12,000 from their personal assets. Ditka and Embs each receive 50% of Boyd's equity. The partners share income equally. Journalize the withdrawal of Boyd.

*Journalize withdrawal paid by personal assets.*
*(SO 6)*

**BE13-9**  Data pertaining to DEB Co. are presented in BE13-8. Instead of payment from personal assets, assume that Boyd receives $32,000 from partnership assets in withdrawing from the firm. Journalize the withdrawal of Boyd.

*Journalize withdrawal paid by partnership assets.*
*(SO 6)*

**BE13-10**  After liquidating noncash assets and paying creditors, account balances in the ARB Co. are Cash $17,000, A Capital (Cr.) $9,000, R Capital (Cr.) $5,000, and B Capital (Cr.) $3,000. The partners share income equally. Journalize the final distribution of cash to the partners.

*Journalize final cash distribution in liquidation.*
*(SO 7)*

# EXERCISES

**E13-1**  Ted Karl has owned and operated a proprietorship for several years. On January 1, he decides to terminate this business and become a partner in the firm of Payne and Karl. Karl's investment in the partnership consists of $15,000 in cash, and the following assets of the proprietorship: accounts receivable $14,000 less allowance for doubtful accounts of $2,000, and equipment $20,000 less accumulated depreciation of $4,000. It is agreed that the allowance for doubtful accounts should be $3,000 for the partnership, and the fair market value of the equipment is $18,000.

*Journalize entry for formation of a partnership.*
*(SO 2)*

**Instructions**
Journalize Karl's admission to the firm of Payne and Karl.

**E13-2**  R. Huma and W. How have capital balances on January 1 of $50,000 and $40,000, respectively. The partnership income sharing agreement provides for (1) annual salaries of $14,000 for Huma and $12,000 for How, (2) interest at 10% on beginning capital balances, and (3) remaining income or loss to be shared 70% by Huma and 30% by How.

*Prepare schedule showing distribution of net income and closing entry.*
*(SO 3)*

**Instructions**
(a) Prepare a schedule showing the distribution of net income, assuming net income is
    (1) $45,000 and (2) $28,000.
(b) Journalize the allocation of net income in each of the situations above.

*Prepare partners' capital statement and partial balance sheet.*
*(SO 4)*

**E13–3** In Salton Co., beginning capital balances on January 1, 1996, are M. Salz $20,000 and C. Toni $18,000. During the year, drawings were Salz $6,000 and Toni $3,000. Net income was $30,000, and the partners share income equally.

**Instructions**
(a) Prepare the partners' capital statement for the year.
(b) Prepare the owners' equity section of the balance sheet at December 31, 1996.

*Journalize admission of a new partner by purchase of an interest.*
*(SO 5)*

**E13–4** T. Halo, K. Rose, and J. Lamp share income on a 5:3:2 basis. They have capital balances of $32,000, $24,000, and $21,000, respectively, when R. Zahn is admitted to the partnership.

**Instructions**
Prepare the journal entry to record the admission of Zahn under each of the following assumptions:

1. Purchase of 50% of Halo's equity for $19,000.
2. Purchase of 50% of Rose's equity for $10,000.
3. Purchase of 33⅓% of Lamp's equity for $9,000.

*Journalize admission of a new partner by investment.*
*(SO 5)*

**E13–5** Joe Keho and Mike McLain share income on a 6:4 basis. They have capital balances of $90,000 and $70,000, respectively, when Ed Kehler is admitted to the partnership.

**Instructions**
Prepare the journal entry to record the admission of Ed Kehler under each of the following assumptions:

1. Investment of $80,000 cash for a 25% ownership interest with bonuses to the existing partners.
2. Investment of $36,000 cash for a 25% ownership interest with a bonus to the new partner.

*Journalize withdrawal of a partner with payment from partners' personal assets.*
*(SO 6)*

**E13–6** Mary Lane, Vera Miles, and Debra Noll have capital balances of $50,000, $30,000, and $20,000, respectively, and their income ratios are 5:3:2. Noll withdraws from the partnership under each of the following independent conditions:

1. Lane and Miles agree to purchase Noll's equity by paying $15,000 each from their personal assets. Each purchaser receives 50% of Noll's equity.
2. Miles agrees to purchase all of Noll's equity by paying $20,000 cash from her personal assets.
3. Lane agrees to purchase all of Noll's equity by paying $23,000 cash from her personal assets.

**Instructions**
Journalize the withdrawal of Noll under each of the assumptions above.

*Journalize withdrawal of a partner with payment from partnership assets.*
*(SO 6)*

**E13–7** Dale Nagel, Keith White, and Dan Neal have capital balances of $95,000, $75,000, and $60,000, respectively. They share income or loss on a 5:3:2 basis. White withdraws from the partnership under each of the following conditions:

1. White is paid $82,000 in cash from partnership assets, and a bonus is granted to the retiring partner.
2. White is paid $68,000 in cash from partnership assets, and bonuses are granted to the remaining partners.

**Instructions**
Journalize the withdrawal of White under each of the assumptions above.

*Prepare cash distribution schedule.*
*(SO 7)*

**E13–8** Baylee Company at December 31 has cash $20,000, noncash assets $100,000, liabilities $55,000, and the following capital balances: Bayer $40,000 and Leech $25,000. The firm is liquidated, and $120,000 in cash is received for the noncash assets. Bayer and Leech income ratios are 60% and 40%, respectively.

**Instructions**
Prepare a cash distribution schedule.

*Journalize transactions in a liquidation.*
*(SO 7)*

**E13–9** Data for the Baylee partnership are presented in E13–8.

**Instructions**
Prepare the entries to record (1) the sale of noncash assets, (2) the allocation of the gain or loss

on liquidation to the partners, (3) payment of creditors, and (4) distribution of cash to the partners.

**E13–10** Prior to the distribution of cash to the partners, the accounts in the MEL Company are: Cash $31,000, M Capital (Cr.) $18,000, E Capital (Cr.) $16,000, and L Capital (Dr.) $3,000. The income ratios are 5:3:2, respectively.

*Journalize transactions with a capital deficiency.*
*(SO 7)*

**Instructions**
(a) Prepare the entry to record (1) L's payment of $3,000 in cash to the partnership and (2) the distribution of cash to the partners with credit balances.
(b) Prepare the entry to record (1) the absorption of L's capital deficiency by the other partners and (2) the distribution of cash to the partners with credit balances.

# PROBLEMS

**P13–1** The post-closing trial balances of two proprietorships on January 1, 1996, are presented below.

*Prepare entries for formation of a partnership and a balance sheet.*
*(SO 2, 4)*

| | Kreal Company | | Donal Company | |
|---|---|---|---|---|
| | Dr. | Cr. | Dr. | Cr. |
| Cash | $ 6,500 | | $ 8,000 | |
| Accounts receivable | 15,000 | | 23,000 | |
| Allowance for doubtful accounts | | $ 2,500 | | $ 4,000 |
| Merchandise inventory | 28,000 | | 17,000 | |
| Equipment | 52,000 | | 30,000 | |
| Accumulated depreciation—equipment | | 24,000 | | 13,000 |
| Notes payable | | 20,000 | | |
| Accounts payable | | 25,000 | | 37,000 |
| R. T. Kreal, Capital | | 30,000 | | |
| A. C. Donal, Capital | | | | 24,000 |
| | $101,500 | $101,500 | $78,000 | $78,000 |

Kreal and Donal decide to form the Donal Kreal Company with the following agreed upon valuations for noncash assets:

| | Kreal Company | Donal Company |
|---|---|---|
| Accounts receivable | $15,000 | $23,000 |
| Allowance for doubtful accounts | 3,500 | 5,000 |
| Merchandise inventory | 30,000 | 21,000 |
| Equipment | 31,000 | 18,000 |

All cash will be transferred to the partnership, and the partnership will assume all the liabilities of the two proprietorships. Further, it is agreed that Kreal will invest $15,000 in cash, and Donal will invest $5,000 in cash.

**Instructions**
(a) Prepare separate journal entries to record the transfer of each proprietorship's assets and liabilities to the partnership.
(b) Journalize the additional cash investment by each partner.
(c) Prepare a balance sheet for the partnership on January 1, 1996.

**P13–2** At the end of its first year of operations on December 31, 1996, the LMN Company's accounts show the following:

*Journalize divisions of net income and prepare a partners' capital statement.*
*(SO 3, 4)*

| Partner | Drawings | Capital |
|---|---|---|
| Lois Lang | $12,000 | $30,000 |
| Mary Mio | 9,000 | 20,000 |
| Sue Norton | 6,000 | 10,000 |

The capital balance represents each partner's initial capital investment. Therefore, net income or net loss for 1996 has not been closed to the partners' capital accounts.

**Instructions**

(a) Journalize the entry to record the division of net income for 1996 under each of the following assumptions:
   1. Net income is $28,000, and income is shared 5:3:2.
   2. Net income is $30,000; Lang and Mio are given salary allowances of $10,000 and $8,000, respectively, and the remainder is shared equally.
   3. Net income is $25,200; each partner is allowed interest of 10% on beginning capital balances; Lang is given a $15,000 salary allowance; and the remainder is shared equally.

(b) Prepare a schedule showing the division of net income under assumption (3) above.

(c) Prepare a partner's capital statement for the year under assumption (3) above.

*Journalize admission of a partner under different assumptions.*
*(SO 5)*

**P13–3**   At April 30, partners' capital balances in the ELM Company are: A. Ellis $50,000, C. Lazzeri $24,000, and W. Matt $16,000. The income sharing ratios are 3:2:1, respectively. On May 1, the ELMO Company is formed by admitting N. Ortiz to the firm as a partner.

**Instructions**

(a) Journalize the admission of Ortiz under each of the following assumptions:
   1. Ortiz purchases 50% of Matt's ownership interest by paying Matt $9,000 in cash.
   2. Ortiz purchases 50% of Lazzeri's ownership interest by paying Lazzeri $16,000 in cash.
   3. Ortiz invests $35,000 cash in the partnership for a 40% ownership interest that includes a bonus to the new partner.
   4. Ortiz invests $30,000 in the partnership for a 20% ownership interest and bonuses are given to the old partners.

(b) Matt's capital balance is $18,000 after admitting Ortiz to the partnership by investment. If Matt's ownership interest is 15% of total partnership capital, what was Ortiz's cash investment and the total bonus to the old partners?

*Journalize withdrawal of a partner under different assumptions.*
*(SO 6)*

**P13–4**   On December 31, the capital balances and income ratios in the ART Company are as follows:

| Partner | Capital Balance | Income Ratio |
|---------|-----------------|--------------|
| E. Atlas | $70,000 | 60% |
| P. Ross | 30,000 | 30 |
| L. Tower | 20,000 | 10 |

**Instructions**

(a) Journalize the withdrawal of Tower under each of the following assumptions:
   1. Each of the remaining partners agrees to pay $12,000 in cash from personal funds to purchase Tower's ownership equity. Each receives 50% of Tower's equity.
   2. Ross agrees to purchase Tower's ownership interest for $18,000 in cash.
   3. From partnership assets, Tower is paid $29,000, which includes a bonus to the retiring partner.
   4. Tower is paid $17,000 from partnership assets, and bonuses to the remaining partners are recognized.

(b) If Ross' capital balance after Tower's withdrawal is $33,000, what was the total bonus to the remaining partners and the cash paid by the partnership to Tower?

*Prepare entries and schedule of cash payments in liquidation of a partnership.*
*(SO 7)*

**P13–5**   The partners in Inland Lakes Company decide to liquidate the firm when the balance sheet shows the following:

**INLAND LAKES COMPANY**
**Balance Sheet**
**April 30, 1996**

| Assets | | Liabilities and Owners' Equity | |
|--------|--|--------------------------------|--|
| Cash | $24,000 | Notes payable | $14,000 |
| Accounts receivable | 18,000 | Accounts payable | 24,000 |
| Allowance for doubtful accounts | (1,000) | Wages payable | 2,000 |
| Merchandise inventory | 30,000 | T. E. Huron, Capital | 24,000 |
| Equipment | 17,000 | P. A. Erie, Capital | 12,800 |
| Accumulated depreciation—equip. | (8,000) | C. R. Lake, Capital | 3,200 |
| Total | $80,000 | Total | $80,000 |

The partners share income and loss 5:3:2. During the process of liquidation, the transactions below were completed in the following sequence:

1. A total of $48,000 was received from converting noncash assets into cash.
2. Liabilities were paid in full.
3. Cash was paid to the partners with credit balances.

**Instructions**
(a) Prepare a cash distribution schedule.
(b) Prepare the entries to record the transactions.
(c) Post to the cash and capital accounts.

# ALTERNATE PROBLEMS

● ● ● ● ● ● ● ● ● ● ● ● ● ● ● ● ● ● ● ● ● ● ● ● ● ● ● ● ● ● ● ● ● ● ● ● ● ● ● ● ● ● ● ● ● ● ● ●

**P13–1A** The post-closing trial balances of two proprietorships on January 1, 1996, are presented below.

*Prepare entries for formation of a partnership and a balance sheet.*
*(SO 2, 4)*

| | Hamp Company | | Vong Company | |
|---|---|---|---|---|
| | Dr. | Cr. | Dr. | Cr. |
| Cash | $ 13,000 | | $16,000 | |
| Accounts receivable | 17,500 | | 26,000 | |
| Allowance for doubtful accounts | | $ 3,000 | | $ 4,400 |
| Merchandise inventory | 26,500 | | 18,400 | |
| Equipment | 45,000 | | 28,000 | |
| Accumulated depreciation—equipment | | 24,000 | | 12,000 |
| Notes payable | | 20,000 | | 15,000 |
| Accounts payable | | 20,000 | | 31,000 |
| L. Hamp, Capital | | 35,000 | | |
| P. Vong, Capital | | | | 26,000 |
| | $102,000 | $102,000 | $88,400 | $88,400 |

Hamp and Vong decide to form the Hamp-Vong Company with the following agreed upon valuations for noncash assets:

| | Hamp Company | Vong Company |
|---|---|---|
| Accounts receivable | $17,500 | $26,000 |
| Allowance for doubtful accounts | 4,500 | 4,000 |
| Merchandise inventory | 28,000 | 20,000 |
| Equipment | 25,000 | 18,000 |

All cash will be transferred to the partnership, and the partnership will assume all the liabilities of the two proprietorships. Further, it is agreed that Hamp will invest $20,000 in cash and Vong will invest $9,000 in cash.

**Instructions**
(a) Prepare separate journal entries to record the transfer of each proprietorship's assets and liabilities to the partnership.
(b) Journalize the additional cash investment by each partner.
(c) Prepare a balance sheet for the partnership on January 1, 1996.

**P13–2A** At the end of its first year of operations on December 31, 1996, HRZ Company's accounts show the following:

*Journalize divisions of net income and prepare a partners' capital statement.*
*(SO 3, 4)*

| Partner | Drawings | Capital |
|---|---|---|
| Sue Horton | $23,000 | $45,000 |
| Tracey Rugen | 14,000 | 30,000 |
| Eileen Zak | 10,000 | 25,000 |

The capital balance represents each partner's initial capital investment; therefore, net income or net loss for 1996 has not been closed to the partners' capital accounts.

*Instructions*

(a) Journalize the entry to record the division of net income for the year 1996 under each of the following assumptions:
  1. Net income is $25,000, and income is shared 6:3:1.
  2. Net income is $34,000; Horton and Rugen are given salary allowances of $15,000 and $10,000, respectively; and the remainder is shared equally.
  3. Net income is $22,000; each partner is allowed interest of 10% on beginning capital balances; Horton is given a $15,000 salary allowance; and the remainder is shared equally.

(b) Prepare a schedule showing the division of net income under assumption (3) above.

(c) Prepare a partners' capital statement for the year under assumption (3) above.

*Journalize admission of a partner under different assumptions.*
*(SO 5)*

**P13–3A**  At April 30, partners' capital balances in NSW Company are: A. Nolan $60,000, D. Spoda $36,000, and T. Wise $14,000. The income sharing ratios are 5:4:1, respectively. On May 1, the NSWO Company is formed by admitting M. Otton to the firm as a partner.

*Instructions*

(a) Journalize the admission of Otton under each of the following assumptions:
  1. Otton purchases 50% of Wise's ownership interest by paying Wise $16,000 in cash.
  2. Otton purchases 33⅓% of Spoda's ownership interest by paying Spoda $15,000 in cash.
  3. Otton invests $60,000 for a 30% ownership interest, and bonuses are given to the old partners.
  4. Otton invests $40,000 for a 30% ownership interest, which includes a bonus to the new partner.

(b) Spoda's capital balance is $30,000 after admitting Otton to the partnership by investment. If Spoda's ownership interest is 20% of total partnership capital, what was Otton's cash investment and the bonus to the new partner?

*Journalize withdrawal of a partner under different assumptions.*
*(SO 6)*

**P13–4A**  On December 31, the capital balances and income ratios in the BAG Company are as follows:

| Partner | Capital Balance | Income Ratio |
|---|---|---|
| R. Beano | $60,000 | 50% |
| D. Alman | 40,000 | 30% |
| P. Garth | 32,000 | 20% |

*Instructions*

(a) Journalize the withdrawal of Garth under each of the following assumptions:
  1. Each of the continuing partners agrees to pay $17,000 in cash from personal funds to purchase Garth's ownership equity. Each receives 50% of Garth's equity.
  2. Alman agrees to purchase Garth's ownership interest for $30,000 cash.
  3. Garth is paid $38,000 from partnership assets, which includes a bonus to the retiring partner.
  4. Garth is paid $28,000 from partnership assets, and bonuses to the remaining partners are recognized.

(b) If Alman's capital balance after Garth's withdrawal is $43,000, what was the total bonus to the remaining partners and the cash paid by the partnership to Garth?

*Prepare entries and schedules of cash payments with a capital deficiency in liquidation of a partnership.*
*(SO 7)*

**P13–5A**  The partners in the JRS Company decide to liquidate the firm when the balance sheet shows the following:

**JRS COMPANY**
**Balance Sheet**
**May 31, 1996**

| Assets | | Liabilities and Owners' Equity | |
|---|---|---|---|
| Cash | $ 27,500 | Notes payable | $ 13,500 |
| Accounts receivable | 24,000 | Accounts payable | 27,000 |
| Allowance for doubtful accounts | (1,000) | Wages payable | 3,800 |
| Merchandise inventory | 34,500 | M. Jagger, Capital | 35,000 |
| Equipment | 21,000 | K. Richards, Capital | 20,000 |
| Accumulated depreciation—equipment | (5,500) | R. Simka, Capital | 1,200 |
| Total | $100,500 | Total | $100,500 |

The partners share income and loss 5:3:2. During the process of liquidation, the following transactions were completed in the following sequence:

1. A total of $53,000 was received from converting noncash assets into cash.
2. Liabilities were paid in full.
3. Simka paid his capital deficiency.
4. Cash was paid to the partners with credit balances.

**Instructions**
(a) Prepare the entries to record the transactions.
(b) Post to the cash and capital accounts.
(c) Assume that Simka is unable to pay the capital deficiency.
    1. Prepare the entry to allocate Simka's debit balance to Jagger and Richards.
    2. Prepare the entry to record the final distribution of cash.

# ▼*B*roadening Your Perspective

## DECISION CASE
••••••••••••••••••••••••••••••••••••••••••••••••••••••••••••••••••••••••

Bart Holmar and Sally Izod, as two professionals in the finance area, have worked for Advanced Leasing for a number of years. Advanced Leasing is a company that leases high-tech medical equipment to hospitals. Bart and Sally have decided that, with their financial expertise, they might start their own company to provide consulting services to individuals interested in leasing equipment. One form of organization they are considering is a partnership.

If they start a partnership, each individual plans to contribute $15,000 in cash. In addition, Bart has a used IBM microcomputer that originally cost $3,800, which he intends to invest in the partnership. The computer has a present market value of $1,800.

Although both Bart and Sally are financial wizards, they do not know a great deal about how a partnership operates. As a result, they have come to you for advice.

**Instructions**
Answer the following questions:

(a) What are the major disadvantages of starting a partnership?
(b) What type of document is needed for a partnership and what should this document contain?
(c) Both Bart and Sally plan to work full-time in the new partnership. Therefore they believe that net income or net loss should be shared equally. However, they are wondering how they can provide compensation to Bart Holman for his additional investment of the microcomputer. What would you tell them?
(d) Bart is not sure how the computer equipment should be reported on his tax return. What would you tell him?
(e) As indicated above, Bart and Sally have worked together for a number of years. Bart's skills complement Sally's and vice versa. If one of them dies, it will be very difficult for the other to maintain the business, not to mention the difficulty of paying the deceased partner's estate for his or her partnership interest. What would you tell them to do?

## COMMUNICATION ACTIVITY
••••••••••••••••••••••••••••••••••••••••••••••••••••••••••••••••••••••••

You are an expert in the field of forming partnerships. Bill Glass and Enid Hall want to establish a partnership to start up "Enid's Pasta Shop," and they are going to meet with you to discuss their plans. Prior to the meeting you will send them a memo discussing the issues they need to consider before their visit.

**Instructions**
Write a memo in good form to be sent to Bill and Enid.

# GROUP ACTIVITY

In groups of five or six students:

*Instructions*

(a) Form a partnership. Decide as a group what you will be selling or providing as a service.

(b) Assume that one member of your group wishes to provide one-half of the total assets of the partnership but does not otherwise wish to participate in the partnership. What would be your partnership's income ratio under this situation?

# ETHICS CASE

Susan and Karen operate a beauty salon as partners who share profits and losses equally. The success of their business has exceeded their expectations and is operating quite profitably. Karen is anxious to maximize profits and schedules appointments from 8 a.m. to 6 p.m. daily, even sacrificing some lunch hours to accommodate regular customers. Susan schedules her appointments from 9 a.m. to 5 p.m. and takes long lunch hours. Susan regularly makes significantly larger withdrawals of cash than Karen does. But, she says, "Karen, you needn't worry, I never make a withdrawal without you knowing about it, so it is properly recorded in my drawing account and charged against my capital at the end of the year." Susan's withdrawals to date are double Karen's.

*Instructions*

(a) Who are the stakeholders in this situation?

(b) Identify the problems with Susan's actions and discuss the ethical considerations of her actions.

(c) How might the partnership agreement be revised to accommodate the differences in Susan's and Karen's work and withdrawal habits?

# CRITICAL THINKING
## ▶ *A Real-World Focus: Texas Meridian Resources*

*Texas Meridian Resources was formed as a limited partnership. It is engaged in the exploration for and development of natural gas properties. It employs state-of-the-art procedures including three-dimensional seismic and computer-aided exploration and work station technology. All of its properties are located in onshore regions of the United States, primarily in Texas and Louisiana.*

The partners of Texas Meridian Resources (TMR) have agreed to a partnership liquidation. The partnership's assets have been sold, and TMR is in the process of determining final distributions and terminating the partnership, which is expected to be completed by or before the end of 1997.

*Instructions*

(a) On what basis will the final cash distributions to the partners be made?

(b) Will final distributions be made to the partners before or after creditor balances are satisfied? Explain.

(c) Will adjusting and closing of the books be performed before or after the liquidation? Explain.

---

*Answers to Self-Study Questions*

1. a    2. b    3. c    4. b    5. c    6. d    7. d    8. d    9. b    10. a

![](Concepts for Review)

Before studying this chapter, you should know or, if necessary, review:

**a.** *The content of the stockholders' equity section of a balance sheet.*
(Ch. 4, p. 154)
**b.** *The content of the owner's equity section of the balance sheet for a pro-prietorship (Ch. 1, pp. 23–24) and for a partnership. (Ch. 13, p. 537)*
**c.** *How to prepare closing entries for a proprietorship (Ch. 4, pp. 141–43) and for a partnership (Ch. 13, pp. 533–34)*

# "Have You Driven a Ford Lately?"

DETROIT, Mich. — A company that has produced such renowned successes as the Model T and the Mustang, and such a dismal failure as the Edsel, would have some interesting tales to tell. Henry Ford was a defiant visionary from the day Ford Motor Company was formed in 1903. His goal from day one was to design a car he could mass-produce and sell at a price that was affordable to the masses. In short order he accomplished this goal, and by 1920 60 percent of all vehicles on American roads were Fords.

Henry Ford was intolerant of anything that stood between himself and success. In the early years Ford issued shares to the public in order to finance the company's exponential growth. In 1916 he decided that, to retain funds to finance expansion, the company would skip a dividend payment to its shareholders. The shareholders sued. Henry Ford's reaction was swift and direct: if the shareholders didn't see things his way, he would get rid of them. In 1919 the Ford family purchased 100 percent of the outstanding shares of Ford, eliminating any outside "interference." It was over 35 years before shares were again issued to the public.

Ford Motor Company has continued to evolve over the years while at the same time it sometimes has appeared to become even more like the company Henry Ford originally dreamed of. Today there are nearly a billion shares of publicly traded Ford stock outstanding, and the President and Chief Executive is not a member of the Ford family.

However, the Ford family still retains a significant stake in Ford. In 1994, in a move Henry Ford might have supported, top management decided to centralize decision-making—that is, to have more key decisions made by top management, rather than by division managers. And, reminiscent of Henry Ford's most famous car, the company is attempting to make a "global car"—a mass-produced car that can be sold around the world with only minor changes. ◀

# CHAPTER 14

# *C*ORPORATIONS: ORGANIZATION AND CAPITAL STOCK TRANSACTIONS

**After studying this chapter, you should be able to:**

1. *Identify and discuss the major characteristics of a corporation.*
2. *Differentiate between paid-in capital and retained earnings.*
3. *Record the issuance of common stock.*
4. *Explain the accounting for treasury stock.*
5. *Differentiate preferred stock from common stock.*
6. *Prepare a stockholders' equity section.*
7. *Compute book value per share.*

Corporations like Ford Motor Company have substantial resources. In fact, the corporation is the dominant form of business organization in the United States in terms of dollar volume of sales, earnings, and employees. All of the 500 largest companies in the United States are corporations. In this chapter we will explain the essential features of a corporation and the accounting for a corporation's capital stock transactions. (In Chapter 15 we will look at other issues related to accounting for corporations.) The content and organization of this chapter are as follows:

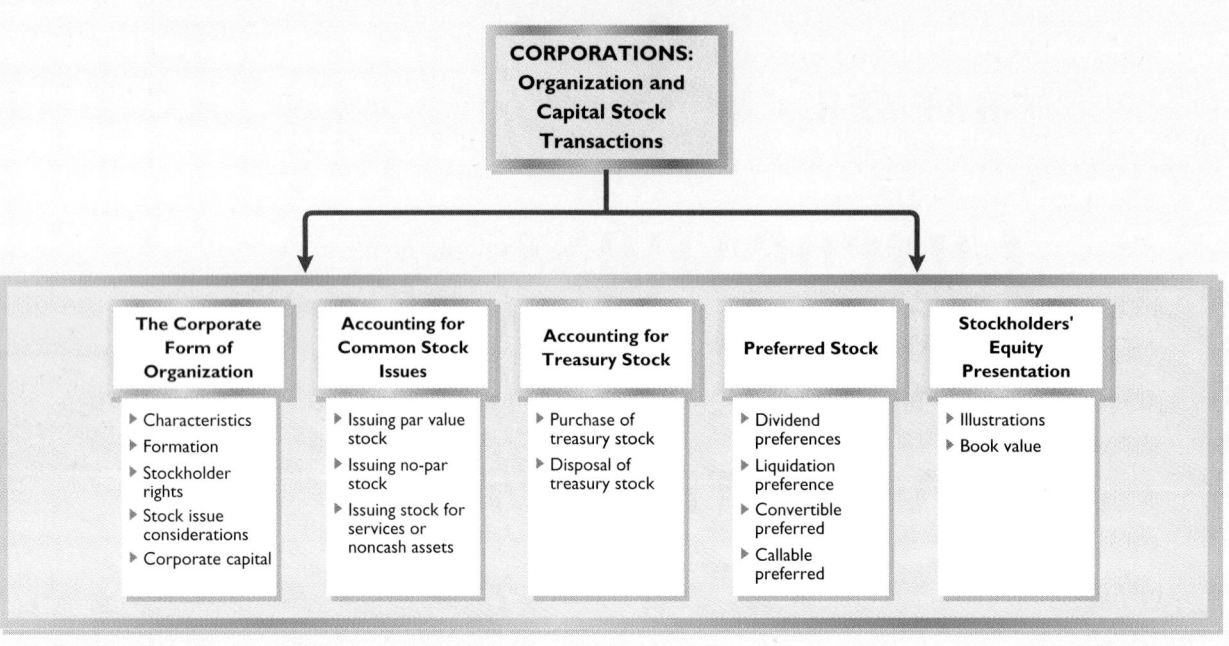

# **T**he Corporate Form of Organization

In 1819, Chief Justice John Marshall defined a corporation as "an artificial being, invisible, intangible, and existing only in contemplation of law." This definition has become the foundation for the prevailing legal interpretation that a corporation is an **entity separate and distinct from its owners**.

A corporation is created by law, and its continued existence depends upon the corporate statutes of the state in which it is incorporated. As a legal entity, a corporation has most of the rights and privileges of a person. The major exceptions relate to privileges that can be exercised only by a living person, such as the right to vote or to hold public office. Similarly, a corporation is subject to the same duties and responsibilities as a person, e.g., it must abide by the laws and it must pay taxes.

Corporations may be classified in a variety of ways. Two common bases are by purpose and by ownership. A corporation may be organized for the **purpose** of making a **profit**, or it may be **nonprofit**. Corporations for profit include such well-known companies as McDonald's, General Motors, and Apple Computer. Nonprofit corporations are organized for charitable, medical, and educational purposes and include the Salvation Army, the American Cancer Society, and the Ford Foundation.

Classification by **ownership** distinguishes between publicly held and privately held corporations. A publicly held corporation may have thousands of stockholders, and its stock is regularly traded on a national securities market such as the New York Stock Exchange. Most of the largest U.S. corporations are publicly held. Examples of publicly held corporations are International Business Machines, Caterpillar Inc., and General Electric. In contrast, a privately held corporation, often referred to as a closely held corporation, usually has only a few stockholders, and does not offer its stock for sale to the general public. Privately held companies are generally much smaller than publicly held companies.

## Characteristics of a Corporation

A number of characteristics distinguish a corporation from proprietorships and partnerships. The most important of these characteristics are explained below.

**STUDY OBJECTIVE**

·········· ▼ ··········

*Identify and discuss the major characteristics of a corporation.*

### *Separate Legal Existence*

As an entity separate and distinct from its owners, the corporation acts under its own name rather than in the name of its stockholders. A corporation may buy, own, and sell property, borrow money, and enter into legally binding contracts in its own name. It may also sue or be sued, and it pays its own taxes.

In contrast to a partnership, in which the acts of the owners (partners) bind the partnership, the acts of the owners (stockholders) do not bind the corporation unless such owners are duly appointed agents of the corporation. For example, if you owned shares of Ford Motor Company stock, you would not have the right to purchase automobile parts for the company unless you were appointed as an agent of the corporation.

Stockholders

**Legal existence separate from owners**

### *Limited Liability of Stockholders*

Since a corporation is a separate legal entity, creditors ordinarily have recourse only to corporate assets to satisfy their claims. The liability of stockholders is normally limited to their investment in the corporation, and creditors have no legal claim on the personal assets of the owners unless fraud has occurred. Thus, even in the event of bankruptcy of the corporation, stockholders' losses are generally limited to their capital investment in the corporation.

Stockholders

**Limited liability of stockholders**

### *Transferable Ownership Rights*

Ownership of a corporation is shown in shares of capital stock, which are transferable units. Stockholders may dispose of part or all of their interest in a corporation simply by selling their stock. In contrast to the transfer of an ownership interest in a partnership, which requires the consent of each owner, the transfer of stock is entirely at the discretion of the stockholder. It does not require the approval of either the corporation or other stockholders. The transfer of ownership rights between stockholders normally has no effect on the operating activities of the corporation or on a corporation's assets, liabilities, and total ownership equity. That is, the enterprise does not participate in the transfer of these ownership rights after it issues the capital stock.

**Transferable ownership rights**

### *Ability to Acquire Capital*

It generally is relatively easy for a corporation to obtain capital through the issuance of stock. Buying stock in a corporation is often more attractive to an investor than investing in a partnership because a stockholder has limited liability and shares of stock are readily transferable. Moreover, many individuals can become stockholders by investing small amounts of money. In sum, the ability of a successful corporation to obtain capital is virtually unlimited.

**Ability to acquire capital**

**Continuous life**

### *Continuous Life*

The life of a corporation is stated in its charter; it may be perpetual or it may be limited to a specific number of years. If it is limited, the period of existence can be extended through renewal of the charter. Since a corporation is a separate legal entity, the life of a corporation and its continuance as a going concern are not affected by the withdrawal, death, or incapacity of a stockholder, employee, or officer. As a result, a successful enterprise can have a continuous and perpetual life.

### *Corporation Management*

Although stockholders legally own the corporation, as in Ford Motor Company, they manage the corporation indirectly through a board of directors they elect. The board, in turn, formulates the operating policies for the company and selects officers, such as a president and one or more vice-presidents, to execute policy and to perform daily management functions.

A typical organization chart showing the delegation of responsibility is shown in Illustration 14-1. The **president** is the chief executive officer with direct responsibility for managing the business. As the organization chart shows, the president delegates responsibility to other officers. The chief accounting officer is the **controller**. The controller's responsibilities include (1) maintaining the accounting records, (2) maintaining an adequate system of internal control, and (3) preparing financial statements, tax returns, and internal reports. The **treasurer** has custody of the corporation's funds and is responsible for maintaining the company's cash position.

**Illustration 14-1**

*Corporation organization chart*

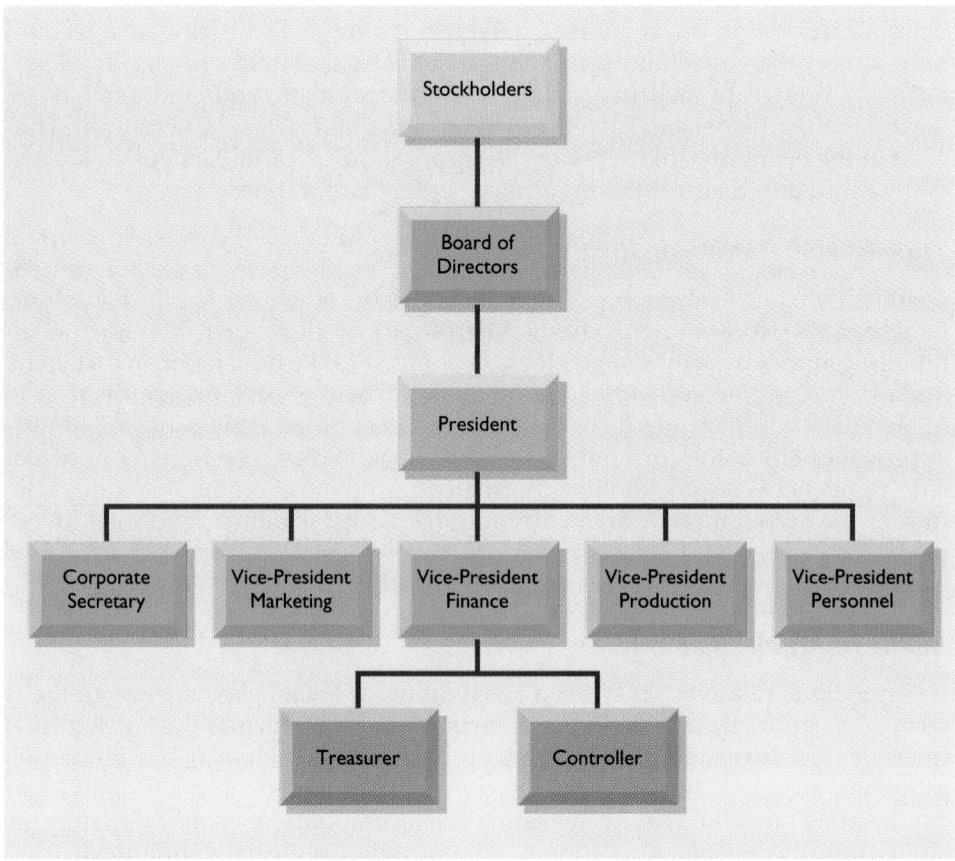

## ►Accounting in Action ► *Business Insight*

An interesting question is: Who runs a corporation—the stockholders or the board of directors? This issue has taken on increased importance because stockholders and boards of directors are often on the opposite sides of the fence these days when potential takeovers occur.

A classic example is the unfriendly takeover bid made by Paramount Communication Inc. for Time Inc. Paramount bid up Time's stock price substantially; many stockholders said sell—but Time's board of directors had other plans. They were in the process of trying to make a friendly deal with Warner Communications. Some stockholders said, "Let's vote on what we should do." But Time decided to proceed without a stockholders' vote, even though the board of directors knew the Warner deal would depress Time's stock price in the short term. They figured that many stockholders would prefer to accept the Paramount bid. The stockholders sued to overturn the deal with Warner Communications but lost. The judge wrote: "Corporation law does not operate on the theory that directors, in exercising their powers to manage the firm, are obligated to follow the wishes of a majority of stockholders. In fact, the directors, not the stockholders, are charged with the duty to manage the firm."

►*Ethics note*

The separation of ownership from management caused by the corporation form of organization can create an ethical dilemma for management. Managers are often compensated based upon the performance of the firm, and thus may be tempted to exaggerate firm performance by inflating income figures.

The organizational structure of a corporation enables a company to hire professional managers to run the business. On the other hand, the separation of ownership and management prevents owners from having an active role in managing the company, which some owners like to have.

### Government Regulations

A corporation is subject to numerous state and federal regulations. For example, state laws usually prescribe the requirements for issuing stock, the distributions of earnings permitted to stockholders, and the effects of retiring stock, as well as other procedures and restrictions. Similarly, federal securities laws govern the sale of capital stock to the general public. Also, most publicly held corporations are required to make extensive disclosure of their financial affairs to the Securities and Exchange Commission through quarterly and annual reports. In addition, when a corporate stock is listed and traded on organized securities markets, the corporation must comply with the reporting requirements of these exchanges.

Government regulations are designed to protect the owners of the corporation. Unlike the owners of most proprietorships and partnerships, most stockholders do not participate in the day-to-day management of the company.

State laws    SEC laws

WKK Corp.

Stock exchange requirements    Federal regulations

**Goverment regulations**

### Additional Taxes

Neither proprietorships nor partnerships pay income taxes. The owner's share of these organizations' earnings is reported on his or her personal income tax return. Taxes are then paid by the individual on this amount. Corporations, on the other hand, must pay federal and state income taxes as a separate legal entity. These taxes are substantial: they can amount to as much as 40% of taxable income.

In addition, stockholders are required to pay taxes on cash dividends, which are pro rata distributions of net income. Thus, many argue that corporate income is **taxed twice (double taxation)**, once at the corporate level, and again at the individual level.

From the foregoing, we can identify the following advantages and disadvantages of a corporation compared to a proprietorship and partnership:

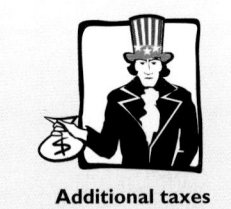

**Additional taxes**

**Illustration 14-2**

*Advantages and disadvan-
tages of a corporation*

| **Advantages** | **Disadvantages** |
|---|---|
| Separate legal existence | Corporation management—separation of |
| Limited liability of stockholders | ownership and management |
| Transferable ownership rights | Government regulations |
| Ability to acquire capital | Additional taxes |
| Continuous life | |
| Corporation management—professional | |
| managers | |

## Forming a Corporation

The initial step in the formation of a corporation is to file an application with the Secretary of State in the state in which incorporation is desired. The application contains the following types of information: (1) the name, purpose, and duration of the proposed corporation; (2) amounts, kinds, and number of shares of capital stock to be authorized; (3) the address of the corporation's principal office; (4) the names and addresses of the incorporators; and (5) the shares of stock to which each has subscribed.

After the incorporation fee is paid and the application approved, a charter is granted. The charter may be an approved copy of the application form or it may be a separate document containing the same basic data. The issuance of the charter, often referred to as the **articles of incorporation**, creates the corporation. Upon receipt of the charter, the corporation develops its by-laws. The by-laws establish the internal rules and procedures for conducting the affairs of the corporation and indicate the powers and relationships of the stockholders, directors, and officers of the enterprise.[1]

## ▲*Accounting in Action* ▸ *Business Insight*

It is not necessary for a corporation to have an office in the state in which it incorporates. In fact, more than 50% of the Fortune 500 corporations are incorporated in Delaware. A primary reason is the Delaware courts' long-standing "business judgment rule." The rule provides that as long as directors exercise "due care" in the interests of stockholders, their actions will not be second-guessed by the courts. The rule has enabled directors to reject hostile takeover offers, even with hefty premiums, or to spurn takeovers simply because they did not want to sell the company. However, new interpretations of the rule appear to be emerging. In a recent case, the state court ruled for the company that made a hostile takeover bid. On appeal, the Delaware Supreme Court ruled for the directors but gave the following guideline to the state courts: "Was the board's response reasonable in the light of the threat posed?"

Regardless of the number of states in which a corporation has operating divisions, it is incorporated in only one state. It is to the company's advantage to incorporate in a state whose laws are favorable to the corporate form of business organization. General Motors, for example, is incorporated in Delaware, whereas USX Corp. is a New Jersey corporation. In fact, some corporations have increasingly been incorporating in states with rules favorable to existing management. For example, Gulf Oil changed its state of incorporation to Delaware to thwart possible unfriendly takeovers. There, certain defensive tactics against

---

[1]Following approval by two-thirds of the stockholders, the by-laws become binding upon all stockholders, directors, and officers. Legally, a corporation is regulated first by the laws of the state, second by its charter, and third by its by-laws. Care must be exercised to ensure that the provisions of the by-laws are not in conflict with either state laws or the charter.

takeovers can be approved by the board of directors alone, without a vote by shareholders.

Corporations engaged in interstate commerce must obtain a license from each state in which they do business. The license subjects the corporation's operating activities to the general corporation laws of the state. Costs incurred in the formation of a corporation are called organization costs. These costs include fees to underwriters for handling stock and bond issues, legal fees, state incorporation fees, and promotional expenditures involved in the organization of the business.

These organization costs are capitalized by debiting an intangible asset entitled Organization Costs. It may be argued that organization costs have an asset life equal to the life of the corporation. Many companies, however, **amortize these costs** over an arbitrary period of time, up to a maximum of 40 years. Because income tax regulations require the amortization of organization costs over a period of at least five years, some companies prefer to use the same period of amortization for accounting purposes. Determining the amount to be recorded when capital stock is used to pay for organization costs is explained later in the chapter.

## Ownership Rights of Stockholders

When chartered, the corporation may begin selling ownership rights in the form of shares of stock. When a corporation has only one class of stock, it is identified as **common stock**. Each share of common stock gives the stockholder the ownership rights pictured in Illustration 14-3. The ownership rights of a share of stock are stated in the articles of incorporation or in the by-laws.

**Illustration 14-3**

*Ownership rights of stockholders*

1. To vote in election of board of directors at annual meeting. To vote on actions that require stockholder approval.

2. To share the corporate earnings through receipt of dividends.

3. To keep same percentage ownership when new shares of stock are issued (**preemptive right**[2]).

4. To share in assets upon liquidation, in proportion to their holdings. Called a **residual claim** because owners are paid with assets remaining after all claims have been paid.

---

[2]A number of companies have eliminated the preemptive right, because they believe it makes an unnecessary and cumbersome demand on management. For example, IBM, by stockholder approval, has dropped its preemptive right for stockholders.

## ▶️Accounting in Action ▸ *International Insight*

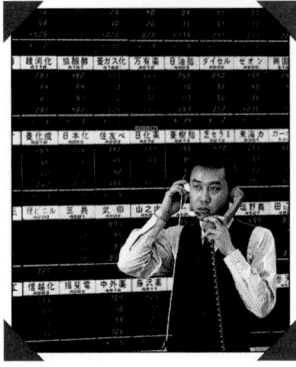

In Japan, stockholders are considered to be far less important to a corporation than employees, customers, and suppliers. Stockholders are rarely asked to vote on an issue, and the notion of bending corporate policy to favor stockholders borders on the heretical in Japan. This attitude toward stockholders appears to be slowly changing, however, as influential Japanese are advocating listening to investors, raising the extremely low dividends paid by Japanese corporations, and improving disclosure of financial information.

**Illustration 14-4**

*A stock certificate*

Proof of stock ownership is evidenced by a printed or engraved form known as a **stock certificate**. As shown in Illustration 14-4, the face of the certificate shows the name of the corporation, the stockholder's name, the class and special features of the stock, the number of shares owned, and the signatures of duly authorized corporate officials. Certificates are prenumbered to facilitate their accountability; they may be issued for any quantity of shares.

## *Before You Go On . . .*

### ▶ *Review It*

1. What are the advantages and disadvantages of a corporation compared to a proprietorship and a partnership?
2. Identify the principal steps in forming a corporation.
3. What rights are inherent in owning a share of stock in a corporation?

## Stock Issue Considerations

In considering the issuance (or sale) of stock, a corporation must resolve a number of basic questions: How many shares should be authorized for sale? How should the stock be issued? At what price should the shares be issued? What value should be assigned to the stock? These questions are answered in the following sections.

## Authorized Stock

The amount of stock that a corporation is **authorized** to sell is indicated in its charter. The total amount of authorized stock at the time of incorporation normally anticipates both initial and subsequent capital needs of a company. As a result, the number of total shares authorized generally exceeds the number of shares initially sold. If all authorized stock is sold, a corporation must obtain consent of the state to amend its charter before it can issue additional shares.

**The authorization of capital stock does not result in a formal accounting entry, since the event has no immediate effect on either corporate assets or stockholders' equity.** However, disclosure of the number of shares of authorized stock is required in the stockholders' equity section. To determine the number of unissued shares that can be issued without amending the charter, the total shares issued are subtracted from the total authorized. For example, if Advanced Micro was authorized to sell 100,000 shares of common stock and issued 80,000 shares, 20,000 shares would remain unissued.

## Issuance of Stock

A corporation has the choice of issuing common stock **directly** to investors or **indirectly** through an investment banking firm (brokerage house) that specializes in bringing securities to the attention of prospective investors. Direct issue is typical in closely held companies, whereas indirect issue is customary for a publicly held corporation.

In an indirect issue, the investment banking firm may agree to **underwrite** the entire stock issue. Under this arrangement, the investment banker buys the stock from the corporation at a stipulated price and resells the shares to investors. The corporation avoids any risk of being unable to sell the shares, and it obtains immediate use of the cash received from the underwriter. The investment banking firm, in turn, assumes the risk of reselling the shares in return for an underwriting fee—the profits expected to be realized from a sales price to the public higher than the price paid to the corporation.[3] For example, Kolff Medical, maker of the Jarvik artificial heart, used an underwriter to help it issue common stock to the public. The underwriter charged a 6.6% underwriting fee on Kolff Medical's approximate $20 million public offering.

How does a corporation set the price for a new issue of stock? Among the factors to be considered are (1) the company's anticipated future earnings, (2) its expected dividend rate per share, (3) its current financial position, (4) the current state of the economy, and (5) the current state of the securities market. The calculation can be complex and is properly the subject of a finance course.

## Market Value of Stock

The stock of publicly held companies is traded on organized exchanges at dollar prices per share established by the interaction between buyers and sellers. In general, the prices set by the marketplace tend to follow the trend of a company's earnings and dividends. However, factors beyond a company's control, such as

▶ *International note*

U.S. and U.K. corporations raise most of their capital through millions of outside shareholders and bondholders. In contrast, companies in Germany, France, and Japan acquire financing from large banks or other institutions. Consequently, in the latter environment, shareholders are less important, and external reporting and auditing receive less emphasis.

---

[3]Alternatively, the investment banking firm may agree only to enter into a **best efforts** contract with the corporation. In such cases, the banker agrees to sell as many shares as possible at a specified price, and the corporation bears the risk of unsold stock. Under a best efforts arrangement, the banking firm is paid a fee or commission for its services.

the imposition of an oil embargo, changes in interest rates, and the outcome of a presidential election, may cause day-to-day fluctuations in market prices.

The volume of trading on national and international exchanges is heavy. Shares in excess of 300 million are often traded daily on the New York Stock Exchange alone. For each listed security the financial press reports the highs and lows of the stock during the year, the total volume of stock traded for a given day, the high and low price for the day, and the closing market price, with the net change for the day. A recent listing for Boeing Aircraft is shown below:

**Illustration 14-5**

*Stock market price information*

| Stock | 52 Weeks | | Sales 3/14 | High | Low | Close | Net Change |
|---|---|---|---|---|---|---|---|
| | High | Low | | | | | |
| Boeing | 50⅛ | 42½ | 27785 | 49¾ | 47⅞ | 48⅞ | +2⅛ |

These numbers indicate that the high and low market prices for the last 52 weeks have been 50⅛ and 42½; the trading volume for March 14 was 2,778,500 shares; the high, low, and closing prices for that date were 49¾, 47⅞, and 48⅞, respectively; and the net change for the day was an increase of 2⅛ or $2.125 per share.

The trading of capital stock on securities exchanges involves the transfer of **already issued shares** from an existing stockholder to another investor. Consequently, these transactions have no impact on a corporation's stockholders' equity section.

## ▸*Technology in Action*

The giant, publicly held corporation could not exist without the organized stock markets, and the stock markets could not exist without massive computerization. Not too many years ago, the NYSE "ticker" would run behind, or trading would even be halted, when sales exceeded 30 million shares or so. Now, with sales sometimes in excess of 300 million shares, the NYSE and its companion exchanges throughout the country operate efficiently with computer technology. Technology has also made possible extended trading hours. An investor in New York, for example, can trade electronically at 3:30 A.M., which is the time in New York when the London Stock Exchange opens. Some predict that 24-hour-trading is not far off.

### *Par and No-Par Value Stocks*

Par value stock is capital stock that has been assigned a value per share in the corporate charter. The par value may be any amount selected by the corporation. Generally, the amount of par value is quite low, because states often levy a tax on the corporation based on par value. For example, International Business Machines has a par of $1.25, Ford Motor Company, $1 par, General Motors Corporation, $1.67, and PepsiCo has 1⅔ cents.

Par value is not indicative of the worth or market value of the stock. As indicated above, IBM has a par value of $1.25, but its recent market price was $85 per share. **The significance of par value is a legal matter.** Par value represents the legal capital per share that must be retained in the business for the protection of corporate creditors. That is, it is not available for withdrawal by stockholders. Thus, most states require the corporation to sell its shares at par or above.

No-par value stock is capital stock that has not been assigned a value in the corporate charter. No-par value stock is often issued because some confusion still exists concerning par value and fair market value. If shares have no par value, the questionable treatment of using par value as a basis for fair market value never arises. The major disadvantage of no-par stock is that some states levy a high tax on the shares issued.

No-par value stock is quite common today. For example, Procter & Gamble and North American Van Lines both have no-par stock. In many states the board of directors is permitted to assign a stated value to the no-par shares, which becomes the legal capital per share. The stated value of no-par stock may be changed at any time by action of the directors. Stated value, like par value, is not indicative of the market value of the stock. When there is no assigned stated value, the entire proceeds received upon issuance of the stock is considered to be legal capital.

The relationship of par and no-par value to legal capital is shown below.

| Stock | Legal Capital per Share |
|---|---|
| Par value ⟶ | Par value |
| No-par value with stated value ⟶ | Stated value |
| No-par value without stated value ⟶ | Entire proceeds |

**Illustration 14-6**

*Relationship of par and no-par value stock to legal capital*

As will be explained later, a common stock account is credited for the legal capital per share each time stock is issued.

## Corporate Capital

Owners' equity is identified as **stockholders' equity, shareholders' equity**, or **corporate capital**. The stockholders' equity section of a corporation's balance sheet consists of: (1) paid-in (contributed) capital, and (2) retained earnings (earned capital). The distinction between paid-in capital and retained earnings is important from both a legal and an economic point of view. Legally, dividends can be declared out of retained earnings in all states, but in many states dividends cannot be declared out of paid-in capital. Economically, management, stockholders, and others look to earnings for the continued existence and growth of the corporation.

**STUDY OBJECTIVE 2**

*Differentiate between paid-in capital and retained earnings.*

### Paid-in Capital

Paid-in capital is the term used to describe the total amount of cash and other assets paid in to the corporation by stockholders in exchange for capital stock. As noted earlier, when a corporation has only one class of stock, it is identified as **common stock**.

### Retained Earnings

Retained earnings is net income retained in a corporation. Net income is recorded in Retained Earnings by a closing entry in which Income Summary is debited and Retained Earnings is credited. For example, assuming that net income for Delta Robotics in its first year of operations is $130,000, the closing entry is:

| | | |
|---|---|---|
| Income Summary | 130,000 | |
|   Retained Earnings | | 130,000 |
|     (To close income summary and transfer net income to retained earnings) | | |

If Delta Robotics has a balance of $800,000 in Common Stock at the end of its first year, its stockholders' equity section is as follows:

| Stockholders' equity | | |
|---|---|---|
| Paid-in capital | | |
| Common stock | $800,000 | |
| Retained earnings | 130,000 | |
| Total stockholders' equity | | $930,000 |

The following illustration compares the owners' equity (stockholders' equity) accounts reported on a balance sheet for a proprietorship, a partnership, and a corporation.

# Before You Go On . . .

## ▸ Review It

1. Of what significance to a corporation is the amount of authorized stock?
2. What alternative approaches may a corporation use in issuing stock?
3. Distinguish between par value and fair market value.

## ▸ Do It

At the end of its first year of operation, Doral Corporation has $750,000 of common stock and net income of $122,000. Prepare (a) the closing entry for net income and (b) the stockholders' equity section at year end.

**Reasoning:** Net income is recorded in Retained Earnings by a closing entry in which Income Summary is debited and Retained Earnings is credited. The stockholders' equity section consists of (1) paid-in capital and (2) retained earnings.

**Solution:**

| (a) Income Summary | 122,000 | |
|---|---|---|
| Retained Earnings | | 122,000 |
| (To close income summary and transfer net income to retained earnings) | | |

(b) Stockholders' equity

| | | |
|---|---:|---:|
| Paid-in capital | | |
| Common stock | $750,000 | |
| Retained earnings | 122,000 | |
| Total stockholders' equity | | $872,000 |

*Related exercise material:* BE14–2, BE14–8, and E14–9.

# Accounting for Common Stock Issues

Let's now look at how to account for issues of common stock. The primary objectives in accounting for the issuance of common stock are to (1) identify the specific sources of paid-in capital and (2) maintain the distinction between paid-in capital and retained earnings. As shown below, **the issue of common stock affects only paid-in capital accounts.**

**STUDY OBJECTIVE**

·········· **3** ··········

*Record the issuance of common stock.*

## Issuing Par Value Common Stock for Cash

As discussed earlier, par value does not indicate a stock's market value. Therefore, the cash proceeds from issuing par value stock may be equal to, greater than, or less than par value. When the issuance of common stock for cash is recorded, the par value of the shares is credited to Common Stock, and the portion of the proceeds that is above or below par value is recorded in a separate paid-in capital account.

To illustrate, assume that Hydro-Slide, Inc. issues 1,000 shares of $1 par value common stock at par for cash. The entry to record this transaction is:

| | | |
|---|---:|---:|
| Cash | 1,000 | |
|    Common Stock | | 1,000 |
|      (To record issuance of 1,000 shares of $1 par common stock at par) | | |

If Hydro-Slide, Inc., issues an additional 1,000 shares of the $1 par value common stock for cash at $5 per share, the entry is:

| | | |
|---|---:|---:|
| Cash | 5,000 | |
|    Common Stock | | 1,000 |
|    Paid-in Capital in Excess of Par Value | | 4,000 |
|      (To record issuance of 1,000 shares of common stock in excess of par) | | |

The total paid-in capital from these two transactions is $6,000, and the legal capital is $2,000. If Hydro-Slide, Inc. has retained earnings of $27,000, the stockholders' equity section is as follows:

| | | |
|---|---:|
| Stockholders' equity | |
|   Paid-in capital | |
|     Common stock | $ 2,000 |
|     **Paid-in capital in excess of par value** | 4,000 |
|     Total paid-in capital | 6,000 |
|   Retained earnings | 27,000 |
|     Total stockholders' equity | $33,000 |

**Illustration 14-9**

*Stockholders' equity—paid-in capital in excess of par value*

When stock is issued for less than par value, the account Paid-in Capital in Excess of Par Value is debited, if a credit balance exists in this account. If a credit balance does not exist, then the amount less than par is debited to Retained Earnings. This situation occurs only rarely: The sale of common stock below par value is not permitted in most states, because stockholders may be held personally liable for the difference between the price paid upon original sale and par value.

## Issuing No-Par Common Stock for Cash

When no-par common stock has a stated value, the entries are similar to those illustrated for par value stock. The stated value represents legal capital and therefore is credited to Common Stock. In addition, when the selling price of no-par stock exceeds stated value, the excess is credited to Paid-in Capital in Excess of Stated Value. For example, assume that instead of $1 par value stock, Hydro-Slide, Inc. has $5 stated value no-par stock and that it issues 5,000 shares at $8 per share for cash. The entry is:

| | | |
|---|---|---|
| Cash | 40,000 | |
|    Common Stock | | 25,000 |
|    Paid-in Capital in Excess of Stated Value | | 15,000 |
|       (To record issue of 5,000 shares of $5 stated value no-par stock) | | |

Paid-in Capital in Excess of Stated Value is reported as part of paid-in capital in the stockholders' equity section.

When no-par stock does not have a stated value, the entire proceeds from the issue become legal capital and are credited to Common Stock. Thus, if Hydro-Slide does not assign a stated value to its no-par stock, the issuance of the 5,000 shares at $8 per share for cash is recorded as follows:

| | | |
|---|---|---|
| Cash | 40,000 | |
|    Common Stock | | 40,000 |
|       (To record issue of 5,000 shares of no-par stock) | | |

The amount of legal capital for Hydro-Slide with a $5 stated value is $25,000; without a stated value, it is $40,000.

## Issuing Common Stock for Services or Noncash Assets

Stock may be issued for services (compensation to attorneys, consultants, and others) or for noncash assets (land, buildings, and equipment). In such cases, a question arises as to the cost that should be recognized in the exchange transaction. To comply with the **cost principle** in a noncash transaction, **cost is the cash equivalent price.** Thus, **cost is either the fair market value of the consideration given up or the fair market value of the consideration received,** whichever is more clearly determinable.

To illustrate, assume that the attorneys for The Jordan Company agree to accept 4,000 shares of $1 par value common stock in payment of their bill of $5,000 for services performed in helping the company to incorporate. At the time of the exchange, there is no established market price for the stock. In this case, the market value of the consideration received, $5,000, is more clearly evident. Accordingly, the entry is:

| | | |
|---|---|---|
| Organization Costs | 5,000 | |
|     Common Stock | | 4,000 |
|     Paid-in Capital in Excess of Par Value | | 1,000 |
|         (To record issuance of 4,000 shares of $1 par value | | |
|         stock to attorneys) | | |

As explained on page 573, organization costs are classified as an intangible asset in the balance sheet.

In contrast, assume that Athletic Research Inc. is a publicly held corporation whose $5 par value stock is actively traded at $8 per share. The company issues 10,000 shares of stock to acquire land recently advertised for sale at $90,000. On the basis of these facts the most clearly evident value is the market price of the consideration given, $80,000. Thus, the transaction is recorded as follows:

| | | |
|---|---|---|
| Land | 80,000 | |
|     Common Stock | | 50,000 |
|     Paid-in Capital in Excess of Par Value | | 30,000 |
|         (To record issuance of 10,000 shares of $5 par value | | |
|         stock for land) | | |

As illustrated in these examples, **the par value of the stock is never a factor in determining the cost of the assets received**. This is also true of the stated value of no-par stock.

## Before You Go On . . .

### ► Review It

1. Explain the accounting for par and no-par common stock issued for cash.
2. Explain the accounting for the issuance of stock for services or noncash assets.

### ► Do It

Cayman Corporation begins operations on March 1 by issuing 100,000 shares of $10 par value common stock for cash at $12 per share. On March 15, it issues 5,000 shares of common stock to attorneys in settlement of their bill of $50,000 for organization costs. Journalize the issuance of the shares assuming the stock is not publicly traded.

**Reasoning:** In issuing shares for cash, common stock is credited for par value per share and any additional proceeds are credited to a separate paid-in capital account. When stock is issued for services, the cash equivalent price should be used. In this case, this price is the value of the attorneys' services.

**Solution:**

| | | | |
|---|---|---|---|
| Mar. 1 | Cash | 1,200,000 | |
| |     Common Stock | | 1,000,000 |
| |     Paid-in Capital in Excess of Par Value | | 200,000 |
| |         (To record issuance of 100,000 shares at $12 | | |
| |         per share) | | |
| | | | |
| Mar. 15 | Organization Costs | 50,000 | |
| |     Common Stock | | 50,000 |
| |         (To record issuance of 5,000 shares for | | |
| |         attorneys' fees) | | |

*Related exercise material:* BE14–3, BE14–4, BE14–5, E14–1, E14–2, E14–3, E14–7, and E14–8.

# Accounting for Treasury Stock

**STUDY OBJECTIVE**

•••••••••• **4** ••••••••••

*Explain the accounting for treasury stock.*

Treasury stock is a corporation's own stock that has been issued, fully paid for, and reacquired by the corporation but not retired. A corporation may acquire treasury stock for the reasons listed below.

1. Reissue the shares to officers and employees under bonus and stock compensation plans.
2. Increase trading of the company's stock in the securities market in the hopes of enhancing its market value.
3. Have additional shares available for use in the acquisition of other companies.
4. Reduce the number of shares outstanding and thereby increase earnings per share.

**Helpful hint** Treasury stock is so named because the company often holds the shares in its treasury for safekeeping.

Another infrequent reason for purchasing treasury shares, as illustrated in the Ford Motor Company opening story, is that management may want to eliminate hostile shareholders.

Many corporations have treasury stock. For example, one survey of 600 companies in the United States found that 64% have treasury stock.[4] Specifically, Kellogg Company recently reported 82.3 million treasury shares, PepsiCo 73.2 million, and Bristol-Meyers Squibb 20.8 million.

## Purchase of Treasury Stock

**The cost method is generally used in accounting for treasury stock.** This method derives its name from the fact that the Treasury Stock account is maintained at the cost of shares purchased. Under the cost method, **Treasury Stock is debited at the price paid to reacquire the shares, and the same amount is credited to Treasury Stock when the shares are sold.** To illustrate, assume that on January 1, 1996, the stockholders' equity section of Mead, Inc. has 100,000 shares of $5 par value common stock outstanding (all issued at par value) and Retained Earnings of $200,000.

The stockholders' equity section before purchase of treasury stock is as follows:

**Illustration 14-10**

*Stockholders' equity with no treasury stock*

| | |
|---|---|
| Stockholders' equity | |
| Paid-in capital | |
| Common stock, $5 par value, 100,000 shares issued and outstanding | $500,000 |
| Retained earnings | 200,000 |
| Total stockholders' equity | $700,000 |

On February 1, 1996, Mead acquires 4,000 shares of its stock at $8 per share. The entry is:

| | | | |
|---|---|---|---|
| Feb. 1 | Treasury Stock | 32,000 | |
| | Cash | | 32,000 |
| | (To record purchase of 4,000 shares of treasury stock at $8 per share) | | |

---

[4]*Accounting Trends & Techniques 1994* (New York: American Institute of Certified Public Accountants).

## ►Accounting in Action ► *Business Insight*

Philip Morris will spend $6 billion over the next three years to buy back a massive amount of stock from its shareholders. The repurchase is second in size to General Electric's $10 billion in the late 1980s. Buying back stock, which tends to increase the value of remaining shares, is not new to Philip Morris; it has at other times bought back stock, because it had few good places to reinvest the cash that it generated. The company also announced it will boost its cash dividend nearly 20%, from 69 cents up to 82½ cents per share.

*Source: USA Today,* September 1, 1994, p. B1.

Note that Treasury Stock is debited for the cost of the shares purchased. The original paid-in capital account, Common Stock, is not affected because the number of issued shares does not change. Treasury stock is deducted from total paid-in capital and retained earnings in the stockholders' equity section.

The stockholders' equity section of Mead, Inc., after purchase of treasury stock is as follows:

> **Helpful hint** Treasury Stock is a contra stockholders' equity account.

> **Illustration 14-11**
>
> *Stockholders' equity with treasury stock*

| | |
|---|---:|
| Stockholders' equity | |
| Paid-in capital | |
| Common stock, $5 par value, 100,000 shares issued and 96,000 shares outstanding | $500,000 |
| Retained earnings | 200,000 |
| Total paid-in capital and retained earnings | 700,000 |
| **Less: Treasury stock (4,000 shares)** | **32,000** |
| Total stockholders' equity | $668,000 |

Thus, the acquisition of treasury stock reduces stockholders' equity.

Both the number of shares issued (100,000) and the number in the treasury (4,000) are disclosed. The difference is the number of shares of stock outstanding (96,000). The term outstanding stock means the number of shares of issued stock that are being held by stockholders.

Some maintain that treasury stock should be reported as an asset because it can be sold for cash. Under this reasoning, unissued stock should also be shown as an asset, clearly an erroneous conclusion. Rather than being an asset, treasury stock reduces stockholder claims on corporate assets. This effect is correctly shown by reporting treasury stock as a deduction from total paid-in capital and retained earnings.

## Disposal of Treasury Stock

Treasury stock is usually sold or retired. The accounting for its sale is different when treasury stock is sold above cost than when it is sold below cost.

### *Sale of Treasury Stock above Cost*

If the selling price of the treasury shares is equal to cost, the sale of the shares is recorded by a debit to Cash and a credit to Treasury Stock. When the selling price of the shares is greater than cost, the difference is credited to Paid-in Capital from Treasury Stock. To illustrate, assume that 1,000 shares of treasury stock of Mead, Inc., previously acquired at $8 per share, are sold at $10 per share on July 1. The entry is as follows:

> **Helpful hint** Treasury stock transactions are classified as capital stock transactions. As in the case of issuing stock, the income statement is not involved.

| July 1 | Cash | 10,000 | |
| | Treasury Stock | | 8,000 |
| | Paid-in Capital from Treasury Stock | | 2,000 |
| | (To record sale of 1,000 shares of treasury stock above cost) | | |

The $2,000 credit in the entry is **not** made to Gain on Sale of Treasury Stock for two reasons: (1) Gains on sales occur when assets are sold and treasury stock is not an asset. (2) A corporation does not realize a gain or suffer a loss from stock transactions with its own stockholders. Thus, paid-in capital arising from the sale of treasury stock should not be included in the measurement of net income. Paid-in Capital from Treasury Stock is listed separately on the balance sheet as a part of paid-in capital.

### Sale of Treasury Stock below Cost

When treasury stock is sold below its cost, the excess of cost over selling price is usually debited to Paid-in Capital from Treasury Stock. Thus, if Mead, Inc. sells an additional 800 shares of treasury stock on October 1 at $7 per share, the entry is as follows:

| Oct. 1 | Cash | 5,600 | |
| | Paid-in Capital from Treasury Stock | 800 | |
| | Treasury Stock | | 6,400 |
| | (To record sale of 800 shares of treasury stock below cost) | | |

Observe from the two sales entries that (1) Treasury Stock is credited at cost in each entry, (2) Paid-in Capital from Treasury Stock is used for the difference between the cost and resale price of the shares, and (3) the original paid-in capital account, Common Stock, again is not affected. **The sale of treasury stock increases both total assets and total stockholders' equity.**

After posting the foregoing entries, the treasury stock accounts will show the following balances on October 1:

**Illustration 14-12**

*Treasury stock accounts*

| Treasury Stock | | | | | Paid-in Capital from Treasury Stock | | | | |
|---|---|---|---|---|---|---|---|---|---|
| Feb. 1 | 32,000 | July 1 | 8,000 | | Oct. 1 | 800 | July 1 | 2,000 |
| | | Oct. 1 | 6,400 | | | | | |
| | | | | | | | Oct. 1 Bal. | 1,200 |
| Oct. 1 Bal. | 17,600 | | | | | | | |

When the credit balance in Paid-in Capital from Treasury Stock is eliminated, any additional excess of cost over selling price is debited to Retained Earnings. To illustrate, assume that Mead, Inc., sells its remaining 2,200 shares at $7 per share on December 1. The excess of cost over selling price is $2,200 [2,200 × ($8 − $7)]. In this case, $1,200 of the excess is debited to Paid-in Capital from Treasury Stock, and the remainder is debited to Retained Earnings. The entry is:

| Dec. 1 | Cash | 15,400 | |
| | Paid-in Capital from Treasury Stock | 1,200 | |
| | Retained Earnings | 1,000 | |
| | Treasury Stock | | 17,600 |
| | (To record sale of 2,200 shares of treasury stock at $7 per share) | | |

## Retiring Treasury Stock

The board of directors may approve the retirement of treasury shares. This decision results in cancellation of the treasury stock and a reduction in the number of shares of issued stock. The accounting effects are similar to the sale of treasury stock except that debits are made to the paid-in capital accounts applicable to the retired shares instead of to cash. For example, if the shares are originally sold at par, Common Stock is debited for the par value per share. If the shares are originally sold at $3 above par value, a debit to Paid-in Capital in Excess of Par Value for $3 per share is also required.

To illustrate, assume that Ottman Company originally issued 10,000 shares of $10 par common stock for $120,000 ($12 per share) on January 2, 1996. Ottman then purchased 1,000 shares of treasury stock for $11,000 ($11 per share) on November 5, 1996. Ottman decides to retire the treasury stock on December 10, 1996. The paid-in capital accounts applicable to the treasury stock are: Common Stock $10,000 (1,000 shares × $10) and Paid-in Capital in Excess of Par Value 2,000 (1,000 shares × $2). Thus, the entry to record the retirement is as follows:

| | | | |
|---|---|---|---|
| Dec. 10 | Common Stock | 10,000 | |
| | Paid-in Capital in Excess of Par Value | 2,000 | |
| |    Treasury Stock | | 11,000 |
| |    Paid-in Capital from Treasury Stock | | 1,000 |
| |     (To record retirement of 1,000 shares of | | |
| |     treasury stock) | | |

In this case, the cost of the treasury stock ($11,000) is less than the applicable paid-in capital ($12,000). Accordingly, the difference is credited to Paid-in Capital from Treasury Stock. If the reverse were true, the excess of applicable paid-in capital over the cost of treasury stock is debited to Paid-in Capital from Treasury Stock until this account has a zero balance. Any additional amount is then debited to Retained Earnings.

## Before You Go On . . .

### ► Review It

1. What is treasury stock, and why do companies acquire it?
2. How is treasury stock recorded?
3. Where is treasury stock reported in the financial statements? Does a company record gains and losses on treasury stock transactions? Explain.

### ► Do It

Santa Anita Inc. purchases 3,000 shares of its $50 par value common stock for $180,000 cash on July 1. The shares are to be held in the treasury until resold. On November 1, the corporation sells 1,000 shares of treasury stock for cash at $70 per share. Journalize the treasury stock transactions.

**Reasoning:** The purchase of treasury stock is recorded at cost. When treasury stock is sold, the excess of the selling price over cost is credited to Paid-in Capital from Treasury Stock.

**Solution:**

| | | | |
|---|---|---|---|
| July 1 | Treasury Stock | 180,000 | |
| |    Cash | | 180,000 |
| |     (To record the purchase of 3,000 shares at | | |
| |     $60 per share) | | |

| | | | |
|---|---|---|---|
| Nov. 1 | Cash | 70,000 | |
| |     Treasury Stock | | 60,000 |
| |     Paid-in Capital from Treasury Stock | | 10,000 |
| |     (To record the sale of 1,000 shares at $70 | | |
| |     per share) | | |

*Related exercise material: BE14–6, E14–2, E14–4, E14–7, and E14–8.*

---

# Preferred Stock

**STUDY OBJECTIVE**
**5**

*Differentiate preferred stock from common stock.*

To appeal to a larger segment of potential investors, a corporation may issue a class of stock in addition to common stock, called preferred stock. Preferred stock has contractual provisions that give it a preference or priority over common stock in certain areas. Typically, preferred stockholders have a priority as to (1) dividends and (2) assets in the event of liquidation. However, they generally do not have voting rights.

Like common stock, preferred stock may be issued for cash or for noncash assets. The entries for these transactions are similar to the entries for common stock. When a corporation has more than one class of stock, each paid-in capital account title should identify the stock to which it relates (e.g., Preferred Stock, Common Stock, Paid-in Capital in Excess of Par Value—Preferred Stock, and Paid-in Capital in Excess of Par Value—Common Stock). Assume that Stine Corporation issues 10,000 shares of $10 par value preferred stock for $12 cash per share. The entry to record the issuance is:

| | | | |
|---|---|---|---|
| Cash | | 120,000 | |
|     Preferred Stock | | | 100,000 |
|     Paid-in Capital in Excess of Par Value—Preferred Stock | | | 20,000 |
|     (To record the issuance of 10,000 shares of $10 par | | | |
|     value preferred stock) | | | |

Preferred stock may have either a par value or no-par value. For example, Walgreen Drug Co. has $0.50 par value preferred and General Motors has three classes of no-par preferred stock, each with a stated value of $100. In the stockholders' equity section, preferred stock is shown first because of its dividend and liquidation preferences over common stock.

## Dividend Preferences

As indicated before, **preferred stockholders have the right to share in the distribution of corporate income before common stockholders.** For example, if the dividend rate on preferred stock is $5 per share, common shareholders will not receive any dividends in the current year until preferred stockholders have received $5 per share. The first claim to dividends does not, however, guarantee dividends. Dividends depend on many factors, such as adequate retained earnings and availability of cash.

The per share dividend amount is stated as a percentage of the par value of preferred stock or as a specified amount. For example, the Crane Company specifies 3¾% dividend on its $100 par value preferred ($100 × 3¾% = $3.75 per share), whereas DuPont has both a $4.50 and a $3.50 series of no-par preferred stock.

## *Cumulative Dividend*

Preferred stock contracts often contain a cumulative dividend feature. This right means that preferred stockholders must be paid both current-year dividends and any unpaid prior-year dividends before common stockholders receive dividends. When preferred stock is cumulative, preferred dividends not declared in a given period are called **dividends in arrears**. To illustrate, assume that Scientific-Leasing has 5,000 shares of 7%, $100 par value cumulative preferred stock outstanding. The annual dividend is $35,000 (5,000 × $7 per share). If dividends are 2 years in arrears, preferred stockholders are entitled to receive the following dividends in the current year before any distribution is made to common stockholders:

| | |
|---|---|
| Dividends in arrears ($35,000 × 2) | $ 70,000 |
| Current-year dividends | 35,000 |
| Total preferred dividends | $105,000 |

**Illustration 14-13**

*Computation of total dividends to preferred stock*

**Dividends in arrears are not considered a liability. No obligation exists until a dividend is declared by the board of directors.** However, the amount of dividends in arrears should be disclosed in the notes to the financial statements. Doing so enables investors to assess the potential impact of this commitment on the corporation's financial position.

Dividends cannot be paid on common stock while any dividend on preferred stock is in arrears. The cumulative feature is often critical in investor acceptance of a preferred stock issue. When preferred stock is noncumulative, a dividend passed in any year is lost forever. Companies that are unable to meet their dividend obligations are not looked upon favorably by the investment community. As a financial officer noted in discussing one company's failure to pay its cumulative preferred dividend for a period of time, "Not meeting your obligations on something like that is a major black mark on your record." The accounting entries for preferred stock dividends are explained in Chapter 15.

## ►Accounting in Action ► *Business Insight*

Dividends in arrears can extend for fairly long periods of time. Long Island Lighting Company's directors voted at one time to make up some $390 million in preferred dividends that had been in arrears since 1984 and to resume normal quarterly preferred payments. The announcement resulted from an agreement between the company and New York State to abandon a nuclear power plant in exchange for sizable rate increases over the next 10 years.

## *Participating Dividend*

Preferred stock may also have a participating dividend feature. This right enables the preferred stockholder to share ratably (proportionately) with common stockholders in any dividends beyond the rate specified on the preferred stock. The participating feature does not apply until common stockholders receive a percentage rate of return on their shares equal to the specified dividend rate on preferred stock. The issuance of participating preferred stock is rare.

## Liquidation Preference

Most preferred stocks have a preference on corporate assets if the corporation fails. This feature provides security for the preferred stockholder. The preference to assets may be for the par value of the shares or for a specified liquidating value. For example, Commonwealth Edison issued preferred stock that entitles the holders to receive $31.80 per share, plus accrued and unpaid dividends, in the event of involuntary liquidation. The liquidation preference is used in litigation pertaining to bankruptcy lawsuits involving the respective claims of creditors and preferred stockholders.

## Convertible Preferred Stock

The attractiveness of preferred stock as an investment is enhanced by adding a conversion privilege. Convertible preferred stock provides for the exchange of preferred stock into common stock at a specified ratio at the stockholder's option.

Convertible preferred stock is purchased by investors who want the greater security of a preferred stock, but who also desire the added option of conversion if the market value of the common stock increases significantly. To illustrate, assume that Ross Industries issues at par value 1,000 shares of $100 par value convertible preferred stock. One share of preferred is convertible into 10 shares of $5 par value common (current price $9 per share). At this point, it would not be advantageous for the holders of the preferred to convert, because they would exchange preferred stock worth $100,000 (1,000 × $100) for common stock worth $90,000 (10,000 × $9). However, if the price of the common stock were to increase above $10 per share, it usually would be advantageous for the preferred holders to convert.

In recording the conversion, it is customary to transfer the amount paid in on the preferred stock to appropriate common stock accounts. To illustrate, assume that the 1,000 shares of Ross Industries preferred issued at $100 par value are converted into 10,000 shares of common stock ($5 par) when the market values per share of the two classes of stock are $101 and $12, respectively. The entry to record the conversion is:

| | | |
|---|---|---|
| Preferred Stock | 100,000 | |
|     Common Stock | | 50,000 |
|     Paid-in Capital in Excess of Par Value—Common Stock | | 50,000 |
|     (To record conversion of 1,000 shares of preferred | | |
|     stock into 10,000 shares of $5 par value common stock) | | |

**The conversion of preferred stock does not result in either gain or loss to the corporation.** If the preferred stock was issued for more than its par value, the paid-in capital in excess of the par value on the preferred stock should be eliminated.

**Note that the market values of the shares at the time of the transaction are not considered in recording the transaction.** The reason is that the exchange of shares is made directly through the corporation and the corporation has not received any assets equal to fair market value.

## Callable Preferred Stock

Many preferred stocks are issued with a call feature. A callable preferred stock grants the issuing corporation the right to purchase the stock from stockholders at specified future dates and prices. The call feature offers some flexibility to a corporation by enabling it to eliminate this type of equity security when it is advantageous to do so. The **call (or redemption) price** is frequently slightly above the par or stated value of the shares. When preferred stock is callable, the call price tends to set a ceiling on the market price of the shares.

# Stockholders' Equity Presentation

In the stockholders' equity section of the balance sheet, paid-in capital and retained earnings are reported, and the specific sources of paid-in capital are identified.

Within paid-in capital, two classifications are recognized:

1. **Capital stock**, which consists of preferred and common stock. Preferred stock is shown before common stock because of its preferential rights. Information as to the par value, shares authorized, shares issued, and shares outstanding is reported for each class of stock.
2. **Additional paid-in capital**, which includes the excess of amounts paid in over par or stated value and paid-in capital from treasury stock.

> **STUDY OBJECTIVE**
> ▼ **6**
> *Prepare a stockholders' equity section.*

## Illustrations

The stockholders' equity section of Connally Inc. shown in Illustration 14-14 includes most of the accounts discussed in this chapter. The disclosures pertaining to Connally's common stock indicate that 400,000 shares are issued, 100,000 shares are unissued (500,000 authorized less 400,000 issued), and 390,000 shares are outstanding (400,000 issued less 10,000 shares in treasury).

| CONNALLY INC. Partial Balance Sheet | | |
|---|---:|---:|
| Stockholders' equity | | |
| Paid-in capital | | |
| Capital stock | | |
| 9% preferred stock, $100 par value, callable at $120, cumulative, 10,000 shares authorized, 6,000 shares issued and outstanding | | $ 600,000 |
| Common stock, no par, $5 stated value, 500,000 shares authorized, 400,000 shares issued, and 390,000 outstanding | | 2,000,000 |
| Total capital stock | | 2,600,000 |
| Additional paid-in capital | | |
| In excess of par value—preferred stock | $ 30,000 | |
| In excess of stated value—common stock | 860,000 | |
| From treasury stock | 140,000 | |
| Total additional paid-in capital | | 1,030,000 |
| Total paid-in capital | | 3,630,000 |
| Retained earnings | | 1,058,000 |
| Total paid-in capital and retained earnings | | 4,688,000 |
| Less: Treasury stock—common (10,000 shares) | | (80,000) |
| Total stockholders' equity | | $4,608,000 |

**Illustration 14-14**

*Stockholders' equity section*

In published annual reports, subclassifications within the stockholders' equity section are seldom presented. Moreover, the individual sources of additional paid-in capital are often combined and reported as a single amount as shown in Illustration 14-15.

**Illustration 14-15**

*Published stockholders'
equity section*

| KNIGHT-RIDDER INC. | |
| --- | --- |
| Stockholders' equity (in millions) | |
| Common stock, $.02½ par value; shares authorized—250,000,000; shares issued—45,720,000 | $      1,143 |
| Additional paid-in capital | 342,201 |
| Retained earnings | 899,825 |
| Total stockholders' equity | $1,243,169 |

In practice, the term "capital surplus" is sometimes used in place of additional paid-in capital and "earned surplus" in place of retained earnings. The use of the term "surplus" suggests that an excess amount of funds is available. Such is not necessarily the case, which is why **the term surplus should not be employed in accounting**. Unfortunately, a number of financial statements still include these terms.

## Book Value—Another Per Share Amount

**STUDY OBJECTIVE**
•••••••••••▼•••••••••••
*Compute book value
per share.*

You have learned about a number of per share amounts in this chapter. Another per share amount of some importance is book value per share. This per share amount represents **the equity a common stockholder has in the net assets of the corporation** from owning one share of stock. Since the net assets of a corporation must be equal to total stockholders' equity, the formula for computing book value per share when a company has only one class of stock outstanding is:

**Illustration 14-16**

*Book value per share formula*

Thus, if the Marlo Corporation has total stockholders' equity of $1,500,000 (Common Stock $1,000,000 and Retained Earnings $500,000) and 50,000 shares of common stock outstanding, book value per share is $30 ($1,500,000 ÷ 50,000).

When a company has both preferred and common stock, the computation of book value is more complex. Since preferred stockholders have a prior claim on net assets over common stockholders, their equity must be deducted from total stockholders' equity to determine the stockholders' equity that applies to the common stock. The computation of book value per share involves the following steps:

**1.** Compute the preferred stock equity. This equity is equal to the sum of the call price of preferred stock plus any cumulative dividends in arrears. If the preferred stock does not have a call price, the par value of the stock is used.

2. Determine the common stock equity by subtracting the preferred stock equity from total stockholders' equity.
3. Divide common stock equity by shares of common stock outstanding to determine book value per share.

### Illustration

We will use the stockholders' equity section of Connally Inc. shown in Illustration 14-14. Connally's preferred stock is callable at $120 per share and cumulative. Assume that dividends on Connally's preferred stock were in arrears for one year, $54,000 (6,000 × $9). The computation of preferred stock equity is:

| | |
|---|---:|
| Call price (6,000 shares × $120) | $720,000 |
| Dividends in arrears (6,000 shares × $9) | 54,000 |
| Preferred stock equity | $774,000 |

**Illustration 14-17**

*Computation of preferred stock equity (Step 1)*

The computation of book value is as follows:

| | |
|---|---:|
| Total stockholders' equity | $4,608,000 |
| Less Preferred stock equity | 774,000 |
| Common stock equity | $3,834,000 |
| Shares of common stock outstanding | 390,000 |
| Book value per share ($3,834,000 ÷ 390,000) | $9.83 |

**Illustration 14-18**

*Computation of book value per share with preferred stock (Steps 2 and 3)*

The call price of $120 was used instead of the par value of $100. Note also that the paid-in capital in excess of par value of preferred stock, $30,000, **is not assigned to the preferred stock equity**. Preferred stockholders ordinarily do not have a right to amounts paid-in in excess of par value. Accordingly, such amounts are assigned to the common stock equity in computing book value.

### Book Value versus Market Value

**Book value per share may not equal market value.** Book value is based on recorded costs; market value reflects the subjective judgment of thousands of stockholders and prospective investors about a company's potential for future earnings and dividends. Market value per share may exceed book value per share, but that fact does not necessarily mean that the stock is overpriced. The correlation between book value and the annual range of a company's market value per share is often remote, as indicated by the following recent data:

| Company | Book Value (year-end) | Market Range (for year) |
|---|---:|---:|
| McDonnell Douglas | $86.84 | $47.88–$118.38 |
| Callaway Golf | $ 6.90 | $17.19–$65.25 |
| Eastman Kodak | $ 8.85 | $40.38–$64.75 |

**Illustration 14-19**

*Book and market values compared*

Book value per share **is** useful in determining the trend of a stockholder's per share equity in a corporation. It is also significant in many contracts and in court cases where the rights of individual parties are based on cost information.

## Before You Go On . . .

1. Identify the classifications within the paid-in capital section and the totals that are stated in the stockholders' equity section of a balance sheet.
2. What is the method for computing book value per share when there is (a) only one class of stock and (b) both preferred and common stock?

### ► A Look Back at Ford Motor Company

Refer back to the opening story about Ford Motor Company, and answer the following questions.

1. Why did Henry Ford originally choose to form a corporation rather than a sole proprietorship?
2. Why did the Ford Motor Company repurchase all of its shares?
3. What advantages and disadvantages of being organized as a corporation are illustrated by Ford?

**Solution:**

1. Henry Ford wanted to take full advantage of mass-production. This would require large factories and many employees, which would in turn require considerable funds. The most efficient way to raise these funds was to issue stock.
2. Ford Motor Company initiated a massive treasury stock purchase when Henry Ford's vision was not consistent with the wishes of the shareholders.
3. The history of Ford Motor Company illustrates a number of the strengths and weaknesses of being formed as a corporation. Forming a corporation allowed for more efficient access to funds, and thus more rapid expansion. This was critical because, in the early 1900s, many companies were trying to build cars for the American market. However, by issuing shares, Henry Ford relinquished his control over the firm. This led to a collision in 1916 when the founder believed that it was in the company's best interest to retain funds in the firm rather than to pay dividends. To the extent that outside shareholders are not as well informed as a corporation's managers, the shareholders may force management to do things that hinder the firm's success.

## ◢ Summary of Study Objectives

**1.** *Identify and discuss the major characteristics of a corporation.* The major characteristics of a corporation are separate legal existence, limited liability of stockholders, transferable ownership rights, ability to acquire capital, continuous life, corporation management, government regulations, and additional taxes.

**2.** *Differentiate between paid-in capital and retained earnings.* Paid-in capital is the total amount paid in on capital stock. It is often referred to as contributed capital. Retained earnings is net income retained in a corporation. It is often referred to as earned capital.

**3.** *Record the issuance of common stock.* When the issuance of common stock for cash is recorded, the par value of the shares is credited to Common Stock and the portion of the proceeds that is above or below par value is recorded in a separate paid-in capital account. When no-par common stock has a stated value, the entries are similar to those for par value stock. When no-par does not have a stated value, the entire proceeds from the issue become legal capital and are credited to Common Stock.

**4.** *Explain the accounting for treasury stock.* The cost method is generally used in accounting for treasury stock. Under this approach, Treasury Stock is debited at the price paid to reacquire the shares, and the same amount is credited to Treasury Stock when the shares are sold. The difference between the sales price and cost is recorded in stockholders' equity accounts, not in income statement accounts. When treasury stock is retired, applicable paid-in capital accounts are debited.

**5.** *Differentiate preferred stock from common stock.* Preferred stock has contractual provisions that give it priority over common stock in certain areas. Typically, preferred stockholders have a preference as to (1) dividends and (2) assets in the event of liquidation. However, they usually do not have voting rights. In addition, preferred stock may be convertible and/or callable. A convertible preferred stock entitles the holder of the preferred stock to convert those shares to common stock in a specified ratio. The callable feature grants to the issuing corporation the right to purchase the stock from stockholders at specified future dates and prices.

**6.** *Prepare a stockholders' equity section.* In the stockholders' equity section, paid-in capital and retained earnings are reported and specific sources of paid-in capital are identified. Within paid-in capital, two classifications are shown:

capital stock and additional paid-in capital. If a corporation has treasury stock, the cost of treasury stock is deducted from total paid-in capital and retained earnings to obtain total stockholders' equity.

**7.** *Compute book value per share.* Book value per share represents the equity a common stockholder has in the net assets of a corporation from owning one share of stock. When there is only common stock outstanding, the formula for computing book value is: Total Stockholders' Equity ÷ Number of Common Shares Outstanding = Book Value per Share.

# GLOSSARY

**Authorized stock**   The amount of stock that a corporation is authorized to sell as indicated in its charter. (p. 575).

**Book value per share**   The equity a common stockholder has in the net assets of the corporation from owning one share of stock. (p. 590).

**By-laws**   The internal rules and procedures for conducting the affairs of a corporation. (p. 572).

**Callable preferred stock**   Preferred stock that grants the issuer the right to purchase the stock from stockholders at specified future dates and prices. (p. 588).

**Charter**   A document that creates a corporation. (p. 572).

**Convertible preferred stock**   Preferred stock that provides for the exchange of preferred stock into common stock at a specified ratio at the stockholder's option. (p. 588).

**Corporation**   A business organized as a legal entity separate and distinct from its owners under state corporation law. (p. 568).

**Cumulative dividend**   A feature of preferred stock entitling the stockholder to receive current and unpaid prior-year dividends before common stockholders receive any dividends. (p. 587).

**Legal capital**   The amount per share of stock that must be retained in the business for the protection of corporate creditors. (p. 576).

**No-par value stock**   Capital stock that has not been assigned a value in the corporate charter. (p. 576).

**Organization costs**   Costs incurred in the formation of a corporation. (p. 573).

**Outstanding stock**   Capital stock that has been issued and is being held by stockholders. (p. 583).

**Paid-in capital**   Total amount of cash and other assets paid in to the corporation by stockholders in exchange for capital stock. (p. 577).

**Par value stock**   Capital stock that has been assigned a value per share in the corporate charter. (p. 576).

**Participating dividend**   A feature of preferred stock enabling the stockholder to share ratably with common stockholders in any dividends beyond the rate specified on the preferred stock. (p. 587).

**Preferred stock**   Capital stock that has contractual preferences over common stock in certain areas. (p. 586).

**Privately held corporation**   A corporation that has only a few stockholders and whose stock is not available for sale to the general public. (p. 569).

**Publicly held corporation**   A corporation that may have thousands of stockholders and whose stock is regularly traded on a national securities market. (p. 569).

**Retained earnings**   Net income retained in the corporation. (p. 577).

**Stated value**   The amount per share assigned by the board of directors to no-par stock that becomes legal capital per share. (p. 577).

**Treasury stock**   A corporation's own stock that has been issued, fully paid for, and reacquired by the corporation but not retired. (p. 582).

# DEMONSTRATION PROBLEM

The Rolman Corporation is authorized to issue 1,000,000 shares of $5 par value common stock. In its first year, the company has the following stock transactions:

Jan. 10   Issued 400,000 shares of stock at $8 per share.

July 1   Issued 100,000 shares of stock for land. The land had an asking price of $900,000. The stock is currently selling on a national exchange at $8.25 per share.

Sept. 1  Purchased 10,000 shares of common stock for the treasury at $9.00 per share.

Dec. 1  Sold 4,000 shares of the treasury stock at $10 per share.

**Instructions**

(a)  Journalize the transactions.

(b)  Prepare the stockholders' equity section assuming the company had retained earnings of $200,000 at December 31.

**Problem-Solving Strategies**

1. When common stock has a par value, Common Stock is always credited for par value.

2. In a noncash transaction, fair market value should be used.

3. The Treasury Stock account is debited and credited at cost.

4. Differences between the cost and selling price of treasury stock are recorded in stockholders' equity accounts, not as gains or losses.

## Solution to Demonstration Problem

(a) 

| | | | | |
|---|---|---|---|---|
| Jan. 10 | Cash | | 3,200,000 | |
| | Common Stock | | | 2,000,000 |
| | Paid-in Capital in Excess of Par Value | | | 1,200,000 |
| | (To record issuance of 400,000 shares of $5 par value stock) | | | |
| July 1 | Land | | 825,000 | |
| | Common Stock | | | 500,000 |
| | Paid-in Capital in Excess of Par Value | | | 325,000 |
| | (To record issuance of 100,000 shares of $5 par value stock for land) | | | |
| Sept. 1 | Treasury Stock | | 90,000 | |
| | Cash | | | 90,000 |
| | (To record purchase of 10,000 shares of treasury stock at cost) | | | |
| Dec. 1 | Cash | | 40,000 | |
| | Treasury Stock | | | 36,000 |
| | Paid-in Capital from Treasury Stock | | | 4,000 |
| | (To record sale of 4,000 shares of treasury stock above cost) | | | |

(b)  Stockholders' equity

| | | | |
|---|---|---|---|
| Paid-in capital | | | |
| Capital Stock | | | |
| Common stock, $5 par value, 1,000,000 shares authorized, 500,000 shares issued, 494,000 shares outstanding | | | $2,500,000 |
| Additional paid-in capital | | | |
| In excess of par value | | $1,525,000 | |
| From treasury stock | | 4,000 | |
| Total additional paid-in capital | | | 1,529,000 |
| Total paid-in capital | | | 4,029,000 |
| Retained earnings | | | 200,000 |
| Total paid-in capital and retained earnings | | | 4,229,000 |
| Less: Treasury stock (6,000 shares) | | | 54,000 |
| Total stockholders' equity | | | $4,175,000 |

# SELF-STUDY QUESTIONS

Answers are at the end of the chapter.

(SO 1)  1. Which of the following is *not* a major advantage of a corporation?

a. Separate legal existence.

b. Continuous life.

c. Government regulations.

d. Transferable ownership rights.

(SO 1)  2. A major disadvantage of a corporation is:

a. limited liability of stockholders.

b. additional taxes.

c. transferable ownership rights.

d. none of the above.

3. Which of the following statements is *false*?  (SO 2)

a. Ownership of common stock gives the owner a voting right.

b. The stockholders' equity section begins with paid-in capital.

c. The authorization of capital stock does not result in a formal accounting entry.

d. Legal capital per share applies to par value stock but not to no-par value stock.

(SO 2) 4. The account, Retained Earnings, is:
a. a subdivision of paid-in capital.
b. net income retained in the corporation.
c. reported as an expense in the income statement.
d. closed to capital stock.

(SO 3) 5. ABC Corporation issues 1,000 shares of $10 par value common stock at $12 per share. In recording the transaction, credits are made to:
a. Common Stock $10,000 and Paid-in Capital in Excess of Stated Value, $2,000.
b. Common Stock $12,000.
c. Common Stock $10,000 and Paid-in Capital in Excess of Par Value $2,000.
d. Common Stock $10,000 and Retained Earnings $2,000.

(SO 4) 6. XYZ, Inc., sells 100 shares of $5 par value treasury stock at $13 per share. If the cost of acquiring the shares was $10 per share, the entry for the sale should include credits to:
a. Treasury Stock $1,000 and Paid-in Capital from Treasury Stock $300.
b. Treasury Stock $500 and Paid-in Capital from Treasury Stock $800.
c. Treasury Stock $1,000 and Retained Earnings $300.
d. Treasury Stock $500 and Paid-in Capital in Excess of Par Value $800.

7. In the stockholders' equity section, the cost of (SO 4) treasury stock is deducted from:
a. Total paid-in capital and retained earnings.
b. Retained earnings.
c. Total stockholders' equity.
d. Common stock in paid-in capital.

8. Preferred stock may have priority over common (SO 5) stock *except* in:
a. dividends.
b. assets in the event of liquidation.
c. conversion.
d. voting.

9. Which of the following is *not* reported under ad- (SO 6) ditional paid-in capital?
a. Paid-in capital in excess of par value.
b. Common stock.
c. Paid-in capital in excess of stated value.
d. Paid-in capital from treasury stock.

10. The ledger of JFK, Inc., shows common stock, com- (SO 7) mon treasury stock, and no preferred stock. For this company, the formula for computing book value per share is:
a. Total paid-in capital and retained earnings divided by the number of shares of common stock issued.
b. Common stock divided by the number of shares of common stock issued.
c. Total stockholders' equity divided by the number of shares of common stock outstanding.
d. Total stockholders' equity divided by the number of shares of common stock issued.

# QUESTIONS

1. Pat Kabza, a student, asks your help in understanding the following characteristics of a corporation: (a) separate legal existence, (b) limited liability of stockholders, and (c) transferable ownership rights. Explain these characteristics to Pat.

2. (a) Your friend T.R. Cedras cannot understand how the characteristic of corporation management is both an advantage and a disadvantage. Clarify this problem for T.R.
(b) Identify and explain two other disadvantages of a corporation.

3. (a) The following terms pertain to the forming of a corporation: (1) charter, (2) by-laws, and (3) organization costs. Explain the terms.
(b) Cary Brant believes a corporation must be incorporated in the state in which its headquarters office is located. Is Cary correct? Explain.

4. What are the basic ownership rights of common stockholders in the absence of restrictive provisions?

5. (a) What are the two principal components of stockholders' equity?
(b) What is paid-in capital? Give three examples.

6. How do the financial statements for a corporation differ from the statements for a proprietorship?

7. The corporate charter of Letterman Corporation allows the issuance of a maximum of 100,000 shares of common stock. During its first two years of operations, Letterman sold 60,000 shares to shareholders and reacquired 7,000 of these shares. After these transactions, how many shares are authorized, issued, and outstanding?

8. Which is the better investment—common stock with a par value of $5 per share or common stock with a par value of $20 per share?

9. What factors help determine the market value of stock?

10. What effect does the issuance of stock at a price above par value have on the issuer's net income? Explain.

11. Why is common stock usually not issued at a price that is less than par value?

12. Land appraised at $80,000 is purchased by issuing 1,000 shares of $20 par value common stock. The market price of the shares at the time of the

exchange, based on active trading in the securities market, is $90 per share. Should the land be recorded at $20,000, $80,000, or $90,000? Explain.

13. For what reasons might a company like IBM repurchase some of its stock (treasury stock)?

14. Wilmor, Inc., purchases 1,000 shares of its own previously issued $5 par common stock for $11,000. Assuming the shares are held in the treasury, what effect does this transaction have on (a) net income, (b) total assets, (c) total paid-in capital, and (d) total stockholders' equity?

15. The treasury stock purchased in question 14, above, is resold by Wilmor, Inc., for $12,500. What effect does this transaction have on (a) net income, (b) total assets, (c) total paid-in capital, and (d) total stockholders' equity?

16. (a) What are the principal differences between common stock and preferred stock?
    (b) Preferred stock may be cumulative or participating or both. Discuss these features.
    (c) How are dividends in arrears presented in the financial statements?

17. A preferred stockholder exercises her right to convert her convertible preferred stock into common stock. What effect does this have on the corporation's (a) total assets, (b) total liabilities, and (c) total stockholders' equity?

18. What is the formula for computing book value per share when a corporation has only common stock?

19. WAT, Inc.'s common stock has a par value of $1, a book value of $29, and a current market value of $15. Explain why these amounts are all different.

20. Indicate how each of the following accounts should be classified in the stockholders' equity section.
    (a) Common stock
    (b) Paid-in capital in excess of par value
    (c) Retained earnings
    (d) Treasury stock
    (e) Paid-in capital from treasury stock
    (f) Paid-in capital in excess of stated value
    (g) Preferred stock

# BRIEF EXERCISES

*Advantages and disadvantages of a corporation.*
(SO 1)

**BE14–1**  Tracy Bono is studying for her accounting midterm examination. Identify for Tracy the advantages and disadvantages of the corporate form of business organization.

*Closing entries for a corporation.*
(SO 2)

**BE14–2**  At December 31, Mile High Corporation reports net income of $400,000. Prepare the entry to close net income.

*Issuance of par value common stock.*
(SO 3)

**BE14–3**  On May 10, Armada Corporation issues 1,000 shares of $10 par value common stock for cash at $14 per share. Journalize the issuance of the stock.

*Issuance of no-par value common stock.*
(SO 3)

**BE14–4**  On June 1, Eagle Inc. issues 2,000 shares of no-par common stock at a cash price of $7 per share. Journalize the issuance of the shares assuming the stock has a stated value of $1 per share.

*Issuance of stock in a noncash transaction.*
(SO 3)

**BE14–5**  Spiro Inc.'s $10 par value common stock is actively traded at a market value of $14 per share. Spiro issues 5,000 shares to purchase land advertised for sale at $80,000. Journalize the issuance of the stock in acquiring the land.

*Treasury stock transactions.*
(SO 4)

**BE14–6**  On July 1, ARB Corporation purchases 500 shares of its $5 par value common stock for the treasury at a cash price of $7 per share. On September 1, it sells 300 shares of the treasury stock for cash at $10 per share. Journalize the two treasury stock transactions.

*Issuance of preferred stock.*
(SO 5)

**BE14–7**  Ozark Inc. issues 5,000 shares of $100 par value preferred stock for cash at $112 per share. Journalize the issuance of the preferred stock.

*Stockholders' equity section.*
(SO 6)

**BE14–8**  Anita Corporation has the following accounts at December 31: Common Stock, $10 par, 5,000 shares issued, $50,000; Paid-in Capital in Excess of Par Value $10,000; Retained Earnings $29,000; and Treasury Stock—Common, 500 shares, $7,000. Prepare the stockholders' equity section of the balance sheet.

*Book value per share.*
(SO 7)

**BE14–9**  The balance sheet for Loren Inc. shows the following: total paid-in capital and retained earnings $860,000, total stockholders' equity $840,000, common stock issued 44,000 shares, and common stock outstanding 40,000 shares. Compute the book value per share.

# EXERCISES

●●●●●●●●●●●●●●●●●●●●●●●●●●●●●●●●●●●●●●●●●●●●●●●●●●●●●●●●●●●●●●●●●●●

**E14–1** During its first year of operations, the Bevis Corporation had the following transactions pertaining to its common stock.

*Journalize issuance of common stock.*
*(SO 3)*

Jan. 10   Issued 80,000 shares for cash at $5 per share.

July  1   Issued 30,000 shares for cash at $7 per share.

**Instructions**
  (a) Journalize the transactions, assuming that the common stock has a par value of $5 per share.
  (b) Journalize the transactions, assuming that the common stock is no-par with a stated value of $1 per share.

**E14–2** Santiago Co. had the following transactions during the current period:

*Entries for issuance of common and preferred stock and purchase of treasury stock.*
*(SO 3, 4, 5)*

Mar.  2   Issued 5,000 shares of $1 par value common stock to attorneys in payment of a bill for $27,000 for services rendered in helping the company to incorporate.

June 12   Issued 60,000 shares of $1 par value common stock for cash of $375,000.

July 11   Issued 1,000 shares of $100 par value preferred stock for cash at $105 per share.

Nov. 28   Purchased 2,000 shares of treasury stock for $80,000.

**Instructions**
Journalize the transactions.

**E14–3** As an auditor for the CPA firm of Bell and Heft, you encounter the following situations in auditing different clients:

*Journalize noncash common stock transactions.*
*(SO 3)*

  1. The Ruth Corporation is a closely held corporation whose stock is not publicly traded. On December 5, the corporation acquired land by issuing 5,000 shares of its $20 par value common stock. The owners' asking price for the land was $120,000, and the fair market value of the land was $110,000.
  2. The Hand Corporation is a publicly held corporation whose common stock is traded on the securities markets. On June 1, it acquired land by issuing 20,000 shares of its $10 par value stock. At the time of the exchange, the land was advertised for sale at $250,000, and the stock was selling at $12 per share.

**Instructions**
Prepare the journal entries for each of the situations above.

**E14–4** On January 1, 1996, the stockholders' equity section of the Margo Corporation shows: Common stock ($5 par value) $1,500,000; Paid-in capital in excess of par value $1,000,000; and Retained earnings $1,200,000. During the year, the following treasury stock transactions occurred:

*Journalize treasury stock transactions.*
*(SO 4)*

Mar. 1   Purchased 50,000 shares for cash at $14 per share.

July 1   Sold 10,000 treasury shares for cash at $16 per share.

Sept. 1   Sold 8,000 treasury shares for cash at $13 per share.

**Instructions**
  (a) Journalize the treasury stock transactions.
  (b) Restate the entry for September 1, assuming the treasury shares were sold at $11 per share.

**E14–5** Talley Corporation is authorized to issue both preferred and common stock. The par value of the preferred is $50. During the first year of operations, the company had the following events and transactions pertaining to its preferred stock:

*Journalize preferred stock transactions and indicate statement presentation.*
*(SO 5, 6)*

Feb. 1   Issued 30,000 shares for cash at $53 per share.

July 1   Issued 10,000 shares for cash at $57 per share.

**Instructions**
  (a) Journalize the transactions.
  (b) Post to the stockholders' equity accounts.
  (c) Indicate the statement presentation of the accounts.

*Journalize conversion of preferred stock.*
(SO 5)

**E14-6** Karen Kerr Corporation has 10,000 shares of $100 par value preferred stock outstanding. Each share is convertible into 5 shares of $15 par value common stock. When the market values of the two classes of stock are $110 and $25, respectively, 3,000 shares of preferred stock are converted into common stock.

**Instructions**

(a) Journalize the conversion of the 3,000 shares.
(b) Repeat (a) assuming that market values at conversion are $105 and $25, respectively.
(c) Repeat (a) assuming each share is convertible into 8 shares of $10 par value common stock.

*Prepare correct entries for capital stock transactions.*
(SO 3, 4, 5)

**E14-7** Anita Ferreri Corporation recently hired a new accountant with extensive experience in accounting for partnerships. Because of the pressure of the new job, the accountant was unable to review what he had learned earlier about corporation accounting. During the first month, the accountant made the following entries for the corporation's capital stock:

| | | | |
|---|---|---|---|
| May 2 | Cash | 144,000 | |
| | Capital Stock | | 144,000 |
| | (Issued 12,000 shares of $5 par value common stock at $12 per share) | | |
| 10 | Cash | 600,000 | |
| | Capital Stock | | 600,000 |
| | (Issued 10,000 shares of $50 par value preferred stock at $60 per share) | | |
| 15 | Capital Stock | 14,000 | |
| | Cash | | 14,000 |
| | (Purchased 1,000 shares of common stock for the treasury at $14 per share) | | |
| 31 | Cash | 7,500 | |
| | Capital Stock | | 2,500 |
| | Gain on Sale of Stock | | 5,000 |
| | (Sold 500 shares of treasury stock at $15 per share) | | |

**Instructions**
On the basis of the explanation for each entry, prepare the entry that should have been made for the capital stock transactions.

*Answer questions about stockholders' equity section.*
(SO 3, 4, 5, 6)

**E14-8** The stockholders' equity section of Kimbria Shumway Corporation at December 31 is as follows:

| | |
|---|---|
| Paid-in capital | |
| Preferred stock, cumulative, 10,000 shares authorized, 6,000 shares issued and outstanding | $ 600,000 |
| Common stock, no par, 750,000 shares authorized, 600,000 shares issued | 1,800,000 |
| Total paid-in capital | 2,400,000 |
| Retained earnings | 1,158,000 |
| Total paid-in capital and retained earnings | 3,558,000 |
| Less: Treasury stock (10,000 common shares) | (64,000) |
| Total stockholders' equity | $3,494,000 |

**Instructions**
From a review of the stockholders' equity section, answer the following questions.

(a) How many shares of common stock are outstanding?
(b) Assuming there is a stated value, what is the stated value of the common stock?
(c) What is the par value of the preferred stock?
(d) If the annual dividend on preferred stock is $48,000, what is the dividend rate on preferred stock?
(e) If dividends of $96,000 were in arrears on preferred stock, what would be the balance reported for Retained Earnings?

*Prepare a stockholders' equity section and compute book value.*
(SO 6, 7)

**E14-9** In a recent year, the stockholders' equity section of the Aluminum Company of America (Alcoa) showed the following (in alphabetical order): Additional (paid-in) Capital $680.5,

Common stock $88.3, Preferred stock $66.0, and Retained earnings $3,750.2. All dollar data are in millions.

The preferred stock has 660,000 shares authorized with a par value of $100 and an annual $3.75 per share cumulative dividend preference. At December 31, all authorized preferred stock is issued and outstanding. There are 300 million shares of $1 par value common stock authorized of which 88.3 million are outstanding at December 31.

**Instructions**
    (a) Prepare the stockholders' equity section, including disclosure of all relevant data.
    (b) Compute the book value per share of common stock, assuming there are no pre-
        ferred dividends in arrears. (Round to two decimals.)

**E14–10**   The ledger of Mintur Corporation contains the following accounts: Common Stock, Preferred Stock, Treasury Stock—Common, Paid-in Capital in Excess of Par Value—Preferred Stock, Paid-in Capital in Excess of Stated Value—Common Stock, Paid-in Capital from Treasury Stock, and Retained Earnings.

*Classify stockholders' equity accounts.*
*(SO 6)*

**Instructions**
Classify each account using the following tabular alignment:

| | Paid-in Capital | | | |
| | Capital | | Retained | |
| Account | Stock | Additional | Earnings | Other |
|---|---|---|---|---|

**E14–11**   At December 31, Kilgora Corporation has total stockholders' equity of $3,000,000. Included in this total are Preferred stock $500,000 and Paid-in capital in excess of par value—Preferred stock $50,000. There are 10,000 shares of $50 par value 10% cumulative preferred stock outstanding. At year end, 200,000 shares of common stock are outstanding.

*Compute book value per share with preferred stock.*
*(SO 7)*

**Instructions**
Compute the book value per share of common stock, under each of the following assumptions:

    (a) There are no preferred dividends in arrears, and the preferred stock does not have a
        call price.
    (b) Preferred dividends are one year in arrears, and the preferred stock has a call price
        of $60 per share.

# PROBLEMS

**P14–1**   The Brazil Corporation was organized on January 1, 1996. It is authorized to issue 20,000 shares of 6%, $50 par value preferred stock, and 500,000 shares of no-par common stock with a stated value of $1 per share. The following stock transactions were completed during the first year:

*Journalize stock transactions, post, and prepare paid-in capital section.*
*(SO 3, 5, 6)*

  Jan. 10   Issued 100,000 shares of common stock for cash at $3 per share.
  Mar.  1   Issued 10,000 shares of preferred stock for cash at $51 per share.
  Apr.  1   Issued 25,000 shares of common stock for land. The asking price of the land was
           $90,000; the fair market value of the land was $85,000.
  May  1   Issued 75,000 shares of common stock for cash at $4 per share.
  Aug.  1   Issued 10,000 shares of common stock to attorneys in payment of their bill for
           $50,000 pertaining to services rendered in helping the company organize.
  Sept. 1   Issued 5,000 shares of common stock for cash at $6 per share.
  Nov.  1   Issued 2,000 shares of preferred stock for cash at $53 per share.

**Instructions**
    (a) Journalize the transactions.
    (b) Post to the stockholders' equity accounts. (Use J1 as the posting reference.)
    (c) Prepare the paid-in capital section of stockholders' equity at December 31, 1996.

**P14–2**   Cole William Sondgeroth Corporation had the following stockholders' equity accounts on January 1, 1996: Common Stock ($1 par) $400,000, Paid-in Capital in Excess of Par

*Journalize treasury stock transactions, post, and prepare stockholders' equity section.*
*(SO 4, 6)*

Value $500,000, and Retained Earnings $100,000. In 1996, the company had the following treasury stock transactions:

Mar. 1   Purchased 5,000 shares at $8 per share.
June 1   Sold 1,000 shares at $10 per share.
Sept. 1   Sold 2,000 shares at $9 per share.
Dec. 1   Sold 1,000 shares at $6 per share.

Cole William Sondgeroth Corporation uses the cost method of accounting for treasury stock. In 1996, the company reported net income of $50,000.

**Instructions**
(a) Journalize the treasury stock transactions, and prepare the closing entry at December 31, 1996, for net income.
(b) Open accounts for (1) Paid-in Capital from Treasury Stock, (2) Treasury Stock, and (3) Retained Earnings. Post to these accounts using J12 as the posting reference.
(c) Prepare the stockholders' equity section for Cole William Sondgeroth Corporation at December 31, 1996.
(d) On May 1, 1997, Cole William Sondgeroth Corporation retires the remaining 1,000 treasury shares. Paid-in capital applicable to the shares was $6 per share. Prepare the entry to record the retirement.

*Journalize and post transactions, prepare stockholders' equity section, and compute book value.*
*(SO 2, 3, 4, 5, 6, 7)*

**P14–3**   The stockholders' equity accounts of Chung Corporation on January 1, 1996, were as follows:

| | |
|---|---:|
| Preferred Stock (10%, $100 par noncumulative, 5,000 shares authorized) | $  300,000 |
| Common Stock ($5 stated value, 300,000 shares authorized) | 1,000,000 |
| Paid-in Capital in Excess of Par Value—Preferred Stock | 15,000 |
| Paid-in Capital in Excess of Stated Value—Common Stock | 400,000 |
| Retained Earnings | 488,000 |
| Treasury Stock—Common (5,000 shares) | 40,000 |

During 1996, the corporation had the following transactions and events pertaining to its stockholders' equity:

Feb.  1   Issued 4,000 shares of common stock for $25,000.
Mar. 20   Purchased 1,000 additional shares of common treasury stock at $8 per share.
June 14   Sold 4,000 shares of treasury stock—common for $34,000.
Sept.  3   Issued 2,000 shares of common stock for a patent valued at $13,000.
Dec. 31   Determined that net income for the year was $215,000.

**Instructions**
(a) Journalize the transactions and the closing entry for net income.
(b) Enter the beginning balances in the accounts and post the journal entries to the stockholders' equity accounts. (Use J1 as the posting reference.)
(c) Prepare a stockholders' equity section at December 31, 1996.
(d) Compute the book value per share of common stock at December 31, 1996, assuming the preferred stock does not have a call price.

*Journalize and post preferred stock transactions and prepare stockholders' equity section.*
*(SO 2, 5, 6)*

**P14–4**   Jackie Remmers Corporation is authorized to issue 10,000 shares of $100 par value, 10% convertible preferred stock and 200,000 shares of $10 par value common stock. On January 1, 1996, the ledger contained the following stockholders' equity balances:

| | |
|---|---:|
| Preferred Stock (4,000 shares) | $400,000 |
| Paid-in Capital in Excess of Par Value—Preferred | 40,000 |
| Common Stock (70,000 shares) | 700,000 |
| Paid-in Capital in Excess of Par Value—Common | 350,000 |
| Retained Earnings | 300,000 |

During 1996, the following transactions occurred:

Feb. 1   Issued 1,000 shares of preferred stock for land having a fair market value of $125,000.
Mar. 1   Issued 1,000 shares of preferred stock for cash at $120 per share.
July 1   Holders of 2,000 shares of preferred stock purchased at $110 per share converted the shares into common stock. Each share of preferred was convertible into 10

shares of common stock. Market values were: preferred stock $122 and common stock $15.

Sept. 1    Issued 400 shares of preferred stock for a patent. The asking price of the patent was $60,000. Market values were: preferred stock $125 and patent, indeterminable.

Dec. 1    Holders of 1,000 shares of preferred stock purchased at $115 per share converted the shares into common stock. Each share of preferred was convertible into 10 shares of common stock. Market values were: preferred stock $125 and common stock $16.

Dec. 31    Net income for the year was $210,000. No dividends were declared.

**Instructions**
 (a) Journalize the transactions and the closing entry for net income.
 (b) Enter the beginning balances in the accounts and post the journal entries to the stock-holders' equity accounts. (Use J2 as the posting reference.)
 (c) Prepare a stockholders' equity section at December 31, 1996.

**P14–5**    The following stockholders' equity accounts arranged alphabetically are in the ledger of Dublin Corporation at December 31, 1996:

*Prepare stockholders' equity section and compute book value.*
*(SO 6, 7)*

| | |
|---|---:|
| Common Stock ($10 stated value) | $1,500,000 |
| Paid-in Capital from Treasury Stock | 6,000 |
| Paid-in Capital in Excess of Stated Value—Common Stock | 900,000 |
| Paid-in Capital in Excess of Par Value—Preferred Stock | 280,000 |
| Preferred Stock (8%, $100 par, noncumulative) | 400,000 |
| Retained Earnings | 1,134,000 |
| Treasury Stock—Common (8,000 shares) | 88,000 |

**Instructions**
 (a) Prepare a stockholders' equity section at December 31, 1996.
 (b) Compute the book value per share of the common stock, assuming the preferred stock has a call price of $110 per share.

**P14–6**    Largent Corporation has been authorized to issue 20,000 shares of $100 par value, 10%, noncumulative preferred stock and 1,000,000 shares of no-par common stock. The corporation assigned a $2.50 stated value to the common stock. At December 31, 1996, the ledger contained the following balances pertaining to stockholders' equity:

*Prepare entries for stock transactions and stockholders' equity section.*
*(SO 3, 4, 5, 6)*

| | |
|---|---:|
| Preferred Stock | $ 120,000 |
| Paid-in Capital in Excess of Par Value—Preferred | 24,000 |
| Common Stock | 1,000,000 |
| Paid-in Capital in Excess of Stated Value—Common | 2,850,000 |
| Treasury Stock—Common (1,000 shares) | 12,000 |
| Paid-in Capital from Treasury Stock | 1,000 |
| Retained earnings | 82,000 |

The preferred stock was issued for land having a fair market value of $144,000. All common stock issued was for cash. In November, 1,500 shares of common stock were purchased for the treasury at a per share cost of $12. In December, 500 shares of treasury stock were sold for $14 per share. No dividends were declared in 1996.

**Instructions**
 (a) Prepare the journal entries for the:
   (1) Issuance of preferred stock for land.
   (2) Issuance of common stock for cash.
   (3) Purchase of common treasury stock for cash.
   (4) Sale of treasury stock for cash.
 (b) Prepare the stockholders' equity section at December 31, 1996.

# ALTERNATE PROBLEMS
••••••••••••••••••••••••••••••••••••••••••••••••••••••••••••

*Journalize stock transactions, post, and prepare paid-in capital section.*
*(SO 3, 5, 6)*

**P14–1A**    The Wetland Corporation was organized on January 1, 1996. It is authorized to issue 10,000 shares of 8%, $100 par value preferred stock, and 500,000 shares of no-par common stock with a stated value of $2 per share. The following stock transactions were completed during the first year:

Jan. 10  Issued 80,000 shares of common stock for cash at $3 per share.
Mar.  1  Issued 5,000 shares of preferred stock for cash at $104 per share.
Apr.  1  Issued 24,000 shares of common stock for land. The asking price of the land was $90,000; the fair market value of the land was $80,000.
May  1  Issued 80,000 shares of common stock for cash at $4 per share.
Aug.  1  Issued 10,000 shares of common stock to attorneys in payment of their bill of $50,000 for services rendered in helping the company organize.
Sept.  1  Issued 10,000 shares of common stock for cash at $5 per share.
Nov.  1  Issued 1,000 shares of preferred stock for cash at $108 per share.

**Instructions**
(a) Journalize the transactions.
(b) Post to the stockholders' equity accounts. (Use J5 as the posting reference.)
(c) Prepare the paid-in capital section of stockholders' equity at December 31, 1996.

*Journalize treasury stock transactions, post, and prepare stockholders' equity section.*
*(SO 4, 6)*

**P14–2A**  Rena Rhoda Corporation had the following stockholders' equity accounts on January 1, 1996: Common Stock ($5 par) $500,000, Paid-in Capital in Excess of Par Value $200,000, and Retained Earnings $100,000. In 1996, the company had the following treasury stock transactions:

Mar. 1  Purchased 5,000 shares at $9 per share.
June 1  Sold 1,000 shares at $12 per share.
Sept. 1  Sold 2,000 shares at $10 per share.
Dec. 1  Sold 1,000 shares at $8 per share.

Rena Rhoda Corporation uses the cost method of accounting for treasury stock. In 1996, the company reported net income of $50,000.

**Instructions**
(a) Journalize the treasury stock transactions and prepare the closing entry at December 31, 1996, for net income.
(b) Open accounts for (1) Paid-in Capital from Treasury Stock, (2) Treasury Stock, and (3) Retained Earnings. Post to these accounts using J10 as the posting reference.
(c) Prepare the stockholders' equity section for Rena Rhoda Corporation at December 31, 1996.
(d) On May 1, 1996, Rena Rhoda Corporation retires the remaining 1,000 treasury shares. Paid-in capital applicable to the shares was $7 per share. Prepare the entry to record the retirement.

*Journalize and post transactions, prepare stockholders' equity section, and compute book value.*
*(SO 2, 3, 4, 5, 6, 7)*

**P14–3A**  The stockholders' equity accounts of the Capozza Corporation on January 1, 1996, were as follows:

| | |
|---|---:|
| Preferred Stock (12%, $50 par cumulative, 10,000 shares authorized) | $ 400,000 |
| Common Stock ($1 stated value, 2,000,000 shares authorized) | 1,000,000 |
| Paid-in Capital in Excess of Par Value—Preferred Stock | 80,000 |
| Paid-in Capital in Excess of Stated Value—Common Stock | 1,400,000 |
| Retained Earnings | 1,816,000 |
| Treasury Stock—Common (10,000 shares) | 40,000 |

During 1996, the corporation had the following transactions and events pertaining to its stockholders' equity:

Feb.  1  Issued 20,000 shares of common stock for $100,000.
Apr. 14  Sold 6,000 shares of treasury stock—common for $28,000.
Sept.  3  Issued 5,000 shares of common stock for a patent valued at $25,000.
Nov. 10  Purchased 1,000 shares of common stock for the treasury at a cost of $6,000.
Dec. 31  Determined that net income for the year was $377,000.

The preferred stock has a call price of $55 per share and no dividends were declared during the year.

*Instructions*

(a) Journalize the transactions and the closing entry for net income.

(b) Enter the beginning balances in the accounts and post the journal entries to the stockholders' equity accounts. (Use J5 for the posting reference.)

(c) Prepare a stockholders' equity section at December 31, 1996, including the disclosure of the preferred dividends in arrears.

(d) Compute the book value per share of common stock at December 31, 1996. (Round to two decimals.)

**P14–4A** Shirley Denison Corporation is authorized to issue 10,000 shares of $100 par value, 10% convertible preferred stock and 125,000 shares of $10 par value common stock. On January 1, 1996, the ledger contained the following stockholders' equity balances:

*Journalize and post preferred stock transactions and prepare stockholders' equity section.*
*(SO 2, 5, 6)*

| | |
|---|---:|
| Preferred Stock (5,000 shares) | $500,000 |
| Paid-in Capital in Excess of Par Value—Preferred | 50,000 |
| Common Stock (70,000 shares) | 700,000 |
| Paid-in Capital in Excess of Par Value—Common | 350,000 |
| Retained Earnings | 300,000 |

During 1996, the following transactions occurred:

Feb. 1  Issued 1,000 shares of preferred stock for land having a fair market value of $125,000.

Mar. 1  Issued 1,000 shares of preferred stock for cash at $120 per share.

July 1  Holders of 2,000 shares of preferred stock purchased at $110 per share converted the shares into common stock. Each share of preferred was convertible into 8 shares of common stock. Market values were: preferred stock $122 and common stock $17.

Sept. 1  Issued 400 shares of preferred stock for a patent. The asking price of the patent was $60,000. Market values were: preferred stock $125 and patent indeterminable.

Dec. 1  Holders of 1,000 shares of preferred stock purchased at $120 per share converted the shares into common stock. Each share of preferred was convertible into 8 shares of common stock. Market values were: preferred stock $125 and common stock $16.

Dec. 31  Net income for the year was $260,000. No dividends were declared.

*Instructions*

(a) Journalize the transactions and the closing entry for net income.

(b) Enter the beginning balances in the accounts and post the journal entries to the stockholders' equity accounts. (Use J2 for the posting reference.)

(c) Prepare a stockholders' equity section at December 31, 1996.

**P14–5A** The following stockholders' equity accounts arranged alphabetically are in the ledger of Hussain Corporation at December 31, 1996:

*Prepare stockholders' equity section and compute book value.*
*(SO 6, 7)*

| | |
|---|---:|
| Common Stock ($5 stated value) | $2,500,000 |
| Paid-in Capital from Treasury Stock | 10,000 |
| Paid-in Capital in Excess of Stated Value—Common Stock | 1,500,000 |
| Paid-in Capital in Excess of Par Value—Preferred Stock | 692,000 |
| Preferred Stock (8%, $50 par, noncumulative) | 800,000 |
| Retained Earnings | 1,958,000 |
| Treasury Stock—Common (10,000 shares) | 130,000 |

*Instructions*

(a) Prepare a stockholders' equity section at December 31, 1996.

(b) Compute the book value per share of the common stock, assuming the preferred stock has a call price of $60 per share.

# ▶*B*roadening Your Perspective

## *F*INANCIAL REPORTING PROBLEM

The stockholders' equity section for PepsiCo, Inc. is shown in the Consolidated Balance Sheet in Appendix A. You will also find data relative to this problem on other pages of the appendix.

### Instructions
Answer the following questions.

(a) What is the par or stated value per share of PepsiCo's common stock?

(b) What percentage of PepsiCo's authorized common stock was issued at December 31, 1994? (Round to nearest full percentage.)

(c) How many shares of common stock were outstanding at December 31, 1994, and at December 25, 1993?

(d) What was book value per share at December 31, 1994, and at December 25, 1993? (Note: The currency translation adjustment is part of stockholders' equity.) Compare your answers with the amounts reported in the Selected Financial Data.

(e) What were the growth rates for book value (shareholders' equity) per share for 1, 5, and 10 years as shown in Selected Financial Data?

(f) What was the closing market price per share at December 31, 1994, and at December 25, 1993, as reported under Capital Stock Information?

(g) How did PepsiCo's stock performance compare with the performance of a leading financial index, Standard & Poor's 500 companies?

(h) What was the low and high quarterly cash dividend during 1994 and 1993? What significant historical facts are stated concerning PepsiCo's dividend policy?

## *D*ECISION CASE

The stockholders' meeting for Mantle Corporation has been in progress for some time. The chief financial officer for Mantle is presently reviewing the company's financial statements and is explaining the items that comprise the stockholders' equity section of the balance sheet for the current year. The stockholders' equity section of Mantle Corporation at December 31, 1996, is as follows:

| | | |
|---|---:|---:|
| Paid-in capital | | |
|   Capital stock | | |
|     Preferred stock, authorized 1,000,000 shares | | |
|       cumulative, $100 par value, $8 per share, 6,000 | | |
|       shares issued and outstanding | | $ 600,000 |
|     Common stock, authorized 5,000,000 shares, $1 par | | |
|       value, 3,000,000 shares issued, and 2,700,000 | | |
|       outstanding | | 3,000,000 |
|     Total capital stock | | 3,600,000 |
|   Additional paid-in capital | | |
|     In excess of par value-preferred stock | $ 50,000 | |
|     In excess of par value-common stock | 25,000,000 | |
|     Total additional paid-in capital | | 25,050,000 |
|     Total paid-in capital | | 28,650,000 |
| Retained earnings | | 900,000 |
|     Total paid-in capital and retained earnings | | 29,550,000 |
| Less: Common treasury stock (300,000 shares) | | 9,300,000 |
|     Total stockholders' equity | | $20,250,000 |

A number of questions regarding the stockholders' equity section of Mantle Corporation's balance sheet have been raised at the meeting.

*Instructions*

Answer the following questions as if you were the chief financial officer for Mantle Corporation.

(a) "What does the cumulative provision related to the preferred stock mean?"

(b) "I thought the common stock was presently selling at $29.75, and yet the company has the stock stated at $1 per share. How can that be?"

(c) "Why is the company buying back its common stock? Furthermore, the treasury stock has a debit balance because it is subtracted from stockholders' equity. Why is treasury stock not reported as an asset if it has a debit balance?"

(d) "Why is it necessary to show additional paid-in capital? Why not just show common stock at the total amount paid in?"

# COMMUNICATION ACTIVITY

Louis P. Brady, your uncle, is an inventor who has decided to incorporate. Uncle Lou knows that you are an accounting major at U.N.O. In a recent letter to you, he ends with the question, "I'm filling out a state incorporation application; can you tell me the difference in the following terms: (1) authorized stock, (2) issued stock, (3) outstanding stock, (4) preferred stock?"

*Instructions*

In a brief note, differentiate for Uncle Lou among the four different stock terms. Write the letter to be friendly, yet professional.

# GROUP ACTIVITY

You are employed as an auditor for the firm of Honest and Accurate. On the last two engagements you encountered the following situations:

1. Larry D. Beaty Corporation is a closely held corporation whose stock is not publicly traded. On May 15 the corporation acquired property (land and building) by issuing 20,000 shares of its $10 par value common stock. The day before the exchange, the property was advertised for sale at $260,000. This listing was based somewhat on a qualified independent appraisal of $240,000 (fair market value), with $50,000 allocable to land and $190,000 to the building.

2. Jea Nea B. Wood Corporation is a publicly held corporation whose common stock is traded on the American Stock Exchange. On September 10, it acquired land by issuing 8,000 shares of $5 par value stock. At the date of the exchange, the land was listed with a real estate firm at an advertised selling price of $175,000, and the stock was selling at $20 a share.

*Instructions*

In groups of five or six people:

(a) Discuss the approach that should be taken or the basis used when recording the above situations.

(b) Prepare the journal entry for each situation.

# ETHICS CASE

The R & D division of Simplex Chemical Corp. has just developed a chemical for sterilizing the vicious Brazilian "killer bees" which are invading Mexico and the southern states of the United States. The president of Simplex is anxious to get the chemical on the market because Simplex's profits need a boost—his job is in jeopardy because of decreasing sales and profits. Simplex has an opportunity to sell this chemical in Central American countries, where the laws are much more relaxed than in the United States.

The director of Simplex's R & D division strongly recommends further testing in the laboratory for side effects of this chemical on other insects, birds, animals, plants, and even humans. He cautions the president, "We could be sued from all sides if the chemical has tragic side effects that we didn't even test for in the labs." The president answers, "We can't wait an additional year for your lab tests. We can avoid losses from such lawsuits by establishing a separate wholly owned corporation to shield Simplex Corp. from such lawsuits. We can't lose any more than our investment in the new corporation, and we'll invest just the patent covering this chemical. We'll reap the benefits if the chemical works and is safe, and avoid the losses from lawsuits if it's a disaster." The following week Simplex creates a new wholly owned corporation called Zoebee Inc., sells the chemical patent to it for $10, and watches the spraying begin.

*Instructions*

    (a) Who are the stakeholders in this situation?

    (b) Are the president's motives and actions ethical?

    (c) Can Simplex shield itself against losses of Zoebee Inc.?

# CRITICAL THINKING

## ▶ *A Real-World Focus: Barrister Information Systems Corporation*

••••••••••••••••••••••••••••••••••••••••••••••••••••••••••••••••••••••••••••••

*Barrister Information Systems Corp. develops, assembles, markets, and services computer systems and local area networks for law firms. Headquartered in Buffalo, N.Y., it has offices in 19 U.S. cities.*

Barrister Information Systems has two classes of preferred stock—A and C—in addition to its common stock. The 1,300 shares of Series A preferred stock are nonvoting, have a 12% cumulative dividend, have liquidation preference rights over the Series C preferred stock and the common stock, and are callable by the company at any time for $1,000 per share plus cumulative unpaid dividends. Each share of Series A preferred stock is convertible into 500 shares of common stock. As of March 31, 1993, the cumulative unpaid dividends on the Series A preferred stock totaled $254,000.

*Instructions*

    (a) Should the $254,000 in dividends not paid be reported as a liability on the balance sheet?

    (b) If the par value of the Class A preferred stock is $100 per share, what dollar amount in dividends can the shareholders expect annually on the Class A preferred stock?

    (c) Are there any features that Barrister's preferred stocks do not possess?

---

**Answers to Self-Study Questions**

1. c    2. b    3. d    4. b    5. c    6. a    7. a    8. d    9. b    10. c

# The "Real Thing" in Total Return

ATLANTA, Ga. — In these days of escalating educational costs, colleges and universities rely heavily on dividend income. Many schools invest their funds in a diversified portfolio of stocks—and rely on dividend income to pay operating costs.

At Emory University in Atlanta, "the dividends we earn are used for operating the university," says Wayne Coon, who oversees the university's endowment fund, made up of bequests or gifts of stocks, bonds, real estate partnerships, and venture capital.

Many years ago, the university received a sizable gift of Coca-Cola stock. Indeed, over half of the school's endowment is made up of this one stock. The university holds over 20 million shares of the Atlanta-based soft drink company. In 1995, Coke was paying a dividend of $0.88 per share. The market price of Coke's stock was as high as $67 per share in 1995. "Our goal for the endowment is total return." The total return is dividends plus the price appreciation of the stock held as an

investment. "If we sold our Coke stock and bought, for example, telephone stock, we would increase our dividend income, but our endowment probably wouldn't grow as fast," explains Coon. He says Coke has returned about 25% per year (dividends plus price appreciation) for the past decade.

One advantage for universities is that, as nonprofit entities, they don't pay income taxes on the dividends they receive on their endowment funds. If they did, they'd receive roughly a third less income. Another good thing about dividend income: it rarely drops, unlike interest income.

"Our long-range investment goal is to beat inflation by 6 percentage points," says Coon. That means that if inflation is 4%, then the school wants to achieve a total return of 10%. ◀

# CHAPTER 15

# *C*ORPORATIONS: DIVIDENDS, RETAINED EARNINGS, AND INCOME REPORTING

▶ STUDY OBJECTIVES ◀

**After studying this chapter, you should be able to:**

1. *Prepare the entries for cash dividends and stock dividends.*
2. *Identify the items that are reported in a retained earnings statement.*
3. *Prepare a comprehensive stockholders' equity section.*
4. *Describe the form and content of corporation income statements.*
5. *Explain the concept of intraperiod tax allocation.*
6. *Indicate the statement presentation of material items not typical of regular operations.*
7. *Compute earnings per share.*

As indicated in the opening story, a corporation like Coca-Cola that is profitable distributes substantial dividends. In addition, it often reinvests a portion of its earnings in the business. This chapter discusses dividends, retained earnings, corporation income statements, and earnings per share. The content and organization of the chapter are as follows:

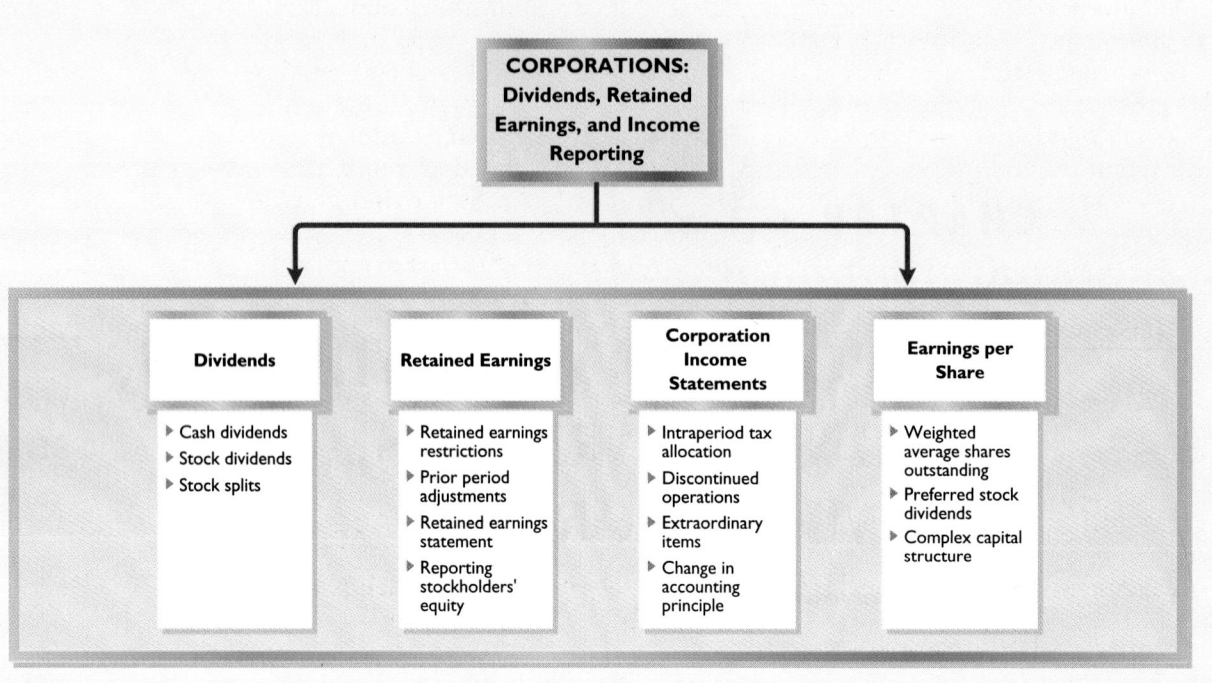

## Dividends

A dividend **is a distribution by a corporation to its stockholders on a pro rata (equal) basis.** Potential buyers and sellers of a corporation's stock are very interested in a company's dividend policies and practices. As indicated by Wayne Coon at Emory University, dividends are used to operate the university. Dividends can take four forms: cash, property, scrip (promissory note to pay cash), or (capital) stock. Cash dividends, which predominate in practice, and stock dividends, which are declared with some frequency, will be the focus of discussion in this chapter.

Dividends may be expressed as a percentage of the par or stated value of the stock or as a dollar amount per share. In the financial press, **dividends are generally reported quarterly as a dollar amount per share**. For example, Dow Chemical Company's quarterly dividend rate is 65 cents a share, J.C. Penney Company's is 42 cents, and PepsiCo's is 18 cents.

### Cash Dividends

A cash dividend is a pro rata distribution of cash to stockholders. For a cash dividend to occur, a corporation must have:

1. **Retained earnings.** The legality of a cash dividend depends on the laws of the state in which the company is incorporated. In general, cash dividends

based on retained earnings are legal, and distributions based on common stock (legal capital) are illegal. Statutory provisions vary considerably with respect to cash dividends based on paid-in capital in excess of par or stated value. Many states permit such dividends. A dividend declared out of paid-in capital is termed a *liquidating dividend*, because the amount originally paid in by stockholders is being reduced or "liquidated."

2.  **Adequate cash.** The legality of a dividend does not indicate a company's ability to pay a dividend. For example, a company such as PepsiCo, with a cash balance of $331 million and retained earnings of $7,739 million, could legally declare a dividend of $7,739 million. However, if it attempted to pay the dividend, it would need to raise additional cash through the sale of other assets or through additional financing. It follows that before declaring a cash dividend, the board of directors must carefully consider both current and future demands on the company's cash resources. In some cases, current liabilities may make a cash dividend inappropriate; in other cases, a major plant expansion program may warrant only a relatively small dividend.

3.  **Declared dividends.** The board of directors has full authority to determine the amount of income to be distributed in the form of a dividend and the amount to be retained in the business. Dividends do not accrue like interest on a note payable, and they are not a liability until declared.

The amount and timing of a dividend are important issues for management to consider. The payment of a large cash dividend could lead to liquidity problems for the enterprise. Conversely, a small dividend or a missed dividend may cause unhappiness among stockholders who expect to receive a reasonable cash payment from the company on a periodic basis. Many companies declare and pay cash dividends quarterly.

## ▶Accounting in Action ▸ *Business Insight*

In order to remain in business, companies must honor their interest payments to creditors, bankers, and bondholders. But the payment of dividends to stockholders is another matter. Many companies can survive, even thrive, without such payouts. In fact, managements might consider dividend payments unnecessary, even harmful to the company. Pay your creditors, by all means. But, fork over perfectly good cash to stockholders as dividends? "Why give money to those strangers?" is the response of one company president.

Investors must keep an eye on the company's dividend policy. For most companies, regular boosts in the face of irregular earnings can be a warning signal. So can the refusal of management to lower dividends when earnings fall or capital requirements rise. Companies with high dividends and rising debt may be borrowing money to pay shareholders. For investors who are seeking high returns on their stock investments, low dividends may mean high returns through market appreciation.

### *Entries for Cash Dividends*

Three dates are important in connection with dividends: (1) the declaration date, (2) the record date, and (3) the payment date. Normally, there is a time span of two to four weeks between each date. Accounting entries are required on two of the dates—the declaration date and the payment date.

On the *declaration date*, the board of directors formally declares (authorizes) the cash dividend and announces it to stockholders. The declaration of a cash dividend **commits the corporation to a binding legal obligation** that cannot be rescinded. Thus, an entry is required to recognize the decrease in retained earnings and the increase in the liability, Dividends Payable. To illustrate, assume that on December 1, 1996, the directors of Media General declare a 50¢ per share cash dividend on 100,000 shares of $10 par value common stock. The dividend is $50,000 (100,000 × 50¢), and the entry to record the declaration is:

**Declaration Date**

| | | | |
|---|---|---|---|
| Dec. 1 | Retained Earnings | 50,000 | |
| |     Dividends Payable | | 50,000 |
| |       (To record declaration of cash dividend) | | |

Dividends Payable is a current liability because it will normally be paid within the next several months. Instead of debiting Retained Earnings, the account Dividends may be debited. This account provides additional information in the ledger. For example, a company may have separate dividend accounts for each class of stock. When a dividend account is used, its balance is transferred to Retained Earnings at the end of the year by a closing entry. Consequently, the effect of the declaration is the same: retained earnings is decreased and a current liability is increased. For homework problems, you should use the Retained Earnings account for recording dividend declarations.

The record date marks the time when ownership of the outstanding shares is determined for dividend purposes. The stockholders' records maintained by the corporation supply this information. The time interval between the declaration date and the record date enables the corporation to update its stock ownership records. Between the declaration date and record date, the number of shares outstanding should remain the same. Thus, the purpose of the record date is to identify the persons or entities that will receive the dividend, not to determine the amount of the dividend liability. For Media General, the record date is December 22. No entry is required on this date because the corporation's liability recognized on the declaration date is unchanged:

**Record Date**

| | | | |
|---|---|---|---|
| Dec. 22 | | | |
| | No entry necessary | | |

## ▶ Technology in Action

A casual glance at *The Wall Street Journal* reveals the vast amount of stock traded on the national and regional stock exchanges. Thousands of shares of a single company's stock may change hands each day. Companies must rely on computers to keep track of the volume of transactions for both ownership and dividend purposes. With dividends, a review of the computer records on the record date would reveal which parties should receive dividend distributions in a timely fashion.

On the payment date, dividend checks are mailed to the stockholders and the payment of the dividend is recorded. Assuming that the payment date is January 20 for Media General, the entry on that date is:

**Payment Date**

| | | | |
|---|---|---|---|
| Jan. 20 | Dividends Payable | 50,000 | |
| |     Cash | | 50,000 |
| |       (To record payment of cash dividend) | | |

Note that payment of the dividend reduces both current assets and current liabilities but has no effect on stockholders' equity. The cumulative effect of the **declaration and payment** of a cash dividend on a company's financial statements is to **decrease both stockholders' equity and total assets**.

### *Allocating Cash Dividends between Preferred and Common Stock*

As explained in Chapter 14, preferred stock has priority over common stock in regard to dividends. That is, cash dividends must be paid to preferred stockholders before common stockholders are paid any dividends.

To illustrate, assume that IBR Inc. has 1,000 shares of 8%, $100 par value cumulative preferred stock and 50,000 shares of $10 par value common stock outstanding at December 31, 1996. The dividend per share for preferred stock is $8 ($100 par value × 8%), and the required annual dividend for preferred stock is $8,000 (1,000 × $8). At December 31, 1996, the directors declare a $6,000 cash dividend. In this case, the entire dividend amount goes to preferred stockholders because of their dividend preference. The entry to record the declaration of the dividend is:

| | | | |
|---|---|---|---|
| Dec. 31 | Retained Earnings | 6,000 | |
| | Dividends Payable | | 6,000 |
| | (To record $6 per share cash dividend to preferred stockholders) | | |

Because of the cumulative feature, dividends of $2 per share are in arrears on preferred stock for 1996. These dividends must be paid to preferred stockholders before any future dividends can be paid to common stockholders. As explained in Chapter 14, dividends in arrears should be disclosed in the financial statements.

At December 31, 1997, IBR declares a $50,000 cash dividend. The allocation of the dividend to the two classes of stock is as follows:

| | | |
|---|---|---|
| Total dividend | | $50,000 |
| Allocated to preferred stock | | |
| Dividends in arrears, 1996 (1,000 × $2) | $2,000 | |
| 1997 dividend (1,000 × $8) | 8,000 | 10,000 |
| Remainder allocated to common stock | | $40,000 |

**Illustration 15-1**

*Allocating dividends to preferred and common stock*

The entry to record the declaration of the dividend is:

| | | | |
|---|---|---|---|
| Dec. 31 | Retained Earnings | 50,000 | |
| | Dividends Payable | | 50,000 |
| | (To record declaration of cash dividends of $10,000 to preferred stock and $40,000 to common stock) | | |

If the preferred stock were not cumulative, preferred stockholders would have received only $8,000 in dividends in 1997 and common stockholders would have received $42,000.

## Stock Dividends

A stock dividend is a pro rata distribution of the corporation's own stock to stockholders. Whereas a cash dividend is paid in cash, a stock dividend is paid in stock. **A stock dividend results in a decrease in retained earnings and an increase in paid-in capital.** Unlike a cash dividend, a stock dividend does not decrease total stockholders' equity or total assets.

To illustrate a stock dividend, assume that you have a 2% ownership interest in Cetus Inc. by virtue of owning 20 of its 1,000 shares of common stock. In a 10% stock dividend, 100 shares (1,000 × 10%) of stock would be issued. You would receive two shares (2% × 100), but your ownership interest would remain at 2% (22 ÷ 1,100). **You now own more shares of stock but your ownership interest has not changed.** Moreover, no cash is disbursed, and no liabilities have been assumed by the corporation.

What then are the purposes and benefits of a stock dividend? Corporations issue stock dividends generally for one or more of the following reasons:

1. To satisfy stockholders' dividend expectations without spending cash.
2. To increase the marketability of its stock by increasing the number of shares outstanding and thereby decreasing the market price per share. Decreasing the market price of the stock makes it easier for smaller investors to purchase the shares.
3. To emphasize that a portion of stockholders' equity has been permanently reinvested in the business and therefore is unavailable for cash dividends.

The size of the stock dividend and the value to be assigned to each dividend share are determined by the board of directors when the dividend is declared. The per share amount must be at least equal to the par or stated value in order to meet legal requirements.

The accounting profession distinguishes between a **small stock dividend** (less than 20–25% of the corporation's issued stock) and a **large stock dividend** (greater than 20–25%). It recommends that the directors assign the **fair market value per share** for small stock dividends. The recommendation is based on the assumption that a small stock dividend will have little effect on the market price of the shares previously outstanding. Thus, many stockholders consider small stock dividends to be distributions of earnings equal to the fair market value of the shares distributed. The amount to be assigned for a large stock dividend is not specified by the accounting profession. However, **par or stated value per share** is normally assigned. Small stock dividends predominate in practice. Thus, we will illustrate only the entries for small stock dividends.

### *Entries for Stock Dividends*

To illustrate the accounting for stock dividends, assume that Medland Corporation has a balance of $300,000 in retained earnings and declares a 10% stock dividend on its 50,000 shares of $10 par value common stock. The current fair market value of its stock is $15 per share. The number of shares to be issued is 5,000 (10% × 50,000) and the total amount to be debited to Retained Earnings is $75,000 (5,000 × $15). The entry to record this transaction at the declaration date is as follows:

| | | |
|---|---:|---:|
| Retained Earnings | 75,000 | |
|    Common Stock Dividends Distributable | | 50,000 |
|    Paid-in Capital in Excess of Par Value | | 25,000 |
|      (To record declaration of 10% stock dividend) | | |

Note that Retained Earnings is debited for the fair market value of the stock issued; Common Stock Dividends Distributable is credited for the par value of the dividend shares (5,000 × $10); and the excess over par (5,000 × $5) is credited to an additional paid-in capital account.

Common Stock Dividends Distributable is a stockholders' equity account; it is not a liability because assets will not be used to pay the dividend. If a balance sheet is prepared before the dividend shares are issued, the distributable account is reported in paid-in capital as an addition to common stock issued, as shown below:

| Paid-in capital | | |
|---|---|---|
| Common stock | $500,000 | |
| Common stock dividends distributable | 50,000 | $550,000 |

When the dividend shares are issued, Common Stock Dividends Distributable is debited and Common Stock is credited as follows:

| | | |
|---|---|---|
| Common Stock Dividends Distributable | 50,000 | |
| Common Stock | | 50,000 |
| (To record issuance of 5,000 shares in a stock dividend) | | |

### Effects of Stock Dividends

How do stock dividends affect stockholders' equity? They **change the composition of stockholders' equity** because a portion of retained earnings is transferred to paid-in capital. However, **total stockholders' equity remains the same**. Stock dividends also have no effect on the par or stated value per share, but the number of shares outstanding increases and the book value per share decreases. These effects are shown below for Medland Corporation.

**Illustration 15-3**

*Stock dividend effects*

| Stockholders' equity | Before Dividend | After Dividend |
|---|---|---|
| Paid-in capital | | |
| Common stock, $10 par | $500,000 | $550,000 |
| Paid-in capital in excess of par value | — | 25,000 |
| Total paid-in capital | 500,000 | 575,000 |
| Retained earnings | 300,000 | 225,000 |
| Total stockholders' equity | $800,000 | $800,000 |
| Outstanding shares | 50,000 | 55,000 |
| Book value per share | $ 16.00 | $ 14.55 |

In this example, total paid-in capital is increased by $75,000 and retained earnings is decreased by the same amount. Note also that total stockholders' equity remains unchanged at $800,000.

## Stock Splits

A stock split, like a stock dividend, involves the issuance of additional shares of stock to stockholders according to their percentage ownership. However, **a stock split results in a reduction in the par or stated value per share.** The purpose of a stock split is to increase the marketability of the stock by lowering its market value per share. This, in turn, makes it easier for the corporation to issue additional stock. The effect of a split on market value is generally inversely proportional to the size of the split. For example, after a 4-for-1 stock split, the market value of IBM stock fell from $284 to approximately $71. In announcing the split,

**Helpful hint** A stock split changes the par value per share but does not affect any balances in stockholders' equity.

the chief executive of IBM said, "We want to make our stock more attractive to the small investor."

In a stock split, the number of shares is increased in the same proportion that par or stated value per share is decreased. For example, in a 2-for-1 split, one share of $10 par value stock is exchanged for two shares of $5 par value stock. **A stock split does not have any effect on total paid-in capital, retained earnings, and total stockholders' equity.** However, the number of shares outstanding increases and book value per share decreases. These effects are shown in Illustration 15-4 for Medland Corporation, assuming that instead of a 10% stock dividend, Medland splits its 50,000 shares of common stock on a 2-for-1 basis.

**Illustration 15-4**

*Stock split effects*

| Stockholders' equity | Before Stock Split | After Stock Split |
|---|---|---|
| Paid-in capital | | |
| Common stock | $500,000 | $500,000 |
| Paid-in capital in excess of par value | –0– | –0– |
| Total paid-in capital | 500,000 | 500,000 |
| Retained earnings | 300,000 | 300,000 |
| Total stockholders' equity | $800,000 | $800,000 |
| Outstanding shares | 50,000 | 100,000 |
| Book value per share | $16.00 | $8.00 |

Because a stock split does not affect the balances in any stockholders' equity accounts, **it is not necessary to journalize a stock split.** Significant differences between stock splits and stock dividends are shown in Illustration 15-5:

**Illustration 15-5**

*Effects of stock splits and stock dividends differentiated*

| Item | Stock Split | Stock Dividend |
|---|---|---|
| Total paid-in capital | No change | Increase |
| Total retained earnings | No change | Decrease |
| Total par value (common stock) | No change | Increase |
| Par value per share | Decrease | No change |

## *Before You Go On . . .*

### ▸ *Review It*

1. What entries are made for cash dividends on (a) the declaration date, (b) the record date, and (c) the payment date?
2. Distinguish between a small and large stock dividend and indicate the basis for valuing each kind of dividend.
3. Contrast the effects of a small stock dividend and a 2 for 1 stock split on (a) stockholders' equity, (b) outstanding shares, and (c) book value per share.

### ▸ *Do It*

Due to 5 years of record earnings at Sing CD Corporation, the market price of its 500,000 shares of $2 par value common stock tripled from $15 per share to $45. During this period, paid-in capital remained the same at $2,000,000, but retained earnings increased from $1,500,000 to $10,000,000. President Joan Elbert is considering either (1) a 10% stock dividend or (2) a 2-for-1 stock split. She asks you to show the before and after effects of each option on (a) retained earnings and (b) book value per share.

**Reasoning:** A stock dividend decreases retained earnings and increases paid-in capital, but total stockholders' equity remains the same. Because additional shares of stock are issued in the dividend, book value per share is decreased. A stock split only changes par value per share and the number of shares outstanding. Thus, this event has no effect on the retained earnings balance, and it decreases book value per share.

**Solution:**

(a) (1) The stock dividend amount is $2,250,000 [(500,000 × 10%) × $45]. The new balance in retained earnings is $7,750,000 ($10,000,000 − $2,250,000).

    (2) The retained earnings balance after the stock split is the same as it was before the split: $10,000,000.

(b) The book value effects are as follows:

| | Original Balances | After Dividend | After Split |
|---|---|---|---|
| Paid-in capital | $ 2,000,000 | $ 4,250,000 | $ 2,000,000 |
| Retained earnings | 10,000,000 | 7,750,000 | 10,000,000 |
| Total stockholders' equity | $12,000,000 | $12,000,000 | $12,000,000 |
| Shares outstanding | 500,000 | 550,000 | 1,000,000 |
| Book value per share | $24 | $21.82 | $12 |

*Related exercise material:* BE15–2, BE15–3, E15–3, E15–4, E15–5, E15–6, and E15–7.

# Retained Earnings

Retained earnings is net income that is retained in the business. The balance in retained earnings is part of the stockholders' claim on the total assets of the corporation. It does not, however, represent a claim on any specific asset. Nor can the amount of retained earnings be associated with the balance of any asset account. For example, a $100,000 balance in retained earnings does not mean that there should be $100,000 in cash. The reason is that the cash resulting from the excess of revenues over expenses may have been used to purchase buildings, equipment, and other assets. Illustration 15-6 shows the relationship of cash to retained earnings in selected companies.

**STUDY OBJECTIVE**
·········· 2 ··········
*Identify the items that are reported in a retained earnings statement.*

| Company | (In Millions) Retained Earnings | Cash |
|---|---|---|
| Amoco Corp. | $12,223 | $ 168 |
| Sears, Roebuck and Co. | 8,163 | 1,864 |
| Bob Evans Farms, Inc. | 211 | 6 |
| The Liposome Company, Inc. | (75) | 5 |

**Illustration 15-6**

*Retained earnings and cash balances*

When expenses exceed revenues, a **net loss** results. In contrast to net income, a net loss is debited to Retained Earnings in preparing closing entries. This is done even if a debit balance results in Retained Earnings. **Net losses are not debited to paid-in capital accounts.** To do so would destroy the distinction between paid-in and earned capital. A debit balance in retained earnings is identified as a deficit and is reported as a deduction in the stockholders' equity section, as shown below:

**Illustration 15-7**

*Stockholders' equity with deficit*

| Stockholders' equity | |
|---|---|
| Paid-in capital | |
| Common stock | $800,000 |
| Retained earnings (deficit) | (50,000) |
| Total stockholders' equity | $750,000 |

## Retained Earnings Restrictions

The balance in retained earnings is generally available for dividend declarations. Some companies state this fact. For example, in the notes to its financial statements, Martin Marietta Corporation states:

> At December 31, retained earnings were unrestricted and available for dividend payments.

In some cases, however, there may be retained earnings restrictions that make a portion of the balance currently unavailable for dividends. Restrictions result from one or more of the following causes: legal, contractual, or voluntary.

1. **Legal restrictions.** Many states require a corporation to restrict retained earnings for the cost of treasury stock purchased. The restriction serves to keep intact the corporation's legal capital that is temporarily being held as treasury stock. When the treasury stock is sold, the restriction is lifted.
2. **Contractual restrictions.** Long-term debt contracts may impose a restriction on retained earnings as a condition for the loan. The restriction limits the use of corporate assets for the payment of dividends. Thus, it enhances the likelihood that the corporation will be able to meet required loan payments.
3. **Voluntary restrictions.** The board of directors of a corporation may voluntarily create retained earnings restrictions for specific purposes. For example, the board may authorize a restriction for the purpose of future plant expansion. By reducing the amount of retained earnings available for dividends, more cash may be available for the planned expansion.

**Retained earnings restrictions** are generally disclosed in the notes to the financial statements. For example, Pratt & Lambert, a leading producer of architectural finishes (paint) has the following note in a recent financial statement:

**Illustration 15-8**

*Disclosure of restriction*

### PRATT & LAMBERT

**Note D  Long-term Debt and Retained Earnings**
   Loan agreements contain, among other covenants, a restriction on the payment of dividends, which limits future dividend payments to $20,565,000 plus 75% of future net income.

## Prior Period Adjustments

Suppose that after the books have been closed and the financial statements have been issued, a corporation discovers that a material error has been made in reporting net income of a prior year. How should this situation be recorded in the accounts and reported in the financial statements? The correction of an error in previously issued financial statements is known as a prior period adjustment. The correction is made directly to Retained Earnings because the effect of the error is now in this account; the net income for the prior period has been recorded in retained earnings through the journalizing and posting of closing entries.

To illustrate, assume that General Microwave discovers in 1996 that it understated depreciation expense in 1995 by $300,000 as a result of computational errors. These errors overstated net income for 1995, and the current balance in retained earnings is also overstated. The entry for the prior period adjustment, assuming all tax effects are ignored, is as follows:

| | | |
|---|---|---|
| Retained Earnings | 300,000 | |
|    Accumulated Depreciation | | 300,000 |
|      (To adjust for understatement of depreciation in a | | |
|      prior period) | | |

A debit to an income statement account in 1996 would be incorrect because the error pertains to a prior year.

Prior period adjustments are reported in the retained earnings statement.[1] They are added (or deducted) from the beginning retained earnings balance to show the adjusted beginning balance. Assuming General Microwave has a beginning balance of $800,000 in retained earnings, the prior period adjustment is reported as follows:

**Illustration 15-9**

*Statement presentation of prior period adjustments*

| (Partial) Retained Earnings Statement | |
|---|---|
| Balance, January 1, as reported | $800,000 |
| Correction for overstatement of net income in prior period | |
|   (depreciation error) | 300,000 |
| Balance, January 1, as adjusted | $500,000 |

Reporting the correction in the current year's income statement would be incorrect because it applies to a prior year's income statement.

## Retained Earnings Statement

The retained earnings statement shows the changes in retained earnings during the year. The statement is prepared from the Retained Earnings account. Transactions and events that affect retained earnings are tabulated in account form as shown in Illustration 15-10.

**Illustration 15-10**

*Debits and credits to retained earnings*

| Retained Earnings | |
|---|---|
| 1. Net loss | 1. Net income |
| 2. Prior period adjustments for overstatement of net income | 2. Prior period adjustments for understatement of net income |
| 3. Cash and stock dividends | |
| 4. Some disposals of treasury stock | |

---

[1]A complete retained earnings statement is shown in Illustration 15-11 on page 620.

As indicated, net income increases retained earnings, and a net loss decreases retained earnings. Prior period adjustments may either increase or decrease retained earnings, whereas both cash and stock dividends decrease retained earnings. The circumstances when treasury stock transactions decrease retained earnings are explained in Chapter 14. The retained earnings statement for Graber Inc., based on assumed data, is as follows:

**Illustration 15-11**

*Retained earnings statement*

| GRABER INC. Retained Earnings Statement For the Year Ended December 31, 1996 | | |
| --- | --- | --- |
| Balance, January 1, as reported | | $1,050,000 |
| Correction for understatement of net income in prior period (inventory error) | | 50,000 |
| Balance, January 1, as adjusted | | 1,100,000 |
| Add: Net income | | 360,000 |
| | | 1,460,000 |
| Less: Cash dividends | $100,000 | |
| Stock dividends | 200,000 | 300,000 |
| Balance, December 31 | | $1,160,000 |

**STUDY OBJECTIVE**

**3**

*Prepare a comprehensive stockholders' equity section.*

## Reporting Stockholders' Equity

The stockholders' equity section of the balance sheet of Graber Inc. is presented in Illustration 15-12. Note that (1) Common Stock Dividends Distributable is shown under capital stock in paid-in capital, and (2) a retained earnings restriction is disclosed in the notes.

**Illustration 15-12**

*Comprehensive stockholders' equity section*

| GRABER INC. Partial Balance Sheet | | |
| --- | --- | --- |
| Stockholders' equity | | |
| Paid-in capital | | |
| Capital stock | | |
| 9% Preferred stock, $100 par value, cumulative, callable at $120, 10,000 shares authorized, 6,000 shares issued and outstanding | | $ 600,000 |
| Common stock, no par, $5 stated value, 500,000 shares authorized, 400,000 shares issued and 390,000 outstanding | $2,000,000 | |
| Common stock dividends distributable | 50,000 | 2,050,000 |
| Total capital stock | | 2,650,000 |
| Additional paid-in capital | | |
| In excess of par value—preferred stock | 30,000 | |
| In excess of stated value—common stock | 1,050,000 | |
| Total additional paid-in capital | | 1,080,000 |
| Total paid-in capital | | 3,730,000 |
| Retained earnings (see Note R) | | 1,160,000 |
| Total paid-in capital and retained earnings | | 4,890,000 |
| Less: Treasury stock—common (10,000 shares) | | 80,000 |
| Total stockholders' equity | | $4,810,000 |

Note R: Retained earnings is restricted for the cost of treasury stock, $80,000.

▸ **International note**

In Switzerland, there are no specific disclosure requirements for shareholders' equity. However, companies typically disclose separate categories of capital on the balance sheet.

Instead of presenting a detailed stockholders' equity section in the balance sheet and a retained earnings statement, many companies prepare a stockholders' equity statement. This statement shows the changes in each stockholders' equity account and in total stockholders' equity that have occurred during the year. An example of a stockholders' equity statement is illustrated in the appendix to this chapter and in PepsiCo's financial statements in Appendix A.

## *Before You Go On . . .*

### ▶ *Review It*

1. How are retained earnings restrictions generally reported?
2. What is a prior period adjustment and how is it reported?
3. What are the principal sources of debits and credits to Retained Earnings?
4. How are stock dividends distributable reported in the stockholders' equity section?

### ▶ *Do It*

Vega Corporation has retained earnings of $5,130,000 on January 1, 1996. During the year, the company earns $2,000,000 of net income and it declares and pays a $250,000 cash dividend. In 1996, Vega records an adjustment of $180,000 that pertains to the understatement of 1995 depreciation expense due to a mathematical error. Prepare a retained earnings statement for 1996.

**Reasoning:** The $180,000 correction of 1995 depreciation is a prior period adjustment. It should be reported as a deduction from the beginning retained earnings balance. Net income is shown as an addition in the statement and dividends are deducted in the statement.

*Solution:*

**VEGA CORPORATION**
**Retained Earnings Statement**
**For the Year Ended December 31, 1996**

| | |
|---|---:|
| Balance, January 1, as reported | $5,130,000 |
| Correction for overstatement of net income in prior period (depreciation error) | 180,000 |
| Balance, January 1, as adjusted | 4,950,000 |
| Add: Net income | 2,000,000 |
| | 6,950,000 |
| Less: Cash dividends | 250,000 |
| Balance, December 31 | $6,700,000 |

*Related exercise material:* BE15–4 and E15–8.

## Corporation Income Statements

Income statements for **corporations are the same as the statements for proprietorships or partnerships except for the reporting of income taxes.** For income tax purposes, corporations are considered to be a separate legal entity. As a result, **income taxes (or income tax expense)** are reported in a separate section of the corporation income statement before net income. The condensed income statement for Leads Inc. in Illustration 15-13 shows a typical presentation. Note that income before income taxes is reported before income tax expense.

**STUDY OBJECTIVE**
••••••••• **4** •••••••••

*Describe the form and content of corporation income statements.*

**Illustration 15-13**

*Income statement with income taxes*

**Helpful hint**   Corporations may also use the single-step form of income statement discussed in Chapter 5.

| LEADS INC.<br>Income Statement<br>For the Year Ended December 31, 1996 | |
| --- | --- |
| Sales | $800,000 |
| Cost of goods sold | 600,000 |
| Gross profit | 200,000 |
| Operating expenses | 50,000 |
| Income from operations | 150,000 |
| Other revenues and gains | 10,000 |
| Other expenses and losses | 4,000 |
| Income before income taxes | 156,000 |
| Income tax expense | 46,800 |
| Net income | $109,200 |

Income tax expense and the related liability for income taxes payable are recorded as part of the adjusting process preceding financial statement preparation. Using the data above for Leads Inc., the adjusting entry for income tax expense at December 31, 1996, would be as follows:

| | | |
| --- | --- | --- |
| Income Tax Expense | 46,800 | |
|     Income Taxes Payable | | 46,800 |
|     (To record income taxes for 1996) | | |

Another illustration of income taxes is presented in the income statement of PepsiCo in Appendix A.

▶ **A**ccounting in **A**ction ▸ *Business Insight*

Net income and its components reported in the income statement measure a company's performance. The amount and trend of net income (earnings) are, therefore, of vital importance to management, stockholders, and creditors. Net income provides an indication of the amount of dividends that a company may distribute, and it results in an increase in retained earnings.

Reported net income has a major effect on the market price of a company's stock at a given point in time. For example, when IBM announced that its net income would be 7.7% lower, the price of its stock dropped $3.875 per share in one day. Conversely, when Eljer Industries Inc. (a Dallas-based maker of plumbing, heating, and ventilation products) reported a sharp improvement in its earnings, the market price of its stock increased 14% in one day.

The income statements we have studied so far provide considerable insight into a company's income-related activities. In studying such statements, the user may ask: (1) Are the results typical for this company? (2) Are the results a reasonable indicator of the company's future earnings?

To provide answers to these questions, accountants have concluded that additional sections should be added to the income statement to **report material items not typical of regular operations**. These items are reported in the income statement immediately before net income. The nontypical items include (1) discontinued operations, (2) extraordinary items, and (3) changes in accounting principle. Each item reported in the income statement should be carefully explained in the notes to the financial statements. The income statement should also report the income tax expense or savings applicable to each item, as explained in the following section.

## Intraperiod Tax Allocation ("Net of Tax")

Intraperiod tax allocation refers to the procedure of associating income taxes with the specific item that directly affects the income taxes for the period. Under intraperiod tax allocation, the applicable income tax expense or tax saving is shown for income before income taxes and each of the three nontypical items identified above. Intraperiod tax allocation provides statement users with informative disclosure as to the income tax effects on these components. The general concept is "let the tax follow the income or loss."

**STUDY OBJECTIVE**
··········**5**··········
*Explain the concept of intraperiod tax allocation.*

To illustrate the importance of intraperiod tax allocation, let's look first at the misleading results that may occur when intraperiod tax allocation is not followed. Assume that Dale Realty Corporation has income before income tax of $250,000, an extraordinary loss from a flood of $80,000, and, therefore, taxable income of $170,000. Both the extraordinary loss and taxable income are subject to a 30% tax rate. Without intraperiod tax allocation, the income statement will show:

| **Partial Income Statement** | |
| --- | --- |
| | **Without Tax Allocation** |
| Income before income taxes | $250,000 |
| Income tax expense ($170,000 × 30%) | 51,000 |
| Income before extraordinary item | 199,000 |
| Extraordinary loss from flood | 80,000 |
| Net income | $119,000 |

**Illustration 15-14**

*Income statement without tax allocation*

This presentation is misleading because income taxes are not directly related to the income or loss. The tax effects of income before income taxes and the extraordinary loss have been combined in reporting income tax expense of $51,000. Thus, income tax expense is understated $24,000 (30% × $80,000), and the effect of the extraordinary loss on net income is overstated by the same amount.

Under intraperiod tax allocation, the tax rate of 30% is applied to income before income taxes of $250,000 to show income taxes of $75,000, and the extraordinary item of $80,000 is reported net of the $24,000 tax saving, or **"net of tax,"** as shown below.

| **Partial Income Statement** | |
| --- | --- |
| | **With Tax Allocation** |
| Income before income taxes | $250,000 |
| Income tax expense ($250,000 × 30%) | 75,000 |
| Income before extraordinary item | 175,000 |
| Extraordinary loss from flood, net of $24,000 income tax saving | 56,000 |
| Net income | $119,000 |

**Illustration 15-15**

*Income statement with tax allocation*

Note that **net income remains unchanged** at $119,000 when intraperiod tax allocation is applied. However, **intraperiod tax allocation matches the tax to the items that affect the tax** and corrects the deficiencies of the first presentation.

**STUDY OBJECTIVE**

••••••••••• **6** •••••••••

*Indicate the statement presentation of material items not typical of regular operations.*

## Discontinued Operations

To downsize its operations, General Dynamics Corp. sold its missile business to Hughes Aircraft Co. for $450 million. In its income statement, General Dynamics was required to report the sale in a separate section entitled "discontinued operations."

Discontinued operations refers to the disposal of a **significant segment** of a business, such as the cessation of an entire activity or the elimination of a major class of customers. Thus, Kmart's decision to terminate its interest in four business activities including PACE Membership Warehouse, Inc., and PayLess Drug Stores Northwest, Inc., were reported as discontinued operations. On the other hand, the phasing out of a model such as the GM Chevette or part of a line of business is not considered to be a disposal of a segment.

When the disposal of a significant segment occurs, the income statement should report both income from continuing operations and income (or loss) from discontinued operations. **The income (loss) from discontinued operations consists of the income (loss) from operations and the gain (loss) on disposal of the segment.** To illustrate, assume that Acro Energy Inc. has revenues of $2.5 million and expenses of $1.7 million from continuing operations in 1996. The company, therefore, has income before income taxes of $800,000. During 1996 the company discontinued and sold its unprofitable chemical division. The loss in 1996 from chemical operations (net of $60,000 taxes) was $140,000, and the loss on disposal of the chemical division (net of $30,000 taxes) was $70,000. Assuming a 30% tax rate on income before income taxes, the income statement presentation is shown below.

**Illustration 15-16**

*Statement presentation of discontinued operations*

**Helpful hint** Observe the dual disclosures: (1) the results of operations of the discontinued division must be eliminated from the results of continuing operations, and (2) the disposal of the operation.

| ACRO ENERGY INC. Partial Income Statement For the Year Ended December 31, 1996 | | |
|---|---:|---:|
| Income before income taxes | | $800,000 |
| Income tax expense | | 240,000 |
| Income from continuing operations | | 560,000 |
| Discontinued operations | | |
| Loss from operations of chemical division, net of $60,000 income tax saving | $140,000 | |
| Loss from disposal of chemical division, net of $30,000 income tax saving | 70,000 | 210,000 |
| Net income | | $350,000 |

Note that the caption "Income from continuing operations" is used and that a section "Discontinued operations" is added. **Within the new section, both the operating loss and the loss on disposal are reported net of applicable income taxes.** This presentation clearly indicates the separate effects of continuing operations and discontinued operations on net income.

## Extraordinary Items

Extraordinary items are events and transactions that meet two conditions: they are (1) **unusual in nature and** (2) **infrequent in occurrence**. To be considered unusual, the item should be abnormal and be only incidentally related to the customary activities of the entity. To be regarded as infrequent, the event or transaction should not be reasonably expected to recur in the foreseeable future. Both criteria must be evaluated in terms of the environment in which the entity operates. Thus, Weyerhaeuser Co. reported the $36 million in damages to its timberland caused by the volcanic eruption of Mount St. Helens as an extraordinary item because the event was both unusual and infrequent. In contrast, Florida Citrus Company does not report frost damage to its citrus crop as an extraordinary item because frost damage is not viewed as infrequent. Illustration 15-17 shows the appropriate classification of extraordinary and ordinary items.

**Illustration 15-17**

*Examples of extraordinary and ordinary items*

| **Extraordinary items** | | **Ordinary items** | |
|---|---|---|---|
| 1. Effects of major casualties (acts of God), if rare in the area. |  | 1. Effects of major casualties (acts of God), frequent in the area. |  |
| 2. Expropriation (takeover) of property by a foreign government. |  | 2. Write-down of inventories or write-off of receivables. |  |
| 3. Effects of a newly enacted law or regulation, such as a condemnation action. |  | 3. Losses attributable to labor strikes. |  |
| | | 4. Gains or losses from sales of property, plant, or equipment. |  |

**Extraordinary items are reported net of taxes in a separate section of the income statement immediately below discontinued operations.** To illustrate, assume that in 1996 a revolutionary foreign government expropriated property held as an investment by Acro Energy Inc. If the loss is $70,000, before applicable income taxes of $21,000, the income statement presentation will show a deduction of $49,000 as shown in Illustration 15-18.

## ►*Accounting in Action* ► *Business Insight*

 In the recession of the early 1990s, many companies closed some of their plants and reduced the size of their work forces. The costs incurred in these activities, called plant restructuring costs, are reported as other expenses and losses in the income statement. These costs are not considered to be an extraordinary item because plant closings are neither unusual nor infrequent in many industries. Plant restructuring costs often have a significant effect on net income as illustrated by the following:

Union Pacific Corp.    $585 million after-tax charge, of which $492 million applies to the disposal of 7,100 miles of the Union Pacific Railroad.

Borden, Inc.    $71.6 million before-tax charge for business reorganization costs as well as severance, relocation, and other employee-related expenses.

**Illustration 15-18**

*Statement presentation of
extraordinary items*

| **ACRO ENERGY INC.**<br>**Partial Income Statement**<br>**For the Year Ended December 31, 1996** | | |
|---|---:|---:|
| Income before income taxes | | $800,000 |
| Income tax expense | | 240,000 |
| Income from continuing operations | | 560,000 |
| Discontinued operations | | |
|   Loss from operations of chemical division, net of $60,000 | | |
|     income tax saving | $140,000 | |
|   Loss from disposal of chemical division, net of $30,000 | | |
|     income tax saving | 70,000 | 210,000 |
| Income before extraordinary item | | 350,000 |
| **Extraordinary item** | | |
|   **Expropriation of investment, net of $21,000 income tax** | | |
|     **saving** | | 49,000 |
| Net income | | $301,000 |

As illustrated, the caption "Income before extraordinary item" is added immediately before the section for the extraordinary item. This presentation clearly indicates the effect of the extraordinary item on net income. If there are no discontinued operations, the third line of the income statement in Illustration 15-18 would be labeled "Income before extraordinary item."

If a transaction or event meets one (but not both) of the criteria for an extraordinary item, it is reported under either "Other revenues and gains" or "Other expenses and losses" at its gross amount (not net of tax). This is true, for example, of gains (losses) resulting from the sale of property, plant, and equipment, as explained in Chapter 10.

## Change in Accounting Principle

For ease of comparison, financial statements are expected to be prepared on a basis **consistent** with that used for the preceding period. That is, where a choice of accounting principles is available, the principle initially chosen should be consistently applied from period to period. A change in an accounting principle occurs when the principle used in the current year is different from the one used in the preceding year. A change is permitted, when (1) management can show that the new principle is preferable to the old principle, and (2) the effects of the change are clearly disclosed in the income statement. Examples of a change in accounting principle include a change in depreciation methods (e.g., declining-balance to straight-line) and a change in inventory costing methods (e.g., FIFO to average cost). The effect of a change in an accounting principle on net income may be significant.

When a change in an accounting principle has occurred,

1. The new principle should be used in reporting the results of operations of the current year.
2. The cumulative effect of the change on all prior year income statements should be disclosed net of applicable taxes in a special section immediately preceding net income.

To illustrate, we will assume that at the beginning of 1996, Acro Energy Inc. changes from the straight-line method of depreciation to the declining-balance method for equipment purchased on January 1, 1993. The cumulative effect on prior year income statements (statements for 1993–1995) is to increase depreciation expense and decrease income before income taxes by $24,000. Assuming a 30% tax rate, the net of tax effect of the change is $16,800 ($24,000 × 70%). The income statement presentation is shown in Illustration 15-19.

| ACRO ENERGY INC.<br>Partial Income Statement<br>For the Year Ended December 31, 1996 | | | |
|---|---:|---:|---:|
| Income before income taxes | | | $800,000 |
| Income tax expense | | | 240,000 |
| Income from continuing operations | | | 560,000 |
| Discontinued operations | | | |
|   Loss from operations of chemical division, net of | | | |
|     $60,000 income tax saving | | $140,000 | |
|   Loss from disposal of chemical division, net of | | | |
|     $30,000 income tax saving | | 70,000 | 210,000 |
| Income before extraordinary item and cumulative effect of | | | |
|   change in accounting principle | | | 350,000 |
| Extraordinary item | | | |
|   Expropriation of investment, net of $21,000 income tax | | | |
|     saving | | | 49,000 |
| **Cumulative effect of change in accounting principle** | | | |
|   **Effect on prior years of change in depreciation method,** | | | |
|     **net of $7,200 income tax saving** | | | **16,800** |
| Net income | | | $284,200 |

**Illustration 15-19**

*Statement presentation of cumulative effect of change in accounting principle*

► *Ethics note*

Changes in accounting principles should result in financial statements that are more informative for statement users. They should not be used to artificially improve the reported performance and financial position of the corporation.

The income statement for Acro Energy will also show depreciation expense for the current year. The amount is based on the new depreciation method. In this case the caption "Income before extraordinary item and cumulative effect of change in accounting principle" is inserted immediately following the effects of discontinued operations. This presentation clearly indicates the cumulative effect of the change on prior years' income. If a company does not have either discontinued operations or extraordinary items, the label, "Income before cumulative effect of change in accounting principle" is used in place of "Income from continuing operations." A complete income statement showing all material items not typical of regular operations is illustrated in the demonstration problem (p. 634–35).

► **Accounting in Action** ► *Business Insight*

Sometimes a change in accounting principle is mandated by the Financial Accounting Standards Board. An example is the change in accounting for interperiod income taxes required by Statement of Financial Accounting Standards 109. Such changes can significantly affect net income. For example, in its 1993 income statement, Consolidated Natural Gas Company reported an increase to income of $17,422,000 under "Cumulative Effect of Accounting Change." An accompanying note explained that the increase in income resulted from a required "change from the deferred method to an asset and liability approach for accounting for and reporting of income taxes."

## *Before You Go On . . .*

### ▶ *Review It*

1. What is the unique feature of a corporation income statement?
2. What is the primary objective of intraperiod tax allocation?
3. What are the similarities and differences in reporting material items not typical of regular operations?

### ▶ *Do It*

In its proposed 1996 income statement, AIR Corporation reports income before income taxes $400,000, extraordinary loss from fire $100,000, income taxes (30%) $90,000, and net income $210,000. Prepare a correct income statement showing intraperiod tax allocation, beginning with income before income taxes.

**Reasoning:**  Under intraperiod tax allocation, the income tax effect of each component is disclosed in the income statement. Thus, the extraordinary loss should be reported net of income taxes.

**Solution:**

### AIR CORPORATION
#### (Partial) Income Statement

| | |
|---|---:|
| Income before income taxes | $400,000 |
| Income tax expense (30%) | 120,000 |
| Income before extraordinary item | 280,000 |
| Extraordinary loss from fire, net of $30,000 income tax saving | 70,000 |
| Net income | $210,000 |

*Related exercise material:* BE15–5, BE15–6, BE15–7, E15–10, and E15–11.

## *E*arnings Per Share

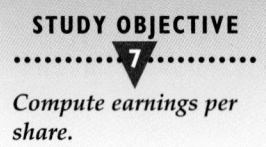

**STUDY OBJECTIVE**

**7**

*Compute earnings per share.*

Earnings per share data are frequently reported in the financial press and are widely used by stockholders and potential investors in evaluating the profitability of a company. Investors, especially, attempt to link earnings per share to the market price per share.[2] Earnings per share (EPS) indicates the net income earned by each share of outstanding common stock. Thus, **earnings per share is reported only for common stock**. The formula for computing earnings per share when there has been no change in outstanding shares during the year is as follows:

**Illustration 15-20**

*Earnings per share formula—no change in outstanding shares*

---

[2]The ratio of the market price per share to the earnings per share is referred to as the *price-earnings (P/E) ratio*. This ratio is reported in *The Wall Street Journal* and other newspapers for common stocks listed on major stock exchanges.

For example, if Modem Inc. has net income of $200,000 and 50,000 shares of common stock outstanding for the year, earnings per share is $4 ($200,000 ÷ 50,000).

Because of the importance of earnings per share (EPS), most companies are required to report it on the face of the income statement. Generally this amount is simply reported below net income on the statement. For Modem Inc. the presentation would be:

| | |
|---|---|
| Net income | $200,000 |
| Earnings per share | $ 4.00 |

**Illustration 15-21**

*Basic earnings per share disclosure*

When the income statement contains any of the three additional sections described earlier in the chapter, EPS should be disclosed for each component. Assuming that Acro Energy had 100,000 shares of common stock outstanding during the year, the additional EPS disclosures for the income statement shown in Illustration 15-19 would be as shown below.

| | |
|---|---|
| Net income | $284,200 |
| Earnings per share | |
|   Income from continuing operations | $5.60 |
|   Loss from discontinued operations | (2.10) |
|   Income before extraordinary item and cumulative effect of change in accounting principle | 3.50 |
|   Extraordinary loss | (.49) |
|   Cumulative effect of change in accounting principle | (.17) |
|   Net income | $2.84 |

**Illustration 15-22**

*Additional earnings per share disclosures*

These disclosures enable decision makers to recognize the effects on EPS of income from continuing operations, as distinguished from income or loss from material items not typical of regular operations. **Earnings per share from continuing operations is generally the most useful per share amount**, because it represents the results of continuing and ordinary business activity. Thus, it provides the best basis for predicting future operating results.

The computation of earnings per share may involve one or all of the following: (1) weighted average shares outstanding, (2) preferred stock dividends, and (3) complex capital structures.

## Weighted Average Shares Outstanding

If there has been any change in the number of shares of common stock outstanding during the year, the weighted average shares outstanding should be used in computing EPS. The **weighted average shares** are computed by determining the time a given number of shares is outstanding during the period. To illustrate, assume that Rally Inc. had 100,000 shares of common stock outstanding on January 1 and issued an additional 10,000 shares of stock on October 1. The weighted average number of shares of stock for the year is computed as follows:[3]

**Illustration 15-23**

*Computation of weighted average shares outstanding*

| | |
|---|---:|
| 100,000 shares × 9/12 of a year | 75,000 |
| 110,000 shares × 3/12 of a year | 27,500 |
| Weighted average shares outstanding | 102,500 |

**Helpful hint** If treasury shares were purchased during the year, then the weighted average shares outstanding are reduced.

The weighted average is used because the issuance or purchase of stock changes the amount of net assets that is available during the period on which to earn revenues.

## Preferred Stock Dividends

Earnings per share relates to earnings per share of **common stock**. When a corporation has both preferred and common stock outstanding, the current year's dividend declared on preferred stock is subtracted from net income to arrive at **income available to common stockholders**. Assuming weighted average common stock is involved, the formula for computing EPS is:

**Illustration 15-24**

*Expanded earnings per share formula*

To illustrate, assume that Rally Inc. reports net income of $211,000 on its 102,500 weighted average common shares. During the year it also declares a $6,000 dividend on its preferred stock. Therefore, Rally has $205,000 ($211,000 − $6,000) available for common stock dividends. Earnings per share is $2 ($205,000 ÷ 102,500). If the preferred stock is cumulative, the dividend for the current year is deducted whether or not it is declared.

## Complex Capital Structure

**Helpful hint**

Complex capital structure = Convertible securities

When a corporation has securities that may be converted into common stock, which, if converted, would reduce or dilute earnings per share, the corporation is said to have a complex capital structure. Two examples of such securities are convertible bonds (discussed in Chapter 16) and convertible preferred stock. The adverse effect that these securities can have on EPS is significant. More important, the effect of convertible securities on EPS would be unexpected unless financial statements in some manner call attention to the potential dilutive effect.

---

[3]An alternative acceptable computation of weighted average shares outstanding is:

| | | |
|---|---:|---|
| 100,000 × 12/12 = | 100,000 | shares outstanding for a full year |
| 10,000 × 3/12 = | 2,500 | shares outstanding for three months annualized |
| | 102,500 | Total weighted average shares outstanding |

Two earnings per share figures are computed and reported when convertible securities have a material effect on EPS.[4] The first EPS figure is referred to as primary earnings per share. It is based on the weighted average common shares outstanding plus shares referred to as common stock equivalents. Common stock equivalents are securities that will probably be converted into common shares. For example, convertible preferred stock might be classified as a common stock equivalent if it is likely to be converted into common stock. Special tests are used to determine whether the convertible security is in substance equivalent to common stock.

The second EPS figure, referred to as fully diluted earnings per share, assumes the maximum dilution possible. It reflects the dilution in earnings per share that would occur if *all* dilutive securities were converted into common shares. Potentially dilutive securities that are not considered a common stock equivalent for computing primary earnings per share are included for computing fully diluted earnings per share. Thus, **fully diluted earnings per share is lower than or equal to primary earnings per share**. The following excerpt from the income statement of the J.C. Penney Company illustrates the statement presentation of primary and fully diluted earnings per share.

| **J.C. PENNEY COMPANY** | |
|---|---|
| Net income (in millions) | $1,057 |
| Earnings per share | |
| Primary | $4.29 |
| Fully diluted | $4.05 |

**Illustration 15-25**

*Primary and fully diluted earnings per share disclosure*

The computations for computing primary and fully diluted earnings per share are complex; they are discussed extensively in advanced accounting courses.

## *Before You Go On . . .*

### ► *Review It*

1. Explain the components of the formula for computing earnings per share when there is only common stock and outstanding shares are unchanged during the year.
2. How are weighted average shares outstanding computed?
3. What effects may preferred stock have on the formula for computing earnings per share?
4. What is the difference between primary and fully diluted earnings per share?

### ► *A Look Back at Emory University*

To answer the following questions, refer to the opening Emory University story.

1. What kind of investments make up the endowment fund of Emory University? Of what significance to Emory's endowment fund are the Coca-Cola shares of stock?
2. Prepare the quarterly journal entry (accounts and amount) recorded by Emory University when it receives a dividend from Coca-Cola.

---

[4]The profession considers material dilutive effect to exist when the potential dilution to earnings per share is 3% or more (*APB Opinion No. 15*, "Earnings Per Share").

3. What is the "total return" on an investment? What total return does Emory University attempt to achieve on its endowment funds? What average annual total return has Emory earned on its Coca-Cola stock over the past decade?

**Solution:**

1. Emory University's endowment fund is made up of bequests and gifts of stocks, bonds, real estate partnerships, and venture capital. The Coca-Cola stock held by Emory University constitutes over half of the school's endowment. The dividend income from those shares provides Emory with approximately $17.6 (20 million × $0.88) million of cash annually.

2. At current dividend payment levels Emory receives approximately $4.4 million from Coca-Cola quarterly ($17.6 million ÷ 4). The entry to record a quarterly dividend is:

| | | |
|---|---|---|
| Cash | 4,400,000 | |
|    Dividend Revenue | | 4,400,000 |
|     (To record dividend revenue) | | |

3. The total return on an investment is the dividends received plus the price appreciation of the investment. As an investment goal, Emory University attempts to beat inflation by 6 percentage points. If inflation is 4%, then it needs a total return of 10% to achieve its 6% goal. The Coca-Cola stock has provided an average annual return of 25% for the past decade—a much more than adequate return!

# ◣ummary of Study Objectives
•••••••••••••••••••••••••••••••••••••••••••••••••••••••••••••••••••••••••••••••

**1.** *Prepare the entries for cash dividends and stock dividends.* Entries for both cash and stock dividends are required at the declaration date and the payment date. At the declaration date the entries are: Cash dividend—debit Retained Earnings and credit Dividends Payable; small stock dividend—debit Retained Earnings, credit Paid-in Capital in Excess of Par (or Stated) Value, and credit Common Stock Dividends Distributable. At the payment date, the entries for cash and stock dividends, respectively, are debit Dividends Payable and credit Cash, and debit Common Stock Dividends Distributable and credit Common Stock.

**2.** *Identify the items that are reported in a retained earnings statement.* Each of the individual debits and credits to retained earnings should be reported in the retained earnings statement. Additions consist of net income and prior period adjustments to correct understatements of prior years' net income. Deductions consist of net loss, adjustments to correct overstatements of prior years' net income, cash and stock dividends, and some disposals of treasury stock.

**3.** *Prepare a comprehensive stockholders' equity section.* A comprehensive stockholders' equity section includes all stockholders' equity accounts. It consists of two sections: paid-in capital and retained earnings. It should also include

notes to the financial statements that explain any restrictions on retained earnings and any dividends in arrears.

**4.** *Describe the form and content of corporation income statements.* The form and content of corporation income statements are similar to the statements of proprietorships and partnerships with one exception: Income taxes or income tax expense must be reported in a separate section before net income in the corporation's income statement.

**5.** *Explain the concept of intraperiod tax allocation.* Intraperiod tax allocation refers to the procedure of associating income taxes with the specific item that directly affects the income taxes for the period.

**6.** *Indicate the statement presentation of material items not typical of regular operations.* Material items not typical of regular operations are reported net of taxes in sections on the income statement immediately before net income. These items include (a) discontinued operations, (b) extraordinary items, and (c) changes in accounting principle.

**7.** *Compute earnings per share.* Earnings per share is computed by dividing net income by the number of common shares outstanding during the period. Additional problems arise when shares outstanding must be weighted and when preferred stock dividends and complex capital structures are involved.

# ▼A PPENDIX ► *Stockholders' Equity Statement*

When balance sheets and income statements are presented by a corporation, changes in the separate accounts comprising stockholders' equity should also be disclosed. Disclosure of such changes is necessary to make the financial statements sufficiently informative for users. The disclosures may be made in an additional statement or in the notes to the financial statements.

Many corporations make the disclosures in a stockholders' equity statement. The statement shows the changes in **each** stockholders' equity account and in **total** stockholders' equity during the year. As shown in Illustration 15A-1 the stockholders' equity statement is prepared in columnar form, with columns for each account and for total stockholders' equity. The transactions are then identified and their effects are shown in the appropriate columns.

In practice, additional columns are usually provided to show the number of shares of issued stock and treasury stock. The stockholders' equity statement for PepsiCo, Inc., for a three-year period is shown in Appendix A. **When this statement is presented, a retained earnings statement is not necessary** because the retained earnings column explains the changes in this account.

> **STUDY OBJECTIVE**
> •••••••••▼•••••••••
>
> *After studying this appendix, you should be able to:*
>
> 8. *Describe the use and content of the stockholders' equity statement.*

**Illustration 15A-1**

*Stockholders' equity statement*

| | HAMPTON CORPORATION Stockholders' Equity Statement For the Year Ended December 31, 1996 | | | | |
|---|---|---|---|---|---|
| | Common Stock ($5 Par) | Paid-in Capital in Excess of Par | Retained Earnings | Treasury Stock | Total |
| Balance January 1 | $300,000 | $200,000 | $650,000 | $(34,000) | $1,116,000 |
| Issued 5,000 shares of common stock at $15 | 25,000 | 50,000 | | | 75,000 |
| Declared a $40,000 cash dividend | | | (40,000) | | (40,000) |
| Purchased 2,000 shares for treasury at $16 | | | | (32,000) | (32,000) |
| Net income for year | | | 240,000 | | 240,000 |
| Balance December 31 | $325,000 | $250,000 | $850,000 | $(66,000) | $1,359,000 |

# ▼S ummary of Study Objective for Chapter 15 Appendix
•••••••••••••••••••••••••••••••••••••••••••••••••••••••••••••••••••

8. *Describe the use and content of the stockholders' equity statement.* Corporations must disclose changes in stockholders' equity accounts and may choose to do so by issuing a separate stockholders' equity statement. This statement, prepared in columnar form, shows changes in each stockholders' equity account and in total stockholders' equity during the accounting period. When this statement is presented, a retained earnings statement is not necessary.

# G LOSSARY
•••••••••••••••••••••••••••••••••••••••••••••••••••••••••••••••••••

**Cash dividend** A pro rata distribution of cash to stockholders. (p. 610).

**Change in accounting principle** The use of a principle in the current year that is different from the one used in the preceding year. (p. 626).

**Complex capital structure** A situation in which a corporation has securities outstanding that may be converted into common stock, which, if converted, would reduce or dilute earnings per share. (p. 630).

**Declaration date** The date the board of directors formally declares the dividend and announces it to stockholders. (p. 611).

**Deficit**   A debit balance in retained earnings. (p. 618).

**Discontinued operations**   The disposal of a significant segment of a business. (p. 624).

**Dividend**   A distribution by a corporation to its stockholders on a pro rata (equal) basis. (p. 610).

**Earnings per share**   The net income earned by each share of outstanding common stock. (p. 628).

**Extraordinary items**   Events and transactions that are unusual in nature and infrequent in occurrence. (p. 624).

**Fully diluted earnings per share**   An amount that shows the maximum dilution possible in earnings per share. (p. 631).

**Intraperiod tax allocation**   The procedure of associating income taxes with the specific item that directly affects the income taxes for the period. (p. 623).

**Liquidating dividend**   A dividend declared out of paid-in capital. (p. 611).

**Payment date**   The date dividend checks are mailed to stockholders. (p. 612).

**Primary earnings per share**   The amount of earnings per

share based on the weighted average common shares outstanding plus common stock equivalents. (p. 631).

**Prior period adjustment**   The correction of an error in previously issued financial statements. (p. 619).

**Record date**   The date when ownership of outstanding shares is determined for dividend purposes. (p. 612).

**Retained earnings**   Net income that is retained in the business. (p. 617).

**Retained earnings restrictions**   Circumstances that make a portion of retained earnings currently unavailable for dividends. (p. 618).

**Retained earnings statement**   A financial statement that shows the changes in retained earnings during the year. (p. 619).

**Stock dividend**   A pro rata distribution of the corporation's own stock to stockholders. (p. 613).

**Stockholders' equity statement**   A statement that shows the changes in each stockholders' equity account and in total stockholders' equity during the year. (p. 621).

**Stock split**   The issuance of additional shares of stock to stockholders according to their percentage ownership, accompanied by a reduction in the par or stated value per share. (p. 615).

# DEMONSTRATION PROBLEM

The events and transactions of the Dever Corporation for the year ending December 31, 1996, resulted in the following data:

| | |
|---|---:|
| Cost of goods sold | $2,600,000 |
| Net sales | 4,400,000 |
| Other expenses and losses | 9,600 |
| Other revenues and gains | 5,600 |
| Selling and administrative expenses | 1,100,000 |
| Income from operations of plastics division | 70,000 |
| Gain on sale of plastics division | 500,000 |
| Loss from tornado disaster (extraordinary loss) | 600,000 |
| Cumulative effect of changing from the straight line depreciation to double-declining-balance (increase in depreciation expense) | 300,000 |

Analysis reveals that

1. All items are before the applicable income tax rate of 30%.
2. The plastics division was sold on July 1.
3. All operating data for the plastics division have been segregated.
4. There were 100,000 shares of common stock outstanding during the year.

*Instructions*

Prepare an income statement for the year, including the presentation of earnings per share data.

## Solution to Demonstration Problem

**DEVER CORPORATION**
**Income Statement**
**For the Year Ended December 31, 1996**

| | | |
|---|---:|---:|
| Net sales | | $4,400,000 |
| Cost of goods sold | | 2,600,000 |
| Gross profit | | 1,800,000 |
| Selling and administrative expenses | | 1,100,000 |
| Income from operations | | 700,000 |
| Other revenues and gains | $ 5,600 | |
| Other expenses and losses | 9,600 | 4,000 |
| Income before income taxes | | 696,000 |
| Income tax expense ($696,000 × 30%) | | 208,800 |
| Income from continuing operations | | 487,200 |
| Discontinued operations | | |
|    Income from operations of plastics division, net of | | |
|      $21,000 income taxes ($70,000 × 30%) | 49,000 | |
|    Gain on sale of plastics division, net of $150,000 | | |
|      income taxes ($500,000 × 30%) | 350,000 | 399,000 |
| Income before extraordinary item and cumulative effect of | | 886,200 |
|    change in accounting principle | | |
| Extraordinary item | | |
|    Tornado loss, net of income tax saving $180,000 | | |
|      ($600,000 × 30%) | | 420,000 |
| Cumulative effect of change in accounting principle | | |
|    Effect on prior years of change in depreciation method, | | |
|      net of $90,000 income tax saving ($300,000 × 30%) | | 210,000 |
| Net income | | $ 256,200 |
| | | |
| Earnings per share | | |
|    Income from continuing operations | | $4.87 |
|    Gain from discontinued operations | | 3.99 |
|    Income before extraordinary item and cumulative effect | | 8.86 |
|      of change in accounting principle | | |
|    Extraordinary loss | | (4.20) |
|    Cumulative effect of change in accounting principle | | (2.10) |
|    Net income | | $2.56 |

**Problem-Solving Strategies**

1. Remember that material items not typical of operations are reported in separate sections net of taxes.
2. Income taxes should be associated with the item that affects the taxes.
3. A corporation income statement will have income tax expense when there is income before income tax.
4. All data presented in determining income before income taxes is the same as for unincorporated companies.

*Note: All **asterisked** Questions, Exercises, and Problems relate to material contained in the appendix to the chapter.

## SELF-STUDY QUESTIONS

Answers are at the end of the chapter.

(SO 1) 1. Entries for cash dividends are required on the:
   a. declaration date and the payment date.
   b. record date and the payment date.
   c. declaration date, record date, and payment date.
   d. declaration date and the record date.

2. Which of the following statements about small (SO 1) stock dividends is true?
   a. A debit to Retained Earnings for the par value of the shares issued should be made.
   b. A stock dividend decreases total stockholders' equity.

c. Market value per share should be assigned to the dividend shares.

d. A stock dividend ordinarily will have no effect on book value per share of stock.

(SO 2)  3. All *but one* of the following is reported in a retained earnings statement. The exception is:
a. cash and stock dividends.
b. net income and net loss.
c. some disposals of treasury stock below cost.
d. sales of treasury stock above cost.

(SO 2)  4. A prior period adjustment is:
a. reported in the income statement as a nontypical item.
b. a correction of an error that is made directly to retained earnings.
c. reported directly in the stockholders' equity section.
d. reported in the retained earnings statement as an adjustment of the ending balance of retained earnings.

(SO 3)  5. In the stockholders' equity section, Stock Dividends Distributable is reported as a(an):
a. deduction from total paid-in capital and retained earnings.
b. addition in additional paid-in capital.
c. deduction from retained earnings.
d. addition in capital stock.

(SO 4)  6. Corporation income statements may be the same as the income statements for unincorporated companies *except* for:
a. gross profit.
b. income tax expense.
c. operating income.
d. net sales.

(SO 5)  7. Intraperiod tax allocation refers to the:
a. association of income taxes with the items that directly affect the income taxes for the period.
b. allocation of income taxes to different accounting periods.

c. system of deferring income taxes to later accounting periods.
d. reporting of income taxes by interim accounting periods.

(SO 6)  8. In reporting discontinued operations, the income statement should show in a special section:
a. gains and losses on the disposal of the discontinued segment.
b. gains and losses from operations of the discontinued segment.
c. Both (a) and (b).
d. Neither (a) nor (b).

(SO 6)  9. The Rand Corporation has income before taxes of $400,000 and an extraordinary loss of $100,000. If the income tax rate is 25% on all items, the income statement should show income before extraordinary items and extraordinary items, respectively, of:
a. $325,000 and $100,000.
b. $325,000 and $75,000.
c. $300,000 and $100,000.
d. $300,000 and $75,000.

(SO 7)  10. The income statement for Nadeen, Inc., shows income before income taxes $700,000, income tax expense $210,000, and net income $490,000. If Nadeen has 100,000 shares of common stock outstanding throughout the year, earnings per share is:
a. $7.00.
b. $4.90.
c. $2.10.
d. no correct answer given.

(SO 8)  *11. When a stockholders' equity statement is presented, it is not necessary to prepare a(an):
a. retained earnings statement.
b. balance sheet.
c. income statement.
d. none of the above.

# QUESTIONS

1. (a) What is a dividend? (b) "Dividends must be paid in cash." Do you agree? Explain.

2. Robin O'Malley maintains that adequate cash is the only requirement for the declaration of a cash dividend. Is Robin correct? Explain.

3. (a) Three dates are important in connection with cash dividends. Identify the dates and explain their significance to the corporation and its stockholders.
   (b) Identify the accounting entries that are made for a cash dividend and the date of each entry.

4. NVC Inc. declares a $45,000 cash dividend on December 31, 1996. The required annual dividend on

preferred stock is $12,000. Determine the allocation of the dividend to preferred and common stockholders assuming the preferred stock is cumulative and dividends are one year in arrears.

5. Contrast the effects of a cash dividend and a stock dividend on a corporation's balance sheet.

6. Jill Simmons asks, "Since stock dividends don't change anything, why declare them?" What is your answer to Jill?

7. Pella Corporation has 10,000 shares of $10 par value common stock outstanding when they announce a 2-for-1 split. Before the split, the stock had a market price of $140 per share. After the

split, how many shares of stock will be outstanding, and what will be the approximate market price per share?

8. The board of directors is considering a stock split or a stock dividend. They understand that total stockholders' equity will remain the same under either action. However, they are not sure of the different effects of the two types of actions on other aspects of stockholders' equity. Explain the differences to the directors.

9. What is a prior period adjustment, and how is it reported in the financial statements?

10. ABC Corporation has a retained earnings balance of $240,000 on January 1. During the year, a prior period adjustment of $90,000 is recorded because of the understatement of depreciation in the prior period. Show the retained earnings statement presentation of these data.

11. What is the purpose of a retained earnings restriction? Identify the possible causes of retained earnings restrictions.

12. How are retained earnings restrictions generally reported in the financial statements?

13. Identify the events that result in credits and debits to retained earnings.

14. Omar Radhah believes that both the beginning and ending balances in retained earnings are shown in the stockholders' equity section. Is Omar correct? Discuss.

15. Ellen Nels, who owns many investments in common stock, says, "I don't care what a company's net income is. The balance sheet tells me everything I need to know!" How do you respond to Ellen?

16. What is the unique feature of a corporation income statement? Illustrate this feature, using assumed data.

17. Define the term "intraperiod tax allocation." Why is this type of allocation important?

18. Why is it important to report discontinued operations separately from income from continuing operations?

19. You are considering investing in Tracey Transportation, which reports 1996 earnings per share of $6.50 on income before extraordinary items and $4.75 on net income. Which EPS figure would you consider more relevant to your investment decision? Why?

20. Iron Inc. reported 1995 earnings per share of $3.26 and had no extraordinary items. In 1996, EPS on income before extraordinary items was $2.99, and EPS on net income was $3.49. Is this a favorable trend?

21. Indicate which of the following items would be reported as an extraordinary item in Corus Corporation's income statement.
   (a) Loss from damages caused by volcano eruption.
   (b) Loss from sale of temporary investments.
   (c) Loss attributable to a labor strike.
   (d) Loss caused when manufacture of a product was prohibited by the Food and Drug Administration.
   (e) Loss from flood damage. (The nearby Black River floods every two to three years.)
   (f) Write-down of obsolete inventory.
   (g) Expropriation of a factory by a foreign government.

22. When studying for an accounting test, a fellow student says, "Changes in accounting principle are reported in the retained earnings statement." Is your friend correct, or should he study harder?

23. Why must preferred stock dividends be subtracted from net income in computing earnings per share?

24. Jean Marin owns 100 shares of Redlands Corporation. She tells you, "The corporation earned net income of $1,000,000 and had 200,000 shares of common stock outstanding. That should be earnings per share of $5.00. But they reported primary earnings per share of $4.10 and fully diluted earnings per share of $3.69." Explain the meaning of these EPS figures to Jean.

*25. What is the purpose of a stockholders' equity statement?

# BRIEF EXERCISES

**BE15–1**  The C-B Corporation has 10,000 shares of common stock outstanding. It declares a $2 per share cash dividend on November 1 to stockholders of record on December 1. The dividend is paid on December 31. Prepare the entries on the appropriate dates to record the declaration and payment of the cash dividend.

*Prepare entries for a cash dividend.*
(SO 1)

**BE15–2**  Patina Corporation has 100,000 shares of $10 par value common stock outstanding. It declares a 10% stock dividend on December 1 when the market value per share is $15. The dividend shares are issued on December 31. Prepare the entries for the declaration and payment of the stock dividend.

*Prepare entries for a stock dividend.*
(SO 1)

*Show before and after effects of a stock dividend.*
(SO 1)

**BE15-3**   The stockholders' equity section of Mertz Corporation consists of common stock ($10 par) $1,000,000 and retained earnings $400,000. A 10% stock dividend (10,000 shares) is declared when the market value per share is $16. Show the before and after effects of the dividend on (a) the components of stockholders' equity, (b) shares outstanding, and (c) book value per share.

*Prepare a retained earnings statement.*
(SO 2)

**BE15-4**   For the year ending December 31, 1996, Maddy Inc. reports net income $182,000 and dividends $85,000. Prepare the retained earnings statement for the year assuming the balance in retained earnings on January 1, 1996, was $220,000.

*Show correct intraperiod tax allocation.*
(SO 4, 5)

**BE15-5**   An inexperienced accountant for Lima Corporation showed the following in the income statement: Income before income taxes and extraordinary item is $300,000, and Extraordinary loss from flood (before taxes) is $80,000. The extraordinary loss and taxable income are both subject to a 30% tax rate. Prepare a correct income statement using intraperiod tax allocation.

*Prepare discontinued operations section of income statement.*
(SO 5, 6)

**BE15-6**   On June 30, Osbern Corporation discontinued its operations in Mexico. During the year, the operating loss was $400,000 before taxes. On September 1, Osbern disposed of the Mexico facility at a pretax loss of $160,000. The applicable tax rate is 30%. Show the discontinued operations section of the income statement.

*Prepare change in accounting principle section of income statement.*
(SO 6)

**BE15-7**   On January 1, 1996, Shirli, Inc., changed from the straight-line method of depreciation to the declining-balance method. The cumulative effect of the change was to increase prior years' depreciation by $50,000 and 1996 depreciation by $8,000. Show the change in accounting principle section of the 1996 income statement, assuming the tax rate is 30%.

*Show earnings per share data in income statement.*
(SO 7)

**BE15-8**   Genoa Corporation's income statement shows: Income from continuing operations $580,000, Loss from discontinued operations $200,000, Extraordinary loss $80,000, and Cumulative effect of a change in accounting principle that increases net income $30,000. Show the earnings per share data in the income statement, assuming there are 100,000 shares of common stock outstanding at December 31.

*Compute earnings per share.*
(SO 7)

**BE15-9**   Darlin Corporation reports net income of $380,000 and a weighted average of 200,000 shares of common stock outstanding for the year. Compute the earnings per share of common stock.

*Compute earnings per share with cumulative preferred stock.*
(SO 7)

**BE15-10**   Income and common stock data for Darlin Corporation are presented in BE15-9. Assume also that Darlin has cumulative preferred stock dividends for the current year of $20,000 that were declared and paid. Compute the earnings per share of common stock.

*Prepare stockholders' equity statement.*
(SO 8)

*BE15-11**   On January 1, 1996, Ritz Corporation had the following stockholders' equity balances: Common Stock $200,000, Paid-in Capital in Excess of Stated Value $300,000, and Retained Earnings $250,000. During 1996, it earned net income of $90,000 and declared a cash dividend of $20,000. Prepare a stockholders' equity statement for the year.

# *E*XERCISES

∙∙∙∙∙∙∙∙∙∙∙∙∙∙∙∙∙∙∙∙∙∙∙∙∙∙∙∙∙∙∙∙∙∙∙∙∙∙∙∙∙∙∙∙∙∙∙∙∙∙∙∙∙∙∙∙∙∙∙∙∙∙∙∙∙∙∙∙∙∙∙∙∙∙∙∙∙∙∙∙∙∙∙

*Journalize cash dividends and indicate statement presentation.*
(SO 1)

**E15-1**   On January 1, Tara Corporation had 75,000 shares of no-par common stock issued and outstanding. The stock has a stated value of $5 per share. During the year, the following occurred:

Apr.  1   Issued 5,000 additional shares of common stock.
June 15   Declared a cash dividend of $1 per share to stockholders of record on June 30.
July 10   Paid the $1 cash dividend.
Dec.  1   Issued 2,000 additional shares of common stock.
      15   Declared a cash dividend on outstanding shares of $1.50 per share to stockholders of record on December 31.

**Instructions**
(a) Prepare the entries, if any, on each of the three dividend dates.
(b) How are dividends and dividends payable reported in the financial statements prepared at December 31?

**E15–2** The Omaha Corporation was organized on January 1, 1994. During its first year, the corporation issued 2,000 shares of $50 par value preferred stock and 100,000 shares of $10 par value common stock. At December 31, the company declared the following cash dividends: 1994 $6,000, 1995 $12,000, and 1996 $30,000.

*Allocate cash dividends to preferred and common stock.*
(SO 1)

*Instructions*
(a) Show the allocation of dividends to each class of stock, assuming the preferred stock dividend is 9% and not cumulative.
(b) Show the allocation of dividends to each class of stock assuming the preferred stock dividend is 10% and cumulative.
(c) Journalize the declaration of the cash dividend at December 31, 1996, under part (b).

**E15–3** On January 1, 1996, Kenya Corporation had $1,500,000 of common stock outstanding that was issued at par and retained earnings of $750,000. The company issued 50,000 shares of common stock at par on July 1 and earned net income of $400,000 for the year.

*Journalize stock dividends.*
(SO 1)

*Instructions*
Journalize the declaration of a 10% stock dividend on December 10, 1996, for the following independent assumptions:
1. Par value is $10 and market value is $16.
2. Par value is $5 and market value is $20.

**E15–4** On October 31, the stockholders' equity section of Sarah Laine Company consists of Common stock $800,000 and Retained earnings $400,000. Sarah is considering the following two courses of action: (1) declaring a 10% stock dividend on the 80,000 $10 par value shares outstanding or (2) effecting a 2-for-1 stock split that will reduce par value to $5 per share. The current market price is $14 per share.

*Compare effects of a stock dividend and a stock split.*
(SO 1)

*Instructions*
Prepare a tabular summary of the effects of the alternative actions on the components of stockholders' equity, outstanding shares, and book value per share. Use the following column headings: Before Action, After Stock Dividend, and After Stock Split.

**E15–5** On October 1, Valentino Corporation's stockholders' equity is as follows:

*Compute book value per share and indicate account balances after a stock dividend.*
(SO 1, 3)

| | |
|---|---:|
| Common stock $10 par value | $200,000 |
| Paid-in capital in excess of par value | 25,000 |
| Retained earnings | 175,000 |
| Total stockholders' equity | $400,000 |

On October 1, Valentino declares and distributes a 10% stock dividend when the market value of the stock is $18 per share.

*Instructions*
(a) Compute the book value per share (1) before the stock dividend and (2) after the stock dividend. (Round to two decimals.)
(b) Indicate the balances in the three stockholders' equity accounts after the stock dividend shares have been distributed.

**E15–6** During 1996, Kettle Corporation had the following transactions and events:

*Indicate the effects on stockholders' equity components.*
(SO 1, 2, 3)

1. Declared a cash dividend.
2. Issued par value common stock for cash at par value.
3. Completed a 3-for-1 stock split in which $15 par value stock was changed to $5 par value stock.
4. Declared a stock dividend when the market value was higher than par value.
5. Made a prior period adjustment for overstatement of net income.
6. Issued the shares of common stock required by the stock dividend declaration in no. 4 above.
7. Paid the cash dividend in no. 1 above.
8. Issued par value common stock for cash above par value.

*Instructions*
Indicate the effect(s) of each of the foregoing items on the subdivisions of stockholders' equity. Present your answer in tabular form with the following columns. Use (I) for increase, (D) for decrease, and (NE) for no effect. Item 1 is given as an example.

|  | Paid-in Capital | | Retained |
|  | Capital | | |
| Item | Stock | Additional | Earnings |
| 1. | NE | NE | D |

*Prepare correcting entries for dividends and a stock split.*
(SO 1)

**E15–7**   Before preparing financial statements for the current year, the chief accountant for DeVito Company discovered the following errors in the accounts:

1. The declaration and payment of $25,000 cash dividend was recorded as a debit to Interest Expense $25,000 and a credit to Cash $25,000.
2. A 10% stock dividend (1,000 shares) was declared on the $10 par value stock when the market value per share was $16. The only entry made was: Retained Earnings (Dr.) $10,000 and Dividend Payable (Cr.) $10,000. The shares have not been issued.
3. A 4-for-1 stock split involving the issue of 400,000 shares of $5 par value common stock for 100,000 shares of $20 par value common stock was recorded as a debit to Retained Earnings $2,000,000 and a credit to Common Stock $2,000,000.

*Instructions*
Prepare the correcting entries at December 31.

*Prepare a retained earnings statement.*
(SO 2)

**E15–8**   On January 1, 1996, Waikiki Corporation had Retained Earnings of $580,000. During the year, Waikiki had the following selected transactions:

1. Declared cash dividends $120,000.
2. Corrected overstatement of 1995 net income because of depreciation error $20,000.
3. Earned net income $310,000.
4. Declared stock dividends $60,000.

*Instructions*
Prepare a retained earnings statement for the year.

*Prepare a stockholders' equity section.*
(SO 3)

**E15–9**   The following accounts appear in the ledger of Ozabal Inc. after the books are closed at December 31.

| | |
|---|---:|
| Common Stock, no par, $1 stated value, 400,000 shares authorized; | |
| 300,000 shares issued | $  300,000 |
| Common Stock Dividends Distributable | 75,000 |
| Paid-in Capital in Excess of Stated Value—Common Stock | 1,200,000 |
| Preferred Stock, $5 par value, 8%, 40,000 shares authorized; | |
| 30,000 shares issued | 150,000 |
| Retained Earnings | 900,000 |
| Treasury Stock (10,000 common shares) | 60,000 |
| Paid-in Capital in Excess of Par Value—Preferred Stock | 244,000 |

*Instructions*
Prepare stockholders' equity section at December 31, assuming retained earnings is restricted for plant expansion in the amount of $100,000.

*Prepare a correct income statement.*
(SO 4, 5, 6)

**E15–10**   For its fiscal year ending October 31, 1996, Dave Grometer Corporation reports the following partial data:

| | |
|---|---:|
| Income before income taxes | $640,000 |
| Income tax expense (30% × $500,000) | 150,000 |
| Income before extraordinary items | 490,000 |
| Extraordinary loss from fire | 140,000 |
| Net income | $350,000 |

The fire loss is considered an extraordinary item. The income tax rate is 30% on all items.

*Instructions*
(a) Prepare a correct income statement, beginning with income before income taxes.
(b) ▭▭▭▭▷ Explain in memo form why the income statement data are misleading.

**E15–11** Dasola Corporation has income from continuing operations of $240,000 for the year ended December 31, 1996. It also has the following items (before considering income taxes): (1) an extraordinary fire loss of $60,000, (2) a gain of $50,000 on the discontinuance of a division, (3) a cumulative change in an accounting principle that resulted in an increase in prior year's depreciation of $30,000, and (4) a correction of an error in last year's financial statements that resulted in a $20,000 understatement of 1995 net income. Assume all items are subject to income taxes at a 30% tax rate.

*Prepare income statement.*
(SO 4, 5, 6)

*Instructions*
(a) Prepare an income statement, beginning with income from continuing operations.
(b) Indicate the statement presentation of any item not included in (a) above.

**E15–12** The Morse Corporation has a simple capital structure. At December 31, 1996, the company has 2,000 shares of $100 par value, 8%, preferred stock outstanding and 100,000 shares of $10 par value common stock issued. Morse's net income for the year is $600,000.

*Compute earnings per share under different assumptions.*
(SO 7)

*Instructions*
Compute the earnings per share of common stock under the following independent situations. (Round to two decimals.)

1. The dividend to preferred stockholders was declared, and there has been no change in the number of shares of common stock outstanding during the year.
2. The dividend to preferred stockholders was declared, and 20,000 shares of common stock were issued on April 1, 1996.
3. The dividend to preferred stockholders was not declared, and 10,000 shares of common treasury stock were held throughout the year. The preferred stock is cumulative.

**\*E15–13** Hartland, Inc. has the following stockholders' equity balances at January 1, 1996: Common Stock ($5 par) $600,000, Paid-in Capital in Excess of Par Value $230,000, and Retained Earnings $160,000. In 1996, the following transactions and events occurred:

*Prepare stockholders' equity statement.*
(SO 8)

1. Issued 10,000 additional shares of common stock for $80,000.
2. Declared and paid a cash dividend of $30,000.
3. Net income was $100,000.

*Instructions*
Prepare a stockholders' equity statement for the year ended December 31, 1996.

# PROBLEMS

**P15–1** On January 1, 1996, O'Brien Corporation had the following stockholders' equity accounts:

*Prepare dividend entries and stockholders' equity section.*
(SO 1, 3)

| | |
|---|---|
| Common Stock ($10 par value, 80,000 shares issued and outstanding) | $800,000 |
| Paid-in Capital in Excess of Par Value | 200,000 |
| Retained Earnings | 540,000 |

During the year, the following transactions occurred:

Jan. 15   Declared a $1 cash dividend per share to stockholders of record on January 31, payable February 15.

Feb. 15   Paid the dividend declared in January.

Apr. 15   Declared a 10% stock dividend to stockholders of record on April 30, distributable May 15. On April 15, the market price of the stock was $13 per share.

May 15   Issued the shares for the stock dividend.

July 1   Announced a 2-for-1 stock split. The market price per share prior to the announcement was $15. (The new par value is $5.)

Dec. 1   Declared a $.50 per share cash dividend to stockholders of record on December 15, payable January 10, 1994.

    31   Determined that net income for the year was $250,000.

**Instructions**

(a) Journalize the transactions and the closing entry for net income.

(b) Enter the beginning balances and post the entries to the stockholders' equity accounts. (*Note:* Open additional stockholders' equity accounts as needed.)

(c) Prepare a stockholders' equity section at December 31.

*Journalize and post transactions, and prepare retained earnings statement and stockholders' equity section.*

*(SO 1, 2, 3)*

**P15–2**  The stockholders' equity accounts of Rodriguez, Inc., at January 1, 1996, are as follows:

| | |
|---|---:|
| Preferred Stock, $100 par, 9% | $400,000 |
| Common Stock, $5 par | 900,000 |
| Paid-in Capital in Excess of Par Value—Preferred Stock | 100,000 |
| Paid-in Capital in Excess of Par Value—Common Stock | 200,000 |
| Retained Earnings | 500,000 |

During 1996, the company had the following transactions and events:

| | | |
|---|---|---|
| July | 1 | Declared a $.50 cash dividend on common stock. |
| Aug. | 1 | Discovered a $72,000 overstatement of 1995 depreciation. Ignore income taxes. |
| Sept. | 1 | Paid the cash dividend declared on July 1. |
| Dec. | 1 | Declared 10% stock dividend on common stock when the market value of the stock was $12 per share. |
| | 15 | Declared a 9% cash dividend on preferred stock payable January 31, 1997. |
| | 31 | Determined that net income for the year was $350,000. |

**Instructions**

(a) Journalize the transactions and the closing entry for net income.

(b) Enter the beginning balances in the accounts and post to the stockholders' equity accounts. (*Note:* Open additional stockholders' equity accounts as needed.)

(c) Prepare a retained earnings statement for the year.

(d) Prepare a stockholders' equity section at December 31, 1996.

*Prepare retained earnings statement and stockholders' equity section and compute earnings per share.*

*(SO 1, 2, 3, 7)*

**P15–3**  The ledger of Reno Corporation at December 31, 1996, after the books have been closed, contains the following stockholders' equity accounts:

| | |
|---|---:|
| Preferred Stock (10,000 shares issued) | $1,000,000 |
| Common Stock (400,000 shares issued) | 2,000,000 |
| Paid-in Capital in Excess of Par Value—Preferred | 200,000 |
| Paid-in Capital in Excess of Par Value—Common | 1,200,000 |
| Common Stock Dividends Distributable | 100,000 |
| Retained Earnings | 2,540,000 |

A review of the accounting records reveals the following:

1. No errors have been made in recording 1996 transactions or in preparing the closing entry for net income.
2. Preferred stock is 10% $100 par value, non-cumulative, and callable at $125. Since January 1, 1995, 10,000 shares have been outstanding; 20,000 shares are authorized.
3. Common stock is no-par with a stated value of $5 per share; 600,000 shares are authorized.
4. The January 1 balance in Retained Earnings was $2,200,000.
5. On October 1, 100,000 shares of common stock were sold for cash at $8 per share.
6. A cash dividend of $400,000 was declared and properly allocated to preferred and common stock on November 1. No dividends were paid to preferred stockholders in 1995.
7. On December 31, a 5% common stock dividend was declared out of retained earnings on common stock when the market price per share was $7.
8. Net income for the year was $880,000.
9. On December 31, 1996, the directors authorized disclosure of a $100,000 restriction of retained earnings for plant expansion. (Use Note A.)

**Instructions**

(a) Reproduce the retained earnings account (T account) for the year.

(b) Prepare a retained earnings statement for the year.

(c) Prepare a stockholders' equity section at December 31.

(d) Compute the earnings per share of common stock using the weighted average shares outstanding for the year.

(e) Compute the allocation of the cash dividend to preferred and common stock.

**P15–4** Tacoma Corporation owns a number of travel agencies and a chain of motels in the Northwest. Its condensed operating results for 1996 show the following:

*Prepare income statement with discontinued operations and an extraordinary loss, and compute earnings per share.*
*(SO 4, 5, 6, 7)*

| | |
|---|---|
| Operating revenues | $14,580,000 |
| Operating expenses | 10,600,000 |
| Income from operations | $ 3,980,000 |

An additional analysis of the data indicate that the travel agencies are very profitable but the motel chain has been unprofitable. Through September 30, the motels lost $500,000 from operating revenues of $4,200,000 and operating expenses of $4,700,000. On October 1, the motel operation was discontinued and sold at a loss of $1,200,000 before taxes. The motel operating results are included in income from operations, but the loss on disposal is not included in the operating results shown above. During the year, the corporation had other expenses and losses of $80,000, which are not included in the operating results. In November, a condemnation action was taken against the company to obtain property for a new national park. As a result, the corporation suffered an extraordinary loss of $800,000 before taxes which is not included in the operating results. The corporation is in a 30% tax bracket.

At December 31, Tacoma has 480,000 shares of $1 par value common stock outstanding, of which 120,000 were issued on September 1.

**Instructions**

(a) Prepare a condensed income statement for the year.

(b) Compute all of the earnings per share amounts that should appear on the income statement. (Round to two decimals.)

**P15–5** The ledger of Gala Corporation at December 31, 1996, contains the following summary data:

*Prepare expanded income statement and compute earnings per share data.*
*(SO 4, 5, 6, 7)*

| | | | |
|---|---|---|---|
| Net sales | $1,500,000 | Cost of goods sold | $800,000 |
| Selling expenses | 110,000 | Administrative expenses | 140,000 |
| Other revenues and gains | 40,000 | Other expenses and losses | 30,000 |

Your analysis reveals the following additional information that is not included in the above data.

1. The entire ceramics division was discontinued on August 31. The loss from operations for this division before income taxes was $150,000. The ceramics division was sold at a gain of $60,000 before income taxes.

2. On July 12, a fire occurred in one plant that resulted in an extraordinary loss of $70,000 before income taxes.

3. During the year, Gala changed its depreciation method from straight-line to declining balance. The cumulative effect of the change on prior years' net income was a decrease of $30,000 before taxes. (Assume that depreciation under the new method is correctly included in the ledger data.)

4. The income tax rate on all items is 30%.

**Instructions**

(a) Prepare an income statement for the year ended December 31, 1996, using the format illustrated in the demonstration problem.

(b) Prepare the earnings per share data that should appear in the income statement, assuming there were 100,000 shares of common stock outstanding throughout the year.

**\*P15–6** On January 1, 1996, Cedeno Inc. had the following stockholders' equity balances:

*Prepare stockholders' equity statement.*
*(SO 8)*

| | |
|---|---|
| Common Stock (500,000 shares issued) | $1,000,000 |
| Paid-in Capital in Excess of Par Value | 500,000 |
| Stock Dividends Distributable | 100,000 |
| Retained Earnings | 600,000 |

During 1996, the following transactions and events occurred:

1. Issued 50,000 shares of $2 par value common stock as a result of 10% stock dividend declared on December 15, 1995.
2. Issued 30,000 shares of common stock for cash at $5 per share.
3. Purchased 20,000 shares of common stock for the treasury at $6 per share.
4. Declared and paid a cash dividend of $100,000.
5. Sold 5,000 shares of treasury stock for cash at $6 per share.
6. Earned net income of $300,000.

*Instructions*
Prepare a stockholders' equity statement for the year.

# ALTERNATE PROBLEMS

*Prepare dividend entries and stockholders' equity section.*
(SO 1, 3)

**P15–1A**  On January 1, 1996, Stengel Corporation had the following stockholders' equity accounts:

| | |
|---|---:|
| Common Stock ($20 par value, 60,000 shares issued and outstanding) | $1,200,000 |
| Paid-in Capital in Excess of Par Value | 200,000 |
| Retained Earnings | 500,000 |

During the year, the following transactions occurred:

Feb.  1  Declared a $1 cash dividend per share to stockholders of record on February 15, payable March 1.

Mar.  1  Paid the dividend declared in February.

Apr.  1  Announced a 4 for 1 stock split. Prior to the split, the market price per share was $36.

July  1  Declared a 5% stock dividend to stockholders of record on July 15, distributable July 31. On July 1, the market price of the stock was $13 per share.

 31  Issued the shares for the stock dividend.

Dec.  1  Declared a $.50 per share dividend to stockholders of record on December 15, payable January 5, 1994.

 31  Determined that net income for the year was $350,000.

*Instructions*
(a) Journalize the transactions and the closing entry for net income.
(b) Enter the beginning balances and post the entries to the stockholders' equity accounts. (*Note:* Open additional stockholders' equity accounts as needed.)
(c) Prepare a stockholders' equity section at December 31.

*Journalize and post transactions, and prepare retained earnings statement and stockholders' equity section.*
(SO 1, 2, 3)

**P15–2A**  The stockholders' equity accounts of Fryman Company at January 1, 1996, are as follows:

| | |
|---|---:|
| Preferred Stock, 9%, $50 par | $300,000 |
| Common Stock, $2 par | 500,000 |
| Paid-in Capital in Excess of Par Value—Preferred Stock | 200,000 |
| Paid-in Capital in Excess of Par Value—Common Stock | 300,000 |
| Retained Earnings | 600,000 |

During 1996, the company had the following transactions and events:

July  1  Declared a $.50 cash dividend on common stock.

Aug.  1  Discovered $45,000 understatement of 1995 depreciation. Ignore income taxes.

Sept.  1  Paid the cash dividend declared on July 1.

Dec.  1  Declared 10% stock dividend on common stock when the market value of the stock was $18 per share.

 15  Declared a 9% cash dividend on preferred stock payable January 15, 1997.

 31  Determined that net income for the year was $385,000.

 31  Recognized a $200,000 restriction of retained earnings for plant expansion.

that at December 31, of the current year, there were 25,554,627 shares of common stock issued and 352,396 shares of common stock held in the treasury.

*Instructions*
   (a) Present the earnings per share data for the company for each year.
   (b) Comment on the relative importance of material nontypical items in each year.
   (c) Prepare a retained earning statement for the current year.
   (d) What was the total dividend per share of common stock for the current year?

# DECISION CASE

General Dynamics develops, produces, and supports innovative, reliable, and highly sophisticated military and commercial products. In July of a recent year, the corporation announced that its Quincy Shipbuilding Division (Quincy) will be closed following the completion of the Maritime Prepositioning Ship construction program.

Prior to discontinuance, the operating results of Quincy were net sales $246.8 million, income from operations before income taxes $28.3 million, and income taxes $12.5 million. The corporation's loss on disposition of Quincy was $5.0 million, net of $4.3 million income tax benefits.

From its other operating activities, General Dynamics' financial results were net sales $8,163.8 million, cost of goods sold $6,958.8 million, and selling and administrative expenses $537.0 million. In addition, the corporation had interest expense of $17.2 million and interest revenue of $3.6 million. Income taxes were $282.9 million.

General Dynamics had an average of 42.3 million shares of common stock outstanding during the year.

*Instructions*
   (a) Prepare the income statement for the year, assuming that the year ended on December 31, 1996. Show earnings per share data on the income statement. All dollars should be stated in millions, except for per share amounts. (For example, $8 million would be shown as $8.0.)
   (b) In the preceding year, Quincy's earnings were $51.6 million before income taxes of $22.8 million. For comparative purposes, General Dynamics reported earnings per share of $0.61 from discontinued operations for Quincy in the preceding year.
      1. What was the average number of common shares outstanding during the preceding year?
      2. If earnings per share from continuing operations was $7.47, what was income from continuing operations during the preceding year? (Round to two decimals.)

# COMMUNICATION ACTIVITY

In the past year, Alameda Corporation declared a 10% stock dividend, and Butte, Inc., announced a 2-for-1 stock split. Your parents own 100 shares of each company's $50 par value common stock. During a recent phone call, your parents ask you, as an accounting student, to explain the difference between the two events.

*Instructions*
Write a letter to your parents that explains the effects of the two events to them as stockholders and the effects of each event on the financial statements of each corporation.

# GROUP ACTIVITY

Among the topics explained in this chapter are (1) prior period adjustments, (2) retained earnings restrictions, (3) intraperiod tax allocation, (4) discontinued operations, (5) extraordinary items, and (6) change in an accounting principle.

*Instructions*
With the class divided into six groups, each group should choose one of the above topics. Each group is to explain its assigned topic to the class and to illustrate how the topic is reported in the financial statements of a corporation.

# ETHICS CASE

Flambeau Corporation has paid 60 consecutive quarterly cash dividends (15 years). The last six months, however, have been a real cash drain on the company, as profit margins have been greatly narrowed by increasing competition. With a cash balance sufficient to meet only day-to-day operating needs, the president, Vince Ramsey, has decided that a stock dividend instead of a cash dividend should be declared. He tells Flambeau's financial vice-president, Janice Rahn, to issue a press release stating that the company is extending its consecutive dividend record with the issuance of a 5% stock dividend. "Write the press release convincing the stockholders that the stock dividend is just as good as a cash dividend," he orders. "Just watch our stock rise when we announce the stock dividend; it must be a good thing if that happens."

*Instructions*
   (a) Who are the stakeholders in this situation?
   (b) Is there anything unethical about Ramsey's intentions or actions?
   (c) What is the effect of a stock dividend on a corporation's stockholders' equity accounts? Which would you rather receive as a stockholder—a cash dividend or a stock dividend? Why?

# CRITICAL THINKING
## ► *A Real-World Focus: Diebold, Inc.*

*Diebold, Incorporated, is a world leader in financial self-service transaction systems, security products, and customer service. The company develops, manufactures, sells, and services automated teller machines (ATMs), electronic and physical security systems, and bank facility equipment. It also designs and markets related application software and integrated systems for global financial and commercial markets. Headquartered in Canton, Ohio, Diebold has offices in five countries and manufacturing facilities in the United States and in China.*

The following note related to stockholders' equity was recently reported in Diebold's annual report:

On February 1, 1994, the Board of Directors declared a 3-for-2 stock split, distributed on February 22, 1994, to shareholders of record on February 10, 1994. Accordingly, all numbers of common shares, except authorized shares and treasury shares, and all per share data have been restated to reflect this stock split in addition to the 3-for-2 stock split declared on January 27, 1993, distributed on February 26, 1993, to shareholders of record on February 10, 1993.
   On the basis of amounts declared and paid, the annualized quarterly dividends per share were $0.80 in 1993, $0.75 in 1992, and $0.71 in 1991.

*Instructions*
   (a) What is the significance of the date of record and the date of distribution?
   (b) Why might Diebold have declared a 3-for-2 stock split?
   (c) What impact does Diebold's stock split have on (1) total stockholders' equity; (2) total par value; (3) outstanding shares, and (4) book value per share?

*Answers to Self-Study Questions*
   1. a    2. c    3. d    4. b    5. d    6. b    7. a    8. c    9. d    10. b    11. a

# UK Builds with Bonds

LEXINGTON, Ky. — Every year, hundreds of college campuses around the country build new buildings. Where do most schools get the money for these expensive projects? From long-term bonds, which are obligations in which the issuer of the bond promises to repay the loan amount plus interest on or before a specified date.

The University of Kentucky (UK) has issued "revenue" bonds to build buildings on the 23,000-student Lexington campus, and on 14 community colleges throughout the state. These bonds pledge the school's revenues as collateral to guarantee payment of the bonds. Recently the outstanding debt on the Lexington campus buildings was $137 million. The total debt on the community college buildings equaled $121 million. The interest rates on the bonds range from 3% (issued in 1970 and guaranteed by a federal program) to 9% (issued in 1983). The bonds generally have maturities ranging from 10 to 20 years.

Additional "guarantees" for bond purchasers are the ratings given the bonds by professional rating agencies. "Our bonds are rated AA − by Standard & Poor's Corp.," says Henry Clay Owen, UK's treasurer. "That's well above investment grade," he says. "We always have a very good market for our bonds. People in Kentucky identify very closely with the university. Even though the bonds are rated AA −, they trade at AAA [the top bond rating] because they're so easy to sell."

One advantage for investors: the bonds are exempt from federal income tax and from state tax for in-state investors. So, an issue offering 6% is the equivalent of 10% to those individuals in the top tax bracket. "I would feel very comfortable buying UK bonds because it's inconceivable to me that there would ever be a default," says Owen. ◀

# CHAPTER 16

# *L*ONG-TERM LIABILITIES

**After studying this chapter, you should be able to:**

1. *Explain why bonds are issued.*
2. *Prepare the entries for the issuance of bonds and interest expense.*
3. *Describe the entries when bonds are redeemed or converted.*
4. *Indicate the entries required for a bond sinking fund.*
5. *Describe the accounting for long-term notes payable.*
6. *Contrast the accounting for operating and capital leases.*
7. *Identify the requirements for the financial statement presentation of long-term liabilities.*

As you can see from the opening story, the University of Kentucky has chosen to issue long-term bonds to fund its building projects. The UK bonds are classified as long-term liabilities because they are obligations that are expected to be paid after one year. In this chapter we will explain the accounting for the major types of long-term liabilities reported on the balance sheet. These liabilities may be bonds, long-term notes, or lease obligations. The content and organization of the chapter are as follows:

## *B*ond Basics

**STUDY OBJECTIVE**
••••••••••▼••••••••••
*Explain why bonds are issued.*

Bonds are a form of interest bearing notes payable issued by corporations, universities, and governmental agencies. Bonds, like common stock, are sold in small denominations (usually a thousand dollars or multiples of a thousand dollars). As a result, bonds attract many investors.

### Why Issue Bonds?

A corporation may use long-term financing other than bonds, such as notes payable and leasing. However, these other forms of financing involve one individual, one company, or a financial institution. Notes payable and leasing are therefore seldom sufficient to furnish the funds needed for plant expansion and major projects like new buildings. To obtain **large amounts of long-term capital**, corporate management usually must decide whether to issue bonds or to use equity financing (common stock).

From the standpoint of the corporation seeking long-term financing, bonds offer the following advantages over common stock:

**Illustration 16-1**

*Advantages of bond financing over common stock*

| Bond Financing | Advantages |
|---|---|
| | 1. **Stockholder control is not affected.**<br>Bondholders do not have voting rights, so current owners (stockholders) retain full control of the company. |
| | 2. **Tax savings result.**<br>Bond interest is deductible for tax purposes; dividends on stock are not. |
| | 3. **Earnings per share on common stock may be higher.**<br>Although bond interest expense reduces net income, earnings per share on common stock often is higher under bond financing because no additional shares of common stock are issued. |

To illustrate the potential effect on earnings per share, assume that Micro-systems, Inc., is considering two plans for financing the construction of a new $5 million plant: Plan A involves issuance of 200,000 shares of common stock at the current market price of $25 per share. Plan B involves issuance of $5 million, 12% bonds at face value. Income before interest and taxes on the new plant will be $1.5 million; income taxes are expected to be 30%. Microsystems currently has 100,000 shares of common stock outstanding. The alternative effects on earnings per share are shown in Illustration 16-2.

**Helpful hint** If a company can earn 15% on money obtained from issuing $1,000,000 bonds at 12%, income before taxes will increase $30,000 (3% × $1,000,000). This phenomenon, known as **leveraging or trading on the equity**, is discussed further in Chapter 19.

**Illustration 16-2**

*Effects on earnings per share—stocks vs. bonds*

| | Plan A<br>Issue stock | Plan B<br>Issue bonds |
|---|---|---|
| Income before interest and taxes | $1,500,000 | $1,500,000 |
| Interest (12% × $5,000,000) | — | 600,000 |
| Income before income taxes | 1,500,000 | 900,000 |
| Income tax expense (30%) | 450,000 | 270,000 |
| Net income | $1,050,000 | $ 630,000 |
| Outstanding shares | 300,000 | 100,000 |
| Earnings per share | $ 3.50 | $ 6.30 |

**Helpful hint** Most corporations have both stock and bonds outstanding.

► **International note**

The priority of bondholders' versus stockholders' rights varies across countries. In Japan, Germany, and France stockholders and employees are given priority, with liquidation of the firm to pay creditors seen as a last resort. In Britain creditors interests are put first—the courts are quick to give control of the firm to creditors.

Note that net income is $420,000 ($1,050,000 − $630,000) less with long-term debt financing (bonds). However, earnings per share is higher because there are 200,000 fewer shares of common stock outstanding.

**The major disadvantages resulting from the use of bonds are that interest must be paid on a periodic basis and the principal (face value) of the bonds must be paid at maturity.** A company with fluctuating earnings and a relatively weak cash position may experience great difficulty in meeting interest requirements in periods of low earnings.

## ▸Accounting in Action ▸ *Business Insight*

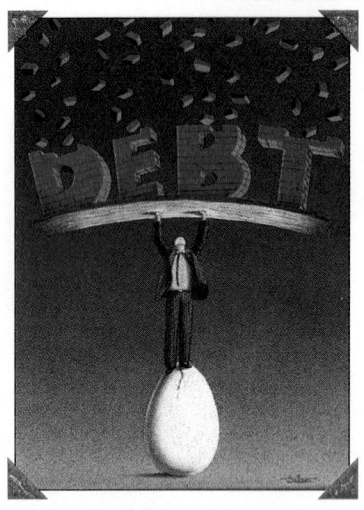

Our discussion of long-term liability in this chapter is relatively traditional. However, it is important to understand that we saw in the late 1980s the leveraging (debt financing) of corporate America. A spectacular group of characters invented ways to take over some of the largest and most prestigious companies in America through the use of debt. Names such as Boone Pickens, Ivan Boesky, Michael Milken, and Carl Icahn became familiar to all those involved in high finance. An obscure firm at one time, Kohlberg Kravis Roberts & Co. (KKR) learned the intricacies of leveraged buyouts (in which management or a third party takes over a company, financing it with debt) so well that it now routinely is involved in takeovers of some of the country's largest corporations.

Why the use of debt? The approach is relatively simple—buy a company's stock using debt, sell off assets to pay off the debt, and then after this procedure issue new stock, and, hopefully, reap a bonanza. Consider the example of Beatrice Cos.: KKR bought Beatrice for a premium of approximately 50% over its initial stock price. What KKR saw in Beatrice was a group of well-known brand names—Playtex undergarments, Samsonite luggage, Tropicana orange juice, La Choy Chinese food, and Hunt's catsup. It then sold off some of these companies and then resold the restructured company to the public at a handsome profit. Although this strategy sometimes works, in other cases what has happened is that the acquired company is saddled with an enormous debt load that has been difficult to pay off from operations. Indeed, as a result, the 1990s have found many companies conserving cash in order to pay these interest costs. Unfortunately conserving cash has led to layoffs, dividend reductions, and in some cases massive restructurings.

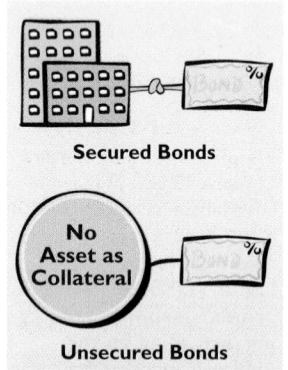

**Secured Bonds**

**Unsecured Bonds**

## Types of Bonds

Bonds may have many different features. Some types of bonds commonly issued are described in the following sections:

### *Secured and Unsecured Bonds*

Secured bonds have specific assets of the issuer pledged as collateral for the bonds. A bond secured by real estate, for example, is called a mortgage bond. A bond secured by specific assets set aside to retire the bonds is called a sinking fund bond. (This type of bond is discussed later in the chapter.) Unsecured bonds are issued against the general credit of the borrower. These bonds, called debenture bonds, are used extensively by large corporations with good credit ratings. For example, in a recent annual report, DuPont reported over $2 billion of debenture bonds outstanding.

**Term Bonds**

**Serial Bonds**

### *Term and Serial Bonds*

Bonds that are due for payment (mature) at a single specified future date are called term bonds. In contrast, bonds that mature in installments are called serial bonds. For example, Caterpillar Inc. debentures due in 2007 are term bonds, and their debentures due between 1996 and 2007 are serial bonds.

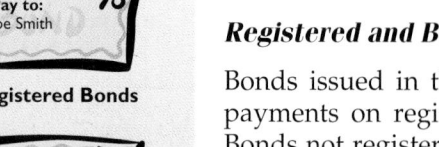

**Registered Bonds**

**Bearer Bonds**

### *Registered and Bearer Bonds*

Bonds issued in the name of the owner are called registered bonds; interest payments on registered bonds are made by check to bondholders of record. Bonds not registered are called bearer (or coupon) bonds; holders are required to send in coupons to receive interest payments. Coupon bonds may be transferred directly to another party. In contrast, the transfer of registered bonds requires cancellation of the bonds by the corporation and the issuance of new bonds. With minor exceptions, most bonds issued today are registered bonds.

### *Convertible and Callable Bonds*

Bonds that can be converted into common stock at the bondholder's option are called convertible bonds. Bonds subject to retirement at a stated dollar amount prior to maturity at the option of the issuer are known as callable bonds.

**Convertible Bonds**

**Callable Bond**

## Issuing Procedures

State laws grant corporations the power to issue bonds. Within the corporation, formal approval by both the board of directors and stockholders is usually required before bonds can be issued. **In authorizing the bond issue, the board of directors must stipulate the total number of bonds to be authorized, total face value, and the contractual interest rate**. The total bond authorization often exceeds the number of bonds originally issued. This is done intentionally to help ensure that the corporation will have the flexibility it needs to meet future cash requirements.

The face value is the amount of principal due at the maturity date. The contractual interest rate, often referred to as the **stated rate**, is the rate used to determine the amount of cash interest the borrower pays and the investor receives. Usually the contractual rate is stated as an annual rate, and interest is generally paid semiannually.

The terms of the bond issue are set forth in a legal document called a bond indenture. In addition to the terms, the indenture summarizes the respective rights and privileges of the bondholders and their trustees, as well as the obligations and commitments of the issuing company. The **trustee** (usually a financial institution) keeps records of each bondholder, maintains custody of unissued bonds, and holds conditional title to pledged property.

**Helpful hint** Do not confuse the terms *indenture* and *debenture.* Indenture refers to the formal bond document (contract). Debenture bonds are unsecured bonds.

After the bond indenture is prepared, **bond certificates** are printed. The indenture and the certificate are separate documents. As shown in Illustration 16-3, a bond certificate provides information such as the following: name of the issuer, the face value of the bonds, the contractual interest rate, and the maturity date of the bonds. Bonds are generally sold through an investment company that specializes in selling securities. In most cases, the issue is underwritten by the investment company. Under an underwriting arrangement, the company sells the bonds to the investment company, which, in turn, sells the bonds to individual investors.

## ►Accounting in Action ► *Business Insight*

Although bonds are generally secured by solid, substantial assets like land, buildings, and equipment, exceptions occur. For example Trans World Airlines Inc. (TWA) at one time decided to issue $300 million of high-yielding 5-year bonds. TWA's bonds would be secured by a grab bag of assets, including some durable spare parts, but also a lot of disposable items that TWA has in its warehouses, such as light bulbs and gaskets. Some are calling the planned TWA bonds "light bulb bonds." As one financial expert noted: "You've got to admit that some security is better than none." However, another noted, "They're digging pretty far down the barrel."

*Source: Wall Street Journal,* June 2, 1989.

## Bond Trading

Corporate bonds, like capital stock, are traded on national securities markets. Thus, bondholders have the opportunity to convert their holdings into cash at any time by selling the bonds at the current market price.

**Bond prices are quoted as a percentage of the face value of the bond, which is usually $1,000.** Thus, a $1,000 bond with a quoted price of 97 means that the

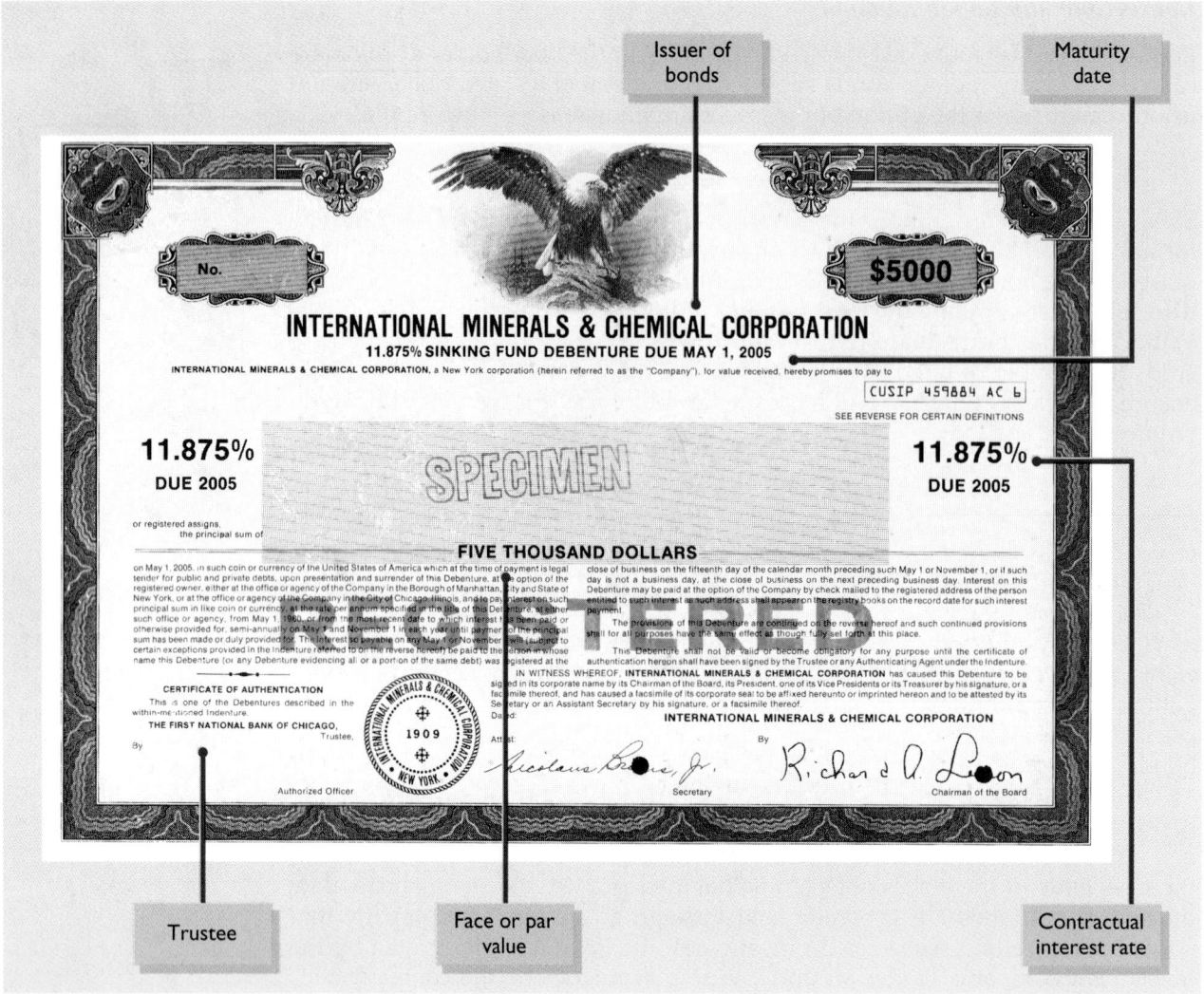

**Illustration 16-3**

*Bond certificate*

selling price of the bond is 97% of face value, or $970 in this case. Bond prices and trading activity are published daily in newspapers and the financial press, as illustrated by the following:

**Illustration 16-4**

*Market information for bonds*

| Bonds | Current Yield | Volume | Close | Net Change |
|---|---|---|---|---|
| Kmart 8⅜ 17 | 8.4 | 35 | 100¼ | +⅞ |

The information in Illustration 16-4 indicates that Kmart Corporation has outstanding 8⅜%, $1,000 bonds maturing in 2017 and currently yielding an 8.4% return. In addition, 35 bonds were traded on this day; and at the close of trading, the price was 100¼% of face value, or $1,002.50. The net change column indicates the difference between the day's closing price and the previous day's closing price.

**Helpful hint**  (1) What is the price of a $1,000 bond trading at 95¼? (2) What is the price of a $1,000 bond trading at 101⅞? Answers: (1) $952.50 and (2) $1,018.75.

Transactions between a bondholder and other investors **are not journalized by the issuing corporation**. If Tom Smith sells bonds that are bought by Faith Jones, the issuing corporation does not journalize the transaction (although it does keep records of the names of bondholders in the case of registered bonds).

A corporation makes journal entries only when it issues or buys back bonds, and when bondholders convert bonds into common stock.

## Determining the Market Value of Bonds

If you were an investor interested in purchasing a bond, how would you determine how much to pay? To be more specific, assume that Coronet, Inc., issues a zero-interest bond (pays no interest) with a face value of $1,000,000 due in 20 years. For this bond, the only cash you receive is a million dollars at the end of 20 years. Would you pay a million dollars for this bond? We hope not, because a million dollars received 20 years from now is not the same as a million dollars received today. The reason you would not pay a million dollars relates to what is called the **time value of money**. If you had a million dollars today, you would invest it and earn interest such that at the end of 20 years, your investment would be worth much more than a million dollars. Thus, if someone is going to pay you a million dollars 20 years from now, you would want to find its equivalent today, or its **present value**. In other words, you would want to determine how much must be invested today at current interest rates to have a million dollars in 20 years.

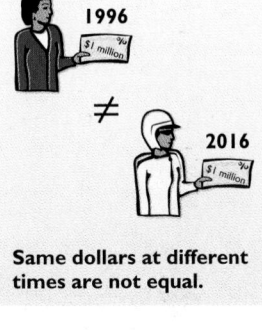

**Same dollars at different times are not equal.**

The market value (present value) of a bond is, therefore, a function of three factors: (1) the dollar amounts to be received, (2) the length of time until the amounts are received, and (3) the market rate of interest. The market interest rate is the rate investors demand for loaning funds to the corporation. The process of finding the present value is referred to as **discounting** the future amounts.

To illustrate, assume that Kimmel Company on January 1, 1996, issues $100,000 of 9% bonds, due in 5 years, with interest payable annually at year-end. The purchaser of the bonds would receive the following two cash payments: (1) **principal** $100,000 to be paid at maturity, and (2) five $9,000 **interest payments** ($100,000 × 9%) over the term of the bonds. The time diagram depicting both cash flows is shown below:

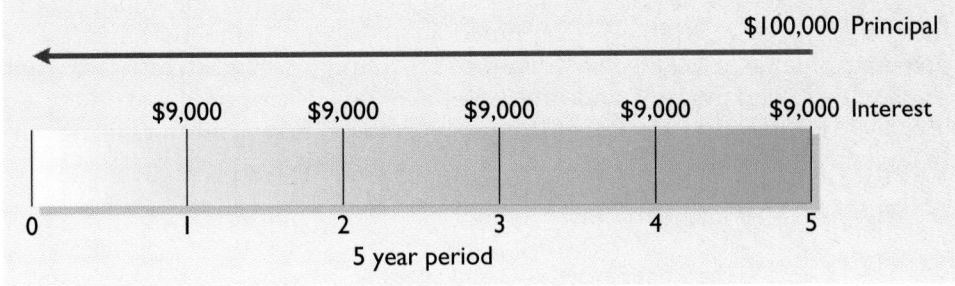

**Illustration 16-5**

*Time diagram depicting cash flows*

The present values of these amounts are as shown in Illustration 16-6.

| Present value of $100,000 received in 5 years | $ 64,993 |
|---|---|
| Present value of $9,000 received annually for 5 years | 35,007 |
| **Market price of bonds** | **$100,000** |

**Illustration 16-6**

*Computing the market price of bonds*

Tables are available to provide the present value numbers to be used, or these values can be determined mathematically.[1] Further discussion of the concepts

[1]For those knowledgeable in the use of present value tables, the computations in this example are: $100,000 × .64993 = $64,993 and $9,000 × 3.88965 = $35,007 (rounded).

and the mechanics of the time value of money computations is provided in Appendix B near the end of the book.

## Before You Go On . . .

### ▶ Review It

1. What are the advantages of bond versus stock financing?
2. What are secured versus unsecured bonds, term versus serial bonds, registered versus bearer bonds, and callable versus convertible bonds?
3. Explain the terms face value, contractual interest rate, and bond indenture.
4. Explain why you would prefer to receive $1 million today rather than 5 years from now.

# *A*ccounting for Bond Issues

Bonds may be issued at face value, below face value (discount), or above face value (premium). They also are sometimes issued between interest dates.

## Issuing Bonds at Face Value

To illustrate the accounting for bonds, assume that Devor Corporation issues 1,000, 10-year, 9%, $1,000 bonds dated January 1, 1996, at 100 (100% of face value). The entry to record the sale is:

| Jan. 1 | Cash | 1,000,000 | |
| | Bonds Payable | | 1,000,000 |
| | (To record sale of bonds at face value) | | |

Bonds payable are reported in the long-term liability section of the balance sheet because the maturity date is January 1, 2006 (more than one year away).

Over the term (life) of the bonds, entries are required for bond interest. Interest on bonds payable is computed in the same manner as interest on notes payable, as explained in Chapter 11. Assuming that interest is payable semiannually on January 1 and July 1 on the bonds described above, interest of $45,000 ($1,000,000 × 9% × 6/12) must be paid on July 1, 1996. The entry for the payment, assuming no previous accrual of interest, is:

| July 1 | Bond Interest Expense | 45,000 | |
| | Cash | | 45,000 |
| | (To record payment of bond interest) | | |

At December 31, an adjusting entry is required to recognize the $45,000 of interest expense incurred since July 1. The entry is:

| Dec. 31 | Bond Interest Expense | 45,000 | |
| | Bond Interest Payable | | 45,000 |
| | (To accrue bond interest) | | |

**Bond interest payable is classified as a current liability**, because it is scheduled for payment within the next year. When the interest is paid on January 1, 1997, Bond Interest Payable is debited and Cash is credited for $45,000.

## Discount or Premium on Bonds

The previous illustrations assumed that the interest rate paid on bonds, often referred to as the contractual (stated) interest rate and the market (effective) interest rate were the same. The contractual interest rate is the rate applied to the face (par) value to arrive at the interest paid in a year. The market interest rate is the rate investors demand for loaning funds to the corporation. When the contractual interest rate and the market interest rate are the same, bonds sell at face value.

However, market interest rates change daily. They are influenced by the type of bond issued, the state of the economy, current industry conditions and the company's individual performance. As a result, the contractual and market interest rates often differ and therefore bonds sell below or above face value.

To illustrate, suppose that investors have one of two options: purchase bonds that have a market rate of interest of 10% or purchase bonds that have a contractual rate of interest of 8%. Assuming that the bonds are of equal risk, investors will select the 10% investment. To make the investments equal, investors will demand a rate of interest higher than the contractual interest rate on the 8% bonds. Because investors cannot change the contractual interest rate, they will pay less than the face value for the bonds. By paying less for the bonds, they can obtain the market rate of interest. In these cases, **bonds sell at a discount**.

Conversely, if the market rate of interest is **lower** than the contractual interest rate, investors will have to pay more than face value for the bonds. That is, if the market rate of interest is 8%, but the contractual interest rate is 9%, the issuer will require more funds from the investor. In these cases, **bonds sell at a premium**. These relationships are shown graphically in Illustration 16-7.

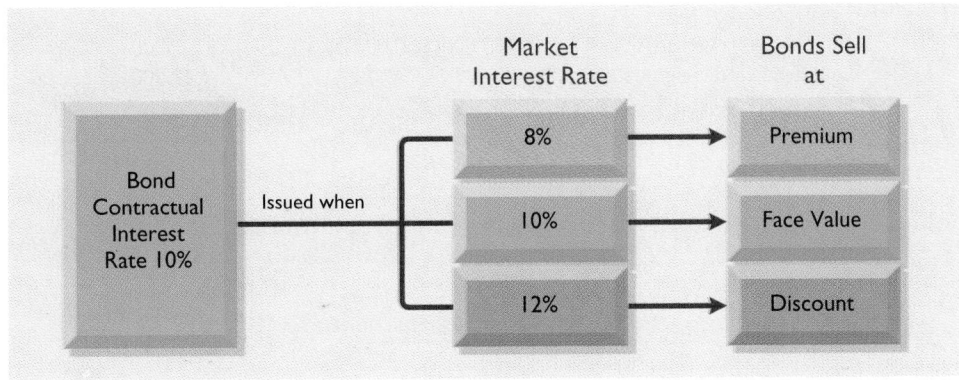

**Illustration 16-7**

*Interest rates and bond prices*

Issuance of bonds at an amount different from face value is quite common. By the time a company prints the bond certificates and markets the bonds, it will be a coincidence if the market rate and the contractual rate are the same. Thus, the issuance of bonds at a discount does not mean that the financial strength of the issuer is suspect. Conversely, the sale of bonds at a premium does not indicate that the financial strength of the issuer is exceptional.

## Issuing Bonds at a Discount

To illustrate the issuance of bonds at a discount, assume that on January 1, 1996, Candlestick, Inc. sells $1 million, 5-year, 10% bonds at 98 (98% of face value) with interest payable on July 1 and January 1. The entry to record the issuance is:

| | | | |
|---|---|---|---|
| Jan. 1 | Cash | 980,000 | |
| | Discount on Bonds Payable | 20,000 | |
| |    Bonds Payable | | 1,000,000 |
| |      (To record sale of bonds at a discount) | | |

Although Discount on Bonds Payable has a debit balance, **it is not an asset**. Rather it is a **contra account**, which is **deducted from bonds payable** on the balance sheet, as illustrated below:

**Illustration 16-8**

*Statement presentation of discount on bonds payable*

| Long-term liabilities | | |
|---|---|---|
| Bonds payable | $1,000,000 | |
| Less: Discount on bonds payable | 20,000 | $980,000 |

**Helpful hint**  Carrying value (book value) of bonds issued at a discount is determined by subtracting the balance of the discount account from the balance of the Bonds Payable account.

The $980,000 represents the **carrying (or book) value** of the bonds. On the date of issue this amount equals the market price of the bonds.

The issuance of bonds below face value causes the total cost of borrowing to differ from the bond interest paid. That is, at maturity the issuing corporation must pay not only the contractual interest rate over the term of the bonds, but also the face value (rather than the issuance price). Therefore, the difference between the issuance price and face value of the bonds—the discount—is an **additional cost of borrowing that should be recorded as bond interest expense over the life of the bonds**. The total cost of borrowing $980,000 for Candlestick, Inc., is $520,000, computed as follows:

**Illustration 16-9**

*Total cost of borrowing— bonds issued at discount*

| **Bonds Issued at a Discount** | |
|---|---|
| Semiannual interest payments | |
| ($1,000,000 × 10% × ½ = $50,000; $50,000 × 10) | $500,000 |
| Add: Bond discount ($1,000,000 − $980,000) | 20,000 |
| Total cost of borrowing | $520,000 |

Alternatively, the total cost of borrowing can be determined as follows:

**Illustration 16-10**

*Alternative computation of total cost of borrowing— bonds issued at discount*

| **Bonds Issued at a Discount** | |
|---|---|
| Principal at maturity | $1,000,000 |
| Semiannual interest payments ($50,000 × 10) | 500,000 |
| Cash to be paid to bondholders | 1,500,000 |
| Cash received from bondholders | 980,000 |
| Total cost of borrowing | $ 520,000 |

### Amortizing Bond Discount

To comply with the matching principle, it follows that bond discount should be allocated systematically to each accounting period benefiting from the use of the cash proceeds.

One method, the straight-line method of amortization, allocates the same amount to interest expense in each interest period.[2] The amount is determined as shown in Illustration 16-11:

---

[2]Another method, the effective-interest method, is discussed in the appendix at the end of this chapter.

**Illustration 16-11**

*Formula for straight-line method of bond discount amortization*

In this example, the bond discount amortization is $2,000 ($20,000 ÷ 10). The entry to record the payment of bond interest and the amortization of bond discount on the first interest date (July 1, 1996) is:

| July 1 | Bond Interest Expense | 52,000 | |
|---|---|---|---|
| | Discount on Bonds Payable | | 2,000 |
| | Cash | | 50,000 |
| | (To record payment of bond interest and amortization of bond discount) | | |

At December 31, the adjusting entry is:

| Dec. 31 | Bond Interest Expense | 52,000 | |
|---|---|---|---|
| | Discount on Bonds Payable | | 2,000 |
| | Bond Interest Payable | | 50,000 |
| | (To record accrued bond interest and amortization of bond discount) | | |

Over the term of the bonds, the balance in Discount on Bonds Payable will decrease annually by the same amount until it has a zero balance at the maturity date of the bonds. Thus, the carrying value of the bonds at maturity will be equal to the face value of the bonds.

Preparing a bond discount amortization schedule as shown in Illustration 16-12 is useful to determine interest expense, discount amortization and the car-

**Illustration 16-12**

*Bond discount amortization schedule*

| Semiannual Interest Periods | (A) Interest to Be Paid (5% × $1,000,000) | (B) Interest Expense to Be Recorded (A) + (C) | (C) Discount Amortization ($20,000 ÷ 10) | (D) Unamortized Discount (D) − (C) | (E) Bond Carrying Value ($1,000,000 − D) |
|---|---|---|---|---|---|
| Issue date | | | | $20,000 | $ 980,000 |
| 1 | $ 50,000 | $ 52,000 | $ 2,000 | 18,000 | 982,000 |
| 2 | 50,000 | 52,000 | 2,000 | 16,000 | 984,000 |
| 3 | 50,000 | 52,000 | 2,000 | 14,000 | 986,000 |
| 4 | 50,000 | 52,000 | 2,000 | 12,000 | 988,000 |
| 5 | 50,000 | 52,000 | 2,000 | 10,000 | 990,000 |
| 6 | 50,000 | 52,000 | 2,000 | 8,000 | 992,000 |
| 7 | 50,000 | 52,000 | 2,000 | 6,000 | 994,000 |
| 8 | 50,000 | 52,000 | 2,000 | 4,000 | 996,000 |
| 9 | 50,000 | 52,000 | 2,000 | 2,000 | 998,000 |
| 10 | 50,000 | 52,000 | 2,000 | –0– | 1,000,000 |
| | $500,000 | $520,000 | $20,000 | | |

Column (A) remains constant because the face value of the bonds ($1,000,000) is multiplied by the semiannual contractual interest rate (5%) each period.

Column (B) is computed as the interest paid (Column A) plus the discount amortization (Column C).

Column (C) indicates the discount amortization each period.

Column (D) decreases each period by the same amount until it reaches zero at maturity.

Column (E) increases each period by the amount of discount amortization until it equals the face value at maturity.

rying value of the bond. As indicated, the interest expense recorded each period is $52,000. Also note that the carrying value of the bond increases $2,000 each period until it reaches its face value $1,000,000 at the end of period 10.

## Issuing Bonds at a Premium

The issuance of bonds at a premium can be illustrated by assuming the Candlestick, Inc. bonds described above are sold at 102 (102% of face value) rather than at 98.

The entry to record the sale is:

| | | | |
|---|---|---|---|
| Jan. 1 | Cash | 1,020,000 | |
| | Bonds Payable | | 1,000,000 |
| | Premium on Bonds Payable | | 20,000 |
| | (To record sale of bonds at a premium) | | |

Premium on bonds payable is **added to bonds payable** on the balance sheet, as shown below:

**Illustration 16-13**

*Statement presentation of bond premium*

| Long-term liabilities | | |
|---|---|---|
| Bonds payable | $1,000,000 | |
| **Add: Premium on bonds payable** | 20,000 | $1,020,000 |

The sale of bonds above face value causes the total cost of borrowing to be **less than the bond interest paid**, because the borrower is not required to pay the bond premium at the maturity date of the bonds. Thus, the premium is considered to be **a reduction in the cost of borrowing** that should be credited to Bond Interest Expense over the life of the bonds. The total cost of borrowing $1,020,000 for Candlestick, Inc., is $480,000, computed as follows:

**Illustration 16-14**

*Total cost of borrowing—bonds issued at a premium*

| **Bonds Issued at a Premium** | |
|---|---|
| Semiannual interest payments | |
| ($1,000,000 × 10% × ½ = $50,000; $50,000 × 10) | $500,000 |
| Less: Bond premium ($1,020,000 − $1,000,000) | 20,000 |
| **Total cost of borrowing** | **$480,000** |

Alternatively, the cost of borrowing can be computed as follows:

**Illustration 16-15**

*Alternative computation of total cost of borrowing—bonds issued at a premium*

| **Bonds Issued at a Premium** | |
|---|---|
| Principal at maturity | $1,000,000 |
| Semiannual interest payments ($50,000 × 10) | 500,000 |
| Cash to be paid to bondholders | 1,500,000 |
| Cash received from bondholders | 1,020,000 |
| **Total cost of borrowing** | **$ 480,000** |

### Amortizing Bond Premium

The formula for determining bond premium amortization under the straight-line method is: bond premium divided by the number of interest periods. Thus, the premium amortization for each interest period is $2,000 ($20,000 ÷ 10). The entry to record the first payment of interest on July 1 is:

| July 1 | Bond Interest Expense | 48,000 | |
|---|---|---|---|
| | Premium on Bonds Payable | 2,000 | |
| | Cash | | 50,000 |
| | (To record payment of bond interest and amortization of bond premium) | | |

At December 31, the adjusting entry is:

| Dec. 31 | Bond Interest Expense | 48,000 | |
|---|---|---|---|
| | Premium on Bonds Payable | 2,000 | |
| | Bond Interest Payable | | 50,000 |
| | (To record accrued bond interest and amortization of bond premium) | | |

Over the term of the bonds, the balance in Premium on Bonds Payable will decrease annually by the same amount until it has a zero balance at maturity.

Preparing a bond premium amortization schedule as shown in Illustration 16-16 is useful to determine interest expense, premium amortized, and the carrying value of the bond. As indicated, the interest expense recorded each period is $48,000. Also note that the carrying value of the bond decreases $2,000 each period until it reaches its face value $1,000,000 at the end of period 10.

**Illustration 16-16**

*Bond premium amortization schedule*

| Semiannual Interest Periods | (A) Interest to Be Paid (5% × $1,000,000) | (B) Interest Expense to Be Recorded (A) − (C) | (C) Premium Amortization ($20,000 ÷ 10) | (D) Unamortized Premium (D) − (C) | (E) Bond Carrying Value ($1,000,000 + D) |
|---|---|---|---|---|---|
| Issue date | | | | $20,000 | $1,020,000 |
| 1 | $ 50,000 | $ 48,000 | $ 2,000 | 18,000 | 1,018,000 |
| 2 | 50,000 | 48,000 | 2,000 | 16,000 | 1,016,000 |
| 3 | 50,000 | 48,000 | 2,000 | 14,000 | 1,014,000 |
| 4 | 50,000 | 48,000 | 2,000 | 12,000 | 1,012,000 |
| 5 | 50,000 | 48,000 | 2,000 | 10,000 | 1,010,000 |
| 6 | 50,000 | 48,000 | 2,000 | 8,000 | 1,008,000 |
| 7 | 50,000 | 48,000 | 2,000 | 6,000 | 1,006,000 |
| 8 | 50,000 | 48,000 | 2,000 | 4,000 | 1,004,000 |
| 9 | 50,000 | 48,000 | 2,000 | 2,000 | 1,002,000 |
| 10 | 50,000 | 48,000 | 2,000 | –0– | 1,000,000 |
| | $500,000 | $480,000 | $20,000 | | |

Column **(A)** remains constant because the face value of the bonds ($1,000,000) is multiplied by the semiannual contractual interest rate (5%) each period.

Column **(B)** is computed as the interest paid (Column A) less the premium amortization (Column C).

Column **(C)** indicates the premium amortization each period.

Column **(D)** decreases each period by the same amount until it reaches zero at maturity.

Column **(E)** decreases each period by the amount of premium amortization until it equals the face value at maturity.

## Issuing Bonds between Interest Dates

Bonds are often issued between interest payment dates. **When this occurs, the issuer requires the investor to pay the market price for the bonds plus accrued interest since the last interest date.** At the next interest date, the corporation will return the accrued interest to the investor by paying the full amount of interest due on outstanding bonds.

To illustrate, assume that Deer Corporation sells $1,000,000, 9% bonds at face value plus accrued interest on March 1. Interest is payable semiannually on July 1 and January 1. The accrued interest is $15,000 ($1,000,000 × 9% × 2/12). The total proceeds on the sale of the bonds, therefore, are $1,015,000, and the entry to record the sale is:

| Mar. 1 | Cash | 1,015,000 | |
|---|---|---|---|
| | Bonds Payable | | 1,000,000 |
| | Bond Interest Payable | | 15,000 |
| | (To record sale of bonds at face value plus accrued interest) | | |

At the first interest date, it is necessary to eliminate the bond interest payable balance and to recognize interest expense for the 4 months (March 1–June 30) the bonds have been outstanding. Interest expense in this example is, therefore, $30,000 ($1,000,000 × 9% × 4/12). The entry on July 1 for the $45,000 interest payment is:

| July 1 | Bond Interest Payable | 15,000 | |
|---|---|---|---|
| | Bond Interest Expense | 30,000 | |
| | Cash | | 45,000 |
| | (To record payment of bond interest) | | |

Why does Deer Corporation collect interest at the time of issuance and then return this interest at the time of payment? The rationale: Collection of accrued interest at the issuance date allows the company to pay a full period's interest to all bondholders at the next interest payment date. Deer Corporation does not have to determine the individual amount of interest due each holder based on the time each bond has been outstanding during the interest period.

In other words, if bonds are not sold "with accrued interest," Deer Corporation would have to keep track of the purchaser and the dates that the bonds were purchased. This procedure would be necessary to ensure that each bondholder received the correct amount of interest. By selling the bonds "with accrued interest," Deer does not have to maintain detailed records and cost savings occur.

## Before You Go On . . .

### ▶ Review It

1. What entry is made to record the issuance of bonds payable of $1 million at 100? at 96? at 102?
2. Why do bonds sell at a discount? at a premium? at face value?
3. Explain the accounting for bonds sold between interest dates.

### ▶ Do It

A bond amortization table shows (a) interest to be paid $50,000, (b) interest expense to be recorded $52,000, and (c) amortization $2,000. Answer the following questions: (1) Were the bonds sold at a premium or a discount? (2) After recording the interest expense, will the bond carrying value increase or decrease?

*Reasoning:* To answer the questions you need to know the effects that the amortization of bond discount and bond premium have on bond interest expense and on the carrying value of the bonds. Bond discount amortization increases both bond interest expense and the carrying value of the bonds. Bond premium amortization has the reverse effect.

**Solution:** The bond amortization table indicates that interest expense is $2,000 greater than the interest paid. This difference is equal to the amortization amount. Thus, the bonds were sold at a discount. The interest entry will decrease Discount on Bonds Payable and increase the carrying value of the bonds.

*Related exercise material:* BE16–2, BE16–3, BE16–4, BE16–5, E16–2, E16–3, E16–4, and E16–5.

# Accounting for Bond Retirements

Bonds may be retired either when they are purchased (redeemed) by the issuing corporation or when they are converted into common stock by bondholders. The appropriate entries for these transactions are explained in the following sections.

## Redeeming Bonds at Maturity

Regardless of the issue price of bonds, the book value of the bonds at maturity will equal their face value. This can be seen in Illustrations 16-12 and 16-16 where the carrying value of the bonds at the end of their 10-year life ($1 million) is equal to the face value of the bonds.

**STUDY OBJECTIVE**

**3**

*Describe the entries when bonds are redeemed or converted.*

Assuming that the interest for the last interest period is paid and recorded separately, the entry to record the redemption of the Candlestick bonds at maturity is:

| | | |
|---|---|---|
| Bonds Payable | 1,000,000 | |
|     Cash | | 1,000,000 |
|       (To record redemption of bonds at maturity) | | |

## Redeeming Bonds before Maturity

Bonds may be redeemed before maturity. A company may decide to retire bonds before maturity to reduce interest cost and remove debt from its balance sheet. A company should retire debt early only if it has sufficient cash resources. When bonds are retired before maturity, it is necessary to: (1) eliminate the carrying value of the bonds at the redemption date, (2) record the cash paid, and (3) recognize the gain or loss on redemption. The carrying value of the bonds is the face value of the bonds less unamortized bond discount or plus unamortized bond premium at the redemption date.

**Helpful hint** Question: If a bond is redeemed prior to its maturity date and its carrying value exceeds its redemption price, will the retirement result in a gain or a loss on redemption? Answer: Gain.

To illustrate, assume at the end of the eighth period Candlestick, Inc. (having sold its bonds at a premium, per Illustration 16-16) retires its bonds at 103 after paying the semiannual interest. The carrying value of the bonds at the redemption date, as shown in the bond premium amortization schedule, is $1,004,000. The entry to record the redemption at the end of the eighth interest period (January 1, 2000) is:

| | | | |
|---|---|---|---|
| Jan. 1 | Bonds Payable | 1,000,000 | |
| | Premium on Bonds Payable | 4,000 | |
| | Loss on Bond Redemption | 26,000 | |
| |     Cash | | 1,030,000 |
| |       (To record redemption of bonds at 103) | | |

Note that the loss of $26,000 is the difference between the cash paid of $1,030,000 and the carrying value of the bonds of $1,004,000. Losses (gains) on bond redemption are reported in the income statement as extraordinary items as required by the accounting profession.

## Converting Bonds into Common Stock

Convertible bonds have features that are attractive both to bondholders and to the issuer. The conversion often gives bondholders an opportunity to benefit if the market price of the common stock increases substantially. Furthermore, until conversion, the bondholder receives interest on the bond. For the issuer, the bonds sell at a higher price and pay a lower rate of interest than comparable debt securities that do not have a conversion option. Many corporations, such as USAir, USX Corp., and Chrysler Corporation, have convertible bonds outstanding.

When bonds are converted into common stocks and the conversion is recorded, the current market prices of the bonds and the stock are ignored. Instead, the **carrying value** of the bonds is transferred to paid-in capital accounts, and **no gain or loss is recognized**. To illustrate, assume that on July 1 Saunders Associates converts $100,000 bonds sold at face value into 2,000 shares of $10 par value common stock. Both the bonds and the common stock have a market value of $130,000. The entry to record the conversion is:

**Helpful hint**  The method of recording this conversion of bonds to stock is called the *book value method* because the amount of the book value of the bonds is removed from the liability accounts and recorded as common stock and related paid-in capital.

| July 1 | Bonds Payable | 100,000 | |
| | Common Stock | | 20,000 |
| | Paid-in Capital in Excess of Par Value | | 80,000 |
| | (To record bond conversion) | | |

Note that the current market price of the bonds and stocks ($130,000) is not considered in making the entry. This method of recording the bond conversion is often referred to as the **carrying (or book) value method**.

## Using a Bond Sinking Fund

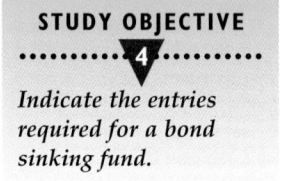

**STUDY OBJECTIVE**
••••••••••**4**••••••••••

*Indicate the entries required for a bond sinking fund.*

Many bond issues require the borrower to make periodic cash contributions to a sinking (redemption) fund over the life of the bonds. A sinking fund is cash or other assets set aside to retire debt. In other words, it is like a savings account that is used to pay back bondholders. **A sinking fund makes the bonds more attractive to investors, because it enhances the likelihood that the bonds will be redeemed at maturity.** For example, Texaco and Alcoa have sinking funds for their debenture bonds. Such bonds are often referred to as **sinking fund bonds**.

Sinking funds are usually under the control of a trustee, such as a bank or a trust company. The trustee may be permitted to invest the periodic deposits in high-quality income-producing securities. **It is expected that the deposits plus the earnings from the investments will equal the face value of the bonds at maturity.** Shortly before the maturity date, the trustee sells the securities and uses the total cash in the fund to redeem the bonds. Any excess cash in the fund is returned to the bond issuer.

To illustrate, assume that Bountiful Corporation issues $1 million face value, 5-year bonds on January 1. The terms of the bond indenture indicate that Bountiful must make annual deposits with a sinking fund trustee, starting at the end of the first year. The amount of the annual cash contribution is $215,000. The entry to record this contribution by Bountiful Corporation at the end of the first year is as follows:

| Dec. 31 | Bond Sinking Fund | 215,000 | |
| | Cash | | 215,000 |
| | (To record annual contribution) | | |

At the end of the second year, Bountiful Corporation records actual earnings on the assets in the sinking fund of $16,500. The entry to record this revenue and the required contribution to the fund is as follows:

| Dec. 31 | Bond Sinking Fund | 231,500 | |
|---|---|---|---|
| | Bond Sinking Fund Revenue | | 16,500 |
| | Cash | | 215,000 |
| | (To record sinking fund revenue and | | |
| | annual contribution) | | |

At the maturity date, sinking fund assets are used to redeem the bonds. The entry to record the redemption, assuming that the sinking fund has $985,000 in cash, is as follows:

| Jan. 1 | Bonds Payable | 1,000,000 | |
|---|---|---|---|
| | Bond Sinking Fund | | 985,000 |
| | Cash | | 15,000 |
| | (To redeem bonds at maturity) | | |

In this case, Bountiful Corporation had to make up for the deficiency by paying an additional $15,000. If the sinking fund had excess cash, it would be returned to Bountiful.

**The bond sinking fund is reported as a single amount in the investment section of the balance sheet.** Bond sinking fund revenue is classified as other revenues and gains in the income statement.

The bond contract may also require the corporation to establish a restriction on its retained earnings. As explained in Chapter 15, this restriction is reported as a note in the financial statements.

 **Accounting in Action** ▸ *International Insight*

Now that you have read about bonds, you may be beginning to realize how significant bond financing can be. A dramatic example of bond financing—which literally changed the course of history—is seen in Britain's struggle for supremacy in the eighteenth and nineteenth centuries. With only a fraction of the population and wealth of France, Britain ultimately humbled its mightier foe through the use of bonds. Because of its effective central bank and a fair system of collecting taxes, Britain developed the capital markets that enabled its government to issue bonds. Britain was able to borrow money at almost half the cost paid by France, and was able to incur more debt as a proportion of the economy than could France. Britain thus could more than match the French navy, raise an army of its own, and lavishly subsidize other armies, eventually destroying Napoleon and his threat to Europe.

*Source:* "How British Bonds Beat Back Bigger France," *Forbes*, March 13, 1995.

## Before You Go On . . .

▶ *Review It*

1. Explain the accounting for redemption of bonds at maturity, before maturity by payment in cash, and by conversion into common stock.
2. What is the purpose of the bond sinking fund? Where is a bond sinking fund reported in the financial statements?

### ▸ *Do It*

R & B Inc. issued $500,000, 10-year bonds at a premium. Prior to maturity, when the carrying value of the bonds is $508,000, the company retires the bonds at 102. Prepare the entry to record the redemption of the bonds.

**Reasoning:** In recording the redemption of bonds before maturity, it is necessary to (1) eliminate the carrying value of the bonds, (2) recognize the cash paid, and (3) recognize the gain or loss equal to the difference between (1) and (2).

**Solution:** There is a loss on redemption because the cash paid, $510,000 ($500,000 × 102), is greater than the carrying value of $508,000. The entry is:

| | | |
|---|---:|---:|
| Bonds Payable | 500,000 | |
| Premium on Bonds Payable | 8,000 | |
| Loss on Bond Redemption | 2,000 | |
|     Cash | | 510,000 |
|       (To record redemption of bonds at 102) | | |

*Related exercise material:* BE16–6, E16–3, E16–4, and E16–6.

# *A*ccounting for Other Long-Term Liabilities

Other common types of long-term obligations are notes payable and lease liabilities. The accounting for these liabilities is explained in the following sections.

## Long-Term Notes Payable

**STUDY OBJECTIVE**

•••••••••**5**•••••••••

*Describe the accounting for long-term notes payable.*

The use of notes payable in long-term debt financing is quite common. Long-term notes payable are similar to short-term interest-bearing notes payable except that the terms of the notes exceed one year. In periods of unstable interest rates, the interest rate on long-term notes may be tied to changes in the market rate for comparable loans. Examples are the 8.03% adjustable rate notes issued by General Motors and the floating rate notes issued by American Express Company.

A long-term note may be secured by a document called a **mortgage** that pledges title to specific assets as security for a loan. Mortgage notes payable are widely used in the purchase of homes by individuals and in the acquisition of plant assets by many small and some large companies. For example, approximately 18% of McDonald's long-term debt relates to mortgage notes on land, buildings, and improvements. Like other long-term notes payable, the mortgage loan terms may stipulate either a fixed or an adjustable interest rate. Typically, the terms require the borrower to make installment payments over the term of the loan. Each payment consists of (1) interest on the unpaid balance of the loan, and (2) a reduction of loan principal. The interest decreases each period, while the portion applied to the loan principal increases.

Mortgage notes payable are recorded initially at face value, and entries are required subsequently for each installment payment. To illustrate, assume that Porter Technology Inc. issues a $500,000, 12%, 20-year mortgage note on December 31, 1996, to obtain needed financing for the construction of a new research laboratory. The terms provide for semiannual installment payments of $33,231 (not including real estate taxes and insurance). The installment payment schedule for the first 2 years is as follows:

| Semiannual Interest Period | (A) Cash Payment | (B) Interest Expense (D) × 6% | (C) Reduction of Principal (A) − (B) | (D) Principal Balance (D) − (C) |
|---|---|---|---|---|
| Issue date | | | | $500,000 |
| 1 | $33,231 | $30,000 | $3,231 | 496,769 |
| 2 | 33,231 | 29,806 | 3,425 | 493,344 |
| 3 | 33,231 | 29,601 | 3,630 | 489,714 |
| 4 | 33,231 | 29,383 | 3,848 | 485,866 |

**Illustration 16-17**

*Mortgage installment payment schedule*

**Helpful hint** Electronic spreadsheet programs can create a schedule of installment loan payments. This allows you to put in the data for your own mortgage loan and get an illustration that really hits home.

The entries to record the mortgage loan and first installment payment are as follows:

| Dec. 31 | Cash | 500,000 | |
| | Mortgage Notes Payable | | 500,000 |
| | (To record mortgage loan) | | |

| June 30 | Interest Expense | 30,000 | |
| | Mortgage Notes Payable | 3,231 | |
| | Cash | | 33,231 |
| | (To record semiannual payment on mortgage) | | |

**In the balance sheet, the reduction in principal for the next year is reported as a current liability, and the remaining unpaid principal balance is classified as a long-term liability.** At December 31, 1997, the total liability is $493,344 of which $7,478 ($3,630 + $3,848) is current, and $485,866 ($493,344 − $7,478) is long-term.

## Lease Liabilities

As indicated in Chapter 10, a lease is a contractual arrangement between the lessor (owner of the property) and a lessee (renter of the property) that grants the right to use specific property for a period of time in return for cash payments. Leasing is big business. For example, an estimated $125 billion of capital equipment was leased in a recent year. This represents approximately one-third of equipment financed that year. The two most common types of leases are operating leases and capital leases.

**STUDY OBJECTIVE**

•••••••••• **6** ••••••••••

*Contrast the accounting for operating and capital leases.*

## ►Accounting in Action ► *Business Insight*

As an excellent example of the magnitude of leasing, leased planes account for nearly 40% of the U.S. fleet of commercial airlines. The reasons for leasing include favorable tax treatment, increased flexibility, and low airline income. As passenger volume is expected to double in the next 20 years, some industry analysts estimate that approximately $400 billion in airplanes will be needed, and it is anticipated that much of the financing will be done through leasing. Leasing is particularly attractive to lessors because airplanes have relatively long lives, a ready secondhand market, and a significant resale value. Or take the commercial truck fleet—over one third of heavy-duty trucks are presently leased.

### *Operating Leases*

The renting of an apartment and the rental of a car at an airport are examples of operating leases. **In an operating lease the intent is temporary use of the prop-**

**erty by the lessee with continued ownership of the property by the lessor.** The lease (or rental) payments are recorded as an expense by the lessee and as revenue by the lessor. For example, assuming that a sales representative for Western Inc. leases a car from Hertz Car Rental at the Los Angeles airport and that Hertz charges a total of $275, the entry by the lessee, Western Inc., is:

| | | |
|---|---|---|
| Car Rental Expense | 275 | |
|    Cash | | 275 |
|      (To record payment of lease rental charge) | | |

In addition, the lessee may incur other costs during the lease period. For example, in the case above, the lessee may be required to pay for gas and oil. These costs are also reported as an expense.

### Capital Leases

**Helpful hint** A capital lease situation is one in which although it is legally a rental case, it is *in substance* an installment purchase by the lessee. Accounting standards require that substance over form be used in such a situation.

In most lease contracts, a periodic payment is made by the lessee and is recorded as rent expense in the income statement. However, in some cases, the lease contract transfers substantially all the benefits and risks of ownership to the lessee, so that the lease is in effect a purchase of the property. This type of lease is called a capital lease because the present value of the cash payments for the lease are capitalized and recorded as an asset.

The lessee must record the lease **as an asset**—that is, as a capital lease—if any **one** of the following conditions exists:

1. **The lease transfers ownership of the property to the lessee.** *Rationale:* If during the lease term, the lessee receives ownership of the asset, the leased asset should be reported as an asset on the lessee's books.

2. **The lease contains a bargain purchase option.** *Rationale:* If during the term of the lease, the lessee can purchase the asset at a price substantially below its fair market value, the lessee will obviously exercise this option. Thus, the lease should be reported as a leased asset on the lessee's books.

3. **The lease term is equal to 75% or more of the economic life of the leased property.** *Rationale:* If the lease term is for much of the asset's useful life, the asset should be recorded by the lessee.

4. **The present value of the lease payments equals or exceeds 90% of the fair market value of the leased property.** *Rationale:* If the present value of the lease payments is equal to or almost equal to the fair market value of the asset, the lessee has essentially purchased the asset. As a result, the leased asset should be recorded on the books of the lessee.

To illustrate, assume that Gonzalez Company decides to lease new equipment. The lease period is 4 years; the economic life of the leased equipment is estimated to be 5 years. The present value of the lease payments is $190,000 which is equal to the fair market value of the equipment. There is no transfer of ownership during the lease term nor is there any bargain purchase option.

In this example, Gonzalez has essentially purchased the equipment. Conditions 3 and 4 have been met: First, the lease term is 75% or more of the economic life of the asset, and second, the present value of cash payments is equal to the equipment's fair market value. The entry to record the transaction is as follows:

| | | |
|---|---|---|
| Leased Asset—Equipment | 190,000 | |
|    Lease Liability | | 190,000 |
|      (To record leased asset and lease liability) | | |

The leased asset is reported on the balance sheet under plant assets. The lease liability is reported as a liability on the balance sheet. **The portion of the lease liability expected to be paid in the next year is reported as a current liability. The remainder is classified as a long-term liability.**

Most lessees do not like to report leases on their balance sheets. The reason is that the lease liability increases the company's total liabilities. This, in turn, may make it more difficult for the company to obtain needed funds from lenders. As a result, companies attempt to keep leased assets and lease liabilities off the balance sheet by not meeting any one of the four conditions mentioned above. This procedure of keeping liabilities off the balance sheet is often referred to as **off-balance sheet financing**.

# Statement Presentation of Long-Term Liabilities

Long-term liabilities are reported in a separate section of the balance sheet immediately following current liabilities, as shown below.

| Long-term liabilities | | |
|---|---:|---:|
| Bonds payable 10% due in 2009 | $1,000,000 | |
| Less: Discount on bonds payable | 80,000 | $ 920,000 |
| Mortgage notes payable, 11%, due in 2015 | | |
| and secured by plant assets | | 500,000 |
| Lease liability | | 540,000 |
| Total long-term liabilities | | $1,960,000 |

**STUDY OBJECTIVE**

**7**

*Identify the requirements for the financial statement presentation of long-term liabilities.*

**Illustration 16-18**

*Balance sheet presentation of long-term liabilities*

Alternatively, summary data may be presented in the balance sheet with detailed data (such as interest rates, maturity dates, conversion privileges, and assets pledged as collateral) shown in a supporting schedule. The current maturities of long-term debt should be reported under current liabilities if they are to be paid from current assets.

# Before You Go On . . .

## ► Review It

1. Explain the accounting for long-term mortgage notes payable.
2. What is the difference in accounting for an operating lease versus a capital lease? Explain the four conditions used to determine whether the lease contract transfers substantially all the benefits and risks of ownership.

## ► A Look Back at the University of Kentucky

Refer to the opening story and answer the following questions:

1. The University of Kentucky's bonds are rated AA− by Standard & Poor's and A1 by Moody's Investor Service. Why is it important to the University of Kentucky that its bonds have a high bond rating?
2. Explain the meaning of the tax-exempt status of the University of Kentucky bonds. What does it mean to say that "a recent issue offering 6% is the equivalent of 10% to those individuals in the top tax bracket"?

3. Why does the state use bonds to finance the buildings rather than taking the funds out of general revenues?

**Solution:**

1. Having a high (good) bond rating is as important to a university as it is to a business corporation. A high bond rating indicates that the bonds are less risky, and thus more attractive, to purchasers of the bonds. Hence a lower interest rate results, and the cost to the issuer of the bonds is less.

2. Because the University of Kentucky bonds are tax exempt, holders of the bonds do not have to pay federal income tax on the interest received on the bonds. To earn an after-tax return of 6%, a person in the maximum tax bracket would have to receive interest equal to approximately 10% on taxable bonds [10% − (40% × 10%)].

3. Financing the buildings through the issuance of bonds spreads the cost of the buildings over many years and more equitably distributes the costs to a broader base of taxpayers. Future taxpayers pay for the buildings as the buildings are used, rather than the taxpayers of one year absorbing the total cost out of general revenues in the year of construction.

# *S*ummary of Study Objectives

**1.** *Explain why bonds are issued.* Bonds may be sold to many investors, and they offer the following advantages over common stock: (a) stockholder control is not affected, (b) tax savings result, (c) earnings per share of common stock may be higher.

**2.** *Prepare the entries for the issuance of bonds and interest expense.* When bonds are issued, Cash is debited for the cash proceeds and Bonds Payable is credited for the face value of the bonds. In addition, Bond Interest Payable is credited if there is accrued interest, and the accounts Premium on Bonds Payable and Discount on Bonds Payable are used to show the bond premium and bond discount. Bond discount and bond premium are amortized by the straight-line method.

**3.** *Describe the entries when bonds are redeemed or converted.* When bonds are redeemed at maturity, Cash is credited and Bonds Payable is debited for the face value of the bonds. When bonds are redeemed before maturity, it is necessary to (a) eliminate the carrying value of the bonds at the redemption date, (b) record the cash paid, and (c) recognize the gain or loss on redemption. When bonds are converted to common stock, the carrying (or book) value of the bonds is transferred to appropriate paid-in capital accounts, and no gain or loss is recognized.

**4.** *Indicate the entries required for a bond sinking fund.* Entries are required for a bond sinking fund to record (a) periodic contributions, (b) annual revenue, and (c) redemption of the bonds.

**5.** *Describe the accounting for long-term notes payable.* Each payment consists of (1) interest on the unpaid balance of the loan, and (2) a reduction of loan principal. The interest decreases each period, while the portion applied to the loan principal increases each period.

**6.** *Contrast the accounting for operating and capital leases.* For an operating lease, lease (or rental) payments are recorded as an expense by the lessee (renter). For a capital lease, the lessee records the asset and related obligation at the present value of the future lease payments.

**7.** *Identify the requirements for the financial statement presentation of long-term liabilities.* The nature and amount of each long-term debt should be reported in the balance sheet or in schedules in the notes accompanying the statements.

# *A*PPENDIX ▸ *Effective-Interest Amortization*

The straight-line method of amortization that you studied in the chapter has a conceptual deficiency: It does not completely satisfy the matching principle. Under the straight-line method, interest expense as a percentage of the carrying value of the bonds varies each interest period. This can be seen by using data

from the first three interest periods of the bond amortization schedule shown in
Illustration 16-12:

**Illustration 16A-1**

*Interest percentage rates
under straight-line method*

| Semiannual Interest Period | Interest Expense to Be Recorded (A) | Bond Carrying Value (B) | Interest Expense as a Percentage of Carrying Value (A) ÷ (B) |
|---|---|---|---|
| 1 | $52,000 | $980,000 | 5.31% |
| 2 | 52,000 | 982,000 | 5.29% |
| 3 | 52,000 | 984,000 | 5.27% |

Note that interest expense as a percentage of carrying value declines in each
interest period. However, to completely comply with the matching principle,
interest expense as a percentage of carrying value should not change over the
life of the bonds. This percentage, referred to as the effective-interest rate, is
established when the bonds are issued and remains constant in each interest
period. The effective-interest method of amortization accomplishes this result.

Under the effective-interest method, the amortization of bond discount or
bond premium results in periodic interest expense equal to a constant percentage
of the carrying value of the bonds. The effective-interest method results in varying amounts of amortization and interest expense per period but a constant percentage rate; the straight-line method results in constant amounts of amortization
and interest expense per period but a varying percentage rate.

The following steps are required under the effective-interest method:

1. Compute the **bond interest expense** by multiplying the carrying value of the
   bonds at the beginning of the interest period by the effective-interest rate.
2. Compute the **bond interest paid** (or accrued) by multiplying the face value
   of the bonds by the contractual interest rate.
3. Compute the **amortization amount** by determining the difference between
   the amounts computed in steps (1) and (2).

These steps are graphically depicted in Illustration 16A-2.

**STUDY OBJECTIVE**

*After studying this
appendix, you should
be able to:*

8. **Contrast the effects
of the straight-line and
effective-interest
methods of amortizing
bond discount and
bond premium.**

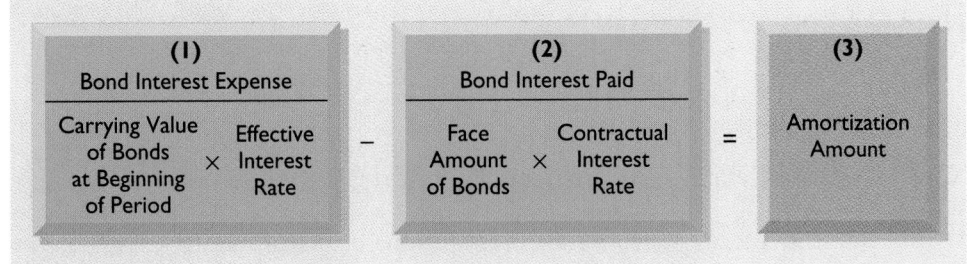

**Illustration 16A-2**

*Computation of amortiza-
tion—effective-interest
method*

**Both the straight-line and effective-interest methods of amortization result
in the same total amount of interest expense over the term of the bonds.** Furthermore, interest expense each interest period is generally comparable in
amount. However, **when the amounts are materially different, the effective-
interest method is required under generally accepted accounting principles
(GAAP)**.

## Amortizing Bond Discount

To illustrate the effective-interest method of bond discount amortization, assume that Wrightway Corporation issues $100,000 of 10%, 5-year bonds on January 1, 1996, with interest payable each July 1 and January 1. The bonds sell for $92,639 (92.639% of face value), which results in bond discount of $7,361 ($100,000 − $92,639) and an effective-interest rate of 12%. (Note that the $92,639 can be proven as shown in Appendix B at the end of this book.) Preparing a bond discount amortization schedule as shown in Illustration 16A-3 facilitates the recording of interest expense and the discount amortization.

**Illustration 16A-3**

*Bond discount amortization schedule*

| | | **WRIGHTWAY CORPORATION** | | | |
|---|---|---|---|---|---|
| | | **Bond Discount Amortization** | | | |
| | | **Effective-Interest Method—Semiannual Interest Payments** | | | |
| | | **10% Bonds Issued at 12%** | | | |
| **Semiannual Interest Periods** | **(A) Interest to Be Paid (5% × $100,000)** | **(B) Interest Expense to Be Recorded (6% × Preceding Bond Carrying Value)** | **(C) Discount Amortization (B) − (A)** | **(D) Unamortized Discount (D) − (C)** | **(E) Bond Carrying Value ($100,000 − D)** |
| Issue date | | | | $7,361 | $ 92,639 |
| 1 | $ 5,000 | $ 5,558 (6% × $92,639) | $ 558 | 6,803 | 93,197 |
| 2 | 5,000 | 5,592 (6% × $93,197) | 592 | 6,211 | 93,789 |
| 3 | 5,000 | 5,627 (6% × $93,789) | 627 | 5,584 | 94,416 |
| 4 | 5,000 | 5,665 (6% × $94,416) | 665 | 4,919 | 95,081 |
| 5 | 5,000 | 5,705 (6% × $95,081) | 705 | 4,214 | 95,786 |
| 6 | 5,000 | 5,747 (6% × $95,786) | 747 | 3,467 | 96,533 |
| 7 | 5,000 | 5,792 (6% × $96,533) | 792 | 2,675 | 97,325 |
| 8 | 5,000 | 5,840 (6% × $97,325) | 840 | 1,835 | 98,165 |
| 9 | 5,000 | 5,890 (6% × $98,165) | 890 | 945 | 99,055 |
| 10 | 5,000 | 5,945* (6% × $99,055) | 945 | -0- | 100,000 |
| | $50,000 | $57,361 | $7,361 | | |

Column **(A)** remains constant because the face value of the bonds ($100,000) is multiplied by the semiannual contractual interest rate (5%) each period.

Column **(B)** is computed as the preceding bond carrying value times the semiannual effective-interest rate (6%).

Column **(C)** indicates the discount amortization each period.

Column **(D)** decreases each period until it reaches zero at maturity.

Column **(E)** increases each period until it equals face value at maturity.

*$2 difference due to rounding.

Note that interest expense as a percentage of carrying value remains constant at 6%.

For the first interest period, the computations of bond interest expense and the bond discount amortization are as follows:

**Illustration 16A-4**

*Computation of bond discount amortization*

| | |
|---|---|
| Bond interest expense ($92,639 × 6%) | $5,558 |
| Contractual interest ($100,000 × 5%) | 5,000 |
| **Bond discount amortization** | **$ 558** |

As a result, the entry to record the payment of interest and amortization of bond discount by Wrightway Corporation on July 1, 1996, is:

| | | | |
|---|---|---|---|
| July 1 | Bond Interest Expense | 5,558 | |
| | Discount on Bonds Payable | | 558 |
| | Cash | | 5,000 |
| | (To record payment of bond interest and amortization of bond discount) | | |

For the second interest period, bond interest expense will be $5,592 ($93,197 × 6%), and the discount amortization will be $592. At December 31, the following adjusting entry is made:

| | | | |
|---|---|---|---|
| Dec. 31 | Bond Interest Expense | 5,592 | |
| | Discount on Bonds Payable | | 592 |
| | Bond Interest Payable | | 5,000 |
| | (To record accrued interest and amortization of bond discount) | | |

Total bond interest expense for 1996 is $11,150 ($5,558 + $5,592). On January 1, payment of the interest is recorded by a debit to Bond Interest Payable and a credit to Cash.

**Helpful hint** When a bond sells for $108,111, it is quoted as 108.111% of face value. Note that $108,111 can be proven as shown in Appendix B.

## Amortizing Bond Premium

The amortization of bond premium by the effective-interest method is similar to the procedures described for bond discount. As an example, assume that Wrightway Corporation issues $100,000, 10%, 5-year bonds on January 1, 1996, with interest payable on July 1 and January 1. In this case, the bonds sell for $108,111, which results in bond premium of $8,111 and an effective-interest rate of 8%. The bond premium amortization schedule is shown in Illustration 16A-5.

**Illustration 16A-5**

*Bond premium amortization schedule*

**WRIGHTWAY CORPORATION**
**Bond Premium Amortization**
**Effective-Interest Method—Semiannual Interest Payments**
**10% Bonds Issued at 8%**

| Semiannual Interest Periods | (A) Interest to Be Paid (5% × $100,000) | (B) Interest Expense to Be Recorded (4% × Preceding Bond Carry Value) | (C) Premium Amortization (A) − (B) | (D) Unamortized Premium (D) − (C) | (E) Bond Carrying Value ($100,000 + D) |
|---|---|---|---|---|---|
| Issue date | | | | $8,111 | $108,111 |
| 1 | $ 5,000 | $ 4,324 (4% × $108,111) | $ 676 | 7,435 | 107,435 |
| 2 | 5,000 | 4,297 (4% × $107,435) | 703 | 6,732 | 106,732 |
| 3 | 5,000 | 4,269 (4% × $106,732) | 731 | 6,001 | 106,001 |
| 4 | 5,000 | 4,240 (4% × $106,001) | 760 | 5,241 | 105,241 |
| 5 | 5,000 | 4,210 (4% × $105,241) | 790 | 4,451 | 104,451 |
| 6 | 5,000 | 4,178 (4% × $104,451) | 822 | 3,629 | 103,629 |
| 7 | 5,000 | 4,145 (4% × $103,629) | 855 | 2,774 | 102,774 |
| 8 | 5,000 | 4,111 (4% × $102,774) | 889 | 1,885 | 101,885 |
| 9 | 5,000 | 4,075 (4% × $101,885) | 925 | 960 | 100,960 |
| 10 | 5,000 | 4,040* (4% × $100,960) | 960 | –0– | 100,000 |
| | $50,000 | $41,889 | $8,111 | | |

Column **(A)** remains constant because the face value of the bonds ($100,000) is multiplied by the semiannual contractual interest rate (5%) each period.

Column **(B)** is computed as the carrying value of the bonds times the semiannual effective-interest rate (4%).

Column **(C)** indicates the premium amortization each period.

Column **(D)** decreases each period until it reaches zero at maturity.

Column **(E)** decreases each period until it equals face value at maturity.

*$2 difference due to rounding.

For the first interest period, the computations of bond interest expense and the bond premium amortization are:

**Illustration 16A-6**

*Computation of bond premium amortization*

| | |
|---|---|
| Bond interest expense ($108,111 × 4%) | $4,324 |
| Contractual interest ($100,000 × 5%) | 5,000 |
| Bond premium amortization | $ 676 |

The entry on the first interest date is:

| July 1 | Bond Interest Expense | 4,324 | |
|---|---|---|---|
| | Premium on Bonds Payable | 676 | |
| | Cash | | 5,000 |
| | (To record payment of bond interest and amortization of bond premium) | | |

For the second interest period, interest expense will be $4,297, and the premium amortization will be $703. Total bond interest expense for 1996 is $8,621 ($4,324 + $4,297).

# ▸Technology in Action

The amortization schedule is an excellent example of an accounting computation efficiently and effectively performed by an electronic spreadsheet. Once the selling price, face amount, contractual rate of interest, effective rate of interest, and number of interest periods are determined and entered into the spreadsheet, all of the computations until maturity can be performed by the computer. Note that all data needed for the adjusting entries can be taken directly from the amortization schedule.

# ◤Summary of Study Objective for Chapter 16 Appendix

**8.** *Contrast the effects of the straight-line and effective-interest methods of amortizing bond discount and bond premium.* The straight-line method of amortization results in a constant amount of amortization and interest expense per period but a varying percentage rate. In contrast, the effective-interest method results in varying amounts of amortization and interest expense per period but a constant percentage rate of interest. The effective-interest method generally results in a better matching of expenses with revenues. When the difference between the straight-line and effective-interest method is material, the use of the effective-interest method is required under GAAP.

# Glossary

**Bearer (coupon) bonds**   Bonds not registered. (p. 655).

**Bond certificate**   A legal document that indicates the name of the issuer, the face value of the bonds, and such other data as the contractual interest rate and maturity date of the bonds. (p. 655).

**Bond indenture**   A legal document that sets forth the terms of the bond issue. (p. 655).

**Bonds**   A form of interest bearing notes payable issued by corporations, universities, and governmental entities. (p. 652).

**Callable bonds**   Bonds that are subject to retirement at a stated dollar amount prior to maturity at the option of the issuer. (p. 655).

**Capital lease**   A contractual arrangement that transfers substantially all the benefits and risks of ownership to the lessee so that the lease is in effect a purchase of the property. (p. 670).

**Convertible bonds** Bonds that permit bondholders to convert them into common stock at their option. (p. 655).

**Contractual interest rate** Rate used to determine the amount of interest the borrower pays and the investor receives. (p. 655).

**Debenture bonds** Bonds issued against the general credit of the borrower. Also called unsecured bonds. (p. 654).

**Effective-interest method of amortization** A method of amortizing bond discount or bond premium that results in periodic interest expense equal to a constant percentage of the carrying value of the bonds. (p. 673).

**Effective-interest rate** Rate established when bonds are issued that remains constant in each interest period. (p. 673).

**Face value** Amount of principal due at the maturity date of the bond. (p. 655).

**Long-term liabilities** Obligations expected to be paid after one year. (p. 652).

**Market interest rate** The rate investors demand for loaning funds to the corporation. (p. 657).

**Mortgage bond** A bond secured by real estate. (p. 654).

**Mortgage note payable** A long-term note secured by a mortgage that pledges title to specific units of property as security for the loan. (p. 668).

**Operating lease** A contractual arrangement giving the lessee temporary use of the property with continued ownership of the property by the lessor. (p. 669).

**Registered bonds** Bonds issued in the name of the owner. (p. 655).

**Secured bonds** Bonds that have specific assets of the issuer pledged as collateral. (p. 654).

**Serial bonds** Bonds that mature in installments. (p. 654).

**Sinking fund** Cash or other assets set aside to retire debt. (p. 666).

**Sinking fund bonds** Bonds secured by specific assets set aside to retire them. (p. 654).

**Straight-line method of amortization** A method of amortizing bond discount or bond premium that allocates the same amount to interest expense in each interest period. (p. 660).

**Term bonds** Bonds that mature at a single specified future date. (p. 654).

**Unsecured bonds** Bonds issued against the general credit of the borrower. Also called debenture bonds. (p. 654).

# DEMONSTRATION PROBLEM 1

Snyder Software Inc. has successfully developed a new spreadsheet program. However, to produce and market the program, the company needed $2.0 million of additional financing. On December 31, 1996, Snyder borrowed money as follows:

1. Snyder issued $500,000, 11%, 10-year convertible bonds. The bonds sold at face value and pay semiannual interest on January 1 and July 1. Each $1,000 bond is convertible into 30 shares of Snyder's $20 par value common stock.

2. Snyder issued $1.0 million, 10%, 10-year bonds for $885,301. Interest is payable semiannually on January 1 and July 1. Snyder uses the straight-line method of amortization.

3. Snyder also issued a $500,000, 12%, 15-year mortgage note payable. The terms provide for semiannual installment payments of $36,324 on June 30 and December 31.

### Instructions

1. For the convertible bonds, prepare journal entries for:
   (a) the issuance of the bonds on January 1, 1997.
   (b) interest expense on July 1 and December 31, 1997.
   (c) the payment of interest on January 1, 1998.
   (d) the conversion of all bonds into common stock on January 1, 1998, when the market value of the common stock was $67 per share.

2. For the 10 year, 10% bonds:
   (a) journalize the issuance of the bonds on January 1, 1997.
   (b) prepare a bond discount amortization schedule for the first six interest periods.
   (c) prepare the journal entries for interest expense and amortization of bond discount in 1997.
   (d) prepare the entry for the redemption of the bonds at 101 on January 1, 2000, after paying the interest due on this date.

3. For the mortgage note payable:
   (a) prepare the entry for the issuance of the note on December 31, 1996.
   (b) prepare a payment schedule for the first four installment payments.
   (c) indicate the current and noncurrent amounts for the mortgage note payable at December 31, 1997.

## Solution to Demonstration Problem 1

1. (a) 1997

| | | | |
|---|---|---|---|
| Jan. 1 | Cash | 500,000 | |
| | Bonds Payable | | 500,000 |
| | (To record issue of 11%, 10-year convertible bonds at face value) | | |

(b) 1997

| | | | |
|---|---|---|---|
| July 1 | Bond Interest Expense | 27,500 | |
| | Cash ($500,000 × 0.055) | | 27,500 |
| | (To record payment of semiannual interest) | | |
| Dec. 31 | Bond Interest Expense | 27,500 | |
| | Bond Interest Payable | | 27,500 |
| | (To record accrual of semiannual bond interest) | | |

(c) 1998

| | | | |
|---|---|---|---|
| Jan. 1 | Bond Interest Payable | 27,500 | |
| | Cash | | 27,500 |
| | (To record payment of accrued interest) | | |

(d) Jan. 1

| | | | |
|---|---|---|---|
| Jan. 1 | Bonds Payable | 500,000 | |
| | Common Stock | | 300,000* |
| | Paid-in Capital in Excess of Par Value | | 200,000 |
| | (To record conversion of bonds into common stock) | | |
| | *($500,000 ÷ $1,000 = 500 bonds; 500 × 30 = 15,000 shares; 15,000 × $20 = $300,000) | | |

2. (a) 1997

| | | | |
|---|---|---|---|
| Jan. 1 | Cash | 885,301 | |
| | Discount on Bonds Payable | 114,699 | |
| | Bonds Payable | | 1,000,000 |
| | (To record issuance of bonds at a discount) | | |

(b)

| Semiannual Interest Period | Interest to Be Paid | Interest Expense to Be Recorded | Discount Amortization | Unamortized Discount | Bond Carrying Value |
|---|---|---|---|---|---|
| Issue date | | | | $114,699 | $885,301 |
| 1 | $50,000 | $55,735 | $5,735 | 108,964 | 891,036 |
| 2 | 50,000 | 55,735 | 5,735 | 103,229 | 896,771 |
| 3 | 50,000 | 55,735 | 5,735 | 97,494 | 902,506 |
| 4 | 50,000 | 55,735 | 5,735 | 91,759 | 908,241 |
| 5 | 50,000 | 55,735 | 5,735 | 86,024 | 913,976 |
| 6 | 50,000 | 55,735 | 5,735 | 80,289 | 919,711 |

(c) 1997

| | | | | |
|---|---|---|---|---|
| July 1 | Bond Interest Expense | | 55,735 | |
| | Discount on Bonds Payable | | | 5,735 |
| | Cash | | | 50,000 |
| | (To record payment of semiannual interest and amortization of bond discount) | | | |

| | | | | |
|---|---|---|---|---|
| Dec. 31 | Bond Interest Expense | | 55,735 | |
| | Discount on Bonds Payable | | | 5,735 |
| | Bond Interest Payable | | | 50,000 |
| | (To record accrual of semiannual interest and amortization of bond discount) | | | |

**Problem-Solving Strategies**

1. Discount on bonds payable is a contra liability account.
2. Amortization of bond discount increases bond interest expense.
3. Bond interest expense is the same each period when the straight-line method is used.
4. Loss on bond redemption occurs when the cash paid is greater than the bond carrying value.

(d) 2000

| | | | | |
|---|---|---|---|---|
| Jan. 1 | Bonds Payable | | 1,000,000 | |
| | Loss on Bond Redemption | | 90,289* | |
| | Discount on Bonds Payable | | | 80,289 |
| | Cash | | | 1,010,000 |
| | (To record redemption of bonds at 101) | | | |
| | *($1,010,000 − $919,711) | | | |

3. (a) 1996

| | | | | |
|---|---|---|---|---|
| Dec. 31 | Cash | | 500,000 | |
| | Mortgage Notes Payable | | | 500,000 |
| | (To record issuance of mortgage note payable) | | | |

**Problem-Solving Strategies**

1. Interest expense decreases each period because the principal is decreasing each period.
2. Each payment consists of (1) interest on the unpaid loan balance and (2) a reduction of the loan principal.

(b)

| Semiannual Interest Period | Cash Payment | Interest Expense | Reduction of Principal | Principal Balance |
|---|---|---|---|---|
| Issue date | | | | $500,000 |
| 1 | $36,324 | $30,000 | $6,324 | 493,676 |
| 2 | 36,324 | 29,621 | 6,703 | 486,973 |
| 3 | 36,324 | 29,218 | 7,106 | 479,867 |
| 4 | 36,324 | 28,792 | 7,532 | 472,335 |

(c) Current liability     $14,638 ($7,106 + $7,532)
    Long-term liability     $472,335.

# *D*EMONSTRATION PROBLEM 2 (Appendix Problem)

Gardner Corporation issues $1,750,000, 10-year, 12% bonds on January 1, 1996, at $1,820,000 to yield 10%. The bonds pay semiannual interest July 1 and January 1. Gardner uses the effective-interest method of amortization.

*Instructions*

(a) Prepare the journal entry to record the issuance of the bonds.
(b) Prepare the journal entry to record the payment of interest on July 1, 1996.

## Problem-Solving Strategies

1. Bond carrying value at beginning of period times effective-interest rate equals interest expense.
2. Credit to cash (or bond interest payable) is computed by multiplying the face value of the bonds by the contractual interest rate.
3. Bond premium or discount amortization is the difference between (1) and (2).
4. Interest expense increases when the effective-interest method is used for bonds issued at a discount. The reason is that a constant percentage is applied to an increasing book value to compute interest expense.

### Solution to Demonstration Problem 2

(a) 1996

| | | | | |
|---|---|---|---|---|
| Jan. 1 | Cash | | 1,820,000 | |
| | Premium on Bonds Payable | | | 70,000 |
| | Bonds Payable | | | 1,750,000 |
| | (To record issuance of bonds at a premium) | | | |
| 1996 | | | | |
| July 1 | Bond Interest Expense | | 91,000* | |
| | Premium on Bonds Payable | | 14,000** | |
| | Cash | | | 105,000 |
| | (To record payment of semiannual interest and amortization of bond premium) | | | |
| | *($1,820,000 × 5%) | | | |
| | **($105,000 − $91,000) | | | |

*Note: All **asterisked** Questions, Exercises, and Problems relate to material contained in the appendix to each chapter.

# SELF-STUDY QUESTIONS

Answers are at the end of the chapter.

(SO 1)  **1.** The term used for bonds that are unsecured is:
   a. callable bonds.
   b. indenture bonds.
   c. debenture bonds.
   d. bearer bonds.

(SO 2)  **2.** Karson Inc. issues 10-year bonds with a maturity value of $200,000. If the bonds are issued at a premium, this indicates that:
   a. the contractual interest rate exceeds the market interest rate.
   b. the market interest rate exceeds the contractual interest rate.
   c. the contractual interest rate and the market interest rate are the same.
   d. no relationship exists between the two rates.

(SO 2)  **3.** On January 1, Hurley Corporation issues $500,000, 5-year, 12% bonds at 96 with interest payable on July 1 and January 1. The entry on July 1 to record payment of bond interest and the amortization of bond discount using the straight-line method will include a:
   a. debit to Interest Expense, $30,000.
   b. debit to Interest Expense, $60,000.
   c. credit to Discount on Bonds Payable, $4,000.
   d. credit to Discount on Bonds Payable, $2,000.

(SO 2)  **4.** For the bonds issued in question 3, above, what is the carrying value of the bonds at the end of the third interest period?
   a. $486,000.
   b. $488,000.
   c. $472,000.
   d. $464,000.

(SO 2)  **5.** When the interest payment dates of a bond are May 1 and November 1, and a bond issue is sold on June 1, the amount of cash received by the issuer will be:
   a. decreased by accrued interest from June 1 to November 1.
   b. decreased by accrued interest from May 1 to June 1.
   c. increased by accrued interest from May 1 to June 1.
   d. increased by accrued interest from June 1 to November 1.

(SO 3)  **6.** Gester Corporation retires its $100,000 face value bonds at 105 on January 1, following the payment of semiannual interest. The carrying value of the bonds at the redemption date is $103,745. The entry to record the redemption will include a:
   a. credit of $3,745 to Loss on Bond Redemption.
   b. debit of $3,745 to Premium on Bonds Payable.
   c. credit of $1,255 to Gain on Bond Redemption.
   d. debit of $5,000 to Premium on Bonds Payable.

(SO 3)  **7.** Colson Inc. converts $600,000 of bonds sold at face value into 10,000 shares of common stock, par value $1. Both the bonds and the stock have a market value of $760,000. What amount should be credited to Paid-in Capital in Excess of Par as a result of the conversion?
   a. $10,000
   b. $160,000
   c. $600,000
   d. $590,000

(SO 4) 8. Sanger Company has a bond sinking fund in the amount of $400,000. Where should this amount be reported on the balance sheet?
  a. investments section
  b. current asset section
  c. current liability section
  d. long-term liability section

|        | Lease A          | Lease B          |
|--------|------------------|------------------|
| a.     | Operating lease  | Capital lease    |
| b.     | Operating lease  | Operating lease  |
| c.     | Capital lease    | Operating lease  |
| d.     | Capital lease    | Capital lease    |

(SO 5) 9. Andrews Inc. issues a $497,000, 10% 3-year mortgage note on January 1. The note will be paid in three annual installments of $200,000, each payable at the end of the year. What is the amount of interest expense that should be recognized by Andrews Inc. in the second year?
  a. $16,567
  b. $49,740
  c. $34,670
  d. $347,600

(SO 6) 10. Lease A does not contain a bargain purchase option, but the lease term is equal to 90 percent of the estimated economic life of the leased property. Lease B does not transfer ownership of the property to the lessee by the end of the lease term, but the lease term is equal to 75 percent of the estimated economic life of the leased property. How should the lessee classify these leases?

*11. On January 1, Besalius Inc. issued $1,000,000, 9% (SO 8) bonds for $939,000. The market rate of interest for these bonds is 10%. Interest is payable annually on December 31. Besalius uses the effective interest method of amortizing bond discount. At the end of the first year, Besalius should report unamortized bond discount of:
  a. $54,900.
  b. $57,100.
  c. $51,610.
  d. $51,000.

*12. On January 1, Dias Corporation issued $1,000,000, (SO 8) 14%, 5-year bonds with interest payable on July 1 and January 1. The bonds sold for $1,098,540. The market rate of interest for these bonds was 12%. On the first interest date, using the effective-interest method, the debit entry to Bond Interest Expense is for:
  a. $60,000.
  b. $76,898.
  c. $65,912.
  d. $131,825.

# QUESTIONS

1. (a) What are long-term liabilities? Give three examples. (b) What is a bond?

2. (a) As a source of long-term financing, what are the major advantages of bonds over common stock? (b) What are the major disadvantages in using bonds for long-term financing?

3. Contrast the following types of bonds: (a) secured and unsecured, (b) term and serial, (c) registered and bearer, and (d) convertible and callable.

4. The following terms are important in issuing bonds: (a) face value, (b) contractual interest rate, (c) bond indenture, and (d) bond certificate. Explain each of these terms.

5. Describe the two major obligations incurred by a company when bonds are issued.

6. Assume that Stoney Inc. sold bonds with a par value of $100,000 for $104,000. Was the market interest rate equal to, less than, or greater than the bonds' contractual interest rate? Explain.

7. Barbara Secord and Jack Dalton are discussing how the market price of a bond is determined. Barbara believes that the market price of a bond is solely a function of the amount of the principal payment at the end of the term of a bond. Is she right? Discuss.

8. If a 10%, 10-year, $600,000 bond is issued at par and interest is paid semiannually, what is the amount of the interest payment at the end of the first semiannual period?

9. If the Bonds Payable account has a balance of $900,000 and the Discount on Bonds Payable account has a balance of $40,000, what is the carrying value of the bonds?

10. Explain the straight-line method of amortizing discount and premium on bonds payable.

11. Moby Corporation issues $200,000 of 8%, 5-year bonds on January 1, 1996, at 104. Assuming that the straight-line method is used to amortize the premium, what is the total amount of interest expense for 1996?

12. Which accounts are debited and which are credited if a bond issue originally sold at a premium is redeemed before maturity at 97 immediately following the payment of interest?

13. Li Su Corporation is considering issuing a convertible bond. What is a convertible bond? Discuss the advantages of a convertible bond from the standpoint of (a) the bondholders and (b) the issuing corporation.

14. The financial statements of Kenota Inc. disclose that it has a bond sinking fund. What is a bond sinking fund? What is its purpose?

15. Doug Bareak, a friend of yours, has recently purchased a home for $125,000, paying $25,000 down and the remainder financed by a 10.5%, 20-year mortgage, payable at $998.38 per month. At the end of the first month, Doug receives a statement from the bank indicating that only $123.38 of principal was paid during the month. At this rate, he calculates that it will take over 67 years to pay off the mortgage. Is he right? Discuss.

16. (a) What is a lease agreement? (b) What are the two most common types of leases? (c) Distinguish between the two types of leases.

17. Marshall Company rents a warehouse on a month-to-month basis for the storage of its excess inventory. The company periodically must rent space when its production greatly exceeds actual sales. What is the nature of this type of lease agreement, and what accounting treatment should be accorded it?

18. Rodriguez Company entered into an agreement to lease 12 computers from Elgin Electronics Inc. The present value of the lease payments is $186,300. Assuming that this is a capital lease, what entry would Rodriguez Company make on the date of the lease agreement?

19. In general, what are the requirements for the financial statement presentation of long-term liabilities?

*20. Julia Amant is discussing the advantages of the effective-interest method of bond amortization with her accounting staff. What do you think Julia is saying?

*21. Summit Corporation issues $400,000 of 9%, 5-year bonds on January 1, 1996, at 104. If Summit uses the effective-interest method in amortizing the premium, will the annual interest expense increase or decrease over the life of the bonds? Explain.

# BRIEF EXERCISES

*Comparison of bond versus stock financing.*
(SO 1)

**BE16–1**  Olga Inc. is considering two alternatives to finance its construction of a new $2 million plant:

(a) Issuance of 200,000 shares of common stock at the market price of $10 per share.
(b) Issuance of $2 million, 8% bonds at par.

Complete the following table and indicate which alternative is preferable.

|  | Issue Stock | Issue Bond |
|---|---|---|
| Income before interest and taxes | $1,000,000 | $1,000,000 |
| Interest expense from bonds |  |  |
| Income before income taxes | $ | $ |
| Income tax expense (30%) |  |  |
| Net income | $ | $ |
| Outstanding shares |  | 700,000 |
| Earnings per share |  |  |

*Journal entries for bonds issued at face value.*
(SO 2)

**BE16–2**  Keystone Corporation issued 1,000, 9%, 5-year, $1,000 bonds dated January 1, 1996, at 100. (a) Prepare the journal entry to record the sale of these bonds on January 1, 1996. (b) Prepare the journal entry to record the first interest payment on July 1, 1996 (interest payable semiannually), assuming no previous accrual of interest. (c) Prepare the adjusting journal entry on December 31, 1996, to record interest expense.

*Journal entries for bonds issued at a discount.*
(SO 2)

**BE16–3**  Dominic Company issues $2 million, 10 year, 9% bonds at 98, with interest payable on July 1 and January 1. The straight-line method is used to amortize bond discount. (a) Prepare the journal entry to record the sale of these bonds on January 1, 1996. (b) Prepare the journal entry to record interest expense and bond discount amortization on July 1, 1996, assuming no previous accrual of interest.

*Journal entries for bonds issued at a premium.*
(SO 2)

**BE16–4**  Hercules Inc. issues $5 million, 5-year, 10% bonds at 103, with interest payable on July 1 and January 1. The straight-line method is used to amortize bond premium. (a) Prepare the journal entry to record the sale of these bonds on January 1, 1996. (b) Prepare the journal entry to record interest expense and bond premium amortization on July 1, 1996, assuming no previous accrual of interest.

**BE16–5** Goodland Inc. has outstanding $1 million, 10-year, 12% bonds with interest payable on July 1 and January 1. The bonds were dated January 1, 1996, but were issued on May 1, 1996, at face value plus accrued interest. (a) Prepare the journal entry to record the sale of the bonds on May 1, 1996. (b) Prepare the journal entry to record the interest payment on July 1, 1996.

*Journal entries for bonds issued between interest dates.*
*(SO 2)*

**BE16–6** The balance sheet for Hathaway Company reports the following information on July 1, 1996:

*Redemption of bonds.*
*(SO 3)*

### Long-term liabilities

| | | |
|---|---|---|
| Bonds payable | $1,000,000 | |
| Less: Discount on bonds payable | 60,000 | $940,000 |

Hathaway decides to redeem these bonds at 102 after paying semiannual interest. Prepare the journal entry to record the redemption on July 1, 1996.

**BE16–7** Frisco Company establishes a sinking fund for its $1 million, 5-year bonds. On January 1, 1996, it makes its first annual cash contribution of $170,000. At the end of 1996, the sinking fund had earned $12,000. (a) Prepare the journal entry to record the contribution made into the sinking fund on January 1, 1996. (b) Prepare the journal entry to record the revenue earned in the sinking fund in 1996.

*Accounting for bond sinking fund.*
*(SO 4)*

**BE16–8** Escobar Inc. issues a $300,000, 10%, 10-year mortgage note on December 31, 1996, to obtain financing for a new building. The terms provide for semiannual installment payments of $24,073. Prepare the entry to record the mortgage loan on December 31, 1996, and the first installment payment.

*Accounting for long-term notes payable.*
*(SO 5)*

**BE16–9** Prepare the journal entries that the lessee should make to record the following transactions:

*Contrast accounting for operating and capital lease.*
*(SO 6)*

1. The lessee makes a lease payment of $80,000 to the lessor in an operating lease transaction.
2. Goldbaum Company leases a new building from Bracer Construction, Inc. The present value of the lease payments is $600,000. The lease qualifies as a capital lease.

**BE16–10** Presented below are long-term liability items for Warner Company at December 31, 1996. Prepare the long-term liabilities section of the balance sheet for Warner Company.

*Financial statement presentation of long-term liabilities.*
*(SO 7)*

| | |
|---|---|
| Bonds payable, due 2001 | $900,000 |
| Lease liability | 50,000 |
| Notes payable, due 2003 | 80,000 |
| Discount on bonds payable | 45,000 |

**\*BE16–11** Presented below is the partial bond discount amortization schedule for Lodge Corp. Lodge uses the effective-interest method of amortization.

*Effective interest method of bond amortization.*
*(SO 8)*

| Semiannual Interest Periods | Interest to Be Paid | Interest Expense to Be Recorded | Discount Amortization | Unamortized Discount | Bond Carrying Value |
|---|---|---|---|---|---|
| Issue date | | | | $62,311 | $937,689 |
| 1 | $45,000 | $46,884 | $1,884 | 60,427 | 939,573 |
| 2 | 45,000 | 46,979 | 1,979 | 58,448 | 941,552 |

**Instructions**

(a) Prepare the journal entry to record the payment of interest and the discount amortization at the end of period 1.
(b) ▭▭▭▶ Explain why interest expense is greater than interest paid.
(c) ▭▭▭▶ Explain why interest expense will increase each period.

# EXERCISES

•••••••••••••••••••••••••••••••••••••••••••••••••••••••••••••••••••••••••

**E16–1** Sundown Airlines is considering two alternatives for the financing of a purchase of a fleet of airplanes. These two alternatives are:

*Compare two alternatives of financing—issuance of common stock vs. issuance of bonds.*
*(SO 1)*

1. Issue 60,000 shares of common stock at $45 per share. (Cash dividends have not been paid nor is the payment of any contemplated.)
2. Issue 13%, 10-year bonds at par for $2,700,000.

It is estimated that the company will earn $900,000 before interest and taxes as a result of this purchase. The company has an estimated tax rate of 30% and has 90,000 shares of common stock outstanding prior to the new financing.

**Instructions**
Determine the effect on net income and earnings per share for these two methods of financing.

*Journal entries for issuance of bonds and payment and accrual of bond interest.*
*(SO 2)*

**E16–2**   On January 1, Laramie Company issued $90,000, 10%, 10-year bonds at par. Interest is payable semiannually on July 1 and January 1. Interest is not accrued on June 30.

**Instructions**
Present journal entries to record:

(a) The issuance of the bonds.
(b) The payment of interest on July 1.
(c) The accrual of interest on December 31.

*Journal entries to record issuance of bonds, payment of interest, amortization of premium, and redemption at maturity.*
*(SO 2, 3)*

**E16–3**   Pueblo Company issued $240,000, 9%, 20-year bonds on January 1, 1996, at 103. Interest is payable semiannually on July 1 and January 1. Pueblo uses straight-line amortization for bond premium or discount. Interest is not accrued on June 30.

**Instructions**
Prepare the journal entries to record:

(a) The issuance of the bonds.
(b) The payment of interest and the premium amortization on July 1, 1996.
(c) The accrual of interest and the premium amortization on December 31, 1996.
(d) The redemption of the bonds at maturity, assuming interest for the last interest period has been paid and recorded.

*Journal entries to record issuance of bonds, payment of interest, amortization of discount, and redemption at maturity.*
*(SO 2, 3)*

**E16–4**   Cotter Company issued $180,000, 11%, 10-year bonds on December 31, 1995, for $172,000. Interest is payable semiannually on June 30 and December 31. Cotter uses the straight-line method to amortize bond premium or discount.

**Instructions**
Prepare the journal entries to record:

(a) The issuance of the bonds.
(b) The payment of interest and the discount amortization on June 30, 1996.
(c) The payment of interest and the discount amortization on December 31, 1996.
(d) The redemption of the bonds at maturity, assuming interest for the last interest period has been paid and recorded.

*Journal entries to record issuance of bonds between interest dates, and payment and accrual of interest.*
*(SO 2)*

**E16–5**   On April 1, Virginia Company issued $72,000, 10%, 10-year bonds dated January 1 at par plus accrued interest. Interest is payable semiannually on July 1 and January 1.

**Instructions**
Present journal entries to record:

(a) The issuance of the bonds.
(b) The payment of interest on July 1. Interest is not accrued on June 30.
(c) The accrual of interest on December 31.

*Journal entries for redemption of bonds and conversion of bonds into common stock.*
*(SO 3)*

**E16–6**   Presented below are three independent situations:

1. Ernst Corporation retired $120,000 face value, 12% bonds on June 30, 1996, at 102. The carrying value of the bonds at the redemption date was $107,500. The bonds pay semiannual interest and the interest payment due on June 30, 1996, has been made and recorded.
2. Young, Inc. retired $150,000 face value, 12.5% bonds on June 30, 1996, at 98. The carrying value of the bonds at the redemption date was $151,000. The bonds pay semiannual interest and the interest payment due on June 30, 1996, has been made and recorded.
3. Lybrand Company has $80,000, 8%, 12-year convertible bonds outstanding. These bonds were sold at face value and pay semiannual interest on June 30 and December

31 of each year. The bonds are convertible into 30 shares of Jefferson $2 par value common stock for each $1,000 worth of bonds. On December 31, 1996, after the bond interest has been paid, $20,000 face value bonds were converted. The market value of Jefferson common stock was $44 per share on December 31, 1996.

**Instructions**
For each independent situation above, prepare the appropriate journal entry for the redemption or conversion of the bonds.

**E16–7**  Shanghai Co. decides to establish a sinking fund for its $6,000,000, 20-year bonds that are outstanding. The trustee indicates that an annual contribution of $163,000 should be made at the end of each year. The sinking fund earned $9,700 in the second year. At the maturity date, the sinking fund had a balance of $5,960,000.

*Journal entries to record sinking fund deposit, revenue earned on fund assets, and redemption of bonds.*
*(SO 4)*

**Instructions**
Prepare the journal entries to record:

(a)  The first contribution by Shanghai Co.
(b)  The actual earnings in the second year and the second contribution.
(c)  The redemption of the bonds at maturity.

**E16–8**  Peyton Co. receives $110,000 when it issues a $110,000, 10%, mortgage note payable to finance the construction of a building at December 31, 1996. The terms provide for semi-annual installment payments of $7,500 on June 30 and December 31.

*Journal entries to record mortgage note and installment payments.*
*(SO 5)*

**Instructions**
Prepare the journal entries to record the mortgage loan and the first two installment payments.

**E16–9**  Presented below are two independent situations.

1.  Ready Car Rental leased a car to Rockefeller Company for one year. Terms of the operating lease agreement call for monthly payments of $500.
2.  On January 1, 1996, Wizard Inc. entered into an agreement to lease 20 computers from Hi-Tech Electronics. The terms of the lease agreement require three annual rental payments of $120,000 (including 10% interest) beginning December 31, 1996. The present value of the three rental payments is $298,422. Wizard considers this a capital lease.

*Journal entries for operating lease and capital lease.*
*(SO 6)*

**Instructions**
(a)  Prepare the appropriate journal entry to be made by Rockefeller Company for the first lease payment.
(b)  Prepare the journal entry to record the lease agreement on the books of Wizard Inc. on January 1, 1996.

**E16–10**  The adjusted trial balance for Viola Corporation at the end of the current year contained the following accounts:

*Statement presentation of long-term liabilities.*
*(SO 7)*

| | |
|---|---|
| Bond interest payable | $  9,000 |
| Lease liability | 59,500 |
| Bonds payable, due 2007 | 120,000 |
| Premium on bonds payable | 32,000 |
| Bond sinking fund | 241,600 |

**Instructions**
(a)  Prepare the long-term liabilities section of the balance sheet.
(b)  Indicate the proper balance sheet classification for the account(s) listed above that do not belong in the long-term liabilities section.

**\*E16–11**  Quebec Corporation issued $260,000, 9%, 10-year bonds on January 1, 1996, for $243,799. This price resulted in an effective interest rate of 10% on the bonds. Interest is payable semiannually on July 1 and January 1. Quebec uses the effective-interest method to amortize bond premium or discount. Interest is not accrued on June 30.

*Journal entries for issuance of bonds payment of interest, and amortization of discount using effective-interest method.*
*(SO 8)*

**Instructions**
Prepare the journal entries to record (round to the nearest dollar):

(a)  The issuance of the bonds.
(b)  The payment of interest and the discount amortization on July 1, 1996.
(c)  The accrual of interest and the discount amortization on December 31, 1996.

*Journal entries for issuance of bonds, payment of interest, and amortization of premium using effective-interest method. (SO 8)*

\*E16–12   Cleveland Company issued $180,000, 11%, 10-year bonds on January 1, 1996, for $191,216. This price resulted in an effective interest rate of 10% on the bonds. Interest is payable semiannually on July 1 and January 1. Cleveland uses the effective-interest method to amortize bond premium or discount. Interest is not accrued on June 30.

**Instructions**

Prepare the journal entries (rounded to the nearest dollar) to record:

    (a)  The issuance of the bonds.
    (b)  The payment of interest and the premium amortization on July 1, 1996.
    (c)  The accrual of interest and the premium amortization on December 31, 1996.

# PROBLEMS

*Prepare journal entries to record issuance of bonds, interest accrual, and amortization for 2 years. (SO 2, 7)*

**P16–1**   Moriarity Company sold $4,000,000, 9%, 20-year bonds on January 1, 1996. The bonds were dated January 1, 1996, and pay interest on January 1 and July 1. Moriarity Company uses the straight-line method to amortize bond premium or discount. The bonds were sold at 97. Assume no interest is accrued on June 30.

**Instructions**

    (a)  Prepare the journal entry to record the issuance of the bonds on January 1, 1996.
    (b)  Prepare a bond discount amortization schedule for the first four interest periods.
    (c)  Prepare the journal entries for interest and the amortization of the discount in 1996 and 1997.
    (d)  Show the balance sheet presentation of the bond liability at December 31, 1997.

*Prepare journal entries to record issuance of bonds, interest, and amortization of bond premium and discount. (SO 2, 7)*

**P16–2**   Beatrice Corporation sold $1,500,000, 8%, 10-year bonds on January 1, 1996. The bonds were dated January 1, 1996, and pay interest on July 1 and January 1. Beatrice Corporation uses the straight-line method to amortize bond premium or discount. Assume no interest is accrued on June 30.

**Instructions**

    (a)  Prepare all the necessary journal entries to record the issuance of the bonds and bond interest expense for 1996, assuming that the bonds sold at 102.
    (b)  Prepare journal entries as in part (a) assuming that the bonds sold at 97.
    (c)  Show balance sheet presentation for each bond issue at December 31, 1996.

*Prepare journal entries to record interest payments, discount amortization, and redemption of bonds. (SO 2, 3)*

**P16–3**   The following is taken from Bermuda Corp. balance sheet at December 31, 1996:

| | | |
|---|---:|---:|
| Current liabilities | | |
|   Bond interest payable (for 6 months | | |
|     from July 1 to December 31) | | $132,000 |
| Long-term liabilities | | |
|   Bonds payable, 11%, due | | |
|     January 1, 2007 | $2,400,000 | |
|   Less: Discount on bonds payable | 84,000 | $2,316,000 |

Interest is payable semiannually on January 1 and July 1. The bonds are callable on any semi-annual interest date. Bermuda uses straight-line amortization for any bond premium or discount. From December 31, 1996, the bonds will be outstanding for an additional 10 years or 120 months. Assume no interest is accrued on June 30.

**Instructions**

(Round all computations to the nearest dollar.)

    (a)  Journalize the payment of bond interest on January 1, 1997.
    (b)  Prepare the entry to amortize bond discount and to pay the interest due on July 1, 1997.
    (c)  Assume on July 1, 1997, after paying interest that Bermuda Corp. calls bonds having a face value of $800,000. The call price is 102. Record the redemption of the bonds.
    (d)  Prepare the adjusting entry at December 31, 1997, to amortize bond discount and to accrue interest on the remaining bonds.

**P16–4** Nankin Electronics issues a $900,000, 10%, 10-year mortgage note on December 31, 1995, to help finance a plant expansion program. The terms provide for semiannual installment payments, not including real estate taxes and insurance of $72,218. Payments are due June 30 and December 31.

*Prepare installment payments schedule and journal entries for a mortgage note payable. (SO 5)*

**Instructions**
(a) Prepare an installment payments schedule for the first 2 years.
(b) Prepare the entries for (1) the mortgage loan and (2) the first two installment payments.
(c) Show how the total mortgage liability should be reported on the balance sheet at December 31, 1996.

**P16–5** Presented below are three different lease transactions in which Manitoba Enterprises engaged in 1996. Assume that all lease transactions start on January 1, 1996. In no case does Manitoba receive title to the properties leased during or at the end of the lease term.

*Analyze three different lease situations and prepare journal entries. (SO 6)*

| | **Lessor** | | |
| --- | --- | --- | --- |
| | Lornegren Associates | Potter Co. | Haskins Inc. |
| Type of property | Bulldozer | Truck | Furniture |
| Bargain purchase option | None | None | None |
| Lease term | 4 years | 6 years | 3 years |
| Estimated economic life | 8 years | 7 years | 5 years |
| Yearly rental | $13,000 | $ 6,000 | $ 4,500 |
| Fair market value of leased asset | $80,000 | $29,000 | $27,500 |
| Present value of the lease rental payments | $48,000 | $27,000 | $12,000 |

**Instructions**
(a) Identify the leases above as operating or capital leases. Explain.
(b) How should the lease transaction for Potter Co. be recorded on January 1, 1996?
(c) How should the lease transactions for Haskins Inc. be recorded in 1996?

**\*P16–6** On July 1, 1996, Global Satellites issued $1,200,000 face value, 9%, 10-year bonds at $1,125,227. This price resulted in an effective-interest rate of 10% on the bonds. Global uses the effective-interest method to amortize bond premium or discount. The bonds pay semiannual interest July 1 and January 1.

*Prepare journal entries to record issuance of bonds, payment of interest, and amortization of bond discount using effective-interest method. (SO 8)*

**Instructions**
(Round all computations to the nearest dollar.)

(a) Prepare the journal entry to record the issuance of the bonds on July 1, 1996.
(b) Prepare the journal entry to record the accrual of interest and the amortization of the discount on December 31, 1996.
(c) Prepare the journal entry to record the payment of interest and the amortization of the discount on July 1, 1997.
(d) Prepare the journal entry to record the accrual of interest and the amortization of the discount on December 31, 1997.
(e) Prepare an amortization table through December 31, 1997 (three interest periods) for this bond issue.

**\*P16–7** On July 1, 1996, Saudi Chemical Company issued $2,000,000 face value, 12%, 10-year bonds at $2,249,245. This price resulted in a 10% effective-interest rate on the bonds. Saudi uses the effective-interest method to amortize bond premium or discount. The bonds pay semiannual interest on each July 1 and January 1.

*Prepare journal entries to record issuance of bonds, payment of interest, and amortization of premium using effective-interest method. In addition, answer questions. (SO 8)*

**Instructions**
(a) Prepare the journal entries to record the following transactions:
(1) The issuance of the bonds on July 1, 1996.
(2) The accrual of interest and the amortization of the premium on December 31, 1996.
(3) The payment of interest and the amortization of the premium on July 1, 1997.

    (4) The accrual of interest and the amortization of the premium on December 31, 1997.
(b) Show the proper balance sheet presentation for the liability for bonds payable on the December 31, 1997, balance sheet.
(c) ▭▭▭▸ Provide the answers to the following questions in letter form.
    (1) What amount of interest expense is reported for 1997?
    (2) Would the bond interest expense reported in 1997 be the same as, greater than, or less than the amount that would be reported if the straight-line method of amortization were used?
    (3) Determine the total cost of borrowing over the life of the bond.
    (4) Would the total bond interest expense be greater than, the same as, or less than the total interest expense if the straight-line method of amortization were used?

# ALTERNATE PROBLEMS

*Prepare journal entries to record issuance of bonds, interest accrual, and amortization for 2 years.*
*(SO 2, 7)*

**P16–1A**   Montego Electric sold $3,000,000, 10%, 10-year bonds on January 1, 1996. The bonds were dated January 1 and pay interest July 1 and January 1. Montego Electric uses the straight-line method to amortize bond premium or discount. The bonds were sold at 104. Assume no interest is accrued on June 30.

*Instructions*
(a) Prepare the journal entry to record the issuance of the bonds on January 1, 1996.
(b) Prepare a bond premium amortization schedule for the first four interest periods.
(c) Prepare the journal entries for interest and the amortization of the premium in 1996 and 1997.
(d) Show the balance sheet presentation of the bond liability at December 31, 1997.

*Prepare journal entries to record issuance of bonds, interest, and amortization of bond premium and discount.*
*(SO 2, 7)*

**P16–2A**   San Diego Company sold $1,500,000, 12%, 10-year bonds on July 1, 1996. The bonds were dated July 1, 1996, and pay interest July 1 and January 1. San Diego Company uses the straight-line method to amortize bond premium or discount. Assume no interest is accrued on June 30.

*Instructions*
(a) Prepare all the necessary journal entries to record the issuance of the bonds and bond interest expense for 1996, assuming that the bonds sold at 102.
(b) Prepare journal entries as in part (a) assuming that the bonds sold at 94.
(c) Show balance sheet presentation for each bond issue at December 31, 1996.

*Prepare journal entries to record interest payments, premium amortization, and redemption of bonds.*
*(SO 2, 3)*

**P16–3A**   The following is taken from the Walenda Oil Company balance sheet at December 31, 1996:

| | | |
|---|---:|---:|
| Current liabilities | | |
|   Bond interest payable (for 6 months | | |
|     from July 1 to December 31) | | $  216,000 |
| Long-term liabilities | | |
|   Bonds payable, 12% due January 1, 2007 | $3,600,000 | |
|   Add: Premium on Bonds Payable | 300,000 | $3,900,000 |

Interest is payable semiannually on January 1 and July 1. The bonds are callable on any semi-annual interest date. Walenda uses straight-line amortization for any bond premium or discount. From December 31, 1996, the bonds will be outstanding for an additional 10 years (120 months). Assume no interest is accrued on June 30.

*Instructions*
(a) Journalize the payment of bond interest on January 1, 1997.
(b) Prepare the entry to amortize bond premium and to pay the interest due on July 1, 1997.
(c) Assume on July 1, 1997, after paying interest, that Walenda Company calls bonds having a face value of $1,800,000. The call price is 101. Record the redemption of the bonds.
(d) Prepare the adjusting entry at December 31, 1997, to amortize bond premium and to accrue interest on the remaining bonds.

**P16–4A** Elite Electronics issues an $800,000, 12%, 10-year mortgage note on December 31, 1995. The proceeds from the note are to be used in financing a new research laboratory. The terms of the note provide for semiannual installment payments, exclusive of real estate taxes and insurance, of $69,748. Payments are due June 30 and December 31.

*Prepare installment schedule and journal entries for a mortgage note payable.*
*(SO 5)*

**Instructions**
(a) Prepare an installment payments schedule for the first 2 years.
(b) Prepare the entries for (1) the loan and (2) the first two installment payments.
(c) Show how the total mortgage liability should be reported on the balance sheet at December 31, 1996.

**P16–5A** Presented below are three different lease transactions that occurred for Brett Inc. in 1996. Assume that all lease contracts start on January 1, 1996. In no case does Brett receive title to the properties leased during or at the end of the lease term.

*Analyze three different lease situations and prepare journal entries.*
*(SO 6)*

| | Lessor | | |
| --- | --- | --- | --- |
| | **Chen Delivery** | **Williams Co.** | **Cecil Auto** |
| Type of property | Computer | Delivery equipment | Automobile |
| Yearly rental | $ 8,000 | $ 4,000 | $ 3,700 |
| Lease term | 6 years | 4 years | 2 years |
| Estimated economic life | 7 years | 7 years | 5 years |
| Fair market value of lease asset | $44,000 | $19,000 | $11,000 |
| Present value of the lease rental payments | $43,000 | $13,000 | $ 6,400 |
| Bargain purchase option | None | None | None |

**Instructions**
(a) Which of the leases above are operating leases and which are capital leases? Explain.
(b) How should the lease transaction for Williams Co. be recorded in 1996?
(c) How should the lease transaction for Chen Delivery be recorded on January 1, 1996?

**\*P16–6A** On July 1, 1996, Mt. Vernon Corporation issued $1,500,000 face value, 12%, 10-year bonds at $1,686,934. This price resulted in an effective-interest rate of 10% on the bonds. Mt. Vernon uses the effective-interest method to amortize bond premium or discount. The bonds pay semiannual interest July 1 and January 1.

*Prepare journal entries to record issuance of bonds, payment of interest, and amortization of bond premium using effective-interest method.*
*(SO 2)*

**Instructions**
(Round all computations to the nearest dollar.)

(a) Prepare the journal entry to record the issuance of the bonds on July 1, 1996.
(b) Prepare the journal entry to record the accrual of interest and the amortization of the premium on December 31, 1996.
(c) Prepare the journal entry to record the payment of interest and the amortization of the premium on July 1, 1997.
(d) Prepare the journal entry to record the accrual of interest and the amortization of the premium on December 31, 1997.
(e) Prepare an amortization table through December 31, 1997 (three interest periods) for this bond issue.

**\*P16–7A** On July 1, 1996, Cherokee Company issued $2,200,000 face value, 10%, 10-year bonds at $1,947,651. This price resulted in an effective-interest rate of 12% on the bonds. Cherokee uses the effective-interest method to amortize bond premium or discount. The bonds pay semiannual interest July 1 and January 1.

*Prepare journal entries to record issuance of bonds, payment of interest, and amortization of discount using effective-interest method. In addition, answer questions.*
*(SO 2, 8)*

**Instructions**
(a) Prepare the journal entries to record the following transactions.
  (1) The issuance of the bonds on July 1, 1996.
  (2) The accrual of interest and the amortization of the discount on December 31, 1996.
  (3) The payment of interest and the amortization of the discount on July 1, 1997.
  (4) The accrual of interest and the amortization of the discount on December 31, 1997.

(b) Show the proper balance sheet presentation for the liability for bonds payable on the December 31, 1997, balance sheet.
(c) ▨▨▨▨▷  Provide the answers to the following questions in letter form.
  (1) What amount of interest expense is reported for 1997?
  (2) Would the bond interest expense reported in 1997 be the same as, greater than, or less than the amount that would be reported if the straight-line method of amortization were used?
  (3) Determine the total cost of borrowing over the life of the bond.
  (4) Would the total bond interest expense be greater than, the same as, or less than the total interest expense that would be reported if the straight-line method of amortization were used?

# ▶*B*roadening Your Perspective

## *F*INANCIAL REPORTING PROBLEM

Refer to the financial statements of PepsiCo, Inc., and the Notes to Consolidated Financial Statements in Appendix A.

*Instructions*
Answer the following questions.

(a) What was PepsiCo's total long-term debt at December 31, 1994? What was the increase/decrease in PepsiCo's total long-term debt from the prior year?
(b) What were the components of total long-term debt on December 31, 1994?
(c) What is the amount of leases that are reported as part of long-term debt?
(d) What amount of the total debt (both short-term and long-term) pays a variable rate? Why is it important to know whether the company is committed to paying variable- or fixed-rate debt?

## *D*ECISION CASE

Presented below is the condensed balance sheet for Construction, Inc., as of December 31, 1996:

### CONSTRUCTION, INC.
### Balance Sheet
### December 31, 1996

| Current assets | $ 800,000 | Current liabilities | $1,200,000 |
| Plant assets | 1,600,000 | Long-term liabilities | 700,000 |
| | | Common stock | 400,000 |
| | | Retained earnings | 100,000 |
| Total | $2,400,000 | Total | $2,400,000 |

Construction has decided that it needs to purchase a new crane for its operations. The new crane costs $900,000 and has a useful life of 15 years. However, Construction's bank has refused to provide any help in financing the purchase of the new equipment, even though Construction is willing to pay an above-market interest rate for the financing.

The chief financial officer for Construction, Lisa Colder, has discussed with the manufacturer of the crane the possibility of a lease arrangement. After some negotiation, the manufacturer of the equipment agrees to lease the crane to Construction under the following terms: length of the lease, 7 years; payments, $100,000 per year. The present value of the lease payments is $548,732.

The board of directors at Construction is delighted with this new lease. They reason that they have the use of the crane for the next 7 years. In addition, Lisa Colder notes that this type of financing is a good deal because it will keep debt off the balance sheet.

*Instructions*
(a) Why do you think the bank decided not to lend money to Construction, Inc.?
(b) How should this lease transaction be reported in the financial statements?
(c) What did Lisa Colder mean when she said "leasing will keep debt off the balance sheet"?

# COMMUNICATION ACTIVITY

Finn Berg, president of the Blue Marlin, is considering the issuance of bonds to finance an expansion of his business. He has asked you to (1) discuss the advantages of bonds over common stock financing, (2) indicate the type of bonds he might issue, and (3) explain the issuing procedures used in bond transactions.

*Instructions*
Write a memorandum to the president, answering his request.

# GROUP ACTIVITY

The text explains that bonds may be issued at (1) face value, (2) a discount, (3) a premium, and (4) a date that is between interest dates.

*Instructions*
With the class divided into four groups, each group should choose one type of bond issue. Your group is to explain, using dollar amounts different from those used in the text: (a) the entry to record the sale of the bonds, (b) the entry at the end of the first interest period after the sale, and (c) the financial statement presentation of the bonds and interest expense at the end of the first interest period.

# ETHICS CASE

Andy Vicks is the president, founder, and majority owner of Custom Medical Corporation, an emerging medical technology products company. Custom is in dire need of additional capital to keep operating and to bring several promising products to final development, testing, and production. Andy, as owner of 51% of the outstanding stock, manages the company's operations. He places heavy emphasis on research and development and long-term growth. The other principal stockholder is Jill Caterino who, as a nonemployee investor, owns 40% of the stock. Jill would like to deemphasize the R&D functions and emphasize the marketing function to maximize short-run sales and profits from existing products. She believes this strategy would raise the market price of Custom's stock.

All of Andy's personal capital and borrowing power is tied up in his 51% stock ownership. He knows that any offering of additional shares of stock will dilute his controlling interest because he won't be able to participate in such an issuance. But, Jill has money and would likely buy enough shares to gain control of Custom. She then would dictate the company's future direction, even if it meant replacing Andy as president and CEO.

The company already has considerable debt. Raising additional debt will be costly, will adversely affect Custom's credit rating, and will increase the company's reported losses due to the growth in interest expense. Jill and the other minority stockholders express opposition to the assumption of additional debt, fearing the company will be pushed to the brink of bankruptcy. Wanting to maintain his control and to preserve the direction of "his" company, Andy is doing everything to avoid a stock issuance and is contemplating a large issuance of bonds, even if it means the bonds are issued with a high effective-interest rate.

*Instructions*

    (a)  Who are the stakeholders in this situation?

    (b)  What are the ethical issues in this case?

    (c)  What would you do if you were Andy?

# CRITICAL THINKING
## ▸ *A Real-World Focus: Apache Corporation*
••••••••••••••••••••••••••••••••••••••••••••••••••••••••••••••••••••••••••••••••••••

*Apache Corporation is an international, independent energy enterprise engaged in the exploration, development, production, gathering, processing, and marketing of natural gas and crude oil. Its corporate headquarters are located in Houston, Texas, and it has operations in 18 states of the U.S. as well as Australia, the Congo, France, Myanmar, and Indonesia.*

The 1994 annual report of Apache Corporation disclosed the following information in its management discussion section:

> In May 1994, Apache issued 9.25% bonds due 2002 in the principal amount of $100 million. The proceeds of $99 million from the offering were used to reduce bank debt, to pay off the 9.5% convertible debentures due 1996, and for general corporate purposes. In December 1994, the company privately placed 3.93% convertible notes due 1997 in the principal amount of $75 million. The notes are not redeemable before maturity and are convertible into Apache common stock at the option of the holders at any time prior to maturity, at a conversion price of $27 per share. Proceeds from the sale of the notes were used for the repayment of bank debt.

*Instructions*

    (a)  Identify the face amount, contractual interest rate, and selling price of the newly issued bonds due in 2002. Explain whether the bonds sold at a premium or a discount.

    (b)  For what purposes has Apache Corporation been incurring more debt?

---

*Answers to Self-Study Questions*

1. c    2. a    3. d    4. a    5. c    6. b    7. d    8. a    9. c    10. d    *11. b
*12. c

## Concepts for Review

**Before studying this chapter, you should know or, if necessary, review:**

**a.** *How to record the issuance of bonds. (Ch. 16, pp. 658–64)*

**b.** *How to compute and record interest. (Ch. 3, pp. 100–1, Ch. 8, pp. 341–3, and Ch. 16, pp. 658–64 and 669)*

**c.** *How to record amortization of bond discount and bond premium using the straight-line method. (Ch. 16, pp. 661–3)*

**d.** *Where temporary and long-term investments are classified on a balance sheet. (Ch. 4, pp. 151–2)*

# They Play the Market for Fun, Profit, and an Education

BEARDSTOWN, Ill. — By day she's a trust officer at the local bank; in her free time Betty Sinnock is the financial planner for the Beardstown Ladies—a fifteen-woman investment club whose success has earned it national attention and air time on "Donahue" and "20/20." The club has attained the public spotlight by earning an average annual return of 23.4% on its investments over the last decade—a return many highly paid mutual fund managers did not come close to equaling during the same period. The National Association of Investors Corporation has six times ranked the group near the top of the 11,000 investment clubs that it follows.

Do these women post a collection of impressive graduate degrees? No—this group of women (twelve of whom are past age 60) is largely self-educated in the ways of Wall Street. The secrets to their investment success are spelled out in a best-selling book, *The Beardstown Ladies Common-Sense Investment Guide*. A central theme of the book is this: "Women need to gain financial information—whether they be young, middle-aged, or old"; they must not "rely on others."

The group's stock-picking methodology combines sound fundamental analysis of financial data with an eye toward innovative products or services. They rely heavily on the information provided by the *Value Line Investment Survey* to determine whether a stock meets their criteria for safety, industry rank, and volatility. But they also look to the products that they purchase themselves: If they think a new product shows promise, they analyze the company as a possible investment.

The fund's investments themselves have made none of the women rich, since each member contributes only $25 a month to the fund. But the women unanimously agree that participation in the club has been "fun" and has allowed them to have confidence in running their own personal financial affairs. As one member put it, she considers the monthly $25 as tuition toward her financial education. ◄

CHAPTER · **17**

# *I*NVESTMENTS

After studying this chapter, you should be able to:

1. *Distinguish between temporary and long-term investments.*
2. *Explain the accounting for debt investments.*
3. *Explain the accounting for stock investments.*
4. *Describe the purpose and usefulness of consolidated financial statements.*
5. *Indicate how debt and stock investments are valued and reported on the financial statements.*

Investment clubs, such as the Beardstown Ladies, represent just one of a vast assortment of ways that investments can be purchased. Investments also can be made by individuals, mutual funds, banks, pension funds, and corporations. In addition, investments can be purchased for a short or a long period of time, as a passive investment, or with the intent to control the firm. As you will see in this chapter, the way in which a company accounts for its investments is determined by a number of factors. The content and organization of this chapter are as follows:

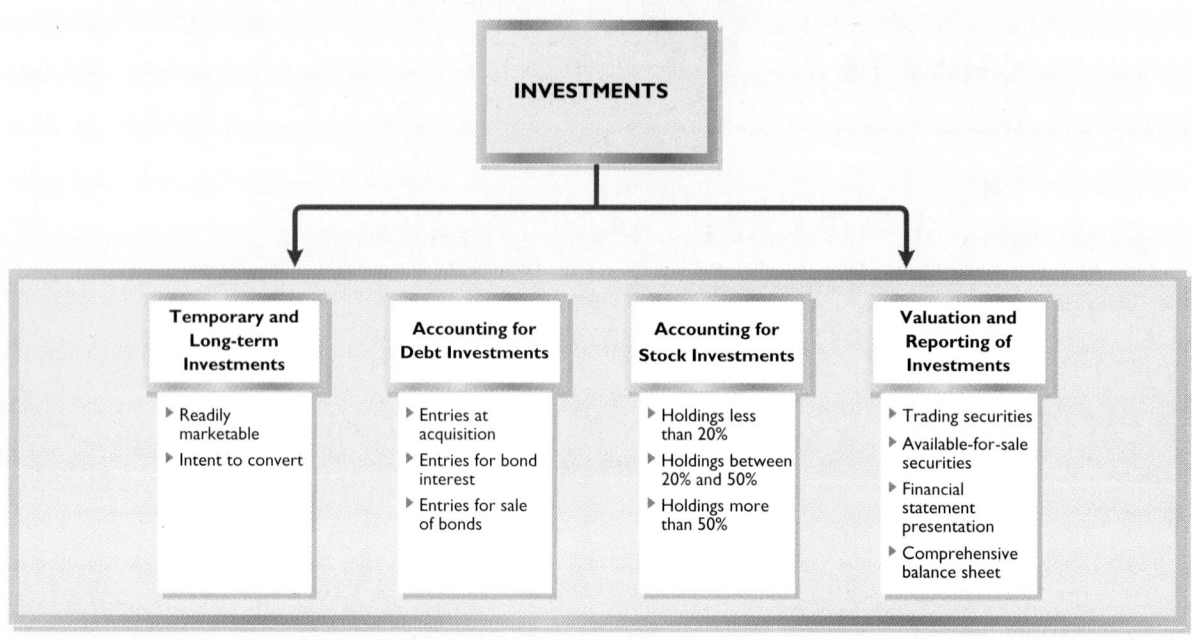

# *T*emporary and Long-Term Investments

**STUDY OBJECTIVE**

••••••••••• **1** •••••••••••

*Distinguish between temporary and long-term investments.*

Many companies experience seasonal fluctuations in sales. A Cape Cod marina will have higher sales in the spring and summer than in the fall and winter, whereas the reverse will be true for an Aspen ski shop. Thus, at the end of their operating cycles, many companies may have cash on hand that is temporarily idle pending the start of another operating cycle. Until the cash is needed in operations, these companies may invest the excess funds to earn interest and dividends. The relationship of temporary investments to the operating cycle is graphically depicted in Illustration 17-1.

**Illustration 17-1**

*Temporary investments and the operating cycle*

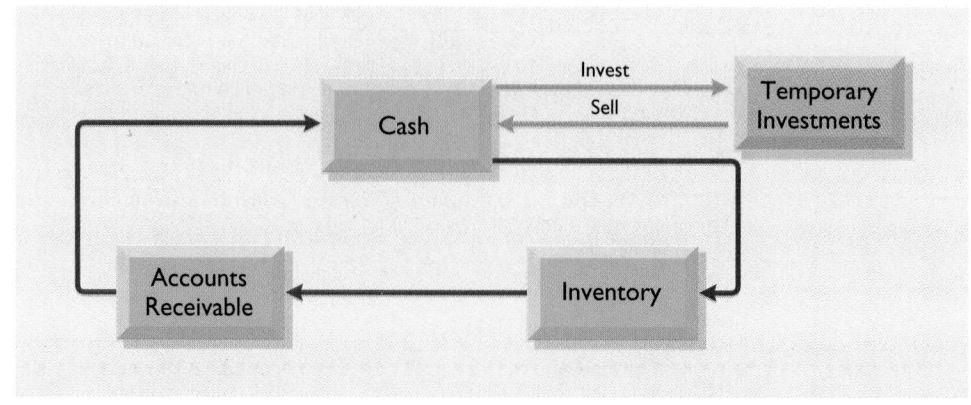

Temporary investments are securities, held by a company, that are (1) **readily marketable** and (2) **intended to be converted into cash** within the next year or operating cycle, whichever is longer. Investments that do not meet **both** criteria are classified as long-term investments.

## Readily Marketable

**An investment is readily marketable when it can be sold easily whenever the need for cash arises.** Short-term paper[1] meets this criterion because it can be sold readily to other investors. Stocks and bonds traded on organized securities markets, such as the New York Stock Exchange, are readily marketable because they can be bought and sold daily. In contrast, there may be only a limited market for the securities issued by small corporations and no market for the securities of a privately held company.

## Intent to Convert

**Intent to convert means that management intends to sell the investment within the next year or operating cycle, whichever is longer.** Generally, this criterion is satisfied when the investment is considered a resource that will be used whenever the need for cash arises. For example, an Aspen ski resort may invest idle cash during the summer months with the intent to sell the securities to buy supplies and equipment shortly before the next winter season. This investment is considered temporary even if lack of snow cancels the next ski season and eliminates the need to convert the securities into cash as intended.

# Accounting for Debt Investments

Debt investments are investments in government and corporation bonds. In accounting for debt investments, entries are required to record (1) the acquisition, (2) the interest revenue, and (3) the sale. **At acquisition, the cost principle applies.** Cost includes all expenditures necessary to acquire these investments, such as the price paid plus brokerage fees (commissions), if any. The entries for debt investments are illustrated below.

**STUDY OBJECTIVE**

••••••••••2••••••••••

*Explain the accounting for debt investments.*

## Entries at Acquisition

Assume that Kuhl Corporation acquires 50 Doan Inc. 12%, 10-year, $1,000 bonds on January 1, 1996, for $54,000, including brokerage fees of $1,000. The entry to record the investment is:

| | | | |
|---|---|---|---|
| Jan. 1 | Debt Investments | 54,000 | |
| |     Cash | | 54,000 |
| |     (To record purchase of 50 Doan Inc. bonds) | | |

## Entries for Bond Interest

The bonds pay interest of $3,000 semiannually on July 1 and January 1 ($50,000 × 12% × ½). The entry for the receipt of interest on July 1 is:

| | | | |
|---|---|---|---|
| July 1 | Cash | 3,000 | |
| |     Interest Revenue | | 3,000 |
| |     (To record receipt of interest on Doan Inc. bonds) | | |

---

[1]Short-term paper includes (1) certificates of deposits (CDs) issued by banks, (2) money market certificates issued by banks and savings and loan associations, (3) Treasury bills issued by the U.S. government, and (4) commercial paper issued by corporations with good credit ratings.

If Kuhl Corporation's fiscal year ends on December 31, it is necessary to accrue the interest of $3,000 earned since July 1. The adjusting entry is:

| Dec. 31 | Interest Receivable | 3,000 | |
|---|---|---|---|
| |     Interest Revenue | | 3,000 |
| |       (To accrue interest on Doan Inc. bonds) | | |

Interest Receivable is reported as a current asset in the balance sheet; Interest Revenue is reported under Other Revenues and Gains in the income statement. When the interest is received on January 1, the entry is:

| Jan. 1 | Cash | 3,000 | |
|---|---|---|---|
| |     Interest Receivable | | 3,000 |
| |       (To record receipt of accrued interest) | | |

A credit to Interest Revenue at this time is incorrect because the interest revenue was earned and accrued in the preceding accounting period.

## Entries for Sale of Bonds

When the bonds are sold, it is necessary to credit the investment account for the cost of the bonds. Any difference between the net proceeds (sales price less brokerage fees) from sale and the cost of the bonds is recorded as a gain or loss. Assume, for example, that Kuhl Corporation receives net proceeds of $58,000 on the sale of the Doan Inc. bonds on January 1, 1997, after receiving the interest due. Since the securities cost $54,000, a gain of $4,000 has been realized. The entry to record the sale is:

| Jan. 1 | Cash | 58,000 | |
|---|---|---|---|
| |     Debt Investments | | 54,000 |
| |     Gain on Sale of Debt Investments | | 4,000 |
| |       (To record sale of Doan Inc. bonds) | | |

The gain on sale of debt investments is reported under Other Revenues and Gains in the income statement.

The accounting for temporary debt investments and for long-term debt investments is similar. The major exception is when bonds are purchased at a premium or discount. For temporary investments, the bond premium or discount is not amortized to interest revenue because the bonds are held for a short period of time and a misstatement of interest revenue for such a period is not considered material. For long-term investments, however, any bond premium or discount is amortized to interest revenue over the remaining term of the bonds. Like the issuer of the bonds, the investor uses either the straight-line or the effective-interest method of amortization. The effective-interest method is required under generally accepted accounting principles when the annual amounts of the two amortization methods are materially different.

## *Before You Go On . . .*

▸ *Review It*

1. What criteria must be met to classify an investment as temporary?
2. What entries are required in accounting for debt investments?
3. How does the accounting for a temporary debt investment differ from that for a long-term debt investment?

## ▶ *Do It*

The Waldo Corporation had the following transactions pertaining to debt investments:

Jan. 1 Purchased 30 10%, $1,000 Hillary Co. bonds for $30,000 plus brokerage fees of $900. Interest is payable semiannually on July 1 and January 1.
July 1 Received semiannual interest on Hillary Co. bonds.
July 1 Sold 15 Hillary Co. bonds for $15,000 less $400 brokerage fees.

(a) Journalize the transactions, and (b) prepare the adjusting entry for the accrual of interest on December 31.

**Reasoning:** Bond investments are recorded at cost. Interest is recorded when received and/or accrued. When bonds are sold, the investment account is credited for the cost of the bonds. Any difference between the cost and the net proceeds is recorded as a gain or loss.

**Solution:**

| | | | | |
|---|---|---|---:|---:|
| (a) | Jan. 1 | Debt Investments | 30,900 | |
| | |     Cash | | 30,900 |
| | |         (To record purchase of 30 Hillary Co. bonds) | | |
| | July 1 | Cash | 1,500 | |
| | |     Interest Revenue ($30,000 × .10 × 6/12) | | 1,500 |
| | |         (To record receipt of interest on Hillary Co. bonds) | | |
| | July 1 | Cash | 14,600 | |
| | | Loss on Sale of Debt Investments | 850 | |
| | |     Debt Investments ($30,900 ÷ 15/30) | | 15,450 |
| | |         (To record sale of 15 Hillary Co. bonds) | | |
| (b) | Dec. 31 | Interest Receivable | 750 | |
| | |     Interest Revenue ($15,000 × .10 × 6/12) | | 750 |
| | |         (To accrue interest on Hillary Co. bonds) | | |

*Related exercise material:* BE17–1 and E17–1.

# Accounting for Stock Investments

Stock investments are investments in the capital stock of corporations. When a company holds stock (or debt) of several different corporations, the group of securities is identified as an investment portfolio. The accounting for investments in common stock is based on the extent of the investor's influence over the operating and financial affairs of the issuing corporation (commonly called the **investee**) as shown in Illustration 17-2. In some cases, depending on the degree of investor influence, net income of the investee is considered to be income to the investor.

The presumed influence may be negated by extenuating circumstances. For example, a company that acquires a 25% interest in another company in a "hostile" takeover may not have any significant influence over the investee.[2] In other

---

[2]Among the factors that should be considered in determining an investor's influence are whether (1) the investor has representation on the investee's board of directors, (2) the investor participates in the investee's policy-making process, (3) there are material transactions between the investor and investee, and (4) the common stock held by other stockholders is concentrated or dispersed.

**STUDY OBJECTIVE**
**3**

*Explain the accounting for stock investments.*

▶ *International note*

A recent study demonstrated the peril of investing overseas. For the same company under different reporting systems, income was $84,600, $260,600, $240,600, and $10,402 in the United States, the United Kingdom, Australia, and West Germany, respectively.

**Illustration 17-2**

*Accounting guidelines for stock investments*

words, companies are required to use judgment instead of blindly following the guidelines. On the following pages we will explain and illustrate the application of each guideline.

## ▸Accounting in Action ▸ *Business Insight*

A corporation may have a variety of motives in purchasing the capital stock of another corporation. Usually, however, the primary reason is to increase its own net income. This may be achieved through (1) the receipt of dividends, (2) appreciation in the market value of the stock, or (3) use of the investment for expanding or diversifying its own operations. For example, at one time Gulf & Western Industries, Inc., had the following investments in common stock that affected its operations:

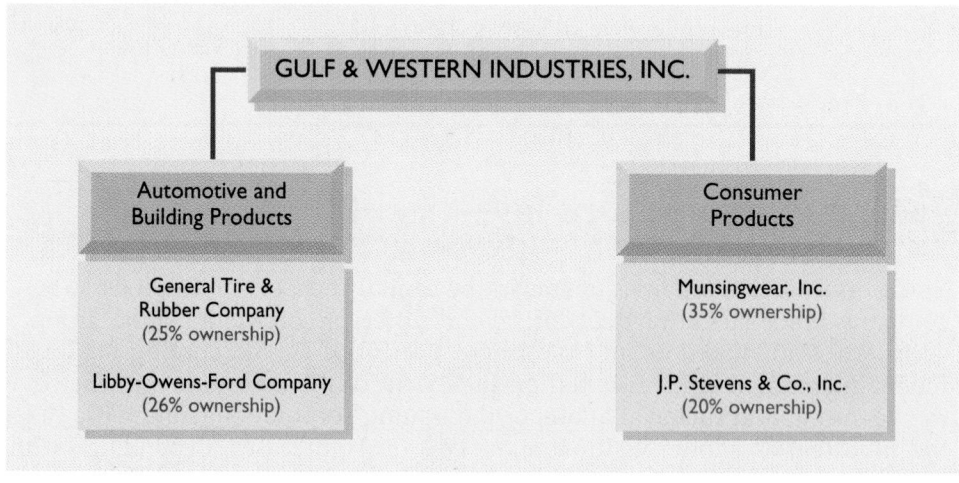

## Holdings Less Than 20%

In accounting for stock investments of less than 20%, the cost method is used. Under the cost method, the investment is recorded at cost and revenue is recognized only when cash dividends are received. At acquisition, the cost principle applies. Cost includes all expenditures necessary to acquire these investments, such as the price paid plus brokerage fees (commissions), if any. The entries for stock investments are illustrated on the next page.

### *Entries at Acquisition*

The starting point in accounting for stock investments is cost. Assume, for example, that on July 1, 1996, Sanchez Corporation acquires 1,000 shares (10% ownership) of Beal Corporation common stock at $40 per share plus brokerage fees of $500. The entry for the purchase is:

| | | | |
|---|---|---|---|
| July 1 | Stock Investments | 40,500 | |
| |     Cash | | 40,500 |
| |         (To record purchase of 1,000 shares of Beal | | |
| |         Corporation common stock) | | |

### *Entries for Dividends*

During the time the stock is held, entries are required for any cash dividends received. Thus, if a $2.00 per share dividend is received by Sanchez Corporation on December 31, the entry is:

| | | | |
|---|---|---|---|
| Dec. 31 | Cash (1,000 × $2) | 2,000 | |
| |     Dividend Revenue | | 2,000 |
| |         (To record receipt of a cash dividend) | | |

Dividend Revenue is reported under Other Revenues and Gains in the income statement. Unlike interest on notes and bonds, dividends do not accrue. Therefore, adjusting entries are not made to accrue dividends.

### *Entries for Sale of Stock*

When stock is sold, the difference between the net proceeds (sales price less brokerage fees) from the sale and the cost of the stock is recognized as a gain or a loss. Assume, for instance, that Sanchez Corporation receives net proceeds of $39,500 on the sale of its Beal stock on February 10, 1997. Because the stock cost $40,500, a loss of $1,000 has been incurred. The entry to record the sale is:

| | | | |
|---|---|---|---|
| Feb. 10 | Cash | 39,500 | |
| | Loss on Sale of Stock Investments | 1,000 | |
| |     Stock Investments | | 40,500 |
| |         (To record sale of Beal common stock) | | |

The loss account is reported under Other Expenses and Losses in the income statement, whereas a gain on sale is shown under Other Revenues and Gains.

## Holdings between 20% and 50%

When an investor owns between 20% and 50% of the common stock of a corporation, it is generally presumed that the investor has significant influence over the financial and operating activities of the investee. **As a result, the investor should record its share of the net income of the investee in the year when it is earned.** To delay recognizing the investor's share of net income until a cash dividend is declared ignores the fact that the investor is better off by the investee's earned income.

    This type of investment in common stock requires the use of the equity method. Under the equity method, the investment in common stock is initially recorded at cost, and the investment account is adjusted annually to show the investor's equity in the investee. Each year, the investor (1) debits the investment account and credits revenue for its share of the investee's net income[3] and

**Helpful hint** The entries for investments in common stock also apply to investments in preferred stock.

---

[3]Conversely, the investor debits a loss account and credits the investment account for its share of the investee's net loss.

(2) credits dividends received to the investment account. The investment account is reduced for dividends received, because the net assets of the investee are decreased when a dividend is paid.

### Entries at Acquisition

Assume that Milar Corporation acquires 30% of the common stock of Beck Company for $120,000 on January 1, 1996. The entry to record this transaction is:

| | | | | |
|---|---|---|---:|---:|
| Jan. 1 | Stock Investments | | 120,000 | |
| | Cash | | | 120,000 |
| | (To record purchase of Beck common stock) | | | |

### Entries for Revenue and Dividends

For 1996, Beck reports net income of $100,000 and declares and pays a $40,000 cash dividend. Milar is required to record (1) its share of Beck's income, $30,000 (30% × $100,000) and (2) the reduction in the investment account for the dividends received, $12,000 ($40,000 × 30%). The entries are:

(1)

| | | | | |
|---|---|---|---:|---:|
| Dec. 31 | Stock Investments | | 30,000 | |
| | Revenue from Investment in Beck Company | | | 30,000 |
| | (To record 30% equity in Beck's 1996 net income) | | | |

(2)

| | | | | |
|---|---|---|---:|---:|
| Dec. 31 | Cash | | 12,000 | |
| | Stock Investments | | | 12,000 |
| | (To record dividends received) | | | |

After posting the transactions for the year, the investment and revenue accounts will show the following:

**Illustration 17-3**

*Investment and revenue accounts after posting*

| **Stock Investments** | | | | **Revenue from Investment in Beck Company** | | |
|---|---|---|---|---|---|---|
| Jan.  1 | 120,000 | Dec. 31 | 12,000 | | Dec. 31 | 30,000 |
| Dec. 31 | 30,000 | | | | | |
| Dec. 31  Bal. | 138,000 | | | | | |

During the year, the investment account has increased by $18,000. This $18,000 is Milar's 30% equity in the $60,000 increase in Beck's retained earnings ($100,000 − $40,000). In addition, Milar will report $30,000 of revenue from its investment, which is 30% of Beck's net income of $100,000. Note that the difference between reported income under the cost method and reported revenue under the equity method can be significant. For example, Milar would report only $12,000 of dividend revenue (30% × $40,000) if the cost method were used.

**STUDY OBJECTIVE**
••••••••• **4** •••••••••

*Describe the purpose and usefulness of consolidated financial statements.*

## Holdings of More Than 50%

A company that owns more than 50% of the common stock of another entity is known as the parent company. The entity whose stock is owned by the parent company is called the subsidiary (affiliated) company. Because of its stock ownership, the parent company has a controlling interest in the subsidiary company.

When a company owns more than 50% of the common stock of another company, consolidated financial statements are usually prepared. **Consolidated financial statements** present the assets and liabilities controlled by the parent company and the aggregate profitability of the subsidiary companies. They are prepared in addition to the financial statements for each of the individual parent and subsidiary companies. **Consolidated statements are especially useful to the stockholders, board of directors, and management of the parent company.** Moreover, consolidated statements inform creditors, prospective investors, and regulatory agencies as to the magnitude and scope of operations of the companies operating under common control. For example, regulators and the courts undoubtedly used the consolidated statements of AT&T to determine whether a breakup of AT&T was in the public interest. Provided below are examples of two companies that prepare consolidated statements and some of the companies they have owned.

**Helpful hint** If parent (A) has three wholly owned subsidiaries (B, C, & D), there are four separate legal entities, but only one economic entity from the viewpoint of the shareholders of the parent company.

| **Beatrice Foods** | **American Brands, Inc.** |
|---|---|
| Tropicana Frozen Juices | American Tobacco Company |
| Switzer Candy Company | Master Lock Company |
| Samsonite Corporation | Pinkerton's Security Service |
| Dannon Yogurt Company | Titleist Golf Company |

The accounting for consolidated financial statements is discussed in the appendix to this chapter.

## ►Accounting in Action ► *Business Insight*

Philip Morris, Inc., for example, owns 100% of the common stock of Kraft General Foods Corporation. The common stockholders of Philip Morris elect the board of directors of the company, who, in turn, select the officers and managers of the company. The board of directors will control the property owned by the corporation, which includes the common stock of Kraft General Foods. Thus, they are in a position to elect the board of directors of Kraft General Foods and, in effect, control its operations. These relationships are graphically illustrated below:

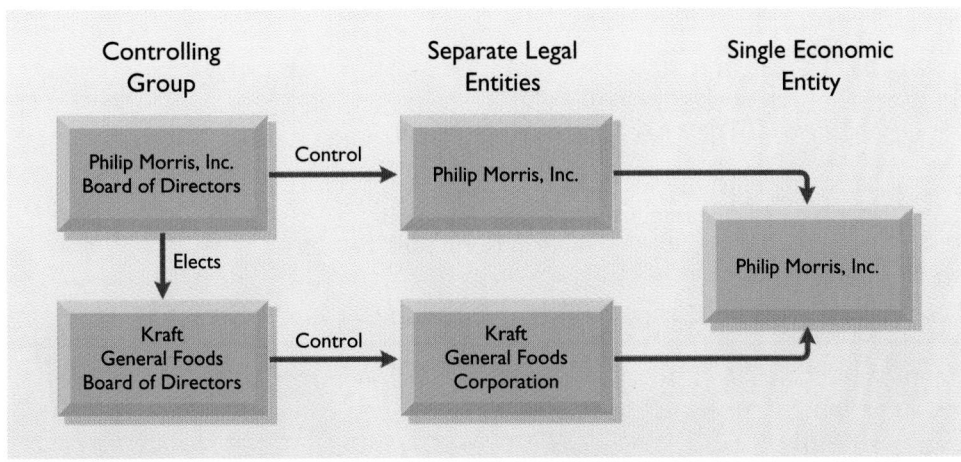

## *Before You Go On . . .*

### ▶ *Review It*

1. What are the accounting entries for investments in stock for which ownership is less than 20%?
2. What entries are made under the equity method when (a) the investor receives a cash dividend from the investee and (b) the investee reports net income for the year?
3. What is the purpose of consolidated financial statements?

### ▶ *Do It*

Presented below are two independent situations:

1. Rho Jean Inc. acquired 5% of the 400,000 shares of common stock of Stillwater Corp. at a total cost of $6 per share on May 18, 1996. On August 30, Stillwater declared and paid a $75,000 dividend. On December 31, Stillwater reported net income of $244,000 for the year.
2. Debbie, Inc., obtained significant influence over North Sails by buying 40% of North Sails' 60,000 outstanding shares of common stock at a cost of $12 per share on January 1, 1996. On April 15, North Sails declared and paid a cash dividend of $45,000. On December 31, North Sails reported a net income of $120,000 for the year.

Prepare all necessary journal entries for 1996 for (1) Rho Jean Inc. and (2) Debbie, Inc.

**Reasoning:** When an investor owns less than 20% of the common stock of another corporation, it is presumed that the investor has relatively little influence over the investee. As a result, net income earned by the investee is not considered a proper basis for recognizing income from the investment by the investor. For investments of 20%–50%, significant influence is presumed and therefore the investor's share of the net income of the investee should be recorded.

#### *Solution:*

| | | | |
|---|---|---|---|
| (1) May 18 | Stock Investments (20,000 × $6) | 120,000 | |
| |     Cash | | 120,000 |
| |       (To record purchase of 20,000 shares of | | |
| |       Stillwater Co. stock) | | |
| | | | |
| Aug. 30 | Cash | 3,750 | |
| |     Dividend Revenue ($75,000 × 5%) | | 3,750 |
| |       (To record receipt of cash dividend) | | |
| | | | |
| (2) Jan. 1 | Stock Investments (60,000 × 40% × $12) | 288,000 | |
| |     Cash | | 288,000 |
| |       (To record purchase of 24,000 shares of | | |
| |       North Sails' stock) | | |
| | | | |
| Apr. 15 | Cash | 18,000 | |
| |     Stock Investments ($45,000 × 40%) | | 18,000 |
| |       (To record receipt of cash dividend) | | |
| | | | |
| Dec. 31 | Stock Investments ($120,000 × 40%) | 48,000 | |
| |     Revenue from Investment in North Sails | | 48,000 |
| |       (To record 40% equity in North Sails' net | | |
| |       income) | | |

*Related exercise material:* BE17–2, BE17–3, E17–1, E17–2, E17–3, E17–4, and E17–5.

# Valuation and Reporting of Investments

The value of debt and stock investments may fluctuate greatly during the time they are held. The Dow-Jones Industrial Average of common stocks illustrates the volatile nature of stock prices. This average, which is based on the stock prices of 30 large companies, may drop drastically with unfavorable economic developments and may jump dramatically with favorable economic events. In light of such price fluctuations, how should investments be valued at the balance sheet date? Valuation could be at cost, at fair value (market value), or at the lower of cost or market value. Fair value offers the best approach because it represents the expected cash realizable value of the securities. Fair value is the amount for which a security could be sold in a normal market.

For purposes of valuation and reporting at a financial statement date, debt and stock investments are classified into three categories of securities, as follows:

Trading securities are securities bought and held primarily for sale in the near term to generate income on short-term price differences.

Available-for-sale securities are securities that may be sold in the future.

Held-to-maturity securities are debt securities that the investor has the intent and ability to hold to maturity.[4]

The valuation guidelines for these securities are as follows:

> **STUDY OBJECTIVE**
> •••••••• ▼**5**▼ ••••••••
>
> *Indicate how debt and stock investments are valued and reported on the financial statements.*

**Illustration 17-4**

*Valuation guidelines*

**Trading**

"We'll sell within ten days."

At fair value with changes reported in net income

**Available-for-sale**

"We'll hold the stock for a while to see how it performs."

At fair value with changes reported in the stockholders' equity section

**Held-to-maturity**

"We intend to hold until maturity."

At amortized cost[4]

The guidelines apply to all debt securities and all stock investments where the holdings are less than 20%.

## Trading Securities

Trading securities are held with the intention of selling them in a short period of time (generally less than a month). Trading means frequent buying and selling. As indicated in Illustration 17-4, trading securities are reported at fair value, and changes from cost are reported as part of net income. The changes are reported as **unrealized gains or losses** because the securities have not been sold. The unrealized gain or loss is the difference between the **total cost** of the securities in the category and their **total fair value**.

---

[4]This category is provided for completeness. The accounting and valuation issues related to held-to-maturity securities are discussed in more advanced accounting courses.

To illustrate, assume that on December 31, 1996, Plano Corporation has the following costs and fair values for its investments classified as trading securities:

**Illustration 17-5**

*Valuation of trading securities*

| Trading Securities, December 31, 1996 | | | |
|---|---|---|---|
| **Investments** | **Cost** | **Fair Value** | **Unrealized Gain (Loss)** |
| Yorkville Company bonds | $ 50,000 | $ 48,000 | $(2,000) |
| Kodak Company stock | 90,000 | 99,000 | 9,000 |
| Total | $140,000 | $147,000 | $ 7,000 |

Plano Corporation has an unrealized gain of $7,000 because total fair value ($147,000) is $7,000 greater than total cost ($140,000).

Fair value and the unrealized gain or loss are recorded through an adjusting entry at the time financial statements are prepared. In the entry, a valuation allowance account, Market Adjustment-Trading, is used to record the difference between the total cost and total fair value of the securities. The adjusting entry for Plano Corporation is:

| | | | |
|---|---|---|---|
| Dec. 31 | Market Adjustment—Trading | 7,000 | |
| | Unrealized Gain—Income | | 7,000 |
| | (To record unrealized gain on trading securities) | | |

The use of a Market Adjustment-Trading account enables the company to maintain a record of the investment cost. Actual cost is needed to determine the gain or loss realized when the securities are sold. The Market Adjustment-Trading balance is added to the cost of the investments to arrive at a fair value for the trading securities.

**The fair value of the securities is the amount reported on the balance sheet.** The unrealized gain is reported on the income statement in the Other Revenues and Gains section. The term income is used in the account title to indicate that the gain affects net income. When the total cost of the trading securities is greater than total fair value, an unrealized loss has occurred. In such a case, the adjusting entry is a debit to Unrealized Loss—Income and a credit to Market Adjustment—Trading. The unrealized loss is reported under Other Expenses and Losses in the income statement.

The market adjustment account is carried forward into future accounting periods. No entries are made to this account during the period. At the end of each reporting period, the balance in the account is adjusted to the difference between cost and fair value. The Unrealized Gain or Loss-Income account is closed at the end of the reporting period.

## Available-for-Sale Securities

As indicated earlier, available-for-sale securities are held with the intent of selling them sometime in the future. If the intent is to sell the securities within the next year or operating cycle, the securities are classified as current assets in the balance sheet. Otherwise, they are classified as long-term assets in the investments section of the balance sheet.

Available-for-sale securities are also reported at fair value. The procedure for determining fair value and the unrealized gain or loss for these securities is the same as for trading securities. To illustrate, assume that Elbert Corporation has two securities that are classified as available-for-sale. Illustration 17-6 provides information on cost, fair value, and the amount of the unrealized gain or loss.

Illustration 17-6

*Valuation of available-for-sale securities*

| **Available-for-Sale Securities, December 31, 1996** | | | |
|---|---|---|---|
| **Investments** | **Cost** | **Fair Value** | **Unrealized Gain (Loss)** |
| Campbell Soup Corporation | | | |
| 8% bonds | $ 93,537 | $103,600 | $ 10,063 |
| Hersey Corporation stock | 200,000 | 180,400 | (19,600) |
| Total | $293,537 | $284,000 | $ (9,537) |

For Elbert Corporation, there is an unrealized loss of $9,537 because total cost ($293,537) is $9,537 more than total fair value ($284,000).

Both the adjusting entry and the reporting of the unrealized gain or loss from available-for-sale securities differ from those illustrated for trading securities. The differences result because these securities are not going to be sold in the near term. Thus, prior to actual sale there is a much greater likelihood of changes in fair value that may reverse either unrealized gains or losses. Accordingly, an unrealized gain or loss is not reported in the income statement. Instead, it is reported as a separate component of stockholders' equity. In the adjusting entry, the market adjustment account is identified with available-for-sale securities, and the unrealized gain or loss account is identified with stockholders' equity. The adjusting entry for Elbert Corporation to record the unrealized loss of $9,537 is as follows:

| | | | |
|---|---|---|---|
| Dec. 31 | Unrealized Loss—Equity | 9,537 | |
| |     Market Adjustment—Available-for-Sale | | 9,537 |
| |     (To record unrealized loss on available-for-sale securities) | | |

**Helpful hint** The entry is the same regardless of whether the securities are considered temporary or long-term.

If total fair value exceeds total cost, the adjusting entry would have a debit to the market adjustment account and a credit to an unrealized gain account. For available-for-sale securities, the unrealized gain or loss account is carried forward to future periods. At each future balance sheet date, it is adjusted with the market adjustment account to show the difference between cost and fair value at that time.

## Financial Statement Presentation

Because of their high liquidity, temporary investments are listed immediately below cash in the current asset section of the balance sheet. Temporary investments are reported at fair value. For example, Plano Corporation would report its trading securities as follows:

| | |
|---|---|
| Current assets | |
|   Cash | $ xx,xxx |
|   Temporary investments, at fair value | 147,000 |

Long-term investments are generally reported in a separate section of the balance sheet immediately below current assets, as shown in Illustration 17-9 on page 709. In this section, long-term investments in available-for-sale securities are reported at fair value, and investments in common stock accounted for under the equity method are reported at equity.

In the income statement, the following items are reported in the nonoperating section:

Illustration 17-7

*Nonoperating items related to investments*

| Other Revenue and Gains | Other Expenses and Losses |
|---|---|
| Interest Revenue | Loss on Sale of Investments |
| Dividend Revenue | Unrealized Loss—Income |
| Gain on Sale of Investments | |
| Unrealized Gain—Income | |

As indicated earlier, an unrealized gain or loss on available-for-sale securities is reported as a separate component of stockholders' equity. To illustrate, assume that Dawson Inc. has common stock of $3,000,000, retained earnings of $1,500,000 and an unrealized loss on available-for-sale securities of $100,000. The statement presentation of the unrealized loss is as follows:

Illustration 17-8

*Unrealized loss in stock-holders' equity section*

| | |
|---|---:|
| Stockholders' equity | |
| Common stock | $3,000,000 |
| Retained earnings | 1,500,000 |
| Total paid-in capital and retained earnings | 4,500,000 |
| Less: Unrealized loss on available-for-sale securities | (100,000) |
| Total stockholders' equity | $4,400,000 |

Note that the presentation of the loss is similar to the presentation of the cost of treasury stock in the stockholders' equity section. An unrealized gain is added in the section. Reporting the unrealized gain or loss in the stockholders' equity section serves two important purposes: (1) It reduces the volatility of net income due to fluctuations in fair value, and (2) it still informs the financial statement user of the gain or loss that would occur if the securities were sold at fair value.

## Comprehensive Balance Sheet

Numerous examples of sections of classified balance sheets have been presented in this and preceding chapters. The balance sheet shown in Illustration 17-9 includes such topics from previous chapters as the issuance of par value common stock, organization costs, restrictions of retained earnings, issuance of long-term bonds, and bond sinking funds. From this chapter, the statement includes (highlighted in red) temporary and long-term investments. The investments in temporary securities are considered trading securities; the long-term investments in stock of less than 20% owned companies are considered available-for-sale securities. Illustration 17-9 also includes a long-term investment reported at equity and descriptive notations within the statement such as the basis for valuing merchandise and two notes to the statement.

Illustration 17-9

*Comprehensive balance sheet*

## PACE CORPORATION
### Balance Sheet
### December 31, 1996

### Assets

| | | |
|---|---:|---:|
| **Current assets** | | |
| Cash | | $   21,000 |
| **Temporary investments, at fair value** | | **60,000** |
| Accounts receivable | 84,000 | |
| Less: Allowance for doubtful accounts | 4,000 | 80,000 |
| Merchandise inventory, at FIFO cost | | 130,000 |
| Prepaid insurance | | 23,000 |
| Total current assets | | 314,000 |
| **Investments** | | |
| Bond sinking fund | 100,000 | |
| **Investments in stock of less than 20% owned** | | |
| **companies, at fair value** | **50,000** | |
| **Investment in stock of 20–50% owned** | | |
| **company, at equity** | **150,000** | |
| Total investments | | 300,000 |
| **Property, plant, and equipment** | | |
| Land | 200,000 | |
| Buildings | $800,000 | |
| Less: Accumulated depreciation | 200,000 | 600,000 |
| Equipment | 180,000 | |
| Less: Accumulated depreciation | 54,000 | 126,000 |
| Total property, plant, and equipment | | 926,000 |
| **Intangible assets** | | |
| Goodwill (Note 1) | 100,000 | |
| Organization costs | 70,000 | |
| Total intangible assets | | 170,000 |
| Total assets | | $1,710,000 |

### Liabilities and Stockholders' Equity

| | | |
|---|---:|---:|
| **Current liabilities** | | |
| Accounts payable | | $185,000 |
| Bond interest payable | | 10,000 |
| Federal income taxes payable | | 60,000 |
| Total current liabilities | | 255,000 |
| **Long-term liabilities** | | |
| Bonds payable, 10%, due 2010 | $  300,000 | |
| Less: Discount on bonds | 10,000 | |
| Total long-term liabilities | | 290,000 |
| Total liabilities | | 545,000 |
| **Stockholders' equity** | | |
| Paid-in capital | | |
| Common stock, $10 par value, 200,000 shares | | |
| authorized, 80,000 shares issued and outstanding | 800,000 | |
| Paid-in capital in excess of par value | 100,000 | |
| Total paid-in capital | 900,000 | |
| Retained earnings (Note 2) | 255,000 | |
| Total paid-in capital and retained earnings | 1,155,000 | |
| **Add: Unrealized gain on available-for-sale** | | |
| **securities** | **10,000** | |
| Total stockholders' equity | | 1,165,000 |
| Total liabilities and stockholders' equity | | $1,710,000 |

Note 1. Goodwill is amortized by the straight-line method over 40 years.

Note 2. Retained earnings of $100,000 is restricted for plant expansion.

## *Before You Go On . . .*

### ► *Review It*

1. What is the proper valuation and reporting of trading and available-for-sale securities on a balance sheet?
2. Explain how the unrealized gain or loss for both trading and available-for-sale securities is reported.
3. Explain where temporary and long-term investments are reported on a balance sheet.

### ► *A Look Back at the Beardstown Ladies*

Refer back to the opening story about the Beardstown Ladies, and answer the following questions:

1. The Beardstown Ladies have averaged a 23.4% annual return over the last decade. Is it more likely that this return has been earned from dividends or from appreciation in share value? Why?
2. Assume that the Beardstown Ladies invest only in stock. If they want to make their investment income look good, what choices might they make in terms of choosing which securities to sell and which to hold?
3. What investment strategies do the Beardstown Ladies employ?

*Solution:*

1. Firms could not consistently pay anywhere near a 23.4% dividend; thus most of the Beardstown Ladies' return must be coming from appreciation in share value.
2. Unrealized losses on available-for-sale securities are not reported in income. In order to maximize reported income the Beardstown Ladies could choose at year-end to sell all securities in the available-for-sale category that have experienced gains, and to hold all such securities that have unrealized losses.
3. They use financial information from *Value Line* to evaluate a security's safety, industry rank, and volatility. In addition, they use good, sound common sense by looking for new products that they think have promising futures.

# Summary of Study Objectives

**1. Distinguish between temporary and long-term investments.** Temporary investments are securities, held by a company, that are readily marketable and intended to be converted to cash within the next year or operating cycle, whichever is longer. Investments that do not meet both criteria are classified as long-term investments.

**2. Explain the accounting for debt investments.** Entries for investments in debt securities are required when the bonds are purchased, interest is received or accrued, and the bonds are sold. The accounting for long-term investments in bonds is the same as for temporary investments in bonds, except that bond premium and bond discount must be amortized.

**3. Explain the accounting for stock investments.** Entries for investments in common stock are required when the stock is purchased, dividends are received, and stock is sold. When ownership is less than 20%, the cost method is used. When ownership is between 20% and 50%, the equity

method should be used. When ownership is more than 50%, consolidated financial statements should be prepared.

**4. Describe the purpose and usefulness of consolidated financial statements.** When a company owns more than 50% of the common stock of another company, consolidated financial statements are usually prepared. These statements are especially useful to the stockholders, board of directors, and management of the parent company.

**5. Indicate how debt and stock investments are valued and reported on the financial statements.** Investments in debt and stock securities are classified as trading, available-for-sale, or held-to-maturity securities for valuation and reporting purposes. Trading securities are reported in current assets at fair value with changes from cost reported in net income. Available-for-sale securities are also reported at fair value with the changes from cost reported in stockholders' equity. Available-for-sale securities are classified as temporary or long-term depending on their expected realization.

# ▼A PPENDIX ▸ *Preparing Consolidated Financial Statements*

## P reparing a Consolidated Balance Sheet

Consolidated balance sheets are prepared from the individual balance sheets of the affiliated companies. They are not prepared from ledger accounts kept by the consolidated entity because only the separate legal entities maintain accounting records.

All items in the individual balance sheets are included in the consolidated balance sheet except amounts that pertain to transactions between the affiliated companies. Transactions between the affiliated companies are identified as intercompany transactions. The process of excluding these transactions in preparing consolidated statements is referred to as intercompany eliminations. These eliminations are necessary to avoid overstating assets, liabilities, and stockholders' equity in the consolidated balance sheet. For example, amounts owed by a subsidiary to a parent company and the related receivable reported by the parent company would be eliminated. The objective in a consolidated balance sheet is to show only obligations to and receivables from parties who are not part of the affiliated group of companies.

To illustrate, assume that on January 1, 1996, Powers Construction Company pays $150,000 in cash for 100% of Serto Brick Company's common stock. Powers Company records the investment at cost, as required by the cost principle. The separate balance sheets of the two companies immediately after the purchase, together with combined and consolidated data, are presented in Illustration 17A-1.[1] The balances in the "combined" column are obtained by adding the items

**Helpful hint**  Eliminations are aptly named because they eliminate duplicate data. They are not adjustments.

**Illustration 17A-1**

*Combined and consolidated data*

| POWERS COMPANY AND SERTO COMPANY<br>Balance Sheets<br>January 1, 1996 | | | | |
|---|---|---|---|---|
| Assets | Powers<br>Company | Serto<br>Company | Combined<br>Data | Consolidated<br>Data |
| Current assets | $ 50,000 | $ 80,000 | $130,000 | $130,000 |
| Investment in Serto Company<br>common stock | 150,000 | | 150,000 | –0– |
| Plant and equipment (net) | 325,000 | 145,000 | 470,000 | 470,000 |
| Total assets | $525,000 | $225,000 | $750,000 | $600,000 |
| **Liabilities and<br>Stockholders' Equity** | | | | |
| Current liabilities | $ 50,000 | $ 75,000 | $125,000 | $125,000 |
| Common stock | 300,000 | 100,000 | 400,000 | 300,000 |
| Retained earnings | 175,000 | 50,000 | 225,000 | 175,000 |
| Total liabilities and<br>stockholders' equity | $525,000 | $225,000 | $750,000 | $600,000 |

---

[1]Condensed data will be used throughout this material to keep details at a minimum.

in the separate balance sheets of the affiliated companies. The combined totals do not represent a consolidated balance sheet, because there has been a double counting of assets and owners' equity in the amount of $150,000.

The Investment in Serto Company common stock that appears on the balance sheet of Powers Company represents an interest in the net assets of Serto. As a result, there has been a double counting of assets. Similarly, there has been a double counting in stockholders' equity, because the common stock of Serto Company is completely owned by the stockholders of Powers Company.

The balances in the consolidated data column are the amounts that should appear in the consolidated balance sheet. The double counting has been eliminated by showing Investment in Serto Company at zero and by reporting only the common stock and retained earnings of Powers Company as stockholders' equity.

## Use of a Work Sheet—Cost Equal to Book Value

**STUDY OBJECTIVE**

▼ **6**

*Describe the content of a work sheet for a consolidated balance sheet.*

**The preparation of consolidated balance sheets is usually facilitated by the use of a work sheet.** As shown in Illustration 17A-2, the work sheet for a consolidated balance sheet contains columns for (1) the balance sheet data for the separate legal entities, (2) intercompany eliminations, and (3) consolidated data. All data in the work sheet relate to the preceding example in which Powers Company acquires 100% ownership of Serto Company for $150,000. In this case, the cost of the investment, $150,000, is equal to the book value $150,000 ($225,000 − $75,000) of the subsidiary's net assets. The intercompany elimination results in a credit to the Investment account maintained by Powers Company for its balance, $150,000, and debits to the Common Stock and Retained Earnings accounts of Serto Company for their respective balances, $100,000 and $50,000.

**Illustration 17A-2**

*Work sheet—Cost equals book value*

### POWERS COMPANY AND SUBSIDIARY
**Work Sheet—Consolidated Balance Sheet**
**January 1, 1996 (Acquisition Date)**

| Assets | Powers Company | Serto Company | Eliminations Dr. | Eliminations Cr. | Consolidated Data |
|---|---|---|---|---|---|
| Current assets | 50,000 | 80,000 | | | 130,000 |
| Investment in Serto Company common stock | 150,000 | | | 150,000 | –0– |
| Plant and equipment (net) | 325,000 | 145,000 | | | 470,000 |
| Totals | 525,000 | 225,000 | | | 600,000 |
| **Liabilities and Stockholders' Equity** | | | | | |
| Current liabilities | 50,000 | 75,000 | | | 125,000 |
| Common stock—Powers Company | 300,000 | | | | 300,000 |
| Common stock—Serto Company | | 100,000 | 100,000 | | –0– |
| Retained earnings—Powers Company | 175,000 | | | | 175,000 |
| Retained earnings—Serto Company | | 50,000 | 50,000 | | –0– |
| Totals | 525,000 | 225,000 | 150,000 | 150,000 | 600,000 |

**Helpful hint** As in the case of the work sheets explained earlier in this textbook, consolidated work sheets are also optional.

**It is important to recognize that intercompany eliminations are made solely on the work sheet to present correct consolidated data. They are not journalized or posted by either of the affiliated companies and therefore do not affect the ledger accounts.** Powers Company's investment account and Serto Company's common stock and retained earnings accounts are reported by the separate entities in preparing their own financial statements.

## ►Technology in Action

The consolidated work sheet is another good spreadsheet application. At this stage in the course, we hope you have familiarized yourself enough with electronic spreadsheets to be able to create your own templates. If not, this is a good work sheet to attempt since the required instructions are very straightforward.

However, computer programs are available that can merge multiple general ledgers for consolidated entities. All you need to do is supply the eliminating information, enter a few command keystrokes, and the consolidated financial statements will come off the printer, ready for distribution.

## Use of a Work Sheet—Cost Above Book Value

The cost of acquiring the common stock of another company may be above or below its book value. The management of the parent company may pay more than book value because it believes (1) the fair market values of identifiable assets such as land, buildings, and equipment are higher than their recorded book values, or (2) the subsidiary's future earnings prospects warrant a payment for goodwill.

To illustrate, assume the same data used above, except that Powers Company pays $165,000 in cash for 100% of Serto's common stock. The excess of cost over book value is $15,000 ($165,000 − $150,000). This amount is separately recognized in eliminating the parent company's investment account, as shown in Illustration 17A-3.

Total assets and total liabilities and stockholders' equity are the same as in the preceding example ($600,000). However, in this case, total assets include $15,000 of Excess of Cost Over Book Value of Subsidiary. The disposition of the excess is explained in the next section.

**Illustration 17A-3**

*Work sheet—Cost above book value*

### POWERS COMPANY AND SUBSIDIARY
### Work Sheet—Consolidated Balance Sheet
### January 1, 1996 (Acquisition Date)

| Assets | Powers Company | Serto Company | Eliminations Dr. | Eliminations Cr. | Consolidated Data |
|---|---|---|---|---|---|
| Current assets | 35,000 | 80,000 | | | 115,000 |
| Investment in Serto Company common stock | 165,000 | | | 165,000 | –0– |
| Plant and equipment (net) | 325,000 | 145,000 | | | 470,000 |
| EXCESS OF COST OVER BOOK VALUE OF SUBSIDIARY | | | 15,000 | | 15,000 |
| Totals | 525,000 | 225,000 | | | 600,000 |
| **Liabilities and Stockholders' Equity** | | | | | |
| Current liabilities | 50,000 | 75,000 | | | 125,000 |
| Common stock—Powers Company | 300,000 | | | | 300,000 |
| Common stock—Serto Company | | 100,000 | 100,000 | | –0– |
| Retained earnings—Powers Company | 175,000 | | | | 175,000 |
| Retained earnings—Serto Company | | 50,000 | 50,000 | | –0– |
| Totals | 525,000 | 225,000 | 165,000 | 165,000 | 600,000 |

Note that a separate line is added to the work sheet for the excess of cost over book value of subsidiary.

## Content of a Consolidated Balance Sheet

**STUDY OBJECTIVE**
••••••••• 7 •••••••••

*Explain the form and content of consolidated financial statements.*

To illustrate a consolidated balance sheet, we will use the work sheet shown in Illustration 17A-3. This work sheet shows an excess of cost over book value of $15,000. In the consolidated balance sheet, this amount is first allocated to specific assets, such as inventory and plant equipment, if their fair market values on the acquisition date exceed their book values. Any remainder is considered to be goodwill. For Powers Company, assume that the fair market value of property and equipment is $155,000. Thus, $10,000 of the excess of cost over book value is allocated to property and equipment, and the remainder, $5,000, is allocated to goodwill.

The condensed consolidated balance sheet of Powers Company is shown in Illustration 17A-4. As explained in Chapter 10, goodwill would be amortized by the straight-line method over the period benefited, but not in excess of 40 years.

**Illustration 17A-4**

*Consolidated balance sheet*

| POWERS COMPANY<br>Consolidated Balance Sheet<br>January 1, 1996 | | |
|---|---|---|
| **Assets** | | |
| Current assets | | $115,000 |
| Plant and equipment (net) | | 480,000 |
| Goodwill | | 5,000 |
| Total assets | | $600,000 |
| **Liabilities and Stockholders' Equity** | | |
| Current liabilities | | $125,000 |
| Stockholders' equity | | |
| Common stock | $300,000 | |
| Retained earnings | 175,000 | 475,000 |
| Total liabilities and stockholders' equity | | $600,000 |

## ▶Accounting in Action ▸ *Business Insight*

Through innovative financial restructuring, the Coca-Cola Company at one time eliminated a substantial amount of non-intercompany debt. It sold to the public 51% of two bottling companies. The "49% solution," as insiders call the strategy, enabled Coca-Cola to keep effective control over the businesses and it swept $3 billion of debt from its consolidated balance sheet. (It no longer consolidated the two bottling companies.) At the same time the new companies obtained independent access to equity markets to satisfy their own voracious appetites for capital.

## Consolidated Income Statement

A consolidated income statement is also prepared for affiliated companies. This statement shows the results of operations of affiliated companies as though they are one economic unit. This means that the statement shows only revenue and expense transactions between the consolidated entity and companies and individuals who are outside the affiliated group. Consequently, all intercompany revenue and expense transactions must be eliminated. Intercompany transactions such as sales between affiliates and interest on loans charged by one affiliate to another must be eliminated. A work sheet facilitates the preparation of consolidated income statements in the same manner as it does for the balance sheet.

## Before You Go On . . .

### ▶ Review It

1. Why are eliminations needed in preparing consolidated financial statements?
2. What eliminations are made for the parent company's investment in the common stock of a subsidiary company?
3. How may the excess of cost over book value be reported in a consolidated balance sheet?

## ◤ Summary of Study Objectives for Chapter 17 Appendix

**6.** *Describe the content of a work sheet and a consolidated balance sheet.* The work sheet for a consolidated balance sheet contains columns for (a) the balance sheet data for the separate entities, (b) intercompany eliminations, and (c) consolidated data.

**7.** *Explain the form and content of consolidated financial statements.* Consolidated financial statements are similar in form and content to the financial statements of an individual corporation. A consolidated balance sheet shows the assets and liabilities controlled by the parent company. A consolidated income statement shows the results of operations of affiliated companies as though they are one economic unit.

**\*Note:** All **asterisked** glossary entries, Questions, Exercises, and Problems relate to material contained in the appendix to the chapter.

## GLOSSARY

**Available-for-sale securities**   Securities that may be sold in the future. (p. 705)

**Consolidated financial statements**   Financial statements that present the assets and liabilities controlled by the parent company and the aggregate profitability of the affiliated companies. (p. 703)

**Controlling interest**   Ownership of more than 50% of the common stock of another entity. (p. 702)

**Cost method**   An accounting method in which the investment in common stock is recorded at cost and revenue is recognized only when cash dividends are received. (p. 700)

**Debt investments**   Investments in government and corporation bonds. (p. 697)

**Equity method**   An accounting method in which the investment in common stock is initially recorded at cost, and the investment account is then adjusted annually to show the investor's equity in the investee. (p. 701)

**Fair value**   Amount for which a security could be sold in a normal market. (p. 705)

**Held-to-maturity securities**   Debt securities which the investor has the intent and ability to hold to their maturity date. (p. 705)

**\*Intercompany eliminations**   Eliminations made to exclude the effects of intercompany transactions in preparing consolidated statements. (p. 711)

**\*Intercompany transactions**   Transactions between affiliated companies. (p. 711)

**Investment portfolio**   A group of stocks in different corporations held for investment purposes. (p. 699)

**Long-term investments**   Investments that are not readily marketable or that management does not intend to convert into cash within the next year or operating cycle, whichever is longer. (p. 697)

**Parent company**   A company that owns more than 50% of the common stock of another entity. (p. 702)

**Stock investments**   Investments in the capital stock of corporations. (p. 699)

**Subsidiary (affiliated) company**   A company in which more than 50% of its stock is owned by another company. (p. 702)

**Temporary investments**   Investments that are readily marketable and intended to be converted into cash within the next year or operating cycle, whichever is longer. (p. 697)

**Trading securities**   Securities bought and held primarily for sale in the near term to generate income on short-term price differences. (p. 705)

# DEMONSTRATION PROBLEM

In its first year of operations, the DeMarco Company had the following selected transactions in stock investments which are considered trading securities:

June  1  Purchased for cash 600 shares of Sanburg common stock at $24 per share plus $300 brokerage fees.

July  1  Purchased for cash 800 shares of Cey common stock at $33 per share plus $600 brokerage fees.

Sept.  1  Received a $1 per share cash dividend from Cey Corporation.

Nov.  1  Sold 200 shares of Sanburg common stock for cash at $27 per share less $150 brokerage fees.

Dec. 15  Received a $.50 per share cash dividend on Sanburg common stock.

At December 31, the fair values per share were: Sanburg $25 and Cey $30.

**Instructions**
(a)  Journalize the transactions.
(b)  Prepare the adjusting entry at December 31 to report the securities at fair value.

**Problem-Solving Strategies**

1. Cost includes the price paid plus brokerage fees.

2. Gain or loss on sales is determined by the difference between net selling price and the cost of the securities.

3. The adjustment to fair value is based on the total difference between cost and fair value of the securities.

## Solution to Demonstration Problem

| | | | | | |
|---|---|---|---|---|---|
| (a) June | 1 | Stock Investments | | 14,700 | |
| | |    Cash | | | 14,700 |
| | |      (To record purchase of 600 shares of Sanburg | | | |
| | |      common stock) | | | |
| July | 1 | Stock Investments | | 27,000 | |
| | |    Cash | | | 27,000 |
| | |      (To record purchase of 800 shares of Cey common | | | |
| | |      stock) | | | |
| Sept. | 1 | Cash | | 800 | |
| | |    Dividend Revenue | | | 800 |
| | |      (To record receipt of $1 per share cash dividend | | | |
| | |      from Cey Corporation) | | | |
| Nov. | 1 | Cash | | 5,250 | |
| | |    Stock Investments | | | 4,900 |
| | |    Gain on Sale of Stock Investments | | | 350 |
| | |      (To record sale of 200 shares of Sanburg common | | | |
| | |      stock) | | | |
| Dec. | 15 | Cash | | 200 | |
| | |    Dividend Revenue | | | 200 |
| | |      (To record receipt of $.50 per share dividend from | | | |
| | |      Sanburg Corporation) | | | |
| (b) Dec. | 31 | Unrealized Loss—Income | | 2,800 | |
| | |    Market Adjustment—Trading | | | 2,800 |
| | |      (To record unrealized loss on trading securities) | | | |

| Investment | Cost | Fair Value | Unrealized Gain (Loss) |
|---|---|---|---|
| Sanburg common stock | $ 9,800 | $10,000 | $  200 |
| Cey common stock | 27,000 | 24,000 | (3,000) |
| Totals | $36,800 | $34,000 | $(2,800) |

# SELF-STUDY QUESTIONS

Answers are at the end of the chapter.

(SO 1)  1. Temporary debt investments must be readily marketable and be expected to be sold within:
   a. 3 months from the date of purchase.
   b. the next year or operating cycle, whichever is shorter.
   c. the next year or operating cycle, whichever is longer.
   d. the operating cycle.

(SO 2)  2. Debt investments are initially recorded at:
   a. cost.
   b. cost plus accrued interest.
   c. fair value.
   d. None of the above.

(SO 2)  3. Hanes Company sells debt investments costing $26,000 for $28,000 plus accrued interest that has been recorded. In journalizing the sale, credits are:
   a. Debt Investments and Loss on Sale of Debt Investments.
   b. Debt Investments, Gain on Sale of Debt Investments, and Bond Interest Receivable.
   c. Stock Investments and Bond Interest Receivable.
   d. No correct answer given.

(SO 3)  4. Pryor Company receives net proceeds of $42,000 on the sale of stock investments that cost $39,500. This transaction will result in reporting in the income statement a:
   a. loss of $2,500 under Other Expenses and Losses.
   b. loss of $2,500 under Operating Expenses.
   c. gain of $2,500 under Other Revenues and Gains.
   d. gain of $2,500 under Operating Revenues.

(SO 3)  5. The equity method of accounting for long-term investments in stock should be used when the investor has significant influence over an investee and owns:
   a. between 20% and 50% of the investee's common stock.
   b. 20% or more of the investee's common stock.
   c. more than 50% of the investee's common stock.
   d. less than 20% of the investee's common stock.

(SO 4)  6. Which of the following statements is *not true*? Consolidated financial statements are useful to:
   a. determine the profitability of specific subsidiaries.
   b. determine the aggregate profitability of enterprises under common control.
   c. determine the breadth of a parent company's operations.
   d. determine the full extent of aggregate obligations of enterprises under common control.

(SO 5)  7. At the end of the first year of operations, the total cost of the trading securities portfolio is $120,000, and total fair value is $115,000. The financial statements should show:

   a. a reduction of an asset of $5,000 and a realized loss of $5,000.
   b. a reduction of an asset of $5,000 and an unrealized loss of $5,000 in the stockholders' equity section.
   c. a reduction of an asset of $5,000 in the current asset section and an unrealized loss in Other Expenses and Losses of $5,000.
   d. a reduction of an asset of $5,000 in the current asset section and a realized loss of $5,000 in Other Expenses and Losses.

(SO 5)  8. In the balance sheet, Unrealized Loss—Equity is reported as a:
   a. contra asset account.
   b. contra stockholders'equity account.
   c. loss in the income statement.
   d. loss in the retained earnings statement.

(SO 6) *9. Pate Company pays $175,000 for 100% of Sinko's common stock when Sinko's stockholders' equity consists of Common Stock $100,000 and Retained Earnings $60,000. In the work sheet for the consolidated balance sheet, the eliminations will include a:
   a. credit to Investment in Sinko Common Stock $160,000.
   b. credit to Excess of Book Value over Cost of Subsidiary $15,000.
   c. debit to Retained Earnings $75,000.
   d. debit to Excess of Cost over Book Value of Subsidiary $15,000.

(SO 6) *10. Which of the following statements about intercompany eliminations is *true*?
   a. They are not journalized or posted by any of the subsidiaries.
   b. They do not affect the ledger accounts of any of the subsidiaries.
   c. Intercompany eliminations are made solely on the work sheet to arrive at correct consolidated data.
   d. All of these statements are true.

(SO 7) *11. Which one of the following statements about consolidated income statements is *false*?
   a. A work sheet facilitates the preparation of the statement.
   b. The consolidated income statement shows the results of operations of affiliated companies as a single economic unit.
   c. All revenue and expense transactions between parent and subsidiary companies are eliminated.
   d. When a subsidiary is wholly owned, the form and content of the statement will differ from the income statement of an individual corporation.

# QUESTIONS

1. Kirk Wholesale Supply owns stock in Xerox Corporation, which it intends to hold indefinitely because of some negative tax consequences if sold. Should the investment in Xerox be classified as a temporary investment? Why?

2. (a) What is the cost of an investment in bonds?
   (b) When is interest on bonds recorded?

3. Ann Adler is confused about losses and gains on the sale of debt investments. Explain to Ann (a) how the gain or loss is computed, and (b) the statement presentation of the gains and losses.

4. Clio Company sells Cross's bonds costing $40,000 for $45,000, including $3,000 of accrued interest. In recording the sale, Clio books a $5,000 gain. Is this correct? Explain.

5. What is the cost of an investment in stock?

6. To acquire Mega Corporation stock, R. L. Duran pays $65,000 in cash plus $1,500 broker's fees. What entry should be made for this investment, assuming the stock is readily marketable?

7. (a) When should a long-term investment in common stock be accounted for by the equity method?
   (b) When is revenue recognized under this method?

8. Malon Corporation uses the equity method to account for its ownership of 35% of the common stock of Flynn Packing. During 1996 Flynn reported a net income of $80,000 and declares and pays cash dividends of $10,000. What recognition should Malon Corporation give to these events?

9. What constitutes "significant influence" when an investor's financial interest is below the 50% level?

10. Distinguish between the cost and equity methods of accounting for investments in stocks.

11. What are consolidated financial statements?

12. What are the valuation guidelines for investments at a balance sheet date?

13. Wendy Walner is the controller of G-Products, Inc. At December 31, the company's investments in trading securities cost $74,000 and have a fair value of $70,000. Indicate how Wendy would report these data in the financial statements prepared on December 31.

14. Using the data in question 13, how would Wendy report the data if the investment were long-term and the securities were classified as available-for-sale?

15. Reo Company's investments in available-for-sale securities at December 31 shows total cost of $192,000 and total fair value of $210,000. Prepare the adjusting entry.

16. Using the data in question 15, prepare the adjusting entry assuming the securities are classified as trading securities.

17. What is the proper statement presentation of the account Unrealized Loss—Equity?

18. What purposes are served by reporting Unrealized Gains (Losses)—Equity in the stockholders' equity section?

*19. (a) What asset and owners' equity balances are eliminated in preparing a consolidated balance sheet for a parent and a wholly owned subsidiary?
   (b) Why are they eliminated?

*20. Weller Company pays $320,000 to purchase all the outstanding common stock of Wood Corporation. At the date of purchase the net assets of Wood have a book value of $290,000. Weller's management allocates $20,000 of the excess cost to undervalued land on the books of Wood. What should be done with the rest of the excess?

# BRIEF EXERCISES

*Journalize entries for debt investments.*
(SO 2)

**BE17–1**   Phelps Corporation purchased debt investments for $41,500 on January 1, 1996. On July 1, 1996, Phelps received cash interest of $2,075. Journalize the purchase and the receipt of interest. Assume that no interest has been accrued.

*Journalize entries for stock investments.*
(SO 3)

**BE17–2**   On August 1, McLain Company buys 1,000 shares of ABC common stock for $35,000 cash plus brokerage fees of $600. On December 1, the stock investments are sold for $38,000 in cash. Journalize the purchase and sale of the common stock.

*Record transactions under the equity method of accounting.*
(SO 3)

**BE17–3**   Harmon Company owns 30% of Hook Company. For the current year Hook reports net income of $150,000 and declares and pays a $50,000 cash dividend. Record Harmon's equity in Hook's net income and the receipt of dividends from Hook.

*Prepare adjusting entry using fair value.*
(SO 5)

**BE17–4**   Cost and fair value data for the trading securities of Michele Company at December 31, 1996, are $62,000 and $59,000, respectively. Prepare the adjusting entry to record the securities at fair value.

**BE17–5**  For the data presented in BE17–4, show the financial statement presentation of the trading securities and related accounts.

*Indicate statement presentation using fair value.* (SO 5)

**BE17–6**  Duggen Corporation holds available-for-sale stock securities costing $72,000 as a long-term investment. At December 31, 1996, the fair value of the securities is $65,000. Prepare the adjusting entry to record the securities at fair value.

*Prepare adjusting entry using fair value.* (SO 5)

**BE17–7**  For the data presented in BE17–6, show the financial statement presentation of the available-for-sale securities and related accounts. Assume the available-for-sale securities are noncurrent.

*Indicate statement presentation using fair value.* (SO 5)

**BE17–8**  Saber Corporation has the following long-term investments: common stock of Sword Co. (10% ownership) held as available-for-sale securities, cost $108,000, fair value $113,000; common stock of Epee Inc. (30% ownership), cost $210,000, equity $250,000; and a bond sinking fund of $150,000. Prepare the investments section of the balance sheet.

*Prepare investment section of balance sheet.* (SO 5)

**\*BE17–9**  Provo Company acquires 100% of the common stock of Stanton Company for $180,000 cash. On the acquisition date, Stanton's ledger shows Common Stock $120,000 and Retained Earnings $60,000. Complete the work sheet for the following accounts: Provo— Investment in Stanton Common Stock, Stanton—Common Stock, and Stanton—Retained Earnings.

*Prepare partial consolidated work sheet when cost equals book value.* (SO 6, 7)

**\*BE17–10**  Data for the Provo and Stanton companies are given in BE17–9. Instead of paying $180,000, assume that Provo pays $200,000 to acquire the 100% interest in Stanton Company. Complete the work sheet for the accounts identified in BE17–9 and for the excess of cost over book value.

*Prepare partial consolidated work sheet when cost exceeds book value.* (SO 6, 7)

# EXERCISES

**E17–1**  Piper Corporation had the following transactions pertaining to debt investments:

*Journalize debt investment transactions and accrue interest.* (SO 2)

Jan. 1  Purchased 60 10%, $1,000 Harris Co. bonds for $60,000 cash plus brokerage fees of $900. Interest is payable semiannually on July 1 and January 1.

July 1  Received semiannual interest on Harris Co. bonds.

July 1  Sold 30 Harris Co. bonds for $32,000 less $400 brokerage fees.

*Instructions*
  (a) Journalize the transactions.
  (b) Prepare the adjusting entry for the accrual of interest at December 31.

**E17–2**  Malea Company had the following transactions pertaining to stock investments:

*Journalize stock investment transactions.* (SO 3)

Feb. 1  Purchased 800 shares of ABC common stock (2%) for $8,200 cash plus brokerage fees of $200.

July 1  Received cash dividends of $1 per share on ABC common stock.

Sept. 1  Sold 300 shares of ABC common stock for $4,000 less brokerage fees of $100.

Dec. 1  Received cash dividends of $1 per share on ABC common stock.

*Instructions*
  (a) Journalize the transactions.
  (b) Explain how dividend revenue and the gain (loss) on sale should be reported in the income statement.

**E17–3**  McCormick Inc. had the following transactions pertaining to investments in common stock:

*Journalize transactions for investments in stocks.* (SO 3)

Jan. 1  Purchased 1,000 shares of Starr Corporation common stock (5%) for $70,000 cash plus $1,400 broker's commission.

July 1  Received a cash dividend of $9 per share.

Dec. 1  Sold 500 shares of Starr Corporation common stock for $37,000 cash less $800 broker's commission.

Dec. 31  Received a cash dividend of $9 per share.

*Instructions*
Journalize the transactions.

*Journalize and post*
*transactions and contrast cost*
*and equity method results.*
(SO 3)

**E17–4**   On January 1 Ranier Corporation purchased a 25% equity in Bellingham Corporation for $150,000. At December 31 Bellingham declared and paid a $60,000 cash dividend and reported net income of $200,000.

**Instructions**
(a) Journalize the transactions.
(b) Determine the amount to be reported as an investment in Bellingham stock at December 31.

*Journalize entries under cost*
*and equity methods.*
(SO 3)

**E17–5**   Presented below are two independent situations:

1. Karen Cosmetics acquired 10% of the 200,000 shares of common stock of Bell Fashion at a total cost of $12 per share on March 18, 1996. On June 30, Bell declared and paid a $75,000 dividend. On December 31, Bell reported net income of $122,000 for the year. At December 31, the market price of Bell Fashion was $15 per share. The stock is classified as available-for-sale.
2. Barb, Inc., obtained significant influence over Diner Corporation by buying 30% of Diner's 30,000 outstanding shares of common stock at a total cost of $9 per share on January 1, 1996. On June 15, Diner declared and paid a cash dividend of $35,000. On December 31, Diner reported a net income of $80,000 for the year.

**Instructions**
Prepare all the necessary journal entries for 1996 for (a) Karen Cosmetics and (b) Barb, Inc.

*Prepare adjusting entry to*
*record fair value and indicate*
*statement presentation.*
(SO 5)

**E17–6**   At December 31, 1996, the trading securities for Nielson, Inc., are as follows:

| Security | Cost | Fair Value |
|---|---|---|
| A | $17,500 | $15,000 |
| B | 12,500 | 14,000 |
| C | 23,000 | 21,000 |
| | $53,000 | $50,000 |

**Instructions**
(a) Prepare the adjusting entry at December 31, 1996, to report the securities at fair value.
(b) Show the balance sheet and income statement presentation at December 31, 1996, after adjustment to fair value.

*Prepare adjusting entry to*
*record fair value and indicate*
*statement presentation.*
(SO 5)

**E17–7**   Data for investments in stock classified as trading securities are presented in E17–6. Assume instead that the investments are classified as available-for-sale securities with the same cost and fair value data. The securities are considered to be a long-term investment.

**Instructions**
(a) Prepare the adjusting entry at December 31, 1996, to report the securities at fair value.
(b) Show the statement presentation at December 31, 1996, after adjustment to fair value.
(c) ▰▰▰▷  J. Arnet, a member of the board of directors, does not understand the reporting of the unrealized gains or losses. Write a letter to Mr. Arnet explaining the reporting and the purposes that it serves.

*Prepare adjusting entries for*
*fair value and indicate*
*statement presentation for two*
*classes of securities.*
(SO 5)

**E17–8**   Felipe Company has the following data at December 31, 1996:

| Securities | Cost | Fair Value |
|---|---|---|
| Trading | $120,000 | $125,000 |
| Available-for-sale | 100,000 | 90,000 |

The available-for-sale securities are held as a long-term investment.

**Instructions**
(a) Prepare the adjusting entries to report each class of securities at fair value.
(b) Indicate the statement presentation of each class of securities and the related unrealized gain (loss) accounts.

*E17–9  On January 1, Swiss Corporation acquires 100% of Arco Inc. for $200,000 in cash. The condensed balance sheets of the two corporations immediately following the acquisition are as follows:

*Prepare consolidated work sheet when cost equals book value.*
*(SO 6)*

| | Swiss Corporation | Arco Inc. |
|---|---|---|
| Current assets | $ 60,000 | $ 40,000 |
| Investment in Arco Inc. common stock | 200,000 | |
| Plant and equipment (net) | 300,000 | 210,000 |
| | $560,000 | $250,000 |
| Current liabilities | $180,000 | $ 50,000 |
| Common stock | 225,000 | 75,000 |
| Retained earnings | 155,000 | 125,000 |
| | $560,000 | $250,000 |

**Instructions**
Prepare a work sheet for a consolidated balance sheet.

*E17–10  Data for the Swiss and Arco corporations are presented in E17–9. Assume that instead of paying $200,000 in cash for Arco Inc., Swiss Corporation pays $215,000 in cash. Thus, at the acquisition date, the assets of Swiss Corporation are: Current assets $45,000, Investment in Arco Inc. Common Stock $215,000, and Plant and Equipment (net) $300,000.

*Prepare consolidated work sheet when cost exceeds book value.*
*(SO 7)*

**Instructions**
Prepare a work sheet for a consolidated balance sheet.

# PROBLEMS

P17–1  The following transactions related to long-term bonds occurred for Lund Corporation:

*Journalize transactions and show financial statement presentation.*
*(SO 2, 5)*

**1996**
Jan. 1   Purchased $50,000 RAM Corporation 10% bonds for $50,000.
July 1   Received interest on RAM bonds.
Dec. 31  Accrued interest on RAM bonds.

**1997**
Jan. 1   Received interest on RAM bonds.
Jan. 1   Sold $25,000 RAM bonds for $27,500.
July 1   Received interest on RAM bonds.

**Instructions**
(a) Journalize the transactions.
(b) Assume that the fair value of the bonds at December 31, 1996, was $57,000. These bonds are classified as available-for-sale securities. Prepare the adjusting entry to record these bonds at fair value.
(c) Show the balance sheet presentation of the bonds and interest receivable at December 31, 1996, and indicate where any unrealized gain or loss is reported in the financial statements.

P17–2  In January 1996, the management of Reed Company concludes that it has sufficient cash to purchase some temporary investments in debt and stock securities. During the year, the following transactions occurred:

*Journalize investment transactions, prepare adjusting entry, and show statement presentation.*
*(SO 1, 2, 3, 5)*

Feb. 1   Purchased 800 shares of IBF common stock for $32,000 plus brokerage fees of $800.
Mar. 1   Purchased 500 shares of RST common stock for $15,000 plus brokerage fees of $500.
Apr. 1   Purchased 60 $1,000, 12% CRT bonds for $60,000 plus $1,200 brokerage fees. Interest is payable semiannually on April 1 and October 1.
July 1   Received a cash dividend of $.60 per share on the IBF common stock.
Aug. 1   Sold 200 shares of IBF common stock at $42 per share less brokerage fees of $350.
Sept. 1  Received a $1 per share cash dividend on the RST common stock.

Oct. 1    Received the semiannual interest on the CRT bonds.

Oct. 1    Sold the CRT bonds for $63,000 less $1,000 brokerage fees.

At December 31, the fair value of the IBF and RST common stocks were $39 and $30 per share, respectively.

**Instructions**

(a) Journalize the transactions and post to the accounts Debt Investments and Stock Investments. (Use the T-account form.)

(b) Prepare the adjusting entry at December 31, 1996, to report the investments at fair value. All securities are considered to be trading securities.

(c) Show the balance sheet presentation of investment securities at December 31, 1996.

(d) Identify the income statement accounts and give the statement classification of each account.

*Journalize transactions and adjusting entry for stock investments.*

*(SO 3, 5)*

**P17–3**    On December 31, 1995, Harmon Associates owned the following securities that are held as long-term investments:

| Common Stock | Shares | Cost |
| --- | --- | --- |
| A Co. | 1,000 | $50,000 |
| B Co. | 6,000 | 36,000 |
| C Co. | 1,200 | 24,000 |

On this date, the total fair value of the securities was equal to its cost. The securities are not held for influence or control over the investees. In 1996, the following transactions occurred:

July  1    Received $1 per share semiannual cash dividend on B Co. common stock.

Aug.  1    Received $.50 per share cash dividend on A Co. common stock.

Sept.  1    Sold 500 shares of B Co. common stock for cash at $8 per share less brokerage fees of $100.

Oct.  1    Sold 400 shares of A Co. common stock for cash at $54 per share less brokerage fees of $600.

Nov.  1    Received $1 per share cash dividend on C Co. common stock.

Dec. 15    Received $.50 per share cash dividend on A Co. common stock.

31    Received $1 per share semiannual cash dividend on B Co. common stock.

At December 31, the fair values per share of the common stocks were: A Co. $47, B Co. $6, and C Co. $18.

**Instructions**

(a) Journalize the 1996 transactions and post to the account Stock Investments. (Use the T-account form.)

(b) Prepare the adjusting entry at December 31, 1996, to show the securities at fair value. The stock should be classified as available-for-sale securities.

(c) Show the balance sheet presentation of the investments at December 31, 1996. At this date, Harmon Associates has common stock $2,000,000 and retained earnings $1,200,000.

*Prepare entries at cost and at equity and prepare memorandum.*

*(SO 3)*

**P17–4**    Cardinal Concrete acquired 20% of the outstanding common stock of Edra, Inc., on January 1, 1996, by paying $1,200,000 for 50,000 shares. Edra declared and paid an $0.80 per share cash dividend on June 30 and again on December 31, 1996. Edra reported net income of $700,000 for the year.

**Instructions**

(a) Prepare the journal entries for Cardinal Concrete for 1996 assuming Cardinal cannot exercise significant influence over Edra. (Use the cost method.)

(b) Prepare the journal entries for Cardinal Concrete for 1996, assuming Cardinal can exercise significant influence over Edra. (Use the equity method).

(c) ▓▓▓▶ The board of directors of Cardinal Concrete is confused about the differences between the cost and equity methods. Prepare a memorandum for the board that (1) explains each method and (2) shows, in tabular form, the account balances under each method at December 31, 1996.

**P17–5** The following are in Hi-Tech Company's portfolio of long-term available-for-sale securities at December 31, 1995:

*Journalize stock transactions and show statement presentation.*
*(SO 3, 5)*

|  | Cost |
|---|---|
| 500 shares of Awixa Corporation common stock. | $26,000 |
| 700 shares of HAL Corporation common stock. | 42,000 |
| 400 shares of Renda Corporation preferred stock. | 16,800 |

On December 31, the total cost of the portfolio equaled total fair value. Hi-Tech had the following transactions related to the securities during 1996:

Jan. 7 Sold 500 shares of Awixa Corporation common stock at $56 per share less brokerage fees of $700.

Jan. 10 Purchased 200 shares, $70 par value common stock of Mintor Corporation at $78 per share, plus brokerage fees of $240.

26 Received a cash dividend of $1.15 per share on HAL Corporation common stock.

Feb. 2 Received cash dividends of $.40 per share on Renda Corporation preferred stock.

10 Sold all 400 shares of Renda Corporation preferred stock at $28.00 per share less brokerage fees of $180.

April 30 Received 700 shares of HAL Corporation common stock as a result of a 2-for-1 stock split.

July 1 Received a cash dividend of $1.00 per share on HAL Corporation common stock.

Aug. 3 Received 20 shares of Mintor Corporation common stock as the result of a 10% stock dividend.

Sept. 1 Purchased an additional 400 shares of the $70 par value common stock of Mintor Corporation at $82 per share, plus brokerage fees of $400.

Dec. 15 Received a cash dividend of $1.50 per share on Mintor Corporation common stock.

At December 31, 1996, the fair values of the securities were:

| HAL Corporation common stock | $32 per share |
|---|---|
| Mintor Corporation common stock | $70 per share |

Hi-Tech uses separate account titles for each investment, such as Investment in HAL Corporation Common Stock.

**Instructions**
(a) Prepare journal entries to record the transactions.
(b) Post to the investment accounts. (Use T accounts.)
(c) Prepare the adjusting entry at December 31, 1996, to report the porfolio at fair value.
(d) Show the balance sheet presentation at December 31, 1996.

**P17–6** The following data, presented in alphabetical order, are taken from the records of Oklahoma Corporation.

*Prepare a balance sheet.*
*(SO 5)*

| | |
|---|---|
| Accounts payable | $ 240,000 |
| Accounts receivable | 110,000 |
| Accumulated depreciation—building | 180,000 |
| Accumulated depreciation—equipment | 52,000 |
| Allowance for doubtful accounts | 6,000 |
| Bonds payable (10%, due 2012) | 400,000 |
| Bond sinking fund | 360,000 |
| Buildings | 900,000 |
| Cash | 92,000 |
| Common stock ($5 par value; 500,000 shares authorized, 300,000 shares issued) | 1,500,000 |
| Discount on bonds payable | 20,000 |
| Dividends payable | 50,000 |
| Equipment | 275,000 |
| Goodwill | 200,000 |
| Income taxes payable | 120,000 |

| | |
|---|---|
| Investment in Houston Inc, stock (30% ownership), at equity | 240,000 |
| Land | 500,000 |
| Temporary stock investment, at fair value | 185,000 |
| Merchandise inventory | 170,000 |
| Notes payable (due 1997) | 70,000 |
| Organization costs | 50,000 |
| Paid-in capital in excess of par value | 200,000 |
| Prepaid insurance | 16,000 |
| Retained earnings | 300,000 |

**Instructions**
Prepare a balance sheet at December 31, 1996.

*Prepare consolidated work sheet and balance sheet when cost exceeds book value. (SO 6, 7)*

**\*P17–7**   Neal Company purchased all the outstanding common stock of Wheaton Company on December 31, 1996. Just before the purchase, the condensed balance sheets of the two companies were as follows:

| | Neal Company | Wheaton Company |
|---|---|---|
| Current assets | $1,476,000 | $379,000 |
| Plant and equipment (net) | 1,882,000 | 353,000 |
| | $3,358,000 | $732,000 |
| | | |
| Current liabilities | $ 868,000 | $ 92,000 |
| Common stock | 1,947,000 | 360,000 |
| Retained earnings | 543,000 | 280,000 |
| | $3,358,000 | $732,000 |

Neal used current assets of $726,000 to acquire the stock of Wheaton. The excess of this purchase price over the book value of Wheaton's net assets is determined to be attributable $30,000 to Wheaton's plant and equipment and the remainder to goodwill.

**Instructions**
(a)  Prepare the entry for Neal Company's acquisition of Wheaton Company stock.
(b)  Prepare a consolidated work sheet at December 31, 1996.
(c)  Prepare a consolidated balance sheet at December 31, 1996.

# ALTERNATE PROBLEMS

• • • • • • • • • • • • • • • • • • • • • • • • • • • • • • • • • • • • • • • • • • • • • • • • • • •

*Journalize transactions and show financial statement presentation. (SO 2, 5)*

**P17–1A**   The following transactions related to long-term bonds occurred for Givarz Corporation.

1996
Jan. 1   Purchased $100,000 Leslye Corporation 9% bonds for $100,000.
July 1   Received interest on Leslye bonds.
Dec. 31   Accrued interest on Leslye bonds.

1997
Jan. 1   Received interest on Leslye bonds.
Jan. 1   Sold $25,000 Leslye bonds for $30,500.
July 1   Received interest on Leslye bonds.

**Instructions**
(a)  Journalize the transactions.
(b)  Assume that the fair value of the bonds at December 31, 1996, was $97,000. These bonds are classified as available-for-sale securities. Prepare the adjusting entry to record these bonds at fair value.
(c)  Show the balance sheet presentation of the bonds and interest receivable at December 31, 1996, and indicate where any unrealized gain or loss is reported in the financial statements.

**P17–2A**  In January, 1996, the management of the Mead Company concludes that it has sufficient cash to permit some temporary investments in debt and stock securities. During the year, the following transactions occurred:

*Journalize investment
transactions, prepare adjusting
entry, and show statement
presentation.*
(SO 1, 2, 3, 5)

Feb. 1  Purchased 600 shares of CBF common stock for $31,800 plus brokerage fees of $600.

Mar. 1  Purchased 800 shares of RSD common stock for $20,000 plus brokerage fees of $400.

Apr. 1  Purchased 50 $1,000, 12% MRT bonds for $50,000 plus $1,000 brokerage fees. Interest is payable semiannually on April 1 and October 1.

July 1  Received a cash dividend of $.60 per share on the CBF common stock.

Aug. 1  Sold 200 shares of CBF common stock at $56 per share less brokerage fees of $200.

Sept. 1  Received a $1 per share cash dividend on the RSD common stock.

Oct. 1  Received the semiannual interest on the MRT bonds.

Oct. 1  Sold the MRT bonds for $51,000 less $1,000 brokerage fees.

At December 31, the fair value of the CBF and RSD common stocks were $55 and $24 per share, respectively.

**Instructions**

(a) Journalize the transactions and post to the accounts Debt Investments and Stock Investments. (Use the T-account form.)

(b) Prepare the adjusting entry at December 31, 1996, to report the investment securities at fair value. All securities are considered to be trading securities.

(c) Show the balance sheet presentation of investment securities at December 31, 1996.

(d) Identify the income statement accounts and give the statement classification of each account.

**P17–3A**  On December 31, 1996, Karen Associates owned the following securities that are held as a long-term investment. The securities are not held for influence or control of the investee.

*Journalize transactions and
adjusting entry for stock
investments.*
(SO 3, 5)

| Common Stock | Shares | Cost |
|---|---|---|
| X Co. | 2,000 | $90,000 |
| Y Co. | 5,000 | 45,000 |
| Z Co. | 1,500 | 30,000 |

On this date, the total fair value of the securities was equal to its cost. In 1997, the following transactions occurred.

July 1  Received $1 per share semiannual cash dividend on Y Co. common stock.

8  Received 4,000 shares of X Co. common stock in a 3 for 1 stock split.

Aug. 1  Received $.50 per share cash dividend on X Co. common stock.

Sept. 1  Sold 700 shares of Y Co. common stock for cash at $8 per share less brokerage fees of $200.

Oct. 1  Sold 600 shares of X Co. common stock for cash at $18 per share less brokerage fees of $500.

Nov. 1  Received $1 per share cash dividend on Z Co. common stock.

Dec. 15  Received $.50 per share cash dividend on X Co. common stock.

31  Received $1 per share semiannual cash dividend on Y Co. common stock.

At December 31, the fair values per share of the common stocks were: X Co. $16, Y Co. $8, and Z Co. $17.

**Instructions**

(a) Journalize the 1997 transactions and post to the account Stock Investments. (Use the T-account form.)

(b) Prepare the adjusting entry at December 31, 1997, to show the securities at fair value. The stock should be classified as available-for-sale securities.

(c) Show the balance sheet presentation of the investments at December 31, 1997. At this date, Karen Associates has common stock $1,500,000 and retained earnings $1,000,000.

*Prepare entries under the cost and equity methods and tabulate differences.*
(SO 3)

**P17–4A**  DFM Services acquired 30% of the outstanding common stock of BNA Company on January 1, 1996, by paying $800,000 for the 40,000 shares. BNA declared and paid $0.20 per share cash dividends on March 15, June 15, September 15, and December 15, 1996. BNA reported net income of $350,000 for the year.

**Instructions**
(a) Prepare the journal entries for DFM Services for 1996 assuming DFM cannot exercise significant influence over BNA. (Use the cost method.)
(b) Prepare the journal entries for DFM Services for 1996, assuming DFM can exercise significant influence over BNA. (Use the equity method.)
(c) In tabular form, indicate the investment and income statement account balances at December 31, 1996, under each method of accounting.

*Prepare a balance sheet.*
(SO 5)

**P17–5A**  The following data, presented in alphabetical order, are taken from the records of Alameda Corporation:

| | |
|---|---:|
| Accounts payable | $ 250,000 |
| Accounts receivable | 120,000 |
| Accumulated depreciation—building | 180,000 |
| Accumulated depreciation—equipment | 52,000 |
| Allowance for doubtful accounts | 6,000 |
| Bonds payable (10%, due 2010) | 500,000 |
| Bond sinking fund | 150,000 |
| Buildings | 950,000 |
| Cash | 92,000 |
| Common stock ($10 par value; 500,000 shares authorized, 150,000 shares issued) | 1,500,000 |
| Dividends payable | 80,000 |
| Equipment | 275,000 |
| Goodwill | 200,000 |
| Income taxes payable | 120,000 |
| Investment in Dodge common stock (10% ownership), at cost | 278,000 |
| Investment in Huston common stock (30% ownership), at equity | 230,000 |
| Land | 500,000 |
| Market adjustment—available-for-sale securities (Dr) | 8,000 |
| Merchandise inventory | 170,000 |
| Notes payable (due 1997) | 70,000 |
| Organization costs | 50,000 |
| Paid-in capital in excess of par value | 200,000 |
| Premium on bonds payable | 40,000 |
| Prepaid insurance | 16,000 |
| Retained earnings | 213,000 |
| Temporary stock investment, at fair value | 180,000 |
| Unrealized gain—available-for-sale securities | 8,000 |

The investment in Dodge common stock is considered to be a long-term available-for-sale security.

**Instructions**
Prepare a balance sheet at December 31, 1996.

*Prepare consolidated work sheet and balance sheet when cost exceeds book value.*
(SO 7)

**\*P17–6A**  Linger Corporation purchased all the outstanding common stock of Chrissy Foods, Inc. on December 31, 1996. Just before the purchase, the condensed balance sheets of the two companies appeared as follows:

| | **Linger Corporation** | **Chrissy Foods, Inc.** |
|---|---:|---:|
| Current assets | $1,480,000 | $ 439,500 |
| Plant and equipment (net) | 2,100,000 | 672,000 |
| | $3,580,000 | $1,111,500 |
| | | |
| Current liabilities | $ 578,000 | $ 92,500 |
| Common stock | 1,950,000 | 525,000 |
| Retained earnings | 1,052,000 | 494,000 |
| | $3,580,000 | $1,111,500 |

Linger used current assets of $1,200,000 to acquire the stock of Chrissy Foods. The excess of this purchase price over the book value of Chrissy Foods' net assets is determined to be attributable $81,000 to Chrissy Foods' plant and equipment and the remainder to goodwill.

**Instructions**
- (a) Prepare the entry for Linger's acquisition of Chrissy Foods, Inc. stock.
- (b) Prepare a consolidated work sheet at December 31, 1996.
- (c) Prepare a consolidated balance sheet at December 31, 1996.

# ▶*Broadening Your Perspective*

# *F*INANCIAL REPORTING PROBLEM
• • • • • • • • • • • • • • • • • • • • • • • • • • • • • • • • • • • • • • • • • • • • • • • • • • •

The annual report of PepsiCo, Inc. is presented in Appendix A.

**Instructions**
Answer the following questions.

- (a) What information about investments is reported in the consolidated balance sheet?
- (b) Based on the information under Assets in Management's Analysis of Financial Condition, what is the nature of PepsiCo, Inc.'s short-term investments?
- (c) Using the information under Interest Expense in Management's Analysis of the Results of Operations, what effect did investments have on Income Before Income Taxes in 1994?
- (d) Using the Statement of Cash Flows, did cash flows from investing activities increase or decrease in 1994, and by how much?
- (e) Based on the information under Investing Activities in Management's Analysis of Cash Flows, what types of investments have been made in (1) recent years and (2) 1994? Does management expect investing activity to increase or decrease in 1995? How much?

# *D*ECISION CASE
• • • • • • • • • • • • • • • • • • • • • • • • • • • • • • • • • • • • • • • • • • • • • • • • • • •

At the beginning of the question and answer portion of the annual stockholders' meeting of Revell Corporation, stockholder Carol Finstrom asks, "Why did management sell the holdings in AHM Company at a loss when this company has been very profitable during the period its stock was held by Revell?"

Since president Larry Wisdom has just concluded his speech on the recent success and bright future of Revell, he is taken aback by this question and responds, "I remember we paid $1,100,000 for that stock some years ago, and I am sure we sold that stock at a much higher price. You must be mistaken."

Finstrom retorts, "Well, right here in footnote number 7 to the annual report it shows that 240,000 shares, a 30% interest in AHM, was sold on the last day of the year. Also, it states that AHM earned $550,000 this year and paid out $150,000 in cash dividends. Further, a summary statement indicates that in past years, while Revell held AHM stock, AHM earned $1,240,000 and paid out $440,000 in dividends. Finally, the income statement for this year shows a loss on the sale of AHM stock of $180,000. So, I doubt that I am mistaken."

Red-faced, president Wisdom turns to you.

**Instructions**
What dollar amount did Revell receive upon the sale of the AHM stock? Explain why both stockholder Finstrom and president Wisdom are correct.

# COMMUNICATION ACTIVITY

Chapperal Corporation has purchased two securities for its portfolio. The first is a stock investment in Sting Ray Corporation, one of its suppliers. Chapperal purchased 10% of Sting Ray with the intention of holding it for a number of years, but has no intention of purchasing more shares. The second investment was a purchase of debt securities. Chapperal purchased the debt securities because its analysts believe that changes in market interest rates will cause these securities to increase in value in a short period of time. Chapperal intends to sell the securities as soon as they have increased in value.

### Instructions
Write a memo to Gils Stiles, the Chief Financial Officer, explaining how to account for each of these investments, and what the implications for reported income are from this accounting treatment.

# GROUP ACTIVITY

Finland Corporation holds a portfolio of debt and equity investments. Although some of the securities in the portfolio have declined in value, the total value of the portfolio is above its total cost. Finn Berge, Finland Corporation's president, has decided to classify all securities in the portfolio that have decreased in value as available-for-sale (the stock investments) or as held-to-maturity (the debt investments). He will classify all securities that have increased in value as trading securities.

### Instructions
In groups of four or five discuss the following:

- (a) What impact will this classification approach have on Finland Corporation's reported results?
- (b) Is this an appropriate approach for classifying these securities?
- (c) What are the implications of this approach for subsequent years?

# ETHICS CASE

Scott Kreiter Financial Services Company holds a large portfolio of debt and stock securities as an investment. The total fair value of the portfolio at December 31, 1996, is greater than total cost, with some securities having increased in value and others having decreased. Vicki Lemke, the financial vice-president, and Ula Greenwood, the controller, are in the process of classifying for the first time the securities in the portfolio.

Lemke suggests classifying the securities that have increased in value as trading securities in order to increase net income for the year. She also wants to classify the securities that have decreased in value as long-term available-for-sale securities so that the decreases in value will not affect 1996 net income.

Greenwood disagrees. She recommends classifying the securities that have decreased in value as trading securities and those that have increased in value as long-term available-for-sale securities. Greenwood argues that the company is having a good earnings year and that recognizing the losses now will help to smooth income for this year. Moreover, for future years, when the company may not be as profitable, the company will have built-in gains.

### Instructions

- (a) Will classifying the securities as Lemke and Greenwood suggest actually affect earnings as each says it will?
- (b) Is there anything unethical in what Lemke and Greenwood propose? Who are the stakeholders affected by their proposals?
- (c) Assume that Lemke and Greenwood properly classify the portfolio. Assume, at year-end, that Lemke proposes to sell the securities that will increase 1996 net income, and that Greenwood proposes to sell the securities that will decrease 1996 net income. Is this unethical?

# CRITICAL THINKING
## ► A Real-World Focus: SPS Technologies, Inc.
...................................................................................

*SPS Technologies, Inc., was formed in 1903 as Standard Pressed Steel. Today the company is engaged in the design, manufacture, and marketing of high-strength mechanical fasteners, superalloys, and magnetic materials for the aerospace, automotive, and off-highway equipment industries. The company owns plants in the United States, United Kingdom, Ireland, Australia, and Spain, and has minority interests in facilities in Brazil and India.*

The following note to the financial statements appears in a recent SPS annual report:

**Investments:** The Company's investments in affiliates consist of a 16.75% interest in Precision Fasteners Ltd., Bombay, India; a 46.49% interest in Metalac S.A. Industria e Comercio, Sao Paulo, Brazil; a 51.0% interest in Pacific Products Limited, Guernsey, Channel Islands, United Kingdom; and a 51.0% interest in National-Arnold Magnetics Company, Adelanto, California, United States. Dividends received from these companies were $42,000, $44,000, and $66,000 in 1993, 1992 and 1991, respectively.

*Instructions*
   (a) Does the investment in these companies represent short- or long-term investments? Are these investments in stocks or in bonds of these companies?
   (b) The ownership percentages in these companies vary. Based upon the information given, which accounting method would appear appropriate for each company? What other information would you like to know before deciding how to account for each investment?
   (c) What is the most likely method used to account for dividends received from Precision Fasteners? From National-Arnolds Magnetics Company?

---

*Answers to Self-Study Questions*
1. c     2. a     3. b     4. c     5. a     6. a     7. c     8. b     9. d     10. d     11. d

# "Cash Is Cash, and Everything Else Is Accounting"

SIOUX FALLS, S.D. — For Gerald Biby, vice president and chief financial officer of Kilian Community College in Sioux Falls, South Dakota, the statement of cash flows was the difference between being able to refinance a mortgage and being turned down by six local banks. "We recently wanted to refinance a $125,000 mortgage on a piece of property that we own," he says. "It was the statement of cash flows that finally showed our lender that we had the cash flow to service the debt."

As he explains, the traditional financial statement for a not-for-profit, educational institution shows revenues and all expenditures, even the capital expenditures. According to this format, which the banks focused on initially, Kilian Community College was just breaking even. "In the business world, if we had spent $250,000 on a computer system, then we would have put that on a depreciation schedule. But in the non-profit arena, it's typical that the entire $250,000 is written off as an expense against the general fund." The statement of cash flows showed the bankers that one of the uses of funds was really the purchase of computer equipment that had several years of life.

The college's statement of cash flows has over 30 classifications including tuition, fees, bookstore revenues, and so on. The school has 250 students, charges $70 a credit hour (12 hours is a full-time schedule), and has five terms each year.

The bankers granted the refinancing when they saw that the college's sources of funds exceeded the loan repayments, including principal and interest, by a ratio of 3-to-1. Not only did the school get the loan, but it did so at a favorable rate. "We were able to cut the mortgage rate to prime plus 1% from prime plus 3%." ◀

# CHAPTER · 18

# *T*HE STATEMENT OF CASH FLOWS

As the story about Kilian Community College indicates, the balance sheet, income statement, and retained earnings statement do not always show the whole picture of the financial condition of a company or institution. In fact, looking at the three traditional financial statements of some well-known companies, a thoughtful investor might have questions like the following: How did Eastman Kodak finance cash dividends of $649 million in a year in which it earned only $17 million? How could Delta Airlines purchase new planes costing $900 million in a year in which it reported a net loss of $86 million? How did Kohlberg Kravis Roberts finance its record-shattering $25 billion purchase of RJR Nabisco? Answers to these and similar questions can be found in this chapter, which presents the **statement of cash flows**. The content and organization of this chapter are as follows:

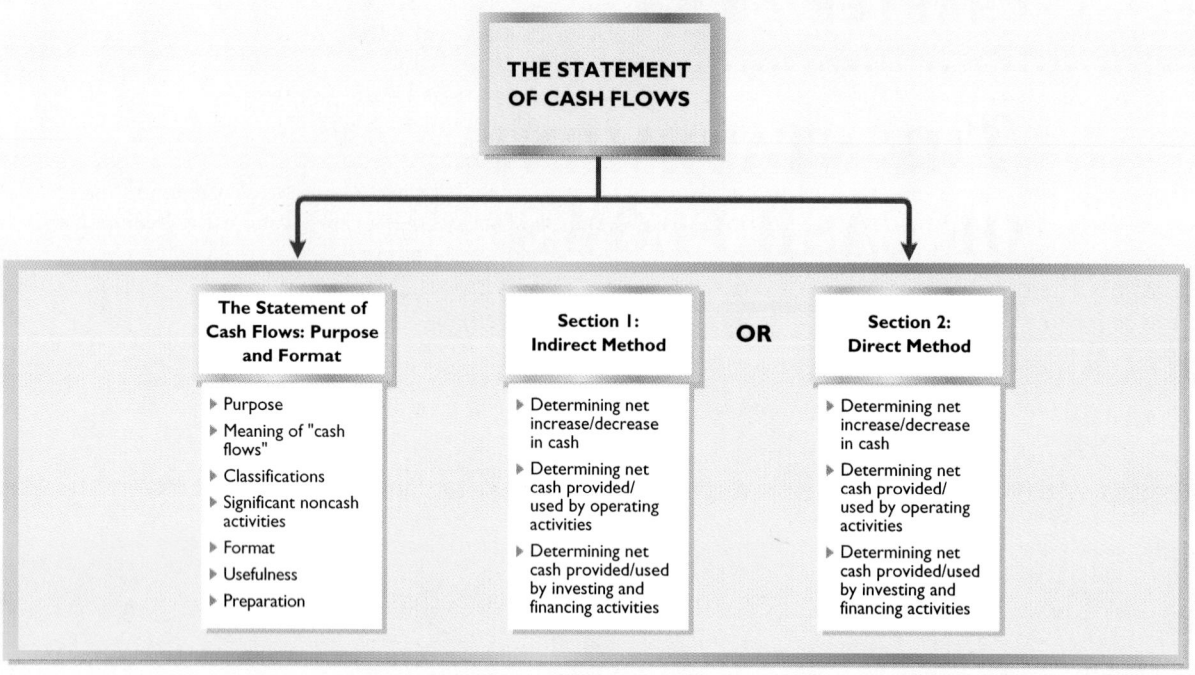

## The Statement of Cash Flows: Purpose and Format

The three basic financial statements we've studied so far present only limited and fragmentary information about a company's cash flows (cash receipts and cash payments). For example, comparative balance sheets show the increase in property, plant, and equipment during the year, but they do not show how the additions were financed or paid for. The income statement shows net income, but it does not indicate the amount of cash generated by operating activities. Similarly, the retained earnings statement shows cash dividends declared but not the cash dividends paid during the year. None of these statements presents a detailed summary of the net change in cash as a result of operating, investing, and financing activities during the period.

**A**ccounting in **A**ction ► *Business Insight*

Libby-Owens-Ford (LOF) Company's mission statement in its annual report emphasizes the importance of cash flow as follows: "LOF stresses the importance of cash flow measurement and performance. Individual companies must analyze the cash flow effects of running their business. Where cash comes from and what cash is used for must be simply and clearly set forth."

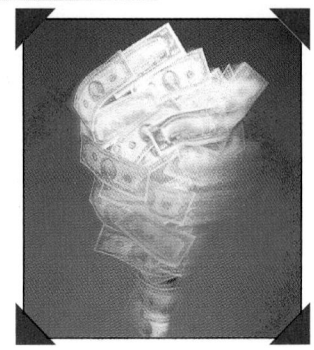

## Purpose of the Statement of Cash Flows

The primary purpose of the statement of cash flows is to provide information about the cash receipts and cash payments of an entity during a period. A secondary objective is to provide information about the operating, investing, and financing activities of the entity during the period.[1] The statement of cash flows reports the cash receipts, cash payments, and net change in cash resulting from the operating, investing, and financing activities of an enterprise during a period in a format that reconciles the beginning and ending cash balances.

Reporting the causes of changes in cash is considered useful because investors, creditors, and other interested parties want to know what is happening to a company's most liquid resource—its cash. As the opening story about Kilian Community College demonstrates, a statement of cash flows helps us understand what is happening. It provides answers to the following simple, but important, questions about the enterprise:

**STUDY OBJECTIVE**
•••••••••▼•••••••••
*Indicate the primary purpose of the statement of cash flows.*

1. Where did the cash come from during the period?
2. What was the cash used for during the period?
3. What was the change in the cash balance during the period?

## Meaning of "Cash Flows"

The statement of cash flows is generally prepared using "**cash and cash equivalents**" as its basis. Cash equivalents are short-term, highly liquid investments that are both:

1. Readily convertible to known amounts of cash, and
2. So near their maturity that their market value is relatively insensitive to changes in interest rates.

Generally, only investments with original maturities of three months or less qualify under this definition. Examples of cash equivalents are Treasury bills, commercial paper (short-term corporate notes), and money market funds. All typically are purchased with cash that is in excess of immediate needs. Note that since cash and cash equivalents are viewed as the same, transfers between cash and cash equivalents are not treated as cash receipts and cash payments—i.e., they are not reported in the statement of cash flows. The term "cash" when used in this chapter includes cash and cash equivalents.

## Classification of Cash Flows

**STUDY OBJECTIVE**
•••••••••▼•••••••••
*Distinguish among operating, investing, and financing activities.*

The statement of cash flows classifies cash receipts and cash payments by operating, investing, and financing activities. Transactions and other events characteristic of each kind of activity are as follows:

---

[1]"Statement of Cash Flows," *Statement of Financial Accounting Standards No. 95* (Stamford, Conn.: FASB, 1987).

1. Operating activities include the cash effects of transactions that create revenues and expenses and thus enter into the determination of net income.
2. Investing activities include (a) acquiring and disposing of investments and productive long-lived assets, and (b) lending money and collecting the loans.
3. Financing activities include (a) obtaining cash from issuing debt and repaying the amounts borrowed, and (b) obtaining cash from stockholders and providing them with a return on their investment.

The category of operating activities is the most important because it shows the cash provided by company operations. This source of cash is generally considered to be the best measure of a company's ability to generate sufficient cash to continue as a going concern.

Illustration 18-1 lists typical cash receipts and cash payments within each of the three classifications. Study the list carefully. It will prove very useful in solving homework exercises and problems.

**Illustration 18-1**

*Typical receipts and payments classified by activity*

**Helpful hint** Operating activities generally relate to changes in current assets and current liabilities. Investing activities generally relate to changes in noncurrent assets. Financing activities relate to changes in noncurrent liabilities and stockholders' equity accounts.

**Types of Cash Inflows and Outflows**

**Operating activities**
  Cash inflows:
    From sale of goods or services.
    From returns on loans (interest received) and on equity securities (dividends received).
  Cash outflows:
    To suppliers for inventory.
    To employees for services.
    To government for taxes.
    To lenders for interest.
    To others for expenses.
**Investing activities**
  Cash inflows:
    From sale of property, plant, and equipment.
    From sale of debt or equity securities of other entities.
    From collection of principal on loans to other entities.
  Cash outflows:
    To purchase property, plant, and equipment.
    To purchase debt or equity securities of other entities.
    To make loans to other entities.
**Financing activities**
  Cash inflows:
    From sale of equity securities (company's own stock).
    From issuance of debt (bonds and notes).
  Cash outflows:
    To stockholders as dividends.
    To redeem long-term debt or reacquire capital stock.

As you can see, some cash flows relating to investing or financing activities are classified as operating activities. For example, receipts of investment revenue (interest and dividends) and payments of interest to lenders are classified as operating activities because these items are reported in the income statement.

Note that, generally, (1) operating activities involve income determination (income statement) items, (2) investing activities involve cash flows resulting from changes in investments and long-term asset items, and (3) financing activities involve cash flows resulting from changes in long-term liability and stockholders' equity items.

## Significant Noncash Activities

Not all of a company's significant activities involve cash. Examples of significant noncash activities are:

1. Issuance of common stock to purchase assets.
2. Conversion of bonds into common stock.
3. Issuance of debt to purchase assets.
4. Exchanges of plant assets.

**Significant financing and investing activities that do not affect cash are not reported in the body of the statement of cash flows.** However, these activities are reported in either a separate schedule at the bottom of the statement of cash flows or in a separate note or supplementary schedule to the financial statements.

The reporting of these activities in a separate note or supplementary schedule satisfies the **full disclosure principle** because it identifies significant noncash investing and financing activities of the enterprise. In solving homework assignments you should present significant noncash investing and financing activities in a separate schedule at the bottom of the statement of cash flows. (See lower section of Illustration 18-2 for an example.)

**Helpful hint** Do not include noncash investing and financing activities in the body of the statement of cash flows. Report this information in a separate schedule at the bottom of the statement.

## Format of the Statement of Cash Flows

The three activities discussed above—operating, investing, and financing—plus the significant noncash investing and financing activities constitute the general format of the statement of cash flows. A widely used form of the statement of cash flows is shown in Illustration 18-2.

Illustration 18-2

*Format of statement of cash flows*

| **COMPANY NAME**<br>**Statement of Cash Flows**<br>**Period Covered** | | |
| --- | --- | --- |
| **Cash flows from operating activities** | | |
| (List of individual items) | XX | |
| Net cash provided (used) by operating activities | | XXX |
| **Cash flows from investing activities** | | |
| (List of individual inflows and outflows) | XX | |
| Net cash provided (used) by investing activities | | XXX |
| **Cash flows from financing activities** | | |
| (List of individual inflows and outflows) | XX | |
| Net cash provided (used) by financing activities | | XXX |
| **Net increase (decrease) in cash** | | XXX |
| **Cash at beginning of period** | | XXX |
| **Cash at end of period** | | XXX |
| **Noncash investing and financing activities** | | |
| (List of individual noncash transactions) | | XXX |

As illustrated, the cash flows from operating activities section always appears first, followed by the investing activities and the financing activities sections. Also, **the individual inflows and outflows from investing and financing activities are reported separately**. Thus, cash outflow for the purchase of property, plant, and equipment is reported separately from the cash inflow from the sale of property, plant, and equipment. Similarly, the cash inflow from the issuance

## ▸Accounting in Action ▸ *Business Insight*

Differences between net income and net cash provided by operating activities are illustrated by the following results from recent annual reports for the same fiscal year (all data are in millions of dollars):

| Company | Net Income | Net Cash from Operations |
|---|---|---|
| Kmart Corporation | $ 296 | $ 76 |
| Wal-Mart Stores, Inc. | 2,681 | 2,906 |
| Woolworth Corporation | 47 | (340) |
| J.C. Penney Company, Inc. | 1,057 | 738 |
| Sears Roebuck & Co. | 1,454 | 1,930 |
| The May Department Stores Company | 782 | 999 |

Note the wide disparity among the companies that engaged in similar types of retail merchandising.

of debt securities is reported separately from the cash outflow for the retirement of debt. If a company did not report the inflows and outflows separately, it would obscure the investing and financing activities of the enterprise and thus make it more difficult to assess future cash flows.

The reported operating, investing, and financing activities result in either net cash **provided or used** by each activity. The net cash provided or used by each activity is totaled to show the net increase (decrease) in cash for the period. The net increase (decrease) in cash for the period is then added to or subtracted from the beginning-of-the-period cash balance to obtain the end-of-the-period cash balance. Finally, any significant noncash investing and financing activities are reported in a separate schedule at the bottom of the statement.

### Usefulness of the Statement of Cash Flows

The information in a statement of cash flows should help investors, creditors, and others assess various aspects of the firm's financial position:

1. **The entity's ability to generate future cash flows.** By examining relationships between such items as sales and net cash provided by operating activities, or cash provided by operations and increases or decreases in cash, investors and others can make predictions of the amounts, timing, and uncertainty of future cash flows better than from accrual basis data.
2. **The entity's ability to pay dividends and meet obligations.** Simply put, if a company does not have adequate cash, employees cannot be paid, debts settled, or dividends paid. Employees, creditors, stockholders, and customers should be particularly interested in this statement, because it alone shows the flows of cash in a business.
3. **The reasons for the difference between net income and net cash provided (used) by operating activities.** Net income is important, because it provides information on the success or failure of a business enterprise. However, some are critical of accrual basis net income because it requires many estimates; as a result, the reliability of the number is often challenged. Such is not the case with cash. Thus, many readers of the financial statement want to know the reasons for the difference between net income and net cash provided by operating activities. Then they can assess for themselves the reliability of the income number.
4. **The cash investing and financing transactions during the period.** By examining a company's investing activities and its financing transactions, a

▸*Ethics note*

Many investors believe that "Cash is cash and everything else is accounting"—that is, cash flow is less susceptible to management manipulation and fraud than traditional accounting measures such as net income. Though we would suggest that reliance on cash flows to the exclusion of accrual accounting is inappropriate, comparing cash from operations to net income can reveal important information about the "quality" of reported net income—that is, the extent to which net income provides a good measure of actual performance.

**Helpful hint**  Income from operations and cash flow from operating activities are different. Income from operations is based on accrual accounting; cash flow from operating activities is prepared on a cash basis.

financial statement reader can better understand why assets and liabilities increased or decreased during the period. In summary, the information in the statement of cash flows is useful in answering the following questions:

How did cash increase when there was a net loss for the period?

How were the proceeds of the bond issue used?

How was the expansion in the plant and equipment financed?

Why were dividends not increased?

How was the retirement of debt accomplished?

How much money was borrowed during the year?

Is cash flow greater or less than net income?

## ►Accounting in Action ► *Business Insight*

Cash flow is also sometimes used to determine the price of a company. Page Net, a company in the telephone beeper business, had an initial public offering (IPO) in which $590 million of stock was sold. In December 1993 the stock had a market value of $1.5 billion. Yet Page Net reported losses in every quarter since it went public. However, its cash flow the year before the IPO was $39 million, $57 million in the IPO year, $75 million in 1992, and approximately $99 million in 1993. As one expert noted, "It is a classic example of a company valued by cash flow."

## Preparing the Statement of Cash Flows

The statement of cash flows is prepared differently from the three other basic financial statements. First, it is not prepared from an adjusted trial balance. Because the statement requires detailed information concerning the changes in account balances that occurred between two periods of time, an adjusted trial balance will not provide the necessary data for the statement. Second, the statement of cash flows deals with cash receipts and payments. As a result, **the accrual concept is not used in the preparation of a statement of cash flows**.

The information to prepare this statement usually comes from three sources:

**Comparative balance sheet.** Information in this statement indicates the amount of the changes in assets, liabilities, and stockholders' equities from the beginning to the end of the period.

**Current income statement.** Information in this statement helps the reader determine the amount of cash provided by or used by operations during the period.

**Additional information.** Additional information includes transaction data that are needed to determine how cash was provided or used during the period.

Preparing the statement of cash flows from these data sources involves three major steps, explained in Illustration 18-3 on page 738.

## Indirect and Direct Methods

In order to perform step 2, the operating activities section of the statement of cash flows **must be converted from an accrual basis to a cash basis**. This conversion may be done by either of two methods: (1) the indirect method or (2) the direct method. **Both methods arrive at the same total amount** for "Net cash provided by operating activities," but they differ in disclosing the items that comprise the total amount.

## Step 1: Determine the net increase/decrease in cash.

The difference between the beginning and ending cash balances can be easily computed from comparative balance sheets.

## Step 2: Determine net cash provided/used by operating activities.

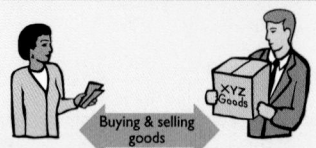

This step involves analyzing not only the current year's income statement but also comparative balance sheets and selected additional data.

## Step 3: Determine net cash provided/used by investing and financing activities.

This step involves analyzing comparative balance sheet data and selected additional information for their effects on cash.

**Illustration 18-3**

*Three major steps in preparing the statement of cash flows*

The indirect method is used extensively in practice, as shown in Illustration 18-4.[2] Companies favor the indirect method for two reasons: (1) it is easier to prepare, and (2) it focuses on the differences between net income and net cash flow from operating activities.

**Illustration 18-4**

*Usage of indirect and direct methods*

▸ **International note**

International accounting requirements are quite similar in most respects with regard to the cash flow statement. Some interesting exceptions: In Japan, operating and investing activities are combined; in Australia, the direct method is mandatory; in Spain, the indirect method is mandatory. Also, in a number of European and Scandinavian countries a cash flow statement is not required at all, although in practice most publicly traded firms provide one.

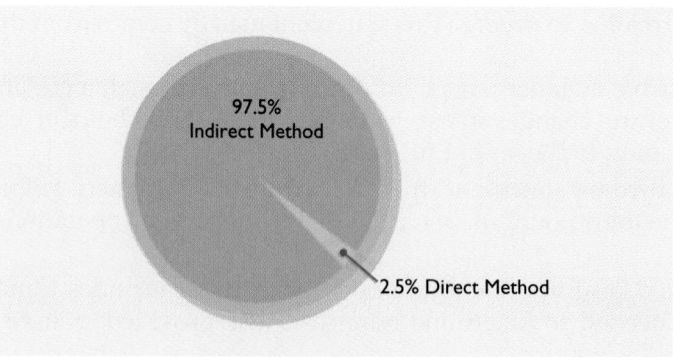

Others, however, favor the direct method. The direct method shows operating cash receipts and payments. Thus, it is more consistent with the objective of a statement of cash flows. The FASB has expressed a preference for the direct method, but allows the use of either method. However, when the direct method is used, the net cash flow from operating activities as computed using the indirect method must also be reported in a separate schedule.

---

[2]*Accounting Trends and Techniques–1994* (New York: American Institute of Certified Public Accountants, 1994).

Section 1 of this chapter illustrates the indirect method; Section 2 illustrates the direct method. These sections are independent of each other; only one or the other need be covered in order to understand and prepare the statement of cash flows.

## *Before You Go On . . .*

### ► *Review It*

1. What is the primary purpose of a statement of cash flows?
2. What are the major classifications of cash flows on the statement of cash flows?
3. What are the three major steps in the preparation of a statement of cash flows?
4. Why is the statement of cash flows useful? What key information does it convey?

### ► *Do It*

During its first week of existence, Plano Molding Company had the following transactions:

1. Issued 100,000 shares of $5 par value common stock for $800,000 cash.
2. Borrowed $200,000 from Sandwich State Bank, signing a 5-year note bearing 8% interest.
3. Purchased two semi-trailer trucks for $170,000 cash.
4. Paid employees $12,000 for salaries and wages.
5. Collected $20,000 cash for services rendered.

Classify by type of cash flow activity each of these transactions.

*Reasoning:* All cash flows are classified into three types of activities for purposes of reporting cash inflows and outflows: operating activities, investing activities, and financing activities. Operating activities include the cash effects of transactions that create revenues and expenses and thus enter into the determination of net income. Investing activities include (a) acquiring and disposing of investments and productive long-lived assets, and (b) lending money and collecting the loans. Financing activities include (a) obtaining cash from issuing debt and repaying the amounts borrowed, and (b) obtaining cash from stockholders and providing them with a return on their investment.

*Solution:*
1. Financing activity.
2. Financing activity.
3. Investing activity.
4. Operating activity.
5. Operating activity.

*Related exercise material: BE18–3, BE18–5, E18–1, and E18–6.*

## ▼**S**ECTION *1* ► *Statement of Cash Flows— Indirect Method*

To explain and illustrate the indirect method, we will use the transactions of the Computer Services Company for two years—1996 and 1997. Annual statements of cash flows will be prepared. Basic transactions will be used in the first year with additional transactions added in the second year.

**STUDY OBJECTIVE**
••••••••▼**3**••••••••
*Prepare a statement of cash flows using the indirect method.*

### First Year of Operations—1996

Computer Services Company started on January 1, 1996, when it issued 50,000 shares of $1.00 par value common stock for $50,000 cash. The company rented its office space and furniture and performed consulting services throughout the first year. The comparative balance sheets at the beginning and end of 1996, showing increases or decreases, appear in Illustration 18-5.

**Illustration 18-5**

*Comparative balance sheet, 1996, with increases and decreases*

**Helpful hint** Note that although each of the balance sheet items of Computer Services increased, their individual effects are not the same. Some of these increases are cash inflows, and some are cash outflows.

**COMPUTER SERVICES COMPANY**
**Comparative Balance Sheet**

| Assets | Dec. 31, 1996 | Jan. 1, 1996 | Change Increase/Decrease |
|---|---|---|---|
| Cash | $34,000 | $ –0– | $34,000 Increase |
| Accounts receivable | 30,000 | –0– | 30,000 Increase |
| Equipment | 10,000 | –0– | 10,000 Increase |
| Total | $74,000 | $ –0– | |

| Liabilities and Stockholders' Equity | | | |
|---|---|---|---|
| Accounts payable | $ 4,000 | $ –0– | $ 4,000 Increase |
| Common stock | 50,000 | –0– | 50,000 Increase |
| Retained earnings | 20,000 | –0– | 20,000 Increase |
| Total | $74,000 | $ –0– | |

The income statement and additional information for Computer Services Company are shown in Illustration 18-6.

**Illustration 18-6**

*Income statement and additional information, 1996*

**COMPUTER SERVICES COMPANY**
**Income Statement**
**For the Year Ended December 31, 1996**

| | |
|---|---|
| Revenues | $85,000 |
| Operating expenses | 40,000 |
| Income before income taxes | 45,000 |
| Income tax expense | 10,000 |
| Net income | $35,000 |

**Additional information:**
(a) Examination of selected data indicates that a dividend of $15,000 was declared and paid during the year.
(b) The equipment was purchased at the end of 1996. No depreciation was taken in 1996.

### Determining the Net Increase/Decrease in Cash (Step 1)

**Helpful hint** You may wish to insert the beginning and ending cash balances and the increase/decrease in cash necessitated by these balances immediately into the statement of cash flows. The net increase/decrease is the target amount. The net cash flows from the three classes of activity must equal the target amount.

To prepare a statement of cash flows, the first step is **determining the net increase or decrease in cash**. This is a simple computation. For example, Computer Services Company had no cash on hand at the beginning of 1996, but had $34,000 on hand at the end of 1996. Thus, the change in cash for 1996 was an increase of $34,000.

### Determining Net Cash Provided/Used by Operating Activities (Step 2)

To determine net cash provided by operating activities under the indirect method, **net income is adjusted for items that did not affect cash**. A useful starting point in determining net cash provided by operating activities is to understand **why** net income must be converted. Under generally accepted accounting principles, most companies use the accrual basis of accounting. As you have learned, this basis requires that revenue be recorded when earned and that expenses be recorded when incurred. Earned revenues may include credit sales that have not been collected in cash and expenses incurred that may not have been paid in cash. Thus, under the accrual basis of accounting, net income does not indicate the net cash provided by operating activities. Therefore, under the indirect method, net income must be adjusted to convert certain items to the cash basis.

The indirect method (or reconciliation method) starts with net income and converts it to net cash provided by operating activities. In other words, **the indirect method adjusts net income for items that affected reported net income but did not affect cash**, as shown in Illustration 18-7. That is, noncash charges in the income statement are added back to net income and noncash credits are deducted to compute net cash provided by operating activities. A useful starting point in identifying the adjustments to net income is the current asset and current liability accounts other than cash. Those accounts—receivables, payables, prepayments, and inventories—should be analyzed for their effects on cash.

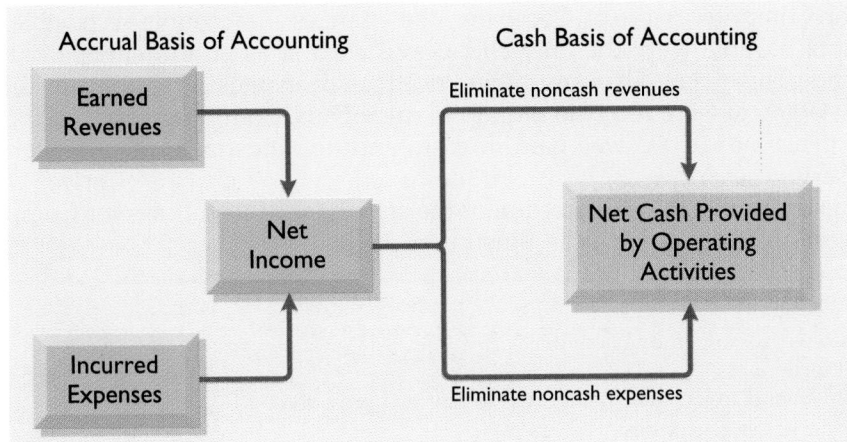

**Illustration 18-7**

*Net income versus net cash provided by operating activities*

**Increase in Accounts Receivable.**   When accounts receivable increase during the year, revenues on an accrual basis are higher than revenues on a cash basis. In other words, operations of the period led to increased revenues, **but not all of these revenues resulted in an increase in cash**; some of the increase in revenues resulted in an increase in accounts receivable.

Illustration 18-8 shows that Computer Services Company had $85,000 in revenues, but it collected only $55,000 in cash. Therefore, to convert net income to net cash provided by operating activities, the increase of $30,000 in accounts receivable must be deducted from net income.

| ACCOUNTS RECEIVABLE | | | |
|---|---|---|---|
| 1/1/96 | Balance | –0– | **Receipts from customers** | 55,000 |
| | Revenues | 85,000 | | |
| 12/31/96 | Balance | 30,000 | | |

**Illustration 18-8**

*Analysis of accounts receivable*

**Increase in Accounts Payable.**   In the first year, operating expenses incurred on account were credited to Accounts Payable. When accounts payable increase during the year, operating expenses on an accrual basis are higher than they are on a cash basis. For Computer Services, operating expenses reported in the income statement were $40,000. However, since Accounts Payable increased $4,000, only $36,000 ($40,000 − $4,000) of the expenses were paid in cash. To adjust net income to net cash provided by operating activities, the increase of $4,000 in accounts payable must be added to net income.

A T-account analysis also indicates that payments to creditors are less than operating expenses.

**Illustration 18-9**

*Analysis of accounts payable*

| ACCOUNTS PAYABLE | | | | |
|---|---|---|---|---|
| **Payments to creditors** | **36,000** | 1/1/96 | Balances | –0– |
| | | | **Operating expenses** | **40,000** |
| | | 12/31/96 | Balance | 4,000 |

For Computer Services Company, the changes in accounts receivable and accounts payable were the only changes in current asset and current liability accounts. This means that any other revenues or expenses reported in the income statement were received or paid in cash. Thus, Computer Services' income tax expense of $10,000 was paid in cash, and no adjustment of net income is necessary.

The operating activities section of the statement of cash flows for Computer Services Company is shown in Illustration 18-10.

**Illustration 18-10**

*Presentation of net cash provided by operating activities, 1996—indirect method*

| | | |
|---|---|---|
| Cash flows from operating activities | | |
| Net income | | $35,000 |
| Adjustments to reconcile net income to net cash provided by operating activities: | | |
| Increase in accounts receivable | $(30,000) | |
| Increase in accounts payable | 4,000 | (26,000) |
| **Net cash provided by operating activities** | | **$ 9,000** |

### Determining Net Cash Provided/Used by Investing and Financing Activities (Step 3)

The third and final step in preparing the statement of cash flows begins with a study of the balance sheet to determine changes in noncurrent accounts. The changes in each noncurrent account are then analyzed using selected transaction data to determine the effect, if any, the changes had on cash.

In Computer Services Company, the three noncurrent accounts are Equipment, Common Stock, and Retained Earnings, and all three have increased during the year. What caused these increases? No transaction data are given for the increases in Equipment of $10,000 and Common Stock of $50,000. In solving your homework, you can conclude that **any unexplained differences in noncurrent accounts involve cash**. Thus, the increase in equipment is assumed to be a purchase of equipment for $10,000 cash. This purchase is reported as a cash outflow in the investing activities section. The increase in common stock is assumed to result from the issuance of common stock for $50,000 cash. It is reported as an inflow of cash in the financing activities section of the statement of cash flows.

The reasons for the net increase of $20,000 in the Retained Earnings account are determined by analysis. First, net income increased retained earnings by

$35,000. Second, the additional information provided below the income statement in Illustration 18-6 indicates that a cash dividend of $15,000 was declared and paid. The $35,000 increase due to net income is reported in the operating activities section. The cash dividend paid is reported in the financing activities section.

This analysis can also be made directly from the Retained Earnings account in the ledger of Computer Services Company as shown in Illustration 18-11:

**Illustration 18-11**

*Analysis of retained earnings*

| **RETAINED EARNINGS** | | | |
|---|---|---|---|
| 12/31/96 Cash dividend | 15,000 | 1/1/96 Balance | –0– |
| | | 12/31/96 Net income | 35,000 |
| | | 12/31/96 Balance | 20,000 |

The $20,000 increase in Retained Earnings in 1996 is a **net** change. When a net change in a noncurrent balance sheet account has occurred during the year, it generally is necessary to report the causes of the net change separately in the statement of cash flows.

### Statement of Cash Flows—1996

Having completed the three steps above, we can prepare the statement of cash flows. The statement starts with the operating activities section, followed by the investing activities section, and then the financing activities section. The 1996 statement of cash flows for Computer Services is shown in Illustration 18-12.

**Illustration 18-12**

*Statement of cash flows, 1996—indirect method*

| **COMPUTER SERVICES COMPANY**<br>**Statement of Cash Flows**<br>**For the Year Ended December 31, 1996** | | |
|---|---|---|
| Cash flows from operating activities | | |
| Net income | | $35,000 |
| Adjustments to reconcile net income to net cash provided by operating activities: | | |
| Increase in accounts receivable | $(30,000) | |
| Increase in accounts payable | 4,000 | (26,000) |
| Net cash provided by operating activities | | 9,000 |
| Cash flows from investing activities | | |
| Purchase of equipment | (10,000) | |
| Net cash used by investing activities | | (10,000) |
| Cash flows from financing activities | | |
| Issuance of common stock | 50,000 | |
| Payment of cash dividends | (15,000) | |
| Net cash provided by financing activities | | 35,000 |
| Net increase in cash | | 34,000 |
| Cash at beginning of period | | –0– |
| Cash at end of period | | $34,000 |

Computer Services' statement of cash flows for 1996 shows that operating activities **provided** $9,000 cash; investing activities **used** $10,000 cash; and financing activities **provided** $35,000 cash. The increase in cash of $34,000 reported in the statement of cash flows agrees with the increase of $34,000 shown as the change in the cash account in the comparative balance sheet.

## Second Year of Operations—1997

Presented in Illustrations 18-13 and 18-14 is information related to the second year of operations for Computer Services Company.

**Illustration 18-13**

*Comparative balance sheet, 1997, with increases and decreases*

**COMPUTER SERVICES COMPANY**
**Comparative Balance Sheet**
**December 31**

| Assets | 1997 | 1996 | Change Increase/Decrease |
|---|---|---|---|
| Cash | $ 56,000 | $34,000 | $ 22,000 Increase |
| Accounts receivable | 20,000 | 30,000 | 10,000 Decrease |
| Prepaid expenses | 4,000 | –0– | 4,000 Increase |
| Land | 130,000 | –0– | 130,000 Increase |
| Building | 160,000 | –0– | 160,000 Increase |
| Accumulated depreciation—building | (11,000) | –0– | 11,000 Increase |
| Equipment | 27,000 | 10,000 | 17,000 Increase |
| Accumulated depreciation—equipment | (3,000) | –0– | 3,000 Increase |
| Total | $383,000 | $74,000 | |
| **Liabilities and Stockholders' Equity** | | | |
| Accounts payable | $ 59,000 | $ 4,000 | $ 55,000 Increase |
| Bonds payable | 130,000 | –0– | 130,000 Increase |
| Common stock | 50,000 | 50,000 | –0– |
| Retained earnings | 144,000 | 20,000 | 124,000 Increase |
| Total | $383,000 | $74,000 | |

**Illustration 18-14**

*Income statement and additional information, 1997*

**COMPUTER SERVICES COMPANY**
**Income Statement**
**For the Year Ended December 31, 1997**

| | | |
|---|---|---|
| Revenues | | $507,000 |
| Operating expenses (excluding depreciation) | $261,000 | |
| Depreciation expense | 15,000 | |
| Loss on sale of equipment | 3,000 | 279,000 |
| Income from operations | | 228,000 |
| Income tax expense | | 89,000 |
| Net income | | $139,000 |

**Additional information:**
(a) In 1997, the company declared and paid a $15,000 cash dividend.
(b) The company obtained land through the issuance of $130,000 of long-term bonds.
(c) A building costing $160,000 was purchased for cash; equipment costing $25,000 was also purchased for cash.
(d) During 1997, the company sold equipment with a book value of $7,000 (cost $8,000, less accumulated depreciation $1,000) for $4,000 cash.

### Determining the Net Increase/Decrease in Cash (Step 1)

To prepare a statement of cash flows from this information, the first step is to **determine the net increase or decrease in cash**. As indicated from the information presented, cash increased $22,000 ($56,000 − $34,000).

## Determining Net Cash Provided/Used by Operating Activities (Step 2)

As in step 2 in 1996, net income on an accrual basis must be adjusted to arrive at net cash provided/used by operating activities. Explanations for the adjustments to net income for Computer Services in 1997 are as follows:

**Decrease in Accounts Receivable.**   Accounts receivable decreases during the period because cash receipts are higher than revenues reported on an accrual basis. To adjust net income to net cash provided by operating activities, the decrease of $10,000 in accounts receivable must be added to net income.

**Increase in Prepaid Expenses.**   Prepaid expenses increase during a period because cash paid for expenses is higher than expenses reported on an accrual basis. Cash payments have been made in the current period, but expenses (as charges to the income statement) have been deferred to future periods. To adjust net income to net cash provided by operating activities, the increase of $4,000 in prepaid expenses must be deducted from net income. An increase in prepaid expenses results in a decrease in cash during the period.

**Increase in Accounts Payable.**   Like the increase in 1996, the 1997 increase of $55,000 in accounts payable must be added to net income to convert to net cash provided by operating activities.

**Depreciation Expense.**   During 1997, Computer Services Company reported depreciation expense of $15,000. Of this amount, $11,000 related to the building and $4,000 to the equipment. These two amounts were determined by analyzing the accumulated depreciation accounts.

> **Helpful hint   Decrease in accounts receivable:** Indicates that cash collections were greater than sales. **Increase in accounts receivable:** Indicates that sales were greater than cash collections. **Increase in prepaid expenses:** Indicates that the amount paid for the prepayments exceeded the amount that was recorded as an expense. **Decrease in prepaid expenses:** Indicates that the amount recorded as an expense exceeded the amount of cash paid for the prepayments. **Increase in accounts payable:** Indicates that expenses incurred exceed the cash paid for expenses that period.

**Increase in Accumulated Depreciation—Building.**   As shown in Illustration 18-13, accumulated depreciation increased $11,000. This change represents the depreciation expense on the building for the year. **Because depreciation expense is a noncash charge, it is added back to net income** in order to arrive at net cash provided by operating activities.

**Increase in Accumulated Depreciation—Equipment.**   The increase in the Accumulated Depreciation—Equipment account was $3,000. This amount does not represent depreciation expense for the year because the additional information indicates that this account was decreased (debited $1,000) as a result of the sale of some equipment. Thus depreciation expense for 1997 was $4,000 ($3,000 + $1,000). This amount is added to net income to determine net cash provided by operating activities. The T-account below provides information about the changes that occurred in this account in 1997.

> **Helpful hint**   Depreciation is similar to any other expense in that it reduces net income. It differs in that it does not involve a current cash outflow; that is why it must be added back to net income to arrive at cash provided by operations.

| ACCUMULATED DEPRECIATION—EQUIPMENT | | | | |
|---|---|---|---|---|
| Accumulated depreciation on equipment sold | 1,000 | 1/1/97 | Balance | –0– |
| | | | Depreciation expense | 4,000 |
| | | 12/31/97 | Balance | 3,000 |

**Illustration 18-15**

*Analysis of accumulated depreciation—equipment*

Depreciation expense on the building of $11,000 plus depreciation expense on the equipment of $4,000 equals the depreciation expense of $15,000 reported on the income statement.

Other charges to expense that do not require the use of cash, such as the amortization of intangible assets and depletion expense, are treated in the same manner as depreciation. Depreciation and similar noncash charges are frequently listed in the statement of cash flows as the first adjustments to net income.

**Loss on Sale of Equipment.**   On the income statement, Computer Services Company reported a $3,000 loss on the sale of equipment (book value $7,000, less cash proceeds $4,000). The loss reduced net income but **did not reduce cash**. Thus the loss is **added to net income** in determining net cash provided by operating activities.[3]

As a result of the previous adjustments, net cash provided by operating activities is $218,000 as computed in Illustration 18-16.

**Illustration 18-16**

*Presentation of net cash provided by operating activities, 1997—indirect method*

| | | |
|---|---:|---:|
| Cash flows from operating activities | | |
| Net income | | $139,000 |
| Adjustments to reconcile net income to net cash provided | | |
| by operating activities: | | |
| Depreciation expense | $15,000 | |
| Loss on sale of equipment | 3,000 | |
| Decrease in accounts receivable | 10,000 | |
| Increase in prepaid expenses | (4,000) | |
| Increase in accounts payable | 55,000 | 79,000 |
| **Net cash provided by operating activities** | | **$218,000** |

## Determining Net Cash Provided/Used by Investing and Financing Activities (Step 3)

After finding net cash provided by operating activities, the next step involves analyzing the remaining changes in balance sheet accounts to determine net cash provided (used) by investing and financing activities.

**Increase in Land.**   As indicated from the change in the land account, land of $130,000 was purchased through the issuance of long-term bonds. Although the issuance of bonds payable for land has no effect on cash, it is a significant noncash investing and financing activity that merits disclosure. As indicated earlier, these activities are disclosed in a separate schedule at the bottom of the statement of cash flows.

**Increase in Building.**   As indicated in the additional data, an office building was acquired using cash of $160,000. This transaction is a cash outflow reported in the investing section.

**Increase in Equipment.**   The equipment account increased $17,000. Based on the additional information, this was a net increase that resulted from two transactions: (1) a purchase of equipment of $25,000 and (2) the sale of equipment costing $8,000 for $4,000. These transactions are classified as investing activities, and each transaction should be reported separately. Thus the purchase of equipment should be reported as an outflow of cash for $25,000 and the sale should

---

[3]If a gain on sale occurs, a different situation results. To allow a gain to flow through to net cash provided by operating activities would be double-counting the gain—once in net income and again in the investing activities section as part of the cash proceeds from sale. As a result, a gain is deducted from net income in reporting net cash provided by operating activities.

be reported as an inflow of cash for $4,000. The T-account below shows the reasons for the change in this account during the year.

| EQUIPMENT | | | |
|---|---|---|---|
| 1/1/97 Balance | 10,000 | Cost of equipment sold | 8,000 |
| Purchase of equipment | 25,000 | | |
| 12/31/97 Balance | 27,000 | | |

**Illustration 18-17**

*Analysis of equipment*

**Increase in Bonds Payable.**   The bonds payable account increased $130,000. As shown in the additional information, land was acquired from the issuance of these bonds. As indicated earlier, this noncash transaction is reported in a separate schedule at the bottom of the statement.

**Increase in Retained Earnings.**   Retained earnings increased $124,000 during the year. This increase can be explained by two factors: (1) net income of $139,000 increased retained earnings and (2) dividends of $15,000 decreased retained earnings. Net income is adjusted to net cash provided by operating activities in the operating activities section. Payment of the dividends is a **cash outflow that is reported as a financing activity**.

**Helpful hint**  When stocks or bonds are issued for cash, it is the amount of the issuance price (proceeds) that will appear on the statement of cash flows as a financing inflow (rather than the amount of par value of the stocks or face value of bonds).

**Helpful hint**  It is the **payment** of dividends, not the declaration, that appears on the cash flow statement.

### Statement of Cash Flows—1997

Combining the previous items, we obtain a statement of cash flows for 1997 for Computer Services Company as presented in Illustration 18-18.

| COMPUTER SERVICES COMPANY<br>Statement of Cash Flows<br>For the Year Ended December 31, 1997 | | |
|---|---:|---:|
| Cash flows from operating activities | | |
| Net income | | $139,000 |
| Adjustments to reconcile net income to net cash provided by operating activities: | | |
| Depreciation expense | $ 15,000 | |
| Loss on sale of equipment | 3,000 | |
| Decrease in accounts receivable | 10,000 | |
| Increase in prepaid expenses | (4,000) | |
| Increase in accounts payable | 55,000 | 79,000 |
| Net cash provided by operating activities | | 218,000 |
| Cash flows from investing activities | | |
| Purchase of building | $(160,000) | |
| Purchase of equipment | (25,000) | |
| Sale of equipment | 4,000 | |
| Net cash used by investing activities | | (181,000) |
| Cash flows from financing activities | | |
| Payment of cash dividends | (15,000) | |
| Net cash used by financing activities | | (15,000) |
| Net increase in cash | | 22,000 |
| Cash at beginning of period | | 34,000 |
| Cash at end of period | | $ 56,000 |
| **Noncash investing and financing activities** | | |
| Issuance of bonds payable to purchase land | | $130,000 |

**Illustration 18-18**

*Statement of cash flows, 1997—indirect method*

**Helpful hint**  Note that in the investing and financing activities sections, positive numbers indicate cash inflows (receipts) and negative numbers indicate cash outflows (payments).

## Summary of Conversion to Net Cash Provided by Operating Activities—Indirect Method

As shown in the previous illustrations, the statement of cash flows prepared by the indirect method starts with net income and adds (or deducts) items not affecting cash to arrive at net cash provided by operating activities. The additions and deductions consist of (1) changes in specific current assets and current liabilities and (2) noncash charges reported in the income statement. A summary of the adjustments for current assets and current liabilities is provided in Illustration 18-19.

**Illustration 18-19**

*Adjustments for current assets and current liabilities*

**Helpful hints**

1. Increase in a current asset is deducted from net income.
2. Decrease in a current asset is added to net income.
3. Increase in a current liability is added to net income.
4. Decrease in a current liability is deducted from net income.

| Current Assets and Current Liabilities | Adjustments to Convert Net Income to Net Cash Provided by Operating Activities | |
| --- | --- | --- |
| | Add to Net Income | Deduct from Net Income |
| Accounts receivable | Decrease | Increase |
| Inventory | Decrease | Increase |
| Prepaid expenses | Decrease | Increase |
| Accounts payable | Increase | Decrease |
| Accrued expenses payable | Increase | Decrease |

Adjustments for the noncash charges reported in the income statement are made as shown in Illustration 18-20.

**Illustration 18-20**

*Adjustments for noncash charges*

| Noncash Charges | Adjustments to Convert Net Income to Net Cash Provided by Operating Activities |
| --- | --- |
| Depreciation expense | Add |
| Patent amortization expense | Add |
| Depletion expense | Add |
| Loss on sale of asset | Add |

## *Before You Go On . . .*

### ▸ *Review It*

1. What is the format of the operating activities section of the statement of cash flows using the indirect method?
2. Where is depreciation expense shown on a statement of cash flows using the indirect method?
3. Where are significant noncash investing and financing activities shown in a statement of cash flows? Give some examples.

### ▸ *Do It*

Presented below is information related to Reynolds Company. Use it to prepare a statement of cash flows using the indirect method.

**REYNOLDS COMPANY**
**Comparative Balance Sheet**
**December 31**

| Assets | 1997 | 1996 | Change Increase/Decrease |
|---|---|---|---|
| Cash | $ 54,000 | $ 37,000 | $ 17,000 Increase |
| Accounts receivable | 68,000 | 26,000 | 42,000 Increase |
| Inventories | 54,000 | -0- | 54,000 Increase |
| Prepaid expenses | 4,000 | 6,000 | 2,000 Decrease |
| Land | 45,000 | 70,000 | 25,000 Decrease |
| Buildings | 200,000 | 200,000 | -0- |
| Accumulated depreciation—buildings | (21,000) | (11,000) | 10,000 Increase |
| Equipment | 193,000 | 68,000 | 125,000 Increase |
| Accumulated depreciation—equipment | (28,000) | (10,000) | 18,000 Increase |
| Totals | $569,000 | $386,000 | |

| Liabilities and Stockholders' Equity | | | |
|---|---|---|---|
| Accounts payable | $ 23,000 | $ 40,000 | $ 17,000 Decrease |
| Accrued expenses payable | 10,000 | -0- | 10,000 Increase |
| Bonds payable | 110,000 | 150,000 | 40,000 Decrease |
| Common stock ($1 par) | 220,000 | 60,000 | 160,000 Increase |
| Retained earnings | 206,000 | 136,000 | 70,000 Increase |
| Totals | $569,000 | $386,000 | |

**REYNOLDS COMPANY**
**Income Statement**
**For the Year Ended December 31, 1997**

| | | |
|---|---|---|
| Revenues | | $890,000 |
| Cost of goods sold | $465,000 | |
| Operating expenses | 221,000 | |
| Interest expense | 12,000 | |
| Loss on sale of equipment | 2,000 | 700,000 |
| Income from operations | | 190,000 |
| Income tax expense | | 65,000 |
| Net income | | $125,000 |

**Additional information:**
(a) Operating expenses include depreciation expense of $33,000 and charges from prepaid expenses of $2,000.
(b) Land was sold at its book value for cash.
(c) Cash dividends of $55,000 were declared and paid in 1997.
(d) Interest expense of $12,000 was paid in cash.
(e) Equipment with a cost of $166,000 was purchased for cash. Equipment with a cost of $41,000 and a book value of $36,000 was sold for $34,000 cash.
(f) Bonds of $10,000 were redeemed at their book value for cash; bonds of $30,000 were converted into common stock.
(g) Common stock ($1 par) of $130,000 was issued for cash.
(h) Accounts payable pertain to merchandise suppliers.

**Reasoning:** As you have learned, the balance sheet and the income statement are prepared from an adjusted trial balance of the general ledger. The statement of cash flows is prepared from an analysis of the content and changes in the balance sheet and the income statement.

**Helpful hint**   To prepare the
statement of cash flows:
1. Determine the net increase/
decrease in cash.
2. Determine net cash pro-
vided/used by operating
activities.
3. Determine net cash pro-
vided/used by investing and
financing activities.
4. Operating activities generally relate to changes in
current assets and current
liabilities.
5. Investing activities generally
relate to changes in non-
current assets.
6. Financing activities generally
relate to changes in non-
current liabilities and stockholders' equity accounts.

**Helpful hint**   You may wish
to insert the beginning and
ending cash balances and the
increase/decrease in cash necessitated by these balances
immediately into the statement
of cash flows. The net in-
crease/decrease is the target
amount. The net cash flows
from the three classes of activities must equal the target
amount.

*Solution:*

**REYNOLDS COMPANY**
**Statement of Cash Flows**
**For the Year Ended December 31, 1997**

| | | | |
|---|---|---:|---:|
| Cash flows from operating activities | | | |
| Net income | | | $125,000 |
| Adjustments to reconcile net income to net cash provided by | | | |
| operating activities: | | | |
| Depreciation expense | | $ 33,000 | |
| Increase in accounts receivable | | (42,000) | |
| Increase in inventories | | (54,000) | |
| Decrease in prepaid expenses | | 2,000 | |
| Decrease in accounts payable | | (17,000) | |
| Increase in accrued expenses payable | | 10,000 | |
| Loss on sale of equipment | | 2,000 | (66,000) |
| Net cash provided by operating activities | | | 59,000 |
| Cash flows from investing activities | | | |
| Sale of land | | 25,000 | |
| Sale of equipment | | 34,000 | |
| Purchase of equipment | | (166,000) | |
| Net cash used by investing activities | | | (107,000) |
| Cash flows from financing activities | | | |
| Redemption of bonds | | (10,000) | |
| Sale of common stock | | 130,000 | |
| Payment of dividends | | (55,000) | |
| Net cash provided by financing activities | | | 65,000 |
| Net increase in cash | | | 17,000 |
| Cash at beginning of period | | | 37,000 |
| Cash at end of period | | | $ 54,000 |
| | | | |
| **Noncash investing and financing activities** | | | |
| Conversion of bonds into common stock | | | $ 30,000 |

*Related exercise material:* BE18–1, BE18–2, BE18–4, E18–2, E18–3, E18–4, and E18–5.

---

# ▼SECTION 2 ▸ *Statement of Cash Flows—*
# *Direct Method*

To explain and illustrate the direct method, we will use the transactions of Juarez
Company for two years, 1996 and 1997. Annual statements of cash flow will be
prepared. Basic transactions will be used in the first year with additional transactions added in the second year.

## First Year of Operations—1996

**STUDY OBJECTIVE**
••••••••• ▼ •••••••••
       4
*Prepare a statement of
cash flows using the
direct method.*

Juarez Company began business on January 1, 1996, when it issued 300,000
shares of $1 par value common stock for $300,000 cash. The company rented
office and sales space along with equipment. The comparative balance sheet at
the beginning and end of 1996 and the changes in each account are shown in
Illustration 18-21. The income statement and additional information for Juarez
Company are shown in Illustration 18-22.

## JUAREZ COMPANY
### Comparative Balance Sheet

| Assets | Dec. 31, 1996 | Jan. 1, 1996 | Change Increase/Decrease |
|---|---|---|---|
| Cash | $159,000 | $-0- | $159,000 Increase |
| Accounts receivable | 15,000 | -0- | 15,000 Increase |
| Inventory | 160,000 | -0- | 160,000 Increase |
| Prepaid expenses | 8,000 | -0- | 8,000 Increase |
| Land | 80,000 | -0- | 80,000 Increase |
| Total | $422,000 | $-0- | |

| Liabilities and Stockholders' Equity | | | |
|---|---|---|---|
| Accounts payable | $ 60,000 | $-0- | $ 60,000 Increase |
| Accrued expenses payable | 20,000 | -0- | 20,000 Increase |
| Common stock | 300,000 | -0- | 300,000 Increase |
| Retained earnings | 42,000 | -0- | 42,000 Increase |
| Total | $422,000 | $-0- | |

**Illustration 18-22**

*Income statement and additional information, 1996*

## JUAREZ COMPANY
### Income Statement
### For the Year Ended December 31, 1996

| | |
|---|---|
| Revenues from sales | $780,000 |
| Cost of goods sold | 450,000 |
| Gross profit | 330,000 |
| Operating expenses | 170,000 |
| Income before income taxes | 160,000 |
| Income tax expense | 48,000 |
| Net income | $112,000 |

**Additional information:**
(a) Dividends of $70,000 were declared and paid in cash.
(b) The accounts payable increase resulted from the purchase of merchandise.

The three steps cited on page 738 for preparing the statement of cash flows are used in the direct method.

### Determining the Net Increase/Decrease in Cash (Step 1)

The comparative balance sheet for Juarez Company shows a zero cash balance at January 1, 1996, and a cash balance of $159,000 at December 31, 1996. Thus, the change in cash for 1996 was a net increase of $159,000.

### Determining the Net Cash Provided/Used by Operating Activities (Step 2)

Under the direct method, net cash provided by operating activities is computed by **adjusting each item in the income statement** from the accrual basis to the cash basis. To simplify and condense the operating activities section, **only major classes of operating cash receipts and cash payments are reported**. The difference between these major classes of cash receipts and cash payments is the net cash provided by operating activities as shown in Illustration 18-23.

An efficient way to apply the direct method is to analyze the revenues and expenses reported in the income statement in the order in which they are listed.

**Illustration 18-23**

*Major classes of cash receipts and payments*

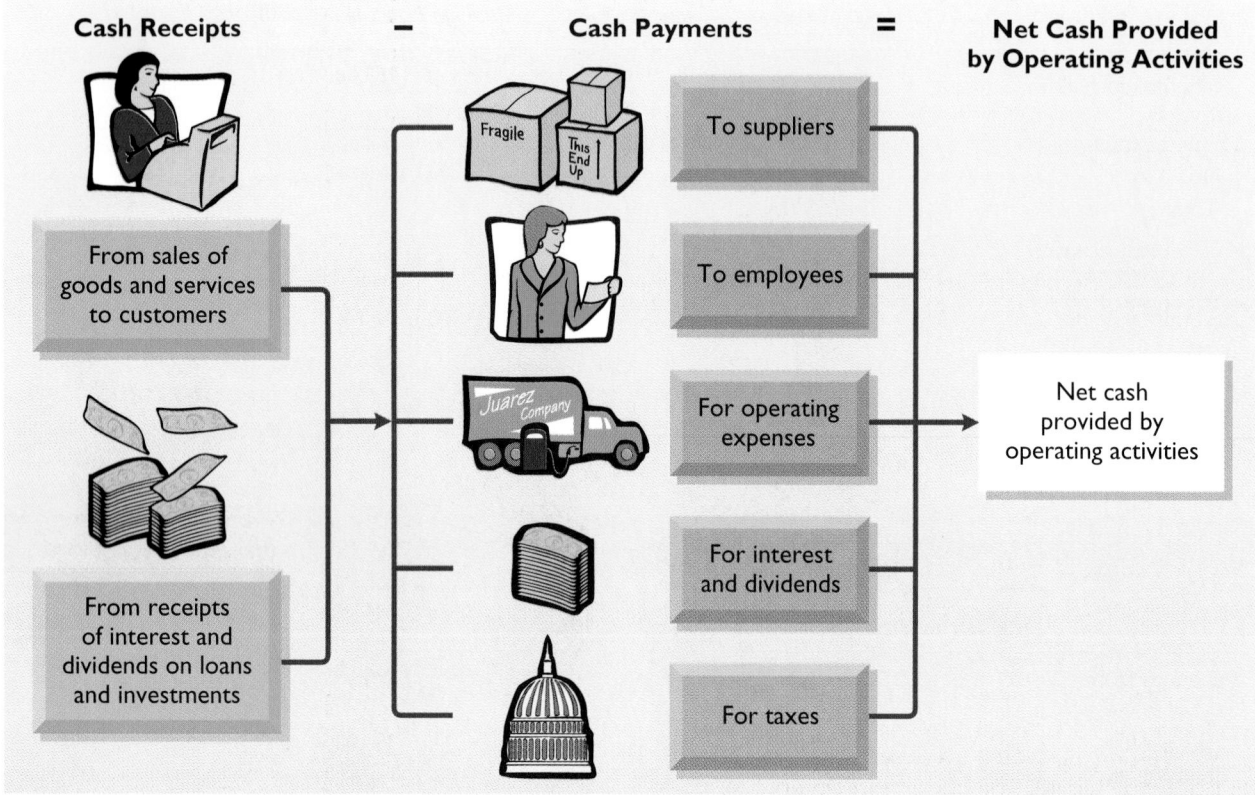

Cash receipts and cash payments related to these revenues and expenses are then determined. The direct method adjustments for Juarez Company in 1996 to determine net cash provided by operating activities are presented in the following sections.

**Cash Receipts from Customers.**   The income statement for Juarez Company reported revenues from customers of $780,000. To determine cash receipts from customers, it is necessary to consider the change in accounts receivable during the year. When accounts receivable increase during the year, revenues on an accrual basis are higher than cash receipts from customers. In other words, operations led to increased revenues, but not all of these revenues resulted in cash receipts. To determine the amount of cash receipts, the increase in accounts receivable is deducted from sales revenues. Conversely, a decrease in accounts receivable is added to sales revenues, because cash receipts from customers then exceed sales revenues.

For Juarez Company, accounts receivable increased $15,000. Thus, cash receipts from customers were $765,000, computed as follows:

**Illustration 18-24**

*Computation of cash receipts from customers*

| | |
|---|---|
| Revenues from sales | $780,000 |
| Deduct: Increase in accounts receivable | 15,000 |
| **Cash receipts from customers** | **$765,000** |

Cash receipts from customers may also be determined from an analysis of the Accounts Receivable account as shown in Illustration 18-25.

| ACCOUNTS RECEIVABLE | | | | |
|---|---|---|---|---|
| 1/1/96 | Balance | –0– | **Receipts from customers** | **765,000** |
| | Revenues from sales | 780,000 | | |
| 12/31/96 | Balance | 15,000 | | |

**Illustration 18-25**

*Analysis of accounts receivable*

**Helpful hint** The T-account shows that revenue less increase in receivables equals cash receipts.

The relationships between cash receipts from customers, revenues from sales, and changes in accounts receivable are shown in Illustration 18-26.

**Illustration 18-26**

*Formula to compute cash receipts from customers— direct method*

**Cash Payments to Suppliers.** Juarez Company reported cost of goods sold on its income statement of $450,000. To determine cash payments to suppliers, it is first necessary to find purchases for the year. To find purchases, cost of goods sold is adjusted for the change in inventory. When inventory increases during the year, it means that purchases this year exceed cost of goods sold. As a result, the increase in inventory is added to cost of goods sold to arrive at purchases.

In 1996, Juarez Company's inventory increased $160,000. Purchases, therefore, are computed as follows:

| Cost of goods sold | $450,000 |
|---|---|
| Add: Increase in inventory | 160,000 |
| **Purchases** | **$610,000** |

**Illustration 18-27**

*Computation of purchases*

After purchases are computed, cash payments to suppliers are determined by adjusting purchases for the change in accounts payable. When accounts payable increase during the year, purchases on an accrual basis are higher than they are on a cash basis. As a result, an increase in accounts payable is deducted from purchases to arrive at cash payments to suppliers. Conversely, a decrease in accounts payable is added to purchases because cash payments to suppliers exceed purchases. Cash payments to suppliers were $550,000, computed as follows:

| Purchases | $610,000 |
|---|---|
| Deduct: Increase in accounts payable | 60,000 |
| **Cash payments to suppliers** | **$550,000** |

**Illustration 18-28**

*Computation of cash payments to suppliers*

Cash payments to suppliers may also be determined from an analysis of the Accounts Payable account as shown in Illustration 18-29.

**Illustration 18-29**

*Analysis of accounts payable*

| ACCOUNTS PAYABLE | | | | |
|---|---|---|---|---|
| **Payments to suppliers** | 550,000 | 1/1/96 | Balance | –0– |
| | | | Purchases | 610,000 |
| | | 12/31/96 | Balance | 60,000 |

**Helpful hint**  The T-account shows that purchases less increase in accounts payable equals payments to suppliers.

The relationship between cash payments to suppliers, cost of goods sold, changes in inventory, and changes in account payable is shown in the following formula:

**Illustration 18-30**

*Formula to compute cash payments to suppliers— direct method*

**Cash Payments for Operating Expenses.**  Operating expenses of $170,000 were reported on Juarez's income statement. To determine the cash paid for operating expenses, this amount must be adjusted for any changes in prepaid expenses and accrued expenses payable. For example, when prepaid expenses increased $8,000 during the year, cash paid for operating expenses was $8,000 higher than operating expenses reported on the income statement. To convert operating expenses to cash payments for operating expenses, the increase of $8,000 must be added to operating expenses. Conversely, if prepaid expenses decrease during the year, the decrease must be deducted from operating expenses.

Operating expenses must also be adjusted for changes in accrued expenses payable. When accrued expenses payable increase during the year, operating expenses on an accrual basis are higher than they are in a cash basis. As a result, an increase in accrued expenses payable is deducted from operating expenses to arrive at cash payments for operating expenses. Conversely, a decrease in accrued expenses payable is added to operating expenses because cash payments exceed operating expenses.

Juarez Company's cash payments for operating expenses were $158,000, computed as follows:

**Illustration 18-31**

*Computation of cash payments for operating expenses*

| | |
|---|---|
| Operating expenses | $170,000 |
| Add: Increase in prepaid expenses | 8,000 |
| Deduct: Increase in accrued expenses payable | (20,000) |
| **Cash payments for operating expenses** | **$158,000** |

The relationships among cash payments for operating expenses, changes in prepaid expenses, and changes in accrued expenses payable are shown in the following formula:

**Illustration 18-32**

*Formula to compute cash payments for operating expenses—direct method*

**Cash Payments for Income Taxes.** The income statement for Juarez shows income tax expense of $48,000. This amount equals the cash paid because the comparative balance sheet indicated no income taxes payable at either the beginning or end of the year.

All of the revenues and expenses in the 1996 income statement have now been adjusted to a cash basis. The operating activities section of the statement of cash flows is as follows:

| | | |
|---|---:|---:|
| Cash flows from operating activities | | |
| Cash receipts from customers | | $765,000 |
| Cash payments: | | |
| To suppliers | $550,000 | |
| For operating expenses | 158,000 | |
| For income taxes | 48,000 | 756,000 |
| **Net cash provided by operating activities** | | **$ 9,000** |

**Illustration 18-33**

*Operating activities section—direct method*

## Determining Net Cash Provided/Used by Investing and Financing Activities (Step 3)

Preparing the investing and financing activities sections of the statement of cash flows begins with a determination of the changes in noncurrent accounts reported in the comparative balance sheet. The change in each account is then analyzed using the additional information to determine the effect, if any, the change had on cash.

> **Helpful hint** This is the same procedure used under the indirect method; the investing and financing activities are measured and reported the same under both methods.

**Increase in Land.** No additional information is given for the increase in land. In such case, you should assume that the increase affected cash. You should also make the same assumption in solving homework problems when the cause of a change in a noncurrent account is not explained. The purchase of land is an investing activity. Thus, an outflow of cash of $80,000 for the purchase of land should be reported in the investing activities section.

**Increase in Common Stock.** As indicated earlier, 300,000 shares of $1 par value stock were sold for $300,000 cash. The issuance of common stock is a financing activity. Thus, a cash inflow of $300,000 from the issuance of common stock is reported in the financing activities section.

**Increase in Retained Earnings.** For the Retained Earnings account, the reasons for the net increase of $42,000 are determined by analysis. First, net income increased retained earnings by $112,000. Second, the additional information section indicates that a cash dividend of $70,000 was declared and paid. The adjustment of revenues and expenses to arrive at net cash provided by operations was done in step 2 above. The cash dividend paid is reported as an outflow of cash in the financing activities section.

> **Helpful hint** It is the **payment** of dividends, not the declaration, that appears on the cash flow statement.

This analysis can also be made directly from the Retained Earnings account in the ledger of Juarez Company as shown in Illustration 18-34.

**Illustration 18-34**

*Analysis of retained earnings*

| RETAINED EARNINGS | | | | |
|---|---|---|---|---|
| 12/31/96 | Cash dividend | 70,000 | 1/1/96  Balance | –0– |
| | | | 12/31/96  Net income | 112,000 |
| | | | 12/31/96  Balance | 42,000 |

The $42,000 increase in Retained Earnings in 1996 is a net change. When a net change in a noncurrent balance sheet account has occurred during the year, it generally is necessary to report the individual items that cause the net change.

### Statement of Cash Flows—1996

The statement of cash flows can now be prepared. The operating activities section is reported first, followed by the investing and financing activities sections. The statement of cash flows for Juarez Company for 1996 is shown in Illustration 18-35.

**Illustration 18-35**

*Statement of cash flows, 1996—direct method*

**JUAREZ COMPANY**
**Statement of Cash Flows**
**For the Year Ended December 31, 1996**

| | | |
|---|---:|---:|
| Cash flows from operating activities | | |
| Cash receipts from customers | | $765,000 |
| Cash payments: | | |
| To suppliers | $550,000 | |
| For operating expenses | 158,000 | |
| For income taxes | 48,000 | 756,000 |
| Net cash provided by operating activities | | 9,000 |
| Cash flows from investing activities | | |
| Purchase of land | (80,000) | |
| Net cash used by investing activities | | (80,000) |
| Cash flows from financing activities | | |
| Issuance of common stock | 300,000 | |
| Payment of cash dividend | (70,000) | |
| Net cash provided by financing activities | | 230,000 |
| Net increase in cash | | 159,000 |
| Cash at beginning of period | | –0– |
| Cash at end of period | | $159,000 |

**Helpful hint**  Note that in the investing and financing activities sections, positive numbers indicate cash inflows (receipts) and negative numbers indicate cash outflows (payments).

The statement of cash flows shows that operating activities provided $9,000 of the net increase in cash of $159,000. Financing activities **provided** $230,000 of cash, and investing activities **used** $80,000 of cash. The net increase in cash for the year of $159,000 agrees with the increase in cash of $159,000 reported in the comparative balance sheet.

## Second Year of Operations—1997

Illustration 18-36 and 18-37 present the comparative balance sheet, the income statement, and additional information pertaining to the second year of operations for Juarez Company.

Illustration 18-36

*Comparative balance sheet, 1997, with increases and decreases*

**JUAREZ COMPANY**
**Comparative Balance Sheet**
**December 31**

| Assets | 1997 | 1996 | Change Increase/Decrease |
|---|---|---|---|
| Cash | $191,000 | $159,000 | $ 32,000 Increase |
| Accounts receivable | 12,000 | 15,000 | 3,000 Decrease |
| Inventory | 130,000 | 160,000 | 30,000 Decrease |
| Prepaid expenses | 6,000 | 8,000 | 2,000 Decrease |
| Land | 180,000 | 80,000 | 100,000 Increase |
| Equipment | 160,000 | –0– | 160,000 Increase |
| Accumulated depreciation—equipment | (16,000) | –0– | 16,000 Increase |
| Total | $663,000 | $422,000 | |
| **Liabilities and Stockholders' Equity** | | | |
| Accounts payable | $ 52,000 | $ 60,000 | $ 8,000 Decrease |
| Accrued expenses payable | 15,000 | 20,000 | 5,000 Decrease |
| Income taxes payable | 12,000 | –0– | 12,000 Increase |
| Bonds payable | 90,000 | –0– | 90,000 Increase |
| Common stock | 400,000 | 300,000 | 100,000 Increase |
| Retained earnings | 94,000 | 42,000 | 52,000 Increase |
| Total | $663,000 | $422,000 | |

Illustration 18-37

*Income statement and additional information, 1997*

**JUAREZ COMPANY**
**Income Statement**
**For the Year Ended December 31, 1997**

| | | |
|---|---|---|
| Revenues from sales | | $975,000 |
| Cost of goods sold | $660,000 | |
| Operating expenses (excluding depreciation) | 176,000 | |
| Depreciation expense | 18,000 | |
| Loss on sale of store equipment | 1,000 | 855,000 |
| Income before income taxes | | 120,000 |
| Income tax expense | | 36,000 |
| Net income | | $ 84,000 |

**Additional information:**
(a) In 1997, the company declared and paid a $32,000 cash dividend.
(b) Bonds were issued at face value for $90,000 in cash.
(c) Equipment costing $180,000 was purchased for cash.
(d) Equipment costing $20,000 was sold for $17,000 cash when the book value of the equipment was $18,000.
(e) Common stock of $100,000 was issued to acquire land.

### Determining the Net Increase/Decrease in Cash (Step 1)

The comparative balance sheet shows a beginning cash balance of $159,000 and an ending cash balance of $191,000. Thus, there was a net increase in cash in 1997 of $32,000.

### Determining Net Cash Provided/Used in Operating Activities (Step 2)

**Cash Receipts from Customers.** Revenues from sales were $975,000. Since accounts receivable decreased $3,000, cash receipts from customers were greater than sales revenues. Cash receipts from customers were $978,000, computed as follows:

| | |
|---|---|
| Revenues from sales | $975,000 |
| Add: Decrease in accounts receivable | 3,000 |
| **Cash receipts from customers** | **$978,000** |

**Cash Payments to Suppliers.**   The conversion of cost of goods sold to purchases and purchases to cash payments to suppliers is similar to the computations made in 1996. For 1997, purchases are computed using cost of goods sold of $660,000 from the income statement and the decrease in inventory of $30,000 from the comparative balance sheet. Purchases are then adjusted by the decrease in accounts payable of $8,000. Cash payments to suppliers were $638,000, computed as follows:

| | |
|---|---|
| Cost of goods sold | $660,000 |
| Deduct: Decrease in inventory | 30,000 |
| Purchases | 630,000 |
| Add: Decrease in accounts payable | 8,000 |
| **Cash payments to suppliers** | **$638,000** |

**Cash Payments for Operating Expenses.**   Operating expenses (exclusive of depreciation expense) for 1997 were reported at $176,000. This amount is then adjusted for changes in prepaid expenses and accrued expenses payable to arrive at cash payments for operating expenses.

As indicated from the comparative balance sheet, prepaid expenses decreased $2,000 during the year. This means that $2,000 was allocated to operating expenses (thereby increasing operating expenses), but cash payments did not increase by that $2,000. To arrive at cash payments for operating expenses, the decrease in prepaid expenses is deducted from operating expenses.

Accrued operating expenses decreased $5,000 during the period. As a result, cash payments were higher by $5,000 than the amount reported for operating expenses. The decrease in accrued expenses payable is added to operating expenses. Cash payments for operating expenses were $179,000, computed as follows:

| | |
|---|---|
| Operating expenses, exclusive of depreciation | $176,000 |
| Deduct: Decrease in prepaid expenses | (2,000) |
| Add: Decrease in accrued expenses payable | 5,000 |
| **Cash payments for operating expenses** | **$179,000** |

**Depreciation Expense and Loss on Sale of Equipment.**   Operating expenses are shown exclusive of depreciation. Depreciation expense in 1997 was $18,000. Depreciation expense is not shown on a statement of cash flows because it is a noncash charge. If the amount for operating expenses includes depreciation expense, operating expenses must be reduced by the amount of depreciation to determine cash payments for operating expenses.

The loss on sale of equipment of $1,000 is also a noncash charge. The loss on sale of equipment reduces net income, but it does not reduce cash. Thus, the loss on sale of equipment is not reported on a statement of cash flows.

Other charges to expense that do not require the use of cash, such as the amortization of intangible assets and depletion expense, are treated in the same manner as depreciation.

**Cash Payments for Income Taxes.**   Income tax expense reported on the income statement was $36,000. Income taxes payable, however, increased $12,000 which means that $12,000 of the income taxes have not been paid. As a result, income taxes paid were less than income taxes reported on the income statement. Cash payments for income taxes were, therefore, $24,000 as shown below.

| | |
|---|---|
| Income tax expense | $36,000 |
| Deduct: Increase in income taxes payable | 12,000 |
| **Cash payments for income taxes** | **$24,000** |

**Illustration 18-41**

*Computation of cash payments for income taxes*

The relationships of cash payments for income taxes, income tax expense, and changes in income taxes payable are shown in the following formula:

**Illustration 18-42**

*Formula to compute cash payments for income taxes— direct method*

## Determining Net Cash Provided/Used by Investing and Financing Activities (Step 3)

**Increase in Land.**   Land increased $100,000. The additional information section indicates that common stock was issued to purchase the land. Although the issuance of common stock for land has no effect on cash, it is a **significant noncash investing and financing transaction**. This transaction requires disclosure in a separate schedule at the bottom of the statement of cash flows.

**Increase in Equipment.**   The comparative balance sheet shows that equipment increased $160,000 in 1997. The additional information in Illustration 18-37 indicates that the increase resulted from two investing transactions: (1) equipment costing $180,000 was purchased for cash, and (2) equipment costing $20,000 was sold for $17,000 cash when its book value was $18,000. The relevant data for the statement of cash flows is the cash paid for the purchase and the cash proceeds from the sale. For Juarez Company, the investing activities section will show: Purchase of equipment $180,000, as an outflow of cash; and sale of equipment $17,000, as an inflow of cash. The two amounts **should not be netted** because one is an outflow of cash and the other is an inflow of cash; **both flows should be shown**.

The analysis of the changes in equipment should include the related Accumulated Depreciation account. These two accounts for Juarez Company are shown in Illustration 18-43.

| EQUIPMENT | | | | |
|---|---|---|---|---|
| 1/1/97 | Balance | –0– | Cost of equipment sold | 20,000 |
| | Cash purchase | 180,000 | | |
| 12/31/97 | Balance | 160,000 | | |

| ACCUMULATED DEPRECIATION—EQUIPMENT | | | | |
|---|---|---|---|---|
| Sale of equipment | 2,000 | 1/1/97 | Balance | –0– |
| | | | Depreciation expense | 18,000 |
| | | 12/31/97 | Balance | 16,000 |

**Increase in Bonds Payable.**   Bonds Payable increased $90,000. The additional information in Illustration 18-37 indicates that bonds with a face value of $90,000 were issued for $90,000 cash. The issuance of bonds is a financing activity. For Juarez Company, there is an inflow of cash of $90,000 from the issuance of bonds.

**Increase in Common Stock.**   The Common Stock account increased $100,000. As indicated from the additional information, land was acquired from the issuance of common stock. This transaction is a **significant noncash investing and financing transaction** that should be reported in a separate schedule at the bottom of the statement.

**Increase in Retained Earnings.**   The net increase in Retained Earnings of $52,000 resulted from net income of $84,000 and the declaration and payment of a cash dividend of $32,000. **Net income is not reported in the statement of cash flows under the direct method.** Cash dividends paid of $32,000 are reported in the financing activities section as an outflow of cash.

### Statement of Cash Flows—1997

The statement of cash flows for Juarez Company is shown in Illustration 18-44.

**Illustration 18-44**

*Statement of cash flows, 1997—direct method*

**JUAREZ COMPANY**
**Statement of Cash Flows**
**For the Year Ended December 31, 1997**

| | | |
|---|---|---|
| Cash flows from operating activities | | |
| Cash receipts from customers | | $978,000 |
| Cash payments: | | |
| To suppliers | $638,000 | |
| For operating expenses | 179,000 | |
| For income taxes | 24,000 | 841,000 |
| Net cash provided by operating activities | | 137,000 |
| Cash flows from investing activities | | |
| Purchase of equipment | (180,000) | |
| Sale of equipment | 17,000 | |
| Net cash used by investing activities | | (163,000) |
| Cash flows from financing activities | | |
| Issuance of bonds payable | 90,000 | |
| Payment of cash dividends | (32,000) | |
| Net cash provided by financing activities | | 58,000 |
| Net increase in cash | | 32,000 |
| Cash at beginning of period | | 159,000 |
| Cash at end of period | | $191,000 |
| **Noncash investing and financing activities** | | |
| Issuance of common stock to purchase land | | $100,000 |

# Before You Go On . . .

## ► Review It

1. What is the format of the operating activities section of the statement of cash flows using the direct method?
2. Where is depreciation expense shown on a statement of cash flows using the direct method?
3. Where are significant noncash investing and financing activities shown on a statement of cash flows? Give some examples.

## ► Do It

Presented below is information related to Reynolds Company. Use it to prepare a statement of cash flows using the direct method.

**REYNOLDS COMPANY**
**Comparative Balance Sheet**
**December 31**

| Assets | 1997 | 1996 | Change Increase/Decrease |
|---|---|---|---|
| Cash | $ 54,000 | $ 37,000 | $ 17,000 Increase |
| Accounts receivable | 68,000 | 26,000 | 42,000 Increase |
| Inventories | 54,000 | -0- | 54,000 Increase |
| Prepaid expenses | 4,000 | 6,000 | 2,000 Decrease |
| Land | 45,000 | 70,000 | 25,000 Decrease |
| Buildings | 200,000 | 200,000 | -0- |
| Accumulated depreciation—buildings | (21,000) | (11,000) | 10,000 Increase |
| Equipment | 193,000 | 68,000 | 125,000 Increase |
| Accumulated depreciation—equipment | (28,000) | (10,000) | 18,000 Increase |
| Totals | $569,000 | $386,000 | |

| Liabilities and Stockholders' Equity | | | |
|---|---|---|---|
| Accounts payable | $ 23,000 | $ 40,000 | $ 17,000 Decrease |
| Accrued expenses payable | 10,000 | -0- | 10,000 Increase |
| Bonds payable | 110,000 | 150,000 | 40,000 Decrease |
| Common stock ($1 par) | 220,000 | 60,000 | 160,000 Increase |
| Retained earnings | 206,000 | 136,000 | 70,000 Increase |
| Totals | $569,000 | $386,000 | |

**REYNOLDS COMPANY**
**Income Statement**
**For the Year Ended December 31, 1997**

| | | |
|---|---|---|
| Revenues | | $890,000 |
| Cost of goods sold | $465,000 | |
| Operating expenses | 221,000 | |
| Interest expense | 12,000 | |
| Loss on sale of equipment | 2,000 | 700,000 |
| Income from operations | | 190,000 |
| Income tax expense | | 65,000 |
| Net income | | $125,000 |

**Additional information:**
(a) Operating expenses include depreciation expense of $33,000 and charges from prepaid expenses of $2,000.
(b) Land was sold at its book value for cash.
(c) Cash dividends of $55,000 were declared and paid in 1997.
(d) Interest expense of $12,000 was paid in cash.
(e) Equipment with a cost of $166,000 was purchased for cash. Equipment with a cost of $41,000 and a book value of $36,000 was sold for $34,000 cash.

(f) Bonds of $10,000 were redeemed at their book value for cash; bonds of $30,000 were converted into common stock.

(g) Common stock ($1 par) of $130,000 was issued for cash.

(h) Accounts payable pertain to merchandise suppliers.

**Reasoning:** The indirect and the direct methods differ primarily in their presentation of the cash flows from the operating activities. The direct method reports cash receipts less cash payments to arrive at net cash provided by operating activities.

**Solution:**

### REYNOLDS COMPANY
### Statement of Cash Flows
### For the Year Ended December 31, 1997

**Helpful hint** To prepare the statement of cash flows:

1. Determine the net increase/decrease in cash.
2. Determine net cash provided/used by operating activities.
3. Determine net cash provided/used by investing and financing activities.
4. Operating activities generally relate to changes in current assets and current liabilities.
5. Investing activities generally relate to changes in noncurrent assets.
6. Financing activities generally relate to changes in noncurrent liabilities and stockholders' equity accounts.

| | | |
|---|---:|---:|
| Cash flows from operating activities | | |
| Cash receipts from customers | | $848,000ª |
| Cash payments: | | |
| To suppliers | $536,000ᵇ | |
| For operating expenses | 176,000ᶜ | |
| For interest expense | 12,000 | |
| For income taxes | 65,000 | 789,000 |
| Net cash provided by operating activities | | 59,000 |
| Cash flows from investing activities | | |
| Sale of land | 25,000 | |
| Sale of equipment | 34,000 | |
| Purchase of equipment | (166,000) | |
| Net cash used by investing activities | | (107,000) |
| Cash flows from financing activities | | |
| Redemption of bonds | (10,000) | |
| Sale of common stock | 130,000 | |
| Payment of dividends | (55,000) | |
| Net cash provided by financing activities | | 65,000 |
| Net increase in cash | | 17,000 |
| Cash at beginning of period | | 37,000 |
| Cash at end of period | | $ 54,000 |
| | | |
| **Noncash investing and financing activities** | | |
| Conversion of bonds into common stock | | $ 30,000 |

*Computations:*
ª$848,000 = $890,000 − $42,000
ᵇ$536,000 = $465,000 + $54,000 + $17,000
ᶜ$176,000 = $221,000 − $33,000 − $2,000 − $10,000

Technically, an additional schedule reconciling net income to net cash provided by operating activities should be presented as part of the statement of cash flows when using the direct method.

*Related exercise material:* BE18–6, BE18–7, BE18–8, E18–7, E18–8, E18–9, and E18–10.

## ▸ *A Look Back at Kilian Community College*
• • • • • • • • • • • • • • • • • • • • • • • • • • • • • • • • • • • • • • • • • • • • • • • • • • • •

Refer to the opening story of Gerald Biby's attempt to refinance Kilian Community College's mortgage, and answer the following questions:

1. How was the purchase of the $250,000 computer system presented on the "traditional educational institution financial statement" so that it negatively affected Biby's ability to refinance the mortgage?
2. How was the purchase of the $250,000 computer system presented on the statement of cash flows? How did the preparation of the statement of cash flows aid Biby in securing the refinancing of the mortgage?

**Solution:**

1. A traditional financial statement for a not-for-profit, educational institution reports receipts as revenues and expenses all expenditures, even capital expenditures such as the $250,000 computer system. That is, the traditional financial statement reported the entire $250,000 as an expense in one year, making it look like the college was just breaking even.
2. When the computer purchase was classified as an investing activity, the statement of cash flows showed the bankers that one of the uses of funds was really the purchase of computer equipment that had several years of life. In addition, the bankers noted from the statement of cash flows "that the college's source of funds exceeded the loan repayments, including principal and interest, by a ratio of 3-to-1."

# Summary of Study Objectives

**1. Indicate the primary purpose of the statement of cash flows.** The primary purpose of the statement of cash flows is to provide information about the cash receipts and cash payments of an entity during a period. A secondary objective is to provide information about the operating, investing, and financing activities of the entity during the period.

**2. Distinguish among operating, investing, and financing activities.** Operating activities include the cash effects of transactions that enter into the determination of net income. Investing activities involve cash flows resulting from changes in investments and long-term asset items. Financing activities involve cash flows resulting from changes in long-term liability and stockholders' equity items.

**3. Prepare a statement of cash flows using the indirect method.** The preparation of a statement of cash flows involves three major steps: (1) determine the net increase or decrease in cash; (2) determine net cash provided (used) by operating activities; and (3) determine net cash flows provided (used) by investing and financing activities. Under the indirect method, accrual basis net income is adjusted to net cash provided by operating activities.

**4. Prepare a statement of cash flows using the direct method.** The preparation of the statement of cash flows involves three major steps: (1) determine the net increase or decrease in cash; (2) determine net cash provided (used) by operating activities; and (3) determine net cash flows provided (used) by investing and financing activities. The direct method reports cash receipts less cash payments to arrive at net cash provided by operating activities.

# ▶ APPENDIX ▶ *Using a Work Sheet for Preparing the Statement of Cash Flows—Indirect Method*

When numerous adjustments of net income are necessary, **a work sheet is often used to assemble and classify the data that will appear on the statement of cash flows.** The work sheet is merely a device that aids in the preparation of the statement; its use is optional. The skeleton format of the work sheet for preparation of the statement of cash flows is shown in Illustration 18A-1.

The following guidelines are important in using a work sheet:

1. In the balance sheet accounts section, **accounts with debit balances are listed separately from those with credit balances**. This means, for example, that Accumulated Depreciation is listed under credit balances and not as a contra account under debit balances. The beginning and ending balances of each account are entered in the appropriate columns. The transactions that caused the change in the account balance during the year are entered as reconciling items in the two middle columns. After all reconciling items have been en-

> **STUDY OBJECTIVE**
> ▼
>
> *After studying this appendix, you should be able to:*
>
> **5. Explain the guidelines and procedural steps in using a work sheet to prepare the statement of cash flows.**

| | End of Last Year Balances | Reconciling Items | | End of Current Year Balances |
|---|---|---|---|---|
| **XYZ COMPANY** **Work Sheet** **Statement of Cash Flows** **For the Year Ended . . .** | | | | |
| Balance Sheet Accounts | | Debits | Credits | |
| Debit balance accounts | XX | XX | XX | XX |
| | XX | XX | XX | XX |
| Totals | XXX | | | XXX |
| Credit balance accounts | XX | XX | XX | XX |
| | XX | XX | XX | XX |
| Totals | XXX | | | XXX |
| Statement of Cash Flows Effects | | | | |
| Operating activities | | | | |
| Net income | | XX | | |
| Adjustments | | XX | XX | |
| Investing activities | | | | |
| Receipts and payments | | XX | XX | |
| Financing activities | | | | |
| Receipts and payments | | XX | XX | |
| Totals | | XXX | XXX | |
| Increase (decrease) in cash | | (XX) | XX | |
| Totals | | XXX | XXX | |

tered, each line pertaining to a balance sheet account should "foot across." That is, the beginning balance plus or minus the reconciling item(s) must equal the ending balance. When this agreement exists for all balance sheet accounts, all changes in account balances have been reconciled.

2. The bottom portion of the work sheet consists of the operating, investing, and financing activities sections. Accordingly, it provides the information necessary to prepare the formal statement of cash flows. **Inflows of cash are entered as debits in the reconciling columns, and outflows of cash are entered as credits in the reconciling columns.** Thus, in this section, the sale of equipment for cash at book value is entered as a debit under investing activities. Similarly, the purchase of land for cash is entered as a credit under investing activities.

3. **The reconciling items shown in the work sheet are not entered in any journal or posted to any account.** They do not represent either adjustments or corrections of the balance sheet accounts. They are used only to facilitate the preparation of the statement of cash flows.

## ▶ Preparing the Work Sheet

As in the case of work sheets illustrated in earlier chapters, the preparation of a work sheet involves a series of prescribed steps. The steps in this case are:

1. Enter in the balance sheet accounts section the balance sheet accounts and their beginning and ending balances.

2. Enter in the reconciling columns of the work sheet the data that explain the changes in the balance sheet accounts other than cash and their effects on the statement of cash flows.

3. Enter on the cash line and at the bottom of the work sheet the increase or decrease in cash. This entry should enable the totals of the reconciling columns to be in agreement.

To illustrate the preparation of a work sheet, we will use the 1997 data for Computer Services Company. Your familiarity with these data should help you understand the use of a work sheet. For ease of reference, the comparative balance sheets, income statement, and selected data for 1997 are presented in Illustrations 18A-2 and 18A-3.

**Illustration 18A-2**

*Comparative balance sheet, 1997, with increases and decreases*

**COMPUTER SERVICES COMPANY**
**Comparative Balance Sheet**
**December 31**

| Assets | 1997 | 1996 | Change Increase/Decrease |
|---|---|---|---|
| Cash | $ 56,000 | $34,000 | $ 22,000 Increase |
| Accounts receivable | 20,000 | 30,000 | 10,000 Decrease |
| Prepaid expenses | 4,000 | –0– | 4,000 Increase |
| Land | 130,000 | –0– | 130,000 Increase |
| Building | 160,000 | –0– | 160,000 Increase |
| Accumulated depreciation—building | (11,000) | –0– | 11,000 Increase |
| Equipment | 27,000 | 10,000 | 17,000 Increase |
| Accumulated depreciation—equipment | (3,000) | –0– | 3,000 Increase |
| Totals | $383,000 | $74,000 | |
| **Liabilities and Stockholders' Equity** | | | |
| Accounts payable | $ 59,000 | $ 4,000 | 55,000 Increase |
| Bonds payable | 130,000 | –0– | 130,000 Increase |
| Common stock | 50,000 | 50,000 | –0– |
| Retained earnings | 144,000 | 20,000 | 124,000 Increase |
| Totals | $383,000 | $74,000 | |

**Illustration 18A-3**

*Income statement and additional information, 1997*

**COMPUTER SERVICES COMPANY**
**Income Statement**
**For the Year Ended December 31, 1997**

| | | |
|---|---|---|
| Revenues | | $507,000 |
| Operating expenses (excluding depreciation) | $261,000 | |
| Depreciation expense | 15,000 | |
| Loss on sale of equipment | 3,000 | 279,000 |
| Income from operations | | 228,000 |
| Income tax expense | | 89,000 |
| Net income | | $139,000 |

**Additional information:**
(a) In 1997, the company declared and paid a $15,000 cash dividend.
(b) The company obtained land through the issuance of $130,000 of long-term bonds.
(c) A building costing $160,000 was purchased for cash; equipment costing $25,000 was also purchased for cash.
(d) During 1997, the company sold equipment with a book value of $7,000 (cost $8,000, less accumulated depreciation $1,000) for $4,000 cash.

## Determining the Reconciling Items

Several approaches may be used to determine the reconciling items. For example, the changes affecting net cash provided by operating activities could be completed first and then the effects of financing and investing transactions could be determined. Alternatively, the balance sheet accounts can be analyzed in the order in which they are listed on the work sheet. We will follow this latter approach for Computer Services, except for cash. As indicated above, **cash is handled last**.

**Accounts Receivable.**   The decrease of $10,000 in accounts receivable means that cash collections from revenues are higher than the revenues reported in the income statement. To convert net income to net cash provided by operating activities, the decrease of $10,000 is added to net income. The entry in the reconciling columns of the work sheet is:

| | | | |
|---|---|---|---|
| (a) | Operating—Decrease in Accounts Receivable | 10,000 | |
| | Accounts Receivable | | 10,000 |

**Prepaid Expenses.**   An increase of $4,000 in prepaid expenses means that expenses deducted in determining net income are less than expenses that were paid in cash. Thus, the increase of $4,000 must be deducted from net income in determining net cash provided by operating activities. The work sheet entry is:

| | | | |
|---|---|---|---|
| (b) | Prepaid Expenses | 4,000 | |
| | Operating—Increase in Prepaid Expenses | | 4,000 |

**Helpful hint**  These amounts are asterisked in the work sheet to indicate that they result from a significant noncash transaction.

**Land.**   The increase in land of $130,000 resulted from a purchase through the issuance of long-term bonds. This transaction should be reported as a significant noncash investing and financing activity. The work sheet entry is:

| | | | |
|---|---|---|---|
| (c) | Land | 130,000 | |
| | Bonds Payable | | 130,000 |

**Building.**   The cash purchase of a building for $160,000 is an investing activity cash outflow. The entry in the reconciling columns of the work sheet is:

| | | | |
|---|---|---|---|
| (d) | Building | 160,000 | |
| | Investing—Purchase of Building | | 160,000 |

**Equipment.**   The increase in equipment of $17,000 resulted from a cash purchase of $25,000 and the sale of equipment costing $8,000. The book value of the equipment was $7,000, the cash proceeds were $4,000, and a loss of $3,000 was recorded. The work sheet entries are:

| | | | |
|---|---|---|---|
| (e) | Equipment | 25,000 | |
| | Investing—Purchase of Equipment | | 25,000 |

| | | | |
|---|---|---|---|
| (f) | Investing—Sale of Equipment | 4,000 | |
| | Operating—Loss on Sale of Equipment | 3,000 | |
| | Accumulated Depreciation—Equipment | 1,000 | |
| | Equipment | | 8,000 |

**Accounts Payable.**   The increase of $55,000 in accounts payable must be added to net income to obtain net cash provided by operating activities. The following work sheet entry is made:

| (g) | Operating—Increase in Accounts Payable | 55,000 | |
|---|---|---|---|
| | Accounts Payable | | 55,000 |

**Bonds Payable.** The increase of $130,000 in this account resulted from the issuance of bonds for land. This is a significant noncash investing and financing activity. Work sheet entry (c) above is the only entry necessary.

**Accumulated Depreciation—Building and Accumulated Depreciation—Equipment.** The increases in these accounts of $11,000 and $4,000, respectively, resulted from depreciation expense. Depreciation expense is a **noncash charge that must be added to net income** in determining net cash provided by operating activities. The work sheet entries are:

| (h) | Operating—Depreciation Expense—Building | 11,000 | |
|---|---|---|---|
| | Accumulated Depreciation—Building | | 11,000 |

| (i) | Operating—Depreciation Expense—Equipment | 4,000 | |
|---|---|---|---|
| | Accumulated Depreciation—Equipment | | 4,000 |

**Retained Earnings.** The $124,000 increase in retained earnings resulted from net income of $139,000 and the declaration of a $15,000 cash dividend that was paid in 1997. Net income is included in net cash provided by operating activities and the dividends are a financing activity cash outflow. The entries in the reconciling columns of the work sheet are:

| (j) | Operating—Net Income | 139,000 | |
|---|---|---|---|
| | Retained Earnings | | 139,000 |

| (k) | Retained Earnings | 15,000 | |
|---|---|---|---|
| | Financing—Payment of Dividends | | 15,000 |

**Disposition of Change in Cash.** The firm's cash increased $22,000 in 1997. The final entry on the work sheet, therefore, is:

| (l) | Cash | 22,000 | |
|---|---|---|---|
| | Increase in cash | | 22,000 |

As shown in the work sheet, the increase in cash is entered in the reconciling credit column as a **balancing** amount. This entry should complete the reconciliation of the changes in the balance sheet accounts. In addition, it should permit the totals of the reconciling columns to be in agreement. When all changes have been explained and the reconciling columns are in agreement, the reconciling columns are ruled to complete the work sheet. The completed work sheet for Computer Services Company is shown in Illustration 18A-4.

# Preparing the Statement

The statement of cash flows is prepared primarily from the data that appear in the work sheet under Statement of Cash Flows Effects. The reconciling columns should also be scanned for any asterisked items that designate significant noncash activities. The formal statement was shown in Illustration 18-16.

**Illustration 18A-4**

*Completed work sheet—*
*indirect method*

| | | COMPUTER SERVICES COMPANY | | |
| | | Work Sheet | | |
| | | Statement of Cash Flows | | |
| | | For the Year Ended December 31, 1997 | | |

| Balance Sheet Accounts | Balance 12/31/96 | Reconciling Items Debit | Reconciling Items Credit | Balance 12/31/97 |
|---|---|---|---|---|
| **Debits** | | | | |
| Cash | 34,000 | (l)  22,000 | | 56,000 |
| Accounts receivable | 30,000 | | (a)  10,000 | 20,000 |
| Prepaid expenses | –0– | (b)   4,000 | | 4,000 |
| Land | –0– | (c) 130,000* | | 130,000 |
| Building | –0– | (d) 160,000 | | 160,000 |
| Equipment | 10,000 | (e)  25,000 | (f)   8,000 | 27,000 |
| Total | 74,000 | | | 397,000 |
| **Credits** | | | | |
| Accounts payable | 4,000 | | (g)  55,000 | 59,000 |
| Bonds payable | –0– | | (c) 130,000* | 130,000 |
| Accumulated depreciation—building | –0– | | (h)  11,000 | 11,000 |
| Accumulated depreciation—equipment | –0– | (f)   1,000 | (i)   4,000 | 3,000 |
| Common stock | 50,000 | | | 50,000 |
| Retained earnings | 20,000 | (k)  15,000 | (j) 139,000 | 144,000 |
| Total | 74,000 | | | 397,000 |
| **Statement of Cash Flows Effects** | | | | |
| Operating activities | | | | |
| Net income | | (j) 139,000 | | |
| Decrease in accounts receivable | | (a)  10,000 | | |
| Increase in prepaid expenses | | | (b)   4,000 | |
| Increase in accounts payable | | (g)  55,000 | | |
| Depreciation expense—building | | (h)  11,000 | | |
| Depreciation expense—equipment | | (i)   4,000 | | |
| Loss on sale of equipment | | (f)   3,000 | | |
| Investing activities | | | | |
| Purchase of building | | | (d) 160,000 | |
| Purchase of equipment | | | (e)  25,000 | |
| Sale of equipment | | (f)   4,000 | | |
| Financing activities | | | | |
| Payment of dividends | | | (k)  15,000 | |
| Totals | | 583,000 | 561,000 | |
| Increase in cash | | | (l)  22,000 | |
| Totals | | 583,000 | 583,000 | |

*Significant noncash investing and financing activity.

# ◤ **S**ummary of Study Objective for Chapter 18 Appendix

•••••••••••••••••••••••••••••••••••••••••••••••••••••••••••••••••••••••••••••••••••••

**5.** *Explain the guidelines and procedural steps in using a work sheet to prepare the statement of cash flows.* When there are numerous adjustments, a work sheet can be a help-ful tool in preparing the statement of cash flows. Key guide-lines for using a work sheet are: (1) list accounts with debit balances separately from those with credit balances; (2) in the reconciling columns in the bottom portion of the work sheet, show cash inflows as debits and cash outflows as credits; (3) do not enter reconciling items in any journal or account but use them only to help prepare the statement of cash flows.

The steps in preparing the work sheet are: (1) enter beginning and ending balances of balance sheet accounts; (2) enter debits and credits in reconciling columns; (3) enter the increase or decrease in cash in two places as a balancing amount.

# GLOSSARY

**Direct method**  A method of determining the "net cash provided by operating activities" by adjusting each item in the income statement from the accrual basis to the cash basis. (p. 751)

**Financing activities**  Cash flow activities that include (a) obtaining cash from issuing debt and repaying the amounts borrowed and (b) obtaining cash from stockholders and providing them with a return on their investment. (p. 734)

**Indirect method**  A method of preparing a statement of cash flows in which net income is adjusted for items that did not affect cash, to determine net cash provided by operating activities. (p. 741)

**Investing activities**  Cash flow activities that include (a) acquiring and disposing of investments and productive long-lived assets and (b) lending money and collecting on those loans. (p. 734)

**Operating activities**  Cash flow activities that include the cash effects of transactions that create revenues and expenses and thus enter into the determination of net income. (p. 734)

**Statement of cash flows**  A basic financial statement that provides information about the cash receipts and cash payments of an entity during a period, classified as operating, investing, and financing activities, in a format that reconciles the beginning and ending cash balances. (p. 733)

# DEMONSTRATION PROBLEM

The income statement for the year ended December 31, 1996, for John Kosinski Manufacturing Company contains the following condensed information:

|  |  |  |
|---|---|---|
| Revenues |  | $6,583,000 |
| Operating expenses (excluding depreciation) | $4,920,000 | |
| Depreciation expense | 880,000 | 5,800,000 |
| Income before income taxes |  | 783,000 |
| Income tax expense |  | 353,000 |
| Net income |  | $  430,000 |

Included in operating expenses is a $24,000 loss resulting from the sale of machinery for $270,000 cash. Machinery was purchased at a cost of $750,000. The following balances are reported on Kosinski's comparative balance sheet at December 31:

|  | 1996 | 1995 |
|---|---|---|
| Cash | $672,000 | $130,000 |
| Accounts receivable | 775,000 | 610,000 |
| Inventories | 834,000 | 867,000 |
| Accounts payable | 521,000 | 501,000 |

Income tax expense of $353,000 represents the amount paid in 1996. Dividends declared and paid in 1996 totaled $200,000.

*Instructions*
(a) Prepare the statement of cash flows using the indirect method.
(b) Prepare the statement of cash flows using the direct method.

**Problem-Solving Strategy**

This demonstration problem illustrates both the direct and indirect methods using the same basic data. Note the similarities and the differences between the two methods. Both methods report the same information in the investing and financing activities sections. The cash flow from operating activities section reports different information, but the amount, net cash provided by operating activities, is the same for both methods.

## Solution to Demonstration Problem

### JOHN KOSINSKI MANUFACTURING COMPANY
### Statement of Cash Flows
### For the Year Ended December 31, 1996

**(a)**                              (Indirect Method)

| | | |
|---|---:|---:|
| Cash flows from operating activities | | |
| Net income | | $ 430,000 |
| Adjustments to reconcile net income to net cash | | |
| provided by operating activities: | | |
| Depreciation expense | $880,000 | |
| Loss on sale of machinery | 24,000 | |
| Increase in accounts receivable | (165,000) | |
| Decrease in inventories | 33,000 | |
| Increase in accounts payable | 20,000 | 792,000 |
| Net cash provided by operating activities | | 1,222,000 |
| Cash flows from investing activities | | |
| Sale of machinery | 270,000 | |
| Purchase of machinery | (750,000) | |
| Net cash used by investing activities | | (480,000) |
| Cash flows from financing activities | | |
| Payment of cash dividends | | (200,000) |
| Net increase in cash | | 542,000 |
| Cash at beginning of period | | 130,000 |
| Cash at end of period | | $672,000 |

**(b)**                              (Direct Method)

| | | |
|---|---:|---:|
| Cash flows from operating activities | | |
| Cash collections from customers | | $6,418,000 * |
| Cash payments for operating expenses | | 4,843,000 ** |
| Income before income taxes | | 1,575,000 |
| Cash payment for income taxes | | 353,000 |
| Net cash provided by operating activities | | 1,222,000 |
| Cash flows from investing activities | | |
| Sale of machinery | $270,000 | |
| Purchase of machinery | (750,000) | |
| Net cash used by investing activities | | (480,000) |
| Cash flows from financing activities | | |
| Payment of cash dividends | | (200,000) |
| Net increase in cash | | 542,000 |
| Cash at beginning of period | | 130,000 |
| Cash at end of period | | $ 672,000 |

### Direct Method Computations

| | |
|---|---:|
| * Computation of cash collections from customers: | |
| Revenues per the income statement | $6,583,000 |
| Less increase in accounts receivable | 165,000 |
| Cash collections from customers | $6,418,000 |
| ** Computation of cash payments for operating expenses: | |
| Operating expenses per the income statement | $4,920,000 |
| Deduct loss from sale of machinery | (24,000) |
| Deduct decrease in inventories | (33,000) |
| Deduct increase in accounts payable | (20,000) |
| Cash payments for operating expenses | $4,843,000 |

*Note: All **asterisked** Questions, Exercises, and Problems relate to material contained in the appendix to the chapter.

# SELF-STUDY QUESTIONS

Answers are at the end of the chapter.

(SO 1) 1. Which of the following is *incorrect* about the statement of cash flows?
   a. It is a fourth basic financial statement.
   b. It provides information about cash receipts and cash payments of an entity during a period.
   c. It reconciles the ending cash account balance to the balance per the bank statement.
   d. It provides information about the operating, investing, and financing activities of the business.

(SO 2) 2. The statement of cash flows classifies cash receipts and cash payments by the following activities:
   a. operating and nonoperating.
   b. investing, financing, and operating.
   c. financing, operating, and nonoperating.
   d. investing, financing, and nonoperating.

(SO 2) 3. An example of a cash flow from an operating activity is:
   a. payment of cash to lenders for interest.
   b. receipt of cash from the sale of capital stock.
   c. payment of cash dividends to the company's stockholders.
   d. none of the above.

(SO 2) 4. An example of a cash flow from an investing activity is:
   a. receipt of cash from the issuance of bonds payable.
   b. payment of cash to repurchase outstanding capital stock.
   c. receipt of cash from the sale of equipment.
   d. payment of cash to suppliers for inventory.

(SO 2) 5. Cash dividends paid to stockholders are classified on the statement of cash flows as:
   a. operating activities.
   b. investing activities.
   c. a combination of the above.
   d. financing activities.

(SO 2) 6. An example of a cash flow from a financing activity is:
   a. receipt of cash from sale of land.
   b. issuance of debt for cash.
   c. purchase of equipment for cash.
   d. none of the above.

(SO 2) 7. Which of the following about the statement of cash flows is **incorrect**?
   a. The direct method may be used to report cash provided by operations.
   b. The statement shows the cash provided (used) for three categories of activity.

   c. The operating section is the last section of the statement.
   d. The indirect method may be used to report cash provided by operations.

**Questions 8 and 9 apply only to the indirect method.**

(SO 3) 8. Net income is $132,000, accounts payable increased $10,000 during the year, inventory decreased $6,000 during the year, and accounts receivable increased $12,000 during the year. Under the indirect method, net cash provided by operations is:
   a. $102,000.
   b. $112,000.
   c. $124,000.
   d. $136,000.

(SO 3) 9. Noncash charges that are added back to net income in determining cash provided by operations under the indirect method do **not** include:
   a. depreciation expense.
   b. an increase in inventory.
   c. amortization expense.
   d. loss on sale of equipment.

**Questions 10 and 11 apply only to the direct method.**

(SO 4) 10. The beginning balance in accounts receivable is $44,000, and the ending balance is $42,000. Sales during the period are $129,000. Cash receipts from customers is:
   a. $127,000.
   b. $129,000.
   c. $131,000.
   d. $141,000.

(SO 4) 11. Which of the following items is reported on a cash flow statement prepared by the direct method?
   a. loss on sale of building.
   b. increase in accounts receivable.
   c. depreciation expense.
   d. cash payments to suppliers.

(SO 3) 12. The statement of cash flows should **not** be used to evaluate an entity's ability to:
   a. earn net income.
   b. generate future cash flows.
   c. pay dividends.
   d. meet obligations.

(SO 5) *13. In a work sheet for the statement of cash flows, a decrease in accounts receivable is entered in the reconciling columns as a credit to Accounts Receivable and a debit in the:
   a. investing activities section.
   b. operating activities section.
   c. financing activities section.
   d. none of the above.

# QUESTIONS

1. (a) What is the statement of cash flows? (b) Alice Weiseman maintains that the statement of cash flows is an optional financial statement. Do you agree? Explain.

2. What questions about cash are answered by the statement of cash flows?

3. What are "cash equivalents"? How do cash equivalents affect the statement of cash flows?

4. Distinguish among the three types of activities reported in the statement of cash flows.

5. What are the major sources (inflows) of cash in a statement of cash flows? What are the major uses (outflows) of cash?

6. Why is it important to disclose certain noncash transactions? How should they be disclosed?

7. Wilma Flintstone and Barny Kublestone were discussing the presentation format of the statement of cash flows of Rock Candy Co. At the bottom of Rock Candy's statement of cash flows was a separate section entitled "Noncash investing and financing activities." Give three examples of significant noncash transactions that would be reported in this section.

8. Why is it necessary to use comparative balance sheets, a current income statement, and certain transaction data in preparing a statement of cash flows?

9. Contrast the advantages and disadvantages of the direct and indirect methods. Are both methods acceptable? Which method is preferred by the FASB? Which method is more popular?

10. When the total cash inflows exceed the total cash outflows in the statement of cash flows, how and where is this excess identified?

11. Describe the indirect method for determining net cash provided by operating activities.

12. Why is it necessary to convert accrual based net income to cash basis income when preparing a statement of cash flows?

13. The president of Aerosmith Company is puzzled. During the last year, the company experienced a net loss of $800,000, yet its cash increased $300,000 during the same period of time. Explain to the president how this situation could occur.

14. Identify five items that are adjustments to reconcile net income to net cash provided by operating activities under the indirect method.

15. Why and how is depreciation expense reported in a statement prepared using the indirect method?

16. Why is the statement of cash flows useful?

17. During 1996, Johnny Carson Company converted $1,700,000 of its total $2,000,000 of bonds payable into common stock. Indicate how the transaction would be reported on a statement of cash flows, if at all.

18. Describe the direct method for determining net cash provided by operating activities.

19. Give the formulas under the direct method for computing (a) cash receipts from customers and (b) cash payments to suppliers.

20. Cindy Crawford Inc. reported sales of $2 million for 1996. Accounts receivable decreased $100,000 and accounts payable increased $300,000. Compute cash receipts from customers, assuming that the receivable and payable transactions related to operations.

21. Why is depreciation expense not reported in the direct-method cash flow from operating activities section?

*22. Why is it advantageous to use a work sheet when preparing a statement of cash flows? Is a work sheet required to prepare a statement of cash flows?

# BRIEF EXERCISES

*Compute cash provided by operating activities—indirect method.*
(SO 3)

**BE18–1**   Crystal, Inc., reported net income of $2.5 million in 1996. Depreciation for the year was $260,000, accounts receivable decreased $350,000, and accounts payable decreased $310,000. Compute net cash provided by operating activities using the indirect approach.

*Compute cash provided by operating activities—indirect method.*
(SO 3)

**BE18–2**   The net income for Sterling Engineering Co. for 1996 was $280,000. For 1996, depreciation on plant assets was $60,000, and the company incurred a loss on sale of plant assets of $9,000. Compute net cash provided by operating activities under the indirect method.

*Indicate statement presentation of selected transactions.*
(SO 2)

**BE18–3**   Each of the following items must be considered in preparing a statement of cash flows for Murphy Co. for the year ended December 31, 1996. For each item, state how it should be shown in the statement of cash flows for 1996.

  (a)  Issued bonds for $200,000 cash.

(b) Purchased equipment for $150,000 cash.
(c) Sold land costing $20,000 for $20,000 cash.
(d) Declared and paid a $50,000 cash dividend.

**BE18–4** The comparative balance sheet for the Rolex Company shows the following changes in noncash current asset accounts: accounts receivable decrease $80,000, prepaid expenses increase $12,000, and inventories increase $30,000. Compute net cash provided by operating activities using the indirect method assuming that net income is $200,000.

*Compute net cash provided by operating activities using indirect method.*
*(SO 3)*

**BE18–5** Classify the following items as an operating, investing, or financing activity. Assume all items involve cash unless there is information to the contrary.

(a) Purchase of equipment.   (d) Depreciation.
(b) Sale of building.   (e) Payment of dividends.
(c) Redemption of bonds.   (f) Issuance of capital stock.

*Classify items by activities.*
*(SO 2)*

**BE18–6** Billy Idol Corporation has accounts receivable of $14,000 at 1/1/96 and $24,000 at 12/31/96. Sales revenues were $480,000 for the year 1996. What is the amount of cash receipts from customers in 1996?

*Compute receipts from customers using direct method.*
*(SO 4)*

**BE18–7** Depeche Mode Corporation reported income taxes of $70,000 on its 1996 income statement and income taxes payable of $12,000 at December 31, 1995, and $9,000 at December 31, 1996. What amount of cash payments were made for income taxes during 1996?

*Compute cash payments for income taxes using direct method.*
*(SO 4)*

**BE18–8** Excel Corporation reports operating expenses of $90,000 excluding depreciation expense of $15,000 for 1996. During the year prepaid expenses decreased $6,600 and accrued expenses payable increased $4,400. Compute the cash payments for operating expenses in 1996.

*Compute cash payments for operating expenses using direct method.*
*(SO 4)*

**BE18–9** The T-accounts for Equipment and the related Accumulated Depreciation for Cindy Trevis Company at the end of 1996 are as follows:

*Determine cash received in sale of equipment.*
*(SO 3, 4)*

**Equipment**

| Beg. bal. | 80,000 | Disposals | 22,000 |
|---|---|---|---|
| Acquisitions | 41,600 | | |
| End. bal. | 99,600 | | |

**Accumulated Depreciation**

| Disposals | 5,500 | Beg. bal. | 44,500 |
|---|---|---|---|
| | | Depr. | 12,000 |
| | | End. bal. | 51,000 |

In addition, Cindy Trevis Company's income statement reported a loss on the sale of equipment of $6,700. What amount was reported on the statement of cash flows as "cash flow from sale of equipment"?

**BE18–10** The following T-account is a summary of the cash account of Anita Baker Company.

*Identify financing activity transactions.*
*(SO 2)*

**Cash (Summary Form)**

| Balance, 1/1/96 | 8,000 | | |
|---|---|---|---|
| Receipts from customers | 364,000 | Payments for goods | 200,000 |
| Dividends on stock investments | 6,000 | Payments for operating expenses | 140,000 |
| Proceeds from sale of equipment | 36,000 | Interest paid | 10,000 |
| Proceeds from issuance of bonds | | Taxes paid | 8,000 |
| payable | 100,000 | Dividends paid | 40,000 |
| Balance, 12/31/96 | 116,000 | | |

For Anita Baker Company what amount of net cash provided (used) by financing activities should be reported in the statement of cash flows?

**\*BE18–11** Using the data in BE18–8, indicate how the changes in prepaid expenses and accrued expenses payable should be entered in the reconciling columns of a work sheet. Assume that beginning balances were: prepaid expenses, $18,600 and accrued expenses payable, $8,200.

*Indicate entries in work sheet.*
*(SO 5)*

# EXERCISES

•••••••••••••••••••••••••••••••••••••••••••••••••••••••••••••••••••••••••••••••••

*Classify transactions by type of activity.*
(SO 2)

**E18–1**   Li Eng Corporation had the following transactions during 1996:

1. Purchased a machine for $30,000, giving a long-term note in exchange.
2. Issued $50,000 par value common stock for cash.
3. Collected $16,000 of accounts receivable.
4. Declared and paid a cash dividend of $25,000.
5. Sold a long-term investment with a cost of $15,000 for $15,000 cash.
6. Issued $200,000 par value common stock upon conversion of bonds having a face value of $200,000.
7. Paid $18,000 on accounts payable.

**Instructions**
Analyze the transactions above and indicate whether each transaction resulted in a cash flow from (a) operating activities, (b) investing activities, (c) financing activities, or (d) noncash investing and financing activities.

*Prepare the operating activities section—indirect method.*
(SO 3)

**E18–2**   Joe Pesci Company reported net income of $195,000 for 1996. Pesci also reported depreciation expense of $35,000, and a loss of $5,000 on the sale of equipment. The comparative balance sheet shows an increase in accounts receivable of $15,000 for the year, an $8,000 increase in accounts payable, and a decrease in prepaid expenses $4,000.

**Instructions**
Prepare the operating activities section of the statement of cash flows for 1996. Use the indirect method.

*Prepare the operating activities section—indirect method.*
(SO 3)

**E18–3**   The current sections of Barth Inc.'s balance sheets at December 31, 1995 and 1996, are presented below.

|  | 1996 | 1995 |
|---|---|---|
| Current assets |  |  |
| Cash | $105,000 | $ 99,000 |
| Accounts receivable | 110,000 | 89,000 |
| Inventory | 171,000 | 186,000 |
| Prepaid expenses | 27,000 | 32,000 |
| Total current assets | $413,000 | $406,000 |
| Current liabilities |  |  |
| Accrued expenses payable | $ 15,000 | $  5,000 |
| Accounts payable | $ 85,000 | $ 92,000 |
| Total current liabilities | $100,000 | $ 97,000 |

Barth's net income for 1996 was $122,000. Depreciation expense was $24,000.

**Instructions**
Prepare the net cash provided by operating activities section of Barth Inc.'s statement of cash flows for the year ended December 31, 1996 using the indirect method.

*Prepare partial statement of cash flows—indirect method.*
(SO 3)

**E18–4**   Presented below are three accounts that appear in the general ledger of Roberta Dupre Corp. during 1996:

| Equipment | | | |
|---|---|---|---|
| Date |  | Debit | Credit | Balance |
| Jan. 1 | Balance |  |  | 160,000 |
| July 31 | Purchase of equipment | 70,000 |  | 230,000 |
| Sept. 2 | Cost of equipment constructed | 53,000 |  | 283,000 |
| Nov. 10 | Cost of equipment sold |  | 45,000 | 238,000 |

### Accumulated Depreciation—Equipment

| Date | | Debit | Credit | Balance |
|------|------|------|------|------|
| Jan. 1 | Balance | | | 71,000 |
| Nov. 10 | Accumulated depreciation on equipment sold | 30,000 | | 41,000 |
| Dec. 31 | Depreciation for year | | 24,000 | 65,000 |

### Retained Earnings

| Date | | Debit | Credit | Balance |
|------|------|------|------|------|
| Jan. 1 | Balance | | | 105,000 |
| Aug. 23 | Dividends (cash) | 14,000 | | 91,000 |
| Dec. 31 | Net income | | 47,000 | 138,000 |

**Instructions**

From the postings in the accounts above, indicate how the information is reported on a statement of cash flows by preparing a partial statement of cash flows using the indirect method. The loss on sale of equipment was $6,000.

**E18–5**  A comparative balance sheet for Oprah Winfrey Company is presented below.

*Prepare a statement of cash flows—indirect method.*
*(SO 3)*

| | December 31 | |
|------|------|------|
| **Assets** | **1996** | **1995** |
| Cash | $ 63,000 | $ 22,000 |
| Accounts receivable | 85,000 | 76,000 |
| Inventories | 180,000 | 189,000 |
| Land | 75,000 | 100,000 |
| Equipment | 260,000 | 200,000 |
| Accumulated depreciation | (66,000) | (42,000) |
| Total | $597,000 | $545,000 |

| **Liabilities and Stockholders' Equity** | | |
|------|------|------|
| Accounts payable | $ 34,000 | $ 47,000 |
| Bonds payable | 150,000 | 200,000 |
| Common stock ($1 par) | 214,000 | 164,000 |
| Retained earnings | 199,000 | 134,000 |
| Total | $597,000 | $545,000 |

Additional information:

1. Net income for 1996 was $105,000.
2. Cash dividends of $40,000 were declared and paid.
3. Bonds payable amounting to $50,000 were redeemed for cash $50,000.
4. Common stock was issued for $50,000 cash.

**Instructions**

Prepare a statement of cash flows for 1996 using the indirect method.

**E18–6**  An analysis of comparative balance sheets, the current year's income statement and the general ledger accounts of Pierce Brosnan Corp. uncovered the following items. Assume all items involve cash unless there is information to the contrary.

*Classify transactions by type of activity.*
*(SO 2)*

(a) Purchase of land.
(b) Payment of dividends.
(c) Sale of building at book value.
(d) Exchange of land for patent.
(e) Depreciation.
(f) Redemption of bonds.
(g) Receipt of interest on notes receivable.
(h) Issuance of capital stock.
(i) Amortization of patent.
(j) Issuance of bonds for land.
(k) Payment of interest on notes payable.
(l) Conversion of bonds into common stock.
(m) Loss on sale of land.
(n) Receipt of dividends on investment in stock.

**Instructions**
Indicate how the above items should be classified in the statement of cash flows using the following four major classifications: operating activity (indirect method), investing activity, financing activity, and significant noncash investing and financing activity.

*Compute cash provided by operating activities—direct method.*
*(SO 4)*

**E18–7**   Kelly McGillis Company has just completed its first year of operations on December 31, 1996. Its initial income statement showed that Kelly McGillis had revenues of $157,000 and operating expenses of $78,000. Accounts receivable and accounts payable at year end were $42,000 and $33,000, respectively. Assume that accounts payable related to operating expenses. Ignore income taxes.

**Instructions**
Compute net cash provided by operating activities using the direct method.

*Compute cash payments—direct method.*
*(SO 4)*

**E18–8**   The income statement for the Garcia Company shows cost of goods sold $355,000 and operating expenses (exclusive of depreciation) $230,000. The comparative balance sheet for the year shows that inventory increased $6,000, prepaid expenses decreased $6,000, accounts payable (merchandise suppliers) decreased $8,000, and accrued expenses payable increased $8,000.

**Instructions**
Using the direct method, compute (a) cash payments to suppliers and (b) cash payments for operating expenses.

*Compute cash flow from operating activities—direct method*
*(SO 2, 4)*

**E18–9**   The 1997 accounting records of Flypaper Airlines reveal the following transactions and events.

| | | | |
|---|---|---|---|
| Payment of interest | $ 6,000 | Collection of accounts receivable | $180,000 |
| Cash sales | 48,000 | Payment of salaries and wages | 68,000 |
| Receipt of dividend revenue | 14,000 | Depreciation expense | 16,000 |
| Payment of income taxes | 16,000 | Proceeds from sale of aircraft | 812,000 |
| Net income | 38,000 | Purchase of equipment for cash | 22,000 |
| Payment of accounts payable for | | Loss on sale of aircraft | 3,000 |
| merchandise | 90,000 | Payment of dividends | 14,000 |
| Payment for land | 74,000 | Payment of operating expenses | 20,000 |

**Instructions**
Prepare the cash flows from operating activities section using the direct method. (Not all of the above items will be used.)

*Calculate cash flows—direct method*
*(SO 4)*

**E18–10**   The following information is taken from the 1997 general ledger of Joan Robinson Company:

| | | |
|---|---|---|
| Rent | Rent expense | $ 31,000 |
| | Prepaid rent, January 1 | 5,900 |
| | Prepaid rent, December 31 | 3,000 |
| Salaries | Salaries expense | $ 54,000 |
| | Salaries payable, January 1 | 5,000 |
| | Salaries payable, December 31 | 8,000 |
| Sales | Revenue from sales | $180,000 |
| | Accounts receivable, January 1 | 12,000 |
| | Accounts receivable, December 31 | 9,000 |

**Instructions**
In each of above cases, compute the amount that should be reported in the operating activities section of the statement of cash flows applying the direct method.

*Prepare a work sheet.*
*(SO 5)*

**\*E18–11**

**Instructions**
Refer to Exercise E18–5 (Oprah Winfrey Company) and use these data to prepare a work sheet for a statement of cash flows for 1996. Enter the reconciling items directly on the work sheet, identifying the entries alphabetically.

# PROBLEMS

**P18-1** The income statement of Breckenridge Company is shown below:

*Prepare the operating activities section—indirect method.*
(SO 3)

### BRECKENRIDGE COMPANY
### Income Statement
### For the Year Ended November 30, 1996

| | | |
|---|---:|---:|
| Sales | | $6,900,000 |
| Cost of goods sold | | |
|   Beginning inventory | $1,900,000 | |
|   Purchases | 4,400,000 | |
|   Goods available for sale | 6,300,000 | |
|   Ending inventory | 1,600,000 | |
|   Cost of goods sold | | 4,700,000 |
| Gross profit | | 2,200,000 |
| Operating expenses | | |
|   Selling expenses | 450,000 | |
|   Administrative expenses | 700,000 | 1,150,000 |
| Net income | | $1,050,000 |

Additional information:

1. Accounts receivable decreased $300,000 during the year.
2. Prepaid expenses increased $150,000 during the year.
3. Accounts payable to suppliers of merchandise decreased $300,000 during the year.
4. Accrued expenses payable decreased $100,000 during the year.
5. Administrative expenses include depreciation expense of $60,000.

*Instructions*
Prepare the operating activities section of the statement of cash flows for the year ended November 30, 1996, for Breckenridge Company, using the indirect method.

**P18-2** Data for the Breckenridge Company are presented in P18-1.

*Prepare operating activities section—direct method.*
(SO 4)

*Instructions*
Prepare the operating activities section of the statement of cash flows using the direct method.

**P18-3** Vail Company's income statement for the year ended December 31, 1996, contained the following condensed information:

*Prepare the operating activities section—direct method.*
(SO 4)

| | | |
|---|---:|---:|
| Revenue from fees | | $840,000 |
| Operating expenses (excluding depreciation) | $624,000 | |
| Depreciation expense | 60,000 | |
| Loss on sale of equipment | 26,000 | 710,000 |
| Income before income taxes | | 130,000 |
| Income tax expense | | 40,000 |
| Net income | | $ 90,000 |

Vail's balance sheet contained the following comparative data at December 31:

| | 1996 | 1995 |
|---|---:|---:|
| Accounts receivable | $47,000 | $55,000 |
| Accounts payable | 41,000 | 33,000 |
| Income taxes payable | 4,000 | 9,000 |

(Accounts payable pertains to operating expenses.)

*Instructions*
Prepare the operating activities section of the statement of cash flows using the direct method.

*Prepare the operating activities section—indirect method*
(SO 4)

**P18–4**

**Instructions**

Using the data from Problem 18–3, prepare the operating activities section of the statement of cash flows using the indirect method.

*Prepare a statement of cash flows—indirect method.*
(SO 3)

**P18–5**   The financial statements of Patrick Swayze Company appear below:

**PATRICK SWAYZE COMPANY**
**Comparative Balance Sheet**
**December 31**

| Assets | 1996 | 1995 |
|---|---|---|
| Cash | $ 29,000 | $ 13,000 |
| Accounts receivable | 28,000 | 14,000 |
| Merchandise inventory | 25,000 | 35,000 |
| Property, plant, and equipment | 60,000 | 78,000 |
| Accumulated depreciation | (20,000) | (24,000) |
| Total | $122,000 | $116,000 |

| Liabilities and Stockholders' Equity | 1996 | 1995 |
|---|---|---|
| Accounts payable | $ 29,000 | $ 23,000 |
| Income taxes payable | 5,000 | 8,000 |
| Bonds payable | 27,000 | 33,000 |
| Common stock | 18,000 | 14,000 |
| Retained earnings | 43,000 | 38,000 |
| Total | $122,000 | $116,000 |

**PATRICK SWAYZE COMPANY**
**Income Statement**
**For the Year Ended December 31, 1996**

| | | |
|---|---:|---:|
| Sales | | $220,000 |
| Cost of goods sold | | 180,000 |
| Gross profit | | 40,000 |
| Selling expenses | $18,000 | |
| Administrative expenses | 6,000 | 24,000 |
| Income from operations | | 16,000 |
| Interest expense | | 2,000 |
| Income before income taxes | | 14,000 |
| Income tax expense | | 4,000 |
| Net income | | $ 10,000 |

The following additional data were provided:

1. Dividends declared and paid were $5,000.
2. During the year equipment was sold for $8,500 cash. This equipment cost $18,000 originally and had a book value of $8,500 at the time of sale.
3. All depreciation expense is in the selling expense category.
4. All sales and purchases are on account.

**Instructions**

Prepare a statement of cash flows using the indirect method.

*Prepare a statement of cash flows—direct method.*
(SO 4)

**P18–6**   Data for the Patrick Swayze Company are presented in P18–5. Further analysis reveals the following:

1. Accounts payable pertain to merchandise suppliers.
2. All operating expenses except for depreciation were paid in cash.

**Instructions**

Prepare a statement of cash flows for Patrick Swayze Company using the direct method.

*Prepare a statement of cash flows—indirect method.*
(SO 3)

**P18–7** Condensed financial data of Fern Galenti, Inc. appear below.

### FERN GALENTI, INC.
### Comparative Balance Sheet
### December 31

| Assets | 1996 | 1995 |
|---|---|---|
| Cash | $ 97,800 | $ 38,400 |
| Accounts receivable | 90,800 | 33,000 |
| Inventories | 112,500 | 102,850 |
| Prepaid expenses | 18,400 | 16,000 |
| Investments | 108,000 | 94,000 |
| Plant assets | 270,000 | 242,500 |
| Accumulated depreciation | (50,000) | (52,000) |
| | $647,500 | $474,750 |

| Liabilities and Stockholders' Equity | | |
|---|---|---|
| Accounts payable | $ 92,000 | $ 67,300 |
| Accrued expenses payable | 16,500 | 17,000 |
| Bonds payable | 85,000 | 110,000 |
| Common stock | 220,000 | 175,000 |
| Retained earnings | 234,000 | 105,450 |
| | $647,500 | $474,750 |

### FERN GALENTI, INC.
### Income Statement Data
### For the Year Ended December 31, 1996

| | | |
|---|---|---|
| Sales | | $342,780 |
| Less: | | |
| Cost of goods sold | $115,460 | |
| Operating expenses (excluding depreciation) | 12,410 | |
| Depreciation expense | 46,500 | |
| Income taxes | 7,280 | |
| Interest expense | 2,730 | |
| Loss on sale of plant assets | 7,500 | 191,880 |
| Net income | | $150,900 |

Additional information:

1. New plant assets costing $85,000 were purchased for cash during the year.
2. Old plant assets having an original cost of $57,500 were sold for $1,500 cash.
3. Bonds matured and were paid off at face value for cash.
4. A cash dividend of $22,350 was declared and paid during the year.

**Instructions**

Prepare a statement of cash flows using the indirect method.

*Prepare a statement of cash flows—direct method.*
(SO 4)

**P18–8** Data for Fern Galenti, Inc., are presented in P18–7. Further analysis reveals that accounts payable pertains to merchandise creditors.

**Instructions**

Prepare a statement of cash flows for Fern Galenti, Inc., using the direct method.

*Prepare a statement of cash flows—indirect method.*
(SO 3)

**P18–9** Presented below is the comparative balance sheet for Cousin Tommy's Toy Company as of December 31:

**COUSIN TOMMY'S TOY COMPANY**
**Comparative Balance Sheet**
**December 31**

| Assets | 1996 | 1995 |
|---|---|---|
| Cash | $ 41,000 | $ 45,000 |
| Accounts receivable | 47,500 | 52,000 |
| Inventory | 151,450 | 142,000 |
| Prepaid expenses | 16,780 | 21,000 |
| Land | 100,000 | 130,000 |
| Equipment | 228,000 | 155,000 |
| Accumulated depreciation—equipment | (45,000) | (35,000) |
| Building | 200,000 | 200,000 |
| Accumulated depreciation—building | (60,000) | (40,000) |
| | $679,730 | $670,000 |

| Liabilities and Stockholders' Equity | | |
|---|---|---|
| Accounts payable | $ 43,730 | $ 40,000 |
| Bonds payable | 250,000 | 300,000 |
| Common stock, $1 par | 200,000 | 150,000 |
| Retained earnings | 186,000 | 180,000 |
| | $679,730 | $670,000 |

Additional information:

1. Operating expenses include depreciation expense of $42,000 and charges from prepaid expenses of $4,220.
2. Land was sold for cash at book value.
3. Cash dividends of $32,000 were paid.
4. Net income for 1996 was $38,000.
5. Equipment was purchased for $95,000 cash. In addition, equipment costing $22,000 with a book value of $10,000 was sold for $8,100 cash.
6. Bonds were converted at face value by issuing 50,000 shares of $1 par value common stock.

**Instructions**
Prepare a statement of cash flows for the year ended December 31, 1996, using the indirect method.

*Prepare a work sheet.*
(SO 5)

**\*P18–10**

**Instructions**
Refer to Problem 18–7 (Fern Galenti, Inc.) and use these data to prepare a work sheet for a statement of cash flows for 1996. Enter the reconciling entries directly on the work sheet, identifying the entries alphabetically.

# ALTERNATE PROBLEMS

••••••••••••••••••••••••••••••••••••••••••••••••••••••••••••••••••••••••••••

*Prepare the operating activities section—indirect method.*
(SO 3)

**P18–1A**   The income statement of Tina Maria Company is shown below:

**TINA MARIA COMPANY**
**Income Statement**
**For the Year Ended December 31, 1996**

| | | |
|---|---|---|
| Sales | | $7,100,000 |
| Cost of goods sold | | |
| Beginning inventory | $1,700,000 | |
| Purchases | 5,430,000 | |
| Goods available for sale | 7,130,000 | |
| Ending inventory | 1,920,000 | |

| | | |
|---|---|---|
| Cost of goods sold | | 5,210,000 |
| Gross profit | | 1,890,000 |
| Operating expenses | | |
| Selling expenses | 400,000 | |
| Administrative expense | 525,000 | |
| Depreciation expense | 75,000 | |
| Amortization expense | 30,000 | 1,030,000 |
| Net income | | $ 860,000 |

**Additional information:**

1. Accounts receivable increased $510,000 during the year.
2. Prepaid expenses increased $170,000 during the year.
3. Accounts payable to merchandise suppliers increased $50,000 during the year.
4. Accrued expenses payable decreased $180,000 during the year.

*Instructions*
Prepare the operating activities section of the statement of cash flows for the year ended December 31, 1996, for Tina Maria Company, using the indirect method.

**P18–2A** Data for the Tina Maria Company are presented in P18–1A.

*Prepare the operating activities section—direct method.*
*(SO 4)*

*Instructions*
Prepare the operating activities section of the statement of cash flows using the direct method.

**P18–3A** The income statement of Hanalei International Inc. for the year ended December 31, 1996, reported the following condensed information:

*Prepare the operating activities section—direct method.*
*(SO 4)*

| | |
|---|---|
| Revenue from fees | $430,000 |
| Operating expenses | 280,000 |
| Income from operations | 150,000 |
| Income tax expense | 47,000 |
| Net income | $103,000 |

Hanalei's balance sheet contained the following comparative data at December 31:

| | 1996 | 1995 |
|---|---|---|
| Accounts receivable | $50,000 | $40,000 |
| Accounts payable | 30,000 | 41,000 |
| Income taxes payable | 6,000 | 4,000 |

Hanalei has no depreciable assets. Accounts payable pertains to operating expenses.

*Instructions*
Prepare the operating activities section of the statement of cash flows using the direct method.

**P18–4A**

*Prepare the operating activities section—indirect method.*
*(SO 3)*

*Instructions*
Using the data from Problem 18–3A, prepare the operating activities section of the statement of cash flows using the indirect method.

**P18–5A** The financial statements of Sean Seymor Company appear below:

*Prepare a statement of cash flows—indirect method.*
*(SO 2, 3)*

### SEAN SEYMOR COMPANY
#### Comparative Balance Sheet
#### December 31

| Assets | | 1996 | | 1995 |
|---|---|---|---|---|
| Cash | | $ 26,000 | | $ 13,000 |
| Accounts receivable | | 18,000 | | 14,000 |
| Merchandise inventory | | 38,000 | | 35,000 |
| Property, plant, and equipment | $70,000 | | $78,000 | |
| Less accumulated depreciation | (30,000) | 40,000 | (24,000) | 54,000 |
| Total | | $122,000 | | $116,000 |

Liabilities and Stockholders' Equity

| | | |
|---|---:|---:|
| Accounts payable | $ 29,000 | $ 33,000 |
| Income taxes payable | 15,000 | 20,000 |
| Bonds payable | 20,000 | 10,000 |
| Common stock | 25,000 | 25,000 |
| Retained earnings | 33,000 | 28,000 |
| Total | $122,000 | $116,000 |

**SEAN SEYMOR COMPANY**
**Income Statement**
**For the Year Ended December 31, 1996**

| | | |
|---|---:|---:|
| Sales | | $240,000 |
| Cost of goods sold | | 180,000 |
| Gross profit | | 60,000 |
| Selling expenses | $28,000 | |
| Administrative expenses | 6,000 | 34,000 |
| Income from operations | | 26,000 |
| Interest expense | | 2,000 |
| Income before income taxes | | 24,000 |
| Income tax expense | | 7,000 |
| Net income | | $ 17,000 |

The following additional data were provided:

1. Dividends of $12,000 were declared and paid.
2. During the year equipment was sold for $10,000 cash. This equipment cost $15,000 originally and had a book value of $10,000 at the time of sale.
3. All depreciation expense, $11,000, is in the selling expense category.
4. All sales and purchases are on account.
5. Additional equipment was purchased for $7,000 cash.

*Instructions*
Prepare a statement of cash flows using the indirect method.

*Prepare a statement of cash flows—direct method.*
(SO 4)

**P18–6A**   Data for the Sean Seymor Company are presented in P18–5A. Further analysis reveals the following:

1. Accounts payable pertains to merchandise creditors.
2. All operating expenses except for depreciation are paid in cash.

*Instructions*
Prepare a statement of cash flows using the direct method.

*Prepare a statement of cash flows—indirect method.*
(SO 3)

**P18–7A**   Condensed financial data of Norway Company appear below:

**NORWAY COMPANY**
**Comparative Balance Sheet**
**December 31**

| | 1996 | 1995 |
|---|---:|---:|
| **Assets** | | |
| Cash | $ 96,700 | $ 47,250 |
| Accounts receivable | 86,800 | 57,000 |
| Inventories | 121,900 | 102,650 |
| Investments | 84,500 | 87,000 |
| Plant assets | 250,000 | 205,000 |
| Accumulated depreciation | (49,500) | (40,000) |
| | $590,400 | $458,900 |

Liabilities and Stockholders' Equity

| | | |
|---|---|---|
| Accounts payable | $ 52,700 | $ 48,280 |
| Accrued expenses payable | 12,100 | 18,830 |
| Bonds payable | 100,000 | 70,000 |
| Common stock | 250,000 | 200,000 |
| Retained earnings | 175,600 | 121,790 |
| | $590,400 | $458,900 |

**NORWAY COMPANY**
**Income Statement Data**
**For the Year Ended December 31, 1996**

| | | |
|---|---|---|
| Sales | | $297,500 |
| Gain on sale of plant assets | | 8,750 |
| | | 306,250 |
| Less: | | |
| Cost of goods sold | $99,460 | |
| Operating expenses (excluding depreciation expense) | 14,670 | |
| Depreciation expense | 49,700 | |
| Income taxes | 7,270 | |
| Interest expense | 2,940 | 174,040 |
| Net income | | $132,210 |

Additional information:

1. New plant assets costing $92,000 were purchased for cash during the year.
2. Investments were sold at cost.
3. Plant assets costing $47,000 were sold for $15,550, resulting in a gain of $8,750.
4. A cash dividend of $78,400 was declared and paid during the year.

*Instructions*
Prepare a statement of cash flows using the indirect method.

**P18–8A** Data for Norway Company are presented in P18–7A. Further analysis reveals that accounts payable pertains to merchandise creditors.

*Prepare a statement of cash flows—direct method.*
*(SO 4)*

*Instructions*
Prepare a statement of cash flows for Norway Company using the direct method.

**P18–9A** Presented below is the comparative balance sheet for Cortina Company at December 31:

*Prepare a statement of cash flows—indirect method.*
*(SO 3)*

**CORTINA COMPANY**
**Comparative Balance Sheet**
**December 31**

| | 1996 | 1995 |
|---|---|---|
| Cash | $ 40,000 | $ 57,000 |
| Accounts receivable | 77,000 | 64,000 |
| Inventory | 132,000 | 140,000 |
| Prepaid expenses | 12,140 | 16,540 |
| Land | 125,000 | 150,000 |
| Equipment | 200,000 | 175,000 |
| Accumulated depreciation—equipment | (60,000) | (42,000) |
| Building | 250,000 | 250,000 |
| Accumulated depreciation—building | (75,000) | (50,000) |
| | $701,140 | $760,540 |
| | | |
| Accounts payable | $ 33,000 | $ 45,000 |
| Bonds payable | 235,000 | 265,000 |
| Common stock, $1 par | 280,000 | 250,000 |
| Retained earnings | 153,140 | 200,540 |
| | $701,140 | $760,540 |

Additional information:

1. Operating expenses include depreciation expense $70,000 and charges from prepaid expenses of $4,400.
2. Land was sold for cash at cost.
3. Cash dividends of $74,290 were paid.
4. Net income for 1996 was $26,890.
5. Equipment was purchased for $65,000 cash. In addition, equipment costing $40,000 with a book value of $13,000 was sold for $14,000 cash.
6. Bonds were converted at face value by issuing 30,000 shares of $1 par value common stock.

**Instructions**
Prepare a statement of cash flows for 1996 using the indirect method.

*Prepare a work sheet*
(SO 5)

**\*P18–10A**

**Instructions**
Refer to Problem 18–7A (Norway Company) and use these data to prepare a work sheet for a statement of cash flows. Enter the reconciling items directly in the work sheet columns, identifying the debit and credit amounts alphabetically.

# ▶*B*roadening *Your Perspective*

# *F*INANCIAL REPORTING PROBLEM

Refer to the financial statements of PepsiCo, Inc., presented in Appendix A and answer the following questions:

(a) What was the amount of net cash provided by operating activities for the year ended December 31, 1994? For the year ended December 25, 1993?
(b) What was the amount of increase or decrease in cash and cash equivalents for the year ended December 31, 1994? For the year ended December 25, 1993?
(c) Which method of computing net cash provided by operating activities does PepsiCo use?
(d) From your analysis of the 1994 statement of cash flows, was the change in notes and accounts receivable a decrease or an increase? Was the change in inventories a decrease or an increase? Was the change in accounts payable a decrease or an increase?
(e) What was the total (gross) outflow of cash for investing activities for 1994?
(f) What was the amount of interest paid in 1994? What was the amount of income taxes paid in 1994?
(g) What significant noncash investing and financing activities did PepsiCo complete in 1994?

# *D*ECISION CASE

Greg Rhoda and Debra Sondgeroth are examining the following statement of cash flows for L.L. Bean Trading Company for the year ended January 31, 1997.

## L.L. BEAN TRADING COMPANY
### Statement of Cash Flows
### For the Year Ended January 31, 1997

| | |
|---|---:|
| Sources of cash | |
| From sales of merchandise | $370,000 |
| From sale of capital stock | 420,000 |
| From sale of investment (purchased below) | 80,000 |
| From depreciation | 55,000 |
| From issuance of note for truck | 20,000 |
| From interest on investments | 6,000 |
| Total sources of cash | 951,000 |
| Uses of cash | |
| For purchase of fixtures and equipment | 340,000 |
| For merchandise purchased for resale | 258,000 |
| For operating expenses (including depreciation) | 160,000 |
| For purchase of investment | 75,000 |
| For purchase of truck by issuance of note | 20,000 |
| For purchase of treasury stock | 10,000 |
| For interest on note payable | 3,000 |
| Total uses of cash | 866,000 |
| Net increase in cash | $ 85,000 |

Greg claims that L.L. Bean's statement of cash flows is an excellent portrayal of a superb first year with cash increasing $85,000. Debra replies that it was not a superb first year, that the year was an operating failure, that the statement was incorrectly presented, and that $85,000 is not the actual increase in cash. The cash balance at the beginning of the year was $140,000.

*Instructions*
(a) With whom do you agree, Greg or Debra? Explain your position.
(b) Using the data provided, prepare a statement of cash flows in proper form using the indirect method. The only noncash items in the income statement are depreciation and the gain from the sale of the investment.

# COMMUNICATION ACTIVITY
................................................................

Arnold Byte, the owner-president of Computer Services Company, is unfamiliar with the statement of cash flows which you, as his accountant, prepared. He asks for further explanation.

*Instructions*
Write him a brief memo explaining the form and content of the statement of cash flows as shown in Illustration 18-12 on page 743.

# GROUP ACTIVITY
................................................................

In groups of four or five, discuss the following questions: What would you expect to observe in the operating, investing, and financing sections of a statement of cash flows of:
(a) a severely financially troubled firm?
(b) a recently formed firm which is experiencing rapid growth?

# ETHICS CASE
................................................................

Puebla Corporation is a medium-sized wholesaler of automotive parts. It has ten stockholders that have been paid a total of $1 million in cash dividends for 8 consecutive years. The

Board of Director's policy requires that in order for this dividend to be declared, net cash provided by operating activities as reported in Puebla's current year's statement of cash flows must be in excess of $1 million. President and CEO Phil Monat's job is secure so long as he produces annual operating cash flows to support the usual dividend.

At the end of the current year, controller Rick Rodgers presents President Monat with some disappointing news—the net cash provided by operating activities is calculated by the indirect method to be only $970,000. The president says to Rick, "We must get that amount above $1 million. Isn't there some way to increase operating cash flow by another $30,000?" Rick answers, "These figures were prepared by my assistant. I'll go back to my office and see what I can do." The president replies, "I know you won't let me down, Rick."

Upon close scrutiny of the statement of cash flows, Rick concludes that he can get the operating cash flows above $1 million by reclassifying a $60,000, 2-year note payable listed in the financing activities section as "Proceeds from bank loan—$60,000." He will report the note instead as "Increase in payables—$60,000" and treat it as an adjustment of net income in the operating activities section. He returns to the president saying, "You can tell the Board to declare their usual dividend. Our net cash flow provided by operating activities is $1,030,000." "Good man, Rick! I knew I could count on you," exults the president.

*Instructions*
  (a)  Who are the stakeholders in this situation?
  (b)  Was there anything unethical about the president's actions? Was there anything unethical about the controller's actions?
  (c)  Are the Board members or anyone else likely to discover the misclassification?

# CRITICAL THINKING
## ▸ *A Real-World Focus: Praxair Incorporated*

*Praxair was founded in 1907 as Linde-Air Products Company and was a pioneer in separating oxygen from air. It was purchased and run as a subsidiary of Union Carbide. In 1992 Praxair became an independent public company. Today, the company is one of the top three largest suppliers of industrial gases worldwide. Praxair has operations in all regions of the world, with a majority of its sales occurring outside of the United States.*

The following management discussion was included in Praxair's 1994 annual report:

**Liquidity, Capital Resources and Other Financial Data**—In 1994, Praxair changed its presentation of the Statement of Cash Flows to the direct method to report major classes of cash receipts and payments from operations. Praxair believes the direct method more clearly presents its operating cash flows. Prior years' cash flow information has been reclassified to conform to the current year presentation.

*Instructions*
  (a)  What method has Praxair changed from?
  (b)  What will the newly prepared cash flow statement show that the former one did not?
  (c)  Will the cash flows from investing and financing appear any differently under the new method of preparation than they did under the old method?

---

*Answers to Self-Study Questions*
1. c    2. b    3. a    4. c    5. d    6. b    7. c    8. d    9. b    10. a    11. d
12. a    13. b

# SAT Scores Help Bring in Loans

CHICAGO, Ill. — When big banks and insurance companies lend millions of dollars to colleges and universities, the lenders understandably want to know that their money is secure. That's why they demand that the schools provide certain financial statement ratios.

At the University of Chicago, John R. Kroll is responsible for putting together some 40 different ratios—ranging from measures of liquidity to qualitative factors such as student SAT scores.

One balance sheet ratio measures the relationship of equity to debt. Kroll says: "A ratio of 1-to-1 says that if a calamity strikes, you could liquidate your net assets and pay off your debt. Your 'A'-rated institutions, as measured by Standard & Poor's, a New York rating agency, have a ratio of 2-to-1. 'AAA' institutions—the highest ranking, have a 4-to-1 ratio. We have a 5.5-to-1 ratio."

Kroll says the good equity-to-debt ratio helped the university bor-row $100 million recently for two new buildings. "Buildings are financed in one of two ways," he says. "Either people give money to build the building, or you have to go out and borrow cash and pay it off over a long period of time."

Another key ratio is the endowment ratio—the ratio of endowment gifts the university has received to the number of students. The more endowment a school has, the less pressure it has to find money from other sources.

Lenders are even interested in SAT scores. The reason: "The stronger the student, the more demand there is to attend your institution," which translates to a healthy financial condition, says Kroll. ◀

# CHAPTER 19

# *F*INANCIAL STATEMENT ANALYSIS

**After studying this chapter, you should be able to:**

1. *Discuss the need for comparative analysis.*
2. *Identify the tools of financial statement analysis.*
3. *Explain and apply horizontal analysis.*
4. *Describe and apply vertical analysis.*
5. *Identify and compute ratios and describe their purpose and use in analyzing a firm's liquidity, profitability, and solvency.*
6. *Recognize the limitations of financial statement analysis.*

If you had excess cash which you wanted to invest, what would you do with it? One of the most popular forms of investments is in stocks or bonds. If stocks are your choice, should you invest in conservative public utility company stocks such as Pacific Gas & Electric Company or in speculative research or high-tech stocks such as Genetic Inc. or Satellite Communications Corp.? If you choose to buy bonds, should you invest in General Electric's quality bonds, which generally have greater stability, less risk, and lower yields, or in Sunshine Mining bonds that offer higher rates of return but are less stable and of greater risk? To answer these types of questions, it is helpful for you to understand how to analyze financial statement information.

Financial statement analysis, the topic of this chapter, enhances the usefulness of published financial statements in making decisions about a company. The content and organization of this chapter are shown below.

# *B*asics of Financial Statement Analysis

Analyzing financial statements involves evaluating three characteristics of a company: its liquidity, its profitability, and its solvency. For example, a **short-term creditor**, such as a bank, is primarily interested in the ability of the borrower to pay obligations when they come due. The liquidity of the borrower in such a case is extremely important in evaluating the safety of a loan. A **long-term creditor**, such as a bondholder, however, looks to indicators such as profitability and solvency that indicate the firm's ability to survive over a long period of time. Long-term creditors consider such measures as the amount of debt in the company's capital structure and the ability to meet interest payments. Similarly, **stockholders** are interested in the profitability and solvency of the enterprise when they assess the likelihood of dividends and the growth potential of the stock.

## Need for Comparative Analysis

Every item reported in a financial statement has significance. For example, when Xerox Corporation reports cash of $35 million on its balance sheet, we know the company had that amount of cash on the balance sheet date. However, we do not know whether the amount represents an increase over prior years or whether the amount is adequate in relation to the company's need for cash. To obtain this information, it is necessary to compare the amount of cash with other financial statement data.

Comparisons can be made on a number of different bases—three are illustrated in this chapter:

1. **Intracompany basis.** This basis compares an item or financial relationship **within a company** in the current year with the same item or relationship in one or more prior years. For example, a comparison of Xerox's cash balance at the end of the current year with last year's balance will show the amount of the increase or decrease. Likewise, Xerox can compare the percentage of cash to current assets at the end of the current year with the percentage in one or more prior years. Intracompany comparisons are useful in detecting changes in financial relationships and significant trends.
2. **Industry averages.** This basis compares an item or financial relationship of a company with **industry averages** (or **norms**) published by financial ratings organizations such as Dun & Bradstreet, Moody's, and Standard & Poor's. For example, Xerox's net income can be compared with the average net income of all companies in the copy-equipment industry. Comparisons with industry averages provide information as to a company's relative performance within the industry.
3. **Intercompany basis.** This basis compares an item or financial relationship of one company with the same item or relationship in **one or more competing companies**. The comparisons are made on the basis of the published financial statements of the individual companies. For example, Xerox's total sales for the year can be compared with the total sales of its major competitors such as Canon or Savin. Intercompany comparisons are useful in determining a company's competitive position.

## Tools of Financial Statement Analysis

Various tools are used to evaluate the significance of financial statement data. Three commonly used tools are these:

**Horizontal analysis** is a technique for evaluating a series of financial statement data over a period of time.

**Vertical analysis** is a technique for evaluating financial statement data that expresses each item in a financial statement in terms of a percent of a base amount.

**Ratio analysis** expresses the relationship among selected items of financial statement data.

Horizontal analysis is used primarily in intracompany comparisons. Two features in published financial statements facilitate this type of comparison: First, each of the basic financial statements is presented on a comparative basis for a minimum of two years. Second, a summary of selected financial data is presented for a series of 5 to 10 years or more. Vertical analysis is used in both intra- and intercompany comparisons. Ratio analysis is used in all three types of comparisons. In the following sections, we will explain and illustrate each of the three types of analysis.

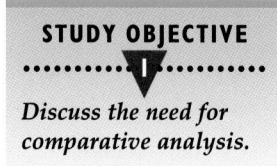

**STUDY OBJECTIVE**
**1**

*Discuss the need for comparative analysis.*

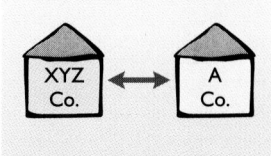

**STUDY OBJECTIVE**
**2**

*Identify the tools of financial statement analysis.*

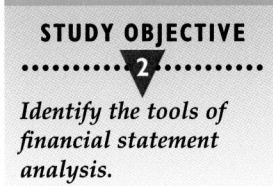

# *H*orizontal Analysis

**STUDY OBJECTIVE**

••••••••••▼3▼••••••••••

*Explain and apply horizontal analysis.*

**Horizontal analysis**, also called **trend analysis**, is a technique for evaluating a series of financial statement data over a period of time. Its purpose is to determine the increase or decrease that has taken place, expressed as either an amount or a percentage. For example, the recent net sales figures of Kellogg Company are as follows:

**Illustration 19-1**

*Kellogg's net sales*

| **KELLOGG COMPANY** (Net Sales Stated in Millions) | | | | |
|---|---|---|---|---|
| 1994 | 1993 | 1992 | 1991 | 1990 |
| $6,562.8 | $6,295.4 | $6,190.6 | $5,786.6 | $5,181.4 |

If we assume that 1990 is the base year, we can measure all percentage increases or decreases from this base period amount as follows:

$$\frac{\text{Current year amount} - \text{Base year amount}}{\text{Base year amount}}$$

For example, we can determine that net sales for Kellogg Company increased approximately 11.7% [($5,786.6 − $5,181.4) ÷ $5,181.4] from 1990 to 1991. Similarly, we can determine that net sales increased over 26.7% [($6,562.8 − $5,181.4) ÷ $5,181.4] from 1990 to 1994. The percentage of the base period for each of the 5 years, assuming 1990 as the base period, is shown in Illustration 19-2.

**Illustration 19-2**

*Horizontal analysis of Kellogg's net sales*

| **KELLOGG COMPANY** (Net Sales Stated in Millions) Base Period 1990 | | | | |
|---|---|---|---|---|
| 1994 | 1993 | 1992 | 1991 | 1990 |
| $6,562.8 | $6,295.4 | $6,190.6 | $5,786.6 | $5,181.4 |
| 127% | 121% | 119% | 112% | 100% |

## Balance Sheet

To further illustrate horizontal analysis, we will use the financial statements of Quality Department Store Inc., a downtown full-line department store in a southeastern city of 55,000 population. Its 2-year condensed balance sheets for 1996 and 1995 showing dollar and percentage changes are presented in Illustration 19-3.

The comparative balance sheet in Illustration 19-3 shows that a number of significant changes have occurred in Quality Department Store's financial structure from 1995 to 1996. In the asset section, plant assets (net) increased $167,500, or 26.5%. In the liabilities section, current liabilities increased $41,500, or 13.7%. In the stockholders' equity section, we find that retained earnings increased $202,600, or 38.6%. This suggests that the company expanded its asset base during 1996 and financed this expansion primarily by retaining income in the business rather than assuming additional long-term debt.

**Illustration 19-3**

*Horizontal analysis of a
balance sheet*

**QUALITY DEPARTMENT STORE INC.**
**Condensed Balance Sheet**
**December 31**

| | 1996 | 1995 | Increase or (Decrease) during 1996 Amount | Increase or (Decrease) during 1996 Percentage |
|---|---|---|---|---|
| **Assets** | | | | |
| Current assets | $1,020,000 | $ 945,000 | $ 75,000 | 7.9% |
| Plant assets (net) | 800,000 | 632,500 | 167,500 | 26.5% |
| Intangible assets | 15,000 | 17,500 | (2,500) | (14.3%) |
| Total assets | $1,835,000 | $1,595,000 | $240,000 | 15.0% |
| **Liabilities** | | | | |
| Current liabilities | $ 344,500 | $ 303,000 | $ 41,500 | 13.7% |
| Long-term liabilities | 487,500 | 497,000 | (9,500) | (1.9%) |
| Total liabilities | 832,000 | 800,000 | 32,000 | 4.0% |
| **Stockholders' Equity** | | | | |
| Common stock, $1 par | 275,400 | 270,000 | 5,400 | 2.0% |
| Retained earnings | 727,600 | 525,000 | 202,600 | 38.6% |
| Total stockholders' equity | 1,003,000 | 795,000 | 208,000 | 26.2% |
| Total liabilities and stockholders' equity | $1,835,000 | $1,595,000 | $240,000 | 15.0% |

**Helpful hint**  It is difficult to comprehend the significance of a change when only the dollar amount of change is examined. When the change is expressed in percentage form, it is easier to grasp the true magnitude of the change.

## Income Statement

Presented in Illustration 19-4 is a 2-year comparative income statement of Quality Department Store Inc. for the years 1996 and 1995 in a condensed format.

**Illustration 19-4**

*Horizontal analysis of an
income statement*

**QUALITY DEPARTMENT STORE INC.**
**Condensed Income Statement**
**For the Years Ended December 31**

| | 1996 | 1995 | Increase or (Decrease) during 1996 Amount | Increase or (Decrease) during 1996 Percentage |
|---|---|---|---|---|
| Sales | $2,195,000 | $1,960,000 | $235,000 | 12.0% |
| Sales returns and allowances | 98,000 | 123,000 | (25,000) | (20.3%) |
| Net sales | 2,097,000 | 1,837,000 | 260,000 | 14.2% |
| Cost of goods sold | 1,281,000 | 1,140,000 | 141,000 | 12.4% |
| Gross profit | 816,000 | 697,000 | 119,000 | 17.1% |
| Selling expenses | 253,000 | 211,500 | 41,500 | 19.6% |
| Administrative expenses | 104,000 | 108,500 | (4,500) | (4.1%) |
| Total operating expenses | 357,000 | 320,000 | 37,000 | 11.6% |
| Income from operations | 459,000 | 377,000 | 82,000 | 21.8% |
| Other revenues and gains Interest and dividends | 9,000 | 11,000 | (2,000) | (18.2%) |
| Other expenses and losses Interest expense | 36,000 | 40,500 | (4,500) | (11.1%) |
| Income before income taxes | 432,000 | 347,500 | 84,500 | 24.3% |
| Income tax expense | 168,200 | 139,000 | 29,200 | 21.0% |
| Net income | $ 263,800 | $ 208,500 | $ 55,300 | 26.5% |

**Helpful hint**  Note that while the amount column is additive (the total is $55,300), the percentage column is not additive (the total is not 26.5%). A separate percentage has been calculated for each item.

Horizontal analysis of the income statements shows the following changes:

1. Net sales increased $260,000, or 14.2% ($260,000 ÷ $1,837,000).
2. Cost of goods sold increased $141,000, or 12.4% ($141,000 ÷ $1,140,000).
3. Total operating expenses increased $37,000, or 11.6% ($37,000 ÷ $320,000).

Overall, gross profit and net income were up substantially. Gross profit, for example, increased 17.1% and net income 26.5%. It appears, therefore, that Quality's profit trend is favorable.

## Retained Earnings Statement

Quality Department Store's comparative retained earnings statement for the years 1996 and 1995 is presented in Illustration 19-5. Analyzed horizontally, net income increased $55,300, or 26.5%, whereas dividends on the common stock increased only $1,200, or 2%. Ending retained earnings, as shown in the horizontal analysis of the balance sheet, increased 38.6%. As indicated earlier, Quality Department Store Inc. retained a significant portion of its net income to finance expenditures for additional plant facilities.

**Illustration 19-5**

*Horizontal analysis of a retained earnings statement*

**QUALITY DEPARTMENT STORE INC.**
**Retained Earnings Statement**
**For the Years Ended December 31**

| | 1996 | 1995 | Increase or (Decrease) during 1996 Amount | Percentage |
|---|---|---|---|---|
| Retained earnings, Jan. 1 | $525,000 | $376,500 | $148,500 | 39.4% |
| Add: Net income | 263,800 | 208,500 | 55,300 | 26.5% |
| | 788,800 | 585,000 | 203,800 | |
| Deduct: Dividends | 61,200 | 60,000 | 1,200 | 2.0% |
| Retained earnings, Dec. 31 | $727,600 | $525,000 | $202,600 | 38.6% |

The measurement of changes from period to period in terms of percentages is relatively straightforward and is quite useful. However, complications can result in making the computations. For example, if an item has no value in a base year or preceding year and a value in the next year, no percentage change can be computed. Similarly, if a negative amount appears in the base or preceding period and a positive amount exists the following year, or vice versa, no percentage change can be computed.

# Vertical Analysis

**STUDY OBJECTIVE**

**▼ 4**

*Describe and apply vertical analysis.*

Vertical analysis, sometimes referred to as **common size analysis**, is a technique for evaluating financial statement data that expresses each item within a financial statement in terms of a percent of a base amount. For example, on a balance sheet we might say that current assets are 22% of total assets (total assets being the base amount). Or on an income statement, we might say that selling expenses are 16% of net sales (net sales being the base amount).

## Balance Sheet

Presented in Illustration 19-6 is the comparative balance sheet of Quality Department Store Inc. for 1996 and 1995, analyzed vertically. The base for the asset items is **total assets**, and the base for the liability and stockholders' equity items is **total liabilities and stockholders' equity**.

**Illustration 19-6**

*Vertical analysis of a balance sheet*

### QUALITY DEPARTMENT STORE INC.
### Condensed Balance Sheet
### December 31

| | 1996 Amount | 1996 Percent | 1995 Amount | 1995 Percent |
|---|---|---|---|---|
| **Assets** | | | | |
| Current assets | $1,020,000 | 55.6% | $ 945,000 | 59.2% |
| Plant assets (net) | 800,000 | 43.6% | 632,500 | 39.7% |
| Intangible assets | 15,000 | .8% | 17,500 | 1.1% |
| Total assets | $1,835,000 | 100.0% | $1,595,000 | 100.0% |
| **Liabilities** | | | | |
| Current liabilities | $ 344,500 | 18.8% | $ 303,000 | 19.0% |
| Long-term liabilities | 487,500 | 26.5% | 497,000 | 31.2% |
| Total liabilities | 832,000 | 45.3% | 800,000 | 50.2% |
| **Stockholders' Equity** | | | | |
| Common stock, $1 par | 275,400 | 15.0% | 270,000 | 16.9% |
| Retained earnings | 727,600 | 39.7% | 525,000 | 32.9% |
| Total stockholders' equity | 1,003,000 | 54.7% | 795,000 | 49.8% |
| Total liabilities and stockholders' equity | $1,835,000 | 100.0% | $1,595,000 | 100.0% |

**Helpful hint** The formula for calculating these balance sheet percentages is:

$$\frac{\text{Each item on B/S}}{\text{Total assets}} = \%$$

In addition to showing the relative size of each category on the balance sheet, vertical analysis may show the **percentage change** in the individual asset, liability, and stockholders' equity items. In this case, even though current assets increased $75,000 from 1995 to 1996, they decreased from 59.2% to 55.6% of total assets. Plant assets (net) have increased from 39.7% to 43.6% of total assets, and retained earnings have increased from 32.9% to 39.7% of total liabilities and stockholders' equity. These results reinforce the earlier observations that Quality is choosing to finance its growth through retention of earnings rather than through the issuance of additional debt.

## Income Statement

Vertical analysis of the comparative income statements of Quality, shown in Illustration 19-7, reveals that cost of goods sold as a percentage of net sales declined 1% (62.1% vs. 61.1%) and total operating expenses declined 0.4% (17.4% vs. 17.0%). As a result, it is not surprising to see net income as a percent of net sales increase from 11.4% to 12.6%. As indicated from the horizontal analysis, Quality appears to be a profitable enterprise that is becoming even more successful.

Illustration 19-7

*Vertical analysis of an income statement*

**QUALITY DEPARTMENT STORE INC.**
**Condensed Income Statement**
**For the Years Ended December 31**

| | 1996 | | 1995 | |
|---|---|---|---|---|
| | Amount | Percent | Amount | Percent |
| Sales | $2,195,000 | 104.7% | $1,960,000 | 106.7% |
| Sales returns and allowances | 98,000 | 4.7% | 123,000 | 6.7% |
| Net sales | 2,097,000 | 100.0% | 1,837,000 | 100.0% |
| Cost of goods sold | 1,281,000 | 61.1% | 1,140,000 | 62.1% |
| Gross profit | 816,000 | 38.9% | 697,000 | 37.9% |
| Selling expenses | 253,000 | 12.0% | 211,500 | 11.5% |
| Administrative expenses | 104,000 | 5.0% | 108,500 | 5.9% |
| Total operating expenses | 357,000 | 17.0% | 320,000 | 17.4% |
| Income from operations | 459,000 | 21.9% | 377,000 | 20.5% |
| Other revenues and gains | | | | |
| Interest and dividends | 9,000 | 0.4% | 11,000 | 0.6% |
| Other expenses and losses | | | | |
| Interest expense | 36,000 | 1.7% | 40,500 | 2.2% |
| Income before income taxes | 432,000 | 20.6% | 347,500 | 18.9% |
| Income tax expense | 168,200 | 8.0% | 139,000 | 7.5% |
| Net income | $ 263,800 | 12.6% | $ 208,500 | 11.4% |

**Helpful hint** The formula for calculating these income statement percentages is:

$$\frac{\text{Each item on Inc. St.}}{\text{Net sales}} = \%$$

An associated benefit of vertical analysis is that it enables you to compare companies of different sizes. For example, Quality's main competitor is a J.C. Penney store in a nearby town. Using vertical analysis, the condensed income statements of the small local retail enterprise, Quality Department Store Inc., can be more meaningfully compared with the income statement of a giant international retailer, J.C. Penney Company, as shown in Illustration 19-8.

Illustration 19-8

*Intercompany income statement comparison*

**CONDENSED INCOME STATEMENTS**

| (in thousands) | Quality Department Store Inc. | | J.C. Penney Company | |
|---|---|---|---|---|
| | Dollars | Percent | Dollars | Percent |
| Net sales | $2,097 | 100.0% | $20,380,000 | 100.0% |
| Cost of goods sold | 1,281 | 61.1% | 13,970,000 | 68.5% |
| Gross profit | 816 | 38.9% | 6,410,000 | 31.5% |
| Selling and administrative expenses | 357 | 17.0% | 4,783,000 | 23.5% |
| Income from operations | 459 | 21.9% | 1,627,000 | 8.0% |
| Other expenses and revenues | | | | |
| (including income taxes) | 195 | 9.3% | 570,000 | 2.8% |
| Net income | $ 264 | 12.6% | $ 1,057,000 | 5.2% |

Although J.C. Penney's net sales are 9,719 times greater than the net sales of relatively tiny Quality Department Store, vertical analysis eliminates this difference in size. The percentages show that Quality's and Penney's gross profit rates were somewhat comparable at 38.9% and 31.5%, although the percentages related to income from operations were significantly different at 21.9% and 8.0%. This disparity can be attributed to Quality's selling and administrative expense percentage (17%) which is much lower than Penney's (23.5%). Although Penney earned net income more than 4,000 times larger than Quality's, Penney's net income as a **percent of each sales dollar** (5.2%) is only 41% of Quality's (12.6%).

## Before You Go On . . .

### ► Review It

1. What are the different tools that might be used to compare financial information?
2. What is horizontal analysis?
3. What is vertical analysis?

### ► Do It

Summary financial information for Rosepatch Company is as follows:

|  | December 31, 1996 | December 31, 1995 |
|---|---|---|
| Current assets | $234,000 | $180,000 |
| Plant assets (net) | 756,000 | 420,000 |
| Total assets | $990,000 | $600,000 |

Compute the amount and percentage changes in 1996 using horizontal analysis, assuming 1995 is the base year.

**Reasoning:** Since 1995 is the base year, the percentage change is found by dividing the amount of the increase by the 1995 amount.

**Solution:**

| | Increase in 1996 | |
|---|---|---|
| | **Amount** | **Percentage** |
| Current assets | $ 54,000 | 30% [($234,000 − $180,000) ÷ $180,000] |
| Plant assets (net) | 336,000 | 80% [($756,000 − $420,000) ÷ $420,000] |
| Total assets | $390,000 | 65% [($990,000 − $600,000) ÷ $600,000] |

*Related exercise material:* BE19–1, BE19–3, BE19–4, BE19–6, E19–1, E19–3, and E19–4.

# Ratio Analysis
. . . . . . . . . . . . . . . . . . . . . . . . . . . . . . . . . . . . . . . . . . . . . . . . . . . . . . . . . . . .

Ratio analysis expresses the relationship among selected items of financial statement data. A ratio expresses the mathematical relationship between one quantity and another. The relationship is expressed in terms of either a percentage, a rate, or a simple proportion. To illustrate, recently IBM Corporation had current assets of $41,338 million and current liabilities of $29,226 million. The relationship is determined by dividing current assets by current liabilities. The alternative means of expression are:

**Percentage:** Current assets are 141% of current liabilities.
**Rate:** Current assets are 1.41 times greater than current liabilities.
**Proportion:** The relationship of current assets to liabilities is 1.41:1.

**STUDY OBJECTIVE**
. . . . . . . . . **5** . . . . . . . . . .

*Identify and compute ratios and describe their purpose and use in analyzing a firm's liquidity, profitability, and solvency.*

**Helpful hint** Each of these is illustrated in the following sections.

## ▶Technology in Action

Many general ledger accounting programs include the generation of financial ratios as routine output. All the ratio computations presented in this chapter can be done with electronic spreadsheets as well. There are also many programs written specifically for financial statement analysis. These packages are written for both general purpose use and use in specific industries. For example, financial institutions routinely use over 60 ratios geared specifically to the banking industry.

For analysis of the primary financial statements, ratios can be classified as follows:

**Illustration 19-9**

*Financial ratio classifications*

**Liquidity Ratios**

Measures of short-term ability of the enterprise to pay its maturing obligations and to meet unexpected needs for cash

**Profitability Ratios**

Measures of the income or operating success of an enterprise for a given period of time

**Solvency Ratios**

Measures of the ability of the enterprise to survive over a long period of time

Ratios can provide clues to underlying conditions that may not be apparent from inspection of the individual components of a particular ratio. However, a single ratio by itself is not very meaningful. Accordingly, in the following discussion we will use:

1. **Intracompany comparisons** covering 2 years for the Quality Department Store.
2. **Industry average comparisons** based on Dun & Bradstreet's median ratios for department stores and Robert Morris Associates' median ratios for department stores.
3. **Intercompany comparisons** based on the J.C. Penney Company, Inc. as Quality Department Store's principal competitor.

## Liquidity Ratios

Liquidity ratios measure the short-term ability of the enterprise to pay its maturing obligations and to meet unexpected needs for cash. Short-term creditors such as bankers and suppliers are particularly interested in assessing **liquidity**. The ratios that can be used to determine the enterprise's short-term debt-paying ability are the current ratio, the acid-test ratio, receivables turnover, and inventory turnover.

## 1. Current Ratio

The current ratio is a widely used measure for evaluating a company's liquidity and short-term debt-paying ability. The ratio is computed by dividing current assets by current liabilities. It is sometimes referred to as the **working capital ratio** because **working capital** is the excess of current assets over current liabilities. The current ratio is a more dependable indicator of liquidity than working capital. Two companies with the same amount of working capital may have significantly different current ratios. The 1996 and 1995 current ratios for Quality Department Store and comparative data are shown in Illustration 19-10.

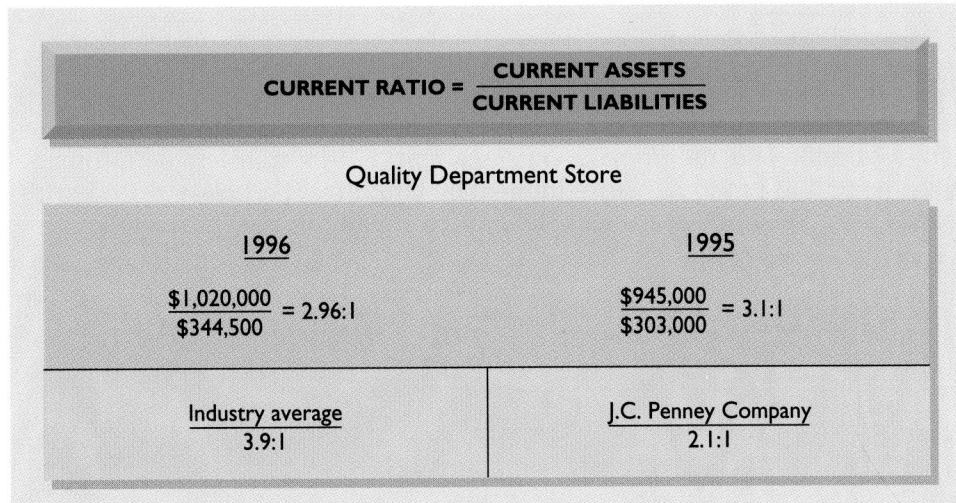

**Illustration 19-10**

*Current ratio*

What does the ratio actually mean? The 1996 ratio of 2.96:1 means that for every dollar of current liabilities, Quality has $2.96 of current assets. Quality's current ratio has decreased in the current year. However, compared to the industry average of 3.9:1, and J.C. Penney Company's 2.1:1 current ratio, Quality appears to be reasonably liquid.

The current ratio is only one measure of liquidity. It does not take into account the composition of the current assets. For example, a satisfactory current ratio does not disclose the fact that a portion of the current assets may be tied up in slow-moving inventory. A dollar of cash is more readily available to pay the bills than is a dollar of slow-moving inventory.

## 2. Acid-Test Ratio

The acid-test ratio is a measure of a company's immediate short-term liquidity, computed by dividing the sum of cash, marketable securities, and net receivables by current liabilities. Thus, it is an important complement to the current ratio. For example, assume that the current assets of Quality Department Store for 1996 and 1995 consist of the following items:

|  | 1996 | 1995 |
|---|---|---|
| Current assets |  |  |
| Cash | $ 100,000 | $155,000 |
| Marketable securities | 20,000 | 70,000 |
| Receivables (net) | 230,000 | 180,000 |
| Inventory | 620,000 | 500,000 |
| Prepaid expenses | 50,000 | 40,000 |
| Total current assets | $1,020,000 | $945,000 |

**Illustration 19-11**

*Current assets of Quality Department Store*

## ▶Accounting in Action ▶ *Business Insight*

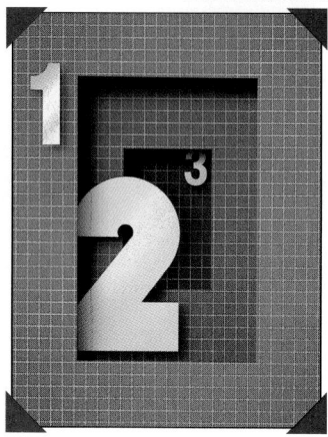

The apparent simplicity of the current ratio can have real world limitations because an addition of equal amounts to both the numerator and the denominator causes the ratio to decrease. Assume, for example, that a company has $2,000,000 of current assets and $1,000,000 of current liabilities; its current ratio is 2:1. If it purchases $1,000,000 of inventory on account, it will have $3,000,000 of current assets and $2,000,000 of current liabilities; its current ratio will decrease to 1.5:1. If, instead, the company pays off $500,000 of its current liabilities, it will have $1,500,000 of current assets and $500,000 of current liabilities, and its current ratio will increase to 3:1. Thus, any trend analysis should be done with care, since the ratio is susceptible to quick changes and is easily influenced by management.

Cash, marketable securities (short-term), and receivables (net) are highly liquid compared to inventory and prepaid expenses. The inventory may not be readily saleable and the prepaid expenses may not be transferable to others. Thus, the acid-test ratio measures **immediate** liquidity. The 1996 and 1995 acid-test ratios for Quality Department Store and comparative data are as follows:

**Illustration 19-12**

*Acid-test ratio*

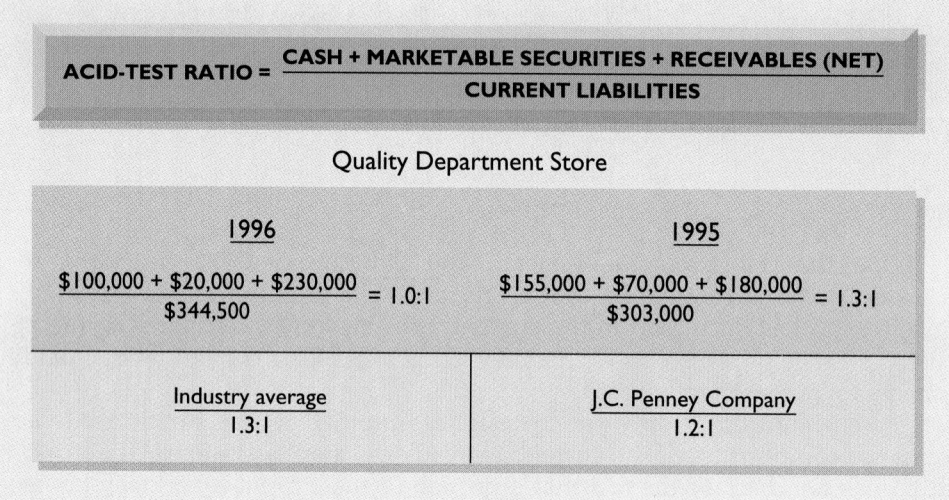

Is an acid-test ratio of 1.0:1 adequate? The ratio has declined in 1996. However, when compared with the industry median of 1.3:1 and J.C. Penney's 1.2:1, Quality's acid-test ratio seems adequate.

### 3. Receivables Turnover

Liquidity may be measured by how quickly certain assets can be converted to cash. How liquid, for example, are the receivables? The ratio used to assess the liquidity of the receivables is the receivables turnover ratio. This ratio measures the number of times, on average, receivables are collected during the period. The receivables turnover ratio is computed by dividing net credit sales (net sales less cash sales) by the average net receivables during the year. Unless seasonal factors are significant, average net receivables outstanding can be computed from the beginning and ending balance of the net receivables.[1]

---

[1]If seasonal factors are significant, the average receivables balance might be determined by using monthly amounts.

Assuming that all sales are credit sales and the balance of accounts receivable (net) at the beginning of 1995 is $200,000, the receivables turnover ratio for Quality Department Store and comparative data are shown in Illustration 19-13. Quality's receivables turnover improved in 1996. The turnover of 10.2 times compares quite favorably with J.C. Penney's 4.1 times and the department store industry's median of 7.0 times.

**Illustration 19-13**

*Receivables turnover*

## ►Accounting in Action ► *Business Insight*

In some cases, receivable turnover may be misleading. Some companies, especially large retail chains, encourage credit and revolving charge sales, and they slow collections in order to earn a healthy return on the outstanding receivables in the form of interest at rates of 18% to 22%. This may explain why J.C. Penney's turnover is only 4.1 times. In general, however, the faster the turnover, the greater the reliance that can be placed on the current and acid-test ratios for assessing liquidity.

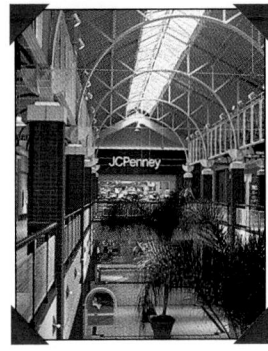

A popular variant of the receivables turnover ratio is to convert it into an **average collection period** in terms of days. This is done by dividing the turnover ratio into 365 days. For example, the receivable turnover in 1996 of 10.2 times is divided into 365 days to obtain approximately 35.8 days. This means that the average collection period for receivables is 36 days, or approximately every 5 weeks. The average collection period is frequently used to assess the effectiveness of a company's credit and collection policies. The general rule is that the collection period should not greatly exceed the credit term period (i.e., the time allowed for payment).

### 4. *Inventory Turnover*

The inventory turnover ratio measures the number of times on average the inventory is sold during the period. Its purpose is to measure the liquidity of the inventory. The inventory turnover is computed by dividing cost of goods sold by the average inventory during the period. Unless seasonal factors are significant, average inventory can be computed from the beginning and ending inventory balances. Assuming that the inventory balance for Quality Department Store at the beginning of 1995 was $450,000, its inventory turnover and comparative data are as shown in Illustration 19-14. Quality's inventory turnover declined slightly in 1996. The turnover ratio of 2.3 times is relatively low compared with the industry average of 3.4 and J.C. Penney's 3.8. Generally, the faster the inventory turnover, the less cash that is tied up in inventory and the less the chance of inventory obsolescence.

**Illustration 19-14**

*Inventory turnover*

$$\text{INVENTORY TURNOVER} = \frac{\text{COST OF GOODS SOLD}}{\text{AVERAGE INVENTORY}}$$

Quality Department Store

| 1996 | 1995 |
|------|------|
| $\dfrac{\$1,281,000}{\left[\dfrac{\$500,000 + \$620,000}{2}\right]} = 2.3$ times | $\dfrac{\$1,140,000}{\left[\dfrac{\$450,000 + \$500,000}{2}\right]} = 2.4$ times |
| Industry average<br>3.4 times | J.C. Penney Company<br>3.8 times |

A variant of the inventory turnover ratio is to compute the **average days to sell the inventory**. For example, the inventory turnover in 1996 of 2.3 times divided into 365 is approximately 159 days. An average selling time of 159 days is also relatively high compared with the industry average of 107 days (365 ÷ 3.4) and J.C. Penney Company's 96 days (365 ÷ 3.8).

## ▶Accounting in Action ▸ *Business Insight*

Inventory turnover ratios vary considerably among industries. For example, grocery store chains have a turnover of 10 times and an average selling period of 37 days. In contrast, jewelry stores have an average turnover of 1.3 times and an average selling period of 281 days. Within a company there may be significant differences in inventory turnover among different types of products. Thus, in a grocery store the turnover of perishable items such as produce, meats, and dairy products will be faster than the turnover of soaps and detergents.

## Profitability Ratios

Profitability ratios measure the income or operating success of an enterprise for a given period of time. Income, or the lack of it, affects the company's ability to obtain debt and equity financing, the company's liquidity position, and the company's ability to grow. As a consequence, creditors and investors alike are interested in evaluating earning power (profitability). Profitability is frequently used as the ultimate test of management's operating effectiveness.

### 5. Profit Margin

The profit margin ratio is a measure of the percentage of each dollar of sales that results in net income. It is computed by dividing net income by net sales for the period. Quality Department Store's profit margin ratios and comparative data are shown in Illustration 19-15.

**Illustration 19-15**

*Profit margin ratio*

**PROFIT MARGIN ON SALES** = $\dfrac{\text{NET INCOME}}{\text{NET SALES}}$

Quality Department Store

| 1996 | 1995 |
|---|---|
| $\dfrac{\$263,800}{\$2,097,000}$ = 12.6% | $\dfrac{\$208,500}{\$1,837,000}$ = 11.4% |
| Industry average<br>3.6% | J.C. Penney Company<br>5.2% |

Quality experienced an increase in its profit margin from 1995 to 1996. Its profit margin is unusually high in comparison with the industry average of 3.6% and J.C. Penney Company's 5.2%.

High-volume (high inventory turnover) enterprises such as grocery stores (Safeway or Kroger) and discount stores (Kmart or Wal-Mart) generally experience low profit margins, whereas low-volume enterprises such as jewelry stores (Tiffany & Co.) or airplane manufacturers (Boeing Aircraft) have high profit margins.

## 6. Asset Turnover

The asset turnover ratio measures how efficiently a company uses its assets to generate sales. It is determined by dividing net sales by average assets for the period. The resulting number shows the dollars of sales produced by each dollar invested in assets. Unless seasonal factors are significant, average total assets can be computed from the beginning and ending balance of total assets. Assuming that the total assets at the beginning of 1995 were $1,446,000, the 1996 and 1995 asset turnover ratios for Quality Department Store and comparative data are as follows:

**Illustration 19-16**

*Asset turnover*

**ASSET TURNOVER** = $\dfrac{\text{NET SALES}}{\text{AVERAGE ASSETS}}$

Quality Department Store

| 1996 | 1995 |
|---|---|
| $\dfrac{\$2,097,000}{\left[\dfrac{\$1,595,000 + \$1,835,000}{2}\right]}$ = 1.2 times | $\dfrac{\$1,837,000}{\left[\dfrac{\$1,446,000 + \$1,595,000}{2}\right]}$ = 1.2 times |
| Industry average<br>2.2 times | J.C. Penney Company<br>1.3 times |

The asset turnover ratio shows that Quality generated sales of $1.22 in 1996 for each dollar it had invested in assets. The ratio changed little from 1995 to 1996. Quality's asset turnover ratio is below the industry median of 2.2 times and J.C. Penney's ratio of 1.3 times.

Asset turnover ratios vary considerably among industries. For example, a large utility company like Union Electric Company (St. Louis) has a ratio of 0.36 times, and the large grocery chain Great Atlantic and Pacific Tea (A&P) has a ratio of 3.6 times.

### 7. Return on Assets Ratio

An overall measure of profitability is the return on assets ratio. This ratio is computed by dividing net income by average assets. The 1996 and 1995 return on assets for Quality Department Store and comparative data are shown below.

**Illustration 19-17**

*Return on assets*

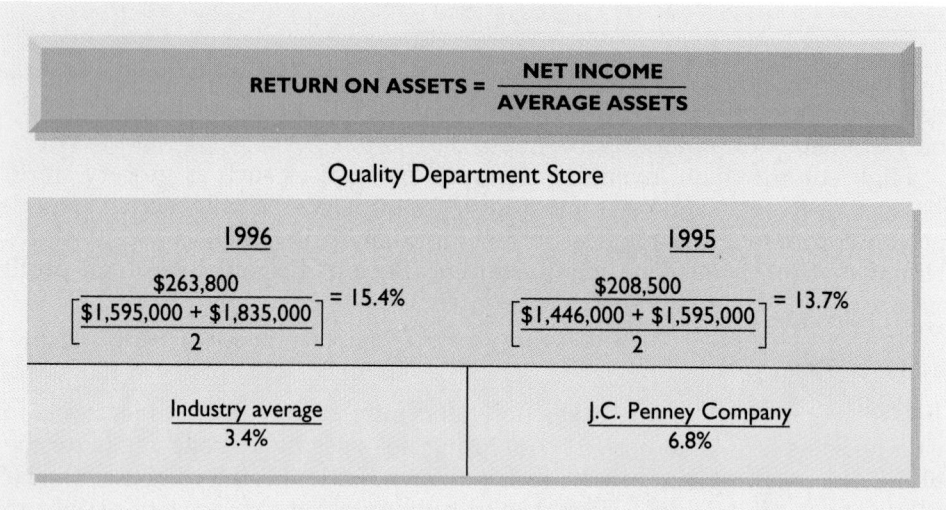

Quality's return on assets improved from 1995 to 1996. Its return of 15.4% is very high, compared with the department store industry median of 3.4% and J.C. Penney Company's 6.8%.

### 8. Return on Common Stockholders' Equity

Another widely used ratio that measures profitability from the common stockholder's viewpoint is return on common stockholders' equity. This ratio shows how many dollars of net income were earned for each dollar invested by the owners. It is computed by dividing net income by average common stockholders' equity. Assuming that common stockholders' equity at the beginning of 1995 was $667,000, the 1996 and 1995 ratios for Quality Department Store and comparative data are shown in Illustration 19-18.

Quality's rate of return on common stockholders' equity is unusually high at 29.3%, considering an industry average of 12.9% and a rate of 19.3% for J.C. Penney Company.

When preferred stock is present, **preferred dividend** requirements are deducted from net income to compute income available to common stockholders. Similarly, the par value of preferred stock (or call price, if applicable) must be

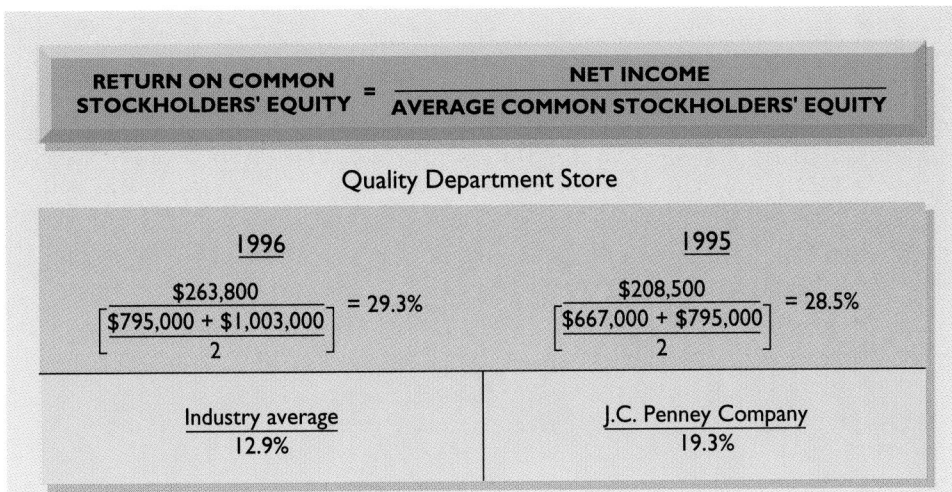

**Illustration 19-18**

*Return on common stock-holders' equity*

deducted from total stockholders' equity to arrive at the amount of common stock equity used in this ratio. The ratio then appears as follows:

$$\text{Rate of return on common stockholders' equity} = \frac{\text{Net income} - \text{Preferred dividends}}{\text{Average common stockholders' equity}}$$

Note that Quality's rate of return on stockholders' equity (29.3%) is substantially higher than its rate of return on assets (15.38%). The reason is that Quality has made effective use of leverage or trading on the equity at a gain. Trading on the equity at a gain means that the company has borrowed money through the issuance of bonds or notes at a lower rate of interest than it is able to earn by using the borrowed money. Leverage is simply trying to use money supplied by nonowners to increase the return to the owners. A comparison of the rate of return on total assets with the rate of interest paid for borrowed money indicates the profitability of trading on the equity. Note that trading on the equity is a two-way street: for example, if you borrow money at 11% and earn only 8% on it, you are trading on the equity at a loss. Quality Department Store earns more on its borrowed funds than it has to pay in the form of interest. Thus the return to stockholders exceeds the return on the assets, benefiting from the positive leveraging.

### 9. Earnings Per Share (EPS)

Earnings per share of stock is a measure of the net income earned on each share of common stock. As explained in Chapter 15, it is computed by dividing net income by the number of weighted average common shares outstanding during the year. Stockholders usually think in terms of the number of shares they own or plan to buy or sell. Reducing net income earned to a per share basis provides a useful perspective for determining profitability. Assuming that there is no change in the number of outstanding shares during 1995 and that the 1996 increase occurred midyear, the net income per share for Quality Department Store for 1996 and 1995 is computed as shown in Illustration 19-20.

Note that no industry or J.C. Penney data are presented. Such comparisons are not meaningful because of the wide variations in the number of shares of

**Illustration 19-20**

*Earnings per share*

outstanding stock among companies. Quality's earnings per share increased 20 cents per share in 1996. This represents a 26% increase over the 1995 earnings per share of 77 cents.

When the term "net income per share" or "earnings per share" is used, it refers to the amount of net income applicable to each share of **common stock**. Therefore, in computing net income per share, if there are preferred dividends declared for the period, they must be deducted from net income to arrive at income available to the common stockholders.

### 10. Price-Earnings Ratio

The price-earnings ratio is an oft-quoted statistic that measures the ratio of the market price of each share of common stock to the earnings per share. The price-earnings (PE) ratio reflects investors' assessments of a company's future earnings. It is computed by dividing the market price per share of the stock by earnings per share. Assuming that the market price of Quality Department Store Inc. stock is $8 in 1995 and $12 in 1996, the price-earnings ratio is computed as follows:

**Illustration 19-21**

*Price-earnings ratio*

In 1996 each share of Quality's stock sold for 12.4 times the amount that was earned on each share. Quality's price-earnings ratio is less than the industry average of 13 times, and it is significantly lower than the ratio of 23 for J.C. Penney Company. The average price-earnings ratio for the stocks that constitute the Dow-Jones industrial average on the New York Stock Exchange in May 1995 was an unusually high 22 times.

## ▶Accounting in Action ▸ *Business Insight*

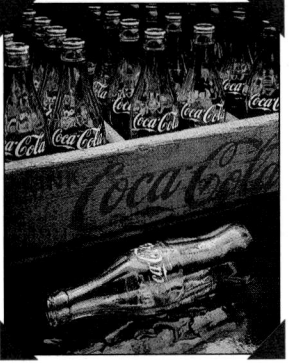

For the stock of some companies, investors are willing to pay over 20 times the current per-share earnings because they feel the future growth in earnings will provide an adequate return on the investment. Examples of companies with price-earnings ratios over 20 are UAL Inc. (38), Coca-Cola (30), and Gillette Co. (26). Examples of companies with low price-earnings ratios are Ford Motor (5), General Motors (7), and Chase Manhattan Bank (8).

### 11. Payout Ratio

The payout ratio measures the percentage of earnings distributed in the form of cash dividends. It is computed by dividing cash dividends by net income. Companies that have high growth rates are characterized by low payout ratios because they reinvest most of their net income into the business. The 1996 and 1995 payout ratios for Quality Department Store are computed as follows:

$$\text{PAYOUT RATIO} = \frac{\text{CASH DIVIDENDS}}{\text{NET INCOME}}$$

Quality Department Store

| 1996 | 1995 |
|---|---|
| $\dfrac{\$61,200}{\$263,800} = 23.2\%$ | $\dfrac{\$60,000}{\$208,500} = 28.8\%$ |
| Industry average | J.C. Penney Company |
| N/A | 39.8% |

**Illustration 19-22**

*Payout ratio*

Quality's payout ratio is comparatively low when compared with J.C. Penney's payout ratio of 39.8%. As indicated earlier, the company has apparently decided to fund its purchase of plant assets through retention of earnings.

## ▶Accounting in Action ▸ *Business Insight*

Many companies with stable earnings have high payout ratios. For example, Pennsylvania Power & Light has had an 86% payout ratio over the last 5 years, and Woolworth Corporation's dividends exceeded net income over the same period. Conversely, companies that are expanding rapidly, such as Toys 'R' Us, Microsoft, and Telecommunications Inc. have never paid a cash dividend.

### Solvency Ratios

Solvency ratios measure the ability of the enterprise to survive over a long period of time. Long-term creditors and stockholders are interested in a company's long-run solvency, particularly its ability to pay interest as it comes due and to repay the face value of the debt at maturity. Debt to total assets and times interest earned are two ratios that provide information about debt-paying ability.

## 12. Debt to Total Assets Ratio

**Helpful hint** A variation of this ratio is the **equity to debt ratio**. This is the ratio used by the University of Chicago in the opening vignette. It is computed by dividing total stockholders' equity by total liabilities. The higher this ratio, the more protection creditors have in a period of financial distress.

The debt to total assets ratio measures the percentage of the total assets provided by creditors (this ratio indicates the degree of leveraging). It is computed by dividing total debt (both current and long-term liabilities) by total assets. This ratio provides some indication of the company's ability to withstand losses without impairing the interests of creditors. The higher the percentage of debt to total assets, the greater the risk that the company may be unable to meet its maturing obligations. The 1996 and 1995 ratios for Quality Department Store and comparative data are as follows:

**Illustration 19-23**

*Debt to total assets*

A ratio of 45.3% means that creditors have provided 45.3% of Quality Department Store's total assets. Quality's 45.3% is above the industry average of 38%, but it is considerably below the 65.3% ratio of J.C. Penney Company. The lower the ratio, the more equity "buffer" there is available to the creditors if the company becomes insolvent. Thus, from the creditors' point of view, a low ratio of debt to total assets is usually desirable.

The adequacy of this ratio is often judged in the light of the company's earnings. Generally, companies with relatively stable earnings, such as public utilities, have higher debt to total assets ratios than cyclical companies with widely fluctuating earnings, such as many high-tech companies. (See Accounting in Action on the next page for examples of debt to total assets ratios for selected companies.)

## 13. Times Interest Earned Ratio

The times interest earned ratio provides an indication of the company's ability to meet interest payments as they come due. It is computed by dividing income before interest expense and income taxes by interest expense. The 1996 and 1995 ratios for Quality Department Store and comparative data are shown in Illustration 19-24. Note that the times interest earned ratio uses income before income taxes and interest expense, because this amount represents the amount available to cover interest. For Quality Department Store the 1996 amount of $468,000 is

## ►**A**ccounting in **A**ction ► *Business Insight*

Examples of debt to total assets ratios for selected companies are:

|  | **Total Debt to Total Assets As a Percent** |
|---|---|
| Advanced Micro Devices | 29% |
| General Motors Corporation | 93% |
| Roberts Pharmaceutical | 23% |
| Callaway Golf Company | 19% |
| Sears Roebuck & Company | 64% |
| Eastman Kodak Company | 83% |

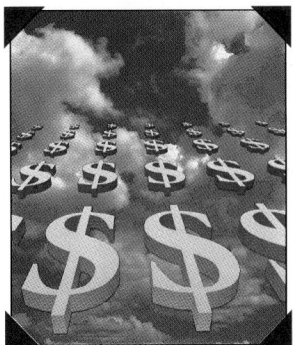

Another means used in practice to measure this same leverage phenomenon is the "debt to equity ratio." It shows the relative use of borrowed funds (total liabilities) as compared to resources invested by the owners. Because this ratio may be computed in several ways, care should be taken when making comparisons. Debt may be defined to include only the noncurrent portion of the liabilities, and intangible assets may be excluded from owner's equity (resulting in tangible net worth).

---

computed by taking the income before income taxes of $432,000 and adding back the $36,000 of interest expense. The interest expense of Quality is well covered at 13 times relative to the industry average of 2.7 times and J.C. Penney Company's 4.7 times.

**Illustration 19-24**

*Times interest earned*

$$\text{TIMES INTEREST EARNED} = \frac{\text{INCOME BEFORE INCOME TAXES AND INTEREST EXPENSE}}{\text{INTEREST EXPENSE}}$$

Quality Department Store

| 1996 | 1995 |
|---|---|
| $\frac{\$468,000}{\$36,000} = 13\text{ times}$ | $\frac{\$388,000}{\$40,500} = 9.6\text{ times}$ |
| Industry average 2.7 times | J.C. Penney Company 4.7 times |

## ►**T**echnology in **A**ction

In terms of the types of financial information that are available and the ratios used by various industries, you should be aware that what can be practically covered in this textbook gives you only the "Titanic approach." That is, you are seeing only the tip of the iceberg compared to the vast data bases and different types of ratio analysis that are available on computers. The availability of information is not a problem. The real trick is to be discriminating enough to perform relevant analysis and to select pertinent comparative data.

## Summary of Ratios

**Illustration 19-25**

*Summary of liquidity, profitability, and solvency ratios*

A summary of the ratios discussed in the chapter is presented in Illustration 19-25. The summary includes the formula and purpose or use of each ratio.

| Ratio | Formula | Purpose or Use |
|---|---|---|
| **Liquidity Ratios** | | |
| 1. Current ratio | $\dfrac{\text{Current assets}}{\text{Current liabilities}}$ | Measures short-term debt-paying ability. |
| 2. Acid-test or quick ratio | $\dfrac{\text{Cash + marketable securities + receivables (net)}}{\text{Current liabilities}}$ | Measures immediate short-term liquidity. |
| 3. Receivables turnover | $\dfrac{\text{Net credit sales}}{\text{Average net receivables}}$ | Measures liquidity of receivables. |
| 4. Inventory turnover | $\dfrac{\text{Cost of goods sold}}{\text{Average inventory}}$ | Measures liquidity of inventory. |
| **Profitability Ratios** | | |
| 5. Profit margin | $\dfrac{\text{Net income}}{\text{Net sales}}$ | Measures net income generated by each dollar of sales. |
| 6. Asset turnover | $\dfrac{\text{Net sales}}{\text{Average assets}}$ | Measures how efficiently assets are used to generate sales. |
| 7. Return on assets | $\dfrac{\text{Net income}}{\text{Average assets}}$ | Measures overall profitability of assets. |
| 8. Return on common stockholders' equity | $\dfrac{\text{Net income}}{\text{Average common stockholders' equity}}$ | Measures profitability of owner's investment. |
| 9. Earnings per share | $\dfrac{\text{Net income}}{\text{Weighted average common shares outstanding}}$ | Measures net income earned on each share of common stock. |
| 10. Price-earnings ratio | $\dfrac{\text{Market price per share of stock}}{\text{Earnings per share}}$ | Measures the ratio of the market price per share to earnings per share. |
| 11. Payout ratio | $\dfrac{\text{Cash dividends}}{\text{Net income}}$ | Measures percentage of earnings distributed in the form of cash dividends. |
| **Solvency Ratios** | | |
| 12. Debt to total assets | $\dfrac{\text{Total debt}}{\text{Total assets}}$ | Measures the percentage of total assets provided by creditors. |
| 13. Times interest earned | $\dfrac{\text{Income before income taxes and interest expense}}{\text{Interest expense}}$ | Measures ability to meet interest payments as they come due. |

## *Before You Go On . . .*

### ▶ *Review It*

1. What are liquidity ratios? Explain the current ratio, acid-test ratio, receivables turnover ratio, and inventory turnover ratio.
2. What are profitability ratios? Explain the profit margin ratio, asset turnover ratio, return on assets ratio, return on common stockholders' equity ratio, earnings per share, price-earnings ratio, and payout ratio.

3. What are solvency ratios? Explain the debt to total assets ratio and times interest earned ratio.

### ▶ *Do It*

Selected financial data for Drummond Company at December 31, 1996, are as follows: cash $60,000; receivables (net) $80,000; inventory $70,000; current liabilities $140,000. Compute the current and acid-test ratios.

**Reasoning:** The formula for the current ratio is: current assets ÷ current liabilities. The formula for the acid-test ratio is: cash + marketable securities + receivables (net) ÷ current liabilities.

**Solution:** The current ratio is 1.5:1 ($210,000 ÷ $140,000). The acid-test ratio is 1:1 ($140,000 ÷ $140,000).

*Related exercise material:* BE19–7, BE19–8, BE19–9, BE19–10, BE19–11, E19–5, E19–6, and E19–7.

# *L*imitations of Financial Analysis

Significant business decisions are frequently made using one or more of the three analytical tools illustrated in this chapter. However, you should be aware of some of the limitations of these tools and of the financial statements on which they are based.

**STUDY OBJECTIVE**

▼ 6

*Recognize the limitations of financial statement analysis.*

## Estimates

Financial statements contain numerous estimates. Estimates, for example, are used in determining the allowance for uncollectible receivables, periodic depreciation, the costs of warranties, and contingent losses. To the extent that these estimates are inaccurate, the financial ratios and percentages are inaccurate.

## Cost

Traditional financial statements are based on cost and are not adjusted for price-level changes. Comparisons of unadjusted financial data from different periods may be rendered invalid by significant inflation or deflation. For example, a 5-year comparison of J.C. Penney's revenues might show a growth of 21%. But this growth trend would be misleading if the general price-level had increased significantly during the same 5-year period.

## Alternative Accounting Methods

Variations among companies in the application of generally accepted accounting principles may hamper comparability. For example, one company may use the FIFO method of inventory costing, whereas another company in the same industry may use LIFO. If inventory is a significant asset to both companies, it is unlikely that their current ratios are comparable. For example, if General Motors Corporation had used FIFO instead of LIFO in valuing its inventories, its inventories would have been 26% higher, significantly affecting the current ratio (and other ratios as well). In addition to differences in inventory costing methods, differences also exist in reporting such items as depreciation, depletion, and amortization. Although these differences in accounting methods might be detectable from reading the notes to the financial statements, adjusting the financial data to compensate for the different methods is difficult, if not impossible in some cases.

▶ *International note*

In many industries competition is global: To evaluate a firm's standing, an investor or analyst must make comparisons to firms from other countries. However, given the many differences in accounting practices, these comparisons can be both difficult and misleading.

## Atypical Data

Fiscal year-end data may not be typical of the financial condition during the year. Firms frequently establish a fiscal year-end that coincides with the low point in operating activity or in inventory levels. Therefore, certain account balances (cash, receivables, payables, and inventories) may not be representative of the balances in the accounts during the year.

## Diversification of Firms

Diversification in American industry also limits the usefulness of financial analysis. Many firms today are so diversified that they cannot be classified by industry. Others appear to be comparable but are not. You might think that PepsiCo, Inc., and Coca-Cola Company would be comparable as soft drink industry competitors. But are they comparable when PepsiCo, in addition to producing Pepsi-Cola, owns Pizza Hut, KFC, Taco Bell, and Frito-Lay; and Coca-Cola, in addition to producing Coke, owns Hi-C (fruit drinks), Minute Maid (frozen concentrate), and Columbia Pictures (motion pictures, TV shows, and commercials)?

▸ *Ethics note*

When investigating diversified firms, investors are often most interested to learn about the results of particular divisions. Firms are required to disclose the results of distinct lines of business separately if they are a material part of operations. Unfortunately, shifting revenues and expenses across divisions to achieve desired results reduces the usefulness of this information for financial statement analysis.

# *Before You Go On . . .*

## ▸ *Review It*

1. What are some limitations of financial analysis?
2. Give examples of alternative accounting methods that hamper compatibility.
3. In what way does diversification limit the usefulness of financial statement analysis?

## ▸ *A Look Back at the University of Chicago*

Refer to the opening story and answer the following questions:

1. What financial ratio(s) helped John R. Kroll of the university receive financing for the school? What other ratios or data are provided by a university when borrowing funds? What relevant information is provided by these ratios or data?
2. What are the sources of funds for a private university?
3. How are educational institutions rated and what equity to debt ratio applies to these ratings? What is the University of Chicago's equity to debt ratio?

*Solution:*

1. John R. Kroll said that its good equity to debt ratio helped the University of Chicago borrow $100 million to build two new buildings. Other ratios or data discussed in the opening story are the endowment ratio and student SAT scores. The endowment ratio is the ratio of gifts the university has received to the number of students; the larger its endowment, the less pressure a school has to generate money from other sources. The higher the SAT scores, the more demand there is to attend that institution.
2. A private university obtains funds from tuition; contributions, gifts, and bequests from alumni, friends, and corporations; grants from foundations, government agencies, and companies; earnings from endowment investments and operating funds; and borrowings.
3. Standard & Poor's ranks educational institutions, as it does corporations, with credit and bond ratings. "A"-rated institutions have a 2:1 equity to debt ratio; "AAA"-institutions—the highest rating—have a 4:1 ratio. The University of Chicago has a 5.5:1 equity to debt ratio.

# Summary of Study Objectives

**1.** *Discuss the need for comparative analysis.* There are three bases of comparison: (1) Intracompany, which compares an item or financial relationship with other data within a company. (2) Industry, which compares company data with industry averages. (3) Intercompany, which compares an item or financial relationship of a company with data of one or more competing companies.

**2.** *Identify the tools of financial statement analysis.* Financial statements may be analyzed horizontally, vertically, and with ratios.

**3.** *Explain and apply horizontal (trend) analysis.* Horizontal analysis is a technique for evaluating a series of data over a period of time to determine the increase or decrease that has taken place, expressed as either an amount or a percentage.

**4.** *Describe and apply vertical analysis.* Vertical analysis is a technique that expresses each item within a financial statement in terms of a percentage of a relevant total or a base amount.

**5.** *Identify and compute ratios and describe their purpose and use in analyzing a firm's liquidity, profitability, and solvency.* The formula and purpose of each ratio is presented in Illustration 19-25.

**6.** *Recognize the limitations of financial statement analysis.* The usefulness of analytical tools is limited by the use of estimates, the cost basis, the application of alternative accounting methods, atypical data at year-end, and the diversification of firms.

# Glossary

**Acid-test ratio**   A measure of a company's immediate short-term liquidity, computed by dividing the sum of cash, marketable securities, and (net) receivables by current liabilities. (p. 799).

**Asset turnover ratio**   A measure of how efficiently a company uses its assets to generate sales, computed by dividing net sales by average assets. (p. 803).

**Current ratio**   A measure used to evaluate a company's liquidity and short-term debt-paying ability, computed by dividing current assets by current liabilities. (p. 799).

**Debt to total assets ratio**   Measures the percentage of total assets provided by creditors, computed by dividing total debt by total assets. (p. 808).

**Earnings per share**   The net income earned by each share of common stock, computed by dividing net income by the weighted average common shares outstanding. (p. 805).

**Horizontal analysis**   A technique for evaluating a series of financial statement data over a period of time to determine the increase (decrease) that has taken place, expressed as either an amount or a percentage. (p. 792).

**Inventory turnover ratio**   A measure of the liquidity of inventory, computed by dividing cost of goods sold by average inventory. (p. 801).

**Liquidity ratios**   Measures of the short-term ability of the enterprise to pay its maturing obligations and to meet unexpected needs for cash. (p. 798).

**Payout ratio**   Measures the percentage of earnings distributed in the form of cash dividends, computed by dividing cash dividends by net income. (p. 807).

**Price-earnings ratio**   Measures the ratio of the market price of each share of common stock to the earnings per share, computed by dividing the market price of the stock by earnings per share. (p. 806).

**Profitability ratios**   Measures of the income or operating success of an enterprise for a given period of time. (p. 802).

**Profit margin ratio**   Measures the percentage of each dollar of sales that results in net income, computed by dividing net income by net sales. (p. 802).

**Ratio**   An expression of the mathematical relationship between one quantity and another. The relationship may be expressed either as a percentage, a rate, or a simple proportion. (p. 797).

**Ratio analysis**   A technique for evaluating financial statements that expresses the relationship among selected financial statement data. (p. 797).

**Receivables turnover ratio**   A measure of the liquidity of receivables, computed by dividing net credit sales by average net receivables. (p. 800).

**Return on assets ratio**   An overall measure of profitability, computed by dividing net income by average assets. (p. 804).

**Return on common stockholders' equity**   Measures the dollars of net income earned for each dollar invested by the owners, computed by dividing net income by average common stockholders' equity. (p. 804).

**Solvency ratios**   Measures of the ability of the enterprise to survive over a long period of time. (p. 807).

**Times interest earned ratio**   Measures a company's ability to meet interest payments as they come due, computed by dividing income before interest expense and income taxes by interest expense. (p. 808).

**Trading on the equity (leverage)**   Borrowing money at a lower rate of interest than can be earned by using the borrowed money. (p. 805).

**Vertical analysis**   A technique for evaluating financial statement data that expresses each item within a financial statement in terms of a percent of a base amount. (p. 794).

# DEMONSTRATION PROBLEM

The condensed financial statements of Kellogg Company for the years 1994 and 1993 are presented below:

### KELLOGG COMPANY
### Balance Sheet
### December 31

#### Assets

| | (In millions) | |
| --- | --- | --- |
| | 1994 | 1993 |
| **Current assets** | | |
| Cash and short-term investments | $ 266.3 | $ 98.1 |
| Accounts receivable (net) | 564.5 | 536.8 |
| Inventories | 396.3 | 403.1 |
| Prepaid expenses and other current assets | 206.4 | 207.1 |
| Total current assets | 1,433.5 | 1,245.1 |
| Property, plant, and equipment (net) | 2,892.8 | 2,768.4 |
| Intangibles and other assets | 141.0 | 223.6 |
| Total assets | $4,467.3 | $4,237.1 |

#### Liabilities and Stockholders' Equity

| | | |
| --- | --- | --- |
| Current liabilities | $1,185.2 | $1,214.6 |
| Long-term liabilities | 1,474.6 | 1,309.1 |
| Stockholders' equity—common | 1,807.5 | 1,713.4 |
| Total liabilities and stockholders' equity | $4,467.3 | $4,237.1 |

### KELLOGG COMPANY
### Income Statement
### For the Year Ended December 31

| | (In millions) | |
| --- | --- | --- |
| | 1994 | 1993 |
| Revenues | $6,562.0 | $6,295.4 |
| **Cost and expenses** | | |
| Cost of goods sold | 2,950.7 | 2,989.0 |
| Selling and administrative expenses | 2,448.7 | 2,237.5 |
| Interest expense | 32.6 | 34.8 |
| Total costs and expenses | 5,432.0 | 5,261.3 |
| Income before income taxes | 1,130.0 | 1,034.1 |
| Income tax expense | 424.6 | 353.4 |
| Net income | $ 705.4 | $ 680.7 |

## Instructions

Compute the following ratios for Kellogg for 1994 and 1993.

(a)  Current ratio.

(b)  Inventory turnover (Inventory 12/31/92, $416.4).

(c)  Profit margin ratio.

(d)  Return on assets (Assets 12/31/92, $4,015.0).

(e)  Return on common stockholders' equity (Equity 12/31/92, $1,945.2).

(f)  Debt to total assets.

(g)  Times interest earned.

## Solution to Demonstration Problem

|  | 1994 | 1993 |
|---|---|---|
| (a)  Current ratio: | | |
| $1,433.5 ÷ $1,185.2 = | 1.2:1 | |
| $1,245.1 ÷ $1,214.6 = | | 1.0:1 |
| (b)  Inventory turnover: | | |
| $2,950.7 ÷ [($396.3 + $403.1) ÷ 2] = | 7.4 times | |
| $2,989.0 ÷ [($403.1 + $416.4) ÷ 2] = | | 7.3 times |
| (c)  Profit margin: | | |
| $705.4 ÷ $6,562.0 = | 10.7% | |
| $680.7 ÷ $6,295.4 = | | 10.8% |
| (d)  Return on assets: | | |
| $705.4 ÷ [($4,467.3 + $4,237.1) ÷ 2] = | 16.2% | |
| $680.7 ÷ [($4,237.1 + $4,015.0) ÷ 2] = | | 16.5% |
| (e)  Return on common stockholders' equity: | | |
| $705.4 ÷ [($1,807.5 + $1,713.4) ÷ 2] = | 40.1% | |
| $680.7 ÷ [($1,713.4 + $1,945.2) ÷ 2] = | | 37.2% |
| (f)  Debt to total assets: | | |
| $2,659.8 ÷ $4,467.3 = | 59.5% | |
| $2,523.7 ÷ $4,237.1 = | | 59.6% |
| (g)  Times interest earned: | | |
| ($705.4 + $424.6 + $32.6) ÷ $32.6 = | 35.7 times | |
| ($680.7 + $353.4 + $34.8) ÷ $34.8 = | | 30.7 times |

### Problem-Solving Strategies

1. Remember that the current ratio includes all current assets; acid-test ratio uses only cash, marketable securities, and net receivables.
2. Use average balances for turnover ratios like inventory, receivables, and assets.
3. Return on assets is greater or smaller than return on common stockholders' equity depending on cost of debt.

# SELF-STUDY QUESTIONS

Answers are at the end of the chapter.

(SO 1)  1. Comparisons of data within a company are an example of the following comparative basis:
  a. Industry averages.
  b. Intracompany.
  c. Intercompany.
  d. Both (b) and (c).

(SO 2)  2. In horizontal analysis, each item is expressed as a percentage of the:
  a. net income amount.
  b. stockholders' equity amount.
  c. total assets amount.
  d. base year amount.

(SO 4)  3. In vertical analysis, the base amount for depreciation expense is generally:
  a. net sales.
  b. depreciation expense in a previous year.
  c. gross profit.
  d. fixed assets.

(SO 4)  4. The following schedule is a display of what type of analysis?

| | Amount | Percent |
|---|---|---|
| Current assets | $200,000 | 25% |
| Property, plant, and equipment | 600,000 | 75% |
| Total assets | $800,000 | |

  a. Horizontal analysis.
  b. Differential analysis.
  c. Vertical analysis.
  d. Ratio analysis.

(SO 3)  5. Leland Corporation reported net sales of $300,000, $330,000, and $360,000 in the years 1994, 1995, and 1996, respectively. If 1994 is the base year, what is the trend percentage for 1996?
  a. 77%.
  b. 108%.
  c. 120%.
  d. 130%.

(SO 5)  6. Which of the following measures is an evaluation of a firm's ability to pay current liabilities?
  a. Acid-test ratio.
  b. Current ratio.
  c. Both (a) and (b).
  d. None of the above.

(SO 5)  7. A measure useful in evaluating the efficiency in managing inventories is:
  a. inventory turnover ratio.
  b. average days to sell inventory.
  c. Both (a) and (b).
  d. None of the above.

(SO 5)  8. Which of the following is *not* a liquidity ratio?
  a. Current ratio.
  b. Asset turnover.

c.  Inventory turnover.
d.  Receivables turnover.

(SO 5)    9.  Plano Corporation reported net income $24,000, net sales $400,000, and average assets $600,000 for 1996. The 1996 profit margin was:
a.  6%.
b.  12%.
c.  40%.
d.  200%.

10.  Which of the following is generally *not* considered    (SO 6)
to be a limitation of financial analysis?
a.  Use of estimates.
b.  Use of ratio analysis.
c.  Use of cost.
d.  Use of alternative accounting methods.

# QUESTIONS

1. (a)  Tia Kim believes that the analysis of financial statements is directed at two characteristics of a company: liquidity and profitability. Is Tia correct? Explain.
   (b)  Are short-term creditors, long-term creditors, and stockholders interested primarily in the same characteristics of a company? Explain.

2. (a)  Distinguish among the following bases of comparison: (1) intracompany, (2) industry averages, and (3) intercompany.
   (b)  Give the principal value of using each of the three bases of comparison.

3.  Two popular methods of financial statement analysis are horizontal analysis and vertical analysis. Explain the difference between these two methods.

4. (a)  If Roe Company had net income of $540,000 in 1996 and it experienced a 24.5% increase in net income for 1997, what is its net income for 1997?
   (b)  If six cents of every dollar of Roe's revenue is net income in 1996, what is the dollar amount of 1996 revenue?

5.  What is a ratio? What are the different ways of expressing the relationship of two amounts? What information does a ratio provide?

6.  Name the major ratios useful in assessing (a) liquidity and (b) solvency.

7.  Tony Robins is puzzled. His company had a profit margin of 10% in 1996. He feels that this is an indication that the company is doing well. Joan Graham, his accountant, says that more information is needed to determine the firm's financial well-being. Who is correct? Why?

8.  What do the following classes of ratios measure? (a) Liquidity ratios. (b) Profitability ratios. (c) Solvency ratios.

9.  What is the difference between the current ratio and the acid-test ratio?

10.  Gerry Bullock Company, a retail store, has a receivables turnover ratio of 4.5 times. The industry average is 12.5 times. Does Bullock have a collection problem with its receivables?

11.  Which ratios should be used to help answer the following questions?
   (a)  How efficient is a company in using its assets to produce sales?
   (b)  How near to sale is the inventory on hand?
   (c)  How many dollars of net income were earned for each dollar invested by the owners?
   (d)  How able is a company to meet interest charges as they fall due?

12.  The price-earnings ratio of McDonnell Douglas (aircraft builder) was 5, and the price-earnings ratio of Microsoft (computer software) was 43. Which company did the stock market favor? Explain.

13.  What is the formula for computing the payout ratio? Would you expect this ratio to be high or low for a growth company?

14.  Holding all other factors constant, indicate whether each of the following changes generally signals good or bad news about a company:
   (a)  Increase in profit margin.
   (b)  Decrease in inventory turnover.
   (c)  Increase in the current ratio.
   (d)  Decrease in earnings per share.
   (e)  Increase in price-earnings ratio.
   (f)  Increase in debt to total assets ratio.
   (g)  Decrease in times interest earned.
   (h)  Increase in book value per share.

15.  The return on total assets for Windsor Corporation is 7.6%. During the same year Windsor's return on common stockholders' equity is 12.8%. What is the explanation for the difference in the two rates?

16.  Which two ratios do you think should be of greatest interest to:
   (a)  A pension fund considering the purchase of 20-year bonds?
   (b)  A bank contemplating a short-term loan?
   (c)  A common stockholder?

17. (a)  What is meant by trading on the equity?
   (b)  How would you determine the profitability of trading on the equity?

18.  Khris Inc. has net income of $270,000, weighted average shares of common stock outstanding of 50,000, and preferred dividends for the period of

$40,000. What is Khris's earnings per share of common stock? Phil Remmers, the president of Khris Inc., believes the computed EPS of the company is high. Comment.

19. Identify and briefly explain five limitations of financial analysis.

20. Explain how the choice of one of the following accounting methods over the other raises or lowers a company's net income during a period of continuing inflation:

(a) Use of FIFO instead of LIFO for inventory costing.

(b) Use of a 6-year life for machinery instead of a 9-year life.

(c) Use of straight-line depreciation instead of accelerated declining-balance depreciation.

# BRIEF EXERCISES*

**BE19–1** Using the following data from the comparative balance sheet of All-State Company, illustrate horizontal analysis:

*Prepare horizontal analysis.*
(SO 3)

|                     | December 31, 1997 | December 31, 1996 |
|---------------------|-------------------|-------------------|
| Accounts receivable | $ 600,000         | $ 400,000         |
| Inventory           | $ 780,000         | $ 600,000         |
| Total assets        | $3,220,000        | $2,800,000        |

**BE19–2** Using the same data presented above in BE19–1 for All-State Company, illustrate vertical analysis.

*Prepare vertical analysis.*
(SO 4)

**BE19–3** Net income was $500,000 in 1995, $420,000 in 1996, and $504,000 in 1997. What is the percentage of change from (1) 1995 to 1996 and (2) 1996 to 1997? Is the change an increase or a decrease?

*Calculate percentage of change.*
(SO 3)

**BE19–4** If Cavalier Company had net income of $672,300 in 1997 and it experienced a 25% increase in net income over 1996, what was its 1996 net income?

*Calculate net income.*
(SO 3)

**BE19–5** Vertical analysis (common size) percentages for Waubons Company's sales, cost of goods sold, and expenses are shown below:

*Calculate change in net income.*
(SO 4)

| Vertical Analysis  | 1997  | 1996  | 1995  |
|--------------------|-------|-------|-------|
| Sales              | 100.0 | 100.0 | 100.0 |
| Cost of goods sold | 59.2  | 62.4  | 64.5  |
| Expenses           | 25.0  | 26.6  | 29.5  |

Did Waubons's net income as a percent of sales increase, decrease, or remain unchanged over the 3-year period presented above? Provide numerical support for your answer.

**BE19–6** Horizontal analysis (trend analysis) percentages for Tilden Company's sales, cost of goods sold, and expenses are shown below:

*Calculate change in net income.*
(SO 3)

| Horizontal Analysis | 1997  | 1996  | 1995  |
|---------------------|-------|-------|-------|
| Sales               | 96.2  | 106.8 | 100.0 |
| Cost of goods sold  | 102.0 | 97.0  | 100.0 |
| Expenses            | 110.6 | 95.4  | 100.0 |

▓▓▓▷ Did Tilden's net income increase, decrease, or remain unchanged over the 3-year period presented above?

---

*Follow the rounding procedures used in the chapter.

*Calculate liquidity ratios.*
(SO 5)

**BE19–7**  Selected condensed data taken from a recent balance sheet of Bob Evans Farms are as follows:

| | |
|---|---:|
| Cash | $ 8,241,000 |
| Marketable securities | 1,947,000 |
| Accounts receivable | 12,545,000 |
| Inventories | 14,814,000 |
| Other current assets | 5,371,000 |
| Total current assets | $42,918,000 |
| Total current liabilities | $44,844,000 |

What are the (1) working capital, (2) current, and (3) acid-test ratios?

*Calculate profitability ratios.*
(SO 5)

**BE19–8**  Boston Patriots Corporation has net income of $15 million and net revenue of $100 million in 1996. Its assets were $12 million at the beginning of the year and $14 million at the end of the year. What are (a) the Patriots' asset turnover ratio and (b) profit margin ratio? (Round to two decimals.)

*Evaluate collection of accounts receivable.*
(SO 5)

**BE19–9**  The following data are taken from the financial statements of Diet-Mite Company:

| | 1997 | 1996 |
|---|---:|---:|
| Accounts receivable (net), end of year | $ 560,000 | $ 540,000 |
| Net sales on account | 5,500,000 | 4,100,000 |
| Terms for all sales are 1/10, n/45. | | |

Compute for each year (1) the receivables turnover and (2) the average collection period. What conclusions about the management of accounts receivable can be drawn from these data? At the end of 1995, accounts receivable (net) was $490,000.

*Evaluate management of inventory.*
(SO 5)

**BE19–10**  The following data were taken from the income statements of Okie Company:

| | 1997 | 1996 |
|---|---:|---:|
| Sales | $6,420,000 | $6,240,000 |
| Beginning inventory | 980,000 | 837,000 |
| Purchases | 4,640,000 | 4,661,000 |
| Ending inventory | 1,020,000 | 980,000 |

▸ Compute for each year (1) the inventory turnover ratio and (2) the average days to sell the inventory. What conclusions concerning the management of the inventory can be drawn from these data?

*Calculate profitability ratios.*
(SO 5)

**BE19–11**  Haymark Products Company has owners' equity of $400,000 and net income of $50,000. It has a payout ratio of 20% and a rate of return on assets of 16%. How much did Haymark Products pay in cash dividends, and what were its average assets?

# *E*XERCISES*

• • • • • • • • • • • • • • • • • • • • • • • • • • • • • • • • • • • • • • • • • • • • • • • • • •

*Prepare horizontal analysis.*
(SO 3)

**E19–1**  Financial information for Merchandise Inc. is presented below:

| | December 31, 1996 | December 31, 1995 |
|---|---:|---:|
| Current assets | $120,000 | $100,000 |
| Plant assets (net) | 400,000 | 330,000 |
| Current liabilities | 91,000 | 70,000 |
| Long-term liabilities | 144,000 | 95,000 |
| Common stock, $1 par | 150,000 | 115,000 |
| Retained earnings | 135,000 | 150,000 |

**Instructions**
Prepare a schedule showing a horizontal analysis for 1996 using 1995 as the base year.

*Follow the rounding procedures used in the chapter.

**E19–2** Operating data for Fleetwood Corporation are presented below:

*Prepare vertical analysis.*
(SO 4)

|  | 1997 | 1996 |
|---|---|---|
| Sales | $800,000 | $600,000 |
| Cost of goods sold | 472,000 | 390,000 |
| Selling expenses | 120,000 | 72,000 |
| Administrative expenses | 80,000 | 54,000 |
| Income tax expense | 38,400 | 25,200 |
| Net income | 89,600 | 58,800 |

*Instructions*
Prepare a schedule showing a vertical analysis for 1997 and 1996.

**E19–3** The comparative balance sheets of Oklahoma Corporation are presented below:

*Prepare horizontal and vertical analyses.*
(SO 3, 4)

**OKLAHOMA CORPORATION**
**Comparative Balance Sheets**
**As of December 31**

|  | 1997 | 1996 |
|---|---|---|
| Assets |  |  |
| Current assets | $ 72,000 | $ 80,000 |
| Property, plant, & equipment (net) | 99,000 | 90,000 |
| Intangibles | 24,000 | 40,000 |
| Total assets | $195,000 | $210,000 |
| Liabilities & stockholders' equity |  |  |
| Current liabilities | $ 40,800 | $ 48,000 |
| Long-term liabilities | 138,000 | 150,000 |
| Stockholders' equity | 16,200 | 12,000 |
| Total liabilities & stockholders' equity | $195,000 | $210,000 |

*Instructions*
(a) Prepare a horizontal analysis of the balance sheet data for Oklahoma Corporation using 1996 as a base. (Show the amount of increase or decrease as well.)
(b) Prepare a vertical analysis of the balance sheet data for Oklahoma Corporation in columnar form for 1997.

**E19–4** The comparative income statements of Olympic Corporation are shown below:

*Prepare horizontal and vertical analyses.*
(SO 3, 4)

**OLYMPIC CORPORATION**
**Comparative Income Statements**
**For the Years Ended December 31**

|  | 1997 | 1996 |
|---|---|---|
| Net sales | $550,000 | $550,000 |
| Cost of goods sold | 440,000 | 450,000 |
| Gross profit | $110,000 | $100,000 |
| Operating expenses | 57,200 | 54,000 |
| Net income | $ 52,800 | $ 46,000 |

*Instructions*
(a) Prepare a horizontal analysis of the income statement data for Olympic Corporation using 1996 as a base. (Show the amounts of increase or decrease.)
(b) Prepare a vertical analysis of the income statement data for Olympic Corporation in columnar form for both years.

**E19–5** Nordstrom, Inc., operates department stores in numerous states. Selected financial statement data in millions of dollars for a recent year are as follows:

*Compute liquidity ratios and compare results.*
(SO 5)

|  | End-of-Year | Beginning-of-Year |
|---|---|---|
| Cash and cash equivalents | $   33 | $   91 |
| Receivables (net) | 676 | 586 |
| Merchandise Inventory | 628 | 586 |
| Prepaid expenses | 61 | 52 |
| Total current assets | $1,398 | $1,315 |
| Total current liabilities | $690 | $627 |

For the year, net sales were $3,894 and cost of goods sold was $2,600.

**Instructions**

(a) Compute the four liquidity ratios at the end of the current year.

(b) Using the data in the chapter, compare Nordstrom's liquidity with (1) J.C. Penney and (2) the industry averages for department stores.

*Perform current and acid-test ratio analysis.*
*(SO 5)*

**E19–6**    Firpo Incorporated had the following transactions occur involving current assets and current liabilities during February 1996:

Feb.  3    Accounts receivable of $15,000 are collected.

  7    Equipment is purchased for $25,000 cash.

  11    Paid $3,000 for a 3-year insurance policy.

  14    Accounts payable of $14,000 are paid.

  18    Cash dividends are declared, $6,000.

Additional information:

1. As of February 1, 1996, current assets were $140,000 and current liabilities were $50,000.
2. As of February 1, 1996, current assets included $15,000 of inventory and $5,000 of prepaid expenses.

**Instructions**

(a) Compute the current ratio as of the beginning of the month and after each transaction.

(b) Compute the acid-test ratio as of the beginning of the month and after each transaction.

*Compute selected ratios.*
*(SO 5)*

**E19–7**    Georgette Company has the following comparative balance sheet data:

|  | December 31, 1996 | December 31, 1995 |
|---|---|---|
| Cash | $ 20,000 | $ 30,000 |
| Receivables (net) | 65,000 | 60,000 |
| Inventories | 60,000 | 50,000 |
| Plant assets (net) | 200,000 | 180,000 |
|  | $345,000 | $320,000 |
| Accounts payable | $ 50,000 | $ 60,000 |
| Mortgage payable (15%) | 100,000 | 100,000 |
| Common stock, $10 par | 140,000 | 120,000 |
| Retained earnings | 55,000 | 40,000 |
|  | $345,000 | $320,000 |

Additional information for 1996:

1. The net income was $25,000.
2. Sales on account were $420,000. Sales returns and allowances amounted to $20,000.
3. Cost of goods sold was $198,000.

**Instructions**

Compute the following ratios at December 31, 1996:

(a) Current.

(b) Acid-test.

(c) Receivables turnover.

(d) Inventory turnover.

**E19–8** Selected comparative statement data for Mighty Products Company are presented below. All balance sheet data are as of December 31.

*Compute selected ratios.*
(SO 5)

|  | 1996 | 1995 |
|---|---|---|
| Net sales | $800,000 | $720,000 |
| Cost of goods sold | 480,000 | 40,000 |
| Interest expense | 7,000 | 5,000 |
| Net income | 56,000 | 42,000 |
| Accounts receivable | 120,000 | 100,000 |
| Inventory | 85,000 | 75,000 |
| Total assets | 600,000 | 500,000 |
| Total common stockholders' equity | 450,000 | 310,000 |

**Instructions**
Compute the following ratios for 1996:

(a) Profit margin.
(b) Asset turnover.
(c) Return on assets.
(d) Return on common stockholders' equity.

**E19–9** The income statement for the year ended December 31, 1996, of Jean LeFay, Inc., appears below.

*Compute selected ratios.*
(SO 5)

| | |
|---|---|
| Sales | $400,000 |
| Cost of goods sold | 230,000 |
| Gross profit | 170,000 |
| Expenses (including $20,000 interest and $24,000 income taxes) | 100,000 |
| Net income | $ 70,000 |

Additional information:

1. Common stock outstanding January 1, 1996, was 30,000 shares. On July 1, 1996, 10,000 more shares were issued.
2. The market price of Jean LeFay, Inc., stock was $15 in 1996.
3. Cash dividends of $21,000 were paid, $5,000 of which were to preferred stockholders.

**Instructions**
Compute the following ratios for 1996.

(a) Earnings per share.
(b) Price-earnings.
(c) Payout.
(d) Times interest earned.

**E19–10** Shaker Corporation experienced a fire on December 31, 1996, in which its financial records were partially destroyed. It has been able to salvage some of the records and has ascertained the following balances:

*Compute amounts from ratios.*
(SO 5)

|  | December 31, 1996 | December 31, 1995 |
|---|---|---|
| Cash | $ 30,000 | $ 10,000 |
| Receivables (net) | 72,500 | 126,000 |
| Inventory | 200,000 | 180,000 |
| Accounts payable | 50,000 | 90,000 |
| Notes payable | 30,000 | 60,000 |
| Common stock, $100 par | 400,000 | 400,000 |
| Retained earnings | 113,500 | 101,000 |

Additional information:

1. The inventory turnover is 3.6 times.
2. The return on common stockholders' equity is 22%. The company had no additional paid-in capital.
3. The receivables turnover is 9.4 times.
4. The return on assets is 20%.
5. Total assets at December 31, 1995, were $605,000.

**Instructions**

Compute the following for Shaker Corporation:

(a) Cost of goods sold for 1996.

(b) Net sales for 1996.

(c) Net income for 1996.

(d) Total assets at December 31, 1996.

# PROBLEMS*

• • • • • • • • • • • • • • • • • • • • • • • • • • • • • • • • • • • • • • • • • • • • • • • • • • • • • • • • • • • •

*Prepare vertical analysis and comment on profitability.*
*(SO 4, 5)*

**P19–1**  Comparative statement data for Chen Company and Couric Company, two competitors, appear below. All balance sheet data are as of December 31, 1996, and December 31, 1995.

|  | Chen Company | | Couric Company | |
|---|---|---|---|---|
|  | **1996** | **1995** | **1996** | **1995** |
| Net sales | $1,549,035 | | $339,038 | |
| Cost of goods sold | 1,080,490 | | 238,006 | |
| Operating expenses | 302,275 | | 79,000 | |
| Interest expense | 6,800 | | 1,252 | |
| Income tax expense | 47,840 | | 7,740 | |
| Current assets | 325,975 | $312,410 | 83,336 | $ 79,467 |
| Plant assets (net) | 521,310 | 500,000 | 139,728 | 125,812 |
| Current liabilities | 66,325 | 75,815 | 35,348 | 30,281 |
| Long-term liabilities | 108,500 | 90,000 | 29,620 | 25,000 |
| Common stock, $10 par | 500,000 | 500,000 | 120,000 | 120,000 |
| Retained earnings | 172,460 | 146,595 | 38,096 | 29,998 |

**Instructions**

(a) Prepare a vertical analysis of the 1996 income statement data for Chen Company and Couric Company in columnar form.

(b) ▣▣▣▭▷ Comment on the relative profitability of the companies by computing the return on assets and the return on common stockholders' equity ratios for both companies.

*Compute ratios from balance sheet and income statement.*
*(SO 5)*

**P19–2**  The comparative statements of Magic Johnson Company are presented below:

**MAGIC JOHNSON COMPANY**
**Income Statement**
**For the Year Ended December 31**

|  | 1996 | 1995 |
|---|---|---|
| Net sales | $1,818,500 | $1,750,500 |
| Cost of goods sold | 1,005,500 | 996,000 |
| Gross profit | 813,000 | 754,500 |
| Selling and administrative expense | 506,000 | 479,000 |
| Income from operations | 307,000 | 275,500 |
| Other expenses and losses | | |
| Interest expense | 18,000 | 19,000 |
| Income before income taxes | 289,000 | 256,500 |
| Income tax expense | 86,700 | 77,000 |
| Net income | $ 202,300 | $ 179,500 |

—————————

*Follow the rounding procedures used in the chapter.

**MAGIC JOHNSON COMPANY**
**Balance Sheet**
**December 31**

| | 1996 | 1995 |
|---|---|---|
| **Assets** | | |
| Current assets | | |
| Cash | $ 60,100 | $ 64,200 |
| Marketable securities | 54,000 | 50,000 |
| Accounts receivable (net) | 107,800 | 102,800 |
| Inventory | 123,000 | 115,500 |
| Total current assets | 344,900 | 332,500 |
| Plant assets (net) | 625,300 | 520,300 |
| Total assets | $970,200 | $852,800 |
| **Liabilities and Stockholders' Equity** | | |
| Current liabilities | | |
| Accounts payable | $150,000 | $145,400 |
| Income taxes payable | 43,500 | 42,000 |
| Total current liabilities | 193,500 | 187,400 |
| Bonds payable | 210,000 | 200,000 |
| Total liabilities | 403,500 | 387,400 |
| Stockholders' equity | | |
| Common stock ($5 par) | 280,000 | 300,000 |
| Retained earnings | 286,700 | 165,400 |
| Total stockholders' equity | 566,700 | 465,400 |
| Total liabilities and stockholders' equity | $970,200 | $852,800 |

On April 1, 1996, 4,000 shares were repurchased and canceled. All sales were on account.

**Instructions**
Compute the following ratios for 1996:

(a) Earnings per share.
(b) Return on common stockholders' equity.
(c) Return on assets.
(d) Current.
(e) Acid-test.

(f) Receivables turnover.
(g) Inventory turnover.
(h) Times interest earned.
(i) Asset turnover.
(j) Debt to total assets.

**P19–3** Condensed balance sheet and income statement data for Pitka Corporation appear below:

*Perform ratio analysis.*
*(SO 5)*

**PITKA CORPORATION**
**Balance Sheet**
**December 31**

| | 1996 | 1995 | 1994 |
|---|---|---|---|
| Cash | $ 25,000 | $ 20,000 | $ 18,000 |
| Receivables (net) | 50,000 | 45,000 | 48,000 |
| Other current assets | 90,000 | 85,000 | 64,000 |
| Investments | 75,000 | 70,000 | 45,000 |
| Plant and equipment (net) | 400,000 | 370,000 | 358,000 |
| | $640,000 | $590,000 | $533,000 |
| Current liabilities | $ 75,000 | $ 80,000 | $ 70,000 |
| Long-term debt | 80,000 | 85,000 | 50,000 |
| Common stock, $10 par | 340,000 | 300,000 | 300,000 |
| Retained earnings | 145,000 | 125,000 | 113,000 |
| | $640,000 | $590,000 | $533,000 |

## PITKA CORPORATION
### Income Statement
### For the Years Ended December 31

|  | 1996 | 1995 |
|---|---|---|
| Sales | $740,000 | $700,000 |
| Less: Sales returns and allowances | 40,000 | 50,000 |
| Net sales | 700,000 | 650,000 |
| Cost of goods sold | 420,000 | 400,000 |
| Gross profit | 280,000 | 250,000 |
| Operating expenses (including income taxes) | 236,000 | 218,000 |
| Net income | $ 44,000 | $ 32,000 |

Additional information:

1. The market price of Pitka's common stock was $4.00, $5.00, and $7.95 for 1994, 1995, and 1996, respectively.
2. All dividends were paid in cash.
3. On July 1, 1996, 4,000 shares of common stock were issued.

*Instructions*
(a) Compute the following ratios for 1995 and 1996:
   (1) Profit margin.
   (2) Asset turnover.
   (3) Earnings per share.
   (4) Price-earnings.
   (5) Payout.
   (6) Debt to total assets.
(b) ▬▭▭▭▷ Based on the ratios calculated, discuss briefly the improvement or lack thereof in financial position and operating results from 1995 to 1996 of Pitka Corporation.

*Compute ratios, commenting on overall liquidity and profitability.*
*(SO 5)*

**P19–4**  Financial information for Caroline Company is presented below:

## CAROLINE COMPANY
### Balance Sheet
### December 31

| Assets | 1996 | 1995 |
|---|---|---|
| Cash | $ 70,000 | $ 65,000 |
| Short-term investments | 45,000 | 40,000 |
| Receivables (net) | 94,000 | 90,000 |
| Inventories | 130,000 | 125,000 |
| Prepaid expenses | 25,000 | 23,000 |
| Land | 130,000 | 130,000 |
| Building and equipment (net) | 190,000 | 175,000 |
|  | $684,000 | $648,000 |
| **Liabilities and Stockholders' Equity** |  |  |
| Notes payable | $100,000 | $100,000 |
| Accounts payable | 45,000 | 42,000 |
| Accrued liabilities | 40,000 | 40,000 |
| Bonds payable, due 1995 | 150,000 | 150,000 |
| Common stock, $10 par | 200,000 | 200,000 |
| Retained earnings | 149,000 | 116,000 |
|  | $684,000 | $648,000 |

## CAROLINE COMPANY
### Income Statement
### For the Years Ended December 31

|  | 1996 | 1995 |
|---|---|---|
| Sales | $850,000 | $790,000 |
| Cost of goods sold | 620,000 | 575,000 |
| Gross profit | 230,000 | 215,000 |
| Operating expenses | 194,000 | 180,000 |
| Net income | $ 36,000 | $ 35,000 |

Additional information:

1. Inventory at the beginning of 1995 was $115,000.
2. Receivables at the beginning of 1995 were $88,000.
3. Total assets at the beginning of 1995 were $630,000.
4. No common stock transactions occurred during 1995 or 1996.
5. All sales were on account.

*Instructions*

(a) Indicate, by using ratios, the change in liquidity and profitability of Caroline Company from 1995 to 1996. (Note: Not all profitability ratios can be computed.)

(b) Given below are three independent situations and a ratio that may be affected. For each situation, compute the affected ratio (1) as of December 31, 1996, and (2) as of December 31, 1997, after giving effect to the situation. Net income for 1997 was $40,000. Total assets on December 31, 1997, were $700,000.

| Situation | Ratio |
|---|---|
| 1. 18,000 shares of common stock were sold at par on July 1, 1997. | Return on common stockholders' equity |
| 2. All of the notes payable were paid in 1997. | Debt to total assets |
| 3. Market price of common stock was $9 and $12.80 on December 31, 1996, and 1997, respectively. | Price-earnings ratio |

**P19–5** Selected financial data of two intense competitors in a recent year are presented below in millions of dollars.

*Compute selected ratios and compare liquidity, profitability, and solvency for two companies.*
*(SO 5)*

|  | Kmart Corporation | Wal-Mart Stores, Inc. |
|---|---|---|
| **Income Statement Data for Year** | | |
| Net sales | $34,025 | $82,494 |
| Cost of goods sold | 25,992 | 65,586 |
| Selling and administrative expenses | 7,701 | 12,858 |
| Interest expense | 494 | 706 |
| Other income (net) | 572 | 918 |
| Income taxes | 114 | 1,581 |
| Net income | $ 296 | $ 2,681 |
| **Balance Sheet Data (End-of-Year)** | | |
| Current assets | $ 9,187 | $15,338 |
| Property, plant, and equipment (net) | 7,842 | 17,481 |
| Total assets | 17,029 | 32,819 |
| Current liabilities | 5,626 | 9,973 |
| Long-term debt | 5,371 | 10,120 |
| Total stockholders' equity | 6,032 | 12,726 |
| Total liabilities and stockholders' equity | $17,029 | $32,819 |
| **Beginning-of-Year Balances** | | |
| Total assets | $17,504 | $26,441 |
| Total stockholders' equity | 6,093 | 10,753 |

**Other Data**

| | | |
|---|---|---|
| Average net receivables | $ 1,570 | $   695 |
| Average inventory | 7,317 | 12,539 |

*Instructions*

(a) For each company, compute the following ratios:

| | |
|---|---|
| (1) Current | (6) Return on assets |
| (2) Receivables turnover | (7) Return on common stockholders' equity |
| (3) Inventory turnover | (8) Debt to total assets |
| (4) Profit margin | (9) Times interest earned |
| (5) Asset turnover | |

(b) Compare the liquidity, profitability, and solvency of the two companies.

*Compute numerous ratios.*
*(SO 5)*

**P19–6**   The comparative statements of Ultra Vision Company are presented below:

### ULTRA VISION COMPANY
### Income Statement
### For Year Ended December 31

| | 1996 | 1995 |
|---|---|---|
| Net sales (all on account) | $600,000 | $520,000 |
| Expenses | | |
| Cost of goods sold | 415,000 | 354,000 |
| Selling and administrative | 120,800 | 114,800 |
| Interest expense | 7,200 | 6,000 |
| Income tax expense | 18,000 | 14,000 |
| Total expenses | 561,000 | 488,800 |
| Net income | $ 39,000 | $ 31,200 |

### ULTRA VISION COMPANY
### Balance Sheet
### December 31

| | 1996 | 1995 |
|---|---|---|
| **Assets** | | |
| Current assets | | |
| Cash | $ 21,000 | $ 18,000 |
| Marketable securities | 18,000 | 15,000 |
| Accounts receivable (net) | 92,000 | 74,000 |
| Inventory | 84,000 | 70,000 |
| Total current assets | 215,000 | 177,000 |
| Plant assets (net) | 423,000 | 383,000 |
| Total assets | $638,000 | $560,000 |
| **Liabilities and Stockholders' Equity** | | |
| Current liabilities | | |
| Accounts payable | $112,000 | $110,000 |
| Income taxes payable | 23,000 | 20,000 |
| Total current liabilities | 135,000 | 130,000 |
| Long-term liabilities | | |
| Bonds payable | 130,000 | 80,000 |
| Total liabilities | 265,000 | 210,000 |
| Stockholders' equity | | |
| Common stock ($5 par) | 150,000 | 150,000 |
| Retained earnings | 223,000 | 200,000 |
| Total stockholders' equity | 373,000 | 350,000 |
| Total liabilities and stockholders' equity | $638,000 | $560,000 |

Additional data:
The common stock recently sold at $19.50 per share.

**Instructions**
Compute the following ratios for 1996:

(a) Current.                          (h) Return on common stockholders' equity.
(b) Acid-test.                        (i) Earnings per share.
(c) Receivables turnover.             (j) Price-earnings.
(d) Inventory turnover.               (k) Payout.
(e) Profit margin.                    (l) Debt to total assets.
(f) Asset turnover.                   (m) Times interest earned.
(g) Return on assets.

**P19–7** Presented below is an incomplete income statement and an incomplete comparative balance sheet of Vienna Corporation:

*Compute missing information given a set of ratios.*
*(SO 5)*

### VIENNA CORPORATION
### Income Statement
### For the Year Ended December 31, 1996

| | |
|---|---:|
| Sales | $11,000,000 |
| Cost of goods sold | ? |
| Gross profit | ? |
| Operating expenses | 1,665,000 |
| Income from operations | ? |
| Other expenses and losses | |
|    Interest expense | ? |
| Income before income taxes | ? |
| Income tax expense | 560,000 |
| Net income | $   ? |

### VIENNA CORPORATION
### Balance Sheet
### December 31

| | 1996 | 1995 |
|---|---:|---:|
| **Assets** | | |
| Current assets | | |
|   Cash | $  450,000 | $  375,000 |
|   Accounts receivable (net) | ? | 950,000 |
|   Inventory | ? | 1,720,000 |
|     Total current assets | ? | 3,045,000 |
| Plant assets (net) | 4,620,000 | 3,955,000 |
| Total assets | $    ? | $7,000,000 |
| **Liabilities and Stockholders' Equity** | | |
| Current liabilities | $    ? | $  825,000 |
| Long-term notes payable | ? | 2,800,000 |
|     Total liabilities | ? | 3,625,000 |
| Common stock, $1 par | 3,000,000 | 3,000,000 |
| Retained earnings | 400,000 | 375,000 |
|     Total stockholders' equity | 3,400,000 | 3,375,000 |
| Total liabilities and stockholders' equity | $    ? | $7,000,000 |

Additional information:

1. The receivables turnover for 1996 is 10 times.
2. All sales are on account.
3. The profit margin for 1996 is 14.5%.
4. Return on assets is 22% for 1996.

5. The current ratio on December 31, 1996, is 3:1.
6. The inventory turnover for 1996 is 4.8 times.

**Instructions**
Compute the missing information given the ratios above. Show computations. (Note: Start with one ratio and derive as much information as possible from it before trying another ratio. List all missing amounts under the ratio used to find the information.)

# ALTERNATE PROBLEMS*

*Prepare vertical analysis and comment on profitability.*
*(SO 4, 5)*

**P19–1A**  Comparative statement data for Brooks Company and Shields Company, two competitors, appear below. All balance sheet data are as of December 31, 1996, and December 31, 1995.

|  | Brooks Company | | Shields Company | |
|---|---|---|---|---|
|  | **1996** | **1995** | **1996** | **1995** |
| Net sales | $250,000 | | $1,200,000 | |
| Cost of goods sold | 160,000 | | 720,000 | |
| Operating expenses | 51,000 | | 252,000 | |
| Interest expense | 3,000 | | 10,000 | |
| Income tax expense | 11,000 | | 65,000 | |
| Current assets | 130,000 | $110,000 | 700,000 | $650,000 |
| Plant assets (net) | 305,000 | 270,000 | 800,000 | 750,000 |
| Current liabilities | 60,000 | 52,000 | 250,000 | 275,000 |
| Long-term liabilities | 50,000 | 68,000 | 200,000 | 150,000 |
| Common stock | 260,000 | 210,000 | 750,000 | 700,000 |
| Retained earnings | 65,000 | 50,000 | 300,000 | 275,000 |

**Instructions**
(a) Prepare a vertical analysis of the 1996 income statement data for Brooks Company and Shields Company in columnar form.
(b) ▭▭▭▷ Comment on the relative profitability of the companies by computing the return on assets and the return on common stockholders' equity ratios for both companies.

*Compute ratios from balance sheet and income statement.*
*(SO 5)*

**P19–2A**  The comparative statements of the Marti Rosen Company are presented below:

**MARTI ROSEN COMPANY**
**Income Statement**
**For the Year Ended December 31**

|  | 1996 | 1995 |
|---|---|---|
| Net sales | $660,000 | $624,000 |
| Cost of goods sold | 440,000 | 405,600 |
| Gross profit | 220,000 | 218,400 |
| Selling and administrative expense | 143,880 | 149,760 |
| Income from operations | 76,120 | 68,640 |
| Other expenses and losses | | |
| Interest expense | 7,920 | 7,200 |
| Income before income taxes | 68,200 | 61,440 |
| Income tax expense | 25,300 | 24,000 |
| Net income | $ 42,900 | $ 37,440 |

*Follow the rounding procedures used in the chapter.

## MARTI ROSEN COMPANY
### Balance Sheet
### December 31

|  | 1996 | 1995 |
|---|---|---|
| **Assets** | | |
| Current assets | | |
| Cash | $ 23,100 | $ 21,600 |
| Marketable securities | 34,800 | 33,000 |
| Accounts receivable (net) | 106,200 | 93,800 |
| Inventory | 72,400 | 64,000 |
| Total current assets | 236,500 | 212,400 |
| Plant assets (net) | 465,300 | 459,600 |
| Total assets | $701,800 | $672,000 |
| **Liabilities and Stockholders' Equity** | | |
| Current liabilities | | |
| Accounts payable | $134,200 | $132,000 |
| Income taxes payable | 25,300 | 24,000 |
| Total current liabilities | 159,500 | 156,000 |
| Bonds payable | 132,000 | 120,000 |
| Total liabilities | 291,500 | 276,000 |
| Stockholders' equity | | |
| Common stock ($10 par) | 140,000 | 150,000 |
| Retained earnings | 270,300 | 246,000 |
| Total stockholders' equity | 410,300 | 396,000 |
| Total liabilities and stockholders' equity | $701,800 | $672,000 |

On July 1, 1996, 1,000 shares were repurchased and canceled. All sales were on account.

**Instructions**
Compute the following ratios for 1996:

(a) Earnings per share.
(b) Return on common stockholders' equity.
(c) Return on assets.
(d) Current.
(e) Acid-test.
(f) Receivables turnover.
(g) Inventory turnover.
(h) Times interest earned.
(i) Asset turnover.
(j) Debt to total assets.

**P19–3A** Condensed balance sheet and income statement data for Los Colinas Corporation appear below: *Perform ratio analysis.* (SO 5)

## LOS COLINAS CORPORATION
### Balance Sheet
### December 31

|  | 1996 | 1995 | 1994 |
|---|---|---|---|
| Cash | $ 40,000 | $ 24,000 | $ 20,000 |
| Receivables (net) | 70,000 | 45,000 | 48,000 |
| Other current assets | 80,000 | 75,000 | 62,000 |
| Investments | 90,000 | 70,000 | 50,000 |
| Plant and equipment (net) | 450,000 | 400,000 | 360,000 |
|  | $730,000 | $614,000 | $540,000 |
| Current liabilities | $ 98,000 | $ 75,000 | $ 70,000 |
| Long-term debt | 97,000 | 75,000 | 65,000 |
| Common stock, $10 par | 400,000 | 340,000 | 300,000 |
| Retained earnings | 135,000 | 124,000 | 105,000 |
|  | $730,000 | $614,000 | $540,000 |

## LOS COLINAS CORPORATION
### Income Statement
### For the Years Ended December 31

|  | 1996 | 1995 |
|---|---|---|
| Sales | $700,000 | $750,000 |
| Less: Sales returns and allowances | 40,000 | 50,000 |
| Net sales | 660,000 | 700,000 |
| Cost of goods sold | 420,000 | 400,000 |
| Gross profit | 240,000 | 300,000 |
| Operating expenses (including income taxes) | 194,000 | 237,000 |
| Net income | $ 46,000 | $ 63,000 |

Additional information:

1. The market price of Los Colinas's common stock was $5.00, $4.50, and $2.30 for 1994, 1995, and 1996, respectively.
2. All dividends were paid in cash.
3. On July 1, 1995, 4,000 shares of common stock were issued and on July 1, 1996, 6,000 shares were issued.

*Instructions*

(a) Compute the following ratios for 1995 and 1996:
   (1) Profit margin.
   (2) Asset turnover.
   (3) Earnings per share.
   (4) Price-earnings.
   (5) Payout.
   (6) Debt to total assets.
(b) ▭▭▭▷ Based on the ratios calculated, discuss briefly the improvement or lack thereof in financial position and operating results from 1995 to 1996 of Los Colinas Corporation.

*Compute ratios, commenting on overall liquidity and profitability.*
*(SO 5)*

**P19–4A**    Financial information for Star Track Company is presented below:

## STAR TRACK COMPANY
### Balance Sheet
### December 31

|  | 1996 | 1995 |
|---|---|---|
| **Assets** |  |  |
| Cash | $  50,000 | $  42,000 |
| Short-term investments | 80,000 | 100,000 |
| Receivables (net) | 100,000 | 87,000 |
| Inventories | 440,000 | 400,000 |
| Prepaid expenses | 25,000 | 31,000 |
| Land | 75,000 | 75,000 |
| Building and equipment (net) | 570,000 | 500,000 |
|  | $1,340,000 | $1,235,000 |
| **Liabilities and Stockholders' Equity** |  |  |
| Notes payable | $ 125,000 | $ 125,000 |
| Accounts payable | 160,000 | 140,000 |
| Accrued liabilities | 50,000 | 50,000 |
| Bonds payable, due 1995 | 200,000 | 200,000 |
| Common stock, $5 par | 500,000 | 500,000 |
| Retained earnings | 305,000 | 220,000 |
|  | $1,340,000 | $1,235,000 |

## STAR TRACK COMPANY
### Income Statement
### For the Years Ended December 31

|  | 1996 | 1995 |
|---|---|---|
| Sales | $1,000,000 | $ 940,000 |
| Cost of goods sold | 650,000 | 635,000 |
| Gross profit | 350,000 | 305,000 |
| Operating expenses | 235,000 | 215,000 |
| Net income | $ 115,000 | $ 90,000 |

Additional information:

1. Inventory at the beginning of 1995 was $350,000.
2. Receivables at the beginning of 1995 were $80,000.
3. Total assets at the beginning of 1995 were $1,175,000.
4. No common stock transactions occurred during 1995 or 1996.
5. All sales were on account.

*Instructions*

(a) Indicate, by using ratios, the change in liquidity and profitability of Star Track Company from 1995 to 1996. (Note: Not all profitability ratios can be computed.)

(b) Given below are three independent situations and a ratio that may be affected. For each situation, compute the affected ratio (1) as of December 31, 1996, and (2) as of December 31, 1997, after giving effect to the situation. Net income for 1997 was $125,000. Total assets on December 31, 1997, were $1,500,000.

| Situation | Ratio |
|---|---|
| (1) 65,000 shares of common stock were sold at par on July 1, 1997. | Return on common stockholders' equity |
| (2) All of the notes payable were paid in 1997. | Debt to total assets |
| (3) Market price of common stock on December 31, 1997, was $6.25. Market price on December 31, 1996, was $5. | Price-earnings ratio |

**P19–5A** Selected financial data of two intense competitors in a recent year are presented below in millions of dollars.

*Compute selected ratios and compare liquidity, profitability, and solvency for two companies.*
*(SO 5)*

|  | Bethlehem Steel Corporation | Inland Steel Company |
|---|---|---|
| **Income Statement Data for Year** | | |
| Net sales | $4,819 | $4,497 |
| Cost of goods sold | 4,548 | 3,991 |
| Selling and administrative expenses | 137 | 265 |
| Interest expense | 46 | 72 |
| Other income (net) | 7 | 0 |
| Income taxes | 14 | 62 |
| Net income | $ 81 | $ 107 |
| **Balance Sheet Data (End-of-Year)** | | |
| Current assets | $1,569 | $1,081 |
| Property, plant, and equipment (net) | 2,759 | 1,610 |
| Other assets | 1,454 | 662 |
| Total assets | 5,782 | 3,353 |
| Current liabilities | 1,011 | 565 |
| Long-term debt | 3,615 | 2,056 |
| Total stockholders' equity | 1,156 | 732 |
| Total liabilities and stockholders' equity | $5,782 | $3,353 |

**Beginning-of-Year Balances**

| | | |
|---|---|---|
| Total assets | $5,877 | $3,436 |
| Total stockholders' equity | 697 | 623 |

**Other Data**

| | | |
|---|---|---|
| Average net receivables | $ 511 | $ 515 |
| Average inventory | 868 | 403 |

*Instructions*

(a) For each company, compute the following ratios:

| | |
|---|---|
| (1) Current | (6) Return on assets |
| (2) Receivables turnover | (7) Return on common stockholders' equity |
| (3) Inventory turnover | (8) Debt to total assets |
| (4) Profit margin | (9) Times interest earned |
| (5) Asset turnover | |

(b) Compare the liquidity, profitability, and solvency of the two companies.

# ▼*B*roadening *Your Perspective*

## *F*INANCIAL REPORTING PROBLEM
........................................................................................

Your parents are considering investing in PepsiCo, Inc., common stock. They ask you, as an accounting expert, to make an analysis of the company for them. Fortunately, excerpts from a current annual report of PepsiCo are presented in Appendix A of this textbook. Note that all amounts omit 000,000's (i.e., all dollar amounts are in millions).

*Instructions*
(Follow the approach in the chapter for rounding numbers.)

(a) Make a 5-year trend analysis, using 1990 as the base year, of (1) net sales and (2) income from continuing operations. Comment on the significance of the trend results.
(b) Compute for 1994 and 1993 the (1) profit margin, (2) asset turnover, (3) return on assets, and (4) return on common stockholders' equity. How would you evaluate PepsiCo's profitability? Total assets at December 30, 1992, were $20,951.2, and total stockholders' equity at December 30, 1992, was $5,355.7.
(c) Compute for 1994 and 1993 the (1) debt to total assets and (2) times interest earned ratio. How would you evaluate PepsiCo's long-term solvency?
(d) What information outside the annual report may also be useful to your parents in making a decision about PepsiCo, Inc.?

## *D*ECISION CASE
........................................................................................

As the CPA for J. Martinez Manufacturing Inc., you have been requested to develop some key ratios from the comparative financial statements. This information is to be used to convince creditors that J. Martinez Manufacturing Inc. is solvent and to support the use of going-concern valuation procedures in the financial statements.

The data requested and the computations developed from the financial statements follow:

|  | 1997 | 1996 |
|---|---|---|
| Current ratio | 3.1 times | 2.1 times |
| Acid-test ratio | .8 times | 1.4 times |
| Asset turnover | 2.8 times | 2.2 times |
| Sales to stockholders' equity | 2.3 times | 2.7 times |
| Net income | Up 32% | Down 8% |
| Earnings per share | $3.30 | $2.50 |
| Book value per share | Up 8% | Up 11% |

**Instructions**

(a) J. Martinez Manufacturing Inc. asks you to prepare a list of brief comments stating how each of these items supports the solvency and going concern potential of the business. The company wishes to use these comments to support its presentation of data to its creditors. You are to prepare the comments as requested, giving the implications and the limitations of each item separately, and then the collective inference that may be drawn from them about J. Martinez's solvency and going-concern potential.

(b) What warnings should you offer these creditors about the limitations of ratio analysis for the purpose stated here?

## COMMUNICATION ACTIVITY

L. R. Stanton is the Chief Executive Officer of Hi-Tech Electronics. Stanton is an expert engineer but a novice in accounting. Stanton asks you, as an accounting major, to explain (1) the bases for comparison in analyzing Hi-Tech's financial statements and (2) the limitations, if any, in financial statement analysis.

**Instructions**

Write a letter to L. R. Stanton that explains the bases for comparison and the limitations of financial statement analysis.

## GROUP ACTIVITY

Three types of analyses are explained in the chapter: horizontal, vertical, and ratio.

**Instructions**

The class should be divided into five groups. Each group will take one of the following topics: horizontal analysis; vertical analysis; ratio analysis—liquidity; ratio analysis—profitability; and ratio analysis—solvency. For horizontal analysis and vertical analysis, the group should explain the analysis and illustrate its application to the balance sheet and income statement. For each category of ratio analysis, the group should state the formula and purpose of each ratio.

## ETHICS CASE

Vern Fairly, president of Fairly Industries, wishes to issue a press release to bolster his company's image and maybe even its stock price, which has been gradually falling. As controller, you have been asked to provide a list of twenty financial ratios along with some other operating statistics relative to Fairly Industries' first quarter financials and operations. Two days after you provide the ratios and data requested, you are asked by Roberto Sanchez, the public relations director of Fairly, to prove the accuracy of the financial and operating data contained in the press release written by the president and edited by Roberto. In the news release, the president highlights the sales increase of 25% over last year's first quarter and the positive change in the current ratio from 1.5:1 last year to 3:1 this year. He also emphasizes that production was up 50% over the prior year's first quarter. You note that the release contains only positive or improved ratios and none of the negative or deteriorated ratios. For instance, no mention is made that the debt to total assets ratio has increased from 35% to 55%, that inventories are up 89%, and that while the current ratio improved, the acid-test ratio fell from 1:1 to .5:1. Nor is there any mention that the reported profit for the quarter would have been a loss had not the estimated lives of Fairly's plant and machinery been increased by 30%. Roberto emphasized, "The Pres wants this release by early this afternoon."

*Instructions*
   (a) Who are the stakeholders in this situation?
   (b) Is there anything unethical in President Fairly's actions?
   (c) Should you as controller remain silent? Does Roberto have any responsibility?

# CRITICAL THINKING
### ▸ *A Real-World Focus: The Coca-Cola Company*
·····················································································

*The Coca-Cola Company provides refreshments to every corner of the world. Four of its brands are among the five best-selling soft drinks in the world, and it ships nearly 11 billion cases of carbonated soft drinks per year. Despite its success, the company believes that great potential still exists—its top 16 markets account for 80% of its sales, but only 20% of the world's population.*

Selected data from the consolidated financial statements for The Coca-Cola Company are presented below. (All dollars are in millions.)

| | |
|---|---:|
| Total current assets (including cash, accounts receivable, and marketable securities totaling $3056) | $ 5,205 |
| Total current liabilities | 6,177 |
| Net sales | 16,172 |
| Cost of goods sold | 6,167 |
| Net income | 2,554 |
| Average receivables for the year | 1,384 |
| Average inventories for the year | 1,048 |
| Average total assets | 12,947 |
| Average common stockholders' equity | 4,910 |

*Instructions*
   (a) Compute the four liquidity ratios for The Coca-Cola Company.
   (b) Compute the four liquidity ratios for PepsiCo, Inc., using the financial statements in Appendix A.
   (c) Comment on the relative liquidity of the two competitors.
   (d) Compute the following profitability ratios for the two companies: profit margin, asset turnover, return on assets, and return on common stockholders' equity.
   (e) Comment on the relative profitability of the two competitors.

# COMPREHENSIVE FINANCIAL REPORTING PROBLEM
·····················································································

Presented below are the income statements, selected balance sheet information, and selected note disclosures from the Annual Report of Sears, Roebuck and Co. for 1993:

**Sears, Roebuck and Co.**
**Consolidated Statements of Income**

| millions, except per common share data | Year Ended December 31, | | |
|---|---:|---:|---:|
| | 1993 | 1992 | 1991 |
| Revenues | $50,837.5 | $52,344.6 | $50,982.9 |
| Expenses | | | |
| Costs and Expenses | 47,233.7 | 52,478.3 | 48,568.2 |
| Restructuring (note 4) | | 3,108.4 | |
| Interest | 1,498.1 | 1,510.9 | 1,680.5 |
| Total Expenses | 48,731.8 | 57,097.6 | 50,248.7 |
| Operating income (loss) | 2,105.7 | (4,753.0) | 734.2 |
| Other income (loss) | 206.0 | (27.2) | 129.6 |
| Gain on the sale of subsidiaries stock | 635.1 | 91.4 | |

**Sears, Roebuck and Co.**
**Consolidated Statements of Income** *(Cont.)*　　　　Year Ended December 31,

| millions, except per common share data | 1993 | 1992 | 1991 |
|---|---|---|---|
| Income (loss) before income taxes (benefit, minority interest, and equity income | 2,946.8 | (4,688.8) | 863.8 |
| Income taxes (benefit) | 400.9 | (2,114.0) | (38.5) |
| Minority interest and equity in net income of unconsolidated companies | (136.9) | 8.0 | 13.3 |
| Income (loss) from continuing operations | 2,409.1 | (2,566.8) | 915.6 |
| Discontinued operations (note 3) | | | |
| 　Operating income, less income tax expense of $167.7, $299.2, and $231.0 | 240.1 | 507.9 | 363.3 |
| 　Loss on disposal, including income tax expense of $22.0 | (64.0) | | |
| Income (loss) before extraordinary loss and cumulative effect of accounting changes | 2,585.2 | (2,058.9) | 1,278.9 |
| Extraordinary loss related to the early extinguishment of debt | (210.8) | | |
| Cumulative effect of accounting changes (note 2) | | (1,873.4) | |
| Net income (loss) | $2,374.4 | ($3,932.3) | $1,278.9 |
| Earnings (loss) per common share, after allowing for dividends on preferred shares | | | |
| 　Income (loss) from continuing operations | $6.22 | ($7.02) | $2.65 |
| 　Discontinued operations | 0.46 | 1.37 | 1.06 |
| Income (loss) before extraordinary loss and cumulative effect of accounting changes | 6.68 | (5.65) | 3.71 |
| 　Extraordinary loss | (0.55) | | |
| 　Cumulative effect of accounting changes | | (5.07) | |
| 　Net income (loss) | $6.13 | ($10.72) | $3.71 |

| **Selected figures from the Sears balance sheets:** | December 31 | |
|---|---|---|
| millions | 1993 | 1992 |
| Total assets | $90,807.8 | $85,490.6 |
| Retail customer receivables | 15,905.6 | 13,877.6 |
| Inventories | 3,518.0 | 4,047.9 |
| Total liabilities | 76,809.7 | 74,423.2 |
| Common shareholders' equity | | |
| 　Common shares ($.75 par) | $293.8 | $290.6 |
| 　Capital in excess of par | 2,353.8 | 2,194.6 |
| 　Retained earnings | 8,162.8 | 8,772.2 |
| 　Less: Treasury stock (at cost) | (1,703.5) | (1,734.3) |
| 　Adjustments | 995.9 | (311.2) |
| 　　Total common shareholders' equity | $10,102.8 | $9,211.9 |

**Selected information from the notes to Sears' financial statements:**
1. Summary of significant accounting policies
   *Inventories:*
   Inventories . . . are valued primarily at the lower of cost (using the last-in, first-out or LIFO method) or market by application of internally developed price indices to estimate the effects of inflation on inventories. . . . If the first-in, first-out (FIFO) method of inventory valuation had been used instead of the LIFO method, inventories would have been $743.7 and $738.4 million higher at December 31, 1993 and 1992, respectively.

*Property and equipment:*

Property and equipment is stated at cost less accumulated depreciation. Depreciation is provided principally by the straight-line method over the estimated useful lives of the related assets.

2. Accounting changes

Effective Jan. 1, 1992, the Company adopted SFAS No. 106, "Employers' Accounting for Postretirement Benefits Other than Pensions," and SFAS No. 112, "Employers' Accounting for Postemployment Benefits," for all domestic and foreign postretirement and postemployment benefit plans by immediately recognizing the transition amounts. The Company previously expensed the cost of these benefits, which consist of health care and life insurance, as claims were incurred.

3. Discontinued operations

In May 1993, the Company entered into separate agreements to sell the Coldwell-Banker Residential business and Sears Mortgage Banking operations. A $64.0 million after-tax loss was recorded in the second quarter of 1993, primarily due to adverse income tax effects related to the sale of Sears Savings Bank. These sales were completed in the fourth quarter of 1993.

4. Restructuring

The Merchandise Group recorded a pretax charge in the fourth quarter of 1992 of $2.65 billion related to discontinuing its domestic catalog operations, offering a voluntary early retirement program to certain salaried associates, closing unprofitable retail department and specialty stores, streamlining or discontinuing various unprofitable merchandise lines, and the writedown of underutilized assets to market value. Corporate also recorded a $23.8 million pretax charge related to offering termination and early retirement programs to certain associates. Additionally, Homart recorded a $326.6 million pretax writedown of land previously held for office development and selected office properties that were to be sold.

During the first quarter of 1992, the Merchandise Group recorded a $106.0 million pretax charge for severance costs related to cost reduction programs for commission sales and headquarters staff in domestic merchandising.

The Merchandise Group and Corporate restructuring charges and Homart [consolidated subsidiary] property writedowns amounted to a combined after-tax expense of $1.95 billion in 1992.

**Instructions**

(a) Calculate the following ratios for 1993:
   (1) Profit margin percentage (return on sales) for both income from continuing operations and net income.
   (2) Return on common stockholders' equity.
   (3) Return on assets.
   (4) Times interest earned.
Evaluate Sears' profitability.

(b) Sears showed a loss of $1.65 billion from Hurricane Andrew in 1992. In what category does a loss appear in Sears' 1992 income statement.

(c) Sears' revenues from its merchandising operations were $26.29 billion and its cost of sales was $18.76 billion in 1993.
   (1) Calculate Sears' inventory turnover for 1993.
   (2) Suppose you wanted to compare Sears' inventory turnover ratio with that of a Canadian company, which under Canadian accounting standards must use FIFO. Would you be able to make such a comparison? If so, how?
   (3) Calculate Sears' receivables turnover for 1993.
   (4) Unlike most retailers, whose fiscal year ends a month into the following year, Sears' year-end is December 31. What effect does Sears' year-end have on the inventory turnover and receivables turnover ratios?
   (5) What effect does Sears' nonstandard year-end (for a retailer) have on the comparability of Sears' ratios with those of other large retailers?

(d) Sears sold two business segments in 1993.
   (1) What did it sell and in what quarter were these sales completed?
   (2) Where does the income or loss from these sales appear on Sears' income statement?

---

*Answers to Self-Study Questions*

1. b    2. d    3. a    4. c    5. c    6. c    7. c    8. b    9. a    10. b

**Before studying this chapter, you should know or, if necessary, review:**

**a.** *The cost principle. (Ch. 1, p. 11)*

**b.** *Ethics in accounting. (Ch. 1, p. 10)*

**c.** *The computation of cost of goods sold. (Ch. 5, p. 192)*

**d.** *The adjusting and closing process used in a merchandising firm. (Ch. 5, pp. 198–200)*

**e.** *The use of a work sheet in the preparation of financial statements. (Ch. 4, pp. 134–40 and Ch. 5, pp. 195–97)*

# Spokesman Says, "Cut the Scrap."

BRENTWOOD, Tenn. — You've heard of the Big Three Automakers—that's shorthand for General Motors, Ford, and Chrysler, the three big domestic car companies. Well, there's also the Big Three U.S. Bicycle makers—Huffy, Murray, and Roadmaster. Like their automotive counterparts, the bike makers have a big challenge: produce domestically a bicycle at a reasonable sticker price when there's a lot of foreign competition.

Murray (short for Murray Ohio Manufacturing Co.) has found a way to keep costs and prices down— and to make a profit. The company manufactures 15,000 bicycles per day at its plant in southern Tennessee. Instead of marketing the bikes to independent bicycle stores, they sell their products to mass merchants such as Sears.

A bicycle's direct materials include steel, tires, spokes, hubs, and brakes. "We take steel and turn it into tubing which, in turn, becomes the bike frame," says Tom Appleton, product manager. "You do have some planned scrap," he says,

because you might want to stamp a round sprocket out of a square piece of steel. "By taking a round part out of a square piece, you've automatically got around 25% scrap," he says, "which we sell to scrap dealers at 5 percent of its original cost. Then, there's unplanned scrap which occurs when one of the workers—to put it bluntly—makes a mistake. We also sell this scrap, but we lose the labor cost."

The direct labor time to make a Murray bike is only about 30 minutes. That's one good reason why an American manufacturer can do well against global competition. "The key is to manage your costs better than the next guy," says Appleton. The most expensive Murray bicycle retails for around $250 and they sold approximately 3 million units to the U.S. market in a recent year. ◄

CHAPTER · **20**

# MANAGERIAL ACCOUNTING

▶ **STUDY OBJECTIVES** ◀

**After studying this chapter, you should be able to:**

1. Explain the distinguishing features of managerial accounting.
2. Identify the three broad functions of management.
3. Define the three classes of manufacturing costs.
4. Distinguish between product and period costs.
5. Explain the difference between a merchandising and a manufacturing income statement.
6. Indicate how cost of goods manufactured is determined.
7. Explain the difference between a merchandising and a manufacturing balance sheet.

Beginning with this chapter, we turn our attention to issues illustrated in the opening story about Murray Ohio Manufacturing Co., such as the costs of materials and labor and the relationship between costs and profits. To this point in the text, we have described the form and content of **financial statements** for **external users** such as stockholders and creditors. These statements represent the principal end-product of financial accounting. The remaining chapters of this textbook focus primarily on the preparation of **reports** for **internal users**, such as the managers and officers of a company. These reports are an integral part of managerial accounting. The content and organization of this chapter are as follows:

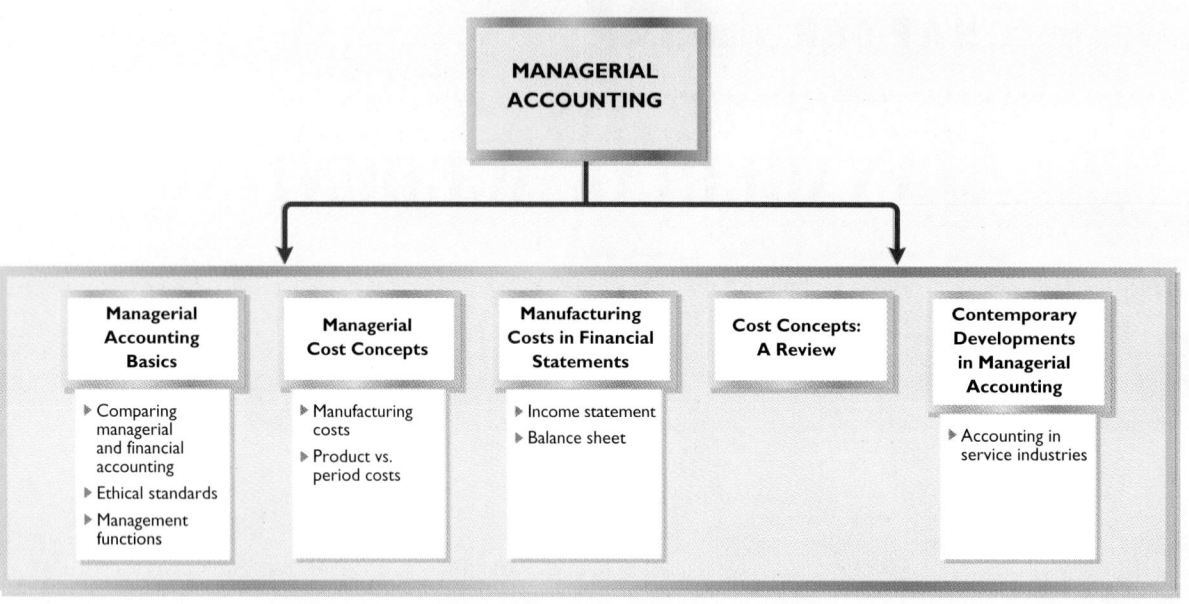

# *M*anagerial Accounting Basics

Managerial accounting, also called management accounting, is a field of accounting that provides economic and financial information for managers and other internal users. The activities that are part of managerial accounting (and the chapters in which they are discussed) are as follows:

1. Explaining manufacturing and nonmanufacturing costs and how they are reported in the financial statements (Chapter 20).
2. Computing the cost of rendering a service or manufacturing a product (Chapters 21 and 22).
3. Determining the behavior of costs and expenses as activity levels change and analyzing cost–volume–profit relationships within a company (Chapter 23).
4. Assisting management in profit planning and formalizing the plans in the form of budgets (Chapter 24).
5. Providing a basis for controlling costs and expenses by comparing actual results with planned objectives and standard costs (Chapters 25 and 26).
6. Accumulating and presenting relevant data for management decision making (Chapter 27).

Managerial accounting applies to all types of businesses—service, merchandising, and manufacturing—and to all forms of business organizations—proprietorships, partnerships, and corporations. Moreover, managerial accounting is needed in not-for-profit entities as well as in profit-oriented enterprises.

## Comparing Managerial and Financial Accounting

There are both similarities and differences between managerial and financial accounting. An important similarity is that each field of accounting deals with the economic events of an enterprise. Thus, their interests overlap. For example, determining the unit cost of manufacturing a product is part of managerial accounting. In contrast, reporting the total cost of goods manufactured and sold is part of financial accounting. In addition, both managerial and financial accounting require that the results of an entity's economic events be quantified and be communicated to interested parties. The diverse needs for economic data among parties interested in an enterprise are responsible for many of the differences between the two fields of accounting.

The principal differences between financial accounting and managerial accounting are summarized in Illustration 20-1.

> **STUDY OBJECTIVE**
> ··········▼··········
> *Explain the distinguishing features of managerial accounting.*

**Illustration 20-1**

*Differences between financial and managerial accounting*

| Financial Accounting | | Managerial Accounting |
|---|---|---|
| • External users, who are stockholders, creditors, and regulatory agencies. | **Primary Users of Reports** | • Internal users, who are officers, department heads, managers, and supervisors in the company. |
| • Classified financial statements. <br> • Issued quarterly and annually. | **Types and Frequency of Reports** | • Internal reports. <br> • Issued as frequently as the need arises. |
| • To provide general-purpose information for all users. | **Purpose of Reports** | • To provide special-purpose information for a particular user for a specific decision. |
| • Pertains to entity as a whole and is highly aggregated (condensed). <br> • Limited to double-entry accounting system and cost data. <br> • Reporting standard is generally accepted accounting principles. | **Content of Reports** | • Pertains to subunits of the entity and may be very detailed. <br> • May extend beyond double-entry accounting system to any type of relevant data. <br> • Reporting standard is relevance to the decision to be made. |
| • Annual independent audit by certified public accountant. | **Verification process** | • No independent audits. |

## Ethical Standards for Managerial Accountants

We have emphasized throughout the textbook the importance of ethics in business and in accounting. Managerial accountants recognize that they have an ethical obligation to their companies and the public. To provide guidance for managerial accountants in the performance of their duties, the Institute of Management Accountants (IMA) has developed a code of ethical standards, entitled *Standards of Ethical Conduct for Management Accountants*, which is shown in Appendix C at the end of the textbook. This code divides the managerial accountants' responsibilities into four areas: (1) competence, (2) confidentiality, (3) integrity, and (4) objectivity. The code states that management accountants should not commit acts in violation of these standards, nor should they condone such acts by others within their organizations. You may wish to review the code to understand the importance of ethics in companies today.

## Management Functions

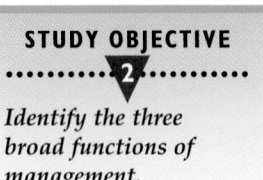

The management of an organization performs three broad functions. They are:

1. Planning.
2. Organizing and directing.
3. Controlling.

In performing these functions, management must make decisions that have a significant impact on the organization.

**Planning** requires management to look ahead and to establish objectives. These objectives are often as diverse as maximizing short-term profits and market share, maintaining a commitment to environmental protection, and contributing to social programs. Today, a key objective of management appears to be to add **value** to the business under its control. Value is usually measured by the trading price of the company's stock and by the potential selling price of the company.

**Organizing and directing** involves coordinating a company's diverse activities and human resources to produce a smooth-running operation. This function relates to the implementation of planned objectives. For example, in companies such as Campbell Soup Company, IBM, General Motors, and Oscar Mayer, purchasing, manufacturing, warehousing, and selling must be coordinated. Similarly, it is necessary to select executives, appoint managers and supervisors, and hire and train employees. Most companies prepare **organization charts** to show the interrelationship of activities and the delegation of authority and responsibility within the company.

## ▶**Accounting in Action** ▸ *Business Insight*

Business researchers have identified different organization types, or "corporate cultures." The ways in which the management function of organizing and directing are carried out differ from one organization type to another:

1. Academies—For the steady climber who must thoroughly master each new job and make one company his or her career home. A classic academy is IBM because as one expert noted: "You don't move ahead until you perform where you are."
2. Clubs—For the individual who strives to fit in. What counts isn't individual achievement, but sincerity, commitment, and doing things for the good of the group. An example is United Parcel Service where one executive noted: "When decisions have to be made we get everyone's opinion, and the company feels like a family to a lot of us."
3. Baseball teams—For those who like to consider themselves free agents. In these situations, companies seek out talent of all ages and experience and reward them by what they produce. They don't care how committed you'll be tomorrow—they want cutting-edge results today. Examples are accounting firms like Price Waterhouse and consulting firms like First Boston Corp.
4. Fortresses—For those who like crisis situations. Many fortresses are companies concerned with survival. Fortresses may be academies, clubs, or baseball teams that have failed in the market place and are struggling to reverse their fortunes. Other fortresses are in a perpetual boom-and-bust cycle, such as natural resources companies.

Companies do change over time. Apple Computer started out as a baseball team but is now becoming an academy. And with deregulation, banks—once clubs—are fast evolving into baseball teams.

*Source:* Adapted from an article by Carol Hymowitz, "Which Corporate Culture Fits You?" *Wall Street Journal*, July 17, 1989.

The third management function, **controlling**, is the process of keeping the firm's activities on track. In controlling operations, management determines whether planned goals are being met and what changes are necessary when there are deviations from targeted objectives.

How do managers achieve control? In small organizations, a manager might use personal observation. A smart manager in a small operation should know the right questions to ask and how to evaluate the answers. But such a system in a large organization would be chaotic. Imagine the president of Ford Motor Company attempting to determine whether planned objectives are being met without some record of what has happened and what is expected to occur. Thus, a formal system of evaluation that includes such items as budgets, responsibility centers, and performance evaluation reports is typically used in large businesses.

As shown by the graphic in the margin, the three functions of management may be depicted as the spokes of a wheel that move around the axle or hub of decision making. Decision making is not a separate management function. Rather, it is the outcome of the exercise of good judgment in planning, organizing and directing, and controlling.

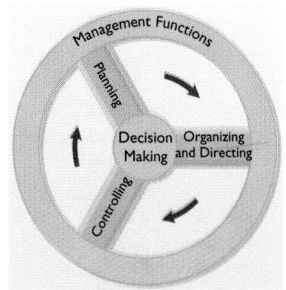

You are now ready to study specific applications of managerial accounting. As you study the managerial chapters, you will encounter many new terms, concepts, and reports. At the same time, you will find some new uses and interpretations of a number of familiar financial accounting terms.

## *Before You Go On . . .*

### ► *Review It*

1. Compare financial accounting and managerial accounting, identifying the principal differences.
2. Give three examples of the expanding role of managerial accounting.
3. Identify and discuss the three broad functions of management.

# *M*anagerial Cost Concepts

To perform the three management functions effectively, management needs information. One very important type of information is related to costs. For example, questions such as the following need answering:

1. What costs are involved in making a product?
2. If production volume is decreased, will costs decrease?
3. What impact will automation have on total costs?
4. How can costs best be controlled in the organization?

To answer these questions, management needs reliable and relevant cost information. We now explain and illustrate the costs that management uses.

## Manufacturing Costs

**Manufacturing** consists of activities and processes that convert raw materials into finished goods. Contrast this type of operation with merchandising, which sells merchandise in the form in which it is purchased. Manufacturing costs are typically classified as follows:

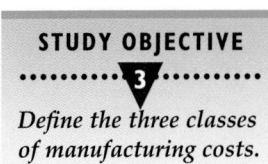

1. Direct materials.
2. Direct labor.
3. Manufacturing overhead.

### Direct Materials

Materials

**Helpful hint** The manufacturer of a product uses masking tape to protect certain sections of the product while other sections are painted. The tape is removed and thrown away when the paint is dry. Should the cost of tape be accounted for as direct or indirect materials?
Answer: Indirect.

To obtain the materials that will be converted into the finished product, the manufacturer purchases raw materials. **Raw materials** represent the basic materials and parts that are to be used in the manufacturing process. For example, steel, plastics, and tires are raw materials in making automobiles.

Raw materials that can be physically and conveniently associated with the finished product during the manufacturing process are called direct materials. Examples include flour in the baking of bread, syrup in the bottling of soft drinks, and steel in the making of automobiles. In the opening story, direct materials for the bicycles included steel, tires, spokes, hubs, and brakes.

Conversely, some raw materials cannot be easily associated with the finished product; these are considered indirect materials. Indirect materials (1) do not physically become part of the finished product, such as lubricants, rosin, and polishing compounds used in the manufacturing process, or (2) cannot be traced because their physical association with the finished product is too small in terms of cost, such as cotter pins, lock washers, and the like. Indirect materials are accounted for as part of **manufacturing overhead**.

### Direct Labor

Factory Labor

The work of factory employees that can be physically and conveniently associated with converting raw materials into finished goods is considered direct labor. In the story about Murray Ohio Manufacturing, it took 30 minutes of direct labor to make a bicycle. Bottlers in a soft drink plant, bakers in a bakery, and typesetters in a print shop are examples of employees whose activities are usually classified as direct labor. In contrast, the wages of maintenance people, timekeepers, and supervisors are usually identified as indirect labor because their efforts have no physical association with the finished product, or it is impractical to trace the costs to the goods produced. Like indirect materials, indirect labor is classified as **manufacturing overhead**.

## ▸Accounting in Action ▸ *Business Insight*

The trend toward more automated and computerized factories will change the way managers and employees interact. For one thing, managers will have fewer direct labor employees to supervise because fewer will be needed on the line. Instead of standing in one spot all day, employees and managers will become more mobile, monitoring the computers that handle the production, and involving themselves in a variety of jobs.

Jobs will be more varied. As machines do more of the repetitive work, employees and managers will need to be more problem-solvers than "cogs in a machine." They will need to be more analytical, to receive more technical training, and to be more highly educated. As a result, they also will be more highly paid.

### Manufacturing Overhead

Manufacturing overhead consists of costs that are indirectly associated with the manufacture of the finished product. These costs may also be defined as manufacturing costs that cannot be classified as either direct materials or direct labor. Manufacturing overhead includes indirect materials, indirect labor, depreciation on factory buildings and machinery, and insurance, taxes, and maintenance on factory facilities.

The magnitude of the three different product costs in terms of the total product cost is provided in the following chart, which covers seven industries:[1]

| PRODUCT COST BY INDUSTRY (Percentage of Total Manufacturing Cost) | | | |
|---|---|---|---|
| **Industry** | **Direct Materials** | **Direct Labor** | **Manufacturing Overhead** |
| Aerospace | 51.7% | 19.3% | 29.0% |
| Computers | 69.9 | 7.5 | 22.5 |
| Electronics | 48.6 | 15.1 | 36.3 |
| Industrial and farm equipment | 46.0 | 12.8 | 41.2 |
| Metal products | 52.0 | 15.7 | 32.3 |
| Motor vehicles and parts | 63.8 | 7.8 | 28.4 |
| Scientific and photographic equipment | 52.3 | 11.3 | 36.5 |
| Average for seven industries | 54.4% | 12.9% | 32.6% |

**Illustration 20-2**

*Product cost components by industry*

Note that the direct labor component is the smallest. This component of product cost is dropping substantially because of automation. In some companies, direct labor has become as little as 5% of the total cost.

## ►*A*ccounting in *A*ction ► *Business Insight*

In valuing inventories, accountants include three types of costs: materials, overhead, and labor. Allocating materials and labor costs to specific products is fairly straightforward. But accountants have big trouble dealing with overhead, a black hole that swallows up everything from the equipment used to fashion a product to the security guard who watches over the plant at night. How much of the purchasing agent's salary is attributable to the semiconductor chip, how much to the typewriter, how much to the hundred other products made in the same plant? What about the grease that keeps the machines humming, or the computers that make sure paychecks come out on time? Boiled down to its simplest form, the question becomes: Which products cause which costs?

## Product versus Period Costs

Each of the manufacturing cost elements (direct materials, direct labor, and manufacturing overhead) are product costs. As the term suggests, product costs are costs that are a necessary and integral part of producing the finished product. These costs do not become expenses under the matching principle until the finished goods inventory is sold. The expense is cost of goods sold. Direct materials and direct labor are often referred to as prime costs because of their direct association with the manufacturing of the finished product. In addition, because direct labor and manufacturing overhead are incurred in converting raw materials into finished goods, these two cost elements are often referred to as conversion costs.

**STUDY OBJECTIVE**

• • • • • • • • • • ▽ **4** • • • • • • • • • • •

*Distinguish between product and period costs.*

---

[1]James A. Hendricks, "Applying Cost Accounting to Factory Automation," *Management Accounting,* December 1988, p. 26.

**Period costs** are costs that are identified with a specific time period rather than with a salable product. These costs relate to nonmanufacturing costs and therefore are not inventoriable costs. Period costs include selling and administrative expenses that are deducted from revenues in the period in which they are incurred.

The foregoing relationships and cost terms are summarized in Illustration 20-3. Our main concern in this chapter is with product costs.

**Illustration 20-3**

*Product versus period costs*

## *Before You Go On . . .*

▸ *Review It*

1. What are the major cost classifications involved in manufacturing a product?
2. What are product and period costs and their relationship to the manufacturing process?

▸ *Do It*

In making bicycles, a company has the following costs: tires, salaries of employees who put tires on the wheels, factory building depreciation, wheel nuts, spokes, salary of factory foreman, handle bars, and salaries of factory maintenance employees. Classify each cost as direct materials, direct labor, or manufacturing overhead.

*Reasoning:* Direct materials are raw materials that can be physically and conveniently associated with the finished product. Direct labor is the work of factory employees that can be physically and conveniently associated with the finished product. Manufacturing overhead are costs that are indirectly associated with the finished product.

*Solution:* Tires, spokes, and handle bars are direct materials. Salaries of employees who put tires on the wheels are direct labor. All of the other costs are manufacturing overhead.

*Related exercise material: BE20–4, BE20–6, BE20–11, E20–1, and E20–2.*

# Manufacturing Costs in Financial Statements
•••••••••••••••••••••••••••••••••••••••••••••••••••••••••••••••••••••

The financial statements of a manufacturing company are very similar to those of a merchandising company. The principal differences pertain to the cost of goods sold section of the income statement and the current assets section of the balance sheet.

## Income Statement

Under a periodic inventory system, the income statements of a merchandising company and a manufacturing company differ in the cost of goods sold section. For a merchandising company, cost of goods sold is computed by adding the beginning merchandise inventory and the **cost of goods purchased** and subtracting the ending merchandise inventory. For a manufacturing company, cost of goods sold is computed by adding the beginning finished goods inventory and **cost of goods manufactured** and subtracting the ending finished goods inventory. The different components are shown graphically below:

**STUDY OBJECTIVE**
•••••••••▼**5**•••••••••
*Explain the difference between a merchandising and a manufacturing income statement.*

**Helpful hint** Cost of goods manufactured in a manufacturing company is like cost of goods purchased in a merchandising company.

**Illustration 20-4**

*Cost of goods sold components*

**Helpful hint** Note that a periodic inventory system is used here.

The cost of goods sold sections for merchandising and manufacturing enterprises presented below illustrate the different presentations:

**Illustration 20-5**

*Cost of goods sold sections of merchandising and manufacturing income statements*

| Merchandise Company<br>Partial Income Statement<br>For the Year Ended December 31, 1996 | | Manufacturing Company<br>Partial Income Statement<br>For the Year Ended December 31, 1996 | |
|---|---|---|---|
| Cost of goods sold | | Cost of goods sold | |
| Merchandise inventory, January 1 | $ 70,000 | Finished goods inventory, January 1 | $ 90,000 |
| Cost of goods purchased | 650,000 | Cost of goods manufactured<br>(see Illustration 20-7) | 370,000 |
| Cost of Goods Available for Sale | 720,000 | Cost of Goods Available for Sale | 460,000 |
| Merchandise inventory, December 31 | 400,000 | Finished goods inventory, December 31 | 80,000 |
| Cost of goods sold | $320,000 | Cost of goods sold | $380,000 |

The other sections of an income statement are similar for both a merchandising and a manufacturing company.

A number of accounts are involved in determining the cost of goods manufactured. To eliminate excessive detail in the income statement, it is customary to show in the income statement only the total cost of goods manufactured and to present the details in a Cost of Goods Manufactured Schedule. The form and content of this schedule are shown in Illustration 20-7 (page 849).

### Determining the Cost of Goods Manufactured

**STUDY OBJECTIVE**
••••••••••**6**••••••••••

*Indicate how cost of goods manufactured is determined.*

An example may be helpful in showing how the cost of goods manufactured for a period is determined. Assume that Ford Motor Company has a number of automobiles in various stages of production on January 1. In total, these partially completed units are called **beginning work in process inventory**. The costs assigned to beginning work in process inventory are based on the **manufacturing costs incurred in the prior period**. In the current year, Ford Motor continues the production of automobiles. The manufacturing costs incurred in the current year are used first to complete the work in process on January 1 and then to start the production of other vehicles. The sum of the direct materials costs, direct labor costs, and manufacturing overhead incurred in the current year is the total manufacturing costs.

**Helpful hint**  Does the amount of "total manufacturing costs for the current year" include the amount of "beginning work in process inventory?"
Answer: No.

We now have two cost amounts: (1) the cost of the beginning work in process and (2) the total manufacturing costs for the current period. The sum of these costs is the total cost of work in process for the year.

At the end of the year, some vehicles may be only partially completed. The costs of these units become the cost of the **ending work in process inventory**. To find the cost of goods manufactured, we subtract this cost from the total cost of work in process. The determination of the cost of goods manufactured is shown graphically in Illustration 20-6.

**Illustration 20-6**

*Cost of goods manufactured formula*

### Cost of Goods Manufactured Schedule

An internal financial schedule called the **cost of goods manufactured schedule** shows each of the cost elements explained in Illustration 20-6. The schedule for Olsen Manufacturing Company using assumed data is shown in Illustration 20-7. Note that detailed data are presented for direct materials and manufacturing overhead.

A review of Illustration 20-6 along with an examination of the cost of goods manufactured schedule, Illustration 20-7, should help you distinguish between "total manufacturing costs" and "cost of goods manufactured." The difference is the effect of the change in work in process during the period.

Illustration 20-7

*Cost of goods manufactured schedule*

### OLSEN MANUFACTURING COMPANY
### Cost of Goods Manufactured Schedule
### For the Year Ended December 31, 1996

| | | | |
|---|---|---|---|
| Work in process, January 1 | | | $ 18,400 |
| Direct materials | | | |
| Raw materials inventory, January 1 | $ 16,700 | | |
| Raw materials purchases | 152,500 | | |
| Total raw materials available for use | 169,200 | | |
| Less: Raw materials inventory, December 31 | 22,800 | | |
| Direct materials used | | $146,400 | |
| Direct labor | | 175,600 | |
| Manufacturing overhead | | | |
| Indirect labor | 14,300 | | |
| Factory repairs | 12,600 | | |
| Factory utilities | 10,100 | | |
| Factory depreciation | 9,440 | | |
| Factory insurance | 8,360 | | |
| Total manufacturing overhead | | 54,800 | |
| Total manufacturing costs | | | 376,800 |
| Total cost of work in process | | | 395,200 |
| Less: Work in process, December 31 | | | 25,200 |
| Cost of goods manufactured | | | $370,000 |

## Balance Sheet

**STUDY OBJECTIVE**

▼ **7**

*Explain the difference between a merchandising and a manufacturing balance sheet.*

Unlike the balance sheet for a merchandising company, which shows just one category of inventory, the balance sheet for a manufacturing company may have three inventory accounts. They are:

**Finished Goods Inventory**, which shows the cost of completed goods on hand.

**Work in Process Inventory**, which shows the cost applicable to units that have been started into production but are only partially completed.

**Raw Materials Inventory**, which shows the cost of raw materials on hand.

Finished Goods Inventory is to a manufacturing enterprise what Merchandise Inventory is to a merchandising firm because it represents the goods that are available for sale.

The current assets sections presented in Illustration 20-8 contrast the presentation of inventories of a merchandising company with those of a manufacturing company. Manufacturing inventories are generally listed in the order of their liquidity—their expected realization in cash. Thus, finished goods inventory is listed first. The remainder of the balance sheet is similar for the two types of companies.

Each step in the accounting cycle for a merchandising company is applicable to a manufacturing company. For example, prior to preparing financial statements, adjusting entries are required. The adjusting entries are essentially the same as those of a merchandising company.

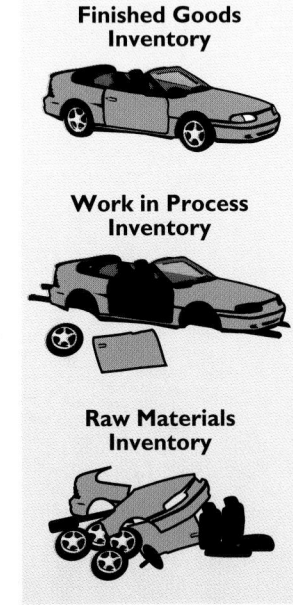

**Finished Goods Inventory**

**Work in Process Inventory**

**Raw Materials Inventory**

**Illustration 20-8**

*Current assets sections of merchandising and manufacturing balance sheets*

| Merchandising Company<br>Balance Sheet<br>December 31, 1996 | | Manufacturing Company<br>Balance Sheet<br>December 31, 1996 | | |
|---|---|---|---|---|
| Current assets | | Current assets | | |
| Cash | $100,000 | Cash | | $180,000 |
| Receivables (net) | 210,000 | Receivables (net) | | 210,000 |
| Merchandise inventory | 400,000 | Inventories: | | |
| Prepaid expenses | 22,000 | Finished goods | $80,000 | |
| Total current assets | $732,000 | Work in process | 25,200 | |
| | | Raw materials | 22,800 | 128,000 |
| | | Prepaid expenses | | 18,000 |
| | | Total current assets | | $536,000 |

The closing entries for a manufacturing company are also similar to those of a merchandising company. The use of a work sheet in the accounting cycle and the journalizing of closing entries for a manufacturing company are illustrated in the appendix at the end of this chapter.

# Cost Concepts—A Review

You have learned a number of cost concepts in this chapter. Because many of these concepts are new, we believe an extended example will be helpful in illustrating how these various cost concepts are used. To illustrate, assume that Northridge Company manufactures and sells pre-hung metal doors. Recently, it has decided to start selling pre-hung wood doors as well. An old warehouse that the company presently owns will be used to manufacture the new product. To manufacture and sell these pre-hung wood doors, Northridge identifies the following costs:

1. The material cost (wood) for each door is $10.
2. Labor costs involved in constructing a wood door are $8 per door.
3. Depreciation on the new equipment used to make the wood door using the straight-line method is $25,000 per year.
4. Property taxes on the old warehouse used to make the wood doors are $6,000 per year.
5. Advertising costs for the pre-hung wood doors total $2,500 per month or $30,000 per year.
6. Sales commissions related to pre-hung wood doors sold are $4 per door.
7. Maintenance salaries for the old warehouse are $28,000.
8. Salary of plant manager in charge of pre-hung wood doors is $70,000.
9. Cost of shipping pre-hung wood doors is $12 per door sold.

These manufacturing and selling costs can be assigned to the various categories shown in Illustration 20-9.

| | Product Costs | | | | | |
|---|---|---|---|---|---|---|
| Cost Item | Direct Materials | Direct Labor | Manufacturing Overhead | Period Costs | Prime Costs | Conversion Costs |
| 1. Material cost ($10) per door | X | | | | X | |
| 2. Labor costs ($8) per door | | X | | | X | X |
| 3. Depreciation on new equipment ($25,000 per year) | | | X | | | X |
| 4. Property taxes ($6,000 per year) | | | X | | | X |
| 5. Advertising costs ($30,000 per year) | | | | X | | |
| 6. Sales commissions ($4 per door) | | | | X | | |
| 7. Maintenance salaries ($28,000 per year) | | | X | | | X |
| 8. Salary of plant manager ($70,000) | | | X | | | X |
| 9. Cost of shipping pre-hung doors ($12 per door) | | | | X | | |

**Illustration 20-9**

*Assignment of costs to cost categories*

Remember that total manufacturing costs are the sum of the product costs—direct materials, direct labor, and manufacturing overhead costs. For example, assume that Northridge Company produces 10,000 pre-hung wood doors the first year. The total manufacturing costs are:

**Illustration 20-10**

*Computation of total manufacturing cost*

| Cost Number and Item | Manufacturing Cost |
|---|---|
| 1. Material cost ($10 × 10,000) | $100,000 |
| 2. Labor cost ($8 × 10,000) | 80,000 |
| 3. Depreciation on new equipment | 25,000 |
| 4. Property taxes | 6,000 |
| 7. Maintenance salaries | 28,000 |
| 8. Salary of plant manager | 70,000 |
| Total manufacturing costs | $309,000 |

If total manufacturing costs are $309,000, then the manufacturing cost per unit (cost to produce one pre-hung wood door) is $30.90 ($309,000 ÷ 10,000 units).

The cost concepts above will be used extensively in subsequent chapters. Study Illustration 20-9 carefully. If you do not understand any of these classifications, go back and reread the appropriate section in this chapter.

# Contemporary Developments in Managerial Accounting

Since the early 1970s, the competitive environment for U.S. businesses has changed significantly. Within the United States, for example, the airline, financial services, and telecommunication industries have been deregulated. Globally, competition from such countries as Japan and Germany has intensified, particularly in the automotive and electronics industries. Consequently, contemporary business managers demand from managerial accountants different and better information than they needed just a few years ago.

Such factors as the following contribute to the expanding role of managerial accounting as we look toward the next century:

- *Importance of quality.* Many companies have installed a total quality control (TQC) system to reduce defects in finished products. This system requires timely data on defective products, rework costs, and the cost of honoring warranty contracts.
- *Automation in the manufacturing process.* Through computer-integrated manufacturing (CIM), many companies can now manufacture products that are untouched by human hands. An example is the use of robotic equipment in the steel and automobile industries. Automation significantly reduces the importance of direct labor costs in some cases, because the worker simply monitors the manufacturing process by watching instrument panels.
- *Expanded use of electronic data processing.* The widespread use of computers has greatly reduced the cost of accumulating, storing, and reporting managerial accounting information. Moreover, computers make it possible to do more detailed costing of products, processes, and services than is possible under manual processing.
- *Innovative inventory systems.* Many companies have changed to inventory systems that significantly lower inventory levels and costs. The smaller inventories have reduced or eliminated the need for extensive perpetual inventory records for manufacturing companies. More will be said about this factor in Chapter 22.
- *Focus on activities for overhead costs.* In order to obtain more accurate product costs, many companies are accounting for overhead costs by the activities used in making the product. Activities include purchasing materials, handling raw materials, and production order scheduling. This development, called activity-based costing, is explained in Chapter 22.
- *Service industry needs.* Managers in service industries are under increasing pressure to determine the cost of their services and to establish prices that are competitive. The bankruptcies of major airlines, such as PanAm and Eastern, underscore the need for more and better cost data.

Not too long ago, the managerial accountant was primarily engaged in **cost accounting**—collecting and reporting manufacturing costs to management. Today, the managerial accountant's responsibilities extend to **cost management**—providing managers with data on the efficient use of company resources in both manufacturing and service industries.

## ▸*T*echnology in *A*ction

The use of computers is as important in managerial accounting as in financial accounting. As one expert on manufacturing recently noted "I am convinced that the manufacturers that survive in the 1990s will be those with an unbelievable amount of automation and computerization. The winners will have true computer-integrated manufacturing (CIM). In such a scenario, computers will do everything. They will design the parts, tell you if they can be built, set up the machines on the line, inspect the products, and pop them out on the loading dock with a computerized bill of lading."

## Managerial Accounting in Service Enterprises

Service industries and companies include the following:

**Illustration 20-11**

*Service industries and companies*

| **Service Industries** | **Service Companies** | **Service Industries** | **Service Companies** |
|---|---|---|---|
| <br>Transportation | Amtrak, American Airlines, Greyhound Bus Co., trucking companies | <br>Professional services | Attorneys, certified public accountants, physicians, architects, engineers |
| <br>Package delivery service | United States Postal Service, Federal Express, United Parcel Service | <br>Financial institutions | Citicorp, Merrill Lynch, mortgage companies, insurance companies |
| <br>Telecommunications | AT&T, cable television companies, radio and television networks | <br>Health care | Blue Cross—Blue Shield, hospitals, outpatient clinics, nursing homes |

Managers of service enterprises have the same need for accurate, relevant, and timely information as managers of manufacturing companies. A primary need in service enterprises is the cost of the service. For example, what is the cost per mile to fly one passenger from New York to Los Angeles? What is the cost per day of intensive care in a cardiology unit of a major hospital? A manager's knowledge of the cost of services is vital in determining the prices to be charged for the services and in assuring that the enterprise will continue as a going concern.

## ►Accounting in Action ► *Business Insight*

 At South Central Bell (Telephone), management accountants have shed their score-keeping image. A corporate reorganization plan challenged the accountants to "show their stuff." The accountants took on the roles of interpreter, advisor, and partner. To do so, the management accountants had to understand what the numbers mean, relate the numbers to business activity, and recommend alternative courses of action. In addition, they evaluate alternatives and make decisions to maximize business efficiency.

*Source: Management Accounting, March 1993, p. 29.*

In some respects, the challenges for managerial accounting are greater in services enterprises than in manufacturing companies. How does a professional firm measure the efficiency and productivity of its professional staff? How does a brokerage firm measure the cost of serving individual customers? What measures can be used to evaluate the quality of services in a hospital or a bank?

Managers of service enterprises look to managerial accounting to answer these questions. In some companies, it may be necessary for the managerial accountant to develop new systems for measuring the cost of serving individual customers and new operating controls to improve the quality and efficiency of specific services.

# *Before You Go On . . .*

## ▸ *Review It*

1. How does the content of an income statement differ between a merchandising company and a manufacturing company?
2. How are the work in process inventories reported in the cost of goods manufactured schedule?
3. How does the content of the balance sheet differ between a merchandising company and a manufacturing company?

## ▸ *A Look Back at Murray Ohio Manufacturing Company*

Refer to the opening story regarding Murray and answer the following questions:

1. What are the similarities in the production processes, general product cost accounts, and cost flows of the car companies and the bicycle makers?
2. Relate the management functions discussed in the chapter to the manufacturing of bicycles.
3. Identify some of the likely manufacturing overhead costs incurred by a bicycle manufacturer.

### Solution:

1. Both car companies and bicycle makers are engaged in a manufacturing process that involves designing, producing, assembling, finishing, and marketing a multi-piece, multi-model product line. Both use general product cost accounts such as direct materials, direct labor, and overhead cost accounts, along with raw material, work in process, and finished goods inventory accounts. The cost flows would also be similar through these accounts.
2. Manufacturing bicycles involves **planning**, that is, establishing production and marketing objectives; **organizing** assets and employees into a production work force; implementing planned objectives by coordinating purchasing, manufacturing, warehousing, and selling functions; and **directing** and **controlling** activities and operations through supervision, training, evaluation, reporting, and analysis.
3. A bicycle manufacturer would likely incur overhead costs such as indirect materials (abrasives, lubricants, etc.); indirect labor (supervisors, maintenance, etc.); depreciation of factory buildings and machinery; and factory insurance, taxes, and utilities.

# *S*ummary of Study Objectives

**1.** *Explain the distinguishing features of managerial accounting.* The distinguishing features of managerial accounting are:

Primary users of reports—internal users, who are officers, department heads, managers, and supervisors in the company.

Type and frequency of reports—internal reports that are issued as frequently as the need arises.

Purpose of reports—to provide special-purpose information for a particular user for a specific decision.

Content of reports—pertains to subunits of the entity and may be very detailed; may extend beyond double-entry accounting systems; the reporting standard is relevance to the decision being made.

Verification of reports—no independent audits.

**2.** *Identify the three broad functions of management.* The three functions are planning, organizing and directing, and

controlling. Planning requires management to look ahead and to establish objectives. Organizing and directing involves coordinating the diverse activities and human resources of a company to produce a smooth-running operation. Controlling is the process of keeping the activities on track.

**3.** *Define the three classes of manufacturing costs.* Manufacturing costs are typically classified as either (1) direct materials, (2) direct labor, or (3) manufacturing overhead. Raw materials that can be physically and conveniently associated with the finished product during the manufacturing process are called direct materials. The work of factory employees that can be physically and conveniently associated with converting raw materials into finished goods is considered direct labor. Manufacturing overhead consists of costs that are indirectly associated with the manufacture of the finished product.

**4.** *Distinguish between product and period costs.* Product costs are costs that are a necessary and integral part of producing the finished product. Product costs are also called inventoriable costs. These costs do not become expenses under the matching principle until the inventory to which they attach is sold. Period costs are costs that are identified with a specific time period rather than with a salable product. These costs relate to nonmanufacturing costs and therefore are not inventoriable costs.

**5.** *Explain the difference between a merchandising and a manufacturing income statement.* The difference between a merchandising and a manufacturing income statement is in the cost of goods sold section. A manufacturing cost of goods sold section shows beginning and ending finished goods inventories and the cost of goods manufactured.

**6.** *Indicate how cost of goods manufactured is determined.* The cost of the beginning work in process is added to the total manufacturing costs for the current year to arrive at the total cost of work in process for the year. The ending work in process is then subtracted from the total cost of work in process to arrive at the cost of goods manufactured.

**7.** *Explain the difference between a merchandising and a manufacturing balance sheet.* The difference between a manufacturing and a merchandising balance sheet is in the current asset section. In the current asset section of a manufacturing company's balance sheet, three inventory accounts are presented: finished goods inventory, work in process inventory, and raw materials inventory.

---

◢**A**PPENDIX ▸ *Accounting Cycle for a Manufacturing Company*

The accounting cycle for a manufacturing company is the same as for a merchandising company when a periodic inventory system is used. Except for the additional manufacturing inventories and manufacturing cost accounts, the journalizing and posting of transactions is the same. Similarly, the preparation of a trial balance and the journalizing and posting of adjusting entries are the same. Some changes, however, occur in the use of a work sheet and in preparing closing entries.

To illustrate the changes in the work sheet, we will use the cost of goods manufactured schedule for Olsen Manufacturing presented in Illustration 20-7 of the chapter and other assumed data. For convenience, the cost of goods manufactured schedule is reproduced below:

**STUDY OBJECTIVE**

▼

*After studying this appendix, you should be able to:*

**8.** *Prepare a work sheet and closing entries for a manufacturing company.*

**Illustration 20A-1**

*Cost of goods manufactured schedule*

| OLSEN MANUFACTURING COMPANY<br>Cost of Goods Manufactured Schedule<br>For the Year Ended December 31, 1996 | | | |
|---|---:|---:|---:|
| Work in process, January 1 | | | $ 18,400 |
| Direct materials | | | |
|   Raw materials inventory, January 1 | $ 16,700 | | |
|   Raw materials purchases | 152,500 | | |
|   Total raw materials available for use | 169,200 | | |
|   Less: Raw materials inventory, December 31 | 22,800 | | |
|   Direct materials used | | $146,400 | |
| Direct labor | | 175,600 | |
| Manufacturing overhead | | | |
|   Indirect labor | 14,300 | | |
|   Factory repairs | 12,600 | | |
|   Factory utilities | 10,100 | | |
|   Factory depreciation | 9,440 | | |
|   Factory insurance | 8,360 | | |
|     Total manufacturing overhead | | 54,800 | |
| Total manufacturing costs | | | 376,800 |
| Total cost of work in process | | | 395,200 |
| Less: Work in process, December 31 | | | 25,200 |
| Cost of goods manufactured | | | $370,000 |

# Work Sheet

Illustration 20A-2

*Partial work sheet*

When a work sheet is used in preparing financial statements, two additional columns are needed for the cost of goods manufactured schedule. As illustrated in the work sheet in Illustration 20A-2, debit and credit columns for this schedule have been inserted before the income statement columns.

**OLSEN MANUFACTURING COMPANY**
**(Partial) Work Sheet**
**For the Year Ended December 31, 1996**

| | Adjusted Trial Balance Dr. | Cr. | Cost of Goods Manufactured Dr. | Cr. | Income Statement Dr. | Cr. | Balance Sheet Dr. | Cr. |
|---|---|---|---|---|---|---|---|---|
| Cash | 42,500 | | | | | | 42,500 | |
| Accounts Receivable (Net) | 71,900 | | | | | | 71,900 | |
| Finished Goods Inv. | 24,600 | | | | 24,600 | 19,500 | 19,500 | |
| Work in Process Inv. | 18,400 | | 18,400 | 25,200 | | | 25,200 | |
| Raw Materials Inv. | 16,700 | | 16,700 | 22,800 | | | 22,800 | |
| Plant Assets | 724,000 | | | | | | 724,000 | |
| Accumulated Depr. | | 278,400 | | | | | | 278,400 |
| Notes Payable | | 100,000 | | | | | | 100,000 |
| Accounts Payable | | 40,000 | | | | | | 40,000 |
| Income Taxes Payable | | 5,000 | | | | | | 5,000 |
| Common Stock | | 200,000 | | | | | | 200,000 |
| Retained Earnings | | 205,100 | | | | | | 205,100 |
| Sales | | 680,000 | | | | 680,000 | | |
| Raw Materials Purchases | 152,500 | | 152,500 | | | | | |
| Direct Labor | 175,600 | | 175,600 | | | | | |
| Indirect Labor | 14,300 | | 14,300 | | | | | |
| Factory Repairs | 12,600 | | 12,600 | | | | | |
| Factory Utilities | 10,100 | | 10,100 | | | | | |
| Factory Depreciation | 9,440 | | 9,440 | | | | | |
| Factory Insurance | 8,360 | | 8,360 | | | | | |
| Selling Expenses | 114,900 | | | | 114,900 | | | |
| Administrative Exp. | 92,600 | | | | 92,600 | | | |
| Income Tax Exp. | 20,000 | | | | 20,000 | | | |
| Totals | 1,508,500 | 1,508,500 | 418,000 | 48,000 | | | | |
| Cost of Goods Manufactured | | | | 370,000 | 370,000 | | | |
| Totals | | | 418,000 | 418,000 | 622,100 | 699,500 | 905,900 | 828,500 |
| Net Income | | | | | 77,400 | | | 77,400 |
| Totals | | | | | 699,500 | 699,500 | 905,900 | 905,900 |

In the cost of goods manufactured columns, the beginning inventories of raw materials and work in process are entered as debits. In addition, all the manufacturing costs are entered as debits. The reason is that each of these amounts increases cost of goods manufactured. Ending inventories for raw materials and work in process are entered as credits in the cost of goods manufactured columns because they have the opposite effect—they decrease cost of goods manufactured. The balancing amount for these columns is the cost of goods manufactured. Note that the amount, $370,000, agrees with the amount reported for cost of goods manufactured in Illustration 20-7. This amount is also entered in the income statement debit column.

The income statement and balance sheet columns for a manufacturing company are basically the same as for a merchandising company. For example, the treatment of the finished goods inventories is identical with the treatment of merchandise inventory. That is, the beginning inventory is entered in the debit column, and the ending finished goods inventory is entered in the income statement credit column and the balance sheet debit column.

As in the case of a merchandising company, financial statements can be prepared from the statement columns of the work sheet. In addition, the cost of goods manufactured schedule can also be prepared directly from the work sheet.

# Closing Entries

The closing entries for a manufacturing company are different than for a merchandising company. **A Manufacturing Summary account is used to close all accounts that appear in the cost of goods manufactured schedule.** The balance of the Manufacturing Summary account is the Cost of Goods Manufactured for the period. Manufacturing Summary is then closed to Income Summary. The closing entries can be prepared from the work sheet. As illustrated below, the closing entries for the manufacturing accounts are prepared first. The closing entries for Olsen Manufacturing are as follows:

| | | | |
|---|---|---:|---:|
| Dec. 31 | Work in Process Inventory (Dec. 31) | 25,200 | |
| | Raw Materials Inventory (Dec. 31) | 22,800 | |
| | **Manufacturing Summary** | | 48,000 |
| | (To record ending raw materials and work in process inventories) | | |
| | | | |
| 31 | **Manufacturing Summary** | 418,000 | |
| | Work in Process Inventory (Jan. 1) | | 18,400 |
| | Raw Materials Inventory (Jan. 1) | | 16,700 |
| | Raw Materials Purchases | | 152,500 |
| | Direct Labor | | 175,600 |
| | Indirect Labor | | 14,300 |
| | Factory Repairs | | 12,600 |
| | Factory Utilities | | 10,100 |
| | Factory Depreciation | | 9,440 |
| | Factory Insurance | | 8,360 |
| | (To close beginning raw materials and work in process inventories and manufacturing cost accounts) | | |
| | | | |
| 31 | Finished Goods Inventory (Dec. 31) | 19,500 | |
| | Sales | 680,000 | |
| | Income Summary | | 699,500 |
| | (To record ending finished goods inventory and close sales account) | | |
| | | | |
| 31 | Income Summary | 622,100 | |
| | Finished Goods Inventory (Jan. 1) | | 24,600 |
| | **Manufacturing Summary** | | 370,000 |
| | Selling Expenses | | 114,900 |
| | Administrative Expenses | | 92,600 |
| | Income Tax Expense | | 20,000 |
| | (To close beginning finished goods inventory, manufacturing summary, and expense accounts) | | |

| 31 | Income Summary | | 77,400 | |
| | Retained Earnings | | | 77,400 |
| | (To close net income to retained earnings) | | | |

After posting, the summary accounts will show the following:

**Manufacturing Summary**

| Dec. 31 | Close | 418,000 | Dec. 31 | Close | 48,000 |
| | | | 31 | Close | 370,000 |

**Income Summary**

| Dec. 31 | Close | 622,100 | Dec. 31 | Close | 699,500 |
| 31 | Close | 77,400 | | | |

These data precisely track the closing entries. It also would be possible to post each account balance to the Manufacturing Summary account.

# Summary of Study Objective for Chapter 20 Appendix

**8.** *Prepare a work sheet and closing entries for a manufacturing company.* Two additional columns are needed in the work sheet for the cost of goods manufactured. In these columns, the beginning inventories of raw materials and work in process are entered as debits and the ending inventories are entered as credits; all manufacturing costs are entered as debits. To close all of the accounts that appear in the cost of goods manufactured schedule, a Manufacturing Summary account is used.

# Glossary

**Conversion costs** Direct labor and manufacturing overhead costs incurred in converting raw materials into finished goods. (p. 845).

**Cost of goods manufactured** Total cost of work in process less the cost of the ending work in process inventory. (p. 848).

**Direct labor** The work of factory employees that can be physically and conveniently associated with converting raw materials into finished goods. (p. 844).

**Direct materials** Raw materials that can be physically and conveniently associated with manufacturing the finished product. (p. 844).

**Indirect labor** Work of factory employees that has no physical association with the finished product, or it is impractical to trace the costs to the goods produced. (p. 844).

**Indirect materials** Raw materials that do not physically become part of the finished product or cannot be traced because their physical association with the finished product is too small. (p. 844).

**Managerial accounting** A field of accounting that provides economic and financial information for managers and other internal users. (p. 840).

**Manufacturing overhead** Manufacturing costs that are indirectly associated with the manufacture of the finished product. (p. 844).

**Period costs** Costs that are identified with a specific time period and charged to expense as incurred. (p. 846).

**Prime costs** Direct materials and direct labor. (p. 845).

**Product costs** Costs that are a necessary and integral part of producing the finished product. (p. 845).

**Total cost of work in process** Cost of the beginning work in process plus total manufacturing costs for the current period. (p. 848).

**Total manufacturing costs** The sum of direct materials, direct labor, and manufacturing overhead incurred in the current period. (p. 848).

# DEMONSTRATION PROBLEM 1

Superior Manufacturing Company has the following cost and expense data for the year ending December 31, 1996.

| | | | |
|---|---|---|---|
| Raw materials, 1/1/96 | $ 30,000 | Insurance, factory | $ 14,000 |
| Raw materials, 12/31/96 | 20,000 | Property taxes, factory building | 6,000 |
| Raw materials purchased | 205,000 | Sales (net) | 1,500,000 |
| Indirect materials | 15,000 | Delivery expenses | 100,000 |
| Work in process, 1/1/96 | 80,000 | Sales commissions | 150,000 |
| Work in process, 12/31/96 | 50,000 | Indirect labor | 90,000 |
| Finished goods, 1/1/96 | 110,000 | Factory machinery rent | 40,000 |
| Finished goods, 12/31/96 | 120,000 | Factory utilities | 65,000 |
| Direct labor | 350,000 | Depreciation, factory building | 24,000 |
| Factory manager's salary | 35,000 | Administrative expenses | 300,000 |

## Instructions

(a) Prepare a cost of goods manufactured schedule for Superior Company for 1996.

(b) Prepare an income statement for Superior Company for 1996.

(c) Assume that Superior Company's ledgers show the balances of the following current asset accounts: Cash, $17,000, Accounts Receivable (net), $120,000, Prepaid Expenses, $13,000, and Short-term Investments, $26,000. Prepare the current assets section of the balance sheet for Superior Company as of December 31, 1996.

## Solution to Demonstration Problem 1

(a)

**SUPERIOR MANUFACTURING COMPANY**
**Cost of Goods Manufactured Schedule**
**For the Year Ended December 31, 1996**

| | | | |
|---|---|---|---|
| Work in process, 1/1 | | | $ 80,000 |
| Direct materials | | | |
| Raw materials inventory, 1/1 | $ 30,000 | | |
| Raw materials purchased | 205,000 | | |
| Total raw materials available for use | 235,000 | | |
| Less: Raw materials inventory, 12/31 | 20,000 | | |
| Direct materials used | | $215,000 | |
| Direct labor | | 350,000 | |
| Manufacturing overhead | | | |
| Indirect labor | 90,000 | | |
| Factory utilities | 65,000 | | |
| Factory machinery rent | 40,000 | | |
| Factory manager's salary | 35,000 | | |
| Depreciation on building | 24,000 | | |
| Indirect materials | 15,000 | | |
| Factory insurance | 14,000 | | |
| Property taxes | 6,000 | | |
| Total manufacturing overhead | | 289,000 | |
| Total manufacturing costs | | | 854,000 |
| Total cost of work in process | | | 934,000 |
| Less: Work in process, 12/31 | | | 50,000 |
| Cost of goods manufactured | | | $884,000 |

## Problem-Solving Strategies

1. Beginning work in process is the first item in the cost of goods manufactured schedule.

2. Total manufacturing costs are the sum of direct materials used, direct labor, and total manufacturing overhead.

3. Total cost of work in process is the sum of beginning work in process and total manufacturing costs.

4. Cost of goods manufactured is total cost of work in process less ending work in process.

5. The cost of goods sold section of the income statement shows beginning and ending finished goods inventory and cost of goods manufactured.

6. In the balance sheet, manufacturing inventories are listed in the order of their expected realization in cash, with finished goods first.

(b)

### SUPERIOR MANUFACTURING COMPANY
### Income Statement
### For the Year Ended December 31, 1996

| | | |
|---|---:|---:|
| Sales (net) | | $1,500,000 |
| Cost of goods sold | | |
| Finished goods inventory, January 1 | $110,000 | |
| Cost of goods manufactured | 884,000 | |
| Cost of goods available for sale | 994,000 | |
| Less: Finished goods inventory, December 31 | 120,000 | |
| Cost of goods sold | | 874,000 |
| Gross profit | | 626,000 |
| Operating expenses | | |
| Administrative expenses | 300,000 | |
| Sales commissions | 150,000 | |
| Delivery expenses | 100,000 | |
| Total operating expenses | | 550,000 |
| Net income | | $   76,000 |

(c)

### SUPERIOR MANUFACTURING COMPANY
### (Partial) Balance Sheet
### December 31, 1996

| | | |
|---|---:|---:|
| Current assets | | |
| Cash | | $ 17,000 |
| Short-term investments | | 26,000 |
| Accounts receivable (net) | | 120,000 |
| Inventories: | | |
| Finished goods | $120,000 | |
| Work in process | 50,000 | |
| Raw materials | 20,000 | 190,000 |
| Prepaid expenses | | 13,000 |
| Total current assets | | $366,000 |

# DEMONSTRATION PROBLEM 2

Giant Company specializes in manufacturing different models of racing bicycles. A new model, the Jaquar, has been well accepted. As a result, the company has established a separate manufacturing facility to produce these bicycles. The company produces 1,000 bicycles per month. Giant's monthly manufacturing cost and other expenses data related to these bicycles are as follows:

1. Rent on manufacturing equipment (lease cost) $2,000/month
2. Insurance on manufacturing building $750/month
3. Raw materials (frames, tires, etc.) $80/bicycle
4. Utility costs for manufacturing facility $1,000/month
5. Supplies for general office $800/month
6. Wages for assembly line workers in manufacturing facility $30/bicycle
7. Depreciation on office equipment $650/month
8. Miscellaneous materials (lubricants, solders, etc.) $1.20/bicycle

9. Property taxes on
manufacturing
building                    $2,400/year
10. Manufacturing
supervisor's salary         $3,000/month

11. Advertising for
bicycles                   $30,000/year
12. Sales commissions          $10/bicycle
13. Depreciation on
manufacturing
building                  $1,500/month

**Instructions**

(a) Prepare an answer sheet with the following column headings:

| Cost Item | Product Costs | | | Period Costs | Prime Costs | Conversion Costs |
|---|---|---|---|---|---|---|
| | Direct Materials | Direct Labor | Manufacturing Overhead | | | |

Enter each cost item on your answer sheet, placing an "X" mark under the appropriate headings.

(b) Compute total manufacturing costs for the month.

## Solution to Demonstration Problem 2

(a)

| Cost Item | Product Costs | | | Period Costs | Prime Costs | Conversion Costs |
|---|---|---|---|---|---|---|
| | Direct Materials | Direct Labor | Manufacturing Overhead | | | |
| 1. Rent on equipment ($2,000/month) | | | X | | | X |
| 2. Insurance on manufacturing building ($750/month) | | | X | | | X |
| 3. Raw materials ($80/bicycle) | X | | | | X | |
| 4. Manufacturing utilities ($1,000/month) | | | X | | | X |
| 5. Office supplies ($800/month) | | | | X | | |
| 6. Wages for workers ($30/bicycle) | | X | | | X | X |
| 7. Depreciation on office equipment ($650/month) | | | | X | | |
| 8. Miscellaneous materials ($1.20/bicycle) | | | X | | | X |
| 9. Property taxes on building ($2,400/year) | | | X | | | X |
| 10. Manufacturing supervisor's salary ($3,000/month) | | | X | | | X |
| 11. Advertising cost ($30,000/year) | | | | X | | |
| 12. Sales commissions ($10/bicycle) | | | | X | | |
| 13. Depreciation on manufacturing building ($1,500/month) | | | X | | | X |

**Problem-Solving Strategies**

1. Remember the definitions of: Prime costs = direct materials + direct labor. Conversion costs = Direct labor + manufacturing overhead costs incurred in converting raw materials into finished goods.
2. Make sure you are doing the computations for the appropriate period: month, year, unit, etc.
3. Period costs are not manufacturing costs and, therefore, are not inventoriable.
4. Product costs are manufacturing costs and are inventoriable.

| (b) | Cost Item | Manufacturing Cost |
|---|---|---|
| | Rent on equipment | $ 2,000 |
| | Insurance | 750 |
| | Raw materials ($80 × 1,000) | 80,000 |
| | Manufacturing utilities | 1,000 |
| | Labor ($30 × 1,000) | 30,000 |
| | Miscellaneous materials ($1.20 × 1,000) | 1,200 |
| | Property taxes ($2,400 ÷ 12) | 200 |
| | Manufacturing supervisor's salary | 3,000 |
| | Depreciation on building | 1,500 |
| | Total manufacturing costs | $119,650 |

***Note:** All **asterisked** Questions, Exercises, and Problems relate to material contained in the appendix to the chapter.

# SELF-STUDY QUESTIONS

Answers are at the end of the chapter.

(SO 1) 1. Managerial accounting:
   a. is governed by generally accepted accounting principles.
   b. places emphasis on special-purpose information.
   c. pertains to the entity as a whole and is highly aggregated.
   d. is limited to cost data.

(SO 1) 2. Which of the following is **not** one of the categories in *Standards of Ethical Conduct for Management Accountants*?
   a. Confidentiality.   c. Integrity.
   b. Competence.       d. Independence.

(SO 2) 3. The management of an organization performs three broad functions. They are:
   a. planning, organizing and directing, and selling.
   b. planning, organizing and directing, and controlling.
   c. planning, manufacturing, and controlling.
   d. organizing and directing, manufacturing, and controlling.

(SO 3) 4. Direct materials are a:

| | Conversion Cost | Manufacturing Cost | Prime Cost |
|---|---|---|---|
| a. | Yes | Yes | No |
| b. | No | Yes | Yes |
| c. | Yes | Yes | Yes |
| d. | No | No | No |

(SO 4) 5. Indirect labor is a:
   a. nonmanufacturing cost.
   b. prime cost.
   c. product cost.
   d. period cost.

(SO 3) 6. Which of the following costs would be included in manufacturing overhead of a computer manufacturer?
   a. the cost of the 3½-inch disk drives.
   b. the wages earned by computer assemblers.
   c. the cost of the memory chips.
   d. depreciation on testing equipment.

(SO 3) 7. Which of the following is **not** an element of manufacturing overhead?
   a. sales manager's salary.
   b. plant manager's salary.
   c. factory repairman's wages.
   d. product inspector's salary.

(SO 5) 8. For the year, Redder Company has cost of goods manufactured of $600,000, beginning finished goods inventory of $200,000, and ending finished goods inventory of $250,000. The cost of goods sold is:
   a. $450,000.   c. $550,000.
   b. $500,000.   d. $600,000.

(SO 6) 9. A cost of goods manufactured schedule shows beginning and ending inventories for:
   a. raw materials and work in process only.
   b. work in process only.
   c. raw materials only.
   d. raw materials, work in process, and finished goods.

(SO 7) 10. In a manufacturing company balance sheet, three inventories may be reported: (1) raw materials, (2) work in process, and (3) finished goods. Indicate in what sequence these inventories generally appear on a balance sheet.
   a. (1), (2), (3)    c. (3), (1), (2)
   b. (2), (3), (1)    d. (3), (2), (1)

# QUESTIONS

1. (a) "Managerial accounting is a field of accounting that provides economic information for all interested parties." Do you agree? Explain.
   (b) Tim Martinez believes that managerial accounting serves only manufacturing firms. Is Tim correct? Explain.

2. Distinguish between managerial and financial accounting as to (a) primary users of reports, (b) types and frequency of reports, and (c) purpose of reports.

3. How does the content of reports and the verification of reports differ between managerial and financial accounting?

4. (a) Identify the four categories of ethical standards for management accountants.
   (b) Is the responsibility of the management accountant limited to only his or her own acts? Explain.

5. Tammy Waslo is studying for the next accounting midterm examination. Summarize for Tammy what she should know about management functions.

6. "Decision making is management's most important function." Do you agree? Why or why not?

7. Pat Wedden is studying for her next accounting examination. Explain to Pat what she should know about the differences between the income statements for a manufacturing company and a merchandising company.

8. Lee Battel is unclear as to the difference between the balance sheets of a merchandising company and a manufacturing company. Explain the difference to Lee.

9. How are manufacturing costs classified?

10. Richard Wey claims that the distinction between direct and indirect materials is based entirely on physical association with the product. Is Richard correct? Why?

11. Alma Jean Ekert is confused about the differences between a product cost and a period cost. Explain the differences to Alma Jean.

12. Karla King asks your help with the terms (a) prime costs and (b) conversion costs. Distinguish between the terms.

13. In Plant Molding Company, direct materials are $12,000, direct labor is $18,000, and manufacturing overhead is $9,000. What is the amount of (a) prime costs and (b) conversion costs?

14. Identify the differences in the cost of goods sold section of an income statement between a merchandising company and a manufacturing company.

15. The determination of the cost of goods manufactured involves the following factors: (A) beginning work in process inventory, (B) total manufacturing costs, and (C) ending work in process inventory. Identify the meaning of x in the following formulas:
    (a) $A + B = x$
    (b) $A + B - C = x$

16. Ammad Manufacturing has beginning raw materials inventory $22,000, ending raw materials inventory $18,000, and raw materials purchases $180,000. What is the cost of direct materials used?

17. Elite Manufacturing Inc. has beginning work in process $27,200, direct materials used $210,000, direct labor $200,000, total manufacturing overhead $120,000, and ending work in process $32,000. What are total manufacturing costs?

18. Using the data in Q17, what are (a) the total cost of work in process and (b) the cost of goods manufactured?

19. In what order should manufacturing inventories be listed in a balance sheet?

*20. How, if at all, does the accounting cycle differ between a manufacturing company and a merchandising company?

*21. What typical account balances are carried into the cost of goods manufactured columns of the manufacturing work sheet?

*22. Prepare the closing entries for (a) ending work in process and raw materials inventories and (b) manufacturing summary. Use XXXs for amounts.

# BRIEF EXERCISES

**BE20–1** Complete the following comparison table between managerial and financial accounting.

*Distinguish between managerial and financial accounting.*
(SO 1)

| | Financial Accounting | Managerial Accounting |
| --- | --- | --- |
| Primary users | | |
| Type of reports | | |
| Frequency of reports | | |
| Purpose of reports | | |

|  | **Financial Accounting** | **Managerial Accounting** |
|---|---|---|
| Reporting standards |  |  |
| Verification |  |  |

*Identify ethical standards.*
(SO 1)

**BE20–2**   The Institute of Management Accountants has promulgated ethical standards for managerial accountants. Identify the four specific standards.

*Identify the three management functions.*
(SO 2)

**BE20–3**   Listed below are three functions of the management of an organization:

(a) Planning   (b) Organizing and directing   (c) Controlling

Identify each of the following statements that best describes each of the above functions.

1. _____ require(s) management to look ahead and to establish objectives. A key objective of management appears to be to add value to the business.
2. _____ involve(s) coordinating the diverse activities and human resources of a company to produce a smooth-running operation. This function relates to the implementation of planned objectives.
3. _____ is the process of keeping the activities on track. Management must determine whether goals are being met and what changes are necessary when there are deviations.

*Classify manufacturing costs.*
(SO 3)

**BE20–4**   Determine whether each of the following costs should be classified as direct materials (DM), direct labor (DL), or manufacturing overhead (MO):

1. _____ Insurance on factory equipment and machinery.
2. _____ Depreciation on factory equipment.
3. _____ Frames and tires used in manufacturing bicycles.
4. _____ Wages paid to production workers.

*Identify product and period costs.*
(SO 4)

**BE20–5**   Identify whether each of the following costs should be classified as product costs or period costs:

1. _____ Advertising expenses.          4. _____ Manufacturing overhead.
2. _____ Direct labor.                  5. _____ Selling expenses.
3. _____ Direct material.               6. _____ Administrative expenses.

*Classify manufacturing costs.*
(SO 3)

**BE20–6**   Indicate whether each of the following costs of an automobile manufacturer would be classified as direct materials, direct labor, or manufacturing overhead:

1. Windshield.                          5. Factory machinery lubricants.
2. Engine.                              6. Tires.
3. Wages of assembly line worker.       7. Steering wheel.
4. Depreciation of factory machinery.   8. Salary of painting supervisor.

*Compute total manufacturing costs and total cost of work in process.*
(SO 6)

**BE20–7**   DuBois Manufacturing Company has the following data: direct labor $260,000, direct materials used $180,000, total manufacturing overhead $208,000, and beginning work in process $25,000. Compute (a) total manufacturing costs and (b) total cost of work in process.

*Prepare current asset section.*
(SO 7)

**BE20–8**   In alphabetical order below are current asset items for Tak Company's balance sheet at December 31, 1996. Prepare the current asset section (including a complete heading).

| | |
|---|---|
| Accounts receivable | $300,000 |
| Cash | 62,000 |
| Finished goods | 75,000 |
| Prepaid expenses | 38,000 |
| Raw materials | 68,000 |
| Work in process | 91,000 |

*Determine missing amounts in computing total manufacturing costs.*
(SO 6)

**BE20–9**   Presented below are incomplete 1996 manufacturing cost data for Inter-Continental Corporation. Determine the missing amounts.

| | Direct Material Used | Direct Labor Used | Factory Overhead | Total Manufacturing Costs |
|---|---|---|---|---|
| 1. | $39,000 | $61,000 | $ 50,000 | ? |
| 2. | ? | $88,000 | $110,000 | $296,000 |
| 3. | $55,000 | ? | $ 95,000 | $300,000 |

**BE20–10** Use the same data from BE20–9 above. Compute the cost of goods manufactured for Inter-Continental Corporation in 1996.

*Determine missing amounts in computing cost of goods manufactured.*
*(SO 6)*

| | Total Manufacturing Costs | Work in Process (1/1) | Work in Process (12/31) | Cost of Goods Manufactured |
|---|---|---|---|---|
| 1. | ? | $120,000 | $86,000 | ? |
| 2. | $296,000 | ? | $98,000 | $308,000 |
| 3. | $300,000 | $480,000 | ? | $715,000 |

**BE20–11** Presented below are Gonzales Company's monthly manufacturing cost data related to its personal computer product:

*Classify manufacturing costs.*
*(SO 3, 4)*

| | | |
|---|---|---|
| (a) | Utilities for manufacturing equipment | $116,000 |
| (b) | Raw material (CPU, chips, etc.) | $ 85,000 |
| (c) | Depreciation on manufacturing building | $880,000 |
| (d) | Wages for production workers | $191,000 |

Enter each cost item on the following table, placing an "X" under the appropriate headings.

| | Product Costs | | | | |
|---|---|---|---|---|---|
| | Direct Material | Direct Labor | Factory Overhead | Prime Costs | Conversion Costs |
| (a) | | | | | |
| (b) | | | | | |
| (c) | | | | | |
| (d) | | | | | |

**\*BE20–12** A work sheet is used in preparing financial statements for Sunbird Manufacturing Company. The following accounts are included in the adjusted trial balance: Finished Goods Inventory $28,000, Work in Process Inventory $21,600, Raw Materials Purchases, $175,000 and Direct Labor $140,000. Indicate the work sheet column(s) to which each account should be extended.

*Identify work sheet columns for selected accounts.*
*(SO 8)*

# EXERCISES

**E20–1** Presented below is a list of costs and expenses usually incurred by Calloway Corporation, a manufacturer of furniture, in its factory:

*Classify costs into three classes of manufacturing costs.*
*(SO 3)*

1. Wages paid to assembly line workers.
2. Factory machinery depreciation.
3. Glue, nails, paint, and other small parts used in production.
4. Factory supervisors' salaries.
5. Wood used in manufacturing furniture.
6. Salaries for assembly-line inspectors.
7. Insurance on factory machines.
8. Property taxes on the factory building.
9. Factory repairs.
10. Upholstery used in manufacturing furniture.

**Instructions**
Classify the above items into the following categories: (a) direct materials, (b) direct labor, and (c) manufacturing overhead.

**E20–2** Sligo Company reports the following costs and expenses in May:

*Determine the total amount of various types of costs.*
*(SO 3, 4)*

| | | | |
|---|---|---|---|
| Factory utilities | $ 9,500 | Direct labor | $79,100 |
| Depreciation on factory equipment | 12,650 | Sales salaries | 49,400 |
| Depreciation on delivery trucks | 3,500 | Property taxes on factory building | 2,500 |
| Indirect factory labor | 48,900 | Repairs to office equipment | 1,300 |
| Indirect materials | 96,200 | Factory repairs | 2,000 |
| Direct materials used | 137,600 | Advertising | 18,000 |
| Factory manager's salary | 8,000 | Office supplies used | 3,000 |

**Instructions**

From the information, determine the total amount of:

(a) Prime costs.
(b) Manufacturing overhead.
(c) Conversion costs.
(d) Product costs.
(e) Period costs.

*Indicate in which schedule or financial statement(s) different cost items will appear.*
*(SO 5, 6, 7)*

**E20–3** Kirkpatrick Manufacturing Company produces blankets. From its accounting records it prepares the following schedule and financial statements on a yearly basis:

(a) Cost of goods manufactured schedule
(b) Income statement
(c) Balance sheet

The following items are found in its ledger and accompanying data:

1. Factory maintenance salaries
2. Cost of goods manufactured
3. Depreciation on delivery equipment
4. Cost of goods available for sale
5. Direct materials used
6. Heat and electricity for factory
7. Repairs to roof of factory building
8. Cost of raw materials purchases
9. Direct labor
10. Raw materials inventory, 1/1
11. Work in process inventory, 12/31
12. Finished goods inventory, 1/1
13. Indirect labor
14. Depreciation on factory machinery
15. Work in process, 1/1
16. Finished goods inventory, 12/31

**Instructions**

List the items (1)–(16). For each item, indicate by using the appropriate letter or letters, the schedule and/or financial statement(s) in which the item will appear.

*Determine the missing amount of different cost items.*
*(SO 6)*

**E20–4** Manufacturing cost data for Tralea Company are presented below:

|  | Case A | Case B | Case C |
|---|---|---|---|
| Direct materials used | (a) | $75,000 | $130,000 |
| Direct labor | $ 60,000 | 86,000 | (g) |
| Manufacturing overhead | 42,500 | 81,600 | 102,000 |
| Total manufacturing costs | 190,650 | (d) | 260,000 |
| Work in process 1/1/97 | (b) | 16,500 | (h) |
| Total cost of work in process | 221,500 | (e) | 317,000 |
| Work in process 12/31/97 | (c) | 9,000 | 70,000 |
| Cost of goods manufactured | 185,275 | (f) | (i) |

**Instructions**

Indicate the missing amount for each letter.

*Determine the missing amount of different cost items and prepare a condensed cost of goods manufactured schedule.*
*(SO 5, 6)*

**E20–5** Incomplete manufacturing cost data for Klondike Company for 1997 are presented as follows:

|  | Direct Materials Used | Direct Labor Used | Manufacturing Overhead | Total Manufacturing Costs | Work in Process 1/1 | Work in Process 12/31 | Cost of Goods Manufactured |
|---|---|---|---|---|---|---|---|
| (1) | $130,000 | $140,000 | $ 77,000 | (a) | $30,000 | (b) | $360,000 |
| (2) | (c) | 200,000 | 130,000 | $450,000 | (d) | $40,000 | 470,000 |
| (3) | 80,000 | 100,000 | (e) | 260,000 | 60,000 | 80,000 | (f) |
| (4) | 70,000 | (g) | 75,000 | 290,000 | 45,000 | (h) | 270,000 |

**Instructions**

(a) Indicate the missing amount for each letter.
(b) Prepare a condensed cost of goods manufactured schedule for situation (1) for the year ended December 31, 1997.

**E20-6** Tipper Corporation has the following cost records for June 1997:

*Prepare a cost of goods manufactured schedule and a partial income statement.*
*(SO 5, 6)*

| | | | |
|---|---|---|---|
| Factory utilities | $ 400 | Indirect factory labor | $ 4,000 |
| Depreciation, factory equipment | 1,700 | Direct materials used | 20,000 |
| Direct labor | 25,000 | Work in process, 6/1/97 | 3,000 |
| Maintenance, factory equipment | 1,300 | Work in process, 6/30/97 | 3,500 |
| Indirect materials | 2,200 | Finished goods, 6/1/97 | 5,000 |
| Factory manager's salary | 3,000 | Finished goods, 6/30/97 | 6,000 |

**Instructions**

(a) Prepare a cost of goods manufactured schedule for June 1997.

(b) Prepare an income statement through gross profit for June 1997 assuming net sales are $98,100.

**E20-7** An analysis of the accounts of Waterway Manufacturing reveals the following manufacturing cost data for the month ended June 30, 1997:

*Prepare a cost of goods manufactured schedule and present the ending inventories of the balance sheet.*
*(SO 5, 6, 7)*

| Inventories: | Beginning | Ending |
|---|---|---|
| Raw materials | $9,000 | $12,000 |
| Work in process | 5,000 | 8,000 |
| Finished goods | 8,000 | 6,000 |

Costs incurred:

Raw materials purchases $64,000, direct labor $50,000, manufacturing overhead $19,200. The specific overhead costs were: indirect labor $5,500, factory insurance $4,000, machinery depreciation $4,000, machinery repairs $1,800, factory utilities $2,400, miscellaneous factory costs $1,500.

**Instructions**

(a) Prepare the cost of goods manufactured schedule for the month ended June 30, 1997.

(b) Show the presentation of the ending inventories on the June 30, 1997, balance sheet.

**E20-8** The cost of goods manufactured schedule shows each of the cost elements. Complete the following schedule for Jupiter Manufacturing Company:

*Determine missing amounts in cost of goods manufactured schedule.*
*(SO 5, 6)*

### JUPITER MANUFACTURING COMPANY
### Cost of Goods Manufactured Schedule
### For the Year Ended December 31, 1997

| | | | |
|---|---|---|---|
| Work in process (1/1) | | | $200,000 |
| Direct materials | | | |
| Raw materials inventory (1/1) | $ ? | | |
| Add: Raw material purchases | 158,000 | | |
| Less: Raw material inventory (12/31) | 6,500 | | |
| Direct materials used | | $190,000 | |
| Direct labor | | ? | |
| Manufacturing overhead | | | |
| Indirect labor | $ 18,000 | | |
| Factory depreciation | 36,000 | | |
| Factory utilities | 68,000 | | |
| Total overhead | | 122,000 | |
| Total manufacturing costs | | | ? |
| Total cost of work in process | | | $ ? |
| Less: Work in process (12/31) | | | 87,000 |
| Cost of goods manufactured | | | $580,000 |

**E20-9** Jaffe Motor Company manufactures automobiles. During September 1997 the company purchased 5,000 head lamps at a cost of $8 per lamp. Wexford withdrew 4,550 lamps from the warehouse during the month. Fifty of these lamps were used to replace the head lamps in autos used by traveling sales staff. The remaining 4,500 lamps were put in autos manufactured during the month.

*Determine the amount of cost to appear in various accounts and indicate in which financial statements these accounts would appear.*
*(SO 5, 6, 7)*

Of the autos put into production during September 1997, 90% were completed and transferred to the company's storage lot. Eighty percent of the cars completed during the month were sold by September 30.

*Instructions*
(a) Determine the cost of head lamps that would appear in each of the following accounts at September 30, 1997: Raw Materials, Work in Process, Finished Goods, Cost of Goods Sold, and Selling Expenses.
(b) ▭▭▭▭▷  Write a short memorandum to the chief accountant, indicating whether and where each of the accounts in (a) would appear on the income statement or on the balance sheet at September 30, 1997.

*Classify various costs into different cost categories.*
(SO 3, 4)

**E20–10**  Yuri Zenko is a manufacturer of personal computers. Various costs and expenses associated with its operations are as follows:

1. Sales commissions paid to sell personal computers.
2. Electrical wiring in assembling computers.
3. Wages of workers assembling personal computers.
4. Soldering materials used on factory assembly lines.
5. Salaries for the night security guards for the factory building.
6. Property taxes on the factory building.
7. Production superintendents' salaries.
8. Memory boards and chips used in assembling computers.
9. Depreciation on the factory equipment.
10. Salaries for assembly-line quality control inspectors.

The company intends to classify these costs and expenses into the following categories: (a) direct materials, (b) direct labor, (c) manufacturing overhead, and (d) period costs.

*Instructions*
List the items (1)–(10). For each item, indicate the cost category to which the item belongs.

*Prepare a partial work sheet of a manufacturing firm.*
(SO 8)

**\*E20–11**

*Instructions*
Using the data in Exercise 20–7, prepare a partial work sheet for Waterway Manufacturing.

# PROBLEMS

*Classify manufacturing costs into different categories and compute the unit cost.*
(SO 3, 4)

**P20–1**  Sabatini Company specializes in manufacturing motorcycles. The model is well accepted by consumers, and the company has a large number of orders to keep the factory production at 1,000 motorcycles per month. Sabatini's monthly manufacturing cost and other expense data are as follows:

| | |
|---|---:|
| Factory manager's salary | $ 5,000 |
| Maintenance costs on factory building | 300 |
| Advertising for motorcycles | 10,000 |
| Sales commissions | 5,000 |
| Depreciation on factory building | 700 |
| Rent on factory equipment | 5,000 |
| Insurance on factory building | 3,000 |
| Raw materials (frames, tires, etc.) | 20,000 |
| Utility costs for factory | 800 |
| Supplies for general office | 200 |
| Wages for assembly line workers | 32,000 |
| Depreciation on office equipment | 500 |
| Miscellaneous materials (lubricants, solders, etc.) | 700 |

*Instructions*
(a) Prepare an answer sheet with the following column headings:

| | Product Costs | | | | | |
|---|---|---|---|---|---|---|
| Cost Item | Direct Materials | Direct Labor | Manufacturing Overhead | Period Costs | Prime Costs | Conversion Costs |

Enter each cost item on your answer sheet, placing the dollar amount under the appropriate headings. Total the dollar amounts in each of the columns.

(b) Compute the cost to produce one motorcycle.

**P20–2** Courier Company, a manufacturer of tennis rackets, started its production in November 1997. For the past 5 years Courier had been a retailer of sports equipment. After a thorough survey of tennis racket markets, Courier Company decided to turn its retail store into a tennis racket factory.

Raw materials cost for a tennis racket will total $20 per racket. Workers on the production lines are on average paid $10 per hour. A racket usually takes two hours to complete. In addition, the rent on the equipment used to produce rackets amounts to $1,000 per month. Additional materials such as glue, paint, and other small parts cost $3 per racket. A supervisor was hired to oversee production; her monthly salary will be $2,000.

Janitorial costs were $1,200 monthly. Advertising costs for the rackets will be $6,000 per month. The factory building depreciation expense is $8,400 per year. Property taxes on the factory building will be $3,600 per year.

*Classify manufacturing costs into different categories and compute the unit cost.*
(SO 3, 4)

**Instructions**

(a) Prepare an answer sheet with the following column headings:

| | Product Costs | | | | | |
| Cost Item | Direct Materials | Direct Labor | Manufacturing Overhead | Period Costs | Prime Costs | Conversion Costs |
| --- | --- | --- | --- | --- | --- | --- |

Assuming that Courier manufactures, on average, 2,000 tennis rackets per month, enter each cost item on your answer sheet, placing the dollar amount per month under the appropriate headings. Total the dollar amounts in each of the columns.

(b) Compute the cost to produce one racket.

**P20–3** Incomplete manufacturing costs, expenses, and selling data for two different cases are as follows:

*Indicate the missing amount of different cost items; prepare a condensed cost of goods manufactured schedule, an income statement, and a partial balance sheet.*
(SO 5, 6, 7)

| | Case | |
| --- | --- | --- |
| | 1 | 2 |
| Direct Materials Used | $ 8,000 | (g) |
| Direct Labor | 3,000 | 4,000 |
| Manufacturing Overhead | 4,000 | 5,000 |
| Total Manufacturing Costs | (a) | 20,000 |
| Beginning Work in Process Inventory | 1,000 | (h) |
| Ending Work in Process Inventory | (b) | 2,000 |
| Sales | 21,500 | (i) |
| Sales Discounts | 1,500 | 1,200 |
| Cost of Goods Manufactured | 13,500 | 21,000 |
| Beginning Finished Goods Inventory | (c) | 3,500 |
| Goods Available for Sale | 16,000 | (j) |
| Cost of Goods Sold | (d) | (k) |
| Ending Finished Goods Inventory | 1,000 | 2,500 |
| Gross Profit | (e) | 6,000 |
| Operating Expenses | 2,700 | (l) |
| Net Income | (f) | 2,200 |

**Instructions**

(a) Indicate the missing amount for each letter.
(b) Prepare a condensed cost of goods manufactured schedule for Case 1.
(c) Prepare an income statement and the current assets section of the balance sheet for Case 1, assuming that in Case 1 the other items in the current assets section are as follows: Cash, $3,000, Receivables (net), $10,000, Raw Materials, $700, and Prepaid Expenses, $200.

*Prepare a cost of goods manufactured schedule, a partial income statement, and a partial balance sheet.*
*(SO 5, 6, 7)*

**P20–4**  The following data were taken from the records of Connecticut Manufacturing Company for the year ended December 31, 1997.

| | | | |
|---|---|---|---|
| Raw Materials | | Factory Insurance | $ 5,400 |
| Inventory 1/1/97 | $ 43,500 | Factory Machinery Depreciation | 7,700 |
| Raw Materials | | Freight-in on Raw Materials Purchased | 3,900 |
| Inventory 12/31/97 | 46,200 | Factory Utilities | 15,900 |
| Finished Goods | | Office Utilities Expense | 8,600 |
| Inventory 1/1/97 | 85,000 | Sales | 475,000 |
| Finished Goods | | Sales Discounts | 3,200 |
| Inventory 12/31/97 | 77,800 | Plant Manager's Salary | 30,000 |
| Work in Process | | Factory Property Taxes | 6,100 |
| Inventory 1/1/97 | 10,200 | Factory Repairs | 800 |
| Work in Process | | Raw Materials Purchases | 64,600 |
| Inventory 12/31/97 | 6,500 | Cash | 28,000 |
| Direct Labor | 145,100 | | |
| Indirect Labor | 19,100 | | |
| Accounts Receivable | 27,000 | | |

**Instructions**

(a) Prepare a cost of goods manufactured schedule.
(b) Prepare an income statement through gross profit.
(c) Prepare the current assets section of the balance sheet at December 31.

*Prepare a cost of goods manufactured schedule and a correct income statement.*
*(SO 5, 6)*

**P20–5**  Huckaboom Company is a manufacturer of toys. Its controller, Ed Belfast, resigned in August 1997. An inexperienced assistant accountant has prepared the following income statement for the month of August 1997.

**HUCKABOOM COMPANY**
**Income Statement**
**For the Month Ended August 31, 1997**

| | | |
|---|---|---|
| Sales (net) | | $670,000 |
| Less: Operating expenses | | |
| Raw materials purchased | $200,000 | |
| Direct labor cost | 150,000 | |
| Advertising expense | 80,000 | |
| Selling and administrative salaries | 70,000 | |
| Rent on factory facilities | 60,000 | |
| Depreciation on sales equipment | 55,000 | |
| Depreciation on factory equipment | 40,000 | |
| Indirect labor cost | 20,000 | |
| Factory utilities | 10,000 | |
| Factory insurance | 5,000 | 690,000 |
| Net loss | | $ (20,000) |

Prior to August 1997, the company had been profitable every month. The company's president is concerned about the accuracy of the income statement above. As a friend of the president, you have been asked to review the income statement and make necessary corrections. After examining other manufacturing cost data, you have acquired additional information as follows:

1. Inventory balances at the beginning and end of August were:

| | August 1 | August 31 |
|---|---|---|
| Raw materials | $18,000 | $33,000 |
| Work in process | 25,000 | 31,000 |
| Finished goods | 40,000 | 62,000 |

2. Only 70% of the utilities expense and 80% of the insurance expense apply to factory operations; the remaining amounts should be charged to selling and administrative activities.

**Instructions**

(a) Prepare a cost goods manufactured schedule for August 1997.

(b) Prepare a correct income statement for August 1997.

*P20–6 Londonberry Manufacturing Company uses a simple manufacturing accounting system. At the end of its fiscal year on August 31, 1997, the adjusted trial balance contains the following accounts.

*Complete a work sheet; prepare a cost of goods manufactured schedule, an income statement, and a balance sheet; journalize and post the closing entries.*
*(SO 8)*

| Debits | | Credits | |
|---|---|---|---|
| Cash | $ 16,700 | Accumulated Depreciation | $ 353,000 |
| Accounts Receivable (net) | 62,900 | Notes Payable | 45,000 |
| Finished Goods Inventory | 56,000 | Accounts Payable | 38,200 |
| Work in Process Inventory | 27,800 | Income Taxes Payable | 9,000 |
| Raw Materials Inventory | 37,200 | Common Stock | 352,000 |
| Plant Assets | 890,000 | Retained Earnings | 205,300 |
| Raw Materials Purchases | 236,500 | Sales | 996,000 |
| Direct Labor | 280,900 | | |
| Indirect Labor | 27,400 | | |
| Factory Repairs | 17,200 | | |
| Factory Depreciation | 19,000 | | |
| Factory Manager's Salary | 40,000 | | |
| Factory Insurance | 11,000 | | |
| Factory Property Taxes | 12,900 | | |
| Factory Utilities | 13,300 | | |
| Selling Expenses | 98,500 | | |
| Administrative Expenses | 115,200 | | |
| Income Tax Expense | 36,000 | | |
| | $1,998,500 | | $1,998,500 |

Physical inventory accounts on August 31, 1997, show the following inventory amounts: Finished Goods $49,600, Work in Process $33,400, and Raw Material $46,500.

**Instructions**

(a) Enter the adjusted trial balance data on a work sheet in financial statement order and complete the work sheet.

(b) Prepare a cost of goods manufactured schedule for the year.

(c) Prepare an income statement for the year and a balance sheet at August 31, 1997.

(d) Journalize the closing entries.

(e) Post the closing entries to Manufacturing Summary and to Income Summary.

# ALTERNATE PROBLEMS

**P20–1A** Utley Company specializes in manufacturing a unique model of bicycle helmet. The model is well accepted by consumers, and the company has a large number of orders to keep the factory production at 10,000 helmets per month (80% of its full capacity). Utley's monthly manufacturing cost and other expense data are as follows.

*Classify manufacturing costs into different categories and compute the unit cost.*
*(SO 3, 4)*

| | |
|---|---|
| Rent on factory equipment | $ 6,000 |
| Insurance on factory building | 1,500 |
| Raw materials (plastics, polystyrene, etc.) | 70,000 |
| Utility costs for factory | 900 |
| Supplies for general office | 300 |
| Wages for assembly line workers | 36,000 |
| Depreciation on office equipment | 800 |
| Miscellaneous materials (lubricants, solders, etc.) | 1,100 |
| Factory manager's salary | 5,700 |
| Property taxes on factory building | 400 |
| Advertising for helmets | 11,000 |
| Sales commissions | 7,000 |
| Depreciation on factory building | 1,500 |

**Instructions**

(a) Prepare an answer sheet with the following column headings:

**Product Costs**

| Cost Item | Direct Materials | Direct Labor | Manufacturing Overhead | Period Costs | Prime Costs | Conversion Costs |
|---|---|---|---|---|---|---|

Enter each cost item on your answer sheet, placing the dollar amount under the appropriate headings. Total the dollar amounts in each of the columns.

(b) Compute the cost to produce one helmet.

*Classify manufacturing costs into different categories and compute the unit cost.*
*(SO 3, 4)*

**P20–2A**   Valdez Company, a manufacturer of stereo systems, started its production in October 1997. For the past 3 years Valdez had been a retailer of stereo systems. After a thorough survey of stereo system markets, Valdez Company decided to turn its retail store into a stereo equipment factory.

Raw materials cost for a stereo system will total $70 per unit. Workers on the production lines are on average paid $12 per hour. A stereo system usually takes five hours to complete. In addition, the rent on the equipment used to assemble stereo systems amounts to $1,200 per month. Additional materials such as solders, paint, and other small parts, cost $5 per system. A supervisor was hired to oversee production; her monthly salary will be $2,400.

Janitorial costs were $1,300 monthly. Advertising costs for the stereo system will be $8,500 per month. The factory building depreciation expense is $7,200 per year. Property taxes on the factory building will be $6,000 per year.

**Instructions**

(a) Prepare an answer sheet with the following column headings:

**Product Costs**

| Cost Item | Direct Materials | Direct Labor | Manufacturing Overhead | Period Costs | Prime Costs | Conversion Costs |
|---|---|---|---|---|---|---|

Assuming that Valdez manufactures, on average, 1,200 stereo systems per month, enter each cost item on your answer sheet, placing the dollar amount per month under the appropriate headings. Total the dollar amounts in each of the columns.

(b) Compute the cost to produce one stereo system.

*Indicate the missing amount of different cost items; prepare a condensed cost of goods manufactured schedule, an income statement, and a partial balance sheet.*
*(SO 5, 6, 7)*

**P20–3A**   Incomplete manufacturing costs, expenses, and selling data for two different cases are as follows.

| | Case 1 | Case 2 |
|---|---|---|
| Direct Materials Used | $ 7,000 | (g) |
| Direct Labor | 6,000 | 8,000 |
| Manufacturing Overhead | 5,000 | 4,000 |
| Total Manufacturing Costs | (a) | 21,000 |
| Beginning Work in Process Inventory | 1,000 | (h) |
| Ending Work in Process Inventory | (b) | 3,000 |
| Sales | 24,500 | (i) |
| Sales Discounts | 2,500 | 1,400 |
| Cost of Goods Manufactured | 16,500 | 22,000 |
| Beginning Finished Goods Inventory | (c) | 3,500 |
| Goods Available for Sale | 18,000 | (j) |
| Cost of Goods Sold | (d) | (k) |
| Ending Finished Goods Inventory | 2,000 | 2,500 |
| Gross Profit | (e) | 7,000 |
| Operating Expenses | 2,500 | (l) |
| Net Income | (f) | 2,800 |

**Instructions**

(a) Indicate the missing amount for each letter.

(b) Prepare a condensed cost of goods manufactured schedule for Case 1.

(c) Prepare an income statement and the current assets section of the balance sheet for Case 1, assuming that in Case 1 the other items in the current assets section are as follows: Cash, $4,000, Receivables (net), $15,000, Raw Materials, $600, and Prepaid Expenses, $400.

**P20–4A** The following data were taken from the records of Tenega Manufacturing Company for the fiscal year ended June 30, 1997.

*Prepare a cost of goods manufactured schedule, a partial income statement, and a partial balance sheet.*
*(SO 5, 6, 7)*

| | | | |
|---|---|---|---|
| Raw Materials | | Accounts Receivable | $ 27,000 |
|   Inventory 7/1/96 | $ 46,500 | Factory Insurance | 4,600 |
| Raw Materials | | Factory Machinery Depreciation | 15,000 |
|   Inventory 6/30/97 | 39,600 | Freight-in on Raw Materials Purchased | 8,600 |
| Finished Goods | | Factory Utilities | 24,600 |
|   Inventory 7/1/96 | 96,000 | Office Utilities Expense | 8,650 |
| Finished Goods | | Sales | 547,000 |
|   Inventory 6/30/97 | 95,900 | Sales Discounts | 3,300 |
| Work in Process | | Plant Manager's Salary | 29,000 |
|   Inventory 7/1/96 | 21,000 | Factory Property Taxes | 9,600 |
| Work in Process | | Factory Repairs | 1,400 |
|   Inventory 6/30/97 | 16,700 | Raw Materials Purchases | 89,800 |
| Direct Labor | 147,250 | Cash | 32,000 |
| Indirect Labor | 24,460 | | |

**Instructions**

(a) Prepare a cost of goods manufactured schedule.

(b) Prepare an income statement through gross profit.

(c) Prepare the current asset section of the balance sheet at June 30, 1997.

**P20–5A** Ballyhigh Company is a manufacturer of computers. Its controller, Mike Reynolds, resigned in October 1997. An inexperienced assistant accountant has prepared the following income statement for the month of October 1997.

*Prepare a cost of goods manufactured schedule and a correct income statement.*
*(SO 5, 6)*

**BALLYHIGH COMPANY**
**Income Statement**
**For the Month Ended October 31, 1997**

| | | |
|---|---|---|
| Sales (net) | | $780,000 |
| Less: Operating expenses | | |
|   Raw materials purchased | $260,000 | |
|   Direct labor cost | 190,000 | |
|   Advertising expense | 90,000 | |
|   Selling and administrative salaries | 75,000 | |
|   Rent on factory facilities | 60,000 | |
|   Depreciation on sales equipment | 45,000 | |
|   Depreciation on factory equipment | 30,000 | |
|   Indirect labor cost | 25,000 | |
|   Factory utilities | 12,000 | |
|   Factory insurance | 8,000 | 795,000 |
| Net Loss | | $ (15,000) |

Prior to October 1997 the company had been profitable every month. The company's president is concerned about the accuracy of the income statement above. As a friend of the president, you have been asked to review the income statement and make necessary corrections. After examining other manufacturing cost data, you have acquired additional information as follows:

1. Inventory balances at the beginning and end of October were:

| | October 1 | October 31 |
|---|---|---|
| Raw materials | $15,000 | $31,000 |
| Work in process | 16,000 | 24,000 |
| Finished goods | 30,000 | 48,000 |

2. Only 80% of the utilities expense and 70% of the insurance expense apply to factory operations; the remaining amounts should be charged to selling and administrative activities.

**Instructions**

(a) Prepare a schedule of cost of goods manufactured for October 1997.

(b) Prepare a correct income statement for October 1997.

# ▶*Broadening Your Perspective*

## DECISION CASE

Guinness Manufacturing Company specializes in producing fashion outfits. On July 31, 1996, a tornado touched down at its factory and general office. The inventories in the warehouse and the factory were totally damaged due to heavy rain and moisture. The general office nearby was completely destroyed. Next morning, through a careful search over the disaster site, however, Pete Olsmon, the company's controller, and Diana Hoffman, the cost accountant, were able to recover a small part of manufacturing cost data for the current month.

"What a horrible experience," sighed Pete. "And the worse part is that we may not have enough records to use in filing an insurance claim."

"It was terrible," replied Diana. "However, I managed to recover some of the manufacturing cost data that I was working on yesterday afternoon. The data indicate that our direct labor cost in July totaled $250,000 and that we had purchased $340,000 of raw materials. In addition, I recall that the raw materials used for July was $350,000. But I'm not sure this information will help; the rest of our records are blown away."

"Well, not exactly," said Pete. "I was working on the year-to-date income statement when the tornado warning was announced. My recollection is that our sales in July were $1,250,000 and our gross profit ratio has been 40% of sales. Also, I can remember that our cost of goods available for sale was $780,000 for July."

"Maybe we can work something out from this information!" exclaimed Diana. "My experience tells me that our manufacturing overhead is usually 60% of direct labor."

"Hey, look what I just found," cried Diana. "It's a copy of this June's balance sheet, and it shows that our inventories as of June 30 are Finished Goods, $36,000, Work in Process, $22,000, and Raw Materials, $19,000."

"Super," yelled Pete. "Let's go work something out."

In order to file an insurance claim Guinness Company must determine the amount of its inventories as of July 31, 1996, the date of the tornado touchdown.

**Instructions**

Determine the amount of cost in the Raw Materials, Work in Process, and Finished Goods inventory accounts as of the date of the tornado touchdown.

## COMMUNICATION ACTIVITY

Refer to Problem 20-5 and add the following requirement:

Prepare a letter to the president of the company, Merlyn Kimmel, describing the changes you made. Explain clearly why net income is different after the changes. Keep the following points in mind as you compose your letter:

1. This is a letter to the president of a company, who is your friend. The style should be generally formal, but you may relax some requirements; for example, you may call the president by her first name.

2. Executives are very busy. Your letter should tell the president your main results first (for example, the amount of net income).

3. You should include brief explanations so that the president can understand the changes you made in the calculations.

# GROUP ACTIVITY

Tennis, Anyone? is a fairly large manufacturing company located in the southern United States. The company manufactures tennis rackets, tennis balls, tennis clothing, and tennis shoes, all bearing the company's distinctive logo, a large green question mark on a white flocked tennis ball. The company's sales have been increasing over the past 10 years. The tennis racket division has recently implemented several advanced manufacturing techniques. Robot arms hold the tennis rackets in place while glue dries, machine vision systems check for defects, and the engineering and design team use computerized drafting and testing of new products. The following managers work in the tennis racket division:

Wayne Gryer, Sales Manager (supervises all sales representatives)

Tommye Stevens, technical specialist (supervises computer programmers)

Martie Lefever, cost accounting manager (supervises cost accountants)

Jack Marler, production supervisor (supervises all manufacturing employees)

Tina Roy, engineer (supervises all new product design teams)

*Instructions*

With the class divided into four or five groups, each group should answer the following questions:

(a) What are the primary information needs of each manager?

(b) Which, if any, financial accounting report(s) is each likely to use?

(c) Name one special-purpose management accounting report that could be designed for each manager. Include the name of the report, the information it contains, and how frequently it should be issued.

# ETHICS CASE

Pascal Margallas, controller for Kasmais Industries, was reviewing production cost reports for the year. One amount in these reports continued to bother him—advertising. During the year, the company had instituted an expensive advertising campaign to sell some of its slower moving products. It was still too early to tell whether the advertising campaign was successful. There had been much internal debate as how to report advertising costs. The Vice-President of Finance argued that advertising costs should be reported as a cost of production, just like direct materials and direct labor. He therefore recommended that this cost be identified as manufacturing overhead and reported as part of inventory costs until sold. Others disagreed. Pascal believed that this cost should be reported as an expense of the current period based on the conservatism principle. Others argued that it should be reported as Prepaid Advertising and reported as a current asset.

The president finally had to decide the issue. He argued that these costs should be reported as inventory. His arguments were practical ones. He noted that the company was experiencing financial difficulty and expensing this amount in the current period might jeopardize a planned bond offering. Also by reporting the advertising costs as inventory rather than as prepaid advertising, less attention would be directed to it by the financial community.

*Instructions*

(a) Who are the stakeholders in this situation?

(b) What are the ethical issues involved in this situation?

(c) What would you do if you were Pascal Margallas?

# CRITICAL THINKING
## ▶ *A Real-World Focus: Anchor Glass Container Corporation*

*In 1983 the managers of the Glass Container Division of Anchor Hocking Corporation purchased the division's assets and formed a separate corporation called the **Anchor Glass Container Corporation**. As a result of a 1989 transaction, the company is currently wholly-owned by a subsidiary of Vitro,*

*Sociedad Anonima, a Mexican firm. The company manufactures and sells a diverse line of various colored and styled glass containers to the food and beverage industries. The company owns seven manufacturing facilities and leases another ten at various locations in the United States.*

The following management discussion appeared in a recent annual report of Anchor Glass:

**Cost of Products Sold**   Cost of products sold as a percentage of net sales was 89.3% in 1992 compared to 87.6% in 1991. The increase in cost of products sold as a percentage of net sales principally reflected the impact of operational problems during the second quarter of 1992 at a major furnace at one of the Company's plants, higher downtime, and costs and expenses associated with an increased number of scheduled capital improvement projects, increases in labor, and certain other manufacturing costs (with no corresponding 1992 selling price increases). Reduced fixed costs from the closing of the Streator, Illinois, plant in June 1992 and productivity and efficiency gains partially offset these cost increases.

**Instructions**
What factors affect the costs of products sold at Anchor Glass Container Corporation?

---

*Answers to Self-Study Questions*
1. b    2. d    3. b    4. b    5. c    6. d    7. a    8. c    9. a    10. d

# "We'd Like It in Red"

CORNELIUS, Oreg. — Western States Fire Apparatus, Inc., of Cornelius, Oregon, is one of the few American companies that makes fire trucks. The company builds about 25 trucks per year. Founded in 1941, the company is run by the children and grandchildren of the original founder.

"We buy the chassis, which is the cab and the frame," says Susan Scott, the company's bookkeeper. "In our computer, we set up an account into which all of the direct material that is purchased for that particular job is charged." Other direct materials include the fire pump—which can cost $10,000—the lights, the siren, ladders, and hoses.

As for direct labor, the production workers fill out job sheets that tell what jobs they worked on. Usually, the company is building four trucks at any one time. On payday, the controller allocates the payroll to the appropriate job record.

Indirect materials, such as nuts and bolts, wiring, lubricants, and abrasives are allocated to each job in proportion to direct material dollars. Other costs, such as insurance and supervisors' salaries, are allocated based on direct labor hours. "We need to allocate overhead in order to know what kind of price we have to charge when we submit our bids," she says.

Western gets orders through a "blind-bidding" process; that is, Western submits its bid without knowing the bid prices made by its competitors. "If we bid too low, we won't make a profit. If we bid too high, we don't get the job."

Regardless of the final price for the truck, the quality had better be first-rate. "The fire departments let you know if they don't like what you did, and you usually end up fixing it." ◀

# CHAPTER 21

# JOB ORDER COST ACCOUNTING

---

**After studying this chapter, you should be able to:**

1. *Explain the characteristics and purposes of cost accounting.*
2. *Describe the flow of costs in a job order cost accounting system.*
3. *Explain the nature and importance of a job cost sheet.*
4. *Indicate how the predetermined overhead rate is determined and used.*
5. *Prepare entries for jobs completed and sold.*
6. *Distinguish between under- and overapplied manufacturing overhead.*

Having read the story about Western States Fire Apparatus, Inc., you should now be familiar with the manufacturing costs used in making a fire truck. This chapter illustrates how these manufacturing costs would be assigned to specific jobs, such as the manufacture of individual fire trucks. We begin the discussion in this chapter with an overview of the flow of costs in a job order cost accounting system. We then use a case study to explain and illustrate the documents, entries, and accounts in this type of cost accounting system. The organization and content of this chapter are as follows:

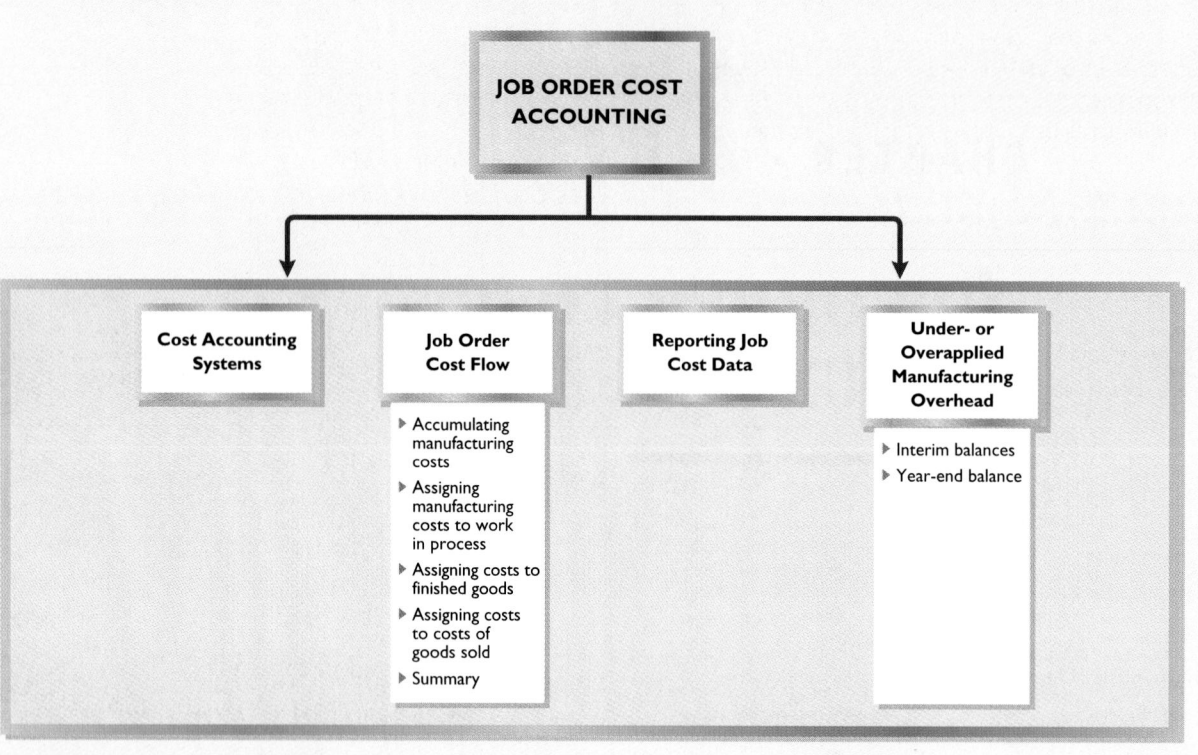

## Cost Accounting Systems

Cost accounting involves the measuring, recording, and reporting of product costs. From the data accumulated, both the total cost and the unit cost of each product is determined.

A cost accounting system consists of manufacturing cost accounts that are fully integrated into the general ledger of a company. **An important feature of a cost accounting system is the use of a perpetual inventory system that provides information immediately on the cost of a product.** There are two basic types of cost accounting systems: (1) a job order cost system and (2) a process cost system. Although cost accounting systems differ widely from company to company, most are based on one of these two traditional product costing systems.

Under a job order cost system, costs are assigned to each **job**, such as the manufacture of a high-speed drilling machine, or to each **batch** of goods, such as 500 wedding invitations. Jobs or batches may be completed to fill a specific customer order or to replenish inventory. An important feature of job order costing is that each job (or batch) has its own distinguishing characteristics. For example, each house is custom built, each motion picture is unique, and each printing job is different. **The objective is to compute the cost per job.** At each point in the manufacturing process, the job and its associated costs can be identified. A job order cost system measures costs for each completed job, rather than for set time periods.

A process cost system is used when a series of connected manufacturing processes or departments produce a large volume of uniform or relatively homogeneous products. Production is continuous to ensure that adequate inventories of the finished product(s) are on hand. A process cost system is used in the manufacture of cereal, the refining of petroleum, and the production of automobiles. Process costing accounts for and accumulates product-related costs **for a period of time** (such as a week or a month) as opposed to assigning costs to specific products or job orders. In process costing, the costs are assigned to or accumulated by departments or processes for a set period of time. The process cost system will be discussed in Chapter 22.

A company may use both types of cost systems. For example, General Motors uses process cost accounting for its standard model cars, such as Chevrolets and Buicks, and job order cost accounting for a custom-made limousine for the President of the United States. The basic flow in each system is shown in Illustration 21-1. The objective of both systems is to provide product unit cost information for product pricing, cost control, inventory valuation, and financial statement presentation. End-of-period inventory values are computed by using product unit cost data.

**Illustration 21-1**

*Job order and process cost systems*

**Job Order Cost System**
Two jobs: Wedding Invitations and Menus

Black ink $
Typesetting $
225 Invitations $
225 Envelopes $
Vellum stock, pure white $
**Job # 9501**

Typesetting $
Lamination $
Yellow stock $
50 Copies $
**Job # 9502**

Each job has distinguishing characteristics and related costs.

**Process Cost System**
Compact Disk Production

1. Oil is pumped.
2. Benzene is removed.
3. The benzene is made into pellets...
4. ...from which compact disks are produced.

Relatively similar products are produced over a specified time period.

## Before You Go On . . .

► **Review It**

1. What is cost accounting?
2. What is a cost accounting system?
3. How does a job order cost system differ from a process cost system?

## ▶Accounting in Action ▸ *Business Insight*

Many companies suffer from poor cost accounting. As a result, companies sometimes make products they ought not to be selling at all and buy others, often from overseas suppliers, that they could more profitably make themselves. Moreover, inaccurate cost data lead companies to misallocate capital and frustrate efforts by plant managers to improve efficiency.

For example, consider a diversified company in the business of rebuilding diesel locomotives. The managers thought they were making money until a consulting firm determined that costs had been seriously underestimated. The company bailed out of the business, and not a moment too soon. Says the consultant who advised the company: "The more contracts it won, the more money it lost."

---

**STUDY OBJECTIVE**
· · · · · · · · · ·**2**· · · · · · · · ·

*Describe the flow of costs in a job order cost accounting system.*

**Illustration 21-2**

*Job order cost accounting system*

# *J*ob Order Cost Flow

The flow of costs (direct materials, direct labor, and manufacturing overhead) in job order cost accounting parallels the physical flow of the materials as they are converted into finished goods. There are two major steps in the flow of costs: (1) **accumulating** the manufacturing costs incurred and (2) **assigning** the accumulated costs to the work done. As shown in Illustration 21-2, manufacturing costs incurred are accumulated in entries 1–3 by debits to Raw Materials Inventory, Factory Labor, and Manufacturing Overhead. No attempt is made when

---

### Job Order Cost Accounting

**Raw Materials Inventory**

| (1) Purchases | (4) Materials used |

**Work in Process Inventory**

| (4) Direct materials used | (7) Cost of completed jobs |
| (5) Direct labor used | |
| (6) Overhead applied | |

**Finished Goods Inventory**

| (7) Cost of completed jobs | (8) Cost of goods sold |

**Factory Labor**

| (2) Factory labor incurred | (5) Factory labor used |

**Cost of Goods Sold**

| (8) Cost of goods sold | |

**Manufacturing Overhead**

| Actual overhead incurred: | (6) Overhead applied |
| (3) Depreciation Insurance Repairs | |
| (4) Indirect materials used | |
| (5) Indirect labor used | |

**Key to Entries:**

| Accumulation | Assignment |
|---|---|
| 1. Purchase raw materials | 4. Raw materials are used |
| 2. Incur factory labor | 5. Factory labor is used |
| 3. Incur manufacturing overhead | 6. Overhead is applied |
| | 7. Completed goods are recognized |
| | 8. Cost of goods sold is recognized |

costs are incurred to associate the costs with specific jobs. The remaining entries (entries 4–8) pertain to the assignment of manufacturing costs incurred. First, as illustrated, costs are assigned to the Work in Process Inventory account. **All debits to this account must also be assigned to specific jobs.** When a job is finished, its cost is transferred to finished goods. Later, when the goods are sold, their cost is transferred to cost of goods sold. We will use a case study to explain and illustrate how a job order system operates.

## Accumulating Manufacturing Costs

In a job order cost system, manufacturing costs are recorded in the period in which they are incurred. To illustrate, we will use the January transactions of Wallace Manufacturing Company, which makes tools and dies.

### *Raw Materials Costs*

**The costs of raw materials purchased are debited to Raw Materials Inventory when materials are received.** This account is debited for the invoice cost and freight costs chargeable to the purchaser. It is credited for purchase discounts taken and purchase returns and allowances. **No effort is made at this point to associate the cost of materials with specific jobs or orders.** The procedures for ordering, receiving, recording, and paying for raw materials are similar to the purchasing procedures of a merchandising company.

To illustrate the purchase of raw materials, assume that Wallace Manufacturing Company purchases 2,000 handles (Stock No. AA2746) at $5 per unit ($10,000) and 800 modules (Stock No. AA2850) at $40 per unit ($32,000) for a total cost of $42,000 ($10,000 + $32,000). The entry to record this purchase on January 4 is:

|  |  (1)  |  |  |
|---|---|---|---|
| Jan. 4 | Raw Materials Inventory | 42,000 | |
| |     Accounts Payable | | 42,000 |
| |     (Purchase of raw materials on account) | | |

**Helpful hint** How does this entry differ for a merchandising company that has a perpetual inventory system? Answer: The debit is to Merchandise Inventory.

**Raw Materials Inventory is a control account.** The subsidiary ledger consists of individual records for each item of raw materials. The records may take the form of accounts (or cards) that are manually or mechanically prepared, or data files maintained electronically on disks or magnetic tape. The records, referred to as **materials inventory records** (or **stores ledger cards**), are similar to the perpetual inventory records illustrated in Chapter 9 for a merchandising company. The card for Stock No. AA2746 following the purchase is shown in Illustration 21-3.

**Illustration 21-3**

*Materials inventory card*

| Item: Handles | | | | | | | Part No: AA2746 | | |
|---|---|---|---|---|---|---|---|---|---|
| | Receipts | | | Issues | | | Balance | | |
| Date | Units | Cost | Total | Units | Cost | Total | Units | Cost | Total |
| 1/4 | 2,000 | $5 | $10,000 | | | | 2,000 | $5 | $10,000 |

Postings are made daily to the subsidiary ledger. After all postings have been completed, the sum of the balances in the raw materials subsidiary ledger should equal the balance in the Raw Materials Inventory control account.

### Factory Labor Costs

The procedures for accumulating factory labor costs are similar to those used in computing the payroll for a merchandising company. For example, time clocks and time cards are used to determine total hours worked; gross and net earnings for each employee are listed in a payroll register; and individual employee earnings records are maintained. To help ensure the accuracy of payroll data, a company should follow the principles of internal control for payrolls described in Chapter 11.

In a manufacturing company, the cost of factory labor consists of (1) gross earnings of factory workers, (2) employer payroll taxes on such earnings, and (3) fringe benefits (such as sick pay, pensions, and vacation pay) incurred by the employer. **Labor costs are debited to Factory Labor when they are incurred.** To illustrate, assume that Wallace Manufacturing incurs $32,000 of factory labor costs, of which $27,000 relates to wages payable and $5,000 relates to payroll taxes payable in January. The entry is:

(2)

| | | | |
|---|---|---|---|
| Jan. 31 | Factory Labor | 32,000 | |
| |     Factory Wages Payable | | 27,000 |
| |     Employer Payroll Taxes Payable | | 5,000 |
| |     (To record factory labor costs) | | |

Factory labor is subsequently assigned to work in process and manufacturing overhead, as explained later in the chapter.

### Manufacturing Overhead Costs

A company may have many types of overhead costs. The accumulation of these costs may be recognized **daily**, as in the case of machinery repairs and the use of indirect materials and indirect labor. Alternatively, overhead costs may be recorded **periodically** through adjusting entries, as in the case of property taxes, depreciation, and insurance. Using assumed data, a summary entry for manufacturing overhead in Wallace Manufacturing Company is:

(3)

| | | | |
|---|---|---|---|
| Jan. 31 | Manufacturing Overhead | 13,800 | |
| |     Utilities Payable | | 4,800 |
| |     Prepaid Insurance | | 2,000 |
| |     Accounts Payable (for repairs) | | 2,600 |
| |     Accumulated Depreciation | | 3,000 |
| |     Property Taxes Payable | | 1,400 |
| |     (To record overhead costs) | | |

**Manufacturing Overhead is a control account.** The subsidiary ledger consists of individual accounts for each type of cost, such as Factory Utilities, Factory Insurance, and Factory Repairs.

### Assigning Manufacturing Costs to Work in Process

> **STUDY OBJECTIVE**
> ••••••••▼3▼••••••••
>
> *Explain the nature and importance of a job cost sheet.*

As shown in the flow chart in Illustration 21-2, assigning manufacturing costs to work in process results in **debits** to Work in Process Inventory and **credits** to Raw Materials Inventory, Factory Labor, and Manufacturing Overhead. Journal entries for the assignment of costs to work in process are usually made and posted **monthly**. An indispensable accounting record in assigning costs to jobs is the job cost sheet, shown in Illustration 21-4. A job cost sheet is a form used to record the costs chargeable to a specific job and to determine the total and

**Illustration 21-4**

*Job cost sheet*

**Job Cost Sheet**

Job No. _____     Quantity _____
Item _____     Date Requested _____
For _____     Date Completed _____

| Date | Direct Materials | Direct Labor | Manufacturing Overhead |
|------|------------------|--------------|------------------------|
|      |                  |              |                        |
|      |                  |              |                        |
|      |                  |              |                        |

Cost of completed job
 Direct materials ............................................ $ _____
 Direct labor ................................................ _____
 Manufacturing overhead ................................ _____
Total cost .................................................... $ _____
Unit cost (total dollars ∏ quantity) .................. $ _____

unit cost of the completed job. **Postings to job cost sheets are made daily**, directly from supporting documentation that shows the cost and job to be charged.

## ►Accounting in Action ► *Business Insight*

At Federal Express, the job order is to deliver the shipper's package to the right customer on time. To make his deliveries, Santa may still rely on Rudolph, but more and more shippers are relying on FedEx. FedEx expects that its 469 planes and 32,560 vans will have their busiest days each year in the week preceding Christmas. In a recent year, for instance, the company handled a record 3 million packages in a single day during that busy preholiday week.

*Source: New York Times,* December 20, 1994, p. D1.

A separate job cost sheet is kept for each job. Job cost sheets constitute the subsidiary ledger for the Work in Process Inventory account. **Each entry to Work in Process Inventory must be accompanied by a corresponding posting to one or more job cost sheets.**

### *Raw Materials Costs*

**Raw materials costs are assigned when the materials are issued by the storeroom.** To achieve effective internal control over the issuance of materials, the storekeeper should obtain a written authorization each time materials are released to production. The authorization for issuing raw materials is made on a prenumbered materials requisition slip signed by an authorized employee such as a department supervisor. Materials may be used directly on a job, or they may be considered to be indirect materials. As shown in Illustration 21-5, the requisition should indicate the quantity and type of materials withdrawn and the account to be charged. The account is Work in Process Inventory for direct materials and Manufacturing Overhead for indirect materials.

**Helpful hint** Approvals are an important part of a materials requisition slip because they help to establish individual accountability over inventory.

**Illustration 21-5**

*Materials requisition slip*

**Helpful hint** The internal control principle is documentation procedures which includes prenumbering to enhance subsequent accountability.

| Wallace Manufacturing Company<br>Materials Requisition Slip | | | | |
|---|---|---|---|---|
| Deliver to: Assembly Department | | | Req. No. R247 | |
| Charge to: Work in Process—Job No. 101 | | | Date: 1/6/96 | |

| Quantity | Description | Stock No. | Cost Per Unit | Total |
|---|---|---|---|---|
| 200 | Handles | AA2746 | $5.00 | $1,000 |
| | | | | |
| | | | | |
| | | | | |

Requested by *Bruce Howart*      Received by *Herb Crowley*

Approved by *Kap Shin*      Costed by *Heather Remmers*

The requisition is prepared in duplicate. A copy is retained in the storeroom as evidence of the materials released; the original is sent to accounting, where the cost per unit and total cost of the materials used are determined. Any of the inventory costing methods (FIFO, LIFO, or average cost) may be used in costing the requisitions; the method selected by management should be followed consistently. After the requisition slips have been costed, they are posted daily to the materials inventory records. In addition, **requisitions for direct materials are posted daily to the individual job cost sheets.**

Periodically, the requisitions are sorted, totaled, and journalized. For example, if $24,000 of direct materials and $6,000 of indirect materials are used in Wallace Manufacturing in January, the entry is:

| | (4) | | |
|---|---|---|---|
| Jan. 31 | Work in Process Inventory | 24,000 | |
| | Manufacturing Overhead | 6,000 | |
| | Raw Materials Inventory | | 30,000 |
| | (To assign materials to jobs and overhead) | | |

The requisition slips show total direct materials costs of $12,000 for Job No. 101, $7,000 for Job No. 102, and $5,000 for Job No. 103. The posting of requisition slip R247 and other assumed postings to the job cost sheets for materials are shown in Illustration 21-6. After all postings have been completed, the sum of the totals of the direct materials columns of the job cost sheets should equal the direct materials debited to Work in Process Inventory.

The materials inventory record for Part No. AA2746, after posting requisition slip R247 and an assumed requisition slip for 760 handles costing $3,800 on January 10 for Job 102, is shown in Illustration 21-7.

### Factory Labor Costs

**Factory labor costs are assigned to jobs on the basis of time tickets prepared when the work is performed.** The time ticket should indicate the employee, the hours worked, the account and job to be charged, and the total labor cost. The

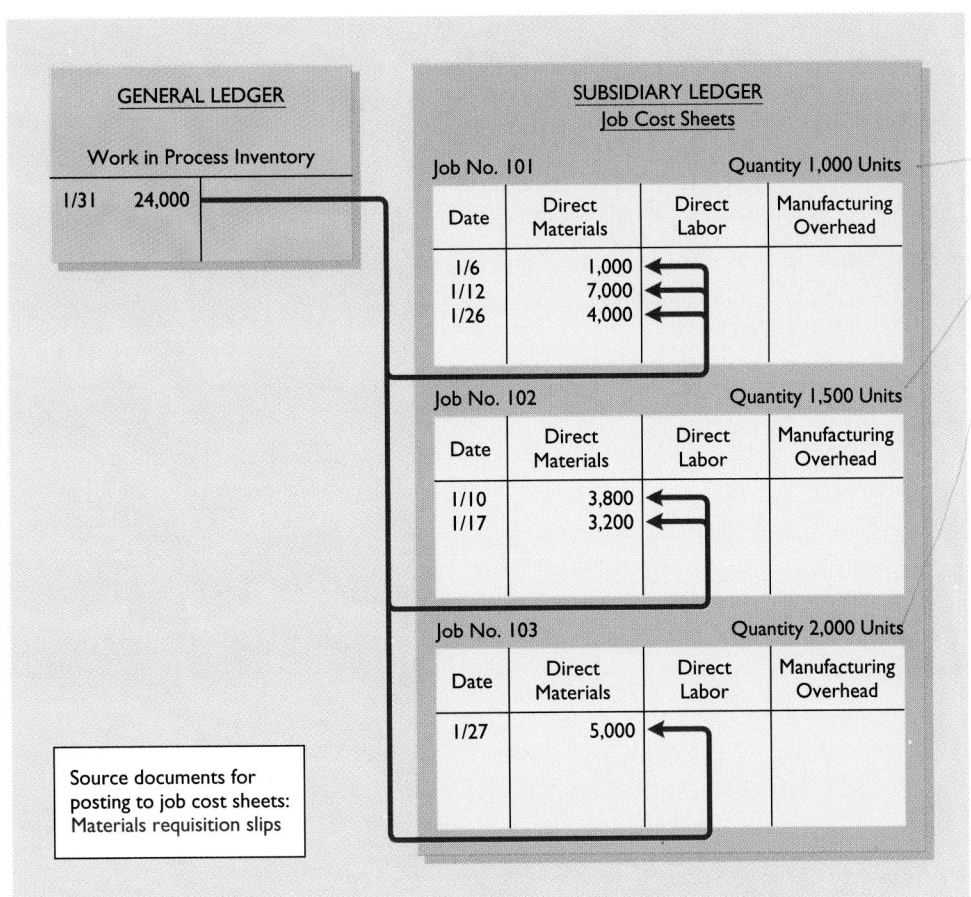

**Illustration 21-6**

*Job cost sheets—direct materials*

*which quantity*

**Illustration 21-7**

*Materials inventory card following issuances*

| Item: Handles | | | | | | | Part No: AA2746 | | | |
|---|---|---|---|---|---|---|---|---|---|---|
| | Receipts | | | Issues | | | Balance | | | |
| Date | Units | Cost | Total | Units | Cost | Total | Units | Cost | Total | |
| 1/4 | 2,000 | $5 | $10,000 | | | | 2,000 | $5 | $10,000 | |
| 1/6 | | | | 200 | $5 | $1,000 | 1,800 | $5 | 9,000 | |
| 1/10 | | | | 760 | $5 | 3,800 | 1,040 | $5 | 5,200 | |

account Work in Process Inventory is debited for direct labor, and Manufacturing Overhead is debited for indirect labor. When direct labor is involved, the job number must be indicated as shown in Illustration 21-8. In some companies, different colored time tickets are used for direct and indirect labor. All time tickets should be approved by the employee's supervisor.

The time tickets are later sent to the payroll department where the total time reported for an employee for a pay period is reconciled with total hours worked, shown on the employee's time card. Then the employee's hourly wage rate is applied and the total labor cost is computed. Subsequently, the time tickets are sorted, totaled, and journalized. For example, if the total factory labor cost in-

**Illustration 21-8**

*Time ticket*

Wallace Manufacturing Company
Time Ticket

| | | | | Date: | 1/6/96 |

Employee: John Nash    Employee No. 124
Charge to: Work in Process    Job No. 101

| Time | | | Hourly Rate | Total Cost |
| Start | Stop | Total Hours | | |
| --- | --- | --- | --- | --- |
| 0800 | 1200 | 4 | 10.00 | 40.00 |

Approved by *Bob Kadler*        Costed by *S. Bono*

curred of $32,000 consists of $28,000 of direct labor and $4,000 of indirect labor, the entry is:

| | (5) | | |
| --- | --- | --- | --- |
| Jan. 31 | Work in Process Inventory | 28,000 | |
| | Manufacturing Overhead | 4,000 | |
| |     Factory Labor | | 32,000 |
| |     (To assign labor to jobs and overhead) | | |

As a result of this entry, Factory Labor is left with a zero balance, and gross earnings are assigned to the appropriate manufacturing accounts.

We will assume that the labor costs chargeable to the three jobs are $15,000, $9,000, and $4,000. The Work in Process Inventory and job cost sheets after posting are shown in Illustration 21-9. As in the case of direct materials, the postings to the direct labor columns of the job cost sheets should equal the posting of direct labor to Work in Process Inventory.

## ▸Technology in Action

A job cost computer program provides summaries of material and labor expenses by job. The program enables the company to accumulate costs by jobs, provide data to accounts receivable for billings, assign overhead costs, and provide up-to-date management reports. The paperwork and reports generated by such systems are basically the same as shown for Wallace Manufacturing Company. The major difference between manual and computerized systems is the time involved in converting data into information and in getting feedback (reports) to management.

**STUDY OBJECTIVE**
••••••••••▼4••••••••••

*Indicate how the predetermined overhead rate is determined and used.*

### Manufacturing Overhead Costs

Unlike direct materials and direct labor that apply to specific jobs, manufacturing overhead relates to production operations as a whole. Consequently, these costs cannot be assigned to specific jobs on the basis of actual costs incurred. Instead, **manufacturing overhead is assigned to work in process and to specific jobs on an estimated basis through the use of a predetermined overhead rate.**

**Illustration 21-9**

*Job cost sheets—direct labor*

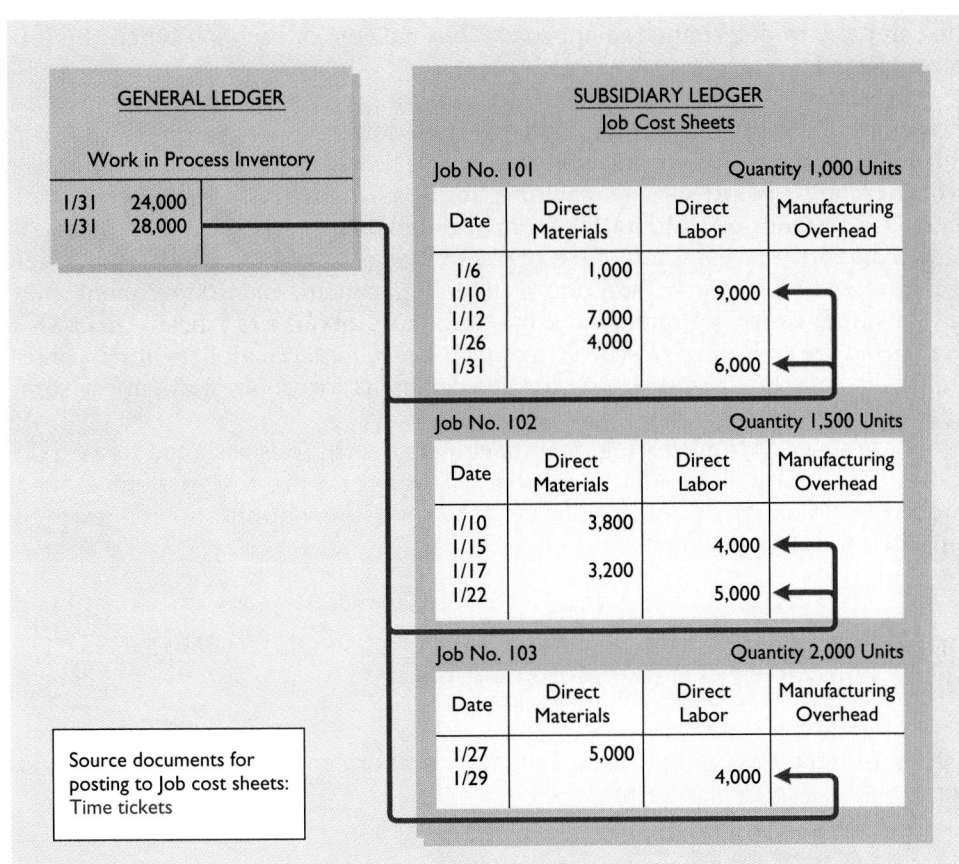

**Helpful hint** Prove the
$28,000 by totaling the
charges by jobs:
101   $15,000
102      9,000
103      4,000
        $28,000

The predetermined overhead rate is based on the relationship between estimated annual overhead costs and expected annual operating activity, expressed
in terms of a common **activity base**. The common activity base may be stated in
terms of direct labor costs, direct labor hours, machine hours, or any other measure that will provide an equitable basis for applying overhead costs to jobs. The
predetermined overhead rate is established at (or prior to) the beginning of the
year. The formula for a predetermined overhead rate is:

**Illustration 21-10**

*Formula for predetermined
overhead rate*

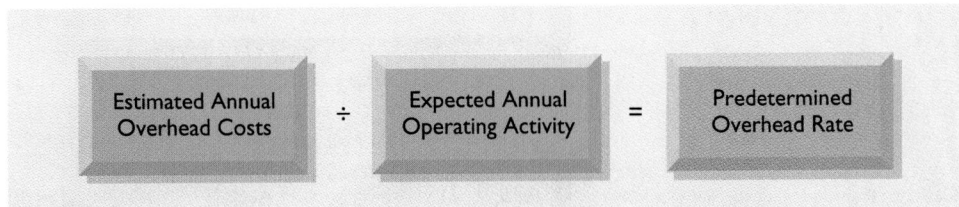

At Wallace Manufacturing, direct labor cost is the activity base. Assuming that
annual overhead costs are expected to be $280,000 and that $350,000 of direct
labor costs are anticipated, the overhead rate is 80%, computed as follows:

$$\$280,000 \div \$350,000 = 80\%$$

This means that for every dollar of direct labor, 80 cents of manufacturing overhead will be assigned to a job. The use of a predetermined overhead rate enables

the company to determine the approximate total cost of each job **when the job is completed**.

Historically, direct labor costs or direct labor hours have often been used as the activity base because of the relatively high correlation between direct labor and manufacturing overhead. In recent years, however, **there has been a significant trend toward use of machine hours as the activity base because of increased reliance on automation in manufacturing operations.**

A company may use more than one activity base. For example, if a job order is manufactured in more than one factory department, each department may have its own overhead rate. In the opening story about fire trucks, two bases were used in assigning overhead to jobs: direct material dollars for indirect materials, and direct labor hours for such costs as insurance and supervisors' salaries.

For Wallace Manufacturing, manufacturing overhead is assigned to work in process and **charged to jobs when direct labor costs are assigned**. Overhead applied for January is $22,400 ($28,000 × 80%), and the application is recorded through the following entry.

|  | (6) |  |  |
|---|---|---|---|
| Jan. 31 | Work in Process Inventory | 22,400 |  |
|  | Manufacturing Overhead |  | 22,400 |
|  | (To assign overhead to jobs) |  |  |

After posting, the Work in Process Inventory account and the job cost sheets will appear as shown in Illustration 21-11.

**Illustration 21-11**

*Job cost sheets—manufacturing overhead applied*

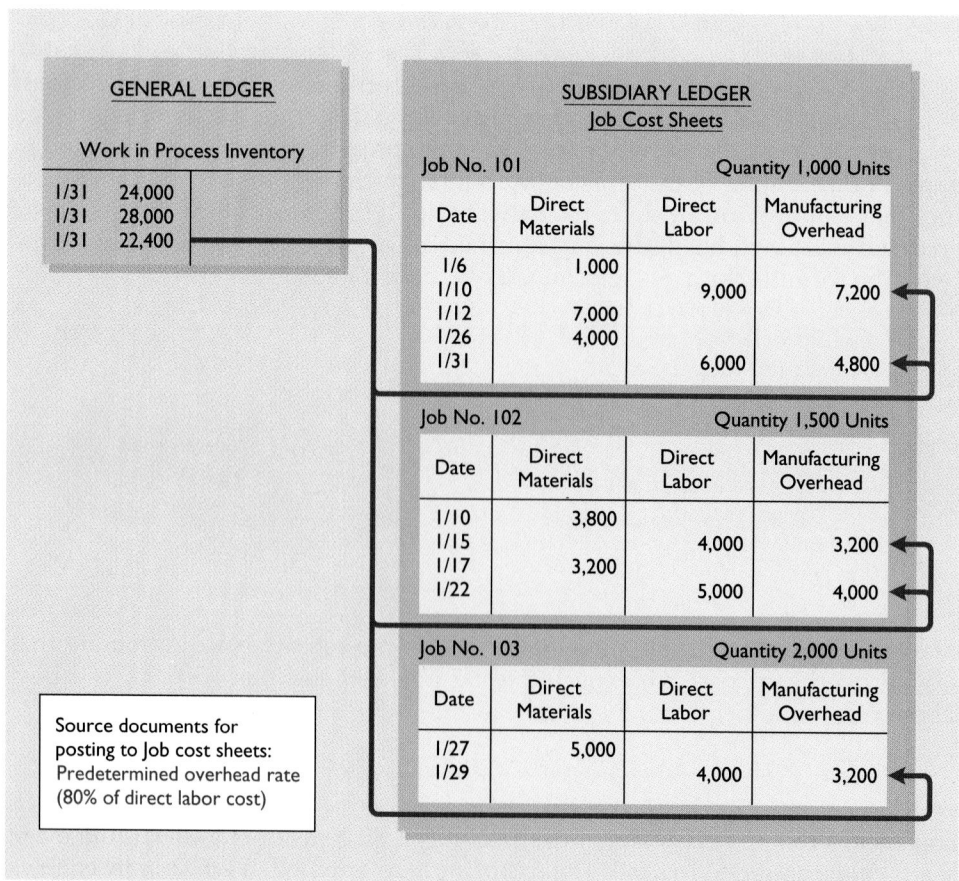

Note that the debit of $22,400 of Work in Process Inventory equals the sum of the overhead assigned to jobs: Job 101 $12,000 + Job 102 $7,200 + Job 103 $3,200.

At the end of each month, the balance in Work in Process Inventory should equal the sum of the costs shown on the job cost sheets of unfinished jobs. Assuming that all jobs are unfinished, proof of the agreement of the control and subsidiary accounts in Wallace Manufacturing is shown below.

**Illustration 21-12**

*Proof of job cost sheets to work in process inventory*

| Work in Process Inventory | | | Job Cost Sheets | |
|---|---|---|---|---|
| Jan. 31 | 24,000 | | No. 101 | $39,000 |
| Jan. 31 | 28,000 | | 102 | 23,200 |
| Jan. 31 | 22,400 | | 103 | 12,200 |
| | 74,400 | ← | | $74,400 |

## Before You Go On . . .

### ▶ Review It

1. What source documents are used in assigning manufacturing costs to Work in Process Inventory?
2. What is a job cost sheet, and what is its primary purpose?
3. What is the formula for computing a predetermined overhead rate?

### ▶ Do It

Danielle Company is working on two job orders. The job cost sheets show the following: direct materials—Job 120 $6,000, Job 121 $3,600; direct labor—Job 120 $4,000, Job 121 $2,000; and manufacturing overhead—Job 120 $5,000, Job 121 $2,500. Prepare the three summary entries to record the assignment of costs to Work in Process from the data on the job cost sheets.

**Reasoning:** Each cost charged to a job must be accompanied by a debit to the control account, Work in Process Inventory. The credits in the summary entries are the accounts debited when the manufacturing costs were accumulated.

**Solution:** The three summary entries are:

| | | |
|---|---|---|
| Work in Process Inventory ($6,000 + $3,600) | 9,600 | |
|    Raw Materials Inventory | | 9,600 |
|      (To assign materials to jobs) | | |
| | | |
| Work in Process Inventory ($4,000 + $2,000) | 6,000 | |
|    Factory Labor | | 6,000 |
|      (To assign labor to jobs) | | |
| | | |
| Work in Process Inventory ($5,000 + $2,500) | 7,500 | |
|    Manufacturing Overhead | | 7,500 |
|      (To assign overhead to jobs) | | |

*Related exercise material: BE21–3, BE21–4, BE21–7, E21–2, E21–3, E21–7, and E21–8.*

## Assigning Costs to Finished Goods

**When a job is completed,** the costs are summarized and the lower portion of the applicable job cost sheet is completed. For example, if we assume that Job No. 101 is completed on January 31, the job cost sheet will show the following:

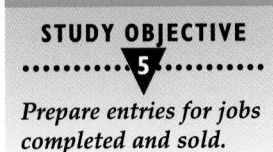

**STUDY OBJECTIVE**

▼ **5**

*Prepare entries for jobs completed and sold.*

**Illustration 21-13**

*Completed job cost sheet*

### Job Cost Sheet

| Job No. | 101 | Quantity | 1,000 |
| Item | Magnetic Sensors | Date Requested | February 5 |
| For | Tanner Company | Date Completed | January 31 |

| Date | Direct Materials | Direct Labor | Manufacturing Overhead |
|------|------------------|--------------|------------------------|
| 1/6 | $ 1,000 | | |
| 1/10 | | $ 9,000 | $ 7,200 |
| 1/12 | 7,000 | | |
| 1/26 | 4,000 | | |
| 1/31 | | 6,000 | 4,800 |
| | $12,000 | $15,000 | $12,000 |

Cost of completed job
Direct materials                  $   12,000
Direct labor                          15,000
Manufacturing overhead                12,000
Total cost                        $   39,000
Unit cost ($39,000 ÷ 1,000)       $      39.00

When a job is finished, an entry is made to transfer its total cost to finished goods inventory. The entry for Wallace Manufacturing is:

| | (7) | | |
|------|-----|-----|-----|
| Jan. 31 | Finished Goods Inventory | 39,000 | |
| | Work in Process Inventory | | 39,000 |
| | (To record completion of Job No. 101) | | |

**Finished Goods Inventory is a control account that controls individual finished goods records** in a finished goods subsidiary ledger. The records are similar to the perpetual inventory records illustrated in Chapter 9. Postings to the receipts columns are made directly from completed job cost sheets. The finished goods inventory record for Job No. 101 is shown below in Illustration 21-14.

**Illustration 21-14**

*Finished goods record*

| Item: Magnetic Sensors | | | | | | | | Job No: 101 | |
|------|------|------|------|------|------|------|------|------|------|
| | Receipts | | | Issues | | | Balance | | |
| Date | Units | Cost | Total | Units | Cost | Total | Units | Cost | Total |
| 1/31 | 1,000 | $39 | $39,000 | | | | 1,000 | $39 | $39,000 |
| 2/2 | | | | 1000 | $39 | $39,000 | | | −0− |

## Assigning Costs to Cost of Goods Sold

Recognition of the cost of goods sold is made when each sale occurs. To illustrate the entries when a completed job is sold, we will assume that on January 31 Wallace Manufacturing sells, on account, Job 101, costing $39,000, for $50,000. The entries are:

| | | (8) | | |
|---|---|---|---|---|
| Jan. 31 | Accounts Receivable | | 50,000 | |
| | Sales | | | 50,000 |
| | (To record sale of Job No. 101) | | | |
| | | | | |
| 31 | Cost of Goods Sold | | 39,000 | |
| | Finished Goods Inventory | | | 39,000 |
| | (To record cost of Job No. 101) | | | |

The units sold, the cost per unit, and the total cost of goods sold for each job sold are recorded in the issues section of the finished goods record as shown in Illustration 21-14.

## Summary of Job Order Cost Flows

A completed flow chart for a job order cost accounting system is shown in Illustration 21-15. All postings are keyed to entries 1–8 in Wallace Manufacturing Company's accounts presented in the cost flow graphic in Illustration 21-2. The graphic also provides a summary of the inventory control accounts, subsidiary ledgers, and source documents for assigning costs to jobs.

## ▸*T*echnology in *A*ction

Many job order cost systems are run by small manufacturers. With the increased sophistication of micro computers, small manufacturers can now use micros to perform (1) computer-aided manufacturing (CAM), (2) computer-aided testing (CAT), (3) computer-aided design (CAD), (4) electronic data interchange (EDI), and (5) materials requirement planning (MRP). As a result of breakthroughs in software development, for a small investment, manufacturers can use software with capabilities only dreamed about a few years ago.

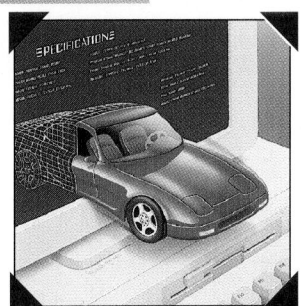

## *R*eporting Job Cost Data

At the end of a period, financial statements are prepared that present aggregate data on all jobs manufactured and sold. The cost of goods manufactured schedule in job order costing is the same as in Chapter 20 with one exception: **Manufacturing overhead applied, rather than actual overhead costs, is added to direct**

**Illustration 21-15**

*Job order cost system—flow of costs and documents*

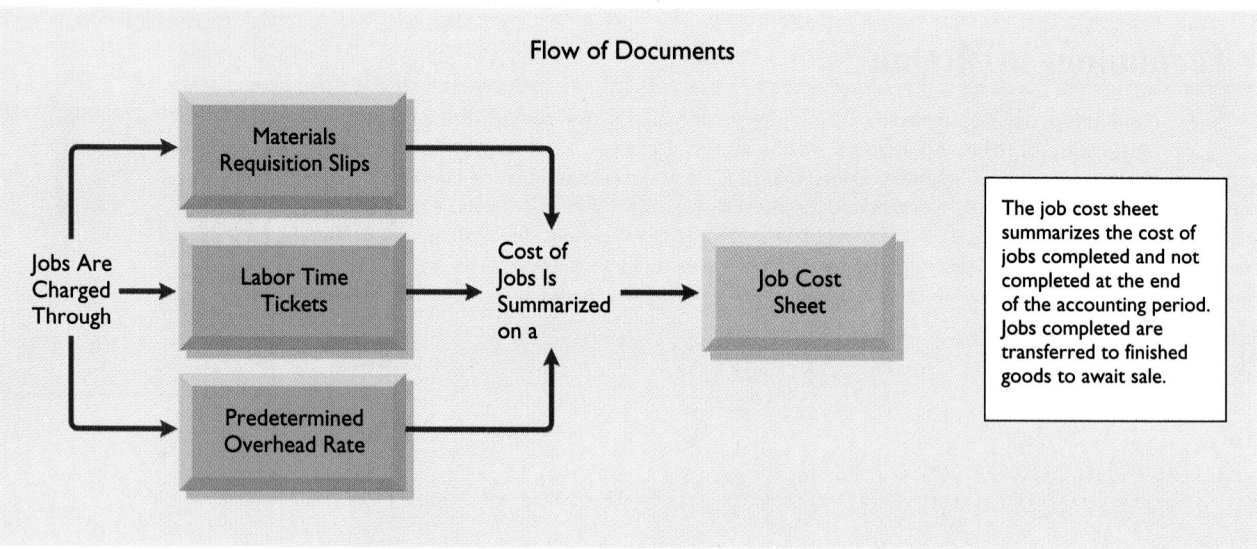

**materials and direct labor in determining total manufacturing costs.** The schedule is prepared directly from the Work in Process Inventory account. A condensed schedule for Wallace Manufacturing Company for January is as follows:

| WALLACE MANUFACTURING COMPANY<br>Cost of Goods Manufactured Schedule<br>For the Month Ended January 31, 1996 | | |
| --- | --- | --- |
| Work in process, January 1 | | $ –0– |
| Direct materials used | $24,000 | |
| Direct labor | 28,000 | |
| Manufacturing overhead applied | 22,400 | |
| Total manufacturing costs | | 74,400 |
| Total cost of work in process | | 74,400 |
| Less: Work in process, January 31 | | 35,400 |
| Cost of goods manufactured | | $39,000 |

**Illustration 21-16**

*Cost of goods manufactured schedule*

Note that the cost of goods manufactured ($39,000) agrees with the amount transferred from Work in Process Inventory to Finished Goods Inventory in journal entry No. 7 in Illustration 21-15.

The income statement and balance sheet are the same as those illustrated in Chapter 20. For example, the partial income statement for Wallace Manufacturing Company for the month of January is as follows:

| WALLACE MANUFACTURING COMPANY<br>Partial Income Statement<br>For the Month Ending January 31, 1996 | | |
| --- | --- | --- |
| Sales | | $50,000 |
| Less: Cost of goods sold | | |
| Finished goods inventory, January 1 | $ –0– | |
| Cost of goods manufactured (See Illustration 21-16) | 39,000 | |
| Cost of goods available for sale | 39,000 | |
| Finished goods inventory, January 31 | –0– | |
| Cost of goods sold | | 39,000 |
| Gross profit | | $11,000 |

**Illustration 21-17**

*Partial income statement*

# Under- or Overapplied Manufacturing Overhead

When Manufacturing Overhead has a **debit balance**, overhead is said to be underapplied. Underapplied overhead means that the overhead assigned to work in process is less than the overhead incurred. Conversely, when manufacturing overhead has a **credit balance**, overhead is overapplied. Overapplied overhead means that the overhead assigned to work in process is greater than the overhead incurred.

The accounting and statement presentation of under- or overapplied overhead depends on whether the balance in Manufacturing Overhead exists at the end of an interim period, such as a month, or at the end of the company's annual accounting period.

**STUDY OBJECTIVE**

·········· **6** ··········

*Distinguish between under- and overapplied manufacturing overhead.*

## Interim Balances

The existence of under- or overapplied overhead at the end of a month usually does not require corrective action by management. If the result is attributable to normal fluctuations in costs and production, no corrective action may even be possible. In Wallace Manufacturing, the predetermined overhead rate was based on expected annual overhead costs of $280,000 and annual direct labor costs of $350,000. This does not mean that each month will have one-twelfth of both factors. For example, $48,000 of utility costs may be anticipated for the year, but variations in heating and air-conditioning costs are expected to produce higher utility costs in the winter and summer months and smaller utility costs in the spring and fall months. Thus, the January costs of $4,800 may be offset by May costs of $3,200. Similarly, January direct labor cost of $28,000, which is slightly below the average monthly cost ($29,167), may be offset by direct labor costs in other months of $30,000 or more. In sum, the existence of under- or overapplied overhead at the end of a month is often expected. It is also anticipated that monthly differences between actual and applied overhead will be offsetting over the course of the year.

When monthly financial statements are prepared, under- or overapplied overhead is reported on the balance sheet. **Underapplied overhead is shown as a prepaid expense in the current asset section. Overapplied overhead is reported as unearned revenue in the current liability section.**

> **Helpful hint** True or false: Underapplied overhead is reported as a current liability in an interim balance sheet. Answer: False; it is reported as a current asset.

## Year-End Balance

At the end of the year, all manufacturing overhead transactions are complete; thus, there is no further opportunity for offsetting events to occur. Accordingly, any balance in Manufacturing Overhead is eliminated by an adjusting entry. Usually, under- or overapplied overhead is considered to be an **adjustment to cost of goods sold**. Thus, **underapplied overhead is debited to Cost of Goods Sold, and overapplied overhead is credited to Cost of Goods Sold**. To illustrate, assume that Wallace Manufacturing has a $2,500 credit balance in Manufacturing Overhead at December 31. The adjusting entry for the overapplied overhead is:

| Dec. 31 | Manufacturing Overhead | 2,500 | |
| |     Cost of Goods Sold | | 2,500 |
| |     (To transfer overapplied overhead to cost of goods sold) | | |

After this entry is posted, Manufacturing Overhead will have a zero balance. In preparing an income statement for the year, the amount reported for cost of goods sold will be the account balance after the adjustment for either under- or overapplied overhead.

## ▶*Accounting in Action* ▶ *Business Insight*

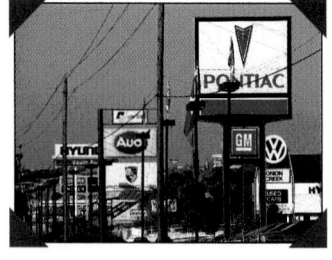

Overhead also applies in nonmanufacturing companies. The State of Michigan found that auto dealers were charging documentary and service fees ranging from $18 to $445 per automobile and inspection fees from $88 to $360. These fees often were charged auto buyers after a base price had been negotiated. The Attorney General of the State of Michigan ruled that auto dealers cannot charge customers additional fees for routine overhead costs. The attorney general said: "Overhead is part of the sales price of a motor vehicle. Processing paper work, dealer incurred costs, and inspection fees to qualify cars for extended warranty plans are ordinary overhead expenses."

Conceptually, it can be argued that under- or overapplied overhead at the end of the year should be allocated among ending work in process, finished goods, and cost of goods sold. However, most management accountants do not believe allocation is worth the cost and effort. The bulk of the under- or overapplied amount will be allocated to cost of goods sold anyway, because most of the jobs will be sold during the year.

## Before You Go On . . .

### ► Review It

1. When are entries made to record the completion and sale of a job?
2. What costs are included in total manufacturing costs in the cost of goods manufactured schedule?
3. How is under- or overapplied manufacturing overhead reported in monthly financial statements?

### ► A Look Back at Western States Fire Apparatus, Inc.

Refer to the opening story, and answer the following questions.
1. Would you expect Western States to use a job order or a process cost system? Why?
2. Is the flow of costs consistent with the cost flow used in the text? Explain.
3. On what basis does Western States allocate its overhead?
4. Why is the allocation of costs important to Western States Fire Apparatus?

**Solution:**

1. Western States uses job cost sheets; thus, the company uses a job order cost system. The use of a job order, rather than process cost, system by Western States makes sense because each job is custom built to fill a specific customer order, and each has its own distinguishing characteristics.
2. Western States follows the approach used in the text: it accumulates material, labor, and overhead costs and then assigns these costs to specific jobs and work in process.
3. Western States' overhead includes indirect materials (such as nuts and bolts, wiring, lubricants, and abrasives), which are allocated to each job in proportion to direct material costs. Its overhead also includes other costs such as insurance and supervisors' salaries, which are assigned based on direct labor hours.
4. Western States engages in blind-bidding to win contracts. In order to avoid over- or underbidding, the firm must have precise knowledge about costs.

## Summary of Study Objectives

**1. Explain the characteristics and purposes of cost accounting.** Cost accounting involves the procedures for measuring, recording, and reporting product costs. From the data accumulated, the total cost and the unit cost of each product is determined.

**2. Describe the flow of costs in a job order cost accounting system.** In job order cost accounting, manufacturing costs are first accumulated in three accounts: Raw Materials Inventory, Factory Labor, and Manufacturing Overhead. The accumulated costs are then assigned to Work in Process Inventory and eventually to Finished Goods Inventory and Cost of Goods Sold.

**3. Explain the nature and importance of a job cost sheet.** A job cost sheet is a form used to record the costs chargeable to a specific job and to determine the total and unit cost of the completed job. Job cost sheets constitute the subsidiary ledger for the Work in Process Inventory control account.

**4. Indicate how the predetermined overhead rate is determined and used.** The predetermined overhead rate is based on the relationship between estimated annual overhead costs and expected annual operating capacity expressed in terms of a common activity base, such as direct labor cost. The rate is used in assigning overhead costs to work in process and to specific jobs.

**5.** *Prepare entries for jobs completed and sold.* When jobs are completed, the cost is debited to Finished Goods Inventory and credited to Work in Process Inventory. When a job is sold the entries are: (a) Debit Cash or Accounts Receivable and credit Sales for the selling price and (b) Debit Cost of Goods Sold and credit Finished Goods Inventory for the cost of the goods.

**6.** *Distinguish between under- and overapplied manufacturing overhead.* Underapplied manufacturing overhead means that the overhead assigned to work in process is less than the overhead incurred. Conversely, overapplied overhead means that the overhead assigned to work in process is greater than the overhead incurred.

# GLOSSARY

**Cost accounting** An area of accounting that involves the measuring, recording, and reporting of product costs. (p. 882).

**Cost accounting system** Manufacturing cost accounts that are fully integrated into the general ledger of a company. (p. 882).

**Job cost sheet** A form used to record the costs chargeable to a job and to determine the total and unit cost of the completed job. (p. 886).

**Job order cost system** A cost accounting system in which costs are assigned to each job or batch. (p. 882).

**Materials requisition slip** A document authorizing the issuance of raw materials from the storeroom to production. (p. 887).

**Overapplied overhead** A situation in which overhead assigned to work in process is greater than the overhead incurred. (p. 897).

**Predetermined overhead rate** A rate based on the relationship between estimated annual overhead costs and expected annual operating activity, expressed in terms of a common activity base. (p. 891).

**Process cost system** A system of accounting used by companies that manufacture relatively homogeneous products through a series of continuous processes or operations. (p. 883).

**Time ticket** A document that indicates the employee, the hours worked, the account and job to be charged, and the total labor cost. (p. 888).

**Underapplied overhead** A situation in which overhead assigned to work in process is less than the overhead incurred. (p. 897).

# DEMONSTRATION PROBLEM

During February, Cardella Manufacturing works on two jobs: Numbers A16 and B17. Summary data concerning these jobs are as follows:

**Manufacturing Costs Incurred:**

Purchased $54,000 of raw materials on account.
Factory labor $76,000 plus $4,000 employer payroll taxes.
Manufacturing overhead exclusive of indirect materials and indirect labor $59,800.

**Assignment of Costs:**

| | |
|---|---|
| Direct materials: | Job A16 $27,000, Job B17 $21,000 |
| Indirect materials: | $3,000 |
| Direct labor: | Job A16 $52,000, Job B17 $26,000 |
| Indirect labor: | $2,000 |

Manufacturing overhead rate 80% of direct labor costs.

Job A16 was completed and sold on account for $150,000. Job B17 was only partially completed.

*Instructions*

(a) Journalize the February transactions in the sequence followed in the chapter.

(b) What was the amount of under- or overapplied manufacturing overhead?

## Solution to Demonstration Problem

(a)

| | | | 1. | | |
|---|---|---|---|---|---|
| Feb. 28 | Raw Materials Inventory | | | 54,000 | |
| | Accounts Payable | | | | 54,000 |
| | (Purchase of raw materials on account) | | | | |

| | | | 2. | | |
|---|---|---|---|---|---|
| 28 | Factory Labor | | | 80,000 | |
| | Factory Wages Payable | | | | 76,000 |
| | Employer Payroll Taxes Payable | | | | 4,000 |
| | (To record factory labor costs) | | | | |

| | | | 3. | | |
|---|---|---|---|---|---|
| 28 | Manufacturing Overhead | | | 59,800 | |
| | Accounts Payable, Accumulated | | | | |
| | Depreciation, and Prepaid Insurance | | | | 59,800 |
| | (To record overhead costs) | | | | |

| | | | 4. | | |
|---|---|---|---|---|---|
| 28 | Work in Process Inventory | | | 48,000 | |
| | Manufacturing Overhead | | | 3,000 | |
| | Raw Materials Inventory | | | | 51,000 |
| | (To assign raw materials to production) | | | | |

| | | | 5. | | |
|---|---|---|---|---|---|
| 28 | Work in Process Inventory | | | 78,000 | |
| | Manufacturing Overhead | | | 2,000 | |
| | Factory Labor | | | | 80,000 |
| | (To assign factory labor to production) | | | | |

| | | | 6. | | |
|---|---|---|---|---|---|
| 28 | Work in Process Inventory | | | 62,400 | |
| | Manufacturing Overhead | | | | 62,400 |
| | (To assign overhead to jobs—80% × $78,000) | | | | |

| | | | 7. | | |
|---|---|---|---|---|---|
| 28 | Finished Goods Inventory | | | 120,600 | |
| | Work in Process Inventory | | | | 120,600 |
| | (To record completion of Job A16: direct materials, $27,000, direct labor $52,000 and manufacturing overhead $41,600) | | | | |

| | | | 8. | | |
|---|---|---|---|---|---|
| 28 | Accounts Receivable | | | 150,000 | |
| | Cost of Goods Sold | | | 120,600 | |
| | Sales | | | | 150,000 |
| | Finished Goods Inventory | | | | 120,600 |
| | (To record sale of Job A16) | | | | |

(b) Manufacturing Overhead has a debit balance of $2,400 as shown below:

**Manufacturing Overhead**

| | | | |
|---|---|---|---|
| (3) | 59,800 | (6) | 62,400 |
| (4) | 3,000 | | |
| (5) | 2,000 | | |
| Bal. | 2,400 | | |

Thus, manufacturing overhead is underapplied for the month.

# SELF-STUDY QUESTIONS

Answers are at the end of the chapter.

(SO 1)   1. Cost accounting involves the measuring, recording, and reporting of:
   a. product costs.
   b. future costs.
   c. manufacturing processes.
   d. managerial accounting decisions.

(SO 2)   2. In accumulating raw materials costs, the cost of raw materials purchased in a perpetual system is debited to:
   a. Raw Material Purchases.
   b. Raw Materials Inventory.
   c. Purchases.
   d. Work in Process.

(SO 2)   3. When incurred, factory labor costs are debited to:
   a. Work in Process.
   b. Factory Wages Expense.
   c. Factory Labor.
   d. Factory Wages Payable.

(SO 3)   4. The source documents for assigning costs to job cost sheets are:
   a. invoices, time tickets, and the predetermined overhead rate.
   b. materials requisition slips, time tickets, and the actual overhead costs.
   c. materials requisition slips, payroll register, and the predetermined overhead rate.
   d. materials requisition slips, time tickets, and the predetermined overhead rate.

(SO 3)   5. In recording the issuance of raw materials in a job order cost system, it would be *incorrect* to:
   a. debit Work in Process Inventory.
   b. debit Finished Goods Inventory.
   c. debit Manufacturing Overhead.
   d. credit Raw Materials Inventory.

(SO 3)   6. The entry when direct factory labor is assigned to jobs is a debit to:
   a. Work in Process Inventory and a credit to Factory Labor.
   b. Manufacturing Overhead and a credit to Factory Labor.
   c. Factory Labor and a credit to Manufacturing Overhead.
   d. Factory Labor and a credit to Work in Process Inventory.

(SO 4)   7. The formula for computing the predetermined manufacturing overhead rate is estimated annual overhead costs divided by an expected annual operating activity, expressed as:
   a. direct labor cost.        c. machine hours.
   b. direct labor hours.       d. any of the above.

(SO 4)   8. In the Cleo Company, the predetermined overhead rate is 80% of direct labor cost. During the month, $210,000 of factory labor costs are incurred, of which $180,000 is direct labor and $30,000 is indirect labor. Actual overhead incurred was $200,000. The amount of overhead debited to Work in Process Inventory should be:
   a. $120,000.       c. $168,000.
   b. $144,000.       d. $160,000.

(SO 5)   9. In BAC Company, Job No. 26 is completed at a cost of $4,500 and later sold for $7,000 cash. A correct entry is:
   a. Debit Finished Goods Inventory $7,000 and credit Work in Process Inventory $7,000.
   b. Debit Cost of Goods Sold $7,000 and credit Finished Goods Inventory $7,000.
   c. Debit Finished Goods Inventory $4,500 and credit Work in Process Inventory $4,500.
   d. Debit Accounts Receivable $7,000 and credit Sales $7,000.

(SO 6)   10. In preparing monthly financial statements, over-applied overhead is reported in the balance sheet as a(an):
   a. prepaid expense.
   b. unearned revenue.
   c. noncurrent asset.
   d. noncurrent liability.

# QUESTIONS

1. Lorna Quay is studying for an accounting midterm examination. What should Lorna know about how management may use job cost data?

2. (a) Nars Holgren is not sure about the differences between cost accounting and a cost accounting system. Explain the difference to Nars. (b) What is an important feature of a cost accounting system?

3. (a) Distinguish between the two types of cost accounting systems. (b) May a company use both types of cost accounting systems?

4. What type of industry is likely to use a job order cost system? Give some examples.

5. What type of industry is likely to use a process cost system? Give some examples.

6. Your roommate asks your help in understanding the major steps in the flow of costs in a job order cost system. Identify the steps for your roommate.

7. There are three inventory control accounts in a job order system. Identify the control accounts and their subsidiary ledgers.

8. What source documents are used in accumulating direct labor costs?

9. Entries to manufacturing overhead normally are only made daily. Do you agree? Explain.

10. Edie Monay is confused about the source documents used in assigning materials and labor costs. Identify the documents and give the entry for each document.

11. What is the purpose of a job cost sheet?

12. Indicate the source documents that are used in charging costs to specific jobs.

13. Differentiate between a "materials inventory record" and a "materials requisition slip" as used in a job order cost system.

14. Paul Abdul believes actual manufacturing overhead should be charged to jobs. Do you agree? Why or why not?

15. What relationships are involved in computing a predetermined overhead rate?

16. How can the agreement of Work in Process Inventory and job cost sheets be verified?

17. Jan Jerome believes that the cost of goods manufactured schedule in job order cost accounting is the same as in manufacturing accounting. Is Jan correct? Explain.

18. Rob Palmer is confused about under- and over-applied manufacturing overhead. Define the terms for Rob and indicate the balance in the manufacturing overhead account applicable to each term.

19. Under- or overapplied overhead is reported in the income statement when monthly financial statements are prepared. Do you agree? If not, indicate the proper presentation.

20. At the end of the year, under- or overapplied overhead is closed to Income Summary. Is this correct? If not, indicate the customary treatment of this account.

# BRIEF EXERCISES

**BE21–1** Premier Tool & Die begins operations on January 1. Because all work is done to customer specifications, the company decides to use a job cost accounting system. Prepare a flow chart of a typical job order system with arrows showing the flow of costs. Identify the eight transactions.

*Prepare a flowchart of a job order cost accounting system, and identify transactions.*
*(SO 2)*

**BE21–2** During the first month of operations, Premier Tool & Die accumulated the following manufacturing costs: raw materials $6,000 on account, factory labor $4,000 of which $3,600 relates to factory wages payable and $400 relates to payroll taxes payable, and utilities payable $2,000. Prepare separate journal entries for each type of manufacturing cost.

*Prepare entries in accumulating manufacturing costs.*
*(SO 2)*

**BE21–3** In January, Premier Tool & Die requisitions raw materials for production as follows: Job 1 $1,000, Job 2 $1,200, Job 3 $1,600, and general factory use $400. Prepare a summary journal entry to record raw materials used.

*Prepare entry for the assignment of raw materials costs.*
*(SO 2)*

**BE21–4** Factory labor data for Premier Tool & Die is given in BE21–2. During January, time tickets show that the factory labor of $4,000 was used as follows: Job 1 $1,200, Job 2 $1,300. Job 3 $900 and general factory use $600. Prepare a summary journal entry to record factory labor used.

*Prepare entry for the assignment of factory labor costs.*
*(SO 2)*

**BE21–5** Data pertaining to job cost sheets for Premier Tool & Die are given in BE21–3 and BE21–4. Prepare the job cost sheets for each of the three jobs. (Note: You may omit the column for Manufacturing Overhead.)

*Prepare job cost sheets.*
*(SO 3)*

**BE21–6** Florita Company estimates that annual manufacturing overhead costs will be $400,000. Estimated annual operating activity bases are: direct labor cost $500,000, direct labor hours 50,000, and machine hours 100,000. Compute the predetermined overhead rate for each activity base.

*Compute predetermined overhead rates.*
*(SO 4)*

*Assign manufacturing overhead to production.*
*(SO 4)*

**BE21–7** During the first quarter, Florita Company incurs the following direct labor costs: January $40,000, February $30,000, and March $50,000. For each month, prepare the entry to assign overhead to production using a predetermined rate of 80% of direct labor cost.

*Prepare entries for completion and sale of completed jobs.*
*(SO 5)*

**BE21–8** In March, Petro Company completes Jobs 10 and 11 costing $25,000 and $32,000, respectively. On March 31, Job 10 is sold to the customer for $35,000 in cash. Journalize the entries for the completion of the two jobs and the sale of Job 10.

*Indicate statement classification of under- or overapplied overhead.*
*(SO 6)*

**BE21–9** On September 30, balances in Manufacturing Overhead are: Florita Company—Debit $2,500, Petro Company—Credit $3,000. Indicate how each company should report its balance at September 30, assuming each company prepares annual financial statements on December 31.

*Prepare adjusting entries for under- and overapplied overhead.*
*(SO 6)*

**BE21–10** At December 31, balances in Manufacturing Overhead are: Florita Company—Debit $1,600, Petro Company—Credit $1,200. Prepare the adjusting entry for each company at December 31, assuming the adjustment is made to cost of goods sold.

# EXERCISES

*Prepare entries for factory labor.*
*(SO 2)*

**E21–1** The gross earnings of the factory workers for Amani Company during the month of January are $95,000. The employer's payroll taxes for the factory payroll are $9,000 and the fringe benefits to be paid by the employer on this payroll are $4,000. Of the total accumulated cost of factory labor, 90% is related to direct labor and 10% is attributable to indirect labor.

**Instructions**
(a) Prepare the entry to record the factory labor costs for the month of January.
(b) Prepare the entry to assign factory labor to production.

*Prepare journal entries for manufacturing costs.*
*(SO 2, 3, 4, 5)*

**E21–2** Liriano Manufacturing uses a job order cost accounting system. On May 1, the company has a balance in Work in Process Inventory of $3,200 and two jobs in process: Job No. 429 $2,000, and Job No. 430 $1,200. During May, a summary of source documents reveals the following:

| For | Materials Requisition Slips | Labor Time Tickets |
|---|---|---|
| Job No. 429 | $2,500 | $ 2,400 |
| Job No. 430 | 2,000 | 3,000 |
| Job No. 431 | 4,400 | 7,600 |
| General use | 800 | 1,200 |
| | $9,700 | $14,200 |

Liriano Manufacturing applies manufacturing overhead to jobs at an overhead rate of 80% of direct labor cost. Job No. 429 is completed during the month.

**Instructions**
(a) Prepare summary journal entries to record the requisition slips, time tickets, the assignment of manufacturing overhead to jobs, and the completion of Job No. 429.
(b) Post the entries to Work in Process Inventory and prove the agreement of the control account with the job cost sheets.

**E21–3**   A job order cost sheet for West Company is shown below.

*Analyze a job cost sheet and prepare entries for manufacturing costs.*
*(SO 2, 3, 4, 5)*

| Job No. 92 | | | For 2,000 Units |
|---|---|---|---|
| Date | Direct Materials | Direct Labor | Manufacturing Overhead |
| 1/ 1 | 5,000 | 6,000 | 4,200 |
| 8 | 6,000 | | |
| 12 | | 8,000 | 6,400 |
| 25 | 2,000 | | |
| 27 | | 4,000 | 3,200 |
| | 13,000 | 18,000 | 13,800 |

| Cost of completed job: | |
|---|---|
| Direct materials | $13,000 |
| Direct labor | 18,000 |
| Manufacturing overhead | 13,800 |
| Total cost | $44,800 |
| Unit cost ($44,800 ÷ 2,000) | $22.40 |

**Instructions**

(a) ▦▤▤▤▷  On the basis of the foregoing data answer the following questions:

(1) What was the balance in Work in Process Inventory on January 1 if this was the only unfinished job?

(2) If manufacturing overhead is applied on the basis of direct labor cost, what overhead rate was used in each year?

(b) Prepare summary entries at January 31 to record the current year's transactions pertaining to Job No. 92.

**E21–4**   Manufacturing cost data for Silva Company, which uses a job order cost system, are presented below:

*Analyze costs of manufacturing and determine missing amounts.*
*(SO 2, 5)*

| | Case A | Case B | Case C |
|---|---|---|---|
| Direct materials | (a) | $83,000 | $ 65,000 |
| Direct labor used | $ 50,000 | 96,000 | (h) |
| Manufacturing overhead applied | 42,500 | (d) | (i) |
| Total manufacturing costs | 180,650 | (e) | 250,000 |
| Work in process 1/1/96 | (b) | 15,500 | 18,000 |
| Total cost of work in process | 201,500 | (f) | (j) |
| Work in process 12/31/96 | (c) | 11,800 | (k) |
| Cost of goods manufactured | 192,300 | (g) | 262,000 |

**Instructions**

Indicate the missing amount for each letter. Assume that in all cases manufacturing overhead is applied on the basis of direct labor cost and the rate is the same.

**E21–5**   Lopez Company applies manufacturing overhead to jobs on the basis of machine hours used. Overhead costs are expected to total $300,000 for the year, and machine usage is estimated at 125,000 hours.

*Compute the manufacturing overhead rate and the amount of under- or overapplied overhead.*
*(SO 4, 6)*

In January, $26,000 of overhead costs are incurred and 10,000 machine hours are used. For the remainder of the year, $294,000 of overhead costs are incurred and 120,000 machine hours are worked.

**Instructions**

(a) Compute the manufacturing overhead rate for the year.

(b) What is the amount of under- or overapplied overhead at January 31? How should this amount be reported in the financial statements prepared on January 31?

(c) What is the amount of under- or overapplied overhead at December 31?

(d) Assuming the under- or overapplied overhead for the year is not allocated to inventory accounts, prepare the adjusting entry to assign the amount to cost of goods sold.

*Analyze job cost sheet and
prepare entry for completed
job.*
(SO 2, 3, 4, 5)

**E21–6**    A job cost sheet of Lai Wong Company is given below:

| Job Cost Sheet | | | |
|---|---|---|---|
| JOB NO.   469 | | Quantity   2,000 | |
| ITEM   White Lion Cages | | Date Requested   7/2 | |
| FOR   Tesla Company | | Date Completed   7/31 | |
| Date | Direct Materials | Direct Labor | Manufacturing Overhead |
| 7/10 | 825 | | |
| 12 | 900 | | |
| 15 | | 440 | 550 |
| 22 | | 360 | 450 |
| 24 | 1,600 | | |
| 27 | 1,500 | | |
| 31 | | 540 | 675 |

Cost of completed job:
   Direct materials    ———
   Direct labor    ———
   Manufacturing overhead    ———
Total cost    ═══
Unit cost    ═══

**Instructions**
(a) ▭▭▭▷ Answer the following questions:
   (1) What are the source documents for direct materials, direct labor, and manufactur-
      ing overhead costs assigned to this job?
   (2) What is the predetermined manufacturing overhead rate?
   (3) What is the total cost and unit cost of the completed job?
(b) Prepare the entry to record the completion of the job.

*Prepare entries for
manufacturing costs.*
(SO 2, 4, 5)

**E21–7**    Anne Scott Corporation incurred the following transactions.

1. Purchased raw materials on account, $45,900.
2. Raw Materials of $36,000 were requisitioned to the factory. An analysis of the materi-
als requisition slips indicated that $8,800 was classified as indirect materials.
3. Factory labor costs incurred were $64,900 of which $59,000 pertained to factory wages
payable and $5,900 pertained to employer payroll taxes payable.
4. Time tickets indicated that $60,000 was direct labor and $4,900 was indirect labor.
5. Overhead costs incurred on account were $80,500.
6. Manufacturing overhead was applied at the rate of 160% of direct labor cost.
7. Goods costing $88,000 were completed and transferred to finished goods.
8. Finished goods costing $68,000 to manufacture were sold on account for $103,000.

**Instructions**
Journalize the transactions. (Omit explanations.)

*Prepare entries for
manufacturing costs.*
(SO 2, 3, 4, 5)

**E21–8**    Kwik Printing Corp. uses a job order cost system. The following data summarize the
operations related to the first quarter's production:

1. Materials purchased on account $172,000 and factory wages incurred, $87,300.
2. Materials requisitioned and factory labor used by job:

| | Materials | Factory Labor |
|---|---|---|
| Job A20 | $ 32,240 | $18,000 |
| Job A21 | 40,920 | 26,000 |
| Job A22 | 36,100 | 15,000 |

| | | |
|---|---|---|
| Job A23 | 39,270 | 25,000 |
| General factory use | 4,470 | 3,300 |
| | $153,000 | $87,300 |

3. Manufacturing overhead costs incurred on account, $39,500.
4. Depreciation on machinery and equipment, $14,550.
5. Manufacturing overhead rate is 80% of direct labor cost.
6. Jobs completed during the quarter: A20, A21, and A23.

*Instructions*
Prepare entries to record the operations summarized above. (Prepare a schedule showing the individual cost elements and total cost for each job in item 6.)

**E21–9** At May 31, the accounts of Mayberry Manufacturing Company show the following:

1. May 1 inventories—finished goods $12,600, work in process $14,700, and raw materials $8,200.
2. May 31 inventories—finished goods $10,500, work in process $16,900, and raw materials, $7,100.
3. Debit postings to work in process were: direct materials $72,400, direct labor $32,000, and manufacturing overhead applied $64,000.
4. Sales totaled $200,000.

*Prepare a cost of goods manufactured schedule and partial financial statements.*
*(SO 2, 5)*

*Instructions*
(a) Prepare a condensed cost of goods manufactured schedule.
(b) Prepare an income statement for May through gross profit.
(c) Indicate the balance sheet presentation of the manufacturing inventories at May 31, 1996.

**E21–10** Strocka Company begins operations on April 1. Information from job cost sheets shows the following:

*Compute work in process and finished goods from job cost sheets.*
*(SO 3, 5)*

| Job Number | Manufacturing Costs Assigned | | |
|---|---|---|---|
| | April | May | June |
| 10 | $5,200 | $4,400 | |
| 11 | 3,100 | 3,900 | $3,000 |
| 12 | 1,200 | | |
| 13 | | 4,700 | 4,500 |
| 14 | | 2,900 | 3,600 |

Job 12 was completed in April. Job 10 was completed in May, and Jobs 11 and 13 were completed in June. Each job was sold for 50% above its cost in the month following completion.

*Instructions*
Answer the following questions:

1. What is the balance in Work in Process Inventory at the end of each month?
2. What is the balance in Finished Goods Inventory at the end of each month?
3. What is the gross profit for May, June, and July?

# PROBLEMS

**P21–1** Vancouver Manufacturing uses a job order cost accounting system. On January 1, the company had Raw Materials Inventory $15,000 and Finished Goods Inventory, represented by Job No. 12, $124,000. During the month, the following summary transactions and events occurred.

*Prepare entries in a job cost system and job cost sheets.*
*(SO 2, 3, 4, 5)*

1. Purchased raw materials on account $225,000.
2. Incurred factory labor $300,000 of which $276,000 relates to factory wages payable and the balance (or $24,000) pertains to employer payroll taxes payable.
3. Incurred manufacturing overhead on account $260,000.
4. Recognized $9,000 of depreciation on factory machinery.
5. Charged direct materials to jobs: No. 13 $110,000 and No. 14 $70,000, and charged in-

direct materials of $50,000 to manufacturing overhead. The jobs call for the production of 20,000 and 10,000 units, respectively.

6. Charged factory labor to jobs on basis of time tickets: No. 13 $180,000 and No. 14 $100,000. The remaining labor was indirect.
7. Charged overhead to jobs at the rate of 120% of direct labor cost.
8. Completed Job No. 13.
9. Sold Job No. 12 on account for $170,000.

**Instructions**
(a) Journalize the transactions and events.
(b) Open accounts for the beginning inventories and post the entries to the job order cost accounts and to the job cost sheets for Jobs 13 and 14.
(c) Reconcile the balance in Work in Process Inventory with the costs of unfinished jobs.

*Prepare entries in a job cost system and partial income statement.*
*(SO 2, 3, 4, 5, 6)*

**P21–2**  For the year ended December 31, 1996, the job cost sheets of Jan Korea Company contained the following data.

| Job Number | Explanation | Direct Materials | Direct Labor | Manufacturing Overhead | Total Costs |
|---|---|---|---|---|---|
| 7650 | Balance 1/1 | $18,000 | $20,000 | $25,000 | $ 63,000 |
|  | Current year's costs | 22,000 | 30,000 | 37,500 | 89,500 |
| 7651 | Balance 1/1 | 12,000 | 18,000 | 22,500 | 52,500 |
|  | Current year's costs | 28,000 | 40,000 | 50,000 | 118,000 |
| 7652 | Current year's costs | 40,000 | 54,000 | 67,500 | 161,500 |

Other data:

1. Raw materials inventory totaled $20,000 on January 1. During the year, $100,000 of raw materials were purchased on account.
2. Finished goods on January 1 consisted of Job No. 7648 for $98,000 and Job No. 7649 for $62,000.
3. Job No. 7650 and Job No. 7651 were completed during the year.
4. Job Nos. 7648, 7649, and 7650 were sold on account for $390,000.
5. Manufacturing overhead incurred on account totaled $115,000.
6. Other manufacturing overhead consisted of indirect materials $12,000, indirect labor $18,000, and depreciation on factory machinery $6,000.

**Instructions**
(a) Journalize the transactions in the sequence followed in the chapter. Credit Factory Wages Payable when recording factory labor.
(b) Prove the agreement of Work in Process Inventory with job cost sheets pertaining to unfinished work.
(c) Prepare the adjusting entry for manufacturing overhead, assuming the balance is allocated entirely to cost of goods sold.
(d) Prepare an income statement for the year through gross profit. (Hint: Show cost of goods sold as one line.)

*Prepare entries in a job cost system and cost of goods manufactured schedule.*
*(SO 2, 3, 4, 5)*

**P21–3**  Kurt Juneau is a contractor specializing in custom-built jacuzzis. On May 1, 1996, his ledger contains the following data:

| | |
|---|---|
| Raw Materials Inventory | $30,000 |
| Work in Process Inventory | 12,200 |
| Manufacturing Overhead | 2,500 (dr.) |

The Manufacturing Overhead account has debit totals of $12,500 and credit totals of $10,000. Subsidiary data for Work in Process Inventory on May 1 include:

**Job Cost Sheets**

| Job By Customer | Direct Materials | Direct Labor | Manufacturing Overhead |
|---|---|---|---|
| Jovi | $2,500 | $2,000 | $1,400 |
| Roth | 2,000 | 1,200 | 840 |
| Nicks | 900 | 800 | 560 |
| | $5,400 | $4,000 | $2,800 |

A summary of materials requisition slips and time tickets for the month of May reveals the following:

| Job by Customer | Materials Requisition Slips | Time Tickets |
|---|---|---|
| Jovi | $ 500 | $ 400 |
| Roth | 600 | 1,000 |
| Nicks | 2,300 | 1,300 |
| Jett | 2,400 | 2,900 |
| | 5,800 | 5,600 |
| General Use | 1,500 | 2,600 |
| | $7,300 | $8,200 |

During May the following costs were incurred: (a) raw materials purchased on account, $5,000, (b) labor paid, $8,200, (c) manufacturing overhead paid $1,400. Overhead was charged to jobs on the basis of direct labor cost at the same rate as in the previous month.

The jacuzzis for customers Jovi, Roth, and Nicks were completed during May. Each jacuzzi was sold for $12,500 cash.

**Instructions**
(a) Prepare journal entries for the May transactions.
(b) Post the entries to Work in Process Inventory.
(c) Reconcile the balance in Work in Process Inventory with the costs of unfinished jobs.
(d) Prepare a cost of goods manufactured schedule for May.

**P21–4**  Skagway Manufacturing uses a job order cost system in each of its three manufacturing departments. Manufacturing overhead is applied to jobs on the basis of direct labor cost in Department A, direct labor hours in Department B, and machine hours in Department C.

In establishing the predetermined overhead rates for 1996 the following estimates were made for the year:

*Compute predetermined overhead rates, apply overhead, and indicate statement presentation of under- or overapplied overhead.*
*(SO 4, 6)*

| | Department | | |
|---|---|---|---|
| | A | B | C |
| Manufacturing overhead | $900,000 | $800,000 | $750,000 |
| Direct labor cost | $600,000 | $100,000 | $600,000 |
| Direct labor hours | 50,000 | 40,000 | 50,000 |
| Machine hours | 100,000 | 120,000 | 150,000 |

During January the job cost sheets showed the following costs and production data:

| | Department | | |
|---|---|---|---|
| | A | B | C |
| Direct materials used | $92,000 | $86,000 | $64,000 |
| Direct labor cost | $48,000 | $35,000 | $50,400 |
| Manufacturing overhead incurred | $76,000 | $67,000 | $64,500 |
| Direct labor hours | 4,000 | 3,500 | 4,200 |
| Machine hours | 8,000 | 10,500 | 12,600 |

**Instructions**
(a) Compute the predetermined overhead rate for each department.
(b) Compute the total manufacturing cost assigned to jobs in January in each department.
(c) Compute the under- or overapplied overhead for each department at January 31.
(d) Indicate the statement presentation of the under- or overapplied overhead at January 31.
(e) If the amount in (d) was the same at December 31, how would it be reported in the year-end financial statements?

*Analyze manufacturing cost*
*accounts and determine*
*missing amounts.*
(SO 2, 3, 4, 5, 6)

**P21–5**   Vanessa Company's fiscal year ends on June 30. The following accounts are found in its job order cost accounting system for the first month of the new fiscal year.

### Raw Materials Inventory

| | | | | | |
|---|---|---|---|---|---|
| July 1 | Beginning balance | 19,000 | July 31 | Requisitions | (a) |
| 31 | Purchases | 88,400 | | | |
| July 31 | Ending balance | (b) | | | |

### Work in Process Inventory

| | | | | | |
|---|---|---|---|---|---|
| July 1 | Beginning balance | (c) | July 31 | Jobs completed | (f) |
| 31 | Direct materials | 72,000 | | | |
| 31 | Direct labor | (d) | | | |
| 31 | Overhead | (e) | | | |
| July 31 | Ending balance | (g) | | | |

### Finished Goods Inventory

| | | | | | |
|---|---|---|---|---|---|
| July 1 | Beginning balance | (h) | July 31 | Cost of goods sold | (j) |
| 31 | Completed jobs | (i) | | | |
| July 31 | Ending balance | (k) | | | |

### Factory Labor

| | | | | | |
|---|---|---|---|---|---|
| July 31 | Factory wages | (l) | July 31 | Wages assigned | (m) |

### Manufacturing Overhead

| | | | | | |
|---|---|---|---|---|---|
| July 31 | Indirect materials | 8,900 | July 31 | Overhead applied | 97,500 |
| 31 | Indirect labor | 16,000 | | | |
| 31 | Other overhead | (n) | | | |

Other data:

1. On July 1, two jobs were in process: Job No. 4085 and Job No. 4086 with costs of $17,000 and $8,200, respectively.
2. During July, Job Nos. 4087, 4088, and 4089, were started. On July 31, only Job No. 4089 was unfinished. This job had charges for direct materials $2,000, direct labor $1,500 plus manufacturing overhead.
3. On July 1, Job No. 4084, costing $135,000, was in the finished goods warehouse. On July 31, Job No. 4088, costing $143,000, was in finished goods.
4. Manufacturing overhead was applied at the rate of 130% of direct labor cost. Overhead was $4,000 underapplied in July.

*Instructions*
List the letters (a) through (n) and indicate the amount pertaining to each letter. Show computations.

# ALTERNATE PROBLEMS

●●●●●●●●●●●●●●●●●●●●●●●●●●●●●●●●●●●●●●●●●●●●●●●●●●●●●●●●●●●●●●●●●●●●●●●●●●●●●●●●●●

*Prepare entries in a job cost*
*system and job cost sheets.*
(SO 2, 3, 4, 5)

**P21–1A**   Lolita Manufacturing uses a job order cost accounting system. On January 1, the company had Raw Materials Inventory $10,000 and Finished Goods Inventory, represented by Job No. 18, $135,000. During the month, the following summary transactions and events occurred.

1. Purchased raw materials on account $270,000.

2. Incurred factory labor $340,000 of which $302,000 relates to factory wages payable and the balance (or $38,000) pertains to employer payroll taxes payable.
3. Incurred manufacturing overhead on account $350,000.
4. Recognized $10,000 of depreciation on factory machinery.
5. Charged direct materials to jobs: No. 19 $150,000 and No. 20 $110,000. The jobs call for the production of 20,000 and 10,000 units, respectively.
6. Charged factory labor to jobs on basis of time tickets: No. 19 $240,000 and No. 20 $90,000. The remaining labor was indirect.
7. Charged overhead to jobs at the rate of 110% of direct labor cost.
8. Completed Job No. 19.
9. Sold Job No. 18 on account for $190,000.

*Instructions*
(a) Journalize the transactions and events.
(b) Open accounts for the beginning inventories and post the entries in (a) to the job order cost accounts and to the job cost sheets.
(c) Reconcile the balance in Work in Process Inventory with the costs of unfinished jobs.

**P21–2A** For the year ended December 31, 1996, the job cost sheets of Bankok Company contained the following data.

*Prepare entries in a job cost system and partial income statement.*
*(SO 2, 3, 4, 5, 6)*

| Job Number | Explanation | Direct Materials | Direct Labor | Manufacturing Overhead | Total Costs |
|---|---|---|---|---|---|
| 7640 | Balance 1/1 | $25,000 | $24,000 | $28,800 | $ 77,800 |
|  | Current year's costs | 34,000 | 36,000 | 43,200 | 113,200 |
| 7641 | Balance 1/1 | 11,000 | 18,000 | 21,600 | 50,600 |
|  | Current year's costs | 40,000 | 48,000 | 57,600 | 145,600 |
| 7642 | Current year's costs | 48,000 | 60,000 | 72,000 | 180,000 |

Other data:

1. Raw materials inventory totaled $15,000 on January 1. During the year, $140,000 of raw materials were purchased on account.
2. Finished goods on January 1 consisted of Job No. 7638 for $87,000 and Job No. 7639 for $92,000.
3. Job No. 7640 and Job No. 7641 were completed during the year.
4. Job Nos. 7638, 7639, and 7641 were sold on account for $530,000.
5. Manufacturing overhead incurred on account totaled $135,000.
6. Other manufacturing overhead consisted of indirect materials $14,000, indirect labor $20,000, and depreciation on factory machinery $8,000.

*Instructions*
(a) Journalize the transactions in the sequence followed in the chapter. (Credit Factory Wages Payable when recording factory labor.)
(b) Prove the agreement of Work in Process Inventory with job cost sheets pertaining to unfinished work.
(c) Prepare the adjusting entry for manufacturing overhead, assuming the balance is allocated entirely to Cost of Goods Sold.
(d) Prepare an income statement for the year through gross profit. (Hint: Show cost of goods sold as one line.)

**P21–3A** Leisure Inc. is a construction company specializing in custom patios. The patios are constructed of concrete, brick, fiberglass, and lumber, depending upon customer preference. On June 1, 1996, the general ledger for Leisure Inc. contains the following data:

*Prepare entries in a job cost system and cost of goods manufactured schedule.*
*(SO 2, 3, 4, 5)*

| | | | |
|---|---|---|---|
| Raw Material Inventory | $4,200 | Manufacturing Overhead Applied | $27,200 |
| Work in Process Inventory | $5,540 | Manufacturing Overhead Incurred | $26,375 |

Subsidiary data for Work in Process Inventory on June 1 are as follows:

## Job Cost Sheets

| | | Customer Job | |
|---|---|---|---|
| Cost Element | Dion | Cole | Kix |
| Direct materials | $ 600 | $ 800 | $ 900 |
| Direct labor | 320 | 540 | 580 |
| Manufacturing overhead | 400 | 675 | 725 |
| | $1,320 | $2,015 | $2,205 |

A summary of materials requisition slips and time tickets for June shows the following:

| Customer Job | Materials Requisition Slips | Time Tickets |
|---|---|---|
| Dion | $ 800 | $ 450 |
| Lock | 2,000 | 1,000 |
| Cole | 500 | 360 |
| Kix | 1,300 | 800 |
| Dion | 300 | 250 |
| | 4,900 | 2,860 |
| General use | 1,500 | 1,200 |
| | $6,400 | $4,060 |

During June, raw materials purchased on account were $3,900 and all wages were paid. Additional overhead costs consisted of depreciation on equipment $700 and miscellaneous costs of $400 incurred on account. Overhead was charged to jobs at the same rate that was used in May. The patios for customers Dion, Cole, and Kix were completed during June and sold for a total of $18,900. Each customer paid in full.

**Instructions**
(a) Journalize the June transactions.
(b) Post the entries to Work in Process Inventory.
(c) Reconcile the balance in Work in Process Inventory with the costs of unfinished jobs.
(d) Prepare a cost of goods manufactured schedule for June.

*Compute predetermined overhead rate, apply overhead and indicate statement presentation of under- or overapplied overhead.*
*(SO 4, 6)*

**P21–4A** San Juan Manufacturing Company uses a job order cost system in each of its three manufacturing departments. Manufacturing overhead is applied to jobs on the basis of direct labor cost in Department X, direct labor hours in Department Y, and machine hours in Department Z.

In establishing the predetermined overhead rates for 1997 the following estimates were made for the year:

| | Department | | |
|---|---|---|---|
| | X | Y | Z |
| Manufacturing overhead | $1,200,000 | $1,500,000 | $900,000 |
| Direct labor cost | $1,500,000 | $1,250,000 | $450,000 |
| Direct labor hours | 100,000 | 125,000 | 40,000 |
| Machine hours | 400,000 | 500,000 | 120,000 |

During January, the job cost sheets showed the following costs and production data:

| | Department | | |
|---|---|---|---|
| | X | Y | Z |
| Direct materials used | $140,000 | $126,000 | $78,000 |
| Direct labor costs | $120,000 | $110,000 | $37,500 |
| Manufacturing overhead incurred | $98,000 | $129,000 | $76,000 |
| Direct labor hours | 8,000 | 11,000 | 3,500 |
| Machine hours | 34,000 | 45,000 | 10,400 |

## Instructions

(a) Compute the predetermined overhead rate for each department.

(b) Compute the total manufacturing costs assigned to jobs in January in each department.

(c) Compute the under- or overapplied overhead for each department at January 31.

(d) Indicate the statement presentation of the under- or overapplied overhead at January 31.

(e) If the amount in (d) was the same at December 31, how would it be reported in the year-end financial statements?

**P21–5A** Barcelona Corporation's fiscal year ends on November 30. The following accounts are found in its job order cost accounting system for the first month of the new fiscal year.

*Analyze manufacturing accounts and determine missing amounts.*
*(SO 2, 3, 4, 5, 6)*

### Raw Materials Inventory

| | | | | | |
|---|---|---|---|---|---|
| Dec. 1 | Beginning balance | (a) | Dec. 31 | Requisitions | 15,850 |
| 31 | Purchases | 17,225 | | | |
| Dec. 31 | Ending balance | 7,975 | | | |

### Work in Process Inventory

| | | | | | |
|---|---|---|---|---|---|
| Dec. 1 | Beginning balance | (b) | Dec. 31 | Jobs completed | (f) |
| 31 | Direct materials | (c) | | | |
| 31 | Direct labor | 8,100 | | | |
| 31 | Overhead | (d) | | | |
| Dec. 31 | Ending balance | (e) | | | |

### Finished Goods Inventory

| | | | | | |
|---|---|---|---|---|---|
| Dec. 1 | Beginning balance | (g) | Dec. 31 | Cost of goods sold | (i) |
| 31 | Completed jobs | (h) | | | |
| Dec. 31 | Ending balance | (j) | | | |

### Factory Labor

| | | | | | |
|---|---|---|---|---|---|
| Dec. 31 | Factory wages | 10,600 | Dec. 31 | Wages assigned | (k) |

### Manufacturing Overhead

| | | | | | |
|---|---|---|---|---|---|
| Dec. 31 | Indirect materials | 1,900 | Dec. 31 | Overhead applied | (m) |
| 31 | Indirect labor | (l) | | | |
| 31 | Other overhead | 1,850 | | | |

Other data:

1. On December 1, two jobs were in process: Job No. 154 and Job No. 155. These jobs had combined direct materials costs of $9,750 and direct labor costs of $12,000. Overhead was applied at a rate that was 80% of direct labor cost.

2. During December, Job Nos. 156, 157, and 158, were started. On December 31, Job No. 158 was unfinished. This job had charges for direct materials $3,800, direct labor $4,400 plus manufacturing overhead. All jobs, except for Job No. 158, were completed in December.

3. On December 1, Job No. 153 was in the finished goods warehouse. It had a total cost of $5,000. On December 31, Job No. 157 was the only job finished that was not sold. It had a cost of $4,000.

4. Manufacturing overhead was $230 overapplied in December.

## Instructions

List the letters (a) through (m) and indicate the amount pertaining to each letter.

# ▼**B**roadening Your Perspective

## Decision Case

Pauline Products Company uses a job order cost system. For a number of months there has been an ongoing rift between the sales department and the production department concerning a special order product, TC-1. TC-1 is a seasonal product that is manufactured in batches of 1,000 units. TC-1 is sold at cost plus a markup of 40% of cost.

The sales department is unhappy because fluctuating unit production costs significantly affect selling prices. Sales personnel complain that this has caused excessive customer complaints and the loss of considerable orders for TC-1.

The production department maintains that each job order must be fully costed on the basis of the costs incurred during the period in which the goods are produced. Production personnel maintain that the only real solution to the problem is for the sales department to increase sales in the slack periods.

Laurie Fiala, president of the company, asks you as the company accountant to collect quarterly data for the past year on TC-1. From the cost accounting system, you accumulate the following production quantity and cost data:

| | Quarter | | | |
|---|---|---|---|---|
| Costs | 1 | 2 | 3 | 4 |
| Direct materials | $100,000 | $220,000 | $ 80,000 | $200,000 |
| Direct labor | 60,000 | 132,000 | 48,000 | 120,000 |
| Manufacturing overhead | 105,000 | 123,000 | 97,000 | 125,000 |
| Total | $265,000 | $475,000 | $225,000 | $445,000 |
| Production in batches | 5 | 11 | 4 | 10 |
| Unit cost (per batch) | $ 53,000 | $ 43,182 | $ 56,250 | $ 44,500 |

**Instructions**
(a) What manufacturing cost element is responsible for the fluctuating unit costs? Why?
(b) What is your recommended solution to the problem of fluctuating unit cost?
(c) Restate the quarterly data on the basis of your recommended solution.

## Communication Activity

You are the management accountant for Abraham Rose Manufacturing. Your company does custom carpentry work and uses a job-order cost accounting system. Abraham Rose sends detailed job cost sheets to its customers, along with an invoice. The job cost sheets show the date materials were used, the dollar cost of materials, and the hours and cost of labor. A predetermined overhead application rate is used, and the total overhead applied is also listed.

Clara Smith is a customer who recently had custom cabinets installed. Along with her check in payment for the work done, she included a letter. She thanked the company for including the detailed cost information but questioned why overhead was estimated. She stated that she would be interested in knowing exactly what costs were included in overhead, and she thought that other customers would, too.

**Instructions**
Prepare a letter to Ms. Smith (address: 123 Loma Linda Lane, Cherryvale, Kansas 66651) and tell her why you did not send her information on exact costs of overhead included in her job. Respond to her suggestion that you provide this information.

# GROUP ACTIVITY

In the course of routine checking of all journal entries prior to preparing month-end reports, Li Chin discovered several strange entries. She recalled that the president's son Jeff had come in to "help out" during an especially busy time and that he had recorded some journal entries. She was relieved that there were only a few of his entries, and even more relieved that he had included rather lengthy explanations. The entries Jeff made were:

| | | |
|---|---|---|
| Work in Process | 20,000 | |
|     Cash | | 20,000 |

(This is for materials put into process. I don't find the record that we paid for these, so I'm crediting cash, because I know we'll have to pay for them sooner or later.)

| | | |
|---|---|---|
| Manufacturing Overhead | 12,000 | |
|     Cash | | 12,000 |

(This is for bonuses paid to salespeople. I know they're part of overhead, and I can't find an account called "non-factory overhead" or "other overhead" so I'm putting it in factory overhead. I have the check stubs, so I know we paid these.)

| | | |
|---|---|---|
| Wages Expense | 120,000 | |
|     Cash | | 120,000 |

(This is for the factory workers' wages. I have a note that payroll taxes are $8,000. I still think that's part of wages expense, and that we'll have to pay it all in cash sooner or later, so I credited cash for the wages and the taxes.)

| | | |
|---|---|---|
| Work in Process | 3,000 | |
|     Raw Materials Inventory | | 3,000 |

(This is for the glue used in the factory. I know we used this to make the products, even though we didn't use very much on any one of the products. I got it out of inventory, so I credited inventory.)

## Instructions

In groups of four to five people each, discuss the following questions:

(a) How should Jeff have recorded each of the four events?

(b) If the entry was not corrected, which financial statements (income statement or balance sheet) would be affected? What balances would be overstated or understated?

# ETHICS CASE

Morgan Printing provides printing services to many different corporate clients. Although Morgan bids most jobs, some jobs, particularly new ones, are often negotiated on a cost plus basis. Cost plus means that the buyer is willing to pay the actual cost plus a return (profit) on these costs to Morgan.

Pamela Smart, controller for Morgan, has recently returned from a meeting where Morgan's president stated that he wanted her to find a way to charge most costs to any project that was on a cost plus basis. The president noted that the company needed more profits to meet its stated goals this period. By charging more costs to the cost plus projects and therefore less cost to the jobs that were bid, the company should be able to increase its profits for the current year.

Pamela knew why the president wanted to take this action. Rumors were that he was looking for a new position and if the company reported strong profits the president's opportunities would be enhanced. Pamela also recognized that she could probably increase the cost of certain jobs by changing the basis used to allocate manufacturing overhead.

*Instructions*

   (a)  Who are the stakeholders in this situation?

   (b)  What are the ethical issues in this situation?

   (c)  What would you do if you were Pamela Smart?

# CRITICAL THINKING
## ▶ *A Real-World Focus: Parlex Company*

*Parlex Company has been located in Massachusetts since its formation in 1970. The company designs, manufactures, and markets products to customers' specifications for use in semiconductors and other components in electronic equipment. Its products include flexible printed circuits, custom-laminated cable, and assemblies of subsystems incorporating one or more of these products. It has a broad range of customers including automotive, communications, computer, military-aerospace, medical, and other industrial electronic industries. Its shares are traded in the over-the-counter market.*

The following information was provided in the annual report of Parlex Company:

> The Company's products are manufactured on a job order basis to customers' specifications. Customers submit requests for quotations on each job, and the Company prepares bids based on its own cost estimates. The Company attempts to reflect the impact of changing costs when establishing prices. However, during the past several years, the market conditions for flexible circuits and the resulting price sensitivity haven't always allowed this to transpire. Although still not satisfactory, the Company was able to reduce the cost of products sold as a percentage of sales to 85% this year versus 87% that was experienced in the two immediately preceding years. Management continues to focus on improving operational efficiency and further reducing costs.

*Instructions*

   (a)  Parlex management discusses the job order cost system employed by their company. What are several advantages of using the job order approach to costing?

   (b)  Contrast the products produced in a job order environment, like Parlex, to those produced when process cost systems are used.

---

*Answers to Self-Study Questions*

1. a    2. b    3. c    4. d    5. b    6. a    7. d    8. b    9. c    10. b

# Ben & Jerry's Tracks Its Mix-Ups

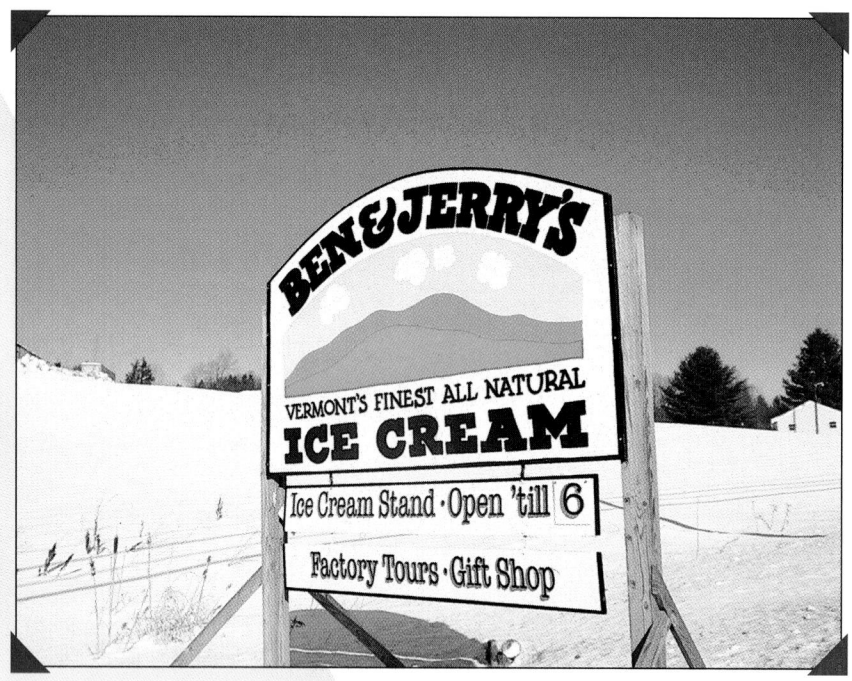

WATERBURY, Vt. — One of the fastest growing companies in the nation is Ben & Jerry's Homemade, Inc., based in Waterbury, Vt. The ice cream company that started out of a garage in 1978 is now a public company with sales exceeding $140 million.

Making ice cream is a process—a movement of product from a mixing department to a prepping department to a pint department. The mixing department is where the ice cream is created. The prep area is where extras such as cherries and walnuts are added to make plain ice cream into "Cherry Garcia." And the pint department is where the ice cream is actually put into containers. As the product is processed from one department to the next, the appropriate materials, labor, and overhead are added to it.

"The incoming ingredients from the shipping and receiving departments are stored in certain locations, either in a freezer or dry warehouse," says Beecher Eurich,

staff accountant. "As ingredients get added, so do the costs associated with them." How much ice cream is actually produced? Running the plant around the clock, 24,000 pints are produced per 8-hour shift, or 72,000 pints per day.

Using the FIFO method, Eurich can tell you how much a certain batch of ice cream costs to make—its materials, labor, and overhead in each of the production depart-

ments. She generates reports for the production department heads, but makes sure not to overdo it. "You can get bogged down in numbers," says Eurich. "If you're generating a report that no one can use, then that's a waste of time." More likely, though, Ben & Jerry's production people want to know how efficient they are. Why? Many own stock in the company. ◀

# CHAPTER · 22

# *P*ROCESS COST ACCOUNTING

▶ STUDY OBJECTIVES ◀

**After studying this chapter, you should be able to:**

1. *Explain the flow of costs in process cost accounting.*
2. *State the end-of-period procedures in process cost accounting.*
3. *Compute the physical units of production.*
4. *Compute equivalent units of production.*
5. *Indicate how unit costs are computed.*
6. *Explain the method and objective of assigning costs to units of output.*
7. *Prepare a production cost report.*
8. *Apply end-of-period procedures to a second process.*
9. *Explain just-in-time (JIT) processing.*
10. *Explain activity-based costing (ABC).*

The cost accounting system used by companies such as Ben & Jerry's is called process cost accounting. In contrast to job order cost accounting, which focuses on the individual job, process cost accounting focuses on the processes involved in producing homogeneous products. The primary objective of this chapter is to explain and illustrate process cost accounting. At the end of the chapter, two contemporary developments, just-in-time (JIT) processing and activity-based costing (ABC) are considered. The content and organization of this chapter are as follows:

# **P**rocess Manufacturing and Accounting

Continuous process manufacturing, sometimes referred to as mass production operations, occurs in producing such items as steel by USX Corp., cereals by Kellogg's, petroleum products by Exxon, and paint by Sherwin-Williams. One characteristic of this type of manufacturing is that **once the production begins, it continues until the finished product emerges**. For example, in a beverage company such as Coca-Cola, the process begins with the blending of the beverage. Next, the beverage is dispensed into bottles that are moved into position by automated machinery. The bottles are then capped, packaged, and forwarded to the finished goods warehouse.

A second characteristic of continuous process manufacturing is that **when the finished product emerges, all units will have been processed in the same manner with precisely the same amount of materials, labor, and overhead**. Each finished unit, such as a bottle of Coke, will therefore be indistinguishable one from another.

A process cost accounting system is used for continuous process manufacturing. In process cost accounting, as in a job order system, it is necessary to record both the accumulation and assignment of manufacturing costs. A distinc-

# ►Accounting in Action ► *Business Insight*

The new General Motors Corporation assembly plants are missing a key element of traditional mass production: the assembly line. Instead, the company utilizes hundreds of automated, unmanned carriers to carry a car as it goes through the assembly process. With the carriers, each car follows a prescribed path, receiving instructions from computers through wires buried in the plant floor. Cars with extensive options are moved out of the main path until the options are installed.

tive feature of process cost accounting, however, is that **individual work in process accounts are maintained for each production department or manufacturing process**. For example, in a beverage company there would be a work in process account for each of the manufacturing processes, as illustrated below:

**Illustration 22-1**

*Manufacturing processes and work in process accounts*

A second feature of process costing is that **costs charged to work in process are summarized in production cost reports rather than in job cost sheets**. There are also significant differences between process and job order cost accounting in determining total manufacturing costs and unit costs. In process cost accounting, **total costs are determined at the end of a period of time**, such as a month, rather than when a job is finished. **Unit costs are computed by dividing total manufacturing costs for the period by the units produced during the period.**

The major differences between job order cost accounting and process cost accounting are summarized in Illustration 22-2.

**Illustration 22-2**

*Differences between job order and process cost accounting*

| Feature | Job Order Cost Accounting | Process Cost Accounting |
|---|---|---|
| • Work in process accounts | One for each job | One for each process |
| • Summary of manufacturing costs | Job cost sheets | Production cost reports |
| • Determination of total manufacturing costs | Each job | Each period |
| • Unit cost computation | Cost of each job ÷ Units produced for the job | Total manufacturing costs ÷ Units produced during the period |

## ▼ Process Cost Flow

**STUDY OBJECTIVE**

••••••••••▼••••••••••

*Explain the flow of costs in process cost accounting.*

Illustration 22-3 shows the flow of costs through various accounts in process cost accounting. Note that separate work in process accounts are provided for each producing department. Ben & Jerry's, in the opening story, would have similar work in process accounts. The other accounts and the flow of costs are the same as in job order cost accounting. For example, manufacturing costs are accumulated by debits to Raw Materials Inventory, Factory Labor, and Manufacturing Overhead. These costs are then assigned to Work in Process, Finished Goods Inventory, and Cost of Goods Sold. The methods of assigning costs, however, differ significantly. These differences are explained and illustrated later in the chapter.

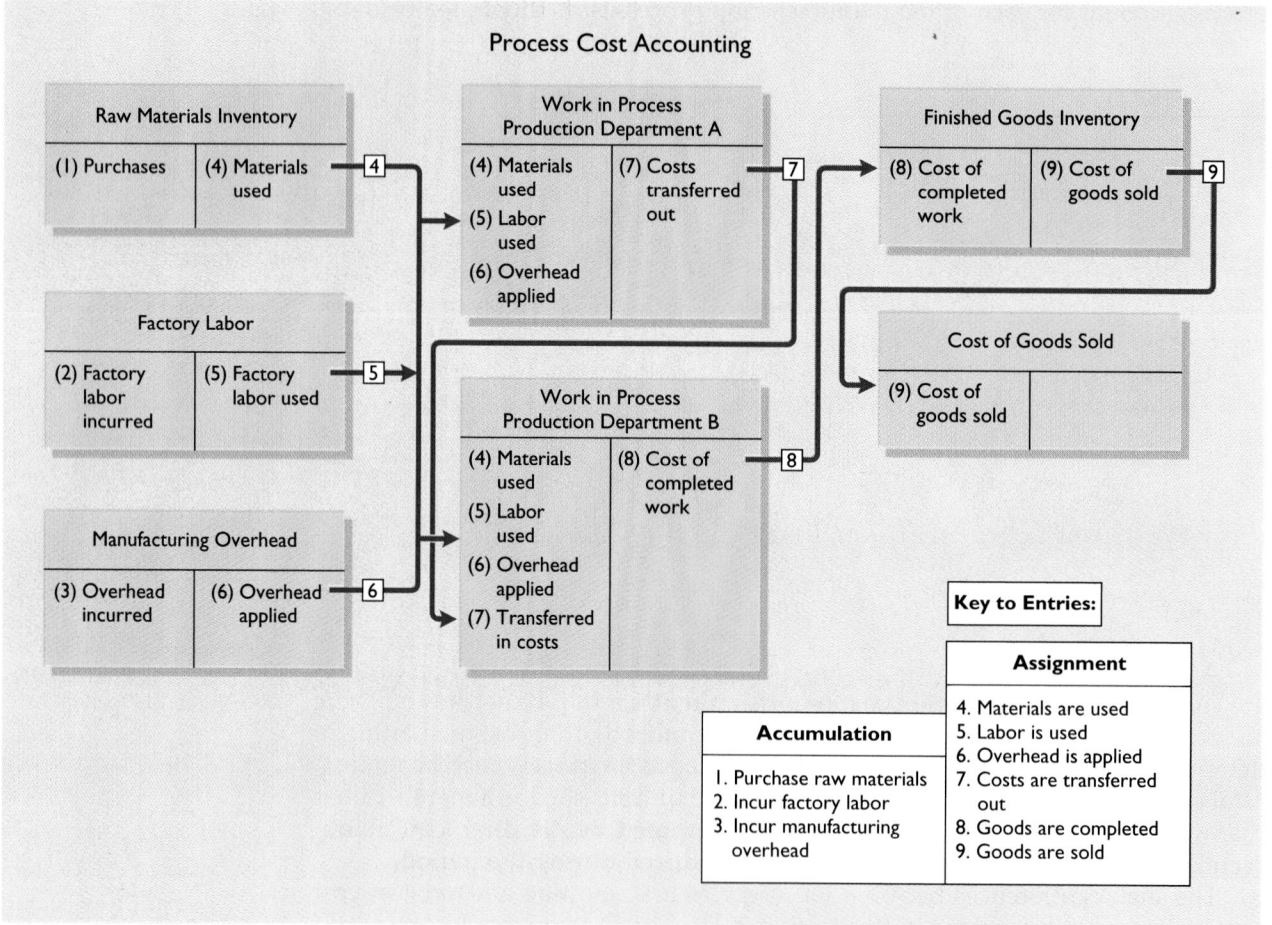

**Illustration 22-3**

*Flow of costs in process cost accounting*

The entries pertaining to the accumulation and assignment of costs are explained in the following pages, using the June transactions of Tyler Manufacturing Company. The entries are keyed to the numbers in Illustration 22-3. Tyler Company manufactures automatic can openers that are sold to retail outlets. Manufacturing consists of two processes: machining and assembly. In the Machining Department, the raw materials are shaped, honed, and drilled. In the Assembly Department, the parts are assembled and packaged. On June 1, the ledger includes the following balances:

| Raw Materials Inventory | $24,000 | Work in Process—Machining | $ –0– |
| Finished Goods Inventory | 6,000 | Work in Process—Assembly | 3,600 |

## Accumulation of Manufacturing Costs

Each of the three manufacturing cost elements presented in Chapter 20—direct materials, direct labor, and overhead—occurs in a process cost system. **The accumulation of the costs of materials and labor is the same in process costing as in job order costing.** All raw materials are debited to Raw Materials Inventory when the materials are purchased. Similarly, all factory labor is debited to Factory Labor when the labor costs are incurred. In the month of June, Tyler Manufacturing purchases $17,000 of raw materials and incurs $20,400 of factory labor. The summary entries for these costs are as follows:

(1)

| June 30 | Raw Materials Inventory | 17,000 | |
|---|---|---|---|
| |     Accounts Payable | | 17,000 |
| |       (To record purchases of raw materials on account) | | |

(2)

| June 30 | Factory Labor | 20,400 | |
|---|---|---|---|
| |     Wages Payable | | 20,400 |
| |       (To record factory labor costs) | | |

The accumulation of manufacturing overhead costs may also be the same as in job order costing. That is, overhead costs are debited to Manufacturing Overhead as they are incurred. During June, overhead costs were $41,800 in Tyler Manufacturing. The summary entry to record these costs is:

(3)

| June 30 | Manufacturing Overhead | 41,800 | |
|---|---|---|---|
| |     Cash (Accounts Payable, etc.) | | 41,800 |
| |       (To record overhead incurred) | | |

## Assignment of Manufacturing Costs

In process accounts the assignment of the three manufacturing cost elements to work in process is different from the assignment of costs in a job order system, as explained below.

### *Materials Costs*

All raw materials issued for production are a materials cost to the producing department. Materials requisition slips may be used in a process cost system, but **fewer requisitions are generally required than in a job order cost system, because the materials are used for processes rather than for specific jobs.** Requisitions are issued less frequently in a process cost system because the requisitions are for larger quantities. When a raw material is used by only one department, it is possible to determine the quantity used by making a physical inventory count.

Materials

Materials are usually added to production at the beginning of the first process. However, in subsequent processes, other materials may be added at various points. For example, in the manufacture of Hershey candy bars, the chocolate and other ingredients are added at the beginning of the first process, and the wrappers and cartons are added at the end of the packaging process. At Tyler Manufacturing, materials are entered at the beginning of each process. During June, materials used are: Machining, $15,000, and Assembly, $4,000. The entry to record the materials used is:

| | (4) | | |
|---|---|---|---|
| June 30 | Work in Process—Machining | 15,000 | |
| | Work in Process—Assembly | 4,000 | |
| |    Raw Materials Inventory | | 19,000 |
| |    (To record materials used) | | |

In our ice cream story at the beginning of the chapter, materials are added in three departments: milk and flavoring in the mixing department; extras such as cherries and walnuts in the prepping department; and cardboard containers in the pinting (packaging) department.

### Factory Labor Costs

Factory Labor

In process costing, as in job order costing, time tickets may be used in determining the cost of labor assignable to the production departments. Since labor costs are assigned to a process rather than a job, the labor cost chargeable to a process can be obtained from the payroll register or departmental payroll summaries.

All labor costs incurred within a producing department are a cost of processing the raw materials. Thus, labor costs for the Machining Department will include the wages of employees who shape, hone, and drill the raw materials. During June, the labor costs in Tyler Manufacturing are: Machining $14,000 and Assembly $6,400. The entry to assign these costs is:

| | (5) | | |
|---|---|---|---|
| June 30 | Work in Process—Machining | 14,000 | |
| | Work in Process—Assembly | 6,400 | |
| |    Factory Labor | | 20,400 |
| |    (To assign factory labor to production) | | |

### Manufacturing Overhead Costs

Manufacturing
Overhead

The objective in assigning overhead in process cost accounting is to allocate the overhead costs to the production departments on an objective and equitable basis. In modern manufacturing, that basis is the activity that "drives" or causes the costs. For most companies, today, the primary driver of overhead costs in continuous manufacturing operations is **machine time used**, not direct labor. Thus, **machine hours are widely used** in allocating manufacturing overhead costs to processing departments.

## ▸Accounting in Action ▸ *Business Insight*

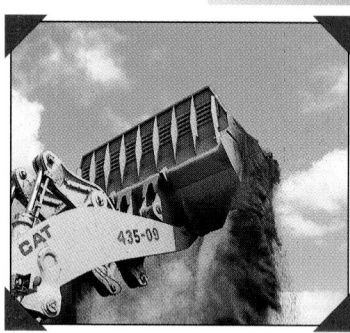

In one of Caterpillar's automated cells, work is fed into the cost center (or cell), processed by numerous robotic machines, and transferred to the next cost center without human intervention. One person tends all of the machines and spends more time on machine maintenance than operating the machines. In such cases, overhead rates based on direct labor hours may be misleading. Surprisingly, in some companies, manufacturing overhead continues to be distributed on the basis of direct labor despite the fact that there is no cause-and-effect relationship between labor and overhead.

To illustrate the assignment of overhead costs, we will assume in Tyler Manufacturing that overhead is charged to production departments at the rate of $10 per machine hour. In June, machine hours were 2,280 in the Machining Department and 1,820 in the Assembly Department. Thus, the entry to allocate overhead to the two processes is:

|  | (6) |  |  |
|---|---|---|---|
| June 30 | Work in Process—Machining | 22,800 |  |
|  | Work in Process—Assembly | 18,200 |  |
|  | Manufacturing Overhead |  | 41,000 |
|  | (To assign overhead to processes) |  |  |

After the foregoing entries are posted, the work in process accounts of Tyler Manufacturing Company show the data indicated in Illustration 22-4. The question marks indicate the amounts that are yet to be determined. The answers to the question marks are obtained through special end-of-period procedures explained in the following sections.

**Helpful hint** When should overhead be applied on the basis of machine hours? Answer: When machine hours "drive" overhead costs; i.e., when there is a cause-and-effect relationship between machine hours and overhead.

**Illustration 22-4**

*Work in process accounts*

**Work in Process—Machining**

| June | 1 | Balance | –0– | June 30 | Transferred to assembly | ? |
|------|---|---------|-----|---------|------------------------|---|
|  | 30 | Materials | 15,000 |  |  |  |
|  | 30 | Labor | 14,000 |  |  |  |
|  | 30 | Overhead applied | 22,800 |  |  |  |
|  | 30 | Balance | ? |  |  |  |

**Work in Process—Assembly**

| June | 1 | Balance | 3,600 | June 30 | Transferred to finished goods | ? |
|------|---|---------|-------|---------|-------------------------------|---|
|  | 30 | Materials | 4,000 |  |  |  |
|  | 30 | Labor | 6,400 |  |  |  |
|  | 30 | Overhead applied | 18,200 |  |  |  |
|  | 30 | Transferred from Machining | ? |  |  |  |
|  | 30 | Balance | ? |  |  |  |

# Before You Go On . . .

## ▶ Review It

1. What type of manufacturing companies might use a process cost accounting system?
2. What are the principal differences between job order cost accounting and process cost accounting?

## ▶ Do It

Ruth Company manufactures ZEBO through two processes: Blending and Bottling. In June, raw materials used were Blending $18,000 and Bottling $4,000; factory labor costs were Blending $12,000 and Bottling $5,000. Journalize the assignment of these costs to the two processes.

*Reasoning:* In process cost accounting, separate work in process accounts are kept for each process. Raw materials are accumulated in the account titled Raw Materials Inventory. Factory labor is accumulated in the account titled Factory Labor. These accounts are credited when the costs are assigned to production.

**Solution:** The entries are:

| | | |
|---|---|---|
| Work in Process—Blending | 18,000 | |
| Work in Process—Bottling | 4,000 | |
|    Raw Materials Inventory | | 22,000 |
|      (To record materials used) | | |
| | | |
| Work in Process—Blending | 12,000 | |
| Work in Process—Bottling | 5,000 | |
|    Factory Labor | | 17,000 |
|      (To assign factory labor to production) | | |

*Related exercise material: BE22–1, BE22–2, BE22–3, and E22–10.*

# End-of-Period Procedures—Machining Department

**STUDY OBJECTIVE**
**2**
*State the end-of-period procedures in process cost accounting.*

By the end of the period, Tyler Manufacturing has accumulated the materials, labor, and overhead costs in each production department's work in process account. Now Tyler must assign these accumulated costs to (1) the units transferred out of each department and (2) the units in the ending work in process in each department. The procedures used in computing and assigning the costs present the most difficult challenge to your understanding of process cost accounting. For each process, it is necessary at the end of the period to perform the following procedures:

1. Compute the physical units.
2. Compute equivalent units of production.
3. Compute unit costs of production.
4. Assign costs to the units transferred and in process.
5. Prepare the production cost report.

We will explain these procedures in detail. First, we will make all of the required computations for the Machining Department of Tyler Manufacturing. Then we will explain the computations for the Assembly Department.

## Computing Physical Units

**STUDY OBJECTIVE**
**3**
*Compute the physical units of production.*

Physical units are the actual units to be accounted for during a period irrespective of any work performed. To keep track of these units, it is necessary to add the units started (or transferred) into production during the period to the units in process at the beginning of the period. This amount is referred to as the total units to be accounted for.

These units then are accounted for by the output of the period, which consists of units transferred out during the period and any units in process at the end of the period. This amount is referred to as the total units accounted for. Illustration 22-5 shows the flow of physical units for Tyler Manufacturing for the month of June for both the Machining and Assembly Departments.

The records indicate that 10,000 units must be accounted for in the Machining Department. Of this sum, 8,000 units were transferred to the Assembly Department and 2,000 units are still in process. A similar record is made in the Assembly Department, where the units to be accounted for include the units transferred in from the Machining Department.

**Illustration 22-5**

*Production data in units*

| Tyler Manufacturing Company | Machining Department | Assembly Department |
|---|---|---|
| Work in process, June 1 | –0– | 500 (40% complete) |
| Started (transferred) into production | 10,000 | 8,000 |
| Total units to be accounted for | 10,000 | 8,500 |
| Transferred out | 8,000 | 8,100 * |
| Work in process, June 30 | 2,000 (60% complete) | 400 (75% complete) |
| Total units accounted for | 10,000 | 8,500 |

*Transferred to finished goods

**Helpful hint** Physical units are always stated in actual units irrespective of any work performed.

The percentages pertaining to the units in work in process in Illustration 22-5 refer to the percentage of completion of the units. The percentages are not relevant in accounting for physical units, but they are needed in the other end-of-period procedures.

## Computing Equivalent Units of Production

Once the physical flow of the units is established, it is necessary to measure each department's productivity in terms of equivalent units of production. **Equivalent units of production are the work done during the period on the physical units of output, expressed in terms of fully completed units.** For example, if a department's output consists entirely of 4,000 units of work in process that are 60% complete, equivalent units of production are 2,400 (4,000 × 60%).

**STUDY OBJECTIVE**

**▼**
**4**

*Compute equivalent units of production.*

## ▲Accounting in Action ► *Business Insight*

An example of equivalent units close to home: Your university probably expresses enrollment statistics in terms of equivalent full-time students, in addition to keeping tabs of the total number of students. For example, a student taking 9 hours of course work when 15 hours is considered full-time would be counted as a 60% equivalent full-time student. Two half-time students would be counted as one equivalent full-time student. This information is of particular use when the school is projecting tuition income and planning departmental staffing needs.

Equivalent units of production are determined by applying the percentage of work done to the physical units of output. Equivalent units are the sum of the work performed to:

1. Finish the units of beginning work in process inventory.
2. Complete the units started into production during the period.
3. Start, but only partially complete, the units in ending work in process inventory.

Normally, in continuous processing, some units will always be in process at both the beginning and end of the period.

### Equivalent Units for Materials

At Tyler Manufacturing, materials are entered at the beginning of each process, and conversion costs (labor and overhead) are incurred uniformly during the process. Thus, two computations of equivalent units are required: one for materials and the other for conversion costs. From the production data given in Illustration 22-5, we know that the 2,000 units in ending work in process are 60% complete. **This percentage pertains only to conversion costs.** The percentage of completion for materials is not stated, because in this case it is 100%. The computation of equivalent units for materials is as follows:

**Illustration 22-6**

*Computation of equivalent units—materials*

| | Machining Department | | |
|---|---|---|---|
| **Production Data** | **Physical Units** | **Materials Added This Period** | **Equivalent Units** |
| Work in process, June 1 | –0– | –0– | –0– |
| Started and finished | 8,000 | 100% | 8,000 |
| Work in process, June 30 | 2,000 | 100% | 2,000 |
| Total | 10,000 | | 10,000 |

In the Machining Department, the equivalent units for materials (10,000) equal the physical units to be accounted for (10,000).

**Helpful hint** If 30,000 units are started into production and 5,000 units are in process at the end of the period, how many units were started and finished? Answer: 25,000 (30,000 − 5,000)

The term units started and finished may be confusing. **It means the number of units that were both started and completed during the period.** As a consequence, the units in work in process at the beginning and at the end of the period are not included in "units started and finished." The easiest way to compute the units started and finished is to determine the units of completed work transferred out of the department and subtract the units in work in process at the beginning of the period. The computation for the Machining Department is as follows:

**Illustration 22-7**

*Computation of units started and finished*

| | |
|---|---|
| Units transferred out | 8,000 |
| Less: Units of work in process, June 1 | –0– |
| **Units started and finished** | 8,000 |

Note that the units in ending work in process are ignored in determining the units started and finished.

### Equivalent Units for Conversion Costs

The computation of equivalent units for conversion costs is basically the same as for material costs, as illustrated below:

**Illustration 22-8**

*Computation of equivalent units—conversion costs*

| | Machining Department | | |
|---|---|---|---|
| **Production Data** | **Physical Units** | **Work Added This Period** | **Equivalent Units** |
| Work in process, June 1 | –0– | –0– | –0– |
| Started and finished | 8,000 | 100% | 8,000 |
| Work in process, June 30 | 2,000 | 60% | 1,200 |
| Total | 10,000 | | 9,200 |

Alternatively, the graphic in Illustration 22-9 may be used in computing the equivalent units of conversion costs:

**Illustration 22-9**

*Equivalent units for conversion costs—graphic illustration*

**Machining Department**

| Production Data | Physical Units | Work Added This Period | % | Equivalent Units |
|---|---|---|---|---|
| Work in process, June 1 | –0– | | –0– | –0– |
| Started and finished | 8,000 | | 100 | 8,000 |
| Work in process, June 30 | 2,000 | | 60 | 1,200 |
| Total | 10,000 | | | 9,200 |

0  20  40  60  80  100

Note in this case, that equivalent units (9,200), do not equal the physical units to be accounted for (10,000).

## Computing Unit Costs of Production

Armed with knowledge of the equivalent units of production, we can now compute the unit production costs. Unit production costs are costs expressed in terms of equivalent units of production. When equivalent units of production are different for materials and conversion costs, three unit costs are computed: (1) materials, (2) conversion, and (3) total manufacturing.

As shown in Illustration 22-4, costs in June for the Machining Department are materials $15,000 and conversion costs $36,800 (labor $14,000 plus overhead $22,800). The formulas and computations of the unit costs are as follows:

**STUDY OBJECTIVE**

· · · · · · · · · · **5** · · · · · · · · · · ·

*Indicate how unit costs are computed.*

**Illustration 22-10**

*Unit cost formulas and computations—Machining Department*

| | | | |
|---|---|---|---|
| (1) | Total Materials Costs | ÷ Equivalent Units of Materials | = Unit Materials Cost |
| | $15,000 | ÷ 10,000 | = $1.50 |
| (2) | Total Conversion Costs | ÷ Equivalent Units of Conversion Costs | = Unit Conversion Cost |
| | $36,800 | ÷ 9,200 | = $4.00 |
| (3) | Unit Materials Cost | + Unit Conversion Cost | = Total Manufacturing Cost per Unit |
| | $1.50 | + $4.00 | = $5.50 |

When equivalent units of production are the same for materials and conversion costs, it is necessary to compute only the total manufacturing cost per unit. The computation is total manufacturing cost divided by equivalent units of production.

## Assigning Costs to Units Transferred and in Process

Our next task is to determine the total cost of the units transferred out in June and the total cost of the units in ending work in process at June 30. To obtain these amounts, unit costs are assigned to the equivalent units of production for the period. The computations for the Machining Department are shown in Illustration 22-11. Note that total manufacturing cost per unit, $5.50, is used in costing the units started and finished. In contrast, the unit cost of materials and the unit cost of conversion are needed in costing the units in process. As indicated in the schedule, **the total costs to be assigned must equal the total costs assigned**.

**Machining Department**

| Costs to be Assigned | Assignment of Costs | Equivalent Units | Unit Cost | | Total Costs Assigned |
|---|---|---|---|---|---|
| Total manufacturing costs | Transferred out | | | | |
| | Work in process, June 1 | –0– | $ –0– | $ –0– | |
| | Started and finished | 8,000 | $5.50 | 44,000 | $44,000 |
| $51,800 | Work in process, June 30 | | | | |
| | Materials | 2,000 | $1.50 | 3,000 | |
| | Conversion costs | 1,200 | $4.00 | 4,800 | 7,800 |
| | | | | | $51,800 |

**Illustration 22-11**

*Assignment of costs—
Machining Department*

When the costs have been assigned, an entry is needed to record the cost of goods transferred out of the department. In this case, the transfer is to the Assembly Department, and the following entry is made:

(7)

| | | | |
|---|---|---|---|
| June 30 | Work in Process—Assembly | 44,000 | |
| | Work in Process—Machining | | 44,000 |
| | (To record transfer of 8,000 units to the Assembly Department) | | |

## Preparing the Production Cost Report

The final end-of-period procedure is the preparation of a production cost report. This is an internal report for management that shows **production quantity and cost data** for a production department. There are five sections in the report: (1) Units charged to department, (2) Units accounted for, (3) Unit costs, (4) Costs charged to department, and (5) Costs accounted for. The production cost report for the Machining Department of Tyler Manufacturing is shown in Illustration 22-12. All of the preceding end-of-period procedures are identified in the report. As shown, the **total physical units accounted for must equal the total units charged to the department**. Similarly, **the total costs accounted for must equal the total costs charged to the department**.

Production cost reports provide a basis for evaluating the productivity of a department. In addition, the cost data can be used to assess whether unit costs and total costs are reasonable. When the quantity and cost data are compared with predetermined goals, top management can also ascertain whether current performance is meeting planned objectives.

In the opening story, the staff accountant prepares the production cost report for each department in Ben & Jerry's.

**Illustration 22-12**

*Production cost report—
Machining Department*

## TYLER MANUFACTURING COMPANY
### Machining Department
### Production Cost Report
### For the Month Ended June 30, 1996

| QUANTITIES | Physical Units (Step 1) | Equivalent Units Materials | Conversion Costs (Step 2) | |
|---|---|---|---|---|
| **Units charged to department** | | | | |
| In process, June 1 | –0– | | | |
| Started into production | 10,000 | | | |
| Total units charged | 10,000 | | | |
| **Units accounted for** | | | | |
| Transferred out | | | | |
| In process, June 1 | –0– | –0– | –0– | |
| Started and finished | 8,000 | 8,000 | 8,000 | |
| Total | 8,000 | 8,000 | 8,000 | |
| In process, June 30 | 2,000 | 2,000 | 1,200 | (2,000 × 60%) |
| Total units accounted for | 10,000 | 10,000 | 9,200 | |

| COSTS | | Materials | Conversion Costs | Total |
|---|---|---|---|---|
| Unit costs (Step 3) | | | | |
| Costs in June | (a) | $15,000 | $36,800 | $51,800 |
| Equivalent units | (b) | 10,000 | 9,200 | |
| Unit costs (a) ÷ (b) | | $1.50 | $4.00 | $5.50 |
| **Costs charged to department** | | | | |
| In process, June 1 | | | | $ –0– |
| Costs in June | | | | 51,800 |
| Total costs charged | | | | $51,800 |
| **Costs accounted for (Step 4)** | | | | |
| Transferred out | | | | |
| In process, June 1 | | | $ –0– | |
| Started and finished (8,000 × $5.50) | | | 44,000 | $44,000 |
| In process, June 30 | | | | |
| Materials (2,000 × $1.50) | | | 3,000 | |
| Conversion costs (1,200 × $4.00) | | | 4,800 | 7,800 |
| Total costs accounted for | | | | $51,800 |

# *E*nd-of-Period Procedures—Assembly Department

## Computing Physical Units

The physical units to be accounted for in the Assembly Department are determined in the same manner as in the Machining Department. From the Tyler Manufacturing production data presented earlier, the physical units for the Assembly Department are shown in Illustration 22-13.

**STUDY OBJECTIVE**

**8**

*Apply end-of-period procedures to a second process.*

**Illustration 22-13**

*Production data in physical units*

**Assembly Department**

| | Units |
|---|---|
| Work in process, June 1 (40% complete) | 500 |
| Transferred in | 8,000 |
| Total units to be accounted for | 8,500 |
| Transferred out | 8,100 |
| Work in process, June 30 (75% complete) | 400 |
| Units accounted for | 8,500 |

In this case the units transferred out (8,100) plus the units in ending work in process (400) equal the total units to be accounted for (8,500).

## Computing Equivalent Units of Production

The equivalent units of production for the Assembly Department are computed in the same way as for the Machining Department. However, the presence of a beginning work in process adds a new dimension to process cost accounting.

When there are units in process at the beginning of the period, it is necessary to **identify the cost flow assumption** to be used. We will use the first-in, first-out (FIFO) costing method in this text and in homework problems. As indicated in the opening story, this is the method used by Ben & Jerry's in costing batches of ice cream. Other methods are discussed in cost accounting courses.

Under the **FIFO costing method,** the computation of equivalent units of production (as well as the computation of unit production costs and the assignment of costs to units transferred out and in process) is done on a first-in, first-out basis. The FIFO cost flow assumption usually corresponds to the actual physical flow of the goods because beginning work in process is normally completed before new work is started. This assumption affects the determination of equivalent units as follows:

1. The first units finished during the current period are the units in beginning work in process. Thus, units started and finished during the current period are the units transferred out minus the units in beginning work in process. For the Assembly Department, units started and finished in June are 7,600 (8,100 − 500).
2. Only the work required to finish the units of beginning work in process is included in the equivalent units of production for the current period.

### Equivalent Units for Materials

Since materials are entered at the beginning of the process, no additional materials costs are required to complete the beginning work in process. In addition, 100% of the materials costs has been incurred on the ending work in process. Thus, the computation of equivalent units for materials is as follows:

**Illustration 22-14**

*Computation of equivalent units—materials*

**Assembly Department**

| Production Data | Physical Units | Materials Added This Period | Equivalent Units |
|---|---|---|---|
| Work in process, June 1 | 500 | –0– | –0– |
| Started and finished | 7,600 | 100% | 7,600 |
| Work in process, June 30 | 400 | 100% | 400 |
| Total | 8,500 | | 8,000 |

Equivalent units can also be determined graphically as shown in Illustration 22-9.

### Equivalent Units for Conversion Costs

The 500 units of beginning work in process were 40% complete in terms of conversion costs. Thus, 300 equivalent units (60% × 500 units) of conversion costs were required to complete the beginning inventory. In addition, the 400 units of ending work in process were 75% complete in terms of conversion costs. Thus the equivalent units for conversion costs is 8,200, computed as follows:

**Illustration 22-15**

*Computation of equivalent units—conversion costs*

**Assembly Department**

| Production Data | Physical Units | Work Added This Period | Equivalent Units |
|---|---|---|---|
| Work in process, June 1 | 500 | 60% | 300 |
| Started and finished | 7,600 | 100% | 7,600 |
| Work in process, June 30 | 400 | 75% | 300 |
| Total | 8,500 | | 8,200 |

## Computing Unit Costs of Production

The production costs chargeable to the Assembly Department in June consist of the following debits to work in process.

**Illustration 22-16**

*Costs charged to Assembly Department*

**Work in Process—Assembly Department**

| | | |
|---|---|---|
| June 1 | Balance | 3,600 |
| 30 | Materials | 4,000 |
| 30 | Labor | 6,400 |
| 30 | Overhead | 18,200 |
| 30 | Transferred from Machining Dept. | 44,000 |
| | Total | 76,200 |

Our objective is to determine the unit costs of production for the month of June. **Under the FIFO method, this determination is based entirely on the production costs incurred on work done during the month.** Thus, the costs in the beginning work in process are not relevant, because they were incurred on work done in the preceding month.

The June costs for the Assembly Department include the same types of costs as in the Machining Department with one exception: the costs tranferred in from

**Helpful hint** In a second department, total materials costs equals the sum of (1) materials added in the department plus (2) costs transferred in.

## ▶Accounting in Action ▸ *Business Insight*

Chrysler Corp.'s low product development costs make it the lowest-cost automotive producer in the world, according to the *Harbour Report* published by Harbour & Associates Inc., a Troy, Michigan, consulting firm. The finding was based on the total cost of both product development and vehicle assembly. Among the Big Three auto makers, Ford leads in efficiency of assembly operations. The comparative costs of assembling a vehicle in 1992 were Ford $1,563, Chrysler $1,872, and GM $2,358.

*Source: Wall Street Journal,* June 23, 1994, p. B10.

the Machining Department. Transferred-in costs **are recognized as materials cost to the receiving department.** At Tyler Manufacturing, these costs are a cost to the Assembly Department. Therefore, total materials costs are $48,000 (materials added by the Assembly Department $4,000 + the transferred-in costs $44,000). Conversion costs total $24,600 (labor $6,400 + overhead $18,200). The computations of unit costs in the Assembly Department are as follows:

**Illustration 22-17**

*Unit cost formulas and computations—Assembly Department*

As shown, the unit costs are $6.00 for materials, $3.00 for conversion costs, and $9.00 for total manufacturing costs.

## Assigning Costs to Units Transferred and in Process

**Under the FIFO method, the first goods to be completed during the period are the units in beginning work in process.** Thus, the cost of the beginning work in process is always assigned to the goods transferred to finished goods (or to the next department). The FIFO method also means that ending work in process will be assigned only production costs that are incurred in the current period. The assignment of the manufacturing costs in the Assembly Department is shown in Illustration 22-18.

**Illustration 22-18**

*Assignment of costs—Assembly Department*

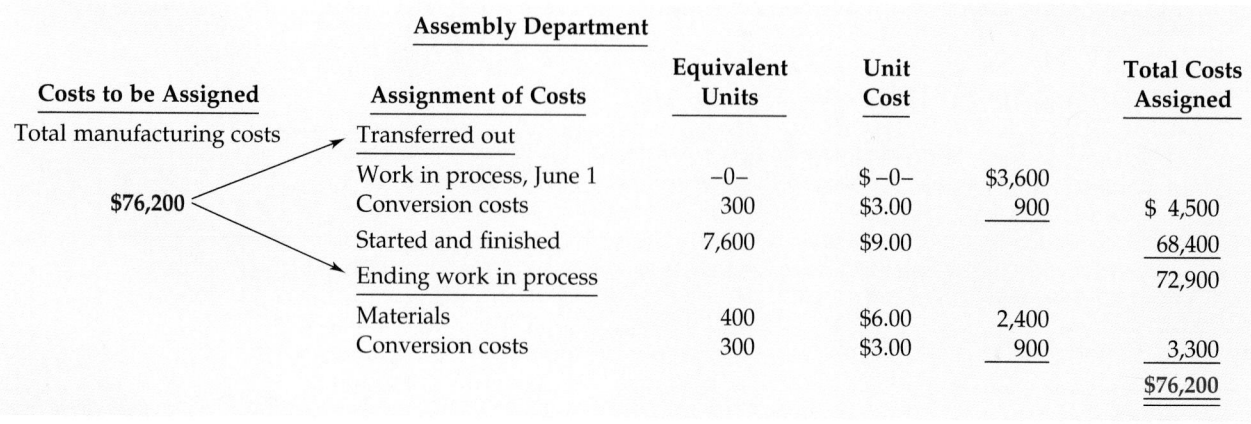

| Costs to be Assigned | Assignment of Costs | Equivalent Units | Unit Cost | | Total Costs Assigned |
|---|---|---|---|---|---|
| Total manufacturing costs | Transferred out | | | | |
| | Work in process, June 1 | –0– | $ –0– | $3,600 | |
| $76,200 | Conversion costs | 300 | $3.00 | 900 | $ 4,500 |
| | Started and finished | 7,600 | $9.00 | | 68,400 |
| | Ending work in process | | | | 72,900 |
| | Materials | 400 | $6.00 | 2,400 | |
| | Conversion costs | 300 | $3.00 | 900 | 3,300 |
| | | | | | $76,200 |

Again, you can see that the costs assigned ($72,900 + $3,300) equal the costs to be assigned ($76,200). In this case, the total costs assigned to units transferred out can be obtained by multiplying the units (8,100) by the unit cost of the goods started and finished ($9.00). This procedure is valid only if there has been no change in unit costs between the preceding and current months. In solving homework problems, the step-by-step approach should be followed.

The units completed in the Assembly Department are transferred to the finished goods warehouse. The entry for this transfer is:

|  | (8) |  |  |
|---|---|---|---|
| June 30 | Finished Goods Inventory | 72,900 | |
| |     Work in Process—Assembly | | 72,900 |
| |     (To record transfer of 8,100 units to finished goods) | | |

## Preparing the Production Cost Report

The procedure for preparing a production report is the same for every department. The report for the Assembly Department is shown in Illustration 22-19. As in the report for the Machining Department, **the total physical units accounted for must equal the units charged to the department**. Similarly, the **total costs accounted for must equal the total costs charged to the department**.

## Process Cost Flow Summary

The flow of costs in process cost accounting was graphically presented in Illustration 22-3 earlier in this chapter. The ledger accounts after posting the nine June transactions of Tyler Manufacturing Company and the flow of documents are shown in Illustration 22-20.

Each posting is based on journal entries illustrated earlier except for the posting pertaining to the cost of goods sold. Data for this entry are obtained from finished goods perpetual inventory records. Assuming 6,000 of the can openers costing $9.00 each are sold in June, the entry to record the cost of goods sold is as follows:

|  | (9) |  |  |
|---|---|---|---|
| June 30 | Cost of Goods Sold | 54,000 | |
| |     Finished Goods Inventory | | 54,000 |
| |     (To record cost of 6,000 units sold) | | |

In addition, an entry would be made to record the sale of the units for $119,700 (6,000 × the selling price of $19.95).

► **Ethics note**

Because production cost reports are used as the basis for evaluating department productivity and efficiency, the units, costs, and computations reported therein should be independently accumulated and analyzed to prevent misstatements by department managers.

## Before You Go On . . .

### ► Review It

1. How do physical units differ from equivalent units of production?
2. What are the formulas for computing unit costs of production?
3. How are costs assigned to units transferred out and in process?
4. What are the five sections of a production cost report?

### ► Do It

In March, Rodayo Manufacturing had the following unit production costs: materials $6 and conversion costs $9. On March 1, it had zero work in process. During March, 12,000 units were transferred out, and 800 units that were 25% completed as to conversion costs were in ending work in process. Assign the costs to the units transferred and in process.

**Illustration 22-19**

*Production cost report—
Assembly Department*

## TYLER MANUFACTURING COMPANY
### Assembly Department
### Production Cost Report
### For the Month Ended June 30, 1996

| | | Equivalent Units | |
| --- | --- | --- | --- |
| | Physical Units (Step 1) | Materials | Conversion Costs (Step 2) |
| **QUANTITIES** | | | |
| Units charged to department | | | |
| In process, June 1 | 500 | | |
| Transferred in | 8,000 | | |
| Total units charged | 8,500 | | |
| Units accounted for | | | |
| Transferred out | | | |
| In process, June 1 | 500 | –0– | 300 (500 × 60%) |
| Started and finished | 7,600 | 7,600 | 7,600 |
| Total | 8,100 | 7,600 | 7,900 |
| In process, June 30 | 400 | 400 | 300 (400 × 75%) |
| Total units accounted for | 8,500 | 8,000 | 8,200 |

| | | | Conversion | |
| --- | --- | --- | --- | --- |
| **COSTS** | | Materials | Costs | Total |
| Unit costs (Step 3) | | | | |
| Costs in June | (a) | $48,000 | $24,600 | $72,600 |
| Equivalent units | (b) | 8,000 | 8,200 | |
| Unit costs (a) ÷ (b) | | $6.00 | $3.00 | $9.00 |
| Costs charged to department | | | | |
| In process, June 1 | | | | $ 3,600 |
| Costs in June | | | | 72,600 |
| Total costs charged | | | | $76,200 |
| Costs accounted for (Step 4) | | | | |
| Transferred out | | | | |
| In process, June 1 | | $ 3,600 | | |
| Conversion costs (300 × $3.00) | | 900 | $ 4,500 | |
| Started and finished (7,600 × $9.00) | | | 68,400 | $72,900 |
| In process, June 30 | | | | |
| Materials (400 × $6.00) | | | 2,400 | |
| Conversion costs (300 × $3.00) | | | 900 | 3,300 |
| Total costs accounted for | | | | $76,200 |

**Illustration 22-20**

*Process cost accounts and document flow*

***Reasoning:*** The units transferred are the 12,000 units started and finished. These units should be assigned the total manufacturing cost of $15 per unit. The assignment of costs to units in process consists of the materials cost and conversion cost based on equivalent units of production.

***Solution:*** The assignment of costs is as follows:

| | | |
|---|---:|---:|
| Transferred out: | | |
| Started and finished (12,000 × $15) | | $18,000 |
| | | |
| Ending work in process: | | |
| Materials (800 × $6) | $4,800 | |
| Conversion costs (200 × $9) | 1,800 | $ 6,600 |

*Related exercise material:* BE22–4, BE22–5, BE22–6, BE22–7, E22–1, E22–2, E22–3, E22–4, and E22–8.

# Contemporary Developments

As indicated in Chapter 20, two contemporary developments in managerial accounting are just-in-time processing and activity-based costing. We explain these innovations in the following sections.

## Just-in-Time Processing

**STUDY OBJECTIVE**

▾ **9**

*Explain just-in-time (JIT) processing.*

Traditionally, continuous process manufacturing has been based on a **just-in-case** philosophy: Inventories of raw materials are maintained **just in case** some items are of poor quality or a key supplier is shut down by a strike. Similarly, subassembly parts are manufactured and stored **just in case** they are needed later in the manufacturing process, and finished goods are completed and stored **just in case** unexpected and rush customer orders are received. This philosophy often results in a **"push approach"** in which raw materials and subassembly parts are pushed through each process. Traditional processing often results in the buildup of extensive manufacturing inventories.

Primarily in response to foreign competition, many U.S. firms have switched to just-in-time (JIT) processing. JIT manufacturing is dedicated to producing the right products (or parts) at the right time as they are needed. Under JIT processing, raw materials are received **just in time** for use in production, subassembly parts are completed **just in time** for use in finished goods, and finished goods are completed **just in time** to be sold. Illustration 22-21 shows the sequence of activities in just-in-time processing.

A primary objective of JIT is to eliminate all manufacturing inventories. Inventories are considered to have an adverse effect on net income because they tie up funds and storage space that could be made available for more productive purposes. JIT strives to eliminate inventories by using a **"pull approach"** in manufacturing. This approach begins at the final process (cell or work station) where a signal is sent via a computer to the next preceding work station indicating the exact materials (parts and subassemblies) needed for a time period, such as four hours or an eight-hour shift, to complete the production of a specified product. The preceding process, in turn, sends its signal to other processes so that there is a smooth continuous flow in the manufacturing process and no buildup of inventories at any point.

**Illustration 22-21**

*Just-in-time processing*

## Elements of JIT Processing

There are three important elements in JIT processing:

1. A company must have dependable suppliers who are willing to deliver on short notice exact quantities of raw materials according to precise quality specifications (even including multiple deliveries within the same day). Suppliers must also be willing to deliver the raw materials at specified work stations rather than at a central receiving department. This type of purchasing requires constant and direct communication with suppliers, which is facilitated by an on-line computer linkage between the company and its suppliers.

2. A multiskilled work force must be developed. Under JIT, machines are often strategically grouped around work cells or centers and much of the work is automated. As a result, one worker may have the responsibility to operate and maintain several different types of machines.

3. A total quality control system must be established throughout the manufacturing operations. Total quality control means **no defects**. Since only required quantities are signaled by the **pull approach**, any defects at any work station will shut down operations at subsequent work stations. Total quality control requires continuous monitoring by both employees and supervisors at each work station.

## Benefits of JIT Processing

The major benefits of JIT processing are:

1. Manufacturing inventories are significantly reduced or eliminated.
2. Product quality is enhanced.

**3.** Rework costs and inventory storage costs are reduced or eliminated.

**4.** Production cost savings are realized from the improved flow of goods through the processes.

One of the major accounting benefits of JIT is the elimination of raw materials and work in process inventory accounts. In place of these accounts is one account, Raw and In-Process Inventory. All materials and conversion costs are charged to this account. Because of the reduction (or elimination) of in-process inventories, the computation of equivalent units of production is simplified.

## ▸Accounting in Action ▸ *Business Insight*

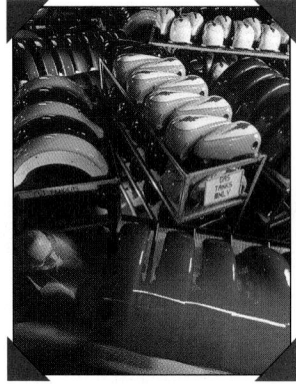

JIT first hit the USA in the early 1980s when it was adopted by automobile companies to meet foreign competition. It is now being successfully used in many companies, including General Electric, Caterpillar, and Harley-Davidson. The effects in most cases have been dramatic. For example, after using JIT for two years, a major division of Hewlett-Packard found that work in process inventories (in dollars) were down 82%, scrap/rework costs were down 30%, space utilization was down 40%, and labor efficiency improved 50%. As indicated, JIT not only reduces inventory but also enables a manufacturer to produce a better product faster and with less waste.

## Activity-Based Costing

**STUDY OBJECTIVE**
·········**10**·········

*Explain activity-based costing (ABC).*

Activity-based costing (ABC) is a development in product costing that has received much attention in recent years. Activity-based costing focuses on the activities performed in producing a product. An ABC system is similar to conventional costing systems in accounting for direct materials and direct labor but differs in regard to manufacturing overhead.

In a conventional cost system, a **single unit-level** basis of allocation is used to allocate overhead costs to products. As explained in this text, the basis may be direct labor or machine hours used to manufacture the product. The assumption in this approach is that as volume of units produced increases, so does the cost of overhead. However, in some cases, the overhead cost is unrelated to the number of units produced.

In ABC, the cost of a product is equal to the sum of the costs of all activities performed to manufacture it. ABC recognizes that to have accurate and meaningful cost data, more than one basis of allocating activity costs to products is needed. In selecting the basis, ABC seeks to identify the **cost drivers** that measure the activities performed on the product. Examples of activities and possible cost drivers are as follows:

**Illustration 22-22**

*Activities and cost drivers in ABC*

| Activity | Cost Driver |
|---|---|
| Ordering raw materials | Ordering hours; number of orders |
| Receiving raw materials | Receiving hours; number of shipments |
| Materials handling | Number of requisitions; weight of materials; handling hours |
| Production scheduling | Number of orders |
| Machine setups | Setup hours; number of setups |
| Machining (fabricating, assembling, etc.) | Machine hours |
| Quality control inspections | Number of inspections |
| Factory supervision | Number of employees |

Two important assumptions must be met in order to obtain accurate product costs under ABC:

1. All overhead costs related to the activity must be driven by the cost driver used to assign costs to products.
2. All overhead costs related to the activity should respond proportionally to changes in the activity level of the cost driver.

For example, if there is little or no correlation between changes in the cost driver and consumption of the overhead cost, inaccurate product costs are inevitable. A case example in the use of ABC is explained and illustrated in the appendix at the end of this chapter.

Activity-based costing may be used with either a job order or a process cost accounting system. The primary benefit of ABC is more accurate and meaningful product costing. Also, improved cost data about an activity can lead to reduced costs for the activity. In sum, ABC makes managers realize that it is activities and not products that determine the profitability of a company.

## ▶ Accounting in Action ▸ *International Insight*

Contrary to popular opinion, ABC was not a Japanese invention. ABC was developed in France in the 1950s, but most Japanese corporations have used a form of ABC since that time. In Japan, ABC is called "target costing." Exhaustive market research is done on a new product to determine a price the market will accept. This becomes the target cost that designers, engineers, and production managers must meet. The use of target costing has resulted in products that are priced properly and profitably and that promptly win market share.

*Source: Chicago Tribune, January 24, 1993, p. 4.*

## *Before You Go On . . .*

### ▶ *Review It*

1. What are the principal accounting effects of just-in-time (JIT) processing?
2. What are the primary differences between activity-based costing (ABC) and traditional costing?

### ▶ *A Look Back at Ben & Jerry's Homemade Inc.*

Refer to the opening story and answer the following questions.

1. How many processes are used by Ben & Jerry's to make ice cream? Identify the processes.
2. Why does Ben & Jerry's use a process costing system rather than a job order system?
3. How does the production report satisfy the needs of the department heads?

**Solution:**

1. The three processes used by Ben & Jerry's to make ice cream are (1) mixing, (2) prepping, and (3) pinting.
2. Ben & Jerry's uses a process costing system because making ice cream is continuous process manufacturing; it is mass production of many homogeneous units. Making ice cream fits the manufacturing characteristics of (1) "once the production begins, it continues until the finished product emerges," and (2) "when the finished product emerges, all units will have been processed in the same manner with precisely the same amount of materials, labor, and overhead." Each finished pint of ice cream is indistinguishable one from another.

3. The production report provides current cost data that can be compared with previous cost data and with budget expectations so that efficiency can be evaluated. The production report shows how much was processed (manufactured) and at what cost. These data are needed by department heads to manage and control production.

# Summary of Study Objectives

**1. *Explain the flow of costs in process cost accounting.*** The cost flow in process cost accounting is basically the same as in job order cost accounting. The accumulation of manufacturing costs (materials, labor, and overhead) is the same in process cost accounting as in job order costing. In process costing, costs are assigned to more than one work in process account, and the method of assigning costs is different.

**2. *State the end-of-period procedures in process cost accounting.*** End-of-period procedures are used to:
(a) Compute the physical units.
(b) Compute equivalent units of production.
(c) Compute unit costs of production.
(d) Assign costs to units transferred and in process.
(e) Prepare the production cost report.

**3. *Compute the physical units of production.*** Keeping track of the physical units of product consists of adding the units started into production during the period to the units in process at the beginning of the period to determine the total units to be accounted for. These units then are accounted for by the output of the period, which consists of units transferred out during the period and any units in process at the end of the period.

**4. *Compute equivalent units of production.*** Equivalent units of production are the sum of the work performed to (a) finish the units of beginning work in process inventory, if any; (b) complete the units started into production during the period; and (c) start, but only partially complete, the units in ending work in process inventory.

**5. *Indicate how unit costs are computed.*** There are two steps in determining unit costs: (a) determine the equivalent units of production, and (b) divide the appropriate costs by the equivalent units. Unit costs are computed for total man-

ufacturing costs and generally it is also necessary to compute unit costs separately for materials and conversion costs.

**6. *Explain the method and objective of assigning costs to units of output.*** Costs are assigned to work done by applying unit costs to the equivalent units of work done. The objective of assigning costs is to determine the costs to be assigned to units transferred out and the units in ending work in process.

**7. *Prepare a production cost report.*** The production cost report contains both quantity and cost data for a production department. There are five sections in the report: (a) Units charged to department, (b) Units accounted for, (c) Unit costs, (d) Costs charged to department, and (e) Costs accounted for.

**8. *Apply end-of-period procedures to a second process.*** For a second process, (a) work done to complete beginning inventory is added in computing equivalent units, (b) costs transferred in are a materials cost, and (c) costs are assigned to beginning work in process in determining the cost of units transferred out.

**9. *Explain just-in-time (JIT) processing.*** JIT is a manufacturing technique that is dedicated to producing the right products at the right time as needed. One of the principal accounting effects is that a Raw and In-Process Inventory account replaces both the raw materials and work in process inventory accounts.

**10. *Explain activity-based costing (ABC).*** ABC is a method of product costing that focuses on the activities performed to produce products. It then assigns the cost of the activities to products by using cost drivers that measure the activities performed. The primary objective of ABC is accurate and meaningful product costs.

# APPENDIX ▸ *Case Example of Traditional Costing versus Activity-Based Costing*

## Production and Cost Data

Atlas Company produces two products, Product X and Product Y. Product X is a high-volume item totaling 25,000 units annually, and Product Y is a low-volume item totaling only 5,000 units per year. Both products require one hour of direct labor for completion. Therefore, total direct labor hours are 30,000 (25,000 + 5,000). Expected annual manufacturing overhead costs are $900,000. Thus, the overhead rate is $30 ($900,000 ÷ 30,000) per direct labor hour.

The direct materials cost per unit is $40 for Product X and $30 for Product Y. The direct labor cost is $12 per unit for each product.

STUDY OBJECTIVE

*After studying this appendix, you should be able to:*

*11. Apply activity-based costing to specific company data.*

## Unit Costs under Traditional Costing

The unit cost for each product under traditional costing is shown below.

**Illustration 22A-1**

*Unit costs—traditional costing*

| Manufacturing Costs | Product X | Product Y |
|---|---|---|
| Direct materials | $40 | 30 |
| Direct labor | 12 | 12 |
| Overhead | 30 | 30 |
| Total unit cost | $82 | $72 |

## Determining Overhead Rates under ABC

Analysis reveals that Atlas Company's expected annual overhead costs of $900,000 relate to three activities—machine setups, machining, and inspections. The cost driver and overhead rate for each activity are shown in Illustration 22A-2.

**Illustration 22A-2**

*Computing overhead rates—ABC*

| Activity | Cost Driver | Total Expected Overhead Cost | Total Expected Use of Driver | Overhead Rate |
|---|---|---|---|---|
| Machine setups | Number of setups | $300,000 | 1,500 | $200 |
| Machining | Machine hours | 500,000 | 50,000 | 10 |
| Inspections | Number of inspections | 100,000 | 2,000 | 50 |

## Assigning Overhead Costs to Products under ABC

In assigning costs, it is necessary to know the expected number of cost drivers for each product. Because of its low volume, Product Y requires more setups and inspections than Product X. The expected number of cost drivers for each product is as follows:

**Illustration 22A-3**

*Expected number of cost drivers*

| Cost Driver | Product X | Product Y | Total Usage |
|---|---|---|---|
| Number of machine setups | 500 | 1,000 | 1,500 |
| Machine hours | 30,000 | 20,000 | 50,000 |
| Number of inspections | 500 | 1,500 | 2,000 |

Using these data, the assignment of the expected annual overhead cost to each product is as follows:

**Illustration 22A-4**

*Assignment of overhead costs to products*

| Activity | Product X Number | Product X Cost | Product Y Number | Product Y Cost | Total Cost |
|---|---|---|---|---|---|
| Machine setups ($200) | 500 | $100,000 | 1,000 | $200,000 | $300,000 |
| Machining ($10) | 30,000 | 300,000 | 20,000 | 200,000 | 500,000 |
| Inspections ($50) | 500 | 25,000 | 1,500 | 75,000 | 100,000 |
| Total assigned costs (a) | | $425,000 | | $475,000 | $900,000 |
| Units produced (b) | | 25,000 | | 5,000 | |
| Overhead cost per unit (a) ÷ (b) | | $17 | | $95 | |

These data show that under ABC, overhead costs are shifted from the high-volume product (Product X) to the low-volume product (Product Y). This shift results in more accurate costing for two reasons:

1. Low-volume products often require more special handling, such as more machine setups and inspections, than high-volume products. This is true for Atlas Company, for example. Thus, the low-volume product frequently is responsible for more overhead costs per unit than a high-volume product.
2. The overhead costs incurred by the low-volume product often are disproportionate to a traditional allocation base such as direct labor hours. Therefore, direct labor hours is usually a poor cost driver for assigning overhead costs to low-volume products. When overhead is properly assigned in ABC, it will usually increase the unit cost of low-volume products.

# Comparing Unit Costs

A comparison of unit manufacturing costs under traditional costing and ABC shows the following significant differences:

**Illustration 22A-5**

*Comparison of unit product costs*

| Manufacturing Costs | Traditional Costing X | Traditional Costing Y | ABC X | ABC Y |
|---|---|---|---|---|
| Direct materials | $40 | $30 | $40 | $ 30 |
| Direct labor | 12 | 12 | 12 | 12 |
| Overhead | 30 | 30 | 17 | 95 |
| Total | $82 | $72 | $69 | $137 |

The comparison shows that unit costs under traditional costing have been significantly distorted. The cost of Product X has been overstated $13 per unit ($82 − $69), and the cost of Product Y has been understated $65 per unit ($137 − $72). The differences are attributable entirely to how manufacturing overhead is assigned. A likely consequence of the differences is that Atlas Company has been

## ►*Technology in Action*

Many software packages designed especially for ABC costing are available for a personal computer or network. EASYABC developed by ABC Technologies includes three modules: overhead, activity, and cost object. The overhead module contains the overhead costs that are to be allocated to activities. In the activity module a user identifies the activities that are consumed by products. In the final module, the user defines the cost object such as a product, a customer, a product line, or any combination of the three. EASYABC also generates reports.

*Source: Cost Management,* Winter 1994, pp. 40–41.

overpricing Product X and possibly losing market share to competitors. In addition, it has been sacrificing profitability by underpricing Product Y.

As illustrated in the above case, ABC involves the following steps:

1. Identify the major activities that pertain to the manufacture of specific products.
2. Accumulate manufacturing overhead costs by activities.
3. Identify the cost driver(s) that accurately measure(s) each activity's contribution to the finished product.
4. Assign manufacturing overhead costs for each activity to products using the cost driver(s).

### Benefits and Limitations of Activity-Based Costing

We have already seen that a primary benefit of ABC is more accurate product costing. In addition, ABC offers the following other benefits:

1. **Control over overhead costs** is enhanced. Many overhead costs are incurred directly by activities. Thus, managers become more aware of their responsibility to control the activities that generate the costs.
2. **Better management decisions** can be made. More accurate product costing should contribute to setting selling prices that will achieve desired product profitability levels. In addition, the cost data should be helpful in deciding whether to discontinue or expand a product line or in deciding whether to make or buy a product component.

## ►*Accounting in Action* ► *Business Insight*

ABC enabled Digital Communications Associates, a computer hardware and software manufacturer, to discover why profit margins slipped from 18.6% to 8% over a 3-year period. Digital boiled down 600 production activities to 136. ABC helped Digital and its 1,300 employees to bring costs under contol.

*Source: Chicago Tribune,* January 24, 1993, p. 4.

The principal disadvantages or limitations of ABC generally focus on two factors. First, **the expense of obtaining the cost data** required by the system is relatively high. ABC requires data that are not normally generated within a company such as the number of setups, inspections, orders placed, and orders received. In addition, numerous computations are involved in assigning overhead costs to individual products.

Second, **ABC does not eliminate arbitrary assignments** of overhead. For example, plant-wide overhead costs such as depreciation, insurance, and property taxes on the factory building should be allocated to the activity centers in determining the cost of a product. These allocations may be more difficult to do accurately than in a traditional cost system because of the increased number of activity centers. As a result, accuracy of product costs could be adversely affected.

# *S*ummary of Study Objective for Chapter 22 Appendix

**11. *Apply activity-based costing to specific company data.*** In applying ABC, it is necessary to compute the overhead rate for each activity by dividing total expected overhead by the total expected usage of the cost driver. The overhead cost for each activity is then assigned to products on the basis of each product's use of the cost driver.

# *G*LOSSARY

**Activity-based costing**   A cost accounting system that focuses on the activities performed in manufacturing a specific product. (p. 938).

**Equivalent units of production**   The work done during the period on the physical units of output expressed in terms of fully completed units. (p. 925).

**Just-in-time processing**   A processing system dedicated to producing the right products (or parts) as they are needed. (p. 936).

**Physical units**   Actual units to be accounted for during a period irrespective of any work performed. (p. 924).

**Production cost report**   An internal report for management that shows both production quantity and cost data for a production department. (p. 928).

**Process cost accounting**   A system of accounting used by companies that manufacture relatively homogeneous prod-

ucts through a series of continuous processes or operations. (p. 918).

**Total units accounted for**   The sum of the units transferred out during the period plus the units in process at the end of the period. (p. 924).

**Total units to be accounted for**   The sum of the units started (or transferred) into production during the period plus the units in process at the beginning of the period. (p. 924).

**Transferred-in costs**   Costs transferred in from a department that are considered to be a materials cost to the receiving department. (p. 932).

**Unit production costs**   Costs expressed in terms of equivalent units of production. (p. 927).

**Units started and finished**   Units both started and completed during the period. (p. 926).

# *D*EMONSTRATION PROBLEM

Karlene Industries produces plastic ice cube trays in two processes: heating and stamping. All materials are added at the beginning of the Heating Department.

On November 1, 1,000 trays were in process in the Heating Department that were 70% complete. During November 12,000 trays were started into production. On November 30, 2,000 trays were in process that were 60% complete.

The following cost information for the Heating Department was also available:

| | | | |
|---|---|---|---|
| Work in process, November 1 | $1,000 | Labor | $2,300 |
| Materials | 3,000 | Overhead | 4,600 |

*Instructions*

(a) Prepare a production cost report for the Heating Department for the month of November 1996.

(b) Journalize the transfer of costs to the Stamping Department.

## Solution to Demonstration Problem

(a)

**KARLENE INDUSTRIES**
**Heating Department**
**Production Cost Report**
**For the Month Ended November 30, 1996**

| | | Equivalent Units | |
| --- | --- | --- | --- |
| | Physical | | Conversion |
| | Units | Materials | Costs |
| Quantities | (Step 1) | | (Step 2) |
| **Units charged to department** | | | |
| In process, November 1 | 1,000 | | |
| Started into production | 12,000 | | |
| Total units charged | 13,000 | | |
| **Units accounted for** | | | |
| Transferred out | | | |
| In process, November 1 | 1,000 | –0– | 300 (1,000 × 30%) |
| Started and finished | 10,000 | 10,000 | 10,000 |
| Total | 11,000 | 10,000 | 10,300 |
| In process, November 30 | 2,000 | 2,000 | 1,200 (2,000 × 60%) |
| Total units accounted for | 13,000 | 12,000 | 11,500 |

**Costs**

| | | Conversion | |
| --- | --- | --- | --- |
| Unit costs (Step 3) | Materials | Costs | Total |
| Costs in November | (a) $ 3,000 | $ 6,900 (1) | $ 9,900 |
| Equivalent units | (b) 12,000 | 11,500 | |
| Unit costs (a) ÷ (b) | $.25 | $.60 | $.85 |

**Costs charged to department**

| | | | |
| --- | --- | --- | --- |
| In process, November 1 | | | $ 1,000 |
| Costs in November | | | 9,900 |
| Total costs charged | | | $10,900 |

**Costs accounted for (Step 4)**

| | | | |
| --- | --- | --- | --- |
| Transferred out | | | |
| In process, November 1 | $ 1,000 | | |
| Conversion costs (300 × $.60) | 180 | $ 1,180 | |
| Started and finished (10,000 × $.85) | | 8,500 | $ 9,680 |
| In process, November 30 | | | |
| Materials (2,000 × $.25) | | 500 | |
| Conversion costs (1,200 × $.60) | | 720 | 1,220 |
| Total costs accounted for | | | $10,900 |

(1) Labor $2,300 plus overhead of $4,600.

| (b) Nov. 30 | Work in Process—Stamping | 9,680 | |
| --- | --- | --- | --- |
| | Work in Process—Heating | | 9,680 |
| | (To record transfer of 11,000 units to Stamping Department) | | |

*Note: All **asterisked** Questions, Exercises, and Problems relate to material contained in the appendix to the chapter.

# SELF-STUDY QUESTIONS

Answers are at the end of the chapter.

(SO 1)   1. Which of the following items is *not* a characteristic of continuous process manufacturing?
   a. Once production begins, it continues until the finished product emerges.
   b. The products produced are heterogeneous in nature.
   c. The focus is on continually producing homogeneous products.
   d. When the finished product emerges, all units have precisely the same amount of materials, labor, and overhead.

(SO 2)   2. End-of-period procedures in process cost accounting do *not* include:
   a. computing physical units of production.
   b. computing equivalent units of production.
   c. assigning costs to units transferred and in process.
   d. preparing a job cost sheet.

(SO 3)   3. In the RYZ Company, there are zero units in beginning work in process, 7,000 units started into production, and 500 units in ending work in process 20% completed. The physical units to be accounted for are:
   a. 7,000.
   b. 7,360.
   c. 7,600.
   d. 7,340.

(SO 4)   4. The Mora Company has 2,000 units in beginning work in process, 20% complete as to conversion costs, 25,000 units started and finished, and 3,000 units in ending work in process, 30% complete as to conversion costs. Equivalent units for materials and conversion costs are, respectively:
   a. 28,000 and 26,600.
   b. 28,000 and 27,500.
   c. 27,000 and 26,200.
   d. 27,000 and 29,600.

(SO 5)   5. KLM Company has no beginning work in process; 9,000 units are started and finished and 3,000 units in ending work in process are one-third finished. If total materials cost is $60,000, the unit materials cost is:
   a. $5.00
   b. $6.00

   c. $6.67 (rounded).
   d. No correct answer given.

(SO 6)   6. Toney Company has unit costs of $10 for materials and $30 for conversion costs. If there are 2,500 units in ending work in process, 40% complete as to conversion costs, the total cost assignable to the ending work in process inventory is:
   a. $45,000.
   b. $55,000.
   c. $75,000.
   d. $100,000.

(SO 7)   7. A production cost report:
   a. is an external report.
   b. shows costs charged to department and costs accounted for.
   c. shows equivalent units of production but not physical units.
   d. contains four sections.

(SO 8)   8. In determining unit costs in a second department:
   a. costs in beginning inventory are added to costs incurred during the period.
   b. only costs incurred on units transferred in are used.
   c. only costs incurred during the period are used.
   d. No correct answer is given.

(SO 9)   9. Just-in-time processing (JIT):
   a. strives to eliminate inventories.
   b. uses a pull approach in manufacturing.
   c. Neither of the above.
   d. Both (a) and (b).

(SO 10)  10. Activity-based costing (ABC):
   a. can be used only in a process cost system.
   b. focuses on units of production.
   c. focuses on activities performed to produce a product.
   d. uses only a single basis of allocation.

(SO 11)  *11. The overhead rate for Machine Setups is $100 per setup. Products A and B have 80 and 60 setups, respectively. The overhead assigned to each product is:
   a. Product A $8,000, Product B $8,000.
   b. Product A $8,000, Product B $6,000.
   c. Product A $6,000, Product B $6,000.
   d. Product A $6,000, Product B $8,000.

# QUESTIONS

1. Contrast the primary focus of job order cost accounting and of process cost accounting.

2. Your roommate is confused about the features of process cost accounting. Identify and explain the four distinctive features for your roommate.

3. Chita Revez believes there are no significant differences in the flow of costs between job order cost accounting and process cost accounting. Is Chita correct? Explain.

4. (a) What source documents are used in assigning (1) materials and (2) labor to production?
   (b) What criterion and basis are commonly used in allocating overhead to processes?

5. In Melbourne Company, overhead is assigned to production departments at the rate of $20 per machining hour. In July, machine hours were 3,000 in the Machining Department and 2,400 in the Assembly Department. Prepare the entry to assign overhead to production.

6. Tina Turner is uncertain about the end-of-period procedures in process cost accounting. State the procedures that are required in the sequence in which they are performed.

7. Kent Krause is confused about computing physical units. Explain to Kent how physical units to be accounted for and physical units accounted for are determined.

8. What is meant by the term "equivalent units of production"?

9. How are equivalent units computed?

10. Marin Company had zero units of beginning work in process. During the period, 8,000 units were completed, and there were 400 units of ending work in process. What were the units started into production?

11. Sandy Co. has zero units of beginning work in process. During the period 9,000 units were completed, and there were 500 units of ending work in process one-fifth complete. What were the equivalent units of production for (a) materials and (b) conversion costs?

12. Cesska Co. started and finished 1,000 units for the period. Its beginning inventory is 600 units one-fourth complete and its ending inventory is 400 units one-fifth complete. How many units were transferred out this period?

13. Hipp Company transfers out 12,000 units and has 2,000 units of ending work in process that are 25% complete. Materials are entered at the beginning of the process and there is no beginning work in process. Assuming unit materials costs of $3 and unit conversion costs of $7, what are the costs to be assigned to units (a) transferred out and (b) in ending work in process?

14. (a) Jane Jelk believes the production cost report is an external report for stockholders. Is Jane correct? Explain.
   (b) Identify the sections in a production cost report.

15. What purposes are served by a production cost report?

16. When units are transferred from one department to another, how should the receiving department handle the costs transferred in?

17. In Gruber Company, there are 800 units of ending work in process that are 100% complete as to materials and 25% complete as to conversion costs. If the unit cost of materials is $4 and the costs assigned to the 800 units is $5,600, what is the per-unit conversion cost?

18. (a) Describe the philosophy and approach of just-in-time processing.
   (b) Identify the major elements of JIT processing.

19. (a) What are the principal differences between activity-based costing (ABC) and traditional product costing?
   (b) What assumptions must be met for ABC costing to be useful?

20. Apex Co. identifies the following activities that pertain to manufacturing overhead: Materials Handling, Machine Setups, Factory Machine Maintenance, Factory Supervision, and Quality Control. For each activity identify an appropriate cost driver.

*21. (a) Identify the steps that pertain to activity-based costing.
   (b) What are the advantages of ABC costing?

# BRIEF EXERCISES

**BE22–1** Table Manufacturing purchases $35,000 of raw materials on account, and it incurs $30,000 of factory labor costs. Journalize the two transactions on March 31 assuming the labor costs are not paid until April.

*Journalize entries for accumulating costs.*
(SO 1)

**BE22–2** Data for Table Manufacturing are given in BE22–1. Supporting records show that (a) the Assembly Department used $14,000 of raw materials and $19,000 of the factory labor, and (b) the Finishing Department used the remainder. Journalize the assignment of the costs to the processing departments on March 31.

*Journalize the assignment of materials and labor costs.*
(SO 1)

**BE22–3** Factory labor data for Table Manufacturing are given in BE22–2. Manufacturing overhead is assigned to departments on the basis of 200% of labor costs. Journalize the assignment of overhead to the Assembly and Finishing Departments.

*Journalize the assignment of overhead costs.*
(SO 1)

*Compute physical units of production.*
(SO 3)

**BE22–4**   Maine Manufacturing Company has the following production data for selected months:

| Month | Beginning Work in Process | Units Started and Finished | Ending Work in Process Units | Ending Work in Process % Complete |
|-------|---------------------------|----------------------------|----------------|-------------|
| Jan. | –0– | 30,000 | 5,000 | 40% |
| March | –0– | 50,000 | 4,000 | 75 |
| July | –0– | 40,000 | 3,000 | 25 |

Compute the physical units for each month.

*Compute equivalent units of production.*
(SO 4)

**BE22–5**   Using the data in BE22–4, compute equivalent units of production for materials and conversion costs, assuming materials are entered at the beginning of the process.

*Compute unit costs of production.*
(SO 5)

**BE22–6**   In Caroline Company, total material costs are $36,000, and total conversion costs are $60,000. Equivalent units of production are materials 12,000 and conversion costs 10,000. Compute the unit costs for materials, conversion costs, and total manufacturing costs.

*Assign costs to units transferred out and in process.*
(SO 6)

**BE22–7**   Sota Company has the following production data for April: units started and finished 30,000, and ending work in process 5,000 units that are 100% complete for materials and 30% complete for conversion costs. If unit materials cost is $8 and unit conversion cost is $12, determine the costs to be assigned to the units transferred out and the units in ending work in process. The total costs to be assigned are $658,000.

*Prepare a partial production cost report.*
(SO 7)

**BE22–8**   Using the data in BE22–7, prepare the cost section of the production cost report for Sota Company.

*Compute unit costs in a second processing department.*
(SO 8)

**BE22–9**   Production costs chargeable to the Finishing Department in June in Madlock Company are materials $8,000, labor $20,000, overhead $18,000, and transferred in costs $52,000. Equivalent units of production are materials 20,000 and conversion costs 19,000. Compute the unit costs for materials and conversion costs.

*Assign costs in a second processing department.*
(SO 8)

**BE22–10**   Data for Madlock Company are given in BE22–9. Production records indicate that 18,000 units were started and finished, and 2,000 units in ending work in process were 50% completed. Show the assignment of costs to the units transferred out and in process.

*Compute overhead rates for activities.*
(SO 11)

**\*BE22–11**   Darlinda Company identifies three activities in its manufacturing process: machine setups, machining, and inspections. Estimated annual overhead cost for each activity is $150,000, $250,000, and $70,000, respectively. The cost driver for each activity and the expected annual usage are: number of setups 1,000, machine hours 25,000, and number of inspections 1,400. Compute the overhead rate for each activity.

# EXERCISES

*Compute physical units and equivalent units of production.*
(SO 3, 4)

**E22–1**   In Kam Company, materials are entered at the beginning of each process. Work in process inventories, with the percentage of work done on conversion costs, and production data for its Sterilizing Department in selected months during 1996 are as follows:

| Month | Beginning Work in Process Units | Beginning Work in Process Conversion Cost % | Units Started and Finished | Ending Work in Process Units | Ending Work in Process Conversion Cost % |
|-------|-------|------|------|------|------|
| January | –0– | — | 8,000 | 1,000 | 60 |
| March | –0– | — | 10,000 | 3,000 | 30 |
| May | –0– | — | 15,000 | 2,500 | 80 |
| July | –0– | — | 9,000 | 1,500 | 40 |

**Instructions**
(a) Compute the physical units for January and May.
(b) Compute the equivalent units of production for (1) materials and (2) conversion costs for each month.

**E22-2** The Cutting Department of Bjerg Manufacturing has the following production and cost data for July:

| Production | Costs | |
|---|---|---|
| 1. Started and finished 8,000 units. | Beginning work in process | $ –0– |
| 2. Started 1,000 units that are 30% | Materials | 45,000 |
| completed at July 31. | Labor | 14,000 |
| | Manufacturing overhead | 19,200 |

Materials are entered at the beginning of the process. Conversion costs are incurred uniformly during the process.

**Instructions**
(a) Determine the equivalent units of production for (1) materials and (2) conversion costs.
(b) Compute unit costs and show the assignment of manufacturing costs to units transferred out and in work in process.

**E22-3** The Sanding Department of Copa Furniture Company has the following production and manufacturing cost data for March 1996:

Production: 12,000 units started and finished; 4,000 units started that are 100% completed as to materials and 25% completed as to conversion costs.

Manufacturing costs: Materials $48,000; labor $30,000; overhead $48,000.

**Instructions**
Prepare a production cost report.

**E22-4** The Smelting Department of Battle Manufacturing Company has the following production and cost data for November:

Production: Beginning work in process 2,000 units that are 100% complete as to materials and 20% complete as to conversion costs; units started and finished 9,000 units; and ending work in process 1,000 units that are 100% complete as to materials and 40% complete as to conversion costs.

Manufacturing costs: Work in process, November 1, $15,200; materials added $50,000; labor and overhead $143,000.

**Instructions**
(a) Compute the equivalent units of production for (1) materials and (2) conversion costs for the month of November.
(b) Compute the unit costs for the month.
(c) Determine the costs to be assigned to the units transferred out and in process.

**E22-5** Larry Lair has recently been promoted to production manager, and so he has just started to receive various managerial reports. One of the reports he has received is the production cost report that you prepared. It showed that his department had 1,500 equivalent units in ending inventory. His department has had a history of not keeping enough inventory on hand to meet demand. He has come to you, very angry, and wants to know why you credited him with only 1,500 units when he knows he had at least twice that many on hand.

**Instructions**
▭▭▭▷ Explain to him why his production cost report showed only 1,500 equivalent units in ending inventory. Write an informal memo. Be kind and explain very clearly why he is mistaken.

**E22-6** The ledger of Tombert Company has the following work in process account:

**Work in Process—Painting**

| | | | | | |
|---|---|---|---|---|---|
| 5/1 | Balance | 3,680 | 5/31 | Transferred out | ? |
| 5/31 | Materials | 4,400 | | | |
| 5/31 | Labor | 1,200 | | | |
| 5/31 | Overhead | 1,400 | | | |
| 5/31 | Balance | ? | | | |

Production records show that there were 800 units in the beginning inventory, 30% complete, 1,100 units started, and 1,300 units transferred out. The units in ending inventory were 40% complete. Materials are entered at the beginning of the painting process.

**Instructions**
Answer the following questions:

(a) How many units are in process at May 31?
(b) What is the unit materials cost for May?
(c) What is the unit conversion cost for May?
(d) What is the total cost of units started in April and completed in May?
(e) What is the total cost of units started and finished in May?
(f) What is the cost of the May 31 inventory?

*Journalize transactions for two processes.*
*(SO 8)*

**E22–7**   Kojak Manufacturing Company has two production departments: Cutting and Assembly. July 1 inventories are Raw Materials $4,200, Work in Process—Cutting $2,900, Work in Process—Assembly $10,600, and Finished Goods $31,000. During July, the following transactions occurred:

1. Purchased $37,600 of raw materials on account.
2. Incurred $56,000 of factory labor. (Credit Wages Payable.)
3. Incurred $70,000 of manufacturing overhead; $42,000 was paid and the remainder is unpaid.
4. Requisitioned materials for Cutting $15,700 and Assembly $8,900.
5. Used factory labor for Cutting $29,000 and Assembly $27,000.
6. Applied overhead at the rate of $20 per machine hour. Machine hours were Cutting 1,740 and Assembly 1,620.
7. Transferred goods costing $67,700 from the Cutting Department to the Assembly Department.
8. Transferred goods costing $134,900 from Assembly to Finished Goods.
9. Sold goods costing $135,000 for $200,000 on account.

**Instructions**
Journalize the transactions. (Omit explanations.)

*Compute equivalent units, unit costs, and costs assigned in a second process.*
*(SO 8)*

**E22–8**   The Polishing Department of Medina Manufacturing Company has the following production and manufacturing cost data for September. Materials are entered at the beginning of the process.

Production: Beginning inventory 2,600 units that are 100% complete as to materials and 30% complete as to conversion costs; units started that came from a prior department 12,000; ending inventory of 3,000 units 10% complete as to conversion costs.

Manufacturing costs: Beginning inventory costs of $63,180; costs transferred into Polishing during the month, $120,000; materials costs added in Polishing during the month, $48,000; labor and overhead applied in Polishing during the month, $100,080 and $300,240, respectively.

**Instructions**

(a) Compute the equivalent units of production for materials and conversion costs for the month of September.
(b) Compute the unit costs for materials and conversion costs for the month.
(c) Determine the costs to be assigned to the units transferred out and in process.

*Prepare a production cost report for a second process.*
*(SO 8)*

**E22–9**   The Welding Department of Tomlin Manufacturing Company has the following production and manufacturing cost data for February 1996. All materials are added at the beginning of the process.

| Manufacturing Costs | | Production Data | |
|---|---|---|---|
| Beginning work in process | $ 32,175 | Beginning work in process | 15,000 units |
| Costs transferred in | 75,000 | | 1/10 complete |
| Materials | 45,000 | Units transferred out | 49,000 |
| Labor | 35,100 | Units transferred in | 60,000 |
| Overhead | 70,300 | Ending work in process | 26,000 |
| | | | 1/5 complete |

**Instructions**
Prepare a production cost report for the Welding Department for the month of February.

**E22–10** MaryLou Company manufactures pizza sauce through two production departments: Cooking and Canning. In each process, materials and conversion costs are incurred evenly throughout the process. For the month of April, the work in process accounts show the following debits:

*Journalize transactions and answer questions for two processes.*
(SO 1, 6, 8)

|  | Cooking | Canning |
|---|---|---|
| Beginning work in process | $   –0– | $ 4,000 |
| Materials | 19,000 | 6,000 |
| Labor | 8,500 | 5,000 |
| Overhead | 29,500 | 21,800 |
| Costs transferred in |  | 54,000 |

**Instructions**
(a) Journalize the April transactions.
(b) If 110,000 units were started into production in Cooking and 100,000 units were transferred to Canning, what is the cost per unit of the goods transferred out?
(c) What is the total materials cost for the Canning Department in April?

**\*E22–11** Allied Instrument Inc. manufactures two products: missile range instruments and space pressure gauges. During January, 50 range instruments and 300 pressure gauges were produced, and overhead costs of $70,000 were incurred. An analysis of overhead costs reveals the following activities:

*Compute overhead rates and assign overhead using ABC.*
(SO 11)

| Activity | Cost Driver | Total Cost |
|---|---|---|
| 1. Materials handling | Number of requisitions | $25,000 |
| 2. Machine setups | Number of setups | 27,000 |
| 3. Quality inspections | Number of inspections | 18,000 |

The cost driver volume for each product was as follows:

| Cost Driver | Instruments | Gauges | Total |
|---|---|---|---|
| Number of requisitions | 400 | 600 | 1,000 |
| Number of setups | 150 | 300 | 450 |
| Number of inspections | 150 | 450 | 600 |

**Instructions**
(a) Determine the overhead rate for each activity.
(b) Assign the manufacturing overhead costs for January to the two products using activity-based costing.
(c) ▭▭▭▭► Write a memorandum to the president of Allied Instrument, explaining the benefits of activity-based costing.

# PROBLEMS
••••••••••••••••••••••••••••••••••••••••••••••••••••••••••••••••••••••

**P22–1** Aquatic Corporation manufactures water skis through two processes: Molding and Packaging. In the Molding Department fiber glass is heated and shaped into the form of a ski. In the Packaging Department, the skis are placed in cartons and sent to the finished goods warehouse. Materials are entered at the beginning of both processes. Labor and manufacturing overhead are incurred uniformly throughout each process. Production and cost data for the Molding Department for January 1996 are presented below.

*Complete end-of-period procedures for first process.*
(SO 3, 4, 5, 6, 7)

| Production Data | January |
|---|---|
| Beginning work in process units | –0– |
| Units started into production | 42,500 |
| Ending work in process units | 2,500 |
| Percent complete—ending inventory | 40% |

**Cost Data**

| | |
|---|---:|
| Materials | $595,000 |
| Labor | 96,000 |
| Overhead | 232,000 |
| Total | $923,000 |

**Instructions**

(a) Compute the physical units of production.

(b) Determine the equivalent units of production for materials and conversion costs.

(c) Compute the unit costs of production.

(d) Determine the costs to be assigned to the units transferred out and in process.

(e) Prepare a production cost report for the Molding Department for the month of January.

*Complete end-of-period procedures for first process.*
*(SO 3, 4, 5, 6, 7)*

**P22–2**  Freedo Corporation manufactures in separate processes refrigerators and freezers for homes. In each process, materials are entered at the beginning and conversion costs are incurred uniformly. Production and cost data for the first process in making two products in two different manufacturing plants are as follows:

| | **Stamping Department** | |
|---|:---:|:---:|
| | **Plant A** | **Plant B** |
| **Production Data—June** | **R12 Refrigerators** | **F24 Freezers** |
| Work in process units, June 1 | –0– | –0– |
| Units started into production | 21,000 | 20,000 |
| Work in process units, June 30 | 4,000 | 2,500 |
| Work in process percent complete | 75 | 60 |

| | | |
|---|:---:|:---:|
| **Cost Data—June** | | |
| Work in process, June 1 | $    –0– | $    –0– |
| Materials | 840,000 | 760,000 |
| Labor | 180,000 | 221,000 |
| Overhead | 420,000 | 292,000 |
| Total | $1,440,000 | $1,273,000 |

**Instructions**

(a) For each plant:

(1) Compute the physical units of production.

(2) Compute equivalent units of production for materials and for conversion costs.

(3) Determine the unit costs of production.

(4) Show the assignment of costs to units transferred out and in process.

(b) Prepare the production cost report for Plant A for June 1996.

*Journalize and post transactions and show assignment of costs.*
*(SO 1, 3, 4, 5, 6)*

**P22–3**  Pepi Company manufactures a nutrient, Everlife, through two manufacturing processes: Blending and Packaging. All materials are entered at the beginning of each process. On August 1, 1996, inventories consisted of Raw Materials $5,000, Work in Process—Blending $0, Work in Process—Packaging $3,945, and Finished Goods $7,500. The beginning inventory for Packaging consisted of 500 units, two-fifths complete as to conversion costs. During August, 9,000 units were started into production in Blending and the following transactions were completed:

1. Purchased $25,000 of raw materials on account.

2. Issued raw materials for production: Blending $16,200 and Packaging $3,690.

3. Incurred labor costs of $17,880.

4. Used factory labor: Blending $13,320 and Packaging $4,560.

5. Incurred $36,500 of manufacturing overhead on account.

6. Applied manufacturing overhead at the rate of $30 per machine hour. Machine hours were Blending 900 and Packaging 300.

7. Transferred 8,200 units from Blending to Packaging at a cost of $54,120. Unfinished units in Blending are 1/4 complete as to conversion costs.

8. Transferred 8,600 units from Packaging to Finished Goods at a cost of $74,490. Unfinished units in the Packaging Department are 3/4 complete as to conversion costs.
9. Sold goods costing $62,000 for $90,000 on account.

**Instructions**
(a) Journalize the August transactions.
(b) Post the entries to the work in process accounts.
(c) Compute the costs assigned to units transferred out and in process in Blending.

**P22–4** Hwang Company has several processing departments. Costs charged to the Assembly Department for October 1996 totaled $1,306,000 as follows:

*Assign costs and prepare production cost report with transferred-in costs.*
(SC 8)

| | | | |
|---|---|---|---|
| Work in process inventory, October 1 | $ 67,500 | Overhead | $121,000 |
| Materials added | 124,500 | Costs transferred in | 913,000 |
| Labor | 80,000 | | |

Production records show that 25,000 units were in beginning work in process 40% complete, 415,000 units were transferred in, and 35,000 units were in ending work in process 20% complete. Materials are entered at the beginning of each process.

**Instructions**
(a) Determine the equivalent units of production and the unit costs for the Assembly Department.
(b) Determine the assignment of costs to goods transferred in and in process.
(c) Prepare a production cost report for the Assembly Department.

**P22–5** The work in process accounts of Crispy Cereal Co. that pertain to the making of "Fast Pops," a new breakfast cereal, during the month of July are presented below.

*Determine equivalent units and unit costs and assign costs for processes with transferred-in costs.*
(SC 8)

**Work in Process—Mixing**

| | | | | | | |
|---|---|---|---|---|---|---|
| July 31 | Materials | 63,000 | | July 31 | Transferred out | 100,000 |
| 31 | Labor | 17,000 | | | | |
| 31 | Overhead | 23,800 | | | | |

**Work in Process—Baking**

| | | | | | | |
|---|---|---|---|---|---|---|
| July 1 | Inventory | 2,200 | | July 31 | Transferred out | 122,400 |
| 31 | Labor | 4,000 | | | | |
| 31 | Overhead | 16,200 | | | | |
| 31 | Transferred in | 100,000 | | | | |

**Work in Process—Packaging**

| | | | | | | |
|---|---|---|---|---|---|---|
| July 1 | Inventory | 7,040 | | July 31 | To Finished Goods | ? |
| 31 | Materials | 40,800 | | | | |
| 31 | Labor | 14,000 | | | | |
| 31 | Overhead | 27,400 | | | | |
| 31 | Transferred in | 122,400 | | | | |

Production and inventory data for the Baking and Packaging Departments are as follows:

| | Inventory, July 1 | | Inventory, July 31 | | Units |
|---|---|---|---|---|---|
| Department | Units | % Complete | Units | % Complete | Transferred Out |
| Baking | 4,000 | 50 | –0– | — | 204,000 |
| Packaging | 8,000 | 40 | 6,000 | 70 | 206,000 |

All materials are entered at the beginning of each process.

**Instructions**
For the Baking and Packaging Departments:
(a) Determine the equivalent units of production for materials and conversion costs.
(b) Determine the unit cost of materials, the unit conversion costs, and the total manufacturing cost per equivalent unit.
(c) Show the assignment of costs to units transferred out and in process.

*Answer questions relating to percentage of completion, unit costs, and costs assigned.*
(SO 4, 5, 6, 8)

**P22–6**   Zion Furniture Company manufactures living room furniture through two departments: Framing and Upholstering. Materials are entered at the beginning of each process. For May, the following cost data are obtained from the two work in process accounts.

|  | Framing | Upholstering |
|---|---|---|
| Work in process, May 1 | $–0– | $   ? |
| Materials | 360,000 | ? |
| Conversion costs | 270,000 | 330,000 |
| Costs transferred in | –0– | 550,000 |
| Costs transferred out | 550,000 | ? |
| Work in process, May 31 | 80,000 | ? |

**Instructions**

Answer the following questions:

(a) If 3,000 sofas were started into production on May 1 and 2,500 sofas were transferred to Upholstering, what was the unit cost of materials for May in the Framing Department?

(b) Using the data in (a) above, what was the per unit conversion cost of the sofas transferred to Upholstering?

(c) Continuing the assumptions in (a) above, what is the percentage of completion of the units in process at May 31 in the Framing Department?

(d) If the materials cost per unit in Upholstering is $350, what was the cost of materials added in Upholstering in May?

(e) If the conversion cost per unit in Upholstering is $150, what are the equivalent units of conversion costs for May?

(f) Assuming there is no beginning work in process in Upholstering, what is the cost of the work in process at May 31 if 800 units are 25% completed?

(g) Assuming the per unit conversion costs for Upholstering in (d) and (e), what is the percentage of completion of 1,000 units of ending work in process inventory if the total costs assigned are $380,000?

(h) If unit costs were the same in April as in May, what is the cost of the May 1 work in process inventory in Upholstering if there are 1,000 units 60% complete?

# ALTERNATE PROBLEMS

• • • • • • • • • • • • • • • • • • • • • • • • • • • • • • • • • • • • • • • • • • • • • • • • • • • • • • • • • • • • • • • • • • •

*Complete end-of-period procedures for first process.*
(SO 3, 4, 5, 6, 7)

**P22–1A**   Bollmor Company manufactures bowling balls through two processes: Molding and Packaging. In the Molding Department, the urethane, rubber, plastics, and other materials are molded into bowling balls. In the Packaging Department, the balls are placed in cartons and sent to the finished goods warehouse. All materials are entered at the beginning of each process. Labor and manufacturing overhead are incurred uniformly throughout each process. Production and cost data for the Molding Department during June 1996 are presented below.

| Production Data | June |
|---|---|
| Beginning work in process units | –0– |
| Units started into production | 22,000 |
| Ending work in process units | 2,000 |
| Percent complete—ending inventory | 45% |

| Cost Data | |
|---|---|
| Materials | $198,000 |
| Labor | 50,400 |
| Overhead | 116,800 |
| Total | $365,200 |

**Instructions**

(a) Prepare a schedule showing physical units of production.

(b) Determine the equivalent units of production for materials and conversion costs.

(c) Compute the unit costs of production.

(d) Determine the costs to be assigned to the units transferred and in process for June.

(e) Prepare a production cost report for the Molding Department for the month of June only.

**P22–2A** Perfecto Industries Inc. manufactures in separate processes furniture for homes. In each process, materials are entered at the beginning, and conversion costs are incurred uniformly. Production and cost data for the first process in making two products in two different manufacturing plants are as follows:

*Complete end-of-period procedures for first process.*
*(SO 3, 4, 5, 6, 7)*

|  | **Cutting Department** | |
|---|---|---|
| | **Plant 1** | **Plant 2** |
| **Production Data—July** | **T12-Tables** | **C10-Chairs** |
| Work in process units, July 1 | –0– | –0– |
| Units started into production | 20,000 | 18,000 |
| Work in process units, July 31 | 1,000 | 500 |
| Work in process percent complete | 60 | 80 |
| **Cost Data—July** | | |
| Work in process, July 1 | $ –0– | $ –0– |
| Materials | 320,000 | 270,000 |
| Labor | 180,000 | 146,000 |
| Overhead | 94,400 | 86,700 |
| Total | $594,400 | $502,700 |

**Instructions**

(a) For each plant:
(1) Compute the physical units of production.
(2) Compute equivalent units of production for materials and for conversion costs.
(3) Determine the unit costs of production.
(4) Show the assignment of costs to units transferred out and in process.

(b) Prepare the production cost report for Plant 1 for July 1996.

**P22–3A** Valu Company manufactures its product, Vitadrink, through two manufacturing processes: Mixing and Packaging. All materials are entered at the beginning of each process. On October 1, 1997, inventories consisted of Raw Materials $26,000, Work in Process—Mixing $0, Work in Process—Packaging $250,000, and Finished Goods $89,000. The beginning inventory for Packaging consisted of 10,000 units that were 50% complete as to conversion costs. During October, 50,000 units were started into production in the Mixing Department and the following transactions were completed:

*Journalize and post transactions and show assignment of costs.*
*(SO 1, 3, 4, 5, 6)*

1. Purchased $300,000 of raw materials on account.
2. Issued raw materials for production: Mixing $200,000 and Packaging $45,000.
3. Incurred labor costs of $238,900.
4. Used factory labor: Mixing $182,500 and Packaging $56,400.
5. Incurred $820,000 of manufacturing overhead on account.
6. Applied indirect manufacturing overhead on the basis of $25 per machine hour. Machine hours were 26,000 in Mixing and 6,600 in Packaging.
7. Transferred 45,000 units from Mixing to Packaging at a cost of $990,000. Unfinished units in Mixing are 25% complete as to conversion costs.
8. Transferred 53,000 units from Packaging to Finished Goods at a cost of $1,455,000. Units unfinished in the Packaging Department are 60% complete as to conversion costs.
9. Sold goods costing $1,460,000 for $2,100,000 on account.

**Instructions**

(a) Journalize the October transactions.
(b) Post the entries to the work in process accounts.
(c) Compute the costs assigned to units transferred out and in process in Mixing.

*Assign costs and prepare
production cost report with
transferred in costs.*
(SO 8)

**P22–4A**   Caproni Company has several processing departments. Costs charged to the Assembly Department for November 1997 totaled $1,999,500 as follows:

| | | | |
|---|---|---|---|
| Inventory, November 1 | $ 75,300 | Overhead | $ 330,880 |
| Materials added | 160,000 | Costs transferred in | 1,312,000 |
| Labor | 121,320 | | |

Production records show that 30,000 units were in beginning work in process 30% complete, 640,000 units were transferred in, and 25,000 units were in ending work in process 40% complete. Materials are entered at the beginning of each process.

**Instructions**
- (a) Determine the equivalent units of production and the units costs for the Assembly Department.
- (b) Determine the assignment of costs to goods transferred out and in process.
- (c) Prepare a production cost report for the Assembly Department.

*Determine equivalent units
and unit costs and assign costs
for processes with transferred
in costs.*
(SO 8)

**P22–5A**   The work in process accounts of Crunchy Cookie Co. that pertain to the making of "Tastee Snacks," a new cookie, during the month of July are presented below.

### Work in Process—Mixing

| | | | | | |
|---|---|---|---|---|---|
| July 31 | Materials | 50,000 | July 31 | Transferred out | 120,000 |
| 31 | Labor | 18,800 | | | |
| 31 | Overhead | 54,400 | | | |

### Work in Process—Baking

| | | | | | |
|---|---|---|---|---|---|
| July 1 | Inventory | 2,700 | July 31 | Transferred out | 183,600 |
| 31 | Labor | 10,600 | | | |
| 31 | Overhead | 50,300 | | | |
| 31 | Transferred in | 120,000 | | | |

### Work in Process—Packaging

| | | | | | |
|---|---|---|---|---|---|
| July 1 | Inventory | 5,370 | July 31 | To Finished Goods | ? |
| 31 | Materials | 24,480 | | | |
| 31 | Labor | 8,740 | | | |
| 31 | Overhead | 28,370 | | | |
| 31 | Transferred in | 183,600 | | | |

Production and inventory data for the Baking and Packaging Departments are as follows:

| | Inventory, July 1 | | Inventory, July 31 | | Units |
|---|---|---|---|---|---|
| Department | Units | % Complete | Units | % Complete | Transferred Out |
| Baking | 24,000 | 25 | –0– | — | 1,224,000 |
| Packaging | 30,000 | 30 | 40,000 | 80 | 1,214,000 |

All materials are entered at the beginning of a process.

**Instructions**
For the Baking and Packaging Departments:

- (a) Determine the equivalent units of production for (1) materials and (2) conversion costs.
- (b) Determine (1) the unit cost of materials, (2) the unit conversion costs, and (3) the total manufacturing cost per equivalent unit.
- (c) Show the assignment of costs to units transferred out and in process.

*Assign overhead to products
using ABC.*
(SO 11)

**\*P22–6A**   Elite Electronics manufactures two large-screen television models: the Royale which sells for $1,500, and a new model, the Majestic, which sells for $1,200. The production cost per unit for each model in 1996 was as follows:

|  | Royale | Majestic |
|---|---|---|
| Direct materials | $ 700 | $420 |
| Direct labor ($20 per hour) | 100 | 80 |
| Manufacturing overhead ($40 per DLH) | 200 | 160 |
| Total per unit cost | $1,000 | $660 |

In 1996, Elite manufactured 30,000 units of the Royale and 10,000 units of the Majestic. The overhead rate of $40 per direct labor hour was determined by dividing total expected manufacturing overhead of $7,600,000 by the total direct labor hours (190,000) for the two models.

The gross profit on the models were: Royale $500 ($1,500 − $1,000) and Majestic $540 ($1,200 − $660). Because of this difference, management is considering phasing out the Royale model and increasing the production of the Majestic model.

Before finalizing its decision, management asks the controller of Elite to prepare an analysis using activity-based costing. The controller accumulates the following information about overhead for the year ended December 31, 1996:

| Activity | Cost Driver | Total Cost | Cost Driver Volume | Overhead Rate |
|---|---|---|---|---|
| Purchase orders | Number of orders | $1,200,000 | 30,000 | $40 |
| Machine setups | Number of setups | 900,000 | 15,000 | 60 |
| Machining | Machine hours | 4,800,000 | 160,000 | 30 |
| Quality control | Number of inspections | 700,000 | 35,000 | 20 |

The cost driver volume for each product was:

| Cost Driver | Royale | Majestic | Total |
|---|---|---|---|
| Purchase orders | 10,000 | 20,000 | 30,000 |
| Machine setups | 5,000 | 10,000 | 15,000 |
| Machine hours | 110,000 | 50,000 | 160,000 |
| Inspections | 10,000 | 25,000 | 35,000 |

**Instructions**
(a) Assign the total 1996 manufacturing overhead costs to the two products using activity-based costing (ABC).
(b) What was the cost per unit and gross profit of each model using ABC costing?
(c) Are management's future plans for the two models sound?

# *B*roadening *Your Perspective*

## DECISION CASE
..................................................................................

West Beach Company manufactures suntan lotion, called Surtan, in 11-ounce plastic bottles. Surtan is sold in a competitive market. As a result, management is very cost-conscious. Surtan is manufactured through two processes: mixing and filling. Materials are entered at the beginning of each process and labor and manufacturing overhead occur uniformly throughout each process. Unit costs are based on the cost per gallon of Surtan using FIFO costing.

On June 30, 1996, Sara Simmons, the chief accountant for the past 20 years, opted to take early retirement. Her replacement, Joe Jacobs, had extensive accounting experience with motels in the area but only limited contact with manufacturing accounting.

During July, Joe correctly accumulated the following production quantity and cost data for the Mixing Department.

Production quantities: Work in process, July 1, 8,000 gallons 75% complete; started into production 100,000 gallons; work in process, July 31, 5,000 gallons 20% complete.

Production costs: Beginning work in process $88,000; incurred in July: materials $500,000, conversion costs $784,000.

Joe then prepared a production cost report on the basis of physical units involved. His report showed a production cost of $14.44 per gallon of Surtan. The management of West Beach was shocked at the high unit cost. The president comes to you, as Sara's top assistant, to review Joe's report and prepare a correct report if necessary.

*Instructions*
  (a) Show how Joe arrived at the unit cost of $14.44 per gallon of Surtan.
  (b) What error(s) did Joe make in preparing his production cost report?
  (c) Prepare a correct production cost report for July.

# COMMUNICATION ACTIVITY

Catherine Harper was a good friend of yours in high school and is from your home town. While you chose to major in accounting when you both went away to college, she majored in marketing and management. You have recently been promoted to accounting manager for the Snack Foods Division of Clark Enterprises, and your friend was promoted to regional sales manager for the same division of Clark. Catherine recently telephoned you. She explained that she was familiar with job cost sheets, which had been used by the Special Projects division where she had formerly worked. She was, however, very uncomfortable with the production cost reports prepared by your division. She faxed you a list of her particular questions. These included the following:

  1. Since Clark occasionally prepares snack foods for special orders in the Snack Foods Divison, why don't we track costs of the orders separately?
  2. What is an equivalent unit?
  3. Why am I getting four production cost reports? Isn't there only one Work in Process account?

*Instructions*
Prepare a memorandum to Catherine. Answer her questions, and include any additional information you think would be helpful. You may write informally, but be careful to use proper grammar and punctuation.

# GROUP ACTIVITY

Logan Company manufactures bird houses in four departments. The first department is Sawing. It is responsible for cutting the pieces of lumber to be used to manufacture the houses. The second department is Construction. In the Construction Department the houses are nailed together; no other materials are added in the Construction Department. The third department is Painting. In the Painting Department, each house receives a primer and then two coats of weather-resistant paint. The fourth and last department is Finishing. Workers in the Finishing Department add trim and pack the bird houses for shipment. Data for March follow:

| | |
|---|---|
| Started by Sawing: | 10,000 units |
| Transferred to Construction | 11,000 |
| Transferred to Painting | 12,000 |
| Transferred to Finishing | 10,000 |
| Transferred to Finished Goods warehouse | 11,000 |

Each department had 2,000 bird houses on hand at the beginning of the month, which were 25% complete as to conversion costs. Each department's ending inventory was 50% complete as to conversion costs.

*Instructions*

In groups of four to five people each:
Compute the physical units for each department, or for only one of the departments, as your instructor directs. Match your results with those of other groups in the class.

# ETHICS CASE

R. B. Robin Company manufactures a high-tech component that passes through two production processing departments, Molding and Assembly. Department managers are partially compensated on the basis of units of products completed and transferred out relative to units of product put into production. This was intended as encouragement to be efficient and to minimize waste.

Bob Guymer is the department head in the Molding Department and Wayne Dermatolis is his quality control inspector. During the month of June, Bob had three new employees who were not yet technically skilled. As a result, many of the units produced in June had minor molding defects. In order to maintain the department's normal high rate of completion, Bob told Wayne to pass through inspection and on to the Assembly Department all units that had defects nondetectable to the human eye. "Company and industry tolerances on this product are too high anyway," says Bob. "Less than 2% of the units we produce are subjected in the market to the stress tolerance we've designed into them. The odds of those 2% being any of this month's units are even less. Anyway, we're saving the company money."

*Instructions*

(a) Who are the potential stakeholders involved in this situation?
(b) What alternatives does Wayne have in this situation? What might the company do to prevent this from occurring?

# CRITICAL THINKING
## ► *A Real-World Focus: General Microwave Corp.*

*General Microwave Corp. is engaged primarily in the design, development, manufacture, and marketing of microwave, electronic, and fiber optic test equipment, components, and subsystems. A substantial portion of the company's microwave product is sold to manufacturers and users of microwave systems and equipment for applications in the defense electronics industry.*

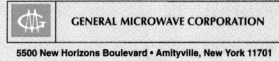

GENERAL MICROWAVE CORPORATION
5500 New Horizons Boulevard • Amityville, New York 11701

General Microwave Corp. reports the following information in one of the notes to its financial statements:

Work in process inventory reflects all accumulated production costs, which are comprised of direct production costs and overhead, reduced by amounts attributable to units delivered. Work in process inventory is reduced to its estimated net realizable value by a charge to cost of sales in the period [in which] excess costs are identified. Raw materials and finished goods inventories are reflected at the lower of cost or market, computed on the first-in, first-out (FIFO) method.

*Instructions*

(a) What types of manufacturing costs are accumulated in the work in process inventory account?
(b) What types of information must General Microwave have to be able to compute equivalent units of production?
(c) How does General Microwave assign costs to the units transferred out of work in process that are completed?

---

*Answers to Self-Study Questions*

1. b  2. d  3. a  4. b  5. a  6. b  7. b  8. c  9. d  10. c  11. b

● ● ● ● ● ● ▶

## Concepts for Review

# Salon Restyles for Larger Profits

PITTSBURGH, Pa. — In manufacturing companies, managers tend to worry a lot. Is the price high enough to make a profit, yet low enough to compete? Are costs low enough to make a profit, yet high enough to ensure quality? Is volume high enough to cover costs and make a profit? At what point do we break even on costs and revenues? Are we running out of capacity?

These questions also apply to service companies. Take the example of Henri's Salon, which offers a wide range of hair, nail, and retail services and products. Henri could not understand why he earned only a small profit last year. He had instituted what he thought were some revenue-enhancing activities and, at the same time, some cost-cutting measures. Unfortunately they did not seem to be working.

Henri consulted an expert, who advised the following: Know the behavior of your costs. You will find that some will remain the same regardless of your revenues, while others will change. Often, the costs that change are easier to control.

You should also analyze your services to determine which are the more profitable. This can be done by identifying the specific costs that are directly associated with each type of service revenue. For example, you may find that hair styling is more profitable than hair cutting. When you have determined the most profitable services, encourage your customers to use those services, through advertising and special-day discount pricing. Other-

wise, look carefully at each cost to determine whether it can be reduced. For example, Henri determined that his cost per towel was $0.15 with an outside service. He was able to reduce that to $0.10 per towel by laundering towels in-house. Henri's expert also told him to stop paying hair stylists a fixed salary and put them on a commission basis. Some hair stylists were taking too long and were more interested in tip income than doing an efficient job. ◀

# COST-VOLUME-PROFIT RELATIONSHIPS

As the opening story indicates, management must understand how costs respond to changes in sales volume and the effect of the interaction of costs and revenues on profits. A prerequisite to understanding cost-volume-profit (CVP) relationships is knowledge of the behavior of costs. In this chapter, we first explain the considerations involved in cost behavior analysis. Then we discuss and illustrate CVP analysis and variable costing. The content and organization of the chapter are as follows:

# Cost Behavior Analysis

**Cost behavior analysis** is the study of how specific costs respond to changes in the level of activity within a company. As you might expect, some costs change and others remain the same. A knowledge of cost behavior helps management plan business operations and decide between alternative courses of action. Cost behavior analysis applies to all types of entities and to segments, such as divisions and departments, as the story about Henri's Salon indicates.

The starting point in cost behavior analysis is measuring the key activities in the company's business. Activity levels may be expressed in terms of sales dollars (in a retail company), miles driven (in a trucking company), room occupancy (in a hotel), or number of customers called on (by a salesperson). Many companies use more than one measurement base. A manufacturing company, for example, may use direct labor hours or units of output for manufacturing costs and sales revenue or units sold for selling expenses.

For an activity level to be useful in cost behavior analysis, there should be correlation between changes in the level or volume of activity and changes in costs. The activity level selected is referred to as the activity (or volume) index. The **activity index** identifies the activity that causes changes in the behavior of costs. Once an appropriate activity index is selected, it is possible to classify the behavior of costs in response to changes in activity levels into three categories: variable, fixed, or mixed.

## Variable Costs

Variable costs are costs that vary **in total** directly and proportionately with changes in the activity level. If the level increases 10%, total variable costs will increase 10%. If the level of activity decreases by 25%, variable costs will be reduced 25%. Examples of variable costs include direct materials and direct labor in a manufacturing company; cost of goods sold, sales commissions, and freight-out in a merchandising company; and gasoline in airline and trucking companies. A variable cost may also be defined as a cost that **remains the same per unit at every level of activity**.

To illustrate the behavior of a variable cost, assume that Damon Company manufactures radios that contain a $10 digital clock. The activity index is the number of radios produced. For each radio manufactured, the total cost of the clocks increases by $10. As illustrated in part (a) of Illustration 23-1, total cost of the clocks will be $20,000 if 2,000 radios are manufactured, and $100,000 when 10,000 radios are produced. The digital clocks can also be used to show that a variable cost remains the same per unit as the level of activity changes. As shown in part (b) of Illustration 23-1, the unit cost of $10 for the clocks is the same whether 2,000 or 10,000 radios are produced.

**STUDY OBJECTIVE**

·········· ▼ ··········

*Distinguish between variable and fixed costs.*

**Illustration 23-1**

*Behavior of total and unit variable costs*

Companies that rely heavily on labor to manufacture a product or to render a service are likely to have many variable costs. In contrast, companies that use a high proportion of machinery and equipment in producing revenue, such as public utilities, may have few variable costs.

## Fixed Costs

Fixed costs are costs that **remain the same in total** regardless of changes in the activity level. Examples include property taxes, insurance, rent, supervisory salaries, and depreciation on buildings and equipment. Because fixed costs remain constant in total as activity changes, it follows that **fixed costs per unit vary inversely with activity. As volume increases, unit cost declines and vice versa.**

To illustrate the behavior of fixed costs, assume that Damon Company leases all of its productive facilities at a cost of $10,000 per month. Total fixed costs of the facilities will remain constant at every level of activity, as shown in part (a) of Illustration 23-2. However, on a per unit basis, the cost of rent will decline as activity increases, as shown in part (b) of Illustration 23-2. At 2,000 units, the unit cost is $5 ($10,000 ÷ 2,000); when 10,000 radios are produced, the unit cost is only $1 ($10,000 ÷ 10,000).

**Illustration 23-2**

*Behavior of total and unit fixed costs*

The trend in many manufacturing companies is to have more fixed costs and fewer variable costs. This development results from increased use of automation and less use of employees. As a result, depreciation and lease charges (fixed costs) increase whereas direct labor costs (variable costs) decrease.

## Relevant Range

**STUDY OBJECTIVE**
................**2**................

*Explain the meaning and importance of the relevant range.*

In Illustrations 23-1 and 23-2, straight lines were drawn throughout the entire activity index for total variable costs and total fixed costs. In essence, the assumption was made that the costs were **linear**. It is now necessary to ask: Is the straight-line relationship realistic? Can the linear assumption produce useful data for CVP analysis?

In most business situations, a straight-line relationship **does not exist** for variable costs throughout the entire range of activity. At abnormally low levels of activity, it may be impossible to be cost efficient, since the scale of operations may not allow the company to obtain quantity discounts in the purchase of raw materials or use specialization of labor. In contrast, at abnormally high levels of activity, labor costs may increase sharply because of overtime pay, and materials costs may jump significantly because of excess spoilage caused by worker fatigue. Consequently, in the real world, the relationship between the behavior of a variable cost and changes in the activity level is often **curvilinear**, as shown in part (a) of Illustration 23-3.

Total fixed costs also do not have a straight-line relationship over the entire range of activity. While some fixed costs will not change, it is possible for management to change other fixed costs. The behavior of total fixed costs through all levels of activity is shown in part (b) of Illustration 23-3.

For most companies, operating at almost zero or at 100% capacity is the exception rather than the rule. Instead, companies often operate over a somewhat

**Illustration 23-3**

*Nonlinear behavior of variable and fixed costs*

narrower range, such as 40–80% of capacity. The range over which a company expects to operate during a year is called the relevant range of the activity index. Within this range, as shown in both diagrams in Illustration 23-4, a straight-line relationship generally exists for both variable and fixed costs.

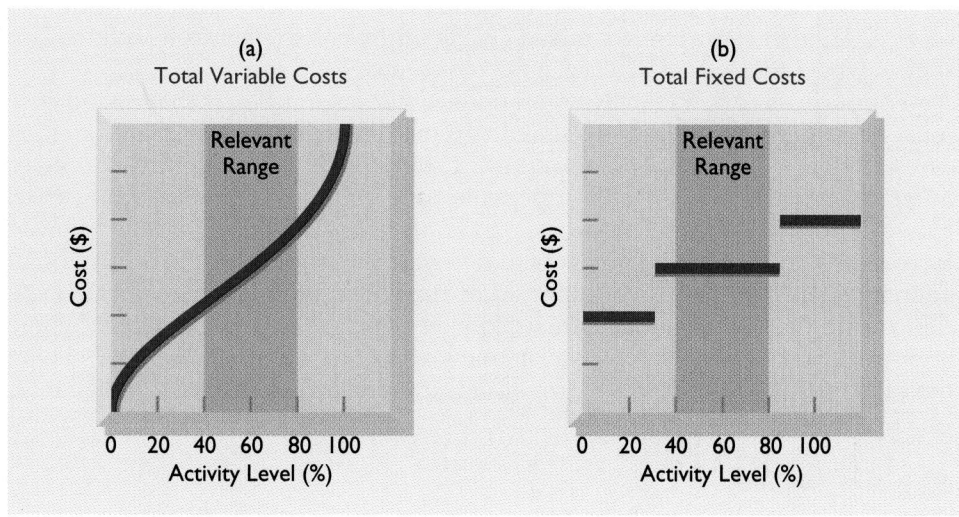

**Illustration 23-4**

*Linear behavior within relevant range*

As you can see, although the straight-line relationship may not be completely realistic, the linear assumption produces useful data for CVP analysis as long as the level of activity remains within the relevant range.

## Mixed Costs

Mixed costs contain both a variable cost element and a fixed cost element. Sometimes called **semivariable costs, mixed costs change in total but not proportionately with changes in the activity level**. The rental of a U-Haul truck is a good example of a mixed cost. To illustrate, assume that local rental terms for a 17-foot truck, including insurance, are $50 per day plus 50 cents per mile. The per diem charge is a fixed cost with respect to miles driven, whereas the mileage charge is a variable cost. The graphic presentation of the rental cost for a one-day rental is as follows:

**Helpful hint** Fixed costs that may be changeable include research such as new product development and management training programs.

STUDY OBJECTIVE
•••••••••3•••••••••

*Explain the concept of mixed costs.*

**Illustration 23-5**

*Behavior of a mixed cost*

In this case, as in others, the fixed cost element is the cost of having the service available, whereas the variable cost element is the cost of actually using the service. Another example of a mixed cost is utility costs (electric, telephone, and so on), where there is a flat service fee plus a usage charge.

For purposes of CVP analysis, an underlying assumption is that **mixed costs must be classified into their fixed and variable elements**. Accordingly, we must ask: How does management make the classification? One possibility is to determine the variable and fixed components each time a mixed cost is incurred. However, because of time and cost constraints, this approach is rarely followed. Instead, the customary approach is to determine variable and fixed costs on an **aggregate basis at the end of a period of time**, using the company's past experience with the behavior of the mixed cost at various levels of activity. Management may use several methods in making the determination. We will explain the **high-low method** here; other methods are more appropriately explained in cost accounting courses.[1]

### High-Low Method

The high-low method is a mathematical method that uses the total costs incurred at the high and low levels of activity. The difference in costs between the high and low levels represents variable costs, since only the variable cost element can change as activity levels change. The steps in computing fixed and variable costs under this method are as follows:

1. **Determine variable cost per unit from the following formula:**

**Illustration 23-6**

*Formula for variable cost per unit using high-low method*

---

[1]Other methods include the scatter diagram method and least squares regression analysis.

To illustrate, assume that Metro Transit Company has the following maintenance costs and mileage data for its fleet of buses over a 4-month period:

**Illustration 23-7**
*Assumed maintenance costs and mileage data*

| Month | Miles Driven | Total Cost | Month | Miles Driven | Total Cost |
|---|---|---|---|---|---|
| January | 20,000 | $30,000 | March | 35,000 | $49,000 |
| February | 40,000 | 48,000 | April | 50,000 | 63,000 |

The high and low levels of activity are 50,000 miles in April and 20,000 miles in January. The maintenance costs at these two levels are $63,000 and $30,000, respectively. The difference in maintenance costs is $33,000 ($63,000 − $30,000) and the difference in miles is 30,000 (50,000 − 20,000). Therefore, for Metro Transit, variable cost per unit is $1.10, computed as follows:

$$\$33,000 \div 30,000 = \$1.10$$

2. **Determine the fixed cost by subtracting the total variable cost at either the high or the low activity level from the total cost at that activity level.**

For Metro Transit, the computations are shown in Illustration 23-8:

**Illustration 23-8**
*High-low method computation of fixed costs*

| | Activity Level | |
|---|---|---|
| | High | Low |
| Total cost | $63,000 | $30,000 |
| Less: Variable costs | | |
| 50,000 × $1.10 | 55,000 | |
| 20,000 × $1.10 | | 22,000 |
| Total fixed costs | $ 8,000 | $ 8,000 |

**Maintenance costs are therefore $8,000 per month plus $1.10 per mile.** For example, at 45,000 miles, estimated maintenance costs would be $49,500 variable (45,000 × $1.10) and $8,000 fixed. The high-low method generally produces a reasonable estimate for analysis. However, it does not produce a precise measurement of the fixed and variable elements in a mixed cost because other activity levels are ignored in the computation.

## Importance of Identifying Variable and Fixed Costs

Why is it important to segregate costs into variable and fixed elements? The answer may become apparent if we look at the following five business decisions:

1. If American Airlines is to make a profit when it reduces all domestic fares by 50%, what reduction in costs or increase in passengers will be required? **Answer:** To make a profit when it cuts domestic fares by 50%, American Airlines will have to increase the number of passengers or cut its variable costs for those flights. Its fixed costs will not change.

2. What increase in sales revenue will be needed to maintain current profit levels if Ford Motor Company meets the United Auto Workers' demands for higher wages? **Answer:** Higher wages to UAW members at Ford Motor Company will increase the variable costs of manufacturing automobiles. To maintain present profit levels, Ford will have to cut other variable costs or increase the price of its automobiles.

3. What level of sales will General Motors need to cover its costs exactly for the Saturn automobile in the next model year? **Answer:** To cover its costs exactly on the Saturn automobile for the next model year, General Motors must determine the sales volume at which sales revenue will equal total costs, both fixed and variable.

4. What will be the effect on the cost of producing one ton of steel at USX Corp. if its program to modernize plant facilities reduces the work force by 50%? **Answer:** The modernizing of plant facilities at USX Corp. changes the proportion of fixed and variable costs of producing one ton of steel. Fixed costs increase because of higher depreciation charges whereas variable costs decrease due to the reduction in the number of steelworkers.

5. What happens if McDonald's Corporation increases its advertising expenses? **Answer:** Sales volume must be increased to cover three items: (1) the increase in advertising, (2) the variable cost of the increased sales volume, and (3) the desired additional net income.

## Before You Go On . . .

### ▶ Review It

1. What are the effects on total cost and per unit cost due to a change in activity on (a) a variable cost and (b) a fixed cost?
2. What is the relevant range and the behavior of costs within this range?
3. What are the steps in applying the high-low method to mixed costs?

### ▶ Do It

Helena Company reports the following total costs at two levels of production:

| | 10,000 units | 20,000 units |
|---|---|---|
| Direct materials | $20,000 | $40,000 |
| Maintenance | 8,000 | 10,000 |
| Depreciation | 4,000 | 4,000 |

Classify each cost as either variable, fixed, or mixed.

**Reasoning:** A variable cost varies in total directly and proportionately with each change. A fixed cost remains the same in total with each change. A mixed cost changes in total but not proportionately with each change.

**Solution:** Direct materials is a variable cost. Maintenance is a mixed cost. Depreciation is a fixed cost.

*Related exercise material:* BE23–1, E23–1, and E23–2.

---

**STUDY OBJECTIVE**

● ● ● ● ● ● ● ● ● ▼**4**● ● ● ● ● ● ● ● ● ●

*State the five components of cost-volume-profit analysis.*

# Cost-Volume-Profit Analysis

Cost-volume-profit (CVP) analysis is the study of the effects of changes in costs and volume on a company's profits. CVP analysis is important in profit planning. It also is a critical factor in such management decisions as setting selling prices, determining the best product mix, and making maximum use of production facilities.

## Basic Components

CVP analysis involves a consideration of the interrelationships among the components shown in Illustration 23-9.

**Illustration 23-9**

*Components of CVP analysis*

| 1. Volume or level of activity | 2. Unit selling prices | 3. Variable cost per unit | 4. Total fixed costs | 5. Sales mix |

The following assumptions underlie each CVP application:

1. The behavior of both costs and revenues is linear throughout the relevant range of the activity index.
2. All costs can be classified as either variable or fixed with reasonable accuracy.
3. Changes in activity are the only factors that affect costs.
4. All units produced are sold.
5. When more than one type of product is sold, total sales will be in a constant sales mix.

When these assumptions are not valid, the results of CVP analysis may be inaccurate.

In the applications of CVP analysis that follow, we will assume that the term "cost" includes **all** costs and expenses pertaining to production and sale of the product. That is, **cost includes manufacturing costs plus selling and administrative expenses**. We will use Vargo Video Company as an example. Relevant data for the videocassette recorders (VCRs) made by this company are as follows:

| | |
|---|---|
| Unit selling price | $500 |
| Unit variable costs | $300 |
| Total monthly fixed costs | $200,000 |

**Illustration 23-10**

*Assumed selling price and cost data for Vargo Video*

## Contribution Margin

One of the key relationships in CVP analysis is contribution margin (CM). **Contribution margin is the amount of revenue remaining after deducting variable costs.** For example, if we assume that Vargo Video sells 1,000 VCRs in one month, sales are $500,000 (1,000 × $500) and variable costs are $300,000 (1,000 × $300). Thus, contribution margin is $200,000 computed as follows:

**STUDY OBJECTIVE**

·········**5**·········

*Indicate the meaning of contribution margin and the ways it may be expressed.*

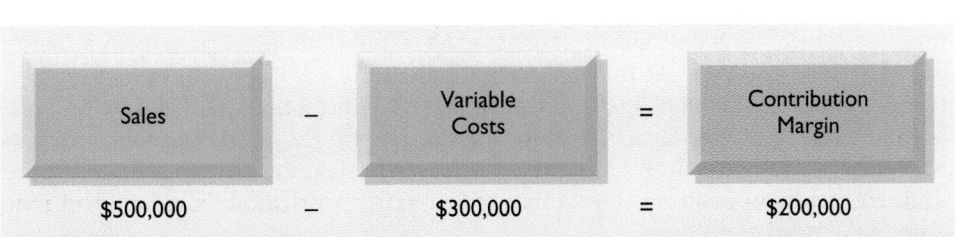

| Sales | − | Variable Costs | = | Contribution Margin |
|---|---|---|---|---|
| $500,000 | − | $300,000 | = | $200,000 |

**Illustration 23-11**

*Formula for and computation of contribution margin*

This contribution margin is then available to cover fixed costs and to contribute income for the company.

Views differ as to the best way to express contribution margin (CM). Some individuals favor a per unit basis. The formula for **contribution margin per unit** is:

Illustration 23-12

*Formula for contribution margin per unit*

At Vargo Video, the contribution margin per unit is $200, computed as follows:

$$\$500 - \$300 = \$200$$

Contribution margin per unit indicates that for every VCR sold, Vargo will have $200 to cover fixed costs and contribute to income. Since fixed costs are $200,000, Vargo Video must sell 1,000 VCRs ($200,000 ÷ $200) before there is any income. Above that sales volume, every sale will contribute $200 to income. Thus, if 1,500 units are sold, income will be $100,000 (500 × $200).

Others prefer to use a **contribution margin ratio**. The formula for this ratio is:

Illustration 23-13

*Formula for contribution margin ratio*

At Vargo Video, the ratio is 40%, as shown below.

$$\$200 \div \$500 = 40\%$$

The CM ratio of 40% means that 40 cents of each sales dollar ($1 × 40%) is available to apply to fixed costs and to contribute to income. This expression of contribution margin is very helpful in determining the effect of changes in sales on income. To illustrate, if the management of Vargo Video wants to know the effect of a $50,000 increase in sales, they simply multiply $50,000 by the CM ratio (40%) to determine that income will increase $20,000.

## Break-Even Analysis

**STUDY OBJECTIVE**

••••••••• **6** •••••••••

*Identify the three ways that the break-even point may be determined.*

A second key relationship in CVP analysis is the level of activity at which total revenues equal total costs, both fixed and variable. This level of activity is called the break-even point. At this volume of sales, the company will realize no income and suffer no loss. Since no income is involved when the break-even point is the objective, the analysis is often referred to simply as **break-even analysis**. Knowledge of the break-even point is useful to management in deciding whether to introduce new product lines, change sales prices on established products, or enter new market areas.

The break-even point can be:

1. Computed from a mathematical equation.
2. Computed by using contribution margin.
3. Derived from a cost-volume-profit (CVP) graph.

The break-even point can be expressed **either in sales dollars or sales units**.

## ►Accounting in Action ► *Business Insight*

It pays to know how break-even is defined. For example, *Forrest Gump*, a highly successful film, provided little to the movie producers initially because of the definitions used for profits. As one producer noted, "The studios do not cheat and they do not lie—they just have very creative accounting methods. A studio, for example, has at least four ways to define 'break-even' and 24 different types of 'gross,' and they're all legitimate." Perhaps the Hollywood bookkeeper is right when he observed, "Most of the creative work in this business is done in the accounting department."

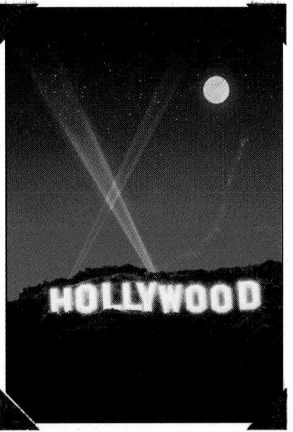

### *Mathematical Equation*

In its simplest form, the equation for break-even sales is:

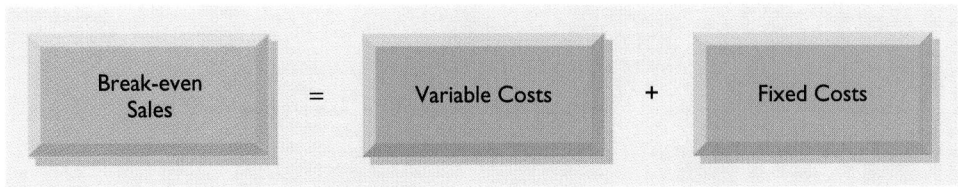

Break-even Sales = Variable Costs + Fixed Costs

**Illustration 23-14**

*Break-even equation*

The break-even point **in dollars** is found by expressing **variable costs as a percentage of unit selling price.** For Vargo Video, the percentage is 60% ($300 ÷ $500). The computation is:

$$X = .60X + \$200,000$$
$$.40X = \$200,000$$
$$X = \$500,000$$

where:

$$X = \text{sales dollars at the break-even point}$$
$$.60X = \text{variable costs as a percentage of unit selling price}$$
$$\$200,000 = \text{total fixed costs}$$

Sales, therefore, must be $500,000 for Vargo Video to break even.

## ▲Accounting in Action ▸ *Business Insight*

As the accompanying chart shows, the level of break-even sales of the Big Three automakers is moving lower. This means Detroit can be expected to pump out profits in the future.

*Source: Fortune,* December 12, 1994, p. 32.

The break-even point **in units** can be computed directly from the mathematical equation by **using unit selling prices** and **unit variable costs**. The computation is:

$$\$500X = \$300X + \$200{,}000$$

$$\$200X = \$200{,}000$$

$$X = 1{,}000 \text{ units}$$

where:

$$\$500X = \text{unit selling price} \times \text{sales volume}$$

$$\$300X = \text{variable cost per unit} \times \text{sales volume}$$

$$\$200{,}000 = \text{total fixed costs}$$

Thus, Vargo Video must sell 1,000 units to break even.

The accuracy of the computations can be proved as follows:

**Illustration 23-15**

*Break-even proof*

| | | |
|---|---|---|
| Sales (1,000 × $500) | | $500,000 |
| Total costs: | | |
|    Variable (1,000 × $300) | $300,000 | |
|    Fixed | 200,000 | 500,000 |
| Net income | | $ –0– |

### Contribution Margin Technique

Because we know that contribution margin equals total revenues less variable costs, it follows that at the break-even point, **contribution margin must equal total fixed costs**. On the basis of this relationship, the break-even point can be computed by using either the contribution margin per unit or the contribution margin ratio.

When the contribution margin per unit is used, the formula to compute break-even point in units is as follows:

For Vargo Video, the contribution margin per unit is $200, as explained above. Thus, the computation is:

$$\$200,000 \div \$200 = 1,000 \text{ units}$$

When the contribution margin ratio is used, the formula to compute break-even point in dollars is:

We know that the contribution margin ratio for Vargo Video is 40%. Thus, the computation is:

$$\$200,000 \div 40\% = \$500,000$$

### Graphic Presentation

An effective way to derive the break-even point is to prepare a break-even graph. Because this graph also shows costs, volume, and profits, it is referred to as the cost-volume-profit (CVP) graph.

In the graph in Illustration 23-18, sales volume is recorded along the horizontal axis. This axis should extend to the maximum level of expected sales. Both total revenues (sales) and total costs (fixed plus variable) are recorded on the vertical axis.

The construction of the graph, using the data for Vargo Video, is as follows:

1. Plot the total revenue line starting at the zero activity level. For every VCR sold, total revenue increases by $500. For example, at 200 units, sales are $100,000, and at the upper level of activity (1,800 units), sales are $900,000. Note that the revenue line is assumed to be linear throughout the full range of activity.

2. Plot the total fixed cost by a horizontal line. For the VCRs, this line is plotted at $200,000, and it is the same at every level of activity.

3. Plot the total cost line starting at the fixed cost line at zero activity and increasing the amount by the variable cost at each level of activity. For each VCR, variable costs are $300. Thus, at 200 units, total variable cost is $60,000 and the total cost is $260,000; at 1,800 units total variable cost is $540,000, and total cost is $740,000. On the graph, the amount of the variable cost can be derived from the difference between the total cost and fixed cost lines at each level of activity.

**Illustration 23-18**

*CVP graph*

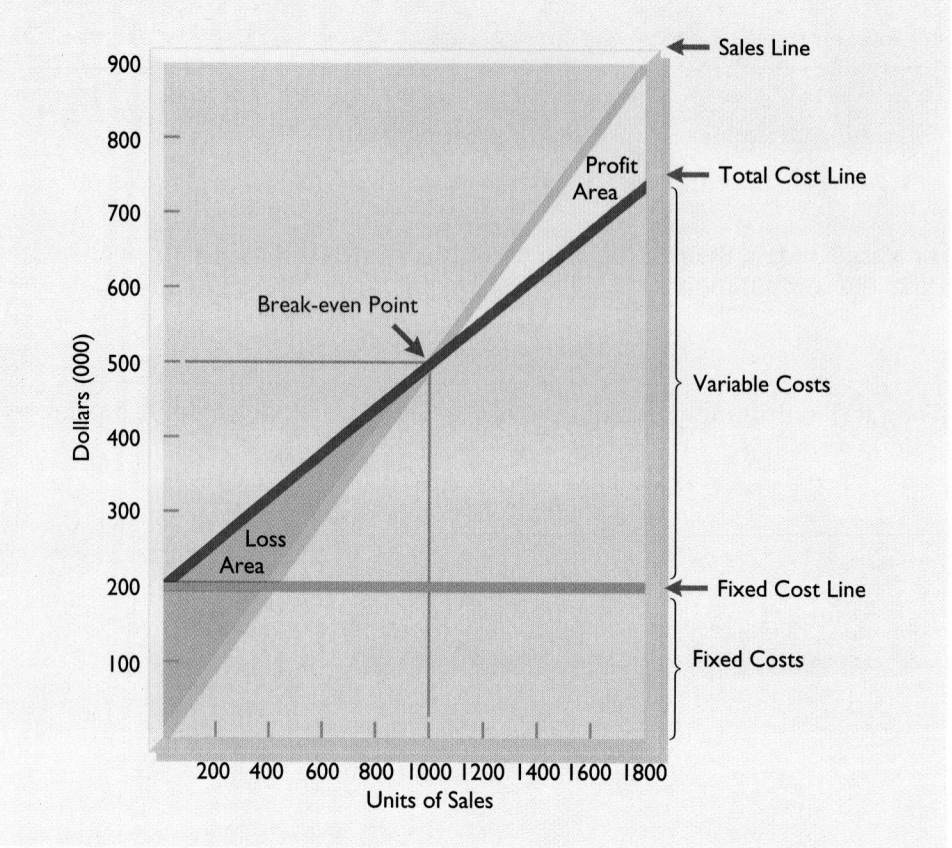

4. Determine the break-even point from the intersection of the total cost line and the total revenue line. The break-even point in dollars is found by drawing a horizontal line from the break-even point to the vertical axis. The break-even point in units is obtained by drawing a vertical line from the break-even point to the horizontal axis. For the VCRs, the break-even point is $500,000 of sales, or 1,000 units. At this sales level, Vargo Video will cover costs but make no profit.

In addition to identifying the break-even point, the CVP graph shows both the net income and net loss areas. Thus, the amount of income or loss at each level of sales can be derived from the total sales and total cost lines.

## ▶**Technology in Action**

 Computer graphics are a valuable companion to an increasing number of computer software packages. Graphs can be instantly changed to provide visual "what if" analysis. This can all be done in color for either video or hard copy output.

While current technology allows for stunning graphs in a variety of different formats (pie charts, bar, stacked bar, two-dimensional, three-dimensional, etc.), care must still be used as to the appropriate situations for the use of graphs. In the appropriate situation, a graph can literally be worth a thousand words. However, just because graphs can be quickly generated does not mean they can convey all the needed information for a management decision.

A CVP graph is especially useful in management meetings because the effects of a change in any element in the CVP analysis can be promptly portrayed. For example, a 10% increase in selling price will change the location of the total revenue line. Likewise, the effects on total costs of wage increases to both office employees and factory workers can be quickly observed.

## Before You Go On . . .

### ► Review It

1. What are the assumptions that underlie each CVP application?
2. What is contribution margin and how may it be expressed?
3. How can the break-even point be determined?

### ► Do It

Lombardi Company has a unit selling price of $400, variable costs per unit of $240, and fixed costs of $160,000. Compute the break-even point in units using (a) a mathematical equation and (b) contribution margin per unit.

   **Reasoning:** The mathematical equation is Break-even Sales = Variable Costs + Fixed Costs. Using contribution margin per unit, the formula is Fixed Costs ÷ Contribution Margin per Unit = Break-even Point in Units.

   **Solution:** (a) The equation is $400X = $240X + $160,000$. Thus, the break-even point in units is 1,000 ($160,000 ÷ $160X). (b) Contribution margin per unit is $160 ($400 − $240). The formula is $160,000 ÷ $160, and the break-even point in units is 1,000.

*Related exercise material:* BE23–5, BE23–6, E23–3, E23–4, E23–5, E23–6, E23–7, and E23–8.

## Margin of Safety

The margin of safety is another relationship that may be calculated in CVP analysis. Margin of safety is the difference between actual or expected sales and sales at the break-even point. This relationship measures the "breathing room" or "cushion" that management has to break even if actual or expected sales fail to materialize. The margin of safety may be expressed in dollars or as a ratio. The formula for stating the **margin of safety in dollars** is:

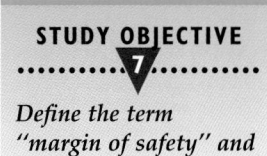

**Illustration 23-19**

*Formula for margin of safety in dollars*

Assuming that actual (expected) sales for Vargo Video are $750,000, the computation is:

$$\$750,000 - \$500,000 = \$250,000$$

In contrast, the formula and computation for determining the **margin of safety ratio** are:

**Illustration 23-20**

*Formula for margin of safety ratio*

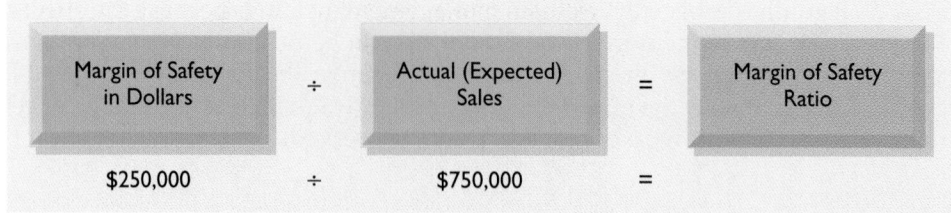

| Margin of Safety in Dollars | ÷ | Actual (Expected) Sales | = | Margin of Safety Ratio |
|:---:|:---:|:---:|:---:|:---:|
| $250,000 | ÷ | $750,000 | = | |

## ►*A*ccounting in *A*ction ► *Business Insight*

Computation of break-even and margin of safety is important for various types of business. Consider how the promoter for the Rolling Stones' tour used the break-even point and margin of safety. For example, one outdoor show should bring 70,000 individuals for a gross of $2.45 million. The promoter guarantees $1.2 million to the Rolling Stones. In addition, 20% of gross or approximately $500,000 goes to the stadium in which the performance is staged. Add another $400,000 for other expenses such as ticket takers, parking attendants, advertising, and so on. This leaves $350,000 per show to the promoter, if it sells out. At 75%, the promoter breaks about even, and at 50%, the promoter loses hundreds of thousands of dollars. However, the promoter also shares in sales of T-shirts and memorabilia for which the promoter will net over $7 million during the tour. If the Rolling Stones' tour is a success, the promoter could make $35 million!

**The higher the dollars or the percentage, the greater the margin of safety.** The adequacy of the margin of safety should be evaluated by management in terms of such factors as the vulnerability of the product to competitive pressures and to downturns in the economy.

### Target Net Income

**STUDY OBJECTIVE**
••••••••• ▼8▼ •••••••••

*Give the formulas for determining sales required to earn target net income.*

Management usually sets an income objective for individual product lines. This objective called target net income is extremely useful to management because it indicates the sales necessary to achieve a specified level of income. The amount of sales necessary to achieve target net income can be determined from each of the approaches used in determining break-even sales.

### *Mathematical Equation*

We know that at the break-even point no profit or loss results for the company. By adding a factor for target net income to the break-even equation, we obtain the following formula for determining required sales:

**Illustration 23-21**

*Formula for required sales to meet target net income*

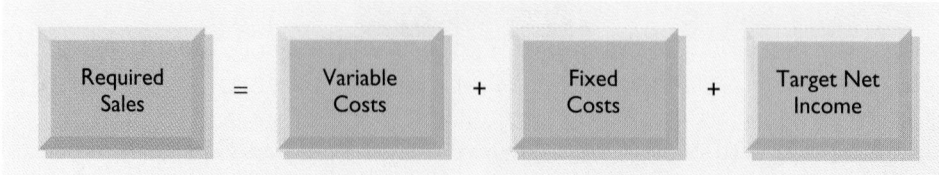

| Required Sales | = | Variable Costs | + | Fixed Costs | + | Target Net Income |
|:---:|:---:|:---:|:---:|:---:|:---:|:---:|

Required sales may be expressed in **either sales dollars or sales units**. Assuming that target net income is $120,000 for Vargo Video, the computation of required sales in dollars is as follows:

$$X = .60X + \$200,000 + \$120,000$$

$$.40X = \$320,000$$

$$X = \$800,000$$

where:

$$X = \text{required sales}$$

$$.60X = \text{variable costs as a percentage of unit selling price}$$

$$\$200,000 = \text{total fixed costs}$$

$$\$120,000 = \text{target net income}$$

The sales volume in units at the targeted income level is found by dividing the sales dollars by the unit selling price ($800,000 ÷ $500) = 1,600 units.

**Helpful hint** Alternatively, the required sales units can be computed directly by using unit prices in the equation: $500X = $300X + $200,000 + $120,000; $200X = $320,000 or 1,600 units.

### Contribution Margin Technique

As in the case of break-even sales, the sales required to meet a target net income can be computed in either dollars or units. The formula using the contribution margin ratio is as follows:

**Illustration 23-22**

*Formula for required sales in dollars using contribution margin ratio*

The computation for Vargo Video is as follows:

$$\$320,000 \div 40\% = \$800,000$$

### Graphic Presentation

The CVP graph presented in Illustration 23-18 can also be used to derive the sales required to meet target net income. In the profit area of the graph, the distance between the sales line and the total cost line at any point equals net income. Required sales are found by analyzing the differences between the two lines until the desired net income is found.

## Sales Mix

In the preceding discussion, we have focused on one product, videocassette recorders. One of the assumptions of CVP analysis is that if more than one product is involved, the sales mix of the products remains constant. Sales mix is the relative combination in which a company's products are sold. For example, if 2 units of Product A are sold for every 1 unit of Product B, the sales mix of the two products is 2:1. Break-even sales can be computed for a mix of two or more products by determining the **weighted average unit contribution margin of all the products**.

To illustrate, we will assume that Vargo Video sells both VCRs and television sets (TVs) at the following per unit data:

**STUDY OBJECTIVE**
•••••••••9•••••••••

*Explain the term "sales mix" and its effects in determining break-even sales.*

**Illustration 23-23**

*Per unit data—sales mix*

| Unit Data | VCRs | TVs |
|---|---|---|
| Selling price | $500 | $800 |
| Variable costs | 300 | 400 |
| Contribution margin | $200 | $400 |
| Sales mix | 3 | 1 |

The **total contribution margin** for this sales mix is $1,000 [($200 × 3) + ($400 × 1)], and the weighted average unit contribution margin is $250 ($1,000 ÷ 4). The break-even formula is as follows:

**Illustration 23-24**

*Break-even formula—sales mix*

The computation of break-even sales in units for Vargo Video, assuming $200,000 of fixed costs, is as follows:

$$\$200,000 \div \$250 = 800 \text{ units}$$

In order to break even with a sales mix of 3:1, Vargo Video must sell 600 VCRs (¾ × 800) and 200 TVs (¼ × 800). This can be verified by the following:

**Illustration 23-25**

*Break-even proof—sales mix*

| Product | Unit Sales | × | Unit CM | = | Total CM |
|---|---|---|---|---|---|
| VCRs | 600 | × | $200 | = | $120,000 |
| TVs | 200 | × | 400 | = | 80,000 |
| | 800 | | | | $200,000 |

Management should continually review the company's sales mix. At any level of units sold, **net income will be greater if more high contribution margin units are sold than low contribution margin units**. For Vargo Video, the television sets produce the higher contribution margin. Consequently, if 300 TVs and 500 VCRs are sold, net income would be higher than in the current sales mix even though total units sold has not changed. An analysis of these relationships shows that a shift from low-margin sales to high-margin sales may increase net income, even though there is a decline in total units sold. Likewise, a shift from high- to low-margin sales may result in a decrease in net income, even though there is an increase in total units sold.

## CVP and Changes in the Business Environment

When the IBM personal computer (PC) was introduced, it sold for $2,500; today the same type of computer sells for much less. When high oil prices fell, the break-even point for airline and trucking companies dropped dramatically. Because of lower prices for imported steel, the demand for domestic steel dropped significantly. The point should be clear: Business conditions change rapidly and management must respond intelligently to these changes. CVP analysis can help.

To illustrate how CVP analysis can be used in responding to change, we will use the following independent situations that might occur at Vargo Video. Each case is based on the original VCR sales and cost data, which were:

Illustration 23-26

*Original VCR sales and cost data*

| | |
|---|---|
| Unit selling price | $500 |
| Unit variable cost | $300 |
| Total fixed costs | $200,000 |
| Break-even sales | $500,000 or 1,000 units |

**Case I.** A competitor is offering a 10% discount on the selling price of its VCRs. Management must decide whether to offer a similar discount. **Question:** What effect will a 10% discount on selling price have on the break-even point for VCRs? **Answer:** A 10% discount on selling price reduces the selling price per unit to $450 [$500 − ($500 × 10%)]. Variable costs per unit remain unchanged at $300. Thus, the contribution margin per unit is $150. Assuming no change in fixed costs, break-even sales are 1,333 units, computed as follows:

Illustration 23-27

*Computation of break-even sales in units*

| Fixed Costs | ÷ | Contribution Margin per Unit | = | Break-even Sales |
|---|---|---|---|---|
| $200,000 | ÷ | $150 | = | 1,333 units (rounded) |

For Vargo Video, this change would require monthly sales to increase by 333 units or 33⅓% in order to break even. In reaching a conclusion about offering a 10% discount to customers, management must determine the likelihood of achieving the increased sales. Also, management should estimate the possible loss of sales if the competitor's discount price is not matched.

**Case II.** To meet the continuing threat of foreign competition, management invests in new robotic equipment that will significantly lower the amount of direct labor required to make the VCRs. It is estimated that total fixed costs will increase 30% and that variable cost per unit will decrease 30%. **Question:** What effect will the new equipment have on the sales volume required to break even? **Answer:** Total fixed costs become $260,000 [$200,000 + (30% × $200,000)], and variable cost per unit is now $210 [$300 − (30% × $300)]. The new break-even point is approximately 900 units, computed as follows:

Illustration 23-28

*Computation of break-even sales in units*

| Fixed Costs | ÷ | Contribution Margin per Unit | = | Break-even Sales |
|---|---|---|---|---|
| $260,000 | ÷ | ($500 − $210) | = | 900 units (rounded) |

These changes appear to be advantageous for Vargo Video because the break-even point is reduced by 10%, or 100 units.

**Case III.** The principal supplier of raw materials has just announced a price increase. It is estimated that the higher cost will increase the variable cost of VCRs by $25 per unit. Management would like to hold the line on the selling price of VCRs. It plans a cost-cutting program that will save $17,500 in fixed costs per month. Vargo is currently realizing monthly net income of $80,000 on sales of 1,400 VCRs. **Question:** What increase in sales will be needed to maintain the same level of net income? **Answer:** The variable cost per unit increases to $325

($300 + $25), and fixed costs are reduced to $182,500 ($200,000 − $17,500). Because of the change in variable cost, the variable cost becomes 65% of sales ($325 ÷ $500). Using the equation for target net income, we find that required sales are $750,000, computed as follows:

**Illustration 23-29**

*Computation of required sales*

$$\text{Required Sales} = \text{Variable Costs} + \text{Fixed Costs} + \text{Target Net Income}$$
$$X = .65X + \$182{,}500 + \$80{,}000$$
$$.35X = \$262{,}500$$
$$X = \$750{,}000$$

To achieve the required sales, 1,500 VCRs will have to be sold ($750,000 ÷ $500), an increase of 100 units. If this does not seem to be a reasonable expectation, management will either have to effect further reductions in costs or accept less net income if the selling price remains unchanged.

# CVP Income Statement

**STUDY OBJECTIVE**
·········▼10··········

*Describe the essential features of a cost-volume-profit income statement.*

As you have learned, cost behavior and contribution margin are key factors in CVP analysis. Because management makes its decisions on these factors, it often wants the results of these decisions reported in a similar format. This has led to the development for **internal use only** of a **CVP** or **contribution margin format** for the income statement. The CVP income statement classifies costs and expenses as variable or fixed and specifically reports contribution margin in the body of the statement. This is in contrast to the income statement traditionally prepared for external use, in which no disclosure is made of the behavior of costs and expenses. In the traditional statement, costs and expenses are classified only by function, such as cost of goods sold, selling expenses, and administrative expenses.

To illustrate the CVP income statement, we will assume that Vargo Video reaches its target net income of $120,000 (see page 977). From an analysis of the transactions, the following information is obtained on the $680,000 of costs that were incurred in June:

**Illustration 23-30**

*Assumed cost and expense data*

|  | Variable | Fixed | Total |
|---|---|---|---|
| Cost of goods sold | $400,000 | $120,000 | $520,000 |
| Selling expenses | 60,000 | 40,000 | 100,000 |
| Administrative expenses | 20,000 | 40,000 | 60,000 |
|  | $480,000 | $200,000 | $680,000 |

The CVP income statement and the conventional income statement based on these data are shown side-by-side for comparative purposes in Illustration 23-31.

Note that net income is the same ($120,000) in both of the statements. The major difference is the format for the expenses. As illustrated, the CVP statement classifies costs and expenses as either variable or fixed. Another difference is that the traditional statement shows gross profit, whereas the CVP statement shows contribution margin. Study the CVP form carefully. It will be used in remaining chapters, and it is often used in business in internal reporting to management.

## VARGO VIDEO COMPANY
### Income Statement
### For the Month Ended June 30, 1996

| Traditional Format | | | CVP Format | | |
|---|---|---|---|---|---|
| Sales | | $800,000 | Sales | | $800,000 |
| Cost of goods sold | | 520,000 | Variable expenses | | |
| Gross profit | | 280,000 |   Cost of goods sold | $400,000 | |
| Operating expenses | | |   Selling expenses | 60,000 | |
|   Selling expenses | $100,000 | |   Administrative expenses | 20,000 | |
|   Administrative expenses | 60,000 | |     Total variable expenses | | 480,000 |
|     Total operating expenses | | 160,000 | **CONTRIBUTION MARGIN** | | 320,000 |
| Net income | | $120,000 | Fixed expenses | | |
| | | |   Cost of goods sold | 120,000 | |
| | | |   Selling expenses | 40,000 | |
| | | |   Administrative expenses | 40,000 | |
| | | |     Total fixed expenses | | 200,000 |
| | | | Net income | | $120,000 |

**Illustration 23-31**

*Traditional versus CVP income statement*

## Before You Go On . . .

### ▶ Review It

1. What is the formula for computing the margin of safety (a) in dollars and (b) as a ratio?
2. State the formula for computing break-even sales in units when a company sells more than one product.
3. How does a CVP income statement differ from a traditional income statement?

### ▶ Do It

At Kimoto Company, variable costs are 65% of sales, fixed costs are $245,000, and target net income is $70,000. Compute the required sales in dollars using the mathematical equation approach.

**Reasoning:** The mathematical equation is Required Sales = Variable Costs + Fixed Costs + Target Net Income.

**Solution:** Required sales are $900,000; the computation is: $X = (.65X + \$245,000 + \$70,000)$.

*Related exercise material: BE23-7, BE23-8, BE23-9, E23-4, E23-6, E23-7, and E23-8.*

## Variable Costing

In the earlier managerial chapters, both variable and fixed manufacturing costs have been classified as product costs. In job order costing, for example, a job is assigned the costs of direct materials, direct labor, and both variable and fixed manufacturing overhead. This costing approach is referred to as full or absorption costing, because all manufacturing costs are charged to, or absorbed by, the product. An alternative approach is to use variable costing. Under variable costing only direct materials, direct labor, and variable manufacturing overhead costs are considered product costs; fixed manufacturing overhead costs are recognized as period costs (expenses) when incurred. The difference between absorption costing and variable costing is graphically shown as follows:

**STUDY OBJECTIVE 11**

*Explain the difference between absorption costing and variable costing.*

**Illustration 23-32**

*Difference between absorption costing and variable costing*

Selling and administrative expenses are period costs under both absorption and variable costing.

To illustrate the computation of unit production cost under absorption and variable costing, assume that Premium Products Corporation manufactures a polyurethane sealant called Fix-it for car windshields. Relevant data for Fix-it in January 1996, the first month of production, is as follows:

**Selling Price:** $20 per unit.

**Units:** Produced 30,000; sold 20,000; beginning inventory zero.

**Variable unit costs:** Manufacturing $9 (direct materials $5, direct labor $3, and variable overhead $1), and selling and administrative expenses $2.

**Fixed costs:** Manufacturing overhead $120,000 and selling and administrative expenses $15,000.

The per unit production cost under each costing approach is:

**Illustration 23-33**

*Computation of per unit production cost*

| Type of Cost | Absorption Costing | Variable Costing |
| --- | --- | --- |
| Direct materials | $ 5 | $5 |
| Direct labor | 3 | 3 |
| Variable manufacturing overhead | 1 | 1 |
| Fixed manufacturing overhead ($120,000 ÷ 30,000 units produced) | 4 | 0 |
| Total unit cost | $13 | $9 |

The difference in total unit cost of $4 ($13 − $9) occurs because fixed manufacturing costs are a product cost under absorption costing and a period cost under variable costing. Based on these data, each unit sold and each unit remaining in inventory is costed at $13 under absorption costing and at $9 under variable costing.

### Effects on Income

The income statements under the two costing approaches are shown in Illustrations 23-34 and 23-35. The conventional income statement format is used with absorption costing, and the cost-volume-profit format is used with variable costing. Computations are inserted parenthetically in the statements to facilitate your understanding of the amounts.

Income from operations under absorption costing shown in Illustration 23-34 is $40,000 higher than under variable costing ($85,000 − $45,000) shown in Illustration 23-35.

As highlighted in the two income statements, there is a $40,000 difference in the ending inventories ($130,000 under absorption costing and $90,000 under variable costing). Under absorption costing, $40,000 of the fixed overhead costs

**Illustration 23-34**

*Absorption costing income statement*

| PREMIUM PRODUCTS COMPANY<br>Income Statement<br>For the Month Ended January 31, 1996<br>(Absorption Costing) | | |
|---|---|---|
| Sales (20,000 units × $20) | | $400,000 |
| Cost of goods sold | | |
| Inventory, January 1 | $ –0– | |
| Cost of goods manufactured (30,000 units × $13) | 390,000 | |
| Cost of goods available for sale | 390,000 | |
| **Inventory, January 31 (10,000 units × $13)** | **130,000** | |
| Cost of goods sold (20,000 units × $13) | | 260,000 |
| Gross profit | | 140,000 |
| Selling and administrative expenses | | |
| (Variable 20,000 units × $2 + fixed $15,000) | | 55,000 |
| **Income from operations** | | **$ 85,000** |

**Illustration 23-35**

*Variable costing income statement*

**Helpful hint** Note the difference in the computation of the ending inventory: $9 per unit here, $13 per unit above.

| PREMIUM PRODUCTS COMPANY<br>Income Statement<br>For the Month Ended January 31, 1996<br>(Variable Costing) | | |
|---|---|---|
| Sales (20,000 units × $20) | | $400,000 |
| Variable expenses | | |
| Variable cost of goods sold | | |
| Inventory, January 1 | $ –0– | |
| Variable manufacturing costs (30,000 units × $9) | 270,000 | |
| Cost of goods available for sale | 270,000 | |
| **Inventory, January 31 (10,000 units × $9)** | **90,000** | |
| Variable cost of goods sold | 180,000 | |
| Variable selling and administrative expenses | | |
| (20,000 units × $2) | 40,000 | |
| Total variable expenses | | 220,000 |
| Contribution margin | | 180,000 |
| Fixed expenses | | |
| Manufacturing overhead | 120,000 | |
| Selling and administrative expenses | 15,000 | |
| Total fixed expenses | | 135,000 |
| **Income from operations** | | **$ 45,000** |

(10,000 units × $4) have been deferred to a future period as a product cost. In contrast, under variable costing the entire fixed manufacturing costs are expensed when incurred.

As shown, when units produced exceed units sold, income under absorption costing is higher than under variable costing. Conversely, when units produced are less than units sold, income under absorption costing is lower than under variable costing. The reason is that the cost of the **beginning inventory will be higher under absorption costing** than under variable costing. For example, if 30,000 units of Fix-it are sold in February and only 20,000 units are produced, income from operations will be $40,000 less under absorption costing than under variable costing because of the $40,000 difference ($130,000 vs. $90,000) in the beginning inventories.

When units produced and sold are the same, income from operations will be equal under the two costing approaches. Since there is no ending inventory, fixed overhead costs of the current period are not deferred to future periods through the ending inventory. The foregoing effects of the two costing approaches on income from operations may be summarized as follows:

**Illustration 23-36**

*Summary of income effects*

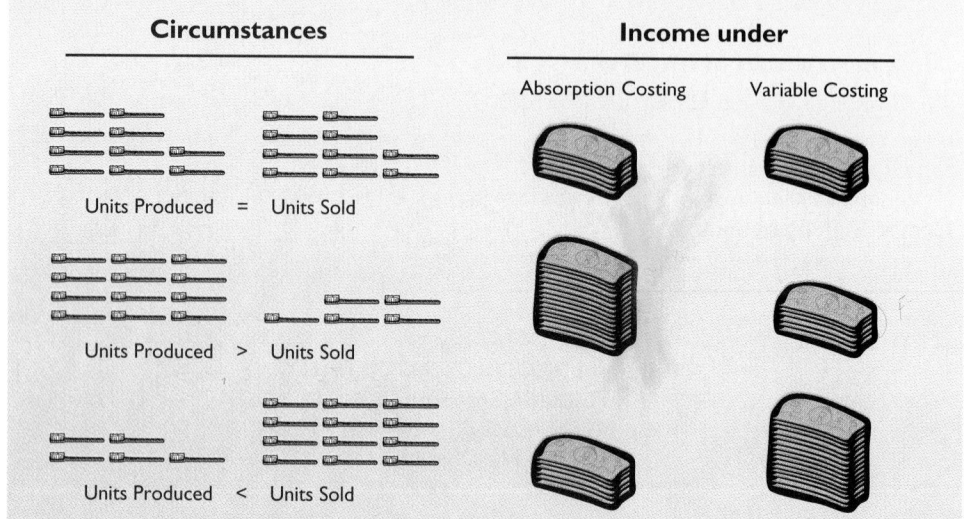

## Rationale for Variable Costing

The rationale for variable costing centers on the purpose of fixed manufacturing costs which is **to have productive facilities available for use**. Conceptually, these costs are incurred whether a company operates at zero or at 100% of capacity. Thus, proponents of variable costing argue that these costs should be expensed in the period in which they are incurred.

Supporters of absorption costing defend the assignment of fixed manufacturing overhead costs to inventory on the basis that these costs are as much a cost of getting a product (such as Fix-it) ready for sale as direct materials or direct labor. Accordingly, these costs should not be matched with revenues until the product is sold.

The use of variable costing in product costing is acceptable **only for internal use by management**. It cannot be used in determining product costs in financial statements prepared in accordance with generally accepted accounting principles because it understates inventory costs. To comply with the matching principle, a company must use absorption costing for its work in process and finished goods inventories. Similarly, absorption costing must be used for income tax purposes.

## *Before You Go On . . .*

### ▶ *Review It*

1. What is variable costing?
2. What is the rationale for variable costing?

## ► *A Look Back at Henri's Salon*

Refer to the opening story and answer the following questions:

(a) What are some variable costs that Henri's Salon might incur?

(b) What are some fixed costs that Henri's Salon might incur?

(c) Why is it important to segregate costs into variable and fixed costs when analyzing profitability?

(d) Why did the management of Henri's Salon change the way compensation was determined for its hair stylists?

### Solution:

(a) Some variable costs are towels, shampoo, cotton, tint, latex gloves, toner, and conditioner.

(b) Some fixed costs are insurance, depreciation, rent, utilities, licenses and taxes, wages and salaries, dues and subscriptions, and maintenance and repairs.

(c) For Henri to determine what went wrong and to decide on a course of corrective action, he must understand how changes in volume affect changes in revenues and costs. For example, when advertising expense is increased, it may increase volume and revenue, or it may increase revenue but not generate any additional profit. By segregating costs into variable and fixed, Henri (probably with the help of an accountant) can determine what dollar impact a change in sales revenue will have on overall profit.

(d) Henri's fixed-salary policy encouraged hair stylists to pamper clients in order to generate tip income. This policy did not motivate them to perform quality services efficiently, which would have been of more help to the salon overall.

## ◣ *Summary of Study Objectives*

**1.** *Distinguish between variable and fixed costs.* Variable costs are costs that vary in total directly and proportionately with changes in the activity index. Fixed costs are costs that remain the same in total regardless of changes in the activity index.

**2.** *Explain the meaning and importance of the relevant range.* The relevant range is the range of activity in which a company expects to operate during a year. It is important in CVP analysis because the behavior of costs is linear throughout the relevant range.

**3.** *Explain the concept of mixed costs.* Mixed costs increase in total but not proportionately with changes in the activity level. For purposes of CVP analysis, mixed costs must be classified into their fixed and variable elements. One method that management may use is the high-low method.

**4.** *State the five components of cost-volume-profit analysis.* The five components of CVP analysis are (a) volume or level of activity, (b) unit selling prices, (c) variable cost per unit, (d) total fixed costs, and (e) sales mix.

**5.** *Indicate the meaning of contribution margin and the ways it may be expressed.* Contribution margin is the amount of revenue remaining after deducting variable costs. It can be expressed as a per unit amount or as a ratio.

**6.** *Identify the three ways that the break-even point may be determined.* The break-even point can be (a) computed from a mathematical equation, (b) computed by using a con-

tribution margin technique, and (c) derived from a CVP graph.

**7.** *Define the term "margin of safety" and give the formulas for computing it.* Margin of safety is the difference between actual or expected sales and sales at the break-even point. The formulas for margin of safety are Actual (Expected) Sales − Break-even Sales = Margin of Safety in Dollars; Margin of Safety in Dollars ÷ Actual (Expected) Sales = Margin of Safety Ratio.

**8.** *Give the formulas for determining sales required to earn target net income.* One formula is: Required Sales = Variable Costs + Fixed Costs + Target Net Income. Another formula is: Fixed Costs + Target Net Income ÷ Contribution Margin Ratio = Required Sales.

**9.** *Explain the term "sales mix" and its effects in determining break-even sales.* Sales mix is the relative combination in which a company's products are sold. Break-even sales are determined by using the weighted average unit contribution margin of all the products.

**10.** *Describe the essential features of a cost-volume-profit income statement.* The CVP income statement classifies costs and expenses as variable or fixed and reports contribution margin in the body of the statement.

**11.** *Explain the difference between absorption costing and variable costing.* Under absorption costing, fixed manufacturing costs are product costs; under variable costing, fixed manufacturing costs are period costs.

# GLOSSARY

**Absorption costing**   A costing approach in which all manufacturing costs are charged to the product. (p. 981).

**Activity index**   The activity that causes changes in the behavior of costs. (p. 962).

**Break-even point**   The level of activity at which total revenues equal total costs. (p. 970).

**Contribution margin (CM)**   The amount of revenue remaining after deducting variable costs. (p. 969).

**Cost behavior analysis**   The study of how specific costs respond to changes in the level of activity within a company. (p. 962).

**Cost-volume-profit (CVP) analysis**   The study of the effects of changes in costs and volume on a company's profits. (p. 968).

**Cost-volume-profit (CVP) graph**   A graph showing the relationship between costs, volume, and profits. (p. 973).

**Cost-volume-profit (CVP) income statement**   A statement for internal use that classifies costs and expenses as fixed or variable and reports contribution margin in the body of the statement. (p. 980).

**Fixed costs**   Costs that remain the same in total regardless of changes in the activity level. (p. 963).

**High-low method**   A mathematical method that uses the total costs incurred at the high and low levels of activity. (p. 966).

**Margin of safety**   The difference between actual or expected sales and sales at the break-even point. (p. 975).

**Mixed costs**   Costs that contain both a variable and a fixed cost element and change in total but not proportionately with changes in the activity level. (p. 965).

**Relevant range**   The range of the activity index over which the company expects to operate during the year. (p. 965).

**Sales mix**   The relative combination in which a company's products are sold. (p. 977).

**Target net income**   The income objective for individual product lines. (p. 976).

**Variable costing**   A costing approach in which only variable manufacturing costs are product costs and fixed manufacturing costs are period costs (expenses). (p. 981).

**Variable costs**   Costs that vary in total directly and proportionately with changes in the activity level. (p. 963).

# DEMONSTRATION PROBLEM

Mabo Company makes pocket calculators that sell for $20 each. For the coming year, management expects fixed costs to total $220,000 and variable costs to be $9.00 per unit.

*Instructions*
(a) Compute break-even sales in dollars using the mathematical equation.
(b) Compute break-even sales using the contribution margin (CM) ratio.
(c) Compute the margin of safety percentage assuming actual sales are $500,000.
(d) Compute the sales required to earn net income of $165,000.

**Problem-Solving Strategies**

1. Know the formulas.
2. Recognize that variable costs change with sales volume; fixed costs do not.
3. Avoid computational errors.
4. Prove your answers.

## Solution to Demonstration Problem

(a) Break-even Sales = Variable Costs + Fixed Costs

$$X = .45X + \$220,000$$
$$.55X = \$220,000$$
$$X = \$400,000$$

(b) Contribution Margin per Unit = Unit Selling Price − Unit Variable Costs
$$= \$11 \ (\$20 - \$9)$$

Contribution Margin Ratio = Contribution Margin per Unit ÷ Unit Selling Price
$$= 55\% \ (\$11 \div \$20)$$

Break-even Sales = Fixed Cost ÷ Contribution Margin Ratio
$$X = \$220,000 \div 55\%$$
$$X = \$400,000$$

(c) Margin of Safety $= \dfrac{\text{Actual Sales} - \text{Break-even Sales}}{\text{Actual Sales}}$

$$= \frac{\$500,000 - \$400,000}{\$500,000}$$
$$= 20\%$$

(d) Required Sales = Variable Costs + Fixed Costs + Net Income
$$X = .45X + \$220,000 + \$165,000$$
$$.55X = \$385,000$$
$$X = \$700,000$$

# SELF-STUDY QUESTIONS

Answers are at the end of the chapter.

(SO 1)  1. Variable costs are costs that:
   a. vary in total directly and proportionately with changes in the activity level.
   b. remain the same per unit at every activity level.
   c. None of the above.
   d. Both (a) and (b) above.

(SO 2)  2. The relevant range is:
   a. the range of activity in which variable costs will be curvilinear.
   b. the range of activity in which fixed costs will be curvilinear.
   c. the range over which the company expects to operate during a year.
   d. usually from zero to 100% of operating capacity.

(SO 3)  3. Mixed costs consist of a:
   a. variable cost element and a fixed cost element.
   b. fixed cost element and a controllable cost element.
   c. relevant cost element and a controllable cost element.
   d. variable cost element and a relevant cost element.

(SO 4)  4. One of the following is *not* involved in CVP analysis. That factor is:
   a. sales mix.
   b. unit selling prices.
   c. fixed costs per unit.
   d. volume or level of activity.

(SO 5)  5. Contribution margin:
   a. is revenue remaining after deducting variable costs.
   b. may be expressed as contribution margin per unit.
   c. None of the above.
   d. Both (a) and (b) above.

(SO 6)  6. Gossen Company is planning to sell 200,000 pliers for $4.00 per unit. The contribution margin ratio is 25%. If Gossen will break even at this level of sales, what are the fixed costs?
   a. $100,000.
   b. $160,000.
   c. $200,000.
   d. $300,000.

(SO 7)  7. Marshall Company had actual sales of $600,000 when break-even sales were $420,000. What is the margin of safety ratio?
   a. 25%.
   b. 30%.
   c. 33⅓%.
   d. 45%.

(SO 8)  8. The mathematical equation for computing required sales to obtain target net income is: Required Sales =
   a. Variable Costs + Target Net Income.
   b. Variable Costs + Fixed Costs + Target Net Income.
   c. Fixed Costs + Target Net Income.
   d. No correct answer is given.

(SO 9)  9. Keynes Company sells both radios and cassette players at the following per unit data:

| Units Data | Radios | Cassette Players |
|---|---|---|
| Selling price | $40 | $70 |
| Variable costs | 35 | 50 |
| Contribution margin | $ 5 | $20 |
| Sales mix | 2 | 1 |

What is the number of radios and cassette players that Keynes must sell in order to break even if fixed costs are $45,000?

| | Radios | Cassette Players |
|---|---|---|
| a. | 1,000 | 500 |
| b. | 1,500 | 750 |
| c. | 2,000 | 1,000 |
| d. | 3,000 | 1,500 |

(SO 10)  10. Cournot Company sells 100,000 wrenches for $12.00 a unit. Fixed costs are $300,000 and net income is $200,000. What should be reported as variable expenses in the CVP income statement?
   a. $700,000.
   b. $900,000.
   c. $500,000.
   d. $1,000,000.

(SO 11)  11. Under variable costing, fixed manufacturing costs are classified as:
   a. period costs.
   b. product costs.
   c. Both (a) and (b).
   d. Neither (a) nor (b).

# QUESTIONS

1. (a) What is cost behavior analysis?
   (b) Why is cost behavior analysis important to management?

2. (a) Sandy Olsen asks your help in understanding the term "activity index." Explain the meaning and importance of this term for Sandy.
   (b) State the two ways that variable costs may be defined.

3. Contrast the effects of changes in the activity level on total and on unit fixed costs.

4. T.J. Ling claims that the relevant range concept is important only for variable costs.
   (a) Explain the relevant range concept.
   (b) Do you agree with T.J.'s claim? Explain.

5. "The relevant range is indispensable in cost behavior analysis." Is this true? Why?

6. Bill Czar is confused. He does not understand why rent on his apartment is a fixed cost and rent on a Hertz rental truck is a mixed cost. Explain the difference to Bill.

7. How should mixed costs be classified in CVP analysis? What approach is used to effect the appropriate classification?

8. At the high and low levels of activity during the month, direct labor hours are 90,000 and 40,000, respectively, and the related costs are $140,000 and $90,000. What are the fixed and variable costs at any level of activity?

9. "Cost-volume-profit (CVP) analysis is based entirely on unit costs." Do you agree? Explain.

10. Paula Dao defines contribution margin as the amount of profit available to cover operating expenses. Is there any truth in this definition? Discuss.

11. In Warrel Company, the Speedo pocket calculator sells for $40, and variable costs per unit are estimated to be $24. What is the contribution margin per unit and the contribution margin ratio?

12. "Break-even analysis is of limited use to management because a company cannot survive by just breaking even." Do you agree? Explain.

13. Total fixed costs are $15,000 for Laser-Tech Inc.; it has a contribution margin per unit of $15, and a contribution margin ratio of 20%. Compute the break-even sales in dollars.

14. Laurie Robey asks your help in constructing a CVP graph. Explain to Laurie how (a) the break-even point is plotted and (b) the level of activity and dollar sales at the break-even point are determined.

15. Define the term "margin of safety." If Telex Company expects to sell 1,250 units of its product at $12 per unit, and break-even sales for the product are $10,000, what is the margin of safety ratio?

16. The Yugo Company's break-even sales are $600,000. Assuming fixed costs are $210,000, what sales dollars are needed to achieve a target net income of $45,000?

17. The sales mix of Oxford Company's two products is 5:2. What does 5:2 mean? What effect, if any, does a company's sales mix have on CVP analysis?

18. Zurhoff Company sells two products, X and Y. Their unit contribution margins are $52 and $70, respectively, and their sales mix is 2:1. What is the weighted average unit contribution margin?

19. What are the similarities and differences between a CVP income statement and a traditional income statement?

20. The traditional income statement for Pacific Company shows sales $900,000, cost of goods sold $500,000, and operating expenses $300,000. Assuming all costs and expenses are 70% variable and 30% fixed, prepare a CVP income statement through contribution margin.

21. Distinguish between absorption costing and variable costing.

22. (a) What is the major rationale for the use of variable costing? (b) Discuss why variable costing may not be used for financial reporting purposes.

# BRIEF EXERCISES

*Classify costs as variable, fixed, or mixed.*
*(SO 1, 3)*

**BE23–1** Monthly production costs in Meghan Company for two levels of production are as follows:

| Cost | 2,000 units | 4,000 units |
| --- | --- | --- |
| Indirect labor | $10,000 | $20,000 |
| Supervisory salaries | 5,000 | 5,000 |
| Maintenance | 3,000 | 3,600 |

Indicate which costs are variable, fixed, and mixed, and give the reason for each answer.

**BE23–2** In Whelan Company, the relevant range of production is 40–80% of capacity. At 40% of capacity, a variable cost is $2,000 and a fixed cost is $3,000. Diagram the behavior of each cost within the relevant range assuming the behavior is linear.

*Diagram the behavior of costs within the relevant range.*
*(SO 2)*

**BE23–3** In Hillard Company, a mixed cost is $40,000 plus $8 per direct labor hour. Diagram the behavior of the cost using increments of 1,000 hours up to 5,000 hours on the horizontal axis and increments of $20,000 up to $80,000 on the vertical axis.

*Diagram the behavior of a mixed cost.*
*(SO 3)*

**BE23–4** Faldo Company accumulates the following data concerning a mixed cost, using miles as the activity level.

*Determine variable and fixed cost elements using the high-low method.*
*(SO 3)*

|  | Miles Driven | Total Cost |  | Miles Driven | Total Cost |
|---|---|---|---|---|---|
| January | 8,000 | $14,200 | March | 8,500 | $15,000 |
| February | 7,500 | 13,400 | April | 8,200 | 14,500 |

Compute the variable and fixed cost elements using the high-low method.

**BE23–5** Determine the missing amounts.

*Determine missing amounts for contribution margin.*
*(SO 5)*

|  | Unit Selling Price | Unit Variable Costs | Contribution Margin per Unit | Contribution Margin Ratio |
|---|---|---|---|---|
| 1. | $250 | $190 | (a) | (b) |
| 2. | $500 | (c) | $125 | (d) |
| 3. | (e) | (f) | $360 | 40% |

**BE23–6** Casan Company has a unit selling price of $400, variable costs per unit of $320, and fixed costs of $120,000. Compute the break-even point using (a) a mathematical equation and (b) contribution margin per unit.

*Compute the break-even point.*
*(SO 6)*

**BE23–7** In Nicole Company actual sales are $1,200,000 and break-even sales are $900,000. Compute (a) the margin of safety in dollars and (b) the margin of safety ratio.

*Compute the margin of safety and the margin of safety ratio.*
*(SO 7)*

**BE23–8** In Novi Company, variable costs are 75% of sales, fixed costs are $180,000, and management's net income goal is $60,000. Compute the required sales needed to achieve management's target net income of $60,000. (Use the mathematical equation approach.)

*Compute sales for target net income.*
*(SO 8)*

**BE23–9** Loos Company sells three units of AA to one unit of BB; the two products have contribution margins of $100 and $200, respectively. Fixed costs are $300,000. Compute the unit sales at the break-even point. How many units of each product must be sold?

*Compute break-even sales units for two products.*
*(SO 9)*

**BE23–10** Zermatt Manufacturing Inc. has sales of $1,900,000 for the first quarter of 1996. In making the sales, the company incurred the following costs and expenses:

*Prepare CVP income statement.*
*(SO 10)*

|  | Variable | Fixed |
|---|---|---|
| Cost of goods sold | $660,000 | $540,000 |
| Selling expenses | 95,000 | 60,000 |
| Administrative expenses | 79,000 | 66,000 |

Prepare a CVP income statement for the quarter ended March 31, 1996.

**BE23–11** ▰▰▰▷ Sheila Company's fixed overhead costs are $6 per unit, and its variable overhead costs are $8 per unit. In the first month of operations, 50,000 units are produced, and 45,000 units are sold. Write a short memorandum to the chief financial officer of Sheila Company explaining which costing approach will produce the higher income and what the difference will be.

*Compute net income under absorption and variable costing.*
*(SO 11)*

# EXERCISES

**E23–1** Niagara Company manufactures a single product. Annual production costs incurred in the manufacturing process are shown below for two levels of production:

*Define and classify variable, fixed, and mixed costs.*
*(SO 1, 3)*

| | Costs Incurred | | | |
|---|---|---|---|---|
| **Production in Units** | **5,000** | | **10,000** | |
| **Production Costs** | **Total Cost** | **Cost/ Unit** | **Total Cost** | **Cost/ Unit** |
| Direct materials | $8,250 | $1.65 | $16,500 | $1.65 |
| Direct labor | 9,500 | 1.90 | 19,000 | 1.90 |
| Utilities | 1,400 | .28 | 2,300 | .23 |
| Rent | 4,000 | .80 | 4,000 | .40 |
| Maintenance | 800 | .16 | 1,100 | .11 |
| Supervisory salaries | 1,000 | .20 | 1,000 | .10 |

**Instructions**

(a) Define the terms variable costs, fixed costs, and mixed costs.

(b) Classify each cost above as either variable, fixed, or mixed.

*Determine fixed and variable costs using the high-low method and prepare graph.*
*(SO 1, 3)*

**E23–2** The controller of Guber Industries has collected the following monthly expense data for use in analyzing the cost behavior of maintenance costs:

| Month | Total Maintenance Costs | Total Machine Hours |
|---|---|---|
| January | $ 2,900 | 3,000 |
| February | 3,000 | 4,000 |
| March | 3,600 | 6,000 |
| April | 4,200 | 7,900 |
| May | 3,200 | 5,000 |
| June | 4,400 | 8,000 |

**Instructions**

(a) Determine the fixed and variable cost components using the high-low method.

(b) Prepare a graph showing the behavior of maintenance costs and identify the fixed and variable cost elements. Use 2,000 unit increments and $1,000 cost increments.

*Compute contribution margin, break-even point, and margin of safety.*
*(SO 5, 6, 7)*

**E23–3** In the month of June, Judy's Beauty Salon gave 2,400 haircuts, shampoos, and permanents at an average price of $25. During the month, fixed costs were $12,000 and variable costs were 60% of sales.

**Instructions**

(a) Determine the contribution margin in dollars, per unit, and as a ratio.

(b) Using the contribution margin technique, compute the break-even point in dollars and in units.

(c) Compute the margin of safety in dollars and as a ratio.

*Prepare a CVP graph and compute break-even point and margin of safety.*
*(SO 6, 7)*

**E23–4** Yale Company estimates that variable costs will be 50% of sales and fixed costs will total $800,000. The selling price of the product is $4.

**Instructions**

(a) Prepare a CVP graph, assuming maximum sales of $3,200,000. (Note: Use $400,000 increments for sales and costs and 100,000 increments for units.)

(b) Compute the break-even point in (1) units and (2) dollars.

(c) Compute the margin of safety in (1) dollars and (2) as a ratio, assuming actual sales are $2.4 million.

*Compute variable cost per unit, contribution margin ratio, and increase in fixed costs.*
*(SO 5)*

**E23–5** In 1996, Argus Company had a break-even point of $350,000 based on a selling price of $7 per unit and fixed costs of $70,000. In 1997, the selling price and the variable cost per unit did not change, but the break-even point increased to $455,000.

**Instructions**

(a) Compute the variable cost per unit and the contribution margin ratio for 1996.

(b) Compute the increase in fixed costs for 1997.

**E23–6** Benoit Company had $90,000 of net income in 1996 when the selling price per unit was $150, the variable costs per unit were $90, and the fixed costs were $510,000. Management expects per unit data and total fixed costs to remain the same in 1997. The president of Benoit Company is under pressure from stockholders to increase net income by $60,000 in 1997.

*Compute various components to derive target net income under different assumptions.*
*(SO 6, 8)*

**Instructions**
(a) Compute the number of units sold in 1996.
(b) Compute the number of units that would have to be sold in 1997 to reach the stockholders' desired profit level.
(c) Assume that Benoit Company sells the same number of units in 1997 as it did in 1996. What would the selling price have to be in order to reach the stockholders' desired profit level?

**E23–7** The following information is selected from the records of Oneida Company, which produces and sells two products:

*Compute sales mix, weighted average unit contribution margin, and break-even point.*
*(SO 5, 6, 9)*

|  | Product A | Product B |
|---|---|---|
| Selling price per unit | $ 9.00 | $ 17.00 |
| Units sold | 100,000 | 50,000 |
| Variable manufacturing cost per unit | $ 4.00 | $ 9.00 |

Fixed manufacturing overhead costs are $248,000, and fixed selling and administrative expenses are $94,000.

**Instructions**
(a) Compute the sales mix for Oneida Company.
(b) Calculate the weighted average unit contribution margin.
(c) Compute the break-even point in units, assuming the sales mix computed in part (a).

**E23–8** The Home Appliance Center sells three models of Super Clean dishwashers. Selling price and variable cost data for the models are as follows:

*Compute and prove the break-even point in units with sales mix.*
*(SO 5, 6, 9)*

|  | Economy | Standard | Deluxe |
|---|---|---|---|
| Unit selling price | $600 | $750 | $1,000 |
| Unit variable costs | $400 | $500 | $ 600 |
| Expected sales volume (units) | 500 | 300 | 200 |

**Instructions**
(a) Compute the break-even point in units, assuming total fixed costs are $229,500.
(b) Prove the correctness of your answer.

**E23–9** Luis Company reports the following operating results for the month of August: Sales $300,000 (units 5,000); variable costs $210,000; and fixed costs $70,000. Management is considering the following independent courses of action to increase net income.

*Compute net income under different alternatives.*
*(SO 8)*

1. Increase selling price by 15% with no change in total variable costs.
2. Reduce variable costs to 60% of sales.
3. Reduce fixed costs by $20,000.

**Instructions**
Compute the net income to be earned under each alternative. Which course of action will produce the highest net income?

**E23–10** Hickory Company had sales in 1996 of $1,500,000 on 60,000 units. Variable costs totaled $720,000, and fixed costs totaled $450,000.

A new raw material is available that will decrease the variable costs per unit by 20% (or $2.40). However, to process the new raw material, fixed operating costs will increase by $50,000. Management feels that one-half of the decline in the variable costs per unit should be passed on to the company's customers in the form of a sales price reduction. The marketing department expects that this sales price reduction will result in a 10% increase in the number of units sold.

*Prepare a CVP income statement before and after changes in business environment.*
*(SO 10)*

**Instructions**
Prepare a CVP income statement for 1996, assuming the changes are made as described.

*Compute total product cost
and prepare an income
statement using variable
costing.*
(SO 11)

**E23–11**   Ellen Equipment Company manufactures and distributes industrial air compressors. The following costs are available for the year ended December 31, 1996. The company has no beginning inventory. In 1996, 1,500 units were produced, but only 1,200 units were sold. The unit selling price was $4,500. Costs and expenses were:

| | | |
|---|---:|---:|
| Variable costs per unit | | |
| Direct materials | $ | 500 |
| Direct labor | | 1,500 |
| Variable manufacturing overhead | | 300 |
| Variable selling and administrative expenses | | 70 |
| Annual fixed costs and expenses | | |
| Manufacturing overhead | | $1,200,000 |
| Selling and administrative expenses | | 100,000 |

*Instructions*
(a) Compute the manufacturing cost of one unit of product using variable costing.
(b) Prepare a 1996 income statement for Ellen Company using variable costing.

# PROBLEMS
••••••••••••••••••••••••••••••••••••••••••••••••••••••••••••••••••••••••••••••

*Determine variable and fixed
costs, compute break-even
point, prepare a CVP graph,
and determine net income.*
(SO 1, 3, 5, 6)

**P23–1**   The Campus Barber Shop employs four barbers. One barber, who also serves as the manager, is paid a salary of $1,200 per month. The other barbers are paid $1,000 per month. In addition, each barber is paid a commission of $4 per haircut. Other monthly costs are: store rent $800 plus 60 cents per haircut, depreciation on equipment $500, barber supplies 40 cents per haircut, utilities $300, and advertising $200. The price of a haircut is $10.

*Instructions*
(a) Determine the variable cost per haircut and the total monthly fixed costs.
(b) Compute the break-even point in units and dollars.
(c) Prepare a CVP graph, assuming a maximum of 1,800 haircuts in a month. Use increments of 300 haircuts on the horizontal axis and $3,000 increments on the vertical axis.
(d) Determine the net income, assuming 1,400 haircuts are given in a month.

*Prepare a CVP income
statement, compute break-even
point, contribution margin
ratio, margin of safety ratio,
and sales for target net
income.*
(SO 5, 6, 7, 8, 10)

**P23–2**   Florida Company bottles and distributes LOKAL, a fruit drink. The beverage is sold for 50 cents per 16-oz. bottle to retailers, who charge customers 70 cents per bottle. At full (100%) plant capacity, management estimates the following revenues and costs.

| | | | | |
|---|---:|---|---:|
| Net sales | $2,000,000 | Selling expenses—variable | $ 90,000 |
| Direct materials | 360,000 | Selling expenses—fixed | 150,000 |
| Direct labor | 450,000 | Administrative expenses— | |
| Manufacturing overhead— | | variable | 30,000 |
| variable | 270,000 | Administrative expenses— | |
| Manufacturing overhead— | | fixed | 70,000 |
| fixed | 280,000 | | |

*Instructions*
(a) Prepare a CVP income statement for the year 1996 based on management's estimates.
(b) Compute the break-even point in (1) units and (2) dollars.
(c) Compute the contribution margin ratio and the margin of safety ratio.
(d) Determine the sales required to earn net income of $220,000.

*Compute break-even point
under alternative courses of
action.*
(SO 5, 6)

**P23–3**   Atlanta Manufacturing had a bad year in 1996. For the first time in its history it operated at a loss. The company's income statement showed the following results from selling 60,000 units of product: Net sales $1,500,000; total costs and expenses $1,740,000; and net loss $240,000. Costs and expenses consisted of the following:

| | Total | Variable | Fixed |
|---|---:|---:|---:|
| Cost of goods sold | $1,200,000 | $780,000 | $420,000 |
| Selling expenses | 420,000 | 75,000 | 345,000 |
| Administrative expenses | 120,000 | 45,000 | 75,000 |
| | $1,740,000 | $900,000 | $840,000 |

Management is considering the following independent alternatives for 1997.

1. Increase unit selling price 20% with no change in costs, expenses, and sales volume.
2. Change the compensation of salespersons from fixed annual salaries totaling $200,000 to total salaries of $40,000 plus a 6% commission on net sales.
3. Purchase new high-tech factory machinery that will change the proportion between variable and fixed cost of goods sold to 50:50.

**Instructions**

(a) Compute the break-even point in dollars for the year 1996.
(b) Compute the break-even point in dollars under each of the alternative courses of action. Which course of action do you recommend?

**P23–4** Cheryl Smith is the advertising manager for Fit-Rite Shoe Store. She is currently working on a major promotional campaign. Her ideas include the installation of a new lighting system and increased display space that will add $41,000 in fixed costs to the $180,000 currently spent. In addition, Cheryl is proposing that a 6⅔% price decrease (from $30.00 to $28.00) will produce an increase in sales volume from 16,000 to 21,000 units. Variable costs will remain at $15.00 per pair of shoes. Management is impressed with Cheryl's ideas but concerned about the effects that these changes will have on the break-even point and the margin of safety.

*Compute break-even point and margin of safety ratio and prepare a CVP income statement before and after changes in business environment.*
*(SO 6, 7, 10)*

**Instructions**

(a) Compute the current break-even point in units, and compare it to the break-even point in units if Cheryl's ideas are used.
(b) Compute the margin of safety ratio for current operations and after Cheryl's changes are introduced. (Round to nearest full percent.)
(c) Prepare a CVP income statement for current operations and after Cheryl's changes are introduced. Would you make the changes suggested?

**P23–5** Precision Electronics manufactures two models of cameras, Superfast and Ultrafast. Unit data for each model are as follows:

*Compute contribution margin ratio, break-even point, and sales to meet target net income and prepare a CVP income statement with a sales mix.*
*(SO 5, 6, 8, 9, 10)*

| | **Superfast** | **Ultrafast** |
|---|---|---|
| Selling price | $240 | $330 |
| Variable costs and expenses: | | |
| Direct materials | 60 | 60 |
| Direct labor | 40 | 70 |
| Manufacturing overhead | 34 | 36 |
| Selling | 20 | 25 |
| Administrative | 26 | 29 |
| Total variable | $180 | $220 |

Monthly fixed costs are: manufacturing overhead $45,000; selling expenses $35,000; and administrative expenses $20,000.

**Instructions**

(a) Compute the contribution margin ratio for each model.
(b) Compute the break-even point in dollars for each model using the contribution margin ratio, assuming fixed costs are divided equally between the products.
(c) Compute the sales necessary to make net income of $25,000 on Superfast and $40,000 on Ultrafast. Each model incurs 50% of the fixed costs.
(d) Assuming unit sales are 1,500 for Superfast and 1,100 for Ultrafast, prepare a CVP income statement for the month ended June 30, 1996 showing the net income on each product line and for the company as a whole. Each model incurs 50% of the fixed costs.

**P23–6** Omaha Metal Company produces the steel wire that goes into the production of paper clips. In 1996, the first year of operations, Omaha produced 40,000 miles of wire and sold 30,000 miles. In 1997, the production and sales results were exactly reversed. In each year, selling price per mile was $80, variable manufacturing costs were 25% of the sales price, variable selling expenses were $8.00 per mile sold, fixed manufacturing costs were $1,200,000, and fixed administrative expenses were $200,000.

*Prepare income statements under absorption and variable costing.*
*(SO 11)*

*Instructions*

    (a)  Prepare comparative income statements for each year using variable costing.

    (b)  Prepare comparative income statements for each year using absorption costing.

    (c)  Reconcile the differences each year in income from operations under the two costing approaches.

    (d)  Comment on the effects of production and sales on net income under the two costing approaches.

# ALTERNATE PROBLEMS

*Determine variable and fixed costs, compute break-even point, prepare a CVP graph, and determine net income.*

*(SO 1, 3, 5, 6)*

**P23–1A**  Ho Hwang owns the Peace Barber Shop. He employs five barbers and pays each a base rate of $800 per month. One of the barbers serves as the manager and receives an extra $400 per month. In addition to the base rate, each barber also receives a commission of $3.50 per haircut.

    Other costs are as follows:

| | |
|---|---|
| Advertising | $200 per month |
| Rent | $600 per month |
| Barber supplies | $.30 per haircut |
| Utilities | $175 per month plus $.20 per haircut |
| Magazines | $25 per month |

Ho currently charges $10 per haircut.

*Instructions*

    (a)  Determine the variable cost per haircut and the total monthly fixed costs.

    (b)  Compute the break-even point in units and dollars.

    (c)  Prepare a CVP graph, assuming a maximum of 1,800 haircuts in a month. Use increments of 300 haircuts on the horizontal axis and $3,000 on the vertical axis.

    (d)  Determine net income, assuming 1,500 haircuts are given in a month.

*Prepare a CVP income statement, compute break-even point, contribution margin ratio, margin of safety ratio, and sales for target net income.*

*(SO 5, 6, 7, 8, 10)*

**P23–2A**  Kalon Company bottles and distributes NOKAL, a diet soft drink. The beverage is sold for 40 cents per 16-oz. bottle to retailers, who charge customers 60 cents per bottle. At full (100%) plant capacity, management estimates the following revenues and costs.

| | | | |
|---|---|---|---|
| Net sales | $1,800,000 | Selling expenses—variable | $80,000 |
| Direct materials | 400,000 | Selling expenses—fixed | 65,000 |
| Direct labor | 460,000 | Administrative expenses— | |
| Manufacturing overhead— | | variable | 20,000 |
| variable | 300,000 | Administrative expenses— | |
| Manufacturing overhead— | | fixed | 52,000 |
| fixed | 183,000 | | |

*Instructions*

    (a)  Prepare a CVP income statement for the year 1996 based on management's estimates.

    (b)  Compute the break-even point in (1) units and (2) dollars.

    (c)  Compute the contribution margin ratio and the margin of safety ratio. (Round to full percents.)

    (d)  Determine the sales required to earn net income of $150,000.

*Compute break-even point under alternative courses of action.*

*(SO 5, 6)*

**P23–3A**  Bavaro Manufacturing's sales slumped badly in 1996. For the first time in its history, it operated at a loss. The company's income statement showed the following results from selling 600,000 units of product: Net sales $2,400,000; total costs and expenses $2,610,000; and net loss $210,000. Costs and expenses consisted of the following:

| | Total | Variable | Fixed |
|---|---|---|---|
| Cost of goods sold | $2,100,000 | $1,440,000 | $  660,000 |
| Selling expenses | 310,000 | 72,000 | 238,000 |
| Administrative expenses | 200,000 | 48,000 | 152,000 |
| | $2,610,000 | $1,560,000 | $1,050,000 |

Management is considering the following independent alternatives for 1997:

1. Increase unit selling price 25% with no change in costs, expenses, and sales volume.
2. Change the compensation of salespersons from fixed annual salaries totaling $210,000 to total salaries of $30,000 plus a 5% commission on net sales.
3. Purchase new automated equipment that will change the proportion between variable and fixed cost of goods sold to 60% variable and 40% fixed.

*Instructions*
(a) Compute the break-even point in dollars for the year 1996.
(b) Compute the break-even point in dollars under each of the alternative courses of action. (Round to full percents.) Which course of action do you recommend?

**P23–4A**  Cheryl Small is the advertising manager for Modern Shoe Store. She is currently working on a major promotional campaign. Her ideas include the installation of a new lighting system and increased display space that will add $34,000 in fixed costs to the $200,000 currently spent. In addition, Cheryl is proposing that a 5% price decrease ($40.00 to $38.00) will produce a 20% increase in sales volume (20,000 to 24,000). Variable costs will remain at $20.00 per pair of shoes. Management is impressed with Cheryl's ideas but concerned about the effects that these changes will have on the break-even point and the margin of safety.

*Compute break-even point and margin of safety ratio and prepare a CVP income statement before and after changes in business environment.*
*(SO 6, 7, 10)*

*Instructions*
(a) Compute the current break-even point in units, and compare it to the break-even point in units if Cheryl's ideas are used.
(b) Compute the margin of safety ratio for current operations and after Cheryl's changes are introduced. (Round to nearest full percent.)
(c) Prepare a CVP income statement for current operations and after Cheryl's changes are introduced. Would you make the changes suggested?

**P23–5A**  Bret Shumway Company manufactures two models of televisions, Superclear and Ultraclear. Unit data for each model are as follows:

*Compute contribution margin ratio, break-even point, and sales to meet target net income and prepare a CVP income statement with a sales mix.*
*(SO 5, 6, 8, 9, 10)*

|  | Superclear | Ultraclear |
|---|---|---|
| Selling price | $360 | $480 |
| Variable costs and expenses: |  |  |
| Direct materials | 90 | 95 |
| Direct labor | 50 | 60 |
| Manufacturing overhead | 60 | 68 |
| Selling | 32 | 36 |
| Administrative | 20 | 29 |
| Total variable | $252 | $288 |

Monthly fixed costs are: manufacturing overhead $72,000; selling expenses $46,000; and administrative expenses $26,000.

*Instructions*
(a) Compute the contribution margin ratio for each model.
(b) Compute the break-even point in dollars for each model using the contribution margin ratio, assuming fixed costs are divided equally between the products.
(c) Compute the sales necessary to make net income of $36,000 on Superclear and $48,000 on Ultraclear. Each model incurs 50% of all fixed costs.
(d) Assuming unit sales are 1,200 for Superclear and 1,000 for Ultraclear, prepare a CVP income statement for the month ended September 30, 1996, showing the net income on each product line and for the company as a whole. Each model incurs 50% of all fixed costs.

# ▼*Broadening Your Perspective*

## DECISION CASE 1

Camero Company has decided to introduce a new product. The new product can be manufactured by either a capital-intensive method or a labor-intensive method. The manufacturing method will not affect the quality of the product. The estimated manufacturing costs by the two methods are as follows:

|  | Capital-Intensive | Labor-Intensive |
|---|---|---|
| Raw materials | $5 per unit | $5.60 per unit |
| Direct labor | $6 per unit | $7.20 per unit |
| Variable overhead | $3 per unit | $4.80 per unit |
| Fixed manufacturing costs | $2,440,000 | $1,320,000 |

Camero's market research department has recommended an introductory unit sales price of $30. The incremental selling expenses are estimated to be $500,000 annually plus $2 for each unit sold, regardless of manufacturing method.

### Instructions

(a) Calculate the estimated break-even point in annual unit sales of the new product if Camero Company uses the:–
   (1) capital-intensive manufacturing method.
   (2) labor-intensive manufacturing method.
(b) Determine the annual unit sales volume at which Camero Company would be indifferent between the two manufacturing methods.
(c) Explain the circumstances under which Camero should employ each of the two manufacturing methods.

(CMA adapted)

## DECISION CASE 2

The condensed income statement for the Ramona and Simon partnership for 1996 is as follows:

**RAMONA AND SIMON COMPANY**
**Income Statement**
**For the Year Ended December 31, 1996**

| | | |
|---|---|---|
| Sales (200,000 units) | | $1,200,000 |
| Cost of goods sold | | 800,000 |
| Gross profit | | 400,000 |
| Operating expenses | | |
|   Selling | 280,000 | |
|   Administrative | 160,000 | 440,000 |
| Net loss | | ($40,000) |

A cost behavior analysis indicates that 75% of the cost of goods sold are variable; 50% of the selling expenses are variable; and 25% of the administrative expenses are variable.

### Instructions

(Round to nearest unit, dollar, and percentage, where necessary. Use the CVP income statement format in computing profits.)

(a) Compute the break-even point in total sales dollars and in units for 1996.
(b) Ramona has proposed a plan to get the partnership "out of the red" and improve its profitability. She feels that the quality of the product could be substantially im-

proved by spending $0.55 more per unit on better raw materials. The selling price per unit could be increased to only $6.50 because of competitive pressures. Ramona estimates that sales volume will increase by 30%. What effect will Ramona's plan have on the profits and the break-even point in dollars of the partnership?

(c) Simon was a marketing major in college. He believes that sales volume can be increased only by intensive advertising and promotional campaigns. He therefore proposed the following plan as an alternative to Ramona's: (1) increase variable selling expenses to $0.85 per unit, (2) lower the selling price per unit by $0.20, and (3) increase fixed selling expenses by $20,000. Simon quoted an old marketing research report that said that sales volume would increase by 50% if these changes were made. What effect will Simon's plan have on the profits and the break-even point in dollars of the partnership?

(d) Which plan should be accepted? Explain your answer.

# COMMUNICATION ACTIVITY

In CVP analysis there are many formulas. Your roommate asks your help on the following questions:

(a) How can the mathematical equation for break-even sales show both sales dollars and sales units?

(b) How do the formulas differ, if at all, for contribution margin per unit and contribution margin ratio?

(c) How can contribution margin be used to determine break-even sales in dollars and in units?

*Instructions*

Write a memorandum to your roommate that states the relevant formulas and the answers to each of the foregoing questions.

# GROUP ACTIVITY

Health-Max, a producer of vitamin supplements, is evaluating several plans to increase net income for the company as a whole. Health-Max currently produces two products. The first is called Vita-Max and is a vitamin supplement made from plant materials, organically grown by Health-Max. The second, called Tranquility, is an herbal tea, also made from organically grown plants. Because of a very strong demand, the company doubled the size of its farm property on which the plants are grown. Health-Max would like to expand its production of Vita-Max and Tranquility, but wants to make certain that the changes will be profitable.

Cost and production information are as follows:

|  | Vita-Max | Tranquility |
|---|---|---|
| Variable costs | $5/bottle | $2/box of tea bags |
| Revenue | $10/bottle | $5/box of tea bags |
| Production | 1/2 capacity | 1/2 capacity |
| Sales volume per month | 10,000 units | 10,000 units |

Fixed costs are $55,000 per month plus $30,000 per month fixed costs related to the new farm property.

The following three projects are under consideration:

1. Double capacity for Vita-Max and Tranquility. If Health-Max does this, Vita-Max will be sold through a distributor, rather than directly to retail outlets. This would mean approximately a 25% decrease in the sales revenue per unit for Vita-Max. Tranquility's sales price would not change.

2. Because Vita-Max is presently earning the most money per unit, Health-Max could use all the new production capacity at the farm to produce an additional 20,000 units of Vita-Max. Since sales have been fairly stable at the retail outlets presently used, there would have to be an advertising campaign, which would increase fixed costs

$15,000 per month. Additional machinery would increase fixed costs an additional $25,000 per month. In addition, variable selling costs would increase by $2.

3. Tranquility could be modified into a new tea called Nature's Lullaby. This would allow the company to increase the selling price of the tea to $6 per box, and would also decrease the variable costs to $1.50, since Nature's Lullaby would use less expensive ingredients. The 10,000 units of Vita-Max would still be sold, and 30,000 boxes of Nature's Lullaby would be sold. No Tranquility would be sold.

*Instructions*

Have groups of four or five students answer the following questions:

(a) What is the net income under each of the alternatives?

(b) Carefully consider each project. Which do you recommend? Include in your answer the advantages and disadvantages of each. Which option, in the opinion of your group, is least risky? Which is most risky?

# ETHICS CASE

••••••••••••••••••••••••••••••••••••••••••••••••••••••••••••••••••••••••••••••••••••••••••

Danny Bern is an accountant for Hot-Chip Company. Early this year Danny made a highly favorable projection of sales and profits over the next 3 years for its hot-selling computer PLEX. As a result of the projections Danny presented to senior management, they decided to expand production in this area. This decision led to dislocations of some plant personnel who were reassigned to one of the company's newer plants in another state. However, no one was fired, and in fact the company expanded its work force slightly.

Unfortunately Danny rechecked his computations on the projections a few months later and found that he had made an error that would have reduced his projections substantially. Luckily, sales of PLEX have exceeded projections so far, and management is satisfied with its decision. Danny, however, is not sure what to do. Should he confess his honest mistake and jeopardize his possible promotion? He suspects that no one will catch the error because sales of PLEX have exceeded his projections, and it appears that profits will materialize close to his projections.

*Instructions*

(a) Who are the stakeholders in this situation?

(b) Identify the ethical issues involved in this situation.

(c) What are the possible alternative actions for Danny? What would you do if in Danny's position?

# CRITICAL THINKING
## ▸ *A Real-World Focus: Biochem Pharma Incorporated*

••••••••••••••••••••••••••••••••••••••••••••••••••••••••••••••••••••••••••••••••••••••••••

**BIOCHEM PHARMA INC.**

*Biochem Pharma is a pharmaceutical company incorporated in Canada and involved in the research and development of therapeutic products related to infectious and other diseases, particularly with respect to viral infections, cancer, immune disorders, and pain control.*

In a recent annual report of Biochem Pharma, the following information was provided:

MANAGEMENT DISCUSSION:
Our product mix improved with higher sales of diagnostics products and lower sales of vaccines. The diagnostic products carry a better contribution margin than the vaccine products.

*Instructions*

(a) What does management mean when it refers to the contribution margin of products?

(b) How can management use the contribution margin information to calculate the break-even point in units?

---

*Answers to Self-Study Questions*

1. d  2. c  3. a  4. c  5. d  6. c  7. b  8. b  9. d  10. a  11. a

# Big Red's Biennial Budget

LINCOLN, Nebr. — Every university has a budget. Usually, there's a capital budget for big projects such as new buildings, and there's an operating budget for the day-to-day expenditures.

At the University of Nebraska, the operating budget request takes up four volumes totaling nearly 900 pages. Because the university is funded by the state of Nebraska, the budget must be submitted to the state legislature for approval. That means the university has to pay lobbyists to plead its case with legislators. The budget is due September 15th of every other year. The lawmakers consider it during their sessions, which begin in January.

As you might expect, increases in expenses are resisted because money is tight. "Roughly 70% of our budget goes toward salaries," says Paula Boroff, budget officer at the

Omaha campus. "A university is a very labor-intensive institution," she observes. The total budget for a recent fiscal year is about $95 million, reflecting a 1% cut in state funds from the prior year.

One budget item of interest to students is the "remission" category. That's where scholarships are

funded. "This year, the budget for honor students and needy students is nearly $2 million—$1,994,488 to be exact," says Boroff, who recently received her MBA from the University of Nebraska graduate school. "Of our 16,000 students, we had 8,274 on some kind of aid," she says. ◀

# CHAPTER 24

# *B*UDGETARY PLANNING

▶ STUDY OBJECTIVES ◀

**After studying this chapter, you should be able to:**

1. *Indicate the benefits of budgeting.*
2. *State the essentials of effective budgeting.*
3. *Identify the budgets that comprise the master budget.*
4. *Describe the sources for preparing the budgeted income statement.*
5. *Explain the principal sections of a cash budget.*
6. *Indicate the applicability of budgeting in nonmanufacturing companies.*

As the story about the University of Nebraska indicates, budgeting is an integral part of our society. As students, you budget your study time and your money. Families budget income and expenses, and governmental agencies budget revenues and expenditures. Business enterprises use budgets in planning and controlling their operations.

Our primary focus in this chapter is budgeting—specifically, how budgeting is used as a *planning tool* by management. Through budgeting, it should be possible for management to maintain enough cash to pay creditors, to have sufficient raw materials to meet production requirements, and to have adequate finished good to meet expected sales. The content and organization of this chapter are as follows:

## **B**udgeting Basics

One of management's major responsibilities is planning. As explained in Chapter 20, **planning** is the process of establishing enterprise objectives. A successful organization establishes both long-term and short-term plans that set forth the objectives of the company and the proposed means of accomplishing them.

A budget is a formal written summary (or statement) of management's plans for a specified future time period, expressed in financial terms. It normally represents the primary means of communicating agreed-upon objectives throughout the business organization. Once adopted, a budget becomes an important basis for evaluating performance. Thus, it promotes efficiency and serves as a deterrent to waste and inefficiency. We consider the role of budgeting as a **control device** in Chapter 25.

## Budgeting and Accounting

Accounting information makes major contributions to the budgeting process. From the accounting records, historical data on revenues, costs, and expenses can be obtained. These data may be helpful in formulating future budget goals.

Normally, accounting has the responsibility for expressing management's budgeting goals in financial terms. In this role, it becomes the translator of management's plans, and it provides the means of communicating the budget to all areas of responsibility. Accounting also prepares periodic budget reports that provide the basis for measuring performance and comparing actual results with planned objectives. The budget itself, and the administration of the budget, however, are entirely management responsibilities.

## ►*T*echnology in *A*ction

In large firms, the computer is an essential tool in the budgeting process. Entire computer programs are designed to aid in budget preparation. These systems can also be integrated into the general ledger and provide a complete reporting package for monitoring budgeted vs. actual results. Packages with similar features are available for microcomputers so even small companies can adopt the budgeting practices found in major companies.

A powerful feature of many spreadsheet packages is the ability to merge and consolidate budget data as they flow up the organizational chain of command.

## The Benefits of Budgeting

The primary benefits of budgeting are:

1. It requires all levels of management to **plan ahead** and to formalize their future goals on a recurring basis.
2. It provides **definite objectives** for evaluating performance at each level of responsibility.
3. It creates an **early warning system** for potential problems. With early warning, management has time to solve the problem before things get out of hand. For example, the cash budget may reveal the need for outside financing several months before an actual cash shortage occurs.
4. It facilitates the **coordination of activities** within the business by correlating the goals of each segment with overall company objectives. Thus, production and sales promotion can be integrated with expected sales.
5. It results in greater **management awareness** of the entity's overall operations and the impact of external factors, such as economic trends, on the company's operations.
6. It contributes to **positive behavior patterns** throughout the organization by motivating personnel to meet planned objectives.

A budget is an aid to management; it is not a substitute for management. A budget cannot operate or enforce itself. The benefits of budgeting will be realized only when budgets are carefully prepared and properly administered by management.

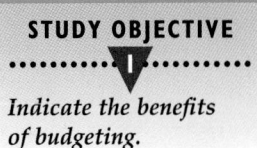

**STUDY OBJECTIVE**

*Indicate the benefits of budgeting.*

## Essentials of Effective Budgeting

In order to be effective management tools, budgets must be based upon a sound organizational structure, research and analysis, and management acceptance of the budget program.

**STUDY OBJECTIVE**

*State the essentials of effective budgeting.*

### *Sound Organizational Structure*

**Effective budgeting depends on an organizational structure in which authority and responsibility over all phases of operations are clearly defined.** The establishment of responsibility is a prerequisite for budgeting. Budgets are prepared by departments, and managers have the responsibility for meeting their budgets. Subsequent comparisons of actual results with budget expectations are made to determine how well managers discharge their responsibilities.

### *Research and Analysis*

A budget based entirely on past performance is ineffective. In today's highly competitive business environment, management must look ahead, or it will fall behind. Research and analysis help determine the feasibility of new products, services, and operating techniques, as well as the market potential of new territories and branches. Research and analysis lead to careful investigation and informed judgments. **Budgets based on research and analysis should result in realistic goals that will contribute to the growth and profitability of a company.**

### *Management Acceptance*

**The effectiveness of a budget program is directly related to its acceptance by all levels of management.** Acceptance of budgets by division managers, department heads, and supervisors is enhanced when these individuals participate fully in the preparation of the budgets. As shown in Illustration 24-1, the input data for budgeting should flow from the lowest level of management responsibility to the highest. The input is reviewed and then consolidated as it moves to each higher level of management. The budget must have the support of top management.

**Illustration 24-1**

*Flow of budget data from bottom to top*

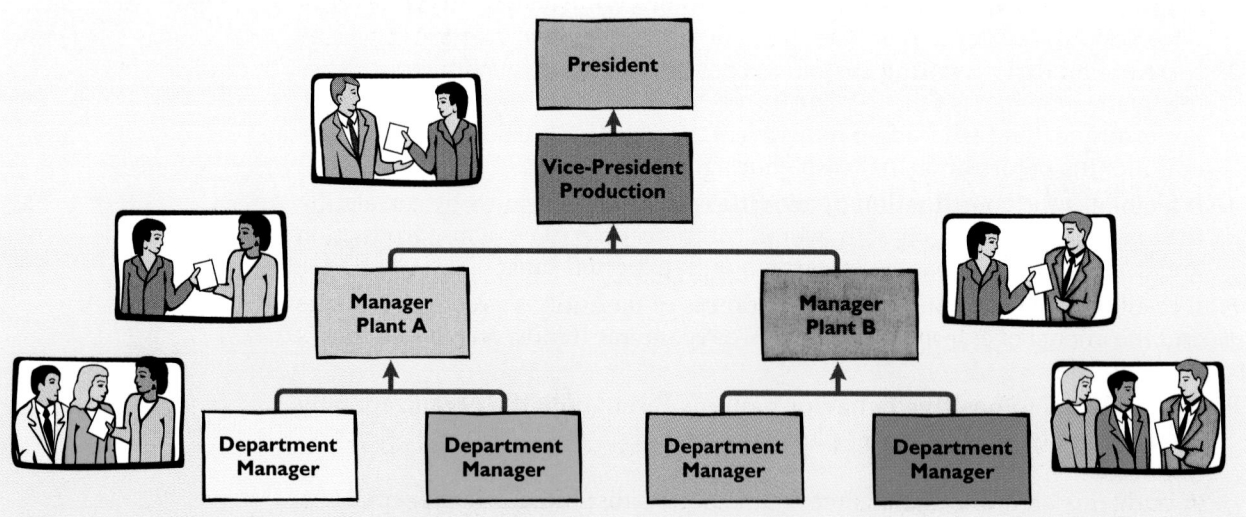

Once the budget has been adopted, it should be an important basis for evaluating performance. Variations between actual and expected results should be systematically and periodically reviewed to determine their cause(s). However, care should be exercised to see that individuals are not held responsible for variations that are beyond their control.

## Length of the Budget Period

As indicated in the opening story about the University of Nebraska budget, the budget period is not necessarily one year in length. **A budget may be prepared for any period of time.** Such factors as the type of budget, the nature of the organization, the need for periodic appraisal, and prevailing business conditions will influence the length of the budget period. For example, cash may be budgeted monthly, whereas a plant expansion program budget may cover a 10-year period.

The budget period should be long enough to provide an attainable goal under normal business conditions. Ideally, the time period should minimize the impact of seasonal and cyclical business fluctuations. On the other hand, the budget period should not be so long that reliable estimates are impossible.

The **most common budget period is one year**. The annual budget, in turn, is often supplemented by monthly and quarterly budgets. Many companies today use **continuous 12-month budgets** by dropping the month just ended and adding a future month. One advantage of continuous budgeting is that it keeps management planning a full year ahead.

## The Budgeting Process

The development of the budget for the coming year generally starts several months before the end of the current year. The budgeting process usually begins with the collection of data from each of the organizational units of the company. Past performance is often the starting point in budgeting, from which future budget goals are formulated.

The budget is developed within the framework of a sales forecast that shows potential sales for the industry and the company's expected share of such sales. Sales forecasting involves a consideration of such factors as (1) general economic conditions, (2) industry trends, (3) market research studies, (4) anticipated advertising and promotion, (5) previous market share, (6) changes in prices, and (7) technological developments. The input of sales personnel and top management are essential in preparing the sales forecast.

## ►*T*echnology in *A*ction

Because a forecast involves many uncertainties, various approaches are taken in an effort to increase the reliability of the forecast. These include a variety of sophisticated statistical and mathematical techniques. Today, many companies use **financial planning models** to forecast sales. A model can express the effects of both internal and external factors on sales.

In many companies, responsibility for coordinating the preparation of the budget is assigned to a budget committee. The committee, often headed by a budget director, ordinarily includes the president, treasurer, chief accountant (controller), and management personnel from each of the major areas of the company, such as sales, production, and research. The budget committee serves as a review board where managers and supervisors can defend their budget goals and requests. After differences are reviewed, modified if necessary, and reconciled, the budget is prepared by the budget committee, put in its final form, and approved. Copies of the budget are subsequently distributed to the various levels of managers who have budget responsibilities.

## Budgeting and Human Behavior

A budget can have a significant effect on human behavior. On the one hand, a budget may have a strong positive influence that inspires a manager to higher levels of performance. On the other hand, a budget may discourage additional effort and have a negative impact on the morale of a manager. Why do these diverse effects occur? The answer is found in the manner in which the budget is developed and administered.

In developing the budget, each level of management should be invited and encouraged to participate. The overall objective is to reach agreement on a budget that the manager considers to be fair and achievable. When this objective is met, the budget will have a positive effect on the manager. In contrast, if the manager views the budget as being unfair and unrealistic, he or she may become discouraged and uncommitted to the budget goals. The risk of having unrealistic budgets is generally greater when the budget is developed from top management down to lower management than vice versa.

Administering the budget relates to the manner in which the budget is used by top management. As explained earlier, the budget should have the complete support of top management. In addition, the budget should be an important basis for evaluating performance. The effect of an evaluation on a manager will be positive when top management tempers criticism with advice and assistance. In contrast, the response of a manager is likely to be negative when the budget is used exclusively to assess blame. Top management should also be sensitive to the behavioral implications of its actions. An understanding and flexible attitude has a positive influence on human behavior. Conversely, a rigid and inflexible attitude has a negative effect on the manager who is being evaluated.

▸ *Ethics note*

Unrealistic budgets can lead to unethical employee behavior such as cutting corners on the job or distorting internal financial reports.

A budget may be used improperly as a pressure device to force improved performance. Alternatively, it can be used as a positive aid in the achievement of projected goals. In sum, a budget can become a friend or a foe to the manager.

The human factor is an important aspect of budgeting. When properly used, budgets can be a positive motivating force within a company.

## Budgeting and Long-Range Planning

In business, you may hear management talk about the need for long-range planning. Budgeting and long-range planning are not the same. One important difference is the **time period involved**. The maximum length of a budget is usually one year, and budgets are often prepared for shorter periods of time, such as a month or a quarter. In contrast, long-range planning usually encompasses a period of at least five years.

A second significant difference is **in emphasis**. Budgeting is concerned with the achievement of specific short-term goals, such as meeting annual profit objectives. Long-range planning, on the other hand, involves the selection of strategies to achieve long-term goals and the development of policies and plans to implement the strategies. In long-range planning, management also considers anticipated trends in the economic and political environment and policies the company should follow to cope with them.

**Helpful hint**  In comparing a budget with a long-range plan: (1) Which has more detail? (2) Which is done for a longer period of time? (3) Which is more concerned with short-term goals? Answer: (1) Budget. (2) Long-range plan. (3) Budget.

The final difference between budgeting and long-range planning pertains to the **amount of detail presented**. Budgets, as you have seen earlier in this chapter, can be very detailed. The detail is needed to provide a basis for control. Long-range plans contain considerably less detail, because the data are intended more for a review of progress toward long-term goals than for an evaluation of specific results to be achieved.

Long-range planning should be a systematic and formalized process. The primary objective of long-range planning is to develop the best strategy to maximize the company's performance over an extended future period. Neither budgeting nor long-range planning can solve all the problems of a manager. Nor can they guarantee the success of the company. However, the two activities should contribute to better planning, control, and decision making by management.

## Before You Go On . . .

▶ **Review It**

1. What are the benefits of budgeting?
2. What are the factors essential to effective budgeting?
3. How does the budget process work?
4. How does budgeting differ from long-range planning?

# The Master Budget

When we discuss a "budget," we actually are using a shorthand term to describe a variety of budget documents, all of which are combined into a master budget. The master budget is a set of interrelated budgets that constitutes a plan of action for a specified time period. The individual budgets included in a master budget for Hayes Company, which sells a single product, Kitchen-mate, are shown in Illustration 24-2.

**STUDY OBJECTIVE**

◂◂◂◂◂◂◂◂◂ ▼3 ◂◂◂◂◂◂◂◂◂

*Identify the budgets that comprise the master budget.*

**Illustration 24-2**

*Components of the master budget*

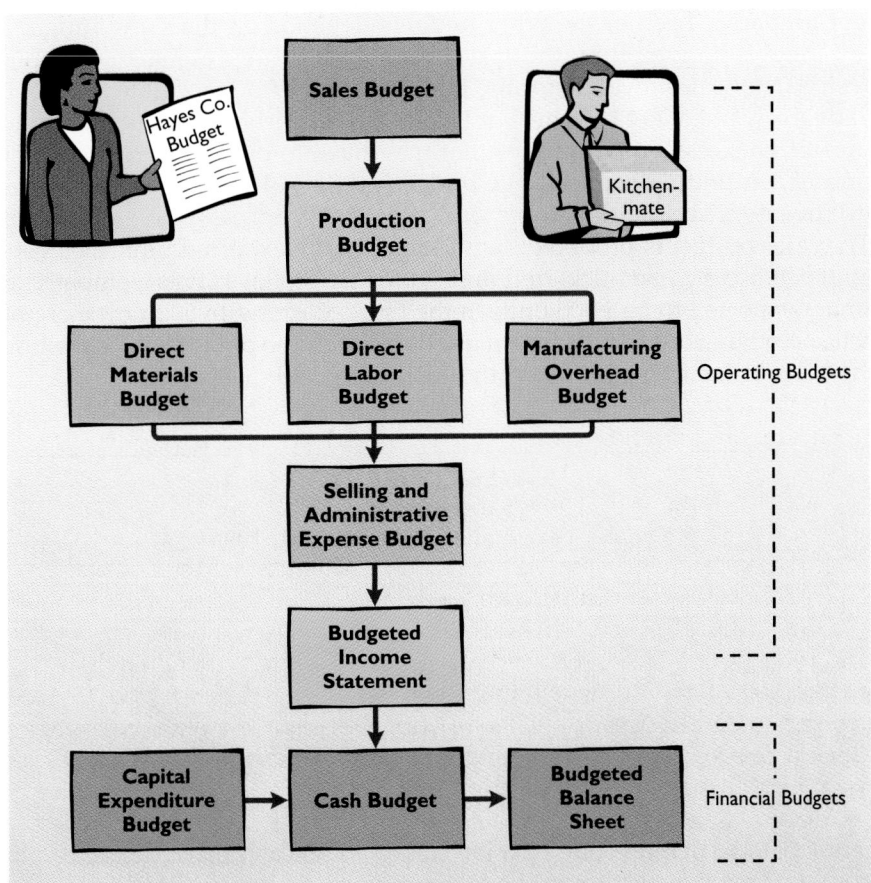

As shown in the illustration, there are two classes of budgets in the master budget. Operating budgets include the individual budgets that culminate in the preparation of the budgeted income statement. The primary objective of these budgets is to establish goals for the company's sales and production personnel. In contrast, financial budgets include the cash budget and the budgeted balance sheet. These budgets focus primarily on the cash resources needed to fund expected operations and planned capital expenditures.

The master budget is prepared in the sequence shown in Illustration 24-2. The operating budgets are developed first beginning with the sales budget. After these budgets have been determined, the financial budgets are prepared. We will explain and illustrate each budget shown in Illustration 24-2 except the capital expenditure budget. This budget is discussed under the topic, Capital Budgeting, in Chapter 27.

# Preparing the Operating Budgets

A case study of Hayes Company will be used in preparing the operating budgets. Hayes Company manufactures and sells a single product, Kitchen-mate. The budgets will be prepared by quarters for the year ending December 31, 1996. Hayes Company begins its annual budgeting process on September 1, 1995, and it completes the budget for 1996 by December 1, 1995.

## Sales Budget

**Helpful hint** For a retail or manufacturing company, what is the starting point in preparing the master budget, and why? Answer: Preparation of the sales budget is the starting point in preparing the master budget because it sets the level of activity for other functions such as production and purchasing.

As shown in the master budget in Illustration 24-2, **the sales budget is the first budget prepared**. Each of the other budgets depends on the sales budget. The sales budget is derived from the sales forecast, and it represents management's best estimate of sales revenue for the budget period. An inaccurate sales budget may adversely affect net income. For example, an overly optimistic sales budget may result in excessive inventories that may have to be sold at reduced prices. In contrast, an unduly conservative budget may result in loss of sales revenue due to inventory shortages.

The sales budget is prepared by multiplying the expected unit sales volume for each product by its anticipated unit selling price. For Hayes Company, sales volume is expected to be 3,000 units in the first quarter with 500-unit increments in each succeeding quarter. Based on a sales price of $60 per unit, the sales budget for the year, by quarters, is shown in Illustration 24-3.

**Illustration 24-3**

*Sales budget*

| | \multicolumn{5}{c}{HAYES COMPANY<br>Sales Budget<br>For the Year Ending December 31, 1996} |
|---|---|---|---|---|---|
| | \multicolumn{5}{c}{Quarter} |
| | 1 | 2 | 3 | 4 | Year |
| Expected unit sales | 3,000 | 3,500 | 4,000 | 4,500 | 15,000 |
| Unit selling price | × $60 | × $60 | × $60 | × $60 | × $60 |
| Total sales | $180,000 | $210,000 | $240,000 | $270,000 | $900,000 |

The anticipated sales revenue may be classified as cash or credit sales and by geographical regions, territories, or salespersons.

## Production Budget

The production budget shows the units that must be produced to meet antici-pated sales. Production requirements are determined from the following formula:[1]

**Illustration 24-4**

*Production requirements formula*

**A realistic estimate of ending inventory is essential in scheduling produc-tion requirements.** Excessive inventories in one quarter may lead to cutbacks in production and layoffs of employees in a subsequent quarter. Conversely, in-adequate inventories may result either in added costs for overtime work or in lost sales in a later period. On the basis of past experience, Hayes Company believes it can meet future sales requirements by maintaining an ending inven-tory equal to 20% of the next quarter's budgeted sales volume. For example, the ending finished goods inventory for the first quarter is 700 units (20% × antic-ipated second-quarter sales of 3,500 units). The production budget is shown in Illustration 24-5.

**Illustration 24-5**

*Production budget*

**HAYES COMPANY**
**Production Budget**
**For the Year Ending December 31, 1996**

| | Quarter | | | | |
| --- | --- | --- | --- | --- | --- |
| | 1 | 2 | 3 | 4 | Year |
| Expected unit sales (Illustration 24-3) | 3,000 | 3,500 | 4,000 | 4,500 | |
| Add: Desired ending finished goods units[a] | 700 | 800 | 900 | 1,000[b] | |
| Total required units | 3,700 | 4,300 | 4,900 | 5,500 | |
| Less: Beginning finished goods units | 600[c] | 700 | 800 | 900 | |
| Required production units | 3,100 | 3,600 | 4,100 | 4,600 | 15,400 |

[a]20% of next quarter's sales
[b]Expected 1997 first quarter sales, 5,000 units × 20%
[c]20% of estimated first quarter 1996 sales units

The production budget, in turn, provides the basis for determining the budgeted costs for each manufacturing cost element, as explained in the following pages.

---

[1]This formula ignores any work in process inventories, which are assumed to be nonexistent in Hayes Company.

## ▶Accounting in Action ▸ *Business Insight*

Wrong move, wrong time, poor planning. Recently, Fruit of the Loom Inc. saw under-wear and apparel sales slowing. It cut back production sharply. Too sharply, in fact: almost overnight, in February, demand soared. Caught with its shorts down, the company hired back thousands of workers and frantically increased production. The mistimed production cuts contributed to a 43% fall in first-quarter profits. For the year, Fruit stood to lose $200 million in sales, and analysts expected an 11% drop in profits for the year.

*Source: Business Week,* June 6, 1994, p. 38.

## Direct Materials Budget

The direct materials budget contains both the quantity and cost of direct materials to be purchased. The quantities of direct materials are derived from the following formula:

**Illustration 24-6**

*Formula for direct materials quantities*

The budgeted cost of direct materials to be purchased is then computed by multiplying the required units of direct materials by the anticipated cost per unit.

**The desired ending inventory is again a critical component in the budgeting process.** For example, inadequate inventories could result in temporary shutdowns of production. Because of its close proximity to suppliers, Hayes Company has found that an ending inventory of raw materials equal to 10% of the next quarter's production is sufficient. The manufacture of each Kitchen-mate requires 2 pounds of raw materials and the expected cost per pound is $4. The direct materials budget is shown in Illustration 24-7.

## ▶*Technology in Action*

The successful manufacturers of the 1990s will be fully computerized. A crucial step on the way is material requirements planning (MRP) systems. Early MRP systems accepted a sales forecast and computed how much materials, inventory, people, and machinery a company needed to manufacture the product. Current MRP systems link the company's manufacturing resource planning with its financial management, creating a powerful system of control over the entire business planning and operating process. With MRP, management can make decisions on facts rather than on "hunches" and "instinct."

**Illustration 24-7**

*Direct materials budget*

**HAYES COMPANY**
**Direct Materials Budget**
**For the Year Ending December 31, 1996**

| | Quarter | | | | |
| --- | --- | --- | --- | --- | --- |
| | 1 | 2 | 3 | 4 | Year |
| Units to be produced (Illustration 24-5) | 3,100 | 3,600 | 4,100 | 4,600 | |
| Direct materials per unit | × 2 | × 2 | × 2 | × 2 | |
| Total pounds needed for production | 6,200 | 7,200 | 8,200 | 9,200 | |
| Add: Desired ending direct materials (pounds)[a] | 720 | 820 | 920 | 1,020[b] | |
| Total materials required | 6,920 | 8,020 | 9,120 | 10,220 | |
| Less: Beginning direct materials (pounds) | 620[c] | 720 | 820 | 920 | |
| Direct materials purchases | 6,300 | 7,300 | 8,300 | 9,300 | |
| Cost per pound | × $4 | × $4 | × $4 | × $4 | |
| Total cost of direct materials purchases | $25,200 | $29,200 | $33,200 | $37,200 | $124,800 |

[a]10% of next quarter's production
[b]Estimated 1997 first quarter pounds needed for production, 10,200 × 10%
[c]10% of estimated first quarter pounds needed for production

## Direct Labor Budget

Like the direct materials budget, the direct labor budget contains the quantity (hours) and cost of direct labor necessary to meet production requirements. Direct labor hours are determined from the production budget. At Hayes Company, two hours of direct labor are required to produce each unit of finished goods, and the anticipated hourly wage rate is $10. These data are shown in Illustration 24-8. The direct labor budget is critical in maintaining a labor force that can meet the expected levels of production.

**Illustration 24-8**

*Direct labor budget*

**HAYES COMPANY**
**Direct Labor Budget**
**For the Year Ending December 31, 1996**

| | Quarter | | | | |
| --- | --- | --- | --- | --- | --- |
| | 1 | 2 | 3 | 4 | Year |
| Units to be produced (Illustration 24-5) | 3,100 | 3,600 | 4,100 | 4,600 | |
| Direct labor time (hours) per unit | × 2 | × 2 | × 2 | × 2 | |
| Total required direct labor hours | 6,200 | 7,200 | 8,200 | 9,200 | |
| Direct labor cost per hour | × $10 | × $10 | × $10 | × $10 | |
| Total direct labor cost | $62,000 | $72,000 | $82,000 | $92,000 | $308,000 |

**Helpful hint** An important assumption here is that the company can add and subtract from its work force as needed so that the $10 per hour labor cost applies to a wide range of possible production activity.

## Manufacturing Overhead Budget

The manufacturing overhead budget shows the expected manufacturing overhead costs for the budget period. As shown in Illustration 24-9, **this budget distinguishes between variable and fixed overhead costs**. From previous experience, Hayes Company expects variable costs to fluctuate with production volume on the basis of the following rates per direct labor hour: indirect materials $1.00, indirect labor $1.40, utilities $0.40, and maintenance $0.20. Thus, for 6,200 direct labor hours, budgeted indirect materials are $6,200 (6,200 × $1), and budgeted indirect labor is $8,680 (6,200 × $1.40). Hayes Company also recognizes that some maintenance is fixed. The amounts reported for fixed costs are assumed.

At Hayes Company, overhead is applied to production on the basis of direct labor hours. Thus, as shown in Illustration 24-9, the annual rate is $8 per hour ($246,400 ÷ 30,800).

**Illustration 24-9**

*Manufacturing overhead budget*

| | | | | | |
|---|---|---|---|---|---|
| **HAYES COMPANY** | | | | | |
| **Manufacturing Overhead Budget** | | | | | |
| **For the Year Ending December 31, 1996** | | | | | |
| | **Quarter** | | | | |
| | 1 | 2 | 3 | 4 | Year |
| Variable costs | | | | | |
| Indirect materials | $ 6,200 | $ 7,200 | $ 8,200 | $ 9,200 | $ 30,800 |
| Indirect labor | 8,680 | 10,080 | 11,480 | 12,880 | 43,120 |
| Utilities | 2,480 | 2,880 | 3,280 | 3,680 | 12,320 |
| Maintenance | 1,240 | 1,440 | 1,640 | 1,840 | 6,160 |
| Total variable | 18,600 | 21,600 | 24,600 | 27,600 | 92,400 |
| Fixed costs | | | | | |
| Supervisory salaries | 20,000 | 20,000 | 20,000 | 20,000 | 80,000 |
| Depreciation | 3,800 | 3,800 | 3,800 | 3,800 | 15,200 |
| Property taxes and insurance | 9,000 | 9,000 | 9,000 | 9,000 | 36,000 |
| Maintenance | 5,700 | 5,700 | 5,700 | 5,700 | 22,800 |
| Total fixed | 38,500 | 38,500 | 38,500 | 38,500 | 154,000 |
| Total manufacturing overhead | $57,100 | $60,100 | $63,100 | $66,100 | $246,400 |
| Direct labor hours | 6,200 | 7,200 | 8,200 | 9,200 | 30,800 |
| Manufacturing overhead rate per direct labor hour ($246,400 ÷ 30,800) | | | | | $8.00 |

## Selling and Administrative Expense Budget

Hayes Company combines its operating expenses into one budget, the selling and administration expense budget. This budget is a projection of anticipated selling and administrative expenses for the budget period. In this budget, as in the preceding budget, expenses are classified as either variable or fixed. In this case, the variable expense rates per unit of sales are sales commissions $3.00, and freight-out $1.00. Variable expenses per quarter are based on the unit sales projected in the sales budget (Illustration 24-3). For example, sales in the first quarter are expected to be 3,000 units. Thus, Sales Commissions Expense is $9,000 (3,000 × $3), and Freight-out is $3,000 (3,000 × $1). Fixed expenses are based on assumed data. The selling and administrative expense budget is shown in Illustration 24-10.

**Illustration 24-10**

*Selling and administrative expense budget*

**HAYES COMPANY**
**Selling and Administrative Expense Budget**
**For the Year Ending December 31, 1996**

| | Quarter | | | | |
|---|---|---|---|---|---|
| | 1 | 2 | 3 | 4 | Year |
| Variable expenses | | | | | |
| Sales commissions | $ 9,000 | $10,500 | $12,000 | $13,500 | $ 45,000 |
| Freight-out | 3,000 | 3,500 | 4,000 | 4,500 | 15,000 |
| Total variable | 12,000 | 14,000 | 16,000 | 18,000 | 60,000 |
| Fixed expenses | | | | | |
| Advertising | 5,000 | 5,000 | 5,000 | 5,000 | 20,000 |
| Sales salaries | 15,000 | 15,000 | 15,000 | 15,000 | 60,000 |
| Office salaries | 7,500 | 7,500 | 7,500 | 7,500 | 30,000 |
| Depreciation | 1,000 | 1,000 | 1,000 | 1,000 | 4,000 |
| Property taxes and insurance | 1,500 | 1,500 | 1,500 | 1,500 | 6,000 |
| Total fixed | 30,000 | 30,000 | 30,000 | 30,000 | 120,000 |
| Total selling and administrative expenses | $42,000 | $44,000 | $46,000 | $48,000 | $180,000 |

## Budgeted Income Statement

The budgeted income statement is the important end-product in preparing operating budgets. This budget indicates the expected profitability of operations for the budget period. Once established, the budgeted income statement provides the basis for evaluating company performance. As you would expect, this budget is prepared from the previous budgets. For example, to find the cost of goods sold, it is first necessary to determine the total unit cost of producing one Kitchen-mate as follows:

**STUDY OBJECTIVE**
**4**

*Describe the sources for preparing the budgeted income statement.*

**Illustration 24-11**

*Computation of total unit cost*

**Cost of One Kitchen-mate**

| Cost Element | Illustration | Quantity | Unit Cost | Total |
|---|---|---|---|---|
| Direct materials | 24-7 | 2 pounds | $ 4.00 | $ 8.00 |
| Direct labor | 24-8 | 2 hours | $10.00 | 20.00 |
| Manufacturing overhead | 24-9 | 2 hours | $ 8.00 | 16.00 |
| Total unit cost | | | | $44.00 |

Cost of goods sold can then be determined by multiplying the units sold by the unit cost. For Hayes Company, budgeted cost of goods sold is $660,000 (15,000 × $44). All data for the statement are obtained from the individual operating budgets except the following: (1) interest expense is expected to be $100 and (2) income taxes are estimated to be $12,000. The budgeted income statement is shown in Illustration 24-12.

**Illustration 24-12**

*Budgeted income statement*

| HAYES COMPANY |
| :-- |
| **Budgeted Income Statement** |
| **For the Year Ending December 31, 1996** |

| | | |
| :-- | --: | --: |
| Sales (Illustration 24-3) | | $900,000 |
| Cost of goods sold (15,000 × $44) | | 660,000 |
| Gross profit | | 240,000 |
| Selling and administrative expenses (Illustration 24-10) | | 180,000 |
| Income from operations | | 60,000 |
| Interest expense | | 100 |
| Income before income taxes | | 59,900 |
| Income tax expense | | 12,000 |
| Net income | | $ 47,900 |

## Preparing the Financial Budgets

As shown in Illustration 24-2, the financial budgets consist of the capital expenditure budget, the cash budget, and the budgeted balance sheet. The capital expenditure budget is discussed in Chapter 27; the other budgets are explained in the following sections.

**STUDY OBJECTIVE**

**5**

*Explain the principal sections of a cash budget.*

### Cash Budget

The cash budget shows anticipated cash flows. Because cash is so vital in a company, this budget is considered to be the most important output in preparing financial budgets. The cash budget contains three sections (cash receipts, cash disbursements, and financing) and the beginning and ending cash balances as shown in Illustration 24-13.

**Illustration 24-13**

*Basic form of a cash budget*

| Cash Budget | |
| :-- | --: |
| Beginning cash balance | $X,XXX |
| Add: Cash receipts (Itemized) | X,XXX |
| Total available cash | X,XXX |
| Less: Cash disbursements (Itemized) | X,XXX |
| Excess (deficiency) of available cash over cash disbursements | X,XXX |
| Financing | X,XXX |
| Ending cash balance | $X,XXX |

The **cash receipts section** includes expected receipts from the company's principal source(s) of revenue such as cash sales and collections from customers on credit sales. This section also shows anticipated receipts of interest and dividends, and proceeds from planned sales of investments, plant assets, and the company's capital stock.

The **cash disbursements section** shows expected payments for direct materials, direct labor, manufacturing overhead, and selling and administrative expenses. This section also includes projected payments for income taxes, dividends, investments, and plant assets.

The **financing section** shows expected borrowings and the repayment of the borrowed funds plus interest. This section is needed when there is a cash deficiency or when the cash balance is below management's minimum required balance.

Data in the cash budget must be prepared in sequence because the ending cash balance of one period becomes the beginning cash balance for the next period. Data for preparing the cash budget are obtained from other budgets and from information provided by management. In practice, cash budgets are often prepared for the year on a monthly basis.

**Helpful hint** Why is the cash budget prepared after the other budgets are prepared? Answer: Because the information generated by the other budgets dictates the need for and the inflows and outflows of cash.

## ▶Accounting in Action ▸ *Business Insight*

Douglas Roberson, president of Atlantic Network, woke up one morning to find that his company was out of cash. At that point, Roberson realized that managing cash flow is different from simply accumulating sales. He says: "If you don't do serious projections about how much cash you will need to handle sales—and how long it will take to collect on invoices—you can end up out of business no matter how fast you are growing." In fact, Roberson says, fast growth exacerbates cash flow problems because the company can be spending cash on supplies and payroll at an accelerated pace while waiting 45 days or longer to collect receivables.

*Source: Inc.*, August 1994, p. 107.

To minimize detail, we will assume that Hayes Company prepares an annual cash budget by quarters. The cash budget for Hayes Company is based on the following assumptions:

1. The January 1, 1996, cash balance is expected to be $38,000.
2. Sales (Illustration 24-3)—60% are collected in the quarter sold and 40% are collected in the following quarter. Accounts receivable of $60,000 at December 31, 1995 are expected to be collected in full in the first quarter of 1996.
3. Marketable securities are expected to be sold for $2,000 cash in the first quarter.
4. Direct materials (Illustration 24-7)—50% are paid in the quarter purchased and 50% are paid in the following quarter. Accounts payable of $10,600 at December 31, 1995, are expected to be paid in full in the first quarter of 1996.
5. Direct labor (Illustration 24-8)—100% is paid in the quarter incurred.
6. Manufacturing overhead (Illustration 24-9) and selling and administrative expenses (Illustration 24-10). All items except depreciation are paid in the quarter incurred.
7. Management plans to purchase a new truck in the second quarter for $10,000 cash.
8. The company makes equal quarterly payments of its estimated annual income taxes.
9. Loans are repaid in the first subsequent quarter in which there is sufficient cash.

Preparing schedules for collections from customers (assumption No. 2, above) and cash payments for direct materials (assumption No. 4, above) is useful in preparing the cash budget. The schedules are shown in Illustrations 24-14 and 24-15.

The cash budget for the Hayes Company is shown in Illustration 24-16. The budget indicates that $3,000 of financing will be needed in the second quarter to maintain a minimum cash balance of $15,000. Since there is an excess of available

**Illustration 24-14**

*Collections from customers*

| **Schedule of Expected Collections from Customers** | | | | |
|---|---|---|---|---|
| | Quarter | | | |
| | 1 | 2 | 3 | 4 |
| Accounts receivable, 12/31/95 | $ 60,000 | | | |
| First quarter ($180,000) | 108,000 | $ 72,000 | | |
| Second quarter ($210,000) | | 126,000 | $ 84,000 | |
| Third quarter ($240,000) | | | 144,000 | $ 96,000 |
| Fourth quarter ($270,000) | | | | 162,000 |
| Total collections | $168,000 | $198,000 | $228,000 | $258,000 |

**Illustration 24-15**

*Payments for direct materials*

| **Schedule of Expected Payments for Direct Materials** | | | | |
|---|---|---|---|---|
| | Quarter | | | |
| | 1 | 2 | 3 | 4 |
| Accounts payable, 12/31/95 | $10,600 | | | |
| First quarter ($25,200) | 12,600 | $12,600 | | |
| Second quarter ($29,200) | | 14,600 | $14,600 | |
| Third quarter ($33,200) | | | 16,600 | $16,600 |
| Fourth quarter ($37,200) | | | | 18,600 |
| Total payments | $23,200 | $27,200 | $31,200 | $35,200 |

**Illustration 24-16**

*Cash budget*

| **HAYES COMPANY** **Cash Budget** **For the Year Ending December 31, 1996** | | | | | |
|---|---|---|---|---|---|
| | | Quarter | | | |
| | Assumption | 1 | 2 | 3 | 4 |
| Beginning cash balance | 1 | $ 38,000 | $ 25,500 | $ 15,000 | $ 19,400 |
| Add: Receipts | | | | | |
| Collections from customers | 2 | 168,000 | 198,000 | 228,000 | 258,000 |
| Sale of securities | 3 | 2,000 | 0 | 0 | 0 |
| Total receipts | | 170,000 | 198,000 | 228,000 | 258,000 |
| Total available cash | | 208,000 | 223,500 | 243,000 | 277,400 |
| Less: Disbursements | | | | | |
| Direct materials | 4 | 23,200 | 27,200 | 31,200 | 35,200 |
| Direct labor | 5 | 62,000 | 72,000 | 82,000 | 92,000 |
| Manufacturing overhead | 6 | 53,300[1] | 56,300 | 59,300 | 62,300 |
| Selling and administrative expenses | 6 | 41,000[2] | 43,000 | 45,000 | 47,000 |
| Purchase of truck | 7 | 0 | 10,000 | 0 | 0 |
| Income tax expense | 8 | 3,000 | 3,000 | 3,000 | 3,000 |
| Total disbursements | | 182,500 | 211,500 | 220,500 | 239,500 |
| Excess (deficiency) of available cash over disbursements | | 25,500 | 12,000 | 22,500 | 37,900 |
| Financing | | | | | |
| Borrowings | | 0 | 3,000 | 0 | 0 |
| Repayments—plus $100 interest | 9 | 0 | 0 | 3,100 | 0 |
| Ending cash balance | | $ 25,500 | $ 15,000 | $ 19,400 | $ 37,900 |

[1]$57,100 − $3,800 depreciation
[2]$42,000 − $1,000 depreciation

cash over disbursements of $22,500 at the end of the third quarter, the borrowing is repaid in this quarter plus $100 interest.

**A cash budget contributes to more effective cash management.** For example, it can show when additional financing will be necessary well before the actual need arises. Conversely, it can indicate when excess cash will be available for investments or other purposes.

## Budgeted Balance Sheet

The budgeted balance sheet is a projection of financial position at the end of the budget period. This budget is developed from the budgeted balance sheet for the preceding year and the budgets for the current year. Pertinent data from the budgeted balance sheet at December 31, 1995, are as follows:

| | | | |
|---|---|---|---|
| Building and equipment | $182,000 | Common stock | $225,000 |
| Accumulated depreciation | $ 28,800 | Retained earnings | $ 46,480 |

The budgeted balance sheet at December 31, 1996, is shown below.

**Illustration 24-17**

*Budgeted balance sheet*

**HAYES COMPANY**
**Budgeted Balance Sheet**
**December 31, 1996**

Assets

| | | |
|---|---|---|
| Cash | | $ 37,900 |
| Accounts receivable | | 108,000 |
| Finished goods inventory | | 44,000 |
| Raw materials inventory | | 4,080 |
| Buildings and equipment | $192,000 | |
| Less: Accumulated depreciation | 48,000 | 144,000 |
| Total assets | | $337,980 |

Liabilities and Stockholders' Equity

| | |
|---|---|
| Accounts payable | $ 18,600 |
| Common stock | 225,000 |
| Retained earnings | 94,380 |
| Total liabilities and stockholders' equity | $337,980 |

The computations and sources of the amounts are explained below.

Cash—Ending cash balance $37,900, shown in the cash budget (Illustration 24-16).

Accounts receivable—40% of fourth quarter sales $270,000, shown in the schedule of expected collections from customers (Illustration 24-14).

Finished goods inventory—Desired ending inventory 1,000 units, shown in production budget (Illustration 24-5) times the total unit cost, $44, shown in Illustration 24-11).

Raw materials inventory—Desired ending inventory 1,020 pounds, times the cost per pound, $4 shown in the direct materials budget (Illustration 24-7).

Buildings and equipment—December 31, 1995, balance $182,000, plus purchase of truck for $10,000.

Accumulated depreciation—December 31, 1995, balance $28,800, plus $15,200 depreciation shown in manufacturing overhead budget (Illustration 24-9) and $4,000 depreciation shown in selling and administrative expense budget (Illustration 24-10).

Accounts payable—50% of fourth quarter purchases $37,200, shown in schedule of expected payments for direct materials (Illustration 24-15).

Common stock—Unchanged from the beginning of the year.

Retained earnings—December 31, 1995, balance $46,480, plus net income, $47,900, shown in budgeted income statement (Illustration 24-12).

# ▸Technology in Action

After the budgeting data are entered into the computer, the various budgets (sales, cash, etc.) can be prepared, as well as the budgeted financial statements. Management can also manipulate the budgets in "what if" (sensitivity) analyses based on different hypothetical assumptions. For example, suppose that sales were budgeted to be 10 percent higher in the coming quarter. What impact would the change have on the rest of the budgeting process and the financing needs of the business? The computer can quickly "play out" the impact of the various assumptions on the budgets. Armed with these analyses, management can make more informed decisions about the impact of various projects and anticipate future problems and business opportunities. Budgeting is one of the top uses of electronic spreadsheets. Template versions of every one of the Hayes Company budgets shown in this chapter could easily be prepared.

## *Before You Go On . . .*

### ▸ *Review It*

1. How may the individual budgets in the master budget be classified?
2. What is the sequence for preparing the budgets that comprise the operating budgets?
3. What are the three principal sections of the cash budget?

### ▸ *Do It*

In Martian Company, management wants to maintain a minimum monthly cash balance of $15,000. At the beginning of March, the cash balance is $16,500, expected cash receipts for March are $210,000, and cash disbursements are expected to be $220,000. How much cash, if any, must be borrowed to maintain the desired minimum monthly balance?

**Reasoning:** The best way to answer this question is to insert the dollar data into the basic form of the cash budget.

**Solution:**

| | |
|---|---:|
| Beginning cash balance | $ 16,500 |
| Add: Cash receipts for March | 210,000 |
| Total available cash | 226,500 |
| Less: Cash disbursements for March | 220,000 |
| Excess of available cash over cash disbursements | 6,500 |
| Financing | 8,500 |
| Ending cash balance | $ 15,000 |

To maintain the desired minimum cash balance of $15,000, $8,500 of cash must be borrowed.

*Related exercise material:* BE24–9 and E24–9.

# Budgeting in Nonmanufacturing Companies

Budgeting is not limited to manufacturing companies. Budgets may also be used in profit planning by merchandising companies, service enterprises, and not-for-profit organizations.

**STUDY OBJECTIVE**

................▼**6**............

*Indicate the applicability of budgeting in nonmanufacturing companies.*

## Merchandising Companies

As in manufacturing operations, the sales budget is both the starting point and the key factor in the development of the master budget for a merchandising company. The major differences between the master budgets of a merchandising company and a manufacturing company are that a merchandiser **(1) uses a merchandise purchases budget instead of a production budget and (2) does not use the manufacturing budgets (direct materials, direct labor, and manufacturing overhead).** The merchandise purchases budget shows the estimated cost of goods to be purchased to meet expected sales. The formula for determining budgeted merchandise purchases is:

**Illustration 24-18**

*Merchandise purchases formula*

To illustrate, assume that the budget committee of Lima Company is preparing the merchandise purchases budget for July. It estimates that budgeted sales will be $300,000 in July and $320,000 in August. Cost of goods sold is expected to be 70% of sales, and the company's desired ending inventory is 30% of the following month's cost of goods sold. Required merchandise purchases for July are $214,200, computed as follows:

**Illustration 24-19**

*Computation of required merchandise purchases*

| | |
|---|---:|
| Budgeted cost of goods sold (budgeted sales for July, $300,000 × 70%) | $210,000 |
| Desired ending merchandise inventory (budgeted cost of goods sold for August, $320,000 × 70% × 30%) | 67,200 |
| Total | 277,200 |
| Less: Beginning merchandise inventory (budgeted sales for July, $300,000 × 70% × 30%) | 63,000 |
| Required merchandise purchases for July | $214,200 |

When the merchandising company is departmentalized, separate budgets are prepared for each department. For example, a grocery store may start by preparing sales budgets and purchases budgets for each of its major departments, such as meats, dairy, and produce. These budgets are then combined into a master budget for the store. When a retailer has branch stores, separate master budgets are prepared for each store. Then these budgets are incorporated into master budgets for the company as a whole.

## Service Enterprises

In service enterprises, such as a public accounting firm, a law office, or a medical practice, the critical factor in budgeting is **coordinating professional staff needs with anticipated services.** If a firm is overstaffed, (1) labor costs will be disproportionately high, (2) profits will be lower because of the additional salaries, and (3) staff turnover may increase because of lack of challenging work. In contrast, if an enterprise is understaffed, revenue may be lost because existing and prospective client needs for service cannot be met, and professional staff may seek other positions because of excessive work loads.

Budget data for service revenue may be obtained from expected output or expected input. When output is used, it is necessary to determine the expected billings of clients for services rendered. In a public accounting firm, for example, output would be the sum of its billings in auditing, tax, and consulting services. When service revenue is derived from input data, each professional staff member is required to project his or her billable time. Billing rates are then applied to billable time to produce expected service revenue.

## ▸*A*ccounting in *A*ction ▸ *Business Insight*

Lucy Carter, managing partner of a small CPA firm in Nashville, uses formal budgets as the principal tool for keeping cash flow on an even keel throughout the year. The firm budgets annually for both revenues and expenses on a month-by-month basis. For example, the revenue budget is derived from chargeable-hour goals set by the staff, with a threshold of 1,800 hours for each staff member and 1,700 hours for each manager. Each month the budget is compared with the financial statements, and adjustments are made if necessary.

*Source: Journal of Accountancy,* August 1993, p. 56.

## Not-for-Profit Organizations

Budgeting is just as important for not-for-profit organizations as for profit-oriented enterprises. The budget process, however, is significantly different. In most cases not-for-profit entities budget **on the basis of cash flows (expenditures and receipts), rather than on a revenue and expense basis.** Further, the starting point in the process is usually expenditures, not receipts. For the not-for-profit entity, management's task generally is to find the receipts needed to support the planned expenditures. This was the case for the University of Nebraska in the opening story. The activity index is also likely to be significantly different. For example, in a not-for-profit entity, such as a university, budgeted faculty positions may be based on full-time equivalent students or credit hours expected to be taught in a department.

For some governmental units, the budget must be approved by voters. In other cases, such as state governments and the federal government, legislative approval is required. After the budget is adopted, it must be strictly followed, and overspending is often illegal. In governmental budgets, authorizations tend to be on a line-by-line basis. That is, the budget for a municipality may have a specified authorization for police and fire protection, garbage collection, street paving, and so on. The line item authorization of governmental budgets significantly limits the amount of discretion management can exercise. The city manager often cannot use savings in one line item, such as street paving, to cover increased spending in another line item, such as snow removal.

## *Before You Go On . . .*

### ► *Review It*

1. What is the formula for computing required merchandise purchases?
2. How does budgeting in service and not-for-profit organizations differ from budgeting in manufacturing and merchandising companies?

### ► *A Look Back at the University of Nebraska*

Refer to the opening story and answer the following questions.

1. How does the length of the budget period for the University of Nebraska compare with the guidelines given for businesses in the chapter?
2. What is the difference between a capital budget and an operating budget?
3. Whom do you believe comprises the budget committee at your college or university?

**Solution:**

1. The University of Nebraska must submit its budget to the state legislature on September 15 *every other year*. Thus, the length of the budget period is 2 years. For businesses, the length of the budget period is normally one year, and for some items, such as cash, monthly budgets may be prepared.
2. A capital budget is for big projects, such as buildings, which span more than a year. An operating budget is established to plan for day-to-day expenditures.
3. The budget committee at many universities consists of key officers and the deans of the various colleges. Key officers would be the president, vice-president for academic affairs (sometimes called the provost), and the vice-president of finance.

## Summary of Study Objectives

**1.** *Identify the benefits of budgeting.* The primary advantages of budgeting are that it (a) requires management to plan ahead, (b) provides definite objectives for evaluating performance, (c) creates an early warning system for potential problems, (d) facilitates coordination of activities, (e) results in greater management awareness, and (f) contributes to positive behavior patterns.

**2.** *Describe the essentials of effective budgeting.* The essentials of effective budgeting are (a) sound organizational structure, (b) research and analysis, and (c) management acceptance.

**3.** *Identify the budgets that comprise the master budget.* The master budget consists of the following budgets: (a) sales, (b) production, (c) direct materials, (d) direct labor, (e) manufacturing overhead, (f) selling and administrative expense, (g) budgeted income statement, (h) capital expenditure budget, (i) cash budget, and (j) budgeted balance sheet.

**4.** *Describe the sources for preparing the budgeted income statement.* The budgeted income statement is prepared from (a) the sales budget, (b) the budgets for direct materials, direct labor, and manufacturing overhead, and (c) the selling and administrative expense budget.

**5.** *Explain the principal sections of a cash budget.* The cash budget has three sections (receipts, disbursements, and financing) and the beginning and ending cash balances.

**6.** *Indicate the applicability of budgeting in nonmanufacturing companies.* Budgeting may be used in merchandising companies for development of a master budget. In service enterprises budgeting is a critical factor in coordinating staff needs with anticipated services. In not-for-profit organizations, the starting point in budgeting is usually expenditures, not receipts.

## Glossary

**Budget** A formal written summary of management's plans for a specified future time period, expressed in financial terms. (p. 1002).

**Budget committee** A group responsible for coordinating the preparation of the budget. (p. 1005).

**Budgeted balance sheet**  A projection of financial position at the end of the budget period. (p. 1017).

**Budgeted income statement**  An estimate of the expected profitability of operations for the budget period. (p. 1013).

**Cash budget**  A projection of anticipated cash flows. (p. 1014).

**Direct labor budget**  A projection of the quantity and cost of direct labor to be incurred to meet production requirements. (p. 1011).

**Direct materials budget**  An estimate of the quantity and cost of direct materials to be purchased. (p. 1010).

**Financial budgets**  Individual budgets that indicate the cash resources needed for expected operations and planned capital expenditures. (p. 1008).

**Long-range planning**  The selection of strategies to achieve long-term goals and the development of policies and plans to implement the strategies. (p. 1006).

**Manufacturing overhead budget**  An estimate of expected manufacturing overhead costs for the budget period. (p. 1011).

**Master budget**  A set of interrelated budgets that constitutes a plan of action for a specific time period. (p. 1007).

**Merchandise purchases budget**  The estimated cost of goods to be purchased in a merchandising company to meet expected sales. (p. 1019).

**Operating budgets**  Individual budgets that culminate in a budgeted income statement. (p. 1008).

**Production budget**  A projection of the units that must be produced to meet anticipated sales. (p. 1009).

**Sales budget**  An estimate of expected sales for the budget period. (p. 1008).

**Sales forecast**  The projection of potential sales for the industry and the company's expected share of such sales. (p. 1005).

**Selling and administrative expense budget**  A projection of anticipated selling and administrative expenses for the budget period. (p. 1012).

# DEMONSTRATION PROBLEM

The Soroco Company is preparing its master budgets for 1996. Relevant data pertaining to its sales and production budgets are as follows:

Sales. Sales for the year are expected to total 1,200,000 units. Quarterly sales are 20%, 25%, 30%, and 25%, respectively. The sales price is expected to be $50 per unit for the first three quarters and $55 per unit beginning in the fourth quarter. Sales in the first quarter of 1997 are expected to be 10% higher than the budgeted sales volume for the first quarter of 1996.

Production. Management desires to maintain ending finished goods inventories at 25% of the next quarter's budgeted sales volume.

### Problem-Solving Strategies

1. For the sales budget, know the form and content.

2. The sales budget is the first budget prepared.

3. Each of the other budgets is dependent on the sales budget.

4. The production budget shows the units that must be produced to meet anticipated sales.

5. The production budget provides the bases for determining the budgeted cost for each manufacturing cost element.

6. Know how to compute the beginning and ending finished goods units.

*Instructions*

Prepare the sales budget and production budget by quarters for 1996.

## Solution to Demonstration Problem

**SOROCO COMPANY**
**Sales Budget**
**For the Year Ending December 31, 1996**

|  | Quarter | | | | |
| --- | --- | --- | --- | --- | --- |
|  | 1 | 2 | 3 | 4 | Year |
| Expected unit sales | 240,000 | 300,000 | 360,000 | 300,000 | 1,200,000 |
| Unit selling price | × $50 | × $50 | × $50 | × $55 | — |
|  | $12,000,000 | $15,000,000 | $18,000,000 | $16,500,000 | $61,500,000 |

**SOROCO COMPANY**
**Production Budget**
**For the Year Ending December 31, 1996**

| | | Quarter | | | |
|---|---|---|---|---|---|
| | 1 | 2 | 3 | 4 | Year |
| Expected unit sales | 240,000 | 300,000 | 360,000 | 300,000 | |
| Add: Desired ending finished goods units | 75,000 | 90,000 | 75,000 | 66,000[1] | |
| Total required units | 315,000 | 390,000 | 435,000 | 366,000 | |
| Less: Beginning finished goods units | 60,000[2] | 75,000 | 90,000 | 75,000 | |
| Units to be produced | 255,000 | 315,000 | 345,000 | 291,000 | 1,206,000 |

[1]Estimated first quarter 1997 sales volume 240,000 + (240,000 × 10%) = 264,000; 264,000 × 25%.
[2]25% of estimated first quarter 1996 sales units.

# SELF-STUDY QUESTIONS

Answers are at the end of the chapter.

(SO 1) 1. The benefits of budgeting include *all but one* of the following:
   a. Management can plan ahead.
   b. An early warning system is provided for potential problems.
   c. It enables disciplinary action to be taken at every level of responsibility.
   d. The coordination of activities is facilitated.

(SO 2) 2. The essentials of effective budgeting do *not* include:
   a. top down budgeting.
   b. management acceptance.
   c. research and analysis.
   d. sound organizational structure.

(SO 2) 3. Compared to budgeting, long-range planning generally has the:
   a. same amount of detail.
   b. longer time period.
   c. same emphasis.
   d. same time period.

(SO 3) 4. A sales budget is:
   a. derived from the production budget.
   b. management's best estimate of sales revenue for the year.
   c. not the starting point for the master budget.
   d. prepared only for credit sales.

(SO 3) 5. The formula for the production budget is budgeted sales in units plus:
   a. desired ending merchandise inventory less beginning merchandise inventory.
   b. beginning finished goods units less desired ending finished goods units.
   c. desired ending direct materials units less beginning direct materials units.

   d. desired ending finished goods units less beginning finished goods units.

(SO 3) 6. Direct materials inventories are kept in pounds in Byrd Company, and the total pounds of direct materials needed for production is 9,500. If the beginning inventory is 1,000 pounds and the desired ending inventory is 2,200 pounds, the total pounds to be purchased is:
   a. 9,400.
   b. 9,500.
   c. 9,700.
   d. 10,700.

(SO 3) 7. The formula for computing the direct labor cost budget is to multiply the direct labor cost per hour by the:
   a. total required direct labor hours.
   b. physical units to be produced.
   c. equivalent units to be produced.
   d. no correct answer is given.

(SO 4) 8. Each of the following budgets is used in preparing the budgeted income statement *except* the:
   a. sales budget.
   b. selling and administrative budget.
   c. capital expenditure budget.
   d. direct labor budget.

(SO 5) 9. Expected direct materials purchases in Read Company are $70,000 in the first quarter and $90,000 in the second quarter. Forty percent of the purchases are paid in cash as incurred, and the balance is paid in the following quarter. The budgeted cash payments for purchases in the second quarter are:
   a. $96,000.
   b. $90,000.
   c. $78,000.
   d. $72,000.

(SO 6) 10. The budget for a merchandising company differs from a budget for a manufacturing company because:
a. a merchandise purchases budget replaces the production budget.

b. the manufacturing budgets are not applicable.
c. None of the above.
d. Both (a) and (b) above.

# QUESTIONS

••••••••••••••••••••••••••••••••••••••••••••••••••••••••••••••••••••••••••••••••••

1. (a) What is a budget?
   (b) How does a budget contribute to good management?

2. Arsenio and Sowinski are discussing the benefits of budgeting. They ask you to identify the primary advantages of budgeting. Comply with their request.

3. Pedro Venzuela asks your help in understanding the essentials of effective budgeting. Identify the essentials for Pedro.

4. (a) "Accounting plays a relatively unimportant role in budgeting." Do you agree? Explain.
   (b) What responsibilities does management have in budgeting?

5. What criteria are helpful in determining the length of the budget period? What is the most common budget period?

6. Kim Bertelli maintains that the only difference between budgeting and long-range planning is time. Do you agree? Why or why not?

7. Distinguish between a master budget and a sales forecast.

8. What budget is the starting point in preparing the master budget? What may result if this budget is inaccurate?

9. "The production budget shows both unit production data and unit cost data." Is this true? Explain.

10. Peru Company has 8,000 beginning finished goods units. Budgeted sales units are 150,000. If management desires 10,000 ending finished goods units, what are the required units of production?

11. In preparing the direct materials budget for Ramero Company, management concludes that required purchases are 50,000 units. If 46,000 direct materials units are required in production and there are 4,000 units of beginning direct materials, what is the desired units of ending direct materials?

12. The production budget of Lucas Company calls for

90,000 units to be produced. If it takes 30 minutes to make one unit and the direct labor rate is $14 per hour, what is the total budgeted direct labor cost?

13. Carrie Company's manufacturing overhead budget shows total variable costs of $186,000 and total fixed costs of $174,000. Total production in units is expected to be 120,000. It takes 15 minutes to make one unit, and the direct labor rate is $15 per hour. Express the manufacturing overhead rate as (a) a percentage of direct labor cost and (b) an amount per direct labor hour.

14. Walsh Company's variable selling and administrative expenses are 10% of net sales and fixed expenses are $50,000 per quarter. The sales budget shows expected sales of $200,000 and $250,000 in the first and second quarters, respectively. What are the total budgeted selling and administrative expenses for each quarter?

15. For Alameda Company, the budgeted cost for one unit of product is direct materials $12, direct labor $20, and manufacturing overhead 75% of direct labor cost. If 25,000 units are expected to be sold at $77 each, what is the budgeted gross profit?

16. Indicate the supporting schedules used in preparing a budgeted income statement through gross profit for a manufacturing company.

17. Identify the three sections of a cash budget. What balances are also shown in this budget?

18. Sinha Company has credit sales of $300,000 in January. Past experience suggests that 40% is collected in the month of sale, 50% in the month following the sale, and 4% in the second month following the sale. Compute the cash collections from January sales in January, February, and March.

19. What is the formula for determining required merchandise purchases in a merchandising company?

20. How may expected revenues in a service enterprise be computed?

# BRIEF EXERCISES

••••••••••••••••••••••••••••••••••••••••••••••••••••••••••••••••••••••••••••••••••

*Prepare a diagram of a master budget.*
(SO 3)

**BE24–1** O'Connell Manufacturing Company uses the following budgets: Balance Sheet, Capital Expenditure, Cash, Direct Labor, Direct Materials, Income Statement, Manufacturing Overhead, Production, Sales, and Selling and Administrative. Prepare a diagram of the interrelationships of the budgets in the master budget. Indicate whether each budget is an operating or a financial budget.

**BE24-2**  Chico Company estimates that unit sales will be 10,000 in quarter 1; 12,000 in quarter 2; 14,000 in quarter 3; and 15,000 in quarter 4. Using a sales price of $50 per unit, prepare the sales budget, by quarters, for the year ending December 31, 1996.

*Prepare a sales budget.*
*(SO 3)*

**BE24-3**  Sales budget data for Chico Company are given in BE24-2. Management desires to have an ending finished goods inventory equal to 20% of the next quarter's expected unit sales. Prepare a production budget, by quarters, for the first 6 months of 1996.

*Prepare a production budget for 2 quarters.*
*(SO 3)*

**BE24-4**  Irene Company has 1,200 pounds of raw materials in its December 31, 1995, ending inventory. Required production for January and February are 4,000 and 5,000 units, respectively. Three pounds of raw materials are needed for each unit, and the estimated cost per pound is $5. Management desires an ending inventory equal to 10% of next month's materials requirements. Prepare the direct materials budget for January.

*Prepare a direct materials budget for one month.*
*(SO 3)*

**BE24-5**  For Kareem Company, units to be produced are 5,000 in quarter 1 and 6,000 in quarter 2. It takes 1.5 hours to make a finished unit, and the expected hourly wage rate is $10 per hour. Prepare a direct labor budget, by quarters, for the 6 months ending June 30, 1996.

*Prepare a direct labor budget for 2 quarters.*
*(SO 3)*

**BE24-6**  For Morgan Marie Sondgeroth, Inc., variable manufacturing overhead costs are expected to be $28,000 in the first quarter of 1996 with $4,000 increments in each of the remaining three quarters. Fixed overhead costs are estimated to be $35,000 in each quarter. Prepare the manufacturing overhead budget, by quarters, for the year.

*Prepare a manufacturing overhead budget.*
*(SO 3)*

**BE24-7**  Norma Company classifies its selling and administrative expense budget into variable and fixed components. Variable expenses are expected to be $21,000 in the first quarter, and $3,000 increments are expected in the remaining quarters of 1996. Fixed expenses are expected to be $30,000 in each quarter. Prepare the selling and administrative expense budget, by quarters, for 1996.

*Prepare a selling and administrative expense budget.*
*(SO 3)*

**BE24-8**  Nashville Company has completed all of its operating budgets. The sales budget for the year shows 50,000 units and total sales of $2,000,000. The total unit cost of making one unit of sales is $30. Selling and administrative expenses are expected to be $200,000, and income taxes are estimated to be $50,000. Prepare a budgeted income statement for the year ending December 31, 1996.

*Prepare a budgeted income statement for the year.*
*(SO 4)*

**BE24-9**  Lurial Industries expects credit sales for January, February, and March to be $200,000, $250,000, and $310,000 respectively. It is expected that 60% of the sales will be collected in the month of sale, and 40% will be collected in the following month. Compute cash collections from customers for each month.

*Prepare data for cash budget.*
*(SO 5)*

**BE24-10**  ASP Wholesalers is preparing its merchandise purchases budget. Budgeted sales are $400,000 for April and $440,000 for May. Cost of goods sold is expected to be 70% of sales, and the company's desired ending inventory is 20% of the following month's cost of goods sold. Compute the required purchases for April.

*Determine required merchandise purchases for one month.*
*(SO 6)*

# EXERCISES

**E24-1**  Dallas Electronics Inc. produces and sells two models of pocket calculators, XQ-103, and XQ-104. The calculators sell for $10 and $15, respectively. Because of the intense competition Dallas faces, management budgets sales semiannually. Its projections for the first 2 quarters of 1996 are as follows:

*Prepare sales budget for 2 quarters.*
*(SO 3)*

**Unit Sales**

| Product | Quarter 1 | Quarter 2 |
|---------|-----------|-----------|
| XQ-103  | 32,000    | 27,000    |
| XQ-104  | 12,000    | 14,000    |

No changes in selling prices are anticipated.

**Instructions**
Prepare a sales budget for the two quarters ending June 30, 1996. List the products and show for each quarter and for the 6 months, units, selling price, and total sales by product and in total.

*Prepare quarterly production budgets.*
(SO 3)

**E24–2**   Saipan Company produces and sells two types of automobile batteries, the heavy-duty HD-240 and the long-life LL-250. The 1996 sales budget for the two products is as follows:

|  | HD-240 | LL-250 |
|---|---|---|
| 1st quarter | 5,000 | 10,000 |
| 2nd quarter | 7,000 | 18,000 |
| 3rd quarter | 8,000 | 20,000 |
| 4th quarter | 10,000 | 35,000 |

The January 1, 1996, inventory of HD-240 and LL-250 units is 4,000 and 8,000, respectively. Management desires an ending inventory each quarter equal to 80% of the next quarter's sales. Sales in the first quarter of 1997 are expected to be 40% higher than sales in the same quarter in 1996.

*Instructions*
Prepare separate quarterly production budgets for each product by quarters for 1996.

*Prepare direct materials purchases budget.*
(SO 3)

**E24–3**   Corona Industries has adopted the following production budget for the first 4 months of 1996.

| Month | Units | Month | Units |
|---|---|---|---|
| January | 10,000 | March | 6,000 |
| February | 8,000 | April | 4,000 |

Each unit requires 6 pounds of raw materials costing $1.20 per pound. On December 31, 1995, the ending raw materials inventory was 36,000 pounds. Management wants to have a raw materials inventory at the end of the month equal to 60% of next month's production requirements.

*Instructions*
Prepare a direct materials purchases budget by months for the first quarter.

*Prepare production and direct materials budgets by quarters for 6 months.*
(SO 3)

**E24–4**   The Villas Company budget committee has reached agreement on the following data for the 6 months ending June 30, 1996:

| Sales units (by quarters): | (1) 5,000, (2) 6,000 |
|---|---|
| Ending raw materials inventory: | 50% of the next quarter's production requirements |
| Ending finished goods inventory: | 25% of the next quarter's expected sales units |

The ending raw materials and finished goods inventories at December 31, 1995, follow the same percentage relationships to production and sales that occur in 1996. Three pounds of raw materials are required to make each unit of finished goods. Raw materials purchased are expected to cost $4 per pound. Sales of 7,000 units and required production of 7,250 units are expected in the third quarter of 1996.

*Instructions*
(a)  Prepare a production budget by quarters for the 6 months.
(b)  Prepare a direct materials budget by quarters for the 6 months.

*Prepare direct labor budget.*
(SO 3)

**E24–5**   Caliente, Inc., is preparing its direct labor budget for 1996 from the following production budget based on a calendar year:

| Quarter | Units | Quarter | Units |
|---|---|---|---|
| 1 | 20,000 | 3 | 35,000 |
| 2 | 25,000 | 4 | 30,000 |

Each unit requires 1.8 hours of direct labor.

*Instructions*
Prepare a direct labor cost budget for 1996. Wage rates are expected to be $14 for the first 2 quarters and $15 for quarters 3 and 4.

*Prepare manufacturing overhead budget for the year.*
(SO 3)

**E24–6**   La Mesa Company is preparing its manufacturing overhead budget for 1996. Relevant data consist of the following:

Units to be produced (by quarters): 10,000; 12,000; 14,000; 16,000.

Direct labor: time—1.5 hours per unit.

Variable overhead costs per direct labor hour: indirect materials $0.70; indirect labor $1.20; and maintenance $0.30.

Fixed overhead costs per quarter: supervisory salaries $25,000; depreciation $8,000; and maintenance $6,000.

**Instructions**
Prepare the manufacturing overhead budget for the year, showing quarterly data.

**E24–7** Quay Company combines its operating expenses for budget purposes in a selling and administrative expense budget. For the first 6 months of 1996, the following data are developed:

*Prepare selling and administrative expense budget for 2 quarters.*
*(SO 3)*

1. Sales: 10,000 units quarter 1; 12,000 units quarter 2.
2. Variable costs per dollar of sales: sales commissions 5%; delivery expense 2%; and advertising 3%.
3. Fixed costs per quarter: sales salaries $10,000; office salaries $6,000; depreciation $4,200; insurance $1,500; utilities $800, and repairs expense $600.
4. Unit selling price $20.

**Instructions**
Prepare a selling and administrative expense budget by quarters, for the first 6 months of 1996.

**E24–8** Shilo Company has accumulated the following budget data for the year 1996:

*Prepare budgeted income statement for the year.*
*(SO 3, 4)*

1. Sales: 25,000 units; unit selling price $80.
2. Cost of one unit of finished goods: direct materials 2 pounds at $5 per pound; direct labor 3 hours at $12 per hour; and manufacturing overhead $6 per direct labor hour.
3. Inventories: raw materials only: beginning, 10,000 pounds; ending, 15,000 pounds.
4. Raw materials cost: $5 per pound.
5. Selling and administrative expenses: $200,000.
6. Income taxes: 30% of income before income taxes.

**Instructions**
Prepare a budgeted income statement for 1996. Show the computation of cost of goods sold.

**E24–9** Hanover Company expects to have a cash balance of $46,000 on January 1, 1996. Relevant monthly budget data for the first 2 months of 1996 are as follows:

*Prepare cash budget for 2 months.*
*(SO 5)*

Collections from customers: January $70,000; February $150,000.

Payments to suppliers: January $40,000; February $75,000.

Direct labor: January $30,000; February $40,000. Wages are paid in the month they are incurred.

Manufacturing overhead: January $21,000; February $30,000. These costs include depreciation of $1,000 per month. All other overhead costs are paid as incurred.

Selling and administrative expenses: January $14,000; February $20,000. These costs are exclusive of depreciation. They are paid as incurred.

Sales of marketable securities in January are expected to realize $10,000 in cash. Hanover Company has a line of credit at a local bank that enables it to borrow up to $25,000. The company wants to maintain a minimum monthly cash balance of $20,000.

**Instructions**
Prepare a cash budget for January and February.

**E24–10** In May 1996, the budget committee of Hill Street Stores assembles the following data in preparation of budgeted merchandise purchases for the month of June.

*Prepare purchases budget and budgeted income statement for a merchandising company.*
*(SO 6)*

1. Expected sales: June $500,000, July $600,000.
2. Cost of goods sold is expected to be 70% of sales.
3. Desired ending merchandise inventory is 30% of the following (next) month's cost of goods sold.
4. The beginning inventory at June 1 will be the desired amount.

**Instructions**
(a) Compute the budgeted merchandise purchases for June.
(b) Prepare the budgeted income statement for June through gross profit on sales.

# PROBLEMS

*Prepare budgeted income statement and supporting budgets.*
*(SO 3, 4)*

**P24–1**  Delta Farm Supply Company manufactures and sells a fertilizer called Basic II. The following data are developed for preparing budgets for Basic II for the first 2 quarters of 1996:

1. Sales: quarter 1, 40,000 bags: quarter 2, 60,000 bags. Selling price is $50 per bag.
2. Direct materials: Each bag of Basic II requires 6 pounds of Crup at a cost of $2 per pound and 10 pounds of Dert at $1.50 per pound.
3. Desired inventory levels:

| Type of Inventory | January 1 | April 1 | July 1 |
|---|---|---|---|
| Basic II (bags) | 10,000 | 15,000 | 20,000 |
| Crup (pounds) | 9,000 | 12,000 | 15,000 |
| Dert (pounds) | 15,000 | 20,000 | 25,000 |

4. Direct labor: direct labor time is 15 minutes per bag at an hourly rate of $10 per hour.
5. Selling and administrative expenses are expected to be 10% of sales plus $150,000 per quarter.
6. Income taxes are expected to be 30% of income from operations.

Your assistant has prepared two budgets: the manufacturing overhead budget that shows expected costs to be 100% of direct labor cost, and the direct materials budget for Dert which shows the cost of Dert to be $682,500 in quarter 1 and $982,500 in quarter 2.

*Instructions*
Prepare the budgeted income statement for the first 6 months of 1996 and all required supporting budgets by quarters. (Note: Use variable and fixed in the selling and administrative expense budget.)

*Prepare sales, production, direct materials, direct labor, and income statement budgets.*
*(SO 3, 4)*

**P24–2**  Leona Inc. is preparing its annual budgets for the year ending December 31, 1996. Accounting assistants furnish the following data:

| | Product LN 35 | Product LN 40 |
|---|---|---|
| Sales budget: | | |
| Anticipated volume in units | 400,000 | 180,000 |
| Unit selling price | $15.00 | $30.00 |
| Production budget: | | |
| Desired ending finished goods units | 30,000 | 25,000 |
| Beginning finished goods units | 20,000 | 5,000 |
| Direct materials budget: | | |
| Direct materials per unit (pounds) | 2 | 3 |
| Desired ending direct materials units | 50,000 | 20,000 |
| Beginning direct materials units | 40,000 | 10,000 |
| Cost per pound | $2.00 | $3.00 |
| Direct labor budget: | | |
| Direct labor time per unit | .5 | .75 |
| Direct labor rate per hour | $8.00 | $8.00 |
| Budgeted income statement: | | |
| Total unit cost | $10.00 | $20.00 |

An accounting assistant has prepared the detailed manufacturing overhead budget and the selling and administrative expense budget. The latter shows selling expenses of $460,000 for product LN 35 and $440,000 for product LN 40, and administrative expenses of $420,000 for product LN 35 and $380,000 for product LN 40. Income taxes are expected to be 30%.

*Instructions*
Prepare the following budgets for the year. Show data for each product. Quarterly budgets should not be prepared.

(a) Sales
(b) Production
(c) Direct materials

(d) Direct labor
(e) Income statement (Note: Income taxes are not allocated to the products.)

**P24–3** Eden Industries had sales in 1996 of $5,250,000 and gross profit of $1,587,500. Management is considering two alternative budget plans to increase its gross profit in 1997.

*Prepare sales and production budgets and compute cost per unit under two plans.*
(SO 3, 4)

Plan A would increase the selling price per unit from $6.00 to $6.60. Sales volume would decrease by 10% from its 1996 level. Plan B would decrease the selling price per unit by 5%. The marketing department expects that the sales volume would increase by 100,000 units.

At the end of 1996, Eastland has 75,000 units on hand. If Plan A is accepted, the 1997 ending inventory should be equal to 87,500 units. If Plan B is accepted, the ending inventory should be equal to 100,000 units. Each unit produced will cost $2.00 in direct materials, $1.00 in direct labor, and $.50 in variable overhead. The fixed overhead for 1997 should be $800,000.

**Instructions**
(a) Prepare a sales budget for 1997 under (1) Plan A and (2) Plan B.
(b) Prepare a production budget for 1997 under (1) Plan A and (2) Plan B.
(c) Compute the cost per unit under (1) Plan A and (2) Plan B. Explain why the cost per unit is different for each of the two plans. (Round to two decimals.)
(d) Which plan should be accepted? (Hint: Compute the gross profit under each plan.)

**P24–4** Joplin Company prepares monthly cash budgets. Relevant data from operating budgets for 1996 are:

*Prepare a cash budget for 2 months.*
(SO 5)

| | January | February |
|---|---|---|
| Sales | $360,000 | $400,000 |
| Direct materials purchases | 100,000 | 110,000 |
| Direct labor | 80,000 | 95,000 |
| Manufacturing overhead | 60,000 | 75,000 |
| Selling and administrative expenses | 75,000 | 85,000 |

All sales are on account. Collections are expected to be 50% in the month of sale, 30% in the first month following the sale, and 20% in the second month following the sale. Forty percent (40%) of direct material purchases are paid in cash in the month of purchase, and the balance due is paid in the month following the purchase. All other items above are paid in the month incurred. Depreciation has been excluded from manufacturing overhead and selling and administrative expenses.

Other data:
(1) Credit sales—November 1995, $200,000; December 1995, $280,000.
(2) Purchases of direct materials—December 1995, $90,000.
(3) Other receipts—January: collection of December 31, 1995, interest receivable $3,000; February: proceeds from sale of securities $5,000.
(4) Other disbursements—February: payment of $20,000 for land.

The company's cash balance on January 1, 1996, is expected to be $60,000. The company wants to maintain a minimum cash balance of $50,000.

**Instructions**
(a) Prepare schedules for (1) expected collections from customers and (2) expected payments for direct materials purchases.
(b) Prepare a cash budget for January and February in columnar form.

**P24–5** The budget committee of Eureka Company collects the following data for its Westwood Store in preparing budgeted income statements for July and August 1996.

*Prepare purchases and income statement budgets for a merchandising company.*
(SO 6)

1. Expected sales: July $400,000, August $450,000, September $500,000.
2. Cost of goods sold is expected to be 72% of sales.
3. Company policy is to maintain ending merchandise inventory at 25% of the following month's cost of goods sold.
4. Operating expenses are estimated to be:

| | |
|---|---|
| Sales salaries | $20,000 per month |
| Advertising | 4% of monthly sales |
| Delivery expense | 2% of monthly sales |
| Sales commissions | 3% of monthly sales |
| Rent expense | $3,000 per month |
| Depreciation | $700 per month |
| Utilities | $500 per month |
| Insurance | $300 per month |

5. Income taxes are estimated to be 30% of income from operations.

**Instructions**

(a) Prepare the merchandise purchases budget for each month in columnar form.

(b) Prepare budgeted income statements for each month in columnar form. Show the details of cost of goods sold in the statements.

*Prepare budgeted income statement and balance sheet.* (SO 3, 4)

**P24–6** Navajo Industries' balance sheet at December 31, 1995, is presented below.

### NAVAJO INDUSTRIES
### Balance Sheet
### December 31, 1995

#### Assets

| | | |
|---|---:|---:|
| Current assets | | |
| Cash | | $ 7,500 |
| Accounts receivable | | 82,500 |
| Finished goods inventory (2,000 units) | | 30,000 |
| Total current assets | | 120,000 |
| Property, plant, and equipment | | |
| Equipment | $40,000 | |
| Less: Accumulated depreciation | 10,000 | 30,000 |
| Total assets | | $150,000 |

#### Liabilities and Stockholders' Equity

| | | |
|---|---:|---:|
| Liabilities | | |
| Notes payable | | $ 25,000 |
| Accounts payable | | 45,000 |
| Total liabilities | | 70,000 |
| Stockholders' equity | | |
| Common stock | $50,000 | |
| Retained earnings | 30,000 | |
| Total stockholders' equity | | 80,000 |
| Total liabilities and stockholders' equity | | $150,000 |

Budgeted data for 1996 include the following:

| | Quarter 4 | Total |
|---|---:|---:|
| Sales budget (8,000 units at $30) | $70,000 | $240,000 |
| Direct materials used | 17,000 | 67,200 |
| Direct labor | 8,500 | 33,600 |
| Manufacturing overhead applied | 10,000 | 42,000 |
| Selling and administrative expenses | 18,000 | 76,000 |

To meet sales requirements and to have 2,400 units of finished goods on hand at December 31, 1996, the production budget shows 8,400 required units of output. The total unit cost of production is expected to be $17. Navajo Industries uses the first-in, first-out (FIFO) inventory costing method. Selling and administrative expenses include $4,000 for depreciation on equipment. Interest expense is expected to be $3,500 for the year. Income taxes are expected to be 30% of income before income taxes.

All sales and purchases are on account. It is expected that 60% of quarterly sales are paid within the quarter and the remainder is paid in the following quarter. Direct materials purchases are paid 50% in the quarter incurred and the remainder in the following quarter. Purchases in the fourth quarter were the same as the materials used. In 1996, the company expects to purchase additional equipment costing $24,000. It expects to pay $8,000 on notes payable plus all interest due and payable to December 31. Accounts payable at December 31 includes amounts due suppliers plus other accounts payable of $7,500. In 1996, the company expects to declare and pay a $2,000 cash dividend. Unpaid income taxes at December 31 will be $5,000. The company's cash budget shows an expected cash balance of $17,150 at December 31, 1996.

**Instructions**

Prepare a budgeted income statement for 1996 and a budgeted balance sheet at December 31, 1996.

# ALTERNATE PROBLEMS

••••••••••••••••••••••••••••••••••••••••••••••••••••••••••••••••••••••

**P24–1A** Ionia Farm Supply Company manufactures and sells a pesticide called Snare. The following data are developed for preparing budgets for Snare for the first 2 quarters of 1997.

1. Sales: quarter 1, 32,000 bags: quarter 2, 48,000 bags. Selling price is $50 per bag.
2. Direct materials: Each bag of Snare requires 6 pounds of Gumm at a cost of $2 per pound and 8 pounds of Tarr at $1.50 per pound.
3. Desired inventory levels:

| Type of Inventory | January 1 | April 1 | July 1 |
|---|---|---|---|
| Snare (bags) | 8,000 | 12,000 | 18,000 |
| Gumm (pounds) | 9,000 | 10,000 | 13,000 |
| Tarr (pounds) | 14,000 | 20,000 | 25,000 |

4. Direct labor: direct labor time is 20 minutes per bag at an hourly rate of $12 per hour.
5. Selling and administrative expenses are expected to be 8% of sales plus $175,000 per quarter.
6. Income taxes are expected to be 30% of income from operations.

Your assistant has prepared two budgets: the manufacturing overhead budget that shows expected costs to be 150% of direct labor cost, and the direct materials budget for Tarr which shows the cost of Tarr to be $441,000 in quarter 1 and $655,500 in quarter 2.

*Prepare budgeted income statement and supporting budgets.*
*(SO 3, 4)*

**Instructions**
Prepare the budgeted income statement for the first 6 months and all required supporting budgets by quarters. (Note: Use variable and fixed in the selling and administrative expense budget.)

**P24–2A** Kankakee Inc. is preparing its annual budgets for the year ending December 31, 1997. Accounting assistants furnish the following data:

*Prepare sales, production, direct materials, direct labor, and income statement budgets.*
*(SO 3, 4)*

| | Product JB 50 | Product JB 60 |
|---|---|---|
| Sales budget: | | |
| Anticipated volume in units | 450,000 | 160,000 |
| Unit selling price | $20.00 | $30.00 |
| Production budget: | | |
| Desired ending finished goods units | 25,000 | 15,000 |
| Beginning finished goods units | 20,000 | 10,000 |
| Direct materials budget: | | |
| Direct materials per unit (pounds) | 2 | 3 |
| Desired ending direct materials units | 30,000 | 15,000 |
| Beginning direct materials units | 40,000 | 10,000 |
| Cost per pound | $3.00 | $4.00 |
| Direct labor budget | | |
| Direct labor time per unit | .4 | .6 |
| Direct labor rate per hour | $10.00 | $10.00 |
| Budgeted income statement: | | |
| Total unit cost | $12.00 | $20.00 |

An accounting assistant has prepared the detailed manufacturing overhead budget and the selling and administrative expense budget. The latter shows selling expenses of $660,000 for product JB 50 and $360,000 for product JB 60 and administrative expenses of $420,000 for product JB 50 and $340,000 for product JB 60. Income taxes are expected to be 30%.

**Instructions**
Prepare the following budgets for the year. Show data for each product. Quarterly budgets should not be prepared.

(a) Sales
(b) Production
(c) Direct materials
(d) Direct labor
(e) Income statement (Note: Income taxes are not allocated to the products.)

*Prepare sales and production budgets and compute cost per unit under two plans.*
(SO 3, 4)

**P24–3A**   Pontiac Industries had sales in 1996 of $6,000,000, and gross profit of $1,500,000. Management is considering two alternative budget plans to increase its gross profit in 1997.

Plan A would increase the selling price per unit from $8.00 to $8.40. Sales volume would decrease by 5% from its 1996 level. Plan B would decrease the selling price per unit by $0.50. The marketing department expects that the sales volume would increase by 150,000 units.

At the end of 1996, Pontiac has 30,000 units of inventory on hand. If Plan A is accepted, the 1997 ending inventory should be equal to 4% of the 1997 sales. If Plan B is accepted, the ending inventory should be equal to 40,000 units. Each unit produced will cost $1.50 in direct labor, $2.00 in direct materials, and $.90 in variable overhead. The fixed overhead for 1997 should be $1,400,000.

**Instructions**

(a) Prepare a sales budget for 1997 under each plan.
(b) Prepare a production budget for 1997 under each plan.
(c) Compute the production cost per unit under each plan. Why is the cost per unit different for each of the two plans? (Round to two decimals.)
(d) Which plan should be accepted? (Hint: Compute the gross profit under each plan.)

*Prepare a cash budget for 2 months.*
(SO 5)

**P24–4A**   Badger Company prepares monthly cash budgets. Relevant data from operating budgets for 1996 are:

|  | January | February |
| --- | --- | --- |
| Sales | $350,000 | $400,000 |
| Direct materials purchases | 120,000 | 130,000 |
| Direct labor | 80,000 | 95,000 |
| Manufacturing overhead | 70,000 | 75,000 |
| Selling and administrative expenses | 79,000 | 86,000 |

All sales are on account. Collections are expected to be 50% in the month of sale, 40% in the first month following the sale, and 10% in the second month following the sale. Fifty percent (50%) of direct material purchases are paid in cash in the month of purchase, and the balance due is paid in the month following the purchase. All other items above are paid in the month incurred except for selling and administrative expenses that includes $1,000 of depreciation per month.

Other data:

(1) Credit sales—November 1995, $260,000; December 1995, $300,000.
(2) Purchases of direct materials—December 1995, $100,000.
(3) Other receipts—January: collection of December 31, 1995, notes receivable $15,000; February: proceeds from sale of securities $6,000.
(4) Other disbursements—February: withdrawal of $5,000 cash for personal use of owner, T. Kempen.

The company's cash balance on January 1, 1996, is expected to be $55,000. The company wants to maintain a minimum cash balance of $50,000.

**Instructions**

(a) Prepare schedules for (1) expected collections from customers and (2) expected payments for direct materials purchases.
(b) Prepare a cash budget for January and February in columnar form.

*Prepare purchases and income statement budgets for a merchandising company.*
(SO 6)

**P24–5A**   The budget committee of Jimenez Company collects the following data for its San Miguel Store in preparing budgeted income statements for May and June 1997.

1. Sales for May are expected to be $600,000. Sales in June and July are expected to be 10% higher than the preceding month.
2. Cost of goods sold is expected to be 75% of sales.
3. Company policy is to maintain ending merchandise inventory at $33\frac{1}{3}$% of the following month's cost of goods sold.

4. Operating expenses are estimated to be:

| | |
|---|---|
| Sales salaries | $30,000 per month |
| Advertising | 5% of monthly sales |
| Delivery expense | 3% of monthly sales |
| Sales commissions | 4% of monthly sales |
| Rent expense | $5,000 per month |
| Depreciation | $800 per month |
| Utilities | $600 per month |
| Insurance | $500 per month |

5. Income taxes are estimated to be 30% of income from operations.

**Instructions**

(a) Prepare the merchandise purchases budget for each month in columnar form.

(b) Prepare budgeted income statements for each month in columnar form. Show the details of cost of goods sold in the statements.

# ►*Broadening Your Perspective*

## DECISION CASE

Kinison Corporation operates on a calendar-year basis. It begins the annual budgeting process in late August when the president establishes targets for the total dollar sales and net income before taxes for the next year.

The sales target is given to the marketing department where the marketing manager formulates a sales budget by product line in both units and dollars. From this budget, sales quotas by product line in units and dollars are established for each of the corporation's sales districts. The marketing manager also estimates the cost of the marketing activities required to support the target sales volume and prepares a tentative marketing expense budget.

The executive vice-president uses the sales and profit targets, the sales budget by product line, and the tentative marketing expense budget to determine the dollar amounts that can be devoted to manufacturing and corporate office expense. The executive vice-president prepares the budget for corporate expenses, and then forwards to the production department the product-line sales budget in units and the total dollar amount that can be devoted to manufacturing.

The production manager meets with the factory managers to develop a manufacturing plan that will produce the required units when needed within the cost constraints set by the executive vice-president. The budgeting process usually comes to a halt at this point because the production department does not consider the financial resources allocated to be adequate.

When this standstill occurs, the vice-president of finance, the executive vice-president, the marketing manager, and the production manager meet together to determine the final budgets for each of the areas. This normally results in a modest increase in the total amount available for manufacturing costs while the marketing expense and corporate office expense budgets are cut. The total sales and net income figures proposed by the president are seldom changed. Although the participants are seldom pleased with the compromise, these budgets are final. Each executive then develops a new detailed budget for the operations in his or her area.

None of the areas has achieved its budget in recent years. Sales often run below the target. When budgeted sales are not achieved, each area is expected to cut costs so that the president's profit target can still be met. However, the profit target is seldom met because costs are not cut enough. In fact, costs often run above the original budget in all functional areas (marketing, production, and corporate office). The president is disturbed that Kinison has not been able to meet the sales and profit targets. He hired a consultant with considerable experience with companies in Kinison's industry. The consultant reviewed the budgets for the past four years. He concluded that the product-line sales budgets were reasonable and that the cost and expense budgets were adequate for the budgeted sales and production levels.

*Instructions*

(a) Discuss how the budgeting process as employed by Kinison Corporation contributes to the failure to achieve the president's sales and profit targets.

(b) Suggest how Kinison Corporation's budgeting process could be revised to correct the problems.

(c) Should the functional areas be expected to cut their costs when sales volume falls below budget? Explain your answer.                          (CMA adapted.)

# COMMUNICATION ACTIVITY

In order to better serve their rural patients, Drs. Martin and Michael Greene (brothers) began giving safety seminars. Especially popular were their "emergency-preparedness" talks given to farmers. Many people asked whether the "kit" of materials the doctors recommended for common farm emergencies was commercially available.

After checking with several suppliers, the doctors realized that no other company offered the supplies they recommended in their seminars, packaged in the way they described. Their wives, Melissa and Gail, agreed to make a test package by ordering supplies from various medical supply companies and assembling them into a "kit" that could be sold at the seminars. When these kits proved a runaway success, the sisters-in-law decided to market them. At the advice of their accountant, they organized this venture as a separate company, called Life Protection Products (LPP), with Melissa Greene as CEO and Gail Greene as Secretary-Treasurer.

LPP soon started receiving requests for the kits from all over the country, as word spread about their availability. Even without advertising, LPP was able to sell its full inventory every month. However, the company was becoming financially strained. Melissa and Gail had about $100,000 in savings, and invested about half that amount initially. They believed that this venture would allow them to make money. However, at the present time, only about $30,000 of the cash remains, and the company is constantly short of cash.

Melissa Greene has come to you for advice. She does not understand why the company is having cash flow problems. She and Gail have not even been withdrawing salaries. However, they have rented a local building and have hired two more full-time workers to help them cope with the increasing demand. They do not think they could handle the demand without this additional help.

Melissa is also worried that the cash problems mean that the company may not be able to support itself. She has prepared the cash budget shown below. All seminar customers pay for their products in full at the time of purchase. In addition, several large companies have ordered the kits for use by employees who work in remote sites. They have requested credit terms and have been allowed to pay in the month following the sale. These large purchasers amount to about 25% of the sales at the present time. LPP purchases the materials for the kits about 2 months ahead of time. Melissa and Gail are considering slowing the growth of the company by simply purchasing less materials, which will mean selling fewer kits.

The workers are paid in cash weekly. Melissa and Gail need about $15,000 cash on hand at the beginning of the month to pay for purchases of raw materials. Right now they have been using cash from their savings, but as noted, only $30,000 is left.

The cash budget that Melissa Greene has given you is as follows:

### LIFE PROTECTION PRODUCTS
### Cash Budget
### For the Quarter Ending June 30, 1997

|                           | April   | May     | June    |
|---------------------------|---------|---------|---------|
| Cash balance, beginning   | $15,000 | $15,000 | $15,000 |
| Cash received             |         |         |         |
| From prior month sales    | 5,000   | 7,500   | 12,500  |
| From current sales        | 15,000  | 22,500  | 37,500  |
| Total cash on hand        | 35,000  | 45,000  | 65,000  |

| Cash payments | | | |
|---|---|---|---|
| To employees | 3,000 | 3,000 | 3,000 |
| For products | 25,000 | 35,000 | 45,000 |
| Miscellaneous expenses | 5,000 | 6,000 | 7,000 |
| Postage | 1,000 | 1,000 | 1,000 |
| Total cash payments | 34,000 | 45,000 | 56,000 |
| | | | |
| Cash balance | $ 1,000 | $     0 | $ 9,000 |
| | | | |
| Borrow from savings | $14,000 | $15,000 | $ 1,000 |
| | | | |
| Borrow from bank? | $     0 | $     0 | $ 7,000 |

## Instructions

Write a response to Melissa Greene. Explain why LPP is short of cash. Will this company be able to support itself? Explain your answer. Make any recommendations you deem appropriate.

# GROUP ACTIVITY

Lowe and Lincoln manufactures ergonomic devices for computer users. Some of their more popular products include glare screens (for computer monitors), keyboard stands with wrist rests, and carousels that allow easy access to floppy disks. Over the past 5 years, they experienced rapid growth, with sales of all products increasing 20% to 50% each year.

Last year, some of the primary manufacturers of computers began introducing new products with some of the ergonomic designs, such as glare screens and wrist rests, already built in. As a result, sales of Lowe and Lincoln's accessory devices have declined somewhat. The company believes that the disk carousels will probably continue to show growth, but that the other products will probably continue to decline. When the next year's budget was prepared, increases were built in to research and development so that replacement products could be developed or the company could expand into some other product line. Some product lines being considered are general-purpose ergonomic devices including back supports, foot rests, and sloped writing pads.

The most recent results have shown that sales decreased more than was expected for the glare screens. As a result, the company may have a shortage of funds. Top management has therefore asked that all expenses be reduced 10% to compensate for these reduced sales. Summary budget information is as follows:

| | |
|---|---|
| Raw materials | $240,000 |
| Direct labor | 110,000 |
| Insurance | 50,000 |
| Depreciation | 90,000 |
| Machine repairs | 30,000 |
| Sales salaries | 50,000 |
| Office salaries | 80,000 |
| Factory salaries (indirect labor) | 50,000 |
| Total | $700,000 |

## Instructions

In groups of four or five people, answer the following questions:

(a) What are the implications of reducing each of the costs? For example, if the company reduces raw materials costs, it may have to do so by purchasing lower quality materials. This may affect sales in the long term.

(b) Based on your analysis in (a), what do you think is the best way to obtain the $70,000 in cost savings requested? Be specific. Are there any costs that cannot or should not be reduced? Why? Select a person from your group to present your results to the class. Be prepared to defend your answer.

# ETHICS CASE

You are an accountant in the budgetary, projections, and special projects department of Axel-Gear Corp., a large manufacturing company. The president, Warner Daggart, asks you on very short notice to prepare some sales and income projections covering the next 2 years of the company's much heralded new product lines. He wants these projections for a series of speeches he is making while on a 2-week trip to eight East Coast brokerage firms. The president hopes to bolster Axel-Gears' stock sales and price.

You work 23 hours in 2 days to compile the projections, hand deliver them to the president, and are swiftly but graciously thanked as he departs. A week later you find time to go over some of your computations and discover a miscalculation that makes the projections grossly overstated. You quickly inquire about the president's itinerary and learn that he has made half of his speeches and has half yet to make. You are in a quandary as to what to do.

*Instructions*
    (a) What are the consequences of telling the president of your gross miscalculations?
    (b) What are the consequences of *not* telling the president of your gross miscalculations?
    (c) What are the ethical considerations to you and the president in this situation?

# CRITICAL THINKING
## ▸ *A Real-World Focus: Network Computing Devices Inc.*

*Network Computing Devices Inc. was founded in 1988 in Mountain View, Calif. The company, which has 375 employees, develops software products such as X-terminals, Z-mail, PC X-ware, and related hardware products.*

Presented below is a discussion by management in its annual report.

MANAGEMENT DISCUSSION:

The Company's operating results have varied significantly, particularly on a quarterly basis, as a result of a number of factors, including general economic conditions affecting industry demand for computer products, the timing and market acceptance of new product introductions by the Company and its competitors, the timing of significant orders from the shipments to large customers, periodic changes in product pricing and discounting due to competitive factors, and the availability of key components, such as video monitors and electronic sub-assemblies, some of which require substantial order lead times. The Company's operating results may fluctuate in the future as a result of these and other factors, including the Company's success in developing and introducing new products, its product and customer mix, and the level of competition which it experiences. The Company operates with a small backlog. Sales and operating results, therefore, generally depend on the volume and timing of orders received, which are difficult to forecast. The Company has experienced slowness in orders from some customers during the first quarter of each calendar year due to budgeting cycles common in the computer industry. In addition, sales in Europe typically are adversely affected in the third calendar quarter as many European customers reduce their business activities during the month of August.

Due to the Company's rapid growth rate and the effect of new product introductions on quarterly revenues, these seasonal trends have not materially impacted the Company's results of operations to date. However, as the Company's product lines mature and its rate of revenue growth declines, these seasonal factors may become more evident. Additionally, the Company's international sales are denominated in U.S. dollars, and an increase or decrease in the value of the U.S. dollar relative to foreign currencies could make the Company's products less or more competitive in those markets.

*Instructions*

(a) Identify the factors that affect the budgeting process at Network Computing Devices Inc.

(b) Explain the additional budgeting concerns created by the international operations of the company.

---

*Answers to Self-Study Questions*

1. c     2. a     3. b     4. b     5. d     6. d     7. a     8. c     9. c     10. d

**Before studying this chapter, you should know or, if necessary, review:**

**a.** *The meaning and scope of the management function of controlling.* (Ch. 20, p. 841)

**b.** *The cost elements that produce a total cost per unit of finished goods.* (Ch. 20, pp. 841–3)

**c.** *How variable costs differ from fixed costs. (Ch. 23, pp. 963–68)*

# "If We're Low on Money, We'll Take the Bus"

LAS VEGAS, Nev. — Virtually every department on a college campus develops a budget and then compares that budget to the amount actually spent. As the school term progresses, the person in charge of the budget can see how well the department is doing compared to expectations.

One of the most expensive departments on campus is the athletic department. That fact usually rankles the academic department heads. They argue that a university exists first and foremost to educate. But the money for sports is often justified because the sports teams— particularly at big schools—generate large incomes from television contracts that can then be used for a variety of educational purposes.

At the University of Nevada, Las Vegas, each athletic team has its own budget and its own financial statements. This financial informa-

tion "shows what the teams have spent for the month and for the year to date, and how the actual expenditures compare to the budget," says Merv Gupton, athletic accounting manager. The biggest budget items: scholarships for student athletes, payroll, and travel costs.

UNLV sports teams include football, basketball, tennis, baseball, softball, soccer, track, cross coun-

try, golf, and swimming. Travel costs are usually the most uncontrollable item in the budget. What if you get two-thirds through the season and run out of money? "One sports team might be able to help out another," says Gupton. Or more likely, "if a coach is running low on money, the team won't fly—it'll take the bus." ◀

# CHAPTER 25

# **B**UDGETARY CONTROL AND RESPONSIBILITY ACCOUNTING

▶ **STUDY OBJECTIVES** ◀

**After completing the study of this chapter, you should be able to:**

1. Describe the concept of budgetary control.
2. Evaluate the usefulness of static budget reports.
3. Explain the development of flexible budgets and the usefulness of flexible budget reports.
4. Describe the concept of responsibility accounting.
5. Indicate the features of responsibility reports for cost centers.
6. Identify the content of responsibility reports for profit centers.
7. Explain the basis and formula used in evaluating performance in investment centers.

The opening story indicates that budgets not only are necessary for an athletic department, but also that they can be used to control the department's activities. For example, if you were the athletic director at UNLV, you might require periodic updates from each coach, showing actual and budgeted expenses.

In contrast to Chapter 24, we now consider how budgets are used by management to control operations. This chapter focuses on two aspects of management control: (1) budgetary control and (2) responsibility accounting. The content and organization of this chapter are as follows:

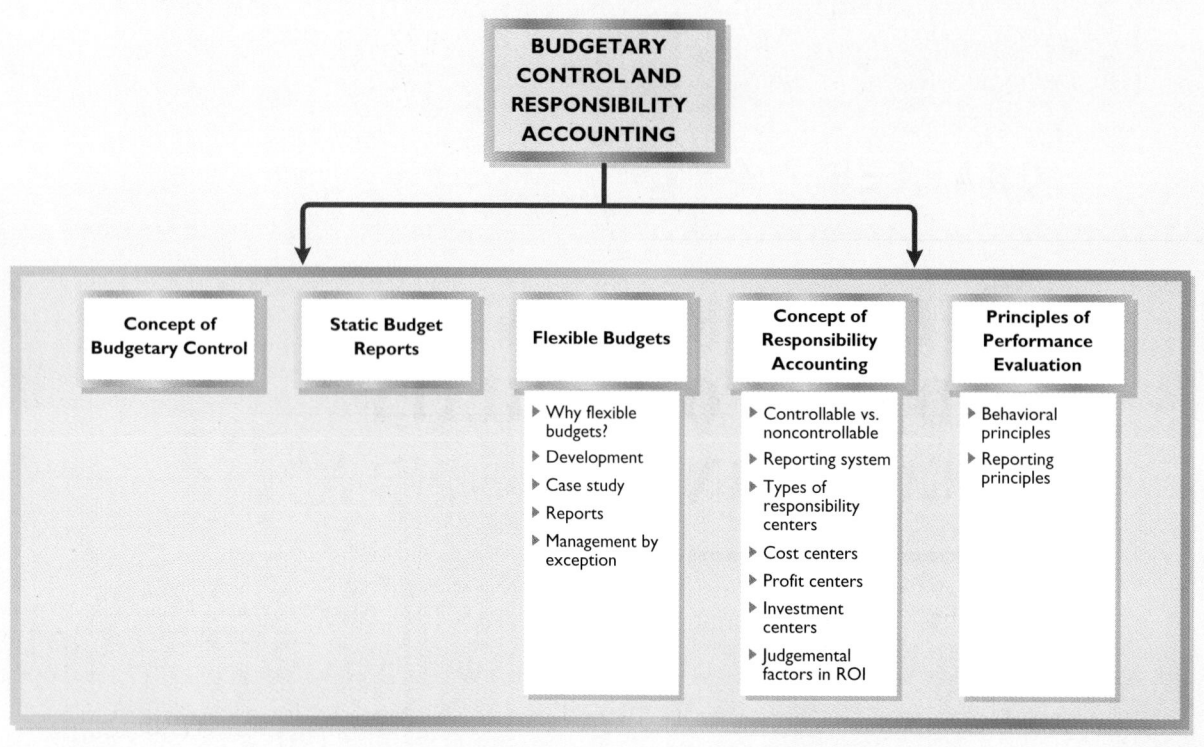

# Concept of Budgetary Control

As stated at the beginning of the managerial accounting chapters, one of management's major functions is controlling the operations of the company. Control was defined as the steps taken by management to see that planned objectives are met. We now ask: How do budgets assist management in controlling operations?

The use of budgets in controlling operations is known as budgetary control. The centerpiece of budgetary control is the use of **budget reports** that compare actual results with planned objectives. The preparation and use of budget reports is based on the belief that planned objectives lose much of their potential value without some monitoring of progress along the way. Just as your professors give midterm examinations to evaluate your progress, so top management requires periodic reports on the progress that department managers are making toward planned annual objectives.

Budget reports provide the feedback needed by management to see whether actual operations are on course. The feedback for a crucial objective, such as having enough cash on hand to pay bills, may be made daily. For other objectives, such as meeting budgeted annual sales and operating expenses, monthly budget reports may suffice. Because of the flexibility of managerial accounting, budget reports can be prepared as frequently as needed. On the basis of the budget reports, management first analyzes any differences between actual and planned results to determine their causes. From this analysis, management may take corrective action, or it may decide to modify future plans.

Budgetary control involves the following:

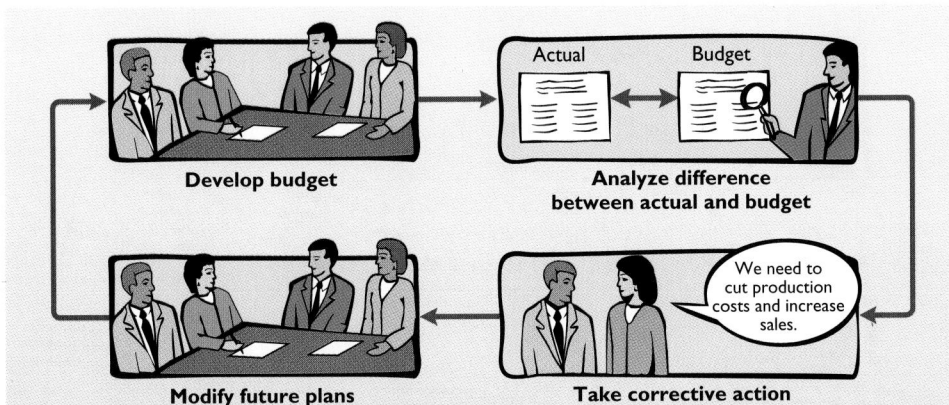

**Illustration 25-1**

*Budgetary control*

Budgetary control works best when a company has a formalized reporting system. The system should (1) identify the name of the budget report, such as the sales budget or the manufacturing overhead budget; (2) state the frequency of the report, such as weekly or monthly; (3) specify the purpose of the report; and (4) indicate the primary recipient(s) of the report. The following schedule illustrates a partial budgetary control system for a manufacturing company. Note the emphasis on control in the reports and the frequency of the reports. For example, there is a daily report on scrap and a weekly report on labor.

**Illustration 25-2**

*Budgetary control reporting system*

| Name of Report | Frequency | Purpose | Primary Recipient(s) |
|---|---|---|---|
| Sales | Weekly | Determine whether sales goals are being met | Top management and sales manager |
| Labor | Weekly | Control direct and indirect labor costs | Vice president of production and production department managers |
| Scrap | Daily | Determine efficient use of materials | Production manager |
| Departmental overhead costs | Monthly | Control overhead costs | Department manager |
| Selling expenses | Monthly | Control selling expenses | Sales manager |
| Income statement | Monthly and quarterly | Determine whether income objectives are being met | Top management |

# Static Budget Reports

You learned in Chapter 24 that the master budget formalizes management's planned objectives for the coming year. When used in budgetary control, each budget included in the master budget is considered to be a static budget. A static budget is a projection of budget data at one level of activity. In such a budget, data for different levels of activity are ignored. As a result, actual results are always compared with budget data at the activity level used in developing the master budget.

**STUDY OBJECTIVE 2**

*Evaluate the usefulness of static budget reports.*

To illustrate the role of a static budget in budgetary control, we will use selected budget data prepared for Hayes Company in Chapter 24. Budget and actual sales data for the Kitchen-mate product in the first and second quarters of 1996 are as follows:

**Illustration 25-3**

*Budget and actual sales data*

| Sales | First Quarter | Second Quarter | Total |
|---|---|---|---|
| Budgeted | $180,000 | $210,000 | $390,000 |
| Actual | 179,000 | 199,500 | 378,500 |
| Difference | $ 1,000 | $ 10,500 | $ 11,500 |

The sales budget report for Hayes Company's first quarter is shown below.

**Illustration 25-4**

*Sales budget report—first quarter*

### HAYES COMPANY
### Sales Budget Report
### For the Quarter Ended March 31, 1996

| Product Line | Budget | Actual | Difference Favorable F Unfavorable U |
|---|---|---|---|
| Kitchen-mate[a] | $180,000 | $179,000 | $1,000 U |

[a]In practice, each product line would be included in the report.

The report shows that sales are $1,000 under budget—an unfavorable result. This difference is less than 1% of budgeted sales ($1,000 ÷ $180,000 = .0056). Top management's analysis of unfavorable differences is often influenced by the materiality (significance) of the difference. Since the difference of $1,000 is immaterial in this case, we will assume that the management of Hayes Company does not investigate the difference and takes no specific action.

The budget report for the second quarter presented in Illustration 25-5 contains one new feature: cumulative year-to-date information. This report indicates that sales for the second quarter were $10,500 below budget, which is 5% of budgeted sales ($10,500 ÷ $210,000). Top management may conclude that the difference between budgeted and actual sales in the second quarter merits investigation.

**Illustration 25-5**

*Sales budget report—second quarter*

### HAYES COMPANY
### Sales Budget Report
### For the Quarter Ended June 30, 1996

| Product Line | Second Quarter | | | Year-to-Date | | |
|---|---|---|---|---|---|---|
| | Budget | Actual | Difference Favorable F Unfavorable U | Budget | Actual | Difference Favorable F Unfavorable U |
| Kitchen-mate | $210,000 | $199,500 | $10,500 U | $390,000 | $378,500 | $11,500 U |

Management's analysis should start by asking the sales manager the cause(s) of the shortfall. The need for corrective action should be considered. For example, management may decide to spur sales by offering sales incentives to customers or by increasing the advertising of Kitchen-mates. On the other hand, if management concludes that a downturn in the economy is responsible for the lower sales, it may decide to modify planned sales and profit goals for the remainder of the year.

From the examples above, you can see that a master sales budget is useful in evaluating the performance of a sales manager. It is now necessary to ask: How appropriate is the master budget for evaluating a manager's performance in controlling costs? Recall that in a static budget, budget data are not modified or adjusted, regardless of changes in activity during the year. It follows, then, that a static budget is appropriate in evaluating a manager's effectiveness in controlling costs when:

Helpful hint   Which of the following is likely to be of little use when costs are variable—the static budget or the flexible budget? Answer: The static budget.

1. The actual level of activity closely approximates the master budget activity level, and/or
2. The behavior of the costs in response to changes in activity is fixed.

A static budget report is, therefore, appropriate for fixed manufacturing costs and fixed selling and administrative expenses. However, as you will see shortly, static budget reports may not be a proper basis for evaluating a manager's performance in controlling variable costs.

# Flexible Budgets

In contrast to a static budget, which is based on one level of activity, a flexible budget projects budget data for various levels of activity. In essence, **the flexible budget is a series of static budgets at different levels of activity**. The flexible budget recognizes that the budgetary process has greater usefulness if it is adaptable to changed operating conditions.

Flexible budgets can be prepared for each of the types of budgets included in the master budget. For example, Marriott Hotels can budget revenues and net income on the basis of 60%, 80%, and 100% of room occupancy. Similarly, American Van Lines can budget its operating expenses on the basis of various levels of truck miles driven. Likewise, the bottling department of Coca-Cola can budget manufacturing costs on the basis of 70%, 80%, and 100% of direct labor costs or machine hours. In the following pages, we will illustrate a flexible budget for manufacturing overhead.

**STUDY OBJECTIVE**
·········▼·········
3

*Explain the development of flexible budgets and the usefulness of flexible budget reports.*

## Why Flexible Budgets?

Assume that you are the manager in charge of manufacturing overhead in the Forging Department of Barton Steel. In preparing the manufacturing overhead budget for 1996, you prepare the following static budget based on a production volume of 10,000 units of steel ingots:

| BARTON STEEL<br>Manufacturing Overhead Budget (Static)<br>Forging Department<br>For the Year Ended December 31, 1996 | |
| --- | --- |
| Budgeted production in units (steel ingots) | 10,000 |
| Budgeted costs | |
| Indirect materials | $  250,000 |
| Indirect labor | 260,000 |
| Utilities | 190,000 |
| Depreciation | 280,000 |
| Property taxes | 70,000 |
| Supervision | 50,000 |
| | $1,100,000 |

**Illustration 25-6**

*Static overhead budget*

Helpful hint   The static budget is the master budget of Chapter 24.

Fortunately for the company, the demand for steel ingots has increased, and 12,000 units are produced during the year, rather than 10,000. You are elated because increased sales means increased profitability, which should mean a large raise for you and the employees in your department. Unfortunately, a comparison of the actual costs incurred with the budgeted costs for the year in the Forging Department has put you on the spot. The budget report is shown below.

**Illustration 25-7**

*Static overhead budget report*

### BARTON STEEL
### Manufacturing Overhead Budget Report (Static)
### Forging Department
### For the Year Ended December 31, 1996

| | Budget | Actual | Difference<br>Favorable F<br>Unfavorable U |
|---|---|---|---|
| Production in units | 10,000 | 12,000 | |
| Costs | | | |
| Indirect materials | $ 250,000 | $ 295,000 | $ 45,000 U |
| Indirect labor | 260,000 | 312,000 | 52,000 U |
| Utilities | 190,000 | 225,000 | 35,000 U |
| Depreciation | 280,000 | 280,000 | –0– |
| Property taxes | 70,000 | 70,000 | –0– |
| Supervision | 50,000 | 50,000 | –0– |
| | $1,100,000 | $1,232,000 | $132,000 U |

**Helpful hint**  A static budget will not work if a company has substantial variable costs.

Note that this comparison is based on budget data based on the original activity level (10,000 steel ingots). The comparison indicates that the Forging Department is significantly **over budget** for three of the six overhead costs. Moreover, there is a total unfavorable difference of $132,000, which is 12% over budget ($132,000 ÷ $1,100,000). Your supervisor is very unhappy! Instead of sharing in the company's success, you may find yourself looking for another job. What would you do in this situation?

When you calm down and carefully examine the manufacturing overhead budget, you identify the problem: The budget data are not relevant! At the time the budget was developed, the company anticipated that only 10,000 units of steel ingots would be produced, **not** 12,000 ingots. As a result, the comparison of actual variable costs with budgeted costs is meaningless. The reason is that as production increases, the budget allowances for variable costs should increase both directly and proportionately. The variable costs in this example are indirect materials, indirect labor, and utilities.

An analysis of the budget data for these costs at 10,000 units produces the following per unit results:

**Illustration 25-8**

*Variable costs per unit*

| Item | Total Cost | Per Unit |
|---|---|---|
| Indirect materials | $250,000 | $25 |
| Indirect labor | 260,000 | 26 |
| Utilities | 190,000 | 19 |
| | $700,000 | $70 |

The budgeted variable costs at 12,000 units, therefore, are as follows:

**Illustration 25-9**

*Budgeted variable costs (12,000 units)*

| Item | Computation | Total |
|---|---|---|
| Indirect materials | $25 × 12,000 | $300,000 |
| Indirect labor | 26 × 12,000 | 312,000 |
| Utilities | 19 × 12,000 | 228,000 |
| | | $840,000 |

Because fixed costs do not change in total as activity changes, the budgeted amounts for these costs remain the same. The budget report based on the flexible budget for 12,000 units of production is shown in Illustration 25-10.

**Illustration 25-10**

*Flexible overhead budget report*

### BARTON STEEL
### Manufacturing Overhead Budget Report (Flexible)
### Forging Department
### For the Year Ended December 31, 1996

| | Budget | Actual | Difference Favorable F Unfavorable U |
|---|---|---|---|
| Production in units | 12,000 | 12,000 | |
| Variable costs | | | |
| Indirect materials | $ 300,000 | $ 295,000 | $5,000 F |
| Indirect labor | 312,000 | 312,000 | –0– |
| Utilities | 228,000 | 225,000 | 3,000 F |
| Total variable | 840,000 | 832,000 | 8,000 F |
| Fixed costs | | | |
| Depreciation | 280,000 | 280,000 | –0– |
| Property taxes | 70,000 | 70,000 | –0– |
| Supervision | 50,000 | 50,000 | –0– |
| Total fixed | 400,000 | 400,000 | –0– |
| Total costs | $1,240,000 | $1,232,000 | $8,000 F |

This report indicates that the Forging Department is below budget—a favorable difference. Instead of worrying about being fired, you may be in line for a raise or a promotion after all! As indicated from the foregoing analysis, the only appropriate comparison is between actual costs at 12,000 units of production and budgeted costs at 12,000 units of production. Flexible budget reports provide this comparison.

## Developing the Flexible Budget

The flexible budget uses the master budget as its basis. To develop the flexible budget, management should take the following steps:

1. Identify the activity index and the relevant range of activity.
2. Identify the variable costs and determine the budgeted variable cost per unit of activity for each cost.
3. Identify the fixed costs and determine the budgeted amount for each cost.

**4.** Prepare the budget for selected increments of activity within the relevant range.

The activity index chosen should be one that significantly influences the costs that are being budgeted. For manufacturing overhead costs, for example, the activity index is usually the same as the index used in developing the predetermined overhead rate—that is, direct labor hours or machine hours. For selling and administrative expenses, the activity index usually is sales or net sales.

The choice of selected increments of activity is largely a matter of judgment. For example, if the relevant range is 8,000 to 12,000 direct labor hours, increments of 1,000 hours may be selected. The flexible budget is then prepared in columnar form for each increment within the relevant range.

## Flexible Budget—A Case Study

To illustrate the preparation of the flexible budget, we will use Fox Manufacturing Company. The management of Fox Manufacturing wants to use the **flexible budget for monthly comparisons** of actual and budgeted manufacturing overhead costs of the Finishing Department. The master budget for the year ending December 31, 1996, shows expected annual operating capacity of 120,000 direct labor hours and the following overhead costs:

**Illustration 25-11**

*Master budget data*

| Variable | | Fixed | |
|---|---|---|---|
| Indirect materials | $180,000 | Depreciation | $180,000 |
| Indirect labor | 240,000 | Supervision | 120,000 |
| Utilities | 60,000 | Property taxes | 60,000 |
| Total | $480,000 | Total | $360,000 |

The application of the four steps is as follows:

**Step 1. Identify the activity index and the relevant range of activity.** The activity index is direct labor hours. Management concludes that the relevant range is 8,000–12,000 direct labor hours per month.

**Step 2. Identify the variable costs and determine the budgeted variable cost per unit of activity for each cost.** There are three variable costs. The variable cost per unit is found by dividing each total budgeted cost by the direct labor hours used in preparing the master budget (120,000 hours). For Fox Manufacturing, the computations are:

**Illustration 25-12**

*Computation of variable costs per direct labor hour*

| Variable Cost | Computation | Variable Cost per Direct Labor Hour |
|---|---|---|
| Indirect materials | $180,000 ÷ 120,000 | $1.50 |
| Indirect labor | 240,000 ÷ 120,000 | 2.00 |
| Utilities | 60,000 ÷ 120,000 | .50 |
| Total | | $4.00 |

**Step 3. Identify the fixed costs and determine the budgeted amount for each cost.** There are three fixed costs. Since Fox Manufacturing desires **monthly budget data**, the budgeted amount is found by dividing each annual budgeted cost by 12. For Fox Manufacturing, the monthly budgeted

fixed costs are: Depreciation $15,000, Supervision $10,000, and Property taxes $5,000.

**Step 4. Prepare the budget for selected increments of activity within the relevant range.** Management decides that the budget be prepared in increments of 1,000 direct labor hours.

The flexible budget is shown in Illustration 25-13.

**Illustration 25-13**

*Flexible monthly overhead budget*

| FOX MANUFACTURING COMPANY<br>Flexible Monthly Manufacturing Overhead Budget<br>Finishing Department<br>For the Year 1996 | | | | | |
|---|---|---|---|---|---|
| **Activity level** | | | | | |
| Direct labor hours | 8,000 | 9,000 | 10,000 | 11,000 | 12,000 |
| **Variable costs** | | | | | |
| Indirect materials | $12,000 | $13,500 | $15,000 | $16,500 | $18,000 |
| Indirect labor | 16,000 | 18,000 | 20,000 | 22,000 | 24,000 |
| Utilities | 4,000 | 4,500 | 5,000 | 5,500 | 6,000 |
| Total variable | 32,000 | 36,000 | 40,000 | 44,000 | 48,000 |
| **Fixed costs** | | | | | |
| Depreciation | 15,000 | 15,000 | 15,000 | 15,000 | 15,000 |
| Supervision | 10,000 | 10,000 | 10,000 | 10,000 | 10,000 |
| Property taxes | 5,000 | 5,000 | 5,000 | 5,000 | 5,000 |
| Total fixed | 30,000 | 30,000 | 30,000 | 30,000 | 30,000 |
| Total costs | $62,000 | $66,000 | $70,000 | $74,000 | $78,000 |

From the budget, the following formula may be used to determine total budgeted costs at any level of activity:

**Illustration 25-14**

*Formula for total budgeted costs*

*Total variable cost per unit times activity level.

For Fox Manufacturing, fixed costs are $30,000, and total variable cost per unit is $4.00. Thus, at 9,000 direct labor hours, total budgeted costs are $66,000 [fixed costs, $30,000 + ($4.00 × 9,000)]. Similarly, at 8,622 direct labor hours, total budgeted costs are $64,488 [$30,000 + ($4.00 × 8,622)].

Total budgeted costs can also be shown graphically, as in Illustration 25-15. In the graph, the activity index is shown on the horizontal axis and costs are indicated on the vertical axis. The graph highlights two of the 1,000 increments (10,000 and 12,000). As shown in Illustration 25-15, total budgeted costs are $70,000 [$30,000 + ($4.00 × 10,000)] and $78,000 [$30,000 + ($4.00 × 12,000)], respectively.

**Helpful hint** Using the data given for the Fox Manufacturing Company, what amount of total costs would be budgeted for 10,600 direct labor hours?
Answer:

| | |
|---|---|
| Fixed | $30,000 |
| Variable (10,600 × $4) | 42,400 |
| Total | $72,400 |

## Flexible Budget Reports

Flexible budget reports represent another type of internal report produced by managerial accounting. The flexible budget report consists of two sections:

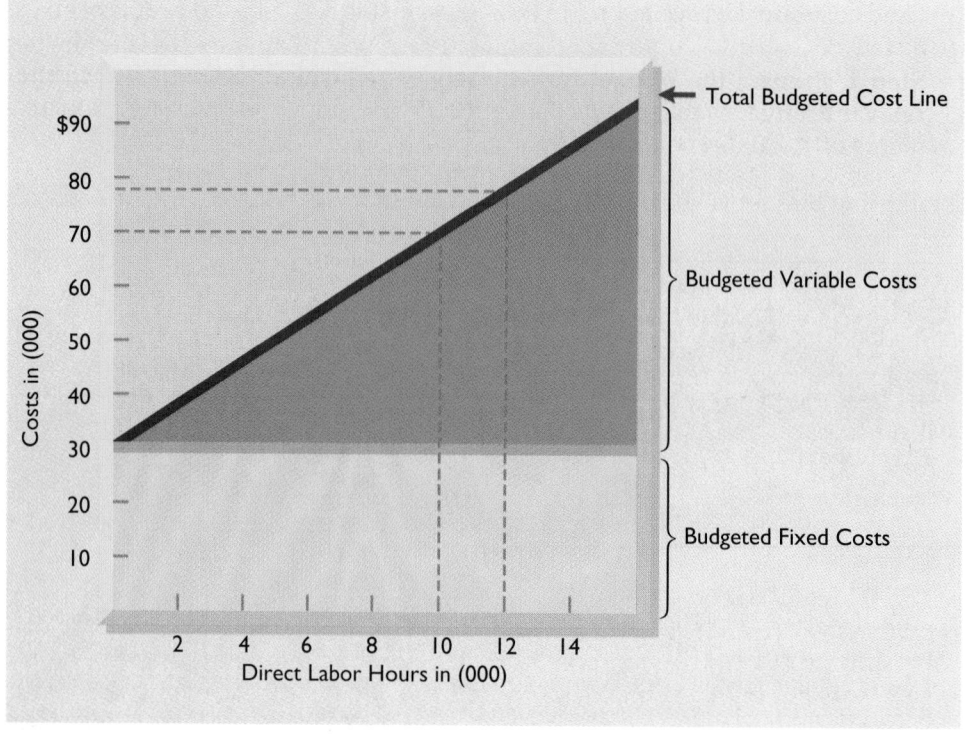

(1) production data such as direct labor hours and (2) cost data for variable and fixed costs. Consequently, the report provides a basis for evaluating a manager's performance in two areas: production control and cost control. Flexible budgets are widely used in production and service departments.

**Helpful hint** An assembly department is a production department and a maintenance department is a service department as explained on page 1054.

A budget report for the Finishing Department of Fox Company for the month of January is shown in Illustration 25-16. In this month, 8,800 direct labor hours were expected but 9,000 hours were worked. The budget data are based on the flexible budget for 9,000 hours in Illustration 25-14. The actual cost data are assumed.

**Illustration 25-16**

*Flexible overhead budget report*

### FOX MANUFACTURING COMPANY
#### Manufacturing Overhead Budget Report (Flexible)
#### Finishing Department
#### For the Month Ended January 31, 1996

| Direct labor hours (DLH) | | Budget at 9,000 DLH | Actual Costs 9,000 DLH | Difference Favorable F Unfavorable U |
|---|---|---|---|---|
| Expected | 8,800 | | | |
| Actual | 9,000 | | | |
| Variable costs | | | | |
| Indirect materials | | $13,500 | $14,000 | $   500 U |
| Indirect labor | | 18,000 | 17,000 | 1,000 F |
| Utilities | | 4,500 | 4,600 | 100 U |
| Total variable | | 36,000 | 35,600 | 400 F |
| Fixed costs | | | | |
| Depreciation | | 15,000 | 15,000 | –0– |
| Supervision | | 10,000 | 10,000 | –0– |
| Property taxes | | 5,000 | 5,000 | –0– |
| Total fixed | | 30,000 | 30,000 | –0– |
| Total costs | | $66,000 | $65,600 | $   400 F |

How appropriate is this report in evaluating the Finishing Department manager's performance in controlling costs? The report clearly provides a reliable basis for this purpose. Both actual and budget costs are based on the activity level worked during January. Since variable costs generally are incurred directly by the department, the difference between the budget allowance for those hours and the actual costs are the responsibility of the department manager.

From the standpoint of production control, the report shows a 200-hour difference between actual direct labor hours and expected hours. This difference is favorable if actual production orders required 9,000 direct labor hours. The difference is unfavorable if actual production orders required only 8,800 direct labor hours. In either case, the budget for purposes of cost control is based on 9,000 direct labor hours.

In subsequent months, other flexible budget reports will be prepared. For each month, the budget data are based on the actual activity level attained. In February that level may be 11,000 direct labor hours, in July, 10,000, and so on.

## Management by Exception

**Management by exception** means that top management's review of a budget report is directed either entirely or primarily to differences between actual results and planned objectives. This approach enables top management to focus on problem areas that need attention. Management by exception does not mean that top management will investigate every difference. For this approach to be effective, there must be some guidelines for identifying an exception. The usual criteria are materiality and controllability of the item.

### *Materiality*

Without quantitative guidelines, management would have to investigate every budget difference regardless of the amount. Materiality is usually expressed as a percentage difference from budget. For example, management may set the percentage difference at 5% for important items and 10% for other items. This means that all differences either over or under budget by the specified percentage will be investigated. Costs over budget warrant investigation to determine why they were not controlled. In contrast, costs under budget merit investigation to determine whether costs critical to the profitability of the division are being curtailed. For example, if maintenance costs are budgeted at $80,000 and only $40,000 is spent, major unexpected breakdowns in productive facilities may occur in the future.

Alternatively, a company may specify a single percentage difference from budget for all items and supplement this guideline with a minimum dollar limit. For example, the exception criteria may be stated at 5% of budget or more than $10,000.

### *Controllability of the Item*

Exception guidelines are more restrictive for controllable items than for items that are not controllable by the manager being evaluated. In fact, there may be no guidelines for noncontrollable items. For example, a large unfavorable difference between actual and budgeted property tax expense may not be flagged by management for investigation because the only possible causes are an unexpected increase in the tax rate or in the assessed value of the property. An investigation into the difference will be useless because the manager cannot control either cause.

## *Before You Go On . . .*

1. What is the meaning of budgetary control?
2. When is a static budget appropriate for evaluating a manager's effectiveness in controlling costs?
3. What is a flexible budget?
4. How is a flexible budget developed?
5. What are the criteria used in management by exception?

Your roommate asks your help in understanding how total budgeted costs are computed at any level of activity. Compute total budgeted costs at 30,000 direct labor hours, assuming that in the flexible budget graph, the fixed cost line and the total budgeted cost line intersect the vertical axis at $36,000 and that the total budget cost line is $186,000 at an activity level of 50,000 direct labor hours.

**Reasoning:** The formula for the computation is: Fixed Costs + Variable Costs (Total Variable Costs per Unit × Activity Level) = Total Budgeted Costs.

**Solution:** Using the graph, fixed costs are $36,000 and variable costs are $3 per direct labor hour [($186,000 − $36,000) ÷ 50,000]. Thus, at 30,000 direct labor hours total budgeted costs are $126,000 [$36,000 + ($3 × 30,000)].

*Related exercise material:* BE25–3, BE25–4, BE25–5, E25–1, E25–2, E25–3, E25–4, E25–5, E25–6, and E25–7.

# Concept of Responsibility Accounting

**STUDY OBJECTIVE**

**· · · · · · · · · ▼4· · · · · · · · · ·**

*Describe the concept of responsibility accounting.*

Like budgeting, responsibility accounting is an important part of management accounting. Responsibility accounting involves accumulating and reporting costs (and revenues, where relevant) on the basis of the individual manager who has the authority to make the day-to-day decisions about the items. Under responsibility accounting, the evaluation of a manager's performance is based on matters directly under that manager's control. Responsibility accounting can be used at every level of management in which the following conditions exist:

1. Costs and revenues can be directly associated with the specific level of management responsibility.
2. The costs and revenues are controllable at the level of responsibility with which they are associated.
3. Budget data can be developed for evaluating the manager's effectiveness in controlling the costs and revenues.

**Helpful hint** All companies use responsibility accounting. Without some form of responsibility accounting, there would be chaos in discharging management's control function.

Responsibility accounting personalizes the managerial accounting system. Under responsibility accounting, any individual who has control and is accountable for a specified set of activities can be recognized as a responsibility center. Thus, responsibility accounting may extend from the lowest level of control to the top strata of management. Once responsibility has been established, the effectiveness of the individual's performance is first measured and reported for the specified activity, and it is then reported upward throughout the organization.

Responsibility accounting is especially valuable in a decentralized company. Decentralization means that the control of operations is delegated by top management to many individuals (managers) throughout the organization. The term segment is sometimes used to identify an area of responsibility in decentralized operations. Under responsibility accounting, reports are prepared periodically such as monthly, quarterly, and annually, to provide a basis for evaluating the performance of each manager.

Responsibility accounting is an essential part of any effective system of budgetary control. The reporting of costs and revenues under responsibility accounting differs from budgeting in two respects:

1. A distinction is made between controllable and noncontrollable items.
2. Performance reports either emphasize or include only items controllable by the individual manager.

Responsibility accounting applies to both profit and not-for-profit entities. The former seek to maximize net income, whereas the latter wish to minimize the cost of providing the service.

## ►*A*ccounting in *A*ction ► *Business Insight*

Since devising the budgeting system, JKL, Inc., a large New York advertising agency, has become aware of which specific accounts are unprofitable and the reasons why. Since the budgeting and control system has been instituted, the agency has resigned several unprofitable accounts that otherwise would have gone unnoticed. Account managers and supervisors now feel responsible for the profitability of their accounts. They carefully monitor actual hours spent on each account to make sure the account is being managed and run as efficiently as possible. For example, an account manager noticed a large amount of supervisory creative time was being spent on an account. Further investigation showed that the supervisors, rather than the creative department, were doing the actual creative work. The account manager pointed this out, and a junior creative team was appointed to the account, saving a great deal of money.

*Source:* William B. Mills, "Drawing Up a Budgeting System for an Ad Agency," *Management Accounting.*

## Controllable versus Noncontrollable Revenues and Costs

All costs and revenues are controllable at some level of responsibility within a company. This truth underscores the adage by the chief executive officer of any organization that "the buck stops here." Under responsibility accounting, the critical issue is **whether the cost or revenue is controllable at the level of responsibility with which it is associated**.

A cost is considered to be controllable at a given level of managerial responsibility if that manager has the power to incur it within a given period of time. From this criterion, it follows that

1. All costs are controllable by top management because of the broad range of its authority.
2. Fewer costs are controllable as one moves down to each lower level of managerial responsibility because of the manager's decreasing authority.

In general, **costs incurred directly by a level of responsibility are controllable at that level**. In contrast, costs incurred indirectly and allocated to a responsibility level are considered to be noncontrollable at that level.

**Helpful hint** Are there more or fewer controllable costs as you move to higher levels of management? Answer: More.

## Responsibility Reporting System

A responsibility reporting system involves the preparation of a report for each level of responsibility shown in the company's organization chart. To illustrate a responsibility reporting system, we will use the partial organization chart and production departments of the Francis Company in Illustration 25-17.

**Illustration 25-17**

*Partial organization chart*

The responsibility reporting system begins with the lowest level of responsibility for controlling costs and moves upward to each higher level, as shown in Illustration 25-18. A brief description of the four reports is as follows:

1. **Report D** is typical of reports that go to managers at the lowest level of responsibility shown in the organization chart—department managers. In this report, additional detail may be presented for manufacturing overhead. Similar reports are prepared for the managers of the Enameling and Assembly Departments.

2. **Report C** is an example of reports that are sent to plant managers. This report shows the costs of the Chicago plant that are controllable at the second level of responsibility. In addition, Report C shows summary data for each department that is controlled by the plant manager. Similar reports are prepared for the Detroit and St. Louis plant managers.

3. **Report B** illustrates the reports at the third level of responsibility. It shows the controllable costs of the vice-president of production and summary data on the three assembly plants for which this officer is responsible.

4. **Report A** is typical of the reports that go to the top level of responsibility— the president. This report shows the controllable costs and expenses of this

**Illustration 25-18**

*Responsibility reporting system*

**REPORT A**

To President                              Month:    January

| Controllable Costs: | Budget | Actual | Fav/Unfav |
|---|---|---|---|
| President | $ 150,000 | $ 151,500 | $ 1,500 U |
| Vice–Presidents: | | | |
| Sales | 185,000 | 187,000 | 2,000 U |
| Production | 1,179,000 | 1,186,300 | 7,300 U |
| Finance | 100,000 | 101,000 | 1,000 U |
| Total | $1,614,000 | $1,625,800 | $11,800 U |

**REPORT B**

To Vice-President Production                    Month:    January

| Controllable Costs: | Budget | Actual | Fav/Unfav |
|---|---|---|---|
| V-P Production | $ 125,000 | $ 126,000 | $ 1,000 U |
| Assembly Plants: | | | |
| Detroit | 420,000 | 418,000 | 2,000 F |
| Chicago | 304,000 | 309,300 | 5,300 U |
| St. Louis | 330,000 | 333,000 | 3,000 U |
| Total | $1,179,000 | $1,186,300 | $ 7,300 U |

**REPORT C**

To Plant Manager-Chicago                        Month:    January

| Controllable Costs: | Budget | Actual | Fav/Unfav |
|---|---|---|---|
| Chicago Plant | $110,000 | $113,000 | $ 3,000 U |
| Departments: | | | |
| Fabricating | 84,000 | 85,300 | 1,300 U |
| Enameling | 62,000 | 64,000 | 2,000 U |
| Assembly | 48,000 | 47,000 | 1,000 F |
| Total | $304,000 | $309,300 | $ 5,300 U |

**REPORT D**

To Fabricating Department Manager               Month:    January

| Controllable Costs: | Budget | Actual | Fav/Unfav |
|---|---|---|---|
| Direct Materials | $ 20,000 | $ 20,500 | $ 500 U |
| Direct Labor | 40,000 | 41,000 | 1,000 U |
| Overhead | 24,000 | 23,800 | 200 F |
| Total | $ 84,000 | $ 85,300 | $ 1,300 U |

office and summary data on the vice-presidents that are accountable to the president.

A responsibility reporting system permits management by exception at each level of responsibility within the organization. In addition to the information shown in Illustration 25-18, each higher level of responsibility can obtain the detailed report for each lower level of responsibility. For example, the vice-president of production in the Francis Company may request the Chicago plant manager's report because this plant is $5,300 over budget.

This type of reporting system also permits comparative evaluations. In Illustration 25-18, the Chicago plant manager can easily rank the department manager's effectiveness in controlling manufacturing costs. Comparative rankings provide further incentive for a manager to control costs. For example, the Detroit plant manager will want to continue to be No. 1 in the report to the vice-president of production, and the Chicago plant manager will not want to remain No. 3 in future reporting periods.

## ▸Technology in Action

Computerized accounting systems can play a major role in increasing the timeliness of performance reports. The computer's speed in processing and reorganizing information has enabled management to receive feedback reports of exceptions much sooner after the exceptions have occurred than would have been possible with a manual system. Efficiency is increased because management's attention is directed to significant deviations requiring corrective action before these deviations get too far "out of hand."

Management has also come to rely on personal computers to increase the timeliness of information receipt. When connected to the main computer system, a manager can "download" financial information and perform additional calculations and manipulations on the information for a decision at hand in a fraction of the time needed to request such information from the EDP Department. Though more timely, accuracy must not be sacrificed, and all calculations should be tested for correctness before being used for decision making.

## ▾Types of Responsibility Centers

There are three basic types of responsibility centers: cost centers, profit centers, and investment centers. These centers indicate the degree of responsibility the manager has for the performance of the center.

A cost center incurs costs (and expenses) but does not directly generate revenues. Managers of cost centers have the authority to incur costs. They are evaluated on their ability to control costs. Cost centers are usually either production departments or service departments. The former participate directly in making the product whereas the latter provide only support services. In a Ford Motor Company automobile plant, the welding, painting, and assembling departments are production departments, and the maintenance, cafeteria, and personnel departments are service departments. All of these departments are cost centers.

A profit center incurs costs (and expenses) but also generates revenues. Managers of profit centers are judged on the profitability of their centers. Examples of profit centers include the individual departments of a retail store, such as clothing, furniture, and automotive products, and branch offices of banks.

Like a profit center, an investment center incurs costs (and expenses) and generates revenues. In addition, an investment center has control over the investment funds available for use. Managers of investment centers are evaluated on the profitability of the center and on the rate of return earned on the funds invested. Investment centers are often associated with subsidiary companies. For example, PepsiCo owns Frito-Lay (potato chips) and Pizza Hut and Kentucky Fried Chicken (restaurants), whereas General Mills owns Parker Brothers (games) and Izod Lacoste (fashions). In each of these instances, the manager of the investment center (segment) is able to control or significantly influence in-

**Helpful hint** (1) Is the jewelry department of Marshall Field's department store a profit center or a cost center? (2) Is the props department of a movie studio a profit center or a cost center? Answers: (1) Profit center. (2) Cost center.

vestment decisions pertaining to such matters as plant expansion and entry into new market areas.

The evaluation of a manager's performance in each type of responsibility center is explained in the remainder of this chapter.

## Responsibility Accounting for Cost Centers

The evaluation of a manager's performance for cost centers is based on the manager's ability to meet budgeted goals for controllable costs. **Responsibility reports for cost centers compare actual controllable costs with flexible budget data.**

A responsibility report is illustrated in Illustration 25-19. The report is adapted from the budget report for Fox Manufacturing Company in Illustration 25-16 on page 1048. It assumes that the Finishing Department manager is able to control all manufacturing overhead costs except depreciation, property taxes, and his own monthly supervisory salary of $6,000. The remaining $4,000 of supervision costs are assumed to apply to other supervisory personnel within the Finishing Department whose salaries are controllable by the manager.

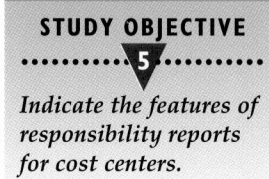

**FOX MANUFACTURING COMPANY**
**Finishing Department**
**Responsibility Report**
**For the Month Ended January 31, 1996**

| Controllable Cost | Budget | Actual | Difference<br>Favorable F<br>Unfavorable U |
|---|---|---|---|
| Indirect materials | $13,500 | $14,000 | $ 500 U |
| Indirect labor | 18,000 | 17,000 | 1,000 F |
| Utilities | 4,500 | 4,600 | 100 U |
| Supervision | 4,000 | 4,000 | –0– |
| | $40,000 | $39,600 | $ 400 F |

*Illustration 25-19*

*Responsibility report for a cost center*

**Only controllable costs are included** in the report, and no distinction is made between variable and fixed costs. As in budget reports, the responsibility report continues the concept of management by exception. In this case, top management may request an explanation of the $1,000 favorable difference in indirect labor and/or the $500 unfavorable difference in indirect materials.

## Responsibility Accounting for Profit Centers

To evaluate the performance of a manager of a profit center properly, detailed information is needed about both controllable revenues and controllable costs. The operating revenues earned by a profit center, such as sales, are controllable by the manager. All variable costs (and expenses) incurred by the center are also controllable by the manager because they vary with sales. However, to determine the controllability of fixed costs, it is necessary to distinguish between direct and indirect fixed costs.

### Direct and Indirect Fixed Costs

A profit center may have both direct and indirect fixed costs. Direct fixed costs are costs that relate specifically to one center and are incurred for the sole benefit of that center. Examples of such costs include the salaries established by the profit center manager for supervisory personnel and the cost of maintaining a time-keeping department for the center's employees. Since these fixed costs can be traced directly to a center, they are also called **traceable costs**. **Most direct fixed costs are controllable by the profit center manager.**

In contrast, indirect fixed costs pertain to a company's overall operating activities and they are incurred for the benefit of more than one profit center. Indirect fixed costs are allocated to profit centers on some type of equitable basis. For example, property taxes on a building occupied by more than one center may be allocated on the basis of square feet of floor space used by each center. Alternatively, the costs of a company's personnel department may be allocated to profit centers on the basis of the number of employees in each center. Because these fixed costs apply to more than one center, they are also called **common costs**. **Most indirect fixed costs are not controllable by the profit center manager.**

### Responsibility Report

**STUDY OBJECTIVE**

**••••••••••6••••••••••**

*Identify the content of responsibility reports for profit centers.*

The responsibility report for a profit center shows budgeted and actual **controllable revenues and costs**. The report is prepared using the cost-volume-profit income statement explained in Chapter 23. In the report:

1. Controllable fixed costs are deducted from contribution margin.
2. The excess of contribution margin over controllable fixed costs is identified as controllable margin.
3. Noncontrollable fixed costs are not reported.

The responsibility report for the manager of the Marine Division, a profit center of Mantle Manufacturing Company, is shown in Illustration 25-20. For the year, the Marine Division also had $60,000 of indirect fixed costs that were not controllable by the profit center manager.

**Illustration 25-20**

*Responsibility report for profit center*

**MANTLE MANUFACTURING COMPANY**
**Marine Division**
**Responsibility Report**
**For the Year Ended December 31, 1996**

|  | Budget | Actual | Difference Favorable F Unfavorable U |
|---|---|---|---|
| Sales | $1,200,000 | $1,150,000 | $50,000 U |
| Variable costs |  |  |  |
| Cost of goods sold | 500,000 | 490,000 | 10,000 F |
| Selling and administrative | 160,000 | 156,000 | 4,000 F |
| Total | 660,000 | 646,000 | 14,000 F |
| Contribution margin | 540,000 | 504,000 | 36,000 U |
| **Controllable fixed costs** |  |  |  |
| Cost of goods sold | 100,000 | 100,000 | –0– |
| Selling and administrative | 80,000 | 80,000 | –0– |
| Total | 180,000 | 180,000 | –0– |
| **Controllable margin** | $  360,000 | $  324,000 | $36,000 U |

Controllable margin is considered to be the best measure of the manager's performance **in controlling revenues and costs**. This report shows that the manager's performance was below budgeted expectations by approximately 10% ($36,000 ÷ $360,000). Top management would likely investigate the causes of this unfavorable result. Note that the report does not show the Marine Division's noncontrollable fixed costs of $60,000. These costs would be included in a report on the profitability of the profit center.

Responsibility reports for profit centers may also be prepared monthly. In addition, they may include cumulative year-to-date results.

►**Ethics note**

Responsibility reports are helpful tools for evaluating the performance of management. Too much emphasis on profits or investments, however, can be harmful because it ignores other important performance issues such as quality and social responsibility.

## *Before You Go On . . .*

### ► *Review It*

1. What conditions are essential for responsibility accounting?
2. What is involved in a responsibility reporting system?
3. What is the primary objective of a responsibility report for a cost center?
4. How does contribution margin differ from controllable margin in a responsibility report for a profit center?

### ► *Do It*

Midwest Division which operates as a profit center reports the following actual results for the year: Sales $1,700,000, variable costs $800,000, controllable fixed costs $400,000, noncontrollable fixed costs $200,000. Annual budgeted amounts were $1,500,000, $700,000, $400,000, and $200,000 respectively. Prepare a responsibility report for the Midwest Division for December 31, 1996.

*Reasoning:* In the responsibility report, variable costs are deducted from sales to show contribution margin. Controllable fixed costs are then deducted to show controllable margin. Noncontrollable fixed costs are not reported.

*Solution:*

**MIDWEST DIVISION**
**Reponsibility Report**
**For the Year Ended December 31, 1996**

| | Budget | Actual | Difference Favorable F Unfavorable U |
|---|---|---|---|
| Sales | $1,500,000 | $1,700,000 | $200,000 F |
| Variable costs | 700,000 | 800,000 | 100,000 U |
| Contribution margin | 800,000 | 900,000 | 100,000 F |
| Controllable fixed costs | 400,000 | 400,000 | –0– |
| Controllable margin | $ 400,000 | $ 500,000 | $100,000 F |

*Related exercise material: BE25–7 and E25–9.*

## Responsibility Accounting for Investment Centers

As explained earlier, an important characteristic of an investment center is that the manager can control or significantly influence the investment funds available for use. Thus, the primary basis for evaluating the performance of a manager of an investment center is return on investment (ROI). The return on investment is considered to be superior to any other performance measurement because it shows the **effectiveness of the manager in utilizing the assets at the manager's disposal**.

**STUDY OBJECTIVE**
··········**7**··········

*Explain the basis and formula used in evaluating performance in investment centers.*

### *Return on Investment (ROI)*

The formula for computing ROI for an investment center, together with assumed illustrative data, is shown in Illustration 25-21. Both factors in the formula are controllable by the investment center manager. Operating assets consist of current assets and plant assets used in operations by the center and controlled by the manager. Nonoperating assets such as idle plant assets and land held for future use are excluded. Average operating assets are usually based on the cost or book value of the assets at the beginning and end of the year.

**Illustration 25-21**

*ROI formula*

### Responsibility Report

The scope of the investment center manager's responsibility significantly affects the content of the performance report. Since an investment center is an independent entity for operating purposes, **all fixed costs are controllable by the investment center manager**. For example, the manager is responsible for depreciation on investment center assets. Accordingly, more fixed costs are identified as controllable in the performance report for an investment center manager than in a performance report for a profit center manager. In addition, the report shows budgeted and actual ROI below controllable margin.

To illustrate the responsibility report, we will now assume that the Marine Division of Mantle Manufacturing Company is an investment center with budgeted and actual average operating assets of $2,000,000. In addition, we will assume that the manager can control the $60,000 of fixed costs that were not controllable when the division was a profit center. The responsibility report is shown in Illustration 25-22.

**Illustration 25-22**

*Responsibility report for investment center*

**MANTLE MANUFACTURING COMPANY**
**Marine Division**
**Responsibility Report**
**For the Year Ended December 31, 1996**

| | Budget | Actual | Difference Favorable F Unfavorable U |
|---|---|---|---|
| Sales | $1,200,000 | $1,150,000 | $50,000 U |
| Variable costs | | | |
| Cost of goods sold | 500,000 | 490,000 | 10,000 F |
| Selling and administrative | 160,000 | 156,000 | 4,000 F |
| Total | 660,000 | 646,000 | 14,000 F |
| Contribution margin | 540,000 | 504,000 | 36,000 U |
| **Controllable fixed costs** | | | |
| Cost of goods sold | 100,000 | 100,000 | –0– |
| Selling and administrative | 80,000 | 80,000 | –0– |
| **Other fixed costs** | 60,000 | 60,000 | –0– |
| Total | 240,000 | 240,000 | –0– |
| **Controllable margin** | $ 300,000 | $ 264,000 | $36,000 U |
| Return on investment | 15% | 13.2% | 1.8% U |
| | (a) | (b) | (c) |

(a) $\dfrac{\$300,000}{\$2,000,000}$   (b) $\dfrac{\$264,000}{\$2,000,000}$   (c) $\dfrac{\$36,000}{\$2,000,000}$

The report shows that the manager's performance based on ROI was 12% below budget expectations (1.8% ÷ 15%). Top management would likely want an explanation of the reasons for this unfavorable result.

### Improving ROI

The manager of an investment center can improve ROI in two ways: (1) increase controllable margin and/or (2) reduce average operating assets. To illustrate, we will use the following assumed data for the Marine Division of Mantle Manufacturing:

**Illustration 25-23**

*Assumed data for Marine Division*

| | |
|---|---|
| Sales | $2,000,000 |
| Variable cost | 1,100,000 |
| Contribution margin (45%) | 900,000 |
| Controllable fixed costs | 300,000 |
| Controllable margin (a) | $ 600,000 |
| Average operating assets (b) | $5,000,000 |
| Return on investment (a) ÷ (b) | 12% |

**Increasing Controllable Margin.** Controllable margin can be increased by increasing sales or by reducing variable and controllable fixed costs as follows:

1. **Increase sales 10%.** Sales will increase $200,000 ($2,000,000 × .10). Assuming no change in the contribution margin percentage of 45%, contribution margin will increase $90,000 ($200,000 × .45). Controllable margin will increase by the same amount because controllable fixed costs will not change. Thus, controllable margin becomes $690,000 ($600,000 + $90,000), and the new ROI is 13.8%, computed as follows:

$$\frac{\$690,000}{\$5,000,000} = 13.8\%$$

**Illustration 25-24**

*ROI computation—increase in sales*

An increase in sales benefits both the investment center and the company if it results in new business. It would not benefit the company if the increase was achieved at the expense of other investment centers.

2. **Decrease variable and fixed costs 10%.** Total costs will decrease $140,000 [($1,100,000 + $300,000) × .10]. This reduction will result in a corresponding increase in controllable margin. Thus, this margin becomes $740,000 ($600,000 + $140,000), and the new ROI is 14.8%, computed as follows:

$$\frac{\$740,000}{\$5,000,000} = 14.8\%$$

**Illustration 25-25**

*ROI computation—decrease in costs*

This course of action is clearly beneficial when waste and inefficiencies are eliminated. However, a reduction in vital costs such as required maintenance and inspections are not likely to be acceptable to top management.

**Reducing Average Operating Assets.** Assume that average operating assets are reduced 10% or $500,000 ($5,000,000 × .10). Average operating assets become

$4,500,000 ($5,000,000 − $500,000). Since controllable margin remains unchanged at $600,000, the new ROI is 13.3%, computed as follows:

**Illustration 25-26**

*ROI computation—decrease in operating assets*

$$\frac{\$600,000}{\$4,500,000} = 13.3\%$$

Reductions in operating assets may or may not be prudent. It is beneficial to eliminate overinvestment in inventories and to dispose of excessive plant assets. However, it is unwise to reduce inventories below expected needs or to dispose of essential plant assets.

### Judgmental Factors in ROI

The return on investment approach includes two judgmental factors.

1. **Valuation of operating assets.** Operating assets may be valued at acquisition cost, book value, appraised value, or market value. The first two bases are readily available from the accounting records.
2. **Margin (income) measure.** This measure may be controllable margin, income from operations, or net income.

Each of the alternative values for operating assets can provide a reliable basis for evaluating a manager's performance as long as it is consistently applied between reporting periods. However, the use of income measures other than controllable margin will not result in a valid basis for evaluating the performance of an investment center manager because they will include some noncontrollable revenues and costs.

# Principles of Performance Evaluation

Performance evaluation is at the center of responsibility accounting. **Performance evaluation** is a management function that compares actual results with budget goals. It is based on internal reports prepared by the managerial accountant. Performance evaluation involves both behavioral and reporting principles.

## Behavioral Principles

The human factor is critical in evaluating performance. Behavioral principles include the following:

1. **Managers of responsibility centers should have direct input into the process of establishing budget goals of their area of responsibility.** Without such input, managers may view the goals as unrealistic or arbitrarily set by top management. Such views adversely affect the managers' motivation to meet the targeted objectives.
2. **The evaluation of performance should be based entirely on matters that are controllable by the manager being evaluated.** Criticism of a manager on matters outside his or her control reduces the effectiveness of the evaluation process. Moreover, it leads to negative reactions by a manager and to doubts about the fairness of the company's evaluation policies.
3. **Top management should support the evaluation process.** As explained earlier, the evaluation process begins at the lowest level of responsibility and

extends upward to the highest level of management. Managers quickly lose faith in the process when top management ignores, overrules, or bypasses established procedures for evaluating a manager's performance.

4. **The evaluation process must allow managers to respond to their evaluations.** Evaluation is not a one-way street. Managers should have the opportunity to defend their performance. Evaluation without feedback is both impersonal and ineffective.

5. **The evaluation should identify both good and poor performance.** Praise for good performance is a powerful motivating factor for a manager. This is especially true when a manager's compensation includes rewards for meeting budget goals.

## Reporting Principles

Performance evaluation under responsibility accounting also involves reporting principles. These principles pertain primarily to the internal reports that provide the basis for evaluating performance. Performance reports should:

1. Contain only data that are controllable by the manager of the responsibility center.
2. Provide accurate and reliable budget data to measure performance.
3. Highlight significant differences between actual results and budget goals.
4. Be tailor-made for the intended evaluation.
5. Be prepared at reasonable intervals.

## *Before You Go On . . .*

### ▶ *Review It*

1. What is the formula for computing return on investment (ROI)?
2. Identify three actions a manager may take to improve ROI.

### ▶ *A Look Back at the University of Nevada, Las Vegas*

Refer to the opening story about the athletic department of UNLV and answer the following questions.

1. Would you expect a static or a flexible budget to be used in comparing actual and budgeted expenditures for each team?
2. Which of the biggest budget items are variable and which are fixed?
3. What is the relationship, if any, of the budgets used at UNLV and the allocation of cash to each team?

**Solution:**

1. At the time of preparing the budget, if a sports team has a fixed schedule of games (meets) along with a fixed number of players and coaches, a static budget might be sufficient. That is, if the predetermined activity level is static or fixed, the budget may be static. However, if the activity level (games/meets along with the roster size, number of scholarships, and coaches) is flexible and not predeterminable, a flexible budget tied to the activity driver is necessary in order to evaluate budget compliance at different activity levels.
2. The biggest variable expense is travel cost, which varies with distance, the number in the traveling party, and number of trips. Once the coaches, trainers, and managers are hired, payroll is a fixed cost for the season. Scholarships, once the number of in-state and out-of-state scholarships has been granted, is also a fixed cost for the season.
3. Once approved, the budget becomes the basis for the appropriation of funds and the allocation of cash to each team. Cash is allocated to each team in accordance with the approved budget. The budget sets the limits and the categories of expenditures.

# Summary of Study Objectives

**1.** *Describe the concept of budgetary control.* Budgetary control consists of (a) preparing periodic budget reports that compare actual results with planned objectives, (b) analyzing the differences to determine their causes, (c) taking appropriate corrective action, and (d) modifying future plans, if necessary.

**2.** *Evaluate the usefulness of static budget reports.* Static budget reports are useful in evaluating the progress toward meeting planned sales and profit goals. They are also appropriate in assessing a manager's effectiveness in controlling fixed costs and expenses when (a) actual activity closely approximates the master budget activity level and/or (b) the behavior of the costs in response to changes in activity is fixed.

**3.** *Explain the development of flexible budgets and the usefulness of flexible budget reports.* To develop the flexible budget it is necessary to:
(a) Identify the activity index and the relevant range of activity.
(b) Identify the variable costs and determine the budgeted variable cost per unit of activity for each cost.
(c) Identify the fixed costs and determine the budgeted amount for each cost.
(d) Prepare the budget for selected increments of activity within the relevant range.

Flexible budget reports permit an evaluation of a manager's performance in controlling production and costs.

**4.** *Describe the concept of responsibility accounting.* Responsibility accounting involves the accumulation and reporting of revenues and costs on the basis of the individual manager who has the authority to make the day-to-day decisions about the items. Under responsibility accounting, the evaluation of a manager's performance is based on the matters directly under the manager's control. In responsibility accounting, it is necessary to distinguish between controllable and noncontrollable fixed costs and to identify three types of responsibility centers: cost, profit, and investment.

**5.** *Indicate the features of responsibility reports for cost centers.* Responsibility reports for cost centers compare actual costs with flexible budget data. The reports show only controllable costs and no distinction is made between variable and fixed costs.

**6.** *Identify the content of responsibility reports for profit centers.* Responsibility reports show contribution margin, controllable fixed costs, and controllable margin for each profit center.

**7.** *Explain the basis and formula used in evaluating performance in investment centers.* The primary basis for evaluating performance in investment centers is return on investment (ROI). The formula for computing ROI for investment centers is: Controllable Margin (in dollars) ÷ Average Operating Assets.

# GLOSSARY

**Budgetary control** The use of budgets to control operations. (p. 1040).

**Controllable costs** Costs that a manager has the authority to incur within a given period of time. (p. 1051).

**Controllable margin** Contribution margin less controllable fixed costs. (p. 1056).

**Cost center** A responsibility center that incurs costs but does not directly generate revenues. (p. 1054).

**Decentralization** Control of operations is delegated by top management to many managers throughout the organization. (p. 1050).

**Direct fixed costs** Costs that relate specifically to a responsibility center and are incurred for the sole benefit of the center. (p. 1055).

**Flexible budget** A projection of budget data for various levels of activity. (p. 1043).

**Indirect fixed costs** Costs that are incurred for the benefit of more than one profit center. (p. 1056).

**Investment center** A responsibility center that incurs costs, generates revenues, and has control over the investment funds available for use. (p. 1054).

**Management by exception** The review of budget reports by top management directed entirely or primarily to differences between actual results and planned objectives. (p. 1049).

**Noncontrollable costs** Costs incurred indirectly and allocated to a responsibility center that are not controllable at that level. (p. 1051).

**Profit center** A responsibility center that incurs costs and also generates revenues. (p. 1054).

**Responsibility accounting** A part of management accounting that involves accumulating and reporting revenues and costs on the basis of the individual manager who has the authority to make the day-to-day decisions about the items. (p. 1050).

**Responsibility reporting system** The preparation of reports for each level of responsibility shown in the company's organization chart. (p. 1051).

**Return on investment (ROI)** A measure of management's effectiveness in utilizing assets at its disposal in an investment center. (p. 1057).

**Segment** An area of responsibility in decentralized operations. (p. 1051).

**Static budget** A projection of budget data at one level of activity. (p. 1041).

# DEMONSTRATION PROBLEM

Glenda Company uses a flexible budget for manufacturing overhead based on direct labor hours. For 1996 the master overhead budget for the Packaging Department at normal capacity of 300,000 direct labor hours was as follows:

| Variable Costs | | Fixed Costs | |
|---|---|---|---|
| Indirect labor | $360,000 | Supervision | $ 60,000 |
| Supplies and lubricants | 150,000 | Depreciation | 24,000 |
| Maintenance | 210,000 | Property taxes | 18,000 |
| Utilities | 120,000 | Insurance | 12,000 |
| | $840,000 | | $114,000 |

During July, 24,000 direct labor hours were worked when 25,000 hours were expected to be worked. The company incurred the following variable costs in July: Indirect labor $30,200, supplies and lubricants $11,600, maintenance $17,500, and utilities $9,200. Actual fixed overhead costs were the same as monthly budgeted fixed costs.

*Instructions*
Prepare a flexible budget report for the Packaging Department for July.

## Solution to Demonstration Problem

**GLENDA COMPANY**
**Manufacturing Overhead Budget Report (Flexible)**
**Packaging Department**
**For the Month Ended July 31, 1996**

| Direct labor hours (DLH) Expected 25,000 Actual 24,000 | Budget 24,000 DLH | Actual Costs 24,000 DLH | Difference Favorable F Unfavorable U |
|---|---|---|---|
| Variable costs | | | |
| Indirect labor | $28,800 | $30,200 | $1,400 U |
| Supplies and lubricants | 12,000 | 11,600 | 400 F |
| Maintenance | 16,800 | 17,500 | 700 U |
| Utilities | 9,600 | 9,200 | 400 F |
| Total variable | 67,200 | 68,500 | 1,300 U |
| Fixed costs | | | |
| Supervision | 5,000 | 5,000 | –0– |
| Depreciation | 2,000 | 2,000 | –0– |
| Property taxes | 1,500 | 1,500 | –0– |
| Insurance | 1,000 | 1,000 | –0– |
| Total fixed | 9,500 | 9,500 | –0– |
| Total costs | $76,700 | $78,000 | $1,300 U |

**Problem-Solving Strategies**
1. Use budget data for actual direct labor hours worked.
2. Classify each cost as variable or fixed.
3. Determine the difference between budgeted and actual costs.
4. Identify the difference as favorable or unfavorable.
5. Determine the difference in total variable costs, total fixed costs, and total costs.

# SELF-STUDY QUESTIONS

Answers are at the end of the chapter.

(SO 1)
1. Budgetary control involves all but one of the following:
   a. modifying future plans.
   b. analyzing differences.
   c. using static budgets.
   d. determining differences between actual and planned results.

(SO 2)
2. A static budget is useful in controlling costs when cost behavior is:
   a. mixed.
   b. fixed.
   c. variable.
   d. linear.

(SO 3)
3. At zero direct labor hours in a flexible budget graph, the total budgeted cost line intersects the

vertical axis at $30,000. At 10,000 direct labor hours, the line drawn from the total budgeted cost line intersects the vertical axis at $90,000. Fixed and variable costs may be expressed as:
a. $30,000 fixed plus $6 per direct labor hour variable.
b. $30,000 fixed plus $9 per direct labor hour variable.
c. $60,000 fixed plus $3 per direct labor hour variable.
d. $60,000 fixed plus $6 per direct labor hour variable.

(SO 3)   4. At 9,000 direct labor hours, the flexible budget for indirect materials is $27,000. If $28,000 of indirect materials costs are incurred at 9,200 direct labor hours, the flexible budget report should show the following difference for indirect materials:
a. $1,000 unfavorable.
b. $1,000 favorable.
c. $400 favorable.
d. $400 unfavorable.

(SO 4)   5. Under responsibility accounting, the evaluation of a manager's performance is based on matters that the manager:
a. directly controls.
b. directly and indirectly controls.
c. indirectly controls.
d. has shared responsibility with another manager.

(SO 4)   6. Responsibility centers include:
a. cost centers.
b. profit centers.

c. investment centers.
d. All of the above.

7. Responsibility reports for cost centers:                (SO 5)
a. distinguish between fixed and variable costs.
b. use static budget data.
c. include both controllable and noncontrollable costs.
d. include only controllable costs.

8. In a responsibility report for a profit center, con-   (SO 6)
trollable fixed costs are deducted from contribution margin to show:
a. profit center margin.
b. controllable margin.
c. net income.
d. income from operations.

9. In the formula for return on investment (ROI), the   (SO 7)
factors for controllable margin and operating assets are, respectively:
a. controllable margin percentage and total operating assets.
b. controllable margin dollars and average operating assets.
c. controllable margin dollars and total assets.
d. controllable margin percentage and average operating assets.

10. A manager of an investment center can improve   (SO 7)
ROI by:
a. increasing average operating assets.
b. reducing sales.
c. increasing variable costs.
d. reducing variable and/or controllable fixed costs.

# QUESTIONS

1. (a) What is budgetary control?
   (b) Roberto Caproni is describing budgetary control. What steps should be included in Roberto's description?

2. The following purposes are part of a budgetary reporting system: (a) determine efficient use of materials, (b) control overhead costs, and (c) determine whether income objectives are being met. For each purpose, indicate the name of the report, the frequency of the report, and the primary recipient(s) of the report.

3. How may a budget report for the second quarter differ from a budget report for the first quarter?

4. Dan Drake questions the usefulness of a master sales budget in evaluating sales performance. Is there justification for Dan's concern? Explain.

5. Under what circumstances may a static budget be an appropriate basis for evaluating a manager's effectiveness in controlling costs?

6. "A flexible budget is really a series of static budgets." Is this true? Why?

7. The static manufacturing overhead budget based on 40,000 direct labor hours shows budgeted indirect labor costs of $56,000. During March, the department incurs $72,000 of indirect labor while working 50,000 direct labor hours. Is this a favorable or unfavorable performance? Why?

8. A static overhead budget based on 40,000 direct labor hours shows Factory Insurance $6,400 as a fixed cost. At the 50,000 direct labor hours worked in March, factory insurance costs were $6,200. Is this a favorable or unfavorable performance? Why?

9. Kim Kinsell is confused about how a flexible budget is prepared. Identify the steps for Kim.

10. Felipe Company has prepared a graph of flexible budget data. At zero direct labor hours, the total budgeted cost line intersects the vertical axis at $25,000. At 12,000 direct labor hours, the line drawn from the total budgeted cost line intersects the vertical axis at $85,000. How may the fixed and variable costs be expressed?

11. The flexible budget formula is fixed costs $40,000 plus variable costs of $3 per direct labor hour. What is the total budgeted cost at (a) 9,000 hours and (b) 12,345 hours?

12. What is management by exception? What criteria may be used in identifying exceptions?

13. What is responsibility accounting? Explain the purpose of responsibility accounting.

14. Alice Waldo is studying for an accounting examination. Describe for Alice what conditions are necessary for responsibility accounting to be used effectively.

15. Distinguish between controllable and noncontrollable costs.

16. How do responsibility reports differ from budget reports?

17. What is the relationship, if any, between a responsibility reporting system and a company's organization chart?

18. Distinguish among the three types of responsibility centers.

19. (a) What costs are included in a performance report for a cost center? (b) In the report, are variable and fixed costs identified?

20. How do direct fixed costs differ from indirect fixed costs? Are both types of fixed costs controllable?

21. Linda Lim is confused about controllable margin reported in an income statement for a profit center. How is this margin computed, and what is its primary purpose?

22. What is the primary basis for evaluating the performance of the manager of an investment center? Indicate the formula for this basis.

23. Explain the ways that ROI can be improved.

24. Indicate two behavioral principles that pertain to (a) the manager being evaluated and (b) top management.

# BRIEF EXERCISES

**BE25–1**   For the quarter ended March 31, 1996, Elaine Company accumulates the following sales data for its product, Garden-Tools: $320,000 budget; $300,000 actual. Prepare a static budget report for the quarter.

*Prepare static budget report.*
*(SO 2)*

**BE25–2**   Data for Elaine Company are given in BE25–1. In the second quarter, budgeted sales were $380,000, and actual sales were $390,000. Prepare a static budget report for the second quarter and for the year to date.

*Prepare static budget report for two quarters.*
*(SO 2)*

**BE25–3**   In DeWitt Company, direct labor is $20 per hour, and the company expects to operate at 10,000 direct labor hours each month. In January 1996, direct labor totaling $210,000 is incurred in working 10,800 hours. Prepare a static budget report and a flexible budget report. Evaluate the usefulness of each report.

*Show usefulness of flexible budgets in evaluating performance.*
*(SO 3)*

**BE25–4**   O'Day Company expects to produce 1,200,000 units of Product XX in 1996. Monthly production is expected to range from 80,000 to 120,000 units. Budgeted variable manufacturing costs per unit are: direct materials $4, direct labor $6, and overhead $3. Prepare a flexible manufacturing budget for the relevant range value using 20,000 unit increments.

*Prepare a flexible budget for variable costs.*
*(SO 3)*

**BE25–5**   Data for O'Day Company are given in BE25–4. In March 1996, the company incurs the following costs in producing 100,000 units: direct materials $415,000, direct labor $590,000, and variable overhead $305,000. Prepare a flexible budget report for March. Were costs controlled?

*Prepare flexible budget report.*
*(SO 3)*

**BE25–6**   In the Assembly Department of Shannon Company, budgeted and actual manufacturing overhead costs for the month of April 1996 were as follows:

|                   | Budget   | Actual   |
|-------------------|----------|----------|
| Indirect materials | $15,000  | $14,000  |
| Indirect labor    | 20,000   | 20,800   |
| Utilities         | 10,000   | 10,600   |
| Supervision       | 5,000    | 5,000    |

All costs are controllable by the department manager. Prepare a responsibility report for April for the cost center.

*Prepare a responsibility report for a cost center.*
*(SO 5)*

**BE25–7**   Milan Manufacturing Company accumulates the following summary data for the year ending December 31, 1996, for its Aqua Division which it operates as a profit center: Sales—$2,000,000 budget, $2,100,000 actual; variable costs—$1,000,000 budget, $1,050,000 actual; and controllable fixed costs—$300,000 budget, $310,000 actual. Prepare a responsibility report for the Aqua Division.

*Prepare a responsibility report for a profit center.*
*(SO 6)*

*Prepare a responsibility report for an investment center.*
*(SO 7)*

**BE25–8**   For the year ending December 31, 1996, Jung Wu Company accumulates the following data for the Plastics Division which it operates as an investment center: contribution margin—$700,000 budget, $715,000 actual; controllable fixed costs—$300,000 budget, $293,000 actual. Average operating assets for the year were $2,000,000. Prepare a responsibility report for the Plastics Division beginning with contribution margin.

*Compute return on investment using the ROI formula.*
*(SO 7)*

**BE25–9**   For its three investment centers, Holland Company accumulates the following data:

|  | I | II | III |
|---|---|---|---|
| Sales | $2,000,000 | $3,000,000 | $ 4,000,000 |
| Controllable margin | 1,200,000 | 2,000,000 | 3,200,000 |
| Average operating assets | 6,000,000 | 8,000,000 | 10,000,000 |

Compute the return on investment (ROI) for each center.

*Compute return on investment under changed conditions.*
*(SO 7)*

**BE25–10**   Data for the investment centers for Holland Company are given in BE25–9. The centers expect the following changes in the next year: (I) increase sales 10%; (II) decrease costs $200,000; (III) decrease average operating assets $400,000. Compute the expected return on investment (ROI) for each center. Assume center I has a contribution margin percentage of 70%.

# EXERCISES

*Prepare flexible manufacturing overhead budget.*
*(SO 3)*

**E25–1**   Paw Paw Company uses a flexible budget for manufacturing overhead based on direct labor hours. Variable manufacturing overhead costs per direct labor hour are as follows:

| | |
|---|---|
| Indirect labor | $1.00 |
| Indirect materials | .50 |
| Utilities | .25 |

Fixed overhead costs per month are: Supervision $3,000, Depreciation $1,500, and Property Taxes $800. The company believes it will normally operate in a range of 7,000–10,000 direct labor hours per month.

**Instructions**
Prepare a monthly flexible manufacturing overhead budget for 1996 for the expected range of activity, using increments of 1,000 direct labor hours.

*Prepare flexible budget reports for manufacturing overhead costs and comment on findings.*
*(SO 3)*

**E25–2**   Using the information in E25–1, assume that in July 1996, Paw Paw Company incurs the following manufacturing overhead costs:

| **Variable** | | **Fixed** | |
|---|---|---|---|
| Indirect labor | $8,700 | Supervision | $3,000 |
| Indirect materials | 4,300 | Depreciation | 1,500 |
| Utilities | 2,100 | Property Taxes | 800 |

**Instructions**
(a) Prepare a flexible budget performance report, assuming that the company worked 9,000 direct labor hours during the month. The company expected to work 9,000 direct labor hours.
(b) Prepare a flexible budget performance report, assuming that the company worked 8,500 direct labor hours during the month. The company expected to work 8,500 direct labor hours.
(c) ▭▭▭▭▷ Comment on your findings.

*Prepare flexible selling expense budget.*
*(SO 3)*

**E25–3**   Lincoln Company uses flexible budgets to control its selling expenses. Monthly sales are expected to range from $170,000 to $200,000. Variable costs and their percentage relationship to sales are: Sales Commissions (6%), Advertising (4%), Traveling (3%), and Delivery (2%). Fixed selling expenses will consist of Sales Salaries $30,000, Depreciation on Delivery Equipment $5,000, and Insurance on Delivery Equipment $1,000.

**Instructions**
Prepare a monthly flexible budget for each $10,000 increment of sales within the relevant range for the year ending December 31, 1996.

**E25–4** The actual selling expenses incurred in March 1996 by Lincoln Company are as follows:

*Prepare flexible budget reports for selling expenses.*
*(SO 3)*

| Variable Expenses | | Fixed Expenses | |
|---|---|---|---|
| Sales Commissions | $10,700 | Sales Salaries | $30,000 |
| Advertising | 7,000 | Depreciation | 5,000 |
| Travel | 5,100 | Insurance | 1,000 |
| Delivery | 3,500 | | |

**Instructions**
(a) Prepare a flexible budget performance report for March using the budget data in E25–3, assuming that March sales were $170,000. Expected and actual sales are the same.
(b) Prepare a flexible budget performance report, assuming that March sales were $180,000. Expected sales and actual sales are the same.
(c) Comment on the importance of using flexible budgets in evaluating the performance of the sales manager.

**E25–5** Huega Company's manufacturing overhead budget for the first quarter of 1996 contained the following data:

*Prepare flexible budget and responsibility report for manufacturing overhead.*
*(SO 3, 5)*

| Variable Costs | | Fixed Costs | |
|---|---|---|---|
| Indirect materials | $12,000 | Supervisory salaries | $30,000 |
| Indirect labor | 10,000 | Depreciation | 7,000 |
| Utilities | 8,000 | Property taxes and insurance | 8,000 |
| Maintenance | 6,000 | Maintenance | 5,000 |

Actual variable costs were: indirect materials $14,200, indirect labor $9,600, utilities $8,700, and maintenance $4,200. Actual fixed costs equaled budgeted costs except for property taxes and insurance, which were $8,100.

All costs are considered controllable by the production department manager except for depreciation, property taxes, and insurance.

**Instructions**
(a) Prepare a flexible overhead budget report for the first quarter.
(b) Prepare a responsibility report for the first quarter.

**E25–6** As sales manager, Greg Potten was given the following static budget report for selling expenses in the Clothing Department of La Salle Company for the month of October.

*Prepare flexible budget report and answer question.*
*(SO 2, 3)*

**LA SALLE COMPANY**
**Clothing Department**
**Budget Report**
**For the Month Ended October 31, 1996**

| | Budget | Actual | Difference Favorable F Unfavorable U |
|---|---|---|---|
| Sales in units | 8,000 | 10,000 | 2,000 F |
| **Variable costs:** | | | |
| Sales commissions | $ 2,000 | $ 2,200 | $ 200 U |
| Advertising expense | 800 | 850 | 50 U |
| Travel expense | 4,000 | 4,900 | 900 U |
| Free samples given out | 1,000 | 1,300 | 300 U |
| Total variable | 7,800 | 9,250 | 1,450 U |
| **Fixed costs:** | | | |
| Rent | 1,500 | 1,500 | –0– |
| Sales salaries | 1,200 | 1,200 | –0– |
| Office salaries | 800 | 800 | –0– |
| Depreciation—autos (sales staff) | 500 | 500 | –0– |
| Total fixed | 4,000 | 4,000 | –0– |
| Total costs | $11,800 | $13,250 | $1,450 U |

As a result of this budget report, Greg was called into the president's office and congratulated on his fine sales performance. He was reprimanded, however, for allowing his costs to get out of control. Greg knew something was wrong with the performance report that he had been given. However, he was not sure what to do, and comes to you for advice.

**Instructions**
(a) Prepare a budget report based on flexible budget data to help Greg.
(b) Should Greg have been reprimanded? Explain.

*State total budgeted cost formulas and prepare flexible budget graph.*
*(SO 3)*

**E25–7**    Gazebo Company has two production departments, Fabricating and Assembling. At a department managers' meeting, the controller uses flexible budget graphs to explain total budgeted costs. Separate graphs based on direct labor hours are used for each department. The graphs show the following:

1. At zero direct labor hours, the total budgeted cost line and the fixed cost line intersect the vertical axis at $40,000 in the Fabricating Department and $38,000 in the Assembling Department.
2. At normal capacity of 50,000 direct labor hours, the line drawn from the total budgeted cost line intersects the vertical axis at $160,000 in the Fabricating Department, and $108,000 in the Assembling Department.

**Instructions**
(a) State the total budgeted cost formula for each department.
(b) Compute the total budgeted cost for each department, assuming actual direct labor hours worked were 53,000 and 47,000, in the Fabricating and Assembling Departments, respectively.
(c) Prepare the flexible budget graph for the Fabricating Department, assuming the maximum direct labor hours in the relevant range is 100,000. Use increments of 10,000 direct labor hours on the horizontal axis and increments of $50,000 on the vertical axis.

*Prepare reports in a responsibility reporting system.*
*(SO 4)*

**E25–8**    Courtney Company's organization chart includes the president; the vice-president of production; three assembly plants—Dallas, Atlanta, and Tucson; and two departments within each plant—Machining and Finishing. Budget and actual manufacturing cost data for July 1996 are as follows:

Finishing Department—Dallas: Direct materials $42,000 actual, $46,000 budget; direct labor $83,000 actual, $82,000 budget; manufacturing overhead $51,500 actual, $49,200 budget.

Machining Department—Dallas: Total manufacturing costs $218,000 actual, $214,000 budget.

Atlanta Plant: Total manufacturing costs $426,000 actual, $421,000 budget.

Tucson Plant: Total manufacturing costs $494,000 actual, $499,000 budget.

The Dallas plant manager's office costs were $95,000 actual and $92,000 budget. The vice-president of production's office costs were $133,000 actual and $130,000 budget. Office costs are not allocated to departments and plants.

**Instructions**
Prepare the reports in a responsibility system for (a) the Finishing Department—Dallas, (b) the plant manager—Dallas, and (c) the vice-president of production. Use the format on page 1053.

*Compute missing amounts in responsibility reports for three profit centers and prepare a report.*
*(SO 6)*

**E25–9**    Sure Shoe Manufacturing Inc. has three divisions which are operated as profit centers. Operating data for the divisions listed alphabetically are as follows:

| Operating Data | Women's Shoes | Men's Shoes | Children's Shoes |
|---|---|---|---|
| Contribution margin | $260,000 | (3) | $160,000 |
| Controllable fixed costs | 100,000 | (4) | (5) |
| Controllable margin | (1) | $ 90,000 | 96,000 |
| Sales | 600,000 | 450,000 | (6) |
| Variable costs | (2) | 300,000 | 250,000 |

**Instructions**
(a) Compute the missing amounts. Show computations.

(b) Prepare a responsibility report for the Women's Shoe Division assuming (1) the data are for the month ended June 30, 1996, and (2) all data equal budget except variable costs which are $20,000 over budget.

**E25–10** The Mastercraft Division of Oakland Company reported the following data for the current year:

*Compute ROI for current year and for possible future changes.*
(SO 7)

| | |
|---|---|
| Sales | $3,000,000 |
| Variable costs | 1,800,000 |
| Controllable fixed costs | 600,000 |
| Average operating assets | 4,000,000 |

Top management is unhappy with the investment center's return on investment (ROI). It asks the manager of the Mastercraft Division to submit plans to improve ROI in the next year. The manager believes it is feasible to consider the following independent courses of action.

1. Increase sales by $320,000 with no change in the contribution margin percentage.
2. Reduce variable costs by $100,000.
3. Reduce average operating assets by 5%.

**Instructions**
(a) Compute the return on investment (ROI) for the current year.
(b) Using the ROI formula, compute the ROI under each of the proposed courses of action. (Round to one decimal.)

# PROBLEMS

**P25–1** Yukon Company estimates that 240,000 direct labor hours will be worked during 1996 in the Assembly Department. On this basis, the following budgeted manufacturing overhead data are computed:

*Prepare flexible budget and budget report for manufacturing overhead.*
(SO 3)

| Variable Overhead Costs | | Fixed Overhead Costs | |
|---|---|---|---|
| Indirect labor | $ 72,000 | Supervision | $ 60,000 |
| Indirect materials | 48,000 | Depreciation | 30,000 |
| Repairs | 24,000 | Insurance | 9,600 |
| Utilities | 14,400 | Rent | 7,200 |
| Lubricants | 9,600 | Property taxes | 6,000 |
| | $168,000 | | $112,800 |

It is estimated that direct labor hours worked each month will range from 18,000 to 24,000 hours.

During January, 20,000 direct labor hours were worked and the following overhead costs were incurred.

| Variable Overhead Costs | | Fixed Overhead Costs | |
|---|---|---|---|
| Indirect labor | $ 6,200 | Supervision | $5,000 |
| Indirect materials | 3,600 | Depreciation | 2,500 |
| Repairs | 1,600 | Insurance | 800 |
| Utilities | 900 | Rent | 700 |
| Lubricants | 830 | Property taxes | 500 |
| | $13,130 | | $9,500 |

**Instructions**
(a) Prepare a monthly flexible manufacturing overhead budget for each increment of 2,000 direct labor hours over the relevant range for the year ending December 31, 1996.
(b) Prepare a manufacturing overhead budget report for January, assuming 20,500 direct labor hours were expected.
(c) Comment on management's efficiency in controlling manufacturing overhead costs in January.

*Prepare flexible budget, budget report, and graph for manufacturing overhead.*
*(SO 3)*

**P25–2**   Zale Manufacturing Company produces one product, Kebo. Because of wide fluctuations in demand for Kebo, the Assembly Department experiences significant variations in monthly production levels.

The master manufacturing overhead budget for the year, based on 300,000 direct labor hours, and the actual overhead costs incurred in July in which 27,500 labor hours were worked, and 27,500 hours were expected to be worked, are as follows:

| Overhead Cost | Master Budget | Actual in July |
|---|---|---|
| Variable: | | |
| Indirect labor | $ 360,000 | $32,000 |
| Indirect materials | 210,000 | 17,000 |
| Utilities | 90,000 | 8,100 |
| Maintenance | 60,000 | 5,400 |
| Fixed: | | |
| Supervision | 150,000 | 12,500 |
| Depreciation | 120,000 | 10,000 |
| Insurance and taxes | 60,000 | 5,000 |
| Total | $1,050,000 | $90,000 |

**Instructions**
(a) Prepare a flexible overhead budget for the year ending December 31, 1996, assuming monthly production levels range from 22,500 to 30,000 direct labor hours. Use increments of 2,500 direct labor hours.
(b) Prepare a budget performance report for July 1996 comparing actual results with budget data based on the flexible budget.
(c) ▉▓▓▓▷ Were costs effectively controlled? Explain.
(d) State the formula for computing the total monthly budgeted costs in Zale Company.
(e) Prepare the flexible budget graph showing total budgeted costs at 25,000 and 27,500 direct labor hours. Use increments of 5,000 on the horizontal axis and increments of $10,000 on the vertical axis.

*State total budgeted cost formula and prepare flexible budget reports for two time periods.*
*(SO 2, 3)*

**P25–3**   Yates Company uses budgets in controlling costs. The May 1996 budget report for the company's Packaging Department is as follows:

### YATES COMPANY
### Budget Report
### Packaging Department
### For the Month Ended May 31, 1996

| Manufacturing Costs | Budget | Actual | Difference Favorable F Unfavorable U |
|---|---|---|---|
| Variable costs: | | | |
| Direct materials | $ 30,000 | $ 32,000 | $2,000 U |
| Direct labor | 40,000 | 43,000 | 3,000 U |
| Indirect materials | 15,000 | 15,200 | 200 U |
| Indirect labor | 12,500 | 13,000 | 500 U |
| Utilities | 7,500 | 7,100 | 400 F |
| Maintenance | 5,000 | 5,200 | 200 U |
| Total variable | 110,000 | 115,500 | 5,500 U |
| Fixed costs: | | | |
| Rent | 7,000 | 7,000 | –0– |
| Supervision | 8,000 | 8,000 | –0– |
| Depreciation | 5,000 | 5,000 | –0– |
| Total fixed | 20,000 | 20,000 | –0– |
| Total costs | $130,000 | $135,500 | $5,500 U |

The budget amounts in the report were on the master budget for the year, which assumed that 600,000 units would be produced. (Hint: The budget amounts above are one-twelfth of the master budget for the year.)

The company president was displeased with the department manager's performance. The department manager, who thought he had done a good job, could not understand the unfavorable results. In May, 55,000 units were produced.

**Instructions**

(a) State the total budgeted cost formula.

(b) Prepare a budget report for May using flexible budget data. Why does this report provide a better basis for evaluating performance than the report based on static budget data? Assume 57,000 units were expected to be produced in the Packaging Department?

(c) In June, 40,000 units were produced when 39,000 were expected. Prepare the budget report using flexible budget data, assuming (1) each variable cost was 20% less in June than its actual cost in May, and (2) fixed costs were the same in the month of June as in May.

**P25–4** Mountain Manufacturing Inc. operates the Home Appliance Division as a profit center. Operating data for this division for the year ended December 31, 1996, are as follows:

*Prepare responsibility report for a profit center.*
*(SO 6)*

|  | Budget | Difference from Budget |
|---|---|---|
| Sales | $2,400,000 | $100,000 U |
| Cost of goods sold |  |  |
| Variable | 1,200,000 | 80,000 U |
| Controllable fixed | 200,000 | 10,000 F |
| Selling and administrative |  |  |
| Variable | 240,000 | 10,000 F |
| Controllable fixed | 60,000 | 6,000 U |
| Noncontrollable fixed costs | 50,000 | 2,000 U |

In addition, Mountain Manufacturing incurs $150,000 of indirect fixed costs that were budgeted at $155,000. Twenty percent (20%) of these costs are allocated to the Home Appliance Division. None of these costs are controllable by the division manager.

**Instructions**

(a) Prepare a responsibility report for the Home Appliance Division for the year.

(b) ▭▭▭▷ Comment on the manager's performance in controlling revenues and costs.

(c) Identify any costs excluded from the responsibility report and explain why they were excluded.

**P25–5** Zukey Manufacturing Company manufactures a variety of garden and lawn equipment. The company operates through three divisions. Each division is an investment center. Operating data for the Lawnmower Division for the year ended December 31, 1996, and relevant budget data are as follows:

*Prepare responsibility report for an investment center and compute ROI.*
*(SO 7)*

|  | Actual | Comparison with Budget |
|---|---|---|
| Sales | $2,800,000 | $200,000 unfavorable |
| Variable cost of goods sold | 1,400,000 | 150,000 unfavorable |
| Variable selling and administrative expenses | 300,000 | 50,000 favorable |
| Controllable fixed cost of goods sold | 270,000 | On target |
| Controllable fixed selling and administrative expenses | 80,000 | On target |

Average operating assets for the year for the Lawnmower Division were $5,000,000 which was also the budgeted amount.

**Instructions**

(a) Prepare a responsibility report (in thousands of dollars) for the Lawnmower Division.

(b) Evaluate the manager's performance. Which items will likely be investigated by top management?

(c) Compute the expected ROI in 1997 for the Lawnmower Division, assuming the following changes:

1. Variable cost of goods sold is decreased by 15%.

2. Average operating assets are decreased by 20%.
3. Sales are increased by $500,000 and this increase is expected to increase contribution margin by $200,000.

*Prepare reports for cost centers under responsibility accounting and comment on performance of managers.*
*(SO 4)*

**P25–6**   Marti Mart Company uses a responsibility reporting system. It has divisions in Denver, Seattle, and San Diego. Each division has three production departments: Cutting, Shaping, and Finishing. The responsibility for each department rests with a manager who reports to the division production manager. Each division manager reports to the vice-president of production. There are also vice-presidents for marketing and finance. All vice-presidents report to the president.

In January 1996, controllable actual and budget manufacturing overhead cost data for the departments and divisions were as follows:

| **Manufacturing Overhead** | **Actual** | **Budget** |
|---|---|---|
| Individual costs—Cutting Department—Seattle: | | |
| Indirect labor | $    73,000 | $    70,000 |
| Indirect materials | 46,700 | 46,000 |
| Maintenance | 21,500 | 18,000 |
| Utilities | 20,100 | 17,000 |
| Supervision | 20,000 | 20,000 |
| | $  181,300 | $  171,000 |
| Total costs: | | |
| Shaping Department—Seattle | $  158,000 | $  148,000 |
| Finishing Department—Seattle | 210,000 | 208,000 |
| Denver division | 676,000 | 673,000 |
| San Diego division | 722,000 | 715,000 |
| | $1,766,000 | $1,744,000 |

Additional overhead costs were incurred as follows: Seattle division production manager—actual costs $52,500, budget $51,000; vice-president of production—actual costs $65,000, budget $64,000; president—actual costs $76,400, budget $74,200. These expenses are not allocated.

The vice-presidents who report to the president, other than the vice-president of production, had the following expenses:

| **Vice-president** | **Actual** | **Budget** |
|---|---|---|
| Marketing | $133,600 | $130,000 |
| Finance | 107,000 | 105,000 |

**Instructions**
(a) Prepare the following responsibility reports:
 (1) Manufacturing overhead—Cutting Department manager—Seattle division.
 (2) Manufacturing overhead—Seattle division manager.
 (3) Manufacturing overhead—vice-president of production.
 (4) Manufacturing overhead and expenses—president. Use the format on page 1053.
(b) Comment on the comparative performances of
 (1) Department managers in the Seattle division.
 (2) Division managers.
 (3) Vice-presidents.

# ALTERNATE PROBLEMS

••••••••••••••••••••••••••••••••••••••••••••••••••••••••••••••••••••••••••••

*Prepare flexible budget and budget report for manufacturing overhead.*
*(SO 3)*

**P25–1A**   Wall Company estimates that 360,000 direct labor hours will be worked during the coming year, 1996, in the Packaging Department. On this basis, the following budgeted manufacturing overhead cost data are computed for the year:

| Fixed Overhead Costs | | Variable Overhead Costs | |
|---|---|---|---|
| Supervision | $ 90,000 | Indirect labor | $144,000 |
| Depreciation | 45,000 | Indirect materials | 90,000 |
| Insurance | 27,000 | Repairs | 54,000 |
| Rent | 36,000 | Utilities | 72,000 |
| Property taxes | 18,000 | Lubricants | 18,000 |
| | $216,000 | | $378,000 |

It is estimated that direct labor hours worked each month will range from 27,000 to 36,000 hours.

During October, 27,000 direct labor hours were worked and the following overhead costs were incurred:

Fixed overhead costs: Supervision $7,500, Depreciation $3,750, Insurance $2,225, Rent $3,000, and Property taxes $1,500.

Variable overhead costs: Indirect labor $11,760, Indirect materials, $6,400, Repairs $4,000, Utilities $5,900, and Lubricants $1,640.

**Instructions**

(a) Prepare a monthly flexible manufacturing overhead budget for each increment of 3,000 direct labor hours over the relevant range for the year ending December 31, 1996.

(b) Prepare a flexible budget report for October, when 27,500 direct labor hours were expected.

(c) Comment on management's efficiency in controlling manufacturing overhead costs in October.

**P25–2A** Hosana Company manufactures tablecloths. Sales have grown rapidly over the past 2 years. As a result, the president has installed a budgetary control system for 1996. The following data were used in developing the master manufacturing overhead budget for the Ironing Department, which is based on an activity index of direct labor hours.

*Prepare flexible budget, budget report, and graph for manufacturing overhead.*
*(SO 3)*

| Variable Costs | Rate per Direct Labor Hour | Annual Fixed Costs | |
|---|---|---|---|
| Indirect labor | $.40 | Supervision | $27,000 |
| Indirect materials | .50 | Depreciation | 18,000 |
| Factory utilities | .30 | Insurance | 12,000 |
| Factory repairs | .20 | Rent | 24,000 |

The master overhead budget was prepared on the expectation that 480,000 direct labor hours will be worked during the year. In June, 42,000 direct labor hours were worked and 42,000 were expected. At that level of activity, actual costs were as follows:

Variable—per direct labor hour: Indirect labor $.42, Indirect materials $.50, Factory utilities $.32, and Factory repairs $.21.

Fixed: same as budgeted.

**Instructions**

(a) Prepare a monthly flexible manufacturing overhead budget for the year ending December 31, 1996, assuming production levels range from 35,000 to 50,000 direct labor hours. Use increments of 5,000 direct labor hours.

(b) Prepare a budget performance report for June comparing actual results with budget data based on the flexible budget.

(c) Were costs effectively controlled? Explain.

(d) State the formula for computing the total budgeted costs for Hosana Company.

(e) Prepare the flexible budget graph, showing total budgeted costs at 35,000 and 45,000 direct labor hours. Use increments of 5,000 direct labor hours on the horizontal axis and increments of $10,000 on the vertical axis.

*State total budgeted cost formula and prepare flexible budget reports for two time periods.*
*(SO 2, 3)*

**P25–3A**   Francisco Company uses budgets in controlling costs. The August 1996 budget report for the company's Assembling Department is as follows:

### FRANCISCO COMPANY
### Budget Report
### Assembling Department
### For the Month Ended August 31, 1996

| Manufacturing | Budget | Actual | Difference<br>Favorable F<br>Unfavorable U |
|---|---|---|---|
| Variable costs: | | | |
| Direct materials | $ 48,000 | $ 47,000 | $1,000 F |
| Direct labor | 72,000 | 68,000 | 4,000 F |
| Indirect materials | 24,000 | 24,200 | 200 U |
| Indirect labor | 18,000 | 17,500 | 500 F |
| Utilities | 15,000 | 14,900 | 100 F |
| Maintenance | 9,000 | 9,200 | 200 U |
| Total variable | 186,000 | 180,800 | 5,200 F |
| Fixed costs: | | | |
| Rent | 12,000 | 12,000 | –0– |
| Supervision | 15,000 | 15,000 | –0– |
| Depreciation | 7,000 | 7,000 | –0– |
| Total fixed | 34,000 | 34,000 | –0– |
| Total costs | $220,000 | $214,800 | $5,200 F |

The budget data in the report are based on the master budget for the year, which assumed that 720,000 units would be produced. The Assembling Department manager is pleased with the report and expects a raise, or at least praise for a job well done. The company president, however, is unhappy with the results for August, because only 58,000 units were produced. (Hint: The budget amounts above are one-twelfth of the master budget.)

**Instructions**
(a)  State the total budgeted cost formula.
(b)  Prepare a budget report for August using flexible budget data. Why does this report provide a better basis for evaluating performance than the report based on static budget data? Assume 62,000 units were expected to be produced.
(c)  In September, 64,000 units were produced when 65,000 were expected. Prepare the budget report using flexible budget data, assuming (1) each variable cost was 10% higher than its actual cost in August, and (2) fixed costs were the same in September as in August.

*Prepare responsibility report for a profit center.*
*(SO 6)*

**P25–4A**   Everglade Manufacturing Inc. operates the Patio Furniture Division as a profit center. Operating data for this division for the year ended December 31, 1996, are as follows:

| | Budget | Difference<br>from Budget |
|---|---|---|
| Sales | $2,500,000 | $50,000 F |
| Cost of goods sold | | |
|    Variable | 1,300,000 | 60,000 F |
|    Controllable fixed | 200,000 | 5,000 U |
| Selling and administrative | | |
|    Variable | 220,000 | 5,000 U |
|    Controllable fixed | 50,000 | 2,000 U |
| Noncontrollable fixed costs | 70,000 | 4,000 U |

In addition, Everglade Manufacturing incurs $180,000 of indirect fixed costs that were budgeted at $175,000. Twenty percent (20%) of these costs are allocated to the Patio Furniture Division.

*Instructions*

(a) Prepare a responsibility report for the Patio Furniture Division for the year.
(b) Comment on the manager's performance in controlling revenues and costs.
(c) Identify any costs excluded from the responsibility report and explain why they were excluded.

**P25–5A**  Houston Manufacturing Company manufactures a variety of tools and industrial equipment. The company operates through three divisions. Each division is an investment center. Operating data for the Home Division for the year ended December 31, 1996, and relevant budget data are as follows:

*Prepare responsibility report for an investment center and compute ROI.*
*(SO 7)*

|  | Actual | Comparison with Budget |
|---|---|---|
| Sales | $1,500,000 | $100,000 favorable |
| Variable cost of goods sold | 700,000 | 100,000 unfavorable |
| Variable selling and administrative expenses | 125,000 | 25,000 unfavorable |
| Controllable fixed cost of goods sold | 170,000 | On target |
| Controllable fixed selling and administrative expenses | 55,000 | On target |

Average operating assets for the year for the Home Division were $2,500,000 which was also the budgeted amount.

*Instructions*

(a) Prepare a responsibility report (in thousands of dollars) for the Home Division.
(b) Evaluate the manager's performance. Which items will likely be investigated by top management?
(c) Compute the expected ROI in 1997 for the Home Division, assuming the following changes:
   1. Variable cost of goods sold is decreased by 6%.
   2. Average operating assets are decreased by 10%.
   3. Sales are increased by 200,000, and this increase is expected to increase contribution margin by $90,000.

# ►*B*roadening *Your Perspective*

## *F*INANCIAL REPORTING PROBLEM
••••••••••••••••••••••••••••••••••••••••••••••••••••••••••••••

PepsiCo, Inc. has three responsibility centers that are called industry segments. They are beverages, snack foods, and restaurants. These segments are operated as investment centers. Refer to the PepsiCo annual report in Appendix A and answer the following questions using the information provided in the Industry Segments section:

(a) How do the segments rank in terms of total (a) net sales and (b) operating profits for 1994? What conclusions do you draw from the rankings?
(b) Does the segment data focus on controllability, profitability, or both? Explain.
(c) Compute the return on investment (ROI) for each segment for 1994 and 1993. Use operating profits as the numerator and identifiable assets (Beverages 1994, $9,566.0, 1993, $9,015.2; Snack Foods 1994, $5,043.9, 1993, $4,994.5; Restaurants 1994, $7,202.9, 1993, $6,412.1) as the denominator in the formula. What conclusions do you draw from the rankings?
(d) Are indirect company fixed costs disclosed in the segment data? Explain.
(e) Within the restaurant segment, how do the chains rank in profitability?

# DECISION CASE

Blu Pastures is a 400-acre farm on the outskirts of the Kentucky Bluegrass, specializing in the boarding of broodmares and their foals. A recent economic downturn in the thoroughbred industry has led to a decline in breeding activities, and it has made the boarding business extremely competitive. To meet the competition, Blu Pastures planned in 1996 to entertain clients, advertise more extensively, and absorb expenses formerly paid by clients such as veterinary and blacksmith fees.

The budget report for 1996 is presented below. As shown, the static income statement budget for the year is based on an expected 21,900 boarding days at $25 per mare. The variable expenses per mare per day were budgeted: Feed $5, Veterinary fees $3, Blacksmith fees $0.30, and Supplies $0.40. All other budgeted expenses were either semifixed or fixed.

During the year, management decided not to replace a worker who quit in March, but it did issue a new advertising brochure and did more entertaining of clients.[1]

## BLU PASTURES
### Static Budget Income Statement
### Year Ended December 31, 1996

|  | Actual | Master Budget | Difference |
|---|---|---|---|
| Number of mares | 52 | 60 | 8* |
| Number of boarding days | 18,980 | 21,900 | 2,920* |
| Sales | $379,600 | $547,500 | $167,900* |
| Less variable expenses: | | | |
| Feed | 104,390 | 109,500 | 5,110 |
| Veterinary fees | 58,838 | 65,700 | 6,862 |
| Blacksmith fees | 6,074 | 6,570 | 496 |
| Supplies | 7,402 | 8,760 | 1,358 |
| Total variable expenses | 176,704 | 190,530 | 13,826 |
| Contribution margin | 202,896 | 356,970 | 154,074* |
| Less fixed expenses: | | | |
| Depreciation | 45,000 | 45,000 | –0– |
| Insurance | 11,000 | 11,000 | –0– |
| Utilities | 12,000 | 14,000 | 2,000 |
| Repairs and maintenance | 10,000 | 11,000 | 1,000 |
| Labor | 88,000 | 96,000 | 8,000 |
| Advertisement | 12,000 | 8,000 | 4,000* |
| Entertainment | 7,000 | 5,000 | 2,000* |
| Total fixed expense | 185,000 | 190,000 | 5,000 |
| Net income | $ 17,896 | $166,970 | $149,074* |

*Unfavorable.

*Instructions*
    (a) Based on the static budget report,
        (1) What was the primary cause(s) of the loss in net income?
        (2) Did management do a good, average, or poor job of controlling expenses?
        (3) Were management's decisions to stay competitive sound?
    (b) Prepare a flexible budget report for the year.
    (c) Based on the flexible budget report, answer the three questions in part (a) above.
    (d) What course of action do you recommend for the management of Blu Pastures?

---

[1]Data for this case are based on Hans Sprohge and John Talbott, "New Applications for Variance Analysis," *Journal of Accountancy*, (AICPA, New York), April 1989, pp. 137–41.

# COMMUNICATION ACTIVITY

The manufacturing overhead budget for Re-Visions contains the following items:

| Variable expenses | |
|---|---|
| Indirect materials | $25,000 |
| Indirect labor | 12,000 |
| Maintenance expenses | 10,000 |
| Manufacturing supplies | 6,000 |
| Total variable | $53,000 |

| Fixed expenses | |
|---|---|
| Supervision | $15,000 |
| Inspection costs | 1,000 |
| Insurance expenses | 2,000 |
| Depreciation | 15,000 |
| Total fixed | $33,000 |

The budget was based on an estimated 2,000 units being produced. During the past month, 1,500 units were produced, and the following costs incurred:

| Variable expenses | |
|---|---|
| Indirect materials | $25,200 |
| Indirect labor | 13,500 |
| Maintenance expenses | 8,200 |
| Manufacturing supplies | 5,100 |
| Total variable | $52,000 |

| Fixed expenses | |
|---|---|
| Supervision | $19,300 |
| Inspection costs | 1,200 |
| Insurance expenses | 2,200 |
| Depreciation | 14,700 |
| Total fixed | $37,400 |

## Instructions

(a) Determine which items would be controllable by Al Jones, the production manager.
(b) How much should have been spent during the month for the manufacture of the 1,500 units?
(c) Prepare a flexible manufacturing overhead budget report for Mr. Jones.
(d) Prepare a responsibility report. Include only the costs that would have been controllable by Mr. Jones. In an attached memo, describe clearly for Mr. Jones the areas in which his performance needs to be improved.

# GROUP ACTIVITY

Lakenvelder Dutch manufactures expensive watch cases sold as souvenirs. Three of its sales departments are: Retail Sales, Wholesale Sales, and Outlet Sales. The Retail Sales Department is a profit center. The Wholesale Sales Department, however, is a cost center, because its managers merely take orders from customers who purchase through the company's wholesale catalog. The Outlet Sales Department is an investment center, because each manager is given full responsibility for an outlet store location. The manager can hire and discharge employees, purchase, maintain, and sell equipment, and in general is fairly independent of company control.

Rena Worthington is a manager in the Retail Sales Department; Winston Hillhouse manages the Wholesale Sales Department; Oscar Hadley manages the Golden Gate Club outlet store in San Francisco. The following are the budget responsibility reports for each of the three departments:

### Budget

| | Retail Sales | Wholesale Sales | Outlet Sales |
|---|---|---|---|
| Sales | $ 750,000 | $ 400,000 | $200,000 |
| **Variable costs** | | | |
| Cost of goods sold | 150,000 | 100,000 | 25,000 |
| Advertising | 100,000 | 30,000 | 5,000 |
| Sales salaries | 75,000 | 15,000 | 3,000 |
| Printing | 10,000 | 20,000 | 5,000 |
| Travel | 20,000 | 30,000 | 2,000 |
| **Fixed costs** | | | |
| Rent | 50,000 | 30,000 | 10,000 |
| Insurance | 5,000 | 2,000 | 1,000 |
| Depreciation | 75,000 | 100,000 | 40,000 |
| Investment in assets | $1,000,000 | $1,200,000 | $800,000 |

### Actual Results

| | Retail Sales | Wholesale Sales | Outlet Sales |
|---|---|---|---|
| Sales | $ 750,000 | $ 400,000 | $200,000 |
| **Variable costs** | | | |
| Cost of goods sold | 195,000 | 120,000 | 26,250 |
| Advertising | 100,000 | 30,000 | 5,000 |
| Sales salaries | 75,000 | 15,000 | 3,000 |
| Printing | 10,000 | 20,000 | 5,000 |
| Travel | 15,000 | 20,000 | 1,500 |
| **Fixed costs** | | | |
| Rent | 40,000 | 50,000 | 12,000 |
| Insurance | 5,000 | 2,000 | 1,000 |
| Depreciation | 80,000 | 90,000 | 60,000 |
| Investment in assets | $1,000,000 | $1,200,000 | $800,000 |

***Instructions***

In groups of four to five people each:

(a) Determine which of the items should be included in the responsibility report for each of the three managers.

(b) Compare the budgeted measures with the actual results. Decide which results should be called to the attention of each manager. Select someone from your group to present your results to the class, and be prepared to defend your answer.

# *E*THICS CASE
••••••••••••••••••••••••••••••••••••••••••••••••••••••••••••••••••••••••••••••••••••••

National Products Corporation participates in a highly competitive industry. In order to meet this competition and achieve profit goals, the company has chosen the decentralized form of organization. Each manager of a decentralized investment center is measured on the basis of profit contribution, market penetration, and return on investment. Failure to meet the objectives established by corporate management for these measures has not been acceptable and usually has resulted in demotion or dismissal of an investment center manager.

An anonymous survey of managers in the company revealed that the managers feel the pressure to compromise their personal ethical standards to achieve the corporate objectives. For example, at certain plant locations there was pressure to reduce quality control to a level which could not assure that all unsafe products would be rejected. Also, sales personnel were encouraged to use questionable sales tactics to obtain orders, including gifts and other incentives to purchasing agents.

The chief executive officer is disturbed by the survey findings. In his opinion such behavior cannot be condoned by the company. He concludes that the company should do something about this problem.

**Instructions**
    (a) Who are the stakeholders (the affected parties) in this situation?
    (b) Identify the ethical implications, conflicts, or dilemmas in the above described situation.
    (c) What might the company do to reduce the pressures on managers and decrease the ethical conflicts?

(CMA adapted)

# CRITICAL THINKING
## ► A Real-World Focus: Computer Associates International, Incorporated
••••••••••••••••••••••••••••••••••••••••••••••••••••••••••••••••••••••••••••••••

*Computer Associates International was incorporated in 1974. Today it designs, develops, markets, and supports standardized computer software products for use with mainframe, midrange, and desktop computers. The company has 6,900 employees who work in its 55 offices in the U.S. or its 62 offices throughout the world including Europe, Asia, Russia, Israel, South America, and New Zealand.*

Presented below is information from the annual report of Computer Associates International:

**MANAGEMENT DISCUSSION:**
The Company has experienced a pattern of business whereby revenue for its third and fourth fiscal quarters reflects an increase over first and second quarter revenue. The Company attributes this increase to clients' increased spending at the end of their calendar year budgetary periods and the culmination of its annual sales plan. Since the Company's costs do not increase proportionately with the third and fourth quarters' increase in revenue, the higher revenue in these quarters results in greater profit margins and income. Fourth-quarter profitability is traditionally affected by significant new hirings, training, and education expenditures for the succeeding year.

**Instructions**
    (a) What type of budgeting seems appropriate for Computer Associate's situation?
    (b) Why don't the company's costs increase proportionately as the revenues increase in the third and fourth quarters?

---

**Answers to Self-Study Questions**
1. c    2. b    3. a    4. d    5. a    6. d    7. d    8. b    9. b    10. d

# Costs Highlight Performance Efficiency

BELLWOOD, Ill. — There's a very good chance that the highlighter you're holding in your hand was made by Sanford Corp., a maker of marking pens and other writing instruments. Sanford, based in Illinois, annually sells in excess of $100 million worth of highlighters, fine-point pens, markers for overhead projectors, and other writing instruments.

Since Sanford makes literally millions of writing utensils per year, the company must keep tight control over manufacturing costs. As a result, a very important part of Sanford's manufacturing process is the determination of how much direct materials, labor, and overhead should cost. These costs are then compared to actual costs to assess performance efficiency.

Raw materials for Sanford's pens include plastic, a barrel, a plug, a cap, a reservoir, and a felt tip. These parts are assembled by machine to produce thousands of units per hour. A major component of manufacturing overhead, then, includes machine maintenance—some fixed, some variable.

There's still a labor component, though: the machine operator. It is this person who makes or breaks Sanford's productivity. "We try to control labor efficiency the best we can," says Bob Stoltz, Sanford's controller. "But excessive labor time is often due to malfunctioning equipment—which is difficult to control."

In contrast, labor rates are more predictable because the hourly workers are covered by a union contract. The story is the same with the fringe benefits and some supervisory salaries. Even volume levels are fairly predictable—demand for the product is high—so that fixed overhead is efficiently absorbed. Raw material standard costs are based on the previous year's actual prices plus any anticipated inflation. Lately, though, inflation has been so low that the company is considering any price increase in raw material to be unfavorable. ◀

# CHAPTER 26

# PERFORMANCE EVALUATION THROUGH STANDARD COSTS

In this chapter we continue the study of controlling costs by considering additional measures that permit the evaluation of performance. The organization and content of this chapter are as follows:

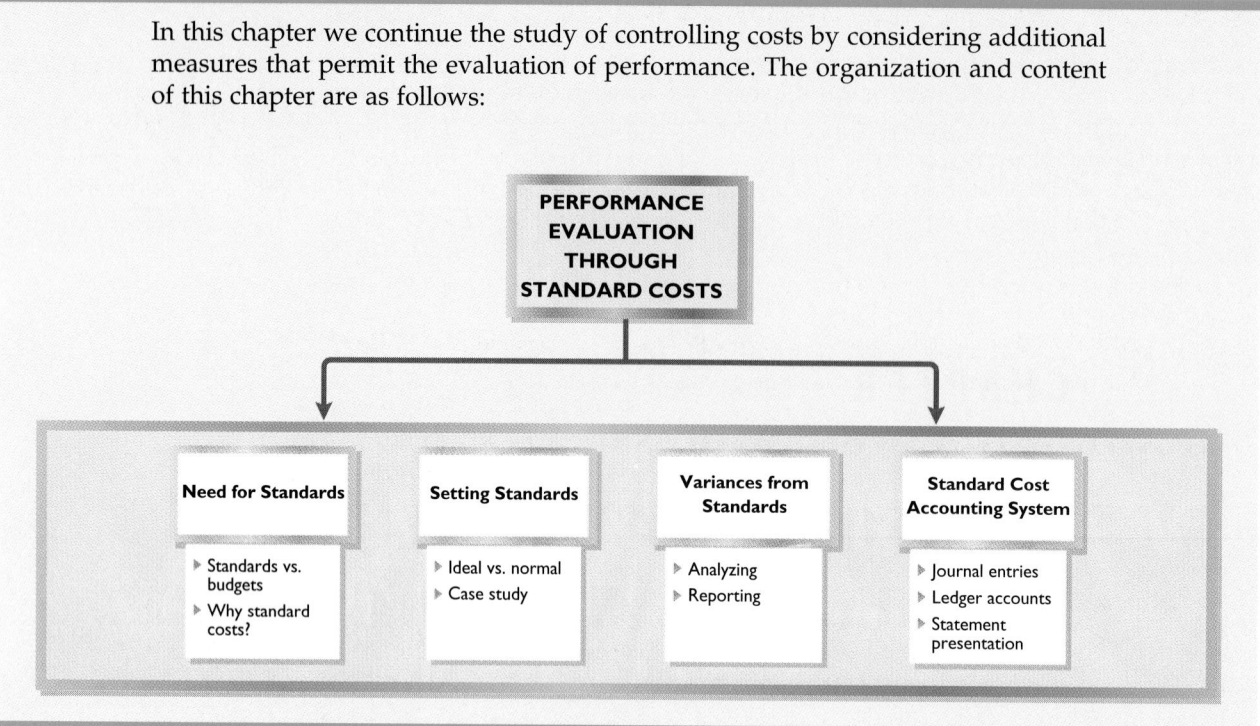

# ▼Need for Standards

Standards are a fact of life. You met the admission standards for the college or university you are attending. The automobile that you drive had to meet certain governmental emissions standards. The hamburgers and salads you eat in a restaurant have to meet certain health and nutritional standards before they can be sold. The reason for standards in these cases is very simple: They help to ensure that the overall quality of the product produced is high. Without standards, quality control is lost.

Standards are also common in business. Those imposed by government agencies are often called **regulations**. They include the Fair Labor Standards Act, the Equal Employment Opportunity Act, and a multitude of environmental standards. Standards established internally by a company may extend to personnel matters, such as employee absenteeism and ethical codes of conduct, quality control standards for products, and standard costs for goods and services. In managerial accounting, standard costs are predetermined unit costs, which are used as measures of performance.

Although we will focus on manufacturing operations in the remainder of this chapter, you should also recognize that standard costs are also applicable to many other types of businesses. For example, a fast-food restaurant such as McDonald's knows not only the price it should pay for pickles, beef, buns, and other ingredients, but also how much time it should take an employee to flip hamburgers. If too much is paid for pickles or too much time is taken to prepare Big Macs, the deviations are noticed and corrective action is taken. Moreover, standard costs may be used in not-for-profit enterprises such as universities, charitable organizations, and governmental agencies.

## Distinguishing between Standards and Budgets

In concept, **standards** and **budgets** are essentially the same. Both are predetermined costs and both contribute significantly to management planning and control. There is a difference, however, in the way the terms are expressed. A standard is a **unit** amount, whereas a budget is a **total** amount. Thus, it is customary to state that the standard cost of direct labor for a unit of product is $10. However, if 5,000 units of the product are produced, the $50,000 of direct labor is the budgeted labor cost. In this context, a standard is the budgeted cost per unit of product. A standard is, therefore, concerned with each individual cost component that makes up the entire budget.

There are important accounting differences between budgets and standards. Except in the application of manufacturing overhead to jobs and processes, budget data are not journalized in cost accounting systems. In contrast, as will be illustrated later in the chapter, standard costs may be incorporated into cost accounting systems. It is also possible for a company to report its inventories at standard cost in its financial statements, but it is not possible to report inventories at budgeted costs.

**STUDY OBJECTIVE**

**1**

*Distinguish between a standard and a budget.*

## Why Standard Costs?

Standard costs offer a number of advantages to an organization, as shown in Illustration 26-1. These advantages will be realized only when standard costs are carefully established and prudently used. Using standards solely as a means of finding fault or placing blame can have a negative effect on managers and employees. In an effort to minimize this effect, many companies offer wage incentives to those who meet their standards.

**STUDY OBJECTIVE**

**2**

*Identify the advantages of standard costs.*

**Illustration 26-1**

*Advantages of standard costs*

Advantages of standard costs

Facilitate management planning

Promote greater economy by making employees more "cost-conscious"

Useful in setting selling prices

Contribute to management control by providing basis for evaluation of cost control

Useful in highlighting variances in management by exception

Simplify costing of inventories and reduce clerical costs

# $S$etting Standard Costs—A Difficult Task

The setting of standard costs to produce a unit of product is a difficult task. It requires input from all persons who have responsibility for costs and quantities. To determine the standard cost of direct materials, management may have to consult the purchasing agents, product managers, quality control engineers, and production supervisors. In setting the cost standard for direct labor, pay rate data are obtained from the payroll department, and the labor time requirements may be determined by industrial engineers. The managerial accountant provides input into the standards-setting process by accumulating historical cost data and by knowing how costs respond to changes in activity levels. The decision as to what the standard cost should be is, of course, a management responsibility.

To be effective in controlling costs, standard costs need to be current at all times. Thus, standards should be under continuous review and should be changed whenever it is determined that the existing standard is not a good measure of performance. Circumstances that may warrant revision of a standard include changed wage rates resulting from a new union contract, a change in product specifications, or the implementation of a new manufacturing method.

## ▸$T$echnology in $A$ction

 Computerized standard cost systems represent one of the most complex accounting systems to develop and maintain. The standard cost system must be fully integrated into the general ledger, allow for the creation and timely maintenance of the data base of standard usage and costs for every product, and perform various variance computations. Such systems must also produce variance reports by product, department, or employee. With the increased use of automation and robotics, the computerized standard cost system may even be tied directly into these systems to gather variance information.

## Ideal versus Normal Standards

Standards may be set at one of two levels: ideal or normal. Ideal standards represent optimum levels of performance under perfect operating conditions. In contrast, normal standards represent efficient levels of performance that are attainable under expected operating conditions.

Some managers believe ideal standards will stimulate the conscientious worker to ever-increasing improvement. However, most managers believe that because these standards are so difficult, if not impossible, to meet, they discourage self-improvement and lower the morale of the entire work force. Very few companies use ideal standards.

Most companies that use standards set them at a normal level. Properly set, normal standards should be **rigorous but attainable**. Normal standards allow for rest periods, machine breakdowns, and other "normal" contingencies in the production process. It will be assumed in the remainder of this chapter that standard costs are set at a normal level.

## A Case Study

To establish the standard cost of producing a product, it is necessary to establish standards for each manufacturing cost element—direct materials, direct labor, and manufacturing overhead. The standard for each element is derived from a consideration of the standard price to be paid and the standard quantity to be used. To illustrate, in the remainder of this section we will look at a case study of how standard costs are set. In this extended example, we will assume that Xonic, Inc., wishes to use standard costs to measure performance in filling an order for 1,000 gallons of Weed-O, a liquid weed killer.

### Direct Materials

The direct materials price standard is the cost per unit of direct materials that should be incurred. This standard should be based on the purchasing department's best estimate of the **cost of raw materials**. This is frequently based on an analysis of current purchase prices. The price standard should also include an amount for related costs such as receiving, storing, and handling. The materials price standard per pound of material for Xonic's weed killer is:

| Item | Price |
|---|---|
| Purchase price, net of discounts | $2.70 |
| Freight | .20 |
| Receiving and handling | .10 |
| Standard direct materials price per pound | $3.00 |

**Illustration 26-2**

*Setting direct materials price standard*

The direct materials quantity standard is the quantity of direct materials that should be used per unit of finished goods. This standard is expressed as a physical measure, such as pounds, barrels, or board feet. In setting the standard, management should consider both the quality and quantity of materials required to manufacture the product. The standard should include allowances for unavoidable waste and normal spoilage. To illustrate, the standard quantity per unit for Xonic, Inc., is as follows:

| Item | Quantity (Pounds) |
|---|---|
| Required materials | 3.5 |
| Allowance for waste | .4 |
| Allowance for spoilage | .1 |
| Standard direct materials quantity per unit | 4.0 |

**Illustration 26-3**

*Setting direct materials quantity standard*

**The standard direct materials cost per unit is the standard direct materials price times the standard direct materials quantity.** For Xonic, Inc., the standard direct material costs per gallon of Weed-O is $12.00 ($3.00 × 4.0 pounds).

### Direct Labor

The direct labor price standard is the rate per hour that should be incurred for direct labor. This standard is based on current wage rates adjusted for anticipated changes, such as cost of living adjustments (COLAs) included in many union contracts. In addition, the price standard generally includes employer payroll taxes and fringe benefits, such as paid holidays and vacations. For Xonic, Inc., the direct labor price standard is as follows:

**Illustration 26-4**

*Setting direct labor price standard*

| Item | Price |
|---|---|
| Hourly wage rate | $ 7.50 |
| COLA | .25 |
| Payroll taxes | .75 |
| Fringe benefits | 1.50 |
| Standard direct labor rate per hour | $10.00 |

The direct labor quantity standard is the time that should be required to make one unit of the product. This standard is especially critical in labor-intensive (as opposed to capital-intensive) companies. Allowances should be made in this standard for rest periods, cleanup, machine setup, and machine downtime. For Xonic, Inc., the direct labor quantity standard is as follows:

**Illustration 26-5**

*Setting direct labor quantity standard*

| Item | Quantity (Hours) |
|---|---|
| Actual production time | 1.5 |
| Rest periods and cleanup | .2 |
| Setup and downtime | .3 |
| Standard direct labor hours per unit | 2.0 |

**The standard direct labor cost per unit is the standard direct labor rate times the standard direct labor hours.** For Xonic, Inc., the standard direct labor cost per gallon of Weed-O is $20 ($10.00 × 2.0 hours).

### Manufacturing Overhead

For manufacturing overhead, a standard predetermined overhead rate is used in setting the standard. This overhead rate is determined by dividing budgeted overhead costs by an expected standard activity index. For example, the index may be standard direct labor hours or standard machine hours. Xonic, Inc., uses standard direct labor hours as the activity index. The company expects to produce 13,200 gallons of Weed-O during the year at normal capacity. Since it takes two direct labor hours for each gallon, total standard direct labor hours are 26,400 (13,200 × 2). At this level of activity, overhead costs are expected to be $132,000, of which $79,200 are variable and $52,800 are fixed. The standard predetermined overhead rates, therefore, are computed as shown in Illustration 26-6:

**Illustration 26-6**

*Computing predetermined overhead rates*

| Budgeted Overhead Costs | Amount | ÷ | Standard Direct Labor Hours | = | Overhead Rate per Direct Labor Hour |
|---|---|---|---|---|---|
| Variable | $ 79,200 | | 26,400 | | $3.00 |
| Fixed | 52,800 | | 26,400 | | 2.00 |
| Total | $132,000 | | 26,400 | | $5.00 |

**The standard manufacturing overhead rate per unit is the predetermined overhead rate times the direct labor quantity standard.** For Xonic, Inc., the standard manufacturing overhead rate per gallon of Weed-O is $10 ($5 × 2 hours).

## Total Standard Cost per Unit

Now that the standard quantity and price have been established per unit of product, the total standard cost can be determined. The total standard cost per unit is the sum of the standard costs of direct materials, direct labor, and manufacturing overhead. For Xonic, Inc., the total standard cost per gallon of Weed-O is $42, as shown on the following standard cost card:

**Illustration 26-7**

*Standard cost per gallon of Weed-O*

| **Product: Weed-O** | | | **Unit Measure: Gallon** | | |
|---|---|---|---|---|---|
| Manufacturing Cost Elements | Standard Quantity | × | Standard Price | = | Standard Cost |
| Direct materials | 4 pounds | | $ 3.00 | | $12.00 |
| Direct labor | 2 hours | | $10.00 | | $20.00 |
| Manufacturing overhead | 2 hours | | $ 5.00 | | $10.00 |
| | | | | | $42.00 |

A standard cost card is prepared for each product. This card provides the basis for determining variances from standards.

## ▶ Accounting in Action ▸ *Business Insight*

Setting standards can be difficult. Consider Susan's Chili Factory, which manufactures and sells chili. The cost of manufacturing Susan's chili consists of the costs of raw materials, labor to convert the basic ingredients to chili, and overhead. We will use material cost as an example. Three standards need to be developed: (1) What should be the formula (mix) of ingredients for one gallon of chili? (2) What should be the normal wastage (or shrinkage) for the individual ingredients? (3) What should be the standard cost for the individual ingredients that go into the chili?

Susan's Chili Factory also illustrates how standard costs can be used by management in controlling costs. Suppose that summer droughts have reduced crop yields and, as a result, prices have doubled for beans, onions, and peppers. In such a case, actual costs will be significantly higher than standard costs, which will cause management to evaluate the situation. Such an evaluation might lead to an increase in the price charged for a gallon of chili, reexamination of the product mix to see if other types of ingredients can be used, or curtailment of production until ingredients can be purchased at or near standard costs. Similarly, assume that poor maintenance procedures caused the onion-dicing blades to become dull. As a result, usage of onions to make a gallon of chili tripled. Because this deviation is quickly highlighted through standard costs, corrective action can be promptly taken.

*Source:* Adapted from David R. Beran, "Cost Reduction Through Control Reporting," *Management Accounting*, April 1982, pp. 29–33.

## *Before You Go On . . .*

### ▶ *Review It*

1. How do standards differ from budgets?
2. What are the advantages of standard costs to an organization?
3. Distinguish between normal standards and ideal standards. Which standard is more widely used? Why?

▸ *Do It*

The management of Arapahoe Company has decided to use standard costs. Management asks you to explain the components used in setting the standard cost per unit for direct materials, direct labor, and manufacturing overhead.

**Reasoning:** Each standard has two components: price and quantity.

**Solution:** The standard direct materials cost per unit is the standard direct materials price times the standard direct materials quantity. The standard direct labor cost per unit is the standard direct labor rate times the standard direct labor hours. The standard manufacturing overhead rate per unit is the predetermined overhead rate times the direct labor quantity standard.

*Related exercise material: BE26–2, BE26–3, and E26–1.*

# Variances from Standards

One of the major management uses of standard costs is to identify variances from standards. Variances are the differences between total actual costs and total standard costs. To illustrate, we will assume that in producing 1,000 gallons of Weed-O in the month of June, Xonic, Inc., incurred the following costs:

**Illustration 26-8**

*Actual production costs*

| | |
|---|---|
| Direct materials | $13,020 |
| Direct labor | 20,580 |
| Variable overhead | 6,500 |
| Fixed overhead | 4,400 |
| Total actual costs | $44,500 |

Total standard costs are determined by multiplying the units produced by the standard cost per unit. The total standard cost of Weed-O is $42,000 (1,000 gallons × $42). Thus, the total variance is $2,500, as shown below:

**Illustration 26-9**

*Computation of total variance*

| | |
|---|---|
| Actual costs | $44,500 |
| Standard costs | 42,000 |
| Total variance | $ 2,500 |

Note that the variance is expressed in total dollars and not on a per unit basis.

When actual costs exceed standard costs, the variance is **unfavorable**. Thus, the $2,500 variance is unfavorable. An unfavorable variance has a negative connotation. It suggests that too much was paid for one or more of the manufacturing cost elements or that the elements were used inefficiently.

If actual costs are less than standard costs, the variance is **favorable**. A favorable variance has a positive inference. It suggests efficiencies in incurring manufacturing costs and in using direct materials, direct labor, and manufacturing overhead. However, be careful: A favorable variance could be obtained by using inferior materials. In printing wedding invitations, for example, a favorable variance could result from using an inferior grade of paper. Similarly, a favorable variance might be achieved in installing tires on an automobile assembly line by tightening only half of the lug bolts. The point should be obvious: A variance is not favorable if quality control standards have been sacrificed.

## Analyzing Variances

To interpret properly the significance of a variance, you must analyze it to determine the underlying factors. Analyzing variances begins with a determination of the cost elements that comprise the variance. **For each manufacturing cost element, a total dollar variance is computed. Then this variance is analyzed into a price variance and a quantity variance.** The relationships are shown graphically as follows:

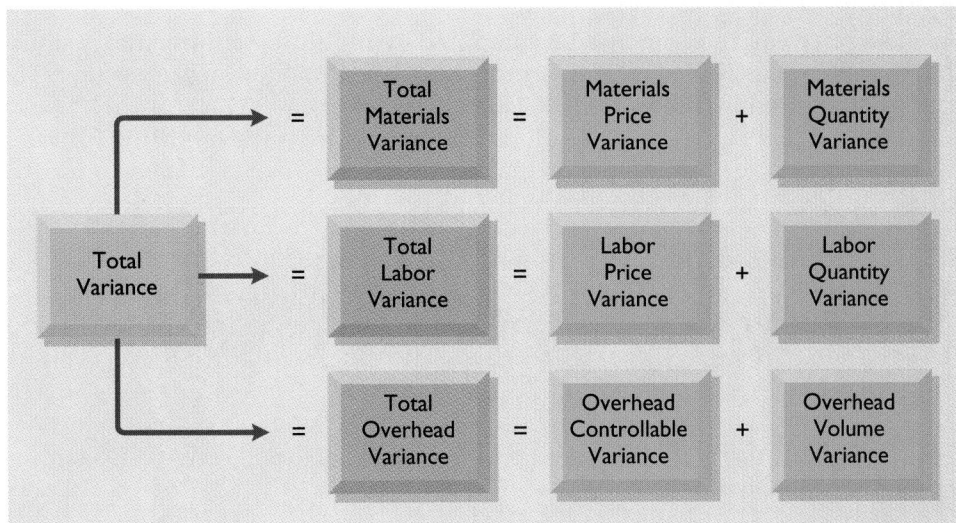

**Illustration 26-10**

*Relationships of variances*

Each of the variances is explained below.

### Direct Materials Variances

In completing the order for 1,000 gallons of Weed-O, Xonic used 4,200 pounds of direct materials purchased at a cost of $3.10 per unit. The total materials variance is computed from the following formula:

**STUDY OBJECTIVE**

............▼............

**4**

*Indicate the formulas for determining direct materials and direct labor variances.*

**Illustration 26-11**

*Formula for total materials variance*

For Xonic, Inc., the total materials variance is $1,020 ($13,020 − $12,000) unfavorable as shown below:

$$(4,200 \times \$3.10) - (4,000 \times \$3.00) = \$1,020 \text{ U}$$

Next, the total variance is analyzed to determine the amount attributable to costs and to quantity (use). The materials price variance is computed from the formula shown in Illustration 26-12.[1]

---

[1]We will assume that all materials purchased during the period are used in production and that no units remain in inventory at the end of the period.

**Illustration 26-12**

*Formula for materials price variance*

For Xonic, Inc., the materials price variance is $420 ($13,020 − $12,600) unfavorable as shown below:

$$(4,200 \times \$3.10) - (4,200 \times \$3.00) = \$420 \text{ U}$$

**Helpful hint** The alternative formula is:

$$\boxed{AQ} \times \boxed{AP - SP} = \boxed{MPV}$$

The price variance can also be computed by multiplying the actual quantity purchased by the difference between the actual and standard price per unit. The computation in this case is 4,200 × ($3.10 − $3.00) = $420 U.

The materials quantity variance is determined from the following formula:

**Illustration 26-13**

*Formula for materials quantity variance*

For Xonic, Inc., the materials quantity variance is $600 ($12,600 − $12,000) unfavorable, as shown below:

$$(4,200 \times \$3.00) - (4,000 \times \$3.00) = \$600 \text{ U}$$

**Helpful hint** The alternative formula is:

$$\boxed{SP} \times \boxed{AQ - SQ} = \boxed{MQV}$$

This variance can also be computed by applying the standard price to the difference between actual and standard quantities used. The computation in this example is $3.00 × (4,200 − 4,000) = $600 U.

The total materials variance of $1,020(U), therefore, consists of the following:

**Illustration 26-14**

*Summary of materials variance*

| | |
|---|---|
| Materials price variance | $  420 U |
| Materials quantity variance | 600 U |
| **Total materials variance** | **$1,020** U |

A matrix is sometimes used to determine and analyze a variance. **When the matrix is used, the formulas for each cost element are computed first and then the variances.** The completed matrix for the direct materials variance for Xonic, Inc. is shown in Illustration 26-15. The matrix provides a convenient structure for determining each variance.

**Causes of Materials Variances.**   What are the causes of a variance? The causes may relate to both internal and external factors. **The investigation of a materials price variance usually begins in the purchasing department.** Many factors affect the price paid for raw materials. These include the delivery method used, availability of quantity and cash discounts, and the quality of the materials requested. To the extent that these factors have been considered in setting the price standard, the purchasing department should be responsible for any variances. However, a variance may be beyond the control of the purchasing department. In a period of inflation, prices may rise faster than expected. Moreover, actions by

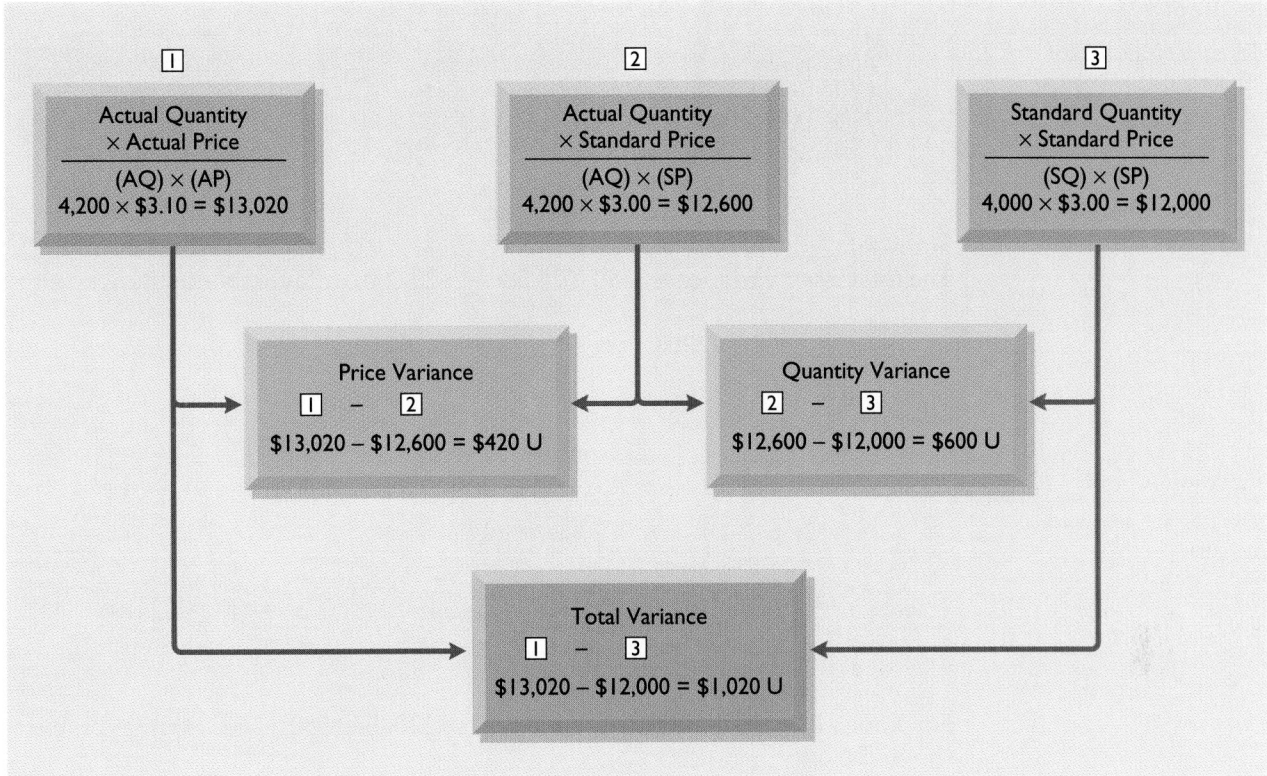

Illustration 26-15

*Matrix for direct materials variance*

groups over which the company has no control, such as the OPEC nations' oil price increases, may cause an unfavorable variance. There are also times when a production department may be responsible for the price variance. This may occur when a rush order forces the company to pay a higher price for the materials.

The starting point for determining the cause(s) of an unfavorable **materials quantity variance** is in the **production department**. If the variances are due to inexperienced workers, faulty machinery, or carelessness, the production department would be responsible. However, if the materials obtained by the purchasing department were of inferior quality, then the purchasing department should be responsible.

## ▶**A**ccounting in **A**ction ▶ *Business Insight*

 If purchase price variances are used as a basis for measuring performance, purchasing departments often will continually search for the lowest cost item. However, this situation can become counterproductive if it leads to late deliveries of the goods or the purchase of inferior quality goods.

### *Direct Labor Variances*

The process of determining direct labor variances is the same as for determining the direct materials variances. In completing the Weed-O order, Xonic, Inc., incurred 2,100 direct labor hours at an average hourly rate of $9.80. The standard hours allowed for the units produced were 2,000 hours (1,000 units × 2 hours) and the standard rate was $10 per hour. The total labor variance is obtained from the following formula:

**Illustration 26-16**

*Formula for total labor variance*

The total labor variance is $580 ($20,580 − $20,000) unfavorable, as shown below:

$$(2,100 \times \$9.80) - (2,000 \times \$10.00) = \$580 \text{ U}$$

The formula for the labor price variance is:

**Illustration 26-17**

*Formula for labor price variance*

For Xonic, Inc., the labor price variance is $420 ($20,580 − $21,000) favorable as shown below.

$$(2,100 \times \$9.80) - (2,100 \times \$10.00) = \$420 \text{ F}$$

**Helpful hint**   The alternative formula is:

$$\boxed{\text{AH}} \times \boxed{\text{AR} - \text{SR}} = \boxed{\text{LPV}}$$

This variance can also be computed by multiplying actual hours worked by the difference between the actual pay rate and the standard pay rate. The computation in this example is 2,100 × ($10.00 − $9.80) = $420 F.

The labor quantity variance is derived from the following formula:

**Illustration 26-18**

*Formula for labor quantity variance*

For Xonic, Inc., the labor quantity variance is $1,000 ($21,000 − $20,000) unfavorable:

$$(2,100 \times \$10.00) - (2,000 \times \$10.00) = \$1,000 \text{ U}$$

**Helpful hint**   The alternative formula is:

$$\boxed{\text{SR}} \times \boxed{\text{AH} - \text{SH}} = \boxed{\text{LQV}}$$

The same result can be obtained by multiplying the standard rate by the difference between actual hours worked and standard hours allowed. In this case the computation is $10.00 × (2,100 − 2,000) = $1,000 U.

The total direct labor variance of $580 U, therefore, consists of:

**Illustration 26-19**

*Summary of labor variances*

| | |
|---|---:|
| Labor price variance | $ 420 F |
| Labor quantity variance | 1,000 U |
| **Total direct labor variance** | $ 580 U |

These results can also be obtained from the matrix in Illustration 26-20.

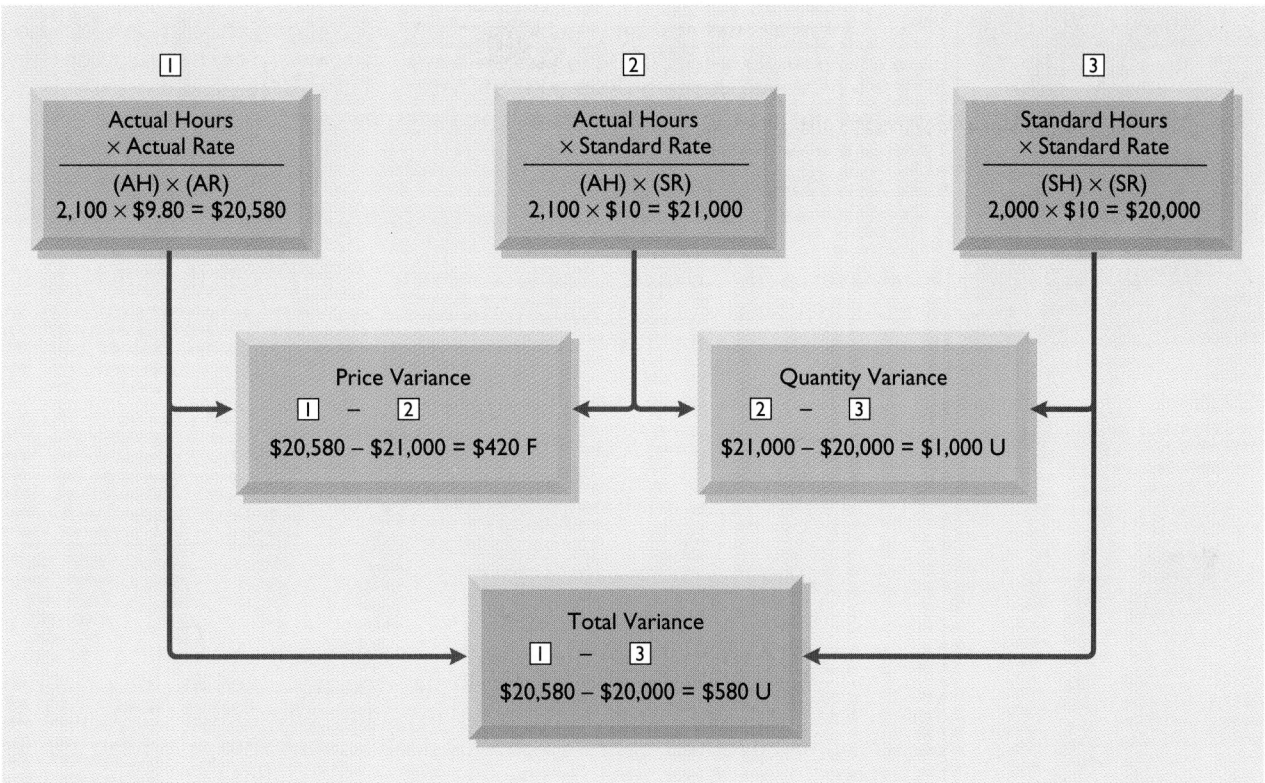

**Illustration 26-20**

*Matrix for direct labor variances*

**Causes of Labor Variances.** **Labor price variances** usually result from two factors: (1) paying workers **higher wages than expected**, and **(2) misallocation of workers**. In companies where pay rates are determined by union contracts, labor price variances should be infrequent. When workers are not unionized, there is a much higher likelihood of such variances. The responsibility for these variances rests with the manager who authorized the wage increase. Misallocation of the work force refers to using skilled workers in place of unskilled workers and vice versa. The use of an inexperienced worker instead of an experienced one will result in a favorable price variance because of the lower pay rate of the unskilled worker. An unfavorable price variance would result if the skilled worker were substituted for the inexperienced employee. The production department generally is responsible for labor price variances resulting from misallocation of the work force.

**Labor quantity variances** relate to the **efficiency of workers**. An investigation of the causes of a quantity variance generally focuses on the production department. The causes of an unfavorable variance may be poor training, worker fatigue, faulty machinery, or carelessness. These causes are the responsibility of the **production department**. However, if the excess time is due to inferior materials, the responsibility falls outside the production department.

### Manufacturing Overhead Variances

The computation of the manufacturing overhead variances is conceptually the same as the computation of the materials and labor variances. However, the task is more challenging for manufacturing overhead because both variable and fixed overhead costs must be considered.

**STUDY OBJECTIVE**
••••••••**5**••••••••

*State the formulas for determining manufacturing overhead variances.*

## ▸Accounting in Action ▸ *Business Insight*

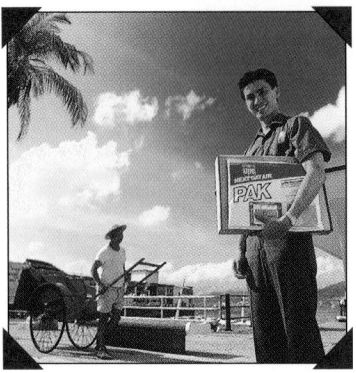

At United Parcel Service (UPS) performance standards are set by industrial engineers for many tasks performed by UPS employees. For example, according to a *Wall Street Journal* article, a UPS driver is expected to walk at a pace of three feet per second when going to a customer's door and knock rather than take the time to look for a doorbell. *The Wall Street Journal* reported that a UPS executive attributes the company's success to its ability to manage and hold labor accountable.

*Source: The Wall Street Journal, April 22, 1986.*

**Total Overhead Variance.** The total overhead variance is the difference between actual overhead costs and overhead costs applied to work done. As indicated earlier, manufacturing overhead costs incurred were $10,900, as follows:

**Illustration 26-21**

*Actual overhead costs*

| | |
|---|---|
| Variable overhead | $ 6,500 |
| Fixed overhead | 4,400 |
| Total actual overhead | $10,900 |

With standard costs, manufacturing overhead costs are applied to work in process on the basis of the **standard hours allowed** for the work done. Standard hours allowed are the hours that should have been worked for the units produced. For the Weed-O order, the standard hours allowed are 2,000 and the predetermined overhead rate is $5 per direct labor hour. Thus, overhead applied is $10,000 (2,000 × $5). Note that actual hours of direct labor (2,100) are not used in applying manufacturing overhead.

The formula for the total overhead variance is:

**Illustration 26-22**

*Formula for total overhead variance*

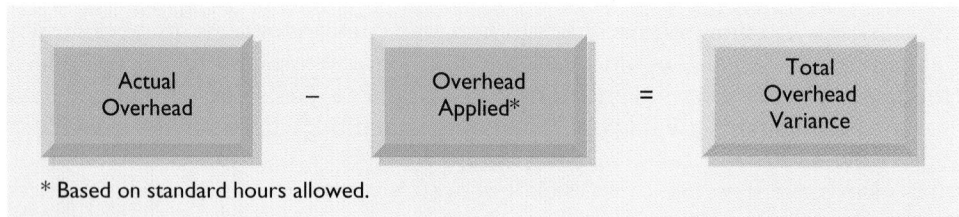

* Based on standard hours allowed.

Thus, for Xonic, Inc., the total overhead variance is $900 unfavorable as shown below:

$$\$10,900 - \$10,000 = \$900 \text{ U}$$

The overhead variance is generally analyzed through a price variance and a quantity variance. The name usually given to the price variance is the **overhead controllable variance**, whereas the quantity variance is referred to as the **overhead volume variance**.

**Overhead Controllable Variance.** The overhead controllable variance shows whether overhead costs were effectively controlled. To compute this variance, actual overhead costs incurred are compared with budgeted costs for the **standard hours allowed**. The budgeted costs are determined from the flexible manufacturing overhead budget. The budget for Xonic, Inc., is as follows:

**Illustration 26-23**

*Flexible budget using standard direct labor hours*

| XONIC, INC.<br>Flexible Manufacturing Overhead Budget | | | | |
|---|---|---|---|---|
| Activity Index | | | | |
| Standard direct labor hours | 1,800 | 2,000 | 2,200 | 2,400 |
| Costs | | | | |
| Variable costs | | | | |
| Indirect materials | $1,800 | $ 2,000 | $ 2,200 | $ 2,400 |
| Indirect labor | 2,700 | 3,000 | 3,300 | 3,600 |
| Utilities | 900 | 1,000 | 1,100 | 1,200 |
| Total variable | 5,400 | 6,000 | 6,600 | 7,200 |
| Fixed costs | | | | |
| Supervision | 3,000 | 3,000 | 3,000 | 3,000 |
| Depreciation | 1,400 | 1,400 | 1,400 | 1,400 |
| Total fixed | 4,400 | 4,400 | 4,400 | 4,400 |
| Total costs | $9,800 | $10,400 | $11,000 | $11,600 |

As shown, the budgeted costs for 2,000 standard hours are $10,400 ($6,000 variable and $4,400 fixed).[2]

The formula for the overhead controllable variance is:

* Based on standard hours allowed.

**Illustration 26-24**

*Formula for overhead controllable variance*

The overhead controllable variance for Xonic, Inc., is $500 unfavorable as shown below:

$$\$10,900 - \$10,400 = \$500 \text{ U}$$

Most controllable variances are associated with variable costs which are controllable costs. Fixed costs are usually known at the time the budget is prepared. In Xonic, Inc., the variance is accounted for by comparing the actual variable overhead costs ($6,500) with the budgeted variable costs ($6,000).

If management desires, actual and budgeted overhead for each manufacturing overhead cost that contributes to the controllable variance can be compared. In addition, cost and quantity variances can be developed for each overhead cost, such as indirect materials and indirect labor.

**Overhead Volume Variance.** The overhead volume variance indicates whether plant facilities were efficiently used during the period. The formula for computing the volume variance is as follows:

---

[2]The flexible budget formula is: fixed costs $4,400 plus variable costs $3 per hour. Thus, total budgeted costs are $4,400 + ($3 × 2,000), or $10,400.

**Illustration 26-25**

*Formula for overhead volume variance*

\* Based on standard hours allowed.

Both the factors in this formula have been explained above. The overhead budgeted is the same as the amount used in computing the controllable variance or $10,400 in our example. Overhead applied of $10,000 is the amount used in determining the total overhead variance. For Xonic Inc., the overhead volume variance is $400 unfavorable as shown below:

$$\$10,400 - \$10,000 = \$400 \text{ U}$$

Further insight into the volume variance can be obtained from a detailed analysis of the two factors. As shown in the flexible manufacturing overhead budget, the budgeted overhead of $10,400 consists of $6,000 variable and $4,400 fixed. As indicated in determining the predetermined overhead rate in Illustration 26-6 (p. 1086), the rate of $5 consists of $3 variable and $2 fixed. The detailed analysis, therefore, is:

**Illustration 26-26**

*Detailed analysis of overhead volume variance*

| | | |
|---|---:|---:|
| Overhead budgeted | | |
| Variable costs | $6,000 | |
| Fixed costs | 4,400 | $10,400 |
| Overhead applied | | |
| Variable costs (2,000 × $3) | 6,000 | |
| Fixed costs (2,000 × $2) | 4,000 | 10,000 |
| Overhead volume variance—unfavorable | | $ 400 |

A careful examination of this analysis indicates that **the overhead volume variance relates solely to fixed costs** (fixed costs budgeted $4,400 − fixed costs applied $4,000). Thus, **the volume variance measures the amount that fixed overhead costs are under- or overapplied**.

We have already established that total fixed costs remain the same at every level of activity within the relevant range. Since a predetermined overhead rate based on normal capacity is used in applying overhead, **it follows that if the standard hours allowed are less than the standard hours at normal capacity, fixed overhead costs will be underapplied**. In contrast, **if production exceeds normal capacity, fixed overhead costs will be overapplied**.

An alternative formula for computing the overhead volume variance is shown in Illustration 26-27.

**Illustration 26-27**

*Alternative formula for overhead volume variance*

In Xonic, Inc., normal capacity is 26,400 hours for the year or 2,200 hours for a month (26,400 ÷ 12), and the fixed overhead rate is $2 per hour. Thus, the volume variance is $400 unfavorable as shown below:

$$\$2 \times (2,200 - 2,000) = \$400 \text{ U}$$

The total overhead variance of $900 unfavorable for Xonic, Inc., therefore, consists of the following:

| | |
|---|---|
| Overhead controllable variance | $500 U |
| Overhead volume variance | 400 U |
| Total overhead variance | $900 U |

**Illustration 26-28**

*Summary of overhead variance*

The results can also be obtained from the matrix in Illustration 26-29.

**Illustration 26-29**

*Matrix for manufacturing overhead variance*

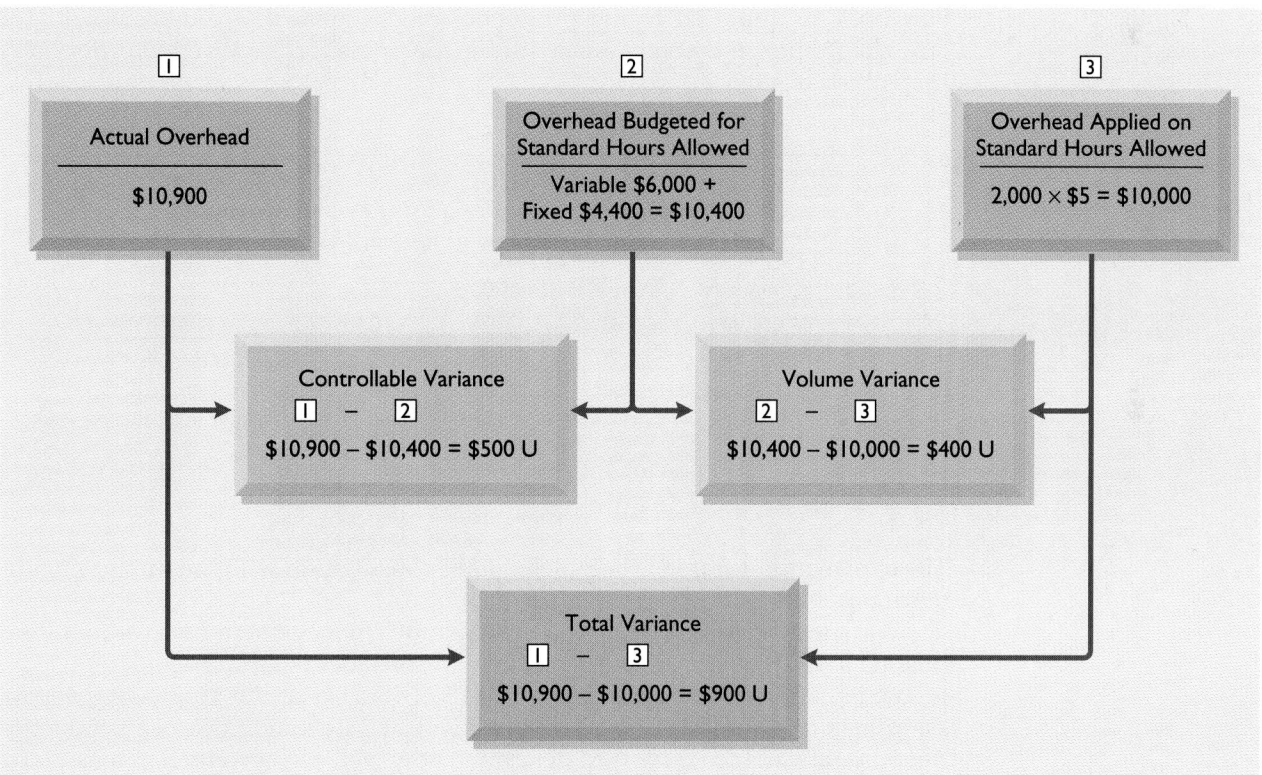

In computing the overhead variances, it is important to remember the following:

1. Standard hours allowed are used in each of the variances.
2. Budgeted costs for the controllable variance are derived from the flexible budget.
3. The controllable variance generally pertains to variable costs.
4. The volume variance pertains solely to fixed costs.

**Causes of Manufacturing Overhead Variances.** Since the **controllable variance** relates to variable manufacturing costs, the responsibility for the variance rests with the **production department**. The cause of an unfavorable variance may be (1) **higher than expected use** of indirect materials, indirect labor, and factory supplies or (2) **increases in indirect manufacturing costs**, such as fuel and maintenance costs.

The **overhead volume variance** is the responsibility of the **production department** if the cause is inefficient use of direct labor or machine breakdowns. However, when the cause is a **lack of sales orders**, the responsibility rests **outside** the production department.

## Reporting Variances

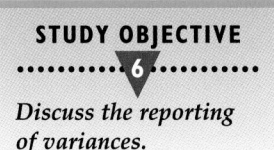

**STUDY OBJECTIVE**

········▼ 6 ▼·········

*Discuss the reporting of variances.*

All variances should be reported to appropriate levels of management as soon as possible. The sooner management is informed, the sooner problems can be evaluated and corrective actions taken if necessary.

The form, content, and frequency of variance reports vary considerably among companies. One approach is to prepare a weekly report for each department that has primary responsibility for cost control. Under this approach, materials price variances are reported to the purchasing department, and all other variances are reported to the production department that did the work. The following report for Xonic, Inc., with the materials for the Weed-O order listed first, illustrates this approach:

**Illustration 26-30**

*Materials price variance report*

### XONIC, INC.
### Variance Report—Purchasing Department
### For Week Ended June 8, 1996

| Type of Materials | Quantity Purchased | Actual Price | Standard Price | Price Variance | Explanation |
|---|---|---|---|---|---|
| X 100 | 4,200 lbs. | $3.10 | $3.00 | $420 U | Rush order. |
| X 142 | 1,200 units | 2.75 | 2.80 | 60 F | Quantity discount. |
| A 85 | 600 doz. | 5.20 | 5.10 | 60 U | Regular supplier on strike. |
| Total price variance | | | | $420 U | |

The explanation column is completed after consultation with the purchasing department manager.

Variance reports facilitate the principle of "management by exception" explained in Chapter 25. For example, the vice-president of purchasing can use the report illustrated above to evaluate the effectiveness of the purchasing department manager. Similarly, the vice-president of production can use production department variance reports to determine how well each production manager is controlling costs. In using variance reports, top management normally looks for **significant variances**. The significance of a variance may be judged on the basis of some quantitative measure, such as more than 10% of the standard or more than $1,000.

# Before You Go On . . .

## ▶ Review It

1. What are the formulas for computing the total, price, and quantity variances for direct materials?
2. What are the formulas for computing the total, price, and quantity variances for direct labor?
3. What are the formulas for computing the total, controllable, and volume variances for manufacturing overhead?

## ▶ Do It

The standard cost of Product XX includes two units of direct materials at $8.00 per unit. During July, 22,000 units of direct materials are purchased at $7.50 and used to produce 10,000 units. Compute the total, price, and quantity variances for materials.

**Reasoning:** It is necessary to know the formulas for computing each of the materials variances. The formulas are:

Total materials variance = (actual quantity × actual price) − (standard quantity × standard price)

Materials price variance = (actual quantity × actual price) − (actual quantity × standard price)

Materials quantity variance = (actual quantity × standard price) − (standard quantity × standard price)

**Solution:** Substituting amounts into the formulas, the variances are:

Total materials variance = (22,000 × $7.50) − (20,000 × $8.00) = $5,000 unfavorable variance

Materials price variance = (22,000 × $7.50) − (22,000 × $8.00) = $11,000 favorable variance

Materials quantity variance = (22,000 × $8.00) − (20,000 × $8.00) = $16,000 unfavorable variance

*Related exercise material:* BE26–4, BE26–5, BE26–6, BE26–7, BE26–8, E26–2, E26–3, E26–4, E26–6, E26–7, E26–8, E26–9, and E26–12.

# Standard Cost Accounting System

A standard cost accounting system is a double-entry system of accounting in which standard costs are used in making entries and variances are formally recognized in the accounts. A standard cost system may be used with either job order or process costing. At this point, we will explain and illustrate a **standard cost, job order cost accounting system**. The system includes two important assumptions: (1) variances from standards are recognized at the earliest opportunity, and (2) the Work in Process account is maintained exclusively on the basis of standard costs. In practice, there are many variations among standard cost systems. However, the system described here should facilitate your transition to a specific company's system.

**STUDY OBJECTIVE**
**▼ 7**

*Enumerate the features of a standard cost accounting system.*

## Journal Entries

The transactions of Xonic, Inc., will be used to illustrate the journal entries. Note as you study the entries that the major difference between the entries here and those for the job order cost accounting system in Chapter 21 is the **variance accounts**.

1. Purchase raw materials on account for $13,020 when the standard cost is $12,600.

| | | |
|---|---|---|
| Raw Materials Inventory | 12,600 | |
| Materials Price Variance | 420 | |
|     Accounts Payable | | 13,020 |
|     (To record purchase of materials) | | |

The inventory account is debited for actual quantities at standard cost. This enables the perpetual materials records to show actual quantities. The price variance, which is unfavorable, is debited to Materials Price Variance.

2. Incur direct labor costs of $20,580 when the standard labor cost is $21,000.

| | | |
|---|---|---|
| Factory Labor | 21,000 | |
|     Labor Price Variance | | 420 |
|     Wages Payable | | 20,580 |
|     (To record direct labor costs) | | |

Like the raw materials inventory account, Factory Labor is debited for actual hours worked at the standard hourly rate of pay. In this case, the labor variance is favorable. Thus, Labor Price Variance is credited.

3. Incur actual manufacturing overhead costs of $10,900.

| | | |
|---|---|---|
| Manufacturing Overhead | 10,900 | |
|     Accounts Payable/Cash/Acc. Depreciation | | 10,900 |
|     (To record overhead incurred) | | |

The controllable overhead variance is not recorded at this time. It depends on standard hours applied to work in process, which is not known at the time overhead is incurred.

4. Issue raw materials for production at a cost of $12,600 when the standard cost is $12,000.

| | | |
|---|---|---|
| Work in Process Inventory | 12,000 | |
| Materials Quantity Variance | 600 | |
|     Raw Materials Inventory | | 12,600 |
|     (To record issuance of raw materials) | | |

Work in Process Inventory is debited for standard materials quantities used at standard prices. The variance account is debited because the variance is unfavorable. Raw Materials Inventory is credited for actual quantities at standard prices.

5. Assign factory labor to production at a cost of $21,000 when standard cost is $20,000.

| | | |
|---|---|---|
| Work in Process Inventory | 20,000 | |
| Labor Quantity Variance | 1,000 | |
|     Factory Labor | | 21,000 |
|     (To assign factory labor to jobs) | | |

Work in Process Inventory is debited for standard labor hours at standard rates, and the unfavorable variance is debited to Labor Quantity Variance. The credit to Factory Labor produces a zero balance in this account.

6. Applying manufacturing overhead to production, $10,000.

| | | |
|---|---|---|
| Work in Process Inventory | 10,000 | |
|     Manufacturing Overhead | | 10,000 |
|       (To assign overhead to jobs) | | |

Work in Process Inventory is debited for standard hours allowed multiplied by the standard overhead rate.

7. Transfer completed work to finished goods, $42,000.

| | | |
|---|---|---|
| Finished Goods Inventory | 42,000 | |
|     Work in Process Inventory | | 42,000 |
|       (To record transfer of completed work to | | |
|       finished goods) | | |

In this example, both inventory accounts are at standard cost.

8. The 1,000 gallons of Weed-O are sold for $60,000.

| | | |
|---|---|---|
| Accounts Receivable | 60,000 | |
| Cost of Goods Sold | 42,000 | |
|     Sales | | 60,000 |
|     Finished Goods Inventory | | 42,000 |
|       (To record sale of finished goods and the cost of | | |
|       goods sold) | | |

Cost of Goods Sold is debited at standard cost. Gross profit, in turn, is the difference between sales and the standard cost of goods sold.

9. Recognize unfavorable overhead variances: controllable, $500; volume, $400.

| | | |
|---|---|---|
| Overhead Controllable Variance | 500 | |
| Overhead Volume Variance | 400 | |
|     Manufacturing Overhead | | 900 |
|       (To recognize overhead variances) | | |

Prior to this entry, a debit balance of $900 existed in Manufacturing Overhead. The above entry therefore produces a zero balance in the Manufacturing Overhead account. The information needed for this entry is often not available until the end of the accounting period.

## Ledger Accounts

The cost accounts for Xonic, Inc., after posting the entries are shown in Illustration 26-31.

**Illustration 26-31**

*Cost accounts with variances*

**Helpful hint**  All debit balances in variance accounts indicate unfavorable variances; all credit balances indicate favorable balances.

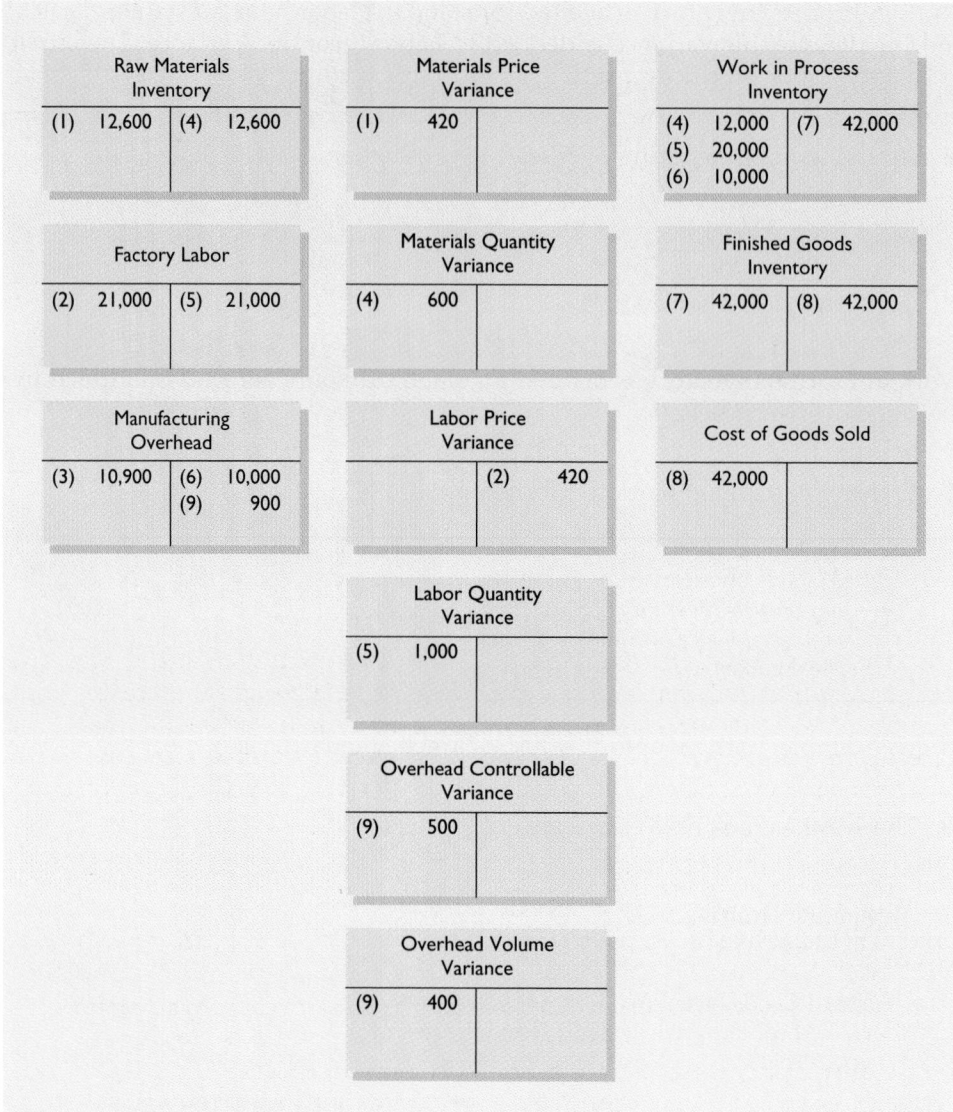

Note that six variance accounts are included in the ledger. The remaining accounts are the same as those illustrated for a job order cost system in Chapter 21 in which only actual costs were used.

## Statement Presentation of Variances

In income statements **prepared for management** under a standard cost accounting system, **cost of goods sold is stated at standard cost and the variances are separately disclosed**, as shown in Illustration 26-32. The statement shown is based entirely on the production and sale of Weed-O and assumes selling and administrative costs of $3,000.

Observe that each variance is shown, as well as the total net variance. In this example, variations from standard costs reduced net income by $2,500.

In financial statements prepared for stockholders and other external users, standard costs may be used. The costing of inventories at standard costs is in accordance with generally accepted accounting principles when there are no significant differences between actual costs and standard costs. Hewlett-Packard and Westinghouse Electric, for example, report their inventories at standard

Illustration 26-32

*Variances in income statement for management*

## XONIC, INC.
### Income Statement
### For the Month Ended June 30, 1996

| | | |
|---|---|---|
| Sales | | $60,000 |
| Cost of goods sold (at standard) | | 42,000 |
| Gross profit (at standard) | | 18,000 |
| Variances | | |
| Materials price | $ 420 | |
| Materials quantity | 600 | |
| Labor price | (420) | |
| Labor quantity | 1,000 | |
| Overhead controllable | 500 | |
| Overhead volume | 400 | |
| Total variance unfavorable | | 2,500 |
| Gross profit (actual) | | 15,500 |
| Selling and administrative expenses | | 3,000 |
| Net income | | $12,500 |

costs. However, if there are significant differences between actual and standard costs, inventories and cost of goods sold must be reported at actual costs.

It is also possible to show the variances in an income statement prepared in the contribution margin format. To do so, it is necessary to analyze the overhead variances into variable and fixed components. This type of analysis is explained in cost accounting textbooks.

## Before You Go On . . .

### ▶ Review It

1. Does a debit balance in a variance account indicate favorable or unfavorable performance?
2. What entry is made to recognize overhead variances in the accounts?
3. How are standard costs and variances reported in income statements prepared for management?

### ▶ A Look Back at Sanford Corporation
. . . . . . . . . . . . . . . . . . . . . . . . . . . . . . . . . . . . . . . . . . . . . . . .

Refer to the data in the opening story and answer the following questions.

1. Should standard unit costs be based on normal or ideal manufacturing activity?
2. What factor is critical in controlling costs? How might Sanford improve its control over this factor?
3. For internal reporting to top management, should Sanford report actual costs, standard costs, or both? Why?
4. In financial statements for stockholders, should Sanford report actual costs, standard costs, or both? Why?

*Solution:*

1. Normal standards are more widely used because they represent an efficient level of performance that is attainable under expected operating conditions. Most managers believe that because ideal standards are so difficult to meet, they discourage self-improvement and lower morale.

2. The critical factor in controlling costs is the efficiency of the machine operator. However, excess labor time is often due to malfunctioning equipment. Management admits that this factor is difficult to control. However, the following steps may reduce or eliminate malfunctions: (1) increase maintenance on the equipment and (2) purchase new equipment.
3. Both standard costs and actual costs should be reported to top management. In addition, differences between the two costs should be reported. Then, by scanning the differences, management can quickly identify those that are significant. This approach follows the principle of "management by exception." When a significant variance is identified, management can investigate the cause and take corrective action.
4. For financial statements, actual costs should be used. Standard costs are permissible but only if standard costs are not significantly different from actual costs. GAAP requires the use of actual costs if standard costs are not current and comparable to actual costs.

# Summary of Study Objectives

**1. Distinguish between a standard and a budget.** Both standards and budgets are predetermined costs. The primary difference is that a standard is a unit amount, whereas a budget is a total amount. A standard may be regarded as the budgeted cost per unit of product.

**2. Identify the advantages of standard costs.** Standard costs offer a number of advantages to an organization. They (a) facilitate management planning, (b) promote greater economy and efficiency, (c) are useful in setting selling prices, (d) contribute to management control, (e) permit "management by exception," and (f) simplify the costing of inventories and reduce clerical costs.

**3. Describe how standards are set.** The direct materials price standard should be based on the delivered cost of raw materials plus an allowance for receiving and handling. The direct materials quantity standard should establish the required quantity plus an allowance for waste and spoilage.

The direct labor price standard should be based on current wage rates and anticipated adjustments such as COLAs. In addition, it generally includes payroll taxes and fringe benefits. Direct labor quantity standards should be based on required production time plus an allowance for rest periods, cleanup, machine setup, and machine downtime.

For manufacturing overhead, a standard predetermined overhead rate is used based on an expected standard activity index such as standard direct labor hours or standard direct labor cost.

**4. Indicate the formulas for determining direct materials and direct labor variances.** The formulas for the direct materials variances are:

$$\begin{pmatrix} \text{Actual quantity} \\ \times \text{ Actual price} \end{pmatrix} - \begin{pmatrix} \text{Standard quantity} \\ \times \text{ Standard price} \end{pmatrix} = \begin{matrix} \text{Total} \\ \text{materials} \\ \text{variance} \end{matrix}$$

$$\begin{pmatrix} \text{Actual quantity} \\ \times \text{ Actual price} \end{pmatrix} - \begin{pmatrix} \text{Actual quantity} \\ \times \text{ Standard price} \end{pmatrix} = \begin{matrix} \text{Materials} \\ \text{price} \\ \text{variance} \end{matrix}$$

$$\begin{pmatrix} \text{Actual quantity} \\ \times \text{ Standard price} \end{pmatrix} - \begin{pmatrix} \text{Standard quantity} \\ \times \text{ Standard price} \end{pmatrix} = \begin{matrix} \text{Materials} \\ \text{quantity} \\ \text{variance} \end{matrix}$$

The formulas for the direct labor variances are:

$$\begin{pmatrix} \text{Actual hours} \\ \times \text{ Actual rate} \end{pmatrix} - \begin{pmatrix} \text{Standard hours} \\ \times \text{ Standard rate} \end{pmatrix} = \begin{matrix} \text{Total} \\ \text{labor} \\ \text{variance} \end{matrix}$$

$$\begin{pmatrix} \text{Actual hours} \\ \times \text{ Actual rate} \end{pmatrix} - \begin{pmatrix} \text{Actual hours} \\ \times \text{ Standard rate} \end{pmatrix} = \begin{matrix} \text{Labor} \\ \text{price} \\ \text{variance} \end{matrix}$$

$$\begin{pmatrix} \text{Actual hours} \\ \times \text{ Standard rate} \end{pmatrix} - \begin{pmatrix} \text{Standard hours} \\ \times \text{ Standard rate} \end{pmatrix} = \begin{matrix} \text{Labor} \\ \text{quantity} \\ \text{variance} \end{matrix}$$

**5. State the formulas for determining manufacturing overhead variances.** The formulas for the manufacturing overhead variances are:

$$\begin{matrix} \text{Actual} \\ \text{overhead} \end{matrix} - \begin{matrix} \text{Overhead} \\ \text{applied} \end{matrix} = \begin{matrix} \text{Total overhead} \\ \text{variance} \end{matrix}$$

$$\begin{matrix} \text{Actual} \\ \text{overhead} \end{matrix} - \begin{matrix} \text{Overhead} \\ \text{budgeted} \end{matrix} = \begin{matrix} \text{Overhead control-} \\ \text{lable variance} \end{matrix}$$

$$\begin{matrix} \text{Overhead} \\ \text{budgeted} \end{matrix} - \begin{matrix} \text{Overhead} \\ \text{applied} \end{matrix} = \begin{matrix} \text{Overhead volume} \\ \text{variance} \end{matrix}$$

**6. Discuss the reporting of variances.** Variances are reported to management in variance reports. The reports facilitate management by exception because significant differences can be highlighted.

**7. Enumerate the features of a standard cost accounting system.** In a standard cost accounting system, standard costs are journalized and posted and separate variance accounts are maintained in the ledger. When differences between actual costs and standard costs do not differ significantly, inventories may be reported at standard costs.

# GLOSSARY

**Direct labor price standard** The rate per hour that should be incurred for direct labor. (p. 1085).

**Direct labor quantity standard** The time that should be required to make one unit of product. (p. 1086).

**Direct materials price standard** The cost per unit of direct materials that should be incurred. (p. 1085).

**Direct materials quantity standard** The quantity of direct materials that should be used per unit of finished goods. (p. 1085).

**Ideal standards** Standards based on the optimum level of performance under perfect operating conditions. (p. 1084).

**Labor price variance** The difference between the actual hours times the actual rate and the actual hours times the standard rate. (p. 1092).

**Labor quantity variance** The difference between actual hours times the standard rate and standard hours times the standard rate. (p. 1092).

**Materials price variance** The difference between the actual quantity times the actual price and the actual quantity times the standard price. (p. 1089).

**Materials quantity variance** The difference between the actual quantity times the standard price and the standard quantity times the standard price. (p. 1090).

**Normal standards** Standards based on an efficient level of performance that are attainable under expected operating conditions. (p. 1084).

**Overhead controllable variance** The difference between

actual overhead incurred and overhead budgeted for the standard hours allowed. (p. 1094).

**Overhead volume variance** The difference between overhead budgeted for the standard hours allowed and the overhead applied. (p. 1095).

**Standard cost accounting system** A double-entry system of accounting in which standard costs are used in making entries and variances are recognized in the accounts. (p. 1099).

**Standard costs** Predetermined unit costs which are used as measures of performance. (p. 1082).

**Standard hours allowed** The hours that should have been worked for the units produced. (p. 1094).

**Standard predetermined overhead rate** An overhead rate determined by dividing budgeted overhead costs by an expected standard activity index. (p. 1086).

**Total labor variance** The difference between actual hours times the actual rate and standard hours times the standard rate for labor. (p. 1091).

**Total materials variance** The difference between the actual quantity times the actual price and the standard quantity times the standard price of materials. (p. 1089).

**Total overhead variance** The difference between actual overhead costs and overhead costs applied to work done. (p. 1094).

**Variances** The difference between total actual costs and total standard costs. (p. 1088).

# DEMONSTRATION PROBLEM

Manlow Company makes a cologne called Allure. The standard cost for one bottle of Allure is as follows:

| Manufacturing Cost Elements | Quantity | | Price | Cost |
|---|---|---|---|---|
| | | **Standard** | | |
| Direct materials | 6 oz. | × | $ .90 | $ 5.40 |
| Direct labor | 0.5 hrs. | × | $12.00 | 6.00 |
| Manufacturing overhead | 0.5 hrs. | × | $ 4.80 | 2.40 |
| | | | | $13.80 |

During the month, the following transactions occurred in manufacturing 10,000 bottles of Allure.

1. 58,000 ounces of materials were purchased at $1.00 per ounce.
2. All the materials purchased were used to produce the 10,000 bottles of Allure.
3. 4,900 direct labor hours were worked at a total labor cost of $56,350.
4. Variable manufacturing overhead incurred was $15,000 and fixed overhead incurred was $10,400.

The manufacturing overhead rate of $4.80 is based on a normal capacity of 5,200 direct labor hours. The total budget at this capacity is $10,400 fixed and $14,560 variable.

**Instructions**

Compute the total variance and the variances for each of the manufacturing cost elements.

**Problem-Solving Strategies**

1. Check to make sure the total variance and the sum of
the individual variances are
equal.
2. Find the price variance first,
then the quantity variance.
3. Budgeted overhead costs
are based on flexible budget
data.
4. Overhead applied is based
on standard hours allowed.
5. Actual hours worked is not
relevant in computing overhead variances.
6. The overhead volume variance relates solely to fixed
costs.

## *Solution to Demonstration Problem*

**Total Variance**

| | |
|---|---|
| Actual costs incurred: | |
| Direct materials | $ 58,000 |
| Direct labor | 56,350 |
| Manufacturing overhead | 25,400 |
| | 139,750 |
| Standard cost (10,000 × $13.80) | 138,000 |
| Total variance | $ 1,750 (U) |

**Direct Materials Variances**

| | | | | | |
|---|---|---|---|---|---|
| Total | = $58,000 | − | $54,000 | = | $4,000 U |
| | (58,000 × $1.00) | | (60,000 × $.90) | | |
| Price | = $58,000 | − | $52,200 | = | $5,800 U |
| | (58,000 × $1.00) | | (58,000 × $.90) | | |
| Quantity | = $52,200 | − | $54,000 | = | $1,800 F |
| | (58,000 × $.90) | | (60,000 × $.90) | | |

**Direct Labor Variances**

| | | | | | |
|---|---|---|---|---|---|
| Total | = $56,350 | − | $60,000 | = | $3,650 F |
| | (4,900 × $11.50) | | (5,000 × $12.00) | | |
| Price | = $56,350 | − | $58,800 | = | $2,450 F |
| | (4,900 × $11.50) | | (4,900 × $12.00) | | |
| Quantity | = $58,800 | − | $60,000 | = | $1,200 F |
| | (4,900 × $12.00) | | (5,000 × $12.00) | | |

**Overhead Variances**

| | | | | | |
|---|---|---|---|---|---|
| Total | = $25,400 | − | $24,000 | = | $1,400 U |
| | ($15,000 + $10,400) | | (5,000 × $4.80) | | |
| Controllable | = $25,400 | − | $24,400 | = | $1,000 U |
| | ($15,000 + $10,400) | | ($14,000 + $10,400) | | |
| Volume | = $24,400 | − | $24,000 | = | $ 400 U |
| | ($14,000 + $10,400) | | (5,000 × $4.80) | | |

# SELF-STUDY QUESTIONS

● ● ● ● ● ● ● ● ● ● ● ● ● ● ● ● ● ● ● ● ● ● ● ● ● ● ● ● ● ● ● ● ● ● ● ● ● ● ● ● ● ● ● ● ● ● ● ● ● ● ● ● ● ● ● ● ● ● ● ● ● ● ● ● ● ● ● ●

Answers are at the end of the chapter.

(SO 1)   1. Standards differ from budgets in that:
   a. budgets may be used in valuing inventories but
      not standards.
   b. budgets may be journalized and posted but not
      standards.
   c. budgets are a total amount and standards are a
      unit amount.
   d. only budgets contribute to management plan-
      ning and control.

(SO 2)   2. The advantages of standard costs include all of the
      following *except*:
   a. management by exception may be used.

   b. management planning is facilitated.
   c. they may simplify the costing of inventories.
   d. management must use a static budget.

3. The setting of standards is:                          (SO 3)
   a. a managerial accountant decision.
   b. a management decision.
   c. a worker decision.
   d. preferably set at the ideal level of performance.

4. Each of the following formulas is correct *except*:   (SO 4)
   a. Labor price variance = (actual hours × actual
      rate) − (actual hours × standard rate).
   b. Overhead controllable variance = actual over-
      head − overhead budgeted.

c. Materials price variance = (actual quantity × actual cost) − (standard quantity × standard cost).

d. Overhead volume variance = overhead budgeted − overhead applied.

(SO 4)   5. In producing product AA, 6,300 pounds of direct materials were used at a cost of $1.10 per pound when the standard was 6,000 pounds at $1 per pound. The direct materials quantity variance is:

a. $330 unfavorable.
b. $300 unfavorable.
c. $600 unfavorable.
d. $630 unfavorable.

(SO 4)   6. In producing product ZZ, 14,800 direct labor hours were used at a rate of $8.20 per hour when the standard was 15,000 hours at $8.00 per hour. Based on these data, the direct labor:

a. quantity variance is $1,600 favorable.
b. quantity variance is $1,600 unfavorable.
c. price variance is $2,960 favorable.
d. price variance is $3,000 unfavorable.

(SO 5)   7. Which of the following is *correct* about overhead variances?

a. The controllable variance generally pertains to fixed overhead costs.

b. The volume variance pertains solely to variable overhead costs.

c. Standard hours actually worked are used in each variance.

d. Budgeted overhead costs are based on the flexible overhead budget.

8. The formula for computing the total overhead variance is:   (SO 5)

a. actual overhead less overhead applied.
b. overhead budgeted less overhead applied.
c. actual overhead less overhead budgeted.
d. no correct answer given.

9. Which of the following is *incorrect* about variance reports?   (SO 6)

a. They facilitate "management by exception."
b. They should only be sent to the top level of management.
c. They should be prepared as soon as possible.
d. They may vary in form, content, and frequency among companies.

10. Which of the following is *incorrect* about a standard cost accounting system?   (SO 7)

a. It is applicable to job order costing.
b. It is applicable to process costing.
c. It is a single-entry system.
d. It keeps separate accounts for each variance.

# QUESTIONS

1. (a) "Standard costs are the expected total cost of completing a job." Is this correct? Explain.
   (b) "A standard imposed by a governmental agency is known as a regulation." Do you agree? Explain.

2. (a) Explain the similarities and differences between standards and budgets.
   (b) Contrast the accounting for standards and budgets.

3. Standard costs facilitate management planning. What are the other advantages of standard costs?

4. Contrast the roles of the management accountant and management in setting standard costs.

5. Distinguish between an ideal standard and a normal standard.

6. What factors should be considered in setting (a) the materials price standard and (b) the materials quantity standard?

7. "The objective in setting the direct labor quantity standard is to determine the aggregate time required to make one unit of product." Do you agree? What allowances should be made in setting this standard?

8. How is the predetermined overhead rate determined when standard costs are used?

9. What is the difference between a favorable cost variance and an unfavorable cost variance?

10. In each of the following formulas, supply the words that should be inserted for each number in parentheses.
    (a) (Actual quantity × (1)) − (standard quantity × (2)) = Total materials variance
    (b) ((3) × actual price) − (actual quantity × (4)) = Materials price variance
    (c) (Actual quantity × (5)) ((6) × standard price) = Materials quantity variance

11. In the direct labor variance matrix, there are three factors: (1) actual hours × actual rate, (2) actual hours × standard rate, and (3) standard hours × standard rate. Using the numbers, indicate the formulas for each of the direct labor variances.

12. Dant Company's standard predetermined overhead rate is $8.00 per direct labor hour. For the month of June, 26,000 actual hours were worked and 27,500 standard hours were allowed. Normal capacity hours were 28,000. How much overhead was applied?

13. If the $8.00 per hour overhead rate in question 12 consists of $5.00 variable, and actual overhead costs were $218,000, what is the overhead controllable variance for June? Is the variance favorable or unfavorable?

14. Using the data in questions 12 and 13, what is the overhead volume variance for June? Is the variance favorable or unfavorable?

15. What is the purpose of computing the overhead volume variance? What is the basic formula for this variance?

16. Helen Henie does not understand why the overhead volume variance indicates that fixed overhead costs are under- or overapplied. Clarify this matter for Helen.

17. Stu Lu Blanc is attempting to outline the important points about overhead variances on a class examination. List four points that Stu should include in his outline.

18. How often should variances be reported to man-agement? What principle may be used with variance reports?

19. What circumstances may cause the purchasing department to be responsible for both an unfavorable materials price variance and an unfavorable materials quantity variance?

20. (a) Explain the basic features of a standard cost accounting system. (b) What type of balance will exist in the variance account when (1) the materials price variance is unfavorable and (2) the labor quantity variance is favorable?

21. (a) How are variances reported in income statements prepared for management? (b) May standard costs be used in preparing financial statements for stockholders? Explain.

# BRIEF EXERCISES

*Distinguish between a standard and a budget.*
(SO 1)

**BE26–1**  Tombo Company uses both standards and budgets. For the year, estimated production of Product X is 500,000 units. Total estimated cost for materials and labor are $1,200,000 and $1,600,000. Compute the estimates for (a) a standard cost and (b) a budgeted cost.

*Set direct materials standard.*
(SO 3)

**BE26–2**  Nurmi Company accumulates the following data concerning raw materials in making one gallon of finished product: (1) Price—net purchase price $3.20, freight-in $0.20 and receiving and handling $0.10; (2) quantity—required materials 2.6 pounds, allowance for waste and spoilage 0.4 pounds. Compute the (a) standard direct materials price per gallon; (b) standard direct materials quantity per gallon and (c) total standard material cost per gallon.

*Set direct labor standard.*
(SO 3)

**BE26–3**  Labor data for making one gallon of finished product in Nurmi Company are as follows: (1) Price—hourly wage rate $10.00, payroll taxes $0.80, and fringe benefits $1.20; (2) Quantity—actual production time 1.2 hours, rest periods and clean up 0.25 hours, and setup and downtime 0.15 hours. Compute the (a) standard direct labor rate per hour, (b) standard direct labor hours per gallon, and (c) the standard labor cost per gallon.

*Compute direct materials variances.*
(SO 4)

**BE26–4**  Nadia Company's standard materials cost per unit of output is $10 (2 pounds × $5.00). During July, the company purchases and uses 3,200 pounds of materials costing $16,320 in making 1,500 units of finished product. Compute the total, price, and quantity materials variances.

*Compute direct labor variances.*
(SO 4)

**BE26–5**  Kimiko Company's standard labor cost per unit of output is $20 (2 hours × $10.00 per hour). During August, the company incurs 1,900 hours of direct labor at an hourly cost of $9.60 per hour in making 1,000 units of finished product. Compute the total, price, and quantity labor variances.

*Compute total manufacturing overhead variance.*
(SO 5)

**BE26–6**  In October, Hilo Company reports 21,000 actual direct labor hours and it incurs $103,000 of manufacturing overhead costs. Standard hours allowed for the work done is 20,000 hours and the predetermined overhead rate is $5.00 per direct labor hour. Compute the total manufacturing overhead variance.

*Compute the manufacturing overhead controllable variance.*
(SO 5)

**BE26–7**  Some overhead data for Hilo Company are given in BE26–6. In addition, the flexible manufacturing overhead budget shows that budgeted costs are $4.00 variable per direct labor hour and $24,000 fixed. Compute the manufacturing overhead controllable variance.

*Compute overhead volume variance.*
(SO 5)

**BE26–8**  Using the data in BE26–6 and BE26–7, compute the manufacturing overhead volume variance.

**BE26–9**  Journalize the following transactions for Nashua Manufacturing:

*Journalize materials variances.*
(SO 7)

1. Purchased 6,000 units of raw materials on account for $12,600 when the standard cost was $12,000.
2. Issued 6,000 units of raw materials for production when the standard units were 5,800.

**BE26-10** Journalize the following transactions for Harlem Manufacturing:

1. Incurred direct labor costs of $24,300 for 3,000 hours when the standard labor cost was $24,000.
2. Assigned 3,000 direct labor hours costing $24,300 to production when standard hours were 3,200.

*Journalize labor variances.*
*(SO 7)*

# EXERCISES

**E26-1** Robin Ritz manufactures and sells homemade wine, and she wants to develop a standard cost per gallon. The following are required for production of a 50-gallon batch:

3,000 ounces of grape concentrate at $0.02 per ounce

55 pounds of granulated sugar at $0.30 per pound

60 lemons at $0.65 each

50 yeast tablets at $0.25 each

50 nutrient tablets at $0.20 each

2,500 ounces of water at $0.004 per ounce

Robin estimates that 4% of the grape concentrate is wasted, 12% of the sugar is lost, and 20% of the lemons cannot be used.

*Compute standard materials costs.*
*(SO 3)*

**Instructions**
Compute the standard cost of the ingredients for one gallon of wine. (Carry computations to three decimal places.)

**E26-2** The standard cost of Product B manufactured by Lum Company includes three units of direct materials at $5.00 per unit. During June, 30,000 units of direct materials are purchased at a cost of $4.70 per unit, and 27,600 units of direct materials are used to produce 9,000 units of Product B.

*Compute materials price and quantity variances.*
*(SO 4)*

**Instructions**
(a) Compute the materials price and quantity variances.
(b) Repeat (a), assuming the purchase price is $5.20 and the quantity used is 26,400 units.

**E26-3** Napier Company's standard labor cost of producing one unit of Product DD is 4 hours at the rate of $12.00 per hour. During August, 40,500 hours of labor are incurred at a cost of $12.20 per hour to produce 10,000 units of Product DD.

*Compute labor price and quantity variances.*
*(SO 4)*

**Instructions**
(a) Compute the labor price and quantity variances.
(b) Repeat (a), assuming the standard is 4.2 hours of direct labor at $12.40 per hour.

**E26-4** Kayjay Inc., which produces a single product, has prepared the following standard cost sheet for one unit of the product.

*Compute materials and labor variances.*
*(SO 4)*

| | |
|---|---|
| Direct materials (8 pounds at $2.50 per pound) | $20.00 |
| Direct labor (3 hours at $12.00 per hour) | $36.00 |

During the month of April, the company manufactures 240 units and incurs the following actual costs:

| | |
|---|---|
| Direct materials (1,900 pounds) | $4,940 |
| Direct labor (700 hours) | $8,120 |

**Instructions**
Compute the total, price, and quantity variances for materials and labor.

**E26-5** Data for Kayjay Inc. are given in E26-4.

*Journalize entries for materials and labor variances.*
*(SO 7)*

**Instructions**
Journalize the entries to record the materials and labor variances.

*Compute the materials and labor variances and list reasons for unfavorable variances.*
(SO 4, 6)

**E26–6**  The following direct materials and direct labor data pertain to the operations of SooTech Manufacturing Company for the month of August.

| Costs | | Quantities | |
|---|---|---|---|
| Actual labor rate | $13.00 per hour | Actual hours incurred and used | 4,200 hours |
| Actual materials price | $128.00 per ton | Actual quantity of materials purchased and used | 1,250 tons |
| Standard labor rate | $12.00 per hour | Standard hours used | 4,300 hours |
| Standard materials price | $130.00 per ton | Standard quantity of materials used | 1,200 tons |

**Instructions**
(a) Compute the total, price, and quantity variances for materials and labor.
(b) ▭▭▭▭▸ Provide two possible explanations for each of the unfavorable variances calculated above and suggest where responsibility for the unfavorable result might be placed.

*Compute manufacturing overhead variances and interpret findings.*
(SO 5)

**E26–7**  The following information was taken from the annual manufacturing overhead cost budget of Fierello Company:

| | |
|---|---|
| Variable manufacturing overhead costs | $33,000 |
| Fixed manufacturing overhead costs | $20,625 |
| Normal production level in hours | 16,500 |
| Normal production level in units | 4,125 |

During the year, 4,000 units were produced, 16,100 hours were worked, and the actual manufacturing overhead was $54,000. Actual fixed manufacturing overhead costs equaled budgeted fixed manufacturing overhead costs. Overhead is applied on the basis of direct labor hours.

**Instructions**
(a) Compute the total, fixed, and variable predetermined manufacturing overhead rates.
(b) Compute the total, controllable, and volume overhead variances.
(c) ▭▭▭▭▸ Briefly interpret the overhead controllable and volume variances computed in (b).

*Compute overhead variances and journalize transactions and adjusting entry.*
(SO 5, 7)

**E26–8**  Manufacturing overhead data for the production of Product H by Parkay Company are as follows:

| | |
|---|---|
| Overhead incurred for 51,000 actual direct labor hours worked | $211,000 |
| Overhead rate (variable $3.00; fixed $1.00) at normal capacity of 54,000 direct labor hours | $    4.00 |
| Standard hours allowed for work done | 52,000 |

**Instructions**
(a) Compute the total, controllable, and volume overhead variances.
(b) Journalize the incurrence of the overhead costs and the application of overhead to the job, assuming a standard cost accounting system is used.
(c) Prepare the adjusting entry for the overhead variances.

*Prepare a variance report for direct labor.*
(SO 4, 6)

**E26–9**  During March 1996, Tenza Tool & Die Company worked on four jobs. A review of direct labor costs reveals the following summary data:

| Job Number | Actual | | Standard | | Total Variance |
|---|---|---|---|---|---|
| | Hours | Costs | Hours | Costs | |
| A257 | 220 | $4,400 | 225 | $4,500 | $  100 F |
| A258 | 450 | 9,900 | 420 | 8,400 | 1,500 U |
| A259 | 300 | 6,150 | 300 | 6,000 | 150 U |
| A260 | 115 | 2,070 | 110 | 2,200 | 130 F |
| Total variance | | | | | $1,420 U |

Analysis reveals that Job A257 was a repeat job. Job A258 was a rush order that required overtime work at premium rates of pay. Job A259 required a more experienced replacement worker on one shift. Work on Job A260 was done for one day by a new trainee when a regular worker was absent.

**Instructions**
Prepare a report for the plant supervisor on direct labor cost variances for March. The report should have columns for (1) Job No., (2) Actual Hours, (3) Standard Hours, (4) Labor Quantity Variance, (5) Actual Rate, (6) Standard Rate, (7) Labor Price Variance, and (8) Explanations.

**E26–10** Augusta Company uses a standard cost accounting system. During January, the company reported the following manufacturing variances:

*Prepare income statement for management.*
(SO 7)

| | | | |
|---|---|---|---|
| Material price variance | $1,250 debit | Labor quantity variance | $ 725 debit |
| Material quantity variance | 700 credit | Overhead controllable | 200 credit |
| Labor price variance | 525 debit | Overhead volume | 1,000 debit |

In addition, 6,000 units of product were sold at $8.00 per unit. Each unit sold had a standard cost of $6.00. Selling and administrative expenses were $7,000 for the month.

**Instructions**
Prepare an income statement for management for the month ending January 31, 1996.

**E26–11** DeSoto Company installed a standard cost system on January 1. Selected transactions for the month of January are as follows:

*Journalize entries in a standard cost accounting system.*
(SO 7)

1. Purchased 18,000 units of raw materials on account at a cost of $3.20 per unit. Standard cost was $3.00 per unit.
2. Issued 18,000 units of raw materials for jobs that required 17,500 standard units of raw materials.
3. Incurred 15,100 actual hours of direct labor at an actual rate of $4.90 per hour. The standard rate is $5.00 per hour. (Credit Wages Payable)
4. Performed 15,100 hours of direct labor on jobs when standard hours were 15,300.
5. Applied overhead to jobs at the rate of 100% of direct labor cost for standard hours allowed.

**Instructions**
Journalize the January transactions.

**E26–12** Los Osis Company uses a standard cost accounting system. Some of the ledger accounts have been destroyed in a fire. The controller asks your help in reconstructing some missing entries and balances.

*Answer questions concerning missing entries and balances.*
(SO 4, 5, 7)

**Instructions**
Answer the following questions:

(a) Materials Price Variance shows a $2,000 favorable balance, and Accounts Payable shows $128,000 of raw materials purchases. What was the amount debited to Raw Materials Inventory for raw materials purchased?
(b) Materials Quantity Variance shows a $3,000 unfavorable balance, and Raw Materials Inventory shows a zero balance. What was the amount debited to Work in Process Inventory for direct materials used?
(c) Labor Price Variance shows a $1,500 unfavorable balance, and Factory Labor shows a debit of $151,000 for wages incurred. What was the amount credited to Wages Payable?
(d) Factory Labor shows a credit of $151,000 for direct labor used, and Labor Quantity Variance shows a $900 unfavorable balance. What was the amount debited to Work in Process for direct labor used?
(e) Overhead applied to Work in Process totaled $168,000. If the total overhead variance was $1,200 unfavorable, what was the amount of overhead costs debited to Manufacturing Overhead?
(f) Overhead Controllable Variance shows a debit balance of $1,400. What was the amount and type of balance (debit or credit) in Overhead Volume Variance?

# PROBLEMS

*Compute variances, and prepare income statement.*
(SO 4, 5, 7)

**P26–1**  Tahoe Manufacturing Company uses a standard cost accounting system. In July 1996, it accumulates the following data relative to jobs started and finished:

| Cost and Production Data | Actual | Standard |
|---|---|---|
| Raw materials | | |
| Units purchased | 17,500 | |
| Units used | 17,500 | 18,000 |
| Unit cost | $3.40 | $3.00 |
| Direct labor | | |
| Hours worked | 2,900 | 3,000 |
| Hourly rate | $11.80 | $12.00 |
| Manufacturing overhead | | |
| Incurred | $87,200 | |
| Applied | | $90,000 |

Manufacturing overhead was applied on the basis of direct labor hours. Normal capacity for the month was 2,800 direct labor hours. At normal capacity, budgeted overhead costs were: variable $56,000 and fixed $28,000.

Jobs finished during the month were sold for $240,000; selling and administrative expenses were $25,000.

**Instructions**
(a) Compute all of the variances for direct materials, direct labor, and manufacturing overhead.
(b) Prepare an income statement for management. Ignore income taxes.

*Compute variances.*
(SO 4, 5)

**P26–2**  Tuxedo Corporation manufactures a single product. The standard cost per unit of product is as follows:

| | |
|---|---|
| Direct materials—2 pounds of plastic at $5.00 per pound | $10.00 |
| Direct labor—2 hours at $12.00 per hour | 24.00 |
| Variable manufacturing overhead | 12.00 |
| Fixed manufacturing overhead | 6.00 |
| Total standard cost per unit | $52.00 |

The master manufacturing overhead budget for the year based on normal productive capacity of 180,000 direct labor hours (90,000 units) shows total variable costs of $1,080,000 and total fixed costs of $540,000. Overhead is applied on the basis of direct labor hours. Actual costs for November in producing 7,600 units were as follows:

| | |
|---|---|
| Direct materials (14,900 pounds) | $ 73,010 |
| Direct labor (14,800 hours) | 180,560 |
| Variable overhead | 90,700 |
| Fixed overhead | 44,000 |
| Total manufacturing costs | $388,270 |

The purchasing department normally buys the quantities of raw materials that are expected to be used in production each month. Raw materials inventories, therefore, can be ignored.

**Instructions**
Compute all of the materials, labor, and overhead variances.

*Compute variances, journalize entries, and identify significant variances.*
(SO 4, 5, 6, 7)

**P26–3**  True-Value Clothiers manufactures women's business suits. The company uses a standard cost accounting system. In March 1996, 12,000 suits were made. The following standard and actual cost data applied to the month of March when normal capacity was 15,000 direct labor hours.

| Cost Element | Standard (per unit) | Actual |
|---|---|---|
| Direct materials | 5 yards at $7.00 per yard | $416,100 for 57,000 yards ($7.30 per yard) |
| Direct labor | 1.0 hours at $12.00 per hour | $123,200 for 11,000 hours ($11.20 per hour) |
| Overhead | 1.0 hours at $9.00 per hour (fixed $6.00; variable $3.00) | $90,000 fixed overhead $48,000 variable overhead |

Overhead is applied on the basis of direct labor hours. At normal capacity, budgeted fixed overhead costs were $90,000 and budgeted variable overhead costs were $45,000.

**Instructions**

(a) Compute the total, price, and quantity variances for (1) materials and (2) labor, and compute the total, controllable, and volume variances for manufacturing overhead.
(b) Journalize the entries to record the variances assuming (1) all purchases of materials were on account and (2) Wages Payable was credited for factory labor incurred.
(c) ▭▭▭▭▷ Which of the materials and labor variances should be investigated if management considers a variance of more than 6% from standard to be significant?

**P26–4** Pomona Manufacturing Company uses standard costs with its job order cost accounting system. In January, an order (Job 84) was received for 4,000 units of Product D. The standard cost of 1 unit of Product D is as follows:

*Journalize and post standard cost entries and prepare income statement.*
*(SO 4, 5, 7)*

| | |
|---|---|
| Direct materials—1.5 pounds at $4.00 per pound | $ 6.00 |
| Direct labor—1 hour at $9.00 per hour | 9.00 |
| Overhead—1 hour (variable $6.00; fixed $10.00) | 16.00 |
| Standard cost per unit | $31.00 |

Overhead is applied on the basis of direct labor hours. Normal capacity for the month of January was 4,500 direct labor hours. During January, the following transactions applicable to Job No. 84 occurred.

1. Purchased 6,250 pounds of raw materials on account at $3.60 per pound.
2. Requisitioned 6,250 pounds of raw materials for production.
3. Incurred 3,900 hours of direct labor at $9.20 hour.
4. Worked 3,900 hours of direct labor on Job No. 84.
5. Incurred $66,650 of manufacturing overhead on account.
6. Applied overhead to Job No. 84 on the basis of direct labor hours.
7. Transferred Job No. 84 to finished goods.
8. Billed customer for Job No. 84 at a selling price of $250,000.
9. Incurred selling and administrative expenses on account $61,000.

**Instructions**

(a) Journalize the transactions.
(b) Post to the job order cost accounts.
(c) Prepare the entry to recognize the overhead variances.
(d) Prepare the income statement for management for January 1996.

**P26–5** Oaks Manufacturing Company uses a standard cost accounting system. In 1996, 33,000 units were produced. Each unit took several pounds of direct materials and 1⅓ standard hours of direct labor at a standard hourly rate of $12.00. Normal capacity was 42,000 direct labor hours. During the year, 130,000 pounds of raw materials were purchased at $0.94 per pound. All pounds purchased were used during the year.

*Answer questions about variances.*
*(SO 4, 5, 7)*

**Instructions**

Answer the following questions:

(a) If the materials price variance was $3,900 unfavorable, what was the standard materials price per pound?
(b) If the materials quantity variance was $1,820 favorable, what was the standard materials quantity per unit?
(c) What were the standard hours allowed for the units produced?

(d) If the labor quantity variance was $9,600 unfavorable, what were the actual direct labor hours worked?

(e) If the labor price variance was $8,960 favorable, what was the actual rate per hour?

(f) If total budgeted manufacturing overhead was $315,000 at normal capacity, what was the predetermined overhead rate?

(g) What was the standard cost per unit of product?

(h) How much overhead was applied to production during the year?

(i) If the fixed overhead rate was $2.50, what was the overhead volume variance?

(j) If the overhead controllable variance was $3,000 favorable, what were the total variable overhead costs incurred?

(k) Using selected answers above, what were the total costs assigned to work in process?

# ALTERNATE PROBLEMS

*Compute variances and prepare income statement.*
(SO 4, 5, 7)

**P26–1A**   Topez Manufacturing Corporation accumulates the following data relative to jobs started and finished during the month of June 1996:

| Costs and Production Data | Actual | Standard |
|---|---|---|
| Raw materials purchases, 10,500 units | $23,100 | $20,000 |
| Raw materials units used | 10,500 | 10,000 |
| Direct labor payroll | $122,100 | $120,000 |
| Direct labor hours worked | 14,800 | 15,000 |
| Manufacturing overhead incurred | $178,200 | |
| Manufacturing overhead applied | | $180,000 |
| Machine hours expected to be used at normal capacity | | 42,500 |
| Budgeted fixed overhead for June | | $42,500 |
| Variable overhead rate per hour | | $3.00 |

Overhead is applied on the basis of standard machine hours. Three hours of machine time are required for each direct labor hour. The jobs were sold for $400,000; selling and administrative expenses were $40,000.

*Instructions*

(a) Compute all of the variances for direct materials, direct labor, and manufacturing overhead.

(b) Prepare an income statement for management. Ignore income taxes.

*Compute variances.*
(SO 4, 5)

**P26–2A**   Li Chin Corporation manufactures a single product. The standard cost per unit of product is shown below:

| | |
|---|---|
| Direct materials—1 pound plastic at $7.00 per pound | $ 7.00 |
| Direct labor—1.5 hours at $12.00 per hour | 18.00 |
| Variable manufacturing overhead | 11.25 |
| Fixed manufacturing overhead | 3.75 |
| Total standard cost per unit | $40.00 |

The predetermined manufacturing overhead rate is $10 per direct labor hour ($15.00 ÷ 1.5). This rate was computed from a master manufacturing overhead budget based on normal production of 90,000 direct labor hours (60,000 units) for the year. The master budget showed total variable costs of $675,000 and total fixed costs of $225,000. Actual costs for October in producing 4,800 units were as follows:

| | |
|---|---|
| Direct materials (5,100 pounds) | $ 37,230 |
| Direct labor (7,000 hours) | 87,500 |
| Variable overhead | 56,170 |
| Fixed overhead | 18,750 |
| Total manufacturing costs | $199,650 |

The purchasing department normally buys the quantities of raw materials that are expected to be used in production each month. Raw materials inventories, therefore, can be ignored.

**Instructions**
Compute all of the materials, labor, and overhead variances.

**P26–3A** Quincy Clothiers is a small company that manufactures tall men's suits. The company has used a standard cost accounting system. In May 1997, 11,250 suits were produced.

The following standard and actual cost data applied to the month of May when normal capacity was 14,000 direct labor hours.

*Compute variances, journalize entries, and identify significant variances.*
*(SO 4, 5, 6, 7)*

| Cost Element | Standard (per unit) | Actual |
|---|---|---|
| Direct materials | 8 yards at $4.50 per yard | $364,000 for 91,000 yards ($4.00 per yard) |
| Direct labor | 1.2 hours at $13.00 per hour | $196,000 for 14,000 hours ($14.00 per hour) |
| Overhead | 1.2 hours at $6.00 per hour (fixed $3.50; variable $2.50) | $49,000 fixed overhead $34,500 variable overhead |

Overhead is applied on the basis of direct labor hours. At normal capacity, budgeted fixed overhead costs were $49,000 and budgeted variable overhead was $35,000.

**Instructions**
(a) Compute the total, price, and quantity variances for (1) materials and (2) labor, and the total, controllable, and volume variances for manufacturing overhead.
(b) Journalize the entries to record the variances assuming (1) all purchases of materials were on account and (2) Wages Payable was credited for factory labor incurred.
(c) ▮▮▮▭▭▷ Which of the materials and labor variances should be investigated if management considers a variance of more than 6% from standard to be significant?

**P26–4A** Ventura Corporation uses standard costs with its job order cost accounting system. In January, an order (Job No. 12) for 2,000 units of Product B was received. The standard cost of 1 unit of Product B is as follows:

*Journalize and post standard cost entries and prepare income statement.*
*(SO 4, 5, 7)*

| | | |
|---|---|---|
| Direct materials | 3 pounds at $1.00 per pound | $ 3.00 |
| Direct labor | 1 hour at $8.00 per hour | 8.00 |
| Overhead | 2 hours (Variable $4.00 per machine hour; fixed $2.00 per machine hour) | 12.00 |
| Standard cost per unit | | $23.00 |

Normal capacity for the month was 4,200 machine hours. During January, the following transactions applicable to Job No. 12 occurred:

1. Purchased 6,100 pounds of raw materials on account at $1.10 per pound.
2. Requisitioned 6,100 pounds of raw materials for Job No. 12.
3. Incurred 2,200 hours of direct labor at a rate of $7.80 per hour.
4. Worked 2,200 hours of direct labor on Job No. 12.
5. Incurred manufacturing overhead on account $24,300.
6. Applied overhead to Job No. 12 on basis of standard machine hours used.
7. Completed Job No. 12.
8. Billed customer for Job No. 12 at a selling price of $70,000.
9. Incurred selling and administrative expenses on account $2,000.

**Instructions**
(a) Journalize the transactions.
(b) Post to the job order cost accounts.
(c) Prepare the entry to recognize the overhead variances.
(d) Prepare the January 1997 income statement for management.

**P26–5A** Ortiz Manufacturing Company uses a standard cost accounting system. In 1997, 30,000 units were produced. Each unit took several pounds of direct materials and 1½ standard hours of direct labor at a standard hourly rate of $12.00. Normal capacity was 50,000 direct labor hours. During the year, 124,000 pounds of raw materials were purchased at $0.96 per pound. All pounds purchased were used during the year.

*Answer questions about variances.*
*(SO 4, 5, 7)*

### Instructions

Answer the following questions:

(a) If the materials price variance was $3,720 favorable, what was the standard materials price per pound?

(b) If the materials quantity variance was $3,960 unfavorable, what was the standard materials quantity per unit?

(c) What were the standard hours allowed for the units produced?

(d) If the labor quantity variance was $7,200 unfavorable, what were the actual direct labor hours worked?

(e) If the labor price variance was $11,400 favorable, what was the actual rate per hour?

(f) If total budgeted manufacturing overhead was $350,000 at normal capacity, what was the predetermined overhead rate?

(g) What was the standard cost per unit of product?

(h) How much overhead was applied to production during the year?

(i) If the fixed overhead rate was $2.00, what was the overhead volume variance?

(j) If the overhead controllable variance is $3,000 unfavorable, what were the total variable overhead costs incurred?

(k) Using one or more answers above, what were the total costs assigned to work in process?

## ▶*Broadening Your Perspective*

### DECISION CASE
..............................................................................................

Planning Professionals, a management consulting firm, specializes in strategic planning for financial institutions. Tom Allam and Beth Moran, partners in the firm, are assembling a new strategic planning model for use by clients. The model is designed for use on most microcomputers and replaces a rather lengthy manual model currently marketed by the firm. To market the new model Tom and Beth will need to provide clients with an estimate of the number of labor hours and computer time needed to operate the model. The model is currently being test marketed at five small financial institutions. These financial institutions are listed below, along with the number of combined computer/labor hours used by each institution to run the model one time.

| Financial Institutions | Computer/Labor Hours Required |
|---|---|
| Midland National | 25 |
| First State | 45 |
| Financial Federal | 40 |
| Pacific America | 30 |
| Lakeview National | 30 |
| Total | 170 |
| Average | 34 |

Any company that purchases the new model will need to purchase user manuals to access and operate the system. Also required are specialized computer forms that are sold only by Planning Professionals. User manuals will be sold to clients in cases of 20, at a cost of $300 per case. One manual must be used each time the model is run because each manual includes a nonreusable computer accessed password for operating the system. The specialized computer forms are sold in packages of 250, at a cost of $50 per package. One application of the model requires the use of 50 forms. This sum includes two forms that are generally wasted in each application due to printer alignment errors. The overall cost of the strategic planning model to user clients is $12,000. Most clients will use the model four times annually.

Planning Professionals must provide its clients with estimates of ongoing costs incurred in operating the new strategic planning model. They would like to provide this information in the form of standard costs.

*Instructions*
(a) What factors should be considered in setting a standard for computer/labor hours?
(b) What alternatives for setting a standard for computer/labor hours might be used?
(c) What standard for computer/labor hours would you select? Justify your answer.
(d) Determine the standard material cost associated with the user manuals and computer forms for each application of the strategic planning model.

# COMMUNICATION ACTIVITY
•••••••••••••••••••••••••••••••••••••••••••••••••••••••••••••••••••••••••••

The setting of standards is critical to the effective use of standards in evaluating performance.

*Instructions*
Explain in a memorandum to your instructor (a) the comparative advantages and disadvantages of ideal versus normal standards, and (b) the factors that should be included in setting the price and quantity standards for direct materials, direct labor, and manufacturing overhead.

# GROUP ACTIVITY
•••••••••••••••••••••••••••••••••••••••••••••••••••••••••••••••••••••••••••

Jake Ryan and Associates is a medium-sized company located near a large metropolitan area in the Midwest. The company manufactures cabinets of mahogany, oak, and other fine woods for use in expensive homes, restaurants, and hotels. Although some of the work is custom, many of the cabinets are a standard size. One such model is called Luxury Base Frame. Standard production is 1,000 units. Each unit has a direct labor hour standard of 5 hours. Overhead is applied to production based on standard direct labor hours. During the most recent month, only 900 units were produced; 4,500 direct labor hours were allowed for standard production, but only 4,000 hours were used. Standard and actual overhead costs were as follows:

|  | Standard (1,000 units) | Actual (900 units) |
|---|---|---|
| Indirect materials | $ 12,000 | $ 12,300 |
| Indirect labor | 43,000 | 51,000 |
| (Fixed) Manufacturing supervisors salaries | 22,000 | 22,000 |
| (Fixed) Manufacturing office employees salaries | 13,000 | 11,500 |
| (Fixed) Engineering costs | 27,000 | 25,000 |
| Computer costs | 10,000 | 10,000 |
| Electricity | 2,500 | 2,500 |
| (Fixed) Manufacturing building depreciation | 8,000 | 8,000 |
| (Fixed) Machinery depreciation | 3,000 | 3,000 |
| (Fixed) Trucks and forklift depreciation | 1,500 | 1,500 |
| Small tools | 700 | 1,400 |
| (Fixed) Insurance | 500 | 500 |
| (Fixed) Property taxes | 300 | 300 |
| Total | $143,500 | $149,000 |

*Instructions*
In groups of four to five:
(a) Determine the overhead application rate.
(b) Determine how much overhead was applied to production.
(c) Calculate the controllable overhead variance and the overhead volume variance.
(d) Decide which overhead variances should be investigated.
(e) Discuss causes of the overhead variances. What can management do to improve its performance next month?

# ETHICS CASE

In Camden Manufacturing Company production workers in the Painting Department are paid on the basis of productivity. The labor time standard for a unit of production is established through periodic time studies conducted by the Manpower Management Department. In a time study, the actual time required to complete a specific task by a worker is observed. Allowances are then made for preparation time, rest periods, and clean up time. Joe Jorken is one of several veterans in the Painting Department.

Joe is informed by Manpower Management that he will be used in the time study for the painting of a new product. The findings will be the basis for establishing the labor time standard for the next 6 months. During the test, Joe deliberately slows his normal work pace in an effort to obtain a labor time standard that will be easy to meet. Because it is a new product, the Manpower Management representative who conducted the test is unaware that Joe did not give the test his best effort.

*Instructions*
    (a) Who was benefited and who was harmed by Joe's actions?
    (b) Was Joe ethical in the way he performed the time study test?
    (c) What measure(s) might the company take to obtain valid data for setting the labor time standard?

# CRITICAL THINKING
## ▸ *A Real-World Focus: Glassmaster Company*

*Glassmaster Co. was incorporated in 1946 as Koolvent Metal Awning Company. Its current name was adopted in 1982 to reflect the more general nature of its products. The company is organized as two divisions, one subsidiary, and one joint venture. One division focuses on the manufacture of filaments such as fishing line and sewing thread; the other division manufactures antennas and specialty fiberglass products. Its subsidiary manufactures flexible steel wire controls and molded control panels. International operations were expanded by forming a joint venture with Filamentos Mexicanos S.A. de C.V which will provide monofilament products to Mexico and South America.*

The annual report of Glassmaster provides the following information:

MANAGEMENT DISCUSSION:
    Gross profit margins for the year improved to 20.9% of sales compared to last year's 18.5%. All operations reported improved margins due in large part to improved operating efficiencies as a result of cost reduction measures implemented during the second and third quarters of the fiscal year and increased manufacturing throughout due to higher unit volume sales. Contributing to the improved margins was a favorable materials price variance due to competitive pricing by suppliers as a result of soft demand for petrochemical based products. This favorable variance is temporary and will begin to reverse itself as stronger worldwide demand for commodity products improves in tandem with the economy. Partially offsetting these positive effects on profit margins were competitive pressures on sales prices of certain product lines. The company responded with pricing strategies designed to maintain and/or increase market share.

*Instructions*
    (a) Is it apparent from the information whether Glassmaster utilizes standard costs?
    (b) Do you think the price variance experienced should lead to changes in standard costs for the next fiscal year?

---

*Answers to Self-Study Questions*
1. c    2. d    3. b    4. c    5. b    6. a    7. d    8. a    9. b    10. c

# What's in a Word?

HOLLYWOOD, Calif. — What's the difference between gross and net? About $20 million if you're Tom Hanks, the actor who played Forrest Gump, or novelist Winston Groom, the creator of the character. Although the movie has grossed over $661 million in box office sales, Paramount Pictures says *Forrest Gump* has lost millions through 1994.

How does Paramount show a loss when it appears to have a real winner? It starts by charging a distribution fee—of nearly a third of the movie's ticket sales—that goes to the studio as almost pure profit. Distribution *expenses*—for everything from making and shipping copies of the film to opening-night parties in posh places—are also added. The costs of actually making the movie have to be accounted for as well, including such costs as office staff, valets and personal trainers for the stars, and even take-out meals from fast-food restaurants. Finally, 50% of each movie's revenues go to theater owners.

For *Forrest Gump*, the distribution fees, expenses, and advertising costs totaled $135 million. The costs of making the movie, including $20 million each to the star and the director, were $112 million. Studio

overhead, computed as about 15% of the cost of making the film, was another $14.5 million. And let's not forget $6 million in interest the studio calculates it *would have earned* if it had put the money it cost to make the movie into the bank—or as some have called it, "interest on money never borrowed."

Thus, accountants for Paramount have managed to make *Forrest Gump* look like a financial loser. Why do that? Because the author and the screenwriter had contracts that provided a fixed percentage of the movie's net profits—repeat, *net*

*profits*. Hanks, knowledgeable to Hollywood's ways, specified that he wanted his contract to be a percentage of *gross profits*—that is, profit before the chicanery.

The author and screenwriter are taking this issue to the courts, where it could be tied up for years. Before the accounting issues are resolved in this and other pending lawsuits, though, the FASB and the American Institute of Certified Public Accountants may adopt new rules, now in the works, that would remove some of the creativity from Hollywood accounting. ◀

# CHAPTER 27

# *I*NCREMENTAL ANALYSIS AND CAPITAL BUDGETING

**After studying this chapter, you should be able to:**

1. *Identify the steps in management's decision-making process.*
2. *Describe the concept of incremental analysis.*
3. *Identify the relevant costs in accepting an order at a special price.*
4. *Indicate the relevant costs in a make-or-buy decision.*
5. *Give the decision rule in deciding whether to sell or process materials further.*
6. *Identify the factors to be considered in retaining or replacing equipment.*
7. *Explain the factors that are relevant in deciding whether to eliminate an unprofitable segment.*
8. *Determine which products to make and sell when a company has limited resources.*
9. *Contrast the annual rate of return and cash payback techniques in capital budgeting.*
10. *Distinguish between the net present value and internal rate of return methods.*

An important purpose of management accounting is to provide management with relevant information for decision making. Examples of these decisions might include:

1. Paramount Picture's decision to produce *Forrest Gump* rather than some other movie.
2. Boeing's decision to spend $5 billion to build a plane for the 21st century—the B-777.
3. Microsoft Corporation's decision to bring out Windows 95, the first major update to Windows, the core software program that runs more than 60 million PCs.

This chapter begins with an explanation of management's decision-making process. It then considers the topics of incremental analysis and capital budgeting. The organization and content of this chapter are as follows:

# ►SECTION *1* ► Incremental Analysis

**STUDY OBJECTIVE**
··········▼··········
*Identify the steps in management's decision-making process.*

Making decisions is an important part of management. Management's decision-making process does not always follow a set pattern, because decisions vary significantly in their scope, urgency, and importance. It is possible, however, to identify some steps that are frequently involved in the process. These steps are graphically shown in Illustration 27-1.

Accounting's contribution to the decision-making process occurs primarily in Steps 4 and 6. In Step 4, for each possible course of action, relevant revenue and cost data are provided to show the expected overall effect on net income. In Step 6, internal reports are prepared that review the actual impact of the decision.

In making business decisions, management ordinarily considers both financial and nonfinancial information. **Financial** information is related to revenues and costs and their effect on the company's overall profitability. **Nonfinancial** information relates to such factors as the effect of the decision on employee turn-

1. Identify the problem and assign responsibility
2. Determine and evaluate possible courses of action
3. Make a decision
4. Review results of the decision

**Illustration 27-1**

*Management's decision-making process*

over, the environment, or the overall image of the company in the community. Although the nonfinancial information can be as important as, and in some cases more important than, the financial information, we will limit our discussion primarily to financial information that is relevant to the decision.

**Decisions involve a choice among alternative courses of action.** Suppose that you were deciding whether to purchase or lease an IBM PC for use in doing your accounting homework. The financial data relate to the cost of leasing versus the cost of purchasing. For example, leasing would involve periodic lease payments; purchasing would require payment of the purchase price. In other words, the financial data relevant to the decision are the data that would vary in the future among the possible alternatives. The process used to identify the financial data that change under alternative courses of action is called incremental analysis. In some cases, you will find that when you use incremental analysis, both costs and revenues will change. In other cases, only costs or revenues will vary.

Just as your decision to buy or lease a PC will affect your future, similar decisions—on a larger scale—will affect a company's future. It follows, therefore, that incremental analysis includes the probable effects of those decisions on future earnings. Such data inevitably involve estimates and uncertainty. Gathering data for incremental analyses may involve market analysts, engineers, and accountants. In quantifying the data, the accountant is expected to exercise professional judgment to produce the most reliable information available at the time the decision must be made.

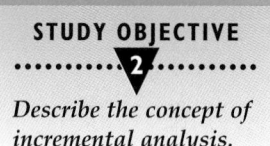

**STUDY OBJECTIVE 2**

*Describe the concept of incremental analysis.*

## *H*ow Incremental Analysis Works

The basic approach in incremental analysis is illustrated in the following example:

| | Alternative A | Alternative B | Net Income Increase (Decrease) |
|---|---|---|---|
| Revenues | $125,000 | $110,000 | $(15,000) |
| Costs | 100,000 | 80,000 | 20,000 |
| Net income | $ 25,000 | $ 30,000 | $ 5,000 |

**Illustration 27-2**

*Basic approach in incremental analysis*

In this example, alternative B is being compared with alternative A. The net income column shows the differences between the alternatives. In this case, incremental revenue will be $15,000 less under alternative B than under alternative

A, but a $20,000 incremental cost saving will be realized.[1] Thus, alternative B will produce $5,000 more net income than alternative A.

In incremental analysis, it is also important to recognize that (1) variable costs may not change under the alternative courses of action, and (2) fixed costs may change. For example, direct labor, normally a variable cost, is not an incremental cost in deciding between two new factory machines if each asset requires the same amount of direct labor. In contrast, rent expense, normally a fixed cost, is an incremental cost in a decision to continue occupancy of a building or to purchase or lease a new building.

# *T*ypes of Incremental Analysis

A number of different types of decisions involve incremental analysis. The more common types of decisions are whether to:

1. Accept an order at a special price.
2. Make or buy.
3. Sell or process further.
4. Retain or replace equipment.
5. Eliminate an unprofitable business segment.
6. Allocate limited resources.

We will consider each of these types of analysis in the following pages.

## Accept an Order at a Special Price

**STUDY OBJECTIVE**

▼ **3**

*Identify the relevant costs in accepting an order at a special price.*

**Helpful hint** This is a good example of different costs for different purposes. In the long-run all costs are relevant, but for this decision only costs that change are relevant.

Sometimes, a company may have an opportunity to obtain additional business if it is willing to make a major price concession to a specific customer. To illustrate, assume that Sunbelt Company produces 100,000 automatic blenders per month, which is 80% of plant capacity. Variable manufacturing costs are $8 per unit, and fixed manufacturing costs are $400,000, or $4 per unit. The blenders are normally sold directly to retailers at $20 each. Sunbelt has an offer from Mexico Co. (a foreign wholesaler) to purchase an additional 2,000 blenders at $11 per unit. Acceptance of the offer would not affect normal sales of the product, and the additional units can be manufactured without increasing plant capacity. What should management do?

If management makes its decision on the basis of the total cost per unit of $12 ($8 + $4), the order would be rejected, because costs ($12) would exceed revenues ($11) by $1 per unit. However, since the units can be produced within existing plant capacity, the special order **will not increase fixed costs**. The relevant data for the decision, therefore, are the variable manufacturing costs per unit of $8 and the expected revenue of $11 per unit. Thus, as shown in Illustration 27-3, Sunbelt will increase its net income by $6,000 by accepting this special order.

**Illustration 27-3**

*Incremental analysis—accepting an order at a special price*

|  | Reject Order | Accept Order | Net Income Increase (Decrease) |
|---|---|---|---|
| Revenues | $–0– | $22,000 | $22,000 |
| Costs | –0– | 16,000 | (16,000) |
| Net income | $–0– | $ 6,000 | $ 6,000 |

---

[1]Although income taxes are sometimes important in incremental analysis, they are ignored in the chapter for simplicity's sake.

Two points should be emphasized: First, it is assumed that sales of the product in other markets would not be affected by this special order. If other sales were affected, then Sunbelt would have to consider the lost sales in making the decision. Second, if Sunbelt is operating at full capacity, it is likely that the special order would be rejected. Under such circumstances, the company would have to expand plant capacity, and, the special order would have to absorb these additional fixed manufacturing costs, as well as the variable manufacturing costs.

## Make or Buy

**STUDY OBJECTIVE**
••••••••••▼4▼••••••••••

*Indicate the relevant costs in a make-or-buy decision.*

When a manufacturer assembles component parts in producing a finished product, management must decide whether to make or buy the components. For example, General Motors Corporation may either make or buy the batteries, tires, and radios used in its cars. Similarly, Zenith Corporation may make or buy the electronic circuitry, cabinets, and speakers for its television sets. The decision to make or buy components should be made on the basis of incremental analysis.

To illustrate the analysis, assume that Baron Company incurs the following annual costs in producing 25,000 ignition switches for motor scooters:

**Illustration 27-4**
___

*Annual product cost data*

| | |
|---|---:|
| Direct materials | $ 50,000 |
| Direct labor | 75,000 |
| Variable manufacturing overhead | 40,000 |
| Fixed manufacturing overhead | 60,000 |
| Total manufacturing costs | $225,000 |
| | |
| Total cost per unit ($225,000 ÷ 25,000) | $9.00 |

Alternatively, Baron Company may purchase the ignition switches from Ignition, Inc., at a price of $8 per unit. The question again is, "What should management do?"

On the one hand, it appears that management should purchase the ignition switches for $8, rather than make them at a cost of $9. However, a review of operations indicates that if the ignition switches are purchased from Ignition, Inc., all of Baron's variable costs but only $10,000 of its fixed manufacturing costs will be eliminated. Thus, $50,000 of the fixed manufacturing costs will remain if the ignition switches are purchased. The relevant costs for incremental analysis, therefore, are as follows:

**Illustration 27-5**
___

*Incremental analysis—make or buy*

► *Ethics note*
___

In the make-or-buy decision it is important for management to take into account the social impact of their choice. For instance, buying may be the most economically feasible solution, but such action could result in the closure of a manufacturing plant that employs many good workers.

| | Make | Buy | Net Income Increase (Decrease) |
|---|---:|---:|---:|
| Direct materials | $ 50,000 | $ –0– | $ 50,000 |
| Direct labor | 75,000 | –0– | 75,000 |
| Variable manufacturing costs | 40,000 | –0– | 40,000 |
| Fixed manufacturing costs | 60,000 | 50,000 | 10,000 |
| Purchase price (25,000 × $8) | –0– | 200,000 | (200,000) |
| Total annual cost | $225,000 | $250,000 | $ (25,000) |

This analysis indicates that Baron Company will incur $25,000 of additional cost by buying the ignition switches. Therefore, Baron should continue to make the ignition switches, even though the total manufacturing cost is $1 higher than the purchase price. The reason is that if the company purchases the ignition switches, it will still have fixed costs of $50,000 to absorb.

The foregoing analysis is complete only if it is assumed that the productive capacity used to make the ignition switches cannot be converted to another purpose. If there is an opportunity to use this productive capacity in some other manner, then this opportunity cost must be considered. Opportunity cost is the potential benefit that may be obtained by following an alternative course of action. To illustrate, assume that through buying the switches, Baron Company can use the released productive capacity to generate additional income of $28,000. This lost income is an additional cost of continuing to make the switches in the make-or-buy decision. This opportunity cost therefore is added to the "Make" column, for comparison. As shown, it is now advantageous to buy the ignition switches.

**Illustration 27-6**

*Incremental analysis—make or buy, with opportunity cost*

|  | Make | Buy | Net Income Increase (Decrease) |
|---|---|---|---|
| Total annual cost | $225,000 | $250,000 | $(25,000) |
| Opportunity cost | 28,000 | –0– | 28,000 |
| Total cost | $253,000 | $250,000 | $ 3,000 |

The qualitative factors in this decision include the possible loss of jobs for employees who produce the ignition switches. In addition, management must assess how long the supplier will be able to satisfy the company's quality control standards at the quoted price per unit.

## ▸Accounting in Action ▸ *Business Insight*

As an example of opportunity cost, one construction company with a heavy load of debt had several pieces of very expensive equipment that had been fully depreciated. The company's books told management that this equipment wasn't tying up any capital. Supposedly it didn't cost the company anything to keep that equipment, except for maintenance expenses. But the equipment could have been sold for a good price. Therefore that zero book value was misleading. The equipment was actually taking up a substantial amount of expensive capital and contributing to the company's weak financial position.

## Sell or Process Further

Many manufacturers have the option of selling products at a given point in the production cycle or continuing to process with the expectation of selling them at a higher price. For example, a bicycle manufacturer such as Schwinn could sell its 10-speed bicycles to retailers either unassembled or assembled, and a furniture manufacturer such as Ethan Allen could sell its dining room sets to furniture stores either unfinished or finished. The sell-or-process further decision should be made on the basis of incremental analysis. The basic decision rule is: **Process further as long as the incremental revenue from such processing exceeds the incremental processing costs.**

Assume, for example, that Woodmasters Inc. makes tables. The cost to manufacture an unfinished table is $35, computed as follows:

**STUDY OBJECTIVE**

**▾5**

*Give the decision rule in deciding whether to sell or process materials further.*

**Illustration 27-7**

*Per unit cost of unfinished table*

| | |
|---|---|
| Direct material | $15 |
| Direct labor | 10 |
| Variable manufacturing overhead | 6 |
| Fixed manufacturing overhead | 4 |
| Manufacturing cost per unit | $35 |

The selling price per unfinished unit is $50. Woodmasters currently has unused productive capacity that is expected to continue indefinitely. Management concludes that some of this capacity may be used to finish the tables and sell them at $60 per unit. For a finished table, it is anticipated that direct materials and direct labor costs will increase $2 and $4, respectively. In addition, variable manufacturing overhead costs will increase by $2.40 (60% of direct labor). No increase is anticipated in fixed manufacturing overhead. The incremental analysis on a per unit basis is as follows:

**Illustration 27-8**

*Incremental analysis—sell or process further*

| | Sell | Process Further | Net Income Increase (Decrease) |
|---|---|---|---|
| Sales per unit | $50.00 | $60.00 | $10.00 |
| Cost per unit | | | |
| Direct materials | 15.00 | 17.00 | (2.00) |
| Direct labor | 10.00 | 14.00 | (4.00) |
| Variable manufacturing overhead | 6.00 | 8.40 | (2.40) |
| Fixed manufacturing overhead | 4.00 | 4.00 | –0– |
| Total | $35.00 | $43.40 | $ (8.40) |
| Net income per unit | $15.00 | $16.60 | $ 1.60 |

**Helpful hint** Current net income is known. Net income from processing further is an estimate. In making its decision, management could add a "risk" factor for the estimate.

As indicated from the analysis, it would be advantageous for Woodmaster to process the tables further. In this case, the incremental revenue of $10.00 from the additional processing is $1.60 higher than the incremental processing costs of $8.40.

## Retain or Replace Equipment

Management often has to decide whether to continue using an asset or replace it. To illustrate, assume that Jeffcoat Company has a factory machine with a book value of $40,000 and a remaining useful life of four years. A new machine is available that costs $120,000 and is expected to have zero salvage value at the end of its 4-year useful life. If the new machine is acquired, variable manufacturing costs are expected to decrease from $160,000 to $125,000 annually and the old unit will be scrapped. The incremental analysis for the 4-year period is as follows:

**STUDY OBJECTIVE**
••••••••••▼6••••••••••
*Identify the factors to be considered in retaining or replacing equipment.*

**Illustration 27-9**

*Incremental analysis—retain or replace equipment*

| | Retain Equipment | Replace Equipment | Net Income Increase (Decrease) |
|---|---|---|---|
| Variable manufacturing costs | $640,000[a] | $500,000[b] | $140,000 |
| New machine cost | | 120,000 | (120,000) |
| Total | $640,000 | $620,000 | $ 20,000 |

[a](4 years × $160,000)
[b](4 years × $125,000)

In this case, it would be to the company's advantage to replace the equipment. The lower variable manufacturing costs due to replacement more than offset the cost of the new equipment.

One other point should be mentioned regarding Jeffcoat's decision: **The book value of the old machine does not affect the decision.** Book value is a sunk cost, which is a cost that cannot be changed by any present or future decision. Sunk costs, therefore, **are not relevant in incremental analysis**. In this example, if the asset is retained, book value will be depreciated over its remaining useful life. On the other hand, if the new unit is acquired, book value will be recognized as a loss of the current period. Thus, the effect of book value on current and future earnings is the same regardless of the replacement decision. **Any trade-in allowance or cash disposal value of the existing asset, however, is relevant** to the decision, because this value will not be realized if the asset is continued in use.

## Eliminate an Unprofitable Segment

**STUDY OBJECTIVE**

••••••••• 7 •••••••••

*Explain the factors that are relevant in deciding whether to eliminate an unprofitable segment.*

Management sometimes needs to decide whether to eliminate an unprofitable business segment. Again, the key is to focus on the data that change under the alternative courses of action. To illustrate, assume that Martina Company manufactures tennis racquets in three models: Pro, Master, and Champ. Pro and Master are profitable lines, whereas Champ (highlighted in color in the table below) operates at a loss. Condensed income statement data are:

**Illustration 27-10**

*Segment income data*

**Helpful hint** A decision to discontinue a segment based solely on the bottom line—net loss—is inappropriate.

|  | Pro | Master | Champ | Total |
|---|---|---|---|---|
| Sales | $800,000 | $300,000 | $100,000 | $1,200,000 |
| Variable expenses | 520,000 | 210,000 | 90,000 | 820,000 |
| Contribution margin | 280,000 | 90,000 | 10,000 | 380,000 |
| Fixed expenses | 80,000 | 50,000 | 30,000 | 160,000 |
| Net income | $200,000 | $ 40,000 | $ (20,000) | $ 220,000 |

It might be expected that total net income will increase by $20,000 to $240,000 if the unprofitable line of racquets is eliminated. However, **it is possible for net income to decrease if the Champ line is discontinued**. The reason is that the fixed expenses allocated to the Champ racquets will have to be absorbed by the other products. To illustrate, assume that the $30,000 of fixed costs applicable to the unprofitable segment are allocated ⅔ and ⅓ to the Pro and Master product lines, respectively. Fixed expenses will increase to $100,000 ($80,000 + $20,000) in the Pro line and to $60,000 ($50,000 + $10,000) in the Master line. The revised income statement is:

**Illustration 27-11**

*Income data after eliminating unprofitable product line*

|  | Pro | Master | Total |
|---|---|---|---|
| Sales | $800,000 | $300,000 | $1,100,000 |
| Variable expenses | 520,000 | 210,000 | 730,000 |
| Contribution margin | 280,000 | 90,000 | 370,000 |
| Fixed expenses | 100,000 | 60,000 | 160,000 |
| Net income | $180,000 | $ 30,000 | $ 210,000 |

Total net income has decreased $10,000 ($220,000 − $210,000). This result is also obtained in the following incremental analysis of the Champ racquets:

**Illustration 27-12**

*Incremental analysis—eliminating an unprofitable segment*

|  | Continue | Eliminate | Net Income Increase (Decrease) |
|---|---|---|---|
| Sales | $100,000 | $ –0– | $(100,000) |
| Variable expenses | 90,000 | –0– | 90,000 |
| Contribution margin | 10,000 | –0– | (10,000) |
| Fixed expenses | 30,000 | 30,000 | –0– |
| Net income | $ (20,000) | $(30,000) | $ (10,000) |

The loss in net income is attributable to the contribution margin ($10,000) that will not be realized if the segment is discontinued.

In deciding on the future status of an unprofitable segment, management should consider the effect of elimination on related product lines. It may be possible for continuing product lines to obtain some or all of the sales lost by the discontinued product line. In addition, management should consider the effect of eliminating the product line on employees who may have to be discharged or retrained.

## Allocate Limited Resources

Everyone's resources are limited. For a company, the limited resource may be floor space in a retail department store, or raw materials, direct labor hours, or machine capacity in a manufacturing company. When a company has limited resources, management must decide which products to make and sell in order to maximize net income.

To illustrate, assume that Collins Company manufactures deluxe and standard pen and pencil sets. The limiting resource is machine capacity, which is 3,600 hours per month. Relevant data consist of the following:

**STUDY OBJECTIVE**
••••••••••**8**••••••••••

*Determine which products to make and sell when a company has limited resources.*

**Illustration 27-13**

*Contribution margin and machine hours*

|  | Deluxe Sets | Standard Sets |
|---|---|---|
| Contribution margin per unit | $8 | $6 |
| Machine hours required | 4 | 2 |

The deluxe sets may appear to be more profitable since they have a higher contribution margin ($8) than the standard sets ($6). However, note that the standard sets take fewer machine hours to produce than the deluxe sets. Therefore, it is necessary to find the **contribution margin per unit of limited resource**. This is obtained by dividing the contribution margin per unit of each product by the number of units of the limited resource required for each product. The computation shows that the standard sets have a higher contribution margin per unit of limited resource.

**Helpful hint** CM alone is not enough in this decision. The key factor is CM per limited resource.

**Illustration 27-14**

*Contribution margin per unit of limited resource*

|  | Deluxe Sets | Standard Sets |
|---|---|---|
| Contribution margin per unit (a) | $8 | $6 |
| Machine hours required (b) | 4 | 2 |
| Contribution margin per unit of limited resource (a) ÷ (b) | $2 | $3 |

If Collins Company is able to increase machine capacity from 3,600 hours to 4,200 hours, the additional 600 hours could be used to produce either the standard or deluxe pen and pencil sets. The total contribution margin under each alternative is found by multiplying the machine hours by the contribution margin per unit of limited resource as shown below.

**Illustration 27-15**

*Incremental analysis—computation of total contribution margin*

|  | Produce Deluxe Sets | Produce Standard Sets |
|---|---|---|
| Machine hours (a) | 600 | 600 |
| Contribution margin per unit of limited resource (b) | $2 | $3 |
| Contribution margin (a) × (b) | $1,200 | $1,800 |

From this analysis, we can see that to maximize net income, all of the increased capacity should be used to make and sell the standard sets.

## *Before You Go On . . .*

### ▸ *Review It*

1. Give three examples of how incremental analysis might be used.
2. What is the decision rule in deciding to sell or process products further?
3. How may the elimination of an unprofitable segment decrease the overall net income of a company?
4. What is the critical factor in allocating limited resources?

### ▸ *Do It*

Cobb Company incurs a cost of $28 per unit, of which $18 is variable, to make a product that normally sells for $42. A foreign wholesaler offers to buy 5,000 units at $25 each. Cobb will incur shipping costs of $1 per unit. Compute the net income (loss) Cobb will realize by accepting the special order, assuming Cobb has excess operating capacity.

**Reasoning:** The decision in this case involves incremental analysis. Thus, Cobb must identify the revenues and costs that change by accepting the special order.

**Solution:**

|  | Reject | Accept | Net Income Increase (Decrease) |
|---|---|---|---|
| Revenues | $–0– | $125,000 | $125,000 |
| Costs | –0– | 95,000* | (95,000) |
| Net income | $–0– | $ 30,000 | $ 30,000 |

*(5,000 × $18) + (5,000 × $1)

*Related exercise material: BE27–2, BE27–3, and E27–1.*

## ▸SECTION 2 ▸ *Capital Budgeting*

Individuals make capital expenditures when they buy a new home, car, or television set. Similarly, businesses make capital expenditures when they modernize plant facilities or expand operations. Examples include the new engine plant to be built in Detroit by Chrysler Corporation and the new baseball stadium built by the Colorado Rockies team.

The amounts spent by companies on capital expenditures each year are substantial. For example, in a recent year, U.S. businesses spent approximately $375 billion on capital expenditures. More specifically, in 1994, Woolworth Corporation spent $218 million, Kmart spent $1.2 billion, and Caterpillar spent $501 million. In business enterprises, as for individuals, the amount of possible capital expenditures usually exceeds the funds available for such expenditures. Thus, the resources available must be allocated (or budgeted) among the competing alternatives. The process of making capital expenditure decisions in business is known as capital budgeting. Capital budgeting involves choosing among various capital projects to find the one(s) that will maximize a company's return on investment.

# Process for Evaluation

Many companies follow a carefully prescribed process in capital budgeting. At least once a year, proposals for projects are requested from each department and plant and from authorized personnel. The proposals are screened by a capital budgeting committee, which submits its findings to the officers of the company. The officers, in turn, select the projects they believe to be most worthy of funding and submit them to the board of directors. Ultimately, the directors approve the capital expenditure budget for the year. The involvement of top management and the board of directors in the process demonstrates the importance of capital budgeting decisions. These decisions often have a significant impact on a company's future profitability. Indeed, poor capital budgeting decisions have led to the bankruptcy of some companies. Accounting data are indispensable in assessing the probable effects of capital expenditures.

To provide management with relevant data for capital budgeting decisions, you should be familiar with the quantitative techniques that may be used. The three most common techniques are: (1) annual rate of return, (2) cash payback, and (3) discounted cash flow. To illustrate the three quantitative techniques, assume that Tappan Company is considering an investment of $130,000 in new equipment. The new equipment is expected to last 10 years and have zero salvage value at the end of its useful life. The straight-line method of depreciation is used for accounting purposes. The expected annual revenues and costs of the new product that will be produced from the investment are:

> **International note**
> The World Bank estimates that Asian, Latin American, and other developing nations will be spending $200 billion annually on infrastructure in the years just ahead. U.S. manufacturers of equipment used to build the infrastructure will benefit greatly.

| | | |
|---|---:|---:|
| Sales | | $200,000 |
| Less: Costs and expenses | | |
| Manufacturing costs (exclusive of depreciation) | $145,000 | |
| Depreciation expense ($130,000 ÷ 10) | 13,000 | |
| Selling and administrative expenses | 22,000 | 180,000 |
| Income before income taxes | | 20,000 |
| Income tax expense | | 7,000 |
| Net income | | $ 13,000 |

**Illustration 27-16**

*Estimated annual net income from capital expenditure*

# Annual Rate of Return

The annual rate of return technique is based directly on accounting data. It indicates **the profitability of a capital expenditure** by dividing expected annual

> **STUDY OBJECTIVE 9**
> Contrast the annual rate of return and cash payback techniques in capital budgeting.

net income by the average investment. The formula for computing annual rate of return is shown in Illustration 27-17.

**Illustration 27-17**

*Annual rate of return formula*

Expected annual net income is obtained from the projected income statement. Tappan Company's expected annual net income is $13,000. Average investment is derived from the following formula:

**Illustration 27-18**

*Formula for computing average investment*

$$\text{Average investment} = \frac{\text{Original investment} + \text{Investment at end of useful life}}{2}$$

The investment at the end of useful life is equal to the asset's salvage value, if any. For Tappan Company, average investment is $65,000 [($130,000 + $0) ÷ 2]. The expected annual rate of return for Tappan Company's investment in new equipment is therefore 20%, computed as follows:

$$\$13,000 \div \$65,000 = 20\%$$

The annual rate of return is then compared with the management's required minimum rate of return for investments of similar risk. The minimum rate of return (also called the **hurdle rate** or **cutoff rate**) is generally based on the company's **cost of capital**. The cost of capital is the rate of return that management expects to pay on all borrowed and equity funds. It does not relate to the cost of funding a specific project. The decision rule is: **A project is acceptable if its rate of return is greater than management's minimum rate of return; it is unacceptable when the reverse is true.** When the rate of return technique is used in deciding among several acceptable projects, **the higher the rate of return for a given risk, the more attractive the investment**.

The principal advantages of this technique of analysis are the simplicity of its calculation and management's familiarity with the accounting terms used in the computation. A major limitation of the annual rate of return approach is that it does not consider the time value of money. For example, no consideration is given as to whether cash inflows from the investment will occur early or late in the life of the investment. As explained in Appendix B, recognition of the time value of money can make a significant difference between the future value and the discounted present value of an investment.

**Helpful hint**  A capital budgeting decision based on only one technique may be misleading. It is often wise to analyze the situation from a number of different perspectives.

# Cash Payback

The cash payback technique identifies the time period required to recover the cost of the capital investment from the annual cash inflow produced by the investment. The formula for computing the cash payback period is:

**Illustration 27-19**

*Cash payback formula*

**Annual cash inflow**, also known as net cash inflow, is approximated by taking net income and adding back depreciation expense. Depreciation expense is added back because depreciation on the capital expenditure does not involve an annual outflow of cash. Accordingly, the depreciation deducted in determining net income must be added back to determine annual cash inflows. In the Tappan Company example, annual cash inflow is $26,000, as shown below.

**Illustration 27-20**

*Computation of annual cash inflow*

| Net income | $13,000 |
|---|---|
| Add: Depreciation expense | 13,000 |
| Annual cash inflow | $26,000 |

The cash payback period in this example is therefore 5 years, computed as follows:

$$\$130,000 \div \$26,000 = 5 \text{ years}$$

The evaluation of the payback period is often related to the expected useful life of the asset. For example, assume that at Tappan Company a project is unacceptable if the payback period is longer than 60% of the asset's expected useful life. The five-year payback period in this case is 50% of the project's expected useful life. Thus, the project is acceptable. It follows that when the payback technique is used to decide among acceptable alternative projects, **the shorter the payback period, the more attractive the investment**. The reason is that: (1) the earlier the investment is recovered, the sooner the cash funds can be used for other purposes, and (2) the risk of loss from obsolescence and changed economic conditions is less in a shorter payback period.

The cash payback technique may be useful as an initial screening tool. It also may be the most critical factor in the capital budgeting decision for a company that desires a fast turnaround of its investment because of a weak cash position. Like the annual rate of return technique, the cash payback technique is relatively easy to compute and understand. However, it should not ordinarily be the only basis for the capital budgeting decision because it ignores the expected profitability of the project. To illustrate, assume that Projects A and B have the same payback period, but Project A's useful life is double the useful life of Project B. Project A's earning power, therefore, is twice as long as Project B's. A further disadvantage of this technique is that it ignores the time value of money.

# Discounted Cash Flow

**STUDY OBJECTIVE**

**10**

*Distinguish between the net present value and internal rate of return methods.*

The discounted cash flow technique is generally recognized as the most informative and best conceptual approach to making capital budgeting decisions. This technique considers both the estimated total cash inflows from the investment and the time value of money. As indicated previously, consideration of the time value of money is critical because of the long-term impact of the capital budgeting decision. The expected total cash inflow consists of the sum of the annual cash inflows plus the estimated liquidation proceeds when the asset is sold for salvage at the end of its useful life. Because liquidation proceeds are generally immaterial, they are ignored in subsequent discussions. Two methods are used with the discounted cash flow technique: (1) net present value and (2) internal rate of return. Before we discuss the methods, we recommend that you examine Appendix B if you need a review of present value concepts.

## Net Present Value Method

Under the net present value method, cash inflows are discounted to their present value and then compared with the capital outlay required by the investment. The difference between these two amounts is referred to as **net present value**. The interest rate to be used in discounting the future cash inflows is the required minimum rate of return. **A proposal is acceptable when net present value is zero or positive**, because this means the rate of return on the investment equals or exceeds the required rate of return. When net present value is negative, the project is unacceptable. Illustration 27-21 shows the net present value decision criteria.

**Illustration 27-21**

*Net present value decision criteria*

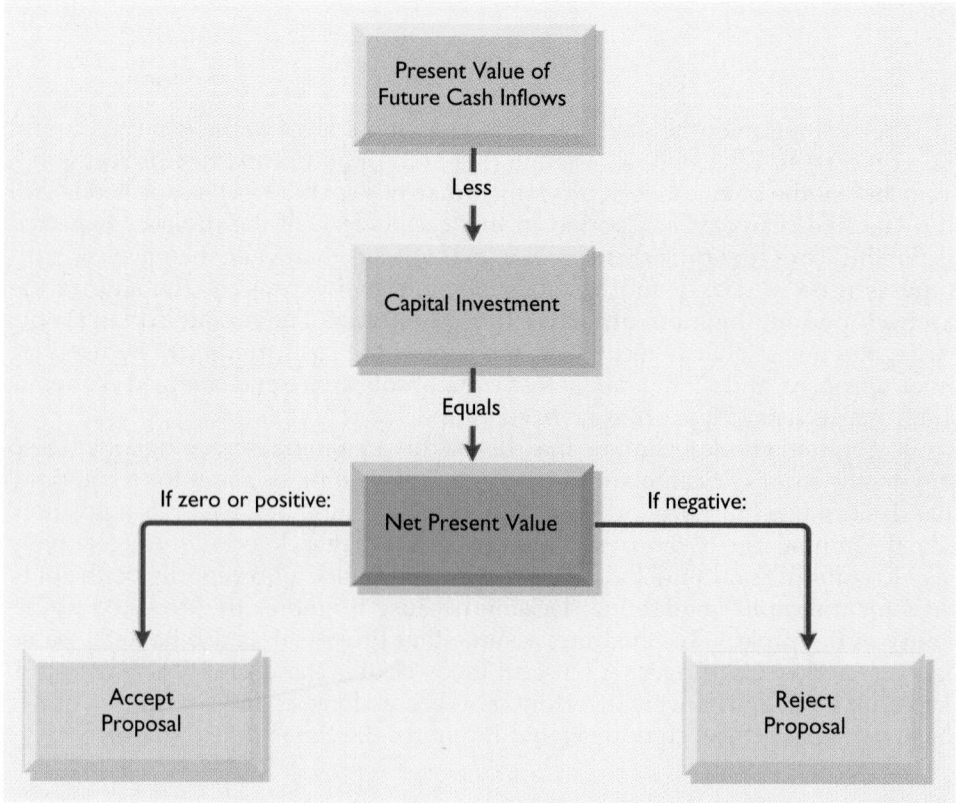

When making a selection among acceptable proposals, **the higher the positive net present value, the more attractive the investment**. The application of this method to two cases is described in the next two sections. In each case, we will assume that the investment has no salvage value at the end of its useful life.

## Equal Annual Cash Flows

Tappan Company's annual cash inflows are $26,000. If we assume this amount **is uniform over the asset's useful life**, the present value of the annual cash inflows can be computed by using the present value of an annuity of 1 for 10 periods (in Table 2, Appendix B). The computations at rates of return of 12% and 15%, respectively, are:

|  | **Present Values at Different Discount Rates** | |
|---|---|---|
|  | 12% | 15% |
| Discount factor for 10 periods | 5.65022 | 5.01877 |
| Present value of cash inflows: | | |
| $26,000 × 5.65022 | $146,906 | |
| $26,000 × 5.01877 | | $130,488 |

**Illustration 27-22**

*Present value of annual cash inflows*

Therefore, the analysis of the proposal by the net present value method is as follows:

|  | 12% | 15% |
|---|---|---|
| Present value of future cash inflows | $146,906 | $130,488 |
| Capital investment | 130,000 | 130,000 |
| Positive (negative) net present value | $ 16,906 | $    488 |

**Illustration 27-23**

*Computations of net present values*

**Helpful hint** The ABC Co. expects equal cash flows over an asset's 5-year useful life. What discount factor should be used in determining present values if management wants (1) a 12% return or (2) a 15% return? Answer: Using Table 2, the factors are (1) 3.60478 and (2) 3.35216.

The proposed capital expenditure is acceptable at a required rate of return of both 12% and 15% because the net present values are positive.

## Unequal Annual Cash Inflows

When annual cash inflows are unequal, it is not possible to use annuity tables to calculate their present value. Instead, tables showing the **present value of a single future amount must be applied to each annual cash inflow**. To illustrate, assume in the Tappan Company that management expects the same aggregate annual cash inflow ($260,000) but a declining market demand for the new product over the life of the equipment. The present value of the annual cash flows is calculated as follows using Table 1 in Appendix B:

| Year | **Assumed Annual Cash Inflows** | **Discount Factor** 12% | 15% | **Present Value** 12% | 15% |
|---|---|---|---|---|---|
|  | (1) | (2) | (3) | (1) × (2) | (1) × (3) |
| 1 | $ 36,000 | .89286 | .86957 | $ 32,143 | $ 31,305 |
| 2 | 32,000 | .79719 | .75614 | 25,510 | 24,196 |
| 3 | 29,000 | .71178 | .65752 | 20,642 | 19,068 |
| 4 | 27,000 | .63552 | .57175 | 17,159 | 15,437 |
| 5 | 26,000 | .56743 | .49718 | 14,753 | 12,927 |
| 6 | 24,000 | .50663 | .43233 | 12,159 | 10,376 |
| 7 | 23,000 | .45235 | .37594 | 10,404 | 8,647 |
| 8 | 22,000 | .40388 | .32690 | 8,885 | 7,192 |
| 9 | 21,000 | .36061 | .28426 | 7,573 | 5,969 |
| 10 | 20,000 | .32197 | .24719 | 6,439 | 4,944 |
|  | $260,000 |  |  | $155,667 | $140,061 |

**Illustration 27-24**

*Computing present value of unequal annual cash inflows*

Therefore, the analysis of the proposal by the net present value method is as follows:

**Illustration 27-25**

*Analysis of proposal using net present value method*

|  | 12% | 15% |
|---|---|---|
| Present value of future cash inflows | $155,667 | $140,061 |
| Capital investment | 130,000 | 130,000 |
| Positive (negative) net present value | $ 25,667 | $ 10,061 |

In this example, the present values of the cash inflows are greater than the $130,000 capital investment. Thus, the project is acceptable at both a 12% and 15% required rate of return. The difference between the present values using the 12% rate under equal cash inflows ($146,906) and unequal cash inflows ($155,667) is due to the pattern of the inflows.

## Internal Rate of Return Method

The internal rate of return method differs from the net present value method in that it results in finding the **interest yield of the potential investment**. The **internal rate of return** is the rate that will cause the present value of the proposed capital expenditure to equal the present value of the expected annual cash inflows. The determination of the internal rate of return involves two steps.

**Step 1. Compute the internal rate of return factor.** The formula for this factor is:

**Illustration 27-26**

*Formula for internal rate of return factor*

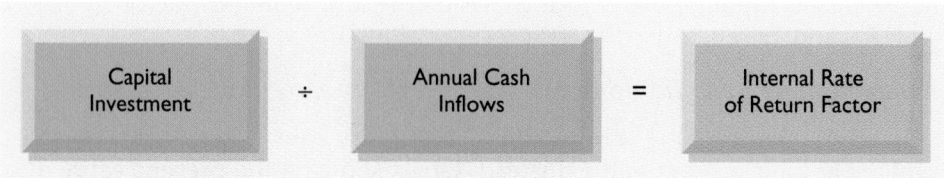

The computation for the Tappan Company, assuming equal annual cash inflows is:

$$\$130,000 \div \$26,000 = 5.0^2$$

**Step 2. Use the factor and the present value of an annuity of 1 table to find the internal rate of return.** Table 2 of Appendix B is used in this step. The internal rate of return is found by locating the discount factor in the table that is closest to the internal rate of return factor for the time period covered by the annual cash flows.

In Tappan Company, the annual cash inflows are expected to continue for 10 years. Thus, it is necessary to read across the period 10 row in Table 2 to find the discount factor. Row 10 is reproduced on the next page for your convenience.

---

[2]When annual cash inflows are equal, the internal rate of return factor is the same as the cash payback period.

**TABLE 2**
**PRESENT VALUE OF AN ANNUITY OF 1**

| (n) Periods | 5% | 6% | 8% | 9% | 10% | 11% | 12% | 15% |
|---|---|---|---|---|---|---|---|---|
| 10 | 7.72173 | 7.36009 | 6.71008 | 6.41766 | 6.14457 | 5.88923 | 5.65022 | 5.01877 |

In this case, the closest discount factor to 5.0 is 5.01877 which represents an interest rate of approximately 15%. The approximate rate can be determined by interpolation, but since we are using estimated annual cash flows such precision is seldom required.

When the internal rate of return has been determined, it is compared to management's required minimum rate of return. The decision rule, therefore, is: **Accept the project when the internal rate of return is equal to or greater than the required rate of return, and reject the project when the internal rate of return is less than the required rate.** These relationships are shown graphically in Illustration 27-27. Assuming the minimum required rate of return is 10% for Tappan Company, the project is acceptable because the 15% internal rate of return is greater than the required rate.

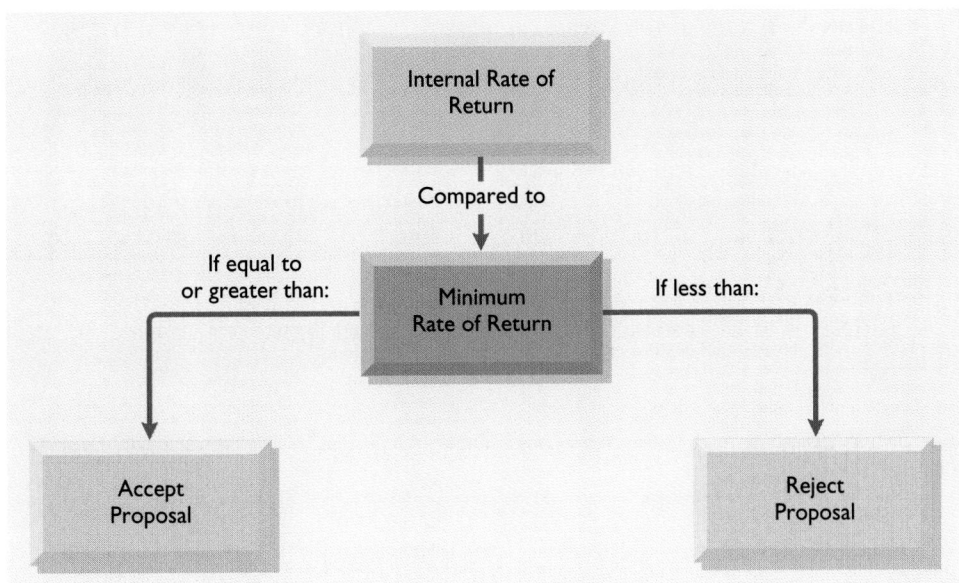

**Illustration 27-27**

*Internal rate of return decision criteria*

The internal rate of return method is widely used in practice. Most managers find the internal rate of return easy to interpret.

## ▶ Accounting in Action ▸ *Business Insight*

Which capital budgeting methods are used the most? One survey asked financial officers which method they used in considering expenditures for factory automation. Internal rate of return and cash payback were the most popular methods. Subjective evaluation—though not, strictly speaking, a capital budgeting method—also turned out to be popular with finance professionals.

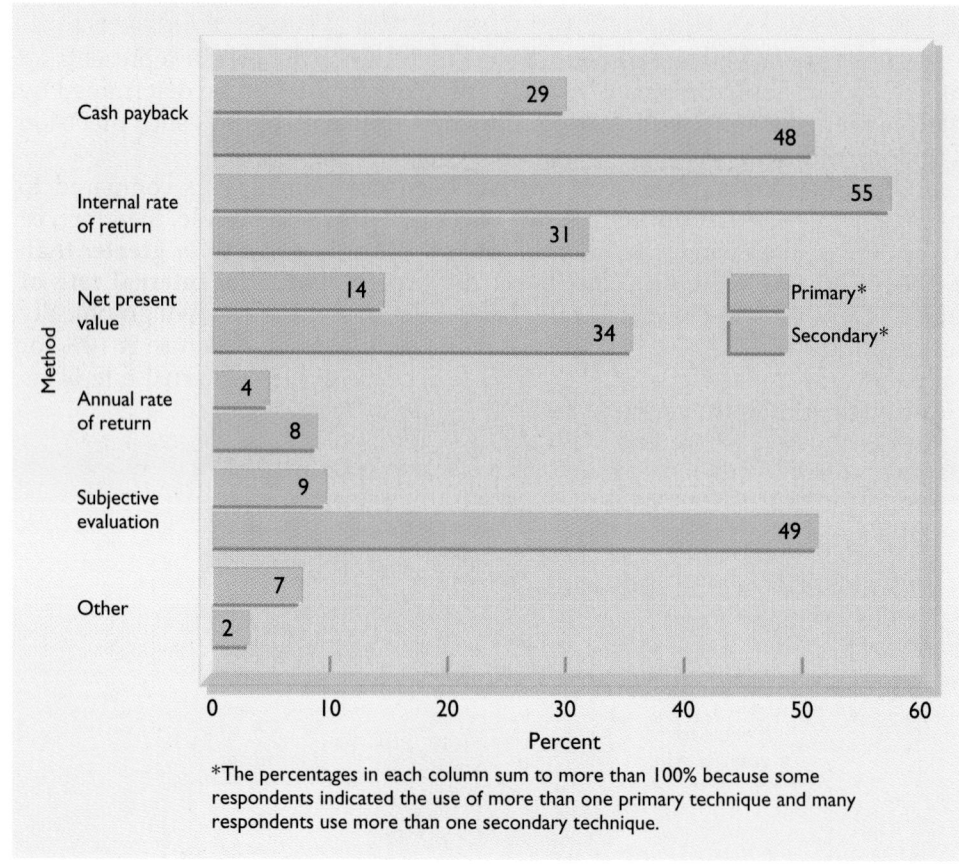

*The percentages in each column sum to more than 100% because some respondents indicated the use of more than one primary technique and many respondents use more than one secondary technique.

*Source:* James A. Hendricks, "Applying Cost Accounting to Factory Automation," *Management Accounting*, December 1988.

## Comparison of Discounted Cash Flow Methods

A comparative summary of the two discounted cash flow methods—net present value and internal rate of return—is presented in Illustration 27-28.

**Illustration 27-28**

*Comparison of discounted cash flow methods*

| Item | Net Present Value | Internal Rate of Return |
|---|---|---|
| 1. Objective | Compute net present value. | Compute internal rate of return. |
| 2. Decision rule | If net present value is zero or positive, accept the proposal; if net present value is negative, reject the proposal. | If internal rate of return is equal to or greater than the minimum required rate of return, accept the proposal; if internal rate of return is less than the minimum rate, reject the proposal. |

When properly used, either method will provide management with relevant quantitative data for making capital budgeting decisions.

## Technology in Action

There are software packages available for each of the decision situations described in the incremental analysis and capital budgeting sections of this chapter. Because of their power and flexibility, spreadsheet programs can also be designed to perform any of these calculations. Thus, businesses often face another decision: Should they purchase packages dedicated only to specific tasks (called a canned approach) or will a general-purpose application package, like a spreadsheet or database program, be better? Management often turns to accountants to help answer such questions. As discussed in Chapter 6, the costs of each alternative should be carefully weighed against the benefits before any purchase is made.

## Before You Go On . . .

### ▶ Review It

1. What is the formula for and the decision rule in using the annual rate of return method?
2. What is the formula for the cash payback method?
3. When is a proposal acceptable under (a) the net present value method and (b) the internal rate of return method?

## ▶ A Look Back at Forrest Gump

Refer back to the story about *Forrest Gump* at the beginning of the chapter, and answer the following questions:

1. What decisions faced by a movie studio might benefit from incremental analysis?
2. Comment on the usefulness of the accounting methods used by Paramount Pictures for incremental analysis.

### Solution:

1. Studio decisions that might benefit from incremental analysis would be: (a) the choice of which two movies to produce (allocation of limited resources); (b) whether to upgrade audio and video equipment (retain or replace); and (c) the sale of distribution rights to a movie (sell or process further).
2. It appears that Paramount Pictures is allocating its costs in a manner that would minimize the payments made on contingent contracts, such as those of the screenwriter and author. If these same accounting methods were employed in deciding whether to produce a movie, some very profitable opportunities might be forgone.

## Summary of Study Objectives

**1. Identify the steps in management's decision-making process.** Management's decision-making process consists of (a) identifying the problem or opportunity, (b) assigning responsibility for the decision, (c) determining possible courses of action, (d) developing data relevant to each course of action, (e) making the decision, and (f) reviewing the results of the decision.

**2. Describe the concept of incremental analysis.** Incremental analysis is the process used to identify financial data that change under alternative courses of action. These data are relevant to the decision because they will vary in the future among the possible alternatives.

**3. Identify the relevant costs in accepting an order at a special price.** The relevant information in accepting an order at a special price is the difference between the variable manufacturing costs to produce the special order and expected revenues.

**4.** *Indicate the relevant costs in a make-or-buy decision.* In a make-or-buy decision, the relevant costs are (a) the variable manufacturing costs that will be saved, (b) the purchase price, and (c) opportunity costs.

**5.** *Give the decision rule in deciding whether to sell or process materials further.* The decision rule in deciding whether to sell or process materials further is: process further as long as the incremental revenue from processing exceeds the incremental processing costs.

**6.** *Identify the factors to be considered in retaining or replacing equipment.* The factors to be considered in determining whether equipment should be retained or replaced are the effects on variable costs and the cost of the new equipment. In addition, any disposal value of the existing asset must be considered.

**7.** *Explain the factors that are relevant in deciding whether to eliminate an unprofitable segment.* In deciding whether to eliminate an unprofitable segment, it is necessary to determine the contribution margin, if any, produced by the segment and the disposition of the segment's fixed expenses.

**8.** *Determine which products to make and sell when a company has limited resources.* When a company has limited resources, it is necessary to find the contribution margin per unit of limited resource. This amount is then multiplied by

the units that could be produced to determine which product maximizes net income.

**9.** *Contrast the annual rate of return and cash payback techniques in capital budgeting.* The annual rate of return is obtained by dividing expected annual net income by the average investment. The higher the rate of return, the more attractive the investment. The cash payback technique identifies the time period to recover the cost of the investment. The formula is: Cost of capital expenditure divided by estimated annual cash inflow equals cash payback period. The shorter the payback period, the more attractive the investment.

**10.** *Distinguish between the net present value and internal rate of return methods.* Under the net present value method, the present value of future cash inflows is compared with the capital investment to determine net present value. The decision rule is: Accept the project if net present value is zero or positive; reject the investment if net present value is negative.

Under the internal rate of return method, the objective is to find the true interest yield of the potential investment. The decision rule is: Accept the project when the internal rate of return is equal to or greater than the required rate of return; reject the project when the internal rate of return is less than the required rate.

# Glossary

**Annual rate of return technique** The determination of the profitability of a capital expenditure by dividing expected annual net income by the average investment. (p. 1131).

**Capital budgeting** The process of making capital expenditure decisions in business. (p. 1131).

**Cash payback technique** A capital budgeting technique that identifies the time period required to recover the cost of a capital investment from the annual cash inflow produced by the investment. (p. 1132).

**Cost of capital** The rate of return that management expects to pay on all borrowed and equity funds. (p. 1132).

**Discounted cash flow technique** A capital budgeting technique that considers both the estimated total cash inflows from the investment and the time value of money. (p. 1133).

**Incremental analysis** The process of identifying the finan-

cial data that change under alternative courses of action. (p. 1123).

**Internal rate of return method** A method used in capital budgeting that results in finding the interest yield of the potential investment. (p. 1136).

**Net present value method** A method used in capital budgeting in which cash inflows are discounted to their present value and then compared to the capital outlay required by the investment. (p. 1134).

**Opportunity cost** The potential benefit that may be obtained from following an alternative course of action. (p. 1126).

**Sunk cost** A cost that cannot be changed by any present or future decision. (p. 1128).

# DEMONSTRATION PROBLEM 1

Juanita Company must decide whether to make or buy some of its components. The costs of producing 50,000 electrical cords for its floor lamps are as follows:

| | | | |
|---|---|---|---|
| Direct materials | $60,000 | Variable overhead | $12,000 |
| Direct labor | 30,000 | Fixed overhead | 8,000 |

Instead of making the electrical cords at an average cost per unit of $2.20 ($110,000 ÷ 50,000), the company has an opportunity to buy the cords at $2.30 per unit. If the cords are purchased all variable costs and one-half of the fixed costs will be eliminated.

**Instructions**

(a) Prepare an incremental analysis showing whether the company should make or buy the electrical cords.

(b) Will your answer be different if the released productive capacity will generate additional income of $25,000?

## Solution to Demonstration Problem 1

(a)

| | Make | Buy | Net Income Increase (Decrease) |
|---|---|---|---|
| Direct materials | $ 60,000 | $ –0– | $ 60,000 |
| Direct labor | 30,000 | –0– | 30,000 |
| Variable manufacturing costs | 12,000 | –0– | 12,000 |
| Fixed manufacturing costs | 8,000 | 4,000 | 4,000 |
| Purchase price | –0– | 115,000 | (115,000) |
| Total cost | $110,000 | $119,000 | $ (9,000) |

**Problem-Solving Strategies**

1. Look for the costs that change.
2. Ignore the costs that do not change.
3. Use the format in the chapter for your answer.
4. Recognize that opportunity cost can make a difference.

This analysis indicates that Juanita Company will incur $9,000 of additional costs if it buys the electrical cords.

(b)

| | Make | Buy | Net Income Increase (Decrease) |
|---|---|---|---|
| Total cost | $110,000 | $119,000 | $ (9,000) |
| Opportunity cost | 25,000 | | 25,000 |
| Total cost | $135,000 | $119,000 | $ 16,000 |

Yes, the answer is different because the analysis shows that net income will be increased by $16,000 if the electrical cords are purchased.

# DEMONSTRATION PROBLEM 2

Sierra Company is considering a long-term capital investment project called ZIP. ZIP will require an investment of $120,000, and it will have a useful life of 4 years. Annual net income is expected to be: Year 1, $12,000; Year 2, $10,000; Year 3, $8,000; and Year 4, $6,000. Depreciation is computed by the straight-line method with no salvage value. The company's cost of capital is 12%.

**Instructions**

(Round all computations to two decimal places.)

(a) Compute the annual rate of return for the project.

(b) Compute the cash payback period for the project. (Round to two decimals.)

(c) Compute the net present value for the project. (Round to nearest dollar.)

(d) Should the project be accepted? Why?

## Solution to Demonstration Problem 2

(a)  $9,000 ($36,000 ÷ 4) ÷ $60,000 ($120,000 ÷ 2) = 15%

(b)  $120,000 ÷ $39,000 ($9,000 + $30,000) = 3.08 years

(c)

| Year | Discount Factor | Cash Inflow | Present Value |
|------|-----------------|-------------|---------------|
| 1 | .89286 | $42,000 | $ 37,500 |
| 2 | .79719 | 40,000 | 31,888 |
| 3 | .71178 | 38,000 | 27,048 |
| 4 | .63552 | 36,000 | 22,879 |
| | | | 119,315 |
| Capital investment | | | 120,000 |
| Negative net present value | | | $  (685) |

(d)  The annual rate of return of 15% is good. However, the cash payback period is 77% of the project's useful life and net present value is negative. The recommendation is to reject the project.

# SELF-STUDY QUESTIONS
••••••••••••••••••••••••••••••••••••••••••••••••••••••••••••••••••••••••••••••••

Answers are at the end of the chapter.

(SO 1)  1. Three of the steps in management's decision process are (1) review results of decision, (2) develop data relevant to each course of action, and (3) make the decision. The steps are prepared in the following order:
a.  (1), (2), (3)
b.  (3), (2), (1)
c.  (2), (1), (3)
d.  (2), (3), (1)

(SO 2)  2. Incremental analysis is the process of identifying the financial data that:
a.  do not change under alternative courses of action.
b.  change under alternative courses of action.
c.  are mixed under alternative courses of action.
d.  No correct answer is given.

(SO 3)  3. It costs a company $14 of variable costs and $6 of fixed costs to produce product A that sells for $30. A foreign buyer offers to purchase 3,000 units at $18 each. If the special offer is accepted and produced with unused capacity, net income will:
a.  decrease $6,000.
b.  increase $6,000.
c.  increase $12,000.
d.  increase $9,000.

(SO 4)  4. In a make-or-buy decision, relevant costs are:
a.  manufacturing costs that will be saved.
b.  the purchase price of the units.
c.  opportunity costs.
d.  All of the above.

(SO 5)  5. The decision rule in a sell-or-process-further decision is: process further as long as the incremental revenue from process exceeds:
a.  incremental processing costs.
b.  variable processing costs.
c.  fixed processing costs.
d.  No correct answer is given.

(SO 6)  6. In a decision to retain or replace equipment, the book value of the old equipment is a (an):
a.  opportunity cost.
b.  sunk cost.
c.  incremental cost.
d.  marginal cost.

(SO 7)  7. If an unprofitable segment is eliminated:
a.  net income will always increase.
b.  variable expenses of the eliminated segment will have to be absorbed by other segments.
c.  fixed expenses allocated to the eliminated segment will have to be absorbed by other segments.
d.  net income will always decrease.

(SO 8)  8. If the contribution margin per unit is $15 and it takes 3.0 machine hours to produce the unit, the contribution margin per unit of limited resource is:
a.  $25.
b.  $5.
c.  $4.
d.  No correct answer is given.

(SO 9)  9. Which of the following is *incorrect* about the annual rate of return technique?
a.  The calculation is simple.

b. The accounting terms used are familiar to management.
c. The timing of the cash inflows is not considered.
d. The time value of money is considered.

(SO 10)  10. A positive net present value means that the:
a. project's rate of return is less than the cutoff rate.

b. project's rate of return exceeds the required rate of return.
c. project's rate of return equals the required rate of return.
d. project is unacceptable.

# QUESTIONS

1. What steps are frequently involved in management's decision-making process?

2. Your roommate contends that accounting contributes to most of the steps in management's decision-making process. Is your roommate correct? Explain.

3. "Incremental analysis involves the accumulation of information concerning a single course of action." Do you agree? Why?

4. Pam Marlin asks your help concerning the relevance of variable and fixed costs in incremental analysis. Help Pam with her problem.

5. What data are relevant in deciding whether to accept an order at a special price?

6. Parton Company has an opportunity to buy parts at $7 each that currently cost $10 to make. What manufacturing costs are relevant to this make-or-buy decision?

7. Define the term "opportunity cost." How may this cost be relevant in a make or buy decision?

8. What is the decision rule in deciding whether to sell a product or process it further?

9. Your roommate is confused about sunk costs. Explain to your roommate the meaning of sunk costs and their relevance to a decision to retain or replace equipment.

10. Diversified Inc. has one product line that is unprofitable. What circumstances may cause overall company net income to be lower if the unprofitable product line is eliminated?

11. How is the contribution margin per unit of limited resources computed?

12. Describe the process a company may use in screening and approving the capital expenditure budget.

13. Your classmate is confused about the factors that are included in the annual rate of return technique. What is the formula for this technique?

14. Stacy Lolb is trying to understand the term "cost of capital." Define the term and indicate its relevance to the decision rule under the annual rate of return technique.

15. Joe Culver claims the formula for the cash payback technique is the same as the formula for the annual rate of return technique. Is Joe correct? What is the formula for the cash payback technique?

16. What are the advantages and disadvantages of the cash payback technique?

17. Two types of present value tables may be used with the discounted cash flow technique. Identify the tables and the circumstance(s) when each table should be used.

18. What is the decision rule under the net present value method?

19. Identify the steps required in using the internal rate of return method.

20. Erkola Company uses the internal rate of return method. What is the decision rule for this method?

# BRIEF EXERCISES

**BE27–1** The steps in management's decision making process are listed in random order below. Indicate the order in which the steps should be executed.

____ Make decision
____ Identify the opportunity or problem
____ Assign responsibility for decision

____ Review results of decision
____ Determine possible courses of action
____ Develop data relevant to each course of action

*Identify the steps in management's decision making process.*
*(SO 1)*

**BE27–2** Elio Company is considering two alternatives. Alternative A will have sales of $150,000 and costs of $100,000. Alternative B will have sales of $185,000 and costs of $125,000. Compare Alternative A to Alternative B showing incremental revenues, costs, and net income.

*Determine incremental changes.*
*(SO 2)*

*Determine whether to accept special order.*
*(SO 3)*

**BE27–3**   In Radford Company it costs $30 per unit ($20 variable and $10 fixed) to make a product that normally sells for $45. A foreign wholesaler offers to buy 4,000 units at $24 each. Radford will incur special shipping costs of $1 per unit. Assuming that Radford has excess operating capacity, indicate the net income (loss) Radford would realize by accepting the special order.

*Determine whether to make or buy a part.*
*(SO 4)*

**BE27–4**   Yumota Manufacturing incurs unit costs of $8 ($5 variable and $3 fixed) in making a sub-assembly part for its finished product. A supplier offers to make 10,000 of the assembly part at $5.80 per unit. If the offer is accepted, Yumota will save all variable costs but no fixed costs. Prepare an analysis showing the total cost saving, if any, Yumota will realize by buying the part.

*Determine whether to sell or process further.*
*(SO 5)*

**BE27–5**   Woodcraft Inc. makes unfinished bookcases that it sells for $60. Production costs are $30 variable and $10 fixed. Because it has unused capacity, Woodcraft is considering finishing the bookcases and selling them for $70. Variable finishing costs are expected to be $9 per unit with no increase in fixed costs. Prepare an analysis on a per unit basis showing whether Woodcraft should sell unfinished or finished bookcases.

*Determine whether to retain or replace equipment.*
*(SO 6)*

**BE27–6**   Stock Company has a factory machine with a book value of $90,000 and a remaining useful life of 4 years. A new machine is available at a cost of $200,000. This machine will have a 4-year useful life with no salvage value. The new machine will lower annual variable manufacturing costs from $600,000 to $410,000. Prepare an analysis showing whether the old machine should be retained or replaced.

*Determine whether to eliminate an unprofitable segment.*
*(SO 7)*

**BE27–7**   Trevino, Inc., manufactures golf clubs in three models. For the year, the Eagle line has a net loss of $20,000 from sales $200,000, variable expenses $180,000, and fixed expenses $40,000. If the Eagle line is eliminated, $32,000 of fixed costs will remain. Prepare an analysis showing whether the Eagle line should be eliminated.

*Show allocation of limited resources.*
*(SO 8)*

**BE27–8**   In Diaz Company, data concerning two products are: Contribution margin per unit—Product A $8, Product B $12; machine hours required for one unit—Product A 2, Product B 3. Compute the contribution margin per unit of limited resource for each product.

*Compute the cash payback period for a capital investment.*
*(SO 9)*

**BE27–9**   Grace Company is considering purchasing new equipment for $200,000. It is expected that the equipment will produce annual net income of $10,000 over its 5-year useful life. Annual depreciation will be $40,000. Compute the payback period.

*Compute net present value of an investment.*
*(SO 10)*

**BE27–10**   Wilkens Company accumulates the following data concerning a proposed capital investment: cash cost $220,000, annual cash inflow $40,000, present value of cash inflows for 10 years 5.65 (rounded). Determine the net present value, and indicate whether the investment should be made.

# EXERCISES

*Make incremental analysis for special order.*
*(SO 3)*

**E27–1**   Geneva Company manufactures toasters. For the first 8 months of 1997, the company reported the following operating results while operating at 75% of plant capacity:

| | |
|---|---|
| Sales (400,000 units) | $4,000,000 |
| Cost of goods sold | 2,400,000 |
| Gross profit | 1,600,000 |
| Operating expenses | 900,000 |
| Net income | $  700,000 |

Cost of goods sold was 70% variable and 30% fixed; operating expenses were 60% variable and 40% fixed.

In September, Geneva Company receives a special order for 15,000 toasters at $6.20 each from Avante Company of Mexico City. Acceptance of the order would result in $3,000 of shipping costs but no increase in fixed operating expenses.

**Instructions**
(a) Prepare an incremental analysis for the special order.
(b) ▭▭▭▷  Should Geneva Company accept the special order? Why or why not?

**E27–2** Delhi Inc. has been manufacturing its own shades for its table lamps. The company is currently operating at 100% of capacity, and variable manufacturing overhead is charged to production at the rate of 50% of direct labor cost. The direct materials and direct labor cost per unit to make the lamp shades are $4.00 and $6.00, respectively. Normal production is 30,000 table lamps per year.

*Make incremental analysis for make-or-buy decision.*
(SO 4) E

A supplier offers to make the lamp shades at a price of $13.80 per unit. If Delhi Inc. accepts the supplier's offer, all variable manufacturing costs will be eliminated, but the $40,000 of fixed manufacturing overhead currently being charged to the lamp shades will have to be absorbed by other products.

**Instructions**
(a) Prepare the incremental analysis for the decision to make or buy the lamp shades.
(b) ▥▭▭▷ Should Delhi Inc. buy the lamps?
(c) ▥▭▭▷ Would your answer be different in (b) if the productive capacity released by discontinuing making the lamp shades could be used to produce income of $35,000?

**E27–3** Diana O'Shea recently opened her own basketweaving studio. She sells finished baskets in addition to the raw materials needed by customers to weave baskets of their own. Diana has put together a variety of raw material kits, each including materials at various stages of completion. Unfortunately, owing to space limitations, Diana is unable to carry all varieties of kits originally assembled and must choose between two basic packages.

*Make incremental analysis for further processing of materials.*
(SO 5) E

The basic introductory kit includes undyed, uncut reeds (with dye included) for weaving one basket. This basic package costs Diana $12 and sells for $27. The second kit, called Stage 2, includes cut reeds that have already been dyed. With this kit the customer need only soak the reeds and weave the basket. Diana is able to produce the second kit by using the basic materials included in the first kit and adding one hour of her own time, which she values at $16 per hour. Because she is more efficient at cutting and dying reeds than her average customer, Diana is able to make two kits of the dyed reeds, in one hour, from one kit of undyed reeds. The kit of dyed reeds sells for $31.

**Instructions**
Determine whether Diana's basketweaving shop should carry the basic introductory kit with undyed reeds or the Stage 2 kit with reeds already dyed. Prepare an incremental analysis to support your answer.

**E27–4** YPSI Enterprises uses a word processing computer to handle its sales invoices. Lately, business has been so good that it takes an extra 3 hours per night, plus every third Saturday, to keep up with the volume of sales invoices. Management is considering updating its computer with a faster model that would eliminate all of the overtime processing.

*Make incremental analysis for retaining or replacing equipment.*
(SO 6) E

|  | **Current Machine** | **New Machine** |
|---|---|---|
| Original purchase cost | $15,000 | $24,000 |
| Accumulated depreciation | 6,000 | — |
| Estimated operating costs | 21,000 | 15,600 |
| Useful life | 5 years | 5 years |

If sold now, the current machine would have a salvage value of $3,000. If operated for the remainder of its useful life, the current machine would have zero salvage value. The new machine is expected to have zero salvage value after five years.

**Instructions**
Should the current machine be replaced? (Ignore the time value of money.)

**E27–5** Lori Samson, a recent graduate of Rolling's accounting program, evaluated the operating performance of Watkin Company's six divisions. Lori made the following presentation to Watkin's Board of Directors and suggested the Hudson Division be eliminated. "If the Hudson Division is eliminated," she said, "our total profits would increase by $16,870."

*Make incremental analysis concerning elimination of division.*
(SO 7) E

|  | The Other Five Divisions | Hudson Division | Total |
|---|---|---|---|
| Sales | $1,664,200 | $ 98,200 | $1,762,400 |
| Cost of goods sold | 978,520 | 76,470 | 1,054,990 |
| Gross profit | 685,680 | 21,730 | 707,410 |
| Operating expenses | 527,940 | 38,600 | 566,540 |
| Net income | $ 157,740 | $(16,870) | $ 140,870 |

In the Hudson Division, cost of goods sold is $62,000 variable and $14,470 fixed, and operating expenses are $12,000 variable and $24,600 fixed. None of the Hudson Division's fixed costs will be eliminated if the division is discontinued.

**Instructions**

▷  Is Lori right about eliminating the Hudson Division? Prepare a schedule to support your answer.

*Compute contribution margin and determine the product to be manufactured.*
*(SO 8)*

**E27–6**  Lorenzo Company manufactures and sells three products. Relevant per unit data concerning each product are given below:

|  | Product | | |
|---|---|---|---|
|  | **A** | **B** | **C** |
| Selling price | $8 | $12 | $14 |
| Variable costs and expenses | $4 | $ 9 | $12 |
| Machine hours to produce | 1 | 1 | 2 |

**Instructions**

(a) Compute the contribution margin per unit of the limited resource for each product.

(b) Assuming 1,200 additional machine hours are available, which product should be manufactured?

(c) Prepare an analysis showing the total contribution margin if the additional hours are (1) divided equally among the products, and (2) allocated entirely to the product identified in (b) above.

*Compute cash payback period and annual rate of return.*
*(SO 9)*

**E27–7**  Waldo Service Center just purchased an automobile hoist for $9,000. The hoist has a 5-year life and an estimated salvage value of $680. Installation costs and freight charges were $2,900 and $580, respectively. Waldo uses straight-line depreciation.

The new hoist will be used to replace mufflers and tires on automobiles. Waldo estimates that the new hoist will enable his mechanics to replace four extra mufflers per week. Each muffler sells for $65 installed. The cost of a muffler is $35 and the labor cost to install a muffler is $10.

**Instructions**

(a) Compute the payback period for the new hoist.

(b) Compute the annual rate of return for the new hoist. (Round to one decimal.)

*Compute cash payback period and net present value.*
*(SO 9, 10)*

**E27–8**  Yeong Manufacturing Company is considering three new projects, each requiring an equipment investment of $21,000. Each project will last for three years and produce the following cash inflows:

| Year | AA | BB | CC |
|---|---|---|---|
| 1 | $ 7,500 | $ 9,500 | $13,000 |
| 2 | 9,000 | 9,500 | 9,000 |
| 3 | 15,000 | 9,500 | 11,000 |
| Total | $31,500 | $28,500 | $33,000 |

The equipment's salvage value is zero, and Karst uses straight-line depreciation. Yeong will not accept any project with a payback period over two years. Yeong's minimum required rate of return is 15%.

## Instructions

(a) Compute each project's payback period, indicating the most desirable project and the least desirable project using this method. (Round to two decimals.)
(b) Compute the net present value of each project. Does your evaluation change? (Round to nearest dollar.)

**E27–9** Erika Company is considering a capital investment of $180,000 in additional productive facilities. The new machinery is expected to have a useful life of 6 years with no salvage value. Depreciation is by the straight-line method. During the life of the investment, annual net income and cash inflows are expected to be $18,000 and $48,000 respectively. Erika has a 15% cost of capital rate which is the minimum acceptable rate of return on the investment.

*Compute annual rate of return, cash payback period, and net present value.*
*(SO 9, 10)*

## Instructions
(Round to two decimals.)

(a) Compute (1) the annual rate of return and (2) the cash payback period on the proposed capital expenditure.
(b) Using the discounted cash flow technique, compute the net present value.

**E27–10** McBride Company is considering three capital expenditure projects. Relevant data for the projects are as follows:

*Determine internal rate of return.*
*(SO 10)*

| Project | Investment | Annual Income | Life of Project |
|---|---|---|---|
| 22A | $240,000 | $18,500 | 6 years |
| 23A | 270,000 | 25,400 | 9 years |
| 24A | 288,000 | 20,000 | 8 years |

Annual income is constant over the life of the project. Each project is expected to have zero salvage value at the end of the project. McBride Company uses the straight-line method of depreciation.

## Instructions

(a) Determine the internal rate of return for each project. Round the internal rate of return factor to three decimals.
(b) If McBride Company's minimum required rate of return is 12%, which projects are acceptable?

# PROBLEMS

**P27–1** Super Sports Inc. manufactures basketballs for the National Basketball Association (NBA). For the first 6 months of 1997, the company reported the following operating results while operating at 90% of plant capacity.

*Make incremental analysis for special order and identify nonfinancial factors in decision.*
*(SO 3)*

| | Amount | Per Unit |
|---|---|---|
| Sales | $4,500,000 | $50.00 |
| Cost of goods sold | 3,600,000 | 40.00 |
| Selling and administrative expenses | 360,000 | 4.00 |
| Net income | $ 540,000 | $ 6.00 |

Fixed costs for the period were: cost of goods sold $900,000, and selling and administrative expenses $180,000.

In July, normally a slack manufacturing month, Super Sports receives a special order for 10,000 basketballs at $33 each from the Italian Basketball Association (IBA). Acceptance of the order would increase variable selling and administrative expenses $.35 per unit because of shipping costs but would not increase fixed costs and expenses.

## Instructions

(a) Prepare an incremental analysis for the special order.
(b) Should Super Sports Inc. accept the special order?

(c) What is the minimum selling price on the special order to produce net income of $2.20 per ball?

(d) ▭▭▭▷ What nonfinancial factors should management consider in making its decision?

*Make incremental analysis related to make or buy; consider opportunity cost, and identify nonfinancial factors. (SO 4)*

**P27–2** The management of LaJolla Manufacturing Company is trying to decide whether to continue manufacturing a part or to buy it from an outside supplier. The part, called WISCO, is a component of the company's finished product.

The following information was collected from the accounting records and production data for the year ending December 31, 1997:

1. 7,000 units of WISCO were produced in the Machining Department.
2. Variable manufacturing costs applicable to the production of each WISCO unit were: direct materials $4.75, direct labor $4.60, indirect labor $0.45, utilities $0.35.
3. Fixed manufacturing costs applicable to the production of WISCO were:

| Cost Item | Direct | Allocated |
|---|---|---|
| Depreciation | $1,600 | $ 900 |
| Property taxes | 400 | 200 |
| Insurance | 900 | 600 |
|  | $2,900 | $1,700 |

All variable manufacturing and direct fixed costs will be eliminated if WISCO is purchased. Allocated costs will have to be absorbed by other production departments.

4. The lowest quotation for 7,000 WISCO units from a supplier is $74,000.
5. If WISCO units are purchased, freight and inspection costs would be $0.30 per unit, and receiving costs totaling $750 per year would be incurred by the Machining Department.

**Instructions**
(a) Prepare an incremental analysis for WISCO. Your analysis should have columns for (1) Make WISCO, (2) Buy WISCO, and (3) Net Income Increase/Decrease.
(b) Based on your analysis, what decision should management make?
(c) Would the decision be different if LaJolla Company has the opportunity to produce $4,000 of net income with the facilities currently being used to manufacture WISCO? Show computations.
(d) ▭▭▭▷ What nonfinancial factors should management consider in making its decision?

*Compute contribution margin and prepare incremental analysis concerning elimination of divisions. (SO 7)*

**P27–3** Bronx Manufacturing Company has four operating divisions. During the first quarter of 1997, the company reported aggregate income from operations of $165,000 and the following divisional results:

|  | **Division** | | | |
|---|---|---|---|---|
|  | **I** | **II** | **III** | **IV** |
| Sales | $490,000 | $410,000 | $300,000 | $200,000 |
| Cost of goods sold | 300,000 | 250,000 | 270,000 | 180,000 |
| Selling and administrative expenses | 60,000 | 80,000 | 35,000 | 60,000 |
| Income (loss) from operations | $130,000 | $ 80,000 | $ (5,000) | $ (40,000) |

Analysis reveals the following percentages of variable costs in each division.

|  | I | II | III | IV |
|---|---|---|---|---|
| Cost of goods sold | 70% | 80% | 75% | 90% |
| Selling and administrative expenses | 40 | 50 | 60 | 70 |

Discontinuance of any division would save 50% of the fixed costs and expenses for that division.

Top management is very concerned about the unprofitable divisions (III and IV). Consensus is that one or both of the divisions should be discontinued.

*Instructions*

(a) Compute the contribution margin for Divisions III and IV.

(b) Prepare an incremental analysis concerning the possible discontinuance of (1) Division III and (2) Division IV. What course of action do you recommend for each division?

(c) Prepare a columnar condensed income statement for Bronx Manufacturing, assuming Division IV is eliminated. Use the CVP format. Division IV's unavoidable fixed costs are allocated equally to the continuing divisions.

(d) Reconcile the total income from operations ($165,000) with the total income from operations without Division IV.

**P27–4** The Kara and Travis partnership is considering three long-term capital investment proposals. Each investment has a useful life of 5 years. Relevant data on each project are as follows:

*Compute rate of return, cash payback, and net present value.*
*(SO 9, 10)*

| | **Project Tic** | **Project Tac** | **Project Toe** |
|---|---|---|---|
| Capital investment | $140,000 | $160,000 | $200,000 |
| Annual net income: | | | |
| Year 1 | 13,000 | 18,000 | 27,000 |
| 2 | 13,000 | 17,000 | 22,000 |
| 3 | 13,000 | 16,000 | 21,000 |
| 4 | 13,000 | 12,000 | 18,000 |
| 5 | 13,000 | 9,000 | 7,000 |
| Total | $ 65,000 | $ 72,000 | $ 95,000 |

Depreciation is computed by the straight-line method with no salvage value. The company's cost of capital is 15%.

*Instructions*

(a) Compute the annual rate of return for each project. (Round to two decimals.)

(b) Compute the cash payback period for each project. (Round to two decimals.)

(c) Compute the net present value for each project. (Round to nearest dollar.)

(d) Rank the projects on each of the foregoing bases. Which project do you recommend?

**P27–5** Jane Kato is an accounting major at a midwestern state university located approximately 60 miles from a major city. Many of the students attending the university are from the metropolitan area and visit their homes regularly on the weekends. Jane, an entrepreneur at heart, realizes that few good commuting alternatives are available for students doing weekend travel. She believes that a weekend commuting service could be organized and run profitably from several suburban and downtown shopping mall locations. Jane has gathered the following investment information:

*Compute annual rate of return, cash payback, and net present value.*
*(SO 9, 10)*

1. Six used vans would cost a total of $67,500 to purchase and would have a 3-year useful life with negligible salvage value. Jane plans to use straight-line depreciation.

2. Ten drivers would have to be employed at a total payroll expense of $48,000.

3. Other annual out of pocket expenses associated with running the commuter service would include Gasoline $12,000, Maintenance $2,800, Repairs $3,500, Insurance $3,200, Advertising $1,500.

4. Jane has visited several financial institutions to discuss funding for her new venture. The best interest rate she has been able to negotiate is 12%. Use this rate for cost of capital.

5. Jane expects each van to make nine round trips weekly and carry an average of five students each trip. The service is expected to operate 30 weeks each year, and each student will be charged $12.00 for a round-trip ticket.

*Instructions*

(a) Determine the annual (1) net income, and (2) cash inflow for the commuter service.

(b) Compute (1) the annual rate of return, and (2) the cash payback period. (Round to two decimals.)

(c) Compute the net present value of the commuter service. (Round to the nearest dollar.)

(d) ▰▰▰▷ What should Jane conclude from these computations?

# ALTERNATE PROBLEMS

∙∙∙∙∙∙∙∙∙∙∙∙∙∙∙∙∙∙∙∙∙∙∙∙∙∙∙∙∙∙∙∙∙∙∙∙∙∙∙∙∙∙∙∙∙∙∙∙∙∙∙∙∙∙∙∙∙∙∙∙∙∙∙∙∙∙∙∙∙∙∙∙∙∙∙∙∙∙∙

*Make incremental analysis for special order and identify nonfinancial factors in decisions.*
(SO 3)

**P27–1A**   Murr Company is currently producing 16,000 units per month, which is 80% of its production capacity. Variable manufacturing costs are currently $11.00 per unit, and fixed manufacturing costs are $48,000 per month. Murr pays a 9% sales commission to its sales people, has $30,000 in fixed administrative expenses per month, and is averaging $320,000 in sales per month.

   A special order received from a foreign company would enable Murr Company to operate at 100% capacity. The foreign company offered to pay 75% of Murr's current selling price per unit. If the order is accepted, Murr will have to spend an extra $2.00 per unit to package the product for overseas shipping. Also, Murr Company would need to lease a new stamping machine to imprint the foreign company's logo on the product, at a monthly cost of $2,500. The special order would require a sales commission of $3,000.

**Instructions**

(a) Compute the number of units involved in the special order and the foreign company's offered price per unit.

(b) What is the manufacturing cost of producing one unit of Murr's product for regular customers?

(c) Prepare an incremental analysis of the special order. Should management accept the order?

(d) What is the lowest price that Murr could accept for the special order to earn net income of $1.20 per unit?

(e) ▭▭▭▭▭▷  What nonfinancial factors should management consider in making its decision?

*Make incremental analysis related to make or buy, consider opportunity cost, and identify nonfinancial factors.*
(SO 4)

**P27–2A**   The management of Morocco Manufacturing Company has asked for your assistance in deciding whether to continue manufacturing a part or to buy it from an outside supplier. The part, called Tropica, is a component of Morocco's finished product.

   An analysis of the accounting records and the production data revealed the following information for the year ending December 31, 1996:

1. The Machinery Department produced 36,000 units of Tropica.

2. Each Tropica unit requires 10 minutes to produce. Three people in the Machinery Department work full time (2,000 hours per year) producing Tropica. Each person is paid $10.00 per hour.

3. The cost of materials per Tropica unit is $2.00.

4. Manufacturing costs directly applicable to the production of Tropica are: indirect labor, $5,500; utilities, $1,300; depreciation, $1,600; property taxes and insurance, $1,000. All of the costs will be eliminated if Tropica is purchased.

5. The lowest price for a Tropica from an outside supplier is $3.50 per unit. Freight charges will be $0.30 per unit, and a part-time receiving clerk at $8,500 per year will be required.

6. If Tropica is purchased, the excess space will be used to store Morocco's finished product. Currently, Morocco rents storage space at approximately $0.50 per unit stored per year. Approximately 4,500 units per year are stored in the rented space.

**Instructions**

(a) Prepare an incremental analysis for the make or buy decision. Should Morocco make or buy the part? Why?

(b) Prepare an incremental analysis, assuming the released facilities can be used to produce $10,000 of net income in addition to the savings on the rental of storage space. What decision should now be made?

(c) ▭▭▭▭▭▷  What nonfinancial factors should be considered in the decision?

*Compute contribution margin and prepare incremental analysis concerning elimination of divisions.*
(SO 7)

**P27–3A**   Northwest Manufacturing Company has four operating divisions. During the first quarter of 1996, the company reported total income from operations of $61,000 and the following results for the divisions:

## Division

| | Denver | Helena | Portland | Seattle |
|---|---|---|---|---|
| Sales | $450,000 | $730,000 | $920,000 | $520,000 |
| Cost of goods sold | 380,000 | 480,000 | 576,000 | 430,000 |
| Selling and administrative expenses | 120,000 | 207,000 | 246,000 | 120,000 |
| Income (loss) from operations | $ (50,000) | $ 43,000 | $ 98,000 | $ (30,000) |

Analysis reveals the following percentages of variable costs in each division.

| | Denver | Helena | Portland | Seattle |
|---|---|---|---|---|
| Cost of goods sold | 95% | 80% | 90% | 90% |
| Selling and administrative expenses | 80 | 60 | 70 | 60 |

Discontinuance of any division would save 60% of the fixed costs and expenses for that division.

Top management is deeply concerned about the unprofitable divisions (Denver and Seattle). The consensus is that one or both of the divisions should be eliminated.

**Instructions**

(a) Compute the contribution margin for the two unprofitable divisions.

(b) Prepare an incremental analysis concerning the possible elimination of (1) the Denver Division and (2) the Seattle Division. What course of action do you recommend for each division?

(c) Prepare a columnar condensed income statement using the CVP format for Northwest Manufacturing Company, assuming (1) the Denver Division is eliminated, and (2) the unavoidable fixed costs and expenses of the Denver Division are allocated 30% to Helena, 50% to Portland, and 20% to Seattle.

(d) Compare the total income from operations with the Denver Division ($61,000) to total income from operations without this division.

**P27–4A** The partnership of Moe and Street is considering three long-term capital investment proposals. Relevant data on each project are as follows:

*Compute rate of return, cash payback, and net present value.*
*(SO 9, 10)*

## Project

| | Brown | Red | Yellow |
|---|---|---|---|
| Capital investment | $180,000 | $225,000 | $250,000 |
| Annual net income: | | | |
| Year 1 | 25,000 | 20,000 | 26,000 |
| 2 | 16,000 | 20,000 | 24,000 |
| 3 | 13,000 | 20,000 | 23,000 |
| 4 | 10,000 | 20,000 | 22,000 |
| 5 | 8,000 | 20,000 | 20,000 |
| Total | $72,000 | $100,000 | $115,000 |

Salvage value is expected to be zero at the end of each project. Depreciation is computed by the straight-line method. The company's minimum rate of return is the company's cost of capital which is 12%.

**Instructions**

(a) Compute the average annual rate of return for each project. (Round to two decimals.)

(b) Compute the cash payback period for each project. (Round to two decimals.)

(c) Compute the net present value for each project. (Round to nearest dollar.)

(d) Rank the projects on each of the foregoing bases. What project do you recommend?

**P27–5A** Teresa Zaire is managing director of the Goodwill day care center. Goodwill is currently set up as a full-time child care facility for children between the ages of 12 months and 6 years. Teresa is trying to determine whether the center should expand its facilities to incorporate a newborn care room for infants between the ages of 6 weeks and 12 months. The

*Compute annual rate of return, cash payback, and net present value.*
*(SO 9, 10)*

necessary space already exists. An investment of $23,000 would be needed, however, to purchase cribs, high chairs, etc. The equipment purchased for the room would have a 5-year useful life with zero salvage value.

The newborn nursery would be staffed to handle 12 infants on a full-time basis. The parents of each infant would be charged $150 weekly, and the facility would operate 52 weeks of the year. Staffing the nursery would require two full-time specialists and five part-time assistants at an annual cost of $74,000. Food, diapers, and other miscellaneous supplies are expected to total $12,500 annually.

***Instructions***
  (a) Determine (1) annual net income and (2) cash inflow for the new nursery.
  (b) Compute (1) the annual rate of return and (2) the cash payback period for the new nursery. (Round to two decimals.)
  (c) Assuming that Goodwill can borrow the money needed for expansion at 12%, compute the net present value of the new room. (Round to the nearest dollar.)
  (d) ▭▭▭▭▶  What should Teresa conclude from these computations?

# ▶*B*roadening Your Perspective

## *F*INANCIAL REPORTING PROBLEM
• • • • • • • • • • • • • • • • • • • • • • • • • • • • • • • • • • • • • • • • • • • • • • • • • • • • • •

Refer to the PepsiCo, Inc. financial statements in Appendix A and answer the following questions:

  (a) Using the chairman's letter to "Dear Friends," what was PepsiCo's total capital spending on its segments in 1994?
  (b) How was the capital spending divided (a) among the segments and (b) between international and domestic?
  (c) From the Industry Segments section (or the Financial Highlights at the beginning of the report) and your answer in question (b) above, how does the capital spending match up with total segment operating profits?
  (d) From the Industry Segments section, what has been the trend in capital spending for each segment and in total from 1989–1994?
  (e) From Investing Activities under Management's Analysis—Cash Flows, what types of capital spending plans does PepsiCo have for 1995?

## *D*ECISION CASE
• • • • • • • • • • • • • • • • • • • • • • • • • • • • • • • • • • • • • • • • • • • • • • • • • • • • • •

Navaro Company is considering the purchase of a new machine. The invoice price of the machine is $115,000, freight charges are estimated to be $4,000, and installation costs are expected to be $6,000. Salvage value of the new equipment is expected to be zero after a useful life of 4 years. Existing equipment could be retained and used for an additional 4 years if the new machine is not purchased. At that time, the salvage value of the equipment would be zero. If the new machine is purchased now, the existing machine would have to be scrapped. Navaro's accountant, Darcy Hank, has accumulated the following data regarding annual sales and expenses with and without the new machine:

  1. Without the new machine, Navaro can sell 11,000 units of product annually at a per unit selling price of $100. If the new unit is purchased, the number of units produced and sold would increase by 20%, and the selling price would remain the same.
  2. The new machine is faster than the old machine, and it is more efficient in its usage of materials. With the old machine the gross profit rate will be 26.5% of sales, whereas the rate will be 28% of sales with the new machine.
  3. Annual selling expenses are $180,000 with the current equipment. Because the new equipment would produce a greater number of units to be sold, annual selling expenses are expected to increase by 10% if it is purchased.

4. Annual administrative expenses are expected to be $100,000 with the old machine, and $113,000 with the new machine.

5. The current book value of the existing machine is $36,000. Navaro uses straight-line depreciation.

6. Navaro's management wants a minimum rate of return of 15% on its investment and a payback period of no more than 3 years.

**Instructions**
(Ignore income tax effects.)

(a) Prepare an incremental analysis for the 4 years showing whether Navaro should keep the existing machine or buy the new machine.

(b) Calculate the annual rate of return for the new machine. (Round to two decimals.)

(c) Compute the payback period for the new machine. (Round to two decimals.)

(d) Compute the net present value of the new machine. (Round to the nearest dollar.)

(e) On the basis of the foregoing data, would you recommend that Navaro buy the machine? Why?

# COMMUNICATION ACTIVITY
•••••••••••••••••••••••••••••••••••••••••••••••••••••••••••••••••••••

Refer back to Exercise 27–7 to address the following:

**Instructions**
Prepare a memo to Mary Ann Griffin, your supervisor. Show your calculations from E27–7, (a) and (b). In one or two paragraphs, discuss important nonfinancial considerations. Make any assumptions you believe to be necessary. Make a recommendation, based on your analysis.

# GROUP ACTIVITY
•••••••••••••••••••••••••••••••••••••••••••••••••••••••••••••••••••••

Electro-More manufactures private-label small electronic products, such as alarm clocks, calculators, kitchen timers, stopwatches, and automatic pencil sharpeners. Some of the products are sold as sets, and others are sold individually. Products are studied as to their sales potential, and then cost estimates are made. The Engineering Department develops production plans, and then production begins. The company has generally had very successful product introduction. Only two products introduced by the company have been discontinued.

One of the products currently sold is a multi-alarm alarm clock. The clock has four alarms that can be programmed to sound at various times and for varying lengths of time. The company has experienced a great deal of difficulty in making the circuit boards for the clocks. The production process has never operated smoothly. The product is unprofitable at the present time, primarily because of warranty repairs and product recalls. Two models of the clocks were recalled, for example, because they sometimes caused an electric shock when the alarms were being shut off. The Engineering Department is attempting to revise the manufacturing process, but the revision will take another 6 months at least.

The clocks were very popular when they were introduced, and since they are private-label, the company has not suffered much from the recalls. Presently, the company has a very large order for several items from Kmart Stores. The order includes 5,000 of the multi-alarm clocks. When the company suggested that Kmart purchase the clocks from another manufacturer, Kmart threatened to rescind the entire order unless the clocks were included.

The company has therefore investigated the possibility of having another company make the clocks for them. The clocks were bid for the Kmart order based on an estimated $5 cost to manufacture:

| | |
|---|---|
| Circuit board, 1 each @ $1.50 | $1.50 |
| Plastic case, 1 each @ $0.50 | 0.50 |
| Alarms, 4 @ $0.10 each | 0.10 |
| Labor, 15 minutes @ $10/hour | 2.50 |
| Overhead, $1.60 per labor hour | 0.40 |

Electro-More could purchase clocks to fill the Kmart order for $10 from Silver Star, a Korean manufacturer with a very good quality record. Silver Star has offered to reduce the price to $7.50 after Electro-More has been a customer for 6 months, placing an order of at least 1,000 units per month. If Electro-More becomes a "preferred customer" by purchasing 15,000 units per year, the price would be reduced still further to $4.50.

Alpha Products, a local manufacturer, has also offered to make clocks for Electro-More. They have offered to sell 5,000 clocks for $3 each. However, Alpha Products has been in business for only 6 months. They have experienced significant turnover in their labor force, and the local press has reported that the owners may face tax evasion charges soon. The owner of Alpha Products is an electronic engineer, however, and the quality of the clocks is likely to be good.

If Electro-More decides to purchase the clocks from either Silver Star or Alpha, all the costs to manufacture could be avoided, except a total of $5,000 in overhead costs for machine depreciation. The machinery is fairly new, and has no alternate use.

### Instructions

In groups of four to five, answer the following questions:

(a) What is the difference in profit under each of the alternatives if the clocks are to be sold for $12.50 each to Kmart?

(b) What are the most important nonfinancial factors that Electro-More should consider when making this decision?

(c) What do you think Electro-More should do in regard to the Kmart order? What should it do in regard to continuing to manufacture the multi-alarm alarm clocks? Be prepared to defend your answer.

# ETHICS CASE

Bristle Brush Company operates in a state where corporate taxes and workmen's compensation insurance rates have recently doubled. Bristle's president has just assigned you the task of preparing an economic analysis and making a recommendation relative to moving the company's entire operation to Missouri. The president is slightly in favor of such a move because Missouri is his boyhood home and he also owns a fishing lodge there.

You have just completed building your dream house, moved in, and sodded the lawn. Your children are all doing well in school and sports and, along with your spouse, want no part of a move to Missouri. If the company does move, so will you because the town is a one-industry community and you and your spouse will have to move to have employment. Moving when everyone else does will cause you to take a big loss on the sale of your house. The same hardships will be suffered by your coworkers, and the town will be devastated.

In compiling the costs of moving versus not moving, you have latitude in the assumptions you make, the estimates you compute, and the discount rates and time periods you project. You are in a position to influence the decision singlehandedly.

### Instructions

(a) Who are the stakeholders in this situation?

(b) What are the ethical issues in this situation?

(c) What would you do in this situation?

# CRITICAL THINKING
## ▸ *A Real-World Focus: Beverly Hills Fan Company*

*Founded in 1983, the **Beverly Hills Fan Company** is located in Woodland Hills, California. With 23 employees and sales of less than $10 million, the company is relatively small. Management feels that there is potential for growth in the upscale market for ceiling fans and lighting. They are particularly optimistic about growth in Mexican and Canadian markets.*

Presented below is information from the President's letter in the company's annual report:

PRESIDENT'S LETTER:

An aggressive product development program was initiated during the past year resulting in new ceiling fan models planned for introduction in 1993. Award winning industrial designer Ron Rezek created several new fan models for the Beverly Hills Fan and L.A. Fan lines, including a new Showroom Collection, designed specifically for the architectural and designer markets. Each of these models has received critical acclaim, and order commitments for 1993 have been outstanding. Additionally, our Custom Color and special order fans continued to enjoy increasing popularity and sales gains as more and more customers desire fans that match their specific interior decors. Currently, Beverly Hills Fan Company offers a product line of over 100 models of contemporary, traditional, and transitional ceiling fans.

*Instructions*
(a) What points did the company management need to consider before deciding to offer the special-order fans to customers?
(b) How would incremental analysis be employed to assist in this decision?

---

*Answers to Self-Study Questions*
1. d    2. b    3. c    4. d    5. a    6. b    7. c    8. b    9. d    10. b

# APPENDIX · A

# SPECIMEN FINANCIAL STATEMENTS

## The Annual Report

Once each year a corporation communicates to its stockholders and other interested parties by issuing a complete set of audited financial statements. The **annual report**, as this communication is called, summarizes the financial results of its operation for the year and its plans for the future. Many such annual reports have become attractive, multicolored, glossy public relations ad pieces containing pictures of corporate officers and directors as well as photos and descriptions of new products and new buildings. Yet the basic function of every annual report is to report financial information, almost all of which is a product of the corporation's accounting system.

The content and organization of corporate annual reports have become fairly standardized. Excluding the public relations part of the report (pictures, products, and propaganda), the following items are the traditional financial portions of the annual report:

Financial Highlights
Letter to the Stockholders
Management's Report
Auditor's Report
Financial Statements (and Management's Analysis)
Notes to the Financial Statements
Supplementary Financial Information

In this appendix we illustrate current financial reporting with a comprehensive set of corporate financial statements that are prepared in accordance with generally accepted accounting principles and audited by an international independent certified public accounting firm. We are grateful for permission to use the actual financial statements and other accompanying financial information from the annual report of a large, publicly held company, PepsiCo, Inc.

**Net Sales**
($ in Millions)

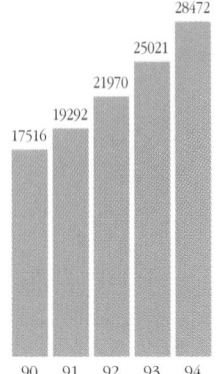

## ◢ *F*inancial Highlights

The financial highlights section, called the **Financial Summary** by PepsiCo, is usually presented inside the front cover or on the first two pages of the annual report. This section generally reports the total or per share amounts for five to ten financial items for the current year and one or more previous years. Financial items from the income statement and the balance sheet that typically are presented are sales, income from continuing operations, net income, net income per share, dividends per common share, and the amount of capital expenditures. The financial highlights section from PepsiCo's **Annual Report** is shown below:

# PepsiCo, Inc.

**Income From
Continuing
Operations**
($ in Millions)

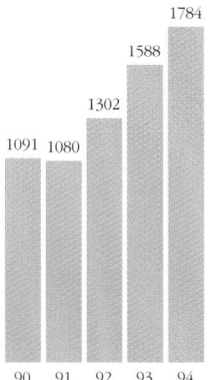

# Financial Highlights

| PepsiCo, Inc. and Subsidiaries<br>(dollars in millions except per share amounts) | **December 31,**<br>**1994** | December 25,<br>1993 | **Percent**<br>**Change** |
|---|---|---|---|
| Net sales | **$28,472** | 25,021 | **+14** |
| Beverages | **$ 9,687** | 8,638 | **+12** |
| Snack foods | **$ 8,264** | 7,027 | **+18** |
| Restaurants | **$10,521** | 9,356 | **+12** |
| Segment operating profits | **$ 3,324** | 3,077 | **+ 8** |
| Beverages | **$ 1,217** | 1,109 | **+10** |
| Snack foods | **$ 1,377** | 1,190 | **+16** |
| Restaurants | **$ 730** | 778 | **– 6** |
| Consolidated operating profit | **$ 3,201** | 2,907 | **+10** |
| Income before cumulative<br>effect of accounting changes | **$ 1,784** | 1,588 | **+12** |
| **Per Share** | **$ 2.22** | 1.96 | **+13** |
| Cumulative effect of accounting changes | **$ (32)** | — | — |
| **Per Share** | **$ (0.04)** | — | — |
| Net income | **$ 1,752** | 1,588 | **(a)** |
| **Per Share** | **$ 2.18** | 1.96 | **(a)** |
| Cash dividends declared | | | |
| **Per Share** | **$ 0.70** | 0.61 | **+15** |
| Net cash provided by operating activities | **$ 3,716** | 3,134 | **+19** |
| Capital spending | **$ 2,288** | 2,008 | **+14** |
| Cash dividends paid | **$ 540** | 462 | **+17** |
| Acquisitions and investments<br>in affiliates | **$ 355** | 1,376 | |
| Purchases of treasury stock | **$ 549** | 464 | |
| Return on average shareholders' equity | **% 27.0** | 27.2 | |

(a)   These comparisons are not meaningful because of two accounting changes in 1994. See Notes 13 and 14.

**Income Per Share
From Continuing
Operations**
(In Dollars)

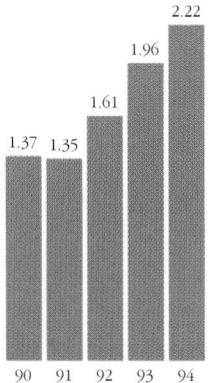

As shown above, PepsiCo chose also to present the percent change from last year to the current year for each of the reported items and net sales and operating profits by segments.

# *L*etter to the Stockholders

Nearly every annual report contains a letter to the stockholders from the Chairman of the Board or the President (or both). This letter typically discusses the company's accomplishments during the past year and highlights significant events such as mergers and acquisitions, new products, operating achievements, business philosophy, changes in officers or directors, financing commitments, expansion plans, and future prospects. The letter to the stockholders ("Dear Friends") signed by Wayne Calloway, Chairman of the Board and Chief Executive Officer of PepsiCo, is shown below:

# Dear Friends:

PepsiCo had a strong year in 1994—for the most part. Sales, earnings and dividends hit all-time highs. Particularly strong were domestic soft drinks and domestic snack foods, our two most profitable businesses.

Our international beverage and snack businesses also had a big year. And across all of our international businesses, sales grew to more than $8 billion. That's bigger than all of PepsiCo was just nine years ago.

On the other hand, our restaurant segment slowed down in 1994. While sales grew a respectable 12% and earnings were nearly three-quarters of a billion dollars, that was still a good bit shy of the remarkable 17% average annual growth our restaurants had posted for well over a decade. In response, we've already realigned and strengthened management and created some promising new programs.

Overall, if you look over at the Financial Highlights page, you'll see it was a good year for PepsiCo, with reported earnings per share growing at 13%. That's faster than the average of our peers in the food, beverage and restaurant businesses. In fact, over the last five years our earnings per share have grown at a compounded annual rate of 14%, faster than the average of our peer companies and a lot faster than the S&P 500.

Looking at our business as a whole, I believe PepsiCo today is strong and healthy. We have some challenges, of course, like getting our restaurants back up to speed and managing the impact of a devalued Mexican peso. Still, we anticipate solid operating profit growth in 1995.

Even better, the opportunity farther out is almost breathtaking. The markets in which we compete add up to over half a trillion dollars, and they're growing. I believe we have a better shot at capturing a big piece of that than any other company on earth, which is exactly what we plan to do.

### Measuring the Business

PepsiCo's ability to turn opportunities into success depends on two things. First, how we respond to changes in the marketplace. Second, the overall health of the company.

Usually in these reports we talk more about how we're pursuing market opportunities by reaching out to consumers—things like new products and new brand strategies. Rest assured we continue to keep a sharp eye on the consumer, and we'll certainly report on some of what we've been doing.

But mostly I'd like to share with you a little about the basic health of PepsiCo. How we measure the business. How we gauge our progress. What we look at to determine if we're on the right track.

In other words, some of the ways we evaluate and manage this big, complex, growing enterprise.

By doing this, I hope to give you a better sense of why I believe PepsiCo will give shareholders a wonderful return on their investment over the long haul.

**Earnings Per Share Growth**
(In Percent. Indexed at 12/31/89)

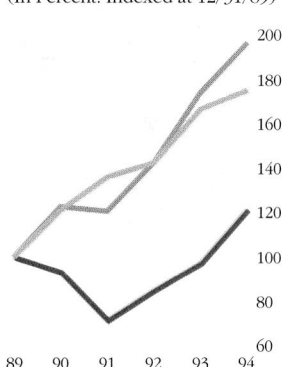

**Cumulative Total Return**
(In Dollars. Indexed at 12/31/89)

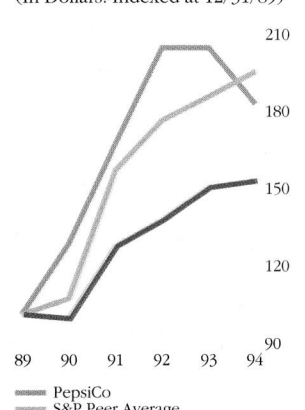

PepsiCo
S&P Peer Average
S&P 500

### Four of Our Yardsticks

There are different ways to look at different businesses. Because PepsiCo is a very large, multi-line, growth-oriented consumer products company, we look primarily at four measurements:

- Volume growth.
- Operating profit growth.
- Cash growth.
- Investment returns.

Here's how I think about them.

### Volume Growth

Other than acquisitions, the only unassailable, completely healthy way for a consumer business to grow year in and year out is to sell more products. In our case this means selling lots more bottles of Pepsi, bags of chips, buckets of chicken. Volume growth is probably the single best gauge of a consumer products company, because it tells us whether we're satisfying consumers and how we're doing against our competitors.

In 1994, volume was up at nearly all our businesses, especially in beverages and snack foods. At Frito-Lay, for example, we had our first year of double-digit volume growth ever, a particularly remarkable feat when you think Frito-Lay already has been one of the most successful food companies in the world for years. International beverages had its strongest volume growth in over a decade. And our oldest business, domestic beverages, bounded along at a 6% rate—its best since 1988.

Even in our restaurants, which had a disappointing year overall, there were some encouraging volume signs. KFC's volume growth was the best in four years. And Taco Bell posted its sixth consecutive year of volume growth. During that time Taco Bell's volume grew at a compounded annual rate of 11%.

So in terms of volume growth, most of our businesses are doing just fine.

### Operating Profit Growth

Now obviously volume has to grow in a way that's profitable. And when you combine our strong volume growth with good profit margins, you're headed for the kind of operating profits that would make any investor smile. Over the last five years, our operating profit margin has been fairly steady, averaging 11%. As a result, our operating profits have grown at a compounded annual rate of 13%.

What's more interesting to the tough-minded among us is that we maintained our profit margins even as we were lowering prices in many of our businesses. The fact is, in competitive businesses like ours, it's pretty hard to raise prices. So to stay competitive and keep our profit margins healthy, we work at improving the way we do things, sometimes in pretty creative ways.

At Taco Bell, for example, we've taken the kitchen, or a good part of it, out of the restaurant. Instead a lot of the food is prepared in central commissaries. That helped Taco Bell to offer top-quality products at terrific prices and achieve operating profit growth greater than almost any big chain for nearly a decade.

So based on operating profit growth, PepsiCo is also in excellent shape.

### Cash Growth

One of my favorite measures of financial strength, and one that says an awful lot about PepsiCo, is cash. I'm talking about what's left after we pay for things like labor and raw materials.

All three of our business segments generate operating cash and plenty of it—totaling nearly $5 billion in 1994. And that's been growing steadily. Our segment

**Volume Growth**
(In Percent)

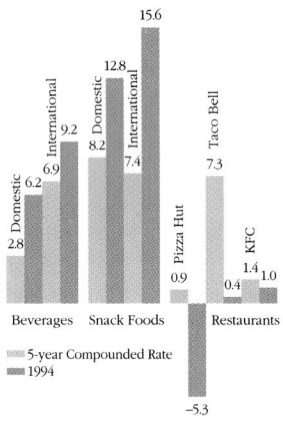

5-year Compounded Rate
1994

**Net Sales
Total: $28,472**
($ in Millions)

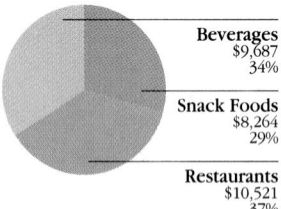

Beverages
$9,687
34%

Snack Foods
$8,264
29%

Restaurants
$10,521
37%

**Segment Operating
Profits Total: $3,324**
($ in Millions)

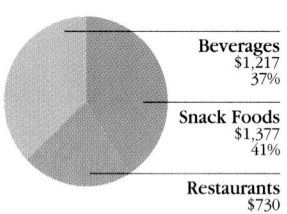

Beverages
$1,217
37%

Snack Foods
$1,377
41%

Restaurants
$730
22%

operating cash grew at 9% in 1994 and at a compounded annual rate of 13% over the past five years.

It's easy to see why a business that produces cash probably has brighter prospects than one that doesn't. But a very strong cash flow, like we produce, gives us the financial muscle to grow year after year. Part of the reason is that a strong cash flow allows us to easily—and comfortably—borrow money if we need it to take advantage of market opportunities.

We have a very deliberate strategy for flexing that financial muscle. Our first priority is to make capital investments in our existing businesses. Second, we acquire new businesses closely related to either beverages, snacks or restaurants. Third, we buy back PepsiCo shares.

Over the last five years with our strong cash flow we've been able to invest over $8 billion in existing businesses, invest nearly $4 billion in new ones, pay $2 billion in dividends and repurchase more than $1 billion worth of PepsiCo stock.

## Investment Returns

Of course when you're investing $3 billion a year, as we did in 1994, it's important to be smart about it. That's where our fourth measurement comes in. We look for our individual investments to produce returns well over our 11% cost of capital. And the higher those returns are, the more value we create for our shareholders.

If you look at our investment in PepsiCo overall, measured by our return on equity, the results are excellent. In 1994 our return on equity was 27%, nearly our best in a decade. And over the last five years it's averaged about 25%.

## Putting It All Together

These four ways we measure and manage our business—volume growth, operating profit growth, cash growth and investment returns—tell me PepsiCo is thriving. I hope you get the same feeling.

Taken all together they offer a clear sign that PepsiCo is strong and growing stronger. Even more important, they tell me that PepsiCo is ready and able to seize the opportunities of its half-trillion-dollar marketplace.

I'll share some more specifics later in this report when I talk about beverages, snacks and restaurants individually.

## Measuring Our People

As important as numbers are to a company, the most important measure is not numerical, it's human.

How well are your executives doing? How about your store managers? Your sales people? Your line workers?

Each year I ask myself if the people who are responsible for our business are getting better. The answer in 1994 is yes, in a big way. All across our company I see talent emerging. Each year I personally review the progress of nearly 800 people in PepsiCo, and my conclusion this year is this: Our people are doing great.

In fact, a recent book on the subject said PepsiCo people are the most sought-after in business, by corporations across America and around the globe. Having met a few thousand of them, I certainly know why. I'd like to thank all our people, all 471,000 of them, for their skill, dedication and hard work. They make my life a joy.

## New Board Member

Speaking of great people I'd like to take this opportunity to introduce Franklin Thomas, the newest member of our Board of Directors. Frank has served 15 years as president of the Ford Foundation, the world's largest philanthropic foundation. Under his

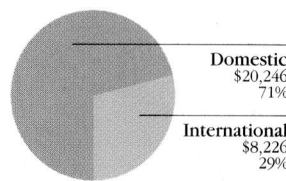

**Net Sales**
**Total: $28,472**
($ in Millions)

Domestic
$20,246
71%

International
$8,226
29%

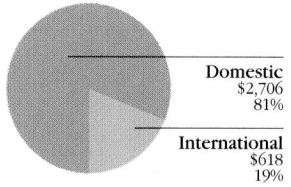

**Segment Operating**
**Profits Total: $3,324**
($ in Millions)

Domestic
$2,706
81%

International
$618
19%

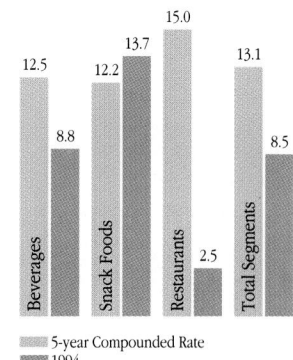

**Segment Operating Cash***
**Growth**
(In Percent)

5-year Compounded Rate
1994

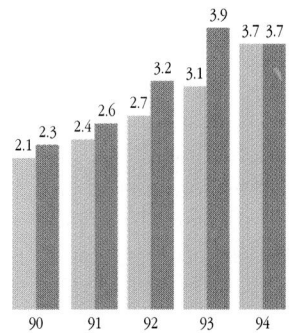

**Consolidated Cash Flows**
($ in Billions)

Consolidated Net Cash Provided by
Operating Activities
Cash Expended for Capital Investments,
Acquisitions, Share Repurchases and
Dividends

**Segment Capital Spending
Total: $2,281**
($ in Millions)

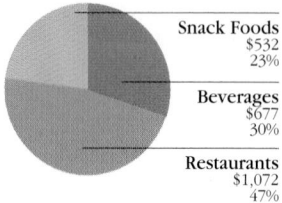

Snack Foods
$532
23%

Beverages
$677
30%

Restaurants
$1,072
47%

**Segment Capital Spending
Total: $2,281**
($ in Millions)

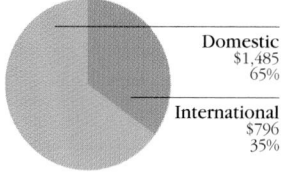

Domestic
$1,485
65%

International
$796
35%

direction, the organization's endowment nearly tripled. Frank's worldwide experience and vision will serve PepsiCo very well. We welcome him to the family.

**A Glorious Future**

So, with opportunities greater than any company on earth—in my unbiased opinion—and nearly a half million bright, talented and resourceful members of the PepsiCo family passionately pursuing them, I'm confident that PepsiCo's future will be even more glorious than its past.

Please read on to learn more about why.

*Wayne Calloway*

Wayne Calloway
Chairman of the Board and Chief Executive Officer

# Management's Report

A relatively recent addition to corporate annual reports is the statement made by management about its role in and responsibility for the accuracy and integrity of the financial statements. PepsiCo's management letter is entitled **Management's Responsibility for Financial Statements**. In it the Chairman of the Board and Chief Executive Officer along with the Chief Financial Officer and the Controller, on behalf of management do the following: (1) assume primary responsibility for the financial statements and the related notes, (2) outline and assess the company's internal control system, (3) declare the financial statements in conformity with generally accepted accounting principles, and (4) comment on the audit by the certified public accountant and the composition and role of the Audit Committee of the Board of Directors. PepsiCo's management report is presented below:

# Management's Responsibility for Financial Statements

To Our Shareholders:

Management is responsible for the reliability of the consolidated financial statements and related notes, which have been prepared in conformity with generally accepted accounting principles and include amounts based upon our estimates and judgments, as required. The financial statements have been audited and reported on by our independent auditors, KPMG Peat Marwick LLP, who were given free access to all financial records and related data, including minutes of the meetings of the Board of Directors and Committees of the Board. We believe that the representations made to the independent auditors were valid and appropriate.

PepsiCo maintains a system of internal control over financial reporting designed to provide reasonable assurance as to the reliability of the financial statements. The system is supported by formal policies and procedures, including an active Code of Conduct program intended to ensure employees adhere to the highest standards of personal and professional integrity. PepsiCo's internal audit function monitors and reports on the adequacy of and compliance with the internal control system, and appropriate actions are taken to address significant control deficiencies and other opportunities for improving the system as they are identified. The Audit Committee of the Board of Directors, which is composed solely of outside directors, provides oversight to the financial reporting process through periodic meetings with our independent auditors, internal auditors and management. Both our independent auditors and internal auditors have free access to the Audit Committee.

Although no cost effective internal control system will preclude all errors and irregularities, we believe our controls as of December 31, 1994 provide reasonable assurance that the financial statements are reliable.

*Wayne Calloway*

Wayne Calloway
Chairman of the Board and Chief Executive Officer

*Robert H Dettmer*

Robert G. Dettmer
Executive Vice President and Chief Financial Officer

*Robert L Carleton*

Robert L. Carleton
Senior Vice President and Controller

February 7, 1995

# Auditor's Report

All publicly held corporations, as well as many other enterprises and organizations (both profit and not-for-profit, large and small) engage the services of independent certified public accountants for the purpose of obtaining an objective, expert report on their financial statements. Based on a comprehensive examination of the company's accounting system and records, and the financial statements, the outside CPA issues the auditor's report.

The standard auditor's report consists of three paragraphs: (1) an introductory paragraph, (2) a scope paragraph, and (3) the opinion paragraph. In the **introductory paragraph**, the auditor identifies who and what was audited and indicates the responsibilities of management and the auditor relative to the financial statements. In the **scope paragraph** the auditor states that the audit was conducted in accordance with generally accepted auditing standards and discusses the nature and limitations of the audit. In the **opinion paragraph**, the auditor expresses an informed opinion as to (1) the fairness of the financial statements and (2) their conformity with generally accepted accounting principles. The **Report of KPMG Peat Marwick Independent Auditors** appearing in PepsiCo's Annual Report is shown below:

# Report of Independent Auditors

Board of Directors and Shareholders
PepsiCo, Inc.

We have audited the accompanying consolidated balance sheet of PepsiCo, Inc. and Subsidiaries as of December 31, 1994 and December 25, 1993, and the related consolidated statements of income, cash flows and shareholders' equity for each of the years in the three-year period ended December 31, 1994. These consolidated financial statements are the responsibility of PepsiCo, Inc.'s management. Our responsibility is to express an opinion on these consolidated financial statements based on our audits.

We conducted our audits in accordance with generally accept-

ed auditing standards. Those standards require that we plan and perform the audit to obtain reasonable assurance about whether the financial statements are free of material misstatement. An audit includes examining, on a test basis, evidence supporting the amounts and disclosures in the financial statements. An audit also includes assessing the accounting principles used and significant estimates made by management, as well as evaluating the overall financial statement presentation. We believe that our audits provide a reasonable basis for our opinion.

In our opinion, the consolidated financial statements referred to above present fairly, in all material respects, the financial position of PepsiCo, Inc. and Subsidiaries as of December 31, 1994 and December 25, 1993, and the results of its operations and its cash flows for each of the years in the three-year period ended December 31, 1994, in conformity with generally accepted accounting principles.

As discussed in Notes 14 and 13 to the consolidated financial statements, PepsiCo, Inc. in 1994 adopted the provisions of the Financial Accounting Standards Board's Statement of Financial Accounting Standards No. 112, "Employers' Accounting for Postemployment Benefits," and changed its method for calculating the market-related value of pension plan assets used in the determination of pension expense, respectively. As discussed in Notes 12 and 17 to the consolidated financial statements,

PepsiCo, Inc. in 1992 adopted the provisions of the Financial Accounting Standards Board's Statements of Financial Accounting Standards No. 106, "Employers' Accounting for Postretirement Benefits Other Than Pensions," and No. 109, "Accounting for Income Taxes," respectively.

*KPMG Peat Marwick LLP*

KPMG Peat Marwick LLP
New York, New York
February 7, 1995

---

The auditor's report above contains a fourth paragraph wherein KPMG Peat Marwick reports that PepsiCo adopted recently issued pronouncements of the FASB, the effects of which are disclosed in notes to the financial statements.

The auditor's report issued on PepsiCo's financial statements is **unqualified** or "clean"; that is, it contains no qualifications or exceptions. In other words, the auditor conformed completely with generally accepted auditing standards in performing the audit, and the financial statements conformed in all material respects with generally accepted accounting principles.

When the financial statements do not conform with generally accepted accounting principles, the auditor must issue a **qualified** opinion and describe the exception. If the lack of conformity with GAAP is sufficiently material, the auditor is compelled to issue an **adverse** or negative opinion. An adverse opinion means that the financial statements do not present fairly the company's financial condition and/or the results of the company's operations at the dates and for the periods reported.

In circumstances where the auditor is unable to perform all the auditing procedures necessary to reach a conclusion as to the fairness of the financial statements, a **disclaimer** must be issued. In these rare instances, the auditor must report the reason for failure to reach a conclusion on the fairness of the financial statements.

Companies strive to obtain an unqualified auditor's report. Hence, only infrequently are you likely to encounter anything other than this type of opinion on the financial statements.

# Financial Statements and Accompanying Notes

The standard set of financial statements consists of: (1) a comparative income statement for 3 years, (2) a comparative balance sheet for 2 years, (3) a comparative statement of cash flows for 3 years, (4) a statement of retained earnings (or stockholders' equity) for 3 years, and (5) a set of accompanying notes that are considered an integral part of the financial statements. The auditor's report, unless stated otherwise, covers the financial statements and the accompanying notes. The financial statements and accompanying notes plus some supplementary data and analyses for PepsiCo, Inc., appear on the following pages.

**Note to the student:** For purposes of consistency PepsiCo uses 52 weeks as its fiscal year in preparing its financial statement. For 6 years in a row 52 weeks is used; every seventh year a 53-week year is adopted to catch up.

# Consolidated Statement of Income

## PepsiCo, Inc.

(in millions except per share amounts)
PepsiCo, Inc. and Subsidiaries
Fifty-three weeks ended December 31, 1994 and fifty-two weeks ended December 25, 1993 and December 26, 1992

|  | 1994 | 1993 | 1992 |
|---|---|---|---|
| **Net Sales** | **$28,472.4** | $25,020.7 | $21,970.0 |
| **Costs and Expenses, net** | | | |
| Cost of sales | **13,715.4** | 11,946.1 | 10,611.7 |
| Selling, general and administrative expenses | **11,243.6** | 9,864.4 | 8,721.2 |
| Amortization of intangible assets | **312.2** | 303.7 | 265.9 |
| **Operating Profit** | **3,201.2** | 2,906.5 | 2,371.2 |
| Gain on joint venture stock offering | **17.8** | — | — |
| Interest expense | **(645.0)** | (572.7) | (586.1) |
| Interest income | **90.4** | 88.7 | 113.7 |
| **Income Before Income Taxes and Cumulative Effect of Accounting Changes** | **2,664.4** | 2,422.5 | 1,898.8 |
| **Provision for Income Taxes** | **880.4** | 834.6 | 597.1 |
| **Income Before Cumulative Effect of Accounting Changes** | **1,784.0** | 1,587.9 | 1,301.7 |
| **Cumulative Effect of Accounting Changes** | | | |
| Postemployment benefits (net of income tax benefit of $29.3) | **(55.3)** | — | — |
| Pension assets (net of income tax expense of $14.5) | **23.3** | — | — |
| Postretirement benefits other than pensions (net of income tax benefit of $218.6) | — | — | (356.7) |
| Income taxes | — | — | (570.7) |
| **Net Income** | **$ 1,752.0** | $ 1,587.9 | $ 374.3 |
| **Income (Charge) Per Share** | | | |
| Before cumulative effect of accounting changes | **$ 2.22** | $ 1.96 | $ 1.61 |
| Cumulative effect of accounting changes | | | |
| Postemployment benefits | **(0.07)** | — | — |
| Pension assets | **0.03** | — | — |
| Postretirement benefits other than pensions | — | — | (0.44) |
| Income taxes | — | — | (0.71) |
| **Net Income Per Share** | **$ 2.18** | $ 1.96 | $ 0.46 |
| Average shares outstanding used to calculate income (charge) per share | **803.6** | 810.1 | 806.7 |

See accompanying Notes to Consolidated Financial Statements.

## Allocation of 1994 Net Sales

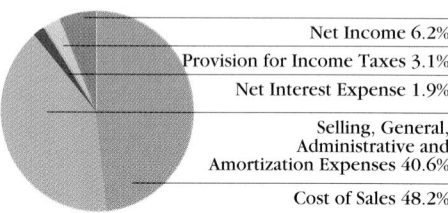

Net Income 6.2%
Provision for Income Taxes 3.1%
Net Interest Expense 1.9%
Selling, General, Administrative and Amortization Expenses 40.6%
Cost of Sales 48.2%

# Management's Analysis—Results of Operations

To improve comparability, Management's Analysis includes analytical data to indicate the impact of beverage and snack food acquisitions, net of operations sold or contributed to joint ventures (collectively, "net acquisitions"). Acquisition impacts represent the results of the acquired businesses for periods in the current year corresponding to the prior year periods that did not include the results of the businesses. Restaurant units acquired, principally from franchisees, and constructed units are treated the same for purposes of this analysis and are collectively referred to as "additional restaurant units." Also, the analysis indicates, as applicable, the impact of the ongoing effects of the 1994 accounting changes (see Notes 13 and 14), the 1994 BAESA gain (see Note 4), the 1993 deferred tax charge due to U.S. tax legislation (see Note 17) and the 1992 restructuring charges (see Note 16), collectively referred to as "the Unusual Items."

Comparisons of 1994 to 1993 were impacted by an additional week's results in 1994 which contributed about $433.5 million or 2 points to growth in Net Sales and increased earnings by about $54.0 million ($34.9 million after-tax or $0.04 per share).

**Net Sales** rose $3.5 billion or 14% in 1994 of which $215 million or 1 point was contributed by net acquisitions. The balance of the increase reflected volume gains of $2.2 billion and $934 million due to additional restaurant units. Sales grew $3.1 billion or 14% in 1993. Net acquisitions contributed $1.1 billion or 5 points to sales growth. The balance of the increase reflected $913 million from additional restaurant units, volume gains that contributed $850 million and higher pricing. International sales grew 23% in 1994 and 24% in 1993 with net acquisitions contributing 1 point and 16 points, respectively. International sales represented 29%, 27% and 25% of total sales in 1994, 1993 and 1992, respectively. The long-term trend of an increasing international component of sales may be interrupted in the near term as a result of the unfavorable impact of the devaluation of the Mexican peso in late 1994 and early 1995 and its related effects.

**Cost of sales** as a percentage of Net Sales was 48.2%, 47.7% and 48.3% in 1994, 1993 and 1992, respectively. The decline in the 1994 gross margin reflected a mix shift to lower-margin businesses in international beverages and worldwide restaurants and lower net pricing in domestic beverages, partially offset by a mix shift to higher-margin packages and products in international snack foods and manufacturing efficiencies in domestic snack foods. The 1993 gross margin improvement was driven by lower product costs (packaging and ingredients) in domestic beverages.

**Selling, general and administrative expenses** rose 14% in 1994 and 13% in 1993, reflecting base business growth. Excluding the Unusual Items, Selling, general and administrative expenses rose 14% in 1994 and 16% in 1993, and as a percentage of Net Sales were 39.6%, 39.4% and 38.8% in 1994, 1993 and 1992, respectively. In 1994, Selling, general and administrative expenses grew at the same rate as sales. In 1993, selling and distribution expenses grew at a faster rate than sales, but marketing expenditures grew at a slower rate. These changes reflect the impact of worldwide bottling acquisitions and flat marketing expenditures in domestic beverages.

**Amortization of intangible assets** rose 3% in 1994 and 14% in 1993. This noncash expense reduced Net Income Per Share by $0.29, $0.28 and $0.24 in 1994, 1993 and 1992, respectively.

**Operating Profit** increased 10% in 1994 and 23% in 1993. Excluding the Unusual Items, operating profit increased $262 million or 9% in 1994 and $342 million or 13% in 1993, driven by combined segment operating profit growth of 7% in 1994 and 14% in 1993. The 1994 increase reflected $850 million from higher volumes and $73 million from additional restaurant units, partially offset by higher operating expenses. Growth in 1993 reflected $425 million from higher volumes and $89 million from additional restaurant units, partially offset by increased operating expenses. International segment profits grew 12% in 1994 and 8% in 1993, reflecting double-digit increases in snack foods and beverages, partially offset by a double-digit decline in restaurants. International profits represented 19%, 18% and 19% of combined segment operating profits in 1994, 1993 and 1992, respectively. This percentage may be affected in the near term due to the devaluation of the Mexican peso and its related effects. Small foreign exchange gains in 1994 compared to 1993's foreign exchange losses, and increased equity in net income of affiliates, which are not included in segment profits, aided 1994 total operating profit growth.

**Gain on Joint Venture Stock Offering** of $17.8 million ($16.8 million after-tax or $0.02 per share) related to the public offering of shares by the BAESA joint venture. See Note 4.

**Interest expense, net of Interest income,** increased 15% in 1994 and 2% in 1993. The 1994 increase reflected higher average borrowings partially offset by higher interest rates on investment balances. The change in 1993 reflected higher average borrowings and lower average short-term investment balances partially offset by lower interest rates. Excluding the impact of net acquisitions, net interest expense increased 10% in 1994 and declined 9% in 1993.

**Provision for Income Taxes** as a percentage of pretax income was 33.0%, 34.5% and 31.4% in 1994, 1993 and 1992, respectively. The 1993 effective tax rate, excluding the Unusual Item, was 33.3%. The slight decline in 1994 reflected reversal of valuation allowances related to deferred tax assets and an increase in the proportion of income taxed at lower foreign rates offset by the absence of 1993's favorable adjustment of certain prior year foreign accruals. The 1993 increase of 1.9 points reflected higher U.S. and foreign effective tax rates, an increase in the proportion of income taxed at the higher U.S. tax rate and higher state taxes, partially offset by the favorable adjustment of prior year accruals.

**Income and Income Per Share Before Cumulative Effect of Accounting Changes** ("income" and "income per share") in 1994 increased 12% to $1.8 billion and 13% to $2.22, respectively, and in 1993 increased 22% to $1.6 billion and 22% to $1.96, respectively. Excluding the Unusual Items, income and income per share rose 8% and 9%, respectively, in 1994 and 13% and 12%, respectively, in 1993. Growth in income per share was depressed by estimated dilution from acquisitions of $0.03 or 1 point in 1994 and $0.05 or 3 points in 1993, primarily due to international beverage acquisitions in both years.

The Mexican peso devaluation may unfavorably impact Net Sales and Net Income in 1995; however, due to many uncertainties in Mexico, we are unable to quantify the impacts.

# Consolidated Balance Sheet

## PepsiCo, Inc.

(in millions except per share amount)
PepsiCo, Inc. and Subsidiaries
December 31, 1994 and December 25, 1993

| | 1994 | 1993 |
|---|---:|---:|
| **ASSETS** | | |
| **Current Assets** | | |
| Cash and cash equivalents | $ 330.7 | $ 226.9 |
| Short-term investments, at cost | 1,157.4 | 1,573.8 |
| | 1,488.1 | 1,800.7 |
| Accounts and notes receivable, less allowance: $150.6 in 1994 and $128.3 in 1993 | 2,050.9 | 1,883.4 |
| Inventories | 970.0 | 924.7 |
| Prepaid expenses, taxes and other current assets | 563.2 | 499.8 |
| **Total Current Assets** | 5,072.2 | 5,108.6 |
| **Investments in Affiliates** | 1,295.2 | 1,090.5 |
| **Property, Plant and Equipment, net** | 9,882.8 | 8,855.6 |
| **Intangible Assets, net** | 7,842.1 | 7,929.5 |
| **Other Assets** | 699.7 | 721.6 |
| **Total Assets** | $24,792.0 | $23,705.8 |
| **LIABILITIES AND SHAREHOLDERS' EQUITY** | | |
| **Current Liabilities** | | |
| Accounts payable | $ 1,451.6 | $ 1,390.0 |
| Accrued compensation and benefits | 753.5 | 726.0 |
| Short-term borrowings | 678.5 | 2,191.2 |
| Income taxes payable | 671.7 | 823.7 |
| Accrued marketing | 546.2 | 400.9 |
| Other current liabilities | 1,168.9 | 1,043.1 |
| **Total Current Liabilities** | 5,270.4 | 6,574.9 |
| **Long-term Debt** | 8,840.5 | 7,442.6 |
| **Other Liabilities** | 1,852.1 | 1,342.0 |
| **Deferred Income Taxes** | 1,972.9 | 2,007.6 |
| **Shareholders' Equity** | | |
| Capital stock, par value 1⅔¢ per share: authorized 1,800.0 shares, issued 863.1 shares | 14.4 | 14.4 |
| Capital in excess of par value | 934.4 | 879.5 |
| Retained earnings | 7,739.1 | 6,541.9 |
| Currency translation adjustment and other | (470.6) | (183.9) |
| | 8,217.3 | 7,251.9 |
| Less: Treasury stock, at cost: 73.2 shares and 64.3 shares in 1994 and 1993, respectively | (1,361.2) | (913.2) |
| **Total Shareholders' Equity** | 6,856.1 | 6,338.7 |
| **Total Liabilities and Shareholders' Equity** | $24,792.0 | $23,705.8 |

See accompanying Notes to Consolidated Financial Statements.

# Management's Analysis—Financial Condition

**Assets** increased $1.1 billion or 5% over 1993. Short-term investments largely represent high-grade marketable securities portfolios held outside the U.S. The portfolio in Puerto Rico, which totaled $853 million at year-end 1994 and $1.3 billion at year-end 1993, arises from the operating cash flows of the centralized concentrate manufacturing facility that operates under a tax incentive grant. The grant provides that the portfolio funds may be remitted to the U.S. without any additional tax. PepsiCo remitted $380 million of the portfolio to the U.S. in 1994 and $564 million in 1993. PepsiCo continually reassesses its alternatives to redeploy its maturing investments in this and other portfolios held outside the U.S., considering other investment opportunities and risks, tax consequences and overall financing strategies.

**Liabilities** rose $569 million or 3% over 1993. Income taxes payable decreased $152 million or 18%, reflecting the prepayment of taxes in 1994 related to a federal tax audit. Other liabilities increased $510 million or 38%, reflecting a reclassification of amounts from Other current liabilities, normal growth in long-term liabilities and recognition of a liability for postemployment benefits under SFAS 112.

At year-end 1994 and 1993, $4.5 billion and $3.5 billion, respectively, of short-term borrowings were classified as long-term, reflecting PepsiCo's intent and ability, through the existence of its unused revolving credit facilities, to refinance these borrowings. PepsiCo's unused credit facilities with lending institutions, which exist largely to support the issuances of short-term borrowings, were $3.5 billion at year-end 1994 and 1993. Effective January 3, 1995, PepsiCo replaced its existing credit facilities with new credit facilities aggregating $4.5 billion, of which $1.0 billion expire in 1996 and $3.5 billion expire in 2000. Annually, these facilities can be extended an additional year upon the mutual consent of PepsiCo and the lending institutions.

**Financial Leverage** is measured by PepsiCo on both a market value and historical cost basis. PepsiCo believes that the most meaningful measure of debt is on a net basis, which takes into account its large investment portfolios held outside the U.S. These portfolios are managed as part of PepsiCo's overall financing strategy and are not required to support day-to-day operations. Net debt reflects the pro forma remittance of the portfolios (net of related taxes) as a reduction of total debt. Total debt includes the present value of operating lease commitments.

PepsiCo believes that market leverage (defined as net debt as a percent of net debt plus the market value of equity, based on the year-end stock price) is an appropriate measure of PepsiCo's financial leverage. Unlike historical cost measures, the market value of equity primarily reflects the estimated net present value of expected future cash flows that will both support debt and provide returns to shareholders. The market net debt ratio was 26% at year-end 1994 and 22% at year-end 1993. The increase was due to a 13% decrease in PepsiCo's stock price as well as an 8% increase in net debt. PepsiCo has established a long-term target range of 20–25% for its market net debt ratio to optimize its cost of capital.

As measured on an historical cost basis, the ratio of net debt to net capital employed (defined as net debt, other liabilities, deferred income taxes and shareholders' equity) was 49% at year-end 1994 and 50% at year-end 1993. The decline was due to a 9% increase in net capital employed, partially offset by the increase in net debt.

Because of PepsiCo's strong cash generating capability and its strong financial condition, PepsiCo has continued access to capital markets throughout the world.

At year-end 1994, about 60% of PepsiCo's net debt portfolio was exposed to variable interest rates, up from about 55% in 1993. In addition to variable rate debt, all net debt with maturities of less than one year is categorized as variable. PepsiCo prefers funding its operations with variable rate debt because it believes that, over the long-term, variable rate debt provides more cost effective financing than fixed rate debt. PepsiCo will issue fixed rate debt if advantageous market opportunites arise. A 1 point change in interest rates on variable rate net debt would impact annual interest expense, net of interest income, by approximately $38 million ($21 million after-tax or $0.03 per share) assuming the level and mix of the December 31, 1994 net debt portfolio was maintained.

PepsiCo's negative operating working capital position, which principally reflects the cash sales nature of its restaurant operations, effectively provides additional capital for investment. Operating working capital, which excludes short-term investments and short-term borrowings, was a negative $677 million and $849 million at year-end 1994 and 1993, respectively. The $172 million decline in negative working capital primarily reflected reclassification of amounts from Other current liabilities to Other Liabilities and base business growth in the more working capital intensive bottling and snack food operations exceeding the growth in restaurant operations.

**Shareholders' Equity** increased $517 million or 8% from 1993. This change reflected an 18% increase in retained earnings due to $1.8 billion in net income less dividends declared of $555 million. This growth was offset by a $448 million increase in treasury stock that reflected share repurchases, net of shares used for stock option exercises and acquisitions, and a $287 million unfavorable change in the currency translation adjustment account (CTA). The CTA change primarily reflected the impact of the devaluation of the Mexican peso in late 1994 on the translation of our peso denominated net assets.

Based on income before cumulative effect of accounting changes, PepsiCo's return on average shareholders' equity (ROAE) was 27.0% in 1994 and 27.2% in 1993. The ROAE was 26.5% in 1994 and 25.3% in 1993, excluding from both income and shareholders' equity the effect of the accounting changes and BAESA gain in 1994 as well as the $29.9 million charge in 1993 due to 1993 U.S. tax legislation.

# Consolidated Statement of Cash Flows

## PepsiCo, Inc.

(in millions)
PepsiCo, Inc. and Subsidiaries
Fifty-three weeks ended December 31, 1994 and fifty-two weeks ended December 25, 1993 and December 26, 1992

|  | 1994 | 1993 | 1992 |
|---|---|---|---|
| **Cash Flows—Operating Activities** | | | |
| Income before cumulative effect of accounting changes | $ 1,784.0 | $ 1,587.9 | $ 1,301.7 |
| Adjustments to reconcile income before cumulative effect of accounting changes to net cash provided by operating activities: | | | |
| Depreciation and amortization | 1,576.5 | 1,444.2 | 1,214.9 |
| Deferred income taxes | (66.9) | 83.3 | (52.0) |
| Other noncash charges and credits, net | 391.1 | 344.8 | 315.6 |
| Changes in operating working capital, excluding effect of acquisitions: | | | |
| Accounts and notes receivable | (111.8) | (161.0) | (45.7) |
| Inventories | (101.6) | (89.5) | (11.8) |
| Prepaid expenses, taxes and other current assets | 1.2 | 3.3 | (27.4) |
| Accounts payable | 30.4 | 143.2 | (102.0) |
| Income taxes payable | 54.4 | (125.1) | (16.9) |
| Other current liabilities | 158.7 | (96.7) | 135.2 |
| Net change in operating working capital | 31.3 | (325.8) | (68.6) |
| **Net Cash Provided by Operating Activities** | 3,716.0 | 3,134.4 | 2,711.6 |
| **Cash Flows—Investing Activities** | | | |
| Acquisitions and investments in affiliates | (315.8) | (1,011.2) | (1,209.7) |
| Capital spending | (2,253.2) | (1,981.6) | (1,549.6) |
| Proceeds from sales of property, plant and equipment | 55.3 | 72.5 | 89.0 |
| Short-term investments, by original maturity: | | | |
| More than three months' purchases | (218.6) | (578.7) | (1,174.8) |
| More than three months' maturities | 649.5 | 846.0 | 1,371.8 |
| Three months or less, net | (9.9) | (8.3) | (249.4) |
| Other, net | (268.3) | (109.4) | (30.8) |
| **Net Cash Used for Investing Activities** | (2,361.0) | (2,770.7) | (2,753.5) |
| **Cash Flows—Financing Activities** | | | |
| Proceeds from issuances of long-term debt | 1,285.2 | 710.8 | 1,092.7 |
| Payments of long-term debt | (1,179.5) | (1,201.9) | (616.3) |
| Short-term borrowings, by original maturity: | | | |
| More than three months' proceeds | 1,303.8 | 3,033.6 | 911.2 |
| More than three months' payments | (1,727.7) | (2,791.6) | (2,062.6) |
| Three months or less, net | 113.8 | 839.0 | 1,075.3 |
| Cash dividends paid | (540.2) | (461.6) | (395.5) |
| Purchases of treasury stock | (549.1) | (463.5) | (32.0) |
| Proceeds from exercises of stock options | 97.4 | 68.6 | 82.8 |
| Other, net | (43.5) | (36.7) | (30.9) |
| **Net Cash (Used for) Provided by Financing Activities** | (1,239.8) | (303.3) | 24.7 |
| **Effect of Exchange Rate Changes on Cash and Cash Equivalents** | (11.4) | (3.4) | 0.4 |
| **Net Increase (Decrease) in Cash and Cash Equivalents** | 103.8 | 57.0 | (16.8) |
| **Cash and Cash Equivalents—Beginning of Year** | 226.9 | 169.9 | 186.7 |
| **Cash and Cash Equivalents—End of Year** | $ 330.7 | $ 226.9 | $ 169.9 |
| **Supplemental Cash Flow Information** | | | |
| **Cash Flow Data** | | | |
| Interest paid | $ 591.1 | 549.5 | 574.7 |
| Income taxes paid | $ 663.1 | 675.6 | 519.7 |
| **Schedule of Noncash Investing and Financing Activities** | | | |
| Liabilities assumed in connection with acquisitions | $ 223.5 | 897.0 | 383.8 |
| Issuance of treasury stock and debt for acquisitions | $ 38.8 | 364.5 | 189.5 |
| Book value of net assets exchanged for investment in affiliates | $ — | 60.8 | 86.7 |

See accompanying Notes to Consolidated Financial Statements.

# Management's Analysis—Cash Flows

Cash flow activity in 1994 reflected strong cash flows from operations of $3.7 billion and $421 million in net proceeds from short-term investment activities. These amounts were used to fund capital spending of $2.3 billion, purchases of treasury stock totaling $549 million, dividend payments of $540 million, acquisition activity of $316 million and net debt repayments of $204 million.

One of PepsiCo's most significant financial strengths is its internal cash generation capability. In fact, after capital spending and acquisitions, each industry segment generated positive cash flows in 1994, with particularly strong results from beverages and snack foods. Net cash flows from PepsiCo's domestic businesses were partially offset by international uses of cash, reflecting strategies to accelerate growth of international operations.

The significant devaluation of the Mexican peso in late 1994 and early 1995 did not materially impact 1994 consolidated cash flows. However, because PepsiCo's operations in Mexico represented approximately 7% of consolidated cash flows from operations in 1994, the devaluation and its related effects are expected to have an unfavorable impact on 1995 cash flows from operations. In addition to the actions taken to mitigate the unfavorable impact on operating profits, the operations in Mexico will defer a portion of their capital spending. Nonetheless, significant uncertainties remain in Mexico and, as a result, it is not possible to quantify the impact on 1995 cash flows. In addition, actions are being taken in other parts of the world intended to mitigate the impact.

**Net Cash Provided by Operating Activities** in 1994 rose $582 million or 19% over 1993, and in 1993 grew $423 million or 16% over 1992. Income before noncash charges and credits rose 6% in 1994 and 24% in 1993. The increases in depreciation and amortization noncash charges of $132 million in 1994 and $229 million in 1993 reflected capital spending and in 1993, acquisitions. The 1994 decrease of $150 million in the deferred income tax provision was primarily due to the effect in 1994 of converting from premium based casualty insurance to self-insurance for most of these risks and adopting SFAS 112 for accounting for postemployment benefits. The 1993 increase of $135 million in the deferred income tax provision was primarily due to the lapping of 1992 effects related to restructuring accruals and pre-funded employee benefit expenses and the impact of 1993 U.S. tax legislation. The cash provided in 1994 from working capital was $357 million better than 1993, reflecting normal increases in accrued liabilities across all of our businesses, lapping the effect of higher income tax payments and a lower provision in 1993 and improved trade receivable collections, partially offset by the impact on accounts payable of the timing of a large year-end payment to prefund employee benefits. The 1993 over 1992 net increase of $257 million in cash used for operating working capital reflected slower collections of domestic accounts receivable, advance domestic purchases of product ingredients, the higher payments of income taxes and the lapping of 1992 and 1991 effects related to restructuring accruals, partially offset by the payment to prefund employee benefits.

**Investing Activities** over the past three years reflected strategic spending in all three industry segments through capital spending, acquisitions and investments in affiliates. PepsiCo seeks investments that generate cash returns in excess of its long-term cost of capital, which is estimated to be approximately 11% at year-end 1994. See Note 5 for a discussion of acquisition activity. About 75% of the total acquisition activity in 1994 represented international transactions, compared to 45% in 1993 and 60% in 1992. PepsiCo continues to seek opportunities to strengthen its position in its domestic and international industry segments through such strategic acquisitions.

Increased capital spending in 1994 was driven by beverages reflecting investments in equipment for new packaging and new products in the U.S. and emerging international markets, primarily Eastern Europe. Capital spending increases in 1993 and 1992 were driven by restaurants, primarily for new units. Restaurants represented about half of the total capital spending in all three years. Restaurants, beverages and snack foods represent 40%, 30% and 30%, respectively, of the estimated $2.4 billion spending in 1995. This reflects a shift primarily from restaurants to snack foods. Beverages and snack foods 1995 capital spending reflects production capacity expansion and equipment replacement, while restaurants is primarily for new units. Restaurant capital spending in 1995 may be further reduced depending upon future decisions. Approximately one-third of the planned 1995 capital spending relates to international businesses, about the same as the prior three years. Cash provided by operations is expected to be sufficient to fund the expected capital spending.

Investment activity in PepsiCo's short-term portfolios, primarily held outside the U.S., provided $421 million in 1994 and $259 million in 1993, respectively, compared to the increased net investment of $52 million in 1992.

**Financing Activities.** The 1994 over 1993 change in cash flows from net financing activities was a use of $937 million, primarily reflecting net repayments of short and long-term debt of $204 million compared to net proceeds of $590 million in 1993. The 1993 over 1992 change in cash flows from financing activities was a use of $328 million, primarily due to increased purchases of treasury stock.

At year-end 1994, PepsiCo had authority to issue $3.4 billion of long-term debt and had facilities in place in the U.S., Europe and Japan to take advantage of marketplace opportunities. The principal purposes of these shelf registrations are for financing growth activities and refinancing borrowings.

Cash dividends declared were $555 million in 1994 and $486 million in 1993. PepsiCo targets a dividend payout of about one-third of the prior year's income from ongoing operations, thus retaining sufficient earnings to provide financial resources for growth opportunities.

Share repurchase decisions are evaluated considering management's target capital structure and other investment opportunities. In 1994, PepsiCo repurchased 15.0 million shares at a cost of $549 million. Subsequent to year-end, PepsiCo repurchased 3.4 million shares through February 7, 1995 at a cost of $121 million. Including these repurchases, 18.8 million shares have been repurchased under the 50 million share repurchase authority granted by PepsiCo's Board of Directors on July 22, 1993.

# Consolidated Statement of Shareholders' Equity

**PepsiCo, Inc.**

(in millions except per share amounts)
PepsiCo, Inc. and Subsidiaries
Fifty-three weeks ended December 31, 1994 and fifty-two weeks ended December 25, 1993 and December 26, 1992

| | Capital Stock | | | | Capital in Excess of Par Value | Retained Earnings | Currency Translation Adjustment and Other | Total |
|---|---|---|---|---|---|---|---|---|
| | Issued | | Treasury | | | | | |
| | Shares | Amount | Shares | Amount | | | | |
| Shareholders' Equity, December 28, 1991 | 863.1 | $ 14.4 | (74.0) | $ (745.9) | $ 476.6 | $ 5,470.0 | $ 330.3 | $ 5,545.4 |
| 1992 Net income | — | — | — | — | — | 374.3 | — | 374.3 |
| Cash dividends declared (per share-$0.51) | — | — | — | — | — | (404.6) | — | (404.6) |
| Currency translation adjustment | — | — | — | — | — | — | (429.3) | (429.3) |
| Shares issued in connection with acquisitions | — | — | 4.3 | 44.2 | 115.3 | — | — | 159.5 |
| Stock option exercises, including tax benefits of $57.5 | — | — | 6.3 | 65.3 | 74.9 | — | — | 140.2 |
| Purchases of treasury stock | — | — | (1.0) | (32.0) | — | — | — | (32.0) |
| Other | — | — | 0.1 | 1.4 | 0.8 | — | — | 2.2 |
| Shareholders' Equity, December 26, 1992 | 863.1 | $ 14.4 | (64.3) | $ (667.0) | $ 667.6 | $ 5,439.6 | $ (99.0) | $ 5,355.7 |
| 1993 Net income | — | — | — | — | — | 1,587.9 | — | 1,587.9 |
| Cash dividends declared (per share-$0.61) | — | — | — | — | — | (485.7) | — | (485.7) |
| Currency translation adjustment | — | — | — | — | — | — | (77.0) | (77.0) |
| Purchases of treasury stock | — | — | (12.4) | (463.5) | — | — | — | (463.5) |
| Shares issued in connection with acquisitions | — | — | 8.9 | 170.2 | 164.6 | — | — | 334.8 |
| Stock option exercises, including tax benefits of $23.4 | — | — | 3.4 | 46.0 | 46.1 | — | — | 92.1 |
| Pension liability adjustment, net of deferred taxes of $5.1 | — | — | — | — | — | — | (7.9) | (7.9) |
| Other | — | — | 0.1 | 1.1 | 1.2 | — | — | 2.3 |
| Shareholders' Equity, December 25, 1993 | 863.1 | $ 14.4 | (64.3) | $ (913.2) | $ 879.5 | $ 6,541.9 | $ (183.9) | $ 6,338.7 |
| 1994 Net income | — | — | — | — | — | 1,752.0 | — | 1,752.0 |
| Cash dividends declared (per share-$0.70) | — | — | — | — | — | (554.8) | — | (554.8) |
| Currency translation adjustment | — | — | — | — | — | — | (294.6) | (294.6) |
| Purchases of treasury stock | — | — | (15.0) | (549.1) | — | — | — | (549.1) |
| Stock option exercises, including tax benefits of $27.1 | — | — | 4.9 | 80.8 | 44.5 | — | — | 125.3 |
| Shares issued in connection with acquisitions | — | — | 0.9 | 15.1 | 13.7 | — | — | 28.8 |
| Pension liability adjustment, net of deferred taxes of $5.1 | — | — | — | — | — | — | 7.9 | 7.9 |
| Other | — | — | 0.3 | 5.2 | (3.3) | — | — | 1.9 |
| **Shareholders' Equity, December 31, 1994** | **863.1** | **$14.4** | **(73.2)** | **$(1,361.2)** | **$934.4** | **$7,739.1** | **$(470.6)** | **$6,856.1** |

See accompanying Notes to Consolidated Financial Statements.

# Notes to Consolidated Financial Statements

## Note 1 - Summary of Significant Accounting Policies

The preparation of the Consolidated Financial Statements requires estimates and assumptions that affect amounts reported and disclosed in the financial statements and related notes. Actual results could differ from those estimates. Certain reclassifications were made to prior year amounts to conform with the 1994 presentation. Significant accounting policies are discussed below, or where applicable, in the Notes that follow.

**Principles of Consolidation.** The financial statements reflect the consolidated accounts of PepsiCo, Inc. and its controlled affiliates. Intercompany accounts and transactions have been eliminated. Investments in affiliates in which PepsiCo exercises significant influence but not control are accounted for by the equity method and the equity in net income is included in Selling, general and administrative expenses.

**Marketing Costs.** Marketing costs are reported in Selling, general and administrative expenses and include costs of advertising, marketing and promotional programs. Promotional discounts are expensed as incurred and other marketing costs not deferred at year-end are charged to expense ratably in relation to sales over the year in which incurred. Marketing costs deferred at year-end consist of media and personal service advertising prepayments, promotional materials in inventory and production costs of future media advertising; these assets are expensed in the year first used.

Promotional discounts to retailers in the beverage segment are classified as a reduction of sales; in the snack food segment, such discounts are generally classified as marketing costs. The difference in classification reflects our historical view that promotional discounts had become so pervasive in the beverage industry, compared to the snack food industry, that they were effectively price discounts and should be classified accordingly. This differing accounting classification was also supported by a survey of the accounting practice of others in the beverage and snack food industries. PepsiCo plans to review its accounting policy in 1995 to determine whether the different accounting classification for beverages and snack foods still reflects the substance of the activity and whether it continues to be consistent with others in our industries. Depending on the outcome of the review, PepsiCo may change its accounting classification of beverage or snack food promotional discounts. Any change will not impact reported earnings as it would only result in a reclassification of the cost of promotional discounts between Net Sales and Selling, general and administrative expenses.

**Cash Equivalents.** Cash equivalents represent funds temporarily invested (with original maturities not exceeding three months) as part of PepsiCo's management of day-to-day operating cash receipts and disbursements. All other investment portfolios, largely held outside the U.S., are primarily classified as short-term investments.

**Net Income Per Share.** Net income per share is computed by dividing net income by the weighted average number of shares and share equivalents outstanding during each year.

**Research and Development Expenses.** Research and development expenses, which are expensed as incurred, were $152 million, $113 million and $102 million in 1994, 1993 and 1992, respectively.

**Fiscal Year.** PepsiCo's fiscal year ends on the last Saturday in December and, as a result, a fifty-third week is added every 5 or 6 years. The fiscal year ending December 31, 1994 consisted of 53 weeks.

## Note 2 - Business Segments

Information regarding industry segments and geographic areas of operations is provided on pages A27 and A28.

## Note 3 - Items Affecting Comparability

The fifty-third week, as described in Note 1, increased earnings in 1994 by approximately $54.0 million ($34.9 million after-tax or $0.04 per share). See Items Affecting Comparability on page A26 for the estimated impact of the fifty-third week on comparability of net sales and operating profits.

The effects of unusual items, primarily restructuring charges, and accounting changes on comparability of operating profits are provided in Items Affecting Comparability on page A26.

Information regarding the 1994 gain from a public share offering by PepsiCo's BAESA joint venture and a 1993 charge to increase net deferred tax liabilities as of the beginning of 1993 for a 1% statutory income tax rate increase due to 1993 U.S. tax legislation are provided in Notes 4 and 17, respectively.

## Note 4 - Joint Venture Stock Offering

In 1993, PepsiCo entered into an arrangement with the principal shareholders of Buenos Aires Embotelladora S.A. (BAESA), a franchised bottler with operations in Argentina and Costa Rica. PepsiCo contributed certain assets, primarily bottling operations in Chile and Uruguay, while the shareholders contributed all of their outstanding shares in BAESA, representing 72.8% of the voting control and 42.5% of the ownership interest. Through this arrangement, PepsiCo's ownership in BAESA, which is accounted for by the equity method, was 25.9%.

On March 24, 1994, BAESA completed a public offering of 2.9 million American Depositary Shares (ADS) at $34.50 per ADS, which are traded on the New York Stock Exchange. In conjunction with the offering, PepsiCo and certain other shareholders exercised options for the equivalent of 1.6 million ADS. As a result of these transactions, PepsiCo's ownership in BAESA declined to 23.8%. The transactions generated cash proceeds for BAESA of $136.4 million. The resulting one-time, noncash gain to PepsiCo was $17.8 million ($16.8 million after-tax or $0.02 per share).

## Note 5 - Acquisitions and Investments in Affiliates

During 1994, PepsiCo completed acquisitions and affiliate investments aggregating $355 million, principally for cash. In addition, approximately $41 million of debt was assumed in these transactions, most of which was subsequently retired. This activity included equity investments in international franchised bottling operations, primarily in Thailand and China, and acquisitions of international and domestic franchised restaurant operations and franchised and independent bottling operations, primarily in India and Mexico.

During 1993, PepsiCo completed acquisitions and affiliate investments aggregating $1.4 billion, principally comprised of $1.0 billion in cash and $335 million in PepsiCo Capital Stock. Approximately $307 million of debt was assumed in these transactions, more than half of which was subsequently retired. This activity included acquisitions of domestic and international franchised restaurant operations, the buyout of PepsiCo's joint venture partners in a franchised bottling operation in Spain and the related acquisition of their fruit-flavored beverage concentrate operation, the acquisition of the remaining 85% interest in a large franchised bottling operation in the Northwestern U.S., the acquisition of a regional Mexican-style casual dining restaurant chain in the U.S. and equity investments in certain franchised bottling operations in Argentina and Mexico.

During 1992, acquisitions and affiliate investment activity aggregated $1.4 billion, principally for cash. In addition, approximately $218 million of debt was assumed in these transactions, most of which was subsequently retired. This activity included acquisitions of international (primarily Canada) and domestic franchised bottling operations and a number of domestic and international franchised restaurant operations, the buyout of PepsiCo's joint venture partner in a Canadian snack food business and an equity investment in a domestic casual dining restaurant chain featuring gourmet pizza. In addition, PepsiCo exchanged certain previously consolidated snack food operations in Europe with a net book value of $87 million for a 60% equity interest in an international snack food joint venture with General Mills, Inc. PepsiCo secured a controlling interest in its Mexican cookie affiliate, Gamesa, through an exchange of certain non-cookie operations of Gamesa for its joint venture partner's interest.

The acquisitions have been accounted for by the purchase method; accordingly, their results are included in the Consolidated Financial Statements from their respective dates of acquisition. The aggregate impact of acquisitions was not material to PepsiCo's net sales, net income or net income per share; accordingly, no related pro forma information is provided.

## Note 6 - Inventories

Inventories are valued at the lower of cost (computed on the average, first-in, first-out or last-in, first-out [LIFO] method) or net realizable value. The cost of 38% of 1994 inventories and 41% of 1993 inventories was computed using the LIFO method. Use of the LIFO method increased the total 1994 and 1993 year-end inventory amounts below by $5.5 million and $8.9 million, respectively.

|  | 1994 | 1993 |
|---|---|---|
| Raw materials and supplies | $454.8 | $463.9 |
| Finished goods | 515.2 | 460.8 |
|  | $970.0 | $924.7 |

See Management's Analysis—Overview, for a discussion of PepsiCo's use of futures contracts to hedge its exposure to market price fluctuations for certain raw materials. Gains and losses on these contracts are deferred and included in the related cost of raw materials when purchased. Gains and losses realized in 1994 or deferred at year-end were not significant. As of December 31, 1994, PepsiCo had various open contracts, generally expiring by December 1995, which were not material.

## Note 7 - Property, Plant and Equipment

Property, plant and equipment are stated at cost. Depreciation is calculated principally on a straight-line basis over the estimated useful lives of the assets. Depreciation expense in 1994, 1993 and 1992 was $1.2 billion, $1.1 billion and $923 million, respectively.

|  | 1994 | 1993 |
|---|---|---|
| Land | $ 1,321.6 | $ 1,186.4 |
| Buildings and improvements | 5,664.1 | 5,017.6 |
| Capital leases, primarily buildings | 451.2 | 402.6 |
| Machinery and equipment | 8,208.1 | 7,175.0 |
| Construction in progress | 485.1 | 468.4 |
|  | 16,130.1 | 14,250.0 |
| Accumulated depreciation | (6,247.3) | (5,394.4) |
|  | $ 9,882.8 | $ 8,855.6 |

## Note 8 - Intangible Assets

Identifiable intangible assets arose from the allocation of purchase prices of businesses acquired and consist principally of reacquired franchise rights and trademarks. Reacquired franchise rights relate to acquisitions of franchised bottling and restaurant operations and trademarks principally relate to acquisitions of international snack food and beverage trademarks. Amounts assigned to such identifiable intangibles were based on independent appraisals or internal estimates. Goodwill represents the residual purchase price after allocation to all identifiable net assets.

Intangible assets are amortized on a straight-line basis over appropriate periods generally ranging from 20 to 40 years. Accumulated amortization, included in the amounts below, was $1.6 billion and $1.3 billion at year-end 1994 and 1993, respectively.

|  | 1994 | 1993 |
|---|---|---|
| Reacquired franchise rights | $3,974.0 | $3,959.7 |
| Trademarks | 768.5 | 849.1 |
| Other identifiable intangibles | 249.7 | 204.1 |
| Goodwill | 2,849.9 | 2,916.6 |
|  | $7,842.1 | $7,929.5 |

The recoverability of carrying amounts of intangible assets is evaluated on a recurring basis. The primary indicators of recoverability are current or forecasted profitability over the estimated remaining life of the intangible assets, measured as the combined operating profit of the acquired business (including amortization of the intangible assets) and existing businesses that are directly related to the acquired business. Consideration is also given to the estimated disposal values of certain identifiable intangible assets compared to their carrying amounts. If recoverability of an intangible asset is unlikely based on the evaluation, the carrying amount is reduced by the amount it exceeds the forecasted operating profits and any disposal value. For the three-year period ended December 31, 1994, there were no significant adjustments to the carrying amounts of the intangible assets resulting from these evaluations.

## Note 9 - Short-term Borrowings and Long-term Debt

| | 1994 | 1993 |
|---|---|---|
| **Short-term Borrowings** | | |
| Commercial paper (5.4% and 3.3%) **(A)** ... | **$ 2,254.4** | $ 3,535.0 |
| Current maturities of long-term debt issuances **(A)** ............ | **987.5** | 1,183.1 |
| Notes (5.4% and 3.5%) **(A)** ........... | **1,492.4** | 394.0 |
| Other borrowings (6.5% and 6.3%) ..... | **444.2** | 529.1 |
| Amount reclassified to long-term debt **(B)** ............. | **(4,500.0)** | (3,450.0) |
| | **$ 678.5** | $ 2,191.2 |
| **Long-term Debt** | | |
| Short-term borrowings, reclassified **(B)** ... | **$ 4,500.0** | $ 3,450.0 |
| Notes due 1995 through 2008 (6.6% and 6.5%) **(A)** .............. | **3,724.7** | 3,873.8 |
| Euro notes, 8% due 1997 ............ | **250.0** | — |
| Zero coupon notes, $795 million due 1995-2012 (14.6% and 14.4% annual yield to maturity) ................ | **219.2** | 327.2 |
| Japanese yen 3.3% bonds due 1997 **(D)** .................... | **200.8** | — |
| Swiss franc perpetual Foreign Interest Payment bonds **(C)** ............... | **213.0** | 212.2 |
| Swiss franc 5¼% bearer bonds due 1995 **(D)** .................... | **99.7** | 90.1 |
| Swiss franc 7⅛% notes due 1994 **(D)** ... | **—** | 69.8 |
| Capital lease obligations (See Note 11) ..................... | **298.2** | 291.4 |
| Other, due 1995-2015 (8.1% and 6.6%) .. | **322.4** | 311.2 |
| | **9,828.0** | 8,625.7 |
| Less current maturities of long-term debt issuances ................... | **(987.5)** | (1,183.1) |
| | **$ 8,840.5** | $ 7,442.6 |

The interest rates in the above table indicate, where applicable, the weighted average rates at year-end 1994 and 1993, respectively.

The carrying amount of long-term debt includes any related discount or premium and unamortized debt issuance costs. The debt agreements include various restrictions, none of which are presently significant to PepsiCo. Subsequent to year-end 1994, PepsiCo issued $150 million of Notes through February 7, 1995.

The annual maturities of long-term debt through 1999, excluding capital lease obligations and the reclassified short-term borrowings, are: 1995-$1.0 billion, 1996-$1.1 billion, 1997-$1.0 billion, 1998-$1.2 billion and 1999-$280 million.

See Management's Analysis—Overview for a discussion of PepsiCo's use of interest rate swaps and currency exchange agreements and its management of the inherent credit risk and Note 10.

**(A)** The following table indicates the notional amount and weighted average interest rates, by category, of interest rate swaps outstanding at year-end 1994 and 1993, respectively. The weighted average variable interest rates that PepsiCo pays, which are indexed primarily to either commercial paper or LIBOR rates, are

based on rates as of the respective balance sheet date and are subject to change. Terms of interest rate swap agreements match the debt they modify and terminate in 1995 through 2008. The differential to be paid or received on interest rate swaps is accrued as interest rates change and is charged or credited to interest expense over the life of the agreements. The carrying amount of each interest rate swap is reflected in the Consolidated Balance Sheet as a receivable or payable under the appropriate current asset or liability caption.

| | 1994 | 1993 |
|---|---|---|
| Receive fixed-pay variable: | | |
| Notional amount ............. | **$1,557.0** | $ 570.0 |
| Weighted average receive rate ... | **5.89%** | 5.96% |
| Weighted average pay rate ...... | **6.12%** | 3.28% |
| Receive variable-pay variable: | | |
| Notional amount ............. | **$1,008.5** | $ 465.0 |
| Weighted average receive rate ... | **4.90%** | 3.81% |
| Weighted average pay rate ...... | **5.99%** | 3.17% |
| Receive variable-pay fixed: | | |
| Notional amount ............. | **$ 215.0** | $ 265.0 |
| Weighted average receive rate ... | **6.56%** | 3.84% |
| Weighted average pay rate ...... | **8.22%** | 7.46% |

The following table identifies the composition of total debt (excluding capital lease obligations and the effect of the reclassified amounts from short-term borrowings) after giving effect to the impact of interest rate swaps. All short-term borrowings are considered variable interest rate debt for purposes of this table.

| | 1994 | | 1993 | |
|---|---|---|---|---|
| | **Carrying Amount** | **Weighted Average Interest Rate** | Carrying Amount | Weighted Average Interest Rate |
| **Variable interest rate debt:** | | | | |
| Short-term borrowings ..... | **$5,178.5** | **6.19%** | $5,641.2 | 4.11% |
| Long-term debt ... | **1,102.5** | **6.25%** | 567.6 | 4.75% |
| | **6,281.0** | **6.20%** | 6,208.8 | 4.17% |
| **Fixed interest rate debt** ............ | **2,939.8** | **6.96%** | 3,133.6 | 6.95% |
| | **$9,220.8** | **6.44%** | $9,342.4 | 5.10% |

**(B)** At year-end 1994 and 1993, PepsiCo had unused revolving credit facilities covering potential borrowings aggregating $3.5 billion. Effective January 3, 1995, PepsiCo replaced its existing credit facilities with new revolving credit facilities aggregating $4.5 billion, of which $1.0 billion expire in 1996 and $3.5 billion expire in 2000. At year-end 1994 and 1993, $4.5 billion and $3.5 billion, respectively, of short-term borrowings were classified as long-term debt, reflecting PepsiCo's intent and ability, through the existence of the unused credit facilities, to refinance these borrowings. These credit facilities exist largely to support the issuances of short-term borrowings and are available for acquisitions and other general corporate purposes.

**(C)** The coupon rate of the Swiss franc 400 million perpetual Foreign Interest Payment bonds issued in 1986 is 7½% through 1996. The bonds have no stated maturity date. At the end of each 10-year period after the issuance of the bonds, PepsiCo and the bondholders each have the right to cause redemption of the bonds. If not redeemed, the coupon rate will be adjusted based on the prevailing yield of 10-year U.S. Treasury Securities. The principal of the bonds is denominated in Swiss francs. PepsiCo can, and intends to, limit the ultimate redemption amount to the U.S. dollar proceeds at issuance, which is the basis of the carrying amount. Interest payments are made in U.S. dollars and are calculated by applying the coupon rate to the original U.S. dollar principal proceeds of $214 million.

**(D)** PepsiCo has entered into currency exchange agreements to hedge its foreign currency exposure on these issues of non-U.S. dollar denominated debt. At year-end 1994, the carrying amount of this debt aggregated $301 million and the receivables and payables under related currency exchange agreements aggregated $50 million and $2 million, respectively, resulting in a net effective U.S. dollar liability of $253 million with a weighted average interest rate of 6.6%. At year-end 1993, the aggregate carrying amount of the debt and the receivables under related currency exchange agreements were $160 million and $41 million, respectively, resulting in a net effective U.S. dollar liability of $119 million with a weighted average fixed interest rate of 6.5%. The carrying amount of each currency exchange agreement is reflected in the Consolidated Balance Sheet as a receivable or payable under the appropriate current and noncurrent asset and liability captions. Changes in the carrying amount of a currency exchange agreement resulting from exchange rate movements are offset by changes in the carrying amount of the related non-U.S. dollar-denominated debt, as both amounts are based on current exchange rates.

### Note 10 - Fair Value of Financial Instruments

The carrying amounts in the following table are included in the Consolidated Balance Sheet under the indicated captions, except for debt-related derivative instruments (interest rate swaps and currency exchange agreements), which are included in the appropriate current or noncurrent asset or liability caption. Investments consist primarily of debt securities and have been classified as held-to-maturity. Noncurrent investments mature at various dates through 2000.

Because of the short maturity of cash equivalents and short-term investments, the carrying amount approximates fair value. The fair value of noncurrent investments is based upon market quotes. The fair value of debt, debt-related derivative instruments and guarantees is estimated using market quotes, valuation models and calculations based on market rates.

See Management's Analysis—Overview and Note 9 for more information regarding PepsiCo's use of interest rate swaps and currency exchange agreements and its management of the inherent credit risk.

| | 1994 | | 1993 | |
|---|---|---|---|---|
| | Carrying Amount | Fair Value | Carrying Amount | Fair Value |
| **Assets** | | | | |
| Cash and cash equivalents | $ 330.7 | $ 330.7 | $ 226.9 | $ 226.9 |
| Short-term investments | $1,157.4 | $1,157.4 | $1,573.8 | $1,573.8 |
| Other assets (noncurrent investments) | $ 48.0 | $ 47.5 | $ 55.5 | $ 55.4 |
| **Liabilities** | | | | |
| Debt: | | | | |
| Short-term borrowings and long-term debt, net of capital leases | $9,220.8 | $9,265.4 | $9,342.4 | $9,626.0 |
| Debt-related derivative instruments: | | | | |
| Open contracts in asset position | (51.3) | (51.4) | (42.4) | (72.7) |
| Open contracts in liability position | 7.9 | 54.1 | 1.2 | 32.8 |
| Net debt | $9,177.4 | $9,268.1 | $9,301.2 | $9,586.1 |
| **Guarantees** | — | $ 2.7 | — | $ 1.7 |

### Note 11 - Leases

PepsiCo has noncancelable commitments under both capital and long-term operating leases, primarily for restaurant units. Certain of these units have been subleased to restaurant franchisees. In addition, PepsiCo is lessee under noncancelable leases covering vehicles, equipment and nonrestaurant real estate. Capital and operating lease commitments expire at various dates through 2088 and, in many cases, provide for rent escalations and renewal options. Most leases require payment of related executory costs which include property taxes, maintenance and insurance.

Future minimum commitments and sublease receivables under noncancelable leases are as follows:

| | Commitments | | Sublease Receivables | |
|---|---|---|---|---|
| | Capital | Operating | Direct Financing | Operating |
| 1995 | $ 58.9 | $ 313.0 | $ 3.2 | $ 9.6 |
| 1996 | 53.9 | 276.4 | 3.0 | 8.8 |
| 1997 | 46.7 | 247.3 | 2.7 | 7.7 |
| 1998 | 65.2 | 228.7 | 2.3 | 6.7 |
| 1999 | 34.4 | 203.3 | 2.0 | 6.0 |
| Later years | 279.0 | 1,072.1 | 7.1 | 24.2 |
| | $538.1 | $2,340.8 | $20.3 | $63.0 |

At year-end 1994, the present value of minimum payments under capital leases was $298 million, after deducting $1 million for estimated executory costs and $239 million representing imputed interest. The present value of minimum receivables under direct financing subleases was $13 million after deducting $7 million of unearned interest income.

Rental expense and income were as follows:

| | 1994 | 1993 | 1992 |
|---|---|---|---|
| **Rental expense** | | | |
| Minimum | **$433.5** | $392.3 | $351.5 |
| Contingent | **31.7** | 27.5 | 27.5 |
| | **$465.2** | $419.8 | $379.0 |
| **Rental income** | | | |
| Minimum | **$ 11.7** | $ 12.2 | $ 10.2 |
| Contingent | **3.5** | 4.4 | 4.5 |
| | **$ 15.2** | $ 16.6 | $ 14.7 |

Contingent rentals are based on sales by restaurants in excess of levels stipulated in the lease agreements.

## Note 12 - Postretirement Benefits Other Than Pensions

PepsiCo provides postretirement health care benefits to eligible retired employees and their dependents, principally in the U.S. Retirees who have 10 years of service and attain age 55 while in service with PepsiCo are eligible to participate in the postretirement benefit plans. The plans are not funded and were largely noncontributory through 1993.

In 1992, PepsiCo adopted Statement of Financial Accounting Standards No. 106, "Employers' Accounting for Postretirement Benefits Other Than Pensions." The cumulative effect of this change in accounting for years prior to 1992 resulted in a non-cash charge of $575.3 million pretax ($356.7 million after-tax or $0.44 per share).

Effective in 1993 and 1994, PepsiCo implemented programs intended to stem rising costs and introduced retiree cost-sharing, including adopting a provision which limits its future obligation to absorb health care cost inflation. These amendments resulted in an unrecognized prior service gain of $191 million, which is being amortized on a straight-line basis over the average remaining employee service period of 10 years as a reduction in postretirement benefit expense beginning in 1993.

The postretirement benefit expense for 1994, 1993 and 1992 included the following components:

| | 1994 | 1993 | 1992 |
|---|---|---|---|
| Service cost of benefits earned | **$ 18.6** | $ 14.7 | $25.5 |
| Interest cost on accumulated postretirement benefit obligation | **41.4** | 40.6 | 50.8 |
| Amortization of prior service (gain) cost | **(19.6)** | (19.6) | 0.1 |
| Amortization of net loss | **5.6** | 0.5 | — |
| | **$ 46.0** | $36.2 | $76.4 |

The decline in the 1993 expense was primarily due to the plan amendments, reflecting reductions in service and interest costs as well as the amortization of the unrecognized prior service gain.

The 1994 and 1993 postretirement benefit liability included the following components:

| | 1994 | 1993 |
|---|---|---|
| Actuarial present value of postretirement benefit obligation: | | |
| Retirees | **$(288.6)** | $(313.8) |
| Fully eligible active plan participants | **(88.1)** | (107.3) |
| Other active plan participants | **(148.0)** | (206.9) |
| Accumulated postretirement benefit obligation | **(524.7)** | (628.0) |
| Unrecognized prior service gain | **(151.9)** | (171.5) |
| Unrecognized net loss | **11.5** | 148.6 |
| | **$(665.1)** | $(650.9) |

The discount rate assumptions used in computing the information above were as follows:

| | 1994 | 1993 | 1992 |
|---|---|---|---|
| Postretirement benefit expense | **6.8%** | 8.2 | 8.9 |
| Accumulated postretirement benefit obligation | **9.1%** | 6.8 | 8.2 |

The year-to-year fluctuations in the discount rate assumptions primarily reflect changes in U.S. interest rates. The discount rate represents the expected yield on a portfolio of high-grade (AA rated or equivalent) fixed-income investments with cash flow streams sufficient to satisfy benefit obligations under the plans when due.

As a result of the plan amendments discussed above, separate assumed health care cost trend rates are used for employees who retire before and after the effective date of the amendments. The assumed health care cost trend rate for employees who retired before the effective date is 9.5% for 1995, declining gradually to 5.5% in 2005 and thereafter. For employees retiring after the effective date, the trend rate is 8.0% for 1995, declining gradually to 0% in 2005 and thereafter. A 1 point increase in the assumed health care cost trend rate would have increased the 1994 postretirement benefit expense by $2.0 million and would have increased the 1994 accumulated postretirement benefit obligation by $20.6 million.

## Note 13 - Pension Plans

PepsiCo sponsors noncontributory defined benefit pension plans covering substantially all full-time domestic employees as well as contributory and noncontributory defined benefit pension plans covering certain international employees. Benefits generally are based on years of service and compensation or stated amounts for each year of service. PepsiCo funds the domestic plans in amounts not less than minimum statutory funding requirements nor more than the maximum amount that can be deducted for federal income tax purposes. International plans are funded in amounts sufficient to comply with local statutory requirements. The plans' assets consist principally of equity securities, government and corporate debt securities and other fixed-income obligations. For 1994 and 1993, the domestic plan assets included 6.9 million shares of

PepsiCo Capital Stock, with a market value of $227.2 million and $265.7 million, respectively. Dividends on PepsiCo Capital Stock of $4.7 million and $4.0 million were received by the domestic plans in 1994 and 1993, respectively.

The international plans presented below are primarily comprised of those in the U.K. and Canada for all three years as well as those in Mexico and Japan for 1994 and 1993. Information for 1992 has not been restated, since complete information for plans in Mexico and Japan was not available. Inclusion of the plans in Mexico and Japan increased the 1994 and 1993 pension expense by $7.9 million and $5.5 million, respectively.

The net pension expense (income) for company-sponsored plans included the following components:

|  | Domestic Plans | | | International Plans | | |
|---|---|---|---|---|---|---|
|  | 1994 | 1993 | 1992 | 1994 | 1993 | 1992 |
| Service cost of benefits earned | $ 69.8 | $ 57.1 | $ 52.3 | $ 15.0 | $ 12.4 | $ 8.6 |
| Interest cost on projected benefit obligation | 84.0 | 75.6 | 72.0 | 15.4 | 15.0 | 10.9 |
| Return on plan assets: | | | | | | |
| Actual loss (gain) | 19.7 | (161.5) | (61.3) | 8.1 | (40.8) | (36.0) |
| Deferred (loss) gain | (130.5) | 70.9 | (26.2) | (32.5) | 20.4 | 18.6 |
|  | (110.8) | (90.6) | (87.5) | (24.4) | (20.4) | (17.4) |
| Amortization of net transition (gain) loss | (19.0) | (19.0) | (19.0) | (0.2) | 0.3 | — |
| Net other amortization | 9.1 | 8.8 | 8.2 | 1.7 | 1.7 | (6.5) |
|  | $ 33.1 | $ 31.9 | $ 26.0 | $ 7.5 | $ 9.0 | $ (4.4) |

Reconciliations of the funded status of the plans to the pension liability are as follows:

|  | Domestic Plans | | | | International Plans | | | |
|---|---|---|---|---|---|---|---|---|
|  | Assets Exceed Accumulated Benefits | | Accumulated Benefits Exceed Assets | | Assets Exceed Accumulated Benefits | | Accumulated Benefits Exceed Assets | |
|  | 1994 | 1993 | 1994 | 1993 | 1994 | 1993 | 1994 | 1993 |
| Actuarial present value of benefit obligation: | | | | | | | | |
| Vested benefits | $ (774.0) | $ (726.0) | $(21.6) | $(192.8) | $(124.4) | $(138.8) | $(22.8) | $(28.0) |
| Nonvested benefits | (97.4) | (99.0) | (1.6) | (28.3) | (2.3) | (3.4) | (7.4) | (5.4) |
| Accumulated benefit obligation | (871.4) | (825.0) | (23.2) | (221.1) | (126.7) | (142.2) | (30.2) | (33.4) |
| Effect of projected compensation increases | (111.1) | (131.6) | (47.6) | (41.7) | (24.1) | (22.9) | (10.1) | (18.4) |
| Projected benefit obligation | (982.5) | (956.6) | (70.8) | (262.8) | (150.8) | (165.1) | (40.3) | (51.8) |
| Plan assets at fair value | 1,133.0 | 1,018.7 | 2.8 | 185.2 | 213.4 | 221.7 | 15.5 | 17.3 |
| Plan assets in excess of (less than) projected benefit obligation | 150.5 | 62.1 | (68.0) | (77.6) | 62.6 | 56.6 | (24.8) | (34.5) |
| Unrecognized prior service cost | 30.6 | 11.7 | 30.0 | 49.9 | 3.5 | 3.2 | 0.3 | 0.5 |
| Unrecognized net (gain) loss | (71.3) | 16.0 | 3.7 | 26.1 | 14.0 | 11.9 | (3.1) | 7.7 |
| Unrecognized net transition (gain) loss | (73.1) | (89.0) | 0.3 | (2.8) | (1.8) | (2.6) | 4.9 | 8.1 |
| Adjustment required to recognize minimum liability | — | — | — | (33.0) | — | — | — | (4.3) |
| Prepaid (accrued) pension liability | $ 36.7 | $ 0.8 | $(34.0) | $ (37.4) | $ 78.3 | $ 69.1 | $(22.7) | $(22.5) |

The assumptions used to compute the information above were as follows:

|  | Domestic Plans | | | International Plans | | |
|---|---|---|---|---|---|---|
|  | 1994 | 1993 | 1992 | 1994 | 1993 | 1992 |
| Discount rate—pension expense | 7.0% | 8.2 | 8.4 | 7.3% | 9.0 | 9.5 |
| Expected long-term rate of return on plan assets | 10.0% | 10.0 | 10.0 | 11.3% | 10.8 | 10.8 |
| Discount rate—projected benefit obligation | 9.0% | 7.0 | 8.2 | 9.3% | 7.4 | 9.0 |
| Future compensation growth rate | 3.3%-7.0% | 3.3-7.0 | 3.3-7.0 | 3.0%-8.5% | 3.5-8.5 | 5.0-7.0 |

The discount rates and rates of return for the international plans represent weighted averages.

The year-to-year fluctuations in the discount rate assumptions primarily reflect changes in interest rates. The discount rates represent the expected yield on a portfolio of high-grade (AA rated or equivalent) fixed-income investments with cash flow streams sufficient to satisfy benefit obligations under the plans when due. The higher assumed discount rates used to measure the 1994 projected benefit obligation compared to the assumed discount rate used to measure the 1993 projected benefit obligation changed the funded status of certain plans from underfunded to overfunded.

In 1994, PepsiCo changed the method for calculating the market-related value of plan assets used in determining the return-on-asset component of annual pension expense and the cumulative net unrecognized gain or loss subject to amortization. Under the previous accounting method, the calculation of the market-related value of assets reflected amortization of the actual capital return on assets on a straight-line basis over a five-year period. Under the new method, the calculation of the market-related value of assets reflects the long-term rate of return expected by PepsiCo and amortization of the difference between the actual return (including capital, dividends and interest) and the expected return over a five-year period. PepsiCo believes the new method is widely used in practice and preferable because it results in calculated plan asset values that more closely approximate fair value, while still mitigating the effect of annual market-value fluctuations. Under both methods, only the cumulative net unrecognized gain or loss which exceeds 10% of the greater of the projected benefit obligation or the market-related value of plan assets is subject to amortization. The change resulted in a noncash benefit in 1994 of $37.8 million ($23.3 million after-tax or $0.03 per share) representing the cumulative effect of the change related to years prior to 1994 and $35.1 million in lower pension expense ($21.6 million after-tax or $0.03 per share) related to 1994 as compared to the previous accounting method. Had this change been applied retroactively, pension expense would have been reduced by $16.4 million ($10.7 million after-tax or $0.01 per share) and $9.5 million ($6.5 million after-tax or $0.01 per share) in 1993 and 1992, respectively.

## Note 14 - Postemployment Benefits Other Than to Retirees

Effective the beginning of 1994, PepsiCo adopted Statement of Financial Accounting Standards No. 112 (SFAS 112), "Employers' Accounting for Postemployment Benefits." SFAS 112 requires PepsiCo to accrue the cost of certain postemployment benefits to be paid to terminated or inactive employees other than retirees. The principal effect to PepsiCo results from accruing severance benefits to be provided to employees of certain business units who are terminated in the ordinary course of business over the expected service lives of the employees. Previously, these benefits were accrued upon the occurrence of an event. Severance benefits resulting from actions not in the ordinary course of business will continue to be accrued when those actions occur. The cumulative effect charge upon adoption of SFAS 112, which relates to years prior to 1994, was $84.6 million ($55.3 million after-tax or $0.07 per share). As compared to the previous accounting method, the current year impact of adopting SFAS 112 was immaterial to 1994 operating profits. PepsiCo's cash flows have been unaffected by this accounting change as PepsiCo continues to largely fund postemployment benefit costs as incurred.

## Note 15 - Franchise Arrangements

Franchise arrangements with restaurant franchisees generally provide for initial fees and continuing royalty payments to PepsiCo based upon a percentage of sales. The arrangements are intended to assist franchisees through, among other things, product development and marketing programs initiated by PepsiCo for both its company-owned and franchised operations. On a limited basis, franchisees have also entered into leases of restaurant properties leased or owned by PepsiCo (See Note 11.) Royalty revenues, initial fees and rental payments from franchisees, which are included in Net Sales, aggregated $407 million, $357 million and $344 million in 1994, 1993 and 1992, respectively. Franchise royalty revenues, which represent the majority of these amounts, are recognized when earned. PepsiCo also has franchise arrangements with beverage bottlers, which do not provide for royalty payments.

## Note 16 - Restructurings

PepsiCo recorded restructuring charges of $193.5 million in 1992 ($128.5 million after-tax or $0.16 per share) and $149.0 million in 1991 ($102.3 million after-tax or $0.13 per share). The 1992 charge related principally to streamlining and reorganizing the domestic beverage business, consolidating the snack food businesses in the U.K. and streamlining an acquired beverage bottling business in Spain. The 1991 charge related to streamlining snack food operations in the U.S. and U.K. and operations at KFC. These charges were classified in Selling, general and administrative expenses and were primarily for costs requiring future cash outlays. The annual accrual activity, including asset valuation allowances, and the related components were as follows:

| | 1994 | 1993 | 1992 |
|---|---|---|---|
| **Annual Accrual Activity** | | | |
| Balance—Beginning of year . . . . . . | **$121.7** | $ 253.2 | $112.6 |
| New restructuring charges . . . . . . . . | — | — | 193.5 |
| New restructuring accruals - purchase price adjustments **(A)** . . | — | — | 41.5 |
| Accretion of interest on net present value of severance . . . . . . | **2.8** | 6.9 | — |
| Cash payments . . . . . . . . . . . . . | **(50.6)** | (122.8) | (83.5) |
| Asset write-offs . . . . . . . . . . . . . | **(4.0)** | (9.1) | (10.3) |
| Change in estimates . . . . . . . . . . . | **(28.7)** | (6.5) | (0.6) |
| Balance—End of year . . . . . . . . . . | **$ 41.2** | $ 121.7 | $253.2 |
| **Accrual Components** | | | |
| Facility closings/fixed asset disposals . . . . . . . . . . . . . . . . . | **$ 3.0** | $ 13.9 | $ 35.3 |
| Employee terminations **(A)** . . . . . . . | **36.1** | 103.2 | 153.9 |
| Relocation of employees and equipment . . . . . . . . . . . . . . | **0.7** | 2.2 | 29.1 |
| Nonrecurring costs of redesigning core business processes **(B)** . . . . . . . . . . . . . . | — | 0.7 | 25.3 |
| Other . . . . . . . . . . . . . . . . . . . . | **1.4** | 1.7 | 9.6 |
| Balance—End of year **(C)** . . . . . . . | **$ 41.2** | $ 121.7 | $253.2 |

**(A)** Included amounts for termination of employees of an acquired beverage bottling business in Spain accounted for as a purchase. The acquired business was formerly accounted for as a 30% owned equity investment. Upon acquisition of the remaining 70%, 30% of the restructuring charge was included in income and 70% was a purchase price adjustment.

**(B)** Included only specific nonrecurring incremental and direct costs for activities clearly identifiable with the redesign of the domestic beverages' core business processes.

**(C)** The 1994 year-end balance of $41 million, which was primarily included in Other current liabilities, represented estimated future cash payments of $26 million, $12 million and $3 million in 1995, 1996 and 1997, respectively.

## Note 17 - Income Taxes

In 1992, PepsiCo adopted Statement of Financial Accounting Standards No. 109 (SFAS 109), "Accounting for Income Taxes." PepsiCo elected to adopt SFAS 109 on a prospective basis, resulting in a noncash tax charge in 1992 of $570.7 million ($0.71 per share) for the cumulative effect of the change related to years prior to 1992. The cumulative effect primarily represented the recording of additional deferred tax liabilities related to identifiable intangible assets, principally acquired trademarks and reacquired franchise rights, that have no tax bases. These deferred tax liabilities would be paid only in the unlikely event the related intangible assets were sold in taxable transactions.

Detail of the provision for income taxes on income before cumulative effect of accounting changes was as follows:

|  |  | 1994 | 1993 | 1992 |
|---|---|---|---|---|
| Current | Federal | $642.0 | $466.8 | $413.0 |
|  | Foreign | 174.1 | 195.5 | 170.4 |
|  | State | 131.2 | 89.0 | 65.7 |
|  |  | 947.3 | 751.3 | 649.1 |
| Deferred | Federal | (63.9) | 78.2 | (18.8) |
|  | Foreign | (1.8) | (12.5) | (33.5) |
|  | State | (1.2) | 17.6 | 0.3 |
|  |  | (66.9) | 83.3 | (52.0) |
|  |  | $880.4 | $834.6 | $597.1 |

In 1993, a charge of $29.9 million ($0.04 per share) was recorded to increase net deferred tax liabilities as of the beginning of 1993 for the 1% statutory income tax rate increase under 1993 U.S. tax legislation. The effect of the higher rate on the 1993 increase in net deferred tax liabilities through the enactment date of the legislation was immaterial.

U.S. and foreign income before income taxes and cumulative effect of accounting changes were as follows:

|  | 1994 | 1993 | 1992 |
|---|---|---|---|
| U.S. | $1,762.4 | $1,633.0 | $1,196.8 |
| Foreign | 902.0 | 789.5 | 702.0 |
|  | $2,664.4 | $2,422.5 | $1,898.8 |

PepsiCo operates centralized concentrate manufacturing facilities in Puerto Rico and Ireland under long-term tax incentives. The foreign amount in the above table includes approximately 50% (consistent with the allocation for tax purposes) of the income from U.S. sales of concentrate manufactured in Puerto Rico.

Reconciliation of the U.S. federal statutory tax rate to PepsiCo's effective tax rate on pretax income, based on the dollar impact of these major components on the provision for income taxes, was as follows:

|  | 1994 | 1993 | 1992 |
|---|---|---|---|
| U.S. federal statutory tax rate | 35.0% | 35.0% | 34.0% |
| State income tax, net of federal tax benefit | 3.2 | 2.9 | 2.3 |
| Effect of lower taxes on foreign income (including Puerto Rico and Ireland) | (5.4) | (3.3) | (5.0) |
| Adjustment to the beginning-of-the-year deferred tax assets valuation allowance | (1.3) | — | — |
| Reduction of prior year foreign accruals | — | (2.0) | — |
| Effect of 1993 tax legislation on deferred income taxes | — | 1.1 | — |
| Nondeductible amortization of domestic goodwill | 0.8 | 0.8 | 0.9 |
| Other, net | 0.7 | — | (0.8) |
| Effective tax rate | 33.0% | 34.5% | 31.4% |

Detail of the 1994 and 1993 deferred tax liabilities (assets) was as follows:

|  | 1994 | 1993 |
|---|---|---|
| Intangible assets other than nondeductible goodwill | $ 1,627.8 | $1,551.0 |
| Property, plant and equipment | 506.4 | 552.3 |
| Safe harbor leases | 171.2 | 177.5 |
| Zero coupon notes | 110.6 | 103.5 |
| Other | 336.7 | 549.0 |
| Gross deferred tax liabilities | 2,752.7 | 2,933.3 |
| Net operating loss carryforwards | (306.0) | (241.5) |
| Postretirement benefits | (248.3) | (268.0) |
| Self-insurance reserves | (71.2) | (10.8) |
| Deferred state income taxes | (69.1) | (39.9) |
| Restructuring accruals | (15.8) | (42.0) |
| Various accrued liabilities and other | (551.2) | (686.8) |
| Gross deferred tax assets | (1,261.6) | (1,289.0) |
| Deferred tax assets valuation allowance | 319.3 | 249.0 |
| Net deferred tax liability | $ 1,810.4 | $ 1,893.3 |
| Included in: |  |  |
| Prepaid expenses, taxes and other current assets | $ (166.9) | $ (138.2) |
| Other current liabilities | 4.4 | 23.9 |
| Deferred income taxes | 1,972.9 | 2,007.6 |
|  | $ 1,810.4 | $ 1,893.3 |

The valuation allowance related to deferred tax assets increased by $70.3 million in 1994 primarily resulting from additions related to current year net operating losses, partially offset by reversals related to prior year net operating losses. The net operating loss carryforwards largely related to a number of state and foreign jurisdictions and generally expire over a range of dates.

Deferred tax liabilities have not been recognized for bases differences related to investments in foreign subsidiaries and joint ventures. These differences, which consist primarily of unremitted earnings intended to be indefinitely reinvested, aggregated approximately $3.8 billion at year-end 1994 and $3.2 billion at year-end 1993, exclusive of amounts that if remitted in the future would result in little or no tax under current tax laws and the Puerto Rico tax incentive grant. Determination of the amount of unrecognized deferred tax liabilities is not practicable.

Tax benefits associated with exercises of stock options of $27.1 million in 1994, $23.4 million in 1993 and $57.5 million in 1992 were credited to shareholders' equity. A change in the functional currency of operations in Mexico from the U.S. dollar to local currency in 1993 resulted in a $19.3 million decrease in the net deferred foreign tax liability that was credited to shareholders' equity.

## Note 18 - Employee Incentive Plans

PepsiCo has established certain employee incentive plans under which stock options are granted. A stock option allows an employee to purchase a share of PepsiCo Capital Stock (Stock) in the future at a price equal to the fair market value on the date of the grant.

Under the PepsiCo SharePower Stock Option Plan, approved by the Board of Directors and effective in 1989, essentially all employees other than executive officers, part-time and short-service employees may be granted stock options annually. The number of options granted is based on each employee's annual earnings. The options generally become exercisable ratably over five years from the grant date and must be exercised within 10 years of the grant date. SharePower options were granted to approximately 128,000 employees in 1994, 118,000 employees in 1993 and 114,000 employees in 1992.

The shareholder-approved 1987 Long-Term Incentive Plan (the 1987 Plan), which has provisions similar to prior plans, provides incentives to eligible senior and middle management employees. In addition to grants of stock options, which are generally exercisable between 1 and 15 years from the grant date, the 1987 Plan allows for grants of performance share units (PSUs) to eligible senior management employees. A PSU is equivalent in value to a share of Stock at the grant date and vests for payment four years from the grant date, contingent upon attainment of prescribed Corporate performance goals. PSUs are not directly granted, as certain stock options granted may be surrendered by employees for a specified number of PSUs within 60 days of the option grant date. During 1994, 1,541,187 stock options were surrendered for 513,729 PSUs. At year-end 1994, 1993 and 1992, there were 629,202, 491,200 and 484,698 outstanding PSUs, respectively.

Grants under the 1987 Plan are approved by the Compensation Committee of the Board of Directors (the Committee), which is composed of outside directors. Payment of awards other than stock options is made in cash and/or Stock as approved by the Committee, and amounts expensed for such awards were $7 million, $5 million and $11 million in 1994, 1993 and 1992, respec-

tively. Under the 1987 Plan, a maximum of 54 million shares of Stock can be purchased or paid pursuant to grants. There were 7 million, 20 million, 22 million and 32 million shares available for future grants at year-end 1994, 1993, 1992 and 1991, respectively. The Committee does not intend to grant future awards under the 1987 Plan.

On May 4, 1994, PepsiCo's shareholders approved the 1994 Long-Term Incentive Plan (the 1994 Plan). The 1994 Plan continues the principal features of the 1987 Plan and authorizes a maximum of 75 million shares of Stock which may be purchased or paid pursuant to grants by the Committee. The first awards under the 1994 Plan were made as of January 1, 1995.

1994, 1993 and 1992 activity for the stock option plans included:

| (options in thousands) | SharePower | Long-Term Incentive |
|---|---|---|
| Outstanding at December 28, 1991 | 23,801 | 27,834 |
| Granted | 8,477 | 12,653 |
| Exercised | (1,155) | (5,155) |
| Surrendered for PSUs | — | (503) |
| Canceled | (2,327) | (1,839) |
| Outstanding at December 26, 1992 | 28,796 | 32,990 |
| Granted | 9,121 | 2,834 |
| Exercised | (1,958) | (1,412) |
| Surrendered for PSUs | — | (96) |
| Canceled | (2,524) | (966) |
| Outstanding at December 25, 1993 | 33,435 | 33,350 |
| Granted | **11,633** | **16,237** |
| Exercised | **(1,820)** | **(3,052)** |
| Surrendered for PSUs | **—** | **(1,541)** |
| Canceled | **(3,443)** | **(2,218)** |
| Outstanding at December 31, 1994 | **39,805** | **42,776** |
| Exercisable at December 31, 1994 | **16,115** | **18,439** |
| Option prices per share: | | |
| Exercised during 1994 | $17.58 to $36.75 | $4.11 to $38.75 |
| Exercised during 1993 | $17.58 to $36.75 | $4.11 to $36.31 |
| Exercised during 1992 | $17.58 to $35.25 | $4.11 to $29.88 |
| Outstanding at year-end 1994 | $17.58 to $36.75 | $7.69 to $42.81 |

## Note 19 - Contingencies

PepsiCo is subject to various claims and contingencies related to lawsuits, taxes, environmental and other matters arising out of the normal course of business. Management believes that the ultimate liability, if any, in excess of amounts already provided arising from such claims or contingencies is not likely to have a material adverse effect on PepsiCo's annual results of operations or financial condition. At year-end 1994 and 1993, PepsiCo was contingently liable under guarantees aggregating $187 million and $276 million, respectively. The guarantees are primarily issued to support financial arrangements of certain PepsiCo joint ventures, and bottling and restaurant franchisees. PepsiCo manages the risk associated with these guarantees by performing appropriate credit reviews in addition to retaining certain rights as a joint venture partner or franchisor. See Note 10 for information related to the fair value of the guarantees.

## Items Affecting Comparability

### Fiscal Year

1994 consisted of 53 weeks and the years 1989 through 1993 consisted of 52 weeks. The estimated favorable impact on net sales of the fifty-third week was $433.5, increasing beverage, snack food and restaurant net sales by $118.9, $142.6 and $172.0, respectively. The estimated favorable impact on operating profits of the fifty-third week was $64.5, increasing beverage, snack food and restaurant operating profits by $16.8, $26.0 and $22.9, respectively, and increasing unallocated expenses, net by $1.2.

### Unusual Items

Unusual charges totaled $193.5 in 1992, $170.0 in 1991 and $83.0 in 1990. These unusual items were as follows:

Beverages - 1992 included $145.0 in charges consisting of $115.4 and $29.6 to reorganize and streamline domestic and international operations, respectively. 1990 included a $10.5 domestic charge for trade receivables exposures.

Snack Foods - 1992 included a $40.3 charge principally to consolidate the Walkers businesses in the U.K. 1991 included $127.0 in charges consisting of $91.4 and $23.6 to streamline domestic and U.K. operations, respectively, and $12.0 to dispose of all or part of a small unprofitable business in Japan. 1990 included a $10.6 domestic charge for trade receivables exposures.

Restaurants - 1991 included $43.0 in charges at KFC consisting of $34.0 to streamline operations and $9.0 related to a delay in the U.S. roll-out of a new product. 1990 included $28.0 in charges consisting of $17.6 for closure of certain underperforming restaurants (Pizza Hut - $9.0, Taco Bell - $4.0 and KFC - $4.6) and $10.4 for reorganization charges for Pizza Hut.

Unallocated Expenses, net - 1992 included an $8.2 charge to streamline operations of the SVE joint venture. 1990 included $33.9 in charges consisting of $18.0 for accelerated contributions to the PepsiCo Foundation and $15.9 to reduce the carrying amount of an international Pizza Hut affiliate.

See Note 16 and Management's Analysis of beverage and snack food performance for additional information on restructurings.

### Accounting Changes

In 1994, PepsiCo adopted a preferred method for calculating the market-related value of plan assets used in determining annual pension expense (see Note 13) and extended the depreciable lives on certain domestic Pizza Hut delivery assets. As compared to the previous accounting methods, these changes increased 1994 operating profit by $49.1, increasing beverage, snack food and restaurant profits by $12.4, $15.5 and $19.6 (almost all domestic), respectively, and decreasing 1994 unallocated expenses, net by $1.6.

In 1992, PepsiCo adopted Statements of Financial Accounting Standards No. 106 and 109, "Employers' Accounting for Postretirement Benefits Other Than Pensions" and "Accounting for Income Taxes," respectively. As compared to the previous accounting methods, these changes reduced 1992 operating profit by $72.8, decreasing beverage, snack food and restaurant profits by $22.4, $30.8 and $15.4, respectively, and increasing 1992 unallocated expenses, net by $4.2. See Notes 12 and 17, respectively.

# Supplementary Financial Information

In addition to the financial statements and the accompanying notes, three items of supplementary financial information typically are presented: business segment information, 5- (or 10-) year summary of related financial data, and quarterly financial data.

## Business Segment Information

To help financial statement users assess the performance of diversified companies that operate in several different industries and lines of business, segmented financial information is required. The required information for each significant segment includes: revenues, income from operations, capital expenditures, identifiable assets, and depreciation and amortization. This information is generally included in the form of notes and schedules in the notes accompanying the financial statements. PepsiCo's note summarizing its business segment information is shown below:

# Business Segments

This information constitutes Note 2 to the Consolidated Financial Statements. (dollars in millions)

PepsiCo operates on a worldwide basis within three industry segments: beverages, snack foods and restaurants. The beverage segment primarily markets its Pepsi, Diet Pepsi, Mountain Dew and other brands worldwide and 7UP internationally, and manufactures concentrates for its brands for sale to franchised bottlers worldwide. The segment also operates bottling plants and distribution facilities located in the U.S. and in various international markets, and manufactures and distributes ready-to-drink Lipton tea products in North America. In addition, under separate distribution and joint venture agreements, the segment distributes certain previously existing, as well as manufactures and distributes new jointly-developed, Ocean Spray juice products in the U.S. and Canada. The snack food segment manufactures, distributes and markets chips and other snacks worldwide, with Frito-Lay representing the domestic business. The international snack food business includes major operations in Mexico, the U.K. and Canada. The restaurant segment consists primarily of the operations of the worldwide Pizza Hut, Taco Bell and KFC chains. PFS, PepsiCo's restaurant distribution operation, supplies company-owned and franchised restaurants, principally in the U.S. Net sales and operating profits of PFS' franchisee operations have been allocated to each restaurant chain.

Unallocated Expenses, net includes the corporate headquarters expenses, minority interests, primarily in the Gamesa (Mexico) and Wedel (Poland) snack food businesses, foreign exchange translation and transaction gains and losses and other corporate items not allocated to the business segments. Corporate Identifiable Assets consist principally of short-term investments held outside the U.S. and investments in affiliates.

PepsiCo has invested in about 75 joint ventures, principally international and all within PepsiCo's three industry segments, in which it exercises significant influence but not control. Equity in net income of these affiliates was $37.8, $30.1, and $40.1 in 1994, 1993 and 1992, respectively. The increase in 1994 primarily reflected increased profits at Snack Ventures Europe (SVE). The decline in 1993 primarily reflected the expansion costs in a beverage affiliate in India and lower profits at SVE. International snack food affiliates, which represented the largest component of equity in net income of affiliates, contributed $34.3, $24.1 and $23.2 in 1994, 1993 and 1992, respectively. Dividends received from affiliates totaled $33.1, $16.4 and $29.6 in 1994, 1993 and 1992, respectively.

PepsiCo's year-end investments in affiliates totaled $1.3 billion in 1994, $1.1 billion in 1993 and $904.9 in 1992. The increase in 1994 reflected advances to California Pizza Kitchen (CPK), a domestic casual dining restaurant chain, and investments in international franchised bottling operations in Thailand and China, partially offset by the translation impact of the late 1994 devaluation of the Mexican peso. Significant investments in affiliates at year-end 1994 included $234.3 in General Bottlers, a U.S. franchised bottler, $162.9 in CPK, $160.2 in a KFC Japan joint venture, $123.2 in BAESA, a franchised bottler with operations in South America, and $80.9 in SVE.

## Industry Segments

(dollars in millions)

| | | Growth Rate 1989 - 1994 | 1994 | 1993 | 1992 | 1991 | 1990 |
|---|---|---|---|---|---|---|---|
| **Net Sales** | | | | | | | |
| Beverages: | Domestic | 7.2% | $ 6,541.2 | $ 5,918.1 | $ 5,485.2 | $ 5,171.5 | $ 5,034.5 |
| | International | 22.2% | 3,146.3 | 2,720.1 | 2,120.4 | 1,743.7 | 1,488.5 |
| | | 10.9% | 9,687.5 | 8,638.2 | 7,605.6 | 6,915.2 | 6,523.0 |
| Snack Foods: | Domestic | 9.3% | 5,011.3 | 4,365.3 | 3,950.4 | 3,737.9 | 3,471.5 |
| | International | 32.0% | 3,253.1 | 2,661.5 | 2,181.7 | 1,512.2 | 1,295.3 |
| | | 15.5% | 8,264.4 | 7,026.8 | 6,132.1 | 5,250.1 | 4,766.8 |
| Restaurants: | Domestic | 13.2% | 8,693.9 | 8,025.7 | 7,115.4 | 6,258.4 | 5,540.9 |
| | International | 26.4% | 1,826.6 | 1,330.0 | 1,116.9 | 868.5 | 684.8 |
| | | 14.9% | 10,520.5 | 9,355.7 | 8,232.3 | 7,126.9 | 6,225.7 |
| **Combined Segments** | | | | | | | |
| | Domestic | 10.1% | 20,246.4 | 18,309.1 | 16,551.0 | 15,167.8 | 14,046.9 |
| | International | 26.6% | 8,226.0 | 6,711.6 | 5,419.0 | 4,124.4 | 3,468.6 |
| | | 13.6% | $28,472.4 | $25,020.7 | $21,970.0 | $19,292.2 | $17,515.5 |
| **By Restaurant Chain** | | | | | | | |
| | Pizza Hut | 12.8% | $ 4,474.4 | $ 4,128.7 | $ 3,603.5 | $ 3,258.3 | $ 2,949.9 |
| | Taco Bell | 18.3% | 3,401.4 | 2,901.3 | 2,460.0 | 2,038.1 | 1,745.5 |
| | KFC | 14.7% | 2,644.7 | 2,325.7 | 2,168.8 | 1,830.5 | 1,530.3 |
| | | 14.9% | $10,520.5 | $ 9,355.7 | $ 8,232.3 | $ 7,126.9 | $ 6,225.7 |
| **Operating Profits** | | | | | | | |
| Beverages: | Domestic | 12.1% | $ 1,022.3 | $ 936.9 | $ 686.3 | $ 746.2 | $ 673.8 |
| | International | 20.0% | 194.7 | 172.1 | 112.3 | 117.1 | 93.8 |
| | | 13.2% | 1,217.0 | 1,109.0 | 798.6 | 863.3 | 767.6 |
| Snack Foods: | Domestic | 8.9% | 1,025.1 | 900.7 | 775.5 | 616.6 | 732.3 |
| | International | 27.1% | 351.8 | 288.9 | 209.2 | 140.1 | 160.3 |
| | | 12.2% | 1,376.9 | 1,189.6 | 984.7 | 756.7 | 892.6 |
| Restaurants: | Domestic | 12.2% | 658.8 | 685.1 | 597.8 | 479.4 | 447.2 |
| | International | 4.3% | 71.5 | 92.9 | 120.7 | 96.2 | 75.2 |
| | | 11.3% | 730.3 | 778.0 | 718.5 | 575.6 | 522.4 |
| **Combined Segments** | | | | | | | |
| | Domestic | 11.1% | 2,706.2 | 2,522.7 | 2,059.6 | 1,842.2 | 1,853.3 |
| | International | 20.6% | 618.0 | 553.9 | 442.2 | 353.4 | 329.3 |
| | | 12.3% | 3,324.2 | 3,076.6 | 2,501.8 | 2,195.6 | 2,182.6 |
| **Equity Income** | | | 37.8 | 30.1 | 40.1 | 32.2 | 30.1 |
| **Unallocated Expenses, net** | | | (160.8) | (200.2) | (170.7) | (116.0) | (170.6) |
| **Operating Profit** | | 12.6% | $ 3,201.2 | $ 2,906.5 | $ 2,371.2 | $ 2,111.8 | $ 2,042.1 |
| **By Restaurant Chain** | | | | | | | |
| | Pizza Hut | 7.5% | $ 294.8 | $ 372.1 | $ 335.4 | $ 314.5 | $ 245.9 |
| | Taco Bell | 18.7% | 270.3 | 253.1 | 214.3 | 180.6 | 149.6 |
| | KFC | 9.0% | 165.2 | 152.8 | 168.8 | 80.5 | 126.9 |
| | | 11.3% | $ 730.3 | $ 778.0 | $ 718.5 | $ 575.6 | $ 522.4 |

## Geographic Areas

| | Net Sales | | | Segment Operating Profits | | | Identifiable Assets | | |
|---|---|---|---|---|---|---|---|---|---|
| | 1994 | 1993 | 1992 | 1994 | 1993 | 1992 | 1994 | 1993 | 1992 |
| United States | $20,246.4 | $18,309.1 | $16,551.0 | $2,706.2 | $2,522.7 | $2,059.6 | $14,218.4 | $13,589.5 | $11,957.0 |
| Europe | 2,177.1 | 1,819.0 | 1,349.0 | 16.7 | 47.4 | 52.6 | 3,062.0 | 2,666.1 | 1,948.4 |
| Mexico | 2,022.8 | 1,613.4 | 1,234.6 | 261.4 | 223.1 | 172.1 | 994.7 | 1,217.1 | 1,054.6 |
| Canada | 1,244.3 | 1,206.1 | 979.6 | 81.6 | 101.7 | 78.9 | 1,342.1 | 1,364.0 | 1,340.6 |
| Other | 2,781.8 | 2,073.1 | 1,855.8 | 258.3 | 181.7 | 138.6 | 2,195.6 | 1,675.1 | 1,282.0 |
| **Combined Segments** | $28,472.4 | $25,020.7 | $21,970.0 | $3,324.2 | $3,076.6 | $2,501.8 | 21,812.8 | 20,511.8 | 17,582.6 |
| Corporate | | | | | | | 2,979.2 | 3,194.0 | 3,368.6 |
| | | | | | | | $24,792.0 | $23,705.8 | $20,951.2 |

## Quarterly Financial Data and Capital Stock Information

Nearly all publicly held companies and many nonpublic companies issue financial information on a quarterly basis to stockholders, regulatory agencies, and others. These quarterly reports are referred to as interim financial reports, for which there are prescribed accounting standards. Quarterly financial data along with capital stock information are frequently summarized in the Annual Report. PepsiCo summarizes its quarterly data and capital stock information as shown below and on page A32.

# Selected Quarterly Financial Data

(in millions except per share amounts, unaudited)
PepsiCo, Inc. and Subsidiaries

| | First Quarter (12 Weeks) | | Second Quarter (12 Weeks) | | Third Quarter (12 Weeks) | | Fourth Quarter (17/16 Weeks) | | Full Year (53/52 Weeks) | |
|---|---|---|---|---|---|---|---|---|---|---|
| | **1994** | 1993 | **1994** | 1993 | **1994** | 1993 | **1994** | 1993 | **1994** | 1993 |
| Net sales | **$5,728.9** | 5,091.6 | **6,557.0** | 5,890.3 | **7,064.0** | 6,316.4 | **9,122.5** | 7,722.4 | **28,472.4** | 25,020.7 |
| Gross profit | **$2,944.4** | 2,641.4 | **3,419.5** | 3,102.8 | **3,684.0** | 3,322.1 | **4,709.1** | 4,008.3 | **14,757.0** | 13,074.6 |
| Operating profit | **$ 550.5** | 506.0 | **785.0** | 750.4 | **961.7** | 851.6 | **904.0** | 798.5 | **3,201.2** | 2,906.5 |
| Income before income taxes and cumulative effect of accounting changes | **$ 438.4** | 391.6 | **672.2** | 635.7 | **830.3** | 736.5 | **723.5** | 658.7 | **2,664.4** | 2,422.5 |
| Provision for income taxes | **$ 155.6** | 131.2 | **225.7** | 208.9 | **288.9** | 278.3 | **210.2** | 216.2 | **880.4** | 834.6 |
| Income before cumulative effect of accounting changes | **$ 282.8** | 260.4 | **446.5** | 426.8 | **541.4** | 458.2 | **513.3** | 442.5 | **1,784.0** | 1,587.9 |
| Cumulative effect of accounting changes | **$ (32.0)** | — | **—** | — | **—** | — | **—** | — | **(32.0)** | — |
| Net income | **$ 250.8** | 260.4 | **446.5** | 426.8 | **541.4** | 458.2 | **513.3** | 442.5 | **1,752.0** | 1,587.9 |
| Income (charge) per share: | | | | | | | | | | |
| Income before cumulative effect of accounting changes | **$ 0.35** | 0.32 | **0.55** | 0.53 | **0.68** | 0.56 | **0.64** | 0.55 | **2.22** | 1.96 |
| Cumulative effect of accounting changes | **$ (0.04)** | — | **—** | — | **—** | — | **—** | — | **(0.04)** | — |
| Net income per share | **$ 0.31** | 0.32 | **0.55** | 0.53 | **0.68** | 0.56 | **0.64** | 0.55 | **2.18** | 1.96 |

# Stock Performance

PepsiCo was formed through the 1965 merger of Pepsi-Cola Company and Frito-Lay, Inc. A $1,000 investment in our stock made at year-end 1984 was worth $9,300 on December 31, 1994, assuming the reinvestment of dividends. This performance represents a compounded annual growth rate of 25%.

The return on PepsiCo Capital Stock compares favorably with the performance of the Standard & Poor's Industrials over the past five years.

The closing price for a share of PepsiCo Capital Stock on the New York Stock Exchange is as reported by the Dow Jones News/Retrieval Service for the end of each fiscal year 1984-1994.

**Total Return to Shareholders**
(In Dollars, assuming reinvestment of dividends)

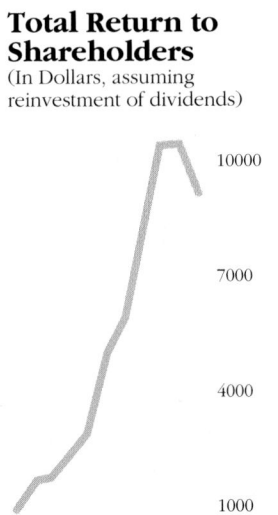

**Comparison of Monthly Market Price Performance**
(Closing Price Indexed at 12/31/89)

**Year-End Market Price of Stock**
(In Dollars)

### Five- or Ten-Year Summary

Usually presented in close proximity to the audited financial statements is a 5- or 10-year summary of selected financial data. From such a summary, one can determine trends and growth patterns over a fairly long period of time. PepsiCo presented the following summary that includes operating data, financial position data, and selected statistics and ratios:

# Selected Financial Data

| (in millions except per share and employee amounts, unaudited) PepsiCo, Inc. and Subsidiaries | Growth Rates | | | | |
|---|---|---|---|---|---|
| | Compounded | | Annual | | |
| | 10-Year 1984-94 | 5-Year 1989-94 | 1-Year 1993-94 | **1994** | 1993 |
| **Summary of Operations** | | | | | |
| Net sales | 15.0% | 13.6% | 13.8% | **$28,472.4** | 25,020.7 |
| Cost of sales and operating expenses | | | | **25,271.2** | 22,114.2 |
| Operating profit | 18.6% | 12.5% | 10.1% | **3,201.2** | 2,906.5 |
| Gain on joint venture stock offering | | | | **17.8** | — |
| Interest expense | | | | **(645.0)** | (572.7) |
| Interest income | | | | **90.4** | 88.7 |
| Income from continuing operations before income taxes and cumulative effect of accounting changes | 19.2% | 14.7% | 10.0% | **2,664.4** | 2,422.5 |
| Provision for income taxes | | | | **880.4** | 834.6 |
| Income from continuing operations before cumulative effect of accounting changes | 20.3% | 14.6% | 12.3% | **$ 1,784.0** | 1,587.9 |
| Cumulative effect of accounting changes | | | | **$ (32.0)** | — |
| Net income | 23.5% | 14.2% | 10.3% | **$ 1,752.0** | 1,587.9 |
| **Per Share Data** | | | | | |
| Income from continuing operations before cumulative effect of accounting changes | 21.0% | 14.5% | 13.3% | **$    2.22** | 1.96 |
| Cumulative effect of accounting changes | | | | **$   (0.04)** | — |
| Net income | 24.2% | 14.0% | 11.2% | **$    2.18** | 1.96 |
| Cash dividends declared | 14.2% | 16.9% | 14.8% | **$   0.700** | 0.610 |
| Average shares and equivalents outstanding | | | | **803.6** | 810.1 |
| **Cash Flow Data** | | | | | |
| Net cash provided by continuing operations | 14.2% | 14.5% | '18.6% | **$ 3,716.0** | 3,134.4 |
| Cash acquisitions and investments in affiliates | | | | **$   315.8** | 1,011.2 |
| Cash capital spending | 15.0% | 19.0% | 13.7% | **$ 2,253.2** | 1,981.6 |
| Cash dividends paid | 13.3% | 17.4% | 17.0% | **$   540.2** | 461.6 |
| **Year-End Position** | | | | | |
| Total assets | 17.7% | 10.4% | 4.6% | **$24,792.0** | 23,705.8 |
| Long-term debt | 29.5% | 7.8% | 18.8% | **$ 8,840.5** | 7,442.6 |
| Total debt | 25.9% | 6.5% | (1.2)% | **$ 9,519.0** | 9,633.8 |
| Shareholders' equity | | | | **$ 6,856.1** | 6,338.7 |
| Per share | 14.8% | 12.0% | 9.3% | **$    8.68** | 7.94 |
| Market price per share | 22.9% | 11.1% | (13.4)% | **$   36¼** | 41⅞ |
| Shares outstanding | | | | **789.9** | 798.8 |
| Employees | 12.1% | 12.1% | 11.3% | **471,000** | 423,000 |
| **Statistics** | | | | | |
| Return on average shareholders' equity | | | | **27.0%** | 27.2 |
| Market net debt ratio | | | | **26%** | 22 |
| Historical cost net debt ratio | | | | **49%** | 50 |

# PepsiCo, Inc.

| 1992 | 1991 | 1990 | 1989 | 1988 | 1987 | 1986 | 1985 | 1984 |
|---|---|---|---|---|---|---|---|---|
| 21,970.0 | 19,292.2 | 17,515.5 | 15,049.2 | 12,381.4 | 11,018.1 | 9,017.1 | 7,584.5 | 7,058.6 |
| 19,598.8 | 17,180.4 | 15,473.4 | 13,276.6 | 11,039.6 | 9,890.5 | 8,187.9 | 6,802.4 | 6,479.3 |
| 2,371.2 | 2,111.8 | 2,042.1 | 1,772.6 | 1,341.8 | 1,127.6 | 829.2 | 782.1 | 579.3 |
| — | — | 118.2 | — | — | — | — | — | — |
| (586.1) | (613.7) | (686.0) | (607.9) | (342.4) | (294.6) | (261.4) | (195.2) | (204.9) |
| 113.7 | 161.6 | 179.5 | 175.3 | 120.5 | 112.6 | 122.7 | 96.4 | 86.1 |
| 1,898.8 | 1,659.7 | 1,653.8 | 1,340.0 | 1,119.9 | 945.6 | 690.5 | 683.3 | 460.5 |
| 597.1 | 579.5 | 563.2 | 438.6 | 357.7 | 340.5 | 226.7 | 256.7 | 180.5 |
| 1,301.7 | 1,080.2 | 1,090.6 | 901.4 | 762.2 | 605.1 | 463.8 | 426.6 | 280.0 |
| (927.4) | — | — | — | — | — | — | — | — |
| 374.3 | 1,080.2 | 1,076.9 | 901.4 | 762.2 | 594.8 | 457.8 | 543.7 | 212.5 |
| 1.61 | 1.35 | 1.37 | 1.13 | 0.97 | 0.77 | 0.59 | 0.51 | 0.33 |
| (1.15) | — | — | — | — | — | — | — | — |
| 0.46 | 1.35 | 1.35 | 1.13 | 0.97 | 0.76 | 0.58 | 0.65 | 0.25 |
| 0.510 | 0.460 | 0.383 | 0.320 | 0.267 | 0.223 | 0.209 | 0.195 | 0.185 |
| 806.7 | 802.5 | 798.7 | 796.0 | 790.4 | 789.3 | 786.5 | 842.1 | 862.4 |
| 2,711.6 | 2,430.3 | 2,110.0 | 1,885.9 | 1,894.5 | 1,334.5 | 1,212.2 | 817.3 | 981.5 |
| 1,209.7 | 640.9 | 630.6 | 3,296.6 | 1,415.5 | 371.5 | 1,679.9 | 160.0 | — |
| 1,549.6 | 1,457.8 | 1,180.1 | 943.8 | 725.8 | 770.5 | 858.5 | 770.3 | 555.8 |
| 395.5 | 343.2 | 293.9 | 241.9 | 199.0 | 172.0 | 160.4 | 161.1 | 154.6 |
| 20,951.2 | 18,775.1 | 17,143.4 | 15,126.7 | 11,135.3 | 9,022.7 | 8,027.1 | 5,889.3 | 4,876.9 |
| 7,964.8 | 7,806.2 | 5,899.6 | 6,076.5 | 2,656.0 | 2,579.2 | 2,632.6 | 1,162.0 | 668.1 |
| 8,671.6 | 8,034.4 | 7,526.1 | 6,942.8 | 4,107.0 | 3,225.1 | 2,865.3 | 1,506.1 | 948.9 |
| 5,355.7 | 5,545.4 | 4,904.2 | 3,891.1 | 3,161.0 | 2,508.6 | 2,059.1 | 1,837.7 | 1,853.4 |
| 6.70 | 7.03 | 6.22 | 4.92 | 4.01 | 3.21 | 2.64 | 2.33 | 2.19 |
| 42¼ | 33¾ | 25¾ | 21⅜ | 13⅛ | 11¼ | 8¾ | 7⅞ | 4⅝ |
| 798.8 | 789.1 | 788.4 | 791.1 | 788.4 | 781.2 | 781.0 | 789.4 | 845.2 |
| 372,000 | 338,000 | 308,000 | 266,000 | 235,000 | 225,000 | 214,000 | 150,000 | 150,000 |
| 23.9 | 20.7 | 24.8 | 25.6 | 26.9 | 26.5 | 23.8 | 23.1 | 15.4 |
| 19 | 21 | 24 | 26 | 24 | 22 | 28 | 15 | 12 |
| 49 | 51 | 51 | 54 | 43 | 41 | 46 | 30 | 17 |

# Capital Stock Information

## Stock Trading Symbol

*PEP*

## Stock Exchange Listings

The New York Stock Exchange is the principal market for PepsiCo Capital Stock, which is also listed on the Chicago, Basel, Geneva, Zurich, Amsterdam and Tokyo Stock Exchanges.

## Shareholders

At year-end 1994, there were approximately 168,000 shareholders of record.

## Dividend Policy

Quarterly cash dividends are usually declared in November, February, May and July and paid at the beginning of January and the end of March, June and September. The dividend record dates for 1995 will be March 10, June 9, September 8 and December 8.

### Dividends Declared Per Share
(In Cents)

Quarterly cash dividends have been paid since PepsiCo was formed in 1965, and dividends paid per share have increased for 22 consecutive years.

Consistent with PepsiCo's current payout target of approximately one-third of the prior year's income from ongoing operations, the 1994 dividends declared represented 34% of 1993 income from ongoing operations:

### Dividends Declared Per Share (in cents)

| Quarter | 1994 | 1993 |
|---|---|---|
| 1 | 16 | 13 |
| 2 | 18 | 16 |
| 3 | 18 | 16 |
| 4 | 18 | 16 |
| Total | 70 | 61 |

## Stock Prices

The high, low and closing prices for a share of PepsiCo Capital Stock on the New York Stock Exchange, as reported by The Dow Jones News/Retrieval Service, for each fiscal quarter of 1994 and 1993 were as follows (in dollars):

| 1994 | High | Low | Close |
|---|---|---|---|
| **Fourth Quarter** | **37³⁄₈** | **32¼** | **36¼** |
| **Third Quarter** | **34⁵⁄₈** | **29¼** | **33¾** |
| **Second Quarter** | **37⁵⁄₈** | **29⁷⁄₈** | **31⅛** |
| **First Quarter** | **42½** | **35¾** | **37⁵⁄₈** |

| 1993 | High | Low | Close |
|---|---|---|---|
| Fourth Quarter | 42⅛ | 37⁵⁄₈ | 41⅞ |
| Third Quarter | 40⅛ | 34⁵⁄₈ | 39 |
| Second Quarter | 43⁵⁄₈ | 34½ | 36½ |
| First Quarter | 43³⁄₈ | 38½ | 42 |

## Cumulative Earnings Growth vs. Change in Stock Price in 1994

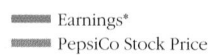

The Stock Market worried that the slow growth in second quarter earnings might be a trend and reacted strongly. However, earnings clearly rebounded in the second half and the stock began to recover.

* Excludes unusual items noted above in notes (c) and (d).

## Year-End Market Price of Stock
(In Dollars)

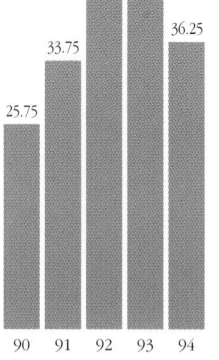

The market price of PepsiCo Capital Stock has grown at a compounded annual rate of 11.1% over the past five years.

# PRESENT VALUE CONCEPTS

Business enterprises borrow and invest large sums of money. Both of these types of transactions involve the use of **present value computations**. A present value computation is based on the concept of the **time value of money**. For example, would you rather be given $1,000 today or be given $1,000 a year from today? If you get the $1,000 today and invest it to earn 10% per year, the $1,000 will accumulate to $1,100 ($1,000 plus the $100 interest) one year from today. The $1,000 received today is the present value amount that is equivalent to $1,100 one year from now. The present value, therefore, is based on three variables: (1) the dollar amount to be received (the future amount), (2) the length of time until the amount is received (the number of periods), and (3) the interest rate (the discount rate). The process of determining the present value is referred to as **discounting the future amount**. The relationship of these fundamental variables is depicted in the following time diagram:

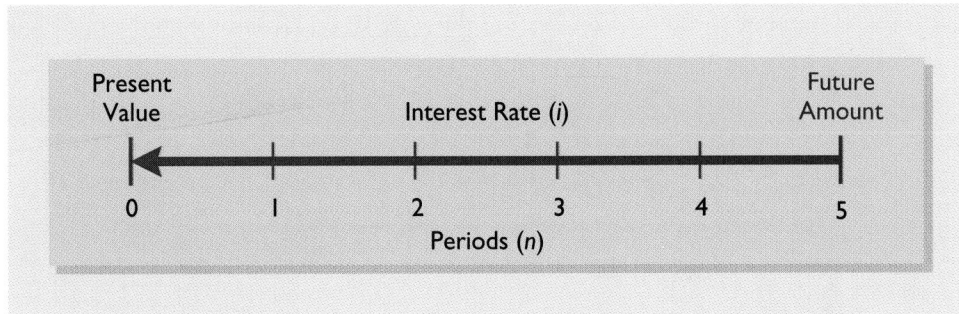

**Illustration B-I**

*Time diagram*

To better understand the variables involved in present value analysis, we encourage you to use time diagrams such as the one in Illustration B-1.

In this textbook, present value computations are used in measuring several items. For example, in Chapter 16, to determine the market price of a bond, the present value of the principal and interest payments is computed. In addition, the determination of the amount to be reported for notes payable and lease liability involves present value computations. And, in Chapter 27, the discounted cash flow technique and the net present value method are used to make capital budget decisions.

## Present Value of a Single Future Amount

To illustrate present value concepts, assume that you are willing to invest a sum of money that will yield $1,000 at the end of one year. In other words, what amount would you need to invest today to have $1,000 one year from now?

If you want a 10% rate of return, the investment or present value is $909.09 ($1,000 ÷ 1.10). The computation of this amount is shown in Illustration B-2.

**Illustration B-2**

*Present value computation— $1,000 discounted at 10% for 1 year*

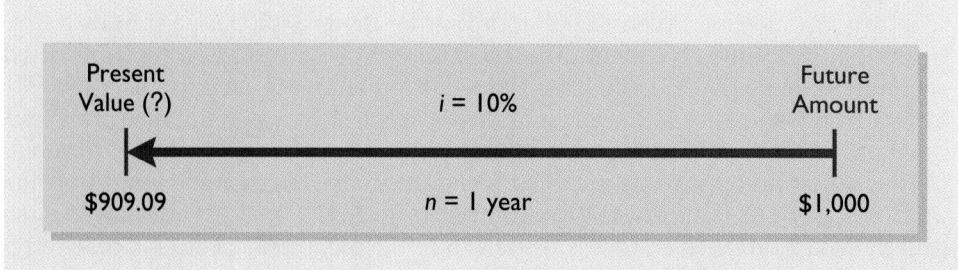

Present value × (1 + interest rate) = Future value
Present value × (1 + 10%)         = $1,000
Present value                     = $1,000 ÷ 1.10
**Present value**                 = **$909.09**

The future amount ($1,000), the discount rate (10%), and the number of periods (1) are known. The variables in this situation can be depicted in the following time diagram:

**Illustration B-3**

*Finding present value if discounted for one period*

Present Value (?)            $i = 10\%$            Future Amount

$909.09            $n = 1$ year            $1,000

If the single future amount of $1,000 is to be received **in 2 years** and discounted at 10%, its present value is $826.45 [($1,000 ÷ 1.10) ÷ 1.10], depicted as follows:

**Illustration B-4**

*Finding present value if discounted for two periods*

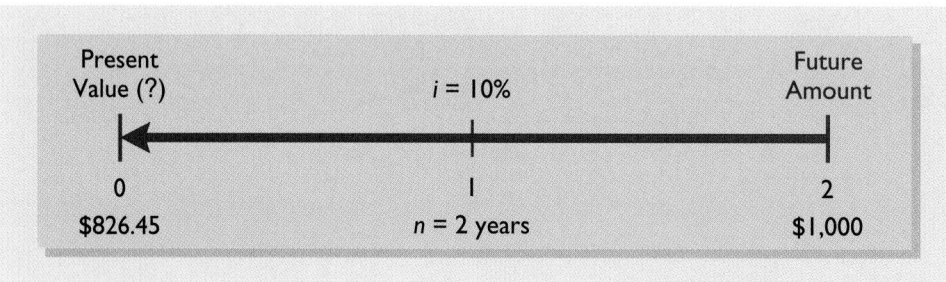

Present Value (?)            $i = 10\%$            Future Amount

0            1            2
$826.45            $n = 2$ years            $1,000

The present value of 1 may also be determined through tables that show the present value of 1 for $n$ periods. In Table B-1 on page B3, $n$ is the number of discounting periods involved. The percentages are the periodic interest rates or discount rates, and the 5-digit decimal numbers in the respective columns are the factors for the present value of 1.

When Table B-1 is used, the future amount is multiplied by the present value factor specified at the intersection of the number of periods and the discount rate. For example, the present value factor for 1 period at a discount rate of 10% is .90909, which equals the $909.09 ($1,000 × .90909) computed in Illustration B-2. For 2 periods at a discount rate of 10%, the present value factor is .82645, which equals the $826.45 ($1,000 × .82645) computed previously.

Note that **a higher discount rate produces a smaller present value**. For example, using a 15% discount rate, the present value of $1,000 due one year from now is $869.57 versus $909.09 at 10%. It should also be recognized that **the further removed from the present the future amount is, the smaller the present**

## TABLE B-1
## PRESENT VALUE OF 1

| (n) Periods | 4% | 5% | 6% | 8% | 9% | 10% | 11% | 12% | 15% |
|---|---|---|---|---|---|---|---|---|---|
| 1 | .96154 | .95238 | .94340 | .92593 | .91743 | .90909 | .90090 | .89286 | .86957 |
| 2 | .92456 | .90703 | .89000 | .85734 | .84168 | .82645 | .81162 | .79719 | .75614 |
| 3 | .88900 | .86384 | .83962 | .79383 | .77218 | .75132 | .73119 | .71178 | .65752 |
| 4 | .85480 | .82270 | .79209 | .73503 | .70843 | .68301 | .65873 | .63552 | .57175 |
| 5 | .82193 | .78353 | .74726 | .68058 | .64993 | .62092 | .59345 | .56743 | .49718 |
| 6 | .79031 | .74622 | .70496 | .63017 | .59627 | .56447 | .53464 | .50663 | .43233 |
| 7 | .75992 | .71068 | .66506 | .58349 | .54703 | .51316 | .48166 | .45235 | .37594 |
| 8 | .73069 | .67684 | .62741 | .54027 | .50187 | .46651 | .43393 | .40388 | .32690 |
| 9 | .70259 | .64461 | .59190 | .50025 | .46043 | .42410 | .39092 | .36061 | .28426 |
| 10 | .67556 | .61391 | .55839 | .46319 | .42241 | .38554 | .35218 | .32197 | .24719 |
| 11 | .64958 | .58468 | .52679 | .42888 | .38753 | .35049 | .31728 | .28748 | .21494 |
| 12 | .62460 | .55684 | .49697 | .39711 | .35554 | .31863 | .28584 | .25668 | .18691 |
| 13 | .60057 | .53032 | .46884 | .36770 | .32618 | .28966 | .25751 | .22917 | .16253 |
| 14 | .57748 | .50507 | .44230 | .34046 | .29925 | .26333 | .23199 | .20462 | .14133 |
| 15 | .55526 | .48102 | .41727 | .31524 | .27454 | .23939 | .20900 | .18270 | .12289 |
| 16 | .53391 | .45811 | .39365 | .29189 | .25187 | .21763 | .18829 | .16312 | .10687 |
| 17 | .51337 | .43630 | .37136 | .27027 | .23107 | .19785 | .16963 | .14564 | .09293 |
| 18 | .49363 | .41552 | .35034 | .25025 | .21199 | .17986 | .15282 | .13004 | .08081 |
| 19 | .47464 | .39573 | .33051 | .23171 | .19449 | .16351 | .13768 | .11611 | .07027 |
| 20 | .45639 | .37689 | .31180 | .21455 | .17843 | .14864 | .12403 | .10367 | .06110 |

**value**. For example, using the same discount rate of 10%, the present value of $1,000 due **in five years** is $620.92 versus the present value of $1,000 due in **one** year, which is $909.09.

The following two demonstration problems (Illustrations B-5 and B-6) illustrate how to use Table B-1.

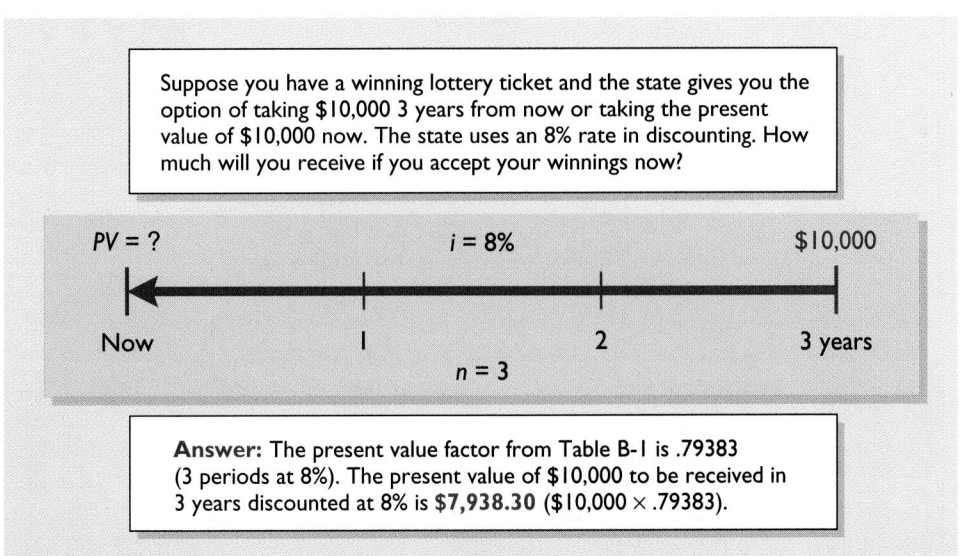

**Illustration B-5**

***Demonstration Problem—*** *Using Table B-1 for PV of 1*

Suppose you have a winning lottery ticket and the state gives you the option of taking $10,000 3 years from now or taking the present value of $10,000 now. The state uses an 8% rate in discounting. How much will you receive if you accept your winnings now?

PV = ?      i = 8%      $10,000

Now    1    2    3 years

n = 3

**Answer:** The present value factor from Table B-1 is .79383 (3 periods at 8%). The present value of $10,000 to be received in 3 years discounted at 8% is **$7,938.30** ($10,000 × .79383).

**Illustration B-6**

*Demonstration Problem—*
*Using Table B-1 for PV of 1*

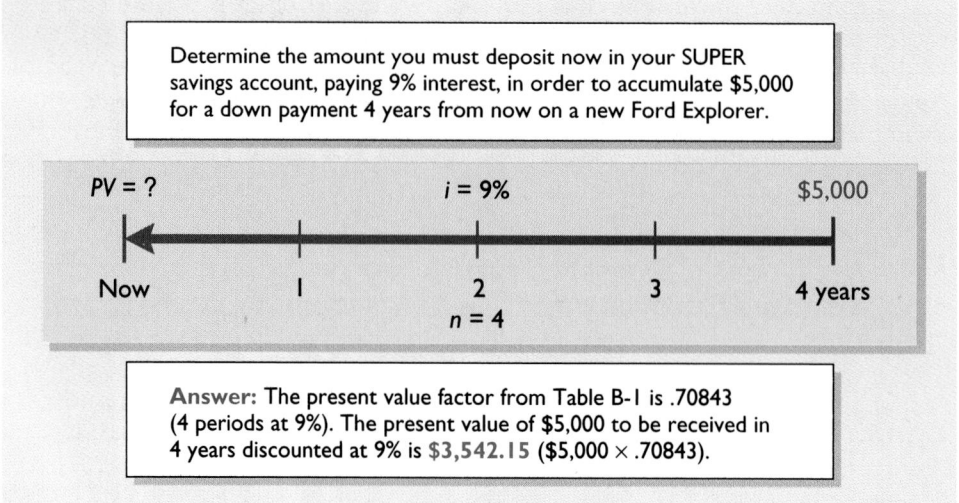

**Present Value of a Series of Future Amounts (Annuities)**

The preceding discussion involved the discounting of only a single future amount. Businesses and individuals frequently engage in transactions in which a series of equal dollar amounts are to be received or paid periodically. Examples of a series of periodic receipts or payments are loan agreements, installment sales, mortgage notes, lease (rental) contracts, and pension obligations. These series of periodic receipts or payments are called **annuities**. In computing the present value of an annuity, it is necessary to know the (1) discount rate, (2) the number of discount periods, and (3) the amount of the periodic receipts or payments. To illustrate the computation of the present value of an annuity, assume that you will receive $1,000 cash annually for 3 years and the discount rate is 10%. This situation is depicted in the following time diagram:

**Illustration B-7**

*Time diagram for a 3-year annuity*

The present value in this situation may be computed as follows:

**Illustration B-8**

*Present value of a series of future amounts computation*

| Future Amount | × | Present Value of 1 Factor at 10% | = | Present Value |
|---|---|---|---|---|
| $1,000 (One year away) | | .90909 | | $ 909.09 |
| 1,000 (Two years away) | | .82645 | | 826.45 |
| 1,000 (Three years away) | | .75132 | | 751.32 |
| | | 2.48686 | | **$2,486.86** |

This method of calculation is required when the periodic cash flows are not uniform in each period. However, when the future receipts are the same in each period, there are two other ways to compute present value. First, the annual cash flow can be multiplied by the sum of the three present value factors. In the example above, $1,000 × 2.48686 equals $2,486.86. Second, annuity tables may be used. As illustrated in Table B-2 below, these tables show the present value of 1 to be received periodically for a given number of periods.

### TABLE B-2
### PRESENT VALUE OF AN ANNUITY OF 1

| (n) Periods | 4% | 5% | 6% | 8% | 9% | 10% | 11% | 12% | 15% |
|---|---|---|---|---|---|---|---|---|---|
| 1 | .96154 | .95238 | .94340 | .92593 | .91743 | .90909 | .90090 | .89286 | .86957 |
| 2 | 1.88609 | 1.85941 | 1.83339 | 1.78326 | 1.75911 | 1.73554 | 1.71252 | 1.69005 | 1.62571 |
| 3 | 2.77509 | 2.72325 | 2.67301 | 2.57710 | 2.53130 | 2.48685 | 2.44371 | 2.40183 | 2.28323 |
| 4 | 3.62990 | 3.54595 | 3.46511 | 3.31213 | 3.23972 | 3.16986 | 3.10245 | 3.03735 | 2.85498 |
| 5 | 4.45182 | 4.32948 | 4.21236 | 3.99271 | 3.88965 | 3.79079 | 3.69590 | 3.60478 | 3.35216 |
| 6 | 5.24214 | 5.07569 | 4.91732 | 4.62288 | 4.48592 | 4.35526 | 4.23054 | 4.11141 | 3.78448 |
| 7 | 6.00205 | 5.78637 | 5.58238 | 5.20637 | 5.03295 | 4.86842 | 4.71220 | 4.56376 | 4.16042 |
| 8 | 6.73274 | 6.46321 | 6.20979 | 5.74664 | 5.53482 | 5.33493 | 5.14612 | 4.96764 | 4.48732 |
| 9 | 7.43533 | 7.10782 | 6.80169 | 6.24689 | 5.99525 | 5.75902 | 5.53705 | 5.32825 | 4.77158 |
| 10 | 8.11090 | 7.72173 | 7.36009 | 6.71008 | 6.41766 | 6.14457 | 5.88923 | 5.65022 | 5.01877 |
| 11 | 8.76048 | 8.30641 | 7.88687 | 7.13896 | 6.80519 | 6.49506 | 6.20652 | 5.93770 | 5.23371 |
| 12 | 9.38507 | 8.86325 | 8.38384 | 7.53608 | 7.16073 | 6.81369 | 6.49236 | 6.19437 | 5.42062 |
| 13 | 9.98565 | 9.39357 | 8.85268 | 7.90378 | 7.48690 | 7.10336 | 6.74987 | 6.42355 | 5.58315 |
| 14 | 10.56312 | 9.89864 | 9.29498 | 8.24424 | 7.78615 | 7.36669 | 6.98187 | 6.62817 | 5.72448 |
| 15 | 11.11839 | 10.37966 | 9.71225 | 8.55948 | 8.06069 | 7.60608 | 7.19087 | 6.81086 | 5.84737 |
| 16 | 11.65230 | 10.83777 | 10.10590 | 8.85137 | 8.31256 | 7.82371 | 7.37916 | 6.97399 | 5.95424 |
| 17 | 12.16567 | 11.27407 | 10.47726 | 9.12164 | 8.54363 | 8.02155 | 7.54879 | 7.11963 | 6.04716 |
| 18 | 12.65930 | 11.68959 | 10.82760 | 9.37189 | 8.75563 | 8.20141 | 7.70162 | 7.24967 | 6.12797 |
| 19 | 13.13394 | 12.08532 | 11.15812 | 9.60360 | 8.95012 | 8.36492 | 7.83929 | 7.36578 | 6.19823 |
| 20 | 13.59033 | 12.46221 | 11.46992 | 9.81815 | 9.12855 | 8.51356 | 7.96333 | 7.46944 | 6.25933 |

From Table B-2 it can be seen that the present value factor of an annuity of 1 for three periods at 10% is 2.48685.[1] This present value factor is the total of the three individual present value factors as shown in Illustration B-8. Applying this amount to the annual cash flow of $1,000 produces a present value of $2,486.85.

The following demonstration problem (Illustration B-9) illustrates how to use Table B-2.

---

[1]The difference of .00001 between 2.48686 and 2.48685 is due to rounding.

**Illustration B-9**

*Demonstration Problem—
Using Table B-2 for PV of
an annuity of 1*

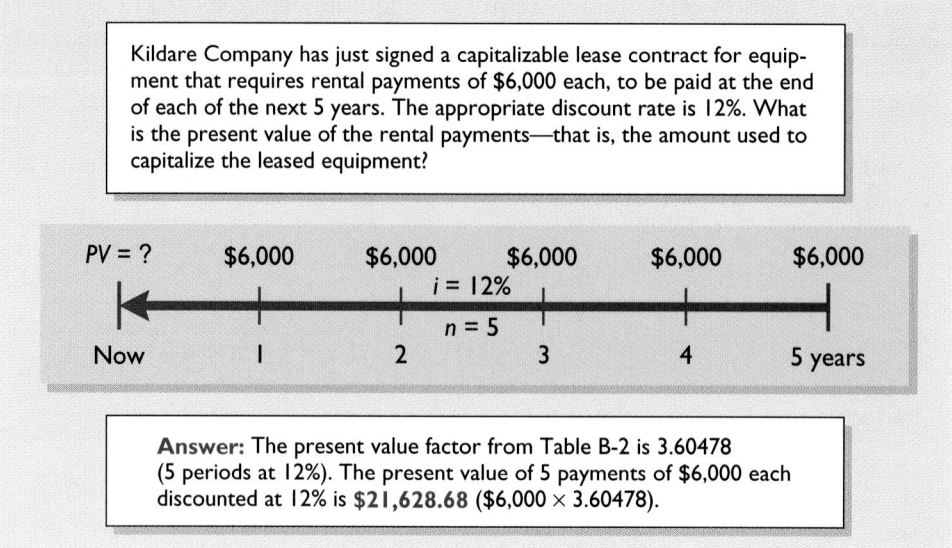

Kildare Company has just signed a capitalizable lease contract for equipment that requires rental payments of **$6,000** each, to be paid at the end of each of the next 5 years. The appropriate discount rate is 12%. What is the present value of the rental payments—that is, the amount used to capitalize the leased equipment?

**Answer:** The present value factor from Table B-2 is 3.60478 (5 periods at 12%). The present value of 5 payments of $6,000 each discounted at 12% is **$21,628.68** ($6,000 × 3.60478).

# Time Periods and Discounting

In the preceding calculations, the discounting has been done on an annual basis using an annual interest rate. Discounting may also be done over shorter periods of time such as monthly, quarterly, or semiannually. When the time frame is less than one year, it is necessary to convert the annual interest rate to the applicable time frame. Assume, for example, that the investor in Illustration B-8 received $500 **semiannually** for 3 years instead of $1,000 annually. In this case, the number of periods becomes 6 (3 × 2), the discount rate is 5% (10% ÷ 2), the present value factor from Table B-2 is 5.07569, and the present value of the future cash flows is $2,537.85 (5.07569 × $500). This amount is slightly higher than the $2,486.86 computed in Illustration B-8 because interest is computed twice during the same year; therefore interest is earned on the first half year's interest.

# Computing the Present Value of a Bond

The present value (or market price) of a bond is a function of three variables: (1) the payment amounts, (2) the length of time until the amounts are paid, and (3) the discount rate.

The first variable (dollars to be paid) is made up of two elements: (1) a series of interest payments (an annuity) and (2) the principal amount (a single sum). To compute the present value of the bond, both the interest payments and the principal amount must be discounted—two different computations. The time diagrams for a bond due in 5 years are shown in Illustration B-10.

When the investor's discount rate is equal to the bond's contractual interest rate, the present value of the bonds will equal the face value of the bonds. To

**Illustration B-10**

*Time diagram for the present value of a bond*

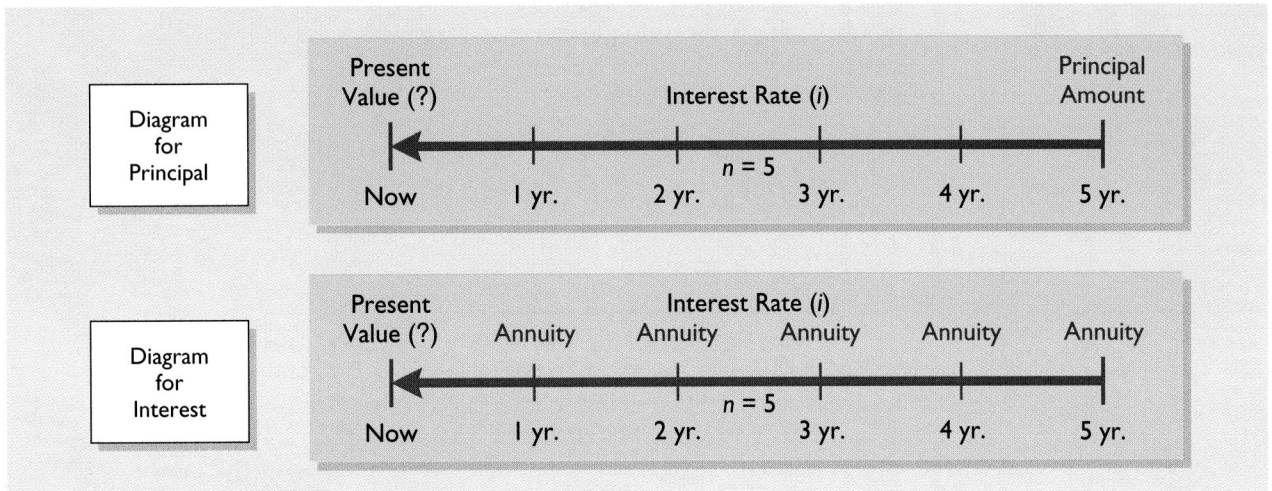

illustrate, assume a bond issue of 10%, 5-year bonds with a face value of $100,000 with interest payable **semiannually** on January 1 and July 1. If the discount rate is the same as the contractual rate, the bonds will sell at face value. In this case, the investor will receive (1) $100,000 at maturity and (2) a series of ten $5,000 interest payments [($100,000 × 10%) ÷ 2] over the term of the bonds. The length of time is expressed in terms of interest periods, in this case, 10, and the discount rate per interest period, 5%. The following time diagram (Illustration B-11) depicts the variables involved in this discounting situation:

**Illustration B-11**

*Time diagram for the present value of a 10%, 5-year bond paying interest semiannually*

The computation of the present value of these bonds is shown below.

**Illustration B-12**

*Present value of principal and interest (face value)*

### 10% Contractual Rate—10% Discount Rate

Present value of principal to be received at maturity
   $100,000 × PV of 1 due in 10 periods at 5%
   $100,000 × .61391 (Table B-1)                                    $ 61,391
Present value of interest to be received periodically
over the term of the bonds
   $5,000 × PV of 1 due periodically for 10 periods at 5%
   $5,000 × 7.72173 (Table B-2)                                      38,609*
Present value of bonds                                              $100,000

*(Rounded).

Now assume that the investor's required rate of return is 12%, not 10%. The future amounts are again $100,000 and $5,000, respectively, but now a discount rate of 6% (12% ÷ 2) must be used. The present value of the bonds is $92,639, as computed below:

**Illustration B-13**

*Present value of principal and interest (discount)*

### 10% Contractual Rate—12% Discount Rate

Present value of principal to be received at maturity
   $100,000 × .55839 (Table B-1)                                    $55,839
Present value of interest to be received periodically
over the term of the bonds
   $5,000 × 7.36009 (Table B-2)                                      36,800
Present value of bonds                                              $92,639

Conversely, if the discount rate is 8% and the contractual rate is 10%, the present value of the bonds is $108,111, computed as follows:

**Illustration B-14**

*Present value of principal and interest (premium)*

### 10% Contractual Rate—8% Discount Rate

Present value of principal to be received at maturity
   $100,000 × .67556 (Table B-1)                                    $ 67,556
Present value of interest to be received periodically
over the term of the bonds
   $5,000 × 8.11090 (Table B-2)                                      40,555
Present value of bonds                                              $108,111

## ▶Technology in Action

As discussed in this appendix, the selling price of the bonds can be determined by present value formulas. Many computer spreadsheets and computer programs can perform the discounting functions given the basic information of the situation.

The above discussion relied on present value tables in solving present value problems. Electronic hand-held calculators may also be used to compute present values without the use of these tables. Some calculators, especially the "business" or "financial" type calculators, have present value (PV) functions that allow you to calculate present values by merely punching in the proper amount, discount rate, periods, and pressing the PV key.

# BRIEF EXERCISES (Use Tables to Solve Exercises)

**BEB–1** For each of the following cases, indicate (a) to what interest rate columns and (b) to what number of periods you would refer in looking up the discount rate.

*Using present value tables.*

1. In Table B-1 (present value of 1):

|  | Annual Rate | Number of Years Involved | Discounts Per Year |
|---|---|---|---|
| a. | 12% | 6 | Annually |
| b. | 10% | 15 | Annually |
| c. | 8% | 8 | Semiannually |

2. In Table B-2 (present value of an annuity of 1):

|  | Annual Rate | Number of Years Involved | Number of Payments Involved | Frequency of Payments |
|---|---|---|---|---|
| a. | 12% | 20 | 20 | Annually |
| b. | 10% | 5 | 5 | Annually |
| c. | 8% | 4 | 8 | Semiannually |

**BEB–2** (a) What is the present value of $10,000 due 8 periods from now, discounted at 8%? (b) What is the present value of $10,000 to be received at the end of each of 6 periods, discounted at 9%?

*Determining present values.*

**BEB–3** Smolinski Company is considering an investment that will return a lump sum of $500,000 5 years from now. What amount should Smolinski Company pay for this investment in order to earn a 15% return?

*Compute the present value of a single-sum investment.*

**BEB–4** Pizzeria Company earns 11% on an investment that will return $875,000 8 years from now. What is the amount Pizzeria should invest now in order to earn this rate of return?

*Compute the present value of a single-sum investment.*

**BEB–5** Shake-A-Soda Company sold a 5-year, noninterest-bearing $27,000 note receivable to Valley Inc. Valley wishes to earn 12% over the remaining 4 years of the note. How much cash will Shake-A-Soda receive upon sale of the note?

*Compute the present value of a single-sum noninterest-bearing note.*

**BEB–6** Roberto Company issues a 3-year, zero-interest-bearing $66,000 note. The interest rate used to discount the zero-interest-bearing note is 8%. What are the cash proceeds that Roberto Company should receive?

*Compute the present value of a single-sum noninterest-bearing note.*

**BEB–7** Kilarny Company is considering investing in an annuity contract that will return $20,000 annually at the end of each year for 15 years. What amount should Kilarny Company pay for this investment if it earns a 6% return?

*Compute the present value of an annuity investment.*

**BEB–8** Zarita Enterprises earns 11% on an investment that pays back $110,000 at the end of each of the next 4 years. What is the amount Zarita Enterprises invested to earn the 11% rate of return?

*Compute the present value of an annuity investment.*

**BEB–9** Hernandez Railroad Co. is about to issue $100,000 of 10-year bonds paying a 12% interest rate, with interest payable semiannually. The discount rate for such securities is 10%. How much can Hernandez expect to receive for the sale of these bonds?

*Compute the present value of bonds.*

**BEB–10** Assume the same information as BEB–9 except that the discount rate is 12% instead of 10%. In this case, how much can Hernandez expect to receive from the sale of these bonds?

*Compute the present value of bonds.*

**BEB–11** Caledonian Taco Company receives a $50,000, 6-year note bearing interest of 11% (paid annually) from a customer at a time when the discount rate is 12%. What is the present value of the note received by Caledonian?

*Compute the present value of a note.*

*Compute the present value of bonds.*

**BEB-12** Galway Bay Enterprises issued 10%, 8-year, $2,000,000 par value bonds that pay interest semiannually on October 1 and April 1. The bonds are dated April 1, 1996, and are issued on that date. The discount rate of interest for such bonds on April 1, 1996, is 12%. What cash proceeds did Galway Bay receive from issuance of the bonds?

*Compute the value of a machine for purposes of making a purchase decision.*

**BEB-13** Barney Googal owns a garage and is contemplating purchasing a tire retreading machine for $16,280. After estimating costs and revenues, Barney projects a net cash flow from the retreading machine of $2,790 annually for 8 years. Barney hopes to earn a return of 11% on such investments. What is the present value of the retreading operation? Should Barney Googal purchase the retreading machine?

*Compute the present value of a note.*

**BEB-14** Hung-Chao Yu Company issues a 10%, 6-year mortgage note on January 1, 1996, to obtain financing for new equipment. Land is used as collateral for the note. The terms provide for semiannual installment payments of $112,825. What were the cash proceeds received from the issuance of the note?

*Compute the maximum price to pay for a machine.*

**BEB-15** Ramos Company is considering purchasing equipment. The equipment will produce the following cash flows: Year 1, $30,000; Year 2, $40,000; Year 3, $50,000. Ramos requires a minimum rate of return of 15%. What is the maximum price Ramos should pay for this equipment?

*Compute the interest rate on a single sum.*

**BEB-16** If Kerry Rodriquez invests $1,827 now, she will receive $10,000 at the end of 15 years. What annual rate of interest will Kerry earn on her investment? (Hint: Use Table B-1.)

*Compute the number of periods of a single sum.*

**BEB-17** Maloney Cork has been offered the opportunity of investing $24,719 now. The investment will earn 15% per year and at the end of that time will return Maloney $100,000. How many years must Maloney wait to receive $100,000? (Hint: Use Table B-1.)

*Compute the interest rate on an annuity.*

**BEB-18** Annie Dublin purchased an investment for $11,469.92. From this investment, she will receive $1,000 annually for the next 20 years, starting one year from now. What rate of interest will Annie's investment be earning for her? (Hint: Use Table B-2.)

*Compute the number of periods of an annuity.*

**BEB-19** Andy Sanchez invests $8,851.37 now for a series of $1,000 annual returns, beginning one year from now. Andy will earn a return of 8% on the initial investment. How many annual payments of $1,000 will Andy receive? (Hint: Use Table B-2.)

# APPENDIX · C

# STANDARDS OF ETHICAL CONDUCT FOR MANAGEMENT ACCOUNTANTS

Management accountants have an obligation to the organizations they serve, their profession, the public, and themselves to maintain the highest standards of ethical conduct. In recognition of this obligation, the Institute of Management Accountants, formerly the National Association of Accountants, has published and promoted the following standards of ethical conduct for management accountants. Adherence to these standards is integral to achieving the *Objectives of Management Accounting*.[1] Management accountants shall not commit acts contrary to these standards nor shall they condone the commission of such acts by others within their organizations.

## Competence

Management accountants have a responsibility to:
- Maintain an appropriate level of professional competence by ongoing development of their knowledge and skills.
- Perform their professional duties in accordance with relevant laws, regulations, and technical standards.
- Prepare complete and clear reports and recommendations after appropriate analyses of relevant and reliable information.

## Confidentiality

Management accountants have a responsibility to:
- Refrain from disclosing confidential information acquired in the course of their work except when authorized, unless legally obligated to do so.
- Inform subordinates as appropriate regarding the confidentiality of information acquired in the course of their work and monitor their activities to assure the maintenance of that confidentiality.

---

[1]Institute of Management Accountants, formerly National Association of Accountants, *Statements on Management Accounting: Objectives of Management Accounting*, Statement No. 1B, June 17, 1982.

- Refrain from using or appearing to use confidential information acquired in the course of their work for unethical or illegal advantage either personally or through third parties.

## Integrity

Management accountants have a responsibility to:

- Avoid actual or apparent conflicts of interest and advise all appropriate parties of any potential conflict.
- Refrain from engaging in any activity that would prejudice their ability to carry out their duties ethically.
- Refuse any gift, favor, or hospitality that would influence or would appear to influence their actions.
- Refrain from either actively or passively subverting the attainment of the organization's legitimate and ethical objectives.
- Recognize and communicate professional limitations or other constraints that would preclude responsible judgment or successful performance of an activity.
- Communicate unfavorable as well as favorable information and professional judgments or opinions.
- Refrain from engaging in or supporting any activity that would discredit the profession.

## Objectivity

Management accountants have a responsibility to:

- Communicate information fairly and objectively.
- Disclose fully all relevant information that could reasonably be expected to influence an intended user's understanding of the reports, comments, and recommendations presented.

# PHOTO CREDITS

● ● ● ● ● ● ● ● ● ● ● ● ● ● ● ● ● ● ● ● ● ● ● ● ● ● ● ● ● ● ● ● ● ● ● ● ● ● ● ● ● ● ●

**Chapter 1**
OPENER: J.L. Bulcao/Gamma Liaison. Page 6: Murray Alcosser/The Image Bank. Page 7: M&C Werner/Comstock, Inc. Page 9: Ann Sates/SABA. Page 12: Michael Keller/FPG International.

**Chapter 2**
OPENER: Antonio M. Rosario/The Image Bank. Page 45: Matthew Borkoski/Index Stock. Page 48: Jonathan Daniel/Allsport. Page 54: Mike Stewart/Sygma Photo News. Page 56: Arthur Meyerson/The Image Bank. Page 66: Nick Koudis/The Stock Market.

**Chapter 3**
OPENER: Joseph Szkodzinski/The Image Bank. Page 90: Jerry Ohlinger. Page 93: Romily Lockyer/The Image Bank. Page 106: Peter Poulides/Tony Stone Images/New York, Inc. Page 108: Frank Steman/Viesti Associates, Inc.

**Chapter 4**
OPENER: Chris Buck/Alexander Griffin Photography. Page 137: Courtesy Lotus Corporation. Page 142: Wal-Mart Stores. Page 150: Chris Cheadle/Tony Stone Images/New York, Inc.

**Chapter 5**
OPENER: Will Crocker/The Image Bank. Page 185: Lorentz Gullachsen/Tony Stone Images/New York, Inc. Page 189: Gregory Heisler/The Image Bank. Page 191: Richard Hutchings/Photo Researchers. Page 192: R. Llewellyn/SUPERSTOCK. Page 198: Romily Lockyer/The Image Bank. Page 203: Comstock, Inc.

**Chapter 6**
OPENER: J.W. Burkey/Tony Stone Images/New York, Inc. Page 240: Deborah Gilbert/The Image Bank. Page 254: Frank Levy/The Stock Market. Page 255: 1992-0- Lightscapes International Communications/The Stock Market. Page 257: Robert Tinney/The Stock Market. Page 258: Garry Gay/The Image Bank. Page 259: Ralph Mercer/Tony Stone Images/New York, Inc. Page 279: Courtesy Alco Standard Corporation.

**Chapter 7**
OPENER: Ken Cooper/The Image Bank. Page 285: Gary Buss/FPG International. Page 287: Mel Digiacomo/The Image Bank. Page 288: R. Michael Stuckey/Comstock, Inc. Page 289: F. Cascioli/The Stock Market. Page 291: Derek Redfearn/The Image Bank. Page 295: Telegraph Colour Library/FPG International. Page 299: Paul Barton/The Stock Market. Page 302 (top): Steve Winter/Black Star. Page 302 (bottom): J.W. Burkey/Tony Stone Images/New York, Inc. Page 303: Comstock, Inc. Page 305: Jay Freis/The Image Bank.

**Chapter 8**
OPENER: Gabe Palmer/The Stock Market. Page 330: Peter Gridley/FPG International. Page 334: G.S.O. Images/The Image Bank. Page 336: Zigy Kaluzny/Tony Stone Images/New York, Inc. Page 337: Brian Smale Photography. Page 338: A. Berliner/Gamma Liaison. Page 343: John Lund/Tony Stone Images/New York, Inc. Page 361: Courtesy Art World Industries.

**Chapter 9**
OPENER: Comstock, Inc. Page 366: Luigi Giordano/The Stock

Market. Page 367: Tom Tracey/FPG International. Page 375: Tommy Ewasko/The Image Bank. Page 376: Bob Krist/Tony Stone Images/New York, Inc. Page 378: Chuck Keeler/Tony Stone Images/New York, Inc.

**Chapter 10**
OPENER: Comstock, Inc. Page 411: International Stock Photo. Page 416: Michael Krasowitz/FPG International. Page 418: Etienne De Malglaive/Gamma Liaison. Page 424: N. Cotton/International Stock Photo. Page 426: Patti McConville/The Image Bank. Page 428: Forrest Anderson/Gamma Liaison. Page 429 (top): Courtesy RJR Nabisco. Page 429 (bottom): Jon Levy/Gamma Liaison. Page 430: Courtesy Grand Met. Page 447: Courtesy Clark.

**Chapter 11**
OPENER: Ralph Mercer/Gamma Liaison. Page 454: Marv Lyons/The Image Bank. Page 456: Peter Gridley/FPG International. Page 459: Joseph Nettis/Photo Researchers. Page 461: Matt/Gamma Liaison. Page 462: Turner and DeVries/The Image Bank. Page 463: Adam Woolfitt/Woodfin Camp & Associates. Page 470: Ron Chapple/FPG International. Page 471: Randy O'Rourke/The Stock Market. Page 489: Courtesy Capitol American Financial Corporation.

**Chapter 12**
OPENER: Kenneth Scallon/The Image Bank. Page 495: Gordon Gahan/Photo Researchers. Page 497: Comstock, Inc. Page 503: Philip M. Prosen/The Image Bank. Page 504: Comstock, Inc. Page 510 (top): Vlastimir Shone/Gamma Liaison. Page 510 (bottom): Cesar Paredes/The Stock Market.

**Chapter 13**
OPENER: Andy Washnik. Page 530: Jim Scruggs/Gamma Liaison. Page 531: Walter Bibikow/The Image Bank. Page 535: Michael Murphy/The Image Bank.

**Chapter 14**
OPENER: Superstock. Page 571: Jacques Chenet/Woodfin Camp & Associates. Page 572: Courtesy Delaware State Travel Service. Page 574: Greg Davis/The Stock Market. Page 576: Dave Wilhelm/The Stock Market. Page 583: Chris Collins/Philip Morris Slide Library. Page 587: Robert Vanmarter/Gamma Liaison. Page 606: Courtesy Barrister Information Systems Corp.

**Chapter 15**
OPENER: Ron Chapple/FPG International. Page 611: Frank White/Gamma Liaison. Page 612: Charles West/The Stock Market. Page 622: Robert Kristofik/The Image Bank. Page 626: Rob Nelson/Black Star. Page 627: Mitchell Funk/The Image Bank. Page 648: Courtesy DIEBOLD Incorporated.

**Chapter 16**
OPENER: Gary Gladstone/The Image Bank. Page 654: E. Salem Krieger/The Image Bank. Page 655: Steven Wilkes/The Image Bank. Page 667: Archiv/Photo Researchers. Page 669: Mitchell Funk/The Image Bank. Page 692: Courtesy Apache Corporation.

**Chapter 17**
OPENER: David Miller/Courtesy Hyperion Press. Page 713:

Douglas Bowles / The Image Bank. Page 714: John Van Hasselt / Sygma. Page 729: Courtesy SPS Technologies.

Chapter 18
OPENER: Vladimir Pcholkin / FPG International. Page 733: R. Rathe / FPG International. Page 736: Lance Nelson / The Stock Market. Page 737: Dick Luria / FPG International.

Chapter 19
OPENER: Bill Losh / FPG International. Page 800: Nora Good / Masterfile. Page 801: Courtesy JC Penney. Page 802: Garry Gay / The Image Bank. Page 807: Michael Skott / The Image Bank. Page 807: Eric Sander / Gamma Liaison. Page 809: Vladimir Pcholkin / FPG International. Page 834: Courtesy The Coca-Cola Company.

Chapter 20
OPENER: John Terence Turner / FPG International. Page 842: Jorgen Vogt / The Image Bank. Page 844: Brownie Harris / The Stock Market. Page 845: Steve Dunwell / The Image Bank. Page 852: Will McIntyre / Photo Researchers. Page 853: Louis H. Jawitz / The Image Bank. Page 875: Courtesy Anchor Glass Container Corp.

Chapter 21
OPENER: Lien / Nibauer Photography Inc. / Gamma Liaison. Page 882: David Plowden / Photo Researchers. Page 885: Courtesy Federal Express. Page 893: Robert Tinney / The Stock Market. Page 896: Bob Daemmrich / The Image Works. Page 914: Courtesy Parlex Corporation.

Chapter 22
OPENER: Peter Miller / The Image Bank. Page 919: James Schnepf / Gamma Liaison. Page 922: Rick Altman / The Stock

Market. Page 925: Mark Scott / FPG International. Page 931: Stephen Simpson / FPG International. Page 938: James Schnepf / Gamma Liaison. Page 939: Ed Taylor Studio / FPG International. Page 943: M & C Werner / Comstock, Inc. Page 959: Courtesy General Microwave Corporation.

Chapter 23
OPENER: Spencer Jones / FPG International. Page 971: Reza Estakhrian / Tony Stone Images / New York, Inc. Page 974: Peter A. Simon / The Stock Market. Page 976: F. Garcia / Retna. Page 998: Courtesy BioChem Pharma Inc.

Chapter 24
OPENER: Shiki / The Stock Market. Page 1010 (top): Peter Zeray / Photonica. Page 1010 (bottom): Peter Vadnai / The Stock Market. Page 1015: Christian Michaels / FPG International. Page 1020: David Blum / Pixel Studios / The Stock Market.

Chapter 25
OPENER: Karl Hentz / The Image Bank. Page 1051: Comstock, Inc. Page 1054: David Chambers / Tony Stone Images / New York, Inc. Page 1079: Courtesy Computer Associates.

Chapter 26
OPENER: Courtesy Sanford Corporation. Page 1087: Naideau / The Stock Market. Page 1091: Michel Tchervkoff / The Image Bank. Page 1094: Courtesy UPS. Page 1118: Courtesy Glassmaster Co.

Chapter 27
OPENER: Photofest. Page 1126: The Telegraph Colour Library / FPG International. Page 1139: Ken Ross / Gamma Liaison.

# COMPANY INDEX

# SUBJECT INDEX